MW00462164

# Harrap's Pocket

## GERMAN

### and

## ENGLISH

### Dictionary

# Harrap's Pocket GERMAN and ENGLISH Dictionary

GERMAN-ENGLISH, ENGLISH-GERMAN
IN ONE VOLUME

Compiled by
LEXUS
with Horst Kopleck,
James Burnett,
and Colin Arthur

National Textbook Company
4255 West Touhy Avenue
Lincolnwood, Illinois 60646-1975 U.S.A.

First published in Great Britain 1988 by HARRAP Ltd,
19–23 Ludgate Hill, London EC4M 7DP

This dictionary is a shortened version of *Harrap's Concise German
and English Dictionary,* edited by Robin Sawers. The project was
carried out for Harrap by LEXUS Ltd.

Dieses Wörterbuch ist eine gekürzte Fassung des *Harrap's Concise
German and English Dictionary,* hrsg. von Robin Sawers. Diese
Kürzung erfolgte unter der Projektleitung von LEXUS Ltd.

Editors/ Mitarbeiter:

Horst Kopleck   Jimmy Burnett   Colin Arthur

Trademarks

Eingetragene Warenzeichen

ISBN 0-245-54573-5

Printed in Great Britain by
Richard Clay Ltd, Bungay

# Preface

## Treatment of entries

As in all other Harrap dictionaries, wide-ranging use is made of a system of 'labels'. These are abbreviations, printed in italics, and positioned before the translation, for example *Sp:* for sport, *Ch:* for chemistry or *Z:* for zoology. As far as possible we have used only easily recognizable short forms. To make the dictionary entries easy to work with we have used Roman numerals (**I.**, **II.** etc.) to subdivide grammatical categories (noun, verb etc.) and Arabic numerals (**1.**, **2.** etc.) and letters ((*a*), (*b*) etc.) to mark differences in meaning.

## Compound nouns

One of the main difficulties in a German-English dictionary lies in the treatment of German compounds. In this dictionary we have, where appropriate, used a system of 'combining form' entries (*comb. fm.*). This shows – with examples – how to translate nouns that form the first part of a compound word. In this way it is possible to include more compounds in the dictionary than would be the case if each compound were given a separate entry. However, if a compound does not fit the pattern shown by the combining form then it is treated as a separate entry.

## Structure of entries

Headwords are given in **bold** type. Main headwords are followed by a phonetic transcription in square brackets. Sub-headwords are only given stress marks unless their pronunciation differs substantially from that of the main headword. There then follows an abbreviation describing the part of speech. Then, if the word is a German noun, come the genitive and the plural ending (with the exception of compounds of which the second element is independently listed as a separate headword). For English nouns we give irregular plurals only. Irregular verbs are given in a separate list and marked up in the text with *irr*. The numbers given with certain irregular German verbs refer to the list of verbs which shows the pattern according to which the parts of these verbs are formed.

Attention should be paid to the use of brackets and obliques. Brackets are used for additional parts of a usage and the bracketed part will also appear in the translation, unless it is superfluous. Obliques are used to indicate alternative elements, for example in a set expression, and corresponding translations are given. Brackets are also used around typical objects of verbs and around nouns that are typically used with adjectives.

## Abbreviation of headwords

In the German-English part of the dictionary a large number of the entries are compounds. Frequently a main headword is split by a vertical stroke (|). This is to show that the first element of the word is not repeated in the following compounds. These compounds consist of the initial letter of the word (big or small), a tilde (~) and the rest of the word, for example: **Förder|band, F~er, f~n** etc. Within the entry the word is abbreviated to its initial letter followed by a full-stop, as long as it is in exactly the same form as given at the beginning of the entry. If the word has a different ending, then the tilde replaces that part of the word at the beginning of the entry up to the vertical stroke. For example, in the entry with the main headword **Durchschlag** we have the verb **d~en** as well as the expression **d~ender Erfolg**. In the English-German part of the dictionary the tilde is not used. Instead all entries are written in full except when they are abbreviated to the initial letter as in example sentences.

## Order of headwords

The headwords are alphabetically ordered with the exception of compounds which are listed under the first element of the compound. Entries like these are not interrupted just to maintain alphabetical order. So, for example, **Bau** is followed by **b~fällig, B~stein, B~werk** etc. and then by **Bauch**. German prefixes such as aus-, bei-, vor-, zu- etc. form an exception to this rule with compounds starting with these prefixes being given separate entries. New headwords run on within an entry are preceded by ◆.

# Vorwort

## Behandlung der Einträge

Wie in allen anderen Harrap-Wörterbüchern finden Sachbereichsangaben weitgehend Verwendung. Hierbei handelt es sich um kursiv gedruckte Abkürzungen, die der Übersetzung vorangestellt sind, wie z.B. *Sp:* für Sport, *Ch:* für Chemie oder *Z:* für Zoologie. Soweit dies möglich war, haben wir uns auf leicht erkennbare Kürzel beschränkt. Um die Einträge übersichtlicher zu gestalten, verwenden wir römische Zahlen (**I., II.** usw.) zur Unterteilung von grammatischen Kategorien (Substantiv, Verb usw.). Bedeutungsunterschiede werden durch arabische Ziffern (**1., 2.** usw.) sowie durch Buchstaben ((*a*), (*b*) usw.) gekennzeichnet.

## Zusammengesetzte Substantive

Eine Hauptschwierigkeit in einem deutsch-englischen Wörterbuch besteht in der Behandlung der deutschen zusammengesetzten Substantive. Wir verwenden in diesem Wörterbuch, wo angemessen, sogenannte 'combining form'-Einträge (*comb. fm.*). Diese zeigen anhand von Beispielen, wie Substantive, die das erste Element einer Zusammensetzung bilden, zu übersetzen sind. Auf diese Weise können mehr Zusammensetzungen aufgenommen werden, als dies bei separaten Einträgen der Fall wäre. Wenn ein zusammengesetztes Wort nicht in das Muster der 'combining form' paßt, wird es als eigener Eintrag angeführt.

## Struktur der Einträge

Stichwörter sind **fett** gedruckt. Einem Hauptstichwort folgt die phonetische Umschrift in eckigen Klammern. Untergeordnete Einträge erhalten lediglich Betonungszeichen, außer wenn die Aussprache abweicht. Hierauf folgt eine Abkürzung, die die grammatische Kategorie bezeichnet. Bei deutschen Substantiven folgen der Genitiv und der Plural (außer bei Zusammensetzungen, bei denen das zweite Wortelement als eigener Eintrag erscheint); bei englischen Substantiven wird der Plural nur angegeben, wenn er unregelmäßig ist. Unregelmäßige Verben sind in einer gesonderten Liste aufgeführt und im Text selbst durch *irr.* gekennzeichnet. Die Zahlenangaben bei einigen unregelmäßigen deutschen Verben verweisen auf Verben in der Liste, deren Formen nach dem gleichen Muster gebildet werden.

Weiterhin ist die Verwendung von Klammern und Schrägstrichen zu beachten. Klammern werden bei zusätzlichen Elementen einer Wendung benutzt, entsprechend erscheint dann auch der Klammerausdruck in der

Übersetzung, es sei denn, er ist überflüssig. Ähnlich bezeichnen auch Schrägstriche Alternativen, etwa bei einer Redewendung, mit Entsprechungen in der Übersetzung. Ebenfalls eingeklammert erscheinen bei Verben typische Objekte sowie bei Adjektiven häufig in Zusammenhang mit diesen verwendete Substantive.

## Abkürzung von Stichwörtern

Im deutsch-englischen Teil besteht ein Großteil der Einträge aus Zusammensetzungen. Häufig wird ein Hauptstichwort durch einen vertikalen Trennstrich (|) unterteilt. Dies zeigt an, daß das Anfangselement des Wortes bei den darauffolgenden Zusammensetzungen nicht wiederholt wird. Diese Zusammensetzungen bestehen aus dem Anfangsbuchstaben des Wortes (groß oder klein), einer Tilde (~) und dem Rest des Wortes, also z.B.: **Förder|band, F~er, f~n** usw. Innerhalb des Eintrags wird das Wort mit seinem Anfangsbuchstaben abgekürzt, dem ein Punkt folgt, solange das Wort die gleiche Form wie das betreffende Stichwort hat. Hat das Wort eine abweichende Endung, ersetzt die Tilde jeweils das Hauptstichwort am Anfang eines Eintrags bis zum Trennstrich, z.B auf den Eintrag mit dem Hauptstichwort **Durchschlag** folgt das Verb **d~en** sowie der Ausdruck **d~ender Erfolg**. Im englisch-deutschen Teil des Wörterbuchs wird die Tilde nicht verwendet; alle Einträge, außer wenn sie in Beispielsätzen durch den Anfangsbuchstaben abgekürzt werden, erscheinen voll ausgeschrieben.

## Folge der Stichwörter

Die Folge der Stichwörter ist alphabetisch, außer bei Zusammensetzungen, die jeweils unter dem ersten Element der Zusammensetzung erscheinen. Ein solcher Eintrag wird nicht durch andere Wörter unterbrochen, nur um die alphabetische Reihenfolge zu wahren: auf **Bau** folgen also **b~fällig, B~stein, B~werk** usw. und erst dann **Bauch**. Eine Ausnahme bilden deutsche Stichwörter mit Präfixen wie aus-, bei-, vor-, zu- usw., die jeweils eigene Einträge haben. Neue Stichwörter innerhalb eines Eintrages sind durch ◆ hervorgehoben.

# Abbreviations and Labels used in the Dictionary
# Im Wörterbuch benutzte Abkürzungen und Bereichsangaben

| | | |
|---|---|---|
| *A:* | archaic | veraltet |
| *abbr.* | abbreviation | Abkürzung |
| *abs.* | absolute use | ohne Akkusativobjekt |
| *acc* | accusative | Akkusativ |
| *adj.* | adjective; adjectival | Adjektiv; adjektivisch |
| *Adm:* | administration; 'officialese' | Verwaltung; Beamtensprache |
| *adv.* | adverb | Adverb |
| *Agr:* | agriculture | Landwirtschaft |
| *Anat:* | anatomy | Anatomie |
| *approx.* | approximately | ungefähr |
| *Arch:* | architecture | Architektur |
| *art.* | article | Artikel |
| *Art:* | art | Kunst |
| *Astr:* | astronomy | Astronomie |
| *Atom.Ph:* | atomic physics | Atomphysik |
| *attrib.* | attributive | attributiv |
| *Aus:* | Austrian | österreichisch |
| *Austral:* | Australia; Australian | Australien; australisch |
| *Aut:* | automobiles, motoring | Automobile |
| *aux.* | auxiliary | Hilfs- |
| *Av:* | aviation; aircraft | Luftfahrt |
| *Biol:* | biology | Biologie |
| *Bot:* | botany | Botanik |
| *Brit:* | British | britisch |
| *Ch:* | chemistry | Chemie |
| *Cin:* | cinema | Kino |
| *Civ.E:* | civil engineering | Tiefbau |
| *Cl:* | clothing | Kleidung |
| *coll.* | collective | kollektiv |
| *Com:* | commerce, business | Handel, Geschäftswelt |
| *comb.fm.* | combining form | Zusammensetzungselement |
| *comp.* | comparative | Komparativ |
| *conj.* | conjunction | Konjunktion |
| *Cu:* | culinary; cooking | Kochkunst |
| *dat* | dative | Dativ |
| *Data-pr:* | data-processing | Datenverarbeitung |
| *decl.* | declined | dekliniert |
| *dem.* | demonstrative | Demonstrativ-, hinweisend |
| *E:* | engineering | Ingenieurwesen |
| *East G:* | East German | ostdeutsch, DDR |
| *Ecc:* | ecclesiastical | kirchlich |
| *e.g.* | for example | zum Beispiel |
| *El:* | electricity | Elektrizität |
| *esp.* | especially | besonders |
| *etc.* | et cetera, and so on | und so weiter |
| *f* | feminine | weiblich |
| *F:* | colloquial(ism) | umgangssprachlich |
| *Fb:* | football | Fußball |
| *Fig:* | figurative | figurativ, übertragen |
| *Fin:* | finance | Finanzwesen |
| *fut.* | future | Futur, Zukunft |
| *G:* | German | deutsch |
| *gen* | genitive | Genitiv |
| *Geog:* | geography | Geographie |
| *Gram:* | grammar | Grammatik |
| *H:* | household | Haushalt |
| *Hist:* | history | Geschichte |
| *Hum:* | humorous | scherzhaft |
| *i.* | intransitive | intransitiv |
| *i.e.* | id est, that is | das heißt |
| *imp.* | imperative | Imperativ |
| *imperf.* | imperfect | Imperfekt |
| *impers.* | impersonal | unpersönlich |
| *Ind:* | industry | Industrie |
| *indef.* | indefinite | unbestimmt |
| *inf.* | infinitive | Infinitiv |
| *insep.* | inseparable | nicht trennbar |
| *int.* | interjection | Ausruf |
| *interrog.* | interrogative | interrogativ |
| *inv.* | invariable | unveränderlich |
| *irr.* | irregular | unregelmäßig |
| *j-d* | | jemand |
| *j-m* | | jemandem |
| *j-n* | | jemanden |
| *j-s* | | jemand(e)s |
| *Jur:* | jurisprudence, law | Rechtswesen |
| *Lit:* | literary usage; literature | gehobener Sprachgebrauch; literarisch |

(ix)

| | | | | | | |
|---|---|---|---|---|---|---|
| *lit.* | literally | wörtlich | | *Rad:* | radio | Rundfunk |
| *m* | masculine | Maskulinum | | *Rail:* | railways, railroads | Eisenbahn |
| *Meas:* | weights and measures | Maße und Gewichte | | *Rec:* | records, recording and hi-fi | Schallplatten, Aufnahmetechnik und Hi-fi |
| *Med:* | medicine | Medizin | | | | |
| *Meteor:* | meteorology | Meteorologie | | *refl.* | reflexive | reflexiv |
| *Mil:* | military; army | militärisch | | *rel.* | relative | relativ |
| *Min:* | mining | Bergbau | | *R.t.m:* | registered trade mark | eingetragenes Warenzeichen |
| *Miner:* | mineralogy | Mineralogie | | | | |
| *Mth:* | mathematics | Mathematik | | | | |
| *Mus:* | music | Musik | | *s.* | substantive, noun | Substantiv |
| | | | | *Sch:* | schools | Schulen |
| *n* | neuter | Neutrum, sächlich | | *Scot:* | Scottish | schottisch |
| *N.Am:* | (North) American | (nord)amerikanisch | | *sep.* | separable | trennbar |
| | | | | *sing.* | singular | Singular |
| *Nau:* | nautical | nautisch, Seefahrt | | *s.o.* | someone | jemand |
| *neg.* | negative | negativ | | *South G:* | South German | süddeutsch |
| *nom* | nominative | Nominativ | | *Sp:* | sport | Sport |
| *North G:* | North German | norddeutsch | | | | |
| | | | | *sth.* | something | etwas |
| *occ.* | occasionally | gelegentlich | | *subj.* | subjunctive | Konjunktiv |
| *Opt:* | optics | Optik | | *suffix* | suffix | Suffix |
| *Orn:* | ornithology, birds | Ornithologie, Vögel | | *superl.* | superlative | Superlativ |
| | | | | *Swiss:* | Swiss | schweizerisch |
| *p.* | (i) participle; (ii) past | (i) Partizip; (ii) Vergangenheit | | *Tchn:* | technical | technisch |
| *P:* | slang | Slang | | *Tel:* | telephones and telegrams | Fernmeldewesen |
| *Pej:* | pejorative | pejorativ, abwertend | | | | |
| | | | | *Th:* | theatre | Theaterwesen |
| *pers., Pers.* | (of) person(s) | (von einer) Person, (von) Personen | | *tr.* | transitive | transitiv |
| | | | | *TV:* | television | Fernsehen |
| *Ph:* | physics | Physik | | | | |
| *Phot:* | photography | Fotografie | | *usu.* | usually | gewöhnlich |
| *pl* | plural | Plural | | *usw.* | (etc.) | und so weiter |
| *Pol:* | politics | Politik | | *v.* | verb | Verb |
| *poss.* | possessive | Possessiv- | | *V:* | vulgar | vulgär |
| *p.p.* | past participle | Partizip Perfekt | | *v.i.* | intransitive verb | intransitives Verb |
| *pred.* | predicate | Prädikat, prädikativ | | | | |
| *prefix* | prefix | Präfix, Vorsilbe | | *v.impers.* | impersonal verb | unpersönliches Verb |
| *prep.* | preposition | Präposition | | | | |
| *pres.* | present (tense) | Präsens | | *v.ind.tr.* | indirectly transitive verb | indirekt transitives Verb |
| *Pr.n.* | proper name | Eigenname | | | | |
| *pron.* | pronoun | Pronomen | | *v.tr.* | transitive verb | transitives Verb |
| *Psy:* | psychology | Psychologie | | *Z:* | zoology, animals | Zoologie, Tiere |

# part 1

# GRAMMAR NOTES

## Articles

The form of the definite article (the) in German depends on whether the noun is masculine, feminine or neuter and on whether it is singular or plural. The forms are:

|   | sing. | pl. |
|---|-------|-----|
| m | *der* | *die* |
| f | *die* | *die* |
| n | *das* | *die* |

For example:

| sing. | pl. |
|-------|-----|
| *der Hund* | *die Hunde* |
| *die Stange* | *die Stangen* |
| *das Heft* | *die Hefte* |

The definite article also changes according to the case it has in the sentence. There are four cases: nominative, accusative, genitive and dative:

|      | m | f | n | pl. |
|------|---|---|---|-----|
| nom. | *der* | *die* | *das* | *die* |
| acc. | *den* | *die* | *das* | *die* |
| gen. | *des* | *der* | *des* | *der* |
| dat. | *dem* | *der* | *dem* | *den* |

For example:

> der Lehrer trat herein
> ich sehe den Lehrer
> die Stimme des Lehrers
> ich habe mit dem Lehrer gesprochen

The indefinite article also varies according to the case and gender of the noun.

|     | m | f | n |
|-----|---|---|---|
| nom | *ein* | *eine* | *ein* |
| acc | *einen* | *eine* | *ein* |
| gen | *eines* | *einer* | *eines* |
| dat | *einem* | *einer* | *einem* |

Examples:

> ein Hund kam gelaufen
> ich sehe einen Hund
> der Kopf eines Hundes
> von einem Hund gebissen werden

## Adjectives

If an adjective is used in front of a noun it is declined. The endings that the adjective will take depends on whether the noun is used with the definite article (der/die/das) or with the indefinite article (ein/eine/ein).

Endings with the definite article:

|      | m | f | n | pl. |
|------|---|---|---|-----|
| nom. | *-e* | *-e* | *-e* | *-en* |
| acc. | *-en* | *-e* | *-e* | *-en* |
| gen. | *-en* | *-en* | *-en* | *-en* |
| dat. | *-en* | *-en* | *-en* | *-en* |

Examples:

> der gute Freund
> den guten Freund
> des guten Freundes
> dem guten Freund
> die guten Freunde

Endings with the indefinite article:

|      | m    | f    | n    |
|------|------|------|------|
| nom. | *-er* | *-e* | *-es* |
| acc. | *-en* | *-e* | *-es* |
| gen. | *-en* | *-en* | *-en* |
| dat. | *-en* | *-en* | *-en* |

Examples:

> ein braves Kind
> ein braves Kind
> eines braven Kindes
> einem braven Kind

Endings when no article is used:

|      | m    | f    | n    | pl.  |
|------|------|------|------|------|
| nom. | *-er* | *-e* | *-es* | *-e* |
| acc. | *-en* | *-e* | *-es* | *-e* |
| gen. | *-en* | *-er* | *-en* | *-er* |
| dat. | *-em* | *-er* | *-em* | *-en* |

Examples:

> feiner Wein
> feinen Wein
> feinen Wein(e)s
> feinem Wein
> feine Weine

If an adjective is used after a noun, it does not change its ending at all, for example:

> der Kaffee ist kalt
> die Frau war schön
> das Haus ist hoch
> die Mäuse waren tot

## Verbs

There are two main groups of verbs: weak and strong. Present and imperfect tense endings for weak verbs are:

*spielen*

| present | imperfect |
|---------|-----------|
| ich spiel-*e* | ich spiel-*te* |
| du spiel-*st* | du spiel-*test* |
| er/sie/es spiel-*t* | er/sie/es spiel-*te* |
| wir spiel-*en* | wir spiel-*ten* |
| ihr spiel-*t* | ihr spiel-*tet* |
| Sie spiel-*en* | Sie spiel-*ten* |
| sie spiel-*en* | sie spiel-*ten* |

Strong verbs are characterized by a vowel change in the verb stem. See the list of irregular German verbs on pages xv-xvi.

Here are two important German verbs: sein (to be) and haben (to have):

*sein*

| present | imperfect |
|---------|-----------|
| ich bin | ich war |
| du bist | du warst |
| er/sie/es ist | er/sie/es war |
| wir sind | wir waren |
| ihr seid | ihr wart |
| Sie sind | Sie waren |
| sie sind | sie waren |

*haben*

| present | imperfect |
|---------|-----------|
| ich habe | ich hatte |
| du hast | du hattest |
| er/sie/es hat | er/sie/es hatte |
| wir haben | wir hatten |
| ihr habt | ihr hattet |
| Sie haben | Sie hatten |
| sie haben | sie hatten |

# List of German Irregular Verbs
## Liste der deutschen unregelmäßigen Verben

| *Infinitive* | *Present Indicative* | *Past Indicative* | *Past Participle* |
|---|---|---|---|
| 1 backen | bäckt | backte | gebacken |
| 2 befehlen | befiehlt | befahl | befohlen |
| 3 beginnen | beginnt | begann | begonnen |
| 4 beißen | beißt | biß | gebissen |
| 5 bergen | birgt | barg | geborgen |
| 6 bewegen | bewegt | bewegte (bewog) | bewegt (bewogen) |
| 7 biegen | biegt | bog | gebogen |
| 8 bieten | bietet | bot | geboten |
| 9 binden | bindet | band | gebunden |
| 10 bitten | bittet | bat | gebeten |
| 11 blasen | bläst | blies | geblasen |
| 12 bleiben | bleibt | blieb | geblieben |
| 13 braten | brät | briet | gebraten |
| 14 brechen | bricht | brach | gebrochen |
| 15 brennen | brennt | brannte | gebrannt |
| 16 bringen | bringt | brachte | gebracht |
| 17 denken | denkt | dachte | gedacht |
| 18 dreschen | drischt | drosch | gedroschen |
| 19 dringen | dringt | drang | gedrungen |
| 20 dürfen | darf | durfte | gedurft |
| 21 erkiesen | erkiest | erkor | erkoren |
| 22 erlöschen | erlischt | erlosch | erloschen |
| 23 erschrecken | erschrickt (erschreckt) | erschrak (erschreckte) | erschrocken (erschreckt) |
| 24 erwägen | erwägt | erwog | erwogen |
| 25 essen | ißt | aß | gegessen |
| 26 fahren | fährt | fuhr | gefahren |
| 27 fallen | fällt | fiel | gefallen |
| 28 fangen | fängt | fing | gefangen |
| 29 fechten | ficht | focht | gefochten |
| 30 fliehen | flieht | floh | geflohen |
| 31 fließen | fließt | floß | geflossen |
| 32 frieren | friert | fror | gefroren |
| 33 gären | gärt | gor | gegoren |
| 34 gebären | gebiert | gebar | geboren |
| 35 geben | gibt | gab | gegeben |
| 36 gehen | geht | ging | gegangen |
| 37 gelten | gilt | galt | gegolten |
| 38 genesen | genest | genas | genesen |
| 39 geschehen | geschieht | geschah | geschehen |
| 40 gleichen | gleicht | glich | geglichen |
| 41 gleiten | gleitet | glitt | geglitten |
| 42 graben | gräbt | grub | gegraben |
| 43 greifen | greift | griff | gegriffen |
| 44 haben | hat | hatte | gehabt |
| 45 halten | hält | hielt | gehalten |
| 46 hängen | hängt | hing | gehangen |
| 47 hauen | haut | haute (hieb) | gehauen |
| 48 heben | hebt | hob | gehoben |
| 49 heißen | heißt | hieß | geheißen |
| 50 helfen | hilft | half | geholfen |
| 51 kennen | kennt | kannte | gekannt |
| 52 klimmen | klimmt | klomm | geklommen |
| 53 kommen | kommt | kam | gekommen |
| 54 können | kann | konnte | gekonnt |

| | | | |
|---|---|---|---|
| 55 kriechen | kriecht | kroch | gekrochen |
| 56 laden | lädt | lud | geladen |
| 57 lassen | läßt | ließ | gelassen |
| 58 laufen | läuft | lief | gelaufen |
| 59 leiden | leidet | litt | gelitten |
| 60 leihen | leiht | lieh | geliehen |
| 61 lesen | liest | las | gelesen |
| 62 liegen | liegt | lag | gelegen |
| 63 lügen | lügt | log | gelogen |
| 64 mahlen | mahlt | mahlte | gemahlen |
| 65 meiden | meidet | mied | gemieden |
| 66 melken | melkt | melkte (molk) | gemolken |
| 67 mögen | mag | mochte | gemocht |
| 68 müssen | muß | mußte | gemußt |
| 69 nehmen | nimmt | nahm | genommen |
| 70 preisen | preist | pries | gepriesen |
| 71 quellen | quillt | quoll | gequollen |
| 72 riechen | riecht | roch | gerochen |
| 73 rinnen | rinnt | rann | geronnen |
| 74 rufen | ruft | rief | gerufen |
| 75 saufen | säuft | soff | gesoffen |
| 76 saugen | saugt | sog (saugte) | gesogen (gesaugt) |
| 77 schaffen | schafft | schuf | geschaffen |
| 78 schallen | schallt | schallte (scholl) | geschallt |
| 79 scheinen | scheint | schien | geschienen |
| 80 schelten | schilt | schalt | gescholten |
| 81 scheren | schert | schor | geschoren |
| 82 schieben | schiebt | schob | geschoben |
| 83 schinden | schindet | schund | geschunden |
| 84 schlafen | schläft | schlief | geschlafen |
| 85 schlagen | schlägt | schlug | geschlagen |
| 86 schleichen | schleicht | schlich | geschlichen |
| 87 schmelzen | schmilzt | schmolz (schmelzte) | geschmolzen (geschmelzt) |
| 88 schreien | schreit | schrie | geschrie(e)n |
| 89 schweigen | schweigt | schwieg | geschwiegen |
| 90 schwimmen | schwimmt | schwamm | geschwommen |
| 91 schwören | schwört | schwor | geschworen |
| 92 sehen | sieht | sah | gesehen |
| 93 sein | ist | war | gewesen |
| 94 senden | sendet | sandte (*Rad:* sendete) | gesandt (*Rad:* gesendet) |
| 95 sieden | siedet | siedete (sott) | gesiedet (gesotten) |
| 96 sinken | sinkt | sank | gesunken |
| 97 sitzen | sitzt | saß | gesessen |
| 98 sollen | soll | sollte | gesollt |
| 99 stecken | steckt | steckte (stak) | gesteckt |
| 100 stehen | steht | stand | gestanden |
| 101 sterben | stirbt | starb | gestorben |
| 102 stinken | stinkt | stank | gestunken |
| 103 stoßen | stößt | stieß | gestoßen |
| 104 treffen | trifft | traf | getroffen |
| 105 treten | tritt | trat | getreten |
| 106 tun | tut | tat | getan |
| 107 wachsen | wächst | wuchs | gewachsen |
| 108 waschen | wäscht | wusch | gewaschen |
| 109 werden | wird | wurde | geworden |
| 110 werfen | wirft | warf | geworfen |
| 111 wissen | weiß | wußte | gewußt |
| 112 wollen | will | wollte | gewollt |
| 113 ziehen | zieht | zog | gezogen |

# German Pronunciation

The stress is shown by means of a stress mark ['] before the accentuated syllable, e.g. **Zucker** ['tsukər], **unmöglich** [un'møːkliç]. Symbols in brackets show an optional sound which is sometimes included and sometimes omitted. We have also used the ʔ to indicate the glottal stop (a slight pause) in transcribing German words.

## Vowels

| Symbol | Examples | Symbol | Examples |
|---|---|---|---|
| [a] | h*a*t, h*a*rt | [ɔ] | P*o*st, *O*rt |
| [ɑː] | B*a*d, B*a*hn, W*aa*ge | [ɔ̃, ɔ̃ː] | Feuille*ton* |
| | | [o] | M*o*ral, Adv*o*kat |
| [ɑ̃, ɑ̃ː] | Abonn*e*m*en*t | [oː] | B*oo*t, l*o*s |
| [ai] | w*ei*ß | [ɔy] | h*eu*te, H*äu*ser |
| [au] | H*au*s | [œ] | g*ö*ttlich, *ö*ffnen |
| [e] | *e*gal, M*e*than | [œ̃] | Parf*um* |
| [eː] | B*ee*t, W*e*h | [ø] | *Ö*konom |
| [ɛ] | B*e*tt, h*ä*tte | [øː] | *Ö*l, sch*ö*n |
| [ɛː] | w*äh*len, sp*ä*t | [u] | B*u*tter, Sch*u*ß |
| [ɛ̃, ẽː] | Terr*ai*n | [uː] | *U*hr, Gr*u*ß |
| [ə] | B*e*hang, halt*e* | [y] | Gl*ü*ck, Ph*y*sik |
| [i] | W*i*nd, m*i*t | [yː] | R*ü*be, f*üh*ren |
| [iː] | v*ie*l, Br*i*se | | |

## Consonants

| Symbol | Examples | Symbol | Examples |
|---|---|---|---|
| [b] | *b*esser | [n] | *n*ein |
| [ç] | i*ch*, trauri*g* | [ŋ] | la*ng*, de*n*ken |
| [x] | Ba*ch*, Lo*ch* | [p] | *P*akt, her*b*, ob*w*ohl |
| [d] | *d*a | | |
| [dʒ] | *G*in | [r] | *r*ot, ze*rr*en, Vate*r* |
| [f] | Fa*ß*, *V*ieh, *Ph*on | | |
| | | [s] | Gra*s*, Ha*s*t, Gru*ß* |
| [g] | *G*eld | [z] | *S*orge, Ro*s*e |
| [h] | *H*aus | [ʃ] | *Sch*ein, *s*pät, sti*ll* |
| [j] | *j*a | [t] | *T*ag, *Th*ron, Ba*d*, Han*d*, Stad*t* |
| [ʒ] | *G*enie, *J*ournal | | |
| [k] | *k*alt, Sar*g*, Ca*f*é, *Ch*or | [ts] | *Z*ar, Hin*z*, Hi*tz*e, Funk*t*ion, *C*äsar |
| [ks] | E*x*zellenz | | |
| [l] | *L*ast, Nabe*l* | [tʃ] | Ma*tsch* |
| [m] | *M*ohn, *m*ein | [v] | *V*ase, *w*eit, et*w*as |

(xvii)

# A

**A, a** [aː], n -/- (the letter) A, a.

**à** [aː], prep. Com: at.

**Aal** [aːl], m -(e)s/-e eel. ◆'**a~en**, v.refl. F: sich a., to lounge about.

**Aas** [aːs], n -es/Äser 1. no pl carrion. 2. V: (Pers.) sod; kein A., not a soul. ◆'**A~geier**, m vulture.

**ab** [ap]. I. prep. + dat from (... onwards); ab 3 Mark, from 3 marks upwards. II. adv. 1. ab und zu, now and then; von nun ab, from now on. 2. off; ab ins Bett! off to bed with you! F: der Knopf ist ab, the button has come off.

'**ab|ändern**, v.tr.sep. to alter (sth.). ◆'**A~ung**, f alteration.

'**Abart**, f variety. ◆'**a~ig**, adj. abnormal.

'**Abbau**, m 1. dismantling. 2. (Senkung) reduction. 3. Min: mining. ◆'**a~en**, v.tr.sep. (a) to take down (a stall, tent etc.); to dismantle (a machine, building); (b) to reduce (expenditure, staff); (c) to work (a mine); to mine (coal etc.).

'**abbeißen**, v.tr.sep.irr.4 to bite (sth.) off.

'**abbekommen**, v.tr.sep.irr.53 (a) to get; (b) etwas/nichts a., to be damaged/undamaged; (Pers.) to be hurt/unhurt.

'**abberufen**, v.tr.sep.irr.74 to recall.

'**abbestellen**, v.tr.sep. to cancel.

'**abbiegen**, v.i.sep.irr.7 (sein) (Straße) to branch off; (Pers., Auto) to turn off; nach rechts/links a., to turn right/left.

'**Abbild**, n image, likeness (of s.o.); portrayal (of sth.). ◆'**a~en**, v.tr. to depict. ◆'**A~ung**, f illustration.

'**abbinden**, v.tr.sep.irr.9 (a) to untie; (b) Med: to ligature.

'**abblasen**, v.tr.sep.irr.11 F: to call off (a strike etc.).

'**abblättern**, v.i.sep. (sein) to peel (off).

'**abblenden**, v.sep. 1. v.tr. die Scheinwerfer a., to dip /N.Am: dim one's headlights. 2. v.i. (haben) Aut: to dip. ◆'**A~licht**, m dipped headlights.

'**abbrechen**, v.sep.irr.14 1. v.tr. (a) to break off (a piece, relations etc.); (beenden) to stop; (b) to demolish (a house); das Lager a., to strike camp. 2. v.i. (haben) to break off.

'**abbremsen**, v.tr.sep. to reduce (speed).

'**abbrennen**, v.i.sep.irr.15 (sein) to burn down; F: abgebrannt sein, to be broke.

'**abbringen**, v.tr.sep.irr.16 j-n von etwas a., to dissuade s.o. from doing sth.

'**Abbruch**, m -(e)s/=e 1. demolition (of a building). 2. breaking off (of negotiations etc.). ◆'**a~reif**, adj. (Haus) condemned.

'**abdanken**, v.i.sep. (haben) to resign; (Herrscher) to abdicate.

'**abdecken**, v.tr.sep. (a) to clear (a table); (b) (zudecken) to cover.

'**abdichten**, v.tr.sep. to seal; Nau: to caulk.

'**abdrehen**, v.sep. 1. v.tr. to turn off. 2.

v.i. (haben) to turn away.

'**Abdruck**, m 1. -(e)s/-e copy. 2. -(e)s/=e imprint. ◆'**a~en**, v.tr.sep. to print.

'**abdrücken**, v.tr.sep. to fire (a gun); abs. to pull the trigger.

**Abend** ['aːbənt]. I. m -s/-e evening; heute a., this evening, tonight; am A., in the evening; es wird A., it is getting dark; zu A. essen, to have supper. II. A~-, comb.fm. evening (suit, sun, star etc.); ◆'**A~brot**, n -s/no pl supper. ◆'**A~essen**, n dinner. ◆'**a~füllend**, adj. full-length (film, programme). ◆'**A~kasse**, f evening box office. ◆'**A~kurs**, m evening class. ◆'**A~land**, n -(e)s/no pl das A., the West. ◆'**a~lich**, adj. (of) evening. ◆'**A~mahl**, n (Holy) Communion. ◆'**A~rot**, n -s/no pl sunset. ◆'**a~s**, adv. in the evening(s); 6 Uhr a., 6 p.m.

**Abenteuer** ['aːbəntɔyər], n -s/- adventure. ◆'**a~lich**, adj. adventurous. ◆'**Abenteurer**, m -s/- adventurer.

**aber** ['aːbər], conj. but; oder a., or else; das ist a. hübsch, that's really pretty. ◆'**A~glaube**, m superstition. ◆'**a~gläubisch**, adj. superstitious. ◆'**a~mals**, adv. again.

'**aberkennen**, v.tr.sep.irr.51 j-m seine Rechte usw. a., to deprive s.o. of his rights etc.

'**abfahren**, v.sep.irr.26 1. v.i. (sein) to leave. 2. v.tr. (a) (Polizei usw.) to patrol (a road etc.); (b) to wear out (tyres). ◆'**A~t**, f 1. (Fahrtbeginn) departure; Sp: start of a rally etc.). 2. (Talfahrt) downward trip. ◆'**A~ts-**, comb.fm. departure (time etc.); starting (signal etc.).

'**Abfall**. I. m 1. (Abnahme) drop; 2. (Lossagung) defection (from a party etc.). 3. (Müll) usu.pl A~e, rubbish, N.Am: garbage. II. A~-, comb.fm. rubbish (heap etc.); Ind: waste (product etc.). ◆'**A~eimer**, m rubbish bin; N.Am: trash can. ◆'**a~en**, v.i.sep.irr.27 (sein) (a) (herunterfallen) to fall, drop (off); (b) (übrigbleiben) to be left over; (c) (sich neigen) to slope (down); (d) (sich lossagen) to break away; (e) (nachlassen) to decline, (schlechter werden) deteriorate; (Druck, Spannung usw.) to drop.

'**abfällig**, adj. adverse (judgement, criticism); disparaging (remark).

'**abfangen**, v.tr.sep.irr.28 (a) to intercept (a letter etc.); to catch (s.o.); (b) to bring (a car etc.) under control.

'**abfärben**, v.i.sep. (haben) (Farbstoff) to run; Fig: to rub off.

'**abfertig|en**, v.tr.sep. (a) to attend to; F: j-n kurz a., to snub s.o.; (b) to turn round (goods, an aircraft etc.); (Zoll) to clear (goods). ◆'**A~ung**, f -/-en turnround; (Zoll) clearance.

'**abfeuern**, v.tr.sep. to fire.

'**abfind|en**, v.tr.sep.irr.9 (a) to pay off (a

creditor); *Jur:* to compensate (s.o.); (b) **sich mit etwas** *dat* **a.**, to resign oneself to sth. ◆'**A~ung**, *f -/-en* settlement.

'**abflauen**, *v.i.sep.* (*Wind*) to drop; (*Interesse usw.*) to flag.

'**abfliegen**, *v.sep.irr.7* **1.** *v.i.* (*sein*) to fly away; *Av:* to take off. **2.** *v.tr.* to patrol.

'**abfließen**, *v.i.sep.irr.31* (*sein*) to flow away.

'**Abflug**, *m* take-off.

'**Abfluß**, *m -sses/-sse* (*Rohr*) waste pipe; (*Öffnung*) outlet. ◆'**A~rinne**, *f* gully. ◆'**A~rohr**, *n* drainpipe.

'**abfragen**, *v.tr. sep.* to question, *Sch:* test (s.o.).

'**Abfuhr**, *f -/no pl* **1.** collection (of rubbish etc.). **2.** (*Abweisung*) rebuff; **j-m eine A. erteilen**, to snub s.o..

'**abführ|en**, *v.sep.* **1.** *v.tr.* (a) to take (s.o.) away; (b) to pay (off) (taxes, debts etc.). **2.** *v.i.* (*haben*) to act as a laxative. ◆'**A~mittel**, *n* laxative.

'**Abgabe**, *f -/-n* **1.** (a) (*Aushändigung*) handing over; (*Einreichen*) handing in; *Sp:* passing; (b) casting (of vote). **2.** (*Geldleistung*) tax; **soziale A.**, social security contribution. ◆'**a~(n)pflichtig**, *adj.* taxable.

'**Abgang**, *m* (a) departure; leaving (*von Schule*); (b) *Th:* exit.

'**Abgas**, *n* exhaust fumes; *Ind:* waste gas.

'**abgearbeitet**, *adj.* worn out (person); worn (hands).

'**abgeben**, *v.tr.sep.irr.36* (a) (*übergeben*) to hand in/over, deliver (a letter, parcel etc.) *Sp:* to pass (the ball) (**an j-n**, to s.o.); (b) (*verkaufen*) to sell (sth.); (c) to cast (one's vote); (d) to generate (heat etc.); (e) *v.refl.* **sich mit j-m/etwas a.**, to go round with sb/in for sth.

'**abgedroschen**, *adj. F:* hackneyed.

'**abgegriffen**, *adj.* worn (coins); well-thumbed (book).

'**abgehen**, *v.sep.irr.36* **1.** *v.i.* (*sein*) (a) to go away; **von der Schule a.**, to leave school; (b) (*ablaufen*) to go off; (c) (*Knopf*) to come off; (d) (*fehlen*) *F:* **ihm geht jedes Gefühl für Humor ab**, he has absolutely no sense of humour. **2.** *v.tr.* to walk along (sth.).

'**abgekartet**, *adj. F:* **a~es Spiel**, put-up job.

'**abgelegen**, *adj.* remote.

'**abgemacht**, *adj.* agreed, understood; **a.!** done! it's a deal!

'**abgeneigt**, *adj.* **a. sein**, to be averse to sth.

**Abgeordnete(r)** ['apgə²ɔrdnətə(r)], *m & f decl. as adj.* Member of Parliament, *U.S:* representative.

'**abgerissen**, *adj.* ragged.

'**Abgesandte(r)**, *m & f decl. as adj.* envoy.

'**abgeschieden**, *adj. Lit:* secluded (position); remote (spot).

'**abgeschmackt**, *adj.* trite.

'**abgesehen**, *adj.* **a. von**, apart from.

'**abgespannt**, *adj.* tired (out).

'**abgestanden**, *adj.* flat (beer); stale (air).

'**abgestorben**, *adj.* numb (limb); dead (tree, tissue etc.).

'**abgewetzt**, *adj. F:* threadbare.

'**abgewinnen**, *v.tr.sep.irr.3* **j-m etwas a.**, to win sth. from s.o.; **etwas** *dat* **Geschmack a.**, to get a taste for sth.

'**abgewöhnen**, *v.tr. sep.* **j-m etwas a.**, to break s.o. (of the habit) of sth.; **ich habe mir das Rauchen abgewöhnt**, I have given up smoking.

'**abgießen**, *v.tr.sep.irr.31* to strain off (water etc.); to drain (potatoes etc.).

'**Abglanz**, *m* reflection.

'**abgleiten**, *v.i.sep.irr.41* (*sein*) to slip/slide off.

'**Abgott**, *m* idol.

'**abgöttisch**, *adv.* **j-n a. lieben**, to idolize s.o.

'**abgrenz|en**, *v.tr.sep.* (a) to mark off; (b) to define (s.o.'s powers, field of action etc.). ◆'**A~ung**, *f -/-en* (a) demarcation; (b) definition.

'**Abgrund**, *m* (a) abyss; (b) *Fig:* (*Verderben*) ruin.

'**abgucken**, *v.tr.sep.* (a) *F:* **j-m etwas a.**, to learn sth. by watching s.o.; (b) *abs. Sch:* to crib.

'**abhaken**, *v.tr.sep.* to tick off.

'**abhalten**, *v.tr.sep.irr.45* (a) to keep (sth.) away; to keep (the rain etc.) off; **j-n von etwas a.**, to prevent s.o. from doing sth.; (b) **eine Sitzung a.**, to hold a meeting.

'**abhand|eln**, *v.tr.sep.* (a) **j-m etwas** *acc* **a.**, to do a deal with s.o. for sth.; (b) (*behandeln*) to deal with (a subject). ◆'**A~lung**, *f* treatise (**über** + *acc*, on).

**ab'handen**, *adv.* **a. kommen**, to get lost.

'**Abhang**, *m* (downward) slope.

'**abhäng|en**, *v.* **1.** *v.i.sep.irr.46* (*haben*) (a) **von j-m, etwas a.**, to depend on s.o., sth.; (b) *Cu:* to hang (until tender). **2.** *v.tr.* (a) *Rail:* to uncouple; (b) *F:* to get rid of (s.o.). ◆'**a~ig**, *adj.* dependent (**von** + *dat*, on); **von einer Bedingung a.**, subject to one condition. ◆'**A~igkeit**, *f -/-en* dependence (**von** + *dat*, on).

'**abhärt|en**, *v.tr.sep.* to harden (s.o.) (**gegen** + *acc*, to). ◆'**A~ung**, *f* hardening (**gegen** + *acc*, to).

'**abhauen**, *v.sep.irr.47* **1.** *v.tr.* to chop off. **2.** *v.i.* (*sein*) *P:* to clear off.

'**abheb|en**, *v.sep.irr.48* **1.** *v.tr.* (a) to take off; *Tel:* to lift (the receiver); **Geld a.**, to draw money; (b) **sich a.**, to stand out. **2.** *v.i.* (*haben*) (a) *Av:* to take off; (*rocket*) to lift off; (b) to cut (the cards). ◆'**A~ung**, *f* withdrawal.

'**abhelfen**, *v.i.sep.irr.50* (*haben*) **etwas** *dat* **a.**, to remedy sth.

'**abhetzen**, *v.tr.sep.* **sich a.**, to wear oneself out.

'**Abhilfe**, *f -/no pl* remedy; **A. schaffen**, to take remedial action.

**abholen**, *v.tr.sep.* (a) to fetch (sth.); to

collect (letters etc.); (b) to pick (s.o.) up.

'**abholzen,** *v.tr.sep.* to cut down.

**abhören** *v.tr.sep.* to tap (a telephone conversation etc.); *Mil:* to intercept (a message).

**Abitur** [abi'tuːr], *n* -s/-e school-leaving examination. ◆**A~ient(in)** [-turi'ent(in)], *m* -en/-en (*f* -/-nen) school-leaving examination candidate.

'**abkaufen,** *v.tr.sep.* j-m etwas a., to buy sth. from s.o; *F:* das kaufe ich dir nicht ab, I don't believe your story for a moment.

**Abkehr** ['apkeːr], *f* -/no pl estrangement; departure (von einer Politik usw., from a policy etc.). ◆**a~en,** *v.tr.* sich von j-m, etwas a., turn one's back on s.o., sth.

'**abklingen,** *v.i.sep.irr.19* (sein) to die down.

'**abknicken,** *v.tr.&i.sep.* (haben) to snap (off).

'**abknöpfen,** *v.tr.sep. F:* j-m Geld a., to sting s.o. for money.

'**abkochen,** *v.tr.sep.* to boil.

'**abkommen. I.** *v.i.sep.irr.53* (sein) vom Wege a., to lose one's way; vom Thema a., to get off the subject. **II. A.,** *n* -s/- agreement.

'**abkömmlich,** *adj.* dispensable.
◆'**A~ling,** *m* -s/-e descendant.

'**abkoppeln,** *v.tr.sep.* to uncouple (a coach etc.), unhitch (a trailer etc.).

'**abkratzen,** *v.sep.* **1.** *v.tr.* to scrape off. **2.** *v.i.* (sein) *P:* to kick the bucket.

'**abkühlen,** *v.sep.* **1.** *v.tr.* to cool. **2.** *v.refl.&i.* (sein) sich a., to cool down; (Wetter) to turn cool. ◆'**A~ung,** *f* cooling.

**abkürzen,** *v.tr.sep.* (abbrechen) to cut short; den Weg a., to take a short cut. ◆'**A~ung,** *f* -/-en (a) (Weg) short cut; (b) abbreviation (of a word etc.).

'**abladen,** *v.tr.sep.irr.56* to unload.

**Ablage** *f* place to put sth.; (Regal) shelf; **A. machen,** to do the filing.

**ablagern,** *v.sep. v.tr.* to deposit; sich a., to settle, form a deposit. ◆'**A~ung,** *f* -/-el deposit.

'**ablassen,** *v.sep.irr.57* **1.** *v.tr.* to let out (water, air etc.); Dampf a., to let off steam. **2.** *v.i.* (haben) von etwas a., to stop doing sth.

'**Ablauf,** *m* **1.** (Rohr usw.) drain. **2.** (Ende) expiry, *N.Am:* expiration. **3.** (Verlauf) A. der Ereignisse, course of events.
◆'**a~en,** *v.sep.irr.58* **1.** *v.i.* (sein) (a) (abfließen) to run away; an etwas dat a., to run down sth.; (b) (Ereignisse usw.) gut/schlecht a., to go well/badly; (c) (Frist usw.) to expire. **2.** *v.tr.* (a) die Geschäfte a., to scour the shops (nach etwas dat, for sth.); (b) (abnutzen) die Sohlen a., to wear out one's soles.

'**ablegen,** *v.sep.* **1.** *v.tr.* (a) (ausziehen) to take off; (b) (aufgeben) to discard (old clothes, cards etc.); to drop (a name etc.); to give up (a habit etc.); (c) to put

down (a burden, the receiver etc.); (d) to file (documents etc.). **2.** *v.i.* (haben) Nau: to cast off. ◆'**a~er,** *m* -s/- (a) shoot, cutting; (b) Com: offshoot (of a firm).

'**ablehnen,** *v.tr.sep.* to refuse (an invitation etc.); to reject (an offer, argument, organ etc.). ◆'**A~ung,** *f* -/-en refusal, rejection.

'**ableiten,** *v.tr.sep.* (a) to divert (a river, traffic etc.); (b) (herleiten) to derive (a word, a formula etc.) (aus/von + dat, from). ◆'**A~ung,** *f* -/-en **1.** no pl (a) diversion; drainage (of water etc.); (b) derivation. **2.** (Wort) derivative.

'**ablenken,** *v.tr.sep.* (a) to turn away, deflect (sth.); (b) to distract (s.o., s.o.'s attention, thoughts etc.); to divert (suspicion etc.). ◆'**A~ung,** *f* -/-en (a) deflection; (b) distraction, diversion. ◆'**A~ungsmanöver,** *n* -s/- diversion.

'**ablesen,** *v.tr.sep.irr.61* to read.

'**ableugnen,** *v.tr.sep.* to deny.

'**abliefern,** *v.tr.sep.* to deliver (goods, *F:* s.o.); (überreichen) to hand over (sth.). ◆'**A~ung,** *f* -/-en delivery.

'**ablösen,** *v.tr.sep.* (a) to remove (sth.) (b) to relieve (s.o.); (c) *Fin:* to redeem (a mortgage etc.). ◆'**A~ung,** *f* -/-en (a) removal; (b) Mil: relief; (c) Fin: redemption.

'**abmachen,** *v.tr.sep.* (a) (entfernen) to remove (sth.); (b) (vereinbaren) to arrange (sth.); to agree on (a date, price etc.); ◆'**A~ung,** *f* -/-en agreement.

'**abmagern,** *v.i.sep.* (sein) to lose weight. ◆'**A~ungskur,** *f* slimming diet.

'**Abmarsch,** *m* departure. ◆'**a~ieren,** *v.i.sep.* (sein) to march off.

'**abmelden,** *v.tr.sep.* to cancel; sich a., to give notice of one's departure; (vom Hotel) to check out. ◆'**A~ung,** *f* -/-en notification of departure.

'**abmessen,** *v.tr.sep.irr.25* to measure. ◆'**A~ung,** *f* dimensions, measurements.

'**abmontieren,** *v.tr. sep.* to take off (a part); to dismantle (a machine etc.).

'**abmühen,** *v.refl.sep.* sich a., to slave away.

'**Abnäher,** *m* -s/- dart.

**Abnahme** ['apnaːmə], *f* -/no pl **1.** removal. **2.** Com: taking delivery (of goods etc.). **3.** (official) inspection (of a machine etc.). **4.** (Nachlassen) decline, decrease.

'**abnehmen,** *v.sep.irr.69* **1.** *v.tr.* (a) to take down (decorations etc.); to take off (a hat, lid etc.); to lift (the receiver); (b) j-m etwas a., to take sth. from s.o.; *F:* das nehme ich dir nicht ab! I don't believe it! (c) Com: to purchase (goods); (d) (prüfen) to inspect (a machine etc.). **2.** *v.i.* (haben) to decrease; (Fieber) to go down; (Kräfte usw.) to decline; (Pers.) to lose weight; (Mond, Interesse usw.) to wane. ◆'**A~er,** *m* -s/- buyer, purchaser.

'**Abneigung,** *f* aversion, dislike.

**abnorm** [ap'nɔrm], *adj.* abnormal.

**'abnutz|en,** *v.tr.sep.* to wear down, *(völlig)* wear *out* (a part, tyres etc.). ◆**'A~ung,** *f* -/-en wear.

**Abonn|ement** [abɔnə'mã:], *n* -s/-s subscription. ◆**A~ent(in)** [-'nɛnt(in)], *m* -en/-en (f -/-nen) subscriber. ◆**a~ieren** [-'ni:rən], *v.tr.* to take out a subscription to (a periodical etc.).

**Abort** [a'bɔrt], *m* -(e)s/-e lavatory, toilet.

**'abpassen,** *v.tr.sep.* to wait for.

**'abpfeifen,** *v.tr.sep.irr.43 (Schiedsrichter)* to blow his whistle. ◆**'Abpfiff,** *m* final whistle.

**'abprallen,** *v.i.sep. (sein) (Ball usw.)* to bounce; *(Geschoß usw.)* to ricochet.

**'abputzen,** *v.tr.sep.* to wipe off.

**'abquälen,** *v.refl.sep.* **sich mit etwas** *dat* a., to struggle with sth.

**'abraten,** *v.tr.&i.sep.irr.13 (haben)* j-m a., to dissuade s.o.

**'abräumen,** *v.tr.sep.* to clear away.

**'abreagieren,** *v.tr.sep.* to work off.

**'abrechn|en,** *v.sep.* **1.** *v.tr. (abziehen)* to deduct (expenses, VAT etc.); ... **abgerechnet,** not counting ... **2.** *v.i. (haben)* to square accounts; *F:* **mit j-m a.,** to get even with s.o. ◆**'A~ung,** *f (Rechnung)* account; *(Schlußa.)* settlement (of accounts).

**'Abreise,** *f* departure. ◆**'a~n,** *v.i.sep. (sein)* to set out.

**'abreiß|en,** *v.sep.* **1.** *v.tr. (a)* to tear (sth.) off; *(b)* to demolish (a building, bridge etc.). **2.** *v.i. (sein)* to stop abruptly.

**'abrichten,** *v.tr.sep.* to train.

**'abriegeln,** *v.tr.sep.* to block (a road); **eine Gegend a.,** to cordon off an area.

**'Abriß,** *m* **1.** *(Übersicht)* outline. **2.** *(Abbruch)* demolition.

**Abruf,** *m* **auf A.** on call; **Waren auf A.,** goods for delivery as required. ◆**'a~en,** *v.tr.sep.irr.74 (a)* to request delivery of (goods ordered); *(b) Data-pr:* to recall (information).

**'abrunden,** *v.tr.sep.* to round off.

**abrupt** [ap'rupt], *adj.* abrupt.

**'abrüst|en,** *v.i.sep. (haben)* to disarm. ◆**'A~ung,** *f* disarmament.

**'abrutschen,** *v.i.sep. (sein)* to slip (off/down).

**'Absage,** *f* -/-n cancellation; refusal (of an invitation etc.). ◆**'a~n,** *v.sep.* **1.** *v.tr.* to cancel (sth.). **2.** *v.i. (haben)* to cry off.

**'Absatz,** *m* **1.** paragraph. **2.** heel (of a shoe). **3.** *no pl Com:* sales. ◆**'A~gebiet,** *n* market.

**abschaffen,** *v.tr.sep.irr.77* to abolish.

**'abschalten,** *v.tr.&i.sep. (haben)* to switch off.

**'abschätz|en,** *v.tr.sep.* to assess (s.o., property etc.); to estimate (value, weight etc.). ◆**'a~ig,** *adj.* adverse (judgment etc.); derogatory (remarks).

**'Abschaum,** *m Pej:* scum.

**'Abscheu,** *m* -(e)s/*no pl* repugnance, loathing; **j-s A. erregen,** to repel/disgust

s.o. ◆**a~lich** [-'ʃɔʏliç], *adj.* revolting (sight, smell etc.); atrocious (deed).

**'abschicken,** *v.tr.sep.* to send off, *(per Post)* post, *N.Am:* mail (a letter etc.).

**'abschieben,** *v.tr.sep.irr.82 (a)* to push (sth.) away; *(b) Jur:* to deport (s.o.).

**Abschied** ['apʃi:t], *m* -(e)s/-e farewell, parting. ◆**'A~s-,** *comb.fm.* farewell (visit, kiss, scene etc.); parting (gift, kiss, tear etc.).

**'abschießen,** *v.tr.sep.irr.31 (a)* to launch (a rocket etc.); *(b)* to shoot down (an aircraft); to shoot (a bird).

**'abschirmen,** *v.tr.sep.* to shield (s.o., sth.) **(gegen** + *acc,* from).

**'abschlag|en,** *v.tr.sep.irr.85 (a)* to knock (sth.) off; *(b)* to refuse (a request etc.). ◆**'A~szahlung,** *f* first instalment.

**abschlägig** ['apʃlɛ:giç], *adj.* unfavourable.

**'abschleifen,** *v.tr.sep.irr.43* to sand (down).

**Abschlepp-** ['apʃlɛp-], *comb.fm.* breakdown (service etc.). ◆**'a~en,** *v.tr.sep.* to tow away.

**'abschließen,** *v.sep. irr.31 v.tr. (a)* to lock; *(b)* to conclude (an agreement etc.), complete (a book, deal etc.).

**'Abschluß,** *m (a)* extremity; *(Rand)* **unterer/oberer A.,** bottom/top edge; *(b) (Ende)* end, conclusion (of a speech etc.); completion (of a deal etc.). **II. 'A~-,** *comb. fm.* final (examination etc.). ◆**'A~bilanz,** *f* final (annual) balancesheet. ◆**'A~feier,** *f* speech day.

**'abschmecken,** *v.tr.sep.* to season.

**'abschneiden,** *v.sep.irr.41* **1.** *v.tr.* to cut off (sth.). **2.** *v.i. (haben)* **gut/schlecht a.,** to make a good/poor showing.

**'Abschnitt,** *m* **1.** *(a)* section; *Mil:* sector (of a front); *(b) (Stadium)* phase; stage (of a journey). **2.** *(abtrennbarer Teil)* stub (of a ticket etc.); *(Bon)* coupon.

**'abschnüren,** *v.tr.sep.* to cut off.

**'abschöpfen,** *v.tr.sep.* to skim off.

**'abschrauben,** *v.tr.sep.* to unscrew.

**'abschreck|en,** *v.tr.sep. (a)* to deter (s.o.); *(b) Cu:* to rinse (spaghetti etc.). ◆**'a~end,** *adj.* deterrent; **a~endes Beispiel,** warning example. ◆**'A~ung,** *f* -/-en deterrent.

**'abschreib|en,** *v.sep.irr.12* **1.** *v.tr. (a) (Abschrift machen)* to copy; *(b) Fin:* to write off (a loss, debt, *F:* a lost friend etc.). **2.** *v.i. (haben) Sch:* to crib **(bei j-m,** from s.o.). ◆**'A~ung,** *f Fin:* writing off (of debts, losses); *(Wertminderung)* depreciation.

**'Abschrift,** *f* copy, transcript.

**'abschürf|en,** *v.tr.sep.* to graze. ◆**'A~ung,** *f* -/-en graze.

**'Abschuß,** *m* **1.** firing (of a gun); launch (of a rocket). **2.** shooting down (of a bird, aircraft).

**abschüssig** ['apʃʏsiç], *adj.* sloping.

**'abschwächen,** *v.tr.sep.* to lessen (an effect etc.); to tone down (one's remarks).

'**abschweifen**, *v.i.sep.* (*sein*) **vom Thema a.**, to digress.

**abseh|bar** [ˈapzeːbaːr], *adj.* foreseeable. ◆'**a~en**, *v.sep.irr.92* 1. *v.tr.* (*a*) to foresee (sth.); **es ist (noch) kein Ende abzusehen**, there is no end in sight; (*b*) **es auf j-n, etwas** *acc* **abgesehen haben**, to be after s.o., sth. 2. *v.i.* (*haben*) (*a*) **von etwas** *dat* **a.**, to ignore/disregard sth.; **abgesehen von** apart from; (*b*) **von einem Plan/Besuch a.**, to abandon a plan/visit.

**abseits**, I. *adv.* **a. vom Wege**, off the road; *Fig:* **sich a. halten**, to keep in the background. II. *A*, *n* offside.

'**absend|en**, *v.tr.sep.irr.94* to send off, (*per Post*) post, *N.Am:* mail (a letter etc.). ◆'**A~er**, *m* sender.

**absetz|bar** [ˈapzɛtsbaːr], *adj. Fin:* (*von der Steuer*) a., (tax) deductible. ◆'**a~en**, *v.sep.* 1. *v.tr.* (*a*) (*abnehmen*) to take off (a hat etc.); (*hinstellen*) to put down (sth. heavy, one's glass etc.); to drop (passengers); (*b*) (*entfernen*) to remove (an official etc.) from office; to depose (a monarch); (*c*) (*ablagern*) **sich a.**, to settle; *Com:* (*verkaufen*) to sell (goods); (*e*) (*abziehen*) **Spesen usw. (von der Steuer) a.**, to deduct expenses etc. (from tax). 2. *v.i.* (*haben*) to stop. ◆'**A~ung**, *f -/-en* (*Entlassung*) dismissal.

'**absicher|n**, *v.tr.sep.* to make safe; **sich gegen etwas a.**, to guard against sth. ◆'**A~ung**, *f -/-en* safeguard.

'**Absicht**, *f -/-en* intention; **mit A.**, intentionally. ◆**a~lich**, [ˈap-], *adj.* intentional.

'**absitzen**, *v.sep.irr.97* 1. *v.i.* (*sein*) to dismount. 2. *v.tr. F:* **eine Strafe a.**, to serve a sentence.

**absolut** [apzoˈluːt], *adj.* absolute.

**absolvieren** [apzɔlˈviːrən], *v.tr.* to complete (a course etc.); to pass (an examination).

'**absonder|n**, *v.tr.sep.* (*a*) to isolate (s.o., oneself), cut (s.o., oneself) off; (*b*) to secrete (bile, sweat etc.). ◆'**A~ung**, *f -/-en* (*a*) isolation; (*b*) *Biol:* secretion.

**absorbieren** [apzɔrˈbiːrən], *v.tr.sep.* to absorb.

'**abspalten**, *v.tr.sep.* to split off (sth.).

'**abspeisen**, *v.tr.sep. F:* **j-n mit Ausreden usw. a.**, to fob s.o. off with excuses etc.

'**absperr|en**, *v.tr.sep.* (*a*) to lock (a door etc.); (*b*) to cordon off (an area). ◆'**A~ung**, *f -/-en* (road) block; barrier.

'**Abspiel**, *n Sp:* (*a*) pass; (*b*) *no pl* passing. ◆'**a~en**, *v.tr.sep.* (*a*) to play (a record); (*b*) *Sp:* to pass (the ball); (*c*) **sich a.**, to take place; (*Buch usw.*) to be set (somewhere).

'**absplittern**, *v.tr.&i.sep.*(*sein*) to splinter (sth.); to chip off (paint).

'**Absprache**, *f* arrangement.

'**absprechen**, *v.tr.sep.irr.14* (*a*) **man kann ihm das Talent nicht a.**, one cannot deny his talent; (*b*) **sich (mit**

**j-m) a.**, to come to an arrangement (with s.o.).

'**abspringen**, *v.i.sep.irr.19* (*sein*) (*a*) to jump, *Sp:* take off; (*b*) (*Farbe, Lack usw.*) to chip off.

'**Absprung**, *m* jump; *Sp:* take-off.

'**abspülen**, *v.tr.sep.* to rinse (plates etc.); to rinse (sth.) off.

'**abstamm|en**, *v.i.sep.* (*sein*) (*Pers.*) to be descended (*Wort*) to be derived. ◆'**A~ung**, *f -/-en* descent, ancestry; derivation.

'**Abstand**, *m* distance, gap; **in gleichen A~en**, at equal intervals; **er ist mit A. der Beste**, he is far and away the best; **von etwas** *dat* **A. nehmen**, to abandon sth.

'**abstatten**, *v.tr.sep.* **j-m einen Besuch a.**, to pay s.o. a visit.

'**abstauben**, *v.tr.sep.* (*a*) to dust (furniture etc.); (*b*) *F:* (*entwenden*) to swipe, pinch (sth.).

'**Abstecher**, *m -s/-* **einen A. machen**, to make a detour.

'**abstehen**, *v.i.sep.irr.100* (*haben*) to stick out.

'**absteigen**, *v.i.sep.irr.89* (*sein*) (*a*) to descend; **in einem Hotel a.**, to put up at a hotel; (*b*) *Sp:* to be relegated.

'**abstell|en**, *v.tr.sep.* (*a*) to put away, store (furniture etc.); to park (a car, cycle etc.); (*b*) (*abschalten*) to stop (a clock, machine etc.); to turn off (gas, water, heating etc.); to switch off (a radio, an engine etc.); (*c*) (*niedersetzen*) to put/set down (a burden). ◆'**A~gleis**, *n* siding. ◆'**A~raum**, *m* store room.

'**abstempeln**, *v.tr.sep.* to stamp.

'**absterben**, *v.i.sep.irr.101* (*sein*) (*Pflanze*) to die (off), wither.

'**Abstieg** [ˈapʃtiːk], *m -(e)s/-e* descent; *Fig:* decline; *Sp:* relegation.

'**abstimm|en**, *v.sep.* 1. *v.tr.* (*a*) to tune (in) (the radio, a circuit etc.) (**auf +** *acc*, to); (*b*) to adjust (sth.) (**auf** *acc*, to suit sth.); **Pläne usw. aufeinander a.**, to co-ordinate/bring into line plans etc. 2. *v.i.* (*haben*) to vote. ◆'**A~ung**, *f* 1. *Rad: TV:* tuning. 2. vote, voting.

**abstinen|t** [apstiˈnɛnt], *adj.* abstemious; (*vom Alkohol*) teetotal. ◆**A~z**, *f /no pl* teetotalism. ◆**A~zler**, *m -s/-* teetotal(l)er.

'**Abstoß**, *m* push (off); *Sp:* goal kick. ◆'**a~en**, *v.tr.sep.irr.103* (*a*) (*mit Stoß bewegen*) to push (s.o., sth.) away/off; *Fig:* **seine Art stößt mich ab**, I find his manner repellent; (*b*) *Com:* **Waren a.**, to sell off goods. ◆'**a~end**, *adj.* repellent.

**abstrakt** [apˈstrakt], *adj.* abstract. ◆**A~ion** [-tsiˈoːn], *f -/-en* abstraction.

'**abstreiten**, *v.tr.sep.* to deny.

'**Abstrich**, *m -(e)s/-e* 1. *Med:* smear. 2. (*Abzug*) deduction, cut.

'**abstufen**, *v.tr.sep.* (*a*) to terrace (land); (*b*) to grade (colours, salaries etc.).

'**Absturz**, *m* plunge; *Av:* crash.

'**abstürzen**, *v.i.sep.* (*sein*) to plunge (down); (*Flugzeug*) to crash.

'**absuchen**, *v.tr.sep.* to search, scour (a district etc.), scan (the horizon).

**absurd** [ap'zurt], *adj.* absurd.

**Abszeß** [aps'tsɛs], *m* -sses/-sse abscess.

**Abt** [apt], *m.* -(e)s/-e abbot.

'**abtasten**, *v.tr.sep.* (*a*) to feel (s.o., sth.) all over; (*Polizei*) to frisk (s.o.); (*b*) *TV:* to scan (an image etc.).

'**abtauen**, *v.tr.sep.* to melt (ice); to defrost (the refrigerator).

**Abtei** [ap'tai], *f* -/-en abbey.

**Ab'teil**, *n* compartment. ◆'**a~en**, *v.tr.sep.* to divide up (a room); to partition off (part of a room). ◆**A~ung**, *f* [ap'tailuŋ] department; *Mil:* detachment. ◆**A~ungsleiter**, *m* head of department/division.

'**abtrag|en**, *v.tr.sep.irr.42* (*a*) to pull down (a building etc.); (*b*) **eine Schuld a.**, to pay a debt; (*c*) to wear out (clothes etc.). **abträglich** ['aptrɛːkliç], *adj.* harmful.

'**abtransportieren**, *v.tr.sep.* to remove.

'**abtreib|en**, *v.sep.irr.12* **1.** *v.tr.* (*a*) to drive (a ship etc.) off course; (*b*) **ein Kind a.**, to procure an abortion. **2.** *v.i.* (*sein*) (*Schiff*) to drift. ◆**A~ung**, *f* -/ -en abortion.

'**abtrenn|en**, *v.tr.sep.* to detach (a counterfoil etc.), to cut off (a button etc.); to divide off (part of a room).

'**abtreten**, *v.sep.irr.105* **1.** *v.tr.* (*a*) (*abnutzen*) to wear out (a step, carpet etc.), wear down (heels); (*b*) (*überlassen*) to relinquish (a right). **2.** *v.i.* (*sein*) (*a*) (*Pers.*) to withdraw; *Mil:* **a.!** dismiss! (*b*) (*Regierung usw.*) to resign.

'**Abtritt**, *m* withdrawal.

'**abtrocknen**, *v.tr.&i.sep.* (*haben*) to dry.

**abtrünnig** ['aptrʏniç], *adj.* renegade.

'**abtun**, *v.tr.sep.irr.106* (*übergehen*) to dismiss (s.o., s.o.'s objections etc.).

'**abverlangen**, *v.tr.sep.* **j-m etwas a.**, to demand sth. from s.o.

'**abwandeln**, *v.tr.sep.* to modify.

'**abwander|n**, *v.i.sep.* (*sein*) to migrate. ◆**A~ung**, *f* migration.

'**abwarten**, *v.tr.sep.* (*haben*) to await, wait for (sth.); **warte ab**, wait and see.

**abwärts** ['apvɛrts], *adv.* down, downwards.

**Abwasch** ['apvaʃ], *m* -es/*no pl F:* washing up. ◆'**a~en**, *v.tr.&i.sep.irr.108* (**das Geschirr**) **a.**, to wash up.

'**Abwasser**, *n* -s/- sewage; *Ind:* effluent.

'**abwechs|eln**, *v.tr.&i.* (*haben*) *sep.* to alternate (two things); (*Pers.*) to take turns (**mit j-m**, with s.o.). ◆'**a~elnd**, *adj.* alternate, alternating. ◆'**A~lung**, *f* -/-en (*a*) alternation; (*b*) variety; **zur A.**, for a change.

'**Abweg**, *m* **auf A~e geraten**, to go astray. ◆'**a~ig**, *adj.* out of the way; obscure (idea etc.); (*verfehlt*) off the point.

'**Abwehr. I.** *f* -/*no pl* (*a*) (*Widerstand*) A. **gegen etwas** *acc*, resistance to sth.; (*b*) *Mil: Sp:* defence. **II.** '**A~-**, *comb.fm.* defensive (measure etc.). ◆'**a~en**, *v.tr.sep.* to ward off (danger, an attack etc.). ◆'**A~spieler**, *m* defender.

'**abweich|en**, *v.i.sep.irr.40* (*sein*) (*verschieden sein*) to differ (**von** + *dat*, from); (*abgehen*) **vom Kurs a.**, to go off course. ◆'**a~end**, *adj.* deviating; divergent (opinion etc.). ◆'**A~ung**, *f* -/-en deviation.

'**abweis|en**, *v.tr.sep.irr.70* (*a*) (*fortschicken*) to turn (s.o.) away; (*b*) (*ablehnen*) to reject, turn down (a candidate, request etc.). ◆'**a~end**, *adj.* a~ende Geste, dismissive gesture.

'**abwenden**, *v.tr.sep.irr.94* (*a*) to turn away (one's eyes, face etc.); **sich a.**, to turn away/aside; (*b*) to ward off (danger); to avert (a disaster etc.).

'**abwerfen**, *v.tr.sep.irr.110* to throw off; to shed (leaves, skin); to drop (bombs, pamphlets etc.).

'**abwert|en**, *v.tr.sep.* to devalue. ◆'**a~end**, *adj.* pejorative.

'**abwesen|d**, *adj.* **1.** absent. **2.** (*zerstreut*) absent-minded. ◆'**A~de(r)**, *m&f decl. as adj.* absentee. ◆'**A~heit**, *f* -/*no pl* absence.

'**abwickeln**, *v.tr.sep.* (*a*) (*abrollen*) to unwind; (*b*) (*erledigen*) to settle (a matter); to organize (an event).

'**abwiegen**, *v.tr.sep.irr.7* to weigh out.

'**Abwurf**, *m* throwing; dropping (of bombs etc.).

'**abzahl|en**, *v.tr.sep.* to pay off. ◆'**A~ung**, *f* instalment.

'**abzählen**, *v.tr.sep.* to count (sth.).

'**Abzeichen**, *n* badge; *Mil: etc:* insignia.

'**abzeichnen**, *v.tr.sep.* (*a*) to draw, sketch (sth.); to copy (a picture etc.); (*b*) **sich gegen etwas** *acc* **a.**, to stand out against sth.

**Abzieh|bild** ['aptsiːbilt], *n* transfer. ◆'**a~en**, *v.sep.irr.113* **1.** *v.tr.* (*a*) to take off (a ring); (*b*) to skin (an animal, a tomato etc.); to strip (a bed, paint etc.); (*c*) to print (a film, negative); (*d*) to deduct (an amount), subtract (a number); (*e*) to withdraw (troops). **2.** *v.i.* (*sein*) (*Nebel, Rauch usw.*) to clear; (*Gewitter*) to pass; (*Truppen*) to withdraw; *F:* (*Pers.*) to go away.

'**abzielen**, *v.i.sep.* (*haben*) **auf etwas** *acc* **a.**, to aim at sth.

'**Abzug**, *m* **1.** deduction; *Com:* (*Rabatt*) discount. **2.** *Phot:* print. **3.** (*Raucha.*) flue. **4.** *Mil:* withdrawal. **5.** trigger (of a gun).

**abzüglich** ['aptsyːkliç], *prep.* + *gen* less.

'**abzweig|en**, *v.tr.&i.sep.* (*sein*) (*a*) (*Straße usw.*) to branch off; (*Auto*) turn off; (*b*) *Com: etc:* to divert (capital). ◆'**A~ung**, *f* -/-en turning (in road); (*Gabelung*) fork.

**ach** [ax], *int.* oh! ah! *F:* **mit A. und Krach**, by the skin of one's teeth.

**Achse** ['aksə], *f* -/-**n 1.** *Aut: etc:* axle. **2.**

*(Mittellinie)* axis.
**Achsel** ['aksəl], *f* -/-n shoulder.
◆'A~**höhle**, *f* armpit. ◆'A~**zucken**, *n* -s/*no pl* shrug.
**acht¹** [axt], *num. adj.* eight; (heute) in a. Tagen, a week today. ◆**a~e(r,s)**, *num. adj.* eighth. ◆'a~**el**, *inv.adj.* eighth (part) of ... ◆'A~**erbahn**, *f* roller coaster. ◆'a~**zehn** *num. adj.* eighteen. ◆'a~**zig**, *num. adj.* eighty. ◆**a~ziger.** I. *inv. adj.* die a. Jahre, the eighties. II. A., *m* -s/- octogenarian. ◆'a~**zigste(r,s)**, *num. adj.* eightieth.
**'acht²**, *in the vbl. phr.* **sich in a. nehmen**, to be careful; **etwas außer a. lassen**, to disregard sth. ◆**a~en**, *v.* 1. *v.tr.* (a) *(respektieren)* to respect (s.o., s.o.'s rights, age); to observe (the law). 2. *v.i.* (haben) **auf etwas acc. a.**, to pay attention to sth. ◆'a~**geben**, *v.i.sep.irr.35* (haben) *(aufpassen)* to pay attention (**auf etwas acc**, to sth.); *(sorgen für)* **auf j-n, etwas acc a.**, to keep an eye on s.o., sth.; **gib acht!** take care! ◆'a~**los**, *adj.* careless, heedless. ◆'a~**sam**, *adj.* heedful (**auf + acc**, of); careful. ◆'a~**ung**, *f -/no pl* 1. *(Aufmerksamkeit)* attention; **A.!** look out! 2. *(Wertschätzung)* respect.
**ächten** ['ɛçtən], *v.tr.* to ostracize (s.o.).
**ächzen** ['ɛçtsən], *v.i.* (haben) *(Pers.)* to moan, groan; *(Dielen usw.)* to creak.
**Acker** ['akər], *m* -s/- field. ◆'A~**bau**, *m* arable farming. ◆'a~**n**, *v.* 1. *v.tr.* to farm (land). 2. *v.i.* (haben) *F:* to slave away.
**Adamsapfel** ['a:dams'apfəl], Adam's apple.
**add|ieren** [a'di:rən], *v.tr.* to add up. ◆A~**ition** [-itsi'o:n], *f -/-en* addition.
**Ad|el** ['a:dəl], *m* -s/*no pl (Klasse)* nobility. ◆'a~**(e)lig**, *adj.* noble (family, descent); titled (person).
**Ader** ['a:dər], *f -/-n* vein; **j-n zur A. lassen**, *A: Med:* to bleed s.o.; *F:* to get money out of s.o.
**Adjektiv** ['atjekti:f], *n* -s/-e adjective.
**Adler** ['a:dlər], *m* -s/- eagle.
**Admiral** [atmi'ra:l], *m* -s/-e admiral.
**adopt|ieren** [adɔp'ti:rən], *v.tr.* to adopt. ◆A~**ion** [-tsi'o:n], *f -/-en* adoption. ◆A~**iv-** [-'ti:f], *comb.fm.* adopted (child); adoptive (parents).
**Adreßbuch** ['a:drɛsbu:x], *n* directory.
**Adress|e** [a'drɛsə], *f -/-n* address; *F:* **an die falsche A. geraten**, to get the wrong person. ◆**a~ieren** [-'si:rən], *v.tr.* to address (**an + acc**, to).
**adrett** [a'drɛt], *adj.* smart.
**Adria** ['a:dria:]. *Pr.n.f* -. **die A.**, the Adriatic.
**Advent** [at'vɛnt], *m* -(e)s/*no pl* Advent. ◆A~**skranz**, *m* advent wreath.
**Adverb** [at'vɛrp], *n* -s/-ien adverb.
**Affäre** [a'fɛ:rə], *f -/-n* affair; *F:* **sich aus der A. ziehen**, to get out of it.
**Aff|e** ['afə], *m* -n/-n 1. *Z:* monkey; *(Menschena.)* ape. ◆'A~**enhitze**, *f -/no*

*pl F:* scorching heat. ◆'a~**ig**, *adj. F:* stuck-up.
**Affekt** [a'fɛkt], *m* -(e)s/-e strong emotion; **im A. begangen**, done in the heat of the moment. ◆**a~iert** [-'ti:rt], *adj.* affected.
**Afrika** ['afrika:]. *Pr.n.n* -s. Africa. ◆A~**ner(in)**, *m* -s/- *(f -/-nen)* African. ◆**a~nisch**, *adj.* African.
**After** ['aftər], *m* -s/- anus.
**Agäis** [ɛ'gɛ:is]. *Pr.n.f* -. **die Ä.**, the Aegean.
**Agent|(in)** [a'gent(in)], *m* -en/-en *(f -/ -nen)* agent. ◆A~**ur** [-'tu:r], *f -/-en* agency.
**Aggregat** [agre'ga:t], *n* -(e)s/-e 1. aggregate. 2. *El:* system.
**Aggress|ion** [agrɛsi'o:n], *f -/-en* aggression. ◆**a~iv** [-'si:f], *adj.* aggressive.
**agil** [a'gi:l], *adj.* agile.
**Agit|ation** [agitatsi'o:n], *f -/-en* agitation. ◆A~**ator** [-'ta:tor], *m* -s/-en agitator.
**Agrar-** [a'gra:r], *comb.fm.* agricultural (product, imports, policy etc.). ◆A~**reform**, *f* land reform. ◆A~**wirtschaft**, *f* farming industry.
**Ägypt|en** [ɛ'gyptən]. *Pr.n.n* -s. Egypt. ◆A~**er(in)**, *m* -s/- *(f -/-nen)* Egyptian. ◆**ä~isch**, *adj.* Egyptian.
**aha** [a'ha:], *int.* (oh) I see!
**Ahn** [a:n], *m* -en/-en *Lit:* ancestor.
**ähneln** ['ɛ:nəln], *v.i.* (haben) **j-m, etwas dat ä.**, to resemble s.o., sth.
**ahn|en** ['a:nən], *v.tr. (Vorgefühl haben)* to have a foreboding of (sth.); to suspect (the truth etc.); **ich habe es geahnt**, I saw it coming. ◆'A~**ung**, *f -/-en* 1. foreboding; **ich habe so eine A., als ob ...**, I have a feeling that ... 2. *(Vermutung)* idea; **hast du eine A.!** fat lot you know about it! ◆'a~**ungslos**, *adj.* unsuspecting.
**ähnlich** ['ɛ:nliç], *adj.* similar; *F:* **das sieht dir ä.!** that's just like you! ◆'A~**keit**, *f -/-en* similarity; *(im Aussehen)* resemblance.
**Ahorn** ['a:hɔrn], *m* -s/-e maple.
**Ähre** ['ɛ:rə], *f -/-n* ear.
**Akadem|ie** [akade'mi:], *f -/-n* academy. ◆A~**ker(in)** [-'de:mikər], *m* -s/- *(f -/ -nen)* university graduate. ◆**a~isch** [-'de:miʃ], *adj.* academic (career etc.); university (education etc.).
**akklimatisieren** [aklimati'zi:rən], *v.refl.* **sich a.**, to become acclimatized.
**Akkord** [a'kɔrt], *m* -(e)s/-e 1. *Mus:* chord. 2. *Ind:* **im A. arbeiten**, to do piecework.
**Akkordeon** [a'kɔrdeɔn], *n* -s/-s accordion.
**Akkusativ** ['akuzati:f], *m* -s/-e accusative (case).
**Akne** ['aknə], *f -/-n* acne.
**Akrobat|(in)** [akro'ba:t(in)], *m* -en/-en *(f -/-nen)* acrobat. ◆**a~isch**, *adj.* acrobatic.

**Akt** [akt]. *m* -(e)s/-e 1. 2. *Art:* nude.

**Akte** ['aktə], *f* -/-n file; *pl* **A~n**, records, files; **etwas zu den A~n legen**, (i) to file sth.; (ii) *F:* to shelve sth. ◆**'A~nschrank**, *m* filing cabinet. ◆**'A~ntasche**, *f* briefcase. ◆**'A~nzeichen**, *n* reference.

**Aktie** ['aktsiə], *f* -/-n share. ◆**'A~n-**, *comb.fm.* share, *N.Am:* stock (index, capital, price etc.); stock (market etc.). ◆**'A~ngesellschaft**, *f* joint-stock company.

**Aktion** [aktsi'o:n], *f* -/-en 1. action; **in A. treten**, to come into action. 2. campaign; *Com:* (sales) drive. ◆**A~är(in)** [-'nɛ:r(in)], *m* -s/-e (*f* -/-nen) shareholder, *N.Am:* stockholder.

**aktiv** [ak'ti:f]. I. *adj.* active; **a~er Soldat**, regular (soldier). II. **A.**, *n* -s/-e active voice. ◆**a~ieren** [-ti'vi:rən], *v.tr.* to get (business etc.) going; to get (people) moving; *Med:* to stimulate (activity). ◆**A~ierung**, *f* -/-en activation, stimulation. ◆**A~ität** [-vi'te:t], *f* -/-en activity. ◆**A~saldo**, *m* credit balance.

**Aktualität** [aktuali'te:t], *f* -/-en topicality. ◆**a~ell** [-'ɛl], *adj.* topical; current (fashion, style etc.); **a~eller Bericht**, up-to-date report.

**Akupunktur** [akupuŋk'tu:r], *f* -/-en acupuncture.

**Akustik** [a'kustik], *f* -/no *pl* acoustics. ◆**a~isch**, *adj.* acoustic.

**akut** [a'ku:t] *adj.* acute.

**Akzent** [ak'tsɛnt], *m* -(e)s/-e accent; *Fig:* stress.

**akzeptabel** [aktsɛp'ta:bəl], *adj.* acceptable. ◆**a~ieren** [-'ti:rən], *v.tr.* to accept (sth.).

**Alarm** [a'larm]. I. *m* -(e)s/-e alarm; *Mil:* alert. II. **A~-**, *comb.fm.* warning (system, device etc.). ◆**a~bereit**, *adj.* on the alert. ◆**A~bereitschaft**, *f* standby. ◆**a~ieren** [-'mi:rən], *v.tr.* (a) (*Alarm geben*) to alert (troops, police etc.); (b) (*aufschrecken*) to alarm (s.o.).

**Allee** [a'le:], *f* -/-n avenue.

**Albanien** [al'ba:niən]. *Pr.n.n* -s. Albania. ◆**A~ier(in)**, *m* -s/- (*f* -/-nen) Albanian. ◆**a~isch**, *adj.* Albanian.

**albern** ['albərn], *adj.* silly (behaviour, person etc.); fatuous (remark). ◆**A~heit**, *f* -/-en silliness.

**Album** ['album], *n* -s/-ben album.

**Algen** ['algən], *fpl* seaweed.

**Algebra** ['algebra], *f* -/no *pl* algebra.

**Algerien** [al'ge:riən]. *Pr.n.n* -s. Algeria. ◆**A~ier(in)**, *m* -s/- (*f* -/-nen) Algerian. ◆**a~isch**, *adj.* Algerian.

**Alibi** ['a:libi], *n* -s/-s alibi.

**Alimente** [ali'mɛntə], *npl* alimony.

**Alkohol** ['alkoho:l], *m* -s/-e alcohol. ◆**a~frei**, *adj.* non-alcoholic, soft (drinks). ◆**A~iker(in)** [-'ho:likər(in)], *m* -s/- (*f* -/-nen) alcoholic. ◆**a~isch** [-'ho:liʃ], *adj.* alcoholic.

**all** [al]. I. *indef. pron.* 1. *sing.* **a~es**, everything; **das ist a~es**, that is all; **a~es in allem**, all in all; **vor a~em**, above all; **bei/trotz a~em**, in spite of everything; **sie war sein ein und a~es**, she was everything to him. 2. *pl* **a~e**, all; (*Pers.*) everybody; **a~e beide**, both (of them). II. *adj.* all; **in a~er Frühe**, bright and early; **a~e Menschen**, all men; **a~e zwei Tage**, every other day. III. *adv.* or *pred. adj. F:* **der Zucker ist a~e**, there is no sugar left. IV. A., *n* -s/ *no pl* **das A.**, the universe. ◆**'a~e'dem**, *indef. pron.* **trotz a.**, in spite of all (that). ◆**'a~e'mal**, *adv.* (a) **ein für a.**, once and for all; (b) *F:* whatever happens. ◆**'a~en'falls**, *adv.* if the worst comes to the worst. ◆**'a~er-**, *comb.fm.* + *superl.* (best, highest, most, most beautiful etc.) at all; very (best, highest etc.). ◆**'a~er'dings**, *adv.* (a) (*bejahend*) certainly; (b) (*einschränkend*) **sie ist ja a. keine Schönheit**, admittedly she is no beauty. ◆**'a~er'hand**, *inv. adj.* of all sorts/kinds; *F:* **das ist ja a.!** that's the limit! ◆**'A~er'heiligen**, *n* -/ *no pl* All Saints' Day. ◆**'a~er'lei**, *inv. adj.* all sorts/kinds of. ◆**'a~er'letzte(r,s)**, *adj.* ◆**'a~er'seits**, *adv.* (a) on all sides; (b) *F:* **guten Morgen a.!** good morning everybody! ◆**'a~'jährlich**, *adj.* annual; *adv.* annually, every year. ◆**'A~tag**, *m* working day; **der A.**, everyday life. ◆**'a~'täglich**, *adj.* (a) (*täglich*) everyday (event etc.); daily (walk etc.); (b) (*durchschnittlich*) ordinary (person, face etc.); mundane (occupation). ◆**'a~tags**, *adv.* on working days/weekdays. ◆**A~tags-**, *comb.fm.* everyday (life, language etc.). ◆**'a~'wissend**, *adj.* omniscient. ◆**'a~'zu-**, *adv. comb.fm.* all too, only too (quickly etc.); far too (long, much etc.); **nicht a~zuviel**, not all that much. ◆**'A~zweck-**, *comb.fm.* all-purpose (tool etc.).

**allein** [a'lain]. I. *adj.& adv.* alone; **sich von a~e schließen**, to shut automatically; **Gedanke ist schrecklich**, the mere thought is terrible. II. **A~-**, *comb.fm.* (*einzig*) sole (proprietor, heir, agency etc.); (*ausschließlich*) exclusive (right, possession etc.). ◆**A~gang**, *m* single-handed effort; **im A.**, on one's own. ◆**A~herrscher**, *m* autocrat. ◆**a~stehend**, *adj.* (a) (*Pers.*) single.

**aller-** *see* all.

**Allergie** [alɛr'gi:], *f* -/-n allergy. ◆**a~isch** [a'lɛrgiʃ], *adj.* allergic.

**alles** *see* all.

**allgemein** [algə'main], *adj.* general; **im a~en**, in general, generally. ◆**A~bildung**, *f* general education; (*A~wissen*) general knowledge. ◆**a~gültig**, *adj.* universal. ◆**A~heit**, *f* -/no *pl* 1. **die A.**, the general public. 2. generality. ◆**a~verständlich**, *adj.*

popular.
**Alli|anz** [ali'ants], f -/-en alliance.
◆a~'iert, adj. allied; **die A~ierten,**
the allies.
**allmählich** [al'mɛ:liç], adj. gradual.
**Alm** [alm], f -/-en alpine meadow.
**Almosen** ['almo:zən], n -s/- alms; F: &
N.Am: hand-out.
**Alp|en** ['alpən]. **I.** Pr.n.pl **die A.,** the
Alps. **II.** '**A~-,** comb.fm. alpine (pass,
plant etc.); ◆**A~enveilchen,** n cycla-
men.
**Alphabet** [alfa'be:t], n -(e)s/-e alphabet.
◆a~isch, adj. alphabetical.
**Alptraum** ['alptraum], m nightmare.
**als** [als], conj. **1.** (a) (zeitlich) when; (b)
(nach Komparativen) than; **ich bin älter
a. er,** I am older than he is; (c) (außer)
but, except; **nichts a.,** nothing but; (d)
(in der Eigenschaft) as; **er kam a. letzter/
erster,** he was the last/first to come. **a.
ob,** as if.
**also** ['alzo], conj. & adv. therefore, so; **da
bist du a.!** so there you are! **a. doch!** so
I was right (after all)! **na a.!** what did I
tell you! **a., ich glaube ...,** well, I think
...
**alt1** [alt], adj. old; **er ist immer noch der
a~e,** he hasn't changed at all; **wir lassen
alles beim a~en,** we are leaving things
just as they are. ◆'**A~bau,** m old
building. ◆**a~be'kannt,** adj. (old and)
familiar. ◆'**a~be'währt,** adj. proven
(remedy, methods); long-standing
(friendship etc.). ◆'**A~eisen,** n scrap
iron. ◆'**a~hergebracht,** adj. traditional. ◆'**a~klug,** adj. precocious
(child). ◆'**a~modisch,** adj. old-
fashioned. ◆'**A~papier,** n waste paper.
◆'**a~sprachlich,** adj. classical (studies). ◆'**A~stadt,** f old (part of a) town.
◆**A~'weibersommer,** m Indian summer.
'**Alt2,** m -s/-e Mus: alto; (weiblich) contralto; ◆'**A~stimme,** f alto/(weiblich) contralto voice.
**Altar** [al'ta:r], m -(e)s/=e altar.
**Alter** [altər], n -s/- age; (a) **im A. von 20,**
at the age of 20; (b) (hohes) **A.,** old age.
◆'**a~n,** v.i. (sein/haben) to age.
◆**A~s-,** comb.fm. (a) age (group etc.);
(b) (of) old age; (care etc.) of old people/
the aged; Med: geriatric (complaints,
medicine etc.). ◆**A~sgrenze,** f age
limit. ◆'**a~sheim,** n old people's
home. ◆'**A~sunterschied,** m difference in age. ◆'**A~tum,** n -s/=er an-
tiquity. ◆'**a~tümlich,** adj. ancient;
(altmodisch) antiquated (dress etc.);
old-world (town etc.).
**ält|er** ['ɛltər], adj. (a) older; elder (son,
brother etc.); **ä. werden,** to grow old; (b)
(ältlich) **ein ä~er Herr,** an elderly gentleman. ◆'**ä~este(r,s),** adj. oldest; eldest (son, brother etc.).
**altern|ativ** [alterna'ti:f], adj. alternative.
◆**A~ative** [-'ti:və], f -/-n alternative.

**Alu|folie** ['a:lufo:liə], f baking foil.
◆**A~minium** [alu'mi:nium], n -s/no pl
aluminium, N.Am: aluminum.
**am** [am], prep. **1.** = **an dem. 2. am deut-
lichsten,** most clearly.
**Amateur** [ama'tø:r], m -s/- amateur.
**Amazonas** [ama'tso:nas]. Pr.n.m -. the
(river) Amazon.
**Amboß** ['ambɔs], m -sses/-sse anvil.
**ambulan|t** [ambu'lant], adj. **j-n a. behan-
deln,** to treat s.o. as an outpatient.
◆**A~z,** f -/-en Med: outpatients' depart-
ment; (b) Aut: ambulance.
**Ameise** ['a:maizə], f -/-n ant.
◆'**A~nsäure,** f formic acid.
**amen** ['a:mən], int. & **A.,** n -s/- amen.
**Amerika** [a'me:rika]. Pr.n.n -s. America.
◆**A~ner** [-'ka:nər], m -s/- American.
◆**A~nerin,** f -/-nen American girl/
woman. ◆**a~nisch,** adj. American.
**Amnestie** [amnɛs'ti:], f -/-n amnesty.
**Ampel** ['ampəl], f -/-n traffic light(s).
**Amput|ation** [amputatsi'o:n], f -/-en am-
putation. ◆**a~ieren** ['ti:rən], v.tr. to
amputate.
**Amsel** ['amzəl], f -/-n blackbird.
**Amt** [amt], n -(e)s/=er **1.** office; **ein A. bekleiden,** to hold an office/a position; **2.**
(a) (Behörde) (government) office/
department; section (of a ministry); (b)
(Gebäude, Raum) (post/tax etc.) office;
Tel: exchange, N.Am: central.
◆**a~ieren** [-'ti:rən], v.i. (haben) to be
in/hold office. ◆'**a~lich,** adj. official.
◆'**A~s-,** comb.fm. official (language, secret etc.); (holder, term, robes, oath etc.)
of office. ◆'**A~sgericht,** n district
court. ◆'**A~srichter,** m district court
judge. ◆'**A~sweg,** m **auf dem A.,**
through official channels.
**Amulett** [amu'lɛt], n -(e)s/-e charm.
**amüs|ant** [amy'zant], adj. amusing.
◆**a~ieren** [-'zi:rən], v.tr. to amuse
(s.o., oneself); **sich über j-n, etwas** acc
**a.,** to be amused at s.o./sth.
**an** [an]. **I.** prep. **1.** + dat (a) (räumlich) at,
on; (neben) by; (b) **an sich,** in itself; as
such; **an und für sich,** strictly speaking;
(c) (zeitlich) on; **am Montag,** on Monday;
**am Tage,** in the daytime. **2.** + acc (a)
(Bemerkung usw.) (directed) to (s.o.); (intended) for (s.o.); (b) **etwas an etwas** acc
**binden/heften/nageln,** to tie/pin/nail sth.
(on)to sth.; (c) (Richtung) at; (gegen) (up)
against. **II.** adv. **1.** **von Köln an,** from
Cologne on(wards); **von heute an,** (as)
from today. **2.** F: **das Licht/Gas/
Radio ist an,** the light/gas/radio is on; (b)
**mit dem Mantel an,** with his/her coat
on.
**analog** [ana'lo:k], adj. analogous
(**zu** + dat, to). ◆**A~ie** [-lo'gi:], f -/-n
analogy.
**Analphabet** [analfa'be:t], m -en/-en illit-
erate.
**Analy|se** [ana'ly:zə], f -/-n analysis.
◆**a~'sieren,** v.tr. to analyse.

**Ananas** ['ananas], *f -/- & -se* pineapple.

**Anarch|ie** [anar'çiː], *f -/-n* anarchy. ◆**A~ist(in)** [-'çist(in)], *m -en/-en (f -/-nen)* anarchist. ◆**a~istisch**, *adj.* anarchic.

**Anatom|ie** [anato'miː], *f -/-n* anatomy. ◆**a~isch** [-'toːmiʃ], *adj.* anatomical.

'**anbahnen**, *v.tr.sep.* to pave the way for (negotiations etc.); *(Sache)* **sich a.**, to be in the offing.

'**Anbau**, *m* 1. *no pl Agr:* cultivation (of wheat etc.). 2. *(Bau)* extension, annexe. ◆'**a~en**, *v.tr.sep.* (a) to grow (plants); (b) to build on (further rooms etc.).

**an'bei**, *adv.* herewith.

'**anbeißen**, *v.tr.sep.* 4 1. *v.tr.* to take a bite out of (an apple etc.); *F:* **zum A. aussehen**, to look adorable. 2. *v.i.* *(haben)* take the bait.

'**anbelangen**, *v.tr. impers. sep.* **was ihn anbelangt**, as far as he is concerned.

'**anbeten**, *v.tr.sep.* to worship.

'**Anbetracht**, *f* **in A.** + *gen*, in consideration of.

'**anbetreffen**, *v.tr.impers.irr.104.* **was mich anbetrifft**, as far as I am concerned.

'**anbiedern**, *v.tr.sep. Pej:* **sich bei j-m a.**, to curry favour with s.o.

'**anbieten**, *v.tr.sep.irr.8* to offer (sth.) (j-m, to s.o.); **sich a.**, to offer one's services.

'**anbinden**, *v.tr.sep.irr.9* to tie up (a boat, an animal etc.) **(an** + *acc*, to).

'**Anblick**, *m* sight. ◆'**a~en**, *v.tr.sep.* to look at (s.o., sth.).

'**anbrechen**, *v.sep.irr.14* 1. *v.tr.* to break into (provisions, stocks etc.); to start (a loaf), open (a bottle). 2. *v.i.* *(sein)* *(Tag)* to dawn; *(Nacht)* to fall.

'**anbrennen**, *v.i.sep.irr.15* *(sein)* (a) to catch fire; (b) *(Essen)* to burn.

'**anbring|en**, *v.tr.sep.* (a) *(befestigen)* to fix, fit (sth.); to put up (curtains, a sign etc.); (b) *(vorbringen)* to put forward (a request, a suggestion); (c) *F: (herbeitragen)* to turn up with (sth.).

'**Anbruch**, *m Lit:* dawn (of a day, era).

**Andacht** ['andaxt], *f -/-en* 1. devotion. 2. *(Gottesdienst)* (short) service. ◆'**andächtig**, *adj.* devout.

'**andauern**, *v.i.sep.* *(haben)* to last. ◆'**a~d**, *adj.* persistent, continuous (rain etc.); constant (questions).

**Anden** ['andən]. *Pr.n.pl* **die A.**, the Andes.

'**Andenken**, *n -s/-* *(Erinnerung)* memory; *(Sache)* souvenir.

**and(e)re(r,s)** ['andərə(r,s)], *adj. & pron.* 1. other; **unter a~m**, among other things; **am a~n Tag/Morgen**, (on) the next day/morning. 2. *(verschieden)* other, different; **jemand/niemand a~r**, somebody/nobody else; **das ist etwas ganz a~s**, that's quite a different matter; **kein a~r als X**, nobody but X. ◆'**a~nfalls**, *adv.* otherwise.

◆'**a~rseits**, *adv.* on the other hand.

**andermal** ['andərmɑːl], *adv.* **ein a.**, another/some other time.

**änder|n** ['ɛndərn], *v.tr.* (a) to change (one's attitude, direction etc.); to alter (plans, a dress, *Nau:* course etc.); **ich kann es nicht ä.**, I cannot help it; **sich ä.**, to change. ◆'**Ä~ung**, *f -/-en* change.

**anders** ['andərs], *adv.* (a) differently, in different ways **(als**, from); (b) *(sonst)* **jemand/niemand a.**, somebody/nobody else; **wer a. als er?** who (else) but he? ◆'**a~artig**, *adj.* different. ◆'**a~wo**, *adv.* elsewhere.

**anderthalb** ['andərt'halp], *inv. adj.* one and a half.

**anderweitig** ['andərvaitiç], *adj.* **a. beschäftigt**, otherwise engaged.

'**andeut|en**, *v.tr. sep.* (a) to indicate (sth.); to outline (a plan). ◆'**A~ung**, *f -/-en* (a) indication; (b) implication.

'**Andrang**, *m -(e)s/no pl* rush **(nach Karten usw.**, for tickets etc.); *(Gedränge)* crush.

'**androhen**, *v.tr.sep.* **j-m etwas a.**, to threaten s.o. with sth.

'**aneign|en**, *v.tr.sep.* (a) **sich** *dat* **etwas a.**, to appropriate sth.; (b) *(lernen)* **sich** *dat* **Kenntnisse usw. a.**, to acquire knowledge etc.

**aneinander** [anai'nandər]. I. *pron. & adv.* by/to one another; **a. vorbei**, past one another; **a. denken**, to think of one another. II. **a~-**, *comb.fm.* (to join, tie etc.) to one another; (to grow, bind etc.) together. ◆**a~geraten**, *v.i.sep.irr.13* *(sein)* *(Parteien, Streitkräfte usw.)* to clash (with one another).

'**anekeln**, *v.tr.sep.* to sicken (s.o.).

'**anerkannt**, *adj.* acknowledged, recognized (expert, authority etc.); established (right, author etc.).

'**anerkenn|en**, *v.tr.sep.&insep.irr.51* (a) *(bestätigen)* to recognize (s.o., a state, s.o.'s merits etc.) **(als**, as); to acknowledge, accept (s.o.'s right, authority etc.); *Com:* to accept (a bill etc.); (b) *(würdigen)* to respect (rules, other people etc.); to appreciate (s.o.'s efforts etc.). ◆'**a~end**, *adj.* approving. ◆'**a~enswert**, *adj.* laudable. ◆'**A~ung**, *f -/-en* recognition, acknowledgment; acceptance; *(Würdigung)* appreciation.

'**anfachen**, *v.tr.sep. Lit:* to fan (flames etc.), stir up (passions etc.).

'**anfahr|en**, *v.sep.irr.26* 1. *v.tr.* (a) *(liefern)* to deliver (coal etc.); (b) *Aut:* to run into (s.o., sth.); (c) *F: (Pers.)* to go for (s.o.). 2. *v.i.* *(sein)* *(Auto usw.)* to start (off).

'**Anfall**, *m* attack. ◆'**a~en**, *v.sep.irr.27* 1. *v.tr.* to attack (s.o.). 2. *v.i.* *(sein)* *(Kosten)* to accrue, *(Arbeit)* accumulate.

**anfä|llig** ['anfeliç], *adj.* prone, *Fig:* vulnerable **(für etwas** *acc*, to sth.).

'**Anfang**, *m -(e)s/⸚e* (a) *(Beginn)* beginning/start; **von A. an**, from the beginning/the start; (b) pl (Ursprünge) the origins. ◆'a~en, v.tr.&i.sep.irr.28 (haben) to begin, start; was soll ich damit a.? what am I to do with it?

**Anfäng|er(in)** ['anfɛnər(in)], m -s/- (f -/ -nen) beginner, learner. ◆'a~lich, adj. initial (hesitation etc.); early (symptoms etc.).

**'anfangs,** adv. at first, to start with. ◆'A~buchstabe, m initial (letter). ◆'A~stadium, n initial stage.

**'anfassen,** v.sep. 1. v.tr. (a) (berühren) to touch (s.o., sth.); (b) Fig: to handle, tackle (a problem etc.); etwas richtig a., to set about sth. the right way. 2. v.i. (haben) mit a., to lend a hand (bei + dat, with).

**'anfechten,** v.tr.sep.irr.29 to contest (an opinion, a statement etc.); to challenge (s.o.'s right etc.).

**'anfertigen,** v.tr.sep. (a) to produce, make (sth.); Ind: to manufacture (goods etc.); (b) to draft (a document etc.).

**'anfeuern,** v.tr.sep. to spur (s.o.) on.

**'anfliegen,** v.sep.irr.17 1. v.tr. Av: (a) (Flugzeug) to approach (an airport etc.); (b) (Fluglinie) to serve (an airport, a city). 2. v.i. (sein) (Vogel) to come flying up.

**'Anflug,** m 1. Av: approach. 2. Fig: (Spur) touch.

**'anforder|n,** v.tr.sep. (a) to demand (sth.); (b) (bestellen) to order (an article). ◆'A~ung, f (a) demand; (b) Com: order (von + dat, for).

**'Anfrage,** f inquiry. ◆'a~n, v.i.sep. (haben) to enquire (wegen + gen, about).

**'anfreunden,** v.refl.sep. sich a., to make friends.

**'anfühlen,** v.tr.sep. to feel (sth.); sich hart/weich a., to feel hard/soft.

**anführ|en,** v.tr.sep. (a) (leiten) to lead; (b) (zitieren) to quote (an author, passage); to state (one's reasons etc.); (c) F: to trick, fool (s.o.). ◆'A~er, m leader, esp. ringleader (of a revolt etc.). ◆'A~ungszeichen, npl quotation marks, inverted commas.

**'Angabe,** f 1. (a) information; Tchn: data; (nähere) A~n, details, particulars; (b) (Erklärung) statement, declaration. 2. (Tennis) service.

**'angeb|en,** v.tr.sep.irr.35 1. v.tr. (a) to give, state (one's name, reasons etc.); (verzollen) to declare (goods); (b) (bestimmen) to set (the pace etc.). 2. v.i. (haben) (a) (Tennis) to serve; (b) F: to show off. ◆'A~er, m -s/- F: show-off. ◆A~e'rei, f -/-en F: showing off. ◆'a~lich, adj. alleged (reason, thief etc.); ostensible (purpose etc.).

**'angeboren,** adj. innate, inborn (qualities etc.).

**'Angebot,** n (a) offer; Com: quotation; (b) (Auswahl) range; (lieferbare Ware) stock, supply; A. und Nachfrage, supply and demand.

**'angebracht,** adj. appropriate; apt (remark).

**'angebunden,** adj. kurz a., curt, offhand.

**'angeheitert,** adj. F: tipsy.

**'angehen,** v.sep.irr.36 1. v.i. (sein) (Pflanze) to take (root); (Licht usw.) to go on; (Maschine, Motor usw.) to start (up); (Feuer) to catch. 2. v.tr. (a) (angreifen) to attack (s.o.); Fig: to tackle (a problem etc.); (b) j-n um Geld, Hilfe usw. a., to turn to s.o. for money, help etc.; (c) (betreffen) to concern, affect (s.o.). ◆a~d, adj. future (teacher, pilot etc.); budding (artist etc.).

**'angehör|en,** v.i.sep. (haben) to belong (dat, to). ◆'A~ige(r), m & f decl. as adj. member.

**'Angeklagte(r),** m & f decl. as adj. Jur: accused; (im Zivilrecht) defendant.

**Ang|el** ['aŋəl]. I. f -/-n 1. (A~elrute) fishing-rod. 2. (Türa.) hinge. II. 'A~el-, comb.fm. fishing (line, gear etc.). ◆'A~elhaken, m fish hook. ◆'a~eln, v. 1. v.i. (haben) to fish. 2. v.tr. to catch. ◆'A~ler, m -s/- angler.

**'Angelegenheit,** f -/-en affair, matter.

**'angemessen,** adj. appropriate, suitable (moment etc.) ( + dat, for); apt (remark); a~er Preis, reasonable price.

**'angenehm,** adj. pleasant; a.! pleased to meet you!

**'angenommen,** see annehmen.

**'angeregt,** adj. lively, spirited.

**'angesehen,** p.p. respected (person); reputable (firm).

**'Angesicht,** n face. ◆'a~s, prep. + gen; in view of.

**'angespannt,** adj. intense (concentration etc.); tense (nerves, situation).

**'angestammt,** adj. hereditary.

**'Angestellte(r),** m & f decl. as adj. (salaried) employee; (bank etc.) clerk; (shop) assistant.

**'angetan,** adj. von j-m, etwas dat a. sein, to be keen on s.o., sth.

**'angetrunken,** adj. tipsy.

**'angewiesen,** adj. auf j-n, etwas acc a. sein, to be dependent on s.o., sth.

**'ange|wöhnen,** v.tr.sep. j-m etwas a., to get s.o. used to sth.; sich dat etwas a., to get into the habit of (doing) sth. ◆'A~wohnheit, f -/-en habit.

**'angleichen,** v.tr.sep.irr.40 to adjust, adapt (sth.).

**'angreifen,** v.tr.sep.irr.43 (a) (überfallen) to attack; (b) (anbrechen) to draw on (reserves etc.); (c) (schädigen) (Krankheit usw.) to affect (s.o.); (Säure usw.) to corrode (metal etc.). ◆'A~er, m -s/- attacker; (Staat) aggressor.

**'Angriff,** m 1. attack; Jur: assault. 2. etwas in A. nehmen, to set about (doing) sth. ◆'A~s-, comb.fm. offensive (weapon etc.); aggressive (spirit etc.).

**Angst** [aŋst], f -/¨e (a) fear; (Sorge) anxiety; A. (vor j-m, etwas) haben, to be afraid/frightened (of s.o., sth.); A. um j-n, etwas haben, to be anxious/worried about s.o., sth.; (b) mir ist/wird a. (und bange), I am scared stiff; j-m a. machen, to scare/frighten s.o. ◆'A~hase, m F: scaredy cat.

ängst|igen ['ɛŋstigən] v.tr. to frighten, scare (s.o.); sich ä., to be frightened (vor + dat, of); (Sorgen haben) to be anxious (um + acc, about). ◆'ä~lich, adj. nervous, (scheu) timid (person, disposition etc.); frightened, scared (look etc.). ◆'A~lichkeit, f -/no pl nervousness; anxiety.

'angucken, v.tr.sep. F: to look at (s.o., sth.).

'anhaben, v.tr.sep.irr.44 (a) to have (sth.) on; (b) F: das Licht a., to have the light on; (c) j-m etwas/nichts a. können, to be able/unable to harm s.o., sth.

'anhalt|en, v.sep.irr.45 1. v.tr. (a) (zum Stehen bringen) to stop (s.o., sth.); to bring (traffic, a train etc.) to a standstill; (b) (ermahnen) j-n zur Arbeit usw. a., to urge s.o. to work etc. 2. v.i. (haben) (a) (Fahrzeug usw.) to stop; (b) (andauern) (Wetter) to continue; (Zustand usw.) to persist. ◆'a~end, adj. lasting (effect); persistent (rain); sustained (interest). ◆'A~er, m -s/- F: hitch-hiker; per A. fahren, to hitch-hike. ◆'A~spunkt, m clue; pl evidence.

an'hand, prep. a. von Beispielen, with the help of examples.

'Anhang, m 1. (in einem Buch usw.) appendix. 2. coll. F: (Gefolge) hangers-on; (Angehörige) relatives; family.

'anhäng|en, v.tr.sep. (a) to hang (sth.) on; (befestigen) to fix, fasten (a label, tag etc.) (an + acc, to); (b) (ankuppeln) to hitch up (a coach, trailer etc.); (c) (hinzufügen) to add on (a paragraph etc.). ◆'A~er, m -s/- 1. trailer. 2. (Schmuck) pendant. 3. (Etikett) tag. 4. (Pers.) adherent (of a belief etc.); supporter (of a party, Sp: club etc.). ◆'A~erschaft, f -/no pl followers, adherents. ◆'a~lich, adj. affectionate; devoted (friend etc.). ◆'A~lichkeit, f -/-en affection. ◆'A~sel, n -s/- appendage.

'anhäuf|en, v.tr.sep. to accumulate (money etc.); (Arbeit usw.) sich a., to pile up. ◆'A~ung, f -/-en accumulation; pile (of work).

'anheben, v.tr.sep.irr.48 to lift, raise (sth.); to jack up (a car).

'anheimelnd ['anhaiməlnt], adj. homely.

'Anhieb, m F: etwas auf A. tun, to do sth. first go.

'Anhöhe, f rise; hillock.

'anhör|en, v.tr.sep. (a) (zuhören) to listen to (s.o., sth.); (b) das hört sich gut an, that sounds good; (c) man hört (es) ihm an, daß ..., one can tell from the way he speaks that ...

animieren [ani'mi:rən], v.tr. (anregen) j-n zum Trinken usw. a., to persuade s.o. to have a drink etc.

Anis [a'ni:s], m -es/-e aniseed.

'Ankauf, m purchase. ◆'a~en, v.tr.sep. to purchase (sth.).

Anker ['aŋkər], m -s/- anchor; vor A. gehen, to drop anchor. ◆'a~n, v.i. (haben) to anchor. ◆'A~platz, m anchorage.

'anketten, v.tr.sep. to chain.

'Anklage, f (a) accusation; Jur: charge; (b) Jur: (auch A~vertretung f) prosecution. ◆'A~bank, dock. ◆'a~n, v.tr.sep. j-n wegen etwas gen a., to accuse s.o. of sth., Jur: charge s.o. with sth. ◆'Ankläger, m Jur: plaintiff.

'Anklang, m 1. (Ähnlichkeit) echo. 2. (bei j-m) A. finden, to meet with (s.o.'s) approval.

'ankleide|n, v.tr.sep. to dress (s.o.); sich a., to dress (oneself). ◆'A~raum, m dressing room, changing room.

'anklopfen, v.i.sep. (haben) bei j-m a., to knock at s.o.'s door.

'anknüpfen, v.sep. 1. v.tr. (a) etwas an etwas acc a., to tie sth. to sth.; (b) to start (a conversation etc.). 2. v.i. (haben) to carry on (where one left off).

'ankommen, v.i.sep.irr.53 (sein) (a) (eintreffen) to arrive. (b) (Erfolg haben) bei j-m (gut) a., to be a success with s.o., (Witz usw.) go down well with s.o.; gegen j-n, etwas acc nicht a. können, to be no match for s.o., sth.; (c) auf j-n, etwas a., to depend on s.o., sth.; F: ich lasse es drauf a.! I'll chance it!

'ankreuzen, v.tr.sep. to mark (sth.) with a cross.

'ankündig|en, v.tr.sep. to announce (sth.); to publicize (an event); Fig: to herald (a new era etc.). ◆'A~ung, f -/-en announcement.

Ankunft ['ankunft], f -/-e arrival.

'Anlage, f 1. (a) installation (of apparatus etc.); (Bau) construction; (b) Fin: investment. 2. (Anordnung) layout; Tchn: system. 3. pl (a) öffentliche A~n, public gardens; (b) Sp: etc: facilities; Ind: plant; sanitäre A~n, lavatories and washrooms. 4. (Beilage) enclosure. 5. (Veranlagung) tendency (zu Allergien usw., to allergies etc.).

Anlaß ['anlas] m -sses/-sse (a) (Grund) reason (zu + dat, for); (b) (Gelegenheit) occasion.

'anlass|en, v.tr.sep.irr.57 (a) to start (up) (an engine, machine); (b) F: to leave (the light, radio etc.) on. ◆'A~er, m -s/- starter.

anläßlich ['anlɛsliç], prep. + gen on the occasion of.

'Anlauf, m 1. Sp: run-up; Fig: im/beim ersten A., at the first attempt. ◆'a~en, v.sep.irr.58 1. v.i. (sein) (a) to run up; (b) (Maschine, Motor usw.) to start (up); (Fahndung usw.) to get under way; (Film) to open; (c) (Scheibe, Brille usw.) to mist up; (Metall) to tarnish; (d) (Pers.) vor Kälte blau a., to go blue with cold. **2.** *v.tr.* **einen Hafen a.,** to call at a port.

**anlege|n**, *v.sep.* **1.** *v.tr.* (a) **etwas an etwas** *acc* **a.,** to put/lay sth. on sth.; (*Pferd usw.*) **die Ohren a.,** to lay back its ears; (b) (*anziehen*) to put on; (c) (*zielen*) **auf j-n a.,** to aim at s.o.; (d) *Fin:* **Geld a.,** to invest/(*ausgeben*) spend money; (e) (*einrichten*) to lay out (a garden etc.); to design, plan (a bridge, road etc.); to draw up (a list, statistics etc.); to install (cables, pipes etc.). **2.** *v.i.* (*haben*) to moor. ◆**'A~platz,** *m* ◆**'A~stelle,** *f* mooring.

**'anlehnen**, *v.tr.sep.* (a) to lean (sth.) (**an etwas** *acc,* against sth.); (*Pers.*) **sich an j-n, etwas a.,** to lean on s.o., sth.; (b) **die Tür/das Fenster a.,** to leave the door/window ajar.

**'Anleihe,** *f* -/-n loan.

**'anleit|en,** *v.tr.sep.* **j-n zu etwas** *dat* **a.,** to train s.o. in sth. ◆**'A~ung,** *f* instruction.

**'anlernen,** *v.tr.sep.* to train.

**'anliege|n. I.** *v.i.sep.irr.*62 (*haben*) (a) (eng) a., to fit closely; (b) (*Arbeit usw.*) to be pending. **II. A.,** *n* -s/- (a) request; **ein A. an j-n haben,** to have a favour to ask of s.o.; (b) (*Sorge*) concern. ◆**'a~end,** *adj.* (a) adjoining (property etc.); (b) (eng) a., close-fitting. ◆**'A~er,** *m* -s/- **A. frei,** access for residents (only).

**'anmachen,** *v.tr.sep.* (a) *Cu:* to dress (the salad); (b) *F:* to switch/turn on (the light, radio etc.).

**'anmaß|en,** *v.tr.sep.* **sich** *dat* **ein Recht usw. a.,** to usurp a right etc. ◆**'a~end,** *adj.* presumptuous; (*hochmütig*) arrogant.

**Anmelde-** ['anmeldə-], *comb.fm.* registration (form, fee etc.). ◆**'a~en,** *v.tr.sep.* (a) to register (a car, birth, death, business etc.); (b) **sich a.,** to register (*polizeilich,* with the police); (*beim Arzt*) to make an appointment (with the doctor); (c) (*ankündigen*) to announce (s.o.). ◆**'A~ung,** *f* (a) registration; announcement; (b) (*Büro*) registration office; (*im Hotel*) reception.

**'anmerk|en,** *v.tr.sep.* **j-m etwas a.,** to notice sth. in s.o.; **laß dir nichts a.!** don't give yourself away! ◆**'A~ung,** *f* -/-en note.

**'Anmut,** *f* -/*no pl* grace. ◆**'a~en,** *v.tr.sep.* **es mutet mich seltsam an,** it strikes me as odd. ◆**'a~ig,** *adj.* graceful; charming (manner etc.).

**'annähen,** *v.tr.sep.* to sew on (sth.).

**'annäher|n,** *v.tr.sep.* **sich** (**etwas** *dat*) **a.,** to come closer to sth. ◆**'a~nd,** *adj.* approximate; *adv.* **nicht a.,** not nearly. ◆**'A~ungsversuch,** *m F:* **bei j-m A~ungsversuche machen,** to make advances/overtures to s.o.

**Annahme** ['annɑːmə], *f* -/-n **1.** (*Annehmen*) acceptance. **2.** (*Aneignung*) adoption (of a name etc.). **3.** (*Vermutung*) assump-

tion.

**annehm|bar** ['anne:mbɑːr], *adj.* acceptable. ◆**'a~en,** *v.tr.sep.irr.*69 (a) to accept (a gift, an invitation, a bill etc.); to take on (a job); to adopt (a resolution, name, attitude etc.); (b) (*vermuten*) to assume, presume (sth.); **angenommen, daß ...,** suppose/supposing that ...; (c) (*kümmern*) **sich j-s/etwas** *gen* **a.,** to take care of s.o./sth. ◆**'A~lichkeiten,** *fpl* amenities.

**Annonc|e** [a'nõːsə], *f* -/-n advertisement. ◆**a~ieren** [-õ'siːrən], *v.tr.&i.* (*haben*) to advertise.

**annullier|en** [anu'liːrən], *v.tr.* to annul (a marriage), cancel (a contract etc.).

**anonym** [ano'nyːm], *adj.* anonymous.

**Anorak** ['anorak], *m* -s/-s anorak.

**'anordn|en,** *v.tr.sep.* (a) to arrange (objects); (b) (*befehlen*) to order. ◆**'A~ung,** *f* -/-en (a) arrangement; (b) order; (*Vorschrift*) regulation.

**'anorganisch,** *adj.* inorganic.

**anormal** ['anormaːl], *adj.* abnormal.

**'anpacken,** *v.tr.sep.* to seize (s.o., sth.); **ein Problem a.,** to tackle a problem.

**'anpass|en,** *v.tr.sep.* to adapt (sth.). ◆**'A~ung,** *f* -/-en adaptation, (**an** + *acc,* to). ◆**'a~ungsfähig,** *adj.* adaptable.

**'Anpfiff,** *m Sp:* kick-off.

**'anpflanzen,** *v.tr.sep.* to plant.

**'anpöbeln,** *v.tr.sep. F:* to shout abuse at (s.o.).

**'anprangern,** *v.tr.sep.* to pillory (s.o.).

**'anpreisen,** *v.tr.sep.irr.*70 to extol.

**'Anprob|e,** *f* -/-n fitting. ◆**'a~ieren,** *v.tr.sep.* to try on.

**'anrechn|en,** *v.tr.sep.* (a) (*berechnen*) **j-m etwas a.,** to charge s.o. for sth.; (b) **j-m etwas als Fehler a.,** to consider sth. as a mistake on s.o.'s part; *Fig:* **wir rechnen ihm seine Hilfe hoch an,** we greatly appreciate his help.

**'Anrecht,** *n* right.

**Anrede,** *f* address; opening (of a letter). ◆**a~n,** *v.tr.sep.* to address (s.o.).

**'anreg|en,** *v.tr.sep.* (a) (*vorschlagen*) to suggest (sth.); (b) (*beleben*) to stimulate (s.o., the circulation etc.). ◆**'a~end,** *adj.* stimulating. ◆**'A~ung,** *f* (a) encouragement; (b) (*Vorschlag*) suggestion.

**'anreichern,** *v.tr.sep.* to enrich.

**'Anreise,** *f* (a) journey (there); (b) (*Ankunft*) arrival. ◆**'a~n,** *v.i.sep.* (*sein*) (a) to travel (there); (b) to arrive.

**'Anreiz,** *m* incentive, inducement.

**'Anrichte,** *f* -/-n sideboard. ◆**'a~n,** *v.tr.sep.* (a) to prepare (a meal, dish); to dress (a salad); (b) to cause (confusion, disaster etc.).

**'anrüchig,** *adj.* disreputable (person etc.); sleazy (night spot etc.).

**'Anruf,** *m* -(e)s/-e call. ◆**'A~beantworter,** *m* answering machine. ◆**'a~en,** *v.tr.sep.irr.*74 (a) to call to (s.o.); (b) **j-n um Hilfe a.,** to appeal to s.o. for help; (c) *Tel:* to ring (s.o.) up, *N.Am:* call (s.o.). ◆'**A**~**er**, *m* -s/- caller.

'**anrühren**, *v.tr.sep.* (a) to mix (a sauce, mortar etc.); (b) (*berühren*) to touch.

**ans** [ans], *prep.* = **an das.**

'**Ansage**, *f* -/-n announcement. ◆'**a**~**n**, *v.tr.sep.* to announce; (b) **er hat sich zum Mittagessen angesagt**, he has told us he is coming to lunch. ◆'**A**~**r(in)**, *m* -s/- (*f* -/-nen) announcer.

'**ansammeln**, *v.tr.sep.* to collect (objects etc.); to accumulate (goods, wealth); **sich a.**, (*Staub usw.*) to collect; (*Menschen*) to gather; (*Vermögen usw.*) to accumulate.

**ansässig** ['anzɛsiç], *adj.* resident.

'**Ansatz**, *m* first sign of (buds etc.); beginning; base (of the neck etc.); **A. des Haars**, hairline. ◆'**A**~**punkt**, *m* starting point.

'**anschaff|en**, *v.tr.sep.* **sich** *dat* **etwas a.**, to acquire sth. ◆'**A**~**ung**, *f* acquisition; (*Kauf*) purchase. ◆'**A**~**ungskosten**, *pl* prime cost.

'**anschalten**, *v.tr.sep.* to turn on.

'**anschau|en**, *v.tr.sep.* to look at. ◆'**a**~**lich**, *adj.* clear (picture); vivid (description). ◆'**A**~**ung**, *f* -/-en opinion, view (**über etwas** *acc*, on sth.). ◆'**A**~**ungsmaterial**, *n* illustrative material; *Sch:* visual aids.

'**Anschein**, *m* appearance, look; (*täuschend*) semblance; **allem A. nach**, to all appearances. ◆'**a**~**end**, *adv.* apparently.

'**Anschlag**, *m* 1. (*Bekanntmachung*) (public) notice. 2. (*Überfall*) attack. 3. touch (of a pianist, piano etc.); **240 A**~**e in der Minute schreiben**, to hit 240 keys per minute. 4. **das Gewehr im A. halten**, to hold the rifle in the aiming position. ◆'**a**~**en**, *v.sep.irr.85* 1. *v.tr.* (a) to put up (a notice, poster etc.); (b) to strike, hit (a note, a key etc.); (c) (*beschädigen*) to chip (a plate, glass etc.). 2. *v.i.* (*haben*) (a) to knock (**an etwas** *acc*, on/against sth.); (b) (*Hund*) to start barking. ◆'**A**~**zettel**, *m* bill.

'**anschließen**, *v.tr.sep.irr.31* (a) to join, attach (sth.); (b) to connect (up) (an appliance); (c) to affiliate (a group); **sich j-m a.**, to join up with s.o.; **sich j-s Meinung a.**, to endorse s.o.'s ideas; (c) (*folgen*) **sich an etwas** *acc* **a.**, to follow (immediately) after sth. ◆'**a**~**d**, *adv.* (immediately) afterwards.

'**Anschluß**, *m* 1. (*Verbindung*) connection. 2. (*Kontakt*) contact; **sie sucht A.**, she wants to make friends. 3. **im A. an** + *acc*, following.

'**anschmieren**, *v.tr.sep.* *F:* to diddle, con (s.o.).

'**anschnall|en**, *v.tr.sep.* to fasten the strap(s) of (a rucksack etc.); to put on (skates, skis); **sich a.**, to put on one's seat belt.

'**anschneiden**, *v.tr.sep.irr.59* (a) to cut

into (a loaf); (b) **ein Thema a.**, to broach a subject.

'**anschreiben**, *v.tr.sep.irr.12* (a) to write (sth.); (b) **etwas a. lassen**, to buy sth. on credit; *Fig:* **bei j-m gut angeschrieben sein**, to be in s.o.'s good books; (c) to write to (s.o., an authority etc.).

'**anschreien**, *v.tr.sep.irr.88* to shout at (s.o.).

'**Anschrift**, *f* address.

'**Anschuldigung**, *f* -/-en accusation; allegation.

'**anschwellen**, *v.i.sep.irr.71* (*sein*) to swell; (*Fluß*) to rise; (*Lärm usw.*) to grow louder.

'**anschwemmen**, *v.tr.sep.* to wash (sth.) up.

'**anseh|en**. I. *v.tr.sep.irr.92* (a) to look at (s.o., sth.); to watch (a programme); **etwas mit a.**, to stand by and watch sth.; **j-m etwas a.**, to see sth. from s.o.'s appearance; (b) **ich sehe es als meine Pflicht an, zu ...**, I regard it as my duty to ... II. **A.**, *n* -s/*no pl* (a) respect. (b) **ohne A. der Person**, regardless of status. ◆'**a**~**nlich**, *adj.* considerable.

'**ansetzen**, *v.sep.* 1. *v.tr.* (a) to place (a tool etc.) in position; to put (a glass) to one's lips; (*festlegen*) to arrange (a meeting etc.); (c) to allow (an amount, a period); (d) (*Eisen*) **Rost a.**, to get rusty, to rust; *F:* **Fett a.**, to put on weight. 2. *v.i.* (*haben*) to start.

'**Ansicht**, *f* -/-en 1. (a) (*Meinung*) opinion; **meiner A. nach**, in my opinion; (b) (*Blick*) view; **eine A. der Stadt Köln**, a view of Cologne. 2. *Com:* **zur A.**, on approval. ◆'**A**~**skarte**, *f* picture postcard. ◆'**A**~**ssache**, *f* matter of opinion.

**an'sonsten**, *adv.* otherwise.

'**anspannen**, *v.tr.sep.* (a) to harness (a horse) (**an** + *acc*, to); (b) to tighten (a rope); to tense (the muscles), strain (one's nerves).

'**anspiel|en**, *v.i.sep.* *v.i.* (*haben*) (a) to start playing; (b) (*hinweisen*) **auf j-n, etwas a.**, to allude to s.o., sth.; (*versteckt*) to hint at sth. ◆'**A**~**ung**, *f* -/-en allusion (**auf** + *acc*, to); (**versteckte**) **A.**, hidden reference.

'**Ansporn**, *m* incentive (**zu etwas** *dat*, to do sth.) ◆'**a**~**en**, *v.tr.sep.* to spur on (one's horse); *Fig:* to spur, urge (s.o.) on.

'**Ansprache**, *f* speech, address.

**ansprech|bar** ['anʃprɛçbaːr], *adj.* (*Pers.*) approachable. ◆'**a**~**en**, *v.sep.irr.14* 1. *v.tr.* to speak to (s.o.) (**auf etwas** *acc*, about sth.); to address (s.o., a crowd etc.). 2. *v.i.* (*haben*) (a) (*reagieren*) to respond; (b) (*gefallen*) to appeal. ◆'**a**~**end**, *adj.* appealing.

'**anspringen**, *v.i.sep.irr.19* (*sein*) (*Motor*) to start.

'**Anspruch**, *m* claim; (**hohe**) **A**~**e stellen**, to make (heavy) demands; **j-n, etwas in**

**A. nehmen,** to make demands upon s.o., sth. ◆'a~**slos,** *adj.* (*bescheiden*) modest; unassuming (person). ◆'a~**svoll,** *adj.* demanding.

'**anstacheln,** *v.tr.sep.* to egg (s.o.) on.

**Anstalt** ['anʃtalt], *f* -/-en **1.** institution. **2.** *pl* **A~en machen, etwas zu tun,** to prepare to do sth.

'**Anstand,** *m* decency. ◆'a~**slos,** *adv.* unhesitatingly.

'**anständig,** *adj.* **1.** proper (conduct etc.); respectable (person, dress etc.). **2.** *F:* (*ziemlich gut/groß*) decent (meal, portion, hotel etc.); (*richtig*) real, proper.

'**anstarren,** *v.tr.sep.* to stare at (s.o., sth.).

**an'statt,** *conj. & prep.* + *gen* instead of.

'**anstechen,** *v.tr.sep.irr.14* to puncture (sth.); **ein Faß a.,** to tap a barrel.

'**ansteck|en,** *v.tr.sep.* (*a*) (*mit Nadel*) to pin (sth.) on; (*b*) (*anzünden*) to set fire to (sth.); to light (a fire, cigarette etc.); (*c*) *Med:* to infect (s.o.). ◆'a~**end,** *adj.* infectious.

'**anstehen,** *v.i.sep.irr.100* (*haben*) to stand in a queue/*N.Am:* line, queue (up).

'**ansteigen,** *v.i.sep.irr.89* to rise.

**an'stelle,** *prep.* + *gen* instead of.

'**anstell|en,** *v.tr.sep.* (*a*) (*Pers.*) **sich a.,** to stand in a queue/*N.Am:* line; to queue (up); (*b*) (*einstellen*) to take (s.o.) on; (*c*) (*in Gang setzen*) to start (machinery); **ich weiß nicht, wie ich es a. soll,** I've no idea how to set about it; (*d*) *F:* **sich geschickt/dumm a.,** to show skill/act stupidly. ◆'A~**ung,** *f* -/-en employment.

**Anstieg** ['anʃti:k], *m* -(e)s/-e (*a*) ascent, climb; (*b*) rise (**der Preise usw.,** in prices etc.).

'**anstift|en,** *v.tr.sep.* to cause (confusion etc.); to instigate (a crime, revolt etc.); **j-n zu etwas** *dat* **a.,** to incite s.o. to (doing) sth. ◆'A~**er,** *m* instigator.

'**anstimmen,** *v.tr.sep.* to strike up (a song); **ein Gelächter a.,** to start laughing.

'**Anstoß,** *m* **1.** (*Anlaß*) impetus; **A. zu etwas geben,** to initiate sth. **2.** (*Ärgernis*) offence. **3.** *Sp:* kick-off. ◆'a~**en,** *v.sep.irr.103* **1.** *v.tr.* (*a*) to give (s.o., sth.) a push/knock; (*mit dem Ellbogen*) to nudge s.o.; (*b*) *abs. Sp:* to kick off. **2.** *v.i.* (*a*) (*sein*) **an etwas** *acc* **a.,** to knock against sth.; (*b*) (*haben*) (**mit den Gläsern**) **a.,** to clink glasses (with s.o.); (*c*) (*haben*) (*angrenzen*) **an etwas** *acc* **a.,** to be adjacent to sth.

**anstößig** ['anʃtø:siç], *adj.* offensive.

'**anstreich|en,** *v.tr.sep.irr.40* (*a*) to paint (sth.); (*b*) to mark (a passage, mistake etc.). ◆'A~**er,** *m* (house) painter.

**anstreng|en** ['anʃtrɛŋən], *v.tr.sep.* (*a*) to strain (one's eyes, voice); **sich a.,** to make an effort (to do sth.); (*körperlich*) to exert oneself. ◆'a~**end,** *adj.* strenuous. ◆'A~**ung,** *f* -/-en effort, exertion; strain (for the eyes etc.).

'**Ansturm,** *m Mil:* assault; (*Andrang*) rush.

**Antarkt|is** [ant'ʔarktis]. *Pr.n.f* -. **die A.,** the Antarctic. ◆**a~isch,** *adj.* antarctic.

'**antasten,** *v.tr.sep.* to touch (an object, money etc.), *Fig:* touch on (a subject).

'**Anteil,** *m* **1.** share, portion; (*im Gemisch*) proportion. **2.** *no pl* **A. an etwas** *dat* **nehmen,** to take an interest in sth., (*besorgt*) be concerned about sth. ◆'A~**mäßig,** *adj.* proportional. ◆'A~**nahme,** *f* -/*no pl* sympathy.

**Antenne** [an'tɛnə], *f* -/-n **1.** aerial. **2.** *pl Z:* antennae, *F:* feelers (of insect).

**Anti-, anti-** [anti-], *prefix* anti-. ◆'A~**alko'holiker(in),** *m, f* teetotaller. ◆'a~**autori'tär,** *adj.* permissive. ◆'A~'**babypille,** *f F:* the pill. ◆A~**biotikum** [-bi'o:tikum], *n* -s/-ka antibiotic. ◆A~**pathie** [-pa'ti:], *f* -/-n antipathy (**gegen** + *acc,* to).

**antik** [an'ti:k], *adj.* (*a*) classical (art, literature); ancient (Greece, Rome); (*b*) antique (furniture etc.). ◆A~**e,** *f* -/-n **die A.,** the ancient world.

**Antilope** [anti'lo:pə], *f* -/-n antelope.

**Antiquar|iat** [antikvari'at], *n* (e)-s/-e secondhand bookshop. ◆**a~isch,** *adj.* secondhand (book, bookshop).

**antiquiert** [anti'kvi:rt], *adj.* antiquated.

**Antiquität** [antikvi'tɛ:t], *f* -/-en *usu. pl* antique. ◆A~**en-,** *comb.fm.* antique (dealer, shop etc.).

**Antrag** ['antra:k], *m* -(e)s/-e (*a*) (*Vorschlag*) proposal; motion; (*b*) *Adm:* application; *Jur:* petition. ◆'A~**steller,** *m* -s/- applicant.

'**antreffen,** *v.tr.sep.irr.104* to find (s.o.).

'**antreiben,** *v.tr.sep.irr.12* to drive.

'**antreten,** *v.sep.irr.105* **1.** *v.tr.* to set out on (a journey); to start (a job); to enter upon (a career); **ein Erbe a.,** to come into an inheritance; **sein Amt a.,** to take up office. **2.** *v.i.* (*sein*) *Mil:* to fall in; *Sp:* **gegen X a.,** to compete against X.

'**Antrieb,** *m* **1.** drive. **2.** *Fig:* motive; **aus eigenem A.,** of one's own accord. ◆'A~**s-,** *comb.fm.* driving (axle, belt, motor etc.).

'**antrinken,** *v.tr.sep.irr.96 F:* **sich** *dat* **Mut a.,** to take a drop of Dutch courage.

'**Antritt,** *m* start (of a journey etc.); taking up (an office). ◆'A~**s-,** *comb.fm.* inaugural (lecture, address etc.).

'**antun,** *v.tr.sep.irr.106* **j-m etwas a.,** to do sth. to s.o.; **sich** *dat* **Zwang a.,** to restrain oneself.

**Antwort** ['antvort], *f* -/-en answer, reply; **um A. wird gebeten,** RSVP. ◆'a~**en,** *v.i.* (*haben*) to answer, reply.

'**anvertrauen,** *v.tr.sep.* (*a*) **j-m etwas a.,** to entrust s.o. with sth.; (*b*) **sich j-m a.,** to confide in s.o.

'**anwachsen,** *v.i.sep.irr.107* (*sein*) (*a*) to grow; (*b*) (*Pflanze*) to take root.

**Anwalt** ['anvalt], *m* -(e)s/-e (*a*) lawyer; (*b*) *Fig:* (*Verfechter*) advocate.

'**Anwandlung,** *f* fit; **in einer A. von Schwäche,** in a weak moment.

**'Anwärter(in),** *m* (*f -/-***nen**) candidate, *Sp:* contender.

**'anweis|en,** *v.tr.sep.irr.70* (*a*) (*zuteilen*) to assign; **j-m einen Platz a.,** to show s.o. to a seat; (*b*) (*anleiten*) to give (s.o.) instructions; to instruct (s.o.) (to do sth.); (*c*) (*überweisen*) to transfer (a sum). ◆**'A~ung,** *f -/-***en** (*a*) assignment; (*b*) instruction; (*c*) (*von Geld*) transfer; (*Schein*) (money) order.

**'anwend|en,** *v.tr.sep.irr.94* to apply (a method, rule, law etc.); (*gebrauchen*) to use (an object, money, force etc.). ◆**'A~ung,** *f -/-***en** application; use.

**'anwesen|d** ['anveːzənt], *adj.* present; **die A~den,** those present. ◆**'A~heit,** *f -/no pl* presence. ◆**'A~heitsliste,** *f* attendance sheet.

**anwidern** ['anviːdərn], *v.tr.sep.* to disgust (s.o.).

**'Anzahl,** *f* number. ◆**'a~en,** *v.tr.sep.* to pay (a sum) as a deposit; to pay a deposit on (a TV etc.). ◆**'A~ung,** *f* deposit.

**'Anzeichen,** *n* indication, sign.

**Anzeige** ['antsaigə], *f -/-***n** **1.** announcement (of a death etc.); (*Inserat*) advertisement; **A. gegen j-n erstatten,** to report s.o. to the authorities. **2.** *Tchn:* reading (on a gauge etc.); *Data-pr:* display. ◆**'a~n,** *v.tr.sep.* (*a*) (*bekanntgeben*) to announce (*melden*) to report (s.o., sth.) to the police. ◆**'A~nteil,** *m* advertisements. ◆**'A~r,** *m* indicator.

**anzetteln,** *v.tr.sep.* to instigate.

**'anzieh|en,** *v.tr.sep.irr.113* (*a*) **die Knie a.,** to draw up one's knees; (*b*) to put on (clothes, shoes etc.); **sich a.,** to put on one's clothes; (*c*) (*Magnet & Fig:*) to attract (s.o., sth.); (*d*) (*festschrauben*) to tighten (a screw etc.). ◆**'a~end,** *adj.* attractive. ◆**'A~ungskraft,** *f -/no pl* attraction; **A. der Erde,** (force of) gravity.

**'Anzug,** *m* **1.** suit. **2.** *no pl;* **im A. sein,** (*Sturm*) to be gathering; (*Gefahr usw.*) to be imminent.

**anzüglich** ['antsyːkliç], *adj.* suggestive.

**'anzünden,** *v.tr.sep.* to light (a cigarette, fire etc.); to set fire to (sth.).

**'anzweifeln,** *v.tr.sep.* to question.

**Apfel** ['apfəl], *m -s/-* apple. ◆**A~sine** [-'ziːnə], *f -/-***n** orange.

**Apostel** [a'pɔstəl], *m -s/-* apostle.

**Apostroph** [apɔ'stroːf], *m -s/-***e** apostrophe.

**Apotheke** [apo'teːkə], *f -/-***n** (dispensing) chemist's (shop); pharmacy. ◆**A~r,** *m -s/-* (dispensing) chemist; pharmacist; *N.Am:* druggist.

**Apparat** [apa'raːt], *m -(e)s/-***e** (*a*) *coll.* apparatus; (*Gerät*) device; (small) machine; (*b*) *Rad: TV:* set; *Phot:* camera; (*c*) telephone; **am A.,** speaking. ◆**A~ur** [apara'tuːr], *f -/-***en** equipment.

**Appartement** [apartə'mãː], *n -s/-***s** luxury apartment.

**Appell** [a'pɛl], *m -s/-***e** (*a*) appeal (*b*) *Mil:* roll-call. ◆**a~ieren** [apɛ'liːrən], *v.i.*

(*haben*) to appeal (**an j-n,** to s.o.).

**Appetit** [ape'tiːt], *m -(e)s/-***e** appetite; **guten A.!** enjoy your food! ◆**a~lich,** *adj.* appetizing.

**applau|dieren** [aplau'diːrən], *v.i.* (*haben*) to applaud (**j-m,** s.o.). ◆**A~s** [a'plaus], *m -es/-***e** applause.

**Aprikose** [apri'koːzə], *f -/-***n** apricot.

**April** [a'pril], *m -(s)/-***e** April. ◆**A~scherz,** *m* April fool joke.

**Aquaplaning** [akva'plaːniŋ], *n -(s)/no pl* aquaplaning.

**Aquarell** [akva'rɛl], *n -s/-***e** water-colour (painting).

**Aquarium** [a'kvaːrium], *n -s/-***rien** aquarium.

**Äquator** [ɛ'kvaːtɔr], *m -s/no pl* equator.

**Ara** ['ɛːra], *f -/-***en** era.

**Arab|er** ['arabər], *m -s/-* Arab. ◆**A~erin** [a'raːbərin], *f -/-***nen** Arab woman. ◆**A~ien** [a'raːbiən]. *Pr.n.n -s-* Arabia. ◆**a~isch** [a'raːbiʃ]. **I.** *adj.* Arabian; Arabic (language, numerals etc.). **II.** **A.,** *n -/no pl* Arabic.

**Arbeit** ['arbait], *f -/-***en** (*a*) work; **sich an die A. machen,** to set to work; **bei der A.,** at work; (*b*) (*Aufgabe*) job. ◆**'a~en,** *v.* **1.** *v.i.* (*haben*) (*a*) to work (**an etwas dat,** on sth.); (*b*) (*Maschine usw.*) to operate. **2.** *v.tr.* to work (metal, wood etc.); *Fig:* **sich nach oben a.,** to work one's way up. ◆**'A~er(in),** *m* (*f*) *-s/- (f -/-***nen**) worker; *Agr: etc:* labourer. ◆**A~er-,** *comb.fm.* labour (movement, shortage etc.); working-class (family etc.). ◆**'A~erschaft,** *f -/no pl* (*a*) workforce (of a firm); (*b*) *coll.* workers. ◆**'A~geber(in),** *m -s/- (f -/-***nen**) employer. ◆**'A~nehmer(in),** *m -s/- (f -/-***nen**) employee. ◆**'A~s-,** *comb.fm.* (*a*) working (clothes, wage, method, day, week, title etc.); (*b*) labour (service, costs, camp, market, minister etc.); work (therapy, process etc.); (*c*) (certificate, contract etc.) of employment; (*d*) industrial (psychology, law, accident etc.). ◆**'A~samt,** *n* employment exchange. ◆**'a~sfähig,** *adj.* (*Pers.*) fit to work. ◆**'A~sfläche,** *f* work top. ◆**'A~sgang,** *m* operation (of a worker); working cycle (of a machine). ◆**'A~sgemeinschaft,** *f* study group. ◆**'A~skraft,** *f* (*a*) worker; *pl* A~skräfte, manpower; (*b*) (s.o.'s) capacity for work. ◆**'a~slos,** *adj.* unemployed; **die A~slosen,** the unemployed. ◆**'A~slosenunterstützung,** *f* unemployment benefit. ◆**'A~slosigkeit,** *f -/no pl* unemployment. ◆**'A~splatz,** *m* (*a*) place of work; (*b*) (*Stelle*) job. ◆**'A~steilung,** *f* division of labour. ◆**'a~sunfähig,** *adj.* unemployable. ◆**'A~szeit,** *f* working hours. ◆**'A~szimmer,** *n* study.

**Archäologie** [arçɛolo'giː] *f -/no pl* archeology.

**Architekt|(in)** [arçi'tɛkt(in)], *m -en/-***en** (*f*

-/-nen) architect. ◆A~ur [-tɛk'tuːr], f
-/-en architecture.
**Archiv** [ar'çiːf], n -s/-e archive.
**arg** [ark], adj. bad (mistake etc.); (unangenehm) nasty (disappointment etc.); a~e
Schmerzen, terrible pains.
**Argentin|ien** [argɛn'tiːniən], Pr.n.n -s.
Argentina. ◆A~ier(in), m -s/- (f -/-nen)
Argentinian. ◆a~isch, adj. Argentinian (meat etc.); Argentine (Republic).
**Ärger** ['ɛrgər], m -s/no pl (a) (Unmut
usw.) annoyance, (Zorn) anger; (b) (Sche-
rerei) trouble. ◆'ä~lich, adj. 1. (Sache)
annoying. 2. (Pers.) annoyed. ◆'ä~n,
v.tr. to annoy; sich über j-n/etwas
schwarz ä., to be hopping mad about
s.o., sth.; ärgere dich nicht! don't let
it upset you. ◆'Ä~nis, n -ses/-se
(a) usu.pl annoyance; (b) öffentliches
Ä., public nuisance.
**arglos** ['arkloːs], adj. unsuspecting; a~e
Bemerkung, innocent remark.
**Argument** [argu'mɛnt], n -(e)s/-e argument. ◆a~ieren [-'tiːrən], v.i. (haben)
to argue.
**Arg|wohn** ['arkvoːn], m -(e)s/no pl suspi-
cion. ◆'a~wöhnisch, adj. mistrustful,
suspicious.
**Arie** ['aːriə], f -/-n aria.
**Aristokrat** [aristo'kraːt], m -en/-en aristocrat. ◆A~ie [-kra'tiː], f -/-n aristocracy. ◆a~isch [-'kraːtiʃ], adj. aristocratic.
**Arkt|is** ['arktis], Pr.n.f -. die A., the Arc-
tic. ◆'a~isch, adj. arctic.
**arm¹** [arm], adj. poor.
**Arm²** [arm], m -(e)s/-e arm; branch (of a
river); j-n auf den A. nehmen, to pull
s.o.'s leg. ◆'A~band, n bracelet;
(Uhra.) watchstrap. ◆'A~banduhr, f
wristwatch.
**Armatur** [arma'tuːr], f -/-en usu. pl
fittings. ◆A~enbrett, n Aut: dashboard; Av: etc: instrument panel.
**Armee** [ar'meː], f -/-n army.
**Ärmel** ['ɛrməl], m -s/- sleeve; F: etwas
aus dem Ä. schütteln, to produce sth.
out of a hat. ◆'A~kanal. Pr.n. m der
Ä., the (English) Channel.
**ärmlich** ['ɛrmliç], adj. poor (family, area
etc.); shabby (house etc.).
**armselig** ['armzeliç], adj. (mittellos) destitute, impoverished; (elend) miserable
(person, state, attempt etc.).
**Armut** ['armuːt], f -/no pl poverty; poorness (of soil etc.).
**Aroma** [a'roːma], n -s/-men (Geruch) aroma; (Geschmack) flavour, taste.
◆a~tisch [aro'maːtiʃ], adj. aromatic.
**Arrang|ement** [arãʒə'mãː], n -s/-s ar-
rangement. ◆a~ieren [-'ʒiːrən], v.tr.
to arrange; sich a. to come to an arrangement.
**Arrest** [a'rɛst], m -(e)s/-e detention.
**arrogan|t** [aro'gant], adj. arrogant.
◆A~z, f -/no pl arrogance.
**Arsch** [arʃ], m -(e)s/-e V: arse, N.Am:

ass.
**Art** [aːrt], f -/-en (a) kind, sort; Z: spe-
cies; Bot: variety; (b) (Weise) way, man-
ner; (c) (Wesen) nature.
**Arterie** [ar'teːriə], f -/-n artery.
◆A~nverkalkung, f arteriosclerosis.
**artig** ['aːrtiç], adj. well-behaved, good
(child etc.).
**Artikel** [ar'tiːkəl], m -s/- article.
**Artillerie** [artilə'riː], f -/-n artillery.
**Artischocke** [arti'ʃɔkə], f -/-n (globe) ar-
tichoke.
**Artist(in)** [ar'tist(in)], m -en/-en (f -/-nen)
(circus) artiste, performer.
**Arznei** [aːrts'nai], f -/-en medicine.
◆A~mittel, n -s/- medicine.
**Arzt** ['aːrtst], m -es/-e doctor.
**Ärzt|in** ['ɛːrtstin], f -/-nen woman doctor.
◆'ä~lich, adj. medical.
**As** [as], n -ses/-se ace.
**Asbest** [as'bɛst], m -(e)s/-e asbestos.
**Asche** ['aʃə], f -/-n ash; ashes (of a fire);
(Schlacke) cinders. ◆'A~nbahn, f cin-
der track. ◆'A~nbecher, m ashtray.
◆'A~nbrödel/'A~nputtel, n -s/-
Cinderella. ◆A~r'mittwoch, m Ash
Wednesday.
**Asi|at(in)** [azi'aːt(in)], m -en/-en (f -/-nen)
Asian. ◆a~'atisch, adj. Asiatic.
◆A~en ['aːziən]. Pr.n.n -s. Asia.
**asozial** ['azotsiaːl], adj. antisocial.
**Aspekt** [a'spɛkt], m -(e)s/-e aspect.
**Asphalt** [as'falt], m -s/-e asphalt.
◆a~ieren [-'tiːrən], v.tr. to surface (a
road) (with asphalt).
**Assistent(in)** [asis'tɛnt(in)], m -en/-en (f
-/-nen) assistant.
**Assozi|ation** [asotsiatsi'oːn], f -/-en asso-
ciation. ◆a~ieren [-tsi'iːrən], v.tr. to
associate.
**Ast** ['ast], m -(e)s/-e branch.
**Aster** ['astər], f -/-n aster.
**Ästhet|ik** [ɛs'teːtik], -/no pl aesthetics.
◆'ä~isch, adj. aesthetic.
**Asthma** ['astma], n -s/no pl asthma.
◆A~tiker, m -s/- asth-
matic. ◆a~tisch [-'maːtiʃ], adj. asth-
matic.
**Astro|loge(-login)** [astro'loːgə(-'loːgin)],
m -n/-n (f -/-nen) astrologer. ◆A~logie
[-lo'giː], f -/no pl astrology. ◆A~naut
[-'naut], m -en/-en astronaut.
◆A~nomie [-no'miː] f -/no pl astronomy. ◆a~nomisch [-'noːmiʃ] adj. as-
tronomical.
**Asyl** [a'zyːl], n -s/-e (a) (politisches) A.,
(political) asylum; (b) (Ort) refuge; (für
Obdachlose) home; Fig: sanctuary.
**Atelier** [atəli'eː], n -s/-s studio.
**Atem** ['aːtəm], m -s/no pl breath; außer
A., out of breath; Fig: A. holen, to
pause for breath. ◆'a~beraubend,
adj. breathtaking. ◆'a~los, adj.
breathless. ◆'A~not, f shortage of
breath. ◆'a~pause, f breathing space.
◆'A~zug, m breath.
**Atheis|mus** [ate'ismus], m -/no pl athe-

ism. ◆**A~t**, *m* **-en/-en** atheist. ◆**a~tisch**, *adj.* atheistic.

**Athen** [a'te:n]. *Pr.n.n* **-s.** Athens.

**Äther** ['ɛ:tər], *m* **-s/-** ether.

**Äthiop|ien** [ɛti'o:piən]. *Pr.n.n* **-s.** Ethiopia. ◆**ä~isch**, *adj.* Ethiopian.

**Athlet|(in)** [at'le:t(in)], *m* **-en/-en** (*f* **-/-nen**) athlete. ◆**A~ik**, *f* **-/no** *pl* athletics. ◆**a~isch**, *adj.* athletic.

**Atlant|ik** [at'lantik]. *Pr.n.m* **-s.** der A., the Atlantic (Ocean). ◆**a~isch**, *adj.* Atlantic.

**Atlas** ['atlas], *m* **-ses/At'lanten** atlas.

**atm|en** ['a:tmən], *v.tr.* & *i.* (*haben*) to breathe. ◆**'A~ung**, *f* **-/no** *pl* respiration.

**Atmosphäre** [atmos'fɛ:rə], *f* **-/-n** atmosphere.

**Atom** [a'to:m]. **I.** *n* **-s/-e** atom. **II.** **A~-**, *comb.fm.* atomic (bomb, weight etc.), nuclear (power station, war etc.). ◆**a~ar** [ato'ma:r], *adj.* atomic. ◆**A~energie**, *f* atomic/nuclear energy. ◆**A~meiler**, *m* atomic pile. ◆**A~müll**, *m* nuclear waste. ◆**A~sprengkopf**, *m* nuclear warhead. ◆**A~waffen**, *fpl* nuclear weapons.

**Attacke** [a'takə], *f* **-/-n** attack.

**Attent|at** [a'tɛnta:t], *n* **-(e)s/-e** assassination (attempt); **ein A. auf j-n verüben,** to make an attempt on s.o.'s life. ◆**A~äter(in)**, *m* **-s/-** (*f* **-/-nen**) (would-be) assassin.

**Attest** [a'tɛst], *n* **-(e)s/-e** certificate.

**Attrakt|ion** [atraktsi'o:n], *f* **-/-en** attraction. ◆**a~iv** ['-'ti:f], *adj.* attractive.

**Attrappe** [a'trapə], *f* **-/-n** dummy.

**Attribut** [atri'bu:t], *n* **-(e)s/-e** attribute. ◆**a~iv** ['-bu'ti:f], *adj.* attributive.

**ätz|en** ['ɛtsən], *v.tr.* to corrode (metal). ◆**'ä~end,** *adj.* corrosive; *Ch: & Fig:* caustic.

**auch** [aux], *adv.* & *conj.* **1.** (*zusätzlich*) (*a*) too, also; **ich bin müde—ich a.!** I am tired—so am I! (*b*) (*mit Negativ*) either; **ich a. nicht,** nor/neither do I; (*c*) (*außerdem*) what's more; **a. das noch!** that's the last straw! **2.** (*a*) (*sogar*) even; **a. wenn du nicht kommst,** even if you don't come; (*b*) (*wirklich*) **was hätte es a. für einen Sinn?** what would be the point anyway? (*c*) **wer/was a. (immer),** whoever/whatever.

**auf** [auf]. **I.** *prep.* **1.** (*räumlich*) + *dat/acc* on; **a. dem Bild/der Welt,** in the picture/the world; **a. der Post,** at the post office; **es hat nichts a. sich,** there's nothing to it; **a. etwas** *acc* **zugehen,** to go towards sth. **2.** (*zeitlich*) + *acc* **a. einige Tage** for a longer period; **a. die Minute genau,** punctual to the minute; **a. einmal war es finster,** suddenly it was dark; **etwas a. morgen verschieben,** to put sth. off until tomorrow; **a. meine Bitte (hin),** at my request. **3. a. dem kürzesten Wege,** by the shortest route; **a. diese Art/Weise,** in this way; **sich a.**

**deutsch unterhalten,** to converse in German. **II.** *adv.* up, upwards; **sich a. und davon machen,** to make off.

**'aufatmen,** *v.i.sep.* (*haben*) to draw a deep breath; (*erleichtert*) to breathe a sigh of relief.

**aufbahren** ['aufba:rən], *v.tr.sep.* to lay out.

**'Aufbau,** *m* **1.** *no* *pl* (*Aufbauen*) construction; erection (of a tent, scaffolding etc.); assembly (of a machine etc.). **2.** (*Zusammenstellung*) composition (of society, a picture etc.); structure (of a building, compound, organization, play etc.). ◆**'a~en,** *v.tr.sep.* (*a*) to construct (a building etc.); to assemble (a machine etc.); to erect (a tent, structure etc.); (*b*) to build up (reserves, a team etc.); **sich** *dat* **eine neue Existenz a.,** to build a new life for oneself; (*c*) (*Theorie usw.*) (**sich**) **auf etwas** *dat* **a.,** to be based on sth.

**'aufbäumen,** *v.tr.sep.* (*Pferd*) **sich a.,** to rear; (*Pers.*) **sich gegen j-n, etwas** *acc* **a.,** to rebel against s.o., sth.

**'aufbauschen,** *v.tr.sep.* to exaggerate.

**'aufbereiten,** *v.tr.sep.* to process.

**'aufbessern,** *v.tr.sep.* to improve (sth.); to raise (a salary etc.).

**'aufbewahr|en,** *v.tr.sep.* to keep (sth.) (safely), (*lagern*) store (luggage, furniture etc.). ◆**'A~ung,** *f* **-/no** *pl* **1.** safekeeping; (*Lagern*) storage. **2.** *Rail: etc:* (*Stelle*) left-luggage office.

**'aufbiet|en,** *v.tr.sep.irr.8* to muster, summon up (all one's tact, strength etc.).

**'aufblasen,** *v.tr. sep.irr.11* to inflate, blow up (a balloon, tyre etc.).

**'aufbleiben,** *v.i.sep.irr.12* (*sein*) (*Pers.*) to stay up; (*Geschäft usw.*) to stay open.

**'aufblicken,** *v.i.sep.* (*haben*) to look up.

**'aufblühen,** *v.i.sep.* (*sein*) (*a*) to blossom; (*b*) *Fig:* (*Handel usw.*) to prosper.

**'aufbrauchen,** *v.tr.sep.* to use up, exhaust.

**'aufbrausen,** *v.i.sep.* (*sein*) (*Pers.*) to flare up. ◆**'a~d,** *adj.* irascible (person), fiery (temperament).

**'aufbrechen,** *v.sep.irr.14* **1.** *v.tr.* to break open (a door etc.), force (a lock etc.). **2.** *v.i.* (*sein*) (*a*) to crack; (*Wunde*) to open, (*Knospe usw.*) burst; (*b*) (*Pers.*) to leave, set out (**nach** + *dat,* for).

**'aufbringen,** *v.tr.sep.irr.16* (*haben*) (*a*) to raise (money); to muster (courage, strength); (*b*) (*reizen*) to anger (s.o.).

**'Aufbruch,** *m* departure, start.

**aufbürden** ['aufbyrdən], *v.tr.sep.* **j-m etwas a.,** to saddle s.o. with sth.

**'aufdeck|en,** *v.tr.sep.* (*a*) to uncover (a bed etc.); (*b*) *Fig:* to expose (a plot, crime etc.), reveal (motives etc.).

**'aufdrängen,** *v.tr.sep.* **j-m etwas a.,** to force sth. on s.o.; **sich j-m a.,** to inflict oneself on s.o.

**'aufdrehen,** *v.tr.sep.* to turn on (a tap, the gas etc.).

**'aufdringlich,** *adj.* persistent, pushy (person); obtrusive (advertisement, object); loud (clothes, colours etc.).

**aufein'ander,** *adv. & comb.fm.* (*a*) (*übereinander*) on top of one another; (*b*) **a. losgehen,** to fly at one another. ◆**a~folgen,** *v.i.sep.* (*sein*) to follow one another. ◆**a~folgend,** *adj.* successive, consecutive. ◆**a~prallen,** *v.i.sep.* (*sein*) (*Autos usw.*) to crash into one another; *Fig:* (*Ansichten*) to clash.

**Aufenthalt** ['auf$\epsilon$nthalt], *m* -(e)s/-e (*a*) stay; (*b*) *Rail: etc:* stop. ◆**'A~serlaubnis,** *f* residence permit. ◆**'A~sraum,** *m* recreation room.

**'auferlegen,** *v.tr.sep.* to impose (taxes, a fine etc.), inflict (a punishment) (j-m, on s.o.).

**'Auferstehung,** *f* -/no pl resurrection.

**'aufessen,** *v.tr.sep.irr.25* to eat (sth.) up.

**'auffahr|en,** *v.sep.irr.26* **1.** *v.i.* (*sein*) (*a*) **auf ein anderes Fahrzeug a.,** to run into (the back of) another vehicle; (*b*) (*Pers.*) **verärgert a.,** to jump up angrily. **2.** *v.tr.sep.* to bring up (the guns). ◆**'A~t,** *f* -/-en drive; (*zur Autobahn*) access road. ◆**'A~unfall,** *m* collision.

**'auffallen,** *v.i.sep.irr.27* (*sein*) to attract attention; **ist Ihnen nichts aufgefallen?** didn't you notice anything? ◆**'a~d,** *adj.* striking (similarity, beauty etc.); marked (difference).

**'auffällig,** *adj.* flashy (dress etc.); showy (person); loud (colours etc.); **a~es Benehmen,** ostentatious behaviour.

**'auffang|en,** *v.tr.sep.irr.28* to catch (s.o., sth. falling); to pick up (words, *Rad:* signals etc.). ◆**'A~lager,** *n* transit camp (for refugees).

**'auffass|en,** *v.tr.sep.* (*a*) to understand, grasp (sth.); (*b*) (*deuten*) to interpret (sth.). ◆**'A~ung,** *f* (*a*) understanding; (*b*) view, opinion.

**'auffindbar,** *adj.* traceable; **nirgends a.,** not to be found anywhere.

**'aufforder|n,** *v.tr.sep.* **j-n a., etwas zu tun,** to call on/(*dringlich*) urge/(*bitten*) ask s.o. to do sth. ◆**'A~ung,** *f* request; **A. zum Tanz,** invitation to dance.

**'auffrisch|en,** *v.sep.* **1.** *v.tr.* to refresh (one's memory); to brush up (one's knowledge). **2.** *v.i.* (*sein/haben*) (*Wind*) to freshen.

**'aufführ|en,** *v.tr.sep.* (*a*) *Th: Mus:* to perform (a play, a piece); to show, put on (a film); (*b*) **sich gut/schlecht a.,** to behave well/badly; (*c*) to list (names, items etc.). ◆**A~ung,** *f* -/-en (*a*) performance; (*b*) listing.

**'Aufgabe,** *f* -/-n **1.** *no pl* (*a*) posting, *N.Am:* mailing; insertion (of an advertisement); *Rail:* registering (luggage); (*b*) (*Verzicht*) giving up; relinquishment (of a right); *Sp:* retirement (from a race etc.). **2.** (*Auftrag*) (*a*) task, job; *Mil: etc:* mission, assignment; (*b*) (*Zweck*) function; (*c*) *Sch:* exercise; *Mth:* problem; **A~n** *pl* (*Hausaufgaben*) homework.

**'Aufgang,** *m* (*a*) rising (of the sun); ascent (of a star); (*b*) (*Treppe*) stairway.

**'aufgeben,** *v.tr.sep.irr.35* (*haben*) (*a*) to post, *N.Am:* mail (a letter); to send (a telegram); **seine Bestellung a.,** to place one's order; **eine Annonce a.,** to put an advertisement in the paper; **sein Gepäck a.,** to register one's luggage; (*b*) **j-m eine Arbeit a.,** to set s.o. a task; (*c*) to give up (a struggle, business etc.); to abandon (an attempt, a plan).

**'Aufgebot,** *n* **1.** array; contingent (of police etc.); *Sp:* (*Mannschaft*) team, squad. **2. unter A. aller Kräfte,** using all one's strength. **3.** *Ecc:* banns.

**'aufgebracht,** *adj.* angry.

**'aufgedreht,** *adj.* *F:* in high spirits.

**'aufgedunsen,** *adj.* puffy (face); bloated (stomach etc.).

**'aufgehen,** *v.i.sep.irr.36* (*sein*) (*a*) (*Sonne, Teig, Vorhang usw.*) to rise; (*b*) (*Tür, Augen usw.*) to open; (*c*) (*Pers.*) **in etwas** *dat* **a.,** to live for sth.

**'aufgeklärt,** *adj.* broad-minded; (**sexuell**) **a. sein,** to know the facts of life.

**'aufgelegt,** *adj.* **gut/schlecht a.,** in a good/bad mood; **zu etwas** *dat* **a. sein,** to be in the mood for sth.

**'aufgeregt,** *adj.* upset; agitated.

**'aufgeschlossen,** *adj.* (*Pers.*) openminded; liberal (views).

**'aufgeschmissen,** *adj.* *F:* **a. sein,** to be in a fix.

**'aufgeweckt,** *adj.* quick-witted; (*klug*) bright (child).

**'aufgießen,** *v.tr.sep.irr.31* to make (tea, coffee).

**'aufgreifen,** *v.tr.sep.irr.43* (*a*) to pick up, catch (a criminal etc.); (*b*) to take up (an idea, a case etc.).

**'aufhaben,** *v.tr.sep.irr.44* *F:* (*a*) (*tragen*) to be wearing (a hat, spectacles etc.); (*b*) *Sch:* to have (sth.) to do as homework.

**'aufhalten,** *v.tr.sep.irr.45* (*a*) to stop (s.o., sth.); to halt (progress etc., *Mil:* an advance); (*b*) (*vorübergehend*) to hold up, delay (s.o., traffic etc.); to obstruct (a development etc.); **sich bei etwas** *dat* **a.,** to dwell on sth.; (*c*) **j-m die Tür a.,** to hold the door open for s.o.; *F:* **die Hand a.,** to hold out one's hand (for money); (*e*) **sich an einem Ort a.,** stay in a place.

**'aufhäng|en,** *v.tr.sep.* (*a*) to hang (sth.) up; to put up (curtains, a poster etc.); to hang (a picture etc.); **j-n/sich a.,** to hang s.o./oneself. ◆**'A~er,** *m* -s/- hanger.

**aufheben. I.** *v.tr.sep.irr.48* (*a*) to lift (s.o., sth.) up; (*vom Boden*) to pick (sth.) up; (*b*) (*aufbewahren*) to keep (sth.); **gut aufgehoben sein,** to be well looked after; (*c*) (*abschaffen*) to lift (a ban, restrictions etc.); to cancel (an order etc.), abolish (a tax etc.); to cancel (out) (an effect). **II. A.,** *n* -s/no pl **viel A~s um j-n, etwas** *acc* **machen,** to make a great fuss about s.o., sth.

**'aufheitern,** *v.tr.sep.* to cheer (s.o.) up;

(*Himmel, Wetter*) **sich a.**, to clear up.

'**aufhellen**, *v.tr.sep.* to lighten (colours etc.); **sich a.**, (*Gesicht*) to light up; (*Wetter*) to clear up.

'**aufhetzen**, *v.tr.sep.* to stir up (people).

'**aufholen**, *v.tr.sep.* (**den Vorsprung**) **a.**, to catch up; **die Verspätung a.**, to make up for lost time.

'**aufhorchen**, *v.i.sep.*(*haben*) to prick up one's ears.

'**aufhören**, *v.i.sep.*(*haben*) to stop; (*Freundschaft usw.*) to come to an end.

'**aufklappen**, *v.tr.sep.* to open (a knife, book etc.), raise (a lid).

'**aufklär**|**en**, *v.tr.sep.* (*a*) to clear up (a misunderstanding, crime etc.); (*b*) **j-n über etwas** *acc* **a.**, to enlighten s.o. about sth.; (**sexuell**) **a.**, to explain the facts of life; (*c*) (*Wetter*) **sich a.**, to clear (up). ◆'**A~ung**, *f* -/-**en** clarification; enlightenment; *Mil:* reconnaissance; (*sexuell*) sex education.

'**Aufkleber**, *m* -**s**/- sticker.

'**aufkochen**, *v.tr.sep.* **etwas** (**kurz**) **a. lassen**, to bring sth. to the boil.

'**aufkommen**, *v.i.sep.irr.53* (*sein*) (*a*) (*Nebel*) to rise; (*Wind*) to spring up; *Fig:* (*Zweifel usw.*) to arise; (*Stil, Mode*) to come in; (*b*) **für j-n, etwas** *acc* **a.**, to be liable for s.o., sth.

'**aufladen**, *v.tr.sep.irr.56* (*haben*) (*a*) to load (baggage etc.); (*b*) *El:* to charge (a battery).

'**Auflage**, *f* -/-**n 1.** (*a*) impression; **überarbeitete A.**, revised edition; (*b*) (*von Zeitung*) circulation. **2.** (*Beschränkung*) condition, restriction.

'**auflassen**, *v.tr.sep.irr.57* (*a*) to leave (the door etc.) open; (*b*) to keep (a hat) on; *F:* to let (children) stay up.

'**auflauern**, *v.i.sep.* (*haben*) **j-m a.**, to waylay s.o.

'**Auflauf**, *m* -(**e**)**s**/**⁀e** (*a*) crowd; (*b*) *Cu:* approx. = soufflé. ◆'**a~en**, *v.i.sep. irr.58* (*sein*) (*a*) to run aground; (*b*) (*sich anhäufen*) to accumulate.

'**aufleben**, *v.i.sep.* (*sein*) (**wieder**) **a.**, to take on a new lease of/*N.Am:* on life; (*Pflanze usw.*) to revive.

'**auflegen**, *v.tr.sep.* (*a*) to put on; *Tel:* (**den Hörer**) **a.**, to hang up; (*b*) **ein Buch neu a.**, to reprint a book.

'**auflehn**|**en**, *v.refl.sep.* **sich a.**, to rebel (**gegen** + *acc*, against). ◆'**A~ung**, *f* -/no *pl* rebellion.

'**auflesen**, *v.tr.sep.irr.61* to pick up.

'**aufleuchten**, *v.i.sep.* (*haben*) (*Licht*) to flash; (*Augen*) to light up.

'**auflockern**, *v.tr.sep.* (*a*) to break up (the soil etc.); (*b*) (*entspannen*) to make (the atmosphere etc.) more relaxed.

'**auflös**|**en**, *v.tr.sep.* (*a*) to dissolve; to untie (knots, one's hair); to close (an account etc.); (*b*) to solve (a riddle etc.); (*c*) **sich a.**, to break up; (*Salz usw.*) to dissolve; (*Menge*) to disperse; (*Nebel, Wolke*) to clear (away). ◆'**A~ung**, *f* -/-**en** (*a*)

disintegration; dissolution; (*b*) *Com:* closing (of an account).

'**aufmach**|**en**, *v.sep.* **1.** *v.tr.* (*a*) to open; to undo (buttons, string etc.); to unfasten (a dress); **ein Geschäft a.**, to set up a business; (*b*) **sich a.**, to set off. **2.** *v.i.* (*haben*) to open. ◆'**A~ung**, *f* -/-**en** appearance (of s.o., sth.); layout (of a page).

'**aufmerksam**, *adj.* (*a*) attentive; (*beobachtend*) observant; (*b*) **auf j-n, etwas** *acc* **a. werden**, to notice s.o., sth.; (*c*) (*höflich*) thoughtful. ◆'**A~keit**, *f* -/-**en** (*a*) attention; (*b*) (*Höflichkeit*) thoughtfulness.

'**aufmöbeln**, *v.tr.sep.* *F:* to do (sth.) up; to buck (s.o.) up.

'**aufmuntern**, *v.tr.sep.* to cheer (s.o.) up; (*Kaffee, Alkohol*) to buck (s.o.) up.

'**Aufnahme** ['aufnɑːmə]. *f* -/-**en 1.** opening (of negotiations etc.); establishment (of relations etc.). **2.** (*Empfang*) reception; admission; **A. beim Publikum**, public reaction. **3.** intake (of food, refugees etc.); **4.** *Phot:* photograph; *Cin: TV:* shot; (*Banda.*) recording. ◆'**a~fähig**, *adj.* receptive. ◆'**A~prüfung**, *f* entrance examination.

'**aufnehmen**, *v.tr.sep.irr.69* (*a*) to pick (sth.) up; (*aufsaugen*) to absorb (water etc.); (*b*) to take up (an idea, the fight etc.); to start (work etc.); (*c*) (*annehmen*) to accept (s.o.) (as a member etc.), include (s.o.) (in a team etc.); (*d*) (*niederschreiben*) to take down (dictation, notes etc.); (*e*) *Phot:* to photograph, take a photograph of (s.o., sth.); (*auf Band*) to record (s.o., sth.).

'**aufopfer**|**n**, *v.tr.sep.* to sacrifice. ◆'**a~nd**, *adj.* self-sacrificial.

'**aufpassen**, *v.i.sep.* (*haben*) (*a*) (*achtgeben*) to pay attention; (*b*) **auf j-n, etwas a.**, to keep an eye on s.o., sth.

'**Aufprall**, *m* impact. ◆'**a~en**, *v.i.sep.* (*sein*) **auf etwas** *acc* **a.**, to strike sth.

'**Aufpreis**, *m* -**es**/-**e** supplement.

'**aufraffen**, *refl.sep.* **sich a.**, to pull oneself together; **ich konnte mich nicht dazu a.**, I could not bring myself to do it.

'**aufräumen**, *v.tr.&i.sep.* (*haben*) to clear up/away (toys etc.); to tidy (a room etc.).

'**aufrecht**, *adj. & adv.* upright. ◆'**a~erhalten**, *v.tr.sep.irr.45* to maintain (order, contact etc.); to uphold (a tradition etc.).

'**aufreg**|**en**, *v.tr.sep.* to excite (s.o.), (*beunruhigen*) upset (s.o.); **sich a.**, to get excited/*F:* worked up. ◆'**a~end**, *adj.* exciting. ◆'**A~ung**, *f* agitation; (*Spannung*) excitement.

'**aufreiben**, *v.tr.sep.irr.12* (*a*) to chafe (the skin); (*b*) (*zermürben*) to wear (s.o.) down, fray (s.o.'s nerves). ◆'**a~d**, *adj.* gruelling.

'**aufreißen**, *v.tr.sep.irr.49* **1.** *v.tr.* to tear/rip (sth.) open; to fling (the door, window) (wide) open; to tear up (the road); **die Augen** (**weit**) **a.**, to stare wide-eyed.

'**aufreizen**, *v.tr.sep.* to provoke. ◆'**a~d**, *adj.* provocative.

'**aufricht|en**, *v.tr.sep.* (*a*) to raise, erect (a mast, pillar etc.); to help (s.o.) up; (*im Bett*) to sit (s.o.) up; (*b*) *Fig:* to console (s.o.). ◆'**a~ig**, *adj.* sincere; upright (conduct); (*offen*) frank (opinion etc.). ◆'**A~igkeit**, *f -/no pl* sincerity; frankness.

'**aufrücken**, *v.i.sep.* (*sein*) (*a*) to move up; (*b*) (*befördert werden*) to be promoted.

'**Aufruf**, *m* (*a*) summons, appeal. ◆'**a~en**, *v.tr.sep.irr.74* to summon; to call out (a name) (s.o., a witness etc.).

'**Aufruhr**, *m -s/no pl* (*a*) (*Tumult*) upheaval, commotion; (*b*) (*Aufstand*) rebellion; (*einer Meute*) riot.

'**Aufrührer**, *m -s/-* rioter; (*Aufständischer*) rebel. ◆**a~isch**, *adj.* rioting (crowd), rebellious (people).

'**aufrunden**, *v.tr.sep.* to round up, *N. Am:* round off.

'**aufrüst|en**, *v.tr.&i.sep.* (*haben*) to (re)arm. ◆'**A~ung**, *f* (re)armament.

'**aufrütteln**, *v.tr.sep.* to shake (s.o.) up.

'**aufsagen**, *v.tr.sep.* to recite.

'**aufsammeln**, *v.tr.sep.* to pick up, collect.

'**aufsässig** ['aufzɛsiç], *adj.* refractory (child); rebellious (people).

'**Aufsatz**, *m -es/-̈e* 1. essay. 2. top (of a dresser etc.).

'**aufsaugen**, *v.tr.sep.irr.76* to absorb (*Schwamm*) soak up.

'**aufschauen**, *v.i.sep.* (*haben*) to look up.

'**aufschieben**, *v.tr.sep.irr.82* (*a*) to slide open (a window etc.); (*b*) (*verschieben*) to postpone (sth.).

'**Aufschlag**, *m* 1. (*Aufprall*) impact (of a bomb etc.). 2. *Sp:* service. 3. *Com:* surcharge. 4. (*Hosena.*) turn-up; (*Ärmela.*) cuff; (*Mantela.*) lapel. ◆'**a~en**, *v.sep.irr.85* 1. *v.i.* (*a*) (*sein*) **auf den Boden (hart) a.**, to hit the ground (hard); (*b*) (*haben*) *Sp:* to serve; (*c*) (*sein*) (*Tür usw.*) to burst open; (*d*) (*haben*) (*Waren usw.*) to go up (in price). 2. *v.tr.* (*a*) to break (sth.) open; to crack (an egg); to open (a book, paper, one's eyes etc.); (*b*) to put up (a tent etc.).

'**aufschließen**, *v.sep.irr.31* 1. *v.tr.* to unlock. 2. *v.i.* (*haben*) (*aufrücken*) to close up.

'**Aufschluß**, *m* **A. über etwas** *acc* **geben**, to provide information about sth. ◆'**a~reich**, *adj.* revealing (facts); (*lehrreich*) informative (talk etc.).

'**aufschnappen**, *v.sep.* 1. *v.tr. F:* (*Pers.*) to catch (s.o.'s words etc.). 2. *v.i.* (*sein*) to spring open.

'**aufschneid|en**, *v.sep.irr.59* 1. *v.tr.* (*a*) to cut (sth.) open; (*b*) to slice (bread etc.). 2. *v.i.* (*haben*) *F:* to brag. ◆'**A~er**, *m -s/- F:* show-off.

'**Aufschnitt**, *m* (selection of) sliced cold meat; *N.Am:* cold cuts.

'**aufschrecken**, *v.sep.* 1. *v.tr.* to startle

(s.o.). 2. *v.i.irr.23* (*sein*) to start (up).

'**Aufschrei**, *m* cry, yell. ◆'**a~en**, *v.i.sep.irr.88* (*haben*) to cry out.

'**aufschreiben**, *v.tr.sep.irr.12* to write (sth.) down.

'**Aufschrift**, *f* writing; (*Etikett*) label.

'**Aufschub**, *m* delay.

'**aufschwatzen**, *v.tr.sep.* **j-m etwas a.**, to talk s.o. into buying sth.

'**Aufschwung**, *m* 1. upward swing. 2. *Fig:* upturn.

'**aufseh|en**. I. *v.i.sep.irr.92* (*haben*) to look up. II. **A.**, *n -s/no pl* **A. erregen/verursachen**, to cause a stir; **ohne A.**, unnoticed. ◆'**a~enerregend**, *adj.* sensational. ◆'**A~er(in)**, *m -s/- (f -/-nen)* supervisor (*im Museum, am Parkplatz*) attendant; (*im Gefängnis*) warder.

'**aufsein**, *v.i.sep.irr.93* (*sein*) (*a*) to be open; (*b*) (*Pers.*) to be up.

'**aufsetzen**, *v.sep.* 1. *v.tr.* (*a*) to put on (a hat, the kettle); (*b*) to draft (a letter, contract etc.); (*c*) (*Pers.*) **sich a.**, to sit up. 2. *v.i.* (*haben*) (*Flugzeug*) to touch down.

'**Aufsicht**, *f no pl* supervision; **A. haben/führen**, to be in charge (of sth.). ◆**A~srat**, *m* board of directors.

'**aufsitzen**, *v.sep.irr.97* (*a*) (*haben*) to sit up; (*b*) (*sein*) (*Reiter, Fahrer*) to get on; (*c*) (*sein*) **j-m, etwas** *dat* **a.**, to be taken in by s.o., sth.

'**aufspannen**, *v.tr.sep.* to put up.

'**aufsparen**, *v.tr.sep.* to save up, keep (sth.).

'**aufsperren**, *v.tr.sep.* (*a*) (*Vogel/Tier*) to open (its beak/mouth) wide; (*b*) to unlock (a door).

'**aufspießen**, *v.tr.sep.* to spear (sth.).

'**aufspringen**, *v.i.sep.irr.19* (*sein*) (*a*) to jump up; **auf etwas** *acc* **a.**, to jump onto sth.; (*b*) (*Deckel usw.*) to spring open; (*Knospen*) to burst; (*Haut*) to crack.

'**aufspüren**, *v.tr.sep.* to trace (s.o., sth.), track down (a criminal).

'**aufstacheln**, *v.tr.sep.* to incite.

'**Aufstand**, *m* revolt, rebellion.

'**aufständisch**, *adj.* rebellious.

'**aufstecken**, *v.tr.sep.* (*a*) to put up (one's hair etc.); (*b*) *F:* to give up (a plan etc.).

'**aufstehen**, *v.i.sep.irr.100* (*a*) (*sein*) to stand up; (*vom Bett*) to get up; (*b*) (*haben*) (*Tür usw.*) to stand open.

'**aufsteigen**, *v.i.sep.irr.89* (*sein*) (*a*) to get on; (*b*) (*Ballon usw.*) to ascend; (*Rauch, Sonne etc.*) to rise; (*Nebel*) to lift.

'**aufstell|en**, *v.tr.sep.* (*a*) to put up (a tent, statue etc.); to set up (a machine); (*b*) to place (chairs, a ladder etc.) in position; (*Pers.*) **sich a.**, to station oneself; (*in Reihen*) to line up; (*c*) to put up (a candidate); (*d*) to form (a team etc.); to set (a record); to draw up (a list, table); to draft (a plan); to lay down (rules, norms); **eine Behauptung a.**, to make a statement. ◆'**A~ung**, *f* 1. (*a*) erection; assembly (of a machine); (*b*) positioning; (*c*) *Parl:* nomination; (*d*) formation (of a team). 2. (*Liste*) list.

**Aufstieg** ['aufʃtiːk], *m* -(e)s/-e 1. climb; ascent (*esp.* of a rocket, balloon). 2. rise (**zur Macht usw.**, to power etc.); (*im Rang*) promotion.

'**aufstoßen**, *v.sep.irr.103* 1. *v.tr.* to push/ (*mit dem Fuß*) kick open (a door etc.). 2. *v.i.* (sein) (*Baby*) to burp; (*Betrunkener usw.*) to belch.

'**Aufstrich**, *m* spread.

'**aufsuchen**, *v.tr.sep.* to look (s.o.) up; to go to see (a doctor).

'**auftakel**|**n**, *v.tr.sep.* (*a*) *Nau:* to rig (a ship); (*b*) *F:* **sich a.**, to doll oneself up.

'**Auftakt**, *m Fig:* opening.

'**auftanken**, *v.tr.&i.sep.* (*haben*) to fill up (a car); to refuel (an aircraft).

'**auftauchen**, *v.i.sep.* (sein) (*a*) to emerge; (*U-Boot, Taucher*) to surface; (*b*) (*Pers., Verlorenes*) to turn up.

'**auftauen**, *v.tr.&i.sep.* (*a*) to thaw (sth.); *Fig:* (*Pers.*) to get going.

'**aufteil**|**en**, *v.tr.sep.* to divide (sth.) up. ◆'**A~ung**, *f* division.

'**auftischen**, *v.tr.sep.* to serve up (food), dish up (a meal, *F:* lies etc.).

**Auftrag** ['auftraːk], *m* -(e)s/-e (*Aufgabe*) task; (*Bestellung*) order; **im A. der Firma X**, on behalf of Messrs X. ◆'**a~en**, *v.tr.sep.irr.85* (*a*) to serve up (a meal); (*b*) to apply, put on (paint, make-up etc.); (*c*) **j-m etwas a.**, to instruct s.o. to do sth. ◆'**A~geber(in)**, *m* (*f*) client.

'**auftreiben**, *v.tr.sep.irr.12 F:* to get hold of (s.o., sth.); to raise (money).

'**auftreten**. I. *v.i.sep.irr.105* (sein) (*a*) (*Pers.*) **leise usw. a.**, to tread softly etc.; (*b*) (*Pers.*) to appear; **selbstbewußt a.**, to behave/act confidently. II. **A.**, *n* -s/*no pl* (*a*) appearance; (*b*) (*Benehmen*) bearing.

'**Auftrieb**, *m* (im *Wasser*) buoyancy; *Av:* lift; *Fig:* impetus.

'**Auftritt**, *m* (*a*) appearance; (*b*) *Th:* scene (of a play).

'**aufwachen**, *v.i.sep.*(sein) to wake up.

'**aufwachsen**, *v.i.sep.irr.107* (sein) to grow up.

**Aufwand** ['aufvant], *m* -(e)s/*no pl* expenditure.

'**aufwärmen**, *v.tr.sep.* (*a*) to warm up (food); *F:* to rehash (a story), rake up (s.o.'s past etc.); (*b*) **sich a.**, to warm oneself up; *Sp:* to warm up.

'**aufwarten**, *v.i.sep.* (*haben*) **mit etwas** *dat* **a.**, to come up with sth.

**aufwärts** ['aufverts]. I. *adv.* upwards. II. '**A~-**, *comb.fm.* upward (movement, trend etc.). ◆'**a~gehen**, *v.i.sep.irr.36* (sein) to get better; **mit ihm geht es aufwärts**, things are looking up for him.

'**aufwecken**, *v.tr.sep.* to wake (s.o.) up.

'**aufweichen**, *v.tr.* to soften (sth.); (*im Wasser*) to leave (sth.) to soak.

'**aufweisen**, *v.tr.sep.irr.70* **etwas a. können**, to have sth. to show for oneself.

'**aufwend**|**en**, *v.tr.sep.* to spend (money, time), use up (material, energy); to de-

vote (effort, time). ◆'**a~ig**, *adj.* lavish; (*kostspielig*) costly.

'**aufwert**|**en**, *v.tr.sep.* to revalue. ◆'**A~ung**, *f* revaluation.

'**aufwiegeln**, *v.tr.sep.* to incite.

'**aufwiegen**, *v.tr.sep.irr.7* to offset (sth.).

'**aufwirbeln**, *v.tr.sep.* to whirl (leaves etc.) into the air; *Fig:* **Staub a.**, to cause a stir.

'**aufwisch**|**en**, *v.tr.sep.* to wipe/mop up.

'**aufzähl**|**en**, *v.tr.sep.* to list. ◆'**A~ung**, *f* list.

'**aufzeichn**|**en**, *v.tr.sep.* (*a*) to sketch (sth.); (*b*) (*festhalten*) to record. ◆'**A~ung**, *f* (*a*) sketch; (*b*) record; recording.

'**aufziehen**, *v.sep.irr.113* 1. *v.tr.* (*a*) to hoist (a sail, flag); (*b*) (*öffnen*) to open (a zip, drawer etc.); to draw back (the curtains); (*c*) to wind up (a clock etc.); (*d*) to bring up (a child), rear (an animal); (*e*) *F:* **j-n a.**, to tease s.o. 2. *v.i.* (sein) (*Sturm, Wolken*) to come up.

'**Aufzug**, *m* 1. procession. 2. (*Fahrstuhl*) lift, *N.Am:* elevator. 3. *Pej: F:* get-up. 4. *Th:* act (of a play).

'**aufzwingen**, *v.tr.sep.irr.19* **j-m etwas a.**, to force sth. on s.o.

**Augapfel** ['aukʔapfəl], *m* eyeball; *Fig:* **er hütet es wie seinen A.**, he keeps it in cotton wool.

**Auge** ['augə], *n* -s/-n eye; **kein A. zutun**, not to sleep a wink; **vor aller A~n**, in public; **unter vier A~n**, in private; **j-n, etwas aus den A~n verlieren**, to lose sight of (s.o., sth.; **etwas mit anderen A~n ansehen**, to view sth. differently; **ein A. zudrücken**, to turn a blind eye to sth. ◆'**A~n-**, *comb.fm.* eye (shade, trouble, drops, lotion etc.); optic (nerve etc.). ◆'**a~nblick**, *m* moment; **im A.**, at the moment. ◆'**a~nblicklich**, *adj.* (*a*) immediate; (*b*) (*derzeitig*) present (situation etc.). ◆'**a~nbraue**, *f* eyebrow. ◆'**a~nfällig**, *adj.* conspicuous; obvious. ◆'**A~nmaß**, *n* visual judgment (of distance). ◆'**A~nschein**, *m Lit:* **dem A. nach.**, to all appearances. ◆'**A~nweide**, *f* sight for sore eyes. ◆'**A~nzeuge**, *m* eyewitness.

**August** [au'gust], *m* -s/-e August.

**Auktion** [auktsi'oːn], *f* -/-en auction. ◆**A~ator** [auktsio'naːtɔr], *m* -s/-en auctioneer.

**Aula** ['aula], *f* -/-len assembly hall.

**aus** [aus]. I. *prep.* + *dat* 1. (*Richtung*) (*a*) out of; **a. dem Haus**, out of the house; (*b*) from; **der Zug kommt a. Hamburg**, the train comes from Hamburg. 2. (*Material*) made of. 3. (*Grund*) from, out of (fear, habit etc.). II. *adv.* (*a*) (*Licht, Feuer*) out; (*Schalter*) off; (*b*) (*vorbei*) over; **es ist a. mit ihm**, it's all up with him; (*c*) **er geht bei ihr ein und a.**, he comes and goes in her house; *Fig:* **er weiß weder a. noch ein**, he is at his wits' end; **auf etwas** *acc* **a. sein**, to be set/bent on sth. **III. A.,** *n -/no pl Sp:* **im/ ins A.,** out of play.

'**ausarbeiten,** *v.tr.sep.* to think out (a plan etc.); draw up (a contract etc.).

'**ausarten,** *v.i.sep.* (*sein*) to degenerate.

'**ausatmen,** *v.tr.&i.sep.* (*haben*) to breathe out, exhale (air).

'**ausbaden,** *v.tr.sep. F:* to carry the can for (s.o.'s mistakes etc.).

'**Ausbau,** *m* **1.** *Tchn:* removal (of a part). **2.** (*Erweiterung*) widening; extension; (*Umbau*) conversion (of an attic etc.). ◆'**a~en,** *v.tr.sep.* (*a*) *Tchn:* to remove (a part, an engine); (*b*) to widen (a road); to extend (a house, network etc.).

'**ausbessern,** *v.tr.sep.* to repair, fix, (*behelfsmäßig*) patch up (sth., damage etc.); to mend (clothes).

'**ausbeulen,** *v.tr.sep.* (*a*) to knock out the dent(s) in (a hat, etc.); (*b*) to make (trousers etc.) baggy.

'**Ausbeut**|**e,** *f* yield; *Fig:* (*Gewinn*) gain. ◆'**a~en,** *v.tr.sep.* (*a*) to exploit (resources etc.), work (a mine etc.); (*b*) (*ausnutzen*) to exploit (s.o.). ◆'**A~er(in),** *m -s/- (f -/-nen)* exploiter; *F:* slave-driver. ◆'**A~ung,** *f -/no pl* exploitation; *Min:* working.

'**ausbild**|**en,** *v.tr.sep.* to train. ◆'**A~er(in),** *m (f)* instructor. ◆'**A~ung,** *f* training; (*further/ university*) education. ◆'**A~ungs-, comb.fm.** training (camp, film, method etc.).

'**ausbitten,** *v.tr.sep.irr.10* **sich** *dat* **etwas a.,** to ask for sth.

'**ausbleiben,** *v.i.sep.irr.12* (*sein*) (*Pers.*) to fail to appear/(*Wirkung, Erwartetes*) materialize; **es konnte nicht a., daß ...,** it was inevitable that ...

'**Ausblick,** *m* (*a*) view; (*b*) *Fig:* prospect.

'**ausbrech**|**en,** *v.i.sep.irr.14* (*sein*) (*a*) (*Feuer, Krieg usw.*) to break out; (*Vulkan*) to erupt; *Fig:* **in Tränen/Gelächter a.,** to burst into tears/laughter; (*b*) (**aus dem Gefängnis**) **a.,** to break out (of prison). ◆'**A~er,** *m -s/-* escaped prisoner.

'**ausbreiten,** *v.tr.sep.* (*a*) to spread out (wares, a map, wings etc.), to open out (a newspaper etc.); (*b*) **sich a.,** to spread.

'**ausbrennen,** *v.tr.sep.irr.15* **1.** *v.tr.* to burn out; *Med:* to cauterize. **2.** *v.i.* (*sein*) to burn out.

'**Ausbruch,** *m* (*a*) (*Beginn*) outbreak; eruption (of a volcano); (*b*) escape (from prison, etc.); (*c*) outburst (of rage etc.).

'**ausbrüten,** *v.tr.sep.* to hatch out (eggs); *Fig:* to think up (a plan).

'**Ausbuchtung,** *f -/-en* bulge.

'**Ausdauer,** *f* staying power; (*Durchhalten*) perseverance. ◆'**a~nd,** *adj.* tenacious.

'**ausdehn**|**en,** *v.tr.sep.* (*a*) to stretch, expand (sth.); to extend (frontiers, contacts etc.); (*b*) **sich a.,** to stretch, extend; (*Stadt, Handel, Ch: Gas*) to expand. ◆'**A~ung,** *f -/-en* (*a*) expansion; (*b*) (*Fläche*) expanse, extent.

'**ausdenken,** *v.tr.sep.irr.17* (*a*) **sich** *dat* **einen Plan usw. a.,** to devise a plan; (*b*) **es ist nicht auszudenken!** it doesn't bear thinking about!

'**ausdrehen,** *v.tr.sep. F:* to turn off.

'**Ausdruck1,** *m -(e)s/-̈e* expression; **zum A. kommen,** to be expressed. ◆'**A~sweise,** *f* mode of expression.

'**Ausdruck2,** *m -(e)s/-e* *Data-pr:* print-out.

'**ausdrück**|**en,** *v.sep.* **1.** *v.tr.* (*a*) to squeeze (out) (water, juice etc.); to stub out (a cigarette); (*b*) to express (an opinion etc.); **anders ausgedrückt,** in other words. ◆'**a~lich,** *adj.* explicit; express (wish, command etc.).

**ausein'ander,** *adv. & comb.fm.* (*a*) apart; (*b*) (*kaputt*) in pieces. ◆**a~bringen,** *v.tr.sep.irr.16* to separate. ◆**a~fallen,** *v.i.sep.irr.27* (*sein*) to fall/come to pieces. ◆**a~gehen,** *v.i.sep.irr.36* (*sein*) (*a*) (*Wege usw.*) to diverge; *Fig:* (*Meinungen usw.*) to differ; (*Paar*) to split up. ◆**a~halten,** *v.tr.sep.irr.45* (*unterscheiden*) to tell (people) apart. ◆**a~nehmen,** *v.tr.sep.irr.69* to take to pieces. ◆**a~setzen,** *v.tr.sep.* (*a*) (*erklären*) to explain (ideas etc.); (*b*) **sich mit einem Problem a.,** to come to terms with a problem; **sich mit j-m a.,** to have it out with s.o. ◆**A~setzung,** *f -/-en* (*a*) discussion; (*b*) (*Streit*) argument.

'**auserlesen,** *adj.* select (people); choice (food, wine); exquisite (taste etc.).

'**ausfahr**|**en,** *v.sep.irr.26* **1.** *v.tr.* (*a*) to take (s.o.) out for a drive; (*b*) *Tchn:* to lower (*Av:* landing gear etc.); to raise (an aerial, periscope etc.). **2.** *v.i.* (*sein*) to drive out; (*Schiff*) to leave harbour. ◆'**A~t,** *f* **1.** (*Abfahrt*) departure. **2.** exit (from a garage, motorway etc.).

'**Ausfall,** *m* **1.** (*a*) (*Verlust*) loss (of hair, earnings etc.); (*b*) (*Absagen*) cancellation; (*c*) (*Versagen*) failure; stoppage (of a factory). **2.** *Mil:* sortie. ◆'**a~en,** *v.i.sep.irr.27* (*sein*) (*a*) (*Zähne, Haare usw.*) to fall out; (*b*) to turn out (well, badly etc.); (*c*) (*Vorstellung, Zug usw.*) to be cancelled; (*d*) (*Maschine usw.*) to break down. ◆'**a~end,** *adj.* impertinent. ◆'**A~straße,** *f* arterial road (out of a town).

'**ausfeilen,** *v.tr.sep.* to file (sth.) to shape; *Fig:* to polish (a speech etc.).

'**ausfertig**|**en,** *v.tr.sep.* to draw up (a contract etc.), make out (a bill etc.); to issue (a passport etc.). ◆'**A~ung,** *f -/-en* (*a*) drawing up, making out; issuing; (*b*) (*Exemplar*) copy.

'**ausfindig,** *adv.* **j-n, etwas a. machen,** to locate s.o., sth.

'**Ausflucht,** *f -/-̈e* excuse, pretext.

'**Ausflug,** *m* excursion.

'**Ausflügler(in)** ['ausfly:glər(in)], *m -s/- (f -/-nen)* day-tripper.

'**Ausfluß,** *m* (*a*) outflow (of water etc.); discharge (of sewage, *Med:* of pus etc.); (*b*) (*Abfluß*) drain, outlet.

'**ausfragen,** *v.tr.sep.* to interrogate, quiz (s.o.).

'**ausfransen,** *v.i.sep.* (sein) to fray (at the edges).

'**ausfressen,** *v.tr.sep.irr.25* F: **was hat er ausgefressen?** what has he been up to?

'**Ausfuhr,** *f -/-en* export.

'**ausführ|bar,** *adj.* **1.** exportable (goods etc.). **2.** (*durchführbar*) feasible. ◆'**a~en,** *v.tr.sep.* (*a*) to export (goods); (*b*) to carry out (an order, a plan, repair etc.); (*c*) to take out (a dog, a girl etc.); (*d*) to elaborate (a question etc.). ◆'**a~lich,** *adj.* detailed; *adv.* in detail. ◆'**A~ung,** *f* **1.** (*Vollzug*) execution; (*Bau*) construction; (*Qualität*) workmanship. **2.** (*Bemerkung*) remark, comment. **3.** *esp. Com:* version; *Aut:* model; (*Lack, Appretur usw.*) finish.

'**ausfüllen,** *v.tr.sep.* (*a*) to fill (up) (a space); to fill in/*N.Am:* fill out (a form); (*b*) to occupy (time, s.o. etc.).

'**Ausgabe,** *f* **1.** (*a*) handing out, (*Verkauf*) sale (of stamps etc.); issue (of shares); (*b*) (*Schalter*) counter. **2.** edition (of a book, news broadcast etc.); issue (of a periodical). **3.** *usu. pl* **A~n,** expenditure.

'**Ausgang,** *m* **1.** way out, exit. **2.** (*a*) **A. haben,** to have time off; (*b*) (*Anfang*) beginning. **3.** (*Ende*) end; (*Ergebnis*) result. ◆'**A~s-,** *comb.fm.* (*a*) starting, initial (position etc.); original (condition, question etc.); (*b*) *El:* output (voltage, stage). ◆'**A~spunkt** *m* starting point, point of departure.

'**ausgeben,** *v.tr.sep.irr.35* (*a*) to hand out, distribute (food etc.); to issue (tickets, *Fin:* shares, notes); (*b*) to spend (money); (*c*) **er gibt sich als Engländer aus,** he pretends to be English.

'**ausgebucht,** *adj.* fully booked.

'**ausgedehnt,** *adj.* extensive; (*riesig*) vast.

'**ausgefallen,** *adj.* off-beat (style etc.); eccentric (taste).

'**ausgeglichen,** *adj.* stable (person, etc.); even (temperament). ◆**A~heit,** *f -/no pl* (good) balance; stability.

'**ausgeh|en,** *v.i.sep.irr.36* (sein) (*a*) to go out; (*b*) **F: der Vorschlag ging von ihm aus,** the suggestion came from him; **gehen wir einmal davon aus, daß ...,** let us assume that ...; (*c*) (*Zähne, Haare usw.*) to fall out; (*Geld usw.*) to run out; (*d*) **die Sache ging gut/schlecht aus,** the affair ended well/badly; (*e*) (*Licht, Feuer*) to go out; (*f*) **auf etwas** *acc* **a.,** to set out to do sth.; **leer a.,** to come away empty-handed. ◆'**A~verbot,** *n* curfew.

'**ausgelassen,** *adj.* exuberant; (*wild*) unruly (child etc.); wild (party).

'**ausgemacht,** *adj.* (*a*) agreed, settled (terms etc.); (*b*) *F:* downright (stupidity etc.).

'**ausgenommen. 1.** *prep. + gen/dat* except (for). **2.** *conj.* **a.** (**wenn**) **es regnet,** unless it rains.

'**ausgeprägt,** *adj.* marked.

'**ausgerechnet,** *adv.* **a. ihm mußte das passieren!** it had to happen to him of all people!

'**ausgeschlossen,** *pred. adj.* out of the question.

'**ausgesprochen,** *adj.* decided (preference etc.); pronounced (talent).

'**ausgestorben,** *adj.* extinct (animal); *Fig:* **wie a.,** (*Stadt usw.*) dead, deserted.

'**Ausgestoßene(r),** *m & f decl. as adj.* outcast.

'**ausgezeichnet,** *adj.* excellent.

**ausgiebig** ['ausgi:biç], *adj.* extensive (discussion etc.); **a. frühstücken/schlafen,** to have a really good breakfast/sleep.

'**Ausgleich,** *m* **-(e)s/no pl 1.** (*Gleichgewicht*) equilibrium, balance. **2.** (*Entschädigung*) compensation. **3.** *Fb:* (*Tor*) equalizer. ◆'**a~en,** *v.tr.sep.irr.40* (*a*) to balance (weights, *Fig:* an account etc.); to reconcile (differences, opposites); to compensate/make up for (a loss, lack etc.); **sich a.,** (*zwei Sachen*) to cancel one another out; (*b*) *Fb:* **a.,** to equalize. ◆'**A~ssport** *m* keep-fit (exercises). ◆'**A~streffer,** *m Fb:* equalizer.

'**ausgrab|en,** *v.tr.sep.irr.42 also Fig:* to dig (sth.) up; to excavate (ruins). ◆'**A~ung,** *f -/-en* excavation, dig.

'**Ausguß,** *m* (*Becken*) sink; (*Abfluß*) plughole.

'**aushaben,** *v.tr.sep.irr.44* F: **ich habe das Buch aus,** I have finished the book.

'**aushalten,** *v.tr.sep.irr.45* (*a*) to bear, stand (s.o., sth.); to endure (pain etc.); (*b*) *F:* to keep (s.o.); **er läßt sich von ihr a.,** he lives off her earnings.

'**aushandeln,** *v.tr.sep.* to negotiate.

**aushändigen** ['aushɛndigən], *v.tr.sep.* to hand (sth.) over, hand out (prizes etc.).

'**Aushang,** *m* notice.

'**aushänge|n,** *v.sep.* **1.** *v.tr.* (*a*) to put up, post (a sign, notice etc.); (*b*) to take (a door) off its hinges. **2.** *v.i.irr.46* (haben) to be displayed. ◆'**A~schild,** *n* sign.

'**ausharren,** *v.i.sep.* (haben) to persevere.

'**aushelfen,** *v.i.sep.irr.50* (haben) (j-m) a., to help (s.o.) out.

'**Aushilf|e,** *f -/-n* (*a*) assistance; (*b*) (*Pers.*) temporary worker. ◆'**A~skraft,** *f* temporary worker, *F:* temp.

'**aushöhlen,** *v.tr.sep.* to hollow out (sth.), scrape out (a melon etc.); to undermine (a river bank etc.).

'**ausholen,** *v.i.sep.* (haben) **mit dem Arm a.,** to raise one's arm; *Fig:* **weit a.,** to go back a long way.

'**aushorchen,** *v.tr.sep.* to sound (s.o.) out.

'**auskennen,** *v.refl.sep.irr.51* **sich a.,** to know what's what/*F:* the ropes; (*in einem Ort*) to know one's way about.

'**auskippen,** *v.tr.sep.* F: to tip out/*N.Am:* dump (a load etc.).

'**ausklammern,** *v.tr.sep.* to leave on one side, exclude (a topic etc.).

'**auskleiden,** *v.tr.sep.* (*a*) *Lit:* to undress (s.o., oneself); (*b*) to line (a wall etc.).

'**ausklingen,** *v.i.sep.irr.19* (*sein*) to come to an end.

'**ausklopfen,** *v.tr.sep.* to beat (a carpet etc.); to knock out (a pipe etc.).

'**auskommen. I.** *v.i.sep.irr.53* (*sein*) (*a*) **mit etwas** *dat* **a.,** to make do/manage with sth.; (*b*) **mit j-m a.,** to get on with s.o. **II. A.,** *n -s/no pl* **er hat ein gutes A.,** he is quite well off.

'**auskundschaften,** *v.tr.sep.* to reconnoitre (an area), spy out (a secret etc.).

**Auskunft** ['auskunft], *f -̈e* (*a*) (item of) information; (*b*) (*Stelle*) information (desk/bureau); *Tel:* Enquiries.

'**auskuppeln,** *v.i.sep.* (*haben*) *Aut:* to let out the clutch.

'**auslachen,** *v.tr.sep.* to laugh at, (*verspotten*) make fun of (s.o.).

'**ausladen,** *v.sep.irr.56* 1. *v.tr.* (*a*) to unload; (*b*) *F:* **einen Gast a.,** to put off a guest. 2. *v.i.* (*haben*) to jut out.

'**Auslage,** *f* 1. *pl.* **A~n,** outlay. 2. (*Schaufenster*) shop window; (*Ausgestelltes*) display.

'**Ausland,** *n* **das A.,** foreign countries; **im/ins A.,** abroad. ◆'**A~s-,** *comb.fm.* (*a*) foreign (business, department etc.); (*b*) international (relations, *Tel:* call etc.). ◆'**A~skorrespondent(in),** *m* (*f*) (*a*) (*Journalist*) foreign correspondent; (*b*) (*Sekretär*) bilingual secretary. ◆'**A~sreise,** *f* trip abroad.

**Ausländer(in)** ['auslɛndər(in)], *m -s/- (f -/-nen)* foreigner. ◆'**a~isch,** *adj.* foreign.

'**auslass|en,** *v.tr.sep.irr.57* (*a*) to let out (steam, water, a dress etc.); (*b*) to leave out, omit (sth.); *F:* to leave off (a piece of clothing); (*c*) *Cu:* to melt (butter); (*d*) **seine schlechte Laune an j-m a.** to take it out on s.o.; **sich über etwas** *acc* **a.,** go on about sth. ◆'**A~ung,** *f -/-en* omission. ◆'**A~ungszeichen,** *n* apostrophe.

'**auslasten,** *v.tr.sep.* to use (a machine, etc.) to capacity; **voll ausgelastet,** fully occupied.

'**Auslauf,** *m* 1. outlet, outflow (for water etc.). 2. **der Hund hat hier keinen A.,** there's no space for the dog to run free here. ◆'**a~en,** *v.sep.irr.58 v.i.* (*sein*) (*a*) (*Flüssigkeit*) to run out, (*durch Leck*) leak; (*Farben*) to run; (*b*) (*Schiff*) to leave harbour; (*c*) (*enden*) to come to an end.

'**Ausläufer,** *m* 1. (*Rand*) fringe; spur (of a mountain). 2. *Bot:* runner. 3. *Meteor:* ridge (of high pressure); trough (of low pressure).

'**ausleeren,** *v.tr.sep.* to empty.

'**ausleg|en,** *v.tr.sep.* (*a*) to display (goods etc.); (*b*) to cover (a surface); (*c*) **für j-n Geld a.,** to lend s.o. money; (*d*) (*deuten*) to interpret (a text, s.o.'s behaviour etc.). ◆'**A~ung,** *f -/-en* interpretation.

'**ausleiern,** *v.tr.sep. F:* to wear out (a mechanism etc.); to stretch (elastic).

'**Ausleihe,** *f -/-n* issue desk (in a library).

◆'**a~en,** *v.tr.sep.irr.60* (*a*) to borrow (money); to take out (a book); (*b*) to lend (sth.) (**an j-n,** to s.o.).

'**Auslese,** *f* 1. *no pl* selection. 2. elite (of society etc.); (*Wein*) wine from specially selected grapes. ◆'**a~n,** *v.tr.sep.irr.61* (*a*) to select (flowers etc.); (*b*) to finish reading (a book etc.).

'**ausliefer|n,** *v.tr.sep.* (*a*) *Com:* to distribute (goods); (*b*) to hand over (s.o.); (*an einen Staat*) to extradite (s.o.). ◆'**A~ung,** *f* 1. *Com:* distribution. 2. handing over; extradition.

'**auslöschen,** *v.tr.sep.* (*a*) to extinguish, put out (a fire, candle etc.); (*b*) to efface (memories); (*c*) to annihilate (a people, lives).

'**auslös|en,** *v.tr.sep.* (*a*) to trigger off (an event etc.); to cause (surprise, joy etc.); to set off (an alarm etc.); (*b*) to redeem (pawned goods); to bail out (a prisoner). ◆'**A~er,** *m -s/-* trigger; *Phot:* (shutter) release.

'**auslosen,** *v.tr.sep.* to draw lots for (sth.).

'**ausmachen,** *v.tr.sep.* (*a*) (*Summe, Zahl*) to amount to (sth.); (*Sachen*) to constitute (a whole, part); (*b*) (*erkennen*) to make out (a ship etc.); (*c*) *F:* (*vereinbaren*) to agree (a time, meeting point etc.); (*d*) *F:* to turn off (the light, radio etc.); to put out (a cigarette etc.); (*e*) *F:* (*bedeuten*) to matter; **macht es Ihnen etwas aus, wenn ich rauche?** do you mind if I smoke?

'**ausmalen,** *v.tr.sep.* (*a*) to paint; (*b*) *Fig:* **sich** *dat* **etwas anders a.,** to imagine sth. differently.

'**Ausmaß,** *m* (*Größe*) size; *Fig:* (*Umfang*) extent (of destruction etc.).

**ausmerzen** ['ausmɛrtsən], *v.tr.sep.* to eliminate.

'**ausmessen,** *v.tr.sep.irr.25* to measure.

**Ausnahm|e** ['ausnaːmə], *f -/-n* exception. ◆'**A~efall,** *m* exception, exceptional case. ◆'**A~ezustand,** *m* state of emergency. ◆'**a~slos,** *adv.* without exception. ◆'**a~sweise,** *adv.* as an exception; for once.

'**ausnehmen,** *v.tr.sep.irr.69* (*a*) to take (sth.) out; to gut (a fish etc.); (*b*) (*ausschließen*) to exclude, exempt (s.o.); (*c*) *P:* (*Geld abnehmen*) to fleece (s.o.); (*d*) *v.refl.* **sich gut/schlecht a.,** (*Pers.*) make a good/bad impression. ◆'**a~d,** *adv.* exceptionally.

'**ausnutz|en,** *v.tr.sep.* (*a*) to exploit (a source of energy etc.); to utilize (time etc.); (*b*) *Pej:* to take advantage of. ◆'**A~ung,** *f -/no pl* exploitation.

'**auspacken,** *v.tr.sep.* to unpack (goods, clothes), unwrap (presents).

'**auspfeifen,** *v.tr.sep.irr.43* to boo.

'**ausplaudern,** *v.tr.sep.* to let out.

'**auspressen,** *v.tr.sep.* to squeeze (a lemon etc.), squeeze out (juice etc.).

'**ausprobieren,** *v.tr.sep.* to try (sth.) out.

'**Auspuff. I.** *m -(e)s/-e* exhaust (system).

II. **'A~-**, *comb.fm.* exhaust (pipe etc.).
◆**'A~topf**, *m* silencer, *N.Am:* muffler.
**'ausradieren**, *v.tr.sep.* to rub out.
**'ausrangieren**, *v.tr.sep.* F: to chuck out.
**'ausrauben**, *v.tr.sep.* to rob (s.o.); to loot (a shop); to empty (the till).
**'ausräumen**, *v.tr.sep.* to turn out (a drawer etc.); to clear (a room).
**'ausrechnen**, *v.tr.sep.* to work out.
**'Ausrede**, *f* excuse. ◆**'a~n**, *v.sep.* **1.** *v.i.* (*haben*) to finish speaking; **laß mich a.!** let me finish! **2.** *v.tr.* **j-m etwas** *acc* **a.**, to talk s.o. out of sth.
**'ausreichen**, *v.i.sep.* (*haben*) (*Vorräte usw.*) to suffice, be enough. ◆**'a~d**, *adj.* sufficient.
**'Ausreise**, *f* departure. ◆**'A~genehmigung**, *f*/**'A~visum**, *m* exit visa. ◆**a~n**, *v.i.sep.* (*sein*) to leave the country.
**'ausreiße|n**, *v.sep.irr.4* **1.** *v.tr.* to pull/tear (sth.) out; to uproot (a plant etc.). **2.** *v.i.* (*sein*) F: to run away (from home etc.), escape (from prison). ◆**'A~r**, *m* **-s/-** runaway.
**'ausrenk|en**, *v.tr.sep.* **sich** *dat* **die Schulter usw. a.**, to dislocate one's shoulder etc.
**'ausrichten**, *v.tr.sep.* (*a*) to align (sth.); (*b*) (*mitteilen*) **j-m etwas a.**, to tell s.o. sth.; **kann ich etwas a.?** can I take a message? (*c*) (*erreichen*) to achieve (sth.).
**'ausrott|en**, *v.tr.sep.* to wipe out (a race etc.); *Fig:* to eradicate (abuses etc.). ◆**'A~ung**, *f* **-/no** *pl* extermination.
**'ausrücken**, *v.i.sep.* (*sein*) *Mil:* to march off; (*Feuerwehr*) to be called out; F: (*Pers.*) to run away.
**'Ausruf**, *m* exclamation. ◆**a~en**, *v.sep.irr.74* **1.** *v.i.* (*haben*) to exclaim. **2.** *v.tr.* (*a*) to call out (names etc.); (*im Hotel usw.*) **j-n a. lassen**, to page s.o.; (*b*) to proclaim (a state of emergency etc.), call (a strike). ◆**'A~ezeichen**, *n* exclamation mark.
**'ausruhen**, *v. refl.* **sich a.**, to rest.
**'ausrüst|en**, *v.tr.sep.* to equip. ◆**'A~ung**, *f* **-/-en** equipment.
**'ausrutschen**, *v.i.sep.* (*sein*) to slide, slip.
**'Aussage** ['ausza:gə], *f* **-/-n** statement. ◆**a~n**, *v.sep.* **1.** *v.tr.* to state (sth.). **2.** *v.i.* (*haben*) to make a statement; **vor Gericht a.**, to give evidence in court.
**Aussätzige(r)** ['auszɛtsigə(r)], *m & f decl. as adj.* leper.
**'ausschacht|en**, *v.tr.sep.* to dig. ◆**'A~ung**, *f* **-/-en** excavation.
**'ausschalten**, *v.tr.sep.* (*a*) to switch/turn off (the light, radio etc.); (*b*) *Fig:* to eliminate (a competitor, mistakes etc.).
**'Ausschank**, *m* **-(e)s/-e** (*a*) sale of alcoholic drinks; (*b*) (*Theke*) bar.
**'Ausschau**, *f* **nach j-m, etwas A. halten**, to keep a lookout for s.o., sth. ◆**a~en**, *v.i.sep.* (*haben*) **nach j-m a.**, to look out for s.o.
**'ausscheid|en**, *v.sep.irr.56* **1.** *v.tr.* to

eliminate (sth. unsatisfactory); to excrete (waste matter). **2.** *v.i.* (*sein*) to retire; *Fig:* **diese Alternative scheidet aus**, this alternative can be eliminated. ◆**'A~ung**, *f* **-/-en 1.** (*Körpera~ung*) excretion. **2.** *Ch:* precipitation. **3.** *Sp:* (*a*) elimination; (*b*) (*A~ungsrunde*) qualifying round. ◆**'A~ungsspiel**, *n* qualifying match/tie.
**'ausschenken**, *v.tr.sep.* to pour out, (*verkaufen*) sell (drinks).
**'ausscheren**, *v.i.sep.* (*sein*) to pull out.
**'ausschlachten**, *v.tr.sep.* (*a*) F: to cannibalize (a car, machine etc.); (*b*) *Pej:* F: exploit (a situation).
**'ausschlafen**, *v.sep.irr.84* **1.** *v.tr.* (*a*) **sich a.**, to have a lie-in; (*b*) **seinen Rausch usw. a.**, to sleep off the effects of alcohol etc. **2.** *v.i.* (*haben*) **ich habe noch nicht ausgeschlafen**, I have not slept enough.
**'Ausschlag**, *m* **1.** *Med:* rash. **2.** Phys: deflection (of a compass needle etc.). **3.** **den A. geben**, to tip the balance. ◆**'a~en**, *v.sep.irr.85* **1.** *v.i.* (*haben*) (*Pferd usw.*) to kick out; (*Pflanzen*) to sprout; (*Kompaßnadel usw.*) to show a deflection. **2.** *v.tr.* (*a*) to knock out (s.o.'s teeth etc.); (*b*) to line (a box etc.); (*c*) (*ablehnen*) to reject, decline (an offer etc.). ◆**'a~gebend**, *adj.* decisive.
**'ausschließ|en**, *v.sep.irr.31* **1.** *v.tr.* (*a*) to lock/shut (s.o.) out; (*b*) **j-n von/aus etwas** *dat* **a.**, to exclude/(*aus Partei*) expel s.o. from sth.; (*c*) to rule out (a possibility etc.). ◆**'a~lich**. **I.** *adj.* exclusive (right etc.). **II.** *prep.* + *gen.* exclusive of. ◆**'A~lichkeit**, *f* **-/no** *pl* exclusivity.
**'Ausschluß**, *m* exclusion; *Pol: Sch:* expulsion; *Sp:* suspension.
**'ausschmück|en**, *v.tr.sep.* to decorate (a room etc.); *Fig:* to embellish (sth.).
**'ausschneiden**, *v.tr.sep.irr.59* to cut (sth.) out.
**'Ausschnitt**, *m* **1.** extract; (*Zeitungsa.*) cutting. **2.** neckline.
**'ausschreiben**, *v.tr.sep.irr.12* (*a*) to write out (a word); to make out (a cheque, prescription etc.); (*b*) to advertise (a post, competition etc.).
**'Ausschreitung**, *f* **-/-en** *esp. pl* **A~en**, excesses.
**'Ausschuß**, *m* **1.** *Pol: etc:* committee. **2.** *no pl Com:* (*also* **A~ware** *f*) rejects.
**'ausschütten**, *v.tr.sep.* (*a*) to pour out; to empty (a bucket etc.); (*b*) *Com:* to pay out (dividends etc.); (*c*) **sich vor Lachen a.**, to fall about laughing.
**'ausschweif|en**, *v.i.sep.* (*sein*) to indulge in excesses. ◆**a~end**, *adj.* dissolute, debauched (life); licentious (thoughts); *Fig:* extravagant (imagination). ◆**'A~ung**, *f* **-/-en** excess.
**'ausschweigen**, *v.refl.sep.irr.89* **sich a.**, to maintain silence.
**'aussehen**. **I.** *v.sep.irr.92* (*haben*) to look; **nach etwas** *dat* **a.**, to look like sth.; **es sieht aus, als ob ...**, it looks as

though ...; *F:* **das Kleid sieht nach nichts aus,** the dress doesn't look anything special; **so siehst du aus!** you can think again! **II. A.,** *n -s/no pl* appearance; *F:* looks.

**außen** ['ausən]. **I.** *adv.* (on the) outside; **nach a. aufgehen,** to open outwards. **II. 'A~-,** *comb.fm.* (a) (*äußere von zwei*) outer (wall, surface etc.); (b) exterior (lighting, angle etc.); outside (pocket, staircase, *Sp:* lane etc.); (c) foreign (trade, policy *Sp:* etc.). ◆**'A~bezirk,** *m* (outer) suburb. ◆**'A~bordmotor,** *m* outboard motor. ◆**'A~dienst,** *m* field work. ◆**'A~handel,** *m* foreign trade. ◆**'A~minister,** *m* foreign minister. ◆**'A~ministerium,** *n* foreign ministry. ◆**'A~politik,** *f* foreign policy. ◆**'a~politisch,** *adj.* with regard to foreign policy. ◆**A~seite,** *f* outside. ◆**'A~seiter,** *m* outsider; *Fig:* (*Pers.*) misfit. ◆**'A~stehende(r),** *m & f* decl. as adj. bystander. ◆**'A~welt,** *f* outside world.

**'aussenden,** *v.tr.sep.irr.94* (a) to send out (s.o., a patrol etc.); (b) to emit (rays, heat).

**außer** ['ausər]. **I.** *prep.* + *dat* 1. out of; **a. Hause essen,** to have a meal out; **a. Betrieb,** not working; *Fig:* (**vor Wut usw.**) **a. sich,** beside oneself (with rage etc.); **a. sich geraten,** to lose one's self-control. 2. (a) except (for); **alle a. einem,** all except one. **II.** *conj.* except; **a. wenn es regnet,** unless it rains. ◆**'a~dem.** **I.** *adv.* (*noch dazu*) in addition, as well. **II.** *conj.* moreover. ◆**'a~ehelich,** *adj.* extra-marital. ◆**'a~gewöhnlich,** *adj.* exceptional. ◆**'a~halb,** *prep.* + *gen & adv.* outside. ◆**'a~ordentlich,** *adj.* extraordinary (situation, session etc.); exceptional (person, etc.). ◆**'a~planmäßig,** *adj.* unscheduled. ◆**a~'stand(e),** *adj.* **a. sein, etwas zu tun,** to be unable/in no position to do sth.

**äußere(r,s)** ['ɔysərə] *adj.* outer (layer, margin etc.); external (circumstances, appearance etc.).

**äußerlich** ['ɔysərliç], *adj.* (a) outward (appearance etc.); external (feature, use etc.); (b) *Fig:* (*oberflächlich*) superficial. ◆**'A~keit,** *f -/-en* outward characteristic; *pl* **Ä~en,** minor matters.

**äußer|n** ['ɔysərn], *v.tr.* (a) to express (an opinion, wish etc.); (b) **sich über etwas** *acc* **ä.,** to comment on sth.; (c) (*Merkmale*) **sich in etwas dat ä.,** to be apparent in sth. ◆**'Ä~ung,** *f -/-en* (a) (*Behauptung*) statement; comment; (b) (*Ausdruck*) expression (of sth.).

**äußerst** ['ɔysərst]. **1.** *adv.* extremely. 2. *adj.* **ä~e(r,s)** (a) (*Ort*) furthest (end, limits etc.); (b) (*höchste*) (absolute) maximum (price, load etc.); extreme (danger, poverty etc.); supreme (effort, concentration); utmost (importance, caution etc.); **zum Ä~en entschlossen,** determined to

try anything; (c) (*schlimmste*) worst; **im ä~en Fall,** if the worst comes to the worst. ◆**'ä~en'falls,** *adv.* at the most/worst.

**'aussetz|en,** *v.sep.* **1.** *v.tr.* (a) to abandon (a child, dog etc.); (b) **j-n/sich einer Gefahr usw. a.,** to expose s.o./oneself to a danger etc.; (c) (*kritisieren*) **etwas an j-m auszusetzen haben,** to find fault with s.o.; (d) *Jur:* to suspend (proceedings etc.). **2.** *v.i.* (*haben*) (a) to stop (suddenly); (*Motor*) to cut out; (b) to make a pause. ◆**'A~ung,** *f -/-en* (a) abandoning; (b) *Jur:* suspension.

**'Aussicht,** *f* (a) view; (b) *Fig:* prospect; *usu. pl* outlook; **j-m etwas in A. stellen,** to promise s.o. sth. ◆**'a~slos,** *adj.* hopeless (situation etc.); doomed (venture etc.). ◆**'A~spunkt,** *m* vantage point. ◆**'a~sreich,** *adj.* promising.

**'aussiedeln,** *v.tr.sep.* to evacuate, resettle.

**'aussöhnen,** *v.tr.sep.* to reconcile; **sich a.,** to become reconciled.

**'aussortieren,** *v.tr.sep.* to sort out (washing etc.), eliminate (unwanted items).

**'ausspannen,** *v.sep.* **1.** *v.tr.* (a) to unhitch (a horse etc.); (b) to spread out (a net, wings etc.); to stretch (a rope etc.); (c) *F:* **j-m den Freund a.,** to steal s.o.'s boyfriend. **2.** *v.i.* (*haben*) to relax.

**'ausspar|en,** *v.tr.sep.* to leave (sth.) empty/(a space) blank; to leave out.

**'aussperr|en,** *v.tr.sep.* to shut/lock (s.o.) out. ◆**'A~ung,** *f -/-en Ind:* lock-out.

**'ausspiel|en,** *v.tr.&i.sep.* (*haben*) (a) (*Kartenspiel*) to lead; (b) **j-n gegen j-n a.,** to play s.o. off against s.o. ◆**'A~ung,** *f -/-en* draw (of a lottery).

**'Aussprache,** *f -/-n* **1.** pronunciation; (*Akzent*) accent. **2.** discussion; **eine offene A.,** a frank exchange of views.

**'aussprechen,** *v.sep.irr.14* **1.** *v.tr.* (a) to pronounce (a word etc.); (b) to express (a wish, one's gratitude etc.); (c) to deliver a judgement); (c) **sich mit j-m a.,** to have a heart-to-heart (talk) with s.o.; **sich für/gegen etwas** *acc* **a.,** to come out in favour of/against sth. **2.** *v.i.* (*haben*) to finish speaking.

**ausstaffieren** ['ausʃtafi:rən], *v.tr.sep.* to rig (s.o, sth.) out.

**'ausstatt|en,** *v.tr.sep.* to provide (s.o., sth.) (**mit etwas** *dat,* with sth.); to equip (an office etc.). ◆**'A~ung,** *f -/-en* (*Ausrüstung*) equipment; (*Kleider usw.*) outfit; (b) *Th:* scenery and costumes.

**'ausstechen,** *v.tr.sep.irr.14* (a) to cut (turf etc.); (b) (*übertreffen*) to outdo (s.o.).

**'ausstehen,** *v.sep.irr.100* **1.** *v.tr.* to endure (pains, anxiety etc.); **ich kann ihn nicht a.,** I can't stand him. **2.** *v.i.* (*haben*) (*Rechnungen usw.*) to be outstanding; (*Entscheidung*) to be pending.

**'aussteigen,** *v.i.sep.irr.89* (*sein*) (a) to get out (of a car), get off (a bus, plane etc.); (b) *F:* to drop out.

**'ausstell|en,** *v.tr.sep.* (a) to display (goods

etc.); to exhibit (pictures, products etc.); (*b*) to issue (a passport etc.); to make out (a cheque, bill etc.). ◆'**A~ung**, *f* 1. display; (*Schau*) show; *Art: etc:* exhibition. 2. *Adm:* issue.

'**aussterben**, *v.i.sep.irr.101* (*sein*) to die out; *Z:* (*Gattungen*) to become extinct.

'**Aussteuer**, *f* dowry.

'**Aussteuer**, *m* -(e)s/-e exit.

'**ausstopfen**, *v.tr.sep.* to pad out (a cushion etc.); to stuff (an animal).

'**Ausstoß**, *m* (*a*) discharge; (*b*) *Ind:* output. ◆'**a~en**, *v.tr.sep.irr.103* (*a*) (*Schlot usw.*) to emit (smoke, fumes etc.); (*b*) to expel, (*aus der Gesellschaft*) ostracize (s.o.).

'**ausstrahl|en**, *v.sep.* 1. *v.tr.* (*a*) to give out; (*b*) *Rad: TV:* to broadcast (a programme). 2. *v.i.* (*sein*) **von/aus etwas** *dat* **a.**, to radiate from sth. ◆'**A~ung**, *f* (*a*) radiation; (*b*) *Rad: TV:* broadcast; (*c*) *Fig:* effect (of an event etc.); charisma (of a person).

'**ausstrecken**, *v.tr.sep.* to stretch out.

'**ausstreichen**, *v.tr.sep.irr.40* to cross out, delete.

'**ausströmen**, *v.sep.* 1. *v.tr.* to give off; *Fig:* to radiate (love etc.). 2. *v.i.* (*sein*) (*Wasser, Gase usw.*) to escape.

'**aussuchen**, *v.tr.sep.* to pick out, select (sth.).

'**Austausch**, *m* (*a*) exchange; (*b*) *Tchn:* replacement (of machine parts etc.). ◆'**a~bar**, *adj.* exchangeable (goods etc.); *Tchn:* interchangeable (parts etc.). ◆'**a~en**, *v.tr.sep.* (*a*) to exchange; (*b*) (*ersetzen*) to replace (*Tchn:* a part, *Sp:* player etc.). ◆'**A~motor**, *m* replacement engine.

'**austeilen**, *v.tr.sep.* to deal out (cards etc.), to distribute (clothes etc.); to dish out (soup, *F:* praise etc.).

'**Auster** ['austər], *f* -/-n oyster.

'**austoben**, *v.refl.sep.* **sich a.**, to let off steam.

'**austragen**, *v.tr. sep.irr.85* (*a*) to hold (a race, contest etc.); (*b*) to settle (a quarrel etc.); (*c*) to deliver (newspapers etc.). ◆'**A~ung**, *f* -/-**en** 1. delivery. 2. *Sp:* staging (of a game etc.).

**Austral|ien** [au'strɑːliən]. *Pr.n.n* -s. Australia. ◆**A~ier(in)**, *m* -s/- (*f* -/-nen) Australian. ◆**a~isch**, *adj.* Australian.

'**austreiben**, *v.tr.sep.irr.12* (*a*) to drive (people etc.) out; (*b*) *Fig:* **j-m eine Unart usw. a.**, to cure s.o. of a bad habit etc.; **böse Geister a.**, to exorcize evil spirits.

'**austreten**, *v.sep.irr.105* 1. *v.tr.* to stamp out (a fire etc.); to wear down (a path, steps etc.). 2. *v.i.* (*sein*) (*a*) (*Gas*) to escape; (*b*) *F:* **a. (gehen)**, to go for a pee; (*c*) **aus der Kirche a.**, to leave the church.

'**austrinken**, *v.tr.sep.irr.96* to drink up; to finish (a drink), drain (a glass etc.).

'**Austritt**, *m* (*a*) escape (of gas); (*b*) resignation, withdrawal (**aus** + *dat*, from).

'**austrocknen**, *v.sep.* 1. *v.tr.* to dry (sth.) thoroughly. 2. *v.i.* (*sein*) to dry out.

'**ausüb|en**, *v.tr.sep.* (*a*) to practise (a profession etc.); to carry on (an activity); (*b*) to exercise, exert (pressure, an influence etc.). ◆'**A~ung**, *f* performance; exercise.

'**Ausverkauf**, *m* (clearance) sale. ◆'**a~en**, *v.tr.sep.* to clear (goods). ◆'**a~t**, *adj.* sold out.

'**Auswahl**, *f* (*a*) choice, selection; (*b*) range, assortment (of goods etc.); (*c*) *Sp:* picked team.

'**auswählen**, *v.tr.sep.* to choose, select.

'**Auswander|er**, *m* emigrant. ◆'**a~n**, *v.i.sep.* (*sein*) to emigrate. ◆'**A~ung**, *f* -/-en emigration.

**auswärt|ig** ['ausvɛrtiç], *adj.* (*a*) non-local; a~ige Besucher, visitors from another town; (*b*) (*ausländisch*) foreign; **das A~ige Amt**, the (West German) foreign ministry. ◆'**a~s**, *adv.* (*a*) away from home; **a. essen**, to eat out; *Sp:* **a. spielen**, to play away; (*b*) **er wohnt a.**, he lives out of town. ◆'**A~sspiel**, *n* away match.

'**auswechseln** *v.tr.sep.* to replace (a part etc.); *Fb:* to substitute (a player).

'**Ausweg**, *m* -(e)s/-e solution; **als letzter A.**, as a last resort. ◆'**a~los**, *adj.* hopeless.

'**ausweichen**, *v.i.sep.irr.40* (*sein*) **j-m, der Versuchung usw. a.**, to avoid s.o., temptation etc.; **einem Auto usw. a.**, to get out of the way of a car etc.; *Fig:* **einem Thema usw. a.**, to evade an issue etc. ◆'**a~end**, *adj.* evasive.

'**ausweinen**, *v.refl.sep.* **sich a.**, to have a good cry.

**Ausweis** ['ausvais], *m* -es/-e identification; (*Personala.*) identity card. ◆'**A~papiere**, *npl* identification papers. ◆'**a~en**, *v.tr.sep.irr.70* (*a*) **j-n, sich a.**, to prove s.o.'s, one's identity; (*b*) (*aus dem Land*) to deport (s.o.). ◆'**A~ung**, *f* -/-en deportation.

'**ausweiten**, *v.tr.sep.* (*a*) to widen (a gap), enlarge (a hole etc.); to stretch (a glove, shoes etc.); (*b*) *Fig:* to expand.

'**auswendig**, *adv.* by heart.

'**auswert|en**, *v.tr.sep.* (*a*) to evaluate (statistics etc.); to utilize (experiences etc.). ◆'**A~ung**, *f* -/-en evaluation; utilization.

'**auswirk|en**, *v.refl.sep.* **sich auf etwas** *acc* **a.**, to have an effect/impact on sth. ◆'**A~ung**, *f* effect, impact.

'**auswischen**, *v.tr.sep.* (*a*) to wipe off (words on a blackboard etc.); (*b*) *F:* **j-m eins a.**, to put one over on s.o.

'**Auswuchs**, *m* *Fig:* esp. *pl* **A~e**, excesses; **das ist ein A. Ihrer Phantasie**, that is a figment of your imagination.

'**auswuchten**, *v.tr.sep.* to balance.

'**auszahlen**, *v.tr.sep.* (*a*) to pay out (money); to pay off (creditors, workmen); to buy out (a business partner); (*b*)

*Fig:* **sich a.**, to be worth it.

'**auszeichn|en**, *v.tr.sep.* (*a*) *Com:* to price (goods); (*b*) to honour (s.o.); (*c*) (*unterscheiden*) to distinguish (s.o.), oneself, sth.). ◆'**A~ung**, *f -/-en* **1.** *Com:* pricing. **2.** (*a*) (*Ehrung*) distinction; award (of a prize etc.); (*b*) (*Preis, Orden*) award.

'**ausziehen**, *v.sep.irr.113* **1.** *v.tr.* (*a*) to pull out (a nail etc.); to extend (a table etc.); (*b*) to take off (clothes); **j-n/sich a.**, to undress s.o./oneself. **2.** *v.i.* (*sein*) to move out (of a house). ◆'**A~tisch**, *m* draw-leaf table.

'**Auszubildende(r)**, *m & f decl. as adj.* trainee.

'**Auszug**, *m* **1.** move, removal (from a house etc.). **2.** (*Ausschnitt*) excerpt, extract. **3.** (*Kontoa.*) statement.

**Auto** ['auto]. **I.** *n -s/-s* car; **A. fahren,** to drive (a car). **II.** '**A~-,** *comb.fm.* (*a*) car (ferry, dealer, tyre, key, insurance etc.); motor (industry, traffic etc.); (*b*) road (at-

las etc.). ◆'**A~bahn**, *f* motorway, *N.Am:* freeway. ◆'**A~bus**, *m* bus; (*für lange Strecken*) coach. ◆'**A~fahrer(in)**, *m* (*f*) driver (of a car), motorist. ◆**A~gramm** [-'gram], *n* autograph. ◆**A~mat** [-'ma:t], *m -en/-en* vending machine. ◆**A~'matik**, *f -/-en* automatic mechanism; *Aut:* automatic transmission. ◆**a~matisch** [-'ma:tiʃ], *adj.* automatic. ◆**a~nom** [-'no:m], *adj.* autonomous. ◆'**A~nummer**, *f* registration number. ◆'**A~radio**, *n* car radio. ◆'**A~rennen**, *n* motor race. ◆'**A~unfall**, *m* car accident. ◆'**A~verleih**, *m* car hire. ◆'**A~werkstatt**, *f* garage.

**Autopsie** [autɔp'siː], *f -/-n* autopsy.

**Autor** ['autɔr], *m -s/-en* [-'to:rən] author. ◆**A~in** [-'to:rin], *f -/-nen* authoress. ◆**a~i'sieren**, *v.tr.* to authorize. ◆**a~itär** [-i'tɛːr], *adj.* authoritarian. ◆**A~ität** [-i'tɛːt], *f -/-en* authority.

**Axt** [akst], *f -/Äxte* axe.

# B

**B, b** [beː], *n -/-* (the letter) B, b.

**Baby** ['beːbi], *n -s/-s* baby.

**Bach** [bax], *m -(e)s/ːe* stream. ◆**B~stelze**, *f* wagtail.

**Back-** [bak-], *comb.fm.* baking (powder etc.). ◆'**B~blech**, *n* baking sheet. ◆'**B~bord**, *n* *Nau:* port (side). ◆**b~en**, *v.tr.irr.* to bake (bread etc.), make (a cake, biscuits etc.). ◆'**B~fisch**, *m* *Cu:* fried fish. ◆'**B~obst**, *n* dried fruit. ◆'**B~ofen**, *m* (baker's/ kitchen) oven. ◆'**B~pflaume**, *f* prune. ◆'**B~rohr**, *n/*◆'**B~röhre**, *f* oven. ◆'**B~stein**, *m* (red) brick. ◆'**B~waren**, *fpl* bakery products.

**Back|e** ['bakə], *f -/-n* **1.** cheek. **2.** *Tchn:* (*a*) jaw (of a vice etc.); (*b*) (*Bremsb.*) brake shoe. ◆'**B~enbart**, *m* sidewhiskers. ◆'**B~enzahn**, *m* molar.

**Bäcker** ['bekər], *m -s/-* baker. ◆**B~ei** [-'rai], *f -/-en* bakery; baker's shop.

**Bad** [baːt], *n -(e)s/ːer* **1.** (*a*) bath; (*b*) (*im Meer usw.*) swim, dip. **2.** (*a*) (*B~ezimmer*) bathroom; (*b*) (*Schwimmb.*) (swimming) pool. **3.** (*Kurort*) spa. ◆**B~e-** ['baːdə-], *comb.fm.* (*a*) bathing (cap, things, beach etc.); (*b*) (*fürs Bad*) bath (mat etc.). ◆'**B~eanstalt**, *f* swimming-baths. ◆'**B~eanzug**, *m* bathing suit. ◆'**B~ehose**, *f* bathing/ swimming trunks. ◆'**B~emantel**, *m* bathrobe. ◆'**B~emeister**, *m* swimming-pool attendant. ◆'**b~en**, *v.* **1.** *v.i.* (*haben*) (*a*) (**kalt/warm**) **b.**, to have a (cold/warm) bath; (*b*) (*schwimmen*) to bathe; (*c*) (**bei/mit etwas** *dat*) **b. gehen,** to come a cropper (with sth.). **2.** *v.tr.* to bath (a baby etc.); to bathe (a wound, eyes etc.). ◆'**B~eort**, *m* **1.** seaside re-

sort. **2.** (*Kurort*) spa. ◆'**B~etuch**, *n* bath towel. ◆'**B~ewanne**, *f* bath tub. ◆'**B~ezimmer**, *n* bathroom.

**baff** [baf], *adj. F:* flabbergasted.

**Bagatelle** [baga'tɛlə], *f -/-n* trifle; trifling matter/(*Geld*) sum.

**Bagger** ['bagər], *m -s/-* (*für das Flußbett*) dredger; (*für Erde*) excavator. ◆'**b~n**, *v.tr. & i.* (*haben*) to excavate. ◆'**B~see**, *m* (water-filled) gravel pit.

**Bahn** [baːn]. **I.** *f -/-en* **1.** way, path; **auf die schiefe B. geraten,** to fall into bad ways. **2.** *Astr:* course (of a star); orbit (of a planet); path (of a comet). **3.** (*a*) *Sp:* (*Rennb.*) (race/running) track; (*b*) (*Fahrb.*) carriageway (of a road). **4.** width (of material, wallpaper etc.). **5.** (*a*) *Rail:* **mit der B. fahren,** to travel by train/rail; (*b*) (*Straßenb.*) tram. **II.** '**B~-,** *comb.fm.* railway, *N.Am:* railroad (worker, official, line); rail (connection). ◆'**b~brechend**, *adj.* revolutionary (idea, discovery etc.). ◆'**B~damm**, *m* railway embankment. ◆'**b~en**, *v.tr.* **sich** *dat* **einen Weg b.**, to clear a way/ path. ◆'**B~hof**, *m* (railway) station. ◆'**B~hofshalle**, *f* station concourse. ◆'**B~hofsvorsteher**, *m* station master. ◆'**B~schranke**, *f* level crossing barrier. ◆'**B~steig**, *m* platform. ◆'**B~übergang**, *m* level crossing. ◆'**B~wärter**, *m* crossing keeper.

**Bahre** ['baːrə], *f -/-n* stretcher; (*für Tote*) bier.

**Bajonett** [bajo'nɛt], *n -(e)s/-e* bayonet.

**Bake** ['baːkə], *f -/-n* beacon.

**Bakterien** [bak'teːriən], *fpl* bacteria, *F:* germs.

**Balanc|e** [ba'lãːsə], *f -/-n* balance. ◆**B~eakt**, *m* balancing act.

◆**b~ieren** [-'siːrən], *v.tr. & i.* (*haben*) to balance.

**bald** [balt], *adv.* **1.** soon; **b. darauf,** shortly afterwards; *F:* **bis b.!** see you soon! **2.** *F:* (*beinahe*) almost. **3. b. ..., b. ...,** now ... now ... ◆**b~ig** ['baldiç], *adj.* speedy.

**Baldrian** ['baldriaːn], *m* -s/-e valerian.

**balgen** ['balgən], *v.refl.* **sich b.,** to tussle, scuffle.

**Balkan** ['balkaːn]. *Pr.n.m* -s. **der B.,** the Balkans.

**Balken** ['balkən], *m* -s/- beam; (*Stahl*) girder.

**Balkon** [bal'kɔŋ], *m* -s/-s *& -e* **1.** balcony. **2.** *Th:* dress circle.

**Ball¹** [bal]. **I.** *m* -(e)s/ᵉe ball. **II.** '**B~**, *comb.fm.* ball (game, boy etc.). ◆**b~en,** *v.tr.* (*a*) to form, press (snow, paper etc.) into a ball; **die (Hand zur) Faust b.,** to clench one's fist; (*b*) **sich b.,** to gather (into a ball); (*Wolken*) to gather, mass. ◆'**B~ung,** *f* -/-en compression; concentration; massing (of clouds etc.). ◆'**B~ungsgebiet,** *n* densely populated (industrial) region.

**Ball²,** *m* -(e)s/ᵉe dance, ball. ◆'**B~saal,** *m* ballroom.

**Ballade** [ba'laːdə], *f* -/-n ballad.

**Ballast** [ba'last, balast], *m* -(e)s/*no pl* ballast; *Fig:* dead wood, lumber. ◆'**B~stoffe,** *mpl* roughage.

**Ballen** ['balən], *m* -s/- **1.** *Com: etc:* bale (of straw, paper etc.). **2.** *Anat:* ball of the hand/foot).

**Ballett** [ba'lɛt], *m* -(e)s/-e ballet. ◆**Ba'llettänzer,** *m* (male) ballet dancer. ◆**Ba'llettänzerin,** *f* ballerina.

**Ballistik** [ba'listik], *f* -/*no pl* ballistics.

**Ballon** [ba'lɔŋ], *m* -s/-s *& -e* balloon.

**Balsam** ['balzaːm], *m* -s/-e balm; *Fig:* balm.

**Bambus** ['bambus], *m* -ses/-se bamboo.

**banal** [ba'naːl], *adj.* commonplace, trite (remark etc.); trivial, banal (story etc.). ◆**B~i'tät,** *f* -/-en (*a*) *no pl* triteness; triviality; (*b*) trite remark.

**Banane** [ba'naːnə], *f* -/-n banana. ◆**B~nschale,** *f* banana skin.

**Banause** [ba'nauzə], *m* -n/-n philistine.

**Band¹** [bant]. **I.** *n* -(e)s/ᵉer **1.** (*a*) tape; (*als Zierde*) ribbon; (*b*) (metal) strip (for packing etc.); hoop (of a barrel); (*c*) *Rec:* (magnetic) tape; (*d*) (*Fließb.*) conveyor belt; *F:* **Fehler am laufenden B.,** one mistake after the other; (*f*) *Anat:* ligament; (*f*) *Rad:* waveband. **2.** *m* -(e)s/ᵉe (*Buch*) volume. **3.** *n* -(e)s/-e (*usu. pl*) *Lit:* bond, tie (of friendship, love etc.). **II.** '**B~**, *comb.fm.* tape (recording etc.). ◆'**B~gerät,** *n* tape recorder. ◆'**B~maß,** *n* tape measure. ◆'**B~säge,** *f* band-saw. ◆'**B~scheibe,** *f* intervertebral disc.

**Band²** [bɛnt, bænd], *f* -s/-s band.

**Bandage** [ban'daːʒə], *f* -/-n bandage. ◆**b~ieren** [-da'ʒiːrən], *v.tr.* to bandage

(a sprained wrist etc.).

**Bande** ['bandə], *f* -/-n (*a*) gang (of thieves, thugs etc.); (*b*) *F:* bunch (of people).

**bändigen** ['bɛndigən], *v.tr.* (*a*) to tame (a wild animal); (*b*) to control (a child, scared animal); *Fig:* to curb (one's anger etc.).

**Bandit** [ban'diːt], *m* -en/-en bandit, gangster.

**bang(e)** ['baŋ(ə)], *adj.* (*a*) anxious; **mir wurde angst und b.,** I got scared. ◆**b~en,** *v.i.* (*haben*) *Lit:* **um j-n, etwas** *acc* **b.,** to be anxious about s.o., sth.

**Bank¹** [baŋk], *f* -/ᵉe **1.** bench. **2.** (*im Meer*) (sand/mud)bank; (oyster)bed.

**Bank²**. **I.** *f* -/-en *Fin:* bank. **II.** '**B~**, *comb.fm.* bank (account etc.). ◆'**B~direktor,** *m* bank manager. ◆**B~ier** [-ki'eː], *m* -s/-s banker. ◆'**B~note,** *f* banknote, *N.Am:* bill. ◆**B~rott** [-'krɔt]. **I.** *m* -s/-e *Jur: & Fig:* bankruptcy; **B. machen,** to go bankrupt. **II. b.,** *adj. Jur:* bankrupt; (*Pers.*) broke. ◆'**B~überfall,** *m* bank robbery.

**Bankett¹** [baŋ'kɛt], *n* -(e)s/-e banquet.

**Bankett²,** *n* -(e)s/-e verge (of road).

**Bann** [ban], *m* -(e)s/-e spell; *Fig:* **j-n in seinen B. ziehen/schlagen,** to cast one's spell over s.o. **2.** *Ecc:* (decree of) excommunication. ◆'**b~en,** *v.tr.* to exorcize (ghosts); *Fig:* to hold (s.o.) spellbound.

**Banner** ['banər], *n* -s/- banner; standard.

**Bar¹** [baːr], *f* -/-s bar. ◆'**B~dame,** *f* barmaid. ◆'**B~hocker,** *m* bar stool. ◆'**B~keeper,** *m* barman.

**bar²**. **I.** *adj.* **1.** **b~es Geld,** cash; (*etwas*) (*in*) **b. bezahlen,** to pay cash (for sth.). **2.** *Lit:* bare (head etc.). **II.** '**B~**, *comb.fm.* cash (payment, sale, transaction, purchase etc.). ◆'**b~fuß,** *adv.* /'**b~füßig,** *adj.* barefoot. ◆'**B~geld,** *n* cash. ◆'**b~geldlos,** *adj.* **b~geldloser Zahlungsverkehr,** credit transactions. ◆'**B~schaft,** *f* -/-en ready money. ◆'**B~scheck,** *m* uncrossed cheque/ *N.Am:* check.

**Bär** [bɛːr], *m* -en/-en bear. ◆'**b~beißig,** *adj.* surly, grumpy.

**Baracke** [ba'rakə], *f* -/-n hut; hutment; *Pej:* shanty.

**barbarisch** [bar'baːriʃ], *adj.* (*a*) barbaric, barbarous; (*b*) *F:* dreadful (cold, hunger etc.).

**Bariton** ['baːritɔn], *m* -s/-e baritone.

**Barkasse** [bar'kasə], *f* -/-n launch.

**barmherzig** [barm'hɛrtsiç], *adj.* merciful; (*mitfühlend*) compassionate. ◆**B~keit,** *f* -/*no pl* mercy, compassion.

**Barometer** [baro'meːtər], *n* -s/- barometer.

**Baron** [ba'roːn], *m* -s/-e baron. ◆**B~in,** *f* -/-nen baroness.

**Barren** ['barən], *m* -s/- **1.** (*Gold usw.*) bar, ingot. **2.** *Sp:* parallel bars.

**Barriere** [bari'ɛːrə], *f* -/-n barrier.

**Barrikade** [bari'kɑːdə], f -/-n barricade.

**barsch**[1] [barʃ], adj. gruff; (kurz angebunden) curt.

**Barsch**[2], m -(e)s/-e perch.

**Bart** ['bɑːrt], m -(e)s/ːe 1. beard. 2. web (of a key).

**bärtig** ['bɛːrtiç], adj. bearded.

**Basar** [ba'zɑːr], m -s/-e bazaar.

**basieren** [ba'ziːrən], v.i. (haben) **auf etwas** dat **b.,** to be based on sth.

**Basis** ['bɑːzis], f -/Basen base; (Grundlage) basis.

**Baskenmütze** ['baskənmytsə], f beret.

**Basketball** ['ba(ː)skətbal], m & n basketball.

**Baß** [bas], m -sses/ːsse 1. bass. 2. (Instrument) double bass.

**Bassin** [ba'sɛn, ba'sɛ̃], n -s/-s pool.

**Bast** [bast], m -(e)s/-e raffia.

**basta** ['basta], int. F: **b.!** enough!

**bastein** ['bastəln], v. 1. v.i. (haben) (a) to do (home) handicrafts; (b) **an etwas** dat **b.,** to tinker (around) with sth. 2. v.tr. to make, F: knock up (sth.). ◆'B~**ler**, m -s/- handicraft enthusiast; (Heimwerker) do-it-yourselfer.

**Batterie** [batə'riː], f -/-n battery.

**Bau** [bau]. I. m 1. -(e)s/no pl (a) construction (of roads, houses etc.); **im B.,** under construction; (b) (Baustelle) building site; (c) Fig: (Aufbau) structure (of a play etc.); (d) (Körperbau) build. 2. -(e)s/-ten building, edifice. 3. -(e)s/-e (a) burrow (of a rabbit); earth (of a fox, badger); couch (of an otter); (b) Min: pit. II. 'B~-, comb.fm. (a) building (firm, costs, material etc.); (b) structural (engineer, steel, drawing etc.). ◆'B~**arbeiter**, m building worker. ◆'B~**art,** f (a) architectural style; (b) = **Bauweise;** (c) Ind: design (of machine etc.). ◆'b~**en,** v. 1. v.tr. (a) to build (houses, a nest etc.); to construct (a machine, model etc.); to make (violins etc.); (Pers.) **kräftig/schmal gebaut sein,** to be of sturdy/slim build; (b) F: **einen Unfall b.,** to have an accident. 2. v.i. (haben) (a) to build; (b) Fig: **auf j-n b.,** to rely on/put one's faith in s.o. ◆'b~**fällig,** adj. dilapidated, tumbledown. ◆'B~**gelände,** n building site. ◆'B~**genehmigung,** f planning permission. ◆'B~**gerüst,** n scaffolding. ◆'B~**herr,** m initiator of a building project. ◆'B~**jahr,** n year of construction/manufacture; Aut: **B.** 1987, 1987 model. ◆'B~**kasten,** m (a) (child's) box of bricks; (Lego usw.) constructional toy; (b) (model) kit. ◆'b~**leiter,** m architect in charge. ◆'b~**lich,** adj. structural. ◆'B~**satz,** m kit (of parts). ◆'B~**sparkasse,** f building society. ◆'B~**stein,** m 1. building brick/stone. 2. Tchn: (Bestandteil) component; (Einheit) unit. ◆'B~**stelle,** f building site; (auf der Straße) roadworks. ◆'B~**unternehmer,** m building contractor.

◆'B~**weise,** f (method of) construction. ◆'B~**werk,** n building, edifice.

**Bauch** [baux]. I. m -(e)s/ːe 1. abdomen; Pej: (dicker B.) paunch; F: (Magen) tummy. 2. (a) belly (of a ship etc.); (b) bulge (of a vase etc.). II. 'B~-, comb.fm. belly (dancer, Av: landing etc.); Anat: abdominal (cavity, region etc.). ◆'b~**ig,** adj. bulbous (vase etc.). ◆'B~**redner,** m ventriloquist. ◆'B~**schmerzen,** mpl stomach ache. ◆'B~**speicheldrüse,** f pancreas.

**Bauer** ['bauər], m -n/-n 1. (a) farmer; (b) Pej: peasant. 2. (Schachspiel) pawn. ◆'B~**nbrot,** n coarse rye bread. ◆'B~**nhaus,** n farmhouse. ◆'B~**nhof,** m farm.

**Bäuer|in** ['bɔyərin], f -/-nen farmer's wife. ◆'b~**lich,** adj. rural; rustic (art etc.).

**Baum** [baum]. I. m -(e)s/ːe tree. II. 'B~-, comb.fm. tree (roots etc.); (group etc.) of trees. ◆'B~**schule,** f (tree) nursery. ◆'B~**stamm,** m tree trunk. ◆'B~**stumpf,** m tree stump. ◆'B~**wolle,** f cotton.

**baumeln** ['baumən], v.i. (haben) to dangle.

**Bausch** ['bauʃ], m -(e)s/ːe ball, wad (of cotton wool etc.); Fig: **in B. und Bogen,** wholesale, indiscriminately. ◆'b~**en,** v.tr. to puff (sth.) out; to fill (a sail); **sich b.,** (Segel, Gardine usw.) to billow (out); (Kleider) to be baggy.

**Bay|er(in)** ['baiər(in)], m -n/-n (f -/-nen) Bavarian. ◆'b~**(e)risch,** adj. Bavarian. ◆'B~**ern.** Pr.n.n -s. Bavaria.

**Bazill|us** [ba'tsilə], f -/-n/B~**us,** m -/-illen bacillus.

**beabsichtigen** [bə'ʔapziçtigən], v.tr. to intend (sth.).

**be'acht|en,** v.tr. (a) to observe (rules, regulations); (b) to heed (a warning etc.); **j-n, etwas nicht b.,** to ignore s.o., sth. ◆b~**lich,** adj. considerable (sum, achievement etc.); important (position). ◆B~**ung,** f -/no pl 1. observation. 2. attention; **B. verdienen,** to be worthy of note.

**Beamt|e(r)** [bə'ʔamtə(r)], m decl. as adj., **B~in,** f -/-nen official; (Funktionär) civil servant.

**beanspruchen** [bə'ʔanʃpruxən], v.tr. (a) to claim (one's share, damages etc.); to take advantage of (s.o.'s help, hospitality etc.); to take up (space, time etc.); (b) to tax, strain (s.o.); Tchn: to stress (a machine etc.); **stark beansprucht,** (Stoff, Teppich usw.) subject to hard wear/Tchn: (Teil) heavy strain.

**beanstand|en** [bə'ʔanʃtandən], v.tr. (a) to object to (sth.); (b) Com: to query (an invoice); to make a complaint about (goods). ◆B~**ung,** f -/-en objection (+to); complaint (+ gen, about).

**beantragen** [bə'ʔantrɑːgən], v.tr. (a) to apply for (a permit etc.); (b) (bei einer

*Sitzung*) to propose (an adjournment etc.); **b.**, **daß** ..., to move that ...; (*c esp. Jur:* to call for, demand (a sentence etc.).

be'antwort|en, *v.tr.* to answer (a question, letter). ◆**B~ung**, *f -/-en* answer.

be'arbeit|en, *v.tr.* (*a*) to work on, (*behandeln*) treat (sth.); *Ind:* to process (raw materials); (*b*) *Adm: Jur: etc:* to deal with, process (an application, a case etc.); (*c*) to edit (a book, text etc.); to adapt (a play etc.); *Mus:* to arrange (a piece). ◆**B~ung**, *f -/-en* **1.** *no pl* treatment; *Ind: Adm:* processing; *Lit:* adapting, revising; *Mus:* arranging; **in B.**, (*Buch usw.*) in preparation; (*Fall*) being dealt with. **2.** (*Ergebnis*) adaptation; (*Neub.*) revision; *Mus:* arrangement.

**Beatmung** [bə'ʔɑːtmuŋ], *f -/no pl* **künstliche B.**, artificial respiration.

beaufsichtig|en [bə'ʔaufziçtigən], *v.tr.* to supervise. ◆**B~ung**, *f -/-en* supervision.

beauftrag|en [bə'ʔauftrɑːgən], *v.tr.* to give (s.o.) the job (**etwas zu tun**, of doing sth.); to commission (an artist etc.); *Jur:* to brief (a lawyer); **j-n mit einer Arbeit b.**, to assign a task to s.o. ◆**B~te(r)**, *m & f decl. as adj.* representative; *Com:* agent.

be'bauen, *v.tr.* (*a*) to build on (a plot, piece of land); **bebautes Gebiet**, built-up area; (*b*) *Agr:* to farm (the land); to cultivate (a garden, field).

beben ['beːbən], *v.i.* (*haben*) to shake.

bebildert [bə'bildərt], *adj.* illustrated.

Becher ['beçər], *m -s/-* (*a*) (*Trinkb.*) beaker; (*aus Glas*) tumbler; (*b*) carton (of cream etc.); tub (of ice cream).

Becken ['bɛkən], *n -s/-* **1.** (*a*) (wash)basin; (kitchen) sink; (*WC*) (lavatory) pan; (*b*) (*Bassin*) (swimming, paddling) pool. **2.** *Mus:* cymbals. **3.** *Anat:* pelvis.

bedacht [bə'daxt], *adj.* (*a*) careful, circumspect; (*b*) (*besorgt*) concerned (**auf** + *acc*, about); **darauf b.**, **etwas zu tun**, intent on doing sth.

bedächtig [bə'dɛçtiç], *adj.* deliberate, slow; (*Pers.*) thoughtful.

be'danken, *v.refl.* **sich b.**, to express one's gratitude; **sich bei j-m** (**für etwas** *acc*) **b.**, to thank s.o. (for sth.).

Bedarf [bə'darf], *m -(e)s/no pl* (*a*) need, *Com:* demand (**an** + *dat*, for); **B. an etwas** *dat* **haben**, to need sth.; **bei B.**, if required; in case of need. ◆**B~sfall** *m*, **im B.**, if necessary. ◆**B~shaltestelle**, *f* request stop.

bedauer|lich [bə'dauərliç], *adj.* regrettable, unfortunate. ◆**b~n. I.** *v.tr.* (*a*) to feel sorry for (s.o.); **er ist zu b.**, he is to be pitied; (*b*) to regret (sth.). **II. B.**, *n -s/no pl* regret; **mit B.**, regretfully. ◆**b~nswert**, *adj.* pitiable (person, condition); deplorable (situation etc.).

be'deck|en, *v.tr.* to cover (sth.); (*Himmel*)

**sich b.** to become overcast. ◆**b~t**, *adj.* covered; overcast (sky).

be'denk|en. **I.** *v.tr.irr.17* (*a*) (*überlegen*) to think (sth.) over; (*b*) (*berücksichtigen*) to bear (sth.) in mind. **II. B.**, *n -s/-* thought, reflection; **ohne B.**, without hesitation; **B. haben** (, **etwas zu tun**), to have doubts/reservations (about doing sth.); **moralische B.**, scruples. ◆**b~lich**, *adj.* **1.** (*Pers.*) thoughtful; doubtful (expression). **2.** (*a*) (*verdächtig*) dubious (transaction etc.); (*b*) (*besorgniserregend*) worrying. ◆**B~zeit**, *f -/no pl* time to think it over.

be'deut|en, *v.tr.* to mean (sth.); **das hat nichts zu b.**, it is of no significance. ◆**b~end**, *adj.* important; distinguished (person); considerable (amount, sum). ◆**b~sam**, *adj.* (*bedeutend*) momentous. ◆**B~ung**, *f -/-en* **1.** (*Sinn*) meaning. **2.** (*Wichtigkeit*) importance. ◆**b~ungslos**, *adj.* (*a*) meaningless; (*b*) unimportant. ◆**b~ungsvoll**, *adj.* significant.

be'dien|en, *v.tr.* (*a*) to serve, attend to (a customer, guest); **bitte b. Sie sich!** (do) help yourself! (*b*) to operate (a machine etc.); (*c*) **sich j-s, etwas** *gen* **b.**, to make use of s.o., sth. ◆**B~stete(r)**, *m & f decl. as adj.* employee. ◆**B~ung**, *f -/no pl* **1.** (*a*) service; (*b*) (*Kellnerin*) waitress. **2.** operation (of a machine). ◆**B~ungsanleitung**, *f* operating instructions.

beding|en [bə'diŋən], *v.tr.* to cause (sth.); to bring (sth.) about. ◆**b~t**, *p.p. & adj.* conditional (permission); qualified (praise, agreement etc.); (*b*) **psychologisch b. sein**, to have psychological causes. ◆**B~ung**, *f -/-en* (*a*) condition, stipulation; **unter der B.**, **daß** ..., on condition that ...; **unter keiner B.**, on no account; (*b*) *pl* (*Verhältnisse*) conditions; (*c*) *pl Com:* terms. ◆**b~ungslos**, *adj.* unconditional (surrender, approval etc.); unquestioning (devotion, faith etc.).

be'drängen, *v.tr.* to press (s.o.) (hard); (*plagen*) to pester (s.o.).

be'droh|en, *v.tr.* to threaten (s.o., sth.). ◆**b~lich**, *adj.* threatening, menacing. ◆**B~ung**, *f* threat (**des Friedens usw.**, to peace etc.).

be'drucken, *v.tr.* to print on (sth.); **bedruckt**, printed (notepaper, cotton).

be'drück|en, *v.tr.* to depress (s.o.); (*Sorgen usw.*) to weigh (heavily) on s.o. ◆**b~end**, *adj.* oppressive. ◆**b~t**, *adj.* depressed; downcast, subdued.

be'dürf|en, *v.tr.irr.20 Lit:* **j-s, etwas b.**, to be in need of s.o., sth. ◆**B~nis**, *n -ses/-se* need, requirement. ◆**B~nisanstalt**, *f* public convenience. ◆**b~nislos**, *adj.* modest (in one's requirements); frugal. ◆**b~tig**, *adj.* needy, poor. ◆**B~tigkeit**, *f -/no pl* neediness, want.

beeiden [bə'ʔaidən], *v.tr.* to declare (sth.) on oath.

**beeilen** [bəˈʔailən], *v.refl.* **sich b.**, to hurry; **sich b., etwas zu tun**, to hasten to do sth.

**beeindrucken** [bəˈʔaindrukən], *v.tr.* to impress (s.o.).

**beeinfluss|en** [bəˈʔainflusən], *v.tr.* to influence. ◆B∼**ung**, *f -/no pl* (use of) influence.

**beeinträchtig|en** [bəˈʔaintrɛçtigən], *v.tr.* to affect (s.o., sth.) (adversely); (*schädigen*) to damage (health etc.), encroach on (rights); (*mindern*) to lessen (effect, value); to impair (judgment etc.). ◆B∼**ung**, *f -/-en* adverse effect (+*gen*, on); damage; encroachment.

**beend(ig)en** [bəˈʔɛnd(ig)ən], *v.tr.* to finish (sth.); to put an end to (a quarrel, s.o.'s career etc.).

**beengen** [bəˈʔɛŋən], *v.tr.* to restrict, hamper (s.o.'s movements, freedom etc.).

**beerdig|en** [bəˈʔɛrdigən], *v.tr.* to bury (a dead person). ◆B∼**ung**, *f -/-en* burial; funeral. ◆B∼**ungsunternehmen**, *n* (firm of) undertakers; *N.Am:* funeral parlor.

**Beere** [ˈbeːrə], *f -/-n* berry.

**Beet** [ˈbeːt], *n -(e)s/-e* (flower etc.) bed.

**befähig|en** [bəˈfɛːigən], *v.tr.* (*Eigenschaft usw.*) to qualify (s.o.); (*Umstände usw.*) to enable (s.o.) (to do sth.). ◆B∼**ung**, *f -/no pl* 1. ability, competence. 2. qualification(s) (**zu** + *dat*, for).

**befahr|bar** [bəˈfaːrbar], *adj.* (*Straße usw.*) passable (for vehicles); **nicht b.**, unfit for traffic. ◆**b∼en**, *v.tr.irr.26* to drive along (a road etc.); **eine stark/wenig b∼e Strecke**, a busy/little-used stretch of road.

**befallen** [bəˈfalən], *v.tr.irr.27* (*a*) (*Krankheit*) to attack (s.o., a plant etc.); (*b*) (*Angst usw.*) to seize, overcome (s.o.).

**be'fangen**, *adj.* 1. (*schüchtern*) shy; (*gehemmt*) self-conscious; (*verlegen*) embarrassed. 2. *esp. Jur:* (*parteiisch*) biased. ◆B∼**heit**, *f -/no pl* 1. shyness; self-consciousness; embarrassment. 2. *esp. Jur:* bias (of a witness).

**be'fassen**, *v.refl.* **sich mit etwas** *dat* **b.**, to concern oneself with sth.; (*untersuchen*) to deal with sth.

**Befehl** [bəˈfeːl], *m -(e)s/-e* (*a*) order; *Data-pr:* instruction; **zu B.!** yes sir! (*b*) *Mil:* command. ◆**b∼en**, *v.tr.irr.* j-m etwas b./j-m b., etwas zu tun, to order/command s.o. to do sth. ◆**b∼igen**, *v.tr. Mil:* to command (an army etc.). ◆B∼**shaber**, *m* commander. ◆B∼**verweigerung**, *f* insubordination.

**be'festig|en**, *v.tr.* (*a*) to fix, attach (sth.); (*b*) to reinforce (a bridge, dam etc.); (*c*) *Mil:* to fortify (a town etc.). ◆B∼**ung**, *f -/-en* 1. *no pl* fixing, attaching. 2. reinforcement. 3. *Mil:* fortification.

**be'feuchten**, *v.tr.* to moisten (sth.), humidify (the air).

**be'find|en**. I. *v.* 1. (*a*) *v.tr.* **etwas für gut/richtig usw. b.**, to judge sth. to be

good/right etc.; *Jur:* **j-n (als/für) schuldig b.**, to find s.o. guilty; (*b*) *refl.* **sich b.**, (*Pers., Sache*) to be; (*Ort, Gebäude usw.*) to be situated. 2. *v.i.* (*haben*) **über etwas** *acc* **b.**, to give a judgement on sth. II. B., *n -s/no pl* 1. (*Meinung*) opinion; judgement. 2. (*Zustand*) state of health.

**be'folgen**, *v.tr.* to follow (advice), comply with (rules etc.).

**be'förder|n**, *v.tr.* (*a*) to transport (s.o., sth.); to convey, (*schicken*) send (letters, goods), *Com:* ship (goods); (*b*) to promote (s.o.) (**zum Direktor**, to the position of director). ◆B∼**ung**, *f -/-en* 1. *no pl* transport(ation), conveyance; *Com:* shipping. 2. promotion.

**be'fragen**, *v.tr.* to ask, question (s.o.); to interrogate (a witness); to consult (a doctor, dictionary etc.).

**be'frei|en** [bəˈfraiən], *v.tr.* (*a*) to release (a prisoner etc.); to free, liberate (s.o., a country etc.); to rescue (s.o.); (*b*) to clear (sth.), rid (s.o.) (**von etwas**, of sth.); (*c*) to exempt (s.o.) (**von Steuern usw.**, from taxes etc.). ◆B∼**er(in)**, *m -s/- (f -/-nen)* liberator; rescuer. ◆B∼**ung**, *f -/no pl* 1. liberation, release (**von** + *dat*, from); emancipation (of women). 2. exemption. ◆B∼**ungs-**, *comb. fm.* freedom (movement etc.).

**befremden** [bəˈfrɛmdən], I. *v.tr.* to take (s.o.) aback, shock (s.o.). II. B., *n -s/no pl* amazement; shock; (*Entrüstung*) indignation.

**befreunden** [bəˈfrɔyndən], *v.refl.* **sich mit etwas** *dat* **b.**, to come to like sth.; **mit j-m (eng) befreundet sein**, to be (great) friends with s.o.

**befriedig|en** [bəˈfriːdigən], *v.tr.* to satisfy (s.o., a need etc.); to fulfil (a desire, demand etc.); **sich (selbst) b.**, to masturbate. ◆**b∼end**, *adj.* satisfactory. ◆B∼**ung**, *f -/no pl* satisfaction; fulfilment.

**befristen** [bəˈfristən], *v.tr.* to limit.

**befruchten** [bəˈfruxtən], *v.tr.* to fertilize (an egg, flower). ◆B∼**ung**, *f -/-en* fertilization; **künstliche B.**, artificial insemination.

**befug|t** [bəˈfuːgt], *adj.* **b. sein, etwas zu tun**, to be authorized to do sth. ◆B∼**nis**, *f -/-se* authority; *pl* B∼**se**, powers.

**Befund** [bəˈfunt], *m* result (of a test etc.); findings (of an inquiry etc.).

**be'fürcht|en**, *v.tr.* to fear. ◆B∼**ung**, *f -/-en* fear; (*Bedenken*) misgiving.

**befürwort|en** [bəˈfyːrvɔrtən], *v.tr.* to support (sth.), advocate (a policy etc.). ◆B∼**er**, *m -s/-* advocate.

**begab|t** [bəˈgɑːpt], *adj.* gifted, talented. ◆B∼**ung**, *f -/-en* gift, talent.

**begatten** [bəˈgatən], *v.tr.* (*Tiere*) to mate with; **sich b.**, to mate.

**be'geben**, *v.refl.irr.35* (*a*) **sich an einen anderen Ort b.**, to proceed to another place; (*b*) *impers. Lit:* **es begab sich, daß**

..., so it happened that ... ◆B~**heit**, *f* /-/-en incident, occurrence.

**begegn|en** [bəˈgeːgnən], *v.i.* (*sein*) (*a*) j-m, etwas *dat* **b.**, to meet s.o. etc.; (*b*) j-m **freundlich/höflich b.**, to treat s.o. kindly/politely. ◆B~**ung**, *f* /-/-en meeting, encounter.

**begeh|bar** [bəˈgeːbaːr], *adj.* passable (road etc.). ◆**b~en**, *v.tr.irr.36* (*a*) to walk along (a path etc.); (*b*) (*feiern*) to celebrate (a birthday etc.); (*c*) (*verüben*) to commit (a crime, blunder etc.); **einen Fehler b.**, to make a mistake.

**begehr|en** [bəˈgeːrən], *v.tr.* to want, covet (sth.); to desire (a woman etc.); (*heftig*) to crave for (sth.). ◆**b~enswert**, *adj.* desirable. ◆**b~t**, *adj.* sought after; popular (dancing partner etc.).

**begeister|n** [bəˈgaistərn], *v.tr.* to arouse enthusiasm in (s.o.); (*Theaterstück usw.*) to delight, thrill (s.o., the audience etc.); **sich (für etwas** *acc*) **b.**, to get enthusiastic/*F:* excited (about sth.). ◆**b~t**, *adj.* enthusiastic, thrilled. ◆B~**ung**, *f /-/no pl* enthusiasm.

**Begier|de** [bəˈgiːrdə], *f* /-/-n desire, (*Gelüste*) craving, (*Sehnsucht*) longing. ◆**b~ig**, *adj.* avid, eager.

**Beginn** [bəˈgin], *m* -(e)s/no pl beginning. ◆**b~en**, *v.irr.* **1.** *v.tr.* to start (a conversation, work etc.); to set about (sth.). **2.** *v.i.* (*haben*) to begin, start.

**beglaubig|en** [bəˈglaubigən], *v.tr.* to authenticate (a document, etc.). ◆B~**ung**, *f* /-/-en authentication.

**be'gleichen**, *v.tr.irr.40* to settle, pay.

**Begleit-** [bəˈglait-], *comb.fm.* accompanying (text etc.); attendant (symptom, circumstances etc.); *Mil: etc:* escort (aircraft, vessel etc.). ◆B~**brief**, *m* accompanying/covering letter; *Com:* advice note. ◆**b~en**, *v.tr.* to accompany (s.o., sth.). ◆B~**er(in)**, *m -s/- (f /-/-nen)* **1.** companion. **2.** *Mus:* accompanist. ◆B~**erscheinung**, *f* side effect. ◆B~**musik**, *f Cin: TV: etc:* background music. ◆B~**ung**, *f /-/-n* **1.** company. **2.** *Mus:* accompaniment.

**beglück|en** [bəˈglykən], *v.tr.* to make (s.o.) happy. ◆**b~wünschen**, *v.tr.* to congratulate.

**begnad|et** [bəˈgnaːdət], *adj.* gifted. ◆**b~igen**, *v.tr.* to pardon (s.o.). ◆B~**igung**, *f /-/-en* (free) pardon.

**begnügen** [bəˈgnyːgən], *v.refl.* **sich mit etwas** *dat* **b.**, to content oneself with sth.

**Begonie** [beˈgoːniə], *f /-/-n* begonia.

**be'graben**, *v.tr.irr.42* to bury (s.o., sth.).

**Begräbnis** [bəˈgrɛːpnis], *n -ses/-se* burial; (*Feier*) funeral.

**begreif|en** [bəˈgraifən], *v.tr.irr.43* to understand (s.o., sth.), grasp (sth.). ◆**b~lich**, *adj.* understandable.

**begrenzen** [bəˈgrɛntsən], *v.tr.* to limit, restrict (sth.).

**Begriff** [bəˈgrif], *m* **1.** concept; (*Ausdruck*) term, expression. **2.** conception, idea; **für**

heutige B~**e**, by present day standards. **3. im B. sein, etwas zu tun**, to be on the point of doing sth. ◆**b~sstutzig**, *adj.* slow on the uptake; *F:* gormless (person, expression).

**be'gründ|en**, *v.tr.* to justify (an action, opinion etc.). ◆**b~et**, *adj.* well-founded (hope, suspicion etc.); reasoned (argument etc.). ◆B~**ung**, *f* seine **B. war ...**, the reasons he gave were ...

**be'grüß|en**, *v.tr.* to greet (s.o.); to welcome (a guest, a suggestion etc.). ◆B~**ung**, *f /-/-en* greeting; welcome.

**begünstig|en** [bəˈgynstigən], *v.tr.* (*a*) to favour (s.o., sth.); (*Umstände usw.*) to further (plans etc.); (*b*) (*bevorzugen*) to give (s.o.) preferential treatment. ◆B~**ung**, *f /-/-en* (*a*) favouring; furtherance; (*b*) preferential treatment; (*c*) *Jur:* aiding and abetting.

**be'gutachten**, *v.tr.* to give a professional opinion on (sth.).

**begütert** [bəˈgyːtərt], *adj.* well-to-do.

**behaart** [bəˈhaːrt], *adj.* hairy.

**behäbig** [bəˈhɛːbiç], *adj.* (*Pers.*) portly (and slow-moving); leisurely (pace etc.).

**behag|en** [bəˈhaːgən], *v.i.* (*haben*) j-m **b.**, to suit s.o. ◆**b~lich**, *adj.* (*a*) comfortable (armchair etc.); cosy (room, restaurant etc.).

**be'halten**, *v.tr.irr.45* to keep; **etwas (im Gedächtnis) b.**, to remember sth.

**Behälter** [bəˈhɛltər], *m* -s/- container, receptacle; (*für Flüssigkeiten*) tank.

**be'hand|eln**, *v.tr.* (*a*) to treat; (*b*) (*Buch, Pers. usw.*) to deal with (a subject). ◆B~**lung**, *f* /-/-en handling (of an affair); (*Patient*) **in B.**, undergoing treatment.

**beharr|en** [bəˈharən]. **I.** *v.i.* (*haben*) to persist; **auf/bei seinem Entschluß b.**, to stick to one's decision. **II. B.**, *n -s/no pl* persistence. ◆**b~lich**, *adj.* persistent; obstinate (silence, refusal etc.); dogged (determination). ◆B~**lichkeit**, *f /-/no pl* persistence; perseverance.

**behaupt|en** [bəˈhauptən], *v.tr.* (*a*) to maintain (sth.); **sich (in einer Position) b.**, to hold one's own; (*b*) to say (sth., the opposite etc.). ◆B~**ung**, *f /-/-en* statement; assertion.

**be'heben**, *v.tr.irr.48* to rectify (an abuse, defect); to repair (damage).

**be'heizen**, *v.tr.* to heat.

**Behelf** [bəˈhɛlf], *m* -(e)s/-e stopgap, makeshift. ◆**b~en**, *v.refl.irr.50* **sich b.**, to manage, make do. ◆**b~smäßig**, *adj.* makeshift.

**behelligen** [bəˈhɛligən], *v.tr.* to bother (s.o.).

**behende** [bəˈhɛndə], *adj. Lit:* nimble; (*geschickt*) deft.

**beherbergen** [bəˈhɛrbərgən], *v.tr.* to put (s.o.) up.

**be'herrsch|en**, *v.tr.* (*a*) to rule (over) (a country etc.); (*b*) (*Pers., Gefühl usw.*) to dominate (s.o., s.o.'s mind/life etc.); (*c*) to be in control of (the situation etc.); to control (oneself, one's feelings etc.); (*d*) to master (an instrument, a language etc.). ◆**B~ung,** *f -/no pl* 1. hold, sway; domination. 2. control. 3. mastery; command (of a language); grasp (of a subject).

**beherz|igen** [bə'hɛrtsigən], *v.tr.* to heed (a warning etc.); to take (s.o.'s advice) to heart.

**beherzt** [bə'hɛrtst], *adj.* courageous.

**behilflich** [bə'hilfliç], *adj.* j-m b. sein, to help s.o. (with sth./to do sth.).

**be'hinder|n**, *v.tr.* to hinder, hamper (s.o.); to obstruct (traffic, *Sp:* an opponent etc.), impede (visibility etc.). ◆**b~t,** *adj.* (mentally/physically) handicapped. ◆**B~ung,** *f -/-en* (*a*) hindrance, impeding; (*Aut: Sp:* obstruction; (*b*) (*Hindernis*) obstacle ( + *gen,* to); (*c*) *Med:* handicap.

**Behörd|e** [bə'hø:rdə], *f -/-n* authority; public body. ◆**b~lich** [-'hø:rtliç], *adj.* official.

**be'hüten**, *v.tr.* to protect (s.o., sth.) (**vor** + *dat*, from).

**behutsam** [bə'hu:tza:m], *adj.* cautious (person, words); gentle (treatment etc.).

**bei** [bai], *prep. + dat* 1. (*Ort*) (*a*) near; (**nahe/dicht**) **bei der Schule,** (right/just) by the school; (*b*) among (a number of people, things); (*c*) at; **bei Tisch,** at table; **bei uns** (**zu Hause**), (i) at our house; (ii) in our country; **bei j-m wohnen,** to live with s.o./in s.o.'s house; **bei einer Firma arbeiten,** to work for a firm; **wie es bei Shakespeare heißt,** as Shakespeare says; **sie hatte kein Geld bei sich,** she didn't have any money with/on her. 2. (*Zeit*) **bei seiner Ankunft,** on his arrival; **when he arrived; er war (gerade) beim Abwaschen,** he was (just) washing up (at that moment); **bei Tag(e)/Nacht,** by day/night. 3. by; **j-n bei der Hand nehmen/beim Namen rufen,** to take s.o. by the hand/call s.o. by name. 4. (*im Falle von*) with, in the case of (s.o., sth.). **bei Regen,** if it rains.

**'beibehalten,** *v.tr.sep.irr.45* to retain (sth.); to keep up (a custom, habit).

**'beibringen,** *v.tr.sep.irr.16* j-m etwas b., to teach s.o. sth.; *F:* **wie soll ich es ihr b.?** how shall I break it to her?

**Beicht|e** ['baiçtə], *f -/-n* confession. ◆**'b~en,** *v.* 1. *v.tr.* to confess (one's sins etc.). 2. *v.i.* (*haben*) to confess; **b. gehen,** to go to confession.

**beide** ['baidə], *adj. & pron.* both; **die b~n Schwestern,** the two sisters; (*betont*) both (of) the sisters; **die b~n,** the two of them; (**alle**) **b.,** both; **b~s,** both; **eins von b~n,** one or the other; **keins von b~n,** neither. ◆**'b~rlei,** *inv. adj.* of both kinds. ◆**'b~rseitig,** *adj.* on both sides; mutual (agreement, satisfaction etc.). ◆**'b~rseits. I.** *prep. + gen* on both sides of (the road etc.). **II.** *adv.* on

both sides; by both sides/parties.

**beiein'ander,** *adv.* (close) together.

**'Beifahrer,** *m* (front-seat) passenger. ◆**'B~sitz,** *m* front seat.

**'Beifall,** *m* 1. applause. 2. (*Billigung*) approval.

**'beifügen,** *v.tr.sep.* (*a*) to enclose (sth.); (*b*) (*hinzufügen*) to add (sth.).

**beige** [bɛ:ʒ], *inv. adj.* beige.

**'beigeben,** *v.sep.irr.36* 1. *v.tr.* (*a*) to add (sth.) (**etwas** *dat,* to sth.); (*b*) to assign (a helper etc.) (j-m, to s.o.). 2. *v.i.* (*haben*) **klein b.,** to give in, *F:* climb down.

**'Beigeschmack,** *m* (slight) taste, flavour (of sth. else); (*scharf*) tang.

**'Beihilfe,** *f* 1. *Adm:* financial aid; (*einmalig*) grant. 2. *Jur:* aiding and abetting.

**Beil** [bail], *n -(e)s/-e* hatchet; (butcher's) cleaver.

**'Beilage,** *f -/-n* 1. supplement. 2. *Cu:* accompaniment(s); **Fleisch mit Nudeln als B.,** meat served with noodles.

**'beiläufig,** *adj.* passing (remark etc.); casual (inquiry, behaviour etc.).

**'beileg|en,** *v.tr.sep.* (*a*) to enclose (sth.); (*b*) to settle (a quarrel, difference etc.). ◆**B~ung,** *f -/-en* settlement.

**bei'leibe,** *adv.* **b. nicht,** certainly not.

**'Beileid,** *n -s/no pl* condolences; **sein B. aussprechen,** to offer one's condolences. ◆**B~s-,** *comb.fm.* (visit, letter etc.) of condolence.

**'beiliegen,** *v.i.sep.irr.62* (*haben*) **einem Brief usw. b.,** to be enclosed with a letter etc. ◆**'b~d,** *adj.* enclosed.

**beim** [baim]=**bei dem.**

**'beimessen,** *v.tr.sep.irr.25* **etwas** *dat* **Wichtigkeit/Bedeutung b.,** to attach importance to sth.

**Bein** [bain], *n -(e)s/-e* leg; **auf den B~en,** on one's feet; (*nach einer Krankheit*) up and about. ◆**'B~bruch,** *m* fracture of the leg.

**beinah(e)** ['bain:(ə)], *adv.* nearly.

**beinhalten** [bə'?inhaltən], *v.tr.* to contain (sth.); (*Begriff usw.*) to cover (sth.); (*Brief usw.*) to say (sth., that ...).

**beipflichten** ['baipfliçtən], *v.i.sep.* (*haben*) j-m b., to agree with s.o.

**'Beirat,** *m* advisory committee.

**beirren** [bə'?irən], *v.tr.* to disconcert (s.o.); **laß dich nicht b.,** don't let yourself be put off.

**beisammen** [bai'zamən], *adv. & comb.fm.* together. ◆**B~sein,** *n -s/no pl* (social) gathering.

**'Beischlaf,** *m* sexual intercourse.

**'Beisein,** *n* **im B. von j-m/in j-s B.,** in the presence of s.o.

**bei'seite,** *adv.* (*auf der Seite*) apart, on one side; *Th:* aside; (*b*) (*an die Seite*) aside, to one side; j-n, etwas b. **schaffen,** to get rid of s.o., sth.

**'beisetz|en,** *v.tr.sep.* to bury (a corpse). ◆**'B~ung,** *f -/-en* burial; (*Feier*) funeral.

**'Beispiel,** *n* example (**für etwas** *acc,* of

sth.); **zum B.**, for example; **sich** *dat* **ein B. an j-m, etwas nehmen**, to take s.o., sth. as one's model. ◆'**b~haft**, *adj.* exemplary. ◆'**b~los**, *adj.* unprecedented. ◆'**b~sweise**, *adv.* for example.

**beiß|en** ['baisən], *v.tr. & i.irr.* (*haben*) (*a*) to bite; (*b*) (*Rauch, Wind usw.*) to burn; *F:* **die Farben b. sich**, the colours clash. ◆'**b~d**, *adj.* biting (cold, wind); acrid (taste, smell, smoke); *Fig:* caustic (wit, remark).

'**Beistand**, *m* assistance; (*Unterstützung*) support.

'**beistehen**, *v.i.sep.irr.100* (*haben*) **j-m b.**, to help/(*in Schwierigkeiten*) stand by s.o.

'**beisteuern**, *v.tr.sep.* to contribute.

'**beistimmen**, *v.i.sep.* (*haben*) **j-m, einem Vorschlag b.**, to agree with s.o., a proposal.

**Beitrag** ['baitra:k], *m -(e)s/-e* contribution; (*Mitgliedsb.*) subscription; (*Versicherungsb.*) premium; (*Zeitungsb.*) article. ◆'**b~en** ['-gən], *v.tr. & i.sep.irr.85* (*haben*) to contribute (sth.).

'**beitreten**, *v.i.sep.irr.105* (*sein*) **einem Verein, einer Partei usw. b.**, to join a club, party etc.

'**Beitritt**, *m* joining (**zu einem Verein usw.**, of a club etc.).

'**Beiwagen**, *m -s/-* sidecar.

'**beiwohnen**, *v.i.sep.* (*haben*) **etwas** *dat* **b.**, to be present at sth.

**Beize** ['baitsə], *f -/-n* **1.** (*a*) corrosive; (*b*) *Cu:* pickle, marinade. **2.** (*für Holz*) stain.

**bei'zeiten**, *adv.* in good time.

**bejahen** [bə'ja:ən], *v.tr.&i.* (*haben*) to say yes to (a question); (*billigen*) to approve of (s.o., sth.). ◆**b~d**, *adj.* positive (attitude); affirmative (answer).

**bejahrt** [bə'ja:rt], *adj.* aged.

**be'jammern**, *v.tr.* to bewail (sth.).

**be'kämpf|en**, *v.tr.* to fight (an opponent, a pest, plan etc.); to combat (an epidemic, evil etc.). ◆**B~ung**, *f -/no pl* fight, battle ( + *gen*, against).

**bekannt** [bə'kant], *adj.* **1.** well-known; (*berühmt*) famous. **2.** (*Tatsache, Person*) known (**j-m**, to s.o.); (*seit langem/von früher*) familiar; **mir ist das schon b.**, I know that already; **sie kam mir b. vor**, she seemed familiar; **darf ich Sie mit meinem Mann b. machen?** may I introduce you to my husband? ◆**B~e(r)**, *m & f decl. as adj.* acquaintance; friend. ◆**B~enkreis**, *m* circle of acquaintances. ◆**B~gabe**, *f* announcement; disclosure. ◆**b~geben**, *v.tr.sep.irr.35* to announce (sth.). ◆**b~lich**, *adv.* as is well known; **er hat b. keine Geduld**, everybody knows he has no patience. ◆**b~machen**, *v.tr.sep.* to publish (findings, a discovery etc.). ◆**B~machung**, *f -/-en* (*a*) publication; (*b*) (*Anschlag*) notice. ◆**B~schaft**, *f no pl* acquaintance.

**be'kehr|en**, *v.tr.* to convert (s.o.). ◆**B~ung**, *f -/-en* conversion.

**be'kenn|en**, *v.tr.irr.51* to admit (one's mistake, guilt); to confess (the truth, one's sins, that ...); **sich zu j-m b.**, to stand by s.o. ◆**B~tnis**, *n* (*Konfession*) denomination.

**be'klag|en**, *v.tr.* (*a*) *Lit:* to grieve over, lament (a loss, death etc.); (*bedauern*) to deplore (sth.); (*b*) **sich b.**, to complain. ◆**B~te(r)**, *m & f decl. as adj.* defendant.

**be'kleid|en**, *v.tr.* (*a*) to dress (s.o.); (*b*) *Lit:* to hold (an office). ◆**B~ung**, *f* **1.** clothing. **2.** tenure (of an office).

**be'klemm|en**, *v.tr.* to oppress. ◆**b~end**, *adj.* oppressive; stifling (atmosphere). ◆**B~ung**, *f -/-en* feeling of oppression/(*Angst*) apprehension.

**beklommen** [bə'kləmən], *adj.* uneasy.

**be'kommen**, *v.irr.53* **1.** *v.tr.* (*a*) to get (sth.); to receive (a letter, permission, money, etc.); **ein Kind b.**, to have a baby; (*b*) (*sich verschaffen*) to obtain (sth.); **den Zug/Bus noch b.**, to catch the train/bus. **2.** *v.i.* (*sein*) **j-m b.** (*Nahrung, Klima usw.*) to agree with s.o.

**bekömmlich** [bə'kœmliç], *adj.* wholesome; **leicht/schwer b.**, easily digestible/indigestible.

**be'kräftig|en**, *v.tr.* to confirm (an opinion, suspicion etc.), strengthen (s.o.). ◆**B~ung**, *f* confirmation.

**be'kümmer|n**, *v.tr.* to trouble, worry (s.o.). ◆**b~t**, *adj.* sorrowful; troubled.

**be'kund|en**, *v.tr.* (*a*) *Lit:* to manifest (one's feelings, intentions etc.); (*b*) *Jur:* to testify (that ...).

**be'lächeln**, *v.tr.* to smile (condescendingly/pityingly) at (s.o., sth.).

**be'laden**, *v.tr. irr.56* to load (s.o., a lorry etc.); **schwer b.**, heavily laden.

**Belag** [bə'la:k], *m -(e)s/-e* **1.** (*Schicht*) coating; (*sehr dünn*) film; *Med:* fur (on the tongue); (*Zahnb.*) plaque. **2.** (*road*) surface; (*floor-*)covering; *Tchn:* lining (of brakes etc.). **3.** *Cu:* filling (for sandwiches etc.).

**be'lager|n**, *v.tr.* to besiege (a town etc.). ◆**B~ung**, *f -/-en* siege.

**Belang** [bə'laŋ], *m -(e)s/-e* **1.** *no pl* **von/ohne B.**, of consequence/no consequence; important/unimportant. **2.** *pl* **B~e**, interests. ◆**b~en**, *v.tr.* to sue, prosecute (s.o.). ◆**b~los**, *adj.* unimportant. ◆**B~losigkeit**, *f -/-en* **1.** *no pl* insignificance. **2.** trifling matter.

**be'lassen**, *v.tr.irr.57* to leave (s.o., sth.).

**belast|en** [bə'lastən], *v.tr.* (*a*) to place a load/strain on (sth.); *Fig:* to burden (oneself, one's memory etc.); (*b*) *Fin:* to debit (an account); (*c*) *Jur:* to incriminate (s.o.). ◆**B~ung**, *f -/-en* **1.** (*a*) load, (*Beanspruchung*) stress; **zulässige B.**, safe (working) load; (*b*) *Fig:* strain. **2.** *Fin:* debiting of an account). **3.** *Jur:* incrimination. ◆**B~ungsprobe**, *f* load test; *Fig:* gruelling test (of s.o.). ◆**B~ungszeuge**, *m* witness for the prosecution.

**be'lästig|en**, *v.tr.* to bother (s.o.), (*Mann*) molest (a girl); to pester (s.o.) (with questions etc.). ◆**B~ung**, *f* -/-en (*a*) *no pl* bothering; molestation; (*b*) (*Besuch usw.*) intrusion; **etwas als B. empfinden**, to find sth. annoying.

**be'laufen**, *v.refl.irr.58* **sich auf 100 DM** *acc* **b.**, to amount to 100 marks.

**be'lauschen**, *v.tr.* to eavesdrop on.

**be'leb|en**, *v.tr.* (*a*) to give life to (s.o., sth.); (*b*) (*lebhafter machen*) to enliven (s.o., sth.); to stimulate (the economy etc.); to brighten (up) (a room etc.); **j-n neu b.**, to revive (s.o.). ◆**b~t**, *adj.* busy (road etc.); animated (conversation).

**Beleg** [bə'le:k], *m* -(e)s/-e (documentary) proof; (*Scheck*) voucher, receipt. ◆**b~en**, *v.tr.* (*a*) (*bedecken*) to cover (sth.); **Brote mit Käse b.**, to put cheese on pieces of bread; **b~te Zunge/Stimme**, coated tongue/husky voice; (*b*) (*reservieren*) to reserve (a seat, table, room); **Vorlesungen b.**, to enrol for lectures; (*c*) (*beweisen*) to substantiate. ◆**B~schaft**, *f* -/-en employees, personnel (of a firm).

**be'lehren**, *v.tr.* to inform, instruct (s.o.).

**beleidig|en** [bə'laidigən], *v.tr.* to offend (s.o., *Fig:* the eye, ear); (*absichtlich*) to insult (s.o.). ◆**B~ung**, *f* -/-en insult; *Jur:* slander; (*schriftlich*) libel.

**be'leucht|en**, *v.tr.* to light (a street, room etc.); *Fig:* to shed light on. ◆**B~ung**, *f* -/-en lighting; (*Licht*) light.

**Belg|ien** ['bɛlgiən]. *Pr.n.n* -s. Belgium. ◆**'B~ier(in)**, *m* -s/- (*f* -/-nen) & ◆**b~isch**, *adj.* Belgian.

**be'licht|en**, *v.tr.* to expose (a photograph etc.). ◆**B~ung**, *f* -/-en exposure. ◆**B~ungsmesser**, *m* light meter.

**be'lieb|ig**, *adj.* 1. *attrib.* any (at all/you like). 2. *adv.* **b. lange/viel**, as long/much as one likes; **etwas b. verändern**, to alter sth. at will. ◆**b~t**, *adj.* popular; **sich bei j-m b. machen**, to get into s.o.'s good books. ◆**B~theit**, *f* -/no pl popularity.

**be'liefern**, *v.tr.* to supply (s.o.).

**bellen** ['bɛlən], *v.i.* (*haben*) to bark.

**be'lohn|en**, *v.tr.* to reward (s.o.), patience etc.). ◆**B~ung**, *f* -/-en reward.

**be'lüften**, *v.tr.* to ventilate (a room etc.).

**be'lügen**, *v.tr.irr.63* to lie to (s.o.).

**be'lustig|en**, *v.tr.* to amuse, entertain (s.o.). ◆**B~ung**, *f* -/-en amusement.

**be'mächtigen**, *v.refl.* **sich j-s, etwas** *gen* **b.**, to seize s.o., sth.

**bemängeln** [bə'mɛŋəln], *v.tr.* to find fault with (s.o., sth.).

**be'mannen**, *v.tr.* to man (a ship etc.).

**bemerk|bar** [bə'mɛrkbɑːr], *adj.* noticeable; **sich b. machen**, to draw attention to oneself/itself. ◆**b~en**, *v.tr.* (*a*) to notice (s.o., sth.); (*b*) (*sagen*) to remark (that ...). ◆**b~enswert**, *adj.* remarkable. ◆**B~ung**, *f* -/-en remark.

**be'messen**, *v.tr.irr.25* to calculate (a price

etc.); **meine Zeit ist knapp b.**, my time is limited.

**be'mitleiden**, *v.tr.* to pity, feel sorry for (s.o.).

**be'müh|en**. **I.** *v.tr.* (*a*) *Lit:* to trouble (s.o.); to call on the services of (a doctor, lawyer etc.); (*b*) **sich b.**, to try (hard); (*c*) (*sich kümmern*) **sich um einen Patienten usw. b.**, to attend to a patient etc. **II. B.**, *n* -s/no pl endeavour; **vergebliches B.**, wasted effort. ◆**B~ung**, *f* -/-en *esp. pl* efforts.

**be'nachbart**, *adj.* neighbouring (town etc.).

**be'nachrichtig|en**, *v.tr.* to inform. ◆**B~ung**, *f* -/-en notification.

**be'nachteilig|en**, *v.tr.* to treat (s.o.) unfairly. ◆**b~t**, *adj.* deprived. ◆**B~ung**, *f* -/-en (*a*) unfair treatment; (*b*) disadvantage.

**be'nehmen**. **I.** *v.refl.irr.69* **sich b.**, to behave. **II. B.**, *n* -s/no pl behaviour; **er hat kein B.**, he has no manners.

**be'neiden**, *v.tr.* to envy (s.o.); **j-n um etwas b.**, to envy s.o. sth. ◆**b~swert**, *adj.* enviable (success etc.); **nicht b.**, not to be envied.

**be'nennen**, *v.tr.irr.51* to name.

**Bengel** ['bɛŋəl], *m* -s/- rascal.

**benommen** [bə'nɔmən], *adj.* dazed, stunned. ◆**B~heit**, *f* -/no pl dazed state.

**be'nötigen**, *v.tr.* to require (sth.).

**be'nutz|en**, *v.tr.* to use. ◆**B~er**, *m* -s/- user. ◆**B~ung**, *f* -/no pl use.

**Benzin** [bɛn'tsiːn], *n* -s/-e petrol; *N.Am:* gas(oline). ◆**B~kanister**, *m* jerry can.

**beobacht|en** [bə'ʔoːbaxtən], *v.tr.* (*a*) to watch, (*kontrollieren*) observe; (*b*) (*bemerken*) to notice (sth.). ◆**B~er**, *m* -s/- observer. ◆**B~ung**, *f* -/-en observation.

**be'pflanzen**, *v.tr.* to plant (a border etc.).

**bequem** [bə'kveːm], *adj.* (*a*) comfortable (chair, shoes etc.); (*b*) easy (route, life, way etc.); **b~e Ausrede**, convenient excuse. ◆**b~en**, *v.refl. esp. F:* **sich (dazu) b., etwas zu tun**, to deign to do sth. ◆**B~lichkeit**, *f* -/-en 1. comfort. 2. *no pl* (*Faulheit*) laziness.

**be'rat|en**, *v.irr.13* 1. *v.tr.* (*a*) to advise (s.o.); **sich b. lassen**, to take advice; **gut b. sein, etwas zu tun**, to be well advised to do sth.; (*b*) (*besprechen*) to debate (sth.). 2. *v.i.* (*haben*) & *refl.* (*sich*) **mit j-m b.**, to confer with s.o.; **sie berieten (miteinander), was zu tun sei**, they discussed what was to be done. ◆**b~er(in)**, *m* -s/- (*f* -/-nen) adviser. ◆**b~schlagen**, *v.i.* (*haben*) to confer. ◆**B~ung**, *f* -/-en 1. advice; *Med: Jur:* consultation. 2. (*Besprechung*) discussion.

**be'rauben**, *v.tr.* to rob (s.o.).

**berech|enbar** [bə'rɛçənbɑːr], *adj.* calculable. ◆**b~nen**, *v.tr.* (*a*) to calculate (sth.); (*schätzen*) to estimate (the price etc.); (*b*) **j-m etwas b.**, to charge s.o. for sth.; **j-m zu viel/wenig b.**, to overcharge/undercharge s.o. ◆b~**nend**, *adj.* calculating. ◆B~**nung**, *f* 1. calculation. 2. *no pl* **mit B.**, deliberately.

**berechtig|en** [bəˈrɛçtigən], *v.tr.* to entitle (s.o.); *(Pers.)* to authorize (s.o.) (to do sth.). ◆b~**t**, *adj.* justified (hope, complaint etc.); legitimate (reason, pride etc.). ◆B~**ung**, *f* -/-en entitlement; right; *(Befugnis)* authorization.

**be'red|en**, *v.tr.* (a) to talk (sth.) over; to discuss (sth.); (b) *(überreden)* to persuade (s.o.). ◆b~**t** [bəˈreːt], *adj.* eloquent.

**Be'reich**, *m* (a) region, area; (b) field of science, art, politics etc.).

**be'reichern**, *v.tr.* (a) to enrich (oneself, a language etc.); to enlarge (a collection); (b) **sich b.**, to grow rich (**an** + *dat*, on).

**be'reinigen**, *v.tr.* to settle (an argument etc.); to clear up (a problem etc.).

**be'reisen**, *v.tr.* to tour (a country).

**bereit** [bəˈrait], *adj.* ready; **sich b. halten**, to hold oneself in readiness; *Mil: etc (einsatzb.)* to stand by; **sich zu etwas** *dat* **b. zeigen**, to show one's willingness to do sth. ◆b~**en**, *v.tr.* **j-m Sorgen/ Kummer b.**, to cause s.o. worry/trouble; **j-m Freude/eine Überraschung b.**, to give s.o. pleasure/a surprise. ◆b~**halten**, *v.tr.sep.irr.45* to have (sth.) ready; *(für Notfälle)* to keep (sth.) handy. ◆b~**legen**, *v.tr.sep.* to put (clothes, a meal etc.) out (ready) (**j-m**, for s.o.). ◆b~**liegen**, *v.i.sep.irr.62 (haben)* to be/lie ready. ◆b~**machen**, *v.tr.sep.* to get (s.o., sth.) ready. ◆b~**s**, *adv.* already. ◆B~**schaft**, *f* -/-en 1. (a) readiness; in **B. sein/stehen**, to be ready/*Mil:* on standby; (b) willingness (**zur Hilfe/zu helfen**, to help). 2. *(Polizeieinheit)* riot squad. ◆B~**schaftsdienst**, *m* emergency service. ◆b~**stehen**, *v.i. sep. irr.100 (haben)* to be ready waiting. ◆b~**stellen**, *v.tr.sep.* to provide (machines, troops etc.); to make (funds etc.) available. ◆b~**willig**, *adj.* willing (etwas zu tun, to do sth.); *adv.* willingly, readily.

**be'reuen**, *v.tr.* to regret (sth., having done sth.).

**Berg** [bɛrk]. I. *m* -(e)s/-e (a) mountain, (high) hill; (b) *Fig:* **jetzt sind wir über den B.**, the worst is behind us; (c) *F:* pile (of work etc.). II. '**B~-**, *comb.fm.* 1. mountain (guide, hut etc.); climbing (boot etc.). 2. mining (engineer etc.). ◆b~'**ab**, *adv.* downhill. ◆'**B~arbeiter**, *m* miner. ◆b~'**auf**, *adv.* uphill. ◆'**B~bau**, *m* mining. ◆'**b~ig**, *adj.* mountainous. ◆'**B~kamm**, *m* mountain ridge. ◆'**B~kette**, *f* mountain range. ◆'**B~mann**, *m* -(e)s/-leute miner. ◆'**b~steigen**. I. *v.i.sep.irr.89 (sein)* to go climbing/ mountaineering. II. **B.**, *n* -s/*no pl* mountaineering. ◆'**B~steiger(in)**, *m* -s/- (f -/-nen) mountaineer, climber.

◆'**B~werk**, *n* mine.

**berg|en** ['bɛrgən], *v.tr.irr.* (a) to salvage (cargo, a vessel); to recover (cargo, a dead body etc.); to rescue (accident victims etc.); (b) *Fig:* **Gefahren in sich b.**, to have hidden dangers. ◆'**B~ung**, *f* -/ -en salvage; recovery; rescue.

**Bericht** [bəˈriçt], *m* -(e)s/e report; account (of an event, journey etc.); **B. erstatten**, to report. ◆b~**en**, *v.tr. & i. (haben)* to report (sth.); **über etwas** *acc* **b.**, to (give a) report on sth. ◆B~**erstatter**, *m* reporter, correspondent.

**berichtig|en** [bəˈriçtigən], *v.tr.* to correct. ◆B~**ung**, *f* -/-en correction.

**beritten** [bəˈritən], *adj.* mounted (policeman etc.).

**Berliner** [bɛrˈliːnər], *m* -s/- *Cu:* doughnut.

**Bernstein** ['bɛrnʃtain], *m* amber.

**bersten** ['bɛrstən], *v.i.* irr.5 *(sein)* to burst; *(Boden usw.)* to develop cracks.

**berüchtigt** [bəˈryçtiçt], *adj.* notorious; disreputable (area, house etc.).

**berücksichtig|en** [bəˈrykziçtigən], *v.tr.* to take (sth.) into account; to consider (feelings, expense, an application etc.). ◆B~**ung**, *f* -/*no pl* consideration.

**Beruf** [bəˈruːf], *m* -(e)s/-e occupation; *(freier B.)* profession; *(handwerklich)* trade. ◆b~**en**. I. *v.tr.irr.74* (a) **j-n zum Nachfolger b.**, to appoint s.o. as one's successor; (b) **sich b. auf** + *acc*, to refer to (s.o., the law etc.). II. *adj.* (a) *(fähig)* competent; (b) **er fühlt sich dazu b.**, he feels he has a vocation for it. ◆b~**lich**, *adj.* vocational (training etc.); professional (duties, advancement etc.); work (problems, prospects etc.). ◆B~**s-**, *comb.fm.* (a) professional (footballer, boxer, criminal, secret etc.); *Mil:* regular (soldier, officer, army); (b) vocational (training, school); (c) occupational (disease etc.); working (clothes etc.). ◆B~**berater(in)**, *m(f)* careers officer/ *Sch:* teacher. ◆B~**beratung**, *f* vocational/careers guidance. ◆b~**s-tätig**, *adj.* working (person). ◆b~**s-verbot**, *n* ban prohibiting a teacher, doctor etc. from practising his profession. ◆B~**ung**, *f* -/-en 1. appointment. 2. *no pl* vocation (**zum Arzt**, to become a doctor). 3. *no pl* reference (**auf** + *acc*, to); **unter B. auf j-n, etwas** *acc*, with reference to s.o., sth. 4. *Jur:* appeal.

**be'ruhen**, *v.i. (haben)* **auf etwas** *dat* **b.**, to be based on sth.; **eine Sache auf sich b. lassen**, to let a matter rest.

**beruhig|en** [bəˈruːigən], *v.tr.* to calm (s.o., the nerves etc.); to reassure (s.o.); to ease (one's conscience, pain etc.); **sich b.**, to calm down. ◆B~**ung**, *f* -/-en *no pl* calming; reassuring; **zur B. der Nerven**, to calm the nerves; (b) reassurance, comfort. ◆B~**ungsmittel**, *n* sedative; *(gegen Depressionen)* tranquillizer.

**berühmt** [bə'ry:mt], *adj.* famous.
◆**B~heit,** *f* -/-en **1.** *no pl* fame. **2.** famous person, celebrity.

**be'rühr|en,** *v.tr.* (*a*) to touch (s.o., sth.); **sich b.,** to come into contact; *Fig:* (*Ideen usw.*) to have something in common; (*b*) to mention (a subject, point etc.); (*c*) to affect (s.o.). ◆**B~ung,** *f* -/-en contact; touch (of s.o.'s hand etc.).

**be'sag|en,** *v.tr.* (*Sache*) to say, mean (sth., nothing). ◆**b~t,** *adj.* aforesaid.

**besänftig|en** [bə'zɛnftigən], *v.tr.* to pacify (s.o.), calm (s.o.'s anger etc.). ◆**B~ung,** *f* -/*no pl* calming.

**Besatzung** [bə'zatsuŋ], *f* (*a*) *Nau: Av:* crew; (*b*) *Mil:* occupying force, (*Garnison*) garrison. ◆**B~s-,** *comb.fm.* occupying (troops etc.); occupied (area etc.).

**beschädig|en** [bə'ʃɛːdigən], *v.tr.* to damage (sth.). ◆**B~ung,** *f* -/-en **1.** *no pl* damaging. **2.** damage.

**be'schaff|en,** *v.tr.* to obtain, *F:* get (sth.). ◆**B~ung,** *f* -/*no pl* obtaining.

**be'schaffen2,** *adj.* **es ist so b., daß ...,** it is so constituted that ... ◆**B~heit,** *f* -/ *no pl* consistency; texture (of skin, material etc.); (*Zustand*) condition; (*Struktur*) composition; (*Art*) nature.

**beschäftig|en** [bə'ʃɛftigən], *v.tr.* to occupy (s.o., oneself); **j-n b.,** to keep (s.o.) busy; (*Problem usw.*) to exercise s.o.'s mind; **die Firma beschäftigt 200 Leute,** the firm employs 200 people. ◆**b~t,** *adj.* (*a*) busy; (*b*) **bei einer Firma b. sein,** to work for a firm. ◆**B~ung,** *f* -/ -en (*Tätigkeit*) occupation; job.

**be'schäm|en,** *v.tr.* to make (s.o.) feel ashamed, to shame (s.o.). ◆**b~end,** *adj.* humiliating; shameful.

**be'schatt|en,** *v.tr.* to tail (s.o.).

**beschau|en,** *v.tr.* to have a look at (sth.). ◆**b~lich,** *adj.* tranquil (life etc.).

**Bescheid** [bə'ʃait], *m* -(e)s/-e **1.** (*a*) information; (*b*) *Adm:* (official) decision. **2.** *F:* **über etwas** *acc* **B. wissen,** to know about sth.; **ich werde Ihnen B. sagen,** I'll let you know.

**be'scheiden,** *adj.* modest. ◆**B~heit,** *f* -/*no pl* modesty.

**be'scheinen,** *v.tr.irr.79* to shine on (s.o., sth.).

**bescheinig|en** [bə'ʃainigən], *v.tr.* to certify (sth.) (in writing); to acknowledge (receipt). ◆**B~ung,** *f* -/-en (*Schein*) certificate; (*Quittung*) receipt.

**be'schenken,** *v.tr.* to give (s.o.) presents.

**Bescherung** [bə'ʃeːruŋ], *f* -/-en giving out of (Christmas) presents; *F:* **eine schöne B.!** a nice mess!

**bescheuert** [bə'ʃɔyərt], *adj. F:* (*Pers.*) dotty.

**be'schießen,** *v.tr.irr.31* to shoot at (sth.); to bombard (a town, *Ph:* nucleus).

**be'schildern,** *v.tr.* to signpost (a road).

**be'schimpf|en,** *v.tr.* to call (s.o.) names. ◆**B~ung,** *f* -/-en abuse.

**Beschlag** [bə'ʃla:k], *m* (*a*) (metal) fittings

(of a door, chest etc.); (*b*) film, mist (on metal, window etc.); (*c*) **j-n, etwas in B. nehmen,** to take s.o., sth. over completely. ◆**b~en. I.** *v.irr.85* **1.** *v.tr.* to put metal fittings on(to) (a door, etc.); to stud (boots etc.); to tip (a stick etc.) with metal; to shoe (a horse). **2.** *v.i.* (*sein*) (*Glas*) to steam/mist up. **II.** *adj.* well-informed; well up. ◆**B~nahme,** *f* -/-n confiscation; *Mil:* requisition. ◆**b~nahmen,** *v.tr.* to confiscate (sth.); *Mil:* to requisition (land, property etc.).

**beschleunig|en** [bə'ʃlɔynigən], *v.* **1.** *v.tr.* to quicken (one's steps etc.); to speed up (work, a process etc.); to hasten (s.o.'s recovery, collapse). **2.** *v.i.* (*haben*) *Aut:* to accelerate. ◆**B~ung,** *f* -/-en **1.** quickening; speeding up. **2.** *Ph: Aut:* acceleration.

**be'schließen,** *v.tr.irr.31* (*a*) to decide (that ...); (*b*) to pass (a bill etc.); (*c*) (*beenden*) to end (a letter, speech etc.).

**Be'schluß,** *m* decision.

**beschmutzen** [bə'ʃmutsən], *v.tr.* to get (sth.) dirty, soil (sth.).

**be'schneiden,** *v.tr.irr.59* (*a*) to trim (a hedge); to prune (a tree, *Fig:* expenditure etc.); (*b*) *Ecc:* to circumcise (s.o.).

**beschönigen** [bə'ʃøːnigən], *v.tr.* to gloss over (a fault etc.).

**beschränk|en** [bə'ʃrɛŋkən], *v.tr.* to limit, restrict (sth.); **sich auf etwas** *acc* **b.,** (i) (*Sache*) to be limited to sth.; (ii) (*Pers.*) to confine oneself to sth. ◆**b~t,** *adj.* (*a*) limited (means, time etc.); (*b*) (*Pers.*) (geistig) b., of limited intelligence; (*c*) (*engstirnig*) narrow-minded. ◆**B~theit,** *f* -/*no pl* **1.** (*a*) limited intelligence; (*b*) narrow-mindedness. **2.** limited nature. ◆**B~ung,** *f* -/-en limitation.

**beschrankt** [bə'ʃraŋkt], *adj.* **b~er Bahnübergang,** level crossing with barriers.

**be'schreib|en,** *v.tr.irr.12* (*a*) to describe (sth.); (*b*) to write on (a piece of paper etc.). ◆**B~ung,** *f* -/-en description.

**beschrift|en** [bə'ʃriftən], *v.tr.* to write (on) (a label etc.); to label (a jar etc.). ◆**B~ung,** *f* -/-en **1.** *no pl* writing; labelling. **2.** (*Aufschrift*) inscription; label.

**beschuldig|en** [bə'ʃuldigən], *v.tr.* **j-n b.,** to charge s.o., accuse s.o. ◆**B~ung,** *f* -/-en accusation.

**be'schütz|en,** *v.tr.* to protect (s.o., sth.). ◆**B~er,** *m* -s/- protector.

**Beschwerde** [bə'ʃveːrdə], *f* -/-n (*a*) complaint; (*b*) *pl* pain, trouble.

**beschwer|en** [bə'ʃveːrən], *v.tr.* (*a*) to weight (down) (a roof, net etc.); (*b*) **sich b.,** to complain. ◆**b~lich,** *adj.* tiring, arduous.

**beschwichtig|en** [bə'ʃviçtigən], *v.tr.* to pacify (s.o.); to placate (s.o., s.o.'s anger etc.); to ease (one's conscience). ◆**B~ung,** *f* -/*no pl* soothing; *esp. Pol:* appeasement; conciliation.

**be'schwindeln,** *v.tr. F:* to swindle; (*belü-*

*gen*) to tell (s.o.) fibs.

**beschwingt** [bəˈʃviŋt], *adj.* gay, lively.

**beschwipst** [bəˈʃvipst], *adj. F:* tipsy.

**be'schwören**, *v.tr.irr.91* (*a*) to swear to (a statement etc.); (*b*) (*anflehen*) to implore (s.o.); (*c*) (*heraufb.*) to invoke (spirits etc.); *Fig:* to evoke (the past, memories etc.).

**beseitig|en** [bəˈzaitigən], *v.tr.* to eliminate (mistakes etc.). to dispose of (rubbish etc.). ◆B~ung, *f -/no pl* elimination; disposal.

**Besen** ['be:zən], *m -s/-* broom. ◆'B~stiel, *m* broomstick.

**besessen** [bəˈzɛsən], *adj.* fanatical; **von einer Idee b.**, obsessed with an idea.

**be'setz|en**, *v.tr.* to occupy (a seat, post, *Mil:* a country etc.); to fill (a space, vacancy, *Th:* part etc.). ◆b~t, *adj.* (*Sitz usw.*) taken; (*Toilette, Tel: Leitung*) engaged. ◆B~tzeichen, *n* engaged tone. ◆B~ung, *f -/-en* 1. (*a*) *Mil:* occupation; (*b*) filling (of a vacancy); *Th:* casting (of a play). 2. *Th:* cast.

**besichtig|en** [bəˈziçtigən], *v.tr.* to look round (a school etc.); to view (a house); to see the sights of (a town). ◆B~ung, *f -/-en* look round; viewing; visit.

**besied|eln** [bəˈziːdəln], *v.tr.* to settle (in) (an area); **dünn/dicht besiedelt,** sparsely/densely populated. ◆B~(e)-lung, *f -/no pl* settlement.

**besiegeln** [bəˈziːgəln], *v.tr.* to seal.

**be'sieg|en**, *v.tr.* (*a*) to defeat; (*b*) *Fig:* to overcome (doubts etc.). ◆B~te(r), *m & f decl. as adj.* loser.

**besinn|en** [bəˈzinən], *v.refl.irr.3* (*a*) **sich b.,** to think, reflect; **sich anders b.,** to change one's mind; (*b*) **sich auf j-n, etwas** *acc* **b.,** to remember s.o., sth. ◆b~lich, *adj.* contemplative. ◆B~ung, *f -/no pl* consciousness; (**wieder**) **zur B. kommen,** to regain consciousness; *Fig:* to come to one's senses. ◆b~ungslos, *adj.* unconscious.

**Be'sitz,** *m -es/no pl* 1. property. 2. (*das B~en*) ownership. ◆b~en, *v.tr.irr.97* (*a*) to possess, own (property etc.); (*b*) to have (talent, courage etc.). ◆B~er(in), *m -s/- (f -/-nen)* owner. ◆B~ergreifung, *f -/no pl* taking possession; (*mit Gewalt*) seizure.

**besohlen** [bəˈzoːlən], *v.tr.* to sole (a shoe etc.).

**Besoldung** [bəˈzɔldung], *f -/-en* salary; *Mil:* pay.

**besonder|e(r, s)** [bəˈzɔndərə(r,s)], *adj.* special; particular (reason, wish, care etc.). ◆B~heit, *f -/-en* peculiarity; special feature. ◆b~s, *adv.* particularly; (e)specially.

**besonnen** [bəˈzɔnən], *adj.* prudent; (*umsichtig*) cautious; (*überlegt*) considered (opinion, judgement). ◆B~heit, *f -/no pl* prudence; caution.

**be'sorg|en,** *v.tr.* (*a*) to get (hold of), (*kaufen*) buy (sth.); (*b*) to see to (sth.).

◆B~nis, *f -/-se* anxiety. ◆b~niserregend, *adj.* worrying. ◆b~t, *adj.* worried, concerned. ◆B~ung, *f -/-en* (*Kauf*) purchase.

**be'sprech|en,** *v.tr.irr.14* (*a*) to discuss, review (a book, film etc.); **sich mit j-m b.,** to confer with s.o.; (*b*) **ein Tonband b.,** to record (one's voice on) a tape. ◆B~ung, *f -/-en* discussion; conference; (*Rezension*) review.

**besser** ['bɛsər], *adj.* better; **b. ist b.,** better safe than sorry; **du hättest b. geschwiegen,** you would have done better to keep quiet; (**oder**) **b. gesagt ...,** or rather ... ◆'b~n, *v.tr.* to improve (sth.); to reform (a criminal etc.); **sich b.,** to get better; (*Pers.*) to mend one's ways. ◆'B~ung, *f -/-en* improvement (+ *gen,* in); reformation; **gute B.!** get well soon! ◆'B~wisser, *m -s/-* know-all.

**best-** ['bɛst-], *comb.fm.* (*a*) best (paid, dressed etc.); (*b*) *F:* most (hated etc.). ◆b~e(r, s), *adj.* best; **im b~n Fall(e),** at best; **b~n Dank!** many thanks; **das b. wäre abzureisen,** it would be best to leave; **der/die/das B.,** the best; **es geschieht zu deinem B~n,** it is in your best interests; **er weiß es am b~n,** he knows best; **einen Witz zum b~n geben,** to tell a joke; **j-n zum b~n halten,** to pull s.o.'s leg. ◆'b~ens, *adv.* at (the) best. ◆'b~ens, *adv.* very well, excellently. ◆'B~leistung, *f* best performance. ◆'b~möglich, *adj.* best possible. ◆'B~zeit, *f* fastest time.

**Be'stand,** *m* 1. *no pl* continued existence, survival (of a nation, firm etc.); **B. haben/von B. sein,** to be enduring. 2. stock (**an etwas** *dat,* of sth.). ◆B~saufnahme, *f* stock-taking. ◆B~teil, *m* component (part); *Fig:* element.

**be'ständig,** *adj.* (*a*) constant; (*b*) enduring (peace, friendship etc.); steadfast (friend etc.); reliable (worker etc.); settled (weather).

**be'stärk|en,** *v.tr.* to confirm (s.o.'s suspicions, doubts etc.).

**bestätig|en** [bəˈʃtɛːtigən], *v.tr.* to confirm (sth.); to verify (a statement etc.), endorse (an opinion etc.), (*bescheinigen*) to certify (sth., that ...). ◆B~ung, *f -/-en* confirmation; verification.

**bestatt|en** [bəˈʃtatən], *v.tr. Lit:* to inter (a corpse); to lay (s.o.) to rest. ◆B~ung, *f -/-en* funeral.

**bestäuben** [bəˈʃtɔybən], *v.tr.* (*a*) to dust (sth.); (*b*) *Bot:* to pollinate (a plant).

**be'staunen,** *v.tr.* to gaze at (s.o., sth.) in amazement/admiration.

**be'stech|en,** *v.tr.irr.14* (*a*) to bribe (s.o.); (*b*) *Fig:* to captivate (s.o.). ◆b~end, *adj.* fascinating (person, appearance etc.). ◆b~lich, *adj.* open to bribery; corruptible. ◆B~ung, *f-/-en* bribery, corruption.

**Besteck** [bə'ʃtɛk], *n* -(e)s/-e **1.** cutlery. **2.** *Med:* (set of instruments.

**be'stehen. I.** *v.irr.100* **1.** *v.i.* (haben) (*a*) to exist; **es besteht ...**, there is ...; (*b*) **b. aus** + *dat*, (i) to be made of (rubber, metal etc.); (ii) to consist of (several parts, two members etc.); **der Unterschied bestand darin, daß ...**, the difference was that ...; (*c*) **auf etwas** *dat* **b.**, to insist (up)on sth.; (*d*) *Sch:* **b.**, to pass the examination. **2.** *v.tr.* to pass (*Sch:* an examination; *Tchn: Fig: etc:* a test). **II. B.**, *n* -s/*no pl* **1.** existence. **2.** insistence (**auf** + *dat*, on).

**be'stehlen**, *v.tr.irr.2* to rob (s.o.).

**be'steigen**, *v.tr.irr.89* to climb (a mountain etc.); to mount, get on(to) (a horse, bicycle etc.); to board (a train etc.); to ascend (the throne).

**Be'stell-**, *comb.fm. Com:* order (book, number etc.). ◆**b~en**, *v.tr.* (*a*) to order (goods, a meal etc.); (*b*) to book (a table, *Th:* seats etc.); (*c*) **j-n zu sich b.**, to summon s.o.; (*d*) (*ausrichten*) **bestell deinem Bruder schöne Grüße von mir**, give my regards to your brother; **kann ich etwas b.?** can I take a message? (*e*) (*ernennen*) to appoint (a representative etc.); (*f*) to cultivate (the land, a garden etc.). ◆**B~schein**, *m* order form. ◆**B~ung**, *f* -/-en *Com:* order.

**be'steuern**, *v.tr.* to tax (s.o., sth.); to rate (a building).

**best'ialisch** [bɛsti'ɑːliʃ], *adj.* bestial, brutal. ◆'**B~ie**, *f* -/-n beast; *Fig: (Pers.)* brute.

**be'stimmen**, *v.* **1.** *v.tr.* (*a*) to fix, decide (on) (a price, time etc.); to lay down (conditions, rules etc.); (*b*) to mean, intend (sth.); **j-n zum/als Nachfolger b.**, to mark out/(*ernennen*) appoint s.o. (as) one's successor; (*c*) (*ermitteln*) to determine (the age, position of sth. etc.); to define (the meaning of a word etc.); *Bot:* to classify (plants); (*d*) to have a decisive influence on (s.o., sth.); (*regeln*) to govern (the amount, size etc.). **2.** *v.i.* (*haben*) (*a*) **über etwas** *acc* (**frei**) **b.**, to be able to do what one likes with sth.; (*b*) (*anordnen*) to give orders. ◆**b~t**, *adj.* **1.** definite (purpose, *Gram:* article); distinct (impression); eine **b~te Summe**, a certain sum; (*b*) *adv.* certainly, definitely; **er wird es b. wissen**, he is sure to know. **2.** particular, special; **hast du etwas B~es vor?** are you doing anything special? **3.** firm, decisive (tone, manner etc.). ◆**B~theit**, *f* -/*no pl* **1.** firmness, decisiveness. **2.** **etwas mit B. wissen/sagen**, to know/say sth. for certain. ◆**B~ung**, *f* -/-en **1.** *no pl* fixing. **2.** *no pl* (*a*) appointment; (*b*) (*Schicksal*) fate, destiny. **3.** (*Ermittlung*) determination (of sth.); definition (of a word etc.). **4.** (*Anordnung*) regulation; clause (of a contract). **5.** *no pl* (*Zweck*) intended purpose.

◆**B~ungs-**, *comb.fm.* (port, country etc.) of destination.

**be'strafen**, *v.tr.* to punish (s.o., sth.). ◆**B~ung**, *f* -/-en punishment.

**be'strahlen**, *v.tr. Med:* to give (s.o.) ray/(*mit Höhensonne*) sunlamp treatment. ◆**B~ung**, *f* ray/sunlamp treatment.

**Be'streben**, *n* -s/*no pl* endeavour; (*Ziel*) aim. ◆**b~t**, *adj.* at pains (to do sth.). ◆**B~ung**, *f* -/-en effort; (*Versuch*) attempt.

**be'streichen**, *v.tr.irr.40* to spread (bread etc.).

**be'streiten**, *v.tr.irr.41* (*a*) to dispute (a statement etc.); to challenge (s.o.'s right etc.); (*leugnen*) to deny (a fact, one's guilt etc.); (*b*) to pay for (sth.); to meet (costs); to provide (entertainment etc.).

**be'streuen**, *v.tr.* to sprinkle (sth.); *Cu:* to powder, dust (a cake etc.).

**be'stürmen**, *v.tr.* (*a*) *Mil: etc:* to storm (the enemy, a town etc.); (*b*) to pester (s.o.) (**mit Fragen usw.**, with questions etc.).

**be'stürzen**, *v.tr.* to dismay, alarm (s.o.), (*erschüttern*) stun (s.o.). ◆**B~ung**, *f* -/*no pl* dismay; alarm.

**Besuch** [bə'zuːx], *m* -(e)s/-e **1.** visit; (*kurz*) call (**bei j-m**, on s.o.); **bei j-m einen B. machen**, to pay s.o. a visit. **2.** **der B. der Schule, Kirche usw.**, attendance at/going to school, church etc. **3. B. bekommen**, to have visitors/a visitor. ◆**b~en**, *v.tr.* (*a*) to visit (s.o., a country etc.); (*kurz*) to call on (s.o.); (*b*) to attend (a meeting etc.); to go to (school, a museum, concert etc.). ◆**B~er(in)**, *m* -s/- (*f* -/-nen) visitor; *Th: etc:* patron. ◆**B~szeit**, *f* -/-en visiting time.

**betätigen** [bə'tɛːtigən], *v.tr.* (*a*) to operate (a machine etc.); (*b*) **sich b.**, to work, be active (**als**, as). ◆**B~ung**, *f* -/-en **1.** *no pl* operation. **2.** activity.

**betäuben** [bə'tɔybən], *v.tr.* (*a*) (*Schlag usw.*) to stun, (*Lärm*) deafen (s.o.); (*b*) *Med:* to anaesthetize (s.o.); (*c*) to deaden (pain, a nerve etc.). ◆**b~end**, *adj.* **1.** *Med:* anaesthetic (effect etc.); narcotic (drug). **2.** (*berauschend*) intoxicating, heady (perfume etc.). ◆**B~ung**, *f* -/*no pl* **1.** daze; dazed/stunned state. **2.** *Med:* anaesthetization; (*Narkose*) anaesthetic. ◆**B~ungsmittel**, *n* anaesthetic.

**Bete** ['beːtə], *f* -/-n **rote B.**, beetroot.

**beteiligen** [bə'tailigən], *v.tr.* **sich b./beteiligt sein an** + *dat*, to take part/participate in (a game, competition etc.); to contribute to (a project, present etc.); **j-n an etwas** *dat* **b.**, to give s.o. a share in sth. ◆**b~te(r)**, *m & f* decl. as adj. person involved; participant; *Jur:* interested party. ◆**B~ung**, *f* -/-en participation; attendance (**an einem Kurs**, at a course).

**beten** ['beːtən], *v.tr. & i.* (haben) to pray.

**beteuern** [bə'tɔyərn], *v.tr.* to declare

(sth.) solemnly; to protest (one's innocence etc.). ◆B~ung, f -/-en declaration; protestation.

**Beton** [be'tɔŋ], m -s/-s & -e concrete. ◆b~ieren [-'to'ni:rən], v.tr. to concrete (a road etc.). ◆b~iert, adj. concrete.

**beton|en** [bə'to:nən], v.tr. to stress. ◆b~t, adj. 1. stressed (syllable etc.). 2. emphatic; studied (indifference, simplicity etc.). ◆B~ung, f -/en emphasis, stress.

**betören** [bə'tø:rən], v.tr. to bewitch, dazzle (s.o.).

**Betracht** [bə'traxt], m j-n, etwas in B. ziehen, (i) (erwägen) to consider (s.o., sth.); (ii) (berücksichtigen) to take s.o., sth. into account; j-n, etwas außer B. lassen, to disregard s.o., sth.; in B. kommen, to be possible. ◆b~en, v.tr. (a) to look at (s.o., sth., Fig: a problem etc.); (b) j-n als seinen Freund usw. b., to regard/look upon s.o. as one's friend etc. ◆B~er, m -s/- onlooker. ◆B~ung, f -/-en 1. no pl observation; bei genauerer B., on closer examination. 2. (Überlegung) reflection, meditation.

**beträchtlich** [bə'trɛçtliç], adj. considerable.

**Betrag** [bə'traːk], m -(e)s/ːe amount, sum (of money). ◆b~en. I. v.tr.irr.85 (a) (Rechnung usw.) to amount to (1000 marks etc.); (b) sich b., to behave. II. B., n -s/no pl behaviour.

**be'treff|en**, v.tr.irr.104 to affect, concern (s.o., sth.); (sich beziehen auf) to refer to (s.o., sth.); Betrifft: ..., re: ... ◆b~end, pres. p. & adj. relevant (person etc.). ◆b~s, prep. + gen concerning, with regard to.

**be'treiben**, v.tr.irr.12 (a) to pursue (a hobby, policy, studies etc.); (b) to run (a business, a machine etc.).

**be'treten**. I. v.tr.irr.105 to enter, go into (a room, house etc.); to walk on (a lawn etc.); to step onto (a bridge etc.); B. verboten! keep out! II. adj. embarrassed, sheepish (smile).

**betreu|en** [bə'trɔyən], v.tr. to take care of (s.o., sth.). ◆B~er(in), m -s/- (f -/ -nen) (a) nurse; (im Hause) home help; (bei Unfällen usw.) relief worker; (b) Sp: coach. ◆B~ung, f -/no pl care.

**Betrieb** [bə'triːp], m -(e)s/-e 1. (Firma) concern, business; (Fabrik) factory, works. 2. no pl running, operation; in B., in use; (nicht defekt) working; außer B., (defekt) out of order. 3. no pl F: bustle; activity; (auf den Straßen) (heavy) traffic. ◆B~s-, comb.fm. (a) operating (costs, El: voltage etc.); working (capital, climate etc.); (b) staff, (Fabriks-) works (canteen, holidays etc.); company (doctor etc.). ◆B~sausflug, m staff outing/ N.Am: trip. ◆b~sfähig, adj. operational; in working order. ◆B~sgeheimnis, n trade secret. ◆B~sleitung, f management.

◆B~srat, m 1. works council. 2. (Pers.) works council member, approx. shop steward. ◆b~ssicher, adj. reliable (in operation). ◆B~sunfall, m accident at work. ◆B~swirt, m business administration graduate. ◆B~swirtschaft, f business administration; management (studies).

**be'trinken**, v.refl.irr.96 sich b., to get drunk.

**betroffen** [bə'trɔfən]. adj. upset; (bestürzt) taken aback; (gekränkt) hurt.

**betrüb|en** [bə'try:bən], v.tr. to sadden (s.o.). ◆b~lich, adj. sad; distressing (news etc.). ◆b~t, adj. sad; gloomy, (face etc.).

**Betrug** [bə'tru:k], m -(e)s/no pl deception; (Betrügerei) cheating; trickery; Jur: fraud.

**betrüg|en** [bə'try:gən], v.irr.63 1. v.tr. to deceive (s.o., oneself); to cheat (s.o.); Jur: to defraud (s.o.). 2. v.i. (haben) to cheat. ◆B~er(in), m -s/- (f -/-nen) deceiver; trickster; (beim Spiel usw.) cheat. ◆b~erisch, adj. deceitful (person); fraudulent (act etc.); in b~erischer Absicht, with intent to deceive.

**betrunken** [bə'truŋkən], adj.pred. drunk; attrib. drunken (man, driver etc.).

**Bett** [bɛt]. I. n -(e)s/-en bed; ins/zu B. gehen, to go to bed. II. 'B~-, comb.fm. bed (jacket, rest etc.); bedtime (reading etc.); bedding (box etc.). ◆'B~bezug, m duvet/quilt cover. ◆'B~decke, f (a) (aus Wolle) blanket; (gesteppt) quilt; (b) (Tagesdecke) bed spread. ◆'b~en, v.tr. to lay, settle (s.o., sth.); sich b., to settle/lie down. ◆'b~lägerig, adj. bed-ridden. ◆'B~nässen, n bedwetting. ◆'Bettuch, n sheet. ◆'B~vorleger, n bedside rug. ◆'B~wäsche, f bed linen. ◆'B~zeug, n F: bedding.

**bettel|arm** ['bɛtəl'arm], adj. desperately poor, destitute. ◆B~ei [-'lai], f -/-en 1. no pl begging. 2. (Flehen) pleading. ◆'b~n, v.i. (haben) to beg.

**Bettler(in)** ['bɛtlər(in)], m -s/- (f -/-nen) beggar.

**betulich** [bə'tu:liç], adj. fussy

**Beug|e** ['bɔygə], f -/-n bend. ◆'b~en, v.tr. (a) to bend (one's arm, leg); to incline (one's head); (b) Lit: to break (s.o.'s will etc.); sich j-m, etwas dat b., to submit to s.o., sth.; (c) Gram: to inflect (a word). ◆'B~ung, f -/-en 1. bending. 2. Gram: inflection.

**Beule** ['bɔylə], f -/-n 1. swelling. 2. (Vertiefung) dent.

**beunruhig|en** [bə'ʔunru:igən], v.tr. to worry (s.o., oneself). ◆B~ung, f -/no pl worry, anxiety.

**beurkund|en** [bə'ʔu:rkundən], v.tr. to register (births etc.); (beglaubigen) to certify (a statement etc.).

**beurlaub|en** [bə'ʔu:rlaubən], v.tr. (a) to grant (s.o.) time off/esp. Mil: leave; (b) Mil:Adm: to suspend (an official etc.).

**beurteil|en** [bə'?u:rtailən], *v.tr.* to judge (s.o., sth.); to assess (value, s.o.'s work etc.). ◆B~**ung**, *f -/-en* **1.** judgement; *(Meinung)* opinion. **2.** *(schriftlich)* assessment.

**Beute** ['bɔytə], *f -/no pl* (a) booty; *Mil:* spoils; (b) *(Opfer)* prey.

**Beutel** ['bɔytəl], *m -s/-* bag; pouch (for tobacco, *Z:* of a kangaroo etc.).

**bevölker|n** [bə'fœlkərn], *v.tr.* (*Pers., Tier*) to inhabit (an area etc.); **ein dicht/dünn bevölkertes Land,** a densely/sparsely populated country. ◆B~**ung**, *f -/-en* population.

**bevollmächtig|en** [bə'fɔlmɛçtigən], *v.tr.* to authorize (s.o.); *Jur:* to give (s.o.) power of attorney. ◆B~**te(r)**, *m & f decl. as adj.* authorized representative/*esp. Com:* agent; *(Beauftragter)* delegate. ◆B~**ung**, *f -/-en* (a) *no pl* authorization; (b) authority; *Jur:* power of attorney.

**bevor** [bə'fo:r], *conj.* before.

**bevormunden** [bə'fo:rmundən], *v.tr.* not to allow (s.o.) to make decisions.

**be'vorstehen,** *v.i.sep.irr.100* *(haben)* **(unmittelbar/nahe) b.,** to be imminent; **ihm steht eine große Enttäuschung bevor,** he is in for a big disappointment. ◆b~**d,** *adj.* forthcoming. **(unmittelbar) b.,** imminent.

**bevorzug|en** [bə'fo:rtsu:gən], *v.tr.* (a) to prefer (s.o., sth.); (b) *(begünstigen)* to give (s.o.) preferential treatment. ◆b~**t,** *adj.* privileged (person, position etc.). ◆B~**ung**, *f -/-en* preferential treatment; priority; **(ungerechte) B.,** favouritism.

**be'wach|en,** *v.tr.* to guard (a house, prisoners etc.). ◆B~**ung**, *f -/no pl* guarding; **unter B.,** under surveillance.

**bewaffn|en** [bə'vafnən], *v.tr.* to arm. ◆B~**ung**, *f -/-en* armament; *(Waffen)* arms, weapons.

**bewahren** [bə'vɑːrən], *v.tr.* (a) to keep, preserve (sth.); (b) **j-n, etwas vor Schaden/einer Gefahr b.,** to preserve/ protect s.o., sth. from harm/danger.

**bewähr|en** [bə'vɛ:rən], *v.refl.* **sich b.,** to prove one's/its worth; *(Einrichtungen usw.)* to prove a success. ◆b~**t,** *adj.* reliable, trustworthy (friend etc.); proven (remedy etc.); established (principle etc.). ◆B~**ung**, *f -/-en Jur:* probation. ◆B~**ungsfrist,** *f Jur:* (period of) probation.

**bewahrheiten** [bə'vɑːrhaitən], *v.refl.* **sich b.,** to prove (to be) true **(an j-m,** in s.o.'s case).

**bewältig|en** [bə'vɛltigən], *v.tr.* to cope with (problems, a pile of work etc.); to overcome (difficulties etc.); to get through (a task, *F:* food etc.).

**bewandert** [bə'vandərt], *adj.* well-versed.

**bewässer|n** [bə'vɛsərn], *v.tr.* to irrigate. ◆B~**ung**, *f -/no pl* irrigation.

**beweg|en¹** [bə've:gən], *v.tr.* (a) *(von der Stelle)* to move (sth.); to shift (sth. large/ heavy); **sich b.,** to move; *(sich rühren)* to stir; (b) *(rühren)* to move (s.o.); **Probleme, die uns alle b.,** problems which exercise all our minds. ◆b~**en²,** *v.tr.irr.* **j-n (dazu) b., etwas zu tun,** to make s.o. do sth. ◆B~**grund,** *m* motive. ◆b~**lich,** *adj.* **1.** movable (parts, feasts etc.); *Mil:* mobile (units, troops). **2.** *(rege)* active, agile (mind, person). ◆B~**lichkeit,** *f -/no pl* **1.** mobility. **2.** (mental/physical) agility. ◆b~**t,** *adj.* (a) *(Pers.)* moved; emotional (words etc.); (b) eventful (times, life etc.). ◆B~**ung**, *f -/-en* **1.** (a) movement; motion; (b) **körperliche B.,** physical exercise; (c) **eine religiöse/politische B.,** a religious/ political movement. **2.** *(Erregung)* emotion. ◆B~**ungsfreiheit,** *f -/no pl* freedom of movement/*Fig:* action; *F:* elbowroom. ◆b~**ungslos,** *adj.* motionless.

**be'weinen,** *v.tr.* to weep for, mourn (s.o., sth.).

**Beweis** [bə'vais], *m -es/-e* (a) proof, *esp. pl.* **B~e,** evidence; *(Zeichen)* sign, token. ◆B~**aufnahme,** *f Jur:* (hearing of) evidence. ◆b~**bar,** *adj.* provable. ◆b~**en** [-zən], *v.tr.irr.70* to prove (a fact, guilt, that ... etc.); to establish (innocence, the truth of sth. etc.). ◆B~**führung,** *f -/no pl* argumentation; (line of) argument. ◆B~**kraft,** *f* conclusiveness, cogency. ◆b~**kräftig,** *adj.* cogent, forceful. ◆B~**mittel,** *n* (piece of) evidence.

**be'wenden,** *v.tr.* **es dabei b. lassen,** to leave it at that.

**be'werb|en,** *v.refl.irr.101* **sich (um eine Stellung) b.,** to apply (for a job). ◆B~**er(in),** *m -s/- (f -/-nen)* applicant; candidate; *Sp:* contender (for a title etc.). ◆B~**ung,** *f -/-en* application.

**bewerkstelligen** [bə'vɛrkʃtɛligən], *v.tr.* to manage, arrange (sth.).

**be'werten,** *v.tr.* to assess; to rate, evaluate (s.o.'s work etc.); *Fin:* to value (sth.).

**bewillig|en** [bə'viligən], *v.tr.* to grant (credit etc.); *(genehmigen)* to approve (a new tax, payment etc.). ◆B~**ung**, *f -/ -en* grant(ing); approval.

**be'wirken,** *v.tr.* to cause (sth.); to effect (a change, cure).

**bewirten** [bə'virtən], *v.tr.* to entertain (guests etc.).

**bewirtschaften** [bə'virtʃaftən], *v.tr.* to run (a farm etc.); to farm (land).

**bewohn|bar** [bə'vo:nbɑːr], *adj.* habitable; fit to live in. ◆b~**en,** *v.tr.* to occupy, live in (a house etc.); to inhabit (a region, country etc.). ◆B~**er,** *m -s/-* occupier, occupant; inhabitant.

**bewölk|t** [bə'vœlkt], *adj.* cloudy, overcast. ◆B~**ung**, *f -/no pl (Wolken)* clouds.

**Bewunder|er** [bə'vundərər], *m -s/-* admirer. ◆b~**n,** *v.tr.* to admire (s.o., sth.). ◆b~**nswert,** *adj.* admirable.

◆B~**ung**, f -/no pl admiration.

**bewußt** [bə'vust], adj. conscious; (a) **sich dat etwas gen b. werden**, to become aware/conscious of sth.; to realize sth.; (b) (absichtlich) deliberate (deception etc.); (c) (erwähnt) aforementioned. ◆**b~los**, adj. unconscious. ◆**B~losigkeit**, f -/no pl (state of) unconsciousness. ◆**B~sein**, n -s/no pl consciousness, awareness; **bei (vollem) B.**, (fully) conscious.

**be'zahl|en**, v.tr.&i. (haben) to pay (s.o., an amount, price, bill etc.); to pay for (goods, Fig: a mistake etc.). ◆**B~ung**, f -/no pl payment.

**be'zaubern**, v.tr. to captivate, enchant (s.o.). ◆**b~d**, adj. enchanting.

**be'zeichn|en**, v.tr. (a) to mark (a spot, path etc.); (b) (nennen) to call (s.o., oneself, sth.) (**als etwas** acc, sth.). ◆**b~end**, adj. characteristic, typical (**für j-n, etwas** acc, of s.o., sth.). ◆**B~ung**, f -/-en 1. marking; indication; **genaue/nähere B.**, specification 2. (Ausdruck) expression.

**be'zeugen**, v.tr. to bear witness to, testify (to) (sth.).

**bezichtigen** [bə'tsiçtigən], v.tr. **j-n eines Verbrechens b.**, to accuse s.o. of a crime. ◆**B~ung**, f -/-en accusation.

**bezieh|bar** [bə'tsi:ba:r], adj. (Wohnung usw.) ready to be moved into, vacant. ◆**b~en**, v.tr.irr.113 (a) to cover, (neu b.) recover (an armchair etc.); **die Betten frisch b.**, to change the bedclothes; (b) to move into (a house, flat etc.); Mil: to take up (a position etc.), Fig: adopt a standpoint; (c) to obtain (goods etc.); to take (a newspaper etc.); to receive (a salary, pension etc.); (d) **etwas auf etwas** acc **b.**, to relate sth. to sth.; (Pers., Bemerkung usw.) **sich auf j-n, etwas b.**, to refer to s.o., sth. ◆**B~ung**, f -/-en 1. (a) pl **freundschaftliche/diplomatische B~en**, friendly/diplomatic relations; **gute B~en zu j-m haben**, to be on good terms with s.o.; (b) pl contacts; (c) (Zusammenhang) connection; **zwei Dinge zueinander in B. setzen**, to connect/link two things. 2. (Verhältnis) relationship. 3. (Hinsicht) **in dieser/jeder B.**, in this/every respect. ◆**b~ungslos**, adj. unrelated, unconnected. ◆**b~ungsweise**, adv. or.

**Bezirk** [bə'tsirk], m -(e)s/-e district.

**Bezug** [bə'tsu:k], m -(e)s/-e 1. cover (of a cushion etc.); loose cover, N.Am: slipcover (of a chair etc.); (pillow-)case. 2. no pl (Erwerb) obtaining; drawing (of a salary etc.). 3. pl **B~e**, salary, income. 4. (Zusammenhang) reference; **mit B./in b. auf j-n, etwas** acc, concerning/regarding s.o., sth. ◆**b~sfertig**, adj. vacant (house etc.); pred. ready to move into. ◆**B~sperson**, f person to whom one relates. ◆**B~spreis**, m purchase/subscription price. ◆**B~squelle**, f

source of supply; supplier.

**bezüglich** [bə'tsy:kliç], prep. + gen concerning, regarding.

**bezwecken** [bə'tsvɛkən], v.tr. to aim at (sth.).

**be'zweifeln**, v.tr. to doubt.

**be'zwing|en**, v.tr.irr.19 to conquer (an enemy, Fig: fear, mountain etc.); to vanquish (an opponent); Fig: to keep (one's curiosity, anger etc.) under control.

**BH** [be'ha:], m -s/-(s) F: bra.

**Bibel** ['bi:bəl], f -/-n Bible.

**Biber** ['bi:bər], m -s/- beaver.

**Biblio|graphie** [bibliogra'fi:], f -/-n bibliography. ◆**B~thek** [-'te:k], f -/-en library. ◆**B~thekar(in)**, [-'te:ka:r(in)], m -s/-e (f -/-nen) librarian.

**biblisch** ['bi:bliʃ], adj. biblical.

**bieder** ['bi:dər], adj. (a) honest, upright; (b) Pej: (spießig) bourgeois.

**bieg|en** ['bi:gən]. I. v.tr. 1. v.tr. to bend (wire, a branch etc.). 2. v.i. (sein) **um die Ecke/in eine Straße usw. b.**, to turn the corner/into a street etc. II. **B.**, n -s/no pl bending, curving; **es geht auf B. oder Brechen**, it's all or nothing. ◆**b~sam**, adj. flexible; pliable (material); supple (body, limbs). ◆**B~ung**, f -/-en bend.

**Biene** ['bi:nə], f -/-n 1. bee. 2. F: (Mädchen) bird. ◆**B~n-**, comb.fm. bee's, bee (sting etc.); (swarm etc.) of bees; bees' (honey). ◆**B~nkönigin**, f queen bee. ◆**B~nkorb**, m (basketwork) beehive. ◆**B~nstich**, m beesting; Cu: plain cake covered in grated almonds and sugar. ◆**B~nstock**, m beehive. ◆**B~nwachs**, m beeswax.

**Bier** [bi:r]. I. n -(e)s/-e beer; **drei B.**, three beers/glasses of beer. II. **'B~-**, comb.fm. beer (barrel, garden etc.). ◆**B~brauer**, m -s/- brewer. ◆**B~deckel**, m beer mat. ◆**B~dose**, f beer can. ◆**B~krug**, m beer mug.

**Biest** [bi:st], n -(e)s/-r (also Fig) beast.

**biet|en** ['bi:tən], v.tr.irr.8 to offer (sth.); to provide (shelter, an opportunity etc.); **(tausend Mark) auf etwas** acc **b.**, to bid (a thousand marks) for sth.; **das lasse ich mir nicht b.!** I won't stand for that.

**Bigamie** [biga'mi:], f -/-n bigamy.

**Bikini** [bi'ki:ni], m -s/-s bikini.

**Bilanz** [bi'lants], f -/-en 1. balance; (schriftlich) balance sheet. 2. Fig: (net) result; **die B. ziehen**, to draw conclusions; (rückblickend) to take stock.

**Bild** [bilt]. I. n -(e)s/-er picture; **das äußere B. der Stadt**, the (outward) appearance of the town; **in B~ern sprechen**, to speak figuratively; **bist du im B~e?** are you in the picture? II. **'B~-**, comb.fm. picture (editor etc.); pictorial (document, book etc.). ◆**B~bericht**, m photo-reportage. ◆**B~erbuch**, n picture book. ◆**B~fläche**, f screen; F: **von der B. verschwinden**, disappear from the scene. ◆**B~hauer**, m sculptor. ◆**b~lich**, adj. 1. pictorial (representation etc.). 2. figurative (expression etc.). ◆'B~nis, n -sses/-sse portrait. ◆'B~platte, f video disc. ◆'B~schärfe, f definition (of the image). ◆'B~schirm, m screen. ◆'b~schön, adj. gorgeous. ◆'B~text, m/'B~unterschrift, f caption.

**bilden** ['bildən], v.tr. (a) to form, (gestalten) shape (sth.); **die b~enden Künste**, the fine arts; Fig: **j-s Charakter b.**, to mould s.o.'s character; (b) (darstellen) to be (sth.); **die Regel/eine Ausnahme b.**, to be the rule/an exception; (c) (erziehen) to educate (s.o., oneself etc.). ◆'B~ung, f -/no pl 1. (Bilden) formation; (Formen) shaping. 2. (Erziehung) education; (general) knowledge, culture. ◆'B~ungs-, comb.fm. educational (policy, reform etc.). ◆'B~ungslücke, f gap in one's education. ◆'B~ungsweg, m type of education; **der zweite B.**, further education.

**Billard** ['biljart]. I. n -s/-e billiards. II. 'B~-, comb.fm. billiard (room etc.). ◆'B~kugel, f billiard ball. ◆'B~queue, n billiard cue.

**billig** ['biliç]. I. adj. 1. (a) cheap; low (price); F: **b. davonkommen**, to get off lightly; (b) (dürftig) poor (goods); **b~e Ausrede**, feeble excuse. 2. **recht und b.**, right and proper. II. 'B~-, comb.fm. cheap (flight, goods); low (price). ◆'b~en [-gən], v.tr. to give (sth.) one's approval; (amtlich) to sanction (sth.). ◆'B~ung, f/no pl approval.

**Billion** [bili'o:n], f -/-en billion; N.Am: trillion.

**bimmeln** ['biməln], v.i. (haben) F: to ring.

**Binde** ['bində], f -/-n (a) bandage; (b) (Armb.) armband; (c) F: (Damenb.) sanitary towel. ◆'B~en, v.tr.irr.9 (a) to tie (a knot, shoelaces, s.o.'s hands etc.); (fesseln) to bind (s.o.), tie (s.o.) up; (zusammenb.) to tie/bind (sth.); to bind (a book, Ch: gases etc.); (b) **ich bin durch/an mein Versprechen gebunden**, I am bound by my promise; **ich will mich noch nicht b.**, I do not want to commit myself/esp. get married yet. ◆'b~end, adj. binding; hard-and-fast (rule). ◆'B~estrich, m hyphen. ◆'B~faden, m string; **ein B.**, a piece of string. ◆'B~ung, f -/-en 1. tie, bond; (gefühlsmäßig) attachment; (Verpflichtung) commitment. 2. (Skib.) binding.

**binnen** ['binən]. I. prep. + dat/occ. gen within; **b. kurzem**, shortly. II. 'B~-, comb.fm. inland (harbour, sea etc.); internal, home (trade etc.). ◆'B~land, n the interior (of a country).

**Binse** ['binzə], f -/-n Bot: rush; F: **in die B~n gehen**, to go west. ◆'B~nweisheit, f truism.

**Bio|graph** [bio'gra:f], m -en/-en biographer. ◆B~graphie [-a'fi:], f -/-en biography. ◆B~loge [-'lo:gə], m -n/-n biologist. ◆B~logie [-lo'gi:], f -/no pl biology. ◆b~'logisch, adj. 1. biological. 2. Agr: organic (cultivation).

**Birke** ['birkə], f -/-n birch (tree).

**Birn|baum** ['birnbaum], m 1. pear tree. 2. (Holz) pearwood. ◆'B~e, f -/-n 1. (a) (Frucht) pear; (b) (Baum) pear tree. 2. El: (light) bulb.

**bis** [bis]. I. prep. + acc 1. until; **b. jetzt**, up to now; so far; **b. heute**, until today; (nachdrücklich) to this day; **von 9 b. 5 Uhr**, from nine to/till five; **von Montag b. Freitag**, from Monday to Friday, N.Am: Monday through Friday; **b. bald/später/morgen usw.**, see you soon/later/tomorrow etc.; **b. in die Nacht (hinein)**, (far) into the night; **b. zum nächsten Mai/zum 1. Mai**, until the next time/May 1st. 2. (nicht später als) by; **b. dahin/Montag**, by then/Monday. 3. (räumlich) as far as; **b. wohin?** how far? **von oben b. unten**, from top to bottom. 4. (+etc.) **b. aufs höchste**, to the utmost; **b. ins kleinste/letzte**, down to the last detail. 5. **b. auf** (a) (inklusive) including; (b) (mit Ausnahme von) **b. auf dich sind alle fertig**, everyone is ready except (for) you. 6. (mit Zahlen) **b. zu**, up to. II. conj. until. ◆b~'her, adv. so far, up to now. ◆b~'herig, adj. existing (up to now). ◆b~'lang, adv. so far, up to now.

**Bischof** ['bifɔf], m -s/=e bishop.

**bischöflich** ['bifø:fliç], adj. episcopal.

**Biskuit** [bis'kvi:t], n & m -(e)s/-s & -e Cu: sponge.

**Biß** [bis], m -sses/-sse bite. ◆'b~chen, inv.s. **ein b.**, a bit.

**Biss|en** ['bisən], m -s/- bite, mouthful (of food). ◆'b~ig, adj. 1. vicious (dog etc.). 2. biting, caustic (remark etc.).

**Bistum** ['bistu:m], n -s/=er bishopric, diocese.

**bisweilen** [bis'vailən], adv. Lit: sometimes, from time to time.

**bitte** ['bitə]. I. adv. please; **ja, b.?** yes? **b. schön!** (etwas anbietend) do have/take one! **vielen Dank!—b. sehr/schön!** thank you very much!—don't mention it/N.Am: you're welcome; **(wie) b.?** pardon? **na b.!** there you are, you see! what did I tell you? II. B~, f -/-n request; (dringend) plea. ◆b~n, v.tr.&i.irr. (haben) **(j-n) um etwas acc b.**, to ask (s.o.) for sth.; **j-n zu sich dat b.**, to ask s.o. to come to see one.

**bitter** ['bitər], adj. bitter; **etwas b. nötig haben**, to need sth. desperately. ◆b~'böse, adj. (wütend) furious, livid; (übel) villainous. ◆'B~keit, f -/no pl bitterness (Verbitterung) rancour; acrimony (of a remark etc.). ◆'b~lich, adv. bitterly.

**Bizeps** ['bi:tseps], m -es/-e biceps.

**bläh|en** ['blɛːən], *v.tr.* (*a*) (*Wind*) to swell (sails); **sich b.**, (*Segel*) to swell, (*Gardine*) billow; (*Nüstern*) to flare; (*b*) *abs.* (*Speisen*) to cause flatulence. ◆**B~ungen**, *fpl* flatulence, *F*: wind.

**blam|abel** [bla'maːbəl], *adj.* humiliating; ignominious (defeat). ◆**B~age** [-'maːʒə], *f* -/-n humiliation. ◆**b~ieren** [-'miːrən], *v.tr.* to make (s.o.) look foolish/small; **sich b.**, to make a fool of oneself.

**blank** [blaŋk], *adj.* **1.** shiny (metal, boots etc.). **2.** (*nackt*) bare (skin, boards etc.). **3.** (*rein*) pure, sheer (nonsense, envy etc.). **4.** *F*: (*pleite*) (stony) broke.

**blanko** ['blaŋko], *inv.adj.* blank. ◆'**B~scheck**, *m* blank cheque.

**Blas|e** ['blaːzə], *f* -/-n **1.** (*a*) bubble; *Tchn*: flaw (in glass etc.); (*b*) *Med*: blister. **2.** *Anat*: bladder. ◆'**B~ebalg**, *m* bellows. ◆'**b~en**, *v.irr.* **1.** *v.tr.* (*a*) to blow; (*b*) *Mus*: to play (a flute, oboe, a tune etc.). **2.** *v.i.* (*haben*) to blow. ◆'**B~instrument**, *n* wind instrument. ◆'**B~kapelle**, *f Mus*: brass band.

**blasiert** [bla'ziːrt], *adj.* blasé.

**blaß** [blas], *adj.* (*a*) pale (face, person, colour etc.); *Fig*: colourless (style, description etc.); (*b*) (*schwach*) faint (hope); vague (memory, idea etc.).

**Blässe** ['blɛsə], *f* -/no pl paleness, pallor; *Fig*: colourlessness.

**bläßlich** ['blɛsliç], *adj.* pallid, rather pale.

**Blatt** [blat], *n* -(*e*)*s/¨er* **1.** leaf. **2.** sheet, leaf (of paper); *Mus*: **vom B. singen/spielen**, to sight-read; *Fig*: **das steht auf einem anderen B.**, that is another matter. **3.** (*Zeitung*) (news)paper. **4.** (*Spielkarte*) (playing) card; **ein gutes B. haben**, to have a good hand. **5.** blade (of an oar, axe, a saw).

**blätter|n** ['blɛtərn], *v.i.* (*a*) (*haben*) **in einem Buch b.**, to leaf/glance through a book; (*b*) (*sein*) (*Farbe usw.*) to flake (off). ◆'**B~teig**, *m* puff pastry.

**blau** [blau]. *adj.* **1.** blue; **ein b~es Auge**, a black eye; **ein b~er Fleck**, a bruise; *Aal/Forelle b.*, boiled eel/trout; **eine Fahrt ins B~e**, a mystery tour. **2.** *F*: (*betrunken*) tight. ◆'**b~äugig**, *adj.* blue-eyed. ◆'**B~beere**, *f* bilberry, *N.Am*: blueberry. ◆'**B~licht**, *n* blue light. ◆'**b~machen**, *v.i.sep.* (*haben*) *F*: to malinger, stay away from work. ◆'**B~pause**, *f* blueprint. ◆'**B~säure**, *f* prussic acid.

**Blech** [blɛç]. **I.** *n* -(*e*)*s/-e* **1.** sheet metal; (*für Dosen usw. & Pej*:) tin. **2.** *no pl Mus*: brass. **3.** *no pl F*: (*Unsinn*) rubbish, rot. **II.** '**B~-**, *comb.fm.* (*a*) tin (drum etc.); metal (shears etc.); (*b*) *Mus*: brass (instrument etc.). ◆'**B~dose**, *f* tin, can. ◆'**b~en**, *v.i.* (*haben*) *F*: to fork out. ◆'**B~schaden**, *m* superficial damage (to the bodywork).

**Blei** [blai], *n* -(*e*)*s/-e* **1.** lead. **2.** (*B~lot*) plumb, lead. ◆'**b~ern**, *adj.* lead.

◆'**b~haltig**, *adj.* containing lead. ◆'**B~stift**, *m* pencil. ◆'**B~stiftspitzer**, *m* pencil sharpener.

**Bleibe** ['blaibə], *f* -/-n *F*: place to stay. ◆'**b~n**, *v.i.irr.* (*sein*) to stay, remain; (*a*) **das bleibt unter uns**, (that's) strictly between ourselves; **bei der Sache b.**, to keep to the point; **b. Sie bitte am Apparat!** hold the line please! (*b*) *F*: **wo bleibst du denn?** what's keeping you? what's happened to you? (*c*) to remain, be left; **es bleibt keine andere Wahl**, there is no other choice (left); (*d*) **bei seiner Meinung b.**, to stick to one's opinion; **es bleibt dabei**, that's settled/final. ◆'**b~nd**, *adj.* permanent (damage etc.); lasting (effect etc.). ◆'**b~nlassen**, *v.tr.sep.irr.57* to leave/let (sth.) alone; **an deiner Stelle würde ich es b.**, I wouldn't do it if I were you.

**bleich** [blaiç], *adj.* pale, white (face etc.). ◆'**b~en**, *v.tr.* to bleach.

**Blend|e** ['blɛndə], *f* -/-n **1.** shield, shade (for the eyes). **2.** *Phot*: diaphragm; (*Öffnung*) aperture, stop. ◆'**b~en**, *v.tr.&i.* (*haben*) (*also Fig*:) to dazzle (s.o.); (*blind machen*) to blind (s.o.). ◆'**b~end**, *adj.* dazzling (beauty etc.); magnificent (sight, spectacle etc.); brilliant (speech, achievements etc.); *adv.* marvellously, wonderfully; **es geht ihm b.**, he's in great form.

**Blick** [blik], *m* -(*e*)*s/-e* **1.** look; (*kurz*) glance; **finsterer B.**, scowl; **die B~e auf sich acc ziehen**, to attract attention; **Liebe auf den ersten B.**, love at first sight. **2.** (*Aussicht*) view. **3.** **einen/keinen B. für etwas acc haben**, to have an/no eye for sth. ◆'**b~en**, *v.* **1.** *v.i.* (*haben*) (*a*) to look; (*b*) *F*: **sich b. lassen**, to show one's face. ◆'**B~fang**, *m* eye-catcher. ◆'**B~feld**, *n* field of vision. ◆'**B~winkel**, *m* point of view.

**blind** ['blint], *adj.* **1.** blind (**für** + *acc*, to); **ein B~er/eine B~e**, a blind man/woman. **2.** cloudy (mirror etc.); dull, tarnished (metal); **b~er Alarm**, false alarm; **b~er Passagier**, stowaway. ◆'**B~darm**, *m* appendix. ◆'**B~darmentzündung**, *f* appendicitis. ◆'**B~en-**, *comb.fm.* (home, school, *Rad*: programme etc.) for the blind. ◆'**B~enhund**, *m* guide dog (for the blind). ◆'**B~enschrift**, *f* braille. ◆'**B~flug**, *m* instrument/blind flight. ◆'**B~gänger**, *m* dud (shell); *P*: (*Pers.*) dud. ◆'**B~heit**, *f* -/no pl blindness. ◆'**b~lings**, *adv.* blindly; **b. rennen/stürzen**, to rush headlong. ◆'**B~schleiche**, *f* -/-n slow-worm. ◆'**b~schreiben**, *v.i.sep.irr.12* (*haben*) to touch-type.

**Blink-** [bliŋk-], *comb.fm.* flashing (light etc.); ◆'**B~anlage**, *f Aut*: hazard warning lights. ◆'**b~en**, *v.i.* (*haben*) (*Stern, fernes Licht usw.*) to twinkle; (*regelmäßig/als Signal*) to flash; *Aut: etc*: to signal. ◆'**B~er**, *m* -*s*/- *Aut*: (flashing) indica-

tor. ◆'B~**licht**, n indicator.
**blinzeln** ['blintsəln], v.i. (haben) to blink; (mit einem Auge) to wink.
**Blitz** [blits]. **I.** m -es/-e **1.** lightning; ein B., a flash of lightning. **2.** Phot: F: flash. **II.** 'B~-, comb.fm. (a) lightning (attack, war etc.); (b) Phot: flash (cube etc.). ◆'B~**ableiter**, m lightning conductor. ◆'b~**en**, v.i. (haben) (a) v. impers. es blitzte, there was a flash of lightning; (b) to flash, sparkle. ◆'B~**gerät**, n flash unit. ◆'B~**licht**, n flash(light). ◆'b~**'schnell**, adj. lightning (movement, reaction etc.); split-second (decision); adv. with lightning speed.
**Block** [blɔk], m -(e)s/-e & -s **1.** (pl -e) block (of stone etc.). **2.** (a) ein B. **Briefpapier**, a writing pad; (b) Pol: bloc; (c) block (of houses). ◆'B~**ade** [-'ka:də], f -/-n blockade. ◆'B~**flöte**, f recorder. ◆'b~**frei**, adj. Pol: non-aligned (state). ◆'B~**hütte**, f log cabin. ◆'b~**ieren** [-'ki:rən], v. **1.** v.tr. to block, obstruct (a road, Rail: line, Fig: decision etc.); to stop (traffic, supplies etc.); to jam (a machine, Tel: lines etc.); Aut: to lock (the wheels); Mil: to blockade (a port). **2.** v.i. (haben) (Räder) to lock; (Motor usw.) to seize. ◆'B~**schrift**, f block capitals.
**blöd(e)** [blø:t, -də], adj. F: (a) silly, daft (person, remark etc.); (b) (ärgerlich) b~e **Situation**, stupid situation. ◆'B~**heit**, f -/-en stupidity; (Äußerung) stupid remark. ◆'B~**sinn**, m F: rubbish; P: crap. ◆'b~**sinnig**, adj. F: nonsensical (chatter); idiotic (behaviour, idea).
**blöken** ['blø:kən], v.i. (haben) (Schafe) to bleat, (Rinder) low.
**blond** [blɔnt], adj. blonde, fair (hair, beard); fair-haired (person). ◆'B~**ine** [-'di:nə], f -/-n blonde (woman).
**bloß** [blo:s], adj. & adv. **1.** bare; mit b~en **Füßen**, barefoot; mit b~em **Auge**, with the naked eye. **2.** (a) mere (supposition, trifle etc.); (b) adv. F: only, just; (verstärkend) **mach das b. nicht wieder!** don't you dare do that again! **was soll ich ihm b. sagen?** what on earth am I going to tell him? ◆'b~**legen**, v.tr.sep. to expose (sth.). ◆'b~**liegen**, v.i.sep.irr. 62 (sein) to be exposed. ◆'b~**stellen**, v.tr.sep. to compromise (s.o., oneself).
**Blöße** ['blø:sə], f -/-n **1.** Lit: nakedness. **2.** sich dat eine B. geben, to show one's weak spot.
**blühen** ['bly:ən], v.i. (haben) (a) to flower, be in bloom/(Bäume) in blossom; (b) Fig: (Pers., Geschäft usw.) to flourish, thrive; F: das kann dir auch noch b., that could happen to you too. ◆'b~d, adj. **1.** (a) Bot: flowering; in flower/bloom; (b) thriving (person, business). **2.** eine b~e Phantasie, a very fertile imagination.
**Blum|e** ['blu:mə], f -/-n **1.** flower. **2.** (a)

bouquet (of wine); (b) froth, head (on beer). ◆'B~**en-**, comb.fm. flower (bed, arrangement, garden, shop etc.); floral (design etc.). ◆'B~**enkohl**, m cauliflower. ◆'B~**enstrauß**, m bunch of flowers, bouquet; (klein) posy. ◆'B~**entopf**, m flowerpot. ◆'B~**enzwiebel**, f bulb. ◆'b~**ig**, adj. flowery.
**Bluse** ['blu:zə], f -/-n blouse.
**Blut** [blu:t]. **I.** n -(e)s/no pl blood; mit B. **befleckt**, bloodstained; F: (nur) ruhig B.! keep calm! keep your hair on! **II.** 'B~-, comb.fm. blood (-bath, group, orange, sausage, transfusion etc.). ◆'B~**alkohol**, m blood alcohol level. ◆'b~**arm**, adj. anaemic. ◆'b~**befleckt**, adj. bloodstained. ◆'B~**bild**, n blood count. ◆'B~**buche**, f copper beech. ◆'B~**druck**, m blood pressure. ◆'B~**egel**, m leech. ◆'b~**en**, v.i. (haben) to bleed. ◆'B~**erguß**, m effusion of blood; haematoma. ◆'b~**ig**, adj. **1.** bloody, gory. **2.** (verstärkend) complete (beginner, layman etc.). ◆'b~**jung**, adj. very young. ◆'B~**probe**, f blood test. ◆'B~**schande**, f incest. ◆'B~**spender**, m blood donor. ◆'B~**ung**, f -/-en bleeding; Med: haemorrhage. ◆'B~**vergiftung**, f blood poisoning.
**Blüte** ['bly:tə], f -/-n **1.** flower, bloom; (von Obstbäumen) blossom. **2.** (Blühen) flowering, blooming; blossoming. **3.** Fig: in der B. seiner Jahre, in the prime of life. **4.** F: dud (bank) note. ◆'B~**nstaub**, m pollen. ◆'b~**n-'weiß**, adj. snow-white. ◆'B~**zeit**, f **1.** flowering period; blossom-time (of a tree). **2.** Fig: (a) period of prosperity; (b) heyday; great period of a culture etc.
**Bö** [bø:], f -/-en gust; (Regenbö) squall.
**Bock** [bɔk], m -(e)s/-e **1.** (a) Z: (Reh, Kaninchen) buck; (Ziegenb.) he-/F: billygoat; (Schafb.) ram; (b) F: der ist ein sturer B., he's as stubborn as a mule. **2.** (Gestell) stand (for tools etc.); trestle (for a table); (Schemel) stool; Sp: (vaulting-)-horse. ◆'b~**en**, v.i. (haben) (Pferd usw.) to dig in its heels; (sich aufbäumen) to rear; F: (Pers.) to be pigheaded; Aut: (Motor) to fire unevenly. ◆'b~**ig**, adj. pigheaded. ◆'B~**shorn**, n F: j-n ins B. jagen, to put the wind up s.o. ◆'B~**wurst**, f large sausage for boiling.
**Boden** ['bo:dən]. **I.** m -s/- **1.** ground; (Erde) soil; (Fußb.) floor; den B. unter den Füßen verlieren, to lose one's footing; (im Wasser) to get out of one's depth; F: ich war am B. zerstört, I was absolutely shattered. **2.** (Grundlage) basis; auf dem B. der Tatsachen stehen, to be firmly based on fact. **3.** bottom (of a box

etc.); **B. des Meeres,** sea bed. **4.** (*Dachb.*) attic, loft. **II. B~-,** *comb.fm.* ground (frost, *Av:* staff etc.); floor (area etc.); *Agr:* land (reform etc.). ◆'**B~heizung,** *f* under-floor heating. ◆'**b~los,** *adj.* abysmal (ignorance etc.); boundless (stupidity etc.). ◆'**B~satz,** *m* -es/*no pl* sediment, *F:* dregs. ◆'**B~schätze,** *mpl* mineral resources. ◆'**B~see.** *Pr.n.m.* **der B.,** Lake Constance. ◆'**B~turnen,** *n* floor exercises.

**Bogen** ['bo:gǝn], *m* -s/- & ¨. **1.** arch (of a bridge etc.); **die Straße macht einen B. nach links,** the road curves round to the left. **2.** (*Waffe*) & *Mus:* bow. **3.** sheet (of paper). ◆'**B~gang,** *m* arcade. ◆'**B~- schießen,** *n* archery. ◆'**B~schütze,** *m* archer.

**Bohle** ['bo:lǝ], *f* -/-n (thick) plank.

**Böhm|en** ['bø:mǝn]. *Pr.n.n* -s. Bohemia. ◆'**b~isch,** *adj.* Bohemian.

**Bohne** ['bo:nǝ], *f* -/-n bean. ◆'**B~nkaffee,** *m* pure/*F:* real coffee. ◆'**B~nstange,** *f* (*a*) beanstick; (*b*) *F:* (*Pers.*) beanpole.

**bohner|n** ['bo:nǝrn], *v.tr.* to polish (a floor). ◆'**B~wachs,** *n* floor polish.

**bohr|en** ['bo:rǝn]. *v.* **1.** *v.tr.* to bore. **2.** *v.i.* (*haben*) (*a*) to drill (*nach* + *dat,* for); **in der Nase b.,** to pick one's nose; *Fig:* **b~ender Schmerz,** gnawing pain; (*b*) *F:* (*drängen*) to keep on; **b~ende Fragen,** probing/persistent questions. ◆'**B~er,** *m* -s/- drill. ◆'**B~insel,** *f* drilling platform/rig. ◆'**B~loch,** *n* bore-hole. ◆'**B~maschine,** *f* power-drill; *Ind:* drilling machine. ◆'**B~turm,** *m* (drilling) derrick.

**böig** ['bø:ɪç], *adj.* gusty; squally.

**Boje** ['bo:jǝ], *f* -/-n buoy.

**Bollwerk** ['bɔlvɛrk], *n* (*also Fig:*) bulwark.

**Bolzen** ['bɔltsǝn], *m* -s/- bolt.

**bomb|ardieren** [bɔmbar'di:rǝn], *v.tr.* to bombard (a town etc.); *F:* s.o. with questions etc.). ◆**B~e** ['bɔmbǝ], *f* -/-n bomb. ◆'**B~en-,** *comb.fm.* **1.** bomb (attack, crater, damage etc.). **2.** *F:* terrific, fantastic (success etc.).

**Bon** [bɔŋ], *m* -s/-s **1.** (*Gutschein*) voucher. **2.** (*Kassenzettel*) receipt.

**Bonbon** [bɔŋ'bɔŋ, bõ'bõ], *m* & *n* -s/-s sweet; *N.Am:* (*sing.* & *pl.*) candy.

**Bonus** ['bo:nʊs], *m* -(ses)/-(se) bonus; extra dividend.

**Bonze** ['bɔntsǝ], *m* -n/-n *F:* big shot/*N.Am:* wheel.

**Boot** [bo:t], *n* -(e)s/-e boat. ◆'**B~s-,** *comb.fm.* boat (builder, hook, race, hire etc.). ◆'**B~ssteg,** *m* landing-stage.

**Bord**[1] [bɔrt], *n* -(e)s/-e shelf.

**Bord**[2], *n* -(e)s/-e **an B.** (**eines Schiffes**), aboard/on board (a ship); **von B. gehen,** to go ashore. ◆'**B~buch,** *n* log (book). ◆'**B~funk,** *m* ship's radio. ◆'**B~- karte,** *f* boarding ticket. ◆'**B~stein,** *m* kerb(stone).

**Bordell** [bɔr'dɛl], *n* -s/-e brothel.

**borgen** ['bɔrgǝn], *v.tr.* (*a*) **j-m etwas b.,** to lend sth. to s.o./lend s.o. sth.; (*b*) **sich** *dat* **etwas (bei/von j-m) b.,** to borrow sth. (from s.o.).

**borniert** [bɔr'ni:rt], *adj.* narrow-minded.

**Börse** ['bœrzǝ], *f* -/-n **1.** *Fin:* stock exchange; (*Warenb.*) commodity market. **2.** (*Geldbeutel*) purse. ◆'**B~nmakler,** *m* stockbroker (on the Exchange).

**Borst|e** ['bɔrstǝ], *f* -/-n bristle. ◆'**b~ig,** *adj.* **1.** bristly. **2.** (*grob*) surly.

**Borte** ['bɔrtǝ], *f* -/-n braid.

**bös** [bø:s], *adj.* = **b~e.** ◆'**b~artig,** *adj.* **1.** vicious (animal); malicious (person, remark etc.). **2.** *Med:* malignant (disease etc.). ◆**b~e** ['bø:zǝ], *adj.* **1.** (*a*) evil, wicked (person, act etc.); **das B~e,** evil; (*b*) bad, nasty (illness); terrible (shock, mistake); **es war nicht b~e gemeint,** no harm was intended. **2.** *F:* (*zornig*) angry, cross. ◆'**B~ewicht,** *m* villain; scoundrel. ◆'**b~willig,** *adj.* (*a*) ill-willed, malicious; (*b*) *Jur:* wilful (damage etc.).

**Böschung** ['bœʃʊŋ], *f* -/-en slope; (*steil*) escarpment; (*Damm*) embankment.

**bos|haft** ['bo:shaft], *adj.* wicked; evil; (*böswillig*) spiteful, malicious. ◆'**B~heit,** *f* -/-en **1.** *no pl* malice, spite. **2.** (*Bemerkung*) malicious remark.

**Boß** [bɔs], *m* -sses/-sse *F:* boss.

**Botan|ik** [bo'ta:nik], *f* -/*no pl* botany. ◆'**b~isch,** *adj.* botanical.

**Bot|e** ['bo:tǝ], *m* -n/-n messenger. ◆'**B~engang,** *m* errand. ◆'**B~- schaft,** *f* -/-en **1.** message. **2.** (*Vertretung*) embassy. ◆'**B~schafter(in),** *m* -s/- (*f* -/-nen) ambassador.

**Bottich** ['bɔtɪç], *m* -s/- tub; (*für Wein usw.*) vat.

**Bouillon** [bul'jõ, -jɔŋ], *f* -/-s broth; clear soup.

**Bowle** ['bo:lǝ], *f* -/-n punch.

**box|en** ['bɔksǝn]. **I.** *v.* **1.** *v.i.* (*haben*) to box; **gegen j-n b.,** to fight s.o. **2.** *v.tr.* to punch (s.o., *F:* sth.). **II. B.,** *n* -s/*no pl* boxing. ◆'**B~er,** *m* -s/- boxer. ◆'**B~kampf,** *m* boxing match; fight. ◆'**B~sport,** *m* boxing.

**Boykott** [bɔy'kɔt], *m* -(e)s/-s & -e boycott. ◆**b~ieren** [-'ti:rǝn], *v.tr.* to boycott (s.o., sth.).

**brachliegen** ['braːxliːgǝn], *v.i.sep.irr.62* (*haben*) to lie fallow.

**Branche** ['brɑ̃:ʃǝ], *f* -/-n branch (of industry etc.); (*Gewerbe*) trade; (line of) business. ◆'**B~nverzeichnis,** *n Tel:* classified directory; *Brit:* Yellow pages.

**Brand** [brant]. **I.** *m* -(e)s/¨-e **1.** fire, blaze; **in B. geraten,** to catch fire. **2.** *no pl Med:* gangrene. **II.** '**B~-,** *comb.fm.* (*a*) fire (-wall etc.); incendiary (bomb etc.); (*b*) burning (smell etc.). ◆'**B~mal,** *n* burn (mark); *Agr:* (*Zeichen*) brand; *Fig:* stigma. ◆'**b~marken,** *v.tr. insep.* to condemn (s.o., sth.) (publicly); to brand

(s.o.). ◆'B~**stifter**, *m* fire-raiser.
◆'B~**stiftung**, *f* arson. ◆'B~**wunde**,
*f* burn.
**brand|en** ['brandən], *v.i.* (*haben*) (*Wellen
usw.*) to break. ◆'B~**ung**, *f* -/no *pl*
surf.
**Branntwein** ['brantvain], *m* spirit; *coll.*
spirits.
**Brasil|ianer(in)** [brazili'ɑːnər(in)], *m* -s/-
(*f* -/-nen) Brazilian. ◆b~i'**anisch**, *adj.*
Brazilian. ◆**B~ien** [bra'ziːljən]. *Pr.n.n*
-s. Brazil.
**Brat-** ['brɑːt-], *comb.fm.* fried (fish etc.);
roast (meat); baked (apple). ◆'b~**en**. I.
*v.tr. & i.irr.* (*haben*) to roast (meat, potatoes etc.); to bake (apples); (*in der
Pfanne*) to fry (meat, potatoes etc.); *Fig:*
(*Pers.*) **in der Sonne b.**, to roast in the
sun. II. **B~en**, *m* -s/- (*gebraten*) roast;
(*auch roh*) joint; **er hat den B~en ge-
rochen**, he got wind of it/(*Unangenehmes*)
smelt a rat. ◆'B~**ensoße**, *f*
gravy. ◆'B~**hähnchen**, *n* roast
chicken. ◆'B~**kartoffeln**, *fpl* fried
potatoes. ◆'B~**pfanne**, *f* frying
pan. ◆'B~**rost**, *m* grill; (*im Freien*) barbecue. ◆'B~**wurst**, *f* fried sausage.
**Bratsche** ['brɑːtʃə], *f* -/-n viola.
**Brauch** ['braux], *m* -(e)s/-e custom; (*im
Geschäft usw.*) practice. ◆'b~**bar**, *adj.*
usable (material, tool etc.); practicable
(idea etc.). ◆'B~**barkeit**, *f* -/no *pl* usa-
bility; practicality. ◆'b~**en**, *v.tr.* (*a*) to
need (sth.); **du brauchst nicht hinzugehen**, you don't have to/need to go there;
(*b*) (*benutzen*) to use (sth.).
**Braue** ['brauə], *f* -/-n (eye)brow.
**brau|en** ['brauən], *v.tr.* to brew.
◆'B~**er**, *m* -s/- brewer. ◆**B~e'rei**, *f*
-/-en brewery.
**braun** [braun], *adj.* brown; bay (horse).
◆b~**gebrannt**, *adj.* sun-tanned.
**Bräun|e** ['brɔynə], *f* -/no *pl* tan.
◆b~**en**, *v.tr. & i.* (*haben*) (*a*) to turn
(sth.) brown; (*in der Sonne*) to tan (s.o.,
skin etc.); (*b*) *Cu:* to brown (meat, onions etc.). ◆'b~**lich**, *adj.* brownish.
◆'B~**ung**, *f* -/no *pl* 1. (*Bräunen*) brown-
ing; tanning. 2. brownness; (*sun*)tan.
**Brause** ['brauzə], *f* -/-n 1. (*a*) (*für Blumen
usw.*) (watering) rose, sprinkler; (*b*)
(*Dusche*) shower. 2. *F:* (*Limonade*) (fizzy)
lemonade. ◆'b~**n**, *v.i.* (*haben*) (*a*) to
roar; (*b*) (*duschen*) to have/take a shower.
◆'B~**pulver**, *n* fizzy lemonade powder;
*Brit:* sherbet.
**Braut** [braut]. I. *f* -/-e bride; (*Verlobte*)
fiancée. II. 'B~-, *comb.fm.* bridal (bouquet, veil etc.). ◆'B~**jungfer**, *f* bridesmaid. ◆'B~**paar**, *n* bridal pair.
**Bräutigam** ['brɔytigam], *m* -s/-e (*a*)
fiancé; (*b*) (*am Hochzeitstag*) bridegroom.
**brav** [brɑːf], *adj.* 1. good, well-behaved
(child etc.). 2. (*bieder*) worthy, honest
(man, citizen etc.).
**Brech|bohne** ['brɛçboːnə], *f* French
bean. ◆'B~**eisen**, *n* crowbar.

◆'b~**en**, *v.irr.* 1. *v.tr.* (*a*) to break
(sth., *Fig:* a record, contract, etc.); to
violate (a truce, an oath etc.); *Med:* to
fracture (a bone); **die Ehe b.**, to commit
adultery; (*b*) *Opt:* to refract, bend (light
rays). 2. *v.i.* (*a*) (*sein*) to break; (*b*) (*sein*)
to burst, break out; (*c*) (*haben*) **mit j-m/
einer Partei usw. b.**, to break with s.o./
break away from a party etc.; (*d*) (*haben*)
*F:* (*sich übergeben*) to vomit, be sick.
◆'B~**reiz**, *m* (feeling of) nausea.
◆'B~**stange**, *f* crowbar.
**Brei** [brai], *m* -(e)s/-e pulp; *Cu:* mash;
(*Haferb.*) porridge.
**breit** [brait], *adj.* wide (street, mouth
etc.); broad (shoulders, grin, base etc.);
**die b~e Masse**, the vast majority; **die
b~e Öffentlichkeit**, the general public.
◆'B~**e**, *f* -/-n 1. width, breadth (of
shoulders etc.). 2. *Geog:* latitude.
◆'B~**engrad**, *m* (degree of) latitude.
◆'b~**ge'fächert**, *adj.* wide-ranging (interests etc.). ◆'b~**machen**, *v.refl.sep.*
*F:* **sich b.**, to take up a lot of room.
◆'b~**schult(e)rig**, *adj* broad-
shouldered. ◆'b~**treten**, *v.tr.sep.irr.*
*105 F:* to flog (a subject), go on about
(sth.); to spread (a story etc.).
◆'B~**wand**, *f* wide screen.
**Brems-** [brɛms-], *comb.fm.* brake (light,
drum etc.). ◆'B~**belag**, *m* brake lining. ◆**B~e** ['brɛmzə], *f* -/-n brake.
◆'b~**en**, *v.* 1. *v.tr.* to slow down (a vehicle, *Fig:* development etc.); to hold
(s.o.) back. 2. *v.i.* (*haben*) to brake.
◆'B~**spur**, *f* braking/tyre marks.
◆'B~**weg**, *m* braking distance.
**brenn|bar** ['brɛnbɑːr], *adj.* combustible;
(*leicht*) **b.**, inflammable. ◆'b~**en**, *v.irr.*
1. *v.i.* (*haben*) (*a*) to burn; (*Haus usw.*) to
be on fire; **es brennt!** fire! *F:* **wo
brennt's denn?** what's (all) the rush? (*b*)
*Fig:* **darauf b., etwas zu tun**, to be dying
to do sth.; (*c*) (*Licht, Lampe*) to be alight;
**das Licht b. lassen**, to leave the light
on; (*d*) (*Wunde, Augen usw.*) to smart,
sting. 2. *v.tr.* to burn (sth., a hole etc.);
to fire (pottery, tiles etc.); to distil
(spirits). ◆'B~**holz**, *n* firewood.
◆'B~**material**, *n* -s/no *pl* fuel.
◆'**Brennessel**, *f* stinging nettle.
◆'B~**punkt**, *m* 1. *Opt: etc:* focal point.
2. *Fig:* centre, focus (of interest etc.).
◆'B~**spiritus**, *m* methylated spirits.
◆'B~**stoff**, *m* fuel.
**brenzlig** ['brɛntsliç], *adj. F:* risky,
dodgy.
**Bretagne** [bre'tanjə]. *Pr.n.f* Brittany.
**Brett** [brɛt], *n* -(e)s/-er 1. board; (*dicker*)
plank. 2. *F: pl:* (*a*) skis; (*b*) *Th:* **die
B~er**, the boards. ◆'B~**erzaun**, *m*
wooden fence. ◆'B~**spiel**, *n* board
game.
**Brezel** ['breːtsəl], *f* -/-n pretzel.
**Brief** [briːf], *m* -(e)s/-e letter.
◆'B~**beschwerer**, *m* -s/- paperweight.
◆'B~**freund(in)**, *m* (*f*) penfriend,

*N.Am:* penpal. ◆'**B~kasten**, *m* letter box, *N.Am:* mailbox. ◆'**B~kopf**, *m* letterhead. ◆'**b~lich**, *adv.* by letter. ◆'**B~marke**, *f* (postage) stamp. ◆'**B~marken-**, *comb.fm.* stamp (collector, album etc.). ◆'**B~papier**, *n* writing paper, notepaper. ◆'**B~porto**, *n* letter rate. ◆'**B~tasche**, *f* wallet, *N.Am:* billfold. ◆'**B~taube**, *f* carrier pigeon. ◆'**B~träger**, *m* postman, *N.Am:* mailman. ◆'**B~trägerin**, *f* postwoman. ◆'**B~umschlag**, *m* envelope. ◆'**B~wahl**, *f* postal vote. ◆'**B~wechsel**, *m* correspondence.

**Brigade** [bri'gɑːdə], *f -/-n* brigade.

**Brikett** [bri'kɛt], *n -s/-s* (coal) briquette.

**brillant** [bril'jant]. **I.** *adj.* brilliant. **II. B.**, *m -en/-en* brilliant, diamond.

**Brille** ['brilə], *f -/-n* **1.** (pair of) spectacles, glasses; **eine B. tragen**, to wear spectacles/glasses. **2.** toilet seat. ◆'**B~n-**, *comb.fm.* spectacle (wearer etc.).

**bringen** ['brɪŋən], *v.tr.irr.* (*a*) to bring, (*wegb.*) take (s.o., sth.); (*b*) to yield (profit, interest etc.); **die Möbel brachten viel Geld**, the furniture fetched a lot of money; *F:* **das bringt nichts**, it doesn't get you anywhere; (*c*) *F: (veröffentlichen)* to publish (an article etc.); *TV:* to screen (a programme etc.); *Rad:Th:* to put on (a play etc.); (*d*) **es zu etwas** *dat* **b.**, to achieve sth.; **es weit b.**, to go far; (*e*) ( + *prep.*) **j-n auf die Idee b.**, to give s.o. the idea; **etwas hinter sich b.**, to get sth. over and done with; **j-n in Gefahr/Verlegenheit b.**, to endanger/embarrass s.o.; **j-n um etwas** *acc* **b.**, to deprive s.o. of sth.; **j-n zum Lachen/zur Verzweiflung b.**, to reduce s.o. to laughter/despair; **j-n dazu b., daß er etwas tut**, to get s.o. to do sth.

**brisan|t** [bri'zant], *adj. Fig:* explosive (question etc.); controversial (book etc.).

**Brise** ['briːzə], *f -/-n* breeze.

**Brit|e** ['briː(t)ə], *m -n/-n*/'**B~in**, *f -/-nen* Briton; *N.Am:* Britisher. ◆**b~isch** ['britiʃ], *adj.* British.

**bröck|(e)lig** ['brœk(ə)liç], *adj.* crumbly, crumbling. ◆'**b~eln**, *v.tr. & i.* (*haben*) to crumble.

**Brocken** ['brɔkən], *m -s/-* bit (of bread, meat etc.); lump (of coal etc.); snatch, *F:* snippet (of a conversation etc.); **ein harter B.**, a tough nut (to crack).

**brodeln** ['broːdəln], *v.i.* (*haben*) to bubble.

**Brokat** [bro'kɑːt], *m -(e)s/-e* brocade.

**Brokkoli** ['brɔkoli], *pl.* broccoli.

**Brombeere** ['brɔmbeːrə], *f -/-n* blackberry.

**bronch|ial** [brɔnçi'ɑːl], *adj.* bronchial. ◆'**b~ien**, *fpl* bronchial tubes. ◆**B~itis** [-'çitis], *f -/no pl* bronchitis.

**Bronze** ['brõːsə], *f -/-n* bronze.

**Brosche** ['brɔʃə], *f -/-n* brooch.

**Broschüre** [brɔ'ʃyːrə], *f -/-n* (*Heft*) booklet; (*Flugschrift*) pamphlet.

**Brot** [broːt], *n -(e)s/-e* bread; **ein B. mit Käse**, a piece of bread and cheese; **belegte B~e**, open sandwiches. ◆'**B~erwerb**, *m* livelihood. ◆'**B~krume**, *f*/'**B~krümel**, *m* breadcrumb. ◆'**b~los**, *adj.* **das ist eine b~e Kunst**, there is no money in that.

**Brötchen** ['brøːtçən], *n -s/-* (bread) roll.

**Bruch** [brux], *m -(e)s/-e* **1.** (*a*) breaking; bursting (of a dike etc.); (*b*) (*B~stelle*) break; fracture (of metal part, *Med:* bone; *Med:* (*Riß*) rupture; (*Eingeweideb.*) hernia; (*c*) breach (of a contract etc.); break (**mit der Tradition**, with tradition); breaking-up (of a friendship etc.); (*Ehe usw.*) **in die B~e gehen**, to break up. **2.** *Mth:* fraction. **3.** *Com:* (*a*) (*B~schaden*) breakage; (*b*) damaged goods; *F:* junk. ◆'**B~bude**, *f* hovel. ◆'**B~landung**, *f* crash-landing. ◆'**B~stelle**, *f* break; (*im Glas usw.*) crack; *Med:* (point of) fracture. ◆'**B~stück**, *n* fragment; snatch (of a song, conversation etc.). ◆'**B~teil**, *m* fraction.

**brüchig** ['bryçiç], *adj.* brittle, (*bröckelig*) crumbly; cracked (leather, *Fig:* voice).

**Brücke** ['brykə], *f -/-n* **1.** bridge. **2.** (*Teppich*) rug.

**Bruder** ['bruːdər], *m -s/-* brother.

**brüder|lich** ['bryːdərliç], *adj.* brotherly, fraternal. ◆'**B~lichkeit**, *f -/no pl* brotherliness. ◆'**B~schaft**, *f -/-en* **1.** **sie tranken B.**, they drank to their friendship (and to calling each other 'du'). **2.** brotherhood.

**Brüh|e** ['bryːə], *f -/-n* **1.** *Cu:* broth; clear soup; (*Grundlage für Suppe*) stock. **2.** *Pej: F:* (*Wasser*) **schmutzige B.**, murky water. ◆'**b~en**, *v.tr. Cu:* to pour boiling water over, scald (meat, vegetables etc.). ◆'**B~würfel**, *m* stock cube.

**brüllen** ['brylən], *v.i.* (*haben*) (*a*) (*Vieh*) to low, (*Stier*) bellow; (*Raubtier*, *Fig: Kanonen usw.*) to roar; (*b*) (*schreien*) to yell, bawl; *F:* (*Baby*) to scream, howl; *F:* **es war zum B.**, it was a scream.

**Brumm|bär** ['brumbɛːr], *m -en/-en F:* grouser, *Hum:* grumbleguts. ◆'**b~en**, *v.* **1.** *v.i.* (*haben*) (*Insekten*) to buzz, drone; (*Bären*) to growl; (*Fig: Motor, Orgel usw.*) (*laut*) to boom; (*leise*) to drone; (*summen*) to hum; **mir brummt der Kopf/Schädel**, my head's throbbing. **2.** *v.tr.&i.* (*haben*) (*a*) to sing (sth.) out of tune; (*b*) to grumble, grouse; (**etwas**) **b.**, to mumble (sth.). ◆'**b~ig**, *adj. F:* grumpy, surly.

**brünett** [bry'nɛt], *adj.* brunette (girl); brown (hair).

**Brunnen** ['brunən], *m -s/-* **1.** well; (*Quelle*) spring. **2.** (*Heilquelle*) spa water(s).

**brüsk** ['brysk], *adj.* brusque, curt. ◆**b~ieren** [-'kiːrən], *v.tr.* to snub (s.o.). ◆**B~ierung**, *f -/-en* snub.

**Brüssel** ['brysəl]. *Pr.n.n* **-s.** Brussels.

**Brust** [brust], *f* -/⁔e **1.** *no pl* chest; *Cu: Fig: & Lit:* breast. **2.** *(der Frau)* breast; **einem Kind die B. geben,** to breastfeed a child. ◆'B~**bein,** *n* breastbone. ◆'B~**korb,** *m* thorax. ◆'B~**schwimmen,** *n* breaststroke. ◆'B~**umfang,** *m* chest measurement. ◆'B~**warze,** *f* nipple.

**brüst|en** ['brystən], *v.refl.* **sich b.,** to boast **(mit etwas** *dat,* about sth.). ◆'B~**ung,** *f* -/-en parapet.

**Brut** [bru:t], *f* -/-en **1.** incubation (of eggs). **2.** brood (of birds, bees). ◆'B~**kasten,** *m* incubator. ◆'B~**reaktor,** *m* breeder (reactor). ◆'B~**stätte,** *f (also Fig:)* breeding-ground.

**brutal** [bru'ta:l], *adj.* brutal, *(grausam)* cruel. ◆B~**ität** [-ali'tɛ:t], *f* -/-en **1.** *no pl* brutality, cruelty. **2.** act of brutality.

**brüt|en** ['bry:tən], *v.* **1.** *v.i.* *(haben) (a) (Vogel)* to brood, *(Henne)* sit (on her eggs); *(b) (Pers.)* **über etwas** *acc* **b.,** to ponder/brood over sth. **2.** *v.tr.* to plot (revenge etc.). ◆'B~**er,** *m* -s/- breeder (reactor).

**brutto** ['bruto], *adv. Com:* gross.

**brutzeln** ['brutsəln], *v.* **1.** *v.i. (haben)* to sizzle. *(Fett etc.)* **2.** *v.tr.* to fry (sausages etc.).

**Bub** [bu:p], *m* -en/-en boy. ◆B~**e** ['-bə], *m* -n/-n *(Spielkarte)* jack, knave.

**Buch** [bu:x], *n* -(e)s/⁔er *(a)* book; *(b) Cin:* script; *(c) Com:* **die B~er führen,** to keep the books/accounts. ◆'B~**binder,** *m* -s/- bookbinder. ◆'B~**drucker,** *m* printer. ◆'B~**führung,** *f* book-keeping, accounts. ◆'B~**halter(in),** *m (f)* bookkeeper. ◆'B~**haltung,** *f* **1.** *no pl* bookkeeping. **2.** accounts department. ◆'B~**handel,** *m* book trade. ◆'B~**händler(in),** *m (f)* bookseller. ◆'B~**handlung,** *f* bookshop, *N.Am:* bookstore. ◆'B~**macher,** *m* bookmaker. ◆'B~**prüfer,** *m* auditor.

**Buch|e** ['bu:xə], *f* -/-n beech (tree). ◆'B~**ecker,** *f* -/-n beechnut. ◆'B~**fink,** *m* chaffinch.

**buchen** ['bu:xən], *v.tr. (a)* to enter (a sum etc.); *(b)* to book (a seat etc.).

**Bücher|bord** ['by:çərbort], *n/* ◆'B~**brett,** *n* bookshelf. ◆'B~**ei** [-'rail], *f* library. ◆'B~**regal,** *n* bookshelves.

**Buchse** ['buksə], *f* -/-n *(a) Tchn:* bush; *(b) El:* socket.

**Büchse** ['byksə], *f* -/-n **1.** *(a) (rund)* tin, *esp. N.Am:* can; *(aus Porzellan usw.) (b) (rechteckig)* small box. **2.** *(Jagdgewehr)* sporting rifle. ◆'B~**n-,** *comb.fm.* tinned, *esp. N.Am:* canned (fruit etc.). ◆'B~**nöffner,** *m* tin/*esp. N.Am:* can opener.

**Buchstab|e** ['bu:xʃta:bə], *m* -ns/-n letter (of the alphabet). ◆**b~ieren** [-ʃta'bi:rən], *v.tr.* to spell (out) (a word). **buchstäblich** ['bu:xʃtɛ:pliç], *usu. adv.* literally.

**Bucht** [buxt], *f* -/-en bay.

**Buchung** ['bu:xuŋ], *f* -/-en **1.** entry. **2.** *(Reservierung)* booking, reservation.

**Buck|el** ['bukəl], *m* -s/- *(a) F:* back; *(b) (krummer B.)* hunchback; **die Katze machte einen B.,** the cat arched its back. ◆'b~**(e)lig,** *adj.* **1.** hunchbacked (person). **2.** *F:* bumpy (road etc.).

**bücken** ['bykən], *v.refl.* **sich b.,** to bend (down), stoop **(nach etwas** *dat,* to pick sth. up).

**Bückling** ['bykliŋ], *m* -s/-e **1.** *F: Hum:* (low) bow. **2.** *(Fisch)* buckling.

**Buddh|ismus** [bu'dizmus], *m* -/*no pl* Buddhism. ◆B~**ist,** *m* -en/-en Buddhist.

**Bude** ['bu:də], *f* -/-n **1.** *(a) (auf dem Markt usw.)* stall, booth; *(b) (Baub.)* site hut. **2.** *F: (Bruchb.)* hovel, dump. **3.** *F: (Mietzimmer)* digs; *(Wohnung)* place, pad.

**Budget** [by'dʒe:], *n* -s/-s budget.

**Büfett** [by'fɛt], *n* -(e)s/-s & -e **1.** sideboard. **2.** *(Theke)* (buffet) counter. **3. kaltes B.,** cold buffet.

**Büffel** ['byfəl], *m* -s/- buffalo.

**büff|eln** ['byfəln], *v. F:* **1.** *v.i. (haben)* to cram, *Brit:* swot. **2.** *v.tr.* to swot/*N.Am:* bone up (a subject).

**Bug** [bu:k], *m* -(e)s/-e *Nau:* bow(s); *Av:* nose.

**Bügel** ['by:gəl], *m* -s/- **1.** *(Kleiderb.)* clothes-/coat-hanger. **2.** *(a) (Steigb.)* stirrup; *(b)* (hacksaw etc.) frame; handle (of a bag etc.). **3.** side-piece of spectacles. ◆'B~**brett,** *n* ironing board. ◆'B~**eisen,** *n* (electric) iron. ◆'B~**falte,** *f* crease (in trousers). ◆'b~**frei,** *adj.* non-iron (material); drip-dry (shirt etc.). ◆'b~**n,** *v.* **1.** *v.tr.* to iron (clothes etc.). **2.** *v.i. (haben)* to do the/some ironing.

**bugsieren** [bu'ksi:rən], *v.tr. F:* to steer (s.o.), manoeuvre (sth.).

**Buh|ruf** ['bu:ru:f], *m* boo. ◆'b~**en,** *v.i. (haben) F:* to boo.

**Bühne** ['by:nə], *f* -/-n **1.** *Th:* stage; *F:* **alles ging glatt über die B.,** everything went off smoothly. **2.** platform; *(Hebeb.)* hydraulic lift. ◆'B~**n-,** *comb.fm. (a)* stage (lighting, version, words etc.); *(b)* dramatic (art etc.). ◆'B~**nbild,** *n* scenery, set. ◆'B~**ntechnik,** *f* production techniques.

**Bukett** [bu'kɛt], *n* -s/-s & -e bouquet (of flowers/wine).

**Bulgar|ien** [bul'ga:riən]. *Pr.n.n* **-s.** Bulgaria. ◆b~**isch,** *adj.* Bulgarian.

**Bull|auge** [bul'ʔaugə], *n Nau:* porthole. ◆'B~**dogge,** *f* bulldog. ◆'B~**e,** *m* -n/-n **1.** bull. **2.** *Pej: P: (Polizist)* rozzer; **die B~en,** the fuzz. ◆'b~**ig,** *adj. F:* **1.** stocky, beefy. **2.** scorching (heat).

**Bumerang** ['bu:məraŋ], *m* -s/-s & -e boomerang.

**Bumm|el** ['buməl], *m* -s/- *F:* stroll. ◆B~**e'lant,** *m* -en/-en *F:* slowcoach; time-waster; *(Nichtstuer)* loafer. ◆B~**e'lei,** *f* -/*no pl* dawdling; idleness.

◆'b~**eln**, v.i. F: (a) (sein) to stroll, saunter; (b) (haben) to dawdle, loiter; (bei der Arbeit) to waste time; (faulenzen) to loaf about. ◆'B~**elstreik**, m go-slow.

◆'B~**elzug**, m F: stopping train.

◆'B~**ler(in)**, m -s/- (f -/-nen) F: 1. stroller. 2. Pej: = B~**elant.**

**Bund¹** [bunt], n -(e)s/-e bundle; bunch (of radishes etc.).

**Bund²**, m -(e)s/-e 1. (a) bond (of friendship etc.); (Verband) association; esp. Pol: confederation; (Bündnis) alliance; **mit j-m im B~e sein**, to be associated/Pej: in league with s.o.; **der B.**, the Federation; (Regierung) the Federal Government. 2. Cl: waistband. ◆'B~**es-**, comb.fm. federal (capital, government, state etc.). ◆'B~**esbahn**, f Federal Railways. ◆'b~**esdeutsch**, adj. West German. ◆'B~**esgebiet**, n -(e)s/no pl federal territory; West G: (territory of the) Federal Republic. ◆'B~**eskanzler**, m Federal Chancellor. ◆'B~**esland**, n West G: Federal State; Aus: Province. ◆'B~**espost**, f (Federal) Post Office. ◆'B~**espräsident**, m President of the Federal Republic. ◆'B~**esrat**, m Upper House (of the Federal Republic). ◆'B~**esrepublik**, f Federal (German) Republic. ◆'B~**esstaat**, m 1. confederation. 2. (Gliedstaat) federal state. ◆'B~**esstraße**, f Federal Highway, main road. ◆'B~**estag**, m the Lower House (of the Federal Republic). ◆'B~**eswehr**, f Federal Armed Forces.

**Bünd|chen** ['byntçən], n -s/- neckband; (an Ärmeln) cuff. ◆'B~**el**, n -s/- bundle; wad (of banknotes). ◆'b~**eln**, v.tr. to tie (wood, banknotes etc.) into a bundle/bundles; to truss (hay, straw). ◆'b~**ig**, adj. 1. valid, convincing (argument etc.); conclusive (proof etc.). 2. (kurz) succinct, terse (answer etc.); precise (style). 3. Tchn: on a level, flush. ◆'B~**nis**, n -ses/-se alliance.

**Bungalow** ['bungalo], m -s/-s bungalow; N.Am: ranch house.

**Bunker** ['buŋkər], m -s/- bunker.

**bunt** [bunt]. I. adj. (a) coloured; (vielfarbig) colourful, multi-coloured; (grell) gaudy (colours, clothes etc.); (b) (gemischt) mixed, varied (programme etc.); (wirr) in a jumble; (c) F: **jetzt wird's mir zu b.!** I've had enough! that's going too far! II. 'B~-, comb.fm. coloured (glass, paper etc.). ◆'B~**stift**, m coloured pencil; crayon. ◆'B~**wäsche**, f coloureds.

**Bürde** ['byrdə], f -/-n burden.

**Burg** [burk], f -/-en castle. ◆'B~**friede(n)**, m truce. ◆'B~**graben**, m moat. ◆'B~**ruine**, f ruined castle.

**Bürg|e** ['byrgə], m -n/-n guarantee; (Pers.)

guarantor. ◆'b~**en**, v.i. (haben) **für j-n, etwas** acc **b.**, to vouch/Fin: stand surety for s.o., sth. ◆'B~**schaft**, f -/-en guarantee, surety.

**Bürger(in)** ['byrgər(in)], m -s/- (f -/-nen) citizen. ◆'B~**initiative**, f (community) pressure group; (Aktion) public campaign. ◆'B~**krieg**, m civil war. ◆'b~**lich**, adj. 1. civil (rights, marriage etc.). 2. (a) middle-class (family etc.); esp. Pej: bourgeois (attitude etc.); (b) (einfach) plain, homely (cooking etc.). ◆'B~**meister**, m mayor. ◆'B~**pflicht**, f duty as a citizen. ◆'B~**recht**, n citizenship; esp. pl B~**rechte**, civil rights. ◆'B~**schaft**, f -/-en 1. citizens, townspeople. 2. (in Hamburg/Bremen) City Parliament. ◆'B~**steig**, m pavement, N.Am: sidewalk. ◆'B~**tum**, n -s/no pl middle class(es), bourgeoisie.

**Büro** [by'ro:], n -s/-s office. ◆'B~**angestellte(r)**, m & f decl. as adj. office worker. ◆'B~**klammer**, f paper clip. ◆'B~**krat** [-o'kra:t], m -en/-en bureaucrat. ◆'B~**kratie** [-a'ti:], f -/-n bureaucracy. ◆'b~**kratisch** [-'kra:tiʃ], adj. bureaucratic. ◆'B~**schluß**, m (office) closing time.

**Bursch|e** ['burʃə], m -n/-n 1. lad, youth. 2. F: (Kerl) chap, bloke; esp. N.Am: guy. ◆'b~**ikos** [-i'ko:s], adj. 1. (Mädchen) (tom)boyish; (Frau) mannish. 2. (salopp) sloppy.

**Bürste** ['byrstə], f -/-n brush. ◆'b~**n**, v.tr. to brush (sth.).

**Bus** [bus], m -ses/-se bus; Brit: (für Ausflüge/längere Strecken) coach.

**Busch** [buʃ], m -(e)s/-e bush. ◆'b~**ig**, adj. 1. bushy (eyebrows etc.). 2. (Gelände) bush-covered. ◆'B~**werk**, n bushes; (Sträucher) shrubbery.

**Büschel** ['byʃəl], n -s/- tuft (of grass, hair); bunch, clump (of flowers etc.); cluster (of blossoms).

**Busen** ['bu:zən], m -s/- bosom. ◆'B~**freund(in)**, m (f) bosom friend.

**Buß** ['bu:s-], comb.fm. (sacrament etc.) of penance/repentance. ◆'B~**e**, f -/-n 1. Ecc: no pl penance. 2. Jur: fine. ◆'B~**geld**, n fine.

**Bussard** ['busart], m -s/-e buzzard.

**büß|en** ['by:sən], v.tr.&i. (haben) **(für) etwas b.**, to pay (the penalty) for (sth.); **für seine Sünden b.**, to atone for one's sins. ◆'B~**er**, m -s/- penitent.

**Büste** ['by:stə], f -/-n bust. ◆'B~**nhalter**, m brassière, F: bra.

**Butter** ['butər], f -/no pl butter; F: **es ist alles in ~** everything's just fine. ◆'B~**blume**, f buttercup. ◆'B~**brot**, n slice of bread and butter. ◆'B~**brotpapier**, n greaseproof paper. ◆'B~**dose**, f butter dish.

# C

**C, c** [tse:], *n* -/- (the letter) C, c.
**Café** [ka'fe:], *n* -s/-s café.
**Camp** [kɛmp], *n* -s/-s camp. ◆**'c~en**,
*v.i.* (*haben*) to camp. ◆**'C~er**, *m* -s/-
(*Pers.*) camper. ◆**'C~ing**, *n* -s/*no pl*
camping. ◆**'C~ingplatz**, *m* camp site/
*N.Am:* ground.
**Caravan** ['karavan], *m* -s/-s (*a*) (motor)
caravan, *N.Am:* camper; (*b*) (*Kombi*) es-
tate car, *N.Am:* station wagon.
**Cell|ist(in)** [tʃe'list(in)], *m* -en/-en (*f* -/
-nen) cellist. ◆**'C~o**, *n* -s/-lli & -s cello.
**Chamäleon** [ka'mɛ:leɔn], *n* -s/-s chameleon.
**Champagner** [ʃam'panjər], *m* -s/- champagne.
**Champignon** ['ʃampinjɔŋ], *m* -s/-s mushroom.
**Chance** ['ʃã:sə], *f* -/-n (*a*) chance; **die
C~n stehen gleich/zwei zu eins**,
the odds are even/two to one; (*b*)
(*Gelegenheit*) opportunity.
**Chaos** ['ka:ɔs], *n* -/*no pl* chaos.
◆**cha'otisch**, *adj.* chaotic.
**Charakter** [ka'raktər], *m* -s/-e [-'te:rə]
character. ◆**c~i'sieren**, *v.tr.* to characterize (s.o., sth.); (*schildern*) to portray,
depict (s.o., sth.); (*kennzeichnen*) to typify (s.o., sth.). ◆**C~istik** [-'ristik], *f* -/
-en characterization; (*C~bild*) character
sketch. ◆**c~istisch** [-'ristiʃ], *adj.* typical, characteristic. ◆**c~lich**, *adj.* (qualities etc.) of character; *adv.* in character.
◆**c~los**, *adj.* insipid (colour, taste);
characterless (person, building).
◆**c~losigkeit**, *f* -/*no pl* insipidness.
◆**c~schwach**, *adj.* spineless, weak-
kneed. ◆**c~stark/c~voll**, *adj.* full of
character; (person) of strong personality.
◆**C~zug**, *m* trait.
**charmant** [ʃar'mant], *adj.* charming; delightful. ◆**Charme** [ʃarm], *m* -s/*no pl*
charm.
**Charter-** ['(t)ʃartər-], *comb.fm.* charter
(flight etc.). ◆**c~n**, *v.tr.* to charter (a
plane etc.).
**Chauffeur** [ʃɔ'fø:r], *m* -s/-e chauffeur;
(taxi) driver.
**Chaussee** [ʃɔ'se:], *f* -/-n [-'se:ən] high
road.
**Chauvin|ismus** [ʃovi'nismus], *m* -/*no pl*
chauvinism. ◆**c~ist**, *m* -en/-en chauvinist. ◆**c~istisch**, *adj.* chauvinist.
**checken** ['tʃekən], *v.tr.&i.* (*haben*) to
check (s.o., sth.).
**Chef(in)** ['ʃɛf(in)]. I. *m* -s/-s (*f* -/-nen)
head (of a firm, school etc.); *F:* boss. II.
**C~-**, *comb.fm.* chief (engineer, editor
etc.). ◆**'C~arzt**, *m* chief consultant,
superintendent (of a hospital).
**Chem|ie** [çe'mi:], *f* -/*no pl* chemistry.
◆**c~iefaser**, *f* man-made fibre.
◆**C~ikalien** [-i'ka:liən], *fpl* chemicals.

◆**'C~iker(in)**, *m* -s/- (*f* -/-nen) chemist.
◆**'c~isch**, *adj.* chemical; **c~ische
Reinigung**, (i) dry cleaning; (ii) (*Geschäft*) dry cleaner's.
**Chicoree** ['ʃikore:], *f* -/*no pl* chicory.
**Chiffr|e** ['ʃifrə], *f* -/-n **1.** number. **2.**
(code) symbol, cipher. **3.** (*Anzeigenc.*)
box number. ◆**c~ieren** [ʃi'fri:rən],
*v.tr.* to encode (a text), put (a message
etc.) into code.
**Chile** ['tʃi:le]. *Pr.n.n* -s. Chile. ◆**C~ne**
[tʃi'le:nə], *m* -n/-n Chilean. ◆**C~nin**, *f*
-/-nen Chilean (woman). ◆**c~nisch**,
*adj.* Chilean.
**Chin|a** ['çi:na]. *Pr.n.n* -s. China.
◆**C~ese** [çi'ne:zə], *m* -n/-n Chinese.
◆**C~esin**, *f* -/-nen Chinese (woman).
◆**c~esisch. I.** *adj.* Chinese. **II. C.,**
-(s)/*no pl* Chinese.
**Chinin** [çi'ni:n], *n* -s/*no pl* quinine.
**Chip** [tʃip], *m* -s/-s **1.** *usu. pl* **C~s**, (pota-
to) crisps/*N.Am:* chips. **2.** (*Spielc.*) chip.
**3.** *Data-pr:* chip.
**Chirurg** [çi'rurk], *m* -en/-en surgeon.
◆**C~ie** [-'gi:], *f* -/-n **1.** *no pl* surgery. **2.**
(*Abteilung*) surgical unit. ◆**c~isch**, *adj.*
surgical.
**Chlor** [klo:r], *n* -s/*no pl* chlorine.
◆**C~oform** [kloro'fɔrm], *n* -s/*no pl*
chloroform.
**Choke** [tʃouk], *m* -s/-s choke.
**Cholera** ['ko(:)ləra], *f* -/*no pl* cholera.
**Choleriker** [ko'le:rikər], *m* -s/- irascible
person.
**Chor** [ko:r]. **I.** *m* -(e)s/-ᵉe choir; (*also Th:*)
chorus; **im C. sprechen**, to speak in unison. **II.** **'C~-**, *comb.fm. Mus:* choral
(concert, music, work etc.); choir (practice etc.). ◆**'C~gestühl**, *n* choir stalls.
◆**'C~knabe**, *m* choirboy.
**Choral** [ko'ra:l], *m* -s/-e chorale.
**Choreograph** [koreo'gra:f], *m* -en/-en
choreographer. ◆**C~ie** [-a'fi:], *f* -/-n
choreography. ◆**c~isch** [-'gra:fiʃ], *adj.*
choreographic.
**Christ|(in)** ['krist(in)], *m* -en/-en (*f* -/-nen)
Christian. ◆**'C~baum**, *m* Christmas
tree. ◆**'C~enheit**, *f* -/*no pl* Christen-
dom. ◆**'C~entum**, *n* -s/*no pl* Christianity. ◆**'C~kind**, *n* **das C.**, the infant
Jesus. ◆**'c~lich**, *adj.* Christian.
◆**'C~us**. *Pr.n.m gen.* Christi. Christ.
**Chrom** [kro:m], *n* -s/*no pl Ch:* chromium;
*Aut: etc: F:* chrome.
**Chromosom** [kromo'zo:m], *n* -s/-en
chromosome.
**Chron|ik** ['kro:nik], *f* -/-en chronicle.
◆**'c~isch**, *adj.* chronic. ◆**c~ologie**
[-olo'gi:], *f* -/-n chronology.
◆**c~ologisch** [-o'lo:giʃ], *adj.* chronological.
**Chrysantheme** [kryzan'te:mə], *f* -/-n
chrysanthemum.

**circa** ['tsirka], *adv.* (*abbr.* **ca.**) about, approximately.
**City** ['siti], *f* -/-s & **Cities** city centre.
**Clique** ['klikə], *f* -/-n clique; gang.
**Clou** [klu:], *m* -s/-s *F:* (*a*) main attraction, highlight; (*b*) **der C.** (**an**) **der Sache ist** ..., the whole point about it is ...
**Clown** [klaun], *m* -s/-s clown.
**Computer** [kɔm'pju:tər], *m* -s/- computer.
**Conferencier** [kõferási'e:], *m* -s/-s compère.
**Container** [kɔn'te:nər]. I. *m* -s/- container. II. **C~-**, *comb.fm.* container (ship, traffic etc.).
**Couch** [kautʃ], *f* -/-(e)s couch, sofa.
**Coupé** [ku'pe:], *n* -s/-s *Aut:* coupé.
**Coupon** [ku'põ:], *m* -s/-s *Com:* voucher, coupon; (*zum Abreißen*) counterfoil.
**Courag|e** [ku'ra:ʒə], *f* -/no pl courage.
◆**c~iert** [-a'ʒi:rt], *adj.* courageous; *F:* plucky.
**Cousin** [ku'zɛ̃], *m* -s/-s (male) cousin.
◆**C~e** [ku'zi:nə], *f* -/-n (female) cousin.
**Crem|e** ['kre:m], *f* -/-s cream.
◆**'c~farben**, *adj.* cream(-coloured).
◆**'c~ig**, *adj.* creamy.
**Curry** ['kœri], *n* -s/-s curry.

# D

**D, d** [de:], *n* -/- **1.** (the letter) D, d.
**da** [da:]. **I.** *adv.* **1.** (*räumlich*) there; **da sind wir,** here we are; **ich bin gleich wieder da,** I'll be back in a minute; **ist noch etwas Brot da?** is there any bread left? **2.** (*zeitlich*) then; **von da an,** from then on; **II.** *conj.* (*Ursache*) as, since.
**dabehalten** ['da:bəhaltən], *v.tr.sep.irr.45* to keep (s.o.) (here, there etc.).
**dabei** [da'bai], *adv.* **1.** (*a*) (*räumlich*) **dicht d.,** close by; (*b*) with it; (*im Paket usw.*) enclosed; (*c*) *F:* **ich habe kein Geld d.,** I have no money on me. **2. d. bleiben,** to stick to one's point; **es bleibt d.,** it's settled; **es ist doch nichts d.!** (i) there's no harm in it! (ii) (*leicht*) there's nothing to it! **was ist schon d.?** what does it matter? **3.** (*a*) (*im Begriff*) **j-n d. erwischen,** to catch s.o. in the act; **d. sein, etwas zu tun,** to be (in the process of) doing sth.; (*b*) (*gleichzeitig*) while doing so; **er hat sich nichts d. gedacht,** he didn't mean anything by it; **d. kam es heraus, daß** ..., in the process it came out that ...; (*c*) (*auch noch*) what is more; (*d*) (*dagegen*) yet; **d. darf man nicht vergessen, daß** ..., at the same time one must not forget that ... ◆**d~bleiben,** *v.i.sep.irr.12* (*sein*) to stay there; (*bei einer Tätigkeit*) to stick to/at it. ◆**d~haben,** *v.tr.sep.irr.44* to have (s.o., sth.) with one. ◆**d~sein,** *v.i.sep.irr.93* (*sein*) to be present (**bei** + *dat*, at).
**'dableiben,** *v.i.sep.irr.12* (*sein*) to stay (here/there).
**Dach** [dax]. **I.** *n* -(e)s/⁼er **1.** roof; **er wohnt unter dem D.,** he lives in the attic; **unter D. und Fach,** under cover; (*sicher*) in safety; (*erledigt*) settled; (*fertig*) finished. **II.** **'D~-**, *comb.fm.* (*a*) roof (beam, gable etc.); (*b*) (*im Dach*) attic (room, flat etc.). ◆**'D~boden,** *m* loft, attic. ◆**'D~decker,** *m* roofer. ◆**'D~first,** *m* ridge (of the roof). ◆**'D~fenster,** *n* dormer window; (*Luke*) skylight. ◆**'D~luke,** *f* skylight. ◆**'D~pappe,** *f* roofing felt. ◆**'D~pfanne,** *f* pantile. ◆**'D~rinne,**

*f* gutter. ◆**'D~schaden,** *m* **1.** roof damage. **2.** *F: Hum:* **er hat einen leichten D.,** he's not quite right in the head. ◆**'D~ziegel,** *m* roof tile.
**Dachs** [daks], *m* -es/-e badger.
**Dackel** ['dakəl], *m* -s/- dachshund.
**dadurch** [da'durç, *emphatic* 'da:durç], *adv.* **1.** (*a*) (*hindurch*) through it/them; (*b*) by it; **was hat er d. gewonnen?** what has he gained by it? **2.** ['da:durç] because of this/that.
**dafür** [da'fy:r, *emphatic* 'da:fy:r], *adv.* **1.** (*a*) for it/them; (*statt dessen*) instead; **ein Beweis d., daß** ..., proof (of the fact) that ...; (*b*) **d. sein,** to be for/in favour of it; **d. spricht, daß** ..., (i) a point in its favour is that ...; (ii) (*Bestätigung*) this is confirmed by the fact that ... **2.** ['da:fy:r] (*a*) **er arbeitet langsam, d. aber gründlich,** he works slowly, but makes up for it in thoroughness; (*b*) **d., daß er noch nicht lange hier ist, beherrscht er die Sprache sehr gut,** considering that he hasn't been here long, he is very good at the language. ◆**d~halten,** *v.i. sep.irr.45* (*haben*) **d., daß** ..., to think/be of the opinion that ... ◆**d~können,** *v.i.sep.irr.54* (*haben*) **er kann nichts dafür,** he can't help it; it's not his fault.
**dagegen** [da'ge:gən, *emphatic* 'da:ge:gən], *adv.* **1.** (*a*) against it/them; **d. hilft nichts,** there's nothing you can do about that; (*b*) opposed to it; **haben Sie etwas d., wenn ich rauche?** do you mind if I smoke? **2. was kann ich d. eintauschen?** what can I exchange for it? **3.** (*im Vergleich*) **dieser ist nichts d.!** this is nothing in comparison. **4.** (*andererseits*) but, on the other hand; ◆**d~halten,** *v.tr.sep.irr.45* to argue, object.
**da'heim,** *adv.* at home; **bei uns d.,** back home.
**daher** [da'he:r, *emphatic* 'da:he:r], *adv.* & *conj.* (*a*) from there. (*b*) (*deshalb*) **d. dieser Brauch,** hence this custom; **d.!** that's why!
**dahin** [da'hin, *emphatic* 'da:hin], *adv.* **1.** (*a*) there, to that place; (*b*) **bis d.,** (i) that

far; (*im Buch usw.*) up to that point; (ii) (*zeitlich*) until then; up to that time; (*Zukunft*) by then; (*c*) (*soweit*) to that point; **j-n d. bringen, daß er etwas tut,** to persuade s.o. to do sth. 2. [da'hin] (*vorbei*) over; (*verloren*) gone; **die Ernte ist d.,** the crops are ruined. ◆**d~gehen,** *v.i.sep.irr.36* (*sein*) to go (along); (*Zeit*) to pass. ◆**d~gehend,** *adv.* to this/that effect. ◆**d~gestellt,** *adv.* **es bleibt d. ob ...,** it remains to be seen whether ...; **es d. sein lassen,** (**ob ...**), to leave it open (whether ...).

**da'hinten,** *adv.* back there; over there.

**dahinter** [da'hintər, *emphatic* 'da:hintər], *adv.* behind it/them; ◆**d~kommen,** *v.i.sep.irr.53* (*sein*) *F:* to get to the bottom of it; **endlich kam ich dahinter, was los war,** I finally got wise to what was going on. ◆**d~stecken,** *v.i.sep.* (*haben*) *F:* to be behind it/(*Pers.*) at the bottom of it. ◆**d~stehen,** *v.i.sep.irr.100* (*haben*) to be behind it, (*unterstützen*) back it.

**Dahlie** ['da:liə], *f* -/-n dahlia.

**'dalassen,** *v.tr.sep.irr.57 F:* to leave (s.o., sth.) (here/there); (*vergessen*) to leave (sth.) behind.

**damalige(r,s)** ['da:ma:ligə(r, s)], *attrib. adj.* of that time; (*fashion etc.*) of the day; **der d. Präsident,** the then president.

**damals** ['da:ma:ls], *adv.* then, at that time; **d., als ...,** (in the days) when ...

**Damast** [da'mast], *m* -(e)s/-e damask.

**Dame** ['da:mə], *f* -/-n **1.** lady; *Sp:* **400 Meter der D~n,** women's 400 metres. **2.** (*Spiel*) draughts, *N.Am:* checkers. **3.** (*Schach, Kartenspiel*) queen. ◆**'D~brett,** *n* draughtboard. ◆**'D~n-,** *comb.fm.* (*a*) lady's (glove, shoe, bicycle etc.); ladies' (hairdresser, tailor, toilet etc.); (*b*) *Sp:* women's (team etc.). ◆**'D~nbinde,** *f* sanitary towel, *N.Am:* napkin. ◆**'d~nhaft,** *adj.* ladylike. ◆**'D~nwahl,** *f* ladies' choice. ◆**'D~nspiel,** *n* draughts, *N.Am:* checkers.

**Damhirsch** ['damhirʃ], *m* fallow deer.

**da'mit** [*emphatic also* 'da:mit]. **I.** *adv.* (*a*) with it; **sie war d. einverstanden,** she agreed to it; *F:* **her d.!** hand it over! **hör auf d.!** stop it! (*b*) **was willst du d. sagen?** what do you mean by that? **d. bewies er seine Unschuld,** he thereby proved his innocence. **II.** *conj.* so that.

**dämlich** ['dɛ:mliç], *adj. F:* silly, stupid.

**Damm** [dam], *m* -(e)s/-̈e embankment (of a road, railway etc.); (*Deich*) dike, *N.Am:* levee; (*im Fluß usw.*) dam; (*Hafend.*) mole; *F:* **nicht (recht) auf dem D.,** under the weather.

**dämmen** ['dɛmən], *v.tr.* to dam (a river).

**dämm(e)rig** ['dɛm(ə)riç], *adj.* dim (light); gloomy (day etc.).

**Dämmerlicht** ['dɛmərliçt], *n* twilight; (*am Abend*) dusk. ◆**d~n,** *v.i.* (*haben*)

to grow light/dark; **es dämmert,** (i) day/dawn is breaking; (ii) dusk is falling; *F:* **jetzt dämmert's bei mir!** now I see! now I'm beginning to get it! ◆**D~ung,** *f -/-en* twilight; (*abends*) dusk; (*morgens*) dawn.

**Dämon** ['dɛ:mɔn], *m -s/-en* [dɛ'mo:nən], demon. ◆**d~isch** [-'mo:niʃ], *adj.* demonic.

**Dampf** [dampf]. **I.** *m* -(e)s/-̈e steam; (**chemische**) **D~e,** vapours; **giftige D~e,** toxic fumes. **II.** **'D~-,** *comb.fm.* steam (power, pressure, pipe, turbine, *H:* iron etc.). ◆**'d~en,** *v.i.* (*a*) (*haben*) (*Suppe, Kessel usw.*) to steam; (*b*) (*sein*) (*Schiff, Zug*) to steam (along). ◆**'D~er,** *m* -s/- steamer. ◆**'D~kochtopf,** *m Cu:* pressure-cooker. ◆**'D~maschine,** *f* steam engine. ◆**'D~schiff,** *n* steamship, steamer. ◆**'D~walze,** *f* steamroller.

**dämpfen** ['dɛmpfən], *v.tr.* (*a*) to deaden, muffle (sound); to soften (light); cushion (a blow etc.); *Fig:* to curb (anger etc.); to dampen (s.o.'s enthusiasm etc.); (*b*) *Cu:* to steam (fish, potatoes); (*c*) *H:* to steam-iron (sth.).

**danach** [da'na:x, *emphatic* 'da:na:x], *adv.* (*a*) (*räumlich*) after it/them; (*dahinter*) behind it/them; (*b*) (*zeitlich*) afterwards; (*c*) (*demgemäß*) in accordance with it/them; (*d*) **ich habe d. gefragt/mich d. erkundigt,** I asked/enquired about it; (*e*) **es sieht (ganz) d. aus,** it looks (very) like it.

**Däne** ['dɛ:nə], *m* -n/-n Dane. ◆**'D~emark.** *Pr.n.n* -s. Denmark. ◆**D~in,** *f* -/-nen Danish girl/woman. ◆**d~isch,** *adj.* Danish.

**daneben** [da'ne:bən, *emphatic* 'da:ne:bən], *adv.* (*a*) beside it/them; **dicht/gleich d.,** right next to it/them; (*b*) (*außerdem*) in addition; (*gleichzeitig*) at the same time; (*c*) (*im Vergleich*) by comparison. ◆**d~gehen,** *v.i.sep.irr.36* (*sein*) (*a*) (*Schuß*) to miss (the target); (*b*) *F:* to go wrong; (*Plan*) to misfire.

**Dank** [daŋk]. **I.** *m* -(e)s/*no pl* thanks, gratitude; **vielen/besten/schönen/herzlichen D.,** thank you very much; many thanks. **II.** **d.,** *prep.* + *gen/occ.* + *dat* thanks to. ◆**d~bar,** *adj.* **1.** grateful; **sich (j-m) d. zeigen/erweisen,** to show one's gratitude. **2.** rewarding, worthwhile (task etc.). ◆**D~barkeit,** *f -/no pl* gratitude; thankfulness. ◆**d~e,** *see* **d~en 1.** (*b*). ◆**d~en,** *v.* **1.** *v.i.* (*haben*) (*a*) to say thank you; **j-m für etwas d.,** to thank s.o. for sth.; **nichts zu d.,** don't mention it; (*b*) **danke (schön/sehr)!** thank you (very much)! **wie geht es Ihnen?—danke gut,** how are you?—very well, thank you. **2.** *v.tr.* **ich habe es ihr zu d.,** I have her to thank for it; **niemand wird es dir d.,** no one will thank you for it. ◆**'d~enswert,** *adj.* deserving (of thanks); **d~e Bemühungen,** commendable efforts. ◆'D~sagung, f -/-en (expression of) thanks.

**dann** [dan], adv. (a) then; **d. und wann,** now and then; **bis d.!** see you (then)! (b) (in dem Fall) in that case; **selbst/nur d., wenn ...,** even/only if ...

**daran** [da'ran, emphatic 'da:ran], adv. **1.** (a) on it/them; onto it/them; (b) at it/them; **er arbeitete lange d.,** he worked at/on it for a long time; (c) **wir gingen d. vorbei,** we went past it; **nahe d.,** close to it/them; **im Anschluß d./d.** anschließend, immediately after that. **2. es ist nichts Wahres d.,** there is no truth in it; **es liegt d., daß ...,** the reason for it is that ...; **mir liegt viel d.,** it is very important to me. ◆**d~gehen,** v.i.sep.irr.36 (sein) **d., etwas zu tun,** to set to work to do sth. ◆**d~setzen,** v.tr.sep. **alles/sein letztes d., um etwas zu erreichen,** to do one's utmost to attain sth.; **sich d.,** to get down to it.

**darauf** [da'rauf, emphatic 'da:rauf], adv. **1.** (a) on it/them; **oben d.,** on top of the pile); (b) **zugehen/losgehen,** to go towards it/them; **d. zielen/schießen,** to aim/shoot at it/them. **2.** after that; **3.** (a) **wie kommst du d.?** what gave you that idea? **ich komme jetzt nicht d.,** I can't think of it at the moment; (b) **d. steht Todesstrafe,** the penalty for that is death; (c) **es kommt d. an,** it all depends. ◆**d~folgend,** adj. next, following. ◆**d~hin,** adv. **1.** (im folgenden) as a result. **2.** (mit Blick darauf) with this in view.

**daraus** [da'raus, emphatic 'da:raus], adv. **1.** (räumlich) from it/them. **2. d. wird nichts,** (i) nothing will come of that; (ii) that's out of the question; **ich mache mir nichts d.,** I'm not keen on it.

**Darbietung** ['da:rbi:tuŋ], f -/-en Th: performance; item (in a programme).

**darin** [da'rin, emphatic 'da:rin], adv. (a) in it/them; inside; (b) (emphatic) there; **d. unterscheiden wir uns,** that's where we differ.

'**darleg|en,** v.tr.sep. to set forth (a plan, reasons); to expound (a theory etc.). ◆'D~ung, f -/-en exposition; demonstration (of a theory).

**Darlehen** ['da:rle:ən], n -s/- loan.

**Darm** [darm]. **I.** m -(e)s/-e **1.** Anat: intestine; pl **D~e,** bowels. **2.** (a) (für Saiten usw.) gut; (b) (sausage) skin. **II.** '**D~-,** comb.fm. Med: intestinal (ulcer, disease, haemorrhage etc.); (cancer etc.) of the bowels. ◆'D~saite, f catgut string.

**darstell|en** ['da:rstelən], v.tr.sep. (a) (bildlich) to portray, (oft symbolisch) represent (s.o., sth.); (b) (in Worten) to portray (s.o., sth.); to present (arguments, facts, etc.); (c) Th: to interpret (a character, part); (spielen) to play the part of (the hero etc.); (d) **sich (als etwas) d.,** to show oneself/itself (to be sth.). ◆'D~er(in), m -s/- (f -/-nen) Th: actor,

actress; interpreter (of a part). ◆'D~ung, f -/-en **1.** representation; portrayal; Th: interpretation (of a part); **bildliche D.,** pictorial representation; **schematische D.,** diagram. **2.** (Schilderung) description; account (of the facts etc.); Jur: **falsche D.** (des Sachverhalts), misrepresentation (of the facts).

**darüber** [da'ry:bər, emphatic 'da:ry:bər], adv. **1.** (a) over it/them; **laufe nicht d.!** don't walk over/across it; (b) **d. hinaus,** beyond (it); (zusätzlich) in addition; **es geht nichts d.,** nothing can touch it; (c) (Zahlen usw.) more; (Preis) higher; **Männer von sechzig Jahren und d.,** men of sixty and over. **2.** (dabei) in the process; **d. vergaß ich meine eigenen Sorgen,** that made me forget my own troubles. **3. sich d. freuen/ärgern,** to be pleased/angry about it.

**darum** [da'rum, emphatic 'da:rum], adv. **1.** (a) round it/them; (b) **d. geht es nicht,** that's not the point; **es geht ihm d., zu ... his** aim is to ... **2.** (mit Verben) (to ask, fight etc.) for it; **d. wetten,** to bet on it. **3.** (Grund) so; (Grund) that's (the reason) why; F: **warum denn?—d.!** but why?—because!

**darunter** [da'runtər, emphatic 'da:runtər], adv. **1.** (a) (räumlich) beneath it/them; (b) (Zahl, Preis) less; (c) (unter mehreren) among(st) them. **2.** (mit Verben) from/by it; **d. kann ich mir nichts vorstellen,** that doesn't mean anything to me.

**das** [das], see **der.**

**dasein** ['da:zain]. **I.** v.i.sep.irr.93 (sein) (a) to be there/(anwesend) present; (b) to exist; **es ist alles schon mal dagewesen,** there is nothing new under the sun; **noch nie dagewesen,** unheard of. **II.** **D.,** n -s/ no pl existence, life.

'**dasitzen,** v.i.sep.irr.97 (haben) to sit (there).

**das'jenige,** see **derjenige.**

**daß** [das], conj. that; **es ist zwei Jahre her, d. wir das Haus gekauft haben,** it is two years since we bought the house; **d. du ja nicht zu spät kommst!** don't you dare be late!

**das'selbe** [das'zelbə], see **derselbe.**

'**dastehen,** v.i.sep.irr.100 (haben) (a) to stand (there); (b) **gut/schlecht d.,** to be in a good/bad position; **jetzt steht er ganz allein da,** now he is all alone in the world.

**Daten** ['da:tən], npl data; (persönliche) **D.,** particulars. ◆'D~bank, f data bank. ◆'D~verarbeitung, f -/no pl data processing.

**datieren** [da'ti:rən], v.tr. & i. (haben) to date (aus + dat, from).

**Dativ** ['da:ti:f], m -s/-e dative (case).

**Dattel** ['datəl], f -/-n date.

**Datum** ['da:tum], n -s/Daten date; **welches D. haben wir heute?** what's the date today? **ohne D.,** undated. ◆'D~s-, comb.fm. date (stamp etc.).

**Dauer** ['dauǝr]. **I.** *f -/no pl* (*a*) length, duration; *Jur:* term (of contract etc.); **es war von kurzer D.**, it did not last long/ (*Begeisterung usw.*) was short-lived; **für die D. eines Jahres**, for (a period of) a year; (*b*) **von D.**, lasting; **auf die D. gewöhnt man sich daran**, you get used to it in the long run. **II. 'D~-**, *comb.fm.* (*a*) permanent (condition, symptom etc.); lasting (success, solution etc.); continuous (rain, *Mil:* fire etc.); constant (speed etc.); (*b*) *Sp: etc:* endurance (run etc.). ◆**'D~auftrag**, *m* standing order. ◆**'d~haft**, *adj.* enduring (peace etc.); durable (material etc.). ◆**'D~haftigkeit**, *f -/no pl* permanence. ◆**'D~karte**, *f* season ticket. ◆**'D~lauf**, *m* (*a*) long-distance run; (*b*) **im D.**, at a jogtrot. ◆**'D~lutscher**, *m F:* lollipop; ◆**'d~n**, *v.i.* (*haben*) to last (an hour etc.); **das dauert (mir) zu lange**, that takes too long (for me). ◆**'d~nd**, *adj.* (*a*) lasting (peace, effect etc.); (*b*) continual; **d. etwas tun**, to keep doing sth.; ◆**'D~ton**, *m* continuous tone. ◆**'D~welle**, *f* permanent wave. ◆**'D~wurst**, *f* hard smoked sausage (*e.g.* salami).

**Daumen** ['daumǝn], *m -s/-* thumb; **j-m den D. drücken/halten**, to keep one's fingers crossed for s.o.

**Daune** ['daunǝ], *f -/-* downy feather; *pl* down. ◆**'D~ndecke**, *f* eiderdown (quilt).

**davon** [da'fɔn, *emphatic* 'da:fɔn], *adv.* **1.** (*Entfernung*) (away) from it/them; **wir sind noch weit d. entfernt**, we still have a long way to go. **2. was habe ich denn d.?** what do I get out of it? **das kommt d.!** that's what you get! **er ist nicht d. betroffen**, he is not affected by it; **3.** (*a*) (*Menge*) of it/them; **das Gegenteil d.**, the opposite (of this); (*b*) (to hear, talk etc.) about it; **d. kann gar keine Rede sein!** that's out of the question! ◆**d~gehen**, *v.i.sep.irr.* (*sein*) to walk/go away; ◆**d~kommen**, *v.i.sep.irr.53* (*sein*) to get away/off; **mit dem Leben/dem Schrecken d.**, to escape with one's life/a fright. ◆**d~laufen**, *v.i.sep.irr.* (*sein*) to run away. ◆**d~machen**, *v.refl.sep.* **sich d.**, to make off. ◆**d~tragen**, *v.tr.sep.irr.85* to carry (s.o., sth.) away; to receive (injuries etc.); **den Sieg/den ersten Preis d.**, to win a victory/first prize.

**davor** [da'fo:r, *emphatic* 'da:fo:r], *adv.* **1.** (*a*) (*Ort*) in front of it/them; (*b*) (*Zeit*) before it/that; (*zunächst*) first; (*c*) **Angst d. haben**, to be afraid of it/them; **j-n d. schützen**, to protect s.o. from it/them.

**dazu** [da'tsu:, *emphatic* 'da:tsu:], *adv.* (*a*) to it/them; **er sah die Menge und stellte sich d.**, he saw the crowd and joined them; (*b*) with it/them; **es wurde Salat d. gereicht**, salad was served with it; (*c*) as well, in addition; **d. kommt, daß ich**

**kein Geld habe**, what's more I haven't any money; (*d*) for it; **sie hat keine Lust d.**, she does not feel like (doing) it; **d. bereit/fähig**, ready to do/capable of it; ◆**d~gehören**, *v.i.sep.* (*haben*) (*a*) to belong to it/them; **es gehört schon einiges dazu**, that takes quite some doing. ◆**d~gehörig**, *adj.* belonging to it/them. ◆**d~kommen**, *v.i.sep.irr.53* (*sein*) (*a*) to come (along), appear (on the scene); (*b*) (*hinzugefügt werden*) to be added. ◆**'d~mal**, *adv. A: & Hum:* in those days. ◆**d~tun**, *v.tr. sep.irr.106* to add (sth.).

**da'zwischen**, *adv.* between them; in between. ◆**d~fahren**, *v.i.sep.irr.26* (*sein*) to intervene (in a quarrel, fight etc.); (*unterbrechen*) to interrupt. ◆**d~kommen**, *v.i.sep.irr.53* (*sein*) (*a*) **wenn nichts dazwischenkommt**, if nothing goes wrong; (*b*) **er ist mit den Fingern dazwischengekommen**, his fingers got caught in it. ◆**d~reden**, *v.i.sep.* (*haben*) to interrupt. ◆**d~treten**, *v.i.sep.irr.105* (*sein*) to intervene.

**Debatt|e** [de'batǝ], *f -/-n* debate; **das steht nicht zur D.**, that's beside the point. ◆**d~ieren** [-'ti:rǝn], *v.tr.&i.* (*haben*) to debate (sth.).

**dechiffrieren** [deʃi'fri:rǝn], *v.tr.* to decipher (a code etc.).

**Deck** [dɛk], *n -s/-s Nau:* deck; **unter D. gehen**, to go below; **alle Mann an D.!** all hands on deck! ◆**'D~adresse**, *f* cover address. ◆**'D~bett**, *n* duvet, continental quilt, *N.Am:* comforter. ◆**'D~e**, *f -/-n* **1.** cover; (*Bettd.*) blanket; (*Bettüberwurf*) bedspread; (*Reised.*) rug; **mit j-m unter einer D. stecken**, to be hand in glove with s.o. **2.** (*Tischtuch*) tablecloth. **3.** (*Zimmerd.*) ceiling; **an die D. gehen**, to hit the roof. ◆**'D~el**, *m -s/-* lid; (*zum Aufschrauben*) screw-top cap; (*Buchd.*) (back/front) cover. ◆**'d~en**, *v.tr.* to cover (sth.); (*a*) **den Tisch d.**, to lay/set the table; **das Dach d.**, (*mit Ziegeln*) to tile/(*mit Stroh*) thatch the roof; (*b*) (*schützen*) to shield (s.o., sth.); *Fig:* to cover up for (s.o., s.o.'s misdemeanours); *Fb: etc:* **einen Spieler d.**, to mark a player; (*c*) **Kosten, seinen Bedarf usw. d.**, to cover expenses, one's needs etc.; (*d*) **sich d.**, (*Berichte, Aussagen*) to tally; (*Ansichten usw.*) to coincide. ◆**'D~en-**, *comb.fm.* ceiling (plaster etc.). ◆**'D~farbe**, *f* opaque paint; body colour. ◆**'D~mantel**, *m Fig:* pretence; cover (*für etwas acc*, for sth.); **unter dem D. der Religion**, disguised as religion. ◆**'D~name**, *m* assumed name; *Lit:* pseudonym; *Mil:* code name. ◆**'D~ung**, *f -/no pl* **1.** covering. **2.** (*a*) *Mil: etc:* cover; (*b*) *Sp:* defence; *Fb:* marking; (*c*) covering up (of a crime etc.). **3.** meeting (of a demand, need). **4.** *Fin:* cover; security (for a sum); guarantee (for a loan etc.). ◆**'d~ungsgleich,**

*adj.* congruent.

**Defekt** [de'fɛkt]. **I.** *m* -(e)s/-e defect; fault (in a machine etc.). **II. d.,** *adj.* defective (part etc.); (*Maschine*) out of order.

**defensiv** [defɛn'ziːf], *adj./***D~-**, *comb.fm.* defensive (warfare, measures etc.). ◆**D~e** [-'ziːvə], *f* -/-n defence.

**defin|ieren** [defi'niːrən], *v.tr.* to define. ◆**D~ition** [-nitsi'oːn], *f* -/-en definition. ◆**d~itiv** [-'tiːf], *adj.* definitive (edition etc.); final (offer, decision etc.).

**Defizit** ['deːfitsit], *n* -s/-e deficit.

**deftig** ['dɛftiç], *adj.* F: **1.** filling (food); **d~e Mahlzeit,** solid/hearty meal. **2.** coarse (jokes).

**Degen** ['deːgən], *m* -s/- sword.

**degenerieren** [degene'riːrən], *v.i.* (*sein*) to degenerate.

**degradieren** [degra'diːrən], *v.tr.* to downgrade (s.o.).

**dehn|bar** ['deːnbaːr], *adj.* (material etc.) that stretches; tensile (metal etc.); expansive (solid etc.); elastic (material, *Fig:* concept, rules etc.); expanding (bracelet etc.). ◆**'D~barkeit,** *f* -/no pl elasticity. ◆**'d~en,** *v.tr.* to stretch (sth.); to lengthen (a vowel etc.); **sich d.,** to stretch. ◆**'D~ung,** *f* -/-en stretching.

**Deich** [daiç], *m* -(e)s/-e dike, seawall.

**Deichsel** ['daiksəl], *f* -/-n (*a*) (*einfach*) pole; (*b*) (*Gabeld.*) shafts of a cart etc.). ◆**'d~n,** *v.tr.* F: to wangle (sth.).

**dein** [dain], *poss. adj.* your. ◆**'d~e(r,s),** *poss. pron.* yours; **sind das d.?** are those yours? **das D.,** (i) your property; (ii) (*Anteil*) your share. ◆**'d~er,** *pers. pron.* (*gen of* **du**) of you. ◆**'d~erseits,** *adv.* on your part. ◆**'d~esgleichen,** *pron.* (of) your (own) kind. ◆**'d~etwegen/ um 'd~etwillen,** *adv.* for your sake; because of you. ◆**'d~ige,** *poss. pron. decl. as adj. Lit:* **der/die/das d.,** yours.

**dekaden|t** [deka'dɛnt], *adj.* decadent. ◆**D~z,** *f* -/no pl decadence.

**Dekan** [de'kaːn], *m* -s/-e dean.

**Dekolleté** [dekɔl'teː], *n* -s/-s (low) neckline, décolleté.

**Dekor** [de'koːr], *m* -s/-s decoration (on glass etc.); *Th: etc:* décor. ◆**D~ateur(in)** [-a'tøːr(in)], *m* -s/- (*f* -/-nen) (*a*) (house) decorator; (*b*) *Com:* window-dresser. ◆**D~ation** [-atsi'oːn], *f* -/-en (*a*) *no pl* decoration; *Com:* (window) dressing; (*b*) (*Auslage*) display; *Th: Cin: etc:* set. ◆**d~a'tiv,** *adj.* decorative. ◆**d~ieren** [-'riːrən], *v.tr.* to decorate (sth., s.o. with a medal); *Com:* to dress (a shop window).

**Delegation** [delegatsi'oːn], *f* -/-en delegation.

**delikat** [deli'kaːt], *adj.* **1.** delicious (dish, fruit etc.). **2.** (*heikel*) delicate (matter, situation). ◆**D~esse** [-'tɛsə], *f* -/-n delicacy. ◆**D~essengeschäft,** *n* delicatessen.

**Delikt** [de'likt], *n* -(e)s/-e *Jur:* (indictable) offence.

**Delle** ['dɛlə], *f* -/-n dent.

**Delphin** [dɛl'fiːn], *m* -s/-e dolphin.

**Delta** ['dɛlta], *n* -s/-s *&* -ten delta.

**dem** [deːm], *dat. sing. of* **der, das** *see* **der.**

**Dementi** [de'mɛnti], *n* -s/-s (official) denial. ◆**d~eren** [-'tiːrən], *v.tr.* to deny (rumours etc.).

**'dem|ent'sprechend,** *adj.* corresponding; (*passend*) suitable; *adv.* accordingly. ◆**'d~ge'mäß,** *adv.* accordingly. ◆**'d~nach,** *adv.* according to that/this; (*also*) so, consequently. ◆**d~'nächst,** *adv.* shortly.

**Demo|krat** [demo'kraːt], *m* -en/-en democrat. ◆**D~kratie** [-a'tiː], *f* -/-n democracy. ◆**d~'kratisch,** *adj.* democratic.

**demolieren** [demo'liːrən], *v.tr.* to wreck (sth.); *F:* to smash up (a car etc.).

**Demonstr|ant(in)** [demɔn'strant(in)], *m* -/-en (*f* -/-nen) *Pol:* demonstrator. ◆**D~ation** [-atsi'oːn], *f* -/-en demonstration. ◆**d~ativ** [-a'tiːf], *adj.* **1.** illuminating (example etc.). **2.** ostentatious (action). **3.** *Gram:* demonstrative. ◆**d~ieren** [-'striːrən], *v.tr. & i.* (*haben*) to demonstrate.

**Demoskopie** [demosko'piː], *f* -/no pl opinion polling/research.

**Demut** ['deːmuːt], *f* -/no pl humility.

**demütig** ['deːmyːtiç], *adj.* humble. ◆**d~en** ['-igən], *v.tr.* to humble (s.o., oneself); (*erniedrigen*) to humiliate (s.o.). ◆**'D~ung,** *f* -/-en humiliation.

**'demzu'folge,** *adv.* consequently, therefore.

**den** [deːn], *acc. of* **der,** *q.v.*

**denen** ['deːnən], *dat.pl of* **der, die, das** *see* **der.**

**Denk|art** ['dɛŋkˀart], *f* -/-en (*a*) way of thinking; (*b*) (*Gesinnung*) mentality. ◆**'d~bar,** *adj.* conceivable. ◆**'d~en. I.** *v.irr.* **1.** *v.tr.* to think (sth., a thought etc.); **das läßt sich d.,** that's understandable; **das kann ich mir d.,** I can well believe it; **er dachte sich nichts Böses dabei,** he meant no harm by it; **das ist für dich gedacht,** this is meant for you. **2.** *v.i.* (*haben*) to think (**an** + *acc,* of; **über** + *acc,* about); *F:* **wo denkst du hin!** what can you be thinking of! **denk mal an!** you don't say! **denkste!** that's what you think! **großzügig/kleinlich d.,** to be of a liberal/petty turn of mind; **ich denke nicht daran, das zu tun,** I wouldn't dream of doing it; **solange ich d. kann,** for as long as I can remember. **II.** **D.,** *n* -s/no pl (way of) thinking; thought. ◆**'D~er,** *m* -s/- thinker. ◆**'d~fähig,** *adj.* capable of thought; rational (being); thinking (person). ◆**'d~faul,** *adj.* mentally lazy. ◆**'D~fehler,** *m* error of logic. ◆**'D~mal,** *n* memorial; (*Plastik usw.*) monument. ◆**'d~würdig,** *adj.* memorable. ◆**'D~zettel,** *m* *F:* (unpleasant) reminder; awful warning.

**denn** [dɛn]. **I.** *conj.* **1.** (*weil*) because; *Lit:* for. **2.** **mehr/besser d. je,** more/better than ever. **II.** *adv.* 1. **was ist d. eigentlich passiert?** what really did happen? **warum d. nicht?** why not? 2. **es sei d. (, daß)** ..., unless ...

**dennoch** ['dɛnɔx], *adv.* nevertheless; however.

**Denunziant(in)** [denuntsi'ant(in)], *m* **-en/-en** (*f* -/-**nen**) informer.

**Deodorant** [deˀodo'rant], *n* **-s/-s** deodorant.

**deponieren** [depo'niːrən], *v.tr.* to deposit (valuables).

**Depot** [de'poː], *n* **-s/-s** depot; (*für Möbel, Waren*) store.

**Depress|ion** [deprɛsi'oːn], *f* -/-en depression. ◆**d~iv** [‑'siːf], *adj.* depressive.

**deprimieren** [depri'miːrən], *v.tr.* to depress (s.o.); **deprimiert,** depressed.

**der** [deːr], *m* (*acc* **den,** *gen* **des,** *dat* **dem**), **die** [diː], *f* (*acc* **die,** *gen/dat* **der**), **das** [das], *n* (*acc* **das,** *gen* **des,** *dat* **dem**), **die,** *pl* (*acc* **die,** *gen* **der,** *dat* **den**). **I.** *def. art.* the; **der Mensch,** man; **die kleine Gabi,** little Gabi; **den Kopf schütteln,** to shake one's head; **zieh dir die Schuhe an,** put your shoes on. **II.** *dem. pron.* (*gen m & n* **dessen;** *gen f & pl* **deren;** *dat pl* **denen**) (*a*) (*Pers.*) he, she; the one; *pl* they; those; the ones; (*Sache*) that; the one; *pl* those; the ones; (*b*) (*betont*) **der/die hat es getan,** 'he/'she did it; **der war es,** it was him; **der/die mit dem grünen Hut,** the one with the green hat; **ach der!** oh him! **der, den ich kenne,** the one (that) I know; (*c*) that; **das ist mein Vater,** that is my father; **das waren Zeiten,** those were the days; **wie dem auch sei,** however that may be; **um und die Zeit,** at such and such time. **III.** *rel. pron.* (*gen m & n* **dessen,** *f & pl* **deren;** *dat pl* **denen**) (*Pers.*) who; *acc* whom; *gen* whose; *dat* to whom; (*Sachen*) which, that; *gen* of which.

**derart** ['deːrˀaːrt], *adv.* (+ *adj.*) so; (*in solchem Maße*) so much, to such an extent. ◆**d~ig,** *adj.* such, like this/that.

**derb** [dɛrp], *adj.* (*grob*) uncouth (person, manners etc.); (*unsanft*) rough (treatment etc.). ◆**'D~heit,** *f* -/no *pl* (*Grobheit*) uncouthness; crudeness.

**deren** ['deːrən], *see* **der, II, III.**

**dergleichen** [deːr'glaiçən], *inv.* **I.** *dem. adj.* such; of this/that kind. **II.** *dem. pron.* things like that; **nichts d.,** nothing of the kind.

**derjenige** ['deːrjeːnigə], *m/***diejenige** *f/* **dasjenige** *n dem. pron.* (*Pers.*) he, she; the one; (*Sachen*) that; the one; *pl* those, the ones.

**dermaßen** ['deːr'mɑːsən], *adv.* so; to such an extent.

**derselbe** [deːr'zɛlbə], *m/***dieselbe** *f/* **dasselbe** *n dem. adj.* the same.

**derzeit** ['deːrtsait], *adv.* at present, at the moment. ◆'**d~ig,** *adj.* present.

---

**des** [dɛs], *see* **der I.**

**Desert|eur** [dezɛr'tøːr], *m* **-s/-e** deserter. ◆**d~ieren** [‑'tiːrən], *v.i.* (*sein/haben*) to desert.

**desgleichen** [dɛs'glaiçən], *adv.* likewise.

**deshalb** ['dɛshalp], *emphatic* dɛs'halp], *adv.* because of this/that; (*also*) therefore.

**Desin|fektion** [dezin-, dɛsˀinfɛktsi'oːn], *f* -/no *pl* disinfection. ◆**D~fektionsmittel,** *n* disinfectant. ◆**d~fi'zieren,** *v.tr.* to disinfect.

**Desinteress|e** ['dɛsˀintərɛsə], *n* **-s/no** *pl* lack of interest; indifference. ◆**d~iert** [‑'siːrt], *adj.* uninterested.

**dessen** ['dɛsən], *see* **der II, III.** ◆**d~'ungeachtet,** *adv.* nevertheless.

**Dessert** [dɛ'seːr], *n* **-s/-s** dessert, *Brit:* sweet.

**Destill|ation** [destilatsi'oːn], *f* -/-en (*a*) no *pl* distilling; (*b*) *Ch:* distillation. ◆**d~ieren** [‑'liːrən], *v.tr.* to distil.

**desto** ['dɛsto], *adv.* (*before comp.*) **je eher, d. lieber,** the sooner, the better.

**destruktiv** [dɛstruk'tiːf], *adj.* destructive.

**deswegen** ['dɛs-, dɛs've:gən], *adv.* = **deshalb.**

**Detail** [de'tai], *n* **-s/-s** detail. ◆**d~liert** [dɛta'jiːrt], *adj.* detailed.

**Detekt|ei** [detɛk'tai], *f* -/-en detective agency. ◆**D~iv** [‑'tiːf], *m* **-s/-e** detective.

**deut|en** ['dɔytən], *v.* 1. *v.tr.* to interpret (a text, dream etc.) (**als,** as); to read (the stars, s.o.'s hand etc.); to foretell (the future). 2. *v.i.* (*haben*) to point (**auf j-n, etwas,** at s.o., sth.); *Fig:* (*Zeichen usw.*) **auf eine Änderung usw. d.,** to point to a change etc. ◆**'d~lich,** *adj.* (*a*) clear; distinct (improvement etc.); (*eindeutig*) explicit; (*grob*) blunt (answer etc.). ◆**'D~lichkeit,** *f* -/no *pl* (*a*) clarity; (*b*) bluntness. ◆**'D~ung,** *f* -/-en interpretation.

**deutsch** [dɔytʃ]. **I.** *adj.* 1. German; **die D~e Demokratische Republik** (*abbr.* **DDR**), the German Democratic Republic (*abbr.* GDR), East Germany. 2. (*a*) **d. sprechen,** to speak German; **d. geschrieben,** written in German; (*b*) **das D~e,** the German language; **ins D~e übersetzen,** to translate into German. 3. **ein D~er/eine D~e,** a German (man/woman); **die D~en,** the Germans; **sie ist D~e,** she is (a) German. **II. D.,** *n* **-(s)/no** *pl* German. ◆**'D~land.** *Pr.n.n* **-s.** Germany.

**Devise** [de'viːzə], *f* -/-n. 1. motto. 2. *pl* **D~n** foreign exchange/currency. ◆**D~nkurs,** *m* rate of exchange.

**Dezember** [de'tsɛmbər], *m* **-(s)/**- December.

**dezent** [de'tsɛnt], *adj.* discreet; (*gedämpft*) subdued (lighting, music); (*geschmackvoll*) tasteful (pattern, furnishings etc.).

**dezimal** [detsi'mɑːl], *adj.* decimal (system etc.). ◆**D~bruch,** *m* decimal (fraction). ◆**D~zahl,** *f* decimal.

**dezimieren** [detsi'mi:rən], *v.tr.* to decimate (a population etc.).

**Dia** ['di:a], *n* -s/-s slide.

**Diabet|iker(in)** [dia'be:tikər(in)], *m* -s/- (*f* -/-nen) *Med:* diabetic. ◆**d~isch**, *adj.* diabetic.

**Diagnose** [dia'gno:zə], *f* -/-n diagnosis.

**diagonal** [diago'nɑ:l], *adj.* diagonal. ◆**D~e**, *f* -/-n diagonal.

**Diagramm** [dia'gram], *n* -s/-e diagram; (statistical) chart.

**Dialekt** [dia'lɛkt], *m* -(e)s/-e dialect. ◆**d~frei**, *adj.* standard (language).

**Dialog** [dia'lo:k], *m* -(e)s/-e dialogue.

**Diamant** [dia'mant], *m* -en/-en diamond. ◆**d~en**, *adj.* diamond (bracelet, *Fig:* wedding etc.).

**Diapositiv** [diapozi'ti:f], *n* -s/-e transparency; (*gerahmt*) slide.

**Diät** [di'ɛ:t]. **I.** *f* -/-en 1. diet. 2. *pl Pol:* allowance. **II. d.**, *adv.* **d. leben/essen**, to be on a diet.

**dich** [diç], 1. *pron. acc of* **du**, *q.v.* you. 2. *refl. pron.* yourself; **wasch(e) d.**, wash (yourself).

**dicht** [diçt], *adj.* 1. dense (fog, forest, traffic, population etc.); thick (hedge, hair, crowd etc.); close (weave etc.); *Fig:* tight, packed (programme etc.); **d. bevölkert/bewohnt**, densely populated. 2. *adv.* (*Lage*) close (**an/bei** + *dat*, to); **d. hintereinander folgen**, to follow in quick succession. 3. leakproof; (*wasserdicht*) waterproof (shoes etc.); watertight (container); *F:* **er ist nicht ganz d.**, he isn't all there. ◆**D~e**, *f* -/-n 1. thickness; density (of population etc.); *Cl:* closeness (of weave). 2. *Ph:* density. ◆**d~en1**, *v.tr.* to make (a roof, tap etc.) watertight; to seal (a joint). ◆**d~halten**, *v.i.sep.irr.45* (*haben*) *F:* to keep one's mouth shut. ◆**D~ung1**, *f* -/-en seal; (*Material*) packing; gasket. ◆**D~ungsring**, *m* -(e)s/-e washer.

**dicht|en2**, *v.* 1. *v.tr.* to write (a poem, novel). 2. *v.i.* (*haben*) to write poetry. ◆**D~er(in)**, *m* -s/- (*f* -/-nen) poet(ess); (*Verfasser*) author(ess); (*Schriftsteller*) writer. ◆**d~erisch**, *adj.* poetic. ◆**D~kunst**, *f* -/no *pl* (art of) poetry. ◆**D~ung2**, *f* -/-en (*a*) (*Lyrik*) poetry; (*b*) fiction.

**dick** [dik], *adj.* thick; fat (person, *F:* book, cigar, *Hum:* salary etc.); **d~e Bohnen**, broad beans; **d. machen**, (*Kleid*) to make one look fat; (*Essen*) to be fattening; **d~e Luft**, stuffy/*Fig:* tense atmosphere; *Fig:* **mit j-m durch d. und dünn gehen**, to go through thick and thin with s.o. ◆**D~darm**, *m* colon, large intestine. ◆**D~e**, *f* -/-n thickness; (*Pers.*) fatness. ◆**d~fellig**, *adj.* *F:* thick-skinned. ◆**D~flüssig**, *adj.* viscous. ◆**D~icht**, *n* -(e)s/-e thicket. ◆**D~kopf**, *m* *F:* pig-headed person. ◆**d~köpfig**, *adj.* *F:* pig-headed. ◆**d~lich**, *adj.* stoutish (person); chub-

by (baby); thickish (liquid). ◆**D~milch**, *f* curd; (*saure Milch*) curdled/sour milk.

**die** [di:], *see* **der**.

**Dieb(in)** ['di:p ('di:bin)], *m* -(e)s/-e (*f* -/-nen) thief; (*Einbrecher*) burglar. ◆**D~esbande**, *f* pack of thieves. ◆**D~esgut**, *n* stolen goods; *F:* loot. ◆**d~isch**, *adj.* impish (delight etc.); **sich d. (über etwas acc) freuen**, to be full of glee (over sth.) ◆**D~stahl**, *m* -(e)s/-e theft; *Jur:* larceny; **geistiger D.**, plagiarism.

**diejenige** ['di:je:nigə], *pron. f see* **derjenige**.

**Diele** ['di:lə], *f* -/-n 1. (floor)board. 2. (*Vorraum*) hall.

**dien|en** ['di:nən], *v.i.* (*haben*) to serve (**j-m** s.o.); *Mil:* to serve (one's time); (*Sache*) **damit ist mir nicht gedient**, that is no help to me; **es dient dem Fortschritt**, it is an aid to progress. ◆**D~er(in)**, *m* -s/- (*f* -/-nen) 1. servant; (*Dienerin*) maid. 2. (*Verbeugung*) bow. ◆**D~erschaft**, *f* -/no *pl* domestic staff. ◆**d~lich**, *adj.* useful; **j-m, einer Sache d. sein**, to be of help to s.o., a cause.

**Dienst** [di:nst]. **I.** *m* -(e)s/-e 1. service; **j-m einen guten/schlechten D. leisten**, to do s.o. a good/bad turn. 2. (*a*) (*Arbeit*) work; (*Stellung*) job; **j-n in D. nehmen**, to engage s.o.; **außer D.**, retired; (*b*) (*öffentlicher*) **D.**, Civil Service; (*c*) *Mil: etc:* duty; **D. tun/haben**, to be on duty; **Offizier vom D.**, Officer of the Day. **II.** '**D~-**, *comb.fm.* official (secret, matter etc.); *esp. Com:* business (trip etc.). ◆**D~abteil**, *n* guard's compartment. ◆**d~bereit**, *adj.* (*Apotheke usw.*) on duty. ◆**D~bote**, *m* (domestic) servant. ◆**d~eifrig**, *adj.* zealous; (*übertrieben*) officious. ◆**D~grad**, *m* grade; *Mil:* rank. ◆**d~habend**, *adj.* (doctor, officer etc.); on duty. ◆**D~leistung**, *f* service (rendered). ◆**D~leistungsgewerbe**, *n* service industry. ◆**d~lich**, *adj.* official (communication, matter); **d. verreist**, away on business. ◆**d~pflichtig**, *adj.* liable for compulsory service. ◆**D~plan**, *m* duty roster. ◆**D~schluß**, *m* end of office hours; **nach D.**, after work. ◆**D~stelle**, *f* (administrative) office; **zuständige D.**, competent authority. ◆**D~stunden**, *fpl* office hours. ◆**d~tauglich**, *adj.* (person) fit for (*Mil:* active) service; able-bodied. ◆**d~tuend**, *adj.* = **d~habend**. ◆**D~weg**, *m* **auf dem D.**, through official channels. ◆**D~zeit**, *f* 1. working hours. 2. *Mil: etc:* term of service.

**Dienstag** ['di:nstɑ:k], *m* Tuesday. ◆**d~s**, *adv.* on Tuesdays.

**dies** [di:s]. **I.** *dem. pron.* this. **II.** *adj.* = **dieses**. ◆**d~bezüglich**, *adj.* relevant (documents etc.); (statement etc.) in this connection. ◆**d~jährig**, *adj.* of this

year; this year's (programme etc.).
◆'d~**mal**, *adv.* this time.
◆'d~**seitig**, *adj.* 1. on this side. 2. *Lit:* earthly. ◆'d~**seits**. I. *prep.* + *gen & adv.* on this side (of). II. D., *n -/no pl Lit:* das D., this earthly life; this world.
**diese(r, s)** ['di:zə(r,s)], *dem. adj. & pron.* I. *adj.* this, *pl* these; **d. Nacht**, (i) tonight; (ii) (*gestern*) last night. II. *pron.* this (one); *pl* these; **d~s und jenes**, this and that.

**Diesel** ['di:zəl], *m -(s)/-* diesel (engine/oil).

**dieselbe** [di:'zɛlbə], *dem. pron. f. see* derselbe.

**diesig** ['di:ziç], *adj.* hazy, misty.

**Dietrich** ['di:triç], *m -s/-e* skeleton key.

**diffamier|en** [difa'mi:rən], *v.tr.* to slander (s.o.). ◆D~**ung**, *f -/-en* defamation; *Pol: etc:* smear.

**Differen|tial** [difərɛntsi'a:l], *m -s/-e Mth:* differential. ◆D~**tialgetriebe**, *n* differential (gear). ◆D~**tialrechnung**, *f* differential calculus. ◆D~**z** [-'rɛnts], *f -/-en* 1. *Mth: etc:* difference; (*Rest*) balance; (*Überschuß*) surplus. 2. *pl* disagreements. ◆d~'**zieren**, *v.tr. & i.* (*haben*) to differentiate. ◆d~'**ziert**, *adj.* varied; discriminating (taste, judgement); sophisticated (method).

**digital** [digi'ta:l], *adj.* digital.

**Dikt|at** [dik'ta:t], *n -(e)s/-e* dictation. ◆D~**ator**, *m -s/-en* dictator. ◆d~**atorisch** [-a'to:riʃ], *adj.* dictatorial. ◆D~**a'tur**, *f -/-en* dictatorship. ◆d~**ieren** [-'ti:rən], *v.tr.* to dictate (letters etc.). ◆D~**iergerät**, *n* dictating machine.

**Dilemma** [di'lɛma], *n -s/-s* dilemma.

**Dilett|ant(in)** [dilɛ'tant(in)], *m -en/-en (f -/-nen)* dilettante. ◆d~**antisch**, *adj.* amateurish.

**Dill** [dil], *m -(e)s/-e* dill.

**Dimension** [dimɛnzi'o:n], *f -/-en* dimension.

**Ding** [diŋ], *n -(e)s/-e* thing; *pl* -e nach Lage der D~e, according to circumstances; **es ist ein D. der Unmöglichkeit**, it's a physical impossibility; **das geht nicht mit rechten D~en zu**, there is something odd about it; *F:* **das ist ja ein D.!** well, honestly! what next! (*Verbrecher*) **ein D. drehen**, to do a job. ◆d~**fest**, *adj.* **j-n d. machen**, to arrest s.o.

**Diphtherie** [difte'ri:], *f -/-n* diphtheria.

**Diplom** [di'plo:m]. I. *n -s/-e* diploma; (*akademischer Grad*) degree. II. D~-, *comb.fm.* holding a diploma, qualified (librarian etc.). ◆D~**ingenieur**, *m* (academically) qualified engineer.

**Diplomat(in)** [diplo'ma:t(in)], *m -en/-en (f -/-nen)* diplomat. ◆D~**ie** [-a'ti:], *f -/ no pl* diplomacy. ◆d~**isch**, *adj.* diplomatic.

**dir** [di:r], *pers. pron. dat of* du (*a*) to/ from/for you; (*b*) *refl.* **tun d. die Füße weh?** do your feet hurt? **nimm d. ein**

**Stück**, help yourself to a piece; **wünsch d. was!** have a wish! (*c*) (*with prep.*) **nach d.!** after you! **bei d.**, at your home.

**direkt** [di'rɛkt], *adj.* 1. direct. ◆D~**heit**, *f -/no pl* directness; (*Offenheit*) frankness. ◆D~**ion** [-tsi'o:n], *f -/ -en* 1. (*Vorstand*) (board of) directors. 2. (*Büro*) director's office. ◆D~**or(in)** [-'rɛktɔr, (-rɛk'to:rin)], *m -s/-en (f -/ -nen)* director; (*von Bank, Theater*) manager; *Sch:* head teacher; *esp. N.Am:* principal. ◆D~**übertragung**, *f* live transmission.

**Dirig|ent** [diri'gɛnt], *m -en/-en* conductor ◆d~**ieren** [-'gi:rən], *v.tr.* (*a*) (*also abs.*) *Mus:* to conduct (an orchestra); (*b*) (*lenken*) to direct (the traffic etc.).

**Dirne** ['dirnə], *f -/-n F:* tart; *N.Am:* tramp.

**Diskont** [dis'kɔnt], *m -s/-e* discount. ◆D~**satz**, *m* discount rate.

**Diskothek** [disko'te:k], *f -/-en* disco(theque).

**Diskrepanz** [diskre'pants], *f -/-en* discrepancy.

**diskret** [dis'kre:t], *adj.* discreet. ◆D~**ion** [-tsi'o:n], *f -/no pl* discretion.

**diskriminieren** [diskrimi'ni:rən], *v.tr.* to discriminate against (s.o.).

**Diskus** ['diskus], *m - & -ses/-se & -ken* discus.

**Diskussion** [diskusi'o:n], *f -/-en* discussion (*über* + *acc*, about, of); (*Debatte*) debate; **zur D. stehen**, to be on the agenda. ◆D~**sbasis**, *f*/D~**sgrundlage**, *f* basis for discussion. ◆D~**steilnehmer(in)**, *m -s/- (f -/-nen)* panellist.

**diskut|abel** [disku'ta:bəl], *adj.* worth discussing; **nicht d.**, out of the question. ◆d~**ieren** [-'ti:rən], *v.tr. & i.* (*haben*) (*über*) etwas *acc* d., to discuss sth.

**disponieren** [dispo'ni:rən], *v.i.* (*haben*) (*a*) to plan (ahead), make arrangements; (*b*) **über j-n, etwas** *acc* **d.**, to have s.o., sth. at one's disposal.

**Disput** [dis'pu:t], *m -(e)s/-e* dispute.

**Disqualifi|kation** [diskvalifikatsi'o:n], *f -/ -en* disqualification. ◆d~**zieren** [-'tsi:rən], *v.tr.* to disqualify (s.o.).

**Dissertation** [dlsɛrtatsi'o:n], *f -/-en* dissertation, (doctoral) thesis.

**Dissident(in)** [disi'dɛnt(in)], *m -en/-en (f -/-nen)* dissident.

**Distanz** [dis'tants], *f -/-en* distance; *Fig:* (*Abstand*) detachment. ◆d~**ieren** [-'tsi:rən], *v.tr.* **sich d.**, to keep one's distance; *Fig:* **sich von j-m, etwas** *dat* **d.**, to dissociate oneself from s.o., sth. ◆d~**iert**, *adj.* detached.

**Distel** ['distəl], *f -/-n* thistle.

**Disziplin** [distsi'pli:n], *f -/-en* discipline. ◆d~**arisch** [-i'na:riʃ], *adj.* disciplinary. ◆d~**ieren** [-i'ni:rən], *v.tr.* to discipline (s.o., oneself). ◆d~**los**, *adj.* undisciplined.

**divers** [di'vɛrs], *adj.* various; (*einzelne*) miscellaneous; (*unterschiedlich*) diverse (opinions etc.).

**Divid|ende** [divi'dɛndə], *f* -/-n dividend. ◆**d~ieren** [-'di:rən], *v.tr.* to divide (a number etc.) (**durch** + *acc*, by).

**Division** [divizi'o:n], *f* -/-en division.

**doch** [dɔx], *conj. & adv.* but; (*dennoch*) yet, however; (*trotzdem*) after all; **es geht d. nicht,** it just won't work/do; **wenn er d. käme!** if only he would come! **du kommst d. (oder?)** you are coming, aren't you? **sei d. ruhig!** do be quiet! **siehst du es nicht?—D.!** can't you see it?—Oh yes, I can; **d. d.,** yes, yes O.K.

**Docht** ['dɔxt], *m* -(e)s/-e wick.

**Dock** [dɔk], *n* -s/-s dock.

**Dogge** ['dɔgə], *f* -/-n (**englische**) **D.,** mastiff; **dänische/deutsche D.,** Great Dane.

**Dogma** ['dɔgma], *n* -s/-men dogma. ◆**d~tisch** [-'ma:tiʃ], *adj.* dogmatic.

**Dohle** ['do:lə], *f* -/-n jackdaw.

**Doktor** ['dɔktɔr], *m* -s/-en doctor. ◆**D~and(in)** [-o'rant (-'randin)], *m* -en/-en (*f* -/-nen) doctoral candidate. ◆**D~arbeit,** *f* doctoral thesis. ◆**D~titel,** *m*/**D~würde,** *f* doctorate.

**Doktrin** [dɔk'tri:n], *f* -/-en doctrine. ◆**d~är** [-tri'nɛ:r], *adj.* doctrinaire.

**Dokument** [doku'mɛnt], *n* -(e)s/-e document. ◆**D~ar-** [-'ta:r-], *comb.fm.* documentary (film, programme). ◆**D~ation** [-tatsi'o:n], *f* -/-en documentation. ◆**d~ieren** [-'ti:rən], *v.tr.* to document (sth.); (*belegen*) to prove (sth.) by documents.

**Dolch** [dɔlç], *m* -(e)s/-e dagger.

**Dollar** ['dɔlar], *m* -s/-s dollar; **5 D.,** five dollars.

**dolmetsch|en** ['dɔlmɛtʃən], *v.tr.&i.* (*haben*) to interpret (a speech etc.). ◆**D~er(in),** *m* -s/- (*f* -/-nen) interpreter.

**Dom** [do:m], *m* -(e)s/-e cathedral. ◆**'D~pfaff,** *m* -en/-en bullfinch.

**domin|ant** [domi'nant], *adj.* dominant. ◆**D~anz,** *f* -/-en dominance. ◆**d~ieren,** *v.tr. & i.* (*haben*) to dominate (s.o., sth.).

**Domizil** [domi'tsi:l], *n* -s/-e abode.

**Dompteur** [dɔmp'tø:r], *m* -s/-e /**Dompteuse** [-'tø:zə], *f* -/-n (animal) tamer.

**Donau** ['do:nau]. *Pr.n.f* -. **die D.,** the (River) Danube.

**Donner** ['dɔnər], *m* -s/- thunder. ◆**d~n,** *v.i.* (*haben*) (a) (also *Fig:*) to thunder; *F:* **an die Tür d.,** to hammer at the door; *Fig:* **d~nder Beifall,** thunderous applause; (b) *F:* (*schimpfen*) to raise hell, fume. ◆**D~wetter,** *n* 1. *F:* (*Rüge*) telling off. 2. *int.* (**zum**) **D.** (**nochmal**)! good heavens!

**Donnerstag** ['dɔnərsta:k], *m* Thursday.

**doof** [do:f], *adj. P:* (a) silly, daft; (b) (*langweilig*) deadly boring.

**Doppel** ['dɔpəl]. I. *n* -s/- 1. (*Zweitschrift*) duplicate. 2. (*Tennis*) doubles. II. '**D~-,** *comb.fm.* (a) double (bed, room, knot, line, window, chin, murder etc.); (b) dual (meaning, *Th:* role etc.). ◆**'D~decker,** *m* -s/- 1. *Av:* biplane. 2. double-decker (bus). ◆**'d~deutig,** *adj.* ambiguous. ◆**'D~gänger,** *m* (*Pers.*) double. ◆**'D~haus,** *n* semi-detached/ *N.Am:* duplex house. ◆**'D~punkt,** *m* colon. ◆**'D~seitig,** *adj.* (a) double-sided; (b) (*in Zeitung*) two-page (advertisement etc.). ◆**'d~sinnig,** *adj.* ambiguous. ◆**'D~stecker,** *m El:* two-way adapter. ◆**'d~t,** *adj.* 1. double; **in d~ter Ausführung,** in duplicate; **d. verglast,** double-glazed. 2. twice the (length, size etc.); **das Buch habe ich d.,** I've got two copies of that book. ◆**'D~verdiener,** *m* 1. person with two sources of income. 2. (*Ehepaar*) **sie sind D.,** they are both earning. ◆**'d~züngig,** *adj.* two-faced.

**Dorf** [dɔrf], *n* -(e)s/-er village. ◆**'D~bewohner(in),** *m* -s/- (*f*-/-nen) villager.

**Dorn** [dɔrn], *m* 1. -(e)s/-en thorn. 2. -(e)s/-e (a) punch, awl; (b) spike (of a running shoe etc.). ◆**'D~busch,** *m* briar, thornbush. ◆**'d~ig,** *adj.* thorny (plant etc.). ◆**D~röschen.** *Pr.n.n* -s. Sleeping Beauty.

**Dörr-** ['dœr-], *comb.fm.* dried (meat, vegetables, fruit).

**Dorsch** [dɔrʃ], *m* -(e)s/-e cod(fish).

**dort** [dɔrt], *adv.* there; **d. oben,** up there; **d. drüben,** over there; **d. herum,** thereabouts. ◆**'d~'her,** *adv.* (**von**) **d.,** from there. ◆**'d~'hin,** *adv.* there; to that place. ◆**'d~ig,** *adj.* in/of that place.

**Dose** ['do:zə], *f* -/-n 1. box; (*für Tabak usw.*) jar; (*für Zucker*) bowl. 2. (*aus Blech*) *esp. N.Am:* can. 3. *El:* socket. ◆**'D~n-,** *comb.fm.* tinned, *esp. N.Am:* canned (meat etc.). ◆**'D~nmilch,** *f pl* evaporated/condensed milk. ◆**'D~nöffner,** *m* tin/ *N.Am:* can opener.

**dös|en** ['dø:zən], *v.i.* (*haben*) *F:* to doze. ◆**'d~ig,** *adj. F:* drowsy; (*stumpfsinnig*) dopey.

**dos|ieren** [do'zi:rən], *v.tr.* to measure out (medicine etc.). ◆**D~is** ['do:zis], *f* -/**Dosen** dose.

**Dotter** ['dɔtər], *m & n* -s/- yolk.

**Dozent(in)** [do'tsɛnt(in)], *m* -en/-en (*f* -/ -nen) lecturer; *N.Am:* assistant professor.

**Drache** [draxə], *m* -n/-n dragon.

**Drachen** ['draxən], *m* -s/- 1. kite. 2. *P:* (*Frau*) shrew. ◆**'D~flieger,** *m* hang-glider.

**Dragée** [dra'ʒe:], *n* -s/-s sugar-coated sweet/*N.Am:* candy/*Med:* pill.

**Draht** [dra:t]. I. *m* -(e)s/-e wire; *Pol:* **heißer D.,** hot line; *F:* **auf D. sein,** to know one's stuff. II. '**D~-,** *comb.fm.* wire (brush, basket, fence etc.). ◆**'D~haar,** *n* wire hair. ◆**'D~haar-,** *comb.fm.* wire-haired (terrier etc.).

◆**'d~ig,** *adj.* wiry (hair, person). ◆**'d~los,** *adj.* wireless (telegraphy etc.). ◆**'D~seil,** *n* (*a*) wire rope; cable; (*b*) (*für Seiltänzer*) tightrope. ◆**'D~seilbahn,** *f* cable railway; (*Kabine*) cable car. ◆**'D~zange,** *f* wire pliers. ◆**'D~zieher,** *m Fig:* string puller.

**drall**¹ [dral], *adj.* plump, buxom (girl, woman).

**Drall**², *m* -(e)s/*occ* -e spin (of a ball, bullet).

**Dram|a** ['drɑːma], *n* -s/-men drama. ◆**D~atiker** [-'mɑːtikər] *m* -s/- dramatist, playwright. ◆**d~atisch** [-'mɑːtiʃ], *adj.* dramatic.

**dran** [dran], *F:* = **daran**; **du bist d.**, it's your turn; **gut d. sein,** to be well off. ◆**'d~bleiben,** *v.i.sep.irr.12* (*sein*) *F:* (**an etwas** *dat*) **d.,** to hold on (to sth.); *Tel:* **bleiben Sie** (**bitte**) **dran!** hold the line please! ◆**'d~kommen,** *v.i.sep.irr.53* (*sein*) *F:* to have one's turn.

**Drang** [draŋ], *m* -(e)s/=e **1.** (*Druck*) pressure. **2.** (*innerer Trieb*) urge; (*plötzlich*) impulse; **D. nach Freiheit,** yearning for freedom.

**drängeln** ['drɛŋəln], *v.tr.&i.* (*haben*) to jostle (s.o.).

**drängen** ['drɛŋən], *v.* **1.** *v.tr.* (*a*) to push, shove (s.o.); (*b*) **j-n zu etwas** *dat* **d./j-n d., etwas zu tun,** urge s.o. to do sth.; **er wollte sie nicht d.,** he didn't want to rush her. **2.** *v.i.* (*haben*) (*a*) (*Menschenmenge usw.*) to push, shove; (*b*) **auf Zahlung usw. d.,** to press for payment etc.; *Fig:* **die Zeit drängt,** time is running short.

**drastisch** ['drastiʃ], *adj.* **1.** drastic (measures etc.). **2.** (*derb, direkt*) uncompromising.

**drauf** [drauf], *F:* = **darauf; d. und dran sein, etwas zu tun,** to be on the point of doing sth. ◆**'D~gänger,** *m* -s/- gogetter; (*waghalsig*) daredevil. ◆**'d~gehen,** *v.i.sep.irr.36* (*sein*) *F:* (*a*) to kick the bucket; (*b*) (*Zeit, Geld*) to be spent. ◆**'d~zahlen,** *v.tr.sep. F:* to pay (sth.) on top.

**draußen** ['drausən], *adv.* outside; (*im Freien*) out of doors; **da d.,** out there.

**Dreck** [drɛk]. **I.** *m* -(e)s/*no pl* **1.** *F:* muck; (*Schlamm*) mud; **j-n, etwas in den D. ziehen,** to run s.o., sth. down. **2.** *P:* (*Sache*) business; (*Kleinigkeit*) trifle. **3.** *P:* **ein D./der letzte D. sein,** to be utterly worthless/(*Pers.*) the lowest of the low. **II.** **'D~,** *comb.fm. F:* dirty, (*stärker*) filthy (work, thing, *Fig:* hole, paw etc.); (*mies*) lousy (weather etc.). ◆**'d~ig,** *adj. F:* dirty (hands, *Fig:* joke etc.); muddy (path etc.); filthy (weather, *Fig:* book etc.); **ihm geht es d.,** he's in a bad way/(*finanziell*) hard up.

**Dreh** [dre:]. **I.** *m* -s/-s *F:* **1.** (*Einfall*) idea; (*Trick*) knack. **2.** (*Drehung*) turn; *Fig:* **einer Geschichte einen D. geben,** to give a story a twist. **II.** **'D~-,** *comb.fm.* (*a*) revolving (door etc.); (*b*) rotary (motion etc.); (*c*) swivel (chair, *Tchn:* joint etc.). ◆**'D~arbeiten,** *fpl* shooting (of a film). ◆**'D~bank,** *f* (turning) lathe. ◆**'d~bar,** *adj.* rotatable; revolving (chair, *Th:* stage etc.); (*schwenkbar*) swivelling. ◆**'D~buch,** *n* (film) script; screenplay. ◆**'d~en,** *v.* **1.** *v.tr.* (*a*) to turn (a key, handle, one's head etc.); (*im Kreis*) to rotate, (*schnell*) spin (a wheel etc.); **sich d.,** to turn, (*im Kreis*) rotate, (*schnell*) spin; **sich um etwas** *acc* **d.,** to revolve around sth., (*Gespräch usw.*) be concerned with sth.; *Fig:* **alles dreht sich um ihn,** he is the centre of everything; (*b*) to roll (a cigarette); *Cin:* to shoot (a film), film (a scene). **2.** *v.i.* (*haben*) (*a*) (*Schiff usw.*) to turn; (*b*) (*Wind*) to change; (*c*) **an etwas** *dat* **d.,** to turn, *Fig:* twist sth. ◆**'D~er,** *m* -s/- turner; lathe operator. ◆**'D~kreuz,** *n* turnstile. ◆**'D~orgel,** *f* barrel organ. ◆**'D~scheibe,** *f* (*a*) turntable; (*b*) (*Töpferei*) potter's wheel. ◆**'D~stuhl,** *m* swivel chair. ◆**'D~ung,** *f* -/-en turn; (*um die Achse*) rotation; (*im Kreis*) gyration. ◆**'D~zahl,** *f* (number of) revolutions; speed. ◆**'D~zahlmesser,** *m* revolution counter.

**drei** [drai]. **I.** *num. adj.* three. **II. D.,** *f* -/ -en (number) three. ◆**'D~eck,** *n* triangle. ◆**'d~eckig,** *adj.* triangular. ◆**'D~eck(s)tuch,** *n* **1.** shawl. **2.** *Med:* triangular bandage. ◆**'D~ecksverhältnis,** *n* ménage à trois. ◆**'D~einigkeit,** *f* -/*no pl* trinity. ◆**'d~er'lei,** *adj.* of three kinds. ◆**'d~fach,** *adj.* threefold, triple; **in d~facher Ausfertigung,** in triplicate; **das D~fache,** three times as much. ◆**'D~faltigkeit,** *f* -/*no pl* trinity. ◆**'d~jährig,** *adj.* three-year-old (child etc.); three-year (appointment etc.). ◆**D~'könige,** *pl*/**D~'königsfest** *m* Epiphany. ◆**'d~mal,** *adv.* three times. ◆**'D~rad,** *n* tricycle; *Aut:* three-wheeler. ◆**'d~ßig,** *num. adj.* thirty. ◆**'d~ßiger,** **I.** *adj.* **die d. Jahre,** the thirties. **II. D.,** *m* -s/- person in his/her thirties. ◆**'d~ßigjährig,** *adj.* thirty-year old (person); thirty years' (war etc.). ◆**'d~ßigste(r,s),** *num. adj.* thirtieth. ◆**'d~stellig,** *adj.* three-figure (number). ◆**'d~teilig,** *adj.* in three parts; *Cl:* three-piece (suit). ◆**'d~'viertel,** *adj.* three quarters; **d. voll,** three-quarters full. ◆**D~viertel'stunde,** *f* three quarters of an hour. ◆**D~'vierteltakt,** *m* three-four time. ◆**'d~zehn,** *adj.* thirteen.

**dreinreden** ['drainre:dən], *v.i.sep.* (*haben*) (*unterbrechen*) to interrupt; (*sich einmischen*) to interfere.

**dreist** ['draist], *adj.* (*kühn*) audacious; (*frech*) impudent. ◆**'D~igkeit,** *f* -/-en audacity; impudence.

**Dresch|e** ['drɛʃə], *f -/no pl F:* thrashing, hiding. ◆'**d~en**, *v.tr.irr.* (a) to thresh (corn etc.); *Fig:* **Phrasen d.**, to talk in platitudes; (b) to thrash (s.o.).

**Dress|eur** [drɛ'sø:r], *m -s/-e* (animal) trainer. ◆**d~ieren** [-'si:rən], *v.tr.* to train (an animal); ◆**D~ur** [-'su:r], *f -/-en* training.

**Drill** [dril], *m -(e)s/no pl* drill. ◆'**D~bohrer**, *m -s/-* (spiral) drill. ◆'**d~en**, *v.tr.* to drill.

**Drilling** ['driliŋ], *m -s/-e* triplet.

**drin** [drin], *F:* = **darin; mehr ist nicht d.**, you can't expect any more.

**dring|en** ['driŋən], *v.i.irr.* (a) *(sein)* **durch etwas** *acc* **d.**, to penetrate sth.; **aus etwas** *dat* **d.**, to break/*(Flüssigkeit)* leak out of sth.; *(Geräusch)* to come from sth.; **bis zu j-m d.**, to get as far as s.o.; (b) *(haben)* **auf etwas** *acc* **d.**, to press for sth. ◆'**d~end**, *adj.* urgent (matter, *Tel:* call etc.); imminent (danger). **d. verdächtig**, strongly suspected. ◆'**d~lich**, *adj.* urgent. ◆'**D~lichkeit**, *f -/no pl* urgency.

**Drink** [driŋk], *m -s/-s* (alcoholic) drink.

**drinnen** ['drinən], *adv.* inside.

**dritt** [drit]. **I.** *adv. phr.* **zu d.**, in a group of three; **wir waren zu d.**, there were three of us. **II.** '**d~-**, *comb.fm.* third (largest, smallest etc.). ◆'**d~e(r,s)**, *adj.* third; **aus d~er Hand**, at third hand; indirectly; *also Jur:* **D~e(r)**, third party; **im Beisein D~er**, in the presence of others. ◆'**D~el**, *n -s/-* third. ◆'**d~eln**, *v.tr.* to divide (sth.) into three. ◆'**d~ens**, *adv.* thirdly.

**Drog|e** ['dro:gə], *f -/-n* drug. ◆**D~enabhängige(r)**, *m & f* drug addict. ◆**D~erie** [drogə'ri:], *f -/-n* (non-dispensing) chemist's shop, *N.Am:* drugstore. ◆**D~ist(in)** [dro'gist(in)], *m -en/-en* (f -/-nen) (non-dispensing) chemist, *N.Am:* druggist.

**Droh|brief** ['dro:bri:f], *m* threatening letter. ◆'**d~en**, *v.i.* *(haben)* to threaten. ◆'**d~end**, *adj.* threatening (attitude etc.); menacing (tone, gesture etc.); imminent (danger). ◆'**D~ung**, *f -/-en* threat.

**dröhnen** ['drø:nən], *v.i.* *(haben)* to boom, *(hallen)* resound; *(sehr laut)* to roar; *(Maschinen usw.)* to throb, *(in der Ferne)* drone.

**drollig** ['droliç], *adj.* funny; *(niedlich)* sweet; *(seltsam)* quaint.

**Drops** ['drops], *m & n -/-* (fruit) drop, boiled sweet; *N.Am:* hard candy.

**Droschke** ['droʃkə], *f -/-n* cab.

**Drossel** ['drosəl], *f -/-n* thrush. ◆'**d~n**, *v.tr.* (a) to throttle (an engine); (b) to cut down (speed, imports etc.).

**drüben** ['dry:bən], *adv.* over there.

**drüber** ['dry:bər], *adv. F:* = **darüber**.

**Druck¹** [druk], *m -(e)s/=e* pressure; squeeze (of s.o.'s hand); *Fig:* **j-n unter D. setzen**, to put pressure on s.o.; *F:*

**in/im D. sein**, to be pressed for time. ◆'**D~knopf**, *m (Verschluß)* press-stud; *(klein)* snap fastener. ◆'**D~luft**, *f -/no pl* compressed air.

**Druck²**. **I.** *m -(e)s/-e* **1.** *no pl* (a) printing; **in D. gehen**, to go to press. **2.** *(Kunst.)* print, engraving. **II.** '**D~-**, *comb.fm.* (a) printing (costs, process etc.); (b) *(gedruckt)* printed (pattern, page, *Cl:* material etc.). ◆'**D~buchstabe**, *m* block letter. ◆'**d~en**, *v.tr.* to print (a book etc.). ◆'**D~er**, *m -s/-* printer. ◆**D~e'rei**, *f -/-en* printing works, *F:* printer's. ◆'**D~erschwärze**, *f -/-n* printer's ink. ◆'**D~fehler**, *m* misprint. ◆'**D~sache**, *f* printed matter. ◆'**D~schrift**, *f* block capitals/letters.

**Drück|eberger** ['drykəbergər], *m -s/- F:* shirker; *Mil:* malingerer. ◆'**d~en**, *v.* **1.** *v.tr.* (a) to press (s.o., sth.); **j-n an sich/an die Brust d.**, to embrace/hug s.o.; **der Schuh drückt (mich)**, this shoe is too tight; (b) *F:* **sich vor etwas** *dat*/**um etwas** *acc* **d.**, to dodge/evade sth. **2.** *v.i.* *(haben)* to press; **auf den Knopf d.**, to press the button. ◆'**d~end**, *adj.* heavy (burden, debt etc.); oppressive (heat etc.). ◆'**D~er**, *m -s/-* (a) door handle; (b) push-button; *F:* **am D. sein/sitzen**, to be in control.

**drum** [drum], *adv. F:* = **darum; mit allem D. und Dran**, with all the trimmings.

**drunter** ['druntər], *adv. F:* = **darunter; d. und drüber**, upside down.

**Drüse** ['dry:zə], *f -/-n* gland. ◆'**D~n-**, *comb.fm.* glandular (fever etc.).

**Dschungel** ['dʒuŋəl], *m -s/-* jungle.

**Dschunke** ['dʒuŋkə], *f -/-n* junk.

**du** [du:]. **I.** *pers. pron.* you; **mit j-m auf du und du stehen/per du sein**, to be on familiar terms with s.o. **II. Du**, *n -(s)/-(s)* you; **j-m das Du anbieten**, to suggest to s.o. that he/she use the familiar form of address.

**Dübel** ['dy:bəl], *m -s/-* wallplug.

**duck|en** ['dukən], *v.tr.* (a) to humble (s.o.); *F:* to do (s.o.) down; (b) **sich d.**, to duck. ◆'**D~mäuser**, *m -s/-* cringer; *F:* yes-man.

**dudel|n** ['du:dəln], *v.* **1.** *v.i.* *(haben)* to tootle, *(Radio usw.)* drone (on). **2.** *v.tr.* to drone out (a song, tune). ◆'**D~sack**, *m* bagpipes.

**Duett** [du'ɛt], *n -(e)s/-e* duet.

**Duft** [duft], *m -(e)s/=e* scent, fragrance (of flowers etc.); aroma (of coffee, a cigar etc.). ◆'**d~en**, *v.i.* *(haben)* to smell, be fragrant. ◆'**d~ig**, *adj.* fine, gauzy (material); light, dainty (dress etc.).

**duld|en** ['duldən], *v.tr.* to bear (pain etc.); to tolerate (injustice etc.); **etwas stillschweigend d.**, to shut one's eyes to sth. ◆'**d~sam**, *adj.* tolerant. ◆'**D~ung**, *f -/-en* toleration.

**dumm** [dum], *adj.* **1.** (a) stupid (person, action); *N.Am:* dumb (person); *(töricht)* foolish, silly; **d~es Zeug reden**, to talk nonsense; (b) **er ist immer der D~e dabei**, he always comes off worst. **2.** *F:* (*unangenehm*) stupid, awkward (business, time etc.); **zu/wie d.!** what a nuisance! **die Sache wird mir zu d.**, that's too much. ◆**'d~dreist**, *adj.* impudent. ◆**'D~heit**, *f* -/-en **1.** *no pl* stupidity; (*Leichtsinn*) silliness, foolishness. **2.** stupid thing, folly. ◆**'D~kopf**, *m F:* fool; ass.

**dumpf** [dumpf], *adj.* dull (sound, *Fig:* pain etc.); (*gedämpft*) muffled (sound).

**Düne** ['dy:nə], *f* -/-n dune.

**Dung** [duŋ], *m* -(e)s/*no pl* dung.

**Düng|emittel** ['dyŋəmitəl], *n* fertilizer. ◆**d'~en**, *v.tr.* to fertilize, manure (a field etc.). ◆**'D~er**, *m* -s/- fertilizer, (*Mist*) manure.

**dunkel** ['duŋkəl]. **I.** *adj.* (a) dark; **d. werden**, to get dark; (*also Fig:*) **im d~n**, in the dark; (b) *Fig:* (*unbestimmt*) vague (idea, memory, suspicion etc.); (*unklar*) obscure (passage etc.); (c) (*zweifelhaft*) **dunkle Geschäfte**, shady deals. **II. D.**, *n* -s/*no pl Lit:* darkness. ◆**'D~heit**, *f -/no pl* darkness. ◆**'D~kammer**, *f* darkroom. ◆**'d~n**, *v.* **1.** *v.i.* (*haben*) to grow dark. **2.** *v.tr.* to darken (colours etc.). ◆**'D~ziffer**, *f* unpublished but suspected figure/statistic.

**Dünkel** ['dyŋkəl], *m* -s/*no pl Lit:* conceit. ◆**'d~haft**, *adj. Lit:* conceited.

**dünn** [dyn], *adj.* thin; (a) slim (figure, volume); spindly (legs); (b) (*schwach*) weak (coffee etc.); *Fig:* **d. gesät**, few and far between. ◆**'D~darm**, *m* small intestine. ◆**'d~flüssig**, *adj.* thin, watery (liquid).

**Dunst** [dunst], *m* -(e)s/-e mist; (*in der Ferne, auch Abgase usw.*) haze; (*Dampf*) vapour. ◆**'d~ig**, *adj.* misty, hazy; (*verräuchert*) smoky.

**dünsten** ['dynstən], *v.tr. Cu:* to steam (fish, vegetables); (*schmoren*) to braise (meat etc.).

**Dünung** ['dy:nuŋ], *f* -/-en swell.

**Duo** ['du:o], *n* -s/-s duo.

**Duplikat** [dupli'ka:t], *n* -(e)s/-e duplicate; (*Abschrift*) copy.

**Dur** [du:r], *n* -/- major (key); **A-D.**, A major.

**durch** [durç]. **I.** *prep. + acc* (a) through; (*mittels*) **d. die Post**, by post; **d. Zufall**, by chance; **etwas d. Lautsprecher bekanntgeben**, to announce sth. over loudspeakers; (b) (*von*) **d. ein Erdbeben zerstört**, destroyed by an earthquake. **II.** *adv.* **1.** (*zeitlich*) (a) **den Sommer d.**, throughout the summer; (b) *F:* (*vorbei*) **es ist schon elf Uhr d.**, it's already gone eleven. **2. d. und d.**, thoroughly.

**'durcharbeiten** *v.sep.* **1.** *v.tr.* to study (sth.) thoroughly. **2.** *v.i.* (*haben*) to work without a break; **die ganze Nacht d.**, to work right through the night.

**'durchatmen**, *v.i.sep.*(*haben*) to breathe deeply.

**durchaus** ['durç(')?aus], *adv.* **1.** (*unbedingt*) absolutely, at all costs. **2. es ist d. möglich/richtig**, it is perfectly possible/correct; **d. nicht**, not at all.

**'durchbeißen**, *v.tr.sep.irr.4* (a) to bite through (sth.); (b) *F:* **sich d.**, to struggle through.

**'durchblättern**, *v.tr.sep.* to glance/thumb through (a book etc.).

**'Durchblick**, *m* **1.** view. **2.** *F:* overall view; **den D. verlieren**, to lose track (of things). ◆**d~en**, *v.i.sep.* (*haben*) (a) to look through (**durch etwas** *acc*, sth.); (b) **etwas d. lassen**, to make sth. clear; **blickst du hier durch?** can you make anything of this?

**Durch'blutung**, *f -/no pl* circulation.

**durch'bohren**, *v.tr. insep.* (*Messer usw.*) to pierce (sth.); *Fig:* **j-n mit seinem Blick d.**, to transfix s.o. with a glance.

**durchbrechen**, *v.irr.14* **1.** ['durçbreçən] *v.tr.sep.* to break (sth.) in two; to break through (a wall etc.). **2.** ['durçbreçən] *v.i.sep.* (*sein*) (a) (*Stock usw.*) to break in two; (b) (*Sonne, Mil: Truppen*) to break through. **3.** [durç'breçən] *v.tr.insep.* to break/burst (through) (sth., a dam etc.).

**'durchbrennen**, *v.i.sep.irr.15* (a) (*haben*) (*Ofen usw.*) to keep burning; (b) (*sein*) **die Sicherung ist durchgebrannt**, the fuse has blown; (c) (*sein*) *F:* to run away.

**'durchbringen**, *v.tr.sep.irr.16* (a) to get (s.o., sth.) through, pull (a patient) through; (b) (*vergeuden*) to squander (money).

**'Durchbruch**, *m* breakthrough; cutting (of teeth).

**durch'denken**, *v.tr.insep.irr.17* to think (sth.) over; **gut durchdacht**, well thought out.

**'durchdrehen**, *v.sep.* **1.** *v.tr.* to put (meat etc.) through the mincer. **2.** *v.i.* (*haben*) (a) (*Räder*) to spin; (b) *F:* (*Pers.*) to panic, go round the bend.

**durchdringen**, *v.irr.19* **1.** ['durçdriŋən], *v.i.sep.* (*sein*) (**durch etwas** *acc*) **d.**, to penetrate (sth.). **2.** [durç'driŋən] *v.tr.insep.* to penetrate (sth.); **j-n d.**, (*Gefühl usw.*) to fill s.o.; (*Idee*) to seize s.o.'s imagination.

**'durchdrücken**, *v.tr.sep.* (a) to press, force (sth.); *F:* to push through (a plan etc.); (b) to straighten (one's knees, back).

**durchein'ander. I.** *adv.* (*Sachen usw.*) jumbled (up); *Pej:* in a mess; **ich bin ganz d.**, I'm all mixed up. **II. D.**, *n* -s/*no pl* disorder; mess; (*Verwechslung usw.*) mix-up. ◆**d~bringen**, *v.tr.sep.irr.16* to confuse (s.o.); to muddle up (papers, words etc.). ◆**d~reden**, *v.i. sep.* (*haben*) **alle redeten durcheinander**, everyone was talking at once.

**durchfahren**, *v. irr.26* **1.** ['durçfa:rən] (*sein*) (a) to drive/travel through (sth.); **der Zug fährt bis X durch**, the train doesn't stop until X. **2.** [durç'fɑːrən] *v.tr.insep.* to travel/*Aut:* drive through (an area, country etc.); *Fig:* (*Schreck, Gedanken usw.*) to pass through (s.o., s.o.'s mind).

'**Durchfahrt**, *f* -/-en sie sind nur auf der **D.**, they are just passing through; **D. verboten**, no thoroughfare.

'**Durchfall**, *m* diarrhoea. ◆'d~en, *v.i.sep.irr.27* (*sein*) (*a*) (**durch etwas**) **d.**, to fall through (sth.); (*b*) *Th:* (*Stück*) to be a flop; (**bei der Prüfung**) **d.**, to fail (the examination); **j-n d. lassen**, to fail s.o.

'**durchfinden**, *v.i. & refl.sep.irr.9* (*haben*) (**sich**) **d.**, to find one's way (through).

**durch'forschen**, *v.tr.insep.* to explore.

**durch'froren**, *adj.* frozen stiff.

'**durchführ|bar**, *adj.* practicable. ◆'d~en, *v.sep.* **1.** *v.i.* (*haben*) **durch etwas d.**, to go through sth. **2.** *v.tr.* (*a*) **j-n** (**durch etwas** *acc*) **d.**, to take s.o. through, show s.o. round (sth.); (*b*) (*verwirklichen*) to carry out (a plan, task, an order etc.); to complete (work etc.); to hold (a meeting); to make (a count). ◆'D~**ung**, *f* -/-en carrying out (*Vollendung*) completion.

'**Durchgang**, *m* -(e)s/-e **1.** passage (through), way through; **D. verboten**, no thoroughfare. **2.** (*Stadium*) phase; *Sp:* round. ◆'D~**s-** *comb.fm.* through (road, station etc.); *esp. Com:* transit (visa, trade etc.). ◆'D~**slager**, *n* transit camp. ◆'D~**sstadium**, *n* transitional stage. ◆'D~**sverkehr**, *m* through traffic.

**durchgängig** ['-gɛniç], *adj.* general; universal (opinion etc.).

'**durchgehen**, *v.irr.sep.36* **1.** *v.i.* (*sein*) (*a*) (**durch etwas** *acc*) **d.**, to walk through (sth.); (*b*) (*Antrag, Gesetz usw.*) to go through; **etwas d. lassen**, to let sth. pass; **j-m etwas d. lassen**, to let s.o. get away with sth.; (*c*) (*Pferd*) to bolt; *F:* (*durchbrennen*) to run away. **2.** *v.tr.* (*sein*) to go/look through (a list, book etc.). ◆'d~**d**, *adj.* **1.** through (train, ticket, carriage etc.). **2.** continuous; **d. geöffnet**, open day and night; (*Geschäft*) no lunchtime closing.

'**durchgreifen**, *v.i.sep.irr.43* (*haben*) (*a*) (**durch etwas** *acc*) **d.**, to reach through (sth.); (*b*) to take (decisive) action.

'**durchhalten**, *v.sep.irr.45* **1.** *v.i.* (*haben*) to hold out. **2.** *v.tr.* to see (sth.) through; **er kann das Tempo nicht d.**, he cannot stand the pace.

'**durchkämpfen**, *v.tr.sep.* (*a*) to fight (sth.) out; *Fig:* to achieve (sth.) (after a struggle); (*b*) **sich** (**durch etwas** *acc*) **d.**, to fight one's way through (sth.).

'**durchkommen**, *v.i.sep.irr.53* (*sein*) (*a*) to come through, (*Regen usw.*) come in; *Tel: etc:* to get through; (*b*) (*Patient*) to pull through; (*c*) to manage/get by (with sth.); *F:* **damit wirst du** (**bei ihm**) **nicht**

**d.**, that won't get you anywhere (with him).

**durch'kreuzen**, *v.tr. insep.* to thwart (s.o.'s plans etc.).

'**durchlassen**, *v.tr.sep.irr.57* to let (s.o., sth.) (pass) through; **Wasser d.**, to leak.

'**durchlässig**, *adj.* (*a*) (*wasserd.*) porous (material, soil etc.); leaky (shoes, roof etc.); (*b*) (*lichtd.*) transparent.

**durchlauf|en**, *v.irr.58* **1.** ['durçlaufən], *v.i.sep.* (**durch etwas** *acc*) **d.**, to run through (sth.). **2.** [durç'laufən] *v.tr.insep.* (*a*) to pass through (stages etc.); (*b*) *Sp:* to cover (a distance). ◆'D~**erhitzer**, *m* constant flow water heater.

'**durchleben**, *v.tr.sep.* to live through (a period), experience (sth.).

'**durchlesen**, *v.tr.sep.irr.61* to read (sth.) through.

**durch'leuchten**, *v.tr.insep.* to X-ray (s.o., sth.); *Fig:* to examine (a case, s.o.'s past etc.); *F:* to screen (s.o.).

**durch'löchern**, *v.tr.insep.* to punch holes in (sth.); **von Kugeln durchlöchert**, riddled with bullets.

'**durchmachen**, *v.tr.sep.* to go through (school, hard times etc.); to undergo (training, a process, an operation etc.).

'**Durchmesser**, *m* -s/- diameter.

**durch'nässen**, *v.tr.insep.* to drench (s.o., sth.), soak (clothes etc.) (through).

'**durchnehmen**, *v.tr.sep.irr.69* *Sch:* to go through, *F:* do (a text, etc.).

'**durchnumerieren**, *v.tr.sep.* to number (pages etc.) consecutively.

'**durchpausen**, *v.tr.sep.* to trace (a picture etc.).

'**durchpeitschen**, *v.tr.sep.* (*a*) to whip (s.o.) soundly; (*b*) to rush (a law etc.) through.

**durchqueren** [durç'kveːrən], *v.tr.insep.* to cross.

'**Durchreiche**, *f* -/-n service hatch. ◆'d~n, *v.tr.sep.* to hand (sth.) through.

'**Durchreise**, *f* -/-n journey through (**durch ein Land usw.**), a country etc.); **auf der D. sein**, to be passing through. ◆'D~**visum**, *n* transit visa.

'**durchringen**, *v.refl.sep.irr.19* **sich zu etwas** *dat* **d.**, to make up one's mind finally to (do) sth.

'**durchrosten**, *v.i.sep.* (*sein*) to rust through.

**durchs** [durçs], *prep.* = **durch das.**

'**Durchsage**, *f* -/-n announcement; *F:* (news)flash.

'**durchsagen**, *v.tr.sep.* to announce (information etc.).

**durch'schau|bar**, *adj.* obvious, transparent (motives etc.); **schwer d.**, puzzling. ◆'d~en, *v.tr.insep.* to see through (s.o., a trick, motives etc.).

'**durchscheinen**, *v.i.sep.irr.79* (*haben*) (*Licht*) to shine through; (*Muster usw.*) to show through. ◆'d~**d**, *adj.* transparent (material).

'**Durchschlag**, *m* -(e)s/-e **1.** carbon copy. **2.** *Cu:* colander; strainer. ◆'**d~en**, *v.sep.irr.85* **1.** *v.tr.* (*a*) to break (sth.) through/in half; (*b*) **sich d.** to struggle through; **sich alleine d.**, to fend for oneself. **2.** *v.i.* (*haben*) (*Tinte, Farbe usw.*) to come/show through. ◆'**d~end**, *adj.* effective (measures etc.); powerful (effect etc.); convincing (argument, evidence); **d~ender Erfolg**, sensational success. ◆'**D~skraft**, *f* -/*no pl* (*a*) penetrating power; penetration (of a shell etc.); (*b*) *Fig:* force (of an idea, argument); effectiveness (of proof etc.).

**durchschneiden**, *v.tr.irr.59* **1.** ['durç-ʃnaidn] *v.sep.* to cut (sth.) through/(in zwei **Teile**) in half. **2.** [durç'ʃnaidn] *v.insep.* to cut through (sth.).

'**Durchschnitt**, *m* **1.** average; **über/unter dem D.**, above/below average. **2.** (*Schnitt*) section (through sth.). ◆'**d~lich**, (*a*) *adj.* average; (*b*) *adv.* on (an) average. ◆'**D~s-**, *comb.fm.* (*a*) average (age, price, speed, temperature etc.); (*b*) ordinary (education etc.). ◆'**D~smensch**, *m* man in the street.

'**Durchschrift**, *f* carbon copy.

'**durchsehen**, *v.sep.irr.92* **1.** *v.i.* (*haben*) (**durch etwas** *acc*) **d.**, to see through (sth.). **2.** *v.tr.* (*a*) to look/go/(*flüchtig*) glance through, (*prüfend*) check (a book, papers etc.).

**durchsetzen** *v.tr.* **1.** ['durçzɛtsən] *v.sep.* (*a*) to get/(*mit Gewalt*) force (a reform, etc.) through; **seinen Willen d.**, to get one's own way; (*b*) **sich d.**, to assert oneself, (*seinen Willen d.*) get one's way; (*Produkt*) to catch on; **er kann sich nicht d.**, he has no authority. **2.** [durç'zɛtsən] *v.insep.* to intersperse (sth.) (with sth.).

'**Durchsicht**, *f* -/*no pl* inspection; **zur D.**, for information. ◆'**d~ig**, *adj.* transparent (material); *Fig:* obvious (plan, deception etc.). ◆'**D~igkeit**, *f* -/*no pl* transparency.

'**durchsickern**, *v.i.sep.* (*haben*) (*Blut usw.*) to seep/trickle through; *Fig:* (*Geheimnis*) to leak out.

'**durchsieben**, *v.tr.sep.* to sieve, sift (flour etc.); *Fig:* to sift through.

'**durchsprechen**, *v.tr.sep.irr.14* to discuss (sth.) (thoroughly).

'**durchstehen**, *v.tr.sep.irr.100* to come through (difficulties, a test etc.); to withstand (pressure); **das Tempo d.**, to stand the pace.

**durch'stöbern**, *v.tr. insep.* to rummage through (drawers, clothes etc.); to ransack (a house, room etc.).

'**durchstreichen**, *v.tr.sep.irr.40* to cross out, delete (a word etc.).

**durch'such|en**, *v.tr.insep.* to search (s.o., a house etc.); (*Polizei*) to frisk (s.o.). ◆**D~ung**, *f* -/-**en** search. ◆**D~ungsbefehl**, *m* search warrant.

'**durchtrainiert**, *adj. Sp:* in top condition.

**durch'tränken**, *v.tr.insep.* to soak (sth.).

**durch'trieben**, *adj.* cunning, sly.

**durch'wachsen**, *adj.* streaky (bacon).

'**durchwählen**, *v.i.sep.* (*haben*) *Tel:* to dial direct.

**durchweg** ['durçvɛk], *adv.* without exception.

'**durchzählen**, *v.tr.sep.* to count (all the people/things).

**durchziehen**, *v.irr.113* **1.** ['durçtsi:ən] *v.tr.sep.* (*a*) **etwas (durch etwas** *acc*) **d.**, to pull sth. through (sth.); (*b*) *F:* to see (sth.) through; to complete (sth.); (*c*) (*Idee, Motiv usw.*) **sich durch ein Werk d.**, to run through a work. **2.** ['durçtsi:ən] *v.i.sep.* (*sein*) to pass/go through; to march through. **3.** [durç'tsi:ən] *v.tr.insep.* to pass/go through (an area, *Fig:* s.o.); (*Motiv usw.*) to run through (a work etc.).

'**Durchzug**, *m* **1.** passage through. **2.** (*Zugluft*) through draught/*N.Am:* draft.

**dürfen** ['dyrfən], *modal aux. vb.* (*a*) **etwas tun d.**, to be allowed to do sth.; **darf ich mitkommen?—ja, du darfst**, may I come too?—yes, you may; **hier darf nicht geraucht werden**, smoking is not permitted here; **darfst du das?** are you allowed to do that? (*b*) (*Höflichkeitsformeln*) **darf ich Sie bitten, mir zu folgen?** would you follow me please? **wenn ich bitten darf**, if you don't mind; please; (*im Geschäft*) **was darf es sein?** can I help you? (*c*) **du darfst dich nicht darüber aufregen**, you mustn't worry about it; **sie darf nichts davon wissen**, she must not know anything about it; **das hätte er nicht tun d.**, he ought not to have done that; (*d*) **das darf doch nicht wahr sein!** it can't be (true)! **er dürfte bald kommen**, he will probably come soon.

**dürftig** ['dyrftiç], *adj.* **1.** poor (dwelling, garment etc.); meagre (wages etc.); (*b*) (*unzulänglich*) inadequate; poor (piece of work, excuse, substitute etc.). ◆'**D~keit**, *f* -/*no pl* (*a*) poverty; meagreness; (*b*) inadequacy; poor quality.

**dürr** [dyr], *adj.* **1.** dry (branches etc.); arid (desert); barren (soil, *Fig:* years). **2.** (*hager*) gaunt (person); scraggy (limb, neck). ◆**D~e**, *f* -/-**n 1.** (*Regenmangel*) drought. **2.** *no pl* aridity; dryness.

**Durst** [durst], *m* -(e)s/*no pl* thirst (**nach** + *dat*/**auf** + *acc*, for); **D. haben**, to be thirsty. ◆'**d~ig**, *adj.* thirsty (**auf** + *acc*, for).

**Dusche** ['du:ʃə], *f* -/-**n** shower. ◆**d~n**, *v.i.* (*haben*) & *refl.* (**sich**) (**kalt/warm**) **d.**, to have a (cold/warm) shower.

**Düse** ['dy:zə], *f* -/-**n** nozzle; jet (of a carburettor). ◆'**D~n-**, *comb.fm. esp. Av:* jet (bomber etc.).

**Dussel** ['dusəl], *m* -s/- *F:* sucker.

**düster** ['dy:stər], *adj.* gloomy (room, light, *Fig:* mood etc.); sombre (colours, landscape etc.). ◆'**D~keit**, *f* -/*no pl* darkness; (*also Fig:*) gloom.

**Dutzend** ['dutsənt], *n* -s/-**e** dozen.

◆'d~ **mal**, *adv.* a dozen times; *F:* dozens of times. ◆'**D~mensch**, *m* run-of-the-mill type. ◆'d~**weise**, *adv.* by the dozen.

**duz|en** ['duːtsən], *v.tr.* j-n d., to call s.o. 'du', be on familiar terms with s.o. ◆'**D~freund(in)**, *m* (*f*) close friend (whom one calls 'du').

**Dynam|ik** [dy'naːmik], *f* -/no pl 1. dynamics. 2. *Fig:* vitality. ◆d~**isch**, *adj.* dynamic.

**Dynamit** [dyna'miːt], *n* -s/no pl dynamite.

**Dynamo** ['dyːnamo], *m* -s/-s dynamo, generator.

**Dynastie** [dynas'tiː], *f* -/-n dynasty.

**D-Zug** ['deːtsuːk], *m* express train.

# E

**E, e** [eː], *n* -/- (the letter) E, e.

**Ebbe** ['ɛbə], *f* -/-n low tide.

**eben** ['eːbən]. **I.** *adj.* flat (surface, country etc.); level (ground); (*glatt*) smooth. **II.** *adv.* **1.** (*verstärkend*) just; (*a*) (*genau*) precisely, exactly; (*b*) simply; **dann muß er e. hier bleiben,** then he'll just have to stay here. **2.** (*gerade*) e. **noch**, only just; **ich komme, wenn ich e. kann,** I'll come if I possibly can; **ich wollte e. gehen,** I was just about to leave. ◆'**E~bild**, *n Lit:* image. ◆e~**bürtig**, *adj.* of equal birth/rank; worthy (opponent). ◆'e~'**da**, *adv.* in that very place; (*bei Zitaten*) ibidem (*usu. abbr.* ibid.). ◆'**E~e**, *f* -/-n 1. *Geog:* plain. 2. *Mth:* (*Fläche*) plane. 3. *Fig:* (*Stufe*) level. ◆'e~**erdig**, *adj.* on the ground/*N.Am:* first floor. ◆'e~**falls**, *adv.* also. ◆'**E~heit**, *f* -/no pl evenness; smoothness. ◆'**E~maß**, *n* -es/no pl harmony; regularity (of features). ◆'e~**so**, *adv.* just as (**wie**, as). ◆'e~**sogut**, *adv.* **er hätte e. hier bleiben können,** he might just as well have stayed here. ◆'e~**soviel**, *adv.* just as much/(*pl*) many. ◆'e~**sowenig**, *adv.* just as little/as few.

**Eber** ['eːbər], *m* -s/- boar.

**ebnen** ['eːbnən], *v.tr.* to level, smooth (ground, a surface etc.).

**Echo** ['ɛço], *n* -s/-s echo.

**echt** [ɛçt], *adj.* (*a*) genuine; real (pearls, silk, leather, *Fig:* problem etc.); true (feelings, friendship etc.); (*b*) *adv. F:* (*verstärkend*) really; **das ist e. Peter!** that's typical of Peter! ◆'**E~heit**, *f* -/no pl sincerity (of feelings etc.); authenticity (of a painting etc.).

**Eck** [ɛk]. **I.** *n* -s/-e(n) = Ecke; übers E., diagonally. **II.** 'E~-, *comb.fm.* corner (house, cupboard, stone, table, room, *Sp:* throw, hit etc.). ◆'**E~ball**, *m* corner (kick). ◆'**E~e**, *f* -/-n (*a*) corner; **es fehlt an allen E~n und Enden,** there is a shortage of everything; (*b*) *Sp:* corner (kick, throw). ◆e~**ig** ['ɛkiç], *adj.* angular; square (brackets etc.); *Fig:* awkward (movements). ◆'**E~zahn**, *m* canine tooth.

**edel** ['eːdəl], *adj.* noble; fine (food, wine); precious (metal, stones). ◆e~**mütig**, *adj.* noble-minded. ◆'**E~stahl**, *m* high-grade steel. ◆'**E~stein**, *m* precious stone.

**Efeu** ['eːfɔy], *m* -s/no pl ivy.

**Effekt** [ɛ'fɛkt]. **1.** *m* -(e)s/-e effect. **2.** **E~en** *pl Fin:* securities; stock. ◆**E~hascherei**, *f* -/no pl straining after effect; *Th: etc:* showmanship. ◆e~**iv** [-'tiːf], *adj.* **1.** (*wirksam*) effective (method, steps etc.). 2. actual (price, weight, value etc.). ◆e~**voll**, *adj.* striking.

**egal** [e'gaːl], *adj.* 1. uniform. 2. *F:* **das ist mir ganz e.,** it's all the same to me; **er muß es machen, e. wie,** he must do it, it doesn't matter how.

**Ego|ismus** [ego'ismus], *m* -/no pl selfishness. ◆E~**ist**, *m* -en/-en egoist. ◆e~**istisch**, *adj.* selfish. ◆e~**zentrisch**, *adj.* self-centred.

**eh** [eː], *adv.* (*a*) *F:* (*sowieso*) anyway; (*b*) **wie eh und je,** as always; **seit eh und je,** since time immemorial.

**ehe**[1] ['eːə], *conj.* before. ◆e~'**dem**, *adv. Lit:* formerly. ◆'e~**malig**, *adj.* former (king, officer, champion etc.). ◆'e~**mals**, *adv. Lit:* formerly. ◆'e~**r**, *adv.* **1.** (*früher*) sooner. **2.** (*wahrscheinlicher*) more likely. **3.** rather; (*a*) (*lieber*) **er würde sich e. umbringen,** he would sooner kill himself; (*b*) (*mehr*) **ich würde das e. als Nachteil ansehen,** I would regard that rather as a disadvantage; (*c*) *F:* (*ziemlich*) somewhat; **e. häßlich,** pretty ugly.

**Ehe**[2]. **I.** *f* -/-n marriage; *Ecc:* matrimony; **die E. schließen,** to get married (**mit** + *dat*, to); **II.** 'E~-, *comb.fm.* (*a*) marriage (partner etc.); (*b*) married (life etc.). ◆'**E~brecher(in)**, *m* (*f*) adulterer; *f* adulteress. ◆'e~**brecherisch**, *adj.* adulterous. ◆'**E~bruch**, *m* adultery. ◆'**E~frau**, *f* wife. ◆'**E~gatte**, *m* spouse. ◆'e~**lich**, *adj.* 1. legitimate (child, descent etc.); **e. geboren,** born in wedlock. 2. marital (harmony, duties etc.); conjugal (rights). ◆'**E~mann**, *m* husband. ◆'**E~paar**, *n* married couple. ◆'**E~ring**, *m* wedding ring. ◆'**E~scheidung**, *f* divorce. ◆'**E~schließung**, *f* marriage.

**Ehr|e** ['eːrə], *f* -/-n honour; **zu seiner E. muß ich sagen, daß...,** to give him his due, I must say that ...; **j-m E. machen/** *Lit:* **zur E. gereichen,** to be a credit to s.o.; **etwas in E~n halten,** to treasure sth.; **was verschafft mir die E.?** to what do I owe the honour of your visit? ◆**'e~en,** *v.tr.* to honour (s.o., sth.). ◆**'E~en-,** *comb.fm.* (a) honorary (member, title etc.); (b) (guest, man etc.) of honour. ◆**'e~enamtlich,** *adj.* honorary (chairman, post etc.). ◆**'E~enbürger,** *m* freeman. ◆**'e~enhaft,** *adj.* honourable. ◆**'e~enrührig,** *adj.* defamatory. ◆**'E~enrunde,** *f* lap of honour. ◆**'E~ensache,** *f* point of honour; **das ist doch E.!** that goes without saying! ◆**'E~entag,** *m* red-letter day. ◆**'e~envoll,** *adj.* honourable. ◆**'E~enwort,** *n* word of honour; *F:* **E.!** honest(ly)! ◆**'e~erbietig,** *adj.* deferential. ◆**'E~furcht,** *f* (*Verehrung*) reverence; (*Scheu*) awe. ◆**'e~fürchtig,** *adj.* reverent. ◆**'E~gefühl,** *n* sense of honour. ◆**'E~geiz,** *m* ambition. ◆**'e~geizig,** *adj.* ambitious. ◆**'e~lich,** *adj.* (a) honest (person, feelings, opinion etc.); fair (dealings etc.); genuine (concern); sincere (wish etc.); **e. gesagt,** quite honestly, to be honest. ◆**'E~lichkeit,** *f* -*/no pl* honesty; sincerity (of feelings etc.). ◆**'E~los,** *adj.* dishonourable. ◆**'E~ung,** *f* -*/-en* 1. honour. 2. *no pl* honouring. ◆**'e~würdig,** *adj.* venerable (old man etc.).

**ei**[1] [ai], *int.* oh! **ei, ei, was seh ich?** aha, what's this?

**Ei**[2] *n* -(e)s/-er 1. egg. 2. *Biol:* ovum. ◆**'Eier-,** *comb.fm.* egg (spoon etc.). ◆**'Eierbecher,** *m* egg cup. ◆**'Eierkuchen,** *m* pancake. ◆**'Eierlikör,** *m* egg flip. ◆**'Eierschale,** *f* eggshell. ◆**'Eierstock,** *m* ovary.

**Eich**[e] ['aiçə], *f* -/-n oak (tree). ◆**'E~el,** *f* -/-n *Bot:* acorn. ◆**'E~en-,** *comb.fm.* oak (leaf, table etc.). ◆**'E~hörnchen,** *n* -s/- squirrel.

**eich**|**en** ['aiçən], *v.tr.* to calibrate (measuring instruments). ◆**'E~maß,** *n* standard measure. ◆**'E~ung,** *f* -/-en standardization; calibration.

**Eid** [ait], *m* -(e)s/-e oath. ◆**'e~esstattlich,** *adj.* **e~esstattliche Erklärung,** statutory declaration.

**Eidechse** ['aidɛksə], *f* -/-n lizard.

**'Eidotter,** *n & m* (egg) yolk.

**Eier-,** *comb.fm. see* **Ei.**

**eiern** ['aiərn], *v.i.* (*haben*) *F:* (*Rad*) to wobble.

**Eif**|**er** ['aifər], *m* -s/*no pl* zeal; (*Begeisterung*) eagerness; *F:* **im E. des Gefechts,** in the heat of the moment. ◆**'E~erer,** *m* -s/- zealot. ◆**'E~ersucht,** *f* jealousy. ◆**'e~ersüchtig,** *adj.* jealous (**auf** j-n, etwas of s.o., sth.). ◆**'e~rig,** *adj.* keen; eager (pupil etc.).

**'Eigelb,** *n* egg yolk(s).

**eigen** ['aigən]. **I.** *adj.* 1. own; **etwas sein e. nennen,** to call sth. one's own; **sich** *dat* **eine Meinung/Theorie zu e. machen,** to adopt an opinion/a theory; **eine Wohnung mit e~em Eingang,** a flat

with its own entrance; **mit dem ihr e~en Charme,** with her characteristic charm. 2. (*seltsam*) odd (ideas etc.); difficult (person). **II. 'E~-,** *comb.fm.* (a) own (property, capital, make etc.); intrinsic (value etc.); (b) self-(financing etc.). ◆**'E~art,** *f* peculiarity; **persönliche E.,** (personal) idiosyncrasy. ◆**'e~artig,** *adj.* (a) **von e~artiger Schönheit,** of singular beauty; (b) (*seltsam*) odd, strange. ◆**'E~bedarf,** *m* own personal requirements. ◆**'E~gewicht,** *n Ph:* specific gravity; *Com:* net weight. ◆**'e~händig,** *adj.* own (signature); personal (letter etc.). ◆**'E~heim,** *n* own home; owner-occupied house. ◆**'E~heit,** *f* -/-en peculiarity (*esp.* of a person). ◆**'E~liebe,** *f* -/*no pl* vanity. ◆**'E~lob,** *n* self-praise. ◆**'e~mächtig,** *adj.* high-handed (person, action etc.); arbitrary (decision); (*unbefugt*) unauthorized (action). ◆**'E~name,** *m* proper name. ◆**'e~nützig,** *adj.* self-interested. ◆**'e~s,** *adv.* expressly. ◆**'E~schaft,** *f* -/-en 1. quality, (*Merkmal*) characteristic (of a person, material); property (of a substance). 2. (*Funktion*) **in seiner E. als Vormund,** in his capacity as guardian. ◆**'E~schaftswort,** *n* adjective. ◆**'E~sinn,** *m* obstinacy. ◆**'e~sinnig,** *adj.* obstinate. ◆**'e~tlich,** *adj.* real; true (value, meaning etc.); **e. sollte ich jetzt arbeiten,** strictly speaking I should be working now; **wie geht es ihm e.?** how is he, I wonder? ◆**'E~tum,** *n* -s/*no pl* property. ◆**'E~tümer,** *m* -s/- owner; proprietor (of a hotel, business etc.). ◆**'e~tümlich,** *adj.* peculiar; **ein e~tümlicher Geruch,** a strange smell. ◆**'E~tumswohnung,** *f* freehold flat; *N.Am:* condominium. ◆**'e~willig,** *adj.* 1. (*e~sinnig*) wilful (child etc.). 2. (*Pers.*) of independent mind; highly individual (interpretation etc.).

**eign**|**en** ['aignən], *v.refl.* to be suitable. ◆**'E~ung,** *f* -/-en suitability.

**Eil-** ['ail-], *comb.fm.* express (messenger, letter etc.). ◆**'E~bote,** *m* carrier. ◆**'E~brief,** *m* express letter. ◆**'E~e,** *f* -/*no pl* hurry, haste; **das hat keine E.,** there's no hurry about that; **j-m zu Hilfe e.,** to rush to s.o.'s aid; (b) (*Sache*) to be urgent. ◆**'e~ig,** *adj.* (a) hurried; **es e. haben,** to be in a hurry; (b) (*dringend*) urgent (business, letter etc.). ◆**'e~igst,** *adv.* posthaste. ◆**'E~zug,** *m* semi-fast train.

**'Eileiter,** *m* -s/- Fallopian tube.

**Eimer** ['aimər], *m* -s/- bucket; *F:* **im E.,** (*Sachen*) up the spout; (*Pers.*) done for.

**ein**[1] [ain]. **I.** *num.adj.* one; **e. für allemal,** once and for all; **er ist ihr e. und alles,** he is everything to her; **eines Tages/Morgens,** one day/morning. **II.** *num.pron.* (a) (*Pers.*) one; someone; **e~er nach dem anderen,** one after another;

**wenn man das sieht, wird e~em schlecht,** it makes you feel ill when you see that; (b) (Sache) one; **ich habe kein Glas, hast du e~(e)s?** I haven't got a glass, have you got one? III. indef.art. a, an; **e. jeder,** each one; IV. **'ein-,** adj.comb.fm. one-(armed, eyed, legged, dimensional etc.). ◆**'e~gleisig,** adj. single-track.

**ein²,** adv. **e. und aus,** in and out; **er weiß weder e. noch aus,** he is at his wit's end.

**einander** [ain'andər], pron.inv. one another; **je im Wege,** in each other's way.

**'einarbeiten,** v.tr.sep. (a) to break (s.o.) in (to a new job); to show (s.o.) the ropes; (b) v.refl. **sich e.,** to settle in (to the work).

**'einatmen,** v.tr.&i.sep. (haben) to breathe in, inhale (sth.).

**'Einbahn-,** comb.fm. one-way (traffic etc.). ◆**'E~straße,** f one-way street.

**'Einband,** m binding.

**'Einbau. I.** m 1. no pl building in; fitting (of a cupboard, engine etc.); installation (of central heating, plumbing etc.); 2. built-in unit. **II. 'E~-,** comb.fm. built-in (shelves etc.). ◆**'e~en,** v.tr.sep. to install (central heating etc.); Fig: incorporate (an episode etc.); to fit (a part, an engine). ◆**'E~küche,** f fitted kitchen. ◆**'E~möbel,** npl built-in furniture.

**'einbegriffen,** adj. included; **alles e.,** altogether.

**'einberuf|en,** v.tr.sep.irr. 74 (a) to summon (a meeting etc.); (b) Mil: **j-n (zum Heer) e.,** to call s.o. up/N.Am: draft s.o. (into the army). **II. 'E~ung,** f -/-en (a) no pl summoning; (b) Mil: conscription; N.Am: draft.

**'einbetten,** v.tr.sep. to embed (sth.).

**'Einbettzimmer,** n single room.

**'einbezieh|en,** v.tr.sep.irr. 113 to include (s.o., sth.), (berücksichtigen) take (sth.) into account. ◆**'E~ung,** f -/no pl inclusion; **unter E. von + dat,** including.

**'einbiegen,** v.i.sep.irr.7 (sein) to turn.

**'einbild|en,** v.refl.sep. (a) **sich dat etwas e.,** to imagine sth.; (b) **was bildest du dir eigentlich ein?** who do you think you are? **darauf brauchst du dir nichts einzubilden!** that's nothing to be proud of! ◆**'E~ung,** f -/-en 1. (Phantasie) imagination; **es ist reine E.,** it is purely imaginary. 2. (Hochmut) conceit. ◆**'E~ungskraft,** f -/no pl imagination.

**'einblenden,** v.tr.sep. to fade in (a scene, music etc.).

**'Einblick,** m insight.

**'einbrech|en,** v.sep.irr.14 1. v.tr. to break in/down (a door etc.); to smash in (a window). 2. v.i. (a) (sein) (Dach usw.) to cave in; (b) (sein/haben) (Einbrecher usw.) to break in; (c) (sein) (Nacht) to fall, (Dämmerung) set in. ◆**'E~er,** m -s/- burglar; (am Tag) housebreaker.

**'einbringen,** v.tr.sep.irr.16 to bring in

(money, the harvest etc.); to earn (money, profit, Fig: a reputation etc.); **es bringt nichts ein,** it doesn't yield any profit.

**'Einbruch,** m 1. (Sturz) collapse (of structure, support etc.); Com: Fin: slump. 2. burglary; **E. in eine Bank,** break-in at a bank. 3. **bei E. der Kälte,** when the cold weather sets in; **bei E. der Dunkelheit,** at nightfall.

**'einbürgern,** v.tr.sep. (a) to naturalize (a foreigner); (b) **sich e.,** (Pers.) to settle down; (Brauch) to become accepted; **es hat sich eingebürgert, daß ...,** it has become the custom that ...

**'Einbuße,** f -/-n loss, Jur: forfeiture (an **Geld usw.,** of money etc.).

**'einbüßen,** v.tr.sep. to lose (money, influence, one's life etc.); to forfeit (one's rights etc.).

**'eindecken,** v.tr.sep. (a) to cover (sth.) up/over; (b) **sich mit etwas e.,** to lay in a supply of sth., stock up with sth.

**'eindeutig,** adj. clear (instructions, defeat etc.); unambiguous (reply, meaning etc.). ◆**'E~keit,** f -/-en clearness; unambiguity.

**'eindring|en. I.** v.i.sep.irr.19 (sein) (a) **e. in + acc,** (also Fig:) to penetrate (sth.); to force one's way into (a room etc.); (Truppen usw.) to invade (a country, town etc.); to infiltrate (enemy lines etc.); Fig: to get to the bottom of (a mystery etc.); (b) **auf j-n e.,** to close in on s.o.; Fig: to urge s.o. **II. E.,** n -s/no pl intrusion; penetration; Mil: invasion. ◆**'e~lich,** adj. urgent (warning etc.); pressing (request etc.); forceful (speech, language etc.). ◆**'E~ling,** m -(e)s/-e intruder.

**'Eindruck,** m impression; **er machte einen unglücklichen E.,** he seemed unhappy. ◆**'e~svoll,** adj. impressive.

**'eindrücken,** v.tr.sep. to press/push in (a knob etc.); (zerdrücken) to crush (a tin, s.o.'s chest etc.).

**'eineinhalb,** num.adj. one and a half.

**'einengen,** v.tr.sep. **j-n e.,** to restrict s.o.'s movements; **eingeengt,** cramped; restricted (space etc.); (b) to restrict (s.o.'s freedom, rights etc.).

**einer** ['ainər], see **ein.** ◆**e~lei. I.** inv.adj. & adv. (egal) immaterial; **das ist mir ganz e.,** that's all the same to me. **II. E.,** n -s/no pl sameness. ◆**'e~seits,** adv. **e. ... andererseits ...,** on the one hand ... on the other hand ...

**einfach** ['ainfax], adj. 1. single (thread, width etc.); Med: simple (fracture); **e. gefaltet,** folded once. 2. (a) (leicht) simple; (b) adv. simply, just. 3. (schlicht) ordinary (people); plain (food); simple (life). ◆**'E~heit,** f -/no pl simplicity.

**'einfädeln,** v.tr.sep. (a) to thread (cotton, film, tape etc.); (b) F: to arrange (sth.).

**'einfahr|en,** v.sep.irr.26 1. v.i. (sein) (ankommen) to arrive. 2. v.tr. to run/N.Am: break in (a car, etc.). ◆**'E~t,** f 1. entry; (*Ankunft*) arrival. 2. (*a*) entrance; **E. freihalten**, keep (entrance) clear; **keine E.!** no entry; (*b*) (motorway/*N.Am:* freeway) access road.

'**Einfall**, *m* 1. idea; **einem plötzlichen E. folgend**, on a sudden impulse. 2. *Ph:* incidence (of light/rays). 3. *Mil:* invasion; (*kurz*) raid. ◆'**e~en**, *v.i.sep.irr.27* (*sein*) (*a*) (*einstürzen*) (*Gebäude*) to collapse; (*b*) (*Licht*) to fall/shine in; (*c*) (*mitmachen*) to join in; (*d*) *Mil:* **in ein Land usw. e.**, to invade a country etc.; (*e*) **dabei fällt mir ein ...**, that reminds me ...; **ihm fiel keine bessere Ausrede ein**, he couldn't think of a better excuse. ◆'**e~slos**, *adj.* unimaginative. ◆'**e~sreich**, *adj.* imaginative; (*klug*) ingenious. ◆'**E~sreichtum**, *m* imaginativeness; ingenuity.

**einfältig** ['ainfɛltiç], *adj.* simple; (*naiv*) naive.

'**Einfamilienhaus**, *n* (undivided) family house; *N.Am:* one-family house.

'**einfangen**, *v.tr.sep.irr.28* to capture.

'**einfarbig**, *adj.* in one colour; plain (material).

'**einfass|en**, *v.tr.sep.* (*a*) to surround (a lawn, plot of land etc.); to edge (a garment, tablecloth etc.); (*b*) to set (a jewel). ◆'**E~ung**, *f* edge; setting.

'**einfinden**, *v.refl.sep.irr.9* **sich e.**, to turn up; (*Menge*) to gather.

'**einfließen**, *v.i.sep.irr.31* (*sein*) **in etwas** *acc* **e.**, to flow into sth.

'**einflößen**, *v.tr.sep.* (*a*) **j-m Arznei/ Wasser e.**, to give s.o. sips of medicine/ water; (*b*) *Fig:* to inspire (respect, admiration etc.).

'**Einfluß**, *m* influence. ◆'**E~bereich**, *m* sphere of influence. ◆'**e~reich**, *adj.* influential.

'**einförmig**, *adj.* uniform. ◆'**E~keit**, *f -/no pl* uniformity.

'**einfrieren**, *v.sep.irr.32* 1. *v.i.* (*sein*) to freeze (up); (*Schiff*) to become icebound. 2. *v.tr.* to freeze.

'**einfüg|en**, *v.tr.sep.* (*a*) **e. in** + *acc*, to fit (an object) into (sth.), insert (a word etc.) into (a text etc.); to add (a remark); (*b*) (*Pers.*) **sich e.**, to fit in. ◆'**E~ung**, *f* insertion.

'**Einfühlungsvermögen**, *n* (power of) empathy.

'**Einfuhr**. I. *f -/-en* (*a*) *no pl* importation (of goods etc.); (*b*) imports (of a country). II. '**E~-**, *comb.fm.* import (regulations, restrictions, licence etc.).

'**einführ|en**, *v.tr.sep.* (*a*) to introduce (s.o.); to bring in (sth. new, a law, reform etc.); (*b*) (*einfügen*) *esp. Med:* to insert (sth.); (*c*) *Com:* to import (goods). ◆'**E~ung**, *f* introduction; insertion. ◆'**E~ungs-**, *comb.fm.* introductory (course, price etc.).

'**Eingabe**, *f* 1. (*Gesuch*) petition; application (**an** *acc*, to). 2. *Data-pr:* input.

'**Eingang**, *m* 1. entrance; **kein E.**, no entry. 2. (*Ankunft*) arrival (of mail etc.); **nach E. Ihres Briefes**, on receipt of your letter. 3. (*Anfang*) beginning. ◆'**e~s. I.** *adv.* at the beginning. **II.** *prep.* + *gen* at the beginning of. ◆'**E~s-**, *comb.fm.* (*a*) entrance (hall etc.); (*b*) opening (words, speech etc.); (*c*) *Com:* (date etc.) of receipt; (*d*) *El:* input (voltage etc.).

'**eingeb|en**, *v.tr.sep.irr.35* (*a*) **j-m eine Medizin usw. e.**, to administer a medicine etc. to s.o.; (*b*) *Data-pr:* to feed (data). ◆'**E~ung**, *f -/-en* inspiration.

'**eingebildet**, *adj.* (*a*) (*Pers.*) conceited; (*b*) imaginary (illness etc.).

'**Eingeborene(r)**, *m & f* decl. as adj. native.

'**eingedenk**, *adv.* + *gen* bearing in mind.

'**eingefleischt**, *adj.* confirmed (bachelor, pessimist etc.); inveterate (opponent etc.).

'**eingehen**, *v.sep.irr.36* 1. *v.i.* (*sein*) (*a*) *esp. Com:* (*Briefe, Gelder*) to come in, be received; (*b*) **in die Geschichte e.**, to go down in history; (*c*) **e. auf** + *acc*, to agree to (a demand, request etc.); (*d*) **auf eine Frage usw. (näher) e.**, to go into a question (more closely); **auf j-n e.**, to take an interest in s.o. (*e*) (*Tier*) to die; (*Firma, Zeitung usw.*) to fold. 2. *v.tr.* (*haben*) to enter into (an alliance, obligation); to take on (a bet); to take (a risk). ◆'**e~d**, *adj.* (*gründlich*) thorough.

'**eingelegt**, *adj.* 1. inlaid (work etc.). 2. *Cu:* marinaded.

'**Eingemachtes**, *n* decl. as adj. preserved/ bottled fruit, vegetables etc.

'**eingemeinden**, *v.tr.sep.* to incorporate.

'**eingenommen**, *adj.* **von etwas e.**, taken with sth.; **gegen j-n, etwas** *acc* **e.**, prejudiced against s.o., sth.

'**eingeschrieben**, *adj.* registered.

'**eingesessen**, *adj.* (old-)established; (*ansässig*) resident.

'**Eingeständnis**, *n* confession; admission.

'**eingestehen**, *v.tr.sep.irr.100* to admit (sth.).

'**Eingeweide** ['aingəvaidə], *npl* viscera, *F:* guts; *Z:* entrails; *Cu:* offal.

'**eingewöhnen**, *v.tr.sep.* **sich e.**, to settle down.

'**eingießen**, *v.tr.sep.irr.31* to pour (a drink).

'**eingliedern**, *v.tr.sep.* to incorporate (sth., a place), insert (details, facts etc.), integrate (s.o.).

'**eingraben**, *v.tr.sep.irr.42* (*a*) to bury (valuables etc.); **sich e.**, to dig in; (*Tier*) to burrow.

'**eingreifen**, *v.i.sep.irr.43* (*haben*) (*a*) to intervene; (*sich einmischen*) to interfere; (*b*) (*Zahnräder usw.*) (**in etwas** *acc*) **e.**, to mesh (with sth.)/engage (sth.).

'**eingrenzen**, *v.tr.sep.* to narrow down (a subject etc.).

'**Eingriff**, *m* 1. intervention. 2. *Med:* operation.

'**einhaken**, *v.tr.sep.* **sich bei j-m e.**, to

link arms with s.o.

**'Einhalt**, *m* etwas *dat* E. **gebieten**, to call a halt to sth. ◆**'e~en**, *v.sep.irr.45* **1.** *v.tr.* (*a*) to keep (a promise, an appointment, one's distance); to keep to (a plan, diet etc.); to follow (a course); to observe (a contract, rule, holiday etc.). **2.** *v.i.* (*haben*) to stop; to pause.

**'einhändig**, *adj.* one-handed; *adv.* with one hand. ◆**'e~en**, *v.tr.sep.* to hand (sth.) over, (*einreichen*) hand (sth.) in.

**'einhängen**, *v.tr.sep.* (*a*) to hang; (**den Hörer**) **e.**, to hang up; (*b*) **sich bei j-m e.**, to link arms with s.o.

**'einheimisch**. *adj.* (*eines Landes*) native (population, plants etc.); domestic (product, market); (*einer Stadt usw.*) local (residents, industry etc.); **die E~en**, the locals.

**Einheit** ['ainhait], *f* -/-en **1.** (*a*) unity (of a nation, party, *Th:* the drama etc.); (*b*) (*Ganzes*) **eine E. bilden**, to form a (homogeneous) whole. **2.** *Meas: Mil: etc:* unit. ◆**'e~lich**, *adj.* uniform; (*a*) homogeneous (whole, work of art etc.); coherent (argument etc.); (*b*) *Com:* standard (price, tariff etc.). ◆**'E~s-**, *comb.fm.* standard (value etc.); uniform (clothing etc.).

**einhellig** ['ainheliç], *adj.* unanimous.

**'einholen**, *v.tr.sep.* (*a*) **e. gehen**, to go shopping; (*b*) **Auskunft e.**, to make inquiries; **j-s Rat/Erlaubnis e.**, to get s.o.'s advice/consent; (*c*) to take in (a sail), draw in (a fishing net); to strike (a flag); (*d*) **j-n/ein Auto e.**, to catch up with s.o./a car; **verlorene Zeit e.**, to make up for lost time.

**'Einhorn**, *n* unicorn.

**'einhüllen**, *v.tr.sep.* to wrap (s.o., sth.) up.

**einig** ['ainiç], *adj.* **1.** (*geeint*) united (nation, people etc.). **2.** (*in Übereinstimmung*) **mit j-m e. sein**, to agree with s.o. ◆**e~en** ['-gən], *v.tr.* (*a*) to unify (a country etc.); (*b*) **sich (mit j-m) e.**, to come to an agreement with s.o. ◆**'E~keit**, *f* -/no *pl* unity; harmony; (*Übereinstimmung*) agreement. ◆**'E~ung**, *f* -/-en (*a*) unification; (*b*) agreement.

**einige(r,s)** [ainigə(r,s)], *indef.pron. & adj.* **1.** *sing.* (*etwas*) some; (*ein bißchen*) a little, a bit of. **2.** *pl* (*a*) (*ein paar*) a few; (*mehrere*) several; (*b*) *pron.* some, a few; **e. wenige**, a few. **3.** (*ziemlich viel*) **e~s kosten**, to cost quite a bit. ◆**e~'mal**, *adv.* a few/several times. ◆**e~r'maßen**, *adv.* to some extent; *F:* **wie geht es dir?—so e.**, how are you?—not too bad/so-so.

**'einjagen**, *v.tr.sep.* **j-m Angst/Schrecken e.**, to give s.o. a real fright/scare.

**'einjährig**, *adj.* (*a*) one-year-old (child, animal etc.); (*b*) *Bot:* **e~e Pflanzen**, annuals.

**'einkalkulieren**, *v.tr.sep.* to take (sth.)

into account, allow for (a possibility, *Fin:* an expense).

**'Einkauf**, *m* (*a*) *no pl* buying; (*b*) purchase; **E~e machen**, to do some shopping. ◆**'e~en**, *v.tr.sep.* to purchase (sth.); **e. gehen**, to go shopping. ◆**'E~s-**, *comb.fm.* shopping (street, basket, bag etc.).

**'einklammern**, *v.tr.sep.* to bracket.

**'Einklang**, *m* harmony (of ideas etc.); **etwas (mit etwas** *dat*) **in E. bringen**, to reconcile sth. (with sth.).

**'einkleiden**, *v.tr.sep.* to clothe (s.o.).

**'einklemmen**, *v.tr.sep.* **etwas (in etwas** *acc*) **e.**, to wedge, jam sth. in(to sth.).

**'einknicken**, *v.tr.&i.sep.* (*haben*) to bend (wire etc.) (at an angle); **seine Knie knickten ein**, his knees gave way.

**'einkochen**, *v.tr.sep.* to preserve, bottle (fruit, vegetables etc.).

**'Einkommen**, *n* -s/- income, earnings; revenue (from estates). ◆**'E~(s)steuer**, *f* -/no *pl* income tax.

**'einkreisen**, *v.tr.sep.* to surround.

**Einkünfte** ['ainkynftə], *pl* earnings; (*Gewinn*) proceeds.

**'einlad|en**, *v.tr.sep.irr.56* **1.** to load (goods) (**in einen Lastwagen usw.**, onto a lorry etc.). **2.** to invite (s.o.); **komm, ich lade dich ein**, come on, I'll treat you. ◆**'e~end**, *adj.* inviting; tempting. ◆**'E~ung**, *f* -/-en invitation.

**'Einlage**, *f* **1.** *Fin:* investment; deposit. **2.** *Cu:* **Suppe mit E.**, soup with added ingredients (noodles, dumplings etc.). **3.** (*in Schuhen*) arch support. **4.** (*Zahne.*) temporary filling. **5.** *Th: etc:* interlude.

**Einlaß** ['ainlas], *m* -sses/-sse **1.** admittance. **2.** *Tchn:* inlet, intake.

**'einlassen**, *v.tr.sep.irr.57* (*a*) to admit (s.o.), let (s.o., sth.) in; (*b*) **e. in** + *acc*, to let (sth.) into (concrete, a wall etc.); (*c*) **sich e. auf** + *acc*, to get involved in (sth.).

**'Einlauf**, *m* **1.** *Sp:* finish. **2.** *Med:* enema. ◆**'e~en**, *v.sep.irr.58* **1.** *v.i.* (*sein*) (*a*) (*Läufer, Pferde usw.*) to come in; (*b*) (*ankommen*) to arrive; (*c*) (*Wasser usw.*) to run/flow in; **das Badewasser e. lassen**, to run the bathwater; (*d*) (*Stoff, Kleidung*) to shrink. **2.** *v.tr.* (*a*) **j-m das Haus e.**, to pester s.o. with requests/troublesome visits; (*b*) to break/wear in (shoes); (*c*) **sich e.**, *Sp:* (*Läufer usw.*) to warm up.

**'einleben**, *v.refl.sep.* **sich e.**, to get used to one's new surroundings.

**'Einleg|earbeit**, *f* -/-en inlaid work. ◆**'e~en**, *v.tr.sep.* (*a*) **etwas in etwas** *acc* **e.**, to insert sth. in sth.; (*b*) *Cu:* to pickle (cucumbers etc.), marinate (fish etc.); (*c*) **eine Pause e.**, to have a break; (*d*) **Protest e.**, to lodge a protest; *Jur:* **Berufung e.**, to appeal; (*e*) **für j-n ein gutes Wort (bei j-m) e.**, to put in a good word for s.o. (with s.o.). ◆**'E~esohle**, *f* inner sole; (loose) insole.

'**einleit|en**, *v.tr.sep.* to begin, start (sth.); to write an introduction to (a book etc.); to initiate (measures); **eine Geburt (künstlich) e.**, to induce a birth. ◆'**e~end**, *adj.* introductory (words); preliminary (measures). ◆'**E~ung**, *f* introduction; initiation; (*Vorspiel*) prelude.

'**einleuchten**, *v.i.sep.* (*haben*) **das leuchtet mir ein**, I can see that. ◆'**e~d**, *adj.* convincing.

'**einliefer|n**, *v.tr.sep.* **j-n ins Gefängnis/ Krankenhaus e.**, to take s.o. to prison/ (the) hospital.

'**einlösen**, *v.tr.sep.* to cash (a cheque); to redeem (securities, sth. from pawn etc.); *Lit:* to make good (one's promise).

'**einmachen**, *v.tr.sep.* to preserve.

'**einmal**, *adv.* 1. (*a*) once; **noch e.**, once again; **noch e. so lang**, twice as long; (*b*) **e. hier, e. da**, now here, now there; (*c*) (*in Zukunft*) **e. wird die Zeit kommen, wo ...**, one/some day the time will come when ...; (*d*) (*zuvor*) (once) before; at one time; **es war e. ...**, once upon a time there was ...; (*e*) **auf e.**, at the same time; (*plötzlich*) suddenly, all at once. 2. (*verstärkend*) **nicht e.**, not even; **das ist nun e. so**, that's the way it is. ◆**E~'eins**, *n* -*/no pl* 1. **das (kleine/ große) E.**, multiplication tables (up to 10/from 10 to 20). 2. rudiments, basics. ◆'**e~ig**, *adj.* 1. (*a*) single (reading etc.); non-recurring (payment etc.); (*b*) (*einzig in seiner Art*) unique (opportunity etc.); unrepeatable (offer); **das war e. schön**, that was absolutely beautiful. ◆'**E~igkeit**, *f* -*/no pl* uniqueness.

**Ein'mannbetrieb**, *m* one-man operation (of buses etc.); *Com:* one-man business.

'**Einmarsch**, *m* marching in; entry. ◆'**e~ieren**, *v.i.sep.* (*sein*) to march in.

'**einmisch|en**, *v.refl.sep.* **sich e.**, to interfere (**in** *etwas acc*, in/with sth.). ◆'**E~ung**, *f* interference.

'**einmünd|en**, *v.i.sep.* (*sein*) **e. in** + *acc*, (*Fluß*) to flow into (the sea); (*Straße*) to lead into, join (another road/street).

**einmütig** ['ainmy:tiç], *adj.* unanimous.

**Einnahme** ['ainna:mə], *f* -*/-n* 1. taking (of a medicine etc.). 2. *Mil:* capture. 3. *usu.pl* **E~n**, earnings; (*Ertrag*) takings. ◆'**E~quelle**, *f* source of income.

'**einnehmen**, *v.tr.sep.irr.69* (*a*) to take (medicine etc.); (*b*) *Com: etc:* to take/ (*verdienen*) make (money); (*c*) *Mil:* to take (a town, fortress etc.); (*d*) to take (one's seat); to take up (a position, *Fig:* standpoint); (*e*) to occupy (space, a position etc.); (*f*) **j-n für sich** *acc* **e.**, to win s.o. over; **j-n gegen sich e.**, to prejudice s.o. against one. ◆'**e~d**, *adj.* captivating, charming.

'**einnicken**, *v.i.sep.* (*sein*) *F:* to nod off.

'**einnisten**, *v.refl.sep.* *F:* **sich bei j-m e.**, to park oneself on s.o.

**Einöde** ['ain?ø:də], *f* desert, wilderness.

'**einordnen**, *v.tr.sep.* to arrange (objects)

in proper order; **sich e.**, (i) (*Pers.*) to fit in; (ii) *Aut:* to get into (the right) lane.

'**einpacken**, *v.sep.* 1. *v.tr.* to pack (sth.); to wrap up (a present etc.). 2. *v.i.* (*haben*) to pack (up), (*also Fig:*) pack one's bags.

'**einpendeln**, *v.refl.sep.* **sich e.**, to level off.

'**einperchen**, *v.tr.sep.* to pen (sheep); to pack (people) (into a small space).

'**einpflanzen**, *v.tr.sep.* to implant (an idea, *Med:* an organ etc.) (**j-m**, in s.o.).

'**einplanen**, *v.tr.sep.* to include (sth.) in one's plans; (*berücksichtigen*) to allow for (sth.).

'**einpräg|en**, *v.tr.sep.* (*a*) to imprint (a mark, design etc.); (*b*) *Fig:* **j-m etwas e.**, to imprint (sth.) on s.o.'s mind; **sich** *dat* **ein Gedicht usw. e.**, to memorize a poem etc. ◆'**e~sam**, *adj.* memorable; catchy (tune).

'**einrahmen**, *v.tr.sep.* to frame (a picture etc.).

'**einrasten**, *v.i.sep.* (*sein*) to snap into position.

'**einräum|en**. **I.** *v.tr.sep.* (*a*) **das Geschirr e.**, to put away the crockery; (*b*) (*gewähren*) **j-m ein Recht**, *Fin:* **einen Kredit usw. e.**, to grant s.o. a right, credit etc.; (*c*) (*zugeben*) to admit.

'**einrechnen**, *v.tr.sep.* to include (sth.).

'**einreden**, *v.tr.sep.* **j-m, sich etwas e.**, to persuade s.o., oneself of sth.

'**einreiben**, *v.tr.sep.irr.12* **sich** *dat* **das Gesicht mit Creme e.**, to rub one's face with cream; **j-m den Rücken e.**, to rub oil etc. on s.o.'s back.

'**einreichen**, *v.tr.sep.* to submit (a petition, an application etc.).

'**einreihen**, *v.tr.sep.* **sich e.**, to take one's place (in a queue etc.); *Fig:* to fall into line.

'**Einreise**, *f* entry (into a country). ◆'**e~n**, *v.i.sep.* (*sein*) (**in ein Land**) **e.**, to enter a country.

'**einreißen**, *v.sep.irr.4* 1. *v.tr.* (*a*) to tear (sth.); to split (one's fingernail etc.); (*b*) (*niederreißen*) to pull down (a house, wall etc.). 2. *v.i.* (*sein*) (*a*) to tear; (*b*) *Fig:* (*Gewohnheit usw.*) to gain a hold.

'**einricht|en**, *v.tr.sep.* (*a*) to furnish (a house, room etc.); to fit out (a kitchen, shop etc.); *F:* **sich häuslich e.**, to make oneself at home; (*b*) (*anordnen*) to arrange (sth.); **sich auf etwas** *acc* **e.**, to make arrangements for sth. ◆'**E~ung**, *f* 1. (*a*) *no pl* furnishing; fitting out; (*b*) equipment; (*Möbel*) furniture. 2. (*Anordnung*) arrangement; set-up of a workshop etc.). 3. (*a*) (*Anstalt*) institution; (*b*) (*Brauch*) practice. 4. *Tchn:* (*Gerät*) device; (*Anlage*) installation.

'**einrosten**, *v.i.sep.* (*sein*) to rust (up); *F:* (*Glieder*) to get stiff; (*Kenntnisse*) to get rusty.

'**einrücken**, *v.sep.* 1. *v.i.* (*sein*) (*a*) (*Truppen*) **in ein Land e.**, to enter a country;

(b) (*einberufen werden*) to be called up (for military service). **2.** *v.tr.* (a) to indent (a line etc.); (b) to insert (an advertisement).

**eins**[1] [ains]. **I.** *num.adj.* one; **um e.**, at one o'clock; **es kommt auf e. heraus**, it comes to the same thing. **II. E.**, f -/-en (figure) one.

**eins**[2], *indef.pron. see* **ein**.

'**einsalzen**, *v.tr.sep.* to salt, cure.

**einsam** ['ainzɑːm], *adj.* (a) lonely, solitary (person, existence); isolated, lonely (place); (b) F: **e~e Spitze**, the tops. ◆'**E~keit**, f -/-en loneliness, solitude.

'**einsammeln**, *v.tr.sep.* to gather (fruit etc.); to collect (money, tickets etc.).

'**Einsatz**, m **1.** (*Teil*) insert, *Tchn:* element (of a filter etc.). **2.** (*Spiele.*) stake; *Fig:* **unter E. des Lebens**, at the risk of one's life. **3.** (a) (*Gebrauch*) use (of labour, machines, police etc.); (b) *Mil:* mission. **4.** *Mus:* entry. ◆**e~bereit**, *adj. Mil:* (*Truppen*) ready for action; **sich e. halten**, to be on standby. ◆'**E~kommando**, *n* task force.

'**einschalten**, *v.tr.sep.* (a) to switch on (a light, radio etc.); to connect (up) (a circuit, battery); *Aut:* to engage (a gear); **sich e.**, to switch itself on/(*Heizung usw.*) come on; (b) (*einfügen*) to insert (a word, sentence etc.); to interpolate (a phrase, remark etc.); (c) to bring in (the police, experts etc.); **sich e.**, to intervene; **sich in ein Gespräch e.**, to join in a conversation.

'**einschärfen**, *v.tr.sep.* **j-m etwas e.**, to impress sth. on s.o.

'**einschätz|en**, *v.tr.sep.* to assess (s.o., sth.); (*bewerten*) to estimate the value of (sth.); **j-n, etwas hoch e.**, to value s.o., sth. highly. ◆'**E~ung**, f assessment; (*Meinung*) opinion; appraisal (of a situation etc.).

'**einschenken**, *v.tr.sep.* to pour out (wine, water etc.) (**j-m**, for s.o.); to fill (a glass, cup etc.).

'**einschicken**, *v.tr.sep.* to send in (sth.).

'**einschieben**, *v.tr.sep.irr.82* (a) **etwas in etwas** *acc* **e.**, to push/*F:* shove sth. into sth.; (b) to insert (a quotation etc.); to add (an extra item etc.).

'**einschiffen**, *v.tr. & refl.sep.* (**sich**) **e.**, to embark.

'**einschlafen**, *v.i.sep.irr.84* (*sein*) to go to sleep.

'**einschläfern**, *v.tr.sep.* to send (s.o.) to sleep; (*töten*) to put (an animal) to sleep. ◆**e~d**, *adj.* soporific.

'**Einschlag**, m **1.** impact (of bomb etc.). **2.** *Fig:* orientalischer E., oriental touch. ◆**e~en**, *v.sep.irr.85* **1.** *v.tr.* (a) to hammer in (a nail, post etc.); (b) to break (a window), knock down (a door); **j-m den Schädel e.**, to smash s.o.'s head in; (c) (*einpacken*) to wrap up (a present etc.) (in paper, cloth etc.); (d) **eine andere Richtung e.**, to change direction; **eine Lauf-**

**bahn e.**, to enter upon a career; (e) (*beim Nähen*) to turn (sth.) over/down. **2.** *v.i.* (*haben*) (a) **der Blitz/die Bombe hat hier eingeschlagen**, the lightning/bomb struck here; *F:* **der Film schlug (gut) ein**, the film was a hit; (b) to shake hands (**auf etwas** *acc*, on sth.); (c) **auf j-n/ein Tier e.**, to shower s.o./an animal with blows.

**einschlägig** ['ainʃlɛːgiç], *adj.* relevant (literature, authority etc.).

'**einschleichen**, *v.refl.sep.irr.86* **sich (in etwas** *acc*) **e.**, to creep in(to sth.); **sich in j-s Vertrauen e.**, to insinuate oneself into s.o.'s confidence.

'**einschließ|en**, *v.tr.sep.irr.31* (a) to lock (s.o., sth.) up; (b) (*umgeben*) to encircle (sth., troops); (c) (*aufnehmen*) to include (s.o., sth.); **X eingeschlossen**, including X. ◆'**e~lich. 1.** *adv.* inclusive. **2.** *prep.* + *gen* including.

'**einschmeicheln**, *v.refl.sep.* **sich bei j-m e.**, to ingratiate oneself with s.o. ◆'**e~d**, *adj.* ingratiating (manners, ways); silky (voice).

'**einschnappen**, *v.i.sep.* (*sein*) (a) to click shut/home; (b) *F:* (*Pers.*) to take offence.

'**einschneiden**, *v.tr. & i.sep.irr.59* (*haben*) (**in**) **etwas** *acc* **e.**, to cut into sth. ◆'**e~d**, *adj.* radical (change); decisive (event).

'**Einschnitt**, m **1.** (a) cut, *esp. Med:* incision; (*Kerbe*) notch; (b) gap (in hills etc.). **2.** *Fig:* turning point.

**einschränk|en**, ['ainʃrɛŋkən], *v.tr.sep.* (a) to restrict (sth.); **sich e.**, to economize; (b) to qualify (a statement, condition etc.). ◆'**E~ung**, f -/-en (a) restriction; (b) qualification; **ohne E.**, without reservation.

'**Einschreib|ebrief**, m registered letter. ◆'**e~en. I.** *v.tr.sep.irr.12* (a) to write (sth.) down; to enter (sth.) (**in eine Liste**, on a list); (b) to register (s.o.); **sich e.**, to enrol; (c) to register (a letter, parcel). **II. E.**, *n* **per E.**, by registered post/*N.Am:* mail. ◆'**E~ung**, f enrolment, registration.

'**einschreiten**, *v.i.sep.irr.41* (*sein*) to intervene.

'**Einschub**, m insertion.

'**einschüchtern**, *v.tr.sep.* to intimidate.

'**einschulen**, *v.tr.sep.* to send (a child) to school (for the first time).

'**einschweißen**, *v.tr.sep.* to shrink-wrap (a book, record).

'**einsehen. I.** *v.tr.sep.irr.92* (a) to inspect, examine (documents, books etc.); (b) to see, realize (one's mistake etc., **that** ...). **II. E.**, *n* **ein E. haben**, (i) (*Verständnis haben*) to show understanding; (ii) (*vernünftig sein*) to listen to reason.

'**einseifen**, *v.tr.sep.* to soap.

**einseitig** ['ainzaitiç], *adj.* (a) unilateral (treaty, decision); (b) *Fig:* one-sided (person, training etc.). ◆'**E~keit**, f -/no pl one-sidedness.

'**einsend|en**, *v.tr.sep.irr.94* to send (sth.) in, submit (an article etc.). ◆'**E~er**, *m* sender. ◆'**E~eschluß**, *m* closing date (for entries). ◆'**E~ung**, *f* entry (for a competition); (*Beitrag*) contribution.

'**einsetzen**, *v.sep.* **1.** *v.tr.* (*a*) to put (sth.) in; to insert (*Cl:* a patch etc.), fill in (the date etc.); (*b*) (*ernennen*) to appoint (s.o., a committee etc.); (*c*) to call in (troops, police etc.); (*anwenden*) to use (a weapon, tactics, all one's strength etc.); *Sp:* bring on (a player); (*d*) to bet (an amount); *Fig:* to risk (one's life); (*e*) **sich für eine Sache e.**, to champion a cause; **sich für j-n e.**, to stand up for s.o. **2.** *v.i.* (*haben*) to start; (*Regen usw.*) to set in; *Mus:* to come in.

'**Einsicht**, *f* **1.** examination. **2.** (*a*) (*Verständnis*) insight; (*Erkenntnis*) realization; (*b*) (*Vernunft*) **E. zeigen**, to show sense. ◆'**e~ig**, *adj.* (*vernünftig*) sensible; (*verständnisvoll*) understanding. ◆'**E~nahme**, *f* -/-n examination; *Jur:* search.

**Einsiedler** ['ainzi:tlər], *m* hermit; recluse.

**einsilbig** ['ainzilbiç], *adj.* monosyllabic (word, person, reply); (*Mensch*) taciturn.

'**einsinken**, *v.i.sep.irr.96* (*sein*) (**in etwas** *acc*) **e.**, to sink in(to sth.); (*Boden usw.*) to subside.

'**Einsitzer**, *m* -s/- single-seater.

'**einspannen**, *v.tr.sep.* (*a*) to clamp (sth.) into position; **ein Blatt Papier e.**, to insert a sheet of paper (into the typewriter); (*b*) to harness (a horse); (*c*) *F:* to rope (s.o.) in (for a job).

'**einsparen**, *v.tr.sep.* to economize on (materials, expenses etc.); to cut down (expenditure etc.).

'**einsperren**, *v.tr.sep.* to lock up, *F:* jail (s.o.).

'**einspielen**, *v.tr.sep.* **sich e.**, (*Musiker*) to practise; (*Sportler*) to warm up; (*Unternehmen*) to get under way; **sie sind gut aufeinander eingespielt**, they work together as a good team.

'**einspringen**, *v.i.sep.irr.19* (*sein*) **für j-n e.**, to stand in for s.o.

'**einspritzen**, *v.tr.sep.* to inject.

'**Einspruch**, *m* objection.

'**einspurig** ['ainʃpuːriç], *adj.* single-track (line, road).

**einst** [ainst], *adv. Lit:* **1.** (*früher*) once, in the past. **2.** (*in Zukunft*) one day.

'**einstampfen**, *v.tr.sep.* to pulp (books).

'**Einstand**, *m* (*beim Tennis*) deuce.

'**einstecken**, *v.tr.sep.* (*a*) to put/stick (sth.) in; to plug in (the radio etc.); to post (a letter); (*b*) to pocket (money, profits etc.); (*c*) (*hinnehmen*) *F:* to suffer (an insult, defeat, criticism etc.), take (blows etc.).

'**einstehen**, *v.i.sep.irr.100* (*sein*) **für j-n, etwas acc e.**, to vouch for s.o., sth.; **für die Folgen e.**, to answer for the consequences.

'**einsteigen**, *v.i.sep.irr.89* (*sein*) to get on (the train, bus etc.); (**in ein Auto**) **e.**, to

get in(to a car).

'**einstell|bar**, *adj.* adjustable. ◆'**e~en**, *v.tr.sep.* (*a*) to put (away) (a vehicle); (*b*) (*beschäftigen*) to take on (s.o.); (*c*) (*aufhören*) to stop (work, smoking etc.); to suspend (payments); (*d*) *Tchn:* to adjust (a machine, screws, volume etc.); **einen Sender e.**, to tune in to a station; *Fig:* (*Pers.*) **sich auf j-n, etwas acc e.**, to adapt oneself to s.o., sth.; (*e*) **sich e.**, (*Pers., Jahreszeit*) to arrive; (*Schmerzen usw.*) to start; (*Zweifel, Schwierigkeiten*) to arise. ◆'**E~ung**, *f* **1.** cessation (of hostilities, production etc.); stoppage (of work); suspension (of payments etc.). **2.** *Tchn:* adjustment. **3.** *Cin: TV:* (*Aufnahme*) take. **4.** (*Haltung*) attitude. **5.** engagement (of staff, workers).

'**Einstieg**, *m* -(e)s/-e entrance (of a bus etc.).

**einstig** ['ainstiç], *adj.* former.

'**einstimm|en**, *v.i.sep.* (*haben*) (*Instrument, Stimme*) to come in; **in den Jubel usw. e.**, to join in the cheering etc. ◆'**e~ig**, *adj.* **1.** *Mus:* unison (singing etc.). **2.** unanimous (decision etc.). ◆'**E~igkeit**, *f* -/no pl unanimity.

**einstöckig** ['ainstœkiç], *adj.* one-storey.

'**einstreichen**, *v.tr.sep.irr.86 F:* to rake in (money, profits etc.).

'**einstudieren**, *v.tr.sep.* to study (a piece of music, *Th:* part etc.); to rehearse (a play).

'**einstürmen**, *v.i.sep.* (*sein*) **auf j-n e.**, to rush at/*Mil:* attack s.o.; *Fig:* (*mit Fragen usw.*) to bombard s.o. (with questions etc.).

'**Einsturz**, *m* collapse; caving in (of ground etc.). ◆'**E~gefahr**, *f* (*Schild*) danger falling masonry.

'**einstürzen**, *v.i.sep.* (*sein*) (*Gebäude usw.*) to collapse; (*Dach*) to cave in.

**einstweil|en** [ainst'vailən], *adv.* (*vorläufig*) for the time being; (*inzwischen*) meanwhile. ◆**e~ig**, *adj.* temporary.

**eintägig** ['aintɛːgiç], *adj.* one-day (visit etc.).

'**eintauchen**, *v.sep.* **1.** *v.tr.* to dip, (*auf längere Zeit*) immerse (sth.). **2.** *v.i.* (*sein*) (**ins Wasser**) **e.**, to dive in(to the water).

'**eintauschen**, *v.tr.sep.* to exchange, *F:* swap (sth.).

'**einteil|en**, *v.tr.sep.* (*a*) to divide (sth.); to classify (animals, plants etc.); (*b*) to map out (one's time, day etc.); (*verteilen*) to distribute (workload, expenditure etc.); (*c*) **j-n zu einer Arbeit e.**, to allot s.o. a task. ◆'**e~ig**, *adj.* one-piece (swimsuit etc.).

**eintönig** ['aintøːniç], *adj.* monotonous. ◆'**E~keit**, *f* -/no pl monotony.

'**Eintopf**, *m* hot-pot; stew.

'**Eintracht**, *f* -/no pl harmony; (*Frieden*) peace.

'**einträchtig**, *adj.* harmonious; peaceful.

'**Eintrag**, *m* -(e)s/-e entry (in a diary, list etc.). ◆'**e~en**, *v.tr.sep.irr.85* (*a*) to put/write (sth.) down; to enter (sth.); (b) to enrol (s.o.) (**als Mitglied,** as a member); to register (a birth, trade mark etc.); **eingetragener Verein,** incorporated society; (*Pers.*) **sich e.,** to enter one's name; (*im Hotel*) to check in. ◆'**E~ung,** *f* **-/-en 1.** (*Eintrag*) entry. **2.** registration.

**einträglich** ['aintrɛ:kliç], *adj.* lucrative.

'**eintreffen,** *v.i.sep.irr.104* (*sein*) (a) (*ankommen*) to arrive; (b) (*Prophezeiung usw.*) to come true; (*Ereignis*) to happen.

'**eintreiben,** *v.tr.sep.irr.12* to recover, collect (outstanding debts, money etc.).

'**eintreten,** *v.sep.irr.105* **1.** *v.i.* (*sein*) (a) (*Pers.*) to enter, come in; **e. in** + *acc,* to enter (the room, a convent, the war etc.); **in einen Verein usw. e.,** to join a club etc.; (b) (*Ereignis*) to occur, take place; (*Zustand*) to set in; (c) **für eine Sache e.,** to support a cause. **2.** *v.tr.* to kick (sth.) in.

'**Eintritt,** *m* **1.** (*Eintreten*) entering; entrance; **E. verboten!** no admittance. **2.** (a) joining (**in einen Verein usw.,** of an association etc.); (b) entry (**in Verhandlungen,** into negotiations); (c) **bei E. der Dunkelheit,** when darkness sets in. ◆'**E~s-,** *comb.fm.* admission (ticket etc.).

'**eintrocknen,** *v.i.sep.* (*sein*) to dry up.

'**einüben,** *v.tr.sep.* to practise (a piece of music, dance step etc.).

**einverleib|en** ['ainfɛrlaibən], *v.tr.sep. & insep.* (a) to incorporate (sth.); (b) *Hum:* (*Pers.*) **sich** *dat* **einen Kuchen usw. e.,** to consume a cake etc.

'**Einvernehmen,** *n* **-s/-** understanding; **im E. mit dem Chef,** with the agreement of the boss.

'**einverstanden,** *pred.adj.* **e. sein,** to be in agreement; **e.!** OK!

'**Einverständnis,** *n* (a) agreement; (*Billigung*) consent; (b) (*Einigkeit*) understanding.

'**Einwand,** *m* **-(e)s/=e** objection (**gegen etwas** *acc,* to sth.). ◆'**e~'frei,** *adj.* satisfactory; (*tadellos*) perfect.

'**Einwander|er,** *m* immigrant. ◆'**e~n,** *v.i.sep.* (*sein*) to immigrate. ◆'**E~ung,** *f* immigration.

**einwärts** ['ainvɛrts], *adv.* inward(s).

'**Einweg-,** *comb.fm.* non-returnable (bottle etc.).

'**einweichen,** *v.tr.sep.* to soak (washing etc.).

'**einweih|en,** *v.tr.sep.* (a) to open (a building, road etc.), consecrate (a church etc.); (b) to initiate (s.o.); **j-n in ein Geheimnis usw. e.,** to let s.o. in on a secret etc. ◆'**E~ung,** *f* **-/-en 1.** official opening; *Ecc:* consecration. **2.** initiation.

'**einweis|en,** *v.tr.sep.irr.70* (a) **j-n ins Krankenhaus usw. e.,** to send s.o. to (the) hospital etc.; (b) **j-n in eine Tätigkeit e.,** to introduce s.o. to a job. ◆'**E~ung,** *f* **-/-en** (a) assignment; **E.**

**ins Krankenhaus,** hospitalization; (b) introduction (**in** + *acc,* to).

'**einwenden,** *v.tr.sep.irr.94* to object; **dagegen läßt sich nichts e.,** there is no objection to that.

'**einwerfen,** *v.tr.sep.irr.110* (a) to throw in (the ball, *Fig:* a remark etc.); to post (a letter); to put in (a coin, money); (b) to smash (a window etc.).

'**einwickeln,** *v.tr.sep.* to wrap up.

'**einwillig|en,** *v.i.sep.* (*haben*) (**in etwas**) *acc* **e.,** to agree(*erlauben*) consent (to sth.). ◆'**E~ung,** *f* **-/-en** agreement; consent.

'**einwirk|en,** *v.i.sep.* (*haben*) **auf j-n, etwas** *acc* **e.,** to have an effect on s.o., sth.; (*beeinflussen*) to influence s.o., sth. ◆'**E~ung,** *f* effect; (*Einfluß*) influence.

'**Einwohner(in),** *m* **-s/-** (*f* **-/-nen**) inhabitant; resident (of a village, estate). ◆'**E~meldeamt,** *n* registration office. ◆'**E~schaft,** *f* **-/no** *pl* resident population.

'**Einwurf,** *m* **1.** *Sp:* throw-in; **E. DM 2,** put 2 marks in the slot. **2.** (*Öffnung*) slot. **3.** (*Bemerkung*) interjection; (*kritisch*) objection.

'**Einzahl,** *f Gram:* singular.

'**einzahl|en,** *v.tr.sep.* to pay in (money) (**auf j-s Konto,** into s.o.'s account). ◆'**E~ung,** *f* **-/-en** payment (into the bank).

'**einzäunen,** *v.tr.sep.* to fence (in) (a plot etc.).

'**einzeichnen,** *v.tr.sep.* to draw in (details).

**Einzel** ['aintsəl]. **I.** *n* **-s/-** (*Tennis*) singles. **II.** '**E~-,** *comb.fm.* (a) separate (question, element, state, edition etc.); (b) single (volume, bed, garage etc.); individual (packaging, *Sp:* contest etc.); (c) (*einzig*) sole; only (child etc.). ◆'**E~gänger(in),** *m* (*f*) (*Pers.*) outsider.); *F:* lone wolf. ◆'**E~haft,** *f* solitary confinement. ◆'**E~handel,** *m* retail trade. ◆'**E~händler,** *m* retailer. ◆'**E~heit,** *f* **-/-en** detail. ◆'**e~n,** *adj.* **1.** (a) (*alleinstehend*) individual, (*gesondert*) separate (parts etc.); **jeder e~ne,** every single one; **e. verpackt,** individually wrapped. **2.** (*einige*) some, a few. **3. das e~ne,** the details; **im e~nen,** in detail. ◆'**E~teil,** *n* component (part). ◆'**E~zimmer,** *n* single room.

'**einziehen,** *v.sep.irr.113* **1.** *v.tr.* (a) to pull/draw in (nets, a rope etc.); to take in (sails, claws etc.); to strike (the flag); to duck (one's head); to retract (the undercarriage); (b) to withdraw (a passport, licence etc.); *Jur:* to seize (s.o.'s property etc.); (c) to collect (debts, taxes etc.); **Erkundigungen über j-n e.,** to make inquiries about s.o.; (d) *Mil:* to call (s.o.) up, *N.Am:* draft (s.o.). **2.** *v.i.* (*sein*) (a) (*Pers.*) (**in eine Wohnung, ein Haus usw.**) **e.,** to move in(to a flat, house etc.); (b) (*Feuchtigkeit usw.*) to be soaked up.

**einzig** ['aintsiç], *adj.* (*a*) only (possibility, child etc.); **nur ein e~es Mal!** just once! **er konnte keine e~e Frage beantworten**, he couldn't answer a single question; (*b*) **e.** (**in seiner Art**), unique. ◆**'e~artig**, *adj.* unique; (*unvergleichlich*) incomparable.

**'Einzug,** *m* (*a*) entrance (of s.o., an army, band); (*b*) moving in; move (**in die neue Wohnung**, into the new flat).

**Eis** [ais]. **I.** *n* -es/*no pl* 1. ice. 2. *Cu:* ice (cream). **II.** **'E~-,** *comb.fm.* (*a*) ice (-hockey, dancing, *Nau:* -breaker etc.); (*b*) ice cream (seller, wafer etc.). ◆**'E~bahn,** *f* ice/skating rink. ◆**'E~bär,** *m* polar bear. ◆**'E~becher,** *m* sundae. ◆**'E~bein,** *n* *Cu:* cured knuckle of pork. ◆**'E~berg,** *m* iceberg. ◆**'E~blume,** *f* frost-flower (on a window). ◆**'E~decke,** *f* frozen surface; (*Schicht*) (layer of) ice. ◆**'E~diele,** *f* ice cream parlour. ◆**e~ig** ['aiziç], *adj.* icy (wind, *Fig:* manner etc.). ◆**'E~kaffee,** *m* iced coffee. ◆**'e~kalt,** *adj.* icy, freezing (room, weather etc.); ice-cold (drink). ◆**'E~kunstlauf,** *m* figure skating. ◆**'E~lauf,** *m* skating. ◆**'e~laufen**, *v.i.sep.irr.58* (*sein*) to skate. ◆**'E~pickel,** *m* ice-axe. ◆**'E~schießen,** *n* *approx.* = curling. ◆**'E~schrank,** *m* refrigerator. ◆**'E~zapfen,** *m* icicle. ◆**'E~zeit,** *f* Ice Age.

**Eisen** ['aizən], *n* -s/- iron. ◆**'E~bahn,** *f* railway, *N.Am:* railroad. ◆**'E~bahn-,** *comb.fm.* railway, *N.Am:* railroad (line, station etc.); rail (journey, network etc.). ◆**'E~bahner,** *m* -s/- *F:* railwayman; *N.Am:* railroader. ◆**'E~erz,** *n* iron ore. ◆**'e~haltig,** *adj.* containing iron; ferrous (compound).

**eisern** ['aizərn], *adj.* (*a*) iron; (*b*) relentless (energy etc.); *F:* **darin bin ich e.,** I won't budge on that.

**eitel** ['aitəl], *adj.* vain. ◆**'E~keit,** *f* -/-en vanity.

**Eiter** ['aitər], *m* -s/*no pl* pus. ◆**'e~n,** *v.i.* (*haben*) to suppurate.

**eitrig** ['aitriç], *adj.* suppurating.

**'Eiweiß,** *n* (*a*) egg-white; (*b*) *Biol:* protein.

**'Eizelle,** *f* ovum.

**Ekel** ['e:kəl]. **1.** *m* -s/*no pl* (*a*) repulsion (**vor** + *dat*, to); **E. über etwas** *acc* **empfinden**, to be sickened by sth. **2.** *n* -s/- *F:* (*Pers.*) beast; (*Mann*) bastard, (*Frau*) bitch. ◆**'e~erregend,** *adj.* nauseating. ◆**'e~haft/'ek(e)lig,** *adj.* (*a*) nauseating (smell etc.); (*b*) (*unangenehm*) beastly (person, job, weather etc.); horrible (sight etc.). ◆**'e~n,** *v.tr.* (*a*) *v.impers.* **es ekelt mich/mir vor ihm,** I am disgusted by him; I loathe him; (*b*) *v.refl.* **sich vor j-m, etwas** *dat* **e.,** to loathe s.o., sth.

**Ekstase** [ɛk'sta:zə], *f* -/-n ecstasy.

**Ekzem** [ɛk'tse:m], *n* -s/-e eczema.

**Elan** [e'lɑ:n], *m* -s/*no pl* vigour.

**elastisch** [e'lastiʃ], *adj.* (*a*) elastic (material, bandage etc.); flexible (wood, metal, *Fig:* person, attitude etc.); (*b*) springy (steps, walk etc.); supple (movements, limbs etc.). ◆**E~izität** [elastitsi'tɛ:t], *f* -/*no pl* elasticity; (*also Fig:*) flexibility; springiness.

**Elch** [ɛlç], *m* -(e)s/-e (European) elk.

**Elefant** [ele'fant], *m* -en/-en elephant.

**elegant** [ele'gant], *adj.* (*a*) elegant; (*b*) *Fig:* neat (solution etc.). ◆**E~z** ['gants], *f* -/*no pl* (*a*) elegance; (*b*) neatness.

**elektrifizieren** [elɛktrifi'tsi:rən], *v.tr.* to electrify (a railway etc.). ◆**E~triker** [e'lɛktrikər], *m* -s/- electrician. ◆**e~trisch** [e'lɛktriʃ], *adj.* electric (shock, razor, current etc.); electrical (appliance etc.). ◆**e~trisieren** [-'zi:rən], *v.tr.* to charge (sth.) with electricity; **sich e.,** to get an electric shock. ◆**E~trizität** [-itsi'tɛ:t], *f* -/*no pl* electricity. ◆**E~trizi'tätswerk,** *n* power station.

**Elektro-** [e'lɛktro-], *comb.fm.* (*a*) *Ph: Ch: etc:* electro-(magnet etc.); (*b*) electrical (industry, engineer etc.); (*c*) electric (boat, drive, vehicle, razor etc.). ◆**E~de** [-'tro:də], *f* -/-n electrode. ◆**E~lyse** [-'tro'ly:zə], *f* -/*no pl* electrolysis. ◆**E~n** [e'lɛktrɔn], *n* -s/-en [-'tro:nən], electron. ◆**E~nen-** [-'tro:nən], *comb.fm.* (*a*) electronic (organ etc.); (*b*) electron (microscope, beam). ◆**E~nik** [-'tro:nik], *f* -/*no pl* electronics. ◆**e~nisch,** *adj.* electronic; *adv.* electronically.

**Element** [ele'mɛnt], *n* -(e)s/-e element; *El:* cell (of a battery). ◆**e~ar** [-'tɑ:r], *adj.* **1.** (*a*) (*wesentlich*) fundamental (needs, requirements); (*b*) (*primitiv*) rudimentary (knowledge etc.). **2.** elemental (force, feeling etc.).

**Elend** ['e:lɛnt]. **I.** *n* -s/*no pl* (*a*) (*Armut*) poverty; (*b*) misery; distress. **II.** **e.,** (*a*) (*jämmerlich*) wretched, (*ärmlich*) poverty-stricken (existence, person etc.); (*b*) (*erbärmlich*) miserable. ◆**'E~sviertel,** *n* slum.

**elf** [ɛlf]. **I.** *num.adj.* eleven. **II.** **E.,** *f* -/-en *Fb:* eleven, team. ◆**E~'meter,** *m* penalty kick.

**Elfe** ['ɛlfə], *f* -/-n elf.

**Elfenbein** ['ɛlfənbain], *n* ivory.

**eliminieren** [elimi'ni:rən], *v.tr.* to eliminate.

**elitär** [eli'tɛ:r], *adj.* elitist. ◆**E~e** [e'li:tə], *f* -/-n elite.

**Ellbogen** ['ɛlbo:gən], *m* -s/- elbow.

**Elle** ['ɛlə], *f* -/-n *Anat:* ulna. ◆**'e~nlang,** *adj.* *F:* interminable.

**Elsaß** ['ɛlzas]. *Pr.n.n* -& -sses Alsace. ◆**Elsässer(in)** ['ɛlzɛsər(in)], *m* -s/- (*f* -/-nen) Alsatian.

**Elster** ['ɛlstər], *f* -/-n magpie.

**elter|lich** ['ɛltərliç], *adj.* parental (home etc.). ◆**E~n** ['ɛltərn], *pl* parents. ◆**'E~nhaus,** *n* (parental) home. ◆**'e~nlos,** *adj.* orphaned. ◆**'E~nteil,** *m* parent.

**Email** [e'maːj], *n* -s/-s/**E~le** [e'maljə], *f* -/-n enamel. ◆**e~lieren** [ema(l)'jiːrən], *v.tr.* to enamel (a vase etc.).

**Emanz|ipation** [emantsipatsi'oːn], *f* -/-en emancipation. ◆**e~i'pieren,** *v.tr.* to emancipate (women etc.).

**Embryo** ['ɛmbryo], *m* -s/-s & **-nen** embryo.

**Emigr|ant** [emi'grant], *m* -en/-en emigrant. ◆**E~ati'on,** *f* -/-en emigration. ◆**e~ieren** [-'griːrən] *v.i.* (*sein*) to emigrate.

**Emotion** [emotsi'oːn], *f* -/-en emotion. ◆**e~al** [-o'naːl], *adj.* emotional.

**Empfang** [ɛm'pfaŋ], *m* -(e)s/¨e receipt (of goods, a letter etc.); reception (of s.o., guests, *TV:* a programme); **in E. nehmen,** to receive (goods, a present etc.), welcome (s.o.). ◆**e~en,** *v.tr.irr.28* (*a*) to receive (money, a gift, letter, an award, orders, *TV:* a programme, the sacrament etc.); (*b*) to welcome (a guest etc.); (*c*) (*Frau*) to conceive (a child). ◆**E~sdame,** *f* receptionist. ◆**E~shalle,** *f* reception area, *N.Am:* lobby (of a hotel).

**Empfäng|er** [ɛm'pfɛŋər], *m* -s/- **1.** (*Pers.*) recipient; addressee. **2.** *Rad: TV:* receiver. ◆**e~lich,** *adj.* **für etwas** *acc* **e.,** susceptible/prone to sth. ◆**E~nis,** *f* -/-se conception. ◆**E~nisverhütung,** *f* contraception.

**empfehl|en** [ɛm'pfeːlən], *v.tr.irr.2* (*a*) to recommend (s.o., sth.); (*b*) (*Pers.*) **sich e.,** to take one's leave; **bitte e. Sie mich Ihrer Gattin,** please remember me to your wife. ◆**e~enswert,** *adj.* to be recommended; (*ratsam*) advisable. ◆**E~ung,** *f* -/-en recommendation.

**empfind|en** [ɛm'pfindən]. **I.** *v.tr.irr.9* to feel (pain, joy etc.). **II. E.,** *n* -s/*no pl* feeling; **meinem E. nach,** in my opinion; the way I feel. ◆**e~lich,** *adj.* (*a*) sensitive (skin etc.) (**gegen** + *acc*, to); *Med:* susceptible; (*b*) (*reizbar*) touchy (person); (*c*) delicate (child, plant, material etc.); (*d*) (*spürbar, hart*) severe (pain, penalty, cold etc.); serious (losses). ◆**E~lichkeit,** *f* -/-en (*a*) sensitivity (**gegen** + *acc*, to); tenderness (of a wound etc.); *Med:* susceptibility; (*b*) touchiness; (*c*) delicacy (of a material etc.). ◆**e~sam** [ɛm'pfintzaːm], *adj.* (*a*) sentimental; (*b*) (*sensibel*) sensitive. ◆**E~ung,** *f* -/-en feeling; sensation (of cold, pain etc.); (*Gemütsbewegung*) sentiment.

**empor** [ɛm'poːr], *adv. Lit:* up(wards). ◆**E~kömmling,** *m* -s/-e upstart. ◆**e~steigen,** *v.tr. & i.sep.irr.89* (*sein*) to rise.

**Empore** [ɛm'poːrə], *f* -/-n gallery.

**empör|en** [ɛm'pøːrən], *v.tr.* to infuriate (s.o.); **sich (über etwas** *acc*) **e.,** to get into a fury (about sth.). ◆**e~end,** *adj.* outrageous (statement etc.); (*schändlich*) shocking. ◆**E~ung,** *f* -/-en indignation.

**emsig** ['ɛmziç], *adj.* busy; (*fleißig*) industrious.

**End-** [ɛnt-], *comb.fm.* final (phase, state, *Sp:* round, spurt etc.); ultimate (purpose etc.). ◆**'E~betrag,** *m* sum total; total amount. ◆**'e~gültig,** *adj.* final (decision, solution etc.); definitive (answer, result etc.); conclusive (proof). ◆**'e~lich. 1.** *adv.* (*a*) at last; (*b*) (*schließlich*) finally. **2.** *adj. Mth: etc:* finite. ◆**'e~los,** *adj.* (*a*) endless; interminable (speech etc.); (*b*) (*unbegrenzt*) boundless (patience etc.). ◆**'E~punkt,** *m* last point (on a scale); end (of a line etc.); destination. ◆**'E~spiel,** *n* final. ◆**'E~station,** *f* last stop; (*Endbahnhof*) terminus; *N.Am:* terminal. ◆**'E~summe,** *f* sum total; total amount.

**End|e** ['ɛndə], *n* -s/-n end; **am E.,** at the end; **E. April,** at the end of April; **sie ist E. Vierzig,** she is in her late forties; **zu E.,** at an end; (*verbraucht*) finished; **zu E. gehen,** to come to an end; (*Vorräte usw.*) to run out; *Fig:* **am E. war er's vielleicht doch nicht,** perhaps it wasn't him after all. ◆**'e~en,** *v.i.* (*haben*) to end; **der Vertrag endet im Mai,** the contract runs out in May. ◆**E~ung,** *f* -/-en ending.

**Energ|ie** [enɛr'giː]. **I.** *f* -/-n energy. **II. E~ie-,** *comb.fm.* energy (requirement etc.); (source etc.) of energy. ◆**e~iegeladen,** *adj.* full of energy; dynamic. ◆**e~ielos,** *adj.* listless. ◆**e~isch** [e'nɛrgiʃ], *adj.* (*a*) forceful (person, character etc.); (*b*) (*entschlossen*) resolute (person, tone, step).

**eng** [ɛŋ], *adj.* (*a*) narrow (street, valley etc.); *Fig:* **hier ist es mir zu e.,** I feel shut in here; (*b*) (*nahe*) close (friend etc.); (*c*) **die Hose ist e.,** the trousers are a tight fit. ◆**E~e** ['ɛŋə], *f* -/-n (*a*) narrowness; (*b*) (*Bedrängnis*) tight corner; **j-n in die E. treiben,** to corner s.o. ◆**'e~herzig,** *adj.* petty, small-minded. ◆**'E~paß,** *m* (*a*) (narrow) pass, defile (between mountains); (*b*) *Fig:* bottleneck. ◆**e~stirnig** ['-ʃtirniç], *adj.* narrow-minded.

**Engage|ment** [ãgaʒə'mãː], *n* -s/-s commitment; *esp. Th:* engagement. ◆**e~ieren** [-'ʒiːrən], *v.tr.* (*a*) to take (s.o.) on, *Th: etc:* engage (s.o.); (*b*) **sich (politisch usw.) e.,** to involve oneself heavily (in politics etc.). ◆**e~iert,** *adj.* committed (person).

**Engel** ['ɛŋəl], *m* -s/- angel. ◆**'e~haft,** *adj.* angelic.

**England** ['ɛŋlant]. *Pr.n.n* -s. England.

**Engländer** ['ɛŋlɛndər], *m* -s/- **1.** Englishman. **2.** *Tchn:* adjustable spanner.

◆'E~in, f -/-nen Englishwoman.
englisch ['ɛŋliʃ]. I. adj. English. II. E., n -(s)/no pl (Sprache) English.
Enkel ['ɛŋkəl], m -s/- grandson.
◆'E~lin, f -/-nen granddaughter.
◆'E~kind, n grandchild.
enorm [e'nɔrm], adj. (a) enormous; (b) F: tremendous; fantastic.
Ensemble [ã'sã:bl], n -s/-s Mus: ensemble; Th: company.
entarten [ɛnt'ʔa:rtən], v.i. (sein) to degenerate.
entbehren [ɛnt'be:rən], v. 1. v.tr. to do without (s.o., sth.). 2. v.i. (haben) + gen Lit: dieses Gerücht entbehrt jeder Grundlage, this rumour is without any foundation. ◆e~lich, adj. superfluous. ◆E~ung, f -/-en privation.
ent'binden v.tr.irr.9 Med: to deliver (a woman) of a child. ◆E~ung, f delivery.
entblößen [ɛnt'blø:sən], v.tr. to bare.
ent'decken, v.tr. to discover (s.o., sth.); to detect (a crime, mistakes etc.). ◆E~er, m -s/- discoverer; (Forscher) explorer. ◆E~ung, f -/-en discovery; (Enthüllung) detection.
Ente ['ɛntə], f -/-n 1. duck. 2. (Zeitungse.) false report.
ent'ehren, v.tr. to dishonour. ◆e~end, adj. degrading.
ent'eignen, v.tr. to dispossess (s.o.); Jur: to expropriate (property).
ent'eisen, v.tr. to defrost (a refrigerator).
ent'erben, v.tr. to disinherit (s.o.).
ent'fachen, v.tr. Lit: to inflame (desire, passions); to provoke (a quarrel etc.).
ent'fallen, v.i.irr.27 (sein) (a) Lit: (Sachen) j-m/j-s Händen e., to slip from s.o.'s hands; Fig: ihr Name ist mir e., her name has slipped my mind; (b) Adm: (auf Formular) entfällt, not applicable; (c) auf j-n e., to fall to s.o.
ent'falten, v.tr. to unfold (a tablecloth, Fig: a plan etc.); sich e., (Blume usw.) to open; (b) (entwickeln) (Pers.) to develop (one's powers, faculties etc.); (c) (zeigen) to display, show (courage, taste etc.). ◆E~ung, f -/no pl (a) unfolding; (b) display (of pomp, courage etc.); (c) development; zur E. kommen, (Plan usw.) to come to fruition; (Schönheit) to blossom.
entfernen [ɛnt'fɛrnən], v.tr. (a) to remove; (herausnehmen) to take (sth.) out; j-n aus dem Amt/Dienst e., to remove/dismiss s.o. from office; (b) to move, carry (s.o., sth.) away; sich e., to go away, leave. ◆e~t, adj. (a) 20 km e., 20 kms away; (b) distant, remote (place, relation); (c) (schwach) faint (resemblance); ich denke nicht im e~testen daran, I haven't the slightest intention of doing it. ◆E~ung, f -/-en (Weite) distance. ◆E~ungsmesser, m rangefinder.
ent'fesseln, v.tr. to unleash (feelings etc.); to provoke (a war, argument etc.).

entflammbar [ɛnt'flambɑ:r], adj. leicht e., inflammable; (Pers.) enthusiastic. ◆e~en, v.tr. (a) to inflame (passions, feelings); to kindle (enthusiasm); to arouse (anger etc.).
ent'fremden, v.tr. to alienate (s.o.).
ent'frosten, v.tr. to defrost.
ent'führen, v.tr. (a) to kidnap, abduct (s.o.); (b) to hijack (an aeroplane, ship etc.). ◆E~er, m (a) kidnapper; (b) hijacker. ◆E~ung, f -/-en (a) kidnapping, abduction; (b) hijacking.
entgegen [ɛnt'ge:gən], adv. & prep. + dat 1. towards. 2. against (the wind etc.); contrary to (s.o.'s wishes, regulations). ◆e~bringen, v.tr.sep.irr.16 j-m, etwas dat Verständnis usw. e., to show understanding etc. for s.o., sth. ◆e~gehen, v.i.sep.irr.36 (sein) j-m e., to go/walk to meet s.o. ◆e~gesetzt, adj. opposite (direction, effect etc.); contrary, opposing (interests etc.). ◆e~halten, v.tr.sep.irr.45 j-m etwas e., to hold sth. out to s.o.; dem ist nichts entgegenzuhalten, there is no objection to that. ◆e~kommen. I. v.i.sep.irr.53 (sein) (a) j-m, etwas dat e., to come towards/approach s.o., sth.; (b) j-m/j-s Wünschen e., to oblige s.o./comply with s.o.'s wishes. II. E., n -s/no pl obligingness; co-operation; (Zugeständnis) concession. ◆e~kommend, adj. 1. oncoming (vehicle, traffic). 2. obliging (person); helpful (suggestion etc.). ◆e~nehmen, v.tr. sep.irr.69 to accept (gifts, orders etc.), take (a telephone call, message etc.); to receive (congratulations, a prize etc.). ◆e~sehen, v.i.sep.irr.92 (haben) j-m e., to look towards s.o./in s.o.'s direction; etwas dat e., to await sth., (mit Freude) look forward to sth. ◆e~setzen, v.tr.sep. (a) j-m, etwas dat Widerstand e., to resist s.o., sth.; diesem Vorwurf habe ich nichts entgegenzusetzen, I have no reply to this reproach; (b) (gegenüberstellen) to contrast (sth.). ◆e~treten, v.i.sep.irr.105 (sein) (a) j-m e., to approach s.o.; dem Feind usw. e., to face the enemy etc.; (b) Vorurteilen usw. e., to oppose prejudices etc. ◆e~wirken, v.i.sep. (haben) etwas dat e., to counteract sth.
entgegnen [ɛnt'ge:gnən], v.tr. to reply. ◆E~ung, f -/-en answer, reply; (schlagfertig) retort, rejoinder.
ent'gehen, v.tr. & i.irr.36 (sein) (a) etwas dat e., to avoid sth.; (b) (unbemerkt bleiben) j-m e., to escape s.o./s.o.'s notice; sie läßt sich dat nichts e. she doesn't miss anything.
entgeistert [ɛnt'gaistərt], adj. dumbfounded; (entsetzt) aghast.
Entgelt ['ɛntgɛlt], n -(e)s/-e payment; gegen E., for a fee.
entgleisen [ɛnt'glaizən], v.i. (sein) (Zug) to be derailed, Fig: (Pers.) to commit a faux pas. ◆E~ung, f -/-en 1. derail-

ment. 2. *Fig:* faux pas; embarrassing slip.

**ent'gräten,** *v.tr.* to bone, fillet (a fish).

**enthaar|en,** *v.tr.* to remove hair from (legs etc.). ◆E~**ungsmittel,** *n* depilatory.

**ent'halt|en,** *v.tr.irr.45* (*a*) to contain (sth.); **im Preis e.,** included in the price; (*b*) **sich der Stimme e.,** to abstain (from voting). ◆**e~sam,** *adj.* abstemious; (*sexuell*) chaste. ◆E~**samkeit,** *f -/no pl* abstinence. ◆E~**ung,** *f Pol: etc:* abstention (from voting).

**ent'härten,** *v.tr.* to soften (water etc.).

**ent'hüllen,** *v.tr.* to reveal (sth., *Fig:* a plot etc.); to unveil (a face, monument etc.).

**Enthusiasmus** [ɛntuzi'asmus], *m -/no pl* enthusiasm.

**ent'kernen,** *v.tr.* to core (apples); to seed (grapes, raisins etc.); to stone (cherries etc.).

**ent'kommen,** *v.i.irr.53* (*sein*) to escape, get away (j-m, from s.o.).

**ent'korken,** *v.tr.* to uncork (a bottle).

**entkräften** [ɛnt'krɛftən], *v.tr.* to weaken (s.o.); *Fig:* to invalidate (an argument).

**ent'laden,** *v.tr.irr.56* to unload (luggage, a rifle, lorry etc.); to discharge (a battery etc.); **sich e.,** (*Gewitter*) to break, burst.

**ent'lang,** *prep. + acc/dat & adv.* along. ◆**e~gehen,** *v.i.sep.irr.36* (*sein*) to walk along.

**entlarven** [ɛnt'larfən], *v.tr.* to unmask (s.o.).

**ent'lass|en,** *v.tr.irr.57* to dismiss (s.o.); to discharge (a patient etc.); (*befreien*) to release (a prisoner). ◆E~**ung,** *f -/-en* 1. (*a*) discharge; release; (*b*) leaving school. 2. dismissal, *F:* firing.

**ent'last|en,** *v.tr.* (*a*) to relieve (the strain etc.) on (s.o., sth.); to ease (traffic, *Fig:* s.o.'s conscience etc.); (*b*) *Jur:* to exonerate. ◆E~**ung,** *f -/-en* relief; easing; *Jur:* **zu j-s E.,** in s.o.'s defence. ◆E~**ungs-,** *comb.fm.* relief (road, train etc.); *Jur:* exonerating (evidence etc.); defence (witness etc.).

**ent'leeren,** *v.tr.* to empty.

**ent'legen,** *adj.* remote; (*einsam*) isolated.

**ent'locken,** *v.tr.* **j-m, etwas** *dat* **etwas e.,** to coax sth. from s.o., sth.

**ent'lüften,** *v.tr.* to ventilate (a room etc.); *Aut:* to bleed (brakes etc.).

**entmutigen** [ɛnt'mu:tigən], *v.tr.* to discourage.

**Entnahme** [ɛnt'na:mə], *f -/-n* taking (**aus** + *dat,* from).

**ent'nehmen,** *v.tr.irr.69* (*a*) **etwas (aus) etwas** *dat* **e.,** to take sth. from/out of sth.; (*b*) (*schließen*) to deduce (sth.).

**ent'puppen,** *v.refl.* **sich als etwas e.,** to turn out to be sth.

**ent'rahmen,** *v.tr.* to (take the) cream off, skim (milk).

**ent'rätseln,** *v.tr.* to puzzle out (a mystery etc.).

**ent'reißen,** *v.tr.irr.4* to snatch (s.o., sth.) away (j-m, from s.o.).

**ent'richten,** *v.tr.* to pay (taxes etc.).

**ent'rinnen,** *v.i.irr.73* (*sein*) to escape, get away (**etwas** *dat,* from sth.).

**ent'rosten,** *v.tr.* to derust (sth.).

**ent'rüst|en,** *v.tr.* to fill (s.o.) with indignation; **sich (über etwas** *acc*) **e.,** to get indignant at sth.; **entrüstet,** indignant (person, face). ◆E~**ung,** *f -/no pl* indignation.

**ent'schädig|en,** *v.tr.* to compensate (s.o.), *Jur:* pay (s.o.) compensation/ (*Schadenersatz*) damages. ◆E~**ung,** *f* compensation; *Jur:* (*Schadenersatz*) damages.

**ent'schärfen,** *v.tr.* to defuse (a bomb, mine etc.); *Fig:* to take the sting out of (a crisis etc.).

**Entscheid** [ɛnt'ʃait], *m -(e)s/-e* decision; *Jur:* ruling. ◆**e~en** [-'ʃaidən], *v.tr. & i.irr.65* (*haben*) to decide (**über** + *acc,* on); **du mußt hier e.,** it's your decision; **sich e.,** (i) (*Pers.*) to decide, make up one's mind; (ii) (*Spiel, Sache usw.*) to be decided. ◆**e~end,** *adj.* decisive (influence, victory, evidence etc.); crucial (point, moment, question); *Sp:* deciding (goal etc.). ◆E~**ung,** *f -/-en* decision; settlement of a question, problem etc.); *Jur: Adm:* ruling.

**entschieden** [ɛnt'ʃi:dən], *adj.* decisive (manner, tone etc.); firm (refusal, denial, supporter, opponent).

**ent'schließen,** *v.refl.irr.31* **sich (zu etwas** *dat*) **e.,** to decide, make up one's mind (to do sth.).

**entschlossen** [ɛnt'ʃlɔsən], *adj.* determined, resolute (person, action, attitude etc.); **er war zu allem e.,** he was ready to do anything. ◆E~**heit,** *f -/no pl* determination; resolution.

**Ent'schluß,** *m* decision. ◆E~**kraft,** *f -/ no pl* determination; initiative.

**entschlüsseln** [ɛnt'ʃlysəln], *v.tr.* to decipher (a code, writing), decode (a message etc.).

**entschuldig|bar** [ɛnt'ʃultba:r], *adj.* excusable, pardonable. ◆**e~igen** [-'ʃuldigən], *v.tr.* (*a*) to excuse (s.o., s.o.'s behaviour etc.); **e. Sie bitte!** excuse me! **e. Sie bitte die Störung,** (I'm) sorry to disturb you; (*b*) (*wegen Abwesenheit*) **j-n e.,** to make s.o.'s excuses; **nicht zu e.,** inexcusable; (*c*) *v.refl.* **sich (bei j-m) e.,** to apologize (bei j-m) um **E. bitten,** to apologize (to s.o.) for s.o.); (**ich bitte um) E.!** I beg your pardon! (I'm) sorry! 2. (*Ausrede*) excuse. ◆E~**igung,** *f -/-en* 1. apology; (j-n/für j-n) um **E. bitten,** to apologize (to s.o./ for s.o.); (**ich bitte um) E.!** I beg your pardon! (I'm) sorry! 2. (*Ausrede*) excuse.

**ent'setz|en.** I. *v.tr.* (*a*) to horrify, appal (s.o.); **sich über j-n, etwas e.,** to be horrified/appalled at s.o., sth.; (*b*) *Mil:* to relieve (a fortress etc.). II. **E.,** *n -s/no pl* horror. ◆**e~lich,** *adj.* (*a*) horrible; appalling (crime); (*b*) *F:* dreadful (weather, person, cold etc.); (*c*) *F:* (*sehr stark*) terrible. ◆**e~t,** *adj.* horrified; appalled; horror-stricken.

**ent'sichern,** *v.tr.* to release the safety catch of (a gun).

**ent'sinnen,** *v.refl.irr.3* **sich (j-s, etwas) e.,** to remember, recollect (s.o., sth.).

**ent'spann|en,** *v.tr. & i. (sein) & refl.* **(sich) e.,** to relax; *Fig:* **die Lage hat sich entspannt,** the situation has eased. ◆**E~ung,** *f -/no pl* relaxation; *Fig:* easing (of a situation etc.); *Pol:* détente (between East and West). ◆**E~ungspolitik,** *f* policy of détente.

**ent'sprech|en,** *v.i.irr.14 (haben) (a)* **den Tatsachen, einer Beschreibung usw. e.,** to correspond to/agree with the facts, a description etc.; *(b) (gleichkommen)* **etwas** *dat* **e.,** to be the equivalent of sth.; *(c) (nachkommen)* **einem Wunsch, einer Bitte usw. e.,** to comply with a wish, request etc.; **j-s Erwartungen usw. e.,** to meet s.o.'s expectations etc. ◆**e~end.** **1.** *adj. (a)* corresponding; *(b) (angemessen)* appropriate (authority, payment etc.); suitable (clothes). **2.** *prep. + dat (je nach)* according to (age, height, size etc.); *(gemäß)* in accordance with (orders, wishes etc.).

**ent'springen,** *v.i.irr.19 (sein) (a) (Fluß)* to rise, have its source; *(b) Fig:* to stem; *(c) (entkommen)* to escape.

**ent'steh|en,** *v.i.irr.100 (sein)* to come into being; *(geschaffen werden)* to be created; *(Wärme usw.)* to be generated; *(Brand)* to start; *(Ideen, Bewegung usw.)* to emerge; *(Freundschaft usw.)* to arise; *(Schaden, Unkosten usw.)* **aus etwas/durch etwas e.,** to result from sth. ◆**E~ung,** *f -/no pl* coming into being (of sth.); emergence (of an idea, a nation etc.).

**ent'stellen,** *v.tr. (a) (verzerren)* to distort (an object, *Fig:* facts, etc.); *(b) (verunstalten)* to disfigure (s.o.'s face, body).

**ent'stören,** *v.tr.* to suppress (interference from) (a radio etc.).

**ent'täusch|en,** *v.tr.* to disappoint (s.o.), dash (s.o.'s hopes), betray (s.o.'s trust). ◆**e~t,** *adj.* disappointed. ◆**E~ung,** *f -/-en* disappointment.

**ent'waffnen,** *v.tr.* to disarm (s.o.).

**Ent'warnung,** *f* all-clear (signal).

**ent'wässer|n,** *v.tr.* to drain (soil, fields etc.). ◆**E~ung,** *f -/-en* drainage.

**entweder** [ɛnt've:dər], *conj. & adv.* **e. ... oder,** either ... or.

**ent'weichen,** *v.i.irr.40 (sein)* to escape.

**ent'wenden,** *v.tr.* to steal.

**ent'werfen** *v.tr.irr.110 (a)* to design (a building, dress, machine, poster etc.); to make a sketch for (a painting, sculpture etc.); *(b)* to draft (a novel, lecture etc.), plan (a programme); to devise (a plan).

**ent'wert|en,** *v.tr. (a)* to devalue (currency); *(b)* to cancel (tickets, postage stamps). ◆**E~er,** *m -s/-* cancelling machine (for tickets).

**ent'wick|eln,** *v.tr.* to develop (sth., *Phot:*

a film), evolve (a plan etc.); to generate (heat etc.). ◆**E~lung,** *f -/-en* development; *esp. Biol:* evolution. ◆**E~lungshilfe,** *f* aid to developing countries. ◆**E~lungsland,** *n* developing country. ◆**E~lungsstufe,** *f* stage (of development).

**entwirren** [ɛnt'virən], *v.tr.* to unravel (thread, a knot etc.); *Fig:* to clarify (a situation), solve (a riddle).

**ent'wischen,** *v.i. (sein) F:* to make off (**mit** + *dat,* with); **j-m e.,** to give s.o. the slip.

**ent'wöhn|en** [ɛnt'vøːnən], *v.tr.* to wean (a child, young animal); to cure (an addict, oneself). ◆**E~ung,** *f -/-en (a)* weaning; *(b)* curing of an addiction.

**ent'würdigen,** *v.tr.* to degrade.

**Ent'wurf,** *m (Konzept)* draft; *(Abriß)* outline (of a plan etc.); *Art:* sketch, study; *(b)* design (of clothes, furniture, machinery); plan (of a building etc.).

**ent'wurzeln,** *v.tr.* to uproot (trees, people).

**ent'zieh|en,** *v.tr.irr.113 (a)* to take (sth.) away, withdraw (one's hand, support, favour etc.) (**j-m,** from s.o.); *(Pflanzen)* **dem Boden Wasser e.,** to draw water from the soil; *(b)* **sich j-m, etwas** *dat* **e.,** to evade s.o., sth. ◆**E~ung,** *f* withdrawal. ◆**E~ungskur,** *f* (course of) treatment for an addiction.

**ent'ziffern,** *v.tr.* to decipher (handwriting, a code etc.), decode (a message).

**ent'zück|en. I.** *v.tr.* to delight (s.o.). **II. E.,** *n -s/no pl* delight, *(Freude)* joy. ◆**e~end,** *adj.* delightful, charming; *(Aussehen)* ravishing.

**Ent'zug,** *m -(e)s/no pl* withdrawal; withholding (of drugs, permission etc.).

**entzünd|en** [ɛnt'tsyndən], *v.tr. (a)* to light (a fire, cigarette etc.), ignite (a substance); **sich e.,** *(Brennstoff usw.)* to ignite; *(Feuer)* to light; *(Heu, Gebäude usw.)* to catch fire; *(b) Fig:* to inflame, excite (passions etc.); *(c) Med: (Wunden usw.)* **sich e.,** to become inflamed. ◆**e~et,** *adj. Med:* inflamed. ◆**E~ung,** *f Med:* inflammation.

**ent'zwei,** *adj.* broken, in pieces. ◆**e~gehen,** *v.i.sep.irr.36 (sein)* to fall apart.

**Enzian** [ˈɛntsiaːn], *m -s/-e* gentian.

**Epidemie** [epideˈmiː], *f -/-n* epidemic.

**Epilepsie** [epilɛˈpsiː], *f -/-n* epilepsy.

**episch** [ˈeːpiʃ], *adj.* epic.

**Episode** [epiˈzoːdə], *f -/-n* episode. ◆**e~nhaft,** *adj.* episodic.

**Epoche** [eˈpɔxə], *f -/-n* period; *Lit:* epoch. ◆**e~machend,** *adj.* epoch-making.

**Epos** [ˈeːpɔs], *n -/Epen* epic.

**er** [eːr], *pers.pron. (Pers.)* he; *(Ding)* it.

**er'achten. I.** *v.tr.* **etwas für/als nötig usw. e.,** to consider sth., necessary etc. **II. E.,** *n* **meines E~s,** in my opinion.

**er'arbeiten,** *v.tr.* to earn enough money

to buy (a house etc.).

**Erb-** ['ɛrp-], *comb.fm.* (*a*) hereditary (disease, title, monarchy etc.); inherited (property, characteristic etc.); (*b*) *Biol:* genetic (research etc.). ◆**E~e¹** ['ɛrbə], *m* -n/-n heir; beneficiary (under a will). ◆**E~e²**, *n* -s/*no pl* inheritance; **geistiges E.**, spiritual heritage. ◆**'e~en**, *v.tr.* to inherit (sth., *Fig:* a characteristic, *F:* old clothes etc.). ◆**'E~faktor**, *m* heredity factor, gene. ◆**'E~folge**, *f Jur:* succession. ◆**E~in** ['ɛrbin], *f -/-nen* heiress. ◆**'e~lich**, *adj.* hereditary. ◆**'E~schaft**, *f -/-en* inheritance. ◆**'E~stück**, *n* heirloom. ◆**'E~sünde**, *f* original sin. ◆**'E~teil**, *n* share in an inheritance.

**erbarm|en** [ɛr'barmən]. I. *v.refl.* **sich j-s e.**, to take pity on s.o. II. **E.**, *n* -s/*no pl* mercy, compassion. ◆**e~ungslos**, *adj.* merciless; remorseless (persecution). ◆**e~ungsvoll**, *adj.* merciful, compassionate.

**erbärmlich** [ɛr'bɛrmliç], *adj.* wretched, miserable; (*a*) (*mitleiderregend*) pitiful (appearance etc.); (*b*) (*sehr schlecht*) dreadful (quality etc.); (*c*) *F:* (*sehr groß, stark*) terrible (thirst, hunger etc.). ◆**E~keit**, *f -/no pl* pitifulness; wretchedness.

**er'bau|en**, *v.tr.* (*a*) to build (sth.), erect (a building); (*b*) *Lit:* **sich (an etwas dat) e.**, to be edified by sth.). ◆**E~er**, *m* -s/- builder. ◆**e~lich**, *adj.* edifying (reading etc.). ◆**E~ung**, *f -/no pl* edification; (moral) uplift.

**erbeuten** [ɛr'bɔytən], *v.tr.* (*a*) *Mil:* to seize (sth.) (as booty); (*b*) (*Dieb usw.*) to make off with (money, jewels etc.).

**erbitter|n** [ɛr'bitərn], *v.tr.* to embitter (s.o.); (*erzürnen*) to anger (s.o.). ◆**e~t**, *adj.* (*a*) (*verbittert*) embittered; (*b*) stubborn (enemy, opponent); fierce (fight, battle).

**erblinden** [ɛr'blindən], *v.i.* (*sein*) to go blind.

**erbos|en** [ɛr'bo:zən], *v.tr.* **sich über j-n, etwas** *acc* **e.**, to get angry about s.o., sth. ◆**e~t**, *adj.* angry.

**er'brechen**, *v.tr. & refl. & i.irr.14* (*haben*) (**sich**) **e.**, to vomit.

**Erbse** ['ɛrpsə], *f -/-n* pea.

**Erd-**, ['ɛːrt-], *comb.fm.* (*a*) earth's (surface, curvature etc.); (axis, interior etc.) of the earth; (*b*) *El:* earth, *N.Am:* ground (lead/wire etc.). ◆**'E~beben**, *n* earthquake. ◆**'E~beere**, *f* strawberry. ◆**'E~boden**, *m* ground, earth. ◆**E~e** ['ɛːrdə], *f -/-n* (*a*) earth; **auf der E.**, on earth; **auf der ganzen E.**, all over the world; (*b*) *El:* earth(-wire), *N.Am:* ground(-wire). ◆**'e~en**, *v.tr. El:* to earth, *N.Am:* ground (an appliance etc.). ◆**'E~gas**, *n* natural gas. ◆**'E~geschoß**, *n* ground/*N.Am:* first floor. ◆**'E~kunde**, *f* geography. ◆**'E~nuß**, *f* peanut. ◆**'E~öl**, *n* (mineral) oil; petroleum. ◆**'E~reich**, *n*

earth, soil. ◆**'E~rutsch**, *m* (*also Fig:*) landslide. ◆**'E~teil**, *m* continent.

**er'denklich**, *adj.* imaginable, conceivable; **alles E~e**, everything possible.

**er'drosseln**, *v.tr.* to choke (s.o.) to death.

**er'drücken**, *v.tr.* to crush, squeeze (s.o.) to death.

**er'dulden**, *v.tr.* to endure (pain, injustice).

**er'eifern**, *v.refl.* **sich über etwas** *acc* **e.**, to get excited/(*zornig*) heated about sth.

**er'eig|nen**, *v.refl.* **sich e.**, to occur; (*Veranstaltung*) to take place. ◆**E~nis**, *n* -sses/-sse event. ◆**e~nisreich**, *adj.* eventful.

**er'fahr|en. I.** *v.tr.&i.irr.26* (*haben*) (*a*) to learn, discover (sth.); **von etwas dat e.**, to hear about sth.; (*b*) (*erleben*) (*Pers.*) to experience (joy, sorrow), meet with (ingratitude, humiliation etc.); to suffer (a defeat, pain etc.). **II.** *adj.* experienced. ◆**E~ung**, *f -/-en* **1.** experience; **schlechte E~en (mit j-m, etwas** *dat*) **machen**, to be let down by s.o., sth. **2. etwas in E. bringen**, to find sth. out. ◆**e~ungsgemäß**, *adv.* judging by (previous) experience.

**er'fass|en**, *v.tr.* (*a*) (*Auto usw.*) to drag (s.o.) along; *Fig:* (*storm*) to overcome (s.o.); (*b*) (*verstehen*) to grasp (sth.); (*c*) (*registrieren*) to list (sth.); **etwas statistisch e.**, to make a statistical survey of sth. ◆**E~ung**, *f* **1.** inclusion. **2.** (*Ermittlung*) record, survey.

**er'find|en**, *v.tr.irr.9* to invent (a machine, *Fig:* stories etc.). ◆**E~er**, *m* -s/- inventor. ◆**e~erisch**, *adj.* inventive; (*findig*) ingenious. ◆**E~ung**, *f -/-en* invention. ◆**E~ungsgabe**, *f* inventiveness.

**Erfolg** [ɛr'fɔlk], *m* -(e)s/-e **1.** (*Resultat*) result, outcome; (*Wirkung*) effect. **2.** (*positives Ergebnis*) success; **E. haben**, to be successful; **viel E.!** good luck! ◆**e~los**, *adj.* unsuccessful; vain; fruitless (attempt etc.). ◆**E~losigkeit**, *f -/no pl* lack of success. ◆**e~reich**, *adj.* successful. ◆**e~versprechend**, *adj.* promising.

**erforder|lich** [ɛr'fɔrdərliç], *adj.* required, (*nötig*) necessary. ◆**e~n**, *v.tr.* (*Sache*) to require (money, time etc.), call for (patience, courage, quick action etc.).

**er'forsch|en**, *v.tr.* (*a*) to explore (a country etc.); (*b*) (*ermitteln*) to investigate (a mystery, s.o.'s motives etc.). ◆**E~ung**, *f* exploration; investigation.

**er'freu|en**, *v.tr.* (*a*) to please, delight (s.o., the eye, ear etc.); (*b*) **sich großer Beliebtheit usw. e.**, to enjoy great popularity etc. ◆**e~lich**, *adj.* pleasing (sight, result etc.); gratifying (achievement); welcome (news). ◆**e~licherweise**, *adv.* fortunately, luckily. ◆**e~t**, *adj.* pleased, glad; **sehr e.!** pleased to meet you!

**er'frieren**, *v.i.irr.32* (*sein*) (*Pers., Tier*) to freeze to death; (*Pflanzen*) to be killed by (the) frost; (*Finger, Zehen usw.*) to be frostbitten.

**er'frisch|en,** v. 1. v.tr. to refresh. ◆e~end, adj. refreshing. ◆E~ung, f -/-en refreshment.

**er'füll|en,** v.tr. (a) to fill (a room etc.); (b) (nachkommen) to perform (a task, duty etc.), fulfil (a promise, condition etc.); **einen Zweck e.,** to serve a purpose; **sich e./erfüllt werden,** (Prophezeiung) to be fulfilled, (Traum) come true, (Hoffnung) be realized. ◆E~ung, f -/no pl -/ fulfilment; (Befriedigung) satisfaction; (b) performance; realization (of a wish, dream etc.).

**ergänz|en** [ɛr'gɛntsən], v.tr. (a) to complement (s.o., sth.); **darf ich noch etwas e.?** may I add something to that? (b) (vervollständigen) to complete (a list, sentence etc.); to fill in (missing words etc.), supply (missing parts). ◆E~ung, f -/ -en no pl complementing; (Vervollständigung) completion; supplying of missing parts, words etc.); (b) complement; (Hinzufügung) addition.

**er'geb|en.** I. v.tr.irr.35 (a) to result in (sth.); to produce (results, proof); (Rechnung) to come to a sum, figure); (b) sich **aus etwas dat e.,** to be the result of sth.; (c) (Schwierigkeit usw.) **sich e.,** to arise, F: crop up; **es hat sich so e.,** it just turned out like that; (d) (Pers., Truppen) **sich e.,** to surrender. II. adj. 1. (a) j-m **e. sein,** to be devoted to s.o. 2. (resignierend) resigned (expression etc.). ◆E~enheit, f -/no pl devotion. ◆E~nis [ɛr'ge:pnis], n -ses/-se result; Mth: (Lösung) solution. ◆e~nislos, adj. without result; inconclusive (negotiations etc.); Sp: drawn (game).

**er'gehen,** v.i.irr.36 (sein) (a) (Verordnung, Befehl usw.) to be issued/(Gesetz) passed; (Einladung) to be sent; **etwas über sich** acc **e. lassen,** to put up with sth.; (b) impers. **es ist ihm/ihr gut, schlecht usw. ergangen,** he/she got on well, badly etc.; (c) refl. **sich in Vermutungen usw.** acc e., to indulge in speculation(s) etc.

**ergiebig** [ɛr'gi:biç], adj. rich (source, harvest etc.) (an + dat, in); productive (discussion, research etc.).

**ergötzen** [ɛr'gœtsən], v.tr. to amuse, (ent-zücken) delight (s.o.).

**er'greifen,** v.tr.irr.43 (a) to seize (s.o., sth., Fig: power etc.); (festnehmen) to capture (a criminal etc.); Fig: (Furcht usw.) to overcome (s.o.); (innerlich bewegen) (Musik usw.) to move (s.o.); **Maßnahmen e.,** to adopt measures/take steps; **einen Beruf e.,** to take up a profession.

**ergriffen** [ɛr'grifən], adj. moved.

**er'gründen,** v.tr. to get to the bottom of (sth., a mystery etc.); to seek out (the cause of sth.).

**Er'guß,** m 1. Med: effusion (of blood). 2. Fig: outpouring; flood (of tears, abuse).

**er'haben,** adj. 1. sublime, lofty (thoughts); exalted (state of mind); mag-

nificent (sight). 2. **über jeden Verdacht usw. e.,** above suspicion etc.

**Er'halt,** m -(e)s/no pl receipt. ◆e~en. I. v.tr.irr.45 (a) (bekommen) to receive, get (sth.); to obtain (permission, access, a substance etc.); (b) to maintain (a building, roads); to keep (the peace, one's freedom etc.); to preserve (a work of art etc.); (ernähren) to support (s.o., a family etc.). II. adj. **gut e.,** well preserved; **e. bleiben,** to survive. ◆E~ung, f -/no pl maintenance, upkeep; preservation (of works of art, one's health etc.).

**erhältlich** [ɛr'hɛltliç], adj. obtainable; **schwer e.,** difficult to obtain.

**er'hängen,** v.refl. **sich e.,** to hang oneself.

**er'härten,** v.tr. to harden; Fig: to support (a statement etc.).

**er'heb|en,** v.tr.irr.48 (a) to raise (one's head, voice, glass etc.); (b) to levy (a tax, toll); (c) **sich e.,** (Pers.) to rise (to one's feet), get up; Fig: (Frage, Problem usw.) to arise, F: crop up. ◆e~lich, adj. considerable.

**erheitern** [ɛr'haitərn], v.tr. to amuse (s.o.).

**erhellen** [ɛr'hɛlən], v.tr. (a) to illuminate (a room, street etc.); **sich e.,** to grow lighter, brighten; (b) to throw light upon (a mystery etc.).

**erhitzen** [ɛr'hitsən], v.tr. (a) to heat (a liquid, metal etc.); **sich e.,** to get hot; (b) (erregen) to excite (s.o., s.o.'s imagination etc.).

**erhöh|en** [ɛr'hø:ən], v.tr. (a) to raise (sth.); (b) (steigern) to increase (prices, speed, Med: the dose etc.); to put up (wages etc.). ◆E~ung, f -/-en 1. raising. 2. increase.

**er'holen,** v.refl. **sich e.,** (a) (Patient usw.) to recover; (b) (sich ausruhen) to have a rest; (nach einer Krankheit) to convalesce. ◆e~sam, adj. restful, relaxing. ◆E~ung, f -/no pl recovery; (Periode) convalescence; (Entspannung) relaxation; (Spiel usw.) recreation. ◆e~ungs-bedürftig, adj. in need of a rest/holiday; run down.

**er'hören,** v.tr. Lit: to answer (a prayer, request etc.).

**Erika** ['e:rika], f -/-ken heather.

**erinner|n** [ɛr'ʔinərn], v.tr. (a) to remind (s.o.) (an j-n, etwas acc, of s.o., sth.); (b) **sich an j-n, etwas** acc **e.,** to remember/recall s.o., sth.; **wenn ich mich recht erinnere,** if I remember rightly. ◆E~ung, f -/-en (a) memory; (b) (Andenken) memento (of s.o.); souvenir (of a visit etc.).

**erkält|en** [ɛr'kɛltən], v.tr. **sich e.,** to catch a cold. ◆E~ung, f -/-en cold.

**erkenn|bar** [ɛr'kɛnbaːr], adj. (a) recognizable; (b) (mit dem Auge) e., visible. ◆e~en, v.tr.irr.51 (a) to recognize (s.o., s.o.'s voice, a danger etc.); to identify (s.o., sth.); (b) (wahrnehmen) to make out (s.o., sth.). ◆e~tlich, adj. sich (j-m) e. zeigen, to show one's gratitude (to s.o.). ◆E~tnis, f -/-se 1. (Wissen) knowledge. 2. (Einsicht) realization, recognition; wissenschaftliche E~tnisse, scientific discoveries. ◆E~ungsdienst, m (police) records department.

Erker ['ɛrkər], m -s/- bay(-window).

erklär|en [ɛr'kle:rən], v.tr. (a) (klarmachen) to explain (sth.); (deuten) to interpret (a text, dream, law etc.); (b) (äußern, bekennen) to declare (sth.); er erklärte sich bereit, es zu tun, he said he was willing to do it. ◆e~end, adj. explanatory. ◆e~lich, adj. explicable; (verständlich) understandable. ◆e~t, adj. declared (enemy etc.). ◆E~ung, f -/-en 1. explanation. 2. declaration.

er'klingen, v.i.irr.19 (sein) to sound; (Glocke, Stimme usw.) to ring out.

erkrank|en [ɛr'kraŋkən], v.i. (sein) to be taken ill/N.Am: sick. ◆E~ung, f -/-en illness.

erkunden [ɛr'kundən], v.tr. to investigate (sth.); Mil: to reconnoitre (the terrain, positions).

erkundig|en [ɛr'kundigən], v.refl. sich e., to enquire (nach j-m, after s.o.; nach etwas dat, about sth.). ◆E~ung, f -/-en enquiry.

er'lahmen, v.i. (sein) (Gespräch usw.) to flag.

er'langen, v.tr. to obtain (sth.), gain (access, popularity etc.).

Erlaß [ɛr'las], m -sses/-sse 1. decree. 2. exemption ( + gen, from); Jur: remission.

er'lass|en, v.tr.irr.57 (a) to issue (a decree, warrant etc.); to enact (a law); (b) to remit (debts, a punishment etc.).

erlauben [ɛr'lauben], v.tr. (a) (j-m) etwas e., to allow (s.o.) sth.; wenn Sie e. ..., if you don't mind ...; (b) sich dat etwas e., to take the liberty of doing sth.; wir können uns kein neues Auto e., we cannot afford a new car. ◆E~nis, f -/no pl permission.

er'läutern, v.tr. to elucidate (a problem etc.). ◆E~ung, f -/-en explanation.

Erle ['ɛrlə], f -/-n alder.

er'leb|en, v.tr. (a) to experience (sth.); to undergo (a change, crisis, hardship etc.); (b) (mite.) to witness (sth.); to live to see (sth., a birthday, year etc.). ◆E~nis, n -ses/-se experience.

erledigen [ɛr'le:digən], v.tr. (a) to deal with (sth.); to get through (one's work, business etc.); to get (a job etc.) done; to settle (a matter, question, problem etc.); sich von selbst e., to take care of itself; (b) F: (vernichten) to do for (s.o.); (finanziell usw.) to ruin (s.o.); (töten) to do (s.o.) in.

erleichter|n [ɛr'laiçtərn], v. 1. v.tr. (a) to lighten (a burden etc.); (b) to relieve (s.o., pain etc.); to ease (s.o.'s conscience, pain, suffering); (c) to facilitate (a task), make (a task, life) easier.

◆e~t, adj. relieved. ◆E~ung, f -/-en relief.

er'leiden, v.tr.irr.59 to suffer (sth.).

er'lernen, v.tr. to learn (a trade, language etc.); to train for (a job).

er'lesen, adj. selected (food, wine etc.); select (company etc.); discerning (taste).

er'leucht|en, v.tr. to illuminate (a room etc.). ◆E~ung, f -/-en (sudden) inspiration.

erlogen [ɛr'lo:gən], adj. false, trumped-up (story etc.).

Erlös [ɛr'lø:s], m -es/-e proceeds.

er'löschen, v.i.irr.22 (sein) (a) (Feuer, Licht usw.) to go out; (b) Lit: (Liebe, Haß, j-s Stimme usw.) to die; (c) (Vertrag usw.) to expire.

er'lös|en, v.tr. (a) to redeem (man, the human soul etc.); (b) to release (s.o.). ◆E~ung, f -/-en (a) release, deliverance; (b) (Erleichterung) relief; (c) Ecc: redemption.

ermächtig|en [ɛr'mɛçtigən], v.tr. j-n zu etwas e., to authorize s.o. to do sth. ◆E~ung, f -/no pl authorization.

er'mahn|en, v.tr. to exhort (s.o.) (zur Vorsicht usw., to be careful etc.); (rügen) to reprimand (s.o.). ◆E~ung, f -/-en admonition; (Rüge) reprimand.

er'mäßig|en, v.tr. to reduce (prices etc.). ◆E~ung, f reduction.

er'messen. I. v.tr.irr.25 to assess, (berechnen) calculate (damage etc.). II. E., n -s/ no pl discretion; judgement.

ermittel|n [ɛr'mitəln], v. 1. v.tr. to establish (facts, the truth, details etc.). 2. v.i. (haben) to investigate, make inquiries. ◆E~lung, f -/-en ascertaining; (Entdeckung) discovery; pl investigations. ◆E~lungsverfahren, n preliminary proceedings.

ermöglichen [ɛr'mø:kliçən], v.tr. to make (sth.) possible (j-m, for s.o.).

er'mord|en, v.tr. to murder (s.o.), assassinate (a king, statesman). ◆E~ung, f -/-en murder; assassination.

ermüd|en [ɛr'my:dən], v. 1. v.tr. to tire (s.o.). 2. v.i. (sein) to tire (s.o.), get tired. ◆E~ung, f -/no pl tiredness, (also Tchn:) fatigue. ◆E~ungserscheinung, f sign of fatigue.

ermunter|n [ɛr'muntərn], v.tr. (a) (ermutigen) to encourage (s.o.); (b) (aufmuntern) to cheer (s.o.) up.

ermutigen [ɛr'mu:tigən], v.tr. to encourage (s.o.).

er'nähr|en, v.tr. (a) to feed (s.o., sth.); (gesund halten) to nourish (s.o., sth.); sich von etwas e., (Pers.) to live on sth.; (Tier, Pflanze) to feed on sth.; (b) (unterhalten) to support (a family etc.). ◆E~er, m -s/- breadwinner. ◆E~ung, f -/no pl (a) (Ernähren) feeding, nourishment (of s.o.); esp. Med: nutrition; (b) (Kost) diet; (c) (Unterhalt) support (of a family etc.).

er'nenn|en, v.tr.irr.51 to appoint (s.o.).

◆**E~ung,** *f* appointment (**zu** + *dat,* as).

**erneuer|n** [ɛr'nɔʏərn], *v.tr.* (*a*) to renovate (a building, furniture); (*b*) (*ersetzen*) to replace (a battery, part etc.); to change (*Med:* a dressing, *Aut:* the oil etc.); to renew (a friendship, relationship etc.). ◆**E~ung,** *f* -/-**en** (*a*) renovation; (*b*) renewal.

**erneut** [ɛr'nɔʏt], *adj.* (*a*) renewed, new; (*b*) *adv.* (*noch einmal*) again.

**erniedrig|en** [ɛr'niːdrigən], *v.* **1.** *v.tr.* (*herabwürdigen*) to degrade (s.o., oneself); (*demütigen*) to humiliate (s.o.). ◆**E~ung,** *f* -/-**en** degradation; humiliation.

**ernst** [ɛrnst]. **I.** *adj.* serious; **meinst du das ä.?** do you really mean that? **II. E.,** *m* -es/*no pl* seriousness; **es ist mein (bitterer) E.,** I am (quite) serious about it; **im E.?** really? honestly? ◆**'E~fall,** *m* (case of) emergency. ◆**'e~gemeint,** *adj.* sincerely meant; genuine (offer, advice). ◆**'e~haft,** *adj.* serious. ◆**'E~haftigkeit,** *f* -/*no pl* seriousness; genuineness. ◆**'e~lich,** *adj.* serious; grave (fault, warning, doubts etc.).

**Ernte** ['ɛrntə], *f* -/-**n** (*Ertrag*) crop, harvest. ◆**E~'dankfest,** *n* harvest festival. ◆**'e~n,** *v.tr.* to harvest (a crop, corn etc.); to pick (fruit); *Fig:* to earn (applause, gratitude, praise).

**er'nüchter|n,** *v.tr.* to sober (s.o.) up; *Fig:* to bring (s.o.) down to earth; (*enttäuschen*) to disillusion (s.o.). ◆**E~ung,** *f* -/-**en** (*a*) sobering up; (*b*) *Fig:* disillusionment.

**Erobe|er** [ɛr'ʔoːbərər], *m* -s/- conqueror. ◆**e~n,** *v.tr.* to conquer (a country, city, *Fig:* s.o.'s heart etc.); to capture (a fortress, city). ◆**E~ung,** *f* -/-**en** *Mil: & Fig:* conquest; capture.

**er'öffn|en,** *v.tr.* to open; **j-m etwas e.,** to disclose sth. to s.o. ◆**E~ung,** *f* -/-**en 1.** opening; (*feierlich*) inauguration; **2.** disclosure. ◆**E~ungs-,** *comb.fm.* opening (ceremony, speech, session etc.).

**erörter|n** [ɛr'ʔœrtərn], *v.tr.* to discuss (a case, problem etc.). ◆**E~ung,** *f* -/-**en** discussion.

**Eroti|k** [e'roːtik], *f* -/*no pl* eroticism. ◆**e~sch,** *adj.* erotic.

**erpicht** [ɛr'piçt], *adj.* **ich bin nicht sehr e. darauf,** I am not very keen on it.

**er'press|en,** *v.tr.* (*a*) to blackmail (s.o.); (*b*) to extort (money, a confession etc.). ◆**E~er,** *m* -s/- blackmailer. ◆**E~ung,** *f* blackmail, extortion.

**er'proben,** *v.tr.* to test, try out (a new machine, remedy etc.); *Fig:* to put (s.o.'s loyalty, honesty etc.) to the test.

**er'raten,** *v.tr.irr.13* to guess (sth.).

**erreg|bar** [ɛr'reːkbaːr], *adj.* excitable; (*reizbar*) irritable. ◆**E~barkeit,** *f* -/*no pl* excitability; irritability. ◆**e~en,** *v.tr.* to excite (s.o., s.o.'s senses); to arouse (envy, suspicion, sympathy, sexual desire etc.); to cause (anxiety, displeasure,

amusement etc.); **sich e.,** to get excited/worked up. ◆**E~er,** *m* -s/- cause (of a disease). ◆**e~t,** *adj.* excited; (*unruhig*) agitated; (*zornig*) heated (argument, words etc.); emotional (voice). ◆**E~theit,** *f* -/*no pl* excitement; (*Unruhe*) agitation. ◆**E~ung,** *f* -/*no pl* (state of) excitement/(*Unruhe*) agitation.

**erreich|bar** [ɛr'raiçbaːr], *adj.* (*a*) within reach; accessible; (*b*) (*Ziel usw.*) attainable; (*c*) (*Pers.*) available. ◆**e~en,** *v.tr.* to reach (s.o., sth., a speed, place etc.); to achieve (a purpose, aim); **schwer zu e.,** difficult to get to; **j-n (telefonisch) e.,** to get through to s.o. (on the telephone).

**er'richten,** *v.tr.* to erect (a building, barricade etc.), put up (scaffolding etc.).

**er'ringen,** *v.tr.irr.19* to gain, win (sth.) (with a struggle).

**erröten** [ɛr'røːtən], *v.i.* (*sein*) to blush.

**Errungenschaft** [ɛr'ruŋənʃaft], *f* -/-**en** achievement; *F:* (*Anschaffung*) acquisition.

**Er'satz. I.** *m* -es/*no pl* (*a*) replacement; substitute; (*Pers.*) stand-in; (*b*) (*Entschädigung*) compensation. **II. E~-,** *comb.fm.* replacement (driver, material etc.); spare (tyre, battery etc.). ◆**E~mann,** *m* stand-in; *Sp:* substitute.

**ersäufen** [ɛr'zɔʏfən], *v.tr. F:* to drown.

**er'schaffen,** *v.tr.irr.77 Lit:* to create (sth.).

**er'schein|en,** *v.i.irr.79* (*sein*) to appear; (*Buch, Zeitschrift*) to come out. ◆**E~ung,** *f* -/-**en** (*a*) (*Aussehen*) appearance; (*b*) (*Sache, Vorgang*) phenomenon; (*Symptom*) symptom; (*Gespenst*) apparition; (*Pers.*) **eine elegante E.,** an elegant figure.

**er'schießen,** *v.tr.irr.31* to shoot (s.o., oneself, an animal) (dead).

**er'schlaffen,** *v.i.* (*sein*) (*Muskeln usw.*) to go limp; (*Haut*) become flabby; (*Pers., Arme usw.*) to become weakened.

**er'schlagen,** *v.tr.irr.85* to kill (s.o.).

**er'schleichen,** *v.tr.irr.86* **sich** *dat* **etwas e.,** to obtain sth. by underhand methods.

**er'schließen,** *v.tr.irr.31* to open up (an area, country, market etc.).

**er'schöpf|en,** *v.tr.* to exhaust (s.o., sth.). ◆**e~t,** *adj.* exhausted; (*Vorräte*) finished; (*Geduld*) at an end. ◆**E~ung,** *f* -/*no pl* exhaustion.

**er'schrecken,** *v.* **1.** *v.i.irr.* (*sein*) (*Angst bekommen*) to get a scare. **2.** *v.tr.* to alarm (s.o.), give (s.o.) a fright; (*plötzlich*) to startle (s.o.); *F:* **sich e.,** to get a fright/shock.

**erschrocken** [ɛr'ʃrɔkən], *adj.* startled, shocked.

**erschütter|n** [ɛr'ʃytərn], *v.tr.* to shake (a building, *Fig:* s.o.'s faith etc.); *Fig:* (*Nachricht usw.*) to shake/(*tief*) shatter (s.o.); ◆**E~ung,** *f* -/-**en 1.** *no pl* shaking; vibration. **2.** (*a*) shock; tremor (of an earthquake); (*b*) (*Ergriffenheit*) (state of) shock.

er'schwer|en, *v.tr.* to make (sth.) more difficult, complicate (a task etc.).

er'schwindeln, *v.tr.* to get (sth.) by trickery.

erschwinglich [ɛr'ʃviŋliç], *adj.* within one's means.

ersetz|bar [ɛr'zɛtsbɑːr], *adj.* replaceable. ◆e~en, *v.tr.* (*a*) to replace (s.o., sth.) (durch j-n, etwas, with s.o., sth.); (*b*) (erstatten) to make good (damage), reimburse (expenses).

ersichtlich [ɛr'ziçtliç], *adj.* obvious.

er'spar|en, *v.tr.* j-m/sich *dat* Geld, Zeit, Mühe usw. e., to save s.o./oneself money, time, trouble etc.; j-m etwas Unangenehmes e., to spare s.o. sth. unpleasant. ◆E~nis, *f -/-se* saving (an/von etwas *dat*, of sth.); *pl* E~nisse, savings; economies.

erst [eːrst], *adv.* (*a*) (zuerst) first; (*b*) (nicht eher als) not … until; (*c*) (nicht mehr als) only; er ist eben e. angekommen, he has only just come; (*d*) (steigernd) wenn du e. einmal so alt bist wie ich, just wait until you're as old as I am; dann wird er e. recht böse sein, then he really will be angry. ◆'E~aufführung, *f* first performance; deutsche E., German premiere. ◆'E~ausgabe, *f* first edition. ◆'e~'beste, *adj.* der/die/das e. = der/die/das e~e beste. ◆'e~'ens, *adv.* first(ly), in the first place. ◆'e~e(r, s), *num.adj.* first; (*a*) im e~en Stock, on the first/*N.Am:* second floor; fürs e., for the time being; in e~er Linie, first and foremost; (*b*) (beste) best; Waren e~er Wahl, top quality goods; (*c*) er nahm das e. beste, he took the first thing he could lay his hands on. ◆'e~malig, *adj.* first. ◆'e~mals, *adv.* for the first time.

er'starren, *v.i.* (sein) (*a*) (Flüssigkeit) to solidify, (frieren) to freeze; (Glieder usw.) to stiffen, (vor Kälte) go numb; (Pers.) vor Schreck erstarrt, petrified with fear.

erstatten [ɛr'ʃtatən], *v.tr.* (*a*) to refund, reimburse (expenses etc.); (*b*) Bericht e., to report.

er'staun|en. I. *v.tr.* to astonish (s.o.); das erstaunt mich nicht, it doesn't surprise me. II. E., *n -s/no pl* astonishment. ◆e~lich, *adj.* astonishing.

er'stechen, *v.tr.irr.14* to stab (s.o.) to death.

er'stehen, *v.tr.irr.100* etwas billig e., to pick sth. up cheap.

er'stick|en, *v.* 1. *v.tr.* to suffocate (s.o.); *Fig:* to stifle (a sound, laugh etc.) to smother (flames). 2. *v.i.* (sein) to suffocate; *F:* ich ersticke in Arbeit, I'm up to my neck in work. ◆E~ung, *f -/no pl* suffocation.

er'streben, *v.tr. Lit:* to strive for (sth.). ◆e~swert, *adj.* desirable; worthwhile (goal).

er'strecken, *v.refl.* sich e., (Gebiet) to stretch; sich auf j-n, etwas *acc* e., to in-

clude, (Gespräch usw.) cover (s.o., sth.); (Vorschrift) to apply to s.o., sth.

er'suchen. I. *v.tr.* j-n um etwas *acc* e., to request sth. from s.o. II. E., *n -s/-* (formal) request.

ertappen [ɛr'tapən], *v.tr.* to catch (s.o.).

er'teilen, *v.tr.* to grant (permission etc.); to place (an order).

ertönen [ɛr'tøːnən], *v.i.* (sein) to be heard; (Sirene usw.) to sound, (Schuß, Schrei) ring out.

Ertrag [ɛr'traːk], *m -(e)s/-e* (*a*) *Agr:* yield; *Min:* output; (*b*) (Gewinn) return(s), profit. ◆E~s-, *comb.fm.* profit (situation, tax etc.).

er'tragen, *v.tr.irr.85* to stand (s.o., sth.), bear (pain, suffering etc.).

erträglich [ɛr'trɛːkliç], *adj.* bearable.

er'tränken, *v.tr.* to drown.

er'träumen, *v.tr.* sich *dat* etwas e., to dream of/imagine sth.

er'trinken, *v.i.irr.96* (sein) to drown.

er'übrigen, *v.tr.* (*a*) to spare (money, time); (*b*) sich e., to be superfluous.

er'wachen, *v.i.* (sein) to awake; *Fig:* (Gefühle usw.) to be aroused.

er'wachsen. I. *v.i.irr.107* (sein) to arise. II. *adj.* grown-up (behaviour etc.). ◆E~e(r), *m & f decl. as adj.* adult.

erwäg|en [ɛr'vɛːɡən], *v.tr.irr.* to consider (sth., whether …), think (sth.) over. ◆E~ung, *f -/-en* consideration; etwas in E. ziehen, to take sth. into consideration.

erwähn|en [ɛr'vɛːnən], *v.tr.* to mention. ◆e~enswert, *adj.* worth mentioning. ◆E~ung, *f -/-en* mention(ing).

er'wärmen, *v.tr.* to warm (up) (a room, liquid etc.); *Fig:* sich für j-n, etwas *acc* e., to warm to s.o., sth.

er'wart|en, *v.tr.* (*a*) (rechnen mit) to expect (s.o., sth., a baby); wider E., contrary to expectation; (*b*) (warten auf) to wait for (s.o., sth.). ◆E~ung, *f -/-en* expectation. ◆e~ungsvoll, *adj.* expectant.

er'wecken, *v.tr. Lit:* to awaken, arouse (s.o., *Fig:* interest, emotions etc.).

er'weichen, *v.tr. & i.* (sein) to soften.

er'weisen, *v.tr.irr.70* (*a*) to prove (s.o.'s innocence etc.); (*b*) j-m einen Dienst, ein Gefallen usw. e., to do s.o. a service, favour etc.

Erwerb [ɛr'vɛrp], *m -s/no pl* (*a*) (Gewerbe) livelihood; (*b*) (Aneignung) acquisition; (Kauf) purchase. ◆e~en ['-bən], *v.tr.irr.101* to acquire, (durch Kauf) purchase (sth.); *Fig:* (gewinnen) to win (fame, respect etc.). ◆e~sfähig, *adj.* (Pers.) capable of gainful employment. ◆e~slos, *adj.* unemployed. ◆e~stätig, *adj.* (gainfully) employed.

erwider|n [ɛr'viːdərn], *v.tr. & i.* (haben) (*a*) to answer; to reply; (*b*) to return a greeting, feeling, visit, *Mil:* fire etc.). ◆E~ung, *f -/-en* 1. answer, reply; (scharf) retort. 2. return (of a feeling

etc.).

**er'wischen,** *v.tr. F:* to catch (s.o., a thief, a bus etc.); **es hat sie erwischt,** (i) *(krank)* she's got it; (ii) *(tot)* she's died; (iii) *(verliebt)* she's got it bad.

**erwünscht** [ɛr'vynʃt], *adj.* desired (effect).

**erwürgen,** *v.tr.* to strangle (s.o.).

**Erz¹** [ɛːrts], *n -es/-e* ore.

**'Erz-, e~-²,** *comb.fm.* (a) *(Rang)* arch(diocese etc.); (b) *(steigernd)* arch-(conservative etc.); complete, utter (fool etc.).

**er'zähl|en,** *v.* 1. *v.tr.* to tell (a story etc.), give an account of (an event). 2. *v.i.* *(haben)* **er kann gut e.,** he is good at telling stories. ◆**e~end,** *adj.* narrative (poem, style etc.). ◆**E~er,** *m -s/-* narrator. ◆**E~ung,** *f -/-en* story, tale.

**er'zeug|en,** *v.tr.* to generate (warmth, electricity, *Fig:* ideas, feelings); to produce (goods, *Fig:* an effect etc.); *Fig:* to engender (interest, hatred etc.); to create (tension etc.). ◆**E~er,** *m -s/-* *(Hersteller)* producer. ◆**E~nis,** *n* product. ◆**E~ung,** *f* generation; *esp. Agr:* production; *Ind:* manufacture.

**er'zieh|en,** *v.tr.irr.113* (in der Familie) to bring up, *Sch:* educate (a child); **streng erzogen werden,** to have a strict upbringing. ◆**e~erisch,** *adj.* educational. ◆**E~ung,** *f -/no pl* upbringing (*Bildung*) education; (*Schulung*) training. ◆**E~ungs-,** *comb.fm.* educational (system, problem etc.); (method etc.) of upbringing. ◆**E~ungsberechtigte(r),** *m & f decl. as adj.* parent or guardian.

**er'zielen,** *v.tr.* to achieve (success, unanimity, a result etc.); *Com:* to realize (a profit, price); *Sp:* to score (a goal).

**er'zwingen,** *v.tr.irr.19* **Geld/ein Versprechen von j-m e.,** to extort money/exact a promise from s.o. (by force); **sich** *dat* **Zutritt in ein Gebäude e.,** to force one's way into a building.

**es** [ɛs], *pron.* it. 1. *subject pron.* *(Sache, Tier)* it; *(Kind)* he; she. 2. *object pron.* (a) it; *(Kind)* him; her.

**Esche** ['ɛʃə], *f -/-n* ash (tree).

**Esel** ['eːzəl], *m -s/-* 1. donkey; ass. 2. *F:* fool, ass. ◆**'E~sbrücke,** *f* *(Gedächtnisstütze)* mnemonic; *Sch:* crib. ◆**'E~sohr,** *n* *Fig:* **Buch mit E~sohren,** dog-eared book.

**Eskalation** [ɛskalatsi'oːn], *f -/-en* escalation. ◆**e~'lieren,** *v.tr.&i.* *(haben)* to escalate (a war etc.).

**Eskimo** ['ɛskimo], *m -(s)/-(s)* Eskimo.

**Eß-** ['ɛs-], *comb.fm.* (a) eating (habits etc.); (b) dining (room etc.). ◆**'eßbar,** *adj.* edible; noch e., still fit to eat/ eatable. ◆**'Eßkastanie,** *f* sweet chestnut. ◆**'Eßlöffel,** *m* tablespoon.

**ess|en** ['ɛsən]. **I.** *v.tr. & i.irr.* *(haben)* to eat; **zu Mittag/Abend e.,** to have lunch/ supper; **wollen wir e. gehen?** shall we go out for a meal? **II. E.,** *n -s/-* 1. *no pl* eat-

ing. 2. *(Nahrung)* food. 3. *(Mahlzeit)* meal; *(offizielles E.)* dinner. ◆**'E~en(s)marke,** *f* meal ticket/ coupon. ◆**'E~enszeit,** *f* mealtime.

**Essenz** [ɛ'sɛnts], *f -/-en* essence.

**Essig** ['ɛsiç], *m -s/-e* vinegar. ◆**'E~gurke,** *f* (pickled) gherkin.

**Estragon** ['ɛstragon], *m -s/no pl* tarragon.

**etabl|ieren** [eta'bliːrən], *v.tr.* to establish, set up (a business etc.); **sich e.,** *(Pers.)* to establish oneself, *Com:* set up in business. ◆**e~iert,** *adj.* (well-)established (firm etc.).

**Etage** [e'taːʒə], *f -/-n* storey, floor; **auf der dritten E.,** on the third/*N.Am:* fourth floor. ◆**E~nbett,** *n* bunk bed. ◆**E~nwohnung,** *f* (self-contained) flat/*N.Am:* apartment (in a block).

**Etappe** [e'tapə], *f -/-n* stage (of a journey etc.); *Sp:* stage, leg (of a race). ◆**e~nweise,** *adv.* by stages.

**Etat** [e'taː], *m -s/-e* budget. ◆**E~jahr,** *n* financial year.

**etepetete** [eːtəpe'teːtə], *adj. F:* *(penibel)* pernickety; *(geziert)* ladida.

**Eth|ik** ['eːtik], *f -/-en* (a) *no pl* ethics; (b) *(Lehre)* ethic. ◆**'e~isch,** *adj.* ethical.

**Etikett** [eti'kɛt], *n -(e)s/-e* label; *(Preisschild)* price tag/ticket. ◆**e~ieren** [-'tiːrən], *v.tr.* to label (sth., *Fig:* s.o.).

**etliche(r,s)** ['ɛtliçə(r,s)], *indef.pron.* some; *pl* several. ◆**e~s,** a number of things.

**Etui** [ɛt'viː], *n -s/-s* (spectacles/cigarette) case.

**etwa** ['ɛtva], *adv.* 1. *(ungefähr)* approximately; **in e. drei Tagen,** in about three days. 2. (a) *(zum Beispiel)* **Länder wie e. Indien,** countries such as India (for example); (b) *(verstärkend)* **er ist doch nicht e. krank?** he isn't ill by any chance? **nicht e., daß ich Angst hätte,** not that I was afraid. ◆**e~ig** ['ɛtva(ː)iç], *adj.* possible.

**etwas** ['ɛtvas]. **I.** *indef.pron.* something; *(in Fragen und Verneinungen)* anything; **nimm dir e. davon,** have some (of it). **II.** *indef.adj.* (a) some; **sie kann e. Englisch,** she knows some English; (b) *adv.* a little; **e. schwierig,** rather difficult; *F:* **ich will noch e. arbeiten,** I want to do a bit more work.

**euch** [ɔyç]. 1. *pers.pron.* *(acc & dat of ihr)* you; **wie geht es e./**(in letter) **E.?** how are you? 2. *refl.pron.* **wascht e.,** wash yourselves.

**euer** ['ɔyər], *poss.adj.* your. ◆**eu(e)re(r,s)** ['ɔyrə(r,s)], *poss.pron.* yours; **ist das eu(e)res?** is that yours/ your one?

**Eule** ['ɔylə], *f -/-n* owl.

**eur|e(r,s)** ['ɔyrə(r,s)], *see* **eu(e)r, euere(r,s).** ◆**'e~erseits,** *adv.* on your part. ◆**'e~esgleichen,** *pron.* (people of) your kind. ◆**'e~etwegen/um 'e~etwillen,** *adv.* for your sake; because of you.

**Europ|a** [ɔy'roːpa]. **I.** *n -s/no pl* Europe.

**II. E~a-,** *comb.fm.* European (*Pol:* Parliament, *Sp:* champion etc.). ◆**E~äer** [-ro'pɛːɐ], *m* **-s/-** European. ◆**e~äisch,** *adj.* European; **die E~äische Gemeinschaft,** the European Community.

**Euter** ['ɔytɐ], *n* **-s/-** udder.

**evakuier|en** [evaku'iːrən], *v.tr.* to evacuate (s.o., an area etc.). ◆**E~ung,** *f* **-/-en** evacuation.

**evangel|isch** [evaŋ'geːliʃ], *adj.* Protestant (church etc.). ◆**E~ium** [-'geːlium], *n* **-s/-ien** gospel.

**eventuell** [evɛntu'ɛl], *adj.* (*a*) possible; (*b*) *adv.* (*vielleicht*) perhaps.

**ewig** ['eːviç], *adj.* 1. (*a*) eternal (life, truth, love etc.); everlasting (peace, joy etc.). 2. *F:* (*ständig*) continual; (*endlos*) endless; **das dauert ja e. (lange)!** this is taking ages! ◆'**E~keit,** *f* **-/-en** eternity.

**exakt** [ɛ'ksakt], *adj.* exact.

**Examen** [ɛ'ksɑːmən], *n* **-s/- &** **-mina** examination; *F:* exam.

**Exemplar** [ɛksɛm'plɑːr], *n* **-s/-e** (*a*) specimen; (*b*) copy (of a paper, book etc.). ◆**e~isch,** *adj.* (*beispielhaft*) exemplary; representative.

**exerzieren** [ɛkser'tsiːrən], *v.i.* (*haben*) to drill.

**Exil** [ɛ'ksiːl], *n* **-s/-e** exile; **im E.,** in exile.

**Existenz** [ɛksis'tɛnts], *f* **-/-en** 1. (*Leben, Dasein usw.*) existence; **es geht um die nackte E.,** it's a matter of life and death. 2. (*Lebensgrundlage*) livelihood. 3. *Pej:* **dunkle E~en,** shady characters; **verkrachte/gescheiterte E.,** failure. ◆**E~kampf,** *m* fight for survival. ◆**E~minimum,** *n* subsistence level; (*Gehalt*) living wage.

**existieren** [ɛksis'tiːrən], *v.i.* (*haben*) to exist; (*leben*) to subsist (**von** + *dat,* on).

**exklusiv** [ɛksklu'ziːf], *adj./***E~-,** *comb.fm.* (*a*) sole (rights etc.); (*b*) (*vornehm*) select (hotel, party etc.). ◆**e~e** [-'ziːvə], *prep.* + *gen esp. Com:* excluding.

**Exot(e)** [ɛ'ksoːt(ə)], *m* **-en/-en** exotic person/plant/animal. ◆**e~isch,** *adj.* exotic.

**Expansion** [ɛkspanzi'oːn], *f* **-/-en** expansion. ◆**E~spolitik,** *f* expansionist policy.

**Expedition** [ɛkspeditsi'oːn], *f* **-/-en** expedition.

**Experiment** [ɛksperi'mɛnt], *n* **-(e)s/-e** experiment (**an** + *dat,* on). ◆**e~ell** [-'tɛl], *adj.* experimental. ◆**e~ieren** [-'tiːrən], *v.i.* (*haben*) to experiment.

**Experte** [ɛks'pɛrtə], *n* **-n/-n** expert.

**explo|dieren** [ɛksplo'diːrən], *v.i.* (*sein*) to explode; (*Kessel usw.*) to burst. ◆**E~sion** [-zi'oːn], *f* **-/-en** explosion; **zur E. bringen,** to detonate (a bomb etc.). ◆**e~siv** [-'ziːf], *adj.* (*also Fig:*) explosive.

**Export** [ɛks'pɔrt], *m* **-(e)s/-e** 1. *no pl* export(ing). 2. exports. ◆**E~eur** [-'tøːr], *m* **-s/-e** exporter. ◆**e~ieren** [-'tiːrən], *v.tr.* to export (goods etc.). ◆**E~kaufmann,** *m* export salesman. ◆**E~land,** *n* exporting country.

**Expreßgut** [ɛks'prɛsguːt], *n Rail:* express parcel(s); *N.Am:* fast freight.

**Expression|ismus** [ɛksprɛsio'nismus], *m* **-/no pl** expressionism.

**extern** [ɛks'tɛrn], *adj.* external.

**extra** ['ɛkstra]. I. *adv.* 1. (*a*) (*gesondert*) separately; (*b*) (*eigens*) (e)specially; (*absichtlich*) **das hast du e. gemacht,** you did that on purpose. 2. (*zusätzlich*) extra; **e. stark,** extra strong. II. *inv.adj.* additional; extra. ◆'**E~blatt,** *n* extra (edition).

**Extrakt** [ɛks'trakt], *m* **-(e)s/-e** extract.

**extravagant** [ɛkstrava'gant], *adj.* flamboyant; (*ausgefallen*) outlandish (person, clothes, taste etc.); far-fetched (idea).

**extrem** [ɛks'treːm]. I. *adj.* extreme. II. **E~,** *n* **-(e)s/-e** extreme.

**extrovertiert** [ɛkstrovɛr'tiːrt], *adj.* extrovert.

**Exzellenz** [ɛkstsɛ'lɛnts], *f* **-/-en Seine/ Eure E.,** His/Your Excellency.

**exzentrisch** [ɛks'tsɛntriʃ], *adj.* eccentric.

**Exzeß** [ɛks'tsɛs], *m* **-zesses/-zesse** excess.

# F

**F, f** [ɛf], *n* **-/-** (the letter) F, f.

**Fabel** ['faːbəl], *f* **-/-n** fable; (*unglaubliche Geschichte*) yarn. ◆'**f~haft,** *adj.* *F:* fabulous. ◆'**F~tier,** *n* mythical beast.

**Fabrik** [fa'briːk]. I. *f* **-/-en** factory. II. **F~-,** *comb.fm.* factory (worker, owner etc.). ◆**F~ant** [fabri'kant], *m* **-en/-en** (*a*) factory owner; (*b*) (*Hersteller*) manufacturer. ◆**F~at** [-i'kɑːt], *n* **-(e)s/-e** make. ◆**F~ation** [-ikatsi'oːn], *f* **-/no pl** manufacture. ◆**F~gelände,** *n* factory site. ◆**f~neu,** *adj.* brand new.

**fabrizieren** [fabri'tsiːrən], *v.tr.* *F:* to concoct.

**Fach** [fax]. I. *n* **-(e)s/=er** 1. compartment (of a drawer etc.). 2. (*a*) *Sch: etc:* subject; (*b*) *Com:* field; line (of business etc.); **ein Meister seines F~es,** a master of his trade; **ein Mann vom F.,** an expert (on the subject). II. **F~-,** *comb.fm.* specialist (bookshop, literature etc.); (*beruflich*) professional (training etc.); (*technisch*) technical (jargon etc.). ◆'**F~arbeiter,** *m* skilled worker. ◆'**F~rzt,** *m/* ◆'**F~ärztin,** *f* specialist (doctor). ◆'**F~ausdruck,** *m* technical term. ◆'**F~bereich,** *m* subject area. ◆'**F~hochschule,** *f* technical/training college. ◆'**f~kundig,** *adj.* expert, with expert knowledge. ◆'**f~lich,** *adj.* tech-

nical; (*beruflich*) professional; **f. qualifiziert,** qualified in one's subject.
◆'**F~mann,** *m* expert (**für** + *acc,* on;
**auf diesem Gebiet,** in this field).
**f~männisch,** *adj.* expert (advice etc.).
◆'**F~schule,** *f* vocational school.
◆'**f~simpeln,** *v.i.* (*haben*) F: to talk
shop. ◆'**F~welt,** *f* **die F.,** the profession; *Com:* the trade. ◆'**F~werkhaus,**
*n* half-timbered house.
**fäch|eln** ['fɛçəln], *v.tr.* to fan (s.o., sth.).
◆'**F~er,** *m* **-s/-** fan.
**Fackel** ['fakəl], *f* **-/-n** torch.
**fad(e)** [faːt ('faːdə)], *adj.* (*a*) tasteless, insipid (food, drink); (*b*) F: boring.
**Faden** ['faːdən], *m* **-s/=** thread; *Fig:* **den
F. verlieren,** to lose the thread.
◆'**F~nudeln,** *fpl* vermicelli.
◆'**f~scheinig,** *adj.* threadbare (garment); flimsy (excuse).
**Fagott** [fa'gɔt], *n* **-(e)s/-e** bassoon.
**fähig** ['fɛːiç], *adj.* (*a*) capable (**zu etwas**
*dat,* of sth.); (*b*) able, competent (teacher
etc.). ◆'**F~keit,** *f* **-/-en** ability.
**fahl** [faːl], *adj.* pale (light etc.); pallid
(complexion etc.).
**fahnd|en** ['faːndən], *v.i.* (*haben*) (*Polizei
usw.*) **nach j-m, etwas** *dat* **f.,** to search/
hunt for s.o., sth. ◆'**F~ung,** *f* **-/-en**
search, hunt (**nach** + *dat,* for).
◆'**F~ungsaktion,** *f* manhunt.
◆'**F~ungsliste,** *f* wanted list.
**Fahne** ['faːnə], *f* **-/-n** (*a*) flag; (*b*)
(*Rauchf.*) trail; *F:* **er hat eine F.,** his
breath reeks of drink. ◆'**F~nflucht,**
*f* desertion. ◆'**F~nmast,** *m/*
'**F~nstange,** *f* flagpole.
**Fahr|ausweis** ['faːrausvais], *m* ticket.
◆'**F~bahn,** *f* **-/-en** carriageway;
(*Straße*) roadway. ◆'**f~bereit,** *adj. Aut:*
in running order. ◆'**f~en,** *v.tr.irr.* **1.** *v.i.*
(*sein*) (*a*) to travel, go; *Aut:* to drive; **mit
der Bahn/dem Auto f.,** to go by train/
car; **er fährt mit meinem Rad,** he's riding my bicycle; **das Auto fährt gut/
schlecht,** the car is running well/badly;
(*b*) (*abfahren*) **wir f. morgen,** we're
going/leaving tomorrow; (*c*) **sich** *dat* **mit
der Hand durch das Haar f.,** to run
one's fingers through one's hair; *F:* **was
ist denn in dich gefahren?** what's got/
*N.Am:* gotten into you? **2.** *v.tr.* to drive
(s.o., a car etc.); to ride (a bicycle etc.);
**das Auto fährt sich gut,** this car is a
pleasure to drive. ◆'**F~er(in),** *m* **-s/-** (*f*
**-/-nen**) driver. ◆'**F~erflucht,** *f* **-/no** *pl*
failure to stop (after an accident); **im
Fall von F.,** a case of hit-and-run driving. ◆'**F~gast,** *m* passenger. ◆**F~-
geld,** *n* fare. ◆'**F~gelegenheit,** *f*
means of transport. ◆'**F~gestell,** *n* **1.**
*Aut:* chassis. **2.** *Av:* undercarriage.
◆'**f~ig,** *adj.* (*geistig*) dithering;
(*physisch*) fidgety. ◆'**F~karte,** *f* ticket.
◆'**F~kartenausgabe,** *f/*'**F~karten-
schalter,** *m* ticket office. ◆'**f~lässig,**
*adj.* careless; *Jur:* negligent; **f~lässige**

**Tötung,** manslaughter. ◆'**F~lässig-
keit,** *f* **-/-en** carelessness; *Jur:* negligence.
◆'**F~lehrer,** *m* driving instructor.
◆'**f~plan,** *m* timetable.
◆'**f~planmäßig,** *adj.* scheduled (service); (departure) as scheduled.
◆'**F~preis,** *m* fare. ◆'**F~prüfung,** *f*
driving test. ◆'**F~rad,** *n* bicycle.
◆'**F~radweg,** *m* cycle track.
◆'**F~schein,** *m* ticket. ◆'**F~schule,** *f*
driving school. ◆'**F~schüler(in),** *m* (*f*)
learner driver. ◆'**F~spur,** *f* traffic lane.
◆'**F~stuhl,** *m* lift, *N.Am:* elevator.
◆'**F~stunde,** *f* driving lesson.
◆'**F~t,** *f* **-/-en** journey, trip; (*im Auto*)
drive; **eine F. ins Blaue,** a mystery tour;
**in voller F.,** (going) at full speed, flat
out. ◆'**F~trichtung,** *f* **-/-en** direction
of travel. ◆'**f~tüchtig,** *adj.* (*a*) (person) fit to drive; (*b*) roadworthy (vehicle).
◆**F~verbot,** *n* driving ban; loss of
one's licence. ◆'**F~wasser,** *n Nau:*
channel, fairway; *Fig:* **in seinem/im richtigen F. sein,** to be in one's element.
◆'**F~zeug,** *n* vehicle.
◆'**F~zeugpapiere,** *npl* (vehicle) registration papers.
**Fähr|mann** ['fɛːrman], ferryman.
◆'**F~schiff,** *n* ferry (boat). ◆'**F~e,** *f*
**-/-n** ferry.
**Fährte** ['fɛːrtə], *f* **-/-n** (*a*) trail; (*b*) *Fig:*
**auf der falschen F.,** on the wrong track.
**Faible** ['fɛːbəl], *n* **-s/-s** *F:* soft spot; weak-
ness.
**fair** [fɛːr], *adj.* fair. ◆'**F~neß,** *f* **-/no** *pl*
fairness.
**Fakten** ['faktən], *pl* facts, data.
**Faktor** ['faktɔr], *m* **-s/-en** [-'toːrən] factor.
**Fakultät** [fakul'tɛːt], *f* **-/-en** faculty.
**Falke** ['falkə], *m* **-n/-n** hawk, *esp.* falcon.
◆'**F~njagd,** *f* hawking.
**Fall** [fal], *m* **-(e)s/=e 1.** fall; *Fig:* **j-n zu F.
bringen,** to bring about s.o.'s downfall.
**2.** *esp. Med: Jur: Gram:* case; **auf jeden
F./alle F~e,** in any case, whatever happens; **auf keinen F.,** under no circumstances; **im F~(e) eines Brandes,** in the
event of a fire; **das ist nicht mein F.,** it's
not my cup of tea; **klarer F.!** sure thing!
◆'**F~beil,** *n* guillotine. ◆'**F~e,** *f* **-/-n**
trap; **in die F. gehen,** to fall into the
trap. ◆'**f~en,** *v.i.irr.* (*sein*) (*a*) to fall;
**sich aufs Bett f. lassen,** to fall/drop onto
the bed; **etwas f. lassen,** to drop sth.;
**das fällt unter diese Kategorie,** that
comes in this category; (*b*) **er ist im 2.
Weltkrieg gefallen,** he was killed in the
Second World War; (*c*) **die Entscheidung
ist gefallen,** the decision has been made.
◆'**f~enlassen,** *v.tr.sep.irr.51* to drop (a
subject, plan, friend, remark etc.).
◆'**F~grube,** *f* pit; *Fig:* pitfall.
◆'**F~obst,** *n* windfalls. ◆'**F~schirm,**
*m* parachute. ◆'**F~schirmjäger,** paratrooper. ◆'**F~schirmspringer,** *m* para-
chutist. ◆'**F~strick,** *m* snare; *Fig:* trap,
pitfall. ◆'**F~tür,** *f* trapdoor.

**fällen** ['fɛlən], *v.tr.* (*a*) to fell, cut down (a tree); (*b*) **ein Urteil f.**, to pass judgement.

**fällig** ['fɛliç], *adj.* due; **der f~e Betrag,** the amount due; **schon längst f.,** long overdue; ◆'**F~keit,** *f -/no pl Fin:* maturity.

**falsch** [falʃ], *adj.* (*a*) (*unecht*) false (teeth, friend, modesty, smile etc.); imitation, *F:* fake (jewellery etc.); forged (banknotes etc.); assumed (name); (*b*) (*nicht korrekt*) wrong; mis-; **wir sind hier f. (gegangen),** we've gone the wrong way; **etwas f. verstehen,** to misunderstand sth. ◆'**F~geld,** *n* counterfeit money. ◆'**F~heit,** *f -/no pl* (*a*) insincerity; (*b*) falsity (of statement etc.). ◆'**F~. meldung,** *f* false report. ◆'**F~spieler,** *m* cheat.

**fälsch|en** ['fɛlʃən], *v.tr.* to forge. ◆'**f~lich,** *adj.* wrong. ◆**f~licher-'weise,** *adv.* by mistake. ◆'**F~ung,** *f -/-en* forgery.

**Falt|blatt** ['faltblat], *n* folder, leaflet. ◆'**F~e,** *f -/-n* (*a*) fold (in material, paper etc.); pleat (in a skirt); crease (in trousers etc.); (*b*) line, wrinkle (in a face). ◆'**f~en,** *v.tr.* (*a*) to fold; (*b*) **sich f.,** to form wrinkles. ◆'**f~enlos,** *adj.* (*a*) (*Rock*) straight; (*b*) (*Gesicht usw.*) smooth. ◆'**F~enrock,** *m* pleated skirt. ◆'**f~ig,** *adj.* (*a*) *Cl:* pleated; (*b*) (*zerknittert*) creased; (*c*) wrinkled (skin).

**Falter** ['faltər], *m -s/-* moth.

**Falz** [falts], *m -es/-e* fold (in paper), (metal) joint.

**familiär** [famili'ɛ:r], *adj.* family (worries etc.); **aus f~en Gründen,** for family reasons.

**Familie** [fa'mi:liə], *f -/-n* family; **er hat F.,** he has children; **zur F. gehören,** to be one of the family. ◆'**F~n-,** *comb.fm.* family (event, planning, life, grave, etc.). ◆'**F~nangehörige(r),** *m & f decl. as adj.* member of the family. ◆'**F~nbetrieb,** *m* family business. ◆'**F~nkreis,** *m* family circle; ◆'**F~n-name,** *m* surname. ◆'**F~noberhaupt,** *n* head of the family. ◆'**F~npackung,** *f* family size/pack. ◆'**F~nstand,** *m* marital status. ◆'**F~nvater,** *m* family man.

**famos** [fa'mo:s], *adj. F:* marvellous.

**Fan** [fɛn], *m -s/-s* fan.

**Fanat|iker** [fa'nɑ:tikər], *m* fanatic. ◆**f~isch** [-'nɑ:tiʃ], *adj.* fanatical.

**Fanfare** [fan'fɑ:rə], *f -/-n* fanfare.

**Fang** [faŋ], *m -(e)s/-e* **1.** *no pl* (*a*) capture (of an animal); catching (of fish); (*b*) (*Beute*) catch; **ein guter F.,** a good catch. **2.** (*a*) *Z:* fang; (*b*) *Orn:* talon. ◆'**f~en,** *v.tr.irr.* to catch (s.o., sth., an animal etc.); to capture (an animal, a prisoner, soldier etc.); **sich f.,** (i) to get caught; (ii) (*beim Fallen*) to regain one's balance; *Fig:* to regain one's composure; ◆'**F~frage,** *f* trick question.

**fantastisch** [fan'tastiʃ], *adj.* fantastic.

**Farb-** ['farp-], *comb.fm.* (*a*) colour (photograph, film, print, etc.); (*b*) paint (pot etc.). ◆'**F~band,** *n* typewriter ribbon. ◆'**F~e** ['-bə], *f -/-n* **1.** colour; **2.** (*Kartenspiel*) suit; **F. bekennen,** to follow suit; *Fig:* to put one's cards on the table. **3.** (*Malerf.*) paint; (*Farbstoff*) dye. ◆'**f~echt,** *adj.* colour-fast. ◆'**f~enblind,** *adj,* colour-blind. ◆'**f~enfroh,** *adj* colourful. ◆'**f~enprächtig,** *adj* dazzlingly colourful. ◆'**F~fernsehen,** *n* colour television. ◆'**f~ig** ['-biç], *adj.* (*a*) coloured (glass etc.); (*b*) colourful (shirt, scene etc.); (*c*) coloured (people); **ein F~iger/eine F~ige,** a coloured man/woman. ◆'**F~kasten,** *m* box of paints. ◆'**f~los,** *adj.* colourless. ◆'**F~losigkeit,** *f -/no pl* colourlessness. ◆'**F~stift,** *m* crayon. ◆'**F~stoff,** *m* dye; (*in Lebensmitteln*) colouring. ◆'**F~ton,** *m* tone, shade (of a colour).

**färb|en** ['fɛrbən], *v.tr.* to dye (material, hair etc.); to colour (a picture etc.); ◆'**F~ung,** *f -/-en* colouring; (*Nuance*) tinge; (*Tendenz*) slant.

**Farce** ['farsə], *f -/-n Th: & Fig:* farce.

**Farm** [farm], *f -/-en* farm. ◆'**F~er,** *m -s/-* farmer.

**Farn** [farn], *m -(e)s/-e/'F~kraut,** *n* fern; bracken.

**Fasan** [fa'za:n], *m -(e)s/-e(n)* pheasant.

**Fasching** ['faʃiŋ], *m -s/-e* carnival.

**Faschis|mus** [fa'ʃismus], *m -/no pl* fascism. ◆**F~t,** *m -en/-en* fascist. ◆**f~tisch,** *adj.* fascist.

**faseln** ['fa:zə'ln], *v.tr. & i.* (*haben*) (*Pers.*) *F:* to blather; **dummes Zeug f.,** to talk crap.

**Faser** ['fa:zər], *f -/-n* fibre. ◆'**f~ig,** *adj.* fibrous; stringy (meat). ◆'**f~n,** *v.i.* (*haben*) to fray; (*Holz*) to splinter.

**Faß** [fas], *n -sses/-sser* barrel; drum (for tar, oil); (butter) churn; (fermentation) vat; **Bier vom F.,** draught beer. ◆'**F~bier,** *n* draught beer.

**Fassade** [fa'sa:də], *f -/-n* facade.

**faßbar** [fas'ba:r], *adj.* (*a*) (*begreiflich*) comprehensible; (*b*) tangible (reason, result).

**fass|en** ['fasən], *v.tr.* (*a*) to take hold of, grasp (s.o., sth.); (*mit Gewalt*) to seize (s.o., sth.); (*Polizei*) to catch, capture (s.o.); (*b*) **sich f.,** to get a hold of oneself; **einen Entschluß f.,** to make a decision; **sich kurz f.,** to express oneself concisely; (*c*) (*begreifen*) to grasp, comprehend (sth.); **sie kann es noch immer nicht f.,** she still can't take it in; (*d*) to set, mount (a jewel); (*e*) to hold (a quantity of sth., people). ◆'**F~ung,** *f -/-en* **1.** (*a*) mount (of a lens etc.); setting (of a jewel); (*b*) frame (for spectacles); (*c*) *El:* socket. **2.** (*Form*) version (of a work, book etc.); draft (of a document); (*Formulierung*) wording, phrasing. **3.** (*Ruhe*) composure; **die F. bewahren/verlieren,**

to keep/lose one's head. ◆'f~ungslos, adj. speechless; (außer sich) beside oneself (vor + dat, with). ◆'F~ungsvermögen, n -s/- 1. capacity. 2. Fig: (powers of) comprehension.

Fasson [fa'sõ:], f -/-s 1. Cl: etc: style, cut; etwas nach seiner F. tun, to do sth. in one's own way. ◆F~schnitt, m fully-styled (hair)cut.

fast [fast], adv. nearly, almost; f. keins, hardly any.

fast|en ['fastən], v.i. (haben) to fast. ◆'F~enzeit, f Lent. ◆'F~nacht, f -/no pl (a) Shrove Tuesday; (b) (Karnevalszeit) carnival.

Faszin|ation [fastsinatsi'o:n], f -/no pl fascination. ◆f~ieren [-'ni:rən], v.tr. to fascinate.

fatal [fa'tɑ:l], adj. awkward (question, situation); embarrassing (consequences etc.); fatal, disastrous (tendency etc.).

fauchen ['fauxən], v.i. (haben) to spit, hiss.

faul [faul], adj. 1. (a) (schlecht) bad; rotten (fruit, egg etc.); stale (air); f. riechen, to smell rotten/foul; (b) Fig: f~e Ausrede, poor/lame excuse; hier ist etwas f., there's something fishy about this. 2. (untätig) lazy. ◆'f~en, v.i. (haben) (Gewebe, Fleisch usw.) to rot; (Zähne usw.) to decay; (Leiche) to decompose. ◆f~enzen ['faulεntsən], v.i. (haben) to laze about. ◆'F~enzer, m -s/- lazy-bones. ◆'F~heit, f -/no pl laziness, idleness. ◆'F~pelz, m F: lazybones. ◆'F~tier, n 1. Z: sloth. 2. F: lazy-bones.

Fäul|e ['fɔʏlə], f -/no pl decay. ◆'F~nis, f -/no pl rot, decay.

Faust [faust], f -/Fäuste fist; Fig: auf eigene F. handeln, to do sth. off one's own bat. ◆F~handschuh, m mitten. ◆'F~regel, f rule of thumb. ◆'F~schlag, m punch.

Favorit(in) [favo'ri:t(in)], m -en/-en (f -/-nen) favourite.

Faxen ['faksən] fpl antics.

Fazit ['fa:tsit], n -s/-e & -s net result.

Februar ['fe:bruɑ:r], m -(s)/-e February.

fecht|en ['fεçtən], I. v.i.irr. (haben) to fence. II. F~, n -s/no pl fencing. ◆'F~er(in), m -s/- (f -/-nen) fencer.

Feder ['fe:dər], I. f -/-n 1. (a) feather; F~n lassen müssen, to suffer in the process; (b) (Schreibgerät) pen. 2. Tchn: spring. II. 'F~-, 'f~-, comb.fm. (a) feather (pillow etc.); plumed (hat etc.); (b) pen-(holder etc.); (c) Tchn: spring (tension etc.). ◆'F~ball, m badminton. ◆'F~bett, n feather bed. ◆'f~führend, adj. in charge. ◆'f~leicht, adj light as a feather. ◆'f~n, v.i. (haben) to spring (Ball usw.) bounce. ◆'F~strich, m stroke of the pen. ◆'F~ung, f -/-en springs; Aut: etc: suspension. ◆'F~vieh, n F: poultry. ◆'F~waage, f spring balanced.

Fee [fe:], f -/-n fairy.

Fege|feuer ['fe:gyfɔʏər], n -s/no pl purgatory. ◆'f~n, v.tr. to sweep (the floor, chimney etc.); to sweep (up/away) (snow, leaves etc.).

Fehde ['fe:də], f -/-n feud.

fehl [fe:l]. I. adj. f. am Platz(e), out of place. II. 'F~-, f~-, comb.fm. wrong (diagnosis, decision etc.); false (Sp: start etc.); invalid (Sp: jump, throw etc.); mis(calculation etc.). ◆'F~anzeige, f -/-n F: (Antwort) negative. ◆'f~betrag, m deficit; (gegenüber dem Geplanten) shortfall. ◆'f~en, v.i. (haben) (a) to be missing; Sch: er fehlt seit einer Woche, he has been absent for a week; (b) es fehlt an Geld, Lehrern, usw., there's a shortage/lack of money, teachers etc.; ihm fehlt jedes Feingefühl, he has no tact at all; (c) F: was fehlt Ihnen? what is the matter with you? (d) sein Auto fehlt ihm sehr, he badly misses his car; das hat mir gerade noch gefehlt! that's all I needed! ◆'f~end, adj. missing; (Pers.) absent. ◆'F~er, m -s/- 1. mistake Sp: fault. 2. defect (in goods, a material etc.); körperliche F~, physical defects. ◆'f~erfrei, adj. faultless. ◆'f~erhaft, adj. faulty; flawed (diamond etc.). ◆'f~erlos, adj. faultless. ◆'F~geburt, f miscarriage. ◆'f~gehen, v.i.sep.irr.36 (sein) to go wrong. ◆'F~griff, m wrong decision. ◆'F~konstruktion, f (i) faulty design; (ii) F: botch-up. ◆'F~schlag, m miss; Fig: failure. ◆'f~schlagen, v.i.sep.irr.85 (sein) to fail. ◆'F~schuß, m miss. ◆'f~tritt, m false step; Fig: lapse. ◆'F~zündung, f misfire.

Feier ['faiər], f -/-n celebration; (private) party; (öffentliche) ceremony. ◆'F~abend, m -s/-e F. machen, to stop work for the day, F: knock off (work); nach F., after hours; F: nun ist aber F.! now that's quite enough of that! ◆'f~lich, adj. solemn; (würdevoll) dignified. ◆'F~lichkeit, f -/-en (a) no pl solemnity; (b) pl F~en, celebrations. ◆'f~n, v. 1. v.tr. & i. (haben) to celebrate. ◆'F~stunde, f ceremony. ◆'F~tag, m holiday.

feig(e) [faik ('faigə)], adj. cowardly; f. sein, to be a coward. ◆'F~heit, f -/no pl cowardice. ◆'F~ling, m -s/-e coward.

Feige ['faigə], f -/-n fig.

Feil|e ['failə], f -/-n file. ◆'f~en, v.tr. to file.

feilschen ['failʃən], v.i. (haben) to bargain, haggle.

fein [fain], adj. (a) fine; delicate (material); Fig: sharp (hearing, sight); (b) (vornehm) refined; sich f. machen, to make oneself smart; (c) (auserlesen) choice, first class (goods). ◆'f~fühlig, adj. sensitive. ◆'F~gefühl, n sensitivity; tact. ◆'F~heit, f -/-en (a) fineness; (Zartheit) delicacy; (*im Geschmack usw.*) refinement; (*b*) *pl* subtleties, finer points. ◆'F~**kost**, *f* -/no *pl* delicatessen (food). ◆'F~**kostgeschäft**, *n* delicatessen. ◆'F~**mechanik**, *f* precision engineering. ◆'F~**schmecker**, *m* gourmet.

**Feind|(in)** ['faint (-din)], *m* -(e)s/-e (*f* -/-nen) enemy. ◆'f~**lich**, *adj.* (*a*) hostile (attitude etc.); (*b*) enemy (troops, positions etc.). ◆'F~**schaft**, *f* -/-en hostility, enmity. ◆'f~**selig**, *adj.* hostile. ◆'F~**seligkeit**, *f* -/-en (*a*) hostility; (*b*) *pl* hostilities.

**feist** [faist], *adj.* podgy.

**Feld** [fɛlt], *n* -(e)s/-er (*a*) field; (*b*) *Sp:* pitch; (*c*) (*bei Brettspielen*) square. ◆'F~**bett**, *n* camp bed. ◆'F~**blume**, *f* wild flower. ◆'F~**flasche**, *f* water bottle. ◆'F~**herr**, *m* commander. ◆'F~**lager**, *n* camp. ◆'F~**stecher**, *m* -s/- fieldglasses. ◆'F~**verweis**, *m Sp:* sending-off. ◆'F~**webel**, *m* -s/- sergeant. ◆'F~**weg**, *m* track, path. ◆'F~**zug**, *m* campaign.

**Felge** ['fɛlgə], *f* -/-n (wheel) rim.

**Fell** [fɛl], *n* -(e)s/-e fur (of a cat etc.); coat (of a dog, horse etc.); fleece (of sheep); **ein dickes F. haben**, to be thick-skinned.

**Fels** [fɛls], *m* -en/-en rock. ◆'F~**block**, *m* large boulder. ◆'F~**en** ['fɛlzən], *m* -s/- rock; (*Felswand*) cliff. ◆'f~**en'fest**, *adj.* unshakable; *adv.* steadfastly. ◆'f~**ig**, *adj.* rocky. ◆'F~**vorsprung**, *m* rocky ledge. ◆'F~**wand**, *f* rock face.

**femin|in** [femi'niːn], *adj.* feminine (clothes etc.); *Pej:* effeminate (man). ◆F~**ist(in)**, *m* -en/-en (*f* -/-nen) feminist. ◆f~**istisch**, *adj.* feminist.

**Fenchel** ['fɛnçəl], *m* -s/no *pl* fennel.

**Fenster** ['fɛnstər], *n* -s/- window. ◆F~**brett**, *n* window ledge. ◆'F~**putzer**, *m* window cleaner. ◆'F~**rahmen**, *m* window frame. ◆'F~**scheibe**, *f* window pane. ◆'F~**sims**, *m* window sill.

**Ferien** ['feːriən]. **I.** *pl* holiday(s); *N.Am:* vacation; **F. machen**, to take one's holiday/vacation. **II.** ◆'F~-, *comb.fm.* holiday, *N.Am:* vacation (house, job, camp etc.). ◆'F~**ort**, *m* (holiday) resort; ◆'F~**wohnung**, *f* holiday home/flat, *N.Am:* vacation apartment. ◆'F~**zeit**, *f* holiday season, *N.Am:* vacation period.

**Ferkel** ['fɛrkəl], *n* -s/- piglet.

**fern** [fɛrn]. **I.** *adj.* far; (*attrib.*) distant (friends etc.); **von f~(e)**, from a long way off. **II.** **F~-**, *comb.fm.* long-distance (driver, transport etc.); long-range (bomber etc.). ◆'F~**bedienung**, *f* remote control. ◆'f~**bleiben**. **I.** *v.i.sep.irr.12* (*sein*) **j-m, etwas dat f.**, to stay away from s.o., sth. **II. F.**, *n* -s/no *pl Sch: etc:* absence. ◆'F~**e**, *f* -/-n distance; **in weiter F.**, a long way off. ◆'f~**er. 1.** *adj.* (*zusätz-*

*lich*) further. **2.** *adv.* **f. möchten wir bestätigen, daß ...**, we should also like to confirm that ... ◆'f~**gelenkt/ 'f~gesteuert**, *adj.* remote-controlled; guided (missile). ◆'F~**gespräch**, *n* long-distance call. ◆'F~**glas**, *n* binoculars. ◆'f~**halten**, *v.tr.sep.irr.45* to keep (s.o., sth.) away, (*schützen*) shield (s.o., sth.). ◆'F~**lenkung**, *f* -/no *pl* remote control. ◆'F~**licht**, *n Aut:* full/*N.Am:* high beam. ◆'f~**liegen**, *v.i. sep.irr.62* (*haben*) **es lag ihm fern, sie zu beleidigen**, he had no intention of offending her ◆'F~**melde-**, *comb.fm.* telecommunications (satellite, service etc.). ◆'f~**mündlich**, *adv.* by telephone. ◆'F~**ost**, *m inv.* in/aus/nach F., in/to/ from the Far East. ◆'f~**'östlich**, *adj.* Far Eastern. ◆'F~**rohr**, *n* telescope. ◆'F~**schreiben**, *n* telex ◆'F~**schreiber**, *m* -s/- telex machine. ◆'F~**seh-**, *comb.fm.* television (aerial, announcer, film, etc.). ◆'F~**sehapparat** *m* television set. ◆'F~**seher**, *m* -s/- **1.** (*Gerät*) *F:* telly, TV. **2.** (*Pers.*) viewer. ◆'F~**sehschirm**, *m* television screen. ◆'F~**sehsender**, *m* television station. ◆'F~**sehzuschauer**, *m* viewer. ◆'f~**sehen**. **I.** *v.i.sep.irr.92* (*haben*) to watch television. **II. F.**, *n* -s/no *pl* television; **im F.**, on (the) television. ◆'F~**sprecher**, *m* telephone. ◆'F~**sprechzelle**, *f* telephone box. ◆'F~**steuerung**, *f* remote control. ◆'F~**studium**, *n* study by correspondence. ◆'F~**unterricht**, *m* **1.** tuition by correspondence. **2.** correspondence course. ◆'F~**ziel**, *n* long-term aim.

**Ferse** ['fɛrzə], *f* -/-n heel.

**fertig** ['fɛrtiç]. **I.** *adj.* (*a*) (*bereit*) ready; (*b*) (*vollendet*) finished; **er ist mit seiner Arbeit f.**, he's finished his work; **mit j-m, etwas dat f. werden**, to cope/deal with s.o., sth.; (*c*) *F:* **ich bin ganz f.**, I'm completely worn out. **II.** **F~-**, *comb.fm.* ready-made (clothes etc.); prefabricated (building, house etc.); *Ind:* finished (product, goods). ◆'f~**bringen**, *v.tr.sep.irr.16* (*a*) to get (sth.) done, complete (a task); (*b*) **es f., etwas zu tun**, to manage to do sth. ◆'f~**en**, *v.tr.* to produce. ◆'F~**keit**, *f* -/-en skill, proficiency (**in** + *dat*, at). ◆'f~**machen**, *v.tr.sep. F:* (*a*) to finish (sth.); (*b*) to get (s.o., sth.) ready; (*c*) (*erschöpfen*) to wear (s.o.) out; (*d*) *P:* to beat (s.o.) up, (*töten*) do (s.o.) in. ◆'f~**stellen**, *v.tr.sep.* to complete. ◆'F~**stellung**, *f* -/no *pl* completion. ◆'F~**ung**, *f* -/no *pl* production.

**Fessel** ['fɛsəl], *f* -/-n bond. ◆'f~**n**, *v.tr.* (*a*) to bind; *Fig:* to tie (s.o.); **ans Bett gefesselt**, confined to bed; (*b*) (*faszinieren*) to enthrall (s.o.). ◆'f~**nd**, *adj.* fascinating; (*spannend*) riveting.

**fest¹** [fɛst], *adj.* firm; (*a*) solid (rock, *Ph:* body etc.); (*unbiegsam*) rigid; (*nicht flüssig*) solid; set (jelly); hard (wood); (*b*)

(stark) strong (material); secure, solid (structure); (unbeweglich) tight (cork, screw etc.); sound (sleep); firm (belief, hope etc.); **eine Tür f. verschließen**, to lock a door securely; **f. davon überzeugt**, firmly convinced (of it); (c) fixed (price, income etc.); firm (offer); set (habits); permanent (home, address); stable (relationship); **f~e Freunde**, firm friends; **eine f~e Vorstellung von etwas** dat, a clear idea of sth.; F: **in f~en Händen sein**, to be spoken for. ◆'**f~angestellt**, adj. permanent. ◆**f~binden**, v.tr.sep.irr.9 to tie (s.o., sth.) up; to lash (s.o., sth.) (**an etwas** acc, to sth.). ◆'**f~fahren**, v.refl.&i.sep.irr.26 (**sein**) (**sich**) **f.**, Aut: to get stuck; Fig: (Verhandlungen) to reach deadlock. ◆'**f~halten**, v.sep.irr.45 **1.** v.i. (**haben**) **an Traditionen usw. f.**, to cling to traditions etc. **2.** v.tr. (a) to keep hold of (s.o., sth.); (b) **sich an etwas** dat **f.**, to hold/hang on to sth.; (c) to record (events); to capture (a scene). ◆'**f~igen**, v.tr. to strengthen (an alliance etc.), consolidate (one's position). ◆'**F~iger**, m -s/- **Haarf.**) setting lotion. ◆**F~igkeit**, f -/no pl firmness, solidity; (Stärke) strength; (Härte) hardness. ◆**f~klammern**, v.tr.sep. to clamp (sth.) (**an etwas** dat, to sth.); **sich an j-m, etwas** dat **f.**, to cling tightly to s.o., sth. ◆**f~klemmen**, v.sep. **1.** v.i. (**sein**) to jam. **2.** v.tr. to jam, wedge (sth.). ◆**F~land**, n mainland. ◆**f~legen**, v.tr.sep. (a) (bestimmen) to lay down (principles), stipulate (conditions, a limit etc.); to fix (a date etc.), decide on (a route, plan); **etwas schriftlich f.**, to put sth. down in writing; (b) to commit (oneself, s.o.) (**auf etwas** acc, to sth.). ◆**f~liegen**, v.i. sep.irr.62 (**sein**) (a) (Schiff) to be aground; (b) (Termin, Preis usw.) to be fixed. ◆**f~machen**, v.tr.sep. (a) to fasten (sth.), tie up (a boat, dog etc.); (**an etwas** dat, to sth.); (b) to settle (a date, price etc.). ◆'**F~nahme**, f -/-n arrest. ◆**f~nehmen**, v.tr.sep.irr.69 to capture, (verhaften) arrest (s.o.). ◆**f~setzen**, v.tr.sep. to settle (a time, date etc.); to fix (a price etc.). ◆**f~stehen**, v.i. sep.irr.3 (**haben**) (Termin, Route usw.) to be decided; **eines steht fest**, one thing is certain. ◆**f~stellen**, v.tr.sep. to establish (a fact etc.); (bemerken) to notice (a change etc.); ◆**F~stellung**, f discovery (of a fact etc.); (Bemerkung) observation. ◆**F~ung**, f -/-en fortress. ◆**f~ziehen**, v.tr.sep. to pull (a knot) tight; to tighten (a belt, screw etc.).
**Fest²**. **I.** n -es/-e **1.** celebration, festivity; (private Gesellschaft) party; **frohes F.!** have a good Christmas! **II.** F~-, comb.fm. festive (evening, dress, mood, decorations etc.); gala (concert, performance). ◆'**F~essen**, n banquet, din-

ner; F: feast. ◆**f~lich**, adj. festive (occasion etc.); dressy (clothes). ◆'**F~saal**, m assembly hall; (für Bälle) ballroom; (für Festessen) banqueting hall. ◆'**F~spiel**, n festival.
**fett** [fɛt]. **I.** adj. (a) (dick) fat; (b) fatty (soup, meal etc.); greasy (hair, skin); F: **f~e Beute**, rich haul; (c) **f. gedruckt**, in bold type. **II.** F., n -(e)s/-e fat. **III.** F~-, f~-, comb.fm. fat (content etc.); grease (mark etc.). ◆**f~arm**, adj. low-fat. ◆'**F~auge**, n speck of fat. ◆'**F~creme**, f skin cream. ◆**f~en**, v.tr. to grease. ◆'**f~ig**, adj. fatty (substance); greasy (hair, dish etc.). ◆'**F~näpfchen**, n F: **ins F. treten**, to put one's foot in it.
**Fetzen** ['fɛtsən], m -s/- scrap.
**feucht** [fɔyçt], adj. damp; moist (lips, earth etc.). ◆'**f~fröhlich**, adj. F: merry. ◆'**F~igkeit**, f -/no pl damp; moisture (in a substance); (von Klima) humidity. ◆'**F~igkeitscreme**, f moisturizing cream.
**feudal** [fɔy'dɑːl], adj. feudal.
**Feuer** ['fɔyər]. **I.** n -s/- fire; (im Freien) bonfire; Fig: fervour; **F. fangen**, to catch fire; **j-m F. geben**, to give s.o. a light; **das F. eröffnen/einstellen**, to open fire/cease firing; **sie war gleich F. und Flamme (dafür)**, she was immediately wild with enthusiasm (about it); **mit dem F. spielen**, to play with fire. **II.** 'F~-, f~-, comb.fm. fire (alarm, -fighting, etc.); (danger etc.) of fire. ◆'**F~eifer**, m ardour, zeal. ◆'**f~fest**, adj. fireproof; Cu: ovenproof. ◆'**f~gefährlich**, adj. inflammable. ◆'**F~leiter**, f fire escape. ◆'**F~löscher**, m fire extinguisher. ◆'**F~melder**, m fire alarm. ◆'**f~n**, v. **1.** v.i. (**haben**) to fire (auf j-n, at s.o.). **2.** v.tr. (a) to stoke (a boiler etc.); (b) F: to fling (sth.); (c) F: to fire (s.o.). ◆'**F~probe**, f Fig: acid test; ordeal. ◆'**f~rot**, adj. fiery (red). ◆'**F~schutz**, m cover. ◆'**F~stein**, m flint. ◆'**F~stelle**, f fireplace. ◆'**F~treppe**, f fire escape. ◆'**F~wehr**, f fire brigade. ◆'**F~wehrauto**, n fire engine. ◆'**F~wehrmann**, m fireman. ◆'**F~werk**, n fireworks. ◆'**F~werkskörper**, m firework. ◆'**F~zange**, f fire tongs. ◆'**F~zeug**, n (cigarette) lighter.
**feurig** ['fɔyriç], adj. fiery (temperament etc.); ardent (lover etc.).
**Fiasko** [fi'asko], n -s/-s fiasco.
**Fichte** ['fiçtə], f -/-n spruce (tree); F: pine (tree).
**fidel** [fi'deːl], adj. F: jolly, cheerful.
**Fieber** ['fiːbər], n -s/- fever. ◆'**f~haft**, adj. feverish. ◆'**f~n**, v.i. (**haben**) to be feverish. ◆'**fiebrig**, adj. feverish.
**fies** [fiːs], adj. F: horrid.
**Figur** [fi'guːr], f -/-en figure; (in Buch) character; (Schachf.) piece.

**Filet** [fi'le:], *n* -s/-s fillet.

**Filial|e** [fili'ɑ:lə], *f* -/-n branch. ◆**F~leiter**, *m* branch manager.

**Film** [film]. **I.** *m* -(e)s/-e film; *N.Am: Cin:* movie. **II. F~-**, *comb.fm.* film, *N.Am:* movie (studio, critic, actor). ◆**'F~aufnahme**, *f* filming. ◆**'f~en**, *v.tr.&i.* (*haben*) to film. ◆**'F~kamera**, *f* cine camera. ◆**'F~star**, *m* film/movie star. ◆**'F~verleih**, *m* film/movie distributors. ◆**'F~vorführer**, *m* projectionist.

**Filter** ['filtər]. **I.** *m* -s/- filter. **II.** ◆**'F~-**, *comb.fm.* filter (paper, bag etc.). ◆**'F~kaffee**, *m* filter coffee. ◆**'f~n**, *v.tr.* to filter. ◆**'F~zigarette**, *f* filter-tipped cigarette.

**Filz** [filts], *m* -es/-e felt. ◆**'f~en**, *v.tr. F:* to frisk (s.o.) ◆**'F~stift**, *m* felt(-tip) pen.

**Fimmel** ['fiməl], *m* -s/no pl *F:* mania, craze.

**Finale** [fi'nɑ:lə], *n* -s/- 1. *Mus:* finale. 2. *Sp:* final.

**Finanz** [fi'nants], *f* -/-en finance. ◆**F~amt**, *n* tax office. ◆**f~iell** [-tsi'ɛl], *adj.* financial. ◆**f~ieren** [-'tsi:rən], *v.tr.* to finance. ◆**F~ierung**, *f* -/-en financing.

**find|en** ['findən], *v.tr.irr.9* (*a*) to find; **er war nirgends zu f.**, he was nowhere to be found; (*b*) (*der Meinung sein*) **f. Sie nicht?** don't you think (so)? (*c*) **sich f.**, (*auftauchen*) to turn up; **es wird sich (schon) alles f.**, everything will be all right. ◆**'F~er(in)**, *m* -s/- (*f* -/-nen) finder. ◆**'F~erlohn**, *m* reward. ◆**'f~ig**, *adj.* resourceful.

**Finesse** [fi'nɛsə], *f* -/-n *F:* trick.

**Finger** ['fiŋər], *m* -s/- finger; **man muß ihnen dauernd auf die F. sehen**, you have to keep an eye on them all the time; **ich kann es mir doch nicht aus den F~n saugen**, I can't produce it out of thin air. ◆**'F~abdruck**, *m* fingerprint. ◆**'f~fertig**, *adj.* deft. ◆**'F~hut**, *m* 1. thimble. 2. *Bot:* foxglove. ◆**'f~n**, *v.i.* (*haben*) **an etwas dat f.**, to finger sth. ◆**'F~nagel**, *m* finger-nail. ◆**'F~spitze**, *f* fingertip. ◆**'F~spitzengefühl**, *n* intuition. ◆**'F~zeig**, *m* -(e)s/-e (*Hinweis*) tip; (*Wink*) sign.

**fingieren** [fiŋ'gi:rən], *v.tr.* to simulate, (*erdichten*) invent (sth.). ◆**f~t**, *adj.* fictitious.

**Fink** [fiŋk], *m* -en/-en finch.

**Finn|e** ['finə], *m* -n/-n/'F~in, *f* -/-nen Finn. ◆**'f~isch**, *adj.* Finnish. ◆**'F~land**. *Pr.n.n* -s. Finland.

**finster** ['finstər], *adj.* (*a*) dark; (*düster*) gloomy; (*unheimlich*) sinister; **im F~n**, in the dark; (*b*) (*zwielichtig*) shady (business etc.); (*c*) **f~e Miene/f~er Blick**, black look. ◆**'F~nis**, *f* -/-se 1. darkness. 2. *Astr:* eclipse.

**Finte** ['fintə], *f* -/-n feint; *Fig:* trick.

**Firm|a** ['firma], *f* -/-men firm; company; ◆**'F~eninhaber**, *m* owner of a/the firm. ◆**'F~enwagen**, *m* company car. ◆**'F~enzeichen**, *n* trade mark.

**firm|en** ['firmən], *v.tr.* to confirm. ◆**'F~ung**, *f* -/-en confirmation.

**Firnis** ['firnis], *m* -ses/-se varnish.

**First** [first], *m* -(e)s/-e ridge.

**Fisch** [fiʃ], *m* -(e)s/-e (*a*) fish; **F~e fangen**, to (catch) fish; (*b*) *Astr:* Pisces; (*c*) *F:* (*Pers.*) **ein großer F.**, a VIP; **kleine F~e**, small fry; (*Sachen*) minor matters. ◆**'f~en**, *v.* 1. *v.tr.* to fish for, (*fangen*) catch; 2. *v.i.* (*haben*) to fish; **f. gehen**, to go fishing; **nach etwas dat f.**, to fish for sth. ◆**'F~er**, *m* -s/- fisherman. ◆**'F~erboot**, *n* fishing boat. ◆**'F~erei**, *f* -/-en fishing. ◆**'F~fang**, *m* fishing. ◆**'F~geschäft**, *n* fishmonger's (shop), *N.Am:* fish store. ◆**'F~gräte**, *f* fishbone. ◆**'F~grätenmuster**, *n* herringbone pattern. ◆**'F~kutter**, *m* fishing boat. ◆**'F~mehl**, *n* fishmeal. ◆**'F~stäbchen**, *n* fish finger, *N.Am:* fishstick. ◆**'F~teich**, *m* fishpond. ◆**'F~zug**, *m* catch.

**fit** [fit], *adj.* fit. ◆**'F~neß**, *f* -/no pl fitness.

**fix** [fiks], *adj.* 1. fixed (prices, salary etc.); 2. (*flink*) quick; sharp-witted (person). 3. *F:* **f. und fertig**, (*a*) (*bereit*) completely finished; (*b*) (*erschöpft*) completely worn out; ◆**'F~n**, *m* -s/- *P:* junkie. ◆**f~ieren**, *v.tr.* (*a*) **etwas schriftlich f.**, to put sth. down in black and white; (*b*) *Phot:* to fix.

**Fjord** [fjɔrt], *m* -(e)s/-e fiord.

**flach** [flax], *adj.* (*a*) flat; (*eben*) level; (*b*) (*niedrig*) low (building, heel etc.); (*c*) (*nicht tief*) shallow (water, dish etc.); *Fig:* superficial (book, conversation etc.). ◆**'F~heit**, *f* -/no pl (*a*) flatness; (*b*) (*also Fig:*) shallowness. ◆**'F~land**, *n* lowland(s).

**Fläch|e** ['flɛçə], *f* -/-n (*a*) (*Oberfläche*) surface; *Mth:* plane (of a figure); (*b*) (*Ausdehnung*) area; expanse (of water etc.). ◆**'F~eninhalt**, *m* area. ◆**'F~enmaß**, *n* square measure.

**Flachs** [flaks], *m* -es/no pl flax.

**flackern** ['flakərn], *v.i.* (*haben*) to flicker.

**Fladen** ['flɑːdən], *m* -s/- fritter.

**Flagg|e** ['flagə], *f* -/-n flag; ◆**'F~schiff**, *n* flagship.

**Flak** [flak], *f* -/-s anti-aircraft gun.

**Flakon** [fla'kõ:], *n* -s/-s phial.

**flämisch** ['flɛ:miʃ], *adj.* Flemish.

**Flamingo** [fla'miŋgo], *m* -s/-s flamingo.

**Flamme** ['flamə], *f* -/-n flame; ◆**'F~nmeer**, *n* mass of flames. ◆**'F~nwerfer**, *m* -s/- flamethrower.

**Flanell** [fla'nɛl], *m* -s/-e flannel.

**Flank|e** ['flaŋkə], *f* -/-n 1. flank. 2. (*a*) (*Turnen*) side vault; (*b*) *Fb:* centre, cross. ◆**f~ieren** [-'ki:rən], *v.tr.* to flank.

**Flasche** ['flaʃə], *f* -/-n 1. bottle; cylinder

(of gas); **eine F. Bier,** a bottle of beer. 2. *F: (Pers.)* useless character. ◆'**F~n-, f~n-,** *comb.fm.* (a) bottle (brush, opener etc.); (b) bottled (beer, wine etc.). ◆**F~nzug,** *m* block and tackle.

**flatter|haft** ['flatərhaft], *adj.* capricious. ◆'**f~n,** *v.i.* (haben) (a) to flutter, flap; (b) *(Vogel)* to flap its wings; *(Hände)* to shake.

**flau** [flau], *adj.* (a) *(schwach)* faint (breeze); (b) *(leblos)* slack (holiday season, business); dull, lifeless (conversation, atmosphere); (c) *F:* **mir ist f. (im Magen),** I feel queasy.

**Flaum** [flaum], *m -(e)s/no pl* down, fluff.

**flauschig** ['flauʃiç], *adj.* fleecy, cuddly (toy etc.).

**Flausen** ['flauzən], *pl F:* nonsense; **er hat nur F. im Kopf,** his head is stuffed with silly ideas.

**Flaute** ['flautə], *f -/-n* **1.** *Nau:* dead calm. **2.** *Com: etc:* slack period.

**Flecht|e** ['flɛçtə], *f -/-n* **1.** *Bot:* lichen. **2.** *Med:* psoriasis. ◆'**f~en,** *v.tr.irr.* to plait, *N.Am:* braid (hair, straw etc.); to weave (a basket etc.). ◆**F~werk,** *n* wickerwork.

**Fleck** [flɛk], *m -(e)s/-e* (a) *(Schmutz)* mark, spot; *(von Wein usw.)* stain; *(Klecks)* blot; **blauer F.,** bruise; (b) *(Stück Boden)* patch (of ground); *(Ort)* spot; **er rührte sich nicht vom F.,** he didn't stir/budge; *F:* **vom F. weg,** on the spot, there and then. ◆'**F~en,** *m -s/- 1.* = **Fleck** (a). **2.** (small) market town. ◆'**f~enlos,** *adj.* spotless. ◆'**F~enwasser,** *n* stain remover. ◆'**f~ig,** *adj.* stained (clothes etc.); blotchy (face).

**Fledermaus** ['fle:dərmaus], *f* bat.

**Flegel** ['fle:gəl], *m -s/-* lout. ◆**F~ei** [-'lai], *f -/-en* rudeness. ◆'**f~haft,** *adj.* loutish. ◆'**F~jahre,** *npl* awkward age.

**flehen** ['fle:ən], *v.i.* (haben) to implore; **bei j-m um etwas** *acc* **f.,** to beg s.o. for sth.

**Fleisch** [flaiʃ]. **I.** *n -(e)s/no pl* (a) flesh; (b) *(Nahrungsmittel)* meat. **II. F~-, ~-,** *comb.fm.* (a) flesh (wound etc.); (b) meat (dish, salad etc.). ◆'**F~brühe,** *f* (a) (beef) stock; (b) *(Suppe)* consommé. ◆'**F~er,** *m -s/-* butcher. ◆**F~e'rei,** *f -/-en* butcher's (shop). ◆'**F~erhaken,** *m* meat hook. ◆'**f~fressend,** *adj.* carnivorous. ◆'**f~ig,** *adj.* meaty (animal); fleshy (face, soft fruit). ◆'**F~käse,** *m* meat loaf. ◆'**F~klößchen,** *n* meat ball. ◆'**f~lich,** *adj.* carnal. ◆'**F~pastete,** *f* meat pie. ◆'**F~wolf,** *m* mincer, *N.Am:* meat grinder.

**Fleiß** [flais], *m -es/no pl* diligence. ◆'**f~ig,** *adj.* hardworking; **f. arbeiten,** to work hard.

**fletschen** ['flɛtʃən], *v.tr.* **die Zähne f.,** to bare one's teeth.

**flex|ibel** ['flɛ'ksi:bəl], *adj.* flexible. ◆**F~ibilität** [-ibili'tɛ:t], *f -/no pl* flexi-

bility.

**flick|en** ['flikən], **f~en. I.** *v.tr.* to mend **II. F.,** *m -s/-* patch. ◆'**F~werk,** *n -(e)s/no pl Pej:* patched up job. ◆'**F~zeug,** *n* (a) *(beim Nähen)* mending things; (b) *(für Fahrrad)* (puncture) repair kit.

**Flieder** ['fli:dər], *m -s/-* lilac.

**Flieg|e** ['fli:gə], *f -/-n* **1.** fly. **2.** *Cl:* bowtie. ◆'**f~en,** *v.tr.&i.irr.30* (sein) to fly; *F:* **alle Mädchen f. auf ihn,** all the girls find him irresistible; *F:* **aus seiner Stellung f.,** to get the sack; *F:* **in die Luft f.,** to explode, blow up. ◆'**f~end,** *adj.* flying; **f~er Händler,** itinerant trader. ◆'**F~enfänger,** *m* flytrap. ◆'**F~engewicht,** *n* flyweight. ◆'**F~er,** *m -s/-* pilot. ◆'**F~eralarm,** *m* air raid warning. ◆'**F~erangriff,** *m* air attack/raid.

**flieh|en** ['fli:ən], *v.i.irr.* (sein) to run away **(vor j-m, etwas** *dat,* from s.o., sth.); *(entkommen)* to escape. ◆'**f~end,** *adj.* **1.** fleeing (troops etc.). **2.** receding (chin, forehead). ◆'**F~kraft,** *f* centrifugal force.

**Fliese** ['fli:zə], *f -/-n* tile.

**Fließ|arbeit** ['fli:sarbait], *f -/no pl* production line work. ◆'**F~band,** *n* conveyor belt. ◆'**f~en,** *v.i.irr.* (sein) to flow; *(Hahn, Nase usw.)* to run. ◆'**f~end,** *adj.* (a) flowing; **Zimmer mit f~em Wasser,** room with running water; (b) **f. deutsch sprechen,** to speak fluent German.

**flimmern** ['flimərn], *v.i.* (haben) *(Sterne)* to twinkle; *(Luft, Hitze)* to shimmer; *(Fernsehen)* to flicker.

**flink** [fliŋk], *adj.* agile (movements, person); nimble (fingers).

**Flinte** ['flintə], *f -/-n* shotgun.

**Flirt** [fleert], *m -s/-s* flirtation. ◆'**f~en,** *v.i.* (haben) to flirt.

**Flitter** ['flitər], *m -s/-* (a) *pl (auf einem Kleid)* sequins; (b) *(Glitzerschmuck)* tinsel. ◆'**F~wochen,** *fpl* honeymoon.

**flitz|en** ['flitsən], *v.i.* (sein) to whizz (along), *(Pers.)* dash.

**Flock|e** ['flɔkə], *f -/-n* flake. ◆'**f~ig,** *adj.* flaky.

**Floh** [flo:]. **I.** *m -(e)s/-̈e* flea; ◆'**F~markt,** *m* flea market; *(Wohltätigkeitsbasar)* jumble sale.

**Flor,** *m -s/-e* **1.** gauze; *(Trauerf.)* crêpe. **2.** *(Teppichf.)* pile.

**florieren** [flo'ri:rən], *v.i.* (haben) *(Geschäft)* to flourish.

**Flora** ['flo:ra], *f -/Floren* flora.

**Florett** [flo'rɛt], *n -(e)s/-e* foil.

**Floskel** ['flɔskəl], *f -/-n* set phrase.

**Floß** [flo:s], *n -/-̈e* raft.

**Flosse** ['flɔsə], *f -/-n* (a) fin; (b) *(Schwimmf.)* flipper.

**Flöt|e** ['flø:tə], *f -/-n* **1.** flute. **2.** champagne flute. ◆**F~ist(in)** [flø'tist(in)], *m -en/-en* (f -/-nen) flautist.

**flott** [flɔt], *adj. F:* (a) *(schnell)* quick, *F:*

speedy (service etc.); (b) (schick) smart (dress, coat etc.); (rasant) sporty (car); (lebendig) lively (music etc.); flamboyant (style); ◆'f~machen, v.tr.sep. to make (a ship, boat) seaworthy/F: (a car) roadworthy.

**Flotte** ['flɔtə], f -/-n fleet. ◆'F~nstützpunkt, m naval base.

**Flöz** [fløːts], n -es/-e seam.

**Fluch** [fluːx], m -(e)s/-e curse. ◆'f~en, v.i. (haben) to curse (auf/über + acc, at, about).

**Flucht**[1] [fluxt]. I. f -/-en escape; **die F. ergreifen**, to take flight; **den Feind in die F. schlagen**, to put the enemy to flight; II. F~-, comb.fm. escape (car etc.). ◆'f~artig, adj. hurried, hasty. ◆'F~versuch, m escape attempt. ◆'F~weg, m escape route.

**Flucht**[2], f -/-en (a) alignment (of buildings etc.); (b) suite (of rooms).

**flücht**[en ['flyçtən], v. 1. v.i. (sein) run away; (sich retten) to escape (vor + dat, from). 2. v.refl. **sich irgendwohin f.**, to take refuge somewhere (vor + dat, from). ◆'f~ig, adj. 1. (flüchtend) fleeing; escaped (prisoner etc.); **f. sein**, to be on the run. 2. (a) (kurz) cursory (acquaintance); fleeting (glance etc.); (b) (oberflächlich) superficial; shoddy (work); **j-n f. kennen**, to know s.o. slightly. ◆'F~igkeitsfehler, m careless mistake. ◆'F~ling, m -s/-e refugee.

**Flug** [fluːk]. I. m -(e)s/-e flight; (Fliegen) flying; **im F.**, in flight; **die Zeit verging (wie) im F~e**, the time flew past. II. F~-, comb.fm. (a) flight (deck, captain etc.); flying (boat, weather etc.); (b) air-(speed, traffic etc.). ◆'F~abwehr, f anti-aircraft defence. ◆'F~abwehrkanone, f anti-aircraft gun. ◆'F~begleiter(in), m (f) steward(ess). ◆'F~blatt, n leaflet, pamphlet. ◆'F~gast, m air passenger. ◆'F~gesellschaft, f airline. ◆'F~hafen, m airport. ◆'F~höhe, f altitude. ◆'F~lotse, m air traffic controller. ◆'F~objekt, n **unbekanntes F.**, unidentified flying object. ◆'F~platz, m airfield. ◆'F~reise, f flight. ◆'f~s [fluks], adv. quickly; at once. ◆'F~steig, m gate (at an airport). ◆'F~zeug, n aeroplane, N.Am: airplane. ◆'F~zeugentführung, f hijacking. ◆'F~zeughalle, f hangar. ◆'F~zeugträger, m aircraft carrier.

**Flügel** ['flyːgəl], m -s/- 1. wing. 2. half (of a window); side (of the lung). 3. sail (of a windmill). Mus: grand piano. ◆'F~schlag, m wing beat. ◆'F~tür, f double door.

**flügge** ['flygə], adj. fully-fledged.

**Flunder** ['flundər], f -/-n flounder.

**flunkern** ['fluŋkərn], v.i. (haben) F: to tell tall stories.

**Fluor** ['fluːɔr], n -s/no pl fluorine.

**Flur**[1] [fluːr], m -(e)s/-e hall.

**Flur**[2], f -/-en (a) Fig: **allein auf weiter F. sein**, to be all alone; (b) Agr: farmland.

**Fluß** [flus]. I. m -sses/-sse 1. river. 2. (Fließen) flow (of water, traffic etc.); **im F. sein**, (Sache) to be in a state of flux. II. 'F~-, comb.fm. river (bed, valley, bank etc.). ◆'F~lauf, m course of a river. ◆'f~'abwärts, adv. downstream. ◆'f~'aufwärts, adv. upstream. ◆'F~pferd, n hippopotamus.

**flüssig** ['flysiç], adj. 1. liquid; molten (metal, lava etc.). 2. (fließend) flowing; fluent (speaker, style etc.). 3. Fin: liquid (capital, assets); ready (money). ◆'F~keit, f -/-en 1. liquid; esp. Anat: etc: fluid. 2. (Eigenschaft) fluency. ◆'f~machen, v.tr.sep. to make available.

**flüster**[n ['flystərn]. I. v.tr. & i. (haben) to whisper. II. F., n -s/no pl whispering; whisper. ◆'F~propaganda, f whispering campaign. ◆'F~ton, m **im F.**, in a whisper.

**Flut** [fluːt], f -/-en 1. no pl high tide; **bei F.**, at high tide; **die F. steigt/fällt**, the tide is coming in/going out. 2. Lit: F~en, waters; **eine F. von Tränen, Briefen usw.**, a flood of tears, letters etc. ◆'F~licht, n floodlight. ◆'F~welle, f tidal wave.

**Fohlen** ['foːlən], n -s/- foal.

**Föhn** [føːn], m -(e)s/-e warm Alpine wind.

**Föhre** ['føːrə], f -/-n pine tree.

**Folg**[e ['fɔlgə], f -/-n 1. consequence; **etwas zur F. haben**, to result in sth. 2. (a) (Reihe) series; sequence; **in rascher F.**, in quick succession; (b) Rad: TV: instalment. 3. **einem Befehl usw. F. leisten**, to obey an order etc.; **einer Einladung F. leisten**, to accept an invitation. ◆'f~en, v.i. (a) (sein) **j-m/etwas dat f.**, to follow s.o., sth.; (b) (sein) (zeitlich) **j-m, etwas dat/auf j-n, etwas acc f.**, to follow from s.o., sth.; **wie folgt**, as follows; **daraus folgt, daß ...**, it follows from this that ...; (c) (haben) (j-m) f., to obey (s.o.). ◆'f~end, adj. following; **am f~en Tag**, the next day; **f~es**, the following. ◆'f~ender'maßen, adv. as follows. ◆'f~enschwer, adj. (action etc.) with far-reaching consequences. ◆'f~erichtig, adj. logical. ◆'f~ern, v.tr. to conclude (**aus** + dat, from). ◆'F~erung, f -/-en conclusion, deduction. ◆'f~lich, adv. & conj. consequently. ◆'f~sam, adj. obedient.

**Folie** ['foːliə], f -/-n (a) (metal) foil; (b) (plastic) film; (Überzug) lamination.

**Folklor**[e ['fɔlk'loːrə], f -/no pl 1. folklore. 2. folk music. ◆f~istisch [-o'ristif], adj. folk, F: folksy.

**Folter** ['fɔltər], f -/-n torture; **j-n auf die F. spannen**, to keep s.o. on tenterhooks. ◆'F~er, m -s/- torturer. ◆'f~n, v.tr. to torture, Fig: torment (s.o.).

**Fön** [fø:n], *m* **-(e)s/-e** *R.t.m.* hairdryer. ◆'**f~en**, *v.tr.* sich *dat* die Haare f., to dry one's hair.

**Fonds** [fõ:], *m* -/- fund.

**foppen** ['fɔpən], *v.tr.* j-n f., to pull s.o.'s leg.

**forcieren** [fɔr'si:rən], *v.tr.* (*a*) **das Tempo f.**, to force the pace; (*b*) to step up (production etc.).

**forder|n** ['fɔrdərn], *v.tr.* (*a*) to demand (rights, money etc.); to claim (*Jur:* damages, *Fig:* lives, victims etc.); **einen hohen Preis f.**, to charge a high price; (*b*) (*herausf.*) to challenge (s.o.). ◆'**F~ung**, *f* -/-en demand.

**Förder|band** ['fœrdərbant], *n* conveyor belt. ◆'**F~er(in)**, *m* -s/- (*f* -/-nen) patron (of the arts etc.); sponsor. ◆'**f~lich**, *adj.* profitable, favourable. ◆'**f~n**, *v.tr.* (*a*) to promote (trade, art, understanding etc.); (*finanziell*) to sponsor, support (a project etc.); to further (development, science etc.); (*b*) *Min:* to extract. ◆'**F~turm**, *m* pithead winding tower. ◆'**F~ung**, *f* -/-en **1.** sponsorship (of art etc.); promotion. **2.** *Min:* production.

**Forelle** [fo'rɛlə], *f* -/-n trout.

**Form** [fɔrm], *f* -/-en **1.** form; (*äußere Gestalt*) shape; (*Plan usw.*) **feste F. annehmen**, to take shape; **in aller F.**, with due ceremony; **die F. wahren**, to keep up appearances. **2.** *Sp:* fitness; **gut/groß in F.**, in good/great form. **3.** (*Gießf.*) mould; (*Backf.*) (baking) tin. ◆**f~al** [fɔr'mɑ:l], *adj.* **1.** formal (structure etc.). **2.** technical (objections, grounds etc.). ◆**F~alität** [-i'tɛːt], *f* -/-en formality. ◆**F~at** [-'mɑːt], *n* -(e)s/-e **1.** size, format (of paper, books etc.). **2.** *no pl* calibre. ◆**F~ation** [-atsi'o:n], *f* -/-en formation. ◆'**f~bar**, *adj.* malleable. ◆'**F~el**, *f* -/-n formula. ◆**f~ell** [-'mɛl], *adj.* formal (agreement etc.). ◆'**f~en**, *v.tr.* to form (a concept, sounds etc.); to shape, mould (a material etc.); (*Gedanken, Stoff usw.*) **sich f.**, to take shape. ◆**f~ieren** [-'mi:rən], *v.tr.* to form; *Mil:* to draw up (troops). ◆'**f~los**, *adj.* **1.** shapeless. **2.** (*zwanglos*) informal; casual (behaviour). ◆'**F~sache**, *f* (reine) F., pure formality; *Adm:* technicality. ◆'**f~schön**, *adj.* beautifully shaped. ◆**F~ular** [-u'lɑ:r], *n* -s/-e *Adm:* form, *N.Am:* blank. ◆**f~u'lieren**, *v.tr.* to formulate. ◆**F~u'lierung**, *f* -/-en formulation; (*Wortlaut*) wording.

**förmlich** ['fœrmlɪç], *adj.* **1.** formal. **2.** (*regelrecht*) real. ◆'**F~keit**, *f* -/-en formality.

**forsch** [fɔrʃ], *adj.* dynamic.

**forsch|en** ['fɔrʃən], *v.i.* (haben) (*a*) **nach j-m, etwas** *dat* **f.**, to search for/ (*fragen nach*) inquire after s.o., sth.; **f~der Blick**, searching glance; (*b*) to (do) research (**auf einem Gebiet**, in an area/into

a subject). ◆'**F~er(in)**, *m* -s/- (*f* -/-nen) **1.** research worker, researcher. **2.** (*F~ungsreisender*) explorer. ◆'**F~ung**, *f* -/-en research. ◆'**F~ungs-**, *comb.fm.* research (work, institute). ◆'**F~ungsreise**, *f* voyage of exploration.

**Forst** [fɔrst], **I.** *m* -(e)s/-e(n) forest. **II.** ◆'**F~-**, *comb.fm.* forestry (officer, administration etc.); ◆'**F~wirtschaft**, *f* forestry.

**Förster** ['fœrstər], *m* -s/- forester, *N.Am:* forest ranger.

**Fort¹** [fo:r], *n* -s/-s fort.

**fort²** [fɔrt], *adv.* **1.** away; **das Buch ist f.**, the book has gone; **sie sind schon f.**, they have already gone/left. **2.** **und so f.**, and so on; **in einem f.**, on and on. ◆'**f~bestehen**, *v.i.sep.irr.100* (haben) to survive. ◆'**f~bewegen**, *v.tr.sep.* to move (sth.); **sich f.**, to move/walk (along). ◆'**f~bilden**, *v.refl.sep.* **sich f.**, to continue one's education/training. ◆'**F~bildung**, *f* further education/ training. ◆'**f~bleiben**, *v.i.sep.irr.12* (sein) to stay away. ◆'**f~bringen**, *v.tr.sep.irr.16* to take (s.o., sth.) away. ◆'**f~dauern**, *v.i.sep.* (haben) to continue. ◆'**f~dauernd**, *adj.* continuous; lasting (effect etc.). ◆'**f~entwickeln**, *v.refl. & i.* (haben) (**sich**) **f.**, to continue to develop. ◆'**f~fahren**, *v.i.sep.irr.26* (*a*) (sein) to drive away/off; (*b*) (haben/ sein) to continue (**in seiner Rede usw.**, speaking etc.). ◆'**f~fallen**, *v.i.sep.irr.27* (sein) to be omitted. ◆'**f~führen**, *v.tr. sep.* to lead/take (s.o., sth.) away; to carry on, continue (sth. begun by s.o. else). ◆'**F~gang**, *m* **1.** (*Verlauf*) course. **2.** *lit:* departure. ◆'**f~gehen**, *v.i.sep.irr.36* (sein) to go away, leave. ◆'**f~geschritten**, *adj.* advanced. ◆'**F~kommen**, *n* -s/*no pl* progress. ◆'**f~können**, *v.i.sep.irr.54* (haben) **er konnte nicht fort**, he could not get away. ◆'**f~laufen**, *v.i.sep.irr.58* (sein) to run away. ◆'**f~laufend**, *adj.* continuous. ◆'**f~müssen**, *v.i.sep.irr.68* (haben) to have to leave. ◆'**f~nehmen**, *v.tr.sep.irr.69* to take (s.o., sth.) away. ◆'**F~pflanzung**, *f* reproduction. ◆'**f~schaffen**, *v.tr.sep.* to remove (s.o., sth.). ◆'**f~schreiten**, *v.i.sep.irr.59* (sein) to progress. ◆'**F~schritt**, *m* progress; **große F~e machen**, to make considerable progress. ◆'**f~schrittlich**, *adj.* advanced (science, student etc.); progressive (person, ideas etc.). ◆'**f~setzen**, *v.tr.sep* to continue (sth.). ◆'**F~setzung**, *f* -/-en **1.** continuation. **2.** (*a*) (*Folge*) instalment; (*b*) (*anschließender Teil*) sequel. ◆'**f~während**, *adj.* incessant. ◆'**f~werfen**, *v.tr.sep.irr.110* to throw (sth.) away. ◆'**f~ziehen**, *v.sep.irr.113* **1.** *v.tr.* to pull, drag (s.o., sth.) away. **2.** *v.i.* (sein) to move away; (*Vögel*) to migrate.

**Fossil** [fɔ'siːl], *n* -s/-ien fossil.

**Foto** ['foːto], **I.** *n* -s/-s photo. ◆'**F~album**, *n* photograph album. ◆'**F~apparat**, *m* camera. ◆**f~gen** [-'geːn], *adj.* photogenic. ◆**F~graf** [-'graːf], *m* -en/-en photographer. ◆**F~grafie** [-a'fiː], *f* -/-n **1.** (*Bild*) photograph. **2.** *no pl* photography. ◆**f~gra'fieren**, *v.tr. & i.* (*haben*) to take a photograph (of s.o., sth.). ◆**f~grafisch** [-'graːfiʃ], *adj.* photographic. ◆**F~ko'pie**, *f* photocopy. ◆**f~ko'pieren**, *v.tr.* to photocopy.

**Foyer** [foa'jeː], *n* -s/-s foyer.

**Fracht** [fraxt], *f* -/-en **1.** freight; (*Ladung*) load, *Av: Nau:* cargo. **2.** (*Transportpreis*) freight. ◆'**F~er**, *m* -s/- freighter. ◆'**F~gut**, *n* freight; *Av: Nau:* cargo. ◆'**F~kosten**, *pl* freight cost. ◆'**F~schiff**, *n* freighter.

**Frack** [frak], *m* -(e)s/-e tails.

**Frag|e** ['fraːgə], *f* -/-n question; (**j-m**) **eine F. stellen**, to ask (s.o.) a question; **außer F. sein/stehen**, to be beyond any doubt; **etwas in F. stellen**, (i) (*Pers.*) to question sth; (ii) (*Sache*) to call sth. into question; **in F. kommen**, to come into consideration; (*Pers.*) to be eligible; **das kommt nicht in F.**, that is out of the question; **ohne F.**, undoubtedly; **nur eine F. der Zeit**, only a matter of time. ◆'**f~ebogen**, *m* questionnaire. ◆'**f~en**, *v.tr. & i.* (*haben*) **j-n etwas f.**, to ask s.o. sth.; **um Rat, Erlaubnis usw. f.**, to ask for advice, permission etc. ◆'**f~end**, *adj.* enquiring (look etc.). ◆'**F~esteller(in)**, *m* -s/- (*f* -/-nen) questioner. ◆'**F~ezeichen**, *n* -s/- question mark. ◆'**f~lich**, *adj.* **1.** questionable. **2. die f~lichen Personen**, the people in question. ◆'**f~los**, *adv.* unquestionably. ◆'**f~würdig**, *adj.* questionable. ◆'**F~würdigkeit**, *f* -/no pl dubiousness.

**Fragment** [frag'mɛnt], *n* -(e)s/-e fragment. ◆**f~arisch** [-'taːriʃ], *adj.* fragmentary.

**Fraktion** [fraktsi'oːn], *f* -/-en *Pol:* parliamentary party; (*innerhalb einer Partei usw.*) faction.

**Franken** ['fraŋkən], *m* -s/- franc.

**frankieren** [fraŋ'kiːrən], *v.tr.* to stamp, *Adm:* frank; **es ist nicht genügend frankiert**, there are not enough stamps on it.

**Frankreich** ['fraŋkraiç], *Pr.n.n* -s. France.

**Franse** ['franzə], *f* fringe.

**Franz|ose** [fran'tsoːzə], *m* -n/-n Frenchman. ◆**F~ösin** [-'tsøːzin], *f* -/-nen Frenchwoman. ◆**f~ösisch. I.** *adj.* French. **II. F.**, *n* -(s)/no pl (*Sprache*) French.

**frapp|ant** [fra'pant], *adj.* striking. ◆**f~ieren**, *v.tr.* to strike; **f~ierende Ähnlichkeit**, striking similarity.

**Fräs|e** ['frɛːzə], *f* -/-n moulding/(*für Metall*) milling machine. ◆'**f~en**, *v.tr.* to

shape (wood); to mill (metal).

**Fratze** ['fratsə], *f* -/-n grimace; **F~n schneiden/ziehen**, to make faces.

**Frau** [frau], *f* -/-en woman; (*Ehef.*) wife; **F. Schmidt**, (i) (*verheiratet*) Mrs. Schmidt; (ii) (*unverheiratet*) Miss Schmidt; **F. Präsident**, Madam President. ◆'**F~enarzt(-ärztin)**, *m* (*f*) gynaecologist. ◆'**F~enbewegung**, *f* feminist movement. ◆'**F~enheld**, *m* lady-killer. ◆'**F~enzeitschrift**, *f* women's magazine. ◆'**F~enzimmer**, *n* -s/-Pej: female. ◆'**f~lich**, *adj.* womanly.

**Fräulein** ['frɔylain], *n* -s/- **1.** young lady. **2. F. Schmidt**, Miss Schmidt.

**frech** [frɛç], *adj.* cheeky, *N.Am:* fresh; barefaced (lie etc.); (*ungezogen*) naughty (children). ◆'**F~dachs**, *m* F: cheeky monkey. ◆'**F~heit**, *f* -/-en (*a*) *no pl* cheek; (*b*) **F~heiten** *pl*, liberties; (*Bemerkungen*) cheeky remarks.

**Fregatte** [fre'gatə], *f* -/-n frigate.

**frei** [frai], *adj.* (*a*) free; **f~er Mitarbeiter/Journalist**, freelance worker/journalist; **f. nach Schiller**, freely adapted from Schiller; **f. erfunden**, entirely fictitious; **f. sprechen**, to speak without notes; (*b*) (*ohne Scheu*) frank (person, play etc.); **F: ich bin so f.!** I'll take the liberty; (*sich bedienen*) I'll help myself; (*c*) (*offen, unbehindert*) open, clear; (*bloß*) bare (torso etc.); **ins F~e gehen**, to go outdoors/into the open (air); **den Oberkörper f. machen**, to strip to the waist; **einen Platz f. machen**, to clear a space; (*d*) (*unbesetzt*) empty (chair etc.); vacant (post); **ist hier noch f.?** is this seat taken? *Com:* **f. Haus**, free delivery; (*f*) **sich** *dat* **einen Tag f. nehmen**, to have a day off; (*g*) **f. von** + *dat*, free of/from. ◆'**F~bad**, *n* open-air swimming pool. ◆'**f~bekommen**, *v.tr.sep.irr.53* (*a*) *F:* to get (a day etc.) off; (*b*) to secure the release of (s.o., sth.). ◆'**f~beruflich**, *adj.* freelance; self-employed. ◆'**F~betrag**, *m* tax allowance. ◆'**F~brief**, *m* justification. ◆'**F~gabe**, *f* -/no pl release. ◆'**f~geben**, *v.tr.sep.irr.35* to release (s.o., a film etc.); to open (a road). ◆'**f~gebig**, *adj.* generous. ◆'**F~gebigkeit**, *f* -/no pl generosity. ◆'**F~gepäck**, *n* (free) baggage allowance. ◆'**f~haben**, *v.tr.&i.sep.irr.44* (*haben*) *F:* to have (time, a day) off. ◆'**f~halten**, *v.tr.sep.irr.45* (*a*) to treat (s.o.); (*b*) to keep (a road, entrance etc.) clear; (*c*) to keep, reserve (a seat). ◆'**F~handelszone**, *f* free trade area. ◆'**f~händig**, *adj.* freehand. **f. radfahren**, to cycle with no hands. ◆'**F~heit**, *f* -/-en freedom; **in F. sein**, to be free/(*Sträfling*) at large; **dichterische F.**, poetic licence. ◆'**f~heitlich**, *adj.* liberal. ◆'**F~heitsentzug**, *m* detention. ◆'**F~heitsstrafe**, prison sentence.

◆'f~he'raus, *adv.* frankly, bluntly.
◆'f~kommen, *v.i.sep.irr.53 (sein)* to be
released. ◆'f~lassen, *v.tr.sep.irr.57* to
release, set free. ◆'F~lassung, *f -/-en*
release. ◆'F~lauf, *m* freewheel; im F.
fahren, to freewheel. ◆'f~legen,
*v.tr.sep.* to expose. ◆'f~lich, *adv.* 1.
(*allerdings*) admittedly. 2. certainly.
◆'F~licht-, *comb.fm.* open-air (theatre,
concert etc.). ◆'f~machen, *v.tr.sep.*
(*a*) to stamp, put a stamp on (a letter);
(*b*) to clear (a road, entrance etc.); to vacate (a seat, building); (*c*) to bare (one's
shoulders etc.); (sich *dat*) den Oberkörper f., to strip to the waist; *Fig:* sich
von etwas *dat* f., to rid oneself of
sth. ◆'f~mütig, *adj.* frank.
◆'f~schaffend, *adj.* freelance, self-
employed. ◆'f~setzen, *v.tr.sep.* to release (workers, *Ch:* gas, energy etc.).
◆'f~sprechen, *v.tr.sep.irr.14* to clear
(s.o.); *Jur:* to acquit (s.o.).
◆'F~spruch, *m* acquittal. ◆'f~
stehen, *v.i.sep.irr.100 (haben)* (*a*) es
steht dir frei, it is up to you; (*b*) (*Gebäude*) to be unoccupied. ◆'f~stellen,
*v.tr.sep.* j-m etwas f., to leave sth. to
s.o.'s discretion. ◆'F~stoß, *m Fb:*
free kick. ◆'F~tod, *m* suicide.
◆'F~umschlag, *m* stamped envelope.
◆'F~wild, *n* easy game. ◆'f~willig,
*adj.* voluntary; sich f. melden, to volunteer. ◆'F~zeichen, *n* ringing tone.
◆'F~zeit, *f* spare time. ◆'F~zeit-,
*comb.fm.* casual, leisure (clothes etc.).
◆'F~zeitgestaltung, *f* planning of
one's leisure. ◆'F~zeitzentrum, *n* leisure centre. ◆'f~zügig, *adj.* 1. (*nicht
ortsgebunden*) (*Pers.*) free to move; noma-
dic (life). 2. (*a*) (*großzügig*) generous;
(*b*) (*liberal*) liberal. ◆'F~zügigkeit,
*f -/no pl* (*a*) generosity; (*b*) permissive-
ness.
**Freitag** ['fraitɑːk], *m* Friday. ◆'f~s,
*adv.* on Fridays.
**fremd** [frɛmt], *adj.* 1. (*ausländisch*) foreign; (*nicht vertraut*) strange, alien; ein
F~er/eine F~e, a stranger/(*Ausländer*)
foreigner; ich bin hier f., I am a stranger
here; Lügen ist ihr f., lying is alien to
her nature. 2. (*andern gehörig*) f~es
Eigentum/Gut, other people's property.
◆'f~artig, *adj.* strange.
◆'F~enführer, *m* (*Pers.*) guide.
◆'F~enlegion, *f* foreign legion.
◆'F~enverkehr, *m* tourism.
◆'F~enzimmer, *n* 1. (hotel) room. 2.
guest/spare room (in a house).
◆'f~gehen, *v.i.sep.irr.36 (sein)* F: to
be unfaithful. ◆'F~körper, *m* foreign
body. ◆'f~ländisch, *adj.* exotic.
◆'F~sprache, *f* foreign language.
◆'f~sprachig, *adj.* (person) speaking a
foreign language; (lessons, literature etc.)
in a foreign language. ◆'F~wort, *n*
word of foreign origin.
**frenetisch** [fre'neːtiʃ], *adj.* frenzied.

**Frequenz** [fre'kvɛnts], *f -/-en Rad: Ph:*
frequency.
**fressen** ['frɛsən], I. *v.tr. & i.irr.25* (*haben*) (*a*) (*Tier*) to eat; *F:* (*Pers.*) to gobble; *Fig:* to eat up (money, petrol etc.);
(*b*) (*Rost usw.*) to corrode. II. F., *n -s/no
pl* food.
**Frettchen** ['frɛtçən], *n -s/-* ferret.
**Freud|e** ['frɔydə], *f -/-n* joy, delight;
(*Vergnügen*) pleasure; es wird mir eine F.
sein, I shall be delighted; j-m (eine) F.
machen, to please s.o., make s.o. happy.
◆'F~enhaus, *n Lit:* brothel.
◆'F~entränen, *fpl* tears of joy.
◆'f~estrahlend, *adj.* beaming.
◆'f~ig, *adj.* joyful, happy; f~iges
Ereignis, happy event; f. überrascht
sein, to be pleasantly surprised.
◆'f~los, *adj.* miserable. ◆'f~voll,
*adj.* joyful, happy.
**freuen** ['frɔyən], *v.tr.* (*a*) to please; es
freut mich, daß ..., I am pleased/glad
that ...; (*b*) sich f., to be pleased/glad; er
freut sich des Lebens, he enjoys life;
sich an Blumen f., to take pleasure in
flowers; sich auf etwas *acc* f., to look
forward to sth.
**Freund** [frɔynt], *m -(e)s/-e* (*a*) friend; (*b*)
(*Verehrer*) boy friend; (*c*) lover (of art,
music etc.); ich bin kein F. davon, I'm
not at all keen on it. ◆'F~eskreis, *m*
circle of friends. ◆'F~in, *f -/-nen* girl
friend. ◆'f~lich, *adj.* 1. (*a*) kind (person, invitation etc.); (*b*) friendly (manner
etc.); mit f~lichen Grüßen, yours sincerely; f. lächeln, to give a friendly
smile. 2 pleasant (area, room etc.); fine
(weather). ◆'f~licherweise, *adv.*
kindly. ◆'F~lichkeit, *f -/no pl* kindness. ◆'F~schaft, *f -/-en* friendship;
mit j-m F. schließen, to make friends
with s.o. ◆'f~schaftlich, *adj.* friendly,
amicable. ◆'F~schaftsspiel, *n* friendly
match.
**Frevel** ['freːfəl], *m -s/- Lit:* iniquity.
◆'f~haft, *adj.* iniquitous.
**Fried|en** ['friːdən], *m -s/no pl* peace; im
F., in peacetime; laß mich in F.! leave
me alone! ◆'F~ens-, *comb.fm.* peace
(movement, plan etc.); ◆'F~ens-
schluß, *m* conclusion of a peace treaty.
◆'F~ensverhandlungen, *fpl* peace
talks. ◆'F~ensvertrag, *m* peace treaty.
◆'F~enszeiten, *pl* peacetime.
◆'f~fertig, *adj.* peaceable.
◆'F~fertigkeit, *f -/no pl* peaceable
nature/behaviour. ◆'F~hof, *m* cemetery. ◆'f~lich, *adj.* 1. peaceful (times,
demonstrations, purposes etc.); peaceable, calm (person, nature). 2. *Lit:* (*ruhig*) peaceful. ◆'f~liebend, *adj.*
peace-loving.
**frieren** ['friːrən], *v.i.irr.* (*a*) (*haben*) to
be/feel (very) cold; ich friere/*impers.*
mich friert (es), I am freezing; draußen
friert es, it is freezing outside; (*b*) (*sein*)
(*Wasser usw.*) to freeze.

**Fries** [fri:s], *m* -es/-e frieze.
**Fries|e** ['fri:zə], *m* -n/-n/**'F~in**, *f* -/-nen Frisian. ◆**'f~isch**, *adj.* Frisian.
**frigid(e)** [fri'gi:t(-də)], *adj.* frigid.
**Frikadelle** [frika'dɛlə], *f* -/-n rissole.
**Frikass|ee** [frika'se:], *n* -s/-s fricassee.
**frisch** [friʃ], *adj.* (*a*) fresh; (*sauber*) clean (clothes etc.); **f. gebackene Eheleute,** a newly married couple; **f. gestrichen!** wet paint! **sich f. machen,** to freshen up, have a wash; *F:* **f. und munter,** fit and well; (*b*) (*kühl*) chilly. ◆**'F~e,** *f* -/no pl freshness. ◆**'F~haltepackung,** *f* vacuum pack. ◆**'F~käse,** *m* curd cheese. ◆**'F~luft,** fresh air.
**Fris|eur** [fri'zø:r], *m* -s/-s hairdresser. ◆**F~euse,** *f* -/-n hairdresser. ◆**f~ieren,** *v.tr.* (*a*) to do (s.o.'s) hair; (*b*) *F:* to dress up (a report); to fiddle (accounts etc.); to soup up (an engine, a car). ◆**F~iertisch,** *m* dressing table.
**Frist** [frist], *f* -/-en (*a*) (*Zeitspanne*) period; **eine Woche F. erhalten,** to receive a week's grace; (*b*) (*Termin*) time-limit; (*äußerste/letzte*) **F.,** deadline. ◆**'f~en,** *v.tr.* **sein Leben/seine Existenz f.,** to scrape a living. ◆**'f~gerecht,** *adj.* punctual. ◆**'f~los,** *adj.* immediate; **f. entlassen,** dismissed without notice.
**Frisur** [fri'zu:r], *f* -/-en hairstyle, *F:* hairdo.
**frivol** [fri'vo:l], *adj.* frivolous; risqué (joke, story).
**froh** [fro:], *adj.* happy, cheerful; **f~e Weihnachten!** happy/merry Christmas! **ich bin f., daß ...,** I am glad/(*erleichtert*) relieved that ... ◆**f~'locken,** *v.i.* (*haben*) *Lit:* to rejoice, (*hämisch*) gloat. ◆**'F~sinn,** *m* cheerfulness.
**fröhlich** ['frø:liç], *adj.* cheerful (person, mood etc.); jolly (party, games etc.); **f~e Weihnachten!** happy Christmas! ◆**F~keit,** *f* -/no pl gaiety; jollity.
**fromm** [frɔm], *adj.* pious.
**Frömm|elei** [frœmə'lai], *f* -/-en no pl bigotry. ◆**'F~igkeit,** *f* -/no pl piety.
**frönen** ['frø:nən], *v.i.* (*haben*) *Lit:* **einem Laster usw. f.,** to indulge a vice etc.
**Fronleichnam** [fro:n'laiçna:m], *m* -s/no pl Corpus Christi.
**Front** [frɔnt]. **I.** *f* -/-en front. **F. gegen j-n/etwas** *acc.* **machen,** to resist s.o., sth; *Sp:* **in F. gehen/liegen,** to take/be in the lead. **II.** **'F~-,** *comb.fm.* (*a*) front (engine etc.); (*b*) *Mil:* front line (experience, troops etc.). ◆**'f~al** [-'ta:l] *adj.* & **F~al-,** *comb.fm.* frontal; **f~aler Zusammenstoß,** head-on collision. ◆**'F~antrieb,** *m* front-wheel drive.
**Frosch** [frɔʃ], *m* -es/-e frog. ◆**'F~mann,** *m* frogman. ◆**'F~schenkel,** *m* frog's leg.
**Frost** [frɔst]. **I.** *m* -(e)s/-e frost. **II.** ◆**'F~-,** *comb.fm.* frost (damage etc.); frosty (night, weather etc.). ◆**'F~beule,** *f* chilblain. ◆**'f~ig,** *adj.* frosty (weather etc.); icy (remark etc.).

◆**'F~schutzmittel,** *n* antifreeze.
**frösteln** ['frœstəln], *v.i.* (*haben*) **mich fröstelt (es),** I feel shivery.
**Frott|ee** [frɔ'te:], *n* -s/-s towelling. ◆**F~eehandtuch,** *n* towel. ◆**f~ieren** [-'ti:rən], *v.tr.* to rub/towel (s.o., oneself) down.
**Frucht** [fruxt]. **I.** *f* -/-e fruit; **F~e tragen,** to bear fruit. **II.** **'F~-,** *comb.fm.* fruit (yoghurt, salad etc.). ◆**'f~bar,** *adj.* fertile (soil, plant, imagination etc.); *Fig:* fruitful (period, talks etc.); prolific (writer). ◆**'F~barkeit,** *f* -/no pl fertility. ◆**'F~fleisch,** *n* fruit flesh. ◆**'f~ig,** *adj.* fruity. ◆**'f~los,** *adj.* fruitless. ◆**'F~saft,** *m* fruit juice.
**früh** [fry:], *adj.* (*a*) early; **er ist f. gestorben,** he died young; **f~er oder später,** sooner or later; (*b*) **f~er,** former (time, enemies); previous (owner etc.); **er war f~er Journalist,** he used to be a journalist; (*c*) (*morgens*) **morgen/heute f.,** tomorrow/this morning; **von f. bis spät,** from dawn till dusk. ◆**'F~aufsteher,** *m* early riser. ◆**'F~e,** *f* -/no pl **in aller F.,** bright and early. ◆**'f~estens,** *adv.* at the earliest. ◆**'F~geburt,** *f* premature birth. ◆**'F~jahr,** *n* spring. ◆**'F~jahrsputz,** *m* -es/no pl spring clean(ing). ◆**'F~ling,** *m* -s/-e spring. ◆**'f~morgens,** *adv.* early in the morning. ◆**'f~reif,** *adj.* precocious. ◆**'F~reife,** *f* precociousness. ◆**'F~schicht,** *f* early shift. ◆**'F~sport,** *m* morning exercises. ◆**'F~stück,** *n* breakfast. ◆**'f~stücken,** *v.* **1.** *v.i.* (*haben*) to have breakfast. **2.** *v.tr.* to have for breakfast. ◆**'f~zeitig,** *adj.* early; (*vorzeitig*) premature.
**Frust** [frust], *m* -(e)s/no pl *F:* frustration. ◆**f~rieren** [-'tri:rən], *v.tr.* to frustrate.
**Fuchs** [fuks], *m* -es/-e fox; (*Pferd*) chestnut. ◆**'F~bau,** *m* fox's earth. ◆**'f~en,** *v.tr.* *F:* to make (s.o.) mad; ◆**'f~ig,** *adj.* *F:* furious, mad. ◆**'F~jagd,** *f* fox-hunt(ing). ◆**'F~schwanz,** *m* handsaw. ◆**'f~teufels'wild,** *adj.* *F:* hopping mad.
**Füchsin** ['fyksin], *f* -/-nen vixen.
**Fucht|el** ['fuxtəl], *f* -/no pl *F:* **unter der F. sein/stehen,** to be kept in check. ◆**'f~eln,** *v.i.* (*haben*) *F:* **mit den Händen f.,** to wave one's hands.
**Fuge** ['fu:gə], *f* -/-n **1.** joint; (*Spalte*) crack; *Fig:* **aus den F~n geraten,** to go to pieces. **2.** *Mus:* fugue.
**füg|en** ['fy:gən], *v.tr.* (*a*) to join (sth.) (**en etwas** *acc*, to sth.), fit (sth.) (**in etwas** *acc,* into sth.); (*b*) **sich j-m, etwas** *dat* **f.,** to give in to s.o., sth.; *Lit:* **sich in sein Schicksal f.,** to resign oneself to one's fate; (*c*) *Lit:* **es fügte sich, daß ...,** it so happened that ... ◆**f~sam,** *adj.* compliant.
**fühl|bar** ['fy:lba:r], *adj.* palpable (loss, re-

lief etc.); tangible, noticeable (difference etc.). ◆'f~en, v.tr. (a) to feel; (b) v.refl. sich krank, betrogen usw. f., to feel ill, deceived etc. ◆'F~er, m -s/- feeler; F: die F. ausstrecken, to put out feelers. ◆'F~ung, f -/no pl contact; mit j-m F. aufnehmen, to get in touch with s.o.

Fuhr|e ['fuːrə], f -/-n cartload. ◆'F~mann, m -(e)s/-leute cart driver. ◆'F~park, m fleet (of vehicles). ◆'F~unternehmer, m haulage contractor. ◆'F~werk, n waggon, cart.

führ|en ['fyːrən], v. 1. v.tr. (a) to lead (s.o.); to take (s.o.) (über die Straße usw., across the road etc.); Hunde müssen an der Leine geführt werden, dogs must be kept on a lead/N.Am: leash; das Glas zum Mund f., to raise the glass to one's lips; (b) (leiten) to command (a regiment etc.); to captain (a team); to run, manage (a business, hotel etc.); Krieg f., to wage war; (c) to carry (water, oil etc.); Com: to stock (goods); er führt kein Geld bei sich, he doesn't have any money on him; (d) (betreiben) to hold (a conversation, talks etc.); to keep (a diary, list etc.); ein elendes Leben f., to lead a miserable life; über etwas acc Buch f., to keep a record of sth.; (e) Adm: to drive (a vehicle); (f) v.refl. sich (gut/schlecht) f., to behave (well/badly). 2. v.i. (haben) to lead; die Straße führt an der Küste entlang, the road runs along the coast; das führt zu weit, that is going too far; unsere Bemühungen führten zu nichts, our efforts got us nowhere. ◆'f~end, adj. leading (newspaper, firm etc.); prominent (personality); in der Entwicklung f. sein, to be in the forefront of development. ◆'F~er(in), m -s/- (f -/-nen) 1. (Pers.) (a) leader; Mil: commander; (b) (im Museum usw.) guide; (c) (Fahrer) driver. 2. (Buch) guidebook. ◆'F~erschein, m driving licence; den F. machen, to take one's driving test; (fahren lernen) to learn to drive. ◆'F~ung, f -/-en 1. no pl Pol: etc: leadership; Com: management; Mil: command. 2. no pl Sp: etc: in F. liegen/gehen, to be in/take the lead. 3. no pl (Betragen) conduct. 4. (Besichtigung) guided tour (durch ein Museum, of a museum). ◆'F~ungszeugnis, n certificate of good conduct.

Füll|e ['fylə], f -/no pl (große Menge) wealth (von Einfällen usw., of ideas etc.). ◆'f~en, v.tr. (a) to fill (sth.); Cu: to stuff; (b) (schütten) to put (sth.) (in Flaschen usw., into bottles etc.); (c) sich f., to fill (up). ◆'F~federhalter/F: ◆'F~er, m -s/- fountain pen. ◆'f~ig, adj. plump. ◆'F~ung, f -/-en 1. filling; (in meat etc.). 2. (Türf.) (door) panel.

fummeln ['fuməln], v.i. (haben) F: to fumble (an etwas dat, with sth.).

Fund [funt], m -(e)s/-e 1. (Finden)

finding. 2. (Gefundenes) find. ◆'F~büro, n lost property/N.Am: lost and found office. ◆'F~grube, f -/-n (Geschäft usw.) goldmine; (Buch usw.) mine of information. ◆'F~ort, m place where it was/they were found. ◆'F~sache, f object found; pl lost property. ◆'F~stätte, f site of a find.

Fund|ament [funda'mɛnt], n -(e)s/-e foundation(s); Fig: basis (of a theory etc.). ◆f~amen'tal, adj. fundamental.

fündig ['fyndiç], adj. f. werden, to make a find.

fünf [fynf], num. adj. five. ◆'F~eck, n pentagon. ◆'f~eckig, adj. five-sided. ◆'f~fach, adj. quintuple; adv. five times. ◆'f~jährig, adj. five-year-old (child, animal); five-year (period). ◆'F~kampf, m pentathlon. ◆'f~mal, adv. five times. ◆'f~stellig, adj. five-figure. ◆'f~t, adv. zu f., in a group of five. ◆'f~te(r, s), num. adj. fifth. ◆'F~tel, n -s/- fifth. ◆'f~tens, adv. fifthly. ◆'f~zehn, num. adj. fifteen. ◆'f~zig, num. adj. fifty.

fungieren [fuŋ'giːrən], v.i. (haben) to officiate; (Gegenstand) f. als, to function as.

Funk [fuŋk]. I. m -s/no pl radio; über F., by radio. II. 'F~-, comb.fm. radio station, contact etc.). ◆'F~e, m -ns/-n spark; glimmer (of hope etc.). ◆'f~eln, v.i. (haben) to sparkle, (Licht, Sterne) twinkle; (Edelstein usw.) to glitter. ◆'f~el'nagel'neu, adj. F: brand new. ◆'f~en. I. v.tr. to radio. II. F., m -s/- = Funke. ◆'F~er, m -s/- radio operator. ◆'F~haus, n radio station. ◆'F~spruch, m radio message. ◆'F~streife, f radio patrol.

Funktion [fuŋktsi'oːn], f -/-en (a) (also Mth:) function; (b) no pl working; außer F., out of action. ◆'F~är [-o'nɛːr], m -s/-e official. ◆f~ieren [-'niːrən], v.i. (haben) to work. ◆F~sstörung, f -/-en malfunction.

Funzel ['funtsəl], f -/-n F: dim/dismal light.

für [fyːr]. I. prep. + acc for; das hat viel f. sich, there is much to be said for it; f. j-n sprechen, to speak on s.o.'s behalf; f~s erste, for now; Tag f. Tag, day by day; Wort f. Wort, word for word; Schritt f. Schritt, step by step; f. sich, alone; ein Volk f. sich, a race apart; an und f. sich, actually; (im Grunde) basically. II. F., n das F. und Wider, the pros and cons. ◆f~ei'nander, adv. for each/one another. ◆'F~sorge, f -/no pl 1. care. 2. (Sozialhilfe) welfare; F: er lebt von der F., he is living on social security. ◆'F~sorger(in), m -s/- (f -/-nen) social worker. ◆'F~sorgeunterstützung, f social security benefit. ◆'f~sorglich, adj. considerate, thoughtful. ◆'F~sprache, f -/no pl plea; (bei j-m) für j-n F. einlegen, to plead (with s.o.) on s.o.'s behalf. ◆'F~**sprecher**, *m* advocate. ◆'F~**wort**, *n* pronoun.

**Furche** ['furçə], *f* -/-n furrow.

**Furcht** ['furçt], *f* -*/no pl* fear; **vor etwas** *dat* **F. haben**, to be afraid of sth.; **aus F. vor Strafe**, for fear of punishment. ◆'f~**bar**, *adj.* terrible, dreadful; **f~baren Hunger haben**, to be terribly hungry. ◆'f~**los**, *adj.* fearless. ◆'F~**losigkeit**, *f* -*/no pl* fearlessness. ◆'f~**sam**, *adj.* timid (person, animal); apprehensive (looks etc.). ◆'F~**samkeit**, *f* -*/no pl* timidity.

**fürcht|en** ['fyrçtən], *v.* 1. *v.tr.* (*a*) to fear, be afraid of; (*b*) **sich f.**, to be afraid/frightened (**vor j-m, etwas** *dat*, of s.o., sth.). 2. *v.i.* (*haben*) to be afraid; **um/für j-n, etwas** *acc* **f.**, to fear for s.o., sth. ◆'f~**erlich**, *adj.* terrifying (sight etc.); *F:* terrible.

**Furnier** [fur'ni:r], *n* -s/-e veneer.

**Furore** [fu'ro:rə], *f & n* **F. machen**, to cause a sensation.

**Fürst** [fyrst], *m* -en/-en prince. ◆'F~**entum**, *n* -s/-er principality. ◆'F~**in**, *f* -/-nen princess. ◆'f~**lich**, *adj.* royal (family etc.); princely (bearing, *Fig:* sum etc.); sumptuous (meal etc.); **f. leben/essen**, to live/eat like a prince.

**Furt** [furt], *f* -/-en ford.

**Fuß** [fu:s], *m* -es/-̈e 1. (*a*) foot; **zu F.**, on foot; **zu F. gehen**, to walk; (**bei**) **F.**! heel! (*also Fig:*) **j-n, etwas mit F~en treten**, to trample s.o., sth. underfoot; (*b*) *Fig:* (**festen**) **F. fassen**, (i) (*Pers.*) to find one's feet; (ii) (*Ideen usw.*) to become established; **auf großem F. leben**, to live like a lord; **mit j-m auf gutem F. stehen**, to be on good terms with s.o. 2. foot, bottom (of a mountain, stairs etc.); base (of a lamp, pillar etc.); stem (of a glass); leg (of a table). ◆'F~**abdruck**, *m* footprint. ◆'F~**angel**, *f* mantrap. ◆'F~**ball**, *m* football. ◆'F~**ball-**, *comb.fm.* football (team stadium etc.). ◆'F~**ballfeld**, *n* football pitch. ◆'F~**ballplatz**, *m* football ground. ◆'F~**ballspiel**, *n* football match. ◆'F~**ballspieler**, *m* footballer. ◆'F~**boden**, *m* floor. ◆'F~**bremse**, *f* footbrake. ◆'f~**en**, *v.i.* (*haben*) (*Argument, Theorien usw.*) to be based (**auf** + *dat*, on). ◆'F~**ende**, *n* foot. ◆'F~**gänger**, *m* -s/- pedestrian. ◆'F~**gänger-**, *comb.fm.* pedestrian (crossing etc.); ◆'F~**gängerzone**, *f* pedestrian precinct. ◆'F~**gelenk**, *n* ankle (joint). ◆'f~**hoch**, *adj.* ankle-deep. ◆'F~**leiste**, *f* skirting board. ◆'F~**marsch**, *m* march. ◆'F~**matte**, *f* doormat. ◆'F~**note**, *f* footnote. ◆'F~**pflege**, *f* -*/no pl* chiropody. ◆'F~**pfleger(in)**, *m* (*f*) chiropodist. ◆'F~**pilz**, *m* athlete's foot. ◆'F~**rücken**, *m* instep. ◆'F~**sohle**, *f* sole of the foot. ◆'F~**stapfen**, *m* -s/- *Fig:* **in j-s F~stapfen treten**, to follow in s.o.'s footsteps. ◆'F~**tritt**, *m* kick. ◆'F~**weg**, *m* footpath.

**Fussel** ['fusəl], *f* -/-n (bit of) fluff. ◆'f~**ig**, *adj.* (*Stoff usw.*) covered in fluff.

**Futter**[1] ['futər], *n* -s/- *Cl: etc:* lining. ◆'F~**stoff**, *m* lining.

**Futter**[2], *n* -*s/no pl* feed. ◆'F~**neid**, *m* professional jealousy.

**Futteral** [futə'ra:l], *n* -s/-e case; (knife) sheath.

**füttern**[1] ['fytərn], *v.tr.* to line (clothes).

**füttern**[2] *v.tr.* to feed (an animal, patient, computer, *F:* machine).

**Futur** [fu'tu:r], *n* -*s/no pl* future (tense).

# G

**G, g** [ge:], *n* -/- (the letter) G, g.

**Gabe** ['ga:bə], *f* -/-n gift.

**Gabel** ['ga:bəl], *f* -/-n (*a*) fork; (*b*) *Tel:* cradle. ◆'g~**n**, *v.refl.* sich g., to fork. ◆'G~**stapler**, *m* -s/- fork lift truck. ◆'G~**ung**, *f* -/-en fork.

**gackern** ['gakərn], *v.i.* (*haben*) to cackle, cluck.

**gaffen** ['gafən], *v.i.* (*haben*) to gape, (*starren*) stare. ◆'G~**er**, *m* -s/- *Pej:* curious bystander.

**Gage** ['ga:ʒə], *f* -/-n fee.

**gähnen** ['gɛ:nən], *v.i.* (*haben*) to yawn; **g~der Abgrund**, gaping chasm.

**Gala** ['ga:la], *f* -*/no pl* evening dress. ◆'G~**vorstellung**, *f* gala performance.

**galant** [ga'lant], *adj.* gallant.

**Galerie** [galə'ri:], *f* -/-n gallery.

**Galgen** ['galgən], *m* -s/- gallows. ◆'G~**frist**, *f* (brief) respite. ◆'G~**humor**, *m* gallows humour.

**Gall|e** ['galə], *f* -/-n (*a*) bile; *Fig:* gall; (*b*) = **Gallenblase**. ◆'G~**enblase**, *f* gall bladder. ◆'G~**enstein**, *m* gall-stone.

**Galopp** [ga'lɔp], *m* -s/-s & -e gallop. ◆'g~**ieren** [-'pi:rən], *v.i.* (*haben/sein*) to gallop.

**Gamasche** [ga'maʃə], *f* -/-n spat.

**gamm|eln** ['gaməln], *v.i.* (*haben*) *F:* to loaf about. ◆'G~**ler(in)**, *m* -s/- (*f* -/-nen) *F:* drop-out.

**gang**[1] [gaŋ], *pred.adj.* **g. und gäbe sein**, to be the usual thing.

**Gang**[2], *m* -(e)s/-̈e 1. (*a*) (*Art zu gehen*) gait; (*b*) **in G. sein**, to be running; *Fig:* **etwas in G. bringen/halten**, to get/keep sth. going; **in G. kommen**, to get under way. 2. (*Lauf*) course (of duties, business etc.). 3. (*Spazierg.*) walk; (*Boteng.*) errand. 4. course (of a meal). 5. *Aut:* gear.

**6.** (*Weg*) path; (*im Gebäude*) corridor; (*Flur*) hallway. ◆'**G~schaltung,** *f Aut:* gearchange, *N.Am:* gearshift.

**Gangster** ['gɛŋstər], *m* -**s**/- gangster.

**gängeln** ['gɛnəln], *v.tr.* to treat (s.o.) like a child.

**gängig** ['gɛniç], *adj.* (*a*) common (opinion, expression); (*b*) *Com:* popular (goods, line).

**Ganove** [ga'noːvə], *m* -**n**/-**n** *P:* crook.

**Gans** [gans], *f* -/**-e** ['gɛnzə] goose.

**Gänse|blümchen** ['gɛnzəblyːmçən], *n* -**s**/- daisy. ◆'**G~braten,** *m* roast goose. ◆'**G~füßchen,** *n* -**s**/- *F:* quotation marks. ◆'**G~haut,** *f F:* goose-pimples; ◆'**G~marsch,** *m* **im G.,** in single file.

**ganz** [gants]. **I.** *adj.* **1.** whole; **von g~em Herzen,** with all one's heart; **g~e Arbeit leisten,** to do a thorough job; **g. Deutschland,** all/the whole of Germany. **meine g~en Sachen,** all my things. **2.** quite; **eine g~e Menge,** quite a lot. **3.** *F:* (*heil*) intact; **etwas wieder g. machen,** to mend sth. **II.** *adv.* **1.** (*völlig*) completely; quite; **er weiß es g. genau,** he knows it perfectly well; **du hast g. recht,** you are quite right; **g. wie du denkst,** just as you think; **sie ist mir g. fremd,** she is a complete stranger to me; **g. und gar,** utterly, completely; **g. und gar nicht,** not by any means. **2.** (*ziemlich*) quite; **es war g. schön,** it was quite nice. ◆'**G~e(s),** *n decl. as adj.* (*a*) **das G.,** the whole (thing); (*Summe*) the total; *Fig:* **aufs G. gehen,** to force the issue; (*b*) **im g~n,** in all, altogether. ◆'**g~jährig,** *adj.* all year (round). ◆'**g~tägig,** *adj.* whole day's (journey etc.); full-time (employment etc.). ◆'**g~tags,** *adv.* **g. arbeiten,** to work full-time.

**gänzlich** ['gɛntslıç], *adj.* complete; *adv.* completely.

**gar** [gaːr]. **I.** *adj. Cu:* **g.** (**gekocht**), (well) cooked, done. **II.** *adv.* (*a*) **g. nicht,** not at all; **g. nicht schlecht,** not at all bad; **g. nichts,** nothing at all; **g. keiner,** nobody at all; (*b*) (*sogar*) **oder g. ...,** or even ...; ◆'**g~aus,** *m* -/no pl *F:* **j-m den G. machen,** to finish s.o. off. ◆'**g~en,** *v.tr.* to cook.

**Garage** [ga'raːʒə], *f* -/-**n** garage.

**Garant|ie** [garan'tiː], *f* -/-**n** guarantee (**auf/für etwas** *acc,* on sth.); **die G. für etwas** *acc* **übernehmen,** to vouch for/ guarantee sth. ◆**g~ieren** [-'tiːrən], *v.tr. & i.* (*haben*) **etwas/für etwas** *acc* **g.,** to guarantee sth. ◆**G~iezeit,** *f* -/-**en** guarantee.

**Garbe** ['garbə], *f* -/-**n** **1.** sheaf. **2.** *Mil:* cone of fire.

**Gard|e** ['gardə], *f* -/-**n** **1. die G.,** the Guards. **2.** *F:* **die alte G.,** the old faithfuls.

**Garderob|e** [gardə'roːbə], *f* -/-**n** **1.** (*Kleider*) clothes. **2.** (*Kleiderablage*) cloakroom, *N.Am:* checkroom. ◆**G~enfrau,** *f* cloakroom/*N.Am:* checkroom attendant.

◆**G~enmarke,** *f* -/-**n** cloakroom ticket, *N.Am:* hat/coat check.

**Gardine** [gar'diːnə], *f* -/-**n** (net)-curtain.

**gären** ['gɛːrən], *v.i.* (*haben*) to ferment.

**Garn** [garn], *n* -(**e**)**s**/-**e** yarn, thread.

**Garnele** [gar'neːlə], *f* -/-**n** shrimp; (**rote**) **G.,** prawn.

**garnier|en** [gar'niːrən], *v.tr.* to garnish. ◆**G~ung,** *f* -/-**en** garnish.

**Garnison** [garni'zoːn], *f* -/-**en** garrison.

**Garnitur** [garni'tuːr], *f* -/-**en** (*a*) set; (*b*) *F:* **erste/zweite G. sein,** to be top-notch/second best.

**garstig** ['garstıç], *adj.* nasty, horrid.

**Garten** ['gartən]. **I.** *m* -**s**/= garden. **II.** ◆'**G~-,** *comb.fm.* garden (wall, path etc.). ◆'**G~arbeit,** *f* gardening. ◆'**G~bau,** *m* horticulture. ◆'**G~fest,** *n* garden party. ◆'**G~gerät,** *n* gardening tool. ◆'**G~laube,** *f* summerhouse. ◆'**G~schau,** *f* flower show. ◆'**G~schere,** *f* secateurs. ◆'**G~zwerg,** *m* -(**e**)**s**/-**e** (*a*) (garden) gnome; (*b*) *Pej:* little squirt.

**Gärt|ner(in)** ['gɛrtnər(ın)], *m* -**s**/- (*f* -/-**nen**) gardener. ◆**G~nerei,** *f* -/-**en 1.** no pl *F:* gardening. **2.** nursery; (*für Gemüse*) market garden.

**Gärung** ['gɛːruŋ], *f* -/-**en** fermentation.

**Gas** [gaːs]. **I.** *n* -**es**/-**e** (*a*) gas; (*b*) *Aut:* **G. geben,** to accelerate. **II.** ◆**G~-,** *comb.fm.* gas (chamber, supply etc.). ◆'**G~brenner,** *m* gas burner. ◆'**G~flasche,** *f* gas cylinder. ◆'**G~hahn,** *m* gas tap. ◆'**G~heizung,** *f* gas(-fired) central heating. ◆'**G~herd,** *m* gas cooker/*N.Am:* range. ◆'**G~kocher,** *m* gas stove. ◆'**G~maske,** *f* gas mask. ◆**G~o-meter** [gazo'meːtər], *m* -**s**/- gasometer. ◆'**G~pedal,** *n* accelerator pedal.

**Gass|e** ['gasə], *f* -/-**n** (*a*) back street, alley; (*b*) *Aus:* street; (*c*) (*durch die Menge*) passage. ◆'**G~enjunge,** *m* street urchin.

**Gast** [gast]. **I.** *m* -(**e**)**s**/-**e** (*a*) guest; **bei j-m zu G. sein,** to be s.o.'s guest; (*b*) (*im Lokal usw.*) patron. **II.** ◆'**G~-,** *comb.fm.* guest (speaker etc.); visiting (professor, *Sp:* team etc.). ◆'**G~arbeiter,** *m* foreign worker. ◆'**g~freundlich,** *adj.* hospitable. ◆'**G~freundschaft,** *f* hospitality. ◆'**G~geber,** *m* -**s**/- host. ◆'**G~geberin,** *f* -/-**nen** hostess. ◆'**G~haus,** *n* small hotel. ◆'**G~hof,** *m* country hotel. ◆**g~ieren** [gas'tiːrən], *v.i.* (*haben*) to make a guest appearance. ◆'**G~land,** *n* host country. ◆'**g~lich,** *adj.* hospitable. ◆'**G~lichkeit,** *f* -/no pl hospitality. ◆'**G~recht,** *n* right to hospitality. ◆'**G~rolle,** *f* guest role. ◆'**G~spiel,** *n* guest performance. ◆'**G~stätte,** *f* restaurant. ◆'**G~wirt,** *m* landlord. ◆'**G~wirtschaft,** *f* **1.** restaurant. **2.** (*Schenke*) public house.

**Gäste|buch** ['gɛstəbuːx], *n* visitors' book.

◆'G~zimmer, *n* spare/guest room.

Gastr|itis ['gas'tri:tis], *f* -/-tiden [-'ti:dən] gastritis. ◆G~onomie [-no'mi:], *f* -/no *pl* gastronomy. ◆g~onomisch, *adj.* gastronomic(al).

Gatt|e ['gatə], *m* -n/-n husband; *Jur:* spouse. ◆G~in, *f* -/-nen wife; *Jur:* spouse. ◆'G~ung, *f* -/-en 1. (a) *Z: Bot:* genus; (b) (*Art*) kind. 2. *Art: Lit:* genre.

Gatter ['gatər], *n* -s/- (a) trellis; (b) (*Eisen*) grating; (c) (*Tor*) gate.

Gauk|elei [gaukə'lai], *f* -/-en *Lit:* trickery. ◆'G~ler, *m* -s/- *Lit:* trickster.

Gaul ['gaul], *m* -(e)s/-e *Pej:* (old) nag.

Gaumen ['gaumən], *m* -s/- palate.

Gauner ['gaunər], *m* -s/- *Pej:* (a) crook; (b) *F:* cunning devil. ◆G~ei [-'rai], *f* -/-en (a) *no pl coll.* crooked dealings; (b) swindle.

Gaze ['ga:zə], *f* -/-n gauze.

Gazelle [ga'tsɛlə], *f* -/-n gazelle.

Gebäck [gə'bɛk], *n* -(e)s/no *pl* pastries.

Gebälk [gə'bɛlk], *n* -(e)s/no *pl* timbers; (*im Dach*) beams.

geballt [gə'balt], *adj.* massed (clouds etc.); clenched (fist); *Fig:* concentrated (power, fury).

gebannt [gə'bant], *adj.* spellbound.

Gebärde [gə'bɛ:rdə], *f* -/-n gesture. ◆g~n, *v.refl. Lit:* sich ... g., to behave ...

Gebaren [gə'ba:rən], *n* -s/no *pl* conduct.

gebär|en [gə'bɛ:rən], *v.tr.irr.34* (a) to give birth to; (b) geboren werden, to be born. ◆G~mutter, *f* womb.

Gebäude [gə'bɔydə], *n* -s/- building; (*Gefüge*) structure.

Gebeine [gə'bainə], *npl* (mortal) remains, bones.

Gebell [gə'bɛl], *n* -(e)s/no *pl* barking.

geben [ge:bən], *v.tr. & i.irr.* (*haben*) (a) to give; j-m etwas g., to give sth. to s.o.; to give s.o. sth.; *F:* es j-m g., (i) (*die Meinung sagen*) to give s.o. a piece of one's mind; (ii) (*verprügeln*) to let s.o. have it; (b) to hold, give (a party, ball etc.); er gibt Geschichte, he teaches history; (c) (die Karten) g., to deal (the cards); (d) viel/wenig auf etwas *acc* g., to set great/little store by sth.; einen Schrei von sich *dat* g., to utter a cry; (e) sich natürlich/freundlich g., to behave naturally/in a friendly way; (f) sich g., (*Schmerz usw.*) to wear off. 2. *v.impers.* es gibt ... *acc*, there is .../are ...; was gibt's? what's the matter?

Gebet [gə'be:t], *n* -(e)s/-e prayer; *F:* j-n ins G. nehmen, to take s.o. to task.

Gebiet [gə'bi:t], *n* -(e)s/-e 1. (a) (*Gegend*) area; (b) (*Staatsg.*) territory. 2. *Fig:* field. ◆g~en, *v.tr.irr. & Lit:* (a) (*befehlen*) j-m g., etwas zu tun, to command s.o. to do sth.; (b) (*erfordern*) to call for, demand. ◆G~er, *m* -s/- lord; (*Herr*) master; (*Herrscher*) ruler. ◆g~isch, *adj.* imperious.

Gebilde [gə'bildə], *n* -s/- structure.

gebildet [gə'bildət], *adj.* (well-)educated; (*kultiviert*) cultured.

Gebirg|e [gə'birgə], *n* -s/- mountains; (*Bergkette*) mountain range. ◆g~ig, *adj.* mountainous. ◆G~s-, *comb.fm.* mountain (pass etc.). ◆G~sland-schaft, *f* mountain scenery. ◆G~szug, *m* mountain range.

Gebiß [gə'bis], *n* -sses/-sse (a) (set of) teeth; (b) (*künstliches*) G., dentures.

Gebläse [gə'blɛ:zə], *n* -s/- blower.

geblümt [gə'bly:mt], *adj.* flowery.

geboren [gə'bo:rən]. *adj.* born; Frau Schmidt, g~e Mayer, Mrs. Schmidt, née Mayer.

ge'borgen, *adj.* safe, sheltered. ◆G~heit, *f* -/no *pl* safety, security.

Gebot [gə'bo:t], *n* -(e)s/-e 1. (a) (*Grundsatz*) principle; *B:* die zehn G~e, the Ten Commandments; (b) *Adm:* regulation; gesetzliches G., legal requirement. 2. bid (at an auction).

Gebrauch [gə'braux], *m no pl* (a) use; von etwas *dat* G. machen, to make use of sth.; (b) usage (of a word etc.). ◆g~en, *v.tr.* to use, make use of; das kann ich gut g., I can make good use of that. ◆G~s-, *comb.fm.* utility (furniture etc.); ◆G~sanweisung, *f* directions for use. ◆G~sartikel, *m* basic commodity. ◆g~sfertig, *adj.* ready for use.

gebräuchlich [gə'brɔyçliç], *adj.* customary (practice, method etc.); common (expression etc.).

gebraucht [gə'brauxt]. *adj.* used, second-hand; (*abgenutzt*) worn; *adv.* etwas g. kaufen, to buy sth. secondhand. ◆G~wagen, *m* secondhand car.

Gebrech|en [gə'brɛçən], *n* -s/- infirmity. ◆g~lich, *adj.* frail.

Gebrüll [gə'bryl], *n* -(e)s/no *pl* roaring (of lion etc.); bawling.

Gebühr [gə'by:r], *f* -/-en 1. charge, fee; (road etc.) toll; *Tel: etc:* charges. 2. über G., unduly. ◆g~en, *v. Lit:* 1. *v.i.* (*haben*) ihm gebührt Bewunderung, he deserves admiration. 2. *v.refl.impers.* wie es sich gebührt, as is fit and proper. ◆g~end, *adj.* due (respect etc.); seemly (behaviour etc.). ◆g~enfrei, *adj.* free of charge. ◆g~enpflichtig, *adj.* subject to a charge.

gebunden [gə'bundən]. *adj.* bound; ◆g~e Ausgabe, hardcover edition.

Geburt [gə'bu:rt], *f* -/-en birth. ◆G~en-, *comb.fm.* birth (rate etc.). ◆G~enkontrolle/G~enregelung, *f* birth control. ◆G~enrate/G~enziffer, *f* birth rate. ◆G~s-, *comb.fm.* birth ...; (date, place etc.) of birth; ◆G~sanzeige, *f* birth notice. ◆G~stag, *m* birthday. ◆G~surkunde, *f* birth certificate. ◆G~swehen, *fpl* labour pains.

gebürtig [gə'byrtiç], *adj.* er ist g~er

**Engländer,** he is English by birth.
**Gebüsch** [gə'byʃ], n -(e)s/-e bushes.
**Gedächtnis** [gə'dɛçtnis]. I. n -ses/-se memory; **etwas im G. behalten,** to remember/retain sth. II. **G~-,** comb.fm. (a) memory (training etc.); (weakness etc.) of memory; (b) (Gedenk-) memorial (service, church etc.). ◆**G~feier,** f commemoration; Ecc: memorial service. ◆**G~lücke,** f gap in one's memory. ◆**G~stütze,** f mnemonic.
**Gedank|e** [gə'daŋkə], m -ns/-n 1. thought (**an** + acc, of); **j-n auf andere G~n bringen,** to distract s.o.; **das habe ich ganz in G~n getan,** I did it without thinking; 2. (Sorgen) **sich dat G~n über j-n, etwas** acc **machen,** to worry about s.o., sth. 3. idea; **G~n austauschen,** to exchange ideas; F: **auf dumme G~n kommen,** to get silly ideas; **mit einem G~n spielen,** to toy with an idea. ◆**G~n,** comb.fm. (a) thought (content, reader etc.); (freedom, chain etc.) of thought; (b) (exchange etc.) of ideas. ◆**G~engang** m, train of thought. ◆**G~engut,** n (stock of) ideas. ◆**g~enlos,** adj. 1. unthinking; adv. etwas g. **tun,** to do sth. without thinking. 2. (zerstreut) absent-minded. ◆**G~enlosigkeit,** f -/-e thoughtlessness; absent-mindedness. ◆**G~enstrich,** m dash. ◆**g~enverloren,** adj. lost in thought. ◆**g~envoll,** adj. pensive, thoughtful.
**Gedärm** [gə'dɛrm], n -(e)s/-e intestines; Z: entrails.
**Gedeck** [gə'dɛk], n -(e)s/-e 1. place (setting). 2. (im Restaurant) set menu.
**Gedeih** [gə'dai], m auf G. **und Verderb,** for better or (for) worse. ◆**g~en.** I. v.i.irr.60 (sein) to thrive, (finanziell) prosper; II. G., n -s/no pl success.
**Gedenk-** [gə'dɛnk-], comb.fm. commemorative (exhibition, concert etc.); memorial (stone, service etc.). ◆**g~en.** I. v.i.irr.17 (haben) Lit: (a) **j-s, einer Sache** gen **g.,** to remember s.o., sth.; (b) (beabsichtigen) to intend. II. G., n -s/no pl memory, remembrance. ◆**G~feier,** f commemoration; Ecc: memorial service. ◆**G~stätte,** f memorial. ◆**G~tafel,** f commemorative plaque; ◆**G~tag,** m commemoration day.
**Gedicht** [gə'diçt], n -(e)s/-e poem.
**gediegen** [gə'di:gən], adj. pure; solid (gold, silver etc.).
**Gedräng|e** [gə'drɛŋə], n -s/no pl 1. (Drängen) pushing, shoving. 2. crush; (Menge) crowd. ◆**g~t,** adj. terse, succinct (style).
**gedrungen** [gə'druŋən], adj. stocky. ◆**G~heit,** f -/no pl stockiness.
**Geduld** [gə'dult], f -/no pl patience (**zu etwas** dat, for sth.); **G. haben (mit j-m),** to be patient (with s.o.); ◆**g~en** [-dən], v.refl. **sich g.,** to be patient. ◆**g~ig** [-diç], adj. patient.

◆**G~sprobe,** f trial of patience.
◆**G~(s)spiel,** n puzzle.
**gedunsen** [gə'dunzən], adj. bloated.
**geeignet** [gə'ʔaignət], adj. (für etwas acc/**zu etwas** dat) **g. sein,** to be suited (to sth.)/suitable (for sth.).
**Gefahr** [gə'faːr], f -/-en danger; **j-n in G. bringen,** to endanger s.o.; **G. laufen, zu ...,** to run the risk of ...; **auf eigene G.,** at one's own risk. ◆**G~en-,** comb.fm. danger (signal etc.); ◆**G~enzulage,** f danger money. ◆**g~los,** adj. safe. ◆**G~losigkeit,** f -/no pl safeness. ◆**g~voll,** adj. perilous.
**gefähr|den** [gə'fɛːrdən], v.tr. to endanger; to jeopardize (the success of sth. etc.). ◆**G~dung,** f -/-en endangering. ◆**g~lich,** adj. dangerous. ◆**G~lichkeit,** f -/no pl dangerous nature.
**Gefährt|e** [gə'fɛːrtə], m -n/-n/**G~in,** f -/-nen companion.
**Gefälle** [gə'fɛlə], n -s/- slope; gradient, N.Am: grade.
**gefallen** [gə'falən]. I. v.i.irr.27 (haben) (a) **j-m g.,** to please s.o.; **das Bild gefällt mir,** I like the picture; F: **sich etwas g. lassen,** to put up with sth. II. G. 1. n -s/no pl pleasure, delight; (sein) **G. an etwas** dat **finden/haben,** to take pleasure in sth. 2. m -s/- favour; **j-m einen G. tun/erweisen,** to do s.o. a favour. ◆**G~e(r),** m decl. as adj. **die G~en,** the dead/fallen.
**gefällig** [gə'fɛliç], adj. 1. (angenehm) pleasant. 2. (hilfsbereit) obliging. ◆**g~st,** adv. (if you) please; **hör g~st zu!** will you please listen! ◆**G~keit,** f -/-en 1. favour. 2. no pl (a) pleasantness; (b) helpfulness.
**Gefangen|e(r)** [gə'faŋənə(r)], m & f decl. as adj. prisoner. ◆**G~enlager,** n prison camp. ◆**g~halten,** v.tr.sep.irr.45 to hold (s.o.) prisoner; to keep (an animal) in captivity. ◆**G~nahme,** f -/no pl capture. ◆**g~nehmen,** v.tr.sep.irr.69 (a) to capture (s.o.), take (s.o.) prisoner; (b) Fig: to captivate. ◆**G~schaft,** f -/no pl captivity.
**Gefängnis** [gə'fɛnnis], n -ses/-se 1. prison; **im G. sitzen,** to be in prison. 2. (G~strafe) imprisonment. ◆**G~strafe,** f prison sentence. ◆**G~wärter,** m prison warder.
**Gefasel** [gə'faːzəl], n -s/no pl F: twaddle, drivel.
**Gefäß** [gə'fɛːs], n -es/-e 1. (Behälter) receptacle. 2. Anat: vessel.
**gefaßt** [gə'fast], adj. 1. composed. 2. **auf etwas** acc **g. sein,** to be prepared for sth.
**Gefecht** [gə'fɛçt], n -(e)s/-e fight; Mil: engagement; **den Gegner außer G. setzen,** to put one's opponent out of action. ◆**G~s-,** comb.fm. combat (training, unit etc.); fighting (strength etc.); battle (line etc.); ◆**g~sbereit** adj. ready for action.
**gefeit** [gə'fait], adj. **gegen etwas** acc **g.**

**sein,** to be immune to sth.
**Gefieder** [gəˈfiːdər], n -s/- plumage, feathers. ◆**g~t,** adj. feathered.
**Geflecht** [gəˈflɛçt], n -(e)s/-e network.
**gefleckt** [gəˈflɛkt], adj. spotted, speckled.
**Geflügel** [gəˈflyːgəl], n -s/no pl poultry. ◆**G~schere,** f poultry shears.
**Geflüster** [gəˈflystər], n -s/- whispering.
**Gefolge** [gəˈfɔlgə], n -s/- **1.** retinue. **2.** Fig: **im G~e** + gen, in the wake of.
**gefragt** [gəˈfraːkt], adj. **(sehr) g.,** (much) in demand.
**gefräßig** [gəˈfrɛːsiç], adj. Pej: greedy.
**Gefreite(r)** [gəˈfraitə(r)], m decl. as adj. lance-corporal; N.Am: private first class.
**Gefrier-** [gəˈfriːr-], comb.fm. (a) frozen (meat etc.); (b) refrigeration (chamber etc.). ◆**g~en,** v.i.irr.32 (sein) to freeze. ◆**G~fach,** n freezer compartment. ◆**G~punkt,** m freezing-point. ◆**g~trocknen,** v.tr.sep. to freeze-dry. ◆**G~truhe,** f -/-n (chest) freezer.
**Gefüge** [gəˈfyːgə], n -s/- structure. ◆**g~ig,** adj. pliant; **j-n g. machen,** to bend s.o. to one's will.
**Gefühl** [gəˈfyːl], n -(e)s/-e feeling; **ich habe kein gutes G. dabei,** I feel uneasy about it; **seinen G~n freien Lauf lassen,** to give vent to one's emotions; **etwas im G. haben,** to know sth. instinctively. ◆**g~los,** adj. **1.** numb (fingers etc.). **2.** unfeeling; (gleichgültig) indifferent. ◆**G~s-,** comb.fm. emotional (content, life, world etc.). ◆**g~sbetont,** adj. emotional. ◆**G~sduselei,** f -/no pl sentimentality. ◆**g~smäßig,** adj. emotional. ◆**g~voll,** adj. sensitive (person); (Musik usw.) emotional.
**gefüllt** [gəˈfylt], adj. filled.
**gegeben** [gəˈgeːbən], adj. (vorhanden) present (circumstances etc.); given (quantity etc.); **im g~en Fall,** in this present case; **zur G~en Zeit,** at the proper time. ◆**g~enfalls,** adv. if necessary.
**gegen** [ˈgeːgən]. **I.** prep. + acc **1.** against; Sp: versus; **ein Mittel g. Husten,** a remedy for coughs. **2.** (in Richtung auf) (a) towards; **g. Osten,** towards the east, eastwards; **etwas g. die Wand lehnen,** to lean sth. against the wall; (zeitlich) **g. Abend/Morgen,** towards evening/morning; (b) (ungefähr) about; **g. Weihnachten,** around Christmas; (c) (gegenüber) to, towards (s.o.); **grausam/höflich g. j-n sein,** to be cruel/polite to s.o. **3.** (verglichen mit) **das ist nichts g. seine Party,** this is nothing compared with his party. **4.** (im Austausch für) in exchange for. **II. G~-,** comb.fm. (a) (entgegengesetzt) opposite (side etc.); (example etc.) of the contrary; opposing (candidate etc.); (b) (entgegenwirkend) counter- (argument, demonstration etc.). ◆'**G~angriff,** m counter-attack. ◆'**G~darstellung,** f **1.** reply (to an article etc.). **2.** conflicting version (of an

event etc.). ◆**g~ei'nander,** adv. against one another/each other. ◆'**G~fahrbahn,** f opposite traffic lane. ◆'**G~frage,** f counter-question. ◆'**G~gewicht,** n counterweight, Fig: counterbalance. ◆'**G~gift,** n antidote. ◆'**G~leistung,** f G., service/favour in return. ◆'**G~mittel,** n remedy (**gegen** + acc, for); (gegen Gift) antidote. ◆'**G~probe,** f cross-check. ◆'**G~satz,** m **1.** contrast (**zu etwas** dat, with sth.); **in scharfem G. zueinander stehen,** to be sharply contrasted. **2.** (Gegenteil) opposite. ◆'**g~sätzlich,** adj. opposing (opinions, forces etc.); opposite, contrary (views, terms etc.). ◆'**G~schlag,** m retaliation. ◆'**g~seitig,** adj. mutual; **sich g. helfen,** to help each other. ◆'**G~seitigkeit,** f -/no pl reciprocity; **auf G. beruhen,** to be mutual. ◆'**G~spieler,** m opponent. ◆'**G~stand,** m (a) (Ding, Objekt) object; (b) (Thema) subject. ◆'**G~stimme,** f protesting voice; Pol: etc: vote against. ◆'**G~stück,** n **1.** (Gegenstand) counterpart (**zu etwas** dat, of sth.). **2.** (G~teil) opposite. ◆'**G~teil,** n **das G.,** the opposite; **im G.,** on the contrary. ◆'**g~teilig,** adj. opposite (opinion etc.); (statement etc.) to the contrary. ◆**g~über. I.** prep. + dat (a) opposite; (b) **er ist mir g. sehr freundlich,** he is very friendly towards/to me; (c) (verglichen mit) compared with. **II.** adv. **das Haus g.,** the house opposite. **III.** G., n -(s)/- person opposite. ◆**g~'überliegen,** v.i.sep.irr.62 (haben) etwas dat g., to be opposite sth.; ◆**g~'überstehen,** v.i.sep.irr.100 (haben) (a) **j-m, etwas** dat g., to be opposite s.o., sth., Fig: to face sth.; (b) **j-m feindlich/freundlich g.,** to have a friendly/hostile attitude to s.o. ◆**g~'überstellen,** v.tr.sep. **j-n einem Zeugen usw. g.,** to confront s.o. with a witness etc.; **zwei Sachen (einander) g.,** to compare two things. ◆**g~'übertreten,** v.i.sep.irr.105 (sein) **j-m (mutig/entschlossen usw.) g.,** to face s.o. (with courage/resolution etc.). ◆'**G~verkehr,** m oncoming traffic. ◆'**G~vorschlag,** m counter-proposal. ◆'**G~wart,** f -/no pl **1. die G.,** the present (time); **2.** (Anwesenheit) presence. ◆'**g~wärtig,** adj. (jetzig) (a) present, current; (b) adv. at present. ◆'**G~wehr,** f -/no pl resistance. ◆'**G~wert,** m equivalent (value). ◆'**G~wind,** m head wind. ◆'**g~zeichnen,** v.tr.sep. to countersign. ◆'**G~zug,** m **1.** countermove. **2.** Rail: oncoming train.
**Gegend** [ˈgeːgənt], f -/-en area.
**geglückt** [gəˈglykt], adj. successful.
**Gegner|(in)** [ˈgeːgnər(in)], m -s/- (f -/-nen) opponent. ◆'**g~isch,** adj. oppos-

ing (team, interests etc.); (feindlich) hostile, Mil: enemy (forces etc.).

**Gehackte(s)** [gə'haktə(s)], n decl. as adj. mince, minced/N.Am: ground meat.

**Gehalt¹** [gə'halt], m -(e)s/-e content. ◆g~voll, adj. substantial (food etc.); (book etc.) rich in content.

**Gehalt²**, n -(e)s/⸗er salary. ◆G~s-, comb.fm. salary (claim, increase etc.) ◆G~sempfänger, m salary earner. ◆G~szulage, f bonus.

**geharnischt** [gə'harniʃt], adj. strongly worded (letter etc.).

**gehässig** [gə'hɛsiç], adj. spiteful, malicious. ◆G~keit, f -/-en 1. no pl spitefulness. 2. spiteful remark.

**Gehäuse** [gə'hɔyzə], n -s/- (a) (clock etc.) case; Rad: TV: cabinet; Tchn: housing; (b) (snail etc.) shell; (c) (Kerng.) core.

**Gehege** [gə'he:gə], n -s/- game preserve; Fig: j-m ins G. kommen, to poach on s.o.'s preserves.

**geheim** [gə'haim]. I. adj. secret; im g~en, in secret, secretly. II. G~-, comb.fm. secret (agreement, agent, organization, police, weapon etc.). ◆G~dienst, m secret service. ◆g~halten, v.tr.sep.irr.45 to keep (sth.) secret. (vor j-m, from s.o.) ◆G~haltung, f -/no pl concealment. ◆G~nis, n -ses/-se 1. secret. 2. (Rätsel) mystery. ◆G~niskräme'rei, f -/no pl F: secretive behaviour. ◆g~nisvoll, adj. mysterious. ◆G~rezept, n secret recipe.

**gehemmt** [gə'hɛmt], adj. inhibited.

**geh|en** ['ge:ən], v.irr. 1. v.i. (sein) (a) to go; (zu Fuß) to walk; ins Ausland/in die Stadt g., to go abroad/into town; Fig: in sich acc g., (i) to take stock of oneself, (ii) to decide to mend one's ways; zum Film g., to go into films; (b) (weggehen) to leave; go; wollen wir g.? shall we go? (c) (funktionieren) (Maschine usw.) to be going; die Uhr geht nicht richtig, the clock is wrong; Com: gut g., (Geschäfte) to be good; (Produkt) to be selling well; (d) (passen) wieviel geht in den Koffer? how much will go/fit into the suitcase? (e) (sich richten nach) er geht nach dem Äußeren, he goes by appearances; wenn es nach mir ginge, if I had anything to do with it; (f) (reichen, sich erstrecken) das Wasser ging ihm bis zum Knie, the water came up to his knees; es geht nichts über ... g., you can't beat ...; es geht auf/gegen Mitternacht, it is nearly midnight; (g) das geht zu weit, that's going too far; die Dinge g. lassen, to let things take their course; sich g. lassen, to lose one's self-control; (h) (möglich sein) das geht nicht, that is impossible; (nicht akzeptabel) that won't do; geht es so? is it all right like that? (i) es geht ihm gut/schlecht, (i) he is well/ill; (ii) (finanziell usw.) he is doing well/badly; wie geht es Ihnen? how are you?; (j) es geht um ...

acc, it is a question of ...; worum geht es? what's it about? es geht ihm nur um das Geld, he is only interested in the money. 2. v.tr. (sein) to walk (a kilometre etc.). ◆'g~enlassen, v.tr. sep.irr.57 (haben) sich g., to lose one's self-control. ◆G~er, m -s/- walker. ◆g~fähig, adj. able to walk. ◆G~steig/ 'G~weg, m pavement, N.Am: sidewalk.

**geheuer** [gə'hɔyər], adj. nicht (ganz) g., eerie; dubious (idea, business).

**Geheul** [gə'hɔyl], n -(e)s/no pl howling.

**Gehilf|e** [gə'hilfə], m -n/-n/G~in, f -/-nen Com: trainee.

**Gehirn** [gə'hirn]. I. n -(e)s/-e brain. II. G~-, comb.fm. brain (surgeon, tumour etc.); cerebral (haemorrhage etc.). ◆G~erschütterung, f concussion. ◆G~hautentzündung, f -/no pl meningitis. ◆G~wäsche, f F: brainwashing.

**gehoben** [gə'ho:bən]. adj. superior (position); elevated (language, style etc.).

**Gehölz** [gə'hœlts], n -es/-e copse.

**Gehör** [gə'hø:r]. I. n -(e)s/no pl 1. hearing; ein feines/empfindliches G., a delicate/sensitive ear. 2. sich dat G. verschaffen, to gain a hearing/(beim Lärm) make oneself heard. ◆g~los, adj. deaf.

**gehorchen** [gə'hɔrçən], v.i. (haben) (+ dat) j-m, etwas dat g., to obey s.o., sth.

**gehören** [gə'hø:rən], v. 1. v.i. (haben) (a) j-m g., to belong to s.o.; (b) (jdm zu) er gehört (mit) zur Familie, he is one of the family; (c) (Teil sein von) es gehört zu meiner Arbeit, it's part of my job; es gehört dazu, it's the done thing; (d) (nötig sein) dazu gehört viel Mut, that takes a lot of courage. 2. v.refl. sich g., to be right; es gehört sich nicht, it isn't done. ◆g~ig, adj. 1. proper (respect, distance etc.). 2. F: (tüchtig) real.

**gehorsam** [gə'ho:rza:m]. I. adj. obedient. II. G~, m -s/no pl obedience.

**Geier** ['gaiər], m -s/- vulture.

**geifern** ['gaifərn], v.i. (haben) to slaver; Fig: gegen j-n, etwas acc g., to bitch about s.o., sth.

**Geige** ['gaigə], f -/-n violin. ◆'g~n, v.tr.&i. (haben) F: to play on the violin. ◆'G~nkasten, m violin case. ◆'G~r(in), m -s/- (f -/-nen) violinist.

**Geigerzähler** ['gaigərtsɛ:lər], m -s/- Geiger counter.

**geil** [gail], adj. lecherous (person, smile etc.). ◆G~heit, f -/no pl lewdness, lechery.

**Geisel** ['gaizəl], f -/-n hostage. ◆G~nahme, f -/-n taking of hostages.

**Geißbock** ['gaisbɔk], m billy-goat.

**Geißel** ['gaisəl], f -/-n scourge. ◆'g~n, v.tr. to denounce.

**Geist** [gaist], m -(e)s/-er 1. (a) mind; großer G., a great mind; hier scheiden sich die G~er, opinions differ on this point; F: von allen guten G~ern verlassen sein, to have taken leave of one's senses;

(b) (*Witz*) wit. 2. (a) spirit; **G. der Zeit,** spirit of the age; *esp. Hum:* **den/seinen G.** aufgeben, to give up the ghost; (b) *Ecc:* **der Heilige G.**, the Holy Ghost/ Spirit; **gute/böse G~er,** good/evil spirits; (c) (*Gespenst*) ghost. ◆'**G~er-**, *comb.fm.* ghost (story, town etc.); ghostly (hand, voice etc.); ◆'**G~erbahn,** f ghost train. ◆'**G~erfahrer,** m F: driver going the wrong way on a dual carriageway. ◆'**g~erhaft,** *adj.* ghostly. ◆'**g~ern,** *v.i.* (*haben/sein*) to wander about like a ghost. ◆'**G~es-**, *comb. fm.* intellectual (work, life etc.); mental (attitude, illness etc.). ◆'**g~esabwesend,** *adj.* absent-minded. ◆'**G~esabwesenheit,** f *-/no pl* absent-mindedness. ◆'**G~esblitz,** m F: flash of inspiration; brainwave. ◆'**G~esgegenwart,** f presence of mind. ◆'**g~esgegenwärtig,** *adj.* quick-witted. ◆'**g~esgestört,** *adj.* mentally deranged. ◆'**g~eskrank,** *adj.* mentally ill. ◆'**G~eswissenschaften,** *fpl* **die G.**, the humanities, the arts. ◆'**G~eszustand,** m mental state; state of mind. ◆'**g~ig,** *adj.* **1.** mental (effort, activity etc.); intellectual (capacity, powers etc.); **g. zurückgeblieben,** mentally retarded. **2.** (*nicht körperlich*) spiritual (beings etc.); **g~e Getränke,** spirits. ◆'**g~lich,** *adj.* religious; (*kirchlich*) (of the) church, ecclesiastical; **g~e Musik,** church music. ◆'**G~liche(r),** m *decl. as adj.* clergyman. ◆'**G~lichkeit,** f *-/no pl* **die G.**, the clergy. ◆'**g~los,** *adj.* stupid. ◆'**g~reich,** *adj.* (a) clever; (b) (*witzig*) witty.

**Geiz** [gaits], m *-es/no pl* miserliness. ◆'**g~en,** *v.i.* (*haben*) **mit etwas** *dat* **g.**, to be stingy with sth. ◆'**G~hals,** m F: miser. ◆'**g~ig,** *adj.* mean.

**Gejammer** [gə'jamər], n *-s/no pl* moaning.

**Gekicher** [gə'kiçər], n *-s/no pl* giggling.

**Gekläff** [gə'klef], n *-(e)s/no pl* yapping.

**Geklapper** [gə'klapər], n *-s/no pl* clatter(ing).

**Geklirr** [gə'klir], n *-(e)s/no pl* rattling (of chains etc.); clinking (of glasses etc.).

**geknickt** [gə'knikt], *adj.* F: downhearted.

**gekonnt** [gə'kɔnt], *adj.* skilful, accomplished.

**gekränkt** [gə'krɛnkt], *adj.* offended, hurt.

**Gekritzel** [gə'kritsəl], n *-s/no pl* scribble, scrawl.

**gekünstelt** [gə'kynstəlt], *adj.* affected (person, behaviour); artificial (smile, laugh).

**Gelächter** [gə'lɛçtər], n *-s/no pl* laughter; **in G. ausbrechen,** to burst out laughing.

**geladen** [gə'laːdən] *adj.* F: (a) (*Atmosphäre*) tense; (b) (*Pers.*) furious.

**Gelage** [gə'laːgə], n *-s/-* banquet.

**Gelände** [gə'lɛndə]. **I.** n *-s/-* **1.** (a) (*Landschaft*) terrain; (b) *Mil:* **G.**

gewinnen/verlieren, to gain/lose ground. **2.** (*Grundstück*) plot; (exhibition, factory) site. **II. G~-**, *comb.fm.* cross-country (drive, run etc.); ◆**g~gängig,** *adj.* *Aut:* suitable for cross-country work. ◆**G~wagen,** m cross-country vehicle.

**Geländer** [gə'lɛndər], n *-s/-* railing; (*Treppeng.*) banisters.

**gelangen** [gə'laŋən], *v.i.* (*sein*) **an etwas** *acc*/**zu etwas** *dat* **g.**, to reach/*Fig:* attain sth.; **in j-s Besitz g.**, to come into s.o.'s possession.

**gelassen** [gə'lasən], *adj.* composed; (*ruhig*) calm (and collected). ◆**G~heit,** f *-/no pl* composure.

**Gelatine** [ʒela'tiːnə], f *-/no pl* gelatine; *N.Am:* gelatin.

**geläufig** [gə'lɔyfiç], *adj.* common; **das Wort ist mir nicht g.**, I am not familiar with this word.

**gelaunt** [gə'launt], *adj.* **gut/schlecht g.**, in a good mood/bad temper.

**gelb** [gelp]. *adj.* yellow, light; *Aut:* **bei G.**, at amber/*N.Am:* yellow. ◆'**g~lich,** *adj.* ◆'**G~sucht,** f jaundice.

**Geld** [gɛlt]. n *-(e)s/-er* **1.** *no pl* money, **es geht ins G.**, it gets expensive. **2.** *pl* **G~er,** *Fin:* funds; *Jur:* moneys. ◆'**G~angelegenheiten,** *fpl* money matters. ◆'**G~anlage,** f investment. ◆'**G~beutel,** m/'**G~börse,** f purse. ◆'**G~buße,** f fine. ◆'**G~gier,** f avarice. ◆'**G~mangel,** m lack of money. ◆'**G~mittel,** *npl* (financial) resources. ◆'**G~schein,** m (bank) note, *N.Am:* bill. ◆'**G~schrank,** m safe. ◆'**G~strafe,** f fine. ◆'**G~stück,** n coin. ◆'**G~wechsel,** m exchange (of money). ◆'**G~wert,** m monetary value.

**Gelee** [ʒe'leː], n & m *-s/-s* jelly.

**Gelege** [gə'leːgə], n *-s/-* clutch (of eggs). ◆**g~n,** *adj.* (a) **schön/ungünstig g.**, pleasantly/awkwardly situated; (b) (*Zeit usw.*) convenient, suitable; **das kommt mir sehr g.**, that suits me very well; (c) **mir ist viel/nichts daran g.**, it matters a great deal/little to me. ◆**G~nheit,** f *-/-en* **1.** opportunity, chance **bei G.**, when there is a chance. **2.** (*Anlaß*) occasion. ◆**G~nheitsarbeiter,** m casual worker. ◆**G~nheitskauf,** m bargain. ◆**g~ntlich. I.** *adj.* occasional. **II.** *adv.* (*manchmal*) occasionally.

**gelehrig** [gə'leːriç], *adj.* quick (to learn). ◆**g~t,** *adj.* learned. ◆**G~te(r),** m & f *decl. as adj.* scholar.

**Geleit** [gə'lait], n *-(e)s/-e* escort; **freies/ sicheres G.**, safe conduct. ◆**g~en,** *v.tr. Lit:* to escort (s.o.). ◆**G~schutz,** m escort.

**Gelenk** [gə'lɛnk], n *-(e)s/-e* joint. ◆**g~ig,** *adj.* supple.

**gelernt** [gə'lɛrnt], *adj.* skilled.

**Geliebte(r)** [gə'liːptə(r)], m & f *decl. as adj.* lover.

**geliefert** [gə'liːfərt], *adj.* F: done for,

ruined.

**gelinde** [gə'lində], *adj.* mild; *adv.* **g. gesagt,** to put it mildly.

**gelingen** [gə'liŋən], I. *v.i.irr.* (*sein*) to succeed, be successful; **es gelang mir/ihm, etwas zu tun,** I/he succeeded in doing sth.

**gellen** ['gɛlən], *v.i.* (*haben*) to sound shrill; (*Schrei usw.*) to ring (out).

**geloben** [gə'lo:bən], *v.tr. Lit:* to vow (sth.).

**Gelöbnis** [gə'lø:pnis], *n -ses/-se* vow.

**gelöst** [gə'lø:st], *adj.* relaxed.

**gelt|en** ['gɛltən], *v.i.irr.* (*haben*) (*a*) (*Gültigkeit haben*) (*Fahrkarte, Paß usw.*) to be valid/(*Gesetz*) in force; (*Regel usw.*) to apply (**für** + *acc*, to); **das gleiche gilt für ihn/von ihm,** the same goes for him; **etwas g. lassen,** to accept sth. (as valid); (*b*) **viel/wenig g.,** to be worth a lot/a little; (*c*) **als etwas** *nom* **g.,** to be considered to be sth.; (*d*) **j-m, etwas** *dat* **g.,** (*Beifall usw.*) to be meant for s.o., sth.; (*Kritik usw.*) to be aimed at s.o., sth.; (*e*) *impers.* **jetzt gilt es, ruhig zu bleiben,** the essential thing now is to remain calm. ◆**g~end,** *adj.* prevailing (opinion, custom etc.) (law) in force; **Rechte, Forderungen usw. g. machen,** to assert rights, demands etc.; **seinen Einfluß g. machen,** to bring one's influence to bear. ◆**G~ung,** *f -/no pl* (*a*) (*Gültigkeit*) validity; **G. haben,** to be valid; (*b*) **etwas zur G. bringen,** to show sth. in its best light; **zur G. kommen,** to have its proper effect; **j-m, etwas** *dat* **G. verschaffen,** to bring s.o., sth. to prominence. ◆**G~ungsbedürfnis,** *n* need for recognition.

**Gelübde** [gə'lypdə], *n -s/-* vow.

**gelungen** [gə'luŋən], *adj.* (*a*) successful; (*b*) *F:* (*drollig*) funny, quaint.

**Gelüst** [gə'lyst], *n -(e)s/-e Lit:* craving (**nach** + *dat*/**auf** + *acc*, for).

**gemächlich** [gə'mɛ(:)çliç], *adj.* leisurely (pace, walk etc.).

**Gemahl** [gə'ma:l], *m -s/-e* (*formal*) spouse; **Ihr Herr G.,** your husband. ◆**G~in,** *f -/-nen* (*formal*) spouse.

**Gemälde** [gə'mɛ:ldə], *n -s/-* painting; *esp. Fig:* picture.

**gemäß** [gə'mɛ:s], I. *prep.* + *dat* in accordance with (regulations, customs etc.); (*je nach*) according to (size etc.). II. *adj.* **j-m, etwas** *dat* **g. sein,** to be right for s.o., sth.

**gemäßigt** [gə'mɛ:sikt], *adj.* moderate; *Geog:* temperate (zone etc.).

**gemein** [gə'main], *adj.* **1.** (*a*) (*grob*) vulgar, (person, speech etc.); (*b*) (*niederträchtig*) mean (person, behaviour etc.); dirty (lie, trick). **2.** (*a*) (*häufig*) common (housefly, sparrow etc.); (*b*) (*allgemein*) common, general; (*c*) (*gemeinsam*) **etwas mit j-m, einer Sache g. haben,** to have sth. in common with s.o., sth. ◆**G~besitz,** *m* public property.

◆**g~gefährlich,** *adj.* dangerous (to the public). ◆**G~gut,** *n* public property. ◆**G~heit,** *f -/-en* **1.** *no pl* (*a*) (*Roheit*) vulgarity; (*b*) (*Niedertracht*) meanness. **2.** mean thing (to do/say). ◆**g~hin,** *adv.* generally. ◆**G~nutz,** *n* common good. ◆**g~nützig,** *adj.* for the common good; non-profitmaking (organization etc.). ◆**G~platz,** *m* platitude. ◆**g~sam,** *adj.* (*a*) common (property, interests); shared (garden etc.); joint (account, ownership, efforts etc.); mutual (friend etc.); **etwas (mit j-m, etwas** *dat*) **g. haben,** to have sth. in common (with s.o., sth.); (**mit j-m**) **g~same Sache machen,** to make common cause (with s.o.); (*b*) *adv.* (*zusammen*) together; **es gehört ihnen g.,** they own it jointly. ◆**G~samkeit,** *f -/-en* **1.** common feature. **2.** *no pl* harmony. ◆**G~schaft,** *f -/-en* community; (business, political etc.) association. ◆**g~schaftlich,** *adj.* common (aim, interest etc.); joint (account, effort etc.). ◆**G~schafts-,** *comb.fm.* (*a*) communal (kitchen, aerial etc.); co-(production, education etc.); joint (task etc.); (*b*) community (spirit, life etc.); social (education etc.). ◆**G~schaftsarbeit** *f,* joint effort; ◆**G~schaftsraum,** *m* recreation room; *Sch:* etc: common room. ◆**G~sinn,** *m* public spirit. ◆**g~verständlich,** *adj.* generally understandable. ◆**G~wesen,** *n* community (structure). ◆**G~wohl,** *n* public welfare.

**Gemeinde** [gə'maində]. I. *f -/-n* **1.** (local) community. **2.** *Ecc:* parish; (*in der Kirche*) congregation. II. **G~-,** *comb.fm.* (*a*) *Adm:* local (election etc.); council (property etc.); (*b*) *Ecc:* parish (centre etc.). ◆**G~mitglied,** *n* parishioner. ◆**G~verwaltung,** *f* local authority.

**Gemenge** [gə'mɛŋə], *n -s/-* mixture (**aus** + *dat*, of); (*Durcheinander*) jumble.

**gemessen** [gə'mɛsən], *adj.* measured.

**Gemetzel** [gə'mɛtsəl], *n -s/-* carnage; **ein G.,** a bloodbath.

**Gemisch** [gə'miʃ], *n -(e)s/-e* mixture (**aus** + *dat*, of). ◆**g~t,** *adj.* mixed.

**Gemse** ['gɛmzə], *f -/-n* chamois.

**Gemunkel** [gə'muŋkəl], *n -s/no pl* gossip.

**Gemurmel** [gə'murməl], *n -s/no pl* murmuring, muttering.

**Gemüse** [gə'my:zə], *n -s/-* vegetable; *usu.coll.* vegetables. ◆**G~händler,** *m* greengrocer. ◆**G~laden,** *m* greengrocer's shop. ◆**G~zwiebel,** *f* Spanish onion.

**Gemüt** [gə'my:t], *n -(e)s/-er* **1.** (*Natur*) disposition; (*Gefühle*) feeling(s), emotion(s); **erhitzte G~er,** frayed tempers; **sich** *dat* **etwas zu G~e führen,** to take sth. to heart. **2.** (*Mensch*) a simple/cheerful soul. ◆**g~lich,** *adj.* (*a*) snug, cosy (room, flat); (*zwanglos*) relaxed (atmosphere etc.); genial (person); **es sich** *dat* **g. ma-**

**chen,** to make oneself comfortable; (b) (*gemächlich*) leisurely (meal, pace etc.). ◆**G~lichkeit,** f -/no pl cosiness; **in aller G.,** at one's leisure. ◆**G~smensch,** m F: unflappable person. ◆**G~sruhe,** f -/no pl equanimity; **in aller G.,** as calmly as you please; (*gemächlich*) at one's leisure. ◆**G~szustand,** m frame of mind. ◆**g~voll,** adj. warm-hearted.

**Gen** [geːn], n -s/-e gene.

**genau** [gə'nau], adj. (a) exact, precise; (clock, scales etc.); **ich kenne ihn g.,** I know exactly what he's like; **das weiß ich ganz g.,** I know that for certain; **g.! exactly!** (b) detailed (description, information etc.); **ich weiß nichts G~es,** I don't know any (of the) details; (c) (*Pers.*) meticulous; **man darf nicht alles so g. nehmen,** you mustn't take everything so seriously; (d) adv. (*gerade*) just; **g. das wollte ich sagen,** that's just/exactly what I was going to say; **er ist g. der Vater,** he is just like his father. ◆**g~genommen,** adv. strictly speaking. ◆**G~igkeit,** f -/no pl (a) exactness; accuracy; (b) meticulousness. ◆**g~so. I.** adv. **g. gut,** just as good/well; **ich hätte es g. gemacht,** I would have done exactly the same. **II. g~so-,** comb.fm. just as (often, far etc.).

**genehmig|en** [gə'neːmigən], v.tr. to grant (an application, request etc.); (*billigen*) to approve (a plan, budget etc.); **j-m etwas g.,** to allow s.o. sth. ◆**G~ung,** f -/-en (a) no pl authorization; (b) (*Schriftstück*) permit, licence.

**geneigt** [gə'naigt], adj. **g. sein, etwas zu tun,** to be inclined to do sth.

**General** [genə'raːl]. **I.** m -s/-e & -e general. **II. G~-,** comb.fm. general (strike etc.); (*großangelegt*) full-scale (attack etc.); ◆**G~direktor,** m managing director. ◆**G~probe,** f dress rehearsal. ◆**G~sekretär,** m secretary-general. ◆**g~überholen,** v.tr.insep. to give (sth.) a thorough overhaul.

**Generation** [genəratsi'oːn], f -/-en generation. ◆**G~sunterschied,** m generation gap.

**Generator** [genə'raːtɔr], m -s/-en [-'toːrən], generator.

**generell** [genə'rɛl], adj. general.

**genes|en** [gə'neːzən], v.i.irr. (*sein*) Lit: to convalesce. ◆**G~ende(r),** m & f decl. as adj. convalescent. ◆**G~ung,** f -/no pl convalescence.

**Genetik** [ge'neːtik], f -/no pl genetics.

**Genf** [gɛnf]. Pr.n.n -s. Geneva.

**genial** [geni'aːl], adj. brilliant. ◆**G~ität** [-iali'tɛːt], f -/no pl genius.

**Genick** [gə'nik], n -(e)s/-e (nape of the) neck.

**Genie** [ʒe'niː], n -s/-s genius.

**genieren** [ʒe'niːrən], v.tr. to bother (s.o.); **sich g.,** to be/feel embarrassed; **sich vor j-m g.,** to be shy of s.o.

**genieß|bar** [gə'niːsbaːr], adj. edible;

(*trinkbar*) drinkable. ◆**g~en,** v.tr.irr.31 (a) to enjoy (rights, s.o.'s respect etc.); (b) to eat, (*trinken*) drink (sth.); F: **sie ist heute nicht zu g.,** she is in a filthy mood today. ◆**G~er,** m -s/- pleasure lover; (*im Essen und Trinken*) gourmet. ◆**g~erisch,** adj. appreciative; adv. with great relish.

**Genitiv** ['geːnitiːf], m -s/-e genitive (case).

**Genoss|e** [gə'nɔsə], m -n/-n Pol: etc: comrade. ◆**G~enschaft,** f -/-en cooperative. ◆**G~in,** f -/-nen Pol: comrade.

**genug** [gə'nuːk], adj. enough; **ich habe g. von seiner Nörgelei,** I've had enough of his moaning. ◆**G~tuung** [-tuːuŋ], f -/no pl satisfaction.

**Genüg|e** [gə'nyːgə], f **zur G.,** sufficiently; Pej: only too well; **j-s Anforderungen G. leisten,** to meet s.o.'s requirements. ◆**g~en,** v.i. (*haben*) (a) to be enough/sufficient (j-m, for s.o.); (b) **Anforderungen usw. g.,** to meet requirements etc. ◆**g~end,** adj. enough, sufficient. ◆**g~sam,** adj. frugal.

**Genuß** [gə'nus], m -sses/-sse 1. consumption; taking (of drugs). 2. (a) (*Vergnügen*) pleasure; enjoyment. (b) **in den G. einer Rente kommen,** to receive a pension. ◆**G~mittel,** n luxury food. ◆**g~süchtig,** adj. self-indulgent.

**genüßlich** [gə'nysliç], adj. pleasurable; adv. with great relish.

**Geo|graphie** [geogra'fiː], f -/no pl geography. ◆**G~loge** [-'loːgə], m -n/-n geologist. ◆**G~logie** [-'loːgiː], f -/no pl geology. ◆**G~metrie** [-me'triː], f -/no pl geometry.

**Gepäck** [gə'pɛk]. **I.** n -(e)s/no pl luggage, esp. N.Am: baggage. **II. G~-,** comb.fm. luggage, esp. N.Am: baggage (check, locker etc.). ◆**G~annahme,** f luggage counter; Av: baggage check-in; ◆**G~ausgabe,** f baggage checkout; ◆**G~netz,** n luggage rack. ◆**G~stück,** n piece of luggage. ◆**G~träger,** m 1. (*Pers.*) porter. 2. (*am Fahrrad*) carrier; Aut: roof rack. ◆**G~wagen,** m luggage van, N.Am: baggage car.

**Gepard** ['geːpart], m -s/-e cheetah.

**gepflegt** [gə'pfleːkt], adj. (a) well-groomed (appearance, person etc.); well cared for (lawn, skin etc.); (b) civilized (atmosphere etc.); (c) high-class (wine, restaurant etc.).

**Gepflogenheit** [gə'pfloːgənhait], f -/-en custom.

**Gepolter** [gə'pɔltər], n -s/no pl banging.

**gequält** [gə'kvɛːlt], adj. pained (expression); forced (smile etc.).

**gerade** [gə'raːdə]. **I.** adj. **1.** even (number). **2.** straight (line etc.); direct (route etc.). **II.** adv. **1.** straight; **g. gegenüber,** straight/directly opposite. **2.** (*zeitlich*) just; **er telefoniert g.,** he is on the phone just at the moment; **g. erst**, only just. **3.** (*verstärkend*) (*a*) (*genau*) exactly; **nicht g. groß/schön**, not exactly large/beautiful; (*b*) (*zufällig*) **er ist g. hier**, he just happens to be here; **g. heute**, today of all days; (*c*) (*besonders*) **g. auf diesem Gebiet**, particularly in this field. **III. G.**, *f* **-n/-n** *Mth:* straight line. ◆**g~'aus**, *adv.* straight ahead. ◆**g~heraus**, *adv. F:* frankly, openly. ◆**g~so**, *adv.* (+ *adj.*) just as (long etc.). ◆**g~stehen**, *v.i.sep.irr.100* (**haben**) (*a*) to stand straight; (*b*) **für etwas** *acc* **g.**, to take the responsibility for sth. ◆**g~wegs**, *adv.* directly. ◆**g~zu**, *adv.* virtually.

**geradlinig** [gə'rɑːtliniç], *adj.* straight; direct (descendant).

**gerammelt** [gə'ramǝlt], *adv. F:* **g. voll**, crammed (full), chock-a-block.

**Geranie** [ge'rɑːniǝ], *f* **-/-n** geranium.

**Gerät** [gə'rɛːt], *n* **-(e)s/-e** (*a*) piece of equipment; (*Werkzeug*) tool; *Cu:* utensil; (*b*) (*Vorrichtung*) device; *esp. El:* appliance; *Rad: TV:* set.

**geraten** [gə'rɑːtǝn], *v.i.irr.13* (**sein**) (*a*) (*irgendwohin*) **in eine Gegend** *acc*/**an einen Ort** *acc* **g.**, to end up in a place; (*b*) **g. in** + *acc*, to get into (difficulties, a situation etc.); **in Vergessenheit, Gefangenschaft usw. g.**, to be forgotten, captured etc.; (*c*) (*zufällig*) **an j-n g.**, to come across s.o.; (*d*) (*gelingen*) **gut/ schlecht g.**, to turn out well/badly; (*e*) **nach j-m g.**, to take after s.o.

**Geratewohl** [gərɑtǝ'voːl], *n* **aufs G.**, on the off chance; (*wahllos*) at random.

**geraum** [gə'raum], *adj.* considerable.

**geräumig** [gə'rɔʏmiç], *adj.* spacious.

**Geräusch** [gə'rɔʏʃ], *n* **-(e)s/-e** noise. ◆**g~los**, *adj.* noiseless. ◆**g~voll**, *adj.* noisy.

**gerb|en** ['gɛrbǝn], *v.tr.* to tan. ◆**'G~er**, *m* **-s/-** tanner. ◆**G~e'rei**, *f* **-/-en** tannery.

**gerecht** [gə'rɛçt], *adj.* **1.** just (**gegen** + *acc*, to); (*unparteiisch*) fair (teacher, treatment etc.). **j-m, etwas** *dat* **g. werden**, to do s.o., sth. justice. **2.** (*berechtigt*) legitimate. ◆**g~fertigt**, *adj.* justified. ◆**G~igkeit**, *f* **-/no pl** justice.

**Gerede** [gə're:dǝ], *n* **-s/no pl** talk.

**ge'regelt** [gə'reːgǝlt], *adj.* orderly.

**ge'reizt** [gə'raitst], *adj.* irritated, irritable; **g~e Atmosphäre**, explosive atmosphere. ◆**G~heit**, *f* **-/no pl** irritation.

**Gericht¹** [gə'riçt], *n* **-(e)s/-e** *Cu:* dish.

**Gericht²**, *n* **-(e)s/-e** *Jur:* court (of law); **vor G.**, in court; **j-n, etwas vor G. bringen**, to take s.o., sth. to court; **über j-n zu G. sitzen**, to sit in judgement on s.o. ◆**g~lich**, *adj.* court (order, decision etc.); (authority, verdict etc.) of the court; legal (proceedings etc.); **gegen j-n g. vorgehen**, to take legal proceedings against s.o. ◆**G~s-**, *comb.fm.* court (records, costs etc.); legal (correspondent, costs etc.); forensic (medicine).

◆**G~sarzt**, *m* forensic expert. ◆**G~shof**, *m* court (of justice). ◆**G~ssaal**, *m* courtroom. ◆**G~sverfahren**, *n* legal proceedings. ◆**G~sverhandlung**, *f* court hearing. ◆**G~svollzieher**, *m* **-s/-** bailiff.

**gerieben** [gǝ'riːbǝn], *adj. F:* crafty.

**gering** [gǝ'riŋ], *adj.* small (number, amount etc.); slight (difference etc.); low (price, temperature, *Fig:* opinion etc.); slim (chance, hope); short distance, duration etc.; **meine g~ste Sorge**, the least of my worries; **nicht im g~sten**, not in the least; **kein G~erer als X**, no less a person than X. ◆**g~fügig**, *adj.* negligible (difference, damage etc.); marginal (improvement); minor (offence, injury etc.). ◆**g~schätzig**, *adj.* disdainful (look); disparaging (remark etc.). ◆**G~schätzung**, *f* contempt, disdain.

**gerinnen** [gǝ'rinǝn], *v.i.irr.73* (**sein**) (*Blut usw.*) to clot; (*Milch*) to curdle.

**Gerippe** [gǝ'ripǝ], *n* **-s/-** skeleton; *Fig:* structure.

**gerissen** [gǝ'risǝn]. *adj. F:* crafty.

**german|isch** [gɛr'mɑːniʃ], *adj.* Germanic. ◆**G~istik**, *f* **-/no pl** German language and literature.

**gern(e)** ['gɛrn(ǝ)], *adj.* **1.** **j-n, etwas g. haben**, to like s.o., sth.; **er spielt g. Tennis**, he likes playing tennis; **ich möchte g. ein Pfund Äpfel**, I'd like a pound of apples; **das glaube ich dir g.**, I can well believe that. ◆**'G~egroß**, *m* **-/-e** *F:* show-off.

**Geröll** [gǝ'rœl], *n* **-(e)s/no pl** pebbles.

**Gerste** ['gɛrstǝ], *f* **-/-n** barley. ◆**'G~nkorn**, *n* sty(e).

**Gerte** ['gɛrtǝ], *f* **-/-n** switch. ◆**'g~n'schlank**, *adj.* slender.

**Geruch** [gǝ'rux], *m* **-(e)s/-e** **1.** smell (**nach/von** + *dat*, of). **2.** *no pl* (*Sinn*) sense of smell. ◆**g~los**, *adj.* odourless. ◆**G~ssinn**, *m* sense of smell.

**Gerücht** [gǝ'ryçt], *n* **-(e)s/-e** rumour; **es geht das G., daß...**, it is rumoured that ...

**geruhsam** [gǝ'ruːzɑːm], *adj.* peaceful; (*erholsam*) relaxing.

**Gerümpel** [gǝ'rympǝl], *n* **-s/no pl** junk.

**Gerüst** [gǝ'ryst], *n* **-(e)s/-e** scaffold(ing); *Fig:* framework.

**ge'salzen**, *adj. F:* steep (prices etc.).

**ge'sammelt**, *adj.* collected.

**gesamt** [gǝ'zamt]. **I.** *adj.* whole, entire. **II. G~-**, *comb. fm.* (*a*) total (number, amount etc.); (*b*) overall (height, length, *Fig:* impression etc.). ◆**G~ausgabe**, *f* complete edition. ◆**g~deutsch**, *adj.* all-German. ◆**G~heit**, *f* **-/no pl** entirety; (the) whole. ◆**G~hochschule**, *f approx.* polytechnic. ◆**G~schule**, *f* comprehensive school.

**Gesandt|e(r)** [gǝ'zantǝr], *m decl. as adj.* envoy. ◆**G~schaft**, *f* **-/-en** legation.

**Gesang** [gǝ'zaŋ], *m* **-(e)s/-e** **1.** *no pl* singing. **2.** (*Lied*) song; *Ecc:* hymn.

◆**G~buch,** *n* hymn book.
◆**G~verein,** *m* choral society.

**Gesäß** [gə'zɛːs], *n* -es/-e *Anat:* buttocks, *F:* bottom.

**Geschäft** [gə'ʃɛft], *n* -(e)s/-e **1.** (*a*) (*Laden*) shop; *esp. N.Am:* store; (*b*) (*Firma*) business. **2.** (*Handel*) business; **mit j-m ins G. kommen,** to (start to) do business with s.o.; **wie gehen die G~e?** how's business? **3.** (*Transaktion*) deal; **ein gutes/schlechtes G. machen,** to get a good/bad deal. **5.** (*Aufgabe*) job, task; **er versteht sein G.,** he knows his job. ◆**G~emacher,** *m* -s/- profiteer. ◆**g~ig,** *adj.* bustling (activity etc.); busy (person). ◆**g~lich,** *adj.* business (matters etc.); **g. verreist,** away on business. ◆**G~s-,** *comb.fm.* **1.** business (letter, woman, friend, secret, life, methods, trip, world etc.). **2.** shopping (street etc.). ◆**g~sführend,** *adj.* managing (director etc.); executive (committee etc.). ◆**G~sführer(in),** *m* (*f*) **1.** *Com:* manager(ess). **2.** secretary (of a society etc.). ◆**G~sführung,** *f* management. ◆**G~sinhaber(in),** *m* (*f*) proprietor. ◆**G~sjahr,** *n* financial year. ◆**G~sleitung,** *f* management. ◆**G~smann,** *m* businessman. ◆**g~smäßig,** *adj.* businesslike. ◆**G~ssinn,** *m* business sense. ◆**G~sstelle,** *f* (*a*) office; (*b*) (*Filiale*) branch. ◆**g~stüchtig,** *adj.* **1.** efficient. **2.** (*gewieft*) smart. ◆**G~sviertel,** *n* shopping area. ◆**G~szeit,** *f* hours of business. ◆**G~szweig,** *m* line of business.

**geschehen** [gə'ʃeːən]. **I.** *v.i.irr.* (*sein*) to happen (j-m, to s.o.); **das geschieht ihm recht,** that serves him right; **es muß etwas g.!** something must be done! **es ist um ihn g.,** he's had it. **II. G.,** *n* -s/- (*a*) happening; (*b*) *coll.* events.

**gescheit** [gə'ʃait], *adj.* clever; *F:* **sei doch g.!** do be sensible!

**Geschenk** [gə'ʃɛŋk], *n* -(e)s/-e present. ◆**G~artikel,** *m usu. pl* gifts, fancy goods. ◆**G~papier,** *n* wrapping paper.

**Geschichte** [gə'ʃiçtə], *f* -/-n **1.** *no pl* history. **2.** (*Erzählung*) story, tale. *F:* **eine dumme/üble G.,** stupid/nasty business. ◆**G~enerzähler,** *m* storyteller. ◆**g~lich,** *adj.* historical. ◆**G~s-,** *comb.fm.* history (book, teacher etc.); historical (research etc.). ◆**G~sschreiber,** *m* -s/- historian.

**Geschick** [gə'ʃik], *n* -(e)s/-e **1.** *Lit:* (*Schicksal*) fate. **2.** *no pl* skill. ◆**G~lichkeit,** *f* -/*no pl* skill (**bei** + *dat,* at, in). ◆**g~t,** *adj.* skilful (**in** + *dat,* at).

**geschieden** [gə'ʃiːdən], *adj.* divorced.

**Geschirr** [gə'ʃir], *n* -(e)s/-e **1.** *no pl* (*a*) crockery, (*Porzellan*) china; (*b*) (dirty) dishes. **2.** (*Pferdeg.*) harness; ◆**G~spülen,** *n* washing up. ◆**G~spülmaschine,** *f* dishwasher.

◆**G~tuch,** *n* tea towel, *N.Am:* dish towel.

**Geschlecht** [gə'ʃlɛçt], *n* -(e)s/-er **1.** sex; *Gram:* gender. **2.** generation; (*Sippe*) family. ◆**g~lich,** *adj.* sexual. ◆**G~s-,** *comb.fm.* sexual (act etc.); sex (life, organ etc.); genital (gland etc.). ◆**G~skrankheit,** *f* venereal disease. ◆**G~steile,** *pl* genitals. ◆**G~sverkehr,** *m* sexual intercourse.

**geschlossen** [gə'ʃlɔsən], *adj.* (*a*) closed; **g~e Gesellschaft/Vorstellung,** private party/performance; **g~e Ortschaft,** built-up area; (*b*) *adv.* unanimously.

**Geschmack** [gə'ʃmak], *m* -(e)s/-e taste; **er findet G. an dem Spiel,** the game appeals to him; **langsam kam er auf den G.,** gradually he acquired a taste for it. ◆**g~los,** *adj.* tasteless; (joke etc.) in bad taste. ◆**G~losigkeit,** *f* -/-en (*a*) *no pl* tastelessness; *Fig:* bad taste; (*b*) (*Bemerkung*) tasteless remark. ◆**G~s-,** *comb.fm.* (question, sense etc.) of taste; ◆**G~ssache,** *f* matter of taste. ◆**g~voll,** *adj.* tasteful.

**geschmeidig** [gə'ʃmaidiç], *adj.* supple; (*biegsam*) pliable.

**Geschmier(e)** [gə'ʃmiːr(ə)], *n* -s/*no pl* **1.** smear. **2.** (*Geschriebenes*) scribble, scrawl.

**Geschöpf** [gə'ʃœpf], *n* -(e)s/-e creature.

**Geschoß** [gə'ʃɔs], *n* -sses/-sse **1.** missile. **2.** (*Stock*) floor, storey.

**geschraubt** [gə'ʃraupt], *adj.* affected (speech etc.); contrived (style, phrase etc.).

**Ge'schrei,** *n* -s/*no pl* (*a*) shouting; (*grell*) screaming; (*b*) **viel G. um etwas** *acc* **machen,** to make a lot of fuss about sth.

**Geschütz** [gə'ʃyts], *n* -es/-e gun; *pl:* artillery; *Fig:* **schweres G. auffahren,** to bring up one's big guns.

**Geschwader** [gə'ʃvaːdər], *n* -s/- squadron.

**Geschwafel** [gə'ʃvaːfəl], *n* -s/*no pl F:* twaddle.

**Geschwätz** [gə'ʃvɛts], *n* -es/*no pl* chatter. ◆**g~ig,** *adj.* garrulous. ◆**G~igkeit,** *f* -/*no pl* garrulity.

**geschweige** [gə'ʃvaigə], *conj.* **g.** (**denn**), let alone.

**geschwind** [gə'ʃvint], *adj.* quick, fast. ◆**G~igkeit,** *f* -/-en speed. ◆**G~igkeits-,** *comb.fm.* speed (check etc.); ◆**G~igkeitsbeschränkung,** *f* speed limit. ◆**G~igkeitsmesser,** *m* speedometer. ◆**G~igkeitsüberschreitung,** *f* exceeding the speed limit.

**Geschwister** [gə'ʃvistər], *n pl* brother(s) and sister(s).

**geschwollen** [gə'ʃvɔlən]. *adj.* pompous.

**Geschworene(r)** [gə'ʃvoːrənər], *m & f decl. as adj.* juror; **die G~n,** the jury.

**Geschwulst** [gə'ʃvulst], *f* -/-e **1.** *Med:* tumour. **2.** (*Schwellung*) swelling.

**geschwungen** [gə'ʃvuŋən], *adj.* curved.

**Geschwür** [gə'ʃvyːr], *n* -s/-e ulcer.

**Gesell|e** [gə'zɛlə], *m* -n/-n 1. skilled worker. 2. *F:* fellow, bloke. ◆**g~en,** *v.refl.* **sich zu j-m g.,** to join s.o. ◆**g~ig,** *adj.* 1. sociable (person, nature etc.). 2. social (evening, gathering etc.). ◆**G~igkeit,** *f* -/-en 1. *no pl* sociability. 2. (*Treffen*) social gathering. ◆**G~schaft,** *f* -/-en 1. society; 2. (*Begleitung, Umgang*) company; **j-m G. leisten,** to keep s.o. company; 3. *Com:* (*Firma*) company. 4. (*Veranstaltung*) party. ◆**g~schaftlich,** *adj.* social. ◆**G~schafts-,** *comb.fm.* social (class, order, novel, criticism etc.). ◆**G~schaftsanzug,** *m* dress suit. ◆**G~schaftsspiel,** *n* party game.

**Gesetz** [gə'zɛts], *n* -es/-e law; *Fig:* **sich *dat* etwas zum G. machen,** to make sth. a rule. ◆**G~blatt,** *n* legal gazette. ◆**G~buch,** *n* statute book. ◆**G~entwurf,** *m* (draft) bill. ◆**G~geber,** *m* -s/- (i) (*Pers.*) legislator; (ii) (*Organ*) legislature. ◆**G~gebung,** *f* -/no pl legislation. ◆**g~lich,** *adj.* legal; (*g. festgelegt*) statutory. ◆**g~los,** *adj.* lawless (person, act etc.). ◆**G~losigkeit,** *f* -/no pl lawlessness. ◆**g~mäßig,** *adj.* (*a*) *Jur: etc:* legal (title, power etc.); legitimate (claim etc.); lawful (right, procedure etc.). ◆**g~widrig,** *adj.* illegal, unlawful.

**gesetzt** [gə'zɛtst]. 1. *adj.* sedate. 2. *conj.* **g. den Fall, (daß) er käme/kommt,** assuming/supposing (that) he comes.

**Gesicht** [gə'zɪçt], *n* -(e)s/-er 1. (*a*) face; **der Wahrheit ins G. sehen,** to face (up to) the truth; **das G. wahren/retten,** to save face; **ein dummes G. machen,** to look stupid; (*b*) (*Aussehen*) look. 2. *no pl* **etwas zu G. bekommen,** to set eyes on sth.; **etwas aus dem G. verlieren,** to lose sight of sth.; **das zweite G. haben,** to have second sight. ◆**G~s-,** *comb.fm.* (*a*) face (powder, cream); facial (massage etc.); (*b*) (field, line etc.) of vision. ◆**G~sausdruck,** *m* expression. ◆**G~sfarbe,** *f* complexion. ◆**G~skreis,** *m* outlook. ◆**G~spunkt,** *m* point of view. ◆**G~szüge,** *mpl* (facial) features.

**Gesindel** [gə'zɪndəl], *n* -s/no pl rabble.

**gesinn|t** [gə'zɪnt], *adj.* **demokratisch g.,** democratically minded; **j-m freundlich/übel g. sein,** to be well/ill disposed towards s.o. ◆**G~ung,** *f* -/-en nature; (*Überzeugungen*) convictions. ◆**g~ungslos,** *adj.* unprincipled. ◆**G~ungslosigkeit,** *f* -/no pl lack of principles. ◆**G~ungswandel,** *m* change of heart/*Pol:* direction.

**gesittet** [gə'zɪtət], *adj.* well-mannered.

**Gesöff** [gə'zœf], *n* -(e)s/-e *P:* evil brew.

**gesondert** [gə'zɔndərt], *adj.* separate.

**Gespann** [gə'ʃpan], *n* -(e)s/-e team. ◆**g~t,** *adj.* 1. taut (rope etc.). 2. *Fig:* (*a*) tense (atmosphere, situation etc.); (*b*)

eager (audience, anticipation); **ich bin g., was er tun wird,** I am curious to know what he will do; **da bin ich aber g.!** I can't wait (for that)! **g. zuhören/zuschauen,** to listen/watch intently.

**Gespenst** [gə'ʃpɛnst], *n* -(e)s/-er 1. ghost. ◆**G~ergeschichte,** *f* ghost story. ◆**g~erhaft/g~isch,** *adj.* ghostly.

**Gespött** [gə'ʃpœt], *n* -(e)s/no pl (*a*) mockery; (*b*) (*Pers.*) laughing-stock.

**Gespräch** [gə'ʃprɛːç], *n* -(e)s/-e 1. conversation, talk; **im G. sein,** to be under discussion; **sie war das G. der ganzen Stadt,** she was the talk of the town. 2. *Tel:* (telephone) call. ◆**g~ig,** *adj.* talkative. ◆**G~igkeit,** *f* -/no pl talkativeness. ◆**G~sstoff,** *m* topic(s) of conversation.

**gesprenkelt** [gə'ʃprɛnkəlt], *adj.* speckled.

**Gespür** [gə'ʃpyːr], *n* -s/no pl feeling.

**Gestalt** [gə'ʃtalt], *f* -/-en 1. (*a*) (*Pers.*) figure; (*b*) *no pl* (*Wuchs*) build; **von zierlicher G. sein,** to be slightly built. 2. (*Form*) shape, form; **G. annehmen/gewinnen,** to take shape. ◆**g~en,** *v.tr.* (*a*) to form, shape (sth., s.o.'s personality etc.); to create (a work of art; to design (a layout etc.); to arrange (a room etc.); to organize (one's time, activities); (*b*) *v.refl.* **sich anders/günstig/ungünstig g.,** to turn out differently/well/badly. ◆**G~ung,** *f* -/-en 1. *no pl* (*Gestalten*) forming; arrangement; creation 2. (*Anordnung*) design; layout.

**geständ|ig** [gə'ʃtɛndɪç], *adj.* confessed (criminal); **g. sein,** to have confessed. ◆**G~nis** [-tnɪs], *n* -ses/-se confession.

**Gestank** [gə'ʃtaŋk], *m* -(e)s/no pl stench.

**gestatten** [gə'ʃtatən], *v.tr.* to allow, permit (sth.); **g. Sie?** may I?

**Geste** ['gɛstə], *f* -/-n gesture.

**ge'stehen,** *v.tr. & i.irr.100* (*haben*) to confess.

**Ge'stein,** *n* -(e)s/-e rock.

**Gestell** [gə'ʃtɛl], *n* -(e)s/-e 1. (*Stütze*) stand, (*für Flaschen usw.*) rack; (*Regal*) shelves. 2. (*Rahmen*) frame (of spectacles etc.); (*Unterbau*) base (of a machine etc.).

**gestern** ['gɛstərn], *adv.* yesterday; **g. abend,** last night; *F:* **er ist nicht von g.,** he wasn't born yesterday.

**Gestik** ['gɛstik], *f* -/no pl gestures. ◆**g~ulieren** [-u'liːrən], *v.i.* (*haben*) to gesticulate.

**Gestirn** [gə'ʃtɪrn], *n* -(e)s/-e *Lit:* star.

**gestochen** [gə'ʃtɔxən]. *adj.* meticulous; **g. scharf,** needle-sharp.

**Gesträuch** [gə'ʃtrɔyç], *n* -(e)s/-e bushes, shrubs.

**gestreift** [gə'ʃtraift], *adj.* striped.

**gestrichen** [gə'ʃtrɪçən]. *adj.* **ein g~er Teelöffel,** a level teaspoonful; **g. voll,** full to the brim.

**gestrig** ['gɛstrɪç], *adj.* 1. yesterday's (paper etc.); **unser g~es Gespräch,** our conversation yesterday; 2. (*altmodisch*)

behind the times.
**Gestrüpp** [gəˈʃtryp], n -(e)s/-e undergrowth; *Fig:* maze.
**Gestüt** [gəˈʃtyːt], n -(e)s/-e stud.
**Gesuch** [gəˈzuːx], n -(e)s/-e petition, *(Antrag)* application (**um/auf** + *acc,* for). ◆**g~t**, *adj.* sought after (items); **sehr g.**, much in demand.
**gesund** [gəˈzunt], *adj.* healthy; **sie ist wieder ganz g.**, she is quite well/fit again; **g. leben**, to lead a healthy life; *Fig:* **der g~e Menschenverstand**, common sense. ◆**G~heit**, f -/no pl health; **auf Ihre G.!** your health! here's to you! **G.!** bless you! ◆**g~heitlich**, *adj.* (relating to) health; (state, reasons etc.) of health; **g. ist er nicht auf der Höhe**, he is not in the best of health. ◆**G~heits-**, *comb.fm.* health (service etc.); (state etc.) of health. ◆**G~heitspflege**, f -/no pl hygiene. ◆**g~heitsschädlich**, *adj.* unhealthy. ◆**G~heitszeugnis**, n health certificate.
**getigert** [gəˈtiːgərt], *adj.* striped.
**Getöse** [gəˈtøːzə], n -s/ no pl din; roar (of waves etc.).
**Getränk** [gəˈtrɛŋk], n -(e)s/-e drink.
**Getreide** [gəˈtraidə]. I. n -s/- grain. II. **G~-**, *comb.fm.* grain (harvest, silo etc.); cereal (product). ◆**G~speicher**, m granary.
**getrennt** [gəˈtrɛnt], *adj.* separate; **g. leben**, to live apart.
**getreu** [gəˈtrɔy], *adj.* (a) faithful (reproduction etc.); (b) *Lit:* loyal (friend etc.).
**Getriebe** [gəˈtriːbə], n -s/- 1. transmission; *Aut:* gearbox. 2. *(Betriebsamkeit)* hustle and bustle.
**getrost** [gəˈtroːst], *adv.* confidently.
**Getto** [ˈgɛto], n -s/-s ghetto.
**Getue** [gəˈtuːə], n -s/ no pl F: fuss.
**Getümmel** [gəˈtyməl], n -s/ no pl tumult.
**getupft** [gəˈtupft], *adj.* spotted.
**geübt** [gəˈyːpt], *adj.* (Pers.) proficient (in + *dat,* at); trained (eye, ear).
**Gewächs** [gəˈvɛks], n -es/-e 1. *(Pflanze)* plant. 2. *Med:* growth. ◆**G~haus**, n greenhouse.
**gewachsen** [gəˈvaksən], *adj.* **einer Sache g. sein**, to be up to sth.; **j-m g. sein**, to be a match for s.o.
**gewagt** [gəˈvaːkt], *adj.* daring.
**gewählt** [gəˈvɛːlt], *adj.* elegant, refined; **sich g. ausdrücken**, to use refined language.
**Gewähr** [gəˈvɛːr], f -/no pl guarantee; *(Verantwortung)* responsibility. ◆**g~en**, *v.tr.* (a) to grant (a request, credit etc.). (b) **j-n g. lassen**, to let s.o. have his way. ◆**g~leisten**, *v.tr.insep.* to guarantee. ◆**G~smann**, m informant. ◆**G~ung**, f -/no pl granting.
**Gewahrsam** [gəˈvaːrzaːm], m -s/no pl *(Obhut)* safekeeping; *(Haft)* custody.
**Gewalt** [gəˈvalt]. I. f -/-en 1. (a) *(Macht)* power; **die G. an sich** acc **reißen**, to seize power; (b) *(Beherrschung)* control;

etwas/sich **in der G. haben**, to be in control of sth./oneself; (c) *(bezwingende Kraft)* force; **G. anwenden**, to use force; *Fig:* **mit aller G.**, with all one's might; *(was auch geschieht)* at all costs. II. **G~-**, *comb.fm.* violent (crime etc.). ◆**G~akt**, m act of violence. ◆**G~anwendung**, f use of force. ◆**G~herrschaft**, f tyranny. ◆**g~ig**, *adj.* colossal (building etc.); tremendous (task, difference etc.); *F:* terrific (quantity, blow, etc.); **da irrst du dich g.!** there you are very much mistaken! ◆**g~los**, *adj.* non-violent. ◆**G~losigkeit**, f -/no pl non-violence. ◆**G~marsch**, m forced march. ◆**g~sam**, *adj.* violent (death, deed etc.); forcible (entry etc.). ◆**g~tätig**, *adj.* violent. ◆**G~tätigkeit**, f 1. no pl violence. 2. esp.pl act of violence.
**Gewand** [gəˈvant], n -(e)s/⸚er robe.
**gewandt** [gəˈvant], *adj.* skilful; confident (manner, style); ◆**G~heit**, f -/no pl skill.
**Gewässer** [gəˈvɛsər], n -s/- stretch of water; *pl.* waters.
**Gewebe** [gəˈveːbə], n -s/- 1. *(Stoff)* fabric. 2. *Anat:* tissue.
**Gewehr** [gəˈveːr], n -(e)s/-e rifle. ◆**G~lauf**, m barrel.
**Geweih** [gəˈvai], n -(e)s/-e antlers.
**Gewerb|e** [gəˈvɛrbə], n -s/- trade; *(Beschäftigung)* occupation; **das graphische G.**, the printing trade. ◆**g~lich**, *adj.* commercial; **g. tätig sein**, to be in business. ◆**g~smäßig**, *adj.* professional; for profit.
**Gewerkschaft** [gəˈvɛrkʃaft], f -/-en trade/N.Am: labor union. ◆**G~(l)er(in)**, m -s/- (f -/-nen) trade/N.Am: labor unionist. ◆**G~s-**, *comb.fm.* union (leader etc.). ◆**G~sbund**, m (German) Trade Union Federation.
**Gewicht** [gəˈviçt], n -(e)s/-e (a) weight; (b) *(Wichtigkeit)* importance; **seine Stimme hat großes G.**, his voice carries a lot of weight. ◆**G~heben**, n -s/no pl weight-lifting. ◆**g~ig**, *adj.* important. ◆**G~s-**, *comb.fm.* (unit etc.) of weight.
**gewieft** [gəˈviːft], *adj.* F: crafty.
**gewillt** [gəˈvilt], *adj.* willing.
**Gewimmel** [gəˈviməl], n -s/no pl swarm.
**Gewinde** [gəˈvində], n -s/- (screw) thread.
**Gewinn** [gəˈvin], m -(e)s/-e 1. (a) *(Ertrag)* profit; **er hat es mit G. verkauft**, he sold it at a profit; (b) *(Vorteil)* benefit. 2. (lottery etc.) prize. ◆**G~beteiligung**, f profit-sharing. ◆**g~bringend**, *adj.* profitable, lucrative. ◆**g~en**, v.tr.73 1. v.tr. (a) to win; (b) to gain (respect, time, control etc.); (c) **j-n für sich/für einen Plan g.**, to win s.o. over to a plan; 2. v.i. *(haben)* (a) to win; (b) **an Bedeutung g.**, to gain in importance; **an Klarheit g.**, to become clearer; ◆**g~end**, *adj.* winning. ◆**G~er**, m -s/- winner.

◆**G~spanne,** f profit margin.
◆**G~ung,** f -/no pl extraction.

**Gewirr** [gə'vir], n -(e)s/-e tangle; maze (of streets etc.); jumble (of sounds etc.).

**gewiß** [gə'vis], adj. certain; seines Sieges g., certain of victory; aber g. (doch)! (but) of course! bis zu einem gewissen Grade, to a certain extent. ◆**gewisser'maßen,** adv. to some/a certain extent. ◆**Ge'wißheit,** f -/no pl certainty; G. (über etwas acc) erlangen, to find out for certain (about sth.).

**Gewissen** [gə'visən], n -s/- conscience; j-n, etwas auf den G. haben, to have s.o., sth. on one's conscience. ◆**g~haft,** adj. conscientious. ◆**G~haftigkeit,** f -/no pl conscientiousness. ◆**g~los,** adj. unscrupulous. ◆**G~s-,** comb.fm. (conflict etc.) of conscience. ◆**G~sbisse,** mpl pangs of conscience; remorse.

**Gewitter** [gə'vitər]. I. n -s/- thunderstorm; Fig: ein häusliches G., a domestic storm. II. G~-, comb.fm. thundery (shower etc.); storm (front, cloud). ◆**g~n,** v.impers. (haben) es gewittert, it is thundering. ◆**g~schwül,** adj. thundery, sultry.

**gewittrig** [gə'vitriç], adj. thundery.

**gewitzt** [gə'vitst], adj. shrewd.

**gewöhnen** [gə'vø:nən], v.tr. j-n an etwas acc g., to get s.o. used to sth.; sich an j-n, etwas acc g., to get used to s.o., sth. ◆**g~lich,** adj. 1. (a) (normal) normal, ordinary; (üblich) usual; adv. usually; wie g., as usual. 2. (ordinär) common. ◆**g~t,** p.p. an etwas acc g. sein, to be used to sth. ◆**G~ung,** f -/no pl G. an etwas acc, becoming accustomed to sth.

**Gewohnheit** [gə'vo:nhait], f -/-en habit; aus G., from (force of) habit; es ist ihm zur G. geworden, it has become a habit with him. ◆**G~heits-,** comb.fm. (a) (matter etc.) of habit; (b) habitual (drinker, criminal etc.). ◆**G~heitsrecht,** n common law. ◆**g~t,** adj. usual; etwas acc g. sein, to be used to sth.

**Gewölbe** [gə'vœlbə], n -s/- 1. vault. 2. (Keller) vaults.

**Gewühl** [gə'vy:l], n -(e)s/no pl (Gewimmel) throng.

**gewunden** [gə'vundən]. adj. twisting.

**Gewürz** [gə'vyrts], n -es/-e spice; (aromatische Zutat) seasoning. ◆**G~gurke,** f -/-n pickled gherkin. ◆**G~nelke,** f clove.

**Gezeiten** [gə'tsaitən]. I. fpl tides. II. G~-, comb.fm. tidal (power station etc.). ◆**G~wechsel,** m turn of the tide.

**gezielt** [gə'tsi:lt], adj. (measure etc.) specific.

**geziert** [gə'tsi:rt], adj. affected. ◆**G~heit,** f -/no pl affectedness.

**Gezwitscher** [gə'tsvitʃər], n -s/no pl twittering.

**gezwungen** [gə'tsvuŋən]. adj. forced.

**Gicht** [giçt], f -/ no pl gout.

**Giebel** ['gi:bəl]. 1. m -s/- gable. II. G~-, comb.fm. gable (window etc.); gabled (roof, house).

**Gier** [gi:r], f -/no pl (Habg.) greed; craving (nach etwas dat, for sth.). ◆**g~ig,** adj. greedy (nach + dat, for).

**gießen** ['gi:sən], v.irr.31 1. v.tr. (a) to pour, (verschütten) spill; (b) to water (plants etc.); (c) to cast (metal etc.); to make (candles). 2. v.i.impers. (haben) F: es gießt (in Strömen), it's pouring (with rain). ◆**G~kanne,** f watering can.

**Gift** [gift]. I. n -(e)s/-e poison; (Schlangeng. & Fig:) venom; darauf kannst du G. nehmen! you can bet your life on that! II. G~-, comb.fm. poisonous (plant, mushroom etc.); poisoned (arrow etc.); poison (gas, cupboard etc.). ◆**g~grün,** adj. bilious green. ◆**g~ig,** adj. poisonous; venomous Fig: remark etc.); Ch: toxic (fumes etc.); Fig: spiteful (person, remark etc.). ◆**G~zahn,** m poison fang.

**Gigant** [gi'gant], m -en/-en giant. ◆**g~isch,** adj. gigantic, colossal.

**Gilde** ['gildə], f -/-n guild.

**Gin** [dʒin], m -s/-s gin.

**Ginster** ['ginstər], m -s/- broom.

**Gipfel** ['gipfəl], m -s/- (Bergg.) summit, top (of a mountain); (also Fig:) peak; esp. Pej: height (of stupidity etc.); F: das ist (doch) der G.! that's the limit! ◆**G~konferenz,** f summit conference. ◆**G~punkt,** m peak; Fig: culmination. ◆**G~treffen,** n summit meeting.

**Gips** [gips], m -es/-e plaster of Paris; Med: plaster. ◆**G~abdruck,** m plastercast. ◆**G~bein,** n F: leg in plaster/N.Am: a cast. ◆**G~verband,** m plastercast.

**Giraffe** [gi'rafə], f -/-n giraffe.

**Girlande** [gir'landə], f -/-n garland.

**Giro** ['ʒi:ro]. I. n -s/-s giro (system); (Überweisung) giro transfer. II. G~-, comb.fm. giro (account etc.).

**Gischt** [giʃt], f -en spray.

**Gitarre** [gi'tarə], f -/-n guitar. ◆**G~ist** ['rist], m -en/-en guitarist.

**Gitter** ['gitər], n -s/- (Stäbe) bars; (Zaun, Geländer) railings; (Drahtg.) wire mesh. ◆**G~fenster,** n barred window. ◆**G~stab,** m bar. ◆**G~zaun,** m lattice-work fence.

**Glacéhandschuh** [gla'se:hantʃu:], m kid glove.

**Gladiole** [gladi'o:lə], f -/-n gladiolus.

**Glanz** [glants], m -es/no pl 1. (a) shine; (halbmatt) sheen; (b) (Helligkeit) brightness; 2. Fig: (Pracht) splendour; Hum: mit G. und Gloria durchfallen, to fail resoundingly. ◆**G~leistung,** f brilliant achievement; Sp: etc: outstanding performance. ◆**g~los,** adj. dull; Fig: lacklustre. ◆**G~stück,** n pièce de résistance. ◆**g~voll,** adj. magnificent (occasion, performance); brilliant (career

etc.). ◆'G~zeit, f heyday.
glänzen ['glɛntsən], v.i. (haben) to shine,
gleam; (Sterne, Lichter) to twinkle; (Hose,
Nase) to be shiny; Fig: (Pers.) to shine.
◆g~d, adj. 1. bright (eyes etc.); shiny
(hair, surface etc.). 2. Fig: brilliant (career, idea etc.).
Glas [glɑːs]. I. n -es/‑er ['glɛːzər]. 1.
glass; zwei G. Bier, two glasses of beer;
ein G. Marmelade, a jar/pot of jam. 2.
(a) (spectacle) lens; (b) (Ferng.) binoculars. II. G~-, comb.fm. glass (eye, roof,
-paper, wool etc.). ◆'G~bläser, m
glass-blower. ◆'G~er, m -s/- glazier.
◆g~'klar, adj. crystal clear.
◆'G~maler, m stained glass artist.
◆G~male'rei, f -/-en stained glass
painting. ◆'G~scheibe, f pane of
glass. ◆'G~scherbe, f piece of (broken) glass.
gläsern ['glɛːzərn], adj. glass.
glas|ieren [gla'ziːrən], v.tr. (a) to glaze
(tiles etc.); (b) Cu: to ice, N.Am: frost
(cakes). ◆g~ig ['glɑːziç], adj. glassy,
glazed. ◆G~ur [gla'zuːr], f -/-en 1.
glaze. 2. Cu: icing, N.Am: frosting.
glatt [glat], adj. 1. (a) smooth; (eben)
even; level (surface, ground etc.); (b)
(glitschig) slippery (road etc.). 2. (eindeutig) clear (victory etc.); downright (lie
etc.); flat (refusal); utter (nonsense); sie
ging g. darüber hinweg, she completely
ignored it; das hatte ich g. vergessen, I
had forgotten all about it. ◆'G~eis, n
(black) ice; Fig: j-n aufs G. führen, to
take s.o. for a ride. ◆'g~gehen,
v.i.sep.irr.36 (sein) to go off without a
hitch. ◆'g~weg, adv. g. ablehnen, to
refuse pointblank; das ist g. erlogen,
that is a downright lie.
Glätte ['glɛtə], f -/-n (a) smoothness; (b)
slipperiness. ◆'g~n, v.tr. to smooth (a
blanket, one's hair etc.); to smooth out
(creases etc.).
Glatz|e ['glatsə], f -/-n bald head; er hat/
bekommt eine G., he is/is going bald.
◆'g~köpfig, adj. bald(-headed).
Glaub|e ['glaubə], m -ns/no pl belief (an
+ acc, in); esp. Ecc: faith; j-m G~n
schenken, to believe s.o. ◆'g~en, v.v.
1. v.tr. to believe; j-m g., to believe s.o.;
das glaube ich dir (gern), I believe you/
what you say; das ist doch kaum zu g.!
it is scarcely credible; ich glaubte, sie
sei in Paris, I thought she was in Paris;
ich glaube nein, I don't think so. 2. v.i.
(haben) to believe (an Gott, Wunder
usw., in God, miracles etc.); (vertrauen)
an j-n, etwas acc g., to have faith in s.o.,
sth. ◆'G~ensbekenntnis, n creed.
◆g~haft ['glaubhaft], adj. plausible.
◆'g~würdig, adj. credible; reliable
(sources). ◆'G~würdigkeit, f -/no pl
credibility.
gläubig ['glɔybiç], adj. 1. (a) believing
(Christian etc.); (b) (fromm) religious. 2.
(vertrauensselig) trusting. ◆'G~e(r), m

& f decl. as adj. believer; die G~en,
the faithful. ◆'G~er, m -s/- creditor.
gleich [glaiç], adj. & adv. 1. (dasselbe) (a)
same; zur g~en Zeit, at the same time;
das kommt auf das g~e hinaus, it
comes/amounts to the same thing; ihr
seid alle g., you are all the same/alike;
sie sehen ziemlich g. aus, they look fairly alike; (b) (g~wertig) equal; zu g~en
Teilen, in equal parts; g. schwer/groß,
equally heavy/large; zweimal zwei (ist) g.
vier, twice two equals four; (c) (gleichgültig) es ist mir g., was er denkt, I don't
care what he thinks; ganz g. wer kommt,
no matter who comes. 2. adv. (a) (sofort)
immediately, at once; bis g.! see you in a
moment! (b) (direkt) g. daneben, right
next to it; g. gegenüber, directly opposite; (c) (fast) es ist g. 9 Uhr, it is
almost/nearly 9 o'clock. ◆'g~alt(e)rig
[-alt(ə)riç], adj. (of) the same age.
◆'g~artig, adj. similar.
◆'g~berechtigt, adj. having equal
rights. ◆G~berechtigung, f -/no pl
equality. ◆'g~bleiben, v.i. sep.irr.12
(sein) (sich dat) g., to remain the same.
◆'g~bleibend, adj. constant; (konsequent) consistent. ◆'g~en, v.i.irr. (haben) j-m/etwas dat g., to be like/resemble
s.o., sth. ◆g~ermaßen, adv. equally.
◆'g~falls, adv. also, likewise; danke
g.! thank you, the same to you!
◆'g~förmig, adj. uniform. ◆'G~-
förmigkeit, f -/no pl uniformity.
◆'g~gesinnt, adj. like-minded.
◆'G~gewicht, n balance; Ph: & Fig:
equilibrium; im G., balanced.
◆'g~gültig, adj. (a) (Pers.) indifferent;
(apathisch) apathetic; (b) (unwichtig) trivial; er ist mir g., he means nothing to
me. ◆'G~gültigkeit, f -/no pl indifference. ◆'G~heit, f -/-en 1. identity (of
interests etc.). 2. no pl (gleiche Stellung)
equality. ◆'g~kommen, v.i.sep.irr.53
(sein) etwas dat g., to be tantamount to
sth.; ◆'g~lautend, adj. identical.
◆'g~machen, v.tr.sep. (a) to make
(people etc.) equal; (b) eine Stadt dem
Erdboden g., to raze a city (to the
ground). ◆'G~maß, n symmetry,
harmony. ◆'g~mäßig, adj. even; regular (breathing, intervals etc.); steady
(pressure, speed etc.); etwas g. verteilen,
to share sth. out equally.
◆'G~mäßigkeit, f -/no pl evenness.
◆'G~mut, m equanimity. ◆'g~-
mütig, adj. calm. ◆'g~namig, adj.
with the same name. ◆'G~nis, n -ses/
-se parable. ◆'g~sam, adv. Lit: as it
were. ◆'g~schalten, v.tr.sep. to bring
(organizations) into line. ◆'G~schritt,
m marching in step. ◆'g~setzen,
v.tr.sep. to equate. ◆'g~stellen,
v.tr.sep. = g~setzen. ◆'G~strom, m
direct current. ◆'g~tun, v.i.sep.irr.106
(haben) es j-m g., to do the same as s.o.
◆'G~ung, f -/-en equation. ◆g~viel,

*adv.* no matter (where, whether … etc.). ◆g~**wertig,** *adj.* of equal value; (*gleich gut*) equally good. ◆'g~**wohl,** *adv.* nevertheless. ◆g~**zeitig,** *adj.* simultaneous; *adv.* at the same time; simultaneously. ◆'g~**ziehen,** *v.i.sep.irr.113* (*haben*) to draw level.

**Gleis** [glais], *n* -**es/-e** line, track; **auf G. 3,** at Platform 3/*N.Am:* on Track 3.

**gleit|en** ['glaitən], *n v.i.irr.* (*sein*) to glide; (*rutschen*) to slip, slide. ◆'G~**flug,** *m* glide. ◆'G~**zeit,** *f* F: flexitime.

**Gletscher** ['glɛtʃər], I. *m* -**s/-** glacier. ◆'G~**spalte,** *f* -/-**n** crevasse.

**Glied** [gli:t], *n* -(**e**)**s/-er** 1. *Anat:* limb; 2. (*Kettengr.*) (*also Fig:*) link. 3. (*Mitglied*) member. 4. *Mil:* rank. ◆'g~**ern** [-dərn], *v.tr.* to order (thoughts, ideas etc.); to plan (an essay, a speech etc.); ◆'G~**erung,** *f* -/-**en** organization. ◆'G~**maßen,** *fpl* limbs.

**glimm|en** ['glimən], *v.i.irr.* (*haben*) to glow. ◆'G~**stengel,** *m* P: fag.

**glimpflich** ['glimpfliç], *adj.* lenient; **g. davonkommen,** to get off lightly.

**glitschig** ['glitʃiç], *adj.* slippery.

**glitzern** ['glitsərn], *v.i.* (*haben*) to glitter, (*Sterne usw.*) twinkle.

**global** [glo'ba:l], *adj.* 1. global (conflict etc.). 2. (*umfassend*) overall (idea etc.).

**Globus** ['glo:bus], *m* - & -**busses/-ben** & -**busse** globe.

**Glocke** ['glɔkə], *f* -/-**n** bell; F: **das brauchst du nicht an die große G. zu hängen,** you needn't tell the whole world about it. ◆'G~**n-,** *comb.fm.* bell (founder etc.); (sound) of a bell/bells. ◆'G~**ngeläut,** *n* ringing/pealing of bells. ◆'G~**nspiel,** *n* 1. (*in Türmen usw.*) carillon. 2. *Mus:* glockenspiel. ◆'G~**nturm,** *m* bell tower; belfry.

**Glosse** ['glɔsə], *f* -/-**n** (satirical) commentary; *F:* (snide) comment.

**glotzen** ['glɔtsen], *v.i.* (*haben*) F: to stare.

**Gluck|e** ['glukə], *f* -/-**n** broody hen. ◆'g~**en,** *v.i.* (*haben*) (*a*) (*Henne*) to cluck; (*b*) (*brüten*) (*also F: Pers.*) to brood. ◆'g~**ern,** *v.i.* (*haben*) to glug, gurgle.

**Glück** [glyk], *n* -(**e**)**s/no pl** 1. (*a*) luck; **G. haben,** to be lucky; **du kannst von G. reden, daß …,** you can count yourself lucky that …; **zu meinem G.,** fortunately for me; **auf gut G.,** on the off chance; (*aufs Geratewohl*) at random; (*b*) (*personifiziert*) fortune; **ihm lächelte/lachte das G.,** fortune smiled on him. 2. (*Zustand*) happiness; **sein G. machen,** to make one's fortune. ◆'g~**en,** *v.i.* (*sein*) to succeed; **nicht g.,** to fail. ◆'g~**lich,** *adj.* happy; **g. ankommen,** to arrive safely; **g. enden,** to end happily; (*c*) *adv. F:* (*endlich*) finally, at last. ◆g~**licher'weise,** *adv.* fortunately, luckily. ◆'G~**s-,** *comb.fm.* lucky (penny number etc.). ◆'G~**sbringer,** *m*

lucky charm. ◆'G~**sfall,** *m* stroke of luck. ◆'G~**spilz,** *m* lucky devil. ◆'G~**ssache,** *f* matter of luck. ◆'G~**sspiel,** *n* gamble. ◆'g~**selig,** *adj.* blissfully happy. ◆'g~**strahlend,** *adj.* radiant. ◆'G~**wunsch,** *m* best wishes; (*Gratulation*) congratulations. ◆'G~**wunsch-,** *comb.fm.* greetings (card, telegram etc.).

**Glüh|birne** ['gly:birnə], *f* light bulb. ◆'g~**en,** *v.i.* (*haben*) to glow. ◆'g~**end,** *adj.* 1. glowing; red-hot (iron, needle etc.); **g. heiß,** scorching hot. 2. *Fig:* fervent; **g~er Verehrer,** ardent admirer. ◆'G~**wein,** *m* mulled wine. ◆G~**würmchen,** *n* -**s/-** glowworm.

**Glut** [glu:t], *f* -/-**en** 1. (*Hitze*) heat; (*Glühen*) glow. 2. *Fig:* fervour, ardour.

**Glyzerin** [glytse'ri:n], *n* -**s/no pl** glycerine.

**Gnade** ['gna:də], *f* -/-**n** 1. favour; **Euer G~n,** Your Grace. 2. (*Barmherzigkeit*) mercy. **G. vor Recht ergehen lassen,** to be lenient. ◆'G~**nfrist,** *f* reprieve. ◆'G~**ngesuch,** *n* plea for clemency. ◆'g~**nlos,** *adj.* merciless. ◆'G~**nstoß,** *m* coup de grâce. ◆'G~**ntod,** *m* mercy killing.

**gnädig** ['gnɛːdiç], *adj.* (*a*) gracious; merciful (God); lenient (judge, sentence etc.); (*b*) (*Anrede*) **g~e Frau,** Madam.

**Gnom** [gno:m], *m* -**en/-en** gnome.

**Gnu** [gnu:], *n* -**s/-s** gnu.

**Gold** [gɔlt]. I. *n* -(**e**)**s/no pl** gold. II. '**G~-,** **g~-,** *comb.fm.* gold (braid, medal, reserves etc.). ◆'G~**ader,** *f* vein of gold. ◆'G~**barren,** *m* gold ingot/bar. ◆'G~**barsch,** *m* ruff. ◆'g~**blond,** *adj.* golden (hair), gold-haired (person). ◆'g~**en** [-dən], *adj.* (*a*) gold; *Fig:* **ein g~enes Herz,** a heart of gold; (*b*) (*g~farbig*) golden; **die g~ene Mitte,** the happy medium. ◆'G~**gräber,** *m* gold-digger. ◆'G~**grube,** *f* goldmine. ◆'g~**ig,** *adj. F:* sweet, lovely, *N.Am:* cute. ◆'G~**rausch,** *m* goldrush. ◆'g~**regen,** *m* *Bot:* laburnum. ◆'g~**richtig,** *adj. F:* absolutely right. ◆'G~**schmied,** *m* goldsmith. ◆'G~**waage,** *f* F: **jedes Wort auf die G. legen,** to weigh every word. ◆'G~**zahn,** *m* gold-capped tooth.

**Golf** [gɔlf], *n* -**s/no pl** golf. ◆'G~**platz,** *m* golf course. ◆'G~**schläger,** *m* golf club. ◆'G~**spieler,** *m* golfer. ◆'G~**strom,** *m* Gulf Stream.

**Gondel** ['gɔndəl], *f* -/-**n** 1. (*Boot*) gondola. 2. cabin (of a cable-car); basket (of a balloon).

**Gong** [gɔn], *m* -**s/-s** gong. ◆'G~**schlag,** *m* stroke of a/the gong.

**gönn|en** ['gœnən], *v.tr.* (*a*) **j-m etwas nicht g.,** to begrudge s.o. sth.; **ich gönne ihm seinen Erfolg,** I don't begrudge him his success; **die Niederlage gönne ich ihm,** I'm not sorry he's been beaten; (*b*) (*gewähren*) **sich** *dat*/**j-m eine Ruhepause**

usw. **g.**, to allow oneself/s.o. a rest etc. ◆**G~er(in)**, *m -s/- (f-/-nen)* benefactor; *Art: etc:* patron. ◆**'g~erhaft**, *adj.* patronizing.

**Gorilla** [go'rila], *m -s/-s* gorilla.

**Gosse** ['gɔsə], *f -/-n* gutter.

**Gott** [gɔt], *m -es/–er* god; *F:* **das wissen die G~er**, heaven knows; **um G~es willen!** for heaven's sake! **G. sei Dank!** thank goodness! **so G. will,** God willing. ◆**G~esdienst**, *m* (church) service. ◆**G~eshaus**, *n* house of God, church. ◆**'g~eslästerlich**, *adj.* blasphemous. ◆**G~eslästerung**, *f* blasphemy. ◆**'G~heit**, *f -/-en* deity. ◆**g~lob**, *int.* thank goodness. ◆**'g~los**, *adj.* godless. ◆**'g~losigkeit**, *f -/no pl* godlessness. ◆**'g~verdammt**, *adj.* damned. ◆**'g~verlassen**, *adj. F:* godforsaken.

**Götterspeise** ['gœtərʃpaizə], jelly.

**Götze** ['gœtsə], *m -n/-n/*◆**G~nbild**, *n* idol.

**Gouvern|ante** [guvɛr'nantə], *f -/-n* governess. ◆**G~eur** [-'nøːr], *m -s/-e* governor.

**Grab** [graːp], *n -(e)s/–er* grave; **bis ans G.**, till/unto death; ◆**'g~en** [-bən]. *v.tr.&i.irr.* to dig. ◆**'G~enkrieg**, *m* trench warfare. ◆**'G~inschrift**, *f* epitaph. ◆**'G~mal**, *n* **1.** monument. **2.** (*G~stätte*) tomb. ◆**'G~rede**, *f* funeral oration. ◆**'G~stätte**, *f* burial place. ◆**'G~stein**, *m* gravestone.

**Grad** [graːt], *m -(e)s/-e (a)* degree; **bis zu einem gewissen G.**, to a certain extent; *(b) Mil:* rank; ◆**'G~einteilung**, *f* calibration. ◆**'G~messer**, *m -s/-* yardstick.

**graduell** [gradu'ɛl], *adj.* **1.** (*allmählich*) gradual (transition etc.). **2.** (difference etc.) of degree.

**Graf** [graːf], *m -en/-en* count; *Brit:* earl. ◆**G~schaft**, *f -/-en* county.

**Gräfin** [ɡrɛ'fin], *f -/-nen* countess.

**Gram** [graːm], *m -(e)s/no pl Lit:* grief.

**grämen** ['grɛːmən], *v.tr. Lit:* **sich g.**, to grieve.

**Gramm** [gram], *n -s/-e* gram.

**Grammat|ik** [gra'matik], *f -/-en* grammar. ◆**g~isch/g~ikalisch** [-i'kaːliʃ], *adj.* grammatical.

**Grammophon** [gramo'foːn], *n -s/-e* gramophone.

**Granat** [gra'naːt], *m -(e)s/-e (Stein)* garnet. ◆**G~apfel**, *m* pomegranate.

**Granate** [gra'naːtə], *f -/-n* shell.

**grandios** [grandi'oːs], *adj.* superb, magnificent.

**Granit** [gra'niːt], *m -s/-e* granite.

**Graph|ik** ['graːfik], *f -/-en* **1.** *no pl* graphic art(s). **2.** (*Druck*) print; (*Stich*) engraving. ◆**G~iker**, *m -s/-* graphic artist. ◆**'g~isch**, *adj.* graphic.

**Gras** [graːs], *n -es/–er* grass; *F:* **ins G. beißen**, to bite the dust; **G. über etwas** *acc* **wachsen lassen**, to let the dust settle on sth. ◆**g~en** ['graːzən], *v.i.* (*haben*)

to graze. ◆**'G~halm**, *m* blade of grass. ◆**'G~land**, *n* grassland. ◆**'G~narbe**, *f* turf.

**grassieren** [gra'siːrən], *v.i.* (*haben*) to be rampant.

**gräßlich** ['grɛsliç], *adj.* ghastly, dreadful.

**Grat** [graːt], *m -(e)s/-e* (*Bergg.*) ridge.

**Gräte** ['grɛːtə], *f -/-n* (fish)bone.

**Gratifikation** [gratifikatsi'oːn], *f -/-en* gratuity; (Christmas) bonus.

**gratis** ['graːtis], *adv.* free (of charge). ◆**'G~probe**, *f -/-n* free sample.

**Gratul|ant** [gratu'lant], *m -en/-en* wellwisher. ◆**G~ation**, *f -/-en* congratulation(s). ◆**g~ieren** [- 'liːrən], *v.i.* (*haben*) j-m (**zu etwas** *dat*) **g.**, to congratulate s.o. (on sth.); **j-m zum Geburtstag g.**, to wish s.o. many happy returns of the day.

**grau** [grau]. **I.** *adj. (a)* grey, *N.Am:* gray; *(b)* (*trostlos*) gloomy (future etc.); *(c)* **in g~er Vorzeit**, in the dim and distant past. ◆**'G~brot**, *n* rye-bread. ◆**'g~haarig**, *adj.* grey-haired. ◆**'g~meliert**, *adj.* greying.

**grauen** ['grauən]. **I.** *v.impers.* **es graut mir/mir graut vor etwas** *dat*, I dread (the thought of) sth. **II. G.**, *n -s/-no pl* dread (**vor dem Tode**, of death). ◆**'g~erregend**, *adj.* horrifying, gruesome. ◆**g~haft/**◆**g~voll**, *adj.* horrifying; *F:* dreadful.

**Graupeln** ['graupəln], *fpl* small (soft) hail.

**Graupen** ['graupən], *fpl* pearl barley.

**graus|am** ['grauzaːm], *adj.* cruel. ◆**'G~amkeit**, *f -/-en* **1.** *no pl* cruelty. **2.** (act of) cruelty; atrocity. ◆**'g~ig**, *adj.* **1.** gruesome. **2.** *F:* dreadful.

**gravier|en** [gra'viːrən], *v.tr.* to engrave. ◆**g~end**, *adj.* serious (mistake, loss etc.); significant (difference etc.). ◆**G~ung**, *f -/-en* engraving.

**Gravur** [gra'vuːr], *f -/-en* engraving.

**graz|il** [gra'tsiːl], *adj.* slender; (*graziös*) graceful. ◆**g~iös** [gratsi'øːs], *adj.* graceful.

**greif|bar** ['graifbaːr], **1.** ready to hand; **in g~barer Nähe**, within (easy) reach. **2.** (*konkret*) tangible (results etc.). ◆**'g~en**, *v.irr.* **1.** *v.tr.* to take hold of (sth.), (*fest*) grasp (sth.), (*schnell*) grab (sth.); **zum G. nah**, (*Berge usw.*) near enough to touch; *Fig:* (*Erfolg usw.*) within one's grasp. **2.** *v.i.* (*haben*) *(a)* **nach etwas** *dat* **g.**, to reach out for sth.; **um sich** *acc* **g.**, (i) to feel around; (ii) (*Feuer, Epidemie usw.*) to spread; *(b)* **zu etwas** *dat* **g.**, to reach out for sth.; **zu einer List g.**, to resort to a trick; *(c) Tchn:* (*Räder, usw.*) to grip, (*Zahnräder*) engage. ◆**'G~vogel**, *m* bird of prey.

**Greis** [grais], *m -es/-e* old man. ◆**'G~enalter**, *n* old age.

**grell** [grɛl], *adj. (a)* glaring (light, sun etc.); garish (colour); *(b)* (*Klang*) shrill.

**Gremium** ['greːmium], *n -s/-ien* committee; panel (of experts etc.).

**Grenz-** ['grɛnts-], *comb.fm.* border, frontier (station, official, town, crossing, traffic etc.). ◆'**G~e**, *f -/-n* **1.** border; (*Stadtg. usw.*) boundary; *Fig:* borderline. **2.** (*Maximum*) *usu. pl* limit; **seiner Macht sind G~en gesetzt**, there is a limit to his power; **seine Begeisterung kannte keine G~en**, his enthusiasm knew no bounds; **sich in G~en halten**, to be limited. ◆'**g~en**, *v.i.* (*haben*) **an etwas** *acc* **g.**, to border (on), (*Raum usw.*) be adjacent to sth.; *Fig:* **das grenzt an Erpressung usw.**, that verges on blackmail etc. ◆'**g~enlos**, *adj.* boundless. ◆'**G~fall**, *m* borderline case. ◆'**G~linie**, *f* boundary (line). ◆'**G~schutz**, *m* (*Polizei*) border police.

**Greuel** ['grɔʏəl], *m -s/- Lit:* horror; **es ist mir ein G.**, I loathe/detest it. ◆'**G~tat**, *f* atrocity.

**Grieben** ['gri:bən], *fpl* greaves.

**Griech|e** ['gri:çə], *m -n/-n* Greek. ◆'**G~enland**, *Pr.n.n -s.* Greece. ◆'**G~in**, *f -/-nen* Greek (woman/girl). ◆'**g~isch**, *adj.* Greek.

**Gries|gram** ['gri:sgrɑ:m], *m -(e)s/-e F:* grouch. ◆'**g~grämig**, *adj. F:* grumpy.

**Grieß** [gri:s], *m -es/no pl* semolina. ◆'**G~brei**, *m* semolina pudding.

**Griff** [grif], *m -(e)s/-e* **1.** (*a*) grasp, hold; *Sp: etc:* grip; *F:* **etwas im G. haben**, to have sth. at one's fingertips/(*unter Kontrolle*) under control; (*b*) (*Handgriff*) movement (of the hand); **2.** handle (of a tool, door etc.). ◆'**g~bereit**, *adj.* handy. ◆'**g~ig**, *adj.* **1.** (*handlich*) handy (tool, etc.). **2.** (*Reifen usw.*) with a good grip.

**Grill** [gril], *m -s/-s* grill; (*im Freien*) barbecue; ◆'**g~en**, *v.tr.* to grill, barbecue (meat etc.).

**Grille** ['grilə], *f -/-n Z:* cricket.

**Grimasse** [gri'masə], *f -/-n* grimace.

**grimmig** ['grimiç], *adj.* (*wütend*) furious; fierce (enemy, animal); grim (humour).

**grinsen** ['grinzən]. **I.** *v.i.* (*haben*) to grin. **II. G.**, *n -s/no pl* grin.

**Grippe** ['gripə], *f -/-n* influenza; *F:* flu.

**Grips** [grips], *m -es/-e F:* gumption.

**grob** [gro:p], *adj.* **1.** coarse (linen, *Fig:* features, language etc.); rough (treatment); uncouth (person, behaviour etc.); **g~e Arbeit**, rough/dirty work; **j-n g. anfahren**, to snap at s.o. **2.** (*ungefähr*) rough (estimate etc.); **g. geschätzt/gerechnet**, roughly, at a rough estimate. **3.** (*schlimm*) gross (violation, injustice, error, insult). ◆'**G~heit**, *f -/-en* **1.** *no pl* coarseness, roughness; rudeness. **2.** rude/coarse remark. ◆**G~ian** ['gro:bia:n], *m -(e)s/-e* boor, brute. ◆'**g~körnig**, *adj.* coarse-grained (sand, film etc.).

**Grog** [grɔk], *m -s/-s* grog. ◆**g~gy** ['grɔgi:], *adj. F:* (*erschöpft*) shattered.

**grölen** ['grø:lən], *v.tr.&i.* (*haben*) *F:* to bawl (out).

**Groll** [grɔl], *m -(e)s/no pl* rancour, resentment; **einen G. gegen j-n hegen**, to bear a grudge against s.o.

**Grönland** ['grø:nlant]. *Pr.n.n -s.* Greenland.

**Gros** [gro:], *n -/-* bulk, majority.

**Groschen** ['grɔʃən], *m -s/-* **1.** *Aus:* groschen (coin). **2.** *F:* ten pfennig (piece). ◆'**G~roman**, *m -s/-e* cheap novel.

**groß** [gro:s]. **I.** *adj.* **1.** (*a*) big, large; (*b*) (*hochgewachsen*) tall; (*c*) (*älter*) elder; (*erwachsen*) grown-up; **meine g~e Schwester**, my big/elder sister; (*d*) (*nicht gering, bedeutend*) great (difficulty etc.; nation etc.); **g~e Angst haben**, to be very frightened. **2.** (*grandios*) grand (style, banquet etc.); **in g~em Rahmen**, on a grand scale; *adv.* **g. feiern/ausgehen**, to celebrate/go out in style. **3. im g~en und ganzen**, on the whole; **g~e Reden schwingen**, to talk big. **II.** ◆'**G~-, g~-,** *comb.fm.* (*a*) large (firm), big (fire, *Z:* cat); *Com:* bulk (order, purchase etc.); (*g~angelegt*) large-scale (attack, industry etc.); (*b*) *Geog:* Great; (*den G~raum bezeichnend*) Greater (Munich etc.); (*c*) (*bei Verwandten*) great-(aunt, uncle etc.). ◆'**G~alarm**, *m* red alert. ◆'**g~angelegt**, *adj.* large-scale (project etc.). ◆'**g~artig**, *adj.* marvellous, splendid; **sich g. amüsieren**, to have a great time. ◆'**G~aufnahme**, *f* close-up. ◆'**G~buchstabe**, *m* capital (letter). ◆**G~britannien**, *n* Great Britain. ◆'**G~einkauf**, *m* bulk buying; *F:* **einen G. machen**, to do a big shop. ◆'**G~einsatz**, *m* large-scale operation. ◆'**G~eltern**, *pl* grandparents. ◆'**G~enkel**, *m* great-grandson. ◆'**G~enkelin**, *f* great-granddaughter. ◆'**G~format**, *n* large size. ◆**G~handel**, *m* wholesale trade. ◆'**G~händler**, *m* wholesale dealer, wholesaler. ◆'**g~jährig**, *adj.* of age. ◆'**G~kapital**, *n* high finance; big business. ◆'**g~macht**, *f* superpower. ◆**G~maul**, *n F:* loudmouth. ◆'**G~mut**, *f* magnanimity. ◆'**g~mütig**, *adj.* magnanimous. ◆'**G~mutter**, *f* grandmother. ◆**G~raum**, *m* large area; **im G. München**, in the Greater Munich area. ◆'**g~räumig** [-rɔʏmiç], *adj.* **1.** spacious (flat, car etc.). **2.** extensive (area etc.). ◆'**g~spurig**, *adj.* self-important; high-sounding (words etc.). ◆'**G~stadt**, *f* (large) city. ◆**G~städter**, *m* city-dweller. ◆'**g~städtisch**, *adj.* city (life etc.). ◆**G~tat**, *f* remarkable feat. ◆**G~teil**, *m* major part; **zum G.**, mainly. ◆'**g~tuerisch**, *adj.* boastful, self-important. ◆'**g~tun**, *v.i.sep.irr.106* (*haben*) to boast (**mit etwas** *dat*, about sth.). ◆'**G~unternehmer**, *m* big busi-

nessman. ◆'G~vater, m grandfather.
◆'G~wild, n big game. ◆'g~ziehen,
v.tr.sep.irr.113 to bring up (a child), rear
(a child, animal). ◆'g~zügig, adj. generous (person etc.); large-scale (planning
etc.). ◆'G~zügigkeit, f -/no pl generosity; spaciousness.

**Größe** ['grø:sə], f -/-n **1.** size; (Höhe)
height; ein Mann mittlerer G., a man of
medium height. **2.** Mth: etc: quantity. **3.**
(a) (Bedeutung) greatness; (b) (Pers.) great
name. ◆'G~enunterschied, m difference in size. ◆'G~enverhältnis, n
proportion. ◆'G~enwahn(sinn), m
megalomania; Hum: delusions of grandeur. ◆'g~enwahnsinnig, adj. megalo-
maniac. ◆'g~er, 'g~te(r,s), adj. comp.
& superl. of groß. ◆'g~ten'teils, adv.
mainly, for the most part.
◆'g~t'möglich, adj. greatest/biggest
possible.

**Grossist** [grɔ'sist], m -en/-en wholesaler.
**grotesk** [gro'tɛsk], adj. grotesque.
**Grotte** ['grɔtə], f -/-n grotto.
**Grube** ['gru:bə], f -/-n pit;
◆'G~narbeiter, m miner, mineworker.
**grüb|eln** ['gry:bə'ln], v.i. (haben) to
brood. ◆'G~ler, m -s/- brooder.
◆'g~lerisch, adj. introspective; brood-
ing.
**Gruft** [gruft], f -/-e burial vault; (Krypta)
crypt.
**grün** [gry:n], adj. green; g~er Salat, lettuce; g~e Bohnen, green beans; ins
G~e fahren, to go for a drive in the
country; Aut: g~e Welle, synchronized
traffic lights; bei G., when the lights are
green; F: das ist dasselbe in G., that
comes to (exactly) the same thing;
◆G~donnerstag, m Maundy Thursday. ◆'g~en, v.i. (haben) Lit: to
become/turn green. ◆'G~fink, m
greenfinch. ◆'g~lich, adj. greenish.
◆'G~schnabel, m greenhorn.
◆'G~span, m verdigris. ◆'G~strei-
fen, m (a) grass verge; (b) (Mittelstreifen)
central reservation.
**Grund** [grunt]. I. m -(e)s/-e **1.** (Erdboden)
ground; von G. auf geändert,
completely/radically altered. **2.** bottom
(of a river, container etc.); (sea/river)
bed; Nau: auf G. laufen, to run
aground; Fig: im G~e seines Herzens,
in his heart of hearts; einer Sache auf
den G. gehen/kommen, to get to the
bottom of sth.; im G~e (genommen),
actually, strictly speaking. **3.** (a) (Ursache) reason; aus taktischen/persön-
lichen G~en, for tactical/personal reasons; aus gutem G., with good reason;
auf G. dieser Tatsache, because of this
fact; (b) (Anlaß) cause (zum Klagen
usw., for complaint etc.); das ist ein G.
zum Feiern, this calls for a celebration.
II. 'G~-, 'g~-, comb.fm. **1.** (a) (grundlegend) basic (equipment, training, right,
rule, wage, Sch: course etc.); funda-

mental (truth, characteristic); (b) (durch
und durch) thoroughly (decent, honest,
bad etc.); completely (different etc.);
◆'G~begriff, m fundamental concept/
principle. ◆'G~besitz, m (a) no pl land
ownership; (b) Jur: real estate.
◆'G~besitzer, m landowner.
◆'G~buch, n land register.
◆'g~falsch, adj. completely/absolutely
wrong. **2.** land (purchase, tax etc.).
◆'G~gebühr, f basic rate; Tel: rental.
◆'G~gesetz, n fundamental law; West
G. Pol: constitution. ◆g~ieren
['-'di:rən], v.tr. to prime. ◆'G~ier-
farbe, f primer. ◆'G~lage, f basis,
foundation; (G~wissen) grounding; (Gerücht usw.) jeder G. entbehren, to be entirely without foundation.
◆'g~legend, adj. fundamental, basic.
◆'g~los, adj. groundless (fear etc.);
unfounded (suspicion); adv. without
(any) reason. ◆'G~mauer, f
foundation(-wall). ◆'G~pfeiler, m cornerstone. ◆'G~riß, m (a) ground plan;
(b) (Abriß) outline. ◆'G~satz, m principle. ◆'g~sätzlich, adj. fundamental;
ich esse g~ keine Schokolade, I never
eat chocolate on principle.
◆'G~schule, f primary school; N.Am:
grade school. ◆'G~stein, m foundation
stone; Fig: cornerstone. ◆'G~stück, n
plot of land. ◆'G~stufe, f Sch: junior
stage (of primary school). ◆G~
wasser, n ground water. ◆'G~züge,
mpl basic/essential features.
**gründ|en** ['gryndən], v.tr. **1.** v.tr. (a) to
found (a university, firm etc.), set up (an
organization etc.), form (a company party etc.); to start (a family etc.); (b) to
base (a verdict etc.) (auf etwas acc, on
sth.). **2.** v.refl. & i. (haben) (sich) auf etwas acc g., to be based on sth.
◆'G~er, m -s/- founder. ◆'g~lich,
adj. thorough. ◆'G~lichkeit, f -/no pl
thoroughness. ◆'G~ung, f -/-en foundation; establishment; formation.
**grunzen** ['gruntsən], v.i. (haben) to
grunt.
**Gruppe** ['grupə], f -/-n group; (Team)
team (of experts etc.). ◆'G~en-,
comb.fm. group (therapy, pictures etc.).
◆'G~enreise, f package tour.
◆'g~enweise, adv. in groups.
◆g~ieren [gru'pi:rən], v.tr. to group
sich g., to form a group/groups.
◆'g~ierung, f -/-en grouping.
**Grusel-** ['gru:zəl-], comb.fm. horror (film,
story etc.). ◆'g~ig, adj. spine-chilling,
F: scary. ◆g~n. I. v.impers. & refl.
ihm gruselte/er gruselte sich, it gave
him the creeps. II. G., n -s/no pl F: the
creeps.
**Gruß** [gru:s], m -es/-e greeting; Mil: salute; einen G. an Ihre Frau! (kind) regards to your wife! mit freundlichen
G~en Ihr ..., yours sincerely ...; liebe
G~e Dein ..., yours ...; love from ...

**grüßen** ['gry:sən], *v.tr. & i.* (*haben*) (*a*) to greet (s.o.), say hello to (s.o.); *Mil:* to salute (an officer); **grüß dich!** hello! **grüß Gott!** good morning/afternoon/evening; (*b*) **g. Sie ihn (herzlich) von mir,** give him my regards.

**Grütze** ['grytsə], *f -/-n* gruel; **rote G.,** red jelly.

**guck|en** ['gukən], *v.i.* (*haben*) *F:* to look; ◆'**G~loch,** *n* peep-hole.

**Gulasch** ['gulaʃ], *n -(e)s/-e & -s* goulash.

**gültig** ['gyltiç], *adj.* valid; (*Gesetz*) in force; **der Fahrplan ist ab 1. Mai g.,** the timetable comes into effect on 1st May. ◆'**G~keit,** *f -/no pl* validity.

**Gummi** ['gumi]. 1. *m & n -s/-s* rubber. 2. (*Harz, Klebstoff*) gum. ◆'**G~band,** *n* rubber/elastic band. ◆'**G~baum,** *m* rubber plant. ◆**g~eren** [gu'mi:rən], *v.tr.* (*a*) to gum (paper etc.); (*b*) to rubberize (fabric etc.). ◆**G~erung,** *f -/-en* 1. (*a*) gumming; (*b*) rubberizing. 2. (*a*) gum (on envelopes etc.); (*b*) rubber coating. ◆'**G~knüppel,** *m* rubber truncheon. ◆'**G~stiefel,** *m* gumboot; *Brit:* wellington. ◆'**G~zelle,** *f* padded cell.

**Gunst** [gunst], *f -/no pl* favour; **zu j-s G~en,** in s.o.'s favour.

**günst|ig** ['gynstiç], *adj.* (*vorteilhaft*) favourable; (*passend*) convenient (time, position etc.); **im g~sten Falle,** at best; **etwas g. kaufen,** to buy sth. at a good price.

**Gurgel** ['gurgəl], *f -/-n* throat. ◆'**g~n,** *v.i.* (*haben*) to gargle.

**Gurke** ['gurkə], *f -/-n* (*Salatg.*) cucumber; **saure/eingelegte G~n,** pickled gherkins.

**gurren** ['gurən], *v.i.* (*haben*) to coo.

**Gurt** [gurt], *m -(e)s/-e* (*Gürtel*) belt; *Aut: Av:* seat belt. ◆'**g~en,** *v.i. Aut:* to put on one's seat belt.

**Gürtel** ['gyrtəl], *m -s/-* belt; (*also Fig:*) **den G. enger schnallen,** to tighten one's belt. ◆'**G~linie,** *f* waistline; **Schlag unter die G.,** blow below the belt. ◆'**G~reifen,** *m* radial(-ply) tyre. ◆'**G~rose,** *f* shingles.

**Guß** [gus], *m -sses/-sse* 1. (*a*) (*Gießen*) founding, casting; (*b*) (*Erzeugnis*) casting. 2. gush, stream (of water etc.); *F:* (*Regeng.*) downpour. 3. *Cu:* icing, *N.Am:* frosting. ◆'**g~eisen,** *n* cast iron. ◆'**g~eisern,** *adj* cast-iron.

**gut1** [gu:t]. **I.** *adj.* good; **g. zu j-m sein,** to be good (*gütig*) kind to s.o.; **sei so gut und mach die Tür zu,** would you mind shutting the door; **sich im g~en einigen,** to come to an amicable agreement; **ihm ist schlecht g.,** he is not feeling well; **wozu ist das g.?** (i) what's the good of that? (ii) what's that for?; **Ende g., alles g.,** all's well that ends well; **g~en Morgen,** good morning; **g~e Reise/Fahrt!** have a good journey! **g~en Appetit!** enjoy your meal! **g~es Neues Jahr,** happy New Year; **so g. wie sicher,** as

good as certain; **so g. wie gar nichts,** hardly anything; **wir wollen es g. sein lassen,** let's leave it at that; **eine g~e Stunde/ein g~es Pfund,** a good hour/ pound; **das G~e daran ist, daß ...,** the good thing about it is that ... **II.** *adv.* well; **eine g. angezogene Frau,** a well-dressed woman; **sie sieht g. aus,** (i) (*schön*) she is good-looking; (ii) (*gesund*) she looks well; **ich fühle mich nicht g.,** I don't feel well; **das kann ich g. verstehen,** I can well understand that; **er hat es g. bei seiner Mutter,** he is well off living with his mother; **das ist g. möglich/kann gut sein,** that could well be; *F:* **mach's g.!** see you! **das riecht/ schmeckt g.,** that smells/tastes good. ◆'**G~achten,** *n -s/-* (expert) opinion, report. ◆'**G~achter,** *m -s/-* expert, consultant. ◆**g~artig,** *adj.* good-natured; *Med:* benign. ◆'**g~aussehend,** *adj.* good-looking. ◆'**g~bürgerlich,** *adj.* solidly middle-class (family etc.); plain (food, accommodation). ◆'**G~dünken,** *n -s/no pl* discretion; **nach (eigenem) G.,** as one thinks fit. ◆'**g~gehen,** *v.i.v.sep.irr.36* (*haben*) (*Sache*) to go well; **es geht mir gut,** (i) I am getting along nicely; (ii) (*gesundheitlich*) I am well. ◆'**g~gelaunt,** *adj.* good-humoured. ◆'**g~gemeint,** *adj.* well-meant. ◆'**g~gläubig,** *adj. Jur:* acting/ (*Sache*) done in good faith. ◆'**G~haben,** *n -s/- Com:* credit. ◆'**g~heißen,** *v.tr. sep.irr.49* to approve. ◆'**g~herzig,** *adj.* kind (-hearted). ◆'**g~machen,** *v.tr.sep.* to make up for (a mistake, wrong etc.) (**an j-m,** to s.o.); to make good, repair (damage). ◆'**g~mütig,** *adj.* good-natured. ◆'**G~mütigkeit,** *f -/no pl* good nature. ◆'**G~schein,** *m* voucher; (*für zurückgegebene Ware*) credit note; (*Geschenkg.*) gift token. ◆'**g~schreiben,** *v.tr.sep.irr.12 Fin:* to credit. ◆'**g~schrift,** *f* credit; (*Bescheinigung*) credit note. ◆'**g~situiert,** *adj.* well off. ◆'**g~tun,** *v.i.v.sep.irr.106* j-m, etwas *dat* **g.,** to do s.o. sth. good. ◆'**g~willig,** *adj.* willing; (*wohlgesinnt*) well-disposed.

**Gut2,** *n -(e)s/-er* 1. (*Besitz*) property; **irdische Güter,** worldly goods. 2. (*Landgut*) estate. ◆'**G~sherr,** *m* landowner. ◆'**G~shof,** *m* estate.

**Güte** ['gy:tə], *f -/no pl* 1. (*Herzensg.*) kindness, goodness; **ein Vorschlag zur G.,** a conciliatory proposal. 2. (*Qualität*) quality. ◆'**G~klasse,** *f Com:* grade (of product).

**Güter-** ['gy:tər-], *comb.fm.* goods, *esp. N.Am:* freight (train, traffic, transport etc.). ◆'**G~abfertigung,** *f* dispatch of goods/freight. ◆'**G~bahnhof,** *m* goods/freight depot. ◆'**G~wagen,** *m* goods wagon; *N.Am:* freight car.

**gütig** ['gy:tiç], *adj.* kind, kind-hearted.

◆'g~lich, *adj.* amicable; *adv.* sich g.
einigen, to come to an amicable agreement.
Gymnasium [gym'nɑ:zium], *n* -s/-ien
*approx.* = grammar/*N.Am:* high
school.

Gymnast|ik [gym'nastik], *f -/no pl* keep-
fit exercises, *Sch:* P.E; (*Turnen*) gymnastics. ◆g~isch, *adj.* gymnastic.
Gynäkolog|e [gyncko'lo:gə], *m* -n/-n gy-
naecologist. ◆G~ie [-lo'gi:], *f -/no pl*
gynaecology.

# H

**H,h** [hɑ:], *n* -/-. (the letter) H, h.
**Haar** [hɑ:r]. I. *n* -(e)s/-e hair; *pl* H~e, (i)
*coll.* hair; (ii) (*einzelne*) hairs; sich *dat*
das H./die H~e waschen, to wash one's
hair; um ein H. wäre ich gestürzt, I
very nearly fell; j-m aufs H. gleichen, to
be the spitting image of s.o. II. 'H~-,
*comb.fm.* hair (dryer etc.). ◆'H~-
bürste, *f* hairbrush. ◆'h~en, *v.i.*
(haben) sich h., to lose hairs.
◆'H~esbreite, *f* um H., by a hair's
breadth. ◆'h~ge'nau, *adj.* precise;
(*detailliert*) in minute detail. ◆'h~ig,
*adj.* 1. hairy. 2. *F:* tricky (business etc.).
◆'H~nadel, *f* hairpin. ◆'h~'scharf,
*adv.* das Auto fuhr h. an ihm vorbei,
the car missed him by a hair's breadth.
◆'H~schnitt, *m* haircut; (*Frisur*) hairstyle. ◆H~spalte'rei, *f -/-en* hairsplit-
ting. ◆'H~spange, *f* hairslide.
◆'h~sträubend, *adj.* (*a*) hair-raising;
(*b*) *Pej:* appalling, (*unglaublich*) incredible.
**Hab|e** ['hɑ:bə], *f -/no pl* belongings.
◆'h~en, *v.tr.irr.* (*a*) to have, (*b*) (*a*) to have
got (children, patience, blue eyes etc.);
Eile/es eilig h., to be in a hurry; was
hast du? what is the matter (with you)?
ich habe Hunger/Durst, I am hungry/
thirsty; (*b*) (*enthalten*) ein Meter hat tausend Millimeter, there are a thousand
millimetres in a metre; (*c*) bei euch hatten wir es gut, we were well off with
you; er hat es nicht leicht, it's not easy
for him; er hat etwas Unheimliches (an
sich), there is something sinister about
him; er hat etwas mit ihr, he is carrying
on with her; er hat nichts davon, he
doesn't get anything out of it; das hat
man davon, that's what comes of it.
◆H~gier ['hɑ:pgi:r], *f -/no pl* greed;
(*für den Besitz anderer*) covetousness.
◆'h~gierig, *adj.* greedy. ◆H~se-
ligkeiten, *fpl* belongings. ◆'H~sucht,
*f Pej:* (obsessive) greed. ◆'h~süchtig,
*adj. Pej:* (obsessively) greedy.
**Habicht** ['hɑ:biçt], *m* -s/-e hawk.
**Hachse** ['haksə], *f -/-n Cu:* knuckle (of
veal/pork).
**Hacke**[1] ['hakə], *f -/-n* 1. *Agr:* hoe, mat-
tock. 2. pickaxe. ◆'h~en, *v.* 1. *v.tr.*
(*a*) to chop (meat, vegetables, wood etc.);
to hack (sth., a hole) (in + *acc*, in); (*b*) to
hoe (the ground). 2. *v.i.* (haben) (*Vogel*)
to peck (nach + *dat* h., at s.o.).
◆'H~fleisch, *n* mince, minced/*N.Am:*

ground meat.
**'Hacke**[2], *f -/-n/*'H~n, *m* -s/- heel.
**Hafen** ['hɑ:fən]. I. *m* -s/= harbour;
(*H~stadt*) port. II. 'H~-, *comb.fm.* harbour (basin etc.); port (authority etc.).
dock (area etc.). ◆'H~arbeiter, *m*
docker. ◆'H~damm, *m* harbour mole.
◆'H~stadt, *f* port.
**Hafer** ['hɑ:fər], *m* -s/no *pl* oats.
◆'H~brei, *m* porridge. ◆'H~-
flocken, *fpl* porridge oats.
**Haft** [haft], *f -/no pl Jur:* custody, detention. ◆'h~bar, *adj. Jur:* liable.
◆'H~befehl, *m* (arrest) warrant.
◆'h~en, *v.i.* (haben) (*a*) an etwas *dat*
h., to stick/(*Staub, Geruch*) cling to sth.
(*b*) für j-n, etwas h., to be liable for s.o.,
sth. ◆'h~enbleiben, *v.i.sep. irr.*12
(*sein*) an etwas *dat* h., to stick/cling to
sth. ◆'H~pflicht, *f* liability.
◆'H~pflichtversicherung, third party
insurance. ◆'H~ung, *f -/-en* 1.
liability. 2. *Tchn:* adhesion.
**Häftling** ['hɛftliŋ], *m* -s/-e detainee.
**Hagebutte** ['hɑ:gəbutə], *f -/-n* rosehip.
**Hagel** ['hɑ:gəl], *m* -s/no *pl* hail.
◆'H~korn, *m* hailstone. ◆'h~n,
*v.i.impers.* (haben) to hail.
**hager** ['hɑ:gər], *adj.* gaunt; scraggy
(neck).
**Hahn** [hɑ:n], *m* -(e)s/=e 1. cock. 2. (*Was-*
*serh. usw.*) tap; *N.Am:* faucet.
**Hai(fisch)** ['hai(fiʃ)], *m* -(e)s/-e shark.
**Häk|chen** ['hɛ:kçən], *n* -s/- (*a*) little
hook; (*b*) (*Zeichen*) tick, *N.Am:* check.
◆h~eln ['hɛ:kəln], *v.tr.* to crochet.
◆'H~elnadel, crochet hook.
**Haken** ['hɑ:kən] *m* -s/- (*a*) hook; peg (for
a hat etc.); (*b*) *Fig:* (*Nachteil*) snag.
◆'H~kreuz, swastika. ◆'H~nase,
hooked nose.
**halb** [halp]. I. *adj. & adv.* half; die h~e
Nacht, half the night; eine h~e Stunde,
half an hour; h. eins, half-past twelve; h.
soviel, half as much. II. 'H~-, 'H~-,
*comb.fm.* (*a*) half-(brother, moon etc.);
(*b*) semi-(darkness etc.). ◆'H~finale, *n*
semi-final. ◆'H~heit, *f -/-en* (*a*) half-
heartedness; (*b*) *esp. pl.* H~en, half-
measures. ◆'h~ieren, *v.tr.* to halve
(sth.); (*schneiden*) to cut (sth.) in half.
◆'H~insel, *f* peninsula. ◆'H~jahr, *n*
half-year. ◆'h~jährlich, *adj.* half-
yearly. ◆'H~kreis, *m* semicircle.
◆'H~kugel, *f* hemisphere. ◆'h~-
lang, *adj.* half-length (skirt etc.).

◆'h~**laut**, *adj.* low (voice).
◆'H~**schuh**, *m* shoe. ◆'H~**starke(r)**, *m decl. as adj.* teddy boy, *N.Am:* hood.
◆'h~**tags**, *adv.* **h. arbeiten**, to work part-time. ◆'H~**tagsarbeit/'H~tagsbeschäftigung**, *f* part-time work.
◆'h~**trocken**, *adj.* medium dry (wine etc.). ◆'h~**wegs**, *adv.* fairly, *N.Am:* halfway. ◆'h~**wüchsig**, *adj* adolescent; **ein H~wüchsiger/eine H~wüchsige**, an adolescent. ◆'H~**zeit**, *f Sp:* half-time; (*Spielhälfte*) half.
**Halde** ['haldə], *f -/-n Min:* tip, slag heap.
**Hälfte** ['hɛlftə], *f -/-n* half; **die H. des Personals**, half the staff.
**Halfter**[1] ['halftər], *m -s/- (Pferdeh.)* halter.
**Halfter**[2], *m -s/- (für eine Pistole)* holster.
**hallen** ['halən], *v.i.* (*haben*) to resound (*widerhallen*) to echo.
**Halle** ['halə], *f -/-n* (*a*) hall, vestibule; (hotel) lobby; (*b*) *Sp:* indoor arena; (*c*) *Av:* hangar. ◆'H~**nbad**, *n* indoor swimming pool.
**hallo** ['halo]. *int.* (*a*) hey! (*b*) *Tel: etc:* hello.
**Halluzination** [halutsinatsi'o:n], *f -/-en* hallucination.
**Halm** [halm], *m -(e)s/-e* blade (of grass); (*Getreideh.*) stalk.
**Hals** [hals], *m -es/ʺe* (*a*) neck; **H. über Kopf verliebt sein**, to be head over heels in love; **j-n auf dem H. haben**, to be saddled with s.o.; (*b*) (*Kehle*) throat; **aus vollem H. schreien**, to shout at the top of one's voice. ◆'H~**band**, *n* (dog etc.) collar. ◆'h~**brecherisch**, *adj.* breakneck (speed etc.). ◆'H~**kette**, necklace. ◆'H~-'**Nasen-'Ohren-Arzt**, *m* ear nose and throat specialist. ◆'H~**schlagader**, *f* carotid artery. ◆'H~**schmerzen**, *mpl* **H. haben**, to have a sore throat. ◆'h~**starrig**, *adj.* obstinate, stubborn, *F:* pigheaded. ◆'H~**tuch**, *n* scarf. ◆'H~**weh**, *n -s/no pl* sore throat.
**Halt**[1] [halt], *m -(e)s/-e* **1.** hold; *Fig:* **keinen H. haben**, to be unstable. **2.** stop, halt; **H. machen**, to stop, (*kurz*) pause. ◆'h~**bar**, *adj.* **1.** (*a*) durable (goods), hard-wearing (clothing etc.); (*b*) (*Essen*) non-perishable. **2.** tenable (argument etc.). ◆'H~**barkeit**, *f -/no pl* durability; keeping quality (of food). ◆'h~**en**, *v. irr.* **1.** *v.tr.* (*a*) to hold (s.o., sth.); (*zurückh.*) to retain (sth.); (*aufh.*) to stop (s.o.); (*b*) (*beibehalten*) to keep, maintain (a distance, course etc.); to hold (prices); (*einh.*) to keep (a promise, one's word); (*c*) (*abh.*) to hold (a meeting); to give (a lecture, talk), make (a speech); (*d*) (*Meinung*) **j-n für ehrlich, usw. h.**, to think s.o. is honest etc.; **ich halte nicht viel davon**, I don't think much of it; (*e*) **sich h.**, (*Essen*) to keep (fresh); (*Blumen*) to last; *Fig:* **sich an j-n h.**, to turn to s.o.;

**sich an die Vorschriften h.**, to stick to the rules. **2.** *v.i.* (*haben*) (*a*) (*Seil, Klebstoff usw.*) to hold, stay (in position); *Fig:* **zu j-m halten**, to remain loyal to s.o.; (*b*) (*Blumen*) to last; (*Wetter*) to stay fine; (*c*) (*haltmachen*) to stop; (**sich**) **links/rechts h.**, to keep left/right. ◆'H~**erung**, *f -/-en Tchn:* mounting; clamp. ◆'H~**estelle**, *f* (bus etc.) stop. ◆'H~**everbot**, *n* parking ban. ◆'h~**los**, *adj.* **1.** (*Pers.*) unstable. **2.** groundless, unfounded (accusation etc.). ◆'h~**machen**, *v.i.* (*haben*) (to make a) halt, stop. ◆'H~**ung**, *f -/-en* **1.** (*des Körpers*) posture. **2.** (*Einstellung*) attitude. **3.** (*Fassung*) composure, poise.
**halt**[2], *adv. South G:* just, simply.
**Halunke** [ha'luŋkə], *m -n/-n* rogue, scoundrel.
**hämisch** ['hɛːmiʃ], *adj.* malicious; malevolent (look).
**Hammel** ['haməl], *m -s/-* (*a*) (male) sheep, ram; (*b*) *Cu:* (*also* **H~fleisch**, *n*) mutton. ◆'H~**keule**, *f* leg of mutton.
**Hammer** ['hamər], *m -s/ʺ* hammer. ◆'H~**werfen**, *n -s/no pl* throwing the hammer.
**hämmern** ['hɛmərn], *v.tr. & i.* to hammer.
**Hämorrhoiden** [hɛmɔro'i:dən], *fpl* piles, haemorrhoids.
**Hampelmann** ['hampəlman], *m* (*a*) jumping jack; (*b*) *Fig:* (*Pers.*) puppet.
**Hamster** ['hamstər], *m -s/-* hamster. ◆'H~**er**, *m -s/-* hoarder. ◆'h~**n**, *v.tr.* to hoard (food etc.).
**Hand** [hant]. **I.** *f -/ʺe* hand; **j-m die H. geben/schütteln**, to shake hands with s.o.; **mit der H. nähen, schreiben usw.**, to sew, write etc. by hand; **etwas in die H~e bekommen**, to get hold of sth.; *Com:* **zu H~en von Herrn X**, for the attention of Mr. X; *Fig:* **unter der H.**, in secret; **sich mit H~en und Füßen wehren**, to fight tooth and nail; **j-n in der H. haben**, to have s.o. at one's mercy; **etwas zur H. haben**, to have sth. on hand/*F:* handy; **das liegt auf der H.**, that is perfectly obvious; **Waren aus zweiter H.**, second-hand goods; **an H. von +** *dat*, by means of (examples etc.); **das ist ohne H. und Fuß**, it doesn't make sense. **II.** '**H~-**, *comb.fm.* (*a*) hand (luggage, -cart, -stand etc.); (*b*) manual (worker, control etc.). ◆'H~**arbeit**, *f* **1.** manual work. **2.** handicraft, *esp.* needlework. ◆'H~**bewegung**, *f* movement of the hand; gesture. ◆'H~**ball**, *m* handball. ◆'H~**bremse**, *f* handbrake. ◆'H~**buch**, *n* handbook, *esp. Tchn:* manual. ◆'h~**fest**, *adj.* **1.** sturdy, robust (person). **2.** substantial (meal); solid (proof); sound (argument); tangible (result). ◆'h~**gearbeitet**, *adj.* handmade. ◆'H~**gelenk**, *n* wrist. ◆'H~**gemenge**, brawl, scuffle. ◆'h~**geschrieben**, *adj.* handwritten. ◆'h~-

**greiflich**, *adj.* 1. manifest, obvious (lie), palpable (proof, success etc.). 2. (*Pers.*) h. **werden**, to become violent. ◆'H~**griff**, *m* operation. ◆'h~**haben**, *v.tr.insep.irr.44* to handle. ◆'H~**habung**, *f* -/-en handling. ◆'H~**langer**, *m* -s/- *Pej:* henchman, F: stooge. ◆'h~**lich**, *adj.* handy, easy to manage. ◆'H~**pflege**, *f* manicure. ◆'H~**schelle**, *f* handcuff. ◆'H~**schlag**, handshake. ◆'H~**schrift**, *f* handwriting. ◆'H~**schuh**, *m* glove. ◆'H~**schuhfach**, *m* glove compartment. ◆'H~**streich**, *m* surprise attack/raid. ◆'H~**tasche**, *f* handbag. ◆'H~**teller**, *m* palm. ◆'H~**tuch**, *n* towel. ◆'H~**voll**, *f* -/*no pl* handful. ◆'h~**warm**, *adj.* lukewarm. ◆'H~**wäsche**, *f* 1. washing by hand. 2. hand-laundry. ◆'H~**werk**, *n* craft; (*Gewerbe*) trade. ◆'H~**werker**, *m* -s/- craftsman. ◆'h~**werklich**, *adj.* (skill etc.) of the craftsman. ◆'H~**werkzeug**, *n* toolkit; *esp. Fig:* tools (of the trade). ◆'H~**zettel**, *m* handbill.

**Händedruck** ['hɛndədruk], *m* handshake.

**Handel** ['handəl], *m* -s/*no pl* (*a*) trade, commerce; (*b*) (business) deal. ◆'h~**n**, *v.i.* (*haben*) (*a*) **mit etwas** *dat* h., to deal/trade in sth.; **um etwas** *acc* h., to bargain for/haggle over sth.; (*b*) to act, take action; (*c*) **wovon handelt dieses Buch?** what is this book about? **um was/worum handelt es sich?** what's it all about? ◆'H~**s-**, *comb.fm.* (*a*) trade (agreement, deficit, register, policy etc.); trading (relations, partner); (*b*) commercial (attaché, law, weight, centre etc.); (*c*) merchant (bank, fleet etc.). ◆'H~**sbilanz**, *f* balance of trade. ◆'h~**seinig**, *adj.* h. **werden/sein**, to agree on terms. ◆'H~**skammer**, *f* Chamber of Commerce. ◆'H~**smarine**, *f* merchant navy. ◆'H~**sreisende(r)**, *m* commercial traveller, *N.Am:* travelling salesman. ◆'H~**sschule**, *f* commercial/*esp.N.Am:* business school. ◆'h~**süblich**, *adj.* customary in the trade; commercial (size). ◆'H~**svertreter**, *m* commercial agent. ◆'H~**svertretung**, *f* trade mission.

**Händler** ['hɛndlər], *m* -s/- dealer.

**Handlung** ['handluŋ], *f* -/-en 1. (*Tat*) action. 2. plot (of a play, novel etc.); storyline. ◆'H~**sweise**, *f* course of action; (*Benehmen*) conduct.

**Hanf** [hanf], *m* -(e)s/*no pl* hemp.

**Hang** [haŋ], *m* -(e)s/-e 1. slope; (*Bergh.*) hillside. 2. *no pl* (*Neigung*) inclination.

**Hänge-** ['hɛŋə-], *comb.fm.* hanging (lamp, cupboard etc.); *Constr:* suspension (bridge etc.). ◆'H~**matte**, *f* hammock. ◆'h~**n**, *v.* 1. *v.i.irr.* (*haben*) (*a*) to hang; **an der Wand/der Decke** *dat* h., to hang on the wall/from the ceiling; (*b*)

(*gern haben*) **an j-m, etwas** *dat* h., to be attached to s.o., sth. 2. *v.tr.* to hang (sth.) (**an/in etwas** *acc*, on/in sth.). ◆'h~**nbleiben**, *v.i.sep.irr.12* (*sein*) (*Kleid usw.*) to catch, get caught (**an etwas** *dat*, on sth.); (*Pers., Bemühungen usw.*) to get stuck; **im Gedächtnis h.**, to stick (in one's mind). ◆'H~**schloß**, *n* padlock.

**Hannover** [ha'no:fər]. *Pr.n.n* -s. Hanover.

**Hänsel|ei** [hɛnzə'lai], *f* -/-en teasing remark(s). ◆'h~**n**, *v.tr.* to tease (s.o.).

**Hantel** ['hantəl], *f* -/-n dumb-bell.

**hantieren** [han'ti:rən], *v.i.* (*haben*) to busy oneself; **mit einem Messer h.**, to handle a knife.

**hapern** ['ha:pərn], *v.i.impers.* (*haben*) **es hapert an etwas** *dat*, there is a shortage/lack of sth.

**Happen** ['hapən], *m* -s/e morsel, mouthful.

**happig** ['hapiç], *adj.* F: steep, stiff (prices etc.).

**Harfe** ['harfə], *f* -/-n harp.

**Harke** ['harkə], *f* -/-n rake. ◆'h~**n**, *v.tr.* to rake (the soil etc.).

**harmlos** ['harmlo:s], *adj.* harmless, innocuous (person, remark etc.); innocent (pleasure, question etc.); slight (cold etc.). ◆'H~**igkeit**, *f* -/*no pl* harmlessness; innocence.

**Harmon|ie** [harmo'ni:], *f* -/-n harmony. ◆h~**ieren** [-'ni:rən], *v.i.* (*haben*) (*Klänge*) to be harmonious; (*Farben*) to match; **mit j-m h.**, to get on (well) with s.o. ◆H~**ika** [-'mo:nika], *f* -/-s (*Mundh.*) mouth-organ, harmonica; (*Ziehh.*) accordion. ◆h~**isch** [-'mo:niʃ], *adj.* harmonious (music, colours, *Fig:* atmosbere etc.).

**Harn** [harn], *m* -(e)s/-e urine. ◆'H~**blase**, *f* bladder.

**Harnisch** ['harniʃ], *m* -(e)s/-e 1. (suit of) armour. 2. **j-n in H. bringen**, to infuriate s.o.

**Harpune** [har'pu:nə], *f* -/-n harpoon.

**harsch** [harʃ]. I. *adj.* harsh. II. H., *m* -s/ *no pl* crusted snow.

**hart** [hart]. I. *adj.* (*a*) hard; (winter etc.); severe (punishment); harsh (law, conditions etc.); (*b*) (*Pers.*) tough. II. 'H~-, 'h~-, *comb.fm.* hard (rubber, cheese etc.). ◆'h~**gekocht**, *adj.* hard-boiled. ◆'h~**herzig**, *adj.* hard-hearted. ◆'h~**näckig**, *adj.* obstinate, stubborn (person, resistance etc.); persistent (attempts). ◆'H~**näckigkeit**, *f* -/*no pl* obstinacy, stubbornness; persistence.

**Härte** ['hɛrtə], *f* -/-n 1. *no pl* (*a*) hardness; toughness; (*b*) harshness; severity. 2. hardship; privation. ◆'h~**n**, *v.tr.* to harden (a metal, etc.), temper (steel).

**Harz** [harts], *n* -es/-e resin.

**Haschisch** ['haʃiʃ] *n* -s/*no pl* hashish.

**Haschee** [ha'ʃe:], *n* -s/-s hash.

**haschen** ['haʃən], *v.tr.* to snatch, seize (sth.).

**Hase** ['hɑːzə], *m* -n/-n hare. ◆'H~**nfuß**, *m F:* coward. ◆'H~**npfeffer**, *m* jugged hare. ◆'H~**nscharte**, *f* harelip.

**Hasel|maus** ['hɑːzəlmaus], *f* dormouse. ◆'H~**nuß**, *f* hazelnut.

**Haspe** ['haspə], *f* -/-n hasp, hook.

**Haß** [has], *m* -sses/*no pl* hate, hatred (**auf/gegen** j-n, **etwas** *acc,* of/towards s.o., sth.).

**hassen** ['hasən], *v.tr.* to hate (s.o., sth.). ◆'h~**swert**, *adj.* odious.

**häßlich** ['hɛslɪç], *adj.* **1.** (*unschön*) ugly. **2.** (*gemein*) mean, nasty. ◆'H~**keit**, *f* -/-en ugliness, nastiness.

**Hast** [hast], *f* -/*no pl* haste, hurry. ◆'h~**ig**, *adj.* hasty; hurried (steps, meal etc.).

**Haube** ['haubə], *f* -/-n **1.** *Cl:* bonnet; (nurse's) cap; *F:* **unter die H. kommen**, to be married off. **2.** *Aut:* bonnet; *N.Am:* hood.

**Hauch** [haux], *m* -(e)s/-e **1.** (*Atem*) breath; (*Lufth.*) (gentle) breeze. **2.** (*Anflug*) tinge, touch. ◆'h~**dünn**, *adj.* wafer-thin; very fine (thread etc.); sheer (stockings). ◆'h~**en**, *v.i.* (*haben*) to breathe. ◆'h~**fein**, *adj.* extremely delicate/fine.

**hauen** ['hauən], **1.** *v.tr.* (*a*) *F:* (*schlagen*) to bash (s.o., sth.); (*prügeln*) to spank (a child etc.); (*b*) (*schneiden*) to cut/hew (rock, steps etc.). **2.** *v.i.* (*haben*) (**mit etwas** *dat*) **an einen Angreifer h.**, to hit out at an attacker (with sth.); **mit der Faust auf den Tisch h.**, to bang on the table with one's fist.

**Haufen** ['haufən], *m* -s/- **1.** pile, (*unordentlich*) heap; **j-n, etwas über den H. rennen/fahren**, to knock/run s.o., sth. down; **Pläne usw. über den H. werfen**, to upset plans etc. **2.** *F:* (*a*) **ein H. Geld**, a lot of money; (*b*) (*Menschen*) crowd; **der ganze H.**, the whole caboodle. ◆'h~**weise**, *adv. F:* in heaps; (*Menschen*) in droves; **er hat h. Geld**, he's got loads of money.

**häuf|en** ['hɔyfən], *v.tr.* to heap up, pile up (sth.); **sich h.**, (*Briefe usw.*) to pile up; (*Abfälle*) to accumulate. ◆'h~**ig**, *adj.* frequent. ◆'H~**igkeit**, *f* -/*no pl* frequency. ◆'H~**ung**, *f* -/-en **1.** accumulation; piling up. **2.** (*Zunahme*) increase; (greater) frequency (of events).

**Haupt** [haupt]. **I.** *n* -(e)s/¨er *Lit:* head. **II.** 'H~-, *comb.fm.* (*a*) main (attraction, entrance, reason, worry, gate, building, meal, difficulty, theme); principal (aim, purpose etc.); (*b*) (*größere*) major (share, part etc.). ◆'H~**bahnhof**, *m* central/main station. ◆'H~**beruf**, *m* chief occupation; main job. ◆'H~**darsteller(in)**, *m(f)*, leading man/lady. ◆'H~**gewinn**, *m* first prize (in a lottery etc.). ◆'H~**mann**, *m* -(e)s/-leute *Mil:* captain. ◆'H~**person**, *f* (*a*) central/principal character (in a play

etc.); (*b*) most important person. ◆'H~**post**, *f* main/central post office. ◆'H~**quartier**, *n* headquarters. ◆'H~**rolle**, *f* leading role; main part. ◆'H~**sache**, *f* main thing; (*Frage*) main point. ◆'h~**sächlich**, *adj.* main, chief (question etc.); *adv.* mainly, chiefly. ◆'H~**saison**, *f* high/full season. ◆'H~**satz**, *m* main clause. ◆'H~**stadt**, *f* capital (city). ◆'H~**straße**, *f* (*a*) main road; (*b*) (*in einer Stadt*) main street. ◆'H~**verkehrszeit**, *f* rush hour. ◆'H~**wort**, *n* noun.

**Häuptling** ['hɔyptlɪŋ], *m* -s/-e chief (of a tribe).

**Haus** [haus]. **I.** *n* -es/¨er **1.** house; (*Gebäude*) building; **nach H~e gehen/kommen**, to go/come home; **zu H~e bleiben**, to stay at home; **außer H. essen**, to eat out; *Fig:* **auf einem Gebiet zu H~e sein**, to be well up in a subject; **aus gutem H~e**, from a good family; **von H~e aus**, by birth; (*ursprünglich*) originally. **2.** *Com:* firm; **er ist nicht im H~e**, he is not on the premises. **3.** *Th:* auditorium. **4.** **H. einer Schnecke**, snail's shell. **II.** 'H~-, *comb.fm.* (*a*) house (arrest, number etc.); (*b*) (*häuslich*) domestic (cat, pig etc.). ◆'H~**angestellte(r)**, *m & f* domestic servant. ◆'H~**apotheke**, *f* medicine chest. ◆'H~**arbeit**, *f* (*a*) housework; (*b*) *Sch:* homework. ◆'H~**arzt**, *m* family doctor. ◆'H~**besetzer**, *m* squatter. ◆'H~**besitzer(in)**, *m(f)* house owner; (*Wirt*) landlord; (*Wirtin*) landlady. ◆'H~**bewohner**, *m* occupier. ◆'h~**en** ['-zən], *v.i.* (*haben*) (*a*) to live, *F:* hang out; (*b*) (*Sturm usw.*) **schlimm h.**, to wreak havoc. ◆'H~**flur**, *m* (entrance) hall; hallway (of flats etc.); (*Gang*) corridor. ◆'H~**frau**, *f* housewife. ◆'h~**gemacht**, *adj.* home-made. ◆'H~**halt**, *m* -(e)s/-e **1.** household. **2.** *Parl:* budget. ◆'h~**halten**, *v.i. sep.irr.45* (*haben*) to be careful (**mit dem Geld usw.**, with one's money etc.); **mit seinen Kräften h.**, to conserve one's energies. ◆'H~**hälterin**, *f* -/-nen housekeeper. ◆'H~**halts-**, *comb.fm.* **1.** household (article, goods, budget etc.); domestic (help etc.). **2.** *Parl:* budget (debate, deficit etc.); budgetary (policy etc.). ◆'H~**haltsgerät**, *n* domestic appliance. ◆'H~**haltsgeld**, *n* housekeeping money. ◆'H~**haltsplan**, *m* budget. ◆'H~**haltung**, *f* **1.** household. **2.** *no pl* (*Führung*) housekeeping. ◆'H~**herr**, *m* householder; master of the house. ◆'h~**hoch**, *adj.* (*a*) towering, huge (flames etc.); (*b*) *Fig:* **haushoher Sieg**, overwhelming victory; **h. gewinnen**, to win hands down. ◆'h~**ieren** ['-ziːrən]. *v.i.* (*haben*) **mit etwas** *dat* **h.**, to sell sth. from door to door. ◆'H~**ierer** ['-ziːrər], *m* -s/- door-to-door salesman.

◆'H~**meister**, *m* caretaker; *N.Am.:* janitor. ◆'H~**ordnung**, *f* house rules. ◆'H~**rat**, *m* -*s*/*no pl* household contents. ◆'H~**schlüssel**, *m* front-door key. ◆'H~**schuh**, *m* slipper. ◆'H~**tier**, *n* domestic animal; (*im Haus*) pet. ◆'H~**suchungsbefehl**, *m* search warrant. ◆'H~**tür**, *f* front door. ◆'H~**verbot**, *n Jur:* order restraining a person from entering (a house etc.). ◆'H~**verwalter**, *m* house agent; property manager. ◆'H~**wirt**, *m* landlord. ◆'H~**wirtin**, *f* landlady. ◆'H~**wirtschaft**, *f* -/*no pl* (*a*) housekeeping; (*b*) (*Fach*) home economics; (*Haushaltsführung*) household management.

**Häus|er-** ['hɔyzər-], *comb.fm.* (block, row etc.) of houses. ◆'H~**ermakler**, *m* estate agent, *N.Am:* realtor. ◆'h~**lich**, *adj.* domestic.

**Haut** [haut], *f* -/*e* (*a*) skin; **mit H. und Haar**, *Fig:* completely, totally; **sich seiner H. wehren**, to put up a stubborn resistance; **aus der H. fahren**, to be hopping mad; (*b*) hide (of a cow, elephant etc.). ◆'H~**arzt**, *m* skin specialist; dermatologist. ◆**h~eng**, *adj.* skin-tight. ◆'H~**farbe**, *f* colour of the skin; (*Teint*) complexion. ◆'h~**nah**, *adj.* **1.** *Sp:* close (marking etc.). **2.** *F:* graphic, sensational (description etc.).

**häuten** ['hɔytən], *v.tr.* (*a*) to skin, flay (an animal); (*b*) **sich h.**, (*Tier*) to shed its skin.

**Haxe** ['haksə], *f* -/-*n* = Hachse.

**Hebamme** ['he:pʔamə], *f* -/-*n* midwife.

**Heb|el** ['he:bəl], *m* -*s*/- lever. ◆'H~**elwirkung**, *f* leverage; purchase. ◆**h~en** ['he:bən], *v.tr.irr.* (*haben*) to lift (s.o., one's hand, a weight etc.), lift up (a child etc.), raise (one's arm, a glass, *Th:* the curtain, *Fig:* one's voice etc.).

**Hecht** [hɛçt], *m* -(*e*)*s*/-*e* pike.

**Heck** [hɛk]. **I.** *n* -(*e*)*s*/-*e & *-*s Nau:* stern; *Av:* tail; *Aut:* rear. **II.** 'H~-, *comb.fm.* *Aut:* etc: rear (drive, engine etc.). ◆'H~**scheibe**, *f* rear window. ◆'H~**tür**, *f* tailgate.

**Hecke** ['hɛkə], *f* -/-*n* hedge. ◆'H~**nrose**, *f* -/-*n* briar/dog rose. ◆'H~**nschere**, *f* garden shears, *esp.* hedge-clippers.

**Heer** [he:r], *n* -(*e*)*s*/-*e* (*a*) *Mil:* army; (*b*) *Fig:* host, multitude, *Pej:* horde (of people, insects etc.).

**Hefe** ['he:fə], *f* -/-*n* yeast. ◆'H~**teig**, *m* leavened dough.

**Heft** [hɛft], *n* -(*e*)*s*/-*e* (*a*) *Sch:* exercise book; (*b*) (*von Zeitschrift*) copy, issue; (*c*) (paper-covered) booklet; (*Prospekt*) brochure. ◆'h~**en**, *v.tr.* (*a*) to tack (a hem etc.); to stitch (a book); (*b*) to fasten, (*mit Klammer*) clip, (*maschinell*) staple, (*mit Nadel*) pin (sheets of paper etc.) together; (*c*) **etwas an etwas** *acc* **h.**, to fasten/clip/pin sth. to sth. ◆'H~**er**,

*m* -*s*/- folder. ◆'H~**klammer**, *f* **1.** staple. **2.** (*Büroklammer*) paper clip. ◆'H~**maschine**, *f* stapler. ◆'H~**pflaster**, *n* sticking plaster. ◆'H~**zwecke**, *f* -/-*n* drawing pin; *N.Am:* thumbtack.

**heftig** ['hɛftiç], *adj.* violent; fierce (argument, blow, storm etc.); heavy (rain, snow); furious, vehement (attack). ◆'H~**keit**, *f* -/-*en* violence, fierceness; fury, ferocity (of a storm, an attack); vehemence.

**hegen** ['he:gən], *v.tr.* (*a*) to conserve, protect (young game etc.); to nurse, tend (plants etc.); (*b*) *Lit:* to harbour (a grudge etc.); cherish (a desire).

**Hehl** [he:l], *m & n* kein(en) H. aus etwas *dat* machen, to make no secret of sth. ◆'H~**er(in)**, *m* -*s*/- (*f* -/-nen) receiver (of stolen goods), *F:* fence.

**Heide**[1] ['haidə], *f* -/-*n* **1.** heath; (*große Fläche*) moor. **2.** = **H~kraut**. ◆'H~**kraut**, *n* heather. ◆'H~**lbeere**, *f* bilberry.

**Heid|e**[2], *m* -*n*/-*n*/'**Heidin**, *f* -/-nen heathen, pagan. ◆'H~**en-**, *comb.fm.* *F:* terrific (noise, fright etc.). ◆'H~**en'angst**, *f F:* **eine H. haben**, to be scared to death. ◆'H~**entum**, *n* -*s*/*no pl* paganism; heathendom. ◆'h~**nisch**, *adj.* heathen, pagan.

**heikel** ['haikəl], *adj.* awkward, tricky (problem, situation etc.); delicate, difficult (matter).

**heil** [hail]. **I.** *adj.* (*a*) unhurt; (*sicher*) safe; (*b*) (*Sache*) intact, undamaged (house etc.); unbroken (cup etc.); *Fig:* **eine h~e Welt**, a perfect world. **II. H.,** *n* -*s*/*no pl Lit:* welfare, well-being; *Ecc:* salvation. **III.** 'H~-, *comb.fm.* healing, *Med:* therapeutic (power, process etc.); medicinal (herbs, plants etc.); (method etc.) of treatment. ◆'H~**and**, *m* -(*e*)*s*/*no pl* Saviour. ◆'h~**bar**, *adj.* curable. ◆'h~**en**, *v.* **1.** *v.tr.* to cure (s.o., a disease), heal (a wound, fracture etc.). **2.** *v.i.* (*sein*) (*Wunde usw.*) to heal. ◆'h~**froh**, *adj.* *F:* **h. sein**, to be mightily relieved. ◆'h~**ig**, *adj.* holy (baptism, land etc.); sacred (songs etc.). ◆'H~**ig'abend**, *m* Christmas Eve. ◆'H~**ige(r)**, *m & f decl.* as *adj.* Saint. ◆'h~**igen**, *v.tr.* to hallow, sanctify (s.o., sth.). ◆'H~**igenschein**, *m* (saint's) halo. ◆'H~**igkeit**, *f* -/*no pl* sanctity; *Ecc:* holiness. ◆'h~**igsprechen**, *v.tr.sep.irr.14 Ecc:* to canonize (s.o.). ◆'H~**igtum**, *n* -*s*/*er* (*a*) holy place; *esp. Fig:* shrine; (*b*) (*Gegenstand*) (sacred) relic. ◆'h~**los**, *adj.* unholy (din, muddle, terror); **h. verschuldet**, hopelessly in debt. ◆'H~**mittel**, *n* remedy, cure (**gegen** + *acc*, for). ◆'H~**praktiker**, *m* (non-professional) practitioner of medicine; healer. ◆'h~**sam**, *adj.* salutary. ◆'H~**s-armee**, *f* Salvation Army. ◆'H~**ung**, *f* *f -/-en* cure; healing.

**Heilbutt** ['hailbut], *m* halibut.

**Heim** [haim]. **I.** *n -(e)s/-e* (*a*) home; (*b*) (*Anstalt*) institution; (*für Geisteskranke*) asylum; (*für Studenten*) hostel. ◆'H~at, *f -/no pl* home; (*Land*) homeland; native country; **in meiner H.**, where I come from. ◆'H~at-, *comb.fm.* home (country, town etc.); local, regional (poet etc.); (place, country) of origin/birth. ◆'h~atlich, *adj.* native (customs etc.). ◆'h~atlos, *adj.* homeless (person etc.); stateless (alien). ◆'H~atvertrie-bene(r), *m & f decl. as adj.* displaced person. ◆'h~fahren, *v.i.* (*sein*) to go/travel/drive home. ◆'H~fahrt, *f* journey home. ◆'h~isch, *adj.* (*a*) native (population), indigenous (plants etc.); local, regional (customs, industry etc.); (*b*) home (surroundings etc.); **sich h. fühlen**, to feel at home. ◆'H~kehr, *f* return home, homecoming. ◆'h~kehren, *v.i.sep.* (*sein*) to return home. ◆'h~lich, *adj.* secret. ◆'H~lichkeit, *f -/no pl* secrecy. ◆'H~reise, *f* journey home. ◆'H~spiel, *n* home game. ◆'h~suchen, *v.tr.* (*a*) *F:* **j-n h.**, to descend on s.o.; (*b*) (*Krankheit usw.*) to afflict (s.o., a country etc.). ◆'h~tückisch, *adj.* malicious; *Fig:* insidious (plans etc.). ◆'H~weg, *m* way home. ◆'H~weh, *n -s/no pl* homesickness; **sie hat H.**, she is homesick. ◆'H~werker, *m -s/-* *F:* do-it-yourselfer, handyman. ◆'h~zahlen, *v.tr.sep.* **j-m (etwas) h.**, to pay s.o. back (for sth.).

**Heirat** ['hairaːt], *f -/-en* marriage. ◆'h~en, *v.tr. & i.* (*haben*) to marry (s.o.), get married (to s.o.). ◆'H~santrag, *m* proposal (of marriage); **j-m einen H. machen**, to propose to s.o.

**heiser** ['haizər], *adj.* hoarse. ◆'H~keit, *f -/no pl* hoarseness.

**heiß** [hais], *adj.* **1.** hot (weather, drink etc.); *Geog:* torrid (zone). **2.** (*a*) (*heftig*) fierce (battle, competition, debate etc.); heated (argument); **h. umstritten/umkämpft**, hotly contested; (*b*) *Sp:* hot (favourite, tip). ◆'h~blütig, *adj.* hot-tempered. ◆'h~ersehnt, *adj.* longed-for; eagerly awaited (moment, letter etc.). ◆'H~hunger, *m* voracious appetite. ◆'h~laufen, *v.i.sep.irr.58* (*sein*) (*Motor usw.*) to run hot; (*übermäßig*) to overheat. ◆'H~luft, *f* hot air. ◆'H~-'wasserbereiter, *m* water-heater.

**heißen** ['haisən], *v.irr.* **1.** *v.i.* (*haben*) (*a*) **wie heißt du?** what's your name? **er heißt Peter**, he is called Peter. **es heißt, er sei krank**, I am told he is ill; (*c*) (*bedeuten*) to mean; **wie heißt es auf Englisch?** what is it (called) in English? **was soll das h.!** what is the meaning of this! *F:* what's this in aid of! **2.** *v.tr.* (*nennen*) to call (s.o. one's friend, a liar etc.); **j-n**

**willkommen h.**, to welcome s.o.

**heiter** ['haitər], *adj.* gay, bright; (*froh*) cheerful (mood, face etc.); fine, bright (day, weather), clear (sky). ◆'H~keit, *f -/no pl* cheerfulness; (*Lachen*) merriment.

**Heiz-** ['haits-], *comb.fm.* heating (costs, element, oil, etc.). ◆'h~bar, *adj.* heatable. ◆'H~decke, *f* electric blanket. ◆'h~en, *v.* **1.** *v.tr.* to heat (a room etc.). **2.** *v.i.* (*haben*) to turn on the heating; (*Feuer machen*) to light a fire; **der Ofen heizt gut**, the stove gives plenty of heat. ◆'H~er, *m -s/-* stoker; *Rail:* fireman. ◆'H~gerät, *n* heater. ◆'H~körper, *m* (*a*) (central heating) radiator; (*b*) heating element. ◆'H~lüfter, *m* fan heater. ◆'H~ung, *f -/-en* heating.

**hektisch** ['hɛktiʃ], *adj.* hectic.

**Held** [hɛlt], *m -en/-en* hero. ◆'H~en-[-dən-], *comb.fm.* heroic (saga, epic, *Mus:* tenor etc.). ◆'h~enhaft, *adj.* heroic. ◆'H~entat *f*, heroic deed. ◆'H~in, *f -/-nen* heroine.

**helf|en** ['hɛlfən], *v.i.irr.* (*haben*) (*a*) **j-m h.**, to help/assist s.o.; **ich kann mir nicht h., aber ...**, I can't help it but ...; **sich zu h. wissen**, to know how to cope; (*b*) (*nützen*) to be good/useful; **es hilft nichts**, it's no use. ◆'H~er(in), *m -s/- (f -/-nen)* helper, assistant. ◆'H~ershelfer, *m* accomplice; henchman.

**Helium** ['heːlium], *n -s/no pl* helium.

**hell** [hɛl]. **I.** *adj.* **1.** (*a*) light; (*blaß*) pale (colour, hair, skin etc.); fair (complexion, hair); (*b*) (*strahlend*) bright (colour, light etc.); **h. erleuchtet**, brightly lit; (*c*) **es wird schon h.**, it is getting light; dawn is breaking. **2.** clear (sound, voice etc.). **II.** 'h~-, *comb.fm.* light (blue, yellow etc.). ◆'h~blond, *adj.* very fair (hair). ◆'H~e, *f -/no pl* light, brightness. ◆'h~hörig, *adj.* **1. h. sein**, to have sharp ears; *F:* **h. werden**, to prick up one's ears. **2.** *Arch:* poorly sound-proofed (walls etc.). ◆'H~igkeit, *f -/no pl* brightness; intensity (of light). ◆'H~seher(in), *m -s/- (f -/-nen)* clairvoyant. ◆'h~'wach, *adj.* wide awake.

**Helm** [hɛlm], *m -(e)s/-e* helmet.

**Hemd** [hɛmt], *n -(e)s/-en* shirt; (*Unterh.*) vest; *N.Am:* undershirt. ◆'H~bluse, *f* shirt blouse.

**Hemisphäre** [heːmi'sfɛːrə], *f* hemisphere.

**hemm|en** ['hɛmən], *v.tr.* (*a*) (*Einhalt gebieten*) to halt, stop, (*vorübergehend*) check (a course of events etc.); to stem (the flow); (*b*) (*einschränken*) to inhibit (s.o., development etc.). ◆'H~ung, *f -/-en Psy: etc:* inhibition; (*Bedenken*) scruple. ◆'h~ungslos, *adj.* uninhibited (person).

**Hengst** [hɛnst], *m -(e)s/-e* stallion.

**Henkel** ['hɛnkəl]. **I.** *m -s/-* handle (of a cup/jug). **II.** 'H~-, *comb.fm.* (basket, jug, pot etc.) with a handle.

**Henker** ['hɛnkər], *m -s/-* executioner;

hangman.

**Henne** ['hɛnə], *f* -/-n hen.

**her** [heːr], *adv.* (*a*) (*Richtung*) here; **h. da-mit!** give it to me! **von weit h.**, from a long way off; (*b*) (*Zeitspanne*) ago, since; **es ist lange h.**, it was long ago.

**herab** [hɛ'rap]. *adv.* down, downwards; **die Treppe h.**, down the stairs. ◆**h~hängen**, *v.i.sep.irr.46* (*haben*) (*a*) to hang down; (*b*) (*Beine*) to dangle; (*Kopf*) to droop. ◆**h~lassen**, *v.tr.sep.irr.57* (*a*) to lower, let down (blinds, a boat etc.); (*b*) **sich zu etwas dat h.**, to condescend to do sth. ◆**h~lassend**, *adj.* condescending. ◆**H~lassung**, *f* -*/no pl* condescension. ◆**h~sehen**, *v.i.sep.irr.92* (*haben*) to look down. ◆**h~setzen**, *v.tr.sep.* (*a*) to reduce (price etc.); (*b*) (*schmälern*) to belittle. ◆**H~setzung**, *f* -/-en (*a*) reduction (**des Preises usw.**, in price etc.); (*b*) disparagement. ◆**h~würdigen**, *v.tr.sep.* (*a*) to speak disparagingly of (s.o.); (*b*) to treat (s.o.) degradingly.

**heran** [hɛ'ran]. *adv.* close; **bis an den Rand h.**, right up to the edge/rim. ◆**h~bilden**, *v.tr.sep.* to train, educate (s.o.). ◆**h~bringen**, *v.tr.sep.irr.16* to bring (s.o., sth.) close (**an + acc**, to). ◆**h~führen**, *v.tr.sep.* (*a*) to lead/take (s.o., sth.) up (**an + acc**, to); (*b*) (*einführen*) to introduce (s.o.) (**an ein Thema**, to a subject). ◆**h~gehen**, *v.i.sep.irr.36* (*sein*) (*a*) (*sich nähern*) **h. an + acc**, to go to/approach (s.o., sth.); (*b*) (*beginnen*) **an die Arbeit usw. h.**, to get down to work etc. ◆**h~kommen**, *v.i.sep.irr.53* (*sein*) (*a*) (*Pers., Ereignis*) to approach; to come up (**an + acc**, to); (*b*) (*ergreifen*) **an etwas acc h.**, to get hold of, (*mit Mühe*) get at sth. ◆**h~lassen**, *v.tr.sep.irr.57* **j-n (nahe) h.**, to let s.o. come close (**an + acc** to). ◆**h~machen**, *v.refl.sep.* (*a*) **sich an eine Arbeit h.**, to get down to a job; (*b*) *F:* **sich an j-n h.**, to make up to s.o. ◆**h~reichen**, *v.i.sep.* (*haben*) **h. an + acc**, to reach (sth.), *Fig:* (*gleichkom-men*) be tantamount to (sth.). ◆**h~treten**, *v.i.sep.irr.105* (*sein*) **h. an + acc**, to come up to, approach (s.o., sth.); (*Probleme, Zweifel*) to beset (s.o.). ◆**h~wachsen**, *v.i.sep.irr.107* (*sein*) to grow up (**zu etwas dat**, into sth.). ◆**h~wachsend**, *adj.* adolescent; rising (generation); **ein H~wachsender/eine H~wachsende**, an adolescent. ◆**h~ziehen**, *v.tr.sep.irr.113* (*a*) to draw/pull (s.o., sth.) up (close); (**an + acc**, to); (*b*) to call in (a specialist etc.); to bring in (foreign workers etc.); to consult (a dictionary etc.).

**herauf** [hɛ'rauf]. *adv.* up, upwards. ◆**h~beschwören**, *v.tr.sep.* (*a*) to conjure up, evoke (memories etc.); (*b*) to cause (a disaster, quarrel etc.). ◆**h~bringen**, *v.tr.sep.irr.16* to bring (s.o., sth.) up(stairs). ◆**h~kommen**,

*v.i.sep.irr.53* (*sein*) to come up/upstairs. ◆**h~setzen**, *v.tr. sep.* to increase (prices etc.). ◆**h~ziehen**, *v.sep.irr.113* **1.** *v.tr.* to pull up (sth.). **2.** *v.i.* (*sein*) (*Tag, Nacht*) to approach; (*Gefahr usw.*) to threaten; **ein Gewitter zieht herauf**, a storm is brewing.

**heraus** [hɛ'raus], *adv.* out; (*a*) **aus einer Notlage h. handeln**, to act from necessity; **aus sich h.**, of one's own accord. ◆**h~bekommen**, *v.tr.sep.irr.53* (*a*) to get (sth.) out (**aus etwas dat**, of sth.); (*b*) (*entdecken*) to find (sth.) out. ◆**h~bringen**, *v.tr.sep.irr.16* (*a*) to bring/take (s.o., sth.) out(side); (*b*) to get (an answer, information) (**aus j-m**, out of s.o.). ◆**h~finden**, *v.tr.sep.irr.19* to find out. ◆**H~forderer**, *m* -s/- challenger. ◆**h~fordern**, *v.tr.sep.* to challenge; ◆**H~forderung** challenge. ◆**h~geben**, *v.tr.sep.irr.35* (*a*) to hand (sth.) over, give (sth.) up; (*b*) (*Geld*) **j-m h.**, to give s.o. change; (*c*) (*veröffentlichen*) to publish, (*redigieren*) edit (a book, periodical etc.); to issue (banknotes, stamps etc.). ◆**H~geber**, *m* -s/- editor. ◆**h~gehen**, *v.i.sep.irr.36* (*sein*) to go out (**aus dem Haus**, of the house); *Fig:* **aus sich dat h.**, to come out of one's shell. ◆**h~halten**, *v.tr.sep.irr.45* to keep (s.o.) out (**aus etwas dat**, of sth.). ◆**h~holen**, *v.tr.sep.* to bring/fetch/(*mit Mühe*) get (s.o., sth.) out. ◆**h~kommen**, *v.i.sep.irr.53* (*sein*) (*a*) to come out (**aus + dat**, of); (*b*) (*Buch usw.*) to come out, appear; (*Briefmarken, Münzen*) to be issued; (*c*) (*Geheimnis, Tatsache*) to come out/to light; (*Plan usw.*) to become known; (*d*) (*sich ergeben*) **es wird nichts Gutes dabei h.**, no good will come of it. ◆**h~lassen**, *v.tr.sep.irr.57* to let (s.o.) out, leave (sth.) out. ◆**h~nehmen**, *v.tr.sep.irr.69* (*a*) to take (sth.) out (**aus etwas dat**, of sth.); (*b*) **sich dat zuviel/Freiheiten h.**, to take liberties. ◆**h~ragen**, *v.i.sep.* (*haben*) to project, jut out; *Fig:* to stand out. ◆**h~reißen**, *v.tr.sep.irr.4* (*a*) to tear (sth.) out (**aus etwas dat**, of sth.); *Fig:* to jolt, startle (s.o.) (**aus seiner Lethargie usw.**, out of his lethargy etc.); (*b*) *F:* (*retten*) **j-n h.**, to come to s.o.'s rescue. ◆**h~rücken**, *v.tr. & i.sep.* (*sein*) *F:* to part with (sth., money) (reluctantly); **mit der Sprache h.**, (i) to speak up; (ii) (*etwas gestehen*) to own up. ◆**h~schauen**, *v.i.sep.* (*haben*) to look out; **zum Fenster h.**, to look out of the window. ◆**h~schlagen**, *v.tr.sep.irr.85* (*a*) to knock out (a tooth, partition etc.); (*b*) *F:* **Geld/Vorteile aus j-m, etwas dat h.**, to make money out of/gain an advantage from s.o., sth. ◆**h~sein**, *v.i.sep.irr.93* to be out; **es ist noch nicht heraus, wer gewonnen hat**, it is not yet known who won. ◆**h~springen**, *v.i.sep.irr.96* (*sein*)

(a) to jump out (**aus etwas** *dat*, of sth.); (b) *F:* **bei der Sache springt nichts für mich heraus**, I'll get nothing out of this affair. ◆**h~stellen**, *v.tr.sep.* (a) to put (sth.) out; (b) (*betonen*) to stress (the importance of sth.); (c) **sich h.**, to turn out (**als falsch, ungenügend usw.**, to be wrong, inadequate etc.). ◆**h~suchen**, *v.tr.sep.* to pick out, select (sth.). ◆**h~wachsen**, *v.i.sep.irr.107* (*sein*) to grow out (**aus etwas** *dat*, of sth.); (*Pers.*) **aus den Kleidern h.**, to outgrow one's clothes.

**herb** [hɛrp], *adj.* bitter (taste, *Fig:* loss etc.); tangy, *Pej:* acrid (smell); dry (wine); (*streng*) harsh (words etc.).

**herbei** [hɛr'bai], *adv.* here. ◆**h~eilen**, *v.i.sep.* (*sein*) hurry up to the spot. ◆**h~führen**, *v.tr.sep.* to bring about (a decision, result etc.); to cause (an accident, death etc.); ◆**h~rufen**, *v.tr.sep.irr.74* to summon (s.o.), help etc.). ◆**h~schaffen**, *v.tr.sep.* to get (s.o., sth.) to the spot, *F:* produce (s.o., sth.).

**herbemühen**, *v.tr.sep.* to ask s.o. to come; **sich h.**, to (be so good as to) come.

**Herberg|e** ['hɛrbɛrgə], *f -/-n* (a) lodging; (b) (*Jugendh.*) (youth) hostel. ◆**H~svater**, *m* warden (of a youth hostel).

**herbitten**, *v.tr.sep.irr.10* to ask (s.o.) to come.

**herbringen**, *v.tr.sep.irr.16* to bring (s.o., sth.) (here).

**Herbst** [hɛrpst]. **I.** *m* -(e)s/-e autumn; *N.Am:* fall. **II.** '**H~~**, *comb.fm.* autumn (holidays, colours etc.); autumnal (air, weather etc.). ◆'**h~lich**, *adj.* autumnal.

**Herd** [heːrt], *m* -(e)s/-e 1. (cooking) stove, *Brit:* cooker. 2. centre (of an earthquake, of unrest etc.); *Med:* seat (of an infection), focus (of a disease). ◆'**H~platte**, *f El:* hotplate.

**Herde** ['heːrdə], *f -/-n* herd (of cattle etc.); flock (of sheep etc.).

**herein** [hɛ'rain], *adv.* (in) here; **h.!** come in! ◆**h~brechen**, *v.i.sep.irr.14* (*sein*) (a) (**in etwas** *acc*) **h.**, to break/ (*Wassermasse*) burst in(to sth.); (b) (*Abend, Winter usw.*) to close in; (*Nacht*) to fall. ◆**h~bringen**, *v.tr.sep.irr.16* to bring (s.o., sth.) in. ◆**h~fallen**, *v.i.sep.irr.27* (*sein*) (a) (**in etwas** *acc*) **h.**, to fall in(to sth.); (*Licht*) to come in; (b) *F:* to be cheated/taken in (**auf j-n**, by s.o.). ◆**h~holen**, *v.tr.sep.* to bring (sth.) in. ◆**h~kommen**, *v.i.sep.irr.53* (*sein*) to come in. ◆**h~lassen**, *v.tr.sep.irr.57* **j-n** (**in das Haus**) **h.**, to let s.o. in/(to the house). ◆**h~legen**, *v.tr.sep.* *F:* to take (s.o.) in, take (s.o.) for a ride. ◆**h~platzen**, *v.i.sep.* (*sein*) *F:* (**in etwas** *acc*) **h.**, to barge in(to) sth.). ◆**h~schauen**, *v.i.sep.* (*haben*) to look in. ◆**h~stürzen**, *v.i.sep.* (*sein*) (**in et-**

**was** *acc*) **h.**, to rush in (to sth.).

'**Herfahrt** *f* journey/*Aut:* drive here.

'**herfallen**, *v.i.sep.irr.27* (*sein*) **über j-n h.**, to pitch into s.o.

'**Hergang**, *m* course of events.

'**hergeben**, *v.tr.sep.irr.35* to surrender (sth.); part with (money etc.); (*überreichen*) to hand (sth.) over; (*zurückgeben*) to give (sth.) back.

'**hergehen**, *v.i.sep.irr.32* (*sein*) (a) **neben/ hinter j-m h.**, to walk next to/behind s.o.; (b) *impers.* **es ging laut/lustig her**, there were noisy/gay goings-on.

'**herhalten**, *v.sep.irr.45* 1. *v.tr.* to hold out (one's hand etc.). 2. *v.i.* (*haben*) **für j-n h. (müssen)**, to have to take the blame for s.o.

**Hering** ['heːriŋ], *m* -s/-e 1. herring. 2. (*Zeltpflock*) tent-peg.

'**her|kommen**, *v.i.sep.irr.53* (*sein*) (a) to come here; to arrive (here); (b) **wo kommst du her?** where do you come from? ◆'**h~kömmlich**, *adj.* conventional; (*üblich*) customary; traditional (belief etc.).

**Herkunft** ['heːrkunft], *f* -/-e origin. ◆'**H~sland**, *n* country of origin.

'**herleiten**, *v.tr.sep.* to derive (a word, theory etc.).

'**hermachen**, *v.tr.sep.* **sich h. über** + *acc*, to fall (up)on, attack (s.o., sth.); *F:* to pitch into (s.o., one's food etc.); to set about, tackle (a job, task etc.).

**Hermelin** [hɛrmə'liːn]. *m* -s/-e (*Pelz*) ermine.

**hermetisch** [hɛr'meːtiʃ], *adj.* hermetic; **h. verschlossen**, hermetically sealed.

**hernach**, *adv.* after(wards); subsequently.

'**hernehmen**, *v.tr.sep.irr.69* to take (sth.).

**Heroin** [hero'iːn], *n* -s/*no pl* heroin.

**heroisch** [he'roːiʃ], *adj.* heroic.

**Herr** [hɛr], *m* -(e)s/-en 1. man; (*formell*) gentleman; **200 Meter der H~en**, men's 200 metres; **meine (Damen und) H~en!** (ladies and) gentlemen! **H. Müller**, Mr Müller; **H. Präsident**, Mr Chairman; **Sehr geehrter H.**, Dear Sir. 2. master (of a servant, dog etc.); **sein eigener H. sein**, to be one's own master; **H. der Lage sein**, to have the situation under control. ◆**H~en-**, *comb.fm.* men's (clothing, fashion etc.); man's (suit, shirt). ◆'**H~enabend**, *m* stag party. ◆'**H~enbesuch**, male visitor. ◆'**h~enlos**, *adj.* (dog etc.) without a master; ownerless (object). ◆'**H~gott**, *m* **der (liebe) H.**, the (good) Lord. ◆'**H~in**, *f -/-nen* lady; mistress (of a dog, servant). ◆'**h~isch**, *adj.* domineering; (*gebieterisch*) imperious. ◆'**h~lich**, *adj.* magnificent (spectacle, view etc.); splendid (food, idea etc.); marvellous (holiday, weather etc.). ◆'**H~lichkeit**, *f -/no pl* magnificence, splendour. ◆'**H~schaft**, *f -/-en* 1. (a) (*Regierung*) rule; (*Macht*) power; sovereignty (of the State); (b) (*Beherrschung*) control (**über etwas** *acc*, of sth.). **2.** *pl* **meine H~en!** ladies and gentlemen! ◆**h~schen**, *v.i.* (haben) (a) to rule, (*Fürst*) reign, *Pol:* (*Partei*) be in power; (b) (*Zustände, Meinung usw.*) to prevail; **überall herrschte Trauer,** there was sadness everywhere. ◆**'h~schend,** *adj.* **1.** reigning (monarch); ruling (class etc.). **2.** (*gegenwärtig*) current, prevailing. ◆**'H~scher,** *m* -s/- ruler; (*Fürst*) monarch, sovereign. ◆**'H~schsucht,** *f* desire to give orders; domineering/*F:* bossy nature. ◆**'h~schsüchtig,** *adj.* domineering,/*F:* bossy.

**'herrichten,** *v.tr.sep.* to prepare (a meal, room).

**'herrühren,** *v.i.sep.* (haben) to derive, originate.

**'hersein,** *v.i.sep.irr.93* (sein) (a) **das dürfte schon Jahre h.,** it must have been years ago; (b) **hinter j-m, etwas** *dat* **h.,** to be after s.o., sth.

**'herstammen,** *v.i.sep.* (haben) **von j-m h.,** to be descended from s.o.; **wo stammen Sie her?** where do you come from?

**'herstell|en,** *v.tr.sep.* (a) *Ind:* to produce, manufacture (goods etc.); (b) to establish (contact, law and order etc.); to create (good relations etc.). ◆**'H~er,** *m* -s/- *Ind:* manufacturer; ◆**'H~ung,** *f* -/no pl *Ind:* manufacture, production. ◆**'H~ungs-,** *comb.fm.* production (fault, costs etc.); manufacturing (process etc.).

**herüber** [hɛ'ry:bər], *adv.* across; over here (to me). ◆**h~fahren,** *v.tr. & i.sep.irr.26* (sein) to drive (s.o.) over.

**herum** [hɛ'rum], *adv.* (a) **um ... acc h.,** (i) round ...; (ii) *Fig:* (etwa) round about; (b) **verkehrt h.,** the wrong way round. ◆**h~ärgern,** *v.refl.sep. F:* **sich mit j-m, etwas** *dat* **h.,** to be constantly irritated by s.o., sth. ◆**h~drehen,** *v.tr.sep.* to turn (s.o., sth.) round. ◆**h~fahren,** *v.i.sep.irr.26* (sein) to travel/*Aut:* drive around. ◆**h~führen,** *v.tr.sep.* (a) **j-n (im Haus usw.) h.,** to take/show s.o. round (the house etc.); (b) **etwas mit sich dat h.,** to take/carry sth. about with one. ◆**h~gehen,** *v.i.sep.irr.36* (sein) (a) (*Pers.*) to go/walk round; **um etwas** *acc* **h.,** to walk round sth.; (b) (*Sache*) to be passed round; *F:* (*Nachricht, Krankheit usw.*) to go the rounds; (c) (*Zeit, Urlaub usw.*) (**schnell**) **h.,** to pass (quickly). ◆**h~kommen,** *v.i.sep.irr.53* (sein) **h. um** + *acc*, to come round (sth.); to get round (an obstacle, *Fig:* a difficulty etc.), get out of (a duty etc.); (b) **er kommt viel herum,** he gets around (a lot). ◆**h~kriegen,** *v.tr. F:* to bring/win (s.o.) round. ◆**h~reden,** *v.i.sep.* (haben) *F:* **um die Sache h.,** to evade the issue. ◆**h~schlagen,** *v.refl.sep.irr.85 F:* **sich (dauernd) mit j-m h.,** to be forever squabbling with s.o.; **sich mit einem Problem h.,** to struggle

with a problem. ◆**h~streiten,** *v.refl.sep.irr.59* **sich mit j-m h.,** to squabble with s.o. ◆**h~treiben,** *v.refl.sep.irr.12 F:* (a) **sich (auf den Straßen usw.) h.,** to roam the streets; (b) (*an einem Ort*) to hang out. ◆**H~treiber,** *m* -s/- *F:* (a) loafer; (b) tramp, vagabond. ◆**h~ziehen,** *v.i.sep.irr.113* (sein) to wander about.

**herunter** [hɛ'runtər], *adv.* down; down here; this way; **die Treppe/Straße h.,** down the stairs/the street. ◆**h~fallen,** *v.i.sep.irr.27* (sein) to fall down/downstairs. ◆**h~gehen,** *v.i.sep.irr.36* (sein) to go down/downstairs; (*Temperatur, Preise*) to drop (**auf** + *acc,* to). ◆**h~gekommen,** *adj.* (*Pers.*) (*materiell*) in reduced circumstances; (*im Aussehen*) down at heel; (*Gebäude*) dilapidated; (*Gesundheit, Firma*) run down. ◆**h~hauen,** *v.tr.sep. F:* **j-m eine h.,** to slap s.o. in the face. ◆**h~holen,** *v.tr.sep.* to get/fetch (sth.) down. ◆**h~kommen,** *v.i.sep.irr.53* (sein) (a) to come down/downstairs; (b) *Fig:* (*Pers.*) (*materiell*) to come down in the world; (*gesundheitlich, auch Firma*) to get run down. ◆**h~lassen,** *v.tr.sep.irr.57* to let (s.o., sth.) down. ◆**h~reißen,** *v.tr.sep.irr.4* to tear down, (*umstoßen*) knock down (sth.). ◆**h~setzen,** *v.tr.sep.* to reduce (prices etc.). ◆**h~stürzen,** *v.i.sep.* (sein) to come hurtling down.

**hervor** [hɛr'fo:r]. *adv.* out; forward; **hinter/unter/zwischen etwas** *dat* **h.,** from behind/under/between sth. ◆**h~brechen,** *v.i.sep.irr.14* (sein) to break/burst out (**aus** + *dat,* from). ◆**h~bringen,** *v.tr.sep.irr.16* to bring (sth.) out; to produce (sth.); to get out (a sound, word etc.). ◆**h~gehen,** *v.i.sep.irr.36* (sein) (a) **aus etwas** *dat* **h.,** to result from sth.; (b) **als Sieger h.,** to emerge victorious. ◆**h~heben,** *v.tr. sep.irr.48* to emphasize (sth.). ◆**h~ragen,** *v.i.sep.* (sein) to jut out (**aus etwas** *dat,* from sth.). ◆**h~ragend,** *adj.* outstanding (achievement etc.); first-rate (quality etc.); excellent (meal, wine etc.); distinguished (actor, artist, scientist etc.). ◆**h~rufen,** *v.tr.sep.irr.74* to cause (sth.); to give rise to (a feeling, misunderstanding etc.). ◆**h~treten,** *v.i.sep.irr.105* (sein) (a) (*Pers.*) to come forward; (b) (*Merkmal*) to show up; (*sich abheben*) to stand out. ◆**h~tun,** *v.refl.sep.irr.106* **sich h.,** (a) to distinguish oneself; (b) *Pej:* to show off.

**'Herweg,** *m* **auf dem H.,** on the way here.

**Herz** [hɛrts]. **I.** *n* -ens/-en heart; **leichten/schweren H~ens,** with a light/heavy heart; **sie sind ein H. und eine Seele,** they are inseparable; **ich bringe es nicht übers H., es zu tun,** I haven't the heart to do it; **sich** *dat* **ein H. fassen**, to pluck up courage; **etwas auf dem H~en haben**, to have sth. on one's mind; **j-n in sein H. schließen**, to become fond of s.o.; **von ganzem H~en**, (i) sincerely; with all one's heart; (ii) wholeheartedly; **im H~en der Stadt**, in the heart of the town; (b) (*Karte*) heart; (*Farbe*) hearts. **II. 'H~-**, *comb.fm.* heart (attack, trouble, surgery, specialist etc.); *Med:* cardiac (infarction, muscle etc.). ◆**'H~ensbrecher**, *m Hum:* ladykiller. ◆**'H~enslust**, *f* **nach H.**, to one's heart's content. ◆**'H~enswunsch**, *m* dearest wish. ◆**'h~ergreifend/'h~erschütternd**, *adj.* heartrending. ◆**'H~fehler**, *m* heart/cardiac defect. ◆**h~haft**, *adj.* hearty. ◆**'H~klopfen**, *n* pounding heart; *Med:* palpitations. ◆**'h~krank**, *adj.* suffering from heart trouble. ◆**'h~lich**, *adj.* cordial, warm (smile, welcome etc.); heartfelt (thanks etc.); hearty (laugh etc.); **h~liches Beileid**, sincere condolences; **h. gern**, with the greatest pleasure; **h. wenig**, precious little. ◆**'H~lichkeit**, *f -/no pl* (a) cordiality, geniality; (b) (*Echtheit*) sincerity. ◆**'h~los**, *adj.* heartless (action etc.); unfeeling (remark etc.). ◆**'H~losigkeit**, *f -/-en* **1.** *no pl* heartlessness. **2.** heartless act. ◆**'H~schlag**, *m* (a) heartbeat; (b) (*H~versagen*) heart failure. ◆**'H~versagen**, *n* heart failure. ◆**'h~zerreißend**, *adj.* heartrending.

**'herziehen**, *v.sep.irr.113* **1.** *v.tr.* **hinter sich** *dat* **h.**, to pull/(*schleppen*) drag (s.o., sth.) along. **2.** *v.i.* (*sein*) *F:* **über j-n, etwas** *acc* **h.**, to pull s.o., sth. to pieces.

**Herzog** ['hɛrtso:k], *m -s/⸚e* duke. ◆**'H~in**, *f -/-nen* duchess. ◆**'H~tum**, *n -s/⸚er* duchy.

**Hess|en** ['hɛsən]. *Pr.n.m -s. Geog:* Hesse. ◆**'h~isch**, *adj.* Hessian, from Hesse.

**'Hetz|e** ['hɛtsə], *f -/-n* **1.** (*Eile*) rush, scramble. **2.** *no pl Pej:* baiting. ◆**'h~en**, *v.* **1.** *v.tr.* (a) to pursue (s.o., sth.) (relentlessly); to hunt (s.o., an animal); *Fig:* to hound (s.o.); (b) (*zur Eile antreiben*) to rush (s.o.); (c) **die Hunde auf j-n h.**, to set the dogs on s.o. **2.** *v.i.* (*haben*) (a) to rush, race; (b) to stir up trouble/hatred (**gegen j-n**, against s.o.). ◆**'H~er**, *m -s/-* agitator, *F:* rabblerouser. ◆**'H~e'rei**, *f -/-en* **1.** (mad) rush. **2.** *F: Pol:* agitation; (*Rede*) (inflammatory) diatribe. ◆**'H~jagd**, *f* (a) chase; (b) *Pol:* witch-hunt.

**Heu** [hɔy], *n -(e)s/no pl* hay; *F:* **Geld wie H. haben**, to be stinking rich. ◆**'H~boden**, *m* hay loft. ◆**'H~gabel**, *f* pitchfork. ◆**'H~haufen**, *m* haystack. ◆**'H~schnupfen**, *m* hayfever. ◆**'H~schrecke**, *f -/-n* grasshopper; (*Wanderh.*) locust.

**Heuch|elei** [hɔyçə'lai], *f -/-en no pl* hypocrisy. ◆**'h~eln**, *v.* **1.** *v.i.* (*haben*) to sham. **2.** *v.tr.* to feign. ◆**'H~ler(in)**,

*m -s/- (f -/-nen)* hypocrite. ◆**'h~lerisch**, *adj.* hypocritical.

**Heuer** ['hɔyər], *f -/-n Nau:* (seaman's) pay. ◆**'h~n**, *v.tr.* to sign on (seamen); to hire (a boat).

**heulen** ['hɔylən], *v.i.* (*haben*) to howl; (*Sirene*) to wail; (*Kind*) bawl (**vor Wut**, with rage); **das ist ja zum H.**, it's enough to make one weep.

**heut|e** ['hɔytə], *adv.* (a) today; **h. morgen**, this morning; **die Zeitung von h.**, today's paper; (b) (*heutzutage*) nowadays; **das Deutschland von h.**, present-day Germany. ◆**'h~ig**, *adj.* today's (paper, post etc.). ◆**'h~zutage**, *adv.* nowadays.

**Hex|e** ['hɛksə], *f -/-n* witch. ◆**'h~en**, *v.i.* (*haben*) to do magic. ◆**'H~enjagd**, *f Fig:* witch-hunt. ◆**'H~enkessel**, *m Fig:* pandemonium. ◆**'H~enmeister**, *m* sorcerer, wizard; (*Zauberer*) magician. ◆**'H~enschuß**, *m* lumbago. ◆**H~e'rei**, *f -/-en* witchcraft; sorcery.

**Hieb** [hi:p], *m -(e)s/-e* **1.** (a) (*Schlag*) blow; (sword) thrust; (b) **H~e bekommen**, to get a hiding/thrashing. **2.** (*also* **H~wunde** *f*) cut, gash. ◆**'h.- und stichfest**, *adj.* watertight (argument, proof etc.).

**hier** [hi:r], *adv.* here. ◆**'h~an**, *adv.* on/onto this; **h. kann man es erkennen**, it can be recognized by this. ◆**'h~auf**, *adv.* (a) onto this; (b) *h.* **verließ er das Zimmer**, hereupon he left the room. ◆**'h~bei**, *adv.* (*währenddessen*) (while) doing this. ◆**'h~durch**, *adv.* (a) through this means; (b) *Fig:* as a result of this; by this means. ◆**'h~für**, *adv.* for this. ◆**'h~gegen**, *adv.* (a) against this; (b) (*im Vergleich*) in comparison with this. ◆**'h~her**, *adv.* here; **bis h.**, as far as this; (up) to here. ◆**'h~hin**, *adv.* **setzen wir uns h.**, let's sit down here; **bis h.**, up to this point; this far. ◆**'h~in**, *adv.* in this; *Fig:* in this connection. ◆**'h~mit**, *adv.* (a) with this; (b) (*hierdurch*) by this means; **h. erkläre ich, daß ...**, I hereby declare that ... ◆**'h~über**, *adv.* above/over here; **h. ist nichts bekannt**, nothing is known about this. ◆**'h~unter**, *adv.* under(neath) this; **h. versteht man ...**, by this is meant ... ◆**'h~von**, *adv.* (a) from here; (b) of/from this; **abgesehen h.**, apart from this. ◆**'h~zu**, *adv.* (a) to this; (b) (*hierüber*) about/concerning this (matter); on this point. ◆**'h~zulande**, *adv.* in this country.

**hiesig** ['hi:zıç], *adj.* local (customs, paper etc.); **er ist kein H~er**, he isn't from here.

**Hilf|e** ['hılfə], *f -/-n* (a) help; assistance; **j-m H. leisten**, to help/assist s.o.; **j-m zu H. kommen**, to come to s.o.'s aid; **etwas zu H. nehmen**, to make use of; **Erste H.**, first aid; (b) (*Sache*) aid; (*Pers.*) help. ◆**'H~eruf**, *m* call for help. ◆**'h~los**, *adj.* helpless; (*ratlos*) at a loss. ◆'H~**losigkeit**, *f* -/no *pl* helplessness. ◆'h~**reich**, *adj.* helpful. ◆'H~s-**aktion**, *f* relief campaign/scheme. ◆'H~s**arbeiter(in)**, *m* (*f*) temporary/ (*ungelernt*) unskilled worker. ◆'h~s-**bedürftig**, *adj.* (*a*) in need of help; (*b*) (*notleidend*) destitute, needy. ◆'h~s**bereit**, *adj.* ready to help; helpful. ◆'H~s**bereitschaft**, *f* readiness to help; helpfulness. ◆'H~s**kraft**, *f* assistant. ◆'H~s**mittel**, *n* aid. ◆'H~s**schule**, *f* special school (for educationally subnormal children). ◆'H~s**werk**, *n* welfare institution; social aid (scheme).

**Himbeer-** ['himbeːr-], *comb.fm.* raspberry (ice, jam etc.). ◆'H~**e**, *f* raspberry.

**Himmel** ['himəl], *m* -s/- (*a*) sky; **unter freiem H.**, in the open; **es kam (wie ein Blitz) aus heiterem H.**, it came out of the blue; **das schreit/stinkt zum H.**, that is an absolute scandal; (*b*) *Ecc:* heaven; **in den H. kommen**, to go to heaven; *Fig:* **im sieb(en)ten H. sein**, to be in (one's) seventh heaven; **um H~s willen!** for goodness' sake! ◆'H~**bett**, *n* four-poster bed. ◆'h~**blau**, *adj.* sky-blue. ◆'H~**fahrt**, *f Ecc:* **Christi H.**, the Ascension. ◆'h~**hoch**, *adj.* skyhigh; towering (peaks etc.). ◆'H~**reich**, *n* Kingdom of Heaven. ◆'h~**schreiend**, *adj.* outrageous. ◆'H~**srichtung**, *f* point of the compass. ◆'h~**weit**, *adj. F:* **ein h~weiter Unterschied**, a world of difference.

**himmlisch** ['himliʃ], *adj. Ecc: & F:* heavenly. **du siehst einfach h. aus**, you look simply divine.

**hin** [hin], *adv.* 1. (*Richtung*) to; towards; there; **ich will nicht h.**, I don't want to go there; **h. und zurück**, there and back; **h. und her**, to and fro; back and forth. 2. *F:* (*verloren, kaputt*) done for.

**hinab** [hi'nap], *adv.* down, downward(s). ◆h~**gehen**, *v.i.sep.irr.36* to go down. ◆h~**sehen**, *v.i. sep.irr.92* to look down.

**hinauf** [hi'nauf], *adv.* upward(s); **den Berg/Fluß h.**, up the mountain/the river. ◆h~**gehen**, *v.i.sep.irr.36* (*sein*) to go up (*die Treppe h.*) upstairs. ◆h~**klettern**, *v.tr.sep.* to climb (a ladder etc.); to clamber/scramble up (a rock etc.) ◆h~**ziehen**, *v.tr.sep.irr.113* to draw/pull (sth.) up.

**hinaus** [hi'naus], *adv.* out; **zum Fenster h.**, out of the window; **nach der Straße h.**, looking onto/facing the street; **über etwas acc h.**, beyond/in addition to sth. ◆h~**fahren**, *v.tr.sep.irr.26* 1. *v.i.* (*sein*) to go/*Aut:* drive out. 2. *v.tr.* to drive/take (the car) out (*aus der Garage*, of the garage). ◆h~**finden**, *v.i.sep.irr.9* (*haben*) to find one's way out (*aus etwas dat*, of sth.). ◆h~**gehen**, *v.i.sep.irr.36* (*sein*) (*a*) to go/walk out (*aus dem Haus usw.*,

of the house etc.); **hier geht es hinaus**, this is the way out; (*b*) **über etwas** *acc* **h.**, to go beyond/exceed sth. ◆h~**laufen**, *v.i.sep.irr.58* (*sein*) (*a*) to run out (-side); (*b*) **auf etwas** *acc* **h.**, to amount to sth. ◆h~**schieben**, *v.tr.sep.irr.82* (*a*) to push sth. (out)side; (*b*) to put off, postpone (an appointment, decision etc.). ◆h~**schmeißen**, *v.tr.sep.irr.4 F:* to chuck (s.o., sth.) out. ◆h~**sehen**, *v.i.sep.irr.92* (*haben*) to look out. ◆h~**tragen**, *v.tr.sep.irr.85* to carry (s.o., sth.) out. ◆h~**wachsen**, *v.i.sep.irr.107* **über etwas** *acc* **h.**, to grow higher than sth.; *Fig:* to outgrow sth. ◆h~**werfen**, *v.tr.sep.irr.110* (*a*) to throw (s.o., sth.) out; (*b*) *F:* to turn/kick (s.o.) out (*aus dem Haus*, of a house); to sack, fire (an employee). ◆h~**wollen**, *v.i.sep.irr.112* (*haben*) (*a*) to want to go out; (*b*) **auf etwas** *acc* **h.**, to have sth. in mind, *F:* be up to sth. ◆h~**ziehen**, *v.sep.irr.113* 1. *v.tr.* (*a*) to pull (s.o., sth.) out(side); (*b*) to drag on; (*Abfahrt usw.*) to be delayed. 2. *v.i.* (*sein*) to move out (*aufs Land usw.*, into the country etc.). ◆h~**zögern**, *v.tr.sep.* to delay, put off (sth.).

**Hinblick** ['hinblik], *m* -s/no *pl* **im H. auf** + *acc*, in view of ...; considering ...

**hinder**|**lich** ['hindərliç], *adj.* **j-m**, **etwas** *dat* **h. sein**, to be in s.o.'s way/in the way of sth. ◆'h~**n**, *v.tr.* (*a*) (*stören*) to hinder (s.o., sth.); (*b*) (*abhalten*) **j-n an etwas** *dat* **h.**, to prevent s.o. from doing sth. ◆'H~**nis**, *n* -ses/-se (*a*) obstacle; (*Schwierigkeit*) difficulty; (*b*) *Sp:* obstacle; (*Hürde*) hurdle. ◆H~**nislauf**, *m* steeplechase; *Fig:* obstacle race.

'**hindeuten**, *v.i.sep.* (*haben*) **auf j-n, etwas** *acc* **h.**, to point to s.o., sth.; (*Symptome usw.*) to suggest, indicate sth.

**hin**'**durch**, *adv.* (*a*) **durch den Wald h.**, through the wood; (*b*) **das ganze Jahr h.**, all through the year.

**hinein** [hi'nain]. *adv.* in, into; **zur Tür h.**, in through the door; (**bis**) **tief in die Nacht h.**, late into the night. ◆h~**bringen**, *v.tr.sep.irr.16* **etwas (ins Zimmer) h.**, to bring sth. in(to the room). ◆h~**fahren**, *v.sep.irr.26* 1. *v.i.* (*sein*) (**in die Stadt usw.**) **h.**, to go/travel/*Aut:* drive (to the town etc.); 2. *v.tr.* **ein Auto (in die Garage) h.**, to drive a car in(to the garage). ◆h~**fallen**, *v.i.sep.irr.27* (*sein*) to fall in. ◆h~**gehen**, *v.i. sep.irr.36* (*sein*) to go in; **ins Zimmer usw. h.**, to go into/enter the room etc. ◆h~**geraten**, *v.i.sep.irr.57* (*sein*) **in etwas** *acc* **h.**, to find oneself/*Fig:* get involved in sth. ◆h~**laufen**, *v.i.sep.irr.58* (*sein*) (**in etwas** *acc*) **h.**, to run in(to sth.). ◆h~**legen**, *v.tr.sep.* **etwas (in etwas** *acc*) **h.**, to put/place sth. inside (sth.). ◆h~**passen**, *v.i.sep.* (*haben*) (**in etwas** *acc*) **h.**, to fit in(to sth.). ◆h~**platzen**, *v.i.sep.* *(sein)* (**ins Zimmer usw.**) h., to burst in(to the room etc.). ◆**h~reden**, *v.i.sep.* *(haben)* *(a)* (**in ein Gespräch**) h., to interrupt (a conversation). ◆**h~stecken**, *v.tr.sep.* to stick/put sth. (**in etwas** *acc*, in sth.). ◆**h~steigern**, *v.refl.sep.* **sich in Wut usw. h.**, to work oneself up into a rage etc. ◆**h~stürzen**, *v.tr.* 1. *v.i.* *(sein)* (**in etwas** *acc*) h., to fall in(to sth.). 2. *v.tr.* **sich in Wasser/***Fig:* **in seine Arbeit h.**, to plunge into the water/*Fig:* one's work. ◆**h~treten**, *v.i.sep.irr.105* *(sein)* (**ins Zimmer usw.**) h., to go/walk in(to the room etc.). ◆**h~ziehen**, *v.tr.sep.irr.113* **in etwas** *acc* h., to pull/drag (s.o., sth.) into sth.; *Fig:* (*verwickeln*) to involve, implicate (s.o.) in sth.

**'hinfahr|en**, *v.i.sep.irr.26* *(sein)* to go/travel/*Aut:* drive there. ◆**H~t**, *f* outward journey/*Nau:* voyage; **auf/bei der H.**, on the way there.

**'hinfallen**, *v.i.sep.irr.27* *(sein)* to fall (down).

**'hinfällig**, *adj.* *(a)* *(Pers.)* infirm; (*gebrechlich*) frail; *(b)* (*ungültig*) invalid.

**'Hin|gabe**, *f* *-/no pl* devotion (**an Gott usw.**, to God etc.); dedication (**an eine Aufgabe**, to a task). ◆**'h~geben**, *v.tr.sep.irr.35* *(a)* to sacrifice (one's life etc.); to give away (one's possessions); *(b)* **sich einer Aufgabe h.**, to devote oneself to a task. ◆**'h~gebungsvoll**, *adj.* devoted.

**hin'gegen**, *adv.* on the other hand.

**'hingehen**, *v.i.sep.irr.36* *(sein)* to go (there).

**'hingerissen**, *adv.* with rapt attention.

**'hinhalt|en**, *v.tr.sep.irr.45* *(a)* to hold (sth.) out; (*bieten*) to offer (sth.); *(b)* (*warten lassen*) to put (s.o.) off.

**'hinhören**, *v.i.sep.* *(haben)* to listen (intently).

**hinken** ['hiŋkən], *v.i.* *(haben)* to limp; *Fig:* **der Vergleich hinkt**, that's a poor comparison.

**'hinknien**, *v.i.* *(haben)* to kneel down.

**'hinkommen**, *v.i.sep.irr.53* *(sein)* *(a)* to arrive; **wo ist es hingekommen?** where has it got to? *(b)* (*hingehören*) to belong, go; *(c)* (*auskommen*) to make do, manage (**mit dem Geld usw.**, with the money etc.).

**'hinlänglich**, *adj.* adequate, sufficient.

**'hinlegen**, *v.tr.sep.* to lay, put (sth.) down; **sich h.**, to lie down; (*sich ausruhen*) to have a rest.

**'hinpassen**, *v.i.sep.* *(haben)* to fit in (there); to be in the right place.

**'hinreichen**, *v.sep.* 1. *v.tr.* **j-m etwas h.**, to hand/pass sth. to s.o. 2. *v.i.* *(haben)* *(a)* **bis zu etwas** *dat* h., to extend as far as sth.; *(b)* (*genügen*) to be enough/adequate. ◆**'h~d**, *adj.* adequate, sufficient.

**'Hinreise**, outward journey; **bei/auf der H.**, on the way there.

**'hinreißen**, *v.tr.sep.irr.43* (*begeistern*) to enthral (s.o.), send (s.o.) into raptures; **sich von seiner Wut usw. h. lassen**, to allow one's anger etc. to get the better of one. ◆**'h~d**, *adj.* enchanting (person, smile), gorgeous (view etc.); enthralling (performance etc.).

**'hinricht|en**, *v.tr.sep.* to execute (s.o.). ◆**'H~ung**, *f* execution.

**'hinschmeißen**, *v.tr.sep.irr.43* *F:* *(a)* to chuck/fling (sth.) down; *(b)* (*aufgeben*) to chuck up, *N.Am:* quit (one's job etc.).

**'hinsehen**, *v.i.sep.irr.92* *(haben)* to look (that way, in that direction); **zu j-m h.**, to look towards s.o.; **bei genauerem H.**, on closer examination.

**'hinsein**, *v.i.sep.irr.93* *F:* *(a)* (*weg sein*) to be gone; *(b)* (*kaputt sein*) **die Vase/Firma ist hin**, the vase/firm has had it; *(c)* *(Pers.)* **ganz h.**, to be all in/(*hingerissen*) in raptures.

**'hinsetzen**, *v.tr.sep.* *(a)* to put (sth.) down; *(b)* **sich h.**, to sit down.

**'Hinsicht**, *f* *-/-en* respect; **in gewisser H.**, in certain respects; **in finanzieller H.**, from a financial point of view. ◆**'h~lich**, *prep.* + *gen* with regard to; concerning.

**'hinstellen**, *v.tr.sep.* *(a)* to put (sth.) down; *(b)* **sich h.**, to stand (there), take up one's position (somewhere); *(c)* (*bezeichnen*) to describe (s.o., sth.).

**'hinstrecken**, *v.tr.sep.* *(a)* **j-m die Hand h.**, to hold out one's hand to s.o.; *(b)* **sich h.**, to stretch oneself out, lie down full length.

**hintan|setzen** [hin'tantsɛtsən] / **h~stellen**, *v.tr. sep.* to disregard; to neglect (one's duty).

**hinten** ['hintən], *adv.* behind; at the rear/the back; **h. im Buch**, at the back of the book; **sie sind noch weit h.**, they are still a long way behind; **nach h.**, backwards; **von h.**, from the rear/behind; **das dritte Haus von h.**, the third house from the end; *F:* **h. und vorn(e)**, in every respect; **nicht wissen, wo h. und vorn(e) ist**, not to know whether one is coming or going. ◆**'h~herum**, *adv.* *F:* *(a)* round the back, the back way; *(b)* *Fig:* by devious means.

**hinter** ['hintər]. I. *prep.* + *dat/acc* behind; **h. j-m herlaufen**, to run after s.o.; **fünf Kilometer h. der Grenze**, five kilometres beyond/the other side of the border; *Fig:* **etwas h. sich** *dat* **haben**, to have got sth. behind one; **eine große Strecke h. sich** *acc* **bringen**, to cover a great distance. II. **'H~-**, *comb.fm.* *(a)* back, rear (axle, wheel, seat, exit, entrance, view etc.); *(b)* *Z:* hind (leg, foot, etc.). ◆**'H~bein**, *n* hind leg; *Fig:* **sich auf die H~e setzen**, to resist. ◆**H~bliebene(r)**, *m & f decl. as adj.* bereaved (person); (surviving) dependent. ◆**'h~e(r,s)**, *adj.* rear; **die h. Seite**, the back; **am h~en Ende**, at the far end. ◆**h~einander**, *adv.* one after the other; (in der Zeit) consecutively; **an drei Tagen h.,** on three consecutive days. ◆'**H**~**gedanke,** m ulterior motive. ◆**h**~'**gehen,** v.tr.insep.irr.36 to deceive, F: doublecross (s.o.). ◆'**H**~**grund,** m background; Fig: **sich im H. halten,** to keep a low profile. ◆'**h**~**gründig,** adj. cryptic (question etc.); enigmatic (smile etc.). ◆'**H**~**halt,** m ambush; **j-n aus dem H. überfallen,** to ambush s.o. ◆'**h**~**hältig,** adj. deceitful, underhand. ◆'**H**~**haus,** n back premises; back of the building. ◆**h**~'**her,** adv. (nachher) afterwards, subsequently. ◆**h**~'**hergehen,** v.i.sep.irr.36 (sein) to walk (behind), follow. ◆**h**~'**herlaufen,** v.i.sep.irr.58 (sein) (j-m) **h.,** to run behind, follow (s.o.); **einem Mädchen usw. h.,** to run after a girl etc. ◆'**H**~**hof,** m backyard. ◆'**H**~**kopf,** m back of the head. ◆**h**~'**lassen,** v.tr.insep.irr.57 (a) to leave (a widow, a fortune, etc.); (b) to leave (behind) (a message, mess etc.). ◆**H**~'**lassenschaft,** f -/-en estate; Fig: legacy. ◆**h**~'**legen,** v.tr.insep. to deposit (documents, money etc.). ◆'**H**~**list,** f cunning; (betrügerische Art) deceitfulness. ◆'**h**~**listig,** adj. cunning, crafty; deceitful. ◆**H**~**mann,** m (a) der **H.,** the man behind; (b) Fig: **die H**~**männer eines Verbrechens usw.,** the brains behind a crime etc. ◆'**H**~**n,** m -s/- F: backside; bottom. ◆'**h**~**rücks,** adv. from behind; Fig: treacherously. ◆'**H**~**seite,** f back, rear (of a building). ◆'**h**~**ste(r,s),** adj. rearmost; last (row etc.); hindmost (person). ◆'**H**~**treffen,** n F: **ins H. geraten/kommen,** to fall/get behind. ◆**h**~'**treiben,** v.tr. insep.irr.12 to foil, frustrate (s.o.'s plans etc.). ◆'**H**~**tür,** f back door; Fig: **durch die H.,** by devious means. ◆**h**~'**ziehen,** v.tr.insep.irr.113 to evade (taxes etc.). ◆**H**~'**ziehung,** f (tax etc.) evasion; (Unterschlagung) embezzlement. ◆'**H**~**zimmer,** n back room.

'**hintreten,** v.i.sep.irr.105 (sein) **vor j-n h.,** to step up to s.o.; to approach s.o.

'**hintun,** v.tr.sep.irr.106 (haben) F: to put (sth.) (somewhere).

**hinüber** [hi'ny:bər], adv. across. ◆**h**~**blicken,** v.i.sep. (haben) to look across. ◆**h**~**fahren,** v.sep.irr.26 1. v.i. (sein) to go/travel/Aut: drive across (**über die Brücke usw.,** the bridge etc.). 2. v.tr. to drive/run (s.o., sth.) across. ◆**h**~**führen,** v.sep. 1. v.tr. to take (s.o.) across (**über die Straße usw.,** the road etc.). 2. v.i. (haben) (Straße usw.) to go across/over, cross (**über etwas acc,** sth.). ◆**h**~**gehen,** v.i.sep.irr.36 (sein) to go over/across (**über den Platz usw.,** the square etc.). ◆**h**~**sehen,** v.i.sep.irr.92 (haben) to look across. ◆**h**~**wechseln,** v.i.sep. (haben) to move over, to change

over.

**hinunter** [hi'nuntər], adv. down; **den Berg/Fluß h.,** down the mountain/river. ◆**h**~**fallen,** v.i.sep.irr.27 (sein) to fall down. ◆**h**~**gehen,** v.i.sep.irr.36 (sein) to go/walk down; (**die Treppe**) **h.,** to go downstairs. ◆**h**~**klettern,** v.i.sep. (sein) to climb down. ◆**h**~**reichen,** v.sep. 1. v.tr. to pass (sth.) down. 2. v.i. (haben) **bis zu etwas dat h.,** to stretch down to sth. ◆**h**~**schlucken,** v.tr.sep. to swallow (food, Fig: anger, an insult etc.). ◆**h**~**sehen,** v.i.sep.irr.92 (haben) to look down. ◆**h**~**spülen,** v.tr.sep. to wash/swill (sth.) down. ◆**h**~**stürzen,** v.sep. 1. v.i. (sein) to tumble/crash down; **die Treppe h.,** to tumble/(eilen) hurtle downstairs. 2. v.tr. (a) to gulp down (food, drink); (b) sich (**von etwas dat**) **h.,** to hurl oneself off (sth.). ◆**h**~**ziehen,** v.tr.sep.irr.113 to pull (s.o., sth.) down.

'**Hinweg¹,** m **auf dem H.,** on the way there.

**hin'weg²,** adv. **über etwas acc h.,** over (the top of) sth.; **über lange Zeit h.,** over a long period. ◆**h**~**gehen,** v.i.sep.irr.36 (sein) **über etwas acc h.,** to pass over/(ignorieren) overlook sth. ◆**h**~**helfen,** v.i.sep.irr.50 (haben) **j-m über etwas acc h.,** to help s.o. to get over sth. ◆**h**~**kommen,** v.i.sep.irr.53 (sein) **über eine Krankheit usw. h.,** to get over an illness etc. ◆**h**~**sehen,** v.i.sep.irr.92 (haben) **über j-n, etwas acc h.,** Fig: to overlook s.o., shut one's eyes to sth. ◆**h**~**sein,** v.i.sep.irr.93 (sein) **über etwas acc h.,** to have got over sth. ◆**h**~**setzen,** v.refl. sep. **sich über j-n, etwas acc h.,** to disregard, turn a blind eye to (sth., sth.).

**Hinweis** ['hinvais], m -es/-e (a) (Wink) hint; **H**~**e für die Benutzung,** instructions/directions for use; (b) (Bemerkung) comment; (Andeutung) indication. ◆'**h**~**en,** v.sep.irr.88 1. v.tr. **j-n auf etwas acc h.,** to draw s.o.'s attention to sth. 2. v.i. (haben) **auf j-n, etwas acc h.,** to point out, indicate s.o., sth.; (erwähnen) to refer to sth.

'**hinwerfen,** v.tr.sep.irr.110 (a) to throw (s.o., sth.) down; (fallenlassen) to drop (sth.); (b) F: (aufgeben) to chuck in, N.Am: quit (one's job etc.).

'**hinziehen,** v.sep.irr.113 1. v.tr. (a) to pull (s.o., sth.); **sich zu j-m, etwas dat hingezogen fühlen,** to feel drawn/attracted to s.o., sth.; (b) **sich h.,** to drag on; (sich verzögern) to be delayed; (sich erstrecken) **sich h.,** to stretch, run. 2. v.i. (sein) to move.

'**hinzielen,** v.i.sep. (haben) **auf etwas acc h.,** to aim at sth.

**hinzu** [hin'tsu:], adv. in addition. ◆**h**~**fügen,** v.tr.sep. to add (sth.) (**etwas dat,** to sth.). ◆**H**~**fügung,** f -/-en addition. ◆**h**~**gesellen,** v.refl.sep. **sich**

**zu j-m h.**, to join s.o. ◆**h~kommen**, *v.i.sep.irr.53 (sein) (a) (Pers.)* (**zur Gruppe**) **h.**, to join the group; **es kamen noch andere Umstände hinzu**, there were additional factors. ◆**h~ziehen**, *v.tr.sep.irr.113* to call in (a specialist etc.).

**Hirn** [hirn]. I. *n* -(e)s/-e brain; *Cu:* brains. II. **'H~-**, *comb.fm.* brain, cerebral (tumour etc.). ◆**'H~gespinst**, *n* fanciful idea; *(eingebildet)* figment of the imagination. ◆**'H~hautentzündung**, *f* meningitis. ◆**h~verbrannt**, *adj.* crackbrained; crazy (idea etc.).

**Hirsch** [hirʃ], *m* -(e)s/-e *(a)* stag; (red) deer; *(b) Cu:* venison. ◆**'H~kuh**, *f* hind.

**Hirse** ['hirzə], *f* -/no pl millet.

**Hirte** ['hirtə], *m* -n/-n shepherd. ◆**'H~n-**, *comb.fm.* shepherd's (song etc.).

**hissen** ['hisən], *v.tr.* to hoist (a flag, sail etc.).

**Histor|iker** [his'to:rikər], *m* -s/- historian. ◆**h~isch**, *adj.* historical (event, novel etc.).

**Hit** [hit], *m* -s/-s *F:* hit (song etc.).

**Hitze** ['hitsə]. I. *f* -/no pl *(a)* heat; *(b)* hot weather; *(c) Fig:* **in der H. des Gefechts**, in the heat of the moment. II. **'H~-**, **'h~-**, *comb.fm.* heat (rash etc.); hot (spell). ◆**h~beständig**, *adj.* heat-resistant. ◆**h~empfindlich**, *adj.* heat-sensitive. ◆**'H~welle**, *f* heat wave.

**hitz|ig** ['hitsiç], *adj. (jähzornig)* hot-tempered (person); heated (argument etc.); *(leidenschaftlich)* fiery (person, temperament). ◆**'H~kopf**, *m* hothead. ◆**h~köpfig**, *adj.* hot-headed; *(jähzornig)* hot-tempered. ◆**'H~schlag**, *m* heat stroke.

**Hobby** ['hɔbi], *n* -s/-s hobby.

**Hobel** ['ho:bəl], *m* -s/- plane; *Cu:* slicer. ◆**'H~bank**, *f* carpenter's bench. ◆**h~n**, *v.tr. (a)* to plane (wood etc.); to polish, smooth (a surface etc.); *(b)* to slice (vegetables etc.). ◆**'H~späne** *mpl* wood/metal shavings.

**hoch** [ho:x]. I. *adj. (a)* high; *(b)* tall (tree etc.); **zwei Meter h.**, two metres high/ *(Schnee)* deep/*(Pers.)* tall; *(c)* high-ranking (officer); **hoher Besuch/Gast**, important guest; **hoher Beamter**, senior official/civil servant; **hohe Ehre**, great honour; *Fig:* **das ist zu h. für mich**, that is above my head/beyond me; *(d)* heavy (penalty, fine); **hohe Summe/Schulden**, large sum/debts; **hohes Alter**, great age. II. *adv. (a)* **h. oben**, high up; **j-m etwas h. anrechnen**, to appreciate greatly sth. that s.o. has done; **etwas h. und heilig versprechen**, to promise sth. solemnly; *(c)* **zu h. geschätzt**, overestimated; *F:* **wenn es h. kommt**, at a pinch. III. **H.**, *n* -s/-s 1. cheer. 2. *Meteor:* high(-pressure area). ◆**h~achten**,

*v.tr.sep.* to have a high regard for (s.o., sth.). ◆**'H~achtung**, *f* (high) esteem. ◆**'h~achtungsvoll**, *adv. Com:* yours faithfully. ◆**'H~adel**, *m* higher nobility. ◆**'H~amt**, *n* High Mass. ◆**'h~arbeiten**, *v.refl.sep.* to work one's way up. ◆**'H~bau**, *m* structural engineering. ◆**'h~begabt**, *adj.* highly/ extremely gifted. ◆**h~be'tagt**, *adj.* advanced in years; aged. ◆**'H~betrieb**, *m F:* frantic activity; **um 5 Uhr ist bei uns H.**, our peak period is around 5 o'clock. ◆**'h~bringen**, *v.tr.sep.irr.16* to bring (s.o., sth.) up/upstairs. ◆**'H~burg**, *f Fig:* stronghold. ◆**H~deutsch**, High German; *F:* proper German. ◆**'H~druck**, *m* high pressure. ◆**'H~ebene**, *f* (high) plateau. ◆**'h~empfindlich**, *adj.* highly sensitive. ◆**'h~erfreut**, *adj.* highly delighted; extremely pleased. ◆**'h~fahren**, *v.i.sep.irr.26 (sein) (a)* to go up (in a lift etc.); *(b)* to jump up, *(ängstlich)* start up. ◆**'h~fliegend**, *adj.* ambitious (plan etc.). ◆**'H~form**, *f esp. Sp:* **in H.**, in top form. ◆**'H~gebirge**, *n* high mountains. ◆**'h~gehen**, *v.i.sep.irr.36 (sein) (a) (Vorhang, Preis usw.)* to go up, rise; *F: (Pers.)* **die Treppe h.**, to go up(stairs); *(b) (also Fig:) (explodieren)* to blow up, explode. ◆**'h~gelegen**, *adj.* high-lying. ◆**'h~geschätzt**, *adj.* held in high esteem. ◆**'h~geschlossen**, *adj.* (shirt etc.) buttoned to the neck; high-necked (dress etc.). ◆**'h~gestochen**, *adj. F:* high falutin; pretentious (style etc.). ◆**'h~gewachsen**, *adj.* tall. ◆**'H~glanz**, *m* high gloss; polish; **etwas auf H. bringen**, to polish sth. until it gleams. ◆**'h~gradig**, *adj.* intense, extreme (anxiety etc.). ◆**'h~halten**, *v.tr.sep.irr.45* to hold up (sth., one's arms, head etc.). ◆**'H~haus**, *n* high-rise building; *Brit:* tower block. ◆**'h~heben**, *v.tr. sep.irr.48* to lift (s.o., sth.) up (high); to raise (one's arms, hand etc.). ◆**'h~interessant**, *adj.* extremely interesting. ◆**'h~kant**, *adv.* 1. **etwas h. stellen**, to put sth. on end. 2. *P:* **j-n h. hinausschmeißen**, to kick s.o. out on his ear. ◆**'h~kommen**, *v.i.sep.irr.53 (sein) F:* to come up/*(im Wasser)* to the surface. ◆**'H~konjunktur**, *f* boom. ◆**'H~kultur**, *f* advanced civilization. ◆**'H~land**, *n* uplands *pl*; Highlands. ◆**'h~leben**, *v.i.sep. (haben)* **j-n, etwas h. lassen**, to give s.o., sth. three cheers. ◆**'H~leistungs-**, *comb.fm.* high output (engine/motor etc.). ◆**h~'mo'dern**, *adj.* ultra-modern. ◆**'H~mut**, *m* pride; arrogance. ◆**'h~mütig**, *adj.* proud; *(herablassend)* arrogant, haughty. ◆**'h~näsig**, *adj. F:* stuck-up, snooty. ◆**'h~nehmen**, *v.tr.sep.irr.69 (a)* to lift/pick (s.o., sth.) up; *(b) F:* **j-n h.**, to pull s.o.'s leg. ◆'H~**ofen**, *m* blast furnace. ◆'H~**parterre**, *n* raised ground floor. ◆'h~**prozentig**, *adj.* containing a high percentage (of alcohol etc.). ◆'h~'**rot**, *adj.* crimson, scarlet. ◆'H~**ruf**, *m* cheer. ◆'H~**saison**, *f* high season. ◆'H~**schul-**, *comb.fm.* university (education etc.). ◆'H~**schullehrer(in)**, *m(f)* university teacher/lecturer. ◆'H~**schule**, *f* university; college (conferring degrees); academy (of drama/music). ◆'H~**seefischerei**, *f* deep sea fishing. ◆'H~**seil**, *n* high wire, tightrope. ◆'H~**sitz**, *m* (elevated) hide. ◆'H~**sommer**, *m* midsummer; high summer. ◆'h~**sommerlich**, *adj.* very summery. ◆'H~**spannung**, *f* (*a*) *El:* high tension; (*b*) *Fig:* (state of) considerable tension. ◆'H~**spannungsleitung**, *f* high tension cable; power line. ◆'H~**spannungsmast**, *m* electricity pylon. ◆'h~**spielen**, *v.tr. sep.* to make great play of (sth.). ◆'H~**sprache**, *f* standard language. ◆'H~**sprung**, *m* high jump. ◆'H~**stape'lei**, *f* -/-en imposture. ◆'H~**stapler**, *m* -s/- impostor, *F:* con man. ◆'H~**stimmung**, *f* elated (*festlich*) festive mood. ◆'H~**tour**, *f* auf H~**touren arbeiten/laufen**, (*Fabrik*) to work at high pressure, (*Motor*) to run at full speed. ◆'h~**tourig**, *adj.* high-speed (engine etc.). ◆'h~**trabend**, *adj.* high-sounding, pompous. ◆'H~**verrat**, *m* high treason. ◆'H~**wasser**, *n* 1. (*Flut*) high tide/(*Fluß*) water. 2. (*Überschwemmung*) flood. ◆'h~**wertig**, *adj.* high-grade (goods, materials). ◆'H~**würden**, *m* -s/- *Ecc:* (*Anrede*) approx. Father; (**seine**) H. X, the Reverend X. ◆'h~**ziehen**, *v.tr.sep.irr.113* to raise (sth); pull up (one's trousers etc.).

**höchst** ['hø:çst]. I. *adv.* most, extremely (exaggerated, unfair). II. 'H~-, *comb.fm.* maximum (amount, weight, price, number etc.); high (level, consumption, etc.); highest (offer, bid etc.). ◆'h~**e(r, s)**, *adj.* (*a*) highest; tallest (building, spire, tree etc.); (*b*) (*h~möglich*) maximum, top (price, speed etc.); greatest (danger etc.); utmost (degree, importance); **es ist h. Zeit**, it is high time. ◆'h~**ens**, *adv.* at most. ◆'h~**fall**, *m* im H., at the most. ◆'H~**geschwindigkeit**, *f* maximum/top speed. ◆'H~**grenze**, *f* upper limit. ◆'H~**maß**, *n* maximum amount. ◆'H~**leistung**, *f* Ind: maximum output; *El:* peak output; *Sp:* best performance. ◆'h~'**möglich**, *adj.* highest/greatest possible. ◆'h~**per'sönlich**, *adj. Hum:* in person. ◆'h~**wahr'scheinlich**, *adv.* most probably.

**Hochzeit** ['hɔxtsait], *f* -/-en wedding. ◆'H~**s-**, *comb.fm.* wedding (guest, present, etc.). ◆'H~**skleid**, *n* wedding dress. ◆'H~**sreise**, *f* honeymoon (trip). ◆'H~**stag**, *m* (*a*) wedding day; (*b*) (*Ju-*

*biläum*) wedding anniversary.

**Hocke** ['hɔkə], *f* -/-n squatting position; **in die H. gehen**, to squat down. ◆'h~**n**, *v.i.* (*haben*) (*a*) to crouch, (*auf dem Boden*) squat; (*b*) *F:* to sit (around). ◆'H~**r**, *m* -s/- stool.

**Höcker** ['hœkər], *m* -s/- hump.

**Hockey** ['hɔki, 'hɔkə], *n* -s/no *pl* hockey.

**Hoden** ['ho:dən], *pl* testicles. ◆'H~**sack**, *m* scrotum.

**Hof** [ho:f]. I. *m* -(e)s/ᵉe 1. yard; courtyard (of a castle etc.); (*Hinterh.*) backyard. 2. (*Fürstenh.*) (royal etc.) court.

**hoff|en** ['hɔfən], *v.tr.&i.* (*haben*) to hope (**auf etwas** *acc*, for sth.); **das will ich h.!** I should hope so! ◆'h~**entlich**, *adv.* it is to be hoped; *esp. N.Am:* hopefully. ◆'H~**nung**, *f* -/-en hope; **er macht sich H~en**, he fancies his chances. ◆'h~**nungslos**, *adj.* hopeless. ◆'H~**nungslosigkeit**, *f* -/no *pl* hopelessness. ◆'H~**nungsschimmer**, *m* glimmer/ray of hope. ◆'h~**nungsvoll**, *adj.* (*a*) hopeful; confident; (*b*) (*vielversprechend*) promising.

**höf|lich** ['hø:fliç], *adj.* polite. ◆'H~**lichkeit**, *f* -/-en (*a*) no *pl* politeness; courtesy; (*b*) polite remark; compliment. ◆'H~**lichkeitsfloskel**, *f* polite formula/phrase.

**Höhe** ['hø:ə], *f* -/-n 1. (*a*) height (of sth.); *esp. Av:* altitude; *F:* **das ist ja die H.!** that's the limit! (*b*) **in die H.**, up; upwards; **auf der H. sein**, to be in good form. 2. (*a*) (*Hügel*) hill; (*b*) *esp. Fig:* (*Gipfel*) peak (of one's career, fame etc.); (*c*) *Rec:* **die H~n**, the treble. 3. (*a*) (*Größe*) level (of income, prices etc.); (*Betrag*) amount (of damages etc.); **ein Schaden in H. von DM 2000** damages to the amount of 2000 marks; (*b*) *Geog:* latitude. ◆'H~**n-**, *comb.fm.* (*a*) altitude (sickness, *Sp:* training etc.); (*b*) mountain (air, climate etc.). ◆'H~**nmesser**, *m* *Av:* altimeter. ◆'H~**nsonne**, *f* *Med:* sun-lamp. ◆'H~**nunterschied**, *m* difference in altitude/height. ◆'H~**nzug**, *m* mountain range. ◆'H~**punkt**, *m* highlight; (*einmalig*) climax; (*Gipfel*) peak (of one's career etc.).

**Hoheit** ['ho:hait], *f* -/-en 1. (*a*) (*Anrede*) Your Highness; (*b*) *Fig:* majesty, dignity. 2. no *pl* sovereignty (of a state). ◆'H~**s-**, *comb.fm.* sovereign (territory, rights etc.). ◆'H~**sgewässer**, *npl* territorial waters. ◆'h~**svoll**, *adj.* dignified, majestic.

**höher** ['hø:ər], *adj.* higher; upper (branches, window etc.); superior (intelligence, rank etc.); **h~e Schule**, secondary school; **h~e Gewalt**, Act of God.

**hohl** [ho:l]. I. *adj.* hollow; *Fig:* dull (sound); *Pej:* empty (phrase etc.). II. 'H~-, *comb.fm.* (*a*) hollow (body etc.); (*b*) (*konkav*) concave (surface, mirror etc.). ◆'H~**kopf**, *m* numbskull. ◆'H~**maß**, *n* measure of capacity; dry measure. ◆'H~raum, m hollow space, cavity.

Höhle ['hø:lə], f -/-n (a) cave; (Schacht) pot-hole; (für Tiere) burrow, lair; (b) Anat: cavity. ◆'H~en-, comb.fm. cave (painting etc.). ◆'H~enbewohner, m cavedweller.

Hohn [ho:n], m -(e)s/no pl scorn, disdain; (Spott) mockery, derision. ◆'H~gelächter, n derisive/scornful laughter. ◆'H~ruf, m jeer.

höhnisch ['hø:niʃ], adj. scornful; (spöttisch) derisive.

hold [hɔlt], adj. Poet: charming, demure.

holen ['ho:lən], v.tr. to fetch (s.o., sth.); to go for (bread etc.); (abholen) to collect; (rufen) to call (the doctor); j-n h. lassen, to send for s.o.; sich dat Rat usw. (bei j-m) h., to get advice etc. (from s.o.); sich dat eine Erkältung, die Grippe usw. h., to catch a cold, the flu etc.

Holland ['hɔlant]. Pr.n.n -s. Holland; the Netherlands. ◆'H~änder [-lɛndər], m -s/- 1. Dutchman. 2. (H~käse) Dutch cheese. ◆'H~änderin, f -/-nen Dutchwoman. ◆'h~ändisch, adj. Dutch.

Hölle ['hœlə], f -/-n hell. ◆'H~en-, comb.fm. F: infernal (noise etc.); hellish (thirst etc.). ◆'H~enangst, f eine H. haben, to be scared to death. ◆'h~isch, adj. infernal (region, F: noise etc.); F: hellish (row etc.); fiendish (task etc.).

holpern ['hɔlpərn], v.i. (haben/sein) (Fahrzeug) to jolt, bump. ◆'h~(e)rig, adj. bumpy.

Holunder [ho'lundər], m -s/- elder. ◆'H~beere, f -/-n elderberry.

Holz [hɔlts]. I. n -es/-er wood; (Bauh.) timber; aus H., wooden. II. 'H~-, comb.fm. (a) (aus H. bestehend) of wood; (vom H.) wood (fibre, wool etc.); (b) (aus H. gemacht) wooden (bridge, house, spoon etc.); (c) Com: timber (trade etc.). ◆'H~fäller, m wood-cutter, N.Am: lumberjack. ◆'H~feuer, n log fire. ◆'H~hammer, m mallet. ◆'h~ig, adj. woody. ◆'H~kohle, f charcoal. ◆'H~kohlengrill, m charcoal grill. ◆'H~kopf, m F: blockhead; clot. ◆'H~schnitzer, m woodcarver. ◆'H~schuh, m clog. ◆'H~weg, m F: auf dem H. sein, to be on the wrong track. ◆'H~wurm, m woodworm.

hölzern ['hœltsərn], adj. wooden.

homogen [homo'ge:n], adj. homogeneous. ◆'H~sexualität, f homosexuality. ◆h~sexu'ell, adj. homosexual; ein H~sexueller, a homosexual.

Honig ['ho:niç], m -s/-e honey. ◆'H~kuchen, m honeycake; (mit Ingwer) gingerbread. ◆'H~wabe, f honeycomb.

Honorar [hono'ra:r], n -s/-e fee (for professional services). ◆h~ieren [-'ri:rən], v.tr. (a) Fig: (belohnen) to reward (an achievement etc.); (b) Fin: to honour (a bill, debt etc.).

Hopfen ['hɔpfən], m -s/- hop, Agr: coll. hops.

hopsen ['hɔpsən], v.i. (sein) F: to hop, skip.

hörbar ['hø:rba:r], adj. audible; (in Hörweite) within earshot. ◆'h~en, v.tr.&i. (haben) (a) to hear; schlecht h., to be hard of hearing; (b) (anhören) to listen to; auf j-n h., to listen to s.o.; sie hört auf den Namen Anna, she answers to the name of Anna; (c) wie ich höre, ist er verreist, I gather/understand that he is away; er läßt nichts von sich h., he hasn't written. ◆'H~ensagen, n vom H., by hearsay. ◆'H~er, m -s/- 1. (a) listener; (die H., the audience; (b) Sch: student (at a lecture). 2. Tel: receiver. ◆'H~gerät, n hearing aid. ◆'h~ig, adj. j-m, etwas dat h. sein, to be enslaved by s.o., sth. ◆'H~saal, m lecture hall. ◆'H~spiel, n radio play.

horchen ['hɔrçən], v.i. (haben) to listen.

Horde ['hɔrdə], f -/-n horde; Pej: mob.

Horizont [hori'tsɔnt], m -(e)s/-e (a) horizon; skyline; (b) Fig: das geht über meinen H., that's beyond me. ◆h~al [-'ta:l], adj. horizontal.

Hormon [hɔr'mo:n], n -s/-e hormone.

Horn [hɔrn], n -(e)s/-er horn. ◆'H~haut, f cornea. ◆H~ist [hɔr'nist], m -en/-en horn-player.

Hörnchen ['hœrnçən], n -s/- small horn; Cu: croissant.

Hornisse [hɔr'nisə], f -/-n hornet.

Horoskop [horo'sko:p], n -s/-e horoscope.

Horror ['hɔrɔr], m -s/no pl dread (vor + dat, of).

Hort [hɔrt], m -(e)s/-e Lit: (a) hoard; (Schatz) treasure; (b) (Zuflucht) refuge; (c) (Kinderh.) children's home. ◆'h~en, v.tr. to hoard (sth.); to stockpile (arms etc.).

Hose ['ho:zə], f -/-n (pair of) trousers, N.Am: pants; eine neue H., a new pair of trousers. ◆'H~n-, comb.fm. trouser (leg, button, pocket, etc.). ◆'H~nanzug, m trouser suit. ◆'H~nträger, mpl braces; N.Am: suspenders.

Hostess/Hosteß [hɔs'tɛs], f -/-ssen hostess; Av: air hostess; esp. N.Am: stewardess.

Hostie ['hɔstiə], f -/-n host; (consecrated) wafer.

Hotel [ho'tɛl], n -s/-s hotel.

Hubraum ['hu:praum], m (cylinder) capacity. ◆'H~schrauber, m helicopter.

hübsch [hypʃ], adj. pretty, (anziehend) attractive (girl, tune etc.); F: nice (evening, house etc.).

huckepack ['hukəpak], adv. F: j-n h. tragen/nehmen, to give s.o. a piggyback.

Huf [hu:f], m -(e)s/-e hoof. ◆'H~eisen, n horseshoe.

Hüft- ['hyft-], comb.fm. hip (joint etc.). ◆'H~e, f -/-n hip. ◆'H~gürtel/

'H~**halter**, *m* girdle. ◆'H~**knochen**, *m* hip-bone. ◆'H~**weite**, *f* hip measurement.

**Hügel** ['hy:gəl], *m* -s/- hill. ◆'h~**ig**, *adj.* hilly. ◆'H~**kette**, *f* line/range of hills.

**Huhn** [hu:n], *n* -(e)s/=er chicken; *(weiblich)* hen.

**Hühner-** ['hy:nər-], *comb.fm.* chicken (broth, liver etc.); hen (house etc.). ◆'H~**auge**, *n* corn. ◆'H~**ei**, *n* hen's egg. ◆'H~**stall**, *m* hencoop.

**huldig|en** ['huldigən], *v.i. (haben) Lit:* j-m, etwas *dat* h., to pay homage/tribute to s.o., sth. ◆'H~**ung**, *f* -/-en *Lit:* tribute, homage.

**Hülle** ['hylə], *f* -/-n *(a)* cover; *(Verpakkung)* wrapping(s); (record) sleeve; *(b) F:* in H. und Fülle, in abundance. ◆'h~**n**, *v.tr.* to wrap (s.o., sth.) in Nebel gehüllt, shrouded in mist.

**Hülse** ['hylzə], *f* -/-n (pea, seed etc.) pod; (rice etc.) husk. ◆'H~**nfrucht**, *f* pulse.

**human** [hu'ma:n], *adj.* humane. ◆h~**itär** [-ni'tɛ:r], *adj.* humanitarian. ◆H~**ität** [-ni'tɛ:t], *f* -/no *pl* humanity; humaneness.

**Hummel** ['huməl], *f* -/-n bumble-bee.

**Hummer** ['humər], *m* -s/- lobster.

**Humor** [hu'mo:r], *m* -s/no *pl* humour; (Sinn für) H. haben, to have a sense of humour. ◆H~**ist** [-'rist], *m* -en/-en humorist. ◆h~**istisch** [-'ristiʃ], *adj.* humorous (writings etc.). ◆h~**los**, *adj.* humourless. ◆h~**voll**, *adj.* humorous.

**humpeln** ['humpəln], *v.i. (a) (haben)* to limp; *(b) (sein)* to hobble (somewhere).

**Humpen** ['humpən], *m* -s/- tankard (with a lid).

**Hund** [hunt], *m* -(e)s/-e *(a)* dog; *(Jagdh.)* hound; *F:* auf den H. kommen, to go to the dogs. ◆'H~**e**-[-də-], *comb.fm.* dog's (tail, *F:* life etc.); dog (bite, breeding, food, racing etc.). ◆'h~**e'elend**, *adj.* mir ist h., I feel rotten. ◆'H~**ehütte**, *f* kennel, *N.Am:* doghouse. ◆'H~**ekuchen**, *m* dog biscuit. ◆'H~**eleine**, *f* (dog) lead, *N.Am:* leash. ◆'H~**emarke**, *f* dog's identity tag. ◆'h~**e'müde**, *adj. F:* dog-tired. ◆'H~**esteuer**, *f* dog licence (fee). ◆'H~**sge'mein**, *adj. P:* filthy, lowdown. ◆'H~**stage**, *mpl* dog-days, high summer.

**hundert** ['hundərt]. *num.adj.* a/one hundred; H~e von Menschen, hundreds of people. ◆'H~**er**, *m* -s/- *F: (a) (Zahl)* hundred; *(b) (Schein)* hundred mark note. ◆'H~'**jahrfeier**, *f* centenary (celebration). ◆'h~**jährig**, *adj.* a hundred years old. ◆'h~**mal**, *adv.* a hundred times. ◆'H~'**meterlauf**, *m* hundred metres. ◆'h~**prozentig**, *adj.* a hundred per cent (alcohol, *F: success etc.*); complete, total (support). ◆'H~**stel**, *n* -s/- hundredth (part). ◆'h~**tausend**, *adj.* a/one hundred thousand.

**Hündin** ['hyndin], *f* -/-nen bitch.

**Hüne** ['hy:nə], *m* -n/-n giant. ◆'h~**nhaft**, *adj.* gigantic.

**Hunger** ['huŋər], *m* -s/no *pl* hunger (auf etwas *acc*, for sth.); H. haben, to be hungry. ◆'H~**lohn**, *m* miserable pittance. ◆'h~**n**, *v.tr. & i. (haben)* to suffer from hunger, starve; *(fasten)* to fast. ◆'H~**snot**, *f* famine. ◆'H~**tuch**, *n Hum:* am H. nagen, to be on the breadline.

**hungrig** ['huŋriç], *adj.* hungry (nach + *dat*, for).

**Hup|e** ['hu:pə], *f* -/-n *Aut:* horn. ◆'h~**en**, *v.i. (haben)* to hoot, *N.Am:* honk.

**hüpfen** ['hypfən], *v.i. (sein)* to hop; *(Ball)* to bounce; das ist gehüpft wie gesprungen, it comes to exactly the same thing.

**Hürde** ['hyrdə], *f* -/-n hurdle. ◆'H~**nlauf**, *m* hurdlerace. ◆'H~**nläufer**, *m* hurdler.

**Hure** ['hu:rə], *f* -/-n *Pej:* whore; *F:* tart.

**hurra** [hu'ra:], *int.* hurra(h), hurray.

**huschen** ['huʃən], *v.i. (sein)* to dart; *(Schatten, Lächeln)* to flit (über + *acc*, across).

**hüsteln** ['hy:stəln], *v.i. (haben)* to give a slight cough, clear one's throat.

**husten** ['hu:stən]. I. *v.* 1. *v.i. (haben)* to cough. 2. *v.tr.* to cough (up) (blood etc.). II. H., *m* -s/no *pl* cough. ◆'H~**anfall**, *m* fit of coughing. ◆'H~**bonbon**, *n* cough sweet/*N.Am:* drop. ◆'H~**reiz**, *m* irritation in the throat. ◆'H~**saft**, *m* cough syrup.

**Hut¹** [hu:t]. I. *m* -(e)s/=e *(a)* hat; *F:* H. ab! well done! *(b) Fig:* verschiedene Interessen usw. unter einen H. bringen, to reconcile different interests etc. ◆'H~**macher**, *m* -s/- hatter.

**Hut²**, *f* -/no *pl* auf der H. sein, to be on one's guard.

**hüt|en** ['hy:tən], *v.tr. (a)* to guard, watch over (s.o., sth.); to keep (a secret); *(aufpassen auf)* to look after, mind (a child, animals etc.); to tend (the fire); *(b)* das Bett/Haus h. müssen, to have to stay in bed/indoors; *(c)* sich vor j-m, etwas *dat* h., to be on one's guard against s.o., sth.; sich h., etwas zu tun, to take care not to do sth.

**Hütte** ['hytə], *f* -/-n 1. hut; *N.Am:* *(Blockh.)* log cabin. 2. *Ind:* foundry; *(ganze Anlage)* iron and steel works. ◆'H~**n-**, *comb.fm.* foundry (worker etc.); iron and steel (plant, industry, works). ◆'H~**nkäse**, *m* cottage cheese.

**Hyäne** [hy'ɛ:nə], *f* -/-n hyena.

**Hyazinthe** [hya'tsintə], *f* -/-n hyacinth.

**Hydrant** [hy'drant], *m* -en/-en hydrant.

**Hydraul|ik** [hy'draulik], *f* -/no *pl* hydraulics. ◆h~**isch**, *adj.* hydraulic (brake etc.).

**Hygien|e** [hygi'e:nə], *f* -/no *pl* hygiene. ◆h~**isch**, *adj.* hygienic.

**Hymne** ['hymnə], *f* -/-n hymn; *(Natio-*

*nalh.*) national anthem.
**Hypno|se** [hyp'no:zə], *f* -/-n hypnosis. ◆**h~tisch**, *adj.* hypnotic. ◆**H~tiseur** [-noti'zøːr], *m* -s/-e hypnotist. ◆**h~tis'ieren**, *v.tr.* to hypnotize.

**Hypothek** [hypo'te:k], *f* -/-en mortgage. **Hypothese** [hypo'te:zə], *f* -/-n hypothesis. **Hyster|ie** [hyste'riː], *f* -/-n hysteria. ◆**h~isch** [hys'te:riʃ], *adj.* hysterical.

# I

**I, i** [iː], *n* -/- (the letter) I, i.
**ich** [iç]. **I.** *pers. pron.* I; **i. selbst,** I myself; **i. bin's,** it's me; **Menschen wie du und i.,** people like you and me; **i. Idiot!** fool that I am! **II. Ich,** *n* -s/*no pl* self; *esp. Psy:* ego. ◆**'ichbezogen,** *adj.* self-centred.
**ideal** [ide'aːl]. **I.** *adj.* ideal. **II.,** *n* -s/-e ideal. ◆**I~fall,** *m* ideal case; **im I.,** ideally. ◆**I~ismus** [-'lismus], *m* -/*no pl* idealism. ◆**I~ist(in)** [-'list(in)], *m* -en/-en (*f* -/-nen) idealist. ◆**i~istisch** [-'listiʃ], *adj.* idealistic.
**Idee** [i'deː], *f* -/-n *(a)* idea; *(b) F:* **eine I. zuviel/zu kurz,** slightly too much/too short. ◆**i~ll** [ide'ɛl], *adj.* theoretical (viewpoint etc.); notional (value, need etc.).
**ident|ifizieren** [identifi'tsiːrən], *v.tr.* to identify (s.o., sth.); **sich i. mit +** *dat,* to identify with (a cause etc.). ◆**i~isch** [i'dɛntiʃ], *adj.* identical. ◆**I~i'tät,** *f* -/-en identity.
**Ideolog|ie** [ideolo'giː], *f* -/-n ideology. ◆**i~isch** [-'loːgiʃ], *adj.* ideological.
**idiomatisch** [idio'maːtiʃ], *adj.* idiomatic.
**Idiot(in)** [idi'oːt(in)], *m* -en/-en (*f* -/-nen) idiot. ◆**i~isch** [-'oːtiʃ], *adj.* idiotic.
**Idol** [i'doːl], *n* -s/-e idol.
**Idyll** [i'dyl], *n* -s/-e/**I~e,** *f* -/-n idyll. ◆**i~isch,** *adj.* idyllic.
**Igel** ['iːgəl], *m* -s/- hedgehog.
**Iglu** ['iːglu], *m & n* -s/-s igloo.
**Ignor|ant** [igno'rant], *m* -en/-en ignoramus. ◆**i~ieren,** *v.tr.* to ignore, take no notice of (s.o., sth.).
**ihm** [iːm], *pers. pron. dat.* of **er/es** *(a)* (+ *verb*) (to) him; (*Sache*) (to) it; **gib's i.,** give it to him; **wie geht es i.?** how is he? *(b)* (+ *prep.*) him, it; **von i.,** from him/it; **ein Freund von i.,** a friend of his.
**ihn** [iːn], *pers. pron. acc.* of **er,** him; (*Sache*) it. ◆**ihnen** [i:nən], *pers. pron. dat.pl.* of **er, sie** *&* **es 1.** (to) them; **ich sagte es i.,** I told them. **2. I.,** (*polite address*) (to) you; **wie geht es I.?** how are you?
**ihr** [iːr]. **I.** *pers. pron.* **1.** *dat.* of **sie** *(a)* (+ *verb*) (to) her; (*Sache*) (to) it; **ich sagte es i.,** I told her; *(b)* (*with prep.*) her; (*Tier*) it; **von i.,** from her/it; its; **ein Freund von i.,** a friend of hers. **2.** *nom.pl* of **du** you. **II.** *poss. pron.* **1.** her; (*Tier/Sache*) its; (*von mehreren*) their; **i~e(r,s)/**Lit: **der/die/das i~e,** her one, hers; (*Tier*) its one; (*von mehreren*) their one, theirs. **2. I.,** your. ◆**'i~erseits,** *adv.* on her/

their/(I.) your part. ◆**'i~esgleichen,** *pron.* **1.** her/(*Sache*) its/*pl* their kind; (*solche Leute*) people like that; **eine Sache, die i. sucht,** something unparalleled/ unequalled. **2. I.,** people like you, your sort. ◆**'i~etwegen/'i~etwillen,** *adv.* **1.** because of her/(*Sache*) it/*pl* them; for her/its/their sake. **2. I.,** for your sake, because of you. ◆**'i~ige,** *poss. pron. Lit:* **der/die/das i.,** hers, its; *pl* theirs.
**Ikone** [i'koːnə], *f* -/-n icon.
**illeg|al** ['ilegaːl], *adj.* illegal. ◆**i~itim** [-i'tiːm], *adj.* illegitimate.
**Illus|ion** [iluzi'oːn], *f* -/-en illusion. ◆**i~orisch** [-'zoːriʃ], *adj. (a)* illusory; *(b)* (*sinnlos*) pointless.
**illustr|ieren** [ilu'striːrən], *v.tr.* to illustrate (a book etc.). ◆**I~ierte** [-'striːrtə], *f* -/-n illustrated magazine.
**Iltis** ['iltis], *m* -ses/-se polecat.
**im** [im], *prep.* = **in dem. 1.** in the. **2.** (*zeitlich*) in; **im Oktober,** in October. **3. im Stehen,** while standing.
**imaginär** [imagi'nɛːr], *adj.* imaginary.
**Imbiß** ['imbis], *m* -sses/-sse snack, light meal. ◆**I~stube,** *f* snack bar.
**Imi|tation** [imitatsi'oːn], *f* -/-en imitation; (*Fälschung*) fake. ◆**i~'tieren,** *v.tr.* to imitate (s.o., sth.).
**Imker** ['imkər], *m* -s/- beekeeper.
**Immatrikulation** [imatrikulatsi'oːn], *f* -/-en matriculation, enrolment.
**immens** [i'mɛns], *adj.* immense; tremendous (achievement etc.).
**immer** ['imər], *adv.* **1.** *(a)* always; **für i.,** for ever, for good; *(b)* (*jedesmal*) every time; **i. wenn,** whenever; **i. wieder,** again and again; *(c)* (*zunehmend*) **i. mehr,** more and more; **i. besser,** better and better; *(d)* **noch i.,** still. **2.** *was/wer/wie/wo* **i.,** whatever/whoever/however/wherever. ◆**'i~grün,** *adj.* evergreen (plant). ◆**'i~hin,** *adv.* (*wenigstens*) at any rate; (*trotzdem*) all the same; **er ist i. dein Vater,** after all he is your father. ◆**'i~zu,** *adv. F:* constantly.
**Immigr|ant(in)** [imi'grant(in)], *m* -en/-en (*f* -/-nen) immigrant. ◆**i~ieren** [-'griːrən], *v.i.* (*sein*) to immigrate.
**Immobilien** [imo'biːliən], *pl* property; *Jur:* real estate.
**immun** [i'muːn], *adj.* immune (**gegen** + *acc,* from); *Fig:* impervious (**gegen Kritik usw.,** to criticism etc.). ◆**i~ität,** *f* -/-en immunity.
**Imperativ** [impera'tiːf], *m* -s/-e imperative (mood).

**Imperfekt** ['ɪmpɛrfɛkt], *n* -s/-e imperfect (tense).

**Imperial|ismus** [imperia'lismus], *m* -/*no pl* imperialism. ◆**I~ist** [-'list], *m* -en/-en *Pej:* imperialist.

**impf|en** ['ɪmpfən], *v.tr.* to inoculate, vaccinate (s.o.). ◆**'I~schein**, *m* vaccination certificate. ◆**'I~stoff**, *m* serum; vaccine. ◆**'I~ung**, *f* -/-en inoculation; vaccination.

**imponieren** [impo'niːrən], *v.i.* (*haben*) j-m i., to impress s.o. ◆**i~d**, *adj.* impressive.

**Impor|t** [ɪm'pɔrt]. **I.** *m* -(e)s/-e **1.** *no pl* import (**von** + *dat*, of). **2.** import, imported article. **II.** **I~-**, *comb.fm.* import (licence, duty, trade etc.). ◆**I~teur** [-'tøːr], *m* -s/-e importer. ◆**I~tfirma**, *f* importing firm, importers. ◆**i~'tieren**, *v.tr.* to import (goods etc.).

**imposant** [impo'zant], *adj.* imposing.

**impoten|t** ['ɪmpotɛnt], *adj.* impotent. ◆**'I~z**, *f* -/-en impotence.

**imprägnieren** [impre'gniːrən], *v.tr.* to impregnate, proof, (*gegen Wasser*) waterproof (a material etc.).

**Improvi|sation** [improvizatsi'oːn], *f* -/-en improvisation. ◆**i~'sieren**, *v.tr. & i.* (*haben*) to improvise (a meal, music etc.); to extemporize (a speech).

**Impul|s** [ɪm'puls], *m* -es/-e impulse; (*treibende Kraft*) impetus; (*Anregung*) stimulus. ◆**i~siv** [-'ziːf], *adj.* impulsive; impetuous.

**imstande** [ɪm'ʃtandə], *adv.* **i. sein, etwas zu tun,** to be capable of doing sth.

**in** [ɪn], *prep.* (*a*) (+ *dat*) in; **in der Stadt,** in town; **in der Schule,** at school; **ich war noch nie in Paris,** I've never been to Paris; **in der Nacht,** in/during the night; **gut in Mathematik,** good at mathematics; (*b*) (+*acc*) into, to; **in die Stadt,** (in)to town; **ins Kino/Theater,** to the cinema/theatre.

**'Inbegriff,** *m* perfect example (of sth.); embodiment (of evil, kindness etc.). ◆**'i~en**, *adj.* included.

**indem** [ɪn'deːm], *conj.* **1.** (*während*) while. **2.** (*Zweck*) **er spart Geld, i. er zu Fuß geht,** he saves money by walking.

**Inder(in)** ['ɪndər(ɪn)], *m* -s/- (*f* -/-nen) Indian.

**indessen** [ɪn'dɛsən], *adv.* meanwhile.

**Indian|er(in)** [ɪndi'aːnər(ɪn)], *m* -s/- (*f* -/-nen) American/*F:* Red Indian. ◆**i~isch,** *adj.* (Red) Indian.

**Indien** ['ɪndiən]. *Pr.n.n* -s. India.

**indigniert** [ɪndɪ'gniːrt], *adj.* indignant.

**Indikat|iv** ['ɪndikatiːf], *m* -s/-e *Gram:* indicative (mood). ◆**I~or** [-'kaːtɔr], *m* -s/-en indicator.

**'indirekt,** *adj.* indirect.

**indisch** ['ɪndiʃ], *adj.* Indian.

**indiskret** ['ɪndiskreːt], *adj.* indiscreet. ◆**I~ion** [-tsi'oːn], *f* -/-en indiscretion.

**indiskutabel** ['ɪndiskutaːbəl], *adj.* out of the question.

**Individu|alist** [individua'list], *m* -en/-en individualist. ◆**I~ali'tät,** *f* -/*no pl* individuality. ◆**i~'ell,** *adj.* individual; personal (style, taste etc.); **das ist i. verschieden,** it varies from case to case. ◆**I~um** [-'viːduum], *n* -s/-duen individual.

**Indiz** [ɪn'diːts], *n* -es/-ien (*a*) *Jur:* relevant circumstances; (*b*) (*Anzeichen*) indication, sign (**für** + *acc*, of). ◆**I~ienbeweis,** *m* circumstantial evidence.

**Indonesien** [indo'neːziən]. *Pr.n.n* -s. Indonesia. ◆**i~isch,** *adj.* Indonesian.

**industrial|isieren** [industriali'ziːrən], *v.tr.* to industrialize (an area). ◆**I~i'sierung,** *f* -/*no pl* industrialization.

**Industrie** [indus'triː]. **I.** *f* -/-n industry; **in der I.,** in industry. **II.** **I~-,** *comb.fm.* industrial (worker, building, product, town, centre etc.). ◆**I~betrieb,** *m* industrial plant. ◆**i~'ell,** *adj.* industrial. ◆**I~gebiet,** *n* industrial area. ◆**I~gewerkschaft,** *f* industrial (trade) union. ◆**I~staat,** *m* industrial nation. ◆**I~zweig,** *m* branch of industry.

**inei'nander,** *adv.* in/into one another. ◆**i~fließen,** *v.i.sep.irr.31* (*sein*) to merge, (*Flüsse*) join; (*Farben*) to run (into one other).

**infam** [ɪn'faːm], *adj.* infamous.

**Infanterie** [infantə'riː], *f* -/-n infantry.

**Infektion** [infɛktsi'oːn], *f* -/-en infection. ◆**I~s-,** *comb.fm.* (*a*) (danger, source etc.) of infection; (*b*) infectious (disease etc.).

**Infinitiv** ['ɪnfinitiːf], *m* -s/-e infinitive.

**infizieren** [ɪnfi'tsiːrən], *v.tr.* to infect (s.o., a wound etc.); **sich i.,** to become infected.

**Inflation** [inflatsi'oːn], *f* -/-en inflation. ◆**i~är** [-tsio'nɛːr], *adj.* inflationary. ◆**I~s-,** *comb.fm.* (*a*) (danger, rate etc.) of inflation; (*b*) inflationary (policy etc.).

**in'folge,** *prep.* + *gen* as a result of. ◆**i~'dessen,** *adv.* consequently.

**Inform|ation** [informatsi'oːn], *f* -/-en (*a*) (piece/item of) information; **I~en,** (items of) information; (*b*) **erkundigen Sie sich bei der I.,** ask at the information desk. ◆**I~ati'ons-,** *comb.fm.* (*a*) information (bureau, service etc.); (source, flow etc.) of information; (*b*) informative; *esp. Pol:* fact-finding (visit etc.). ◆**i~a'tiv,** *adj.* informative. ◆**i~ieren** [-'miːrən], *v.tr.* to inform (s.o.); **sich über etwas** *acc* **i.,** to gather information/find out about sth.

**infrarot** ['ɪnfraroːt], *adj.* infra-red.

**Infusion** [infuzi'oːn], *f* -/-en infusion, drip.

**Ingenieur** [inʒeni'øːr], *m* -s/-e engineer. ◆**I~schule,** *f* college of engineering.

**Ingwer** ['ɪŋvər], *m* -s/*no pl* ginger.

**Inhaber(in)** ['ɪnhaːbər(ɪn)], *m* -s/- (*f* -/-nen) holder (of a document, office, *Sp:* record etc.); occupant (of a house, post etc.); (*Besitzer*) owner (of a business

etc.).

**inhaftieren** [inhaf'ti:rən], *v.tr. Jur:* to take (s.o.) into custody.

**inhalieren** [inha'li:rən], *v.tr.* to inhale.

**Inhalt** ['inhalt], *m* -(e)s/-e **1.** contents (of a bottle etc.); (*Fassungsvermögen*) capacity; *Mth:* volume. **2.** (*Stoff*) content, subject matter (of a book etc.); (*I~s-verzeichnis*) contents (list). ◆'i~**lich**, *adv.* as far as the content is concerned. ◆'I~**sangabe**, *f* synopsis. ◆'i~**slos**, *adj.* empty (life, speech etc.). ◆'I~**sverzeichnis**, *n* contents list.

**Initiat|ive** [initsia'ti:və], *f* -/-n initiative. ◆I~**or** [-'a:tɔr], *m* -s/-en initiator.

**Injektion** [injɛktsi'o:n], *f* -/-en injection.

**inklusive** [inklu'zi:və], *adv.* i. **Porto,** including postage; **bis zum 20. März** i., until March 20th inclusive.

**inkognito** [in'kɔgnito], *adv.* incognito.

**'inkonsequent**, *adj.* inconsistent.

**'Inland**, *n* **1.** home country; **im In- und Ausland,** at home and abroad. **2.** interior (of a country). ◆'I~**s-**, *comb.fm.* inland (letter etc.); domestic (flight, *Com:* trade etc.); home (market etc.). ◆'I~**sporto**, *n* inland postage rates.

**inländisch** ['inlɛndiʃ], *adj.* indigenous (goods); home (product etc.); domestic, internal (affairs etc.); inland (mail etc.).

**in'mitten**, *prep. & adv. Lit:* i. + *gen*/i. **von** + *dat*, amidst.

**inne|haben** ['inəha:bən], *v.tr.sep.irr.44* to hold (an office, a title etc.), occupy (a position etc.). ◆'i~**halten**, *v.i.sep.irr.45 v.i.* (*haben*) to pause. ◆'i~**wohnen**, *v.i.sep.* (*haben*) **etwas** *dat* i., to be inherent in sth.

**innen** ['inən]. **I.** *adv.* inside; **nach** i., inwards; **von** i., from inside/within. **II.** '**I~-**, *comb.fm.* (*a*) inner (harbour, courtyard, *Fig:* life etc.); (*b*) inside (pocket etc.); (*c*) interior (lighting, wall, *Aut:* mirror etc.); (*im Hause*) indoor (aerial, temperature etc.). ◆'I~**architekt**, *m* interior designer/decorator. ◆'I~**minister**, *m* Minister for the Interior/ Home Affairs. ◆'I~**politik**, *f* domestic policy. ◆'i~**politisch**, *adj.* concerning domestic policy. ◆'I~**raum**, *m* (*a*) interior; (*b*) (*Platz*) space inside. ◆'I~**stadt**, *f* town/city centre.

**inner|e(r,s)** ['inərə(r,s)], *adj.* **1.** inner (edge, circle, room etc.); internal (organization, *Pol:* affairs, *Med:* injury, organs etc.); *Fig:* inner, inward (calm, voice etc.). **2. das I.,** the interior; the inner being (of s.o.); **im tiefsten I~n,** deep down (inside). ◆I~**eien** [-'raiən], *fpl Cu:* offal. ◆'i~**halb**. **I.** *prep.* + *gen* inside (the house etc.); within (an area, a time, the family etc.). **II.** *adv.* within. ◆'i~**lich**, *adj.* internal (bleeding etc.); i. **unbeteiligt,** emotionally detached; i. **lachen,** to laugh inwardly. ◆'i~**örtlich**, *adj.* within a built-up area. ◆'i~**parteilich**, *adj.* within the party.

◆'i~**städtisch**, *adj.* inner city (area etc.). ◆'i~**ste(r,s)**, *adj.* (*a*) innermost (circle etc.); (*b*) *Fig:* inmost (being etc.); deepest (conviction etc.); **im I~sten getroffen,** cut to the quick.

**innig** ['iniç], *adj.* deep, warm; (*echt*) sincere (feelings etc.); intimate (friendship etc.); **j-n i. lieben,** to love s.o. with all one's heart.

**Innung** ['inuŋ], *f* -/-en guild, corporation.

**'inoffiziell**, *adj.* unofficial; informal (discussions etc.).

**ins** [ins], *prep.* = **in das;** i. **Theater gehen,** to go to the theatre.

**Insass|e** ['inzasə], *m* -n/-n/'I~**in**, *f* -/-nen inmate; *Aut:* occupant, passenger.

**insbe'sond(e)re**, *adv.* especially, particularly.

**'Inschrift**, *f* inscription.

**Insekt** [in'zɛkt], *n* -s/-en insect. ◆I~**en-**, *comb.fm.* insect (powder etc.). ◆I~**enstich**, *m* insect bite/sting. ◆I~**envertilgungsmittel**, *n* insecticide.

**Insel** ['inzəl], *f* -/-n island. ◆'I~**bewohner(in)**, *m(f)* islander. ◆'I~**gruppe**, *f* group of islands.

**Inser|at** [inze'ra:t], *n* -(e)s/-e (small) advertisement, *F:* (small) ad. ◆I~'**ent**, *m* -en/-en advertiser. ◆i~'**ieren**, *v.tr. & i.* (*haben*) to advertise.

**insge'heim**, *adv.* in secret, secretly; *F:* on the quiet/*N.Am:* sly.

**insge'samt**, *adv.* in all; all told.

**inso'fern** [in'zo:fern], *adv.* to this extent; i. **als ...,** in so far as .... ◆i~'**weit. I.** [in'zo:vait], *adv.* = **insofern. II.** [inzo'vait], *conj.* as far as; (*solange*) as long as.

**Inspekt|ion** [inspɛktsi'o:n], *f* -/-en inspection; *Aut:* (*Wartung*) service. ◆I~**or(in)** [in'spɛktɔr (-'to:rin)], *m* -s/-en (*f* -/-nen) inspector.

**Inspir|ation** [inspiratsi'o:n], *f* -/-en inspiration. ◆i~**ieren** [-'ri:rən], *v.tr.* to inspire (s.o.).

**inspizieren** [inspi'tsi:rən], *v.tr.* to inspect (troops, a school etc.); to survey (a building).

**Install|ateur** [instala'tø:r], *m* -s/-e (gas etc.) fitter; (*Elektriker*) electrician; (*Klempner*) plumber. ◆i~**ieren** [-'li:rən], *v.tr.* to install, put in (central heating etc.).

**instand** [in'ʃtant], *adv.* i. **halten,** to keep up (a house etc.), maintain (a car etc.); i. **setzen,** to put (a machine etc.) into working order; to restore (furniture etc.). ◆I~**haltung**, *f* maintenance, upkeep. ◆I~**setzung**, *f* -/-en repair; restoration.

**'inständig**, *adj.* urgent (request etc.); fervent (prayer).

**Instanz** [in'ʃtants], *f* -/-en authority; *Jur:* court; **erste/zweite I.,** first/second instance.

**Instinkt** [in'ʃtiŋkt], *m* -(e)s/-e instinct. ◆i~**iv** [-'ti:f], *adj.* instinctive.

**Institut** [insti'tu:t], *n* -(e)s/-e institute. ◆I~**ion** [-tutsi'o:n], *f* -/-en institution.

**instruieren** [instru'i:rən], *v.tr.* to instruct, brief (s.o.).

**Instrument** [instru'mɛnt], *n* -(e)s/-e instrument; (*Werkzeug*) tool, implement. ◆I~**al-** [-'ta:l], *comb.fm.* instrumental (music etc.).

**Insulin** [inzu'li:n], *n* -s/*no pl* insulin.

**inszenier|en** [instse'ni:rən], *v.tr.* to stage, put on (a play etc.); to produce (a play, film etc.). *Fig:* to engineer (a scandal etc.). ◆I~**ung**, *f* -/-en *Th:* production.

**intakt** [in'takt], *adj.* intact.

**Integration** [integratsi'o:n], *f* -/-en integration. ◆i~**rieren** [-'gri:rən], *v.tr.* to integrate (s.o., sth.). ◆I~**rität** [-gri'tɛ:t], *f* -/*no pl* integrity.

**Intellekt** [intɛ'lɛkt], *m* -(e)s/*no pl* intellect. ◆i~**ektu'ell**, *adj.* intellectual; **ein I~er/eine I~e**, an intellectual. ◆I~**igenz** [-i'gɛnts], *f* -/-en intelligence.

**Intendant** [intɛn'dant], *m* -en/-en artistic (and administrative) director; *Th:* theatre manager.

**Intensität** [intɛnzi'tɛ:t], *f* -/*no pl* intensity; strength. ◆i~**iv** [-'zi:f], *adj.* intensive (talks etc.); intense (feelings etc.). ◆i~**ivieren** [-zi'vi:rən], *v.tr.* to intensify (sth.). ◆I~**ivstation** [-'zi:f-], *f* intensive care unit.

**inter-** [intər-], *adj.prefix* inter-(continental etc.). ◆i~**natio'nal**, *adj.* international.

**interess|ant** [intərɛ'sant], *adj.* interesting; **das ist für mich nicht i.**, that is of no interest to me. ◆i~**anter'weise**, *adv.* interestingly enough. ◆I~**e** [-'rɛsə], *n* -s/-n interest; **I. für j-n, etwas *acc* haben**, to be interested in s.o., sth. ◆I~**ent** [-'sɛnt], *m* -en/-en interested party; prospective buyer/(*Kunde*) customer. ◆i~**ieren** [-'si:rən], *v.tr.* to interest (s.o.) (**für etwas** *acc* in sth.); **das interessiert mich nicht**, I am not interested in that. ◆i~**iert** [-'si:rt], *adj.* interested (**an +** *dat*, in); **politisch i.**, interested in politics.

**intern** [in'tɛrn], *adj.* internal. ◆I~**at** [-'na:t], *n* -(e)s/-e boarding school. ◆i~**ieren** [-'ni:rən], *v.tr.* to intern (prisoners of war). ◆I~**ierung**, *f* -/-en internment. ◆I~**ist** [-'nist], *m* -en/-en *Med:* specialist in internal diseases, internist.

**Interpret(in)** [intərpre:t(in)], *m* -en/-en (*f* -/-nen) interpreter. ◆I~**ation** [-pretatsi'o:n], *f* -/-en interpretation. ◆i~**ieren** [-'ti:rən], *v.tr.* to interpret.

**Interpunktion** [intərpuŋktsi'o:n], *f* -/-en punctuation.

**Intervall** [intər'val], *n* -s/-e interval.

**interven|ieren** [intɛrve'ni:rən], *v.i.* (*haben*) to intervene (**in +** *dat*, in). ◆I~**tion** [-vɛntsi'o:n], *f* -/-en intervention.

**Interview** [intər'vju:], *n* -s/-s interview.

◆i~**en**, *v.tr.* to interview (s.o.).

**intim** [in'ti:m], *adj.* intimate; private (thoughts etc.). ◆I~**ität** [intimi'tɛ:t], *f* -/-en intimacy. ◆I~**sphäre**, *f* privacy.

**intoler|ant** ['intolerant], *adj.* intolerant. ◆I~**anz**, *f* -/-en intolerance.

**intransitiv** ['intranziti:f], *adj.* intransitive.

**Intri|gant(in)** [intri'gant(in)], *m* -en/-en (*f* -/-nen) intriguer; schemer. ◆I~**ge** [-'tri:gə], *f* -/-n intrigue. ◆i~**gieren**, *v.i.* (*haben*) to plot.

**introvertiert** [introver'ti:rt], *adj.* introverted.

**Intui|tion** [intuitsi'o:n], *f* -/-en intuition. ◆i~**tiv** [-'ti:f], *adj.* intuitive.

**Invalid|e** [inva'li:də], *m* -n/-n invalid, disabled worker/*Mil:* serviceman. ◆I~**ität** [-lidi'tɛ:t], *f* -/*no pl* disability; (*Zustand*) disablement.

**Invasion** [invazi'o:n], *f* -/-en invasion.

**Invent|ar** [invɛn'ta:r], *n* -s/-e (*a*) goods and chattels; assets; (*Lagerbestand*) stock; (*b*) (*Verzeichnis*) inventory. ◆I~**ur** [-'tu:r], *f* -/-en stocktaking; **I. machen**, to take stock.

**invest|ieren** [invɛs'ti:rən], *v.tr.* to invest (money, *Fig:* time etc.). ◆I~**ition** [-titsi'o:n], *f* -/-en capital investment.

**inwendig** ['invɛndiç], *adj.* inside; **j-n, etwas in- und auswendig kennen**, to know s.o., sth. inside out.

**inwiefern** [invi'fɛrn], *adv.* in what way.

**inwieweit** [invi'vait], *adv.* to what extent.

**in'zwischen**, *adv.* meanwhile.

**Ion** [i'o:n], *n* -s/-en ion.

**Irak** [i'ra:k]. *Pr.n.m* -s. Iraq. ◆I~**er(in)**, *m* -s/- (*f* -/-nen) Iraqi. ◆i~**isch**, *adj.* Iraqi.

**Iran** [i'ra:n]. *Pr.n.m* -s. Iran. ◆I~**er(in)**, *m* -s/- (*f* -/-nen) Iranian. ◆i~**isch**, *adj.* Iranian.

**ird|en** ['irdən], *adj.* earthenware. ◆i~**isch**, *adj.* earthly (goods etc.); worldly (pleasures etc.).

**Ire** ['i:rə], *m* -n/-n Irishman. ◆**'Irin**, *f* -/-nen Irishwoman. ◆**'irisch**, *adj.* Irish. ◆**'Irland**. *Pr.n.n* -s. Ireland; (*Republik*) Eire.

**irgend** ['irgənt], *adv.* **1.** **i. jemand**, someone; **i. etwas**, something; **hat er i. etwas gesagt?** did he say anything? **nicht i. etwas gesagt**, not (just) anybody. **2.** **wenn es i. möglich ist**, if it is at all possible. ◆i~**'ein**, *indef. pron.* **1.** some; (+ *neg./interrog.*) any. **2.** **i~er**, someone; **besser als i. anderer**, better than anyone else. ◆i~**'wann**, *adv.* sometime (or other). ◆i~**'was**, *indef. pron. F:* something; **kannst du i. tun?** can you do anything? ◆i~**'wer**, *indef. pron. F:* someone, somebody. ◆i~**'wie**, *adv.* somehow. ◆i~**'wo**, *adv.* somewhere. ◆i~**'wo'hin**, *adv.* **i. fahren**, to drive somewhere/anywhere.

**Iron|ie** [iro'ni:], *f* -/-n irony. ◆i~**isch** [i'ro:niʃ], *adj.* ironic.

**irr(e)** ['ɪr(ə)], adj. crazy. ◆**I~e¹**, m & f decl. as adj. lunatic; F: wie ein I~r, like mad. ◆**I~e²**, f j-n in die I. führen = i~eführen. ◆**i~eführen**, v.tr. to mislead (s.o.); (täuschen) to deceive (the public etc.). ◆**I~eführung**, f deception. ◆**i~en**, v.i. (haben) & refl. (a) sich in j-m, etwas dat i., to be mistaken about s.o., sth.; **wenn ich (mich) nicht irre**, if I am not mistaken; **ich habe mich in der Zeit geirrt**, I got the time wrong; (b) to wander, stray; **durch die Straßen i.**, to roam the streets. ◆**I~enhaus**, n lunatic asylum; F: madhouse. ◆**I~fahrt**, f roundabout journey; pl wanderings. ◆**i~ig**, adj. mistaken; false (supposition etc.). ◆**I~licht**, n will-o'-the-wisp. ◆**I~sinn**, m insanity; madness. ◆**i~sinnig**, adj. 1. insane; crazy. 2. F: terrific, tremendous; **i. komisch**, screamingly funny. ◆**I~tum**, m -s/¨er error; mistake; **im I. sein**, to be mistaken. ◆**i~tümlich**, adj. erroneous (assertion etc.), mistaken (opinion etc.); adv. by mistake. ◆**I~weg**, m wrong track.

**irritieren** [iri'ti:rən], v.tr. to distract; (ärgern) to irritate.

**Ischias** ['ɪʃias], m -/no pl sciatica.

**Islam** [is'la:m], m -s/no pl Islam. ◆**i~isch**, adj. Islamic.

**Island** ['i:slant]. Pr.n.n -s. Iceland. ◆**isländisch**, adj. Icelandic.

**Isol|ation** [izolatsi'o:n], f -/-en isolation; El: insulation. ◆**I~ator**, m -s/-en El: etc: (a) insulator; (b) insulating material. ◆**I~ier-** [-'li:r-], comb.fm. insulating (material etc.). ◆**i~ieren**, v.tr. (a) to isolate (a person); Med: to quarantine (a patient); (b) to insulate (wires etc., a pipe, wall etc.). ◆**I~ierstation**, f isolation ward. ◆**I~ierung**, f -/-en Med: & Fig: isolation; El:etc: insulation.

**Israel** ['israe:l]. Pr.n.n -s. Israel. ◆**I~i** [-'e:li], m -s/-s Israeli. ◆**i~isch**, adj. Israeli.

**Italien** [i'ta:liən]. Pr.n.n -s. Italy. ◆**I~er(in)** [itali'e:nər(in)], m -s/- (f -/-nen) Italian. ◆**i~isch. I.** adj. Italian. **II. I.**, n -s/no pl (Sprache) Italian.

# J

**J, j** [jɔt], n -/- (the letter) J, j.

**ja** [ja:], adv. 1. (Antwort) yes; **mit Ja antworten**, to answer 'yes'; **wenn ja**, if so. 2. F: **sag ja nichts**, don't you dare say anything; **du kennst ihn ja**, you know what he's like; **ich geh ja schon**, don't worry, I'm going; **du bleibst doch, ja?** you will stay, won't you? **ja, dann ...!** of course, in that case ...! ◆**ja'wohl**, adv. (bejahend) yes, indeed; (natürlich) certainly. ◆**'Jawort**, n consent; **sein J. geben**, to say yes.

**Jacht** [jaxt], f -/-en yacht.

**Jacke** ['jakə], f -/-n jacket; (aus Wolle) cardigan. ◆**J~tt** [ʒa'kɛt], n -s/-s jacket.

**Jagd** [ja:kt]. **I.** f -/-en **1.** (nach Wild) hunting, (Schießen) shooting (auf + acc, of); **auf die J. gehen**, to go hunting. 2. (Verfolgung) chase. **II.** 'J~d-, comb.fm. 1. hunting. 2. Av: fighter (aircraft, squadron etc.). ◆**'J~beute**, f quarry. ◆**'J~gewehr**, n hunting/sporting gun. ◆**'J~revier**, n shoot; esp. Fig: hunting ground.

**jagen** ['ja:gən], v. 1. v.tr. (a) to hunt; (b) (verfolgen) to chase; to drive (s.o.) **aus dem Hause usw.**, out of the house etc.); (hetzen) to hound (s.o.); F: **damit kannst du mich j.!** you can keep it! (c) to drive (a knife, ball etc.). 2. v.i. (haben) (a) to hunt; to go hunting; (b) (rasen) (Pers.) to dash, rush; (Pferd) to gallop; (Motor) to race; (c) Fig: **nach Ruhm, Geld usw. j.**, to pursue fame, fortune etc.

**Jäger** ['jɛ:gər], m -s/- 1. (a) hunter; (b) (Verfolger) pursuer. 2. (Aufseher) gamekeeper. 3. Av: F: fighter (plane).

**jäh** [jɛ:], adj. (a) (plötzlich) sudden; abrupt (ending etc.); (b) sheer (drop etc.). ◆**j~lings** ['jɛ:liŋs], adv. suddenly, abruptly.

**Jahr** [ja:r], n -(e)s/-e year; **in den fünfziger J~en**, in the fifties; **1000 Mark im J.**, 1000 marks a year; **in die J~e kommen**, to be getting on in years; **in den besten J~en**, in the prime of life. ◆**j~'aus**, adv. j., **jahrein**, year in, year out. ◆**j~elang**, adj. (lasting) for years; **in j~em Studium**, in years of study. ◆**'J~es-**, comb.fm. (a) year's (turnover, salary etc.); (beginning, end etc.) of the year; (b) (wiederholt) annual (report, meeting etc.). ◆**'J~eswechsel**, m/ **'J~eswende**, f turn of the year. ◆**'J~eszeit**, f season; time of year. ◆**'J~gang**, m **1.** age group; **der J. 1970**, those born in 1970; **er ist mein J.**, he was born the same year as I was. 2. (Wein usw.) **ein guter J.**, a good vintage. 3. (Zeitschrift) year's issues. ◆**'J~'hundert**, n -s/-e century. ◆**'J~'hundertfeier**, f centenary. ◆**'J~markt**, m fair. ◆**'J~'zehnt**, n -(e)s/-e decade.

**jährlich** ['jɛ:rlix], adj. yearly, annual; **einmal j.**, once a year.

**Jähzorn** ['jɛ:tsɔrn], m violent temper.

**Jalousie** [ʒalu'zi:], f -/-n blind.

**Jammer** ['jamər], m -s/no pl (Elend) misery; F: **es ist ein J.**, it's a crying shame. ◆**'j~n**, v.i. (haben) to complain, F: moan **über** (+ acc, about); **die Kinder j. nach der Mutter**, the children are crying for their mother. ◆**j~'schade**, pred.

*adj.* **es ist j.**, it's a crying shame.
**jämmerlich** ['jɛmərlix], *adj.* **1.** miserable (state etc.); pitiful (cry etc.); wretched (conditions); **er sieht j. aus**, he is a pitiful sight. **2.** *F:* (*a*) miserable (work, effort); (*b*) terrible (fear, pain).
**Januar** ['januɑːr], *m* **-(s)/-e** January.
**Japan** ['jɑːpan]. *Pr.n.n* **-s.** Japan. ◆**J~er(in)** [ja'pɑːnər(in)], *m* **-s/-** (*f -/ -nen*) Japanese. ◆**j~isch** [ja'pɑːnif], *adj.* Japanese.
**japsen** ['japsən], *v.i.* (*haben*) *F:* to gasp (**nach Luft**, for air).
**Jargon** [ʒar'gõː], *m* **-s/-s** jargon.
**Jasmin** [jas'miːn], *m* **-s/-e** jasmine.
**jäten** ['jɛːtən], *v.tr.* to weed.
**Jauche** ['jauxə], *f* **-/-** liquid manure. ◆**J~grube**, *f* cesspit.
**jauchzen** ['jauxtsən], *v.i.* (*haben*) to rejoice (**über etwas** *acc*, over sth.); (**vor Wonne**) **j.**, to shout for joy.
**jaulen** ['jaulən], *v.i.* (*haben*) to howl.
**je** [jeː]. **I.** *adv.* (*a*) (*jemals*) ever; (*b*) (*jeweils*) at a time; each; (*c*) **je nach** according to; **je nach Belieben**, just as/however you like (it); **je nachdem**, as the case may be; (*Antwort*) it all depends; (*d*) **das hat er seit (eh und) je gehabt**, he's always had that. **II.** *prep.* + *acc*; **je zwei Meter Stoff**, (for) every two metres of material; **die Kosten je Teilnehmer**, the cost for each/per participant. **III.** *conj.* **je ..., desto ...**, the ..., the ....
**Jeans** [dʒiːnz], *pl* jeans. ◆**J~stoff**, *m* denim.
**jede(r,s)** ['jeːdə(r,z)], *indef. pron.* **1.** *adj.* every, (*j~s einzelne*) each; **j-n zweiten Tag**, every other day; (*b*) (*j~s beliebige*) any. **2.** *s.* (*a*) **j~(r)**, everybody, everyone; (*Sache*) each (one); **j~r** (*einzelne*) **von uns**, each (and every) one of us; **j~r** (**von den beiden**, each/both of them; (*b*) **j~(r)** (**beliebige**), anybody, anyone; (*Sache*) anything. ◆**j~nfalls** ['jeːdənfals], *adv.* (*was auch geschieht*) in any case; (*wenigstens*) at least. ◆**j~rmann**, *indef. pron.* everybody, everyone. ◆**j~rzeit**, *adv.* (at) any time. ◆**j~smal**, *adv.* each/ every time.
**jedoch** [je'dɔx], *conj. & adv.* however.
**jeher** [jeː'heːr], *adv.* **von/seit j.**, always; all along.
**jemals** ['jeːmɑːls], *adv.* ever.
**jemand** ['jeːmant], *indef. pron.* (*a*) someone, somebody; **j. anders**, somebody else; (*b*) (*fragend/unbestimmt*) anybody; anyone; **ist hier j.?** is (there) anybody here?
**jen|e(r,s)** ['jeːnə(r,s)], *dem. pron.* that; *pl* those. ◆**j~seitig**, *adj.* far, opposite (bank etc.). ◆**j~seits. I.** *prep.* + *gen* beyond; **j. des Flusses**, on the other side of the river. **II.** *s.*, *n -/no pl Ecc:* **das J.**, the life hereafter.
**Jesus** ['jeːzus]. *Pr.n.m* **-.** Jesus. ◆**J~kind**, *n* **das J.**, the Infant Jesus.
**jetzig** ['jɛtsiç], *adj.* present.

**jetzt** [jɛtst], *adv.* now; **er kommt j. gleich**, he'll be coming in a moment.
**jeweil|ig** ['jeːvailiç], *adj.* (*a*) particular; **der j~e Präsident usw.**, the president etc. in office/power at the time; (*b*) (*in Frage kommend*) relevant (authority etc.); **sie wurden an die j~en Besitzer zurückerstattet**, they were returned to their respective owners. ◆**j~s**, *adv.* in each case; **Sie erhalten j. 50 Mark**, you each receive 50 marks.
**Job** [dʒɔp], *m* **-s/-s** *F:* job. ◆**j~ben** [-bən], *v.i.* (*haben*) *F:* to take a job.
**Joch** [jɔx], *n* **-(e)s/-e** yoke.
**Jockei** ['dʒɔki, -keɪ], *m* **-s/-s** jockey.
**Jod** [joːt], *n* **-(e)s/no pl** iodine.
**jodeln** ['joːdəln], *v.i.* (*haben*) to yodel.
**Joga** ['joːgɑː], *n -/no pl* yoga.
**Joghurt** ['joːgurt], *m & n* **-s/-s** yoghurt.
**Johannisbeere** [jo'hanisbeːrə], *f -/-n* **schwarze/rote J.**, blackcurrant/redcurrant.
**johlen** ['joːlən], *v.i.* (*haben*) to bawl, yell.
**Jolle** ['jɔlə], *f -/-n* dinghy.
**Jong|leur** [dʒɔŋ'gløːr], *m* **-s/-e** juggler. ◆**j~lieren** [-'liːrən], *v.i.* (*haben*) to juggle.
**Joppe** ['jɔpə], *f -/-n* loden jacket.
**Jordan|ien** [jɔr'dɑːniən]. *Pr.n.n* **-s.** Jordan. ◆**J~ier** [-'dɑːniər], *m* **-s/-** Jordanian.
**Jota** ['joːta], *n -(s)/-s F:* **er wich (um) kein J.**, he wouldn't budge an inch.
**Journal** [ʒur'nɑːl], *n* **-s/-e** journal. ◆**J~ismus** [-a'lismus], *m -/no pl* journalism. ◆**J~ist(in)**, *m* **-en/-en** (*f -/-nen*) journalist.
**Jubel** ['juːbəl], *m* **-s/no pl** jubilation, rejoicing; (*J~rufe*) cheering. ◆**J~jahr**, *n F:* **alle J~e** (**ein)mal**, once in a blue moon. ◆**j~n**, *v.i.* (*haben*) to rejoice (**über etwas** *acc*, at sth.); (*rufen*) to cheer.
**Jubi|lar(in)** [jubi'lɑːr(in)], *m* **-s/-e** (*f -/ -nen*) man/woman celebrating an anniversary. ◆**J~läum** [-'lɛːum], *n* **-s/-läen** jubilee; **150-jähriges J.**, 150th anniversary.
**jucken** ['jukən], *v.tr. & i.* (*haben*) (*a*) to irritate; **es juckt (mich) am ganzen Körper**, my whole body is itching; *Fig:* **das juckt mich nicht**, I couldn't care less; (*b*) *F:* **sich j.**, to scratch oneself.
**Jude** ['juːdə], *m -n/-n* Jew. ◆**J~ntum**, *n -s/no pl* Judaism.
**Jüd|in** ['jyːdin], *f -/-en* Jewish woman. ◆**j~isch**, *adj.* Jewish.
**Jugend** ['juːgənt]. **I.** *f -/no pl* **1.** (*Alter*) youth; (*13–18*) adolescence; **von J. an**, from an early age. **2.** (*junge Leute*) young people. **II.** **'J~-**, *comb./Im.* (*a*) youth (club, orchestra etc.); juvenile (court etc.); *Sp:* junior (champion etc); (*b*) (*von seiner J.*) youthful (writings etc.); (*memory*, *friend* etc.) of one's youth. ◆**'J~buch**, *n* book for young people. ◆**'j~frei**, *adj.* (book etc.) suitable for young people; *Cin:* = U-certificate/ *N.Am:* G/PG-rated (film). ◆**j~gefährdend**, *adj.* (literature) tending to

corrupt youth; *Cin:* X-certificate/*N.Am:* R-rated (film). ◆'J~**heim**, *n* (residential) youth club. ◆'J~**herberge**, *f* youth hostel. ◆'J~**kriminalität**, *f* juvenile delinquency. ◆'j~**lich**, *adj.* youthful. ◆'J~**liche(r)**, *f(m) decl. as adj.* young person; *Jur:* juvenile. ◆'J~**stil**, *m* art nouveau. ◆'J~**weihe**, *f East G:* dedication of youth. ◆'J~**zeit**, *f* youth.

**Jugoslaw|e** [juːgosˈlɑːvə], *m* -n/-n Yugoslav. ◆**J~ien**. *Pr.n.n* -s. Yugoslavia. ◆**J~in**, *f* -/-nen Yugoslav (woman). ◆**j~isch**, *adj.* Yugoslavian.

**Juli** ['juːli], *m* -s/-s July.

**jung** [juŋ]. I. *adj.* young. II. '**J~-**, *comb.fm.* young (farmer, animal etc.). ◆**J~e**, *m* -n/-n 1. boy. 2. *F: (junger Mann)* lad; **schwerer J.**, tough guy; *(Verbrecher)* hard case. 3. *int. F:* **J., J.!** I'll be blowed! wow! ◆'**J~e(s)**, *n decl. as adj.* *(Tier)* young one; (wolf, bear etc.) cub. ◆**J~en-**, *comb.fm.* boy's (voice etc.); *pl* boys' (school etc.). ◆'j~**enhaft**, *adj.* boyish. ◆'J~**fer**, *f* -/-n *Pej:* (alte) J., spinster; old maid. ◆'J~**fern-**, *comb.fm.* maiden (flight, speech etc.). ◆'J~**fernfahrt**, *f* maiden voyage. ◆'J~**frau**, *f* 1. virgin; **die (Heilige) J. Maria**, the (Holy) Virgin Mary. 2. *Astr:* Virgo. ◆'J~**geselle**, *m* bachelor. ◆'J~**lehrer(in)**, *m(f)* student teacher.

**jünger** ['jyŋər]. I. *adj.* (a) younger; (b) *(ziemlich jung)* fairly young, youngish; (c) recent (occurence, history etc.). II. **J.**, *m*

-s/- disciple.

**Jüngling** ['jyŋliŋ], *m* -s/-e *Lit: & Pej:* youth.

**jüngste(r,s)** ['jyŋstə(r,s)], *adj.* (a) youngest (child etc.); *F:* **sie ist nicht mehr die J.**, she's no spring chicken; (b) latest (events etc.); *Ecc:* **der J. Tag**, Doomsday; **das J. Gericht**, the Last Judgement.

**Juni** ['juːni], *m* -s/-s June.

**junior** ['juːniɔr]. I. *adj.* **Robert Schmidt j.**, Robert Schmidt junior. II. **J.**, *m* -s/-en (a) *(Sohn)* offspring; (b) *no pl Com:* junior director/partner; (c) *Sp:* junior.

**Jura** ['juːra], *s.inv.* **J. studieren**, to study law.

**Jurist(in)** [juˈrist(in)], *m* -en/-en (*f* -/-nen) lawyer.

**Jury** ['ʒyːri], *f* -/-s panel of judges.

**justieren** [jusˈtiːrən], *v.tr.* (a) to adjust, regulate; (b) to justify (a line).

**Justiz** [jusˈtiːts], *f* -/no pl 1. (administration of) justice. 2. *(Behörden)* judiciary. ◆**J~beamte(r)**, *m* officer of the law. ◆**J~irrtum**, *m* miscarriage of justice. ◆**J~minister**, *m* Minister of Justice; approx. Attorney General.

**Jute** ['juːtə], *f* -/no pl jute.

**Juwel** [juˈveːl], *n & m* -s/-en 1. *n & m* jewel, precious stone. 2. *n (pl* **J~e**) *Fig:* gem. ◆**J~ier** [juveˈliːr], *m* -s/-e jeweller.

**Jux** [juks], *m* -es/-e (practical) joke; **aus J.**, for fun/*F:* kicks.

# K

**K, k** [kɑː], *n* -/- (the letter) K, k.

**Kabarett** [kabaˈrɛt], *n* -s/-s cabaret, satirical revue. ◆**K~ist(in)** [-'tist(in)], *m* -en/-en (*f* -/-nen) cabaret/revue artist.

**Kabel** ['kɑːbəl]. I. *n* -s/- *El:* *(größeres)* cable; *(Leitung)* lead. II. '**K~-**, *comb.fm.* cable (television etc.).

**Kabeljau** ['kɑːbəljau], *m* -s/-e & -s cod.

**Kabine** [kaˈbiːnə], *f* -/-n *(Schiffsk.)* cabin; *(im Schwimmbad, beim Friseur usw.)* cubicle; (telephone) booth.

**Kabinett** [kabiˈnɛt], *n* -s/-e *Pol:* cabinet. ◆**K~s-**, *comb.fm. Pol:* cabinet (minister etc.). ◆**K~ssitzung**, *f* cabinet meeting.

**Kabriolett** [kabrioˈlɛt], *n* -s/-s convertible.

**Kachel** ['kaxəl], *f* -/-n tile. ◆'k~**n**, *v.tr.* to tile. ◆'K~**ofen**, *m* tiled stove.

**Kadaver** [kaˈdɑːvər], *m* -s/- carcass.

**Kader** ['kɑːdər], *m* -s/- cadre (of an army etc.); *Pol:* hard core, nucleus (of a party).

**Kadett** [kaˈdɛt], *m* -en/-en cadet.

**Käfer** ['kɛːfər], *m* -s/- beetle.

**Kaff** [kaf], *n* -s/-s *F:* (deadly) hole, dump.

**Kaffee** ['kafe, ka'feː]. I. *m* -s/-s coffee; **zwei K.**, two coffees. II. '**K~-**, *comb.fm.*

coffee (bean, cup etc.). ◆'K~**kanne**, *f* coffee pot. ◆'K~**klatsch**, *m* (women's) afternoon coffee party. ◆'K~**löffel**, *m* (a) (large) coffee spoon; (b) *Meas:* teaspoonful. ◆'K~**maschine**, *f* coffeemaker. ◆'K~**mühle**, *f* coffee-grinder. ◆'K~**pause**, *f* coffee break. ◆'K~**satz**, *m* coffee grounds.

**Käfig** ['kɛːfiç], *m* -s/-e cage.

**kahl** [kɑːl], *adj.* (a) *(haarlos)* bald; (b) *(schmucklos)* bare (room, tree, rock etc.); bleak (landscape etc.). ◆'k~**fressen**, *v.tr.sep.irr.* (Tiere) to strip (a tree etc.). ◆'k~**geschoren**, *adj.* shorn, shaven. ◆'k~**köpfig**, *adj.* bald-headed. ◆'K~**schlag**, *m* clearing (in a forest).

**Kahn** [kɑːn], *m* -(e)s/-e (a) *(Ruderboot)* rowing boat, *N.Am:* rowboat; (b) *(Lastk.)* barge.

**Kai** [kai], *m* -s/-s quay. ◆'K~**anlage**, *f* wharf.

**Kaiser** ['kaizər]. I. *m* -s/- emperor. II. **K~-**, *comb.fm.* imperial (crown, palace etc.). ◆'K~**in**, *f* -/-nen empress. ◆'k~**lich**, *adj.* imperial. ◆'K~**reich**, *n* empire. ◆'K~**schnitt**, *m Med:* Caesarean (section).

**Kajak** ['ka:jak], *m* -s/-s kayak.
**Kajüte** [ka'jy:tə], *f* -/-n cabin.
**Kakadu** ['kakadu:], *m* -s/-s cockatoo.
**Kakao** [ka'kau], *m* -s/-s cocoa.
**Kakerlak** ['ka:kərlak], *m* -s & -en/-en cockroach.
**Kaktee** [kak'te:ə], *f* -/-n/**Kaktus** ['kaktus], *m* -/-teen & -tusse cactus.
**Kalb** [kalp], *n* -(e)s/-er (a) calf; (b) Cu: veal. ◆'**k~en** [-bən], *v.i.* (haben) (Kuh usw.) to calve. ◆'**K~fleisch**, *n* veal. ◆'**K~s-**, comb.fm. Cu: (a) calf's, (liver etc.); (b) veal (steak etc.); (breast etc.) of veal. ◆'**K~sbraten**, *m* roast veal. ◆'**K~sleder**, *n* calf (leather); calfskin.
**Kalender** [ka'lɛndər], *m* -s/- 1. calendar. 2. (Taschenk.) diary.
**Kali** ['ka:li]. *n* -s/-s potash; Ch: potassium.
**Kaliber** [ka'li:bər], *n* -s/- calibre.
**Kalium** ['ka:lium], *n* -s/no pl potassium.
**Kalk** [kalk], *m* -(e)s/-e (a) lime; ungelöschter K., quicklime; (b) (K~stein) limestone; (c) (Knochensubstanz) calcium. ◆'**K~stein**, *m* limestone.
**Kalkul|ation** [kalkulatsi'o:n], *f* -/-en calculation; Com: estimate. ◆**k~ieren** [-'li:rən], *v.tr.* to calculate (sth.).
**Kalorie** [kalo'ri:], *f* -/-n [-ən] calorie. ◆**k~narm**, adj. low-calorie (food).
**kalt** [kalt], adj. cold; mir ist (es) k., I am cold; etwas k. stellen, to put sth. to cool; Cu: k~e Platte, plate of cold meats; das läßt mich k., it leaves me cold. ◆'**k~blütig**, adj. cold-blooded; adv. in cold blood. ◆'**K~blütigkeit**, *f* -/no pl coolness; Pej: cold-bloodedness. ◆'**K~miete**, *f* basic rent (without heating). ◆'**K~schale**, *f* fruit purée/whip; (Vorspeise) sweet soup. ◆'**k~schnäuzig**, adj. F: cold; (grausam) callous. ◆'**k~stellen**, v.tr.sep. F: to reduce (s.o.) to impotence.
**Kälte** ['kɛltə], *f* -/no pl 1. cold; (unter Null) frost; 10 Grad K., 10 degrees below freezing. 2. Fig: coldness, coolness. ◆'**K~grad**, *m* (degree of) coldness. ◆'**K~welle**, *f* cold spell.
**Kalzium** ['kaltsium], *n* -s/no pl calcium.
**Kamel** [ka'me:l], *n* -s/-e 1. Z: camel. 2. (Pers.) idiot.
**Kamera** ['kamərə], *f* -/-s camera. ◆'**K~mann**, *m* cameraman.
**Kamerad(in)** [kamə'ra:t (-'ra:din)], *m* -en/-en (*f* -/-nen) comrade, companion; F: mate; N.Am: buddy. ◆**K~schaft**, *f* -/no pl comradeship; companionship. ◆**k~schaftlich**, adj. comradely; friendly (relationship).
**Kamille** [ka'milə], *f* -/-n camomile. ◆**K~ntee**, *m* camomile tea.
**Kamin** [ka'mi:n], *m* -(e)s/-e fireplace; (Schornstein) chimney. ◆**K~kehrer**, *m* -s/- chimney-sweep. ◆**K~sims**, *m* mantelpiece.
**Kamm** [kam], *m* -(e)s/-e 1. comb. 2. crest (of a wave); ridge (of a mountain). 3. Z:

crest (of a bird); comb (of a cock).
**kämmen** ['kɛmən], *v.tr.* to comb (hair, wool etc.); sich k., to comb one's hair.
**Kammer** ['kamər]. I. *f* -/-n 1. (Abstellraum) boxroom; (für Haushaltsgeräte) broom cupboard. 2. Pol: Com: chamber (of parliament, trade). II. K~-, comb.fm. Mus: chamber (music etc.). ◆'**K~konzert**, *n* concert of chamber music. ◆'**K~spiele**, npl intimate theatre.
**Kampagne** [kam'panjə], *f* -/-n campaign.
**Kampf** [kampf]. I. *m* -(e)s/-e (a) fight; schwere K~e, heavy fighting; (b) Sp: (Wettkampf) contest; (c) Fig: struggle, (Aktion) campaign; etwas dat den K. ansagen, to declare war on sth. II. 'K~-, comb.fm. fighting (troops etc.); battle (song etc.); Mil: combat (zone, troops etc.). ◆'**k~bereit**, adj. ready for action; esp. Fig: ready for the fray. ◆'**K~handlungen**, fpl fighting, (military) action. ◆'**K~kraft**, *f* fighting strength. ◆'**k~los**, adj. without a fight. ◆'**k~lustig**, adj. belligerent. ◆'**K~richter**, *m* -s/- Sp: judge. ◆'**k~unfähig**, adj. (Soldat) unfit for active service; (Panzer usw.) out of action. ◆'**K~verband**, *m* fighting/combat force.
**kämpf|en** ['kɛmpfən], *v.* 1. *v.i.* (haben) to fight; um etwas acc k., to fight/esp. Fig: struggle for sth.; Fig: mit sich k., to struggle with oneself. 2. *v.refl.* sich durch etwas acc k., to fight one's way through sth. ◆'**K~er**, *m* -s/- fighter; Fig: crusader. ◆'**k~erisch**, adj. fighting (spirit, mood etc.).
**Kampfer** ['kampfər], *m* -s/no pl camphor.
**Kanad|a** ['kanada]. Pr.n.n -s. Canada. ◆**K~ier(in)** [ka'na:diər(in)], *m* -s/- (*f* -/-nen) Canadian. ◆**k~isch** [ka'na:diʃ], adj. Canadian.
**Kanal** [ka'na:l], *m* -s/-e 1. (für Schiffe) canal; Geog: der K., the (English) Channel. 2. (für Abwässer) drain, sewer. 3. Rad: TV: channel. ◆**K~isation** [kanalizatsi'o:n], *f* -/-en (für Abwässer) sewerage (system); main drainage. ◆**k~i'sieren**, v.tr. (a) to canalize (a river); (b) to provide (a town etc.) with sewers/drains.
**Kanarienvogel** [ka'na:riənfo:gəl], canary.
**Kandi|dat** [kandi'da:t], *m* -en/-en candidate; (Bewerber) applicant. ◆**K~datur** [-da'tu:r], *f* -/-en candidature. ◆**k~'dieren**, *v.i.* (haben) to be a candidate; Pol: etc: to stand; N.Am: run.
**kand|ieren** [kan'di:rən], *v.tr.* Cu: to candy (fruit). ◆'**K~iszucker**, *m* -s/no pl candy sugar.
**Känguruh** ['kɛnguru], *n* -s/-s kangaroo.
**Kaninchen** [ka'ni:nçən], *n* -s/- rabbit.
**Kanister** [ka'nistər], *m* -s/- canister; (aus Blech) tin; (für Wasser) water carrier.
**Kanne** ['kanə], *f* -/-n (a) (Krug) jug; (b)

(*mit Deckel*) (milk) churn, (*klein*) can; (coffee, tea) pot; (*c*) (*Gießk.*) (watering-)-can.

**Kannibal|e** [kani'bɑːlə], *m* -n/-n cannibal. ◆**K~ismus** [-a'lismus], *m* -/no pl cannibalism.

**Kanon** ['kɑːnɔn], *m* -s/-s *Mus:* canon; (*Lied*) round.

**Kanone** [ka'noːnə], *f* -/-n **1.** *Mil:* (field etc.) gun; *Hist:* cannon. **2.** *F:* (*Pers.*) *esp. Sp:* ace, champ. ◆**K~nkugel**, *f* cannon ball.

**Kantate** [kan'tɑːtə], *f* -/-n cantata.

**Kant|e** ['kantə], *f* -/-n edge. ◆**'k~ig**, *adj.* angular (stone etc.); squared (timber etc.); square (chin etc.).

**Kantine** [kan'tiːnə], *f* -/-n canteen.

**Kanu** ['kɑːnu, ka'nuː], *n* -s/-s canoe; **K. fahren**, to canoe.

**Kanz|el** ['kantsəl], *f* -/-n **1.** *Ecc:* pulpit. **2.** *Av:* cockpit. ◆**'K~ler**, *m* -s/- *Pol:* chancellor.

**Kap** [kap], *n* -s/-s cape, headland.

**Kapazität** [kapatsi'tɛːt], *f* -/-en **1.** capacity. **2.** (*Pers.*) **eine K. auf diesem Gebiet**, an authority in this field.

**Kapelle** [ka'pɛlə], *f* -/-n **1.** *Ecc:* chapel. **2.** *Mus:* band.

**Kaper** ['kɑːpər], *f* -/-n caper.

**kapern** ['kɑːpərn], *v.tr.* to seize (a ship etc.) (as a prize).

**kapieren** [ka'piːrən], *v.tr. F:* to understand, get (sth.).

**Kapital** [kapi'tɑːl], *n* -s/-e & -ien capital; *Fig:* asset. **II. K~-**, *comb.fm.* capital (*Fin:* investment, market etc.; *Jur:* crime etc.). ◆**K~gesellschaft**, *f* -/-en joint stock company. ◆**K~ismus** [-ta'lismus], *m* -/no pl capitalism. ◆**K~ist** [-ta'list], *m* -en/-en capitalist. ◆**k~istisch**, *adj.* capitalist.

**Kapitän** [kapi'tɛːn], *m* -s/-e (*a*) *Nau: Av:* captain; master (of a merchant vessel); (*b*) *Sp: etc:* team leader.

**Kapitel** [ka'pitəl], *n* -s/- chapter.

**Kapitul|ation** [kapitulatsi'oːn], *f* -/-en capitulation, surrender. ◆**k~ieren** [-'liːrən], *v.i.* (*haben*) to capitulate.

**Kaplan** [kap'lɑːn], *m* -s/-e chaplain; (*Hilfsgeistlicher*) curate.

**Kappe** ['kapə], *f* -/-n cap. ◆**'k~n**, *v.tr.* to chop (sth.); to top (a tree).

**Kapsel** ['kapsəl], *f* -/-n (*Behälter*) capsule.

**kaputt** [ka'put], *adj.* (*Sache*) bust; broken (cup, *Hum:* leg etc.); *F:* (*Auto*) smashed up; (*nicht funktionierend*) on the blink; *Fig:* ruined (firm, marriage etc.). ◆**k~gehen**, *v.i.sep.irr.36* (*sein*) *F:* to bust, (*Teller usw.*) break; (*Uhr usw.*) to go on the blink; (*Birne usw.*) to go; (*Kleider, Schuhe usw.*) to fall to pieces. ◆**k~lachen**, *v.refl.sep. F:* **sich k.**, to laugh one's head off. ◆**k~machen**, *v.tr.sep. F:* to bust (sth.); *Fig:* to ruin (s.o., a firm etc.); (*erschöpfen*) to wear (s.o.) out.

**Kapuze** [ka'puːtsə], *f* -/-n hood.

**Karaffe** [ka'rafə], *f* -/-n decanter; (*im Restaurant*) carafe.

**Karambolage** [karambo'lɑːʒə], *f* -/-n *F: Aut:* smash; (*Massenk.*) pile-up.

**Karamel** [kara'mɛl], *m* -s/no pl caramel.

**Karat** [ka'rɑːt], *n* -(e)s/-e carat.

**Karawane** [kara'vɑːnə], *f* -/-n caravan (of camels etc.).

**Kardinal** [kardi'nɑːl], *m* -(e)s/-e cardinal. ◆**'K~zahl**, *f* cardinal number.

**Karfreitag** [kar'fraitɑːk], *m* Good Friday.

**karg** [kark], *adj.* (*a*) scanty (vegetation etc.); frugal (meal); (*b*) poor (soil etc.).

**kärglich** ['kɛrkliç], *adj.* scanty (vegetation etc.); frugal (meal); niggardly (sum).

**Kargo** ['kargo], *m* -s/-s cargo.

**Karib|ik** [ka'riːbik]. *Pr.n.f.* -. **die K.**, the Caribbean. ◆**k~isch**, *adj.* Caribbean.

**kariert** [ka'riːrt], *adj.* check (pattern etc.); *Sp:* chequered (flag).

**Karies** ['kɑːriɛs], *f* -/no pl caries.

**Karik|atur** [karika'tuːr], *f* -/-en caricature; (*political etc.*) cartoon. ◆**K~aturist** [-tu'rist], *m* -en/-en caricaturist, cartoonist.

**karitativ** [karita'tiːf], *adj.* charitable.

**Karneval** ['karnəval], *m* -s/-s carnival.

**Karo** ['kɑːro]. **I.** *n* -s/-s (*a*) (*Viereck*) square; (*b*) (*Muster*) check; (*c*) (*Karte*) diamond; (*Farbe*) diamonds. **II. K~-**, *comb.fm.* (*a*) check (pattern etc.); (*b*) (ace, king, queen etc.) of diamonds.

**Karosse** [ka'rɔsə], *f* -/-n (state) coach. ◆**K~rie** [-'riː], *f* body(work).

**Karotte** [ka'rɔtə], *f* -/-n carrot.

**Karpfen** ['karpfən], *m* -s/- carp.

**Karre** ['karə], *f* -/-n = **Karren**.

**Karree** [ka'reː], *n* -s/-s square.

**Karren** ['karən], *m* -s/- **1.** cart; (*Handk.*) barrow. **2.** *Pej:* (*Auto*) jalopy.

**Karriere** [kari'eːrə], *f* -/-n career; **K. machen**, to get to the top (of one's profession). ◆**K~macher**, *m Pej:* careerist.

**Karte** ['kartə], *f* -/-n **1.** (*a*) card; *esp.* postcard; (*b*) (visiting) card; (*c*) (*Speisek.*) menu. **2.** (*Fahrk., Eintrittsk.*) ticket. **3.** (*Spielk.*) (playing) card; **K~n geben**, to deal; **K~n legen**, to tell fortunes from the cards; **alles auf eine K. setzen**, to put all one's eggs in one basket. **4.** (*Landk.*) map. ◆**'K~n-**, *comb. fm.* (*a*) card (player, table etc.); (*b*) map(-reading etc.). ◆**'K~spiel**, *n* (*a*) pack of cards; (*b*) game of cards.

**Kartei** [kar'tai], *f* -/-en card index. ◆**K~karte**, *f* index/file card.

**Kartell** [kar'tɛl], *n* -s/-e cartel.

**Kartoffel** [kar'tɔfəl]. **I.** *f* -/-n potato. **II. K~-**, *comb.fm.* potato (salad etc.). ◆**K~käfer**, *m* Colorado beetle, *N.Am:* potato bug. ◆**K~knödel**, *m* potato dumpling. ◆**K~puffer**, *m* potato pancake/fritter. ◆**K~püree**, *n* mashed potatoes.

**Karton** [kar'tɔŋ], *m* -s/-s **1.** (*Material*) card, cardboard. **2.** (*Schachtel*) cardboard box, carton.

**Karussell** [karu'sɛl], n -s/-s roundabout, merry-go-round.
**Karwoche** ['kɑːrvɔxə], f -/no pl Holy Week.
**kaschieren** [ka'ʃiːrən], v.tr. to conceal.
**Käse** ['kɛːzə], m -s/- cheese. ◆'K~blatt, n F: Pej: rag. ◆'K~kuchen m, cheese-cake.
**Kasern|e** [ka'zɛrnə], f -/-n barracks. ◆K~enhof, m barrack square.
**Kasino** [ka'ziːno], n -s/-s 1. casino. 2. Mil: officer's mess.
**Kasse** ['kasə], f -/-n 1. (a) (Behälter) cash register, till; (Zahlstelle) cash desk; (im Supermarkt) check-out; (b) Th: Cin: etc: box office. 2. (a) F: gut/knapp bei K. sein, to be flush (with money)/short of cash; (b) (Spielk.) pool, F: kitty. 3. F: (a) (Spark.) savings bank; (b) (Krankenk.) health insurance (scheme). ◆'K~n-bestand, m cash balance. ◆'K~n-sturz, m F: K. machen, to count one's worldly wealth. ◆'K~nzettel, m receipt, sales slip.
**Kasserolle** [kasə'rɔlə], f -/-n cast-iron frying pan.
**Kassette** [ka'sɛtə], f -/-n 1. (a) (Kästchen) small box; (Schmukk.) case, casket; (b) (Buchk.) slipcase. 2. Phot: Rec: cassette. ◆K~nrecorder, m -s/- cassette recorder.
**kassier|en** [ka'siːrən], v.tr. to take (in) (money from customers etc.); to collect (rent etc.); (Kellner usw.) darf ich bitte k.? can I give you the bill? ◆K~er(in), m -s/- (f -/-nen) cashier; Th: etc: box-office clerk.
**Kastagnetten** [kastan'jɛtən], fpl castanets.
**Kastanie** [kas'tɑːnjə], f chestnut. ◆K~nbaum, m chestnut tree.
**Kästchen** ['kɛstçən], n -s/- small box; casket.
**Kaste** ['kastə], f -/-n caste.
**Kasten** ['kastən], m -s/- box; (Briefk.) letter/N.Am: mail box; (Schauk.) show-case; (für Brot) bin; ein K. Bier, a crate of beer. ◆'K~wagen, m box cart/Rail: car/Aut: van.
**kastrieren** [kas'triːrən], v.tr. to castrate (a man); to neuter, F: doctor (a pet).
**Katalog** [kata'loːk], m -(e)s/-e catalogue.
**Katapult** [kata'pult], n -(e)s/-e catapult.
**Katarrh** [ka'tar], m -s/-e catarrh.
**katastroph|al** [katastro'faːl], adj. cata-strophic, disastrous. ◆K~e [katas'troːfə], f -/-n catastrophe, disaster. ◆K~engebiet, n disaster area.
**Kategor|ie** [katego'riː], f -/-n category. ◆k~isch [-'goːriʃ], adj. categorical (denial etc.); flat (refusal).
**Kater** ['kaːtər], m -s/- 1. Z: tom cat. 2. F: einen K. haben, to have a hangover.
**Katheder** [ka'teːdər], m -s/- (lecturer's) reading desk; Sch: teacher's desk.
**Kathedrale** [kate'draːlə], f -/-n cathedral.
**Kathode** [ka'toːdə], f -/-n cathode.

**Kathol|ik(in)** [kato'liːk(in)], m -en/-en (f -/-nen) (Roman) Catholic. ◆k~isch [-'toːliʃ], adj. (Roman) Catholic.
**Kätzchen** ['kɛtsçən], n -s/- 1. kitten. 2. Bot: catkin.
**Katze** ['katsə], f -/-n Z: cat, esp. she-cat; die K. aus dem Sack lassen, to let the cat out of the bag; F: das ist alles für die Katz, that's a waste of effort. ◆'K~nauge, n 1. cat's eye. 2. Aut: etc: reflector. ◆'k~nhaft, adj. catlike, fe-line (movements etc.). ◆'K~njammer, m hangover. ◆'K~nsprung, m F: es ist nur ein K. (von hier), it's only a stone's throw (from here). ◆'K~n-wäsche, f F: lick and a promise.
**Kauderwelsch** ['kaudərvɛlʃ], n -(e)s/no pl F: gibberish, double Dutch.
**kau|en** ['kauən], v.tr. & i. (haben) (a) to chew (food); (b) an den Nägeln k., to bite one's fingernails. ◆'K~gummi, n chewing gum.
**kauern** ['kauərn], v.i. (haben) & v.refl. (sich) k., (Pers.) to squat, (Pers., Tier) crouch (down).
**Kauf** [kauf]. I. m -(e)s/-e (a) purchase; Fig: etwas (mit) in K. nehmen, to put up with sth.; (b) (Sache) ein guter/ günstiger K., a good buy/bargain. II. 'K~-, comb.fm. purchase (price etc.); (conditions etc.) of purchase. ◆'k~en, v.tr. to buy (sth.); regelmäßig bei X k., to shop regularly at X's. ◆'K~haus, n department store. ◆'k~lustig, adj. eager to buy. ◆'K~mann, m (a) business man; (Händler) dealer; (b) A: shop-keeper; zum K. gehen, to go to the gro-cer's. ◆'k~männisch, adj. commercial (training, firm etc.); k~männischer Angestellter, (clerical) employee in a busi-ness firm. ◆'K~vertrag, m contract of purchase; Jur: deed of sale.
**Käuf|er(in)** ['kɔyfər(in)], m -s/- (f -/-nen) buyer; (Eink.) shopper. ◆'k~lich, adj. for sale.
**Kaulquappe** ['kaulkvapə], f -/-n tadpole.
**kaum** [kaum], adv. hardly; sie ist k. acht, she is barely eight.
**Kaution** [kautsi'oːn], f -/-en Jur: security, guarantee; (für einen Gefangenen) bail.
**Kautschuk** ['kautʃuk], n -s/-e (india) rub-ber.
**Kauz** [kauts], m -es/-e 1. (small) owl. 2. F: komischer K., odd bird, N.Am: screwball.
**Kavalier** [kava'liːr], m -s/-e gentleman. ◆K~sdelikt, n trivial offence.
**Kavaller|ie** [kavalə'riː], f -/-n cavalry. ◆K~ist, m -en/-en cavalryman, troop-er.
**Kaviar** ['kaːviar], m -s/-e caviar.
**keck** [kɛk], adj. saucy, (frech) cheeky; (vorlaut) forward; (forsch) bold.
**Kegel** ['keːgəl], m -s/- 1. Mth: cone. 2. (Spielk.) skittle; (bowling) pin. ◆'K~bahn, f skittle/N.Am: bowling al-ley. ◆'k~förmig, adj. conical.

◆'k~n, *v.i.* *(haben)* to play skittles, *N.Am:* to bowl.

**Kehl|e** ['keːlə], *f* -/-n throat. ◆'K~kopf, *m* larynx. ◆'K~kopfentzündung, *f* laryngitis.

**Kehr|e** ['keːrə], *f* -/-n *(Kurve)* sharp bend, *esp.* hairpin. ◆'k~en¹, *v.tr.* etwas nach außen, oben usw. k., to turn sth. outwards, upwards etc.; *(Pers.)* in sich gekehrt, withdrawn, lost in thought. ◆'k~en², *v.tr. & i.* *(haben)* to sweep. ◆'K~icht, *m & n* -s/*no pl* sweepings. ◆'K~maschine, *f* (carpet, street) sweeper. ◆'K~reim, *m* refrain. ◆'K~seite, *f* -/-n *(Rückseite)* reverse (of a coin etc.). ◆'k~tmachen, *v.i.sep.* *(haben)* to turn on one's heel.

**keifen** ['kaifən], *v.i.* *(haben)* to scold, bicker.

**Keil** [kail], *m* -(e)s/-e wedge. ◆'k~en, *v.tr.* to split (sth.) with a wedge. ◆'K~riemen, *m* V-belt.

**Keiler** ['kailər], *m* -s/- wild boar.

**Keim** [kaim], *m* -(e)s/-e *Bot: & Fig:* germ; *Biol:* embryo; *Fig:* etwas im K. ersticken, to nip sth. in the bud. ◆'k~en, *v.i.* *(haben)* to germinate. ◆'k~frei, *adj.* sterile. ◆'k~tötend, *adj.* germicidal, antiseptic.

**kein** [kain]. **I.** *indef.art.* no, not any; **ich habe k. Geld**/k~e Zeit, I've no money/time, I haven't any money/time; **k. Wort mehr**, not another word. **II.** *indef.pron.* **1.** **k~e(r)**, nobody, no one; **k~er von beiden**, neither (of them); **ich kenne k~en**, I do not know anyone/anybody. **2.** *(Sache)* **k~er/k~e**/k~es, none, not one; **ich habe k~e(s) (mehr)**, I haven't got any (more). ◆'k~es'falls, *adv.* on no account. ◆'k~es'wegs, *adv.* by no means; *(überhaupt nicht)* not in the least.

**Keks** [keːks], *m* -es/-e biscuit, *N.Am:* cookie.

**Kelch** [kɛlç], *m* -(e)s/-e **1.** goblet. **2.** *Bot:* calyx.

**Kelle** ['kɛlə], *f* -/-n **1.** *H:* ladle (for soup etc.). **2.** *(Maurerk.)* trowel. **3.** *Rail:* signalling disc.

**Keller** ['kɛlər], *m* -s/- cellar, *(bewohnbar)* basement. ◆'K~assel, *f* woodlouse.

**Kellner** ['kɛlnər], *n* -s/- waiter, *Nau: Rail:* steward. ◆'K~in, *f* -/-nen waitress.

**keltern** ['kɛltərn], *v.tr.* to press (grapes, fruit etc.).

**kenn|en** ['kɛnən], *v.tr.irr.* to know (s.o., sth.); **er kennt keine Rücksicht**, he has no idea of consideration (for others); **wir k. uns schon**, we have already met. ◆'k~enlernen, *v.tr.sep.* to get to know (s.o., sth.); *(treffen)* to meet (s.o.); **wir haben uns in Rom kennengelernt**, we met in Rome. ◆'K~er, *m* -s/- expert, authority ( + *gen*/von + *dat*, on). ◆'k~tlich, *adj.* recognizable; etwas k. machen, to mark/identify sth. ◆'K~tnis, *f* -/-se knowledge; etwas zur

**K. nehmen**, to take note of sth. ◆'K~wort, *n* *Mil:* etc: password. ◆'K~zeichen, *n* (a) *(Merkmal)* (distinguishing) feature; (b) *(Zeichen)* mark; *(Abzeichen)* badge; *Aut:* (polizeiliches) K., registration number; *N.Am:* licence number. ◆'k~zeichnen, *v.tr.sep.* (a) *(markieren)* to mark (goods, parts etc.); (b) *(charakterisieren)* to characterize, distinguish (sth.). ◆'K~ziffer, *f* code number; *Com:* reference number.

**kentern** ['kɛntərn], *v.tr. & i.* *(sein)* to capsize.

**Keramik** [ke'raːmik], *f* -/-en **1.** *no pl* ceramics, pottery. **2.** eine K., a piece of pottery.

**Kerb|e** ['kɛrbə], *f* -/-n notch; slot (for a peg etc.). ◆'K~holz, *n* *F:* etwas auf dem K. haben, to have blotted one's copybook.

**Kerker** ['kɛrkər], *m* -s/- *Hist:* dungeon; *A: & Aus:* prison.

**Kerl** [kɛrl], *m* -s/-e *F:* chap, fellow; *P:* bloke; *esp. N.Am:* guy.

**Kern** [kɛrn]. **I.** *m* -(e)s/-e **1.** (nut) kernel; pip (of an orange, apple, grape); stone, *N.Am:* pit (of a cherry etc.). **2.** *Ph: Biol:* nucleus. **3.** *Fig:* core; heart (of a city etc.). **II.** 'K~-, *comb.fm.* (a) *Ph:* nuclear (fuel, energy etc.); (b) *Fig:* central (problem, idea etc.); crucial (question, point). ◆'K~forschung, *f* nuclear research. ◆'K~gehäuse, *n* core (of an apple etc.). ◆'k~gesund, *adj.* healthy, as sound as a bell. ◆'k~ig, *adj.* earthy (words etc.); robust (person, style etc.). ◆'K~kraftwerk, *n* nuclear power station. ◆'K~obst, *n* apple-like fruit(s); pomes. ◆'K~physik, *f* nuclear physics. ◆'K~spaltung, *f* nuclear fission. ◆'K~waffe, *f* nuclear weapon.

**Kerze** ['kɛrtsə], *f* -/-n **1.** candle. **2.** *Aut:* (sparking) plug. ◆'k~nge'rade, *adj.* bolt upright. ◆'K~nhalter, *m* candleholder. ◆'K~nständer, *m* candlestick.

**keß** [kɛs], *adj.* jaunty (hat); pert (girl, answer).

**Kessel** ['kɛsəl], *m* -s/- **1.** (a) *(Teek.)* kettle; (b) *(großer Topf)* cauldron; (c) *(Heizk., Dampfk.)* boiler. **2.** *(Talk.)* basin-shaped valley, hollow. ◆'K~treiben, *n* *Fig:* round-up (of a gang); *Pol:* witchhunt.

**Kett|e** ['kɛtə], *f* -/-n (a) chain; (b) *(Halsk.)* necklace; string (of pearls); (gold, silver etc.) chain; (c) *Fig:* series, succession (of events etc.). ◆'k~en¹, *v.tr.* an j-n, etwas *acc* gekettet sein, to be bound/tied to s.o., sth. ◆'K~en-², *comb.fm.* (a) chain (drive, *Fig:* reaction, smoker etc.); (b) tracked (vehicle).

**Ketzer** ['kɛtsər], *m* -s/- heretic. ◆'k~isch, *adj.* heretical.

**keuch|en** ['kɔyçən], *v.i.* *(haben)* to pant. ◆'K~husten, *m* whooping cough.

**Keule** ['kɔylə], *f* -/-n **1.** club. **2.** *Cu:* leg.

**keusch** [kɔyʃ], *adj.* chaste. ◆'K~heit, *f*

-/no pl chastity.

**kichern** ['kiçərn], v.i. (haben) to giggle, titter.

**kidnappen** ['kitnɛpən], v.tr. to kidnap.

**Kiebitz** ['ki:bits], m -es/-e Orn: lapwing.

**Kiefer¹** ['ki:fər], f -/-n pine (tree). ◆'K~nholz, n pinewood.

**Kiefer²**, m -s/- Anat: jaw.

**Kiel** [ki:l], m -(e)s/-e 1. shaft (of a feather). 2. Nau: keel. ◆'K~wasser, n wake.

**Kieme** ['ki:mə], f -/-n gill.

**Kies** [ki:s], m -es/-e gravel. ◆'K~grube, f gravel pit. ◆'K~weg, m gravel path.

**Kiesel** ['ki:zəl], m -s/- pebble. ◆'K~stein, m pebble.

**Kilo** ['ki:lo], n -s/-(s) kilo. ◆'K~gramm, n kilogram. ◆K~meter [kilo'me:tər], m -s/- kilometre. ◆K~'metergeld, n mileage allowance. ◆K~'meterzähler, m mileometer. ◆'K~watt, n kilowatt.

**Kimme** ['kimə], f -/-n notch (in a rifle sight).

**Kind** [kint], n -(e)s/-er (a) child; von K. auf, from childhood; (b) (Kleink.) baby; sie bekommt ein K., she's having a baby. ◆'K~er- ['kindər-], comb.fm. children's (book, shoes, choir, home etc.); (love etc.) of children; child's (voice, toy etc.). ◆'K~erarzt, m/'K~erärztin, f paediatrician. ◆'K~erbett, n junior bed. ◆K~e'rei, f -/-en (a) childish behaviour; (b) triviality. ◆'K~ergarten, m kindergarten, nursery school. ◆'K~ergeld, n child allowance. ◆'K~erkrippe, f crèche, N.Am: day care (nursery). ◆'K~erlähmung, f infantile paralysis, F: polio. ◆'k~er'leicht, adj. F: dead easy. ◆'k~erlos, adj. childless. ◆'K~erlosigkeit, f -/no pl childlessness. ◆'k~ermädchen, n nursemaid. ◆'k~erreich, adj. large (family). ◆'K~erspiel, n (a) children's game; (b) F: pushover, cinch. ◆'K~erstube, f Fig: er hat keine K., he has no manners. ◆'K~erteller, m dish for children. ◆'K~erwagen, m pram, N.Am: baby carriage. ◆'K~esalter, n -s/no pl infancy, childhood; im K., in childhood. ◆K~heit, f -/no pl childhood. ◆'k~isch [-diʃ], adj. childish (person, behaviour). ◆k~lich ['kintliç], adj. childlike (behaviour). ◆K~skopf ['kints-], m F: childish person.

**Kinn** [kin], n -(e)s/-e chin. ◆'K~haken, m hook (to the chin).

**Kino** ['ki:no], n -s/-s cinema, N.Am: movie theatre. ◆'K~besucher, m cinemagoer, N.Am: moviegoer.

**Kiosk** [ki'ɔsk], m -(e)s/-e kiosk.

**Kipp|e** ['kipə], f -/-n 1. (Müllk.) dump, tip. 2. F: es steht auf der K., (Gegenstand) it's balanced precariously; Fig: (Erfolg usw.) it's touch and go. 3. F: (Stummel) fag-end, N.Am: cigarette- butt.

◆'k~en, v. 1. v.i. (sein) (Schrank, Stoß Bücher usw.) to tilt, (umfallen) topple (over). 2. v.tr. (a) to tilt (sth.); (b) to tip (rubbish, gravel etc.). ◆'K~schalter, m tumbler switch.

**Kirch|e** ['kirçə], f -/-n church; in die K. gehen, to go to church. ◆'K~en-, comb.fm. church (choir, music etc.). ◆'K~enlied, n hymn. ◆'K~gänger(in), m -s/- (f -/-nen) churchgoer. ◆'K~hof, m churchyard. ◆'k~lich, adj. church (holiday, wedding etc.); ecclesiastical (office, dignitary etc.). ◆'K~turm, m church tower, steeple.

**Kirsch-** ['kirʃ-], comb.fm. cherry (tree, cake etc.). ◆'K~kern, m cherry-stone/ N.Am: pit. ◆'K~e, f -/-n cherry. ◆'K~wasser, n kirsch.

**Kissen** ['kisən], n -s/- cushion; (Kopfk.) pillow. ◆'K~bezug, m cushion cover; (Kopfk.) pillow case.

**Kiste** ['kistə], f -/-n crate; box (of cigars etc.).

**Kitsch** [kitʃ], m -(e)s/no pl kitsch. ◆'k~ig, adj. kitschy.

**Kitt** [kit], m -(e)s/-e (adhesive) cement; (für Fenster, Risse) putty. ◆'k~en, v.tr. to glue (broken china etc.); to fix (a pane etc.) with putty.

**Kittchen** ['kitçən], n -s/- F: clink, jug.

**Kittel** ['kitəl], m -s/- (a) (workman's) overall; (b) housecoat; (doctor's etc.) (white) coat.

**Kitz** [kits], n -es/-e Z: kid (of a deer, goat).

**Kitz|el** ['kitsəl], m -s/no pl tickle. ◆'k~(e)lig, adj. ticklish; Fig: tricky (situation). ◆'k~eln, v.tr. to tickle.

**Kladde** ['kladə], f -/-n (Heft) (rough) notebook; scribbling pad.

**klaffen** ['klafən], v.i. (haben) (Loch, Wunde usw.) to gape; (Abgrund usw.) to yawn.

**kläffen** ['klɛfən], v.i. (haben) (Hund) to yap, yelp.

**Klage** ['kla:gə], f -/-n (a) (Beschwerde) complaint; (b) Jur: action, suit. ◆'k~n, v.i. (haben) (a) to complain; (b) Jur: to take legal action; auf Schadenersatz usw. k., to sue for damages etc.; (c) Lit: über j-s Tod k., to mourn s.o.'s death. **Kläg|er(in)** ['klɛ:gər(in)], m -s/- (f -/-nen) Jur: (Privatrecht) plaintiff. ◆'k~lich, adj. (a) (mitleiderregend) pitiful, piteous (sight, crying etc.); (b) (erbärmlich) wretched; miserable (performance, result etc.); k. versagen, to fail miserably.

**klamm** [klam], adj. (a) numb, stiff (hands etc.); (b) cold and damp, clammy (clothes etc.).

**Klammer** ['klamər], f -/-n 1. (paper etc.) clip; (Heftk.) (wire) staple; Tchn: clamp; H: (Wäschek.) (clothes) peg, N.Am: clothespin. 2. (Schriftzeichen) bracket. ◆'k~n, v.tr. (a) to clip (things) together; (b) sich an j-n, etwas acc k., to cling to s.o., sth.

**Klang** [klaŋ], m -(e)s/-e sound; (Klang-

*farbe)* tone. ◆'K~**farbe,** *f* tone; timbre. ◆'k~**voll,** *adj.* sonorous (voice, language etc.); *Fig:* k~**voller Name,** illustrious name.

**Klapp-** ['klap-], *comb.fm.* folding (bed, seat etc.); hinged (lid). ◆**K~e** ['klapə], *f* -/-n *(a)* flap; drop-leaf (of a table); drop-front (of a desk etc.); *Anat:* valve; *(b) P: (Mund)* trap. ◆'k~**en,** *v.* 1. *v.i. (haben) (a) (Tür usw.)* to bang; *(b) Fig: (Plan, Versuch usw.)* to work, come off; *(Unternehmen usw.)* to go well; **nicht k.,** to go wrong. 2. *v.tr.* **nach oben k.,** to turn up (a collar etc.); to lift up (a flap etc.), tip up (a cinema seat etc.). ◆'K~**messer,** *n* jack-knife. ◆'K~**stuhl,** *m* folding chair/stool.

**Klapp|er** ['klapər], *f* -/-n (child's) rattle. ◆'k~**erkasten,** *m F:* rattletrap. ◆'k~**ern,** *v.i. (haben)* to clatter; *(lose Gegenstände usw.)* rattle. ◆'K~**er-schlange,** *f* rattlesnake. ◆'k~**(e)rig,** *adj. F: (Pers.)* shaky; ramshackle (vehicle etc.).

**Klaps** [klaps], *m* -es/-e smack, slap.

**klar** [kla:r], *adj.* clear; **ich bin mir darüber (völlig) im k~en, daß ...,** I am (perfectly) aware/(fully) realize that ... **ja k.!** yes, of course! *N.Am:* sure thing! *Mil: etc:* **k. zum Gefecht,** ready for action. ◆'K~**heit,** *f -/no pl* clarity; lucidity. ◆'k~**machen,** *v.tr.sep.* **j-m etwas k.,** to make sth. clear to s.o. ◆'k~**sehen,** *v.i.sep.irr.92 (haben) F:* to see daylight. ◆'K~**sichtfolie,** *f* transparent foil. ◆'k~**stellen,** *v.tr.sep.* to clarify; **k., daß ...,** to make it clear that ...

**Klär|anlage** ['klɛːr²anlɑːgə], *f* sewage works. ◆'k~**en,** *v.tr.* to clarify (a liquid, *Fig:* problem); to treat (sewage); **sich k.,** to become clear. ◆'K~**ung,** *f -/no pl* clarification.

**Klarinette** [klari'nɛtə], *f* -/-n clarinet.

**Klasse** ['klasə]. **I.** *f* -/-n class; **ein Hotel/ Rail: eine Fahrkarte erster K.,** a first-class hotel/*Rail:* ticket; *F: (Spieler)* **er ist große K.!** he's great stuff! **II. k.,** *adj. F:* smashing, *N.Am:* swell. ◆'K~**n-,** 'k~**n-,** *comb.fm.* class (hatred, distinctions, *Sch:* teacher etc.). ◆'K~**narbeit,** *f* (written) class test. ◆'k~**nbewußt,** *adj.* class-conscious. ◆'k~**nbuch,** *n* class register. ◆'K~**nkamerad(in),** *m(f)* classmate. ◆'K~**nkampf,** *m* class struggle. ◆'k~**nlos,** *adj.* classless. ◆'K~**nsprecher(in),** *m(f)* class captain. ◆'K~**nzimmer,** *n* classroom.

**Klassif|ikation** [klasifikatsi'oːn], *f -/-en* classification. ◆'k~**i'zieren,** *v.tr.* to classify.

**Klass|ik** ['klasik], *f -/no pl* classicism; *(Zeit)* classical period. ◆'K~**iker,** *m -s/-* classical author/artist/*Mus:* composer. ◆'k~**isch,** *adj. (a)* classical; *(b) (vorbildlich)* classic (example).

**Klatsch** [klatʃ], *m* -es/-e **1.** *(Geräusch)* smack; *(aufs Wasser)* splash; *(Schlag)*

slap. **2.** *no pl F:* gossip. ◆'K~**base,** *f F: (Pers.)* gossip. ◆'K~**e,** *f* -/-n (fly) swatter. ◆'k~**en,** *v.tr. & i. (haben) (a)* to slap (sth.); *(b)* to clap; **j-m Beifall k.,** to applaud s.o.; *(c) F:* to gossip. ◆'K~**mohn,** *m* field/corn poppy. ◆'k~**naß,** *adj. F:* soaking wet (clothes etc.); *(Pers.)* soaked to the skin. ◆'K~**spalte,** *f* gossip column.

**Klaue** ['klauə], *f* -/-n **1.** *Orn: Z:* claw; talon (of bird of prey). **2.** *F: (Hand)* paw. **3.** *F: (Schrift)* scrawl, scribble. ◆'k~**n,** *v.tr. F:* to pinch, swipe (sth.) (j-m/von j-m, from s.o.); to crib (an idea etc.).

**Klausel** ['klauzəl], *f Jur: etc:* clause.

**Klausur** [klau'zuːr], *f* written examination/test.

**Klaviatur** [klavia'tuːr], *f -/-en* keyboard.

**Klavier** [kla'viːr], *n -s/-e* piano.

**kleb|en** ['kleːbən], *v.* 1. *v.tr.* to stick, *(mit Klebstoff)* glue (sth.). 2. *v.i. (haben)* to stick, *(Kleider usw.)* cling **(an/auf etwas dat,** to sth.). ◆'K~**estreifen,** *m* adhesive/*F:* sticky tape. ◆'k~**rig,** *adj.* sticky. ◆'K~**stoff,** *m* adhesive, *esp.* glue.

**kleck|ern** ['klɛkərn], *v.tr. & i. (haben)* to spill (soup etc.). ◆'K~**s,** *m* -es/-e (ink) blot; blob, dab (of paint); splodge (of dirt etc.). ◆'k~**sen,** *v.i. (haben)* to make blots.

**Klee** [kleː], *m* -s/*no pl* clover. ◆'K~**blatt,** *n* clover-leaf.

**Kleid** [klait], *n* -(e)s/-er *(a)* dress; *(b) pl* **K~er,** clothes. ◆'k~**en** [-dən], *v.tr. (a)* to dress, clothe (s.o.); **sich sportlich usw. k.,** to wear sporting etc. clothes; **der Mantel kleidet dich gut,** the coat suits you. ◆'K~**erbügel,** *m* coat hanger. ◆'K~**erbürste,** *f* clothes brush. ◆'K~**erschrank,** *m* wardrobe, *N.Am:* clothes closet. ◆'k~**sam,** *adj.* becoming. ◆'K~**ung,** *f -/no pl* clothes, clothing.

**Kleie** ['klaiə], *f -/-n* bran.

**klein** [klain]. **I.** *adj. (a)* small; *esp. F:* little; **mein k~er Finger,** my little finger; **ein k. wenig,** a little bit; **unser K~er/ unsere K~e,** our youngest son/daughter; **von k. an/auf,** from childhood; *(b)* low (number, figure, cost etc.); **ein Wort k. schreiben,** to write a word with a small (initial) letter; *(c) (unbedeutend)* minor (problem etc.); slight (misfortune, illness etc.); **das k~ere Übel,** the lesser evil; **meine k~ste Sorge,** the least of my worries. **II. K~-,** *comb.fm.* small (shareholder, car etc.). ◆'K~**anzeige,** *f* small ad. ◆'K~**arbeit,** *f* detail/painstaking work. ◆'K~**bildkamera,** *f* miniature camera. ◆'k~**bürgerlich,** *adj. Pej:* petty bourgeois. ◆'K~**format,** *n* small size. ◆'k~**gedruckt,** *attrib.adj.* in small print. ◆'K~**geld,** *n* (small/loose) change. ◆'K~**holz,** *n* (chopped) firewood; *F:* **aus j-m K. machen,** to make mincemeat of s.o. ◆'K~igkeit, f -/-en trifle; minor matter; F: (zum Verschenken/Essen) a little something. ◆'k~kariert, adj. (a) (material etc.) in a small check; (b) F: Pej: narrow-minded (views etc.). ◆'K~kind, n small child. ◆'K~kram, m F: (a) bits and pieces; (b) Pej: trivia. ◆'k~kriegen, v.tr.sep. F: to smash (sth.) up; j-n k., to squash s.o. ◆'k~laut, adj. subdued, meek. ◆'k~lich, adj. petty; (engstirnig) small-minded. ◆'K~lichkeit, f -/no pl pettiness. ◆'k~mütig, adj. faint-hearted, pusillanimous. ◆'K~od [klaino:t], n -(e)s/-e & -ien Lit: jewel, gem. ◆'k~schneiden, v.tr.sep.irr.59 to chop (onions, parsley etc.). ◆'K~st-, comb.fm. smallest possible (amount etc.). ◆'K~stadt, f small town. ◆'k~städtisch, adj. small-town, provincial.

Kleister ['klaistər], m -s/- (wallpaper etc.) paste. ◆'k~n, v.tr. to paste, F: plaster (sth.).

Klemm|e ['klɛmə], f -/-n 1. clamp, clip. 2. F: tight spot; in der K. sitzen, to be in a fix. ◆'k~en, v. 1. v.tr. (a) (zwängen) to wedge, jam (sth.); (b) to clip (sth.); (c) F: sich hinter etwas acc k., (i) to get down to sth.; (ii) (weitermachen) to get on with sth. 2. v.i. (haben) (Schublade usw.) to jam, stick. Klempner ['klɛmpnər], m -s/- plumber.

Klerus ['kle:rus], m -/no pl clergy. Klette ['klɛtə], f -/-n Bot: burr. Kletter- ['klɛtər-], comb.fm. climbing (plant, pole, shoes etc.). ◆'K~er, m -s/-climber. ◆'k~n, v.i. (sein) to climb; (Pers.) (mit Mühe) to clamber, scramble. ◆'K~tour, f climbing trip.

klicken ['klikən], v.i. (haben) to click. Klient(in) [kli'ɛnt(in)], m -en/-en (f -/-nen) Jur: client. Klima ['kli:ma], n -s/-s & -te climate. ◆'K~anlage, f air-conditioning (system). ◆'k~tisch [kli'ma:tiʃ], adj. climatic. ◆'K~wechsel, m change of climate/air.

klimpern ['klimpərn], v.i. (haben) (a) Pej: (Pers.) to strum; (b) (Münzen usw.) to chink.

Klinge ['kliŋə], f -/-n blade. Kling|el ['kliŋəl], f -/-n (bicycle, door etc.) bell. ◆'K~elknopf, m bellpush. ◆'k~eln, v.i. (haben) (Klingel, Telefon usw.) to ring; (Pers.) to ring the bell (nach j-m, for s.o.); es klingelt, s.o./the doorbell is ringing. ◆'k~en, v.i.irr. (haben) (a) (Glocke, Gläser usw.) to ring; (Stimme, Musikinstrument) to sound; (b) (+ adj.) to sound (good, sad etc.). Klin|ik ['kli:nik], f -/-en clinic. ◆'k~isch, adj. clinical. Klinke ['kliŋkə], f -/-n (Griff) (door)handle; latch. klipp [klip], adj. k. und klar, clear as daylight; ich habe es ihm k. und klar ge-

sagt, I told him straight. Klippe ['klipə], f -/-n rock (in the sea). klirren ['klirən], v.i. (haben) (Gläser, Tassen usw.) to clink, chink; k~de Kälte, tingling cold. Klischee [kli'ʃe:], n -s/-s (Wendung) cliché. ◆K~vorstellung, f hackneyed idea. Klo [klo:], n -s/-s F: loo, N.Am: john. Kloake [klo'a:kə], f -/-n sewer; (Senkgrube) cesspool. klobig ['klo:biç], adj. clumsy. klopf|en ['klɔpfən], v. 1. v.i. (haben) (a) to knock; es hat geklopft, there was a knock; (b) j-m auf die Schulter k., to tap s.o. on the shoulder; (c) (Herz) (heftig) k., to pound (vor + dat, with); (d) (Motor) to knock, F: pink, N.Am: ping. 2. v.tr. (schlagen) to knock, drive a nail etc.) (in + acc, into); to beat (a carpet etc.). ◆'K~er, m -s/- (a) (door) knocker; (b) H: carpet-beater. ◆'K~zeichen, n tap, knock. Klöppel ['klœpəl], m -s/- clapper (of a bell). Klops [klɔps], m -es/-e meatball. Klosett [klo'zɛt], n -s/-s & -e lavatory, toilet. Kloß [klo:s], m -es/-e 1. Cu: dumpling. 2. F: einen K. im Hals haben, to have a lump in one's throat. Kloster ['klo:stər], n -s/- (a) (für Mönche) monastery; (b) (für Nonnen) convent. Klotz [klɔts], m -es/-e block of wood; (zum Brennen) log; F: einen K. am Bein haben, to have a millstone round one's neck. Klub [klup], m -s/-s club. ◆'K~sessel, m big armchair. Kluft¹ [kluft], f -/-e 1. (Felsspalte) cleft (in rock). 2. Fig: gulf (between parties etc.). Kluft², f -/-en F: Cl: outfit, gear. klug [klu:k], adj. (a) (gescheit) clever, bright; N.Am: smart (child, idea etc.); intelligent (person, animal etc.); daraus/aus ihm werd ich nicht k., I can't make it/him out; (b) (einsichtig) wise; k~er Rat, good advice. ◆'K~heit, f -/no pl (a) cleverness; astuteness; (b) prudence. Klump|en ['klumpən], m -s/- lump; Min: nugget (of gold etc.). ◆'k~ig, adj. lumpy (sauce etc.). knabbern ['knabərn], v.tr. & i. (haben) to nibble (an + dat, at). Knabe ['kna:bə], m -n/-n A: & Lit: boy. ◆'K~nchor, m boys' choir. ◆'k~nhaft, adj. boyish. Knack [knak], m -(e)s/-e crack. ◆'k~en, v. 1. v.i. (haben) (Zweige usw.) to crack. 2. v.tr. (a) to crack (a nut etc.); (b) F: to pick (a lock), crack (a safe). ◆'k~ig, adj. F: crisp (salad), crunchy (roll etc.). ◆'K~s, m -es/-e F: (a) (Geräusch, Sprung) crack; (b) defect. ◆'K~wurst, f pork sausage. Knäckebrot ['knɛkəbro:t], n crispbread. Knall [knal], m -(e)s/-e (a) bang; crack (of a shot, whip etc.); pop (of a cork); (b) F: **K. und Fall**, at once; (auf der Stelle) on the spot; (c) F: (Pers.) **einen K. haben**, to be crackers. ◆'**K~bonbon**, n (party) cracker, N.Am: favor. ◆'**K~effekt**, m sensation; sensational part. ◆'**k~en**, v. 1. v.i. (haben) to (go) bang; (Peitsche) to crack; (Sektkorken) to pop; (sein) F: to crash (in/gegen etwas acc, into/against sth.). 2. v.tr. to slam (sth.); F: **j-m eine k.**, to clout s.o. ◆'**k~'hart**, adj. F: tough (business etc.); (Pers.) hard as nails; Sp: (shot etc.) like a bullet. ◆'**k~ig**, adj. F: glaring (colour); flashy (dress etc.). ◆'**k~'rot**, adj. F: bright scarlet.

**knapp** [knap], adj. 1. Cl: tight, closefitting. 2. (a) (Waren) scarce, Com: in short supply; meagre (portion, pay etc.); (b) (etwas weniger) just under; **eine k~e Stunde**, barely an hour; (c) Sp: etc: **k~er Sieg**, narrow win. 3. (kurz) brief (summary etc.); terse (style etc.). ◆'**K~heit**, f -/no pl (a) scantiness; shortage (**an Nahrungsmitteln usw.**, of provisions etc.); (b) terseness.

**knarren** ['knarən], v.i. (haben) to creak.

**Knast** [knast], m -(e)s/-e P: clink.

**knattern** ['knatərn], v.i. (haben) (Gewehr, Motorrad) to bang away, (MG) crackle.

**Knäuel** ['knɔyəl], n -s/- ball (of wool etc.).

**Knauf** [knauf], m -(e)s/-e knob (of a door etc.).

**knauserig** ['knauzəriç], adj. stingy, tight-fisted. ◆'**k~n**, v.i. (haben) to skimp.

**knautsch|en** ['knautʃən], v.tr. & i. (haben) to crumple (material, paper etc.). ◆'**K~zone**, f Aut: crumple zone.

**Knebel** ['kne:bəl], m -s/- gag. ◆'**k~n**, v.tr. to gag (s.o.).

**Knecht** [knɛçt], m -(e)s/-e 1. A: farmhand. 2. Pej: Fig: slave.

**kneif|en** ['knaifən], v.irr. 1. v.tr. to pinch (s.o.). 2. v.i. (haben) F: **vor etwas dat k.**, to back out of sth. ◆'**K~zange**, f (pair of) pincers.

**Kneipe** ['knaipə], f -/-n F: pub; N.Am: bar.

**kneten** ['kne:tən], v.tr. to knead (dough etc.).

**Knick** [knik], m -(e)s/-e kink, sharp bend; (Falte) fold, crease. ◆'**k~en**, v. 1. v.tr. (a) to bend (wire etc.); to crease (paper etc.); (b) (brechen) to snap (a twig etc.); **einen geknickten Eindruck machen**, to look dejected. 2. v.i. (sein) to bend (at an angle); (brechen) to snap.

**Knicks** [kniks], m -es/-e curtsey; **einen K. machen**, to curtsey.

**Knie** [kni:], n -s/- ['kni:ə], knee. ◆'**K~beuge**, f knees-bend, N.Am: knee-bend. ◆'**k~fall**, m **einen K. tun**, to go down on one's knees (**vor j-m**, to s.o.). ◆'**K~gelenk**, n knee joint. ◆'**K~kehle**, f hollow of the knee.

◆**k~n** ['kni:ən], v.refl. & i. (haben) to kneel. ◆'**K~scheibe**, f knee-cap. ◆'**K~strumpf**, m knee-length sock.

**Kniff** [knif], m -(e)s/-e 1. crease (in paper, material etc.). 2. F: knack (of doing sth.). ◆'**k~lig**, adj. fiddly (task etc.); (heikel) tricky (question etc.).

**knipsen** ['knipsən], v.tr. (a) to punch (a ticket etc.); (b) to flick (a switch etc.); (c) Phot: F: to snap.

**Knirps** [knirps], m -es/-e 1. F: little chap, Brit: titch. 2. R.t.m: folding umbrella.

**knirschen** ['knirʃən], v.i. (haben) to grate, grind; (Sand, Schnee usw.) to crunch; **mit den Zähnen k.**, to grind/gnash one's teeth.

**knistern** ['knistərn], v.i. (haben) (Feuer usw.) to crackle.

**knitter|frei** ['knitərfrai], adj. creaseresistant. ◆'**k~n**, v.i. (haben) to crease.

**Knoblauch** ['kno:plaux], m -(e)s/no pl garlic.

**Knöchel** ['knœçəl], m -s/- (a) (Fußk.) ankle; (b) (Fingerk.) knuckle.

**Knoch|en** ['knɔxən], m -s/- bone. ◆'**K~enbruch**, m (bone) fracture. ◆'**K~enmark**, n (bone) marrow. ◆'**k~ig**, adj. bony.

**Knödel** ['knø:dəl], m -s/- dumpling.

**Knolle** ['knɔlə], f -/-n Bot: corm, tuber.

**Knopf** [knɔpf], m -(e)s/-e (a) button; (b) knob (on radio etc.). ◆'**K~loch**, m buttonhole.

**knöpfen** ['knœpfən], v.tr. to button (up) (a jacket etc.).

**Knorp|el** ['knɔrpəl], m -s/- 1. Anat: cartilage. 2. Cu: gristle. ◆'**k~(e)lig**, adj. (a) cartilaginous (tissue etc.); (b) gristly (meat etc.).

**knorrig** ['knɔriç], adj. gnarled (tree etc.).

**Knospe** ['knɔspə], f -/-n bud. ◆'**k~n**, v.i. (haben) (Baum usw.) to bud.

**Knot|en** ['kno:tən], m -s/- (also Nau:) knot; Bot: node (on a stem); Med: lump (in the breast etc.). II. **k.**, v.tr. to knot (string etc.). ◆'**K~enpunkt**, m junction, intersection (of roads, railway lines etc.).

**knüll|en** ['knylən], v.tr. to crease, crumple (material etc.). ◆'**K~er**, m -s/- F: (a) (smash) hit; (Zeitungsartikel) sensation; (b) fantastic idea.

**knüpfen** ['knypfən], v.tr. (a) to knot (a tie, carpet etc.); to tie (shoelaces); (b) Fig: to attach (hopes, condition etc.) (**an** + acc, to).

**Knüppel** ['knypəl], m -s/- 1. club, cudgel; (policeman's) truncheon. 2. Av: joystick; Aut: gear lever. ◆'**k~n**, v.tr. to beat (s.o.) with a club/truncheon.

**knurren** ['knurən], v.i. (haben) (a) (Hund usw.) to growl, snarl; (Magen) to rumble; (b) to grumble.

**knusprig** ['knuspriç], adj. crisp, crunchy (biscuit etc.); crusty (bread etc.).

**k.o.** [ka:'o:], pred.adj. (a) knocked out; (b) F: **ich bin völlig k.o.**, I'm completely whacked.

**Koalition** [koalitsi'o:n], *f* -/-en *Pol: etc:* coalition.

**Kobalt** ['ko:balt], *n* -(e)s/*no pl* cobalt.

**Kobold** ['ko:bɔlt], *m* -(e)s/-e goblin, imp.

**Kobra** ['ko:bra], *f* -/-s cobra.

**Koch** [kɔx], *m* -(e)s/-e cook. ◆'K~**buch**, *n* cookery book, *N.Am:* cookbook. ◆**k~en**, *v.* 1. *v.tr.* (*a*) to cook (meat, vegetables, a meal etc.); (*b*) (*sieden lassen*) to boil (water etc.); to make (tea, coffee etc.). 2. *v.i.* (*haben*) (*a*) to cook, do the cooking; **gut/schlecht k.**, to be a good/bad cook; (*b*) (*Wasser usw.*) to boil. ◆**k~end**, *adj.* boiling. ◆**K~gelegenheit**, *f* cooking facilities. ◆'K~**herd**, *m* cooker, *N.Am:* stove. ◆'K~**kunst**, *f* art of cooking, cooking. ◆'K~**löffel**, *m* wooden (mixing) spoon. ◆'K~**nische**, *f* kitchenette. ◆'K~**platte**, *f* ring, *esp. N.Am:* hot plate. ◆'K~**salz**, *n* (common) salt. ◆'K~**topf**, *m* saucepan.

**Köchin** ['kœçin], *f* -/-nen (woman) cook.

**Köder** ['kø:dər], *m* -s/- bait. ◆'k~**n**, *v.tr.* to lure, entice (fish, *Fig:* s.o.).

**Koexistenz** ['ko:ɛksis'tɛnts], *f* -/-en coexistence.

**Koffein** [kɔfe'i:n], *n* -s/*no pl* caffeine. ◆**k~frei**, *adj.* decaffeinated.

**Koffer** ['kɔfər], *m* -s/- suitcase, case. ◆'K~**radio**, *n* portable radio. ◆'K~**raum**, *m* boot, *N.Am:* trunk.

**Kognak** ['kɔnjak], *m* -s/-s brandy, cognac.

**Kohl** [ko:l], *m* -(e)s/-e cabbage. ◆'K~**dampf**, *m P:* ravenous hunger. ◆'K~**rabi**, *m* -(s)/-(s) kohlrabi. ◆'K~**rübe**, *f* swede, *N.Am:* rutabaga.

**Kohle** ['ko:lə], *f* -/-n 1. (*a*) coal; (*b*) (*Zeichenk.*) charcoal. 2. *P:* (*Geld*) *M/s:* cash, dough. ◆'K~**ehydrat**, *n* carbohydrate. ◆'K~**en-**, *comb.fm.* (*a*) coal (bunker, heating, industry etc.); (*b*) *Ch:* carbon (dioxide, monoxide etc.). ◆'K~**enbergwerk**, *n*/'K~**engrube**, *f* coalmine. ◆'K~**ensäure**, *f* (*a*) *Ch:* carbonic acid; (*b*) (*in Getränken*) gas. ◆'K~**enstoff**, *m* carbon. ◆'K~**epapier**, *n* carbon paper. ◆'K~**ezeichnung**, *f* charcoal drawing.

**Köhler** ['kø:lər], *m* -s/- charcoal-burner.

**Koje** ['ko:jə], *f* -/-n *Nau:* bunk, berth.

**Kokain** [koka'i:n], *n* -s/*no pl* cocaine.

**kokett** [ko'kɛt], *adj.* coquettish, flirtatious. ◆**k~ieren** [-'ti:rən], *v.i.* (*haben*) to flirt.

**Kokos-** [ko:kɔs-], *comb.fm.* coconut (fibre, mat, palm etc.). ◆'K~**nuß**, *f* coconut.

**Koks** [ko:ks], *m* -es/-e coke.

**Kolben** ['kɔlbən], *m* -s/- 1. *Tchn:* piston. 2. (*Gewehr.*) rifle butt. 3. *Ch:* (laboratory) flask. 4. *Bot:* (corn) cob.

**Kolchose** [kɔl'ço:zə], *f* -/-n collective farm.

**Kolibri** ['ko:libri], *m* -s/-s humming bird.

**Kolik** ['ko:lik], *f* -/-en colic.

**Kollaps** ['kɔlaps], *m* -es/-e collapse.

**Kolleg** [kɔ'le:k], *n* -s/-s course of lectures. ◆**K~mappe**, *f* slim briefcase.

**Kolleg|e** [kɔ'le:gə], *m* -n/-n colleague. ◆**k~ial** [-legi'a:l], *adj.* helpful, friendly (attitude etc.). ◆**K~in** [-'le:gin], *f* -/-nen (female) colleague.

**Kollekt|e** [kɔ'lɛktə], *f* -/-n collection. ◆**K~i'on** [-tsi'o:n], *f* -/-en collection (*esp.* of dresses, shoes etc.); *Com:* range; selection. ◆**k~iv** [-'ti:f], *adj.* collective.

**kolli|dieren** [kɔli'di:rən], *v.i.* (*sein*) to collide. ◆**K~sion** [-zi'o:n], *f* -/-en collision; *Fig:* clash.

**Köln** [kœln]. *Pr.n.n* -s. Cologne. ◆'k~**isch**, *adj.* (of) Cologne; **K. Wasser**, eau de Cologne.

**kolon|ial** [koloni'a:l], *adj.* colonial. ◆**K~i'alwaren**, *fpl* (*esp.* imported) groceries. ◆**K~ie** [-'ni:], *f* -/-n colony. ◆**k~i'sieren**, *v.tr.* to colonize (a country etc.).

**Kolonne** [ko'lɔnə], *f* -/-n column (of vehicles, troops, *Mth:* figures); *Aut:* string (of vehicles); line (of traffic); *Mil:* convoy; *Ind:* gang (of workers).

**Kol|oß** [ko'lɔs], *m* -sses/-sse giant. ◆**k~ossal** [-'sa:l], *adj.* colossal, gigantic (building etc.); *F:* terrific (luck etc.).

**Koma** ['ko:ma], *n* -s/-s & -ta coma.

**Kombi|nation** [kɔmbinatsi'o:n], *f* -/-en combination; *Fb: etc:* (concerted) move; *Cl:* overalls. ◆**k~'nieren**, *v.tr.* to combine (qualities etc.). ◆'K~**wagen**, *m Aut:* estate car; *N.Am:* station wagon. ◆'K~**zange**, *f* combination pliers.

**Komet** [ko'me:t], *m* -en/-en comet.

**Komfort** [kɔm'fo:r], *m* -s/*no pl* comfort; (*Luxus*) luxury; **Haus mit allem K.**, house with all mod. cons. ◆**k~abel** [-fɔr'ta:bəl], *adj.* comfortable.

**Kom|ik** ['ko:mik], *f* -/*no pl* comedy, comic effect. ◆'K~**iker**, *m* -s/- comedian. ◆'k~**isch**, *adj.* funny.

**Komitee** [komi'te:], *n* -s/-s committee.

**Komma** ['kɔma], *n* -s/-s comma; **vier K. fünf**, four point five.

**Kommand|ant** [kɔman'dant], *m* -en/-en commanding officer; commandant (of a fort etc.). ◆**K~eur** [-'dø:r], *m* -s/-s commander (of a large unit). ◆**k~ieren** [-'di:rən], *v.tr. Mil: etc:* to command (an army etc.); *Nau:* to captain (a ship); *F:* to order (s.o.) about. ◆**K~o** [-'mando], *n* -s/-s 1. (word of) command, order. 2. *Mil:* command; **das K. haben/führen**, to be in command (**über** + *acc*, of). 3. (*Verband*) squad, detachment.

**kommen** ['kɔmən]. I. *v.i.v.irr.53* (*sein*) (*a*) to come; (*ankommen*) to arrive; **wann k. wir nach Graz?** when do we get to Graz? **sie kommt immer zu spät**, she is always late; **angekrochen k.**, to come crawling along; **ins Gefängnis/in den Himmel k.**, to go to prison/heaven; **jetzt k. Sie an die Reihe**, now it's your turn; **der Regen**

kommt durch diesen Riß, the rain comes (in) through this crack; **die Kisten k. in den Keller,** the crates go in the cellar; **woher kommt es, daß ...?** how is it that ...? *F:* **das kommt davon!** that's what happens! it serves you/him/her/them right! **einen Installateur usw. k. lassen,** to send for a plumber etc.; **etwas k. lassen,** to have sth. sent; *(bestellen)* to order sth.; *(b)* *(impers.)* *(geschehen)* to happen; *(sich ergeben)* to result; **es kam zu einer Vereinbarung,** agreement was reached; **es kam ganz anders (als erwartet),** it turned out quite differently (from what we had expected); *(c)* *(es schaffen)* **ich komme nicht mehr in dieses Kleid,** I can't get into this dress any more; **er kommt einfach nicht dazu,** he just doesn't get round to it; *(d)* *(kosten)* **wie teuer kommt diese Vase?** how much is this vase? **wenn es hoch kommt,** at the most; *(e)* **j-m grob/frech k.,** to be rude/cheeky to s.o.; **j-m gelegen/ungelegen k.,** to come at the right/wrong moment for s.o.; **zu etwas** *dat* **k.,** to get hold of sth.; **zu sich** *dat* **k.,** to regain consciousness, *F:* come round; **in Schwierigkeiten usw. k.,** to get into difficulties etc.; **wie bist du darauf gekommen?** what made you think of that? **um etwas** *acc* **k.,** to lose/be deprived of sth. **II. K.,** *n* **-s/** *no pl* coming, arrival; **im K. sein,** *(Pers., Firma)* to be on the way up; *(modisch werden)* to become fashionable. ◆**'k~d,** *adj.* coming; **k~de Generationen,** future generations.

**Kommentar** [kɔmɛn'tɑːr], *m* **-s/-e** commentary **(zu** + *dat,* on); *(Bemerkung)* comment. ◆**K~ator** [-'tɑːtɔr], *m* **-s/-en** commentator. ◆**k~ieren** [-'tiːrən], *v.tr.* to comment on (sth.).

**kommerziell** [kɔmɛrtsi'ɛl], *adj.* commercial.

**Kommilitone** [kɔmili'toːnə], *m* **-n/-n** fellow student.

**Kommiß** [kɔ'mis], *m* **-sses/** *no pl F:* army (life).

**Kommissar** [kɔmi'saːr], *m* **-s/-e** *(a)* (government) commissioner; *(b)* (police) superintendent.

**Kommission** [kɔmisi'oːn], *f* **-/-en** commission; board (of examiners etc.); *Com:* **(Waren) in K.,** (goods) on sale or return.

**Kommode** [kɔ'moːdə], *f* **-/-n** chest of drawers, *N.Am:* dresser.

**Kommun|al-** [kɔmu'nɑːl-]. *comb.fm.* local (politics, election etc.). ◆**K~ikation** [-ikatsi'oːn], *f* **-/-en** communication. ◆**K~ion** [-ni'oːn], *f* **-/-en** Communion. ◆**K~iqué** [-yni'keː], *n* **-s/-s** communiqué. ◆**K~ismus** [-u'nismus], *m* **-/** *no pl* communism. ◆**K~ist(in),** *m* **-en/-en** *(f* **-/-nen)** Communist. ◆**k~istisch,** *adj.* Communist.

**Komödie** [kɔ'møːdiə], *f* **-/-n** comedy.

**kompakt** [kɔm'pakt], *adj.* compact.

**Kompanie** [kɔmpa'niː], *f* **-/-en** company.

**Komparativ** ['kɔmparatiːf], *m* **-s/-e** com-

parative.

**Kompaß** ['kɔmpas], *m* **-sses/-sse** compass.

**kompet|ent** [kɔmpe'tɛnt], *adj.* competent (authority etc.). ◆**K~enz,** *f* **-/-en** authority; competence.

**komplett** [kɔm'plɛt], *adj.* complete.

**komplex** [kɔm'plɛks]. **I.** *adj.* complex. **II. K.,** *m* **-es/-e** *also Psy:* complex.

**Kompli|kation** [kɔmplikatsi'oːn], *f* **-/-en** complication. ◆**k~'ziert,** *adj.* complicated (problem etc.); *(knifflig)* tricky (job etc.).

**Kompliment** [kɔmpli'mɛnt], *n* **-(e)s/-e** compliment.

**Komplize** [kɔm'pliːtsə], *m* **-n/-n** accomplice.

**Komplott** [kɔm'plɔt], *n* **-(e)s/-e** plot, *(Verschwörung)* conspiracy.

**kompo|nieren** [kɔmpo'niːrən], *v.tr.* to compose (a piece); to write (a song). ◆**K~'nist,** *m* **-en/-en** composer.

**Kompost** [kɔm'pɔst], *m* **-(e)s/-e** compost. ◆**K~haufen,** *m* compost heap.

**Kompott** [kɔm'pɔt], *n* **-(e)s/-e** stewed fruit.

**Kompress|e** [kɔm'prɛsə], *f* **-/-n** compress. ◆**K~or** [-'prɛsɔr], *m* **-s/-en** compressor.

**Komprom|iß** [kɔmpro'mis], *m* **-sses/-sse** compromise. ◆**k~ißlos,** *adj.* uncompromising.

**Konden|sation** [kɔndɛnzatsi'oːn], *f* **-/-en** condensation. ◆**K~sator** [-'zaːtɔr], *m* **-s/-en** condenser. ◆**k~'sieren,** *v.tr.* to condense (vapour etc.). ◆**K~smilch** [-'dɛns-], *f* evaporated milk.

**Kondition** [kɔnditsi'oːn], *f* **-/-en** **1.** *Com: usu.pl* **K~en,** terms, conditions. **2.** *no pl Sp:* (physical) fitness. ◆**K~sschwäche,** *f Sp:* lack of fitness. ◆**K~straining,** *n* fitness training.

**Konditor** [kɔn'diːtɔr], *m* **-s/-en** confectioner; *(Tortenbäcker)* pastrycook. ◆**K~ei** [-dito'rai], *f* **-/-en** (confectionery and) cake/*N.Am:* pastry shop.

**Kondom** [kɔn'doːm], *n* **-s/-s** condom.

**Konfekt** [kɔn'fɛkt], *n* **-(e)s/-e** confectionery, *N.Am:* candy.

**Konfektion** [kɔnfɛktsi'oːn], *f* **-/-en** ready-to-wear clothes.

**Konfer|enz** [kɔnfe'rɛnts], *f* **-/-en 1.** *(Sitzung)* (business) meeting. **2.** *(Tagung)* conference. ◆**k~ieren** [-e'riːrən], *v.i.* *(haben)* to confer.

**Konfession** [kɔnfesi'oːn], *f* **-/-en** (religious) denomination. ◆**k~ell** [-io'nɛl], *adj.* denominational. ◆**k~slos,** *adj.* belonging to no religious denomination. ◆**K~sschule,** *f* denominational school.

**Konfetti** [kɔn'fɛti], *n* **-s/** *no pl* confetti.

**Konfirm|and(in)** [kɔnfir'mant(-din)], *m* **-en/-en** *(f* **-/-nen)** confirmation candidate. ◆**K~ation** [-atsi'oːn], *f* **-/-en** confirmation. ◆**k~ieren** [-'miːrən], *v.tr.* to confirm (s.o.).

**konfiszieren** [kɔnfis'tsiːrən], *v.tr.* to confiscate (property).

**Konfitüre** [kɔnfi'ty:rə], *f* -/-n jam.

**Konflikt** [kɔn'flikt], *m* -(e)s/-e conflict; *Ind:* dispute.

**konform** [kɔn'fɔrm], *adj.* concurring (views etc.); **mit j-m k. gehen**, to concur with s.o.

**Konfront|ation** [kɔnfrɔntatsi'o:n], *f* -/-en confrontation. ◆**k~ieren** [-'ti:rən], *v.tr.* to confront (s.o.).

**konfus** [kɔn'fu:s], *adj.* confused, muddled.

**Kongreß** [kɔn'grɛs], *m* -sses/-sse congress.

**König** ['kø:niç], *m* -s/-e king. ◆**'K~in** [-gin], *f* -/-nen queen. ◆**'k~lich** [-lɪç], *adj.* royal; *F:* **sich k. amüsieren**, to have a whale of a time. ◆**'K~reich**, *n* kingdom. ◆**'K~s-**, *comb.fm.* royal (crown, palace etc.); king's (son, daughter etc.).

**konisch** ['ko:nɪʃ], *adj.* conical.

**Konjug|ation** [kɔnjugatsi'o:n], *f* -/-en conjugation. ◆**k~ieren** [-'gi:rən], *v.tr.* to conjugate (a verb).

**Konjunktion** [kɔnjuŋktsi'o:n], *f* -/-en conjunction.

**Konjunktiv** ['kɔnjuŋktif], *m* -s/-e subjunctive (mood).

**Konjunktur** [kɔnjuŋk'tu:r]. **I.** *f* -/-en **1.** economic situation. **2.** (*Hochk.*) boom. **II.** **'K~-**, *comb.fm.* business (report etc.); economic (policy etc.).

**konkav** [kɔn'ka:f], *adj.* concave.

**konkret** [kɔn'kre:t, kɔŋ-], *adj.* concrete (proposal, example etc.); actual (situation etc.).

**Konkurr|ent(in)** [kɔnku'rɛnt(in)], *m* -en/ -en (*f* -/-nen) competitor. ◆**k~enz** [-'rɛnts], *f* -/no pl competition; **j-m/sich** *dat* **K. machen**, to compete with s.o./one another; **unsere K.**, our competitors. ◆**k~enzfähig**, *adj. Com:* competitive. ◆**'K~enzkampf**, *m* rivalry. ◆**k~ieren** [-'ri:rən], *v.i.* (*haben*) to compete.

**Konkurs** [kɔn'kurs, kɔŋ-], *m* -es/-e bankruptcy; **K. machen/in K. geraten**, to go bankrupt/(*Firma*) into liquidation.

**könn|en** ['kœnən]. **I.** *v.irr.* **1.** *v.tr.* to know (how to do) (sth.); to be able to do (sth.); **k. Sie Deutsch?** can/do you speak German? **lesen k.**, to know how to/be able to read; **ich kann nichts dafür,** I can't help it; *F:* **er kann nichts für den Unfall**, the accident was not his fault. **2.** *modal aux.* (*a*) to be able to; **ich kann (nicht) kommen,** I can/can't come; (*b*) (*möglich sein*) **es könnte verloren gegangen sein**, it could/might have got lost; **man kann nie wissen**, you never know; **kann sein!** maybe! possibly! (*c*) **er kann nicht anders**, he cannot do anything else; *P:* **du kannst mich (mal)!** get stuffed! (*d*) (*dürfen*) **kann ich jetzt gehen?** can/may I go now? **II. K.**, *n* -s/no pl ability. ◆**'K~er**, *m* -s/- person of ability; expert.

**konsequ|ent** [kɔnze'kvɛnt], *adj.* (*a*) (*folgerichtig*) consistent (behaviour etc.); (*b*) (*unbeirrbar*) persistent, single-minded (person, efforts etc.). ◆**K~enz**, *f* -/-en (*a*) consistency; logic; (*b*) persistence; (*c*) (*Folge*) consequence.

**konserv|ativ** [kɔnzerva'ti:f], *adj.* conservative. ◆**K~atorium** [-va'to:rium], *m* -s/-ien *Mus:* conservatoire, *N.Am:* conservatory. ◆**K~e** [-'zɛrvə], *f* -/-n **1.** (*Büchse*) tin, *esp. N.Am:* can. **2.** *pl* **K~n**, tinned/canned food. ◆**K~endose**, *f* tin, *esp. N.Am:* can. ◆**k~ieren** [-'vi:rən], *v.tr.* to can, (*im Glas*) preserve (meat, fruit etc.). ◆**K~ierungsmittel**, *n* preservative.

**Konsonant** [kɔnzo'nant], *m* -en/-en consonant.

**konstant** [kɔn'stant], *adj.* constant (velocity, number etc.); consistent (treatment, *Sp:* form etc.).

**Konstitution** [kɔnstitutsi'o:n], *f* -/-en constitution. ◆**k~ell** [-o'nɛl], *adj.* constitutional.

**konstru|ieren** [kɔnstru'i:rən], *v.tr.* to construct, *Tchn:* (*entwerfen*) design (sth.); *Pej:* to fabricate (a story etc.). ◆**K~ktion** [-ruktsi'o:n], *f* -/-en construction; (*Bauweise*) design (of an engine, car etc.). ◆**k~ktiv** [-'ti:f], *adj.* constructive.

**Konsul** ['kɔnzul], *m* -s/-n consul. ◆**K~at** [-'lu:t], *n* -(e)s/-e consulate.

**konsultieren** [kɔnzul'ti:rən], *v.tr.* to consult (a doctor, dictionary etc.).

**Konsum** [kɔn'zu:m], *m* -s/no pl consumption. ◆**K~gesellschaft**, *f* consumer society.

**Kontakt** [kɔn'takt], *m* -(e)s/-e contact; **mit j-m K. aufnehmen/haben**, to get/be in touch with s.o. ◆**k~arm**, *adj.* unable to make friends easily. ◆**k~freudig**, *adj.* sociable. ◆**K~linse**, *f* contact lens.

**Konter-** ['kɔntər-], *comb.fm.* counter-(attack, revolution etc.). ◆**'k~n**, *v.tr. & i.* to counter.

**Kontinent** [kɔnti'nɛnt], *m* -(e)s/-e continent.

**Kontingent** [kɔntiŋ'gɛnt], *n* -(e)s/-e quota (of goods); *Mil:* contingent.

**kontinuierlich** [kɔntinu'i:rliç], *adj.* continuous.

**Konto** ['kɔnto]. **I.** *n* -s/-s & -ten account. **II.** **'K~-**, *comb.fm.* account (number etc.). ◆**K~auszug**, *m* statement of account. ◆**'K~inhaber(in)**, *m(f)*, account-holder. ◆**'K~stand**, *m* balance of an account.

**Kontra** ['kɔntra], *n* -s/-s (*im Spiel*) double. ◆**'K~baß**, *n* double-bass. ◆**K~'hent**, *m* -en/-en **1.** opponent. **2.** *Jur: etc:* party to a contract.

**Kontrast** [kɔn'trast], *m* -(e)s/-e contrast.

**Kontroll-** [kɔn'trɔl-], *comb.fm.* control (room, *Av:* tower etc.); check (list etc.).

◆**K~e,** f -/-n **1.** check; (*Überprüfung*) inspection (of goods, machinery etc.); checking (of tickets etc.); (*Zollk.*) customs check/control. **2.** *no pl* (*Beherrschung*) control (**über j-n, etwas** *acc,* of s.o., sth.). ◆**K~eur** [-'lø:r], *m* -s/-e supervisor, inspector; *Rail: etc:* ticket inspector. ◆**k~ieren** [-'li:rən], *v.tr.* (*a*) to check (baggage, weight, quality etc.); to supervise, (s.o., s.o.'s work); to inspect (tickets, papers); (*b*) to control (a company, the market etc.).

**Kontroverse** [kɔntro'vɛrzə], f -/-n dispute.

**Kontur** [kɔn'tu:r], f -/-en contour, outline.

**Konvention** [kɔnvɛntsi'o:n], f -/-en (social) convention. ◆**k~ell** [-o'nɛl], *adj.* conventional.

**Konversation** [kɔnvɛrzatsi'o:n], f -/-en conversation. ◆**K~slexikon,** *n* popular encyclopedia.

**konvex** [kɔn'vɛks], *adj.* convex.

**Konvoi** ['kɔnvɔy], *m* -s/-s convoy.

**Konzentr|ation** [kɔntsɛn'tratsi'o:n], f -/-en concentration. ◆**K~ati'onslager,** *n* concentration camp. ◆**k~ieren** [-'tri:rən], *v.tr. & refl.* to concentrate.

**Konzept** [kɔn'tsɛpt], *n* -(e)s/-e (*a*) (*Entwurf*) rough copy, draft (of an essay etc.); (*b*) (*Begriff*) concept, idea; **das paßt ihm nicht ins K.,** it doesn't fit in with his plans/ideas.

**Konzern** [kɔn'tsɛrn], *m* -s/-e *Ind:* combine, *N.Am:* conglomerate; group (of companies etc.).

**Konzert** [kɔn'tsɛrt], *n* -(e)s/-e **1.** concert. **2.** (*Stück*) concerto.

**Konzession** [kɔntsɛsi'o:n], f -/-en **1.** *Com:* (trading, publican's etc.) licence. **2.** (*Zugeständnis*) concession.

**Konzil** [kɔn'tsi:l], *n* -s/-e council.

**konzipieren** [kɔntsi'pi:rən], *v.tr.* to draw up, draft (a document etc.).

**Kooperat|ion** [ko:operatsi'o:n], f -/-en co-operation. ◆**k~iv** [-'ti:f], *adj.* co-operative.

**Koordin|ation** [ko:ɔrdinatsi'o:n], f -/-en co-ordination. ◆**k~ieren** [-'ni:rən], *v.tr.* to co-ordinate (measures etc.).

**Kopf** [kɔpf], *m* -(e)s/-e head; **K. an K. liegen,** to be neck and neck; **K. hoch!** chin up! **den K. riskieren,** to risk one's neck; **aus dem K.,** from memory; **sich** *dat* **über etwas** *acc* **den K. zerbrechen,** to rack one's brains over sth.; **ich muß es mir durch den K. gehen lassen,** I'll have to think it over; **den K. verlieren,** to lose one's head; **den K. voll haben,** to have a lot on one's mind; **seinen eigenen K. haben,** to have a will of one's own; **sich** *dat* **etwas** *acc* **in den K. setzen,** to take sth. into one's head; **das mußt du dir aus dem K. schlagen,** you must put it right out of your head; **pro K.,** per head. ◆'**K~ball,** *m Fb:* header. ◆'**K~bedeckung,** f headgear.

◆'**K~geld,** *n* reward (for s.o.'s capture). ◆'**K~haut,** f scalp. ◆**K~hörer,** *m* (pair of) headphones. ◆'**K~jäger,** *m* headhunter. ◆'**K~kissen,** *n* pillow. ◆'**k~los,** *adj.* headless; (*Pers.*) **k.** (**vor Angst**), panic-stricken; *adv.* in a state of panic. ◆'**K~rechnen,** *n* mental arithmetic. ◆'**K~salat,** *m* cabbage lettuce. ◆'**K~schmerzen,** *mpl* headache. ◆'**K~schütteln,** *n* shake of the head. ◆'**K~sprung,** *m* header, (straight) dive. ◆'**K~stand,** *m* head stand. ◆'**k~stehen,** *v.i.sep.irr.100* (*haben*) *F:* to be at sixes and sevens. ◆'**K~steinpflaster,** *n* cobbled surface, cobbles. ◆'**K~stoß,** *m Fb:* header. ◆'**K~tuch,** *n* headscarf. ◆'**k~über,** *adj.* head first, headlong. ◆'**K~weh,** *n* -s/*no pl* headache. ◆'**K~zerbrechen,** *n* -s/*no pl* **sich** *dat* **K. machen,** to rack one's brains.

**köpfen** ['kœpfən], *v.tr.* (*a*) to behead (s.o.); to cut off the head of (an animal); (*b*) *Fb:* to head (the ball).

**Kopie** [ko'pi:], f -/-n [-ən] copy; (*Doppel*) duplicate; (*Nachbildung*) replica; *Phot:* (*Abzug*) print. ◆**k~ren** [-'pi:rən], *v.tr.* to copy (s.o., sth.), to duplicate (a document). ◆**K~rgerät,** *n* (photo)copier.

**Kopilot** ['ko:pilo:t], *m* -en/-en co-pilot.

**Kopp|el¹** ['kɔpəl], f -/-n (enclosed) pasture; (*für Pferde*) paddock. ◆**K~²,** *n* -s/- *Mil:* leather belt. ◆'**k~eln,** *v.tr.* to couple.

**Koralle** [ko'ralə], f -/-n coral. ◆**K~nriff,** *n* coral reef.

**Korb** [kɔrp], *m* -(e)s/-e basket. ◆'**K~ball,** *m* basketball. ◆'**K~sessel,** *m* wicker chair.

**Kord** [kɔrt], *m* -(e)s/-e corduroy.

**Kordel** ['kɔrdəl], f -/-n cord (of a dressing gown etc.); (*Schnur*) string.

**Kordon** [kɔr'dõ], *m* -s/-s (police etc.) cordon.

**Korea** [ko're:a]. *Pr.n.n* -s. Korea. ◆**K~ner(in)** [-re'a:nər(in)], *m* -s/- (f -/-nen) Korean. ◆**k~nisch** [-re'a:niʃ], *adj.* Korean.

**Korinthe** [ko'rintə], f -/-n currant.

**Kork** [kɔrk], *m* -(e)s/*no pl* cork. ◆'**K~en,** *m* -s/- cork (stopper). ◆'**K~enzieher,** *m* -s/- corkscrew.

**Korn¹** [kɔrn], *n* -(e)s/-er *& -e* **1.** (*a*) (*pl* **K~er**) (*Samenk.*) grain (of sand, salt etc.); (*b*) *no pl* (*Getreidek.*) grain, corn. **2.** (*pl* -e) (front) sight (of a rifle etc.); *Fig:* **j-n, etwas aufs K. nehmen,** to hit out at s.o., sth. ◆**Korn²,** *m* -(e)s/-e grain spirit. ◆'**K~blume,** f cornflower.

**Körn|chen** ['kœrnçən], *n* -s/- small grain; granule. ◆'**k~ig,** *adj.* granular.

**Körper** ['kœrpər], *m* -s/- body. ◆'**K~bau,** *m* build, physique. ◆'**K~behinderte(r),** *m & f* (physically) disabled/handicapped person.

◆'**K~geruch,** *m* body odour. ◆'**K~haltung,** *f* posture. ◆'**k~lich,** *adj.* physical. ◆'**K~pflege,** *f* personal hygiene. ◆'**K~schaft,** *f* -/-en *Jur: etc:* corporation. ◆'**K~teil,** *m* part of the body. ◆'**K~verletzung,** *f* physical injury; *Jur:* bodily harm.

**Korps** [kɔːr], *n* -/- *Mil:* corps.

**korpulent** [kɔrpu'lent], *adj.* corpulent.

**korrekt** [kɔ'rekt], *adj.* correct; (*Pers.*) **sehr k.,** very proper. ◆**K~heit,** *f* -/-en correctness. ◆**K~ur** [-'tuːr], *f* -/-en correction.

**Korrespond|ent(in)** [kɔrespɔn'dent(in)], *m* -en/-en (*f* -/-nen) correspondent. ◆**K~enz** [-'dents], *f* -/-en correspondence. ◆**k~ieren** [-'diːrən], *v.i.* (*haben*) to correspond.

**Korridor** ['kɔridoːr], *m* -s/-e corridor, passage.

**korrigieren** [kɔri'giːrən], *v.tr.* to correct.

**korrupt** [kɔ'rupt], *adj.* corrupt. ◆**K~ion** [-tsi'oːn], *f* -/-en corruption.

**Korsett** [kɔr'zet], *n* -s/-e corset.

**Kose|name** ['koːzənaːmə], *m* pet name. ◆'**K~wort,** *n* term of endearment.

**Kosmet|ik** [kɔs'meːtik], *f* -/no pl beauty culture, cosmetics. ◆**K~ikerin,** *f* -/-nen beautician. ◆**k~isch,** *adj.* cosmetic.

**kosm|isch** ['kɔsmiʃ], *adj.* cosmic. ◆**K~onaut** [-o'naut], *m* -en/-en cosmonaut. ◆**K~opolit** [-opo'liːt], *m* -en/-en cosmopolitan (person). ◆**K~os,** *m* -/no pl cosmos.

**Kost** [kɔst], *f* -/no pl food; (*Verpflegung*) board. ◆'**k~en1,** *v.tr.* to taste, sample (food, wine etc.). ◆**K~probe,** *f* sample, taste.

**kost|bar** ['kɔstbaːr], *adj.* precious, valuable. ◆**K~barkeit,** *f* -/-en **1.** no pl preciousness; high value. **2.** treasure, valuable item. ◆'**k~en2.** **I.** *v.tr.* to cost; **was/wieviel kostet das Buch?** how much is the book? **II.** **K.,** *pl* cost, expense; (*Auslagen*) expenses; *Jur: etc:* costs; **es geht auf meine K.,** it is at my expense/ *F:* on me; *F:* **auf seine K. kommen,** to get one's money's worth. ◆'**k~enlos,** *adj.* free (sample etc.); *adv.* free of charge. ◆'**K~envoranschlag,** *m* preliminary estimate/*Brit:* costing. ◆'**k~spielig,** *adj.* expensive, costly.

**köstlich** ['kœstliç], *adj.* (*a*) delicious, luscious (food, wine etc.); (*b*) delightful (humour etc.); **sich k. amüsieren,** to enjoy oneself immensely.

**Kostüm** [kɔs'tyːm], *n* -s/-e (*a*) (woman's) suit; (*b*) *Th:* costume; (*c*) (*Maske*) fancy dress costume. ◆**K~fest,** *n* fancy dress ball. ◆**k~ieren** [-y'miːrən], *v.tr.* & *refl.* to dress (s.o., oneself) up (in a costume).

**Kot** [koːt], *m* -(e)s/no pl excrement; droppings (of animals, birds etc.). ◆'**K~flügel,** *m* wing, *N.Am:* fender.

**Kotelett** [kɔt'let], *n* -s/-s chop; (*vom Hals*) cutlet. ◆**K~en,** *fpl* sideburns.

**Köter** ['køːtər], *m* -s/- *F: Pej:* wretched hound; (*Mischung*) mongrel, *N.Am:* mutt.

**Krabbe** ['krabə], *f* -/-n (*a*) crab; (*b*) (*Garnele*) shrimp.

**krabbeln** ['krabəln], *v.i.* (*sein*) (*Insekten*) to scuttle; (*Baby*) to crawl.

**krach** [krax]. **I.** *int.* crash! bang! **II.** **K.,** *m* -(e)s/-s & -̈e **1.** (*Lärm*) row, racket. **2.** *F:* (*Streit*) row; **K. miteinander haben,** to quarrel/have a row (with one another). ◆'**k~en,** *v.i.* (*a*) (*haben*) (*Donner usw.*) to crash; (*b*) (*sein*) to crash, smash.

**krächzen** ['kreçtsən], *v.i.* (*haben*) (*Rabe*) to caw, *F:* (*Pers.*) to croak.

**Krad** [kraːt], *n* -(e)s/-er motorcycle.

**Kraft** [kraft]. **I.** *f* -/-̈e **1.** (*Stärke*) (*a*) strength; **mit aller K.,** with all one's might; **bei K~en sein,** to be well/in good health; (*b*) force (of a blow, wind, *Fig:* an argument etc.); power (of an engine etc.); (*c*) (*Vorschrift usw.*) in **K. treten,** to come into effect/force. **2.** (*Arbeiter*) *Ind:* worker; *Com:* employee. **II. k.,** *prep* + *gen* by virtue of (one's authority etc.). ◆'**K~ausdruck,** *m* swearword. ◆'**K~fahrer,** *m* driver. ◆'**K~fahrzeug,** *n* motor vehicle. ◆'**k~los,** *adj.* weak, feeble; powerless (hand, arm etc.). ◆'**K~probe,** *f* trial of strength; showdown. ◆'**K~stoff,** *m* fuel (for an engine). ◆'**k~voll,** *adj.* powerful. ◆'**K~wagen,** *m* motor car, *N.Am:* automobile. ◆'**K~werk,** *n* power station.

**kräft|ig** ['kreftiç], *adj.* strong (person, arms, voice etc.); sturdy (child, plant etc.); vigorous (growth etc.); heavy (rain); nutritious (food, soup). ◆'**k~igen,** *v.tr.* to strengthen (s.o., the body etc.). ◆'**K~igung,** *f* -/no pl strengthening; improvement (in one's health).

**Kragen** ['kraːgən], *m* -s/- collar. ◆'**K~weite,** *f* collar size.

**Krähe** ['kreːə], *f* -/-n crow. ◆'**k~n,** *v.i.* (*haben*) (*Hahn*) to crow; (*Baby*) to coo.

**Krake** ['kraːkə], *m* -n/-n octopus.

**krakeelen** [kra'keːlən], *v.i.* (*haben*) *F:* to brawl.

**krakeln** ['kraːkəln], *v.tr. F:* to scrawl (words).

**Kralle** ['kralə], *f* -/-n claw; (*Raubvogel*) talon. ◆'**k~n,** *v.tr.* **sich an etwas** *dat* **k.,** to cling to sth. (*Z:* with its claws).

**Kram** [kraːm], *m* -(e)s/no pl *F:* junk; *Fig:* **der ganze K.,** the whole business. ◆'**k~en,** *v.i.* (*haben*) *F:* **nach etwas** *dat* **k.,** to rummage about for sth.

**Krampf** [krampf], *m* -(e)s/-̈e (*a*) cramp; (*b*) convulsion; spasm. ◆'**K~ader,** *f* varicose vein. ◆'**k~haft,** *adj.* convulsive (twitch etc.); forced, desperate (laugh); *Fig:* frantic (effort etc.).

**Kran** [kraːn], *m* -(e)s/-̈e **1.** crane. **2.** (*Wasserk.*) tap.

**Kranich** ['kraːniç], *m* -s/-e crane.

**krank** [kraŋk], *adj.* (*a*) ill, *esp. N.Am:* sick; **ein K~er,** an invalid; (*unter Behandlung*) a patient; (*b*) diseased (organ, plant); weak (heart). ◆'K~**enbesuch,** *m* visit to a sick person; (doctor's) call on a patient. ◆'K~**enbett,** *n* sickbed. ◆'K~**engeld,** *n* sickness benefit. ◆'K~**enhaus,** *n* hospital. ◆'K~**enkasse,** *f* (national/private) health insurance scheme. ◆'K~**enpfleger(in),** *m(f)* male (female) nurse. ◆'K~**enschein,** *m* treatment form; certificate entitling a patient to treatment. ◆'K~**enschwester,** *f* nurse. ◆'K~**enversicherung,** *f* health insurance. ◆'K~**enwagen,** *m* ambulance. ◆'k~**haft,** *adj.* pathological (growth, state etc.); *Fig:* obsessive (jealousy, ambition etc.). ◆'K~**heit,** *f* -/-en illness, disease. ◆'K~**heitserreger,** *m* germ.

**kränk|en** ['krɛŋkən], *v.tr.* to hurt, offend (s.o.). ◆'k~**lich,** *adj.* sickly. ◆'K~**ung,** *f* -/-en slight.

**Kranz** [krants], *m* -es/-e wreath.

**Kränzchen** ['krɛntsçən], *n* -s/- 1. small wreath. 2. ladies' (coffee etc.) circle.

**Krapfen** ['krapfən], *m* -s/- (*a*) (meat etc.) fritter; (*b*) doughnut.

**kraß** [kras], *adj.* glaring (example, mistake); blatant (lie, injustice); **krasser Außenseiter,** rank outsider.

**Krater** ['kraːtər], *m* -s/- crater.

**Kratz|bürste** ['krats bʏrstə], *f* -/-n *F:* little shrew/vixen. ◆'k~**en,** *v.tr. & i.* (*haben*) to scratch; (*Pullover usw.*) to prickle; **das Eis vom Fenster k.,** to scrape the ice off/from the window. ◆'K~**er,** *m* -s/- 1. *Tchn:* scraper. 2. *F:* scratch. ◆'k~**ig,** *adj.* prickly, scratchy (wool etc.).

**kraulen**[1] ['kraulən], *v.i.* (*haben*) *Sp:* to (do the) crawl.

'**kraulen**[2], *v.tr.* to fondle (a cat, dog etc.) (with one's fingertips), ruffle (a cat's fur etc.).

**kraus** [kraus], *adj.* (*a*) fuzzy, crinkly (hair); creased, wrinkled (dress, brow); (*b*) *Fig:* muddled (thoughts etc.). ◆K~**e** ['krauzə], *f* -/-n *F:* tight perm.

**kräuseln** ['krɔyzəln], *v.tr.* (*a*) to curl, crimp (hair); (*Stoff*) to gather (a skirt etc.); *Fig:* (*Wind*) to ruffle, ripple (water etc.); (*b*) **sich k.,** (*Haare usw.*) to curl; (*Wasser*) to ripple.

**Kraut** [kraut], *n* -(e)s/-er 1. herb. 2. *no pl* (*Blätter*) leaves; tops (of turnips etc.). 3. *no pl* (*Kohl*) cabbage.

**Kräuter-** ['krɔytər-], *comb.fm.* herb (vinegar, tea etc.); herbal (liqueur etc.); (butter, cheese etc.) containing herbs.

**Krawall** [kra'val], *m* -(e)s/-e (*a*) (*Tumult*) riot; (*b*) *F:* (*Lärm*) racket, row.

**Krawatte** [kra'vatə], *f* -/-n tie. ◆K~**nnadel,** *f* tiepin.

**Krea|tion** [kreatsi'oːn], *f* -/-en creation. ◆k~**tiv** [-a'tiːf], *adj.* creative. ◆K~**tur** [a'tuːr], *f* -/-en creature.

**Krebs** [kreːps], *m* -es/-e 1. *Z:* crab;

(*Flußk.*) crayfish. 2. *Astr:* Cancer. 3. *Med:* cancer. ◆'K~**kranke(r),** *m & f* *decl. as adj.* cancer patient.

**Kredit** [kre'diːt], *m* -(e)s/-e credit; **auf K.,** on credit. ◆K~**karte,** *f* credit card.

**Kreide** ['kraidə], *f* -/-n chalk. ◆'k~**bleich,** *adj.* as white as a sheet.

**kreieren** [kre'iːrən], *v.tr.* to create (a fashion, *Th:* a part etc.).

**Kreis** [krais]. I. *m* -es/-e (*a*) circle; **sich im K. bewegen,** to revolve; (*also Fig: Gespräch usw.*) to go round and round (in circles); *Fig:* (*Affäre*) **K~e ziehen,** to have repercussions; **weite K~e der Bevölkerung,** large sections of the population; (*b*) *Adm:* administrative district. II. 'K~-, *comb.fm.* 1. (*a*) circular (motion, line etc.); (*b*) *Mth:* (area, arc etc.) of a circle. 2. *Adm:* district (authority, administration etc.). ◆k~**en** [k'raizən], *v.i.* (*haben*) (*Vogel, Flugzeug usw.*) to circle; (*Planeten, Fig: Gedanken usw.*) **um etwas** *acc* **k.,** to revolve around sth. ◆'k~**förmig,** *adj.* circular (movement etc.). ◆'K~**lauf,** *m* circulation (of blood, money etc.); *Fig:* cycle (of life, seasons etc.). ◆'K~**laufstörung,** *f* circulatory disorder. ◆'K~**säge,** *f* circular saw. ◆'K~**stadt,** *f* chief town of a district. ◆'K~**verkehr,** *m* (traffic) roundabout, *N.Am:* traffic circle.

**kreischen** ['kraiʃən], *v.i.* (*haben*) to screech; to shriek.

**Kreisel** ['kraizəl], *m* -s/- (*Spielzeug*) top.

**Krem** [kreːm], *f* -/-s cream. ◆'k~**ig,** *adj.* creamy.

**Krematorium** [krema'toːrium], *n* -s/-ien crematorium, *N.Am:* crematory.

**Krempe** ['krɛmpə], *f* -/-n brim (of a hat).

**Krempel** ['krɛmpəl], *m* -s/*no pl* *F:* stuff, junk.

**krepieren** [kre'piːrən], *v.i.* (*sein*) (*a*) (*Bombe usw.*) to burst; (*b*) *F:* (*Tier, P: Pers.*) to die a miserable death.

**Krepp** [krɛp], *m* -s/-s crêpe. ◆'K~**papier,** *n* crêpe paper. ◆'K~**sohle,** *f* crêpe-(rubber) sole.

**Kresse** ['krɛsə], *f* -/-n cress.

**Kreta** ['kreːta]. *Pr.n.n* -s. Crete.

**Kreuz** [krɔyts]. I. *n* -es/-e 1. cross. 2. *Anat:* small of the back. 3. (*Karte*) club; (*Farbe*) clubs. II. **k.,** *adv.* **k. und quer,** higgledy-piggledy; (*hin und her*) this way and that. III. 'K~-, *comb.fm.* (*a*) cross- (stitch etc.); (*b*) (ace, king etc.) of clubs. ◆'k~**en,** *v. i.* 1. *v.tr.* (*a*) (*Linie, Straße usw.*) to cross, intersect (another line, road etc.); **sich k.,** (*Straßen, Linien*) to cross; (*b*) to cross (animals, plants etc.). 2. *v.i.* (*haben*) *Nau:* to cruise. ◆'K~**er,** *m* -s/- cruiser. ◆'K~**fahrt,** *f Nau:* cruise. ◆'K~**feuer,** *n* crossfire. ◆'k~**igen,** *v.tr.* to crucify (s.o.). ◆'K~**igung,** *f* -/-en crucifixion. ◆'K~**otter,** *f* adder, common viper. ◆'K~**ung,** *f* -/-en 1. intersection (of roads, railways); (*Straßenk.*) (road) junc-

tion, crossroads; (*Übergang*) crossing. **2.**
*Bot: Z:* (*a*) crossing (of animals, plants);
(*b*) (*Tier, Pflanze*) cross. ◆'K~**verhör**,
*n* cross-examination. ◆'K~**worträtsel**,
*n* crossword puzzle. ◆'K~**zug**, *m* crusade.

**kribbel|ig** ['kribəliç], *adj. F:* edgy; (*unruhig*) fidgety (child etc.). ◆'K~**n**, *n -s/no
pl* tingling; pins and needles.

**kriech|en** ['kri:çən], *v.i.irr.55* (*sein*) to
crawl, (*sehr langsam*) creep; **vor j-m k.**, to
grovel/toady to s.o. ◆'K~**er**, *m -s/- Pej:*
crawler, creep. ◆'k~**erisch**, *adj. Pej:*
obsequious, grovelling. ◆'K~**spur**, *f*
crawler lane. ◆'K~**tier**, *n* reptile.

**Krieg** [kri:k], *m -(e)s/-e* war. ◆K~**er**
['kri:gər], *m -s/-* warrior. ◆'k~**erisch**,
*adj.* warlike (attitude, people etc.); martial (bearing etc.). ◆'k~**führend**, *adj.*
belligerent. ◆'K~**führung**, *f* warfare.
◆'K~**s-**, *comb.fm.* war (service, damage, crime etc.); (outbreak, costs, state
etc.) of war. ◆'K~**sbemalung**, *f*
warpaint. ◆'K~**sbeschädigt**, *adj.*
(war) disabled. ◆'K~**sdienstverweigerer**, *m* conscientious objector.
◆'K~**serklärung**, *f* declaration of war.
◆'K~**sfall**, *m* **im K.**, in the event of
war. ◆'K~**sfuß**, *m F:* **mit j-m auf K.
stehen/leben**, to be at loggerheads with
s.o. ◆'K~**sgebiet**, *n* war zone.
◆'K~**sgefangene(r)**, *m & f decl. as
adj.* prisoner of war.
◆'K~**sgefangenschaft**, *f* captivity.
◆'K~**sgericht**, *n* court martial.
◆'K~**srecht**, *n* martial law.
◆'K~**sschauplatz**, *n* theatre of war.
◆'K~**sschiff**, *n* warship.
◆'K~**steilnehmer**, *m* combatant.
◆'k~**sversehrt**, *adj.* (war) disabled.

**kriegen** ['kri:gən], *v.tr. F:* to get (sth.);
to catch (a train, criminal, cold etc.).

**Krimi** ['krimi], *m -s/-s F:* detective story,
whodunnit.

**Kriminal|beamte(r)** [krimi'nɑ:lbɛamtə(r)], *m* criminal investigator.
◆K~**film**, *m* crime/detective film.
◆K~**ität** [-nali'tɛ:t], *f -/no pl* crime
(rate). ◆K~**polizei**, *f* criminal investigation department. ◆K~**roman**, *m*
crime/detective novel.

**kriminell** [krimi'nɛl], *adj.* criminal.
◆K~**e(r)**, *m & f decl. as adj.* criminal.

**Kringel** ['kriŋəl], *m -s/-* curl (of smoke
etc.). ◆'k~**n**, *v.tr.* to coil, curl (sth.);
(*Rauch usw.*) **sich k.**, to curl.

**Kripo** ['kri:po], *f -/no pl F:* = **Kriminalpolizei**.

**Krippe** ['kripə], *f -/-n* **1.** crib, manger. **2.**
(*Kinderk.*) day nursery.

**Krise** ['kri:zə], *f -/-n* crisis. ◆'K~**nherd**,
*m* storm centre, trouble spot.

**Kristall** [kris'tal]. **I.** *m -s/-e* crystal. **II.** *n
-s/no pl* crystal (glass). ◆k~**i'sieren**,
*v.tr. & i.* (*haben*) to crystallize.

**Kriterium** [kri'te:rium], *n -s/-ien* criterion.

**Krit|ik** [kri'ti:k], *f -/-en* (*a*) (*Rezension*) notice, review; (*b*) *no pl* (*allgemein*) criticism; *F:* **unter aller/jeder K.**, beneath
contempt. ◆K~**iker** ['kri:tikər], *m -s/-*
critic. ◆k~**iklos** [kri'ti:klo:s], *adj.* uncritical. ◆k~**isch** ['kri:tiʃ], *adj.* critical. ◆k~**isieren** [kriti'zi:rən], *v.tr.* to
criticize.

**kritteln** ['kritəln], *v.i.* (*haben*) to find fault
(**an** + *dat*, with).

**Kritzel|ei** [kritsə'lai], *f -/-en* scrawl, scribble. ◆'k~**n**, *v.tr.&i.* (*haben*) to scribble, scrawl (sth.).

**Krokodil** [kroko'di:l], *n -s/-e* crocodile.

**Krokus** ['kro:kus], *m -/- &* -se crocus.

**Kron|e** ['kro:nə], *f -/-n* crown.
◆'K~**enkorken**, *m* crown cap.
◆'K~**leuchter**, *m* chandelier.
◆'K~**prinz**, *m* crown prince.

**krön|en** ['krø:nən], *v.tr.* to crown (s.o.,
*Fig:* sth.). ◆'K~**ung**, *f -/-en* (*a*) coronation; (*b*) *Fig:* consummation, crowning
achievement.

**Kropf** [krɔpf], *m -(e)s/-̈e* **1.** crop. **2.** *Med:*
goitre.

**Kröte** ['krø:tə], *f -/-n* toad.

**Krücke** ['krykə], *f -/-n* crutch.

**Krug** [kru:k], *m -(e)s/-̈e* jug.

**Krümel** ['kry:məl], *m -s/-* crumb.
◆'k~**n**, *v.tr.* to crumble (bread, cake
etc.).

**krumm** [krum], *adj.* **1.** twisted, out of
shape; warped (wood); bent (nail etc.);
curved (line, spine etc.); crooked (stick,
nose, etc.). **2.** *F:* (*unehrlich*) **eine k~e
Sache drehen**, to do sth. crooked.
◆'k~**beinig**, *adj.* bow-legged, bandylegged; (*Dackel usw.*) with bent/bandy
legs. ◆'k~**nehmen**, *v.tr.sep.irr.69* to
take (sth.) amiss.

**krümm|en** ['krymən], *v.tr.* to bend (a
wire, one's back etc.), crook (one's
finger); **sich k.**, to bend, twist; (*Fluß,
Pfad*) to wind. ◆'K~**ung**, *f -/-en* bend;
curve (of an arch, road etc.); curvature
(of the spine etc.).

**Krüppel** ['krypəl], *m -s/-* cripple.

**Kruste** ['krustə], *f -/-n* crust.

**Kruzifix** [krutsi'fiks], *n -es/-e* crucifix.

**Kuba** ['ku:ba]. *Pr.n.n* -s. Cuba.
◆K~**ner(in)** [ku'ba:nər(in)], *m -s/-
(-nen)* Cuban.

**Kübel** ['ky:bəl], *m -s/-* bucket, tub (for
plants etc.); bin (for rubbish).

**Kubik-** [ku'bi:k-], *comb.fm. Meas:* cubic
(metre, centimetre etc.).

**Küche** ['kyçə], *f -/-n* **1.** kitchen. **2.**
(*Kochen*) cooking; **kalte K.**, hot/cold
food. ◆'K~**n-**, *comb.fm.* kitchen (towel,
furniture, chair, knife etc.).
◆'K~**nchef**, *m* chef. ◆'K~**ngerät**, *n*
kitchen utensil/*coll.* utensils.
◆'K~**nherd**, *m* kitchen range.
◆'K~**nmaschine**, *f* (electric) mixer.
◆'K~**nschabe**, *f -/-n* cockroach.

**Kuchen** ['ku:xən], *m -s/-* cake.
◆'K~**blech**, *n* baking sheet.

◆'**K~form,** f cake tin/N.Am: pan.
◆'**K~gabel,** f cake/pastry fork.
◆'**K~teig,** m cake mixture.

**Kuckuck** ['kukuk], m -s/-e (a) cuckoo; (b) P: **zum K.!** damn it! **das weiß der K.!** goodness knows! ◆'**K~suhr,** f cuckoo clock.

**Kufe** ['ku:fə], f -/-n runner (of a sledge etc.); Av: skid.

**Kugel** ['ku:gəl], f -/-n **1.** ball; Mth: sphere; Sp: shot. **2.** (Geschoß) bullet. ◆'**k~förmig,** adj. spherical. ◆'**K~kopf,** m golfball. ◆'**K~lager,** n ball bearing. ◆'**k~n,** v.refl. F: **sich k.,** to roll about. ◆'**k~'rund,** adj. F: round as a ball, tubby. ◆'**K~schreiber,** m ballpoint pen. ◆'**k~sicher,** adj. bullet-proof.

**Kuh** [ku:], f -/-e cow. ◆'**K~haut,** f cowhide; F: **das geht auf keine K.!** it's absolutely staggering! ◆'**K~stall,** m cowshed.

**kühl** [ky:l], adj. **1.** (frisch) cool; (unangenehm) chilly. **2.** Fig: cool (reception, head etc.). ◆'**K~e,** f -/no pl coolness; cool (of the evening etc.); chilliness (of night etc.). ◆'**k~en,** v.tr. to cool (sth.). ◆'**K~er,** m -s/- Aut: radiator. ◆'**K~erhaube,** f bonnet, N.Am: hood. ◆'**K~raum,** m cold store. ◆'**K~schrank,** m refrigerator. ◆'**K~tasche,** f cooler bag. ◆'**K~truhe,** f (chest) freezer. ◆'**K~turm,** m cooling tower. ◆'**K~ung,** f -/-en (a) (refreshing) coolness; (b) Tchn: cooling.

**kühn** [ky:n], adj. bold; (gewagt) daring (escape etc.). ◆'**K~heit,** f -/no pl boldness, daring.

**Küken** ['ky:kən], n -s/- chick.

**kulant** [ku'lant], adj. obliging, reasonable.

**Kuli¹** ['ku:li], m -s/-s coolie.

**Kuli²,** m -s/-s F: ballpoint (pen).

**Kulisse** [ku'lisə], f -/-n (a) Th: piece of scenery; pl **K~n,** (Seite der Bühne) wings; (b) Fig: background; **hinter den K~n,** behind the scenes.

**Kult** [kult], m -(e)s/-e (a) (form of) worship, rite; (b) Fig: idolization. ◆**k~ivieren** [-'vi:rən], v.tr. to cultivate (land, plants, Fig: taste etc.). ◆**k~i'viert,** adj. refined, cultivated (taste etc.); cultured (person, mind etc.).

**Kultur** [kul'tu:r]. I. f -/-en **1.** (a) culture, civilization; (b) no pl culture; **ohne K.,** uncultured (person). **2.** (a) Agr: etc: cultivation; (b) plantation (of trees etc.). II. **K~-,** comb.fm. **1.** cultural (agreement, policy, centre etc.). **2.** Agr: cultivated (plants, land, area etc.). ◆'**K~ell** [-'tu'rɛl], adj. cultural. ◆**K~geschichte,** f cultural history; history of civilization.

**Kümmel** ['kyməl], m -s/- caraway.

**Kummer** ['kumər], m -s/no pl grief, sorrow; (Sorge) worry, distress.

**kümmerlich** ['kymərliç], adj. miserable,

wretched (conditions, quarters etc.); puny (plant, efforts etc.); paltry, meagre (salary, result etc.). ◆**k~n** (a) to bother, concern (s.o.); **was kümmert dich das?** what concern is that of yours? (b) **sich um j-n, etwas** acc **k.,** to take care of s.o., sth.; **ich kümmere mich nicht um diesen Klatsch,** I don't take any notice of this gossip.

**Kumpan** [kum'pa:n], m -s/-e F: mate, chum, N.Am: buddy; Pej: crony.

**Kumpel** ['kumpəl], m -s/- mate, N.Am: buddy.

**Kunde¹** ['kundə], m -n/-n customer; (zu Beratender) client. ◆'**K~endienst,** m customer service; (für Käufer) after-sales service. ◆'**K~enkreis,** m clientele. ◆'**K~in,** f -/-nen woman customer/ client. ◆'**K~schaft,** f -/no pl **1.** (Kundenkreis) clientele. **2.** custom.

**Kunde²,** f -/-n A: & Lit: tidings. ◆**k~geben** ['kunt-], v.tr.sep.irr.35 Lit: to announce, make known (one's views etc.). ◆'**K~gebung,** f -/-en demonstration, rally. ◆'**K~ig** [-diç], adj. knowledgeable; expert (advice, mechanic etc.).

**kündbar** ['kyntba:r], adj. Jur: etc: terminable. ◆**k~igen** ['kyndigən], v.tr. (a) to terminate, cancel (an agreement, contract etc.); (b) v.tr. & i. (haben) (Firma usw.) **j-m k.,** to give s.o. notice; (Angestellter) **(die Stellung) k.,** to hand in one's notice. ◆'**K~igung,** f -/-en (a) termination, cancellation; (b) (employer's/employee's) notice; (landlord's) notice to quit. ◆'**K~igungsfrist,** f period of notice.

**künftig** ['kynftiç], adj. future; prospective (candidate); coming (event etc.); (b) adv. in future.

**Kunst** [kunst]. I. f -/-e **1.** art. **2.** (Fähigkeit) skill; F: **das ist keine K.,** there is nothing to it. II. **'K~-,** comb.fm. **1.** artificial (manure, limb etc.); synthetic (resin etc.). **2.** art (gallery, lover, collector etc.). ◆'**K~akademie,** f art college/school. ◆'**K~faser,** f synthetic fibre. ◆'**k~fertig,** adj. skilful. ◆'**K~fertigkeit,** f skilfulness. ◆'**K~geschichte,** f art history. ◆'**K~gewerbe,** n arts and crafts. ◆'**k~gewerblich,** adj. craftsmanmade. ◆'**K~griff,** m trick, dodge. ◆'**K~händler,** m art dealer. ◆'**K~seide,** f artificial silk, rayon. ◆'**K~stoff,** m plastic. ◆'**K~stück,** n trick, stunt; (Glanzleistung) feat; F: **K.!** no wonder! ◆'**K~turnen,** n (competitive) gymnastics. ◆'**K~verstand,** m artistic judgment. ◆'**k~voll,** adj. highly artistic; elaborate (carving etc.); ingenious (machine etc.). ◆'**K~werk,** n work of art.

**Künstler(in)** ['kynstlər(in)], m -s/- (f -/ -nen) artist. ◆'**k~lerisch,** adj. artistic. ◆'**K~lername,** m stage name. ◆'**k~lich,** adj. artificial.

**kunterbunt** ['kuntərbunt], *adj.* very varied, mixed.
**Kupfer** ['kupfər], *n* -s/no pl copper. ◆'K~n, *adj.* (made of) copper. ◆'K~stich, *m* copper(-plate) engraving.
**Kuppe** ['kupə], *f* -/-n 1. brow (of a hill). 2. (*a*) (*Fingerk.*) fingertip; (*b*) rounded head (of a nail etc.).
**Kuppel** ['kupəl], *f* -/-n dome.
**Kupp|elei** [kupə'lai], *f* -/-en *Jur:* procuring. ◆'k~eln, *v.* 1. *v.tr.* to couple (sth.). 2. *v.i.* (*haben*) (*a*) *Jur:* to procure; (*b*) *Aut:* to declutch. ◆'K~ler(in), *m* -s/- (*f* -/-nen) *Jur:* procurer. ◆'K~lung, *f* -/-en *Tchn:* coupling; *Aut:* clutch.
**Kur** [ku:r], *f* -/-en cure, treatment (*esp.* at a spa). ◆'K~gast, *m* patient at/visitor to a spa. ◆k~ieren [ku'ri:rən], *v.tr.* to cure, heal (s.o., a disease etc.). ◆'K~ort, *m* health resort, spa. ◆'K~pfuscher, *m* -s/- *Pej:* quack.
**Kür** [ky:r], *f* -/-en *Sp:* free skating; (*Turnen*) voluntary exercise. ◆'K~lauf, *m* *Sp:* free skating.
**Kurbel** ['kurbəl], *f* -/-n crank. ◆'k~n, *v.tr.* **in die Höhe k.,** to winch up (a load), wind up (a car window etc.). ◆'K~welle, *f* crankshaft.
**Kürbis** ['kyrbis], *m* -ses/-se pumpkin; (*Flaschenk.*) (vegetable) marrow; *esp.* *N.Am:* squash.
**Kurier** [ku'ri:r], *m* -s/-e courier.
**kurios** [kuri'o:s], *adj.* queer (story, idea etc.); quaint (person, object etc.).
**Kurs** [kurs], *m* -es/-e 1. (*a*) course; (*b*) *Fig:* policy, line. 2. (*Börsenk.*) price; *Fin:* rate of exchange. 3. *Sch:* course, syllabus; *N.Am:* program. ◆'K~buch, *n* railway timetable. ◆'K~wagen, *m* *Rail:* through coach.
**kurs|ieren** [kur'zi:rən], *v.i.* (*haben*) to circulate. ◆k~iv [-'zi:f], *adj.* italic. ◆K~us ['kurzus], *m* -/Kurse course.
**Kurve** ['kurvə], *f* -/-n curve; bend (of a road, river etc.). ◆'k~nreich, *adj.* (*Straße*) winding, twisting.
**kurz** [kurts], *adj.* short; **k. dahinter,** just behind it; *Fig:* **alles k. and klein schlagen,** to smash everything to pieces; **den k~eren ziehen,** to come off worst; *adv.* **zu k. kommen,** to lose out; **vor k~em,**

recently; **k. anhalten,** to stop briefly. ◆'K~arbeit, *f* short-time work. ◆'k~ärmelig, *adj.* short-sleeved. ◆'k~atmig, *adj.* (*Pers.*) short-winded. ◆'k~er'hand, *adv.* without hesitation/delay. ◆'K~fassung, *f* abridged version (of a book etc.). ◆'k~fristig, *adj.* short-term (credit etc.). ◆'K~geschichte, *f* short story. ◆'k~haarig, *adj.* short-haired. ◆'k~halten, *v.tr.sep.irr.45* to keep (s.o.) short (of money, food etc.). ◆'k~lebig, *adj.* short-lived; ephemeral (insect, plant etc.). ◆'K~nachrichten, *fpl* news summary. ◆'K~schluß, *m El:* short-circuit, *F:* short. ◆'K~schrift, *f* shorthand. ◆'k~sichtig, *adj.* (*also Fig:*) short-sighted, *N.Am:* near-sighted. ◆'k~'um, *adv.* in short. ◆'K~waren, *fpl* haberdashery, *N.Am:* notions. ◆'K~welle, *f* *Rad:* short wave.
**Kürz|e** ['kyrtsə], *f* -/no pl (*a*) shortness; brevity (of a description etc.); briefness (of a visit etc.); (*b*) (*Knappheit*) conciseness. ◆'k~en, *v.tr.* (*a*) (*kürzer machen*) to shorten (sth.); (*b*) (*verringern*) to cut, reduce (taxes, expenses etc.). ◆k~lich, *adj.* recently, a short time ago. ◆'K~ung, *f* -/-en reduction, cut (**des Einkommens usw.,** in income etc.).
**kusch|elig** ['kuʃəliç], *adj.* cuddly. ◆'k~eln, *v.refl.* **sich an j-n k.,** to cuddle/snuggle up to s.o.
**Kusine** [ku'zi:nə], *f* -/-n (female) cousin.
**Kuß** [kus], *m* -sses/-sse kiss.
**küssen** ['kysən], *v.tr.* to kiss.
**Küste** ['kystə], *f* -/-n coast. ◆'K~n-, *comb.fm.* coastal (area etc.). ◆'K~ngewässer, *n* coastal/inshore waters. ◆'K~nlinie, *f* coastline. ◆'K~nwache, *f* coastguard service.
**Kutsche** ['kutʃə], *f* -/-n (horsedrawn) coach, carriage. ◆'K~er, *m* -s/- coachdriver, coachman.
**Kutte** ['kutə], *f* -/-n monk's habit.
**Kutter** ['kutər], *m* -s/- cutter; (*Fischk.*) fishing boat.
**Kuvert** [ku've:r], *n* -s/-s 1. envelope. 2. (*Gedeck*) cover (at table).

# L

**L, l** [ɛl], *n* -/- (the letter) L, l.
**laben** ['la:bən], *v.tr.* to refresh (s.o.).
**labil** [la'bi:l], *adj.* unstable (situation, character etc.); delicate (health etc.).
**Labor** [la'bo:r], *n* -s/-s & -e laboratory, *F:* lab. ◆L~ant(in) [-o'rant(in)], *m* -en/-en (*f* -/-nen) laboratory assistant. ◆L~atorium [-a'to:rium] *n* -s/-rien laboratory.
**Labyrinth** [laby'rint], *n* -(e)s/-e maze.
**Lache** ['la:xə], *f* -/-n puddle.

**lach|en** ['laxən]. I. *v.tr. & i.* (*haben*) to laugh (**über** + *acc*, at); *F:* **er hat nichts zu l.,** he has a hard time (of it); **das wäre ja gelacht, wenn ...,** it'd be ridiculous if ... II. L., *n* -s/no pl laugh; *coll* laughter; **es ist zum L.,** it's ridiculous; **es ist nicht zum L.,** it's no laughing matter. ◆'L~gas, *n* laughing gas. ◆'l~haft, *adj.* ludicrous. ◆'L~krampf, *m* fit of laughter.
**läch|eln** ['lɛçəln]. I. *v.i.* (*haben*) to smile

(über etwas *acc*, at sth.; über j-n, about s.o.). II. L., *n* -s/- smile. ◆'l~**erlich**, *adj.* ridiculous; j-n l. **machen**, to make s.o. look a fool. ◆'L~**erlichkeit**, *f* -/-en absurdity.

**Lachs** [laks], *m* -es/-e salmon. ◆'l~**farben**, *adj.* salmon pink. ◆'L~**forelle**, *f* -/-n salmon trout.

**Lack** [lak], *m* -(e)s/-e 1. (*farblos*) varnish. 2. *Aut:* paintwork, finish. ◆'L~**affe**, *m* F: conceited ass. ◆'l~**ieren** [·'kiːrən], *v.tr.* to varnish (wood, fingernails etc.). ◆'L~**schuh**, *m* patent leather shoe.

**Lackmuspapier** ['lakmuspapiːr], *n* -s/*no pl* litmus paper.

**Lad**|**e**-, *comb.fm.* (a) loading (crane etc.); (b) *El:* charging (voltage, current etc.). ◆'L~**egerät**, *n* (battery) charger. ◆'l~**en**[1], *v.tr.irr.* (a) to load (goods, cargo etc.) (**auf** + *acc*, onto); (b) to load (a gun etc.); *El:* to charge (a battery etc.); (c) **Verantwortung usw. auf sich** l., to burden oneself with responsibility. (d) *Jur:* **einen Zeugen (vor Gericht)** l., to summon a witness. ◆'L~**eraum**, *m* load/cargo space; *Nau:* hold. ◆'L~**ung**, *f* -/-en 1. load; *Nau:* cargo. 2. *E.:* charge. 3. *Jur:* L. (vor Gericht), summons.

**Laden**[2] ['laːdən], *m* -s/= 1. shop, *N.Am:* store. 2. F: business. 3. (*Fenster*.) shutter. ◆'L~**besitzer(in)**, *m & f* shopkeeper. ◆'L~**dieb(in)**, *m & f* shoplifter. ◆'L~**diebstahl**, *m* (case of) shoplifting. ◆'L~**hüter**, *m* -s/- slow-moving article. ◆'L~**preis**, *m* retail price. ◆'L~**schluß** *m* (shop-)closing time. ◆'L~**tisch**, *m* (shop) counter.

**Lafette** [la'fetə], *f* -/-n gun carriage.

**Lage** ['laːgə], *f* -/-n 1. position, situation; **versetze dich mal in meine L.**, just put yourself in my position/F: in my shoes; **L. der Dinge**, (present) state of affairs; F: **die L. peilen**, to find out how the land lies; **in der L. sein, etwas zu tun**, to be in a position to do sth. 2. (*Schicht*) layer (of sand etc.). ◆'L~**bericht**, *m* *Mil:* etc: report on the situation. ◆'L~**plan**, *m* plan (of a town etc.).

**Lager** ['laːgər]. I. *n* -s/- 1. *Mil:* etc: camp. 2. (a) *Com:* store; (*L~haus*) warehouse; (b) (*Vorrat*) stock; **einen Artikel auf L. haben**, to have sth. in stock. 3. *Tchn:* bearing. II. **L~**-, *comb.fm.* (a) camp (fire, leader etc.); (b) (*für Lagerung*) storage (charge, costs etc.); (c) *Tchn:* bearing (metal etc.). ◆'L~**arbeiter**, *m* warehouseman. ◆'L~**bestand**, *m* stock. ◆'L~**haus**, *n* warehouse. ◆'l~**n**, *v.* 1. *v.tr.* (a) to place, lay (s.o., sth.) (somewhere); (b) to store (goods, provisions etc.). 2. *v.i.* (*haben*) (a) *Mil:* etc: to camp; (b) (*Waren usw.*) to be in store; (c) (*Wein*) to age. ◆'L~**ung**, *f* -/-en 1. storing, storage (of goods). 2. *Tchn:* mounting in a bearing/bearings.

**Lagune** [la'guːnə], *f* -/-n lagoon.

**lahm** [laːm], *adj.* (a) (*Pers.*) lame; (b) F: feeble, limp (handshake); *Fig:* lame, feeble (joke, excuse etc.). ◆'l~**en**, *v.i.* (*haben*) (*Tier*) to be lame. ◆'l~**legen**, *v.tr.* to bring (production, traffic etc.) to a standstill.

**lähm**|**en** ['lɛːmən], *v.tr.* (a) (*Gift*) to paralyse (a muscle), numb (a nerve); *Fig:* to cripple (industry etc.); (b) (*Angst usw.*) to petrify, paralyse (s.o.); (*Schock usw.*) to numb (s.o.). ◆'L~**ung**, *f* -/-en *Med: & Fig:* paralysis; *Fig:* immobilization (of industry etc.).

**Laib** [laip], *m* -(e)s/-e **ein L. Brot**, a loaf of bread.

**Laich** [laiç], *m* -(e)s/-e spawn. ◆'l~**en**, *v.i.* (*haben*) to spawn.

**Laie** ['laiə], *m* -n/-n *also Ecc:* layman; *Th: Mus: etc:* amateur; ◆'l~**nhaft**, *adj. Pej:* amateurish (performance etc.). ◆'L~**n**-, *comb.fm.* (a) *Th: Mus: etc:* amateur (actor, choir, painter etc.); (b) *esp. Ecc:* lay (brother, preacher etc.).

**Lakai** [la'kai], *m* -en/-en (a) lackey, footman; (b) *Fig: Pej:* bootlicker.

**Lake** ['laːkə], *f* -/-n *Cu:* brine (for pickling).

**Laken** ['laːkən], *n* -s/- sheet.

**lakonisch** [la'koːniʃ], *adj.* laconic.

**Lakritze** [la'kritsə], *f* -/-n liquorice.

**lallen** ['lalən], *v.tr. & i.* (*haben*) (*Betrunkene usw.*) to babble (incoherently).

**Lama** ['laːma], *n* -s/-s *Z:* llama.

**Lamelle** [la'mɛlə], *f* -/-n 1. thin plate/ (*Scheibe*) disc; (*Jalousienl.*) slat; (*Kühlerl.*) gill; 2. (*Pilzl.*) gill, lamella.

**lamentieren** [lamɛn'tiːrən], *v.i.* (*haben*) F: to moan.

**Lametta** [la'mɛta], *n* -s/*no pl* tinsel.

**Lamm** [lam], *n* -(e)s/=er lamb. ◆'L~**fell**, *n* lambskin. ◆'l~'**fromm**, *adj.* F: as meek as a lamb. ◆'L~**wolle**, *f* lambswool.

**Lampe** ['lampə], *f* -/-n (a) lamp; (*Deckenl.*) light; (b) (*Birne*) lightbulb. ◆'L~**nfieber**, *n* stage fright. ◆'L~**nschirm**, *m* lampshade.

**Lampion** [lampi'ɔŋ], *m & n* -s/-s Chinese lantern.

**Land** [lant]. I. *n* -(e)s/=er 1. land; *Nau:* **an L. gehen**, to go ashore; 2. (*nicht Stadt*) country; **auf dem L./L~e**, in the country. 3. (a) *Pol:* country; (b) *Adm:* West G: Land, state; *Aus:* province. II. 'L~-, *comb.fm.* (a) (*vom Lande*) country (doctor, house, life, people, air etc.); (*ländlich*) rural (population etc.); (b) land (warfare, forces etc.); ◆'L~**arbeiter**, *m* farmhand. ◆'l~'**aus**, *adv.* l., **landein**, far and wide. ◆'L~**besitz**, *m* landed property, real estate. ◆'L~**besitzer**, *m* landowner. ◆**L~e**- ['landə-], *comb.fm.* landing (*Av:* light, flap, *Nau:* place etc.); ◆'L~**ebahn** *f*, (landing) runway; ◆'L~**eerlaubnis**, *f* permission to land. ◆'l~'**einwärts**, *adv.* (further) inland. ◆'l~**en**, *v.* 1. *v.tr. & i.* (*sein*) to land.

◆'L~enge, f -/-n isthmus. ◆L~es-['landəs-], comb.fm. 1. national (custom, frontier, colours, flag etc.); state (police etc.); (language etc.) of a/the country; 2. West G: Land/state, Aus: provincial (boundary, government etc.); ◆'l~esüblich, adj. customary in a/the country. ◆'L~esverrat, m high treason. ◆'L~esverräter, m traitor (to one's country). ◆'L~eswährung, f currency of the country. ◆'L~flucht, f drift from the country to the town. ◆'L~friedensbruch, m Jur: breach of the peace. ◆'L~gut n country estate. ◆'L~karte, f map. ◆'L~kreis, m country/rural district. ◆'l~läufig, adj. popular, widespread (opinion, view etc.). ◆'L~plage, f plague (of insects); ◆'L~regen, n steady rain. ◆'l~schaft, f -/-en landscape; coll scenery; die L. um Bonn, the countryside round Bonn. ◆'l~schaftlich, adj. (a) regional (custom, culture etc.); (b) das Dorf liegt l. sehr schön, the village is beautifully situated. ◆'L~sitz, m country seat. ◆'L~smann, m -(e)s/-leute fellow-countryman. ◆'L~smännin, f -/-nen fellow-countrywoman. ◆'L~straße, f country road; (kleinere) minor road. ◆'L~streicher(in), m -s/- (f -/-nen) tramp, N.Am: hobo. ◆'L~strich m tract of country. ◆'L~tag, m West G. Pol: Land/State parliament. ◆'L~ung, f -/-en Av: Nau: landing; Av: touchdown. ◆'L~ungsbrücke, f jetty, pier. ◆'L~vermesser m, land surveyor. ◆'L~weg, m auf dem L., overland. ◆'L~wein, m local wine. ◆'L~wirt(in), m & f farmer. ◆'L~wirtschaft, f -/-en farming, agriculture. ◆'l~wirtschaftlich adj. / ◆'L~wirtschafts-, comb.fm. agricultural. ◆'L~zunge, f tongue of land. **Länd|ereien** [lɛndəˈraiən], fpl estates, landed properties. ◆'L~erspiel, n Sp: international match. ◆'l~lich, adj. rural.

**lang** [laŋ], adj. long; F: ein l~er Kerl, a tall fellow; vor l~er Zeit, a long time ago; er wartete drei Jahre l., he waited for three years; sein Leben l., all his life. ◆'l~atmig, adj. long-winded (speech etc.); lengthy (explanation etc.). ◆'l~e, adv. a long time; das ist schon l. her, that was a long time ago; wie l. (dauert es) noch? how much longer (does it take)? (noch) l. nicht fertig, not nearly ready. ◆L~e'weile, f -/no pl boredom. ◆'L~finger, m F: pilferer; (Taschendieb) pickpocket. ◆'l~fristig, adj. long-term (loan etc.). ◆'l~haarig, adj. long-haired. ◆'l~jährig, adj. long (experience etc.), long-standing (friendship etc.). ◆'l~lauf, m cross-country skiing. ◆'l~lebig, adj. long-lived (person etc.); durable (material). ◆'l~sam,

adj. slow; (allmählich) gradual (development, change etc.); es wird l. Zeit zu gehen, it is about time to go. ◆'L~samkeit, f -/no pl slowness. ◆'L~schläfer(in), m(f) late riser. ◆'L~spielplatte, f -/-n long-playing record. ◆'L~strecken-, comb.fm. long-distance (flight, runner etc.); long-range (rocket, aircraft etc.). ◆'l~weilen, v.tr. to bore (s.o.); sich l., to be bored. ◆'l~weilig, adj. boring; dull (landscape, person). ◆'L~welle, f Rad: etc: long wave. ◆'l~wierig, adj. lengthy, protracted.

**Läng|e** ['lɛŋə], f -/-n (a) length; F: height (of a person); (b) Geog: longitude. ◆'L~engrad, m degree of longitude. ◆'L~enmaß, n longitudinal measure. ◆'l~lich, adj. oblong. ◆'L~s-, comb.fm. longitudinal (stripe, axis etc.). ◆'l~st, adv. (schon) l., a long time ago; F: ages ago; (noch) l. nicht so viel, nothing like as much; F: das reicht l., that is more than enough. ◆'l~ste(r, s), adj. longest.

**langen** ['laŋən], v.i. (haben) (a) to reach; nach der Zuckerdose l., to reach for the sugar; (b) F: (Geld, Nahrung usw.) to be enough; jetzt langt's mir aber! now I've had enough!

**Languste** [laŋ'gustə], f -/-n spiny lobster.

**Lanz|e** ['lantsə], f -/-n lance. ◆L~ette [-'tsɛtə], f -/-n lancet.

**lapidar** [lapi'doːr], adj.pithy, terse.

**Lappalie** [la'poːliə], f -/-n trifle.

**Lapp|en** ['lapən], m -s/- rag, cloth. **läppisch** ['lɛpiʃ], adj. silly; (kindisch) childish.

**Lapsus** ['lapsus], m -/- slip.

**Lärche** ['lɛrçə], f -/-n (common) larch.

**Lärm** [lɛrm], m -s/no pl (loud) noise. ◆'L~belästigung, f noise pollution. ◆'l~empfindlich, adj. sensitive to noise. ◆'l~en, v.i. (haben) to make a noise; (Radio usw.) to blare. ◆'l~end, adj. noisy.

**Larve** ['larfə], f -/-n larva.

**lasch** [laʃ], adj. F: (a) listless (person); limp (handshake etc.); (b) (fade) tasteless (food).

**Lasche** ['laʃə], f -/-n 1. tongue (of a shoe); Cl: flap. 2. Tchn: joint.

**Laser** ['leizər], m -s/- laser. ◆'L~strahl, m laser beam.

**lassen** ['lasən], v.tr.irr. (a) j-n etwas tun l., (i) (erlauben) to let s.o. do sth.; (ii) (heißen) to get s.o. to do sth.; ich ließ es mir schicken, I had it sent; laß dich nicht stören, don't let me disturb you; das läßt sich machen, that can be done; j-m freie Hand l., to allow s.o. a free hand; (b) (zurücklassen) to leave (s.o., sth.); laß mich in Ruhe/Frieden! leave me alone/in peace! (c) (unterlassen) to stop (doing sth.); laß das (sein/bleiben)! stop it! l. wir es dabei/gut sein, let's leave it at that.

**lässig** ['lɛsiç], *adj.* casual; (*unbekümmert*) nonchalant. ◆'L~keit, *f -/no pl* casualness; nonchalance.

**Lasso** ['laso], *m & n -s/-s* lasso.

**Last** [last], *f -/-en* load; *esp. Fig:* burden; **unter der L. des Schnees,** under the weight of the snow; *Fig:* **j-m zur L. fallen,** to be a burden to s.o.; **j-m etwas zur L. legen,** to accuse s.o. of sth. ◆'L~auto, *n* lorry, *N.Am:* truck. ◆'l~en, *v.i.* (*haben*) (*Sorge, Verantwortung usw.*) **auf j-m l.,** to weigh on s.o. ◆'L~enaufzug, *m* goods lift, *N.Am:* freight elevator. ◆'L~er1, *m -s/-/* ◆'L~(kraft)wagen, *m* lorry, *N.Am:* truck.

**Laster2,** *n -s/-* vice. ◆'l~haft, *adj.* wicked.

**läster|lich** ['lɛstərliç], *adj.* blasphemous (words etc.). ◆'l~n, *v.i.* (*haben*) (*a*) *F:* **über j-n l.,** to run s.o. down (behind his back); (*b*) **Gott l.,** to blaspheme.

**lästig** ['lɛstiç], *adj.* troublesome (cough etc.); irksome (task); tiresome (child, visitor etc.); **l. werden,** to become a nuisance.

**Latein** [la'tain], *n -(s)/no pl* Latin. ◆L~amerika. *Pr.n.n -s.* Latin America. ◆'l~amerikanisch, *adj.* Latin American. ◆l~isch, *adj.* Latin.

**latent** [la'tɛnt], *adj.* latent (talent, ability); potential (danger).

**Laterne** [la'tɛrnə], *f -/-n* (*a*) lantern; (*b*) (*Straßenl.*) streetlamp. ◆L~npfahl, *m* lamppost.

**Latrine** [la'tri:nə], *f -/-n* latrine.

**Latsche** ['latʃə], *f -/-n* dwarf pine.

**latschen** ['lɑːtʃən]. **I.** *v.i.* (*sein*) *F:* (*a*) (*schlürfen*) to shuffle (along); (*b*) **wir latschten durch die ganze Stadt,** we traipsed through the whole town. **II. L.,** *m -s/-* *F:* (worn-out) old shoe.

**Latte** [latə], *f -/-n* (*a*) (wooden) slat; *Tchn etc:* batten; rail (of a fence); (*b*) *Sp:* bar; *Fb:* crossbar. ◆'L~nzaun, *m* paling (fence).

**Latz** [lats], *m -es/-e* bib. ◆L~hose, *f* *Cl:* dungarees, *N.Am:* overalls.

**Lätzchen** ['lɛtsçən], *n -s/-* (child's) bib, feeder.

**lau** [lau], *adj.* (*a*) mild (breeze, weather); balmy (air, evening etc.); (*b*) lukewarm (water).

**Laub** [laup], *n -(e)s/no pl* leaves, foliage. ◆'L~baum, *m* deciduous tree. ◆'L~frosch, *m* treefrog. ◆'L~säge, *f* fretsaw. ◆'L~wald, *m* deciduous forest.

**Laube** ['laubə], *f -/-n* summer-house.

**Lauch** [laux], *m -(e)s/-e* leek.

**Lauer** [lauər], *f -/no pl* **auf der L. liegen/sein,** (*Tier*) to lie in wait; *F:* (*Pers.*) to be on the lookout. ◆'l~n, *v.i.* (*haben*) (*Pers., Fig: Gefahren usw.*) to lurk (somewhere); **auf j-n, etwas** *acc* **l.,** to lie in wait for s.o., sth.; *F:* to look out for s.o., sth.

**Lauf** [lauf], *m -(e)s/-e* **1.** (*a*) *no pl* (*das Laufen*) running; (*b*) *Sp:* race; **der 200-Meter-L.,** the 200 metres. **2.** *no pl* (*Verlauf*) course (of a river; *Fig:* of events etc.); **der L. der Dinge** the way things go; **im L~e des Tages,** during the day; **im L~e von wenigen Stunden,** within a few hours. **3.** *no pl* running (of a machine, an engine etc.). **4.** (*Gewehrl.*) barrel (of a rifle etc.). ◆'L~bahn, *f* career. ◆'l~en, *v.irr.* **1.** *v.i.* (*sein*) (*a*) to run; **j-m über den Weg l.,** to run/*F:* bump into s.o.; **den Motor l. lassen,** to run the engine; (*b*) (*gehen*) to walk; (*c*) **der Film läuft im Fernsehen,** the film is being shown on television; (*d*) (*fließen*) **das Wasser/den Hahn l. lassen,** to run the water/the tap. **2.** *v.tr.* to run (a distance, race etc.). ◆'l~end, *adj.* (*a*) running (commentary); current (account, expenses, tax year etc.); present (month); (*regelmäßig*) regular (payments); **l. steigen,** to increase continually; (*b*) **auf dem l~en sein/bleiben,** to be well-informed/up-to-date. ◆'l~enlassen, *v.tr.sep.irr.57* to let (s.o., an animal) go; to set (a prisoner, an animal) free. ◆'L~feuer, *n -s/-* *Fig:* **sich wie ein L. verbreiten,** to spread like wildfire. ◆'L~kundschaft, *f* casual customers. ◆'L~masche, *f* ladder, *pus: N.Am:* run (in a stocking/tights). ◆'L~paß, *m* *F:* **j-m den L. geben,** to give s.o. the push. ◆'L~schritt, *m* **im L.,** at the double. ◆'L~steg, *m* catwalk; walkway. ◆'L~stall, *m* playpen. ◆'L~werk, *n -(e)s/-e* (*a*) running gear (of a vehicle etc.); (*b*) clockwork (mechanism); (*c*) *Rec:* turntable unit. ◆'L~zettel, *m* circular; distribution sheet.

**Läufer** ['lɔyfər], *m -s/-* **1.** (*a*) *Sp:* runner; (*b*) *Fb:* half-back. **2.** *H:* (strip of) carpet, runner; (*Treppenl.*) stair-carpet. **3.** (*Schach*) bishop.

**läufig** ['lɔyfiç], *adj.* (*Hündin, Katze*) on heat.

**Lauge** ['laugə], *f -/-n* **1.** (*Waschl.*) soapy water. **2.** *Ch:* lye, alkaline solution.

**Laun|e** ['launə], *f -/-n* (*a*) mood; **bei guter/schlechter L.,** in a good mood/a bad temper; (*b*) (*Einfall*) **das war nur so eine L. von ihm,** that was just one of his whims. ◆'l~isch, *adj.* moody, petulant.

**Laus** [laus], *f -/-e* louse. ◆'L~bub, *m -en/-en* *Hum:* little rascal.

**lausch|en** ['lauʃən], *v.i.* (*haben*) to listen; (*heimlich*) to eavesdrop. ◆'l~ig, *adj.* (*gemütlich*) snug, cosy; (*ruhig*) quiet (spot etc.).

**laut1** [laut], *prep.* + *gen/dat* in accordance with; **l. Bericht,** according to reports.

**laut2. I.** *adj.* (*a*) loud (voice, shout etc.); noisy (area, children etc.); (*b*) **Klagen, Zweifel usw. wurden l.,** complaints, doubts etc. were voiced. **II. L.,** *m -(e)s/*

-e sound. ◆**'l~en**, v.i. (haben) **genau lautet der Befehl** ..., the exact wording of the order is ...; **das Schreiben lautet wie folgt:** ..., the letter reads as follows: ... ◆**'l~hals**, adv. at the top of one's voice. ◆**'l~los**, adj. silent (mechanism, footsteps); deep (silence). ◆**'l~malend**, adj. onomatopoeic. ◆**'l~schrift**, f phonetic transcription. ◆**'L~sprecher**, m loudspeaker. ◆**'l~stark**, adj. vociferous, noisy. ◆**'L~stärke**, f loudness; volume.

**Laute** ['lautə], f -/-n lute.

**läuten** ['lɔytən], v. 1. v.i. (haben) (Klingel, Telefon) to ring; (Wecker) to go off. 2. v.tr. to ring (the bell).

**lauter** ['lautər], adj. inv. sheer, utter (despair, greed); pure (joy, pleasure); **l. Steine**, nothing but stones.

**läuter|n** ['lɔytərn], v.tr. to purify (liquids); to refine (metals, glass). ◆**'L~ung**, f -/no pl purification; refinement.

**lauwarm** ['lauvarm], adj. lukewarm.

**Lava** ['lɑːva], f -/Laven lava.

**Lavendel** [la'vɛndəl], m -s/- lavender.

**lavieren** [la'viːrən], v.i. (haben) Fig: (Pers.) to manoeuvre.

**Lawine** [la'viːnə], f -/-n avalanche. ◆**l~nartig**, adj. like an avalanche; ◆**L~ngefahr**, f -/no pl danger of avalanches.

**lax** [laks], adj. lax (morals, principles etc.); slack (leadership, attitude).

**Lazarett** [latsa'rɛt], n -(e)s/-e military hospital.

**leb|en** ['leːbən]. I. v.i. (haben) to live; **seine Mutter lebt noch**, his mother is still alive; **er lebt nur für die Wissenschaft**, his life is dedicated to science; **von Wasser und Brot l.**, to live on bread and water. II. L., n -s/- life; **am L.**, alive; **ums L. kommen**, to lose one's life; Fig: **etwas ins L. rufen**, to bring sth. into being; **mein L. lang**, all my life; F: **nie im L.!** not on your life! ◆**'l~end**, adj. living (person, organism); live (fish, animals). ◆**l~endig** [le'bɛndiç], adj. (a) (am Leben) living; pred. alive; (b) (lebhaft) lively (child, story). ◆**L~endigkeit**, f liveliness. ◆**'L~ens-**, **'l~ens-**, comb.fm. (necessities, experience, form etc.) of life; living (conditions etc.). ◆**'L~ensabend**, m old age. ◆**'L~ensalter**, n age. ◆**'L~ensdauer**, f lifespan; Tchn: working life. ◆**'L~enserwartung**, f expectation of life. ◆**'l~ensfähig**, adj. (baby etc.) capable of survival; Biol: & Fig: viable (life-form etc.). ◆**'L~ensfreude**, f zest; **voller L.**, full of the joys of life. ◆**'L~ensgefahr**, f danger to life; **er schwebt in L.**, his life is in danger. ◆**'l~ensgefährlich**, adj. extremely dangerous (undertaking); critical (illness, injury). ◆**'L~ensgefährte**, m/

◆**'L~ensgefährtin**, f partner for life. ◆**'L~ensgröße**, f -/no pl actual size; **in L.**, lifesize. ◆**'L~enshaltungskosten**, pl cost of living. ◆**'L~enslage**, f situation. ◆**'l~enslänglich**, adj. life (imprisonment, membership). ◆**'L~enslauf**, m curriculum vitae. ◆**'L~ensmittel**, npl food; (Vorräte) provisions. ◆**'L~ensmittelgeschäft**, n food shop/esp. N.Am: store. ◆**'l~ensmüde**, adj. tired of life. ◆**'l~ensnah**, adj. realistic, true to life. ◆**'l~ensnotwendig**, adj. essential, vital. ◆**'L~ensstandard** m standard of living. ◆**'L~ensunterhalt**, m livelihood; **seinen L. verdienen**, to earn one's living. ◆**'L~ensversicherung** f life insurance/assurance. ◆**'L~enswandel**, m way of life. ◆**'L~ensweise**, f way of life. ◆**'L~enswerk**, n **sein L.**, his life's work. ◆**'l~enswichtig**, adj. vitally important, essential. ◆**'L~enszeichen**, n sign of life. ◆**'L~enszeit**, f lifetime; **auf L.**, for life. ◆**'L~ewesen**, n (living) being, creature. ◆**L~e'wohl**, n -(e)s/-e goodbye, A: & Hum: farewell. ◆**l~haft** ['leːphaft], adj. lively; animated (discussion etc.); vivid (colours, description); keen (interest); brisk (business etc.); busy (traffic). ◆**'L~haftigkeit**, f -/no pl liveliness; vivacity; vividness; keenness (of interest); briskness (of business). ◆**'l~los**, adj. lifeless; inanimate (object). ◆**'L~zeiten**, fpl lifetime; **zu seinen L.**, in/during his lifetime.

**Leber** ['leːbər], f -/-n liver. ◆**L~fleck**, m F: mole. ◆**L~käse**, m -s/no pl (spiced) meat loaf. ◆**'L~knödel**, m liver dumpling. ◆**'L~pastete**, f Cu: liver pâté. ◆**'L~tran**, m cod-liver oil. ◆**'L~wurst**, f (continental) liver sausage.

**Lebkuchen** ['leːpkuːxən], m (kind of) gingerbread.

**leck** [lɛk]. I. adj. leaky, leaking. II. L., n -(e)s/-s leak. ◆**l~en1**, v.i. (haben) to leak.

**lecken2** ['lɛkən], v.tr. & i. to lick.

**lecker** ['lɛkər], adj. delicious, tasty. ◆**'L~bissen**, m -s/- tasty morsel, titbit; (Delikatesse) delicacy. ◆**L~eien** [-'raiən], fpl good things (to eat), esp. sweets/N.Am: candy. ◆**'L~maul**, n F: **ein L. sein**, to have a sweet tooth.

**Leder** ['leːdər], n -s/- leather. ◆**'L~hose**, f esp.pl leather shorts, lederhosen. ◆**'L~jacke**, f -/-n leather jacket. ◆**'l~n**, adj. leather (gloves etc.). ◆**'L~waren**, fpl leather goods.

**ledig** ['leːdiç], adj. unmarried, single. ◆**l~lich** ['leːdikliç], adv. merely, solely.

**leer** [leːr], adj. (a) (ohne Inhalt) empty; flat (battery); (menschenleer) deserted, empty (streets); **l~es Blatt**, blank sheet; (b) Fig: empty, idle (talk, threats etc.).

l~er Blick, blank look; (Miene) vacant expression. ◆'L~e, f -/no pl emptiness. ◆'l~en, v.tr. to empty (a glass etc.), clear (a letter box, dustbin); (Saal usw.) sich l., to empty. ◆'L~gewicht, n weight unladen. ◆'L~lauf, m idling; Brit: tickover. ◆'l~stehend, adj. empty, vacant (room, flat etc.). ◆'L~taste, f space-bar.

legal [le'ga:l], adj. legal; legitimate (government, means etc.). ◆l~i'sieren, v.tr. (haben) to legalize (a practice etc.), authenticate (a document, signature). ◆L~i'tät, f -/no pl legality.

leg|en ['le:gən], v.tr. (a) (hinlegen) to put/lay (s.o., sth.) down; (Henne) Eier l., to lay (eggs); (b) etwas auf/in/unter etwas acc l., to put sth. on/in/under sth.; (c) sich l., (Wind, Fig: Aufregung usw.) to die down; (Lärm, Schmerz) to subside. legend|är [legɛn'dɛ:r], adj. legendary. ◆L~e [le'gɛndə], f -/-n legend.

leger [le'ʒe:r], adj. casual, relaxed.
legier|en [le'gi:rən], v.tr. to alloy (metals); ◆L~ung, f -/-en alloy.
legitim [legi'ti:m], adj. legitimate. ◆L~ation [-timatsi'o:n], f -/-en (Ausweis) proof of identity. ◆l~ieren [-ti'mi:rən], v.tr. (a) to authorize (s.o. to do sth.); (b) sich l., to show proof of one's identity.

Lehm [le:m], m -(e)s/-e clay (soil); Agr: loam.
Lehn|e ['le:nə], f -/-n (Rückenl.) back, (Arml.) arm (of a chair). ◆'l~en, v.tr. & i. (haben) to lean (sth.) (gegen/an + acc, against); ◆'L~stuhl, m armchair.
Lehr- ['le:r-], comb.fm. teaching (staff, method etc.); ◆'L~buch, n Sch: textbook. ◆'L~e1, f -/-n 1. Ind: etc: apprenticeship; kaufmännische L., commercial training. 2. (a) (Gelehrtes) die L. Christi/Hegels, the teachings of Christ/ Hegel; (b) Fig: (Lektion) lesson; moral (of a story); das soll dir eine L. sein! let that be a lesson to you! ◆'l~en, v.tr. to teach (a subject); ◆'L~er, m -s/- Sch: teacher; N.Am: & Sp: etc: instructor. ◆'l~erin, f -/-nen Sch: (woman) teacher; (school)mistress; Sp: etc: instructress. ◆'L~erzimmer, n Sch: staff room. ◆'L~gang, m course of instruction); N.Am: program. ◆'L~jahr, n year of apprenticeship. ◆'L~junge, m (boy) apprentice. ◆'L~kraft, f teacher. ◆'L~ling, m -s/-e apprentice; (Auszubildender) trainee. ◆'L~plan, m syllabus. ◆'l~reich, adj. instructive, informative. ◆'L~satz, m Mth: theorem; Ecc: dogma. ◆'L~stelle, f place for an apprentice. ◆'L~stuhl, m chair, professorship. ◆'L~zeit, f -/no pl (term of) apprenticeship.
Lehre2 ['le:rə], f -/-n Tchn: gauge.
Leib [laip], m -(e)s/-er (a) esp. Lit: body; mit L. und Seele dabei sein, to put one's (whole) heart into it; ich hielt ihn

mir vom L~e, I kept him at arm's length. ◆'L~eserziehung, f physical education. ◆'L~eskräfte, f aus L~n, with all one's might. ◆'L~esübungen, fpl physical exercises/training. ◆'L~gericht, n favourite dish. ◆l~'haftig, adj. personified; (devil etc.) incarnate; adv. as large as life. ◆'l~lich, adj. (a) physical (pleasure, needs etc.); (b) l~licher Bruder, real/full brother. ◆'L~wächter, m bodyguard.

Leich|e ['laiçə], f -/-n (dead) body, corpse; Fig: über L~en gehen, to stop at nothing. ◆'L~enbestatter, m undertaker, N.Am: also: mortician. ◆'L~enhalle, f mortuary. ◆'L~enschau, f post mortem (examination). ◆'L~enstarre, f -/no pl rigor mortis. ◆'L~enwagen, m hearse. ◆'L~nam, m -s/-e Lit: (dead) body, corpse.

leicht [laiçt]. I. adj. 1. light (load, touch, Mil: artillery etc.); lightweight (material etc.); l. gebaut, lightly built. 2. (einfach) easy (job, decision, life etc.); light (reading, music etc.); er hat es nicht l., things aren't easy for him; das ist l. möglich, that's perfectly possible; l. zerbrechlich, very fragile. 3. (gering) slight (accent, error, exaggeration etc.); light (food, rain etc.); (im Geschmack) mild (cigar etc.); l~e Grippe, mild attack of flu; l. irritiert, slightly irritated. II. comb.fm. 1. 'l~-, adj. (a) lightly (dressed, Mil: armed etc.); (b) easily (movable etc.); (c) slightly (damaged etc.). 2. 'L~-, light (metal, industry etc.); lightweight (concrete etc.). ◆'L~athlet(in), m(f) (track/field) athlete. ◆'L~athletik, f -/ no pl (track and field) athletics. ◆'l~fallen, v.i.sep.irr.27 (sein) es ist ihm nicht leichtgefallen, he didn't find it easy. ◆'l~fertig, adj. rash (decision etc.); thoughtless, (action, talk); sein Leben l. aufs Spiel setzen, to risk one's life recklessly; ◆'L~fertigkeit, f -/no pl rashness; thoughtlessness. ◆'l~gläubig, adj. gullible (person). ◆'l~'hin, adv. casually. ◆'L~igkeit, f -/no pl 1. lightness. 2. easiness (of a task etc.); mit L., easily, with ease. ◆'l~lebig, adj. happy-go-lucky. ◆'l~machen, v.tr.sep. to make (sth.) easy; er macht es sich dat leicht, he's making things easy for himself. ◆'L~metall, n light metal, esp. alloy. ◆'l~nehmen, v.tr.sep.irr.69 to take (sth.) lightly; not to take (work, life etc.) seriously; ◆'L~sinn, m rashness; (Gefahr gegenüber) recklessness. ◆'l~sinnig, adj. careless (mistake etc.); (zu gewagt) reckless (behaviour etc.); foolhardy (action, person etc.); rash (remark etc.).

leid [lait]. I. adj. (a) (es) tut mir l., I'm sorry; er tut mir l., I feel sorry for him; (b) j-n, etwas acc l. sein, to be tired of s.o., sth. **II. L.,** *n* -(e)s/*no pl esp. Lit:* grief, sorrow; (*Leiden*) suffering; **dir wird kein L. geschehen,** no harm will come to you. ◆**'l~en. I.** *v.tr.* 59 1. *v.i.* (*haben*) to suffer (**an einer Krankheit,** from an illness; **die Rosen haben durch den Frost (stark) gelitten,** the roses were (badly) damaged by the frost. 2. *v.tr.* (*a*) to suffer (thirst, pain etc.); (*b*) **j-n, etwas (nicht) l. können/mögen,** to (dis)like s.o., sth. **II. L.,** *n* -s/- (*a*) suffering; **nach langem L.,** after a long illness; (*b*) *Med:* (*Gebrechen*) complaint. ◆**'L~enschaft,** *f* -/-en passion; (*Begeisterung*) fervour, enthusiasm. ◆**'l~enschaftlich,** *adj.* passionate (person, nature, interest etc.); ardent, (admirer etc.); fervent (speech etc.); *F:* **er geht l. gern in die Oper,** he adores going to the opera. ◆**l~er** ['laidər], *adv.* unfortunately; **er ist l. krank,** I'm afraid he's ill. ◆**l~ig** ['laidiç], *adj.* nasty (problem, etc.); tiresome (business). ◆**'l~lich,** *adj.* reasonable (number, weather, knowledge etc.); passable (food etc.). ◆**'l~tragend,** *adj.* suffering; **die L~en,** (i) those who suffer; (ii) (*nach einem Todesfall*) the bereaved/(*Trauernde*) mourners. ◆**'L~wesen,** *n* **zu meinem, seinem usw. L.,** to my, his etc. regret.

**Leier** ['laiər], *f* -/-n 1. *Mus:* lyre. 2. *F:* **immer die alte L.,** always the same old story. ◆**'L~kasten,** *m* barrel-organ. ◆**'l~n,** *v.tr.* (*haben*) *F:* (*a*) to wind (a handle etc.); (*b*) to drone through (a poem, song etc.).

**Leih-** ['lai-], *comb.fm.* lending (fee etc.). ◆**'L~bibliothek,** *f* lending library. ◆**'l~en,** *v.tr.irr.* (*a*) to lend (money, books etc.); to loan (an exhibit etc.); (*b*) **ich habe (mir) bei/von ihm Geld geliehen,** I borrowed money from him. ◆**'L~gabe,** *f esp. Art:* loan. ◆**'L~haus,** *n* pawnshop. ◆**'L~wagen,** *m* hire/*N.Am:* rental car. ◆**'l~weise,** *adv.* on loan.

**Leim** [laim], *m* -(e)s/-e (*a*) glue; *F:* **aus dem L. gehen,** (*Gegenstand*) to come to pieces; (*b*) *F:* **j-m auf den L. gehen,** to fall for s.o.'s tricks. ◆**'l~en,** *v.tr.* (*a*) to glue (sth.); (*b*) *F:* to take (s.o.) in.

**Lein|e** ['lainə], *f* -/-n 1. line; (*b*) (*Hundel.*) leash, lead. ◆**'l~en. I.** *adj.* linen (sheets etc.). **II. L.,** *n* -s/- linen. ◆**'L~en-,** *comb.fm.* linen (dress, paper etc.). ◆**'L~öl,** *n* linseed oil. ◆**'L~samen,** *m* linseed. ◆**'L~tuch,** *n* (*esp.* linen) sheet. ◆**'L~wand,** *f* (*a*) *Art:* canvas; (*b*) *Cin:* screen.

**leise** ['laizə], *adj.* (*a*) faint (steps, noise etc.); quiet (voice etc.); soft (music); **l. sprechen,** to talk quietly/in a low voice; **das Radio l~r stellen,** to turn the radio down; (*b*) light, gentle (rain, breeze, touch etc.); slight (mist, *Fig:* hope, doubt etc.); vague, faint (suspicion etc.).

**Leiste** ['laistə], *f* -/-n (edging) strip;

(*Zierl.*) moulding; *Aut: etc:* trim; (*Fußl.*) skirting board.

**'leist|en,** *v.tr.* (*a*) (*vollbringen*) to achieve, accomplish (sth.); to perform (a task etc.); **gute Arbeit l.,** to do good work; (*b*) to render (a service, help etc.); (*c*) *F:* **sich** *dat* **etwas l.,** to treat oneself to sth.; **er kann sich keine Fehler mehr l.,** he can't afford to make any more mistakes. ◆**'L~ung,** *f* -/-en (*a*) (*Errungenschaft*) achievement (sth.); (*b*) (*Niveau*) **nach L. bezahlen,** to pay by results/*Ind:* productivity; (*c*) (*Ausstoß*) output (of a machine, factory); power (of an engine etc.); performance (of a part, car engine etc.); (*d*) (*Zahlung*) payment (of a sum, damages etc.). ◆**'L~ungs-,** *comb.fm.* (*a*) *Sp:* performance (test etc.); (*b*) *Tchn:* power (output, reactor etc.); (*c*) *Ind:* productivity (check etc.). ◆**'L~ungsdruck,** *m Sch:* pressure (on a pupil/student) to reach a high standard. ◆**'l~ungsfähig,** *adj.* (*a*) efficient (worker, machine); powerful, high performance (car, engine); (*b*) (*Pers.*) fit. ◆**'L~ungsfähigkeit,** *f* -/*no pl* efficiency; productivity; *Ind:* output; *Aut:* performance; *Tchn:* power. ◆**'L~ungsprämie, 'L~ungszulage,** *f* productivity bonus.

**Leit-** ['lait-], *comb.fm.* (*a*) leading (currency etc.); guiding (star etc.); (*b*) main, central (idea, concept etc.). ◆**'L~artikel,** *m* leading article, leader. ◆**'L~bild,** *n* ideal. ◆**'l~en,** *v.tr.* (*a*) (*führen*) to lead (an expedition, discussion etc.); to manage (a firm etc.); to run (a hotel, shop etc.); to chair (a meeting); *Mus:* to conduct (an orchestra, choir etc.); *Sp:* to referee (a game); (*b*) to lead, guide (s.o.); (*lenken*) to divert (traffic etc.); (*c*) *Ph: etc:* to conduct (electricity, heat etc.). ◆**'l~end,** *adj.* guiding (principle etc.); managerial (position, function); leading (personality, part); top-ranking (official etc.). ◆**'L~er1,** *m* -s/- 1. (*Pers.*) (*also* **L~in** *f*) leader (of a group etc.); director (of a firm); manager, *f* manageress (of a shop etc.); head (of a department etc.); *Mus:* conductor. 2. *Ph:* conductor. ◆**'L~faden,** *m* (*Buch*) manual, guide; ◆**'L~fähigkeit,** *f Ph:* conductivity. ◆**'L~motiv,** *n* main theme; *Mus:* leitmotif. ◆**'L~planke,** *f* crash barrier, *N.Am:* guardrail. ◆**'L~spruch,** *m* motto. ◆**'L~stelle,** *f* control point. ◆**'L~ung,** *f* -/-en 1. (*Leiten*) *no pl* leadership; *Com:* management; direction (of a project etc.); administration, control (of finances etc.); chairmanship (of a committee, discussion); *Mus:* **unter (der) L. von X** conducted by X; *N.Am:* X conducting. 2. *Com:* (*Leitende*) management. 3. (*a*) *El:* cable; (*für Geräte*) wire, lead; (*b*) *Tel:* line; **er hat eine lange L.,** he's slow on the uptake; (*c*) (*Rohr*) (water, gas etc.) pipe; (*Hauptl.*) main, *N.Am:* line.

◆'L~ungsmast, m (a) Tel: telegraph pole; (b) mast/pylon (for electric cables). ◆'L~ungsrohr, n (water, gas etc.) pipe. ◆'L~ungswasser, n tap water.
Leiter² ['laitər], f -/-n ladder.
Lek|tion [lɛktsi'o:n], f -/-en Sch: lesson, unit (in a book). ◆L~türe ['tyːrə], -/ -n 1. (Lesen) no pl reading. 2. reading matter.
Lende ['lɛndə], f -/-n Anat: & Cu: loin. ◆'L~nbraten, m loin; (Rind) sirloin.
lenk|bar ['lɛŋkbaːr], adj. steerable; (steuerbar) controllable; manageable (child). ◆'l~en, v.tr. (a) to steer (a vehicle), turn (a horse etc.); to guide (s.o., a missile etc.); to direct (traffic, a conversation etc.); (b) (regeln) to control (the press, economy etc.); to rule (a state). ◆'L~er, m -s/- 1. (Pers.) driver. 2. Aut: steering wheel; (von Fahrrad) handlebars. ◆'L~rad, n Aut: steering wheel. ◆'L~stange, f (von Fahrrad) handlebars. ◆'L~ung, f -/-en 1. Aut: steering. 2. control of the economy etc.).
Leopard [leo'part], m -en/-en leopard.
Lepra ['leːpra], f -/no pl leprosy.
Lerche ['lɛrçə], f -/-n lark.
Lern- ['lɛrn-], comb.fm. (a) learning (method, process etc.); educational (aim etc.); (b) teaching (programme etc.). ◆'l~bar, adj. learnable; leicht/schwer l., easy/difficult to learn. ◆'l~begierig, adj. eager to learn. ◆'l~en, v.tr. to learn (sth., to do sth.); Klavier spielen l., to learn to play the piano; einen Beruf l., to train for a career; er lernt es nie, he'll never learn.
les|bar ['leːsbaːr], adj. legible (writing etc.); readable (book, style). ◆L~e-1 ['leːzə-], comb.fm. reading (lamp, circle, desk etc.). ◆'l~en1, v.irr. v.tr. & i. to read. hier ist zu l., daß ..., it says here that ... in ihren Augen war zu l., daß ..., you could tell from her eyes that ... ◆'l~enswert, adj. worth reading. ◆'L~er(in), m -s/- (f -/-nen) reader. ◆'L~erbrief, m reader's letter. ◆'l~erlich, adj. legible. ◆'L~esaal, m reading room (of a library). ◆'L~ezeichen, n bookmark. ◆'L~ung, f -/-en reading.
Lesb|ierin ['lɛsbiərin], f -/-nen Lesbian. ◆'l~isch, adj. Lesbian.
Lese² ['leːzə], f -/-n harvest, esp. (Weinl.) grape harvest. ◆'l~n2, v.tr. to pick, gather (grapes, berries etc.).
letzt- ['lɛtst-], comb.fm. last(-born, possible etc.). ◆'l~e(r,s), adj. last; (neueste) latest (news etc.). in l~er Zeit, of late, recently; er wurde als l~er bedient, he was served last; er wurde l~er he came last; F: der Film ist das L., the film is hopeless; sein L~es hergeben, to do one's utmost; bis ins l., to the last detail; ◆'l~emal, adv. das l., the last time; zum l~enmal, for the last time. ◆'l~ens, adv. (a) lastly; (b) (neulich)

recently. ◆'l~jährig, adj. last year's. ◆'l~lich, adv. (a) after all, when it comes to the point; (b) (zum Schluß) finally.
Leucht- ['lɔyçt-], comb.fm. luminous (dial etc.); fluorescent (screen etc.); (mit L~stoffröhren) neon (writing etc.). ◆'L~e, f -/-n light. ◆'l~en, v.i. (haben) (Mond, Licht usw.) to shine; (Farben, Himmel usw.) to glow; (Meer usw.) in der Sonne l., to gleam in the sun; ◆'l~end, adj. luminous, glowing (colours etc.); vivid (green etc.); shining (eyes etc.). ◆'L~er, m -s/- chandelier; (Kerzenständer) candlestick. ◆'L~farbe, f luminous paint. ◆'L~feuer, n light beacon. ◆'L~kugel, f flare. ◆'L~rakete, f signal rocket. ◆'L~reklame, f neon (advertising) sign. ◆'L~turm, m lighthouse.
leugnen ['lɔygnən], v.tr. to deny (sth.).
Leukämie [lɔykɛ'miː], f -/no pl leukaemia.
Leukoplast [lɔyko'plast], n -(e)s/-e R.t.m. (plain) sticking plaster.
Leumund ['lɔymunt], m -(e)s/no pl (personal) reputation.
Leute ['lɔytə], pl. people.
Leutnant ['lɔytnant], m -s/-s second lieutenant.
leutselig ['lɔytzeːlik], adj. affable. ◆'L~keit, f -/no pl affability.
Lexikon ['lɛksikɔn], n -s/-ka (a) encyclopedia. (b) (Wörterbuch) dictionary.
Liban|ese [liba'neːzə], m -n/-n Lebanese. ◆L~esin, f -/-nen Lebanese (woman). ◆'l~esisch, adj. Lebanese. ◆L~on ['liːbanɔn]. Pr.n.m -s. Lebanon.
Libelle [li'bɛlə], f -/-n dragonfly.
liberal [libe'raːl], adj. liberal. ◆L~ismus [-ra'lismus], m -/no pl liberalism.
Lib|yen ['liːbjən]. Pr.n.n -s. Libya. ◆'L~yer(in), m -s/- (f -/-nen) Libyan. ◆'l~ysch ['liːbyʃ], adj. Libyan.
Licht¹ [liçt]. I. n -(e)s/-er light; L. machen, to turn the light(s) on; Fig: ans L. kommen, to come to light. II. 'L~-, 'l~- comb.fm. light (year, source, conditions etc.); (patch, speed, strip etc.) of light. ◆'L~bild, n (passport-size) photograph. ◆'L~blick, m Fig: bright spot. ◆'l~durchlässig, adj. translucent. ◆'l~empfindlich, adj. light-sensitive. ◆'l~er'loh, adv. blazing; adv. l. brennen, to be blazing fiercely. ◆'L~hupe, f flasher. ◆'L~maschine, f Aut: etc: dynamo. ◆'L~schalter, m light switch. ◆'l~scheu, adj. Fig: shady (character etc.).
licht², adj. 1. (hell) light (room, sky, colour etc.); am l~en Tag, in broad daylight; 2. thin, sparse (hair, vegetation). ◆'l~en1, v.tr. to thin (out) (trees, undergrowth etc.); sich l., (Wald usw.) to thin out; (Haare) to (get) thin; (Nebel) to clear. ◆'L~ung, f -/-en

clearing.
**lichten**², *v.tr.* den Anker l., to weigh anchor.

**Lid** [li:t], *n* -(e)s/-er (eye)lid.
◆**'l~schatten,** *m* eye shadow.

**lieb** [li:p], *adj.* **1.** (*a*) dear; **l~e Grüße, Dein X,** kind regards, X; *F:* with love from X; **2.** (*a*) (*nett*) kind, *F:* nice (**zu j-m,** to s.o.); (*b*) (*brav*) good; **sei l.!** be a good boy/girl! **3.** welcome (guest etc.); **mehr als mir l.** war, more than I wanted. ◆**'l~äugeln,** *v.i.insep.* (*haben*) **l. mit** + *dat,* to fancy (sth.), have one's eye on (sth.); to toy/flirt with (an idea). ◆**L~e** ['li:bə], *f* -/-n love (**zu etwas** *dat,* of sth.; **zu j-m,** of/for s.o.). ◆**'l~ebedürftig,** *adj.* in need of love. ◆**L~e'lei,** *f* -/-en flirtation. ◆**'l~en,** *v.tr.* to love (s.o., sth.); **sie l. sich,** they are in love. ◆**'l~enswert,** *adj.* lovable (person); endearing, engaging (manner, smile etc.). ◆**'l~enswürdig,** *adj.* kind (**zu j-m,** to s.o.). ◆**L~enswürdigkeit,** *f* -/-en kindness. **2.** kind remark. ◆**'l~er,** *adv.* **1.** er möchte l. gehen, he would prefer to/would rather go; **er fährt l. als ich,** he likes driving more than I do; **es wäre mir l., wenn ...,** I would prefer it if ... **2.** (*besser*) **wir wollen l. gehen,** we had better go. ◆**L~es-,** *comb.fm.* love (letter, story, life, scene etc.); (need, declaration etc.) of love. ◆**L~esdienst,** *m* (act of) kindness, good turn. ◆**L~eskummer,** *m* heartache; **sie hat L.,** she is unhappily in love. ◆**L~espaar,** *n* courting couple; (pair of) lovers. ◆**'l~evoll,** *adj.* loving, affectionate (embrace, look etc.); (*fürsorglich*) devoted (care etc.). ◆**'l~gewinnen** [li:p-], *v.tr.sep.irr.3* to grow fond of (s.o., sth.). ◆**'l~haben,** *v.tr.sep. irr.44* to love (s.o., sth.), (*mögen*) be fond of (s.o., sth.). ◆**L~haber,** *m* -s/- **1.** (*Geliebter*) lover. **2.** (also **L~haberin** *f*) lover (of art etc.); (*Sammler*) collector; *Sp:* enthusiast. ◆**'l~kosen** [li:p'ko:zən], *v.tr.insep. Lit:* to caress (s.o.). ◆**'l~lich** ['li:bliç], *adj.* (*a*) sweet; (*b*) (*sanft*) gentle (landscape etc.); mellow (wine). ◆**'L~ling,** *m* -s/-e (*a*) darling; (*Kind*) pet; (*b*) (*Bevorzugte*) favourite. ◆**'L~lings-,** *comb.fm.* favourite (occupation, food, colour etc.). ◆**'l~los,** *adj.* loveless (childhood etc.); unloving (person, nature etc.); unkind (words etc.). ◆**'L~losigkeit,** *f* -/*no pl* unkindness; lack of care. ◆**'l~ste(r,s),** *adj.* dearest (friend etc.); favourite (toy etc.).

**Lied** [li:t], *n* -(e)s/-er song; *Ecc:* hymn. ◆**'L~ermacher(in),** *m* -s/- (*f* -/-nen) writer and performer) of topical songs.

**liederlich** ['li:dərliç], *adj.* slovenly; slipshod (piece of work etc.); (*ausschweifend*) dissolute, debauched.

**Liefer-** ['li:fər-], *comb.fm. Com:* delivery (contract, service etc.); (terms etc.) of delivery. ◆**L~ant** [-ə'rant], *m* -en/-en supplier. ◆**'l~bar,** *adj. Com:* available. ◆**'l~n,** *v.tr.* (*a*) (*Firma*) (*verkaufen*) to supply (goods, spare parts etc.) (j-m, to s.o.); (*zustellen*) to deliver (goods); (*b*) to provide (food, *Fig:* evidence etc.); (*Tier*) to yield (milk etc.); ◆**'L~schein,** *m* delivery/advice note. ◆**L~ung,** *f* -/-en *Com:* (*a*) supply; (*Zustellung*) delivery; (*b*) (*Warensendung*) consignment, shipment. ◆**'L~wagen,** *m* van; (*offen*) pick-up truck. ◆**L~zeit,** *f* period for delivery.

**Lieg|e** ['li:gə], *f* -/-n day-bed, divan. ◆**'l~en,** *v.i.irr.* (*haben*) (*a*) to lie; (*b*) (*Stadt, Haus usw.*) to be (situated); **das Zimmer liegt nach Süden,** the room faces south. *Fig:* **so wie die Dinge l.,** as things are; (*c*) (*sich befinden*) to be; **auf dem Tisch lag Staub,** there was dust on the table; (*d*) **er/es liegt mir,** he/it appeals to me; **es liegt mir viel/nichts daran,** it is very important/of no importance to me; **es liegt an ihm,** (i) (*Entscheidung*) it is up to him; (ii) (*ist seine Schuld*) it is his fault. ◆**'l~enbleiben,** *v.i.sep.irr.12* (*sein*) (*a*) to stay in bed; (*b*) (*Schnee*) to settle; (*c*) (*übrigbleiben*) to be left/ (*liegenlassen*) left behind; (*Arbeit*) to be left undone. ◆**'l~enlassen,** *v.tr.sep.irr.57* (*a*) to leave (s.o., sth.) (lying somewhere); (*b*) (*vergessen*) to leave (sth.) behind. ◆**L~esitz,** *m* reclining seat. ◆**'L~estuhl,** *m* deckchair. ◆**'L~estütz,** *m* -es/-e press-up, *N.Am:* push-up. ◆**'L~ewagen,** *m* couchette car.

**Lift** [lift], *m* -(e)s/-e & -s lift.

**Liga** ['li:ga], *f* -/Ligen league.

**Likör** [li'kø:r], *m* -s/-e liqueur.

**lila** ['li:la], *inv.adj.* lilac; (*tief*) mauve.

**Lilie** ['li:liə], *f* -/-n lily.

**Liliput|aner** [lilipu'ta:nər], *m* -s/- dwarf. ◆**L~ne** [li'mo:nə], *f* -/-n lime.

**Limo|nade** [limo'na:də], *f* -/-n fizzy drink, mineral; (*Zitronenl.*) lemonade.

**Limousine** [limu'zi:nə], *f* -/-n *Aut:* (large) saloon, *N.Am:* sedan; (*mit Trennwand*) limousine.

**Linde** ['lində], *f* -/-n lime tree.

**linder|n** ['lindərn], *v.tr.* to ease, relieve (pain, suffering etc.); to soothe (pain etc.). ◆**L~ung,** *f* -/*no pl* relief.

**Lineal** [line'a:l], *n* -s/-e ruler.

**Linie** ['li:niə], *f* -/-n line; **in erster L.,** first of all, primarily; **in zweiter L.,** secondarily; *F:* **auf die (schlanke) L. achten,** to watch one's figure. ◆**L~nrichter,** *m* linesman. ◆**L~nschiff,** *m* liner.

**linieren** [li'ni:rən], *v.tr.* to rule lines on (paper etc.); **liniertes Papier,** lined paper.

**linke(r,s)** ['liŋkə(r,s)], *adj.* **1.** (*a*) left (arm, side etc.); **auf der l~en Seite/zur L~en,** on the lefthand side/the left; (*b*) *Pol:* left-wing (politician, views etc.); left (wing); **die L.,** the left; (*c*) (*von Klei-*)

*dung*) 1. **Seite,** wrong side; 1. **Masche,** purl stitch. 2. *P:* shady, doubtful (dealings, character etc.). ◆**'l~isch,** *adj.* clumsy; (*gehemmt*) awkward. ◆**'l~s,** *adv.* (*a*) on the left; **die zweite Straße l.,** the second on the left; **l. von mir** to my left; **von/nach l.,** from/to the left; **j-n l.** **liegenlassen,** to cold-shoulder s.o.; (*b*) *Pol:* 1. **stehen/***F:* **sein,** to be leftwing. ◆**'L~saußen,** *m Fb:* outside left. ◆**'l~sherum,** *adv.* to the left, anticlockwise. ◆**'l~sradikal,** *adj.* with radical/extreme leftwing views. ◆**'L~sverkehr,** *m* lefthand rule of the road.

**Linoleum** [li'no:leum], *n* **-s/***no pl* linoleum.

**Linse** ['linzə], *f* **-/-n** 1. *Bot:* lentil. 2. *Opt:* lens.

**Lippe** ['lipə], *f* **-/-n** lip. ◆**'L~n-bekenntnis,** *n* lip-service. ◆**'L~nstift,** *m* lipstick.

**liquidieren** [likvi'di:rən], *v.tr.* to liquidate (a firm, opponent etc.); to wind up (a firm).

**lispeln** ['lispəln], *v.tr.&i.* (*haben*) to lisp (sth.).

**List** ['list], *f* **-/-en** 1. *no pl* cunning, craft(iness); guile. 2. trick; subterfuge. ◆**'l~ig,** *adj.* cunning, crafty; (*schlau*) sly.

**Liste** ['listə], *f* **-/-n** list.

**Litanei** [lita'nai], *f* **-/-en** 1. *Ecc:* litany. 2. *F:* rigmarole.

**Liter** ['li(:)tər], *m & n* **-s/-** litre.

**liter|arisch** [litə'ra:riʃ], *adj.* literary. ◆**L~atur** [-a'tu:r]. I. *f* **-/-en** literature. II. **L~-,** *comb.fm.* literary (criticism, language, prize etc.); (history etc.) of literature.

**Litfaßsäule** ['litfaszɔylə], *f* advertisement pillar.

**Liturg|ie** [litur'gi:], *f* **-/-n** liturgy. ◆**l~isch** [-'turgiʃ], *adj.* liturgical.

**Litze** ['litsə], *f* **-/-n** (*gedreht*) cord; (*geflochten*) braid.

**live** [laif]. I. *inv.adj. & adv.* live. II. **'L~-,** *comb.fm.* live (broadcast etc.).

**Livree** [li'vre:], *f* **-/-n** [-ɛ:ən] livery.

**Lizenz** [li'tsents], *f* **-/-en** licence.

**Lob** [lo:p], *n* **-(e)s/-e** praise. ◆**l~en** ['lo:bən], *v.tr.* to praise (s.o.); **das lobe ich mir,** that's what I like to see. ◆**'l~enswert,** *adj.* praiseworthy, laudable. ◆**'L~lied,** *n* song of praise; *Fig:* **ein L. auf j-n anstimmen,** to sing s.o.'s praises. ◆**'L~rede,** *f* eulogy.

**löblich** ['lø:pliç], *adj.* praiseworthy, laudable.

**Loch** [lɔx], *n* **-(e)s/**⁼**er** (*a*) hole; gap (in a hedge etc.); (*b*) *Billiards:* pocket. ◆**'l~en,** *v.tr.* to punch (a ticket, *Datapr:* card etc.). ◆**'L~er,** *m* -s/- punch (for paper etc.). ◆**'L~karte,** *f* punched card. ◆**'L~streifen,** *m* punched tape.

**löcherig** ['lœçəriç], *adj.* full of holes.

**Lock|e** ['lɔkə], *f* **-/-n** curl. ◆**'l~en¹,** *v.tr.*

to curl (s.o.'s hair); (*Haare*) **sich l.,** to curl. ◆**'L~enwickler,** *m* **-s/-** curler; (*dicker*) roller. ◆**'l~ig,** *adj.* curly.

**lock|en²,** *v.tr.* (*a*) to attract (a bird etc.); to lure (s.o., an animal); (*b*) (*reizen*) to tempt; **ein l~des Angebot,** a tempting offer. ◆**'L~mittel,** *n* bait, lure. ◆**'L~ruf,** *m* mating call. ◆**'L~ung,** *f* **-/-en** lure, attraction; (*Versuchung*) temptation. ◆**'L~vogel,** *m* (*Vogel, Pers.*) decoy.

**locker** ['lɔkər], *adj.* loose; light (soil, mixture); relaxed (posture); *Fig:* casual (relationship etc.); *Pej:* lax (morals, discipline). ◆**'l~lassen,** *v.i.sep.irr.57* (*haben*) *F:* **nicht l.,** to keep at it. ◆**'l~n,** *v.tr.* to loosen (a screw etc.); to slacken (a rope etc.); to relax (one's grip, discipline etc.); **in gelockerter Stimmung,** in a relaxed mood; **sich l.,** (*Zahn, Schraube usw.*) to work loose; (*Nebel*) to lift; (*Disziplin usw.*) to relax; (*Spannung usw.*) to ease. ◆**'L~ung,** *f* **-/**no pl loosening; slackening, relaxation; easing (of tension).

**lodern** ['lo:dərn], *v.i.* (*haben*) (*Flamme*) to flare (up); (*Feuer*) to blaze.

**Löffel** ['lœfəl], *m* **-s/-** spoon; ◆**'l~n,** *v.tr.* to spoon (sth.) (up). ◆**'l~weise,** *adv.* by the spoonful.

**Logbuch** ['lɔkbu:x], *n* log(book).

**Loge** ['lo:ʒə], *f* **-/-n** 1. *Th:* box. 2. (porter's/masonic) lodge.

**logieren** [lo'ʒi:rən], *v.i.* (*haben*) to stay, (*als Untermieter*) lodge, *N.Am:* room (**bei j-m,** with s.o.).

**Log|ik** ['lo:gik], *f* **-/**no pl logic. ◆**'l~isch,** *adj.* logical.

**Lohn** [lo:n]. I. *m* **-(e)s/**⁼**e** (*a*) wage; *coll:* pay; (*b*) (*Belohnung*) reward. II. **'L~-,** *comb.fm.* wage (increase etc.); wages (office, book); pay (increase, pause, round etc.). ◆**'L~empfänger,** *m* wage earner. ◆**'L~steuer,** *f* income tax (on earned income). ◆**'L~stopp,** *m* wage freeze. ◆**'L~tüte,** *f* wage/pay packet.

**lohnen** ['lo:nən], *v.* 1. *v. refl. & i.* (*haben*) (**sich**) **l.,** to be worthwhile/worth it. 2. *v.tr. Lit:* **j-m etwas l.,** to reward s.o. for sth. ◆**'l~d,** *adj.* worthwhile; rewarding (job, experience etc.).

**Lok** [lɔk], *f* **-/-s** *F:* engine. ◆**L~führer,** *m* engine driver, *N.Am:* engineer.

**lokal** [lo'ka:l]. I. *adj.* local. II. **L.,** *n* **-(e)s/-e** (*Kneipe*) *Brit:* pub, *N.Am:* bar; (*Speisel.*) restaurant. III. **L~-,** *comb.fm.* local (newspaper etc.) ◆**L~termin,** *m* *Jur:* visit to the scene of the crime.

**Lokomotiv|e** [lokomo'ti:və], *f* **-/-n** locomotive, engine. ◆**L~führer** [-'ti:f-fyrər], *m* engine driver, *N.Am:* engineer.

**Lorbeer** ['lɔrbe:r], *m* **-s/-en** laurel, bay; (*L~kranz*) laurel wreath; laurels. ◆**'L~baum,** *m* bay (tree). ◆**'L~blatt,** *n esp. Cu:* bay leaf.

**Lore** ['lo:rə], *f* **-/-n** *Min: etc:* truck.

**Los¹** [loːs], *n* -es/-e 1. (*Schein*) lottery/
raffle ticket; *also Fig:* **das Große L. zie-**
**hen,** to hit the jackpot. 2. (*Schicksal*) lot,
fate.

**los².** I. *pred.adj.* (*a*) (*Hund usw.*) free,
loose; **der Knopf ist l.,** the button has
come off; *F:* **ich bin ihn/es l.,** I have got
rid of him/it; (*b*) **was ist hier l.?** what is
going on here? **was ist (mit dir) l.?**
what's the matter (with you?) **in dieser**
**Stadt ist nichts l.,** nothing ever happens
in this town. II. *adv.* 1. *int.* come on!
hurry up! 2. **ich muß (schon) l.,** I must
go. ◆**l~binden,** *v.tr.* to untie.
◆**l~brechen,** *v.tr. & i. sep.irr.14* (*sein*)
to break (sth.) off; (*Sturm usw.*) to break
out; (*Tumult usw.*) to break out.
◆**l~fahren,** *v.i.sep.irr.26* (*sein*) (*a*) (*ab-*
*fahren*) to start; (*Fahrzeug*) to move/*Aut:*
drive off. ◆**l~gehen,** *v.i.sep.irr.36*
(*sein*) (*a*) (*aufbrechen*) to set off (on foot);
(*b*) (*angreifen*) **auf j-n l.,** to go for s.o.; (*c*)
*F:* (*anfangen*) to start; **jetzt geht's los!**
here goes! this is it! (*d*) *F:* (*sich lösen*) to
come off; (*e*) (*Mine usw.*) to go off.
◆**l~kaufen,** *v.tr.sep.* to buy the release
of (a prisoner), ransom (s.o.).
◆**l~kommen,** *v.i.sep.irr.53* (*sein*) to
get away. ◆**l~lassen,** *v.tr.sep.irr.57* (*a*)
to let go of (sth.); **laß mich los!** let me
go! take your hands off me! (*b*) to release
(a prisoner, one's hold, *Aut:* the brake
etc.); **die Hunde auf j-n l.,** to set the
dogs on s.o.; (*c*) *F:* to deliver oneself of
(a speech, joke etc.). ◆**l~legen,**
*v.i.sep.* (*haben*) *F:* (*mit der Arbeit*) **l.,** to
get cracking/*Brit:* stuck in. ◆**l~lösen,**
*v.tr.sep.* to remove, detach (sth.).
◆**l~reißen,** *v.tr.sep.irr.4* to tear/pull
(sth.) off; **sich l.,** (*Tier*) to break free/
loose. ◆**l~sagen,** *v.refl.sep.* **sich von**
**j-m, einer Partei usw. l.,** to break with
s.o., a party etc. ◆**l~schießen,**
*v.i.sep.irr.31* *F:* (*a*) (*sein*) (*wegrasen*) to
shoot off; (*b*) *Fig:* (*reden*) to fire away.
◆**l~sprechen,** *v.tr.sep.irr.14* to absolve
(s.o.) (**von einer Schuld usw.,**
from blame etc.). ◆**l~werden,**
*v.tr.sep.irr.109* (*sein*) to get rid of (s.o.,
sth.). ◆**l~ziehen,** *v.i.sep.irr.113* (*sein*)
*F:* (*a*) to set out; (*b*) (*kritisieren*) **gegen**
**j-n l.,** to pull s.o. to pieces.

**lösbar** ['løːsbaːr], *adj.* soluble (problem).

**Löschblatt** ['lœʃblat], *n* (sheet of) blotting paper. ◆**l~en¹,** *v.tr.* (*a*) to extinguish, put out (a fire, candle etc.); (*b*) to
quench (one's thirst); (*c*) (*beseitigen*) to
delete (an entry etc.); to erase (a tape recording); (*d*) to blot (ink). ◆**L~papier,**
*n* blotting paper.

**löschen²,** *v.tr.* *Nau:* to unload, discharge
(a ship, cargo etc.).

**lose** ['loːzə], *adj.* loose; slack (rope etc.);
casual (acquaintance etc.).

**Lösegeld** ['løːzəgɛlt], *n* ransom.
◆**l~en,** *v.tr.* (*a*) (*entfernen*) to remove,
get off (dirt etc.); **sich l.,** (*Tapete,*

*Schmutz usw.*) to come off; (*Pers.*) to
detach/free oneself; (*b*) (*lockern*) to loosen
(a screw, one's belt, grip etc.); to undo (a
knot etc.), to relieve (tension etc.); **sich**
**l., (***Schraube usw.***)** to work loose, (*los-*
*kommen*) come undone; (*Spannung usw.*)
to be relieved; (*c*) to cancel, terminate (a
contract etc.); to break (ties, connections
etc.); **seine Verlobung l.,** to break off
one's engagement; (*d*) to solve (a problem, puzzle etc.); (*e*) to buy (a ticket).
◆**l~lich,** *adj.* soluble. ◆**L~ung,** *f*
-/-en (*also Ch:*) solution;
◆**L~ungsmittel,** *n* solvent.

**losen** ['loːzən], *v.i.* (*haben*) to draw lots
(**um etwas** *acc,* for sth.).

**Losung** ['loːzuŋ], *f* -/-en 1. *Mil: etc:* password. 2. *Pol: etc:* (*Parole*) slogan, watch-
word.

**Lot** [loːt], *n* -(e)s/-e plumb line; *Nau:*
(sounding) lead. ◆**l~en,** *v.tr.* to plumb
(a wall etc.); *Nau:* to sound (depth of
water). ◆**l~recht,** *adj.* vertical, perpendicular.

**löten** ['løːtən], *v.tr.* to solder (sth.).
◆**L~kolben,** *m* soldering iron.

**Lothringen** ['loːtriŋən]. *Pr.n.n* -s. Lor-
raine.

**Lotse** ['loːtsə], *m* -n/-n *Nau: etc:* pilot.
◆**l~n,** *v.tr.* to pilot (a ship etc.); to
guide (an aircraft, s.o.).

**Lotterie** [lɔtə'riː], *f* -/-n lottery.

**Lotto** ['lɔto], *n* -s/-s (*esp.* state) lottery.

**Löwe** ['løːvə], *m* -n/-n lion.
◆**L~enanteil,** *m* **der L.,** the lion's
share. ◆**L~enmäulchen,** *n* -s/- snap-
dragon. ◆**L~enzahn,** *m* dandelion.
◆**L~in,** *f* -/-nen lioness.

**loyal** [loa'jaːl], *adj.* loyal. ◆**L~ität**
[-jali'tɛːt], *f* -/-en loyalty.

**Luchs** [luks], *m* -es/-e lynx.

**Lücke** ['lykə], *f* -/-n gap; (*im Formular*
*usw.*) blank (space). ◆**L~nbüßer,** *m*
-s/- (*Pers., Sache*) stopgap. ◆**l~nhaft,**
*adj.* (*a*) with gaps; (*b*) incomplete; fragmentary (knowledge etc.). ◆**l~nlos,**
*adj.* complete (set etc.); comprehensive
(knowledge).

**Luder** ['luːdər], *n* -s/- *P:* (*a*) (*Mädchen*)
**ein kleines/faules L.,** a little/lazy so-
and-so; (*b*) *Pej:* (*gemeines*) **L.,** (*Mann*)
bastard; (*Frau*) bitch.

**Luft** [luft]. I. *f* -/ᵉe (*a*) air; **in die L. ge-**
**hen,** to blow up, explode; *F:* (*Pers.*) to
blow one's top; *Fig:* **etwas liegt in der**
**L.,** there is sth. in the air; **die Geschich-**
**te ist völlig aus der L. gegriffen,** the
story is pure invention; **er behandelte**
**mich wie L.,** he behaved as if I wasn't
there; (*b*) (*Atem*) breath; **tief L. holen,** to
take a deep breath; **er bekam keine L.,**
he could not breathe; *F:* **mir blieb die L.**
**weg,** it took my breath away; (*c*) *F:*
(*freier Raum*) space (between objects
etc.). II. **'L~-,** *comb.fm.* air (freight,
hole, cooling, offensive, rifle, battle,
traffic etc.); (change etc.) of air.

◆'L~**angriff,** m air raid. ◆'L~**ballon,** m balloon. ◆'L~**blase,** f air bubble/ *Min:* pocket. ◆'l~**dicht,** adj. airtight. ◆'L~**druck,** m (a) atmospheric pressure; (b) (*Druckwelle*) blast. ◆'L~**fahrt,** f aviation. ◆'L~**feuchtigkeit,** f humidity. ◆'l~**gekühlt** adj. air-cooled. ◆'L~**hauch,** m breath of air. ◆'l~**ig,** adj. (a) airy (room etc.); (b) cool, light (dress etc.). ◆'L~**kissenfahrzeug,** n hovercraft. ◆'L~**kurort,** m climatic health resort. ◆'l~**leer,** adj. containing no air; l~**leerer Raum,** vacuum. ◆'L~**linie,** f 100 km L., 100 m as the crow flies. ◆'L~**matratze,** f airbed. ◆'L~**pirat,** m hijacker (of aircraft). ◆'L~**post,** f airmail; **per/mit L.,** by airmail. ◆'L~**raum,** m air space (of a country). ◆'L~**röhre,** f windpipe, trachea. ◆'L~**schiff,** n airship. ◆'L~**schlange,** f streamer. ◆'L~**schutz-,** comb.fm. air-raid (shelter, siren etc.). ◆'L~**sprung,** m leap, jump (in the air). ◆'L~**verschmutzung,** f air pollution. ◆'L~**waffe,** f air force. ◆'L~**weg,** m air route; **auf dem L.,** by air. ◆'L~**zufuhr,** f air supply. ◆'L~**zug,** m draught, N.Am: draft (of air).

**lüft|en** ['lyftən], v. 1. v.tr. (a) to air (a room, bed); (b) Fig: to reveal (a secret etc.). 2. v.i. (*haben*) to let in some air. ◆'L~**ung,** f -/ no pl airing; ventilation.

**Lüg|e** ['ly:gə], f -/-n lie; **j-n L~en strafen,** (i) to prove s.o. a liar; (ii) Fig: to prove s.o. wrong. ◆'l~**en,** v.i.irr. (*haben*) to lie. ◆'L~**ner(in),** m -s/- (f -/ -nen) liar.

**Luke** ['lu:kə], f -/-n (a) (*im Dach*) skylight; (b) Nau: etc: hatch.

**Lümmel** ['lyməl], m -s/- Pej: lout, P: slob. ◆'l~**haft,** adj. loutish. ◆'l~**n,** v.refl. F: sich l., to loll, sprawl.

**Lump** [lump], m -s/-n F: Pej: scoundrel, P: swine. ◆'l~**en.** I. v.i. (*haben*) F: sich nicht l. lassen, to be openhanded. II. L., m -s/- rag. ◆'l~**ig,** adj. F: measly, paltry (salary, sum etc.).

**Lunge** ['luŋə], f -/-l lung. ◆'L~**n-,** comb.fm. lung (disease, cancer etc.). ◆'L~**nentzündung,** f pneumonia. ◆'l~**nkrank,** adj. suffering from tuberculosis.

**Lunte** ['luntə], f F: L. **riechen,** to sense trouble.

**Lupe** ['lu:pə], f -/-n magnifying glass; F: **j-n, etwas unter die L. nehmen,** to investigate s.o., sth. closely. ◆'l~**nrein,** adj. flawless (diamond etc.).

**Lupine** [lu'pi:nə], f -/-n lupin.

**Lurch** [lurç], m -(e)s/-e amphibian.

**Lust** [lust], f -/-e (a) no pl desire (**etwas zu tun,** to do sth.); **ich hatte keine L. (dazu),** I didn't feel like/fancy it; (b) no pl (*Freude*) pleasure; **etwas mit L. und Liebe tun,** to love doing sth.; (c) Lit: (*Begierde*) lust, (carnal) desire; (*Wollust*) (sensual) pleasure. ◆'l~**ig,** adj. (a) (*munter*) jolly; gay (person, colour etc.); (b) (*komisch*) funny, amusing (person, story etc.); **sich über j-n, etwas acc l. machen,** to make fun of s.o., sth. ◆'l~**los,** adj. (Pers. usw.) apathetic, listless; adv. half-heartedly. ◆'L~**mord,** m sex murder. ◆'L~**spiel,** n comedy.

**Lüster** ['lystər], m -s/- chandelier.

**lüstern** ['lystərn], adj. (a) lascivious, lecherous; l~**er Blick,** leer; (b) (*gierig*) greedy (**nach** + dat/**auf** + acc, for).

**lutsch|en** ['lutʃən], v.tr. & i. (*haben*) **etwas/an etwas** dat l., to suck sth. ◆'l~**er,** m -s/- lollipop.

**lux|uriös** [luksuri'ø:s], adj. luxurious. ◆L~**us** ['luksus], m -/no pl luxury; L. **treiben/im L. leben,** to live a life of luxury. ◆'L~**us-,** comb.fm. luxury (article, flat, hotel etc.); de luxe (model, edition etc.).

**lynch|en** ['lynçən], v.tr. to lynch (s.o.). ◆'L~**justiz,** f lynch law.

**Lyr|ik** ['ly:rik], f -/no pl lyric poetry. ◆'L~**iker,** m -s/- lyric poet. ◆'l~**isch,** adj. l. lyric (verse, Mus: tenor). 2. (*gefühlvoll*) lyrical (mood etc.).

# M

**M, m** [ɛm], n -/- (the letter) M, m.

**Maat** [mɑ:t], m -(e)s/-e(n) (ship's) mate.

**Mach|art** ['max²ɑ:rt], f Cl: etc: style. ◆'m~**bar,** adj. feasible. ◆'M~**e,** f -/ no pl **das ist alles nur M.,** that's all just show/put on. ◆'m~**en,** v. 1. v.tr. (a) (*schaffen, herstellen*) to make (sth.); **aus Holz gemacht,** made of wood; **ein Examen/Foto m.,** to take an exam/a photo; **das Essen m.,** to get the meal; **j-n zum General/zu seiner Frau m.,** to make s.o. a general/one's wife; (b) (*tun, ausführen*) to do (sth., nothing, one's homework etc.); **was macht er?** (i) what

is he doing? (ii) (*beruflich*) what does he do (for a living)? **so etwas macht man nicht,** that isn't done; **was macht deine Mutter/deine Arbeit?** how is your mother/your work getting on? F: (*Abschiedsgruß*) **mach's gut!** cheerio! good luck! (c) **das macht zusammen drei Mark,** that comes to three marks (altogether); (d) (*verursachen*) to cause (sth.); **salzige Speisen m. Durst,** salty food makes you thirsty; **er macht mir viele Sorgen,** he causes me a lot of worry; **das macht mir Freude,** it gives me pleasure; (e) F: **das macht nichts!** that doesn't matter! **mach dir nichts daraus**, don't take it to heart; (*f*) *F:* to act as (referee etc.); (*g*) *F:* **sich m.**, (*Pers.*) to do well, (*Kranker*) get well; (*Sache*) to turn out well; (*Wetter*) to improve; **sich an die Arbeit m.**, to get down to work; **sich auf den Weg m.**, to set off, *F:* get going; **sich bemerkbar m.**, (*Sache*) to become noticeable; (*Pers.*) to make one's presence felt. 2. *v.i.* (*haben*) (*a*) **laß ihn nur m.!** let him do as he pleases; (*b*) *F:* **mach' schon/schnell!** hurry up! **macht, daß ihr bald zurück seid!** see that you are back soon.

**Macht** [maxt]. I. *f* -/¨e power; (*Stärke*) strength; force (of a blow etc.); **mit aller M.**, with all one's might; **die M. der Gewohnheit**, force of habit; **an die M. kommen/an der M. sein**, to come to/be in power; **die verbündeten M~e**, the allied powers. II. **'M~**, *comb.fm.* power (politics etc.); (position etc.) of strength. ◆**'M~bereich**, *m* sphere of influence. ◆**'M~haber**, *m* -s/- ruler. ◆**'m~los**, *adj.* powerless. ◆**'M~losigkeit**, *f* -/no *pl* powerlessness; helplessness. ◆**'M~probe**, *f* trial of strength. ◆**'m~voll**, *adj.* powerful (ruler etc.). ◆**'M~wort**, *n* ein M. sprechen, to put one's foot down.

**mächtig** ['mɛçtiç], *adj.* 1. powerful (ruler, enemy etc.); mighty (nation, fleet, river etc.); strong, powerful (blow, build, voice); massive (building etc.); **sich m. freuen**, to be terribly pleased. 2. **einer Sprache m. sein**, to be able to speak a language.

**Machwerk** ['maxvɛrk], *n* concoction.

**Macke** ['makə], *f* -/-n *F:* (*Tick*) quirk; **eine M. haben**, to be nutty.

**Mädchen** ['mɛːtçən]. I. *n* -s/- girl; *F:* **M. für alles**, maid of all work; *Hum:* girl Friday. II. **'M~**, *comb.fm.* girl's (voice etc.); girls' (voices, school etc.). ◆**'m~haft**, *adj.* girlish. ◆**'M~name**, *m* (i) girl's name; (ii) (*vor der Ehe*) maiden name.

**Made** ['maːdə], *f* -/-n maggot. ◆**'m~ig**, *adj.* maggoty.

**Magazin** [maga'tsiːn], *n* -s/-e 1. (*a*) (*Lager*) warehouse; storeroom; *Mil:* (storage) depot; (*b*) (*Behälter*) magazine (of a gun etc.). 2. (*Zeitschrift*) magazine.

**Magen** ['maːgən]. I. *m* -s/¨ & - stomach; **mir dreht sich der M. um**, I feel quite sick. II. **'M~**, *comb.fm.* stomach (complaint, acid etc.); (cancer etc.) of the stomach; gastric (region, juice, acid etc.). ◆**'M~beschwerden**, *fpl* stomach trouble. ◆**'M~geschwür**, *n* gastric ulcer. ◆**'M~grube**, *f* pit of the stomach. ◆**'M~schmerzen**, *mpl* stomach ache.

**mager** ['maːgər], *adj.* 1. (*dünn*) thin, lean (person, face etc.). 2. (*ohne Fett*) lean (meat); *Agr:* poor (soil, harvest); *Fig:* meagre. ◆**'M~keit**, *f* -/no *pl* 1. thin-

ness. 2. (*a*) leanness; low-fat content; (*b*) *Agr:* poorness (of soil etc.).

**Mag|ie** [ma'giː], *f* -/no *pl* magic. ◆**M~ier** ['maːgiər], *m* -s/no *pl* magician. ◆**'m~isch**, *adj.* magic (spell etc.).

**Magistrat** [magis'traːt], *m* -(e)s/-e *Adm:* city council.

**Magnet** [ma'gneːt]. I. *m* -en & -s/-en & -e magnet. II. **M~-**, *comb.fm.* magnetic (field, compass, needle, *Rec:* head etc.). ◆**m~isch**, *adj.* magnetic.

**Mahagoni** [maha'goːni], *n* -s/no *pl* mahogany.

**Mäh|drescher** ['mɛːdrɛʃər], *m* -s/- combine harvester. ◆**'m~en**, *v.tr.* to mow (a lawn); to cut (grass etc.), (*ernten*) reap (corn etc.). ◆**'M~er**, *m* -s/-/ **'M~maschine**, *f* (*für Gras*) mower; (*für Getreide*) reaper.

**Mahl** [maːl], *n* -(e)s/¨-e meal. ◆**'M~zeit**, *f* meal; *int.* **M.!** (i) I hope you enjoy your meal; (ii) (*Gruß am Mittag*) hello! *F:* **Prost M.!** that's a fine mess!

**mahl|en** ['maːlən], *v.tr.&i. irr.* (*haben*) to grind (coffee, corn etc.).

**mahn|en** ['maːnən], *v.tr.* (*erinnern*) to remind (s.o.) (**wegen etwas** *gen*, about sth.; **an etwas** *acc*, of sth.); (*warnen*) to warn (s.o.); (*auffordern*) to urge (s.o.) (**zur Vorsicht usw.**, to be careful etc.). ◆**'M~mal**, *n* memorial. ◆**'M~ung**, *f* -/-en (*a*) (*Aufforderung*) reminder; (*b*) warning.

**Mähne** ['mɛːnə], *f* -/-n mane.

**Mai** [mai], *m* -(e)s/-e May. ◆**'M~baum**, *m* maypole. ◆**'M~feier**, *f* May Day celebration. ◆**'M~glöckchen**, *n* -s/- lily of the valley. ◆**'M~käfer**, *m* cockchafer, maybug.

**Mailand** ['mailant]. *Pr.n.n* -s. Milan.

**Mais** [mais], *m* -es/no *pl* (*a*) maize; *N.Am:* corn; (*b*) *Cu:* (*als Gemüse*) sweet corn. ◆**'M~kolben**, *m* corn-cob; *Cu:* corn on the cob.

**Majestät** [majɛs'tɛːt], *f* -/-en 1. majesty. 2. **Seine/Ihre M.**, His/Her Majesty. ◆**m~isch**, *adj.* majestic.

**Major** [ma'joːr], *m* -s/-e 1. *Mil:* major. 2. *Av:* squadron leader.

**Majoran** [majo'raːn], *m* -s/-e marjoram.

**makaber** [ma'kaːbər], *adj.* macabre.

**Makel** ['maːkəl], *m* -s/- (*Fehler*) blemish (on fruit/*Fig:* s.o.); *Lit:* (*Schmach*) stain, taint. ◆**'m~los**, *adj.* flawless (skin, articles etc.); spotless (appearance, condition); *Fig:* untarnished (reputation); **m. sauber**, spotlessly clean.

**mäkeln** ['mɛːkəln], *v.i.* (*haben*) *F:* **an etwas** *dat* **m.**, to find fault with sth.

**Makkaroni** [maka'roːni], *pl* macaroni.

**Makler** ['maːklər], *m* -s/- 1. (*Börsenm.*) broker. 2. (*Grundstücksm.*) estate agent. ◆**'M~gebühr**, *f* brokerage; broker's commission.

**Makrele** [ma'kreːlə], *f* -/-n mackerel.

**Makrone** [ma'kroːnə], *f* -/-n macaroon.

**Mal¹** [mɑːl]. I. *n* -(e)s/-e time; **zum ersten/letzten M.**, for the first/last time; **mit einem M~(e)**, all at once; **kein einziges M.**, not once. II. **m.**, *adv.* 1. *Mth:* **acht m. zwei ist sechzehn**, eight times two equals sixteen; **das Zimmer ist acht m. fünf Meter (groß)**, the room is eight metres by five. 2. *F:* (= *einmal*) once; **warst du schon m. dort?** have you ever been there? **m. hier, m. dort**, sometimes here, sometimes there; **stell dir das m. vor**, just imagine that; **hör m.!** (just) listen!

**Mal²**, *n* -(e)s/-e 1. mark; (*Mutterm.*) birthmark; (*braun*) mole. 2. *Sp:* marker; base; (*also* **M~feld** *n*) touch.

**Malaria** [ma'lɑːria], *f* -/no *pl* malaria.

**mal|en** ['mɑːlən]. I. *v.tr.* (*a*) to paint (sth.); (*Kind*) to draw (sth.); (*b*) *Fig:* (*schildern*) to portray (sth.). II. **M.**, *n* -s/ no *pl* painting. ◆**'M~er(in)**, *m* -s/- (*f* -/-nen) painter; (*Kunstm.*) artist. ◆**M~er-**, *comb.fm.* (*a*) *Art:* artist's (studio, canvas etc.); (*b*) painting and decorating (business, work etc.). ◆**M~e'rei**, *f* -/-en painting. ◆**'m~erisch**, *adj.* 1. picturesque (area, place); quaint (house etc.). 2. artistic (talent). ◆**'M~kasten**, *m* paintbox. ◆**'M~stift**, *m* crayon.

**Malheur** [ma'løːr], *n* -s/-e & -s *F:* mishap.

**Mallorca** [ma'jɔrka]. *Pr.n.n* -s. Majorca.

**Malt|a** ['malta]. *Pr.n.n* -s. Malta. ◆**M~eser(in)** [-'teːzər(in)], *m* -s/- (*f* -/-nen) Maltese.

**Malz** [malts], *n* -es/no *pl* malt. ◆**'M~bier**, *n* (non-alcoholic) malt beer.

**Mammut** ['mamut]. I. *n* -s/-e & -s *Z:* mammoth. II. **'M~-**, *comb.fm.* mammoth (programme, enterprise etc.); gigantic (building etc.).

**man** [man], *indef.pron.* (*a*) one; you; **das sagt m. nicht**, one doesn't/you don't say that; **das tut m. nicht**, that isn't done; **das trägt m. wieder**, that is being worn again; (*b*) people; somebody; **m. sagt, daß ...**, they say that ...; it is said that ...

**Manager** ['mɛnidʒər], *m* -s/- *Com: Th: etc:* manager; *Com:* executive.

**manch** [manç], *indef.pron. & adj.* (*a*) *sing.* many (a), several; **in m~em hat er recht**, he is right about quite a few things; (*b*) *pl* (*mehrere*) **m~e (der) Kandidaten**, some/several of the candidates; (*c*) *inv. Lit:* **m. einer**, many a person. ◆**'m~erlei**, *adj.* various (kinds of); **m. Dinge**, various things. ◆**'m~mal**, *adv.* sometimes.

**Mandant(in)** [man'dant(in)], *m* -en/-en (*f* -/-nen) *Jur:* client.

**Mandarine** [manda'riːnə], *f* -/-n mandarin (orange); (*flach*) tangerine.

**Mandat** [man'dɑːt], *n* -(e)s/-e 1. power of attorney. 2. (*Parlamentsm.*) (member's) mandate, seat.

**Mandel** ['mandəl], *f* -/-n 1. almond. 2. tonsil. ◆**'M~entzündung**, *f* tonsillitis.

**Mandoline** [mando'liːnə], *f* -/-n mandolin(e).

**Manege** [ma'neːʒə], *f* -/-n circus ring.

**Mangel¹** ['maŋəl]. I. *m* -s/- 1. *no pl* (*Fehlen*) lack (**an** + *dat*, of); (*nicht genug*) shortage (**an Lebensmitteln usw.**, of food etc.); **aus M.** an Erfahrung/ Beweisen, due to lack of experience/ evidence. 2. *usu.pl* (*Fehler*) shortcoming. II. **'M~-**, *comb.fm. Med:* deficiency (disease, symptom etc.). ◆**M~beruf**, *m* understaffed profession. ◆**'m~haft**, *adj.* (*a*) (*fehlerhaft*) defective, faulty (goods etc.); (*b*) (*schlecht*) poor (light, memory etc.); *Sch: unsatisfactory.* ◆**'m~n¹**, *v.i.* (**haben**) *esp. Lit:* **es mangelt an etwas dat**, there is a lack/shortage of sth. ◆**'M~ware**, *f* scarce commodity; **M. sein**, to be in short supply.

**Mangel²**, *f* -/-n mangle. ◆**'m~n²**, *v.tr.* to mangle (washing etc.).

**Manie** [ma'niː], *f* -/-n mania; obsession.

**Manier** [ma'niːr], *f* -/-en 1. *no pl* (*Art*) manner; *Art:* style. 2. *usu.pl* (**gute/ schlechte**) **M~en**, (good/bad) manners. ◆**m~lich**, *adj.* (*a*) well-behaved (child); proper (appearance etc.); *adv.* **sich m. benehmen**, to behave properly; (*b*) *F:* reasonable, decent (quality etc.).

**Manifest** [mani'fɛst], *n* -es/-e manifesto.

**Maniküre** [mani'kyːrə], *f* -/-n 1. *no pl* manicure. 2. (*Pers.*) manicurist.

**Manipul|ation** [manipulatsi'oːn], *f* -/-en manipulation. ◆**m~ieren** [-'liːrən], *v.tr.* to manipulate (s.o., a situation etc.); *F:* to rig (an election etc.).

**Manko** ['maŋko], *n* -s/-s 1. disadvantage; drawback. 2. *Fin:* deficit.

**Mann** [man], *m* -(e)s/-er (*a*) man; **M. für M.**, one by one; **Gespräch von M. zu M.**, man-to-man/frank talk; **fünf Mark pro M.**, five marks per person; **seinen M. stehen**, to hold one's own; *F:* **an den M. bringen**, to find a taker for (sth.); (*b*) *Mil: Ind:* **hundert M.**, a hundred men; *Nau:* **alle M. an Deck!** all hands on deck! (*c*) (*Ehemann*) husband. ◆**'m~haft**, *adj.* manly (deed etc.); courageous (deed, decision etc.); stout (resistance). ◆**'M~sbild**, *n F: Pej:* male. ◆**'M~schaft**, *f* -/-en *Sp: & Fig:* team; (*Besatzung*) crew. ◆**'M~schafts-**, *comb.fm.* team (game, sport, race, captain etc.). ◆**'m~shoch**, *adj.* as tall/ high as a man. ◆**'m~stoll**, *adj. F:* nymphomaniac.

**Männ|chen** ['mɛnçən], *n* -s/- 1. little man, dwarf. 2. *Z:* male; *Orn:* cock. 3. (*Hund*) **M. machen**, to sit up (and beg). ◆**'M~er-**, *comb.fm.* man's (trousers, voice etc.); men's (clothing, ward, club etc.); male (voice, *Ecc:* order etc.). ◆**'M~ersache**, *f* a man's work/ business. ◆**'M~erchor**, *m* male voice choir. ◆**'m~lich**, *adj.* (*a*) male (sex, line, animal etc.); *Gram:* masculine (noun etc.); (*b*) masculine (behaviour, features etc.). ◆**'M~lichkeit**, *f -/no pl* manliness, masculinity; (*Potenz*) virility.

**Mannequin** ['manəkɛ́], *n -s/-s* (fashion) model.

**mannig|fach** ['maniçfax], *adj. esp. Lit:* numerous, manifold. ◆**'m~faltig**, *adj. Lit:* diverse.

**Manöv|er** [ma'nø:vər], *n -s/-* **1.** manoeuvre. **2.** *Pej: F:* gambit; trick. ◆**m~rieren** [-ø'vri:rən], *v.tr. & i.* (*haben*) to manoeuvre (a car, ship etc.); *Fig:* to steer (s.o.). ◆**m~rierfähig**, *adj.* manoeuvrable.

**Mansarde** [man'zardə], *f -/-n* attic room. ◆**M~nwohnung**, *f* attic flat/*N.Am:* apartment.

**Manschette** [man'ʃɛtə], *f -/-n* (*a*) *Cl:* cuff; (*b*) paper wrapper (around flowers etc.). ◆**M~nknopf**, *m* cuff-link.

**Mantel** ['mantəl], *m -s/-* **1.** coat; (*Winterm.*) overcoat; *Fig:* cloak (of secrecy etc.). **2.** *Tchn:* outer covering.

**manuell** [manu'ɛl], *adj.* manual.

**Manuskript** [manu'skript], *n -(e)s/-e* script; manuscript (of a book).

**Mappe** ['mapə], *f -/-n* **1.** (*Aktenm.*) briefcase; (*Schulm.*) satchel; (*Schreibm.*) writing case. **2.** (*Sammelm.*) folder; (*Ordner*) file, (loose-leaf) binder.

**Marathon-** ['ma:raton], *comb.fm.* marathon (*Sp:* runner, course, *F:* sitting, film etc.). ◆**'M~lauf**, *m* marathon.

**Märchen** ['mɛ:rçən]. **I.** *n -s/-* **1.** fairy tale. **2.** *F:* tall story; (*Lüge*) fib. **II.** '**M~-**, *comb.fm.* fairy-tale (opera, castle, world etc.). ◆**'m~haft**, *adj.* (*a*) fairy-tale (world, play etc.); (*b*) *F:* fabulous (job, journey etc.); *adv.* **er spielt m.**, he plays like a dream. ◆**'M~land**, *n* fairy-land; wonderland. ◆**'M~prinz**, *m esp. Hum:* Prince Charming.

**Marder** ['mardər], *m -s/-* marten.

**Margarine** [marga'ri:nə], *f -/-n* margarine.

**Marienkäfer** [ma'ri:ənkɛ:fər], *m* ladybird, *N.Am:* ladybug.

**Marihuana** [marihu'a:na], *n -s/no pl* marijuana, *P:* grass.

**Marinade** [mari'na:də], *f -/-n* *Cu:* (*a*) marinade; (*b*) (*Salatsoße*) salad dressing.

**Marine** [ma'ri:nə]. **I.** *f -/no pl* navy. **II.** **M~-**, *comb.fm.* naval (officer, forces etc.). ◆**m~blau**, *adj.* navy blue. ◆**M~soldat**, *m* marine.

**Marionette** [mario'nɛtə], *f -/-n* marionette; puppet. ◆**M~n-**, *comb.fm.* puppet (theatre, *Pol:* government).

**Mark¹** [mark], *n -(e)s/no pl* **1.** (*Knochenm.*) marrow. **2.** (*a*) (*Fruchtm.*) pulp; (*b*) *Cu:* (*Tomatenm. usw.*) purée. ◆**'M~knochen**, *m* marrowbone.

**Mark²** [mark], *f* (*Geld*) mark; **sechs M.**, six marks. ◆**'M~stück**, *n* one-mark piece.

**markant** [mar'kant], *adj.* striking, distinctive.

**Marke** ['markə], *f -/-n* **1.** (*Briefm.*) stamp. **2.** *Com:* brand (of cigarettes, coffee etc.); make (of car, radio etc.); (*b*) (*Warenzeichen*) trade mark. **3.** (*a*) (*Bon*) voucher; (*Lebensmittelm.*) coupon; (*b*) (*Spielm.*) counter, chip; (*c*) (*Hundem. usw.*) identity disc; (cloakroom etc.) tag. **4.** (*Zeichen*) mark (showing level etc.). ◆**'M~n-**, *comb.fm. Com:* branded (article, goods etc.). ◆**'M~nfabrikat**, *n* proprietary brand. ◆**'M~nname**, *m* brand/trade name.

**markier|en** [mar'ki:rən], *v.tr.* (*a*) (*also Fig:*) to mark (sth.); (*b*) *F:* (*vortäuschen*) to sham, fake (sth.). ◆**M~ung**, *f -/-en* (*a*) *no pl* marking; (*b*) (*Kennzeichen*) marking; (identification) mark.

**Markise** [mar'ki:zə], *f -/-n* sun (blind); awning (of a shop).

**Markt** [markt]. **I.** *m -(e)s/-e* (*also Com:*) market; (*M~platz*) market place; **ein Produkt auf den M. bringen**, to market/launch a product. **II.** '**M~-**, *comb.fm.* market (price, value, town, day etc.). ◆**'M~bude**, *f* market stall. ◆**'M~platz**, *m* market place/square. ◆**'M~forschung**, *f* market research. ◆**'M~lage**, *f* state of the market. ◆**'M~lücke**, *f* gap in the market. ◆**'M~wirtschaft**, *f* (**freie) M.**, free market economy.

**Marmelade** [marmə'la:də], *f -/-n* jam.

**Marmor** ['marmɔr]. **I.** *m -s/-e* marble. **II.** '**M~-**, *comb.fm.* marble (bust, pillar, *Cu:* cake etc.); (block etc.) of marble.

**marokk|anisch** [marɔ'ka:niʃ], *adj.* Moroccan. ◆**M~o** [ma'rɔko]. *Pr.n.n. -s.* Morocco.

**Marone** [ma'ro:nə], *f -/-n* sweet chestnut.

**Marotte** [ma'rɔtə], *f -/-n* whim; fad.

**Marsch** [marʃ]. **I.** *m -(e)s/-e* march; (*Wanderung*) hike, walk; **j-m den M. blasen**, to give s.o. a piece of one's mind. **II.** *F:* **m. ins Bett!** off to bed with you! **III.** '**M~-**, *comb.fm. Mil:* marching (song, step etc.). ◆**'M~befehl**, *m* marching orders. ◆**'m~bereit**, *adj.* ready to march. ◆**m~ieren** [-'ʃi:rən], *v.i.* (*sein*) to march; (*wandern*) to walk, hike.

**Marter** ['martər], *f -/-n* torment, agony. ◆**'m~n**, *v.tr.* to torment (s.o.).

**Märtyrer(in)** ['mɛrtyrər(in)], *m -s/- (f -/ -nen)* martyr.

**Marx|ismus** [mar'ksismus], *m -/no pl Pol:* Marxism. ◆**M~ist(in)**, *m -en/-en (f -/ -nen)* Marxist. ◆**m~istisch**, *adj.* Marxist.

**März** [mɛrts], *m -(es)/-e* March.

**Marzipan** [martsi'pa:n], *n -s/no pl* marzipan.

**Masche** ['maʃə], *f -/-n* **1.** stitch. **2.** mesh (of a net); *Fig:* **durch die M. schlüpfen**, to slip through the net. **3.** *F:* (*Trick*) ploy; gimmick. ◆**'M~ndraht**, *m* wire netting.

**Maschin|e** [ma'ʃi:nə], *f -/-n* **1.** (*a*)

machine; (b) F: Aut: (Motor) engine. 2. (a) (Flugzeug) plane; (b) F: (Motorrad) machine; (c) (Schreibm.) typewriter; **mit/ auf der M. geschrieben**, typewritten. ◆m~**ell** [maʃi'nɛl], adj. 1. (production etc.) by machine; adv. **m. hergestellt**, machine-made. 2. mechanical (process etc.). ◆M~**en-**, comb.fm. machine (part etc.). ◆'M~**enschlosser**, m machine fitter. ◆'M~**enfabrik**, f engineering works. ◆M~**enbau**, m -(e)s/no pl (Fach) mechanical engineering. ◆M~**engewehr**, n machine gun. ◆M~**enpistole**, f sub-machine gun; tommy gun. ◆M~**enraum**, m Nau: engine room. ◆M~**enschaden**, m mechanical breakdown; Aut: etc: engine trouble. ◆M~**enschrift**, f typescript; **in M.**, typewritten. ◆M~**e'rie**, f -/-n (a) no pl machinery; (b) (Apparat) mechanism. ◆M~**ist** [-i'nist], m -en/-en 1. Ind: machinist, machine operative. 2. Nau: (ship's) engineer.

**Maser** ['mɑːzər], f -/-n vein (in wood). ◆'M~**ung**, f -/-en texture, grain.

**Masern** ['mɑːzərn], pl Med: measles.

**Mask|e** ['maskə], f -/-n mask; (Verkleidung) disguise. ◆'M~**enball**, m masked/fancy-dress ball. ◆'M~**enbildner(in)**, m -s/- (f -/-nen) Th: etc: make-up artist. ◆M~**erade** [-ə'rɑːdə], f -/-n dressing up; Fig: masquerade, pretence. ◆m~**ieren** [-'kiːrən], v.tr. (verkleiden) to disguise (s.o., oneself).

**Maß¹** [mɑːs]. I. n -es/-e 1. (Einheit) measure; Fig: **mit zweierlei M. messen**, to apply double standards. 2. (Größe) measurement, dimension; **ein Anzug usw. nach M.**, a tailor-made/made-to-measure suit. 3. (Grad) extent, degree; **ein hohes M. an Vertrauen**, a high degree of trust; **in beschränktem/gewissem/hohem M~e**, to a limited/certain/large extent; **alles mit M.!** everything in moderation! **über alle M~en glücklich sein**, to be happy beyond measure; **ohne M. und Ziel**, to excess. II. 'M~-, comb.fm. Cl: made-to-measure (suit etc.). ◆'M~**arbeit**, f **das ist M.**, f: that's cutting it fine. ◆'M~**einheit**, f unit of measure. ◆'m~**gebend**/'m~**geblich**, adj. (a) authoritative (book, statement etc.); (b) leading (authority etc.); (ausschlaggebend) decisive (factor, influence etc.). ◆'m~**geschneidert**, adj. made-to-measure, tailor-made. ◆'m~**halten**, v.i.sep. irr.45 (haben) to be moderate (**in etwas** dat, in sth.). ◆'m~**los**, adj. uncontrolled, unrestrained (anger, emotions etc.); excessive (demands etc.); boundless (zeal, curiosity etc.); **ich habe mich m. übertrieben, grossly exaggerated; **ich habe mich m. geärgert**, I was absolutely furious. ◆'M~**nahme**, f -/-n measure. ◆'m~**regeln**, v.tr. to reprimand (s.o.).

◆'M~**stab**, m 1. scale (of map, plan etc.). 2. (Norm) standard; criterion. ◆'m~**stab(s)getreu**, adj. (map etc.) (drawn) to scale. ◆'m~**voll**, adj. restrained (behaviour etc.); reasonable (demand etc.).

**Maß²**, f -/-e South G: litre (of beer). ◆'M~**krug**, m one litre beer mug.

**Massage** [ma'sɑːʒə], f -/-n massage.

**Massak|er** [ma'sɑːkər], n -s/- massacre. ◆m~**rieren** [-a'kriːrən], v.tr. to massacre (people).

**Masse** ['masə], f -/-n 1. mass. 2. (Menge) crowd; (Mehrheit) majority; **die breite M.**, the masses; F: **eine M. Leute/Geld**, masses of people/money. ◆'M~**n-**, comb.fm. mass (unemployment, demonstration, grave, murder etc.). ◆'M~**nartikel**, m mass-produced article. ◆m~**nhaft**, adj. a vast number/F: masses of; F: **wir haben m. Zeit**, we've got heaps of time. ◆'M~**nmedien**, pl mass media.

**Mass|eur** [ma'søːr], m -s/-e masseur. ◆M~**euse** [-'søːzə], f -/-n masseuse. ◆m~**ieren** [-'siːrən], v.tr. to massage (s.o., s.o.'s back etc.).

**massig** ['masiç], adj. massive, huge; F: **m. Arbeit**, loads of work.

**mäßig** ['mɛːsiç], adj. (a) moderate (speed, income, demands etc.); (b) mediocre (work, pupil etc.); limited (intelligence, ability etc.). ◆'m~**en** [-gən], v.tr. esp. Lit: to moderate (one's language, views etc.); to curb (one's impatience etc.); **sich m.**, to restrain/(beherrschen) control oneself. ◆'M~**ung**, f -/no pl moderation; reduction (of speed).

**massiv** [ma'siːf]. I. adj. 1. (a) solid (gold etc.); (b) massive, solidly built (statue etc.); 2. heavy, massive (attack, demands etc.); severe, grave (threat, accusation etc.). II. M., n -s/-e massif.

**Mast¹** [mast], m -(e)s/-e & -en mast; Tel: etc: (telegraph etc.) pole; El: pylon.

**Mast²**. I. f -/-en Agr: fattening (of animals). II. 'M~-, comb.fm. fattened (duck, ox etc.). ◆'M~**darm**, m rectum.

**mästen** ['mɛstən], v.tr. to fatten (an animal).

**Material** [materi'ɑːl], n -s/-ien material; Mil: (Ausrüstung) equipment. ◆M~**ismus** [-a'lismus], m -/no pl materialism. ◆M~**ist** [-a'list], m -en/-en materialist. ◆m~**istisch** [-a'listiʃ], adj. materialistic.

**Materie** [ma'teːriə], f -/-n 1. no pl matter. 2. (Thema) subject matter. ◆m~**ll** [materi'ɛl], adj. (a) material, (finanziell) financial; (b) Pej: materialistic (person etc.).

**Mathematik** [matəma'tiːk], f -/no pl mathematics. ◆M~**matiker** [-'mɑːtikər], m -s/- mathematician. ◆m~**'matisch**, adj. mathematical.

**Matratze** [ma'tratsə], f -/-n mattress.

**Matrize** [ma'tri:tsə], f -/-n (a) (für Ab-
züge) stencil; (b) Rec: etc: matrix.
**Matrose** [ma'tro:zə], m -n/-n sailor.
**Matsch** [matʃ], m -(e)s/no pl 1. (a)
(Schneem.) slush; (b) (Schlamm) mud,
sludge. 2. (Brei) mush. ◆'m~ig, adj.
F: (a) slushy (snow); soggy (ground etc.);
(b) mushy, squashy (fruit).
**matt** [mat], adj. 1. (a) (Pers.) exhausted,
worn out; drained of energy; weary
(limbs); (b) weak, feeble (smile, voice
etc.); lifeless (performance). 2. (glanzlos)
dull (colour, shine, eyes); matt (paint
etc.); pearl (bulb). 3. (Schach, Fig:) j-n
m. setzen, to checkmate s.o.
◆'M~scheibe, f F: TV: screen.
**Matte** ['matə], f -/-n mat.
**Mauer** ['mauər], f -/-n wall.
◆'M~blümchen, n -s/- Fig: (Pers.)
wallflower. ◆'M~werk, m -(e)s/no pl
masonry, brickwork.
**Maul** [maul], n -(e)s/⁼er 1. Z: mouth. 2.
P: (Mund) trap, gob; halt's M.! shut up!
shut your trap! j-m das M. stopfen, to
shut s.o. up; sich dat das M. über j-n
zerreißen, to take s.o. to pieces.
◆'m~en, v.i. (haben) F: to grumble,
moan. ◆'M~esel, m mule.
◆'M~korb, m muzzle. ◆'M~tier, n
mule. ◆'M~- und 'Klauenseuche, f
foot-and-mouth disease. ◆'M~wurf, m
mole. ◆'M~wurfshaufen, m molehill.
**Maurer** ['maurər], m -s/- bricklayer; mason.
**Maus** [maus], f -/⁼e ['mɔyzə], 1. mouse.
2. F: pl M~e, (Geld) cash, Brit:
lolly. ◆'M~efalle ['mauzə-], f mousetrap. ◆'m~e'tot, adj. F: dead as a doornail.
◆'m~grau, adj. mousy (grey).
**Mäuschen** ['mɔysçən], n -s/- little mouse.
◆'m~'still, adj. (Pers.) as quiet as a
mouse; es war m., one could have heard
a pin drop.
**mausern** ['mauzərn], v.refl. F: (Pers.)
sich (zu etwas dat) m., to blossom (into
sth.).
**maxi|mal** [maksi'ma:l], adj. maximum.
◆M~mum ['maksimum], n -s/-ima
maximum.
**Maxime** [ma'ksi:mə], f -/-n maxim.
**Mayonnaise** [majo'nɛ:zə], f -/-n mayonnaise.
**Mechan|ik** [me'ça:nik], f -/-en 1. no pl
(science of) mechanics. 2. (Mechanismus)
mechanism. ◆M~iker, m -s/- mechanic. ◆m~isch, adj. mechanical;
Fig: automatic (action, movement).
◆M~ismus [-a'nismus], m -/-men
mechanism; F: works (of a watch etc.).
**meckern** ['mɛkərn], v.i. (haben) (a)
(Ziege) to bleat; (b) F: (nörgeln) to grumble, grouse; (Frau) to nag.
**Medaill|e** [me'daljə], f -/-n medal.
◆M~on [-dal'jõ], m -s/-s (also Cu:) medallion; (Schmuck) locket.
**Medikament** [medika'mɛnt], n -(e)s/-e

medicine; (Droge) drug.
**Medit|ation** [meditatsi'o:n], f -/-en medi-
tation. ◆m~ieren [-'ti:rən], v.i. (haben) to meditate (über + acc, on).
**Medium** ['me:dium], n -s/-ien medium;
die Medien, the media.
**Medizin** [medi'tsi:n]. I. f -/-en medicine.
II. M~-, comb.fm. medicine (ball etc.);
medical (student etc.). ◆M~studium
n, study of medicine. ◆m~isch, adj. 1.
medical (research, knowledge etc.). 2.
(mit Heilwirkung) medicinal (preparation
etc.).
**Meer** [me:r], n -(e)s/-e (a) sea; auf dem
M., at sea; am M., at the seaside; 1000
Meter über dem M., 1,000 metres above
sea level; (b) Fig: sea, mass (of houses
etc.); flood (of light). ◆'M~busen, m
gulf. ◆'M~enge, f strait, sound.
◆'M~es-, comb.fm. sea (coast, air etc.);
marine (climate, plants, animals etc.).
◆'M~esfrüchte, fpl seafood.
◆'M~esgrund, m sea bed; ocean floor.
◆'M~esspiegel, m über dem M.,
above sea level. ◆'M~esstrand, m
seashore. ◆'M~esströmung, f ocean
current. ◆'M~jungfrau, f mermaid.
◆'M~rettich, m horseradish.
◆'M~schweinchen, n guinea pig.
◆'M~wasser, n sea water.
**Mega-** [mega-], comb.fm. mega-.
◆M~phon [-'fo:n], n -s/-e megaphone;
(mit Verstärker) loudhailer.
**Mehl** [me:l], n -(e)s/-e 1. flour; (grobes)
meal. 2. (Pulver) powder. ◆'m~ig, adj.
mealy. ◆'M~speise, f dessert.
**mehr** [me:r]. I. pron. & adv. more; m.
als, more than; m. denn je, more than
ever; was willst du m.? what more do
you want? um so m., all the more; das
ist ein Grund m., that is yet another reason; nicht m., no more/longer; es dauert
nicht m. lange, it won't be much longer;
es ist nichts m. da, there is nothing left;
nie m., never again. II. M~, n -(s)/no pl
ein M. an Kosten, additional costs. III.
'M~-, 'm~-, comb.fm. (a) (zusätzlich)
additional, extra (expenditure, costs,
amount etc.); (überschüssig) excess
(weight, profit etc.); (b) adj. multi-
(layered, coloured etc.); in several
(volumes, parts). ◆'M~arbeit, f
extra work; (Überstunden) overtime.
◆'m~deutig, adj. ambiguous.
◆'M~deutigkeit, f -/no pl ambiguity;
polysemy. ◆'m~ere, adj. several; aus
m~eren Gründen, for various reasons;
m~eres, adv. several things.
◆'m~fach, adj. multiple; (wiederholt)
repeated (attempts etc.); m~facher Mil-
lionär, multimillionaire; in m~facher
Hinsicht, in more than one respect; m.
vergrößert, magnified several times.
◆'M~familienhaus, n detached house
divided into flats. ◆'m~geschossig,
adj. multi-storey. ◆'M~heit, f -/-en
majority. ◆'m~jährig, adj. 1. several

years' (experience etc.); (stay etc.) of/
lasting several years. **2.** *Bot:* perennial.
◆'m~**malig**, *adj.* repeated.
◆'m~**mals**, *adv.* on several occasions.
◆'m~**sprachig**, *adj.* multilingual;
(*Pers.*) polyglot. ◆'m~**stimmig**, *adj.
Mus:* in several parts. ◆'m~**stündig**,
*adj.* lasting several hours. ◆'m~**tägig**,
*adj.* lasting several days.
◆'**M**~**wertsteuer**, *f* value-added tax.
◆'**M**~**zahl**, *f* **1.** majority. **2.** *Gram:*
plural. ◆'**M**~**zweck**-, *comb.fm.* multi-
purpose (vehicle, furniture etc.).
**meiden** ['maidən], *v.tr.irr.65* to avoid.
**Meile** ['mailə], *f* -/-n mile. ◆'**M**~**n**-
**stein**, *m Fig:* milestone. ◆'m~**n'weit**,
*adv.* miles; **m. von hier entfernt**,
miles away.
**mein** [main], *poss.adj.* my. ◆'m~**e(r,s)**,
*poss.pron.* mine; **ich habe das M. getan**,
I have done my share; **die M~en**, my
people. ◆'m~**er**, *pers.pron.* (*gen of* **ich**)
of me; **er erinnerte sich m.**, he remembered me. ◆'m~**er'seits**, *adv.* as far as
I am concerned; for my part; (*Antwort*)
**ganz m.**, the pleasure is mine.
◆'m~**es'gleichen**, *pron.* people like
me. ◆'m~**et'wegen**, *adv.* **1.** (*mir zuliebe*) because of me; for my sake. **2.** *F:*
for all I care; **m. kannst du gehen**, it's
all right with me/I don't mind if you go.
◆'m~**ige**, *poss.pron. decl. as adj. Lit:*
**der/die/das m.**, mine.
**Meineid** ['main²ait], *m* perjury.
**mein|en** ['mainən], *v.tr.* (*a*) to think
(sth., that ...); **das will ich** (aber) **m.!** I
should think so too! **wenn du meinst**, if
you think so; (*b*) to mean (s.o., sth.); **du
warst nicht gemeint**, the remark was not
aimed at you; **wie meinst du das?** what
do you mean by that? **es ehrlich/böse
m.**, to have honest/evil intentions; **er
meint es gut mit uns**, he has our interests at heart; (*c*) (*sagen*) to say (sth.); **was
m. Sie?** what did you say? ◆'**M**~**ung**,
*f* -/-en opinion (**über** + *acc*/**von** + *dat*, of/
about); **meiner M. nach**, in my opinion;
**ich bin ganz Ihrer M.**, I quite agree with
you; *F:* **ich habe ihm gehörig meine M.
gesagt**, I really gave him a piece of my
mind. ◆'**M**~**ungs**-, *comb.fm.* opinion
(research etc.); (exchange etc.) of views.
◆'**M**~**ungsumfrage**, *f* opinion poll.
◆'**M**~**ungsverschiedenheit**, *f* difference of opinion.
**Meise** ['maizə], *f* -/-n tit.
**Meißel** ['maisəl], *m* -s/- chisel. ◆'m~**n**,
*v.tr.* to chisel (stone etc.).
**meist** [maist]. **I.** *adj.* most (of); **die
m~en** (Leute), most people; **er hat das
m~e Geld**, he has (the) most money;
**die m~e Zeit**, most of the time; **das
m~e davon**, most of it. **II.** *adv.* (*a*) =
**m~ens**; (*b*) **am m~en**, the most. **III.**
'm~-, *comb.fm.* most (loved etc.); most
often (read, bought etc.). ◆'m~**ens**,
*adv.* mostly; **er ist m. pünktlich**, he is

usually on time.
**Meister** ['maistər], *m* -s/- **1.** master. **2.**
*Sp: etc:* champion. ◆'m~**haft**, *adj.*
masterly; *adv.* **m. spielen**, to play bril-
liantly. ◆'**M**~**hand**, *f* **von M.**, from/by
the hand of a master. ◆'**M**~**leistung**,
*f* masterly feat/achievement. ◆'m~**n**,
*v.tr.* to master (a subject, situation etc.);
to control (feelings, oneself etc.).
◆'**M**~**schaft**, *f* -/-en **1.** *no pl* mastery.
**2.** *Sp: etc:* championship. ◆'**M**~**werk**,
*n* masterpiece.
**Melancholie** [melaŋko'li:], *f* -/no pl
melancholy. ◆m~**isch** [-'ko:liʃ], *adj.*
melancholy.
**Melasse** [me'lasə], *f* -/-n molasses.
**Meld|e**- ['mɛldə-], *comb.fm. Adm:* regis-
tration (office, fee etc.). ◆'m~**en**, *v.tr.*
(*a*) to report (sth.); **sich m.**, to report
(**zum Dienst**, for duty; **krank**, sick); to
register (**bei der Polizei**, with the police);
**sich (freiwillig) zu einer Arbeit m.**, to
volunteer for a job; **sich (zu Wort) m.**,
to indicate that one wants to speak; (*b*)
(*ankündigen*) to announce (s.o., a train
etc.); *Meteor:* to forecast (rain, snow
etc.); *Lit:* **der Herbst meldet sich**, there
are signs of autumn; (*c*) **er hat sich** (**bei
mir**) **lange nicht gemeldet**, he hasn't
been in touch (with me) for a long time;
*Tel:* **eine fremde Stimme meldete
sich**, a strange voice answered.
◆'**M**~**epflicht**, *f* obligation to register/
report (a disease etc.). ◆'m~**e-
pflichtig**, *adj.* (*a*) (*Pers.*) obliged
to register; (*b*) notifiable (disease etc.).
◆'**M**~**ung**, *f* -/-en **1.** *TV: Rad:* report;
(*Nachricht*) news (item). **2.** *Adm:* notification; registration (of a birth, death etc.).
**meliert** [me'li:rt], *adj.* mottled, speckled
(material etc.); (**grau**) **m~es Haar**, hair
streaked with grey.
**melken** ['mɛlkən], *v.tr.irr.* to milk (a
cow, goat etc.).
**Melod|ie** [melo'di:], *f* -/-n melody; tune
(of a song etc.). ◆m~**isch** [me'lo:diʃ],
*adj.* tuneful (music etc.); melodious
(voice etc.).
**Melone** [me'lo:nə], *f* -/-n **1.** *Bot:* melon.
**2.** *F:* bowler (hat).
**Membran** [mɛm'bra:n], *f* -/-en *Tchn:* diaphragm.
**Memoiren** [memo'a:rən], *pl* memoirs.
**Menge** ['mɛŋə], *f* -/-n **1.** (*a*) quantity,
amount; (*b*) (*eine* (*ganze*)) **M.**, a great
deal, *F:* a lot; *F:* **eine M. Leute**, a lot/
lots of people; **jede M. Äpfel**, any
amount/heaps of apples. **2.** (*Menschenm.*)
crowd. ◆'**M**~**nlehre**, *f Mth:* theory of
sets. ◆'m~**nmäßig**, *adj.* quantitative;
(turnover etc.) in numbers/units.
◆'**M**~**nrabatt**, *m* bulk discount.
**mengen** ['mɛŋən], *v.tr.* to mix (liquids,
foods etc.) (**mit** + *dat*, with).
**Mensa** ['mɛnza], *f* -/-s & -sen student's
refectory/*N.Am:* cafeteria.
**Mensch** [mɛnʃ], *m* -en/-en **1.** man; hu-

man being; der M., man. 2. person; **junge** M~en, young people; **unter die** M~en kommen, to mix with other people; jeder M., everybody, everyone; **es erschien kein M.**, not a soul turned up. 3. *int. F:* M., **war das eine Hitze!** gosh, it was hot! ◆'M~en-, *comb.fm.* human (life, sacrifice, dignity etc.). ◆'M~enaffe, *m* ape. ◆'M~enalter, *n* lifetime. ◆'M~enfeind, *m* misanthropist. ◆'m~enfeindlich, *adj.* misanthropic; anti-social. ◆'M~enfresser, *m* -s/- cannibal. ◆'M~enfreund, *m* philanthropist; humanitarian. ◆'m~enfreundlich, *adj.* humanitarian. ◆'M~engedenken, *n* seit M., as long as anyone can remember. ◆'M~enkenner, *m* (good) judge of character. ◆'M~enkenntnis, *f* knowledge of human nature. ◆'m~enleer, *adj.* deserted, empty. ◆'M~enliebe, *f* philanthropy; love of one's fellow men. ◆'M~enmenge, *f* crowd. ◆'m~en'möglich, *adj.* humanly possible. ◆'M~enrechte, *pl* human rights. ◆'m~enscheu, *adj.* shy, unsociable. ◆'M~enschlag, *m* -(e)s/*no pl* breed (of people). ◆'m~enunwürdig, *adj.* (a) degrading (behaviour etc.); (b) inhumane (treatment etc.). ◆'M~enverstand, *m* human understanding; **gesunder M.**, common sense. ◆'m~enwürdig, *adj.* (a) (behaviour etc.) worthy of a human being; (b) humane (treatment etc.). ◆'M~heit, *f* -/*no pl* (*alle Menschen*) humanity; mankind. ◆'m~lich, *adj.* 1. human (nature, society, body etc.). 2. (*human*) humane; **sich m. zeigen**, to show sympathy. ◆'M~lichkeit, *f* -/*no pl* humanity; human qualities; **aus reiner M.**, for purely humanitarian reasons.

**Menstruation** [mɛnstruatsi'oːn], *f* -/-en menstruation.

**Mentalität** [mɛntali'tɛːt], *f* -/-en mentality.

**Menthol** [mɛn'toːl], *n* -s/*no pl* menthol.

**Menü** [me'nyː], *n* -s/-s menu.

**Menuett** [menu'ɛt], *n* -(e)s/-e minuet.

**merk|bar** ['mɛrkbaːr], *adj.* noticeable. ◆'M~blatt, *n Adm:* (explanatory) leaflet. ◆'m~en, *v.tr.* (a) to notice (sth.); **kaum zu m.**, hardly noticeable; (b) to tell, see (sth.) (an + *dat*, from); **man merkt an seiner Aussprache(, daß ...)**, one can tell from his accent (that ...); (c) **sich** *dat* **etwas m.**, to make a (mental) note of sth.; **das kann ich mir nie m.**, I can never remember that. ◆'m~lich, *adj.* noticeable, marked; **m. kühler**, noticeably cooler. ◆'M~mal, *n* feature; (*Zug*) characteristic, trait. ◆'m~würdig, *adj.* remarkable; (*seltsam*) strange. ◆M~würdigkeit, *f no pl* oddness, strangeness.

**Meß-** ['mɛs-], *comb.fm.* measuring (instrument etc.). ◆'m~bar, *adj.* measurable. ◆'M~diener, *m* server. ◆'M~ge-

**wand**, *n* (Mass) vestment, *esp.* chasuble.

**Messe¹** ['mɛsə], *f* -/-n *Ecc:* mass; **M. halten**, to say mass.

**Messe²**, *f* -/-n (trade) fair. ◆'M~gelände, *n* exhibition site.

**Messe³**, *f* -/-n *Mil:* mess.

**mess|en** ['mɛsən], *v.irr.* 1. *v.tr.* (a) to measure (sth.); (b) to compare (s.o., sth.) (an + *dat*, with); **sich mit j-m m.**, to match oneself against s.o., take s.o. on. 2. *v.i.* (*haben*) to measure; **er mißt 1,80 m**, he is 6 feet tall. ◆'M~ung, *f* -/-en measurement.

**Messer** ['mɛsər]. **I.** *n* -s/- (a) knife; (b) blade (of a mower etc.); cutter (of a mincer etc.); (c) (*Rasierm.*) cut-throat razor. **II.** M~-, *comb.fm.* knife (blade etc.). ◆'m~scharf, *adj.* razor-sharp (edge etc.); *Fig:* **m~scharfer Verstand**, keen/acute mind. ◆'M~spitze, *f* point of a knife; *Cu:* **eine M. Salz**, a pinch of salt. ◆'M~stich, *m* stab (with a knife); (*Wunde*) knife wound.

**Messing** ['mɛsɪŋ], *n* -s/*no pl* brass.

**Metall** [me'tal], *n* -s/-e metal. ◆M~arbeiter, *m* metalworker. ◆m~isch, *adj.* metallic. ◆m~verarbeitend, *adj.* metalworking.

**Metapher** [me'tafər], *f* -/-n metaphor.

**Metaphysik** [metafy'ziːk], *f* metaphysics.

**Meteor** [mete'oːr], *n* -s/-e meteor. ◆M~it [-o'riːt], *m* -s/-e meteorite. ◆M~ologe [-o'loːgə], *m* -n/-n meteorologist. ◆m~ologisch [-o'loːgɪʃ], *adj.* meteorological.

**Meter** ['meːtər], *m & n* -s/- metre. ◆'M~maß, *n* metric tape measure/(*Stab*) measuring rod.

**Method|e** [me'toːdə], *f* -/-n method. ◆m~isch, *adj.* 1. methodical, systematic. 2. (difficulties etc.) of method. ◆M~ist [-o'dɪst], *m* -en/-en Methodist.

**Metier** [meti'eː], *n* -s/-s profession; *F:* speciality.

**Metri|k** ['meːtrɪk], *f* -/-en metre. ◆'m~sch, *adj.* 1. *Mus:* metrical. 2. *Meas:* metric (system etc.).

**Metro|nom** [metro'noːm], *n* -s/-e metronome. ◆M~'pole, *f* -/-n metropolis.

**Mett** [mɛt], *n* -(e)s/*no pl* raw minced/*N.Am:* ground pork. ◆'M~wurst, *f* smoked (pork/beef) sausage.

**Metzger** ['mɛtsgər], *m* -s/- butcher. ◆M~ei [-'rai], *f* -/-en butcher's (shop).

**Meuchel|mord** ['mɔyçəlmɔrt], *m* foul murder. ◆'M~mörder(in), *m* foul murderer.

**Meute** ['mɔytə], *f* -/-n pack (of hounds); *Fig:* mob (of people). ◆M~'rei, *f* -/-en mutiny; (*im Gefängnis usw.*) revolt, riot. ◆'M~rer, *m* -s/- mutineer. ◆'m~rn, *v.i.* (*haben*) to mutiny, (*Gefangene usw.*) riot.

**Mexik|aner(in)** [mɛksi'kaːnər(in)], *m* -s/- (*f* -/-nen) Mexican. ◆m~anisch, *adj.* Mexican. ◆'M~o. *Pr.n.n* -s. Mexico.

**miauen** [mi'auən], *v.i.* (*haben*) to miaow.

**mich** [miç]. **I.** *pers.pron.* (*acc. of* **ich**) me. **II.** *refl.pron.* myself.

**mickerig** ['mikəriç], *adj.* F: (*Pers.*) puny; measly (present, helping etc.).

**Mieder** ['mi:dər], *n* -s/- bodice.

**Mief** [mi:f], *m* -(e)s/*no pl* P: fug.

**Miene** ['mi:nə], *f* -/-n (facial) expression; **eine finstere M. machen,** to look grim. ◆'M~**nspiel,** *n* (range of) facial expressions.

**mies** [mi:s], *adj.* P: rotten, lousy; **mir ist m.,** I feel rotten. ◆'m~**machen,** *v.tr.sep.* F: to run s.o., sth. down; **j-m etwas m.,** to spoil sth. for s.o. ◆'M~**macher,** *m* -s/- F: killjoy.

**Miet**- ['mi:t-], *comb.fm.* (*a*) (*zu mieten*) (house etc.) to rent; (boat etc.) for hire; (*gemietet*) rented (house etc.); hired (boat etc.); (*b*) rent (increase, allowance etc.); (loss, payment etc.) of rent. ◆'M~**e,** *f* -/-n **1.** renting (of a house etc.); hire (of a boat etc.); **zur M. wohnen,** to live in rented accommodation. **2.** (*Betrag*) rent. ◆'m~**en,** *v.tr.* to rent (a flat, room etc.); to hire (a car, boat etc.). ◆'M~**er(in),** *m* -s/- (*f* -/-**nen**) (*a*) tenant; (*Untermieter*) lodger; (*b*) hirer of a car etc.). ◆'M~**shaus,** *n* block of (rented) flats/*N.Am:* apartments. ◆'M~**vertag,** *m* lease; rental agreement. ◆'M~**wagen,** *m* hire(d) car. ◆'M~**wohnung,** *f* rented flat/*N.Am:* apartment.

**Migräne** [mi'grɛ:nə], *f* -/-n migraine.

**Mikro**- ['mi:kro-], *comb.fm.* micro-. ◆'M~**film,** *m* microfilm. ◆M~'**phon,** *n* -s/-e microphone. ◆M~'**skop** [-'sko:p], *n* -s/-e microscope. ◆m~'**skopisch,** *adj.* microscopic; **etwas m. untersuchen,** to examine sth. under the microscope. ◆'M~**wellenherd,** *m* microwave oven.

**Milbe** ['milbə], *f* -/-n mite.

**Milch** [milç]. **I.** *f* -/*no pl* milk. **II.** 'M~-, *comb.fm.* (*a*) milk (bar, tooth etc.); (*b*) dairy (products, cow etc.). ◆'M~**brötchen,** *n* *approx.* bun. ◆'M~**glas,** *n* opaque glass. ◆'m~**ig,** *adj.* milky (fluid etc.). ◆'M~**kaffee,** *m* white coffee, *N.Am:* coffee with milk. ◆'M~**kanne,** *f* milk churn; (*kleiner*) milk can. ◆'M~**pulver,** *n* dried milk. ◆'M~**reis,** *m* rice pudding. ◆'M~**straße,** *f* galaxy; **die M.,** the Milky Way. ◆'M~**tüte,** *f* milk carton.

**mild** [milt], *adj.* mild (weather, taste, cigar, criticism etc.); temperate (climate etc.); balmy (air etc.); lenient (sentence, judge etc.); **m. gewürztes Essen,** lightly seasoned food; **m~e Gabe,** charitable gift; (*Almosen*) alms. ◆'M~**e** ['mildə]. **I.** *f* -/*no pl* leniency; clemency (**gegen j-n,** towards s.o.). **II. m.,** *adj.* = **mild; m. gesagt,** to put it mildly. ◆'m~**ern,** *v.tr.* to relieve (pain, tension etc.); to calm (anger etc.); to tone down (contrasts etc.); to reduce (intensity etc.); *Jur:*

**m~de Umstände,** mitigating/extenuating circumstances. ◆'m~**tätig,** *adj.* charitable.

**Milieu** [mil'jø:], *n* -s/-s environment.

**militant** [mili'tant], *adj.* militant.

**Militär** [mili'tɛ:r]. **I.** *n* -s/*no pl* (*Heer*) army; (*Streitkräfte*) armed forces; (*Truppen*) troops. **II. M~-,** *comb.fm.* military (airport, parade, police etc.). ◆'M~**dienst,** *m* military service. ◆M~**gericht,** *n* court-martial. ◆m~**isch,** *adj.* military.

**Militar|ismus** [milita'rismus], *m* -/*no pl* militarism. ◆M~**ist,** *m* -en/-en militarist.

**Miliz** [mi'li:ts], *f* -/-en militia.

**Milli|arde** [mili'ardə], *f* -/-n thousand million; *N.Am:* billion. ◆'M~**gramm,** *n* milligram. ◆M~'**meter,** *m & n* millimetre.

**Million** [mili'o:n], *f* -/-en million; **zwei M~en Einwohner,** two million inhabitants. ◆M~**är(in)** [-o'nɛ:r(in)], *m* -s/-e (*f* -/-nen) millionaire; *f* millionairess. ◆M~**enstadt,** *f* city of (over) a million people.

**Milz** [milts], *f* -/-en spleen.

**Mim|e** ['mi:mə], *m* -n/-n *esp. Hum:* actor. ◆'m~**en,** *v.tr.* F: to act (the hero etc.). ◆'M~**ik,** *f* -/*no pl* mimicry.

**Mimose** [mi'mo:zə], *f* -/-n *Bot:* mimosa. ◆m~**nhaft,** *adj.* hypersensitive.

**minder** ['mindər], *adv.* -n/-n *esp. Hum:* less. ◆'m~**bemittelt,** *adj.* (*a*) of limited means; (*b*) F: **geistig m.,** not very bright. ◆'M~**heit,** *f* -/-en minority. ◆'m~**jährig,** *adj.* under age. ◆'M~**jährigkeit,** *f* -/*no pl* minority. ◆'m~**n,** *v.tr.* Lit: to diminish (pain, strength etc.). ◆'M~**ung,** *f* -/-en decrease; easing (of pain). ◆'m~**wertig,** *adj.* inferior; third-rate (literature etc.). ◆'M~**wertigkeit,** *f* inferiority; *Com:* inferior quality. ◆'M~**wertigkeitskomplex,** *m* inferiority complex.

**Mindest**- ['mindəst-], *comb.fm.* minimum (distance, age, weight, wage etc.). ◆'m~**e,** *adj.* least, slightest; **nicht im m~n,** not in the least. ◆'m~**ens,** *adv.* at least. ◆'M~**maß,** *n* minimum (amount/extent).

**Mine** ['mi:nə], *f* -/-n **1.** *Mil:* mine. **2.** refill (for a ballpoint pen); (pencil) lead. ◆'M~**nfeld,** *n* minefield. ◆'M~**nsuchboot,** *n* minesweeper.

**Mineral** [minə'ra:l], *n* -s/-e & -ien mineral. ◆m~**isch,** *adj.* mineral. ◆M~**quelle,** *f* mineral spring. ◆M~**wasser,** *n* mineral water.

**Mini**- ['mini-], *comb.fm.* mini-. ◆'M~**rock,** *m* miniskirt.

**mini|mal** [mini'ma:l]. **I.** *adj.* minimal. **II.** M~-, *comb.fm.* minimum (price, weight etc.). ◆M~**mum** ['mi:nimum], *n* -s/-ma minimum (**an** + *dat,* of).

**Minister** [mi'nistər]. **I.** *m* -s/- *Pol:* minister (**für Handel usw.,** of trade etc.). **II.**

**M~-**, *comb.fm.* ministerial (office, conference). ◆**m~i'ell**, *adj.* ministerial. ◆**M~ium** [-'te:rium], *n* **-s/-rien** ministry; *N.Am:* department. ◆**M~präsident**, *m* prime minister.

**minus** ['mi:nus]. **I.** *adv.* minus; (*Temperatur*) m. 4 Grad, 4 degrees below zero. **II. M.**, *n -/-* **1.** *Mth:* minus (sign). **2.** *Com:* (*also* **M~betrag** *m*) deficit. **3.** *F:* (*Nachteil*) drawback; shortcoming; **das ist ein M. für mich**, that's a point against as far as I am concerned. ◆**'M~pol**, *m* negative pole/terminal. ◆**'M~punkt**, *m Sp: etc:* minus point; *F:* disadvantage. ◆**'M~zeichen**, *n Mth:* minus sign.

**Minute** [mi'nu:tə], *f -/-n* minute; in letzter M., at the last minute. ◆**m~nlang**, *adj.* lasting for several minutes. ◆**M~nzeiger**, *m* minute hand.

**mir** [mi:r], *pers.pron. dat of* **ich**. **1.** (to) me; **gib's m.**, give it to me; **er half m.**, he helped me; **m. nichts, dir nichts**, just like that; **mit m.**, with me; **bei m.**, at my home/*F:* place; **ein Freund von m.**, a friend of mine. **2.** *refl.* myself; **m. läuft die Nase**, my nose is running.

**Mirabelle** [mira'bɛlə], *f -/-n* small yellow plum; mirabelle.

**Misch-** ['miʃ-], *comb.fm.* (*a*) mixing (drum, vessel etc.); (*b*) mixed (vegetables, fruit etc.). ◆**'m~en**, *v.tr.* (*a*) to mix (drinks, colours etc.); to blend (coffee, tobacco etc.); to shuffle (cards); (*b*) (*Pers.*) **sich in etwas acc m.**, to interfere in sth. ◆**'M~ling**, *m -s/-e* **1.** (*Pers.*) half-caste. **2.** *Biol:* hybrid. ◆**'M~masch**, *m -(e)s/-e F:* hotchpotch. ◆**'M~ung**, *f -/-en* mixture; blend (of coffee, tea etc.).

**miserabel** [mizə'ra:bəl], *adj. F:* awful; **sie fühlt sich m.**, she feels rotten. ◆**M~e** [mi'ze:rə], *f -/-n* (*Lage*) miserable position.

**mißachten** [mis'axtən], *v.tr.* to disregard. ◆**M~ung**, *f -/no pl* disregard; (*Geringschätzung*) disrespect (of s.o.).

**'Mißbehagen**, *n -s/no pl* uneasiness.

**'Mißbildung**, *f -/-en* deformity, abnormality.

**miß'billigen**, *v.tr.* to disapprove of (sth.).

**'Mißbrauch**, *m* abuse; (*falscher Gebrauch*) misuse. ◆**m~en** [mis'brauxən], *v.tr.* to abuse (power, s.o. etc.); to misuse (drugs etc.); to indulge in (alcohol etc.) to excess.

**'Mißerfolg**, *m* failure.

**miß'fallen**. **I.** *v.i.irr.27* (*haben*) **es mißfällt mir**, it displeases me. **II. M.** ['mis-], *n -s/no pl* displeasure; **M. erregen**, to meet with disapproval.

**'Mißgeschick**, *n -(e)s/-e* (*Pers.*) misfortune; (*Malheur*) mishap.

**'mißgestaltet**, *adj.* deformed, misshapen.

**miß'glücken**, *v.i.* (*sein*) (*Versuch, Plan usw.*) to fail, be unsuccessful.

**miß'gönnen**, *v.tr.* j-m etwas m., to begrudge s.o. sth.

**'Mißgriff**, *m* false move, mistake.

**'Mißgunst**, *f -/no pl* envy; resentment (at s.o.'s success).

**miß'handeln**, *v.tr.* to ill-treat (s.o., sth.). ◆**M~lung**, *f -/-en* ill-treatment.

**Mission** [misi'o:n], *f -/-en* mission; **in geheimer M.**, on a secret mission. ◆**M~ar** [-'o'na:r] *m -s/-e* missionary.

**'Mißklang**, *m Mus:* discord; *Fig:* discordant/jarring note.

**'Mißkredit**, *m* in j-n, etwas *acc* in M. bringen, to discredit s.o., sth.

**mißliebig** ['misli:biç], *adj.* unpopular.

**mißlingen** [mis'liŋən], *v.i.irr.9* (*sein*) to fail, (*Plan*) miscarry; (*Überraschung*) to fall flat.

**'Mißmut**, *m* bad mood/temper. ◆**'m~ig**, *adj.* sullen.

**miß'raten**, *v.i.irr.13* (*sein*) (*a*) (*Ernte*) to fail; (*b*) (*Kind*) to turn out badly; **m~er Sohn**, black sheep of the family.

**'Mißstand**, *m* anomaly; (*Schande*) disgrace; (*Zustand*) deplorable state of affairs.

**'Mißstimmung**, *f* ill-feeling; discord.

**'Mißton**, *m Mus:* dissonance; *Fig:* discordant note.

**miß'trauen**. **I.** *v.i.* (*haben*) j-m, etwas dat m., to mistrust s.o., sth. **II. M.** ['mis-], *n -s/no pl* (*a*) mistrust (**gegen** + *acc*, of); (*b*) (*Verdacht*) suspicion. ◆**'M~ensvotum**, *n Pol:* vote of no confidence. ◆**'m~isch**, *adj.* suspicious (**gegen** + *acc*, of); mistrustful.

**'Mißverhältnis**, *n* disproportion.

**'Mißverständnis**, *n* misunderstanding. ◆**'m~verstehen**, *v.tr.irr.100* to misunderstand.

**Mist** [mist], *m -(e)s/no pl* **1.** (*a*) dung; (*b*) *Agr:* (farmyard) manure. **2.** *F:* rubbish; (*a*) (*Unsinn*) rot; (*b*) (*Sachen*) junk, trash; (*c*) **mach keinen M.!** don't do anything stupid; (*d*) **so ein M.!** verdammter M.! damn it all! ◆**'M~haufen**, *m* manure heap, dungheap. ◆**'M~stück**, *n P:* (*Mann*) bastard; (*Frau*) bitch. ◆**'M~wetter**, *n F:* lousy/rotten weather.

**Mistel** ['mistəl], *f -/-n* mistletoe.

**mit** [mit]. **I.** *prep.* + *dat* **1.** with. **2.** (*mittels*) by; **m. dem Zug fahren**, to go by train; **m. der Post**, by post; **m. Scheck bezahlen**, to pay by cheque; **m. lauter Stimme**, in a loud voice; **m. anderen Worten**, in other words. **3.** **m. 20** (*Jahren*), at (the age of) 20; **m. 100 Stundenkilometern**, at 100 kilometres per hour. **II.** *adv.* also, as well; **das gehört m. dazu**, that belongs to it.

**'Mitarbeit**, *f -/no pl* collaboration, co-operation; (*Hilfe*) assistance; (*Beteiligung*) participation; **unter M. von X** *dat*, with the collaboration/assistance of X. ◆**'m~en**, *v.i.sep.* (*haben*) **an/bei etwas** *dat* **m.**, to collaborate on sth. ◆**'M~er(in)**, *m(f)* (*a*) collaborator (**an einem Projekt usw.**, on a project etc.);

freier **M.**, freelance worker/ journalist; (b) (Arbeitskollege) colleague; fellow worker; (Betriebsangehöriger) member of staff, employee.

'**mitbekommen**, v.tr.sep.irr.53 (a) to be given (sth.) (für die Reise, for the journey; (b) to catch, (aufnehmen) take in (a remark etc.); (c) **von etwas** dat **nichts m.**, to miss out on sth.

'**mitbestimm**|**en**, v.i.sep. (haben) to have a say (**in etwas** dat, in sth.). ◆'**M~ung**, f -/no pl participation in decision-making.

'**mitbring**|**en**, v.tr.sep.irr.16 to bring (s.o., sth.) (with one). ◆**M~sel** ['mitbriŋzəl], n -s/- little present (brought back from holiday etc.).

'**Mitbürger(in)**, m(f) fellow citizen.

**miteinander** [mitai'nandər], adv. with each other/one another; (zusammen) together; **m. bekannt werden**, to get to know one another; **alle m.**, all together.

'**miterleben**, v.tr.sep. to witness (sth.); F: **werde ich das noch m.?** will I live to see that?

'**Mitesser**, m -s/- blackhead.

'**mitfahr**|**en**, v.i.sep.irr.26 (sein) to go/come too (by car etc.). ◆'**M~er**, m passenger.

'**mitführen**, v.tr.sep. to carry (documents etc.) with one.

'**mitgeben**, v.tr.sep.irr.35 j-m etwas m., to give s.o. sth. (to take with him).

'**Mitgefühl**, n sympathy.

'**mitgehen**, v.i.sep.irr.36 (sein) to go/come (along) too.

**mitgenommen** ['mitgənɔmən], adj. battered; (Pers.) run down, worn out.

'**Mitgift**, f -/-en dowry.

'**Mitglied**, n member. ◆**M~sbeitrag**, m membership fee; subscription. ◆'**M~schaft**, f -/no pl membership.

'**mithalten**, v.i.sep.irr.45 (haben) to hold one's own; (schritthalten) to keep up.

'**mit**|**helfen**, v.i.sep.irr.50 (haben) to help, lend a hand. ◆'**M~hilfe**, f assistance; co-operation.

'**mithören**, v.tr.sep. to listen (in) to (sth.).

'**mitkommen**, v.i.sep.irr.53 (sein) (a) to come (along) too; (b) (schritthalten) to keep up; F: (verstehen) **da komme ich nicht ganz mit**, I'm not quite with you.

'**Mitläufer**, m Pol: etc: sympathizer, hanger-on; (Kommunist usw.) fellow traveller.

'**Mitleid**, n pity; (Mitgefühl) sympathy, compassion; **M. mit j-m haben**, to feel sorry for s.o.; **take** pity on s.o. ◆'**M~enschaft**, f -/no pl j-n, etwas in M. ziehen, to affect s.o., sth. (as well). ◆'**m~erregend**, adj. pitiful, pathetic. ◆'**m~ig** [-diç], adj. sympathetic; pitying. ◆'**m~(s)los**, adj. unpitying (look), unfeeling, pitiless (person); ruthless (action).

'**mitmachen**, v.sep. 1. v.tr. (a) to join in (a dance etc.); to take part in (a course,

war etc.); **die Mode m.**, to follow the fashion; (b) to go through (difficult times, experiences etc.); **viel m. müssen**, to suffer a lot. 2. v.i. (haben) to join in (**bei** + dat, in).

'**Mitmensch**, m fellow man.

'**mitnehmen**, v.tr.sep.irr.69 (a) to take (s.o., sth.) with one; **j-n (im Auto) m.**, to give s.o. a lift; (b) **j-n schwer/sehr m.**, (Erlebnis usw.) to hit s.o. hard; (Reise, Krankheit usw.) to take it out of one.

'**mitreden**, v.i.sep. (haben) to join in (the conversation); **sie will überall m.**, she wants a say in everything.

'**mitreisen**, v.i.sep. (sein) **mit j-m m.**, to travel with s.o. ◆'**M~de(r)**, m & f decl. as adj. fellow traveller/passenger.

'**mitreiß**|**en**, v.tr.sep.irr.4 to carry (s.o., sth.) away. ◆**m~end**, adj. thrilling (game etc.), stirring, rousing (speech etc.).

**mit**'**samt**, prep. + dat together with.

'**Mitschuld**, f -/no pl complicity. ◆'**m~ig**, adj. **an etwas** dat **m. sein**, to be partly responsible for sth.

'**Mitschüler(in)**, m & f schoolmate.

'**mitsingen**, v.sep.irr.19 1. v.tr. to join in (a song). 2. v.i. (haben) to join in the singing; **in einem Chor m.**, to sing in a choir.

'**mitspiel**|**en**, v.i.sep. (haben) (a) to join in a game; (b) to play (in a team, orchestra etc.); to act (in a play, film etc.); (c) (Gefühle, Gründe usw.) to play a part. ◆'**M~er(in)**, m & f participant (in a game); Sp: (team) member.

'**Mitspracherecht**, n right to have a say.

**Mittag** ['mitɑːk]. I. m -s/-e noon; midday; **zu M.**, at noon/lunchtime; **zu M. essen**, to have lunch. II. m., adv. **heute/morgen m.**, at midday today/tomorrow. ◆'**M~essen**, n lunch, midday meal. ◆'**m~s**, adv. at midday/noon. ◆'**M~spause**, f lunch hour. ◆'**M~sruhe**, f (time of) quiet after lunch. ◆'**M~sschlaf**, m siesta, afternoon nap. ◆**M~szeit**, f lunchtime; midday.

'**Mittäter(in)**, m & f accomplice.

**Mitte** ['mitə], f -/no pl middle (of a room, road, week etc.); centre (of a town, circle etc.); **M. Mai**, in the middle of May; **er ist M. fünfzig**, he is in his mid-fifties; **in unserer M.**, in our midst; amongst us.

'**mitteil**|**en**, v.tr.sep. **j-m etwas m.**, to inform s.o. of sth., tell s.o. sth.; **es wurde amtlich mitgeteilt, daß ...**, it was officially announced that ... ◆'**m~sam**, adj. communicative, forthcoming. ◆'**M~ung**, f -/-en communication (**an** j-n, to s.o.); (Bericht) report; **amtliche M.**, official announcement.

**Mittel** ['mitəl]. I. n -s/- 1. means, way; **M. und Wege**, ways and means; **mit drastischen M~n vorgehen**, to use drastic methods; **als letztes M.**, as a last resort. 2. Med: preparation; (Heilm.) cure; (zum

*Einnehmen*) medicine. **3.** *pl* (*Geldm.*) means, funds; **öffentliche M.**, public money. **4.** (*Durchschnitt*) average (**aus** + *dat*, of). **II.** **'M~-**, **'m~-**, *comb.fm.* central (part, piece etc.); Central (America, Europe, European etc.); middle (ear, finger etc.); centre (parting, *Fb:* circle etc.). **◆'M~alter, das M.**, the Middle Ages. **◆'m~alterlich**, *adj.* (*also Fig:*) medieval. **◆'M~ding**, *n* cross. **◆'M~feld**, *n Fb: etc:* midfield. **◆'m~fristig**, *adj.* medium-term. **◆'m~groß**, *adj.* medium-sized; (*Pers.*) of medium height. **◆'m~los**, *adj.* penniless, destitute. **◆'M~maß**, *n* average (standard). **◆'m~mäßig**, *adj.* (*a*) (*durchschnittlich*) middling, average; (*b*) *Pej:* mediocre, indifferent. **◆'M~meer**. *Pr.n.n* **das M.**, the Mediterranean (Sea). **◆'M~punkt**, *m* centre, central point; *Fig:* hub. **◆'M~s**, *prep.* + *gen* by means of. **◆'M~stand**, *m* middle class. **◆'M~strecken-**, *comb.fm.* (*a*) *Sp:* middle-distance (race, runner); (*b*) *Av: etc:* medium-range (aircraft, rocket etc.). **◆'M~streifen**, *m* central reservation. **◆'M~stürmer**, *m* centre forward. **◆'M~welle**, *f* medium wave.

**mitten** ['mitən], *adv.* **m. auf der Straße/ in der Nacht**, in the middle of the road/ night; **m. in der Luft**, in mid-air; **m. durch die Stadt**, right through the centre of the town. **◆'m~'durch**, *adv. F:* (right) through the middle (of it/them).

**Mitternacht** ['mitərnaxt], *f* midnight.

**mittler|e(r,s)** ['mitlərə(r,s)], *adj.* (*a*) middle (house, window etc.); central (part, area etc.); (*b*) medium (size, quality etc.); moderate (speed, temperature etc.); medium-sized (town etc.). **◆'m~-'weile**, *adv.* meanwhile.

**Mittwoch** ['mitvɔx], *m* -(e)s/-e Wednesday. **◆'m~s**, *adv.* on Wednesdays.

**mit'unter**, *adv.* occasionally; from time to time.

**'mitverantwortlich**, *adj.* jointly responsible.

**'Mitverfasser**, *m* co-author.

**'Mitwelt**, *f* -/no *pl* **die M.**, one's fellow men/(*Zeitgenossen*) contemporaries.

**'mitwirk|en**, *v.i.sep.* (*haben*) (*a*) **an/bei etwas** *dat* **m.**, (*Pers.*) to help with sth.; (*Faktoren usw.*) to play a part in sth.; (*b*) *Th: etc:* to take part; **die M~enden**, the performers/*Th:* cast/*Mus:* players. **◆'M~ung**, *f* co-operation.

**Mix|becher** ['miksbɛçər], *m* (cocktail) shaker. **◆'m~en**, *v.tr.* to mix (drinks). **◆'M~er**, *m* -s/- *Cu:* liquidizer. **◆'M~getränk**, *n* mixed drink; cocktail. **◆M~'tur**, *f* -/-en mixture.

**Möbel** ['mø:bəl]. **I.** *n* -s/- piece of furniture; *usu.pl* **die M.**, the furniture. **II.** **'M~-**, *comb.fm.* furniture (shop, industry, polish etc.). **◆'M~stück**, *n* piece of furniture. **◆'M~wagen**, *m* furniture/removal/*N.Am:* moving van.

**mobil** [mo'bi:l], *adj.* **1.** (*a*) mobile (shop etc.); (*b*) *Mil:* mobilized (troops etc.). **2.** *F:* lively (child). **◆M~iar** [mobili'a:r], *n* -s/no *pl* furniture and fittings.

**möblier|en** [mø'bli:rən], *v.tr.* to furnish (a room, flat etc.). **◆m~t**, *adj.* furnished; *adv.* **m. wohnen**, to live in furnished accommodation.

**Mode** ['mo:də]. **I.** *f* -/-n fashion; (**in**) **M. sein/aus der M. (gekommen) sein**, to be fashionable/out of fashion. **II.** **'M~-**, *comb.fm.* (*a*) fashion (photographer, drawing etc.); (*b*) (*modisch*) fashionable (profession, colour, illness etc.). **◆'M~(n)schau**, *f* fashion show/parade. **◆'M~schmuck**, *m* -(e)s/no *pl* costume jewellery. **◆'M~schöpfer(in)**, *m(f)* fashion/dress designer.

**Modell** [mo'dɛl]. **I.** *n* -s/-e model; *Art:* **j-m M. sitzen/stehen**, to sit/pose for s.o. **II.** **'m~-**, *comb.fm.* model (aeroplane, railway, dress etc.). **◆M~baukasten**, *m* modelling kit. **◆m~ieren** [-'li:rən], *v.tr.* to model (a statue, vase etc.); to mould (clay, wax etc.).

**Moder** ['mo:dər], *m* -s/no *pl* mould.

**modern** [mo'dɛrn], *adj.* modern; (*modisch*) fashionable; (*fortschrittlich*) progressive (ideas etc.); up-to-date (methods etc.). **◆m~i'sieren**, *v.tr.* to modernize (sth.).

**Modif|ikation** [modifikatsi'o:n], *f* -/-en modification. **◆m~i'zieren**, *v.tr.* to modify (sth.).

**modisch** ['mo:diʃ], *adj.* fashionable, *F:* trendy.

**Mofa** ['mo:fa], *n* -s/-s (low-powered) moped.

**mogeln** ['mo:gəln], *F: v.i.* (*haben*) to cheat.

**mögen** ['mø:gən], *v.tr.irr.* & *modal aux.* to like (s.o., sth.); **was möchten Sie?** what would you like? **ich möchte kommen**, I would like to come; **es mag sein, daß...**, it may well be that ...; **und wie sie alle heißen m.**, and whatever their names might be; **mag kommen, was will**, come what may.

**möglich** ['mø:kliç], *adj.* possible; **sobald es Ihnen m. ist**, as soon as you can; **das ist doch nicht m.!** it can't be! *F: er* **sprach über alles m~e**, he talked about all sorts of things. **◆'M~er'weise**, *adv.* possibly, perhaps. **◆'M~keit**, *f* -/-en (*a*) possibility; **nach M.**, if possible; (*möglichst*) as much/far as possible; (*b*) (*Chance*) chance, opportunity. **◆'m~st**, *adv.* **1.** (*a*) as ... as possible; **m. viel/ schnell**, as much/quickly as possible; (*b*) (*wenn möglich*) if possible. **2.** **sein m~stes tun**, to do one's utmost.

**Mohn** [mo:n], *m* -(e)s/-e (*a*) *Bot:* poppy; (*b*) *Cu:* (*Samen*) poppy-seed. **◆'M~blume**, *f* poppy.

**Möhre** ['mø:rə], **-/-n**, **Mohrrübe** ['mo:rry:bə], *f* carrot.

**Mokka** ['mɔka], *m* -s/-s strong black coffee.

**Molch** [mɔlç], *m* -(e)s/-e newt.

**Mole** ['moːlə], *f* -/-n mole, breakwater.

**Molekül** [mole'kyːl], *n* -s/-e molecule.

**Molke** ['mɔlkə], *f* -/no pl whey. ◆**M~e'rei**, *f* -/-en dairy.

**Moll** [mɔl], *n* -s/no pl minor (key).

**mollig** ['mɔlɪç], *adj.* **1.** (*dick*) plump, chubby. **2.** (*bequem*) cosy, snug.

**Moment¹** [mo'mɛnt], *m* -(e)s/-e moment; **im M.**, at the moment; **M. mal!** hang on a minute! (*halt!*) hold it! ◆**m~an** [-'taːn], *adj.* (*a*) present (situation etc.); (*b*) (*flüchtig*) momentary, fleeting.

**Moment²**, *n* -(e)s/-e factor, element.

**Monarch(in)** [mo'narç(in)], *m* -en/-en (*f* -/-nen) monarch. ◆**M~ie** [-'çiː], *f* -/-n monarchy.

**Monat** ['moːnat], *m* -(e)s/-e month; **im M. Juli**, in the month of July; *F:* **sie ist im vierten M.**, she's four months pregnant. ◆**m~elang**, *adj.* lasting several months; **m. warten**, to wait for (several) months. ◆**m~lich**, *adj.* monthly; **m. einmal**, once a month. ◆**M~s-**, *comb.fm* (*a*) monthly (rent, salary etc.); (*b*) (beginning, end etc.) of the month. ◆**M'~skarte**, *f* monthly season (ticket). ◆**M'~srate**, *f* monthly instalment.

**Mönch** [mœnç], *m* -(e)s/-e monk.

**Mond** [moːnt]. **I.** *m* -(e)s/-e moon. **II.** '**M~~**, *comb.fm.* lunar (landscape etc.); moon (rock, landing etc.). ◆'**M~bahn**, *f* lunar orbit. ◆'**M~fähre**, *f* lunar module. ◆'**M~finsternis**, *f* lunar eclipse; eclipse of the moon. ◆'**m~'hell**, *adj.* moonlit. ◆'**M~schein**, *m* moonlight. ◆'**m~süchtig**, *adj.* somnambulant.

**Monitor** ['moːnitɔr], *m* -s/-en monitor.

**mono** ['moːno, 'mɔno]. **I.** *adj.* mono. **II.** '**M~-**, *comb.fm.* mono (recording etc.).

**Monogramm** [mono'gram], *n* -s/-e monogram.

**Monolog** [mono'loːk], *m* -(e)s/-e monologue.

**Monopol** [mono'poːl], *n* -s/-e monopoly.

**monoton** [mono'toːn], *adj.* monotonous. ◆**M~ie** [-o'niː], *f* -/-n monotony.

**Monstrum** ['mɔnstrum], *n* -s/-ren monster.

**Monsun** [mɔn'zuːn], *m* -s/-e monsoon.

**Montag** ['moːntaːk], *m* -(e)s/-e Monday. ◆'**m~s**, *adv.* on Mondays.

**Montage** [mɔn'taːʒə], *f* -/-n (*a*) assembly; fitting (of a part); (*b*) *Art:* montage. ◆**M~eur** [-'tøːr], *m* -s/-e fitter, mechanic. ◆**m~ieren** [-'tiːrən], *v.tr.* (*a*) to assemble, set up (a machine etc.); to put together (a collage etc.); (*b*) (*anbringen*) to fit (tyres, a handle etc.), mount (a gun, light etc.); to install (sth.).

**Monument** [monu'mɛnt], *n* -(e)s/-e monument. ◆**m~al** [-'taːl], *adj.* monumental.

**Moor** [moːr], *n* -(e)s/-e fen; (*Sumpf*) bog. ◆'**M~bad**, *n* mud-bath.

**Moos** [moːs], *n* -es/-e **1.** *Bot:* moss. **2.** *no* *pl F:* (*Geld*) cash, lolly; *N.Am:* dough. ◆'**m~grün**, *adj.* moss green.

**Mop** [mɔp], *m* -s/-s mop.

**Moped** ['moːpɛt], *n* -s/-s moped.

**Mops** [mɔps], *m* -es/-e *Z:* pug (dog). ◆'**m~en**, *v.tr. F:* to pinch, swipe (sth.).

**Moral** [mo'raːl], *f* -/no pl **1.** morals; morality. **2.** moral (of a story etc.). **3.** morale (of troops etc.). ◆**m~isch**, *adj.* moral. ◆**M~predigt**, *f Pej:* lecture, homily.

**Moräne** [mo'rɛːnə], *f* -/-n moraine.

**Morast** [mo'rast], *m* -(e)s/-e (*a*) bog; quagmire; (*b*) (*Schlamm*) mire, mud.

**Mord** [mɔrt]. **I.** *m* -(e)s/-e murder, *esp. N.Am:* homicide (**an j-m,** of s.o.); *F:* **es gibt M. und Totschlag,** all hell will be let loose. **II.** '**M~~**, *comb.fm.* murder (case etc.). ◆'**M~kommission**, *f* murder/*N.Am:* homicide squad. ◆'**M~verdacht**, *m* suspicion of murder. ◆'**M~versuch**, *m* attempted murder. ◆'**M~s-**, '**m~s-**, *comb.fm. F:* (*schrecklich*) terrible, awful (noise, heat etc.). ◆'**m~smäßig**, *adj. F:* terrible (noise etc.); terrific (fun etc.).

**Mörder(in)** ['mœrdər(in)], *m* -s/- (*f* -/-nen) murderer, *f* murderess. ◆'**m~isch**, *adj.* murderous (weapon, plan etc., *F:* task, pace, heat etc.); *F:* breakneck (speed).

**morgen** ['mɔrgən]. **I.** *adv.* **1.** tomorrow; **m. früh,** tomorrow morning. **2. heute/ gestern m.,** this/yesterday morning. **II. M.,** *m* -s/- **1.** morning; **am M.,** in the morning. **2.** *Meas:* acre. **III.** '**M~~**, *comb.fm.* morning (star, newspaper etc.). ◆'**M~dämmerung**, *f* dawn. ◆'**m~dlich**, *adj.* morning (stillness, walk etc.). ◆'**M~grauen**, *n* dawn. ◆'**M~mantel**, *m*/'**M~rock**, *m* housecoat; (*Schlafrock*) dressing gown. ◆'**M~rot**, *n* red (morning) sky. ◆'**m~s**, *adv.* in the morning; every morning; **von m. bis abends,** from morning to night.

**morgig** ['mɔrgiç], *adj.* tomorrow's (weather etc.).

**Morphium** ['mɔrfium], *n* -s/no pl morphine.

**morsch** [mɔrʃ], *adj.* rotten (wood etc.).

**Morsealphabet** ['mɔrzəʔalfabeːt], *n* Morse (code). ◆'**m~n**, *v.tr.* to send (a message etc.) in Morse.

**Mörser** ['mœrzər], *m* -s/- *Cu: & Mil:* mortar.

**Mörtel** ['mœrtəl], *m* -s/- mortar; (*Putz*) plaster.

**Mosaik** [moza'iːk], *n* -s/-en & -e mosaic.

**Moschee** [mɔ'ʃeː], *f* -/-n mosque.

**Mosel** ['moːzəl]. *Pr.n.f* -. Moselle.

**Moskau** ['mɔskau]. *Pr.n.n* -s. Moscow.

**Moskito** [mɔs'kiːto], *m* -s/-s mosquito.

**Most** [mɔst], *m* -(e)s/-e **1.** must. **2.** (*Apfelm.*) (rough) cider.

**Motiv** [mo'tiːf], *n* -s/-e **1.** (*Grund*) motive.

**2.** (a) *Mus: Lit:* motif, theme; (b) *Art: Phot:* subject. ◆**M~ation** [-ivatsi'oːn], f ~/-en motivation. ◆**m~ieren** [-'viːrən], v.tr. to motivate (a pupil etc.).

**Motor** ['moːtor]. **I.** m -s/-en engine; *El:* motor. **II.** '**M~-**, comb.fm. (a) (eines M~s) engine (oil, noise etc.); (b) (mit einem M.) motor (mower, scooter, vessel etc.); power (pump, saw etc.). ◆'**M~boot**, n motorboat. ◆'**M~haube**, f -/-n *Aut: etc:* bonnet, N.Am: hood. ◆**m~i'siert**, adj. motorized (troops etc.); motor (traffic); (visitors etc.) in cars. ◆**M~rad** [moˈtoːrraːt], n motorcycle. ◆**M~radfahrer**, m motorcyclist. ◆'**M~schaden**, m engine trouble.

**Motte** ['mɔtə], f -/-n moth. ◆'**M~nkugel**, f mothball.

**Motto** ['mɔto], n -s/-s motto.

**Möwe** ['møːvə], f -/-n gull.

**Mücke** ['mykə], f -/-n mosquito; (kleine M.) midge. ◆'**M~nstich**, m mosquito bite.

**Mucks** [muks], m -es/-e F: (a) slight(est) sound; (b) (Bewegung) **keinen M. tun/ machen**, not to stir/budge. ◆**m~en**, v.i. (haben) & refl. usu.neg. F: (sich) m., to make a sound; (sich rühren) to budge. ◆'**m~mäuschenstill**, adj. F: as quiet as a mouse.

**müde** ['myːdə], adj. tired; weary (smile, movement etc.); **ich bin es m.**, I am tired of it. ◆'**M~igkeit**, f -/no pl tiredness; weariness.

**Muff** [muf], m -(e)s/-e muff.

**Muff|el** ['mufəl], m -s/- F: (Pers.) sourpuss, crosspatch. ◆'**m~(el)ig**, adj. F: sulky, grumpy.

**muffig** ['mufiç], adj. F: (moderig) musty, stale.

**muhen** ['muːən], v.i. (haben) to moo.

**Müh|e** ['myːə], f -/-n trouble; (Anstrengung) effort; **er scheut keine M.**, he spares no effort; **sich** dat **M. geben/ machen**, to take trouble/try hard; **mit M. und Not**, with great difficulty; (gerade noch) only just. ◆'**m~elos**, adj. effortless (action etc.); easy (victory etc.). ◆'**m~evoll**, adj. laborious; (schwierig) difficult (task, work etc.). ◆'**m~sam**, adj. arduous (life etc.); laborious, (schwierig) uphill (task etc.). ◆'**m~selig**, adj. Lit: arduous.

**Mühle** ['myːlə], f -/-n mill; (für Kaffee usw.) grinder.

**Mulde** ['muldə], f -/-n hollow; dip (in the road).

**Mull** [mul], m -(e)s/-e muslin; *Med:* gauze.

**Müll** [myl]. **I.** m -s/no pl rubbish, refuse; N.Am: garbage. **II.** '**M~-**, comb.fm. refuse, rubbish, N.Am: garbage (heap etc.). ◆'**M~abfuhr**, f refuse collection (service). ◆'**M~beutel**, m dustbin liner. ◆'**M~eimer**, m -s/- dustbin;

N.Am: garbage can; (im Haus) waste bin. ◆'**M~halde** f/'**M~kippe**, f rubbish/ refuse tip. ◆'**M~mann**, m F: dustman, N.Am: garbage man. ◆'**M~schlucker**, m rubbish chute. ◆'**M~tonne**, f dustbin, N.Am: garbage can.

**mulmig** ['mulmiç], adj. F: (a) tricky, precarious (situation etc.); (b) **mir ist m. zumute**, I feel uneasy/(schlecht) queasy.

**multi-** ['multi-], comb.fm. multi- (millionaire etc.). ◆**m~pli'zieren**, to multiply (figures etc.).

**Mumie** ['muːmiə], f -/-n mummy.

**Mumm** [mum], m -s/no pl F: spunk.

**Mumps** [mumps], m -/no pl mumps.

**Mund** [munt], m -(e)s/-er mouth; **halt den M.!** shut up! pipe down! **j-m über den M. fahren**, to cut s.o. short. ◆'**M~art**, f dialect. ◆'**M~harmonika**, f harmonica; F: mouth organ. ◆'**M~stück**, n mouthpiece; tip (of a cigarette). ◆'**M~wasser**, n -s/-: mouthwash. ◆'**M~werk**, n -(e)s/no pl F: mouth. ◆'**M~winkel**, m corner of the mouth. ◆'**M~-zu-'M~-Beatmung**, f mouth-to-mouth resuscitation; F: kiss of life.

**Mündel** ['myndəl], n -s/- *Jur:* ward.

**münd|en** ['myndən], v.i. (sein) (Fluß) to flow; (Straße) to lead. ◆'**M~ung**, f -/-en 1. (Flußm.) mouth, estuary. 2. (Gewehrm.) muzzle.

**mündig** ['myndiç], adj. of age; **m. werden**, to come of age. ◆'**M~keit**, f -/no pl majority.

**mündlich** ['myntliç], adj. oral.

**Munition** [munitsi'oːn], f -/no pl ammunition. ◆**M~slager**, n -s/- ammunition depot.

**munkeln** ['muŋkəln], v.tr. & i. (haben) to whisper furtively; **man munkelt, (daß ...)**, it is rumoured that...

**munter** ['muntər], adj. (a) (lebhaft) lively (person, eyes, game etc.); (b) (heiter) gay, cheerful; (c) (wach) awake. ◆'**M~keit**, f -/no pl liveliness; cheerfulness.

**Münz|e** ['myntsə], f -/-n coin. ◆**m~en**, v.tr. (a) to mint, coin (silver, gold etc.); (b) **auf j-n/etwas** acc **gemünzt sein**, to be aimed/directed at s.o., sth.

**mürb|e** ['myrbə], adj. (a) crumbly (cake, pastry etc.); crunchy (apple); mellow (fruit etc.); (b) (morsch) rotten (wood, rope etc.); (c) Fig: **j-n m. machen**, to wear s.o. down. ◆'**M~teig**, m short (crust) pastry.

**Murks** [murks], m -es/no pl F: botchup.

**Murmel** ['murməl], f -/-n marble.

**murmeln** ['murməln]. **I.** v.tr. & i. (haben) to murmur (sth.). **II.** M., n -s/no pl F: murmur.

**Murmeltier** ['murməltiːr], n marmot; **wie ein M. schlafen**, to sleep like a log.

**murren** ['murən], v.i. (haben) to grumble, moan.

**mürrisch** ['myrif], adj. grumpy; sulky.

**Mus** [muːs], n -es/-e purée.

**Muschel** ['muʃəl], *f -/-n* **1.** (*a*) (*Schale*) (sea) shell; (*b*) (*Miesm.*) mussel. **2.** *Tel:* (*Sprechm.*) mouthpiece; (*Hörm.*) earpiece.

**Museum** [mu'ze:um], *n -s/-seen* museum.

**Musical** [mju:zikəl], *n -s/-s* musical.

**Musik** [mu'zi:k]. **I.** *f -/no pl* **1.** music. **2.** *F:* (*M~kapelle*) band. **II.** **M~-**, *comb.fm.* (*a*) musical (instrument, scene etc.); (*b*) music (lesson, teacher, critic etc.); (school, history etc.) of music. ◆**m~alisch** [-'ka:liʃ], *adj.* musical. ◆**M~ant** [-'kant], *m -en/-en* (street etc.) musician. ◆**M~box**, *f* juke-box. ◆**M~er(in)** ['muzikər(in)], *m -s/- (f -/-nen)* musician. ◆**M~kapelle**, *f* band.

**musisch** ['mu:ziʃ], *adj.* artistic; **er ist m. veranlagt**, he has an artistic disposition.

**musizieren** [muzi'tsi:rən], *v.i.* (*haben*) to make music.

**Muskat** [mus'ka:t], *m -(e)s/-e* (*also* **M~nuß** *f*) nutmeg.

**Muskel** ['muskəl]. **I.** *m -s/-n* muscle. **II.** **M~-**, *comb.fm.* muscular (pain etc.); muscle (fibre etc.). ◆**M~kater**, *m* (**einen**) **M. haben**, to be stiff (as a result of physical effort). ◆**M~zerrung**, *f* pulled muscle.

**muskulös** [musku'lø:s], *adj.* muscular.

**Muße** ['mu:sə], *f -/no pl Lit:* leisure. ◆**M~stunde**, *f* leisure/spare time.

**müssen** ['mysən], *v.irr. modal aux. & v.i.* (*haben*) to have to; **ich muß jetzt gehen**, I must/have to/*F:* I've got to go now; **wenn es sein muß**, if it's really necessary; **du mußt es ja wissen**, you should know; **Geld müßte man haben!** it would be nice to be rich; **ich muß in die Stadt**, I must go into town; **er mußte zum Arzt**, he had to go to the doctor.

**müßig** ['my:sıç], *adj. Lit:* **1.** idle. **2.** (*sinnlos*) futile.

**Muster** ['mustər]. **I.** *n -s/-* **1.** (*a*) (*Vorlage*) pattern; (*b*) (*Vorbild*) model. **2.** (*Dessin*) pattern, design. **3.** (*Warenprobe*) sample, specimen. **II.** '**M~-**, *comb.fm.* **1.** model (letter, pupil etc.); perfect (marriage etc.). **2.** *Com:* pattern, sample (book etc.). ◆**m~gültig/m~haft**, *adj.* exemplary, model (behaviour, pupil etc.); perfect (example etc.); *adv.* in an exem-

plary fashion. ◆**m~n**, *v.tr.* (*a*) to eye, study (s.o.); (*b*) *Mil:* to inspect (troops etc.); (*auf Tauglichkeit*) **gemustert werden**, to have a medical. ◆**M~ung**, *f -/-en* **1.** inspection, scrutiny (of s.o.). **2.** *Mil:* medical examination. **3.** (*Stoff usw.*) pattern, design.

**Mut** [mu:t], *m -(e)s/no pl* courage; (*Tapferkeit*) bravery; (*Kühnheit*) boldness; **den M. verlieren**, to lose heart; **j-m M. machen/den M. nehmen**, to encourage/discourage s.o. ◆**m~ig**, *adj.* courageous, brave. ◆**m~los**, *adj.* fainthearted; (*entmutigt*) despondent.

**mutmaß|lich** ['mu:tma:slıç], *adj.* probable (result, verdict etc.); suspected (murderer etc.). ◆**M~ung**, *f -/-en* speculation.

**Mutter¹** ['mutər]. **I.** *f -/-* mother. **II.** *comb.fm.* (*a*) maternal, motherly (love, instinct etc.); mother's (milk, Day etc.); (*b*) mother (country, ship etc.). ◆**M~boden**, *m/'M~erde*, *f* topsoil. ◆**M~gesellschaft**, *f* parent company. ◆**M~leib**, *m* womb. ◆'**m~los**, *adj.* motherless. ◆'**M~mal**, *n* birthmark; (*braun*) mole. ◆**M~schaft**, *f -/no pl* motherhood. ◆**M~seelen\|allein**, *adj.* all alone. ◆**M~sprache**, *f* mother tongue, native language. ◆**M~tier**, *n* dam.

**Mutter²**, *f -/-n Tchn:* nut.

**mütterlich** ['mytərlıç], *adj.* motherly (love, woman, type etc.); maternal (instincts, care etc.). ◆'**m~erseits**, *adv.* on one's mother's side.

**Mutti** ['muti], *f -/-s F:* mummy, mum.

**Mutwill|e** ['mu:tvilə], *m* wilfulness; (*Bosheit*) wilful malice. ◆'**m~ig**, *adj.* wilful (behaviour etc.); wanton (damage).

**Mütze** ['mytsə], *f -/-n* cap; (*Wollm.*) woolly hat.

**mysteriös** [mysteri'ø:s], *adj.* mysterious.

**Mystik** ['mystik], *f -/no pl* mysticism. ◆**m~isch**, *adj* (*a*) mystic (symbol, ceremony); (*b*) *F:* (*geheimnisvoll*) mysterious.

**Myth|ologie** [mytolo'gi:], *f -/-n* mythology. ◆**m~ologisch** [-o'lo:gıʃ], *adj.* mythological. ◆**M~os** ['my:tɔs], *m -/* **Mythen** myth.

# N

**N, n** [ɛn], *n -/-* (the letter) N, n.

**na** [na], *int. F:* well; (*also*) so; **na so was!** well I never! I say! **na und?** so what? **na, also!** there you are! what did I tell you? **na gut!** all right then!

**Nabe** ['na:bə], *f -/-n* hub.

**Nabel** ['na:bəl], *m -s/-* navel. ◆'**N~schnur**, *f* umbilical cord.

**nach** [na:x]. **I.** *prep. + dat* **1.** (*räumlich*) (*a*) to; **n. links/rechts**, to the left/right; **n. allen Richtungen**, in all directions; (*b*)

**n. etwas greifen, streben usw.**, to reach out, strive etc. for sth. **2.** (*zeitlich, Folge*) after; **n. der Schule**, after school; **fünf (Minuten) n. drei**, five (minutes) past three; **bitte n. Ihnen!** after you! **3.** (*gemäß*) according to; **n. dem, was Sie sagen**, going by/from what you say; **wenn es n. mir ginge**, if I had my way; **n. Litern gemessen**, measured in litres; **etwas n. Gewicht verkaufen**, to sell sth. by weight. **II.** *adv.* (*a*) **n. wie vor**, as was always the case; **n. und n.**, gradually; by degrees; (b) **mir n.!** follow me!

'**nachahm|en**, v.tr.sep. usu. Pej: to ape, mimic (s.o., sth.).

'**nachahm|en**, v.tr.sep. to imitate, copy, (nachäffen) mimic (s.o., sth.). ◆'**N~er**, m -s/- imitator; mimic. ◆'**N~ung**, f -/-en imitation.

'**nacharbeiten**, v.tr. & i. sep. (haben) to make up for (lost time); **zwei Stunden n.**, to do two extra hours' work.

**Nachbar|(in)** ['naxbɑːr(in)]. **I.** m -s/-n (f -/-nen) neighbour. **II. N~-**, comb.fm. neighbouring (country etc.); adjoining (building, room etc.); nextdoor (house, garden); next (table, town etc.). ◆'**n~lich**, adj. neighbourly (relations etc.). ◆'**N~schaft**, f -/no pl neighbourhood; **unsere N.**, our neighbourhood/ (Nachbarn) neighbours.

'**nachbestell|en**, v.tr.sep. to order some more of (sth.). ◆'**N~ung**, f Com: repeat order.

'**nachbild|en**, v.tr.sep. to reproduce, copy (sth.). ◆'**N~ung**, f reproduction, copy.

'**nachblicken**, v.i.sep. (haben) **jdm. n.** to gaze after s.o.

'**nachdatieren**, v.tr.sep. to backdate (a form, cheque etc.).

**nach'dem**, conj. (a) (zeitlich) after, when; (b) (kausal) **n. die Preise gestiegen sind,** since prices have risen.

'**nachdenk|en**. **I.** v.i.sep.irr.17 (haben) to think (carefully) (**über** + acc, about); **denk mal nach**, try and think; **er dachte (darüber) nach, ob ...,** he wondered whether .... **II. N.**, n -s/no pl thought, meditation. ◆'**n~lich**, adj. pensive.

'**Nachdruck**, m **1.** no pl emphasis; **mit N.**, emphatically. **2.** (Neudruck) reprint. ◆'**n~en**, v.tr.sep. to reprint.

**nach'drücklich** ['naːxdryklɪç], adj. emphatic.

'**nacheifern**, v.i.sep. (haben) **j-m n.**, to emulate s.o.

**nachei'nander**, adv. one after the other; **drei Tage n.**, three days running.

'**nachempfinden**, v.tr.sep.irr.9 **j-s Leid, Freude usw. n.**, to share s.o.'s sorrow, joy etc.; **das kann ich dir n.**, I understand how you feel.

'**Nacherzählung**, f Sch: reproduction.

'**Nachfahre**, m -n/-n Lit: descendant.

'**Nachfolge**, f succession (**in einem Amt,** to an office). ◆'**n~n**, v.i.sep. (sein) **j-m n.**, to follow s.o., (im Amt) succeed s.o. ◆'**N~r(in)**, m -s/- (f -/-nen) successor.

'**nachforsch|en**, v.i.sep. (haben) to make enquiries. ◆'**N~ungen**, fpl enquiries, investigations.

'**Nachfrage**, f **1.** Com: demand (**nach** + dat, for). **2.** F: **danke der N.!** how kind of you to ask! ◆'**n~n**, v.i. sep. (haben) to inquire, make inquiries; **bei j-m n.**, to ask s.o.

'**nachfühlen**, v.tr.sep. to understand (s.o.'s disappointment etc.).

'**nachfüllen**, v.tr.sep. (a) to refill (a glass etc.); to top up (a radiator etc.); (b) to top up with (petrol etc.).

'**nachgeben**, v.i.sep.irr.35 (haben) (a) (Pers.) to give in, yield (**etwas** dat, to sth.); **j-s Wünschen n.**, to bow to s.o.'s wishes; (b) (Material, Seil) to give, yield; (Boden usw.) to give way; Fin: (Preise, Kurse) to weaken.

'**Nachgebühr**, f postage due (payment); surcharge.

'**Nachgeburt**, f afterbirth.

'**nachgehen**, v.i.sep.irr.36 (sein) **j-m, etwas** dat **n.**, to follow s.o., sth.; **einem Problem n.**, to look into a problem; **seiner Arbeit n.**, to go about one's work; (Uhr) (**fünf Minuten usw.**) **n.**, to be (five minutes etc.) slow.

'**nachgemacht**, p.p. as adj. imitation (jewellery etc.); counterfeit (money, signature).

'**Nachgeschmack**, m aftertaste.

**nachgiebig** ['naːxgiːbɪç], adj. (a) flexible, pliant (material etc.); (b) yielding, compliant (person). ◆'**N~keit**, f -/no pl (a) flexibility; (b) compliance, yielding nature; indulgence (of parents etc.).

'**Nachhall**, m echo; reverberation. ◆'**n~en**, v.i.sep. (haben) to echo, reverberate.

'**nachhaltig**, adj. lasting; **n. wirken**, to have a lasting effect/influence.

**Nachhauseweg** [naːx'hauzəveːk], m way home.

'**nachhelfen**, v.i.sep.irr.50 (haben) (**j-m**) **n.**, to lend (s.o.) a hand, help (s.o.); **etwas** dat **n.**, to help sth. along.

**nachher** [nax'heːr], adv. afterwards; (später) later; **bis n.!** see you later.

'**Nachhilfe**, f (also **N~unterricht** m) Sch: coaching; **N. bekommen**, to be coached. ◆'**N~stunde**, f extra (private) lesson.

'**nachhinein**, adv. **im n.**, afterwards; (nachträglich) after the event.

'**nachholen**, v.tr.sep. (a) to make up for (lost time etc.); to catch up on (sleep, work etc.); (b) to do (an examination etc.) later.

'**Nachkomm|e**, m -n/-n descendant. ◆'**n~en**, v.i.sep.irr.53 (sein) (a) to come, follow (on) later; **j-m, etwas** dat **n.**, to follow s.o., sth.; (b) (Schritt halten) to keep up; (c) (erfüllen) **einem Versprechen usw. n.**, to keep a promise etc.

'**Nachkriegs-**, comb.fm. post-war (generation etc.); ◆'**N~zeit**, f post-war period.

**Nachlaß** ['naːxlas], n -lasses/-lässe **1.** (Erbschaft) estate (of a dead person). **2.** Com: (Preisn.) discount; reduction.

'**nachlassen**, v.sep.irr.57 **1.** v.i. (haben) (a) to lessen; (Wind) to drop; (Sturm, Schmerz, Druck usw.) to ease, let up; (Fieber) to go down; (Gehör, Augen usw.) to (begin to) fail; (Interesse usw.) to wane, fall off; (Wirkung) to wear off; (b) (aufgeben) to give up; **nicht n.!** keep it up! **2.**

*v.tr. Com:* etwas vom Preis n., to deduct sth. from the price.

'nachlässig, *adj.* careless; slipshod (person, work etc.); lax, casual (behaviour etc.). ◆'N~keit, *f* -/-en carelessness, negligence; *F:* sloppiness.

'nachlaufen, *v.i.sep.irr.58* (sein) j-m, etwas *dat* n., to run after s.o., sth.; *F:* einem Mädchen n., to chase a girl.

'nachlegen, *v.tr.sep.* to put more (wood etc.) on (the fire).

'nachlesen *v.tr.sep.irr.61* (nachschlagen) to look/read (sth.) up.

'nachmachen, *v.tr.sep. F:* (a) to copy, (nachäffen) mimic (s.o., sth.); to reproduce, copy (period furniture etc.); (unerlaubt) to forge (a signature etc.), counterfeit (money etc.); (b) (nachholen) to catch up on (sth.) later.

'Nachmittag. I. *m* afternoon; am N., in the afternoon. II. n., *adv.* heute/gestern n., this/yesterday afternoon. ◆'n~s, *adv.* in the afternoon/(jeden N.) afternoons.

'Nachnahme, *f* -/-n etwas per/mit N. schicken, to send sth. cash on delivery/ *abbr.* C.O.D.

'Nachname, *m* surname.

'Nachporto, *n* postage due.

'nachprüfen, *v.tr.sep.* to check, verify (a fact, statement etc.).

'nachrechnen, *v.tr.sep.* to check (a sum etc.).

'Nachrede, *f Jur:* üble N., defamation, slander.

'Nachricht ['nɑːxrɪçt], *f* -/-en news; eine N., a piece of news/information; eine N. hinterlassen, to leave a message; j-m N. geben, to inform s.o.; *Rad: TV:* die N~en, the news. ◆'N~en-, *comb.fm.* news (magazine etc.). ◆'N~enagentur, *f* news agency. ◆'N~endienst, *m esp. Mil:* intelligence (service). ◆'N~ensprecher(in), *m(f),* newsreader, *N.Am:* newscaster. ◆'N~entechnik, *f* (tele)communications.

'nachrücken, *v.i.sep.* (sein) (Pers., Mil: Truppen) to move up.

'Nachruf, *m* obituary.

'nachsagen, *v.tr.sep.* j-m etwas n., to say sth. of s.o.; j-m Gutes/Böses n., to speak well/badly of s.o.

'Nachsaison, *f* off/low season.

'nachschicken, *v.tr.sep.* to forward, send on (a letter etc.) (j-m, to s.o.).

'nachschlag|en, *v.sep.irr.85* 1. *v.tr.* to look (sth.) up. 2. *v.i.* (haben) in einem Wörterbuch usw. n., to consult a dictionary etc. ◆'N~ewerk, *n* reference work.

'Nachschlüssel, *m* duplicate key.

'Nachschub, *m* -(e)s/no pl Mil: supply (an Proviant usw., of food etc.); *coll.* der N., supplies. ◆'N~linie, *f*/'N~weg, *m* supply line.

'nachsehen. I. *v.sep.irr.92* 1. *v.i.* (haben)

(a) j-m, etwas *dat* n., to look/gaze after s.o., sth.; (b) (kontrollieren) to have a look, check up. 2. *v.tr.* (a) to look (sth.) up (in a book etc.); (b) (kontrollieren) to check (homework etc.); (c) j-m seine Fehler usw. n., to overlook s.o.'s mistakes etc. II. N., *n* -s/no pl das N. haben, to come off badly.

'nachsenden, *v.tr.sep.irr.94* to forward, send on (a letter etc.).

'Nachsicht, *f* -/no pl leniency; N. üben, to be lenient, show forbearance. ◆'n~ig, *adj.* lenient (gegen j-n, towards s.o.); forbearing, charitable (attitude etc.).

'nachsitzen. I. *v.i.sep.irr.97* (haben) n. müssen, to be kept in. II. N., *n* -s/no pl detention.

'Nachspeise, *f* dessert, *Brit:* sweet.

'Nachspiel, *n* 1. *Th:* epilogue. 2. (Folgen) consequences; es wird noch ein N. geben, there will be repercussions. ◆'n~en, *v.tr.sep. Fb: etc:* fünf Minuten n. lassen, to allow five minutes injury time.

'nachsprechen, *v.tr.sep.irr.14* to repeat (s.o.'s words etc.).

nächst [nɛːçst]. I. *prep.* + *dat Lit:* next to. II. n~-, *comb.fm.* next (largest, highest, smallest, possible etc.). ◆'n~e(r, s), *adj.* next; (nächstgelegen) nearest; das n. Geschäft, the nearest shop; die n~en Verwandten, the closest relatives; in den n~en Tagen, in the next few days; wer kommt als n~er? whose turn is it next? ◆'n~beste, *adj.* (a) next best; (b) the first (hotel etc.) one comes across; *F:* any old (restaurant etc.). ◆'n~emal, *adv.* das n./beim nächstenmal, (the) next time. ◆'N~enliebe, *f* charity. ◆'n~ens, *adv.* shortly, soon. ◆'n~gelegene, *attrib. adj.* nearest (town, house etc.). ◆'n~liegende(r, s), *adj.* most obvious, first (question, etc.).

'nachstehen, *v.i.sep.irr.100* (haben) j-m an etwas *dat* n., to be inferior to s.o. in sth. ◆'n~d, *adj.* following; *adv.* below.

'nachstellen, *v.sep.* 1. *v.tr.* (a) to adjust (brakes etc.); (b) *Gram:* to postpone (a verb etc.). 2. *v.i.* (haben) *F:* einem Mädchen n., to pursue a girl.

'nachsuchen, *v.tr.sep.* (haben) (a) to search; (b) um etwas n. to ask for sth.

Nacht [naxt]. I. *f* -/¨e night; bei N., at night; bei N. und Nebel, under cover of darkness; (heimlich) furtively; über N., overnight. II. n., *adv.* heute n., (i) last night; (ii) tonight; Dienstag n., on Tuesday night. III. 'N~-, *comb.fm.* night (work, blindness, club, flight, life, train etc.; *Cin: TV:* late-night (programme, performance etc.). ◆'N~hemd, *n* nightshirt; (Frauenn.) nightdress, *F:* nightie. ◆'N~lokal, *n* nightspot. ◆'N~portier, *m* night porter. ◆'N~quartier, *n* shelter/

accommodation for the night. ◆'N~**ruhe**, f night's sleep. ◆'n~**s**, adv. at night; **n. um 3 (Uhr)**, at 3 (o'clock) in the morning. ◆'N~**schicht**, f night shift. ◆'N~**schwester**, f night nurse. ◆'N~**tisch**, m bedside table. ◆'N~**topf**, m chamber pot. ◆'N~**wache**, f night watch. ◆'N~**wächter**, m night watchman. ◆'N~**zeit**, f night-time; **zur N.**, at night.

'**Nachteil**, m disadvantage, drawback. ◆'n~**ig**, adj. disadvantageous; (schädlich) detrimental, damaging.

**nächt|elang** ['nɛçtəlaŋ], adj. lasting several nights; adv. night after night. ◆'n~**lich**, adj. nocturnal (habits, visit etc.); (darkness, stillness) of the night; night-time (theft etc.).

'**Nachtigall** ['naxtigal], f -/-en nightingale.

'**Nachtisch**, m dessert, Brit: sweet; **zum N.**, as dessert, Brit: F: for afters.

'**Nachtrag**, m -(e)s/-e supplement; postscript (to a report etc.). ◆'n~**en**, v.tr.sep.irr.85 (a) **j-m etwas n.**, (i) to walk behind s.o. carrying sth.; (ii) refuse to forgive s.o. for sth.; (b) (hinzufügen) to add (sth.).

**nachträglich** ['na:xtrɛkliç], adj. subsequent (remark, apology etc.); belated (greetings etc.); adv. later; subsequently.

'**nachtrauern**, v.i.sep. (haben) **j-m, etwas dat n.**, to bemoan the loss of s.o., sth.

'**Nachuntersuchung**, f Med: (postoperative etc.) checkup.

'**Nachwehen**, pl Med: afterpains.

'**Nachweis**, m -es/-e proof, evidence. ◆'n~**bar**, adj. demonstrable; Med: detectable (disease etc.); **es ist nicht n.**, it cannot be proved. ◆'n~**en**, v.tr.sep.irr.70 to prove (a fact, one's identity etc.); **man konnte ihm nichts n.**, it was impossible to pin anything on him.

'**Nachwelt**, f die N., posterity.

'**Nachwirkung**, f after-effect.

'**Nachwort**, n postscript (to a book).

'**Nachwuchs**. I. m 1. F: (Kinder) offspring. 2. (a) **musikalischer/wissenschaftlicher N.**, rising generation of musicians/scientists; (b) Com: trainees (in a firm etc.). II. N~-, comb.fm. (a) young, up and coming (player, actor, author etc.); (b) Com: trainee (salesman etc.).

'**nachzahl|en**, v.tr.sep. to pay (sth.) later/ (zusätzlich) extra. ◆'N~**ung**, f 1. subsequent payment. 2. back-payment.

'**nachzählen**, v.tr.sep. to re-count (money, votes etc.); to check (change etc.).

**Nachzügler** ['na:xtsy:klɐ], m -s/- latecomer; straggler (on a hike etc.).

**Nacken** ['nakən], m -s/- (nape of the) neck; Fig: **j-m im N. sitzen**, to breathe down s.o.'s neck; **er hatte die Polizei im N.**, the police were hard on his heels.

**nackt** [nakt]. I. adj. (a) naked (person,

body etc.); bare (arms, wall etc.); Art: etc: nude (model etc.); **mit n~em Oberkörper**, stripped to the waist; **sich n. ausziehen**, to strip (naked); (b) bare (facts, existence etc.); stark (poverty etc.); undisguised (hatred); **die n~e Wahrheit**, the plain truth. II. 'N~-, comb.fm. nude (bathing, photograph, dancer etc.). ◆'N~**heit**, f -/no pl nakedness, nudity. ◆'N~**kultur**, f nudism.

**Nadel** ['na:dəl]. I. f -/-n needle; (Steckn., Hutn., Haarn.) pin; Rec: stylus. II. 'N~-, comb.fm. (a) needle (size etc.); pin-(head etc.); (b) Bot: coniferous (forest etc.). ◆'N~**baum**, m coniferous tree, conifer. ◆'N~**kissen**, n pincushion. ◆'N~**stich**, m (i) pinprick; (ii) (Nähstich) stitch. ◆'N~**streifen**, mpl pinstripe.

**Nagel** ['na:gəl]. I. m -s/- nail; seine Stellung usw. **an den N. hängen**, to chuck in one's job etc.; **sich dat etwas unter den N. reißen**, to make off with sth. II. 'N~-, comb.fm. nail(-brush, -file etc.). ◆'N~**lack**, m nail varnish. ◆'n~**n**, v.tr. to nail (sth.) (**an etwas acc**, to sth.). ◆'n~**neu**, adj. F: brand-new. ◆'N~**schere**, f nail scissors.

**nag|en** ['na:gən], v. 1. v.i. (haben) (Tier) to gnaw, (Pers.) nibble (**an etwas dat**, at sth.); Fig: (Kummer, Zweifel usw.) **an j-m n.**, to prey on s.o.; **n~de Zweifel**, nagging doubt. 2. v.tr. to gnaw (sth.). ◆'N~**er**, m -s/-/'N~**etier**, n rodent.

**nah(e)** ['na:(ə)], adj. 1. (örtlich) near; **j-m, etwas dat n~(e)**, close to s.o., sth.; **n~e (gelegen)**, nearby (town, house etc.); **n~(e) bei der Kirche**, near the church. 2. (zeitlich) close, impending (event etc.); near (future); imminent (danger, departure etc.); **n~e bevorstehen**, to be imminent; (b) **den Tränen n~e**, on the verge of tears. 3. (eng, vertraut) close (relative, contact etc.); adv. **n~e verwandt**, closely related. ◆'N~**aufnahme**, f close-up. ◆'n~**e'bei**, adv. near/close by. ◆'n~**e'gehen**, v.i.sep.irr.36 (sein) to affect s.o. deeply. ◆'n~**e'kommen**, v.i.sep.irr.53 (sein) (a) **etwas dat n.**, to come close to sth.; (b) **j-m n.**, to get to know s.o. well. ◆'n~**e'legen**, v.tr.sep. **j-m etwas n.**, to recommend sth. (strongly) to s.o. ◆'n~**e'liegen**, v.i.sep.irr.62 (haben) to seem likely; (Idee usw.) to suggest itself. ◆'n~**e'liegend**, adj. likely; fair (assumption etc.); **aus n~eliegenden Gründen**, for obvious reasons. ◆'n~**en**, v.i. (sein) Lit: to draw near, approach. ◆'n~**e'stehen**, v.i.sep.irr.100 (haben) **j-m n.**, to be close to s.o./(sympathisieren) in sympathy with s.o. ◆'n~**e'zu**, adv. almost, nearly. ◆'N~**kampf**, m Mil: close combat. ◆'N~**ost**, inv. the Near East.

◆'N~verkehr, m Rail: Aut: local traffic. ◆'N~ziel, n short-term aim.

**Näh-** ['nɛː-], comb.fm. sewing (needle, silk, lesson, table etc.). ◆'n~en, v.tr. & i. (a) to sew; to make (a dress, curtains etc.); (b) to stitch up (a wound etc.). ◆'N~erin, f -/-nen needlewoman. ◆'N~garn, n sewing cotton. ◆'N~korb, m sewing basket, workbasket. ◆'N~maschine, f sewing machine.

**Nähe** ['nɛːə], f -/no pl nearness, proximity; **etwas aus der N. betrachten,** to have a close look at sth.; **in der N.,** nearby; **in der N. der Stadt,** near/close to the town; **in meiner N.,** near me/where I live. ◆'n~r, adj. (a) nearer, closer; shorter (route etc.); **n~re Verwandtschaft,** close relatives; adv. **j-n n. kennenlernen,** to get to know s.o. better; (b) (genauer) more detailed (examination etc.); **N~es/n~e Auskünfte,** further details/information. ◆'n~rkommen, v.i.sep.irr.53 (sein) **j-m n.,** to get to know s.o. better. ◆'n~rn, v.tr. (a) to move/bring sth. closer (**etwas dat,** to sth.); (b) **sich n.,** to come up (**j-m, etwas dat,** to s.o., sth.).

**nähren** ['nɛːrən], v.tr. (a) to feed (s.o., a baby etc.); **gut/schlecht genährt,** well-fed/undernourished; (b) Lit: to nurture (suspicion etc.). ◆'N~mittel, npl cereal products. ◆'N~stoff, m nutrient. ◆'N~wert, m food value.

**nahr|haft** ['naːrhaft], adj. nourishing, nutritious. ◆'N~ung, f -/no pl food. ◆'N~ungsmittel. I. n food item; pl foodstuffs. II. 'N~-, comb.fm. food (industry etc.).

**Naht** [naːt], f -/-e seam; Med: suture; **aus allen N~en platzen,** to burst at the seams. ◆'n~los, adj. seamless; Fig: smooth (transition etc.).

**naiv** [na'iːf], adj. naive. ◆N~ität [naivi'tɛːt], f -/no pl naiveté, ingenuousness.

**Nam|e** ['naːmə], m -ns/-n name; **nur dem N~en nach,** only by name; (nicht wirklich) nominally, in name only; **sich dat einen N~en machen,** to make a name for oneself. ◆'N~en-, comb.fm. (list, register etc.) of names. ◆'n~enlos, adj. unnamed, nameless (person, thing); unknown (hero etc.). ◆'n~ens, adv. by the name of, called. ◆N~ensschild, n nameplate. ◆'N~enstag, m name-day. ◆'N~ensvetter, m namesake. ◆'N~enszug, m signature. ◆'n~entlich, adv. 1. **j-n n. nennen,** to mention s.o. by name. 2. (besonders) especially, particularly. ◆'n~haft, adj. (a) renowned, celebrated (artist etc.); (b) (ansehnlich) considerable (sum, part etc.); (c) Jur: **den Täter n. machen,** to name the offender.

**nämlich** ['nɛːmliç], adv. namely; **er**

**konnte nicht kommen, er ist n. krank,** he couldn't come as he is ill.

**nanu** [na'nuː], int. well! well I never!

**Napf** [napf], m -(e)s/-e dish, bowl (for a dog etc.).

**Narb|e** ['narbə], f -/-n Med: scar. ◆'n~ig, adj. scarred.

**Narkose** [nar'koːzə], f -/-n narcosis; (N~mittel) anaesthetic. ◆'N~arzt, m anaesthetist.

**Narr** [nar], m -en/-en fool; **j-n zum N~en halten,** to make a fool of s.o. ◆'n~ensicher, adj. F: foolproof. ◆'n~ensicher, adj. (verrückt) mad, crazy (person, idea etc.).

**närrisch** ['nɛrɪʃ], adj. (verrückt) mad, crazy (person, idea etc.).

**Narzisse** [nar'tsɪsə], f -/-n narcissus; **gelbe N.,** daffodil.

**naschen** ['naʃən], v.tr. & i. (haben) to nibble (a cake etc.); **an etwas dat n.,** to nibble at sth.; **gerne n.,** to have a sweet tooth. ◆'n~haft, adj. fond of nibbling; sweet-toothed.

**Nase** ['naːzə], f -/-n nose; **immer der N. nach,** just follow your nose; (direkt) **vor der N.,** (right) under one's nose; F: **auf die N. fallen,** to fall flat on one's face; also Fig: to come a cropper; **von j-m, etwas dat die N. voll haben,** to be fed up with s.o., sth.; **j-n an der N. herumführen,** to pull the wool over s.o.'s eyes; **es ging nicht nach meiner N.,** things didn't go the way I wanted. ◆'N~en-, comb.fm. nose (drops etc.); (tip etc.) of the nose; nasal (spray etc.). ◆'N~enbein, n nasal bone. ◆'N~enbluten, n nose-bleed. ◆'N~enhöhle, f nasal cavity. ◆'N~enloch, n nostril. ◆'N~enrücken, m bridge of the nose. ◆'n~eweis. I. adj. precocious. II. N., m -es/-e know-all. ◆'N~horn, n rhinoceros.

**näseln** ['nɛːzəln], v.i. (haben) to speak through one's nose.

**naß** [nas], adj. wet. ◆'n~kalt, adj. cold and damp.

**Nässe** ['nɛsə], f -/no pl wetness; **bei N.,** in the wet; when wet. ◆'n~n, v.tr. to wet (one's bed etc.).

**Nation** [natsi'oːn], f -/-en nation. ◆n~al [-o'naːl]. I. adj. national. II. N~al-, comb.fm. national (flag, park, sport, pride etc.). ◆'N~alhymne f, national anthem. ◆'n~alisieren [-ali'ziːrən], v.tr. to nationalize (an industry etc.). ◆N~alisierung, f -/-en nationalization. ◆N~a'lismus, m -/no pl nationalism. ◆n~a'listisch, adj. nationalistic. ◆N~ali'tät, f -/-en nationality. ◆'N~almannschaft, f national team. ◆'N~alsozialismus, m National Socialism, Nazism. ◆'N~alsozialist, m National Socialist, Nazi.

**Natter** ['natər], f -/-n (esp. non-poisonous) snake, Z: colubrid; (Ringeln.) grass snake.

**Natur** [na'tuːr]. I. f -/-en 1. no pl nature; (Landschaft) countryside. 2. (a) (Wesen) nature; disposition; **die menschliche N.,** human nature; **sie ist von N. aus schüchtern,** she is shy by nature; (b) (*Mensch*) character. **II. N~-, n~-,** *comb.fm.* (a) natural (colour, law, talent, landscape, product etc.); (b) nature (description etc.). **◆N~alien** [-'rɑːliən], *pl* (a) natural produce; (b) **in N. bezahlen,** to pay in kind. **◆N~a'lismus,** *m -/no pl* naturalism. **◆n~a'listisch,** *adj.* naturalistic. **◆N~ell** [-u'rɛl], *n -s/-e* temperament, disposition. **◆N~erscheinung,** *f* natural phenomenon. **◆N~forscher,** *m* naturalist. **◆n~gemäß,** *adj.* 1. natural (way of life etc.). 2. *adv.* (*von sich aus*) by its very nature. **◆N~katastrophe,** *f* natural disaster. **◆n~rein,** *adj.* pure, unadulterated (honey, fruit-juice etc.). **◆N~schutz,** *m* nature conservation; **unter N. stehen,** to be a protected species. **◆N~schutzgebiet,** *n* nature reserve. **◆N~wissenschaft,** *f* (natural) science. **◆N~wissenschaftler(in),** *m(f)* scientist. **◆n~wissenschaftlich,** *adj.* scientific.

**natürlich** [na'tyːrliç], *adj.* (a) natural; (*ungekünstelt*) unaffected; **sich n. benehmen,** to behave naturally; (b) *adv.* of course, naturally. **◆'n~er'weise,** *adv.* naturally. **◆N~keit,** *f -/no pl* naturalness.

**Naut|ik** ['nautik], *f -/no pl* navigation, nautical science. **◆'n~isch,** *adj.* nautical.

**Navig|ation** [navigatsi'oːn], *f -/no pl* navigation. **◆N~ator** [-'gaːtɔr], *m -s/-en* [-ga'toːrən] navigator.

**Naz|i** ['naːtsi], *m -s/-s* Nazi. **◆N~ismus** [-'tsismus], *m -/no pl* Nazism.

**Nebel** ['neːbəl]. **I.** *m -s/-* fog; (leichter) N., mist; **bei N.,** in fog. **II. 'N~-, 'n~-,** *comb.fm.* (a) fog (bell, lamp etc.); (b) foggy (day, weather). **◆'N~horn,** *n* foghorn. **◆'n~ig = neblig.**

**neben** ['neːbən]. **I.** *prep.* 1. next to, beside; (a) (+) **er saß n. mir,** he sat next to/beside me; (b) (+) **er setzte sich n. mich,** he sat down next to/beside me. 2. (+) (*zusätzlich zu*) apart from, in addition to. 3. (+ *dat*) (*verglichen mit*) compared to/with. **II. N~-,** *comb.fm.* (a) (*zusätzlich*) extra, additional (work etc.); (b) (*untergeordnet*) subsidiary, secondary (meaning, form etc.); minor (figure etc.); (*beiläufig*) incidental, passing (remark etc.); (c) (*benachbart*) next (table, room etc.); nextdoor (house). **◆'n~amtlich,** *adj.* second, additional (employment etc.); **er macht das n.,** he does that as a spare-time job/*F:* sideline. **◆'n~an,** *adv.* next door; **im Zimmer n.,** in the next room. **◆'n~bei,** *adv.* 1. (*zusätzlich*) in addition; as well. 2. **n. bemerkt,** incidentally; **etwas n. erwähnen,** to mention sth. in passing. **◆'n~beruflich,** *adj.* spare-time (work); second (job).

**◆'N~beschäftigung,** *f* second job; (*in der Freizeit*) spare-time job. **◆'N~buhler(in),** *m -s/- (f -/-nen)* rival. **◆'n~einander,** *adv.* next to each other; side by side; **friedlich n. wohnen,** to live together in harmony. **◆'N~eingang,** *m* side entrance. **◆'N~fach,** *n* subsidiary/*N.Am:* minor subject. **◆'N~fluß,** *m* tributary. **◆'N~geräusch,** *n* background noise. **◆'n~her,** *adv.* in addition; as well. **◆'N~kosten,** *pl* additional expenditure/costs. **◆'N~mann,** *m* neighbour (at table etc.). **◆'N~produkt,** *n* by-product. **◆'N~rolle,** *f* minor/supporting part. **◆'N~sache,** *f* minor matter. **◆'n~sächlich,** *adj.* unimportant. **◆'N~satz,** *m* subordinate clause. **◆'N~straße,** *f* secondary/minor road; (*in der Stadt*) side street. **◆'N~verdienst,** *m* additional income. **◆'N~wirkung,** *f esp. Med:* side effect; *Fig:* spin-off.

**neblig** ['neːbliç], *adj.* foggy, misty.

**Necessaire** [nesɛ'sɛːr], *n -s/-s* 1. (*Reisen.*) toilet bag. 2. (*Näh.*) sewing kit.

**neck|en** ['nɛkən], *v.tr.* to tease (s.o.). **◆N~e'rei,** *f -/-en* 1. teasing. 2. teasing remark. **◆'n~isch,** *adj.* teasing (remark, manner etc.).

**Neffe** ['nɛfə], *m -n/-n* nephew.

**negativ** ['neːgatiːf]. **I.** *adj.* negative. **II. N.,** *n -s/-e Phot:* negative.

**Neger** ['neːgər], *m -s/-* negro. **◆'N~in,** *f -/-nen* negress.

**negieren** [ne'giːrən], *v.tr.* to negate (a fact etc.).

**nehmen** ['neːmən], *v.tr.irr.* to take (s.o., sth.); (a) **ich nehme ein Omelett,** I'll have an omelette; **Verantwortung auf sich n.,** to take on responsibility; **etwas an sich n.,** to take care of sth.; **etwas zu sich n.,** to eat sth.; **j-n zu sich n.,** to take s.o. in; **sich dat die Zeit für etwas n.,** to make time for sth.; *F:* **wie man's nimmt,** it depends how you look at it; (b) **j-m etwas n.,** to take sth. away from s.o.; **er nahm ihr die Sorgen,** he freed her of her worries; **sich dat etwas n.,** to help oneself to sth.; **was n. Sie pro Stunde?** how much do you charge per hour?

**Neid** [nait], *m -(e)s/no pl* envy, jealousy. **◆N~er** ['naidər], *m -s/-* **er hat viele N.,** there are many who envy him. **◆'n~isch** [-dɪʃ], *adj.* envious, jealous (**auf** j-n, **etwas** *acc,* of s.o., sth.). **◆'n~los,** *adj.* without envy.

**neig|en** ['naigən], *v.* 1. *v.tr.* to slant, incline (a surface etc.); to tilt (a glass, bottle etc.); (*beugen*) to bow, bend (one's head, body etc.); **sich n.,** to take sth. away from s.o.; **er nahm ihr die Sorgen,** he freed her of her worries; **sich dat etwas n.,** to help oneself to sth.; **was n. Sie pro Stunde?** how much do you charge per hour?

lean, tilt; (*Hang*) (downward) slope. **2.** (*a*) tendency, inclination (**zu** + *dat*, to); (*Anfälligsein*) susceptibility, (pre)disposition (**zur Trunksucht usw.**, to alcoholism etc.); (*b*) liking, (*Vorliebe*) predilection (**zu** + *dat*, for); **N. zu j-m spüren/fühlen**, to feel attracted to s.o. ◆'**N~ungswinkel**, *m* angle of inclination; rake.

**nein** [nain], *adv.* no; **mit (einem) N. antworten**, to answer in the negative. ◆'**N~stimme**, *f Pol:* no (vote).

**Nelke** ['nɛlkə], *f -/-n* **1.** *Bot:* carnation. **2.** *Cu:* (*Gewürzn.*) clove.

**nenn|en** ['nɛnən], *v.tr.irr.* (*a*) to name (a child, town etc.); to call (s.o. sth.); **sich ... n.**, (*Pers.*) to call oneself ..., (*Sache*) be called ...; (*b*) to give, state (one's name, a reason, price etc.); **ein Beispiel n.**, to give/quote an example. ◆'**n~enswert**, *adj.* significant, appreciable. ◆'**N~er**, *m -s/-* (*a*) *Mth:* denominator; (*b*) **etwas auf einen (gemeinsamen) N. bringen**, to reduce sth. to a common denominator. ◆'**N~ung**, *f -/-en* naming; mention. ◆'**N~wert**, *m Fin:* nominal/face value.

**Neon-** ['neːɔn-], *comb.fm.* neon- (light, tube etc.). ◆'**N~reklame**, *f* neon sign.

**Nepp** [nɛp], *m -s/no pl F:* daylight robbery. ◆'**n~en**, *v.tr. F:* to fleece (s.o.), rook (s.o.).

**Nerv** [nɛrf], *m -s/-en* nerve; **die N~en verlieren**, to lose one's nerve; **j-m den N. töten**, to drive s.o. mad; **es geht ihm auf die N~en**, it gets on his nerves. ◆'**N~en-, 'n~en-**, *comb.fm.* (*a*) (*nervlich*) nervous (illness, system etc.); (*b*) *Anat:* nerve (centre, cell etc.). ◆'**N~enarzt**, *m* neurologist. ◆'**N~enbündel**, *n* bundle of nerves. ◆'**N~enkitzel**, *m F:* thrill. ◆'**N~ensäge**, *f F:* pain in the neck; trial. ◆'**N~enzusammenbruch**, *m* nervous breakdown. ◆'**n~lich**, *adj.* nervous (strain etc.); **n. völlig am Ende sein**, to be a nervous wreck. ◆**n~ös** [nɛr'vøːs], *adj.* restless, fidgety (person); highly-strung (person, horse etc.); **dieser Lärm macht mich n.**, this noise gets on my nerves.

**Nervosität** [nɛrvozi'tɛːt], *f -/no pl* state of nerves; restlessness; irritability.

**Nerz** [nɛrts], *m -es/-e* (*a*) *Z:* mink; (*b*) (*N~mantel*) mink coat.

**Nessel** ['nɛsəl], *f -/-n* nettle.

**Nest** [nɛst], *n -(e)s/-er* **1.** nest. **2.** *F: Pej:* (*kleiner Ort*) **armseliges N.**, miserable hole. ◆'**N~häkchen**, *n F:* baby of the family; pet. ◆'**N~wärme**, *f Fig:* love and security (of a home).

**nesteln** ['nɛstəln], *v.i.* (*haben*) to fumble (**an etwas** *dat*, with sth.).

**nett** [nɛt], *adj.* nice; **n., daß du anrufst**, it's nice of you to call; **seien Sie bitte so n.**, would you please be so kind.

**netto** ['nɛto]. **I.** *adv. Com:* net. **II.** '**N~-**,

comb. fm. net (weight, income, profit etc.).

**Netz** [nɛts]. **I.** *n -es/-e* **1.** net; (*Spinnenn.*) (spider's) web; *Fig:* web (of lies etc.); **j-m ins N. gehen**, to fall into s.o.'s trap. **2.** system, network (of roads, railways etc.); *El: etc:* mains. **II.** '**N~-**, *comb.fm. El:* mains (connection, voltage etc.). ◆'**N~haut**, *f Anat:* retina. ◆'**N~karte**, *f -/-n Rail: etc:* area season ticket.

**neu** [nɔy]. **I.** *adj.* (*a*) new; **n.**, as good as/like new; **das ist mir n.**, that's news to me; **er ist ein n~er Mensch geworden**, he is a different person/a changed man; (*b*) (*erneut*) fresh (start, hope etc.); (*noch ein*) another; **aufs n~e/von n~em**, afresh; (*von vorn*) from scratch; **n. anfangen**, to start (all over) again; **es muß n. gestrichen werden**, it will have to be re-painted; (*c*) **die n~esten Nachrichten/Moden**, the latest news/fashions; **weißt du das N~este?** do you know the latest? **n. verheiratet**, newly married. **II.** '**N~-**, 'n~-, *comb.fm.* (*a*) new (start, snow, creation etc.); (*b*) (*erneut*) re-(orientation etc.). ◆'**N~anschaffung**, *f* (*Sache*) new acquisition. ◆'**n~artig**, *adj.* novel, of a new kind. ◆'**N~auflage**, *f* reprint; (*N~bearbeitung*) new edition. ◆'**N~bau**, *m* **1.** *no pl* rebuilding, reconstruction. **2.** new building/house. ◆'**n~erdings**, *adv.* lately; recently; **n. geht er allein zur Schule**, he recently started going to school by himself. ◆'**N~eröffnung**, *f* reopening. ◆'**N~erscheinung**, *f* new publication/ (*Platte*) release. ◆'**N~erung**, *f -/-en* innovation. ◆'**n~geboren**, *adj.* **n~geborenes Kind**, new-born baby; **sich wie n. fühlen**, to feel a different person. ◆'**N~heit**, *f -/-en* **1.** *no pl* newness; novelty (of an idea, design etc.). **2.** innovation, novelty. ◆'**N~igkeit**, *f -/ -en* (piece) of news. ◆'**N~jahr**, *n* New Year's Day; **pros(i)t N.!**, happy New Year! ◆'**n~lich**, *adv.* recently; the other day. ◆'**N~ling**, *m -s/-e* (*a*) novice, tyro; (*b*) newcomer. ◆'**n~modisch**, *adj.* highly fashionable (clothes etc.); ultra-modern (design etc.); *Pej:* newfangled (idea, machine etc.). ◆'**N~mond**, *m* new moon. ◆'**N~ordnung**, *f* reorganization. ◆'**N~regelung**, *f* revision; *Jur:etc:* reform. ◆'**n~reich**, *adj. Pej:* nouveau riche. ◆**N~'seeland**. *Pr.n.* -s. New Zealand. ◆**n~'seeländisch**, *adj.* New Zealand. ◆'**N~wert**, *m* value when new; *Com:* replacement value. ◆'**n~wertig**, *adj.* (as good) as new. ◆'**N~zeit**, *f* modern times. ◆'**n~zeitlich**, *adj.* up-to-date, modern (building, thinking etc.).

**Neugier** ['nɔygiːr], *f* curiosity. ◆'**n~ig**, *adj.* curious, *F:* nosey (person) (**auf j-n, etwas** *acc*, about s.o., sth.); inquisitive (glance etc.).

**neun** [nɔyn], *num.adj.* nine. ◆**'n~mal**, *adv.* nine times. ◆**'n~malklug**, *adj. F:* too clever by half. ◆**'n~te(r, s)**, *num.adj.* ninth. ◆**'N~tel**, *n -s/-* ninth. ◆**'n~zehn**, *num.adj.* nineteen. ◆**'n~zig**, *num.adj.* ninety.

**Neur|ologe** [nɔyro'lo:gə], *m -n/-n* neurologist. ◆**N~ologie** [-olo'gi:], *f -/no pl* neurology. ◆**N~ose** [-'ro:zə], *f -/-n* neurosis. ◆**n~otisch** [-'ro:tiʃ], *adj.* neurotic.

**neutral** [nɔy'trɑːl], *adj.* 1. neutral. 2. *Gram:* neuter. ◆**n~isieren** [-ali'ziːrən], *v.tr.* to neutralize (a country, acid etc.). ◆**N~i'tät**, *f -/no pl* neutrality.

**Neutrum** ['nɔytrum], *n -s/-tra & -tren Gram:* neuter noun.

**nicht** [niçt]. **I.** *adv.* not; **sie raucht n.**, she does not/*F:* doesn't smoke; (*momentan*) she is not/*F:* isn't smoking; (**bitte**) **n. füttern!** (please) do not feed! **ich auch n.**, nor I; **n. besser als**, no better than; **n. mehr und n. weniger**, neither more nor less; **n. doch!** don't! **bitte n.!** please don't! **es ist schön hier, n. (wahr)?** it's nice here, isn't it? **II.** **'N~-**, **'n~-**, *comb.fm.* non-(swimmer, member, recognition etc.). ◆**'N~achtung**, *f* disregard (of sth.); ignoring (of s.o.). ◆**'n~amtlich**, *adj.* unofficial. ◆**N~'angriffspakt**, *m* non-aggression treaty. ◆**'N~beachtung**, *f* disregard, ignoring. ◆**'n~ig**, *adj.* **1.** *Jur:* void, invalid. **2.** *Lit:* trivial, insignificant. ◆**'n~leitend**, *adj. El:* non-conducting. ◆**'N~raucher**, *m* non-smoker.

**Nichte** [niçtə], *f -/-n* niece.

**nichts** [niçts]. **I.** *indef.pron. & adj.* nothing; **ich weiß n. darüber**, I don't know anything about it; **das macht n.**, that doesn't matter; **ich habe n. dagegen**, I don't mind; **n. als Ärger**, nothing but trouble; **das ist n. für dich**, it is not your cup of tea/all wrong for you; **das führt zu n.**, it doesn't get you anywhere; *F:* **n. zu machen!** it can't be helped! **mir n., dir n.**, without so much as a by your leave; **n. da!** nothing doing! **n. Besonderes**, nothing special. **II.** **N.**, *n -/no pl* **1.** nothingness; (*Leere*) void; **wie aus dem N. auftauchen**, to appear from nowhere. **2.** (*Pers.*) a nonentity. ◆**'n~ahnend**, *adj.* unsuspecting. ◆**n~desto-'weniger**, *adv.* nevertheless. ◆**'n~nutzig**, *adj.* useless. ◆**'n~sagend**, *adj.* meaningless (remark etc.); blank (expression). ◆**'N~tun**, *n -s/no pl* idleness.

**Nickel** ['nikəl], *n -s/no pl* nickel.

**nick|en** ['nikən], *v.i.* (*haben*) to nod; **mit dem Kopf n.**, to nod one's head. ◆**'N~erchen**, *n -s/- F:* snooze, nap; **ein N. machen**, to have forty winks.

**nie** [niː], *adv.* never; **noch n.**, never before; **fast n.**, hardly ever; **n. mehr**, never again; **n. und nimmer**, never in a thousand years; *int.* (*ablehnend*) not on your

life!

**nieder** ['niːdər]. **I.** *adj.* low (wall, price, rank etc.); **n~e Beamte**, minor officials; low-grade civil servants. **II.** **N~-**, **n~-** *comb.fm.* low (pressure, frequency etc.); (to kneel, rain, sink etc.) down. ◆**'n~beugen**, *v.tr. sep.* **sich n~beugen**, to bend/bow down. ◆**'N~gang**, *m no pl Lit:* decline. ◆**'n~gehen**, *v.i.sep.irr.36* (*sein*) (*a*) (*Flugzeug usw.*) to land, touch down; (*b*) (*Boxer*) to go down, be floored; (*c*) (*Regen usw.*) to come down; (*Gewitter*) to burst. ◆**'n~geschlagen**, *adj.* dispirited, depressed. ◆**'N~geschlagenheit**, *f -/no pl* depression, dejection. ◆**'N~lage**, *f* defeat. ◆**'N~lande**. *Pr.n.pl* **die N.**, the Netherlands. ◆**'n~ländisch**, *adj.* (*a*) (*holländisch*) Dutch; Netherlands (government etc.); (*b*) *Hist:* (art etc.) of the Netherlands. ◆**'n~lassen**, *v.refl. sep.irr.57* (*a*) **sich (in einem Ort) n.**, to settle (in a place); (*b*) *Lit:* **sich (in einem Stuhl) n.**, to sit down (in a chair). ◆**'N~lassung**, *f -/-en* **1.** *no pl* settlement (of s.o., a tribe etc.); *Com:* establishment (of a firm etc.). **2.** *Com:* (*Zweign.*) branch. ◆**'n~legen**, *v.tr.sep.* (*a*) to lay down (one's arms etc.); **die Arbeit n.**, to down tools; **das Amt n.**, to resign; (*b*) **sich n.**, to lie down; (*c*) **etwas (schriftlich) n.**, to put sth. down (in writing). ◆**'n~machen**, *v.tr.sep. F:* to slaughter (people etc.). ◆**'N~sachsen**. *Pr.n.n -s.* Lower Saxony. ◆**'N~schlag**, *m Meteor:* precipitation; (*Regen*) rainfall; **radioaktiver N.**, (radioactive) fallout. ◆**'n~schlagen**, *v.tr. sep.irr.85* (*a*) to knock (s.o.) down; (*senken*) to lower (one's eyes); (*b*) **sich n.**, *Ch:* to precipitate; *Fig:* (*Erlebnisse, Gefühle usw.*) to find expression; (*c*) to suppress (a revolt, strike etc.). ◆**'n~schreiben**, *v.tr.sep.irr.12* to write (sth.) down. ◆**'N~schrift**, *f* (*a*) writing down, recording; (*b*) written record; (*Protokoll*) minutes. ◆**'n~setzen**, *v.tr.sep.* to put (sth.) down; **sich n.**, to sit down. ◆**'n~trächtig**, *adj.* base, vile; (*gemein*) mean, low (trick, lie etc.). ◆**'n~trächtigkeit**, *f -/-en* (*a*) *no pl* vileness, baseness; (*b*) mean trick. ◆**'N~ung**, *f -/-en* (piece of) low ground; (*Mulde*) hollow; **in den N~ungen**, on lower ground.

**niedlich** ['niːtliç], *adj.* sweet, dear (little); *N.Am:* cute.

**niedrig** ['niːdriç], *adj.* low; **von n~er Geburt/Herkunft**, of low birth/humble origins; **n~e Arbeit**, menial work. ◆**'n~wasser**, *n* low water.

**niemals** ['niːmɑːls], *adv.* never.

**niemand** ['niːmant]. **I.** *indef.pron.* nobody, no one; **von uns spricht n. Französisch**, none of us speaks French; **n. anders als**, none other than; **sonst n.**, nobody else. **II.** **N.**, *m -s/no pl* **ein N.**, a nobody/nonentity. ◆'N~sland, n no man's land.

**Niere** ['niːrə], f -/-n kidney. ◆'N~n-, comb.fm. kidney (stone, transplant etc.); renal (disease etc.). ◆'n~nförmig, adj. kidney-shaped.

**niesel|n** ['niːzəln], v.impers. es nieselt, it is drizzling. ◆'N~regen, m drizzle.

**niesen** ['niːzən], v.i. (haben) to sneeze.

**Niet** [niːt], m & n -(e)s/-e/'N~e¹, f -/-n Tchn: rivet; Cl: stud (on jeans etc.). ◆'n~en, v.tr. to rivet (metal sheets etc.).

**Niete²** ['niːtə], f -/-n 1. (Los) blank. 2. F: (Mißerfolg) flop, washout; (Pers.) dead loss.

**Nikotin** [niko'tiːn], n -s/no pl nicotine. ◆n~arm, adj. with a low nicotine content.

**Nil** [niːl]. Pr.n.m -s. the (river) Nile. ◆'N~pferd, n hippopotamus.

**nimmersatt** ['nimərzat]. I. adj. F: insatiable. II. N., m -(e)s/-e F: greedy-guts.

**nippen** ['nipən], v.i. (haben) to (take a) sip (an einem Glas, from a glass).

**Nippes** ['nip(ə)s], pl knick-knacks.

**nirgend|s** ['nirgənts]/'n~wo, adv. nowhere, not anywhere.

**Nische** ['niːʃə], f -/-n recess, alcove.

**nist|en** ['nistən], v.i. (haben) to nest. ◆'N~kasten, m nesting box.

**Nitrat** [ni'traːt], n -(e)s/-e Ch: nitrate.

**Niveau** [ni'voː], n -s/-s level; die Schüler haben ein hohes/niedriges N., the students' standard is high/low; N. haben, to have class/high standards.

**Nixe** ['niksə], f -/-n water nymph.

**nobel** ['noːbəl], adj. (edel) noble, high-minded; F: (großzügig) generous (tip etc.).

**noch** [nɔx]. I. adv. (a) still; n. nicht, not yet; es regnet kaum n., it is hardly raining any more; hast du n. Geld? do you have any money left? n. gestern habe ich ihn gesehen, I saw him only yesterday; (b) even; n. wärmer als gestern, even warmer than yesterday; (c) (zusätzlich) as well; (mit Zahlen) another; wer war n. da? who else was there? n. ein Bier bitte, another beer please; n. einmal, once more; again; sonst n. Fragen? (are there) any more questions? n. etwas, something else, another thing; (d) sei es n. so klein, however small it may be. II. conj. weder heute n. gestern, neither today nor yesterday. ◆'n~malig, adj. repeat, fresh (attempt etc.); (zusätzlich) further, additional. ◆'n~mals, adv. (once) again.

**Nockenwelle** ['nɔkənvɛlə], f camshaft.

**Nomad|e** [no'maːdə], m -n/-n nomad.

**Nomin|ativ** ['nominatiːf], m -s/-e Gram: nominative (case). ◆n~ieren [-'niːrən], v.tr. to nominate (a candidate etc.); Sp: to name (a team etc.).

**Nonne** ['nɔnə], f -/-n nun. ◆'N~n-kloster, n nunnery; convent.

**Nord** [nɔrt]. I. m north; aus/von N., from the north. II. 'N~-, 'n~-, comb.fm. (a) north (coast, side, bank, wind etc.); Geog: North (America, Germany, Pole etc.); (b) (nördlich) northern (frontier, edge, shore etc.); Northern (Ireland, England etc.). ◆'n~deutsch, adj. North German. ◆N~en ['nɔrdən], m -s/no pl north; nach N., northwards. ◆'n~isch, adj. Nordic (type, landscape etc.). ◆'N~'ost(en), m north-east. ◆n~'östlich. I. adj. north east(ern) (district etc.); north-easterly (wind, direction etc.). II. prep. + gen n. der Stadt, (to the) north-east of the town. ◆'N~see, f North Sea. ◆'N~stern, m pole star. ◆N~'west(en) m north-west. ◆n~'westlich. I. adj. north-west(ern) (district etc.); north westerly (wind, direction etc.). II. prep. + gen n. der Stadt, (to the) north-west of the town.

**nördlich** ['nœrtliç]. I. adj. northern (border, hemisphere etc.); northerly (wind, direction etc.); n. von Berlin, (to the) north of Berlin. II. prep. + gen n. der Stadt, (to the) north of the town.

**Nörg|elei** [nœrgə'lai], f -/-en grumbling, grousing. ◆'n~eln, v.i. (haben) to grumble, grouse, (kleinlich) niggle (an j-m, etwas dat, about s.o., sth.). ◆'N~ler, m -s/- grumbler.

**Norm** [nɔrm], f -/-en norm; standard (of behaviour, Ind: for a product etc.); moralische N~en, moral standards. ◆n~al [-'maːl]. I. adj. normal; (genormt) standard (size, measurement etc.). II. N~al-, comb.fm. (a) (genormt) standard (weight, size, format etc.); (b) normal (state, temperature etc.). ◆'N~al(benzin) n regular/two-star petrol; N.Am: low-octane gas. ◆n~alisieren [-ali'ziːrən], v.tr. to normalize (a situation etc.); (Lage usw.) sich n., to return to normal. ◆N~ali'tät, f -/no pl normality. ◆'n~en/n~ieren [-'miːrən], v.tr. to standardize (a product etc.). ◆'N~ung, f -/-en standardization.

**Norweg|en** ['nɔrveːgən]. Pr.n.n -s. Norway. ◆'N~er(in), m -s/- (f -/-nen) Norwegian. ◆'n~isch, adj./N., n -/no pl (Sprache) Norwegian.

**Nostalg|ie** [nɔstal'giː], f -/-n nostalgia. ◆n~isch [-'talgiʃ], adj. nostalgic.

**Not** [noːt]. I. f -/-e 1. no pl (a) need; (N~lage) predicament, plight; (Notwendigkeit) necessity; zur N., in a case of necessity/an emergency; (b) (Elend) hardship; (Armut) poverty; N. leiden, to suffer hardship; (c) (Bedrängnis) distress; seelische N., mental anguish. 2. (Schwierigkeit) difficulty; in N~en, in difficulties/trouble; mit knapper N., by the skin of one's teeth. II. 'N~-, comb.fm. emergency (lighting, service, operation, switch etc.); (behelfsmäßig) makeshift, temporary (solution, quarters etc.). ◆'**N~ausgang**, *m* emergency exit. ◆'**N~behelf**, *m* temporary measure; makeshift. ◆'**N~bremse**, *f* emergency brake; *Rail:* communication cord. ◆'**N~durft**, *f* -/no pl seine N. verrichten, to relieve oneself. ◆'**n~dürftig**, *adj.* scanty (clothing etc.); makeshift (repair, shelter etc.); etwas n. reparieren, to do a makeshift repair on sth. ◆'**N~fall**, *m* emergency; für den N., in case of need; im N., in an emergency. ◆'**n~falls**, *adv.* if need be. ◆'**n~gedrungen**, *adv.* out of necessity. ◆'**N~lage**, *f* plight; predicament. ◆'**n~landen**, *v.i.insep.* (sein) to make a forced landing. ◆'**N~landung**, *f* emergency/forced landing. ◆'**n~leidend**, *adj.* needy, destitute. ◆'**N~lüge**, *f* white lie. ◆'**N~ruf**, *m* emergency/*Nau: Av:* mayday call; (*Nummer*) emergency services number. ◆'**N~signal**, *n* distress signal. ◆'**N~stand**, *m* emergency; desperate situation; *Pol:* state of emergency. ◆'**N~verband**, *m* temporary bandage. ◆'**N~wehr**, *f* -/no pl self-defence. ◆'**n~wendig**, *adj.* necessary (operation, qualities, evil etc.); essential (equipment etc.); das N~ste, the bare essentials. ◆'**N~wendigkeit**, *f* -/-en necessity.

**Notar** [no'taːr], *m* -s/-e *Jur:* notary (public). ◆**n~i'ell**, *adj.* notarial; *adv.* by a notary.

**Note** ['noːtə], *f* -/-n 1. note; *pl* **N~n**, *Mus:* (printed/sheet) music; **N~n lesen**, to read music. 2. *Sch:* mark; *N.Am:* grade. 3. (*Merkmal*) character, aura; (*Stimmung*) atmosphere; persönliche N., personal touch. ◆'**N~nblatt**, *n* sheet of music. ◆'**N~nschlüssel**, *m Mus:* clef. ◆'**N~nständer**, *m* music stand.

**notier|en** [no'tiːrən], *v.* 1. *v.tr.* to make a note of (sth.); *Fb: etc:* den Namen eines Spielers n., to book a player. 2. *v.i.* (*haben*) *Com:* to be quoted (mit/zu + *dat*, at). ◆**N~ung**, *f* -/-en *Com:* quotation.

**nötig** ['nøːtiç], *adj.* necessary (zu + *dat*, for); j-n, etwas n. haben, to need s.o., sth.; hast du das n.? do you have to? ◆'**n~en**, *v.tr.* to force, compel (s.o.); ich sah mich genötigt, einzugreifen, I felt compelled to intervene; laß dich nicht n.! don't wait to be asked! ◆'**N~ung**, *f* -/-en *Jur:* intimidation (zu etwas *dat*, to commit sth.).

**Notiz** [no'tiːts], *f* -/-en 1. (*a*) note, memo; sich *dat* N~en machen, to take notes; (*b*) (*Zeitungsn.*) (short) article, item. 2. von j-m, etwas *dat* (keine) N. nehmen, to take (no) notice of s.o., sth. ◆**N~block**, *m* memo pad, jotter. ◆**N~buch**, *n* notebook.

**notorisch** [no'toːriʃ], *adj.* notorious.

**Nougat** ['nuːgat], *m & n* -s/-s nougat.

**Novelle** [no'vɛlə], *f* -/-n 1. novella, long

short story. 2. *Jur:etc:* amendment (to a law).

**November** [no'vɛmbər], *m* -(s)/- November.

**Nu** [nuː], *n F:* im N., in a jiffy/flash.

**Nuance** [ny'ãsə], *f* -/-n nuance.

**nüchtern** ['nʏçtərn], *adj.* (*nicht betrunken*) sober; (*sachlich*) matter-of-fact; (*vernünftig*) level-headed (person, appraisal etc.); n. betrachtet, viewed dispassionately; etwas auf n~en Magen trinken, to drink sth. on an empty stomach. ◆'**N~heit**, *f* -/no pl sobriety, level-headedness.

**Nudel** ['nuːdəl], *f* -/-n 1. *Cu:* noodle; *pl* **N~n**, pasta. 2. *F:* (*Pers.*) eine (komische) N., a funny creature. ◆'**N~holz**, *n* rolling pin. ◆'**N~suppe**, *f* noodle soup. ◆'**N~teig**, *m* pasta dough.

**nuklear** [nukle'aːr], *adj.* nuclear.

**null** [nʊl]. I. *num.adj.* nought, *esp. N.Am:* zero; n. Fehler, no/zero mistakes; n. Uhr, midnight; n. Komma fünf (0,5), nought point five (0·5); n. Grad, zero (degrees); *Sp:* zwei zu n., two-nil; (*Tennis*) dreißig-n., thirty-love; *Jur:* n. und nichtig, null and void. II. N., *f* -/-en (*a*) (*Ziffer*) nought, *N.Am:* zero; (*b*) no *pl* (*Zahl*) zero; fünf Grad unter N., five degrees below zero; seine Chancen sind gleich N., his chances are nil; (*c*) *Pej:* (*Pers.*) eine N., a nonentity. ◆'**N~diät**, *f* starvation diet. ◆'**N~punkt**, *m* zero (point).

**numer|ieren** [numə'riːrən], *v.tr.* to number (pages, tickets etc.). ◆**n~isch** [nu'meːriʃ], *adj.* numerical.

**Nummer** ['nʊmər], *f* -/-n (*a*) number; *Aut:* eine Bonner N., a Bonn registration/*N.Am:* plate; (*b*) issue, copy (of a magazine etc.); (*c*) size (of shoes etc.); (*d*) (*Darbietung*) number, item; (*im Zirkus usw.*) act. ◆'**N~nschild**, *n Aut:* number/*N.Am:* license plate.

**nun** [nuːn], *adv.* (*a*) now; was n.? what now/next? n. gerade! now more than ever! das ist n. mal so, that's just the way it is; (*b*) well; n., wie geht's? well now, how are you? n. gut/schön, all right then.

**nur** [nuːr], *adv.* only; warum hat er das n. getan? why ever did he do that? n. keine Angst! just don't you worry! wenn sie n. käme! if only she would come! ich bin nicht krank, n. müde, I'm not ill, just tired.

**Nürnberg** ['nʏrnbɛrk]. *Pr.n.n* -s. Nuremberg.

**nuscheln** ['nʊʃəln], *v.i.* (*haben*) *F:* to mumble.

**Nuß** [nʊs], *f* -/Nüsse nut. ◆'**N~baum**, *m* walnut tree. ◆'**N~knacker**, *m* -s/- nut-cracker. ◆'**N~schale**, *f* (*a*) nutshell; (*b*) *Fig:* (*Boot*) tiny little tub.

**Nüster** ['nyːstər], *f* -/-n *usu.pl* **N~n**, nostrils.

**Nut** [nuːt], *f* -/-en/'**N~e**, *f* -/-n *Tchn:* groove, slot.

**Nutte** ['nutə], *f -/-n P:* tart; *N.Am:* broad.

**nutz|bar** ['nutsbɑːr], *adj.* usable, exploitable (resources etc.). ◆**n~en. I.** *v.tr. & i.* (*haben*) = **nützen. II. N.,** *m -s/no pl* use; **wenig N. haben,** to be of little use/benefit; (**j-m**) **von N. sein,** to be useful/of use (to s.o.). ◆**'n~los,** *adj.* useless; futile, pointless (conversation etc.); vain, futile (attempts, efforts etc.). ◆**'N~losigkeit,** *f -/no pl* uselessness; pointlessness; futility. ◆**'N~nießer,** *m -s/-* exploiter. ◆**'N~ung,** *f -/-en* exploitation (of land, resources).

**nütz|e** ['nytsə], *adj.* (**zu**) **etwas/nichts n. sein,** to be some/no use. ◆**'n~en,** *v.* **1.** *v.i.* (*haben*) to be of use/useful (j-m, to s.o.); **das nützt nichts,** that's no use. **2.** *v.tr.* to make use of (sth.); to take advantage of (an opportunity etc.); to exploit (land, water power etc.). ◆**'n~lich,** *adj.* useful (j-m, to s.o.); helpful (person, advice etc.). ◆**'N~lichkeit,** *f -/no pl* usefulness.

**Nymph|e** ['nymfə], *f -/-n* nymph. ◆**N~omanin** [-'oːmaːnin], *f -/-nen* nymphomaniac.

# O

**O, o** [oː], *n -/-* (the letter) O, o.

**Oase** [o'ɑːzə], *f -/-n* oasis.

**ob** [ɔp], *conj.* whether; (*a*) **ob er wohl kommt?** I wonder if he will come? (*b*) **als ob,** as if/though; (*c*) *F:* (**na**) **und ob!** and how! sure thing! **und ob ich's gelesen habe!** you bet I've read it!

**Obacht** ['oːbaxt], *f -/no pl* attention; **auf etwas** *acc* **O. geben,** to pay attention to sth.

**Obdach** ['ɔpdax], *n -(e)s/no pl* shelter. ◆**'o~los,** *adj.* homeless. ◆**'O~losigkeit,** *f -/no pl* homelessness.

**Obduktion** [ɔpduktsi'oːn], *f -/-en* post mortem.

**O-Beine** ['oːbainə], *npl* bow-legs.

**oben** ['oːbən], *adv.* (*a*) at the top; (*o~drauf*) on top; (**an der Oberfläche**) on the surface; **das dritte von o.,** the third from the top; **von o. bis unten,** from top to bottom; (*Pers.*) from head to foot; (*b*) (**über dem Sprecher**) above, overhead; **hier/dort o.,** up here/there; **hoch o.,** high up/above; (*c*) (*Richtung*) **nach o.,** upwards; **mit dem Gesicht nach o.,** face up; (*d*) (**im Buch**) **siehe o.,** see above. ◆**'o~'an,** *adv.* at the top. ◆**'o~'auf,** *adv.* (*a*) on (the) top; (*b*) *Fig:* (*Pers.*) **o. sein,** to be in good form. ◆**'o~'drein,** *adv.* besides; what is more. ◆**'o~genannt,** *adj.* above-mentioned.

**Ober¹** ['oːbər], *m -s/-* waiter.

**Ober-²,** *comb.fm.* (*a*) upper (arm, deck, jaw, lip etc.); (*b*) (*Rang*) senior (*Sch:* classes etc.); (*leitend*) chief (inspector etc.). ◆**'O~arzt,** *m* senior registrar. ◆**'O~befehlshaber,** *m* supreme commander. ◆**'O~begriff,** *m* generic term. ◆**'O~bekleidung,** *f* outer garments. ◆**'O~bürgermeister,** *m* first mayor of a city). ◆**'o~e(r,s),** *adj.* upper; (*höchste*) top. ◆**'O~fläche,** *f* surface. ◆**'o~flächlich,** *adj.* superficial. ◆**'O~flächlichkeit,** *f -/no pl* superficiality. ◆**'O~geschoß,** *n* upper storey. ◆**'o~halb,** *prep.* + *gen.* above. ◆**'O~haupt,** *n* head of state, the family etc.). ◆**'O~haus,** *n Pol:* Upper

House. ◆**'O~hemd,** *n* (man's) shirt. ◆**'O~in,** *f -/-nen* (*a*) *Ecc:* mother superior; (*b*) *Med:* matron. ◆**'O~kellner,** *m* head waiter. ◆**'O~körper,** *m* (upper) torso. ◆**'O~leitung,** *f El:* overhead wires. ◆**'O~licht,** *n* (*Fenster*) skylight. ◆**'O~schenkel,** *m* thigh. ◆**'O~schwester,** *f* ward sister. ◆**'O~seite,** *f* upper side; right side (of cloth, wallpaper etc.). ◆**'O~st,** *m -en & -s/-en* colonel. ◆**'o~ste(r,s),** *adj.* (*a*) top, uppermost; (*b*) supreme, highest (rank). ◆**'O~teil,** *n Cl: etc:* top (part). ◆**'O~wasser,** *n Fig:* **O. haben** to be in a strong position.

**obgleich** [ɔp'glaiç], *conj.* although.

**Obhut** ['ɔphuːt], *f -/no pl Lit:* care; *Jur:* custody (of a child etc.); **er ist in guter O.,** he is well looked after.

**Objekt** [ɔp'jɛkt], *n -(e)s/-e* object; *Com:* (*Verkaufso.*) item.

**Objektiv¹** [ɔpjɛk'tiːf], *n -s/-e Phot:* lens.

**objektiv²,** *adj.* objective; actual (conditions, facts etc.). ◆**O~ität** [-tivi'tɛːt], *f -/no pl* objectivity.

**Oblate** [o'blaːtə], *f -/-n Ecc:* wafer.

**obligatorisch** [ɔbliga'toːriʃ], *adj.* compulsory.

**Oboe** [o'boːə], *f -/-n* oboe.

**Obrigkeit** ['oːbriçkait], *f -/-en* *A: & Hum:* **die O.,** the powers that be.

**ob'schon,** *conj.* although.

**obskur** [ɔps'kuːr], *adj.* obscure; (*zwielichtig*) dubious, shady (figure etc.).

**Obst** [oːpst]. **I.** *n -(e)s/no pl coll.* fruit. **II.** **'O~-,** *comb.fm.* fruit (juice, knife, salad, tree etc.). ◆**'O~garten,** *m.* orchard. ◆**'O~händler,** *m* fruiterer. ◆**'O~kuchen,** *m*/**'O~torte,** *f* fruit flan/*N.Am:* pie.

**obszön** [ɔps'tsøːn], *adj.* obscene. ◆**O~ität** [-tsøni'tɛːt], *f -/-en* obscenity.

**ob'wohl,** *conj.* although.

**Ochs|e** ['ɔksə], *m -n/-n* **1.** ox. **2.** *F:* (*Pers.*) fool, oaf. ◆**'O~enschwanz,** *m* oxtail. ◆**'O~enzunge,** *f* ox tongue.

**Ocker** ['ɔkər], *m -s/no pl* ochre.

**Öde** ['ø:də]. **I.** f -/no pl (a) desert, waste-land; (b) Fig: desolation, solitude. **II.** ö., adj. barren (landscape); desolate (place, Fig: existence etc.).

**oder** ['o:dər], conj. or; F: **das magst du doch, o.?** you like that, don't you?

**Ofen** ['o:fən], m -s/- (a) (zum Heizen) stove; **(elektrischer) O.**, electric fire; (b) Ind: furnace, kiln; (c) Cu: (Backo.) oven. ◆**'O~rohr**, n stovepipe.

**offen** ['ɔfən], adj. (a) open; (nicht abgeschlossen) unlocked; (Haare) loose, untied; o~e Weine, wines by the glass; auf o~er Strecke, on an open stretch (of road/rail); o~e Stellen, vacant posts, vacancies; (b) (Pers.) frank, candid; o. gesagt/gestanden, frankly; to be frank. ◆**'o~bar**, adj. obvious. ◆**o~'baren**, v.tr. insep. to reveal (a secret, oneself etc.) (j-m, to s.o.). ◆**O~'barung**, f -/-en Ecc. revelation. ◆**'o~halten**, v.tr.sep.irr.45 to hold (a door etc.) open (j-m, for s.o.); to keep (one's eyes, a shop etc.) open. ◆**'O~heit**, f -/no pl openness, frankness. ◆**o~herzig**, adj. 1. open-hearted, unreserved. 2. Hum: (dress) with a plunging neckline. ◆**'o~kundig**, adj. obvious. ◆**'o~lassen**, v.tr.sep.irr.57 (a) to leave (sth.) open; (b) to leave (a space etc.) blank; (c) to leave (a question) undecided. ◆**'o~sichtlich**, adj. obvious, evident. ◆**'o~stehen**, v.i.irr.sep.100 (haben) (a) (Tür usw.) to be open; (b) (Rechnung usw.) to be outstanding/unpaid.

**offensiv** [ɔfɛn'zi:f], adj. Mil: offensive (weapons etc.); Sp: attacking (game). ◆**O~e** [-'zi:və], f -/-n Mil: offensive; Sp: attack.

**öffentlich** ['œfəntliç], adj. public; Pol: etc: open (session); etwas ö. erklären, to state sth. publicly. ◆**'O~keit**, f -/no pl die (breite) Ö., the (general) public; unter Ausschluß der Ö., behind closed doors; etwas an die Ö. bringen, to publicize sth.

**Offerte** [ɔ'fɛrtə], f -/-n offer.

**offiziell** [ɔfitsi'ɛl], adj. official.

**Offizier** [ɔfi'tsi:r], m -s/-e officer.

**öffn|en** ['œfnən], v.tr. (a) to open (sth.); to undo (a zip), unbutton (a coat etc.); (b) j-m ö., to open the door to s.o.; (c) (Tür usw.) sich ö., to open. ◆**'Ö~er,** m s/- opener. ◆**'O~ung,** f -/-en (a) opening; (b) hole, gap (in a wall etc.). ◆**'O~ungszeiten,** fpl hours of opening/Com: business.

**oft** [ɔft], adv. often, frequently; des öfteren, repeatedly.

**ohne** ['o:nə]. **I.** prep. + acc. (a) without; o. mich! count me out! (b) excluding; o. den Fahrer waren wir sechs Personen, there were six of us, not counting the driver; (c) F: nicht o., not bad; (schwierig) pretty tough. **II.** conj. sie tat es, o. daß er es merkte, she did it without him noticing. ◆**'o~gleichen**, pred.adj.

matchless, incomparable. ◆**'o~'hin**, adv. anyway, in any case.

**Ohnmacht** ['o:nmaxt], f -/-en (a) powerlessness, impotence; (b) Med: faint; (Zustand) unconsciousness; in O. fallen, to faint.

**ohnmächtig** ['o:nmɛçtiç], adj. (a) powerless; (b) Med: unconscious; o. werden, to faint/pass out.

**Ohr** [ø:r], n -(e)s/-e eye (of a needle etc.).

**Ohr** [o:r], n -(e)s/-en (a) ear; ganz O. sein, to be all ears; es ist mir zu O~en gekommen, daß ..., it has come to my attention that ...; j-m eins hinter die O~en hauen, to box s.o.'s ears; sich aufs O. legen, to take a nap; (b) j-n übers O. hauen, to rip s.o. off. ◆**'O~enarzt**, m. ear (nose and throat) specialist. ◆**'o~enbetäubend**, adj. ear-splitting. ◆**'O~ensausen**, n noises/singing in the ears. ◆**'O~feige**, f slap in the face. ◆**'o~feigen**, v.tr. to slap (s.o.) (in the face). ◆**'O~läppchen**, n -s/- earlobe. ◆**'O~ring**, m earring. ◆**'O~wurm**, m 1. earwig. 2. F: (catchy) hit tune.

**Ökolog|ie** [økolo'gi:], f -/no pl ecology. ◆**ö~isch** [-'lo:gif], adj. ecological.

**Ökonomie** [økono'mi:], f -/-n 1. economics. 2. (Sparsamkeit) economy. ◆**ö~isch** [-'no:mif], adj. 1. economic. 2. (sparsam) economical.

**Oktave** [ɔk'ta:və], f -/-n octave.

**ökumenisch** [øku'me:nif], adj. ecumenical.

**Öl** [ø:l]. **I.** n -(e)s/-e oil. **II.** 'Öl-, comb.fm. oil-(field, -firing, -can, Aut: change etc.). ◆**'Olheizung,** f oil-fired (central) heating. ◆**'ölig,** adj. oily. ◆**'Olmeßstab,** m Aut: dipstick. ◆**'Olquelle,** f oilwell. ◆**'Olsardine,** f tinned sardine (in oil). ◆**'Olschicht,** f film of oil. ◆**'Olstand,** m oil level. ◆**'Olteppich,** m oil slick. ◆**'Olung,** f -/-en anointment; Ecc: die letzte Ö., extreme unction. ◆**Ölzeug,** n oilskins.

**Oliv|e** [o'li:və], f -/-n olive. ◆**O~en-,** comb.fm. olive (tree, oil etc.). ◆**o~grün,** adj. olive-green.

**Olympiade** [olympi'a:də], f -/-n Sp: Olympic Games. ◆**o~isch,** adj. Olympic.

**Oma** ['o:ma], f -/-s F: granny.

**Omelett** [ɔm(ə)'lɛt], n -(e)s/-e & -s omelette.

**Omen** ['o:mən], n -s/- omen.

**ominös** [omi'nø:s], adj. ominous; (verdächtig) suspicious, odd (taste etc.).

**Omnibus** ['ɔmnibus], m -ses/-se bus; Brit: (für lange Strecken) coach.

**Onkel** ['ɔŋkəl], m -s/- uncle.

**Opa** ['o:pa], m -s/-e F: grandpa.

**Opal** [o'pa:l], m -s/-e opal.

**Oper** ['o:pər], f -/-n 1. opera. 2. (Gebäude) opera house. ◆**'O~n-,** comb.fm. operatic (aria, composer etc.); opera (guide, singer, house etc.). ◆**'O~n-**

**glas,** *n* opera glasses.

**Operation** [operatsi'o:n], *f -/-en Med: Mil: etc:* operation. ◆**O~s-,** *comb.fm.* (*a*) *Mil:* (area, plan etc.) of operations; (*b*) *Med:* operating (team, table etc.). ◆**O~ssaal,** *m* operating theatre/*N.Am:* room.

**Operette** [opə'rɛtə], *f -/-n* operetta.

**operieren** [opə'ri:rən], *v.* 1. *v.i.* (*haben*) *Med: Mil: etc:* to operate. 2. *v.tr. Med:* to operate on (s.o.); **er wurde gestern operiert,** he had an operation yesterday.

**Opfer** ['ɔpfər], *n -s/-* (*a*) sacrifice; (*b*) victim (of an accident etc.); **einer Täuschung usw. zum O. fallen,** to be the victim of a deception etc. ◆**o~n,** *v.tr.* to sacrifice (*Fig:* one's health etc.), give up (one's free time etc.); **sein Leben o.,** to lay down one's life. ◆**O~-stock,** *m Ecc:* offertory box.

**Opium** ['o:pium], *n -s/no pl* opium.

**opportun** [opɔr'tu:n], *adj.* opportune. ◆**O~ist** [-'nist], *m -en/-en* opportunist.

**Opposition** [ɔpozitsi'o:n], *f -/-en* opposition (**gegen** + *acc,* to); **in O. zu j-m, etwas** *dat* **stehen,** to be opposed to s.o., sth.

**Optik** ['ɔptik], *f -/no pl* optics. ◆**O~er,** *m -s/-* optician.

**optimal** [ɔpti'ma:l], *adj.* optimum. ◆**O~ismus** [-'mismus], *m -/no pl* optimism. ◆**O~ist(in),** *m -en/-en* (*f -/-nen*) optimist. ◆**o~istisch,** *adj.* optimistic.

**optisch** ['ɔptiʃ], *adj.* 1. optical (system, illusion etc.). 2. visual (impression, signal etc.).

**Orakel** [o'ra:kəl], *n -s/-* oracle.

**Orange** [o'raŋʒə], *f -/-n* orange. ◆**o~(farben),** *adj* orange(-coloured). ◆**O~at** [-'ʒa:t], *n -s/-e* candied orange peel. ◆**O~nschale,** *f* orange peel.

**Orchester** [ɔr'kɛstər]. I. *n -s/-* orchestra. II. **O~-,** *comb.fm.* orchestral (concert, music etc.).

**Orchidee** [ɔrçi'de:(ə)], *f -/-n* orchid.

**Orden** ['ɔrdən], *m -s/-* 1. *Ecc:* order. 2. *Mil: etc:* decoration, medal.

**ordentlich** ['ɔrdəntliç], *adj.* 1. (*a*) neat, tidy (person, room etc.); (*b*) (*anständig*) respectable (family etc.); (*c*) **o~es Mitglied,** ordinary/full member (of an association etc.); **o~er Professor,** (full) professor. 2. *F:* (*richtig*) proper (meal etc.); **eine o~e Tracht Prügel,** a sound thrashing.

**ordinär** [ɔrdi'nɛ:r], *adj.* common, vulgar (person etc.).

**ordnen** ['ɔrdnən], *v.tr.* to put (sth.) into order; to order, arrange (sth.).

**Ordner** ['ɔrdnər], *m -s/-* 1. file, *esp.* ring binder. 2. (*Pers.*) steward.

**Ordnung** ['ɔrdnuŋ], *f -/-en* (*a*) order; (*b*) orderliness, tidiness; **O. schaffen,** to tidy up; (*c*) **in O.,** all right; (*Papiere usw.*) in order. ◆**O~samt,** *n* Public Order Office (issuing passports, permits etc.).

◆**'o~sgemäß,** *adj.* correct, according to the regulations. ◆**'o~swidrig,** *adj.* contrary to the regulations. ◆**'O~s-zahl,** *f* ordinal number.

**Organ** [ɔr'ga:n], *n -s/-e* 1. *Anat:* organ. 2. (*a*) publication; (*b*) *Pol:* **das ausführende O.,** the executive body. ◆**o~isch,** *adj.* organic (disease etc.). ◆**O~ismus** [-ga'nismus], *m. -/-men* organism; *Anat:* system.

**Organisation** [ɔrganizatsi'o:n], *f -/-en* organization. ◆**O~ator** [-'za:tɔr], *m -s/en* organizer. ◆**o~ieren** [-'zi:rən], *v.tr.* to organize (a conference etc.); **sich o.,** to form an organization/*Ind:* a union.

**Organist(in)** [ɔrga'nist(in)], *m -en/-en* (*f -/-nen*) organist.

**Orgel** ['ɔrgəl], *f -/-n* organ. ◆**'O~konzert,** *n* organ recital.

**Orgie** ['ɔrgiə], *f -/-n* orgy.

**Orient** ['o:riɛnt], *m -s/no pl* **der O.,** the Orient. ◆**O~ale** [orien'ta:lə], *m -n/-n* (*Pers.*) Oriental. ◆**o~alisch,** *adj.* oriental.

**orientier|en** [orien'ti:rən], *v.tr.* (*a*) **j-n/sich über etwas** *acc* **o.,** to inform s.o./oneself about sth.; **gut orientiert,** well-informed; (*b*) **sich o.,** to get one's bearings. ◆**O~ung,** *f -/-en* (*a*) orientation; (*O~ssinn*) sense of direction; (*b*) *Pol: etc:* alignment. ◆**O~ungspunkt,** *m* landmark.

**Original** [origi'na:l]. I. *n -s/-e* (*a*) original; (*b*) *Fig:* **er ist ein O.,** he is quite a character. II. **o.,** *adj.* (*a*) original; (*b*) (*echt*) **o. indischer Tee,** genuine Indian tea. ◆**O~ausgabe,** *f* first edition. ◆**O~fassung,** *f* original version; ◆**O~ität** [-nali'tɛ:t], *f -/no pl* originality; (*Echtheit*) authenticity. ◆**O~übertragung,** *f Rad: TV:* live transmission.

**originell** [origi'nɛl], *adj.* original.

**Orkan** [ɔr'ka:n], *m -(e)s/-e* hurricane.

**Ornament** [ɔrna'mɛnt], *n -(e)s/-e* ornament.

**Ort** [ɔrt], *m -(e)s/-e* (*a*) (*Stelle*) place; **an O. und Stelle,** (i) in the proper place; (ii) (*sogleich*) on the spot; **am O. des Verbrechens,** at the scene of the crime; (*b*) (*Ortschaft*) locality; (*Dorf*) village; (*Stadt*) town; **sie wohnen am O.,** they live locally. ◆**'o~en,** *v.tr.* to locate, pinpoint the position of (a ship, aircraft etc.). ◆**'O~s-,** *comb.fm.* local (knowledge, traffic, time etc.). ◆**'O~schaft,** *f -/-en* village; (*Stadt*) town. ◆**'o~sfremd,** *adj.* **ich bin hier o.,** I am a stranger here. ◆**'O~sgespräch,** *n* local call. ◆**'O~sname,** *m* place name. ◆**'O~snetz,** *n* local telephone system. ◆**'O~sschild,** *n* place-name sign. ◆**'O~sung,** *f -/no pl* position-finding, location.

**örtlich** ['œrtliç], *adj.* local. ◆**Ö~keit,** *f -/-en* locality.

**orthodox** [ɔrto'dɔks], *adj.* orthodox.

**Orthograph|ie** [ɔrtogra'fi:], *f -/no pl*

orthography, spelling. ◆o~isch ['graːfiʃ], adj. orthographical; o~ischer **Fehler,** spelling mistake.

**Orthopäd|e** [ɔrtoˈpɛːdə], m -n/-n orthopaedic surgeon; o~isch, adj. orthopaedic.

**Öse** ['øːzə], f -/-n **Haken und Ö.,** hook and eye.

**Ost-** [ɔst-], comb.fm. (a) east (coast, side, bank, wind etc.); East (Germany, Indies etc.); (b) (östlich) eastern (frontier etc.). ◆'O~block, m Pol: Eastern Bloc. ◆'o~deutsch, adj. East German. ◆'O~en, m -s/no pl east; aus dem/von **O.,** from the east; nach **O.,** eastwards; (Lage) in the east. ◆'O~politik, f policy towards Eastern Europe. ◆'O~see, Pr.n.f -. die **O.,** the Baltic. ◆'o~wärts, adv. eastwards.

**Oster-** ['ɔstər-], comb.fm. Easter (Sunday, Monday, rabbit etc.). ◆'O~ei, n

Easter egg. ◆'O~glocke, f daffodil. ◆'O~n, n -/- Easter; zu **O.,** at Easter.

**Österreich** ['øːstərraiç], Pr.n.n -s. Austria. ◆'ö~isch, adj. Austrian.

**östlich** ['œstliç]. I. adj. eastern (border, France etc.); easterly (wind, direction etc.); ö. von Bonn, (to the) east of Bonn. II. prep. + gen ö. der **Stadt,** to the east of the town.

**Otter¹** [ɔtər], m -s/- Z: otter.

**Otter²,** f -/-n Z: & Fig: viper.

**Ouvertüre** [uvɛrˈtyːrə], f -/-n overture.

**Oval** [oˈvaːl]. I. n -s/-e oval. II. o., adj. oval.

**Ovation** [ovatsiˈoːn], f -/-en ovation.

**Oxyd** [ɔkˈsyːt], n -(e)s/-e oxide. ◆o~ieren [-yˈdiːrən], v.tr. & i. (haben) to oxidize.

**Ozean** ['oːtseaːn], m -s/-e ocean.

**Ozon** [oˈtsoːn], n -s/no pl ozone.

# P

**P, p** [peː], n -/- (the letter) P, p.

**Paar** [paːr]. I. n -(e)s/-e pair; (Mann und Frau) couple. II. p., inv. adj. ein p., a few; **alle p. Tage,** every few days; **vor ein p. Tagen,** a few/couple of days ago. ◆'p~en v.tr. (a) to mate (animals, birds); die Vögel p. sich, the birds are mating; (b) to combine (qualities etc.). ◆'P~lauf, m pairs skating. ◆'p~mal, adv. ein p., a few times. ◆'P~ung, f -/-en (a) Z: Orn: mating; (Kreuzung) crossing; (b) coupling. ◆'p~weise, adv. in pairs; two by two.

**Pacht** [paxt], f -/-en lease. ◆'p~en, v.tr. to lease, rent (a farm etc.). ◆'P~vertrag, m lease, tenancy agreement.

**Pächter** ['pɛçtər], m -s/- leaseholder, tenant.

**Pack¹** [pak], m -(e)s/-e package, bundle (of papers). ◆**Pack²,** n -(e)s/no pl Pej: rabble, riffraff. ◆'P~eis, n pack-ice. ◆'p~en. I. v.tr. (a) to pack (one's clothes, goods, a suitcase etc.); to wrap up (a parcel etc.); (b) to grab, seize (s.o.) (am Kragen usw., by the collar etc.), grasp (s.o.'s hand etc.); Fig: to thrill (an audience etc.); Fig: von Angst gepackt, gripped/seized with fear; (c) F: p. wir's noch? will we make it? II. 'P~en, m -s/- (large) pack, bundle (of washing etc.). ◆'p~end, adj. gripping, riveting; thrilling (spectacle). ◆'P~er(in), m (f -/-nen) packer. ◆'P~esel, m F: (Pers.) beast of burden; drudge. ◆'P~papier, n (brown) wrapping paper. ◆'P~ung, f -/-en 1. packet, esp. N.Am: pack (of cigarettes etc.); 2er-P., double pack. 2. Med: pack. ◆'P~zettel, m packing slip.

**Päckchen** ['pɛkçən], n -s/- packet, esp.

N.Am: pack; (Paket) small parcel.

**Pädagog|e** [pɛdaˈgoːgə], m -n/-n (Lehrer) educator, N.Am: instructor. ◆P~ik, f -/no pl educational theory; pedagogy. ◆p~isch, adj. educational, teaching (methods etc.); p~ische Hochschule, teacher training college.

**Paddel** ['padəl], n -s/- paddle. ◆'P~boot, n canoe. ◆'p~n, v.i. (haben/sein) to paddle, canoe.

**paffen** ['pafən], v.tr. & i. (haben) to puff (smoke, steam).

**Page** ['paːʒə], m -n/-n page boy. ◆'P~nkopf, m page-boy hairstyle.

**Paket** [paˈkeːt]. I. n -(e)s/-e parcel; N.Am: package. II. 'P~-, comb.fm. parcel (post etc.); parcels (counter etc.). ◆P~annahme, f parcels counter.

**Pakistaner(in)** [paːkiˈstaːnər(in)], m -s/- (f -/-nen) Pakistani. ◆p~isch, adj. Pakistani.

**Pakt** [pakt], m -(e)s/-e Pol: etc: pact, (Vertrag) treaty.

**Palast** [paˈlast], m -(e)s/=e palace.

**Palästin|a** [palɛsˈtiːna]. Pr.n.n -s. Geog: Palestine. ◆P~enser [-ˈnɛnzər], m -s/- & p~ensisch, adj. Palestinian.

**Palaver** [paˈlaːvər], n -s/- endless discussion, palaver. ◆p~n, v.i. (haben) to discuss endlessly.

**Palette** [paˈlɛtə], f -/-n 1. Art: palette. 2. Ind: Rail: pallet.

**Palme** ['palmə], f -/-n palm (tree); F: j-n **auf die P. bringen,** to drive s.o. up the wall.

**Pampelmuse** [pampəlˈmuːzə], f -/-n grapefruit.

**pampig** ['pampiç], adj. F: (frech) rude, stroppy.

**panieren** [paˈniːrən], v.tr. to bread.

**Pani|k** ['paːnik], f -/no pl panic. ◆'p~sch, adj. panic-stricken, frantic;

p~sche Angst haben to be terrified.
**Panne** ['panə], f -/-n (a) Tchn: & Fig:
breakdown; (b) F: (Fehler) cock-up.
**Panorama** [pano'rɑːma], n -s/-men panorama.
**pan(t)schen** ['pan(t)ʃən], v. 1. v.tr. to
adulterate, F: (wine, milk etc.). 2.
v.i. F: (Kind) to splash about.
**Panther** ['pantər], m -s/- Z: panther.
**Pantoffel** [pan'tɔfəl], m -s/-n (bedroom)
slipper. ◆P~held, m F: henpecked
husband.
**Pantomime** [panto'miːmə]. 1. f -/-n
mime (show). 2. m -n/-n (Pers.) mime.
**Panzer** ['pantsər]. I. m -s/- 1. Hist: armour; ein P., a suit of armour. 2. Mil:
tank. 3. Z: shell (of a crab etc.). II.
P~-, comb.fm. (gepanzert) armoured
(Nau: cruiser, Mil: brigade, division,
corps, regiment etc.). ◆P~faust, f
Mil: bazooka. ◆P~glas, n bullet-proof
glass. ◆'p~n, v.tr. to armour-plate (a
ship, vehicle). ◆P~ung, f -/-en
armour(-plating). ◆P~wagen, n armoured car.
**Papa** [pa'pɑː], m -s/-s F: papa, daddy.
**Papagei** [papa'gai], m -s/-en parrot.
**Papier** [pa'piːr]. I. n -s/-e 1. no pl paper.
2. pl papers, documents. II. P~-,
comb.fm. paper (money etc.). ◆P~-
fabrik, f papermill. ◆P~korb, m waste
paper basket. ◆P~krieg, m F: (yards
of) red tape. ◆P~schlangen, fpl paper
streamers. ◆P~taschentuch, n paper
handkerchief; tissue.
**Papp|(en)deckel** ['pap(ən)dɛkəl], m card-
board. ◆P~e, f -/-n cardboard; F:
nicht von P. sein, to be quite something.
◆'p~en, v.tr. & i. (haben) F: to stick,
(mit Klebstoff) glue (sth.). ◆'P~enstiel,
m F: das ist keinen P. wert! I wouldn't
give twopence for it! für einen P., for a
song. ◆p~erla'papp, int. nonsense!
◆p~ig, adj. (klebrig) sticky; (breiig)
mushy.
**Pappel** ['papəl], f -/-n poplar.
**Paprika** ['paprika], m -s/-(s) (a) (sweet)
pepper; (b) (Gewürz) paprika.
◆'P~schote, f (single) pepper.
**Papst** [pɑːpst], m -(e)s/-e pope.
**päpstlich** ['pɛːpstliç], adj. papal.
**Parade** [pa'rɑːdə], f -/-n Mil: parade,
march-past. ◆P~stück, n showpiece.
**Paradies** [para'diːs], n -es/-e paradise.
◆p~isch [-'diːzif], adj. heavenly; delightful.
**paradox** [para'dɔks], adj. paradoxical.
**Paragraph** [para'grɑːf], m -en/-en Jur:
section, article (of a law); clause (of a
contract).
**parallel** [para'leːl]. I. adj. & adv. parallel
(mit/zu etwas dat, with/to sth.). II. P~-,
comb.fm. parallel (case, Sch: class etc.).
◆P~e, f -/-n parallel. ◆P~ogramm
[-elo'gram], n -s/-e parallelogram.
◆P~straße, f street running parallel.
**Paranuß** ['pɑːranus], f brazil nut.

**Parasit** [para'ziːt], m -en/-en parasite.
**parat** [pa'rɑːt], adj. & adv. ready.
**Pärchen** ['pɛːrçən], n -s/- (esp. young)
couple.
**Pardon** [par'dõː], m -s/-s P.! sorry! excuse me!
**Parfüm** [par'fyːm], n -s/-e perfume;
scent. ◆p~ieren [-fy'miːrən], v.tr. to
perfume (sth.).
**parieren** [pa'riːrən], v. 1. v.tr. to ward off
(an attack etc.), parry (a blow). 2. v.i.
(haben) F: to toe the line.
**Parität** [pari'tɛːt], f -/-en parity.
◆p~isch, adj. with equal rights.
**Park** [park]. I. m -s/-s park. II. 'P~-,
comb.fm. Aut: parking (light, fee, disc
etc.). ◆'p~en, v.tr. & i. (haben) Aut:
(Pers.) to park (a car); (Auto) to be
parked. ◆'P~haus, n multi-storey car
park. ◆'P~lücke, f parking space.
◆'P~platz, m (a) car park, N.Am:
parking lot; (b) (P~lücke) parking space.
◆'P~uhr, f parking meter. ◆'P~-
verbot, n parking ban; hier ist P.,
there's no parking here.
**Parkett** [par'kɛt], n -(e)s/-e 1. (P~boden)
parquet floor; (Tanzp.) dance floor. 2.
Th: Cin: stalls.
**Parlament** [parla'mɛnt], n -(e)s/-e parliament. ◆p~arisch [-'tɑːriʃ], adj. parliamentary. ◆P~s-, comb.fm. parliamentary (committee, elections etc.); parliament (building etc.). ◆P~smitglied n,
member of parliament.
**Paro|die** [paro'diː], f -/-n parody (auf et-
was acc, of sth.). ◆p~'dieren, v.tr. to
parody (s.o., sth.).
**Parole** [pa'roːlə], f -/-n (a) Mil: etc: password; (b) Pol: etc: slogan.
**Partei** [par'tai]. I. f -/-en 1. side; Pol:
Jur: Com: party; für/gegen j-n P. ergreifen, to side with/against s.o. 2. (Mieter)
tenant. II. P~-, comb.fm. party
(leadership etc.). ◆p~isch, adj. biased,
prejudiced. ◆p~los, adj. independent.
◆p~politisch, adj. party political.
◆P~programm, n party manifesto.
◆P~tag, m party conference/N.Am:
convention.
**Parterre** [par'tɛr]. I. n -s/-s 1. ground/
N.Am: first floor. 2. Th: stalls. II. p.,
adv. on the ground/N.Am: first floor.
**Partie** [par'tiː], f -/-n 1. part. 2. (a) (Spiel)
game (of chess, tennis etc.); round (of
golf etc.); (b) Com: batch (of goods); (c)
eine gute/schlechte P., a good/bad
match; (d) F: mit von der P. sein, to be
in on it.
**Partikel** [par'tiːkəl], n -s/- particle.
**Partisan** [parti'zɑːn], m -s & -en/-en partisan, guer(r)illa.
**Partitur** [parti'tuːr], f -/-en Mus: score.
**Partizip** [parti'tsiːp], n -s/-ien Gram: participle.
**Partner(in)** ['partnər(in)], m -s/- (f -/
-nen) partner. ◆'P~schaft, f -/-en
partnership. ◆'P~schaftlich, adj.

p~schaftliches Verhältnis, partnership.
◆'P~stadt, f twin town.

Party ['pɑːrti], f -/-s party.

Parzelle [par'tsɛlə], f -/-n plot (of land),
N.Am: lot.

Paß [pas]. I. m -sses/-sse 1. passport. 2.
(mountain etc.) pass. 3. Fb: etc: pass. II.
'P~-, comb.fm. passport (office, control
etc.). ◆P~bild, n passport photograph.
◆P~straße, f (road leading over a)
pass.

passabel [pa'saːbəl], adj. reasonable,
tolerable; adv. reasonably well.

Passag|e [pa'saːʒə], f -/-n passage.
◆P~ier [-a'ʒiːr], m -s/-e passenger.
◆P~ierschiff, n -(e)s/-e passenger
liner.

Passant [pa'sant], m -en/-en passer-by.

passen ['pasən], v. 1. v.i. (haben) (a) (die
richtige Größe haben) to fit; das Kleid
paßt (dir) gut, the dress fits (you)/is a
good fit (on you); (b) (geeignet sein) to be
suitable (zu j-m, etwas dat, for s.o.,
sth.); der Hut paßt zum Kleid, the hat
matches/goes with the dress; sie p./p.
nicht zueinander, (Pers.) they are well/
ill-matched; (c) (gelegen sein) to be convenient (j-m, for s.o.); heute paßt (es) mir
besser, today is better for me; dein Benehmen paßt ihm nicht, he doesn't like
your behaviour; das könnte dir so p.!
you'd like that, wouldn't you! (d) (Kartenspiel) (ich) passe, (I) pass; no bid; F:
da muß ich p., there you have me. 2.
v.tr. (einfügen) to insert (sth.). ◆p~d,
adj. (a) (geeignet) suitable; appropriate
(behaviour, gift etc.); opportune (moment etc.); apt, fitting (remark etc.);
right, proper (place, time, words etc.);
(b) matching (colour, hat, tie etc.).

passier|bar [pa'siːrbaːr], adj. passable.
◆p~en, v. 1. v.tr. (a) to pass (a house,
s.o.); to pass through (a town etc.); to
pass over, cross (a bridge, frontier etc.);
(b) Cu: to strain (soup etc.). 2. v.i. (sein)
to happen; ihm ist nichts passiert, he's
all right/unhurt. ◆P~schein, m pass;
permit.

Passion [pasi'oːn], f -/-en (a) passion; (b)
Ecc: Passion. ◆p~iert [-o'niːrt], adj.
enthusiastic, keen.

passiv ['pasif]. I. adj. passive; non-active
(member etc.); Com: adverse (balance of
trade). II. P~, Gram: passive (voice).

Paste ['pastə], f -/-n paste.

Pastell [pas'tɛl]. I. n -(e)s/-e Art: pastel
(drawing). II. P~-, comb.fm. pastel
(colour, painting etc.).

Pastete [pas'teːtə], f -/-n Cu: 1. (meat
etc.) pie; (Königinp.) vol-au-vent. 2. (Le-
berp.) pâté.

pasteurisieren [pastøri'ziːrən], v.tr. to
pasteurize (milk etc.).

Pastille [pas'tilə], f -/-n pastille, lozenge.

Pastor ['pastor], m -s/-en pastor, minister.

Pat|e ['paːtə], m -n/-n godfather; pl P~n,
godparents. ◆P~enkind, n godchild.

◆'P~enonkel, m godfather. ◆'P~en-
sohn, m godson. ◆'P~entochter, f
goddaughter. ◆'P~in, f -/-nen godmother.

Patent [pa'tɛnt]. I. n -(e)s/-e Jur: patent.
II. p., adj. F: neat, ingenious; p~er
Kerl, great guy; (Mädchen) good sort.
III. P~-, comb.fm. patent (law etc.);
P~amt n, Patent Office. ◆p~ieren
[-'tiːrən], v.tr. to patent (an invention).

Pater ['paːtər], m -s/- & Patres Ecc:
father.

path|etisch [pa'teːtiʃ], adj. emotional,
passionate (speech etc.). ◆P~os
['paːtɔs], n -/no pl emotionalism.

Patholog|e [pato'loːgə], m -n/-n patholo-
gist. ◆P~ie [-lo'giː], f -/-n pathology.
◆p~isch [-'loːgiʃ], adj. pathological.

Patience [pasi'ɑ̃s], f -/-n (Spiel) patience;
P~n legen, to play patience.

Patient(in) [patsi'ɛnt(in)], m -en/-en (f -/
-nen) patient.

Patriot|(in) [patri'oːt(in)], m -en/-en (f -/
-nen) patriot. ◆p~isch, adj. patriotic.
◆P~ismus [-o'tismus], m -/no pl patriotism.

Patron(in) [pa'troːn(in)], m -s/- (f -/-nen)
Ecc: patron saint.

Patrone [pa'troːnə], f -/-n cartridge.

Patrouill|e [pa'truljə], f -/-n Mil: etc:
patrol. ◆p~ieren [-ul'jiːrən], v.i. (haben)
to (go on) patrol.

patsch [patʃ], int. splash! (Schlag) slap!
◆'P~e, f -/-n F: mess; in der P.
sitzen/stecken, to be in a jam.
◆'p~en, v.i. (haben/occ. sein) F: (a) (im
Wasser) to splash; (b) (klatschen) to
smack. ◆'p~naß, adj. F: soaking wet.

patz|en ['patsən], v.i. (haben) F: to make
a slip, boob. ◆'P~er, m -s/- F: slip.
◆'p~ig, adj. F: impudent.

Pauk|e ['paukə], f -/-n Mus: kettledrum;
pl P~n, timpani; Fig: mit P~n und
Trompeten, Hum: resoundingly; F: auf
die P. hauen, (i) to paint the town red;
(ii) (prahlen) to blow one's own trumpet.
◆'p~en, v. 1. v.i. (haben) Sch: F: to
cram, swot. 2. v.tr. Sch: F: to swot (sth.)
up. ◆'P~er, m -s/- Sch: F: (Lehrer)
teacher; Pej: crammer.

pausbäckig ['pausbɛkiç], adj. chubby-
faced.

pauschal [pau'ʃaːl], adj. & P~-,
comb.fm. (einheitlich) flat-rate (fee etc.);
(inklusiv) lump (sum etc.); all-in (price);
Fig: general, Pej: sweeping (judgment
etc.). ◆P~e, f -/-n lump sum.
◆P~reise, f package tour.

Paus|e1 ['pauzə], f -/-n pause; Sch: break;
Th: interval; Cin: N.Am: intermission;
Mus: rest. ◆'p~enlos, adj. ceaseless,
incessant; p. arbeiten, to work non-stop.
◆p~ieren [-'ziːrən], v.i. (haben) to
take a break/rest.

Paus|e2, f -/-n tracing. ◆'P~papier, n
tracing paper.

Pavian ['paːviaːn], m -s/-e Z: baboon.

**Pavillon** [pavil'jɔn], *m* -s/-s pavilion, annexe (of a school, hospital).

**Pazifi|k** [pa'tsi:fik]. *Pr.n.m* -s. **der P.**, the
Pacific. ◆**p~sch**, *adj.* **der P~sche
Ozean**, the Pacific (Ocean). ◆**P~smus**
[-i'fismus], *m* -/*no* *pl* pacifism.
◆**P~st(in)**, *m* -en/-en (*f* -/-nen) &
**p~stisch**, *adj.* pacifist.

**Pech** [pɛç], *n* -s/*no* *pl* **1.** pitch. **2.** bad
luck; **P. haben**, to be unlucky.
◆'p~'schwarz, *adj.* pitch-black (darkness etc.); jet-black (hair etc.).
◆'P~strähne, *f* run of bad luck.
◆'P~vogel, *m* unlucky person.

**Pedal** [pe'daːl], *n* -s/-e pedal.

**Pedant** [pe'dant], *m* -en/-en pedant.
◆**P~e'rie**, *f* -/-n pedantry. ◆**p~isch**,
*adj.* pedantic.

**Pediküre** [pedi'ky:rə], *f* -/-n *no* *pl* chiropody; pedicure.

**Pegel** ['pe:gəl], *m* -s/- water level indicator. ◆**P~stand**, *m* water level.

**peilen** ['pailən], *v.tr. & i.* (*haben*) *Nau:
Av:* to take a bearing on a point etc.;
*Rad:* to detect (the direction of) (sth.).

**Pein** [pain], *f* -/*no* *pl* *Lit:* anguish; (mental) agony. ◆'p~igen, *v.tr.* to torment
(s.o.). ◆'p~lich, *adj.* embarrassing,
awkward (moment, silence etc.); painful
(scene etc.); **es ist mir sehr p.**, I feel
very embarrassed about it; **p. genau**,
scrupulously exact; painstaking. ◆'P~-
lichkeit, *f* -/-en awkwardness, embarrassment.

**Peitsch|e** ['paitʃə], *f* -/-n whip.
◆'p~en, *v.tr. & i.* (*haben*) to whip
(s.o., an animal); *Fig:* (*Regen usw.*) to
lash (**gegen** + *acc.*, against).

**Pekinese** [peki'ne:zə], *m* -n/-n pekinese.

**Pelikan** ['pe:likɑːn], *m* -s/-e pelican.

**Pell|e** ['pɛlə], *f* -/-n peel (of potatoes,
fruit); (sausage) skin; *F:* **j-m auf die P.
rücken**, (*bedrängen*) to pester s.o.
◆'p~en, *v.tr.* to peel (potatoes etc.); to
shell (an egg); (*Haut*) **sich p.**, to peel.
◆'P~kartoffeln, *fpl* potatoes boiled in
their skins.

**Pelz** [pɛlts]. **I.** *m* -es/-e fur. **II.** 'P~-,
*comb.fm.* fur (jacket, coat etc.).
◆'P~jäger, *m* trapper. ◆'P~tier, *n*
animal with a valuable fur.

**Pendel** ['pɛndəl], *n* -s/- pendulum.
◆'p~n, *v.i.* (*a*) (*haben*) to swing (to
and fro); *Fig:* to vacillate; (*b*) (*sein*)
(*Pers.*) to commute. ◆'P~uhr, *f* pendulum clock. ◆'P~verkehr, *m Rail: etc:*
shuttle service; (*für Pendler*) commuter
service.

**Pendler** ['pɛndlər], *m* -s/- commuter.

**penetrant** [pene'trant], *adj.* penetrating;
(*also Fig: Pers:*) overpowering.

**penibel** [pe'ni:bəl], *adj.* (*übergenau*) pedantic.

**Penis** ['pe:nis], *m* -/-se & *Penes* penis.

**pennen** ['pɛnən], *v.i.* (*haben*) *P:* to kip,
have a kip.

**Pension** [pɑ̃zi'oːn], *f* -/-en **1.** (*a*) (*Rente*)

pension; (*b*) (*Ruhestand*) **in P.**, retired. **2.**
(*a*) (*Hotel*) boarding-house, guesthouse;
(*b*) (*Kost*) **volle/halbe P.**, full/half board.
◆**P~är(in)** [-io'nɛːr(in)], *m* -s/-e (*f* -/-
nen) pensioner. ◆**p~ieren** [-o'ni:rən],
*v.tr.* to retire (s.o.). ◆**P~s-**, *comb.fm.*
retirement (age etc.).

**Pensum** ['pɛnzuːm], *n* -s/-sen & -sa (allotted) material, (*Aufgabe*) task.

**per** [pɛr], *prep.* + *acc* (*a*) by; **p. Post, Zug
usw.**, by post, train etc.; (*b*) *Com:* (*ab*) as
from.

**perfekt** [pɛr'fɛkt]. **I.** *adj.* (*a*) perfect;
faultless (French etc.); (*b*) (*abgemacht*)
settled. **II. P.**, *n* -s/-e *Gram:* perfect
(tense). ◆**P~ion** [-tsi'oːn], *f* -/*no* *pl*
perfection.

**Perfor|ation** [pɛrforatsi'oːn], *f* -/-en per-
foration. ◆**p~ieren** [-'ri:rən], *v.tr.* to
perforate (sth.).

**Pergament** [pɛrga'mɛnt], *n* -(e)s/-e
parchment. ◆**P~papier**, *n* greaseproof
paper.

**Period|e** [peri'oːdə], *f* -/-n period.
◆**p~isch**, *adj.* periodical.

**Peripherie** [perife'riː], *f* -/-n periphery;
(*Stadtrand*) outskirts.

**Perl|e** ['pɛrlə], *f* -/-n pearl; (*Glas*-,
*Holz*p. *usw.*) bead; *Fig:* gem. ◆'p~en,
*v.i.* (*haben*) (*Sekt usw.*) to bubble; (*Tropfen*) to run down. ◆'P~en-, *comb.fm.*
pearl (fisher, diver etc.). ◆'P~enkette
*f*, pearl necklace. ◆**P~mutt** [pɛrl'mut],
*n* -s/*no* *pl* mother of pearl. ◆'P~wein,
*m* sparkling wine.

**perplex** [pɛr'plɛks], *adj.* perplexed,
puzzled.

**Pers|er** ['pɛrzər], *m* -s/- (*a*) (*Pers.*) Per-
sian; (*b*) (*Teppich*) Persian carpet.
◆'P~erin, *f* -/-nen Persian woman.
◆'P~erteppich, *m* Persian carpet.
◆**P~ianer** [-zi'ɑːnər], *m* -s/- Persian
lamb (skin/coat). ◆'p~isch, *adj.* Persian.

**Person** [pɛr'zoːn], *f* -/-en (*a*) person; **die
Geduld in P.**, patience personified; **ich
für meine P.**, as for me; for my part;
(*b*) **pl zehn P~en**, ten people; (*c*) *Th:
Lit:* character. ◆**P~al** [-zo'nɑːl], *n* -s/
*no* *pl* staff; personnel. ◆**P~al-**,
*comb.fm.* **1.** personnel (department etc.);
staff (costs etc.). **2.** personal (description,
*Gram:* pronoun etc.). ◆**P~alausweis**,
*m* identity card. ◆**P~alchef(in)** *m* (*f*)
personnel manager. ◆**P~alien**
[-o'nɑːliən], *fpl* personal data.
◆**P~en-**, *comb.fm.* passenger (vehicle
etc.). ◆**P~enaufzug**, *m* passenger lift/
*N.Am:* elevator. ◆**P~enkraftwagen**,
*m* passenger/private car. ◆**P~enzug**, *m* stopping train; *N.Am:* local train.
◆**p~ifi'zieren**, *v.tr.* to personify (beauty etc.).

**persönlich** [pɛr'zøːnliç], *adj.* personal; **p.
erscheinen**, to appear in person.
◆**P~keit**, *f* -/-en personality.

**Perspektive** [pɛrspɛk'tiːvə], *f* -/-n perspective; (*Blickpunkt*) viewpoint.
**Peru** [pe'ruː]. *Pr.n.n* -s. Peru. ◆**P~aner(in)** [-u'ɑːnər(in)], *m* -s/- (*f* -/-nen) & **p~anisch**, *adj.* Peruvian.
**Perücke** [pe'rykə], *f* -/-n wig.
**pervers** [pɛr'vɛrs], *adj.* perverse. ◆**P~sion** [-zi'oːn], *f* -/-en perversion. ◆**P~sität** [-zi'tɛːt], *f* -/-en perversity.
**Pessimis|mus** [pɛsi'mismus], *m* -/no pl pessimism. ◆**P~t(in)**, *m* -en/-en (*f* -/-nen) pessimist. ◆**p~tisch**, *adj.* pessimistic.
**Pest** [pɛst], *f* -/no pl Med: plague; **er haßt sie wie die P.**, he hates her guts.
**Petersilie** [petər'ziːliə], *f* -/-n parsley.
**Petroleum** [pe'troːleum], *n* -s/no pl paraffin, N.Am: kerosene. ◆**P~lampe**, *f* oil lamp.
**Petunie** [pe'tuːniə], *f* -/-n petunia.
**petzen** ['pɛtsən], *v.tr. & i.* (*haben*) Sch: F: to tell tales.
**Pfad** [pfɑːt], *m* -(e)s/-e path. ◆**P~finder**, *m* -s/- boy scout.
**Pfahl** [pfɑːl], *m* -(e)s/-e post. ◆**P~bau**, *m* pile dwelling.
**Pfalz** [pfalts], *f* -/-en **die P.**, the Palatinate.
**Pfand** [pfant], *n* -(e)s/-er (*Bürgschaft*) security; (*Flaschenp. usw.*) deposit; (*Spielp.*) forfeit. ◆**P~haus**, *n* 'P~leihe, *f* -/-en pawnshop. ◆**P~leiher**, *m* -s/- pawnbroker.
**pfänd|en** ['pfɛndən], *v.tr.* to seize (property etc.) as security. ◆**P~erspiel**, *n* (game of) forfeits. ◆**P~ung**, *f* -/-en *Jur:* seizure.
**Pfann|e** ['pfanə], *f* -/-n Cu: (frying) pan. ◆'**P~kuchen**, *m* -s/- pancake; **Berliner P.**, doughnut.
**Pfarr-** ['pfar-], *comb.fm. Ecc:* parish (district, church etc.). ◆**P~er**, *m* -s/- vicar; parson; (*katholischer P.*) (parish) priest. ◆**P~haus**, *n* vicarage.
**Pfau** [pfau], *m* -(e)s/-en peacock. ◆'**P~enauge**, *n* peacock butterfly.
**Pfeffer** ['pfɛfər], *m* -s/- 1. pepper. 2. F: (*Schwung*) pep. ◆'**P~korn**, *n* peppercorn. ◆**P~kuchen**, *m* approx. = gingerbread. ◆'**P~minz(bonbon)**, *n* -es/-e peppermint (sweet). ◆'**P~minze**, *f* peppermint. ◆'**P~mühle**, *f* peppermill. ◆'**p~n**, *v.tr.* to pepper (food); *Fig:* to spice (a speech etc.) (with jokes etc.).
**Pfeif|e** ['pfaifə], *f* -/-n 1. whistle; pipe (of an organ). 2. (*Tabaksp.*) pipe. ◆'**p~en**, *v.irr.* 1. *v.tr.* to whistle (a tune etc.); to play (a tune) on a (penny) whistle. 2. *v.i.* (*haben*) (*a*) to whistle; (*b*) *P:* **ich pfeife auf dein Geld!** you can keep your money! ◆'**P~en-**, *comb.fm.* pipe (smoker, cleaner, tobacco etc.). ◆'**P~er**, *m* -s/- whistler; *Mus:* piper. ◆'**P~konzert**, *n* chorus of whistles/catcalls.
**Pfeil** [pfail], *m* -(e)s/-e arrow.

◆'**p~'schnell**, *adj.* as quick as lightning.
**Pfeiler** ['pfailər], *m* -s/- pillar; (*Brückenp.*) pier.
**Pfennig** ['pfɛniç], *m* -s/-e pfennig; *Fig:* penny. ◆'**P~absatz**, *m* stiletto heel.
**pferchen** ['pfɛrçən], *v.tr.* to cram, stuff (people, animals) (in + *acc*, into).
**Pferd** [pfeːrt], *n* -(e)s/-e (*a*) horse; (*b*) *Sp:* (vaulting) horse; (*c*) (*Schach*) knight. ◆**P~efleisch**, *n* horsemeat. ◆**P~erennen**, *n* (i) horse racing; (ii) (*einzelnes*) horse race. ◆**P~eschwanz**, *m* (*Frisur*) ponytail. ◆'**P~esport**, *m* equestrian sport. ◆'**P~estall**, *m* stable. ◆**P~estärke**, *f* horsepower. ◆'**P~ewagen**, *m* horse-drawn carriage.
**Pfiff** [pfif], *m* -(e)s/-e (*a*) whistle; (*b*) *F:* trick; **der letzte P.**, the final touch.
**Pfifferling** ['pfifərliŋ], *m* -s/-e 1. chanterelle. 2. *F:* **das ist keinen P. wert**, it isn't worth a bean.
**pfiffig** ['pfifiç], *adj.* smart (child etc.); knowing (face).
**Pfingst-** ['pfiŋst-], *comb.fm.* Whit (Sunday, Monday); Whitsun (holiday, week). ◆**P~en**, *n* -s/- Whitsun. ◆**P~rose**, *f* peony.
**Pfirsich** ['pfirziç], *m* -s/-e peach.
**Pflanz|e** ['pflantsə], *f* -/-n plant. ◆'**P~en**, *v.tr.* to plant. ◆'**P~en-**, *comb.fm.* plant (milk, protection etc.); vegetable (fibre, fat etc.). ◆'**P~enreich**, *n* vegetable kingdom. ◆'**P~enwelt** *f*, plant life. ◆'**P~enfresser**, *m* -s/- herbivore. ◆'**P~enkunde**, *f* botany. ◆'**p~lich**, *adj.* vegetable (fat etc.). ◆'**P~ung**, *f* -/-en 1. no pl planting. 2. plantation.
**Pflaster** ['pflastər], *n* -s/- 1. Med: (sticking) plaster. 2. (*Fahrbahnbelag*) road surface; (*aus Steinen*) pavement, paving; **ein gefährliches P.**, a dangerous spot. ◆'**p~n**, *v.tr.* to surface (the road etc.). ◆'**P~stein**, *m* paving stone; (*runder P.*) cobble(stone).
**Pflaume** ['pflaumə], *f* -/-n plum. ◆'**P~nkuchen**, *m* plumtart.
**Pflege** ['pfleːgə]. I. *f* -/-n care (of s.o., sth.); maintenance (of parks, buildings etc.); cultivation (of the arts etc.); (*ärztliche*) P., medical care, nursing; **ein Kind in P. geben/nehmen**, to put/take a child into care. II. '**P~-**, *comb.fm.* foster-(child, mother etc.). ◆'**p~bedürftig**, *adj.* in need of care/Med: nursing. ◆**P~eltern**, *pl* foster parents. ◆'**P~fall**, *m* person in need of nursing. ◆'**p~n**, *v.* 1. *v.tr.* (*a*) to care for, look after (s.o., sth.); to nurse (a sick person); (*b*) to cultivate (the arts, friendship etc.). 2. *v.i.* (*haben*) **montags pflegt er ins Kino zu gehen**, he usually goes to the cinema on Mondays. ◆'**P~r(in)**, *m* -s/- (*f* -/-nen) (*Krankenp.*) nurse.
**Pflicht** [pfliçt]. I. *f* -/-en duty; **es ist P.**, it is compulsory/obligatory. II. '**P~-**,

*comb.fm.* compulsory (contribution, *Sp:* exercise, *Sch:* reading etc.). ◆'p~**bewußt**, *adj.* dutiful; conscientious. ◆'P~**fach**, *n Sch:* compulsory subject. ◆'P~**gefühl**, *n* sense of duty. ◆'p~**gemäß**, *adj.* dutiful; due (care, respect etc.). ◆'p~**vergessen**, *adj.* neglectful of one's duty.

**Pflock** [pflɔk], *m -(e)s/-e* (tent etc.) peg; *(für Tiere)* post, stake.

**pflück|en** ['pflykən], *v.tr.* to pick (flowers, fruit). ◆'P~**er(in)**, *m -s/- (f -/ -nen)* picker.

**Pflug** [pfluːk], *m -(e)s/-e* plough, *N.Am:* plow.

**pflüg|en** ['pflyːgən], *v.tr. & i. (haben)* to plough (a field).

**Pforte** ['pfɔrtə], *f -/-n (Tor)* gate; *(Tür)* door.

**Pförtner** ['pfœrtnər], *m -s/- Sch: etc:* porter; doorman.

**Pfosten** ['pfɔstən], *m -s/- post; (wall)* stud; *Fb:* goalpost, upright.

**Pfote** ['pfoːtə], *f -/-n* paw.

**Pfropfen** ['pfrɔpfən]. I. *m -s/- stopper, (Korken)* cork; bung (of a barrel etc.). II. *p., v.tr. (a)* to cork, stopper (a bottle), bung (a barrel etc.); *(b)* to cram, stuff (sth.) *in etwas acc,* into sth.).

**pfui** [pfui], *int. p. (Teufel)!* ugh, how disgusting!

**Pfund** [pfunt], *n -(e)s/-e* pound; **zwei P. Zucker,** two pounds of sugar. ◆'p~**weise**, *adv.* by the pound.

**pfusch|en** ['pfuʃən], *v.i. (haben)* to bungle (it). ◆'P~**er**, *m -s/- bungler.* ◆P~**e'rei**, *f -/no pl* bungling.

**Pfütze** ['pfytsə], *f -/-n* puddle.

**Phänomen** [fɛnoˈmeːn], *n -s/-e* phenomenon. ◆p~**al** [-meˈnɑːl], *adj.* phenomenal; stupendous.

**Phant|asie** [fantaˈziː], *f -/-n* imagination; **eine schmutzige P.,** a dirty mind. ◆p~**a'sielos**, *adj.* unimaginative. ◆p~**a'sieren**, *v.i. (haben) (a)* to fantasize; to dream (von Erfolg usw., of success etc.); *(b) Med:* **(im Fieber) p.,** to be delirious. ◆p~**a'sievoll**, *adj.* imaginative. ◆p~**astisch**, *adj.* fantastic. ◆P~**om** [-ˈtoːm], *n -s/-e* phantom.

**pharma|zeutisch** [farmaˈtsɔytiʃ], *adj.* pharmaceutical. ◆P~**'zie**, *f -/no pl* pharmacy.

**Phase** ['faːzə], *f -/-n* phase.

**Philanthrop** [filanˈtroːp], *m -en/-en* philanthropist. ◆p~**isch** [-ˈtroːpiʃ], *adj.* philanthropic.

**Philatelie** [filateˈliː], *f -/no pl* philately.

**Philolog|e** [filoˈloːgə], *m -n/-n* student of language and literature. ◆P~**ie** [-oˈgiː], *f -/no pl* study of language and literature.

**Philosoph** [filoˈzoːf], *m -en/-en* philosopher. ◆P~**ie** [-oˈfiː], *f -/-n* philosophy. ◆p~**isch** [-ˈzoːfiʃ], *adj.* philosophical.

**Phlegma|tiker** [flɛgˈmɑːtikər], *m -s/- lethargic person.* ◆p~**tisch**, *adj.* lethar-

gic, stolid.

**Phosphor** ['fɔsfɔr], *m -s/-e* phosphorus.

**Photo** ['foːto]. I. *n & m -s/-s* = Foto. II. **P~-,** *comb.fm.* = Foto-.

**Phrase** ['fraːzə], *f -/-n (a)* phrase; *(b) Pej: (Gemeinplatz)* platitude; trite remark. ◆P~**ndrescher**, *m -s/- Pej:* windbag, speechifier.

**Physik** [fyˈziːk], *f -/no pl* physics. ◆p~**alisch** [-iˈkɑːliʃ], *adj.* physical (laws etc.); physics (institute, experiment etc.). ◆'P~**er**, *m -s/-* physicist.

**Physio|loge** [fyzioˈloːgə], *m -n/-n* physiologist. ◆P~**logie** [-loˈgiː], *f -/no pl* physiology. ◆p~**logisch** [-ˈloːgiʃ], *adj.* physiological.

**physisch** ['fyːziʃ], *adj.* physical.

**Pianist(in)** [piaˈnist(in)], *m -en/-en (f -/ -nen)* pianist.

**Pickel** ['pikəl], *m -s/- 1. (Spitzhacke)* pickaxe; *(Eisp.)* ice-pick. 2. pimple, spot. ◆'p~**ig**, *adj.* spotty (face etc.).

**picken** ['pikən], *v.tr. & i. (haben)* to peck; **nach etwas p.,** to peck at sth.

**Picknick** ['piknik], *n -s/-s* picnic. ◆'p~**en**, *v.i. (haben)* to picnic.

**piep|en** ['piːpən], *v.i. (haben) (a) (Vögel)* to peep, chirp; *Rad:* to bleep; *(b)* **bei dir piept's wohl?** you must be off your rocker! ◆'p~**sen**, *v.i. (haben)* to peep, squeak, *Rad:* bleep.

**Pietät** [pieˈtɛːt], *f -/no pl* reverence; (reverential) respect. ◆p~**los**, *adj.* irreverent.

**Pik** [piːk]. I. *n -s/-s (Kartenspiel) (Farbe)* spades; *(Karte)* spade. II. 'P~-, *comb.fm.* (ace, king etc.) of spades.

**pikant** [piˈkant], *adj.* spicy (food, *Fig:* story etc.); *(schlüpfrig)* suggestive (joke etc.).

**pikiert** [piˈkiːrt], *adj. (Pers)* put out, needled; *N.Am:* miffed; *(gekränkt)* injured.

**Pilger** ['pilgər], *m -s/-* pilgrim. ◆'P~**fahrt**, *f* pilgrimage.

**Pille** ['pilə], *f -/-n* pill.

**Pilot(in)** [piˈloːt(in)], *m -en/-en (f -/-nen)* pilot.

**Pils** [pils], *n -/-* Pilsener (beer).

**Pilz** [pilts], *m -es/-e* fungus; *(eßbarer)* P., (edible) mushroom; *giftiger* P., toadstool. ◆'P~**krankheit,** *f* mycosis.

**pingelig** ['piŋəliç], *adj. F:* pernickety, fussy.

**Pinguin** ['piŋguiːn], *m -s/-e* penguin.

**Pinie** ['piːniə], *f -/-n* pine.

**Pinkel** ['piŋkəl], *m -s/- P: (feiner)* P., toff, swell; *N.Am:* dude. ◆p~**n**, *v.i. (haben)* P: to (have a) pee.

**Pinscher** ['pinʃər], *m -s/-* pinscher.

**Pinsel** ['pinzəl], *m -s/-* brush, esp. paintbrush. ◆'p~**n**, *v.tr. & i. (haben)* F: to paint (sth.).

**Pinzette** [pinˈtsɛtə], *f -/-n* tweezers.

**Pionier** [pioˈniːr], *m -s/-e* 1. *(Bahnbrecher)* pioneer. 2. *Mil:* engineer, sapper.

**Pirat** [piˈrɑːt], *m -en/-en* pirate.

◆**P~en-**, *comb.fm.* pirate (ship etc.);
**P~ensender**, *m Rad:* pirate station.
**Pirsch** [pirʃ], *f -/no pl* (deer-)stalking.
◆**'p~en**, *v.i.* (*haben*) to stalk.
**Piste** ['pistə], *f -/-n Sp:* track; (*Skip.*) run,
piste; *Av:* runway.
**Pistole** [pis'to:lə], *f -/-n* pistol.
**pläd|ieren** [plɛ'di:rən], *v.i.* (*haben*) to
plead, put the case. ◆**P~oyer**
[-doa'je:], *n -s/-s Jur:* (counsel's) sum-
ming up; *Fig:* plea.
**Plage** ['pla:gə], *f -/-n* nuisance; (*Schwie-*
*rigkeiten*) trouble; **es macht ihm das**
**Leben zur P.**, it makes his life a
misery. ◆**'p~n**, *v.tr.* (*a*) to plague,
torment (s.o.); (*b*) **sich p.**, to slave away
(**mit etwas** *dat*, at sth.); to struggle
(**mit einem Problem**, with a problem).
**Plakat** [pla'ka:t], *n -(e)s/-e* poster; (*auf*
*Pappe*) placard.
**Plakette** [pla'kɛtə], *f -/-n* (*a*) (*Gedenktafel*)
plaque; (*b*) (*Abzeichen*) badge.
**Plan** [pla:n]. **I.** *m -(e)s/¨e* (*a*) plan; (*b*)
(*Karte*) (town etc.) map, plan. **II.** '**P~**,
*comb.fm.* planned (economy etc.).
◆**'p~en**, *v.tr.* to plan (sth.). ◆**'P~er**,
*m -s/-* planner. ◆**'p~los**, *adj.* haphazard, unsystematic (procedure etc.); aimless (search etc.). ◆**'p~mäßig**, *adj.* (*a*)
planned (development etc.); scheduled
(arrival etc.); *adv.* according to plan/
schedule; (*b*) systematic (search etc.).
◆**'P~soll**, *n* planned (output) target.
◆**'P~stelle**, *f Adm:* established post.
◆**'P~ung**, *f -/no pl* planning; **in der P.**,
in the planning stage.
**Plane** ['pla:nə], *f -/-n* tarpaulin.
**Planet** [pla'ne:t], *m -en/-en* planet.
◆**P~en-**, *comb.fm.* planetary (orbit,
system).
**planier|en** [pla'ni:rən], *v.tr.* to level.
◆**P~raupe**, *f* bulldozer.
**Planke** ['plaŋkə], *f -/-n* plank.
**Plansch|becken** ['planʃbɛkən], *n -s/-*
paddling pool. ◆**'p~en**, *v.i.* (*haben*) to
splash about.
**Plantage** [plan'ta:ʒə], *f -/-n* plantation.
**plappern** ['plapərn], *v.i.* (*haben*) *F:* to
chatter.
**Plast|ik** ['plastik]. **I.** *f -/-en Art:* sculp-
ture. **II.** *n -s/no pl* plastic. **III.** '**P~ik-**,
*comb.fm.* plastic (cup, bomb etc.).
◆**P~ikbeutel**, *m* plastic/polythene bag.
◆**P~ikfolie**, *f* plastic film; polythene
sheet. ◆**'p~isch**, *adj.* **1.** three-
dimensional; *Fig:* graphic (description
etc.). **2.** (*formbar*) malleable.
**Platane** [pla'ta:nə], *f -/-n* plane tree.
**Platin** ['pla:tin], *n -s/no pl* platinum.
**platschen** ['platʃən], *v.i.* (*haben/sein*) *F:*
to splash.
**plätschern** ['plɛtʃərn], *v.i.* (*haben*) to
splash; (*Bach*) to babble; (*Wellen*) to lap
(**an** + *acc*, against).
**platt** [plat]. **I.** *adj.* (*a*) flat (roof, nose
etc.); **etwas p. drücken**, to flatten sth.;
(*b*) *Fig:* trite (conversation etc.); (*c*) *F:*

**ich war einfach p.!** you could have
knocked me down with a feather! **II. P.**,
*n -(s)/no pl.*/'**P~deutsch**, *n -(s)/no pl*
Low German. ◆**'P~e**, *f -/-n* (*a*) plate,
sheet (of metal, glass etc.); (*Holzp.*) panel, board; (*Steinp.*) slab; (*Fliese*) tile; (*b*)
(*Kochp.*) ring (of a cooker); (*c*) *Rec:* (gramophone) record; (*d*) (*großer Teller*)
(large) plate, dish; *Cu:* **eine kalte P.**, a
plate of cold meats. ◆**P~en-**, *comb.fm.*
record (album, collection etc.).
◆**'P~enhülle** *f*, record sleeve.
◆**'P~enspieler** *m*, record player.
◆**'P~enteller** *m*, (record) turntable.
◆**'P~form**, *f* (*a*) platform; (*b*) *Fig:* basis (for discussion). ◆**'P~fuß**, *m* flat
foot. ◆**'P~heit**, *f -/-en* (*a*) *no pl* triteness; (*b*) (*Bemerkung*) platitude.
**plätten** ['plɛtən], *v.tr.* to iron (clothes
etc.).
**Platz** [plats], *m -es/¨e* **1.** (*a*) (*Stelle*) place;
**sonniger P.**, sunny spot; **fehl am P~e**,
in the wrong place/(*Pers.*) job; *F:* out of
place; (*b*) (*Rang*) position; *Sp:* place; **auf**
**P. drei**, in third place; (*c*) (*Sitzp.*) seat;
(*am Tisch*) place; **P. nehmen**, to sit
down. **2.** (*a*) (*Marktp. usw.*) square; (*b*)
*Sp:* (sports/football) ground; (golf)
course; (tennis) court. **3.** *no pl* (*Raum*)
space; **j-m P. machen**, to make way for
s.o. ◆**'P~angst**, *f F:* claustrophobia.
◆**'P~anweiser(in)**, *m* (*f*) usher, *f* ush-
erette. ◆**'P~karte**, *f Rail:* seat ticket/
reservation. ◆**'P~mangel**, *m* lack of
space. ◆**'P~verweis**, *m Sp:* sending
off. ◆**'P~wechsel**, *m* change of position.
**Plätzchen** ['plɛtsçən], *n -s/-* **1.** (little)
place, spot. **2.** (round) biscuit; *N.Am:*
cookie.
**platz|en** ['platsən], *v.i.* (*haben*) (*a*) to
burst (**vor** + *dat*, with); (*Bombe*) to explode; (*Naht*) to split; **vor Lachen p.**, to
split one's sides with laughter; **vor Wut**
**p.**, to be seething with rage; (*b*) *F:* (*Vor-*
*haben*) to fall through. ◆**'P~patrone**, *f*
blank cartridge. ◆**'P~regen**, *m* cloudburst; downpour.
**Plauder|ei** [plaudə'rai], *f -/-en* chat.
◆**'p~n**, *v.i.* (*haben*) to (have a) chat.
**plausibel** [plau'zi:bəl], *adj.* comprehensible; plausible (explanation).
**plazieren** [pla'tsi:rən], *v.tr.* to place (s.o.,
an advertisement, *Sp:* the ball etc.); to
position (guards, players etc.); **sich p.**, to
place oneself; *Sp:* to be placed.
**pleite** ['plaitə]. **I.** *adj. F:* broke, *Brit:*
skint; (*Firma*) **p. gehen**, to go bust. **II.**
**P.**, *f -/no pl F:* (*a*) bankruptcy; **P. ma-**
**chen**, to go bust; (*b*) (*Mißerfolg*) flop,
washout.
**Plenar-** [ple'na:r-], *comb.fm.* plenary (session, assembly).
**Pleuelstange** ['plɔyəlʃtaŋə], *f* connecting
rod.
**Plexiglas** ['plɛksigla:s], *n R.t.m.* = per-
spex, *N.Am:* plexiglass.

**Plomb|e** ['plɔmbə], f -/-n 1. (Zahnp.) filling. 2. lead seal. ◆p~**ieren** [-'biːrən], v.tr. (a) to fill (a tooth); (b) to seal (a crate etc.).

**plötzlich** ['plœtsliç], adj. sudden; abrupt (change, stop etc.).

**plump** [plump], adj. (a) (dick) tubby; podgy (fingers etc.); (massig) bulky (shape etc.); (b) (ungeschickt) awkward; (c) Pej: blatant (lie etc.); crude (joke etc.). ◆'p~**sen**, v.i. (haben/sein) to (fall/land with a) thump.

**Plunder** ['plundər], m -s/no pl junk.

**Plünder|er** ['plyndərər], m -s/- plunderer, looter. ◆'p~**n**, v.tr. & i. (haben) to loot (a shop, house etc.); Hum: to raid, rifle (the larder etc.), plundering; Hist: pillaging. ◆P~**ung**, f -/no pl looting; plundering; Hist: pillaging.

**Plural** ['pluːraːl], m -s/-e plural.

**Plus** [plus]. I. n -/- 1. (Vorteil) plus, asset. 2. (Gewinn) profit. II. p., adv. & prep. + dat plus. ◆'P~**pol**, m El: positive pole/terminal. ◆'P~**punkt**, m plus; Sp: point; Fig: advantage. ◆'P~**quamperfekt** [-kvam-], n Gram: pluperfect (tense).

**Plüsch** [plyːʃ], m -(e)s/-e plush. ◆'P~**tier**, n soft/F: cuddly toy, N.Am: stuffed animal.

**pneumatisch** [pnɔy'maːtiʃ], adj. pneumatic.

**Po** [poː], m -s/-s P: bottom, behind.

**Pöbel** ['pøːbəl], m -s/no pl Pej: mob; rabble.

**pochen** ['pɔxən], v.i. (haben) to knock; (Herz) to pound, thump.

**Pocken** ['pɔkən], pl Med: smallpox.

**Podest** [po'dɛst], n & m -(e)s/-e (low) rostrum, platform.

**Podium** ['poːdium], n -s/-dien (speaker's) rostrum, platform.

**Poesie** [poe'ziː], f -/-ien poetry.

**Poet** [po'eːt], m -en/-en poet. ◆p~**isch**, adj. poetic.

**Pointe** [po'ɛ̃tə], f -/-n point (of a joke etc.).

**Pokal** [po'kaːl], m -s/-e goblet; Sp: cup. ◆P~**sieger**, m cup winner. ◆P~**spiel**, n Sp: cup tie.

**Pökel|fleisch** ['pøːkəlflaiʃ], n salt meat. ◆'p~**n**, v.tr. to cure, pickle, (mit Salz) salt (fish, meat).

**Pol** [poːl], m -s/-e pole; Fig: der ruhende P., the constant factor. ◆p~**ar** [po'laːr]. I. adj. polar (region etc.); (cold air etc.) from the Arctic. II. P~**ar-**, comb.fm. polar (expeditions, ice, region etc.); arctic (cold, fox etc.). ◆P~**arkreis**, m Arctic Circle.

**Pol|e** ['poːlə], m -n/-n Pole. ◆'P~**en**. Pr.n.n -s. Poland. ◆'P~**in**, f -/-nen Polish woman.

**Polemi|k** [po'leːmik], f -/-en polemics. ◆p~**sch**, adj. polemical (attack etc.); provocative, controversial (statement etc.).

**Police** [po'liːsə], f -/-n (Versicherungsp.) policy.

**Polier¹** [po'liːr], m -s/-e foreman.

**Polier-²**, comb.fm. polishing (brush, cloth). ◆p~**en**, v.tr. to polish (sth.).

**Poliklinik** ['poːliklinik], f outpatients' department.

**Politesse** [poli'tɛsə], f -/-n (female) traffic warden.

**Polit|ik** [poli'tiːk], f -/-en (a) no pl (Bereich) politics; (b) (bestimmte P.) policy; auswärtige P., foreign policy. ◆P~**iker(in)** [-'liːtikər(in)], m -s/- (f -/-nen) politician. ◆p~**isch** [-'liːtiʃ], adj. political; p. tätig, active in politics. ◆p~**i'sieren**, v.i. (haben) to talk politics.

**Politur** [poli'tuːr], f -/-en polish.

**Polizei** [poli'tsai]. I. f -/-en (a) no pl police; (b) police force. II. P~-, comb.fm. police (operation, dog, state etc.); (chief etc.) of police. ◆P~**beamte(r)** m, police officer. ◆p~**lich**, adj. police (procedure etc.); sich p. anmelden, to register with the police. ◆P~**präsident**, m chief of police; Brit: Chief Constable. ◆P~**präsidium**, n police headquarters. ◆P~**revier**, n (i) (Bezirk) police district/N.Am: precinct; (ii) (Wache) police station. ◆P~**spitzel**, m (police) informer. ◆P~**streife**, f police patrol. ◆P~**stunde**, f closing time (for bars etc.).

**Polizist** [poli'tsist], m -en/-en policeman. ◆P~**in**, f -/-nen policewoman.

**polnisch** ['pɔlniʃ], adj. & P., n -(s)/no pl Polish.

**Polo** ['poːlo], m -s/no pl Sp: polo. ◆'P~**hemd**, n T-shirt with collar.

**Polster** ['pɔlstər]. I. n -s/- (a) (auf Stühlen usw.) upholstery; Cl: pad, padding; (b) Fig: (Geldreserve) cushion. II. P~-, comb.fm. upholstered (furniture, chair etc.). ◆'P~**er**, m -s/- upholsterer. ◆'p~**n**, v.tr. to upholster (furniture); Cl: to pad (shoulders etc.); F: (Pers.) gut gepolstert, well-padded. ◆'P~**ung**, f -/no pl upholstery; (Watte usw.) stuffing.

**Polter|abend** ['pɔltərʔaːbənt], m wedding-eve party (with breaking of crockery). ◆'p~**n**, v.i. (haben/sein) (a) (Pers.) to make a racket; to bang/thump about; (b) (sein) (im Fallen) to crash, clatter (down); (Karren) to clatter (along); (c) (schelten) to rant, bluster.

**polygam** [poly'gaːm], adj. polygamous. ◆P~**gamie** [-ga'miː], f -/no pl polygamy.

**Polyp** [po'lyːp], m -en/-en 1. Z: (a) polyp; (b) F: (Krake) octopus. 2. P: cop, rozzer.

**Pomade** [po'maːdə], f -/-n hair cream.

**Pommes frites** [pɔm'frit], pl (potato) chips; esp. N.Am: French fries.

**Pomp** [pɔmp], m -(e)s/no pl pomp; splendour; Pej: ostentation. ◆p~**ös** [-'pøːs], adj. lavish, ostentatious.

**Pony** ['pɔni]. I. n -s/-s pony. II. m -s/-s

*(Haar)* fringe, *N.Am:* bangs.

**Pop-** ['pɔp-], *comb.fm.* pop (group, music etc.).

**Popelin** [popə'liːn], *m* -s/-e poplin.

**Popo** [po'poː], *m* -s/-s *P:* bottom.

**poppig** ['pɔpiç], *adj. F:* jazzy.

**populär** [popu'lɛːr], *adj.* popular.

**Por|e** ['poːrə], *f* -/-n pore. ◆**p~ös** [po'røːs], *adj.* porous.

**Porno** ['pɔrno]. I. *m* -s/-s *F:* porn. II. '**P~-**, *comb.fm.* pornographic (film etc.). ◆**p~'graphisch**, *adj.* pornographic.

**Porree** ['pɔre], *m* -s/-s leek.

**Portal** [pɔr'taːl], *n* -s/-e porch.

**Portemonnaie** [pɔrt(ə)mɔ'neː], *n* -s/-s purse.

**Portier** [pɔr'jeː], *m* -s/-s (hall) porter; doorman.

**Portion** [pɔrtsi'oːn], *f* -/-en helping, portion; *F:* *(Pers.)* **eine halbe P.**, a midget/ *Brit:* titch.

**Porto** ['pɔrto], *n* -s/-s postage. ◆'**p~frei**, *adj.* post free, *N.Am:* post paid.

**Porträt** [pɔr'trɛː], *n* -s/-s portrait. ◆**p~ieren** [-ɛ'tiːrən], *v.tr.* j-n **p.**, to paint s.o.'s portrait; *Fig:* to portray s.o.

**Portu|gal** ['pɔrtugal]. *Pr.n.n* -s. Portugal. ◆**P~'giese**, *m* -n/-n/**P~'giesin**, *f* -/-nen Portuguese (man/woman). ◆**p~'giesisch**, *adj.* & *n* -(s)/no pl Portuguese.

**Portwein** ['pɔrtvain], *m* port.

**Porzellan** [pɔrtsə'laːn]. I. *n* -s/-e *(a)* *(Werkstoff)* porcelain; *(b)* *(Geschirr)* china. II. **P~-**, *comb.fm.* china (figure, cup etc.).

**Posaun|e** [po'zaunə], *f* -/-n trombone.

**Pos|e** ['poːzə], *f* -/-n pose. ◆**p~ieren** [po'ziːrən], *v.i.* *(haben)* to pose.

**Position** [pozitsi'oːn], *f* -/-en position; *(a)* *(Stellung)* post; *(b)* *Com: etc: (Posten)* item. ◆**P~slicht**, *n Nau: Av:* navigation light.

**positiv** ['poːzitiːf]. I. *adj.* positive; *(günstig)* favourable; **eine p~e Antwort geben**, to answer in the affirmative; *F:* **ich weiß es p.**, I know it for certain. II. **P.**, *n* -s/-e *Phot:* positive.

**Positur** [pozi'tuːr], *f* -/-en posture.

**Poss|e** ['pɔsə], *f* -/-n *Th:* burlesque, farce. ◆**p~ierlich** [-'siːrliç], *adj.* (delightfully) comical.

**possessiv** ['pɔsəsiːf], *adj. Gram:* possessive. ◆**P~pronomen**, *n* -s/- *Gram:* possessive pronoun.

**Post** [pɔst]. I. *f* -/no pl *(a)* *(Briefe usw.)* post, *N.Am:* mail; **mit der P.**, by post/ mail; *(b)* *(P~amt)* post office. II. '**P~-**, *comb.fm.* *(a)* postal (address, district etc.); *(b)* post office (employee, administration etc.); *(c)* mail (steamer, coach, train etc.). ◆'**P~amt**, *n* post office. ◆**P~anweisung**, *f* postal/money order. ◆'**P~bote**, *m* postman, *N.Am:* mailman. ◆**P~fach**, *n* post office box, *usu. abbr.* P.O. Box. ◆'**P~karte**, *f* -/-n

postcard. ◆'**p~lagernd**, *adj.* poste restante. ◆'**P~leitzahl**, *f* postal/*N.Am:* zip code. ◆'**P~scheckkonto**, *n* postal cheque/giro account. ◆'**P~sparkasse**, *f* post office savings bank. ◆'**P~stempel**, *m* postmark. ◆'**p~wendend**, *adj.* by return (of post), *N.Am:* by return mail. ◆'**P~wertzeichen**, *n* postage stamp.

**Posten** ['pɔstən], *m* -s/- 1. *Mil:* *(a)* *(Stelle)* post; *F:* **auf dem P. sein**, (i) to feel fit; (ii) *(wachsam)* to be on the alert; *(b)* *(Wachtp.)* sentry. 2. *(Stellung)* post, job. 3. *Com:* item, entry; *(Waren)* lot, batch.

**poten|t** [po'tɛnt], *adj.* potent. ◆**P~tial** [-tsi'aːl], *n* -s/-e potential. ◆**p~tiell** [-tsi'ɛl], *adj.* potential. ◆**P~z** [po'tɛnts], *f* -/-en 1. *no pl* (sexual) potency; *Fig:* strength. 2. *Mth:* power.

**Potpourri** ['pɔtpuri], *n* -s/-s *Mus:* medley.

**Poularde** [pu'lardə], *f* -/-n pullet.

**Pracht** [praxt]. I. *f* -/no pl magnificence, splendour. II. '**P~-**, *comb.fm.* magnificent (building etc.). ◆'**P~exemplar** *n*/ '**P~stück**, *n* magnificent specimen, *F:* beauty. ◆'**p~voll**, *adj.* magnificent, gorgeous (colours etc.).

**prächtig** ['prɛçtiç], *adj.* magnificent, gorgeous (colours etc.); *(großartig)* marvellous (weather etc.).

**Prädikat** [prɛdi'kaːt], *n* -(e)s/-e 1. rating, assessment; **Wein mit P.**, high-quality wine. 2. *Gram:* predicate.

**präg|en** ['prɛːgən], *v.tr.* *(a)* to mint (money, coins); to stamp (metal); *(b)* *(schöpfen)* to coin (a new phrase, word etc.); *(c)* to form (s.o.'s character etc.); to characterize (a period, style etc.). ◆'**P~ung**, *f* -/no pl coining, minting; stamping.

**pragmatisch** [prag'maːtiʃ], *adj.* pragmatic.

**prägnan|t** [prɛg'nant], *adj.* concise, succinct; *(kernig)* pithy. ◆**P~z**, *f* -/no pl conciseness; incisiveness.

**prahl|en** ['praːlən], *v.i.* *(haben)* to boast, brag **(mit** + *dat,* about). ◆**P~e'rei**, *f* -/-en (constant) boasting.

**Prakt|ik** ['praktik], *f* -/-en practice. ◆**P~i'kant(in)**, *m* -en/-en *(f* -/-nen) student trainee. ◆'**P~ikum**, *n* -s/-ka practical training. ◆'**p~isch**, *adj.* practical; *(zweckmäßig)* convenient; *(handlich)* handy (tool etc.); **p~ischer Arzt**, general practitioner; **p. unmöglich**, virtually/ practically impossible. ◆**p~i'zieren**, *v.i.* *(haben)* to practise **(als Arzt**, as a doctor).

**Praline** [pra'liːnə], *f* -/-n chocolate; **Schachtel P~n**, box of chocolates.

**prall** [pral]. I. *adj.* 1. bulging (muscles, briefcase etc.); well-rounded (breasts etc.); **p. gefüllt**, filled to bursting. 2. blazing (sun). II. **P.**, *m* -(e)s/-e impact. ◆'**p~en**, *v.i.* *(haben)* **auf/gegen j-n, etwas** *acc* **p.**, to bump/(mit Wucht) crash into s.o., sth.; (*Ball*) to bounce against s.o., sth.

**Präm|ie** ['prɛːmiə], *f -/-n* (*bei Lotterien*) prize; (*Versicherungsp.*) premium; *Ind:* bonus. ◆**p~ieren** [prɛ'miːrən], *v.tr.* to give (s.o.) an award/a prize; to award (a film etc.) a prize.

**Pranke** ['praŋkə], *f -/-n* (lion's etc.) paw.

**Präpar|at** [prɛpa'rɑːt], *n -(e)s/-e Med: Ch:* preparation. ◆**p~ieren**, *v.tr.* to prepare (a material, work, oneself etc.).

**Präposition** [prɛpozitsi'oːn], *f -/-en* preposition.

**Prärie** [prɛ'riː], *f -/-n* prairie.

**Präsen|s** ['prɛːzəns], *n -/-'sentia* present (tense). ◆**p~t** [prɛ'zɛnt], *adj.* present; **etwas p. haben**, to have sth. at one's fingertips. ◆**p~'tieren**, *v.tr.* to present.

**Präservativ** [prɛzɛrva'tiːf], *n -s/-e* condom.

**Präsid|ent** [prɛzi'dɛnt], *m -en/-en* president. ◆**P~entschaft**, *f -/no pl* presidency. ◆**P~entschaftskandidat**, *m* presidential candidate. ◆**P~ium** [-'ziːdium], *n -s/-ien* 1. (*a*) (*Amt*) chairmanship; (*b*) (*Gremium*) management committee. 2. (*Polizeip.*) (police) headquarters.

**prasseln** ['prasəln], *v.i.* (*haben*) (*a*) (*Feuer*) to crackle; (*b*) (*Regen usw.*) to drum, patter.

**prassen** ['prasən], *v.i.* (*haben*) to indulge oneself, *F:* live it up.

**Präteritum** [prɛ'teritum], *n -s/-ta* preterite, past tense.

**Präventiv-** [prɛvɛn'tiːf-], *comb.fm.* preventive (measure etc.).

**Praxis** ['praksis], *f -/-xen* 1. *no pl* practice; (*Erfahrung*) experience; **in der P.**, in (actual) practice. 2. (*a*) (doctor's/lawyer's) practice; (*b*) (*Raum*) (doctor's) surgery, consulting room, *N.Am:* doctor's office; (lawyer's) office.

**Präzedenzfall** [prɛtse'dɛntsfal], *m* precedent.

**präzis|(e)** [prɛ'tsiːs (-iːzə)], *adj.* precise. ◆**P~ion** [-izi'oːn], *f -/no pl* precision. ◆**P~i'ons-**, *comb.fm.* precision (work, instrument etc.).

**predig|en** ['preːdigən], *v.tr. & i.* (*haben*) to preach. ◆**P~er**, *m -s/-* preacher. ◆**P~t**, *f -/-en* (*a*) *Ecc:* sermon; (*b*) *F:* lecture.

**Preis** [prais]. I. *m -es/-e* 1. price; **zum halben P.**, at half-price; **um jeden/keinen P.**, at any/not at any price. 2. (*bei Wettbewerb usw.*) prize. II. **'P~-**, **'p~-**, *comb.fm.* 1. price (rise, limit, list etc.). 2. prize (question etc.). ◆**'P~ausschreiben**, *n* (prize) competition. ◆**'P~gabe**, *f -/no pl* abandonment, betrayal. ◆**'p~geben**, *v.tr.sep.irr.35* to abandon, give up (s.o., sth.), *Mil:* surrender (ground); (*verraten*) to betray (s.o., a secret). ◆**'p~gekrönt**, *adj.* prizewinning. ◆**'p~günstig**, *adj.* attractively priced; reasonable; *adv.* at a

low price. ◆**'P~lage**, *f* price range. ◆**'p~lich**, *adj.* in price; *adv.* with regard to price. ◆**'P~nachlaß**, *m* discount. ◆**'P~richter**, *m* competition judge; adjudicator. ◆**'P~schild**, *n* price tag. ◆**'P~senkung**, *f* price concession/reduction. ◆**'P~sturz**, *m* slump in prices. ◆**'P~träger**, *m* prizewinner. ◆**'P~verleihung**, *f* prize ceremony. ◆**'p~wert**, *adj.* reasonably priced.

**Preiselbeere** ['praizəlbeːrə], *f -/-n F:* cranberry.

**preisen** ['praizən], *v.tr. Lit:* to praise, extol (s.o., sth.).

**prekär** [pre'kɛːr], *adj.* awkward; precarious.

**Prell|bock** ['prɛlbɔk], *m Rail:* buffer. ◆**p~en**, *v.tr.* to hit (sth.) hard; *F:* **die Zeche p.**, to leave without paying (the bill). ◆**'P~ung**, *f -/-en* contusion; bruise.

**Premier|e** [premi'ɛːrə], *f -/-n* first performance; *Th:* first night. ◆**P~minister** [prəmi'eː-], *m* Prime Minister.

**Press|e** ['prɛsə]. I. *f -/-n* press. II. **'P~e-**, *comb.fm.* press (report, ticket, conference etc.); (freedom etc.) of the press. ◆**'P~eagentur**, *f* press/news agency. ◆**'p~en**, *v.tr.* to press (s.o., sth., flowers, oneself etc.); to squeeze (s.o.'s hand, a lemon etc.); (*stopfen*) to cram (sth.) (**in etwas** *acc*, into sth.). ◆**p~ieren** [-'siːrən], *v.i.* (*haben*) *South G: etc:* to be urgent.

**Preßluft** ['prɛsluft], *f* compressed air. ◆**P~bohrer**, *m* pneumatic drill.

**Prestige** [prɛs'tiːʒə], *n -s/no pl* prestige.

**Preuß|e** ['prɔysə], *m -n/-n* Prussian. ◆**'P~en**. *Pr.n.* **-s**. Prussia. ◆**'p~isch**, *adj.* Prussian.

**prickeln** ['prikəln], *v.i.* (*haben*) (*a*) to tingle; *Fig:* **p~de Spannung**, electric tension; (*b*) (*Sekt*) to bubble.

**Priester** ['priːstər], *m -s/-* priest.

**prima** ['priːma]. I. *adj.* (*a*) prime (quality); first-class (goods etc.); (*b*) *F:* first-rate; tip-top (condition); **das ist p.!** that's great! **mir geht's p.**, I'm fine. II. **P.**, *f -/Primen Sch:* top form (in a *Gymnasium*).

**primär** [pri'mɛːr], *adj.* primary (stage etc.); prime (importance).

**Primel** ['priːməl], *f -/-n* primrose; (*Gartenp.*) primula.

**primitiv** [primi'tiːf], *adj.* (*a*) primitive (conditions, culture, art etc.); (*b*) (*sehr einfach*) simple, basic; rough and ready (method etc.).

**Prinz** [prints], *m -en/-en* prince. ◆**P~essin** [-'tsɛsin], *f -/-nen* princess.

**Prinzip** [prin'tsiːp], *n -s/-ien* principle; **aus P.**, on principle; **im P.**, in principle; **ein Mann mit P~ien**, a man of principles. ◆**p~iell** [-ipi'ɛl], *adj.* fundamental (difference, importance etc.); (question etc.) of principle; *adv.* (to agree etc.) in principle; (*grundsätzlich*) on principle.

**Priorität** [priɔri'tɛːt], f -/-en priority.

**Prise** ['priːzə], f -/-n pinch (of salt, tobacco etc.).

**privat** [pri'vaːt]. I. adj. private (entrance, life etc.); personal (opinion, reasons etc.); **das sage ich dir ganz p.**, I am telling you this in confidence; **j-n p. sprechen**, to speak to s.o. privately/in private. II. **P~-**, comb.fm. private (matter, detective, property, life, patient, lessons etc.); personal (matter, use etc.). ◆**P~adresse**, f private/home address. ◆**P~gespräch**, n Tel: personal/private call. ◆**p~isieren** [-ati'ziːrən], v.tr. to transfer (a business etc.) to private ownership. ◆**P~recht**, n civil law.

**Privileg** [privi'leːk], n -s/-ien privilege. ◆**p~iert** [-le'giːrt], adj. privileged.

**pro** [proː]. I. prep. + acc per; **p. Jahr**, per annum; **einmal p. Tag**, once a day; 5 Mark p. Stück, 5 marks each. II. n **das P. und Kontra**, the pros and cons.

**Probe** ['proːbə]. I. f -/-n 1. (a) (Versuch) test; **auf/zur P.**, on trial; (Angestellter) on probation; (Waren) on approval; **j-n, etwas auf die P. stellen**, to put s.o., sth. to the test; **die P. bei einer Rechnung machen**, to check a calculation; (b) Th: Mus: rehearsal. 2. (Muster) sample; Med: specimen (of blood etc.). II. **'P~-**, comb.fm. test (recording, drilling, flight etc.); trial (order, shot, lesson etc.); probationary (year etc.); esp. Sp: practice (jump, throw etc.). ◆**'P~exemplar**, n specimen copy. ◆**'p~fahren**, v.irr.26 v.tr. to test drive (a car). ◆**'P~fahrt**, f test/trial run. ◆**'p~n**, v.tr. & i. (haben) to rehearse (a concert, play etc.). ◆**'p~weise**, adv. as a test; **j-n p. anstellen**, to employ s.o. on a trial basis. ◆**'P~zeit**, f trial/probationary period.

**probier|en** [pro'biːrən], v.tr. (a) to try, sample (a dish, drink etc.); (b) (ausprobieren) to try (out) (sth.).

**Problem** [pro'bleːm], n -s/-e problem. ◆**P~atik** [-e'maːtik], f -/no pl (range of) problems. ◆**p~atisch**, adj. problematic; (zweifelhaft) doubtful. ◆**p~los**, adj. problem-free; adv. without any problems.

**Produkt** [pro'dukt], n -(e)s/-e (also Fig:) product; **landwirtschaftliche P~e**, farm produce. ◆**P~ion** [-duktsi'oːn], f -/-en production; (Menge) output. ◆**P~i'ons-**, comb.fm. production (costs, manager, process etc.); (volume etc.) of production. ◆**p~iv** [-'tiːf], adj. productive; prolific (writer). ◆**P~ivität** [-tivi'tɛːt], f -/no pl productivity.

**Produ|zent** [produ'tsɛnt], m -en/-en producer; Ind: manufacturer. ◆**p~zieren**, v.tr. to produce (goods, food etc.).

**profan** [pro'faːn], adj. (alltäglich) mundane.

**professionell** [profesio'nɛl], adj. professional.

**Professor** [pro'fɛsɔr], m -s/-en 1. professor (**für Biologie**, of biology). 2. Aus: Gymnasium teacher.

**Profi** ['proːfi]. I. m -s/-s Sp: F: pro. II. **'P~-**, comb.fm. professional (boxer etc.).

**Profil** [pro'fiːl], n -s/-e (a) profile; (Umriß) outline; (b) Aut: tread (of a tyre). ◆**p~ieren** [-i'liːrən], v.tr. (Pers.) **sich p.**, to make one's mark.

**Profit** [pro'fiːt], m -(e)s/-e profit. ◆**p~ieren** [-i'tiːrən], v.i. (haben) to (make a) profit, benefit (**bei/von** + dat, from).

**Prognose** [pro'gnoːzə], f -/-n forecast.

**Programm** [pro'gram]. I. n -s/-e programme; N.Am: program; (a) plan, schedule; agenda (of a conference); **auf dem P. stehen**, to be on the agenda/planned; (b) (Sender) Rad: station; TV: channel; (c) (gedrucktes P.) programme, N.Am: playbill; (d) Com: (Angebot) range (of furniture etc.). II. **P~-**, comb.fm. programme (control etc.); (change etc.) of programme. ◆**p~gemäß**, adj. according to plan/schedule. ◆**p~ieren** [-a'miːrən], v.tr. to set up a schedule for (a visitor etc.), programme (a computer etc.). ◆**P~ierer**, m -s/- Data-pr: programmer.

**progressiv** [progrɛ'siːf], adj. progressive.

**Projekt** [pro'jɛkt], n -(e)s/-e project. ◆**P~or** [-'jɛktɔr], m -s/-en projector.

**projizieren** [proji'tsiːrən], v.tr. to project (slides).

**Prokla|mation** [proklamatsi'oːn], f -/-en proclamation. ◆**p~'mieren**, v.tr. to proclaim (sth.).

**Prokurist** [proku'rist], m -en/-en Jur: attorney; Com: approx. company secretary.

**Prolet** [pro'leːt], m -en/-en Pej: F: prole, peasant. ◆**P~ariat** [-letari'aːt], n -(e)s/no pl proletariat. ◆**P~arier** [-'taːriər], m -s/- proletarian. ◆**p~arisch** [-ta'riːʃ], adj. proletarian.

**Prolog** [pro'loːk], m -(e)s/-e prologue.

**Promen|ade** [promə'naːdə], f -/-n promenade. ◆**P~adenmischung**, f Hum: mongrel.

**Promille** [pro'milə], n -(s)/- thousandth part (esp. of alcohol in the blood).

**prominen|t** [promi'nɛnt], adj. prominent. ◆**P~z**, f -/-en **die P.**, the top people.

**promovieren** [promo'viːrən], v.i. (haben) to receive one's doctor's degree.

**prompt** [prɔmpt], adj. prompt; F: adv. (sogleich) promptly, immediately.

**Pronomen** [pro'noːmən], n -s/- & -mina pronoun.

**Propag|anda** [propa'ganda], f -/no pl Pol: etc: propaganda; Com: publicity. ◆**p~ieren** [-'giːrən], v.tr. to propagate (an idea).

**Propeller** [pro'pɛlər], m -s/- propeller.

**Prophet** [pro'feːt], m -en/-en prophet. ◆**p~ezeien** [-fe'tsaiən], v.tr. to prophesy, predict (sth.).

**Proportion** [proportsi'oːn], f -/-en proportion. ◆**p~al** [-io'naːl], adj. propor-

tional; proportionate (**zu** + *dat*, to).
**Prosa** ['pro:za], *f -/no pl* prose.
**prosit** ['pro:zit], *int.* cheers! your health!
**p. Neujahr!** happy New Year!
**Prospekt** [pro'spɛkt], *m -(e)s/-e*
(*Broschüre*) leaflet; brochure.
**prost** [pro:st], *int.* = **prosit**.
**Prostata** ['prɔstata], *f -/-ae* prostate
(gland).
**Prostitu|ierte** [prostitu'i:rtə], *f decl. as
adj.* prostitute. ◆**P~tion** [-tutsi'o:n], *f
-/no pl* prostitution.
**Protest** [pro'tɛst], *m -(e)s/-e* protest.
◆**P~ant(in)** [-ɛs'tant(in)], *m -en/-en* (*f
-/-nen*) *Ecc:* Protestant. ◆**p~antisch**,
*adj.* Protestant. ◆**p~ieren** [-'ti:rən],
*v.i.* (*haben*) to protest.
**Prothese** [pro'te:zə], *f -/-n* artificial limb;
(*Zahnp.*) dentures.
**Protokoll** [proto'kɔl], *n -s/-e* **1.** *Adm: etc:*
written record; minutes (of a meeting
etc.); **etwas zu P. geben/nehmen**, to
make/take down a statement. **2.** (*Zeremoniell*) (diplomatic) protocol. ◆**p~ieren**
[-'li:rən], *v.* **1.** *v.i.* (*haben*) to keep the
minutes. **2.** *v.tr.* to enter (sth.) in the
minutes/records; to record (a statement
etc.).
**protzen** ['prɔtsən], *v.i.* (*haben*) *F:* to
show off; *Brit:* to swank (**mit** + *dat*,
about). ◆**p~ig**, *adj. F:* ostentatious;
flashy (car etc.).
**Proviant** [provi'ant], *m -s/no pl* provisions; (food) supplies.
**Provinz** [pro'vints], *f -/-en* province; *Pej:*
**die hinterste P.**, the back of beyond.
◆**p~i'ell**, *adj. usu. Pej:* provincial.
**Provision** [provizi'o:n], *f -/-en Com:* commission.
**provisorisch** [provi'zo:riʃ], *adj.* provisional.
**provozieren** [provo'tsi:rən], *v.tr.* to provoke (s.o., an attack). ◆**p~d**, *adj.* provocative.
**Prozedur** [protse'du:r], *f -/-en* (lengthy/
complicated) procedure.
**Prozent** [pro'tsɛnt], *n -(e)s/-e* per cent.
◆**P~satz**, *m* percentage (**an** + *dat*, of).
◆**p~u'al**, *adj.* percentage (share etc.);
*adv.* in percentage terms.
**Prozeß** [pro'tsɛs], *m -sses/-sse* (*a*) (*Vorgang*) process; (*b*) *Jur:* (*Verfahren*) trial;
**den P. gewinnen/verlieren**, to win/lose a
case; *F:* **mit etwas** *dat* **kurzen P. machen**, to make short work of sth.
◆**P~kosten**, *pl Jur:* legal costs.
**prozessieren** [protse'si:rən], *v.i.* (*haben*)
to be engaged in litigation (**mit**
**j-m**, with s.o.).
**Prozession** [protsɛsi'o:n], *f -/-en esp. Ecc:*
procession.
**prüde** ['pry:də], *adj.* (*in der Moral usw.*)
straitlaced. ◆**P~'rie**, *f -/no pl* prudish-
ness; prudery.
**Prüf-** ['pry:f-], *comb.fm. Tchn:* test (report, load, procedure etc.); testing (apparatus, process etc.). ◆**'p~en**, *v.tr.* (*a*)

to test (s.o., s.o.'s knowledge, skill etc.)
(**auf etwas** *acc*, for sth.); *Sch: Univ:* to
examine (a candidate); (*b*) (*auf Richtigkeit
hin*) to check (a bill etc.); (*c*) (*untersuchen*)
to examine (a document etc.); to investigate (a case etc.); **p~ender Blick**,
searching glance. ◆**'P~er**, *m -s/- Sch:
etc:* examiner. ◆**'P~ling**, *m -s/-e* exami-
nee; examination candidate. ◆**P~-
stein**, *m Fig:* touchstone. ◆**'P~ung**, *f
-/-en* (*a*) test; *Sch: etc:* (*formell*) examination, *F:* exam; **eine P. ablegen/machen**,
to take an examination/exam; (*b*) checking; (*c*) examination; investigation.
◆**P~ungsausschuß**, *m/***P~ungskom-
mission**, *f* board of examiners.
**Prügel** ['pry:gəl], *m -s/-* **1.** (*Knüppel*)
club, cudgel. **2.** *pl* beating; **eine gehörige
Tracht P.**, a sound thrashing. ◆**P~ei**
[-'lai], *f -/-en* brawl(ing); fight(ing).
◆**'p~n**, *v.tr.* to beat, thrash (s.o.); **sich
p.**, to (have a) fight. ◆**'P~strafe**, *f* cor-
poral punishment.
**Prunk** [pruŋk], *m -(e)s/no pl* (great) splendour; sumptuousness; (*beim Zeremoniell*)
pomp, spectacle. ◆**'P~stück**, *n* showpiece. ◆**'p~voll**, *adj.* sumptuous; flamboyant (style etc.).
**Psalm** [psalm], *m -s/-en* psalm.
**Pseudonym** [psɔydo'ny:m], *n -s/-e* pseudonym.
**Psych|iater** [psyçi'a:tər], *m -s/-* psychia-
trist. ◆**'p~isch**, *adj.* psychological
(illness, reasons etc.); **unter p~ischem
Druck**, under emotional stress;
**p. bedingt**, of a psychological nature.
**Psycho-** ['psyço-], *comb.fm.* psy-
cho(therapy etc.). ◆**P~ana'lyse**, *f* psychoanalysis. ◆**P~loge** [-'lo:gə], *m -n/-
n* psychologist. ◆**P~logie** [-lo'gi:], *f -/
no pl* psychology. ◆**p~logisch**
[-'lo:giʃ], *adj.* psychological.
**Pubertät** [puber'tɛ:t], *f -/no pl* puberty.
**publik** [pu'bli:k], *adj.* public; **etwas p.
machen**, to announce (sth.) (publicly).
◆**P~ikum** ['pu:blikum], *n -s/no pl* (*a*)
(*Zuhörer*) audience; (*Zuschauer*) spectators. ◆**p~izieren** [-bli'tsi:rən], *v.tr.* to
publish (an article etc.).
**Pudding** ['pudiŋ], *m -s/-e & -s Cu: approx.* blancmange.
**Pudel** ['pu:dəl], *m -s/-* poodle.
◆**p~'wohl**, *adv. F:* **sich p. fühlen**, to
feel on top of the world.
**Puder** ['pu:dər], *m & n -s/-* powder.
◆**'P~dose**, *f* powder compact.
◆**'p~n**, *v.tr.* to powder (a baby, oneself
etc.). ◆**'P~zucker**, *m* icing/*N.Am:*
powdered sugar.
**Puff** [puf]. **1.** *m -s/-e & -e F:* (*Schlag*)
punch; jab, poke. **2.** *m -s/-s* pouffe,
*N.Am:* hassock; (*Wäschep.*) padded
linen-basket. **3.** *m & n -s/-s P:* brothel.
◆**'P~er**, *m -s/- Rail:* buffer.
◆**'P~erzone**, *f Pol:* buffer-zone.
◆**'P~reis**, *m* puffed rice.
**Pull|over** [pu'lo:vər], *m -s/-/F:* **Pulli**

['puli], m -s/-s pullover, sweater.
◆P~under [-'lundər], m -s/- sleeveless
sweater, Brit: slipover.

**Puls** [puls], m -es/-e pulse; **j-m den P.
fühlen**, to take s.o.'s pulse. ◆p~ieren
[-'i:rən], v.tr. (haben) to pulsate, throb.
◆'P~schlag, m pulse (beat).

**Pult** [pult], n -(e)s/-e desk.

**Pulver** ['pulfər, -vər], n -s/- powder;
(Schießp.) gunpowder. ◆p~isieren
[-i'zi:rən], v.tr. to grind (sth.) to powder.
◆'P~kaffee, m instant coffee.
◆'P~schnee, m powdery snow.

**pummelig** ['puməliç], adj. F: chubby,
tubby (person).

**Pump** [pump], m -(e)s/-e F: credit; **auf
P.**, on credit/Brit: F: tick. ◆'P~e, f -/
-n 1. pump. 2. F: (Herz) ticker.
◆'p~en, v.tr.&i. (haben) (a) to pump
(air, water etc.); (b) F: **sich dat Geld
usw. bei j-m p.**, to borrow money etc.
from s.o.

**Punkt** [puŋkt], m -(e)s/-e 1. spot; Gram:
full stop, N.Am: period; **P. auf dem i**,
dot on the i; **P. drei Uhr**, on the stroke
of three. 2. (Thema) subject, topic; point
(in a debate etc.); **P. auf der Tagesord-
nung**, item on the agenda. 3. Sp: etc:
point. ◆'P~sieger, m winner on
points. ◆'P~zahl, f number of points.

**pünktlich** ['pyŋktliç], adj. punctual;
prompt (payment etc.); **p. ankommen**, to
arrive on time. ◆'P~keit, f -/no pl
punctuality.

**Punsch** [punʃ], m -(e)s/-e (hot) punch.

**Pupille** [pu'pilə], f -/-n pupil (of the eye).

**Puppe** ['pupə], f -/-n 1. doll; (Marionette)
puppet, marionette. 2. (von Insekt) chrysalis; cocoon (of a silkworm). ◆'P~n-,
comb.fm. doll's (house, face, furniture
etc.). ◆'P~spieler, m puppeteer.

**pur** [pu:r], adj. pure (gold etc.); sheer
(nonsense etc.); Whisky p., neat whisky.

**Püree** [py're:], n -s/-s Cu: purée, mash;
(Kartoffelp.) mashed potatoes.

**Purpur** ['purpur], m -s/no pl (royal) purple; (sattes P~rot) crimson. ◆'p~rot,
adj. purple; (sattrot) crimson, scarlet.

**Purzel|baum** ['purtsəlbaum], m somer-
sault. ◆'p~n, v.i. (sein) to (take a)
tumble.

**Puste** ['pu:stə], f -/no pl P: puff; **außer
P.**, puffed, out of breath. ◆'P~blume,
f F: dandelion-clock. ◆'p~n, v.i. (haben) F: to blow (in + acc, into).

**Put|e** ['pu:tə], f -/-n turkey (hen).
◆'P~er, m -s/- turkey (cock).
◆'p~er'rot, adj. crimson, scarlet.

**Putz** [puts], m -es/no pl 1. (an Wand) plas-
ter(work). 2. **in vollem P.**, all dressed/F:
dolled up. ◆'p~en, v.tr. (saubermachen)
to clean, (polieren) polish (sth.); **sich dat
die Zähne p.**, to brush one's teeth.
◆'P~frau, f cleaner, Brit: charwoman.
◆'p~ig, adj. cute. ◆'P~lappen, m
cleaning rag; floorcloth.

**Puzzlespiel** ['pazəlʃpi:l], n jigsaw puzzle.

**Pyjama** [py'dʒa:ma], m -s/-s (pair of) pyjamas.

**Pyramide** [pyra'mi:də], f -/-n pyramid.

**Pyrenäen** [pyre'nɛ:ən], Pr.n.pl die P.,
the Pyrenees.

**Pythonschlange** ['py:tɔnʃlaŋə], f
python.

# Q

**Q, q** [ku:], n -/- (the letter) Q, q.

**quabb(e)lig** ['kvab(ə)liç], adj. jelly-like;
flabby (flesh).

**Quacksalber** ['kvakzalbər], m -s/- quack
(doctor).

**Quader** ['kva:dər], m -s/- 1. Arch: stone
block, ashlar. 2. Math: rectangular solid.

**Quadrat** [kva'dra:t], I. n -(e)s/-e Mth:
etc: square; **4 im Q.**, 4 squared. II. Q~-,
comb.fm. square (metre, kilometre, number etc.).

**quaken** ['kva:kən], v.i. (haben) (Frosch)
to croak; (Ente) to quack.

**quäken** ['kvɛ:kən], v.i. (haben) to
screech, (Baby usw.) squawk.

**Qual** [kva:l], f -/-en agony; (seelisch) torment; Q~en, sufferings; (seelisch) anguish; **sie machte ihm das Leben zur
Q.**, she made his life a misery.
◆'q~voll, adj. agonizing; excruciating
(pain).

**quäl|en** ['kvɛ:lən], v.tr. to torment, (fol-
tern) torture (s.o., an animal); (plagen) to
plague, pester (s.o.); **Tiere q.**, to be
cruel to animals; **sich q.**, (sich abmühen)
to struggle. ◆'q~end, adj. agonizing;
excruciating (pain, thirst etc.); nagging
(though, doubt). ◆Q~e'rei, f -/-en
(Schmerz) agony; torment; (Folter) torture; (Grausamkeit) cruelty. ◆'Q~-
geist, m F: (Kind usw.) pest; perfect
nuisance.

**Qualifi|kation** [kvalifikatsi'o:n], f -/-en
qualification; (Fähigkeit) ability.
◆Q~kati'ons-, comb.fm. Sp: qualifying
(round, game etc.). ◆q~'zieren, v.tr.
& i. to qualify; **sich q.**, to become qualified.

**Quali|tät** [kvali'tɛ:t], f -/-en quality; (von)
**schlechter Q.**, of poor quality.
◆Q~'täts-, comb.fm. (a) quality (control etc.); (b) high-quality (wine etc.).
◆'Q~tätsware, f (high-) quality product.

**Qualle** ['kvalə], f -/-n jellyfish.

**Qualm** ['kvalm], m -(e)s/no pl (clouds of)
dense smoke. ◆'q~en, v. 1. v.i. (haben) (a) (Feuer usw.) to give off clouds of
smoke. 2. v.tr. to puff away at (a cigarette etc.). ◆'q~ig, adj. smoky; (room

etc.) full of smoke.

**Quanten** ['kvantən], *npl Hum: (Füße)* (great big) hooves. ◆'**Q~theorie**, *f Ph:* quantum theory.

**Quant|ität** [kvanti'tɛ:t], *f -/-en* quantity. ◆**q~itativ** [-ta'ti:f] *adj.* quantitative; *adv.* in quantity/numbers. ◆'**Q~um**, *n -s/Quanten* amount; (*Anteil*) share (**an** + *dat*, of).

**Quarantäne** [karan'tɛ:nə], *f -/-n* quarantine.

**Quark** [kvark], *m -s/no pl* **1.** *Cu:* curd cheese. **2.** *F:* **red keinen Q.!** don't talk rot!

**Quarta** ['kvarta], *f -/-ten Sch:* approx. third form/year; *Aus:* fourth form/year.

**Quartal** [kvar'tɑ:l], *n -s/-e* quarter (of a year). ◆**Q~ssäufer**, *m F:* habitual drinker, dipso.

**Quarte** ['kvartə], *f -/-n Mus:* fourth.

**Quartett** [kvar'tɛt], *n -(e)s/-e* **1.** *Mus:* quartet. **2.** (*Spiel*) Happy Families.

**Quartier** [kvar'ti:r], *n -s/-e (also Mil:)* quarters; accommodation.

**Quarz** [kvɑ:rts], *m -es/-e* quartz.

**quasi** ['kvɑ:zi], *adv.* more or less, as good as.

**Quassel|ei** [kvasə'lai], *f -/-en F:* (endless) jabbering, chatter. ◆'**q~n**, *v.i.* (*haben*) *F:* to jabber (away), chatter.

**Quaste** ['kvastə], *f -/-n Cl: etc:* tassel.

**Quatsch** [kvatʃ], *m -(e)s/no pl F:* (*a*) (*dummes Gerede*) rubbish, nonsense; (*b*) (*dumme Späße*) tomfoolery; **Q. machen,** to fool around; (*c*) (*Torheit*) **mach keinen Q.!** don't do anything stupid! ◆'**q~en**, *v.tr. & i. (haben) F:* (*a*) (*Unsinn*) q., to talk rubbish/nonsense; (*b*) (*schwatzen*) to chat, (*abfällig*) gossip, (*dauernd*) chatter (away). ◆'**Q~kopf**, *m F:* windbag.

**Quecksilber** ['kvɛksilbər], *n -s/no pl* mercury; quicksilver.

**Quell|e** ['kvɛlə], *f -/-n* source; heiße **Q~n,** hot springs; **aus sicherer/ zuverlässiger Q.,** from a reliable source/ on good authority; *F:* **an der Q. sitzen,** to be on the spot; to have direct access (to information, goods etc.). ◆'**q~en,** *v.i.irr.* (*sein*) (*a*) (*Wasser usw.*) to well up; (*Rauch*) to billow (out); (*Tränen, Fig: Menschen usw.*) to stream, pour; (*b*) (*Holz, Cu: Reis usw.*) to swell. ◆'**Q~wasser,** *n* spring water.

**queng|elig** ['kvɛŋəliç], *adj. F:* whining. ◆'**q~eln,** *v.i.* (*haben*) to whine.

**quer** [kve:r]. **I.** *adv.* crosswise; (*rechtwinklig*) at right angles; **das Kleid ist q. gestreift,** the dress has horizontal stripes; **q. auf dem Bett liegen,** to lie across the bed; **der Anhänger stand q. auf der Straße,** the trailer was at an angle across the road. **II.** '**Q~-, Q~~-,** *comb.fm.* transverse (axis, motion, flute, *Cl:* pleat

etc.); horizontal (stripe etc.). ◆'**Q~balken,** *m* crossbeam; (door, window) transom; *Fb: etc:* crossbar. ◆'**Q~e,** *f -/no pl F:* **j-m in die Q. kommen,** to get in s.o.'s way, (*Auto usw.*) block s.o.'s path; (*hindern*) to thwart s.o. ◆**Q~feld'ein-,** *comb.fm.* cross-country (race, course etc.). ◆**q~gestreift,** *adj.* with transverse/horizontal stripes. ◆'**Q~kopf,** *m F:* awkward customer. ◆'**q~köpfig,** *adj. F:* perverse. ◆'**Q~latte,** *f Fb:* crossbar. ◆'**Q~schiff,** *n Ecc.Arch:* transept. ◆'**Q~schnitt,** *m* **1.** *Mth: etc:* (cross-)section; *Tchn:* transverse/cross section. **2.** (*Auswahl*) cross-section (of the population etc.). ◆'**q~schnittsgelähmt,** *adj.* paraplegic. ◆'**Q~straße,** *f* road/street crossing another; (*Abzweigung*) turning. ◆'**Q~verbindung,** *f* direct link/ connection (between two places/*Fig:* two facts).

**Querulant** [kveru'lant], *m -en/-en* (eternal) moaner.

**quetsch|en** ['kvɛtʃən], *v.tr. F:* (*a*) to squeeze (s.o., sth., *Cu:* lemons etc.); (*b*) (*verletzen*) to bruise (sth.), (*zerquetschen*) crush (a foot etc.). ◆'**Q~ung** *-/-en/* '**Q~wunde,** *f* bruise.

**quicklebendig** [kvikle'bɛndiç], *adj.* sprightly; *F:* full of beans.

**quieken** ['kvi:kən], *v.i.* (*haben*) to squeal, (*Maus*) squeak.

**quietsch|en** ['kvi:tʃən], *v.i.* (*haben*) (*Tür usw.*) to squeak; (*Reifen usw.*) to screech; (*Kind*) **vor Vergnügen q.,** to squeal with delight. ◆'**q~ver'gnügt,** *adj. F:* cheery, chirpy.

**Quinta** ['kvinta], *f -/-ten Sch:* approx. second form/year, *Aus:* fifth form/year.

**Quint|(e)** [kvint(ə)], *f -/-en (-/-n) Mus:* fifth. ◆'**Q~essenz,** *f -/-en* quintessence. ◆**Q~ett** [kvin'tɛt], *n -(e)s/-e Mus:* quintet.

**Quirl** [kvirl], *m -(e)s/-e* **1.** *Cu:* (star-shaped) beater. **2.** *Fig:* (*Kind*) live wire.

**quitt** [kvit], *pred.adj. F:* **mit j-m q. sein,** to be quits/even with s.o.

**Quitte** ['kvitə], *f -/-n* quince.

**quitt|ieren** [kvi'ti:rən], *v.tr. Com:* to give a receipt (for a bill etc.); to acknowledge (receipt of a delivery etc.); **eine Bemerkung mit einem Lächeln q.,** to greet/ answer a remark with a smile. ◆'**Q~ung,** *f -/-en* **1.** *Com: etc:* receipt (über eine **Summe,** for a sum). **2.** *Fig:* **das ist die Q. für dein schlechtes Benehmen,** that's what you get for your bad behaviour.

**Quiz** [kvis], *n -/-* quiz.

**Quote** ['kvo:tə], *f -/-n* quota.

**Quotient** [kvotsi'ɛnt], *m -en/-en* quotient.

# R

**R, r** [ɛr], *n -/-* (the letter) R, r.
**Rabatt** [ra'bat], *m -(e)s/-e Com:* discount;
◆**R~marke,** *f Com:* trading stamp.
**Rabatte** [ra'batə], *f -/-n* (flower) border.
**Rabe** ['raːbə], *m -n/-n Orn:* raven.
◆**'R~nmutter,** *f* cruel mother.
◆**'r~n'schwarz,** *adj.* jet-black.
**rabiat** [rabi'aːt], *adj. (aggressiv)* violent;
*(roh)* brutal; *(rücksichtslos)* ruthless.
**Rach|e** ['raxə], *f -/no pl* revenge, *Lit:* vengeance **(an j-m für etwas** *acc,* on s.o. for
sth.); *(Vergeltung)* retaliation.
◆**'R~eakt,** *m* act of revenge.
◆**'r~süchtig,** *adj. Lit:* vengeful.
**Rachen** ['raxən], *m -s/-* *Anat:* *(Kehle)*
throat; *Med:* pharynx.
**rächen** ['rɛçən], *v.tr.* *(a)* *(Pers.)* to avenge
(s.o., sth.); **sich r.,** to take one's revenge, *F:* get one's own back **(an j-m,** on
s.o.); *(b)* *(Sache)* **sich r.,** to take its toll;
**dein Leichtsinn wird sich noch r.,** you
will have to pay (the penalty) for your
recklessness.
**Rachitis** [ra'xiːtis], *f -/no pl* rickets.
**Rad** [raːt]. **I.** *n -(e)s/-er* **1.** wheel; *(Zahnrad)* gear. **2.** *F:* *(Fahrrad)* bike. **II.** **'R~-,**
*comb.fm.* **1.** wheel (rim etc.). **2.** cycle
(race etc.); cycling (tour etc.). ◆**'r~eln,**
*v.i.* *(sein)* *F:* to ride a bike, *(irgendwohin)*
go by bike. ◆**'r~fahren,** *v.i.sep.irr.*
*(sein)* to cycle; **er kann r.,** he can ride a
bicycle. ◆**'R~fahrer,** *m* cyclist.
◆**'R~kappe,** *f Aut:* hub cap. ◆**'R~-
ler,** *m -s/-* cyclist. ◆**'R~rennbahn,** *f*
cycle racing track. ◆**'R~sport,** *m* cycling. ◆**'R~weg,** *m* cycle track.
**Radar** ['raːdar, ra'daːr], *m & n -s/no pl*
radar. ◆**R~anlage,** *f* radar installation.
**Radau** [ra'dau], *m -s/no pl* *F:* row, racket.
**Rädchen** ['rɛːtçən], *n -s/-* small wheel.
**radebrechen** ['raːdəbrɛçən], *v.tr.irr.* to
mangle (a language); **Englisch/Deutsch
r.,** to speak broken English/German.
**Rädelsführer** ['rɛːdəlsfyːrər], *m* ringleader.
**Räderwerk** ['rɛːdərvɛrk], *n* mechanism,
*F:* works (of a clock etc.); *Fig:* machinery (of justice etc.).
**radier|en** [ra'diːrən], *v.tr.&i.* *(haben)* *(a)*
to erase, rub (sth.) out; *(b)* *Art:* to etch (a
landscape etc.). ◆**R~gummi,** *m & n*
(india)- rubber, eraser. ◆**R~ung,** *f*
*-/-en* etching.
**Radieschen** [ra'diːsçən], *n -s/-* (red) radish.
**radikal** [radi'kaːl], *adj.* radical (change,
*Pol:* idea, etc.); drastic (action, measures
etc.); ruthless (pursuit of aims etc.); *Pol:*
**ein R~er,** a radical; **etwas r. ausrotten,**
to eradicate sth. completely.
**Radio** ['raːdio], *n -s/-s* radio; **im R.,** on
the radio. ◆**r~aktiv** [-ak'tiːf], *adj.*
radioactive. ◆**R~aktivität** [-tivi'tɛːt], *f*

radioactivity. ◆**'R~apparat,** *m* radio
(set).
**Radium** ['raːdium], *n -s/no pl* radium.
**Radius** ['raːdius], *m -/-ien* radius.
**raffen** ['rafən], *v.tr.* *(a)* to snatch, grab
(sth.) (up); to amass (money); *(b)* *Cl:* to
gather (material etc.).
**Raffin|ade** [rafi'naːdə], *f -/-n* refined sugar. ◆**R~erie** [-ə'riː], *f -/-n* refinery.
◆**R~esse** [-fi'nɛsə], *f -/-n* **1.** *(Schlauheit)* cunning; ingenuity (of a plan etc.).
**2.** refinement. ◆**r~iert,** *adj.* **1.** refined
(sugar etc.). **2.** *(a)* *(schlau)* crafty, cunning; *(b)* *(fein)* subtle (flavour etc.); sophisticated (system etc.); refined (taste).
**ragen** ['raːgən], *v.i.* *(haben)* to rise, tower
(up).
**Rahm** [raːm], *m -(e)s/no pl* *South G:*
cream. ◆**'R~käse,** *m -s/no pl* cream
cheese.
**rahmen** ['raːmən]. **I.** *v.tr.* to frame (a
picture etc.). **II. R., *m -s/-* *(a)* frame;
*Aut:* chassis (frame); *(b)* *Fig:* framework
(of a story etc.); *(Kulisse)* setting; *(Textzusammenhang)* context; **im R. bleiben,**
to keep within bounds; **aus dem R. fallen,** to be out of place/*(nicht normal)* out
of the ordinary.
**Rakete** [ra'keːtə], *f -/-n* rocket; *Mil:*
*(Geschoß)* missile. ◆**'R~nwerfer,** *m*
*Mil:* rocket launcher.
**rammen** ['ramən], *v.tr.* to ram (a car,
ship etc.).
**Rampe** ['rampə], *f -/-n* **1.** ramp. **2.**
*(Startr.)* launching pad. ◆**'R~nlicht,** *n*
*Th:* footlights; *Fig:* **im R. stehen,** to be
in the limelight.
**ramponier|en** [rampo'niːrən], *v.tr.* *F:* to
knock about (furniture etc.). ◆**r~t,** *adj.*
*F:* battered; *(ruiniert)* ruined.
**Ramsch** [ramʃ], *m -(e)s/-e* *F: Pej:* junk.
◆**'R~laden,** *m Pej:* junk shop.
**ran** [ran], *adv. F:* =**heran.**
**Rand** [rant]. **I.** *m -(e)s/-er* edge; *(a)* rim
(of a plate etc.); lip (of a cup etc.); brim
(of a hat, glass etc.); *(b)* **am R~(e) der
Stadt,** on the outskirts of the town; *(c)*
brink (of a precipice, *Fig:* of ruin etc.);
*(d)* margin (of a page); *Fig:* **etwas am
R~e erwähnen,** to mention sth. in passing; *(e)* *F:* **außer R. und Band,** *(Kinder)*
out of hand. **II. 'R~-,** *comb.fm.* peripheral (zone, *Fig:* problem, figure etc.).
◆**'R~bemerkung,** *f* marginal note;
*(nebenbei)* incidental remark. ◆**'R~er-
scheinung,** *f* item/aspect of peripheral
importance. ◆**'r~los,** *adj.* rimless.
◆**'r~voll,** *adj.* full (to the brim).
**randalieren** [randa'liːrən], *v.i.* *(haben)* to
rampage, *(lärmen)* make a racket.
**Rang** [raŋ], *m -(e)s/-e* **1.** rank; **alles, was
R. und Namen hat,** everybody who is
anybody. **2.** *(Qualität)* quality. **3.** *Sp:*

place. **4.** *Th:* **erster/zweiter R.**, dress/upper circle, *N.Am:* first/second balcony. ◆'R~**älteste(r)**, *m & f decl. as adj.* senior officer. ◆'R~**ordnung,** *f* order of precedence.

**Rangier|bahnhof** [raŋ'ʒiːrbɑːnhoːf], *m Rail:* marshalling yard, *N.Am:* switchyard. ◆r~**en** [-'ʒiːrən], *v.* **1.** *v.i.* (*haben*) to rank, be classed. **2.** *v.tr. Rail:* to shunt, *N.Am:* switch (a train etc.). ◆R~**gleis,** *n* siding.

**Rank|e** ['raŋkə], *f -/-n Bot:* tendril. ◆'r~**en,** *v.refl. & i.* (*haben*) (*Pflanze*) to shoot, send out tendrils; (**sich**) **r.,** to climb.

**Ränke** ['rɛŋkə], *pl.* **R. schmieden,** to scheme, hatch plots.

**Ranzen** ['rantsən], *m -s/-* **1.** *Sch:* satchel. **2.** *P:* (*Bauch*) paunch, belly.

**ranzig** ['rantsiç], *adj.* rancid.

**rapid(e)** [ra'piːt (-iːdə)], *adj.* rapid.

**Raps** [raps], *m -es/-e* rape.

**rar** [rɑːr], *adj.* scarce (commodity etc.); rare (stamp); *F:* **er macht sich r.,** he rarely puts in an appearance. ◆R~**ität** [rari'tɛːt], *f -/-en* rarity.

**rasant** [ra'zant], *adj. F:* (*schnell*) meteoric (development etc.); *Aut:* very fast, hairy (car, driving); (*im Aussehen*) racy (car, styling); **r~es Tempo,** breakneck speed.

**rasch** [raʃ], *adj.* quick (movement etc.); swift (decisions, action etc.).

**rascheln** ['raʃəln], *v.i.* (*haben*) to rustle.

**rase|n**[1] ['rɑːzən], *v.i.* (*haben*) (*Pers., Fig: Sturm usw.*) to rage; (*Verrückter*) to rave; (*b*) (*sein*) (*Auto, Fahrer*) to tear/(*Pers.*) dash along. ◆'r~**nd,** *adj.* (*a*) (*schnell*) very fast; (*b*) raging (fury etc.); raving (madman etc.); (*c*) (*heftig*) violent (jealousy, pain etc.); **r~nde Kopfschmerzen,** a splitting headache; **r~nder Beifall,** tumultuous applause. ◆R~'**rei,** *f -/no pl* (*a*) raving; (*Wut*) rage, fury; (*b*) mad rush/*Aut:* speed.

**Rasen**[2] ['rɑːzən]. **I.** *m -s/-* coll. grass; (*also* **R~fläche** *f*) lawn. **II.** '**R~,** comb.fm. lawn (fertilizer etc.); (piece etc.) of grass. ◆'R~**mäher,** *m* lawn mower.

**Rasier-** [ra'ziːr-], comb.fm. shaving (mirror, cream, soap etc.). ◆R~**apparat,** *m* razor; **elektrischer R.,** electric shaver. ◆r~**en** [ra'ziːrən], *v.tr.* to shave (s.o., one's chin etc.); **sich r.,** to shave. ◆R~**klinge,** *f* razor blade. ◆R~**messer,** *n* cut-throat razor. ◆R~**pinsel,** *m* shaving brush; ◆R~**wasser,** *n* after-shave (lotion).

**Rass|e** ['rasə], *f -/-n* (*a*) (*Menschenr.*) (human) race; (*b*) *Z:* breed. ◆'R~**ehund,** *m* pedigree dog. ◆'R~**en-,** comb.fm. racial (discrimination, characteristic etc.). ◆'R~**enhaß,** *m,* racial/race hatred. ◆'R~**entrennung** *f* racial segregation. ◆'R~**epferd,** *n* thoroughbred (horse). ◆'r~**ig,** *adj.* vivacious (woman etc.); fiery (wine, temperament etc.).

◆'r~**isch,** *adj.* racial. ◆R~**ismus** [-'sismus], *m -/no pl* racism, racialism. ◆R~**ist** [-'sist], *m -en/-en* racist. ◆r~**istisch,** *adj.* racist.

**Rassel** ['rasəl], *f -/-n* rattle. ◆'r~**n,** *v.i.* (*haben*) to rattle (**mit etwas** *dat,* sth.); (*Ketten*) to clank.

**Rast** [rast], *f -/-en* rest. ◆'R~**e,** *f -/-n Tchn:* catch. ◆'r~**en,** *v.i.* (*haben*) to (take a) rest, have a break (on a journey). ◆'R~**haus,** *n* roadhouse; *esp.* motorway restaurant. ◆'r~**los,** *adj.* ceaseless; (*unermüdlich*) tireless; (*unruhig*) restless. ◆'R~**stätte,** *f* service area.

**Rasur** [ra'zuːr], *f -/-en* shave.

**Rat** [rɑːt], *m -(e)s (pl* **R~schläge)** (piece of) advice; **ich weiß mir keinen R. (mehr),** I am at my wit's end; **j-n/ein Buch zu R~e ziehen,** to consult s.o./a book. **2.** *Adm:* (*Gremium*) council; (*R~smitglied*) councillor. ◆'r~**en,** *v.tr. & i.irr.* (*haben*) (*a*) **j-m (etwas) r.,** to advise s.o. (to do sth.); **das würde ich dir auch r.!** you better had (do that)! (*b*) (*erraten*) to guess (an answer etc.). ◆'R~**geber,** *m -s/-* adviser. ◆'R~**haus,** *n* town hall. ◆'r~**los,** *adj.* helpless (look etc.). ◆'R~**losigkeit,** *f -/no pl* helplessness, perplexity. ◆'r~**sam,** *pred. adj.* advisable; (*weise*) prudent. ◆'R~**schlag,** *m* piece of advice. ◆'R~**sherr,** *m* councillor.

**Rate** ['rɑːtə], *f -/-n Com:* instalment. ◆'r~**nweise,** *adv.* in/by instalments.

**ratifizier|en** [ratifi'tsiːrən], *v.tr.* to ratify (a treaty etc.). ◆R~**ung,** *f -/-en* ratification.

**Ration** [ratsi'oːn], *f -/-en* ration. ◆r~**ieren** [-o'niːrən], *v.tr.* to ration (sth.).

**rational** [ratsio'nɑːl], *adj.* rational. ◆r~**isieren** [-nali'ziːrən], *v.tr.* to rationalize.

**rationell** [ratsio'nɛl], *adj.* efficient; (*wirtschaftlich*) economical.

**Rätsel** ['rɛːtsəl], *n -s/-* (*a*) (*Wortr.*) riddle; (*b*) (*Geheimnis*) mystery; **es ist mir ein R., wie ...,** it is a mystery to me how ... ◆'r~**haft,** *adj.* baffling (problem); enigmatic (person), mysterious (circumstances etc.).

**Ratte** ['ratə], *f -/-n* rat. ◆'R~**ngift,** *n* rat poison.

**rattern** ['ratərn], *v.i.* (*a*) (*haben*) (*Maschinengewehr usw.*) to chatter; (*b*) (*sein*) (*Auto usw.*) to rattle, clatter (along).

**Raub** [raup], *m -(e)s/no pl* **1.** robbery. **2.** (*Beute*) loot, booty. ◆'R~**bau,** *m* overexploitation (of natural resources); **mit seiner Gesundheit R. treiben,** to abuse one's health. ◆r~**en** ['raubən], *v.tr.* (*a*) **j-m etwas r.,** to rob/deprive s.o. of sth.; (*b*) (*entführen*) to kidnap (a child etc.). ◆'r~**gierig,** *adj.* rapacious. ◆'R~**mord,** *m* robbery with murder. ◆'R~**mörder,** *m* robber and murderer.

◆'R~**tier**, *n* beast of prey. ◆'R~**überfall**, *m* (bank etc.) raid; holdup.
◆'R~**vogel**, *m* bird of prey.

**Räuber** ['rɔybər], *m* **-s/-** robber. ◆'R~**bande**, *f* gang of thieves/robbers.

**Rauch** [raux]. I. *m* **-(e)s/no pl** smoke; (*Dämpfe*) fumes. II. 'R~~, *comb.fm.* (*a*) smoke (bomb, cartridge, ring, signal etc.); (cloud etc.) of smoke; (*b*) (*geräuchert*) smoked (meat, glass etc.); (*c*) (*für Raucher*) smoking (room, tobacco etc.); smoker's (table etc.). ◆'r~**en**. I. *v.tr. & i.* (*haben*) to smoke. II. R., *n* **-s/no pl** smoking; **R. verboten!** no smoking. ◆'R~**er**, *m* **-s/-** 1. (*Pers.*) smoker. 2. F: *Rail:* (*also* **R~erabteil** *n*) smoking compartment, *f:* smoker. ◆'r~**ig**, *adj.* smoky. ◆'R~**verbot** *n* smoking ban.

**Räucher-** ['rɔyçər], *comb.fm.* smoked (eel, ham etc.). ◆'R~**hering**, *m* smoked herring; kipper. ◆'R~**kerze**, *f* aromatic candle. ◆'r~**n**, *v.tr.* to smoke (fish, meat etc.).

**räudig** ['rɔydiç], *adj.* mangy.

**rauf** [rauf], *adv. F:* = **herauf/hinauf.**

**Rauf|bold** ['raufbɔlt], *m* **-(e)s/-e** *Pej:* ruffian. ◆'r~**en**, *v.* 1. *v.tr. Fig:* **sich** *dat* **die Haare r.**, to tear one's hair. 2. *v.refl. & i.* (*haben*) (**sich**) **r.**, to fight, scrap. ◆R~**e'rei**, *f* **-/-en** fight, scrap; (*Handgemenge*) brawl. ◆'r~**lustig**, *adj.* pugnacious.

**rauh** [rau]. I. *adj.* 1. (*a*) rough (surface, hands etc.); coarse (cloth etc.); harsh (texture, sound); (*b*) (*heiser*) hoarse (voice). 2. (*unwirtlich*) (*a*) rough (sea); (*b*) raw (climate); biting (wind); severe (winter, weather etc.). 3. (*grob*) uncouth (manners, person etc.). 4. **in r~en Mengen**, in vast quantities. ◆'R~**fasertapete**, *f* rough-textured wallpaper. ◆'R~**haardackel**, *m* wire-haired dachshund. ◆'r~**haarig**, *adj.* wire-haired (dog). ◆'R~**reif**, *m* hoar frost.

**Raum** [raum]. I. *m* **-(e)s/-e** (*a*) space; (*b*) (*Gebiet*) *Geog:* area; (*c*) (*Zimmer*) room. II. 'R~~, *comb.fm.* 1. space (flight, station etc.). 2. room, interior (acoustics etc.). ◆'R~**fahrt**, *f* space travel. ◆'R~**inhalt**, *m* volume, cubic capacity. ◆'R~**maß**, *n* cubic measure. ◆'R~**pflegerin**, *f* (woman) cleaner. ◆'R~**schiff**, *n* spaceship. ◆'R~**sonde**, *f* space probe.

**räum|en** ['rɔymən], *v.tr.* (*a*) to vacate (a house, one's seat etc.); to evacuate (a building, *Mil:* position etc.); (*b*) (*wegr.*) to clear away (snow, rubble, dishes etc.); (*c*) (*leeren*) to clear (a space, road, table etc.). ◆'r~**lich**, *adj.* spatial; three-dimensional (effect etc.). ◆'R~**ung**, *f* **-/-en** (*a*) (*also Com:*) clearance; (*b*) vacating; evacuation. ◆'R~**ungsbefehl**, *m* eviction order. ◆'R~**ungsverkauf**, *m* *Com:* clearance sale.

**raunen** ['raunən], *v.tr. & i.* (*haben*) to murmur (sth.).

**Raupe** ['raupə], *f* **-/-n** 1. caterpillar. 2. tracked vehicle, *esp.* bulldozer. ◆'R~**nkette**, *f* (caterpillar) track. ◆'R~**nschlepper**, *m* caterpillar tractor.

**raus** [raus], *adv. F:* = **heraus/hinaus.** ◆'r~**schmeißen**, *v.tr.sep.irr.4* (*a*) to chuck (s.o., sth.) out; (*b*) (*entlassen*) to fire (s.o.).

**Rausch** [rauʃ], *m* intoxication; **einen R. haben**, to be drunk. ◆'r~**en**. I. *v.i.* (*haben*) to make a rushing sound; (*leise*) to rustle, (*Bach*) murmur; *Rad: etc:* to hiss; **r~der Beifall**, enthusiastic applause; *Fig:* **r~de Feste**, exhilarating parties; (*b*) (*sein*) to rush (along). II. R., *n* **-s/no pl** rushing (sound); (*leise*) rustle; *Rad: etc:* hiss. ◆'R~**gift**, *n* (narcotic) drug, *F:* dope. ◆'R~**gifthändler**, *m* drug pedlar/pusher. ◆'r~**giftsüchtig**, *adj.* drug-addicted; **ein R~giftsüchtiger**, a drug addict.

**räuspern** ['rɔyspərn], *v.refl.* **sich r.**, to clear one's throat.

**Raute** ['rautə], *f* **-/-n** diamond (shape); *Mth:* rhombus.

**Razzia** ['ratsia], *f* **-/-ien** (police) raid, swoop.

**Reag|enzglas** [rea'gɛntsgla:s], *n* test tube. ◆'r~**ieren** [-'gi:rən], *v.i.* (*haben*) to react, (*Pers.*) respond (**auf etwas** *acc*, to sth.).

**Reaktion** [reaktsi'o:n], *f* **-/-en** reaction, response (**auf etwas** *acc*, to sth.). ◆r~**är** [-o'nɛ:r], *adj.* reactionary. ◆R~**sfähigkeit**, *f* **-/-en** ability to react (quickly); reactions.

**Reaktor** [re'aktɔr], *m* **-s/-en** reactor.

**real** [re'a:l]. I. *adj.* real, actual (value etc.). II. R~~, *comb.fm.* real (income, wages, value etc.). ◆r~**i'sieren**, *v.tr.* (*a*) to realize (hopes), put (a plan, ideas etc.) into practice; (*b*) (*einsehen*) to realize (one's mistakes etc.). ◆R~**ismus** [-a'lismus], *m* **-/no pl** realism. ◆R~**ist**, *m* **-en/-en** realist. ◆r~**istisch**, *adj.* realistic. ◆R~**i'tät**, *f* **-/-en** reality. ◆R~**schule**, *f* modern secondary school.

**Rebe** ['re:bə], *f* **-/-n** 1. vine-shoot. 2. (*Weinstock*) vine.

**Rebhuhn** ['re:phu:n], *n* partridge.

**Rebell|(in)** [re'bɛl(in)], *m* **-en/-en** (*f* **-/-nen**) rebel. ◆r~**ieren** [-'li:rən], *v.i.* (*haben*) to rebel. ◆R~**ion** [-li'o:n], *f* **-/-en** rebellion. ◆r~**isch** [-'belɪʃ], *adj.* rebellious.

**Rechen** ['rɛçən], *m* **-s/-** rake. ◆R~**aufgabe**, *f* arithmetical problem. ◆R~**maschine**, *f* calculator. ◆'R~**schaft**, *f* **-/no pl** account; **von j-m R. fordern**, to demand an explanation from s.o.; **j-n zur R. ziehen**, to call s.o. to account. ◆'R~**zentrum**, *n* computer centre.

**rechn|en** ['rɛçnən]. 1. *v.i.* (*haben*) (*a*) to calculate; **gut r. können**, to be good at figures; **vom 1. April an gerechnet**, taking April 1st as a starting point; (b) (*haushalten*) **mit jedem Pfennig** r., to count every penny; (c) (*erwarten*) **r. mit** + *dat*, to be prepared for (sth.); (d) (*sich verlassen*) **auf ihn kann man nicht** r., one cannot rely on him. 2. *v.tr.* (a) (*schätzen*) to estimate, allow (sth.); **grob gerechnet**, at a rough estimate; (b) (*zählen*) to count, include (s.o., sth.) (**zu** + *dat*, among); **das Trinkgeld nicht gerechnet**, not counting the tip. ◆**R~er**, *m* -s/- (*Gerät*) calculator; *Data-pr:* computer. ◆**'R~ung**, *f* -/-en **1.** calculation. **2.** bill; *Com:* invoice; **das geht auf meine** R., this is on me; *Fig:* **j-m, einer Sache** R. **tragen**, to take s.o., sth. into account. ◆**'R~ungsjahr**, *n* financial year. ◆**'R~ungsprüfer**, *m* auditor.

**recht**[1] [rɛçt], *adj.* right; (a) (*richtig*) **nach dem R~en sehen**, to see that all is well; (**völlig**) r. **haben**, to be (perfectly) right; **ich muß dir r. geben**, I am forced to admit you are right; r. **so!** that's the idea! that's right! **das ist mir** r., that's all right with me; (b) (*gerecht*) fair; just; **es ist nicht r. von dir**, it's wrong/unfair of you; **es geschieht dir r.**, it serves you right; (c) (*echt*) real (pity etc.); **ich habe keine r~e Lust**, I don't really feel like it; r. **traurig**, really sad; r. **gut**, pretty good.

**Recht**[2], *n* -(e)s/-e **1.** *no pl* law; R. **und Ordnung**, law and order; R. **sprechen**, to administer justice; *Fig:* **im** R. **sein**, to be in the right; **mit** R., rightly, justifiably. **2.** (*Anspruch usw.*) right (**auf** + *acc*, to). ◆**'r~fertigen**, *v.tr.* to justify (s.o., oneself, sth.). ◆**'R~fertigung**, *f* -/-en justification. ◆**'r~haberisch**, *adj.* opinionated (person). ◆**'r~lich**, *adj.* legal (question, success etc.); legitimate (claim etc.). ◆**'r~mäßig**, *adj.* legal, lawful (practice etc.); legitimate (claim etc.); rightful (owner). ◆**'R~s-**, *comb.fm.* (a) legal (matter, question, claim, protection etc.); (principle etc.) of law; (b) (sense etc.) of justice. ◆**'R~sanwalt**, *m* lawyer; *Brit:* solicitor; *N.Am:* attorney. ◆**'R~sbrecher**, *m* law-breaker. ◆**'r~schaffen**, *adj.* upright, decent; (*ehrlich*) honest. ◆**'R~schreib-**, *comb.fm.* spelling (reform, mistake etc.). ◆**'R~schreibung**, *f* orthography, (correct) spelling. ◆**'r~skräftig**, *adj.* (decision etc.) with the force of law. ◆**'R~sprechung**, *f* -/-en jurisdiction, administration of justice. ◆**'R~sstreit**, *m* legal action, lawsuit. ◆**'r~swidrig**, *adj.* illegal, against the law. ◆**'r~zeitig**, *adj.* in time; timely (intervention etc.); r. **ankommen/abfahren**, to arrive/leave on time.

**recht|e(r, s)** ['rɛçtə(r,s)], *adj.* (a) right (arm, shoe, angle etc.); **zu meiner** R~en, on my right; (b) *Pol:* rightwing (politician, views etc.); right (wing). ◆**'R~eck**, *n* rectangle. ◆**'r~eckig**, *adj.* rectangular. ◆**r~s**, *adv.* (a) on the right; **von/nach** r., from/to the right; **die erste Straße** r., the first on the right; r. **abbiegen**, to turn right; (b) *Pol:* r. **stehen/F: sein**, to be right-wing. ◆**'R~saußen**, *m Fb:* outside right. ◆**'r~sherum**, *adv.* (round) to the right, clockwise. ◆**'r~sradikal**, *adj.* with radical/extreme rightwing views. ◆**'R~sverkehr**, *m* righthand rule of the road. ◆**r~winkl(e)lig**, *adj.* rightangled.

**Reck** [rɛk], *n* -(e)s/-e horizontal bar. ◆**'r~en**, *v.tr.* to crane (one's neck); **sich** r., to stretch oneself.

**Redakt|eur(in)** [redakt'ø:r(in)], *m* -s/-e (*f* -/-nen) editor. ◆**R~tion** [-tsi'o:n], *f* -/-en **1.** *no pl* editing. **2.** (a) editorial staff; (b) (*Abteilung*) editorial department.

**Rede** ['re:də], *f* -/-n (a) speech; (b) **wovon ist die** R.? what are you talking about? what is it all about? **davon kann keine** R. **sein**, that is out of the question; (c) *Gram:* **direkte/indirekte** R., direct/indirect speech; (d) **j-n zur** R. **stellen**, to demand an explanation from s.o. ◆**'r~gewandt**, *adj.* eloquent. ◆**r~n** ['re:dən], *v.* **1.** *v.i.* (*haben*) to talk, speak; (*eine Rede halten*) to make a speech; **du hast gut** r., it's easy for you to talk; **er läßt mit sich** r., he is open to persuasion. **2.** *v.tr.* (nonsense etc.), speak (the truth etc.); **er redete kein Wort**, he didn't say a word. ◆**'R~nsart**, *f* saying. ◆**'R~wendung**, *f* phrase.

**redlich** ['re:tliç], *adj.* honest, sincere; (*rechtschaffen*) upright.

**Redner** ['re:dnər], *m* -s/- speaker.

**redselig** ['re:tze:liç], *adj.* talkative. ◆**R~keit**, *f* -/*no pl* talkativeness.

**reduzier|en** [redu'tsi:rən], *v.tr.* to reduce (prices, staff etc.). ◆**R~ung**, *f* -/-en reduction.

**Reede** ['re:də], *f* -/-n *Nau:* roads. ◆**'R~r**, *m* -s/- shipowner. ◆**R~'rei**, *f* -/-en shipping company.

**reell** [re'ɛl], *adj.* **1.** honest, straight (deal etc.); r~e **Preise**, reasonable/realistic prices. **2.** (*wirklich*) real, genuine (chance etc.).

**Refer|at** [refe'ra:t], *n* -(e)s/-e **1.** (*Aufsatz*) paper; (*Bericht*) report. **2.** *Adm:* (*Abteilung*) department. ◆**R~ent(in)** [-'rɛnt(in)], *m* -en/-en (*f* -/-nen) **1.** author of a paper; (*Redner*) speaker. **2.** (*Berater*) consultant. ◆**r~ieren** [-'ri:rən], *v.i.* (*haben*) to report, read a paper (**über** + *acc*, on).

**reflektieren** [reflɛk'ti:rən], *v.* **1.** *v.tr.* to reflect (sth.). **2.** *v.i.* (*haben*) to meditate (**über** + *acc*, on).

**Reflex** [re'flɛks], *m* -es/-e reflex. ◆**r~iv** [-ɛ'ksi:f], *adj. Gram:* reflexive.

**Reform** [re'fɔrm], *f* -/-en reform. ◆**R~ati'on**, *f* -/-en Reformation. ◆**R~haus**, *n* health-food shop. ◆**r~ieren** [-'mi:rən], *v.tr.* to reform

(sth.)
**Refrain** [rəˈfrɛ:], *m* -s/-s refrain.
**Regal** [reˈgɑːl], *n* -s/-e (set of) shelves;
(*Bücher.*) bookcase.
**Regatta** [reˈgata], *f* -/-ten regatta.
**rege** [ˈreːgə], *adj.* (*a*) active (person etc.);
busy (traffic, trade etc.); brisk (business,
demand etc.); (*b*) (*lebhaft*) lively (person,
imagination, discussion etc.).
**Regel** [ˈreːgəl], *f* -/-n **1.** rule; (scientific)
law; (*Vorschrift*) regulation; **in der R.,** as
a rule. **2.** *Med:* period (of a woman).
◆'r~los, *adj.* disorderly. ◆'r~
mäßig, *adj.* regular; symmetrical (features). ◆'R~mäßigkeit, *f* -/no pl regularity; symmetry, orderliness. ◆r~n
[ˈreːgəln], *v.tr.* (*a*) to regulate (speed,
temperature etc.), control (volume,
prices, traffic etc.); (*b*) to put (affairs
etc.) in order; (*erledigen*) to deal with,
sort out (a matter). ◆'r~recht, *adj.*
downright, *F:* out-and-out. ◆'R~ung,
*f* -/-en **1.** regulation, control. **2.** settlement; (*Lösung*) solution. **3.** (*Beschluß*)
ruling. ◆'r~widrig, *adj.* against the
rules/regulations; irregular (conduct, procedure etc.).
**regen¹** [ˈreːgən], *v.tr.* (*a*) to move (one's
arm etc.); (*b*) **sich** *r.,* to move, (*Gefühle*)
stir.
**Regen²**, *m* -s/no pl rain. ◆'R~bogen, *m*
rainbow. ◆'R~bogenhaut, *f* iris (of
the eye). ◆'R~fälle, *mpl* rainfall.
◆'R~guß, *m* downpour. ◆'R~man-
tel, *m* raincoat. ◆'r~reich, *adj.* wet,
rainy. ◆'R~schauer, *m* shower of rain.
◆'R~schirm *m* umbrella. ◆'R~tag,
*m* rainy day. ◆'R~tropfen, *m* raindrop. ◆'R~wetter, *n* rain/wet weather.
◆'R~wurm, *m* earthworm.
◆'R~zeit, *f* rainy season.
**Regent** [reˈgɛnt], *m* -en/-en ruler, sovereign. ◆R~schaft, *f* -/-en reign.
**Regie** [reˈʒiː], *f* -/-n *Cin: TV:* direction;
*Th: Rad:* production; **R. führen,** to
direct/produce; **unter staatlicher R.,** under state control.
**regier|en** [reˈgiːrən], *v.* **1.** *v.tr.* to rule,
govern (a country). **2.** *v.i.* (*haben*) to rule
(**über** + *acc,* over). ◆R~ung, *f* -/-en
government; (*Tätigkeit*) rule; reign (of a
king etc.). ◆R~ungs-, r~ungs-,
*comb.fm.* government (official, circles,
spokesman etc.); (change etc.) of government. ◆R~ungschef, *m* head of government.
**Regime** [reˈʒiːm], *n* -s/- [-mə] regime.
**Regiment** [regiˈmɛnt], *n* **1.** -(e)s/-er *Mil:*
regiment. **2.** -(e)s/-e (*Herrschaft*) rule.
**Region** [regiˈoːn], *f* -/-en region; *Lit:*
sphere.
**Regisseur** [reʒiˈsøːr], *m* -s/-e *Cin: TV:*
director; *Th: Rad:* producer.
**Regist|er** [reˈgistər], *n* -s/- **1.** (*alphabe-
tisch*) index. **2.** *Adm:* register (of births
etc.). ◆r~rieren [-ˈtriːrən], *v.tr.* (*a*) to
register (a birth etc.); (*eintragen*) to enter

(sth.) (in + *dat,* in); (*b*) *Tchn:* (*Meßgerät*)
to record (temperature etc.); (*c*) (*zur
Kenntnis nehmen*) to note (sth.).
◆R~rierkasse, *f* cash register.
**Reglement** [regləˈmãː], *n* -s/-s regulations, rules.
**Regler** [ˈreːglər], *m* -s/- regulator; (*Hebel*)
lever.
**reglos** [ˈreːkloːs], *adj.* motionless.
**reg|nen** [ˈreːgnən], *v.impers.* to rain.
◆'r~nerisch, *adj.* rainy.
**regsam** [ˈreːkzɑːm], *adj.* active, lively.
**regul|är** [reguˈlɛːr], *adj.* (*vorschriftsmäßig*)
according to the regulations, regular
(troops etc.); proper (time, price etc.).
◆r~ieren [-ˈliːrən], *v.tr.* to regulate
(temperature, a watch etc.), control
(speed, prices etc.); (*einstellen*) to adjust
(volume, mixture etc.).
**Regung** [ˈreːguŋ], *f* -/-en *Lit:* **1.** (*Bewegung*) movement; stirring (of leaves, air
etc.). **2.** (*Gefühl*) feeling; (*Anwandlung*)
impulse. ◆r~slos, *adj.* motionless.
**Reh** [reː], *n* -(e)s/-e **1.** roe (deer). **2.** *Cu:*
(roe) venison. ◆'R~bock, *m* roebuck.
◆'R~kitz, *n* fawn. ◆'R~rücken, *m*
*Cu:* saddle of venison.
**rehabilitieren** [rehabiliˈtiːrən], *v.tr.* to rehabilitate (s.o.).
**Reib|e** [ˈraibə], *f* -/-n *Cu:* grater.
◆'r~en, *v. irr.* **1.** *v.tr.* (*a*) to rub (sth.);
(*b*) *Cu:* to grate (nuts, cheese etc.). **2.**
*v.i.* (*haben*) (*Riemen usw.*) to rub, chafe.
◆R~e'rei, *f* -/-en *usu. pl.* friction.
◆'R~fläche, *f* striking surface (of a
matchbox). ◆'R~ung, *f* -/-en rubbing;
*Tchn: Fig:* friction. ◆'R~ungs-
*comb.fm.* frictional (electricity, heat etc.).
◆'r~ungslos, *adj.* smooth (flow etc.);
*Tchn:* frictionless; *adv.* r. verlaufen, to
go off without a hitch.
**reich¹** [raiç], *adj.* (*a*) rich; **die R~en,** the
rich/wealthy; (*b*) r~e Ausstattung,
lavish/opulent furnishings (of a house); r.
geschmückt, richly decorated; (*c*)
(*r~haltig*) copious (selection, knowledge
etc.); lavish (meal); plentiful (harvest
etc.). ◆'r~haltig, *adj.* extensive, (*umfassend*) comprehensive; substantial (meal
etc.); rich (fauna etc.). ◆'r~lich, *adj.*
ample (means, meal etc.); abundant (supply etc.); liberal (helping, tip etc.); **das
ist etwas r.,** that's a bit too much; r.
spät, jolly late. ◆'R~tum, *m* -s/-er
wealth, *esp. Fig:* richness (an + *dat,* in);
affluence (of s.o., society etc.).
**Reich²**, *n* -(e)s/-e (*a*) *Hist:* empire; **das
Dritte R.,** the Third Reich; (*b*) *Fig:*
realm (of the arts etc.); the world (of
dreams etc.); **das R. der Tiere,** the animal kingdom.
**reich|en** [ˈraiçən], *v.* **1.** *v.tr.* j-m etwas r.,
to hand/pass s.o. sth. **2.** *v.i.* (*haben*) (*a*)
to reach, extend; (*b*) (*genügen*) to be
enough/sufficient; (*Vorrat usw.*) to last;
*F:* jetzt reicht es mir aber! I've had enough! that's the end! ◆'R~weite, *f*

reach (of s.o.); range (of vision, *Mil:* a gun, *Av:* an aircraft etc.).

**reif¹** [raif], *adj.* ripe (fruit, cheese etc.); mature (wine, *Fig:* personage, views etc.). ◆'**R~e**, *f -/no pl* ripeness; *esp. Fig:* maturity. ◆'**r~en¹**, *v.i.* (*sein*) to ripen; (*Wein, Fig: Pers. usw.*) to mature. ◆'**R~eprüfung**, *f* school-leaving examination. ◆'**R~ezeugnis**, *n* school-leaving certificate.

**Reif²**, *m -(e)s/no pl* hoarfrost.

**Reifen²** ['raifən]. **I.** *m -s/-* **1.** (barrel etc.) hoop. **2.** *Aut: etc:* tyre, *N.Am:* tire. **3.** (*Schmuck*) bangle. **II.** '**R~-**, *comb.fm.* tyre, *N.Am:* tire (pressure, change etc.). ◆'**R~panne**, *f* flat tyre, puncture.

**Reihe** ['raiə], *f -/-n* **1.** row; *Fig:* **ein Verräter in den eigenen R~n**, a traitor in one's own ranks. **2.** (*a*) **ich bin an der R./komme an die R.**, it is my turn; **der R. nach**, one after another, in turn; (*b*) (*Folge*) (*also Mth:*) series; **seit einer R. von Jahren**, for a number of years. ◆'**r~n**, *v.tr.* (*a*) to string (beads etc.); (*b*) **ein Fest reihte sich ans andere**, one celebration followed another. ◆'**R~nfolge**, *f* order; sequence. ◆'**R~nhaus**, *n* terraced house, *N.Am:* row house. ◆'**r~nweise**, in rows; *F:* in great numbers.

**Reiher** ['raiər], *m -s/- Orn:* heron.

**Reim** [raim], *m -(e)s/-e* rhyme. ◆'**r~en**, *v.* **1.** *v.tr.* & *i.* (*haben*) to rhyme (words etc.). **2.** *v.refl.* '**klein' reimt sich auf 'fein'**, 'klein' rhymes with 'fein'.

**rein¹** [rain], *adv. F:* = **herein/hinein.** ◆'**R~fall**, *m F:* (*Pleite*) washout, flop; (*Enttäuschung*) let-down. ◆'**r~legen**, *v.tr.sep. F:* to take (s.o.) for a ride.

**rein²**. **I.** *adj.* **1.** (*a*) pure (gold, silk, race etc.); unadulterated (wine etc.); *Com:* **r~er Gewinn**, net/clear profit; (*b*) (*nichts als*) sheer (imagination, coincidence etc.); (*bloß*) mere (thought etc.); *F:* (*völlig*) utter (madness etc.); **r. private Angelegenheit**, purely/strictly personal matter. **2.** (*a*) (*sauber*) clean (clothes, air etc.); *Fig:* clear (conscience etc.); pure (voice etc.); (*b*) **etwas ins r~e schreiben**, to make a fair copy of sth.; **ein Mißverständnis usw. ins r~e bringen**, to clear up a misunderstanding etc. **II.** '**R~-**, '**r~-**, *comb.fm. Com: etc:* net (amount, weight, profit etc.). ◆'**R~haltung**, *f -/no pl* keeping (a room etc.) clean. ◆'**R~heit**, *f -/no pl* **1.** purity. **2.** (*Sauberkeit*) cleanness. ◆'**r~igen**, *v.tr.* to clean (sth.); to cleanse (skin, blood etc.). ◆'**R~igung**, *f -/-en* **1.** cleaning; purification. **2.** (*chemische*) **R.**, (dry) cleaner's. ◆'**R~igungscreme**, *f* cleansing cream. ◆'**r~lich**, *adj.* (immaculately) clean; spotless (clothes, house etc.). ◆'**R~lichkeit**, *f -/no pl* cleanness, cleanliness. ◆'**R~(e)machefrau**, *f* cleaner, *Brit:* charwoman. ◆'**r~rassig**, *adj.* **1.** pedigree, purebred (dog etc.); thor-

oughbred (horse etc.). **2.** pure-blooded (person). ◆'**R~schrift**, *f* fair copy. ◆'**r~waschen**, *v.tr.sep.irr.108 F:* to whitewash (s.o.).

**Reis** [rais], *m -es/-e* rice. ◆'**R~korn**, *n* grain of rice.

**Reise** ['raizə]. **I.** *f -/-n* journey; (*auch hin und zurück*) trip; **R. zur See**, sea voyage; **auf R~n sein**, to be away (on a trip). **II.** '**R~-**, *comb.fm.* (*a*) travelling (companion, expenses etc.); travel (sickness, brochure etc.); (*b*) (*Urlaubs-*) holiday (traffic, weather etc.). ◆'**R~andenken**, *n* souvenir. ◆'**R~bericht**, *m* travelogue. ◆'**R~büro**, *n* travel agency/agent's. ◆'**r~fähig**, *adj.* fit to travel. ◆'**R~führer**, *m* (*a*) (*Buch*) guide book; (*b*) (*Pers.*) (travel) guide. ◆'**R~gepäck**, *n* (hand) luggage, *esp. N.Am:* baggage. ◆'**R~gesellschaft**, *f* party of tourists. ◆'**R~leiter(in)**, *m(f)* tour leader. ◆'**r~n**, *v.i.* (*sein*) to travel; **nach Italien, in den Urlaub usw. r.**, to go to Italy, on holiday etc. ◆'**R~nde(r)**, *m & f decl. as adj.* traveller. ◆'**R~paß**, *m* passport. ◆'**R~route**, *f* itinerary. ◆'**R~scheck**, *m* traveller's cheque. ◆'**R~tasche**, *f* travelling bag. ◆'**R~ziel**, *n* destination.

**Reisig** ['raiziç], *n -s/no pl* brushwood.

**Reiß**|**aus** [rais'?aus], *m F:* **R. nehmen**, to scram, hop it. ◆'**R~brett**, *n* drawing board. ◆'**r~en** ['raisən], *v.irr.* **1.** *v.tr.* (*a*) to tear (sth.); *Fig:* **die Macht usw. an sich r.**, to seize power etc.; **j-n zu Boden r.**, to pull/drag s.o. to the ground; (*b*) *F:* **sich um etwas** *acc* **r.**, to be dead keen on (doing) sth; (*c*) **Witze r.**, to crack jokes. **2.** *v.i.* (*a*) (*sein*) (*Papier, Stoff*) to tear, rip; (*Seil usw.*) to break, snap; (*b*) (*haben*) **an etwas** *dat* **r.**, to pull on/at sth. ◆'**r~end**, *adj.* torrential (stream, river etc.); searing (pain); *Com:* **r~en Absatz finden**, to sell like hot cakes. ◆'**R~er**, *m -s/- Pej: F:* (*Roman, Film usw.*) cheap thriller. ◆'**r~erisch**, *adj.* sensational (advertising etc.). ◆'**R~leine**, *f* (parachute) ripcord. ◆'**R~verschluß**, *m* zip(-fastener), *N.Am:* zipper. ◆'**R~zwecke**, *f* drawing pin, *N.Am:* thumb tack.

**Reit**- ['rait-], *comb.fm.* riding (instructor, whip, school, boot etc.); *R~hose f*, riding breeches. ◆'**r~en**, *v.irr.* & *i.* (*sein, occ. haben*) to ride. ◆'**R~er**, *m -s/-* (*Pers.*) rider, horseman; *Mil:* cavalryman. ◆**R~e'rei**, *f -/-en Mil:* cavalry. ◆'**R~erin**, *f -/-nen* horsewoman. ◆'**R~pferd**, *n* saddle-horse. ◆'**R~turnier**, *n* horse show.

**Reiz** [raits], *m -es/-e* **1.** *Psy: etc:* stimulus. **2.** (*a*) attraction; lure (des Unbekannten, of the unknown); (*b*) *usu.pl* **R~e**, charms. ◆'**r~bar**, *adj.* irritable, touchy. ◆'**R~barkeit**, *f -/no pl* irritability; sensitiveness. ◆'**r~en**, *v.tr.* to excite, rouse (s.o.); to arouse (curiosity, desire etc.); to stimulate (feelings); **einen Hund r.**, to tease a dog; **der Rauch reizt die Augen**, smoke irritates the eyes; (b) (anziehen) to attract (s.o.); **das reizt mich nicht**, that doesn't appeal to me; (c) also v.i. (haben) (im Skat) to bid (sth.). ◆'r~**end**, adj. charming; enchanting (girl etc.). ◆'R~**husten**, m dry (tickling) cough. ◆'r~**los**, adj. unattractive. ◆'R~**ung**, f -/-en Med: irritation. ◆'r~**voll**, adj. delightful, charming; r~**volle Aufgabe**, attractive/fascinating task. ◆'R~**wäsche**, f sexy underwear.

**rekeln** ['re:kəln], v.refl. F: **sich r.**, to stretch; (im Stuhl usw.) to sprawl.

**Reklam|ation** [reklamatsi'o:n], f -/-en complaint. ◆R~**e** [re'kla:mə]. I. f -/-n 1. (Werbung) advertising, publicity; **R. für etwas acc machen**, to advertise/ promote/F: push sth. 2. F: (Anzeige) advertisement, (Plakat) poster; Rad: TV: commercial. II. **R~e-**, comb.fm. publicity (film, purpose etc.); advertising (sign etc.). ◆R~**esendung**, f Rad: TV: commercial. ◆r~**ieren** [-a'mi:rən], v. 1. v.tr. (a) Com: etc: to complain about (a lost parcel, damaged goods etc.); (b) to reclaim, claim back (money etc.). 2. v.i. (haben) to complain; to protest.

**rekonstruieren** [rekɔnstru'i:rən], v.tr. to reconstruct (sth.).

**Rekord** [re'kɔrt]. I. m -(e)s/-e Sp: etc: record. II. **R~-**, comb.fm. record (attendance, attempt, time etc.). ◆R~**halter**, m record holder.

**Rekrut** [re'kru:t], m -en/-en Mil: recruit. ◆r~**ieren** [-u'ti:rən], v.tr. to recruit (staff, A: soldiers).

**Rektor** ['rɛktɔr], m -s/-en [-'to:rən] (a) (Universität) rector; Brit: vice-chancellor, N.Am: president; (b) Sch: headmaster, N.Am: principal.

**Relais** [rə'lɛ:], n -/- [-'lɛ:(s)] relay.

**relativ** [rela'ti:f], adj. relative; **es geht mir r. gut**, I am fairly/reasonably well. ◆R~**ität** [-ivi'tɛ:t], f -/-en relativity.

**Relief** [reli'ɛf], n -s/-e & -s relief.

**Religi|on** [religi'o:n], f -/-en religion; (Konfession) denomination; (Schulfach) religious education, R.E. ◆R~'**ons-**, comb.fm. religious (freedom, war etc.); (history etc.) of religion. ◆R~'**onsstunde**, f R.E./scripture lesson. ◆r~**ös** [-gi'ø:s], adj. religious.

**Reling** ['re:liŋ], f -/-s & -e (deck) rail.

**Remis** [re'mi:], n -/- & -en drawn game, draw.

**Rempel|ei** [rɛmpə'lai], f -/-en F: jostling; Fb: pushing. ◆'r~**n**, v.tr. to jostle, Fb: push (s.o.).

**Ren** [rɛn], n -s/-s reindeer.

**Rendezvous** [rãde'vu:], n -/- [-'vu:(s)] rendezvous.

**Renn-** ['rɛn-], comb.fm. racing (boat, season, Aut: tyres etc.); race(-day etc.). ◆'R~**bahn**, f race course/track. ◆'r~**en**. I. v.i.irr. (sein) to run, (eilen)

rush. II. **R.**, n -s/- 1. no pl running, racing. 2. Sp: (Wettbewerb) race; F: **das R. machen**, to win the race; Fig: to come out on top. ◆'R~**rad**, n racing cycle. ◆'R~**sport**, m racing. ◆'R~**strecke**, f racing circuit; race course.

**renovier|en** [reno'vi:rən], v.tr. (a) to renovate (a building etc.); (b) to redecorate (a room etc.). ◆R~**ung**, f -/-en (a) renovation; (b) redecoration.

**rent|abel** [rɛn'ta:bəl], adj. profitable. ◆R~**abilität** [-tabili'tɛ:t], f -/no pl profitability. ◆'R~**e**, f -/-n pension. ◆'R~**enversicherung**, f pension (insurance) scheme. ◆r~**ieren** [-'ti:rən], v.refl. **sich r.**, to be profitable/(sich lohnen) worth while. ◆'R~**ner(in)**, m -s/- (f -/-nen) (old-age) pensioner.

**Rentier** ['rɛnti:r], n reindeer.

**reparabel** [repa'ra:bəl], adj. repairable.

**Repar|atur** [repara'tu:r], f -/-en repair. ◆r~**a'turbedürftig**, adj. in need of repair. ◆R~**a'turwerkstatt**, f (repair) workshop. ◆r~**ieren** [-'ri:rən], v.tr. to repair (sth.), mend (shoes etc.).

**Repertoire** [reper'toa:r], n -s/-s Mus: etc: repertoire; Th: repertory.

**Report** [re'pɔrt], m -(e)s/-e report. ◆R~**age** [-'ta:ʒə], f -/-n (a) (esp. eyewitness) report; TV: documentary; (b) Rad: etc: (running) commentary. ◆R~**er** [re'pɔrtər], m -s/- (a) reporter; (b) Rad: etc: commentator.

**Repräsent|ant** [reprɛzɛn'tant], m -en/-en Pol: etc: representative. ◆r~**ativ** [-ta'ti:f], adj. 1. prestige (car, address, building etc.). 2. (typisch) representative. ◆r~**ieren** [-'ti:rən], v.tr. to represent (sth.).

**Repress|alie** [reprɛ'sa:liə], f -/-n reprisal. ◆R~**ion** [-si'o:n], f -/-en repression. ◆r~**iv** [-'si:f], adj. repressive.

**Reprodu|ktion** [reproduktsi'o:n], f reproduction. ◆r~'**zieren**, v.tr. to reproduce (a painting etc.).

**Reptil** [rɛp'ti:l], n -s/-ien reptile.

**Republik** [repu'bli:k], f -/-en Pol: republic. ◆R~**aner** [-i'ka:nər], m -s/- republican. ◆r~**anisch** [-i'ka:niʃ], adj. republican.

**Requiem** ['re:kviɛm], n -s/-s requiem.

**Requisiten** [rekvi'zi:tən], npl Th: (stage) properties, F: props.

**Reserv|at** [rezɛr'va:t], n -(e)s/-e reservation (for an ethnic group etc.). ◆R~**e** [re'zɛrvə]. I. f -/-n reserve; Mil: **die R.**, the reserves; **j-n aus seiner R. locken**, to make s.o. come out of his shell. II. **R~-**, comb.fm. spare (battery etc.); reserve (Mil: officer, Aut: tank etc.). ◆R~**erad**, n spare wheel. ◆r~**ieren** [-'vi:rən], v.tr. to reserve (a table etc.). ◆r~**iert**, adj. reserved. ◆R~**ierung**, f -/-en reservation. ◆R~**ist**, m -en/-en Mil: reservist. ◆R~**oir** [-'voa:r], n -s/-e reservoir.

**Residenz** [rezi'dɛnts], f -/-en (prince's)

residence.

**Resign|ation** [rezignatsi'o:n], *f -/-en* resignation. ◆**r~ieren** [-'gni:rən], *v.i.* (*haben*) to resign oneself, give up.

**resolut** [rezo'lu:t], *adj.* resolute, determined. ◆**R~ion** [-tsi'o:n], *f -/-en* resolution.

**Resonanz** [rezo'nants], *f -/-en* **1.** *Ph: etc:* resonance. **2.** *Fig:* response.

**Respekt** [re'spɛkt], *m -(e)s/no pl* respect. ◆**r~abel** [-'ta:bəl], *adj.* **1.** respectable (size etc.). **2.** reasonable (decision, grounds etc.). ◆**r~ieren** [-'ti:rən], *v.tr.* to respect. ◆**r~los,** *adj.* disrespectful. ◆**R~sperson,** *f* person commanding respect. ◆**r~voll,** *adj.* respectful.

**Ressort** [rɛ'so:r], *n -s/-s Adm:* (government etc.) department.

**Rest** [rɛst], *m -(e)s/-e* rest; *Fin:* balance (of a sum); *pl* **R~e,** leftovers, scraps (of food etc.); remains (of a castle etc.); *Fig:* **j-m den R. geben,** to finish s.o. off. ◆**'R~bestand,** *m Com: etc:* remaining stock. ◆**'R~betrag,** *m* balance. ◆**'r~lich,** *attrib. adj.* remaining. ◆**'r~los,** *adj.* complete (confidence, satisfaction etc.); total, utter (exhaustion etc.).

**Restaurant** [rɛsto'rɑ̃:], *n* restaurant.

**Restaur|ation** [rɛstauratsi'o:n], *f -/-en* restoration. ◆**r~ieren** [-'ri:rən], *v.tr.* to restore (a building etc.).

**Resultat** [rezul'ta:t], *n -(e)s/-e* result.

**Resümee** [rezy'me:], *n -s/-s* summary.

**Retorte** [re'tortə], *f -/-n* retort. ◆**R~nbaby,** *n* test-tube baby.

**rett|en** ['rɛtən], *v.tr.* to save, rescue (s.o., an animal etc.); to salvage (a ship etc.); to retrieve (one's honour); **r~der Gedanke,** solution, way out; *F:* **bist du noch zu r.?** are you out of your mind? **sich vor Anfragen nicht r. können,** to be swamped with enquiries. ◆**'R~er(in),** *m -s/- (f -/-nen)* rescuer. ◆**'R~ung,** *f -/ -en* rescue; *F:* **du bist meine letzte R.,** you are my only hope; **das war seine R.,** that was his salvation. ◆**'R~ungs-comb.fm.** rescue (operation, service etc.). ◆**'R~ungsboot,** *n* lifeboat. ◆**'r~ungslos,** *adj.usu.adv.* beyond all hope; **er ist r. verloren,** there is no hope for him. ◆**'R~ungsring,** *m* lifebelt.

**retuschieren** [retu'ʃi:rən], *v.tr. Phot: etc:* to retouch, touch up (a picture etc.).

**Reu|e** ['rɔyə], *f -/no pl* remorse; (*also Ecc:*) repentance. ◆**'r~en,** *v.tr. Lit:* (*Tat usw.*) to fill (s.o.) with remorse; **es reut mich, daß ...,** I regret that ... ◆**'r~ig,** *adj. Lit:* penitent, repentant. ◆**'r~mütig,** *adj. esp. Hum:* remorseful, rueful.

**Revanch|e** [re'vɑ̃:ʃ(ə)], *f -/-n* (*a*) revenge; (*b*) *Sp: etc:* return match/game. ◆**r~ieren** [-'ʃi:rən], *v.refl.* **sich r.,** to take one's revenge, *F:* get one's own back (**an j-m,** on s.o.); **sich bei j-m (für seine Güte usw.) r.,** to reciprocate (s.o.'s

kindness etc.).

**Revers** [re'vɛ:r], *n -/- Cl:* lapel.

**revidieren** [revi'di:rən], *v.tr.* (*ändern*) to revise (one's opinion etc.).

**Revier** [re'vi:r], *n -s/-e* **1.** (*Bereich*) territory (of an animal, gang etc.); (policeman's etc.) beat, *F:* patch; (*Kohlenr.*) mining district; (*Jagdr.*) shoot; hunt. **2.** (*Polizeiwache*) police station.

**Revision** [revizi'o:n], *f -/-en* **1.** (*Prüfung*) checking; *Com:* audit. **2.** *Jur:* appeal.

**Revol|te** [re'voltə], *f -/-n* revolt. ◆**R~ution** [-olutsi'o:n], *f -/-en* revolution. ◆**R~utionär** [-o'nɛ:r], *m -s/-e* revolutionary. ◆**r~utio'nieren,** *v.tr.* to revolutionize (a country, ideas etc.).

**Revolver** [re'volvər], *m -s/-* revolver.

**Rezens|ent** [retsɛn'zɛnt], *m -en/-en* (book etc.) reviewer; *Th: Mus:* critic. ◆**r~ieren** [-'zi:rən], *v.tr.* to review (a book, play etc.). ◆**R~ion** [-zi'o:n], *f -/ -en* review.

**Rezept** [re'tsɛpt], *n -(e)s/-e* **1.** *Med:* prescription; *Fig:* cure, remedy. **2.** *Cu: & Fig:* recipe. ◆**R~ion** [-tsi'o:n], *f -/-en* reception (desk). ◆**r~pflichtig,** *adj.* obtainable only on prescription.

**rezitieren** [retsi'ti:rən], *v.tr.* to recite (a poem etc.).

**Rhabarber** [ra'barbər], *m -s/no pl* rhubarb.

**Rhapsodie** [rapzo'di:, raps-], *f -/-n* rhapsody.

**Rhein** [rain]. *Pr.n.m -s.* **der R.,** the Rhine. ◆**'r~isch,** *adj.* Rhenish. ◆**'R~land.** *Pr.n.n -s.* **das R.,** the Rhineland.

**Rhetori|k** [re'to:rik], *f -/no pl* rhetoric. ◆**r~sch,** *adj.* rhetorical.

**Rheuma** ['rɔyma], *n -s/no pl*/**R~'tismus,** *m -/-men* rheumatism.

**Rhinozeros** [ri'no:tserɔs], *n -ses/-se* rhinoceros.

**rhythm|isch** ['rytmiʃ], *adj.* rhythmical. ◆**'R~us,** *m -/-men* rhythm.

**Richt-** ['riçt-], *comb.fm.* guide, guiding (value, figure etc.); (*empfohlen*) recommended (price etc.). ◆**'R~antenne,** *f* directional antenna. ◆**'r~en,** *v.tr.* (*a*) to aim, point (a gun, telescope etc.) (**auf +** *acc,* at); to direct (an aerial, *Fig:* efforts etc.), turn (one's eyes etc.) (**auf +** *acc,* towards); **eine Frage an j-n r.,** to put/ address a question to s.o.; (*b*) (*zurechtmachen*) to straighten (teeth, wire etc.); to prepare (a meal etc.); (*c*) (*Urteil fällen*) to judge, pass sentence on (s.o.); (*d*) **sich nach etwas** *dat* **r.,** to comply/adhere to sth.; (*auf etwas ankommen*) to depend on sth.; **danach kann man sich nicht r.,** you cannot go by that; ◆**'R~er(in),** *m -s/- (f -/-nen)* judge. ◆**R~geschwindigkeit,** *f* recommended (maximum) speed. ◆**'R~linie,** *f* guideline, guiding principle. ◆**'R~ung,** *f -/-en* (*a*) direction; (*b*) *Fig:* direction, line (of thought, research etc.); *Art: Pol:* movement, trend. ◆'R~ungsanzeiger, *m Aut:* direction indicator.

**richtig** ['riçtiç], *adj.* **1.** *(nicht falsch)* right, correct (answer, assumption etc.); **das ist genau das R~e!** that's just the job! **ich halte es für das r~ste,** I think it would be the best thing; **etwas r. machen,** to do sth. correctly; **er kam gerade r.,** he came at just the right moment; **(sehr) r.!** quite right! **2.** *(echt)* proper (meal, job etc.); real (name, mother, *F:* coward etc.). ◆'R~**keit,** *f -/no pl* correctness; accuracy (of a statement etc.); rightness (of a decision etc.). ◆'r~**stellen,** *v.tr.sep.* to correct (a statement etc.), rectify (a mistake etc.). ◆'R~**stellung,** *f -/-en* correction.

**riechen** ['riçən], *v.tr. & i.irr.* (haben) to smell; **das konnte ich wirklich nicht r.,** how was I to know? *F:* **ich kann ihn nicht r.,** I can't stand him.

**Ried** [ri:t], *n -(e)s/-e* reeds.

**Riege** ['ri:gə], *f -/-n* squad.

**Riegel** ['ri:gəl], *m -s/-* **1.** bolt (of a door etc.). **2.** bar (of soap, chocolate).

**Riemen** ['ri:mən], *m -s/-* **1.** strap; *(Gürtel)* belt. **2.** *Nau:* *(Ruder)* oar.

**Ries|e** ['ri:zə], *m -n/-n* giant. ◆'R~**en-,** *comb.fm.* (a) giant (wheel, firm, *Ski:* slalom, *Z:* tortoise etc.); enormous, gigantic (building, portion etc.); (b) *F:* tremendous (success, fun etc.); (c) *F: Pej:* terrible (mistake, stupidity etc.). ◆'r~**en-'groß,** *adj. F:* gigantic, enormous; colossal (stupidity). ◆'R~**enschlange,** *f* (giant) boa constrictor. ◆'r~**ig,** *adj.* enormous, gigantic; tremendous (strength etc.).

**rieseln** ['ri:zəln], *v.i.* (a) (sein) (Wasser, Sand usw.) to trickle; (b) (haben) (Regen) to drizzle, (Schnee) fall lightly.

**Riff** [rif], *n -(e)s/-e* reef.

**rigoros** [rigo'ro:s], *adj.* rigorous, severe.

**Rille** ['rilə], *f -/-n* groove.

**Rind** [rint], *n -(e)s/-er* **1.** *(Stier)* bull; *(Kuh)* cow. **2.** *Cu:* beef. ◆'R~**er-** ['rindər-], *comb.fm.* **1.** *Cu:* beef (goulash etc.). **2.** *Agr:* (herd etc.) of cattle. ◆'R~**erbraten,** *m* roast beef. ◆'R~**erfilet,** *n* fillet of beef. ◆'R~**fleisch,** *n* beef. ◆'R~**sleder,** *n* cowhide. ◆'R~**vieh,** *n* **1.** *coll.* cattle. **2.** *F: (pl* **R~viecher)** ass, twit.

**Rinde** ['rində], *f -/-n* **1.** *(Baumr.)* bark. **2.** *(Brotr.)* crust; *(Käser. usw.)* rind.

**Ring** [riŋ], *m -(e)s/-e* ring; circle (of people etc.). ◆'r~**förmig,** *adj.* ringshaped, annular. ◆'R~**richter,** *m Sp:* referee.

**ringeln** ['riŋəln], *v.tr.* to curl (hair), coil (a tail etc.); **sich r.,** to curl, form curls. ◆'R~**natter,** *f* grass snake.

**ring|en** ['riŋən]. **I.** *v.i.irr.* (haben) to wrestle; *esp. Fig:* to struggle; **nach Atem/Luft r.,** to gasp/struggle for breath. **II. R~en,** *n -s/no pl Sp:* wrestling; *Fig:* struggle. ◆'R~**kampf,** *m* wrestling bout.

**rings** [riŋs], *adv.* round about, all around. ◆'r~**he'rum/r~um'her,** *adv.* all around, all the way round.

**Rinn|e** ['rinə], *f -/-n* *(also Nau:)* channel; *(Rinnstein, Dachr.)* gutter. ◆'r~**en,** *v.i.irr.* (sein) (Regen, Tränen usw.) to flow, run; (Sand) to trickle. ◆'R~**sal,** *n -(e)s/-e* trickle; *(Bächlein)* rivulet. ◆'R~**stein,** *m* gutter.

**Ripp|chen** ['ripçən], *n -s/-* *Cu:* *(esp.* spare) rib (of pork). ◆'R~**e,** *f -/-n* rib. ◆'R~**enbruch,** *m* broken rib. ◆'R~**enfellentzündung,** *f* pleurisy.

**Risiko** ['ri:ziko], *n -s/-s & -ken* risk. ◆'r~**los,** *adj.* safe, without any risk.

**risk|ant** [ris'kant], *adj.* risky, hazardous. ◆r~**ieren** [-'ki:rən], *v.tr.* to risk (sth.).

**Riß** [ris], *m -sses/-sse* *(im Stoff, Papier usw.)* tear; *(im Felsen)* fissure, cleft; *Fig: (zwischen Freunden)* rift; *Pol:* split.

**rissig** ['risiç], *adj.* cracked; chapped (skin).

**Rist** [rist], *m -(e)s/-e* *(am Fuß)* instep; *(an der Hand)* back of the hand.

**Ritt** [rit], *m -(e)s/-e* ride (on a horse etc.). ◆'R~**er,** *m -s/-* knight. ◆'r~**erlich,** *adj.* chivalrous; *Hist:* knightly. ◆'R~**ersporn** *m -(e)s/-e* larkspur, delphinium.

**Rit|ual** [ritu'a:l], *n -s/-e & -ien* ritual. ◆r~**u'ell,** *adj.* ritual.

**Ritz** [rits], *m -es/-e* scratch. ◆'R~**e,** *f -/-n* crack; *(im Vorhang usw.)* gap, chink. ◆'r~**en,** *v.tr.* to scratch (sth.), *(schneiden)* cut (glass etc.); to carve (one's name etc.).

**Rival|e** [ri'va:lə], *m -n/-n/R~in,** *f -/-nen* rival; *esp. Sp:* competitor. ◆R~**i'tät,** *f -/-en* rivalry.

**Rizinusöl** ['ri:tsinus?ø:l], *n* castor oil.

**Robbe** ['rɔbə], *f -/-n* seal.

**Roboter** ['rɔbɔtər], *m -s/-* robot.

**robust** [ro'bust], *adj.* robust (material, health etc.); strong, sturdy (person, table etc.).

**röcheln** ['ræçəln], *v.i.* (haben) to breathe stertorously; *(Sterbende)* to give the death rattle.

**Rochen** ['rɔxən], *m -s/-* ray.

**Rock** [rɔk], *m -(e)s/-e* skirt.

**rodeln** ['ro:dəln], *v.i.* (sein/haben) to toboggan. ◆'R~**schlitten,** *m* toboggan.

**roden** ['ro:dən], *v.tr.* to clear (woodland).

**Rogen** ['ro:gən], *m -s/-* (hard) roe.

**Roggen** ['rɔgən], *m -s/-* rye. ◆'R~**brot,** *n* rye bread.

**roh** [ro:]. **I.** *adj.* **1.** (a) raw (hide, silk etc.); raw, uncooked (food); (b) crude (oil); unrefined (sugar); (c) rough, uncut (diamond). **2.** *(ungenau)* rough (sketch, shaping estimate). **3.** *(grob)* coarse, uncouth (person, manners etc.); **mit r~er Gewalt,** with brute force. **II.** 'R~, *comb.fm.* raw (vegetables, silk etc.); uncut (diamond); crude (ore, oil). ◆'R~**bau,** *m* shell. ◆'R~**eisen,** *n* pig-iron. ◆'R~**kost,** *f* raw (vegetarian

food. ◆'R~ling, m -s/-e (Pers.) brute.
◆'R~material, n/'R~stoff, m raw material. ◆'R~zustand, m natural/Ind: crude state.

Rohr [ro:r], n -(e)s/-e 1. (Schilfr.) reed; coll. reeds; (Zuckerr., Bambusr.) cane. 2. (a) tube; (R~leitung) (water etc.) pipe; (b) (Geschützr.) (gun) barrel. ◆'R~bruch, m burst pipe. ◆'r~förmig, adj. tubular. ◆'R~geflecht, n wickerwork. ◆'R~leitung, f (water/gas) pipe, main. ◆'R~post, f pneumatic tube post. ◆'R~stock, m cane (stick). ◆'R~zucker, m cane sugar.

Röhre ['rø:rə], f -/-n 1. (a) Tchn: tube; (für Wasser usw.) pipe; (b) Rad: valve, N.Am: tube. 2. Cu: oven. ◆'r~nförmig, adj. tubular.

Rokoko ['rokoko], n -s/no pl rococo.

Roll|bahn ['rolba:n], f -/-en Av: runway. ◆'R~e, f -/-n 1. roll (of paper, film, money etc.); (Garnr.) reel, N.Am: spool (of thread). 2. Tchn: (Walze) roller. 3. Th: Cin: etc: part; esp. Fig: role; Fig: (bei etwas dat) eine große R. spielen, to play an important part/figure prominently (in sth.). ◆'r~en, v. 1 v.i. (sein) to roll; (Fahrzeug) to move, Av: taxi; ins R. kommen, to start to move, (also F: Sache) get under way. 2. v.tr. to roll (a ball, barrel etc.). ◆'R~er, m -s/- 1. (child's) scooter. 2. (Welle) (heavy) roller. ◆'R~feld, n Av: airfield. ◆'R~film, m roll film. ◆'R~kragen, m polo neck/N.Am: collar. ◆'R~mops, m pickled herring, rollmops. ◆'R~schuh, m roller skate. ◆'R~schuhläufer, m roller-skater. ◆'R~splitt, m (rolled) loose chippings. ◆'R~stuhl, m wheelchair. ◆'R~treppe, f escalator.

Rom [ro:m]. Pr.n.n -s. Rome.

Roman [ro'ma:n], m -s/-e novel. ◆R~cier [romāsi'e:], m -s/-s/R~schriftsteller, m novelist.

Roman|tik [ro'mantik], f -/no pl romanticism. ◆r~tisch, adj. romantic. ◆R~ze, f -/-n romance.

Römer|er ['rø:mər], m -s/- 1. (Pers.) Roman. 2. (Weinglas) large goblet (with green/brown stem). ◆'R~erin, f -/-nen Roman (woman/girl). ◆'r~isch, adj. Roman, of Rome. ◆'r~isch-katholisch, adj. Roman Catholic.

Rommé ['rome], n -s/-s rummy.

röntgen ['rœntgən]. I. v.tr. to X-ray (s.o., sth.); sich r. lassen, to have an X-ray. II. 'R~-, comb.fm. X-ray (treatment, examination etc.). ◆'R~aufnahme, f X-ray (picture). ◆'R~strahlen, mpl X-rays.

rosa ['ro:za], inv.adj. pink. ◆'r~farben/'r~farbig, adj. pink. ◆'r~rot, adj. (esp. deep) pink.

Rose ['ro:zə], f -/-n rose. ◆'R~n-, 'r~n-, comb.fm. rose (garden, hedge, oil, water etc.); (scent, bunch etc.) of roses. ◆'R~nkohl, m (Brussels) sprouts.

◆'R~nkranz, m rosary; den R. beten, to say the rosary. ◆'R~n'montag, m Shrove Monday.

rosig ['ro:ziç], adj. rosy (cheeks, Fig: prospects etc.).

Rosine [ro'zi:nə], f -/-n raisin.

Roß [ros], n -sses/-sse & -sser Lit: steed. ◆'R~kastanie, f horse-chestnut. ◆'R~kur, f F: drastic/kill-or-cure treatment.

Rost¹ [rost], m -(e)s/-e grid (iron), grating; (Feuerstelle) grate; Cu: grill. ◆'R~braten, m grilled steak.

Rost², m -(e)s/no pl rust. ◆'r~en, v.i. (haben/sein) to rust. ◆'r~frei, adj. rustproof; stainless (steel). ◆'r~ig, adj. rusty. ◆'r~rot, adj. rust-red. ◆'R~schutzmittel, n anti-rust preparation.

rösten ['rœstən], v.tr. Cu: to grill (meat), roast (coffee), fry (potatoes), toast (bread etc.). ◆'R~er, m -s/- (für Brot) toaster.

rot [ro:t]. I. adj. red; sie wurde r., she went red (in the face)/blushed; das R~e Meer, the Red Sea; das R~e Kreuz, the Red Cross; r~e Beete/Rübe, beetroot. II. R., n -s/- (a) red; (b) Aut: (Ampel) bei R., when the lights are red. III. R~-, 'r~-, comb.fm. red (light, wine etc.). ◆'R~barsch, m rosefish; N.Am: ocean perch. ◆'r~blond, adj. ginger (hair); ginger-haired (person). ◆'r~haarig, adj. red-haired. ◆'R~käppchen. Pr.n.n -s. Little Red Riding Hood. ◆'R~kehlchen, n -s/- robin (redbreast). ◆'R~kohl, m red cabbage. ◆'r~sehen, v.i.sep.irr. 92 (haben) F: to see red, go into a rage. ◆'R~wild, n red deer.

Rotation [rotatsi'o:n], f -/-en rotation.

rotieren [ro'ti:rən], v.i. (haben) to rotate.

Röt|e ['rø:tə], f -/no pl redness; (im Gesicht) blush; flush (of anger). ◆'R~eln, pl German measles. ◆'r~en, v.tr. to redden (sth.). ◆'r~lich, adj. reddish; ruddy (cheeks etc.).

Rotz [rots], m -es/-e P: snot; ◆'r~näsig [-ne:ziç], adj. F: (a) snotty-nosed; (b) (frech) cheeky.

Roulade [ru'la:də], f -/-n beef olive.

Route ['ru:tə], f -/-n route.

Routin|e [ru'ti:nə], f -/no pl (a) routine; (b) (Erfahrung) experience. ◆r~emäßig, adj. routine (examination etc.). ◆'r~iert [-ti'ni:rt], adj. experienced (driver, lecturer etc.); expert (card player etc.).

Rowdy ['raudi], m -s/-s rowdy, hooligan.

Rübe ['ry:bə], f -/-n beet; weiße R., turnip; gelbe R., carrot; rote R., beetroot. ◆'R~nzucker, m beet sugar.

Rubel ['ru:bəl], m -s/- rouble.

rüber ['ry:bər], adv. F: = herüber/hinüber; komm r.! come over (to us)!

Rubin [ru'bi:n], m -s/-e ruby. ◆r~rot, adj. ruby(-red).

Rubrik [ru'bri:k], f -/-en heading; (Spalte) column.

**Ruck** |ruk|, *m* -(e)s/-e jerk; (*Stoß*) jolt; (*Zug*) tug, yank; **einen R. geben,** to jerk, (*Fahrzeug*) lurch; *F:* **in einem R.,** in one go. ◆'r~**artig,** *adj.* jerky (movement etc.); sudden (braking etc.); *adv.* suddenly, with a jerk. ◆'R~**sack,** *m* rucksack. ◆'r~**weise,** *adv.* in fits and starts.

**Rück-, rück-** |'ryk-|, *comb.fm.* 1. (*hintere, nach hinten*) rear, back (wall etc.); rear (light etc.). 2. return (flight, flow, march, *Tel:* call etc.). ◆'R~**antwort** *f* reply. ◆'R~**blick,** *m* review (of past events); **im R.,** in retrospect. ◆'r~**blickend,** *adj.* retrospective; *adv.* looking back, in retrospect. ◆'r~**erstatten,** *v.tr.insep.* to refund (expenses, taxes etc.) (j-m, s.o.); to return (property). ◆'R~**erstattung,** *f* refund; return (of property). ◆'R~**fahrkarte,** *f* return ticket. ◆'R~**fahrt,** *f* return journey. ◆'R~**fall,** *m Med: etc:* relapse; *F: (in alte Gewohnheiten)* backsliding. ◆'r~**fällig,** *adj.* r. werden, to have a relapse; *Fig:* to go back to one's old ways/*Jur:* a life of crime. ◆'R~**frage,** *f* (further) question, query. ◆'r~**fragen,** *v.i. sep.* (*haben*) **bei j-m r.,** to check with s.o. ◆'R~**gabe,** *f* return (of money etc.). ◆'R~**gang,** *m* decrease, decline (in population etc.); drop, fall (in prices etc.); **R. an Geburten,** drop in the number of births. ◆'r~**gängig,** *adj.* **etwas r. machen,** to cancel sth. ◆'R~**grat,** *n Anat:* spine; *Fig:* backbone (of a country etc.); *F:* **j-m das R. brechen,** to break s.o.'s will/resistance. ◆'R~**griff,** *m* recourse (**auf** + *acc,* to). ◆'R~**halt,** *m (Unterstützung)* support, backing. ◆'r~**haltlos,** *adj.* unreserved (admiration etc.); complete (support etc.). ◆'R~**kehr,** *f -/no pl* return. ◆'R~**lage,** *f Fin: esp.pl* **R~lagen,** reserves. ◆'r~**läufig,** *adj.* declining (number, production etc.); *Com:* downward (tendency etc.). ◆'r~**lings,** *adv.* (*von hinten*) from behind/the rear; **er fiel r. hin,** he fell (over) backwards. ◆'R~**nahme,** *f -/no pl Com: etc:* taking back; withdrawal (of a statement etc.). ◆'R~**porto,** *n* return postage. ◆'R~**reise,** *f* return journey. ◆'R~**schau,** *f -/-en* review (**auf** + *acc,* of). ◆'R~**schlag,** *m* setback. ◆'R~**schluß,** *m* conclusion. ◆'R~**schritt,** *m* retrograde step. ◆'r~**schrittlich,** *adj.* reactionary. ◆'R~**seite,** *f* back; reverse (of a coin). ◆'R~**sendung,** *f* return (of a letter etc.). ◆'R~**sicht,** *f* consideration; **auf j-n R. nehmen,** to show consideration for s.o. ◆'r~**sichtslos,** *adj.* (*a*) inconsiderate; (*gefährlich*) reckless; (*b*) (*schonungslos*) ruthless. ◆'r~**sichtsvoll,** *adj.* considerate. ◆'R~**sitz,** *m* back seat. ◆'R~**spiegel,** *m* rear view mirror. ◆'R~**spiel,** *n* return match.

◆'R~**sprache,** *f* consultation. ◆'R~**stand,** *m* 1. (*Rest*) remains; *Ch:* residue. 2. backlog (of work etc.); *Fin:* arrears; **im R. sein,** to be behind. ◆'r~**ständig,** *adj.* 1. backward (country etc.); old-fashioned, outdated (equipment etc.). 2. (*Zahlung*) overdue, outstanding; (*Pers.*) in arrears. ◆'R~**stau,** *m Aut:* tailback. ◆'R~**strahler,** *m Aut: etc:* (rear) reflector. ◆'R~**taste,** *f* back spacer. ◆'R~**tritt,** *m* (*a*) resignation; (*Abdankung*) abdication; (*b*) withdrawal (**von einem Vertrag,** from a contract). ◆'R~**vergütung,** *f* (partial) refund. ◆'r~**wärtig,** *adj.* back (door, room etc.); rear (part, section etc.). ◆'r~**wärts,** *adv.* backwards; **von r.,** from behind. ◆'R~**wärtsgang,** *m Aut:* reverse gear. ◆'R~**weg,** *m* way back; (*nach Hause*) way home. ◆'r~**wirkend,** *adj. Jur: etc:* retrospective. ◆'R~**wirkung,** *f -/-en* repercussion (**auf** + *acc,* on). ◆'R~**zahlung,** *f* repayment. ◆'R~**zug,** *m* retreat.

**rücken¹** |'rykən|, *v.* 1. *v.tr.* to move, shift (a table etc.). 2. *v.i.* (*sein*) to move, (*stückweise*) edge; **mit dem Stuhl näher r.,** to pull up one's chair; **an j-s Stelle r.,** to take over from s.o.

**Rücken²** I. *m* -s/- (*a*) back (of s.o., sth.); (*b*) (*Bergr.*) (mountain) ridge. **'R~-,** *comb.fm.* back, *Anat:* dorsal (muscle etc.). ◆'R~**deckung,** *f* 1. *Mil: etc:* rear cover. 2. *Fig:* backing, support. ◆'R~**lehne,** *f* back (of a chair). ◆'R~**schwimmen,** *n* backstroke. ◆'R~**wind,** *m* tail/following wind. ◆'R~**wirbel,** *m* dorsal vertebra.

**rüde¹** |'ry:də|, *adj.* uncouth.

**Rüde²,** *m* -n/-n dog; male (fox/wolf).

**Rudel** |'ru:dəl|, *n* -s/- herd (of deer etc.); pack (of wolves); pride (of lions).

**Ruder** |'ru:dər|. I. *n* -s/- 1. oar. 2. *Nau:* (*Steuer:*) rudder; *esp. Fig:* helm; *Pol: etc:* **ans R. kommen,** to come to power. II. '**R~-,** *comb.fm.* rowing (club, regatta etc.). ◆'R~**boot,** *n* rowing boat, *N.Am:* rowboat. ◆'R~**er,** *m* -s/- oarsman, rower. ◆'r~**n.** I. *v.* 1. *v.i.* (*sein/haben*) to row. 2. *v.tr.* to row (s.o., a boat etc.). II. **R.,** *n* -s/no pl rowing.

**Ruf** |ru:f|, *m* -(e)s/-e 1. call (of s.o., a bird); (*Schrei*) cry, shout; *Fig:* **R. nach Freiheit,** call/demand for freedom. 2. reputation; **von R.,** of renown/repute. ◆'r~**en,** *v.irr.* 1. *v.i.* (*haben*) (*Pers., Vogel*) to call (**nach etwas** *dat,* for sth.); (*schreien*) to cry, shout. 2. *v.tr.* to call (s.o., an animal etc.). ◆'R~**mord,** *m* character assassination. ◆'R~**name,** *m* Christian name (*by which one is generally known*). ◆'R~**nummer,** *f* telephone number.

**Rüge** |'ry:gə|, *f -/-n* reprimand, rebuke; (*Kritik*) criticism. ◆'r~**n,** *v.tr.* to reprimand, rebuke (s.o.); to criticize, censure (an attitude etc.).

**Ruhe** ['ru:ə], *f -/no pl* (*a*) (*Stille*) quiet, silence; (*b*) (*Gelassenheit*) calmness, composure; *F:* **immer mit der R.!** take it easy! (*c*) (*Ungestörtheit*) peace; **R. und Ordnung,** law and order; *F:* **laß mich in R.!** leave me alone/in peace! (*d*) rest; (*Schlaf*) sleep; **angenehme R.!** sleep well! ◆'R~**gehalt,** *n* pension. ◆'r~**los,** *adj.* restless; unsettled (times etc.). ◆'r~**n,** *v.i.* (*haben*) (*a*) to rest; (*b*) (*zum Stillstand kommen*) (*Produktion, Verkehr usw.*) to have stopped, be at a standstill; (*Geschütze*) to be silent. ◆'R~**pause,** *f* break (from work). ◆'R~**stand,** *m* retirement; **in den R. treten/versetzt werden,** to retire/be retired. ◆'R~**stätte,** *f Lit:* (*letzte*) **R.,** last resting place. ◆'R~**störung,** *f* disturbance of the peace.

**ruhig** ['ru:iç], *adj.* (*a*) (*ohne Bewegung*) calm, still (water, air etc.); calm (weather, sea); smooth (crossing, flight); **r. sitzen/liegen,** to sit/lie still; (*b*) (*ohne Lärm*) quiet; (*c*) (*friedlich*) peaceful (life etc.); (*d*) (*gelassen*) calm (voice etc.); steady (hand, voice); **man kann das Kind r. allein lassen,** it's quite all right to leave the child alone.

**Ruhm** [ru:m], *m -(e)s/no pl* fame. ◆'r~**reich/'r~voll,** *adj. esp. Mil:* glorious (campaign, history etc.); famous (regiment etc.).

**rühmen** ['ry:mən], *v.tr. Lit:* to praise, extol (s.o., sth.); **sich einer Sache r.,** to pride oneself on sth.

**Ruhr** [ru:r], *f -/no pl Med:* dysentery.

**Rühr|ei** ['ry:r²ai], *n* scrambled eggs. ◆'r~**en. 1.** *v.tr.* (*a*) to stir (soup, paint etc.); (*b*) (*bewegen*) to move (an arm, leg etc.); **sich r.,** to move; (*Luft usw.*) to stir; *Fig:* (*Pers.*) (*aktiv sein*) to be up and doing; **rührt euch!** (i) *Mil:* (stand) at ease! (ii) *F:* (*beeilt euch*) get a move on! (*c*) (*innerlich bewegen*) to move, touch (s.o.); **es rührte ihn gar nicht,** it left him quite unmoved. **2.** *v.i.* (*haben*) (*a*) **im Kaffee r.,** to stir one's coffee; (*b*) *Lit:* **r. an** + *acc,* to touch (sth.), *Fig:* touch on (a subject). ◆'r~**end,** *adj.* touching. ◆'r~**ig,** *adj.* active; enterprising, go-ahead (businessman etc.). ◆'r~**selig,** *adj.* (sickeningly) sentimental; maudlin, *F:* tear-jerking (play etc.). ◆'R~**ung,** *f -/no pl* emotion.

**Ruin** [ru'i:n], *m -s/no pl* ruin. ◆R~**e** [ru'i:nə], *f -/-n* ruin(s). ◆r~**ieren** [-i'ni:rən], *v.tr.* to ruin (s.o., sth.); to wreck (s.o.'s nerve, hopes etc.).

**rülpsen** ['rylpsən], *v.i.* (*haben*) *F:* to belch.

**Rum** [rum], *m -s/-s* rum.

**Rumän|e** [ru'mɛ:nə], *m -n/-n* Romanian, R(o)umanian. ◆R~**ien.** *Pr.n.n -s.* Romania, R(o)umania. ◆r~**isch,** *adj.* Romanian, R(o)umanian.

**Rummel** ['ruməl], *m -s/no pl* (*a*) (*Trubel*) hustle and bustle; (*mit Lärm*) commotion; (*viel Aufsehen*) fuss, to-do; (*b*) (*Jahrmarkt*) fair. ◆'R~**platz,** *m* fairground.

**rumoren** [ru'mo:rən], *v.i.* (*haben*) *F:* to bang about, make a noise.

**Rumpel|kammer** ['rumpəlkamər], *f F:* lumber room, boxroom. ◆'r~**n,** *v.i.* (*haben/sein*) to rumble; (*Pers.*) to bang about.

**Rumpf** [rumpf], *m -(e)s/⸚e* **1.** *Anat:* trunk; torso. **2.** *Av:* fuselage; *Nau:* hull.

**rümpfen** ['rympfən], *v.tr.* **die Nase r.,** to turn up one's nose (**über etwas** *acc,* at sth.).

**rund** [runt]. **I.** *adj.* (*a*) round; **ein r~es Dutzend,** a good dozen. **II.** *adv.* **1. r. um** + *acc,* (a)round; **r. um die Welt,** all (a)round the world. **2. r. 50 Mark,** about/approximately 50 marks. **III.** '**R~-,** *comb.fm.* circular (building, tent etc.); round (arch, file, pillar etc.). ◆'R~**brief,** *m* circular letter. ◆R~**e** ['rundə], *f -/-n* (*a*) round; circle (of friends etc.); **eine R. Bier usw.,** a round of beer etc.; **R. durch die Stadt,** tour of the town; **eine R. machen,** (*spazieren*) to go round the block; (*b*) *Sp:* (*Durchgang*) round (of a competition etc.); (*bei Rennen*) lap. ◆'r~**en,** *v.tr.* to round (sth.), one's lips, back etc.); **sich r.,** to become round, fill out. ◆'R~**fahrt,** *f* circular tour. ◆'R~**frage,** *f* survey, questionnaire. ◆'R~**funk,** *m* radio; **im R.,** on the radio. ◆'R~**funk-,** *comb.fm.* radio (programme, announcer, technology etc.); ◆'R~**funkgebühr,** *f* radio licence fee. ◆'R~**funksender,** *m* radio station. ◆'R~**funksendung,** *f* radio broadcast. ◆'R~**gang,** *m* **1.** round (of a postman, night-watchman etc.); tour of inspection. **2.** (*in einer Burg usw.*) circular gallery/walk. ◆'r~**he'raus,** *adv.* straight out, bluntly; (*offen*) frankly. ◆'r~**he'rum,** *adv.* all round; *F:* (*völlig*) completely, thoroughly. ◆'r~**lich,** *adj.* plump, chubby. ◆'r~**weg,** *adv.* totally.

**runter** ['runtər], *adv. F:* = **herunter/hinunter.**

**Runz|el** ['runtsəl], *f -/-n* wrinkle. ◆'r~**(e)lig,** *adj.* wrinkled. ◆'r~**eln,** *v.tr.* **die Stirn r.,** to knit one's brows, frown; **sich r.,** to wrinkle.

**Rüpel** ['ry:pəl], *m -s/-* lout. ◆'r~**haft,** *adj.* loutish, uncouth.

**rupfen** ['rupfən], *v.tr.* to pluck (a chicken etc.); to pull up (grass, weeds etc.).

**ruppig** ['rupiç], *adj.* (*grob*) uncouth; gruff (answer).

**Rüsche** ['ry:ʃə], *f -/-n* frill.

**Ruß** [ru:s], *m -es/no pl* soot. ◆'r~**en,** *v.i.* (*haben*) to form soot. ◆'r~**ig,** *adj.* sooty.

**Russ|e** ['rusə], *m -n/-n* Russian. ◆'R~**in,** *f -/-nen* Russian woman. ◆'r~**isch,** *adj. &* **R.,** *n -(s)/no pl* Russian.

**Rüssel** ['rysəl], *m -s/-* (elephant's) trunk;

(pig's) snout.
**Rußland** ['ruslant]. *Pr.n.n* **-s.** Russia.
**rüst|en** ['rystən], *v.* **1.** *v.i.* (*haben*) to arm
(**zum Krieg**, for war). **2.** *v.refl.* **sich zu
etwas** *dat* **r.**, to prepare for sth.
◆'**r~ig**, *adj.* active, sprightly (elderly
person). ◆'**R~ung**, *f* -/-**en 1.** *no pl*
armament; (*Waffen*) arms, armaments. **2.**
*Hist:* (suit of) armour. ◆'**R~ungs-,
comb.fm.** arms (control, factory etc.);
armaments (industry etc.). ◆'**R~ungs-
beschränkung**, *f* arms limitation.
◆'**R~zeug**, *n* (*a*) (right) tools/
equipment for the job; (*b*) (*Wissen*)
know-how.
**rustikal** [rusti'kɑːl], *adj.* rustic.

**Rute** ['ruːtə], *f* -/-**n** (*esp.* birch) rod;
(*Gerte*) switch; (*Angelr.*) fishing rod.
**Rutsch** [rutʃ], *m* -(*e*)**s/-e** slip, slide;
(*Erdr.*) landslide; *F:* **auf einen R.**, in one
go; **guten R. (ins neue Jahr)!** Happy
New Year! ◆'**R~bahn**, *f* slide.
◆'**R~e**, *f* -/-**n** *Ind:* chute. ◆'**r~en**,
*v.i.* (*sein*) to slide; (*Pers.*, *Tchn: Kupplung
usw.*) to slip; (*Auto*) to skid. ◆'**r~fest**,
*adj.* non-slip (mat etc.). ◆'**r~ig**, *adj.*
slippery.
**rütteln** ['rytəln], *v.* **1.** *v.tr.* to shake (s.o.,
sth.). **2.** *v.i.* (*haben/sein*) (*a*) to shake,
(*Fahrzeug*) jolt; **an der Tür r.**, to rattle at
the door; (*b*) *Fig:* **daran ist nicht zu r.**,
that is irrefutable/(*Entschluß*) irrevocable.

# S

**S, s** [ɛs], *n* -/- (the letter) S, s.
**Saal** [zɑːl], *m* -(*e*)**s/Säle** hall.
**Saat** [zɑːt], *f* -/-**en 1.** *no pl* (*Säen*) sowing.
**2.** *coll.* (*Samen*) seed. **3.** *coll.* (*Pflanzen*)
seedlings, *Agr:* young crops. ◆'**S~gut**,
*n coll.* seed(s).
**sabbern** ['zabərn], *v.i.* (*haben*) *F:* to slobber, (*Baby*) dribble.
**Säbel** ['zɛːbəl], *m* -**s/-** sabre.
**Sabot|age** [zabo'tɑːʒə], *f* -/-**n** sabotage.
◆'**S~eur** [-'tøːr], *m* -**s/-e** saboteur.
◆**s~ieren** [-'tiːrən], *v.tr.* to sabotage.
**Sach|bearbeiter** ['zaxbəʔarbaitər], *m*
person/*Adm:* official responsible.
◆'**S~beschädigung**, *f* damage to
property. ◆'**S~buch**, *n* (*esp.* popularly
written) non-fiction book. ◆'**s~dien-
lich**, *adj.* relevant, helpful (information
etc.). ◆'**S~e**, *f* -/-**n 1.** *usu. pl* **S~n**,
things. **2.** (*Angelegenheit*) (*a*) matter, affair; **eine schlimme S.**, a bad business;
**er hat die ganze S. erfunden**, he made
up the whole thing; (*b*) **das ist ihre S.**,
that's her business/affair; **seine S. verstehen**, to know one's job/*F:* stuff; **das gehört nicht/tut nichts zur S.**, that is beside the point; **zur S. kommen**, to come
to the point; (*c*) (*wofür man sich einsetzt*)
cause. ◆'**S~gebiet**, *n* (subject) area,
field. ◆'**s~gemäß**, *adj.* proper, appropriate. ◆'**S~kenntnis**, *f* expertise;
*F:* know-how. ◆'**s~kundig**, *adj.* expert
(advice etc.); knowledgeable (person).
◆'**S~lage**, *f* -/*no pl* state of affairs;
(current) situation. ◆'**s~lich**, *adj.* (*a*)
(*faktisch*) factual (details etc.); practical
(reasons etc.); (*b*) (*nüchtern*) matter-of-
fact (person, attitude, tone etc.); businesslike (person, manner etc.). ◆'**S~-
schaden**, *m* material damage. ◆'**S~-
verhalt**, *m* -(*e*)**s/-e** facts (of the matter).
◆'**S~verständige(r)**, *m & f decl.* as
*adj.* expert.
**sächlich** ['zɛçliç], *adj.* neuter (noun etc.).
**Sachse** ['zaksə], *m* -**n/-n** Saxon. ◆'**S~n**.
*Pr.n.n* -**s.** Saxony.

**Sächs|in** ['zɛksin], *f* -/-**nen** Saxon girl/
woman. ◆'**s~isch**, *adj.* Saxon.
**sacht** [zaxt], *adj.* gentle; (*leise*) soft; (*vorsichtig*) cautious (movement etc.); *F:*
**s~e, s~e!** easy does it.
**Sack** [zak], *m* -(*e*)**s/-e** sack; *F:* **mit S. und
Pack**, with bag and baggage.
◆'**S~bahnhof**, *m* terminus. ◆'**s~en**,
*v.i.* (*sein*) (*Boden, Gebäude etc.*) to subside, sink; (*Pers.*) to slump (**in einen
Stuhl usw.**, into a chair etc.).
◆'**S~gasse**, *f* cul-de-sac; *Fig:* dead
end. ◆'**S~leinen**, *n* sackcloth.
**Sadis|mus** [za'dismus], *m* -/*no pl* sadism.
◆**S~t**, *m* -**en/-en** sadist. ◆**s~tisch**,
*adj.* sadistic.
**säen** ['zɛːən], *v.tr.* to sow (seeds, corn,
*Fig:* discord); *Fig:* **dünn gesät**, few and
far between.
**Safari** [za'fɑːri], *f* -/-**s** safari.
**Safe** [seːf], *m* -**s/-s** safe (in a bank etc.).
**Saft** [zaft], *m* -(*e*)**s/-e** juice (of fruit, *Cu:*
meat); *Bot:* sap (of a tree etc.). ◆'**s~ig**,
*adj.* (*a*) juicy (fruit, meat etc.); (*b*) lush
(plant, grass etc.). ◆'**s~los**, *adj.* juice-
less.
**Sage** ['zɑːgə], *f* -/-**n** saga; (*klassische*) legend. ◆'**s~n**, *v.tr.* to say (sth.); **die
Wahrheit s.**, to speak the truth; **wie sagt
man das auf Englisch?** what is the English for that? *F:* **das kann man wohl s.!**
that's very true! **was Sie nicht s.!** you
don't say! **das ist nicht gesagt**, you can't
bank on it; **j-m etwas s.**, (*mitteilen*) to
tell s.o. sth.; **er läßt sich das nichts s.**,
he won't listen; **j-m seine Meinung s.**, to
give s.o. a piece of one's mind; *F:* **wem
sagst du das!** you're telling me! **was
wollen Sie damit s.?** what do you mean
by that? **sagt dir das etwas?** does it
mean anything to you? **das hat nichts zu
s.**, it's of no consequence; **s. Sie ihm, er
soll kommen**, tell him to come; *F:* **er
hat nichts zu s.**, he has no say (in the
matter). ◆'**s~nhaft**, *adj.* (*a*) legendary;
(*b*) *F:* fabulous; **s. teuer**, terribly expen-

sive.

**Säge** ['zɛːgə]. **I.** *f* -/-n saw. **II.** **'S~-**, *comb.fm.* saw (tooth etc.). ◆**'s~n**, *v.tr.* to saw (wood, metal etc.). ◆**'S~werk**, *n* sawmill.

**Sahn|e** ['zaːnə], *f* -/no *pl* cream; *(Schlags.)* whipped cream. ◆**'S~e-bonbon**, *m & n* toffee. ◆**'s~ig**, *adj.* creamy.

**Saison** [zɛˈzɔŋ]. **I.** *f* -/-s season; *Fig:* S. haben, to be popular/in vogue. **II.** **'S~-**, *comb.fm.* seasonal (work, worker, business etc.). ◆**s~bedingt**, *adj.* seasonal.

**Saite** ['zaitə], *f* -/-n string. ◆**'S~ninstrument**, *n* string instrument.

**Sakko** ['zako], *m & n* -s/-s sports jacket.

**sakral** [zaˈkraːl], *adj.* religious (art, music etc.).

**Sakrament** [zakraˈmɛnt], *n* -(e)s/-e sacrament.

**Salami** [zaˈlaːmi], *f* -/-s salami.

**Salat** [zaˈlaːt], *m* -(e)s/-e **1.** *(Kopfs.)* lettuce. **2.** *Cu:* salad. **3.** *F: (Unordnung)* mess; **der ganze S.,** the whole caboodle/ *(Sache)* business. ◆**S~blatt**, *n* lettuce leaf. ◆**S~soße**, *f* salad dressing.

**Salb|e** ['zalbə], *f* -/-n ointment. ◆**'S~ung**, *f* -/-en anointing. ◆**'s~ungsvoll**, *adj.* unctuous.

**Salbei** ['zalbai], *m* -s/no *pl* sage.

**Saldo** ['zaldo], *m* -s/-s & -den balance.

**Salmiak** [zalmiˈak], *m & n* -s/no *pl* ammonium chloride.

**Salon** [zaˈlɔŋ], *m* -s/-s **1.** drawing-room. **2.** *(Geschäft)* hairdresser's/beauty salon. ◆**s~fähig**, *adj.* socially acceptable (behaviour); respectable (clothes etc.).

**salopp** [zaˈlɔp], *adj.* casual; *(schlampig)* slipshod (dress, manner); easy-going (behaviour etc.).

**Salpeter** [zalˈpeːtər], *m* -s/no *pl* saltpetre. ◆**S~säure**, *f* nitric acid.

**Salto** ['zalto], *m* -s/-s & -ti somersault.

**Salut** [zaˈluːt], *m* -(e)s/-e *Mil: etc:* (gun) salute. ◆**s~ieren** [-uˈtiːrən], *v.i. (haben)* **(vor j-m) s.,** to salute (s.o.).

**Salve** ['zalvə], *f* -/-n salvo.

**Salz** [zalts]. **I.** *n* -es/-e salt. **II.** **'S~-**, *comb.fm.* salt (mine, content, lake etc.); *Cu:* salted (meat, herring). ◆**'s~en**, *v.tr.* to salt (food). ◆**'s~ig**, *adj.* salty. ◆**'S~kartoffeln**, *fpl* boiled potatoes. ◆**'s~los**, *adj.* salt-free. ◆**'S~säure**, *f* hydrochloric acid. ◆**'S~streuer**, *m* salt shaker. ◆**'S~wasser**, *n* salt/*Cu:* salted water.

**Samen** ['zaːmən]. **I.** *m* -s/- seed; *Anat:* sperm. **II.** **'S~-**, *comb.fm.* *(a)* seed (shop, capsule etc.); *(b)* *Anat:* sperm (bank, cell etc.); seminal (fluid etc.).

**Sammelband** ['zaməlbant], *m* omnibus (volume). ◆**'S~elbecken**, *n* reservoir. ◆**'S~elbestellung**, *f* joint order. ◆**'s~eln**, *v.tr.* to collect (money, stamps, wood, facts, *Fig:* one's thoughts etc.); to gather (berries etc.); **neue Kräf-**

te s., to build up one's strength; **sich s.,** *(Menschen, Truppen usw.)* to gather, assemble; *Fig: (Pers.)* to collect oneself/ one's thoughts. ◆**S~el'surium**, *n* -s/no *pl F:* conglomeration. ◆**'S~ler**, *m* -s/- *(Pers.)* collector. ◆**'S~lung**, *f* -/-en collection; *Fig: (Konzentration)* composure.

**Samstag** ['zamstaːk], *m* Saturday.

**Samt¹** [zamt]. **I.** *m* -(e)s/-e velvet. **II.** **'S~-**, *comb.fm.* *(aus S.)* velvet (ribbon, suit, glove etc.); *(samtig)* velvety (green, skin, paw etc.). ◆**'s~ig**, *adj.* velvety (skin etc.).

**samt²**. **I.** *prep.* + *dat* together/*F:* complete with. **II.** *adv.* **s. und sonders,** all (without exception).

**sämtlich** ['zɛmtliç], *adj.* all; **s~es vorhandene Material,** all the material available.

**Sanatorium** [zanaˈtoːrium], *n* -s/-ien sanatorium.

**Sand** [zant]. **I.** *m* -(e)s/-e **1.** sand; *(für Straßen usw.)* grit. **II.** **'S~-**, *comb.fm.* sand (-dune, -storm etc.); *(sandig)* sandy (beach, soil etc.). ◆**'S~bank**, *f* sandbank. ◆**'s~ig**, *adj.* sandy. ◆**'S~kasten**, *m* *(für Kinder)* sandpit, *N.Am:* sandbox. ◆**'S~kuchen**, *m* Madeira cake. ◆**'S~papier**, *n* sandpaper. ◆**'S~uhr**, *f* hour-glass; *(für Eier)* egg-timer.

**Sandale** [zanˈdaːlə], *f* -/-n sandal.

**Sandelholz** ['zandəlhɔlts], *n* sandalwood.

**sanft** [zanft], *adj.* gentle; *(leise)* soft (sound, voice etc.); *(friedlich)* peaceful (sleep etc.). ◆**'S~heit**, *f* -/no *pl* gentleness; softness. ◆**'S~mut**, *f* gentleness, meekness. ◆**'s~mütig**, *adj.* gentle, meek.

**Sänger|(in)** ['zɛŋər(in)], *m* -s/-s *(f* -/-nen) singer.

**sanier|en** [zaˈniːrən], *v.tr.* *(a)* to renovate (bad housing etc.); to develop (a district etc.), clear (slums); to clean up (a river etc.); *(b)* *Com:* to put (a firm) back on its feet. ◆**S~ung**, *f* -/-en redevelopment; slum clearance.

**sani|tär** [zaniˈtɛːr], *adj.* sanitary; **s~täre Anlagen,** sanitation; *(Toiletten)* lavatories. ◆**S~'täter**, *m* -s/- first-aid man; *(im Krankenwagen)* ambulance man; *Mil:* medical orderly. ◆**S~'tätsauto**, *n* ambulance.

**Sanktion** [zaŋktsiˈoːn], *f* -/-en sanction. ◆**s~ieren** [-oˈniːrən], *v.tr.* to sanction (a law, plan etc.).

**Saphir** ['zaːfir], *m* -s/-e *Rec:* sapphire stylus.

**Sardelle** [zarˈdɛlə], *f* -/-n anchovy.

**Sardine** [zarˈdiːnə], *f* -/-n sardine.

**Sarg** [zark], *m* -(e)s/-e coffin.

**Sarkas|mus** [zarˈkasmus], *m* -/-men sarcasm. ◆**s~tisch**, *adj.* sarcastic.

**Satan** ['zaːtan], *m* -s/-e Satan. ◆**s~isch** [zaˈtaːnif], *adj.* satanic.

**Satellit** [zatɛˈliːt], *m* -en/-en satellite. ◆**S~en-**, *comb.fm.* satellite (state, town

etc.).

**Satin** [za'tɛn], *m* -s/-s satin.

**Satir|e** [za'ti:rə], *f* -/-n satire. ◆**S~iker**, *m* -s/- satirist. ◆**s~isch**, *adj.* satirical.

**satt** [zat], *adj.* **1.** (*a*) (*Pers.*) well-fed, satisfied; *F:* full; **sich s. essen**, to eat one's fill; **bist du s.?** have you had enough (to eat)? **das macht s.**, that's filling; (*b*) *F:* **j-n, etwas s. sein/haben**, to be fed up with/sick of s.o., sth. **2.** rich, deep (colour, blue etc.).

**Satt|el** [za'tɛl], *m* -s/= saddle; *Fig:* **fest im S. sitzen**, to be secure in one's position. ◆**S~eldach**, *n* saddleback roof. ◆**'s~elfest**, *adj.* **s. sein**, to know one's job. ◆**'s~eln**, *v.tr.* to saddle (a horse etc.). ◆**S~elschlepper**, *m* tractor of an articulated lorry/*N.Am:* truck). ◆**'S~eltasche**, *f* saddlebag.

**sättig|en** ['zɛtigən], *v.tr.* (*a*) to satisfy (s.o.), *Fig:* s.o.'s curiosity etc.); (*Essen*) **sehr s~end**, very filling; (*b*) to saturate (*Ch:* an acid, *Com:* the market etc.). ◆**'S~ung**, *f* -/-en (*a*) satisfaction (of hunger); (*b*) *Ch: etc:* saturation.

**Satz** [zats], *m* -es/=e **1.** (*a*) *Gram:* sentence; **abhängiger S.**, subordinate clause; (*b*) (*These*) thesis; *Mth:* theorem. **2.** *Mus:* movement (of a symphony etc.). **3.** (*Gruppe*) set (of stamps, glasses etc.); kit (of tools etc.); (*Porzellan*) service. **4.** (*Tennis*) set. **5.** (*Tarif*) rate. **6.** (*Rückstand*) sediment; (*Kaffees*) (coffee) grounds. **7.** (*Sprung*) leap; **mit einem S.**, with one bound. ◆**'S~teil**, *m* clause. ◆**'S~ung**, *f* -/-en *usu.* pl **S~en**, *Jur:* articles (of association); regulations. ◆**'S~zeichen**, *n* punctuation mark.

**Sau** [zau]. **I.** *f* **1.** -/=e (*a*) *Z:* sow; *P:* **unter aller S.**, bloody awful, lousy; (*b*) *P:* (*Pers.*) (dirty) swine, (*Frau*) bitch. **2.** -/ -en female (wild) boar. **II.** '**S~-**, '**s~-**, *comb.fm. P:* filthy (weather etc.); bloody awful (job etc.); damn, bloody (stupid, rude, cold etc.). ◆**'S~bohne**, *f* broad bean. ◆**S~e'rei**, *f* -/-en *F:* (*a*) (*Ärgernis*) absolute scandal; (*b*) (*Unordnung, Schmutz*) awful mess; (*c*) (*Anstößiges*) smut. ◆**'S~haufen**, *m* scruffy bunch. ◆**'s~mäßig**, *adj. P:* filthy (weather etc.); lousy (pay etc.); frightful (bad luck); **s. kalt**, frightfully cold. ◆**'S~stall**, *m* pigsty. ◆**'s~'wohl**, *adj. F:* **sich s. fühlen**, to be on top of the world.

**sauber** ['zaubər], *adj.* (*a*) (*schmutzfrei*) clean; (*b*) (*ordentlich*) neat (handwriting, appearance etc.); (*c*) (*anständig*) decent. ◆**'s~halten**, *v.tr.sep.irr.45 F:* to keep (sth.) clean. ◆**'S~keit**, *f* -/no pl (*a*) cleanness; neatness; (*b*) decency. ◆**'s~machen**, *v.tr.sep.* to clean (a room etc.).

**säuber|lich** ['zɔybərlıç], *adj.* accurate (copying etc.); (**fein**) **s. verpackt**, neatly/ carefully packed. ◆**'s~n**, *v.tr.* (*a*) to clean (a room, shoes, wound etc.); (*b*)

*Pol:* to purge (a party). ◆**'S~ung**, *f* -/ -en cleaning; *Pol:* purge.

**Saudi-Arabien** [zaudi'a:rɑːbiən]. *Pr.n.n.* -s. Saudi Arabia.

**sauer** ['zauər], *adj.* sour (fruit, taste etc.), *Fig:* face etc.); *Ch: etc:* acid (solution, soil etc.); *Cu:* (*in Essig usw.*) pickled (cucumber, herrings etc.); **s. verdientes Geld**, hard earned money; *F:* **er ist s. auf mich**, he's cross with/mad at me. ◆**'S~braten**, *m* roast marinated beef. ◆**'S~kirsche**, *f* sour cherry. ◆**'S~kraut**, *n* sauerkraut. ◆**'S~stoff**, *m* oxygen. ◆**'S~teig**, *m* leaven.

**säuerlich** ['zɔyərlıç], *adj.* (slightly) sour.

**sauf|en** ['zaufən], *v.tr. & i. irr.* (*haben*) (*Tier*) to drink (water etc.); *F:* **wir haben die ganze Nacht gesoffen**, we were boozing all night. ◆**S~e'rei**, *f* -/-en *F:* (*a*) no pl boozing; (*b*) booze-up. **Säufer** ['zɔyfər], *m* -s/- *F:* boozer.

**saug|en** ['zaugən], *v.tr. & i. irr.* (*haben*) (*a*) to suck (sth.); (*b*) (*staubsaugen*) to hoover, vacuum (a room etc.). ◆**'S~er**, *m* -s/- teat, *N.Am:* nipple (on baby's bottle). ◆**'S~fähig**, *adj.* absorbent (paper etc.). ◆**'S~wirkung**, *f* suction.

**säug|en** ['zɔygən], *v.tr.* to suckle (a baby, *Z:* young). ◆**'S~etier**, *n* mammal. ◆**'S~ling**, *m* -s/-e baby.

**Säule** ['zɔylə], *f* -/-n column, (round) pillar. ◆**'S~ngang**, *m* colonnade.

**Saum** [zaum], *m* -(e)s/=e hem; *Fig:* edge. ◆**'s~selig**, *adj. Lit:* dilatory.

**säumen** ['zɔymən], *v.tr.* (*a*) to hem (a garment); (*b*) *Fig:* to line (a road etc.).

**Sauna** ['zauna], *f* -/-s sauna (bath).

**Säure** ['zɔyrə], *f* -/-n **1.** *Ch:* acid. **2.** no pl acidity (of wine etc.); sourness (of unripe fruit etc.).

**säuseln** ['zɔyzəln], *v.i.* (*haben*) (*Wind usw.*) to whisper; (*Blätter*) to rustle.

**sausen** ['zauzən], *v.i.* (*a*) (*haben*) (*Wind usw.*) to rush, roar; (*Ohren, Kopf usw.*) to buzz; (*b*) *F:* (*eilen*) (*sein*) (*Pers., Wagen usw.*) to dash, rush (somewhere); (*c*) (*sein*) *P:* **durchs Examen s.**, to plough/ flunk the exam; (*d*) *F:* **etwas s. lassen**, to give sth. a miss.

**Saxophon** [zakso'fo:n], *n* -s/-e saxophone.

**S-Bahn** ['ɛsbɑːn], *f* urban railway.

**Schabe** ['ʃːbə], *f* -/-n *Z:* cockroach.

**Schab|en** ['ʃɑːbən], *v.tr.* to scrape (sth.). ◆**'S~er**, *m* -s/- scraper.

**Schabernack** ['ʃɑːbərnak], *m* -(e)s/-e practical joke, prank.

**schäbig** ['ʃɛːbıç], *adj.* (*a*) shabby (clothes, room etc.); tatty (clothes, car etc.); seedy (hotel etc.); (*b*) measly (present etc.).

**Schablon|e** [ʃa'blo:nə], *f* -/-n (*a*) *Tchn:* template; (*für eine Zeichnung*) stencil; (*b*) *Fig:* fixed pattern. ◆**s~enhaft**, *adj.* stereotyped.

**Schach** [ʃax], *n* -s/no pl chess; *Fig:* **j-n in S. halten**, to keep s.o. under control.

◆'S~brett, n chessboard. ◆'S~-figur, f chessman. ◆'s~'matt. I. int. checkmate. II. adj. 1. j-n s. setzen, to checkmate s.o. 2. F: (erschöpft) dead beat. ◆'S~zug, m (also Fig:) move.

schachern ['ʃaxərn], v.i. (haben) to haggle (um den Preis usw., over the price etc.).

Schacht [ʃaxt], m -(e)s/-e (mine, lift etc.) shaft; (Brunnen:) well; (für Kohlen usw.) chute.

Schachtel ['ʃaxtəl], f -/-n 1. box; S. Zigaretten, packet/N.Am: pack of cigarettes. 2. F: (Frau) alte S., old bag.

schade ['ʃɑːdə], adj. (a) (bedauerlich) es ist (sehr) s., it's a (great) pity/shame (um + acc, about); (b) (wertvoll) es ist zu s. zum Wegwerfen, it is too good to throw away; für diese Arbeit ist er sich zu s., he considers this kind of work beneath him.

Schädel ['ʃɛːdəl], m -s/- skull. ◆'S~-bruch, m fracture of the skull.

schad|en ['ʃɑːdən]. I. v.i. (haben) to do harm/damage; das schadet der Gesundheit sehr, that is very bad for one's health; F: das schadet ihm nichts, that won't do him any harm/(geschieht ihm recht) serves him right. II. S., m -s/- damage; (Verletzung) injury; (Mangel) defect; (Verlust) loss; (Nachteil) harm, detriment; j-m S. zufügen, to do s.o. harm; es soll dein S. nicht sein, you won't lose by it. ◆'S~enersatz, m compensation (for damage/injury). ◆'S~enfreude, f malicious pleasure (over s.o.'s misfortune). ◆'s~enfroh, adj. gloating, (maliciously) gleeful. ◆'s~haft, adj. defective, faulty (part etc.); (beschädigt) damaged (goods etc.). ◆'s~los, adj. sich an j-m s. halten, to take advantage of s.o. (für etwas acc, to make up for sth.).

schäd|igen ['ʃɛːdigən], v.tr. to do harm to, harm (one's health, eyes, reputation etc.); to damage (s.o., s.o.'s interests etc.). ◆'S~igung, f -/-en harm, damage. ◆'s~lich, adj. harmful, damaging (effect, influence etc.); unhealthy (climate etc.); noxious (chemicals). ◆'S~ling, m -s/-e pest. ◆'S~lings-bekämpfungsmittel, n pesticide.

Schaf [ʃɑːf], n -(e)s/-e sheep. ◆'S~-bock, m ram. ◆'S~fell, n sheepskin. ◆'S~herde, f flock of sheep. ◆'S~hirt, m shepherd. ◆'S~skäse, m sheep's milk cheese.

Schäf|chen ['ʃɛːfçən], n -s/- little sheep, lamb. ◆'S~chenwolken, fpl fleecy clouds. ◆'S~er, m -s/- shepherd. ◆'S~erhund, m -(e)s/-e sheepdog; (Deutscher) S., Alsatian.

schaffen¹ ['ʃafən]. I. v.tr.irr. to create (sth.); to establish (connections, relationships, order etc.); sie sind für einander geschaffen, they were made for each other. II. S., n -s/no pl (Vorgang) creation; (Tätigkeit) activity. ◆'S~skraft, f

creativity.

schaffen², v. 1. v.tr. (a) to manage (sth.), get (sth.) done; to manage to catch (a train etc.); to pass (an exam); das schaffe ich nie, I can never (manage to) do that; (zeitlich) I'll never make it; (b) (bringen) to take, get (s.o., sth.) (somewhere); (c) F: (erschöpfen) j-n s., to wear s.o. out, finish s.o. off, (nervlich) get on s.o.'s nerves. 2. v.i. (haben) (a) (arbeiten) to work; (b) (Sorge machen) j-m zu s. machen, to cause s.o. difficulty/trouble; (c) sich dat zu s. machen, to busy oneself.

Schaffner ['ʃafnər], m -s/- (bus/tram) conductor; Rail: ticket inspector. ◆'S~in, f -/-nen (bus/tram) conductress.

Schaft [ʃaft], m -(e)s/-e shaft (of a column, axe etc.); shank (of a bolt, tool); leg (of a boot). ◆'S~stiefel, m jackboot.

Schakal [ʃa'kɑːl], m -s/-e jackal.

schäkern ['ʃɛːkərn], v.i. (haben) A: & Hum: to tease, flirt; (scherzen) to joke.

Schal¹ [ʃɑːl], m -s/-s & -e scarf; (für die Schulter) shawl.

schal², adj. flat (beer etc.); Fig: stale (joke etc.).

Schale ['ʃɑːlə], f -/-n 1. (Hülle) (a) (hart) shell (of an egg etc.); (b) (des Obstes) skin; (abgeschält) peel (of an apple, potato etc.); (Rinde) rind (of a lemon etc.). 2. (Schüssel) bowl; (shallow) dish; pan (of scales). ◆'S~ntiere, npl molluscs.

schälen ['ʃɛːlən], v.tr. (a) to peel (potatoes, apples etc.), skin (tomatoes, almonds); (b) sich s., to peel.

Schall [ʃal], m -(e)s/-e sound. ◆'s~-dicht, adj. soundproof. ◆'S~dämpfer, m Aut: silencer; N.Am: muffler. ◆'s~en, v.i. (haben) to resound. ◆'s~end, adj. resounding (applause, blow), ringing (laughter). ◆'S~geschwindigkeit, f speed of sound. ◆'S~mauer, f sound barrier. ◆'S~platte, f (gramophone) record. ◆'S~platten-, comb.fm. record (album, archive, shop etc.).

Schalt|bild ['ʃaltbilt], n wiring/circuit diagram. ◆'S~brett, n switchboard. ◆'s~en, v. 1. v.tr. (haben) (a) Aut: to change gear; (b) El: etc: to switch; (c) F: (begreifen) to catch on, click; (reagieren) to react; (d) s. und walten, to do as one pleases. 2. v.tr. El: to switch (an oven etc.), turn (a switch). ◆'S~er, m -s/- 1. El: switch. 2. Rail: Th: ticket-window; (in Postamt usw.) (counter) position. ◆'S~erhalle, f Rail: booking hall. ◆'S~erstunden, fpl counter hours. ◆'S~hebel, m Aut: gear lever. ◆'S~jahr, n leap year. ◆'S~plan, m El: circuit/wiring diagram. ◆'S~tafel, f switchboard, control panel; Ind: console. ◆'S~ung, f -/-en 1. El: (a) connection; (b) (alle Bauteile) circuit. 2. Aut: gearchange, N.Am: gearshift.

**Scham** [ʃɑːm]. I. f -/no pl shame; **ohne S.,** unashamed. II. '**S**~-, comb.fm. Anat: pubic (hair, region etc.). ◆'**S**~**bein,** n pubic bone. ◆'**S**~**gefühl,** n sense of shame. ◆'s~**los,** adj. shameless; (unanständig) indecent; unscrupulous (trick etc.). ◆'**S**~**losigkeit,** f -/-en shamelessness; indecency.

**schämen** ['ʃɛːmən], v.tr. **sich (wegen) etwas** gen **s.,** to be ashamed of sth.; **s. Sie sich!** shame on you!

**Schand|e** ['ʃandə], f -/no pl disgrace; **j-m S. machen,** to bring shame on s.o. ◆'**S**~**fleck,** m blot (**in der Landschaft usw.,** on the landscape etc.). ◆'**S**~**tat,** f villainous deed.

**schänd|en** ['ʃɛndən], v.tr. (a) to disgrace (a family's name etc.); (entweihen) to desecrate (a church, grave etc.). ◆'s~**lich,** adj. disgraceful (behaviour etc.); shameful (deed etc.).

**Schank|erlaubnis** ['ʃaŋkɛrlaupnis], f (publican's) licence, N.Am: excise licence. ◆'**S**~**tisch,** m bar (counter).

**Schanze** ['ʃantsə], f -/-n Sp: ski jump, hill.

**Schar** [ʃɑːr], f -/-en crowd (of people); troop (of children etc.); flock (of birds); **in (hellen) S**~**en,** in droves/hordes. ◆'s~**en,** v.refl. **sich um j-n, etwas** acc **s.,** to flock/cluster round s.o., sth. ◆'s~**enweise,** adv. in droves/hordes.

**scharf** [ʃarf], adj. **1.** (a) sharp (knife, frost, Fig: eyes etc.); keen (edge, wind, Fig: observation etc.); **s. nachdenken/ hinsehen,** to think/look hard; (b) (deutlich) clear-cut (outlines etc.); sharp (photograph etc.); **nicht s.,** unclear, (verschwommen) blurred; (c) (hart, streng) harsh (criticism, measures etc.); **s. durchgreifen/vorgehen,** to take strong/ severe measures. **2.** (stark) (a) Cu: spicy (food); hot (curry etc.); strong (mustard); pungent (smell); **s. gewürzt,** highly seasoned; (b) strong (drink). **3.** (a) (heftig) fierce (resistance, protest); (b) live (ammunition). **4.** F: **auf j-n, etwas** acc **s. sein,** to be keen on s.o., sth. ◆'**S**~**blick,** m perspicacity. ◆'s~**machen,** v.tr. F: to incite, rouse (s.o.). ◆'**S**~**richter,** m executioner. ◆'**S**~**schütze,** m sharpshooter, marksman. ◆'**S**~**sinn,** m shrewdness, astuteness. ◆'s~**sinnig,** adj. shrewd, astute.

**Schärfe** ['ʃɛrfə], f -/-n **1.** (a) sharpness; keenness (of the wind etc.); Fig: acuteness (of mind etc.); quickness (of hearing); (b) clarity, Phot: etc: definition; (c) harshness, severity. **2.** (Stärke) strength; pungency; Cu: spiciness, hotness. **3.** (Heftigkeit) fierceness. ◆'s~**n,** v.tr. to sharpen (a knife etc.).

**Scharlach** ['ʃarlax], m -s/no pl **1.** (Farbe) scarlet. **2.** Med: scarlet fever. ◆'s~**rot,** adj. scarlet.

**Scharlatan** ['ʃarlatan], m -s/-e charlatan, quack.

**Scharnier** [ʃar'niːr], n -s/-e hinge.

**Schärpe** ['ʃɛrpə], f -/-n sash.

**scharren** ['ʃarən], v.i. (haben) to scrape, scratch.

**Scharte** ['ʃartə], f -/-n notch (on a blade etc.).

**Schaschlik** ['ʃaʃlik], n -s/-s kebab.

**Schatt|en** ['ʃatən], m -s/- (a) shadow (of s.o., sth.); (b) no pl shade (of a tree etc.); **30° im S.,** 30° C in the shade; Fig: **j-n, etwas in den S. stellen,** to overshadow s.o., sth. ◆'s~**enhaft,** adj. shadowy (figures etc.). ◆'**S**~**enriß,** m silhouette. ◆'**S**~**enseite,** f -/-n **1.** shady side (of a house etc.). **2.** (Nachteil) drawback, negative aspect; dark side (of life). ◆s~**ieren** [ʃa'tiːrən], v.tr. to shade (background etc.). ◆**S**~**ierung,** f -/-en (a) no pl shading; (b) also Fig: nuance. ◆'s~**ig,** adj. shady.

**Schatulle** [ʃa'tulə], f -/-n casket.

**Schatz** [ʃats], m -es/-e **1.** treasure. **2.** F: (Kind, netter Mensch) darling. ◆'**S**~**kammer,** f treasure house/ chamber. ◆'**S**~**meister,** m treasurer. ◆'**S**~**sucher,** m treasure hunter.

**schätz|en** ['ʃɛtsən], v.tr. (a) to estimate (sth.); to judge (a distance etc.); (taxieren) to assess, value (a house etc.); **grob geschätzt,** at a rough estimate; **wie alt s. Sie ihn?** how old would you say he is? **ich schätze, daß er bald kommt,** I reckon/N.Am: guess he'll come soon; (b) (achten) to think highly of (s.o.); (würdigen) appreciate (s.o., wine etc.), value (s.o.'s advice etc.). ◆'**S**~**ung,** f -/-en estimate, (Vorgang) estimation; valuation (of a house etc.). ◆'s~**ungsweise,** adv. at a rough estimate. ◆'**S**~**wert,** m assessment, valuation.

**Schau** [ʃau]. I. f -/-en (fashion, theatre etc.) show; **etwas zur S. stellen/tragen,** to display sth. II. '**S**~-, comb.fm. (a) show (business, Pol: trial etc.); Com: display (pack etc.). ◆'**S**~**bild,** n diagram. ◆'s~**en,** v.i. (haben) to look; **nach j-m, etwas** dat **s.,** to look after s.o., sth. ◆'**S**~**fenster,** n shop/N.Am: store window. ◆'**S**~**fensterbummel:** **einen S. machen,** to go window-shopping. ◆'**S**~**fensterdekoration,** f window dressing. ◆'**S**~**fensterpuppe,** f window dummy. ◆'s~**lustig,** adj. curious, inquisitive. ◆'**S**~**platz,** m setting (of a novel etc.); scene (of an accident, crime etc.); Sp: venue. ◆'**S**~**spiel,** n Th: play, drama; Fig: Lit: spectacle. ◆'**S**~**spieler,** m actor. ◆'**S**~**spielerin,** f actress. ◆'s~**spielerisch,** adj. acting (ability etc.). ◆'**S**~**spielhaus,** n theatre. ◆'**S**~**steller,** m (travelling) showman. ◆'**S**~**tafel,** f wall chart.

**Schauder** ['ʃaudər], m -s/- shiver; (vor Angst usw.) shudder. ◆'s~**haft,** adj. F: dreadful, appalling. ◆'s~**n. I.** v.tr. & i. (haben) (frösteln) to shiver; (vor Angst *usw.*) to shudder, tremble. **II. S.,** *n -s/ no pl* shiver; (*Grauen*) (feeling of) horror.

**Schau|er** ['ʃauər]. **I.** *m -s/-* shower (of rain etc.). **II. 'S~-,** *comb.fm.* horror (play etc.). ◆**'s~erlich,** *adj.* ghastly, gruesome (crime, sight etc.); spine-chilling (story). ◆**'S~ermärchen,** *n* horror story, spine-chiller. ◆**'s~rig,** *adj.*=s~erlich; **s. schön,** eerily beautiful.

**Schaufel** ['ʃaufəl], *f -/-n* **1.** shovel. **2.** *Tchn:* (wheel) paddle; blade (of a turbine etc.). ◆**'s~n,** *v.tr.* to shovel (coal, snow etc.).

**Schaukel** ['ʃaukəl], *f -/-n* (child's) swing. ◆**'s~n,** *v.* **1.** *v.i.* (*haben*) (*auf einer Schaukel usw.*) to (have a) swing; (*im Schaukelstuhl usw.*) to rock. **2.** *v.tr.* to rock (a baby, cradle etc.). ◆**'S~pferd,** *n* rocking horse. ◆**'S~stuhl,** *m* rocking chair.

**Schaum** [ʃaum], *m -(e)s/ᴈe* foam; froth (on beer etc.); (*Seifens.*) lather. ◆**'S~gebäck,** *n* meringues. ◆**'S~gummi,** *n* foam rubber. ◆**'s~ig,** *adj.* frothy (liquid); foamy (sea etc.); **Eier s. schlagen,** to beat eggs (until frothy). ◆**'S~krone,** *f* white horse (on a wave). ◆**'S~schläger,** *m F:* (*Pers.*) show-off. ◆**'S~stoff,** *m* plastic foam. ◆**'S~wein,** *m* sparkling wine.

**schäumen** ['ʃɔymən], *v.i.* (*haben*) to foam; (*Bier usw.*) to froth; (*Seife*) to lather; (*Sekt usw.*) to sparkle.

**Scheck** [ʃɛk]. **I.** *m -s/-s* cheque, *N.Am:* check. **II. 'S~-,** *comb.fm.* cheque, *N.Am:* check (card etc.). ◆**'S~buch/ 'S~heft,** *n* cheque/*N.Am:* check book.

**scheckig** ['ʃɛkiç], *adj.* dappled (horse, cow); piebald (horse); blotchy (skin etc.).

**scheel** [ʃeːl], *adj. F:* **s. ansehen,** to give s.o. an old-fashioned look.

**scheffeln** ['ʃɛfəln], *v.tr. F:* **Geld s.,** to rake in money.

**Scheibe** ['ʃaibə], *f -/-n* **1.** (*rund*) disc; *Sp:* (*Schießs.*) target. **2.** (*Schnitte*) slice. **3.** (*Glas*) (window etc.) pane. ◆**'S~nbremse,** *f* disc brake. ◆**'S~nwaschanlage,** *f* windscreen/*N.Am:* windshield washer. ◆**'S~nwischer,** *m* windscreen/*N.Am:* windshield wiper.

**Scheich** [ʃaiç], *m -s/-s* sheikh, sheik.

**Scheid|e** ['ʃaidə], *f -/-n* **1.** sheath (for a sword etc.). **2.** *Anat:* vagina. ◆**'s~en,** *v.irr.65* **1.** *v.tr.* (*a*) *Lit:* (*trennen*) to separate, divide (two things/people); (*b*) *Jur:* to dissolve (a marriage), divorce (a married couple); **sich s. lassen,** to get a divorce. **2.** *v.i.* (*sein*) *Lit:* to part. ◆**'S~ung,** *f -/-en* (*a*) separation; (*b*) *Jur:* divorce. ◆**'S~ungsgrund,** *m* grounds for divorce. ◆**'S~ungsprozeß,** *m* divorce proceedings.

**Schein** [ʃain]. **I.** *m -(e)s/-e* **1.** *no pl* (*Licht*) light. **2.** *no pl* (*Anschein*) appearance, pretence; **er tut es nur zum S.,** he only pre-tends to do it. **3.** (*a*) (*Bescheinigung*) certificate; (*Zettel*) chit; (*Führers. usw.*) licence; (*b*) (*Gelds.*) (bank)note, *N.Am:* bill. **II. 'S~-,** *comb.fm.* sham, mock (at-tack etc.); specious (argument, reason). ◆**'s~bar,** *adj.* apparent (contradiction etc.); ostensible (reasons etc.); *adv.* seemingly. ◆**'s~en,** *v.i.irr.* (*haben*) (*a*) (*leuchten*) to shine; (*b*) (*Eindruck erwecken*) to seem, appear; **mir scheint, daß ...,** it seems to me that ... ◆**'s~heilig,** *adj. F:* hypocritical. ◆**'S~tod,** *m* suspended animation. ◆**'S~werfer,** *m -s/- Aut:* headlight; *Th: etc:* spotlight; *Mil: etc:* (*Suchs.*) search-light.

**Scheiß-** ['ʃais-], *comb.fm. P:* bloody, blasted (work etc.). ◆**'S~e,** *f -/no pl & int. V:* shit. ◆**'s~e'gal,** *adj. P:* **das ist mir s.!** I don't give a damn! ◆**'S~kerl,** *m V:* bastard.

**Scheitel** ['ʃaitəl], *m -s/-* (*a*) crown, top (of the head); (*b*) (*Haars.*) parting. ◆**'s~n,** *v.tr.* **das Haar s.,** to part one's hair. ◆**'S~punkt,** *m* apex.

**Scheiter|haufen** ['ʃaitərhaufən], *m -s/- Hist:* (funeral) pyre. ◆**'s~n.** **I.** *v.i.* (*sein*) to fail (utterly); (*Verhandlungen usw.*) to break down (**an etwas** *dat*, due to sth.); (*Ehe*) to break up. **II. S.,** *n -s/no pl* failure; breakdown.

**Schelle** ['ʃɛlə], *f -/-n* (small) bell. ◆**'s~n,** *v.i.* (*haben*) to ring.

**Schellfisch** ['ʃɛlfiʃ], *m* haddock.

**Schelm** [ʃɛlm], *m -(e)s/-e* scallywag, rogue. ◆**'s~isch,** *adj.* roguish, mischie-vous.

**Schelte** ['ʃɛltə], *f -/-n* scolding. ◆**'s~n,** *v.tr. & i. irr.* (*haben*) to scold, chide (s.o.).

**Schema** ['ʃeːma], *n -s/-s & -ta* (*a*) (*Entwurf*) draft; (*Zeichnung*) diagram; (*b*) (*Muster, Norm*) pattern. ◆**s~tisch** [ʃeˈmaːtiʃ], *adj.* (*a*) diagrammatic; **s. ab-gebildet,** illustrated in a diagram; (*b*) *Pej:* routine, mechanical (work etc.).

**Schemel** ['ʃeːməl], *m -s/-* stool.

**Schenke** ['ʃɛŋkə], *f -/-n* tavern.

**Schenkel** ['ʃɛŋkəl], *m -s/-* **1.** *Anat:* thigh. **2.** *Mth:* side (of an angle).

**schenk|en** ['ʃɛŋkən], *v.tr.* **j-m etwas s.,** to give s.o. sth. (as a present); **j-m Auf-merksamkeit s.,** to pay attention to s.o.; **j-m Vertrauen s.,** to trust s.o.; *F:* **das können wir uns s.,** we can do without that. ◆**'S~ung,** *f -/-en* donation.

**Scherbe** ['ʃɛrbə], *f -/-n* broken piece/ fragment (of china, glass etc.).

**Scher|e** ['ʃeːrə], *f -/-n* (*a*) pair of scissors/(*größer*) shears; (*b*) *usu. pl* **S~n,** claws, pincers (of a crab etc.). ◆**'s~en1,** *v.tr.irr.* to shear (sheep etc.). ◆**'s~en2,** *v.refl.* **er schert sich nicht/ darum,** he doesn't care/*F:* give a damn about it; **s. dich zum Teufel!** get lost!

**Scherflein** ['ʃɛrflain], *n* **sein S. beitra-gen,** to make one's little contribution.

**Scherz** [ʃɛrts], *m* -es/-e joke; **etwas im S. sagen,** to say sth. jokingly/in fun. ◆'S~**artikel,** *m* novelty (article). ◆'s~**en,** *v.i.* (*haben*) to joke; **damit ist nicht zu s.,** that's no laughing matter. ◆'S~**frage,** *f* (comic) catch question. ◆'s~**haft,** *adj.* jocular; (*leichtfertig*) flippant (remark etc.).

**scheu** [ʃɔy]. **I.** *adj.* shy. **II. S.,** *f* -/no *pl* shyness; (*Hemmung*) inhibition; (*Angst*) awe (vor j-m, of s.o.). ◆'s~**en,** *v.tr.* (a) to shun (publicity etc.), avoid (risks etc.); **keine Mühe/Kosten s.,** to spare no pains/expense; (b) **sich vor etwas** *dat* **s.,** to be afraid of sth./to do sth. ◆'S~**klappen,** *fpl* (horse's) blinkers.

**Scheuer|bürste** [ʃɔyərbyrstə], *f* scrubbing brush. ◆'s~**lappen,** *m* floorcloth. ◆'s~**n,** *v.tr.* (a) to scour (pots etc.), scrub (a floor etc.); (b) (*Schuh, Riemen usw.*) to chafe. ◆'S~**tuch,** *n* floorcloth.

**Scheune** [ʃɔynə], *f* -/-n barn.

**Scheusal** ['ʃɔyzaːl], *n* -s/-e *Pej:* (*Pers.*) **du S.!** you beast!

**scheußlich** ['ʃɔyslɪç], *adj.* (*häßlich*) hideous (sight, building etc.); (*gräßlich*) monstrous (crime etc.); *F:* **s. kalt,** frightfully/terribly cold. ◆'S~**keit,** *f* -/-en hideous appearance; monstrousness.

**Schi** [ʃiː], *m* -s/-er = **Ski.**

**Schicht** [ʃɪçt]. **I.** *f* -/-en **1.** layer; coat of paint). **2.** *Ind:* shift. **3.** (social) class. **II. 'S~-,** *comb.fm. Ind:* shift (work, worker etc.). ◆'s~**en,** *v.tr.* to stack (wood, bricks etc.). ◆'s~**weise,** *adv.* **1.** in layers. **2.** *Ind:* in shifts.

**schick** [ʃik], *adj.* smart, stylish.

**schick|en** ['ʃikən], *v.tr.* (a) to send (sth.); (b) **sich** *dat* **in etwas** *acc* **s.,** to resign oneself to sth.; (c) *impers.* **es schickt sich nicht,** it is not done/proper. ◆'s~**lich,** *adj. Lit:* proper; seemly.

**Schicksal** ['ʃikzaːl], *n* -s/-e fate. ◆'s~**haft,** *adj.* fateful. ◆'S~**sschlag,** *m* blow of fate.

**Schieb|edach** ['ʃiːbədax], *n*, sliding roof, sunroof. ◆'s~**en,** *v.tr.* **1.** *v.tr.* (a) to push (s.o., sth.); to wheel (a bicycle etc.); (b) **die Schuld auf j-n s.,** to lay the blame on s.o. **2.** *v.i.* (*haben*) (a) to push; (b) **mit Rauschgift usw. s.,** to push drugs etc. ◆'S~**er,** *m* -s/- **1.** (baby's) pusher. **2.** (*zum Absperren usw.*) slide. **3.** *F:* (*Pers.*) racketeer. ◆'S~**ung,** *f* -/-en *F:* (*S~ergeschäft*) racket, fiddle; **das ist alles S.!** the whole thing's a fiddle!

**Schieds|gericht** ['ʃiːtsɡərɪçt], *n* court of arbitration. **1.** ◆'S~**richter,** *m* **1.** arbitrator. **2.** *Sp:* umpire; *Fb: etc:* referee. ◆'S~**spruch,** *m* arbitration award.

**schief** [ʃiːf], *adj.* (a) (*nicht gerade*) not straight; crooked; (*geneigt*) slanting (wall etc.); (*zur Seite geneigt*) leaning; *F:* lopsided (post etc.); *Mth:* oblique (angle); inclined (plane); **j-n s. ansehen,** to look askance at s.o.; (b) (*falsch*) false, distorted (picture, view). ◆'s~**gehen,**

*v.i.sep.irr.36* (*sein*) *F:* (*Unternehmen usw.*) to go wrong. ◆'s~**lachen,** *v.sep.refl. F:* **sich s.,** to laugh oneself silly. ◆'s~**liegen,** *v.i.sep.irr.62* (*haben*) *F:* to be mistaken.

**Schiefer** ['ʃiːfər], *m* -s/- slate. ◆'S~**tafel,** *f* slate.

**schielen** ['ʃiːlən], *v.i.* (*haben*) (a) *Med:* to squint; (b) *F:* **auf etwas** *acc* **s.,** to cast a beady eye on sth.

**Schienbein** ['ʃiːnbain], *n* shin(bone).

**Schiene** ['ʃiːnə], *f* -/-n (a) *Rail: etc:* rail; (b) track (for curtains etc.); (c) *Med:* splint. ◆'s~**n,** *v.tr. Med:* to splint (a limb). ◆'S~**nstrang,** *m* (stretch of) railway/*N.Am:* railroad track.

**schier** [ʃiːr], *adj.* **1.** sheer, pure (stupidity etc.). **2.** *adv.* almost; **s. unmöglich,** all but impossible.

**Schieß|bude** ['ʃiːsbuːdə], *f* shooting gallery. ◆'s~**en,** *v.irr.31* **1.** *v.i.* to shoot/fire at s.o., sth.; *F:* **schieß los!** fire away! **in die Höhe/aus der Erde s.,** to shoot up. **2.** *v.tr.* (a) to shoot (sth.); (b) *Fb:* **ein Tor s.,** to score a goal. ◆**S~e'rei,** *f* -/-en shoot-out. ◆'S~**pulver,** *n* gunpowder. ◆'S~**scharte,** *f* embrasure; arrow slit. ◆'S~**stand,** *m* rifle/shooting range.

**Schiff** [ʃif], *n* -(e)s/-e **1.** ship. **2.** *Ecc:* (*Mittels.*) nave; (*Seitens.*) aisle. ◆'**Schiffahrt,** *f* -/no *pl* (*Schiffe*) shipping; (b) (*Fahren*) navigation. ◆'**Schiffahrts-,** *comb.fm.* shipping (company etc.). ◆'**Schiffahrtslinie,** *f* shipping route/(*Gesellschaft*) line. ◆'s~**bar,** *adj.* navigable (river etc.). ◆'S~**bau,** *m* shipbuilding. ◆'S~**bruch,** *m* shipwreck; **S. erleiden,** to be shipwrecked; *Fig:* (*Pläne usw.*) to fail. ◆'s~**brüchig,** *adj.* shipwrecked. ◆'S~**er,** *m* -s/- boatman; (*Kapitän*) skipper. ◆'S~**s-,** *comb.fm.* ship's (boy, captain, papers etc.); shipping (agent etc.). ◆'S~**sfracht,** *f* ship's cargo. ◆'S~**schaukel,** *f* swing-boat.

**Schikan|e** [ʃiˈkaːnə], *f* -/-n **1.** (*usu.* petty) victimization; (bloody-minded) harassment. **2.** *F: Aut: etc:* **mit allen S~n,** with all the extras/trimmings (s.o.). ◆s~**ieren** [-aˈniːrən], *v.tr.* to victimize (s.o.).

**Schild**[1] [ʃilt], *m* -(e)s/-e *Mil: Tchn: etc:* shield; *F:* **was führt er im S~e?** what's he after? ◆'S~**drüse,** *f* thyroid gland. ◆'S~**kröte,** *f* (*Wassers.*) turtle; (*Lands.*) tortoise.

**Schild**[2], *n* -(e)s/-er sign (*Wegweiser*) signpost; (*große Tafel*) signboard (of a firm etc.); (*Etikett*) label. ◆'s~**ern,** *v.tr.* to describe (an occurrence, one's impressions etc.); (*bildhaft*) to depict (s.o., a scene). ◆'S~**erung,** *f* -/-en description, portrayal.

**Schilf(rohr)** ['ʃilf(roːr)], *n* -(e)s/-e reed.

**schillern** ['ʃilərn], *v.i.* (*haben*) to shimmer, (*Diamant usw.*) sparkle.

**Schimmel** ['ʃiməl], *m* -s/- 1. white horse. 2. *no pl* (*Fäulnis*) mould (on food etc.). ◆'s~ig, *adj.* mouldy. ◆'s~n, *v.i.* (*sein*) to go mouldy.

**Schimmer** ['ʃimər], *m* -s/*no pl* 1. gleam, glint. 2. (*Anflug*) hint, suspicion. ◆'s~n, *v.i.* (*haben*) to gleam, glint; (*Perlen, Seide usw.*) to shimmer.

**Schimpanse** [ʃim'panzə], *m* -n/-n chimpanzee.

**schimpf|en** ['ʃimpfən], *v.* 1. *v.i.* (*haben*) (*a*) to curse, *F:* carry on, *Brit:* create (*auf/über* j-n, etwas *acc*, about s.o., sth.); **mit** j-m s., to tell s.o. off. 2. *v.tr. Lit:* **j-n einen Lügner usw. s.**, to call s.o. a liar etc. ◆'S~**wort**, *n* swearword.

**Schindel** ['ʃindəl], *f* -/-n shingle.

**schind|en** ['ʃindən], *v.irr.* 1. *v.tr.* (*a*) to drive (s.o.) hard, *F:* slave-drive (s.o.); (*grausam*) to ill-treat (animals, prisoners etc.); (*b*) **Zeit** s., to play for time; **Eindruck** s., to try to impress. ◆'S~**er**, *m* -s/- slave-driver. ◆**S~e'rei**, *f* -/-en *F:* hard slog, grind. ◆'S~**luder**, *n F:* **mit** j-m, etwas *dat* **S. treiben**, to abuse s.o., sth.

**Schinken** ['ʃiŋkən]. I. *m* -s/- *Cu:* ham. II. ◆'S~-, *comb.fm.* ham (roll, sausage etc.).

**Schippe** ['ʃipə], *f* -/-n shovel; *F:* **j-n auf die S. nehmen**, to pull s.o.'s leg.

**Schirm** [ʃirm], *m* -(e)s/-e 1. (*a*) (*Regens.*) umbrella; (*Sonnens.*) sunshade. 2. (*gegen Hitze usw.*) screen; (*gegen Licht*) shade; *Cl:* peak (of a cap). ◆'S~**herr**, *m* patron. ◆'S~**herrschaft**, *f* patronage.

**schizophren** [ʃitso'fre:n], *adj.* schizophrenic.

**Schlacht** [ʃlaxt], *f* -/-en battle (**um** + *acc*, for). ◆'s~**en**, *v.tr.* to slaughter (animals). ◆'S~**er**, *m* -s/- butcher. ◆'S~**feld**, *n* battlefield. ◆'S~**hof**, *m* slaughterhouse. ◆'S~**plan**, *m* plan of battle/*Fig:* campaign. ◆'S~**schiff**, *n* battleship. ◆'S~**ung**, *f* -/*no pl* slaughter(ing).

**Schlacke** ['ʃlakə], *f* -/-n clinker; (*Erzs.*) slag.

**Schlaf** [ʃla:f]. I. *m* -(e)s/*no pl* sleep. II. 'S~-, *comb.fm.* sleeping (tablet, pill, sickness etc.). ◆'S~**anzug**, *m* pyjamas, *N.Am:* pajamas. ◆'s~**en**, *v.i.irr.* (*haben*) to sleep; (*Zustand*) to be asleep; **s. gehen**, to go to bed. ◆'S~**engehen**, *n* -s/*no pl* going to bed. ◆'S~**enszeit**, *f* bedtime. ◆'s~**los**, *adj.* sleepless. ◆'S~**gelegenheit**, *f* sleeping accommodation. ◆'S~**losigkeit**, *f* -/*no pl* sleeplessness, insomnia. ◆'S~**mittel**, *n* sleeping tablet/drug. ◆'S~**saal**, *m* dormitory. ◆'S~**sack**, *m* sleeping bag. ◆'S~**wagen**, *m* sleeping car, sleeper. ◆'S~**wandler(in)**, *m* -s/- (*f* -/-nen) sleepwalker, *Med:* somnambulist. ◆'S~**zimmer**, *n* bedroom.

**Schläf|er(in)** ['ʃlɛːfər(in)], *m* -s/- (*f* -/- -nen) sleeper. ◆'s~**rig**, *adj.* sleepy, drowsy.

**Schläfe** ['ʃlɛːfə], *f* -/-n temple.

**schlaff** [ʃlaf], *adj.* (*locker*) slack (rope etc.); flabby (skin, muscles); (*Pers.*) listless; *Fig:* lax (discipline, morals).

**Schlag** [ʃla:k], *m* -(e)s/ᵈe 1. blow; (*a*) (*Treffer*) hit; (*Fausts.*) punch; (*mit einem Stock usw.*) stroke; **S~e bekommen**, to get a hiding/thrashing; **mit einem S.**, with one blow; *Fig:* at one fell swoop; **S. auf S.**, in quick succession; (*b*) (*Geräusch*) chime (of a clock, bell etc.); beat (of a drum, heart, waves etc.); (*c*) (*Stroms.*) (electric) shock; *Med: F:* (*Anfall*) stroke. 2. *F:* (*Portion*) **ein S. Suppe**, a helping of soup. 3. (*Menschens.*) type; **ein anderer S. (von Menschen)**, another breed. ◆'S~**ader**, *f* artery. ◆'S~- **anfall**, *m* apoplexy; *F:* stroke. ◆'s~**artig**, *adj.* sudden; *adv.* all of a sudden. ◆'S~**baum**, *m* barrier (across the road). ◆'s~**en**, *v.irr.* 1. *v.tr.* (*a*) to hit, strike (s.o., sth.); (*dreschen*) to beat, thrash (s.o., an animal); (*b*) **sich (mit** j-m) **s.**, to fight (s.o.); (*c*) (*klopfen*) to knock, (*hämmern*) hammer (a nail etc.); (*d*) *Cu:* to whip (cream), whisk (egg-whites); (*e*) (*Uhr*) to strike (the hour); (*f*) (*besiegen*) **den Gegner s.**, to beat/defeat one's opponent/(*Feind*) enemy; (*g*) (*wickeln*) to wrap (sth.). 2. *v.i.* (*a*) (*haben*) (*Pers.*) to strike (a blow); **nach** j-m **s.**, to lash/hit out at s.o.; (*Vogel*) **mit den Flügeln s.**, to beat/flap its wings; (*b*) (*haben*) (*Regen usw.*) to beat, (*Wellen usw.*) pound, (*Tür*) bang; (*c*) (*sein*) (*Flammen*) to shoot, leap; (*Blitz*) **in etwas** *acc* **s.**, to strike sth.; (*d*) (*haben*) (*Uhr*) to strike, chime; (*Glocke*) to toll; (*Herz usw.*) to beat; (*e*) (*sein*) **nach** j-m **s.**, to take after s.o. ◆'s~**end**, *adj.* 1. (*überzeugend*) convincing (proof, argument etc.). 2. *Min:* **s~e Wetter**, firedamp. ◆'S~**er**, *m* -s/- *F:* (*Lied*) pop song; (*Erfolg*) hit; (*Ware*) best-selling line. ◆'S~**er- sänger**, *m* pop singer. ◆'s~**fertig**, *adj.* quick-witted. ◆'S~**fertigkeit**, *f* -/*no pl* quick-wittedness. ◆'S~**instrument**, *n* percussion instrument. ◆'S~**loch**, *n* pot-hole. ◆'S~**sahne**, *f* whipped cream. ◆'S~**seite**, *f Nau:* list; **S. haben**, (*Schiff*) to list; *F:* (*Pers.*) to be sloshed. ◆'S~**wort**, *n* slogan, catchword. ◆'S~**zeile**, *f* headline. ◆'S~**zeug**, *n* percussion.

**Schläger** ['ʃlɛːgər], *m* -s/- 1. *Sp:* (*Gerät*) (golf) club; (hockey) stick; (tennis) racket; (cricket, baseball) bat. 2. *Pej:* ruffian, rowdy. ◆'S~**ei**, *f* -/-en brawl, *F:* punch-up, *N.Am:* fist-fight.

**Schlamassel** [ʃla'masəl], *m* -s/- *F:* mess.

**Schlamm** [ʃlam], *m* -(e)s/-e mud. ◆'s~**ig**, *adj.* muddy.

**Schlampe** ['ʃlampə], *f* -/-n *F:* slut. ◆**S~e'rei**, *f* -/-en *F:* (*a*) slovenly work/behaviour; (*b*) *no pl* slovenliness.

◆'s~**ig**, *adj.* slovenly; slipshod (work etc.); sluttish (woman etc.).

**Schlange** ['ʃlaŋə], *f -/-n* **1.** *Z:* snake. **2.** (*lange Reihe*) queue, *N.Am:* line (of people, cars); **S. stehen**, to queue up, *N.Am:* stand in line. ◆'**S~nbiß**, *m* snakebite. ◆'**S~ngift**, *n* (snake's) venom. ◆'**S~nlinie**, *f* wavy line. ◆'**S~nmensch**, *m* contortionist.

**schlängeln** ['ʃlɛŋəln], *v.refl.* **sich s.**, (*Fluß, Weg usw.*) to wind, meander; (*Pers.*) to worm one's way.

**schlank** [ʃlaŋk], *adj.* slim, slender. ◆'**S~heit**, *f -/no pl* slimness, slenderness. ◆'**S~heitskur**, *f* slimming diet.

**schlapp** [ʃlap], *adj.* limp, weak. ◆'**S~e**, *f -/-n* setback. ◆'**S~hut**, *m* squash hat. ◆'**s~machen**, *v.i.* *sep.* (*haben*) *F:* (*Sportler usw.*) to fall by the wayside. ◆'**S~schwanz**, *m* *F:* drip, wet.

**Schlaraffenland** [ʃla'rafənlant], *n* land of milk and honey.

**schlau** [ʃlau], *adj.* (*a*) (*listig*) cunning, crafty; (*b*) *usu.* *F:* (*klug*) clever (person, plan etc.). ◆'**S~heit**, *f -/no pl* = **Schläue.**

**Schlauch** [ʃlaux], *m -(e)s/-e* **1.** hose(pipe). **2.** *Aut:* etc: (inner) tube. ◆'**S~boot**, *n* rubber dinghy. ◆'**s~los**, *adj.* tubeless.

**Schläue** ['ʃlɔyə], *f -/no pl* cunning; cleverness.

**Schlaufe** ['ʃlaufə], *f -/-n* loop; *Cl:* (*Aufhänger*) hanger.

**schlecht** ['ʃlɛçt], *adj.* (*a*) bad; **s~es Gehalt**, low salary; **sie ist s. in Englisch**, she is bad at English; **s. über j-n reden**, to speak ill of s.o.; **s~er werden**, to get worse, worsen; (*b*) *adv.* badly, not well; (*mit Mühe*) with difficulty; **ich informiert**, badly/ill-informed; **er hat es immer s. gehabt**, he has always had a hard time of it; **sich s. und recht durchschlagen**, to manage as best one can; **es paßt mir heute s.**, it isn't very convenient for me today; (*c*) *F:* **mir ist s.**, I feel ill/ (*Brechreiz*) sick; **es steht s. um ihn**, he is in a bad way; (*Milch, Fleisch usw.*) **s. werden**, to go off, *N.Am:* spoil. ◆'**s~gehen**, *v.i.sep.irr.36* (*sein*) **es geht ihm schlecht**, (i) he is up against it/ having a hard time; (ii) (*gesundheitlich*) he is ill/unwell. ◆'**S~igkeit**, *f -/-en* **1.** *no pl* badness. **2.** bad/evil deed. ◆'**s~machen**, *v.tr.sep.* to run (s.o., sth.) down.

**schlecken** ['ʃlɛkən], *v.tr. & i.* (*haben*) **an etwas** *dat* **s.**, to lick sth.

**Schlehe** ['ʃleːə], *f -/-n* sloe.

**schleich|en** ['ʃlaiçən], *v.i.irr.* (*sein*) to creep, steal; (*langsam*) to crawl. ◆'**s~end**, *adj.* creeping (inflation etc.); *Med:* insidious (disease). ◆'**S~weg**, *m* secret path; *Fig:* **auf S~wegen**, by surreptitious means.

**Schleie** ['ʃlaiə], *f -/-n* tench.

**Schleier** ['ʃlaiər], *m -s/-* **1.** (*also Fig:*) veil.

**2.** (*Dunst*) haze. ◆'**S~eule**, *f* barn owl. ◆'**s~haft**, *adj.* *F:* **es ist mir s.**, it's a mystery to me.

**Schleif|e** ['ʃlaifə], *f -/-n* **1.** (*Knoten*) bow (in hair etc.). **2.** (*Biegung*) U-turn. ◆'**s~en1**, *v.tr.irr.43* to grind, sharpen (a knife etc.); to grind (metal, glass etc.). ◆'**s~en2**, *v.tr.* (*a*) to drag (s.o., sth.) (in/über etwas *acc*, into/across sth.); (*b*) *Aut:* **die Kupplung s. lassen**, to slip the clutch. ◆'**S~stein**, *m* grindstone.

**Schleim** [ʃlaim], *m -(e)s/-e* slime; *Med:* mucus. ◆'**S~haut**, *f* mucous membrane. ◆'**s~ig**, *adj.* slimy; mucous (membrane etc.).

**schlemmen** ['ʃlɛmən], *v.tr. & i.* (*haben*) to feast (on sth.), *F:* stuff (sth.).

**schlendern** ['ʃlɛndərn], *v.i.* (*sein*) to saunter, stroll (along).

**schlenkern** ['ʃlɛnkərn], *v.tr. & i.* (*haben*) to swing, dangle (one's legs etc.).

**Schlepp|e** ['ʃlɛpə], *f -/-n* *Cl:* train. ◆'**s~en**, *v.tr.* (*a*) (*hinter sich herziehen*) to tow (a car, ship etc.); (*schleifend*) to drag (sth., *F:* s.o.) along; *Fig:* (*Prozeß usw.*) **sich über viele Jahre s.**, to drag on for many years; (*b*) (*tragen*) to lug, cart (sth. heavy). ◆'**s~end**, *adj.* slow (service, sales etc.); long drawn out (process); sluggish (tempo etc.). ◆'**S~er**, *m -s/-* **1.** *Aut:* tractor. **2.** *Nau:* towboat, tug (boat). ◆'**S~tau**, *n* **ein Schiff/***F:* **j-n ins S. nehmen**, to take a ship/*F:* s.o. in tow.

**Schleuder** ['ʃlɔydər], *f -/-n* **1.** catapult, *N.Am:* slingshot. **2.** *H:* (*Wäsches.*) spindrier. ◆'**s~n**, *v.* **1.** *v.tr.* (*a*) to fling, hurl (sth.); (*b*) to spin-dry (clothes etc.). **2.** *v.i.* (*sein*) (*Auto usw.*) to skid. ◆'**S~preis**, *m* *F:* giveaway price. ◆'**S~sitz**, *m* ejector seat.

**schleunigst** ['ʃlɔynikst], *adv.* with all possible haste; (*sofort*) instantly.

**Schleuse** ['ʃlɔyzə], *f -/-n* (*a*) (*zum Regulieren*) sluice; (*b*) (*für Schiffe*) lock. ◆'**s~n**, *v.tr.* (*a*) to lock (a boat etc.); (*b*) to guide, steer (s.o.). ◆'**S~ntor**, *n* lock-gate.

**Schliche** ['ʃliçə], *mpl* **j-m auf die S. kommen**, to get wise to s.o.'s tricks.

**schlicht** [ʃliçt], *adj.* simple (dress, style etc.); plain (food, *Fig:* truth); (*bescheiden*) modest, unpretentious (house etc.). ◆'**s~en**, *v.* **1.** *v.tr.* to settle (a dispute etc.). **2.** *v.i.* (*haben*) to arbitrate. ◆'**S~er**, *m -s/-* arbitrator. ◆'**S~ung**, *f -/no pl* arbitration, conciliation.

**Schlick** [ʃlik], *m -(e)s/-e* silt.

**Schließ|e** ['ʃliːsə], *f -/-n* clasp. ◆'**s~en**, *v.irr.31* **1.** *v.tr.* (*a*) to close, shut (a door, one's eyes etc.); to do up (a dress etc.); **sich s.**, to close; (*b*) to conclude (an agreement etc.); **ein Bündnis s.**, to form an alliance; (*c*) (*beenden*) to end, conclude (a letter, article etc.); (*d*) (*folgern*) to conclude (that...) (**aus etwas** *dat*, from sth.). **2.** *v.i.* (*haben*) (*a*) to close, shut; (*Ge-*

*schäft usw.) (endgültig)* to close down; *(b) (enden)* to end; *(c)* **sein Benehmen läßt auf ein hitziges Temperament s.**, his behaviour suggests a fiery temperament. ◆'S~**fach**, *n* Rail: (luggage) locker; *(in Bank)* safe-deposit box. ◆'s~**lich**, *adv.* *(a)* finally; *(endlich)* at last; *(b)* **er ist s. mein Bruder**, after all, he is my brother. ◆'S~**ung**, *f* -/-en *(a)* closing down (of a shop etc.); closure (of a pit, factory, school etc.); *(b)* conclusion (of an agreement).

**Schliff** [ʃlif], *m* -(e)s/-e cut (of a gem, glass etc.); *(Vorgang)* cutting; *Fig:* **etwas** *dat* **den letzten S. geben,** to put the finishing touch to sth.

**schlimm** [ʃlim], *adj.* *(a)* bad (mistake, news, cold etc.); serious (accident etc.); nasty (illness, wound); **im s~sten Fall,** at the worst; **es könnte s~er kommen,** things could get worse; *(b)* **(böse)** wicked, *(unartig)* naughty (person, child); *(c)* F: *(krank)* **mein s~es Bein,** my bad leg. ◆'s~**sten'falls,** *adv.* if the worst comes to the worst; *(höchstens)* at the worst.

**Schlinge** [ʃliŋə], *f* -/-n loop; *(zum Zuziehen)* noose; Med: *(Binde)* sling; *(Falle)* snare. ◆'s~**n,** *v.irr.19* 1. *v.tr.* to wind, wrap (sth.). 2. *v.tr. & i. (haben)* F: to gobble, bolt (one's food).

**Schlingel** [ʃliŋəl], *m* -s/- rascal.

**schlingern** [ʃliŋərn], *v.i. (haben)* to roll.

**Schlips** [ʃlips], *m* -es/-e F: tie.

**Schlitt|en** [ʃlitən], *m* -s/- sledge, *N.Am:* sled; **S. fahren,** to toboggan. ◆'s~**ern,** *v.i. (haben)* to slide (on the ice). ◆'S~**schuh,** *m* skate; **S. laufen,** to skate. ◆'S~**schuhläufer(in),** *m (f)* skater.

**Schlitz** [ʃlits], *m* -es/-e slit; *(Einwurf)* slot (for coins etc.); *Cl:* vent (of a jacket etc.); *(Hosens.)* fly. ◆'s~**äugig,** *adj.* slit-eyed. ◆'S~**ohr,** *n* F: sly devil.

**Schloß** [ʃlɔs], *n* -sses/=sser 1. *(a) (Türs.)* lock; *(Vorhänges.)* padlock; *(b) (Schließe)* clasp. 2. *(Herrenhaus)* mansion, stately home; *(Palast)* palace; *(Burg)* castle.

**Schlosser** [ʃlɔsər], *m* -s/- *(a)* locksmith; *(b) (Metallarbeiter)* metalworker.

**Schlot** [ʃloːt], *m* -(e)s/-e *(Fabriks.)* (factory) chimney.

**schlottern** [ʃlɔtərn], *v.i. (haben) (Pers.)* to shake, shiver *(vor + dat,* with).

**Schlucht** [ʃluxt], *f* -/-en gully, ravine.

**schluchz|en** [ʃluxtsən], *v.i. (haben)* to sob.

**Schluck** [ʃluk], *m* -(e)s/-e gulp; **in kleinen S~en,** in small mouthfuls/sips. ◆'S~**auf,** *m* -s/no *pl* hiccups. ◆'s~**en,** *v.tr.* to swallow (water, a pill etc.; *Fig:* an insult etc.); *Fig:* to swallow up (savings etc.). ◆'S~**impfung,** *f* oral vaccination. ◆'s~**weise,** *adv.* in sips.

**schludern** [ʃluːdərn], *v.i. (haben)* F: to do slipshod work.

**Schlummer** [ʃlumər], *m* -s/no *pl* Lit: slumber. ◆'s~**n,** *v.i. (haben)* Lit: to

slumber.

**Schlund** [ʃlunt], *m* -(e)s/=e 1. back of the throat. 2. *Fig: (Abgrund)* abyss.

**schlüpf|en** [ʃlypfən], *v.i. (sein)* to slip; *(Vogel)* **(aus dem Ei) s.,** to hatch. ◆'S~**er,** *m* -s/- knickers. ◆'s~**rig,** *adj.* *(a)* slippery (road, floor etc.); *(b) (anstößig)* lewd (joke etc.). ◆'S~**rigkeit,** *f* -/-en *(a)* slipperiness; *(b)* lewdness.

**Schlupfloch** [ʃlupflɔx], *n* hideout, hiding-place.

**schlurfen** [ʃlurfən], *v.i. (sein)* to shuffle, shamble (along).

**schlürfen** [ʃlyrfən], *v.tr.* to slurp, *(vorsichtig)* sip (soup etc.).

**Schluß** [ʃlus]. I. *m* -sses/=sse 1. *(Ende)* end; ending (of a play, piece of music etc.); **zum/am S.,** at the end; **zum S. sagte er...,** finally/in conclusion he said...; *F:* **S. machen,** *(mit der Arbeit)* to knock off, call it a day; **mit dem Rauchen usw. S. machen,** to give up/stop smoking etc.; **S. damit!** stop it! 2. *(Folgerung)* conclusion; **S~e ziehen,** to draw conclusions *(aus etwas dat,* from sth.). II. **'S~-,** *comb.fm.* final (result, round, scene etc.); last (minute, *Th:* act; *Sp:* runner etc.); closing (remark, speech etc.). ◆'S~**folgerung,** *f* logical conclusion. ◆'S~**licht,** *n (a)* Aut: etc: tail light; *(b)* F: *Sp:* tailender. ◆'S~**strich,** *m* unter etwas *dat* **einen S. ziehen,** to put an end to sth. ◆'S~**verkauf,** *m* Com: (end of season) sale. ◆'S~**wort,** *n* closing remarks.

**Schlüssel** [ʃlysəl]. I. *m* -s/- *(also Fig:)* key; *Tchn:* spanner; *Mus:* clef. II. **'S~-,** *comb.fm.* key (ring, *Fig:* figure, industry, position etc.). ◆'S~**bein,** *n* collarbone. ◆'S~**blume,** *f* primrose, cowslip. ◆'S~**bund,** *m & n* bunch of keys. ◆'S~**loch,** *n* keyhole.

**schlüssig** [ʃlysiç], *adj.* conclusive (evidence, proof).

**schmachten** [ʃmaxtən], *v.i. (haben)* to languish **(nach** + *dat,* for sth.).

**schmächtig** [ʃmɛçtiç], *adj.* slight; *Pej:* weedy.

**schmackhaft** [ʃmakhaft], *adj.* tasty (food); *Fig:* **j-m etwas s. machen,** to make sth. palatable to s.o.

**schmäh|en** [ʃmɛːən], *v.tr.* to abuse, revile (s.o.). ◆'s~**lich,** *adj.* disgraceful (treatment etc.); ignominious (defeat etc.).

**schmal** [ʃmaːl], *adj.* *(a)* narrow (street, bridge, hips etc.); slender (figure, hands etc.); thin (lips, face); *(b) (gering)* meagre (income, diet etc.). ◆'S~**film,** *m* 8 mm *or* 16 mm cine film. ◆'S~**spur-,** *comb.fm.* 1. narrow-gauge (railway, track). 2. *F:* small-time (academic etc.).

**schmälern** [ʃmɛːlərn], *v.tr.* to diminish (values etc.); *(Pers.)* to belittle (s.o.'s achievements etc.).

**Schmalz**[1] [ʃmalts], *n* -es/-e lard.

**Schmalz²**, *m* **-es**/*no pl F:* schmaltz.
◆'**s~ig**, *adj. F:* schmaltzy, sentimental.
**schmarotz|en** [ʃma'rɔtsən], *v.i. (haben) F:* **bei j-m s.**, to sponge on s.o.
◆**S~er**, *m* **-s**/- *also Fig:* parasite; *F: (Pers.)* sponger.
**Schmarren** ['ʃmarən], *m* **-s**/- **1.** *Aus: Cu:* fried strips of pancake. **2.** *F: Pej: (Unsinn)* trash.
**schmatzen** ['ʃmatsən], *v.i. (haben)* **beim Essen s.**, to eat noisily.
**schmecken** ['ʃmɛkən], *v.tr. & i. (haben)* to taste; **es schmeckt nach nichts**, it's tasteless; **schmeckt's Ihnen?** are you enjoying it? is it to your liking? **es hat geschmeckt!** it was delicious!
**Schmeich|elei** [ʃmaiçə'lai], *f* **-/-en** flattery. ◆'**s~elhaft**, *adj.* flattering.
◆'**s~eln**, *v.i. (haben)* to flatter.
◆'**S~ler**, *m* **-s**/- flatterer.
**schmeiß|en** ['ʃmaisən], *v.tr. & i.irr.4 (haben) F:* (a) to chuck (sth.). **mit Steinen s.**, to throw stones; **aus der Schule geschmissen werden**, to be kicked out of school. ◆'**S~fliege**, *f* bluebottle.
**Schmelz** [ʃmɛlts], *m* **-es**/*no pl (esp. dental)* enamel. ◆'**s~en**, *v.irr.* **1.** *v.i. (sein) (Schnee, Eis usw.)* to melt; *Fig: (Vermögen)* to shrink. **2.** *v.tr. Tchn:* to smelt (ore). ◆'**S~käse**, *m* (soft) processed cheese. ◆'**S~punkt**, *m* melting point. ◆'**S~tiegel**, *m Fig:* melting pot. ◆'**S~wasser**, *n* melted snow/ice.
**Schmerz** [ʃmɛrts], *m* **-es**/**-en 1.** pain; *(dumpf, anhaltend)* ache; **wo haben Sie S~en?** where does it hurt? **2.** *(Kummer)* sorrow. ◆'**s~empfindlich**, *adj.* sensitive (to pain). ◆'**s~en**, *v.tr. & i. (haben)* to hurt (s.o.); **mir schmerzt der Kopf**, my head aches. ◆'**S~ensgeld**, *n Jur:* compensation for personal suffering. ◆'**s~haft**, *adj.* painful. ◆'**s~lich**, *adj.* painful. ◆'**s~los**, *adj.* painless.
◆'**S~losigkeit**, *f* **-/**no pl freedom from pain. ◆'**s~stillend**, *adj.* ◆**s~es Mittel**, painkiller.
**Schmetter|ling** ['ʃmɛtərliŋ], *m* **-s**/**-e** butterfly. ◆'**s~n**, *v.tr. (a)* to hurl (sth.); *(b) (Trompete usw.)* to blare out (a signal etc.); *Hum: (Pers.)* to bawl out (a song).
**Schmied** [ʃmiːt], *m* **-(e)s**/**-e** smith, *esp.* blacksmith. ◆**S~e** [ʃmiːdə], *f* **-/-n** (smith's) forge, smithy. ◆'**s~eeisern**, *adj.* wrought-iron (gate etc.). ◆**s~en**, *v.tr.* to forge (steel etc., *Fig:* plans).
**schmieg|en** ['ʃmiːgən], *v.refl. (Pers., Tier usw.)* **sich an j-n, etwas** *acc* **s.**, to snuggle close up to s.o., sth. ◆'**s~sam**, *adj.* supple (leather, *Fig:* body etc.).
**Schmier|e** [ʃmiːrə], *f* **-/-n 1.** lubricant. **2.** *F: (Pers.)* **S. stehen**, to act as a lookout.
◆'**s~en**, *v.* **1.** *v.tr. (a)* to lubricate, *(mit Fett)* grease (moving parts); *(b) (streichen)* to apply (ointment, grease etc.), spread (butter, jam etc.); *(c) F:* to scrawl (a note, word etc.). **2.** *v.i. (haben) (Pers.)* to scrawl. ◆**S~e'rei**, *f* **-/-en** scribble;

*(Parolen)* graffiti; *(Gemälde)* daub.
◆'**S~fett**, *n* lubricating grease.
◆'**S~fink**, *m F:* (a) scrawler; (b) *(schmutziges Kind)* filthy brat.
◆'**s~geld**, *n F:* bribe. ◆'**s~ig**, *adj.* **1.** greasy, *(schmutzig)* grubby (hand, book). **2.** *F: Pej:* smarmy (person, manner etc.). ◆'**S~seife**, *f* soft soap.
**Schmink|e** ['ʃmiŋkə], *f* **-/-n** make-up; *Th:* greasepaint. ◆'**s~en**, *v.tr.* to make up (one's face, eyes etc.), make (s.o.) up; **sich s.**, to put on make-up.
◆'**S~tisch**, *m* make-up table.
**schmirgel|n** ['ʃmirgəln], *v.tr.* to rub down, sand (a surface). ◆'**S~papier**, *n* emery paper; *(Sandpapier)* sandpaper.
**Schmiß** [ʃmis], *m* **-sses**/*no pl F:* pep, verve. ◆**schmissig** [ʃmisiç], *adj. F:* rousing (music etc.).
**Schmöker** ['ʃmøːkər], *m* **-s**/- *F:* tome.
◆'**s~n**, *v.tr. & i. (haben) F:* to browse.
**schmollen** ['ʃmɔlən], *v.i. (haben)* to sulk.
**Schmor|braten** ['ʃmoːrbraːtən], *m* braised beef, pot roast. ◆'**s~en**, *v.tr. & i. (haben) Cu:* to braise (meat, vegetables etc.); *Fig:* **j-n s. lassen**, to leave s.o. to stew in his own juice.
**Schmuck** [ʃmuk], *m* **-(e)s**/*no pl* **1.** *(S~stücke)* jewellery. **2.** *(Verzierung)* decoration; *Arch: etc:* ornamentation.
◆'**s~los**, *adj.* unadorned; *(kahl)* bare.
◆'**S~losigkeit**, *f* **-/**no pl plainness; bareness. ◆'**S~sachen**, *fpl* jewellery.
◆'**S~stück**, *n* piece of jewellery; *Fig:* gem (of a collection etc.).
**schmücken** ['ʃmykən], *v.tr.* to decorate (sth.), *Fig:* to embellish (a speech etc.).
**schmuddelig** ['ʃmudəliç], *adj. F:* mucky.
**Schmugg|el** ['ʃmugəl], *m* **-s**/*no pl* smuggling. ◆'**s~en**, *v.tr.* to smuggle (s.o., sth.). ◆'**S~ler**, *m* **-s**/- smuggler.
**schmunzeln** ['ʃmuntsəln], *v.i. (haben)* to smile to oneself.
**schmusen** ['ʃmuːzən], *v.i. (haben) F: (Liebespaar)* to kiss and cuddle.
**Schmutz** [ʃmuts], *m* **-es**/*no pl* dirt.
◆'**S~fink**, *m F:* filthy brat.
◆'**S~fleck**, *m* dirty mark. ◆'**s~ig**, *adj.* dirty; **sich s. machen**, to get dirty; **ein s~iges Geschäft**, a shady/crooked deal.
**Schnabel** ['ʃnaːbəl], *m* **-s**/∗ **1.** beak. **2.** *F: (Mund)* trap; **den S. halten**, to keep quiet.
**Schnake** ['ʃnaːkə], *f* **-/-n 1.** crane-fly, *F:* daddy-long-legs. **2.** *F: (Mücke)* gnat.
**Schnalle** ['ʃnalə], *f* **-/-n** buckle.
**schnalzen** ['ʃnaltsən], *v.i. (haben) (Pers.)* **mit der Zunge s.**, to click one's tongue; **mit den Fingern s.**, to snap one's fingers.
**schnapp|en** ['ʃnapən], *v.* **1.** *v.tr. (a) (sich dat)* **etwas s.**, to snatch/grab sth.; *(b) (gefangennehmen)* to catch, nab (a thief etc.). **2.** *v.i. (haben) (a)* **nach etwas s.**, *(Pers.)* to grab at/*(Hund usw.)* snap at sth. ◆'**S~schuß**, *m* snapshot.

**Schnaps** [ʃnaps], *m* -es/=e schnaps; *F:* (*Spirituosen*) hard stuff/*N.Am:* liquor.

**schnarchen** ['ʃnarçən], *v.i.* (*haben*) to snore.

**schnarren** ['ʃnarən], *v.i.* (*haben*) to rattle, clatter; (*Klingel usw.*) to buzz; (*Stimme*) to rasp.

**schnattern** ['ʃnatərn], *v.i.* (*haben*) to gabble; *F:* (*Frau, Kind*) to chatter away.

**schnauben** ['ʃnaubən], *v.i.* (*haben*) to snort.

**schnaufen** ['ʃnaufən], *v.i.* (*haben*) (*Pers., Lok usw.*) to puff.

**Schnauz|bart** ['ʃnautsbɑːrt], *m* large/*esp.* walrus moustache. ◆'**S~e,** *f* -/-n **1.** snout (of a bear, fox, fish etc.); muzzle (of a dog); (*Maul*) mouth. **2.** *P:* (*Mund*) gob; (**halt die**) **S.!** shut your trap! **3.** *F:* nose (of a car etc.).

**Schnecke** ['ʃnɛkə], *f* -/-n snail; (*ohne Gehäuse*) slug. ◆'**S~nhaus,** *n* snail-shell. ◆'**S~ntempo,** *n* **F: im S.,** at a snail's pace.

**Schnee** [ʃneː], *m* -s/*no pl* snow. ◆'**S~ball,** *m* snowball. ◆'**S~fall,** *m* snowfall; fall of snow. ◆'**S~flocke,** *f* snowflake. ◆'**S~gestöber,** *n* snow flurry. ◆'**S~glöckchen,** *n* snowdrop. ◆'**S~kette,** *f* snow chain. ◆'**S~mann,** *m* snowman. ◆'**S~pflug,** *m* snowplough. ◆'**S~regen,** *m* sleet. ◆'**S~sturm,** *m* snowstorm. ◆'**s~weiß,** snow-white.

**Schneid** [ʃnait], *m* -(e)s/*no pl F:* guts.

**Schneid|brenner** ['ʃnaitbrenər], *m* cutting torch. ◆'**S~e** [-'ʃnaidə], *f* -/-n (*cutting*) edge, blade. ◆'**s~en,** *v.irr.59* **1.** *v.tr.* (*a*) to cut (sth.); (*in Scheiben*) to slice (bread, sausage etc.); (*b*) (*Pers.*) **sich s.,** to cut oneself; **sich** *dat* **in den Finger s.,** to cut one's finger; (*c*) (*ignorieren*) to cut s.o. dead; (ii) *Aut:* to cut in on s.o.; (*d*) (*Straßen, Linien usw.*) to cut across; **sich s.,** to intersect. **2.** *v.i.* (*haben*) to cut. ◆'**s~end,** cutting edge, *Fig:* tone etc.); biting (wind, cold etc.). ◆'**S~er,** *m* -s/- tailor. ◆'**S~erin,** *f* -/-nen dressmaker. ◆'**s~ern,** *v.tr.* to make (a dress, coat etc.); to tailor (a suit etc.). ◆'**S~ezahn,** *m* incisor. ◆'**s~ig,** *adj.* (*Pers.*) dashing; rousing (music).

**schneien** ['ʃnaiən], *v.i.* (*haben*) to snow.

**Schneise** ['ʃnaizə], *f* -/-n firebreak; *Av:* flight path/lane.

**schnell** [ʃnɛl]. **I.** *adj.* quick (movement, worker, service etc.); fast (car, train, road, journey, runner etc.); **s. laufen,** to run fast/quickly; *F:* **mach s.!** hurry up! **II.** '**S~-,** '**s~-,** *comb.fm.* express (service, etc.); high-speed (railway, bus etc.); fast(-growing etc.). ◆'**s~en,** *v.i.* (*sein*) **in die Höhe s.,** to leap up; (*Preise*) to shoot up. ◆'**S~hefter,** *m* loose-leaf binder. ◆'**S~igkeit,** *f* -/*no pl* (*a*) quickness; rapidity (of progress etc.); (*b*) (*Geschwindigkeit*) speed. ◆'**S~imbiß,** *m*

snack bar. ◆'**S~kochtopf,** *m* pressure cooker. ◆'**s~stens,** *adv.* as quickly as possible. ◆'**S~straße,** *f* expressway. ◆'**S~zug,** *m* fast/(*Fernschnellzug*) express train.

**schneuzen** ['ʃnɔytsən], *v.refl.* **sich s.,** to blow one's nose.

**schnipp|en** ['ʃnipən], *v.* **1.** *v.tr.* to flick (sth.) with one's finger etc. **2.** *v.i.* (*haben*) **mit dem Finger s.,** to snap one's finger. ◆'**s~isch,** *adj.* pert, cheeky.

**Schnipsel** ['ʃnipsəl], *m* -s/- *F:* snippet.

**Schnitt** [ʃnit], *m* -(e)s/-e **1.** cut (in one's hand, in cloth etc.). **2.** *no pl* cutting. **3.** (*S~muster*) pattern. **4.** *Mth:* section. **5.** *F:* (*Durchs.*) average. ◆'**S~blumen,** *fpl* cut flowers. ◆'**S~e,** *f* -/-n (*a*) open sandwich; (*b*) (*Scheibe*) slice. ◆'**S~fläche,** *f* (*a*) cut surface; (*b*) *Mth: etc:* section. ◆'**s~ig,** *adj.* (car, boat) with racy/sleek lines. ◆'**S~lauch,** *m* chives. ◆'**S~muster,** *n* pattern. ◆'**S~wunde,** *f* cut.

**Schnitz|el** ['ʃnitsəl], *n* -s/- **1.** *Cu:* escalope. **2.** scrap, shred (of paper etc.). ◆'**s~en,** *v.tr.* to carve (wood, a figure etc.). ◆'**S~er,** *m* -s/- **1.** carver. **2.** *F:* **einen (groben) S. machen,** to make a (bad) blunder.

**schnodderig** ['ʃnɔdəriç], *adj.* brash.

**schnöde** ['ʃnøːdə], *adj.* base, despicable; **j-n s. behandeln,** to treat s.o. with contempt.

**Schnorchel** ['ʃnɔrçəl], *m* -s/- snorkel.

**Schnörkel** ['ʃnœrkəl], *m* -s/- curlicue; (*schriftlich*) flourish; *F:* squiggle. ◆'**s~ig,** *adj.* ornate; flowery (style); *F:* squiggly (handwriting etc.).

**schnorr|en** ['ʃnɔrən], *v.tr. & i.* (*haben*) *F:* to scrounge, cadge (sth.). ◆'**S~er(in),** *m* -s/- (*f* -/-nen) scrounger, cadger.

**schnüff|eln** ['ʃnyfəln], *v.i.* (*haben*) (*a*) (*Hund*) to sniff (**an** + *dat,* at); (*b*) (*Pers.*) to snoop. ◆'**S~ler,** *m* -s/- *F:* snooper; *Pej:* nosy parker.

**Schnuller** ['ʃnulər], *m* -s/- (baby's) dummy, *N.Am:* pacifier.

**Schnulze** ['ʃnultsə], *f* -/-n *F:* tearjerker.

**Schnupfen** ['ʃnupfən], *m* -s/*no pl Med:* head cold.

**schnuppern** ['ʃnupərn], *v.i.* (*haben*) **an etwas** *dat* **s.,** to sniff at sth.

**Schnur** [ʃnuːr], *f* -/-e **1.** string. **2.** *El:* flex. ◆'**s~ge'rade,** *adj.* dead straight.

**schnür|en** ['ʃnyːrən], *v.tr.* to lace (sth.); to tie, lace (up) (shoes etc.). ◆'**S~schuh,** *m* lace-up shoe. ◆'**S~senkel,** *m* -s/- shoelace.

**Schnurr|bart** ['ʃnurbɑːrt], *m* moustache. ◆'**s~en,** *v.i.* (*haben*) (*Katze*) to purr.

**Schock** [ʃɔk], *m* -(e)s/-s shock; **unter S. stehen,** to be in a state of shock. ◆'**s~ieren** [-'kiːrən], *v.tr.* to shock, scandalize (s.o.). ◆'**s~ierend,** *adj.* shocking, scandalous.

**Schöff|e** ['ʃœfə], *m* -n/-n lay judge (in a

S~ngericht). ◆'S~engericht, n district court composed of two lay judges and a professional judge.

**Schokolade** [ʃokoˈluːdə], f -/-n chocolate. ◆S~ntorte, f chocolate gateau.

**Scholle** [ˈʃɔlə], f -/-n 1. (a) Agr: clod (of earth); (b) (Eiss.) ice floe. 2. (Fisch) plaice.

**schon** [ʃoːn], adv. (a) (bereits) already; s. im Jahre 1900, as early as 1900; s. damals, even at that time; (b) (endlich) komm s.! come on! (c) (allein) just; (sogar) even; s. der Gedanke daran ist schrecklich, the mere thought of it is terrible; s. deshalb/aus diesem Grund, for this reason alone; (d) (gewiß) certainly; really; (wohl) probably; das ist s. möglich, that is quite possible; ja s., aber..., yes of course, but...; es wird s. besser werden, it will get better, don't worry; s. recht! OK! ich glaube s., I think so.

**schon|en** [ˈʃoːnən], v.tr. to spare, save (one's strength, s.o.'s feelings etc.); (Pers.) to go/(Sache) be easy on (the brakes, eyes etc.); (schützen) to protect (one's hands, clothes); sich s., to take things gently. ◆'S~end, adj. gentle (für + acc, to); mild (detergent etc.). ◆'S~kost, f light food. ◆'S~ung, f -/-en 1. no pl sparing, saving; (Schutz) protection, care. 2. (im Wald) young plantation. ◆'s~ungslos, adj. ruthless, (unbeirrt) relentless. ◆'S~zeit, f close season.

**schön** [ʃøːn], adj. 1. beautiful; s~es Wetter, fine weather. 2. (a) (angenehm) pleasant, F: nice (surprise, holiday etc.); (b) s~e Feiertage/ein s~es Wochenende! have a good holiday/a nice weekend! er läßt s. grüßen, he sends his best wishes; (c) (gut) wie s., daß Sie gekommen sind, how nice of you to come; zu s., um wahr zu sein, too good to be true; F: das war nicht sehr s. von ihr, that wasn't very nice of her. 3. F: (beträchtlich) handsome (sum, profit); great (success etc.); wir mußten ganz s. arbeiten, we had to work jolly hard; s. langsam, nice and slowly. ◆'S~heit, f -/-en beauty. ◆'S~heits-, comb.fm. beauty (queen, contest etc.); cosmetic (surgery etc.). ◆'S~heitsfehler, m blemish, Fig: minor/F: cosmetic defect. ◆'s~machen, v.tr.sep. sich s., to smarten oneself up. ◆'s~tun, v.i.sep.irr. 106 (haben) F: j-m s., to suck up to s.o.

**Schoner** [ˈʃoːnər], m -s/- Nau: schooner.

**schöpf|en** [ˈʃœpfən], v.tr. (a) Wasser aus einem Brunnen usw. s., to draw water from a well etc.; Suppe s., to ladle out soup; (b) Lit: frische Luft s., to get some fresh air; Fig: neue Hoffnung s., to gain fresh hope. ◆'S~er, m -s/- creator. ◆'s~erisch, adj. creative. ◆'S~kelle, f/'S~löffel, m ladle.

◆'S~ung, f -/-en creation.

**Schorf** [ʃɔrf], m -(e)s/-e scab (on a wound).

**Schornstein** [ˈʃɔrnʃtain], m -s/-e chimney; Nau: funnel. ◆'S~feger, m -s/- chimney sweep.

**Schoß** [ʃoːs], m -es/-e 1. (a) lap; (b) (Mutterleib) womb. 2. Cl: (Rocks.) (coat) tail. ◆'S~hund, m lap-dog.

**Schote** [ˈʃoːtə], f -/-n pod.

**Schott|e** [ˈʃɔtə], m -n/-n Scot, Scotsman. ◆'S~in, f -/-nen Scotswoman. ◆'S~isch, adj. Scots, Scottish. ◆'S~land. Pr.n.n -s. Scotland.

**Schotter** [ˈʃɔtər], m -s/- gravel; Rail: ballast. ◆'S~straße, f (loose) gravel road.

**schraff|ieren** [ʃraˈfiːrən], v.tr. to hatch (a drawing etc.).

**schräg** [ʃrɛːk], adj. sloping (ground, surface etc.); slanting (eyes, writing etc.); s. gegenüber, diagonally opposite. ◆'S~e [ˈ·ɡə], f -/-n slant; (Fläche) slope; pitch (of a roof). ◆'S~schrift, f italics.

**Schramme** [ˈʃramə], f -/-n scratch. ◆'s~n, v.tr. to scratch (sth., oneself).

**Schrank** [ʃraŋk], m -(e)s/-e cupboard; (Kleiders.) wardrobe, N.Am: closet; (Büros.) filing cabinet. ◆'S~koffer, m, clothes trunk. ◆'S~wand, f cupboard (wall) unit.

**Schrank|e** [ˈʃraŋkə], f -/-n (a) (Sperre) barrier; (Bahns.) level-crossing gates; (b) Fig: usu.pl S~en, limits; sich in S~en halten, to restrain oneself. ◆'s~enlos, adj. unlimited (freedom etc.). ◆'S~enwärter, m crossing keeper.

**Schraube** [ˈʃraubə], f -/-n screw; (mit eckigem Kopf) bolt. ◆'s~en, v.tr. to screw. ◆'S~enmutter, f nut. ◆'S~enschlüssel, m spanner, N.Am: wrench. ◆'S~enzieher, m screwdriver. ◆'S~stock, m vice, N.Am: vise. ◆'S~verschluß, m screw top.

**Schrebergarten** [ˈʃreːbərɡartən], m allotment (usu. with summerhouse).

**Schreck** [ʃrɛk], m -(e)s/no pl fright, shock. ◆'S~en. I. m -s/- (a) no pl (Schreck) fright, shock; (b) die S. des Krieges, the horrors of war. II. s. v.tr. to give (s.o.) a fright. ◆'s~enerregend, adj. terrifying. ◆'S~ens-, comb.fm. terrifying (sight, news etc.); (night, cry etc.) of terror. ◆'S~gespenst, n (a) (Pers.) bogeyman; (b) (Sache) nightmare. ◆'s~haft, adj. easily frightened/scared. ◆'s~lich, adj. terrible. ◆'S~lichkeit, f -/no pl terribleness. ◆'S~schuß, m warning shot.

**Schrei** [ʃrai], m -(e)s/-e cry (of a person, bird); (gellender) scream; die S~e der Zuschauer, the shouts of the spectators. ◆'s~en, v.tr.&i.irr. (haben) (a) (Pers.) to shout, (laut) yell (abuse, curses, one's name etc.); F: das ist zum S~en, it's a scream; (b) (Eule, Affe usw.) to screech; (Möwe, Baby) to cry. ◆'s~end, adj. glaring, garish (colour); Fig: flagrant glaring (injustice etc.). ◆'S~hals, m F: noisy lout; (Kind) yelling child.

**schreib|en** ['ʃraibən]. **I.** v.tr.&i.irr.12 (haben) (a) to write (sth.); (b) (buchstabieren) wie schreibt man dieses Wort? how does one spell this word? **II. S.,** n -s/- (Brief) letter. ◆'S~er(in), m -s/- (f -/-nen) writer. ◆'s~faul, adj. lazy about writing letters. ◆'S~fehler, m slip of the pen. ◆'S~heft, n exercise book. ◆'S~kraft, f clerical assistant; usu. shorthand typist. ◆'S~maschine, f typewriter. ◆'S~stube, f Mil: orderly room. ◆'S~tisch, m (writing) desk. ◆'S~waren, fpl stationery. ◆'S~warenhändler, m stationer. ◆'S~weise, f 1. spelling. 2. (Stil) written style.

**Schreiner** ['ʃrainər], m -s/- joiner.

**schreiten** ['ʃraitən], v.i.irr.41 (sein) (a) to stride (along); (b) Lit: zu etwas dat s., to proceed with sth.

**Schrift** [ʃrift], f -/-en 1. (a) (Alphabet) script; (b) (Geschriebenes) writing; (Handschrift) (hand)writing. 2. (Abhandlung) report, paper. ◆'S~art, f fount; type. ◆'S~führer(in), m (f) secretary. ◆'s~lich, adj. written; j-m etwas s. mitteilen, to inform s.o. of sth. in writing. ◆'S~setzer, m typesetter. ◆'S~sprache, f written language. ◆'S~steller(in), m -s/- (f -/-nen) writer. ◆'S~stück, n document, Jur: deed. ◆'S~tum, n -s/no pl literature. ◆'S~wechsel, m Adm: correspondence.

**schrill** [ʃril], adj. shrill, strident.

**Schritt** [ʃrit], m -(e)s/-e 1. (a) step; S~e hören, to hear footsteps; einen S. machen/tun, to take a step; auf S. und Tritt, at every turn; wherever one goes; Fig: mit j-m, etwas dat S. halten, to keep up with s.o., sth.; (b) (Gangart) gait; (im) S. fahren, to drive at walking pace. 2. Cl: (Hosens.) crotch. ◆'S~macher, m -s/- pacemaker. ◆'Schritttempo, n im S., at a walking pace. ◆'s~weise, adv. step by step, gradually.

**schroff** [ʃrɔf], adj. (a) sheer, precipitous (rock face etc.); (b) abrupt (manner, change etc.); in s~em Gegensatz, in sharp/stark contrast.

**schröpfen** ['ʃrœpfən], v.tr. F: to fleece (s.o.), bleed (s.o.) white.

**Schrot** [ʃro:t], m -(e)s/-e 1. (Munition) (small) shot. 2. no pl whole-corn meal, wholemeal. ◆'S~kugel, f pellet.

**Schrott** [ʃrɔt], m -(e)s/-e scrap (metal). ◆'S~händler, m scrap dealer. ◆'S~haufen, m scrapheap. ◆'s~reif, adj. fit for the scrapheap.

**schrubbe|n** ['ʃrubən], v.tr. to scrub (a floor etc.). ◆'S~r, m -s/- scrubbing brush (with a long handle).

**Schrulle** ['ʃrulə], f -/-n 1. (Einfall) cranky/crackpot idea; (Laune) odd whim.

2. (Frau) old crone. ◆'s~ig, adj. dotty, cranky.

**schrumpfen** ['ʃrumpfən], v.i. (sein) to shrink; (Äpfel usw.) to shrivel.

**Schub** [ʃu:p], m -(e)s/-e ['ʃy:bə]. 1. (Stoß) push, shove. 2. (Gruppe) batch (of bread, people etc.). ◆'S~fach, n = S~lade. ◆'S~karre, f/'S~karren, m wheelbarrow. ◆'S~lade, f drawer. ◆'S~s [ʃups], m -es/-e F: push, shove. ◆'s~sen ['ʃupsən], v.tr. F: to shove (s.o., sth.). ◆'s~weise, adv. in batches, a few at a time.

**schüchtern** ['ʃʏçtərn], adj. shy (person, smile, manner etc.); (zaghaft) diffident (request, attempt). ◆'S~heit, f -/no pl shyness.

**Schuft** [ʃuft], m -(e)s/-e F: scoundrel. ◆'s~en, v.i. (haben) F: to slave away.

**Schuh** [ʃu:]. **I.** m -(e)s/-e shoe. **II.** ◆'S~-, comb.fm. shoe (brush, nail etc.); (heel, sole) of a shoe. ◆'S~creme, f shoe polish. ◆'S~größe, f shoe size. ◆'S~löffel, m shoehorn. ◆'S~macher, m shoemaker; (für Reparaturen) shoe repairer.

**Schul-** ['ʃu:l-], comb.fm. school (age, bus, friend, class, year, teacher, sport etc.). ◆'S~arbeit, f (a) schoolwork; (b) (Hausaufgabe) homework. ◆'S~besuch, f school attendance. ◆'S~bildung, f schooling. ◆'S~buch, n schoolbook. ◆'S~e, f -/-n 1. school; in die/zur S. gehen, to go to school; S. machen, to set a precedent. ◆'s~en, v.tr. to train (s.o., a horse, troops etc.). ◆'S~fach, n school subject. ◆'S~ferien, pl school holidays/ N.Am: vacation. ◆'S~frei, adj. morgen ist s., there is no school tomorrow. ◆'S~funk, m school broadcasting. ◆'S~hof, m school yard/(Spielplatz) playground. ◆'S~junge, m schoolboy. ◆'S~leiter, m head teacher, N.Am: principal. ◆'S~mädchen, n schoolgirl. ◆'S~pflicht, f obligation to attend school. ◆'s~pflichtig, adj. im s~pflichtigen Alter, of school age. ◆'S~schiff, n training ship. ◆'S~stunde, f (school) lesson. ◆'S~ung, f -/-en training; (Lehrgang) training course. ◆'S~weg, m way to/ from school. ◆'S~zeit, f schooldays. ◆'S~zeugnis, n school report.

**Schuld** [ʃult]. **I.** f -/-en [ʃuldən]. 1. no pl (a) (Verantwortlichkeit) blame; es ist meine S./die S. liegt bei mir, it is my fault; I am to blame; (b) (Unrecht) guilt. 2. Fin: debt. **II. s.,** adj. er ist/hat s. (daran), he's to blame (for it); it's his fault. ◆'s~bewußt, adj. guilty (look, expression etc.). ◆'s~en [ʃuldən], v.tr. j-m Geld, Fig: eine Erklärung usw. s., to owe s.o. money, Fig: an explanation etc. ◆'s~enfrei, adj. (Pers.) clear of debt. ◆'S~gefühl, n guilty feeling, sense of guilt. ◆'s~ig ['ʃuldiç], adj. 1. Jur: etc:

guilty; **der/die S~ige,** the guilty person; the culprit. **2. j-m Geld/**Fig: **eine Erklärung/Dank s. sein,** to owe s.o. money/Fig: an explanation/a debt of gratitude; **sie blieb mir die Antwort s.,** she could not give me an answer. ◆**'S~igkeit,** f -/no pl duty. ◆**'s~los,** adj. innocent (**an** + dat, of). ◆**'S~ner** ['ʃuldnər], m -s/-debtor. ◆**'S~schein,** m I.O.U. ◆**'S~spruch,** m verdict of guilty.

**Schüler** ['ʃyːlər], m -s/- (a) Sch: schoolboy; (in der Oberstufe) student; pupil (of a school, a teacher etc.); pl schoolchildren; pupils (of a school); (b) Art: etc: pupil. ◆**'S~in,** f -/-nen schoolgirl, (girl) pupil.

**Schulter** ['ʃultər], f -/-n shoulder. ◆**'S~blatt,** n shoulder blade. ◆**'s~n,** v.tr. to shoulder (a rifle etc.). ◆**'S~tasche,** f shoulder bag.

**schummeln** ['ʃuməln], v.i. (haben) F: to cheat.

**Schund** [ʃunt]. **I.** m -(e)s/no pl F: junk, rubbish; (Buch usw.) trash. **II. 'S~-,** comb.fm. F: rubbishy (goods etc.); trashy (literature).

**Schupp|e** ['ʃupə], f -/-n (a) Z: etc: scale; (b) flake of skin); pl (Haars~n) dandruff. ◆**'s~en¹,** v.tr. to scale (fish); (Haut) **sich s.,** to flake. ◆**'s~ig,** adj. scaly.

**Schuppen²** ['ʃupən], m -s/- shed; (Scheune) barn.

**Schur** [ʃuːr], f -/-en shearing (of sheep etc.). ◆**'S~wolle,** f clipped wool; **reine S.,** pure new wool.

**schür|en** ['ʃyːrən], v.tr. to poke (the fire); Fig: to stir up (hatred). ◆**'S~haken,** m poker.

**schürfen** ['ʃyrfən], v. **1.** v.tr. **sich** dat **den Ellbogen usw. s.,** to graze one's elbow etc. **2.** v.i. (haben) **nach Gold usw. s.,** to prospect for gold etc.

**Schurke** ['ʃurkə], m -n/-n rogue.

**Schürze** ['ʃyrtsə], f -/-n apron. ◆**'s~n,** v.tr. (a) to gather/tuck up (one's skirt etc.). ◆**'S~njäger,** m F: womanizer.

**Schuß** [ʃus], m -sses/-sse ['ʃysə]. **1.** shot; **S. aufs Tor,** shot at goal. **2.** (a) dash (of rum etc.). **3.** Fig: **in S. sein,** to be in fine fettle/(Haus usw.) shipshape. ◆**'S~linie,** f line of fire. ◆**'S~waffe,** f firearm. ◆**'S~wunde,** f gunshot wound.

**Schüssel** ['ʃysəl], f -/-n bowl; (serving etc.) dish.

**Schuster** ['ʃuːstər], m -s/- shoemaker.

**Schutt** [ʃut], m -(e)s/no pl rubble. ◆**'S~abladeplatz,** m (refuse) tip, dump. ◆**'S~haufen,** m heap of rubble.

**Schüttel|frost** ['ʃytəlfrɔst], m (violent) shivering. ◆**'s~n,** v.tr. to shake (s.o., sth., one's head, fist etc.); (Pers.) **sich vor Ekel s.,** to shudder with disgust.

**schütt|en** ['ʃytən], v.tr. to tip (ash etc.), pour (a liquid etc.).

**schütter** ['ʃytər], adj. sparse, thin (hair etc.).

**Schutz** [ʃuts]. **I.** m -es/no pl protection (**vor** + dat, from; **gegen** + acc, against); (Zuflucht) shelter; (Abschirmung) shield (**gegen Strahlung,** against radiation); **zum S. gegen Ansteckung,** as a safeguard against infection; **j-n in S. nehmen,** to stand up for s.o.; Fig: **unter dem/im S. der Dunkelheit,** under cover of darkness. **II. 'S~-,** comb.fm. protective (helmet, layer, film, Z: colouring etc.). ◆**'S~anzug,** m protective clothes. ◆**'S~befohlene(r),** m & f decl. as adj. Jur: charge, ward. ◆**'S~blech,** n guard; (am Fahrrad) mudguard. ◆**'S~engel,** m guardian angel. ◆**'S~gebiet,** n conservation area; (also Hist:) protectorate. ◆**'S~haft,** f protective custody. ◆**'S~impfung,** f vaccination. ◆**'s~los,** adj. unprotected, insecure. ◆**'S~maßnahme,** f precaution.

**Schütz|e** ['ʃytsə], m -n/-n **1.** (a) marksman; **ein guter S.,** a good shot; (b) Fb: scorer. **2.** Astr: Sagittarius. ◆**'s~en,** v. **1.** v.tr. to protect (s.o., sth.) (**vor etwas** dat, from sth.); to shelter (s.o.) (**vor dem Regen,** from the rain). **2.** v.i. (haben) to provide protection/shelter (**vor** + dat, from). ◆**'s~end,** adj. protective. ◆**'S~ling,** m protégé.

**Schwabe** ['ʃvaːbə], m -n/-n Swabian. ◆**'S~n.** Pr.n.n -s. Swabia.

**schwäbisch** ['ʃvɛːbiʃ], adj. Swabian.

**schwach** [ʃvax], adj. (a) weak; poor (hearing, sight, memory etc.); delicate (child, health etc.); frail (old person); (b) (gering) faint (light, resemblance, hope etc.); **ein s~er Trost,** a slight/Pej: poor consolation; **s~e Leistungen/Arbeit,** poor/inferior work; **s. in Englisch,** bad at English. ◆**'S~heit,** f -/no pl weakness. ◆**'S~kopf,** m Pej: dimwit. ◆**'S~sinn,** m mental deficiency. ◆**'s~sinnig,** adj. mentally deficient; F: Pej: moronic. ◆**'S~strom,** m El: low-voltage current.

**Schwäche** ['ʃvɛçə], f -/-n (a) weakness; (b) (Mangel) fault, shortcoming (of a book etc.); deficiency (of a plan etc.); (c) no pl (Vorliebe) **eine S. für j-n, etwas** acc **haben,** to have a soft spot for s.o., sth. ◆**'s~en,** v.tr. to weaken (s.o., sth.). ◆**'s~lich,** adj. sickly. ◆**'S~ling,** m -s/-e weakling. ◆**'S~ung,** f -/no pl weakening.

**Schwaden** ['ʃvaːdən], m -s/- cloud (of smoke etc.).

**schwafeln** ['ʃvaːfəln], v.i. (haben) F: to blather, (Unsinn reden) drivel.

**Schwager** ['ʃvaːgər], m -s/⁼ brother-in-law.

**Schwägerin** ['ʃvɛːgərin], f -/-nen sister-in-law.

**Schwalbe** ['ʃvalbə], f -/-n swallow.

**Schwall** [ʃval], m -(e)s/-e (Bewegung) surge; (große Menge) torrent (of water,

*Fig:* words).

**Schwamm** [ʃvam], *m* -(e)s/�=e **1.** sponge; *F:* **S. drüber!** (let's) forget it! **2.** (*Hauss.*) dry rot. ◆**'s~ig,** *adj.* (a) spongy; (b) *Pej:* puffy (face etc.).

**Schwan** [ʃvaːn], *m* -(e)s/�=e swan; ◆**'s~en,** *v.i.* (*haben*) **mir schwant nichts Gutes!** I fear the worst!

**schwanger** [ˈʃvaŋər], *adj.* pregnant. ◆**'S~schaft,** *f* -/-en pregnancy. ◆**'S~schaftsabbruch,** *m* termination of pregnancy.

**schwängern** [ˈʃvɛŋərn], *v.tr.* to make (s.o.) pregnant.

**Schwank** [ʃvaŋk], *m* -(e)s/ˆe comical tale; *Th:* farce. ◆**'s~en,** *v.i.* (*haben*) (a) (*Grashalme usw.*) to sway, wave; (*Gebäude, Boot usw.*) to rock; (*Betrunkener usw.*) to sway, (*taumeln*) stagger, reel; (b) (*Preise, Kurse usw.*) to fluctuate; (*Pers.*) to waver. ◆**'S~ung,** *f* -/-en (a) swaying; (b) fluctuation, variation.

**Schwanz** [ʃvants], *m* -es/ˆe tail.

**schwänze|n** [ˈʃvɛntsən], *v.i.* (*haben*) **die Schule s.,** to play truant/*N.Am:* *F:* hooky. ◆**'s~r,** *m* -s/- truant.

**Schwarm** [ʃvarm], *m* -(e)s/ˆe **1.** swarm (of bees, insects, *Fig:* people); flock (of birds); shoal (of fish). **2.** *no pl Fig:* (*Pers.*) heart-throb.

**schwärm|en** [ˈʃvɛrmən], *v.i.* (a) (*haben/ sein*) (*Bienen usw.*) to swarm; (b) (*haben*) (*Pers.*) **für j-n, etwas** *acc* **s.,** to be smitten with s.o., sth.; **von j-m, etwas** *dat* **s.,** to rave about s.o., sth.; ◆**S~e'rei,** *f* -/ -en enthusiasm; (*Verzückung*) rapture. ◆**'s~erisch,** *adj.* effusive; gushing (girl).

**Schwarte** [ˈʃvartə], *f* -/-n **1.** rind (of bacon); *Cu:* crackling (of pork).

**schwarz** [ʃvarts], *adj.* black; **ein S~er/ eine S~e,** a black man/woman; a negro/ negress; **ins S~e treffen,** to score a bull's-eye, *Fig:* hit the mark; *F:* **sich s. ärgern,** to be fuming/hopping mad; **s. über die Grenze gehen,** to cross the border illegally. ◆**'S~arbeit,** *f* work on the side (not declared for tax). ◆**'S~brot,** *n* black bread. ◆**s~fahren,** *v.i.sep. irr.26* (*sein*) (a) to travel without a ticket; (b) *Aut:* to drive without a licence. ◆**S~handel,** *m* illicit trade, black market. ◆**'S~händler,** *m* black marketeer. ◆**'s~hören,** *v.i.sep.* (*haben*) to listen to the radio without a licence. ◆**'s~sehen,** *v.i.sep. irr.92* (*haben*) (a) to take a pessimistic view; (b) to watch television without a licence. ◆**'S~seher,** *m* -s/- **1.** confirmed pessimist. **2.** *TV:* viewer who has no licence. ◆**s~'weiß,** *adj.* black and white (film etc.). ◆**'S~wald,** *m* Black Forest.

**Schwärze** [ˈʃvɛrtsə], *f* -/no *pl* blackness. ◆**'s~n,** *v.tr.* to blacken (shoes etc.).

**schwatz|en** [ˈʃvatsən], *v.* **1.** *v.i.* (*haben*) to chatter, natter. **2.** *v.tr.* **dummes Zeug**

**s.,** to talk rubbish. ◆**'s~haft,** *adj.* garrulous, talkative.

**schwätz|en** [ˈʃvɛtsən], *v.* = **schwatzen.** ◆**'S~er(in),** *m* -s/- (*f* -/-nen) *Pej:* talker, windbag.

**Schwebe** [ˈʃveːbə], *f Fig:* **in der S. sein/ hängen,** to hang in the balance/be undecided. ◆**'S~bahn,** *f* suspension railway. ◆**'S~balken,** *m* (balance) beam. ◆**s~n,** *v.i.* (*haben*) (*an einem Seil usw.*) to hang, dangle; (*Ballon, Wolken*) to float; **zwischen Leben und Tod s.,** to hover between life and death; **in Gefahr s.,** to be in danger.

**Schwed|e** [ˈʃveːdə], *m* -n/-n Swede. ◆**'S~en.** *Pr.n.n* -s. Sweden. ◆**'S~in,** *f* -/-nen Swedish woman. ◆**'s~isch,** *adj.* Swedish.

**Schwef|el** [ˈʃveːfəl], *m* -s/no *pl* sulphur. ◆**'s~(e)lig,** *adj.* sulphurous. ◆**'S~el- säure,** *f* sulphuric acid.

**Schweif** [ʃvaif], *m* -(e)s/-e tail (of a lion, comet etc.). ◆**'s~en,** *v.i.* (*sein*) (*Blick usw.*) to roam, wander.

**Schweig|egeld** [ˈʃvaigəgɛlt], *n* hushmoney. ◆**'s~emarsch,** *m* silent protest march. ◆**'s~en.** **I.** *v.i.irr.* (*haben*) to be silent; (*Pers.*) to say nothing. **kannst du s.?** can you keep a secret? **II.** **S.,** *n* -s/no *pl* silence; **j-n zum S. bringen,** to silence s.o., *F:* shut s.o. up. ◆**'s~end,** *adj.* silent. ◆**'s~sam,** *adj.* taciturn. ◆**'S~samkeit,** *f* -/no *pl* taciturnity.

**Schwein** [ʃvain], *n* -(e)s/-e **1.** pig. **2.** *F:* (*Pers.*) **armes S.,** poor devil; **kein S.,** not a soul; **3.** *F:* (*Glück*) **S. haben,** to be dead lucky. ◆**'S~e-,** *comb.fm.* (a) pig (breeding etc.); (b) *Cu:* pork (chop, fillet etc.); (belly etc.) of pork. ◆**'S~ebraten,** *m* joint of pork; roast pork. ◆**'S~ehund,** *m* -(e)s/-e *P:* bastard, swine. ◆**S~e'rei,** *f* -/-en *F:* (a) (*Schmutz*) filthy mess; (b) (*Gemeinheit*) mean trick; scandal; (c) (*Unanständigkeit*) obscenity; (*Witz*) dirty joke. ◆**'S~efleisch,** *n* pork. ◆**'S~estall,** *m* pigsty. ◆**'s~isch,** *adj. F: Pej:* lewd (joke, behaviour etc.). ◆**'S~sleder,** *n* pigskin.

**Schweiß** [ʃvais], *m* -es/no *pl* sweat; (*nur vom Menschen*) perspiration. ◆**'S~brenner,** *m* welding torch. ◆**'S~drüse,** *f* sweat gland. ◆**'s~en,** *v.tr.* to weld (metals, plastics etc.). ◆**'S~er,** *m* -s/- welder. ◆**'S~füße,** *fpl* sweaty feet. ◆**'s~gebadet,** *adj.* bathed in sweat. ◆**'S~naht,** *f* welded seam.

**Schweiz** [ʃvaits]. *Pr.n.f* - **die S.,** Switzerland. ◆**'S~er.** **I.** *m* -s/- Swiss. **II.** *adj.* Swiss. ◆**'S~erin,** *f* -/-nen Swiss woman. ◆**'S~erdeutsch,** *n* Swiss German. ◆**'s~erisch,** *adj.* Swiss (town etc.).

**schwelen** [ˈʃveːlən], *v.i.* (*haben*) to smoulder.

**schwelgen** [ˈʃvɛlgən], *v.i.* (*haben*) to in-

dulge (in food, *Fig:* memories etc.).
**Schwelle** ['ʃvɛlə], *f* -/-n (*also Fig:*) thresh-
hold.
**schwell|en** ['ʃvɛlən], *v.tr. & i.irr.* (*sein*)
to swell. ◆'S~**ung**, *f* -/-en swelling.
**Schwengel** ['ʃvɛŋəl], *m* -s/- (*a*) (bell)
clapper; (*b*) handle (of a pump etc.).
**Schwenk** [ʃvɛnk], *m* -(e)s/-s (*a*) swing;
(*b*) *Phot:* pan. ◆'S~**bar**, *adj.* swivelling. ◆'s~**en**, *v.* 1. *v.tr.* (*a*) to wave
(one's hat, arms, a flag etc.); (*b*) to swivel (sth.); *Phot:* to pan (a camera). 2. *v.i.*
(*haben*) to swing, *Mil:* wheel. ◆'S~**er**,
*m* -s/- brandy glass. ◆'S~**ung**, *f* -/-en
swing; change of direction; *Mil:* wheel;
*Phot:* panning.
**schwer** [ʃveːr], *adj.* 1. (*nicht leicht*) heavy;
**s. beladen**, heavily loaded. 2. (*a*) (*hart*)
hard (work, job, life, fate etc.); severe
(punishment etc.); **s. arbeiten**, to work
hard; (*b*) (*schwierig*) difficult (problem,
task, decision, language etc.); **es ist s. zu
begreifen**, it is hard/difficult to understand; **s. hören**, to be hard of hearing; **s.
atmen**, to breathe with difficulty; **es s.
haben**, to have a hard/difficult time. 3.
(*schlimm*) serious, bad (accident, injuries,
mistake etc.); serious (harm, offence
etc.); **s. krank sein**, to be seriously ill.
◆'S~**arbeit**, *f* hard (physical) work.
◆'S~**athlet**, *m* weight lifter, wrestler
*or* boxer. ◆'s~**bewaffnet**, *adj.* heavily
armed. ◆'S~**e**, *f* -/no *pl* 1. heaviness;
(*Gewicht*) weight. 2. (*Schwierigkeit*) difficulty. 3. (*Ausmaß*) severity; seriousness.
◆'s~**elos**, *adj.* weightless. ◆'S~**e-
losigkeit**, *f* -/no *pl* weightlessness.
◆'s~**er'ziehbar**, *adj.* s~**erziehbares
Kind**, problem child. ◆'s~**fallen**, *v.i.
sep.irr.27* (*sein*) **die Arbeit fällt ihm
schwer**, he finds the work difficult.
◆'s~**fällig**, *adj.* ponderous.
◆'S~**gewicht**, *n* 1. *Sp:* heavyweight.
2. *Fig:* (*Betonung*) (main) stress.
◆'s~**hörig**, *adj.* hard of hearing.
◆'S~**hörigkeit**, *f* -/no *pl* hardness of
hearing. ◆'S~**industrie**, *f* heavy industry. ◆'S~**kraft**, *f* (force of) gravity.
◆'s~**krank**, *adj.* gravely/critically ill.
◆'s~**lich**, *adv.* hardly. ◆'s~**machen**,
*v.tr.sep.* to make (life, work etc.) difficult
(j-m, for s.o.). ◆'s~**mütig**, *adj.* melancholy. ◆'s~**nehmen**, *v.tr.sep.irr.69*
to take (life etc.) (too) seriously.
◆'S~**punkt**, *m* 1. *Ph:* centre of gravity. 2. *Fig:* (main) emphasis. ◆'s~**tun**,
*v.refl.sep.irr.106 F:* **sich** *dat* **mit etwas
dat s.**, to have difficulties with sth.
◆'S~**verbrechen**, *n* major crime.
◆'S~**verbrecher**, *m* dangerous criminal. ◆'s~**verdaulich**, *adj.* indigestible.
◆'s~**verletzt**, *adj.* seriously wounded.
◆'s~**wiegend**, *adj.* weighty (decisions,
reason etc.).
**Schwert** [ʃveːrt], *n* -(e)s/-er sword.
◆'S~**lilie**, *f* iris.
**Schwester** ['ʃvɛstər], *f* -/-n 1. sister. 2.

(*Krankens.*) (female) nurse. ◆'s~**lich**,
*adj.* sisterly.
**Schwieger|eltern** ['ʃviːgər'ɛltərn], *pl*
parents-in-law. ◆'S~**mutter**, *f*
mother-in-law. ◆'S~**sohn**, *m* son-in-
law. ◆'S~**tochter**, *f* daughter-in-law.
◆'S~**vater**, *m* father-in-law.
**Schwiele** ['ʃviːlə], *f* -/-n callus.
**schwierig** ['ʃviːrɪç], *adj.* difficult.
◆'S~**keit**, *f* -/-en difficulty.
**Schwimm|bad** ['ʃvɪmbaːt], *n* swimming
pool/(*Hallenbad*) baths. ◆'S~**becken**,
*n* swimming pool. ◆'s~**en**, *v.i.irr.90*
(*sein/haben*) (*a*) (*sein*) (*Pers., Tier*) to
swim; (*Sache*) to float; (*Pers.*) **S. ist gesund**, swimming is good for you; *F:* **im
Geld s.**, to be rolling in money; (*b*) (*haben*) *F:* (*überschwemmt sein*) **der ganze
Boden schwimmt**, the whole floor is
awash; (*c*) (*verschwimmen*) to blur; (*d*) *F:*
(*Redner usw.*) **er ist ins S. geraten**, he
floundered/came unstuck. ◆'S~**er**, *m*
-s/- (*Pers.*) swimmer. ◆'S~**lehrer(in)**,
*m* (*f*) swimming
instructor. ◆'S~**weste**, *f* lifejacket.
**Schwind|el** ['ʃvɪndəl], *m* -s/no *pl* 1. giddi-
ness; *Med:* vertigo. 2. (*Betrug*) swindle,
cheat. ◆'s~**elerregend**, *adj.* vertigi-
nous (heights etc.). ◆'s~**elfrei**, *adj.*
(*Pers.*) free from giddiness/dizziness.
◆'s~**eln**, *v.i.* (*haben*) (*a*) *Pej:* (*lügen*) to
tell stories, *F:* fib; (*b*) **mir/mich schwin-
delt es**, I feel dizzy; **s~elnde Höhen**,
dizzy heights. ◆'S~**ler(in)**, *m* -s/- (*f* -/-
*nen*) swindler; (*Lügner*) liar. ◆'s~**lig**,
*adj.* dizzy, giddy; **mir ist s.**, I feel dizzy/
giddy.
**schwind|en** ['ʃvɪndən], *v.i.irr.9* (*haben*)
(*a*) *Lit:* (*Kräfte, Vorräte usw.*) to dwindle;
(*Schönheit, Einfluß usw.*) to wane;
(*Hoffnung usw.*) to fade; (*b*) (*verschwinden*) to disappear.
**schwing|en** ['ʃvɪŋən], *v.irr.19* 1. *v.tr.* to
swing (one's arm, a hammer etc.);
(*schwenken*) to wave (a flag etc.). 2. *v.i.*
(*haben*) (*a*) to swing; (*b*) (*Saite usw.*) to
vibrate. ◆'S~**ung**, *f* -/-en *Ph:* oscilla-
tion, vibration.
**Schwips** [ʃvɪps], *m* -es/-e *F:* **einen S. haben**, to be tipsy.
**schwirren** ['ʃvɪrən], *v.i.* (*a*) (*sein*) (*Insekten usw.*) to buzz (along); (*Pfeil usw.*) to
whirr; (*b*) (*haben*) **die Stadt schwirrt von
Gerüchten**, the town is buzzing with rumours.
**schwitzen** ['ʃvɪtsən], *v.i.* (*haben*) (*Pers.
usw.*) to sweat, perspire.
**schwören** ['ʃvøːrən], *v.tr. & i.irr.* (*haben*)
to swear (an oath, loyalty etc.); *F:* **auf
ein Medikament usw. s.**, to swear by a
remedy etc.
**schwul** [ʃvuːl], *adj. F:* gay (man, magazine etc.).
**schwül** [ʃvyːl], *adj.* sultry. ◆'S~**e**, *f* -/
no *pl* sultriness.
**Schwulst** [ʃvʊlst], *m* -(e)s/no *pl Pej:*
bombast.

**Schwund** [ʃvunt], *m* -(e)s/*no pl* decrease; *Com:* wastage, loss in weight.

**Schwung** [ʃvuŋ], *m* -(e)s/ːe 1. (*Bewegung*) swing (of the arms, a pendulum etc.); **S. holen**, to get a good swing. 2. (*a*) (*Antrieb*) momentum; **in S. kommen**, to get under way, (*Party*) warm up; (*Pers.*) to get into one's stride; (*b*) (*Elan*) verve, *F:* zip. ◆'**S~rad**, *n* flywheel. ◆'**s~voll**, *adj.* vivid (performance etc.); lively, spirited (music, speech etc.).

**Schwur** [ʃvuːr], *m* -(e)s/ːe oath. ◆'**S~gericht**, *n G.Jur:* court composed of professional and lay judges; (*mit Geschworenen*) jury court.

**sechs** [zɛks], *num.adj.* six. ◆'**S~eck**, *n* hexagon. ◆'**s~eckig**, *adj.* hexagonal. ◆'**s~mal**, *adv.* six times. ◆'**s~ste(r, s)**, *num.adj.* sixth. ◆'**S~tel**, *n* -s/- sixth. ◆'**s~tens**, *adv.* sixthly.

**sech|zehn** ['zɛçtseːn], *num.adj.* sixteen. ◆'**s~zig**, *num.adj.* sixty. ◆'**s~ziger**, *inv.adj.* **die s.** Jahre, the sixties.

**See** [zeː]. I. *m* -s/-n lake. II. *f* -/-n sea; **auf S.**, at sea; **an der S.**, at the seaside. ◆'**S~bad**, *n* seaside resort. ◆'**S~fahrt** *f* 1. *no pl* seafaring, navigation. 2. voyage. ◆'**S~gang**, *m* swell. ◆'**S~hund**, *m* seal. ◆'**s~krank**, *adj.* seasick. ◆'**S~krankheit**, *f* seasickness. ◆'**S~macht**, *f* naval/maritime power. ◆'**S~mann**, *m* -(e)s/'**S~leute** seaman, sailor. ◆'**S~ngebiet**, *n* lake district. ◆'**S~not**, *f* distress at sea. ◆'**S~pferdchen**, *n* sea-horse. ◆'**S~räuber**, *m* pirat. ◆'**S~rose**, *f* water-lily. ◆'**S~stern**, *m* starfish. ◆'**S~tang**, *m* seaweed. ◆'**s~tüchtig**, *adj.* seaworthy. ◆'**S~weg**, *m* sea route; **auf dem S.**, by sea. ◆'**S~zunge**, *f* sole.

**Seele** ['zeːlə], *f* -/-n soul; **das ist mir aus der S. gesprochen**, that's just what I feel. ◆'**S~nfriede**, *m* peace of mind. ◆'**S~nruhe**, *f* -/*no pl* complete calm.

**seel|isch** ['zeːliʃ], *adj.* psychological (illness etc.); emotional (balance, state etc.); **s. bedingt**, with psychological causes. ◆'**S~sorge**, *f* pastoral work. ◆'**S~sorger**, *m* -s/- pastor, clergyman.

**Segel** ['zeːgəl]. I. *n* -s/- sail. II. *S~*, *comb.fm.* sailing (boat, ship, club etc.). ◆'**S~fahrt**, *f* -/-en sail (trip). ◆'**S~fliegen**, *n* gliding. ◆'**S~flieger**, *m* glider pilot. ◆'**S~flugzeug**, *n* glider. ◆'**s~n**. I. *v.tr.&i.* (*haben/sein*) to sail (a boat, distance etc.); *Av:* to glide. II. **S.**, *n* -s/*no pl* sailing. ◆'**S~sport**, *m* sailing. ◆'**S~tuch**, *n* canvas.

**Segen** ['zeːgən], *m* -s/*no pl* blessing. ◆'**s~sreich**, *adj.* beneficial.

**Segment** [zɛg'mɛnt], *n* -(e)s/-e segment.

**segn|en** ['zeːgnən], *v.tr.* to bless (s.o., sth.). ◆'**S~ung**, *f* -/-en blessing.

**seh|en** ['zeːən], *v.irr.* 1. *v.tr.* (*a*) to see; **niemand war zu s.**, there was nobody to be seen; (*b*) (*schätzen*) to regard, judge (sth.); **etwas anders s.**, to look at sth. differently; **sich gezwungen/veranlaßt s., etwas zu tun**, to feel bound to do sth.; **das werden wir ja gleich s.**, we'll soon find out; (*c*) **er hat sich lange nicht s. lassen**, there hasn't been any sign of him for a long time; **etwas gern/ungern s.**, to like/dislike sth.; **sie ist stets gern gesehen**, she is always welcome; **sich s. lassen können**, (i) to look attractive/ (*repräsentativ*) respectable; (ii) *Fig:* (*Leistung usw.*) to be pretty good. 2. *v.i.* (*haben*) (*a*) to see; **gut/schlecht s.**, to have good/bad eyesight; (*b*) (*blicken*) to look (**aus dem Fenster, in den Spiegel usw.**, out of the window, in the mirror etc.); **lassen Sie mich/laß (mich) mal s.**, let me have a look; (*c*) **auf Pünktlichkeit s.**, to be particular about punctuality. ◆'**s~enswert**, *adj.* worth seeing. ◆'**S~enswürdigkeit**, *f* -/-en sight (worth seeing). ◆'**S~er(in)**, *m* -s/- (*f* -nen) seer, prophet. ◆'**S~fehler**, *m* eye defect. ◆'**S~schwäche**, *f* poor eyesight. ◆'**S~test**, *m* eye test. ◆'**S~vermögen**, *n* eyesight.

**Sehn|e** ['zeːnə], *f* -/-n tendon. ◆'**s~ig**, *adj.* sinewy; stringy (meat etc.).

**sehn|en** ['zeːnən], *v.refl.* **sich nach etwas dat s.**, to yearn/long for sth. ◆'**s~lich**, *adj.* ardent (wish etc.). ◆'**S~sucht**, *f* -/*no pl* longing (**nach** + *dat*, for). ◆'**s~süchtig**, *adj.* longing; wistful (expression etc.).

**sehr** [zeːr], *adv.* very; **s. viel**, very much; **s. viel Geld**, a great deal of money; **das tue ich s. gern**, I like doing that very much; **sich s. bemühen**, to try very hard; **danke s.**, thank you very much; **es gefiel ihr so s., daß ...**, she liked it so much that ...

**seicht** [zaiçt], *adj.* shallow (water); *Fig:* superficial (book etc.).

**Seid|e** ['zaidə], *f* -/-n silk. ◆'**s~en**, *adj.* silk. ◆'**S~enpapier**, *n* tissue paper. ◆'**s~nweich**, *adj.* soft and silky. ◆'**s~ig**, *adj.* silky.

**Seidel** ['zaidəl], *n* -s/- beer mug.

**Seif|e** ['zaifə], *f* -/-n soap. ◆'**S~en-**, *comb.fm.* soap (powder, dish etc.); soapy (water). ◆'**S~nlauge**, *f* soap suds. ◆'**S~nschaum**, *m* (soapy) lather. ◆'**s~ig**, *adj.* soapy.

**seihen** ['zaiən], *v.tr.* to strain (a liquid etc.).

**Seil** [zail], *n* -(e)s/-e rope; (*Hochs.*) tightrope. ◆'**S~bahn**, *f* cable railway. ◆'**s~springen**, *v.i.* to skip. ◆'**S~tänzer(in)**, *m* (*f*) tightrope walker.

**sein**[1] [zain], *poss.pron.* his; (*Tier, Sache*) its; **das ist s~er/s~e/s~es**, that's his (one)/(*Tier*) its one; **er hat das S~e dazu beigetragen**, he has done his bit; **jedem das S~e**, to each his own. ◆'**s~er**, *pers.pron.* *gen of* **er/es** of him/it. ◆'**s~erseits**, *adv.* on his part.

◆'s~**erzeit**, adv. (damals) at that time.
◆'s~**es'gleichen**, pron. (a) people like him; (b) ein Buch, das s. sucht, a unique book. ◆'s~**etwegen/um 's~etwillen**, adv. because of him; (für ihn) for his sake. ◆'s~**ige**, poss.pron. Lit: der/die/das s., his/its one.

**sein²**. I. v.i.irr. (sein) to be; (a) sei brav! be good! du warst es! it was you! keiner will es gewesen sein, nobody will admit to it; (b) es ist an dir zu ..., it is up to you to ...; wie dem auch sei, be that as it may; es sei denn, morgen regnet es, unless it rains tomorrow; wie wäre es mit einem Spaziergang? how about a walk? (c) mir ist kalt, schlecht usw., I feel cold, ill etc.; (d) F: (passieren) wenn etwas ist, if anything happens; ist was? is anything wrong? er ist nicht gewesen wäre, if it had not been for him. II. S., s -s/no pl Lit: existence.
◆'s~**lassen**, v.tr.sep.irr.57 F: to stop (doing) sth., (aufgeben) drop (sth.).

**seit** [zait], prep. + dat & conj. (a) since; ich bin s. vier Tagen krank, I have been ill for four days now; s. wann weißt du das? how long have you known this? ich weiß es erst s. kurzem, I only learnt about it recently; s. wir hier sind, since we have been here. ◆s~'**dem**. I. adv. since then; II. conj. since. ◆'s~**her**, adv. = seitdem I.

**Seit|e** ['zaitə], f -/-n (a) side; face (of a coin, dice etc.); Mil: flank; zur S. treten, to step aside; S. an S., side by side; F: seine schwache/starke S., his weak spot/strong point; auf der einen S...., auf der anderen S. ..., on the one hand ..., on the other hand ...; er stand auf ihrer S., he took her side; Sp: die S~n wechseln, to change ends; (b) (Buch:) page. ◆'S~**nansicht**, f side view; profile. ◆'S~**nblick**, m side/sidelong glance. ◆'S~**nhieb**, m side-swipe (auf + acc, at). ◆'s~**nlang**, adj. going on for (several) pages. ◆'s~**ns**, prep. + gen on the part of. ◆'S~**nschiff**, n side aisle. ◆'S~**nsprung**, m (extramarital) escapade. ◆'S~**nstechen**, n stitch (in one's side). ◆'S~**nstraße**, f side street. ◆'S~**nstreifen**, m verge (of a road). ◆'s~**nverkehrt**, adj. the wrong way round; (picture etc.) in mirror image. ◆'S~**nzahl**, f number of pages.
**seit|lich** ['zaitliç]. I. adj. side (entrance etc.); s. von mir, to one side of me. II. prep. + gen to one side of, beside. ◆'s~**wärts**, adv. sideways.

**Sekre|tär** [zekre'tɛːr], m -s/-e 1. (Pers.) secretary. 2. H: (fall-front) secretary. ◆S~**tariat** [-tari'aːt], n -(e)s/-e (a) administrative office; (b) Pol: secretariat. ◆S~**'tärin**, f -/-nen (female) secretary.
**Sekt** [zɛkt], m -(e)s/-e (German) champagne.
**Sekte** ['zɛktə], f -/-n sect.

**Sektion** [zɛktsi'oːn], f -/-en Adm: section, department.
**Sektor** ['zɛktɔr], m -s/-en (Bereich) sector.
**Sekund|a** [ze'kunda], f -/-den Sch: sixth and seventh years/second (highest) form (in a Gymnasium). ◆S~**är** [-'dɛːr] adj. secondary. ◆S~**e** [-'kundə], f -/-n second. ◆S~**enzeiger**, m second hand.
**selber** ['zɛlbər], dem.pron. F: = selbst.
**selbst** [zɛlpst]. I. dem.pron. ich s., I myself; du/Sie s., you yourself; er s., he himself; sie s., she herself; pl they themselves; wir s., we ourselves; Ihr/Sie s., you yourselves; die Tür geht von s. zu, the door closes itself/automatically; das versteht sich von s., that goes without saying. II. adv. even; s. wenn, even if. ◆'S~**achtung**, f self-esteem. ◆'S~**auslöser**, m Phot: automatic release. ◆'S~**bedienung**, f self-service. ◆'S~**befriedigung**, f masturbation. ◆'S~**beherrschung**, f self-control. ◆'s~**bewußt**, adj. self-confident, self-possessed. ◆'S~**bewußtsein**, n self-confidence. ◆'S~**erhaltung**, f self-preservation. ◆'s~**gefällig**, adj. smug, complacent. ◆'S~**gespräch**, n soliloquy. ◆'s~**herrlich**, adj. high-handed, autocratic. ◆'S~**kostenpreis**, m cost price. ◆'s~**los**, adj. unselfish. ◆'S~**losigkeit**, f -/no pl unselfishness. ◆'S~**mord**, m (act of) suicide. ◆'S~**mörder(in)**, m (f) (Pers.) suicide. ◆'s~**sicher**, adj. self-assured. ◆'s~**süchtig**, adj. selfish. ◆'s~**tätig**, adj. automatic. ◆'s~**verständlich**, adj. (offensichtlich) self-evident, obvious (truth, fact etc.); adv. of course. ◆'S~**verteidigung**, f self-defence. ◆'S~**vertrauen**, n self-confidence. ◆'S~**verwaltung**, f self-administration/government. ◆'S~**zufrieden**, adj. self-satisfied. ◆'S~**zweck**, m end in itself.
**selbständig** ['zɛlpʃtɛndiç], adj. independent; (mit eigenem Betrieb) self-employed (person). ◆'S~**keit**, f -/no pl independence.
**selektiv** [zelɛk'tiːf], adj. selective.
**selig** ['zeːliç], adj. (a) blissful; (Pers.) overjoyed, F: on cloud nine; (b) Ecc: blessed.
**Sellerie** ['zɛləri], m -s/-(s) & f -/- celeriac; (Stangens.) celery.
**selten** ['zɛltən], adj. (a) rare (books, plants etc.); ich sehe ihn nur s., I seldom/hardly ever see him. ◆'S~**heit**, f -/no pl rarity.
**seltsam** ['zɛltzaːm], adj. strange. ◆'s~**er'weise**, adv. strangely/oddly enough. ◆'S~**keit**, f no pl strangeness.
**Semester** [ze'mɛstər], n -s/- semester, (six-monthly) term. ◆S~**ferien**, pl vacation.
**Semikolon** [zemi'koːlɔn], n -s/-s & -la semicolon.
**Seminar** [zemi'naːr], n -s/-e 1. seminar;

*(Abteilung)* department. 2. *Ecc:* seminary.
**Semmel** ['zɛməl], *f* -/-n *South G:* (crusty) roll.
**Senat** [ze'naːt], *m* -(e)s/-e senate. ◆**S~or** [-'naːtɔr], *m* -s/-en [-'toːrən] senator.
**send|en** ['zɛndən], *v.tr. & i.* 1. *v.irr.* *(haben)* to send; to dispatch (goods etc.). 2. *(haben) Rad: TV:* to transmit, broadcast (signals, a programme etc.). ◆**'S~epause,** *f Rad: TV:* interlude. ◆**'S~er,** *m* -s/- (broadcasting) station; *(Gerät)* transmitter. ◆**'S~ereihe,** *f* radio/television series. ◆**'S~esaal,** *m* broadcasting studio. ◆**'S~eschluß,** *m* end of broadcasting, close-down. ◆**'S~ung,** *f* -/-en 1. *(a) no pl* dispatch (of goods); *(b)* *(das Gesandte)* consignment; *(Paket usw.)* package. 2. *Rad: TV: (a) no pl* broadcasting (of a programme); *(b)* broadcast; programme. 3. *Fig: (Aufgabe)* mission.
**Senf** [zɛnf], *m* -(e)s/*no pl* mustard.
**sengen** ['zɛŋən], *v.tr.&i.* *(haben)* to scorch, singe (sth.). ◆**'s~d,** *adj.* scorching, sweltering (sun, heat etc.).
**senil** [ze'niːl], *adj.* senile.
**Senior** ['zeːniɔr]. I. *m* -s/-en *Sp:* senior; *(ältestes Mitglied)* veteran. ◆**'S~chef,** *m* boss of a family firm. ◆**S~en-** [zeni'oːrən-], *comb.fm. (a) Sp: etc:* senior (team etc.); *(b)* old people's (home, club etc.).
**Senk|blei** ['zɛŋkblai], *n* lead, plummet. ◆**'S~e,** *f* -/-n hollow, dip (in a landscape). ◆**'S~el,** *m* -s/- shoelace. ◆**'s~en,** *v.tr.* to lower (one's eyes, voice, arms etc.); to bow (one's head); to reduce (taxes, prices etc.); **sich s.,** to sink; *(Boden)* to fall (away), drop; *(Schranke, Vorhang)* to descend. ◆**'S~fuß,** *m* fallen arches. ◆**'s~recht,** *adj.* vertical. ◆**'S~rechte,** *f* -n/-n *Mth:* perpendicular. ◆**'S~ung,** *f* -/-en *(a)* *(Abfall)* drop, dip (in the terrain, road etc.); *(b)* *(Verminderung)* lowering (of prices etc.) *(um + acc,* by).
**Sensation** [zɛnzatsi'oːn], *f* -/-en sensation. ◆**s~ell** [-o'nɛl], *adj.* sensational.
**Sense** ['zɛnzə], *f* -/-n scythe.
**sensi|bel** [zɛn'ziːbəl], *adj.* sensitive. ◆**S~bilität** [-ibili'tɛːt], *f* -/*no pl* sensitivity, sensitiveness.
**sentimental** [zɛntimɛn'taːl], *adj.* sentimental. ◆**S~ität** [-tali'tɛːt], *f* -/-en sentimentality.
**separat** [zepa'raːt], *adj.* separate; **s~e Wohnung,** self-contained flat.
**September** [zɛp'tɛmbər], *m* -s/- September.
**Serenade** [zere'naːdə], *f* -/-n serenade.
**Serie** ['zeːriə], *f* -/-n series; *Com:* line (of goods etc.); *Aut: etc:* range (of models); *Ind:* **in S. hergestellt,** mass-produced. ◆**'S~nproduktion,** *f* series/mass production. ◆**'s~nweise,** *adj.* in series.
**seriös** [zeri'øːs], *adj.* respectable (person etc.); sound (firm); **ein s~es Angebot,** a

genuine offer.
**Serpentine** [zɛrpɛn'tiːnə], *f* -/-n zigzag (line, road).
**Serum** ['zeːrum], *n* -s/-en serum.
**Serv|ice** [zɛr'viːs], *n* -s/- (tea etc.) service. ◆**s~ieren** [-'viːrən], *v.tr. & i. (haben)* to serve (sth.). ◆**S~iererin,** *f* -/-nen waitress. ◆**S~iette** [-vi'ɛtə], *f* -/-n (table) napkin.
**Servus** ['zɛrvus], *int. F: South G: & Aus: (a)* hello! N.Am: hi! *(b)* *(Abschiedsgruß)* so long! see you!
**Sesam** ['zeːzam], *m* -s/-s *(a)* sesame; *(b)* *(Samen)* sesame seeds.
**Sessel** ['zɛsəl], *m* -s/- (upholstered) armchair. ◆**'S~lift,** *m* chair lift.
**seßhaft** ['zɛshaft], *adj.* *(Pers., Leben)* settled; **s. werden,** to settle down.
**Set** [sɛt], *m & n* -s/-s 1. *(Satz)* set. 2. table mat.
**setz|en** ['zɛtsən], *v.* 1. *v.tr. (a)* to put (sth. somewhere); **etwas auf eine Liste s.,** to enter/put sth. on a list; **sein Geld auf etwas** *acc* **s.,** to put/stake one's money on sth.; *(b)* *(festlegen)* to set (limits, a target etc.); *(c)* **sich s.,** to sit down; *(d)* to plant (a tree etc.); *(e)* **j-m ein Denkmal s.,** to put up a monument to s.o.; **die Segel s.,** to set/hoist the sails; *(f)* to set (a book etc.). 2. *v.i. (a)* *(sein)* **über eine Hecke s.,** to jump/leap over a hedge; **die Fähre setzte über den Fluß,** the ferry crossed the river; *(b)* *(haben)* to bet; **auf ein Pferd s.,** to back a horse. ◆**S~er,** *m* -s/- typesetter, compositor. ◆**'S~ling,** *m* -s/-e seedling.
**Seuche** ['zɔyçə], *f* -/-n epidemic.
**seufze|n** ['zɔyftsən], *v.i. (haben)* to sigh. ◆**'S~r,** *m* -s/- sigh.
**Sex** [sɛks], *m* -es/*no pl* sex. ◆**s~istisch** [se'ksistiʃ], *adj.* sexist.
**Sexta** ['zɛksta], *f* -/-ten *Sch:* first form/year (in a *Gymnasium*).
**Sextett** [zɛks'tɛt], *n* -(e)s/-e *Mus:* sextet.
**Sexu|al-** [zɛksu'aːl-], *comb.fm.* sex (life, crime etc.). ◆**S~alität** [-ali'tɛːt], *f* -/*no pl* sexuality. ◆**s~ell** [-u'ɛl], *adj.* sexual.
**sezier|en** [ze'tsiːrən], *v.tr.* to dissect (a corpse etc.).
**Shampoo** [ʃam'puː], *m* -s/-s shampoo.
**Show** [ʃəu], *f* -/-s show. ◆**'S~geschäft,** *n* show business.
**siam|esisch** [zia'meːziʃ], *adj.* Siamese. ◆**S~katze** [ziːam-], *f* Siamese cat.
**Sibir|ien** [zi'biːriən]. *Pr.n.n* -s. Siberia. ◆**s~isch,** *adj.* Siberian (climate etc.).
**sich** [ziç], *refl.pron. (a) 3rd pers. sing. m* himself, *f* herself, *n* itself; *pl* themselves; *2nd pers. polite form* yourself, *pl* yourselves; *indef.* oneself; **das Problem löste s. von selbst,** the problem solved itself; **er gab s. (selbst) die Schuld,** he blamed himself; *(b)* *(einander)* each other, one another; **sie helfen s.** dat, they help one another; *(c)* **sie denkt nur an s.,** she only thinks of herself; **er hat es hinter s.,** he has this behind him; **haben Sie Geld bei**

s.? have you any money on you?
**Sichel** ['ziçəl], *f -/-n* sickle.
**sicher** ['ziçər], *adj. (a)* safe (place etc.);
secure (job, investment etc.); **vor Gefahr
s. sein,** to be safe/protected from danger;
**s. ist s.,** better safe than sorry; *(b)* sure
(sign, judgement etc.); *(gewiß)* certain;
*(zuverlässig)* reliable (method, evidence
etc.); **sind Sie s.?** are you sure/certain?
**das ist s. richtig,** that is certainly true;
**aber s.!** of course! *(c)* steady (hand etc.);
confident (belief, manner etc.).
◆'**S~gehen,** *v.i.sep.irr.36* (*sein*) to play
safe; **um sicherzugehen,** to be on the
safe side, make sure. ◆'**S~heit,** *f -/-en*
**1.** *no pl (a)* safety; security (of the state
etc.); *(b) (Gewißheit)* certainty; **er kommt
mit S.,** he is sure to come; *(c) (Selbsts.)*
confidence, assurance. **2.** *Fin:* security.
◆'**S~heits-,** *comb.fm. (a)* safety (factor,
glass, device etc.); safe (car, distance
etc.); *(b)* security (officer, service, forces,
police, risk etc.). ◆'**S~heitsgurt,** *m*
safety belt; *Av: Aut:* seat belt.
◆'**s~heitshalber,** *adj.* for safety's
sake. ◆'**S~heitsnadel,** *f* safety pin.
◆'**S~heitsschloß,** *n* safety lock.
◆'**s~lich,** *adv.* certainly. ◆'**s~n,** *v.tr.
(a)* to safeguard, *(schützen)* protect (sth.)
*(vor etwas dat,* from sth.); *(b) (verschaffen)* to secure (sth.); **sich dat einen guten
Platz s.,** to make sure of a good seat; *(c)*
to put the safety catch on (a gun).
◆'**s~stellen,** *v.tr.sep. (a) (beschlagnahmen)* to seize, confiscate (goods etc.); *(b)*
to safeguard (a position, service etc.).
◆'**S~ung,** *f -/-en* **1.** *no pl (Schutz)* protection, safeguard(ing). **2.** *(a) El:* fuse;
*(b) (von Pistole)* safety catch.

**Sicht** [ziçt], *f -/no pl* visibility; **die S. versperren,** to obstruct/block one's view;
**außer S.,** out of sight; *Com:* **auf/nach
S.,** on/after sight; *Fig:* **auf kurze/lange
S.,** in the short/long run; **aus meiner S.,**
from my point of view. ◆'**s~bar,** *adj.*
visible. ◆'**S~barkeit,** *f -/no pl* visibility. ◆'**s~en,** *v.tr.* to sight (a ship etc.).
◆'**S~gerät,** *n Data-pr:* visual display
unit. ◆'**s~lich,** *adj.* visible, evident
(pleasure, relief etc.). ◆'**S~verhält-
nisse,** *npl* visibility. ◆'**S~vermerk,** *m*
visa (in a passport etc.). ◆'**S~weite,** *f
-/no pl* range of visibility.
**sickern** ['zikərn], *v.i.* (*sein*) to seep, ooze.
**sie** [zi:], *pers.pron.* **1.** *(Frau usw.)* (*nom.*)
she, *(acc)* her, *(Ding)* it; *pl* they, *(acc)*
them. **2.** **S~** you.
**Sieb** [zi:p], *n -(e)s/-e* strainer, sieve.
◆**s~en1** ['zi:bən], *v.tr.* to sieve (flour
etc.).
**sieben2** ['zi:bən], *num.adj.* seven.
◆'**s~fach,** *adj.* sevenfold. ◆'**s~mal,**
*adv.* seven times. ◆'**S~'sachen,** *fpl F:*
(personal) belongings.
**sieb|te(r,s)** ['zi:ptə(r,s)], *num.adj.* se-
venth. ◆'**S~tel,** *n -s/-* seventh.
◆'**s~tens,** *adv.* seventhly. ◆'**s~-**

**zehn,** *num.adj.* seventeen. ◆'**s~zig,**
*num.adj.* seventy. ◆'**s~ziger. I.**
*inv.adj.* **die s. Jahre,** the seventies. **II.**
**S~(in),** *m -s/- (f -/-nen)* seventy-year
old.
**sied|eln** ['zi:dəln], *v.i.* (*haben*) to settle
(somewhere). ◆'**S~ler,** *m -s/-* settler.
◆'**S~lung,** *f -/-en* **1.** housing estate/
*N.Am:* development. **2.** *esp. Hist:* settlement.
**siede|n** ['zi:dən], *v.tr.&i.* (*haben*) to boil
(sth.); **s~nd heiß,** boiling hot.
◆'**S~punkt,** *m* boiling point.
**Sieg** [zi:k], *m -(e)s/-e* victory; *Sp:* win.
◆'**s~en,** *v.i.* (*haben*) to win a victory;
*Sp: Pol: etc:* to win; *Fig:* to triumph.
◆'**S~er(in)** [-gər(in)], *m -s/- (f -/-nen)*
victor; *Sp: etc:* winner. ◆'**S~er-
ehrung,** *f Sp:* prize-giving ceremony.
◆'**s~esgewiß/'s~essicher,** *adj.* confident of victory. ◆'**S~eszug,** *m*
triumphant/victorious progress. ◆'**s~-
reich,** *adj.* victorious.
**Siegel** ['zi:gəl], *n -s/-* seal; *(Stempel)*
stamp. ◆'**S~lack,** *m & n* sealing wax.
◆'**S~ring,** *m* signet ring.
**siezen** ['zi:tsən], *v.tr.* to address (s.o.)
formally/as *Sie.*
**Signal** [zi'gna:l], *n -s/-e* signal.
◆**s~i'sieren,** *v.tr.* to signal (a message
etc.); *Fig:* to indicate (sth.).
**Sig|natur** [zigna'tu:r], *f -/-en* signature.
◆**s~'nieren,** *v.tr.* to sign (sth.).
**Silbe** ['zilbə], *f -/-n* syllable.
**Silber** ['zilbər]. **I.** *n -s/no pl* silver; **das S.
putzen,** to polish the silver. **II.** '**S~-,**
*comb.fm.* silver (foil, fox, medal, coin,
paper etc.). ◆'**s~n,** *adj.* silver (bracelet, wedding etc.); *(silbrig)* silvery (sheen
etc.).
**silbrig** ['zilbriç], *adj.* silvery.
**Silhouette** [zilu'ɛtə], *f -/-n* silhouette.
**Silizium** [zi'li:tsium], *n -s/no pl* silicon.
**Silo** ['zi:lo], *m -s/-s* silo.
**Silvester** [zil'vɛstər], *n -s/-* New Year's
Eve; *Scot:* Hogmanay.
**simpel** ['zimpəl], *adj.* simple (fact, solution); *Pej: (einfältig)* simple-minded (person etc.).
**Sims** [zims], *m & n -es/-e (Fensters. usw.)*
ledge, sill; *Arch:* cornice.
**simulieren** [zimu'li:rən], *v.* **1.** *v.tr.* to
sham (an illness etc.); *Tchn:* to simulate
(processes etc.). **2.** *v.i.* (*haben*) to sham,
pretend.
**simultan** [zimul'ta:n], *adj.* simultaneous.
**Sinfoni|e** [zinfo'ni:], *f -/-n* symphony.
◆**s~sch** [-'fo:niʃ], *adj.* symphonic.
**sing|en** ['ziŋən], *v.tr. & i.irr.19* (*haben*) to
sing (a song, alto etc.). ◆'**S~vogel,** *m*
song bird.
**Singular** ['ziŋgula:r], *m -s/-e* singular.
**sinken** ['ziŋkən], *v.i.irr.* (*sein*) *(a) (Schiff,
Wasserspiegel usw.)* to sink; *(Sonne)* to
set; *(b) (Temperatur, Preise usw.)* to drop,
fall; *(Wert, Einfluß usw.)* to decline, diminish; **in j-s Achtung s.,** to go down in

s.o.'s estimation.

**Sinn** [zin], *m* -(e)s/-e 1. *no pl* (*Bedeutung*) sense (of a term, phrase etc.); meaning (of s.o.'s words etc.); (*Zweck*) point; **im S~e des Gesetzes**, within the meaning of the law. 2. *no pl* (*a*) (*Geist*) mind; **es kam mir plötzlich in den S.**, I suddenly thought of it; **es ist nicht nach meinem S.**, it is not to my liking; (*b*) (*Gefühl, Verständnis*) feeling; **er hat S. für Humor**, he has a sense of humour. 3. sense (of hearing etc.); **bist du von S~en?** are you out of your mind? ◆**'S~bild**, *n* symbol. ◆**'s~bildlich**, *adj.* symbolic. ◆**'s~en**, *v.i.irr.73* (*haben*) *Lit:* **über etwas** *acc* **s.**, to meditate on/brood over sth. ◆**'S~esorgan**, *n* sense organ. ◆**'S~estäuschung**, *f* -/-en hallucination. ◆**'s~gemäß**, *adj.* **s~gemäße Wiedergabe einer Geschichte**, rendering giving the gist of a story. ◆**'s~ig**, *adj.* apt, *F:* clever (present, action etc.). ◆**'s~lich**, *adj.* sensual (pleasures, love, person, etc.); (*sexuell*) sexual (attraction, desire etc.); **s~liche Wahrnehmung**, sensory perception. ◆**'S~lichkeit**, *f* -/ *no pl* sensuality; sensuousness. ◆**'s~los**, *adj.* pointless (enterprise etc.); **s~lose Wut**, blind rage; **s. betrunken**, dead drunk. ◆**'S~losigkeit**, *f* -/*no pl* pointlessness, futility. ◆**'s~voll**, *adj.* 1. meaningful (sentence, *Fig:* activity etc.); satisfying, fulfilling (work etc.). 2. (*vernünftig*) sensible; wise (undertaking, use etc.).

**Sintflut** ['zintfluːt], *f* die **S.**, the Flood.

**Sinus** ['ziːnus], *m* -/-se sine.

**Siphon** ['ziːfɔn], *m* -s/-s (soda etc.) siphon.

**Sippe** ['zipə], *f* -/-n (whole) family; clan; (*bei Naturvölkern*) tribe. ◆**'S~schaft**, *f* -/-en *usu.Pej:* clan, tribe.

**Sirene** [zi'reːnə], *f* -/-n siren.

**Sirup** ['ziːrup], *m* -s/-e syrup.

**Sisal** ['ziːzal], *m* -s/*no pl* sisal.

**Sitte** ['zitə], *f* -/-n (*a*) custom; **nach alter S.**, in the old way; (*b*) **die gute S./gute S~en**, good manners; etiquette. ◆**'s~enstreng**, *adj.* puritanical, straitlaced. ◆**'s~enwidrig**, *adj.* immoral (action etc.); morally offensive (advertising etc.). ◆**'s~lich**, *adj.* moral. ◆**'S~lichkeit**, *f* -/*no pl* morality. ◆**'S~lichkeitsverbrechen**, *n* sexual assault. ◆**'s~sam**, *adj.* demure (girl, behaviour), well-behaved (children).

**Situation** [zituatsi'oːn], *f* -/-en situation.

**Sitz** [zits], *m* -es/-e 1. seat. 2. *Cl: & Tchn:* fit. ◆**'s~en**, *v.i.irr.* (*haben*) (*a*) to sit; **bitte bleiben Sie s.!** please don't get up! **er saß vier Jahre** (**im Gefängnis**), he spent four years in jail; (*b*) *F:* **die Bemerkung/der Hieb saß!** that remark/ blow went home; **die Vokabeln s.**, the words have been well memorized/*F:* have stuck; (*c*) (*Kleidung*) to fit. ◆**'s~enbleiben**, *v.i.sep.irr.12* (*sein*) (*a*)

*Sch: F:* to stay down, repeat a class/ *N.Am:* grade; (*b*) *Com: F:* **der Kaufmann blieb auf seinen Waren s~en**, the shopkeeper was stuck with his goods. ◆**'s~enlassen**, *v.tr.sep.irr.57* *F:* to leave (s.o.) in the lurch; to desert (a fiancé(e), wife, husband); to jilt (a girl). ◆**'S~gelegenheit**, *f* seat, place to sit down. ◆**'S~platz**, *m* seat. ◆**'S~ung**, *f* -/-en session (of a court, conference etc.).

**Sizilianer(in)** [zitsili'aːnər(in)], *m* -s/- (*f* -/-nen) Sicilian. ◆**S~en** [zi'tsiːliən]. *Pr.n.n* -s. Sicily.

**Skala** ['skaːla], *f* -/-len (*a*) scale (of sounds, *Mus:* notes etc.); range (of colours, ability etc.); (*b*) *Meas:* scale, dial (of an instrument).

**Skalpell** [skal'pɛl], *n* -s/-e scalpel.

**Skandal** [skan'daːl], *m* -s/-e scandal; ◆**s~ös** [-da'løːs], *adj.* scandalous (behaviour etc.). ◆**S~presse**, *f* gutter press.

**Skandinavien** [skandi'naːviən]. *Pr.n.n* -s. Scandinavia. ◆**S~vier(in)**, *m* -s/- (*f* -/-nen) Scandinavian. ◆**s~visch**, *adj.* Scandinavian.

**Skelett** [ske'lɛt], *n* -(e)s/-e skeleton.

**Skepsis** ['skɛpsis], *f* -/*no pl* scepticism. ◆**'S~tiker**, *m* -s/- sceptic. ◆**'s~tisch**, *adj.* sceptical.

**Ski** [ʃiː]. I. *m* -s/-er ski; **S. laufen/fahren**, to ski. II. **'S~-**, *comb.fm.* ski (lift, boots, stick etc.); skiing (area, club, competition etc.). ◆**'S~fahren/'S~laufen**, *n* skiing. ◆**'S~fahrer/'S~läufer**, *m* skier. ◆**'S~lehrer**, *m* skiing instructor. ◆**'S~piste**, *f* ski run. ◆**'S~springen**, *n* ski jumping.

**Skizze** ['skitsə], *f* -/-e sketch. ◆**s~ieren** [-'tsiːrən], *v.tr.* (*a*) to sketch, make a sketch of (sth.); to outline (a subject); (*b*) (*entwerfen*) to draft (a plan etc.).

**Sklave** ['sklaːvə], *m* -n/-n slave. ◆**'S~enarbeit**, *f* slave-labour, slavery. ◆**S~e'rei**, *f* -/*no pl* slavery. ◆**'S~in**, *f* -/-nen (female) slave. ◆**'s~isch**, *adj.* slavish.

**Skonto** ['skɔnto], *n & m* -s/-s *Com:* discount.

**Skorpion** [skɔrpi'oːn], *m* -s/-e scorpion; *Astr:* Scorpio.

**Skrupel** ['skruːpəl], *m* -s/- *usu.pl* scruple. ◆**'s~los**, *adj.* unscrupulous. ◆**'S~losigkeit**, *f* -/*no pl* unscrupulousness.

**Skulptur** [skulp'tuːr], *f* -/-en sculpture.

**skurril** [sku'riːl], *adj.* bizarre.

**Slalom** ['slɔːlɔm], *m* -s/-s slalom.

**Slawe** ['slaːvə], *m* -n/-n Slav. ◆**'S~in**, *f* -/-nen Slav (woman). ◆**'s~isch**, *adj.* Slav.

**Smaragd** [sma'rakt], *m* -(e)s/-e emerald.

**Smoking** ['smoːkiŋ], *m* -s/-s dinner jacket; *N.Am:* tuxedo.

**Snob** [snɔp], *m* -s/-s snob. ◆**S~ismus**

[sno'bismus], *m* -/*no pl* snobbery.
**so** [zo:]. **I.** *int. F:* so! right! that's that!
so? really? ach so! oh I see! so that's
what/how it is! **II.** *adv.* **1.** (*a*) (*auf diese
Weise*) in this/that way; like this/that; **laß
es so, wie es ist,** leave it as it is; **so oder
so,** one way or the other; (*b*) (*in solchem
Maße*) **sei so gut,** be so kind; (*mit einer
Geste*) **es ist so lang,** it's this long; **das
ist so gut wie sicher,** that's as good as/
virtually certain; **es ärgerte ihn so
(sehr), daß ...,** it annoyed him so much
that ...; **das ist gar nicht so einfach,** it's
not that easy; (*c*) *F:* such; **so ein langes
Buch,** such a long book; **so ein Pech/
Unsinn!** what bad luck/nonsense! **na so
was!** well really! what next! **2.** *F:* (*ungefähr*) about; **so um drei Uhr,** (*somewhere*) around three o'clock.
**sobald** [zo'balt], *conj.* as soon as.
**Socke** ['zɔkə], *f* -/-n sock.
**Sockel** ['zɔkəl], *m* -s/- base; *Arch: Art:*
pedestal; plinth (of a statue).
**Soda** ['zo:da], *n* -s/*no pl* 1. *Ch:* soda. 2.
(*also* S~**wasser**) soda water.
**Sodbrennen** ['zo:tbrɛnən], *n* heartburn.
**soeben** [zo'e:bən], *adv.* just (now).
**Sofa** ['zo:fa], *n* -s/-s sofa, couch.
**sofern** [zo'fɛrn], *conj.* **s. es euch paßt,** as
long as it suits you.
**sofort** [zo'fɔrt], *adv.* immediately, at
once. ◆'s~**ig,** *adj.* immediate.
**Sog** [zo:k], *m* -(e)s/-e undertow (of waves
etc.); *Tchn:* suction.
**sogar** [zo'ga:r], *adv.* even.
**sogenannt** ['zo:gənant], *adj.* so-called.
**sogleich** [zo'glaiç], *adv.* immediately.
**Sohle** ['zo:lə], *f* -/-n (*a*) sole (of a foot or
shoe); (*b*) bottom (of a ditch etc.); (*c*)
*Min:* pit level.
**Sohn** [zo:n], *m* -(e)s/=e son.
**Sojabohne** ['zo:jabo:nə], *f* -/-n soya bean.
**solang(e)** [zo'laŋ(ə)], *conj.* as long as.
**solch** [zɔlç], *dem.pron.* such; **ein s~er
Mensch,** such a man; a man like that; **s.
herrliches Wetter,** such wonderful
weather; **ein paar s~e,** a few of those;
**die Musik als s~e,** the music as such.
**Sold** [zɔlt], *m* -(e)s/-e (soldiers') pay.
**Soldat** [zɔl'da:t], *m* -en/-en soldier.
◆**s~isch,** *adj.* soldierly.
**Söldner** ['zœldnər], *m* -s/- mercenary.
**solidar|isch** [zoli'da:riʃ], *adj.* **s. handeln,**
to act with complete solidarity; to show a
united front; **sich mit j-m s. erklären,** to
identify fully with s.o.'s aims; to give
s.o. full support. ◆S~**ität** [-dari'tɛːt],
*f* -/*no pl* solidarity.
**solide** [zo'li:də], *adj.* solid (shoes, material, building); sound (craftsmanship, firm
etc.); (*anständig*) respectable (person
etc.).
**Solist(in)** [zo'list(in)], *m* -en/-en (*f* -/-nen)
soloist.
**Soll** [zɔl], *n* -s/*no pl* 1. *Com:* debit. 2. *Ind:*
(production etc.) target. ◆'s~**en.** **1.**
*modal aux.* (*p.p.* **sollen**) (*a*) (*Pflicht*) **ich**

**soll Hamlet spielen,** I am to play Hamlet; **das hättest du nicht sagen s.,** you
should not have said that; (*b*) (*Zukunft*)
**was soll man da machen?** what is to be
done? **niemand soll sagen, daß ...,** let it
not be said that ...; (*c*) (*laut Bericht usw.*)
to be supposed to; **der Film soll sehr gut
sein,** the film is supposed to be very
good; **was soll das heißen?** (i) what is
that supposed to mean? (ii) *F:* what's all
this in aid of? (*d*) (*konditional*) **sollten Sie
ihn sehen,** should you/if you see him. **2.**
*v.i.* (*haben*) (*p.p.* **gesollt**) (*a*) **ich weiß
nicht, ob ich soll/sollte,** I don't know if
I should; (*b*) **was soll (denn) das?** what's
all this for/*F:* in aid of?
**Solo** ['zo:lo], *n* -s/-li solo.
**somit** [zo'mit], *adv.* hence, consequently.
**Sommer** ['zɔmər]. **I.** *m* -s/- summer. **II.**
S~-, *comb.fm.* summer (clothes, coat,
month, term, weather etc.); (*beginning
etc.*) of summer. ◆'s~**lich,** *adj.* summer (temperatures, heat etc.); summery,
*F:* summery (weather, clothes etc.); **sich
s. kleiden,** to wear summer clothes.
◆S~**'schlußverkauf,** *m* summer sale.
◆'S~**sprosse,** *f* freckle. ◆'S~**zeit,** *f*
(*Jahreszeit*) summertime; (*Uhrzeit*) summer time.
**Sonate** [zo'na:tə], *f* -/-n sonata.
**Sonde** ['zɔndə], *f* -/-n probe.
**Sonder-** ['zɔndər-], *comb.fm.* special
(agreement, report, subject, training,
mission, stamp, train etc.).
◆'S~**angebot,** *n* special offer.
◆'s~**bar,** *adj.* odd, strange.
◆'S~**fahrt,** *f* special journey; (*Ausfahrt*)
excursion. ◆'S~**fall,** *m* special case.
◆'s~**gleichen,** *adv.* unparalleled, unprecedented. ◆'s~**lich,** *adj.* **1.** (*bei Verneinungen*) particular; **ohne s~liche
Mühe,** without any great effort. **2.** (*seltsam*) strange. ◆'S~**ling,** *m* -s/-e eccentric, crank. ◆'S~**schule,** *f* school for
retarded children.
**sondern** ['zɔndərn], *conj.* but; **nicht nur
kalt, s. auch naß,** not only cold but wet.
**sondieren** [zɔn'di:rən], *v.tr.* to sound out
(s.o., public opinion etc.), explore (a situation etc.).
**Sonett** [zo'nɛt], *n* -(e)s/-e sonnet.
**Sonnabend** ['zɔn'a:bənt], *m* Saturday.
**Sonne** ['zɔnə], *f* -/-n sun. ◆'s~**n,** *v.refl.*
**sich s.,** to sun oneself/bask in the sun.
◆'S~**n-,** *comb.fm.* (*a*) sun-(worshipper,
god, hat, oil etc.); (orbit, surface etc.) of
the sun; (*b*) solar (energy, radiation etc.).
◆'S~**naufgang,** *m* sunrise. ◆'S~**n-
baden,** *n* sunbathing. ◆'S~**nblume,** *f*
sunflower. ◆'S~**nbrille,** *f* sunglasses.
◆'S~**nfinsternis,** *f* eclipse of the sun.
◆'S~**nschein,** *m* sunshine.
◆'S~**nschirm,** *m* parasol.
◆'S~**nschutzmittel,** *n* suntan lotion.
◆'S~**nstich,** *m* sunstroke. ◆'S~**n-
strahl,** *m* sunbeam. ◆'S~**nsystem,** *n*
solar system. ◆'S~**nuhr,** *f* sundial.

◆'S~nuntergang, m sunset. ◆'S~n-
wende, f solstice.
sonnig ['zɔniç], adj. (also Fig:) sunny.
Sonn|tag ['zɔntɑːk], m -(e)s/-e Sunday.
◆'s~tags¹, adv. on Sundays.
◆'S~tags-², comb.fm. Sunday (driver,
school, clothes etc.).
sonst [zɔnst], adv. (a) otherwise; (b) (zusätzlich) s. noch Fragen? any more questions? s. noch etwas/jemand? anything/
anybody else? (c) (gewöhnlich) usually;
wie s., as usual. ◆'s~ige(r,s), adj.
other; (gewöhnlich) normal. ◆'s~
jemand, indef.pron. someone/(ein Beliebi-
ger) anyone else. ◆'s~wer, indef.pron.
F: = s~jemand. ◆'s~wie, adv. F: in
some/any (other) way. ◆'s~wo, adv.
F: somewhere/anywhere else.
◆'s~wohin, adv. F: anywhere.
sooft [zo'ɔft], conj. whenever.
Sopran [zo'prɑːn], m -s/-e soprano.
◆S~istin, f -/-nen soprano.
Sorge ['zɔrgə], f -/-n (a) worry; sie
machte sich dat S~n um ihn, she was
worried about him; keine S.! don't worry! (b) no pl (Fürsorge) care (um/
für + acc, for). ◆'s~n, v.i. (haben) (a)
für j-n, etwas acc s., to take care of/be
responsible for s.o., sth.; dafür s., daß
..., to ensure that ..., s. Sie für Ruhe,
make sure everything is quiet; (b) sich
um j-n, etwas acc s., to be worried about
s.o., sth. ◆'s~nfrei, adj. carefree.
◆'S~nkind, n problem child.
◆'s~nvoll, adj. worried, anxious.
Sorg|falt ['zɔrkfalt], f -/no pl care;
(Gründlichkeit) thoroughness. ◆'s~
fältig, adj. careful; (gewissenhaft) conscientious. ◆'s~los, adj. (a) lighthearted, nonchalant (person); carefree
(life); (b) (ohne Sorgfalt) careless (treatment etc.). ◆'s~sam, adj. careful
(handling etc.).
Sor|te ['zɔrtə], f -/-n 1. sort, type;
(Marke) brand. 2. Fin: pl S~ten, foreign
currency. ◆s~'tieren, v.tr. to sort (letters etc.).
Sortiment [zɔrti'mɛnt], n -(e)s/-e Com:
assortment, range.
sosehr [zo'zeːr], conj. however much; s.
ich mich auch bemühte, however hard I
tried.
Soße ['zoːsə], f -/-n sauce; (Bratens.) gravy.
Souff|leur [zu'fløːr], m -s/-e/S~leuse, f
-/-n Th: prompter. ◆s~lieren
[-'fliːrən], v.i. (haben) Th: to prompt, act
as prompter.
Souterrain [zute'rɛ̃ː], n -s/-s basement.
Souvenir [zuvə'niːr], n -s/-s souvenir.
souverän [zuvə'rɛːn], adj. sovereign
(state etc.); die Lage s. beherrschen, to
be in complete control. ◆S~ität
[-rɛni'tɛːt], f -/no pl sovereignty.
soviel [zo'fiːl]. I. adv. so/as much (wie,
as); doppelt s., twice as much. II. conj.
s. ich weiß, as far as I know.

soweit [zo'vait]. I. adv. 1. generally. 2.
(a) s. wie möglich, as far as possible; (b)
F: ich bin s., I am finished/(bereit) ready.
II. conj. as far as.
sowenig [zo'veːniç], adv. s. wie, no more
than; s. wie möglich, as little as possible.
sowie [zo'viː], conj. 1. as well as. 2. (sobald) as soon as. ◆s~so [-'viːzoː], adv.
F: anyway, in any case.
Sowjet|union [zɔ'vjɛt?unioːn], f the So-
viet Union. ◆s~isch, adj. Soviet.
sowohl [zo'voːl], conj. s. A als auch B,
both A and B.
sozial [zotsi'ɑːl]. I. adj. social; (Pers.)
public-spirited; s~e Unterschiede,
social/class differences. II. S~, comb.fm.
social (work, worker, policy, studies
etc.); welfare (work, state etc.).
◆S~abgaben, fpl social security con-
tributions. ◆S~demokrat(in), m(f) Social Democrat. ◆s~demokratisch,
adj. Social Democratic (party etc.).
◆S~ismus [-a'lismus], m -/no pl socialism. ◆S~ist [-a'list], m -en/-en socialist. ◆s~istisch [-a'listiʃ], adj. socialist. ◆S~versicherung, f social security.
Soziolo|ge [zotsio'loːgə], m -n/-n/S~gin,
f -/-nen sociologist. ◆S~gie [-loːgiː], f
-/no pl sociology. ◆s~gisch [-'loːgiʃ],
adj. sociological.
Sozius ['zoːtsius], m -/-se Com: partner.
◆'S~sitz, m pillion.
sozusagen [zoːtsu'zaːgən], adv. so to
speak; as it were.
Spachtel ['ʃpaxtəl], m -s/- (a) Med: spatula; (b) (für Mörtel usw.) putty knife.
◆'s~n, v. 1. v.tr. to smooth (a surface). 2. v.i. (haben) F: to dig/tuck in.
Spagat [ʃpa'gaːt], m -(e)s/-e S. machen,
to do the splits/N.Am: a split.
späh|en ['ʃpeːən], v.i. (haben) to peer
(aus dem Fenster usw., out of the window). ◆'S~er, m -s/- lookout; scout.
Spalier [ʃpa'liːr], n -s/-e (a) (Gitter) trellis; (b) Fig: S. stehen, to form a guard of
honour /a lane.
Spalt [ʃpalt], m -(e)s/-e crack; (im Vorhang) chink. ◆'s~bar, adj. Atom.Ph:
fissile, fissionable. ◆'S~e, f -/-n 1.
crack; (Gletschers.) crevasse. 2 (Zeitungss.)
column. ◆'s~en, v.tr. to split (wood,
Ph: atoms, Fig: hairs etc.); Fig: to divide
(a country, party). ◆'S~ung, f -/-en
(a) splitting, division; Atom.Ph: fission;
(b) Fig: split.
Span [ʃpaːn], m -(e)s/-e chip, shaving (of
wood); filing (of metal). ◆'S~ferkel, n
sucking pig. ◆'S~platte, f chipboard.
Spange ['ʃpaŋə], f -/-n clasp; (am Schuh)
buckle; (Haars.) grip; (Zahns.) brace.
Span|ien ['ʃpaːniən]. Pr.n.n -s. Spain.
◆'S~ier(in), m -s/- (f -/-nen) Spaniard.
◆'s~isch, adj. Spanish.
Spann [ʃpan], m -(e)s/-e Anat: instep.
◆'S~beton, m pressed concrete.

◆'S~e, f -/-n (a) (Zeits.) length of time; (Zwischenzeit) interval; (b) Com: margin; (Preisunterschied) price difference. ◆'s~en, v. 1. v.tr. to stretch, tauten (a rope etc.), tighten (the violin strings etc.), tense (muscles etc.), draw (a bow). 2. v.i. (haben) Cl: etc: to be (too) tight. ◆'s~end, adj. exciting, thrilling (story etc.). ◆'S~kraft, f -/no pl vigour, resilience. ◆'S~ung, f -/-en 1. no pl (a) tightness; (b) El: voltage; (c) Fig: tension; (Erwartung) suspense. 2. (psychische) S~ungen, (psychological) strains/tensions.

Spar- ['ʃpaːr-], comb.fm. (a) savings (book, account etc.); (b) economy (measure etc.). ◆'S~büchse, f money box. ◆'s~en, v. 1. v.tr. to save (money, time, one's strength etc.); sich dat die Mühe s., to save/spare oneself the trouble. 2. v.i. (haben) to save (up); an Material, Zutaten usw. s., to economize on materials, ingredients etc. ◆'S~er, m -s/- saver. ◆'S~kasse, f savings bank. ◆'s~sam, adj. economical (use of sth. etc.); mit etwas dat s. umgehen, to be sparing with sth. ◆'S~samkeit, f -/no pl economy; thrift. ◆'S~schwein, n piggy bank.

Spargel ['ʃpargəl], m -s/no pl asparagus.

spärlich ['ʃpɛːrlɪç], adj. meagre (rations, applause); scanty, sparse (vegetation etc.), thin (hair etc.); s. bekleidet, scantily dressed.

Sparte ['ʃpartə], f -/-n branch (of sport, industry etc.); in meiner S., in my field/area.

Spaß [ʃpaːs], m -es/ˆe (a) (Scherz) joke; (Streich) lark; er versteht keinen S., he has no sense of humour; (b) no pl fun; aus/zum S., for fun; es macht S., it's fun; die Arbeit macht ihm keinen S., he doesn't enjoy the work; S. beiseite, joking apart; viel S.! have fun/a good time! ◆'s~en, v.i. (haben) to joke; mit ihm ist nicht zu s., he stands no nonsense. ◆'s~eshalber, adv. F: for fun/kicks. ◆'s~ig, adj. funny, comical. ◆'S~macher, m -s/- joker; clown. ◆'S~vogel, m joker, legpuller.

spät [ʃpɛːt], I. adj. late; wie s. ist es? what's the time/what time is it? II. 'S~-, comb.fm. late (summer, shift etc.). ◆'s~er, adj. later. ◆'s~estens, adv. at the latest.

Spaten ['ʃpaːtən], m -s/- spade.

Spatz [ʃpats], m -en/-en Orn: sparrow.

Spätzle ['ʃpɛtslə], npl (esp. home-made) noodles.

spazier|en [ʃpa'tsiːrən], v.i. (sein) to stroll, (go for a) walk. ◆s~enfahren, v.i.sep.irr.26 (sein) to go for a drive. ◆s~engehen, v.i.sep.irr.36 (sein) to go for a walk. ◆S~fahrt, f outing, drive. ◆S~gang, m walk, stroll; einen S. machen, to go for a walk. ◆S~gänger(in), m -s/- (f -/-nen) walker.

◆S~stock, m walking stick.

Specht [ʃpɛçt], m -(e)s/-e woodpecker.

Speck [ʃpɛk], m -(e)s/-e (a) Cu: (fatty) bacon; (b) F: fat. ◆'s~ig, adj. greasy.

Spedi|teur [ʃpedi'tøːr], m -s/-e shipper; (im Straßenverkehr) carrier, haulage contractor; (Möbels.) (furniture) remover/N.Am: mover. ◆S~tion [-itsi'oːn], f (also S~sbetrieb m) shippers, carriers; haulage/(Möbels.) removal/N.Am: moving firm.

Speer [ʃpeːr], m -(e)s/-e spear; Sp: javelin. ◆'S~werfen, n -s/no pl Sp: javelin (throwing).

Speiche ['ʃpaiçə], f -/-n spoke.

Speichel ['ʃpaiçəl], m -s/no pl saliva.

Speicher ['ʃpaiçər], m -s/- (a) store(house); (für Getreide) silo, granary; (für Wasser) reservoir; (b) (Dachs.) attic, loft; (c) Data-pr: memory. ◆'s~n, v.tr. to store (goods, data etc.).

speien ['ʃpaiən], v.irr.88 1. v.tr. to spit, bring up (blood etc.); (Vulkan usw.) to belch (fire). 2. v.i. (haben) to spit; (sich übergeben) to vomit.

Speis|e ['ʃpaizə], f -/-n food; (Gericht) warme S~en, hot food. ◆'S~eeis, n ice cream. ◆'S~ekammer, f larder. ◆'S~ekarte, f menu. ◆'s~en, v. 1. v.i. (haben) Lit: to have a meal, dine. 2. v.tr. to feed (a reservoir etc.). ◆'S~eröhre, f oesophagus, gullet. ◆'S~esaal, m dining hall/(im Hotel) room. ◆'S~ewagen, m dining car.

Spektak|el [ʃpɛk'taːkəl], n -s/no pl F: noise, racket. ◆s~ulär [-aku'lɛːr], adj. spectacular.

Spektrum ['ʃpɛktrum], n -s/-tren Ph: & Fig: spectrum.

Spekul|ant [ʃpeku'lant], m -en/-en speculator. ◆S~ation [-tsi'oːn], f -/-en speculation. ◆s~ieren [-'liːrən], v.i. (haben) to speculate; F: auf etwas acc s., to hope for sth.

Spelunke [ʃpe'luŋkə], f -/-n Pej: low dive.

spendabel [ʃpɛn'daːbəl], adj. F: generous, open-handed.

Spende ['ʃpɛndə], f -/-n donation; (Beitrag) contribution. ◆'s~n, v.tr. to contribute, donate (money etc.), give (blood, warmth, shade etc.). ◆'S~r, m -s/- 1. (Pers.) donor. 2. (Maschine) dispenser.

spendieren [ʃpɛn'diːrən], v.tr. F: j-m ein Eis usw. s., to treat s.o. to an ice etc.

Sperling ['ʃpɛrlɪŋ], m -s/-e sparrow.

Sperr|e ['ʃpɛrə], f -/-n (a) Rail: etc: barrier; Tchn: locking device; (b) (Verbot) ban; Sp: suspension. ◆'s~en, v. 1. v.tr. (a) to block (a road etc.); to close (a road, border etc.); Sp: to obstruct (a player); (b) sich gegen etwas acc s., to resist/object to sth. (strongly); (c) to cut off (the electricity, telephone etc.); to place a ban/an embargo on (imports etc.), block (an account); Sp: to suspend (a player); (d) j-n ins Gefängnis, ein

**Tier in einen Käfig usw. s.**, to lock s.o. in prison, an animal in a cage etc. **2.** *v.i.* *(haben)* *(Tür usw.)* to jam, stick; *(Räder usw.)* to lock. ◆**'S~holz,** *n* plywood. ◆**'s~ig,** *adj.* unwieldy, bulky (object, package etc.). ◆**'S~müll,** *m* bulky refuse. ◆**'S~sitz,** *m* *(im Zirkus)* front seat; *Cin:* rear stall. ◆**'S~stunde,** *f* closing time; *Mil:* curfew.

**Spesen** ['ʃpeːzən], *pl* expenses.

**Spezial-** [ʃpetsiˈaːl-], *comb.fm.* special (training, subject, mission etc.); specialist (dictionary etc.). ◆**S~gebiet,** *n* special field. ◆**S~isieren** [-ali'ziːrən], *v.refl.* **sich auf etwas** *acc* **s.**, to specialize in sth. ◆**S~ist(in)** [-a'list(in)], *m* *-en/-en* *(f* *-/-nen)* specialist. ◆**S~ität** [-ali'tɛːt], *f* *-/-en* speciality *esp. N.Am:* specialty.

**speziell** [ʃpetsi'ɛl], *adj.* special.

**spezifisch** [ʃpe'tsiːfiʃ], *adj.* specific.

**Sphäre** ['sfɛːrə], *f* *-/-n* sphere.

**spick|en** ['ʃpikən], *v.tr. Cu:* to lard (meat etc.); *Fig:* **mit Fehlern gespickter Aufsatz,** essay riddled with mistakes. ◆**S~zettel,** *m* *F:* crib.

**Spiegel** ['ʃpiːgəl], *m* *-s/-* **1.** mirror. **2.** *(a)* surface (of the sea etc.); *(b)* *(Wasserstand)* level. ◆**'S~bild,** *n* reflection; mirror image. ◆**'s~bildlich,** *adj.* in mirror image. ◆**'S~ei,** *n* *Cu:* fried egg. ◆**'s~n,** *v.* **1.** *v.i.* *(haben)* *(a)* to reflect; *(b)* *(glänzen)* to shine. **2.** *v.refl.* **sich im Wasser s.**, to be reflected in the water. ◆**'S~schrift,** *f* mirror writing. ◆**'S~ung,** *f* *-/-en* reflection.

**Spiel** [ʃpiːl]. **I.** *n* *-(e)s/-e* **1.** *no pl (a)* play(ing) (of children etc.); *(b)* movement, play (of colours, lights, waves etc.). **2.** *Sp: etc:* game (of tennis, cards, chess etc.); *(als Wettkampf)* match. **3.** *Th:* *(Stück)* play. **4.** *(Satz)* set; **ein S. Karten,** a pack of cards. **5.** *Tchn:* slack, clearance. **6.** *Fig:* **auf dem S. stehen,** to be at stake; **etwas aufs S. setzen,** to risk sth. **II.** **'S~-,** *comb.fm.* *(a)* play (street etc.); playing (area, card etc.); *(b)* gambling (casino, debt etc.). ◆**'S~automat,** *m* fruit machine; *Hum:* one-armed bandit. ◆**'s~en,** *v.* **1.** *v.i.* *(haben)* to play; *(um Geld)* s., to gamble; **das Stück spielt in der Gegenwart,** the play is set in the present; **mit dem Gedanken s.**, to toy with the idea. **2.** *v.tr.* to play (a game, *Mus:* an instrument, *Th:* a part etc.); to perform (a play, opera etc.). ◆**'s~end,** *adv. F:* easily. ◆**'S~er(in),** *m* *-s/- (f* *-/-nen)* *(a)* player; *(b)* *(um Geld)* gambler. ◆**S~e'rei,** *f* *-/-en (a) no pl* playing/*Pej:* fooling around; *(Zeitvertreib)* amusement, diversion; *(b)* *(etwas Leichtes)* trifle, child's play. ◆**'s~erisch,** *adj.* **1.** playful (movements etc.). **2.** *Sp:* playing, *Th:* acting (ability etc.). ◆**'S~feld,** *n* *Sp:* pitch. ◆**'S~film,** *m* feature film. ◆**'S~halle,** *f* amusement arcade. ◆**'S~marke,** *f* (gaming) chip.

◆**'S~plan,** *m* *Th:* repertory, programme. ◆**'S~platz,** *m* playground. ◆**'S~raum,** *m* room to move, *also Fig:* elbow-room; *Tchn:* (free) play, clearance. ◆**'S~regeln,** *fpl* rules (of the game). ◆**'S~sachen,** *fpl* toys. ◆**'S~verderber(in),** *m* *-s/- (f* *-/-nen)* spoilsport. ◆**'S~waren,** *fpl* toys. ◆**'S~zeit,** *f* *Th: Sp: (a) (Saison)* season; *(b)* *(S~dauer)* duration of a performance/game. ◆**'S~zeug,** *n* *(a)* toy; *(b)* coll. toys.

**Spieß** [ʃpiːs], *m* *-es/-e* *(a)* *(Waffe)* spear; *F:* **den S. umdrehen,** to turn the tables; *(b)* *Cu:* skewer; *(Brats.)* spit. ◆**'S~bürger,** *m* *Pej:* (ultra-conservative) bourgeois (prig). ◆**'s~en,** *v.tr.* to skewer (meat etc.). ◆**'S~er,** *m* *-s/-* = **S~bürger.** ◆**'S~rute,** *f* **S~ruten laufen,** to run the gauntlet.

**Spikes** [ʃpaiks, sp-], *pl (a) Sp:* spikes; *(b)* *Aut:* studded (snow) tyres.

**Spinat** [ʃpi'naːt], *m* *-(e)s/-e* spinach.

**Spind** [ʃpint], *n* *-(e)s/-e* locker.

**Spindel** ['ʃpindəl], *f* *-/-n* spindle. ◆**'s~dürr,** *adj.* thin as a rake.

**Spinn|e** ['ʃpinə], *f* *-/-n* spider. ◆**'s~en,** *v.irr.73* **1.** *v.tr.* to spin (wool etc.). **2.** *v.i.* *(haben)* *F:* to be crackers/nuts. ◆**'S~(en)gewebe,** *n* cobweb. ◆**'S~ennetz,** *n* spider's web. ◆**'S~er(in),** *m* *-s/- (f* *-/-nen)* *F:* **er ist ein S.**, he is a crackpot/*Brit:* nutter. ◆**'S~rad,** *n* spinning wheel.

**Spion(in)** [ʃpi'oːn(in)], *m* *-s/-e (f* *-/-nen)* *(a)* spy; *(b)* *(Guckloch)* peephole (in door). ◆**S~age** [-o'naːʒə]. **I.** *f* */no pl* espionage, spying. **II.** **S~-,** *comb.fm.* spy (film, trial, ring etc.). ◆**s~ieren** [-o'niːrən], *v.i.* *(haben)* to spy.

**Spirale** [ʃpi'raːlə], *f* */-n* spiral; *Med:* coil.

**Spirituosen** [ʃpiritu'oːzən], *fpl* spirits, hard drinks. ◆**S~us** ['ʃpiritus], *m* */no pl* (surgical) spirit.

**Spital** [ʃpi'taːl], *n* *-s/-er* *A: & Aus:* hospital.

**Spitz¹** [ʃpits], *m* *-es/-e* *Z:* Pomeranian (dog).

**spitz²,** *adj.* pointed (shoes, arch, *Fig:* remark etc.); sharp (pencil, *Fig:* tongue etc.); **s~er Winkel,** acute angle. ◆**'S~bart,** *m* pointed beard. ◆**'S~bube,** *m Pej: & Hum:* rogue. ◆**'S~e,** *f* *-/-n* **1.** *(a)* point (of a needle, pencil), tip (of a pen, the nose etc.); (cigar/cigarette) holder; *(b)* *(oberes Ende)* top (of a tree etc.); *(Gipfel)* peak; *Fig: (Höchstwert)* maximum; *F:* **er/sie/es ist (absolute/einsame) S.**, he/she/it is (absolutely) super/fantastic; *(c)* *(Führung)* head (of a procession, train, organization etc.); leadership (of a party), management (of a firm); *Sp:* **an der S. liegen,** to be in the lead; *(d)* *(Anzüglichkeit)* dig, tilt *(gegen* **j-n,** at s.o.). **2.** *(Stoff)* lace. ◆**'S~el,** *m* *-s/-* informer; *(Spion)* spy, undercover agent. ◆**'s~en,** *v.tr.* to sharpen (a pencil etc.). ◆'S~**en-**, *comb.fm.* **1.** *(a)* top (speed, team, quality etc.); top-quality, first-class (product, wine etc.); *(b)* (*Höchst-*) maximum (amount, output etc.); peak (load, value etc.). **2.** *Cl:* lace (blouse, collar, trimming etc.). ◆'S~**enreiter**, *m* leader; number one. ◆'s~**findig**, *adj.* tortuous (argument etc.); niggling, pedantic (person). ◆'S~**hacke**, *f* pick-axe. ◆'S~**name**, *m* nickname.

**Splitter** ['ʃplitər], *m* -s/- splinter. ◆'S~**gruppe**, *f* -/-n splinter group. ◆'s~**n**, *v.i.* (*sein*) to splinter. ◆'s~'**nackt**, *adj. F:* stark naked.

**spontan** [ʃpɔn'tɔːn], *adj.* spontaneous (response etc.); impulsive (action).

**sporadisch** [ʃpo'raːdiʃ], *adj.* sporadic.

**Sporen** ['ʃpoːrən], *mpl* spurs.

**Sport** [ʃpɔrt]. **I.** *m* -(e)s/*no pl* *(a)* sport; *Sch:* physical education, games; *(b)* hobby. **II.** 'S~-, *comb.fm.* *(a)* sports (badge, report, fan, club, news etc.); *(b)* sporting (event, accident etc.). ◆'S~**art**, *f* (type of) sport. ◆'S~**lehrer(in)**, *m* (*f*) P.E. teacher, *Brit:* games master/mistress. ◆'S~**ler(in)**, *m* -s/- (*f* -/-nen) sportsman, *f* sportswoman. ◆'s~**lich**, *adj.* *(a)* sporting (occasion, career etc.); casual (clothes); (*Pers.*) good at games; sporty; *(b)* (*fair*) sportsmanlike (behaviour etc.). ◆'S~**platz**, *m* sports ground, playing field. ◆'S~**wagen**, *m* (i) sports car; (ii) (*für Kinder*) pushchair, *N.Am:* stroller.

**Spott** [ʃpɔt], *m* -(e)s/*no pl* mockery, ridicule. ◆'s~'**billig**, *adj. F:* dirt-cheap. ◆'s~**en**, *v.i.* (*haben*) to mock; **über j-n, etwas** *acc* **s.**, to poke fun at/(*höhnisch*) sneer at s.o., sth.

**Spött|er** ['ʃpœtər], *m* -s/- mocker; **er ist ein S.**, he pokes fun at everything. ◆'s~**isch**, *adj.* mocking, quizzical (smile etc.); **s~ische Bemerkung**, snide remark.

**Sprach-** [ʃpraːx-], *comb.fm.* linguistic (research, exercise etc.); language (course, teacher, school etc.). ◆'S~**begabung**, *f* gift for languages. ◆'S~**e**, *f* -/-n **1.** language; **in englischer S.**, in English. **2.** *no pl* speech; **das kam auch zur S.**, that was also mentioned. ◆'S~**fehler**, *m* speech defect. ◆'s~**lich**, *adj.* linguistic; grammatical (errors etc.). ◆'s~**los**, *adj.* speechless (**vor** + *dat*, with); (*erstaunt*) dumbfounded. ◆'S~**raum**, *m* language area. ◆'S~**rohr**, *n* (*a*) megaphone; (*b*) *Fig:* (*Pers.*) mouthpiece.

**Spray** [ʃpreː], *m* & *n* -s/-s spray.

**Sprech|anlage** ['ʃprɛçʔanlaːgə], *f F:* intercom. ◆'s~**en**, *v.irr.14* **1.** *v.tr.* (*a*) to speak (a language, the truth etc.); to say (a word, prayer etc.); *Jur:* to pronounce (judgement); **er sprach kein Wort**, he didn't say a word; (*b*) to speak to (s.o.); **er ist nicht/für niemanden zu s.**, he cannot see anybody. **2.** *v.i.* (*haben*) to speak (**über** + *acc*/**von** + *dat*, about); **mit j-m s.**,

to talk to s.o.; **es spricht ...**, the speaker is ...; *Fig:* **das spricht für ihn**, that's a point in his favour. ◆'S~**er(in)**, *m* -s/- (*f* -/-nen) speaker; (*Wortführer*) spokesman; *Rad: TV:* announcer. ◆'S~**stunde**, *f Med:* consulting/*Brit:* surgery hours. ◆'S~**stundenhilfe**, *f* (doctor's) receptionist. ◆'S~**zimmer**, *n* consulting room.

**spreizen** ['ʃpraitsən], *v.tr.* to splay (one's legs etc.), spread (wings etc.).

**spreng|en** ['ʃprɛŋən], *v.tr.* (*a*) to blast (rock etc.), blow up (a bridge etc.); (*b*) to burst (chains, a lock etc.); (*c*) to sprinkle (washing, water etc.). ◆'S~**kopf**, *m* warhead. ◆'S~**körper**, *m* explosive device. ◆'S~**ladung**, *f* explosive charge. ◆'S~**stoff**, *m* explosive. ◆'S~**ung**, *f* -/-en explosion, blasting.

**Spreu** [ʃprɔy], *f* -/*no pl* chaff.

**Sprich|wort** ['ʃpriçvɔrt], *n* proverb. ◆'s~**wörtlich**, *adj.* proverbial.

**Spring|brunnen** ['ʃpriŋbrunən], *m* -s/- fountain. ◆'s~**en**, *v.i.irr.19* (*sein*) (*a*) to jump, (*mit einem großen Satz*) leap; (*b*) (*Glas usw.*) to crack. ◆'S~**er**, *m* -s/- (*a*) jumper; (*b*) (*Schach*) knight; (*c*) *Ind:* stand-in. ◆'S~**reiten**, *n* -s/*no pl* show jumping.

**Sprit** [ʃprit], *m* -s/*no pl* *F:* juice, *N.Am:* gas.

**Spritz|e** ['ʃpritsə], *f* -/-n **1.** (*Gerät*) spray; (*Düse*) nozzle; *Med: etc:* syringe. **2.** *Med:* injection, jab. ◆'s~**en**, *v.* **1.** *v.tr.* (*a*) to spray (crops, water, paint, a car etc.); (*b*) (*injizieren*) to inject (a drug etc.). **2.** *v.i.* (*haben*) (*Flüssigkeiten*) to splash, (*in einem Strahl*) squirt; (*Fett usw.*) to spatter. ◆'S~**er**, *m* -s/- **1.** splash (of water etc.); blob (of paint etc.). ◆'s~**ig**, *adj.* tangy (perfume, wine); lively, sparkling (wit, performance etc.); racy (car, style). ◆'S~**pistole**, *f* spraygun. ◆'S~**tour**, *f F:* **eine S. machen**, to go for a joyride/*Aut:* spin.

**spröde** ['ʃprøːdə], *adj.* (*a*) brittle (metal, wood, hair etc.); dry, chapped (skin); (*b*) (*Pers.*) standoffish.

**Sproß** [ʃprɔs], *m* -sses/-sse (*a*) *Bot:* sprout, shoot; (*b*) offspring.

**Sprosse** ['ʃprɔsə], *f* -/-n ladder rung; slat (of a chair).

**Sprößling** ['ʃprœsliŋ], *m* -s/-e *F:* offspring.

**Sprotte** ['ʃprɔtə], *f* -/-n sprat.

**Spruch** [ʃprux], *m* -(e)s/ᵉe (*a*) saying; maxim; (*Parole*) slogan; (*b*) *Jur:* (*Urteil*) sentence, ruling; (*c*) *Pej: F:* S~e, empty words, hot air.

**Sprudel** ['ʃpruːdəl], *m* -s/- (*effervescent*) mineral water. ◆'s~**n**, *v.i.* (*haben*) (*Flüssigkeiten*) to effervesce, *F:* fizz; (*Blasen bilden*) to bubble. ◆'S~**wasser**, *n* = **Sprudel**.

**Sprüh|dose** ['ʃpryːdoːzə], *f* spray, aerosol. ◆'s~**en**, *v.* **1.** *v.tr.* to spray (water etc.); to give off (sparks etc.). **2.** *v.i.*

(sein) (a) to spray, (Gischt) shower; (b) Fig: (Pers.) to sparkle, scintillate (vor Witz usw.), with wit etc.). ◆'S~regen, m drizzle.

Sprung [ʃprʊŋ], m -(e)s/ᵉe 1. jump, (großer) leap. 2. (Riß) crack. ◆'S~brett, n springboard. ◆'S~feder, f spring. ◆'s~haft, adj. (a) spasmodic, erratic (movement etc.); (b) sudden (change); rapid (increase). ◆'S~schanze, f jumping hill, ski jump. ◆'S~tuch, n jumping sheet.

Spuck|e ['ʃpʊkə], f -/no pl F: saliva, spit. ◆'s~en, v.tr.&i. (haben) to spit.

Spuk [ʃpuːk], m -(e)s/no pl 1. haunting; ghostly apparition. 2. Fig: ghastly business, nightmare. ◆'s~en, v.i. (haben) to haunt; hier spukt es, this place is haunted. ◆'s~haft, adj. ghostly.

Spül|becken ['ʃpyːlbɛkən], n//'S~e, f -/-n sink. ◆'s~en, v.tr.&i. (haben) to rinse (out) (one's mouth, washing etc.); (auf der Toilette) to flush; (Geschirr) s., to wash up, F: & N.Am: do the dishes; etwas an Land s., to wash sth. ashore. ◆'S~maschine, f dishwasher. ◆'S~mittel, n washing-up/N.Am: dishwashing liquid/powder. ◆'S~tuch, n dishcloth. ◆'S~wasser, n dishwater.

Spule ['ʃpuːlə], f -/-n (a) spool, bobbin; (b) El: coil. ◆'s~n, v.tr. to wind (sth.) onto a spool.

Spur [ʃpuːr], f -/-en 1. (a) (im Boden) track(s) (of a person, animal, tyre etc.); (Fährte) trail; (Fig: Rest) trace; (b) F: eine S. Pfeffer, a trace of pepper; von Takt keine S., not a sign/scrap of tact; eine S. zu hart, slightly/a shade too hard. 2. (Fahrs.) lane. 3. Rec: track. ◆'s~en, v.i. (haben) F: to toe the line. ◆'s~los, adj. esp. adv. without a trace. ◆'S~weite, f Aut: track.

spür|bar ['ʃpyːrbaːr], adj. noticeable; (deutlich) distinct. ◆'s~en, v.tr. to feel (pain, the heat etc.), sense (s.o.'s fear etc.). ◆'S~hund, m (a) tracker dog, pointer; (b) F: (Detektiv) sleuth. ◆'S~sinn, m (Instinkt) sixth sense.

Spurt [ʃpʊrt], m -(e)s/-s spurt, sprint. ◆'s~en, v.i. (sein) to spurt, sprint.

Staat [ʃtaːt], m -(e)s/-en 1. state; (Land) country. 2. F: (festliche Kleidung) finery. ◆'s~enlos, adj. stateless. ◆'s~lich, adj. state, government (grant, control etc.); (sovereignty, interests etc.) of the state; s. anerkannt, officially/state-approved. ◆'S~s-, comb.fm. (a) state (visit, secret, reception, theatre etc.); (affair etc.) of state; (s~eigen) state-owned (business etc.); national (debt, government etc.); (b) government (expenditure, employee etc.); public (property, enemy etc.). ◆'S~sangehörige(r), m & f decl. as adj. national. ◆'S~sangehörigkeit, f -/no pl nationality, citizenship. ◆'S~sanwalt, m public prosecutor; N.Am: district attorney.

◆'S~sbürger(in), m (f) citizen. ◆'S~sdienst, m civil service. ◆'S~smann, m statesman. ◆'S~soberhaupt, n head of state. ◆'S~ssekretär, m permanent secretary; N.Am: secretary of state. ◆'S~sstreich, m coup (d'état).

Stab [ʃtaːp], m -(e)s/ᵉe 1. (a) rod, pole; (Stock) stick; (b) (aus Eisen) bar (of a cage etc.). 2. (Personal) staff. ◆'S~hochsprung, m pole vault. ◆'S~soffizier, m staff officer.

Stäbchen ['ʃtɛːpçən], n -s/- (Eßb.) chopstick.

stabil [ʃta'biːl], adj. (a) stable (currency etc.); (b) sturdy, robust (structure etc.). ◆s~i'sieren, v.tr. to stabilize (prices etc.). ◆S~ität [-ili'tɛːt], f -/no pl stability; sturdiness, solidity.

Stachel ['ʃtaxəl], m -s/-n (a) (Insektens.) sting; (b) spine, quill (of a porcupine etc.); Bot: thorn; (c) barb (of barbed wire etc.). ◆'S~beere, f gooseberry. ◆'S~draht, m barbed wire. ◆'s~ig, adj. prickly. ◆'S~schwein, n porcupine.

Stadion ['ʃtaːdiɔn], n -s/-ien stadium.

Stadium ['ʃtaːdium], n -s/-ien stage, phase.

Stadt [ʃtat]. I. f -/ᵉe town, (Großs.) city. II. 's~-, comb.fm. town (wall, gate etc.); city (fathers, wall, gate, state etc.); urban (motorway/N.Am: freeway, population, district, guerilla etc.); municipal (administration, park, library, theatre etc.). ◆'s~bekannt, adj. well-known, Pej: notorious. ◆'S~plan, m town plan/(street) map. ◆'S~rand, m outskirts of the town. ◆'S~teil, m part/district of the town. ◆'S~zentrum, n town/city centre, N.Am: downtown (area).

Städt|chen ['ʃtɛːtçən], n -s/- small town. ◆'S~ebau, m town planning. ◆'S~er(in), m -s/- (f -/-nen) town/city dweller. ◆'s~isch, adj. urban (life, transport etc.); city (clothes etc.); Adm: municipal (authorities etc.).

Staffel ['ʃtafəl], f -/-n (a) Sp: relay team; (b) Av: squadron. ◆S~ei [-ə'lai], f -/-en Art: easel. ◆'s~n, v.tr. to stagger (Ind: hours etc.), grade (wages).

stagnieren [ʃtag'niːrən], v.i. (haben) to stagnate.

Stahl [ʃtaːl]. I. m -(e)s/ᵉe steel. II. 'S~-, 's~-, comb.fm. steel (blue, industry, works, helmet etc.). ◆'s~hart, adj. hard as steel/Fig: (Pers.) as nails.

Stall [ʃtal], m -(e)s/ᵉe stable; (Kuhs.) cowshed; (Kaninchens.) hutch.

Stamm [ʃtam]. I. m -(e)s/ᵉe 1. (Baums.) trunk (of a tree). 2. (Volkss.) tribe. 3. Gram: stem, root. II. 'S~-, comb.fm. (a) favourite (café etc.); (b) regular (guest etc.). ◆'S~baum, m family tree; Z: & Hum: pedigree. ◆'s~en, v.i. (haben) (a) s. aus + dat, to come from (a place, an old family etc.); die Worte s. nicht von mir, those are not my words. **◆'S~halter,** *m Hum:* son and heir.

**stammeln** ['ʃtaməln], *v.tr. & i.* (*haben*) to stammer (sth.).

**stämmig** ['ʃtɛmiç], *adj.* burly, stocky.

**stampfen** ['ʃtampfən], *v.i.* (*a*) (*haben*) to stamp; (*Maschine, Motor usw.*) to pound; (*b*) (*sein*) **er stampfte durch den Schnee,** he tramped/stomped through the snow.

**Stand** [ʃtant], *m -(e)s/-̈e* **1.** (*a*) *no pl* standing position; stance; (*b*) (*für Taxis*) stand, rank; (*am Markt usw.*) stall; (*Messes.*) stand. **2.** *no pl* (*Lage*) position; (*Stadium*) stage; (*Zustand*) state (of finances, a game etc.); **S. der Dinge,** state of affairs; position. **◆'S~bild,** *n* statue. **◆'S~esamt** ['ʃtandəs-], *n* registry office. **◆'S~esbeamte,** *m* registrar (of births etc.). **◆'s~esgemäß,** *adj.* in keeping with social status. **◆'s~fest,** *adj.* steady, stable (table etc.); *Fig:* steadfast. **◆'S~gericht,** *n* summary court martial. **◆'s~haft,** *adj.* steadfast, unwavering (person etc.); stout (denial etc.). **◆'S~haftigkeit,** *f -/no pl* steadfastness, staunchness. **◆'s~halten,** *v.i.sep.* (*haben*) (*Pers.*) to stand firm; **einem Angriff s.,** to hold out against an attack; **Druck usw. s.,** to withstand/stand up to pressure etc. **◆'S~licht,** *n Aut:* parking light(s). **◆'S~ort,** *m* location; position (of a plant, ship etc.); site of a firm etc.); *Mil:* garrison. **◆'S~punkt,** *m* point of view, standpoint. **◆'S~recht,** *n* martial law.

**Standard** [ʃtandart], *m -s/-s* norm, standard.

**Ständ|er** ['ʃtɛndər], *m -s/-* stand (for music, hats etc.). **◆'s~ig** ['ʃtɛndiç], *adj.* permanent (residence etc.); constant (companion etc.); steady, continuous (noise etc.).

**Stange** ['ʃtaŋə], *f -/-n* (*Holzs.*) pole; (*Metalls.*) rod, bar; (*Kleiders.*) clothes rail; *F:* **Kleider von der S.,** clothes off the peg; *F:* **eine S. Geld,** a pretty penny. **◆'S~nbrot,** *n* (loaf of) French bread.

**Stanniol** [ʃtani'o:l], *n -s/-e* tin foil. **◆S~papier,** *n* silver paper.

**Stanze** ['ʃtantsə], *f -/-n* punch, punching machine. **◆'s~n,** *v.tr.* to punch (holes); (*prägen*) to stamp (metal etc.).

**Stapel** ['ʃta:pəl], *m -s/-* **1.** stack, pile (of books, wood etc.). **2.** (*beim Schiffbau*) stocks; **vom S. laufen,** to be launched. **◆'S~lauf,** *m* launching (of a ship). **◆'s~n,** *v.tr.* to stack, pile up (goods etc.).

**stapfen** ['ʃtapfən], *v.i.* (*sein*) to trudge.

**Star¹** [ʃtaːr], *m -(e)s/-e* **1.** *Orn:* starling. **2.** *Med:* cataract.

**Star²,** *m -s/-s Cin: etc:* star.

**stark** [ʃtark], *adj.* (*a*) strong (man, coffee, drink, current etc.); powerful (engine, voice etc.); (*b*) (*zahlenmäßig*) big (army, *Sp:* field etc.); (*heftig*) violent (storm); in-

tense (pain etc.); heavy (traffic, demand, rain etc.); **s~e Beteiligung,** large attendance/number of people participating; (*c*) *adv.* (*viel*) a lot; (+ *adj.*) very; **s. übertrieben/vergrößert,** greatly exaggerated/enlarged. **◆'S~strom,** *m* high voltage/power current.

**Stärk|e** ['ʃtɛrkə], *f -/-n* **1.** (*a*) *no pl* (*Kraft*) strength (of a person, party, *Fig:* s.o.'s faith etc.); (*Leistung*) power (of an engine etc.); violence, intensity (of pain, a storm, reaction etc.); **mit voller S.,** with full force; (*b*) *Fig:* strong point; (*c*) (*Dicke*) thickness; (*d*) (*Größe*) size (of an army etc.); amount (of traffic etc.). **2.** *Cu:* starch. **◆'s~en,** *v.tr.* (*a*) to strengthen (s.o., s.o.'s position etc.); (*b*) to starch (shirt collars etc.). **◆'S~ung,** *f -/-en* strengthening, boosting; (*b*) (*Erfrischung*) refreshment. **◆'S~ungsmittel,** *n* restorative, tonic.

**starr** [ʃtar], *adj.* rigid; (*steif*) stiff (attitude etc.); **s~er Blick,** fixed stare; **s. vor Kälte,** frozen stiff. **◆'s~en,** *v.i.* (*haben*) (*a*) to stare; (*b*) **vor Schmutz s.,** to be absolutely filthy. **◆'s~köpfig,** *adj.* obdurate, obstinate; (*eigensinnig*) self-willed. **◆'S~sinn,** *m* obduracy, obstinacy. **◆'s~sinnig,** *adj.* = s~köpfig.

**Start** [ʃtart], *m -(e)s/-s* (*a*) *Sp: & Fig:* start; (*b*) *Av:* take-off; launch (of a rocket). **II. 'S~-,** *comb.fm.* starting (block, line, signal etc.). **◆'S~bahn,** *f Av:* (take-off) runway. **◆'s~bereit,** *adj.* ready to go/*Av:* for take-off. **◆'s~en,** *v.* **1.** *v.tr.* to start (a race, an engine etc.); to launch (a rocket, *F:* a campaign etc.). **2.** *v.i.* (*sein*) to start (in a race etc.); *Av:* to take off.

**Station** [ʃtatsi'o:n], *f -/-en* **1.** (bus/train/tram) stop; **S. machen,** to break one's journey, *esp. N.Am:* stop over. **2.** *Rad:* station. **3.** *Med:* ward. **◆s~är** [-o'nɛːr], *adj. Med:* (treatment) as an in-patient. **◆s~ieren** [-o'ni:rən], *v.tr.* to station (troops etc.).

**Statist** [ʃta'tist], *m -en/-en Th: Cin:* extra. **◆S~ik,** *f -/-en coll.* statistics. **◆S~iker,** *m -s/-* statistician. **◆s~isch,** *adj.* statistical.

**Stativ** [ʃta'ti:f], *n -s/-e* tripod.

**statt** [ʃtat], *conj. & prep. + gen* instead of; **s. dessen,** instead (of this). **◆'s~finden,** *v.i.sep.irr.9* (*haben*) to happen, take place. **◆'s~haft,** *adj.* permissible. **◆'s~lich,** *adj.* stately, imposing (house, person etc.); magnificent (figure, building etc.); impressive (collection); considerable (number, sum etc.).

**Stätte** ['ʃtɛtə], *f -/-n Lit:* place; site (of an event).

**Statu|e** ['ʃta:tuə], *f -/-n* statue. **◆S~r** [ʃta'tu:r], *f -/no pl* stature, build. **◆S~s** ['ʃta:tus], *m -/no pl* status. **◆S~t** [ʃta'tu:t], *n -(e)s/-en* statute.

**Stau** [ʃtau], *m -(e)s/-s* **1.** *no pl* = S~ung **1. 2.** tailback (of traffic). **◆'S~damm,**

*m* barrage, dam. ◆'s~**en**, *v.tr.* to dam (a river etc.), staunch (blood); **sich s.,** to accumulate; (*Leute*) form a crowd, (*Autos*) form a tailback. ◆'S~**see,** *m* artificial lake, reservoir. ◆'S~**ung,** *f -/ -en* **1.** *no pl* damming-up, staunching (of blood). **2.** congestion; snarl-up (of traffic etc.).

**Staub** [ʃtaup], *m -(e)s/no pl* dust; ◆**s~en** [ʃtaubən], *v.i.* (*haben*) to make dust. ◆**s~ig** [ʃtaubiç], *adj.* dusty. ◆'S~**korn,** *n* speck of dust. ◆'s~**saugen,** *v.tr.sep.* to hoover, vacuum (a carpet etc.). ◆'S~**sauger,** *m* vacuum cleaner. ◆'S~**tuch,** *n* duster.

**Staude** [ʃtaudə], *f -/-n* (perennial) herbaceous plant; (*Strauch*) shrub.

**staunen** [ʃtaunən], *v.i.* (*haben*) to be astonished/amazed (**über etwas** *acc,* at sth.).

**stech|en** [ʃtɛçən]. **I.** *v.irr.14* **1.** *v.tr.* (*haben*) (*a*) (*Insekt*) to sting, (*Mücke usw.*) bite (s.o.); (*Messerspitze, Dolch usw.*) to stab (s.o.), pierce (holes in sth.); (*b*) to cut (peat, asparagus etc.); (*c*) *Art:* **ein Bild (in Kupfer) s.,** to engrave a picture; (*d*) (*Kartenspiel*) to trump (a card). **2.** *v.i.* (*haben*) (*Sonne*) to blaze/beat down. **II. S.,** *n -s/no pl* (*a*) stinging, pricking; (*b*) *Sp:* deciding contest/round. ◆'s~**end,** *adj.* stinging, stabbing (pain etc.), pungent (smell); penetrating (gaze, smell etc.). ◆'S~**mücke,** *f* gnat, mosquito. ◆'S~**palme,** *f* holly. ◆'S~**uhr,** *f* time clock.

**Steck|brief** [ʃtɛkbriːf], *m* personal description (*für:* of s.o. wanted). ◆'S~**dose,** *f* socket. ◆'s~**en,** *v.* **1.** *v.i.* (*haben*) to be, (*fests.*) be stuck. **2.** *v.tr.* (*a*) to put (sth.) (**in etwas** *acc,* into sth.); to stick (a pin etc.) (**in etwas** *acc,* into sth.); to fix/fasten (**mit Nadeln**) pin (a brooch etc.) (**an**+*acc,* to); (*b*) to plant (onions etc.). ◆'s~**enbleiben,** *v.i. sep.irr.12* (*sein*) to get stuck (**im Schlamm usw.,** in the mud etc.); (*Redner usw.*) to dry up; (*Gräte usw.*) **im Halse s.,** to stick in one's throat. ◆'S~**enpferd,** *n* **1.** hobby horse. **2.** hobby; (*Thema*) pet subject. ◆'S~**er,** *m -s/-* plug. ◆'S~**nadel,** *f* pin. ◆'S~**rübe,** *f* turnip. ◆'S~**schloß,** *n* mortice lock.

**Steg** [ʃteːk], *m -(e)s/-e* (narrow) footbridge; *Nau:* (*Brett*) gangplank; (*Bootss.*) jetty. ◆'S~**reif,** *m* **aus dem S.,** impromptu.

**steh|en** [ʃteːən], *v.i.irr.* (*haben*) (*a*) (*aufrechts.*) (*Pers., Gebäude usw.*) to stand; **im S./s~end arbeiten,** to work standing up; **zu j-m/seinem Versprechen s.,** to stand by s.o./one's promise; (*b*) (*stills.*) (*Uhr usw.*) to have stopped; (*Verkehr usw.*) to be stationary/at a standstill; **zum S. kommen,** to come to a standstill; (*c*) (*sich befinden*) to be (somewhere); **das Auto steht vor der Tür,** the car is (standing)

at the door; (*d*) (*geschrieben s.*) **es steht in der Zeitung,** it's in the paper; **auf dem Schild steht, daß ...,** the notice says that ...; (*e*) (*Stellung*) **die Uhr steht auf 6,** the clock says 6; **gut/schlecht s.,** (*Währung usw.*) to be strong/weak; (*Sache*) to be going well/ badly; **es steht schlecht um ihn,** things look bad for him; (*gesundheitlich*) he is in a bad way; *Sp:* **das Spiel steht 2:1,** the score is 2–1; (*f*) (*passen*) **die Jacke steht dir,** the jacket suits you/ looks good on you. ◆'s~**enbleiben,** *v.i.sep.irr.12* (*sein*) (*a*) to stop; (*Pers., Fig: Zeit*) to stand still; (*Motor*) to stall; (*b*) to remain, be left. ◆'s~**enlassen,** *v.tr.sep.57* (*a*) to leave (sth.) behind; (*vergessen*) to forget (sth.); (*nicht essen*) to leave (food) (untouched); (*b*) **sich** *dat* **einen Bart s.,** to grow a beard. ◆'S~**lampe,** *f* standard lamp. ◆'S~**platz,** *m Th: etc:* (space in the) standing room; (*im Bus*) space to stand; *pl* **S~plätze,** standing room.

**stehlen** [ʃteːlən], *v.tr.irr.2* to steal (sth.) (**j-m,** from s.o.).

**steif** [ʃtaif], *adj.* stiff; *Fig:* stiff, formal (reception, style etc.); **etwas s. und fest behaupten,** to insist stubbornly on sth.

**Steig|bügel** [ʃtaikbyːgəl], *m* stirrup. ◆'S~**eisen,** *n* crampon. ◆'s~**en,** *v.i.irr.89* (*sein*) (*a*) to climb; **auf einen Berg s.,** to climb a mountain; **in ein Flugzeug, einen Bus usw. s.,** to board/ get on a plane, bus etc.; (*b*) (*Flut, Sonne, Temperatur usw.*) to rise; (*Nebel*) to lift; (*Preise usw.*) to go up, increase; (*Spannung, Schulden*) to mount; (*Chancen, Stimmung*) to improve. ◆'s~**ern,** *v.tr.* to increase; to step up (production, demands etc.); (*verbessern*) improve a performance, an offer etc.); **sich s.,** to increase; *Gram:* **Adjektive s.,** to form the comparative and superlative of adjectives. ◆'S~**erung,** *f -/-en* increase; intensification, enhancement; *Gram:* comparison (of adjectives). ◆'S~**ung,** *f -/-en* (upward) gradient; *N.Am:* grade; (*Hang*) slope.

**steil** [ʃtail], *adj.* steep; *Fig:* rapid (increase etc.); mercurial (career).

**Stein** [ʃtain], *m -(e)s/-e* stone. ◆'s~'**alt,** *adj. F:* (*Pers.*) ancient. ◆'S~**bock,** *m Z:* ibex; *Astr:* Capricorn. ◆'S~**bruch,** *m* quarry. ◆'S~**butt,** *m* turbot. ◆'s~**ern,** *adj.* stone; *Fig:* (heart) of stone; stony (expression). ◆'S~**gut,** *n -(e)s/no pl* earthenware. ◆'s~'**hart,** *adj.* rock-hard. ◆'s~**ig,** *adj.* stony (ground etc.). ◆'s~**igen,** *v.tr.* to stone (s.o.). ◆'S~**kohle,** *f* (hard) coal. ◆'S~**metz,** *m -es/-e* stone mason. ◆'S~**obst,** *n* stone fruit. ◆'S~**pilz,** *m* edible boletus. ◆'S~**reich,** *adj. F:* rolling (in money). ◆'S~**zeit,** *f* Stone Age.

**Steißbein** [ʃtaisbain], *n* coccyx.

**Stell|dichein** [ʃtɛldiçʔain], *n -s/-* rendezvous. ◆'S~**e,** *f -/-n* **1.** (*a*) place; **kahle**

S., bare patch; **wunde S.**, sore spot; *Fig:* **auf der S.**, (*sofort*) immediately; (*hier*) here and now; **zur S. sein**, to be on hand; (*b*) position; **an der richtigen S.**, in the right position/place; **an S. von +** *dat*, instead/in lieu of; **an dieser S. der Geschichte**, at this point in the story. **2.** (*Arbeitss.*) job, post. **3.** (*Diensts.*) office; (*Behörde*) authority. **4.** *Mth:* digit; (*Dezimals.*) (decimal) place. ◆**'s~en**, *v.tr.* (*a*) to put (s.o., sth.); (*b*) (*Pers.*) **sich s.**, to place oneself, take up position (somewhere); **stell dich neben mich**, come (and stand) next to me; **wie s. Sie sich dazu?** what is your view on this? (*c*) to set (a trap, switch etc.); to put (the clock) right; **den Wecker auf 7 Uhr s.**, to set the alarm for 7 o'clock; **das Gas höher/niedriger s.**, to turn the gas up/down; (*d*) (*beschaffen, geben*) to provide (wine, workers etc.); to put forward (a demand), put (a question); **j-m eine Aufgabe s.**, to set s.o. a task; (*e*) to corner (an animal, a criminal); **sich (der Polizei) s.**, to give oneself up to the police; **sich einem Gegner s.**, to meet an opponent; (*f*) **sich krank, taub usw. s.**, to pretend to be ill, deaf etc. ◆**'S~enangebot**, *n* offer of a post; (*in Zeitung*) **S~enangebote**, situations vacant. ◆**'S~engesuch**, *n* application for a post; (*in Zeitung*) **S~engesuche**, situations wanted. ◆**'S~envermittlung**, *f* employment agency. ◆**'s~enweise**, *adv.* here and there. ◆**'S~ung**, *f* -/-en (*a*) position; (*b*) (*Körperhaltung*) posture; (*c*) *Mil:* **feindliche S~ungen**, enemy positions/lines; (*d*) (*Posten*) post, job; (*e*) (*Haltung*) attitude (**zu +** *dat*, to); **zu etwas** *dat* **S. nehmen**, to express an opinion on sth. ◆**'S~ungnahme**, *f* -/-n view, comment. ◆**'S~ungssuche**, *f* job-hunting. ◆**'s~vertretend**, *adj.* deputy; (*vorübergehend*) acting. ◆**'S~vertreter(in)**, *m* (*f*) deputy; (*Ersatzmann*) substitute; (*an einem anderen Ort*) representative. ◆**S~werk**, *n* signal box.

**Stelze** ['ʃtɛltsə], *f* -/-n *pl* **S~n**, stilts.

**Stemm|bogen** ['ʃtɛmboːgən], *m* *Sp:* stem turn. ◆**'S~eisen**, *n* crowbar. ◆**'s~en**, *v.tr.* (*a*) to lift (a weight etc.) above one's head; (*b*) to press (one's knee etc.); **sich gegen etwas** *acc* **s.**, to brace oneself against sth., *Fig:* to resist sth.

**Stempel** ['ʃtɛmpəl], *m* -s/- **1.** stamp; (*auf Silber usw.*) hallmark; (*Posts.*) postmark. **2.** *Bot:* pistil. ◆**'S~kissen**, *n* inkpad. ◆**'s~n**, *v.* **1.** *v.tr.* to stamp (a document etc.), postmark (a letter), cancel (a stamp), hallmark (precious metals). **2.** *v.i.* (*haben*) *F:* **s. gehen**, to be on the dole.

**Stengel** ['ʃtɛŋəl], *m* -s/- *Bot:* stem.

**Steno|gramm** [ʃteno'gram], *n* -(e)s/-e shorthand version/text. ◆**s~gra'phieren**, *v.tr.* to take (sth.) down in shorthand. ◆**S~ty'pist(in)**, *m* -en/-en

(*f* -/-nen) shorthand-typist.

**Stepp|decke** ['ʃtɛpdɛkə], *f* -/-n quilt. ◆**'S~e**, *f* -/-n (*in Asien*) steppes; *N.Am:* prairie; *S.Am:* pampas. ◆**'s~en**, *v.tr.* to machine-stitch (clothes), quilt (material).

**Sterb|e-** ['ʃtɛrbə-], *comb.fm.* death (certificate etc); (hour, date, place etc.) of death. ◆**'S~ebett**, *n* deathbed. ◆**'S~efall**, *m* death. ◆**'s~en**, *v.i.irr.* (*sein*) to die (**an etwas** *dat*, of sth.); **im S. liegen**, to be dying. ◆**'s~ens'krank**, *adj.* mortally ill. ◆**'s~lich**, *adj.* mortal (remains etc.); **ein gewöhnlicher S~licher**, an ordinary mortal. ◆**'S~lichkeit**, *f* -/no *pl* mortality. ◆**'S~lichkeitsrate**, *f* death rate.

**Stereo-** ['ʃteːreo-, 'st-], *comb.fm.* stereo (record, tape recorder etc.). ◆**'S~anlage**, *f* stereo system, *F:* stereo.

**steril** [ʃte'riːl], *adj.* sterile. ◆**S~isation** [-rilizatsi'oːn], *f* -/-en sterilization. ◆**s~i'sieren** [-'ziːrən], *v.tr.* to sterilize (s.o., sth.), neuter (a cat).

**Stern** [ʃtɛrn], *m* -(e)s/-e star. ◆**'S~bild**, *n* constellation. ◆**'S~enbanner**, *n* das **S.**, the stars and stripes. ◆**'s~förmig**, *adj.* star-shaped. ◆**'S~kunde**, *f* -/no *pl* astronomy. ◆**'S~schnuppe**, *f* -/-n shooting star. ◆**'S~stunde**, *f* great moment. ◆**'S~warte**, *f* observatory.

**stet|ig** ['ʃteːtiç], *adj.* steady, constant (increase, decrease etc.). ◆**'s~s**, *adv.* always.

**Steuer¹** ['ʃtɔyər], *n* -s/- *Aut:* steering wheel; *Nau:* rudder; *Av: etc:* controls; **am S.**, at the wheel/*Av:* controls/*Nau:* helm. ◆**'S~bord**, *n* starboard. ◆**'S~gerät**, *n* *Rad:* control unit. ◆**'S~knüppel**, *m* *Aut: Av:* (control) stick. ◆**'S~mann**, *m* helmsman. ◆**'s~n**, *v.* **1.** *v.tr.* (*a*) to steer (a car, ship, course etc.), navigate (a ship), pilot (an aircraft); (*b*) *Tchn:* (*regulieren*) to control (a machine, speed, *Fig:* a firm etc.). **2.** *v.i.* to steer, be at the controls/*Nau:* helm. ◆**'S~rad**, *n* steering wheel. ◆**'S~ung**, *f* -/-en *a) no pl* steering; *Av:* piloting; *Tchn: & Fig:* control; (*b*) steering (mechanism); *Av:* controls.

**Steuer²**. **I.** *f* -/-n tax. **II.** **'S~-**, *comb.fm.* tax (increase, collector, group, offence etc.); fiscal (law, policy, secrecy, year etc.). ◆**'S~behörde**, *f* tax authorities. ◆**'S~berater**, *m* tax consultant. ◆**'S~erklärung**, *f* tax return. ◆**'S~flucht**, *f* tax evasion (by going abroad). ◆**'s~frei**, *adj.* tax-free, untaxed (goods etc.). ◆**'S~hinterziehung**, *f* tax evasion. ◆**'s~pflichtig**, *adj.* taxable (income etc.). ◆**'S~satz**, *m* tax rate; rate of assessment. ◆**'S~zahler**, *m* taxpayer.

**Stewardeß** [stjuːar'dɛs], *f* -/-ssen stewardess; *Av:* air hostess.

**stibitzen** [ʃti'bitsən], *v.tr.* *F:* to pinch, nick (sth.).

**Stich** [ʃtiç], m -(e)s/-e 1. (a) prick (of a needle); stab (of a knife, dagger etc.); (S~wunde) stab wound; (b) sting, bite (of an insect). 2. (Nähs.) stitch. 3. Art: engraving. 4. (Kartenspiel) **einen S. machen,** to take a trick. 5. **das Kleid hat einen S. ins Rötliche,** the dress has a reddish tinge. 6. **j-n im S. lassen,** to let s.o. down, (verlassen) leave s.o. in the lurch. ◆**S~e'lei,** f -/-en F: (a) snide remark; gibe; (b) no pl sneering, gibing. ◆**'s~eln,** v.i. (haben) **gegen j-n s.,** to gibe at s.o., make snide remarks about s.o. ◆**'S~flamme,** f leaping flame; jet of flame. ◆**'s~haltig,** adj. sound, valid (reason, argument etc.). ◆**'S~probe,** f spot check. ◆**'S~waffe,** f stabbing weapon. ◆**'S~wahl,** f final ballot. ◆**'S~wort,** n -(e)s 1. (pl ˭er) headword (in a dictionary etc.). 2. (pl -e) (a) Th: cue; (b) Mus: f notes. ◆**'S~wunde,** f stab (wound). ◆**'S~wortverzeichnis,** n index.

**stick|en** ['ʃtikən], v.tr. to embroider (a cushion etc.). ◆**'s~e'rei,** f -/-en embroidery. ◆**'s~ig,** adj. stuffy (air, room), close (atmosphere). ◆**'S~stoff,** m nitrogen.

**Stief-** ['ʃtiːf-], comb.fm. step (-mother, -father, -brother etc.). ◆**'S~kind,** n stepchild; Fig: poor cousin. ◆**'S~mütterchen,** n -s/- pansy.

**Stiefel** ['ʃtiːfəl], m -s/- boot.

**Stiege** ['ʃtiːgə], f -/-n (narrow/steep) stairs.

**Stiel** [ʃtiːl], m -(e)s/-e stalk (of a plant etc.); stem (of a glass etc.); handle (of a broom etc.).

**Stier** ['ʃtiːr], m -(e)s/-e bull; Astr: Taurus. ◆**'S~kampf,** m bullfight. ◆**'S~kämpfer,** m bullfighter.

**stieren** ['ʃtiːrən], v.i. (haben) to stare fixedly.

**Stift**[1] [ʃtift], m -(e)s/-e 1. pin; (Nagel) tack; (Holzs.) peg. 2. (Bleis.) pencil; (Farbs.) crayon. 3. F: (Lehrling) apprentice.

**Stift**[2], n -(e)s/-e (endowed) religious foundation, esp. seminary. ◆**'s~en,** v.tr. (a) to endow, found (a convent etc.); (spenden) to donate (a prize etc.); (b) (bewirken) to cause (confusion, disaster etc.); to bring about (peace etc.). ◆**'S~er(in),** m -s/- (f -/-nen) founder; (Spender) donor (of a prize etc.). ◆**'S~ung,** f -/-en (a) foundation; (Schenkung) donation, bequest (to a museum etc.); (b) (charitable/religious) foundation, institution.

**Stil** [ʃtiːl]. I. m -(e)s/-e style; **im großen S.,** in the grand manner; on a grand scale. II. **'S~-,** comb.fm. stylistic (analysis, level, exercise etc.); (question, dictionary etc.) of style. ◆**'S~blüte,** f stylistic blunder. ◆**'S~bruch,** m (incongruous) change of style. ◆**'S~gefühl,** n sense of style. ◆**'s~istisch,** adj. stylis-

tic. ◆**'s~los** ['ʃtiːlloːs], adj. lacking in style/taste. ◆**'S~möbel,** npl period furniture. ◆**'s~voll,** adj. stylish, tasteful.

**still** [ʃtil], adj. (lautlos) quiet, silent; (ohne Bewegung) still; (ruhig) quiet (area, life, person etc.), calm (sea); peaceful (day, village etc.); private (hope, wish); **sie blieb s.,** she said nothing; **im s~en,** secretly, privately; **s~er Teilhaber,** sleeping partner. ◆**'S~e,** f -/no pl silence, quiet(ness); stillness; **in aller S. heiraten,** to have a quiet wedding. ◆**'s~en,** v.tr. (a) to nurse, breastfeed (a baby); (b) to quench (one's thirst), satisfy (one's hunger, curiosity, desires etc.); (c) to staunch (blood); to stop (pain etc.). ◆**'s~halten,** v.i. sep.irr.45 (haben) to keep still/Fig: quiet. ◆**'S~leben,** n -s/- Art: still life. ◆**'s~stillegen,** v.tr.sep. to shut down (a factory, railway line etc.). ◆**'S~schweigen,** n silence. ◆**'s~schweigend,** adj. silent, unspoken; **s~schweigendes Einverständnis,** tacit agreement; **etwas s. übergehen,** to pass over sth. in silence. ◆**'S~stand,** m standstill. ◆**'s~stehen,** v.i.sep.irr.100 (haben) to stand still, (Verkehr, Produktion usw.) be at a standstill; (Maschinen usw.) to be idle.

**Stimm|abgabe** ['ʃtimʔapgaːbə], f voting. ◆**'S~bänder,** npl vocal cords. ◆**'s~berechtigt,** adj. entitled to vote. ◆**'S~bruch,** m **er ist im S.,** his voice is breaking. ◆**'S~e,** f -/-n 1. (a) voice; **die S. des Volkes,** public opinion. 2. Mus: (Partie) part. 3. Pol: etc: **seine S. abgeben,** to (cast one's) vote. ◆**'s~en,** v. 1. v.tr. (a) **die Nachricht stimmte ihn glücklich,** the news made him happy; (b) Mus: to tune (an instrument). 2. v.i. (haben) (a) to be right/correct; **da stimmt etwas nicht,** there is something wrong/(suspekt) fishy there; (b) Pol: etc: **für/gegen j-n s.,** to vote for/against s.o. ◆**'S~enthaltung,** f abstention from voting. ◆**'S~gabel,** f tuning fork. ◆**'s~haft,** adj. voiced (consonant etc.). ◆**'S~lage,** f (vocal) register. ◆**'s~los,** adj. unvoiced. ◆**'S~ung,** f -/-en (a) (Laune) mood; **die S. des Volkes,** public feeling; F: **sie waren in S.,** they were in high spirits; (b) atmosphere. ◆**'s~ungsvoll,** adj. full of atmosphere, evocative. ◆**'S~zettel,** m voting/ballot paper.

**stimu|lieren** [ʃtimu'liːrən], v.tr. to stimulate (s.o.).

**Stink|bombe** ['ʃtiŋkbɔmbə], f -/-n stink-bomb. ◆**'s~en,** v.i.irr. (haben) to stink. ◆**'s~'faul,** adj. F: bone-idle. ◆**'S~tier,** n skunk.

**Stipendium** [ʃti'pɛndiʊm], n -s/-ien scholarship, grant.

**Stirn** [ʃtirn], f -/-en forehead, brow; Fig: **j-m die S. bieten,** to stand up to/defy s.o.; **er hatte die S., mir zu sagen ...,** he had the effrontery/nerve to tell me ...

◆'S~höhle, f (frontal) sinus.
◆'S~runzeln, n frown.
stöbern ['ʃtøːbərn], v.i. (haben) to rummage (about).
stochern ['ʃtɔxərn], v.i. (haben) to poke (about).
Stock¹ [ʃtɔk], m -(e)s/=e 1. stick; (zum Prügeln) cane; Mus: baton. 2. no pl storey; im ersten S., on the first/N.Am: second floor. ◆'S~werk, n floor, storey.
stock-², adj.comb.fm. F: completely and utterly (stupid, normal etc.); arch-(-conservative etc.). ◆'s~'dunkel, adj. pitch dark. ◆'s~'taub, adj. stone-deaf.
stock|en ['ʃtɔkən], v.i. (haben) (Pers.) to falter, hesitate; (Gespräch) to flag; (Verkehr usw.) to be held up, proceed in fits and starts. ◆'s~end, adj. faltering, hesitant. ◆'S~ung, f -/-en hesitation; hold-up (of traffic etc.).
Stoff [ʃtɔf], m -(e)s/-e 1. material. 2. (a) Ch: etc: substance; pflanzliche S~e, vegetable matter; (b) Lit: material; (Thema) subject; subject-matter (of a book etc.). ◆'S~wechsel, m metabolism.
stöhnen ['ʃtøːnən], v.i. (haben) to groan, moan.
stoisch ['ʃtoːiʃ], adj. stoic.
Stollen ['ʃtɔlən], m -s/- 1. Min: tunnel; gallery. 2. Cu: (Christmas) fruit loaf, stollen.
stolpern ['ʃtɔlpərn], v.i. (sein) to stumble.
stolz [ʃtɔlts]. I. adj. proud (auf etwas acc, of sth.); eine s~e Leistung, a splendid achievement. II. S., m -es/no pl pride. ◆s~ieren [-'tsiːrən], v.i. (sein) to swagger, strut.
Stopf- ['ʃtɔpf-], comb.fm. darning (thread, wool, needle etc.). ◆'s~en, v. 1. v.tr. (a) to darn (socks etc.); (b) to fill (a pipe, sausage etc.), stuff (a pillow, one's pockets etc.); ein Loch/Leck s., to plug a hole/leak. 2. v.i. (haben) to cause constipation.
Stopp [ʃtɔp], m -s/-s 1. (Halt) stop. 2. (Sperre) ban (für + acc, on); (wage etc.) freeze. II. 'S~-, comb.fm. stop (sign etc.). ◆'s~en, v.tr. (a) to stop (s.o., sth.); Fb: etc: to tackle (a player); (b) to time (s.o.) (with a stopwatch). ◆'S~straße, f minor road. ◆'S~uhr, f stopwatch.
Stoppel ['ʃtɔpəl], f -/-n stubble.
Stöpsel ['ʃtœpsəl], m -s/- plug; stopper (in a bottle).
Stör¹ [ʃtøːr], m -(e)s/-e sturgeon.
Stör-², comb.fm. disruptive (action, factor, manoeuvre etc.); Mil: harrassing (action, fire etc.). ◆'s~en, v. 1. v.tr. (a) to disturb (s.o.), interfere with (a plan, Rad: reception etc.); (unterbrechen) to interrupt (a conversation etc.); (b) (beunruhigen) to bother, worry (s.o.); stört es Sie, wenn ...? do you mind if ...? 2. v.i. (haben) störe ich? am I interrupting/in the way? ◆'s~end, adj. disturbing; disruptive

(effect, influence); (lästig) troublesome. ◆'S~enfried, m -(e)s/-e disruptive element. ◆'S~sender, m jamming transmitter. ◆'S~ung, f -/-en (a) disturbance; interruption, disruption (of proceedings etc.); hold-up (of traffic); (b) Tchn: (Fehler) fault; Rad: interference; Med: disorder.
störrisch ['ʃtœriʃ], adj. stubborn, pigheaded.
Stoß [ʃtoːs], m -es/=e 1. (a) push; j-m einen S. mit dem Fuß/der Faust versetzen, to kick/punch s.o.; ein S. mit dem Dolch, a thrust/stab with the dagger; (b) (Anprall) impact, (kräftig) shock; (Erds.) tremor. 2. (Stapel) pile (of washing, books etc.). ◆'S~dämpfer, m shock absorber. ◆'s~en, v.irr. 1. v.tr. to push (s.o., sth.); (schlagen) to hit, (mit dem Fuß) kick; (zufällig) to knock, (plötzlich) jolt (s.o., sth.); to thrust (a knife etc.); sich (an etwas dat) s., to knock oneself (on sth.); Fig: sich an j-s Benehmen usw. s., to take exception to s.o.'s behaviour etc. 2. v.i. (sein) (a) er ist an/gegen das Bett gestoßen, he bumped into/knocked against the bed; nach j-m s., to lunge at/(Stier usw.) butt s.o.; (b) (grenzen) to border (an etwas acc, on sth.); (c) auf etwas acc s., to come across sth.; auf j-n s., to run into s.o. ◆'s~fest, adj. shockproof. ◆'S~stange, f bumper. ◆'S~verkehr, m rush-hour traffic. ◆'S~zeit, f rush hour.
Stotter|er ['ʃtɔtərər], m -s/- stammerer. ◆'s~n, v.tr. & i. (haben) to stammer.
stracks [ʃtraks], adv. straight, directly.
Straf- ['ʃtraːf-], comb.fm. (a) penal (colony etc.); criminal (court, proceedings etc.); (b) Sp: penalty (bench, points etc.). ◆'S~anstalt, f penal institution, prison. ◆'S~anzeige, f charge. ◆'S~arbeit, f Sch: imposition. ◆'s~bar, adj. Jur: punishable, criminal (action etc.); sich s. machen, to commit an offence. ◆'S~e, f -/-n punishment, penalty; (Gelds.) fine; (Freiheitss.) sentence; zur S., as a punishment. ◆'s~en, v.tr. to punish/(prügeln) beat (s.o.). ◆'s~fällig, adj. s. werden, to commit a criminal offence. ◆'s~frei, adj. unpunished; s. ausgehen, to be let off. ◆'S~gefangene(r), m & f decl. as adj. convict, prisoner. ◆'S~gericht, n criminal court. ◆'S~gesetzbuch, n penal/criminal code. ◆'S~mandat, n (esp. parking) ticket. ◆'s~mildernd, adj. mitigating. ◆'S~porto, n surcharge. ◆'S~predigt, f F: j-m eine S. halten, to give s.o. a good talking to. ◆'S~prozeß, m criminal proceedings/case. ◆'S~recht, n criminal law. ◆'S~raum, m penalty area. ◆'S~stoß, m penalty kick. ◆'S~tat, f criminal act. ◆'S~täter, m offender. ◆'S~vollzug, m execution of a sen-

tence. ◆'S~zettel, m F: = S~mandat.

**straff** [ʃtraf], adj. taut (rope etc.); tight (reins, trousers, Fig: organization); Fig: strict (discipline). ◆'s~en, v.tr. to tighten (a rope etc.), Fig: tighten up (organization etc.).

**sträf|lich** [ʃtrɛːfliç], adj. criminal (negligence etc.). ◆'S~ling, m -s/-e convict.

**Strahl** [ʃtraːl], m -(e)s/-en (a) ray (of light, the sun, Fig: hope etc.); beam (of a torch etc.); (b) jet (of water etc.). ◆'s~en, v.i. (a) to shine, (glänzen) gleam; (b) Fig: (Pers.) to beam (vor Freude usw., with joy etc.). ◆'S~en-, comb.fm. ray (treatment etc.); radiation (damage etc.). ◆'s~end, adj. radiant (beauty, appearance, face, smile etc.); brilliant (sun, weather etc.); shining, sparkling (eyes etc.). ◆'S~entherapie, f radiotherapy. ◆'S~ung, f -/-en radiation.

**Strähn|e** [ʃtrɛːnə], f -/-n strand (of hair etc.). ◆'s~ig, adj. straggly (hair etc.).

**stramm** [ʃtram], adj. (a) (aufrecht) upright; (b) (straff) tight (elastic etc.). ◆'s~stehen, v.i.sep.irr.100 (haben) Mil: to stand to attention.

**strampeln** [ʃtrampəln], v.i. (haben) (Baby) to kick.

**Strand** [ʃtrant], m -(e)s/-e beach; shore (of a lake). ◆'S~bad, n (am Fluß/See) bathing place; (am Meer) bathing beach. ◆'s~en, v.i. (sein) (Schiffe) to run aground. ◆'S~gut, n flotsam and jetsam. ◆'S~korb, m roofed wickerwork beach chair. ◆'S~promenade, f promenade, sea front.

**Strang** [ʃtraŋ], m -(e)s/-e (a) (Seil) rope; (b) über die S~e schlagen, to kick over the traces; (c) Rail: section (of track).

**Strapaz|e** [ʃtraˈpaːtsə], f -/-n (physical) strain. ◆s~ieren [-aˈtsiːrən], v.tr. to be hard on (shoes, clothes, skin etc.); to tax/put a strain on (s.o., sth.); to take it out of (s.o.). ◆s~ier'fähig, adj. hardwearing, durable. ◆s~i'ös, adj. exhausting, gruelling.

**Straße** [ʃtraːsə], f -/-n **1.** (a) street; (b) (Lands.) road. **2.** (Meeress.) straits. ◆'S~n-, comb.fm. road (dirt, vehicle, map, network, race, conditions etc.); street (corner, fighting, musician, name, cleaning, theatre etc.). ◆'S~nbahn, f tram; N.Am: streetcar. ◆'S~nbau, m road building/construction. ◆'S~nbeleuchtung, f street lighting. ◆'S~ncafe, n pavement cafe. ◆'S~nkehrer, m road/street sweeper. ◆'S~nkreuzer, m -s/- F: large swanky car. ◆'S~nkreuzung, f road junction, crossroads. ◆'S~nrand, m roadside. ◆'S~nschild, road/street sign. ◆'S~nseite, f side of the street. ◆'S~nsperre, f road block. ◆'S~nverkehr, m (road) traffic; im S., on the road. ◆'S~nverkehrsordnung,

f traffic regulations.

**Strate|ge** [ʃtraˈteːgə], m -n/-n strategist. ◆S~gie [-teˈgiː], f -/-n strategy. ◆s~gisch [-ˈteːgiʃ], adj. strategic.

**sträuben** [ʃtrɔybən], v.tr. (a) (Vogel) to ruffle (its feathers); (Haare) sich s., to stand on end; (b) (Pers.) sich gegen etwas acc s., to rebel/fight against sth.

**Strauch** [ʃtraux], m -(e)s/-er bush, shrub.

**Strauß¹** [ʃtraus], m -es/-e ostrich.

**Strauß²**, m -es/-e bunch (of flowers).

**Streb|e** [ʃtreːbə], f -/-n brace. ◆'s~en, v.i. (a) (haben) to strive (nach + dat, for). ◆'S~er, m -s/- F: pusher; Sch: swot, N.Am: grind. ◆s~sam [ʃtreːpzam], adj. ambitious; eager to get on; (fleißig) industrious.

**Streck|e** [ʃtrɛkə], f -/-n (a) (Abschnitt) stretch (of road etc.); Rail: section (of track); Mth: die S. AB, the straight line AB; (b) (Entfernung) distance; Fig: auf der S. bleiben, to retire (from a race). Fig: j-n zur S. bringen, to hunt down (and capture) s.o. ◆'s~en, v.tr. (a) to stretch (sth., one's arms, legs etc.); crane (one's neck); sich s., to stretch (out); (b) to eke out (supplies etc.); (c) j-n zu Boden s., to knock down/ floor s.o.; (d) Fig: die Waffen s., to give up. ◆'s~enweise, adv. in parts.

**Streich¹** [ʃtraiç], m -(e)s/-e prank; j-m einen S. spielen, to play a practical joke/Fig: (Gedächtnis usw.) play tricks on s.o.

**Streich-²**, comb.fm. (a) Mus: string (instrument, orchestra etc.); (b) Cu: (sausage etc.) for spreading. ◆'s~eln, v.tr. to stroke (s.o., a cat etc.). ◆'s~en, v.irr.40 **1.** v.tr. (a) to spread (butter, a roll, face cream etc.); (b) to stroke (s.o.'s face etc.); (c) to paint (a room etc.); (d) (auss.) to delete (a word etc.), strike off (a name etc.). **2.** v.i. (a) (haben) to stroke; (b) (sein) (umhergehen) to wander, roam. ◆'S~er, mpl Mus: strings. ◆'s~fähig, adj. easy to spread; (cheese etc.) for spreading. ◆'S~holz, n match. ◆'S~holzschachtel, f matchbox. ◆'S~ung, f -/-en deletion.

**Streif|e** [ʃtraifə], f -/-n (army/police) patrol. ◆'s~en¹, v. **1.** v.tr. (a) to touch (s.o., sth.) (lightly), brush against (s.o., sth.); Fig: j-n mit dem Blick/den Augen s., to glance at s.o. **2.** v.i. (sein) (umherziehen) to wander, roam (about). ◆'S~en², m -s/- (a) stripe (of colour etc.); (b) S. Stoff, Land usw., strip of cloth, land etc.; (c) F: (Film) movie. ◆'S~enwagen, m (police) patrol car. ◆'S~schuß, m grazing shot. ◆'S~zug, m reconnaissance; pl (ohne Ziel) wanderings.

**Streik** [ʃtraik], m -(e)s/-s strike. ◆'S~brecher, m strike-breaker; F: blackleg; N.Am: scab. ◆'s~en, v.i. (haben) (a) to strike; (b) F: (Pers.) (nicht mitmachen) to go on strike; (Gerät) to pack up. ◆'S~**ende(r)**, m & f decl. as adj. striker. ◆'S~**posten**, m picket.

**Streit** [ʃtrait], m -(e)s/no pl quarrel, (heftig) row; (zwischen Parteien usw.) dispute. ◆'s~**bar**, adj. quarrelsome. ◆'s~**en**, v.irr.41.refl. & i. (haben) (**sich**) **über etwas** acc **s.**, to quarrel/argue about sth.; to have an argument/(Eheleute) a row about sth. ◆'S~**fall**, m (a) dispute, controversy; (b) Jur: case. ◆'S~**frage**, f matter in dispute, issue (in an argument). ◆'s~**ig**, adj. **j-m etwas s. machen**, to question s.o.'s right to sth. ◆'S~**igkeiten**, fpl quarrels, disputes. ◆'S~**kräfte**, fpl armed forces. ◆'s~**lustig**, adj. pugnacious, argumentative. ◆'S~**punkt**, m point at issue. ◆'S~**sucht**, f quarrelsomeness. ◆'s~**süchtig**, adj. quarrelsome.

**streng** [ʃtrɛŋ], adj. strict (parent, rule etc.); severe (measure, penalty, expression etc.); hard (winter, frost); strong (taste, smell). ◆'S~**e**, f -/no pl strictness, severity, harshness (of treatment etc.); Fig: austerity. ◆'s~**genommen**, adv. strictly speaking. ◆'s~**gläubig**, adj. orthodox. ◆'s~**stens**, adv. s. **verboten**, strictly forbidden.

**Streß** [ʃtrɛs], m -sses/no pl stress.

**Streu** [ʃtrɔy], f -/no pl bed of straw/occ. leaves. ◆'s~**en**, v. 1. v.tr. to scatter (seeds etc.), (unordentlich) strew (paper, flowers etc.), spread (dung, Fig: rumours etc.), sprinkle (sugar etc.). 2. v.i. (haben) (mit Sand) to grit. ◆'S~**er**, m -s/- sprinkler; (für Salz) salt cellar.

**streunen** ['ʃtrɔynən], v.i. (sein) (Tier, Hum: Pers.) to roam; s~**de Katze**, stray cat.

**Streusel** ['ʃtrɔyzəl], m -s/- crumble. ◆'S~**kuchen**, m yeast cake with crumble.

**Strich** [ʃtriç], m -(e)s/-e 1. (Linie) line; (Gedankens.) dash; stroke (of the pen etc.); F: **S. drunter!** let's forget it! F: **es geht (mir) gegen den S.**, it goes against the grain. 3. F: **auf den S. gehen**, to walk the streets. ◆'s~**weise**, adv. s. **Regen**, rain in places.

**Strick** [ʃtrik], m -(e)s/-e cord, (Seil) rope. II. 'S~-, comb.fm. (a) knitting (needle, machine etc.); (b) (gestrickt) knitted (dress etc.). ◆'s~**en**, v.tr. & i. (haben) to knit (a pullover etc.). ◆'S~**jacke**, f cardigan. ◆'s~**leiter**, f rope ladder.

**Striemen** ['ʃtriːmən], m -s/- weal.

**strikt** [ʃtrikt], adj. strict (orders etc.), severe (measures etc.).

**strittig** ['ʃtritiç], adj. contentious; s~**er Punkt**, point at issue.

**Stroh** [ʃtroː], n -(e)s/no pl straw. ◆'S~**blume**, f everlasting flower. ◆'S~**dach**, n thatched roof. ◆'S~**halm**, m (a) (blade of) straw; (b) (drinking) straw. ◆'S~**hut**, m straw hat. ◆'S~**mann**, m -(e)s/-er dummy;

Fig: front man. ◆'S~**witwe(r)**, f (m) F: grass widow(er).

**Strolch** [ʃtrɔlç], m -(e)s/-e (a) Pej: tramp, N.Am: bum; (b) F: (Kind) rascal.

**Strom** [ʃtroːm]. I. m 1. -(e)s/-e (a) (large) river; (b) stream (of blood, Fig: people etc.); **es goß in S~en**, it poured with rain. 2. (Strömung) current. 3. no pl El: current; (Elektrizität) electricity; **unter S. stehen**, to be live. II. 'S~-, comb.fm. electricity (bill, consumption etc.); power (cable, source etc.); electric (cable etc.). ◆'s~'**abwärts**, adv. downstream. ◆'s~'**aufwärts**, adv. upstream. ◆'s~**linienförmig**, adj. streamlined.

**ström|en** ['ʃtrøːmən], v.i. (haben) (Wasser, Fig: Menschen usw.) to stream, pour. ◆'S~**ung**, f -/-en (a) current (in water/air); (b) Art: Pol: etc: movement; (Tendenz) trend.

**Strophe** ['ʃtroːfə], f -/-n verse (of a poem etc.).

**strotzen** ['ʃtrɔtsən], v.i. (haben) **vor Energie usw. s.**, to be full of/bursting with energy etc.

**Strudel** ['ʃtruːdəl], m -s/- 1. whirlpool; Fig: whirl (of events etc.). 2. Cu: strudel.

**Struk|tur** [ʃtruk'tuːr], f -/-en structure. ◆s~**turell** [-u'rɛl], adj. structural.

**Strumpf** [ʃtrumpf], m -(e)s/-e stocking. ◆'S~**band**, n garter. ◆'S~**hose**, f tights.

**Strunk** [ʃtruŋk], m -(e)s/-e stalk; (Baums.) trunk.

**struppig** ['ʃtrupiç], adj. shaggy.

**Stube** [ʃtuːbə], f -/-n room. ◆'S~**narrest**, m F: (Kind usw.) **S. haben**, to be confined to one's room. ◆'S~**nhocker**, m F: stay-at-home. ◆'s~**nrein**, adj. house-trained.

**Stuck** [ʃtuk], m -s/no pl stucco.

**Stück** [ʃtyk], n -(e)s/-e 1. piece; **S. Papier/Kuchen**, piece of paper/cake; (Wurst, Käse usw.) **am/im S.**, in a piece, unsliced; **fünf Mark pro/das S.**, five marks apiece/each; **ein S. aus dem Buch**, a passage from the book; **S. für S.**, bit by bit; (eins nach dem anderen) one by one; Fig: **aus freien S~en**, voluntarily; F: **das ist ein starkes S.!** that's going too far! what a cheek! 2. (a) Th: play; (b) Mus: piece. 3. (Gegenstand) item; **mein bestes S.**, my most precious possession; ◆'S~**arbeit**, f piecework. ◆'S~**chen**, n -s/- little bit; scrap (of paper etc.). ◆'S~**lohn**, m piece rate. ◆'S~**preis**, m unit price. ◆'s~**weise**, adv. one by one; individually; (nach und nach) bit by bit. ◆'S~**werk**, n S. **sein/bleiben**, to be/remain fragmentary.

**Student|(in)** [ʃtu'dɛnt(in)], m -en/-en (f -/-nen) student. ◆S~**(en)heim**, n student hostel. ◆s~**isch**, adj. student (customs etc.).

**Stud|ie** ['ʃtuːdiə], f -/-n (a) study; (b) Art:

sketch, study. ◆**s~ieren** [-'di:rən], v.
1. v.tr. to study (sth.). 2. v.i. (haben) to
study; to be a student/at university.
◆**S~ierzimmer**, n study.
**Studio** ['ʃtu:dio], n -s/-s studio.
**Studium** ['ʃtu:dium], n -s/-ien course of
study, studies.
**Stuf|e** ['ʃtu:fə], f -/-n 1. step; (im Hause)
stair. 2. stage (of a rocket, Fig: development etc.); (Niveau) level. ◆**'s~en**,
v.tr. (a) to terrace (a slope etc.); (b) to
grade (wages etc.). ◆**'S~enleiter**, f stepladder; Fig: hierarchy. ◆**'s~enlos**,
adj. Tchn: infinitely variable.
◆**'s~enweise**, adv. step by step, in
stages.
**Stuhl** [ʃtu:l], m -(e)s/-e chair.
◆**'S~gang**, m movement of the bowels.
**stülpen** ['ʃtylpən], v.tr. etwas nach
oben/innen/außen/unten s., to turn sth.
up/in/out/down.
**stumm** [ʃtum], adj. dumb (person);
(schweigend) silent (person, prayer etc.).
◆**'S~film**, m silent film.
**Stummel** ['ʃtuməl], m -s/- stump, stub;
(Zigarettens.) (cigarette) butt.
**Stümper** ['ʃtympər], m -s/- bungler,
botcher. ◆**S~ei** [-'rai], f -/-en bungled
job/coll. work. ◆**'s~haft**, adj. botched,
bungled (job etc.).
**Stumpf1** [ʃtumpf], m -(e)s/-e stump.
**stumpf2**, adj. (a) blunt (knife, pencil
etc.); Mth: truncated (cone, pyramid);
s~er Winkel, obtuse angle; (b) (glanzlos)
matt, dull (surface, colour etc.); Fig:
apathetic, impassive (look etc.).
◆**'S~heit**, f -/no pl bluntness; dullness;
Fig: apathy. ◆**'S~sinn**, m (a) (Zustand)
apathy; (b) dullness (of a job etc.).
◆**'s~sinnig**, adj. (a) apathetic (person,
behaviour etc.); (b) soul-destroying (job
etc.).
**Stund|e** ['ʃtundə], f -/-n 1. hour; zu spä-
ter S., at a late hour; bis zur S., until
now. 2. Sch: lesson, period. ◆**'s~en**,
v.tr. j-m einen Betrag, die Miete usw.
s., to give s.o. time to pay a sum, the
rent etc. ◆**S~engeschwindigkeit**, f
average speed (in k.p.h.). ◆**'S~en-
kilometer**, mpl 40 S., 40 kilometres per
hour/abbr. k.p.h. ◆**'s~enlang**, adj.
lasting for hours; s. warten, to wait for
hours. ◆**'S~enlohn**, m hourly wage
rate. ◆**'S~enplan**, m timetable.
**stündlich** ['ʃtyntliç], adj. hourly; sich s.
verändern, to change from hour to hour.
**stupid|(e)** [ʃtu'pi:t(-də)], adj. Pej: point-
less, soul-destroying (work etc.).
**Stups** [ʃtups], m -es/-e F: nudge, jog.
◆**'s~en**, v.tr. to nudge, jog (s.o.).
◆**'S~nase**, f F: snub nose.
**stur** [ʃtu:r], adj. F:Pej: dour; (unnachgiebig) pig-headed, stubborn (person).
◆**'S~heit**, f -/no pl F:Pej: pig-
headedness.
**Sturm** [ʃturm]. I. m -(e)s/-e 1. storm;

(Wind) gale. 2. Mil: no pl assault, storming (auf + acc, of). II. **'S~-**, comb.fm.
storm (damage etc.); stormy (night,
weather etc.); Nau: gale (warning etc.).
◆**'S~angriff**, m assault; storming.
◆**'S~flut**, f storm tide. ◆**'S~schritt**,
m im S., at the double.
**stürm|en** ['ʃtyrmən], v. 1. v.tr. Mil: to
storm (a fortress etc.); Fig: to besiege (a
shop etc.). 2. v.i. (a) (haben) (Wind) to
blow hard; es stürmt, there is a gale
blowing; (b) (sein) er stürmte ins Zimmer, he stormed/rushed into the room.
◆**'S~er**, m -s/- Fb: etc: forward, striker. ◆**'s~isch**, adj. (a) stormy (sea,
weather etc.); rough (sea, crossing etc.);
Fig: turbulent (time); (b) (lautstark) tu-
multuous (applause etc.); vociferous, vehement (protest etc.).
**Sturz** [ʃturts], m -es/-e fall; (in die Tiefe)
plunge; Fig: collapse, fall (of a government etc.). ◆**'S~flug**, m nose-dive.
◆**'S~flut**, f torrent. ◆**'S~helm**, m
crash helmet.
**stürzen** ['ʃtyrtsən], v. 1. v.i. (sein) (a) to
fall; Lit: (in die Tiefe) to plunge, plum-
met; Fig: (Regierung usw.) to collapse,
fall; (Preise usw.) to drop sharply, slump;
(b) (Pers.) (eilen) to rush, dash. 2. v.tr.
(a) (werfen) to hurl (s.o., sth.); to plunge
(s.o., sth.); sich auf j-n s., to pounce on
s.o.; (b) to bring down, (durch Gewalt)
overthrow (a government etc.).
**Stute** ['ʃtu:tə], f -/-n mare.
**stutz|en** ['ʃtutsən], v. 1. v.tr. to trim,
clip (a beard, hedge etc.), prune, lop (a
tree, bush), dock (a dog's tail). 2. v.i.
(haben) to stop (short). ◆**'s~ig**, adj. da
wurde ich s., I became suspicious.
**Stütz-** ['ʃtyts-], comb.fm. Tchn: supporting (beam, wall, bar etc.). ◆**'S~e**, f -/-
n support, prop; Fig: (Pers.) mainstay (of
the family etc.); (Hilfe) helper.
◆**'s~en**, v.tr. to support, (stärker) brace
(sth.); sich auf etwas acc s., (Pers.) to
lean on sth.. ◆**'S~punkt**, m Mil: etc:
base.
**Subjekt** [zup'jɛkt], n -(e)s/-e subject.
◆**s~iv** [-'ti:f], adj. subjective.
**Substantiv** ['zupstanti:f], n -s/-e noun.
**Substanz** [zup'stants], f -/-en substance.
**subtil** [zup'ti:l], adj. subtle (distinction
etc.), refined (methods). ◆**S~ität**
[-tili'tɛ:t], f -/no pl subtlety.
**subtrahieren** [zuptra'hi:rən], v.tr. to subtract (a number).
**Subvention** [zupvɛntsi'o:n], f -/-en subsidy, grant. ◆**s~ieren** [-'o:niːrən], v.tr.
to subsidize (theatres etc.).
◆**S~ierung**, f no pl subsidization.
**subversiv** [zupvɛr'zi:f], adj. subversive
(elements etc.).
**Such|aktion** ['zu:xˀaktsio:n], f -/-n
(large-scale) search. ◆**S~e**, f -/no pl
search (nach + dat, for). ◆**s~en**, v. 1.
v.tr. (a) to look/(angestrengt) search for
(sth.); (Polizei) to hunt for (a criminal);

to seek (shelter, protection, advice etc.);
**Verkäuferin gesucht**, sales lady wanted.
2. *v.i.* (*haben*) to search, look (**nach j-m**,
**etwas** *dat*, for s.o., sth.). ◆'**S~er**, *m*
-*s*/- *Phot:* viewfinder. ◆'**S~trupp**, *n*
search party.

**Sucht** [zuxt], *f* -*/e* addiction (**nach** + *dat*,
to); *Fig:* **S. nach Erfolg**, craving for success.

**süchtig** ['zʏçtiç], *adj.* addicted
(**nach** + *dat*, to); **ein S~er/eine S~e**, an
addict.

**Süd** [zy:t]. I. *m* south; **aus/von S.**, from
the south. II. '**S~-**, '**s~-**, *comb.fm.* (*a*)
south (coast, side, bank, wind etc.);
*Geog:* South (Africa, America, Germany,
Pole etc.); (*b*) (*südlich*) southern (frontier,
edge, shore etc.); *Geog:* Southern (Italy
etc.). ◆**S~afri'kaner(in)** *m(f)*/
**s~afri'kanisch**, *adj* South African.
◆**S~en** ['zy:dən], *m* -*s/no pl* south;
**nach S.**, southwards. ◆'**S~früchte**, *fpl*
tropical fruit. ◆'**s~ländisch**, *adj.*
mediterranean (climate etc.); Latin (temperament etc.). ◆'**s~lich**. I. *adj.* (*a*)
southern (border, hemisphere, region
etc.); southerly (wind, direction etc); (*b*)
*adv.* **s. von München**, south of Munich.
II. *prep.* + *gen* **s. der Alpen**, (to the)
south of the Alps. ◆'**S~'ost(en)**, *m*
south-east. ◆'**s~'östlich**. I. *adj.*
south-eastern (district etc.); south-
easterly (wind, direction). II. *prep.* + *gen*
**s. der Stadt**, (to the) south-east of the
town. ◆'**S~'west(en)**, *m* south-west.
◆'**s~'westlich**. I. *adj.* south-western
(district etc.); south-westerly (wind, direction). II. *prep.* + *gen* **s. der Stadt**, (to
the) south-west of the town.

**Sudan** [zu'dɑːn]. *Pr.n.m* **-s. der S.**, the
Sudan. ◆**s~esisch**, *adj.* Sudanese.

**süffig** ['zʏfiç], *adj.* F: very drinkable,
(wine) which goes down well.

**süffisant** [zʏfi'zant], *adj.* smug, complacent.

**sugge|rieren** [zuge'riːrən], *v.tr.* **j-m et-
was s.**, to put sth. into s.o.'s head.
◆**S~stion** [-gɛsti'oːn], *f* -*/-en* insinua-
tion, suggestion; (*Überredung*) (hidden)
persuasion. ◆**s~stiv** [-'tiːf], *adj.* suggestive (power); insinuating (remark
etc.).

**Sühn|e** ['zyːnə], *f* -*/no pl Lit:* atonement;
(*Strafe*) penalty. ◆'**s~en**, *v.tr. & i.* (*haben*) *Lit:* to atone, pay the penalty (for a
crime etc.).

**Sultan** ['zultɑːn], *m* -*s/-e* sultan.
◆**S~ine** [-a'niːnə], *f* -*/-n* sultana (raisin).

**Sülze** ['zʏltsə], *f* -*/-n* brawn.

**Summe** ['zumə], *f* -*/-n* sum.

**summen** ['zumən], *v.* 1. *v.tr.* to hum (a
melody etc.). 2. *v.i.* (*haben*) to hum;
(*Biene usw.*) to buzz.

**summieren** [zu'miːrən], *v.tr.* to add up
(numbers etc.); **sich s.**, to accumulate,
add up (to quite a lot).

**Sumpf** [zumpf], *m* -(*e*)*s/-e* swamp, bog.
◆'**s~ig**, *adj.* boggy, marshy.

**Sund** [zunt], *m* -(*e*)*s/-e* sound, straits.

**Sünd|e** ['zʏndə], *f* -*/-n* sin. ◆'**S~en-
bock**, *m* scapegoat. ◆'**S~er(in)**, *m* -*s/*
(*f* -*/-nen*) sinner. ◆'**s~haft**, *adj.* sinful
(thoughts, life etc.); *F:* **s. teuer**, frightfully expensive. ◆'**s~ig**, *adj.* sinful.
◆'**s~igen**, *v.i.* (*haben*) to sin.

**Super** ['zuːpər], *n* -*s/no pl F:* super (petrol). ◆**S~lativ** ['zuːpərlatiːf], *m* -*s/-e*
superlative. ◆'**S~markt**, *m* supermarket.

**Suppe** ['zupə], *f* -*/-n* soup. ◆'**S~ngrün**,
*n* (bunch of) soup-flavouring vegetables
and herbs. ◆'**S~nhuhn**, *n* boiling
fowl. ◆'**S~nwürfel**, *m* stock cube.

**Surfbrett** ['sɔːfbrɛt], *n* -(*e*)*s/-er* surfboard.

**Surreal|ismus** [zurea'lismus], *m* -*/no pl
Art:* Surrealism. ◆**s~istisch**, *adj.* sur-
realist (picture etc.).

**surren** ['zurən], *v.i.* (*sein*) **durch die Luft
s.**, (*Insekt usw.*) to buzz/(*Kugel*) whizz
through the air.

**suspekt** [zus'pɛkt], *adj.* suspect.

**süß** [zyːs], *adj.* sweet. ◆'**S~e**, *f* -*/no pl*
sweetness. ◆'**s~en**, *v.tr.* to sweeten
(dishes, drinks etc.). ◆'**S~igkeiten**, *fpl*
sweets, *N.Am:* candy. ◆'**s~lich**, *adj.*
sickly, cloying (taste, *Fig:* smile etc.).
◆'**S~speise**, *f* sweet (dish), pudding.
◆'**S~stoff**, *m* sweetener. ◆'**S~-
waren**, *fpl* confectionery. ◆'**S~-
wasser**, *n* freshwater.

**Sylvester** [zyl'vɛstər], *n* -*s/no pl* = **Silvester**.

**Symbol** [zym'boːl], *m* -*s/-e* symbol.
◆**s~isch**, *adj.* symbolic. ◆**s~isieren**
[-oli'ziːrən], *v.tr.* to symbolize (sth.).

**symmetrisch** [zy'meːtriʃ], *adj.* symmetrical.

**Sympath|ie** [zympa'tiː], *f* -*/-n* sympathy.
◆**S~isant** [-ti'zant], *m* -*en/-en Pol:
etc:* sympathizer. ◆**s~isch** [-'paːtiʃ],
*adj.* congenial, likeable (person etc.); **er
ist mir s.**, I like him. ◆**s~isieren**
[-pati'ziːrən], *v.i.* (*haben*) **mit j-m s.**, to
sympathize with s.o.

**Symphon|ie** [zymfo'niː], *f* -*/-n Mus:*
symphony. ◆**s~isch** [-'foːniʃ], *adj.*
symphonic (poem etc.).

**Symptom** [zymp'toːm], *n* -*s/-e Med:*
symptom; *Fig:* (*Anzeichen*) sign, indication. ◆**s~atisch** [-o'maːtiʃ], *adj.*
symptomatic, indicative (**für etwas** *acc*,
of sth.).

**Synagoge** [zyna'goːgə], *f* synagogue.

**synchron** [zyn'kroːn], *adj.* /**S~-**,
*comb.fm.* synchronous (movements, motor etc.). ◆**s~isieren** [-oni'ziːrən],
*v.tr.* to synchronize (movements etc.); to
dub (a film).

**Syndikat** [zyndi'kɑːt], *n* -(*e*)*s/-e* syndicate.

**Syndrom** [zyn'droːm], *n* -*s/-e* syndrome.

**Synode** [zy'noːdə], *f* -*/-n* synod.

**Synonym** [zyno'ny:m]. **I.** *n -s/-e* synonym. **II. s.,** *adj.* synonymous (word etc.).

**Syntax** ['zyntaks], *f -/no pl* syntax.

**synthetisch** [zyn'te:tiʃ], *adj.* synthetic; artificial (flavour etc.); man-made (fibres etc.).

**Syphilis** ['zyfilis], *f -/no pl* syphilis.

**Syr|ien** ['zy:riən]. *Pr.n.n* **-s.** *Geog:* Syria.

◆**'S~(i)er(in),** *m -s/- (f -/-nen)* Syrian.

◆**'s~isch,** *adj.* Syrian.

**System** [zys'te:m], *n -s/-e* system. ◆**s~atisch** [-e'ma:tiʃ], *adj.* systematic, methodical.

**Szen|e** ['stse:nə], *f -/-n* scene. ◆**S~e'rie,** *f -/-n* scenery (*Schauplatz*) setting. ◆**'s~isch,** *adj. Th:* with regard to the scenery/setting.

# T

**T, t** [te:], *n -/-* (the letter) T, t.

**Tabak** ['ta(:)bak], *m -s/-e* tobacco. ◆**'T~laden,** *m* tobacconist's (shop). ◆**'T~sbeutel,** *m* tobacco pouch. ◆**'T~sdose,** *f* tobacco tin. ◆**'T~waren,** *pl* tobacco products.

**tabell|arisch** [tabe'la:riʃ], *adj.* tabulated; *adv.* in tabular form. ◆**T~e** [ta'bɛlə], *f -/-n* table (of contents, statistics etc.). ◆**T~enführer,** *m* league leaders.

**Tablett** [ta'blɛt], *n -(e)s/-s & -e* tray.

**Tablette** [ta'blɛtə], *f -/-n* tablet, pill.

**tabu** [ta'bu:]. **I.** *adj.* taboo. **II. T.,** *n -s/-s* taboo.

**Tacho** ['taxo], *m -s/-s Aut: F:* speedo. ◆**T~'meter,** *m* speedometer.

**Tadel** ['ta:dəl], *m -s/-* reproach, (*Verweis*) rebuke; (*Kritik*) censure, criticism. ◆**'t~los,** *adj.* perfect (accent, *Cl:* fit etc.); impeccable, irreproachable (behaviour etc.). ◆**'t~n,** *v.tr.* to reproach, (*scharf*) rebuke, reprimand (s.o.). ◆**'T~nswert,** *adj.* reprehensible.

**Tafel** ['ta:fəl]. **I.** *f -/-n* **1.** (wooden) board, panel; (stone) slab; (*Gedenkt.*) (memorial) tablet, plaque; (*Anzeiget.*) notice board; (*Schild*) sign; *Sch:* blackboard; *El:* (*Schaltt.*) control panel; **eine T. Schokolade,** a bar of chocolate. **2.** (*Bild*) plate. **3.** *A: & Lit:* (*Tisch*) table. **II. T~-,** *comb.fm.* table (salt, silver, wine etc.). ◆**'t~n,** *v.i.* (*haben*) to dine/(*üppig*) feast. ◆**'T~wasser,** *n* mineral/table water.

**täf|eln** ['tε:fəln], *v.tr.* to panel (a wall, ceiling). ◆**'T~(e)lung,** *f -/-en* panelling.

**Taft** [taft], *m -(e)s/-e* taffeta.

**Tag** [ta:k], *m -(e)s/-e* day; **am/bei T~e,** in the daytime; **am (hellichten) T~e,** in (broad) daylight; **es wird schon T.,** it is getting light; **etwas an den T. bringen,** to bring sth. to light; **Interesse, Eifer usw. an den T. legen,** to display interest, eagerness etc.; *Min:* **über/unter T~e,** above/below ground; **eines T~es,** one day; **T. für T.,** daily, every day; **(guten) T.!** good morning/afternoon! *F:* hello! *N.Am:* hi! (*bei Vorstellung*) how do you do? ◆**t~'aus,** *adv.* **t., tagein,** day in, day out. ◆**'T~ebuch,** *n* diary; *Lit:* journal. ◆**'T~edieb,** *m* lazybones, loafer. ◆**'T~egeld,** *n* daily allowance.

◆**'t~elang,** *adj.* lasting for days; *adv.* for days (on end). ◆**'t~en,** *v.i.* (*haben*) (*a*) (*Konferenz*) to meet; (*Gericht usw.*) to sit; (*b*) *Lit:* **es tagt,** the day is dawning/breaking. ◆**'T~es-,** *comb.fm.* (events, politics, news, *Mil:* order etc.) of the day; day's (work, march, journey etc.). ◆**'T~esanbruch,** *m* **bei T.,** at daybreak. ◆**'T~eskarte,** *f (a)* day ticket; (*b*) menu for the day. ◆**'T~eslicht,** *n* daylight; **ans T. kommen,** to come to light. ◆**'T~esmutter,** *f* child minder. ◆**'T~esordnung,** *f* agenda. ◆**'T~eszeit,** *f* time of (the) day. ◆**'T~eszeitung,** *f* daily newspaper. ◆**'t~'hell,** *adj.* as bright as day. ◆**'t~s,** *adv.* **t. darauf/zuvor,** the day after/before; the next/previous day. ◆**'T~schicht,** *f* day shift. ◆**'t~süber,** *adv.* during the day. ◆**'T~ung,** *f -/-en* conference.

**täglich** ['tɛ:kliç], *adj.* daily; **dreimal t.,** three times a day.

**Taifun** [tai'fu:n], *m -s/-e* typhoon.

**Taill|e** ['taljə], *f -/-n* waist. ◆**t~iert** [ta'ji:rt], *adj. Cl:* close-fitting at the waist; fully fashioned (shirt etc.).

**Takel** ['ta:kəl], *n -s/- Nau:* tackle. ◆**'T~age** [takə'la:ʒə], *f -/-n Nau:* rigging. ◆**'t~n,** *v.tr.* to rig (a ship).

**Takt** [takt], *m -(e)s/-e* **1.** *Mus:* time; rhythm (of a waltz etc.). **2.** *no pl* tact, tactfulness. ◆**'T~gefühl,** *n* (sense) of tact. ◆**'t~los,** *adj.* tactless. ◆**'T~losigkeit,** *f -/-en* **1.** *no pl* tactlessness. **2.** tactless act, indiscretion. ◆**'T~stock,** *m* (conductor's) baton. ◆**'t~voll,** *adj.* tactful.

**Takt|ik** ['taktik], *f -/-en Mil: etc:* tactics. ◆**'t~isch,** *adj.* tactical.

**Tal** [ta:l], *n -(e)s/-er* valley. ◆**T~fahrt,** *f* downhill trip/(*Ski*) run; descent. ◆**'T~kessel,** *m* valley basin. ◆**'T~sohle,** *f* valley floor/bottom. ◆**'T~sperre,** *f* dam.

**Talar** [ta'la:r], *m -s/-e* gown; *Jur:* robe.

**Talent** [ta'lɛnt], *n -(e)s/-e* talent; **er ist ein großes T.,** he is extremely talented. ◆**t~iert** [-'ti:rt], *adj.* talented, gifted.

**Talg** [talk], *m -(e)s/-e* tallow; *Cu:* suet.

**Talisman** ['ta:lisman], *m -s/-e* talisman.

**Tamburin** [tambu'ri:n], *m -s/-e* tambourine.

**Tampon** ['tampɔn], *m* -s/-s tampon.

**Tandem** ['tandɛm], *n* -s/-s tandem.

**Tang** [taŋ], *m* -(e)s/-e seaweed.

**Tang|ente** [taŋ'gɛntə], *f* -/-n 1. tangent. 2. (*Straße*) by-pass, ring road. ◆t~**ieren** [-'giːrən], *v.tr.* (*a*) *Mth:* to form a tangent to (a curve etc.); (*b*) to affect (s.o.).

**Tango** ['taŋgo], *m* -s/-s tango.

**Tank** [taŋk], *m* -s/-s tank. ◆t~**en** ['taŋkən], *v.* 1. *v.i.* (*haben*) to refuel, fill up. 2. *v.tr.* **Benzin usw. t.,** to fill up with petrol etc. ◆'T~**er,** *m* -s/- tanker. ◆'T~**stelle,** *f* filling station; *N.Am:* gas station. ◆'T~**wart,** *m* pump attendant.

**Tann|e** ['tanə], *f* -/-n fir (tree). ◆'T~**enbaum,** *m* fir tree. ◆'T~**enzapfen,** *m* fir cone.

**Tante** ['tantə], *f* -/-n aunt.

**Tanz** [tants]. I. *m* -es/⸚e dance. II. 'T~-, *comb.fm.* dance (music, orchestra, step etc.); dancing (song, partner, school etc.). ◆'t~**en,** *v.tr. & i.* (*haben*) to dance. ◆'T~**lokal,** *n* dance hall. ◆'T~**saal,** *m* ballroom. ◆'T~**stunde,** *f* dancing lesson.

**Tänzer(in)** ['tɛntsər(in)], *m* -s/- (*f* -/-nen) dancer.

**Tapete** [ta'peːtə], *f* -/-n wallpaper. ◆'T~**nwechsel,** *m F:* change of scenery.

**tapezier|en** [tape'tsiːrən], *v.tr.* to (wall)paper (a room etc.). ◆T~**er,** *m* -s/- paperhanger. ◆T~**tisch,** *m* (paperhanger's) trestle table.

**tapfer** ['tapfər], *adj.* brave; (*kühn*) bold. ◆'T~**keit,** *f* -/no pl bravery, boldness.

**tappen** ['tapən], *v.i.* (*sein*) to blunder, stumble; (*im Dunkeln*) to grope one's way.

**täppisch** ['tɛpiʃ], *adj.* awkward, clumsy.

**Tarif** [ta'riːf], *m* -s/-e (*a*) (*Gebühr*) rate; charge; (*b*) (*Verzeichnis*) tariff; table of (fixed) charges; (*c*) *Ind:* (wage/salary) scale. ◆T~**lohn,** *m* standard wage(s). ◆T~**verhandlungen,** *fpl* collective bargaining. ◆T~**vertrag,** *m* (collective) wage agreement.

**Tarn-** ['tarn-], *comb.fm. esp. Mil:* camouflage (paint, net etc.). ◆'t~**en,** *v.tr.* to camouflage (sth.); *Fig:* to disguise (s.o., oneself). ◆'T~**ung,** *f* -/-en camouflage; disguise.

**Tasche** ['taʃə], *f* -/-n 1. pocket. 2. (*zum Tragen*) bag. ◆'T~**n-,** *comb.fm.* pocket (lighter, dictionary etc.). ◆'T~**nbuch,** *n* paperback (book). ◆'T~**ndieb(in),** *m* (*f*) pickpocket. ◆'T~**ngeld,** *n* pocket money. ◆'T~**nlampe,** *f* (electric) torch, *N.Am:* flashlight. ◆'T~**nmesser,** *n* penknife. ◆'T~**nrechner,** *m* pocket calculator. ◆'T~**nspieler,** *m* conjurer, juggler. ◆'T~**ntuch,** *n* handkerchief.

**Tasse** ['tasə], *f* -/-n cup.

**Tast|atur** [tasta'tuːr], *f* -/-en keyboard.

◆'T~**e,** *f* -/-n (piano, typewriter etc.) key; (*Druckt.*) push-button. ◆'t~**en,** *v.* 1. *v.i.* (*haben*) to feel; **nach dem Lichtschalter usw. t.,** to feel/grope for the light switch etc. 2. *v.tr.* to feel (sth.), examine (sth.) by touch. ◆'T~**entelefon,** *n* push-button telephone. ◆'T~**sinn,** *m* sense of touch.

**Tat** [taːt], *f* -/-en action; *esp. Lit:* deed. ◆'T~**bestand,** *m* facts of the case; (*Sachlage*) state of affairs. ◆'T~**enlos,** *adj.* inactive, idle; *adv.* without doing anything. ◆'T~**kraft,** *f* energy, vigour. ◆'t~**kräftig,** *adj.* energetic, active. ◆'T~**ort,** *m* scene (*esp. Jur:* of the crime). ◆'T~**sache,** *f* fact. ◆t~**sächlich** [-'zɛçliç], *adj.* (*a*) real (reason, circumstances etc.); actual (time, costs etc.); (*b*) *adv.* actually, really. ◆'T~**verdacht,** *m* suspicion (of having committed a crime).

**Tät|er** ['tɛːtər], *m* -s/- culprit; **die T.,** those responsible. ◆'t~**ig,** *adj.* (*a*) active (person, volcano, co-operation etc.); (*b*) **als Lehrer t. sein,** to work as a teacher etc. ◆'T~**igkeit,** *f* -/-en (*a*) activity; (*Beschäftigung*) occupation; (*Beruf*) profession, job; (*Arbeit*) work; (*b*) *no pl* **in/außer T.,** in/out of operation. ◆'T~**igkeitsbereich,** *m* field/sphere of activity. ◆'t~**lich,** *adj.* violent, physical (assault etc.); *Jur:* **t~licher Angriff,** assault (and battery). ◆'T~**lichkeiten,** *fpl* violence.

**tätowier|en** [tɛto'viːrən], *v.tr.* to tattoo (s.o.). ◆T~**ung,** *f* -/-en tattooing; (*Bild*) tattoo.

**tatt(e)rig** ['tat(ə)riç], *adj. F:* shaky, trembling (hand etc.); doddery (old man etc.).

**Tatze** ['tatsə], *f* -/-n paw.

**Tau¹** [tau], *n* -(e)s/-e *esp. Nau:* (heavy) rope, hawser. ◆'T~**ziehen,** *n* -s/no pl tug-of-war.

**Tau²,** *m* -(e)s/no pl dew. ◆'t~**en,** *v.tr. & i.* (*haben/sein*) to thaw, melt (snow etc.). ◆'t~**frisch,** *adj.* dewy, fresh (as the dew). ◆'T~**tropfen,** *m* dewdrop. ◆'T~**wetter,** *n* thaw.

**taub** [taup], *adj.* 1. deaf (**auf einem Ohr,** in one ear); **die T~en,** the deaf. 2. (*ohne Empfinden*) numb (**vor Kälte,** with cold); **mein Fuß ist t.,** my foot has gone to sleep. 3. empty (nut, ear of grain). ◆'T~**heit,** *f* -/no pl 1. deafness. 2. numbness. ◆'t~**stumm,** *adj.* deaf and dumb; **ein T~**stummer/eine T~**stumme,** a deaf-mute.

**Taube** ['taubə], *f* -/-n 1. pigeon, dove. 2. *Fig:* (*Pers.*) dove. ◆'T~**nschlag,** *m* dovecote.

**Tauch|boot** ['tauxboːt], *n* submarine (for short dives). ◆t~**en** [tauxən]. I. *v.* 1. *v.i.* (*haben/sein*) (*a*) to dive; (*b*) (*im Flug*) to dip. 2. *v.tr.* (*kurz*) to dip (s.o., sth.); (*auf länger*) to immerse, steep (sth.). II. **T.,** *n* -s/no pl diving. ◆'T~**er,** *m* -s/-

diver. ◆'T~er-, *comb.fm.* diver's (suit, helmet etc.); diving (bell etc.). ◆'T~sieder, *m* -s/- (small) coil immersion heater.

Tauf|becken ['taufbɛkən], *n* font. ◆'T~e, *f* -/-n baptism, *Ecc:* christening. ◆'t~en, *v.tr.* (*a*) to baptize, *Ecc:* christen (s.o.); (*b*) (*nennen*) to name (a dog, ship etc.). ◆'T~name, *m* Christian/*N.Am:* given name. ◆'T~pate, *m* godfather. ◆'T~patin, *f* godmother. ◆'T~schein, *m* certificate of baptism. ◆'T~zeuge, *m* godparent.

taug|en ['taugən], *v.i.* (*haben*) (*a*) etwas t., to be good/of use, useful; wenig/nichts t., to be little/no use; zu etwas *dat* t., to be suitable for sth. ◆'T~enichts, *m* -(es)/-e good-for-nothing. ◆t~lich ['tauklıç], *adj.* useful, suitable (zu + *dat*, for); *Mil:* fit (for service). ◆'T~lichkeit, *f* -/no *pl* usefulness, suitability; *Mil:* fitness.

Taum|el ['tauməl], *m* -s/no *pl* (feeling of) giddiness; (*Benommenheit*) grogginess; (*Rausch*) ecstasy, rapture. ◆t~eln, *v.i.* (haben/sein) (*a*) to reel, totter; (*b*) (*Falter*) to flutter.

Tausch [tauʃ], *m* -(e)s/-e exchange. ◆'t~en, *v.* 1. *v.tr.* to exchange (sth.) (für/gegen etwas *acc*, for sth.). 2. *v.i.* (haben) to swap. ◆'T~geschäft, *n* exchange (transaction). ◆'T~handel, *m* barter.

täusch|en ['tɔyʃən], *v.* 1. *v.tr.* (*a*) to deceive (s.o., oneself); sich t., to delude oneself/(*sich irren*) be mistaken/wrong; ich habe mich in ihm getäuscht, I am disappointed in him. 2. *v.i.* (haben) der Schein täuscht, appearances are deceptive. ◆'t~end, *adj.* deceptive (appearance); sie sehen sich t. ähnlich, one can hardly tell them apart. ◆'T~ung, *f* -/-en 1. deception. 2. (*Sinnest.*) illusion; optische T., optical illusion. ◆'T~ungsmanöver, *n* diversion.

tausend ['tauzənt], *num. adj.* a/one thousand; T~e von Menschen, thousands of people. ◆'T~er, *m* -s/- *F:* (*Schein*) thousand mark note. ◆'t~fach, *adj.* a thousandfold; *adv.* in a thousand different ways; (*tausendmal*) a thousand times. ◆'T~füßler, *m* -s/- centipede. ◆'t~'mal, *adv.* a thousand times. ◆'t~ste(r,s), *num.adj.* thousandth. ◆'T~stel, *n* -s/- thousandth (part).

Tax|e ['taksə], *f* -/-n 1. (*Gebühr*) charge, fee; (*Ortst.*) tax. 2. = Taxi. ◆t~ieren [ta'ksi:rən], *v.tr.* to estimate (the value etc. of sth.).

Taxi ['taksi], *n* -s/-s taxi, *N.Am:* cab. ◆'T~fahrer, *m* taxi/*N.Am:* cab driver. ◆'T~stand, *m* taxi/*N.Am:* cab stand.

Teak [ti:k], *n* -s/no *pl*/'T~holz, *n* teak.

Team [ti:m], *n* -s/-s team.

Techn|ik ['tɛçnik], *f* -/-en 1. no *pl* (*a*) technology; (*b*) (*Fach*) engineering. 2. (*a*) (*Methode*) technique; (*b*) *Tchn:* (*Aufbau*)

mechanics, *F:* works (of a machine). ◆'T~iker(in), *m* -s/- (*f* -/-nen) technician; (*Ingenieur*) engineer. ◆'t~isch, *adj.* technical; t. begabt, technically minded; with a technical flair. ◆'T~ologe [-o'lo:gə], *m* -n/-n technologist. ◆'T~ologie [-olo'gi:], *f* -/-n technology. ◆t~o'logisch, *adj.* technological.

Tee [te:], *m* -s/-s tea. ◆'T~beutel, *m* teabag. ◆'T~kanne, *f* teapot. ◆'T~löffel, *m* teaspoon. ◆'T~sieb, *n* tea strainer. ◆'T~stunde, *f* teatime. ◆'T~tasse, *f* teacup. ◆'T~wagen, *m* tea trolley.

Teer [te:r], *m* -(e)s/-e tar. ◆'t~en, *v.tr.* to tar (a road etc.).

Teich [taiç], *m* -(e)s/-e pond.

Teig [taik], *m* -(e)s/-e dough; (*Mürbt.*) pastry. ◆'t~ig [-giç], *adj.* doughy; soggy (cake etc.). ◆'T~rolle, *f* rolling pin. ◆'T~waren, *fpl* pasta.

Teil [tail]. I. *m & n* -(e)s/-e 1. (*a*) *m* part; der vierte/fünfte T. davon, a quarter/fifth of it; zum T., partly, to some extent; zum größten T., for the most part, mostly; (*b*) *n esp. Tchn:* component, part. 2. (*Anteil*) share, portion; sein T. beitragen, to do one's bit. II. 'T~-, 't~-, *comb.fm.* partial (success, result, solution etc.); part (consignment etc.). ◆'t~bar, *adj.* divisible. ◆'T~bereich, *m* section. ◆'T~betrag, *m* part of an amount; (*Rate*) instalment. ◆'T~chen, *n Ph:* particle. ◆'t~en, *v.* 1. *v.tr.* (*a*) (*trennen*) to divide (sth.); sich t., to divide, separate; (*Weg*) to fork; (*Gruppe*) to split up; (*Meinungen*) to differ; 20 geteilt durch 5 ist 4, 20 divided by 5 is 4; (*b*) (*teilhaben an*) to share (a room, profits, *Fig:* opinion, feelings etc.); to divide, split (up) (the profit, booty etc.). 2. *v.i.* (haben) to share. ◆'t~nehmen, *v.i.sep.irr.44* (haben) an etwas *dat* t., to participate/have a share in sth. ◆'T~haber(in), *m* -s/- (*f* -/-nen) *Com:* partner. ◆'T~nahme, *f* -/no *pl* 1. participation (an + *dat*, in). 2. (*Interesse*) interest (an + *dat*, in); *Lit:* (*Mitgefühl*) sympathy. ◆'t~nahmslos, *adj.* indifferent, apathetic (person); expressionless (face). ◆'T~nahmslosigkeit, *f* -/no *pl* indifference; apathy. ◆'t~nehmen, *v.i.sep.irr.69* (haben) (*a*) an etwas *dat* t., to take part in sth.; (*b*) an j-s Freude/Schmerz t., to share in s.o.'s joy/pain. ◆'T~nehmer, *m* -s/- participant; *Sp: etc:* competitor; *Tel:* subscriber. ◆'t~s, *adv.* in part, partly; *F:* wie geht's? t., t., how are you? so-so. ◆'T~stück, *n* fragment. ◆'T~ung, *f* -/-en division. ◆'t~weise, *adj.* partial; *adv.* partly; (*da und dort*) in places; (*ab und zu*) now and then. ◆'T~zahlung, *f* part payment; (*Rate*) instalment; etwas auf T. kaufen, to buy sth. on hire purchase. ◆'T~zeitbeschäftigung, *f* part-time job.

**Teint** [tɛ̃ː], *m* -s/-s complexion.

**Telefon** [tele'fo:n], *n* -s/-e telephone; ◆**T~anruf**, *m* telephone call. ◆**T~at** [-o'na:t], *n* -(e)s/-e telephone call. ◆**T~buch**, *n* telephone directory. ◆**t~ieren** [-o'ni:rən], *v.i.* (*haben*) to telephone, F: phone, make a phone call. ◆**t~isch**, *adj.* (enquiry etc.) on the telephone; **j-n t. benachrichtigen**, to inform s.o. by telephone. ◆**T~ist(in)** [-o'nist(in)], *m* -en/-en (*f* -/-nen) telephone operator; telephonist. ◆**T~nummer**, *f* telephone number. ◆**T~zelle**, *f* (tele)phone box. ◆**T~zentrale**, *f* telephone exchange.

**Telegraf** [tele'gra:f], *m* -en/-en telegraph. ◆**T~enmast**, *m* telegraph pole. ◆**T~ie** [-a'fi:], *f* -/no *pl* telegraphy. ◆**t~ieren** [-'fi:rən], *v.i.* (*haben*) (j-m) **t.**, to send (s.o.) a telegram/(*nach Übersee*) cable. ◆**t~isch** [-'gra:fiʃ], *adj.* telegraphic (message, remittance etc.); (reply) by telegram.

**Telegramm** [tele'gram]. I. *n* -s/-e telegram, (*nach Übersee*) cable. II. **T~-,** *comb.fm.* telegram (form etc.); telegraphic (address, style).

**Teleobjektiv** ['te:le?ɔpjekti:f], *n* telephoto lens.

**Telepath|ie** [telepa'ti:], *f* -/no *pl* telepathy. ◆**t~isch** [-'pa:tiʃ], *adj.* telepathic.

**Telephon** [tele'fo:n], *n* -s/-e = Telefon.

**Teleskop** [tele'sko:p], *n* -s/-e telescope.

**Telex** ['te:lɛks], *n* -/-e *pl* telex.

**Teller** ['tɛlər], *m* -s/- plate. ◆**'t~förmig**, *adj.* plate-shaped (disc etc.). ◆**'T~wäscher**, *m* dishwasher.

**Tempel** ['tɛmpəl], *m* -s/- temple.

**Temperament** [tɛmpera'mɛnt], *n* -(e)s/-e 1. (*Gemütsart*) temperament, disposition. 2. (a) (*Schwung*) vivacity; high spirits; (b) (*Leidenschaft*) fire. ◆**t~los**, *adj.* spiritless, phlegmatic. ◆**t~voll**, *adj.* spirited; (*feurig*) fiery, hot-blooded; ardent (lover etc.).

**Temperatur** [tɛmpera'tu:r], *f* -/-en temperature. ◆**T~abfall**, *m* drop in temperature. ◆**T~anstieg**, *m* rise in temperature. ◆**T~regler**, *m* thermostat.

**Tempo** ['tɛmpo], *n* -s/-s 1. speed; **ein gemächliches T.**, a leisurely pace. 2. *pl* **Tempi** *Mus:* tempo; **das T. angeben**, to beat/mark time; *Sp: etc:* to set the pace.

**Tendenz** [tɛn'dɛnts], *f* -/-en tendency; (*Neigung*) inclination; **allgemeine T.**, general trend. ◆**t~iell**, *adv.* in keeping with the trend. ◆**t~iös**, *adj.* tendentious; (politically etc.) biased.

**Tender** ['tɛndər], *m* -s/- tender.

**tendieren** [tɛn'di:rən], *v.i.* (*haben*) to tend, have a tendency; **nach rechts/links t.**, to have right-/leftwing leanings.

**Tennis** ['tɛnis]. I. *n* -/no *pl* (lawn) tennis. II. **'T~-,** *comb.fm.* tennis (ball, club, shoes, player etc.). ◆**'T~platz**, *m* tennis court. ◆**'T~schläger**, *m* tennis racket.

**Tenor** [te'no:r], *m* -s/-e tenor.

**Teppich** ['tɛpiç], *m* -s/-e carpet. ◆**T~boden**, *m* fitted carpet. ◆**'T~klopfer**, *m* -s/- carpet beater.

**Termin** [tɛr'mi:n]. I. *m* -s/-e date; (*Zeit*) time; (*beim Arzt usw.*) appointment. ◆**t~gemäß/t~gerecht**, *adj.* on time/ schedule. ◆**t~ieren** [-i'ni:rən], *v.tr.* to fix the date for (sth.). ◆**T~kalender**, *m* -s/- engagements book.

**Termin|ologie** [tɛrminolo'gi:], *f* -/-n [-ən] terminology. ◆**T~us** ['tɛrminus], *m* -/ -ni term, expression.

**Termite** [tɛr'mi:tə], *f* -/-n termite, white ant.

**Terpentin** [tɛrpen'ti:n], *n* -s/-e turpentine.

**Terrain** [tɛ'rɛ̃ː], *n* -s/-s *esp. Mil:* terrain; **T. gewinnen**, to gain ground.

**Terrasse** [tɛ'rasə], *f* -/-n terrace.

**Terrier** ['tɛriər], *m* -s/- terrier.

**Terrine** [tɛ'ri:nə], *f* -/-n tureen.

**Territorium** [tɛri'to:rium], *n* -s/-rien territory.

**Terror** ['tɛrɔr]. I. *m* -s/no *pl* terrorism; (*also* **T~herrschaft** *f*) reign of terror; (*Druck*) intimidation. II. **T~-,** *comb.fm.* terrorist (act, attack, methods etc.). ◆**t~isieren** [-i'zi:rən], *v.tr.* to terrorize (a community etc.). ◆**T~ismus** [-'rismus], *m* -/no *pl* terrorism. ◆**T~ist** [-'rist], *m* -en/-en terrorist. ◆**t~istisch**, *adj.* terrorist.

**Tertia** ['tɛrtsia], *f* -/-ien fourth and fifth years (in a *Gymnasium*).

**Terz** [tɛrts], *f* -/-en third.

**Test** [tɛst]. I. *m* -(e)s/-s & -e test. II. **'T~-,** *comb.fm.* test (picture, drive, flight, pilot etc.); trial (game etc.). ◆**t~en**, *v.tr.* to test (s.o., sth.). ◆**'T~stopp**, *m* (atomic) test ban.

**Testament** [tɛsta'mɛnt], *n* -(e)s/-e 1. *Jur:* will. 2. **das Alte/Neue T.**, the Old/New Testament. ◆**t~arisch** [-'ta:riʃ], *adj.* testamentary (legacy etc.). ◆**T~svollstrecker**, *m* executor.

**Tetanus** ['te:tanus], *m* -/no *pl* tetanus, lockjaw.

**teuer** ['tɔyər], *adj.* 1. expensive; (*wertvoll*) valuable; **wie t. ist dieser Stoff?** how much does this material cost? 2. *Lit:* (*lieb*) dear (friend etc.). ◆**'T~ung**, *f* -/ -en rise in prices.

**Teufel** ['tɔyfəl], *m* -s/- devil; *F: int.* **pfui T.!** ugh! how disgusting! **zum T. (nochmal)!** damn it all! **wer zum T. hat das gesagt?** who on earth said that? ◆**'T~saustreibung** *f* exorcism. ◆**'T~skerl**, *m* *F:* daredevil. ◆**'T~skreis**, *m* vicious circle.

**teuflisch** ['tɔyfliʃ], *adj.* diabolical, devilish (plan etc.); fiendish (smile etc.).

**Text** [tɛkst], *m* -(e)s/-e (a) text; (*Stückt.*) passage; (b) (*Bildt.*) caption; (c) *Mus:* words (of a song); (*Opernt.*) libretto.

◆t~en ['tɛkstən], v.tr. (a) Mus: to write lyrics; (b) (Werbung etc.) to write copy. ◆'T~er, m -s/- (a) Mus: lyrics writer; (b) (Werbet. etc.) copywriter. ◆'T~stelle, f passage.

Textil- [tɛks'tiːl-], comb.fm. textile (industry, worker). ◆T~ien [-'tiːliən], pl textiles.

Thai|land ['tailant]. Pr.n.n -s. Thailand. ◆'T~länder(in), m -s/- (f -/-nen) Thai (man/woman). ◆'t~ländisch, adj. Thai.

Theater [te'aːtər]. I. n -s/- 1. theatre, N.Am: theater; T. spielen, to act. 2. (Getue) fuss. II. T~-, comb.fm. theatrical (agency, performance etc.); theatre (ticket, critic, programme etc.); drama (group, critic etc.). ◆T~besucher, m playgoer. ◆'T~kasse, f theatre box office. ◆T~stück, n (stage) play.

theatralisch [tea'trɑːliʃ], adj. theatrical.

Theke ['teːkə], f -/-n bar; (Ladentisch) counter.

Them|a ['teːma], n -s/-men & -mata (a) subject; (Gesprächst.) topic; (b) Mus: theme. ◆t~'atisch, adj. with regard to the subject.

Themse ['tɛmzə]. Pr.n.f -. die T., the (River) Thames.

Theolog|e [teo'loːgə], m -n/-n theologian. ◆T~ie [-o'giː], f -/-n [-ən] theology. ◆t~isch, adj. theological.

Theor|etiker [teo're:tikər], m -s/- theorist. ◆t~etisch [-'reːtiʃ], adj. theoretical. ◆T~ie [teo'riː], f -/-n [-ən] theory.

Therap|eut(in) [tera'pɔʏt(in)], m -en/-en (f -/-nen) therapist. ◆t~eutisch, adj. therapeutic. ◆T~ie [-'piː], f -/-n [-ən] therapy.

Therm|albad [tɛr'mɑlbaːt], n thermal bath. 2. (Ort) thermal spa. ◆T~ometer [-o'meːtər], n thermometer. ◆'T~osflasche, f R.t.m. thermos (flask). ◆T~ostat [-o'stɑːt], m -(e)s & -en/-e(n) thermostat.

These ['teːzə], f -/-n thesis.

Thrombose [trɔm'boːzə], f -/-n thrombosis.

Thron [troːn], m -(e)s/-e throne. ◆'t~en, v.i. (haben) to sit in state. ◆'T~erbe, m heir to the throne. ◆'T~folge, f (line of) succession. ◆'T~folger(in), m -s/- (f -/-nen) successor to the throne.

Thunfisch ['tuːnfiʃ], m tuna.

Thüring|en ['tyːriŋən]. Pr.n.n -s. Thuringia. ◆'T~er(in), m -s/- (f -/-nen) Thuringian.

Thymian ['tyːmiaːn], m -s/-e thyme.

Tibet ['tiːbɛt]. Pr.n.n -s. Tibet. ◆T~aner(in) [tibe'tɑːnər(in)], m -s/- (f -/-nen) Tibetan.

Tick [tik], m -(e)s/-s F: quirk; einen T. haben, (i) to be a bit crazy; (ii) to have an obsession (mit + dat, about). ◆'t~en, v.i. (haben) to tick.

tief [tiːf]. I. adj. 1. (a) deep (gorge, water,

roots, Fig: silence, sleep, voice etc.); zwei Meter t., two metres deep; t. atmen, to breathe deeply, take a deep breath; (b) (sehr stark) intense (hate, pain etc.); im t~sten Winter, in the depth of winter; bis t. in die Nacht, far into the night. 2. (niedrig) low (cloud, blow, Mus: note etc.); t. ausgeschnittenes Kleid, low-cut dress; Av: t. fliegen, to fly low. II. T., n -s/-s Meteor: depression. III. comb.fm. 1. 'T~-, (a) deep (drilling, ploughing etc.); (b) low (pressure, flying etc.). 2. 't~-, adj. (a) deeply (offended, moved, felt etc.); (b) (Farben) deep (blue, red etc.). ◆'T~bau, m civil engineering; underground and surface level construction. ◆T~druckgebiet, n Meteor: depression. ◆T~e ['tiːfə], f -/-n (a) depth; aus der T., from far below; (b) (Tiefgründigkeit) profundity, depth (of insight, thoughts etc.); (c) (Stärke) intensity (of love, pain etc.). ◆'T~ebene, f lowland, low plain. ◆'T~enpsychologie, f depth psychology. ◆'T~enschärfe, f Phot: depth of focus. ◆'T~flug, m low-level flight. ◆'T~gang, m Nau: draught, N.Am: draft. ◆'T~garage, f underground car park. ◆'t~greifend, adj. far-reaching, radical (changes etc.); thorough (investigation etc.). ◆'t~gründig, adj. profound (observation etc.). ◆'t~kühlen, v.tr.sep. (a) (deep) freeze (fruit, vegetables etc.). ◆'T~kühlfach, n freezer compartment. ◆'T~kühlkost, f frozen food. ◆'T~kühltruhe, f deepfreeze, chest freezer. ◆'T~land, n lowland plain; pl lowlands. ◆'T~punkt, m low (point); Fig: low ebb. ◆'T~schlag, m blow below the belt. ◆'t~schürfend, adj. penetrating, thorough-going. ◆'T~see, f deep sea. ◆'T~sinn, m profundity (of thought etc.). ◆'t~sinnig, adj. (a) profound; (b) (grüblerisch) pensive. ◆'t~sitzend, adj. deep-seated. ◆'T~st-, comb.fm. lowest, minimum (price, temperature etc.). ◆'T~stand, m (also Fig:) low watermark; Com:etc: low (point). ◆'t~stapeln, v.i.sep. (haben) F: to understate a case.

Tiegel ['tiːgəl], m -s/- 1. Cu: shallow saucepan. 2. Tchn: crucible.

Tier [tiːr]. I. n -(e)s/-e animal. II. 'T~-, comb.fm. animal (book, story, world etc.); animals' (home etc.). ◆'T~arzt, m veterinary surgeon, F: vet. ◆'T~freund, m animal lover. ◆'T~garten, m zoo. ◆'t~isch, adj. (a) animal (fat, protein etc.); (b) Pej: bestial, brutal (behaviour etc.); (c) F: adv. t. ernst, deadly serious. ◆'T~kreiszeichen, n sign of the zodiac. ◆'T~kunde, f zoology. ◆'t~lieb, adj. fond of animal. ◆'T~liebe, f love of animals. ◆'T~park, m (large) zoo. ◆'T~quälerei, f cruelty to animals. ◆'T~-

**reich,** n animal kingdom. ◆'T~**schutz-verein,** m society for the prevention of cruelty to animals.

**Tiger** ['ti:gər], m -s/- tiger.

**tilg|en** ['tilgən], v.tr. (a) Fin: to pay off, repay (a debt etc.); (b) Lit: to eradicate, erase (a mistake etc.), obliterate, efface (memories, Fig: traces etc.); ◆'T~**ung,** f -/-en (a) Fin: repayment; (b) Lit: eradication, obliteration.

**Tint|e** ['tintə], f -/-n ink. ◆'T~**enfisch,** m squid; (Krake) octopus. ◆'T~**enklecks,** m ink blot. ◆'T~**enstift,** m indelible pencil.

**Tip** [tip], m -s/-s tip.

**tipp|en¹** ['tipən], v.tr. & i. (haben) (a) j-m, j-n auf die Schulter t., to tap s.o. on the shoulder; (b) F: to type (sth.). ◆'T~**fehler,** m typing mistake.

'**tipp|en²,** v.i. (haben) (a) **ich tippe darauf, daß** ..., it's my guess that ...; (b) (wetten) to have a flutter; (im Toto) to fill in the pools. ◆'T~**zettel,** m lottery/ (Toto) pools coupon.

**tipptopp** ['tip'tɔp], adj. F: tip-top, spotless.

**Tirol** [ti'ro:l]. Pr.n.n -s. T., the Tyrol.

**Tisch** [tiʃ]. I. m -(e)s/-e table; **am T. sitzen,** to sit at the table; F: **es fiel unter den T.,** it went by the board; **diese Sache muß vom T.,** this matter must be dealt with. II. 'T~-, comb.fm. table (leg, lamp, manners etc.); (ledge etc.) of the table; (neighbour etc.) at table; dinner (guest etc.). ◆'T~**decke,** f tablecloth. ◆'T~**ler,** m -s/- joiner; (Kunstt.) cabinet-maker; (Baut.) carpenter. ◆T~**le'rei,** f -/-en 1. no pl joinery; carpentry. 2. joiner's/carpenter's workshop. ◆'T~**rede,** f after-dinner speech. ◆'T~**tennis,** n table tennis.

**Titel** ['ti:təl]. I. m -s/- title. II. 'T~-, comb.fm. title (figure, Th: role, Sp: holder etc.). ◆'T~**bild,** n frontispiece; cover picture (of a magazine). ◆'T~**blatt,** n title page. ◆'T~**verteidiger,** m defender (of the title), defending champion.

**Toast** [to:st], m -(e)s/-e & -s 1. Cu: (piece of) toast. 2. (Trinkspruch) toast. ◆'t~**en,** v.tr. to toast (bread).

**tob|en** ['to:bən], v.i. (a) (haben) (Pers., Fig: Meer usw.) to rage; (Pers.) to rave, rant (**gegen** j-n, at s.o.); (b) (haben/sein) (Kinder) to romp (about). ◆'T~**sucht,** f -/no pl frenzy, raving madness. ◆'t~**süchtig,** adj. raving mad.

**Tochter** ['tɔxtər], f -/- daughter. ◆'T~**gesellschaft,** f subsidiary (company).

**Tod** [to:t], m -(e)s/-e death. ◆'t~**bringend,** adj. deadly (poison), fatal (illness); lethal (weapons etc.). ◆'t~**ernst,** adj. F: deadly serious. ◆T~**es-** ['to:dəs-] comb.fm. death (blow, cell etc.); (year, time, cause etc.) of (s.o.'s) death; fatal (blow etc.).

◆'T~**esangst,** f (a) fear of death; (b) (große Angst) mortal fear. ◆'T~**esanzeige,** f notice of death, obituary. ◆'T~**esfall,** m death, fatality. ◆'T~**eskampf,** m death throes/agony. ◆'T~**esopfer,** n casualty. ◆'T~**esstrafe,** f death penalty. ◆'T~**estag,** m day/(Jubiläum) anniversary of (s.o.'s) death. ◆'T~**esurteil,** n death sentence. ◆'T~**esverachtung,** f (a) contempt for death; (b) utter contempt. ◆'T~**feind,** m mortal/deadly enemy. ◆'t~**krank,** adj. fatally ill. ◆'t~**langweilig,** adj. F: deadly boring. ◆'t~**müde,** adj. F: dead tired. ◆'t~**sicher,** adj. F: (a) dead certain; sure-fire (method etc.); (b) (untrüglich) unerring (instinct etc.). ◆'T~**sünde,** f deadly/Ecc: mortal sin. ◆'t~**unglücklich,** adj. F: dreadfully unhappy.

**tödlich** ['tø:tliç], adj. fatal (illness, accident, wound etc.); deadly (blow, weapon, poison etc.); lethal (dose etc.); **t. verunglücken,** to die in an accident; **t. beleidigt,** mortally offended.

**Toilette** [toa'lɛtə], f -/-n 1. (Abort) lavatory, toilet; N.Am: john. 2. (a) (Ankleiden usw.) toilet; (b) (Kleidung) dress. ◆T~**n-,** comb.fm. toilet (article, paper, soap, water etc.). ◆T~**ntisch,** m dressing table, N.Am: dresser.

**toler|ant** [tole'rant], adj. tolerant. ◆T~**anz** ['rants], f -/no pl tolerance. ◆t~**ieren** [-'ri:rən], v.tr. to tolerate (s.o., sth.).

**toll** [tɔl], adj. 1. (ausgelassen) wild, (verrückt) crazy (pranks, ideas). 2. F: (großartig) super, terrific (idea etc.), smashing (girl), stunning (woman). ◆'T~**heit,** f/no pl craziness, madness. ◆'T~**kirsche,** f deadly nightshade, belladonna. ◆'t~**kühn,** adj. foolhardy, reckless. ◆'T~**wut,** f rabies.

**Tolpatsch** ['tɔlpatʃ], m -(e)s/-e F: clumsy fellow.

**Tölpel** ['tœlpəl], m -s/- F: blockhead. ◆'t~**haft,** adj. silly.

**Tomate** [to'ma:tə], f -/-n tomato. ◆T~**n-,** comb.fm. tomato (juice, sauce etc.). ◆T~**nmark,** m tomato puree.

**Tombola** ['tɔmbola], f -/-s & -len raffle, tombola.

**Ton¹** [to:n]. I. m -(e)s/-e clay. II. 'T~-, comb.fm. clay (pit, pipe, pigeon etc.); earthenware (pot etc.). ◆'T~**waren,** fpl earthenware.

**Ton².** I. m -(e)s/=e 1. (a) sound; F: **große T~e reden/spucken,** to talk big; (b) Mus: note; Fig: **den T. angeben,** to call the tune; (c) (Betonung) stress. 2. (a) (Redeweise, Tonfall) tone (of voice); (b) **der gute T.,** good form/manners. 3. (Farbt.) tone, shade. II. 'T~-, comb.fm. sound (film, camera, quality etc.). ◆'T~**abnehmer,** m cartridge. ◆'t~**angebend,** adj. trend-setting.

◆'T~arm, m pickup (arm). ◆'T~art, f Mus: key. ◆'T~band, n (recording) tape. ◆'T~bandgerät, n tape recorder. ◆'T~fall, m (a) intonation; (Akzent) accent; (b) (Redeweise) tone of voice. ◆'T~höhe, f pitch (of a note). ◆'T~kopf, m recording head. ◆'T~lage, f pitch. ◆'T~leiter, f scale. ◆'t~los, adj. soundless; toneless (voice etc.). ◆'T~stärke, f volume. ◆'T~techniker, m sound engineer.

tön|en ['tø:nən], v. 1. v.i. (haben) (a) to sound, (Glocke) ring; (b) F:.(prahlen) to boast. 2. v.tr. to tint (hair etc.). ◆'T~ung, f -/-n tint, shade.

tönern ['tø:nərn], adj. clay.

Tonne ['tɔnə], f -/-n 1. (Faß) barrel; (Regent.) butt; (Müllt.) dustbin. 2. Meas: ton.

Topf [tɔpf]. I. m -(e)s/⁼e pot; Cu: (sauce)pan. II. 'T~-, comb.fm. pot (plant etc.); potted (flower, plant); pan (lid, cleaner etc.). ◆'T~lappen, m oven cloth.

Töpfer ['tœpfər], m -s/- potter. ◆T~ei [-'rai], f -/-en (Werkstatt) pottery. ◆'t~n, v.i. (haben) to make pottery. ◆'T~scheibe, f potter's wheel. ◆'T~waren, fpl pottery.

Topographie [topogra'fi:], f -/-n topography.

Tor¹ [to:r]. I. n -(e)s/-e 1. gate; door (of a garage etc.). 2. Fb: etc: goal. II. 'T~-, comb.fm. Fb: etc: goal (difference, line etc.); scoring (chance etc.). ◆'T~bogen, m archway. ◆'T~hüter, m Fb:etc: goalkeeper. ◆'T~pfosten, m Sp: goalpost. ◆'T~schlußpanik, f last-minute panic. ◆'T~schütze, m goal scorer. ◆'T~wart, m goalkeeper.

Tor², m -en/-en fool. ◆'T~heit, f -/-en folly.

Torf [tɔrf], m -(e)s/no pl peat.

töricht ['tø:riçt], adj. foolish, (dumm) stupid.

torkeln ['tɔrkəln], v.i. (sein) F: to reel, stagger.

torped|ieren [tɔrpe'di:rən], v.tr. to torpedo (a ship, Fig: plan). ◆T~o [-'pe:do], m -s/-s torpedo.

Torte ['tɔrtə], f -/-n (a) cream cake, gateau; (b) (Obstt.) (fruit) flan. ◆'T~nboden, m flan case.

Tortur [tɔr'tu:r], f -/-en agony, torture.

tosen ['to:zən], v.i. (haben) to roar, (Sturm) rage.

Toskana [tɔs'ka:na]. Pr.n.f -. die T., Tuscany.

tot [to:t], adj. (a) dead; mein t~er Onkel, my late uncle; (b) Fig: lifeless, dull (eyes etc.); deserted (city etc.); t~er Winkel, blind spot; (c) t~er Punkt, impasse, deadlock; (Stillstand) standstill; (Pers.) einen t~en Punkt haben, to be at a low ebb; Sp: t~es Rennen, dead heat. ◆'t~arbeiten, v.refl. F: sich t., to work oneself to death. ◆'T~e(r), m

& f decl. as adj. dead person; (Todesopfer) casualty; die T~n, the dead. ◆'T~en-, comb.fm. death(-bed, mask etc.). ◆'t~en'blaß, adj. deathly pale. ◆'T~engräber, m gravedigger. ◆'T~enhemd, n shroud. ◆'T~enkopf, m death's head, skull. ◆'T~enmesse, f requiem (mass). ◆'T~enschein, m death certificate. ◆'T~enstarre, f rigor mortis. ◆'t~en'still, adj. dead still/silent. ◆'T~enstille, f dead silence. ◆'T~entanz, m dance of death. ◆'t~geboren, adj. ein t~geborenes Kind, (i) a stillborn child; (ii) F: a doomed/abortive enterprise. ◆'T~geburt, f stillbirth; (Kind) stillborn child. ◆'t~kriegen, v.tr.sep. F: er/es ist nicht totzukriegen, he/it just goes on and on. ◆'t~lachen, v.refl.sep. sich t., to split one's sides laughing. ◆'T~schlag, m manslaughter, homicide. ◆'t~schlagen, v.tr. sep.irr.85 to kill (s.o., F: time, sth.). ◆'T~schläger, m -s/- 1. (Pers.) killer. 2. (Stock) life-preserver. ◆'t~schweigen, v.tr.sep.irr.89 to hush up (sth.), ignore (s.o.) completely. ◆'t~stellen, v.refl.sep. sich t., to pretend to be dead.

total [to'ta:l], adj. total. ◆T~isator [-ali'za:tɔr], m -s/-en totalizator, F: tote. ◆t~i'tär, adj. totalitarian. ◆T~schaden, m (Fahrzeug) T. haben, to be a write-off.

töt|en ['tø:tən], v.tr. to kill (s.o., oneself, an animal, a nerve). ◆'T~ung, f -/no pl killing; Jur: homicide.

Toto ['to:to], n & m -s/-s (football) pool(s). ◆'T~schein, m pools coupon.

Toupet [tu'pe:], n -s/-s toupet. ◆t~ieren [-'pi:rən], v.tr. to back-comb (one's hair).

Tour [tu:r], f -/-en 1. (Ausflug) excursion, tour; (Fahrt) trip. 2. F: (a) (Art und Weise) way; auf die dumme/langsame T., stupidly/slowly; (b) (Trick) ploy; krumme T~en, shady dealings. 3. Tchn: (Umdrehung) revolution; auf vollen T~en laufen, to be running flat out; (Aktion) to be in full swing; F: j-n auf T~en bringen, to spur s.o. into action; in einer T., incessantly; without stopping. ◆'T~ismus [-'rismus], m -/no pl tourism. ◆T~ist [-'rist], m -en/-en tourist. ◆T~isten-, comb.fm. tourist (hotel, class, traffic etc.). ◆T~nee [tur'ne:], f -/-n tour.

Trab [tra:p], m -(e)s/no pl trot; F: j-n auf T. bringen, to make s.o. get a move on. ◆t~en ['tra:bən], v.i. (sein) to trot. ◆'T~er, m -s/- trotter, trotting horse. ◆'T~rennen, n trotting race.

Trabant [tra'bant], m -en/-en satellite. ◆T~enstadt, f satellite town.

Tracht [traxt], f -/-en 1. traditional costume; (Amtskleidung) official dress, (nurse's) uniform. 2. F: eine T. Prügel, a sound thrashing. ◆'t~en, *v.i.* (*haben*) *Lit:* nach etwas *dat* t., to strive for sth.; j-m nach dem Leben t., to make an attempt on s.o.'s life.

**trächtig** ['trɛçtiç], *adj.* pregnant (animal).

**Tradi|tion** [traditsi'oːn], *f* -/-en tradition. ◆t~tio'nell, *adj.* traditional.

**Trafo** ['traːfo], *m* -s/-s transformer.

**Trag|bahre** ['traːkbaːrə], *f* -/-en stretcher. ◆'t~bar, *adj.* (*a*) portable; *Cl:* fit to wear, wearable; (*b*) (*erträglich*) bearable; (*annehmbar*) acceptable (für + *acc*, to). ◆t~en ['traːgən], *v.irr.85* 1. *v.tr.* (*a*) to carry (s.o., sth.); (*irgendwohin*) to take (sth.) (somewhere); (*Baum usw.*) to bear (fruit); *Fig:* to bear (responsibility, a name, *Fin:* losses, costs etc.); **die Schuld an etwas** *dat* t., to be guilty of sth.; (*b*) (*ertragen*) to bear (suffering, one's fate etc.); (*c*) to wear (clothes, spectacles, a ring etc.); to have (a beard); (*d*) *refl.* **sich mit einem Gedanken** t., to toy with an idea. 2. *v.i.* (*haben*) (*a*) **das Eis trägt nicht**, the ice won't take your weight; (*b*) (*Baum*) **gut/schlecht** t., to produce a good/bad crop. ◆'T~etasche, *f* carrier bag. ◆'t~fähig, *adj.* capable of supporting a load. ◆'T~fähigkeit, *f* buoyancy (of water). ◆'T~fläche, *f Av:* wing. ◆'T~flächenboot, *n* hydrofoil. ◆'T~weite, *f* 1. range. 2. *Fig:* (*Bedeutung*) significance; (*Folgen*) consequences (of an action/decision).

**träge** ['trɛːgə], *adj.* sluggish; (*Pers.*) lethargic; *Ph:* t. **Masse**, inert mass.

**Träger(in)** ['trɛːgər(in)], *m* -s/- (*f* -/-nen) 1. (*Pers.*) (*a*) carrier (of a load, illness etc.); bearer (of a load, news, a title etc.); (*b*) wearer (of clothing); (*c*) holder (of a prize, office etc.). 2. *Tchn:* beam; (*aus Stahl*) girder; (*Stütze*) support. 3. *Cl:* (shoulder) strap; (*Hosent.*) braces, *N.Am:* suspenders. ◆'T~rakete, *f* launch vehicle.

**Trägheit** ['trɛːkhait], *f* -/no *pl* sluggishness; lethargy; *Ph: etc:* inertia.

**Trag|ik** ['traːgik], *f* -/no *pl* tragedy. ◆'t~ikomisch, *adj.* tragicomic. ◆'T~ikomödie, *f* tragicomedy. ◆'t~isch, *adj.* tragic. ◆T~ödie [tra'gøːdiə], *f* -/-n tragedy.

**Train|er** ['trɛːnər], *m* -s/- *Sp:* trainer; *Fb:* (trainer-)manager. ◆t~ieren [-'ɛː'niːrən], *v.tr.&i.* (*haben*) to train (s.o., a team, horse etc.); to exercise (muscles). ◆T~ing ['trɛːnɪŋ], *n* -s/-s training. ◆'T~ings-, *comb.fm.* training (camp, method, facilities etc.). ◆'T~ingsanzug, *m* track suit.

**Trakt** [trakt], *m* -(e)s/-e tract. ◆T~at [-'taːt], *m & n* -(e)s/-e (scientific etc.) treatise. ◆t~ieren [-'tiːrən], *v.tr.* (*a*) to give (s.o.) a rough time; (*b*) (*plagen*) to plague, torment (s.o.).

**Traktor** ['traktor], *m* -s/-en tractor.

**trällern** ['trɛlərn], *v.tr.* & *i.* (*haben*) to warble (a tune etc.).

**tramp|eln** ['trampəln], *v.* 1. *v.i.* (*a*) (*haben*) (*stampfen*) to stamp (one's feet); (*b*) (*sein*) to stamp, stomp (along). 2. *v.tr.* to trample (s.o., sth.). ◆t~en ['trɛmpən], *v.i.* (*sein*) *F:* to hitchhike. ◆T~olin ['trampoliːn], *n* -s/-e trampoline.

**Tran** [traːn], *m* -(e)s/-e 1. train oil. 2. *F:* **im** T., dopey.

**Trance** ['trɑ̃ːs(ə)], *f* -/-n trance.

**Tranchier-** [trã'fiːr-], *comb.fm.* carving (knife etc.). ◆'T~besteck, *n* carving set. ◆t~en, *v.tr.* to carve (meat).

**Träne** ['trɛːnə], *f* -/-n tear. ◆'t~n, *v.i.* (*haben*) to water. ◆'T~ngas, *n* tear gas. ◆'t~nüberströmt, *adj.* tearstained.

**Tränke** ['trɛŋkə], *f* -/-n watering place; (*Trog*) drinking trough. ◆'t~n, *v.tr.* (*a*) to water (animals); (*b*) to soak (sth.) (**mit** + *dat*, with).

**Transform|ator** [transfɔr'maːtɔr], *m* -s/-en transformer. ◆t~ieren [-'miːrən], *v.tr.* to transform (current etc.).

**Transistor** [tran'zistɔr], *m* -s/-en (*a*) *El:* transistor; (*b*) (*also* T~gerät *n*) transistor radio.

**Transit-** [tran'ziːt-, tranzit-], *comb.fm.* transit (goods, traffic etc.). ◆t~iv ['tranzitiːf], *adj.* transitive (verb).

**transparent** [transpa'rɛnt]. I. *adj.* transparent. II. T., *n* -(e)s/-e banner.

**Transpiration** [transpiratsi'oːn], *f* -/-en perspiration.

**Transplant|ation** [transplantatsi'oːn], *f* -/-en transplant; (skin) graft. ◆t~ieren [-'tiːrən], *v.tr.* to transplant (an organ); to graft (tissue, skin).

**Transport** [trans'pɔrt]. I. *m* -(e)s/-e 1. (*Transportieren*) transport; *Aut: Rail:* haulage (of goods, people). 2. consignment, shipment (of goods). II. T~-, *comb.fm.* transport (worker, vehicle, aircraft etc.); carriage, freight (costs, charges, insurance etc.). ◆t~abel [-'taːbəl], *adj.* transportable. ◆T~er, *m* -s/- transport vehicle. ◆t~fähig, *adj.* movable. ◆t~ieren [-'tiːrən], *v.tr.* to transport, (*per Schiff*) ship (goods, people); to move (a patient). ◆T~mittel, *n* means of transport/transportation. ◆T~unternehmen, *n* transport/haulage company.

**Transvestit** [transvɛs'tiːt], *m* -en/-en transvestite.

**Trapez** [tra'peːts], *n* -es/-e 1. trapeze. 2. *Mth.* trapezium.

**Trasse** ['trasə], *f* -/-n (marked-out) line, route (for a road etc.).

**Tratsch** [traːtʃ], *m* -(e)s/no *pl F: Pej:* gossip. ◆t~en, *v.i.* (*haben*) to gossip.

**Tratte** ['tratə], *f* -/-n *Com:* draft.

**trau|en** ['trauən], *v.* 1. *v.tr.* to marry (a couple). 2. *v.i.* (*haben*) j-m, etwas *dat* t., to trust s.o., sth. 3. *v.refl.* **sich** t., to dare (etwas **zu tun**, to do sth.). ◆'T~ring, *m* wedding ring. ◆'T~schein, *m* marriage certificate.

◆'**T~ung**, f -/-en wedding/marriage ceremony. ◆'**T~zeuge**, m/'**T~zeugin**, f witness.

**Traube** ['traubə], f -/-n **1.** grape. **2.** Fig: cluster (of people etc.). ◆'**T~nernte** fl '**T~nlese**, f grape harvest. ◆'**T~nsaft**, m grape juice. ◆'**T~nzucker**, m glucose.

**Trauer** ['trauər]. **I.** f -/no pl **1.** sorrow, grief; **T. um den Verstorbenen,** sorrow/mourning for the deceased. **2.** (a) (T~zeit) (period of) mourning; (b) (T~kleidung) **T. tragen,** to wear mourning. **II.** '**T~-,** comb.fm. mourning (veil, period etc.); (house, year etc.) of mourning; funeral (service, march etc.). ◆'**T~fall**, m bereavement. ◆'**T~feier**, f funeral/burial service. ◆'**t~n**, v.i. (haben) (a) to grieve, mourn (**um** + acc, for). ◆'**T~spiel**, n tragedy. ◆'**T~weide**, f weeping willow. ◆'**T~zug**, m funeral procession.

**träufeln** ['trɔyfəln], v. **1.** v.tr. to let (sth.) drip/trickle. **2.** v.i. (haben/sein) to drip, trickle.

**traulich** ['traulıç], adj. intimate, cosy.

**Traum** [traum], m -(e)s/⸗e dream. ◆'**T~bild**, n vision. ◆'**t~haft**, adj. **1.** dreamlike. **2.** F: (wunderbar) fabulous, fantastic.

**Trauma** ['trauma], n -s/-men trauma. ◆**t~tisch** [-'mɑːtıʃ], adj. traumatic.

**träum|en** ['trɔymən], v.tr.&i. (haben) to dream (sth.); **das hätte ich mir nie t. lassen,** I would never have imagined that possible. ◆'**T~er,** m -s/- dreamer. ◆**T~e'rei,** f -/-en daydream.

**traurig** ['trauriç], adj. sad. ◆'**T~keit**, f -/no pl sadness.

**Treck** [trɛk], m -s/-s trek; (Zug) trail (of refugees etc.).

**Treff** [trɛf], m -s/-s F: (a) get-together; (b) = **T~punkt** m. ◆'**t~en. I.** v.tr. **1.** v.tr. (a) (schlagen) to hit (s.o., a target etc.); **vom Blitz getroffen,** struck by lightning; Fig: **dieser Vorwurf traf ihn schwer,** this reproach hurt him deeply; (b) (richtig erfassen) to get (sth.) right; to hit on (the right thing/tone etc.); (c) refl. **es trifft sich gut/schlecht, daß ...,** it is convenient/inconvenient that ...; **es traf sich so, daß ...,** it so happened that ...; **wie es sich so trifft,** as chance would have it; (d) (begegnen) to meet (s.o.); **wo wollen wir uns t.?** where shall we meet? **ihre Blicke trafen sich,** their eyes met; (e) (zustande bringen) to make (arrangements, preparations, a choice, decision etc.). **2.** v.i. (a) (haben) to hit the mark/target; (b) (sein) **auf j-n, etwas** acc **t.,** to meet s.o./come across sth.; **auf Widerstand usw. t.,** to meet with/encounter resistance etc. **II. T.,** n -s/- meeting. ◆'**t~end,** adj. fitting, apt. ◆'**T~er,** m -s/- **1.** Sp: hit; Fb: etc. goal. **2.** (Lotteriegewinn) winner; F: (Glücksfall) lucky strike. ◆'**T~punkt**, m meeting place,

rendezvous. ◆'**t~sicher,** adj. unerring, accurate; (Bemerkung) to the point. ◆'**T~sicherheit**, f accuracy; (good) marksmanship.

**Treib-** ['traip-], comb.fm. (a) floating (mine etc.); drift (-ice, -wood etc.); (b) (antreibend) driving (wheel, belt etc.); fuel (gas, oil etc.). ◆**t~en** ['traibən]. **I.** v.irr.12 **1.** v.tr. (a) to drive (s.o., cattle, snow, a machine etc.); (b) (sich beschäftigen mit) to pursue, carry on (a business etc.); to go in for (sport etc.); **sein Spiel mit j-m t.,** to play a game with s.o. **2.** v.i. (a) (sein) (Schiff, Wolke usw.) to drift; **die Dinge t. lassen,** to let things take their course; (b) (haben) (Pflanzen) to sprout, (Knospen) burst; Cu: (Teig) to rise. **II. T.,** n -s/no pl goings-on, doings; (geschäftig) bustle. ◆'**T~haus,** n hothouse. ◆'**T~jagd,** f battue; Pol: witchhunt. ◆'**T~sand**, m quicksand. ◆'**T~stoff**, m fuel.

**Trend** [trɛnt], m -s/-s trend.

**trenn|bar** ['trɛnbaːr], adj. separable (prefix etc.); detachable (part etc.). ◆'**t~en**, v.tr. (a) to separate (s.o., sth., objects) (**von** + dat, from); (lösen) to detach, take off (a collar etc.); (b) (aufteilen) to divide (sth.); to break/split (sth.) up (**in seine Bestandteile,** into its component parts); **sie leben getrennt,** they are separated; (c) **sich t.,** to separate/part; (Abschied nehmen) to say goodbye; **sie trennte sich von ihm,** she parted company with/left him; **sich von etwas** dat **t.,** to part with sth.; (aufgeben) to give sth. up. ◆'**T~ung**, f -/-en separation; (in Teile) division (of a room, word etc.); segregation (of races etc.); distinction (**zwischen Begriffen,** between concepts). ◆'**T~wand**, f partition (wall).

**trepp|auf** [trɛp⁊'auf], adv. **t., treppab laufen,** to run up and down the stairs. ◆'**T~e,** f -/-n staircase, (flight of) stairs; (außen) (flight of) steps. ◆'**T~engeländer,** n banisters. ◆'**T~enhaus,** n stairwell. ◆'**T~enstufe,** f stair, step.

**Tresor** [tre'zoːr], m -s/-e safe, strongbox; (T~raum) strong room.

**Tret-** ['treːt-], comb.fm. pedal (car, boat etc.). ◆'**T~eimer,** m pedal bin. ◆'**t~en,** v.irr. **1.** v.i. (a) (sein) (Pers.) to step (**nach vorn, auf die Seite usw.,** forward, aside etc.); **ins Zimmer t.,** to enter/come into the room; (b) (sein) (kommen) to come (**aus** + dat, out of), go (**hinter** + dat, behind; **in** + acc, into); Fig: **in Aktion/Kraft t.,** to come into effect; (c) (haben) to kick; **gegen die Tür t.,** to kick the door. **2.** v.tr. (a) to kick (s.o., the ball etc.); (b) (trampeln) to tread (sth., water etc.); to trample (sth., a path).

**Treu** [trɔy], adj. faithful (husband, wife etc.); loyal (subject, friend, servant etc.); **sich selber t.,** true to oneself; **seinen Grundsätzen t. bleiben,** to stick to one's principles. ◆'**T~e,** f -/no pl loyalty;

faithfulness. ◆'T~händer, m -s/- trustee. ◆'T~handgesellschaft, f trust company. ◆'t~herzig, adj. ingenuous; innocently trusting. ◆'t~los, adj. faithless. ◆'T~losigkeit, f -/no pl faithlessness.

**Triangel** ['tri:aŋəl], m -s/- Mus: triangle.

**Tri|bunal** [tribu'nɑ:l], n -s/-e tribunal. ◆T~büne [-'by:nə], f -/-n (Podium) platform, rostrum; (Zuschauert.) grandstand. ◆T~but [-'bu:t], m -(e)s/-e tribute.

**Trichter** ['trictər], m -s/- 1. funnel. 2. (Granatt.) crater. ◆'t~förmig, adj. funnel-shaped.

**Trick** [trik], m -s/-s trick; (List) ploy, dodge. ◆'T~film, m trick film; (gezeichneter) T., animated cartoon film. ◆'t~reich, adj. artful.

**Trieb** [tri:p], m -(e)s/-e 1. (Drang) urge; (innerer Antrieb) impulse; (Verlangen) desire. 2. Bot: sprout, shoot. ◆'T~feder, f mainspring (of a watch etc.); Fig: driving force. ◆'t~haft, adj. impulsive, instinctive (actions etc.). ◆'T~kraft, f motive force. ◆'T~täter/'T~verbrecher, m sexual offender, sex maniac. ◆'T~wagen, m tramcar; Rail: railcar.

**trief|en** ['tri:fən], v.i. (a) (sein) (Regen, Schweiß usw.) to drip; (b) (haben) (tropfend naß sein) (von/vor Nässe) t., to be dripping wet; (Nase, Auge) to run. ◆'t~'naß, adj. dripping/sopping wet.

**triftig** ['triftiç], adj. valid; (zwingend) cogent (reason, argument etc.).

**Trigonometrie** [trigonome'tri:], f -/no pl trigonometry.

**Trikot** [tri'ko:], n -s/-s Sp: singlet; Fb: shirt.

**Triller** ['trilər], m -s/- Mus: trill. ◆'t~n, v.i. (haben) Mus: to trill; (Lerche usw.) to warble. ◆'T~pfeife, f bird whistle.

**trimmen** ['trimən], v.tr. (a) to trim, clip (a dog); (b) F: to train (s.o.); (c) Sp: F: sich t., to get oneself into shape.

**Trink-** ['triŋk-], comb.fm. drinking (vessel, glass, song, chocolate, water etc.). ◆'t~en, v.tr. & i. irr.96 (haben) to drink (sth.). ◆'T~er, m -s/- heavy drinker, alcoholic. ◆'t~fest, adj. F: t. sein, to hold one's drink well. ◆'T~geld, n tip. ◆'T~halle, f refreshment stall. ◆'T~spruch, m toast.

**Trio** ['tri:o], n -s/-s trio.

**trippeln** ['tripəln], v.i. (sein) to trip, mince along; (Baby) to toddle.

**trist** [trist], adj. dismal (weather, life etc.); dreary (houses etc.); bleak (prospects).

**Tritt** [trit], m -(e)s/-e (a) (Schritt) step; (b) (Fußt.) kick. ◆'T~brett, n running board. ◆'T~leiter, f (short) stepladder.

**Triumph** [tri'umf], m -(e)s/-e triumph. ◆t~al [-'fɑ:l], adj. triumphant. ◆T~bogen, m triumphal arch. ◆t~ieren [-'fi:rən], v.i. (haben) to

triumph/(schadenfroh) gloat (über etwas acc, over sth.).

**trivial** [trivi'ɑ:l], adj. commonplace, trite; (unbedeutend) trivial, insignificant. ◆T~literatur, f light fiction; Pej: trashy literature.

**trocken** ['trɔkən]. I. adj. (a) dry; im T~en, in the dry; under cover; F: auf dem trocknen sitzen, to be stuck/(pleite) broke; (b) (langweilig) dull, tedious (work etc.); dry-as-dust (book, lecture etc.). II. 'T~-, comb.fm. (a) dry (battery, dock, ice, weight, cleaning etc.); (b) (getrocknet) dried (vegetables, milk, fruit etc.). ◆T~boden, m drying loft. ◆'T~element, n dry cell. ◆'T~haube, f drying hood; drier. ◆'T~heit, f -/no pl 1. dryness; Fig: dullness. 2. (Dürre) drought. ◆'T~kurs, m preparatory (indoor) course. ◆'t~legen, v.tr.sep. (a) ein Baby t., to change a baby's nappies; (b) to drain (a swamp etc.). ◆'T~rasierer, m dry/electric shaver.

**trockn|en** ['trɔknən], v.tr.&i. (sein/haben) to dry. ◆'T~er, m -s/- drier.

**Troddel** ['trɔdəl], f -/-n tassel.

**Tröd|el** ['trø:dəl], m -s/no pl F: lumber, junk. ◆T~e'lei, f -/no pl F: dawdling. ◆'T~elmarkt, m flea market; (für Wohltätigkeitszwecke) jumble sale. ◆'t~eln, v.i. (haben/sein) F: to dawdle. ◆'T~ler, m -s/- 1. junk dealer. 2. F: dawdler, slowcoach, N.Am: slowpoke.

**Trog** [tro:k], m -(e)s/ːe trough.

**Trommel** ['trɔməl], f -/-n drum. ◆'T~bremse, f drum brake. ◆'T~fell, n Anat: eardrum. ◆'T~feuer, n barrage. ◆'t~n, v.i. (haben) to drum.

**Trommler** ['trɔmlər], m -s/- drummer.

**Trompete** [trɔm'pe:tə], f -/-n trumpet. ◆'T~r, m -s/- trumpeter.

**Tropen** ['tro:pən]. I. pl die T., the tropics. II. 'T~-, comb.fm. tropical (suit, fever, disease etc.). ◆'t~fest, adj. tropicalized. ◆'T~helm, m sun helmet, topee.

**Tropf** [trɔpf], m -(e)s/ːe 1. F: armer T., poor beggar. 2. (pl -e) Med: drip. ◆'T~en, I. m -s/- drop; (herunterfallend) drip. II. t., v.tr.&i. (haben) to drip (sth.). ◆'T~enfänger, m drip catcher. ◆'T~enweise, adv. drop by drop. ◆'t~'naß, adj. dripping wet. ◆'T~steinhöhle, f cave with stalactites/stalagmites.

**tröpfeln** ['trœpfəln], v.i. (haben) to trickle; (Regen) es tröpfelt, it's spitting.

**Trophäe** [tro'fɛ:ə], f -/-n trophy.

**tropisch** ['tro:piʃ], adj. tropical.

**Trost** [tro:st], m -(e)s/no pl consolation; comfort; F: nicht ganz/recht bei T. sein, to be off one's rocker. ◆'t~bedürftig, adj. in need of consolation. ◆'t~los, adj. bleak, cheerless (countryside, weather etc.); miserable

(conditions); hopeless (situation etc.).
◆'T~**losigkeit,** f -/no pl bleakness, cheerlessness; hopelessness, desperation. ◆'T~**preis,** m consolation prize. ◆'t~**reich,** adj. comforting.

**tröst|en** ['trøːstən], v.tr. to console, comfort (s.o., oneself); **sich damit t., daß** ..., to console oneself with the thought that ... ◆'t~**lich,** adj. comforting, consoling. ◆'T~**ung,** f -/-en consolation, comfort.

**Trott** [trɔt], m -(e)s/-e 1. trot. 2. Fig: routine. ◆'T~**el,** m -s/- F: idiot. ◆'t~**elig,** adj. F: dithering. ◆'t~**en,** v.i. (sein) to trot; F: (Pers.) to trudge (along). ◆'T~**oir** [trɔtoˈaːr], n -s/-e & -s pavement, N.Am: sidewalk.

**trotz** [trɔts]. I. prep. + gen in spite of; t. **Regen/des Regens,** in spite of the rain. II. **T.,** m -es/no pl defiance; (Eigensinn) obstinacy; **j-m zum T.,** in defiance of s.o.; **aller Vernunft zum T.,** contrary to all reason. ◆'t~**dem,** adv. nevertheless. ◆'t~**en,** v.i. (haben) (a) j-m/etwas dat t., to defy s.o., sth.; **einer Gefahr t.,** to brave a danger; (b) (trotzig sein) to be obstinate/(Kind) rebellious. ◆'t~**ig/'t~köpfig,** adj. defiant; (Kind usw.) pigheaded; (widerspenstig) rebellious. ◆'T~**kopf,** m pigheaded person/esp. child.

**trüb|e** ['tryːbə], adj. (a) cloudy (liquid, sky etc.); dull (weather, day, eyes etc.); dim (light); (b) (traurig) gloomy (person, times, thoughts, mood etc.); grim (prospect, experience). ◆'t~**en,** v.tr. (a) to cloud (a liquid); to dull (a window etc.); **sich t.,** to become cloudy/dull; (b) to cast a cloud over (s.o.'s mood etc.); to spoil, mar (a good relationship/atmosphere etc.). ◆T~**heit** ['tryːphait], f -/no pl (a) cloudiness; dullness; dimness, sombreness; (b) gloominess. ◆'T~**sal,** f -/-e Lit: affliction; (Trauer) grief; F: **T. blasen,** to be down in the dumps. ◆'t~**selig,** adj. gloomy (person, mood etc.). ◆'T~**sinn,** m melancholy. ◆'t~**sinnig,** adj. gloomy, dejected. ◆'T~**ung,** f -/-en (a) (also Fig:) clouding; dimming; tarnishing; (b) (Beeinträchtigung) marring.

**Trubel** ['truːbəl], m -s/no pl bustle, hurly-burly.

**trudeln** ['truːdəln], v.i. (sein) to spiral, Av: spin.

**Trüffel** ['tryfəl], f -/-n truffle.

**Trug** [truːk], m -(e)s/no pl Lit: deception. ◆'T~**bild,** n hallucination. ◆'T~**schluß,** m wrong conclusion; fallacy.

**trüg|en** ['tryːgən], v.irr.63 1. v.tr. to deceive (s.o.); **wenn mich nicht alles trügt,** if I am not much mistaken. 2. v.i. (haben) **der Schein trügt,** appearances are deceptive. ◆'t~**erisch,** adj. deceptive.

**Truhe** ['truːə], f -/-n chest.

**Trümmer** ['trymər], pl debris; (von Gebäuden) rubble; Nau: Av: wreckage.

◆'T~**haufen,** m heap of rubble.

**Trumpf** [trumpf], m -(e)s/-e trump (card); Fig: **alle T~e in der Hand haben,** to hold all the trumps. ◆'t~**en,** v.tr.&i. (haben) to trump (a card).

**Trunk** [truŋk], m -(e)s/-e Lit: (a) drink; (b) (T~sucht) drinking. ◆'T~**enheit,** f -/no pl drunkenness; **T. am Steuer,** drunken driving. ◆'T~**sucht,** f alcoholism.

**Trupp** [trup], m -s/-s gang (of workers etc.); detachment, squad (of police etc.); group (of people). ◆'T~**e,** f -/-n 1. (a) no pl army; (b) (Verband) unit; (c) pl **T~en,** troops. 2. Th: etc: company, troupe (of acrobats etc.); Sp: squad. ◆'T~**en-,** comb.fm: troop (movement, transport etc.); military (parade etc.). ◆'T~**enführer,** m unit commander. ◆'T~**enteil,** m unit. ◆'T~**enübung,** f troop manoeuvre, field exercise. ◆'T~**enübungsplatz,** m military training area.

**Truthahn** ['truːthaːn], m turkey(-cock).

**Tschech|e** ['tʃɛçə], m -n/-n Czech. ◆'T~**in,** f -/-nen Czech woman. ◆'t~**isch,** adj. Czech. ◆T~**oslowakei** [-oslovaˈkai]. Pr.n.f -. Czechoslovakia.

**tschüs** [tʃyːs], int. F: bye now! so long!

**Tub|a** ['tuːba], f -/-ben tuba. ◆'T~**e,** f -/-n tube.

**Tuberkulose** [tubɛrkuˈloːzə], f -/-n tuberculosis.

**Tuch** [tuːx], n -(e)s/-er cloth; (Halst.) scarf; (Kopft.) head scarf; (Staubt.) duster.

**tüchtig** ['tyçtiç], adj. 1. (fähig) able, competent; (leistungsfähig) efficient; (fleißig) hardworking (person). 2. (beträchtlich) sizeable (piece, portion); big (gulp etc.); hard (blow); healthy (appetite). ◆'T~**keit,** f -/no pl ability, competence; efficiency; excellence (of work); (Fleiß) industry.

**Tück|e** ['tykə], f -/-n 1. no pl treachery; Fig: fickleness (of fate). 2. (Handlung) trick, ruse; Fig: danger; **seine T~n haben,** (Maschine) to be temperamental/ (Berg, Fluß usw.) treacherous. ◆'t~**isch,** adj. treacherous, pernicious (illness); malicious (glance etc.).

**tuckern** ['tukərn], v.i. (haben/sein) (Boot) to chug.

**Tugend** ['tuːgənt], f -/-en virtue. ◆'t~**haft,** adj. virtuous.

**Tüll** [tyl], m -(e)s/-e tulle.

**Tülle** ['tylə], f -/-n spout.

**Tulpe** ['tulpə], f -/-n tulip. ◆'T~**nzwiebel,** f tulip bulb.

**tummeln** ['tuməln], v.refl. **sich t.,** (Kinder) to romp (about).

**Tumor** ['tuːmɔr], m -s/-en ['tumoːrən] tumour.

**Tümpel** ['tympəl], m -s/- pond.

**Tumult** [tuˈmult], m -(e)s/-e tumult, commotion; pl **T~e,** disturbances.

**tun** [tu:n]. **I.** *v.irr.* **1.** *v.tr.* (*a*) to do (sth., a job, favour, one's duty etc.); to make (a vow, remark etc.), take (a step); **so etwas tut man nicht,** that sort of thing isn't done; (*b*) (*antun*) **was hat er dir getan?** what did he do to you? **der Hund tut dir nichts,** the dog won't hurt you; (*c*) *F*: (*stellen*) to put (sth.) (somewhere); (*d*) **das tut's auch,** that would do; **das hat damit nichts zu t./tut nichts zur Sache,** that has nothing to do it/is quite irrelevant; **es mit j-m zu t. haben,** to have dealings with s.o.; **was tut das schon?** what does it matter? **es tut sich etwas** there is something going on. **2.** *v.i.* (*haben*) (*a*) **ich habe zu t.,** I have work to do/(*Geschäfte*) business to attend to; (*b*) **freundlich t.,** to act/behave in a friendly way; **tu doch nicht so!** stop pretending/putting it on! **so t., als ob...,** to act/behave as if ...; (*c*) **mit j-m zu t. haben,** to have dealings with s.o.; **mit etwas** *dat* **zu t. haben,** to be concerned/connected with sth. **II. T.,** *n -s/no pl* doings. ◆'**t~lichst,** *adv.* if at all possible.

**Tünche** ['tynçə], *f -/-n* whitewash; *Fig:* (*äußerer Schein*) veneer. ◆'**t~n,** *v.tr.* to whitewash (sth.).

**Tundra** ['tundra], *f -/-dren* tundra.

**Tunesien** [tu'ne:ziən]. *Pr.n.n* **-s.** Tunisia. ◆**t~isch,** *adj.* Tunisian.

**Tunke** ['tuŋkə], *f -/-n esp.* sauce; (*Bratent.*) gravy. ◆'**t~n,** *v.tr.* to dip (sth.).

**Tunnel** ['tunəl], *m -s/- &* **-s** tunnel.

**Tüpfel|chen** ['typfəlçən], *n -s/-* tiny spot; (*gedruckt usw.*) dot. ◆'**t~n,** *v.tr.* to spot (sth.).

**tupf|en** ['tupfən]. **I.** *v.tr.* (*a*) to dab (sth.) (**auf etwas** *acc,* onto sth.); (*b*) (**blau**) **getupftes Kleid,** dress with (blue) polka dots. **II. T.,** *m -s/-* spot; dot. ◆'**T~er,** *m -s/-* **1.** dot. **2.** *Med:* swab.

**Tür** [ty:r]. *f -/-en* door; **j-n vor die T. setzen,** to throw s.o. out; **Weihnachten steht vor der T.,** Christmas is just round the corner. **II.** '**T~-,** *comb.fm.* door (chain, lock, key etc.). ◆'**T~angel,** *f* door hinge. ◆'**T~flügel,** *m* (lefthand/righthand) door (of a pair). ◆'**T~klingel,** *f* doorbell. ◆'**T~öffner,** *m* (electric) door opener. ◆'**T~rahmen,** *m* doorframe. ◆'**T~schwelle,** *f* doorsill, threshold.

**Turban** ['turba:n], *m -s/-e* turban.

**Turb|ine** [tur'bi:nə], *f -/-n* turbine. ◆'**T~omotor,** *m* turbocharged engine.

**turbulen|t** [turbu'lɛnt], *adj.* turbulent. ◆**T~z,** *f -/-en* turbulence.

**Türk|e** ['tyrkə], *m -n/-n* Turk. ◆**T~ei** [-'kai]. *Pr.n.f -.* **die T.,** Turkey.

◆'**T~in,** *f -/-nen* Turkish woman. ◆'**t~isch,** *adj.* Turkish.

**Türkis** [tyr'ki:s], *m -es/-e* turquoise. ◆**t~(farben),** *adj.* turquoise.

**Turm** [turm], *m -(e)s/⁀e* (*a*) tower; (*spitzer Kirct.*) steeple; (*b*) (*Schach*) castle; (*c*) (*Sprungt.*) diving platform. ◆'**t~hoch,** *adj.* towering (waves etc.). ◆'**T~spitze,** *f* spire. ◆'**T~uhr,** *f* tower/*esp.* (*am Kirct.*) church clock.

**Türm|chen** ['tyrmçən], *n -s/-* small tower, turret. ◆'**t~en,** *v.tr.* to pile, stack (books etc.); **sich t.,** to pile. **2.** *v.i.* (*sein*) *F:* to clear out, *Brit:* to do a bunk.

**Turn-** ['turn-], *comb.fm.* gymnastic (apparatus, exercise etc.); *Sch:* gym/P.E. (teacher, lesson etc.). ◆'**t~en. I.** *v.i.* (*haben*) to do gymnastics/*F:* gym/*Sch:* P.E. **II. T.,** *n -s/no pl Sp:* gymnastics; *Sch: F:* gym; P.E. ◆'**T~er(in),** *m -s/-* (*f -/-nen*) gymnast. ◆'**T~halle,** *f* gymnasium, *F:* gym. ◆'**T~hemd,** *n* singlet. ◆'**T~hose,** *f* gym shorts. ◆'**T~schuhe,** *mpl* gym shoes, *N.Am:* sneakers. ◆'**T~verein,** *m* gymnastics club. ◆'**T~zeug,** *n* gym kit.

**Turnier** [tur'ni:r]. **I.** *n -s/-e* tournament; (*Reitt.*) (horse) show; (*Tanzt.*) (dancing) competition. **II.** '**T~-,** *comb.fm.* tournament (winner etc.); show (horse, rider etc.); competition (dancing, winner etc.).

**Turnus** ['turnus], *m -/-se* rota; **im T.,** in rotation.

**Turteltaube** ['turtəltaubə], *f* turtledove.

**Tusch** [tuʃ], *m -(e)s/-e Mus:* flourish.

**Tusch|e** ['tuʃə], *f -/-n* Indian ink. ◆'**T~zeichnung,** *f* pen-and-ink drawing.

**tuscheln** ['tuʃəln], *v.tr. & i.* (*haben*) to whisper (sth.).

**Tüte** ['ty:tə], *f -/-n* (*a*) (paper/plastic) bag; (*b*) (*Eist.*) ice-cream cone/cornet.

**tuten** ['tu:tən], *v.i.* (*haben*) to toot, hoot.

**Tutor** ['tu:tor], *m -s/-en* [tu'to:rən] tutor.

**Typ** [ty:p], *m -s/-en* type; (*a*) **sie ist nicht mein T.,** she is not my type/sort; (*b*) *F:* (*Pers.*) character, *N.Am:* guy; (*c*) (*Modell*) type, model. ◆'**T~e,** *f -/-n* **1.** character; *pl* **T~n,** type. **2.** *F:* (*Pers.*) queer bird, odd character. ◆'**t~isch,** *adj.* typical (**für j-n, etwas** *acc,* of s.o., sth.); *F:* **t. Frau/Mann!** how typical of a woman/man!

**Typhus** ['ty:fus], *m -/no pl* typhoid (fever).

**Typus** ['ty:pus], *m -/-pen* type.

**Tyrann** [ty'ran], *m -en/-en* tyrant; *Fig:* (*Chef usw.*) bully. ◆**T~ei** [-'nai], *f -/-en* tyranny. ◆**t~isch,** *adj.* tyrannical, bullying. ◆**t~i'sieren,** *v.tr.* to bully (s.o.), tyrannize (a country etc.).

# U

**U, u** [uː], n -/- (the letter) U, u.
**U-Bahn** ['uːbaːn], f underground (railway), N.Am: subway. ◆'**U**~**-Station,** f underground/N.Am: subway station.
**übel** ['yːbəl]. **I.** adj. (a) (schlecht) bad; (moralisch schlecht) wicked, evil; (b) (unangenehm) nasty, (stärker) foul (weather, smell etc.); **j-m ü. mitspielen,** to play a nasty trick on s.o.; (c) **mir ist/wird ü.,** I feel sick. **II. Ü.,** n -s/- evil; (Mißstand) anomaly; **zu allem Ü. ...,** to crown it all/make matters worse ... ◆'**ü**~**gelaunt,** adj. grumpy. ◆'**ü**~**nehmen,** v.tr.sep.irr.69 to take (sth.) amiss, take offence at (sth.). ◆'**ü**~**riechend,** adj. evil-smelling. ◆'**Ü**~**täter,** m wrongdoer. ◆'**ü**~**wollen,** v.i.sep.irr.112 (haben) **j-m ü.,** to be ill-disposed towards s.o.
**üben** ['yːbən], v.tr. & i. (haben) to practise; **sich (in etwas** dat) **ü.,** to practise (sth.).
**über** ['yːbər]. **I.** prep. **1.** (Lage) + dat above, over; **er wohnt ü. uns,** he lives above us/on the next floor; **ü. dem Durchschnitt,** above average. **2.** + acc over; **ü. einen Graben springen,** to jump over/across a ditch; **ü. München fahren,** to go via Munich; **ü. Fernschreiber,** by telex; **ein Scheck ü. DM 100,** a cheque for 100 marks; **das geht ü. meinen Verstand,** it's beyond my comprehension; **ü. j-n herrschen/Macht haben,** to rule/have power over s.o.; **Fehler ü. Fehler machen,** to make one mistake after the other; **übers Wochenende,** over/for the weekend. **3.** + acc (betreffend) about; **ein Buch ü. Kunst,** a book about/on art. **II.** adv. **1.** (mehr als) over, more than; **seit ü. einem Jahr,** for more than a year. **2.** **das ganze Jahr ü.,** all (the) year round; **ü. und ü.,** all over. **III.** adj. F: **j-m ü. sein,** to be superior to/more than a match for s.o.
**über'all,** adv. everywhere, esp. N.Am: all over.
**über'anstrengen,** v.tr.insep. to over-exert (s.o., oneself); to overstrain (one's heart etc.).
**über'arbeiten,** v.tr.insep. (a) to rework, revise (a text etc.); (b) **sich ü.,** to overwork; **überarbeitet,** overworked.
**überaus,** adv. extremely, exceedingly.
**über'backen,** v.tr.insep.irr.1 Cu: to brown (cauliflower etc.); **mit Käse ü.,** au gratin.
**über'bieten,** v.tr.insep.irr.8 (a) (bei einer Auktion) to outbid (s.o.); (b) to excel/surpass (s.o., oneself etc.); **einen Rekord ü.,** to break a record.
**'Überbleibsel** [-blaipsəl], n -s/- remnant; pl remains.
**'Überblick,** m (a) panoramic/Fig: overall view (**über etwas** acc, of sth.); (b) (Vor-

trag usw.) survey. ◆**ü**~**en** [-'blikən], v.tr.insep. to overlook, have a view of (sth.); Fig: to grasp, take in (a situation etc.).
**über'bringen,** v.tr.insep.irr.16 to deliver.
**über'brücken,** v.tr.insep. to get/(mit Geld) tide over (a period); **Gegensätze ü.,** to reconcile differences.
**über'dauern,** v.tr.insep. to outlast (sth.), (überstehen) survive (wars etc.).
**über'denken,** v.tr.insep.irr.17 to think (sth.) over.
**überdimensional** [yːbərdimɛnziʲoˈnaːl], adj. huge, outsize.
**'Überdosis,** f overdose.
**'Überdruck,** m Ph: excess pressure.
**Überdruß** ['yːbərdrus], m -sses/no pl. surfeit, (Müdigkeit) weariness (**an etwas** dat, of sth.). ◆**ü**~**drüssig** [-'drysiç], adj. **j-s, einer Sache** gen **ü.,** tired of/fed up with s.o., sth.
**'überdurchschnittlich,** adj. above average.
**'übereifrig,** adj. overeager.
**über'eilen,** v.tr.insep. to rush (matters etc.); to do (sth.) too hastily. ◆**ü**~**t,** adj. over/hasty, (leichtsinnig) rash.
**überei'nander,** adv. & comb.fm. (a) on top of one another; one above the other; (b) **ü. reden,** to talk about one another.
**über'ein|kommen,** v.i.sep.irr.53 (sein) Lit: to agree, reach agreement. ◆**Ü**~**kunft,** f -/-e agreement, understanding. ◆**ü**~**stimmen,** v.i.sep. (haben) to agree, (Aussagen usw.) tally, (Farben) match (**mit etwas** dat, sth.). ◆**ü**~**stimmend,** adj. concurring (reports etc.); **ü. mit** + dat, in conformity with. ◆**Ü**~**stimmung,** f agreement.
**'überempfindlich,** adj. over-sensitive.
**über'fahr|en,** v.tr.insep.irr.26 (a) to run over (s.o., an animal); (b) to drive across (a line etc.), drive through (traffic lights). ◆'**Ü**~**t,** f Nau: crossing.
**'Überfall,** m (surprise) attack (**auf** + acc, on); (auch von Räubern) raid (**auf eine Bank,** on a bank). ◆**ü**~**en** [-'falən], v.tr.insep.irr.27 to attack (s.o., sth.) (suddenly); to raid, hold up (a bank etc.).
**'überfällig,** adj. overdue.
**über'fliegen,** v.tr.insep.irr.7 to fly over.
**'Überfluß,** m abundance; (zu groß) surplus, excess (**an etwas** dat, of sth.); **im Ü. leben,** to live in luxury.
**'überflüssig,** adj. superfluous; (unnötig) unnecessary.
**über'fluten,** v.tr.insep. to flood over.
**über'fordern,** v.tr.insep. to ask too much of (s.o.); to strain, overtax (the heart, Fig: s.o.'s patience etc.).
**über'führ|en,** v.tr.insep. (a) to transport, convey (s.o., sth.); (b) Jur: **j-n (eines Verbrechens) ü.,** to find s.o. guilty (of a

crime). ◆Ü~ung, f -/-en 1. transport(ation). 2. *Jur:* conviction. 3. (*Brücke*) flyover, *esp. N.Am:* overpass.

**überfüllt** [-'fylt], *adj.* crammed full; overcrowded (schools, buses etc.); congested (roads).

**'Übergabe**, f -/no pl handing over; *esp. Mil:* surrender (**an** + *acc*, to).

**'Übergang**, m 1. (*a*) no pl crossing; (*b*) (*Brücke*) footbridge. 2. (*Wechsel*) transition (**auf/in** + *acc*, to). ◆'Ü~s-, *comb.fm.* interim (regulation, solution etc.); transitional (stage etc.). ◆'Ü~szeit, f transitional period/season.

**über'geben**, *v.tr.insep.irr.35* (*a*) to hand (s.o., sth.) over, (*liefern*) deliver (sth.), (*anvertrauen*) entrust (sth.); to pass on (a message etc.); *Mil:* to surrender (a town etc.); (*b*) **sich ü.**, to vomit, be sick.

**übergehen**, *v.irr.36* 1. ['y:bərge:ən] *v.i.sep.* (*sein*) (*a*) **ins feindliche Lager/zu einer anderen Partei ü.**, to go over to the enemy/another party; (*b*) (*Besitz*) **auf j-n ü.**, to pass to s.o.; (*c*) **zu etwas (anderem) ü.**, to proceed/pass on to sth. (else); (*d*) **in etwas ü.**, to change (gradually) into sth. 2. [y:bər'ge:ən] *v.tr.insep.* to ignore (s.o., sth.); (*bei der Beförderung usw.*) to pass (s.o.) over; (*auslassen*) to skip (a chapter etc.).

**'übergeschnappt**, *adj. F:* round the bend.

**'Übergewicht**, n excess weight/(*Gepäck*) baggage; **Ü. haben**, to be overweight.

**übergießen** [-'gi:sən], *v.tr.insep.irr.31* **etwas mit Wasser ü.**, to pour water over sth.

**'überglücklich**, *adj.* overjoyed.

**'übergreifen**, *v.i.sep.irr.43* (*haben*) (*Brand usw.*) to spread (**auf** + *acc*, to).

**'Übergriff**, m infringement; encroachment (**auf** + *acc*, on); *Mil:* incursion (**auf** + *acc*, into).

**'übergroß**, *adj.* oversize, outsize.

**'Übergröße**, f Cl: outsize.

**über'handnehmen**, *v.i.sep.irr.69* (*haben*) to increase/multiply out of all proportion; (*Unkraut usw.*) to get out of hand.

**über'häufen**, *v.tr.insep.* to inundate (s.o.).

**über'haupt**, *adv.* 1. (*im allgemeinen*) altogether. 2. **ü. nicht/nichts**, not/nothing at all; **ü. nicht möglich**, completely impossible; **wie war es ü. möglich?** how was it at all possible?

**über'heblich**, *adj.* arrogant; (*eingebildet*) conceited, self-important. ◆Ü~keit, f -/no pl arrogance; conceit.

**über'holen** *v.tr.insep.* (*a*) to overtake, pass (s.o., a car); (*b*) *Tchn:* (*instandsetzen*) to overhaul (an engine etc.). ◆ü~t, *adj.* obsolete; (*veraltet*) old-fashioned, out of date. ◆Ü~verbot, n overtaking ban; (*auf Verkehrsschild*) no overtaking.

**über'hören**, *v.tr.insep.* not to hear (sth.); (*absichtlich*) to ignore (sth.).

**'überirdisch**, *adj.* supernatural; heavenly

(beauty).

**'überkochen**, *v.i.sep.* (*sein*) (*Milch usw.*) to boil over.

**über'lagern**, *v.tr.insep.* to cover, overlie, (*teilweise*) overlap (sth.); **sich ü.**, to overlap.

**über'lassen**, *v.tr.insep.irr.57* **j-m etwas ü.**, to leave sth. to s.o.; (*abtreten*) to relinquish/yield sth. to s.o.

**über'lasten** *v.tr.insep.* to overload (a lorry etc.), overstrain (the heart).

**'überlaufen**, *v.irr.58* 1. ['y:bərlaufən] *v.i.sep.* (*sein*) (*a*) (*Bad, Topf usw.*) to overflow; (*b*) (*Soldaten usw.*) **zum Gegner ü.**, to go over to the enemy/other side. 2. [y:bər'laufən] *v.tr.insep.* **es überläuft mich kalt, wenn ...**, shivers run down my spine when ...; **von Touristen ü.**, overrun/(*stark*) inundated with tourists.

**'Überläufer**, m turncoat, renegade.

**über'leben**, *v.tr.insep.* (*a*) to survive (an accident etc.); (*b*) to outlive (s.o.) (**um 2 Jahre**, by 2 years). ◆Ü~de(r), m & f decl. as adj. survivor.

**über'leg|en**. I. *v.tr. & i.insep.* (*haben*) (**etwas**) **ü.**, to think (about sth.), consider (sth.); **er hat es sich anders überlegt**, he has changed his mind. II. *adj.* superior (j-m, to s.o.); (**in Kraft usw.**, in strength etc.); **ein ü~ener Sieg**, a clear victory. ◆Ü~enheit, f -/no pl superiority. ◆Ü~ung, f -/-en (*a*) consideration; (*b*) pl deliberations.

**'überleit|en**, *v.i.sep.* (*haben*) **zu etwas** *dat* **ü.**, to lead/go on to sth. (else). ◆'Ü~ung, f transition.

**über'liefer|n**, *v.tr.insep.* to hand (sth.) down. ◆Ü~ung, f tradition; (*Brauch*) old custom.

**überlisten** [-'listən], *v.tr.insep.* to outwit (s.o.).

**überm** ['y:bərm] = **über dem**.

**'Übermacht**, f -/no pl superiority, superior strength/(*zahlenmäßig*) numbers.

**'übermächtig**, *adj.* (*a*) superior (in strength); (*b*) *Fig:* overwhelming (desire etc.).

**übermannen** [-'manən], *v.tr.insep.* (*Gefühle usw.*) to overcome (s.o.).

**'Übermaß**, n excess (**an Arbeit usw.**, of work etc.).

**'übermäßig**, *adj.* excessive.

**'Übermensch**, m superman. ◆ü~lich, *adj.* superhuman.

**Übermüdung** [-'my:duŋ], f overtiredness.

**übermittel|n** [-'mitəln], *v.tr.insep.* to transmit, pass on (a message etc.). ◆Ü~lung, f transmission.

**'übermorgen**, *adv.* the day after tomorrow.

**'Übermut**, m exuberance, high spirits.

**'übermütig**, *adj.* high-spirited, boisterous; frisky, (*frech*) cocky (child etc.).

**'übernächste(r,s)**, *adj.* (the) next (house etc.) but one; the (week, year etc.) after next.

**über'nacht|en,** *v.i.insep.* *(haben)* to stay/ spend the night (**bei j-m,** with s.o.). ◆**U~ung,** *f* -/-en overnight stay.

**über'nächtigt,** *adj.* bleary-eyed.

**'Übernahme,** *f* -/-n taking over; under- taking (of a task etc.); acceptance (of re- sponsibility etc.).

**'übernatürlich,** *adj.* supernatural.

**über'nehmen,** *v.tr.insep.69* (*a*) to take over (a business, job etc.); (*selbst anwen- den*) to adopt, F: borrow (ideas, a pas- sage); (*auf sich nehmen*) to undertake, take on (a task, *Jur:* case etc.); to accept (responsibility etc.); (*b*) **sich ü.,** to over- do it/things; (*beruflich/finanziell*) to take on too much.

**über'prüf|en,** *v.tr.insep.* (*a*) to check (s.o., sth.); to screen, vet (suspects); (*b*) (*von neuem prüfen*) to review (a decision etc.). ◆**U~ung,** *f* (*a*) check(ing); screening; (*b*) review.

**über'queren,** *v.tr.insep.* to cross (a street etc.).

**über'ragen,** *v.tr.insep.* (*a*) to tower above (s.o., sth.); (*b*) *Fig:* to outclass (s.o.).

**überrasch|en** [y:bər'raʃən], *v.tr.insep.* to surprise (s.o.); **j-n beim Stehlen ü.,** to catch s.o. stealing. ◆**ü~end,** *adj.* sur- prising; (*unerwartet*) unexpected (visit etc.); **es kam ü.,** it came as a surprise. ◆**U~ung,** *f* -/-en surprise. ◆**U~ungs-,** *comb.fm.* surprise (attack, victory, winner etc.).

**über'reden,** *v.tr.insep.* to persuade (s.o.).

**über'reichen,** *v.tr.insep.* to hand over, (*feierlich*) present (sth.).

**überreizt** [-'raitst], *adj.* overexcited, over- wrought.

**'Überrest,** *m* remnant; (*Spur*) relic (of a civilization etc.); *esp. pl* remains, ruins.

**über'rumpeln,** *v.tr.insep.* to take (s.o.) by surprise.

**übers** ['y:bərs] = **über das.**

**'Überschall-,** *comb.fm.* supersonic (speed, aircraft etc.).

**über'schätzen,** *v.tr.insep.* to overesti- mate.

**über'schau|bar,** *adj.* (*Szene*) visible at a glance; (*Sache*) easy to grasp. ◆**ü~en,** *v.tr.insep.* = **übersehen** (*a*).

**über'schlafen,** *v.tr.insep.irr.84 F:* to sleep on (a decision).

**überschlag|en** *v.irr.85* 1. [y:bər'ʃla:gən], *v.tr.insep.* (*a*) (*auslassen*) to skip, miss out (a passage, lunch etc.); (*b*) (*berechnen*) to estimate (roughly), tot up (costs etc.); (*c*) **sich ü.,** (*Pers.*) to somersault; (*Auto*) to overturn; *Fig:* **seine Stimme überschlug sich,** his voice cracked/broke. 2. ['y:bərʃla:gən] *v.tr.sep.* to cross (one's legs etc.). 3. ['y:bərʃla:gən] *v.i.sep.* (*sein*) (*Funken usw.*) to jump across; (*Wellen*) to break.

**über'schneiden,** *v.refl.insep.irr.59* **sich ü.,** (*Linien usw.*) to intersect; *Fig:* (*The- men usw.*) to overlap; (*zeitlich*) (*Ereignisse usw.*) to coincide, clash.

**über'schreiben,** *v.tr.insep.irr.12* (*a*) to head (a chapter etc.); (*b*) (*übertragen*) to make over (property).

**über'schreiten,** *v.tr.insep.irr.41* to cross (a frontier etc.); *Fig:* to exceed (a limit, one's authority etc.); to pass (its peak); to infringe (a regulation).

**'Überschrift,** *f* heading, title.

**'Überschuß,** *m* (*a*) surplus (**an Frauen usw.,** of women etc.); (*b*) (*Gewinn*) profit.

**überschüssig** [y:bər-ʃysiç], *adj.* surplus (heat, energy, goods etc.); excess (profits etc.).

**über'schütten,** *v.tr.insep.* to cover (s.o., sth.); *Fig:* **j-n mit Geschenken usw. ü.,** to shower s.o. with presents etc.

**über'schwemm|en,** *v.tr.insep.* to flood. ◆**U~ung,** *f* -/-en 1. *no pl* overflowing (of a river etc.); (*also Fig:*) flooding. 2. (*Hochwasser*) flood.

**überschwenglich** ['y:bərʃvɛŋliç], *adj.* ef- fusive; extravagant (style, praise etc.).

**'Übersee.** I. *inv.* overseas; **aus/von Ü.,** from overseas; **nach Ü. gehen,** to go overseas. II. **'Ü~-,** *comb.fm.* overseas (trade, traffic etc.).

**über'seh|bar,** *adj.* easily surveyed; *Fig:* clear (situation); foreseeable (conse- quences). ◆**ü~en,** *v.tr.insep.irr.92* (*a*) to overlook (a valley etc.); *Fig:* to have an overall view of (a situation etc.); (*b*) (*nicht sehen*) to overlook; **es ist nicht zu ü.,** you can't miss it.

**über'senden,** *v.tr.insep.irr.94* **j-m etwas ü.,** to send sth. to s.o.

**übersetz|en,** *v.* 1. [y:bər'zɛtsən] *v.tr.&i.insep.* (*haben*) (*a*) to translate (sth.) (**ins Deutsche usw.,** into German etc.). 2. ['y:bərzɛtsən] *v.i.sep.* (*haben/ sein*) to cross (over). ◆**ü~er** [-'zɛtsər], *m* translator. ◆**U~ung** [-'zɛtsuŋ], *f* -/-en 1. translation. 2. *Tchn:* gearing; (*Ü~ungsverhältnis*) gear ratio.

**'Übersicht,** *f* 1. overall view. 2. (*Abriß*) outline, survey (**über** + *acc,* of); (*Tabelle*) table. ◆**ü~lich,** *adj.* easily surveyed; *Fig:* clear, lucid (description etc.). ◆**'Ü~lichkeit,** *f* -/*no pl* openness; *Fig:* clarity.

**übersiedeln,** *v.i.sep.* ['y:bərzi:dəln] & *in- sep.* [y:bər'zi:dəln] (*sein*) (*Pers., Firma*) to (re)move.

**'übersinnlich,** *adj.* supernatural (powers etc.).

**über'spannen,** *v.tr.insep.* (*a*) (*Brücke, Dach*) to span (a river, space etc.); (*be- spannen*) to cover (sth.); (*b*) (*zu stark*) to overtighten (a bow etc.).

**über'spitzt,** *adj.* exaggerated; (*allzu fein*) oversubtle.

**über'springen,** *v.tr.sep.irr.19* (*a*) to jump over (sth.), clear (a fence, *Sp:* height etc.); (*b*) (*auslassen*) to skip (a class, chapter etc.).

**überstehen,** *v.irr.100* 1. ['y:bərʃte:ən] *v.i.sep.* (*haben*) to project, jut out. 2.

[y:bər'ʃteːən] v.tr.insep. to get over, recover from (an illness etc.); to overcome, surmount (a danger, difficulties); to weather (a storm, crisis etc.); (überleben) to survive (a catastrophe, the winter etc.); to come through (an operation etc.).

**über'steigen,** v.tr.insep.irr.89 (a) to climb over (sth.); (b) to exceed (a sum, expectations).

**über'stimmen,** v.tr.insep. to outvote (s.o.).

**'Überstunden,** fpl overtime.

**über'stürz|en,** v.tr.insep. to rush (into) (sth.); (Ereignisse usw.) **sich ü.,** to follow in rapid succession. ◆**ü~t,** adj. overhasty.

**über'tönen,** v.tr.insep. to drown (a voice etc.).

**Übertrag** ['y:bərtraːk], m -(e)s/-e sum carried forward. ◆**ü~bar** [-'traːkbaːr], adj. transferable (**auf** + acc, to); Med: infectious, (durch Berührung) contagious. ◆**ü~en** [-'traːgən], v.tr.insep.irr.85 (a) to transfer (sth.) (**auf etwas** acc, to sth.); to transmit (Med: a disease, Tchn: power etc.) (**auf** + acc, to); to assign (a task etc.) (b) (übersetzen) to translate (a text); **in ü~ener Bedeutung,** in a figurative sense, figuratively; (c) Rad: TV: to broadcast, transmit (a programme). ◆**U~ung,** f -/-en (a) transfer; Med: Tchn: transmission; (b) translation; transcription; (c) Rad: TV: transmission, broadcast.

**über'treffen,** v.tr.insep.irr.104 (a) to surpass, outdo; **er hat sich selbst übertroffen,** he excelled himself; (b) (übersteigen) to exceed (expectations etc.).

**über'treib|en,** v.tr. & i.insep.irr.12 (haben) to exaggerate (sth.), carry (demands etc.) too far. ◆**U~ung,** f -/-en exaggeration.

**übertret|en,** v.irr.105 1. ['y:bərtreːtən] v.i.sep. (sein) **zur Opposition usw. ü.,** to go over to the opposition etc.; **zum katholischen Glauben ü.,** to be converted to the Catholic faith. 2. [y:bər'treːtən] v.tr.insep. to break (a law, rule etc.), infringe (a regulation). ◆**U~ung,** f -/-en infringement; offence; Jur: misdemeanour.

**über'trieben,** adj. exaggerated.

**'Übertritt,** m changeover; Ecc: conversion.

**übervölker|t** [y:bər'fœlkərt], adj. overpopulated. ◆**U~ung,** f -/no pl overpopulation.

**'übervoll,** adj. overfull.

**über'vorteilen,** v.tr.insep. to cheat (s.o.).

**über'wach|en,** v.tr.insep. to supervise; (Polizei) to shadow (s.o.), control (traffic etc.). ◆**U~ung,** f -/no pl supervision; control.

**überwältigen** [y:bər'vɛltigən], v.tr.insep. (also Fig:) to overwhelm (s.o.). ◆**ü~d,** adj. overwhelming (victory etc.).

**über'weis|en,** v.tr.insep.irr.70 to pay, transfer (money). ◆**U~ung,** f -/-en remittance, payment; transfer (of money).

**über'wiegen,** v.insep.irr.7 1. v.i. (haben) to predominate, (Meinung usw.) prevail. 2. v.tr. to outweigh (sth.). ◆**ü~d,** adj. (a) predominant (feature, tone etc.); (b) substantial (majority); (b) adv. mainly.

**überwinden** [y:bər'vindən], v.tr.insep.irr.9 to overcome (difficulties, one's fear), surmount (an obstacle etc.), get over (shyness, a crisis etc.); **sich ü., etwas zu tun,** to bring oneself to do sth. ◆**U~ung,** f -/no pl willpower, strength of mind.

**'Überzahl,** f majority.

**überzählig** ['y:bərtsɛːliç], adj. superfluous; Com: etc: surplus (to requirements).

**über'zeug|en,** v.tr.insep. to convince (s.o.), oneself (**von etwas** dat, of sth.); **ü. Sie sich selbst!** see for yourself! ◆**ü~end,** adj. convincing (argument, proof etc.); compelling (reason). ◆**U~ung,** f -/no pl conviction.

**überziehen,** v.tr.irr.113 1. ['y:bərtsiːən] v.sep. to put on (a coat etc.) (on top). 2. [y:bər'tsiːən] v.insep. (a) to cover (sth.); Ind: to coat (sth.); (b) Fin: to overdraw (one's account).

**'Überzug,** m 1. coating (of sugar etc.); coat (of varnish etc.). 2. (Bezug) (chair etc.) cover.

**üblich** ['y:pliç], adj. usual.

**'U-Boot,** n submarine.

**übrig** ['y:briç], adj. (a) attrib. (andere) remaining, other (parts, things etc.); **das ü~e,** the rest; **die ü~en,** the others; the rest of them; **alles ü~e,** everything else; **im ü~en,** for the rest; otherwise; (b) pred. left (over); (c) **er hat viel für sie ü.,** he likes her a lot. ◆**'ü~bleiben,** v.i. sep.irr.12 (sein) to remain, be left; **mir bleibt nichts anderes ü. als zu...,** I have no alternative but to... ◆**ü~ens** [-gəns], adv. by the way, incidentally. ◆**ü~lassen,** v.tr.sep.irr.57 to leave (sth.).

**Übung** ['y:buŋ], f -/-en 1. practice; Mil: Sp: training. 2. (Aufgabe) exercise. ◆**Ü~s-,** comb.fm. practice (flight etc.); training (area etc.).

**Ufer** ['u:fər], n -s/- (Seeu.) shore; (Flußu.) (river) bank. ◆**'u~los,** adj. endless; (grenzenlos) boundless. ◆**'U~straße,** f riverside/lakeside road.

**Uhr** [u:r], f -/-en clock; (Armbandu./Taschenu.) watch; **acht U.,** eight o'clock; **wieviel U. ist es/haben Sie?** what time is it/do you make it? ◆**'U~(arm)band,** n watch strap. ◆**'U~macher,** m watchmaker; clockmaker. ◆**'U~werk,** n clockwork. ◆**'U~zeiger,** m watch/clock hand. ◆**'U~zeigersinn,** m im U., clockwise; **entgegen dem U.,** anticlockwise.

**Uhu** ['u:hu:], m -s/-s eagle owl.

**Ulk** [ulk], *m* -(e)s/-e joke; (*Streich*) lark. ◆**'u~ig**, *adj. F:* comical, funny; (*seltsam*) odd.

**Ulme** ['ulmə], *f* -/-n elm.

**Ultimatum** [ulti'mɑːtum], *n* -s/-ten & -s ultimatum.

**Ultra-** ['ultra-], *comb.fm.* ultra(-conservative, -modern etc.). ◆**U~'kurzwelle**, *f Rad:* very high frequency. ◆**'U~schall-**, *comb.fm.* ultrasonic (frequency, wave etc.).

**um** [um]. I. *prep.* + *acc* 1. (*räumlich*) (a)round; **um sich schlagen**, to lash out in all directions. 2. (*Zeitpunkt*) (a) (*genau*) **um 20 Uhr**, at 8 p.m.; (b) (*ungefähr*) around; (c) (*Folge*) **Tag um Tag/Stunde um Stunde**, day after day/hour after hour. 3. (a) (*Zweck*) for; **um Geld spielen**, to play for money; (b) (*wegen*) about; **sich um etwas streiten**, to quarrel over/about sth. 4. (*Maß*) by; **um einen Kopf größer**, taller by a head; **um vieles besser**, far better. II. *conj.* 1. **um zu** + *infin.*, (in order) to. 2. **um so besser/weniger**, all the better/less. III. *adv.* (*vorbei*) over. IV. *prep.* + *gen* **um ... willen**, for the sake of...

**'umänder|n**, *v.tr.sep.* to alter (sth.). ◆**'U~ung**, *f* -/-en alteration.

**'umarbeit|en**, *v.tr.sep.* to remake, remodel (a dress etc.); to revise, rewrite (a book etc.). ◆**'U~ung**, *f* -/-en revision; adaptation; *Cl:* remodelling.

**um'arm|en**, *v.tr.insep.* to embrace, (*fest*) hug (s.o.). ◆**U~ung**, *f* -/-en embrace, hug.

**'Umbau**, *m* (structural) alteration(s); conversion. ◆**'u~en**, *v.tr.sep.* to alter, make structural alterations in (a building).

**'umbiegen**, *v.tr.sep.irr.7* to bend (sth.) over/back.

**'umbild|en**, *v.tr.sep.* to transform (sth.); *Pol:* to reshuffle (a cabinet). ◆**'U~ung**, *f* transformation; reshuffle.

**'umblättern**, *v.tr. & i.sep.* (*haben*) to turn over (the page).

**'umblicken**, *v.refl.sep.* **sich u.**, to look round.

**'umbringen**, *v.tr.sep.irr.16* to kill, (*ermorden*) murder (s.o.); **sich u.**, to kill oneself, commit suicide.

**'Umbruch**, *m esp. Pol:* radical change; upheaval.

**'umbuchen**, *v.tr.sep.* to change the reservation for (one's flight etc.).

**'umdreh|en**, *v.sep.* 1. *v.tr.* (a) (*auf die andere Seite*) to turn over (a stone, page, record etc.); to turn (a mattress etc.); (b) (*um seine Achse*) to turn (sth.) round; to turn (a key); **sich u.**, (*Pers.*) to turn round; (c) **j-m den Hals u.**, to wring s.o.'s neck. 2. *v.i.* (*sein*) to turn back. ◆**U~ung** [-'dreːuŋ], *f* turn; *Ph: Astr:* rotation; *Tchn:* revolution.

**umei'nander**, *adv.* (a) around each other; (b) **sie kümmern sich nicht u.**, they don't bother about each other.

**umfahren**, *v.tr.irr.26* 1. ['umfaːrən] *v.sep. Aut: etc:* to knock (s.o., sth.) down. 2. [um'faːrən] *v.sep.* to go/*Aut:* drive/*Nau:* sail round (an obstacle etc.), bypass (a town etc.).

**'umfallen**, *v.i.sep.irr.27* (*sein*) to fall over/ (*zum Boden*) down; (*zusammenbrechen*) to collapse.

**'Umfang**, *m* -(e)s/*no pl* 1. circumference (of a tree, circle etc.). 2. (*Größe*) size; (*Fläche*) area (of an estate etc.); (*Ausmaß*) extent (of a book etc.); volume (of business etc.); range (of a voice etc.). ◆**'u~reich**, *adj.* extensive; long (book).

**um'fassen**, *v.tr.insep.* (a) to put one's arm round (s.o., s.o.'s waist); (*mit Händen*) to clasp (sth.); (b) (*umgeben*) to surround; (c) (*enthalten*) to contain (200 pages etc.), comprise (four volumes etc.). ◆**u~d**, *adj.* comprehensive (knowledge, powers etc.); full (confession, description etc.).

**'umform|en**, *v.tr.sep.* to revise, recast (a sentence etc.). ◆**'U~er**, *m* -s/- *El:* converter.

**'Umfrage**, *f* (public) opinion poll; survey.

**'umfüllen**, *v.tr.sep.* to pour (sth.) (into another container); to decant (wine).

**'umfunktionieren**, *v.tr.sep.* to change the function/purpose of (sth.); to convert (sth.).

**'Umgang**, *m* association, contact (**mit** j-m, with s.o.); **mit j-m U. haben/ pflegen**, to associate with s.o.; **schlechten U. haben**, to keep bad company; **der U. mit Büchern/Tieren**, working with books/dealing with animals. ◆**'umgänglich** [-gɛŋliç], *adj.* sociable, affable. ◆**U~sformen**, *fpl* manners, social graces. ◆**'U~ssprache**, *f* colloquial speech. ◆**'u~ssprachlich**, *adj.* colloquial.

**um'geb|en**, *v.tr.insep.irr.35* to surround (s.o., oneself, sth.); (*einschließen*) to enclose (sth.). ◆**U~ung**, *f* -/-en (a) surroundings; (*Gegend*) neighbourhood; **in der (näheren) U.**, in the vicinity; (b) (*Umkreis*) circle.

**umgeh|en**, *v.irr.36* 1. ['umgeːən] *v.i.sep.* (*sein*) (a) to circulate; (*Gerücht usw.*) *F:* to go the rounds; **die Grippe geht wieder um**, there's (a lot of) flu about again; (b) **mit j-m, etwas** *dat* **u.**, to handle s.o., sth.; (*behandeln*) to treat (s.o., sth.); (*verkehren*) to associate with s.o.; **er versteht mit Kindern umzugehen**, he knows how to handle children. 2. [um'geːən] *v.tr.insep.* (a) to go round (sth.); *Aut:* to bypass (a town); (b) (*vermeiden*) to avoid (a difficulty etc.); (*nicht beachten*) to evade/get round (a law, regulation). ◆**'u~end**, *adj.* **u~ende Antwort**, reply by return. ◆**U~ung** [um'geːuŋ], *f* -/*no pl* (a) bypassing; (b) avoidance, evasion. ◆**U~ungsstraße**, *f* bypass.

**'umgekehrt**, *adj.* opposite; reverse (order

etc.); **es ist gerade u.!** it's exactly the opposite.

**um'grenzen,** *v.tr.insep.* to border, *(Zaun)* enclose (a field etc.).

**'Umhang,** *m* wrap, cape.

**'umhängen,** *v.tr.sep.* (*a*) to hang (sth.) somewhere else; (*b*) **j-m, sich** *dat* **etwas u.,** to put sth. round s.o.'s/one's shoulders.

**um'her,** *adv. & comb.fm.* (to wander, drive etc.) around; (to look etc.) about. ◆**u~gehen,** *v.i.sep.irr.36* (*sein*) to go/walk around.

**um'hinkönnen,** *v.i.sep.irr.54* (*haben*) **ich kann nicht umhin, es zu tun,** I cannot help/get out of (doing) it.

**'umhören,** *v.refl.sep.* **sich u.,** to ask around.

**um'hüllen,** *v.tr.insep.* to wrap (s.o., sth.) up. ◆**U~ung,** *f -/-en* wrapper, wrapping.

**'Umkehr,** *f -/no pl* (*a*) turning back; (*b*) *Pol: etc:* about-face. ◆**u~bar,** *adj.* reversible. ◆**u~en,** *v.sep.* **1.** *v.i.* (*sein*) to turn back. **2.** *v.tr.* (*a*) to turn (pockets etc.) inside out; (*b*) to reverse (the order, a development etc.). ◆**U~ung,** *f -/no pl* reversal.

**'umkippen,** *v.* **1.** *v.i.sep.* (*sein*) (*a*) to fall over; *(Auto usw.)* to overturn; *(Boot)* to capsize; (*b*) *F: (ohnmächtig werden)* to faint; (*c*) *F: (seine Meinung ändern)* to give way (under pressure), change one's tune. **2.** *v.tr.* to tip (sth.) over, upset (a vase etc.).

**um'klammern,** *v.tr.insep.* to clasp, cling to (s.o., sth.).

**'Umkleidekabine,** *f* changing cubicle. ◆**u~n,** *v.refl.sep.* **sich u.,** to change (one's clothes). ◆**U~raum,** *m* changing room.

**'umkommen,** *v.i.sep.irr.53* to die, be killed.

**'Umkreis,** *m -es/no pl (Nähe)* vicinity, neighbourhood; **im U. von drei Kilometer(n),** within a radius of three kilometres. ◆**u~en** [um'kraizən], *v.tr.insep.* to circle (around) (sth.); *(Planet)* to revolve around, *(Satellit)* orbit (a star).

**'Umlauf,** *m* circulation (of blood, money etc.); **im U. sein,** *(Geld)* to be in circulation; *Fig: (Gerüchte usw.)* to circulate. ◆**U~bahn,** *f Astr:* orbit.

**'Umlaut,** *m* umlaut.

**'umlegen,** *v.tr.sep.* (*a*) **j-m/sich** *dat* **einen Mantel usw. u.,** to put a coat etc. round s.o./oneself; (*b*) to transfer, move (a cable, patient etc.); (*c*) *F: (erschießen)* to bump (s.o.) off.

**'umleiten,** *v.tr.sep.* to divert (traffic etc.). ◆**U~ung,** *f* diversion.

**um'nachtet,** *adj. Lit:* **geistig u.,** mentally deranged.

**um'rahmen,** *v.tr.insep.* to frame (a picture, *Fig:* face etc.); *Fig:* **von Wäldern umrahmt,** ringed by woods.

**'umrechnen,** *v.tr.sep. Mth:* to convert **(Mark in Pfund usw.,** marks into pounds etc.). ◆**'U~ung,** *f* conversion. ◆**'U~ungskurs,** *m* rate of exchange.

**um'reißen,** *v.tr.insep.irr.4* to outline (a situation etc.).

**um'ringen,** *v.tr.insep.* to surround (s.o., sth.).

**'Umriß,** *m* contour, outline.

**'umrühren,** *v.tr.sep.* to stir (soup, paint etc.).

**ums** [ums] = **um das.**

**'umsatteln,** *v.i.sep.* (*haben*) *F:* to change jobs.

**'Umsatz,** *m* turnover. ◆**'U~steuer,** *f* turnover/*N.Am:* sales tax.

**'umschalten,** *v.sep.* **1.** *v.tr.* to switch (the TV, radio etc.) (over) **(auf** + *acc,* to); to move (a switch, lever etc.) **(auf** + *acc,* to). **2.** *v.i.* (*haben*) to change, switch over, *TV: Rad:* retune **(auf** + *acc* to).

**'Umschau,** *f -/no pl* look round; **nach j-m, etwas** *dat* **U. halten,** to be on the lookout for s.o., sth. ◆**'u~en,** *v.refl.sep.* **sich u.** = **sich umsehen.**

**'Umschlag,** *m* **1.** (dust) jacket (of a book). **2.** *(Brie fu.)* envelope. **3.** *Med:* compress. **4.** *Cl:* cuff; *(Hosenu.)* turn-up, *N.Am:* cuff (of trousers); *(Saum)* hem. **5.** *(Wetteru. usw.)* sudden change. ◆**'u~en** [-gən], *v.sep.irr.85* **1.** *v.tr.* (*a*) *(umwenden)* to turn over (pages etc.), fold back (the carpet), turn up (one's sleeves); (*b*) *(umhauen)* to knock (sth.) down, fell (a tree etc.). **2.** *v.i.* (*sein*) (*a*) *(Auto usw.)* to overturn, *(Boot)* capsize; (*b*) *(Wetter, Fig: Stimmung)* to change abruptly; *(Wind)* to veer (round).

**umschreiben,** *v.tr.irr.12* **1.** ['umʃraibən] *v.sep.* (*a*) to rewrite, redraft (a text); (*b*) **etwas auf js/ein Konto u.,** to transfer sth. to s.o./an account. **2.** [um'ʃraibən] *v.insep.* (*genau*) to define (duties etc.); *(mit anderen Worten)* to paraphrase (a term etc.).

**'umschulen,** *v.tr.sep.* (*a*) to move (a child) to another school; (*b*) *(umerziehen)* to re-educate (s.o.); *Ind:* to retrain (s.o.).

**'Umschweife,** *pl* **etwas ohne U. sagen,** to say sth. bluntly/straight out.

**'Umschwung,** *m* reversal (of fortunes, public opinions etc.), about-turn.

**'umsehen,** *v.refl.sep.irr.92* **sich u.,** to look round/back; **sich nach einem passenden Geschenk u.,** to be looking/on the lookout for a suitable present.

**'umseitig,** *adj.* overleaf.

**'umsetzen,** *v.tr.sep. Com:* to sell/turn over (goods).

**'Umsicht,** *f* circumspection, discretion, prudence. ◆**'u~ig,** *adj.* circumspect; *(klug)* prudent.

**'umsiedeln,** *v.tr.&i.sep.* (*sein*) to resettle (refugees etc.).

**um'sonst,** *adv.* for nothing; *(vergeblich)* in vain.

**um'spannen,** *v.tr.insep.* to clasp, *(mit den*

*Armen*) reach round (sth.); *Fig:* to en-compass (an area), span (a period).

**Umstand** ['umʃtant], *m* 1. (*a*) circum-stance; **ein entscheidender U.**, a decisive factor; (*b*) *pl* **unter diesen/keinen U~en**, in these/no circumstances; (*c*) **in anderen U~en**, in the family way. 2. *pl* (*Mühe*) bother; trouble; **ohne U~e**, without cer-emony; (*sogleich*) without further ado. ◆**'U~skleid**, *n* maternity dress.

**umständelhalber** ['umʃtɛndəhalbər], *adv.* due to circumstances. ◆**'u~lich**, *adj.* awkward, (*übergenau*) fussy (person, manner etc.); complicated, involved (de-scription etc.).

**'umsteigen** *v.i.sep.irr.89* (*sein*) to change (trains/buses).

**umstellen**, *v.tr.* 1. ['umʃtɛlən] *v.sep.* (*a*) to shift round, rearrange (furniture etc.); (*b*) (*neu einstellen*) to readjust (sth.), reset (a switch, clock etc.); (*c*) (*ändern*) to change (one's diet etc.). 2. [um'ʃtɛlən] *v.insep.* to surround (a house etc.). ◆**'U~ung**, *f* (*a*) rearrangement; rede-ployment; (*b*) readjustment, resetting; (*c*) changeover, conversion.

**'umstimmen**, *v.tr.sep.* (*überreden*) to make (s.o.) change his/her mind; to win (s.o.) round.

**'umstoßen**, *v.tr.sep.irr.103* to knock (s.o., a vase etc.) over; *Fig:* to upset, wreck (a plan, calculations etc.).

**um'stritten**, *adj.* disputed (thesis etc.); controversial (subject, issue etc.).

**'Umsturz**, *m Pol:* overthrow (of a re-gime); coup.

**'umstürzen**, *v.sep.* 1. *v.tr.* to knock over (chairs, tables etc.). 2. *v.i.* (*sein*) to fall over, (*Mauer usw.*) fall down.

**'Umtausch**, *m* exchange. ◆**'u~en**, *v.tr.sep.* to exchange (sth.) (**gegen etwas** *acc*, for sth.); to change (money).

**'Umtriebe**, *mpl* machinations, intrigues.

**'umwandeln**, *v.tr.sep.* (*a*) to transform (s.o.'s character etc.); (*b*) *Ph: Ch:* to con-vert (sth.) (**in** + *acc*, into). ◆**'U~lung**, *f* transformation; conversion.

**'Umweg**, *m* detour.

**'Umwelt**. I. *f* -/*no pl* environment. II. **'U~-**, **'u~-**, *comb.fm.* environmental (factor, question etc.); *Biol: etc:* ecologi-cal (policy etc.). ◆**'u~freundlich**, *adj.* harmless to the environment. ◆**'U~schutz**, *m* conservation. ◆**'U~schützer**, *m* conservationist. ◆**'U~verschmutzung**, *f* (environ-mental) pollution.

**'umwenden**, *v.tr.sep.irr.94* to turn over (a page etc.), (*Pers.*) **sich u.**, to turn round.

**'umwerfen**, *v.tr.sep.irr.110* to knock over (s.o., a vase etc.), overturn (a table); *Fig:* to upset, wreck (plans). ◆**'u~d**, *adj.* stupendous (success etc.); stunning (beauty).

**um'zäunen**, *v.tr.insep.* to fence in/round (a plot etc.).

**'umziehen**, *v.sep.irr.113* 1. *v.i.* (*sein*) to

move (**nach X**, to X). 2. *v.tr.* **ein Kind/ sich u.**, to change a child's/one's clothes.

**umzingeln** [um'tsiŋəln], *v.tr.insep.* to sur-round, encircle (the enemy, a town etc.).

**Umzug** ['umtsu:k], *m* 1. move, removal (**nach** + *dat* to). 2. procession.

**unabänderlich** [un²ap'²ɛndərliç], *adj.* unalterable (fact etc.); irrevocable (deci-sion etc.).

**'unabhängig**, *adj.* independent. ◆**'U~keit**, *f* -/*no pl* independence.

**unab'kömmlich**, *adj.* indispensable.

**unablässig** ['un²aplɛsiç], *adj.* incessant, constant (complaints etc.); unremitting (efforts).

**unab'sehbar**, *adj.* (*a*) unforeseeable (con-sequences etc.); (*b*) (*unermeßlich*) immea-surable (loss etc.).

**'unabsichtlich**, *adj.* unintentional.

**unabwendbar** [un²ap'vɛntba:r], *adj.* un-avoidable, inevitable.

**'unachtsam**, *adj.* (*nachlässig*) careless, negligent (action etc.).

**'unähnlich**, *adj.* dissimilar; **j-m u.**, unlike s.o.

**'unangebracht**, *adj.* inappropriate, out-of-place (remark etc.).

**'unangemessen**, *adj.* inappropriate.

**'unangenehm**, *adj.* unpleasant; (*peinlich*) embarrassing, awkward (question etc.).

**unan'nehmbar**, *adj.* unacceptable. ◆**'U~lichkeit**, *f* -/-en *usu.pl* **j-m U~lichkeiten bereiten**, to cause s.o. difficulties/trouble.

**'unansehnlich**, *adj.* plain (girl etc.); shabby (clothes etc.).

**'unanständig**, *adj.* indecent (behaviour, language, dress etc.); dirty (joke etc.), rude (word).

**unan'tastbar**, *adj.* sacrosanct; *Jur:* inviol-able (rights etc.).

**'unappetitlich**, *adj.* unappetizing (food etc.); *Fig:* unsavoury.

**Unart** ['una:rt], *f* bad habit. ◆**'u~ig**, *adj.* naughty.

**'unauffällig**, *adj.* inconspicuous; unobtru-sive (colour, behaviour etc.).

**unauf'findbar**, *adj.* nowhere to be found.

**'unaufgefordert**, *adj.* of one's own ac-cord.

**unaufhaltsam** [un²auf'haltza:m], *adj.* ir-resistible, inexorable.

**unaufhörlich** [un²auf'hø:rliç], *adj.* incess-ant, ceaseless.

**'unaufmerksam**, *adj.* inattentive.

**'unaufrichtig**, *adj.* insincere.

**unaufschiebbar** [-'ʃi:pba:r], *adj.* urgent, pressing.

**unausbleiblich** [un²aus'blaipliç], *adj.* in-evitable.

**'unausgeglichen**, *adj.* unbalanced, *Fig:* (*Pers.*) unstable.

**unaus'löschlich**, *adj.* indelible (impres-sion etc.).

**unaus'sprechlich**, *adj.* inexpressible; un-utterable; unspeakable (misery etc.).

**unausstehlich** [-'ʃte:liç], *adj.* insufferable.

**unbändig** ['unbɛndiç], *adj.* uncontrollable; unruly (child); **sich u. freuen,** to be jumping for joy.

'**unbarmherzig,** *adj.* merciless.

'**unbeabsichtigt,** *adj.* unintentional.

'**unbeachtet,** *adj.* unnoticed; unheeded (warning etc.).

'**unbedenklich,** *adj.* harmless (proposal etc.).

'**unbedeutend,** *adj.* insignificant; minor (damage, poet etc.); trivial (matter).

unbe'dingt [*stressed* 'un-], *adj.* absolute (loyalty, obedience etc.); **kommst du? ja, u.!** are you coming? yes, definitely; **nicht u.,** not necessarily; **das müssen Sie sich u. anschen,** you really must see that.

'**unbefangen,** *adj.* 1. (*unparteiisch*) unbiased; impartial. 2. (*natürlich*) unaffected, natural.

'**unbefriedigend,** *adj.* unsatisfactory.

'**unbefugt,** *adj.* unauthorized.

'**unbegabt,** *adj.* untalented, ungifted.

**unbegreiflich** [unbə'graifliç], *adj.* incomprehensible.

'**unbegrenzt,** *adj.* unlimited.

'**unbegründet,** *adj.* unfounded (optimism etc.); groundless (accusation, fear etc.).

**Unbehag|en,** *n* -*s/no pl* uneasiness; (*körperlich*) discomfort. ◆'**u~lich,** *adj.* uncomfortable (atmosphere etc.); uneasy (feeling etc.).

'**unbeherrscht,** *adj.* (*Pers.*) lacking/ without self-control.

'**unbeholfen,** *adj.* awkward, clumsy.

**unbeirr|bar** [unbə'ʔirbɑːr], *adj.* unwavering, unswerving. ◆**u~t** [-'ʔirt], *adv.* unswervingly; without wavering.

'**unbekannt,** *adj.* unknown; **ein U~er/ eine U~e,** a stranger.

'**unbekleidet,** *adj.* undressed.

**unbekümmert,** *adj.* unconcerned; easygoing (person, manner).

**unbelehrbar** [unbə'leːrbɑːr], *adj.* not open to reason.

'**unbeliebt,** *adj.* unpopular. ◆'**U~heit,** *f* unpopularity.

'**unbemannt,** *adj.* unmanned (satellite etc.).

**unbe'merkt,** *adj.* unnoticed, unobserved.

'**unbequem,** *adj.* (*a*) uncomfortable (shoe, chair etc.); (*b*) (*peinlich*) awkward (person, questions etc.).

**unbe'rechenbar,** *adj.* unpredictable.

'**unberechtigt,** *adj.* unjustified (criticism, claim etc.).

'**unberührt,** *adj.* untouched; unspoilt (countryside); **u~es Mädchen,** virgin.

'**unbescheiden,** *adj.* immodest, presumptuous.

'**unbeschränkt,** *adj.* unlimited.

**unbeschreiblich** [unbə'fraipliç], *adj.* indescribable.

'**unbeschwert,** *adj.* carefree; lighthearted (mood).

**unbe'sehen,** *adj.* unseen, unexamined; **etwas u. kaufen,** to buy sth. sight unseen.

**unbesieg|bar** [unbə'ziːkbɑːr], *adj.* invincible; *Sp:* unbeatable. ◆**u~t,** *adj. Sp:* unbeaten.

'**unbesonnen,** *adj.* thoughtless, imprudent; (*übereilt*) rash.

'**unbesorgt,** *adj.* unconcerned; **seien Sie u.,** don't worry.

'**unbeständig,** *adj.* changeable (weather etc.); unsettled (weather, *Fin:* market etc.); fluctuating (prices etc.); *Fig:* (*Pers.*) inconsistent.

'**unbestechlich,** *adj.* incorruptible.

**unbe'stimm|bar,** *adj.* indeterminate (age etc.); indefinable (feeling etc.). ◆'**u~t,** *adj.* indefinite (period, future, *Gram:* article); indeterminate (age); (*unsicher*) uncertain; (*unklar*) vague (feeling etc.). ◆'**U~theit,** *f* indefiniteness; uncertainty; vagueness.

**unbe'streitbar,** *adj.* incontestable, indisputable.

'**unbestritten,** *adj.* uncontested, undisputed.

'**unbeteiligt,** *adj.* not involved; (*gleichgültig*) detached (observer etc.).

**unbeugsam** [un'bɔykzɑːm], *adj.* uncompromising; unshakable (will etc.).

**unbeweg|lich,** *adj.* (*a*) (*nicht zu bewegen*) immovable, fixed (joint, part etc.); (*b*) (*ganz still*) motionless, immobile (figures etc.). ◆'**u~t,** *adj.* motionless; calm, still (sea etc.); *Fig:* (*unberührt*) unmoved.

'**unbewiesen,** *adj.* unproved, (*Schuld*) unproven.

**unbe'wohn|bar,** *adj.* uninhabitable. ◆'**u~t,** *adj.* uninhabited (region etc.); unoccupied (house).

'**unbewußt,** *adj.* unconscious.

**unbe'zahl|bar,** *adj.* 1. prohibitively expensive. 2. priceless (painting etc.). ◆'**u~t,** *adj.* unpaid.

'**unblutig,** *adj.* bloodless (revolution etc.).

'**unbrauchbar,** *adj.* useless (work, person etc.); unusable, (*defekt*) unserviceable (apparatus etc.).

**und** [unt], *conj.* and; *F:* **u. ob!** you bet! and how! **na u.?** well? what then? (*wenn schon*) so what!

'**Undank,** *m Lit:* ingratitude. ◆'**u~bar,** *adj.* ungrateful (**gegen j-n,** to s.o.); **u~bare Aufgabe,** thankless task. ◆'**U~barkeit,** *f* -*/no pl* ingratitude.

**un'denkbar,** *adj.* unthinkable, inconceivable.

'**undeutlich,** *adj.* unclear; indistinct.

'**undicht,** *adj.* leaky, leaking.

'**Unding,** *n* es ist ein **U., zu ...,** it is absurd/preposterous to ...

'**unduldsam,** *adj.* intolerant.

**undurch'führbar,** *adj.* impracticable.

'**undurchlässig,** *adj.* impermeable, impervious.

**undurch'schaubar,** *adj.* unfathomable; (*Pers.*) inscrutable, baffling.

'**undurchsichtig,** *adj.* opaque; *Fig:* baffling; (*suspekt*) shady.

'**uneben,** *adj.* uneven (surface etc.); (*holperig*) bumpy, rough (road etc.).
'**unecht,** *adj.* imitation (leather, pearls etc.); artificial (flowers); false (hair etc.).
'**unehelich,** *adj.* illegitimate (child).
'**unehrlich,** *adj.* dishonest, (*betrügerisch*) deceitful.
'**uneigennützig,** *adj.* unselfish, selfless. ◆'**U~keit,** *f* unselfishness.
'**uneinig,** *adj.* (*Gruppe*) divided; **u. sein,** to disagree/be at loggerheads (**mit j-m,** with s.o.). ◆'**U~keit,** *f* disagreement, dissension.
**uneins** ['un²ains], *adj.* = **uneinig.**
'**unempfindlich,** *adj.* insensitive (**gegen** + *acc,* to); (*abgehärtet*) hardened, inured. ◆'**U~keit,** *f* insensitivity.
**un'endlich,** *adj.* infinite; (*Zeit, Weg*) endless; **u. groß/hoch,** enormously large/high. ◆**U~keit,** *f -/no pl* endlessness; infinity; (*Ewigkeit*) eternity.
**unent'behrlich,** *adj.* indispensable.
**unentgeltlich** [un²ɛnt'gɛltliç], *adj.* gratis, free.
'**unentschieden. I.** *adj.* undecided; (*Frage*) unsettled; *Sp:* drawn (game); **u~es Rennen,** dead heat. **II. U.,** *n -s/-* *Sp:* draw.
'**unentschlossen,** *adj.* undecided; (*allgemein*) irresolute, indecisive.
**unentwegt** [un²ɛnt've:kt], *adj.* (*unaufhörlich*) incessant, uninterrupted; (*unermüdlich*) tireless (fighter etc.); (*wiederholt*) constant.
**unerbittlich** [un²ɛr'bitliç], *adj.* unrelenting (critic, struggle etc.); inexorable (fate, law); **u. bleiben,** to remain adamant.
'**unerfahren,** *adj.* inexperienced. ◆'**U~heit,** *f* inexperience.
'**unerfreulich,** *adj.* unpleasant, disagreeable.
**uner'gründlich,** *adj.* unfathomable.
'**unerheblich,** *adj.* insignificant (quantity etc.).
**unerhört** [un²ɛr'hø:rt], *adj.* (*a*) (*noch nie dagewesen*) unheard of, unprecedented (achievement etc.); (*b*) (*skandalös*) outrageous, scandalous (behaviour etc.); exorbitant (prices).
**uner'klärlich,** *adj.* inexplicable.
**unerläßlich** [un²ɛr'lɛsliç], *adj.* indispensable.
'**unerlaubt,** *adj.* not allowed, prohibited; (*unbefugt*) unauthorized.
**uner'meßlich,** *adj.* immeasurable, immense.
**unermüdlich** [un²ɛr'my:tliç, 'un-], *adj.* untiring, tireless.
**uner'reich|bar,** *adj.* unattainable (goal etc.); inaccessible (place etc.). ◆**u~t,** *adj.* unequalled (performance etc.).
**unersättlich** [un²ɛr'zɛtliç], *adj.* insatiable.
**unerschöpflich** [-'ʃœpfliç], *adj.* inexhaustible.
'**unerschrocken,** *adj.* intrepid, fearless.
**unerschütterlich** [-'ʃytərliç], *adj.* un-

shakable (will etc.).
**uner'schwinglich,** *adj.* exorbitant, prohibitive (price etc.).
**unersetzlich** [un²ɛr'zɛtsliç], *adj.* irreplaceable.
**uner'träglich,** *adj.* intolerable, unbearable.
'**unerwartet,** *adj.* unexpected.
'**unerwünscht,** *adj.* unwanted; unwelcome (visit, visitor etc.).
'**unerzogen,** *adj.* badly behaved/brought up.
'**unfähig,** *adj.* (*a*) *pred.* incapable (**zu etwas** *dat,* of sth.); (*b*) (*untauglich*) incompetent. ◆'**U~keit,** *f* (*a*) inability; (*b*) incompetence.
**Unfall** ['unfal]. **I.** *m* accident. **II.** '**U~-,** *comb.fm.* accident (insurance etc.). ◆'**u~frei,** *adj.* accident-free. ◆'**U~-ort,** *m* scene of the accident.
**unfaßbar** [un'fasba:r], *adj.* incomprehensible.
**unfehlbar** [un'fe:lba:r], *adj.* infallible. ◆**U~keit,** *f -/no pl* infallibility.
'**unfolgsam,** *adj.* disobedient.
'**unfreiwillig,** *adj.* involuntary; (*unbeabsichtigt*) unintentional (joke etc.).
'**unfreundlich,** *adj.* (*a*) unfriendly; unkind (words etc.); unwelcoming (face); *Pol:* hostile (act); (*b*) (*trüb*) cheerless (room etc.); unpleasant, inclement (weather etc.). ◆'**U~keit,** *f* (*a*) unfriendliness; unkindness; (*b*) cheerlessness; inclemency.
'**unfruchtbar,** *adj.* (*a*) infertile (animal, soil); sterile (person); (*b*) *Fig:* fruitless (discussion etc.).
**Unfug** ['unfu:k], *m -(e)s/no pl* mischief; *F:* monkey business; (*Unsinn*) nonsense, rubbish; *Jur:* **grober U.,** public nuisance.
**Ungar|(in)** ['ungar(in)], *m -n/-n (f -/-nen)* Hungarian (man/woman). ◆**u~isch,** *adj.* Hungarian. ◆'**U~n.** *Pr.n. n. -s.* Hungary.
**ungeachtet** ['ungə²axtət], *prep.* + *gen Lit:* notwithstanding; (*trotz*) despite.
**unge'ahnt,** *adj.* unsuspected.
'**ungebeten,** *adj.* unasked, uninvited.
'**ungeboren,** *adj.* unborn.
'**ungebräuchlich,** *adj.* not usual; (*selten*) uncommon.
'**ungedeckt,** *adj.* uncovered, *F:* dud (cheque etc.).
'**Ungeduld,** *f* impatience. ◆'**u~ig,** *adj.* impatient.
'**ungeeignet,** *adj.* unsuitable; wrong, inappropriate (tool, method); inopportune (moment).
**ungefähr** ['ungəfɛ:r]. **1.** *adj.* approximate, rough. **2.** *adv.* approximately; about.
'**ungefährlich,** *adj.* safe, not dangerous; harmless (animal, drug etc.).
'**ungehalten,** *adj.* annoyed; (*entrüstet*) indignant.
**ungeheuer** ['ungəhɔyər]. **I.** *adj.* im-

mense, enormous (size, height, wealth etc.); tremendous (strength, luck etc.); (*schrecklich*) terrible (pain etc.); **u. groß,** tremendously large; **u. heiß,** terribly hot. **II. U.,** *n* -**s**/- monster. ◆'**u**~**lich,** *adj.* monstrous (accusation, crime etc.); outrageous (remark).

'**ungehindert,** *adj.* unhindered; (*ungestört*) undisturbed.

'**ungehörig,** *adj.* unseemly, improper. ◆'**U**~**keit,** *f* -/-**en** impropriety.

'**ungehorsam. I.** *adj.* disobedient. **II. U.,** *m* disobedience.

'**ungeklärt,** *adj.* not cleared up; unsolved (problem, mystery); unsettled (question).

'**ungekürzt,** *adj.* unabridged.

'**ungeladen,** *adj.* uninvited (guest etc.).

'**ungelegen,** *adj.* inopportune (remark, proposal etc.); inconvenient (time etc.).

'**ungelernt,** *adj.* unskilled (worker).

'**ungemein,** *adj.* extraordinary, prodigious (effort, progress etc.); *adv.* exceedingly.

'**ungemütlich,** *adj.* (*a*) uninviting, cheerless (room etc.); uncomfortable (atmosphere etc.); (*b*) unpleasant (situation, meeting etc.); unfriendly (person).

'**ungenau,** *adj.* inaccurate (measurement, calculation etc.).

**ungeniert** ['unʒeniːrt], *adj.* unconcerned, nonchalant; (*ungehemmt*) uninhibited, free and easy (behaviour etc.); **etwas u. aussprechen,** to say sth. quite openly.

**unge'nießbar,** *adj.* inedible, uneatable (food); undrinkable (wine etc.); *F:* (*Pers.*) unbearable.

'**ungenügend,** *adj.* inadequate; (*nicht genug*) insufficient; (*mangelhaft*) unsatisfactory.

'**ungenutzt,** *adj.* unused.

'**ungeordnet,** *adj.* out of order, in disorder.

'**ungepflegt,** *adj.* unkempt; *F:* scruffy (person, appearance etc.).

'**ungerade,** *adj.* odd, uneven (number).

'**ungerecht,** *adj.* unjust (**gegen j-n,** to s.o.); unfair. ◆'**u**~**fertigt,** *adj.* unjustified. ◆'**U**~**igkeit,** *f* injustice.

'**ungern,** *adv.* unwillingly; (*widerwillig*) reluctantly.

'**ungerührt,** *adj.* unmoved; impassive (face etc.).

'**Ungeschick,** *n*/'**U**~**lichkeit,** *f* clumsiness; ineptitude. ◆'**u**~**t,** *adj.* (*a*) clumsy, inept; *F:* ham-fisted; (*b*) (*taktlos*) tactless.

'**ungeschminkt,** *adj.* without make-up; *Fig:* **die u**~**e Wahrheit,** the plain/unvarnished truth.

'**ungeschützt,** *adj.* unprotected; unsheltered.

'**ungesetzlich,** *adj.* illegal. ◆'**U**~**keit,** *f* illegality.

'**ungesittet,** *adj.* improper, uncivilized.

'**ungestört,** *adj.* undisturbed; uninterrupted (development).

'**ungestraft,** *adj.* unpunished; **u. davonkommen,** to get off scot-free.

'**ungesund,** *adj.* unhealthy.

'**ungeteilt,** *adj.* undivided; united (country etc.); (*einmütig*) unanimous (approval etc.).

'**ungetrübt,** *adj.* perfect (happiness), blissful, unspoilt (days).

**Ungetüm** ['ungəty:m], *n* -**(e)s**/-**e** monster.

'**ungewiß,** *adj.* uncertain. ◆'**U**~**heit,** *f* uncertainty.

'**ungewöhnlich,** *adj.* unusual; exceptional (performance, talent etc.).

'**ungewohnt,** *adj.* unaccustomed; **diese Arbeit ist mir u.,** I am not used to this work.

'**ungewollt,** *adj.* unwanted (pregnancy etc.); (*unbeabsichtigt*) unintentional, inadvertent.

**Ungeziefer** ['ungətsiːfər], *n* -**s**/no *pl* vermin.

'**ungezogen,** *adj.* badly behaved, naughty (child); (*frech*) cheeky.

'**ungezwungen,** *adj.* (*Pers.*) natural, unaffected; informal, free and easy (conversation, atmosphere etc.).

'**unglaub**|**haft,** *adj.* incredible, unconvincing. ◆**u**~**lich** [un'glauplɪç], *adj.* incredible; (*unerhört*) appalling (conditions etc.). ◆'**u**~**würdig,** *adj.* unbelievable, implausible (story); untrustworthy.

'**ungleich,** *adj.* **1.** unequal (size, struggle etc.); (*unähnlich*) dissimilar; **u**~**es Paar,** ill-assorted couple. **2.** *adv.* **u. schwerer,** far more difficult. ◆'**U**~**heit,** *f* inequality; dissimilarity. ◆'**u**~**mäßig,** *adj.* irregular (pulse etc.); uneven, unequal (distribution etc.).

'**Unglück,** *n* (*a*) misfortune; (*Pech*) bad luck; (*Elend*) distress, misery; **zum U.,** unfortunately; (*b*) (*Unfall*) accident; (*Mißgeschick*) mishap. ◆'**u**~**lich,** *adj.* (*a*) (*ungünstig*) unfortunate, unlucky (person, coincidence, choice etc.); (*b*) (*traurig*) unhappy (person, ending etc.). ◆'**u**~**licher'weise,** *adv.* unfortunately. ◆'**u**~**selig,** *adj.* hapless (person); ill-starred, ill-fated (affair etc.); unfortunate (affair, liking etc.). ◆'**U**~**sfall,** *m* (great) misfortune; (*Unfall*) (serious) accident.

'**Ungnade,** *f* **bei j-m in U. fallen,** to fall out of favour with s.o.

'**ungültig,** *adj.* invalid.

'**ungünstig,** *adj.* unfavourable; adverse (conditions); (*ungelegen*) inconvenient (time).

'**ungut,** *adj.* bad (impression, memory etc.); **ein u**~**es Gefühl haben,** to have misgivings/feel uneasy; **nichts für u.!** no hard feelings!

'**unhaltbar,** *adj.* **1.** untenable (assertion etc.). **2.** (*unerträglich*) intolerable (conditions etc.). **3.** *Sp:* unstoppable (ball, shot).

'**unhandlich,** *adj.* unwieldy, cumbersome.

'**Unheil,** *n Lit:* **1.** disaster, misfortune; (*Schaden*) damage; **großes U. anrichten,**

to cause havoc. **2.** (*Böses*) evil.
◆'u∼**bar**, *adj.* incurable (disease, person). ◆'u∼**voll**, *adj.* disastrous (consequences etc.); malign (influence).

**'unheimlich**, *adj.* **1.** eery, uncanny (experience, atmosphere, feeling etc.); weird (person, story etc.); sinister (appearance). **2.** *F:* (*riesig*) terrific, tremendous (appetite, amount etc.); **u. schnell**, incredibly fast.

**'unhöflich**, *adj.* impolite; (*absichtlich*) rude. ◆'U∼**keit**, *f* impoliteness; rudeness.

**'unhygienisch**, *adj.* unhygienic.

**Uniform** [uni'fɔrm], *f* -/-en uniform. ◆u∼**iert** [-'miːrt], *adj.* uniformed, in uniform.

**'uninteressant**, *adj.* uninteresting; (*gleichgültig*) immaterial. ◆'u∼**iert**, *adj.* uninterested (**an etwas** *dat*, in sth.); bored (face).

**Union** [uni'oːn], *f* -/-en union.

**universal** [univɛr'zaːl], *adj.* universal. ◆U∼**alerbe**, *m* sole heir. ◆u∼**ell** [-'zɛl], *adj.* universal. ◆U∼**ität** [-zi'tɛːt], *f* -/-en university. ◆U∼**um** [-'vɛrzum], *n* -s/no pl universe.

**'unkenntlich**, *adj.* unrecognizable; (*Text*) undecipherable. ◆'U∼**nis**, *f* ignorance.

**'unklar**, *adj.* unclear; cloudy (liquid etc.); indistinct (outline etc.); **j-n über etwas** *acc* **im u∼en lassen**, to leave s.o. in the dark about sth. ◆'U∼**heit**, *f* lack of clarity; vagueness, indistinctness; **darüber herrscht U.**, it is uncertain.

**'unklug**, *adj.* imprudent, unwise.

**'unkompliziert**, *adj.* uncomplicated.

**'Unkosten**, *pl* expenses.

**'Unkraut**, *n* (*a*) *no pl coll* weeds; (*b*) (type of) weed.

**'unkritisch**, *adj.* uncritical.

**'unlängst**, *adv.* recently, not long ago.

**'unleserlich**, *adj.* illegible, unreadable (handwriting).

**'unliebsam** ['unliːpzaːm], *adj.* unpleasant (surprise etc.).

**'unlogisch**, *adj.* illogical.

**un'lösbar**, *adj.* **1.** inseparable (union, bond etc.). **2.** insoluble (problem etc.); impossible (task).

**'Unlust**, *f* disinclination, reluctance; **mit U.**, reluctantly.

**'Unmasse**, *f* *F:* mass; **U∼n/eine U. (von) Geld**, masses/loads of money.

**'unmäßig**, *adj.* immoderate, excessive; inordinate (desire).

**'Unmenge**, *f* mass (**an/von** + *dat*, of); **eine U. Geld**, masses of money.

**'Unmensch**, *m* brute; *F:* **ich bin ja kein U.**, I'm not inhuman. ◆u∼**lich**, *adj.* **1.** brutal; inhuman (cruelty); (*menschenunwürdig*) subhuman (conditions etc.). **2.** *F:* (*schrecklich*) terrible (heat etc.).

**un'merklich**, *adj.* imperceptible.

**'unmißverständlich**, *adj.* unmistakable.

**'unmittelbar**, *adj.* direct (connection, consequence etc.); immediate (surround-

ings, superior etc.).

**'unmöbliert**, *adj.* unfurnished (room etc.).

**'unmodern**, *adj.* old-fashioned, unfashionable.

**unmöglich** ['un-, *stressed* un'møːkliç], *adj.* (*a*) impossible; **ich kann u. kommen**, I cannot possibly come; (*b*) *F:* ridiculous, absurd (hat, dress etc.); **sich u. benehmen**, to behave outrageously.

**'unmoralisch**, *adj.* immoral.

**'Unmut**, *m* *Lit:* displeasure.

**unnachahmlich** ['unnaːxˀaːmliç], *adj.* inimitable.

**'unnachgiebig**, *adj.* unyielding, inflexible.

**unnahbar** [un'naːbaːr], *adj.* unapproachable, *F:* standoffish (person).

**'unnatürlich**, *adj.* unnatural.

**'unnötig**, *adj.* unnecessary; needless (anger, worry). ◆'u∼**er'weise**, *adv.* unnecessarily.

**'unnütz**, *adj.* useless; (*sinnlos*) pointless; wasted (effort, expenditure).

**'unordentlich**, *adj.* untidy (person, room, desk etc.); (*nachlässig*) slipshod (work, style etc.).

**'Unordnung**, *f* disorder, mess.

**'unparteiisch**, *adj.* impartial, unbiased; *Sp:* **der U∼e**, the referee.

**'unpassend**, *adj.* unsuitable, inept (remark); (*ungelegen*) inconvenient, inopportune.

**unpäßlich** ['unpɛsliç], *pred.adj.* poorly, under the weather.

**'unpersönlich**, *adj.* impersonal; (*Pers.*) distant, aloof.

**'unpolitisch**, *adj.* non-political; (*Pers.*) unpolitical.

**'unpraktisch**, *adj.* impractical; impracticable (plan etc.).

**'unproblematisch**, *adj.* problem-free; (*einfach*) straightforward, uncomplicated.

**'unpünktlich**, *adj.* unpunctual. ◆'U∼**keit**, *f* lack of punctuality, lateness.

**'unrasiert**, *adj.* unshaven.

**'Unrat**, *m* -(e)s/no pl refuse, *N.Am:* trash.

**'unrealistisch**, *adj.* unrealistic.

**'unrecht. I.** *adj.* wrong. **II. U.**, *n* (*a*) injustice, wrong; **im U. sein**, to be in (the) wrong/mistaken; **mit/zu U.**, unjustly, wrongly; (*b*) **u. haben**, to be wrong; **damit tust du ihm u.**, there you are doing him an injustice. ◆'u∼**mäßig**, *adj.* illegal, unlawful.

**'unredlich**, *adj.* dishonest.

**'unregelmäßig**, *adj.* irregular (pulse, *Gram:* verb etc.); uneven (surface etc.). ◆'U∼**keit**, *f* **1.** *no pl* irregularity; unevenness. **2.** *esp.pl* U∼**en**, irregularities.

**'unreif**, *adj.* unripe; *Fig:* immature (person etc.). ◆'U∼**e**, *f* -/no pl unripeness; *Fig:* immaturity.

**'unrein**, *adj.* unclean (shirt etc.); dirty (water etc.); impure (alcohol etc.); blemished (skin).

**'unrentabel**, *adj.* unprofitable.

'**unrichtig,** *adj.* incorrect, wrong.
**Unruh** ['unruː], *f -/-en* balance wheel.
'**Unruh|e,** *f* 1. *no pl (Ruhelosigkeit)* restlessness; *(Unbehagen)* uneasiness; *(Besorgnis)* anxiety, disquiet; **U. stiften,** to stir up trouble. 2. *Pol: etc: usu.pl* **U~n,** disturbances, *esp.* riots. ◆'**U~eherd,** *m* trouble spot. ◆'**U~estifter,** *m* troublemaker, agitator. ◆'**u~ig,** *adj.* restless (person, people, life etc.); troubled, fitful (sleep); *(besorgt)* anxious, worried; *(nervös)* jittery.
**uns** [uns], *pers.pron.* 1. *(a) acc* us; *(b) dat* (to) us; **das gehört u.,** that belongs to us; **ein Freund von u.,** a friend of ours; **bei u.,** (i) at our home/*F:* place; (ii) *(in der Heimat)* where we come from. 2. *refl.* ourselves; *(einander)* each other, one another.
'**unsach|gemäß,** *adj.* improper, inexpert. ◆'**u~lich,** *adj.* subjective (standpoint etc.); *(nicht zur Sache)* irrelevant (remarks etc.).
**un'sagbar**/*Lit:* **unsäglich** [un'zɛːkliç], *adj.* inexpressible, unutterable; beyond expression.
'**unsanft,** *adj.* rough; abrupt (push etc.).
'**unsauber,** *adj.* 1. *(schmutzig)* dirty; *Fig:* blurred (sound). 2. *(unordentlich)* untidy (handwriting etc.). 3. *(fragwürdig)* shady (practices etc.).
'**unschädlich,** *adj.* harmless; **u. machen,** to render (sth.) harmless; defuse (a bomb); *(ausschalten)* to eliminate (s.o.).
'**unscharf,** *adj.* blurred, fuzzy; *Phot:* out of focus; *Fig:* woolly (definition etc.).
**unschätzbar** [un'ʃɛtsbaːr], *adj.* inestimable (value etc.); invaluable (services etc.).
'**unscheinbar,** *adj.* inconspicuous; nondescript.
**un'schlagbar,** *adj.* unbeatable (team etc.).
'**unschlüssig,** *adj.* undecided; irresolute.
**Unschuld** ['unʃult], *f -/no pl* innocence; *(Jungfräulichkeit)* virginity. ◆'**u~ig,** *adj. (a)* innocent (**an etwas** *dat,* of sth.); *Jur:* **sich u. bekennen,** to plead not guilty; *(b)* **sie ist noch u.,** she is still a virgin.
'**unschwer,** *adv.* easily, without difficulty.
'**unselbständig,** *adj.* dependent (on others); lacking in independence.
**unser** ['unzər], *poss.adj.* our. ◆'**u~e(r,s),** *poss.pron.* ours. ◆'**u~eins,** *indef.pron. F:* people like you and me; the likes of us. ◆'**u~erseits,** *adv.* for our part. ◆'**u~esgleichen,** *inv.indef.pron.* our equals, people like ourselves. ◆'**u~(e)twegen,** *adv.* for our sake, on our account.
'**unsicher,** *adj.* 1. *(gefährlich)* unsafe, dangerous; *(bedroht)* insecure (jobs etc.). 2. *(zweifelhaft)* uncertain; *(nicht selbstsicher)* unsure (of oneself); unsteady, shaky (hand etc.); *Pol: etc:* unstable, unsettled (conditions etc.). ◆'**U~heit,** *f* 1. un-

safeness, insecurity. 2. uncertainty; unsteadiness.
'**unsichtbar,** *adj.* invisible.
**Unsinn** ['unzin], *m* nonsense, rubbish; *(Unfug)* tomfoolery. ◆'**u~ig,** *adj. (sinnlos)* senseless, foolish, stupid (talk, ideas etc.).
'**Unsitt|e,** *f* bad habit/*(Brauch)* practice. ◆'**u~lich,** *adj.* immoral.
'**unsozial,** *adj.* anti-social (laws etc.).
'**unsportlich,** *adj.* 1. unsporting (behaviour etc.); unfair (play). 2. **er ist sehr u.,** he is not at all the sporting type.
**unsre** ['unzrə] = **unsere.**
**un'sterblich,** *adj.* immortal. ◆**U~keit,** *f* immortality.
'**unstet,** *adj.* restless (person, nature etc.); wandering (glance); unsettled (life).
**unstillbar** [un'ʃtilbaːr, 'un-], *adj.* insatiable (desire); unquenchable (thirst).
'**Unstimmigkeit,** *f -/-en (a)* difference (of opinion); *(b) (Fehler)* inconsistency, discrepancy.
'**Unsumme,** *f* enormous sum, fortune.
'**unsympathisch,** *adj.* uncongenial, disagreeable; **er ist mir u.,** I don't like him.
'**Untat,** *f* atrocity, monstrous crime.
'**untätig,** *adj.* inactive; idle.
'**untauglich,** *adj.* unsuitable, wrong; *(nutzlos)* useless; *Mil: (Pers.)* unfit for military service.
**un'teilbar,** *adj.* indivisible.
**unten** ['untən], *adv. (a) (an der Unterseite)* underneath; **u. im Faß/auf der Seite,** at the bottom of the barrel/page; **nach u. hin/zu,** towards the bottom; *F:* **er ist bei mir u. durch,** I'm through with him; *(b) (unterhalb)* (down) below; **hier/dort u.,** down here/there; *(c) (Richtung)* **nach u.,** downwards; *(d) (im Haus)* downstairs.
**unter** ['untər], *prep. + dat/acc* under; *(tiefer als)* below; **u. seiner Würde,** beneath his dignity; **eine Abteilung u. sich haben,** to be in charge of a department; *(mitten)* **u.,** among(st); amidst; **u. anderem,** among other things; **u. uns gesagt,** between you and me; **u. sich sein,** to be in private/undisturbed; **u. der Woche,** during the week; **was versteht man u. diesem Ausdruck?** what is meant by this expression?
'**unterbelichtet,** *adj.* underexposed.
'**unterbewußt,** *adj.* subconscious (motive etc.). ◆'**U~sein,** *n Psy:* subconscious (mind).
**unter'bieten,** *v.tr.insep.irr.8 (a) Com:* to undercut (prices); to undersell (the competition); *(b) Sp:* to beat (a record, time).
**unter'binden,** *v.tr.insep.irr.9* to put a stop to, prevent (sth.).
**unter'bleiben,** *v.i.insep.irr.12 (sein)* **das muß u.,** that must not happen again.
'**Unterbodenschutz,** *m* underseal.
**unter'brech|en,** *v.tr.insep.irr.14 (a)* to interrupt (s.o., sth.); *(b) El:* to disconnect, switch off (current); to break (a circuit); *(c) Sp:* to stop (play); *Med:* to terminate

(a pregnancy). ◆**U**~**ung**, *f* -/-**en** interruption; (*Pause*) break.

**unter'breiten**, *v.tr.insep.* **j-m etwas u.**, to submit sth. to s.o.

'**unterbringen**, *v.tr.sep.irr.16* to accommodate (s.o., sth.); (*lagern*) to store, *N.Am:* stash (sth.) (away); to fit in (sth. extra etc.).

**unter'dessen**, *adv.* meanwhile, in the meantime.

'**Unterdruck**, *m Ph:* subatmospheric pressure; vacuum.

**unter'drück|en**, *v.tr.insep.* (*a*) to suppress (a sigh, feelings, news etc.); to stifle (a yawn etc.); to choke back (one's anger); (*b*) to oppress (people etc.). ◆**U**~**ung**, *f* -/**no** *pl* suppression; oppression.

'**unterdurchschnittlich**, *adj.* below average.

'**untere(r,s)**, *adj.* lower.

**unterei'nander**, *adv.* **1.** (*Lage*) one below/beneath the other. **2.** (*miteinander*) with one another; **das müssen Sie u. ausmachen**, you must decide that amongst yourselves.

'**unterentwickelt**, *adj.* underdeveloped.

'**unterernährt**, *adj.* undernourished.

'**Unterernährung**, *f* malnutrition.

**Unter'fangen**, *n* -**s**/**no** *pl* undertaking.

**Unter'führung**, *f* underpass; (*für Fußgänger*) subway.

'**Untergang**, *m* **1.** (*a*) sinking (of a ship); (*b*) setting (of the sun/moon). **2.** downfall (of a person etc.); end (of the world).

**unter'geben**, *adj.* **j-m u.**, subordinate to/under s.o.

'**untergehen**, *v.i.sep.irr.36* (*sein*) (*a*) (*Schiff usw.*) to sink; (*Pers.*) to go under; *Fig:* **im Lärm u.**, to be drowned by the noise; (*b*) (*Sonne usw.*) to set; (*c*) *Lit:* (*Volk usw.*) to perish; (*Welt*) to come to an end.

'**Untergeschoß**, *n* basement.

'**Untergewicht**, *n* **U. haben**, to be underweight.

**unter'graben**, *v.tr.insep.irr.42* to undermine (public order, one's health etc.).

'**Untergrund**, *m* **1.** *m Agr:* subsoil. **2.** (*Farbe*) undercoat. **3.** *Pol:* underground. **II.** '**U**~-, *comb.fm.* underground (railway, movement etc.).

'**unterhalb**. **I.** *prep.* + *gen* underneath; (*tiefer als*) below. **II.** *adv.* **u. von** + *dat*, below.

'**Unterhalt**, *m* -(**e**)**s**/**no** *pl* **1.** support (of a wife, a family); (*U*~**sbeitrag**) maintenance, alimony. **2.** (*Instandhaltung*) upkeep. ◆**u**~**en** [-'haltən], *v.tr.insep.irr.45* (*a*) to support, keep (a family, one's parents etc.); to operate, run (a business etc.); (*instandhalten*) to maintain (roads, *Pol: etc:* relations etc.); (*b*) (*erfreuen*) to entertain, amuse (s.o., oneself); **wir haben uns prächtig u.**, we enjoyed ourselves immensely; we had a splendid time; (*c*) **sich mit j-m über etwas** *acc* **u.**, to (have a) talk to s.o. about

sth. ◆**u**~**sam**, *adj.* entertaining, amusing. ◆'**U**~**s**-, *comb.fm.* maintenance (costs, payment etc.). ◆**U**~**ung**, *f* **l.** *no pl* (*Pflege*) maintenance, upkeep. **2.** (*Gespräch*) conversation, talk. **3.** entertainment, amusement; **gute U.!** enjoy yourselves!

'**Unterhändler**, *m* -**s**/- negotiator; (*Vermittler*) mediator.

'**Unterhemd**, *n* vest; *N.Am:* undershirt.

'**Unterholz**, *n* undergrowth.

'**Unterhose**, *f* (*für Männer*) (pair of) underpants, *Brit:* pants.

'**unterirdisch**, *adj.* underground, subterranean.

'**Unterkiefer**, *m* lower jaw.

'**unterkommen**, *v.i.sep.irr.53* (*sein*) (*a*) to find accommodation; (*b*) *F:* (*eine Stelle finden*) to get a job.

**unter'kühlt**, *adj. Med:* suffering from hypothermia; *Fig:* cold, detached.

'**Unterkunft**, *f* -/-**e** accommodation; *Mil:* quarters.

'**Unterlage**, *f* **1.** underlay; (*Grundlage*) base. **2.** *pl* **U**~**n**, (supporting) documents, records.

'**Unterlaß** [-las], *m* **ohne U.**, incessantly.

**unter'lass|en**, *v.tr.insep.irr.57* (*a*) to refrain from (doing) (sth.); (*b*) (*versäumen*) to omit (sth.). ◆**U**~**ung**, *f* -/-**en** omission, failure (to do sth.); *Jur:* default.

**unter'laufen**. **I.** *v.i.insep.irr.58* (*sein*) **ihm sind einige Fehler u.**, he has made several mistakes. **II.** *adj.* **mit Blut u.**, bloodshot (eye).

**unterlegen**. **I.** *v.tr.* ['untərle:gən] *v.sep.* to put (sth.) under(neath). **II.** [untər'le:gən], *adj.* **1.** inferior (j-m, to s.o.; **an Stärke usw.**, in strength etc.). **2.** (*besiegt*) defeated; *Sp:* losing (team etc.).

'**Unterleib**, *m* (*a*) lower abdomen; (*b*) (*der Frau*) womb, uterus.

**unter'liegen**, *v.i.insep.irr.62* (*sein*) (*a*) (*geschlagen werden*) to be defeated/beaten (j-m, by s.o.); (*b*) (*unterworfen sein*) to be subject to (rules, censorship etc.).

**unterm** ['untərm], *F:* = **unter dem**.

'**Untermiete**, *f* -/**no** *pl* **in/zur U. wohnen**, to be a subtenant. ◆'**U**~**r(in)**, *m(f)* subtenant, lodger.

**unter'nehm|en**. **I.** *v.tr.insep.irr.69* to undertake (a journey etc.); to take (a walk, measures etc.); to make (an attempt etc.); **viel zusammen u.**, to do a lot together. **II. U.**, *n* -**s**/- **1.** (*Vorhaben*) enterprise; *esp. Mil:* operation; **gewagtes U.**, risky undertaking, bold venture. **2.** *Com:* (*Betrieb*) enterprise, business concern. ◆**U**~**er**, *m* -**s**/- *Com:* entrepreneur; *Ind:* industrialist; (*Arbeitgeber*) employer. ◆**u**~**ungslustig**, *adj.* enterprising, go-ahead; (*kühn*) adventurous.

'**Unteroffizier**, *m* **1.** non-commissioned officer, NCO. **2.** (*Feldwebel*) sergeant.

'**unterordnen**, *v.tr.sep.* to subordinate (interests etc.); **sich u.**, to accept a subordinate role.

**Unter'redung,** f -/-en (formal) conversation, discussion.

**Unterricht** ['untərriçt], m -(e)s/-e teaching; (privat) tuition; (Stunden) lessons; **j-m U. erteilen,** to teach s.o.; **im U.,** in class. ◆**u~en** [-'riçtən], v.tr.insep. (a) to teach (s.o., a subject); (b) (informieren) to inform, notify (s.o.); **sich u.,** to inform oneself, (laufend) keep oneself informed. ◆'**U~sstunde,** f lesson.

'**Unterrock,** m petticoat, slip.

**unters** ['untərs], F: = unter das.

**unter'sagen,** v.tr.insep. **j-m etwas u.,** to forbid s.o. to do sth.

**Untersatz,** m stand; (für Gläser) mat, coaster; (Untertasse) saucer.

**unter'schätzen,** v.tr.insep. to underestimate.

**unter'scheid|en,** v.insep.irr.65 1. v.tr. (a) to distinguish (two things), tell (two people/things) apart; (b) **sich (von j-m, etwas** dat**) u.,** to differ (from s.o., sth.). 2. v.i. (haben) to distinguish, make a distinction. ◆**U~ung,** f -/-en distinction; discrimination.

**Unterschied** ['untərʃiːt], m -(e)s/-e 1. difference. 2. (Unterscheidung) distinction; **im U. zu ihm,** in contrast with/unlike him. ◆'**u~lich,** adj. different; (schwankend) varying, variable. ◆'**u~slos,** adj. indiscriminate.

**unter'schlag|en,** v.tr.insep.irr.85 to embezzle (money); to suppress (news, evidence etc.). ◆**U~ung,** f -/-en embezzlement.

'**Unterschlupf,** m -(e)s/-e 1. (Versteck) hiding-place, hide-out. 2. (Obdach) shelter.

**unter'schreiben,** v.tr. & i.insep.irr.12 (haben) to sign (sth.).

'**Unterschrift,** f signature.

'**Unterseeboot,** n submarine.

'**Unterseite,** f bottom, underside.

'**Untersetz|er,** m mat, coaster. ◆**u~t** [-'zɛtst], adj. stocky, thickset.

'**unterste(r, s),** adj. lowest; bottom (floor, class etc.).

**unterstehen,** v.irr.100. 1. ['untərʃteːən] v.i.sep. (haben) to take shelter. 2. [untər'ʃteːən] v.i.insep. (haben) **j-m u.,** to be/come under s.o., be subordinate to s.o. 3. [untər'ʃteːən], v.refl.insep. **sich u., etwas zu tun,** to have the audacity to do sth.; **untersteh dich!** don't you dare!

**unterstell|en,** v.tr. 1. ['untərʃtɛlən] v.sep. (a) to put, (lagern) store (sth. somewhere); (in einer Garage) to garage (a car); **sich unter einem Balkon u.,** to take shelter under a balcony. 2. [untər'ʃtɛlən] v.insep. (a) **j-m eine Abteilung usw. u.,** to put s.o. in charge of a department etc.; (b) (annehmen) to assume (sth.). ◆**U~ung** [-'ʃtɛluŋ], f -/-en 1. subordination; placing under supervision. 2. imputation; insinuation.

**unter'streichen,** v.tr.insep.irr.40 to underline (a word etc.); Fig: (betonen) to emphasize, stress (s.o.'s merits etc.).

**unter'stütz|en,** v.tr.insep. to support; (finanziell) to back. ◆**U~ung,** f -/-en (a) no pl support; (Hilfe) assistance, aid; backing (of a project etc.); (b) Adm: benefit (payment).

**unter'such|en,** v.tr.insep. to investigate, look into (sth.); (durchsuchen) to search (s.o., luggage etc.); to examine (an object, a document, Med: patient etc.); (nachprüfen) to check; **sich ärztlich u. lassen,** to have a medical (examination)/checkup. ◆**U~ung,** f -/-en investigation; examination; (Durchsuchung) search; (Kontrolle) check, inspection. ◆**U~ungsausschuß,** m fact-finding committee; committee of enquiry. ◆**U~ungshaft,** f imprisonment awaiting trial. ◆**U~ungsrichter,** m approx. examining magistrate.

**untertan** ['untərtaːn]. I. adj. **j-m u. sein,** to be s.o.'s creature/servant. II. **U.,** m -s & -en/-en A: subject.

'**Untertasse,** f saucer.

'**untertauchen,** v.i.sep. (sein) to dive (under water); Fig: (verschwinden) to disappear.

'**Unterteil,** n & m lower/bottom part. ◆**u~en** [-'tailən], v.tr.insep. to subdivide (an area, text etc.). ◆**U~ung,** f subdivision.

'**Untertitel,** m subtitle.

'**Unterton,** m undertone.

**Unter'treibung,** f -/-en understatement.

**unter'wandern,** v.tr.insep. Pol: to infiltrate (a party etc.).

'**Unterwäsche,** f underwear.

**Unter'wasser-,** comb.fm. underwater (photography, camera, massage etc.).

**unter'wegs,** adv. on the way; **er ist immer/viel u.,** he is always on the move/travels a lot.

**unter'weis|en,** v.tr.insep.irr.70 **j-n (in etwas** dat**) u.,** to instruct s.o. (in sth.), teach s.o. (sth.). ◆**U~ung,** f -/-en instruction, teaching.

'**Unterwelt,** f underworld.

**unter'werf|en,** v.tr.insep.irr.110 to subjugate (a people etc.); **sich u.,** (i) to surrender; (ii) (sich fügen) to submit (der **Disziplin usw.,** to discipline etc.). ◆**U~ung,** f -/no pl subjugation; subjection, submission.

**unterwürfig** [untər'vyrfiç], adj. servile, obsequious.

**unter'zeichnen,** v.tr.insep. to sign (a treaty, contract etc.).

**unter'ziehen,** v.tr.insep.irr.113 **j-n, etwas einer Prüfung** dat **u.,** to subject s.o., sth. to an examination; **sich einer Prüfung, Operation usw. u.,** to undergo an examination, operation etc.

'**Untiefe,** f shallow, shoal.

**un'tragbar,** adj. intolerable (conditions etc.).

**un'trennbar,** adj. inseparable.

'**untreu,** adj. unfaithful. ◆'**U~e,** f -/no

*pl* unfaithfulness; (conjugal) infidelity.

un'tröstlich, *adj.* inconsolable.

'Untugend, *f* bad habit; (*Laster*) vice.

'überlegt, *adj.* ill-considered (action), rash (action, person).

unüber'sehbar, *adj.* vast (forest, crowd etc.); inestimable (difficulties etc.).

unüber'troffen, *adj.* unsurpassed, unmatched.

unum'gänglich, *adj.* unavoidable, inevitable; (*unentbehrlich*) indispensable.

unumschränkt [unum'frɛnkt], *adj.* unlimited, absolute (power etc.).

unum'stritten, *adj.* undisputed, unchallenged.

'ununterbrochen, *adj.* unbroken, continuous (succession, flow etc.); incessant (rain, chatter etc.); sie redet u., she talks non-stop/incessantly.

unver'änder|lich, *adj.* unchanging. ◆'u~t, *adj.* unchanged, unaltered.

unver'antwortlich, *adj.* irresponsible.

unver'besserlich, *adj.* incorrigible (optimist etc.).

'unverbindlich, *adj.* 1. *Com:* not binding; (*Angebot usw.*) without obligation. 2. non-committal (words); (*reserviert*) detached (attitude, person etc.).

unver'blümt, *adj.* blunt, downright (manner etc.).

'unverdaulich, *adj.* indigestible.

'unverdient, *adj.* undeserved.

'unverdünnt, *adj.* undiluted; neat (whisky etc.).

unver'einbar, *adj.* incompatible, irreconcilable.

'unverfänglich, *adj.* harmless, innocent.

unverfroren ['unfɛrfro:rən], *adj.* impudent, insolent.

unver'geßlich, *adj.* unforgettable.

unver'gleichlich, *adj.* incomparable; (*einmalig*) unique, matchless.

'unverheiratet, *adj.* unmarried, single.

unverhofft ['unfɛrhɔft], *adj.* unexpected.

'unverkäuflich, *adj.* not for sale.

unver'kennbar, *adj.* unmistakable.

unver'meidbar, *adj.* unavoidable (encounter, collision etc.); inevitable (happening etc.).

'unvermindert, *adj.* undiminished; unabated (fury etc.).

'Unvermögen, *n* inability.

'unvermutet, *adj.* unexpected (visit etc.); unsuspected (talents etc.).

'Unver|nunft, *f* unreasonableness; (*Torheit*) stupidity. ◆'u~nünftig, *adj.* unreasonable; (*töricht*) stupid, foolish.

'unverschämt, *adj.* outrageous; (*frech*) impertinent, insolent (remark, behaviour etc.). ◆'U~heit, *f* -/-en (*a*) *no pl* outrageousness; (*Frechheit*) insolence; (*b*) impertinence.

unversehens ['unfɛrze:əns], *adv.* unexpectedly; (*plötzlich*) all of a sudden.

'unversehrt, *adj.* (*Pers.*) unhurt; (*heil*) unscathed, safe and sound.

'unversöhnlich, *adj.* irreconcilable (en-

emies, opinions etc.).

'unverständ|lich, *adj.* incomprehensible; (*undeutlich*) unintelligible. ◆'U~nis, *n* auf U. stoßen, to meet with incomprehension.

'unversucht, *adj.* nichts u. lassen, to try everything.

'unverträglich, *adj.* (*a*) (*Pers.*) cantankerous; (*b*) incompatible (ideas, drugs etc.), indigestible (food).

unver'wechselbar, *adj.* unmistakable.

unver'wüstlich [unfɛr'vy:stliç], *adj.* durable; *Fig:* indefatigable (person); irrepressible (humour).

unver'zeihlich, *adj.* inexcusable; unforgivable.

unverzüglich [unfɛr'tsy:kliç], *adj.* immediate; instant (reaction etc.).

'unvollendet, *adj.* unfinished.

'unvollkommen, *adj.* (*a*) imperfect (performance etc.); (*b*) (*unvollständig*) incomplete.

'unvollständig, *adj.* incomplete.

'unvorbereitet, *adj.* unprepared (auf + *acc*, for); impromptu (speech, lecture).

'unvoreingenommen, *adj.* unprejudiced, unbiased.

'unvorhergesehen, *adj.* unforeseen; unexpected (visit etc.).

'unvorsichtig, *adj.* unwary (step); unguarded (remark); (*leichtsinnig*) careless (driving etc.).

unvor'stellbar, *adj.* unimaginable, inconceivable.

'unvorteilhaft, *adj.* unfavourable (conditions etc.); unbecoming (dress etc.).

'unwahr, *adj.* untrue, false. ◆'U~heit, *f* 1. untruth, falsehood. 2. *no pl* untruthfulness, falseness. ◆'u~scheinlich, *adj.* (*a*) unlikely, improbable (story etc.); (*b*) *F:* (*unglaublich*) incredible, fantastic (luck etc.).

unweigerlich [un'vaigərliç], *adj.* inevitable; das wird u. eintreten, it is bound to happen.

'unweit, *adv.* u. + *gen*/u. von + *dat*, not far from.

'Unwesen, *n* curse; public nuisance; sein U. treiben, to be up to (one's) mischief.

'unwesentlich, *adj.* insignificant.

'Unwetter, *n* (bad) storm, (*Gewitter*) thunderstorm.

'unwichtig, *adj.* unimportant, insignificant.

unwider'legbar, *adj.* irrefutable.

unwider'ruflich, *adj.* irrevocable (decision etc.).

unwider'stehlich, *adj.* irresistible.

'Unwill|e, *m* indignation, anger. ◆'u~ig, *adj.* (*a*) indignant, angry; (*b*) (*widerwillig*) reluctant. ◆u~'kürlich, *adj.* involuntary.

'unwirklich, *adj.* unreal.

unwirsch ['unvi:rʃ], *adj.* gruff, surly.

'unwirt|lich, *adj. esp. Fig:* inhospitable. ◆'u~schaftlich, *adj.* wasteful (person etc.); *esp. Com:* uneconomic (method).

'unwissen|d, *adj.* ignorant (person). ◆'U~heit, *f -/no pl* ignorance.

'unwohl, *pred.adj.* unwell; mir ist/ich fühle mich u., I feel unwell/*Fig:* (*unbehaglich*) uneasy. ◆'U~sein, *n* indisposition.

'unwürdig, *adj.* unworthy (+ *gen*, of).

'Unzahl, *f* eine U. von + *dat*, an enormous number/a whole host of.

unzählig [un'tsɛ:lɪç], *adj.* innumerable.

Unze ['untsə], *f -/-n* ounce.

unzer'brechlich, *adj.* unbreakable.

unzer'störbar, *adj.* indestructible.

unzer'trennlich, *adj.* inseparable (friends etc.).

'Unzucht, *f* sexual offence.

'unzüchtig, *adj.* lewd (remark), obscene (literature etc.).

'unzufrieden, *adj.* dissatisfied. ◆'U~heit, *f* dissatisfaction; discontent.

'unzulänglich, *adj.* insufficient, inadequate.

'unzulässig, *adj.* inadmissible.

'unzumutbar, *adj.* unreasonable (demand etc.).

'unzurechnungsfähig, *adj.* not responsible for his/her actions.

'unzureichend, *adj.* insufficient, inadequate.

'unzutreffend, *adj.* incorrect, untrue; U~es bitte streichen, delete if not applicable.

'unzuverlässig, *adj.* unreliable.

'unzweideutig, *adj.* unequivocal, unambiguous.

üppig ['ypɪç], *adj.* (*a*) luxuriant (vegetation etc.); lush (grass etc.); thick (beard, hair); (*b*) (*reichlich*) lavish (meal etc.); (*c*) opulent (figure, blonde etc.).

Ur-, ur- ['u:r-], *prefix* 1. (*ursprünglich*) original (form, text etc.). 2. (*bei Verwandtschaften*) great-(grandmother, grandfather etc.).

ur'alt, *adj.* extremely old, ancient.

Uran [u'ra:n], *n -s/no pl* uranium.

'Uraufführung, *f* premiere; first performance.

urbar ['u:rba:r], *adj.* u. machen, to reclaim, cultivate (land, a swamp etc.).

'Ureinwohner, *m* original inhabitant;

*Austral:* aborigine.

'Urenkel(in), *m(f)* great-grandson/granddaughter.

'Urgroßeltern, *pl* great-grandparents.

'Urheber(in), *m -s/- (f -/-nen)* originator (of an idea etc.); (*Schöpfer*) creator; (*Autor*) author.

Urin [u'ri:n], *m -s/-e* urine.

ur'komisch, *adj.* extremely funny, hilarious.

Urkund|e ['u:rkundə], *f -/-n* document; *Jur:* legal instrument; deed (of ownership etc.). ◆u~lich ['-kuntlɪç], *adj.* documentary (evidence etc.); u. erwähnt, recorded, documented.

Urlaub ['u:rlaup], *m -(e)s/-e (Ferien)* holiday(s), *N.Am:* vacation; *Mil: Adm: etc:* leave (of absence); auf/im/in U., on holiday/*N.Am:* vacation/*Mil:* leave. ◆'U~er, *m -s/-* holidaymaker, *N.Am:* vacationist. ◆'U~szeit, *f* holiday/*N.Am:* vacation season.

Urne ['urnə], *f -/-n* 1. urn. 2. *Pol:* ballot box.

'Ursache, *f -/-n* cause; (*Grund*) reason.

'Ursprung, *m* origin; (*Quelle*) source (of a river, *Fig:* tradition etc.).

ursprünglich ['ursprynlɪç], *adj.* (*a*) original (form etc.); initial (reaction); (*b*) (*unverdorben*) natural, pristine (state).

Urteil ['urtail], *n -s/-e Jur: etc:* judgement; (*Meinung*) opinion; (*Befund*) findings; (*Strafe*) sentence; *Jur:* ein U. über j-n fällen, to pronounce/pass sentence on s.o. ◆'u~en, *v.i.* (*haben*) to judge; wie u. Sie darüber? what is your opinion on/of this? ◆'U~sfähigkeit/'U~skraft, *f* ability to judge; judgement; discrimination. ◆'U~sspruch, *m* verdict; (*Strafe*) sentence.

'Urwald, *m* primeval forest; (*tropischer U.*) jungle.

urwüchsig ['u:rvy:ksɪç], *adj.* unpolished, unsophisticated (manners etc.); untouched, (*rauh*) rugged (landscape).

Utensil [utɛn'zi:l], *n -s/-ien* utensil, implement.

Utop|ie [uto'pi:], *f -/-n* Utopia. ◆u~isch [u'to:pɪʃ], *adj.* utopian.

# V

V, v [fau], *n -/-* (the letter) V, v.

Vagabund [vaga'bunt], *m -en/-en Lit:* vagabond; (*Landstreicher*) vagrant.

vag(e) ['va:g(ə)], *adj.* vague.

Vakuum ['va:kuum], *n -s/-kuen* vacuum. ◆'v~verpackt, *adj.* vacuum-packed.

Vampir [vam'pi:r], *m -s/-e* vampire.

Vandalismus [vanda'lismus], *m -/no pl* vandalism.

Vanill|e [va'nɪl(j)ə], *f -/no pl* vanilla. ◆V~egeschmack, *m* vanilla flavour.

vari|abel [vari'a:bəl], *adj.* variable.

◆V~ation [-atsi'o:n], *f -/-en* variation. ◆V~eté [-ie'te:], *n -s/-s (a)* (*Vorstellung*) variety show; (*b*) (*also* V~theater *n*) variety theatre, music hall. ◆v~'ieren, *v.tr. & i.* (*haben*) to vary.

Vase ['va:zə], *f -/-n* vase.

Vater ['fa:tər], *m -s/-* father. ◆'V~land, *n* home/native country; (*Deutschland*) fatherland. ◆'V~landsliebe, *f* patriotism. ◆'v~los, *adj.* fatherless. ◆'V~schaft, *f -/no pl* fatherhood; *Jur:* paternity. ◆'V~stadt, *f* home town.

◆V~'**unser**, n -s/- Lord's Prayer.

**väterlich** ['fɛːtərliç], adj. 1. (wie ein Vater) fatherly, paternal (advice, interest etc.). 2. (des Vaters) the/one's father's (house, business etc.). ◆'**v~erseits**, adv. on the/one's father's side.

**Vatikan** [vati'kaːn]. Pr.n.m -s. der V., the Vatican.

**Veget|arier** [vege'taːriər], m -s/- vegetarian. ◆v~**arisch**, adj. vegetarian. ◆V~**ation** [-atsi'oːn], f -/-en vegetation.

**Veilchen** ['failçən], n -s/- violet.

**Vene** ['veːnə], f -/-n vein.

**Venedig** [ve'neːdiç]. Pr.n.n -s. Venice.

**Venez|olaner(in)** [venetso'laːnər(in)], m -s/- (f -/-nen)/v~**o'lanisch**, adj. Venezuelan. ◆V~**uela** [-tsu'eːla]. Pr.n.n -s. Venezuela.

**Ventil** [vɛn'tiːl], n -s/-e valve. ◆V~**ation** [-ilatsi'oːn], f -/-en ventilation (system). ◆V~**ator** [-i'laːtɔr], m -s/-en [-'toːrən] ventilator, (electric) fan.

**ver'abred|en**, v.tr. to arrange, fix (a meeting, time etc.); **sich mit j-m v.**, to make an appointment with s.o. ◆V~**ung**, f -/-en arrangement; appointment; (mit Freund/Freundin) date.

**ver'abscheuen**, v.tr. to detest, loathe (s.o., sth.).

**ver'abschieden**, v.tr. (a) **sich (von j-m) v.**, to take one's leave (of s.o.), say goodbye (to s.o.); (b) to discharge (an officer etc.); (c) Pol: to pass (a bill).

**ver'acht|en**, v.tr. to despise (s.o., sth.). ◆V~**ung**, f -/no pl contempt, disdain.

**verächtlich** [fɛr'ʔɛçtliç], adj. disdainful (gesture etc.); disparaging (remark).

**verallgemeiner|n** [fɛr'ʔalgəˈmainərn], v.tr. & i. (haben) to generalize (about sth.). ◆V~**ung**, f -/-en generalization.

**veraltet** [fɛr'ʔaltət], adj. out of date, obsolete.

**Veranda** [ve'randa], f -/-den veranda; N.Am: porch.

**veränder|lich** [fɛr'ʔɛndərliç], adj. changeable (weather etc.); inconstant (nature, behaviour). ◆v~**n**, v.tr. to change, alter (s.o., sth.); **sich v.**, to change. ◆V~**ung**, f alteration, change.

**verängstigt** [fɛr'ʔɛŋstiçt], adj. frightened; scared.

**veranlag|t** [fɛr'ʔanlaːkt], adj. **künstlerisch v. sein**, to have an artistic disposition; **praktisch v.**, practically minded. ◆V~**ung**, f -/-en disposition; (Hang) tendency; **künstlerische V.**, artistic bent.

**ver'anlass|en**, v.tr. (a) to arrange for (sth.); **das Nötige v.**, to take the necessary steps; (b) **j-n v., etwas zu tun**, to make s.o. do sth.; **sich veranlaßt sehen/fühlen, es zu tun**, to feel obliged to do it. ◆V~**ung**, f -/-en cause (zu + dat, of); (Grund) reason (zu + dat, for); **auf seine V. hin**, at his instigation.

**veranschaulichen** [fɛr'ʔanʃauliçən], v.tr. to illustrate (sth.).

**veranstalt|en** [fɛr'ʔanʃtaltən], v.tr. to organize (sth.); to mount, F: put on (a concert, exhibition etc.). ◆V~**er**, m -s/- organizer. ◆V~**ung**, f -/-en (a) organization; (b) (Vorstellung) performance, presentation; **öffentliche V.**, public function.

**verantwort|en** [fɛr'ʔantvɔrtən], v.tr. to answer for, take the responsibility for (an action etc.); **sich v.**, to defend/justify oneself. ◆v~**lich**, adj. responsible. ◆V~**ung**, f -/-en responsibility. ◆v~**ungsbewußt**, adj. conscientious. ◆v~**ungslos**, adj. irresponsible. ◆v~**ungsvoll**, adj. responsible; trustworthy.

**ver'arbeit|en**, v.tr. (a) Ind: to process (raw material etc.); (b) to digest (Fig: facts etc.). ◆V~**ung**, f -/no pl (a) processing; (b) digestion.

**ver'ärgern**, v.tr. to annoy, irritate (s.o.).

**Verb** [vɛrp], n -s/-en verb.

**Verband** [fɛr'bant], m -(e)s/ːe 1. (a) (Vereinigung) association; (b) Mil: formation; force. 2. Med: bandage, dressing. ◆V~**(s)kasten**, m first-aid box/kit.

**ver'bann|en**, v.tr. to exile (s.o.); to banish (Hist: s.o., Fig: a thought etc.). ◆V~**ung**, f -/-en exile; banishment.

**verbarrikadieren** [fɛrbarika'diːrən], v.tr. to barricade (sth., oneself) (in).

**ver'bergen**, v.tr.irr.5 to conceal, hide (s.o., sth.) (vor j-m, from s.o.); **sich v.**, to hide.

**ver'besser|n**, v.tr. to improve (s.o., sth.); (korrigieren) to correct (a mistake, text etc.); **sich v.**, (i) (Pers., Sache) to improve; (seine Lage v.) to better oneself; (ii) (Pers.) (beim Sprechen) to correct oneself. ◆V~**ung**, f -/-en (a) improvement; (b) correction.

**ver'beug|en**, v.refl. **sich v.**, to bow. ◆V~**ung**, f -/-en bow.

**ver'biegen**, v.tr.irr.7 to bend (sth.) (out of shape).

**ver'bieten**, v.tr.irr.8 to forbid, Adm: prohibit (sth.); Adm: to ban (a demonstration, play etc.), suppress (a publication); **Rauchen verboten**, no smoking.

**ver'billigen**, v.tr. to reduce (sth.) (in price).

**ver'bind|en**, v.tr.irr.9 (a) to connect (two parts/places etc.); to join (two things); (gleichzeitig) to combine (two articles/Ch: substances); (vereinen) to unite (people, nations); **damit sind Gefahren usw. verbunden**, that involves danger etc.; (b) Tel: to connect (s.o.), put (s.o.) through; **(Sie sind) falsch verbunden**, (you've got the) wrong number; (c) Med: to bandage (a wound etc.). ◆v~**lich**, adj. (a) (entgegenkommend) obliging; friendly (smile, words etc.); (b) (bindend) binding (agreement etc.). ◆V~**ung**, f -/-en (a) connection; (b) Tel: Rail: communication; Tel: **schlechte V.**, bad line; (c) (Kombination) combination; Ch: compound; Fig: association (of ideas); *Fig:* **j-n mit etwas** *dat* **in V. bringen,** to link/associate s.o. with sth.; (*d*) (*Verein*) association; (*e*) (*Beziehung*) contact; **sich mit j-m in V. setzen,** to get in touch with s.o.

**verbissen** [fɛr'bisən], *adj.* dogged, grim.

**ver'bitten,** *v.tr.irr.10* **das verbitte ich mir!** I won't stand for that!

**ver'bittern,** *v.tr.* to embitter (s.o.).

**verblassen** [fɛr'blasən], *v.i.* (*sein*) (*also Fig:*) to fade.

**Verbleib** [fɛr'blaip], *m* -(e)s/*no pl* whereabouts. ◆**v~en** [-bən], *v.i.irr.12* (*sein*) to remain.

**verblüff|en** [fɛr'blyfən], *v.tr.* (*erstaunen*) to amaze, (*ratlos machen*) baffle (s.o.). ◆**V~ung,** *f* -/*no pl* amazement, stupefaction.

**ver'blühen,** *v.i.* (*sein*) to fade, wither.

**ver'bluten,** *v.i.* (*sein*) to bleed to death.

**ver'borgen** *adj.* hidden (danger, feeling etc.); secluded (place); **im v~en,** secretly, in secret.

**Verbot** [fɛr'bo:t], *n* -(e)s/-e prohibition; ban (**des Rauchens usw.,** on smoking etc.). ◆**V~sschild,** *n* prohibition sign.

**Ver'brauch,** *m* -(e)s/*no pl* consumption (**an/von** + *dat*, of). ◆**v~en,** *v.tr.* to consume, use (fuel etc.); to spend (time, money etc.); (*erschöpfen*) to use up (reserves, provisions etc.). ◆**v~t,** *adj.* worn (out) (article etc.); stale (air); exhausted (battery etc.). ◆**V~er,** *m* -s/- consumer.

**Ver'brech|en,** *n* -s/- crime. ◆**V~er(in),** *m* -s/- (*f* -/-nen) criminal. ◆**v~erisch,** *adj.* criminal.

**verbreit|en** [fɛr'braitən], *v.tr.* to spread (news, a disease etc.); to give out (light, heat etc.); **sich v.,** to spread. ◆**v~ern,** *v.tr.* to widen (a road etc.). ◆**v~et,** *adj.* common, widespread. ◆**V~ung,** *f* -/*no pl* spreading; giving out (heat/light).

**verbrenn|en** *v.irr.15* **1.** *v.tr.* to burn (sth., oneself); to cremate (a corpse); **ich habe mir die Finger/Zunge verbrannt,** I burnt my fingers/tongue. **2.** *v.i.* (*sein*) to burn; (*Pers.*) to burn to death. ◆**V~ung,** *f* -/-en (*a*) *no pl* burning; cremation; *Tchn:* combustion; (*b*) (*Brandwunde*) burn. ◆**V~ungsmotor,** *m* combustion engine.

**ver'bringen,** *v.tr.irr.16* to spend (time, one's holidays etc.).

**ver'brüh|en,** *v.tr.* to scald (s.o., sth.). ◆**V~ung,** *f* -/-en (*a*) *no pl* scalding; (*b*) scald.

**ver'buchen,** *v.tr.* to enter (an amount etc.); *Fig:* **einen Erfolg v.,** to score a success.

**verbunden** [fɛr'bundən], *adj.* connected; **ich bin Ihnen sehr v.,** I am much obliged to you.

**verbünde|n** [fɛr'byndən], *v.refl.* **sich v.,** to enter into an alliance. ◆**V~te(r),** *m & f* decl. as adj. ally.

**ver'bürgen,** *v.tr.* to guarantee (sth.); **sich**

**für etwas** *acc* **v.,** to vouch for sth.

**Verdacht** [fɛr'daxt], *m* -(e)s/*no pl* suspicion; **j-n in/im V. haben,** to suspect s.o.

**verdächtig** [fɛr'dɛçtiç], *adj.* suspicious; **sich v. machen,** to arouse suspicion. ◆**v~en** [-gən], *v.tr.* to suspect (s.o.) (**des Mordes usw.,** of murder etc.). ◆**V~ung,** *f* -/-en suspicion; (*Beschuldigung*) accusation.

**ver'damm|en,** *v.tr.* to condemn (s.o., sth.). ◆**v~t,** *adj. P:* damned, blasted, *N.Am:* doggone.

**ver'dampfen,** *v.i.* (*sein*) to vaporize.

**ver'danken,** *v.tr.* **j-m etwas v.,** to be indebted to s.o. for sth.; **das habe ich dir zu v.,** I have you to thank for that.

**verdau|en** [fɛr'dauən], *v.tr.* to digest (sth.). ◆**v~lich,** *adj.* digestible; **leicht v.,** easy to digest. ◆**V~ung,** *f* -/*no pl* digestion. ◆**V~ungsstörung,** *f* indigestion.

**Verdeck** [fɛr'dɛk], *n* -(e)s/-e **1.** *Nau:* top deck. **2.** *Aut:* hood; (*fest*) hardtop. ◆**v~en,** *v.tr.* to cover (sth.) (up); (*verbergen*) to conceal (sth.).

**ver'denken,** *v.tr.irr.17* **man kann es ihm nicht v.,** one cannot hold it against him.

**verderb|en** [fɛr'dɛrbən]. **I.** *v.irr.101* **1.** *v.i.* (*sein*) to deteriorate; (*Essen*) to go bad/off. **2.** *v.tr.* to spoil (a child, food, s.o.'s pleasure, one's health etc.), (*völlig*) ruin (an evening, s.o.'s enjoyment etc.); (*moralisch*) to corrupt (s.o., s.o.'s character); **es mit j-m v.,** to fall out with s.o., get on the wrong side of s.o. **II. V.,** *n* -s/*no pl Lit:* ruin; **j-n ins V. stürzen,** to ruin s.o. ◆**v~lich,** *adj.* (*a*) perishable (food); (*b*) pernicious (influence etc.).

**verdeutlichen** [fɛr'dɔytliçən], *v.tr.* to clarify (sth.).

**ver'dichten,** *v.tr.* to compress (a gas, *Fig:* events etc.); **sich v.,** (*Nebel usw.*) to become dense.

**ver'dien|en,** *v.tr. & i.* (*haben*) (*a*) to earn (money etc.); **gut v.,** to have a good income; (*b*) (*zu Recht bekommen*) to deserve (sth.). ◆**V~st. 1.** *m* -(e)s/-e (*Einkommen*) earnings, income; (*Gehalt*) salary. **2.** *n* -(e)s/-e merit; **es ist dein V.,** it is (entirely) due/owing to you. ◆**v~t,** *adj.* deserving (person); (well-)deserved, just (praise etc.); **sich um sein Land v. machen,** to render great services to one's country. ◆**v~ter'maßen,** *adv.* deservedly.

**ver'doppel|n,** *v.tr.* to double (sth.); to redouble (one's efforts); **sich v.,** to double (in number/size). ◆**V~ung,** *f* -/-en doubling, duplication.

**verdorben** [fɛr'dɔrbən], *adj.* spoiled; gone off/bad (food); foul, polluted (air); upset (stomach); corrupt (morals etc.).

**verdorren** [fɛr'dɔrən], *v.i.* (*sein*) to dry up, (*Pflanze*) wither.

**ver'dräng|en,** *v.tr.* to push/thrust (s.o., sth.) aside; (*vertreiben*) to oust (s.o.); *Fig:* to repress (an emotion etc.). ◆**V~ung,**

f **-**/no pl ousting; Psy: repression.

**ver'drehen**, v.tr. (also Fig:) to twist (sth.); Fig: to distort (the meaning etc.); **j-m den Kopf v.**, to turn s.o.'s head.

**verdreifachen** [fɛr'draifaxən], v.tr. to treble (sth.); **sich v.**, to treble.

**verdrieß|en** [fɛr'driːsən], v.tr.irr.31 to annoy (s.o.). ◆**v~lich**, adj. grumpy; bad-tempered (person, expression).

**verdrossen** [fɛr'drɔsən], adj. morose, sullen.

**ver'drücken**, v.tr. F: (a) to tuck away (food); (b) **sich v.**, to slink away.

**Verdruß** [fɛr'drus], m **-sses/-sse** Lit: annoyance.

**ver'duften**, v.i. (sein) F: (Pers.) to make off; **verdufte!** hop it!

**ver'dunkeln**, v.tr. to darken (a colour, room etc.); to dim (a lamp etc.); **sich v.**, to darken.

**verdünnen** [fɛr'dynən], v.tr. to dilute (a liquid), water down (wine etc.), thin (paint etc.).

**ver'dunsten**, v.i. (haben) to evaporate.

**ver'dursten**, v.i. (sein) to die/be dying of thirst.

**verdutzt** [fɛr'dutst], adj. taken aback; (perplex) nonplussed, puzzled.

**ver'ehr|en**, v.tr. to admire, look up to (s.o.), (mit Liebe) venerate (s.o. older); (anbeten) to worship (s.o., a saint). ◆**V~er(in)**, m **-s/-** (f **-/-nen**) admirer; F: fan. ◆**V~ung**, f **-**/no pl admiration, veneration; Ecc: worship.

**vereidig|en** [fɛr'ʔaidigən], v.tr. to swear (s.o.) in. ◆**V~ung**, f **-**/no pl swearing in.

**Verein** [fɛr'ʔain], m **-(e)s/-e** society; Sp: etc: club. ◆**v~bar**, adj. compatible, (Aussage) consistent. ◆**v~baren**, v.tr. (a) to agree (on) (sth.), fix (a date etc.); (b) to reconcile (facts, opinions etc.). ◆**V~barung**, f **-/-en** agreement, arrangement; **nach V.**, by arrangement/(Termin) appointment. ◆**v~igen**, v.tr. to unite (nations etc.); to bring together (a family etc.); to combine (functions, tasks etc.); **sich v.**, to unite, combine (**zu etwas** dat, to form sth.); (Firmen usw.) to merge; **die Vereinigten Staaten**, the United States. ◆**V~igung**, f **-/-en 1.** union; combination; Pol: unification; Com: merger. **2.** (Organisation) organization.

**ver'einfach|en**, v.tr. to simplify (sth.). ◆**v~ung**, f **-/-en** simplification.

**ver'einheitlichen**, v.tr. to standardize (a product etc.), unify (a system etc.).

**ver'einsam|en**, v.i. (sein) to grow lonely. ◆**V~ung**, f **-**/no pl isolation.

**vereinzelt** [fɛr'ʔaintsəlt], adj. occasional; scattered (showers etc.).

**vereis|en** [fɛr'ʔaizən], v.i. (sein) (Straße) to become icy; (Fenster usw.) to ice up. ◆**v~t**, adj. icy (road etc.); Av: iced up.

**vereiteln** [fɛr'ʔaitəln], v.tr. to foil, thwart (a plan etc.), frustrate (efforts etc.).

**ver'enden**, v.i. (sein) (Tiere) to die (miserably).

**verengen** [fɛr'ʔɛŋən], v.tr. to narrow (sth.); **sich v.**, to narrow; (Pupille) to contract.

**ver'erb|en**, v.tr. to leave, bequeath (sth.); to pass on (qualities etc.); **sich v.**, to be hereditary. ◆**v~lich**, adj. hereditary. ◆**V~ung**, f **-**/no pl heredity.

**ver'fahren. I.** v.tr.irr.26 **1.** v.i. (sein) to proceed, act; **mit j-m streng v.**, to deal severely with s.o. **2.** v.refl. **sich v.**, to lose one's way. **II.** adj. hopelessly bungled. **III. V.**, n **-s/-** (a) procedure; Tchn: process; (b) Jur: proceedings.

**Verfall** [fɛr'fal], m **-(e)s/no pl 1.** decay, dilapidation; decline (of civilization etc.). **2.** Jur: expiry (of a period etc.). ◆**v~en**, v.i.irr.27 (sein) (a) (Gebäude) to (fall into) decay, become dilapidated; (Zivilisation, Moral usw.) to (go into) decline; (b) (ungültig werden) to expire; (Fin: Wechsel usw.) to lapse; (c) **v. in** + acc, to lapse into (silence etc.); (d) **j-m v.**, (Pers.) to fall under s.o.'s spell; **dem Alkohol v.**, to become addicted to drink; (e) **auf einen Plan usw. v.**, to hit on a plan etc.

**ver'fälschen**, v.tr. to falsify (documents etc.), distort (facts, truth etc.).

**verfänglich** [fɛr'fɛŋliç], adj. awkward, compromising.

**ver'färben**, v.refl. **sich v.**, to change colour, (Stoff usw.) discolour.

**ver'fass|en**, v.tr. to write (sth.). ◆**v~er**, m **-s/-** author, writer. ◆**v~ung**, f **-/-en** (a) (Zustand) condition, state; (b) Pol: constitution. ◆**v~ungswidrig**, adj. unconstitutional.

**ver'faulen**, v.i. (sein) to decay, (Obst, Holz) rot.

**ver'fecht|en**, v.tr.irr.29 to champion (a theory etc.). ◆**v~er**, m **-s/-** advocate, champion.

**ver'fehl|en**, v.tr. to miss (s.o., sth., one's way). ◆**v~t**, adj. mistaken, misguided.

**verfeiner|n** [fɛr'fainərn], v.tr. to refine, improve (methods etc.). ◆**v~t**, adj. refined, sophisticated.

**ver'film|en**, v.tr. to film, make a film of (a novel etc.). ◆**V~ung**, f **-/-en** film version.

**ver'fliegen**, v.i.irr.30 (haben) to evaporate, (verschwinden) vanish; (Zeit) to fly past.

**ver'fluch|en**, v.tr. to curse (s.o., sth.). ◆**v~t**, adj. F: confounded, damned; int. damn! blast!

**ver'folg|en**, v.tr. to pursue (s.o., an aim, etc.); to shadow (a suspect etc.); to follow (events, progress etc.) closely; esp. Pol: to persecute (s.o., a minority etc.). ◆**v~er**, m **-s/-** pursuer; Pol: persecutor. ◆**V~ung**, f **-/-en** pursuit; Pol: persecution.

**ver'formen**, v.tr. to distort (sth.); **sich v.**, to get out of shape, (Holz) warp.

**verfrachten** [fɛr'fraxtən], v.tr. to ship (goods).

**verfroren** [fɛr'froːrən], adj. frozen (hands etc.).

**verfrüht** [fɛr'fryːt], adj. premature; untimely (death).

**verfüg|bar** [fɛr'fyːkbɑːr], adj. available. ◆**V~barkeit**, f -/no pl availability. ◆**v~en** [-gən], v. **1.** v.tr. to decree (, daß..., that...); to order (sth.). **2.** v.i. (haben) **über etwas** acc v., to have sth. at one's disposal; **über sein Geld frei v. können**, to do as one likes with one's money. ◆**V~ung**, f -/-en (a) Jur: Adm: (Befehl) decree, order; (Anordnung) instruction; (b) **ich stehe Ihnen zur V.**, I am at your service/disposal; **mein Auto steht Ihnen jederzeit zur V.**, you can use my car whenever you like.

**ver'führ|en**, v.tr. to lead (s.o.) astray; to seduce (a girl); esp. Hum: (verlocken) to tempt (s.o.). ◆**V~er**, m -s/- seducer. ◆**v~erisch**, adj. seductive (smile, look etc.); tempting (offer etc.). ◆**V~ung**, f -/-en seduction; enticement.

**ver'gammeln**, v.i. (sein) F: (Speisen) to go bad; (Pers.) to go to seed.

**vergangen** [fɛr'gaŋən], adj. past (generations etc.); **im v~en Jahr**, last year. ◆**V~heit**, f -/no pl past; Gram: past tense.

**vergänglich** [fɛr'gɛŋliç], adj. transitory, fleeting. ◆**V~keit**, f -/no pl transitoriness.

**vergas|en** [fɛr'gɑːzən], v.tr. to vaporize (a liquid); to gas (s.o., an animal). ◆**V~er**, m -s/- carburettor.

**ver'geb|en**, v.tr.irr.35 (a) (verzeihen) j-m **etwas** v., to forgive s.o. sth.; (b) (überreichen) to give, award (a prize, scholarship etc.); **ein Amt an j-n v.**, to appoint s.o. to an office; **seine Tochter ist schon v.**, his daughter is already spoken for; (c) Sp: to miss (a chance, goal etc.). ◆**v~ens**, adv. in vain. ◆**v~lich**, adj. futile, vain. ◆**V~ung**, f -/no pl forgiveness.

**ver'gehen. I.** v.irr.36 **1.** v.i. (sein) (a) (Zeit, Schmerz usw.) to pass; (Gefühl usw.) to disappear, go; (b) **vor Angst, Scham usw.** v., to die of fright, shame etc. **2.** v.refl. **sich v.**, to commit an offence; **sich an j-m v.**, to assault s.o. (sexually). **II. V.**, n -s/- offence.

**vergelt|en** [fɛr'gɛltən], v.tr.irr.37 to repay, (belohnen) reward (a kindness etc.); (sich rächen) to retaliate for (a wrong). ◆**V~ung**, f -/no pl retaliation, Mil: reprisals pl.

**vergessen** [fɛr'gɛsən], v.tr.irr.25 to forget; (liegenlassen) to leave (sth.) behind. ◆**V~heit**, f -/no pl oblivion; **in V. geraten**, to fall into oblivion.

**vergeßlich** [fɛr'gɛsliç], adj. forgetful. ◆**V~keit**, f -/no pl forgetfulness.

**vergeuden** [fɛr'gɔydən], v.tr. to squander, waste (money, time etc.).

**vergewaltig|en** [fɛrgə'valtigən], v.tr. to rape (a woman); Fig: to do violence to (language etc.). ◆**V~ung**, f -/-en rape; Fig: violation.

**vergewissern** [fɛrgə'visərn], v.refl. **sich v.**, to make sure.

**ver'gießen**, v.tr.irr.31 to spill (sth.); Lit: to shed (blood, tears).

**vergiften** [fɛr'giftən], v.tr. to poison (s.o., sth., oneself).

**vergilben** [fɛr'gilbən], v.i. (sein) to turn yellow.

**Vergißmeinnicht** [fɛr'gismainniçt], n -s/-(e) forget-me-not.

**verglasen** [fɛr'glɑːzən], v.tr. to glaze (a window).

**Vergleich** [fɛr'glaiç], m -(e)s/-e **1.** comparison; **im V. zu** + dat, compared with/to. **2.** Jur: (Einigung) settlement. ◆**v~bar**, adj. comparable. ◆**v~en**, v.tr.irr.40 (a) to compare (s.o., sth.); **es ist nicht zu v. mit...**, you cannot compare it with...; (b) Jur: **sich mit j-m v.**, to settle with s.o. ◆**v~sweise**, adv. comparatively.

**vergnüg|en** [fɛr'gnyːgən]. **I.** v.refl. **sich v.**, to enjoy oneself, have a good time. **II. V.**, n -s/no pl pleasure; (Freude) delight; **viel V.!** enjoy yourself! **es war mir ein V.**, I was pleased to do it/meet you. ◆**v~lich**, adj. enjoyable, pleasant. ◆**v~t**, adj. cheerful; (Pers.) in good spirits. ◆**V~ung**, f -/-en entertainment, F: jollification. ◆**V~ungs-**, comb.fm. entertainment (industry, tax etc.); amusement (park etc.); pleasure (steamer etc.). ◆**V~sreise**, f pleasure trip. ◆**v~ssüchtig**, adj. pleasure-seeking.

**ver'golden**, v.tr. to gold-plate, (mit Blattgold) gild (sth.).

**ver'gönnen**, v.tr. j-m **etwas** v., to grant s.o. sth.

**vergöttern** [fɛr'gœtərn], v.tr. to idolize, worship (s.o.).

**ver'graben**, v.tr.irr.42 to bury.

**ver'greifen**, v.refl.irr.43 (a) **sich v.**, to make a mistake; **sich im Ausdruck usw.** v., to choose the wrong term etc.; (b) **sich an etwas** dat v., to misappropriate (sth.); **sich an j-m v.**, to lay hands on s.o., (sexuell) violate s.o.

**vergriffen** [fɛr'grifən], adj. unavailable; (Buch) out of print.

**vergrößer|n** [fɛr'grøːsərn], v.tr. to enlarge (a photograph etc.); to expand (a business etc.); to increase (a number, danger etc.); **sich v.**, to expand, increase (in size); (Menge) to swell. ◆**V~ung**, f -/-en increase (in size); esp. Phot: enlargement; expansion; extension. ◆**V~ungsglas**, n magnifying glass.

**Vergünstigung** [fɛr'gynstiguŋ], f -/-en privilege; concession.

**vergüt|en** [fɛr'gyːtən], v.tr. to refund, reimburse (expenses). ◆**V~ung**, f -/-en refund.

**ver'haft|en**, v.tr. to arrest (s.o.).

◆**V~ung,** f -/-en arrest.
**ver'hallen,** v.i. (sein) to die away.
**ver'halten. I.** v.tr.irr.45 **sich v.,** to behave/(handeln) act; **sich richtig v.,** to do the right thing; **es verhält sich so,** this is how matters stand; **wie verhält es sich mit...?** what is the position regarding...? **II. V.,** n -s/no pl behaviour, conduct. ◆**V~s-,** comb.fm. behaviour (pattern etc.); behavioural (research, psychology etc.). ◆**V~sweise,** f (kind of) behaviour.
**Verhältnis** [fɛr'hɛltnis], n -ses/-se **1.** (a) Mth: etc: ratio; Fig: **im V. zu früher,** compared with earlier times; **in keinem V. zu etwas dat stehen,** to bear no relation to sth.; (b) relationship (**zu j-m,** with s.o.); (c) F: (Liebesv.) affair. **2.** pl **V~se,** conditions, (Umstände) circumstances; **über seine V~se leben,** to live beyond one's means; **aus ärmlichen V~sen,** from a poor background/family. ◆**v~mäßig,** adv. comparatively, relatively.
**ver'hand|eln,** v.tr. & i. (haben) to negotiate; Jur: to hear, try (a case). ◆**V~lung,** f -/-en negotiation, discussion; pl **V~lungen,** negotiations, talks; Jur: (legal) proceedings.
**ver'häng|en,** v.tr. to impose (a fine etc.). ◆**V~nis,** n -ses/-se disaster; (Schicksal) fate; **j-m zum V. werden,** to be s.o.'s downfall. ◆**v~nisvoll,** adj. disastrous, fatal (mistake etc.); fateful (day etc.).
**ver'harren,** v.i. (haben) **bei/in etwas dat v.,** to persist in sth.
**ver'härten,** v.tr. & refl. to harden.
**verhaßt** [fɛr'hast], adj. hateful, odious; (Pers.) hated.
**verhauen,** v.tr.irr.47 F: to beat (s.o.) up, (verdreschen) thrash (s.o.).
**verheerend** [fɛr'heːrənt], adj. devastating (storm etc.); disastrous (fire, consequences etc.); appalling (conditions etc.).
**ver'heilen,** v.i. (sein) to heal.
**verheimlichen** [fɛr'haimliçən], v.tr. to keep (sth.) secret, conceal (sth.) (j-m, from s.o.).
**ver'heiratet** [fɛr'hairaːtət], adj. married (man, woman).
**ver'heiß|en,** v.tr.irr.49 Lit: to promise (sth.). ◆**v~ungsvoll,** adj. promising, auspicious.
**ver'helfen,** v.i.irr.50 (haben) **j-m zu etwas dat v.,** to help s.o. to get to sth.
**verherrlichen** [fɛr'hɛrliçən], v.tr. to glorify (s.o., deeds etc.).
**ver'hindern,** v.tr. to prevent (sth.); **verhindert sein,** to be prevented from coming/going.
**verhöhnen** [fɛr'høːnən], v.tr. to deride, jeer at (s.o., sth.).
**Verhör** [fɛr'høːr], n -(e)s/-e (police etc.) interrogation; Jur: hearing. ◆**v~en,** v.tr. (a) to interrogate, question (a witness etc.); (b) **sich v.,** to hear wrongly.
**ver'hüllen,** v.tr. to cover (one's head, face etc.).

**ver'hungern,** v.i. (sein) to starve (to death).
**ver'hüt|en,** v.tr. to prevent, avert (sth.). ◆**V~ungsmittel,** n contraceptive.
**verirr|en** [fɛr'ʔirən], v.refl. **sich v.,** to get lost. ◆**v~t,** adj. lost; stray (bullet etc.).
**ver'jagen,** v.tr. to chase (s.o., sth.) away.
**verjüngen** [fɛr'jyŋən], v.tr. (a) to rejuvenate (s.o.), make (s.o., oneself) look younger; (b) **sich v.,** (schmaler werden) to taper.
**verkalken** [fɛr'kalkən], v.i. (sein) (a) to calcify, (Arterien) harden; (b) F: (Pers.) to become senile; (c) (Kessel usw.) to fur up.
**verkalku'lieren,** v.refl. **sich v.,** to miscalculate.
**Verkauf** [fɛr'kauf], m sale. ◆**v~en,** v.tr. to sell (sth.); **zu v.,** for sale. ◆**V~spreis,** m selling/retail price.
**Verkäuf|er(in)** [fɛr'kɔyfər(in)], m -s/- (f -/-nen) (a) seller; (b) (Angestellter) shop assistant, N.Am: sales clerk. ◆**v~lich,** adj. saleable; **gut/schlecht v.,** easy/hard to sell.
**Verkehr** [fɛr'keːr], m -s/no pl **1.** traffic. **2.** (Umgang) association; (social) contact; (geschäftlich) dealings; (Geschlechtsv.) (sexual) intercourse; **er ist kein V. für dich,** he's not suitable company for you. ◆**v~en,** v. **1.** v.i. (haben) (a) (Zug, Bus usw.) to run, (Schiff) ply; (b) (Pers.) to have contact, associate, (geschlechtlich) have (sexual) intercourse. **2.** v.tr. to turn (sth.) (**ins Gegenteil usw.,** into the opposite etc.). ◆**V~s-,** comb.fm. (a) traffic (chaos, density, check, police, policeman, conditions etc.); (b) road (safety, accident etc.); (c) transport (minister, network, system etc.). ◆**V~sampel,** f traffic light(s). ◆**V~sdelikt,** n traffic offence. ◆**V~sfluß,** m traffic flow. ◆**V~smittel,** n means of transport. ◆**V~sregel,** f traffic regulation. ◆**V~sstau,** m traffic jam. ◆**V~ssteilnehmer,** m road user. ◆**V~szeichen,** n traffic/road sign.
**verkehrt** [fɛr'keːrt], adj. wrong (end etc.); **v. herum,** the wrong way round.
**ver'kennen,** v.tr. to mistake (motives etc.); to misjudge (s.o., sth.); Hum: **verkanntes Genie,** unrecognized/misunderstood genius.
**ver'klagen,** v.tr. Jur: to sue (s.o.) (**wegen etwas dat,** for sth.).
**ver'kleid|en,** v.tr. (a) to disguise (s.o., oneself); (b) Tchn: to face (an outer wall), (täfeln) panel (an inner wall etc.). ◆**V~ung,** f (a) disguise; (b) facing; panelling.
**verkleinern** [fɛr'klainərn], v.tr. to make (sth.) smaller, reduce (size, volume etc.).
**ver'klingen,** v.i.irr.96 (sein) to die away.
**verkneifen** [fɛr'knaifən], v.tr.irr.43 F: **sich dat das Lachen usw. v.,** to suppress one's laughter etc.

**ver'knüpfen**, *v.tr.* (*a*) to knot, tie (string etc.); (*b*) (*verbinden*) to combine (two actions, sth, with sth.); (*in Gedanken usw.*) to associate, connect (s.o., sth.).

**ver'kommen. I.** *v.i.irr.53* (*sein*) (*Pers.*) to go downhill, (*stärker*) go to the dogs; (*Obst usw.*) to go bad; (*Gebäude usw.*) to decay, (*Garten*) to go wild. **II.** *adj.* dilapidated (building etc.); (*moralisch*) depraved (person); sleazy (hotel etc.). ◆**V~heit**, *f* -/no *pl* dilapidated state; depravity.

**verkörpern** [fɛr'kœrpərn], *v.tr.* to embody, personify (an idea, quality).

**verkraften** [fɛr'kraftən], *v.tr.* to manage (a task etc.); to cope with (the amount of work/traffic); (*bewältigen*) to get over (an experience).

**verkrampft** [fɛr'krampft], *adj.* clenched (fingers etc.); tense (person); forced (laughter).

**ver'kriechen**, *v.refl.irr.55* **sich v.**, to crawl, creep; (*sich verstecken*) to hide.

**ver'krümmen**, *v.tr.* to bend (sth.).

**verkrüppelt** [fɛr'krypəlt], *adj.* crippled.

**verkrusten** [fɛr'krustən], *v.i.* (*sein*) to form a crust/(*Blut*) scab.

**ver'kühlen**, *v.refl.* **sich v.**, to catch cold.

**ver'kümmern**, *v.i.* (*sein*) (*Pflanze, Glied*) to become stunted; (*Tier*) to waste away.

**verkünd|en** [fɛr'kyndən], *v.tr. Lit:* to proclaim (sth.); *Jur:* to pronounce (judgement). ◆**V~(ig)ung**, *f* -/-en announcement; proclamation; *Jur:* pronouncement.

**ver'kürz|en**, *v.tr.* to shorten (sth.); to cut (travelling/working time, a script etc.). ◆**v~t**, *adj.* shortened; abridged (book etc.); abbreviated (word, name).

**verladen**, *v.tr.* to load (goods etc.).

**Verlag** [fɛr'laːk], *m* -(e)s/-e publisher(s); publishing house/firm.

**ver'lagern**, *v.tr. & refl.* to shift.

**verlangen** [fɛr'laŋən]. **I. v. 1.** *v.tr.* (*fordern*) to demand (sth.); (*bitten um*) to ask for (the bill etc.); (*wollen*) to want (sth.); (*Aufgabe usw.*) to call for (patience, time etc.); **du wirst am Telefon verlangt**, you are wanted on the telephone. **2.** *v.i.* (*haben*) **v. nach** + *dat*, to ask for (the doctor, a drink etc.). **II. V.**, *n* -s/no *pl* (*a*) *Lit:* desire (**nach** + *dat*, for); (*b*) **auf V.**, on demand; **auf j-s V.** (**hin**), at s.o.'s request.

**verläng|ern** [fɛr'lɛŋərn], *v.tr.* to lengthen (sth.); to extend (a fence, journey, passport etc.). ◆**V~ung**, *f* -/-en extension; *Sp:* extra time. ◆**V~ungsschnur**, *f* extension lead.

**verlangsamen** [fɛr'laŋzaːmən], *v.tr.* to slow down (traffic etc.); **das Tempo v.**, to slow down.

**Verlaß** [fɛr'las], *m* **auf ihn/sie ist kein V.**, there is no relying on him/her.

**ver'lassen. I.** *v.tr.irr.57* (*a*) to leave (s.o., sth.); (*im Stich lassen*) to abandon, desert (one's family etc.); (*b*) **sich auf j-n, et-** **was** *acc* **v.**, to rely on s.o., sth. **II.** *adj.* deserted (house, person etc.); abandoned (vehicle); (*öde*) desolate (place etc.). ◆**V~heit**, *f* -/no *pl* desolation.

**verläßlich** [fɛr'lɛsliç], *adj.* reliable, dependable. ◆**V~keit**, *f* -/no *pl* reliability.

**Ver'lauf**, *m* -(e)s/no *pl* course; **den weiteren V. abwarten**, to await further developments. ◆**v~en**, *v.i.irr.58* (*sein*) (*a*) (*Ereignis usw.*) to go (off); (*vergehen*) (*Tage usw.*) to pass (slowly etc.); (*b*) (*Linie, Straße usw.*) to run (parallel, straight etc.); (*c*) (*Butter, Farbe usw.*) to run; (*d*) **sich v.**, to lose one's way; (*Menge*) to disperse.

**verlautbaren** [fɛr'lautbaːrən], *v.tr. Adm:* to make (sth.) known.

**ver'leben**, *v.tr.* to spend (holidays, one's youth etc.).

**ver'leg|en. I.** *v.tr.* (*a*) to move, transfer (people, one's quarters etc.); (*b*) (*verschieben*) to put off (an appointment etc.) (**auf** + *acc*, until); (*c*) (*verlieren*) to mislay (a key etc.); (*d*) to lay (a cable etc.); (*e*) (*herausgeben*) to publish (a book etc.); (*f*) **sich auf etwas** *acc* **v.**, to specialize in sth.; *Pej:* to resort to sth. **II.** *adj.* (*Pers.*) embarrassed; **er ist nie um eine Antwort v.**, he is never at a loss for an answer. ◆**V~enheit**, *f* -/no *pl* embarrassment. ◆**V~er**, *m* -s/- publisher.

**Verleih** [fɛr'lai], *m* -(e)s/-e (*a*) hire, *esp. N.Am:* rental; (*b*) (*Firma*) hire/rental service; *Cin:* (film) distributors. ◆**v~en**, *v.tr.irr.60* (*a*) to lend (sth.); (*b*) (*überreichen*) to award (a prize); to confer (an honour, title etc.) (**j-m**, on s.o.); (*c*) (*geben*) **j-m Mut, Kraft usw. v.**, to give s.o. courage, strength etc. ◆**V~ung**, *f* -/-en (*a*) lending; (*b*) award.

**ver'leiten**, *v.tr.* to lead (s.o.) astray/on; **j-n zu etwas** *dat* **v.**, to induce/(*verlocken*) tempt s.o. to do sth.

**ver'lernen**, *v.tr.* to unlearn, forget (sth.).

**ver'lesen**, *v.tr.irr.61* (*a*) to read out (sth.); (*b*) **sich v.**, to make a mistake (while reading).

**verletz|bar** [fɛr'lɛtsbaːr], *adj.* vulnerable. ◆**v~en**, *v.tr.* (*a*) to hurt, injure, *esp. Mil:* wound (s.o., oneself, *Fig:* s.o.'s pride etc.); to injure (one's arm, foot etc.); (*b*) to offend against (decency, good taste etc.); to violate (an agreement etc.), infringe (a law, patent). ◆**v~end**, *adj.* hurtful, wounding (manner, remark etc.). ◆**v~t**, *adj.* (*also Fig:*) hurt, injured; wounded (pride, vanity); **ein V~ter**, a casualty. ◆**V~ung**, *f* -/-en (*a*) injury; (*Wunde*) wound; (*b*) infringement; violation.

**ver'leugnen**, *v.tr.* to deny (a fact etc.); to disown (a friend etc.).

**verleumd|en** [fɛr'lɔymdən], *v.tr.* to slander, (*schriftlich*) libel (s.o.). ◆**v~erisch**, *adj.* slanderous; libellous. ◆**V~ung**, *f* -/-en slander; (*schriftlich*) libel. ◆**V~ungskampagne**, *f* smear campaign.

**ver'lieb|en**, *v.refl.* **sich v.**, to fall in love (in j-n, with s.o.). ◆**v~t**, *adj.* in love (in + *acc*, with); amorous (couple, glances etc.). ◆**V~theit**, *f -/no pl* (state of) being in love.

**verlier|en** [fɛrˈliːrən], *v.irr.32 v.tr. & i.* (*haben*) to lose (s.o., sth.); **sich v.**, (*Pers.*) to get lost; (*Angst, Spur usw.*) to disappear, vanish; *F:* **ihr habt hier nichts verloren**, you've got no business (to be) here. ◆**V~er**, *m -s/-* loser.

**Verlies** [fɛrˈliːs], *n -es/-e* dungeon.

**ver'lob|en**, *v.refl.* **sich v.**, to get engaged. ◆**V~te(r)**, *m & f decl. as adj.* (*Mann*) fiancé; (*Frau*) fiancée. ◆**V~ung**, *f -/-en* engagement. ◆**V~ungs-**, *comb.fm.* engagement (ring etc.).

**ver'lock|en**, *v.tr.* to entice, lure (s.o.). ◆**v~end**, *adj.* tempting. ◆**V~ung**, *f -/-en* temptation, enticement.

**verlogen** [fɛrˈloːgən], *adj.* untruthful; hypocritical (morals etc.).

**verloren** [fɛrˈloːrən], *adj.* lost (person, object etc.); vain (effort, hope etc.); j-n, etwas **v. geben**, to give s.o., sth. up for lost. ◆**v~gehen**, *v.i.sep.irr.36* (*sein*) to get lost; (*Zeit*) to be wasted.

**verlos|en** [fɛrˈloːzən], *v.tr.* to draw lots for, (*durch Tombola*) raffle (sth.). ◆**V~ung**, *f -/-en* draw, raffle.

**verlotter|n** [fɛrˈlɔtərn], *v.i.* (*sein*) to go to the dogs. ◆**v~t**, *adj.* dissipated, dissolute.

**Verlust** [fɛrˈlʊst], *m -(e)s/-e* loss. ◆**V~geschäft**, *n* loss-making deal.

**ver'|machen**, *v.tr. F:* **j-m etwas v.**, to leave sth. to s.o. (in one's will). ◆**V~'mächtnis**, *n -ses/-se* bequest, legacy.

**vermählen** [fɛrˈmɛːlən], *v.refl. Lit:* **sich v.**, to get married.

**ver'mehren**, *v.tr.* to increase (an amount, wages etc.); **sich v.**, to increase, (*Tiere*) breed, (*Pflanzen*) propagate.

**vermeiden**, *v.tr.* to avoid (sth.).

**vermeintlich** [fɛrˈmaintlɪç], *adj.* supposed (gangster etc.); alleged (father etc.).

**Vermerk** [fɛrˈmɛrk], *m -(e)s/-e* note; (*Eintrag*) entry. ◆**v~en**, *v.tr.* to make a note of (sth.).

**ver'mess|en. I.** *v.tr.* to survey (land etc.). **II.** *adj.* presumptuous; impudent (request etc.). ◆**V~enheit**, *f -/no pl* presumption, temerity. ◆**V~er**, *m -s/-* surveyor.

**ver'miet|en**, *v.tr.* to let (a flat, house etc.), lease (buildings, land etc.); to hire (out) (a boat, car etc.). ◆**V~er(in)**, *m -s/- (f -/-nen)* (*a*) landlord, (*Frau*) landlady; (*b*) hirer. ◆**V~ung**, *f -/-en* (*a*) letting; (*b*) hire, hiring.

**ver'minder|n**, *v.tr.* to reduce (sth.); **sich v.**, to lessen; (*Einfluß usw.*) to decrease. ◆**V~ung**, *f -/no pl* reduction, decrease.

**ver'mischen**, *v.tr.* to mix (colours, *Cu:* ingredients etc.); **sich v.**, to mix, (*Farben*) blend, (*Personen*) mingle.

**vermissen** [fɛrˈmisən], *v.tr.* to miss (s.o., sth.); **ein Vermißter**, a missing person.

**vermitt|eln** [fɛrˈmitəln], *v.* 1. *v.i.* (*haben*) to mediate. 2. *v.tr.* (*a*) to obtain, procure (sth.) (j-m, for s.o.); to negotiate (a deal etc.); (*b*) (*übertragen*) to convey (an idea, a picture etc.); to pass on (one's knowledge); *Tel:* to put through (a call). ◆**V~ler**, *m -s/-* (*a*) (*Schlichter*) mediator; (*b*) agent. ◆**V~lung**, *f -/-en* 1. *no pl* (*Schlichtung*) mediation. 2. (*Stelle*) agency; *Tel:* exchange.

**ver'mögen. I.** *v.tr.irr.67 Lit:* **etwas zu tun v.**, to be able to do sth. **II. V.**, *n -s/-* 1. (*Können*) ability. 2. (*Besitz*) property, (*Reichtum*) fortune, wealth; *F:* **das kostet ein V.**, it costs a fortune. ◆**v~d**, *adj.* wealthy, well-off.

**vermut|en** [fɛrˈmuːtən], *v.tr.* to suspect (sth.); (*annehmen*) to assume (sth.). ◆**v~lich**, *adj.* presumable, probable (result etc.). ◆**V~ung**, *f -/-en* supposition.

**vernachlässig|en** [fɛrˈnaːxlɛsigən], *v.tr.* to neglect (sth.). ◆**V~ung**, *f -/no pl* neglect.

**vernehm|en. I.** *v.tr.irr.69* (*a*) to hear (a sound etc., that ...); (*b*) (*Polizei usw.*) to question (a witness etc.). **II. V.**, *n* **dem V. nach**, from what one hears. ◆**V~ung**, *f -/-en* questioning.

**vernein|en** [fɛrˈnainən], *v.tr.&i.* (*haben*) to say no (to a question etc.); to deny (the truth of sth.). ◆**V~ung**, *f -/-en* (*a*) negative answer; (*b*) *Gram:* negation.

**vernicht|en** [fɛrˈniçtən], *v.tr.* to destroy (sth., *Fig:* hopes etc.), to exterminate (a pest, weeds etc.), wipe out (an army, a species etc.). ◆**v~end**, *adj.* crushing (blow, defeat etc.); devastating (criticism etc.); **j-n v. schlagen**, to crush s.o., *Sp:* beat s.o. hollow. ◆**V~ung**, *f -/no pl* destruction; extermination.

**Vernunft** [fɛrˈnʊnft], *f -/no pl* reason; **V. annehmen/zur V. kommen**, to see reason/come to one's senses.

**vernünftig** [fɛrˈnʏnftiç], *adj.* (*a*) sensible, sound (argument etc.); **sei doch v.!** do be reasonable/sensible! (*b*) *F:* (*ordentlich*) decent; (*richtig*) proper (job etc.).

**veröffentlich|en** [fɛrˈʔœfəntliçən], *v.tr.* to publish (a book, report). ◆**V~ung**, *f -/-en* publication.

**ver'ordn|en**, *v.tr. Med:* to prescribe (a treatment, rest etc.). ◆**V~ung**, *f* order, ruling.

**ver'pachten**, *v.tr.* to let (sth.) (out), lease (a farm, land etc.).

**ver'pack|en**, *v.tr.* to pack, *Com:* package (sth.); (*einwickeln*) to wrap (up) (a present, parcel). ◆**V~ung**, *f* packing, packaging.

**ver'passen**, *v.tr.* (*a*) to miss (a train, chance etc.); (*b*) *F:* (*geben*) **j-m einen Tritt usw. v.**, to give s.o. a kick etc.

**verpesten** [fɛrˈpɛstən], *v.tr.* to poison, pollute (the air etc.).

**ver'pfleg|en**, *v.tr.* to feed (s.o., oneself). ◆**V~ung**, *f -/no pl* catering; (*Mahlzeiten*) meals; (*im Hotel usw.*) board; *Mil:* rations.

**verpflicht|en** [fɛr'pfliçtən], *v.tr.* (*a*) to oblige, (*durch Eid usw.*) bind (s.o.); to commit (s.o.) (**zu einer Zahlung,** to make a payment); **j-m (zu Dank) verpflichtet,** obliged/indebted to s.o.; **sich zu etwas** *dat* **v.,** to commit oneself to sth.; to undertake to do sth.; (*b*) (*engagieren*) to engage, sign on (an actor etc.). ◆**V~ung**, *f -/-en* (*a*) obligation (**j-m gegenüber,** to s.o.); **eine V. eingehen,** to take on a commitment; (*b*) *Th:* engagement.

**ver'pfuschen**, *v.tr. F:* to bungle, ruin (one's life etc.).

**verpönt** [fɛr'pøːnt], *adj.* disapproved of, taboo.

**ver'prügeln**, *v.tr.* to beat (s.o.) up; (*zur Strafe*) to beat/thrash (s.o.).

**Verputz** [fɛr'puts], *m* plaster; (*Rauhputz*) roughcast. ◆**v~en**, *v.tr.* (*a*) to plaster, (*außen* render, (*mit Rauhputz*) roughcast (a wall); (*b*) *F:* to polish off (food).

**Verrat** [fɛr'raːt], *m -(e)s/no pl* betrayal (**eines Geheimnisses,** of a secret); (*Landesv.*) treason. ◆**v~en**, *v.tr.irr.13* (*a*) to betray (s.o., one's country etc.), give away (a secret etc.); **sich v.,** to give oneself away; (*b*) (*mitteilen*) **j-m etwas v.,** to tell s.o. sth. (in confidence).

**Verräter** [fɛr'rɛːtər], *m -s/-* traitor, betrayer. ◆**V~in,** *f -/-nen* traitress. ◆**v~isch,** *adj.* treacherous; *Fig:* telltale, giveaway (look etc.).

**ver'rechn|en**, *v.tr.* (*a*) to charge/ (*gutschreiben*) credit (a sum) to account; to clear (a cheque); **etwas mit etwas dat v.,** to offset/balance one thing with another; (*b*) (*also Fig:*) **sich v.,** to miscalculate. ◆**V~ungsscheck,** *m* nonnegotiable/crossed cheque.

**verregnet** [fɛr'reːgnət], *adj.* spoilt by rain.

**ver'reisen**, *v.i.* (*sein*) to go away (on a journey/trip).

**ver'reißen**, *v.tr.irr.4* to tear (a book, play) to pieces, *F:* slate (a book, play).

**verrenk|en** [fɛr'rɛŋkən], *v.tr.* to dislocate (one's shoulder etc.); to crick (one's neck); **sich** *dat* **den Fuß v.,** to twist one's ankle. ◆**V~ung,** *f -/-en* dislocation; contortion.

**ver'richten**, *v.tr.* to carry out, perform (a duty, task etc.).

**verringer|n** [fɛr'riŋərn], *v.tr.* to reduce (sth.); **sich v.,** to decrease, diminish. ◆**V~ung,** *f -/-en* reduction; cut (in output, wages etc.).

**ver'rost|en**, *v.i.* (*sein*) to rust. ◆**v~et,** *adj.* rusty.

**verrotten** [fɛr'rɔtən], *v.i.* (*sein*) to rot, (*Gebäude*) decay.

**ver'rückt** [fɛr'rykt], *adj.* crazy, mad (**auf** +*acc,* about); (*geistesgestört*) insane; **ein V~er/eine V~e,** a lunatic. ◆**v~heit,**

*f -/-en* **1.** *no pl* insanity; *esp. Fig:* madness. **2.** folly; crazy idea.

**Ver'ruf,** *m* **in V. kommen,** to fall into disrepute. ◆**v~en,** *adj.* disreputable.

**Vers** [fɛrs], *m -es/-e* verse (in the bible/of a hymn); (*Zeile*) line.

**ver'sag|en. I.** *v.* **1.** *v.tr.* **j-m/sich** *dat* **etwas v.,** to deny s.o./oneself sth. **2.** *v.i.* (*haben*) (*Pers., Ding*) to fail; (*Motor usw.*) to break down. **II. V.,** *n -s/no pl* failure; **menschliches V.,** human error/fallibility. ◆**V~er,** *m -s/-* failure; *F:* flop.

**ver'salzen. I.** *v.tr.irr.* to put too much salt in (sth.); *Fig:* **j-m etwas v.,** to spoil sth. for s.o. **II.** *adj.* too salty.

**ver'samm|eln,** *v.tr.* to assemble (people), gather (people) together; **sich um j-n, den Kamin usw. v.,** to gather round s.o., the fire etc. ◆**V~lung,** *f -/-en* assembly; (*weniger formell*) gathering.

**Versand** [fɛr'zant], *m -s/no pl* dispatch. ◆**V~haus,** *n* mail order firm.

**versäum|en** [fɛr'zɔymən], *v.tr.* to miss (a chance, train etc.); to lose (time etc.); to neglect (one's duty). ◆**V~nis,** *n -ses /-se* neglect; (*Pflichtv.*) omission.

**ver'schaffen,** *v.tr.* **sich** *dat*/**j-m etwas v.,** to get (hold of) sth. for oneself/s.o.; **j-m eine Arbeit v.,** to provide s.o. with a job; **sich** *dat* **einen Vorteil usw. v.,** to gain an advantage etc.

**verschämt** [fɛr'ʃɛːmt], *adj.* bashful; shamefaced.

**verschandeln** [fɛr'ʃandəln], *v.tr. F:* to disfigure (sth.), spoil (a dress etc.).

**verschanzen** [fɛr'ʃantsən], *v.refl.* **sich v.,** to dig oneself in; (*in Deckung*) to take cover.

**ver'schärfen,** *v.tr.* to heighten, increase (contrast, tension etc.); to tighten up (censorship, checks etc.); to stiffen (a penalty); to step up (speed, tempo); **sich v.,** to be heightened/increased.

**ver'schätzen,** *v.refl.* **sich v.,** to miscalculate.

**ver'schenken,** *v.tr.* to give (sth.) away, throw away (a chance).

**ver'scheuchen,** *v.tr.* to chase away (s.o., an animal, *Fig:* worries etc.).

**ver'schicken,** *v.tr.* to send out (invitations etc.); to send (s.o.) away.

**verschieben,** *v.tr.irr.82* (*a*) to move, shift (cargo, furniture etc.); *Rail:* to shunt (wagons); (*b*) (*auf später*) to postpone, put off (sth.) (**auf** + *acc,* until).

**verschieden** [fɛr'ʃiːdən], *adj.* (*a*) (*unterschiedlich*) different, distinct; **v. groß/ schwer,** of different sizes/weights; (*b*) **pl aus v~en Gründen,** for various reasons; **V~es,** miscellaneous (items); sundries. ◆**v~artig,** *adj.* diverse, of various kinds. ◆**V~heit,** *f -/-en* difference, dissimilarity. ◆**v~tlich,** *adv.* on various occasions.

**ver'schimmeln,** *v.i.* (*sein*) to go mouldy.

**ver'schlafen. I.** *v.irr.84* **1.** *v.refl.* & *i.* (*haben*) (**sich**) **v.,** to oversleep. **2.** *v.tr.* to sleep away (the day, time etc.); *F:* **seinen Zug usw. v.**, to miss one's train etc. by oversleeping. **II.** *adj.* sleepy (person, village etc.).

**Ver'schlag**, *m* shack, shed; *(Kiste)* crate. ◆**v~en. I.** *v.tr.irr.85* (*a*) to board up (an opening etc.); (*b*) **es verschlug ihm die Sprache**, he was struck dumb. **II.** *adj.* sly, underhand (person). ◆**V~enheit**, *f -/no pl* craftiness; slyness.

**verschlechter|n** [fɛr'ʃlɛçtərn], *v.tr.* to make (sth.) worse; **sich v.**, to worsen; *(Gesundheit)* to deteriorate. ◆**V~ung**, *f -/no pl* worsening, deterioration.

**verschleiern** [fɛr'ʃlaiərn], *v.tr.* to veil (one's face); *Fig: (verbergen)* to conceal (one's intentions).

**Verschleiß** [fɛr'ʃlais], *m -es/-e* wear and tear; *(Verbrauch)* consumption (**an** + *dat*, of). ◆**v~en**, *v.tr. & i.irr.4* (*sein*) to wear (sth., *Fig:* s.o.) out.

**ver'schleppen**, *v.tr.* (*a*) to take (s.o.) away by force; *(entführen)* to abduct (s.o.); (*b*) to drag out (a discussion etc.).

**ver'schleudern**, *v.tr.* (*a*) to squander (one's fortune etc.); (*b*) *Com:* to sell (goods) at giveaway prices.

**ver'schließ|bar**, *adj.* lockable. ◆**v~en**, *v.tr.irr.31* to lock (a door etc.), lock up (a house etc.); **sich Argumenten v.**, to close one's mind to arguments.

**verschlimm|ern** [fɛr'ʃlimərn], *v.tr.* to make (sth.) worse, aggravate (a situation etc.); **sich v.**, to get worse, deteriorate. ◆**V~erung**, *f -/no pl* worsening, deterioration.

**ver'schlingen**, *v.tr.irr.95* (*a*) to devour (food, *Fig:* a book etc.); *esp. Fig:* to swallow (s.o., sth.), *Lit: (Wellen usw.)* engulf (s.o., sth.); (*b*) *(ineinander)* to entwine (threads etc.).

**ver'schlissen**, *adj.* worn; *(völlig)* worn out.

**verschlossen** [fɛr'ʃlɔsən], *adj.* (*a*) locked; (*b*) *(zurückhaltend)* reserved, reticent. ◆**V~heit**, *f -/no pl* reserve.

**ver'schlucken**, *v.tr.* to swallow (food, words); **sich v.**, to choke.

**Ver'schluß**, *m -sses/-üsse* (*a*) (door etc.) catch; *Cl:* fastener; *(Flaschenv.)* stopper, bottle top; **hinter/unter V.**, under lock and key; (*b*) *Phot:* shutter.

**ver'schmähen**, *v.tr.* to disdain, spurn (help, an offer etc.).

**ver'schmerzen**, *v.tr.* to get over (a loss etc.).

**ver'schmieren**, *v.tr.* to besmear, *(bekritzeln)* scrawl over (sth.).

**verschmutz|en** [fɛr'ʃmutsən], *v.tr.* to soil (clothes, a carpet etc.); to pollute (air, water etc.). ◆**V~ung**, *f -/no pl* pollution.

**ver'schnaufen**, *v.refl.* **sich v.**, to pause for breath.

**verschneit** [fɛr'ʃnait], *adj.* covered with snow.

**Ver'schnitt**, *m* blend.

**verschnupft** [fɛr'ʃnupft], *adj.* suffering from a cold.

**ver'schnüren**, *v.tr.* to tie up (a parcel etc.).

**verschollen** [fɛr'ʃɔlən], *adj.* missing (person etc.).

**ver'schonen**, *v.tr.* to spare (s.o., sth.) *(von/mit* + *dat*, from).

**verschönern** [fɛr'ʃøːnərn], *v.tr.* to beautify (s.o., sth.), embellish (a dress, story etc.).

**verschränken** [fɛr'ʃrɛŋkən], *v.tr.* to fold (one's arms), cross (one's legs).

**ver'schreiben**, *v.tr.irr.88* (*a*) *Med:* to prescribe (a medicine); (*b*) **sich v.**, to make a slip of the pen; (*c*) **sich etwas** *dat* **v.**, to devote oneself to sth.

**verschroben** [fɛr'ʃroːbən], *adj.* eccentric (person); cranky, crackpot (ideas).

**verschrotten** [fɛr'ʃrɔtən], *v.tr.* to scrap (a car etc.).

**ver'schuld|en. I.** *v.tr.* to be responsible for (an accident etc.). **II. V.**, *n -s/no pl* fault, blame; **ohne mein V.**, through no fault of mine. ◆**v~et**, *adj.* in debt; insolvent (firm).

**ver'schütten**, *v.tr.* (*a*) to spill (sth.); (*b*) *(Lawine usw.)* to bury (people, a village etc.).

**ver'schweigen**, *v.tr.irr.89* to keep (sth.) secret; to conceal (news, the truth etc.) (**j-m**, from s.o.).

**verschwend|en** [fɛr'ʃvɛndən], *v.tr.* to waste (effort, money etc.). ◆**V~er**, *m -s/-* spendthrift. ◆**v~erisch**, *adj.* extravagant, wasteful; lavish (costumes, feast etc.). ◆**V~ung**, *f -/no pl* (*a*) waste (of sth.); (*b*) wastefulness, extravagance.

**verschwiegen** [fɛr'ʃviːgən], *adj.* discreet (person); secluded (place etc.). ◆**V~heit**, *f -/no pl* discretion, seclusion.

**ver'schwimmen**, *v.i.irr.90* (*sein*) to become blurred/*(dunstig)* hazy.

**ver'schwinden. I.** *v.i.irr.9* (*sein*) to disappear, vanish; *F:* **verschwinde!** get lost! **II. V.**, *n -s/no pl* disappearance.

**verschwitzt** [fɛr'ʃvitst], *adj.* soaked in perspiration; sweaty.

**verschwommen** [fɛr'ʃvɔmən], *adj.* blurred (photograph etc.); hazy (outline etc.); vague, woolly (idea etc.).

**ver'schwör|en**, *v.refl.irr.91* **sich v.**, to conspire. ◆**V~er(in)**, *m -s/- (f -/-nen)* conspirator. ◆**V~ung**, *f -/-en* conspiracy, plot.

**ver'sehen. I.** *v.tr.irr.92* (*a*) to provide (s.o.) (**mit** + *dat*, with); (*b*) to perform (a duty etc.); (*c*) **sich v.**, to make a mistake; (*d*) **ehe man sich versieht**, before you know where you are. **II. V.**, *n -s/-* slip, oversight; *(Fehler)* (careless) mistake; **aus V.**, inadvertently. ◆**v~tlich**, *adv.* inadvertently.

**Versehrte(r)** [fɛr'zeːrtə(r)], *m & f decl. as adj.* disabled (person).

**ver'senden**, *v.tr.irr.94* to send out (circulars etc.), dispatch (goods etc.).

**versenk|en**, *v.tr.* to sink (a ship etc.), submerge (ship etc.); *Fig:* **sich in ein Buch v.**, to bury/immerse oneself in a book. ◆**V~ung**, *f* sinking; submersion; *Fig:* (self-)absorption; *F:* **in der V. verschwinden**, to disappear from the scene.

**versessen** [fɛr'zɛsən], *adj.* **auf j-n, etwas acc v.**, crazy/mad about s.o., sth.

**ver'setz|en**, *v.tr.* (*a*) to move (sth.) (somewhere); to transfer (sth., an employee etc.) (**nach** + *dat*, to); *Sch:* to move up, *N.Am:* promote (a pupil); (*b*) **v. in** + *acc*, to set (sth.) in (motion etc.); to put (s.o.) into a (good/bad mood); **v. Sie sich in meine Lage**, put yourself in my shoes; (*c*) **j-m einen Schlag/Stoß v.**, to hit/push s.o.; (*d*) (*verpfänden*) to pawn (a watch etc.). ◆**V~ung**, *f* -/-en (*a*) move, transfer; *Sch:* moving up, promotion; (*b*) pawning.

**verseuch|en** [fɛr'zɔyçən], *v.tr.* to contaminate (water etc.). ◆**V~ung**, *f* -/no pl contamination.

**ver'sicher|n**, *v.tr.* (*a*) to insure (s.o., oneself etc.); (*b*) **j-m v., daß ...**, to assure s.o. that...; **sich j-s, einer Sache v.**, to make sure of s.o., sth. ◆**V~ung**, *f* 1. insurance. 2. (*Erklärung*) assurance. ◆**V~ungs-**, *comb.fm.* insurance (agent, claim, company, card, cover etc.). ◆**V~spolice**, *f* insurance policy. ◆**V~sprämie**, *f* (insurance) premium.

**ver'siegeln**, *v.tr.* to seal (sth.).

**ver'siegen**, *v.i.* (*sein*) to run dry, (*Brunnen usw.*) dry up.

**versiert** [vɛr'ziːrt], *adj.* experienced, (well) versed.

**ver'sinken**, *v.i.irr.96* (*sein*) to sink, (*Sonne usw.*) go down.

**versklav|en** [fɛr'sklɑːvən], *v.tr.* to enslave (s.o.). ◆**V~ung**, *f* -/no pl enslavement.

**versöhn|en** [fɛr'zøːnən], *v.tr.* to reconcile (s.o.); **sich v.**, to become reconciled; **sie haben sich versöhnt**, they have made it up. ◆**v~lich**, *adj.* conciliatory (mood etc.); forgiving (person). ◆**V~ung**, *f* -/-en reconciliation.

**ver'sorg|en**, *v.tr.* (*a*) to provide, supply (s.o., an area etc.); (*b*) (*sorgen für*) to look after (children etc.); to provide for (a family etc.). ◆**V~ung**, *f* -/no pl (*a*) supply; (*b*) (*Pflege*) care (of the old, sick etc.); **die V. einer Familie**, looking after/providing for a family.

**verspät|en** [fɛr'ʃpeːtən], *v.refl.* **sich v.**, to be late. ◆**v~et**, *adj.* late (arrival etc.); belated (thanks etc.). ◆**V~ung**, *f* -/-en lateness; *Rail:Av:etc:* delay; **mit (10 Minuten) V.**, (10 minutes) late.

**ver'sperren**, *v.tr.* to block (an entrance, road etc.), obstruct (a view etc.).

**ver'spiel|en**, *v.tr.* to gamble away (money, chances etc.). ◆**v~t**, *adj.* playful (kitten etc.); cheerful (tune, pattern).

**ver'spotten**, *v.tr.* to mock at, deride

(s.o., sth.).

**ver'sprech|en. I.** *v.tr.irr.104* (*a*) **j-m etwas v.**, to promise s.o. sth.; **sich dat viel von einer Sache v.**, to have high hopes of sth.; (*b*) **sich v.**, to make a slip of the tongue. **II. V.**, *n* -s/no pl promise. ◆**V~er**, *m* slip of the tongue. ◆**V~ungen**, *fpl* leere V., empty promises.

**ver'spüren**, *v.tr.* to feel (cold, fear, hunger etc.).

**verstaatlich|en** [fɛr'ʃtɑːtliçən], *v.tr.* to nationalize (an industry etc.). ◆**V~ung**, *f* -/no pl nationalization.

**Verstand** [fɛr'ʃtant], *m* -(e)s/no pl (*Geist*) mind, intellect; (*Vernunft*) sense; sanity; **bei V.**, sane, of sound mind; **den V. verlieren**, to go insane; **wieder zu V. kommen**, to come to one's senses; **nimm doch V. an!** be reasonable! ◆**v~esmäßig** [-dəs-], *adj.* rational (process); intellectual (superiority etc.). ◆**V~esmensch**, *m* rational person.

**verständig** [fɛr'ʃtɛndiç], *adj.* intelligent, (*vernünftig*) sensible. ◆**v~en**, *v.tr.* (*a*) to inform, notify (s.o.); (*b*) **sich v.**, to make oneself understood; **sich (mit j-m) v.**, (i) to communicate (with s.o.); (ii) (*sich einigen*) to come to an understanding (with s.o.). ◆**V~ung**, *f* -/-en (*a*) informing, notification; (*b*) (*sich verständigen*) communication; (*c*) (*Übereinkunft*) agreement, understanding.

**verständ|lich** [fɛr'ʃtɛntliç], *adj.* comprehensible; (*begreiflich*) understandable; **leicht/schwer v.**, easy/difficult to grasp; **sich v. machen**, to make oneself understood/(*bei Lärm*) heard. ◆**V~lichkeit**, *f* -/no pl comprehensibility, intelligibility; (*Klarheit*) clarity. ◆**V~nis** [-'ʃtentnis], *n* -ses/no pl understanding; **für Unzuverlässigkeit habe ich kein V.**, I have no time for unreliable people. ◆**v~nislos**, *adj.* uncomprehending. ◆**v~nisvoll**, *adj.* understanding, sympathetic.

**ver'stärk|en**, *v.tr.* to strengthen (sth.); to reinforce (a material, *Mil:* garrison etc.); (*steigern*) to intensify (pressure, effect etc.); to amplify (*Rad:* a signal etc.); **sich v.**, to increase; (*Sturm usw.*) to grow stronger. ◆**V~er**, *m* -s/- amplifier. ◆**V~ung**, *f* (*a*) *Tchn: etc:* strengthening, reinforcement; (*b*) increase (des Verkehrs usw.), in traffic etc.); (*c*) *esp. Mil:* (*Truppen*) reinforcements.

**ver'staub|en**, *v.i.* (*sein*) to get dusty. ◆**v~t**, *adj.* dusty.

**ver'stauchen**, *v.tr.* **sich dat den Fuß/die Hand v.**, to sprain one's ankle/wrist.

**ver'stauen**, *v.tr.* to stow (sth., *Hum:* s.o.), pack (books etc.).

**Versteck** [fɛr'ʃtɛk], *n* -(e)s/-e hiding-place. ◆**v~en**, *v.tr.* to hide (s.o., sth.); to conceal (one's embarrassment etc.); **sich v.**, to hide, (*Verfolgte usw.*) go into hiding. ◆**V~spiel**, *n* (game of) hide-

and-seek. ◆**v~t**, *adj.* hidden; (*heimlich*) secret.

ver'**stehen**, *v.tr. & i.irr.100* (*haben*) to understand (s.o., sth.); **versteh mich nicht falsch**, don't get me wrong; **was v. Sie darunter?** what do you mean by that? **er versteht nichts davon**, he doesn't know anything about it; **er versteht sich auf Autos**, he knows all about cars; **es versteht sich (von selbst)**, it goes without saying.

ver'**steifen**, *v.tr.* to stiffen (sth.), brace (a structure etc.); **sich v.**, to stiffen, (*Haltung*) harden.

ver'**steiger|n**, *v.tr.* to auction (sth.). ◆**V~ung**, *f -/-en* auction (sale).

ver'**stell|bar**, *adj.* adjustable. ◆**v~en**, *v.tr.* (*a*) (*versperren*) to block (a road etc.); (*b*) to shift (sth.); (*falsch*) to put (sth.) in the wrong place; (*einstellen*) to adjust; (*Pers.*) **sich v.**, to pretend, playact. ◆**V~ung**, *f* pretence, play-acting; disguise.

ver'**stimm|t** [fɛr'ʃtimt], *adj.* (*a*) *Mus:* out of tune; (*b*) (*Pers.*) in a bad mood; disgruntled. ◆**V~ung**, *f -/-en* strained atmosphere; (*Unwillen*) ill-feeling.

ver**stockt** [fɛr'ʃtɔkt], *adj.* obdurate, stubborn. ◆**V~heit**, *f -/no pl* obduracy.

ver**stohlen** [fɛr'ʃtoːlən], *adj.* furtive (glance); stealthy (footstep etc.).

ver'**stopf|en**, *v.tr.* to close (up), plug (a crack, hole etc.); to block, choke (a drain, pipe etc.). ◆**v~t**, *adj.* blocked, congested (street); *F:* bunged up (drain, nose etc.). ◆**V~ung**, *f -/-en* (*im Rohr usw.*) obstruction; (*in den Straßen*) congestion; *Med:* constipation.

ver**storben** [fɛr'ʃtɔrbən], *adj.* **der/die V~e**, the deceased.

ver**stört** [fɛr'ʃtøːrt], *adj.* distraught, bewildered.

Ver'**stoß**, *m* infringement, violation (**gegen** + *acc.* of). ◆**v~en**, *v.irr.103* 1. *v.tr.* to drive (s.o.) away; to disown (a child). 2. *v.i.* (*haben*) **v. gegen** + *acc*, to infringe (regulations etc.), break (the law).

ver'**streichen**, *v.irr.59* 1. *v.tr.* to spread (butter etc.). 2. *v.i.* (*sein*) *Lit:* (*Zeit*) to pass (by).

ver'**streut** [fɛr'ʃtrɔyt], *adj.* scattered.

ver'**stricken**, *v.tr. Fig:* to involve (s.o.) (**in** + *acc*, in); **sich in etwas** *acc* **v.**, to get involved in sth.

ver**stümmeln** [fɛr'ʃtyməln], *v.tr.* to mutilate (s.o., *Fig:* a text).

ver**stummen** [fɛr'ʃtumən], *v.i.* (*sein*) to fall silent; (*Lärm*) to stop.

Ver**such** [fɛr'zuːx], *m -(e)s/-e* 1. attempt. 2. *Ph: etc:* experiment; (*Probe*) test. ◆**v~en**, *v.tr.* (*a*) to try (sth., to do sth.); to attempt (flight, a climb, the impossible etc.); **es mit j-m v.**, to give s.o. a try; **sich an/in etwas** *dat* **v.**, to try one's hand at sth.; (*b*) to tempt (s.o.); **versucht, etwas zu tun**, tempted to do

sth. ◆**V~s-**, *comb.fm.* experimental (stage, purposes etc.); test (drilling, drive etc.). ◆**V~skaninchen**, *n F:* experimental subject, *F:* guinea-pig. ◆**v~sweise**, *adv.* on a trial basis. ◆**V~ung**, *f -/-en* temptation; **in V. kommen**, to be tempted.

ver'**süßen**, *v.tr.* to sweeten (sth.).

ver'**tagen**, *v.tr.* to adjourn (a debate etc.), (*verschieben*) defer (a decision etc.).

ver'**tauschen**, *v.tr.* (*a*) to exchange (one thing) (**mit** + *dat*, for); (*b*) (*verwechseln*) to mix up (hats etc.).

verteidig|en [fɛr'taidigən], *v.tr. & i.* (*haben*) to defend (s.o., oneself, sth.). ◆**V~er**, *m -s/-* defender; *Jur:* advocate, counsel for the defence. ◆**V~ung**, *f -/ no pl* defence. ◆**V~ungs-**, *comb.fm.* defence (alliance, budget, system, weapon etc.); (line, minister etc.) of defence.

ver'**teil|en**, *v.tr.* to distribute (food, the load etc.), (*verstreuen*) to scatter, spread (sand, sugar etc.); to allocate (duties, subsidies etc.); **die Rollen v.**, *Th:* to cast the parts; *Fig:* to allocate tasks. ◆**V~er**, *m -s/-* distributor. ◆**V~ung**, *f* distribution.

ver**teufelt** [fɛr'tɔyfəlt], *adj. F:* (*verzwickt*) extremely awkward; *adv.* devilishly (awkward, difficult etc.); fiendishly (clever, cold etc.).

ver'**tief|en** [fɛr'tiːfən], *v.tr.* to deepen (a channel, *Fig:* rift etc.); *Fig:* to extend (one's knowledge, etc.); **sich in etwas** *acc* **v.**, to become engrossed in sth. ◆**V~ung**, *f -/-en* 1. depression; (*Mulde*) hollow. 2. *no pl* deepening; extension.

ver**tikal** [verti'kaːl], *adj.* vertical (plane etc.).

ver**tilgen** [fɛr'tilgən], *v.tr.* to exterminate (vermin etc.); *F:* to demolish (a cake etc.).

ver'**tippen**, *v.refl.* **sich v.**, to make a typing mistake.

ver'**tonen**, *v.tr.* to set (a poem etc.) to music.

Ver**trag** [fɛr'traːk], *m -(e)s/⁺e* contract; *Pol: etc:* treaty. ◆**v~en** [-gən], *v.tr.irr.85* (*a*) (*aushalten*) to bear, stand (s.o., noise, pain etc.); *F:* to take (criticism etc.); **Alkohol v.**, to hold one's drink/*N.Am:* liquor; **sie verträgt keinen Kaffee**, coffee doesn't agree with her; (*b*) **sich mit j-m v.**, to get on (well) with s.o. ◆**v~lich**, *adj.* contractual. ◆**V~s-bruch**, *m* breach of contract. ◆**V~spartner**, *m* partner to a contract.

ver**träglich** [fɛr'trɛːkliç], *adj.* (*a*) (*Pers.*) easy to get on with; (*friedlich*) peaceable, good-natured; (*b*) (*Essen*) easy to digest. ◆**V~keit**, *f -/no pl* 1. easy-going nature. 2. digestibility.

ver'**trauen**. I. *v.i.* (*haben*) **j-m, etwas** *dat* **v.**, to trust s.o., sth.; **v. auf** + *acc*, to place one's trust in (God, justice etc.). II. **V.**, *n -s/no pl* confidence, trust (**zu** + *dat*, in). ◆**v~erweckend**, *adj.* dependable, inspiring confidence. ◆**V~sbruch**, *m* breach of trust. ◆**v~sselig**, *adj.* too trusting, gullible. ◆**v~svoll**, *adj.* trustful, trusting. ◆**v~swürdig**, *adj.* trustworthy.

**ver'traulich**, *adj.* (*a*) confidential (report etc.); (*b*) (*familiär*) familiar, F: pally. ◆**V~keit**, *f* **-/en 1.** *no pl* confidential nature. 2. familiarity.

**ver'traut**, *adj.* (*a*) intimate (circle etc.); (*b*) (*bekannt*) familiar (face, tune etc.); **sich mit etwas** *dat* **v. machen**, to familiarize oneself with sth. ◆**V~heit**, *f* -/ -en (*a*) intimacy; (*b*) familiarity, intimate knowledge.

**ver'treiben**, *v.tr.irr.12* (*a*) to drive/chase away (s.o., an animal, clouds etc.); (*aus dem Land*) to exile (s.o.); (*b*) *Fig:* to get rid of (a cold, cough etc.); **sich** *dat* **die Zeit v.**, to while away/pass the time; (*c*) *Com:* to sell (goods) (wholesale).

**vertret|bar** [fɛr'treːtbɑːr], *adj.* tenable (standpoint); defensible (costs, risk etc.). ◆**v~en**, *v.tr.irr.105* (*a*) (*zeitweise ersetzen*) to stand in/deputize for (s.o.); (*Interessen wahrnehmen*) to represent (s.o., a country etc.); (*verteidigen*) to advocate (an idea etc.); **die Ansicht v., daß ...**, to take the view that ...; (*b*) *F:* **sich** *dat* **die Beine v.**, to stretch one's legs. ◆**V~er(in)**, *m* -s/- (*f* -/-nen) (*also Com:*) (*a*) representative; (chairman's, minister's etc.) deputy; (*b*) (*Verfechter*) advocate. ◆**V~ung**, *f* -/-en (*a*) *Jur: Pol: etc:* representation; *Com:* agency; **j-s V. übernehmen**, to stand in for s.o.

**Vertrieb** [fɛr'triːp], *m* -(e)s/-e sales, marketing. ◆**V~s-**, *comb.fm.* sales (department etc.); marketing (costs, organization etc.). ◆**V~sleiter**, *m* sales manager.

**ver'trocknen**, *v.i.* (*sein*) to dry up, (*Brot usw.*) go dry.

**ver'trödeln**, *v.tr.* to dawdle away, waste (time).

**ver'trösten**, *v.tr.* to string (s.o.) along (with promises etc.).

**ver'tun**, *v.tr.* (*a*) to waste (money, time); (*b*) *F:* **sich v.**, to make a slip.

**ver'tuschen**, *v.tr.* to cover up (an error etc.).

**verüben** [fɛr'ʔyːbəln], *v.tr.* **j-m etwas v.**, to hold sth. against s.o.

**ver'üben**, *v.tr.* to commit (a crime etc.).

**verunglücken** [fɛr'ʔunglykən], *v.i.* (*sein*) (*Pers.*) to have an accident; (*Auto, Zug usw.*) to crash; **tödlich v.**, to be killed in an accident.

**ver'unreinigen**, *v.tr.* to pollute (air, water etc.); to soil (clothes etc.).

**verunstalten** [fɛr'ʔunʃtaltən], *v.tr.* to disfigure (s.o., sth.).

**veruntreuen** [fɛr'ʔuntrɔyən], *v.tr.* to embezzle (money).

**verursachen** [fɛr'ʔuːrzaxən], *v.tr.* to cause (sth.).

**ver'urteil|en**, *v.tr.* to condemn (s.o., sth.); *Jur:* to sentence (s.o.) (**zu** + *dat*, to). ◆**V~ung**, *f* -/-en *Jur:* conviction; *Fig:* condemnation.

**vervielfachen** [fɛr'fiːlfaxən], *v.tr.* to increase (production etc.) considerably.

**vervielfältig|en** [fɛr'fiːlfɛltigən], *v.tr.* to duplicate, make copies of (a text etc.). ◆**V~ung**, *f* -/-en duplication, copying.

**vervollkommnen** [fɛr'fɔlkɔmnən], *v.tr.* to perfect (sth.).

**vervollständigen** [fɛr'fɔlʃtɛndigən], *v.tr.* to complete (sth.).

**ver'wackelt**, *adj.* shaky, blurred (photograph).

**ver'wahr|en**, *v.tr.* (*a*) to keep (sth.) safely; (*b*) **sich gegen etwas** *acc* **v.**, to protest against sth. ◆**v~losen** [-'vɑːrloːzən], *v.i.* (*sein*) to be neglected; (*Garten, Fig: Pers.*) to go to seed. ◆**V~ung**, *f* -/no pl (safe) keeping; custody (of s.o.); **etwas in V. geben/nehmen**, to hand over/accept sth. for safe keeping.

**verwaist** [fɛr'vaist], *adj.* orphaned.

**ver'walt|en**, *v.tr.* to administer (sth.); to manage, run (a business, hotel etc.). ◆**V~er**, *m* -s/- administrator; (*Leiter*) manager; (*Treuhänder*) trustee. ◆**V~ung**, *f* -/-en **1.** *no pl* administration; (*Leitung*) management, running. 2. (*Behörde*) (local etc.) authority. ◆**V~ungs-**, *comb.fm.* administrative (district, costs etc.). ◆**V~sbeamte(r)**, *m* administrative official; civil servant.

**ver'wand|eln**, *v.tr.* to change, transform (s.o., sth.) (**in** + *acc*, into); **sich in etwas** *acc* **v.**, to change/turn into sth. ◆**V~lung**, *f* change, transformation.

**verwandt** [fɛr'vant], *adj.* related (**mit** + *dat*, to). ◆**V~e(r)**, *m & f decl. as adj.* relative, relation. ◆**V~schaft**, *f* -/-en **1.** relationship. 2. *no pl* relatives, relations.

**ver'warn|en**, *v.tr.* to caution (s.o.), warn (*Sp:* a player etc.). ◆**V~ung**, *f* warning, caution.

**ver'waschen**, *adj.* washed out, faded.

**ver'wässern**, *v.tr.* to water down (wine, *Fig:* an idea etc.).

**ver'wechs|eln**, *v.tr.* to confuse, mix up (people, things); to mistake (s.o., sth.) (**mit j-m, etwas** *dat*, for s.o., sth.). ◆**V~lung**, *f* -/-en confusion, *F:* mix-up; mistake.

**verwegen** [fɛr've:gən], *adj.* bold, daring. ◆**V~heit**, *f* -/no pl audacity, daring.

**ver'wehren**, *v.tr.* **j-m etwas v.**, to refuse s.o. sth.

**verweichlichen** [fɛr'vaiçliçən], *v.tr.* to make (s.o.) soft, *F:* mollycoddle (a child).

**ver'weigern**, *v.tr.* (**j-m**) **etwas v.**, to refuse (s.o.) sth.; **den Befehl v.**, to refuse to obey orders.

**verweilen** [fɛr'vailən], *v.i.* (*sein*) *Lit:* to stay, (*länger als nötig*) linger.

**Verweis** [fɛr'vais], *m* -es/-e **1.** (*Tadel*) reprimand, rebuke. 2. (*Hinweis*) reference.

◆**v~en** [-zən], *v.tr.irr.70* (a) to expel (s.o.) (**aus/von** + *dat*, from); **j-n des Landes v.**, to deport s.o.; *Sp:* **einen Spieler des Platzes v.**, to send a player off (the field); (b) (*hinweisen*) **j-n auf etwas** *acc* **v.**, to refer s.o. to sth.

ver'**welken**, *v.i.* (*sein*) to wilt, wither.

ver'**wend|en**, *v.tr.irr.94* to use (s.o., sth.); to spend (care, effort, time etc.). ◆**V~ung**, *f -/-en* use. ◆**v~ungsfähig**, *adj.* fit for use, (*geeignet*) suitable. ◆**V~ungszweck**, *m* purpose, application.

ver'**werf|en**, *v.tr.irr.110* to reject, turn down (a plan etc.); to dismiss (a complaint etc.). ◆**v~lich**, *adj.* reprehensible.

ver'**wert|en**, *v.tr.* to make (good) use of (sth.), put (sth.) to good use; to utilize (resources etc.). ◆**V~ung**, *f* utilization, exploitation.

ver**wes|en** [fɛr'veːzən], *v.i.* (*sein*) (*Leiche*) to decompose. ◆**V~ung**, *f -/no pl* decomposition.

ver'**wick|eln**, *v.tr.* (a) to involve (s.o.); **sich v.**, (*Fäden, Wolle*) to get into a tangle; (*also Pers.*) **sich in etwas** *acc/dat* **v.**, to get entangled/mixed up in sth. ◆**v~elt**, *adj.* complex, involved. ◆**V~lung**, *f -/-en* **1.** *no pl* entanglement; involvement. **2.** (*Komplikation*) complication.

ver**wildern** [fɛr'vildərn], *v.i.* (*sein*) to go wild; (*Pflanze*) to grow wild.

ver**wirklichen** [fɛr'virkliçən], *v.tr.* to realize (an ambition, idea etc.); to put (a plan) into effect.

ver**wirr|en** [fɛr'virən], *v.tr.* (a) to entangle (threads etc.); to tousle (hair); (b) to bewilder, (*durcheinanderbringen*) confuse. ◆**V~ung**, *f -/-en* confusion; (*Fassungslosigkeit*) bewilderment; **j-n in V. bringen**, to confuse/fluster s.o.; **geistige V.**, distraught state.

ver'**wischen**, *v.tr.* to smudge.

ver'**wittern**, *v.i.* (*sein*) to weather.

ver**witwet** [fɛr'vitvət], *adj.* widowed.

ver**wöhn|en** [fɛr'vøːnən], *v.tr.* to spoil, (*verhätscheln*) pamper (s.o.). ◆**v~t**, *adj.* spoilt (child etc.); fastidious (taste etc.).

ver**worfen** [fɛr'vɔrfən], *adj.* depraved. ◆**V~heit**, *f -/no pl* depravity.

ver**worren** [fɛr'vɔrən], *adj.* confused; (*verwickelt*) involved.

ver**wund|bar** [fɛr'vuntbaːr], *adj.* vulnerable. ◆**v~en**, *v.tr.* to wound (s.o.). ◆**V~ete(r)**, *m & f decl. as adj.* wounded (man/woman), casualty. ◆**V~ung**, *f -/-en* **1.** *no pl* wounding. **2.** wound.

ver'**wunder|lich**, *adj.* surprising; (*seltsam*) strange, odd. ◆**v~n**, *v.tr.* to surprise (s.o.). ◆**V~ung**, *f -/no pl* surprise; amazement.

ver'**wünschen**, *v.tr.* to curse (s.o., sth.).

ver**wüst|en** [fɛr'vyːstən], *v.tr.* to devastate, ravage (a country etc.).

◆**V~ung**, *f -/-en* devastation, ravages.

ver**zagen** [fɛr'tsaːgən], *v.i.* (*haben*) to lose heart, give up (hope).

ver'**zählen**, *v.refl.* **sich v.**, to miscount.

ver'**zaubern**, *v.tr.* to bewitch, enchant (s.o., sth.).

ver**zehr** [fɛr'tseːr], *m -(e)s/no pl* consumption. ◆**v~en**, *v.tr.* to consume (food, drink).

ver'**zeich|nen**, *v.tr.irr.60* to record (sth.), take (sth.) down; (*aufführen*) to list (items, names etc.). ◆**V~nis**, *n -sses/ -sse* list; (*Register*) index.

ver**zeih|en** [fɛr'tsaiən], *v.tr.irr.60* to forgive (sth.); (*entschuldigen*) to excuse (a fault etc.); **ich verzeihe es dir**, I'll forgive you (for that). ◆**v~lich**, *adj.* excusable, pardonable. ◆**V~ung**, *f -/no pl* forgiveness; **V.!** sorry!

ver'**zerren**, *v.tr.* to distort (a picture, sound, facts etc.).

ver**zicht** [fɛr'tsiçt], *m -(e)s/-e* renunciation, (*Opfer*) sacrifice (**auf** + *acc*, of). ◆**v~en**, *v.i.* (*haben*) to do without, abstain; **v. auf** + *acc*, (*aufgeben*) to give (sth.) up; to waive, relinquish (a claim, right etc.); to abstain from (alcohol, comment etc.).

ver'**ziehen**, *v.irr.113* **1.** *v.tr.* (a) to screw up (one's face, mouth); **er verzog das Gesicht**, he pulled a face; (b) (*verwöhnen*) to spoil (a child); (c) **sich v.**, (*die Form verlieren*) to get out of shape; (*verschwinden*) to disappear. **2.** *v.i.* (*sein*) to move (house).

ver'**zier|en**, *v.tr.* to decorate (sth.). ◆**V~ung**, *f -/-en* decoration.

ver**zins|en** [fɛr'tsinzən], *v.tr.* to pay interest on (a loan etc.). ◆**v~lich**, *adj.* bearing interest.

ver'**zöger|n**, *v.tr.* to delay (sth.); (*verlangsamen*) to retard, slow down (development etc.); **sich v.**, to be delayed/held up. ◆**V~ung**, *f -/-en* **1.** *no pl* delaying; slowing down. **2.** delay.

ver'**zollen**, *v.tr.* to pay duty on (sth.); **haben Sie etwas zu v.?** have you anything to declare?

ver**zück|t** [fɛr'tsykt], *adj.* ecstatic; *adv.* **v. zuhören**, to listen entranced. ◆**V~ung**, *f -/no pl* (state of) ecstasy.

**Ver'zug**, *m -(e)s/no pl* delay; *Fin:* **in V. sein**, to be in arrears.

ver'**zweif|eln**, *v.i.* (*sein*) to despair. ◆**v~elt**, *adj.* desperate; despairing (look etc.). ◆**V~lung**, *f -/no pl* despair.

ver**zweigen** [fɛr'tsvaigən], *v.refl.* **sich v.**, (*Baum, Straße*) to branch, divide; *Fig:* (*System usw.*) to ramify.

ver**zwickt** [fɛr'tsvikt], *adj. F:* tricky; ticklish (problem etc.).

**Veto** ['veːto], *n -s/-s* veto. ◆**V~recht**, *n* (power of) veto.

**Vetter** ['fɛtər], *m -s/-* cousin. ◆**V~nwirtschaft**, *f* nepotism.

**Viadukt** [via'dukt], *m -(e)s/-e* viaduct.

**Vibr|ation** [vibratsi'oːn], *f -/-en* vibration.

◆**v~ieren** [vi'briːrən], *v.i.* *(haben)* to vibrate.

**Video** ['video]. **I.** *n* -s/*no pl* video. **II.** '**V~-**, *comb.fm.* video (tape, cassette etc.). ◆**V~recorder**, *m*, video (tape) recorder.

**Vieh** [fiː]. **I.** *n* -(e)s/*no pl* **1.** *Agr:* livestock, *esp.* cattle. **2.** *Pej:* F: *(a)* *(Tier)* creature; *(b)* *(Pers.)* beast. **II.** '**V~-**, *comb.fm.* *Agr:* livestock, *esp.* cattle (trader, dealer, market etc.). ◆'**v~isch**, *adj.* brutal, bestial. ◆'**V~zucht**, *f* cattle/stock breeding.

**viel** [fiːl]. **1.** *adj.* much; *pl* many; v~e Freunde, many/a lot of friends; **das** v~e Geld, all that money; **v. Zeit**, a lot of time; **nicht v. Geld**, not much money. **2.** *adv.* **v. arbeiten/lachen**, to work/laugh a lot; **v. größer**, much bigger. **3.** *pron.* *(a)* *inv.* **er sagt v./nicht v.**, he says a lot/not much; **einer zu v.**, one too many; **gleich v.**, the same (amount); *(b)* **v~es**, a lot of things; **in v~em**, in many respects; **um v~es jünger/besser**, much younger/better; *(c)* **v~e**, many, a lot; *(Menschen)* a lot of people. ◆'**v~deutig**, *adj.* ambiguous. ◆'**V~deutigkeit**, *f* -/-en ambiguity. ◆**v~er'lei**, *inv. adj.* many (different) kinds of, a great variety of. **2.** *pron.* all kinds of things; a great many things. ◆'**v~fach**, *adj.* *(a)* multiple; many different (ways); **auf v~fachen Wunsch**, by popular demand; **um ein V~faches**, many times; *(b)* *adv.* many times (over); *(häufig)* frequently. ◆'**V~falt**, *f -/no pl* diversity; (great) variety. ◆'**v~fältig**, *adj.* diverse (problems etc.); multifarious (activities, duties etc.). ◆'**V~fraß**, *m* -es/-e glutton. ◆**v~leicht** [fi'laiçt], *adv.* perhaps; *F:* **das war v. ein Schreck!** that (really) was some shock! ◆'**v~mals**, *adv.* many times; **danke v.**, a thank you very much. ◆'**v~mehr**, *conj. & adv.* (or) rather; *(genauer gesagt)* to be more precise; *(im Gegenteil)* on the contrary. ◆'**v~sagend**, *adj.* meaning(ful) (look etc.). ◆'**v~schichtig**, *adj.* manylayered; *Fig:* many-faceted. ◆'**v~seitig**, *adj.* versatile (person, tool etc.); all-round (abilities); varied, wide (experience, interests etc.). ◆'**V~seitigkeit**, *f -/no pl* versatility. ◆'**v~versprechend**, *adj.* very promising. ◆'**v~zahl**, *f -/no pl* multiplicity, enormous number. ◆'**V~zweck-**, *comb.fm.* multi-purpose.

**vier** [fiːr], *num.adj.* four; **auf allen v~en**, on all fours; **unter v. Augen**, confidentially, in private. ◆'**V~beiner**, *m* -s/- *Hum:* four-footed friend. ◆'**v~beinig**, *adj.* four-legged. ◆'**V~eck**, *n* quadrilateral; *(Rechteck)* rectangle; *(mit gleichen Seiten)* square. ◆'**v~eckig**, *adj.* rectangular; square; *Mth:* quadrilateral. ◆'**v~erlei**, *adj.* of four kinds. ◆'**v~fach**, *adj.* *(a)* fourfold; quadruple; **das V~fache**, four times as much; *(b)*

*adv.* four times. ◆'**v~jährig**, *adj.* four-year-old (child etc.); four-year (period etc.). ◆'**v~mal**, *adv.* four times. ◆'**v~malig**, *adj.* (repeated) four times. ◆'**v~stellig**, *adj.* four-figure (number). ◆'**V~taktmotor**, *m* four-stroke engine. ◆'**v~te(r,s)**, *num.adj.* fourth. ◆'**v~teilig**, *adj.* in four parts. ◆**V~tel** ['fiːrtəl], *n* -s/- quarter; **V. nach vier**, quarter past four. ◆'**V~telfinale**, *n* quarter final. ◆'**V~teljahr**, *n* quarter (of a year). ◆'**v~teljährlich**, *adj. & adv.* quarterly; *adv.* every quarter. ◆'**v~teln**, *v.tr.* to quarter (sth.). ◆'**V~telnote**, *f* crotchet. ◆'**V~telstunde**, *f* quarter of an hour. ◆'**v~tens**, *adj.* fourthly. ◆'**v~türig**, *adj.* *Aut:* four-door. ◆'**v~zehn**, *num.adj.* fourteen. ◆'**v~zehntägig**, *adj.* fortnight's (holiday etc.). ◆'**v~zehntäglich**, *adj.* fortnightly. ◆'**v~zehnte(r,s)**, *num.adj.* fourteenth. ◆'**v~zig**, *num.adj.* forty.

**Vikar** [vi'kaːr], *m* -s/-e curate.

**Vill|a** ['vila], *f -/Villen* detached house. ◆'**V~enviertel**, *n* smart residential district.

**violett** [vio'lɛt], *adj.* violet.

**Viol|ine** [vio'liːnə], *f* -/-n violin. ◆**V~inkonzert**, *n* violin concerto. ◆**V~oncello** [violɔn'tʃɛlo], *n* cello.

**Virus** ['viːrus], *m* -/Viren virus.

**Visier** [vi'ziːr], *n* -s/-e *Mil:* gun sight.

**Vision** [vizi'oːn], *f* -/-en vision.

**Visit|e** [vi'ziːtə], *f* -/-n *Med:* (doctor's) round (in a hospital). ◆**V~enkarte**, *f* visiting card.

**visuell** [vizu'ɛl], *adj.* visual.

**Visum** ['viːzum], *n* -s/Visa & Visen visa.

**vital** [vi'taːl], *adj.* *(Pers. usw.)* dynamic; full of life.

**Vitamin** [vita'miːn], *n* -s/-e vitamin. ◆**V~mangel**, *m* vitamin deficiency.

**Vitrine** [vi'triːnə], *f* -/-n glass case; *(Schaukasten)* show/display case.

**Vize-** ['fiːtsə-], *comb.fm.* vice-(admiral, chancellor etc.). ◆'**V~präsident**, *m* vice-president.

**Vlies** [fliːs], *n* -es/-e fleece.

**Vogel** ['foːgəl], *m* -s/- bird; *F:* *(Pers.)* **komischer/seltsamer V.**, queer bird/customer; **einen V. haben**, to be cuckoo; **j-m den/einen V. zeigen**, to tap one's forehead. ◆'**V~bauer**, *n* birdcage. ◆'**V~futter**, *n* bird feed. ◆'**V~kunde**, *f -/no pl* ornithology. ◆'**V~perspektive**, *f* bird's eye view.

**Vokab|el** [vo'kaːbəl], *f* -/-n word; *pl* **V~n**, vocabulary. ◆**V~ular** [-abu'laːr], *n* -s/-e (personal) vocabulary.

**Vokal** [vo'kaːl], *m* -s/-e vowel.

**Volk** [fɔlk], *n* -(e)s/"er *(a)* people; nation; *(b)* F: V., crowds of people.

**Völker-** ['fœlkər-], *comb.fm.* international (friendship, understanding etc.). ◆'**V~kunde**, *f -/no pl* ethnology. ◆'**V~mord**, *m* genocide. ◆'**V~recht**, *n* international law. ◆'v~**rechtlich**, *adj.* in/according to international law.

**Volks-** ['fɔlks-], *comb.fm.* (*a*) popular (edition, custom, front, hero, art etc.); national (income, day of mourning etc.); (enemy, voice etc.) of the people; *esp. Pol:* people's (army, party, republic, representative etc.); (*b*) (*öffentlich*) public (library, health, welfare etc.); (*c*) *Mus: Lit: etc:* folk (ballad, epic, music, dance etc.). ◆'V~**abstimmung**, *f* national referendum. ◆'V~**fest** *n*, (local) public festival; (*Jahrmarkt*) funfair. ◆'V~**gruppe**, *f* ethnic minority. ◆'V~**hochschule**, *f* adult/her further education college. ◆'V~**lied**, *n* folksong. ◆'V~**schule**, *f* basic primary (and secondary) school. ◆'v~**tümlich**, *adj.* popular; (*traditionell*) traditional; *Pej:* folksy. ◆'V~**wirtschaft**, *f* economics; political economy. ◆'v~**wirtschaftlich**, *adj.* economic.

**voll** [fɔl], *adj.* (*a*) full; v. von/mit etwas *dat*, full of sth.; (*b*) (*ganz*) whole (truth etc.); complete (success, certainty); in v~em Ernst, in all seriousness; *Fig:* j-n nicht für v. nehmen, not to take s.o. seriously; v. und ganz, completely. ◆v~'**auf**, *adv.* fully. ◆'v~**automatisch**, *adj.* fully automatic. ◆'V~**bart**, *m* full beard. ◆'V~**blut**, *n* thoroughbred. ◆'v~'**bringen**, *v.tr.insep.irr.16 Lit:* to accomplish (sth.), perform (a task etc.). ◆'v~'**enden**, *v.tr.insep.* to complete (a task etc.). ◆v~**ends** ['fɔlɛnts], *adj.* completely; (*erst recht*) especially. ◆'V~'**endung**, *f -/no pl* **1.** (*Abschluß*) accomplishment. **2.** (*Vollkommenheit*) perfection. ◆'v~**er**, *inv.adj.* ein Korb v. Früchte, a basket (full) of fruit. ◆'v~'**führen**, *v.tr.insep.* to perform (a deed, trick etc.). ◆'V~**gas**, *n* full throttle. V. geben, to open right up. ◆'v~**jährig**, *adj.* of age. ◆'V~**jährigkeit**, *f -/no pl* majority. ◆'V~**kaskoversicherung**, *f* comprehensive insurance. ◆v~'**kommen**, *adj.* perfect; flawless (beauty); *adv.* completely. ◆'V~**kornbrot**, *n* coarse wholemeal bread; (*Schwarzbrot*) black bread. ◆'V~**macht**, *f* authority; *Jur:* power of attorney. ◆'V~**mond**, *m* full moon. ◆'V~**pension**, *f* full board. ◆'v~**schlank**, *adj.* buxom, plump. ◆'v~**ständig**, *adj.* complete. ◆v~'**strecken**, *v.tr.insep. Jur:* to execute (a judgment, will etc.), carry out (a sentence). ◆'V~'**streckung**, *f -/no pl Jur:* execution; enforcement. ◆'v~**tanken**, *v.tr. & i.sep.* (*haben*) *Aut:* to fill up (a car). ◆'V~**treffer**, *m Mil: etc:* direct hit; *Fig:* (*Schlager*) smash hit. ◆'v~**versammlung**, *f* full/general assembly. ◆'v~**zählig**, *adj.* complete (set etc.); full (turnout). ◆v~'**ziehen**, *v.tr. insep.irr.113* to carry out (an order etc.);

sich v., to take place. ◆V~'**zug**, *m -(e)s/no pl* execution.

**völlig** ['fœliç], *adj.* complete; sheer (madness, nonsense); **du hast v. recht,** you are absolutely right/perfectly correct.

**Volleyball** ['vɔlibal], *m* volleyball.

**Volt** [vɔlt], *n -s/-* volt.

**Volumen** [vo'luːmən], *n -s/-* volume.

**vom** [fɔm], *prep.* = von dem.

**von** [fɔn], *prep. + dat.* **1.** from; **v. mir aus,** I don't mind; please yourself; **v. jetzt an,** from now on. **2. ein Gedicht v. Heine,** a poem by Heine; **müde v. der Reise,** tired from the journey; **v. selbst,** by oneself/itself; automatically. **3. eine Frau v. 40 Jahren,** a woman of 40; **der König v. Spanien,** the King of Spain; **ein Freund v. mir,** a friend of mine; **v. etwas erzählen/sprechen,** to talk about sth. ◆v~**ei'nander,** *adv.* from one another/each other. ◆v~**statten** [-'ʃtatən], *adv.* v. gehen, to take place, (*verlaufen*) proceed.

**vor** [foːr], *prep.* **1.** (*räumlich*) (+ *dat/acc*) in front of; **v. allem/allen Dingen,** above all. **2.** (*zeitlich*) (+ *dat*) before; **fünf Minuten v. sieben,** five minutes to seven; (**heute**) **v. einem Jahr,** a year ago (today). **3.** (+) **v. Kälte, Angst, Zorn usw. zittern,** to tremble with cold, fear, rage etc.; **v. Hunger sterben,** to die of hunger.

'**Vorabend,** *m* evening before.

'**Vorahnung,** *f* premonition.

**voran** [fo'ran], *adv.* (*a*) first, in front; (*b*) (*vorwärts*) forwards. ◆v~**gehen,** *v.i.sep.irr.36* (*sein*) (*a*) (*Pers.*) to lead (the way); to go on ahead (j-m, of s.o.); (*Sache*) etwas *dat* v., to precede sth.; (*b*) (*Arbeit usw.*) to make progress. ◆v~**kommen,** *v.i.sep.irr.53* (*sein*) to make headway/progress.

'**Voranmeldung,** *f* advance booking.

'**Voranschlag,** *m* estimate.

'**Vorarbeit,** *f* preparatory work, ground work. ◆'V~**er,** *m* foreman.

**voraus** [fo'raus], *adv.* (*a*) ahead, in front (+ *dat*, of); (*b*) ['foːraus] **im v.,** in advance. ◆v~**berechnen,** *v.tr.sep.* to estimate (costs etc.); to forecast (a result etc.). ◆'V~**sage,** *f -/-n* prediction, forecast. ◆v~**sagen,** *v.tr.sep.* to forecast, predict (sth.). ◆v~**sehen,** *v.tr.sep.irr.92* to foresee, anticipate (sth.). ◆v~**setzen,** *v.tr.sep.* to presuppose (sth.), take (sth.) for granted; (*Stellung*) to require (sth.); **vorausgesetzt, daß ...,** provided that ... ◆V~**setzung,** *f -/-en* requirement; qualification (for a job); **falsche V.,** wrong assumption/premise; **unter der V., daß ...,** on the condition/understanding that ... ◆'V~**sicht,** *f* foresight; **aller V. nach,** in all probability. ◆v~**sichtlich,** *adj.* expected (date, time etc.); **er kommt v. am Montag,** he is expected on Monday.

'**Vorbedingung,** *f* precondition, prerequisite.

**'Vorbehalt,** *m* -(e)s/-e reservation; *(Bedenken)* misgiving. ◆**'v~en,** *v.tr.sep.irr.45* sich *dat* etwas v., to reserve the right to sth.; **alle Rechte v.,** all rights reserved. ◆**'v~los,** *adj.* unconditional; *adv.* unreservedly.

**vorbei** [for'bai], *adv. (a) (räumlich)* past; *(b) (zeitlich)* over, past; **3 Uhr v.,** past/*F:* gone 3 o'clock. ◆**v~fahren,** *v.i.sep.irr.26 (sein)* to go/*Aut:* drive past. ◆**v~gehen,** *v.i.sep.irr.36 (sein) (a) (Pers., Fig: Zeit usw.)* to pass; **v. an +** *dat,* to go/*(zu Fuß)* walk past (s.o., sth.); *(Schuß)* to miss (the target); **im V.,** in passing; *(b) (besuchen) F:* to drop in (**bei** j-m, on s.o.).

**'vorbereit|en,** *v.tr.sep.* to prepare (s.o., sth.). ◆**'V~ung,** *f* -/-en preparation. ◆**'V~ungs-,** *comb.fm.* preparatory (work, measures etc.).

**'vorbestell|en,** *v.tr.sep.* to order (goods etc.) in advance; to book, reserve (a room, seats etc.). ◆**'V~ung,** *f* advance order; *Th:etc:* booking, reservation.

**'vorbestraft,** *adj. Jur:* (zweimal/mehrfach) v., with (two/several) previous convictions.

**'vorbeug|en,** *v. 1. v.i. (haben)* etwas *dat* v., to prevent sth.; **v~de Maßnahmen,** preventive measures. *2. v.refl.* sich v., to bend forward. ◆**'V~ung,** *f* -/-en prevention.

**'Vorbild,** *n* model, example. ◆**'v~lich,** *adj.* exemplary (behaviour etc.); model (pupil etc.).

**'Vorbote,** *m esp. Fig:* herald.

**'vorbringen,** *v.tr.sep.irr.16* to put forward (an argument, a claim etc.); to offer (an excuse, proof).

**Vorder-** ['fordər-], *comb.fm.* front (axle, wheel, seat, paw, tooth etc.); fore(-deck etc.). ◆**v~e(r,s)** ['fordərə(r,s)], *adj.* front. ◆**'V~grund,** *m* foreground; *Fig:* etwas in den V. stellen, to give sth. prominence/emphasis. ◆**'v~gründig,** *adj.* obvious, transparent (motive etc.); *(oberflächlich)* superficial (treatment etc.). ◆**'V~mann,** *m* -es/-er man in front. ◆**'V~seite,** *f* front; obverse (of a coin). ◆**'v~ste(r,s),** *adj.* foremost; very first (row etc.).

**'vordring|en,** *v.i.sep.irr.19 (sein)* to advance. ◆**'v~lich,** *adj.* urgent.

**'Vordruck,** *m* printed form, *N.Am:* blank.

**'vorehelich,** *adj.* pre-marital.

**'voreilig,** *adj.* (over)hasty, rash.

**'voreingenommen,** *adj.* biased, prejudiced. ◆**'V~heit,** *f* -/no pl bias, prejudice.

**'vorenthalten,** *v.tr.sep.irr.45* to withhold (information etc.) (j-m, from s.o.).

**'vorerst,** *adj.* for the time being.

**'Vorfahr,** *m* -en/-en ancestor. ◆**'v~en,** *v.tr. & i.sep.irr.26 (sein) (vorausfahren)* to drive on ahead. ◆**'V~t,** *f* right of way, priority. ◆**'V~t(s)straße,** *f* major

road.

**'Vorfall,** *m* incident, occurrence. ◆**'v~en,** *v.i.sep.irr.27 (sein) (geschehen)* to happen, occur.

**'Vorfilm,** *m* supporting film.

**'vorfinden,** *v.tr.sep.irr.96* to find (s.o., sth.) (waiting for one).

**'Vorfreude,** *f* pleasurable anticipation.

**'vorführ|en,** *v.tr.sep. (a) (aufführen)* to put on (an act, show etc.); to show (a film, play etc.); *(b) (ausstellen)* to display (goods etc.), model (clothes); **dem Richter vorgeführt werden,** to be brought before the judge. ◆**'V~raum,** *m Cin:* projection room. ◆**'V~ung,** *f* presentation; *Cin:* showing; *Th:* performance.

**'Vorgabe,** *f -/no pl Sp:* handicap.

**'Vorgang,** *m* course of events; *(Verfahren) Tchn: Biol: etc:* process; *Tchn:* operation.

**'Vorgänger(in),** *m* -s/- (f -/-nen) predecessor.

**'Vorgarten,** *m* front garden.

**'vorgeb|en,** *v.tr.sep.irr.35 (a) (zum Vorwand)* to pretend (**krank zu sein usw.,** to be ill etc.); *(b) (festlegen)* to prescribe, lay down (sth.). ◆**'v~lich,** *adj.* alleged; ostensible (reason).

**'Vorgebirge,** *n* -s/- foothills.

**'vorgefaßt,** *adj.* v~e Meinung, preconceived idea.

**'Vorgefühl,** *n* presentiment.

**'vorgehen. I.** *v.i.sep.irr.36 (sein) (a)* to go forward; *(vorausgehen)* to go on ahead; *(Uhr)* to be fast; *(b) (Vorrang haben)* to take precedence (**allem anderen,** over everything else); *(c) (geschehen)* to happen, *(stattfinden)* take place; *(d) (handeln)* to act, take action. **II. V.,** *n* -s/no pl action.

**'vorgerückt,** *adj.* late (hour), advanced (age, stage etc.).

**'Vorgeschmack,** *m* foretaste.

**'Vorgesetzte(r),** *m & f* decl. as adj. superior; *Mil:* superior officer.

**'vorgestern,** *adv.* the day before yesterday.

**'vorgreifen,** *v.i.sep.irr.43 (haben)* to anticipate (**j-m, einer Entscheidung usw.,** s.o., a decision etc.).

**'vorhaben. I.** *v.tr.sep.irr.44* to have (sth.) in mind; to plan (sth.); **hast du heute abend etwas vor?** have you got anything on tonight? **II. V.,** *n* -s/- plan, *Com:* project; *(Absicht)* intention.

**'vorhalt|en,** *v.sep.irr.45* **1.** *v.tr. (a)* to hold up (a dress, *Fig:* s.o. as an example etc.); *(b)* **j-m einen Fehler usw. v.,** to reproach s.o. with a mistake etc. **2.** *v.i. (haben) F: (Vorrat usw.)* to last (out). ◆**'V~ung,** *f* remonstration.

**'vorhanden** [fo:r'handən], *adj.* existing; *(verfügbar)* available; *Com: (Ware)* in stock. ◆**'V~sein,** *n* -s/no pl existence.

**'Vorhang,** *m* -(e)s/-e curtain.

**'Vorhängeschloß,** *n* padlock.

**vorher** ['fo:rhe:r], *adv.* before; *(im voraus)* beforehand, in advance. ◆**v~gehen,**

*v.i.sep.irr.36* (*sein*) **etwas** *dat* **v.**, to pre-cede sth. ◆**v~gehend**, *adj.* preceding; previous (chapter etc.). ◆**v~ig** [foːrˈheːriç], *adj.* previous (evening etc.); prior (warning, agreement etc.). ◆**V~sage**, *f -/-n* prediction; (weather etc.) forecast. ◆**v~sagen**, *v.tr.sep.* to predict, forecast (sth.). ◆**v~sehen**, *v.tr.sep.irr.92* to foresee (sth.).

'**Vorherr|schaft**, *f -/no pl* predominance; *Pol:etc:* supremacy. ◆'**v~schen**, *v.i.sep.* (*haben*) to predominate; (*Meinung usw.*) to prevail.

'**vorhin**, *adv.* a moment ago, just now. ◆'**v~ein**, *adv.* **im v.**, beforehand, in advance.

**vorig** [ˈfoːriç] *adj.* last (month, year etc.); previous (chapter, paragraph etc.); for-mer, previous (boss, job etc.).

'**Vorjahr**, *n* previous year. ◆'**vorjährig**, *adj.* previous year's (fashion etc.).

'**Vorkämpfer(in)**, *m(f)* pioneer.

'**Vorkehrungen**, *fpl* precautions.

'**vorkomm|en**. **I.** *v.i.sep.irr.53* (*sein*) (*a*) (*geschehen*) to happen; (*sich finden*) (*Pflanzen, Tiere usw.*) to occur, be found (somewhere); (*b*) (*scheinen*) **j-m komisch, verdächtig v.**, to strike s.o. as odd, sus-picious etc.; **ich kam mir überflüssig vor**, I felt unwanted; (*c*) to come to the front; (*hervorkommen*) to come out. **II. V.**, *n -s/no pl* occurrence. ◆'**V~nis**, *n -sses/-sse* incident, occurrence.

'**Vorkriegs-**, *comb.fm.* prewar.

'**vorlad|en**, *v.tr.sep.irr.56 Jur:* to sum-mon(s) (s.o.), *esp N.Am:* subpoena (s.o.). ◆'**V~ung**, *f Jur:* summons, *esp. N.Am:* subpoena.

'**Vorlage**, *f -/-n* (*Muster*) pattern; *Lit:* model; (*Gesetzesv.*) bill; *Fb:* forward pass.

'**vorlassen**, *v.tr.sep.irr.57* to let (s.o.) go first; *Aut: Sp:* to let (s.o.) overtake.

'**Vorläuf|er(in)**, *m -s/-* (*f -/-nen*) forerun-ner. ◆'**v~ig**, *adj.* provisional; interim (measure, report etc.); temporary (ap-pointment etc.).

'**vorlaut**, *adj.* cheeky; too full of himself/herself.

'**vorleg|en**, *v.tr.sep.* to present (sth.); to produce, show (one's passport etc.); to submit (evidence, a question etc.). ◆'**V~er**, *m -s/-* mat, rug.

'**vorles|en**, *v.tr.&i.sep.irr.61* (*haben*) to read (sth.) aloud; **soll ich (es) dir v.?** shall I read (it) to you? ◆'**V~ung**, *f -/-en* lecture.

'**vorletzte(r,s)**, *adj.* last but one; penulti-mate (syllable etc.); **im v~n Jahr**, the year before last.

'**Vorlieb|e**, *f -/no pl* predilection, prefer-ence. ◆'**v~nehmen** [-ˈliːpneːmən], *v.i.sep.irr.69* (*haben*) to make do.

'**vorlieg|en**, *v.i.sep.irr.62* (*haben*) to be on hand/(*zur Verfügung*) available; **j-m, dem Gericht usw. v.**, to be in s.o.'s hands, the hands of the court etc.; **es liegt/**

**liegen ... vor**, there is/are ... ◆'**v~end**, *adj.* available; **im v~enden Fall**, in this/the present case.

'**vormachen**, *v.tr.sep. F:* (*a*) **j-m etwas v.**, to show s.o. how to do sth.; (*b*) **j-m/sich** *dat* **etwas v.**, to kid s.o./oneself.

'**Vormachtstellung**, *f* supremacy.

'**vormals**, *adv.* formerly.

'**Vormarsch**, *m* advance.

'**vormerken**, *v.tr.sep.* to make a note of (sth.); to book (a room etc.).

'**Vormittag**. **I.** *m -s/-e* (late) morning. **II. v.**, *adv.* **heute/gestern/morgen v.**, this/yesterday/tomorrow morning. ◆'**v~s**, *adv.* in the morning.

'**Vormund**, *m -(e)s/-e* guardian. ◆'**V~schaft**, *f -/no pl* guardianship.

**vorn(e)** [fɔrn(ˈfɔrnə)], *adv.* in/at the front; (*vor mir/uns*) ahead; **von v.**, (i) (seen) from the front; (ii) (*am Anfang*) at the beginning; (*von neuem*) all over again. ◆**v~he'rein**, *adv.* **von v.**, from the start.

'**Vorname**, *m* Christian name, *N.Am:* gi-ven name.

**vornehm** [ˈfoːrneːm], *adj.* (*a*) distin-guished (circles, family, appearance etc.); gentlemanly, ladylike (manner); (*b*) (*ele-gant, modisch*) smart (resort, area, school etc.); (*c*) (*kultiviert*) refined (taste etc.); elegant (dress, interior).

'**vornehmen**, *v.tr.sep.irr.69* (*a*) (*ausführen*) to carry out (an alteration etc.); (*b*) *F:* (*vorknöpfen*) **den werde ich mir v.!** I'll give him a piece of my mind! (*c*) **sich** *dat* **etwas v.**, to decide to do sth.; (*d*) *F:* **sich** *dat* **ein Buch usw. v.**, to take up/start a book etc.

'**Vorort**. **I.** *m* suburb. **II. V~(s)-**, *comb.fm.* suburban (traffic, train etc.).

'**Vorrang**, *m -(e)s/no pl* precedence, prior-ity (**vor +** *dat*, over). ◆'**v~ig**, *adj.* of prime importance.

'**Vorrat**, *m -(e)s/-e* stock, supply (**an +** *dat*, of). ◆'**V~s-**, *comb.fm.* store, *Com:* stock (room etc.).

**vorrätig** [ˈfoːrɛːtiç], *adj.* in stock, avail-able.

'**Vorrecht**, *n* privilege, prerogative.

'**Vorrichtung**, *f -/-en* apparatus, ap-pliance; (*Gerät*) device.

'**vorrücken**, *v.sep.* **1.** *v.tr.* to move (sth.) forward. **2.** *v.i.* (*sein*) to move up; *Mil:* to advance.

'**vorsagen**, *v.tr.* to recite (a poem etc.); to dictate (sth.); *Sch:* to whisper (the an-swer).

'**Vorsatz**, *m -es/-e* resolution; **gute V~e**, good intentions.

**vorsätzlich** [ˈfoːrzɛtsliç], *adj.* deliberate (insult etc.); premeditated (action); mal-icious (damage etc.); wilful (murder).

'**Vorschau**, *f -/-en* preview, *esp. Cin:* trai-ler.

'**Vorschein**, *m* **zum V. kommen**, to emerge.

'**vorschieben**, *v.tr.sep.irr.82* (*a*) to push

(sth.) forward; to push (a bolt) across; (b) to give (sth.) as an excuse.

'**Vorschlag**, m suggestion, proposal; (*Angebot*) offer; **auf j-s V. (hin)**, at s.o.'s suggestion. ◆'**v~en**, *v.tr.sep.irr.85* to suggest (s.o., sth.); to propose (s.o.). ◆'**V~hammer**, m sledgehammer.

'**vorschnell**, adj. hasty, rash.

'**vorschreiben**, *v.tr.sep.irr.88 (fordern)* to dictate, lay down (conditions, conduct etc.), *(Gesetz usw.)* decree (that...); **j-m etwas v.**, to order/tell s.o. to do sth.

'**Vorschrift**, f -/-en regulation, rule; *(Befehl)* order, decree; **j-m V~en machen**, to give s.o. orders. ◆'**v~smäßig**, adj. prescribed; adv. as directed; according to regulations.

'**Vorschuß**, m advance (payment).

'**vorschweben**, *v.i.sep.* *(haben)* **mir schwebt ... vor**, I have ... in mind.

'**vorseh|en**, *v.sep.irr.92* 1. *v.tr.* (a) to plan (improvement etc.); *(berücksichtigen)* to provide/allow for (an eventuality etc.); **das Gesetz sieht vor, daß ...**, the law provides that ...; (b) **sich v.**, to take care; to look out/watch **(vor + dat,** for). 2. *v.i.* *(haben)* to look out; *(Unterrock usw.)* to show. ◆'**V~ung**, f -/no pl providence.

'**vorsetzen**, *v.tr.* (a) to move (s.o., sth.) forward; (b) to put (sth.) in front **(j-m,** of s.o.).

'**Vorsicht**, f -/no pl care; *(Behutsamkeit)* caution; discretion; **V.!** look out! **V. Stufe!** mind the step; **V. Hochspannung!** danger high voltage. ◆'**v~ig**, adj. careful; *(behutsam)* cautious; conservative (estimate). ◆'**v~shalber**, adv. as a precaution. ◆'**V~smaßnahme**, f precaution, safeguard.

'**Vorsilbe**, f prefix.

'**Vorsitz**, m chairmanship. ◆'**V~ende(r)**, m & f decl. as adj. chairman; f chairwoman; *(bei Sitzungen)* chairperson.

'**Vorsorg|e**, f -/no pl provision, precaution. ◆'**v~en**, *v.i.* *(haben)* to make provision. ◆'**v~lich**, adv. as a precaution.

'**Vorspeise**, f hors d'oeuvre, F: starter.

'**Vorspiel**, n Mus: & Fig: prelude; Th: prologue. ◆'**v~en**, *v.sep.* 1. *v.tr.* (a) Mus: to play, Th: act (a piece); (b) *(vortäuschen)* to pretend (sth.). 2. *v.i.* *(haben)* **j-m v.**, to play/Th: act for s.o.

'**vorsprechen**, *v.sep.irr.37* 1. *v.tr.* **j-m etwas v.**, (i) to say sth. for s.o. to repeat; (ii) *(vortragen)* to recite sth. to s.o. 2. *v.i.* *(haben)* (a) Th: to audition; (b) **bei j-m v.**, to call to see s.o.

'**Vorsprung**, m -(e)s/=e 1. projection. 2. Sp: & Fig: lead **(vor j-m,** over s.o.).

'**Vorstadt**. I. f suburb. II. '**V~-**, *comb.fm.* suburban (theatre, cinema etc.).

'**Vorstand**, m -(e)s/=e (a) board (of directors/management); governing body (of an institution); (b) *(Pers.)* chairman. ◆'**V~s-**, *comb.fm.* Com: board (member etc.).

'**vorstehen**, *v.i.sep.irr.100* *(haben)* (a) to project, jut out; *(Ohren, Zähne usw.)* to stick out; (b) **etwas dat v.**, to be in charge of/Com: manager of sth.

'**vorstell|bar**, adj. conceivable, imaginable. ◆'**v~en**, *v.tr.sep.* (a) to move (sth.) forward; to put (a clock) forward/on; (b) *(bekanntmachen)* to introduce (s.o., oneself, sth.); (c) **sich dat j-n, etwas v.**, to imagine s.o., sth.; (d) *(darstellen)* to portray, represent (s.o., sth.). ◆'**V~ung**, f 1. introduction (of s.o., sth.). 2. Th:Cin: performance; Cin: showing. 3. *(Begriff)* idea; *(Phantasie)* imagination. ◆'**V~ungsgespräch**, n (job) interview. ◆'**V~ungsvermögen**, n (powers of) imagination.

'**Vorstoß**, m Mil: & Fig: advance. ◆'**v~en**, *v.sep.irr.103* 1. *v.tr.* to push/thrust (s.o., sth.) forward. 2. *v.i.* *(sein)* Mil: & Fig: to advance.

'**Vorstrafe**, f previous conviction.

'**vorstrecken**, *v.tr.sep.* (a) to stretch out (one's arms etc.), crane (one's head); (b) to advance (money).

'**Vorstufe**, f preliminary stage.

'**Vortag**, m previous day; day before.

'**vortäusch|en**, *v.tr.sep.* to sham, simulate (sth.); **j-m v., daß...**, to pretend to s.o. that ... ◆'**V~ung**, f pretence.

'**Vorteil**, m advantage; **von V.**, advantageous; **gegenüber j-m, etwas dat im V. sein**, to have the advantage over s.o., sth.; **die Vor- und Nachteile**, the pros and cons. ◆'**v~haft**, adj. advantageous, favourable (offer, terms, position etc.).

'**Vortrag**, m -(e)s/=e 1. *(Rede)* talk; *(wissenschaftlich)* lecture. 2. *(Darbietung)* performance; recital (of music); recitation (of poetry); *(Art und Weise)* delivery. ◆'**v~en**, *v.tr.sep.irr.56* (a) to recite a poem etc.); to perform (music etc.); (b) *(mitteilen)* to submit (a request etc.), convey (one's reasons etc.), express (a wish etc.). ◆'**V~sreise**, f lecture tour.

vor'**trefflich**, adj. excellent, first-rate.

'**vortreten**, *v.i.sep.irr.105* *(sein)* (a) to step forward; (b) *(hervorragen)* to project, stick out.

vor**über** [fo'ry:bər], adv. = vorbei. ◆**v~gehen**, *v.sep.irr.36* *(sein)* = vorbeigehen (a); *(Krankheit usw.)* **nicht spurlos an j-m v.**, to leave its mark on s.o. ◆**v~gehend**, adj. passing (phase, symptom etc.); momentary (lapse etc.); temporary (spell etc.).

'**Vorurteil**, n prejudice. ◆'**v~sfrei**/'**v~slos**, adj. unprejudiced; unbiased (opinion etc.).

'**Vorverkauf**, m Th: etc: advance booking; **im V.**, in advance.

'**vorverlegen**, *v.tr.sep.* to move/*(zeitlich)* bring (sth.) forward.

'**Vorwahl**, f (a) Pol: preliminary election; N.Am: primary; (b) Tel: dialling code.

'**Vorwand**, m -(e)s/=e pretext, excuse.

**vorwärts** ['fo:rverts]. I. adv. forwards.

**II. V~-,** *comb.fm.* forward (movement, *Aut:* gear etc.). ◆'v~**gehen,** *v.i.sep.irr.36 (sein) F:* to progress, make progress. ◆'v~**kommen,** *v.i.sep.irr.53 (sein)* to (make) progress; *(beruflich usw.)* to get on.

**vorweg** [for'vɛk], *adv.* (a) beforehand; *(im voraus)* in advance; (b) *(räumlich)* first, in front. ◆**V~nahme,** *f -/no pl* anticipation. ◆**v~nehmen,** *v.tr.sep.irr.69* to anticipate (sth., a result etc.).

'**vorweisen,** *v.tr.sep.irr.60* to show (one's passport, knowledge of sth. etc.).

'**vorwerfen,** *v.tr.sep.irr.110* (a) to throw (food) **(einem Tier,** to an animal); (b) j-m etwas v., to reproach s.o. with sth., *(beschuldigen)* accuse s.o. of (doing) sth.; **ich habe mir nichts vorzuwerfen,** I have nothing on my conscience.

'**vorwiegend,** *adv.* predominantly.

'**Vorwort,** *n* foreword, preface.

'**Vorwurf,** *m* reproach; *(Beschuldigung)* accusation; **j-m V~e machen,** to reproach/blame s.o. ◆'v~**svoll,** *adj.* reproachful.

'**Vorzeichen,** *n* (a) omen, sign; (b) *Med: etc:* (advance) symptom.

'**vorzeigen,** *v.tr.sep.* to produce, show (a passport, ticket etc.).

'**Vorzeit,** *f* prehistoric times, remote past. ◆'v~**ig,** *adj.* premature.

'**vorziehen,** *v.tr.sep.irr.113* (a) to pull (sth.) forward/*(hervor)* out; to pull (a curtain) across; (b) *(lieber mögen)* to prefer (s.o., sth.).

'**Vorzug,** *m (Vorrang)* preference; *(Vorteil)* advantage; *(gute Eigenschaft)* merit, virtue; **etwas dat den V. geben,** to give sth. preference. ◆'V~**s-,** *comb.fm.* preferential (treatment, position etc.). ◆**V~spreis,** *m* preferential rate; special price. ◆'v~**sweise,** *adv.* preferably, for preference.

**vorzüglich** [fo:r'tsy:kliç], *adj.* excellent, first-rate.

**vulgär** [vul'gɛːr], *adj.* vulgar.

**Vulkan** [vul'kaːn], *m -s/-e* volcano. ◆**V~ausbruch,** *m* volcanic eruption. ◆**v~isch,** *adj.* volcanic. ◆**v~isieren** [-ani'ziːrən], *v.tr.* to vulcanize (rubber etc.).

# W

**W, w** [veː], *n -/-* (the letter) W, w.

**Waag|e** [ˈvaːɡə], *f -/-n* **1.** (pair of) scales. **2.** *Astr:* Libra. ◆'w~**(e)recht,** *adj.* horizontal (line, plane etc.); level (surface etc.).

**wabb(e)lig** [ˈvab(ə)liç], *adj. F:* wobbly.

**Wabe** [ˈvaːbə], *f -/-n* honeycomb.

**wach** [vax], *adj.* (a) awake; **w. werden,** to wake up; **j-n w. machen,** to wake s.o. up; (b) *(rege)* alert (mind, senses etc.). ◆'W~**e,** *f -/-n* **1.** (a) *Mil:* (Posten) sentry; *(also coll.)* guard; (b) *(Dienst) Mil:* guard (duty); *esp. Nau:* watch; **auf W.,** on guard; **(bei j-m) W. halten,** to keep watch/guard (over s.o.). **2.** *(Gebäude)* (police) station. ◆'w~**en,** *v.i.* (haben) (a) **bei einem Kranken w.,** to sit up with a sick person; (b) **über j-n, etwas** *acc* **w.,** to watch/keep an eye on s.o., sth. ◆'w~**hund,** *m* watchdog, guard-dog. ◆'w~**rufen,** *v.tr.sep.irr.74 Fig:* to awaken (memories, feelings etc.). ◆'w~**sam,** *adj.* watchful, vigilant. ◆'W~**samkeit,** *f -/no pl* watchfulness, vigilance.

**Wacholder** [va'xɔldər], *m -s/-* juniper (bush).

**Wachs** [vaks], *n -es/-e* wax. ◆'W~**bohne,** *f -/-n* wax bean. ◆'w~**en,** *v.tr.* to wax (a floor etc.).

**wachs|en²** [ˈvaksən], *v.i.irr.* (sein) to grow; *(zunehmen)* to increase; **sich** *dat* **einen Bart/die Haare w. lassen,** to grow a beard/one's hair. ◆'W~**tum,** *n -s/no pl* growth; *(Zunahme)* increase.

**Wächter** [ˈvɛçtər], *m -s/-* guard; (night) watchman; (museum) attendant; (park) keeper; *Fig:* guardian.

**Wacht|meister** [ˈvaxt-maistər], *m Brit:* (police-)constable. ◆'W~**posten,** *m* guard; *Mil:* sentry.

**wackel|ig** [ˈvakəliç], *adj.* (a) wobbly; *(im Bau)* rickety; unsteady (ladder etc.); (b) *F:* (Pers.) w. **(auf den Beinen),** shaky. ◆'W~**kontakt,** *m El:* loose connection. ◆'w~**n,** *v.i.* (haben) to wobble; *(beben)* to shake.

**wacker** [ˈvakər], *adj.* *(tapfer)* bold; *(ordentlich)* hearty (eater etc.).

**Wade** [ˈvaːdə], *f -/-n* calf.

**Waffe** [ˈvafə], *f -/-n* weapon; *pl* **W~n,** arms. ◆'W~**n-,** *comb.fm.* arms (trade etc.); weapons (system). ◆'W~**n-schein,** *m* firearms licence. ◆'W~**n-stillstand,** *m* armistice.

**Waffel** [ˈvafəl], *f -/-n* waffle; *(Keks)* wafer.

**Wag|emut** [ˈvaːɡəmuːt], *m* daring, audacity. ◆'w~**emutig,** *adj.* daring, audacious. ◆'w~**en¹,** *v.tr.* to risk (one's life etc.); **es w., etwas zu tun,** to dare to do sth. ◆'w~**halsig,** *adj.* daring. ◆'W~**nis,** *n -ses/-se* hazardous enterprise; *(Gefahr)* risk.

**Wagen²** [ˈvaːɡən]. **I.** *m -s/-* (a) *Aut:* car; (b) *(Pferdew.)* cart, waggon; (c) *Rail:* *(für Pers.)* coach; *(für Güter)* truck; waggon; *N.Am:* car. **II.** 'W~-, *comb.fm. Aut:* car (roof, care etc.); (column etc.) of cars. ◆'W~**heber,** *m* (car) jack. ◆'W~**ladung,** *f* lorryload, *N.Am:* truckload; *Rail:* waggonload.

**Wahl** [vaːl]. **I.** *f -/-en* **1.** choice; **sie hat-**

ten nur zwei zur W., they only had two to choose from; **ich hatte keine andere W.,** I had no alternative. **2.** *Pol: etc:* election; **zur W. gehen,** to go to the polls. **3.** *Com:* **Güter erster/zweiter W.,** top quality goods/second grade goods. **II. 'W~-,** *comb.fm. Pol:* election (defeat, slogan, speech, victory etc.); electoral (reform, system etc.); polling (day etc.). ◆**'w~berechtigt,** *adj.* entitled to vote. ◆**'W~beteiligung,** *f* turn-out, poll. ◆**'W~ergebnis,** *n* election result. ◆**'W~fach,** *n Sch:* optional subject. ◆**'W~kampf,** *m* election campaign. ◆**'W~kreis,** *m* constituency. ◆**'W~lokal,** *n* polling station. ◆**'w~los,** *adj.* indiscriminate; *adv.* at random. ◆**'W~recht,** *n* (*aktives*) franchise; **allgemeines W.,** universal suffrage. ◆**'W~spruch,** *m* motto.

**wähl|en** ['vɛːlən], *v.tr.&i.* (*haben*) (*a*) to choose; (*b*) *Tel:* to dial (a number); (*c*) *Pol: etc:* to elect (s.o., a party); (*stimmen*) to vote; **wen haben Sie gewählt?** for whom did you vote? ◆**'W~er,** *m* -s/- voter, elector. ◆**'w~erisch,** *adj.* choosy, particular. ◆**'W~erschaft,** *f no pl* electorate.

**Wahn** [vaːn], *m* -(e)s/*no pl* delusion; (*Manie*) mania. ◆**'W~sinn,** *m* insanity; *F:* (*Verrücktheit*) madness. ◆**'w~sinnig,** *adj.* (*a*) mad, insane; (*b*) *F:* terrible (pain etc.); terrific (shock etc.); **w. schnell,** incredibly fast. ◆**'W~vorstellung,** *f* delusion; *F:* crazy idea.

**wahr** [vaːr], *adj.* (*a*) true (story etc.); **w. werden,** to come true; **es ist etwas W~es daran,** there is some truth in it; (*b*) (*wirklich*) real (reason, feeling etc.); (*richtig*) genuine (art etc.); *Lit:* true (love, friend etc.); *F:* **das ist nicht das W~e,** it's not quite the thing. ◆**'w~haben,** *v.tr.* **etwas nicht w. wollen,** to refuse to admit/believe sth. ◆**'w~haft,** *adj. Lit:* true; (*wirklich*) real. ◆**w~'haftig,** *adj. Lit:* truthful; *adv.* really, truly; (*ehrlich*) honestly. ◆**'W~heit,** *f* -/-en truth; **in W.,** in reality. ◆**'w~heitsgemäß,** *adj.* truthful (statement etc.). ◆**'w~nehmbar,** *adj.* perceptible. ◆**'w~nehmen,** *v.tr.sep.irr.69* (*a*) (*merken*) to notice; (*b*) (*nutzen*) to avail oneself of (an opportunity etc.); (*c*) (*vertreten*) to look after (s.o.'s interests). ◆**'W~nehmung,** *f* -/-en **1.** perception, awareness. **2.** seizing (of a chance). ◆**'w~sagen,** *v.tr. & i.sep. & insep.* (*haben*) to predict (the future, that ...). ◆**'W~sager(in),** *m* -s/- (*f* -/-nen) fortune-teller. ◆**w~'scheinlich,** *adj.* probable; *adv.* probably. ◆**W~'scheinlichkeit,** *f* -/-en probability; **aller W. nach,** in all probability. ◆**'W~zeichen,** *n* symbol, emblem (of a town etc.).

**wahr|en** ['vaːrən], *v.tr.* (*a*) to protect (interests, rights); (*b*) to keep (a secret,

one's distance etc.), maintain (one's dignity etc.). ◆**'W~ung,** *f* -/no pl (*a*) protection; (*b*) keeping, maintaining.

**währ|en** ['vɛːrən], *v.i.* (*haben*) *Lit:* to last. ◆**'w~end** [-ənt]. **I.** *prep.* + *gen* during. **II.** *conj.* **1.** while. **2.** (*wohingegen*) whereas, while. ◆**w~end'dessen,** *adv.* meanwhile, in the meantime.

**Währung** ['vɛːruŋ], *f* -/-en currency.

**Waise** ['vaizə], *f* -/-n orphan. ◆**'W~nhaus,** *n* orphanage.

**Wal** [vaːl], *m* -(e)s/-e whale. ◆**'W~fang,** *m* whaling.

**Wald** [valt], *m* -(e)s/-er wood; (*große Fläche*) forest. ◆**'W~brand,** *m* forest fire. ◆**'W~meister,** *m* woodruff.

**Walis|er** ['vaːliːzər], *m* -s/- Welshman; **die W.,** the Welsh. ◆**'W~erin,** *f* -/-nen Welshwoman. ◆**'w~isch,** *adj.* Welsh.

**Wall** [val], *m* -(e)s/-e rampart.

**Wall|fahrer(in)** ['valfaːrər(in)], *m* (*f*) pilgrim. ◆**'W~fahrt,** *f* pilgrimage.

**Wallon|e** [va'loːnə], *m* -n/-n/**W~in,** *f* -/-nen Walloon. ◆**'w~isch,** *adj.* Walloon.

**Walnuß** ['valnus], *f* walnut.

**Walroß** ['valrɔs], *n* walrus.

**walten** ['valtən], *v.i.* (*haben*) *Lit:* **Vorsicht w. lassen,** to exercise caution.

**Walz|e** ['valtsə], *f* -/-n roller; cylinder (of a musical box). ◆**'w~en,** *v.tr.* to roll (metal etc.).

**wälz|en** ['vɛltsən], *v.tr.* (*a*) to roll, heave (sth. heavy); (*b*) *sich w.,* to roll; (*im Schlamm*) to wallow; (*schlaflos*) to toss and turn; (*c*) *F:* **Gedanken, Probleme usw. w.,** to turn over thoughts, problems etc. in one's mind; **Bücher w.,** to pore over books. ◆**'w~er,** *m* -s/- *F:* weighty tome.

**Walzer** ['valtsər], *m* -s/- waltz.

**Wand,** *f* -/-e wall; (*Trennw.*) partition; (*Seitenw.*) side (of a crate etc.); (*rock* etc.) face. ◆**'W~schrank,** *m* built-in cupboard. ◆**'W~tafel,** *f* blackboard. ◆**'W~teppich,** *m* tapestry. ◆**'W~verkleidung,** *f* wall-covering/ (*Täfelung*) panelling.

**Wandel** ['vandəl], *m* -s/no pl change. ◆**'w~bar,** *adj.* changeable. ◆**'w~n,** *v.i.* (*sein*) **1.** *Lit:* to wander, stroll. **2.** *v.tr.* to change (s.o., sth.); **sich w.,** to change.

**Wander-** ['vandər-], *comb.fm.* **1.** travelling (exhibition, circus etc.); itinerant (preacher etc.); *Med:* floating (kidney, liver). **2.** walking (shoes, stick etc.); hiking, rambling (club etc.). ◆**'W~bühne,** *f* touring company. ◆**'W~er,** *m* -s/- hiker, rambler. ◆**'w~n,** *v.i.* (*sein*) (*a*) to hike, ramble; (*b*) (*Tiere*) to migrate; (*ziellos*) (*Pers., Fig: Blicke usw.*) to wander, roam. ◆**'W~pokal,** *m* challenge cup/trophy. ◆**'W~schaft,** *f* -/no pl travels; **auf W.,** on one's travels. ◆**'W~ung,** *f* -/-en hike, ramble. ◆**'W~weg,** *m* footpath.

**Wandlung** ['vandluŋ], *f* -/-en change,

transformation.
**Wange** ['vaŋə], f -/-n Lit: cheek.
**wank|elmütig** ['vaŋkəlmy:tiç], adj. Lit: irresolute, vacillating. ◆'w~en, v.i. (a) (sein) to stagger, totter; (Betrunkener) to reel; (b) (haben) Fig: to waver.
**wann** [van], adv. when.
**Wanne** ['vanə], f -/-n (bath-)tub, bath.
**Wanze** ['vantsə], f -/-n bug.
**Wappen** ['vapən], n -s/- (coat of) arms.
**wappnen** ['vapnən], v.refl. sich gegen etwas acc w., to prepare to face sth.
**Ware** ['va:rə], f -/-n commodity, article; (Erzeugnis) product; W~n, goods. ◆'W~nhaus, n (department) store. ◆'W~nprobe, f sample. ◆'W~n-zeichen, n trade mark.
**warm** [varm], adj. warm; hot (meal, drink, bath etc.); **Essen w. machen,** to heat/warm up food; **w. essen/duschen,** to have a hot meal/shower. ◆'w~herzig, adj. warm-hearted. ◆'w~laufen, v.i.sep.irr.58 (sein) Aut: (Motor) to warm up. ◆'W~miete, f rent including heating. ◆W~'wasser-, comb.fm. hot-water (heating, supply etc.).
**Wärm|e** ['vɛrmə], f -/no pl (also Fig:) warmth; Ph: etc: heat. ◆'w~en, v. 1. v.tr. to warm (one's hands, oneself etc.); to warm up (food). 2. v.i. (haben) to warm one up; to make/keep one warm. ◆'W~flasche, f hot-water bottle. ◆'w~stens, adv. very/most warmly.
**Warn-** ['varn-], comb.fm. warning (cry, light, shot, signal etc.). ◆'W~blinkanlage, f Aut: hazard warning lights. ◆'W~dreieck, n hazard warning/accident triangle. ◆'w~en, v.tr. to warn (s.o.) (vor + dat, of/against). ◆'W~streik, m token strike. ◆'W~ung, f -/-en warning (vor + dat, of/against).
**Warschau** ['varʃau]. Pr.n.n -s. Warsaw.
**Warte¹** ['vartə], f -/no pl 1. Fig: standpoint. 2. (a) Meteor: weather-station; (b) Astr: observatory.
**'Warte-²**, comb.fm. waiting (list etc.). ◆'W~saal, m/'W~zimmer, n waiting room.
**wart|en** ['vartən], v. 1. v.i. (haben) to wait (auf + acc, for); jmdn. w. lassen, to keep s.o. waiting; auf sich w. lassen, to take a long time, (Pers.) take one's time. 2. v.tr. to service (a machine, car). ◆'W~ung, f -/-en 1. no pl servicing. 2. service.
**Wärter(in)** ['vɛrtər(in)], m -s/- (f -/-nen) attendant; (zoo/lighthouse) keeper; (Gefängnisw.) (prison) warder/f wardress.
**warum** [va'rum], adv. why.
**Warze** ['vartsə], f -/-n wart.
**was** [vas]. I. interrog. & rel.pron. what; w. für ein Lärm! what a noise! F: w. stehst du so blöd da? why do you just stand there and look stupid? gut, w.? not bad, eh? das, w. er sagt, what he says; alles/

vieles, w. ..., everything/much that ...
II. indef.pron. F: (etwas) something; (in Fragen/Verneinungen) anything; w. Neues, something new; ist w.? is anything wrong?
**Wasch|bär** ['vaʃbɛ:r], m racoon. ◆'W~becken, n washbasin. ◆'w~echt, adj. 1. colour-fast (material), fast (colours). 2. Fig: genuine, F: pukka (Berliner etc.). ◆'w~en, v.tr.&i.irr. (haben) to wash (s.o., sth.); sich dat die Hände/Haare w., to wash one's hands/hair; (Wäsche) w., to do the washing; sich w., to wash (oneself); W. und Legen, shampoo and set. ◆'W~küche, f laundry room. ◆'W~lappen, m 1. face flannel, N.Am: washcloth. 2. F: (Pers.) cissy, wet; (Schwächling) weed. ◆'W~maschine, f washing machine. ◆'W~mittel, n detergent. ◆'W~pulver, n washing powder. ◆'W~salon, m laundrette. ◆'W~straße, f automatic car wash.
**Wäsche** ['vɛʃə], f -/no pl 1. washing; (Schmutzw.) laundry. 2. (a) (Unterw.) underwear; (b) (Bettw./Tischw.) (bed-/table-)linen. ◆'W~klammer, f clothes peg/N.Am: pin. ◆'W~leine, f clothes-/washing-line. ◆'W~'rei, f -/-en laundry. ◆'W~trockner, m clothes drier, esp. tumble drier.
**Wasser** ['vasər], n -s/- water; Fig: sich über W. halten, to keep one's head above water; er kann ihr nicht das W. reichen, he can't hold a candle to her; das Fest fiel ins W., the party fell through; F: er ist mit allen W~n gewaschen, he wasn't born yesterday; W. lassen, to pass water. ◆'W~ball, m water polo. ◆'w~dicht, adj. waterproof (coat etc.); watertight (container etc.). ◆'W~fall, m waterfall. ◆'W~farbe, f water colour. ◆'w~gekühlt, adj. water-cooled. ◆'W~hahn, m water tap, N.Am: faucet. ◆'W~leitung, f water pipe. ◆'W~mann, m Astr: Aquarius. ◆'w~n, v.i. (haben) Av: to land on the water, ditch; (Raumschiff) to splash down. ◆'w~scheu, adj. afraid of water. ◆'W~spülung, f flush (of a WC). ◆'W~ski, m water ski; (Sport) water skiing. ◆'W~stand, m water level. ◆'W~stoff, m hydrogen. ◆'W~versorgung, f water supply. ◆'W~vogel, m waterfowl. ◆'W~waage, f spirit level. ◆'W~werfer, m water cannon. ◆'W~werk, n waterworks. ◆'W~zeichen, n watermark.
**wässer|ig** ['vɛsəriç], adj. watery. ◆'w~n, v. 1. v.tr. (a) to water down (wine etc.); (b) to water (a plant etc.) thoroughly. 2. v.i. (haben) (Augen usw.) to water.
**wäßrig** ['vɛsriç], adj. = wässerig.
**waten** ['va:tən], v.i. (sein) to wade.
**Watt¹** [vat], n -s/- El: watt.

**Watt²**, *n -s/-en North G*: mudflats.

**Watt|e** ['vatə], *f -/no pl* cotton wool. ◆**'W~ebausch**, *m* wad of cotton wool. ◆**w~ieren** [-'tiːrən], *v.tr.* to pad, line (a garment etc.).

**web|en** ['veːbən], *v.tr. & i. (haben)* to weave. ◆**'W~er(in)**, *m -s/- (f -/-nen)* weaver. ◆**W~e'rei**, *f -/-en* **1.** *no pl* weaving. **2.** weaving mill. ◆**'W~stuhl**, *m* loom.

**Wechsel** ['vɛksəl], *m -s/-* **1.** change; *(sich wiederholend)* rotation (of the seasons, crop etc.); *(Abwechslung)* alternation (of day and night etc.); *(Spielerw.)* substitution. **2.** *Fin:* bill of exchange. ◆**'W~beziehung**, *f* correlation. ◆**'W~geld**, *n* change. ◆**'w~haft**, *adj.* changeable. ◆**'W~jahre**, *npl* change of life, menopause. ◆**'W~kurs**, *m* rate of exchange. ◆**'w~n**, **1.** *v.tr. & i. (haben)* to change; **die Wohnung w.**, to move (house); **den Platz, Briefe usw. mit j-m w.**, to exchange places, letters etc. with s.o. **2.** *v.i. (haben)* to change; *(Tag und Nacht usw.)* to alternate. ◆**'w~nd**, *adj.* changeable (weather etc.); variable (wind etc.); varying (success etc.). ◆**'w~seitig**, *adj.* mutual, reciprocal. ◆**'W~spiel**, *n* interplay. ◆**'W~strom**, *m* alternating current. ◆**'W~stube**, *f* exchange office. ◆**'w~weise**, *adv.* alternately, in turn. ◆**'W~wirkung**, *f* interaction.

**weck|en** ['vɛkən], *v.tr.* to wake (s.o.) (up); *Fig:* to awaken, arouse (s.o.'s feelings, memories etc.). ◆**'W~er**, *m -s/-* alarm (clock).

**Wedel** ['veːdəl], *m -s/- (Staubw.)* (feather) duster. ◆**'w~n**, *v.i. (haben)* **w. mit + dat**, *(Hund usw.)* to wag (its tail); *(Pers.)* to wave (a hand, paper etc.).

**weder** ['veːdər], *conj.* **w. ... noch ...**, neither ... nor ...

**Weg¹** [veːk], *m -(e)s/-e (a) (Gehw.)* path; *(Fahrw.)* track; **ich würde ihm nicht über den W. trauen**, I wouldn't trust him an inch; *(b) (Route)* way, route; *(Strecke)* distance; **auf den kürzesten W.**, by the shortest route; **auf halbem W~e**, halfway; **sich auf den W. machen**, to set off; **etwas in die W~e leiten**, to get sth. under way; *(c)* **du bist/stehst mir im W.**, you're in my way; **j-n, etwas aus dem W. räumen**, to get rid of/eliminate s.o., sth.; **der Gefahr aus dem W. gehen**, to keep clear of danger; *(d) (Weise)* **auf diesem W~e**, in this way; **auf diplomatischem W~e**, through diplomatic channels. ◆**'W~bereiter**, *m -s/-* forerunner. ◆**'W~strecke**, *f* stretch; *(Entfernung)* distance. ◆**'W~weiser**, *m -s/-* signpost.

**weg²** [vɛk], *adv.* away, off; **weit w.**, far away; **Hände w.!** hands off! **das muß w.**, that must go. ◆**'w~bleiben**, *v.i.sep.irr.12 (sein)* to stay away. ◆**'w~bringen**, *v.tr.sep.irr.16* to take/

get (s.o., sth.) away, remove (furniture etc.). ◆**'w~fallen**, *v.i.sep.irr.27 (sein)* to be discontinued/*(ausgelassen)* omitted; *(aufhören)* to cease, stop. ◆**'w~gehen**, *v.i.sep.irr.36 (sein) (a) (Pers.)* to leave, go away/*(ausgehen)* out; *(Fleck)* to come out; *(b)* **wie warme Semmeln w.**, to sell like hot cakes. ◆**'w~kommen**, *v.i.sep.irr.53 (sein) (Pers.)* to get away; *(verlorengehen)* to be lost, disappear. ◆**'w~lassen**, *v.tr.sep.57* to leave out, omit (s.o., sth.); to let (s.o.) go. ◆**'w~laufen**, *v.i.sep.irr.58* to run away. ◆**'w~legen**, *v.tr.sep.* to put (sth.) away/*(beiseite)* aside. ◆**'w~machen**, *v.tr.sep. F:* to remove (dirt, a spot etc.). ◆**'w~müssen**, *v.i.sep.irr.68 (haben)* to have to go; **ich muß weg**, I must leave/be off. ◆**'W~nahme**, *f -/no pl* taking away, removal. ◆**'w~nehmen**, *v.tr.sep.irr.69* to take (sth.) away, remove (sth.) (j-m, from s.o.); to take up (light, space, s.o.'s time etc.). ◆**'w~räumen**, *v.tr.sep* to clear (sth.) away. ◆**'w~schaffen**, *v.tr.sep.* to do away with/*(entfernen)* remove (sth.). ◆**'w~schnappen**, *v.tr.sep.* to snatch (sth.) away. ◆**'w~tun**, *v.tr.sep.irr.106* to clear/*(wegwerfen)* throw (sth.) away. ◆**'W~werf-**, *comb.fm.* disposable (bottle, nappy etc.). ◆**'w~werfen**, *v.tr.sep.irr.100* to throw (rubbish, one's life etc.) away, throw out (old clothes etc.). ◆**'w~werfend**, *adj.* disparaging. ◆**'w~wischen**, *v.tr.sep.* to wipe (sth.) away/(a word etc.) out; to dismiss (objections etc.). ◆**'w~wollen**, *v.i.sep. (haben)* to want to get away/*(ausgehen)* go out. ◆**'w~ziehen**, *v.tr.sep.irr.113* **1.** *v.tr.* to pull (s.o., sth.) away. **2.** *v.i. (sein)* to move (away) (**aus/von + dat**, from).

**wegen** ['veːgən], *prep. + gen/F: + dat* because of; owing to; **w. mir**, on my account; **von Rechts w.**, by right; *F:* **von w.!** it's nothing of the sort! *(kommt nicht in Frage)* nothing doing!

**weh** [veː], *adj. F:* painful, sore (finger etc.); hurting (feet etc.); **j-m/sich** *dat* **w. tun**, to hurt s.o./oneself; **mir tut der Fuß w.**, my foot is hurting. ◆**'w~(e)**, *int.* alas! **w. dir, wenn ...!** it'll be the worse for you, if ... ◆**'W~en¹**, *fpl* labour pains; **in den W. liegen**, to be in labour. ◆**'W~klage**, *f Lit:* lament(ation). ◆**'w~leidig**, *adj.* plaintive (voice etc.); **sei doch nicht so w.**, don't make such a fuss. ◆**'W~mut**, *f -/no pl* melancholy, *(Sehnsucht)* longing. ◆**'w~mütig**, *adj.* melancholy; wistful (smile etc.).

**Wehe** ['veːə], *f -/-n* (snow etc.) drift. ◆**'w~n²**, *v.* **1.** *v.i. (haben) (Wind)* to blow; *(Fahne usw.)* to wave, flutter; *(Haare)* to blow about. **2.** *v.tr.* to blow (sth.).

**Wehr** [veːr]. **1.** *f* **sich zur W. setzen**, to resist, put up a fight. **2.** *n -(e)s/-e* weir.

◆'W~**dienst**, *m* military service.
◆'W~**dienstverweigerer**, *m* conscientious objector. ◆'w~**en**, *v.refl.* **sich w.**, to fight back; to defend oneself (**gegen etwas**, against sth.). ◆'w~**los**, *adj.* defenceless. ◆'W~**macht**, *f* armed forces. ◆'W~**pflicht**, *f* conscription; compulsory military service. ◆'w~-**pflichtig**, *adj.* liable to military service.

**Weib** [vaip], *n* -(e)s/-er [-bər] *Pej:* female; *N.Am:* broad. ◆'W~**chen**, *n* -s/- *Orn: Z:* female. ◆'w~**isch**, *adj. Pej:* effeminate, womanish. ◆'W~**lich**, *adj.* (a) female (sex etc.); *Gram:* feminine (gender); (b) (*frauenhaft*) feminine (characteristic etc.). ◆'W~**lichkeit**, *f -/no pl* femininity.

**weich** [vaiç], *adj.* soft; tender (meat etc.); (*w~gekocht*) soft-boiled (egg); **w. liegen**, to lie on something soft. ◆'W~**heit**, *f -/no pl* softness; tenderness. ◆'w~**lich**, *adj.* soft (thing, person); weak (character); (*weibisch*) effeminate. ◆'W~**ling**, *m* -s/-e weakling; *F:* softy, sissy. ◆'W~**spüler**, *m* -s/- (fabric) conditioner.

**Weiche** ['vaiçə], *f -/-n Rail:* points, *N.Am:* switch; **die W~n stellen**, to set the points/*Fig:* the course. ◆'w~**n**, *v.i.irr.* (*sein*) to give way, yield (**j-m**, **etwas** *dat* to s.o., sth.); (*Feind*) to fall back, retreat (**vor** + *dat*, from).

**Weide**[1] ['vaidə], *f -/-n* pasture, meadow. ◆'W~**land**, *n* pastureland, pasturage. ◆'w~**n**, *v.tr. & i.* (*haben*) to graze, pasture (sheep etc.); *Fig:* **sich an etwas** *dat* **w.**, to take delight in/(*Augen usw.*) feast on sth.

**Weide**[2] *f -/-n/*'W~**nbaum**, *m* willow tree.

**weiger|n** ['vaigərn], *v.refl.* **sich w.**, to refuse (to do sth.). ◆'W~**ung**, *f -/-en* refusal.

**Weih|e** ['vaiə], *f -/-n Ecc: etc:* consecration; **W. zum Priester**, ordination. ◆'w~**en**, *v.tr.* to consecrate (ground, a church etc.); to ordain (s.o.); *Fig:* **dem Tode geweiht**, doomed to die. ◆'W~**nachten** [-naxtən] *n* Christmas. ◆'w~**nachtlich**, *adj.* like Christmas; *F:* Christmassy. ◆'W~**nachts-**, *comb.fm.* Christmas (tree, card, present etc.). ◆'W~**nachtsabend**, *m* Christmas Eve. ◆'W~**nachtsfest**, *n* Christmas (holiday). ◆'W~**nachtslied**, *n* Christmas carol. ◆'W~**nachtsmann**, *m* Father Christmas. ◆'W~**nachtstag**, *m* **erster W.**, Christmas Day; **zweiter W.**, Boxing Day. ◆'W~**nachtszeit**, *f* Christmas period. ◆'W~**rauch**, *m* incense. ◆'W~**wasser**, *n* holy water.

**Weiher** ['vaiər], *m* -s/- pond.

**weil** [vail], *conj.* because; (*da*) since.

**Weile** ['vailə], *f -/no pl* while, (space of) time.

**Wein** [vain]. **I.** *m* -(e)s/-e (a) wine; (b) (*W~reben*) vines; **W. ernten/lesen**, to pick grapes. **II.** '**W~-**, *comb.fm.* (a) wine (vinegar, bottle, glass, cellar, cooler etc.); (b) (*vom W~stock*) vine (leaf etc.). ◆'W~**bau**, *m* wine-growing. ◆'W~**(bau)gebiet**, *m* wine-growing area. ◆'W~**beere**, *f* grape. ◆'W~**berg**, *m* (terraced) vineyard. ◆'W~**bergschnecke**, *f* (edible) snail. ◆'W~**brand**, *m* brandy. ◆'W~**geist**, *m* pure alcohol, spirit. ◆'W~**karte**, *f* wine list. ◆'W~**lese**, *f* grape harvest, vintage. ◆'W~**probe**, *f* wine-tasting. ◆'w~**rot**, *adj.* burgundy. ◆'W~**stein**, *m* tartar. ◆'W~**stock**, *m* grapevine. ◆'W~**stube**, *f* wine bar/parlour. ◆'W~**traube**, *f* grape.

**wein|en** ['vainən], *v.i.* (*haben*) to cry, weep (**vor** + *dat*, from; **um** + *acc*, over). ◆'w~**erlich**, *adj.* tearful; *Pej:* whining (child etc.).

**weise**[1] ['vaizə], *adj.* wise; (*umsichtig*) prudent.

'**Weise**[2], *f -/-n* **1.** manner, way; **auf diese W.**, in this way/manner; **auf keine/in keiner W.**, by no means. **2.** *Mus:* melody, tune.

'**weis|en**, *v.tr.irr.70* **j-m den Weg, die Tür usw. w.**, to show s.o. the way, door etc.; **etwas von sich** *dat* **w.**, to reject sth. completely. ◆'W~**ung**, *f -/-en* direction, instruction.

**Weis|heit** ['vaishait], *f -/no pl* wisdom. ◆'W~**heitszahn**, *m* wisdom tooth. ◆'w~**machen**, *v.tr.sep.* **j-m etwas w.**, to make s.o. believe sth. ◆'w~**sagen**, *v.tr.insep.* to prophesy (disaster etc.).

**weiß** [vais], *adj.* white. ◆'W~**brot**, *n* white bread/(*Laib*) loaf. ◆'w~**en**, *v.tr.* to whiten (shoes); to whitewash (a room, wall etc.). ◆'w~**haarig**, *adj.* white-haired. ◆'W~**kohl**, *m* white cabbage. ◆'W~**wäsche**, *f* household linen. ◆'W~**wein**, *m* white wine. ◆'W~**wurst**, *f* veal sausage.

**weit** [vait], *adj.* (a) wide (expanse, sleeve etc.); extensive (area, view etc.); **im w~esten Sinne**, in the broadest sense; **w. geöffnet**, wide open; (b) (*lang*) long (way, journey etc.); **in w~er Ferne**, far in the distance; **w. und breit**, far and wide; **haben Sie es noch w.?** have you much further to go? **das geht zu w.!** that's going too far/the limit! (c) *adv.* (*erheblich*) **w. größer/besser**, far larger/better; **bei w~em**, by far; **bei w~em nicht genug**, not nearly enough. ◆'w~**aus**, *adv.* far (better etc.); by far, much (the best etc.). ◆'W~**blick**, *m* far-sightedness, vision. ◆'W~**e**, *f -/-n* (a) (*Fläche*) extent; (b) (*Breite*) width; (c) *esp. Sp:* (*Entfernung*) distance. ◆'w~**en**, *v.tr.* to widen (sth.), stretch (shoes etc.). ◆'w~**er**, *adj.* further (news, orders etc.); (*zusätzlich*) additional (expense, worry etc.); **bis auf w~eres**, until further notice; **im w~eren**, in the following; **w. niemand/nichts**, nobody/

nothing else; **und so w.,** and so on; **ohne w~eres,** easily; without any trouble. ◆'**W~erbildung,** f further education. ◆'**w~erempfehlen,** v.tr.sep.irr.2 to recommend (s.o., sth.) to others. ◆'**w~ererzählen,** v.tr.sep. to pass on (news etc.); to tell (news etc.) to others. ◆'**w~ergeben,** v.tr.sep.irr.35 to pass on (a message, book etc.). ◆'**w~ergehen,** v.i.sep.irr.36 (sein) to go/walk on; (Pers., Sache) to continue. ◆'**w~erhin,** adv. (künftig) further, in future; (außerdem) moreover, furthermore; **etwas w. tun,** to continue doing/to do sth. ◆'**w~erkommen,** v.i.sep. irr.53 (sein) to get on, progress. ◆'**w~erlaufen,** v.i.sep.irr.58 (sein) to go on running; (Zahlungen usw.) to continue. ◆'**w~erleiten,** v.tr.sep. to pass on (a request etc.), send on (mail). ◆'**w~ermachen,** v.tr.&i.sep. (haben) **mit etwas** dat **w.,** to carry on/continue sth. ◆'**w~este(r,s),** adj. furthest, most distant (point etc.); **am w~esten,** farthest (away). ◆'**w~gehend,** adj. extensive, far-reaching (changes etc.); wide (powers etc.); adv. largely. ◆'**w~läufig,** adj. (a) extensive, spacious (grounds etc.); (b) distant (relative). ◆'**w~reichend,** adj. far-reaching. ◆'**w~schweifig,** adj. long-winded, rambling. ◆'**W~sicht,** f Fig: farsightedness, vision. ◆'**w~sichtig,** adj. Med: long-sighted; Fig: far-sighted. ◆'**W~springer,** m long-jumper. ◆'**W~sprung,** m long jump. ◆'**w~verbreitet,** adj. widespread, common. ◆'**W~winkelobjektiv,** n wide-angle lens.

**Weizen** ['vaitsən], m -s/no pl wheat.

**welch** [vɛlç], pron. Lit: **w. ein Segen!** what a blessing! ◆'**w~e(r,s),** pron. 1. interrog. **w~er von ihnen?** which (one) of them? 2. rel. (Pers.) who, (Sache/Sachen) which. 3. indef. some; **hast du w~es?** have you got some/any? F: **was für w~es?** what sort?

**welk** [vɛlk], adj. wilting, (verblaßt) faded (flowers etc.). ◆'**w~en,** v.i. (sein) to wilt, fade.

**Well|blech** ['vɛlblɛç], n corrugated iron. ◆'**W~e,** f -/-n 1. wave. 2. Tchn: shaft. ◆'**w~en,** v.tr. to wave (hair), corrugate (tin, paper); **sich w.,** (Haar) to form waves, be wavy; (Teppich usw.) to get ridges. ◆'**W~enbrecher,** m breakwater. ◆'**W~enlänge,** f (also Fig:) wavelength. ◆'**W~enlinie,** f wavy line. ◆'**W~enreiten,** n surfriding, surfing. ◆'**W~enreiter,** m surfrider, surfer. ◆'**W~ensittich,** m budgerigar. ◆'**w~ig,** adj. wavy (hair etc.); bumpy (road, ground etc.). ◆'**W~pappe,** f corrugated cardboard.

**Welpe** ['vɛlpə], m -n/-n whelp.

**Welt** [vɛlt]. I. f -/-en world; **etwas aus der W. schaffen,** to do away with/

(bereinigen) clear up sth.; **ein Mann von W.,** a man of the world; F: **es kostet nicht die W.,** it doesn't cost the earth; **alle W.,** everybody. II. '**W~-,** '**w~-,** comb.fm. (a) world (atlas, peace, literature, market, order etc.); international (politics etc.); (map etc.) of the world; (b) (weltweit) worldwide (reputation etc.). ◆'**W~all,** n universe; cosmos. ◆'**W~anschauung,** f ideology; philosophy (of life). ◆'**w~fremd,** adj. unworldly. ◆'**W~fremdheit,** f unworldliness. ◆'**W~klasse,** f world's best/elite; **W. sein,** to be world class. ◆'**W~krieg,** m world war. ◆'**w~lich,** adj. worldly (pleasures etc.); mundane (outlook etc.); (nicht religiös) secular (education, art etc.). ◆'**W~macht,** f world power. ◆'**w~männisch,** adj. sophisticated, urban. ◆'**W~meer,** n ocean. ◆'**W~meister(in),** m(f) world champion. ◆'**W~meisterschaft,** f world championship. ◆'**W~raum,** m (outer) space. ◆'**W~raumfahrt,** f space travel. ◆'**W~reich,** n empire. ◆'**W~reise,** f world tour. ◆'**W~rekord,** m world record. ◆'**W~ruf,** m world-wide renown; international reputation. ◆'**W~stadt,** f metropolis. ◆'**W~untergang,** m end of the world. ◆'**w~weit,** adj. world-wide. ◆'**W~wunder,** n wonder of the world.

**wem** [ve:m], pron. 1. (to) whom? 2. F: (jemandem) (to) someone.

**wen** [ve:n], pron. 1. whom? 2. F: (jemanden) someone.

**Wend|e** ['vɛndə], f -/-n turning point; **W. zum Guten/Schlechten,** change for the better/worse. ◆'**W~ekreis,** m 1. Geog: tropic. 2. Aut: lock; turning circle. ◆'**W~eltreppe,** f spiral staircase. ◆'**w~en,** v. 1. v.tr.irr.94 to turn; **sich w.,** (Pers.) to turn (round); **sich an j-n/ eine Behörde w.,** to turn to s.o. (for help)/apply to an authority (**um** + acc, for); **sich zum Guten/Schlechten w.,** to take a turn for the better/worse. 2. v.i. (haben) to turn (round). ◆'**W~epunkt,** m turning point. ◆'**W~ung,** f -/-en 1. turn. 2. = **Redewendung.**

**wenig** ['ve:niç], pron. & adj. 1. sing. little; **das w~e Geld,** the small amount of money; **w. bekannt,** little known; **w. erfreulich,** not very pleasant; **ein w. Schnee,** a bit of/a little snow. 2. pl (a) few; **mit w~en Worten,** in few/(ein paar) a few words; **nicht w~e,** not a few; quite a number. ◆'**w~er,** comp. adj. & pron.inv. 1. less; pl fewer; **w. Geld,** less money. 2. Mth: 4 **w.** 2, 4 minus 2. ◆'**W~keit,** f -/no pl trifle; Hum: **meine W.,** yours truly. ◆'**w~ste(r,s),** superl. adj. sing. least; pl fewest. ◆'**w~stens,** adv. at least.

**wenn** [vɛn], conj. 1. if; **w. schon!** what of it! F: so what! **w. er nur käme!** if only he would come! 2. (zeitlich) when; **w. er**

kommt, **frage ich ihn,** I'll ask him when he arrives; **immer w.,** whenever. ◆**'w~gleich,** *conj.* although. ◆**'w~schon,** *conj.* w., **dennschon,** in for a penny, in for a pound.

**wer** [veːr]. **1.** *interr.pron.* who; **w. von euch,** which of you? **2.** *rel.pron.* anyone who; **w. mitkommen will,** anyone who/ whoever wants to come. **3.** *indef.pron. F:* (*jemand*) **falls w. auftaucht,** if anyone turns up.

**Werbe-** ['verbə-], *comb.fm.* advertising (agent, agency, costs, film etc.); commercial (broadcast etc.). ◆**'W~kampagne,** *f* advertising campaign. ◆**'W~fernsehen,** *n* TV commercials. ◆**'W~geschenk,** *n* free sample. ◆**'w~n,** *v.irr.101* **1.** *v.tr.* to enlist, recruit (members etc.); to canvass, *Hum:* woo (customers etc.). **2.** *v.i.* (*haben*) to campaign (**für eine Partei usw.,** for a party etc.); *Com:* to advertise (**für etwas** *acc,* sth.); **um j-s Vertrauen w.,** to try to gain s.o.'s trust. ◆**'W~spot,** *m* -s/-s commercial. ◆**'w~wirksam,** *adj.* **w. sein,** to be good publicity/have plenty of pull.

**Werbung** ['verbʊŋ], *f* -/-en **1.** recruitment (of members etc.). **2.** *no pl Com:* advertising, publicity; promotion (**für** + *acc,* of).

**Werdegang** ['veːrdəgaŋ], *m* development; (*Laufbahn*) career.

**werden** ['veːrdən], *v.i.irr.* (*sein*) **1.** to become (sth., angry, old etc.); to go (blind, mad, red etc.); to turn (pale, sour etc.); to grow (longer, shorter etc.); to get (wet, warm etc.); **gesund/krank w.,** to get well/fall ill; **mir wurde schlecht,** I began to feel ill; **zu etwas** *dat* **w.,** to turn into sth.; **daraus wird nichts,** nothing will come of that; **was wird, wenn er nicht kommt?** what will happen if he doesn't come? **2.** *v.aux.* (*a*) (*Futur*) **er wird kommen,** he will come; (*b*) (*Konditional*) **er würde kommen, wenn ...,** he would come if ... (*c*) (*Passiv*) **geliebt w.,** to be loved; **er würde gewählt,** he was chosen. ◆**'w~d,** *adj.* growing, budding (doctor etc.); **w~de Mutter,** expectant mother.

**werfen** ['verfən], *v.tr.irr.* (*a*) to throw (sth.); to cast (*Fig:* a glance, shadow etc.); (*b*) **Blasen/Falten w.,** to form bubbles/creases.

**Werft** [verft], *f* -/-en shipyard.

**Werk** [verk], *n* -(e)s/-e **1.** work; *coll.* (artistic etc.) works, output; **am W.,** at work. **2.** *Tchn:* mechanism, *F:* works. **3.** *Ind:* works; plant; **ab W.,** ex works. ◆**'W~bank,** *f* workbench. ◆**'W~seigen,** *adj.* company(-owned). ◆**'W~statt** *f* -/-stätten workshop; *Art:* studio. ◆**'W~stoff,** *m* material. ◆**'W~stück,** *n* workpiece. ◆**'W~student,** *m* working student. ◆**'W~tag,** *m* working day. ◆**'w~tags,** *adv.* on working days. ◆**'w~tätig,** *adj.* working (population

etc.). ◆**'W~tisch,** *m* workbench. ◆**'W~zeug,** *n* (*also Fig: Pers.*) tool; *coll.* toolkit, tools. ◆**'W~zeugkasten,** *m* tool box/chest.

**Wermut** ['veːrmuːt], *m* -(e)s/*no pl* **1.** *Bot:* wormwood. **2.** (*Wein*) vermouth.

**wert** [veːrt]. **I.** *adj.* **1.** (*a*) ( + *nom*) **viel/wenig/1000 Mark w.,** worth a lot/a little/1000 marks; **nichts w.,** worthless; **der Film ist es w., daß man ihn sieht,** the film is worth seeing; (*b*) ( + *gen*) worthy of ...; **der Mühe w.,** worth the trouble. **2.** *Lit:* esteemed, valued; *Com:* **Ihr w~es Schreiben,** your kind letter. **II. W.,** *m* -(e)s/-e (*a*) value; **im W~(e) von,** to the value of; (*b*) *esp. Fig:* worth (of s.o., sth.); **ohne jeden W.,** valueless, worthless; **das hat keinen W.,** it's pointless/ useless; **auf etwas** *acc* (**großen/viel**) **W. legen,** to lay (great) stress on/attach (great) importance to sth.; (*c*) *pl* **W~e,** values; (*W~sachen*) valuables. **III.** **'W~-,** *comb.fm.* value (judgement etc.; (standard etc.) of value. ◆**'W~angabe,** *f* declaration of value. ◆**'W~arbeit,** *f* quality workmanship. ◆**'w~beständig,** *adj.* retaining its value; stable (currency, prices). ◆**'w~en,** *v.tr.* to assess, calculate (a development etc.); to rate (a performance etc.); *Sp:* **es wird nicht gewertet,** it does not count. ◆**'w~los,** *adj.* valueless, worthless. ◆**'W~losigkeit,** *f* -/*no pl* worthlessness. ◆**'W~marke,** *f* stamp, coupon. ◆**'W~papier,** *n* security; *pl* **W~papiere,** stocks and shares. ◆**'W~sache,** *f* article of value; *pl* valuables. ◆**'W~ung,** *f* -/-en (*a*) assessment, evaluation; (*b*) *Sp:* score, points. ◆**'w~voll,** *adj.* valuable.

**Wesen** ['veːzən], *n* -s/- **1.** *no pl* nature; (*das Wesentliche*) essence. **2.** (*Lebewesen*) being; (*Geschöpf*) creature. ◆**'w~tlich,** *adj.* (*a*) essential; **im w~tlichen,** essentially; in the main; (*b*) (*grundlegend*) basic, fundamental (quality etc.); (*c*) (*erheblich*) substantial (difference etc.).

**weshalb** [vɛsˈhalp]. **I.** *interrog.adv.* why. **II.** *conj.* (which is) why.

**Wespe** ['vɛspə], *f* -/-n wasp. ◆**'W~n-,** *comb.fm.* wasp's (nest etc.). ◆**'W~nstich,** *m* wasp sting.

**wessen** ['vɛsən], *interrog.pron.* whose; **w. Buch?** whose book?

**West-** [vɛst-], *comb.fm.* (*a*) west (coast, side, bank, wind etc.); West (Germany, Africa, Berlin etc.); (*b*) (*westlich*) western (frontier etc.); Western (Europe, France etc.). ◆**'w~deutsch,** *adj.* West German. ◆**'W~en,** *m* -s/*no pl* west; **aus dem/von W.,** from the west; **nach W.,** westwards; (*Lage*) to the west. ◆**W~ern** ['vɛstən], *m* -s/- *Cin: F:* western. ◆**W~falen** ['fuːlən]. *Pr.n.n* -s. Westphalia. ◆**w~fälisch** [-ˈfɛːliʃ], *adj.* Westphalian. ◆**'w~lich. I.** *adj.* western (hemisphere, border, sky etc.); westerly (wind, direction etc.); **w. von Bonn,** (to the) west of Bonn. **II.** *prep.* + *gen* **w. der Stadt,** to the west of the town. ◆**'W~mächte,** *fpl* Western Powers. ◆**'w~wärts,** *adj.* westwards.

**Weste** ['vɛstə], *f* -/-n waistcoat, *N.Am:* vest; *Fig:* **eine weiße W. haben,** to have a clean record.

**weswegen** [vɛs've:gən], *interrog.pron.* = **weshalb.**

**wett** [vɛt], *adj.* even, *F:* quits. ◆**'W~bewerb,** *m* -(e)s/-e competition; *Sp:* contest, event. ◆**'W~büro,** *n* betting office/shop. ◆**'W~e,** *f* -/-n bet; **sie liefen/fuhren um die W.,** they raced each other (on foot/in cars). ◆**'w~eifer,** *m* competitive spirit. ◆**'w~eifern,** *v.i.* (*haben*) to vie, contend (**um etwas** *acc,* for sth.). ◆**'w~en. I.** *v.i.* (*haben*) to bet (**mit j-m um etwas** *acc,* s.o. sth.); **auf ein Pferd usw. w.,** to bet on/back a horse etc. **II. W.,** *n* -s/*no pl* betting. ◆**'W~er1(in),** *m* -s/- (*f* -/-nen) better. ◆**'W~kampf,** *m Sp:* contest, match. ◆**'W~kämpfer,** *m* competitor; contestant. ◆**'W~lauf,** *m* race. ◆**'w~machen,** *v.tr.sep.* to make good (an error, a loss etc.); to offset (a deficiency etc.). ◆**'W~rennen,** *n* race. ◆**'W~rüsten,** *n* -s/*no pl* arms race. ◆**'W~streit,** *m* contest.

**Wetter2** ['vɛtər]. **I.** *n* -s/- weather; **bei jedem W.,** in all weathers; *F:* **was ist für W.?** what's the weather like? **II. 'W~-,** **'w~-,** *comb.fm.* weather (service, situation, satellite, conditions etc.); meteorological (office etc.). ◆**'W~bericht,** *m* weather report. ◆**'w~fest,** *adj.* weatherproof. ◆**'W~karte,** *f* weather map/chart. ◆**'W~leuchten,** *n* sheet lightning. ◆**'w~n,** *v.i.* (*haben*) *Fig:* **gegen j-n, etwas** *acc* **w.,** to fulminate against s.o., sth. ◆**'W~vorhersage,** *f* weather forecast. ◆**'W~warte,** *f* weather/meteorological station.

**wetzen** ['vɛtsən], *v.* **1.** *v.tr.* to sharpen, grind (a knife etc.). **2.** *v.i.* (*sein*) *F:* to shoot, rush (along).

**Whisky** ['viski], *m* -s/-s whisk(e)y.

**wichtig** ['viçtiç], *adj.* important; **sich/etwas w. nehmen,** to take oneself/sth. seriously; **sich w. machen,** to be full of one's own importance. ◆**'W~keit,** *f* -/*no pl* importance.

**Wick|el** ['vikəl], *m* -s/- (*a*) (*Haarw.*) roller, curler; (*b*) *Med:* compress. ◆**'w~eln,** *v.tr.* to wind (thread, wire, a bandage etc.); to coil (wire); to put (hair) in curlers; (*einw.*) to wrap (sth., oneself); **ein Baby w.,** to put a nappy/*N.Am:* diaper on a baby. ◆**'W~eltisch,** *m* (baby's) changing table. ◆**'W~ler,** *m* -s/- (hair) curler.

**Widder** ['vidər], *m* -s/- *Z:* ram; *Astr:* Aries.

**wider** ['vi:dər], *prep.* + *acc* against; **w. Erwarten,** contrary to expectation.

◆**w~'fahren,** *v.i.insep.*26 (*sein*) to happen (j-m, to s.o.). ◆**'W~haken,** *m* barb, barbed hook. ◆**w~'legen,** *v.tr.insep.* to refute, disprove (sth.). ◆**W~'legung,** *f* -/*no pl* refutation. ◆**w~'lich,** *adj.* loathsome (person, behaviour etc.); obnoxious (spectacle, smell etc.); odious (task etc.). ◆**w~'natürlich,** *adj.* unnatural, perverted. ◆**'w~rechtlich,** *adj.* unlawful; wrongful (arrest, dismissal). ◆**'W~rede,** *f* contradiction; **ohne W.!** unquestioningly; **keine W.!** don't argue! ◆**'W~ruf,** *m* cancellation, revocation; withdrawal; **bis auf W.,** until further notice. ◆**w~'rufen,** *v.tr.insep.irr.*74 to cancel, revoke (an order etc.); to withdraw (a statement). ◆**'W~sacher,** *m* -s/- adversary. ◆**w~'setzen,** *v.refl.insep.* **sich j-m, etwas** *dat* **w.,** to oppose/resist s.o., sth. ◆**'w~sinnig,** *adj.* senseless, absurd. ◆**'w~spenstig,** *adj.* rebellious; unruly, unmanageable (child, hair); (*störrisch*) obstinate, stubborn. ◆**'W~spenstigkeit,** *f* -/-en rebelliousness; unruliness; obstinacy. ◆**'w~spiegeln,** *v.tr.sep.* also *Fig:* to reflect, mirror (sth.). ◆**w~'sprechen,** *v.i.insep.irr.*14 (*haben*) to contradict (j-m, etwas *dat,* s.o., sth.); (*Aussagen usw.*) **sich w.,** to be contradictory; to conflict. ◆**w~'sprechend,** *adj.* conflicting. ◆**'W~spruch,** *m* contradiction; **ohne W.,** without protest. ◆**'w~spruchslos,** *adv.* unprotestingly. ◆**'w~sprüchlich** [-ʃpryçlıç], *adj.* contradictory, inconsistent. ◆**'W~stand,** *m* -(e)s/*no pl* (*also El:*) resistance; (j-m, etwas *dat*) **W. leisten,** to resist (s.o., sth.). ◆**'W~stands-,** *comb.fm.* resistance (movement etc.). ◆**'W~standskämpfer,** *m* resistance fighter. ◆**'w~standsfähig,** *adj.* resistant (**gegen** + *acc,* to); (*stark*) tough (person, clothing); hardy (plant). ◆**'w~standslos,** *adj.* unresisting. ◆**w~'stehen,** *v.i.insep.irr.*100 (*haben*) **einem Angriff,** *Fig:* **der Versuchung usw. w.,** to resist an attack, *Fig:* temptation etc.; (*Material*) (**dem**) **Druck usw. w.,** to withstand pressure etc. ◆**'W~streit,** *m Lit:* conflict. ◆**w~'wärtig,** *adj.* = **widerlich.** ◆**'W~wille,** *m* aversion (**gegen** + *acc,* to); (*Ekel*) disgust, repugnance. ◆**'w~willig,** *adj.* reluctant, grudging.

**widm|en** ['vitmən], *v.tr.* to dedicate (a book etc.) (j-m, to s.o.); **sich/seine Zeit usw. etwas** *dat* **w.,** to devote oneself/one's time etc. to sth. ◆**'W~ung,** *f* -/-en dedication.

**widrig** ['vi:drıç], *adj.* adverse.

**wie** [vi:], *adv. interrog.* how? *F:* **und w.!** and how! not half! **w.! du hast es vergessen!** what! you've forgotten it! **II.** *conj.* (*a*) *comp.* as; (*ähnlich w.*) like; **so groß w. du,** as big as you; **w. sein Va-**

ter, like his father; **w. wenn ...**, as if ...; **w. gesagt**, as has been said; as I have said before; (b) how; **du weißt, w. es ist**, you know how it is; **w. reich er auch sein mag**, however rich he may be.

**wieder** ['vi:dər], *adv.* again, once more; **er ging w. ins Haus**, he went back into the house. ◆**W~'aufbau**, *m* rebuilding, reconstruction. ◆**W~'aufnahme**, *f* resumption; renewal; readmission (**in einen Verein usw.**, to a club etc.). ◆**w~'aufnehmen**, *v.tr.sep.irr.69* to resume (work, discussions etc.); *Jur:* to re-open (a case). ◆**'W~beginn**, *m* recommencement; resumption. ◆**w~bekommen**, *v.tr.sep.irr.53* to get (sth.) back. ◆**'w~bringen**, *v.tr.sep.irr.16* to bring back. ◆**'w~entdeckung**, *f* rediscovery. ◆**w~erinnern**, *v.refl. sep.* **sich an etwas acc w.**, to recall sth. ◆**'w~erkennen**, *v.tr.sep.irr.51* to recognize (s.o., sth.). ◆**'w~erlangen**, *v.tr.sep.* to recover, regain (sth.). ◆**'w~finden**, *v.tr.sep.irr.9* to find (s.o., sth.) again. ◆**W~gabe**, *f* 1. reproduction; (*Übersetzung, Aufführung*) rendering; (*Schilderung*) account, description. 2. (*Rückgabe*) return. ◆**'w~geben**, *v.tr.sep.irr.35* (a) to give back, return (sth.); (b) (*vortragen, übersetzen*) to render (a song, text etc.); (*schildern*) to give an account of (a conversation, event etc.). ◆**'w~gewinnen**, *v.tr.sep.irr.90* to recover (one's equilibrium etc.). ◆**w~'gutmachen**, *v.tr.sep.* to make good, (*entschädigen*) compensate for (damage); to make up for (a mistake etc.), redress (a wrong). ◆**W~'gutmachung**, *f -/no pl* compensation; *Pol:* reparations. ◆**w~'herstellen**, *v.tr.sep.* to restore (sth.); to re-establish (contact etc.). ◆**w~'holen**, *v.tr.insep.* to repeat (sth.); *Sp:* to replay (a match), re-run (a race); **sich w.**, (*Pers.*) to repeat oneself; (*Ereignis*) to recur. ◆**w~'holt**, *adj.* repeated. ◆**W~'holung**, *f -/-en* repetition; reiteration; (*Sendung usw.*) repeat; *Sp:* replay, re-run. ◆**W~'holungsspiel**, *n Sp:* replay. ◆**'W~hören**, *n -s/no pl* **auf W.**, goodbye. ◆**'W~kehr**, *f -/no pl* return; recurrence; (*Jubiläum*) anniversary. ◆**'w~kehren**, *v.i.sep.* (*sein*) to return, come back. ◆**'w~kommen**, *v.i.sep.irr.53* (*sein*) to come back/(*noch einmal*) again. ◆**'w~sehen**. **I.** *v.tr.sep.irr.92* to see (s.o., sth.) again. **II. W.**, *n -s/-* reunion; **auf W.**, goodbye. ◆**'w~um**, *adv.* (a) *Lit:* again; (b) (*andererseits*) on the other hand. ◆**'W~vereinigen**, *v.tr.sep.* to reunite. ◆**'W~vereinigung**, *f* reunification. ◆**'W~verkauf**, *m* resale. ◆**'W~wahl**, *f* re-election. ◆**'w~wählen**, *v.tr.sep.* to re-elect.

**Wiege** ['vi:gə], *f -/-n* (*also Fig:*) cradle. ◆**'w~n¹**, *v.tr.* to rock (a baby, boat

etc.); *Fig:* **sich in Sicherheit w.**, to be lulled into a false sense of security. ◆**'W~nlied**, *n* lullaby, cradle-song.

**wiegen²**, *v.tr.&i.irr.7* (*haben*) to weigh (s.o., sth., oneself etc.); *Fig:* (*Argument usw.*) **schwer w.**, to carry a lot of weight.

**wiehern** ['vi:ərn], *v.i.* (*haben*) to neigh.

**Wien** [vi:n]. *Pr.n.n -s.* Vienna. ◆**'W~er**, *adj.* Viennese.

**Wiese** ['vi:zə], *f -/-n* meadow; (*Weide*) pasture.

**Wiesel** ['vi:zəl], *n -s/-* weasel.

**wie'so**, *interrog. adv.* why?

**wie'viel**, *interrog.adv.* how much? how many? **w. Geld das kostet!** what a lot of money it costs! ◆**w~te(r,s)**, *interrog.adj.* which (number, date etc.); **den w~ten haben wir heute?** what is the date today?

**wild** [vilt]. **I.** *adj.* (a) wild; savage (tribe etc.); rugged (landscape etc.); fierce, ferocious (battle, dog etc.); *F:* **das ist halb so w.**, it's not as bad as all that; **wie w. arbeiten**, to work like mad; (b) (*unerlaubt*) unauthorized (bathing, parking etc.); **w~er Streik**, wildcat strike; **in w~er Ehe leben**, to cohabit, *F:* live in sin. **II. W.**, *n -(e)s/no pl* game. ◆**'W~bret**, *n -s/no pl* game. ◆**'W~erer**, *m -s/-* poacher. ◆**'w~ern**, *v.tr. & i.* (*haben*) to poach (game). ◆**W~fang**, *m* (little) scamp; (*Mädchen*) tomboy. ◆**'w~'fremd**, *adj. F:* completely strange; **w~fremder Mensch**, total stranger. ◆**'W~hüter**, *m* gamekeeper. ◆**'w~lebend**, *adj.* living in the wild. ◆**'W~leder**, *n* suede. ◆**'W~nis**, *f -/-se* wilderness; (*Wüste*) desert. ◆**'W~schwein**, *n* wild bear. ◆**'W~wechsel**, *m* game path/crossing.

**Wille** ['vilə], *m -ns/-n* will; **mein fester W.**, my firm intention; **bei/mit gutem W~n**, given enough goodwill; **beim besten W~n**, with the best will in the world; **seinen W~n durchsetzen**, to get one's own way; **ich mußte wider W~n lachen**, I couldn't help laughing. ◆**'w~n**, *prep. + gen* **um j-s/des Friedens usw. w.**, for s.o.'s sake/the sake of peace etc. ◆**'w~nlos**, *adj.* weak-willed. ◆**'W~nskraft**, *f* willpower. ◆**'w~nsstark**, *adj.* strong-willed, strong-minded. ◆**'w~ntlich**, *adv.* deliberately, intentionally.

**will|ig** ['viliç], *adj.* willing, docile (animal etc.). ◆**w~'kommen**. **I.** *adj.* welcome; **j-n w. heißen**, to welcome s.o. **II. W.**, *n -s/-* welcome. ◆**'W~kür**, *f -/no pl* arbitrariness; (*Launen*) capriciousness. ◆**'w~kürlich**, *adj.* arbitrary.

**wimmeln** ['viməln], *v.i.* (*haben*) to be teeming/crawling (**von + dat**, with).

**wimmern** ['vimərn], *v.i.* (*haben*) to whimper.

**Wimper** ['vimpər], *f -/-n* (eye)lash; *Fig:* **ohne mit der W. zu zucken**, without batting an eyelid. ◆**'W~ntusche**, *f* mascara.

**Wind** [vint], *m* -(e)s/-e wind; *Fig:* **W. bekommen/haben von** + *dat*, to get wind of sth.; **etwas in den W. schlagen**, to turn a deaf ear to sth.; **viel W. machen**, to make a lot of noise, (*prahlen*) brag. ◆'**W~beutel**, *m Cu:* cream puff. ◆'**W~eseile** [-dəs-], *f -/no pl* lightning speed; **sich mit W. verbreiten**, to spread like wildfire. ◆'**W~hund**, *m* greyhound. ◆'**w~ig**, *adj.* 1. windy. 2. *F:* dubious (business). ◆'**W~licht**, *n* storm lantern. ◆'**W~mühle**, *f* windmill. ◆'**W~pocken**, *fpl* chickenpox. ◆'**W~röschen**, *n* -s/- anemone. ◆'**W~rose**, *f Nau:* compass rose. ◆'**W~schatten**, *m* lee (side). ◆'**W~schutzscheibe**, *f* windscreen, *N.Am:* windshield. ◆'**W~stärke**, *f* wind force. ◆'**w~still**, *adj.* windless, calm. ◆'**W~stille**, *f* calm. ◆'**W~stoß**, *m* gust of wind.

**Wind|e** ['vində], *f -/-n* 1. winch, *Nau:* capstan. 2. *Bot:* bindweed, convolvulus. ◆'**w~en**, *v.tr.irr.9* (*a*) (*hochw.*) to winch (up), hoist (a load etc.); (*b*) (*flechten*) to bind, weave (a wreath etc.); (*c*) **sich w.**, (*Pers.*) to wind (one's way) (**durch** + *acc*, through); to writhe (**vor Schmerzen**, with pain); (*Wurm usw.*) to wriggle; (*Pfad, Fluß usw.*) to twist, wind.

**Windel** ['vindəl], *f -/-n* (baby's) nappy, *N.Am:* diaper. ◆'**w~'weich**, *adj. F:* **j-n w. schlagen**, to beat s.o. to a pulp.

**Wink** [viŋk], *m* -(e)s/-e (*a*) (*mit der Hand*) wave, sign; (*mit den Augen*) wink; (*Kopfnicken*) nod; (*b*) (*Hinweis*) hint; pointer. ◆'**w~en**, *v.* 1. *v.i.* (*haben*) to wave (j-m, to s.o.); **einem Taxi w.**, to hail a taxi; *Fig:* **ihm winkt eine Belohnung**, he has a reward coming to him. 2. *v.tr.* **j-n zu sich** *dat* **w.**, to beckon/signal to s.o. to come over.

**Winkel** ['viŋkəl], *m* -s/- (*a*) *Mth:* angle; (*b*) *Tchn:* (set) square; (*c*) (*Ecke*) corner. ◆'**W~eisen**, *n* angle iron. ◆'**w~ig**, *adj.* full of corners. ◆'**W~messer**, *m* protractor.

**winseln** ['vinzəln], *v.i.* (*haben*) (*Hund*) to whine.

**Winter** ['vintər]. I. *m* -s/- winter. II. '**W~-**, *comb.fm.* (*a*) winter (suit, clothes, months etc.); winter's (night, day); (beginning etc.) of winter; (*b*) (*winterlich*) wintry (weather etc.). ◆'**w~fest**, *adj.* winterproof, *N.Am:* winterized; *Bot:* hardy. ◆'**w~lich**, *adj.* wintry. ◆'**W~reifen**, *m* snow tyre. ◆'**W~schlaf**, *m* hibernation; **W. halten**, to hibernate. ◆'**W~schlußverkauf**, *m* winter sale. ◆'**W~sport**, *m* winter sports.

**Winzer** ['vintsər], *m* -s/- wine grower.

**winzig** ['vintsiç], *adj.* tiny; **w. klein**, minute.

**Wipfel** ['vipfəl], *m* -s/- treetop.

**Wippe** ['vipə], *f -/-n* seesaw.

**wir** [viːr], *pers. pron.* we; **w. beide**, both of us; **w. waren es**, it was us.

**Wirbel** ['virbəl], *m* -s/- 1. (*in Wasser, Luft*) eddy; *Fig:* whirl (of activity etc.); (*Aufruhr*) commotion. 2. *Anat:* vertebra. ◆'**w~n**, *v.i.* (*haben/sein*) (*Wasser, Rauch usw.*) to eddy, swirl; (*Pers.*) to whirl. ◆'**W~säule**, *f* spinal column, spine. ◆'**W~sturm**, *m* cyclone, tornado. ◆'**W~tier**, *n* vertebrate. ◆'**W~wind**, *m* whirlwind.

**wirk|en** ['virkən], *v.* 1. *v.i.* (*haben*) (*a*) (*tätig sein*) to work, be active (**als Arzt usw.**, as a doctor etc.); (*b*) (*Wirkung haben*) to have an effect (**auf j-n**, on s.o.); (*Arznei*) to be effective; (*Mitteilung usw.*) **beruhigend w.**, to have a soothing effect; (*Pers.*) **müde/nervös w.**, to seem tired/on edge. 2. *v.tr. Lit:* to work (wonders). ◆'**w~lich**, *adj.* real; actual (fact, state of affairs etc.); (*echt*) genuine (artist, friend etc.); *adv.* really. ◆'**W~lichkeit**, *f -/-en* reality; **in W.**, in actual fact. ◆'**w~sam**, *adj.* effective; (*Vorschrift usw.*) **w. werden**, to come into effect/force. ◆'**W~samkeit**, *f -/no pl* effectiveness. ◆'**W~ung**, *f -/-en* effect, impression. ◆'**W~ungskreis**, *m* sphere of activity; *Pol: etc:* influence. ◆'**W~ungslos**, *adj.* ineffective; **w. bleiben**, to have no effect. ◆'**W~ungsweise**, *f* (mode of) operation. ◆'**w~ungsvoll**, *adj.* effective.

**wirr** [vir], *adj.* confused (person); (*verfilzt*) dishevelled (hair); **w~es Zeug reden**, to talk incoherently. ◆'**W~warr**, *m* -s/no *pl* chaos; (*Lärm*) hubbub.

**Wirsing** ['virziŋ], *m* -s/no *pl* savoy (cabbage).

**Wirt** [virt], *m* -(e)s/-e (*Gastwirt, Vermieter*) landlord. ◆'**W~in**, *f -/-nen* landlady. ◆'**W~schaft**, *f -/-en* 1. economy; (*freie W.*, free enterprise. 2. (*a*) (*Haushalt*) household, housekeeping; (*b*) *F:* **eine saubere/schöne W.**, a fine mess. 3. (*Gastw.*) *Brit:* = public house, *F:* pub; *N.Am:* = saloon. ◆'**w~schaften**, *v.i.* (*haben*) to manage (well, badly etc.); (*Haushalt führen*) to keep house. ◆'**W~schafterin**, *f -/-nen* housekeeper. ◆'**w~schaftlich**, *adj.* 1. economic (development, growth etc.). 2. (*sparsam*) economical (car etc.); thrifty (housewife etc.). ◆'**W~schafts-**, *comb.fm.* economic (relations, history, aid, policy, system etc.); business (life, school etc.); trade (agreement, delegation etc.); industrial (sabotage, espionage etc.). ◆'**W~schaftsgeld**, *n* housekeeping money. ◆'**W~schaftsgemeinschaft**, *f* economic community. ◆'**W~schaftslage**, *f* economic situation. ◆'**W~schaftsminister**, *m* minister for economic affairs. ◆'**W~schaftsprüfer**, *m* accountant; (*Buchprüfer*) auditor. ◆'**W~schaftswunder**, *n* economic miracle. ◆'**W~shaus**, n Brit: public house, F: pub, N.Am: saloon.

**Wisch** [viʃ], m -(e)s/-e F: scrap of paper. ◆'**w~en**, v.tr. to wipe (sth.). ◆'**W~er**, m -s/- Aut: etc: wiper. ◆'**W~tuch**, n (floor etc.) cloth.

**wispern** ['vispərn], v.tr.&i. (haben) to whisper (sth.) (hurriedly).

**Wißbegier|de** ['visbəgi:r(də)], f -/no pl thirst for knowledge; curiosity. ◆'**w~ig**, adj. eager to learn.

**wissen** ['visən]. I. v.tr. & i.irr. (haben) to know (sth.); **das mußt du w.,** that's up to you; **weißt du noch?** do you remember? **nicht, daß ich wüßte,** not that I am aware of; **ich will nichts von ihm/davon w.,** I will have nothing to do with him/it; **oder was weiß ich,** or something of the sort. II. **W.,** n -s/no pl knowledge; **meines W~s,** to my knowledge. ◆'**W~schaft,** f -/-en science. ◆'**W~schaftler,** m -s/- scientist. ◆'**w~schaftlich,** adj. scientific (discovery, method etc.); (akademisch) academic (work, education etc.). ◆'**w~swert,** adj. worth knowing; valuable (information). ◆'**w~tlich,** adj. deliberate; adv. deliberately, knowingly.

**witter|n** ['vitərn], v.tr. to scent, get wind of (prey, Fig: danger etc.). ◆'**W~ung,** f -/no pl (Wetter) weather (conditions).

**Witwe** ['vitvə], f -/-n widow. ◆'**W~nrente,** f widow's pension. ◆'**W~r,** m -s/- widower.

**Witz** [vits], m -es/-e (a) joke; (b) no pl (Geist) wit. ◆'**W~blatt,** n comic magazine. ◆'**W~bold,** m -(e)s/-e joker. ◆'**w~eln,** v.i. (haben) to make jokes. ◆'**W~figur,** f figure of fun. ◆'**w~ig,** adj. witty; (spaßig) funny. ◆'**w~los,** adj. unfunny; (sinnlos) pointless.

**wo** [vo:]. I. interrog. & rel.adv. where; F: (irgendwo) somewhere; **wo immer (auch),** wherever; **der Tag, wo ...,** the day when ... II. conj. **wo nicht,** if not; **wo du gerade da bist,** seeing you're here. ◆**w~'anders,** adv. elsewhere, somewhere else. ◆**w~'bei** [vo:'bai], adv. 1. interrog. at what? doing what? 2. rel. in/in doing which; in the course of which.

**Woche** ['vɔxə], f -/-n week. ◆'**W~n-ende,** n weekend. ◆'**w~nlang,** adj. for weeks. ◆'**W~nschau,** f Cin: newsreel. ◆'**W~ntag,** m weekday. ◆'**w~ntags,** adv. on weekdays.

**wöchentlich** ['vœçəntliç], adj. weekly (report etc.); **einmal w.,** once a week.

**Wodka** ['vɔtka], m -s/-s vodka.

**wo'durch,** adv. 1. interr. by what means? how? 2. rel. through/as a result of which.

**wo'für,** adv. 1. interrog. for what? what ... for? 2. rel. (in return) for which.

**Woge** ['vo:gə], f -/-n wave.

**wo'gegen,** adv. 1. interrog. against what? 2. rel. against which.

**wo'her,** interrog. & rel.adv. from where(?); where from(?); **w. weißt du** das? how do you know that?

**wo'hin,** interrog. & rel.adv. where (to); **w. damit?** where shall I put it? ◆**w~'gegen,** conj. whereas.

**wohl** [vo:l]. I. adv. 1. well; **sich w. fühlen,** to feel well/(wie zu Hause) at home/comfortable; **ist dir nicht w.?** aren't you well? **w. oder übel,** willy nilly; whether I/you like it or not; **das kann man w. sagen!** you can say that again! **es kann w. sein,** it may well be (true). 2. (vermutlich) presumably, I suppose; **es wird w. besser sein ...,** it will probably be better ...; **w. kaum,** hardly likely. 3. (zwar) perhaps; **er hat es w. gut gemeint, aber ...,** he may have meant well, but ... II. **W.,** n -(e)s/no pl well-being; welfare; **auf j-s W. trinken,** to drink s.o.'s health; **zum W.!** cheers! ◆**w~'auf,** pred.adj. well, in good health. ◆**W~befinden,** n well-being. ◆**W~behagen,** n (feeling of) well-being, pleasure. ◆**w~behalten,** adj. (Pers.) safe and sound; (Objekt) in good condition. ◆**W~fahrt,** f welfare. ◆'**W~fahrts-,** comb.fm. welfare (state etc.); charity (organization etc.). ◆'**W~geruch,** m pleasant smell, fragrance. ◆**w~habend,** adj. well-to-do, affluent. ◆**w~ig,** adj. cosy; contented (sigh etc.). ◆**w~meinend,** adj. well-meaning. ◆**w~schmeckend,** adj. pleasant-tasting, tasty. ◆'**W~stand,** m prosperity, affluence. ◆'**W~stands-gesellschaft,** f affluent society. ◆'**W~tat,** f (a) good deed; (b) (Erleichterung) relief; (Segen) boon. ◆'**W~täter(in),** m(f) benefactor, f benefactress. ◆**w~tätig,** adj. charitable. ◆**W~tätigkeit,** f charity. ◆**w~tuend,** adj. beneficial (effect etc.); refreshing (breeze etc.); (lindernd) soothing. ◆**w~tun,** v.i.sep.irr.106 (haben) (j-m) w., to do (s.o.) good. ◆**w~überlegt,** adj. well-considered. ◆**w~verdient,** adj. well-deserved, well-earned. ◆'**w~weislich,** adv. very wisely. ◆**W~wollen,** n -s/no pl goodwill. ◆**w~wollend,** adj. benevolent; kindly (smile etc.).

**Wohn|block** ['vo:nblɔk], m block of flats, N.Am: apartment house. ◆**w~en,** v.i. (haben) to live. ◆**W~gemeinschaft,** f group sharing a house/flat; commune. ◆**w~haft,** adj. Adm: resident. ◆**W~haus,** n residential building, dwelling. ◆**W~heim,** n residential home/hostel; (Studentenw.) hall of residence. ◆'**w~lich,** adj. cosy, home-like. ◆'**W~ort,** m (place of) residence. ◆'**W~raum,** m living space. ◆'**W~sitz,** m (place of) residence; **ohne festen W.,** of no fixed abode. ◆'**W~ung,** f -/-en (a) home; Adm: residence; (Unterkunft) accommodation; (b) (Etagenw.) flat, N.Am: apartment. ◆'**W~ungsnot,** f housing shortage.

◆'W~ungssuche, f house-/flat-hunting. ◆'W~wagen, m caravan; *N.Am:* trailer. ◆'W~zimmer, n living room.

wölb|en ['vœlbən], *v.tr.* to curve (sth.); to arch (one's back, brows etc.); sich w., to curve, (*Bauch usw.*) bulge; (*Brücke usw.*) to arch (**über** + *acc*, across). ◆'W~ung, f -/-en curve; curvature (of the spine).

Wolf [vɔlf], m -(e)s/=e 1. Z: wolf. 2. *Cu:* mincer.

Wölf|in ['vœlfin], f -/-nen she-wolf. ◆'w~isch, adj. wolfish.

Wolk|e ['vɔlkə], f -/-n cloud; **aus allen W~n fallen,** to come down to earth with a bump. ◆'W~en-, *comb.fm.* cloud (bank, formation etc.); (layer, wall etc.) of cloud. ◆'W~enbruch, m cloud-burst. ◆'W~enkratzer, m -s/- skyscraper. ◆'w~enlos, adj. cloudless. ◆'w~ig, adj. cloudy.

Woll|decke ['vɔldekə], f woollen blanket/(*Reisedecke*) rug. ◆'W~jacke, f woollen cardigan. ◆'W~knäuel, m ball of wool. ◆'W~e, f -/-n wool. ◆'w~en¹, adj. wool, woollen.

wollen² ['vɔlən], *v.tr.&v.irr.* (*haben*) to want (sth., to do sth.); to wish (**daß** ..., that ...); **ich will, er doesn't** want to; **ich will, daß du hier bleibst,** I want you to stay here; **w. wir aufstehen?** shall we get up?

wo'mit, adv. 1. *interrog.* with what? what ... with? 2. *rel.* with what.

wo'möglich, adv. possibly.

wo'nach, adv. 1. *interrog.* after what? according to what? 2. *rel.* after/according to which.

Wonne ['vɔnə], f -/-n delight; **vor W.,** with joy.

wo'ran, adv. 1. *interrog.* at what? **w. arbeiten Sie?** what are you working on? 2. *rel.* about/at/on which.

wo'rauf, adv. 1. *interrog.* on what? 2. *rel.* (up)on which; (*wonach*) whereupon, after which.

wo'raus, adv. 1. *interrog.* out of what? from what? 2. *rel.* out of/of/from which.

wo'rin, adv. 1. *interrog.* in what? 2. *rel.* in which, wherein.

Wort [vɔrt], n -(e)s/-e *& (Vokabeln)* =er word; **j-m aufs W. glauben/gehorchen,** to believe/obey s.o.'s every word; **mit anderen W~en,** in other words; **mir fehlen die W~e,** words fail me; **j-m ins W. fallen,** to interrupt s.o.; **das W. haben/führen,** to speak; **zu W. kommen,** to get a chance to speak; **j-m das W. geben/erteilen,** to let s.o. speak; **j-n beim W. nehmen,** to take s.o. at his word. ◆'W~art, f part of speech. ◆'W~bruch, m breaking one's word; breach of promise. ◆'w~brüchig, adj. **w. werden,** to break one's word. ◆'W~führer, m spokesman. ◆'w~karg, adj. taciturn. ◆'W~laut,

m wording. ◆'w~los, adj. silent; adv. without a word. ◆'w~reich, adj. wordy, verbose. ◆'W~schatz, m vocabulary. ◆'W~spiel, n play on words, pun. ◆'W~wahl, f choice of words. ◆'W~wechsel, m heated exchange, altercation. ◆'w~'wörtlich, adv. verbatim, word for word; quite literally.

Wört|erbuch ['vœrtərbuːx], n dictionary. ◆'w~lich, adj. literal (translation etc.); verbatim (account etc.); adv. word for word; **etwas w. nehmen,** to take sth. literally.

wo'rüber, adv. 1. *interrog.* (a) about what? (b) (*Lage*) over what? 2. *rel.* (a) about which; (b) over which.

wo'rum, adv. 1. *interrog.* (a) about what? (b) (*Lage*) round what? 2. *rel.* (a) about which; (b) round which.

wo'runter, adv. 1. *interrog.* under/among what? 2. *rel.* under/among which.

wo'von, adv. 1. *interrog.* from/of what. 2. *rel.* from/of/about which.

wo'vor, adv. 1. *interrog.* before what? **w. hat er Angst?** what is he afraid of? 2. *rel.* before/(*räumlich*) in front of which.

wo'zu, adv. 1. *interrog.* to what? (*warum*) why? for what (purpose)? 2. *rel.* to which.

Wrack [vrak], n -(e)s/-e wreck.

wringen ['vriŋən], *v.tr.* to wring (out) (washing).

Wucher ['vuːxər]. I. m -s/no pl profiteering, extortion. II. 'W~-, *comb.fm.* exorbitant, extortionate (rent, price etc.). ◆'W~er, m -s/-/'W~in, f -/-nen profiteer. ◆'w~isch, adj. profiteering (practices); exorbitant (prices etc.). ◆'w~n, *v.i.* (*haben*) (a) (*Pflanzen usw.*) to grow profusely; (b) (**mit etwas dat**) **w.,** to profiteer (with sth.). ◆'W~ung, f -/-en *Bot:* rank/rampant growth; *Med:* growth, *esp.* proud flesh.

Wuchs [vuːks], m -es/=e growth; (*Körperbau*) build.

Wucht [vuxt], f -/no pl 1. force, impact (of a blow etc.). 2. *F:* **das ist eine W.!** that's terrific!

wühl|en ['vyːlən], *v.i.* (*haben*) to dig, (*Tier*) burrow; (*suchend*) to rummage (**nach etwas** *dat,* for sth.). ◆'W~maus, f *Z:* vole.

Wulst [vulst], m -es/=e bulge, roll (of fat etc.); (*im Stoff*) (thick) fold.

wund [vunt], adj. sore. ◆'W~e, f -/-n wound. ◆'W~starrkrampf, m tetanus.

Wunder ['vundər], n -s/- miracle; W. **tun/wirken,** to work miracles/*Fig:* (*Arznei usw.*) wonders; **kein/was W., daß ...,** no wonder (that) ...; **ein W. an Genauigkeit,** a miracle of precision. ◆'w~bar, adj. (a) (*wie ein Wunder*) miraculous; (b) (*herrlich*) marvellous, wonderful. ◆'W~kerze, f sparkler. ◆'W~kind, n child prodigy. ◆'w~lich, adj. odd, strange; weird (ideas etc.). ◆'W~mittel, n miracle cure, *Hum:*

magic potion. ◆'w~n, v.tr. to surprise (s.o.); **sich über j-n, etwas** acc **w.,** to be surprised about/at s.o., sth. ◆'w~'schön, adj. (very) beautiful, lovely. ◆'w~voll, adj. wonderful, marvellous. ◆'W~welt, f magic world, wonderland. ◆'W~werk, n marvel.

**Wunsch** [vunʃ], m -(e)s/ːe wish; (Verlangen) desire; (Bitte) request; **auf j-s W.,** at s.o.'s request; **nach W.,** as desired/required. ◆'w~gemäß, adv. as requested/desired. ◆'W~konzert, n (musical) request programme. ◆'w~los, adj. w. glücklich, perfectly happy. ◆'W~traum, m pipe-dream. ◆'W~zettel, m list of wants.

**Wünschelrute** ['vynʃəlruːtə], f divining rod.

**wünschen** ['vynʃən], v.tr. to wish; **ich wünsche Sie zu sprechen,** I wish to speak to you; **es wäre sehr zu w.,** it would be highly desirable; **etwas/viel zu w. übrig lassen,** to leave something/much to be desired; **sich** dat **etwas w.,** to want/(bitten um) ask for/(im stillen) wish for sth. ◆'w~swert, adj. desirable.

**Würd|e** ['vyrdə], f -/-n 1. no pl dignity. 2. title, (Rang) rank. ◆'w~elos, adj. undignified. ◆'W~elosigkeit, f -/no pl lack of dignity. ◆'W~enträger, m dignitary. ◆'w~evoll, adj. dignified; adv. with dignity. ◆'w~ig, adj. worthy; **j-s/des Vertrauens w. sein,** to be worthy of s.o./of trust. ◆'w~igen, v.tr. to appreciate (s.o., sth.), (erkennen) recognize (s.o.'s merits etc.); **ohne mich eines Blickes zu w.,** without deigning to look at me. ◆'W~igung, f -/en appreciation; (Huldigung) tribute.

**Wurf** [vurf], m -(e)s/ːe 1. (a) throw, toss (of the coin); (b) no pl (Werfen) throwing. 2. Z: litter (of puppies etc.). ◆'W~pfeil, m dart. ◆'W~sendung, f direct mailing.

**Würfel** ['vyrfəl], m -s/- (a) Mth:etc: cube; (b) (Spielw.) dice. ◆'W~becher, m dice shaker. ◆'w~n, v. 1. v.i. (haben) to play/throw dice (**um etwas** acc, for sth.). 2. v.tr. Cu: to dice (carrots, meat etc.). ◆'W~spiel, n game of dice.

◆'W~zucker, m cube/lump sugar.

**Würg|egriff** ['vyrgəgrif], m stranglehold. ◆'w~en, v. 1. v.tr. to strangle, throttle (s.o.); (Kragen usw.) to choke (s.o.). 2. v.i. (haben) to choke (**an etwas** dat, on sth.).

**Wurm** [vurm], m -(e)s/ːer worm. ◆'w~en, v.tr. F: **es wurmt mich,** it rankles with me. ◆'W~fortsatz, m appendix. ◆'w~ig/'w~stichig, adj. worm-eaten.

**Wurst** [vurst]. I. f -/ːe sausage; F: **jetzt geht's um die W.!** it's now or never! II. adv. F: **das ist mir (völlig) w.,** it's all the same to me; I couldn't care less (about that). ◆'W~waren, fpl (cold meats and) sausage products. ◆'W~zipfel, m sausage end.

**Würstchen** ['vyrstçən], n -s/- small sausage, esp. Frankfurter.

**Würze** ['vyrtsə], f -/-n seasoning; (also Fig:) spice.

**Wurzel** ['vurtsəl], f -/-n root; **W~n schlagen,** to take root; (esp. Fig: Pers.) to put down roots.

**würz|en** ['vyrtsən], v.tr. to season, spice (food); Fig: to add spice to (a story etc.). ◆'w~ig, adj. spicy, well-seasoned. ◆'W~stoff, m flavouring, seasoning.

**wuschel|ig** ['vuʃəliç], adj. fuzzy; (zerzaust) tousled. ◆'W~kopf, m mop of (fuzzy) hair.

**Wust** [vuːst], m -(e)s/no pl F: jumble.

**wüst** [vyːst], adj. (a) (öde) barren, desert (area etc.); (b) (ausschweifend) wild, dissolute (person, life etc.); **w~es Durcheinander,** utter confusion/chaos. ◆'W~e, f -/-n desert. ◆'W~ling, m -s/-e libertine; rake.

**Wut** [vuːt], f -/no pl fury, rage; **aus/vor W.,** with rage; **eine W. auf j-n haben,** to be furious with s.o.; **in W. geraten,** to fly into a rage. ◆'W~anfall, m fit of rage. ◆'W~ausbruch, m outburst of rage. ◆'w~entbrannt, adj. burning/filled with rage.

**wüt|en** ['vyːtən], v.i. (haben) (Pers., Fig: Sturm usw.) to rage; Fig: (Feuer usw.) to wreak havoc. ◆w~end, adj. furious (**auf j-n,** with s.o.); fuming, irate; **j-n w. machen,** to enrage/infuriate s.o.

## X

**X, x** [iks], n -/- (the letter) X, x. ◆'X-Beine, npl knock-knees. ◆'x-beinig, adj. knock-kneed. ◆'x-be'liebig, adj. F: any old. ◆'x-mal, adv. F: umpteen times. ◆'x-te(r, s), adj. F: umpteenth.

**Xanthippe** [ksan'tipə], f -/-n F: shrew.
**Xeroko|pie** [kseroko'piː], f -/-n Xerox copy. ◆x~'pieren, v.tr. to xerox (a document etc.).
**Xylophon** [ksylo'foːn], n -s/-e xylophone.

# Y

**Y, y** ['ypsilɔn], *n -/-* (the letter) Y, y. | **Ypsilon** ['ypsilɔn], *n -(s)/-s* (the letter) Y.

# Z

**Z, z** [tsɛt], *n -/-* (the letter) Z, z.

**Zack|e** ['tsakə], *f -/-n* point; tooth (of a saw, comb etc.); prong (of a fork); (*Bergz.*) jagged peak. ◆'z~**ig**, *adj. (a)* jagged (rocks etc.); *(b) F:* smart, dashing (soldier etc.); brisk (movements, music).

**zaghaft** ['tsɑːkhaft], *adj.* timid; (*zögernd*) hesitant. ◆'Z~**igkeit**, *f -/no pl* timidity.

**zäh** [tsɛː], *adj. (a)* tough (meat, *Fig:* person etc.); *Fig:* tenacious (resistance etc.); *(b) =* **zähflüssig**; (*schleppend*) slow, laboured (conversation etc.). ◆'z~**flüssig**, *adj.* glutinous (liquid); viscous (oil); slow-moving (traffic). ◆'**Zähigkeit**, *f -/no pl* toughness (of a person); tenacity.

**Zahl** [tsɑːl], *f -/-en* number; **in Z~en geschrieben**, written in figures; **in großer Z.**, in large numbers. ◆'z~**bar**, *adj.* payable. ◆'z~**en**, *v.tr.&i. (haben)* to pay (a bill, debt, sum etc.); **z. bitte/ ich möchte z.**, may I have the bill/ *N.Am:* check please? ◆'Z~**karte**, *f* paying-in form for postal giro. ◆'z~**los**, *adj.* innumerable. ◆'z~**reich**, *adj.* numerous; large (family, audience etc.). ◆'Z~**tag**, *m* payday. ◆'Z~**ung**, *f -/-en* payment; **etwas in Z. nehmen**, to take sth. in part exchange. ◆'Z~**ungsempfänger**, *m* payee. ◆'z~**ungsfähig**, *adj. Com:* (*Firma*) solvent. ◆'Z~**ungsmittel**, *n* means of payment. ◆'z~**ungsunfähig**, *adj.* unable to pay, insolvent. ◆'Z~**wort**, *n* numeral.

**zähl|en** ['tsɛːlən], *v.* 1. *v.i. (haben) (a)* to count; *(b)* **z. zu** + *dat*, to belong to (a group etc.), rank among/with (the best etc.); *(c)* **auf j-n, etwas** *acc* **z.**, to count on s.o., sth. 2. *v.tr.* to count (people, money etc.); **seine Tage sind gezählt**, his days are numbered. ◆'Z~**er**, *m -s/-* 1. counter; *El: etc:* meter. 2. *Mth:* numerator. ◆'Z~**ung**, *f -/-en* count.

**zahm** [tsɑːm], *adj.* tame.

**zähmen** ['tsɛːmən], *v.tr. (a)* to tame (an animal); *(b) Fig:* to restrain (one's impatience etc.).

**Zahn** [tsɑːn], *m -(e)s/ːe* tooth; *F:* **j-m auf den Z. fühlen**, to sound s.o. out, (*streng*) put s.o. through it. ◆'Z~**arzt**, *m* dentist. ◆'z~**ärztlich**, *adj.* dental (treatment etc.). ◆'Z~**belag**, *m* plaque. ◆'Z~**bürste**, *f* toothbrush. ◆'z~**en**, *v.i. (haben)* to cut teeth. ◆'Z~**ersatz**, *m* denture. ◆'Z~**fäule**, *f* dental decay/ caries. ◆'Z~**fleisch**, *n* gum; *coll.* gums.

◆'z~**los**, *adj.* toothless. ◆'Z~**pasta**, *f* toothpaste. ◆'Z~**rad**, *n* gearwheel; (*für Ketten*) sprocket (wheel). ◆'Z~**radbahn**, *f* rack-railway. ◆'Z~**schmelz**, *m* enamel. ◆'Z~**schmerzen**, *mpl* toothache. ◆'Z~**spange**, *f* brace. ◆'Z~**stein**, *m* tartar. ◆'Z~**stocher**, *m* toothpick.

**zähneknirschend** ['tsɛːnəknirʃənt], *adv.* under protest, with a bad grace.

**Zander** ['tsandər], *m -s/-* zander.

**Zange** ['tsaŋə], *f -/-n* (sugar etc.) tongs; *Tchn:* pliers; *Med:* forceps; *Z:* (lobster's etc.) pincers. ◆'Z~**ngeburt**, *f* forceps delivery.

**Zank** [tsaŋk], *m -(e)s/no pl* squabble, row (**um/über** + *acc*, over). ◆'Z~**apfel**, *m Fig:* bone of contention. ◆'z~**en**, *v.refl.* **sich z.**, to squabble, have a row (**um** + *acc*, over). ◆Z~**e'rei**, *f -/-en* squabbling.

**zänkisch** ['tsɛŋkiʃ], *adj.* quarrelsome.

**Zäpfchen** ['tsɛpfçən], *n -s/-* 1. *Anat:* uvula. 2. *Med:* suppository.

**Zapf|en** ['tsapfən]. I. *m -s/-* 1. *Bot:* (pine etc.) cone. 2. bung, spigot (of a barrel). II. **z.**, *v.tr.* to tap, draw off (beer etc.). ◆'Z~**enstreich**, *m Mil:* last post. ◆'Z~**säule**, *f* petrol/*N.Am:* gas pump.

**zappel|ig** ['tsapəliç], *adj.* fidgety, wriggly. ◆'z~**n**, *v.i. (haben)* (*Kind usw.*) to fidget, wriggle.

**Zar** [tsɑːr], *m -en/-en* tsar.

**zart** [tsɑːrt], *adj.* tender (meat etc.); soft (skin, *Fig:* sound, colour etc.); gentle (touch etc.); (*empfindlich*) delicate (child, material etc.). ◆'z~**besaitet**, *adj.* hypersensitive. ◆'Z~**heit**, *f -/no pl* tenderness; softness; delicacy.

**zärtlich** ['tsɛːrtliç], *adj.* affectionate. ◆'Z~**keit**, *f -/-en* 1. tenderness, affection. 2. *esp. pl* endearments; (*Liebkosungen*) caresses.

**Zauber** ['tsaubər], *m -s/no pl* magic; (*Bann*) spell; *Fig:* (*Reiz, Faszination*) charm (of a person). ◆'Z~**er**, *m -s/-* magician. ◆'z~**haft**, *adj.* enchanting, delightful. ◆'Z~**künstler**, *m* conjurer, magician. ◆'z~**n**, *v.* 1. *v.i. (haben)* to do magic/(*Zauberkünstler*) conjuring tricks. 2. *v.tr.* to conjure up (sth.). ◆'Z~**spruch**, *m* magic spell. ◆'Z~**stab**, *m* magic wand. ◆'Z~**trick**, *m* conjuring trick.

**zaudern** ['tsaudərn], *v.i. (haben)* to procrastinate.

**Zaum** [tsaum], *m -(e)s/ːe* bridle; *Fig:*

**sich/seinen Zorn im Z. halten,** to restrain oneself/one's anger.

**Zaun** [tsaun], *m* -(e)s/⸚e fence; *Fig:* **einen Streit vom Z. brechen,** to start a quarrel. ◆**'Z~gast,** *m* onlooker. ◆**'Z~-könig,** *m* wren. ◆**'Z~pfahl,** *m* fence-post; *Fig:* **Wink mit dem Z.,** broad hint.

**Zebra** ['tse:bra], *n* -s/-s *Z:* zebra. ◆**'Z~streifen,** *m* zebra crossing.

**Zech|e** ['tseçə], *f* -/-n **1.** (*Rechnung*) bill; *also Fig:* **die Z. bezahlen müssen,** to have to foot the bill. **2.** *Min:* (*esp.* coal) pit, mine. ◆**'z~en,** *v.i.* (*haben*) *A: & Hum:* to tipple, knock it back. ◆**'Z~er,** *m* -s/- *A: & Hum:* tippler.

**Zecke** ['tsɛkə], *f* -/-n tick.

**Zeh** [tse:], *m* -s/-en toe. ◆**'Z~e,** *f* -/-n **1.** toe. **2.** *Bot:* clove (of garlic). ◆**'Z~ennagel,** *m* toenail. ◆**'Z~enspitzen,** *fpl* **auf Z.,** on tiptoe.

**zehn** [tse:n], *num.adj.* ten. ◆**'Z~er,** *m* -s/- *F:* ten mark note. ◆**'z~fach,** *adj.* tenfold; *adv.* ten times. ◆**'z~jährig,** *adj.* ten-year-old (child etc.); ten-year (period etc.). ◆**'Z~kampf,** *m Sp:* decathlon. ◆**'z~mal,** *adv.* ten times. ◆**'z~te(r, s),** *num.adj.* tenth. ◆**'Z~tel,** *n* -s/- tenth (part).

**zehren** ['tse:rən], *v.i.* (*haben*) (*a*) **an j-s Kräften z.,** to sap s.o.'s strength; (*b*) (*Pers.*) **von Ersparnissen usw. z.,** to live on savings etc.

**Zeichen** ['tsaiçən], *n* -s/- (*a*) sign; (*Wink usw.*) signal (**zum Anfang usw.,** to start etc.); (*b*) (*Markierung*) mark; (*c*) (*Symbol*) sign (of the Zodiac, cross etc.). **II.** **'Z~-,** *comb.fm.* drawing (board, pen, materials, paper, table etc.); *Sch:* art (teacher etc.). ◆**'Z~erklärung,** *f* legend (on a map); key. ◆**'Z~setzung,** *f* -/-en punctuation. ◆**'Z~sprache,** *f* sign language. ◆**'Z~trickfilm,** *m* cartoon film.

**zeichn|en** ['tsaiçnən]. **I.** *v.* **1.** *v.tr.* (*a*) to draw (s.o., sth., a picture etc.); (*b*) (*kennz.*) to mark (laundry, trees etc.). **2.** *v.i.* (*haben*) (*a*) to draw; (*b*) *A: & Com:* to sign. **II.** **Z.,** *n* -s/*no pl* drawing. ◆**'Z~er,** *m* -s/- *Art: & Ind:* draughtsman. ◆**'Z~ung,** *f* -/-en (*a*) drawing; (*b*) (*Kennz.*) markings.

**Zeig|efinger** ['tsaigəfiŋər], *m* -s/- forefinger, index finger. ◆**'z~en,** *v.* **1.** *v.tr.* (*a*) to show; (*b*) **sich z.,** to appear; **das wird sich z.,** we shall see. **2.** *v.i.* (*haben*) to point. ◆**'Z~er,** *m* -s/- pointer; (*Uhrz.*) (watch/clock) hand. ◆**'Z~e-stock,** *m* pointer.

**Zeile** ['tsailə], *f* -/-n (*a*) line; (*b*) (*Häuserz.*) (long) row of houses. ◆**'Z~nabstand,** *m* line spacing.

**Zeisig** ['tsaiziç], *m* -s/-e siskin.

**Zeit** [tsait]. **I.** *f* -/-en time; (*a*) *no pl* **sich *dat* Z. für etwas *acc* nehmen,** to make time for sth.; **nimm/laß dir Z.,** take your time; **das hat Z.,** that can wait; (*b*) **mit der Z. gehen,** to move with the times; **in**

**der nächsten Z.,** in the near future; (*c*) (*Zeitpunkt*) **zur Z.,** at present; **in letzter Z.,** lately; **von Z. zu Z.,** from time to time. **II.** **z.,** *prep.+gen* **z. meines/seines/ihres Lebens,** in my/his/her lifetime. **III.** **'Z~-,** *comb.fm.* **1.** (*a*) time (bomb, difference etc.); (*b*) (question, problem, lack etc.) of time. **2.** *Com:* (*zeitweilig*) temporary (work etc.). ◆**'Z~alter,** *n* age, era. ◆**'Z~druck,** *m* **in Z. sein/unter Z. stehen,** to be pressed for time. ◆**'z~gemäß,** *adj.* in keeping with the period; (*modern*) up-to-date; contemporary (views), topical (theme). ◆**'Z~genosse,** *m* contemporary. ◆**'z~genössisch,** *adj.* contemporary. ◆**'Z~geschehen,** *n* **das Z.** current events. ◆**'z~ig,** *adj.* in good time; **z. aufstehen,** to get up early. ◆**'Z~lang,** *f* **eine Z.,** for a while. ◆**'z~lebens,** *adv.* all one's life. ◆**'z~lich,** *adj.* in **z~licher Reihenfolge,** in chronological order; **z. begrenzt sein,** to have a time limit. ◆**'z~los,** *adj.* timeless (beauty etc.). ◆**'Z~lupe,** *f* **in Z.,** in slow motion. ◆**'Z~lupentempo,** *n* snail's pace, crawl. ◆**'Z~not,** *f* **in Z. sein,** to be pressed for time. ◆**'Z~punkt,** *m* time; (*Augenblick*) moment. ◆**'Z~raffer,** *m* -s/- **im Z.,** speeded up. ◆**'z~raubend,** *adj.* time-consuming. ◆**'Z~rechnung,** *f* calendar. ◆**'Z~schrift,** *f* periodical; (*Illustrierte*) magazine. ◆**'Z~verschwendung,** *f* waste of time. ◆**'Z~vertreib,** *m* pastime. ◆**'z~weilig,** *adj.* temporary. ◆**'z~weise,** *adv.* at times. ◆**'Z~wort,** *n* verb. ◆**'Z~zeichen,** *n Rad:* time signal. ◆**'Z~zünder,** *m* time fuse.

**Zeitung** ['tsaituŋ], *f* -/-en newspaper, *F:* paper. ◆**'Z~shändler,** *m* newsagent.

**Zell|e** ['tsɛlə], *f* -/-n cell. ◆**'Z~kern,** *m* nucleus. ◆**'Z~stoff,** *m* cellulose.

**Zellophan** [tsɛlo'fa:n], *n* -s/*no pl* cellophane.

**Zelt** [tsɛlt], *n* -(e)s/-e tent. ◆**'Z~bahn,** *f* canvas; (*Plane*) tarpaulin. ◆**'z~en,** *v.i.* (*haben*) to camp. ◆**'Z~lager,** *n* camp. ◆**'Z~platz,** *m* camp site.

**Zement** [tse'mɛnt], *m* -(e)s/-e cement. ◆**z~ieren** [-'ti:rən], *v.tr.* to cement.

**zens|ieren** [tsɛn'zi:rən], *v.tr.* (*a*) *Sch:* to mark (work); (*b*) to censor (a book, film). ◆**Z~ur** [-'zu:r], *f* -/-en **1.** *Sch:* mark. **2.** censorship.

**Zent|imeter** ['tsɛntime:tər], *m* centimetre. ◆**'Z~ner,** *m* -s/- hundredweight.

**zentral** [tsɛn'tra:l]. **I.** *adj.* central; *adv.* **z. gelegen,** centrally situated. **II.** **Z~-,** *comb.fm.* central (committee, government etc.); *Geog:* Central (Asia etc.). ◆**Z~e,** *f* -/-n central/head office; (*Hauptquartier*) headquarters (of police etc.); *Tel:* telephone exchange. ◆**Z~heizung,** *f* central heating. ◆**z~i'sieren,** *v.tr.* to centralize (power etc.).

**zentri|fugal** [tsɛntrifu'gɑːl], *adj.* centrifugal. ◆**Z~fuge** [-'fuːgə], *f* **-/-n** *Tchn:* centrifuge.

**Zentrum** ['tsɛntrum], *n* **-s/-tren** centre; (*Stadtz.*) town/city centre, *N.Am:* downtown.

**Zepter** ['tsɛptər], *n* **-s/-** sceptre.

**zer'brech|en**, *v.tr. & i.* (*sein*) *irr.14* to break; *Fig:* (*Freundschaft usw.*) to break up. ◆**z~lich**, *adj.* fragile.

**zer'bröckeln**, *v.tr. & i.* (*sein*) to crumble.

**zer'drücken**, *v.tr.* to crush (sth.); (*zu Brei*) to mash (potatoes etc.); *F:* to crumple (clothes).

**Zeremoni|e** [tseremo'niː], *f* **-/-n** ceremony. ◆**z~ell** [-moni'ɛl]. **I.** *adj.* ceremonial, formal. **II. Z.**, *n* **-s/-e** ceremonial.

**zer'fahren**, *adj.* (*Pers.*) distracted.

**Zer'fall**, *m* **-s/**no pl disintegration; decay (of buildings, *Fig:* culture etc.). ◆**z~en. I.** *v.i.sep.irr.27* (*sein*) (*a*) to disintegrate; (*Gebäude usw.*) to fall into ruins; (*Ph:* Atomkern, *Fig:* Reich usw.) to decay; (*b*) (*sich teilen*) **in drei Kapitel z.**, to be divided into three chapters. **II.** *adj.* tumbledown; in ruins.

**zer'fetz|en**, *v.tr.* to tear (sth.) up/to pieces. ◆**z~t**, *adj.* torn (to pieces); *Cl:* tattered.

**zer'fließen**, *v.i.irr.31* (*sein*) (*Eis, Fig:* Geld) to melt (away); (*Farben*) to run, (*Konturen*) blur.

**zer'gehen**, *v.i.irr.36* (*sein*) to dissolve, (*schmelzen*) melt.

**zer'kleinern**, *v.tr.* to cut/chop up (meat etc.); to crush (rock etc.).

**zer'klüftet**, *adj.* deeply fissured (rock etc.).

**zer'knirscht**, *adj.* (*Pers.*) rueful, remorseful.

**zer'knittern**, *v.tr.* to crease (a dress).

**zer'kochen**, *v.tr. & i.* (*sein*) to overcook.

**zer'kratzen**, *v.tr.* to scratch (sth.), (*ganz*) cover (sth.) in scratches.

**zer'leg|bar**, *adj.* collapsible; **leicht z.**, easy to dismantle. ◆**z~en**, *v.tr.* to take (sth.) apart; *Cu:* to carve up (an animal etc.).

**zer'lumpt**, *adj.* ragged, tattered (clothes); (beggar etc.) in rags.

**zer'malmen**, *v.tr.* to crush (s.o., sth.).

**zer'mürb|en**, *v.tr.* to wear down (s.o., s.o.'s resistance etc.). ◆**z~end**, *adj.* wearing, trying.

**zer'platzen**, *v.i.* (*sein*) to burst.

**zer'quetschen**, *v.tr.* to squash (a fly etc.), crush (s.o.'s leg etc.).

**Zerrbild** ['tsɛrbilt], *n* distorted picture.

**zer'reiben**, *v.tr.irr.12* to crush, (*zu Pulver*) pulverize (sth.).

**zer'reißen**, *v.irr.4* **1.** *v.tr.* (*a*) to tear up (a letter etc.); (*b*) to tear (stockings etc.). **2.** *v.i.* (*sein*) to tear; (*Seil, Kette usw.*) to break.

**zerr|en** ['tsɛrən], *v.* **1.** *v.i.* (*haben*) **an etwas** *dat* **z.**, to tug at sth. **2.** *v.tr.* (*a*) to tug, drag (s.o., sth.); (*b*) **sich** *dat* **eine Sehne/einen Muskel z.**, to pull a tendon/muscle. ◆**'Z~ung**, *f Med:* pull.

**zer'rinnen**, *v.i.irr.73* (*sein*) = **zerfließen**.

**zer'rütten** [tsɛr'rytən], *v.tr.* to ruin (s.o.'s nerves etc.), wreck (a marriage etc.).

**zer'schellen**, *v.i.* (*sein*) to be dashed to pieces.

**zer'schlagen**, *v.tr.irr.85* (*a*) to break, smash (china etc.); (*b*) **sich z.**, (*Plan usw.*) to fall through; (*Hoffnungen*) to be shattered.

**zer'schmettern**, *v.tr.sep.* to smash, shatter (sth.).

**zer'schneiden**, *v.tr.sep.irr.59* to cut up (a cake etc.).

**zer'setz|en**, *v.tr.sep.* (*a*) to corrode (metal); (*Leiche*) **sich z.**, to decompose; (*b*) *Fig:* to undermine (morale etc.). ◆**Z~ung**, *f* -/no pl (*a*) corrosion; decomposition; (*b*) *Fig:* undermining.

**zer'splittern**, *v.tr. & i.* (*sein*) to splinter; (*Glas usw.*) to shatter.

**zer'springen**, *v.i.irr.19* (*sein*) to shatter.

**zer'stäub|en**, *v.tr.* to atomize, spray (a liquid, perfume etc.). ◆**Z~er**, *m* -s/- atomizer; spray.

**zer'stör|en**, *v.tr.* to destroy (sth.); to wreck (a marriage etc.). ◆**Z~er**, *m* -s/- destroyer. ◆**Z~ung**, *f* destruction.

**zer'streu|en**, *v.tr.* (*a*) to scatter, disperse (leaves, a crowd etc.); *Fig:* to dispel (fears, doubts etc.); (*Menge*) **sich z.**, to disperse; (*b*) (*ablenken*) **j-n/sich z.**, to take s.o.'s/one's mind off things; (*unterhalten*) to entertain s.o./oneself. ◆**z~t**, *adj.* (*a*) (*Pers.*) distracted; absent-minded, *F:* scatterbrained; (*b*) scattered (villages etc.). ◆**Z~theit**, *f* -/no pl absentmindedness. ◆**Z~ung**, *f* -/-en (*a*) no pl dispersal, scattering; *Fig:* dispelling; (*b*) (*Unterhaltung*) diversion; entertainment.

**zer'stückeln**, *v.tr.* to divide (sth.) up, dismember (a body).

**zer'teilen**, *v.tr.* to divide (sth.) up.

**Zertifikat** [tsɛrtifi'kɑːt], *n* **-(e)s/-e** certificate.

**zer'treten**, *v.tr.irr.105* to trample on (flowers, grass etc.).

**zer'trümmern**, *v.tr.sep.* to smash up (crockery etc.), wreck (a building etc.); to shatter (glass).

**zer'zaus|en**, *v.tr.sep.* to ruffle (hair etc.). ◆**z~t**, *adj.* dishevelled, tousled.

**Zettel** ['tsɛtəl], *m* -s/- piece/slip of paper; (*Notizz.*) note; (*Handz.*) leaflet.

**Zeug** [tsɔʏk], *n* **-(e)s/**no pl *F:* (*a*) usu. *Pej:* stuff; (*Kleider usw.*) things; (*b*) *F:* (*Unsinn*) **wirres Z. reden**, to ramble, talk incoherently; (*c*) *Fig:* **sich ins Z. legen**, to go hard at it; to do one's utmost (**für j-n**, for s.o.); (*d*) (*Anlage*) **er hat das Z. zum Arzt**, he has the makings of a doctor.

**Zeug|e** ['tsɔʏgə], *m* -n/-n witness. ◆**'z~en**, *v.* **1.** *v.tr.* to reproduce (offspring); to father (a child). **2.** *v.i.* (*haben*) *Jur:* **für/gegen j-n z.**, to give evidence for/against s.o.; (*Sache*) **von etwas** *dat* **z.**,

to testify to/show sth.
◆'Z~enaussage, f testimony.
◆'Z~enbank, f = witness box/N.Am: stand. ◆'Z~in, f -/-nen (female) witness. ◆'Z~nis, n -ses/-se (a) (Beweise) evidence; Jur: etc: testimony; Z. ablegen, to give evidence; (b) Com: testimonial; (c) Sch: report. ◆'Z~ung, f -/-en procreation, reproduction; fathering. ◆'z~ungsunfähig, adj. sterile, impotent.

Zickzack ['tsiktsak], m -s/-e zigzag; im Z. laufen/verlaufen, to zigzag.

Ziege ['tsi:gə], f -/-n Z: goat. ◆'Z~nbock, m he-/F: billy goat. ◆'Z~nkäse, m goat's milk cheese. ◆'Z~npeter, m -s/- Med: mumps.

Ziegel ['tsi:gəl], m -s/- brick; (Dachz.) tile. ◆Z~ei [-'lai], f -/-en brickworks. ◆'Z~stein, m brick.

zieh|en ['tsi:ən], v.irr. 1. v.tr. (a) to pull (sth.); Med: to extract (a tooth); to draw (a card, lottery ticket, Fig: conclusions etc.); die Blicke auf sich acc z., to attract attention; Folgen nach sich dat z., to have consequences; etwas acc ins Lächerliche z., to turn sth. into a joke; (b) (züchten) to breed (cattle, pigs etc.); (c) sich z., to run, stretch (in die Ferne, into the distance); (in die Länge) z., to go on and on; (d) to draw (a line etc.). 2. v.i. (a) (+ haben) to pull, (zerren) tug (an etwas dat, on/at sth.); an einer Pfeife/Zigarre z., to puff on a pipe/cigar; (b) (+ sein) to move, go, (marschieren) march; (umherstreifen) to wander, roam; (Vögel) to migrate; er zog zu seinen Kindern, he moved to live with his children; (c) (+ haben) impers. es zieht, there is a draught/N.Am: draft; (d) (+ haben) Cu: (Tee) to draw. ◆'Z~harmonika, f accordion. ◆'Z~ung, f -/-en draw (of a lottery).

Ziel [tsi:l]. I. n -(e)s/-e 1. (a) (Reisez.) destination; (b) Sp: finish; (c) Mil: etc: target. 2. (Zweck) aim, goal; sich etwas zum Z. setzen, to set oneself sth. as one's target. II. 'Z~-, comb.fm. (a) target (group etc.); (b) Sp: finishing (line etc.). ◆'Z~bewußt, adj. purposeful. ◆'z~en, v.i. (haben) to aim (auf + acc, at). ◆'Z~fernrohr, n telescopic sight. ◆'Z~foto, n Sp: photofinish photograph. ◆'z~los, adj. aimless. ◆'Z~scheibe, f -/-n (practice) target; Fig: (Pers.) butt. ◆'z~strebig, adj. single-minded.

ziemlich ['tsi:mliç], adj. considerable (number, effort etc.); eine z~e Strecke, quite a distance; z. kalt, quite/rather/F: pretty cold; so z. alles, more or less everything; so z. das gleiche, much the same.

Zier- ['tsi:r-], comb.fm. ornamental (fish, garden, plant etc.). ◆'Z~de, f -/-n ornament. ◆'z~en, v.tr. (a) to decorate, Lit: & Fig: adorn (sth.); Fig: (Namen

usw.) to grace (sth.); (b) sich z., to make a fuss. ◆'z~lich, adj. dainty; slight (build etc.). ◆'Z~lichkeit, f -/no pl daintiness.

Ziffer ['tsifər], f -/-n 1. numeral, digit. 2. Jur: clause, sub-section. ◆'Z~blatt, n dial (of a clock etc.).

zig [tsiç], inv.adj. F: umpteen. ◆'z~mal, adv. F: umpteen times.

Zigarette [tsiga'rɛtə], f -/-n cigarette. ◆Z~n-, comb.fm. cigarette (machine, paper, smoker etc.). ◆Z~nstummel, m cigarette end.

Zigarillo [tsiga'rilo], m & n -s/-s small cigar, cigarillo.

Zigarre [tsi'garə], f -/-n cigar.

Zigeuner(in) [tsi'gɔynər(in)], m -s/- (f -/ -nen) gipsy.

Zimmer ['tsimər]. I. n -s/- room. II. 'Z~-, comb.fm. (a) room (number, service, temperature etc.); (b) indoor (aerial etc.). ◆'Z~mädchen, n chambermaid. ◆'z~mann, m carpenter. ◆'z~n, v. 1. v.tr. to make (sth.) from wood. 2. v.i. (haben) to do carpentry, work in wood. ◆'Z~pflanze, f indoor/house plant. ◆'Z~vermittlung, f room/ accommodation agency.

zimperlich ['tsimpərliç], adj. Pej: (a) (prüde) prudish, N.Am: prissy; (b) (feige) cowardly; sei nicht so z.! don't make such a fuss/be so soft!

Zimt [tsimt], m -(e)s/-e cinnamon.

Zink [tsiŋk], n -(e)s/no pl zinc.

Zinke ['tsiŋkə], f -/-n prong; tooth (of a comb etc.).

Zinn [tsin]. I. m -(e)s/no pl 1. tin. 2. (Z~geschirr) pewter (ware). II. 'Z~-, comb.fm. (a) tin (mine, soldier etc.); (b) pewter (dish, plate etc.).

Zinnober [tsi'no:bər], m -s/- (Farbe) vermilion. ◆z~rot, adj. vermilion.

Zins [tsins], m -es/-e(n) esp. pl Fin: Z~en, interest. ◆'Z~eszins, m compound interest. ◆'z~los, adj. interest-free. ◆'Z~fuß/'Z~satz, m interest rate.

Zipfel ['tsipfəl], m -s/- corner (of a cloth etc.); end (of sausage etc.); (Spitze) tip. ◆'Z~mütze, f (long) pointed cap.

zirka ['tsirka], adv. about, approximate.

Zirkel ['tsirkəl], m -s/- pair of compasses.

Zirkul|ation [tsirkulatsi'o:n], f -/-en circulation. ◆z~ieren [-'li:rən], v.i. (haben) to circulate.

Zirkus ['tsirkus], m -/-se circus. ◆'Z~zelt, n circus tent, big top.

zisch|eln ['tsiʃəln], v.tr. & i. (haben) to whisper (sth.). ◆'z~en, v.i. (haben) to hiss; (Fett usw.) to sizzle.

Zitadelle [tsita'dɛlə], f -/-n citadel.

Zit|at [tsi'ta:t], n -(e)s/-e quotation. ◆z~ieren [-'ti:rən], v.tr. (a) to quote (s.o., sth.); (b) (vorladen) to summon (s.o.).

Zither ['tsitər], f -/-n zither.

Zitron|at [tsitro'na:t], n -(e)s/no pl candied lemon peel. ◆**Z~e** [tsi'tro:nə], *f* -/-en lemon. ◆**Z~en-**, *comb. fm.* lemon (tree, juice etc.). ◆'**Z~enlimonade**, *f* lemonade. ◆**Z~enpresse**, *f* lemon squeezer. ◆**Z~ensäure**, *f* citric acid.

**Zitrusfrucht** ['tsitrusfruxt], *f* citrus fruit.

**zitt(e)rig** ['tsit(ə)riç], *adj.* shaky; tremulous, quavering. ◆'**z~ern**, *v.i.* (*haben*) to tremble (**vor** + *dat*, with); (*vor Kälte*) to shiver; (*Gebäude*) to shake; (*Stimme*) to quaver; **um j-n, etwas** *acc* **z.**, to be very worried about s.o., sth.

**Zitze** ['tsitsə], *f* -/-n teat.

**zivil** [tsi'vi:l]. **I.** *adj.* (*a*) civil; (*nicht militärisch*) civilian (life, population etc.); (*b*) (*anständig*) reasonable (terms, prices etc.). **II. Z.**, *n* -s/*no pl* in Z., (*Soldat usw.*) in civilian/(*Polizist*) in plain clothes. **III. Z~-**, *comb.fm.* (*a*) civilian (authority, population, life etc.); (*b*) *Jur:* civil (court, law etc.). ◆**Z~courage**, *f* courage of one's convictions. ◆**Z~dienst**, *m* community service (for conscientious objectors). ◆**Z~isation** [-ilizatsi'o:n], *f* -/-en civilization. ◆**Z~isati'onskrankheiten**, *fpl* diseases of modern society. ◆**z~i'sieren**, *v.tr.* to civilize (a people etc.). ◆**Z~ist(in)** [-i'list(in)], *m* -en/en (*f* -/-nen) civilian.

**zögern** ['tsø:gərn], *v.i.* (*haben*) to hesitate; **mit etwas** *dat* **z.**, to delay sth. ◆'**z~d**, *adj.* hesitant.

**Zölibat** [tsøli'ba:t], *n* -(e)s/*no pl* celibacy.

**Zoll**[1] [tsɔl], *m* -(e)s/- *Meas:* inch. ◆'**Z~stock**, *m* folding rule.

**Zoll**[2]. **I.** *m* -s/=e **1**. (*Abgabe*) (customs) duty. **2**. *no pl* customs. **II.** '**Z~-**, *comb.fm.* customs (declaration, frontier, union etc.). ◆'**Z~abfertigung**, *f* customs clearance. ◆'**Z~amt**, *n* customs house. ◆'**Z~beamte(r)**, *m* customs officer. ◆'**Z~frei**, *adj.* duty-free. ◆'**Z~kontrolle**, *f* customs examination. ◆'**z~pflichtig**, *adj.* dutiable (goods).

**Zone** ['tso:nə], *f* -/-n zone.

**Zoo** [tso:], *m* -s/-s zoo. ◆**z~'logisch**, *adj.* zoological.

**Zopf** [tsɔpf], *m* -(e)s/=e pigtail; *F:* alter Z., antiquated view/custom.

**Zorn** [tsɔrn], *m* -(e)s/*no pl* anger. ◆'**z~ig**, *adj.* angry (**auf j-n**, with s.o.).

**zott(el)ig** ['tsɔt(ə)liç], *adj.* shaggy.

**zu** [tsu:]. **I.** *prep.* + *dat* to; **zur Stadt hin**, towards the town; **zu beiden Seiten**, on both sides; **zu Weihnachten**, at Christmas; **zum ersten Mal**, for the first time; **zu Fuß/Pferd**, on foot/horseback; **zu etwas werden**, to turn into/become sth.; **j-n zum Vorbild nehmen**, to take s.o. as a model; **nehmen Sie Milch zum Kaffee?** do you take milk with your coffee? **er kommt zum Essen**, he is coming for lunch; **ein Lappen zum Putzen**, a rag for cleaning; **was sagst du zu dem Vorschlag?** what do you say about/to the proposal? **zum halben Preis**, for half the price; **drei zu eins**, (*Chancen*) three to

one; *Sp:* (*Ergebnis*) three-one (3–1). **II.** *adv.* **1. zu alt**, too old; **zu sehr**, too much. **2.** *F:* (*geschlossen*) closed, shut.

**zu'aller'erst**, *adv.* first of all. ◆**z~'letzt**, *adv.* last of all.

**Zubehör** ['tsu:bəhø:r], *n* -(e)s/-e fittings; (*zusätzlich*) accessories.

**zubereit|en**, *v.tr.sep.* to prepare (a meal etc.). ◆'**Z~ung**, *f* -/*no pl* preparation.

'**zubring|en**, *v.tr.sep.irr.16* to spend (time, the night etc.). ◆'**Z~er**, *m* -s/- (*Z~straße*) feeder road.

**Zucchini** [tsu'ki:ni], *f* -/- courgette.

**Zucht** [tsuxt]. **I.** *f* -/-en **1**. (*a*) *no pl* (*Züchten*) Z: breeding; *Bot:* cultivation; (*b*) (*Rasse*) breed. **2**. *no pl* (*Disziplin*) discipline; **j-n in Z. halten**, to keep s.o. under control. **II.** '**Z~-**, *comb.fm.* breeding (bull, animal etc.). ◆'**Z~haus**, *n* (long-stay) prison, *N.Am:* penitentiary.

**zücht|en** ['tsyçtən], *v.tr.* to breed (animals); to grow (roses etc.); to cultivate (pearls, bacteria etc.). ◆'**Z~er**, *m* -s/- breeder; grower (of roses etc.). ◆'**z~igen**, *v.tr.* to beat, *Lit:* chastise (s.o.). ◆'**Z~igung**, *f* -/-en corporal punishment.

**zuck|en** ['tsukən], *v.tr. & i.* (*haben*) to twitch; (*Blitz, Fig: Gedanke*) to flash; **mit den Achseln z.**, to shrug one's shoulders. ◆'**Z~ung**, *f* -/-en twitch.

**zücken** ['tsykən], *v.tr.* to draw (a sword etc.); *Hum:* to whip out (one's cheque book etc.).

**Zucker** ['tsukər], *m* -s/*no pl* sugar; *Med: F:* **Z. haben**, to be diabetic. ◆'**Z~dose**, *f* sugar basin/bowl. ◆'**Z~guß**, *m* icing, *N.Am:* frosting. ◆'**z~krank**, *adj.* diabetic. ◆'**z~n**, *v.tr.* to sugar (coffee etc.). ◆'**Z~rohr**, *n* sugar cane. ◆'**Z~rübe**, *f* sugar beet. ◆'**Z~stange**, *f* stick of rock. ◆'**z~süß**, *adj.* (*a*) as sweet as sugar; (*b*) *Pej:* sugary (smile etc.). ◆'**Z~watte**, *f* candyfloss. ◆'**Z~würfel**, *m* sugar lump, lump of sugar. ◆'**Z~zange**, *f* sugar tongs.

'**zudecken**, *v.tr.sep.* to cover up (s.o., sth.).

'**zudrehen**, *v.tr.sep.* to turn off (a tap etc.).

'**zudringlich**, *adj.* pushing, pushy; **z. werden**, to make advances.

**zuei'nander**, *adv.* to one another; **z. gehören**, to belong together.

'**zuerkennen**, *v.tr.sep.irr.51* to award (a right, damages etc.) (**j-m**, to s.o.).

**zu'erst**, *adv.* (*a*) first; (*b*) (*anfangs*) at first, to start with.

'**Zufahrt**, *f* access; (*Einfahrt*) drive. ◆'**Z~sstraße**, *f* access road.

'**Zufall**, *m* coincidence. ◆'**z~en**, *v.i.sep.irr.27* (*sein*) (*a*) (*Tür usw.*) to slam shut; (*b*) **j-m z.**, (*Aufgabe usw.*) to fall to s.o. ◆'**Z~streffer**, *m* lucky hit, *F:* fluke.

'**zufällig**, *adj.* accidental; **weißt du z., wo**

er ist? do you know by any chance where he is?

'**Zuflucht,** f refuge (**vor** + dat, from). ◆'**Z~sort,** m (place of) refuge.

'**Zufluß,** m flow, supply (of water); influx (of capital etc.); (*Nebenfluß*) tributary.

**zu'folge,** prep. + dat (*laut*) according to.

**zu'frieden,** adj. content; attrib. contented (face, person etc.). ◆'**Z~heit,** f -/no pl contentment. ◆**z~stellen,** v.tr. to satisfy (s.o., s.o.'s wishes etc.); **z~stellende Antwort,** satisfactory answer.

**zufrieren,** v.i.sep.irr.32 (sein) to freeze over.

'**zufügen,** v.tr.sep. to inflict (sth.) (**j-m,** on s.o.); **j-m Leid z.,** to do s.o. harm.

'**Zufuhr,** f -/-en supply; (*Nachschub*) supplies; Meteor: influx (of cold air etc.).

'**zuführen,** v.sep. 1. v.tr. **j-m, einem Gebäude, einer Stadt usw. etwas z.,** to supply s.o., a building, town etc. with sth. 2. v.i. (*haben*) (*Straße*) **z. auf** + acc, to lead to (a town etc.).

**Zug** [tsu:k], m -(e)s/-e 1. (*Bahn*) train. 2. (*Kolonne*) column; (*Umzug*) procession; Mil: platoon. 3. (*Ziehen*) (a) pull (**nach unten usw.,** downwards etc.); (b) Orn: etc: migration. 4. (*Vorrichtung*) (bell, light etc.) pull. 5. (*Luftzug*) draught, N.Am: draft (of air/a chimney). 6. (a) (*Schluck*) gulp; **in einem Z.,** in one gulp; Fig: in one go; (b) (*Atemzug*) breath; F: **in den letzten Z~en liegen,** to be at one's last gasp; Fig: **etwas in vollen Z~en genießen,** to enjoy sth. to the full; (c) **Z. an einer Pfeife/Zigarette usw.,** puff at a pipe, cigarette etc. 7. (a) usu.pl (*Gesichtsz~e*) features; (b) (*Charakterzug*) characteristic, trait. 8. (a) (*beim Schreiben/Schwimmen*) stroke; (b) (*Spielz.*) move; Fig: **zum Z. kommen,** to get a chance. ◆'**Z~brücke,** f drawbridge. ◆'**z~ig,** adj. draughty. ◆'**Z~führer,** m (chief) train guard/N.Am: conductor. ◆'**z~kräftig,** adj. with popular/a strong appeal. ◆'**Z~luft,** f draught, N.Am: draft. ◆'**Z~maschine,** f tractor. ◆'**Z~verkehr,** m train/rail services. ◆'**Z~vogel,** m migratory bird.

'**Zugabe,** f 1. Com: free gift. 2. Mus: encore.

'**Zugang,** m (a) access (**zu** + dat, to); (b) (*Eingang*) entrance.

**zugänglich** ['tsu:gɛŋliç], adj. accessible, (*offen*) open (+ dat to); (*Pers.*) approachable.

'**zugeben,** v.tr.sep.irr.35 (a) to give (sth.) as a bonus/Com: free gift; Cu: to add (salt etc.); (b) (*gestehen*) to admit.

'**zugehen,** v.i.sep.irr.36 (sein) (a) **auf j-n, etwas** acc **z.,** to walk one to/also Fig: approach s.o., sth.; **dem Ende z.,** to draw to a close; (b) F: (*Tür usw.*) to shut; (c) v.impers. **es ging lebhaft zu,** things went with a swing.

'**zugehörig,** adj. belonging to (it); matching (colour etc.). ◆'**Z~keit,** f -/no pl

membership (**zu** + dat, of).

'**zugeknöpft,** adj. F: tight-lipped, reserved.

**Zügel** ['tsy:gəl], m -s/- rein. ◆'**z~los,** adj. unrestrained; (*unzüchtig*) licentious. ◆'**Z~losigkeit,** f -/no pl lack of restraint; licentiousness. ◆'**z~n,** v.tr. to rein in (a horse); Fig: to check, restrain (oneself, one's temper etc.).

'**Zugeständnis,** n concession (**an** + acc, to).

'**zugestehen,** v.tr.sep.irr.100 (a) **j-m ein Recht,** Com: **Rabatt usw. z.,** to grant s.o. a right, Com: discount etc.; (b) **z., daß ...,** to admit that...

**zügig** ['tsy:giç], adj. swift, rapid.

**zu'gleich,** adv. at the same time.

'**zugreifen,** v.i.sep.irr.43 (*haben*) (a) (*sich festhalten*) to grab hold; (b) (*bei einem Angebot*) to jump at it; (*beim Essen*) **bitte greifen Sie zu,** please help yourself.

**zu'grunde,** adv. (a) **z. gehen,** (*Pers.*) to be ruined; (*sterben*) to die; **eine Firma usw. z. richten,** to ruin a firm etc.; (b) **etwas** dat **z. liegen,** to be the basis of sth.

**zu'gunsten,** prep. + gen in favour of.

**zu'gute,** adv. **j-m etwas z. halten,** to make s.o. due allowance for sth.; **j-m, etwas** dat **z. kommen,** to prove beneficial to/benefit s.o., sth.

'**zuhalten,** v.sep.irr.45 1. v.tr. to keep (sth.) shut; **sich** dat **die Nase z.,** to hold one's nose. 2. v.i. (*haben*) **auf etwas** acc **z.,** to make for sth.

'**Zuhälter,** m -s/- pimp.

**Zuhause** [tsu'hauzə], n -s/no pl home.

**Zu'hilfenahme,** f -/no pl use (as an aid); **unter Z. von** + dat, with the aid of.

'**zuhör|en,** v.i.sep. (*haben*) to listen (**j-m, etwas** dat, to s.o., sth.). ◆'**Z~er,** m listener. ◆'**Z~erschaft,** f -/no pl audience.

'**zujubeln,** v.i.sep. (*haben*) **j-m z.,** to cheer s.o.

'**zukleben,** v.tr.sep. to seal (a letter etc.).

'**zuknöpfen,** v.tr.sep. to button up (a coat etc.).

'**zukommen,** v.i.sep.irr.53 (*sein*) (a) **auf j-n z.,** to come towards/approach s.o.; **die Dinge auf sich** acc **z. lassen,** to take things as they come; (b) **j-m etwas z. lassen,** to send s.o. sth.; (c) (*gebühren*) **j-m z.,** to be befitting for s.o.

**Zukunft** ['tsu:kunft], f -/no pl future. ◆'**Z~saussichten,** fpl fears/prospects for the future. ◆'**Z~smusik,** f F: pie in the sky. ◆'**z~sweisend,** adj. forward-looking.

'**zukünftig,** adj. future; adv. in future.

'**Zulage,** f (additional) allowance, bonus.

'**zulass|en,** v.tr.sep.irr.57 (a) to allow, permit (sth.); (*dulden*) to tolerate (injustice etc.); (b) to admit, accept (s.o.) (**als Mitglied usw.,** as a member etc.); to license, register (a motor vehicle, s.o. as a doctor etc.); (c) F: to leave (a window etc.)

shut. **◆'Z~ung**, *f* admission (**zum Studium usw.**, to follow a course etc.); authorization, licensing; *Aut:* registration.

**'zulässig**, *adj.* permissible.

**'Zulauf**, *m* **großen Z. haben**, to be very popular. **◆'z~en**, *v.i.irr.58 (sein) (a)* **z. auf** + *acc*, (*Pers.*) to run towards (s.o., sth.); (*Straße, Weg*) to lead to (sth.); (*b*) **die Katze ist uns zugelaufen**, the cat just came to us/adopted us; (*c*) **spitz z.**, to end in a point.

**zulegen**, *v.sep. F:* **1.** *v.tr.* **sich** *dat* **ein Auto usw. z.**, to get oneself a car etc. **2.** *v.i.* (**haben**) to get moving.

**zu'leide**, *adv.* **j-m etwas z. tun**, to harm/hurt s.o.

**zuleiten**, *v.tr.sep.* (*a*) to supply (water, electricity etc.) (**einer Fabrik usw.**, to a factory etc.); (*b*) to pass on (a message etc.) (**j-m**, to s.o.).

**zu'letzt**, *adv.* (*a*) last; (*b*) (*schließlich*) finally; (*c*) **nicht z. wegen, weil ...**, not least because ...

**zu'liebe**, *adv.* **ich tat es ihm z.**, I did it for his sake.

**zum** [tsum], *prep.* = **zu dem**.

**zumachen**, *v.sep.* **1.** *v.tr.* to shut, close (a door etc.); to do up (a coat etc.). **2.** *v.i.* (**haben**) to shut.

**zu'mal**, *conj.* especially as.

**zu'meist**, *adv.* mostly, mainly.

**zu'mindest**, *adv.* at least.

**zumut|bar** ['tsu:mu:tba:r], *adj.* reasonable (load etc.). **◆z~e** [tsu'mu:tə], *adv.* **ihm ist traurig z.**, he feels sad. **◆z~en** ['tsu:mu:tən], *v.tr.sep.* **j-m etwas z.**, to expect/ask sth. of s.o.; **sich** *dat* **zuviel z.**, to take on too much. **◆'Z~ung**, *f -/no pl* (unreasonable) demand.

**zu'nächst**, *adv.* at first.

**'Zunahme**, *f -/-n* increase (*gen/*an + *dat*, in).

**'Zuname**, *m* surname.

**zünd|en** ['tsyndən], *v.tr. & i.* (**haben**) to ignite; *Fig:* **eine z~ende Rede**, a rousing speech. **◆'Z~er**, *m -s/-* fuse, detonator. **◆'Z~holz**, *n* match. **◆'Z~kerze**, *f* sparking plug. **◆'Z~schlüssel**, *m* ignition key. **◆'Z~schnur**, *f* fuse. **◆'Z~ung**, *f -/-en* ignition.

**'zunehmen**, *v.i.sep.irr.69* (**haben**) (*a*) to increase (**an** + *dat*, in); (*b*) (*Pers.*) (**an Gewicht**) **z.**, to put on weight. **◆z~d**, *adj.* (*a*) increasing (influence etc.); **z~der Mond**, waxing moon; (*b*) *adv.* increasingly.

**'zuneig|en**, *v.i.sep.* (**haben**) **einer Ansicht usw. z.**, to incline to an opinion etc. **◆'Z~ung**, *f* fondness, affection.

**zünftig** ['tsynftiç], *adj.* professional; *F:* (*richtig*) proper, pukkah; sound (thrashing etc.).

**Zunge** ['tsuŋə], *f -/-n* tongue. **◆'Z~nbrecher**, *m* tongue-twister. **◆'z~nfertig**, *adj.* glib.

**zu'nichte**, *adv.* **Pläne usw. z. machen**, to ruin plans etc.

**zu'nutze**, *adv.* **sich** *dat* **etwas z. machen**, to take advantage of/(*verwenden*) make use of sth.

**zu'oberst**, *adv.* at the top; on top.

**'zupacken**, *v.i.sep.* (**haben**) (*a*) to grab hold; (*b*) (*arbeiten*) to get/knuckle down to it.

**zupf|en** ['tsupfən], *v.tr.* to pluck (eyebrows, *Mus:* a string etc.); to pull up (weeds etc.). **◆'Z~instrument**, *n* plucked instrument.

**zur** [tsu:r], *prep.* = **zu der**.

**'zurechnungsfähig**, *adj.* of sound mind, sane.

**zurecht|finden** [tsu'rɛçtfindən], *v.refl.sep. irr.9* **sich z.**, to find one's way about/around. **◆z~kommen**, *v.i.sep.irr.53* (*sein*) (*a*) to cope (**mit j-m, etwas** *dat*, with s.o., sth.); (*b*) (*rechtzeitig*) (**gerade noch**) **z.**, to arrive just in time. **◆z~legen**, *v.tr.sep.* to put/place (sth.) ready. **◆z~machen**, *v.tr.sep. F:* to get (a meal, bed etc.) ready, prepare (a salad etc.); **sich z.**, to get oneself ready. **◆z~weisen**, *v.tr.sep.irr.70* to reprimand (s.o.). **◆'Z~weisung**, *f -/-en* reprimand.

**'zureden**, *v.i.sep.* (**haben**) **j-m z.**, to try to persuade s.o.

**'zurichten**, *v.tr.sep.* (*a*) to prepare (a meal etc.); (*b*) **j-n übel z.**, to beat s.o. up.

**zurück** [tsu'ryk]. **I.** *adv.* (*a*) back; (*b*) *F:* (*im Rückstand*) behind. **II.** **Z.**, *n* **es gibt kein Z.**, there is no going back. **◆z~behalten**, *v.tr.sep.irr.45* to keep back (money etc.). **◆z~bekommen**, *v.tr.sep.irr.53* to get (sth.) back. **◆z~bleiben**, *v.i.sep.irr.12* (*sein*) to stay behind; **hinter j-m z.**, to fall/drop behind s.o.; **hinter den Erwartungen z.**, not to come up to expectations. **◆z~bringen**, *v.tr.sep.irr.16* to take/bring (sth.) back. **◆z~drängen**, *v.tr.sep.* to push/force back (s.o., sth.). **◆z~erobern**, *v.tr.sep.* to recapture (a town etc.). **◆z~erstatten**, *v.tr.sep.* to refund (s.o.'s expenses). **◆z~fahren**, *v.sep.irr.26* **1.** *v.i.* (*sein*) to return. **2.** *v.tr.* to drive (s.o., a car etc.) back. **◆z~fallen**, *v.i.sep.irr.27* (*sein*) to fall back/(*Sp: Läufer usw.*) behind; *Fig:* **in alte Gewohnheiten usw. z.**, to relapse into old habits etc. **◆z~finden**, *v.i.sep.irr.9* (**haben**) to find one's way back. **◆z~fordern**, *v.tr.sep.* to ask for (sth.) back, reclaim (one's property). **◆z~führen**, *v.tr.sep.* (*a*) to lead/take (s.o.) back; (*b*) **etwas auf seinen Ursprung z.**, to trace sth. back to its origins. **◆z~geben**, *v.tr.sep.irr.35* to return (sth.), give (sth.) back. **◆z~geblieben**, *adj.* backward; **geistig z.**, mentally retarded. **◆z~gehen**, *v.i.sep.irr.36* (*sein*) (*a*) to go back; *Fig:* (*herstammen*) **es geht auf seine Kindheit**

**zurück**, it goes back to his childhood; (b) (*abnehmen*) to go down; (*Einnahmen usw.*) to fall off. ◆**z~gezogen**, *adj.* secluded, retired; *adv.* z. leben, to live a secluded existence. ◆**z~halten**, *v.i.sep.irr.45* 1. *v.tr.* to hold (s.o., sth.) back; to keep (anger etc.) in check, restrain (feelings); **sich z.**, to restrain oneself. 2. *v.i.* (*haben*) **mit etwas** *dat* **z.**, to withhold sth. ◆**z~haltend**, *adj.* restrained; (*reserviert*) reserved. ◆**Z~haltung**, *f* -/*no pl* restraint; reserve. ◆**z~kehren**, *v.i.sep.* (*sein*) to return. ◆**z~kommen**, *v.i. sep.irr.53* (*sein*) to come/get back; to return (**nach Hause**, home). ◆**z~lassen**, *v.tr.sep.irr.57* to leave (s.o., sth.) behind. ◆**z~legen**, *v.tr.sep.* (*a*) to put (sth.) back; (b) (*beiseitelegen*) to put aside, put by (money); (c) (*hinter sich bringen*) to cover (a distance etc.). ◆**z~liegen**, *v.i. sep.irr.62* (*haben*) (*a*) *Sp:* **zehn Sekunden usw. z.**, to be ten seconds etc. behind; (b) **das liegt schon lange zurück**, that was a long time ago. ◆**z~nehmen**, *v.tr.sep.irr.69* to take back (goods, a remark etc.); to withdraw (an offer etc.). ◆**z~rufen**, *v.tr.sep.irr.74* 1. *v.tr.* to call (s.o.) back; **j-m etwas ins Gedächtnis z.**, to remind s.o. of sth. 2. *v.i.* (*haben*) *Tel:* to call back. ◆**z~schrecken**, *v.i.sep.* (*sein*) to start back, recoil (in fright); to flinch (**vor** + *dat*, from); **er schreckt vor nichts zurück**, he stops at nothing. ◆**z~setzen**, *v.tr.sep.* (*a*) to put (sth.) back (in its place); to move (a table etc.) back; *Aut:* to reverse (a car etc.); (b) (*benachteiligen*) to place (s.o.) at a disadvantage. ◆**z~stehen**, *v.i. sep.irr.100* (*haben*) (*a*) (*Gebäude usw.*) to be set back; (b) **hinter j-m z.**, to be inferior/take second place to s.o. ◆**z~stellen**, *v.tr.sep.* (*a*) to put (sth.) back (in its place); (b) (*reservieren*) to reserve (an article etc.); (c) (*verschieben*) to postpone (plans etc.); (*beiseite legen*) to set (personal wishes etc.) on one side. ◆**z~treten**, *v.i.sep.irr.105* (*sein*) (*a*) (*Pers.*) to step back (**von** + *dat*, from); (b) (**von seinem Amt**) z., to resign (one's post); (c) *Fig:* **hinter etwas** *dat* **z.**, to take second place to sth. ◆**z~weichen**, *v.i.sep.irr.86* (*sein*) to step/(*ängstlich*) shrink back; (*Hochwasser usw.*) to recede. ◆**z~weisen**, *v.tr.sep.irr.70* (*a*) to turn (s.o.) away/(*an der Grenze usw.*) back; (b) (*ablehnen*) to refuse, reject (an offer, a request etc.). ◆**z~zahlen**, *v.tr.sep.* to pay back (an amount); to repay (a loan etc.). ◆**Z~zahlung**, *f* repayment. ◆**z~ziehen**, *v.tr.sep.irr.113* (*a*) to pull (sth.) back; to withdraw (one's hand etc., *Mil:* troops); **sich z.**, to withdraw; to retire (**vom Geschäft**, from business); *Mil:* to retreat; (b) (*rückgängig machen*) to withdraw (a statement, an offer, application etc.); *Jur:* to drop (an action etc.).

'**Zuruf**, *m* shout. ◆'**z~en**, *v.tr.sep.irr.74* **j-m etwas z.**, to shout sth. to s.o.

**Zusage** ['tsuːzaːgə], *f* -/-*n* (*a*) acceptance (of an invitation); (b) (*Versprechen*) promise. ◆'**z~n**, *v.sep.* 1. *v.tr.* **j-m Hilfe usw. z.**, to promise s.o. help etc. 2. *v.i.* (*haben*) (*a*) to accept (an/the invitation); (b) (*gefallen*) **j-m z.**, to appeal to/(*Klima usw.*) agree with s.o.

**zusammen** [tsuˈzamən], *adv.* (*a*) together; (b) (*insgesamt*) in all, altogether; **das macht z. 10 Mark**, altogether that makes 10 marks. ◆**z~arbeit**, *f* co-operation. ◆**z~arbeiten**, *v.i.sep.* (*haben*) to co-operate (**an etwas** *dat*, on sth.). ◆**z~bauen**, *v.tr.sep.* to assemble (a radio etc.). ◆**z~beißen**, *v.tr.sep.irr.4* to clench (one's teeth). ◆**z~bleiben**, *v.i.sep.irr.12* to stay together. ◆**z~brechen**, *v.i.sep.irr.14* (*sein*) (*Gerüst, Brücke, Pers. usw.*) to collapse; (*Pers., Verhandlungen usw.*) to break down; (*Verkehr*) to come to a standstill. ◆**z~bringen**, *v.tr.sep.irr.16* (*a*) to bring together, unite (people); (b) to find (money). ◆**Z~bruch**, *m* collapse, breakdown (of negotiations, a system etc.); (*Nervenz.*) (nervous) breakdown. ◆**z~fallen**, *v.i.sep.irr.27* (*sein*) (*a*) to collapse; (b) (*Pers.*) (*schwächer werden*) to become enfeebled; (c) (*gleichzeitig geschehen*) to coincide, (*zum Teil*) overlap; (*Termine*) to clash. ◆**z~fassen**, *v.tr.sep.* (*a*) (*vereinigen*) to combine, unite (clubs etc.) (**zu** + *dat*, in); (b) to summarize (a speech etc.); **z~fassend läßt sich feststellen, daß ...**, to sum up it can be said that ... ◆**Z~fassung**, *f* 1. combination. 2. summing-up, summary. ◆**z~finden**, *v.refl.sep.irr.9* **sich z.**, to come together, meet. ◆**z~fließen**, *v.i.sep.irr.31* to flow together/into one another. ◆**Z~fluß**, *m* confluence. ◆**z~fügen**, *v.tr.sep.* to join (parts) together. ◆**z~führen**, *v.tr.sep.* to bring (people) together. ◆**z~gehören**, *v.i.sep.* (*haben*) to belong together; (*zueinander passen*) to match, go together. ◆**z~gesetzt**, *adj. Gram:* compound (word); complex (sentence). ◆**Z~halt**, *m* cohesion; *Fig:* solidarity. ◆**z~halten**, *v.i.sep.irr.45* 1. *v.tr.* to hold (sth.) together, keep (people) together. 2. *v.i.* (*haben*) (*Freunde usw.*) to stick together. ◆**Z~hang**, *m* connection; (*im Text*) context; **der Satz ist aus dem Z. gerissen**, the sentence is out of context. ◆**z~hängen**, *v.i.sep.irr.46* (*haben*) to be connected. ◆**z~hanglos**, *adj.* disjointed; incoherent. ◆**z~klappbar**, *adj.* collapsible. ◆**z~klappen**, *v.sep.* 1. *v.tr.* to fold up (a chair etc.), close (a knife etc.). 2. *v.i.* (*sein*) *F:* (*Pers.*) to crack up. ◆**z~kommen**, *v.i.sep.irr.53* (*sein*) (*Freunde usw.*) to meet, get together. ◆**Z~kunft**, *f* -/-*e* meeting, get-together. ◆**z~laufen**, *v.i.sep.irr.58* (*sein*)

(*Menschen*) to come together, gather; (*Ströme, Linien usw.*) to meet, (*Straßen*) converge. ◆**z~legen**, *v.sep.* **1.** *v.tr.* (*vereinigen*) to combine (classes etc.), amalgamate (businesses etc.); to pool (money, ideas etc.). **2.** *v.i.* (*haben*) to club together. ◆**z~nehmen**, *v.tr.sep.irr.69* (*a*) to collect (one's thoughts); to summon up (strength, courage); (*b*) **sich z.**, to pull oneself together; (*c*) **alles zusammengenommen**, all things considered. ◆**z~passen**, *v.i.sep.* (*haben*) to match, go together; (*Menschen*) to suit one another. ◆**z~prallen**, *v.i.sep.* (*sein*) to collide, crash. ◆**z~reißen**, *v.refl.sep.irr.4* F: **sich z.**, to pull oneself together. ◆**z~schlagen**, *v.tr.sep.irr.85* F: to smash up (furniture etc.), beat (s.o.) up. ◆**z~schließen**, *v.refl.sep.irr.31* **sich z.**, to join forces; (*Firmen*) to merge. ◆**Z~schluß**, *m* amalgamation; *Com:* merger; *Pol:* union. ◆**z~schreiben**, *v.tr.sep.irr.12* to write (sth.) in one word. ◆**z~schrumpfen**, *v.i.sep.* (*sein*) to shrivel up. ◆**Z~sein**, *n* get-together. ◆**z~setzen**, *v.tr.sep.* (*a*) to put together, assemble (parts, a model etc.), **sich z. aus** + *dat*, to be composed/made up of (sth.); (*b*) (*Pers.*) **sich z.**, (*sich treffen*) to get together, meet. ◆**Z~setzung**, *f -/-en* **1.** assembly. **2.** composition. ◆**Z~spiel**, *n* (*a*) *Sp: etc:* teamwork; (*b*) interaction (of forces etc.). ◆**z~stellen**, *v.tr.sep.* to put together (sth.); to assemble (a collection etc.); to compile (a list, book etc.). ◆**Z~stellung**, *f* putting together; assembly; compilation. ◆**Z~stoß**, *m* **1.** *Aut: etc:* crash, collision. **2.** F: (*Auseinandersetzung*) clash. ◆**z~stoßen**, *v.i.sep.irr.103* (*sein*) (*Autos usw.*) to collide. ◆**z~stürzen**, *v.i.sep.* (*sein*) to collapse. ◆**z~tragen**, *v.tr.sep.irr.85* to collect (material etc.). ◆**z~treffen**, *v.i.sep.irr.104* (*a*) **mit alten Bekannten usw. z.**, to meet up with old friends etc.; (*b*) (*Ereignisse usw.*) to coincide. ◆**z~treten**, *v.i.sep.irr.105* (*sein*) to assemble, meet. ◆**z~wachsen**, *v.i.sep.irr.107* (*sein*) to grow together; (*Wunde*) to heal. ◆**z~zählen**, *v.tr.sep.* to add up (figures etc.). ◆**z~ziehen**, *v.sep.irr.113* **1.** *v.tr.* (*a*) to pull/draw (a loop etc.) together; **sich z.**, to contract, (*schrumpfen*) shrink; (*b*) to add up (figures etc.); to concentrate, mass (troops etc.). **2.** *v.i.* (*sein*) F: **mit j-m z.**, to move in with s.o. ◆**z~zucken**, *v.i.sep.* (*sein*) to give a start; (*vor Schmerz*) to wince.

'**Zusatz. I.** *m* (*a*) addition; (*b*) (*also* **Z~stoff** *m*) additive. **II.** '**Z~**-, *comb.fm.* additional (clause etc.); supplementary (agreement, insurance etc.).

**zusätzlich** ['tsuːzɛtsliç], *adj.* additional, extra; *adv.* in addition.

'**zuschaue**|**n**, *v.i.sep.* (*haben*) = **zusehen**. ◆'**Z~r(in)**, *m -s/-* (*f -/-nen*) onlooker, (*Beistehender*) bystander; *Sp: etc:* spectator; *Th: etc:* member of the audience. ◆'**Z~rraum**, *m* auditorium.

'**zuschicken**, *v.tr.sep.* to send (a letter, goods etc.) (j-m, to s.o.).

'**zuschießen**, *v.sep.irr.31* **1.** *v.i.* (*sein*) **auf j-n z.**, to shoot/rush towards s.o. **2.** *v.tr.* (*a*) F: to contribute (money); (*b*) Fb: to shoot, pass (the ball) (j-m, to s.o.).

'**Zuschlag** *m* **1.** (*Gebühr*) surcharge; *Rail: etc:* supplementary fare, supplement. **2.** (*zum Gehalt usw.*) bonus. **3.** (*bei Versteigerungen*) knocking down. ◆'**z~en**, *v.sep.irr.85* **1.** *v.tr.* (*a*) to shut, (*mit Wucht*) slam shut (a door, book etc.); (*mit Nägeln*) to nail down (a crate etc.); (*b*) *Sp:* to hit (the ball) (j-m, to s.o.). **2.** *v.i.* (*haben*) (*a*) to hit out; (*Feind, Schicksal usw.*) to strike; (*b*) (*Tür usw.*) to slam shut. ◆'**Z~karte**, *f* supplementary fare ticket. ◆'**z~pflichtig**, *adj.* subject to a supplement.

'**zuschließen**, *v.tr.sep.irr.31* to lock.

'**zuschnappen**, *v.i.sep.* (*a*) (*sein*) to snap/click shut; (*b*) (*haben*) (*Hund*) to snap viciously.

'**zuschneiden**, *v.tr.sep.irr.59* to cut (timber etc.) to size; to cut out (a suit, dress etc.); *Fig:* **auf etwas** *acc* **zugeschnitten**, tailormade for sth.

'**zuschnüren**, *v.tr.sep.* to tie up (a parcel, shoes etc.).

'**zuschrauben**, *v.tr.sep.* to screw (a lid etc.) tight, screw on the lid of (a bottle etc.).

'**zuschreiben**, *v.tr.sep.irr.12* **j-m etwas** *acc* **z.**, to attribute sth. to s.o.; **das hast du dir selbst zuzuschreiben**, you only have yourself to blame for that.

'**Zuschrift**, *f* reply (**auf eine Annonce usw.**, to an advertisement etc.).

**zu'schulden**, *adv.* **sich** *dat* **etwas z. kommen lassen**, to do wrong, F: blot one's copybook.

'**Zuschuß**, *m* allowance; (**staatlicher**) **Z.**, subsidy.

'**zuschütten**, *v.tr.sep.* (*a*) to fill in (a ditch etc.); (*b*) F: to add (water etc.).

'**zusehen**, *v.i.sep.irr.92* (*haben*) (*a*) to look on, watch; **bei genauerem/näherem Z.**, on closer examination; (*b*) (*aufpassen*) zu, **daß ...**, to see/take care that ... ◆'**z~ds**, *adv.* noticeably, visibly.

'**zusein**, *v.i.sep.irr.93* (*sein*) to be shut/closed.

'**zusetzen**, *v.sep.* **1.** *v.tr.* (*a*) to add (sth.) (**einem Getränk usw.**, to a drink etc.); (*b*) (*einbüßen*) to lose (one's money). **2.** *v.i.* (*haben*) **j-m z.**, (i) (*Pers.*) to go on at s.o.; (*plagen*) to pester/plague s.o.; (ii) (*Krankheit*) to take it out of s.o.; (*j-s Tod usw.*) to affect (s.o.) deeply.

'**zusicher**|**n**, *v.tr.sep.* **j-m etwas z.**, to promise s.o. sth. ◆'**Z~ung**, *f* promise, guarantee.

'**zuspielen**, *v.tr.sep. Sp:* to pass (the ball) (j-m, to s.o.).

'**zuspitzen**, *v.tr.sep.* to sharpen (sth.); **sich z.**, to come to a point; *Fig: (Lage usw.)* to worsen, get critical.

'**zusprechen**, *v.tr. & i.sep.irr.14 (haben)* (a) **j-m Mut/Trost z.**, to give s.o. (words of) encouragement/comfort; (b) *(genießen)* **dem Wein/Essen z.**, to do justice to the wine/food.

'**Zuspruch**, *m* 1. words (*esp.* of encouragement). 2. **großen Z. haben**, to be very popular.

'**Zustand**, *m (a) no pl* condition, state; (b) *usu.pl* **unhaltbare Z~e**, intolerable conditions/state of affairs. ◆'**z~e** [tsu'ʃtandə], *adv.* **etwas z. bringen**, to bring about/manage sth.; **z. kommen**, to come about, *(stattfinden)* take place.

'**zuständig**, *adj.* relevant, competent (authority etc.); *(verantwortlich)* responsible. ◆'**Z~keit**, *f -/no pl* competence; responsibility.

**zu'statten**, *adv.* **j-m z. kommen**, to be useful/an advantage for s.o.

'**zustehen**, *v.i.sep.irr.100 (haben)* **das Geld steht ihm zu**, he is entitled to the money.

'**zustell|en**, *v.tr.sep. (a) (versperren)* to block (a doorway etc.); (b) to deliver (mail etc.). ◆'**Z~ung**, *f* delivery.

'**zustimm|en**, *v.i.sep. (haben)* **(etwas dat) z.**, to agree, *(einwilligen)* consent (to sth.). ◆'**Z~ung**, *f* agreement; consent.

'**zustoßen**, *v.i.sep.irr.103 (sein)* to happen; **hoffentlich ist ihr nichts zugestoßen**, I hope nothing has happened to her.

'**Zustrom**, *m* stream (of visitors, *Meteor:* warm air etc.).

**zu'tage**, *adv.* **z. treten**, to come to light, be revealed.

'**Zutat**, *f usu.pl* **Z~en**, *Cu: etc:* ingredients.

'**zuteilen**, *v.tr.sep.* to allot, allocate (sth.) (j-m, to s.o.).

**zu'tiefst**, *adv.* extremely, deeply.

'**zutragen**, *v.tr.sep.irr.42 (a)* **j-m etwas** *acc* **z.**, to take/*(erzählen)* report sth. to s.o.; (b) *Lit:* **sich z.**, to occur.

'**zuträglich**, *adj.* wholesome (food); beneficial (j-m, etwas *dat*, to s.o.).

'**zutrau|en. I.** *v.tr.sep.* **j-m etwas z.**, to believe s.o. capable of sth.; **dem ist alles zuzutrauen!** I wouldn't put anything past him! **II. Z.**, *n -s/no pl* confidence (zu j-m, in s.o.). ◆'**z~lich**, *adj.* trusting (child etc.); friendly (animal).

'**zutreffen**, *v.i.sep.irr.104 (haben)* to be correct; **z. auf** + *acc*, to apply to (s.o., sth.). ◆'**z~d**, *adj.* correct; applicable (**auf** + *acc*, to).

'**zutreten**, *v.i.sep.irr.105 (sein)* **auf j-n z.**, to approach, come up to s.o.

'**zutrinken**, *v.i.sep.irr.96* **j-m z.**, to raise one's glass to s.o.

'**Zutritt**, *m* admittance, admission.

'**Zutun**, *n* **es geschah ohne mein Z.**, I had no hand in it.

**zu'unterst**, *adv.* (right) at the bottom.

'**zuverlässig**, *adj.* reliable, dependable. ◆'**Z~keit**, *f -/no pl* reliability.

'**Zuversicht**, *f -/no pl* confidence, optimism. ◆'**z~lich**, *adj.* confident, optimistic.

**zu'viel**, *indef.pron.* too much.

**zu'vor**, *adv.* before; *(erst einmal)* first. ◆**z~kommen**, *v.i.sep.irr.53 (sein)* **j-m z.**, to forestall s.o.; to get in first (before s.o.). ◆**z~kommend**, *adj.* obliging; *(hilfsbereit)* helpful, thoughtful.

'**Zuwachs**, *m -es/⁼e* increase (**an Macht usw.**, in power etc.); growth (**an Bevölkerung usw.**, of population etc.); *Hum:* **Meyers haben Z. bekommen**, the Meyers have had an addition to the family. ◆'**z~en**, *v.i.sep.irr.107 (sein) (a) (Wunde)* to heal; (b) **mit Efeu usw. zugewachsen**, overgrown with ivy etc.

'**Zuwander|er**, *m -s/-* immigrant. ◆'**z~n**, *v.i. (sein)* to immigrate.

**zu'wege**, *adv.* **etwas z. bringen**, to bring sth. about, achieve sth.

**zu'weilen**, *adv.* occasionally, sometimes.

'**zuweis|en**, *v.tr.sep.irr.70* to assign (a task etc.), allocate (a room, money etc.) (j-m, to s.o.). ◆'**Z~ung**, *f -/-en* assignment, allocation.

'**zuwend|en**, *v.tr.sep.irr.94 (a)* **j-m sein Gesicht z.**, to turn one's face towards s.o.; **sich j-m z.**, to turn to s.o.; (b) *(widmen)* **seine Aufmerksamkeit j-m, etwas** *dat* **z.**, to turn one's attention to s.o., sth. ◆'**Z~ung**, *f -/-en (a)* payment, *(Beitrag)* contribution; (b) *(Fürsorge)* attention, care.

**zu'wenig**, *indef.pron.* too little.

'**zuwerfen**, *v.tr.sep.irr.110* **j-m etwas z.**, to throw/toss sth. to s.o.

**zu'wider. I.** *adv.* **j-m z. sein**, to be repugnant to s.o. **II.** *prep.* + *dat* contrary to.

'**zuwinken**, *v.i.sep. (haben)* **j-m z.**, to wave to s.o.

'**zuziehen**, *v.tr.sep.irr.113 (a)* to pull (a door) shut/(a knot) tight; to draw (curtains); (b) *Fig:* to consult, bring in (a specialist etc.); (c) **sich** *dat* **eine Krankheit z.**, to catch an illness.

**zuzüglich** ['tsu:tsy:kliç], *prep.* + *gen Com:* plus.

**Zwang** [tsvaŋ], *m -(e)s/⁼e* compulsion; **körperlicher Z.**, physical force; **wirtschaftliche Z~e**, economic pressures; **Z. auf j-n ausüben**, to put pressure on s.o.; **tu dir keinen Z. an!** *(tu es)* go ahead! feel free! ◆'**z~los**, *adj.* informal; free and easy; **z. über etwas** *acc* **sprechen**, to speak openly/freely about sth. ◆'**Z~losigkeit**, *f -/no pl* informality. ◆'**Z~s-**, *comb.fm. (a)* compulsory (loan, auction etc.); (en)forced (stay, sale etc.); (b) coercive (measure etc.). ◆'**Z~sarbeit**, *f* forced labour.

◆'Z~**sjacke**, f straitjacket. ◆'Z~s-**lage**, f predicament. ◆'z~**släufig**, adj. inevitable. ◆'z~**sweise**, adv. compulsory; (zwangsläufig) inevitably.

**zwängen** ['tsvɛŋən], v.tr. to force, squeeze (sth.).

**zwanzig** ['tsvantsiç], num.adj. twenty. ◆'z~**jährig**, adj. twenty year-old (person etc.); twenty-year (period etc.). ◆'z~**ste(r,s)**, num.adj. twentieth.

**zwar** [tsvɑːr], adv. (a) (freilich) it's true, admittedly; **es ist z. schön, aber auch teuer**, it is very beautiful of course, but also very expensive; (b) **und z.**, in fact; **... und z. sofort!** ... and I mean immediately!

**Zweck** [tsvɛk], m -(e)s/-e (a) purpose; (Ziel) aim; **zu diesem Z.**, for this purpose, with this aim (in view); **ein wohltätiger Z.**, a charitable cause; (b) (Sinn) point; **es hat keinen Z. (, das zu tun)**, there is no point (in doing that). ◆'z~**dienlich**, adj. esp. Adm: appropriate; relevant, helpful (information etc.). ◆'z~**los**, adj. pointless. ◆'z~**mäßig**, adj. appropriate; functional, suitable (for the purpose). ◆'Z~**mäßigkeit**, f -/no pl appropriateness, fitness of purpose. ◆z~s [tsvɛks], prep. + gen for the purpose of. ◆'z~**widrig**, adj. inappropriate.

**zwei** [tsvai], num.adj. two. ◆'z~**beinig**, adj. two-legged. ◆'Z~**bettzimmer**, n twin-bedded room. ◆'z~**deutig**, adj. ambiguous; **z~deutige Bemerkung**, suggestive remark. ◆'z~**dimensional**, adj. two-dimensional. ◆'z~**erlei**, adj. two sorts/kinds of (material, cheese etc.); two different (possibilities etc.); **das ist z.**, those are two different things. ◆'z~**fach**, adj. double (crime etc.); in **z~facher Ausfertigung**, in duplicate. ◆'Z~**fa'milienhaus**, n two-family house. ◆'z~**jährig**, adj. two-year-old (child, wine etc.); biennial (plant); two-year (period). ◆'Z~**kampf**, m duel. ◆'z~**mal**, adv. twice; two times. ◆'z~**motorig**, adj. twin-engined. ◆'Z~**rad**, n two-wheeler; (Fahrrad) bicycle. ◆'Z~**reiher**, m -s/- double-breasted suit. ◆'z~**schichtig**, adj. double-layered. ◆'z~**schneidig**, adj. double-edged. ◆'z~**seitig**, adj. two-sided; reversible (coat etc.); adv. on both sides; (b) bilateral (agreement etc.). ◆'Z~**sitzer**, m -s/- two-seater. ◆'z~**sprachig**, adj. bilingual. ◆'z~**spurig**, adj. two-lane (motorway etc.). ◆'z~**stellig**, adj. two-figure (number). ◆'z~**stimmig**, adj. Mus: for two voices; in two parts. ◆'z~**stöckig**, adj. two-storey. ◆z~t [tsvait], adv. **zu z.**, (i) (als Paar) as a couple; (in Gesellschaft) with someone else; (ii) (in Paaren) in twos; **wir waren zu z.**, there were two of us. ◆'Z~t-, 'z~t-, comb.fm. second (car etc.); second-(best,

largest, highest, fastest etc.). ◆'Z~**taktmotor**, m two-stroke engine. ◆'z~**te(r, s)**, adj. second; **aus z~ter Hand**, secondhand; **jeden z~ten Tag**, every other day; on alternate days. ◆'z~**teilen**, v.tr.sep. to divide (sth.) in two. ◆'z~**teilig**, adj. Cl: two-piece (dress etc.). ◆'z~**tens**, adv. secondly. ◆'z~**tklassig/'z~trangig**, adj. second-rate. ◆'z~**türig**, adj. two-door (car). ◆'Z~**twohnung**, f second home. ◆'z~**wöchig**, adj. two-week (period); a fortnight's (holiday etc.).

**Zweifel** ['tsvaifəl], m -s/- doubt; **Z. an etwas dat haben**, to be doubtful about sth.; **über etwas acc im Z. sein**, to be uncertain about sth.; **das steht außer Z.**, that is beyond doubt/question. ◆'z~**elhaft**, adj. doubtful, questionable; (anrüchig) dubious (business etc.). ◆'z~**ellos**, adv. undoubtedly; without any doubt. ◆'z~**eln**, v.i. (haben) (an etwas dat) z., to doubt (sth.). ◆'Z~**elsfall**, m doubtful case; **im Z.**, in case of doubt. ◆'z~**els'ohne**, adv. undoubtedly.

**Zweig** [tsvaik], m -(e)s/-e twig; (Trieb) shoot; (Ast) branch. ◆'Z~**geschäft**, n branch (shop). ◆'Z~**stelle**, f branch office.

**Zwerchfell** ['tsvɛrçfɛl], n diaphragm.

**Zwerg** [tsvɛrk]. I. m -(e)s/-e dwarf. II. 'Z~-, comb.fm. miniature (tree, form, dog etc.); tiny (state, school etc.).

**Zwetsch(g)e** ['tsvɛtʃ(g)ə], f -/-n damson plum.

**zwicken** ['tsvikən], v.tr. to pinch (s.o., sth.). ◆'Z~**mühle**, f **in einer Z. sein/ sitzen**, to be in a dilemma.

**Zwieback** ['tsviːbak], m -(e)s/-e rusk.

**Zwiebel** ['tsviːbəl], f -/-n onion; (Blumenz.) bulb. ◆'Z~**kuchen**, m (kind of) onion tart. ◆'Z~**schale**, f onion skin. ◆'Z~**turm**, m onion tower.

**Zwie|gespräch** ['tsviːgəʃprɛːç], n Lit: dialogue. ◆'z~**licht**, n twilight. ◆'z~**lichtig**, adj. shady (character etc.). ◆'Z~**spalt**, m (a) (inner) conflict; (b) (Uneinigkeit) discord. ◆'z~**spältig**, adj. conflicting (feelings etc.); unbalanced (character etc.). ◆'Z~**tracht**, f -/no pl Lit: discord.

**Zwilling** ['tsviliŋ], m -s/-e twin; Astr: **Z~e**, Gemini.

**zwing|en** ['tsviŋən], v.tr.irr.19 to force (s.o., oneself) (**zu etwas dat**, into sth./to do sth.). ◆'z~**end**, adj. compelling; cogent (reasons etc.); conclusive (proof etc.). ◆'Z~**er**, m -s/- kennel(s).

**zwinkern** ['tsviŋkərn], v.i. (haben) to blink, (als Zeichen) wink.

**Zwirn** [tsvirn], m -(e)s/-e (twisted) yarn; twine.

**zwischen** ['tsviʃən], prep. + dat/(mit Bewegung) acc between; (mitten) amongst, in the middle of. ◆'Z~**bemerkung**, f interjection.

◆'Z~**bilanz,** *f* interim balance. ◆'Z~**ding,** *n F:* cross. ◆'z~'**durch,** *adv.* **1.** (*a*) at intervals; (*b*) (*inzwischen*) in the meantime; in between (times). **2.** (*räumlich*) here and there. ◆'Z~**ergebnis,** *n* interim/provisional result; *Sp:* latest score. ◆'Z~**fall,** *m* incident. ◆'Z~**frage,** *f* interposed question. ◆'Z~**gericht,** *n Cu:* entrée. ◆'Z~**geschoß,** *n* mezzanine. ◆'Z~**händler,** *m* middleman. ◆'Z~**landung,** *f* intermediate landing, stopover. ◆'Z~**mahlzeit,** *f* snack (between meals). ◆'z~**menschlich,** *adj.* between people; personal (relations etc.). ◆'Z~**raum,** *m* gap; space; (*Abstand*) distance. ◆'Z~**ruf,** *m* interjection; Z~**rufe,** interruptions; *Pol:* heckling. ◆'Z~**spiel,** *n 1. Mus: & Th:* intermezzo. **2.** *Fig:* interlude. ◆'z~**staatlich,** *adj.* international. ◆'Z~**station,** *f* intermediate stop, stopover. ◆'Z~**stecker,** *m* adapter. ◆'Z~**summe,** *f* subtotal. ◆'Z~**wand,** *f* partition. ◆'Z~**zeit,** *f* interim (period); **in der Z.,** in the meantime.

**Zwist** [tsvist], *m* **-es/-e** *Lit:* strife; (*Fehde*) feud.

**zwitschern** ['tsvitʃərn], *v.i.* (*haben*) to twitter, chirp.

**Zwitter** ['tsvitər], *m* **-s/-** hermaphrodite.

**zwölf** [tsvœlf], *num.adj.* twelve. ◆'z~**te(r, s),** *num.adj.* twelfth.

**Zyklus** ['tsy:klus], *m* **-/-klen** cycle.

**Zylind|er** [tsi'lindər], *m* **-s/-** **1.** *Tchn: etc:* cylinder. **2.** *Cl:* (*also* Z~**erhut** *m*) top hat. ◆z~**risch,** *adj.* cylindrical.

**Zyn|iker** ['tsy:nikər], *m* **-s/-** cynic. ◆'z~**isch,** *adj.* cynical. ◆Z~**ismus** [tsy'nismus] *m* **-/no pl** cynicism.

**Zyp|ern** ['tsy:pərn]. *Pr.n.n* **-s.** Cyprus. ◆Z~**riote** [tsypri'o:tə], *m* **-n/-n** Cypriot. ◆z~**ri'otisch,** *adj.* Cypriot.

**Zypresse** [tsy'prɛsə], *f* **-/-n** cypress.

**Zyste** ['tsystə], *f* **-/-n** cyst.

# part 2

# GRAMMATISCHE HINWEISE

## 1. Plural der Substantive

(1) **Allgemeine Regel**. In der Regel wird der Plural eines Substantivs durch Anhängen von -s geformt, z.B. cat, cats; table, tables.

(2) Substantive mit den Endungen -s, -sh, -ch und -x bilden den Plural durch Anhängen von -es, z.B. glass, glasses; brush, brushes; church, churches; box, boxes.

(3) Die meisten Substantive, die in -o enden, formen den Plural durch Anhängen von -s, einige jedoch durch Anhängen von -es, z.B. potato, potatoes. In diesen Fällen ist die Pluralform im Wörterbuch angegeben.

(4) Substantive mit Endung -y ersetzen das 'y' bei der Bildung des Plurals durch -ies, außer wenn das 'y' auf einen Vokal folgt. In diesem Fall wird der Plural einfach durch Anhängen von -s gebildet, also: army, armies; fly, flies; story, stories; aber: boy, boys; storey, storeys; valley, valleys.

(5) Substantive mit Endung auf -f bilden den Plural normalerweise durch Anhängen von -s, einige jedoch verwenden die Pluralform -ves, z.B. calf, calves; knife, knives. Diese abweichenden Formen sind im Wörterbuch angegeben.

(6) Ebenfalls bei den jeweiligen Einträgen angegeben sind unregelmäßige Pluralformen wie: foot, feet; mouse, mice; child, children usw. Zur Beachtung: policeman, policemen; aber: German, Germans.

(7) Folgende Maß- und Mengenbezeichnungen erscheinen ohne Pluralform, wenn sie auf eine Zahlenangabe folgen: **dozen, hundred, hundredweight, million, stone, thousand**; also: he weighs ten stone; two dozen eggs; aber: dozens of people.

(8) **Zusammensetzungen**. Der Plural eines zusammengesetzten Substantivs wird normalerweise durch Anhängen von -s an das letzte Element der Zusammensetzung gebildet, also: ticket collector, ticket collectors; forget-me-not, forget-me-nots. Bei einigen Zusammensetzungen jedoch, insbesondere solchen, die mit **man** und **woman** beginnen, bilden beide Wortelemente den Plural: manservant, menservants; woman doctor, women doctors.

Bei einigen zusammengesetzten Substantiven erscheint nur das erste Element im Plural: father-in-law, fathers-in-law; governor-general, governors-general; commander-in-chief, commanders-in-chief.

## 2. Konjugation der Verben

(1) **Regelmäßige Verben**. Regelmäßige Verben bilden Imperfekt und Perfekt durch Anhängen von -ed an den Infinitiv, z.B.: walk, walked. Endet der Infinitiv in -e, wird lediglich -d angehängt, z.B. dance, danced. Endet der Infinitiv in -y, verändert sich die Endung für die Vergangenheitsformen in -ied, also: marry, married; try, tried. Das Partizip Präsens wird durch Anhängen von -ing gebildet: walk, walking. Endet der Infinitiv in -e, entfällt das -e: dance, dancing; Ausnahme: singe, singeing (im Gegensatz zu: sing, singing). Bei den Verben auf -ie verändert sich die Endung in -ying, also: die, dying; lie, lying.

(2) Einsilbige Verben, die auf einen Einzelkonsonanten enden, ebenso Verben, die auf einen Vokal + 1 enden, bilden die Vergangenheit und das Partizip Perfekt unter Verdopplung des Endkonsonanten, z.B.: hop, hopped; step, stepped; travel, travelled.

(3) **Unregelmäßige Verben**. Die Stammformen der hauptsächlichen unregelmäßigen Verben sind im folgenden in alphabetischer Reihenfolge zusammengefaßt. Unregelmäßige Verben sind im Text durch *irr.* gekennzeichnet.

*Zur Beachtung: (a)* **to be**: *pres.* I am; he is; we, you, they are; *p.* I, he was; we, you, they were; *Partizip Perfekt:* been; *Partizip Präsens:* being.

*(b) Modale Hilfsverben:* Diese Verben bilden weder Infinitiv noch Partizip Perfekt und werden (mit Ausnahme von **ought**) von einer Infinitivform ohne **to** gefolgt.

**can**, *p.* could (für Infinitiv wird 'to be able to' und für das Partizip Perfekt 'been able' verwendet).

**may**, *p.* might.

**must**, *(gefolgt von Infinitiv, keine Vergangenheitsform)*.

**ought**, *(gefolgt von Infinitiv, keine Vergangenheitsform)*.

**shall**, *p.* should.

**will**, *p.* would.

# Liste der englischen unregelmäßigen Verben
# List of English irregular verbs

| *Infinitive* | *Past Tense* | *Past Participle* |
|---|---|---|
| abide | abode, abided | abode, abided |
| arise | arose | arisen |
| be | was, were | been |
| bear | bore | borne |
| beat | beat | beaten |
| become | became | become |
| begin | began | begun |
| bend | bent | bent |
| beseech | besought | besought |
| bet | bet, betted | bet, betted |
| bid | bade, bid | bidden, bid |
| bind | bound | bound |
| bite | bit | bitten |
| bleed | bled | bled |
| blow | blew | blown |
| break | broke | broken |
| breed | bred | bred |
| bring | brought | brought |
| broadcast | broadcast | broadcast |
| build | built | built |
| burn | burnt, burned | burnt, burned |
| burst | burst | burst |
| buy | bought | bought |
| cast | cast | cast |
| catch | caught | caught |
| choose | chose | chosen |
| cling | clung | clung |
| come | came | come |
| cost | cost | cost |
| creep | crept | crept |
| cut | cut | cut |
| deal | dealt | dealt |
| dig | dug | dug |
| dive | dived, *N.Am:* dove | dived |
| do | did | done |
| draw | drew | drawn |
| dream | dreamed, dreamt | dreamed, dreamt |
| drink | drank | drunk |
| drive | drove | driven |
| dwell | dwelt | dwelt |
| eat | ate | eaten |
| fall | fell | fallen |
| feed | fed | fed |
| feel | felt | felt |
| fight | fought | fought |
| find | found | found |
| fling | flung | flung |
| fly | flew | flown |
| forbid | forbad(e) | forbidden |
| forecast | forecast | forecast |
| foresee | foresaw | foreseen |
| foretell | foretold | foretold |
| forget | forgot | forgotten |
| forgive | forgave | forgiven |

| | | |
|---|---|---|
| forsake | forsook | forsaken |
| freeze | froze | frozen |
| get | got | got, *N.Am:* gotten |
| give | gave | given |
| go | went | gone |
| grind | ground | ground |
| grow | grew | grown |
| hang | hung, hanged | hung, hanged |
| have | had | had |
| hear | heard | heard |
| hide | hid | hidden |
| hit | hit | hit |
| hold | held | held |
| hurt | hurt | hurt |
| keep | kept | kept |
| kneel | knelt, kneeled | knelt, kneeled |
| know | knew | known |
| lay | laid | laid |
| lead | led | led |
| lean | leant, leaned | leant, leaned |
| leap | leapt, leaped | leapt, leaped |
| learn | learnt, learned | learnt, learned |
| leave | left | left |
| lend | lent | lent |
| let | let | let |
| lie | lay | lain |
| light | lit, lighted | lit, lighted |
| lose | lost | lost |
| make | made | made |
| mean | meant | meant |
| meet | met | met |
| mow | mowed | mown, mowed |
| overcome | overcame | overcome |
| overhear | overheard | overheard |
| overtake | overtook | overtaken |
| pay | paid | paid |
| prove | proved | proved, proven |
| put | put | put |
| quit | quit, quitted | quit, quitted |
| read | read [red] | read [red] |
| rid | rid | rid |
| ride | rode | ridden |
| ring | rang | rung |
| rise | rose | risen |
| run | ran | run |
| saw | sawed | sawn, sawed |
| say | said | said |
| see | saw | seen |
| seek | sought | sought |
| sell | sold | sold |
| send | sent | sent |
| set | set | set |
| sew | sewed | sewn, sewed |
| shake | shook | shaken |
| shed | shed | shed |
| shine | shone | shone |
| shoe | shod | shod |
| shoot | shot | shot |
| show | showed | shown, showed |
| shrink | shrank | shrunk |

| shut | shut | shut |
| sing | sang | sung |
| sink | sank | sunk |
| sit | sat | sat |
| slay | slew | slain |
| sleep | slept | slept |
| slide | slid | slid |
| sling | slung | slung |
| slit | slit | slit |
| smell | smelt, smelled | smelt, smelled |
| sow | sowed | sown, sowed |
| speak | spoke | spoken |
| speed | sped, speeded | sped, speeded |
| spell | spelt, spelled | spelt, spelled |
| spend | spent | spent |
| spill | spilt, spilled | spilt, spilled |
| spin | spun | spun |
| spit | spat | spat |
| split | split | split |
| spoil | spoilt, spoiled | spoilt, spoiled |
| spread | spread | spread |
| spring | sprang | sprung |
| stand | stood | stood |
| steal | stole | stolen |
| stick | stuck | stuck |
| sting | stung | stung |
| stink | stank | stunk |
| stride | strode | stridden |
| strike | struck | struck |
| string | strung | strung |
| strive | strove | striven |
| swear | swore | sworn |
| sweep | swept | swept |
| swell | swelled | swollen, swelled |
| swim | swam | swum |
| swing | swung | swung |
| take | took | taken |
| teach | taught | taught |
| tear | tore | torn |
| tell | told | told |
| think | thought | thought |
| throw | threw | thrown |
| thrust | thrust | thrust |
| tread | trod | trodden |
| undergo | underwent | undergone |
| understand | understood | understood |
| undertake | undertook | undertaken |
| undo | undid | undone |
| upset | upset | upset |
| wake | woke | woken |
| wear | wore | worn |
| weave | wove | woven |
| weep | wept | wept |
| win | won | won |
| wind | wound | wound |
| withdraw | withdrew | withdrawn |
| withhold | withheld | withheld |
| withstand | withstood | withstood |
| wring | wrung | wrung |
| write | wrote | written |

# Englische Aussprache

Die Betonung wird durch ein Betonungszeichen ['] vor der zu betonenden Silbe angegeben, z.B. **sugar** ['sugər], **impossible** [im'pɔsibl]. Eingeklammerte Zeichen deuten auf Laute, die manchmal ausgesprochen werden und manchmal nicht.

## Vokale

| Zeichen | Beispiele | Zeichen | Beispiele |
|---------|-----------|---------|-----------|
| [æ] | bat, add | [i:] | he, sea, bee, fever, police |
| [ɑ:] | bath, cart | | |
| [ɑ̃, ɑ̃:] | ensemble | [iə] | beer, real |
| [ai] | life, fly, aisle, height | [ɔ] | lot, wasp, what |
| | | [ɔ:] | all, haul, short, saw |
| [au] | fowl, house | | |
| [e] | bet, said, bury | [ɔi] | boil, toy, loyal |
| [ɛə] | bare, air, there | [əu] | boat, low, rope, no |
| [ei] | hate, day, nail | | |
| [ə] | annoy, butter, photograph | [ʌ] | cut, son, cover, rough |
| [(ə)] | nation, ocean, reason, sudden | [u] | put, wool, would |
| [ə:] | learn, whirl, burn | [u:] | shoe, prove, too, true |
| [i] | wind, added, physics | [uə] | surely, tourist |

## Konsonanten

| Zeichen | Beispiele | Zeichen | Beispiele |
|---------|-----------|---------|-----------|
| [b] | better | [r] | red, break, hurry |
| [d] | dud | [r] | father, sailor |
| [dʒ] | rage, edge, jet, digit | [s] | sat, mouse, less |
| [f] | fat, laugh, photo | [z] | houses, fuse, buzz, zinc |
| [g] | gold, egg, rogue | [ʃ] | sham, dish, pressure, ocean, machine, nation |
| [gz] | exact | | |
| [h] | house | | |
| [j] | yet | | |
| [ʒ] | pleasure, vision | [t] | top, bat |
| [k] | cold, kick, ache | [ts] | tsar, hints |
| [ks] | except, axe, accident | [tʃ] | match, chat, rich |
| [l] | log, able | [θ] | thatch, breath, ether |
| [m] | mast, prism | | |
| [n] | nine | [ð] | that, breathe, other |
| [ŋ] | song, think | [v] | vase, have |
| [p] | part, bump | [w] | wigwam |

# A

**A, a¹** [ei], s. (der Buchstabe) A, a n.

**a²** *before a vowel* **an** [ə/ən], *indef. art.*
ein(e); **five pence a pound,** fünf Pence
das Pfund; **five pounds a head,** fünf
Pfund pro Kopf; **three times a week,**
dreimal in der Woche; **not a,** kein, keine; **what a,** was für ein(e); **he is a doctor,** er ist Arzt.

**aback** [ə'bæk], *adv.* **to be taken a.,**
überrascht/(*puzzled*) verblüfft sein.

**abandon** [ə'bændən], *v.tr.* (j-n, etwas)
verlassen; (einen Plan) aufgeben.

**abashed** [ə'bæʃt], *adj.* verlegen.

**abate** [ə'beit], *v.i.* nachlassen.

**abattoir** ['æbətwɑːr], s. Schlachthaus n.

**abbey** ['æbi], s. Abtei f.

**abbot** ['æbət], s. Abt m.

**abbreviate** [ə'briːvieit], *v.tr.* abkürzen.
◆**abbrevi'ation,** s. Abkürzung f.

**abdicate** ['æbdikeit], *v.i.* (*of king etc.*) abdanken. ◆**abdi'cation,** s. Abdankung f.

**abdomen** ['æbdəmen], s. Bauch m; (*esp.
of woman*) Unterleib m. ◆**abdominal**
[-'dɔminəl], *adj.* abdominal.

**abduct** [æb'dʌkt], *v.tr.* entführen.
◆**ab'duction,** s. Entführung f.

**aberration** [æbə'reiʃ(ə)n], s. **mental a.,**
geistige Verwirrung f; (*slip*) Versehen n.

**abet** [ə'bet], *v.tr.* **to (aid and) a. s.o.,** j-m
Beihilfe leisten.

**abeyance** [ə'beiəns], s. **in a.,** unentschieden.

**abhor** [əb'hɔːr], *v.tr.* verabscheuen.

**abide** [ə'baid], *v.irr.* **1.** *v.i.* **to a. by a
promise,** bei seinem Versprechen blei-
ben. **2.** *v.tr.* **I can't a. him,** ich kann ihn
nicht ausstehen.

**ability** [ə'biliti], s. Fähigkeit f.

**abject** ['æbdʒekt], *adj.* elend; **a. despair,**
tiefste Verzweiflung.

**ablaze** [ə'bleiz], *adv. & adj.* in Flammen.

**able** [eibl], *adj.* fähig; (*efficient*) tüchtig;
**to be a. to do sth.,** etwas tun können.
◆**able-'bodied,** *adj.* gesund; *Mil:*
tauglich. ◆**'ably,** *adv.* (*adroitly*) geschickt; (*well*) tüchtig.

**abnormal** [æb'nɔːməl], *adj.* abnorm;
(*pathological*) krankhaft; (*more than usual*)
überdurchschnittlich.

**aboard** [ə'bɔːd]. **I.** *adv.* an Bord. **II.** *prep.*
**a.** (a) **ship,** an Bord eines Schiffes; **all a.!**
alles einsteigen!

**abolish** [ə'bɔliʃ], *v.tr.* abschaffen.
◆**abo'lition,** s. Abschaffung f.

**abominable** [ə'bɔminəbl], *adj.* abscheulich.

**aborigine** [æbə'ridʒiniː], s. Ureinwohner
m.

**abortion** [ə'bɔːʃ(ə)n], s. Abtreibung f.
◆**a'bortive,** *adj.* mißlungen.

**abound** [ə'baund], *v.i.* reichlich vorhanden sein; **to a. in/with sth.,** sehr reich an
etwas *dat* sein.

**about** [ə'baut], *adv. & prep.* **1.** (*around*)
(a) um + *acc,* um ... *acc* herum; (b)
**there's something unusual a. him,** es ist
etwas Ungewöhnliches an ihm. **2.** (*of
boat*) **to go a.,** wenden; *Mil:* **a. turn!**
kehrt machen! **3.** (*approximately*) ungefähr, etwa; **he came a. three o'clock,** er
kam gegen drei Uhr. **4.** (*concerning*)
über + *acc.* **5. to be a. to do sth.,** im Begriff sein, etwas zu tun.

**above** [ə'bʌv]. **I.** *prep.* über + *dat.* **II.**
*adv.* oben; **from a.,** von oben; **a. all,** vor
allem. ◆**a'bove'board,** *adj.* ehrlich.

**abreast** [ə'brest], *adv.* Seite an Seite; **to
keep a. of developments etc.,** mit Entwicklungen usw. Schritt halten.

**abridge** [ə'bridʒ], *v.tr.* kürzen.

**abroad** [ə'brɔːd], *adv.* **to go a.,** ins Ausland fahren; **to live a.,** im Ausland wohnen.

**abrupt** [ə'brʌpt], *adj.* abrupt; (*sudden*)
plötzlich; (*of manner*) schroff; (*of drop,
ending*) jäh.

**abscess,** *pl.* **-es** ['æbses,-iz], s. Abszeß m.

**abscond** [əb'skɔnd], *v.i.* entfliehen; (*furtively*) (von zu Hause, vom Internat)
durchbrennen.

**absence** ['æbs(ə)ns], s. Abwesenheit f.
◆**absent** ['æbs(ə)nt], *adj.* abwesend; **to
be a.,** fehlen. ◆**absentee** [æbs(ə)n'tiː],
s. Abwesende(r) f(m). ◆**absen'teeism,**
s. Fernbleiben n vom Arbeitsplatz.
◆**absent-'minded,** *adj.* geistesabwe-
send.

**absolute** ['æbsəl(j)uːt], *adj.* absolut; **a.
power,** unbeschränkte Macht; **-ly,** *adv.*
völlig; **a. essential,** unbedingt notwendig; **a. fantastic!** einfach fantastisch!
(*affirmative*) **a.!** genau! ◆**absolve**
[əb'zɔlv], *v.tr.* freisprechen.

**absorb** [əb'sɔːb], *v.tr.* (a) (eine Flüssigkeit, usw.) absorbieren; (b) (einen Stoß
usw., *Fig:* Einwanderer usw.) aufnehmen; (Wissen, Eindrücke) in sich aufnehmen; (c) **to be absorbed in a book,**
in ein Buch vertieft sein. ◆**ab'sorbent,**
*adj.* absorbierend.

**abstain** [əb'stein], *v.i.* sich enthalten
(**from,** *gen*); (*from voting*) sich der
Stimme enthalten. ◆**abstemious**
[əb'stiːmiəs], *adj.* enthaltsam.
◆**abstention** [əb'stenʃ(ə)n], s. (*in voting*) Stimmenthaltung f. ◆**abstinence**
['æbstinəns], s. Enthaltsamkeit f; (*from
alcohol*) Abstinenz f.

**abstract** ['æbstrækt]. **I.** *adj.* abstrakt. **II.**
s. Abriß m.

**abstruse** [æb'struːs], *adj.* abstrus.

**absurd** [əb'sɔːd], *adj.* absurd; (*ridiculous*)
unsinnig. ◆**ab'surdity,** s. Absurdität f;
(*nonsense*) Unsinn m.

**abundant** [ə'bʌndənt], *adj.* reichlich
(vorhanden). ◆**a'bundance,** s. Reich-

tum *m* (of, an + *dat*).

**abuse. I.** *s.* [ə'bju:s]. **1.** (*practice*) Mißbrauch *m.* **2.** (*cursing*) Beschimpfung *f.* **II.** *v.tr.* [ə'bju:z]. (seine Macht, j-s Vertrauen) mißbrauchen; (j-n) mißhandeln. ◆**a'busive,** *adj.* beleidigend.

**abysmal** [ə'bizm(ə)l], *adj.* miserabel; **a. ignorance,** bodenlose Unwissenheit.

**abyss** [ə'bis], *s.* Abgrund *m.*

**academic** [ækə'demik], *adj.* akademisch; *Fig:* **a purely a. question,** eine rein theoretische Frage. ◆**academy** [ə'kædəmi], *s.* Akademie *f.*

**accelerate** [æk'seləreit], *v.tr. & i.* (einen Vorgang usw.) beschleunigen. ◆**accele'ration,** *s.* Beschleunigung *f.* ◆**ac'celerator,** *s.* Gaspedal *n.*

**accent** ['æksənt], *s.* Akzent *m.* ◆**accentuate** [æk'sentjueit], *v.tr.* betonen; (*emphasize*) hervorheben. ◆**accentu'ation,** *s.* Akzentuierung *f.*

**accept** [ək'sept], *v.* **1.** *v.tr.* (eine Einladung, ein Amt usw.) annehmen; (j-n, sein Schicksal, ein Geschenk usw.) akzeptieren; (j-n als Mitglied usw.) aufnehmen. **2.** *v.i.* zusagen. ◆**ac'ceptable,** *adj.* annehmbar. ◆**ac'ceptance,** *s.* Annahme *f.*

**access** ['ækses], *s.* Zutritt *m*; (*road, drive*) Zufahrt *f.* ◆**ac'cessible,** *adj.* (*also Fig:*) zugänglich.

**accessory** [æk'sesəri], *s.* **1.** Zusatz *m*; accessories, Zubehör *n.* **2.** *Jur:* Mitschuldige(r) *f(m).*

**accident** ['æksidənt], *s.* (*a*) Unfall *m*; (*serious*) *a.,* Unglück *n*; (*b*) (*chance*) Zufall *m*; **by a.,** zufällig. ◆**acci'dental,** *adj.* zufällig; (*by mistake*) versehentlich.

**acclaim** [ə'kleim]. **I.** *v.tr.* (j-m) zujubeln. **II.** *s.* Beifall *m.*

**acclimatize** [ə'klaimətaiz], *v.tr.* to become acclimatized, sich akklimatisieren. ◆**acclimati'zation,** *s.* Akklimatisation *f.*

**accommodate** [ə'kɔmədeit], *v.tr.* (*a*) (*assist*) (j-m) entgegenkommen; (*b*) (*put up*) (j-n) unterbringen. ◆**a'commodating,** *adj.* (of pers.) entgegenkommend. ◆**accommo'dation,** *s.* Unterkunft *f.*

**accompany** [ə'kʌmp(ə)ni], *v.tr.* begleiten. ◆**a'ccompaniment,** *s.* Begleitung *f.*

**accomplice** [ə'kʌmplis], *s.* Komplize *m,* Komplizin *f.*

**accomplish** [ə'kʌmpliʃ], *v.tr.* erzielen. ◆**a'ccomplished,** *adj.* vollendet; (*of pers.*) gewandt. ◆**a'ccomplishment,** *s.* Leistung *f.*

**accord** [ə'kɔ:d], *s.* Zustimmung *f*; **of one's own a.,** aus eigenem Antrieb. ◆**a'ccordance,** *s.* **in a. with,** gemäß + *dat.* ◆**a'ccording,** *adv.* **a. to,** laut + *dat*; **-ly,** *adv.* **to act a.,** entsprechend handeln.

**accordion** [ə'kɔ:diən], *s.* Akkordeon *n.*

**accost** [ə'kɔst], *v.tr.* (j-n) ansprechen.

**account** [ə'kaunt]. **I.** *s.* **1.** (*a*) (*with bank,* firm*)* Konto *n*; **the accounts (of a firm),** die Bücher *npl* (einer Firma); (*b*) (*invoice*) Rechnung *f.* **2. of no a.,** ohne Bedeutung; **to take sth. into a.,** etwas berücksichtigen; **on a. of,** wegen + *gen*; **on his a.,** seinetwegen; **on no/not on any a.,** keinesfalls. **3.** (*description*) Beschreibung *f*; (*report*) Bericht *m*; **by all accounts,** nach allem, was man hört. **II.** *v.i.* **to a. for sth.,** für etwas acc Rechenschaft ablegen; (*explain*) etwas erklären. ◆**a'ccountable,** *adj.* verantwortlich (**for,** für + *acc*; **to,** gegenüber + *dat*). ◆**a'ccountant,** *s.* Buchhalter *m*; (**chartered**) **a.,** Wirtschaftsprüfer *m.*

**accumulate** [ə'kju:mjuleit], *v.* **1.** *v.tr.* (*collect*) ansammeln; (*amass*) (Geld, Vorräte) anhäufen. **2.** *v.i.* (*pile up*) sich anhäufen; (*collect*) sich ansammeln.

**accurate** ['ækjurit], *adj.* genau, exakt; (*with no mistakes*) fehlerfrei. ◆**a'ccuracy** [-əsi], *s.* Genauigkeit *f*; Präzision *f* (eines Instruments).

**accuse** [ə'kju:z], *v.tr.* (j-n) anklagen; (j-n) beschuldigen (**of a crime,** eines Verbrechens; **of doing sth.,** etwas getan zu haben). ◆**accu'sation,** *s.* Anklage *f.* ◆**a'ccused,** *s.* *Jur:* **the a.,** der/die Angeklagte.

**accustom** [ə'kʌstəm], *v.tr.* **to a. s.o. to sth.,** j-n an etwas *acc* gewöhnen. ◆**a'ccustomed,** *adj.* **1. to be a. to sth./to doing sth.,** an etwas *acc* gewohnt sein/gewohnt sein, etwas zu tun; **to get a. to sth.,** sich an etwas *acc* gewöhnen. **2.** (*usual*) gewohnt.

**ace** [eis], *s.* As *n.*

**ache** [eik]. **I.** *s.* Schmerz *m*; **I have a stomach a.,** ich habe Magenschmerzen *pl.* **II.** *v.i.* schmerzen; **my back aches,** mir tut der Rücken weh.

**achieve** [ə'tʃi:v], *v.tr.* (*a*) (eine Großtat usw.) vollbringen; (*b*) (etwas, ein Ziel) erreichen; (Erfolg) erzielen. ◆**a'chievement,** *s.* **1.** (*action*) Erreichen *n*; Vollendung *f* (eines Plans). **2.** Leistung *f*; **achievements,** Errungenschaften *fpl.*

**acid** ['æsid], *s.* Säure *f*; **the a. test,** die Feuerprobe. ◆**acidity** [ə'siditi], *s.* Säuregehalt *m.*

**acknowledge** [ək'nɔlidʒ], *v.tr.* (*a*) (*recognize*) anerkennen; (*b*) (*admit*) (Schuld usw.) eingestehen; (*c*) (einen Gruß usw.) erwidern; **to a. (receipt of) a letter,** den Eingang eines Briefes bestätigen. ◆**ack'nowledgement,** *s.* Anerkennung *f*; Bestätigung *f* (eines Briefes).

**acne** ['ækni], *s.* Akne *f.*

**acorn** ['eikɔ:n], *s.* Eichel *f.*

**acoustic** [ə'ku:stik], *adj.* akustisch. ◆**a'coustics,** *s.pl.* Akustik *f.*

**acquaint** [ə'kweint], *v.tr.* (*a*) (*inform*) **to a. s.o./oneself with sth.,** j-n/sich über etwas *acc* informieren; (*b*) **to be acquainted with s.o.,** j-n kennen. ◆**a'cquaintance,** *s.* **1. to make the a. of s.o.,** j-n kennenlernen. **2.** (*pers.*) Bekannte(r) *f(m)*.

**acquiesce** [ækwi'es], *v.i.* einwilligen (**in sth.**, in etwas *acc*).

**acquire** [ə'kwaiər], *v.tr.* erwerben. ◆**acquisition** [ækwi'ziʃ(ə)n], *s.* **1.** (*action*) Erwerb *m.* **2.** (*object*) Anschaffung *f.* ◆**acquisitive** [ə'kwizitiv], *adj.* habgierig.

**acquit** [ə'kwit], *v.tr.* (*a*) freisprechen (**of a crime**, von einem Verbrechen); (*b*) **to a. oneself well/badly**, gut/schlecht abschneiden. ◆**a'cquittal**, *s.* Freispruch *m.*

**acre** ['eikər], *s.* Morgen *m.*

**acrid** ['ækrid], *adj.* beißend.

**acrimonious** [ækri'məuniəs], *adj.* bissig.

**acrobat** ['ækrəbæt], *s.* Akrobat(in) *m(f)*. ◆**acrobatic**, *adj.* akrobatisch.

**across** [ə'krɔs]. **I.** *prep.* **1.** (*motion*) über + *acc.* **2.** (*position*) **a. the river is a small town**, auf der anderen Seite des Flusses ist eine kleine Stadt. **II.** *adv.* hinüber; **the river is 100 metres a.**, der Fluß ist 100 Meter breit.

**act** [ækt]. **I.** *s.* **1.** (*a*) Handlung *f*; (*deed*) Tat *f*; **to catch s.o. in the a.**, j-n auf frischer Tat ertappen; (*b*) **A. of Parliament**, (verabschiedetes) Gesetz *n.* **2.** *Th:* (*a*) Akt *m* (eines Stückes); (*b*) Nummer *f* (eines Artisten). **II.** *v.* **1.** *v.tr.* (ein Stück, eine Rolle) spielen. **2.** *v.i.* (*a*) handeln; (*b*) (*behave*) sich benehmen; (*c*) (*function*) **to a. as**, fungieren/dienen als; (*d*) *Th: Cin:* spielen. ◆'**acting. I.** *adj.* (*deputy*) stellvertretend. **II.** *s. Th:* Spielen *n.* ◆**action** ['ækʃ(ə)n], *s.* **1.** Handlung *f*; **to take a.**, handeln; **to bring/put sth. into a.**, etwas in Gang setzen; **out of a.**, außer Betrieb. **2.** (*movement*) Bewegung *f.* **3.** (*effect*) Wirkung *f* (**on**, auf + *acc*). **4.** *Jur:* Verfahren *n*; (*trial*) Prozeß *m.* **5.** *Mil:* Gefecht *n.* ◆'**actionable**, *adj.* klagbar.

**active** ['æktiv], *adj.* aktiv; (*of mind, imagination, interest*) rege; (*of old pers.*) rüstig. ◆**ac'tivity**, *s.* **1.** (*bustle*) Tun *n.* **2.** Tätigkeit *f.*

**actor** ['æktər], *s.* Schauspieler *m.* ◆'**actress**, *s.* Schauspielerin *f.*

**actual** ['æktju(ə)l], *adj.* eigentlich; (*real*) tatsächlich; **in a. fact**, in Wirklichkeit. **-ly**, *adv.* eigentlich; **he a. said ...**, (i) er ging so weit zu sagen, ...; (ii) was er eigentlich sagte, war ...

**acute** [ə'kju:t], *adj.* **1.** (*of observer, mind*) scharf. **2.** (*of problem, shortage etc.*) akut; (*of pain*) heftig.

**ad** [æd], *s. F:* Anzeige *f*; **small ad**, Kleinanzeige *f*, Inserat *n.*

**Adam** ['ædəm]. *Pr.n.* **A's apple**, Adamsapfel *m.*

**adamant** ['ædəmənt], *adj.* unnachgiebig.

**adapt** [ə'dæpt], *v.tr.* (sich, etwas) anpassen (**to sth.**, etwas *dat*/an etwas *acc*). ◆**adapta'bility**, *s.* Anpassungsfähigkeit *f.* ◆**a'daptable**, *adj.* anpassungsfähig. ◆**adap'tation**, *s. Th: etc:* Bearbeitung

*f.* ◆**a'daptor**, *s. El:* Zwischenstecker *m.*

**add** [æd], *v.* **1.** *v.tr.* (*a*) (etwas) hinzufügen; (*b*) **to a. up**, (Zahlen, eine Rechnung) addieren. **2.** *v.i.* **to a. to sth.**, etwas vermehren. ◆**addition** [ə'diʃ(ə)n], *s.* (*sth. added*) Zusatz *m*; **in a.**, zusätzlich. ◆**a'dditional**, *adj.* zusätzlich. ◆'**additive**, *s.* Zusatz *m.*

**adder** ['ædər], *s.* Kreuzotter *f.*

**addict** ['ædikt], *s.* Süchtige(r) *f(m)*; **drug a.**, Rauschgiftsüchtige(r) *f(m)*. ◆**a'ddicted** [ə'diktid], *adj.* süchtig; **a. to heroin**, heroinsüchtig. ◆**a'ddiction**, *s.* Sucht *f.*

**address** [ə'dres]. **I.** *s.* **1.** Adresse *f*; **a. book**, Adreßbuch *n.* **2.** (*speech*) Ansprache *f*; **public a.** (**system**), Lautsprecheranlage *f.* **II.** *v.tr.* (*a*) **to a. a letter** (**to s.o.**), einen Brief (an j-n) adressieren; (*b*) (j-n) ansprechen. ◆**addressee** [ædre'si:], *s.* Empfänger *m.*

**adenoids** ['ædənɔidz], *s.pl.* adenoide Wucherungen *fpl.*

**adept** ['ædept], *adj.* geschickt (**at/in**, in + *dat*).

**adequate** ['ædikwət], *adj.* hinreichend; **to be a.**, genügen.

**adhere** [əd'hiər], *v.i.* (*a*) (*of thing*) kleben (**to sth.**, an etwas *dat*); (*b*) (*of pers.*) festhalten (**to sth.**, an etwas *dat*). ◆**ad'herence** [ə'hiər], *s.* Festhalten *n* (**to sth.**, an etwas *dat*). ◆**adhesive** [-'hi:z-]. **I.** *adj.* klebend; **a. tape**, Klebestreifen *m*; **a. plaster**, Heftpflaster *n.* **II.** *s.* Klebstoff *m.*

**adjacent** [ə'dʒeis(ə)nt], *adj.* angrenzend; **a. to**, direkt neben + *dat.*

**adjective** ['ædʒiktiv], *s.* Adjektiv *n.*

**adjoining** [ə'dʒɔiniŋ], *adj.* angrenzend.

**adjourn** [ə'dʒə:n], *v.tr.* vertagen (**to/until**, auf + *acc*).

**adjudicate** [ə'dʒu:dikeit], *v.i.* entscheiden. ◆**a'djudicator**, *s.* Preisrichter *m.*

**adjust** [ə'dʒʌst], *v.tr.* (*a*) (sich, etwas) einstellen (**to**, auf + *acc*); (*adapt*) (sich, etwas) anpassen (**to**, *dat*/an + *acc*); (*b*) (einen Mechanismus) einstellen; (Schrauben usw.) justieren; (eine Uhr usw.) regulieren; (Bremsen) nachstellen; (*c*) (den Hut, den Kragen usw.) zurechtrücken. ◆**a'djustable**, *adj.* regulierbar. ◆**a'djustment**, *s.* Regulierung *f.*

**administer** [əd'ministər], *v.tr.* (*a*) (ein Geschäft usw.) verwalten; (*b*) **to a. a drug**, eine Droge verabreichen. ◆**adminis'tration**, *s.* Verwaltung *f*; **the Kennedy a.**, die Regierung Kennedy. ◆**ad'ministrative**, *adj.* verwaltend. ◆**administrator**, *s.* Verwalter *m.*

**admiral** ['ædm(ə)rəl], *s.* Admiral *m.*

**admire** [əd'maiər], *v.tr.* bewundern. ◆**admirable** ['ædm(ə)rəbl], *adj.* bewundernswert; (*excellent*) großartig. ◆**admiration** [ædmə'reiʃən], *s.* Bewunderung *f.* ◆**ad'mirer**, *s.* Bewunderer *m*; Bewunderin *f*; Verehrer *m* (einer Dame).

**admission** [əd'miʃ(ə)n], *s.* **1.** (*a*) Eintritt

*m* (**to**, in + *acc*); (*access*) Zutritt *m* (**to**, zu + *dat*); (*b*) (*fee*) Eintrittspreis *m*; (*c*) Einlieferung *f* (ins Krankenhaus). 2. Eingeständnis *n* (**of a crime** etc., eines Verbrechens usw.). ◆**admit** [əd'mit], *v.tr.* (*a*) (*let in*) (j-n, Luft usw.) einlassen; (j-m) Eintritt gewähren; **to be admitted to hospital**, ins Krankenhaus eingeliefert werden; (*b*) (*allow*) (Beweise usw.) zulassen; (*c*) (*concede*) (Schuld usw.) zugeben. ◆**ad'mittance**, *s.* Eintritt *m* (**to**, in + *dat*); Zutritt *m* (**to**, zu + *dat*); **no a.**, Eintritt verboten. ◆**ad'mittedly**, *adv.* allerdings.

**ado** [ə'du:], *s.* **without (any) more a.**, ohne weitere Umstände.

**adolescence** [ædə'les(ə)ns], *s.* Reifezeit *f*. ◆**ado'lescent**. I. *adj.* jugendlich. II. *s.* Jugendliche(r) *f(m)*.

**adopt** [ə'dɔpt], *v.tr.* (*a*) (ein Kind) adoptieren; (*b*) (einen Plan, Kandidaten) annehmen; (Maßnahmen) ergreifen; (eine Handlungsweise) wählen. ◆**a'dopted**, *adj.* adoptiert; **a. son**, Adoptivsohn *m*. ◆**a'doption**, *s.* 1. Adoption *f*. 2. Annahme *f*.

**adore** [ə'dɔ:r], *v.tr.* (j-n) anbeten; (für etwas *acc*) schwärmen. ◆**a'dorable**, *adj.* entzückend. ◆**ado'ration**, *s.* Anbetung *f*.

**adorn** [ə'dɔ:n], *v.tr.* (etwas) schmücken.

**adrift** [ə'drift], *adv.* treibend.

**adulation** [ædju'leiʃ(ə)n], *s.* Schmeichelei *f*.

**adult** ['ædʌlt]. I. *adj.* erwachsen. II. *s.* Erwachsene(r) *m(f)*.

**adulterate** [ə'dʌltəreit], *v.tr.* verfälschen.

**adulterer** [ə'dʌltərər], **-eress** [ə'dʌltərər, -əres], *s.* Ehebrecher(in) *m(f)*. ◆**a'dultery**, *s.* Ehebruch *m*.

**advance** [əd'vɑ:ns]. I. *s.* 1. (*a*) *Mil: etc:* Vormarsch *m*; (*b*) **in a.**, im voraus; **a. booking**, Vorverkauf *m*. 2. Fortschritt *m* (der Wissenschaft usw.); (*improvement*) Verbesserung *f*. II. *v.* 1. *v.tr.* (*further*) (eine Sache) fördern; **to a. s.o. money**, j-m Geld vorschießen. 2. *v.i.* (*a*) *Mil: etc:* vorrücken; (*b*) (*progress*) Fortschritte machen. ◆**ad'vanced**, *adj.* (*a*) (*of age, stage*) vorgerückt; (*b*) (*of standard*) fortgeschritten; (*c*) (*of ideas* etc.) fortschrittlich. ◆**ad'vancement**, *s.* Beförderung *f* (im Rang); Förderung *f* (der Wissenschaft).

**advantage** [əd'vɑ:ntidʒ], *s.* Vorteil *m* (**over s.o.**, j-m gegenüber); (*use*) Nutzen *m*; **to take a. of s.o., sth.**, j-n, etwas ausnutzen. ◆**advantageous** [ædvən'teidʒəs], *adj.* vorteilhaft.

**advent** ['ædvənt], *s.* 1. *Ecc:* **A.**, Advent *m*, Adventszeit *f*. 2. *Fig:* Kommen *n*.

**adventure** [əd'ventʃər], *s.* Abenteuer *n*. ◆**ad'venturous**, *adj.* abenteuerlich; (*of pers.*) abenteuerlustig.

**adverb** ['ædvə:b], *s.* Adverb *n*.

**adverse** ['ædvə:s], *adj.* ungünstig.

◆**adversary** ['ædvəs(ə)ri], *s.* Gegner(in) *m(f)*. ◆**ad'versity**, *s.* Unglück *n*.

**advertise** ['ædvətaiz], *v.tr. & i.* (*a*) (für ein Produkt) werben; **to a. a post**, eine Stelle ausschreiben; (*b*) (in einer Zeitung) inserieren (**for**, um + *acc*). ◆**advertisement** [əd'və:tismənt], *s.* Anzeige *f*. ◆**'advertising**, *s.* Werbung *f*; **a. agency**, Werbeagentur *f*.

**advice** [əd'vais], *s.* (*no pl.*) Rat *m*; **piece of a.**, Ratschlag *m*. ◆**ad'visable**, *adj.* ratsam. ◆**advise** [əd'vaiz], *v.tr.* (*a*) (j-n) beraten; **to a. s.o. to do sth.**, j-m raten, etwas zu tun; **to a. s.o. against sth.**, j-m von etwas *dat* abraten; (*b*) (*recommend*) (etwas) empfehlen. ◆**ad'viser**, *s.* (*professional*) Berater *m*; (*personal*) Ratgeber *m*. ◆**ad'visory**, *adj.* beratend.

**advocate** I. ['ædvəkeit] *v.tr.* befürworten. II. ['ædvəkət] *s.* (*champion*) Verfechter *m*; Befürworter *m*.

**aerial** ['ɛəriəl]. I. *adj.* Luft-. II. *s.* *Rad: TV:* Antenne *f*.

**aero-** ['ɛərəu-], *prefix* Luft-; Flug-. ◆**aero'batics**, *s.pl.* Kunstflug *m*. ◆**'aerodrome**, *s.* Flugplatz *m*. ◆**aerody'namics**, *s.pl.* Aerodynamik *f*. ◆**'aerofoil**, *s.* *Aut:* Heckflügel *m*. ◆**aero'nautics**, *s.pl.* Luftfahrt *f*. ◆**'aeroplane**, *s.* Flugzeug *n*. ◆**'aerosol**, *s.* (*a*) Sprühdose *f*; (*b*) *Ch:* Aerosol *n*.

**affable** ['æfəbl], *adj.* leutselig.

**affair** [ə'fɛər], *s.* 1. Angelegenheit *f*; Sache *f*. 2. (*love*) **a.**, Liebesverhältnis *n*.

**affect**¹ [ə'fekt], *v.tr.* (*pretend*) vortäuschen. ◆**a'ffected**, *adj.* affektiert. ◆**affec'tation**, *s.* 1. *no pl* Affektiertheit *f*. 2. (*habit*) affektierte Angewohnheit *f*.

**affect**² [ə'fekt], *v.tr.* (*a*) (*influence*) (auf etwas *acc*) wirken; (im Ergebnis, eine Lage usw.) beeinflussen; (*b*) (*move*) (j-n) bewegen. ◆**a'ffection**, *s.* Liebe *f* (**for**, zu + *dat*). ◆**a'ffectionate**, *adj.* liebevoll.

**affidavit** [æfi'deivit], *s.* beeidigte Erklärung *f*.

**affinity** [ə'finiti], *s.* Verwandtschaft *f*; (*similarity*) Ähnlichkeit *f*.

**affirm** [ə'fə:m], *v.tr.* (*confirm*) bestätigen; (*state*) erklären. ◆**affirmation** [æfə(:)'meiʃ(ə)n], *s.* Bestätigung *f*. ◆**af'firmative**, *adj.* positiv; **to answer sth. in the a.**, etwas bejahen.

**afflict** [ə'flikt], *v.tr.* heimsuchen. ◆**a'ffliction**, *s.* (*physical*) Leiden *n*; (*psychological*) Kummer *m*.

**affluence** ['æfluəns], *s.* Reichtum *m*. ◆**'affluent**, *adj.* wohlhabend; **a. society**, Wohlstandsgesellschaft *f*.

**afford** [ə'fɔ:d], *v.tr.* sich *dat* (etwas) leisten.

**affront** [ə'frʌnt], *s.* Beleidigung *f*.

**afloat** [ə'fləut], *adv. & adj.* schwimmend; (*of ship*) flott.

**afoot** [ə'fut], *adv.* im Gange.

**afraid** [ə'freid], *adj.* **to be a.**, sich fürchten, Angst haben (**of** s.o., **sth.**, vor j-m, etwas *dat*); **I am a.** he's not here, er ist leider nicht hier.

**afresh** [ə'freʃ], *adv.* von neuem.

**Africa** ['æfrikə]. *Pr. n.* Afrika *n.*
◆**'African. I.** *adj.* afrikanisch. **II.** *s.* Afrikaner(in) *m(f)*.

**aft** [ɑːft], *adv. Nau:* achtern.

**after** ['ɑːftər]. **I.** *prep.* nach + *dat*; **to run a.** s.o., j-m nachlaufen; **the police are a. him**, die Polizei ist hinter ihm her; **day a. day**, Tag für Tag; **the day a. tomorrow**, übermorgen; **the week a. next**, übernächste Woche; **a. all**, schließlich; **called Brian a. his father**, nach seinem Vater Brian genannt. **II.** *adv.* danach; **the week a.**, die folgende Woche. **III.** *conj.* nachdem. ◆**'aftereffect**, *s.* Nachwirkung *f.* ◆**'aftermath**, *s.* Nachspiel *n;* (*effects*) Nachwirkungen *fpl.* ◆**'after'noon**, *s.* Nachmittag *m;* **good a.!** guten Tag! ◆**'afters**, *s.pl.* Nachtisch *m.* ◆**'afterthought**, *s.* nachträglicher Einfall *m.* ◆**'afterwards**, *adv.* später.

**again** [ə'gen], *adv.* **1.** wieder; (*once more*) noch einmal; **a. and a.**, immer wieder; **now and a.**, ab und zu. **2.** (*what is more*) außerdem.

**against** [ə'genst], *prep.* gegen + *acc.*

**age** [eidʒ] **I.** *s.* **1.** Alter *n;* **to be under a.**, minderjährig sein; **to come of a.**, großjährig werden; **a. group**, Altersgruppe *f;* **a. limit**, Altersgrenze *f;* **old a.**, hohes Alter. **2.** Zeitalter *n;* **the Middle Ages**, das Mittelalter; **I haven't seen him for ages**, ich habe ihn schon ewig nicht gesehen. **II.** *v.* **1.** *v.i.* altern. **2.** *v.tr.* (j-n) alt werden lassen. ◆**'aged**, *adj.* **a. twenty**, 20 Jahre alt. ◆**'ag(e)ing**, *adj.* alternd.

**agency** ['eidʒənsi], *s. Com:* Vertretung *f;* **travel a.**, Reisebüro *n.* ◆**agent** ['eidʒənt], *s. Com:* Vertreter *m;* (**secret**) **a.**, Geheimagent *m.*

**aggravate** ['ægrəveit], *v.tr.* (*a*) (ein Problem, die Lage) verschlimmern; (*b*) (j-n) reizen. ◆**'aggravating**, *adj.* ärgerlich. ◆**aggra'vation**, *s.* **1.** Verschlimmerung *f.* **2.** (*general*) Ärger *m;* (*instance*) Ärgernis *n.*

**aggregate** ['ægrigit], *s.* Summe *f; Mth:* Aggregat *n.*

**aggression** [ə'greʃ(ə)n], *s.* Aggression *f.* ◆**a'gressive**, *adj.* aggressiv.

**aggrieved** [ə'griːvd], *adj.* gekränkt.

**aghast** [ə'gɑːst], *adj.* entsetzt (**at**, über + *acc*).

**agile** ['ædʒail], *adj.* flink; (*of mind etc.*) rege. ◆**agitate** ['ædʒiteit], *v.* **1.** *v.tr.* (j-n) aufregen. **2.** *v.i.* **to a. for/against sth.**, für/gegen etwas *acc* Propaganda machen. ◆**'agitated**, *adj.* aufgeregt. ◆**agi'tation**, *s.* **1.** *Pol: etc:* Aufwiegelung *f.* **2.** (*of pers.*) Aufregung *f.* ◆**'agitator**, *s.* Aufwiegler *m.*

**ago** [ə'gəu], *adv.* vor; **ten years a.**, vor zehn Jahren; **a little while a.**, vor kur-

zem; **it is long a.**, es ist lange her.

**agonizing** ['ægənaiziŋ], *adj.* (*of pain*) quälend; (*of spectacle*) qualvoll. ◆**'agony**, *s.* Qual *f.*

**agree** [ə'griː], *v.* **1.** *v.i.* (*a*) einwilligen (**to sth.**, in etwas *acc*); (*b*) sich einigen (**on sth.**, über etwas *acc*); **to a. on a time**, einen Termin ausmachen; (*c*) (*approve*) einverstanden sein; (*d*) (*of things*) übereinstimmen; (*of pers.*) gleicher Meinung sein; (*e*) **oysters do not a. with me**, Austern vertrage ich nicht. **2.** *v.tr.* (einen Preis, Termin usw.) vereinbaren; **he agreed to come**, er erklärte sich bereit zu kommen. ◆**a'greeable**, *adj.* (*a*) (*of pers.*) einverstanden; (*b*) (*pleasant*) angenehm. ◆**a'greement**, *s.* **1.** (*document*) Vereinbarung *f;* (*contract*) Vertrag *m; Pol:* Abkommen *n.* **2.** (*a*) (*consent*) Zustimmung *f;* (*b*) (*accord*) Übereinstimmung *f;* **to be in a. with s.o., sth.**, mit j-m, etwas *dat* übereinstimmen.

**agriculture** ['ægrikʌltʃər], *s.* Landwirtschaft *f.* ◆**agri'cultural**, *adj.* landwirtschaftlich.

**aground** [ə'graund], *adv.* **to run a.**, stranden.

**ahead** [ə'hed] *adv.* **the town was straight a. of us**, die Stadt lag direkt vor uns; **he went on a.**, er ging vor; **to be two hours a.** (**of s.o.**), zwei Stunden Vorsprung (vor j-m) haben; **a. of time**, vorzeitig.

**aid** [eid]. **I.** *v.tr.* (j-m) helfen; (j-n, ein Land usw.) unterstützen. **II.** *s.* (*a*) Hilfe *f;* **in a. of**, zugunsten + *gen;* (*b*) (*device*) Hilfsmittel *n.*

**ailment** ['eilmənt], *s.* Leiden *n; pl* Beschwerden *fpl.*

**aim** [eim]. **I.** *v.* **1.** *v.tr.* (etwas) richten (**at s.o., sth.**, auf j-n, etwas *acc*). **2.** *v.i.* (*a*) **to a. at sth.**, (i) (*with weapon*) auf etwas *acc* zielen; (ii) (*intend*) etwas im Auge haben. **II.** *s.* **1.** Ziel *n;* **to take a.** zielen. **2.** (*purpose*) Zweck *m.* ◆**'aimless**, *adj.* ziellos.

**air** [ɛər]. **I.** *v.tr.* (*a*) (ein Zimmer, Betten usw.) lüften; (*b*) (eine Meinung) äußern; **to a. grievances**, Beschwerden vorbringen. **II.** *s.* **1.** Luft *f;* **in the open a.**, im Freien; **by a.**, auf dem Luftweg; **a. hostess**, Stewardeß *f.* **2.** (*look*) Aussehen *n;* (*of pers.*) Miene *f.* ◆**'airbase**, *s.* Luftstützpunkt *m.* ◆**'airborne**, *adj.* in der Luft. ◆**'air-con'ditioning**, *s.* Klimaanlage *f.* ◆**'air-cooled**, *adj.* luftgekühlt. ◆**'aircraft**, *s.* Flugzeug *n;* **a. carrier**, Flugzeugträger *m.* ◆**'aircrew**, *s.* Flugzeugbesatzung *f.* ◆**'airfield**, *s.* Flugplatz *m.* ◆**'airforce**, *s.* Luftwaffe *f.* ◆**'airlift**, *s.* Luftbrücke *f.* ◆**'airline**, *s.* Fluggesellschaft *f.* ◆**'airliner**, *s.* Verkehrsflugzeug *n.* ◆**'airlock**, *s.* Lufteinschluß *m.* ◆**airmail**, *s.* Luftpost *f;* **by a.**, mit Luftpost. ◆**'airman**, **-men**, *s.* Flieger *m.* ◆**'airplane**, *s. N.Am:* Flugzeug *n.* ◆**'airpocket**, *s.* Luftloch *n.* ◆**'airport**, *s.* Flughafen *m.* ◆**'air-raid**, *s.* Fliegerangriff *m.* ◆**'air-sickness**,

Luftkrankheit f. ◆'airstrip, s. Av: Landestreifen m. ◆'airtight, adj. luftdicht. ◆'air-traffic, s. Flugverkehr m; a.-t. control, Flugsicherung f; a.-t. controller, Fluglotse m.

aisle [ail], s. Th: Av: etc: Gang m.

ajar [ə'dʒɑːr], adv. angelehnt.

alarm [ə'lɑːm]. I. v.tr. erschrecken; to be alarmed at sth., über etwas acc beunruhigt sein. II. s. Alarm m; to give/sound the a., Alarm schlagen; (device) Alarmanlage f; a. (clock), Wecker m. ◆a'larming, adj. alarmierend; (frightening) erschreckend; (worrying) beängstigend. ◆a'larmist, s. Schwarzseher m.

alas [ə'lɑːs], int. ach!

Albania [æl'beinjə]. Pr. n. Albanien n.

albatross ['ælbətrɔs], s. Albatros m.

album ['ælbəm], s. Album n.

alcohol ['ælkəhɔl], s. Alkohol m. ◆alco'holic, I. adj. alkoholisch. II. s. (pers.) Alkoholiker(in) m(f).

alcove ['ælkəuv], s. Nische f.

ale [eil], s. Ale n; pale a., helles Bier.

alert [ə'ləːt]. I. adj. wachsam; (of mind) rege, aufgeweckt. II. s. Alarm(zustand) m; to be on the a., (i) alarmbereit sein; (ii) Fig: auf der Hut sein. ◆a'lertness, s. Wachsamkeit f.

alfresco [æl'freskəu], adj. & adv. im Freien.

algebra ['ældʒibrə], s. Algebra f.

Algeria [æl'dʒiəriə]. Pr. n. Algerien n.

alias ['eiliəs], adv. sonst … genannt.

alibi ['ælibai], s. Alibi n.

alien ['eiliən]. I. adj. (a) (foreign) ausländisch; (b) (strange) fremd. II. s. Ausländer m. ◆alienate ['eiliəneit], v.tr. entfremden.

alight¹ [ə'lait], v.i. (of pers.) aussteigen; (of bird) sich niederlassen.

alight², adj. to be a., brennen; to set sth. a., etwas anzünden.

alignment [ə'lainmənt], s. Aufstellung f in einer geraden Linie; political a., politische Orientierung f.

alike [ə'laik], adj. & adv. gleich; (similar) ähnlich; teachers and children a., Lehrer sowie Kinder.

alimentary [æli'mentəri], adj. a. canal, Verdauungskanal m.

alimony ['æliməni], s. Alimente npl.

alive [ə'laiv], adj. lebendig; he is still a., er lebt noch.

alkali ['ælkəlai], s. Alkali n.

all [ɔːl], adj. pron. & adv. 1. (a) adj. (sing.) ganz; (pl) alle; a. his life, sein ganzes Leben lang; (b) (pers.) alle; a. of us, wir alle; we a. love him, wir haben ihn alle gern; Sp: five a., fünf zu fünf; (c) (things) alles; a. that, das alles. 2. once and for a., ein für allemal; for a. I know, soviel ich weiß; not at a., überhaupt nicht; a. but, fast, beinahe; a. in a./a. things considered, alles in allem. 3. adv. ganz; a. in black, ganz in schwarz; a. the better, umso besser; a.

right, in Ordnung; he enjoyed it a. the same, er hat es trotzdem genossen; a. the same, you might have told me, das hättest du mir immerhin sagen können; a. at once, (i) (suddenly) plötzlich; (ii) (at one time) zugleich. ◆'all(-)'clear, s. Entwarnung f. ◆'all-'in, adj. (of pers.) erschöpft; a.-in price, Inklusivpreis m. ◆'all-'out, adj. maximal; to go a.-o. for sth., alles auf etwas acc setzen. ◆'all-'purpose, adj. Allzweck-. ◆'all-'round, adj. umfassend. ◆'all-'rounder, s. Sp: Allroundsportler m. ◆'all-'time, adj. absolut; a.-t. low, absoluter Tiefstand.

allege [ə'ledʒ], v.tr. (a) behaupten; (b) (pretend) vorgeben. ◆allegation [æli'geiʃ(ə)n], s. Anschuldigung f. ◆a'lleged, adj. angeblich.

allegiance [ə'liːdʒ(ə)ns], s. Treue f (to, gegenüber + dat).

allergy ['ælədʒi], s. Allergie f. ◆a'llergic, adj. allergisch (to, gegen + acc).

alleviate [ə'liːvieit], v.tr. (Schmerzen) lindern; (ein Problem) erleichtern.

alley ['æli], s. (enge) Gasse f.

alliance [ə'laiəns], s. Pol: Bündnis n. ◆allied ['ælaid], adj. 1. Pol: alliiert, verbündet (to/with, mit + dat). 2. (related) verwandt.

alligator ['æligeitər], s. Alligator m.

allocate ['æləkeit], v.tr. to a. a task, j-m eine Aufgabe zuteilen/Adm: zuweisen; to a. a sum to sth., eine Summe für etwas acc zur Verfügung stellen. ◆allo'cation, s. 1. (act) Zuteilung f. 2. Quote f; (money) zugeteilter Betrag m.

allot [ə'lɔt], v.tr. to a. sth. to s.o., j-m etwas zuteilen; in its allotted place, an seinem vorgeschriebenen Platz. ◆a'llotment, s. (ground) Schrebergarten m.

allow [ə'lau], v.tr. (permit) (a) to a. s.o. sth., j-m etwas erlauben; to be allowed to do sth., etwas tun dürfen; (b) to a. (oneself) enough time for sth., (sich dat) genug Zeit zu etwas dat lassen; (c) to a. for sth., etwas berücksichtigen. ◆a'llowance, s. 1. (a) Quote f; (b) (money) Zuwendung f; (addition to salary) Zuschuß m; child a., Kinderbeihilfe f. 2. to make a. for sth., etwas berücksichtigen/esp. Tchn: einkalkulieren; you have to make allowances for small children, man muß bei kleinen Kindern ein schon Verständnis haben.

alloy ['ælɔi], s. Legierung f.

allude [ə'l(j)uːd], v.i. to a. to s.o., sth., auf j-n, etwas acc anspielen.

alluring [ə'l(j)uəriŋ], adj. verlockend.

allusion [ə'l(j)uːʒ(ə)n], s. Anspielung f.

ally. I. [ə'lai], v.tr. & i. (etwas, sich) vereinigen (to/with, mit + dat). II. ['ælai], s. (pl. 'allies). Verbündete(r) f(m), Alliierte(r) f(m).

almanac ['ɔːlmənæk], s. Almanach m.

**almighty** [ɔːlˈmaɪtɪ]. **I.** *adj.* allmächtig. **II.** *s.* **the A.,** der Allmächtige.

**almond** [ˈɑːmənd], *s.* Mandel *f*.

**almost** [ˈɔːlməust], *adv.* beinahe, fast.

**alms** [ɑːmz], *s. sing. or pl.* Almosen *n*.

**alone** [əˈləun], *adj.* allein; **to leave s.o., sth. a.,** (i) etwas in Ruhe lassen; (ii) etwas sein lassen.

**along** [əˈlɔŋ]. **I.** *prep.* (etwas *acc*) entlang. **II.** *adv.* **to move a.,** sich fortbewegen; **come a.!** komm doch! **a. with,** zusammen mit + *dat.* ◆**a'long'side. I.** *prep.* (a) neben + *dat*; (b) (*compared with*) verglichen mit + *dat.* **II.** *adv.* daneben; *Nau:* längsseits.

**aloof** [əˈluːf], *adv. & adj.* zurückhaltend; **to remain a.,** sich fernhalten. ◆**a'loofness,** *s.* Zurückhaltung *f*.

**aloud** [əˈlaud], *adv.* laut.

**alp** [ælp], *s.* **the Alps,** die Alpen.

**alphabet** [ˈælfəbet], *s.* Alphabet *n*. ◆**alpha'betical,** *adj.* alphabetisch.

**alpine** [ˈælpaɪn], *adj.* alpin; **a. plants,** Alpenpflanzen *fpl*.

**already** [ɔːlˈredɪ], *adv.* schon. ◆**Alsatian** [ælˈseɪʃ(ə)n], *s.* (*dog*) Schäferhund *m*.

**Alsace** [ælˈsæs]. *Pr.n.* Elsaß *n*.

**also** [ˈɔːlsəu], *adv.* auch, ebenfalls.

**altar** [ˈɔːltər], *s.* Altar *m*.

**alter** [ˈɔːltər], *v.* **1.** *v.tr.* ändern; (Kleider) umändern. **2.** *v.i.* sich ändern; (*in appearance*) sich verändern. ◆**alte'ration,** *s.* (a) Änderung *f*; (b) *Tchn: etc:* Umbau *m*.

**alternate. I.** [ɔːlˈtəːnɪt], *adj.* **1.** abwechselnd; **on a. days,** jeden zweiten Tag. **2.** *N.Am:* **an a. date,** ein anderer Termin. **II.** [ˈɔːltəneɪt], *v.* **1.** *v.tr.* (zwei Sachen) abwechseln lassen. **2.** *v.i.* abwechseln. ◆**'alternating,** *adj.* abwechselnd; *El:* **a. current,** Wechselstrom *m*. ◆**alternative** [ɔːlˈtəːnətɪv]. **I.** *adj.* alternativ. **II.** *s.* Alternative *f*; **to have no a.,** keine Wahl haben; **-ly,** *adv.* andernfalls.

**although** [ɔːlˈðəu], *conj.* obwohl.

**altitude** [ˈæltɪtjuːd], *s.* Höhe *f*.

**altogether** [ɔːltəˈgeðər], *adv.* (a) (*wholly*) völlig; (b) (*on the whole*) alles in allem; **how much does that come to a.?** was macht das alles zusammen?

**aluminium** [æljuˈmɪnɪəm], *N.Am:* **aluminum** [əˈluːmɪnəm], *s.* Aluminium *n*.

**always** [ˈɔːlwɪz, -weɪz], *adv.* immer.

**amalgam** [əˈmælgəm], *s. Fig:* Mischung *f*. ◆**amalgamate** [əˈmælgəmeɪt], *v.* **1.** *v.tr.* zusammenschließen, (*combine*) vereinigen. **2.** *v.i.* sich zusammenschließen. ◆**amalga'mation,** *s.* Zusammenschluß *m*.

**amass** [əˈmæs], *v.tr.* anhäufen.

**amateur** [ˈæmətər], *s.* Amateur *m*; *Pej:* Dilettant *m*. ◆**'amateurish,** *adj.* dilettantisch.

**amaze** [əˈmeɪz], *v.tr.* erstaunen. ◆**a'mazed,** *adj.* erstaunt. ◆**a'mazement,** *s.* Erstaunen *n*. ◆**a'mazing,** *adj.* erstaunlich.

**ambassador** [æmˈbæsədər], *s.* Botschafter(in) *m(f)*.

**amber** [ˈæmbər], *s.* **1.** Bernstein *m*. **2.** (*colour*) Bernsteinfarbe *f*; *Aut:* gelbes Licht.

**ambiguous** [æmˈbɪgjuəs], *adj.* zweideutig. ◆**ambi'guity,** *s.* Zweideutigkeit *f*.

**ambition** [æmˈbɪʃ(ə)n], *s.* (*general*) Ehrgeiz *m*; (*particular*) Ambition *f*. ◆**am'bitious,** *adj.* ehrgeizig.

**amble** [ˈæmbl], *v.i.* **to a. (along),** dahinschlendern.

**ambulance** [ˈæmbjuləns], *s.* Krankenwagen *m*.

**ambush** [ˈæmbuʃ]. **I.** *v.tr.* (j-n) aus dem Hinterhalt überfallen. **II.** *s.* Hinterhalt *m*.

**amen** [ˈɑːmən], *int.* amen.

**amenable** [əˈmiːnəbl], *adj.* zugänglich (**to,** *dat*).

**amend** [əˈmend], *v.tr.* (a) ändern; (b) (*correct*) (einen Text usw.) verbessern. ◆**a'mendment,** *s.* (a) Änderung *f*; (b) Verbesserung *f*. ◆**a'mends,** *s.pl.* **to make a. for sth.,** etwas wiedergutmachen.

**amenity** [əˈmiːnɪtɪ], *s.* Annehmlichkeit *f*.

**America** [əˈmerɪkə]. *Pr.n.* Amerika *n*. ◆**A'merican. I.** *s.* Amerikaner(in) *m(f)*. **II.** *adj.* amerikanisch.

**amethyst** [ˈæmɪθɪst], *s.* Amethyst *m*.

**amiable** [ˈeɪmjəbl], *adj.* liebenswürdig.

**amicable** [ˈæmɪkəbl], *adj.* freundlich; (*of relations, feelings*) freundschaftlich; **-ably,** *adv.* auf gütlichem Wege.

**amid(st)** [əˈmɪd(st)], *prep.* mitten in + *dat*; (*with pl.*) mitten unter + *dat.*

**amiss** [əˈmɪs], *adv. & adj.* **to take sth. a.,** etwas übelnehmen.

**ammonia** [əˈməunjə], *s.* Ammoniak *n*.

**ammunition** [æmjuˈnɪʃ(ə)n], *s.* Munition *f*.

**amnesia** [æmˈniːzɪə], *s.* Gedächtnisschwund *m*.

**amnesty** [ˈæmnɪstɪ], *s.* Amnestie *f*.

**among(st)** [əˈmʌŋ(st)], *prep.* (mitten) unter; **a. other things,** unter anderem.

**amorous** [ˈæmərəs], *adj.* zärtlich; (*in love*) verliebt.

**amount** [əˈmaunt]. **I.** *s.* **1.** (*money*) Betrag *m*. **2.** (*quantity*) Menge *f*. **II.** *v.i.* **to a. to £200,** 200 Pfund betragen; **that amounts to the same thing,** das kommt auf das gleiche hinaus; **he'll never a. to much,** er wird es nie sehr weit bringen.

**amphibian** [æmˈfɪbɪən], *s.* Amphibie *f*. ◆**am'phibious,** *adj.* amphibisch.

**amphitheatre** [ˈæmfɪθɪətər], *s.* Amphitheater *n*.

**ample** [ˈæmpl], *adj.* (a) reichlich; (b) **an a. figure,** eine volle Figur.

**amplify** [ˈæmplɪfaɪ], *v.tr.* (ein Signal usw.) verstärken. ◆**'amplifier,** *s.* Verstärker *m*.

**amputate** [ˈæmpjuteɪt], *v.tr.* amputieren. ◆**ampu'tation,** *s.* Amputation *f*.

**amuse** [əˈmjuːz], *v.tr.* (j-n, sich) unterhalten. ◆**a'musement,** *s.* Unterhaltung f; (*pleasure*) Vergnügen *n*; (*pastime*) Zeitvertreib *m*; **a. park**, Vergnügungspark *m*; **a. arcade**, Spielhalle *f*. ◆**a'musing**, *adj.* amüsant.

**an** *see* a².

**anaemia** [ə'niːmiə], *s.* Anämie *f*, Blutarmut *f*. ◆**a'naemic**, *adj.* blutarm.

**anaesthetic** [ænis'θetik], *s.* Betäubungsmittel *n*; **under a.**, in Narkose; **local a.**, örtliche Betäubung. ◆**anaes'thetist** [ə'niːsθətist], *s.* Narkosearzt *m*, Narkoseärztin *f*.

**analogy** [ə'nælədʒi], *s.* Analogie *f*. ◆**analogous** [ə'næləgəs], *adj.* analog (**to/with**, + *dat*).

**analyse** ['ænəlaiz], *v.tr.* analysieren. ◆**analysis**, *pl.* **-ses** [ə'nælisis, -siːz], *s.* Analyse *f*. ◆**'analyst**, *s.* Analytiker *m*; *esp. N.Am:* Psychoanalytiker *m*. ◆**ana'lytic**, *adj.* analytisch.

**anarchy** ['ænəki], *s.* Anarchie *f*. ◆**'anarchist**, *s.* Anarchist(in) *m(f)*.

**anathema** [ə'næθəmə], *s.* **it's a. to me**, es ist mir ein Greuel.

**anatomy** [ə'nætəmi], *s.* Anatomie *f*. ◆**anatomical** [ænə'tɔmik(ə)l], *adj.* anatomisch.

**ancestor** ['ænsestər], *s.* Vorfahr *m*. ◆**an'cestral**, *adj.* angestammt; **his a. home**, sein Stammsitz *m*. ◆**ancestry** ['ænsistri], *s.* **1.** (*origin*) Abstammung *f*. **2.** *coll.* Vorfahren *mpl.*

**anchor** ['æŋkər]. **I.** *s.* Anker *m*. **II.** *v.* **1.** *v.tr.* verankern; **to be anchored,** vor Anker liegen. **2.** *v.i.* ankern. ◆**'anchorage**, *s.* Ankerplatz *m*.

**anchovy** ['æntʃəvi], *s.* Sardelle *f*.

**ancient** ['einʃ(ə)nt], *adj.* sehr alt; *esp. F:* uralt.

**and** [ænd, ənd], *conj.* und; **better a. better,** immer besser.

**anecdote** ['ænikdəut], *s.* Anekdote *f*.

**anemone** [ə'neməni], *s.* Anemone *f*.

**angel** ['eindʒel], *s.* Engel *m*. ◆**angelic** [æn'dʒelik], *adj.* engelhaft.

**anger** ['æŋgər], *s.* Zorn *m*.

**angle¹** ['æŋgl], *s.* (*a*) Winkel *m*; **at an a.,** schräg (**to,** zu + *dat*); (*b*) (*aspect*) Gesichtspunkt *m*.

**angle²**, *v.i.* angeln.

**Anglican** ['æŋglikən]. **I.** *s.* Anglikaner(in) *m(f)*. **II.** *adj.* anglikanisch.

**angry** ['æŋgri], *adj.* zornig; **a. with s.o. about sth.,** böse auf j-n wegen etwas *gen*; **to make s.o. a.,** j-n ärgern.

**anguish** ['æŋgwiʃ], *s.* Qual *f*.

**angular** ['æŋgjulər], *adj.* eckig; (*of features*) knochig.

**animal** ['ænim(ə)l]. **I.** *s.* Tier *n*. **II.** *adj.* Tier-; *Pej:* tierisch.

**animate** ['ænimeit], *v.tr.* beleben. ◆**'animated**, *adj.* lebhaft; **a. cartoon,** Zeichentrickfilm *m*. ◆**ani'mation**, *s.* Lebhaftigkeit *f*.

**animosity** [æni'mɔsiti], *s.* Feindseligkeit *f*; (*hatred*) Haß *m*.

**aniseed** ['ænisiːd], *s.* Anis *m*.

**ankle** ['æŋkl], *s.* Knöchel *m*.

**annex** [ə'neks], *v.tr.* (ein Land usw.) annektieren. ◆**annex(e)** ['æneks], *s.* Anbau *m*.

**annihilate** [ə'naiəleit], *v.tr.* vernichten. ◆**annihi'lation**, *s.* Vernichtung *f*.

**anniversary** [æni'vəːs(ə)ri], *s.* Jahrestag *m*; **wedding a.,** Hochzeitstag *m*.

**annotate** ['ænəteit], *v.tr.* mit Anmerkungen versehen.

**announce** [ə'nauns], *v.tr.* (*a*) (eine Nachricht) bekanntgeben; *Rad: TV:* (ein Programm) ansagen; (*b*) (etwas Zukünftiges) ankündigen. ◆**a'nnouncement**, *s.* Meldung *f*; *Rad: TV:* Ansage *f*; (*also over loudspeaker*) Durchsage *f*; (*small ad*) Anzeige *f*. ◆**a'nnouncer**, *s. Rad: TV:* Ansager(in) *m(f)*.

**annoy** [ə'nɔi], *v.tr.* (*a*) (*irritate*) ärgern; **to be annoyed,** sich ärgern (**at, about sth.,** über etwas *acc*; **with s.o.,** über j-n); (*b*) (*inconvenience*) belästigen. ◆**a'nnoyance**, *s.* Ärger *m*. ◆**a'nnoyed**, *adj.* verärgert. ◆**a'nnoying**, *adj.* ärgerlich.

**annual** ['ænju(ə)l]. **I.** *adj.* jährlich; Jahres-. **II.** *s.* (*a*) *Bot:* einjährige Pflanze *f*; (*b*) (*book*) Jahrbuch *n*.

**annuity** [ə'njuːiti], *s.* Jahresrente *f*.

**annul** [ə'nʌl], *v.tr.* annulieren.

**anomaly** [ə'nɔməli], *s.* Anomalie *f*; (*situation*) Mißstand *m*. ◆**a'nomalous**, *adj.* anomal.

**anonymous** [ə'nɔniməs], *adj.* anonym. ◆**ano'nymity**, *s.* Anonymität *f*.

**anorak** ['ænəræk], *s.* Anorak *m*.

**another** [ə'nʌðər], *adj. & pron.* **1.** (*an additional*) noch ein(e); **a. (one),** noch einer/eine/eines; **a. ten years,** noch zehn Jahre. **2.** (*a different*) ein anderer, eine andere, ein anderes; **one way or a.,** auf irgendeine Weise. **3. one a.,** einander; **they greeted one a.,** sie grüßten sich.

**answer** ['ɑːnsər]. **I.** *s.* **1.** Antwort *f* (**to a question,** auf eine Frage). **2.** Lösung *f* (**to a problem,** eines Problems). **II.** *v.* **1.** *v.tr.* (einen Brief usw.) beantworten; (j-m) antworten; **to a. the telephone,** (den Hörer) abnehmen; **to a. an advertisement,** auf eine Anzeige antworten; **to a. the door,** aufmachen. **2.** *v.i.* antworten; **to a. to the name of X,** auf den Namen X hören; **to a. for sth.,** für etwas *acc* verantwortlich sein; **to a. (s.o.) back,** (j-m) frech antworten. ◆**'answerable**, *adj.* **to be a. to s.o. for sth.,** j-m für etwas *acc* verantwortlich sein.

**ant** [ænt], *s.* Ameise *f*.

**antagonize** [æn'tægənaiz], *v.tr.* sich *dat* (j-n) zum Gegner machen. ◆**an'tagonism**, *s.* Antagonismus *m* (**to,** gegen + *acc*). ◆**an'tagonist,** *s.* Gegner *m*. ◆**antago'nistic**, *adj.* feindselig (**to,** gegen + *acc*).

**antarctic** [ænt'ɑːktik]. **I.** *adj.* antarktisch; **the A. Ocean,** das Südliche Polarmeer. **II.** *s.* **the A.,** die Antarktis.

**antedate** ['ænti'deit], *v.tr.* (*a*) (einem Ereignis) vorausgehen; (*b*) (ein Dokument usw.) nachdatieren.

**antelope** ['æntiloup], *s.* Antilope *f.*

**antenatal** ['ænti'neitl], *adj.* vor der Geburt.

**antenna,** *pl.* **-ae** [æn'tenə,-iː], *s.* 1. *Z:* Fühler *m.* 2. *Rad: TV:* Antenne *f.*

**anthem** ['ænθəm], *s.* **national a.,** Nationalhymne *f.*

**anthology** [æn'θɔlədʒi], *s.* Anthologie *f.*

**anthropology** [ænθrə'pɔlədʒi], *s.* Anthropologie *f.* ◆**anthro'pologist,** *s.* Anthropologe *m,* Anthropologin *f.*

**anti-** ['ænti], *prefix* anti-, gegen-. ◆**'anti-'aircraft,** *adj.* Fliegerabwehr-. ◆**'antibi'otic,** *s.* Antibiotikum *n.* ◆**'antibody,** *s.* Antikörper *m.* ◆**'anti'climax,** *s.* Enttäuschung *f.* ◆**'anti'clockwise,** *adv.* gegen den Uhrzeigersinn. ◆**'anti'cyclone,** *s.* Hoch(druckgebiet) *n.* ◆**'anti-'dazzle,** *adj.* Blendschutz-. ◆**'antidote,** *s.* Gegenmittel *n;* Gegengift *n.* ◆**'antifreeze,** *s.* Frostschutzmittel *n.* ◆**'anti-se'mitic,** *adj.* antisemitisch. ◆**'anti'septic, I.** *adj.* antiseptisch. **II.** *s.* Antiseptikum *n.* ◆**'anti'social,** *adj.* unsozial.

**anticipate** [æn'tisipeit], *v.tr.* (*a*) vorwegnehmen; (den Ereignissen) vorauseilen; (*b*) (*expect*) erwarten. ◆**antici'pation,** *s.* Erwartung *f;* Vorwegnahme *f.*

**antics** ['æntiks], *s.pl.* Possen *fpl.*

**antipathy** [æn'tipəθi], *s.* Antipathie *f* (to, gegen + *acc*); Abneigung *f.*

**antiquarian** [ænti'kweəriən], *adj.* **a. bookseller,** Antiquar *m.* ◆**antique** [æn'tiːk]. **I.** *adj.* antik; **a. furniture,** antike Möbel. **II.** *s.* Antiquität *f;* **a. dealer,** Antiquitätenhändler *m.* ◆**'antiquated,** *adj.* veraltet. ◆**an'tiquity,** *s.* (*period*) Altertum *n,* Antike *f.*

**antithesis** [æn'tiθisis], *pl.* **-es** [-iːz], *s.* Gegensatz *m* (to/of, zu + *dat*).

**antler** ['æntlər], *s.* **the antlers,** das Geweih.

**anus** ['einəs], *s.* After *m.*

**anvil** ['ænvil], *s.* Amboß *m.*

**anxiety** [æn'zaiəti], *s.* (*a*) (*fear*) Angst *f;* (*b*) (*worry*) Sorge *f* (for, um + *acc*); (*state*) Besorgtheit *f.*

**anxious** ['æŋ(k)ʃəs], *adj.* 1. (*a*) (*of pers.*) (*afraid*) ängstlich; (*disturbed*) unruhig (about, wegen + *gen*); (*worried*) besorgt (about, um + *acc*); (*b*) (*of time*) sorgenvoll. 2. **to be a. to do sth,** darauf aus sein, etwas zu tun; **-ly,** *adv.* 1. besorgt. 2. (*impatiently*) gespannt.

**any** ['eni]. **I.** *adj.* 1. (*a*) (*interrog. sing.* irgendein(e), *pl.* irgendwelche; **have you a. milk?** haben Sie (etwas) Milch? **have you a. eggs?** haben Sie Eier? (*b*) *neg.* **not a.,** kein(e). 2. (*no matter which*) jeder, jede, jedes; **at a. time,** jederzeit; **in a. case,** jedenfalls. **II.** *pron.* (*a*) **have you a. left?** (i) (*sing.*) haben Sie noch davon? (ii) (*pl.*)

haben Sie noch welche? (*b*) *neg.* **I can't find a.,** ich kann keine/keine/keines finden. **III.** *adv.* **is he a. better?** geht es ihm etwas besser? **if it gets a. hotter,** wenn es noch wärmer wird; **she doesn't dance a. more,** sie tanzt nicht mehr. ◆**'anybody/'anyone,** *pron.* 1. (irgend) jemand. 2. **not a.,** niemand. 3. (*no matter who*) jeder. ◆**'anyhow. I.** *adv.* **to do sth.** (just) a., etwas recht und schlecht machen. **II.** *conj.* (*concessive*) immerhin; (*whatever happens*) sowieso. ◆**'anything,** *pron.* (irgend) etwas; **not ... a.,** nichts; **he eats a.,** er ißt alles. ◆**'anyway,** *adv.* & *conj.* =anyhow. ◆**'anywhere,** *adv.* 1. irgendwo; **you can buy it a.,** du kannst es überall kaufen. 2. **not ... a.,** nirgends; nirgendwo.

**apart** [ə'pɑːt], *adv.* 1. (*a*) (*of two people*) **to live a.,** getrennt leben; **you can't tell them a.,** man kann die beiden nicht auseinanderhalten; (*b*) (*to pieces*) auseinander. 2. **a. from,** abgesehen von + *dat;* joking a., Spaß beiseite.

**apartment** [ə'pɑːtmənt], *s.* Wohnung *f.*

**apathy** ['æpəθi], *s.* Teilnahmslosigkeit *f.* ◆**apathetic** [-'θetik], *adj.* teilnahmslos.

**ape** [eip]. **I.** *s.* Menschenaffe *m.* **II.** *v.tr.* nachäffen.

**aperitif** [ə'peritif], *s.* Aperitif *m.*

**aperture** ['æpətjuər, -tʃər], *s.* 1. Öffnung *f.* 2. *Phot:* Blende *f.*

**apex,** *pl.* **-exes, -ices** ['eipeks, -eksiz, -isiːz], *s.* Spitze *f.*

**aphrodisiac** [æfrəu'diziæk], *s.* Aphrodisiakum *n.*

**apiece** [ə'piːs], *adv.* pro Stück; (*pers.*) pro Kopf/Person.

**aplomb** [ə'plɔm], *s.* Selbstbewußtsein *n;* **with a.,** selbstsicher.

**apocryphal** [ə'pɔkrif(ə)l], *adj.* (*of story*) erfunden.

**apologetic** [əpɔlə'dʒetik], *adj.* **to be a.** (for/about sth.), sich (für etwas *acc*) entschuldigen. ◆**apologize** [ə'pɔlədʒaiz], *v.i.* **to a. to s.o. for sth.,** sich bei j-m für etwas *acc* entschuldigen. ◆**a'pology,** *s.* Entschuldigung *f.*

**apoplexy** ['æpəpleksi], *s.* Schlaganfall *m.*

**apostle** [ə'pɔsl], *s.* Apostel *m.*

**apostrophe** [ə'pɔstrəfi], *s.* Apostroph *m.*

**appal(l)** [ə'pɔːl], *v.tr.* entsetzen. ◆**a'ppalling,** *adj.* entsetzlich.

**apparatus** [æpə'reitəs], *s.* Apparat *m.*

**apparent** [ə'pærənt], *adj.* 1. (*clear*) offenbar. 2. (*seeming*) scheinbar; **-ly,** *adv.* anscheinend.

**apparition** [æpə'riʃ(ə)n], *s.* Erscheinung *f.*

**appeal** [ə'piːl]. **I.** *s.* 1. Appell *m* (to reason, an die Vernunft); *Jur:* Berufung *f.* 2. (*a*) Aufforderung *f* (for calm, zur Ruhe); (*b*) Bitte *f* (for funds, um Spenden). 3. (*attraction*) Reiz *m.* **II.** *v.i.* (*a*) appellieren (to s.o., sth., an j-n, etwas *acc*); **to a. for help,** (dringend) um Hilfe bitten; *Jur:* **to a. against a sentence,** Berufung gegen ein Urteil einlegen; (*b*) (of thing) gefallen (**to**, *dat*). ◆**a'ppealing**, *adj.* reizvoll.

**appear** [ə'piər], *v.i.* (*a*) (*become visible, be published etc.*) erscheinen; (*on stage etc.*) auftreten; (*b*) (*seem*) scheinen. ◆**a'ppearance**, *s.* 1. Erscheinen *n*; Auftritt *m*; **to put in an a.**, sich (kurz) zeigen. 2. (*look*) Aussehen *n*; (*semblance*) Schein *m*.

**appease** [ə'pi:z], *v.tr.* beschwichtigen.

**appendix** [ə'pendiks], *pl.* **-ixes, -ices** [-isi:z], *s.* 1. Anhang *m* (eines Buches). 2. *Anat:* Blinddarm *m*. ◆**appendi'citis**, *s.* Blinddarmentzündung *f*.

**appetite** ['æpitait], *s.* Appetit *m* (**for sth.**, auf etwas *acc*). ◆**'appetizing**, *adj.* appetitlich; (*delicious*) lecker.

**applaud** [ə'plɔːd], *v.tr. & i.* (*a*) (j-m) applaudieren; (*clap*) klatschen; (*b*) *Fig:* (einen Entschluß usw.) begrüßen. ◆**a'pplause**, *s.* Beifall *m*.

**apple** ['æpl], *s.* Apfel *m*.

**appliance** [ə'plaiəns], *s.* Gerät *n*.

**apply** [ə'plai], *v.* 1. *v.tr.* (*a*) (etwas) auflegen (**to sth.**, auf etwas *acc*); (einen Verband) anlegen; (Farbe usw.) auftragen; (*b*) (*use*) (Kraft, eine Vorschrift usw.) anwenden; (*c*) **to a. one's mind to sth.**, sich etwas *dat* widmen. 2. *v.i.* (*a*) *impers.* gelten (**to**, für + *acc*); (*b*) **to a. to s.o. (for sth.)**, sich an j-n (um etwas *acc*) wenden; (*request*) **to a. for sth.**, etwas beantragen; **to a. for a job**, sich um eine Stellung bewerben. ◆**applicable** [ə'plikəbl, 'æplik-], *adj.* (*usable*) anwendbar; (*relevant*) zutreffend. ◆**applicant** ['æplikənt], *s.* Bewerber(in) *m(f)*. ◆**application** [æpli'keiʃ(ə)n], *s.* 1. (*use*) Anwendung *f* (von etwas *dat*). 2. (*concentration*) Fleiß *m*. 3. (*written*) Antrag *m* (**for sth.**, auf etwas *acc*); Bewerbung *f* (**for a job**, um eine Stellung). ◆**a'pplied**, *adj.* **a. linguistics**, angewandte Linguistik.

**appoint** [ə'pɔint], *v.tr.* (j-n zu etwas *dat*) ernennen; **to a. a new headmaster**, einen neuen Schuldirektor anstellen. ◆**a'ppointed**, *adj.* 1. (*agreed*) vereinbart. 2. (*of house*) **well a.**, gut ausgestattet. ◆**a'ppointment**, *s.* 1. (*meeting*) Verabredung *f*; *Com: etc.* Termin *m*; **to make an a.**, sich anmelden; **by a.**, nach Vereinbarung. 2. Ernennung *f* (**to a post**, zu einem Posten usw.).

**appreciate** [ə'priːʃieit], *v.* 1. *v.tr.* (*a*) (etwas) zu schätzen wissen; **I would a. your help**, ich wäre für Ihre Hilfe sehr dankbar; (*b*) (*recognize*) erkennen. 2. *v.i.* im Wert steigen. ◆**a'ppreciable**, *adj.* merklich; (*considerable*) bedeutend; (*esp. with neg.*) nennenswert. ◆**appreci'ation**, *s.* 1. (*a*) Würdigung *f*; (*b*) (*gratitude*) Dankbarkeit *f*; (*recognition*) Anerkennung *f*; (*c*) (*understanding*) Verständnis *n* (**of**, für + *acc*). 2. *Fin:* Wertsteigerung *f*. ◆**a'ppreciative** [-ʃjətiv], *adj.* (*of review, opinion*) positiv; (*of pers.*)

dankbar.

**apprehend** [æpri'hend], *v.tr.* festnehmen. ◆**appre'hension**, *s.* 1. Festnahme *f*. 2. (*fear*) Befürchtung *f*. ◆**appre'hensive**, *adj.* ängstlich; (*concerned*) besorgt.

**apprentice** [ə'prentis], *s.* Lehrling *m*. ◆**a'pprenticeship**, *s.* Lehre *f*.

**approach** [ə'prəutʃ]. **I.** *s.* 1. (*a*) Nahen *n* (einer Person, des Frühlings usw.); (*b*) (*attitude*) Einstellung *f* (**to**, zu + *dat*); (*introduction*) Einführung *f*. 2. Zugang *m* (zu einem Haus); Zufahrt *f* (zu einer Stadt usw.); *Av:* Anflug *m*. **II.** *v.* 1. *v.i.* nahen; (*of pers.*) sich nähern. 2. *v.tr.* (*a*) sich (einem Ort) nähern; (*b*) sich (an j-n) wenden (**with a proposal etc.**, mit einem Vorschlag usw.); (*c*) **to a. a question**, an eine Frage herangehen. ◆**a'pproachable**, *adj.* leicht zugänglich.

**appropriate**. **I.** [ə'prəuprieit] *v.tr.* sich *dat* (etwas) aneignen. **II.** [ə'prəupriət] *adj.* angemessen.

**approve** [ə'pruːv], *v.* 1. *v.tr.* (eine Handlung) billigen; *Adm:* (ein Ansuchen usw.) genehmigen. 2. *v.i.* **to a. of sth.**, etwas gutheißen; **I don't a. of your friends**, ich bin mit deinen Freunden nicht einverstanden. ◆**a'pproval**, *s.* Zustimmung *f*; *Com:* **on a.**, zur Ansicht.

**approximate**. **I.** [ə'prɔks(i)mit], *adj.* ungefähr; **-ly**, *adv.* etwa. ◆**approxi'mation**, *s.* Annäherung *f* (**to**, an + *acc*); (*figure*) ungefähre Angabe *f*.

**apricot** ['eiprikɔt], *s.* Aprikose *f*.

**April** ['eipril], *s.* April *m*.

**apron** ['eiprən], *s.* Schürze *f*.

**apt** [æpt], *adj.* 1. (*suitable*) passend, geeignet; (*of remark*) treffend. 2. (*tending*) (*of pers.*) **to be a. to do sth.**, geneigt sein, etwas zu tun. ◆**'aptitude**, *s.* Eignung *f* (**for sth.**, zu etwas *dat*).

**aqualung** ['ækwəlʌŋ], *s.* Preßlufttauchgerät *n*.

**aquarium** [ə'kweəriəm], *s.* Aquarium *n*.

**Aquarius** [ə'kweəriəs]. *Pr.n.* Wassermann *m*.

**aquatic** [ə'kwætik], *adj.* Wasser-.

**aqueduct** ['ækwidʌkt], *s.* Aquädukt *m*.

**Arab** ['ærəb], *s.* Araber(in) *m(f)*. ◆**A'rabian**, *adj.* arabisch. ◆**Arabic** ['ærəbik], **I.** *adj.* arabisch. **II.** *s.* Arabisch *n*.

**arable** ['ærəbl], *adj.* urbar; **a. land**, Ackerland *n*.

**arbitrate** ['ɑːbitreit], *v.* 1. *v.tr.* (einen Streit) schlichten. 2. *v.i.* einen Schiedsspruch fällen. ◆**'arbitrary**, *adj.* willkürlich. ◆**arbi'tration**, *s.* Schlichtung *f*; (*by tribunal*) Schiedsgerichtsverfahren *n*. ◆**'arbitrator**, *s.* Schlichter *m*.

**arc** [ɑːk], *s.* *Mth:etc:* Bogen *m*; *El:* Lichtbogen *m*.

**arcade** [ɑː'keid], *s.* (*a*) Arkade *f*; (*b*) **shopping a.**, Einkaufspassage *f*.

**arch¹** [ɑːtʃ]. **I.** *v.tr.* (den Rücken) krümmen. **II.** *s.* Bogen *m*; (*vault*) Gewölbe *n*.

**arch²**, *adj.* Erz-; **a. enemy**, Erzfeind *m.* ◆**archangel** ['ɑːkeindʒ(ə)l], *s.* Erzengel *m.* ◆**archbishop** ['ɑːtʃ'biʃəp], *s.* Erzbischof *m.*

**arch(a)eology** [ɑːki'ɔlədʒi], *s.* Archäologie *f.* ◆**arch(a)e'ologist**, *s.* Archäologe *m*, Archäologin *f.*

**archaic** [ɑː'keiik], *adj.* altertümlich; (*out of date*) altmodisch.

**archery** ['ɑːtʃəri], *s.* Bogenschießen *n.*

**archipelago** [ɑːki'peləgəu, -əuz], *s.* Archipel *n.*

**architect** ['ɑːkitekt], *s.* Architekt(in) *m(f).* ◆**archi'tectural** [-tʃərəl], *adj.* architektonisch. ◆**'architecture** [-tʃər], *s.* Architektur *f.*

**archives** ['ɑːkaivz], *s.pl.* Archiv *n.*

**arctic** ['ɑːktik]. **I.** *adj.* arktisch; **A. Ocean**, Nordpolarmeer *n.* **II.** *s.* **the A.**, die Arktis.

**ardent** ['ɑːdənt], *adj.* feurig; (*of supporter etc.*) leidenschaftlich. ◆**'ardour** ['ɑːdər], *s.* **1.** (*enthusiasm*) Begeisterung *f.* **2.** (*passion*) Leidenschaft *f.*

**arduous** ['ɑːdjuəs], *adj.* (*of task etc.*) mühsam; (*strenuous*) anstrengend.

**area** ['ɛəriə], *s.* **1.** (*measurement*) Fläche *f.* **2.** (*region, also Fig:*) Gebiet *n.*

**arena** [ə'riːnə], *s.* Arena *f.*

**Argentina** [ɑːdʒ(ə)n'tiːnə]. *Pr. n.* Argentinien *n.* ◆**Argentinian** [ɑːdʒən'tiniən]. **I.** *adj.* argentinisch. **II.** *s.* Argentinier(in) *m(f).*

**argue** ['ɑːgjuː], *v.* **1.** *v.tr.* (eine Frage usw.) lebhaft diskutieren. **2.** *v.i.* argumentieren; **to a. that ...**, behaupten, daß ...; **to a. with s.o., about sth.**, mit j-m über etwas *acc* streiten; **to a. for/against sth.**, für/gegen etwas *acc* eintreten. ◆**'arguable**, *adj.* **it is a.**, das könnte man schon behaupten. ◆**'argument**, *s.* **1.** (*reasons*) Argument *n.* **2.** (*quarrel*) Streit *m;* **they had an a.**, sie stritten sich. ◆**argu'mentative**, *adj.* streitlustig.

**arid** ['ærid], *adj.* dürr.

**Aries** ['ɛəriːz]. *Pr.n. Astr:* Widder *m.*

**arise** [ə'raiz], *v.i.irr.* (*a*) (*get up*) aufstehen; (*b*) (*occur*) auftreten; **should the occasion a.**, sollte sich die Gelegenheit ergeben; (*c*) (*originate*) herrühren.

**aristocrat** ['æristəkræt], *s.* Aristokrat(in) *m(f).* ◆**aristocracy** [-'tɔkrəsi], *s.* Aristokratie *f; coll.* Adel *m.* ◆**aristo'cratic**, *adj.* aristokratisch.

**arithmetic** [ə'riθmətik], *s.* Rechnen *n.*

**ark** [ɑːk], *s.* **Noah's A.**, die Arche Noah.

**arm¹** [ɑːm], *s.* **1.** Arm *m.* **2.** Armlehne *f* (eines Sessels). ◆**'arm'chair**, *s.* Sessel *m.* ◆**'armful**, *adj.* Armvoll *m.* ◆**'armhole**, *n.* Ärmelloch *n.* ◆**'armpit**, *s.* Achselhöhle *f.*

**arm²** [ɑːm], *v.* **1.** *v.tr.* bewaffnen. **II.** *s.* **1.** *usu. pl.* Waffen *fpl;* **the arms race**, das Wettrüsten *n.* **2.** (**coat of) arms**, Wappen *n.* ◆**'armed**, *adj.* bewaffnet; **the a. forces**, die Streitkräfte *fpl.* ◆**'armour**, *s.* (*a*) *Mil:* **a.** (**plate**), Panzerung *f;* (*b*)

(**suit of) a.**, Rüstung *f.* ◆**'armoured**, *adj.* gepanzert; **a. car**, Panzerwagen *m.* ◆**'armoury**, *s.* Arsenal *n.* ◆**'army**, *s.* (*particular*) Armee *f;* (*general*) Militär *n.*

**armistice** ['ɑːmistis], *s.* Waffenstillstand *m.*

**aroma** [ə'rəumə], *s.* Aroma *n.* ◆**aromatic** [ærəu'mætik], *adj.* aromatisch.

**around** [ə'raund]. **I.** *adv.* ringsumher. **II.** *prep.* (*a*) (rund)um + *acc;* um ... *acc* herum; (*b*) (*approx.*) **he paid a. £400**, er hat ungefähr £400 bezahlt.

**arouse** [ə'rauz], *v.tr.* (Gefühle usw.) erregen.

**arrange** [ə'rein(d)ʒ], *v.tr.* (*a*) (*set in order*) (Bücher) ordnen; (Möbel) stellen; (*b*) (*plan beforehand*) (eine Zeit, einen Treffpunkt usw.) festlegen; **to a. with s.o. to do sth.**, mit j-m vereinbaren, etwas zu tun. ◆**a'rrangement**, *s.* **1.** Anordnung *f;* Einteilung *f* (eines Hauses); (*putting in order*) Ordnung *f;* **to make arrangements**, Anordnungen/(*preparations*) Vorbereitungen treffen. **2.** (*agreement*) Vereinbarung *f;* **by a.**, nach Vereinbarung.

**array** [ə'rei], *s.* Aufgebot *n* (**of sth.**, an etwas *dat*).

**arrears** [ə'riəz], *s.pl.* Rückstände *mpl;* **to be in a.**, im Rückstand sein.

**arrest** [ə'rest]. **I.** *s.* Verhaftung *f* **II.** *v.tr.* (*a*) (einen Verbrecher) verhaften; (*b*) (Fortschritt usw.) hemmen.

**arrival** [ə'raiv(ə)l], *s.* Ankunft *f;* (*of pers., thing*) Eintreffen *n.* ◆**arrive** [ə'raiv], *v.i.* (*a*) ankommen; eintreffen; (*b*) **to a. at an agreement**, zu einer Vereinbarung kommen.

**arrogant** ['ærəgənt], *adj.* (*haughty*) hochmütig; (*conceited*) eingebildet. ◆**'arrogance**, *s.* Arroganz *f.*

**arrow** ['ærəu], *s.* Pfeil *m.*

**arsenal** ['ɑːsən(ə)l], *s.* Arsenal *n.*

**arsenic** ['ɑːs(ə)nik], *s.* Arsen *n.*

**arson** ['ɑːs(ə)n], *s.* Brandstiftung *f.*

**art** [ɑːt], *s.* Kunst *f;* **arts subjects**, geisteswissenschaftliche Fächer. ◆**'artful**, *adj. Pej:* listig. ◆**'artist**, *s.* Künstler(in) *m(f).* ◆**ar'tistic**, *adj.* künstlerisch; (*of pers.*) kunstverständig. ◆**'artless**, *adj.* **1.** natürlich. **2.** naiv. ◆**'arty**, *adj. F: usu. Pej:* (gewollt) künstlerisch; **a. type**, Bohemien *m.*

**artery** ['ɑːtəri], *s.* Arterie *f.*

**arthritis** [ɑː'θraitis], *s.* Arthritis *f.*

**artichoke** ['ɑːtitʃəuk], *s.* (**globe**) **a.**, Artischocke *f;* **Jerusalem a.**, Erdartischocke *f.*

**article** ['ɑːtikl], *s.* **1.** (*paragraph*) Abschnitt *m;* (*in treaty*) Artikel *m.* **2.** (**newspaper**) **a.**, Zeitungsartikel *m;* Beitrag *m.* **3.** (*object*) Gegenstand *m; Com:* Ware *f;* **a. of clothing**, Kleidungsstück *n.* **4.** *Gram:* Artikel *m.*

**articulate**. **I.** [ɑː'tikjuleit] *v.tr.* (Worte) artikulieren. **II.** [ɑː'tikjulit] *adj.* (*of language, pers.*) leicht verständlich, deutlich (im Ausdruck). ◆**ar'ticulated,** adj. a. lorry, Sattelschlepper m.

**artificial** [ɑːtiˈfiʃ(ə)l], adj. 1. künstlich. 2. unnatürlich.

**artillery** [ɑːˈtiləri], s. Artillerie f.

**artisan** [ɑːtiˈzæn, ˈɑːti-], s. Handwerker m.

**as** [æz,əz]. I. adv. so; **you're not as tall,** du bist nicht so groß; **as from the 15th,** ab dem fünfzehnten; **as for that,** was das anbetrifft. II. conj. & rel. adv. 1. (comparison) wie; **you are as tall as him,** du bist so groß wie er; **as well as,** sowie, sowohl ... wie; **much as I would like to,** so gern ich es auch möchte; **as if/though,** als ob, als wenn. 2. (manner) (a) wie; **as (is) usual,** wie gewöhnlich; (b) als; **to consider s.o. as a friend,** j-n als Freund betrachten. 3. (time) während. 4. (reason) da. III. rel. pron. wie; **beasts of prey (such) as the lion,** Raubtiere wie etwa der Löwe.

**asbestos** [æsˈbestəs], s. Asbest m.

**ascend** [əˈsend], v. 1. v.i. (empor)steigen. 2. v.tr. besteigen. ◆**A'scension,** s. Ecc: (Christi) Himmelfahrt f. ◆**a'scent,** s. (a) Aufstieg m; (b) Besteigung f (eines Berges).

**ascertain** [æsəˈtein], v.tr. (etwas) feststellen, (die Wahrheit) ermitteln.

**ascetic** [əˈsetik], adj. asketisch.

**ascribe** [əˈskraib], v.tr. zuschreiben (**to s.o., sth.,** j-m, etwas dat); zurückführen (**to sth.,** auf etwas acc).

**ash¹** [æʃ], s. Bot: Esche f.

**ash²** s. Asche f. ◆**'ashtray,** s. Aschenbecher m. ◆**'Ash 'Wednesday,** s. Aschermittwoch m.

**ashamed** [əˈʃeimd], adj. **to be/feel a.** (**of sth.**), sich (etwas gen) schämen.

**ashore** [əˈʃɔːr], adv. an Land.

**Asia** [ˈeiʃə]. Pr.n. Asien n. ◆**'Asian, Asiatic** [eiʃiˈætik]. I. adj. asiatisch. II. s. Asiate m, Asiatin f.

**aside** [əˈsaid], adv. (a) beiseite; **to put sth. a.,** etwas beiseite legen; **to stand a.,** zur Seite treten; (b) **a. from,** abgesehen von + dat.

**ask** [ɑːsk], v.tr. & i. (a) (j-n etwas) fragen; **to a. s.o. the way,** j-n nach dem Weg fragen; **to a. s.o. a question,** j-m eine Frage stellen; **to a. £6 for sth.,** für etwas acc 6 Pfund verlangen; (c) (request) **to a. s.o. to do sth.,** j-n bitten, etwas zu tun; **to a. to do sth.,** um Erlaubnis bitten, etwas zu tun; (d) (enquire) **to a. about sth.,** sich nach etwas dat erkundigen; **to a. s.o. about sth.,** j-n wegen etwas gen fragen; **to a. after s.o.,** sich nach j-m erkundigen; (e) **to a. for sth.,** um etwas acc bitten; (f) (invite) **to a. s.o. to lunch,** j-n zum Mittagessen einladen. ◆**'asking,** s. **it's yours for the a.,** Sie brauchen nur ein Wort zu sagen.

**askance** [əˈskæns], adv. **to look a. at s.o.,** j-n schief ansehen.

**askew** [əˈskjuː], adv. schief.

**asleep** [əˈsliːp], adj. & adv. eingeschlafen; **to be a.,** schlafen; **to fall a.,** einschlafen.

**asparagus** [əsˈpærəgəs], s. Spargel m.

**aspect** [ˈæspekt], s. 1. (appearance) Aussehen n. 2. Aspekt m (eines Problems).

**aspersion** [əˈspɜːʃ(ə)n], s. **to cast aspersions upon s.o.,** j-n verleumden.

**asphalt** [ˈæsfælt, -fɔlt], s. Asphalt m.

**asphyxiate** [æsˈfiksieit], v.tr. ersticken.

**aspire** [əˈspaiər], v.i. streben (**to,** nach + dat). ◆**aspiration** [-pəˈreiʃ(ə)n], s. Bestreben n. ◆**a'spiring,** adj. ehrgeizig.

**aspirin** [ˈæsp(ə)rin], s. Aspirin n.

**ass** [æs], s. Z: & F: Esel m.

**assailant** [əˈseilənt], s. Angreifer(in) m(f).

**assassin** [əˈsæsin], s. Mörder(in) m(f). ◆**a'ssassinate,** v.tr. ermorden. ◆**assassi'nation,** s. Mord m.

**assault** [əˈsɔːlt]. I. v.tr. (j-n) (tätlich) angreifen; (indecently) (j-n) unsittlich belästigen, (rape) vergewaltigen. II. s. (a) Mil: Sturm m; (b) Angriff m; Jur: indecent a., unsittliche Belästigung.

**assemble** [əˈsembl], v. 1. v.tr. (a) (Menschen) versammeln; (eine Sammlung) zusammenstellen; (b) (eine Maschine usw.) zusammenbauen. 2. v.i. sich versammeln; (of parliament) zusammentreten. ◆**a'ssembly,** s. 1. Versammlung f. 2. Montage f (einer Maschine usw.); a. line, Fließband n.

**assent** [əˈsent]. I. v.i. zustimmen. II. s. Zustimmung f.

**assert** [əˈsɜːt], v.tr. (a) (state) behaupten; (b) (ein Recht) geltend machen; **to a. oneself,** sich durchsetzen. ◆**a'ssertion,** s. Behauptung f. ◆**a'ssertive,** adj. selbstbewußt.

**assess** [əˈses], v.tr. bewerten; (den Wert von etwas) schätzen; Jur: (Schadenersatz usw.) festlegen. ◆**a'ssessment,** s. Einschätzung f. ◆**a'ssessor,** s. Schätzer m.

**asset** [ˈæset], s. 1. Vorteil m. 2. Fin: assets, Aktiva pl; Jur: Güter pl.

**assiduous** [əˈsidjuəs], adj. fleißig.

**assign** [əˈsain], v.tr. zuweisen (**to s.o.,** j-m). ◆**a'ssignment,** s. (task) Aufgabe f.

**assimilate** [əˈsimileit], v.tr. (in sich) aufnehmen. ◆**assimi'lation,** s. Aufnahme f.

**assist** [əˈsist], v.tr. & i. helfen. ◆**a'ssistance,** s. Unterstützung f. ◆**a'ssistant,** s. Hilfskraft f; Assistent m; shop a., Verkäufer(in) m(f).

**associate.** I. [əˈsəuʃieit], v. 1. v.tr. (etwas) assoziieren. 2. v.i. **to a. with s.o.,** mit j-m verkehren. II. [əˈsəuʃiət]. 1. s. Kollege m; Mitarbeiter m; business a., Geschäftspartner m. 2. adj. Mit-. ◆**associ'ation,** s. (a) Verbindung f; (b) Umgang m (mit usw.); (organization) Verband m; (club) Verein m.

**assorted** [əˈsɔːtid], adj. gemischt.

◆**a'ssortment,** s. Mischung f; (selection) Auswahl f; Com: (samples) Sortiment n.

**assume** [ə'sju:m], v.tr. (a) (ein Amt, die Verantwortung) übernehmen; (b) (etwas) annehmen, (suppose) vermuten.
◆**a'ssumed,** adj. a. name, falscher Name. ◆**a'ssumption,** s. Annahme f; on the a. that ..., in der Annahme, daß ...

**assure** [ə'ʃuər], v.tr. to a. s.o. that ..., j-m versichern, daß ...; you can rest assured that ..., Sie können sicher sein, daß ... ◆**a'ssurance,** s. 1. Versicherung f. 2. Selbstbewußtsein n.
◆**a'ssured,** adj. (a) (certain) sicher; (b) (pers.) selbstbewußt. ◆**a'ssuredly** [-idli], adv. ganz gewiß.

**asterisk** ['æst(ə)risk], s. Sternchen n.

**astern** [ə'stə:n], adv. achtern.

**asthma** ['æsmə], s. Asthma n. ◆**asth'matic. I.** adj. asthmatisch. **II.** s. Asthmatiker(in) m(f).

**astonish** [ə'stɔniʃ], v.tr. erstaunen; to be astonished at sth., über etwas acc erstaunt sein. ◆**a'stonishing,** adj. erstaunlich. ◆**a'stonishment,** s. Erstaunen n.

**astound** [ə'staund], v.tr. in Erstaunen setzen. ◆**a'stounding,** adj. erstaunlich.

**astray** [ə'strei], adj. & adv. to go a., sich verlaufen; (of letter) verlorengehen; to lead s.o. a., j-n irreführen.

**astride** [ə'straid], adv. & prep. rittlings (auf + dat).

**astrology** [ə'strɔlədʒi], s. Astrologie f. ◆**a'strologer,** s. Astrologe m, Astrologin f.

**astronaut** ['æstrənɔ:t], s. Astronaut(in) m(f).

**astronomy** [ə'strɔnəmi], s. Astronomie f. ◆**a'stronomer,** s. Astronom m. ◆**astro'nomic(al),** adj. astronomisch.

**astute** [əs'tju:t], adj. scharfsinnig; (of mind) klug.

**asylum** [ə'sailəm], s. 1. Asyl n; to grant s.o. a., j-m Asyl gewähren. 2. (institution) Anstalt f.

**at** [æt], prep. 1. (place) an + dat, bei + dat; (with town) in; at school, in der Schule; at work, bei der Arbeit; at home, zu Hause; at the Schmidts', bei Schmidts; at the tailor's, beim Schneider. 2. (time) at 5 o'clock, um 5 Uhr. 3. (price) at twenty pence a pound, (zu) zwanzig Pence das Pfund. 4. (age) at (the age of) eighty, im Alter von 80. 5. (speed) bei, mit + dat; to drive at (a speed of) 100 kph, mit 100 Kilometern fahren. 6. at my request, auf meine Bitte hin; she's at it again, sie tut es schon wieder; while we are at it, wenn wir einmal dabei sind.

**atheism** ['eiθiizm], s. Atheismus m. ◆**'atheist,** s. Atheist m.

**Athens** ['æθinz]. Pr. n. Athen n.

**athlete** ['æθli:t], s. Athlet(in) m(f). ◆**athletic** [-'letik], adj. athletisch.

◆**ath'letics,** s.pl. Leichtathletik f.

**Atlantic** [ət'læntik], adj. & s. the Atlantic (Ocean), der Atlantik.

**atlas** ['ætləs], s. Atlas m.

**atmosphere** ['ætməsfiər], s. Atmosphäre f.

**atom** ['ætəm], s. Atom n; a. bomb, Atombombe f. ◆**atomic** [ə'tɔmik], adj. atomar; a. energy, Atomenergie f. ◆**'atomizer,** s. Zerstäuber m.

**atone** [ə'təun], v.i. to a. for sth., etwas sühnen.

**atrocious** [ə'trəuʃəs], adj. entsetzlich; F: scheußlich; (of crime) gräßlich. ◆**atrocity** [ə'trɔsiti], s. Greueltat f.

**attach** [ə'tætʃ], v.tr. to a. sth. to sth., etwas an etwas acc befestigen/(permanently) anbringen; to a. importance to sth., auf etwas acc Wert legen. ◆**attaché** [ə'tæʃei], s. Attaché m; a. case, Aktentasche f. ◆**a'ttached,** adj. to be very a. to s.o., sth., j-m etwas dat sehr zugetan sein. ◆**a'ttachment,** s. 1. (affection) Zuneigung f (für j-n). 2. Zusatzgerät n (zu einer Maschine usw.).

**attack** [ə'tæk]. **I.** v.tr. angreifen, (mug etc.) überfallen; (ein Problem) in Angriff nehmen. **II.** s. 1. Angriff m. 2. Med: Anfall m. ◆**a'ttacker,** s. Angreifer m.

**attain** [ə'tein], v.tr. erzielen. ◆**a'ttainable,** adj. erreichbar.

**attempt** [ə'tem(p)t]. **I.** v.tr. versuchen. **II.** s. Versuch m.

**attend** [ə'tend], v. 1. v.i. (a) dabei sein; (b) to a. to s.o., sth., sich um j-n, etwas acc kümmern; (c) (pay attention) aufpassen. 2. v.tr. (einer Versammlung usw.) beiwohnen; (an einem Kurs usw.) teilnehmen; to a. school, die Schule besuchen. ◆**a'ttendance,** s. Besuch m; Beteiligung f (an einem Kurs usw.); in a., anwesend. ◆**a'ttendant. I.** s. Diener(in) m(f); (in museum, zoo etc.) Wärter m. **II.** adj. damit verbunden.

**attention** [ə'tenʃ(ə)n], s. 1. Aufmerksamkeit f; to pay a. to sth., auf etwas acc achten; Com: for the a. of Mr. X, zu Händen von Herrn X; a. to detail, Berücksichtigung f von Einzelheiten; (b) (repair) needing a., reparaturbedürftig. 2. Mil: a.! stillgestanden! ◆**attentive** [ə'tentiv], adj. aufmerksam.

**attic** ['ætik], s. Dachgeschoß n.

**attire** [ə'taiər], s. Kleidung f; Lit: Gewand n.

**attitude** ['ætitju:d], s. Haltung f.

**attorney** [ə'tə:ni], s. N.Am: Rechtsanwalt m; District A., = Staatsanwalt m; A. General, Brit: erster Kronanwalt m; U.S: approx. = Justizminister m; power of a., Vollmacht f.

**attract** [ə'trækt], v.tr. anziehen; to be attracted to s.o., sich zu j-m hingezogen fühlen. ◆**a'ttraction,** s. Reiz m. ◆**a'ttractive,** adj. attraktiv, reizvoll. ◆**a'ttractiveness,** s. Reiz m.

**attribute. I.** v.tr. [ə'tribju:t], to a. a work

etc. to s.o., j-m ein Werk usw. zuschreiben. **II.** s. ['ætribjuːt], Eigenschaft f.
**attrition** [ə'trɪʃ(ə)n], s. war of a., Zermürbungskrieg m.
**aubergine** ['əubəʒiːn], s. Aubergine f.
**auburn** ['ɔːbən], adj. (of hair) kupferrot.
**auction** ['ɔːkʃ(ə)n]. **I.** v.tr. (etwas) versteigern. **II.** s. Auktion f, Versteigerung f. ◆**auctio'neer**, s. Auktionator m.
**audacious** ['ɔːdeiʃəs], adj. kühn, verwegen. ◆**audacity** [ɔː'dæsiti], s. 1. Wagemut n. 2. Pej: Frechheit f.
**audible** ['ɔːdibl], adj. hörbar.
**audience** ['ɔːdjəns], s. 1. Th: Rad: etc: Publikum n; TV: Zuschauer mpl; (in a concert) Zuhörer mpl. 2. (interview) Audienz f (with, bei + dat).
**audio-visual** ['ɔːdiəu'viʒuəl], adj. audiovisuell.
**audit** ['ɔːdit]. **I.** v.tr. prüfen. **II.** s. Buchprüfung f. ◆**'auditor,** s. Buchprüfer m.
**auditorium** [ɔːdi'tɔːriəm], s. Auditorium n.
**audition** [ɔː'diʃ(ə)n]. **I.** s. Th: Vorsprechen n. **II.** v. 1. v.i. Th: vorsprechen. 2. v.tr. Th: (j-n) vorsprechen lassen.
**augment** [ɔːg'ment], v.tr. (etwas) vergrößern; (eine Zahl) vermehren.
**augur** ['ɔːgər], v.i. it augurs well for him, es sieht gut für ihn aus.
**August** ['ɔːgəst], s. August m.
**aunt** [ɑːnt], F: **auntie** ['ɑːnti], s. Tante f.
**au pair** [əu'pɛər], adj. & s. a. p. (girl), Au-pair-Mädchen n.
**auspices** ['ɔːspisiz], s.pl. under the a. of ..., unter der Schirmherrschaft von ... dat. ◆**au'spicious** [-ʃəs], adj. günstig; (promising) verheißungsvoll.
**austere** [ɔs'tiər], adj. (severe) streng; (plain) nüchtern. ◆**austerity** [-'teriti], s. Strenge f; Nüchternheit f; time of a., Zeit f der (wirtschaftlichen) Einschränkungen.
**Australia** [ɔs'treiliə]. Pr.n. Australien n. ◆**Aus'tralian. I.** adj. australisch. **II.** s. Australier(in) m(f).
**Austria** ['ɔstriə]. Pr.n. Österreich n. ◆**'Austrian. I.** adj. österreichisch. **II.** s. Österreicher(in) m(f).
**authentic** [ɔː'θentik], adj. authentisch, echt. ◆**au'thenticate,** v.tr. beglaubigen. ◆**authenticity** [-'tisiti], s. Echtheit f.
**author** ['ɔːθər], s. Autor(in) m(f).
**authoritative** [ɔː'θɔritativ], adj. 1. (of tone, manner) gebieterisch. 2. (of statement) maßgebend. ◆**au'thority,** s. 1. Autorität f; to have a. over s.o., über j-n gebieten. 2. Ermächtigung f (, etwas zu tun); (document) Vollmacht f. 3. Experte m (on, über + acc); on good a., aus glaubwürdiger Quelle. 4. the authorities, die Behörden f pl. ◆**authorize** ['ɔːθəraiz], v.tr. bewilligen; to a. s.o. to do sth., j-n ermächtigen, etwas zu tun. ◆**authori'zation,** s. Ermächtigung f.

◆**'authorized,** adj. autorisiert.
**auto-** ['ɔːtəu-], prefix auto-, selbst-.
◆**autobi'ography,** s. Autobiographie f. ◆**'autocrat,** s. Autokrat m. ◆**auto'cratic,** adj. selbstherrlich. ◆**'autograph. I.** s. Autogramm n. **II.** v.tr. (ein Buch usw.) signieren. ◆**'automate,** v.tr. automatisieren. ◆**auto'matic,** adj. automatisch; Aut: a. transmission, Automatik f. ◆**auto'mation,** s. Automation f. ◆**'automobile,** s. esp. N.Am: Auto n. ◆**autonomous** [ɔː'tɔnəməs], adj. autonom. ◆**au'tonomy,** s. Autonomie f. ◆**autopsy** ['ɔːtɔpsi], s. Obduktion f.
**autumn** ['ɔːtəm], s. Herbst m. ◆**autumnal** [ɔː'tʌmnəl], adj. herbstlich.
**auxiliary** [ɔːg'ziljəri]. **I.** adj. Hilfs-. **II.** s. Helfer m.
**avail** [ə'veil]. **I.** v.tr. to a. oneself of sth., sich einer Sache bedienen. **II.** s. it's of no a., es ist nutzlos. ◆**availa'bility,** s. Verfügbarkeit f. ◆**a'vailable,** adj. verfügbar; Com: vorrätig.
**avalanche** ['ævəlɑːnʃ], s. Lawine f.
**avantgarde** ['ævä(ŋ)'gɑːd], s. Avantgarde f.
**avarice** ['ævəris], s. Habgier f. ◆**ava'ricious,** adj. habgierig.
**avenge** [ə'ven(d)ʒ], v.tr. (etwas, sich) rächen (on s.o., an j-n).
**avenue** ['ævinjuː], s. Allee f.
**average** ['ævəridʒ]. **I.** s. Durchschnitt m; on (an) a., im Durchschnitt. **II.** adj. durchschnittlich; above a., überdurchschnittlich; below a., unterdurchschnittlich; the a. Englishman, der Durchschnittsengländer. **III.** v.tr. & i. durchschnittlich betragen; we averaged 120 kph, wir hatten ein Durchschnittstempo von 120 Stundenkilometern.
**averse** [ə'vəːs], adj. to be a. to sth., etwas dat abgeneigt sein. ◆**a'version,** s. Abneigung f (to, gegen + acc).
**avert** [ə'vəːt], v.tr. (a) (den Blick) abwenden; (b) (prevent) verhindern.
**aviary** ['eiviəri], s. Vogelhaus n.
**aviation** [eivi'eiʃ(ə)n], s. Luftfahrt f. ◆**'aviator,** s. Flieger m.
**avid** ['ævid], adj. begierig (for, auf + acc).
**avocado** [ævə'kɑːdəu], s. a. (pear), Avocado f.
**avoid** [ə'vɔid], v.tr. (a) (j-n, etwas) meiden; (etwas) vermeiden; to a. doing sth., es vermeiden, etwas zu tun; (b) (einer Gefahr usw.) entgehen. ◆**a'voidable,** adj. vermeidbar. ◆**a'voidance,** s. Vermeidung f; tax a., Steuerhinterziehung f.
**await** [ə'weit], v.tr. (j-n) erwarten; (wait for) (auf j-n, etwas acc) warten.
**awake** [ə'weik]. **I.** v.irr. 1. v.i. erwachen. 2. v.tr. (j-n) wecken. **II.** adj. wach; wide a., hellwach. ◆**a'waken,** v. 1. v.tr. (a) (Gefühle usw.) erwecken; (b) (j-n) wecken. 2. v.i. Lit: aufwachen.

◆a'wakening, s. Erwachen n; rude a., unsanftes Erwachen.

award [ə'wɔːd]. I. v.tr. (j-m einen Preis usw.) verleihen. II. s. Auszeichnung f; (prize) Preis m.

aware [ə'wɛər], adj. bewußt; to be a. of sth., sich dat etwas gen bewußt sein. ◆a'wareness, s. Bewußtsein n.

away [ə'wei], adv. (a) weg, fort, davon; to go a., weggehen; five paces a., fünf Schritte entfernt; (b) (absent) abwesend; when he is a., wenn er nicht da ist; a. match, Auswärtsspiel n.

awe [ɔː], s. Ehrfurcht f. ◆'awe-inspiring, adj. ehrfurchtgebietend. ◆'awful, adj. furchtbar.

awkward ['ɔːkwəd], adj. 1. (a) (clumsy)

ungeschickt; (b) (ill at ease) verlegen. 2. (a) (unpleasant) peinlich. (b) (difficult) schwierig; (of shape) unhandlich. ◆'awkwardness, s. 1. (a) Ungeschicklichkeit f; (b) Verlegenheit f. 2. Peinlichkeit f.

awning ['ɔːniŋ], s. Plane f; (of shop) Markise f.

awry [ə'rai], adv. & adj. schief; to go (all) a., schiefgehen.

axe [æks]. I. s. Axt f, Beil n. II. v.tr. (ein Projekt) fallenlassen.

axis pl. -es ['æksis, 'æksiːz], s. Achse f.

axle ['æksl], s. Achse f; (shaft) Welle f.

aye [ai]. I. int. ja. II. s. Parl: Ja-stimme f.

azalea [ə'zeiljə], s. Azalee f.

# B

B, b [biː], s. (der Buchstabe) B, b n.

babble ['bæbl]. I. s. Geplapper n. II. v.i. (a) plappern; (b) (of stream) murmeln.

baboon [bə'buːn], s. Pavian m.

baby ['beibi], s. Baby n; to have a b., ein Kind bekommen; F: to be holding the b., die Verantwortung (für etwas acc) tragen; F: that's your b.! das ist deine Sache!; b. sister, kleine Schwester f. ◆'babyish, adj. babyhaft, kindisch. ◆'babysit, v.i. babysitten. ◆'baby-sitter, s. Babysitter m.

bachelor ['bætʃələr], s. Junggeselle m.

back ['bæk]. I. s. 1. Rücken m; b. to front, verkehrt; to do sth. behind s.o.'s b., etwas hinter j-s Rücken tun; to break one's b., sich dat das Rückgrat brechen; Fig: to break the b. of the work, den größten Teil der Arbeit erledigen. 2. (a) (of paper, house etc.) Rückseite f; (of chair) Rückenlehne f; (b) he knows London like the b. of his hand, er kennt London wie seine Westentasche; (c) Aut: in the b., hinten; auf dem Rücksitz; (d) at the b., hinten; at the b. of sth./ N.Am: to do sth., hinter etwas dat. 3. Fb: Verteidiger m. II. adj. (a) hintere(r,s), Hinter-; b. door, Hintertür f; b. seat, Rücksitz m; b. wheel, Hinterrad n; to take a b. seat, eine untergeordnete Rolle spielen. III. adv. zurück; to hit b., zurückschlagen; to call s.o. b., j-n zurückrufen; when will you be b.? wann kommst du zurück? some years b., vor einigen Jahren. IV. v. 1. v.i. (a) rückwärts gehen/Aut: fahren; (b) (of house) to b. onto sth., hinten an etwas acc grenzen. 2. v.tr. (a) (support) (j-n) unterstützen; (b) to b. a horse, (Geld) auf ein Pferd setzen; (c) (einen Wagen) rückwärts fahren. ◆'backache, s. Rückenschmerzen mpl. ◆'back-'bencher, s. Brit: Pol: Parlamentsabgeordnete(r) f (m), die (der) nicht zur Führung seiner Partei gehört. ◆'backbiter, s. Verleum-

der(in) m(f). ◆'backbone, s. (a) Rückgrat n; (b) Fig: Stütze f. ◆'back'dated, adj. a rise b. to April 1st, eine Gehaltserhöhung rückwirkend vom 1. April an. ◆'back 'down, v.i. einen Rückzieher machen. ◆'backer, s. Unterstützer m; Com: Fin: Geldgeber m. ◆'back'fire, v.i. (of plan etc.) fehlschlagen; Aut: fehlzünden. ◆'background, m. Hintergrund m; what's his family b.? aus welchen Familienverhältnissen stammt er? ◆'backhand, s. Rückhand f. ◆'back'handed, adj. b. compliment, zweifelhaftes Kompliment. ◆'backing, s. (finanzielle) Unterstützung f. ◆'backlash, s. Fig: starke Gegenreaktion f. ◆'backlog, s. Rückstände mpl. ◆'back 'out, v.i. to b. out of a deal etc., aus einem Geschäft usw. aussteigen. ◆'backside, s. Hintern m. ◆'back 'up, v. 1. v.tr. (a) (support) (j-n) unterstützen; (eine Aussage) bestätigen; (b) N.Am: (einen Wagen) rückwärts fahren. 2. v.i. rückwärts fahren. ◆'backward. I. adj. (a) b. motion, Rückwärtsbewegung f; (b) (of child) zurückgeblieben; (of country etc.) unterentwickelt. II. adv. backward(s), rückwärts. ◆'backwardness, s. (of child) Zurückgebliebenheit f; (of country) Rückständigkeit f. ◆'backwater, s. (stiller) abgelegener Ort m.

bacon ['beik(ə)n], s. Speck m.

bacterium [bæk'tiəriəm], s. (pl bacteria) Bakterie f.

bad [bæd], adj. schlecht; (serious) (of accident etc.) schwer, schlimm; (of food) to go b., schlecht werden; he's in a b. way, es geht ihm gar nicht gut; things are going from b. to worse, es wird immer schlimmer; a b. boy, ein schlimmer Junge; b. smell, übler Geruch; b. tempered, schlecht gelaunt; to have a b. cold, einen starken Schnupfen haben; that's too b.! Pech gehabt! my b. leg, mein

schlimmes Bein; **-ly**, *adv.* schlecht;
**b. wounded**, schwer verwundet; **to
want sth. b.**, (i) etwas sehr gerne wollen;
(ii) (*need*) etwas dringend brauchen.
**badge** [bædʒ], *s.* Abzeichen *n.*
**badger¹** ['bædʒər], *s.* Dachs *m.*
**badger²** ['bædʒər], *v.tr.* (j-n) belästigen.
**baffle** ['bæfl], *v.tr.* verblüffen.
**bag** [bæg], *s.* **1.** (*handbag*) Tasche *f;* (**paper**) **b.**, Tüte *f;* **plastic b.**, (*small*) Pla-
stiktüte *f,* (*large*) Plastiksack *m.* **2.** *F:*
(*woman*) **old b.**, alte Zicke. ◆'**baggy**,
*adj.* (*of clothes*) bauschig; (*of trousers*) aus-
gebeult.
**baggage** ['bægidʒ], *s.* Reisegepäck *n.*
**bagpipes** ['bægpaips], *s.pl.* Dudelsack *m.*
**bail¹** [beil], *s.* Kaution *f;* (**released**) **on
b.**, gegen Kaution freigelassen.
◆'**bailiff**, *s.* Gerichtsvollzieher *m.*
**bail²** [beil], *v.tr. Nau:* **to b. out**, (Wasser)
ausschöpfen; (ein Boot) leerschöpfen.
**bait** [beit], *s.* Köder *m.*
**bake** [beik], *v.tr. & i.* backen. ◆'**baker**,
*s.* Bäcker *m;* **b.'s** (**shop**), Bäckerei *f.*
◆'**bakery**, *s.* Bäckerei *f.* ◆'**baking-
powder**, *s.* Backpulver *n.*
**balance** ['bæləns]. **I.** *s.* **1.** (*scales*) Waage
*f;* **on b.**, alles in allem. **2.** Gleichgewicht
*n;* **to lose one's b.**, das Gleichgewicht
verlieren; **b. of power**, politisches
Gleichgewicht. **3.** *Com:* (*in hand*) Saldo
*m;* (*amount due*) Restbetrag *m; Fin:* **b. of
payments**, Zahlungsbilanz *f;* **b. sheet**,
Bilanz *f.* **II.** *v.* **1.** *v.tr.* (*a*) (etwas) ausba-
lancieren; (*b*) (eine Rechnung, ein Kon-
to) ausgleichen; **to b. the books**, die Bilanz machen. **2.** *v.i.* (*a*) (*of accounts*) sich
ausgleichen; (*b*) (*of pers.*) balancieren.
◆'**balanced**, *adj.* ausgeglichen.
**balcony**, *pl* **-ies** ['bælkəni, -iz], *s.* Balkon
*m.*
**bald** [bɔːld], *adj.* **1.** glatzköpfig. **2.** (*of
statement*) unverblümt. ◆'**baldness**, *s.*
Kahlheit *f.*
**bale¹** [beil], *s.* Ballen *m.*
**bale²** [beil], *v.i.* **to b. out**, (mit dem Fallschirm) abspringen.
**balk** [bɔːk], *v.i.* **to b. at sth.**, vor etwas
*dat* stutzen.
**ball** [bɔːl], *s.* **1.** Ball *m;* **billiard b.**, Billard-
kugel *f.* ◆'**ball-'bearing**, *s.* Kugellager
*n.* ◆'**ballcock**, *s.* Schwimmerhahn *m.*
◆'**ballpoint**, *s.* **b.** (**pen**), Kugelschrei-
ber *m.*
**ballad** ['bæləd], *s.* Ballade *f.*
**ballast** ['bæləst], *s.* Ballast *m.*
**ballet** ['bælei], *s.* Ballett *n;* **b. dancer**,
Balletttänzer(in) *m(f).*
**balloon** [bə'luːn], *s.* (*child's*) Luftballon
*m; Av:* Ballon *m.*
**ballot** ['bælət], *s.* (**secret**) **b.**, geheime
Abstimmung/Wahl; **b. box**, Wahlurne *f.*
**ballroom** ['bɔːlruːm], *s.* Ballsaal *m.*
**Baltic** ['bɔːltik], *adj. & s.* **the B.** (**Sea**),
die Ostsee.
**balustrade** ['bæləs'treid], *s.* Balustrade *f.*
**bamboo** [bæm'buː], *s.* Bambus *m.*

**ban** [bæn]. **I.** *s.* Verbot *n.* **II.** *v.tr.* verbieten.
**banal** [bə'nɑːl], *adj.* banal.
**banana** [bə'nɑːnə], *s.* Banane *f.*
**band¹** [bænd], *s.* Band *n;* **elastic/rubber
b.**, Gummiband *n.*
**band²**. **I.** *s.* **1.** (*gang*) Bande *f.* **2.** *Mus:*
Band *f.* **II.** *v.i.* **to b. together**, sich zusammenrotten. ◆'**bandstand**, *s.* Musik-
pavillon *m.* ◆'**bandwagon**, *s.* **to jump
on the b.**, sich einer erfolgreichen Sache
anschließen; (*habitually*) seine Fahne
nach dem Wind hängen.
**bandage** ['bændidʒ]. **I.** *s.* Verband *m,*
Bandage *f.* **II.** *v.tr.* verbinden.
**bandit** ['bændit], *s.* Bandit *m.*
**bandy¹** ['bændi], *v.tr.* (Worte mit j-m)
wechseln.
**bandy,²** *adj.* **b. legs**, O-Beine *npl.*
◆'**bandy-legged**, *adj.* O-beinig.
**bang** [bæŋ]. **I.** *s.* Knall *m;* **to go b.**, knallen. **II.** *int.* bums! peng! *F:* **b. goes my
money!** futsch ist mein Geld! **III.** *v.* **1.**
*v.i.* knallen. **2.** *v.tr.* (eine Tür usw.) zuknallen. ◆'**banger**, *s. F:* **1.** (*sausage*)
Würstchen *n.* **2.** (*firework*) Knallfrosch *m.*
**3.** (*car*) **old b.**, alte Kiste *f.*
**banish** ['bæniʃ], *v.tr.* (j-n) verbannen.
**banisters** ['bænistəz], *s.pl.* Treppen-
geländer *n.*
**banjo**, *pl.* **-oes**/*N.Am:* **-os** ['bændʒəu,
-əuz], *s.* Banjo *n.*
**bank¹** [bæŋk]. **I.** *s.* (*embankment*) Wall *m;*
(*of river*) Ufer *n;* (*slope*) Hang *m.* **II.** *v.i.
Av:* sich in die Kurve legen.
**bank²** [bæŋk]. **I.** *s.* Bank *f;* **b. account**,
Bankkonto *n; Brit:* **b. holiday**, gesetz-
licher Feiertag. **II.** *v.i.* (*a*) **to b. with the
X Bank**, ein Konto bei der X Bank ha-
ben; (*b*) *F:* **to b. on sth.**, auf etwas *acc*
bauen. ◆'**banker**, *s.* Bankier *m.*
◆'**banking**, *s.* Bankgeschäft *n,* Bankwe-
sen *n.* ◆'**banknote**, *s.* Banknote *f.*
◆'**bankrupt**. **I.** *adj.* bankrott; **to go b.**,
Bankrott machen. **II.** *s.* (*pers.*) Bankrot-
teur *m.* ◆'**bankruptcy**, *s.* Bankrott *m.*
**banner** ['bænər], *s.* Banner *n;* (*in demonstration*) Transparent *n.*
**banns** [bænz], *s.pl.* Aufgebot *n.*
**banquet** ['bæŋkwit], *s.* Festessen *n; Lit:*
Bankett *n.*
**baptize** [bæp'taiz], *v.tr.* (j-n) taufen.
◆'**baptism**, *s.* Taufe *f.*
**bar** [bɑːr]. **I.** *s.* **1.** (*a*) (*metal*) Stange *f;* (*on
door*) Riegel *m;* (*b*) (*of chocolate*) Tafel *f;*
(*of soap*) Stück *n;* (*of gold, silver*) Barren
*m;* (*c*) **bars** *pl,* Gitter *n;* **to be behind
bars**, hinter Gittern sitzen. **2.** (*obstacle*)
Hindernis *n.* **3.** *Jur:* **to be called to the
b.**, als plädierender Anwalt zugelassen
werden. **4.** (*a*) (*premises*) Bar *f;* (*b*) (*counter*) Theke *f.* **II.** *v.tr.* (*a*) (den Weg) versperren; (eine Tür) verriegeln; (*b*) (j-n)
ausschließen. **III.** *prep.* (*also* '**barring**)
ausgenommen; **b. none**, ohne Ausnahme.
**barbarian** [bɑː'bɛəriən], *s.* Barbar(in)
*m(f).* ◆**barbaric** [-'bærik], *adj.* barba-

risch. ◆**bar'barity**, s. Barbarei f.
◆**'barbarous** [-ərəs], adj. barbarisch;
(cruel) grausam.

**barbecue** ['bɑ:bikju:], s. (a) Grill m; (b)
(party) Grillparty f.

**barbed** [bɑ:bd], adj. **b. wire**, Stacheldraht m; **b. remark**, spitze Bemerkung.

**barber** ['bɑ:bər], s. Herrenfriseur m.

**bare** [beər]. I. adj. 1. (a) (uncovered)
nackt; (b) (barren) kahl. 2. **b. majority**,
knappe Mehrheit; **-ly**, adv. kaum. II.
v.tr. entblößen; (die Zähne) blecken.
◆**'bareback**, adv. **to ride b.**, ohne Sattel reiten. ◆**'barefaced**, adj. schamlos.
◆**'barefoot**, adv. barfuß.

**bargain** ['bɑ:gin]. I. s. (a) (transaction)
Geschäft n; **into the b.**, obendrein; (b)
(cheap purchase) Gelegenheitskauf m; **at
b. price**, zu einem sehr günstigen Preis.
II. v.i. **to b. with s.o.**, mit j-m
(ver)handeln; **I didn't b. for that!** damit
hatte ich nicht gerechnet!

**barge** [bɑ:dʒ]. I. s. Lastkahn m; (if
towed) Schleppkahn m. II. v.i. F: **to b.
in**, hereinplatzen.

**baritone** ['bæritəun], s. Bariton m.

**bark¹** [bɑ:k], s. Baumrinde f.

**bark²** [bɑ:k]. I. s. Bellen n. II. v.i. bellen. ◆**'barking**, s. Bellen n.

**barley** ['bɑ:li], s. Gerste f; **b. sugar**, (esp.
Bonbons aus) Gerstenzucker m.

**barmaid** ['bɑ:meid], s. Bardame f.

**barman**, pl **-men** ['bɑ:mən, -men], s.
Barkeeper m.

**barn** [bɑ:n], s. Scheune f.

**barnacle** ['bɑ:nəkl], s. Entenmuschel f.

**barometer** [bə'rɔmitər], s. Barometer n.

**baron** ['bærən], s. Baron m. ◆**'baroness**, s. Baronin f.

**barrack** ['bærək], s. (usu.pl.) Kaserne f.

**barrage** ['bærɑ:ʒ], s. 1. Staudamm m;
(across valley) Talsperre f. 2. Mil: Sperr-
feuer n.

**barrel** ['bærəl], s. 1. Faß n; (large) Tonne
f. 2. (of small gun) Lauf m; (of large gun)
Rohr n.

**barren** ['bærən], adj. unfruchtbar.

**barricade** ['bærikeid]. I. s. Barrikade f.
II. v.tr. (etwas) verbarrikadieren.

**barrier** ['bæriər], s. 1. Schranke f; (ticket
b. etc.) Sperre f. 2. (obstacle) Hindernis
n.

**barrister** ['bæristər], s. Brit. plädierender
Rechtsanwalt m.

**barrow** ['bærəu], s. (wheel-)b., Schubkar-
ren m.

**barter** ['bɑ:tər], s. Tauschhandel m.

**base** [beis]. I. s. 1. (a) Basis f; (b) (of
statue etc.) Sockel m; (small) Fuß m. 2.
(place) Standort m; Mil: Stützpunkt m.
II. v.tr. (etwas) gründen (on, auf + acc);
**to be based on sth.**, sich auf etwas acc
stützen. ◆**'baseless**, adj. grundlos.
◆**'basement**, s. Kellergeschoß n.

**baseball** ['beisbɔ:l], s. Baseball m.

**bash** [bæʃ]. I. s. F: **to have a b. at sth.**,
etwas mal probieren. II. v.tr. F: **to b.**

**sth. in**, etwas einbeulen; **to b. s.o.
about**, j-n verprügeln.

**bashful** ['bæʃf(u)l], adj. schüchtern.

**basic** ['beisik], adj. grundsätzlich; **b.
wage**, Grundlohn m.

**basin** ['beisn], s. (a) (pudding) b., Schüssel f; (b) (wash-)b., Waschbecken n.

**basis** ['beisis], s. Basis f.

**bask** [bɑ:sk], v.i. sich sonnen.

**basket** ['bɑ:skit], s. Korb m.
◆**'basketball**, s. Basketball m.

**Basle** [bɑ:l]. Pr.n. Basel n.

**bass** [beis]. I. adj. Baß-. II. s. Baß m.

**bassoon** [bə'su:n], s. Fagott m.

**bastard** ['bɑ:stəd, 'bæstəd], s. Scheißkerl
m.

**baste** [beist], v.tr. begießen.

**bat¹** [bæt], s. Fledermaus f.

**bat²** [bæt]. I. s. Sp: Schläger m; Fig: **to
do sth. off one's own b.**, etwas auf eigene Faust tun. II. v.tr. F: **he didn't b. an
eyelid**, er hat nicht mit der Wimper ge-
zuckt. ◆**'batsman**, pl **-men**, s. Schläger m.

**batch** [bætʃ], s. Ladung f; (of letters) Stoß
m.

**bated** ['beitid], adj. **with b. breath**, mit
angehaltenem Atem.

**bath**, pl **baths** [bɑ:θ, bɑ:ðz]. I. s. 1. Bad
n; **to take/have a b.**, baden. 2. Badewanne f. II. v.tr. baden. ◆**'bathmat**, s. Ba-
dematte f. ◆**'bathroom**, s. Badezimmer
n. ◆**'bath(-)towel**, s. Badetuch n.

**bathe** [beið], v.tr. & i. baden.
◆**'bather**, s. Badende(r) f(m).
◆**'bathing**, s. Baden n; **b. costume/
suit**, Badeanzug m.

**baton** ['bæt(ə)n,-tɔ̃], s. Stab m; Mus:
Taktstock m.

**battalion** [bə'tæljən], s. Bataillon n.

**batter¹** ['bætər], s. Cu: (flüssiger) Teig m.

**batter²** ['bætər], v.tr. schlagen.
◆**'battered**, adj. stark beschädigt; **b.
wife**, vom Ehemann verprügelte Frau; **b.
baby**, mißhandeltes Kind.

**battery** ['bæt(ə)ri], s. Batterie f; **b.
charger**, Batterieladegerät n.

**battle** ['bætl]. I. s. Schlacht f. II. v.i. **to
b. with s.o. for sth.**, mit j-m um etwas
acc kämpfen. ◆**'battlefield**, s. Schlacht-
feld n. ◆**'battlements**, s.pl. Zinnen fpl.
◆**'battleship**, s. Schlachtschiff n.

**Bavaria** [bə'veəriə]. Pr.n. Bayern n.
◆**Ba'varian**. I. adj. bay(e)risch. II. s.
Bayer(in) m(f).

**bawl** [bɔ:l], v.tr. & i. brüllen.

**bay¹** [bei], s. **b. leaf**, Lorbeerblatt n.

**bay²** [bei], s. Geog: Bucht f. ◆**'bay-
'window**, s. Erkerfenster n.

**bay³** [bei], s. **at b.**, gestellt; **to keep s.o.
at b.**, j-n in Schach halten.

**bayonet** ['beiənit], s. Bajonett n.

**bazaar** [bə'zɑ:r], s. Basar m.

**be** [bi:], v.irr. I. v.i. sein; **how are you?**
wie geht es dir? **the town is in the valley**, die Stadt liegt im Tal; **how much is
that together?** was macht das zusammen?

there is/there are, es gibt; there were twelve of us, wir waren zwölf; be that as it may, wie dem auch sei; is it you? – yes, it's me, sind Sie es? – ja, ich bin's. **II.** *v.aux.* 1. (*continuous tense*) **I am living in London,** ich wohne in London. 2. (*a*) (*passive*) werden; **he was killed,** er wurde getötet; (*b*) (*with infin.*) sollen; **I am to tell you ...,** ich soll Ihnen sagen, ... ◆**'being. I.** *adj.* for the time b., vorläufig. **II.** *s.* 1. **to come into b.,** entstehen. 2. (*creature*) Wesen *n*; **human b.,** Mensch *m*.

**beach** [biːtʃ]. **I.** *s.* Strand *m.* **II.** *v.tr.* (ein Boot) auf den Strand setzen. ◆**'beachwear,** *s.* Strandkleidung *f.*

**beacon** ['biːk(ə)n], *s. Av:* Funkfeuer *n; Nau:* b. (light), Leuchtbake *f.*

**bead** [biːd], *s.* Perle *f.*

**beak** [biːk], *s.* Schnabel *m.*

**beaker** ['biːkər], *s.* Trinkbecher *m.*

**beam** [biːm]. **I.** *s.* 1. (*of wood, steel*) Balken *m.* 2. (*ray*) Strahl *m.* **II.** *v.i.* strahlen. ◆**'beaming,** *adj.* (freude)strahlend.

**bean** [biːn], *s.* Bohne *f.*

**bear¹** ['bɛər], *s.* Bär *m.*

**bear²** [bɛər], *v.tr. & i.* (*a*) (eine Last, einen Namen, ein Datum) tragen; (*b*) (Schmerz usw.) ertragen; **to b. with s.o.,** mit j-m Geduld haben; (*c*) *Aut: etc:* **to b. (to the) right,** sich rechts halten; (*d*) **to b. a child,** ein Kind gebären; **to b. fruit,** Früchte tragen. ◆**'bearable,** *adj.* erträglich. ◆**'bearer,** *s.* Träger *m.* ◆**'bearing,** *s.* (*a*) *E:* Lager *n;* (*b*) (*usu.pl.*) Orientierung *f.* ◆**'bear 'out,** *v.tr.* bestätigen.

**beard** [biəd], *s.* Bart *m.* ◆**'bearded,** *adj.* bärtig.

**beast** [biːst], *s.* 1. (wildes) Tier *n.* 2. (*of pers.*) **F:** what a b.! was für ein Biest! ◆**'beastly,** *adj.* (*of pers., action*) gemein; *F:* eklig; **what b. weather!** was für ein scheußliches Wetter!

**beat** [biːt]. **I.** *v.tr. & i.irr.* schlagen; **to b. time,** (den) Takt schlagen; **that beats everything!** das schlägt dem Faß den Boden aus! **it beats me,** ich begreife es nicht. **II.** *s.* 1. (*a*) Schlag *m;* (*heart*) Herzschlag *m;* (*b*) *Mus:* Taktschlag *m.* 2. Runde *f* (eines Polizisten). ◆**'beat 'down,** *v.tr.* **to b. s.o. down,** j-n (im Preis) drücken. ◆**'beaten,** *adj.* **to be off the b. track,** abseits liegen. ◆**'beating,** *s.* 1. Schlagen *n;* Klopfen *n* (des Herzens). 2. (*a*) (*thrashing*) Prügel *f;* (*b*) (*defeat*) Niederlage *f.* ◆**'beat 'off,** *v.tr.* (einen Angriff) abwehren. ◆**'beat 'up,** *v.tr.* (*a*) *Cu:* (Eier usw.) schlagen; (*b*) *F:* (j-n) zusammenschlagen.

**beautiful** ['bjuːtif(u)l], *adj.* schön; (*emphatic*) wunderschön. ◆**'beautify,** *v.tr.* verschönern. ◆**'beauty,** *s.* Schönheit *f.*

**beaver** ['biːvər], *s.* Biber *m.*

**because** [bi'kɔz]. **I.** *conj.* weil. **II.** *prep. phr.* **b. of,** wegen + *gen.*

**beckon** ['bek(ə)n], *v.i.* winken; **to b. to**

s.o., j-m Zeichen geben.

**become** [bi'kʌm], *v.i.irr.* werden; **what's b. of him?** was ist aus ihm geworden? ◆**be'coming,** *adj.* kleidsam; **her hat is very b.,** der Hut steht ihr sehr gut.

**bed** [bed], *s.* 1. Bett *n;* **to go to b.,** ins Bett gehen; **to get out of b.,** aufstehen; **b. and breakfast,** Übernachtung *f* mit Frühstück. 2. **river b.,** Flußbett *n;* **flower b.,** Blumenbeet *n.* ◆**'bedclothes,** *s.pl.* Bettzeug *n.* ◆**'bedding,** *s.* Bettzeug *n.* ◆**'bedridden,** *adj.* bettlägerig. ◆**'bedroom,** *s.* Schlafzimmer *n.* ◆**'bedside,** *s.* **at the b.,** neben dem Bett; **b. table,** Nachttisch *m;* **b. lamp,** Nachttischlampe *f.* ◆**'bed-'sitting room,** *F:* **'bed-'sitter/'bed-'sit,** *s.* Wohn-Schlafzimmer *n.* ◆**'bedspread,** *s.* Bettüberwurf *m.* ◆**'bedtime,** *s.* Schlafenszeit *f;* **b. story,** Geschichte *f* vor dem Einschlafen.

**bedlam** ['bedləm], *s.* Chaos *n.*

**bee** [biː], *s.* Biene *f.* ◆**'beehive,** *s.* Bienenstock *m.* ◆**'beeline,** *s.* **to make a b. for sth.,** geradewegs auf etwas *acc* zusteuern.

**beech** [biːtʃ], *s.* Buche *f.*

**beef** [biːf], *s.* Rindfleisch *n;* **roast b.,** Rinderbraten *m.* ◆**'beefy,** *adj. F:* kräftig.

**beer** ['biər], *s.* Bier *n.*

**beet** [biːt], *s.* **sugar b.,** Zuckerrübe *f.* ◆**'beetroot,** *s.* rote Rübe/*North G:* Bete *f.*

**beetle** ['biːtl], *s.* Käfer *m.*

**before** [bi'fɔːr]. **I.** *adv.* vorher; **the day b.,** am Tag vorher; **never b.,** noch nie; **I have seen him b.,** ich habe ihn schon mal gesehen. **II.** *prep.* vor + *dat;* **the day b. yesterday,** vorgestern; **the week b. last,** vorletzte Woche; **b. long,** bald; **b. leaving he gave me this,** ehe er wegging, gab er mir das. **III.** *conj.* bevor. ◆**be'forehand,** *adv.* im voraus.

**befriend** [bi'frend], *v.tr.* **to b. s.o.,** sich mit j-m anfreunden.

**beg** [beg], *v.* 1. *v.i.* betteln. 2. *v.tr.* (j-n) (dringend) bitten (**for sth.,** um etwas *acc*).

**beggar** ['begər], *s.* Bettler *m.*

**begin** [bi'gin], *v.tr. & i.* beginnen, anfangen; **to b. with,** zunächst. ◆**be'ginner,** *s.* Anfänger(in) *m(f).* ◆**be'ginning,** *s.* Anfang *m;* **at the b.,** am Anfang; **from the b.,** von Anfang an.

**behalf** [bi'hɑːf], *s.* **on b. of s.o.,** im Namen von j-m.

**behave** [bi'heiv], *v.i.* sich benehmen. ◆**be'haved,** *adj.* **well(-)b.,** (*of child*) artig; **badly(-)b.,** ungezogen. ◆**be'haviour,** *s.* (*a*) Benehmen *n;* (*b*) (*of things*) Verhalten *n.*

**behead** [bi'hed], *v.tr.* enthaupten.

**behind** [bi'haind]. **I.** *adv.* hinten; **to stay/remain b.,** zurückbleiben; **to be b. with one's work,** mit der Arbeit im Rückstand sein. **II.** *prep.* hinter + *dat & acc; Fig:* **to be b. s.o.,** j-n unterstützen.

**III.** *s. F:* Hintern *m.*
**beige** [beiʒ], *adj.* beige.
**belated** [bi'leitid], *adj.* verspätet.
**belch** [belt]ʃ]. **I.** *v.* **1.** *v.i.* rülpsen. **2.**
*v.tr.* **to b. (forth) smoke/flames,** Rauch/
Flammen ausspeien. **II.** *s.* Rülpser *m.*
**belfry** ['belfri], *s.* Glockenturm *m.*
**Belgian** ['beldʒən]. **I.** *adj.* belgisch. **II.** *s.*
Belgier(in) *m(f).* ◆**Belgium** ['beldʒəm].
*Pr.n.* Belgien *n.*
**belief** [bi'li:f], *s.* (*a*) Glauben *m* (**in,**
an + *acc*); (*b*) (*personal b.*) Überzeugung
*f.*
**believe** [bi'li:v], *v.* **1.** *v.tr.* glauben; **to b.**
**s.o.,** j-m glauben. **2.** *v.i.* **to b. in sth.,** an
etwas *acc* glauben. ◆**be'lievable,** *adj.*
glaubhaft. ◆**be'liever,** *s.* (*a*) **to be a**
**great b. in sth.,** auf etwas *acc* schwören;
(*b*) *Ecc:* Gläubige(r) *f(m).*
**belittle** [bi'litl], *v.tr.* (j-s Leistungen)
schmälern; (j-n) herabsetzen.
**bell** [bel], *s.* Glocke *f; (doorbell)* Klingel *f;*
(*small handbell etc.*) Schelle *f;* **to ring the**
**b.,** klingeln; **I:** **that rings a b.,** das
kommt mir bekannt vor.
**belligerent** [bi'lidʒər(ə)nt], *adj.* (*of coun-*
*try etc.*) kriegführend; (*of pers.*) angriffs-
lustig.
**bellow** ['beləu], *v.i.* brüllen.
**bellows** ['beləuz], *s.pl.* **(pair of) b.,** Bla-
sebalg *m.*
**belly,** *pl.* **-ies** ['beli, -iz], *s.* Bauch *m.*
**belong** [bi'lɔŋ], *v.i.* (*a*) gehören (**to s.o.,**
j-m); (*b*) (*be appropriate*) **put it back**
**where it belongs,** stellen Sie es wieder
dorthin, wo es hingehört; (*c*) (*be part of*)
**to b. to sth.,** zu etwas *dat* gehören; **to b.**
**to a society,** einer Gesellschaft angehö-
ren. ◆**be'longings,** *s.pl.* Habe *f.*
**beloved** [bi'lʌvid], *s.* Geliebte(r) *f(m).*
**below** [bi'ləu]. **I.** *adv.* unten. **II.** *prep.*
unter + *dat; (level)* unterhalb + *gen;* **10°**
**b. (zero),** 10 Grad unter Null.
**belt** [belt]. **I.** *s.* **1.** Gürtel *m; (seat) b.,* Sicherheitsgurt *m.* **2.** *E:* Riemen *m; con-*
*veyor b.,* Förderband *n.* **II.** *v.tr.* **to b.**
**s.o.,** j-n verprügeln. ◆**'belt 'up,** *v.i.*
*P:* **b. up!** halt die Klappe!
**bench** [ben(t)ʃ], *s.* **1.** (*a*) (*seat*) Bank *f; (b)*
*Jur:* **the B.,** (i) der Richterstuhl *m;* (ii)
(*the judges*) das Richterkollegium. **2.**
(**work**) **b.,** Werkbank *f.*
**bend** [bend]. **I.** *v.irr.* **1.** *v.tr.* (das Knie
usw.) beugen; (den Rücken) krümmen;
(etwas) biegen. **2.** *v.i.* (*a*) (*of pers.*) sich
bücken; (*b*) (*of thing*) sich biegen; (*of*
*road, river etc.*) eine Biegung machen. **II.**
*s.* **1.** Biegung *f;* Krümmung *f* (in einem
Rohr); Kurve *f* (einer Straße); *F:* **round**
**the b.,** bekloppt. **2.** *Med:* **the bends,**
Druckluftkrankheit *f.* ◆**'bend 'down,**
*v.i.* (sich) bücken. ◆**bent. I.** *adj.* **1.** (*a*)
gebogen; (*b*) **(out of shape),** verbogen; (*b*)
*F:* korrupt. **2. to be b. on doing sth.,**
darauf erpicht sein, etwas zu tun. **II.** *s.*
Neigung *f* (**for sth.,** zu etwas *dat*).
**beneath** [bi'ni:θ]. **I.** *adv.* darunter. **II.**

*prep.* unter + *dat;* unterhalb + *gen.*
**benefactor** ['benifæktər], *s.* Wohltäter(in)
*m(f).* ◆**beneficial** [beni'fiʃ(ə)l], *adj.*
wohltuend; (*to advantage*) vorteilhaft.
◆**beneficiary,** *pl.* **-ies** [beni'fiʃəri, -iz],
*s.* Nutznießer(in) *m(f);* Begünstigte(r)
*f(m).*
**benefit** ['benifit]. **I.** *s.* **1.** Nutzen *m.* **2.**
*Adm:* Unterstützung *f;* **unemployment**
**b.,** Arbeitslosenunterstützung *f;* **sickness**
**b.,** Krankengeld *n.* **II.** *v.* **1.** *v.i.* **to b.**
**by/from sth.,** von etwas *dat* profitieren/
Nutzen ziehen. **2.** *v.tr.* **to b. s.o.,** j-m
nützen.
**benevolence** [bi'nevələns], *s.* Wohlwol-
len *n.* ◆**be'nevolent,** *adj.* wohlwollend.
**benign** [bi'nain], *adj.* gutmütig.
**bequeath** [bi'kwi:ð], *v.tr.* **to b. sth. to**
**s.o.,** j-m etwas hinterlassen.
◆**be'quest,** *s.* Vermächtnis *n.*
**bereaved** [bi'ri:vd], *s.pl.* **the b.,** die Leidtragenden. ◆**be'reavement,** *s.* Trauer-
fall *m; (state)* Verlassenheit *f* (der Witwe
usw.).
**beret** ['berei], *s.* Baskenmütze *f.*
**berry** ['beri], *s.* Beere *f.*
**berth** [bə:θ], *s.* **1. to give s.o., sth. a**
**wide b.,** um j-n, etwas *acc* einen großen
Bogen machen. **2.** Liegeplatz *m.*
**beseech** [bi'si:tʃ], *v.tr.irr.* anflehen.
**beside** [bi'said], *prep.* neben + *dat & acc;*
**to be b. oneself (with joy),** außer sich
(vor Freude) sein.
**besides** [bi'saidz]. **I.** *adv.* außerdem. **II.**
*prep.* außer + *dat;* **nobody b. him had**
**seen it,** niemand außer ihm hatte es gesehen.
**besiege** [bi'si:dʒ], *v.tr.* belagern.
**bespoke** [bi'spəuk], *adj.* **b. tailor,** Maß-
schneider *m.*
**best** [best]. **I.** *adj. & s.* beste(r,s); **b. man**
*approx.* = Brautführer *m;* **to do one's b.,**
sein Bestes tun; *F:* **all the b.!** alles Gute!
**at (the) b.,** bestenfalls. **II.** *adv.* am besten. ◆**'best'seller,** *s.* Bestseller *m.*
**bestial** ['bestjəl], *adj.* bestialisch.
**bet** [bet]. **I.** *s.* Wette *f.* **II.** *v.* **1.** *v.tr.* (eine
Summe) setzen (**on sth.,** auf etwas *acc*).
**2.** *v.i.* wetten. ◆**'betting,** *s.* Wetten *n;*
**b. shop,** Wettbüro *n.*
**betray** [bi'trei], *v.tr.* verraten.
◆**be'trayal,** *s.* Verrat *m.*
**better** ['betər]. **I.** *adj. s. & adv.* besser;
**so much the b.,** um so besser; **to get the**
**b. of s.o.,** j-n übervorteilen; **to think b.**
**of it,** sich eines besseren besinnen; **I'd b.**
**go now,** es ist besser, ich gehe jetzt. **II.**
*v.tr.* (*a*) **to b. oneself,** sich verbessern;
(*b*) (*improve on*) (etwas) übertreffen.
**between** [bi'twi:n]. **I.** *prep.* **1.** (*b. two*)
zwischen + *dat & acc.* **2.** (*b. several*)
unter + *dat;* **b. friends,** unter Freunden.
**II.** *adv.* (**in b.**), dazwischen.
**beverage** ['bevəridʒ], *s.* Getränk *n.*
**beware** [bi'wɛər], *v.i.* sich hüten (**of sth.,**
vor etwas *dat*); **b. of the dog!** Vorsicht,
bissiger Hund!

**bewilder** [bi'wildər], *v.tr.* verwirren. ◆**be'wildered**, *adj.* verwirrt. ◆**be'wildering**, *adj.* verwirrend.

**bewitching** [bi'witʃiŋ], *adj.* bezaubernd.

**beyond** [bi'jɔnd]. **I.** *adv.* darüber hinaus. **II.** *prep.* jenseits + *gen*; über … *acc* hinaus; **it's b. me**, das geht über meinen Horizont. **III.** *s. F:* **at the back of b.**, am Ende der Welt.

**bias** ['baiəs], *s.* Voreingenommenheit *f*; (*prejudice*) Vorurteil *n*; *Jur:* Befangenheit *f*. ◆**'biased**, *adj.* voreingenommen; (*esp. against sth.*) parteiisch; *Jur:* befangen.

**bib** [bib], *s.* Latz *m*; (*baby's*) Lätzchen *n*.

**Bible** ['baibl], *s.* Bibel *f*. ◆**biblical** ['biblikl], *adj.* biblisch.

**bibliography** [bibli'ɔgrəfi], *s.* Bibliographie *f*.

**bicarbonate** [bai'kɑːbənit], *s.* **b. of soda**, doppeltkohlensaures Natrium *n*.

**biceps** ['baiseps], *s.* Bizeps *m*.

**bicker** ['bikər], *v.i.* (sich) zanken.

**bicycle** ['baisikl], *s.* Fahrrad *n*.

**bid** [bid]. **I.** *v.tr. & i.irr.* (*at auction*) bieten. **II.** *s.* (*at auction*) Gebot *n*; **to make a b. for freedom**, zu entkommen versuchen. ◆**'bidder**, *s.* Bieter *m*. ◆**'bidding**, *s.* **1. to do s.o.'s b.**, j-s Befehle ausführen. **2.** Bieten *n*.

**bide** [baid], *v.tr.* **to b. one's time**, (eine Gelegenheit) abwarten.

**bifocal** [bai'fəuk(ə)l], *adj.* **b. spectacles/** *F:* **bifocals**, Bifokalbrille *f*.

**big** [big], groß. ◆**'bighead**, *s. F:* eingebildeter Kerl *m*.

**bigamy** ['bigəmi], *s.* Bigamie *f*.

**bigot** ['bigət], *s.* (*a*) *Ecc:* Frömmler *m*; (*b*) engstirniger Fanatiker *m*. ◆**'bigoted**, *adj.* intolerant; (*narrow*) engstirnig. ◆**'bigotry**, *s.* **1.** *Ecc:* Frömmelei *f*. **2.** Fanatismus *m*.

**bigwig** ['bigwig], *s. F:* hohes Tier *n*.

**bike** [baik], *s. F:* Rad *n*.

**bikini** [bi'kiːni], *s.* Bikini *m*.

**bilberry** ['bilbəri], *s.* Heidelbeere *f*.

**bile** [bail], *s.* Galle *f*.

**bilge** [bildʒ], *s. Nau:* Bilge *f*.

**bilingual** [bai'liŋgw(ə)l], *adj.* zweisprachig.

**bill¹** [bil], *s.* Schnabel *m* (eines Vogels).

**bill²** [bil], *s.* **1.** *Com:* Rechnung *f.* **2.** (*a*) *N.Am:* Banknote *f*; (*b*) *Fin:* **b. of exchange**, Wechsel *m*. **3.** *Th:* **double b.**, Doppelprogramm *n*. **4. b. of fare**, Speisekarte *f*. **5.** *Pol:* Gesetzentwurf *m*. ◆**'billfold**, *s. N.Am:* Brieftasche *f*.

**billet** ['bilit]. **I.** *v.tr.* einquartieren. **II.** *s.* Quartier *n*.

**billiard** ['biljəd], *s.* **1.** *pl.* **billiards**, Billard *n*. **2. b. cue**, Queue *n*.

**billion** ['biljən], *s.* (*a*) Billion *f*; (*b*) *N.Am:* (*thousand million*) Milliarde *f*.

**bin** [bin], *s.* Kasten *m*; (**waste**) **b.**, Abfalleimer *m*; **bread b.**, Brotkasten *m*.

**bind** [baind], *v.tr.irr.* (*a*) binden; **to b. (up) a wound**, eine Wunde verbinden;

(*b*) (*oblige*) verpflichten. ◆**'binding**. **I.** *adj.* verbindlich. **II.** *s.* **1.** (*of ski*) Bindung *f*. **2.** (*of book*) Einband *m*.

**binoculars** [bi'nɔkjuləz], *s.pl.* Fernglas *n*.

**biodegradable** ['baiəudi'greidəbl], *adj.* biologisch abbaubar.

**biography** [bai'ɔgrəfi], *s.* Biographie *f*. ◆**bi'ographer**, *s.* Biograph *m*.

**biology** [bai'ɔlədʒi], *s.* Biologie *f*. ◆**biological** [baiə'lɔdʒikl], *adj.* biologisch. ◆**bi'ologist**, *s.* Biologe *m*, Biologin *f*.

**birch** [bəːtʃ], *s.* **1.** Birke *f*. **2. b.(-rod)**, Rute *f*.

**bird** [bəːd], *s.* **1.** Vogel *m*; **to kill two birds with one stone**, zwei Fliegen mit einer Klappe schlagen. **2.** *P:* (*girl*) Biene *f*. ◆**'bird's-eye**, *adj.* **b.-e. view**, Vogelperspektive *f*.

**birth** [bəːθ], *s.* Geburt *f*; **b. certificate**, Geburtsurkunde *f*; **b. control**, Geburtenregelung *f*; **to give b. to a child**, ein Kind zur Welt bringen. ◆**'birthday**, *s.* Geburtstag *m*. ◆**'birthmark**, *s.* Muttermal *n*. ◆**'birthplace**, *s.* Geburtsort *m*; (*house*) Geburtshaus *n*. ◆**'birthrate**, *s.* Geburtenziffer *f*.

**biscuit** ['biskit], *s.* Keks *m*.

**bishop** ['biʃəp], *s.* **1.** *Ecc:* Bischof *m*. **2.** (*in chess*) Läufer *m*.

**bit¹** [bit], *s.* (*horse's*) Gebiß *n*.

**bit²** [bit], *s.* Stückchen *n*; **a b. (of)**, ein wenig/bißchen.

**bitch** [bitʃ], *s.* **1.** Hündin *f*. **2.** *P:* (*woman*) Luder *n*.

**bite** [bait]. **I.** *v.tr.irr.* beißen; (*of insect*) stechen; *Fig:* **to b. off more than one can chew**, sich dat zuviel zumuten; *F:* **to b. s.o.'s head off**, j-m den Kopf abreißen. **II.** *s.* **1.** Biß *m*; (*of insect*) Stich *m*. **2.** (*of food*) Bissen *m*. ◆**'biting**, *adj.* schneidend.

**bitter** ['bitər]. **I.** *adj.* bitter; (*of taste*) herb; (*of wind*) scharf; (*pers.*) verbittert. **II.** *s.* Bitterbier *n*. ◆**'bitterness**, *s.* (*a*) Bitterkeit *f*; (*b*) (*of pers.*) Verbitterung *f*.

**bizarre** [bi'zɑːr], *adj.* bizarr.

**black** [blæk]. **I.** *adj.* schwarz; **b. ice**, Glatteis *n*; **b. and white photograph**, Schwarzweißfoto *n*; **to beat s.o. b. and blue**, j-n grün und blau schlagen; **b. pudding**, Blutwurst *f*; **b. eye**, blaues Auge. **II.** *v.tr. Ind:* boykottieren. ◆**'blackberry**, *s.* Brombeere *f*. ◆**'blackbird**, *s.* Amsel *f*. ◆**'blackboard**, *s.* Wandtafel *f*. ◆**'black'currant**, *s.* schwarze Johannisbeere *f*. ◆**'blacken**, *v.tr.* schwärzen; *Fig:* anschwärzen. ◆**'blackhead**, *s.* Mitesser *m*. ◆**'blackleg**, *s.* Streikbrecher *m*. ◆**'blacklist**, *v.tr.* **to b. s.o.**, j-n auf die schwarze Liste setzen. ◆**'blackmail. I.** *s.* Erpressung *f*. **II.** *v.tr.* erpressen. ◆**'blackmailer**, *s.* Erpresser(in) *m(f)*. ◆**'blackout**, *s.* **1.** Verdunkelung *f*. **2.** (*faint*) Ohnmachtsanfall *m*. **3. news b.**, Nachrichtensperre *f*.

◆'blacksmith, s. Schmied m.
bladder ['blædər], s. Blase f.
blade [bleid], s. 1. (grass) Halm m. 2. (knife) Klinge f.
blame [bleim]. I. s. Schuld f; to take the b., die Schuld auf sich acc nehmen. II. v.tr. (j-m) die Schuld geben (for sth., an etwas acc); he's to b., er ist schuld daran. ◆'blameless, adj. schuldlos.
blanch [blɑːn(t)ʃ], v. 1. v.tr. Cu: blanchieren. 2. v.i. (of pers.) erbleichen.
blancmange [blə'mɒnʒ], s. Pudding m.
bland [blænd], adj. mild; (of taste) neutral; (of style) charakterlos.
blank [blæŋk]. I. adj. 1. (of paper) leer; (of tape) unbespielt; to leave sth. b., etwas freilassen; b. cheque, Blankoscheck m. 2. b. look, ausdrucksloser Blick; to look b., verdutzt dreinblicken. II. s. 1. (a) N.Am: Formular n; (b) (in document) leere Stelle; (c) my mind's a b., ich habe alles vergessen; F: ich habe Mattscheibe. 2. b. (cartridge), Platzpatrone f.
blanket ['blæŋkit], s. Decke f.
blare ['blɛər], v.i. (of trumpet) schmettern; the radio is blaring away, das Radio plärrt.
blasé ['blɑːzei], adj. blasiert.
blaspheme [blæs'fiːm], v.tr. & i. (Gott) lästern. ◆'blasphemous [-fəməs], adj. gotteslästerlich. ◆'blasphemy [-fəmi], s. Gotteslästerung f.
blast [blɑːst]. I. s. 1. b. of air, heftiger Windstoß; to be going full b., auf Hochtouren laufen. 2. (explosion) Explosion f. II. v.tr. P: b. it! verdammt! ◆'blast-furnace, s. Hochofen m. ◆'blast-off, s. Start m.
blatant ['bleit(ə)nt], adj. eklatant.
blaze [bleiz]. I. s. 1. Feuer n; (house etc.) Brand m. 2. b. of colour, Farbenpracht f. II. v.i. (of fire) lodern; (of sun) strahlen.
blazer ['bleizər], s. Blazer m.
bleach [bliːtʃ]. I. v.tr. & i. bleichen. II. s. Bleichmittel n.
bleak [bliːk], adj. 1. (of place) öde; (bare) kahl. 2. (of weather) rauh. 3. Fig: trübe; b. prospects, trostlose Aussichten.
bleary ['bliəri], adj. b. eyes, trübe/(on waking) verschlafene Augen.
bleat [bliːt], v.i. (of sheep) blöken; (of goat) meckern.
bleed [bliːd], v.irr. 1. v.i. bluten; to b. to death, verbluten. 2. v.tr. Aut: to b. the brakes, die Bremsen entlüften. ◆'bleeding, adj. 1. blutend. 2. P: verdammt.
blemish ['blemiʃ], s. 1. Makel m. 2. Fig: Schandfleck m.
blend [blend]. I. v. 1. v.tr. (Kaffee, Tee usw.) mischen; (etwas) vermengen. 2. v.i. sich (ver)mischen (with, mit + dat); (match) zusammenpassen. II. s. Mischung f (von Kaffee, Tee); Verschnitt m (von Whisky usw.).
bless [bles], v.tr. segnen; b. you! Gesund-

heit!
blessed ['blesid], adj. (a) Ecc: the B. Virgin Mary, die Heilige Jungfrau Maria; (b) F: that b. boy, dieser verflixte Junge. ◆'blessing, s. Segen m; to count one's blessings, mit dem zufrieden sein, was man hat.
blight [blait]. I. s. 1. Bot: Brand m; (on potatoes) Kartoffelfäule f. 2. Fig: schädlicher Einfluß m. II. v.tr. (Hoffnungen usw.) zunichte machen.
blind¹ [blaind]. I. adj. blind; b. spot, Aut: etc: toter Winkel; to turn a b. eye, ein Auge zudrücken; b. alley, Sackgasse f; -ly, adv. blindlings. II. v.tr. blenden. ◆'blindfold. I. v.tr. (j-m) die Augen verbinden. II. adj. & adv. mit verbundenen Augen. ◆'blindness, s. Blindheit f.
blind² [blaind], s. (roller) b., Rollo n; Venetian b., Jalousie f.
blink [bliŋk]. I. v.i. blinzeln. II. s. F: to be on the b., kaputt sein. ◆'blinkers, s.pl. Scheuklappen fpl.
bliss [blis], s. Seligkeit f. ◆'blissful, adj. selig; -ly, adv. b. ignorant/unaware, völlig ahnungslos/unbewußt.
blister ['blistər]. I. s. Blase f; (small) Bläschen n. II. v.i. Blasen bekommen; (of paint) Blasen werfen.
blithe ['blaið], adj. fröhlich.
blitz [blits], s. F: to have a b. on a room, ein Zimmer radikal aufräumen.
blizzard ['blizəd], s. Schneesturm m.
bloated ['bləutid], adj. (of face) aufgedunsen; (of belly) aufgebläht.
blob [blɒb], s. (of colour) Fleck m; (of ink) Klecks m.
bloc [blɒk], s. Block m.
block [blɒk]. I. s. 1. (of marble etc.) Block m; (of wood) Klotz m. 2. b. of flats, Wohnblock m; to walk round the b., um den Block gehen. 3. (a) road b., Straßensperre f; (b) to have a mental b., eine Sperre haben. 4. b. capitals, Blockbuchstaben mpl. II. v.tr. blockieren. ◆blo'ckade. I. s. Blockade f. II. v.tr. blockieren. ◆'blockage, s. Verstopfung f. ◆'block 'up, v.tr. zustopfen.
blonde [blɒnd]. I. adj. blond. II. s. Blondine f.
blood [blʌd], s. Blut n; in cold b., kaltblütig; industry needs new b., die Industrie braucht Nachwuchs; b. pressure, Blutdruck m; b. vessel, Blutgefäß n; b. transfusion, Blutübertragung f; b. test, Blutprobe f; b. donor, Blutspender m; b. group, Blutgruppe f. ◆'blood-curdling, adj. markerschütternd. ◆'bloodhound, s. Bluthund m. ◆'bloodless, adj. unblutig. ◆'bloodshed, s. Blutvergießen n. ◆'bloodshot, adj. b. eyes, blutunterlaufene Augen. ◆'bloodstained, adj. blutbefleckt. ◆'bloodthirsty, adj. blutrünstig. ◆'bloody, adj. 1. blutig; (of tyrant) blutrünstig. 2. P: (a) adj. ver-

dammt, verflucht; (b) adv. **it's b.** hot, es ist verdammt heiß. ◆'**bloody-'minded,** adj. P: boshaft.

**bloom** [blu:m]. I. s. Blüte f. II. v.i. blühen.

**blossom** ['blɔsəm]. I. s. Blüte f. II. v.i. blühen.

**blot** [blɔt]. I. s. (a) Fleck m; (of ink) Klecks m; (b) Pej: **b. on the landscape,** Schandfleck m (in der Landschaft). II. v.tr. (a) (etwas) beflecken; Fig: **to b. one's copybook,** sich blamieren; (b) (Tinte) aufsaugen; (Geschriebenes) löschen. ◆'**blotter,** s. Schreibunterlage f. ◆'**blotting 'paper,** s. Löschpapier n; (sheet) Löschblatt n.

**blotchy** ['blɔtʃi], adj. fleckig.

**blouse** [blauz], s. Bluse f.

**blow**[1] [bləu], v.irr. **1.** v.i. blasen; **it's blowing a gale,** es stürmt. **2.** v.tr. (a) blasen; **to b. one's nose,** sich dat die Nase putzen; (b) El: **to b. a fuse,** eine Sicherung durchhauen; (c) F: **b. the expense!** zum Teufel mit den Kosten! ◆'**blow a'way,** v.tr. wegblasen. ◆'**blow 'down,** v.tr. umwehen. ◆'**blow 'in,** v.tr. (ein Fenster usw.) eindrücken. ◆'**blowlamp,** s. Lötlampe f. ◆'**blow 'off,** v. **1.** v.tr. (einen Hut usw.) wegwehen. **2.** v.i. weggeblasen werden. ◆'**blow 'out,** v. **1.** v.tr. ausblasen. **2.** v.i. ausgehen. ◆'**blow-out,** s. geplatzter Reifen m. ◆'**blow 'over,** v.i. (of storm) vorübergehen; (of scandal etc.) in Vergessenheit geraten. ◆'**blow 'up,** v. **1.** v.i. in die Luft gehen. **2.** v.tr. (a) (einen Luftballon usw.) aufblasen, (with a pump) aufpumpen; (b) (explode) sprengen; (c) (enlarge) vergrößern.

**blow**[2] [bləu], s. **1.** (with fist) Schlag m; (with stick) Hieb m. **2.** Fig: Enttäuschung f.

**blue** [blu:]. I. adj. blau; **to feel b.,** niedergeschlagen sein; F: (of language, jokes) schlüpfrig; **b. film,** Pornofilm m. II. s. out of the b., unerwartet. ◆'**bluebell,** s. Glockenblume f. ◆'**bluebottle,** s. Schmeißfliege f. ◆'**blue-print,** s. 1. Blaupause f. **2.** Fig: (model) Vorbild f. ◆'**blue-stocking,** s. Blaustrumpf m.

**bluff**[1] [blʌf], adj. (of manner) rauh aber herzlich.

**bluff**[2] [blʌf]. I. s. Bluff m. II. v.tr. & i. bluffen.

**blunder** ['blʌndər]. I. s. Schnitzer m. II. v.i. einen Schnitzer machen.

**blunt** [blʌnt], adj. **1.** (of knife etc.) stumpf. **2.** (of manner) schroff; **-ly,** adv. **to put it b.,** um es offen zu sagen. ◆'**bluntness,** s. **1.** Stumpfheit f. **2.** Unverblümtheit f.

**blur** [blə:r], v.tr. verschwommen machen. ◆'**blurred,** adj. verschwommen.

**blurb** [blə:b], s. Klappentext m.

**blurt** [blə:t], v.tr. **to b. out** a secret etc., mit einem Geheimnis usw. herausplatzen.

**blush** [blʌʃ], v.i. erröten. ◆'**blushing,**

adj. errötend; (demure) züchtig.

**boar** [bɔ:r], s. Eber m; **wild b.,** Wildschwein n.

**board** [bɔ:d]. I. s. **1.** (a) Brett n; (floor) **b.,** Diele f; (b) Sch: etc: Tafel f; (notice) Schild n. **2.** Verpflegung f; (full) **b.,** Vollpension f; **b. and lodging,** Unterkunft und Verpflegung. **3. b. of enquiry,** Untersuchungsausschuß m; **b. of directors,** Adm: Aufsichtsrat m; Com: Vorstand m. **4. on b.,** an Bord; **on b. a ship,** an Bord eines Schiffes. II. v.tr. (a) **to b. a ship/aircraft,** an Bord eines Schiffes/eines Flugzeugs gehen; **to b. a train/bus,** in einen Zug/Bus einsteigen; (b) **to b. up (a window etc.),** (ein Fenster usw.) mit Brettern verschlagen. ◆'**boarder,** s. Mieter(in) m(f); (in boarding house) Pensionsgast m; Sch: Internatsschüler(in) m(f). ◆'**boarding,** s. **b. house,** Pension f; **b. school,** Internat n.

**boast** [bəust], v. **1.** v.i. prahlen. **2.** v.tr. sich (etwas gen) rühmen. ◆'**boastful,** adj. angeberisch. ◆'**boastfulness,** s. Angeberei f. ◆'**boasting,** s. Prahlerei f.

**boat** [bəut], s. Boot n; (ship) Schiff n; **we are all in the same b.,** wir sitzen alle in einem Boot; **to miss the b.,** den Anschluß verpassen; **b. race,** Bootsrennen n; **b. train,** Zug m mit Schiffsanschluß. ◆'**boathouse,** s. Bootshaus n.

**bob** [bɔb], v.i. **to b. (up and down),** sich auf und ab bewegen, tänzeln.

**bobbin** ['bɔbin], s. Spule f.

**bodice** ['bɔdis], s. (a) Mieder n; (b) Oberteil n (eines Kleides).

**body** ['bɔdi], s. **1.** (a) Körper m; (b) (dead) **b.,** Leiche f. **2.** Adm: Körperschaft f; **public b.,** Behörde f. **3.** (main part) Substanz f (eines Dokumentes); (b) Aut: Karosserie f. ◆'**bodily.** I. adj. körperlich. II. adv. **to remove s.o. b.,** j-n wegschleppen. ◆'**bodyguard,** s. Leibwächter m. ◆'**bodywork,** s. Karosserie f.

**bog** [bɔg]. I. s. **1.** Sumpf m. **2.** P: (lavatory) Klo n. II. v.tr. **to get bogged down,** ins Stocken geraten; steckenbleiben. ◆'**boggy,** adj. sumpfig.

**boggle** ['bɔgl], v.i. F: **to b. at sth.,** vor etwas dat stutzen; **the mind boggles!** da staunt man!

**bogus** ['bəugəs], adj. falsch.

**boil**[1] [bɔil], s. Med: Furunkel m & n.

**boil**[2] [bɔil], v. **1.** v.i. kochen. **2.** v.tr. kochen lassen; **boiled potatoes,** Salzkartoffeln fpl; **boiled sweet,** Lutschbonbon m & n. ◆'**boil a'way,** v.i. verkochen. ◆'**boil 'down,** v.tr. F: **what it boils down to is that...,** im Endeffekt heißt es, daß... ◆'**boiler,** s. Heizkessel m; **b. suit,** Schlosseranzug m. ◆'**boiling.** I. s. Kochen m; **b. point,** Siedepunkt m. II. adj. kochend; adv. **b. hot,** kochend/siedend heiß. ◆'**boil 'over,** v.i. überkochen.

**boisterous** ['bɔist(ə)rəs], adj. ungestüm;

(*of child*) ausgelassen.

**bold** [bəuld], *adj.* **1.** (*of pers.*) kühn; (*of action*) gewagt; (*of colours*) kräftig. **2.** (*type*) fett gedruckt. ◆'**boldness,** *s.* Kühnheit *f*.

**bolshy** ['bɔlʃi], *adj. F:* störrisch.

**bolster** ['bəulstər], *s.* Kissen *n;* (*round*) Schlummerrolle *f*.

**bolt** [bəult]. **I.** *s.* **1.** (*of door*) Riegel *m.* **2.** *E:* Bolzen *m.* **II.** *v.* **1.** *v.i.* (*of horse*) durchgehen. **2.** *v.tr.* (*a*) (sein Essen) herunterschlingen; (*b*) (eine Tür) verriegeln. **III.** *adv.* **b. upright,** kerzengerade.

**bomb** [bɔm]. **I.** *s.* Bombe *f;* **b. disposal,** (i) (*removal*) Bombenräumung *f;* (ii) (*exploding*) Bombensprengung *f.* **II.** *v.tr.* (*a*) bombardieren; (*b*) (auf ein Gebäude usw.) ein Bombenattentat machen. ◆**bom'bard,** *v.tr.* bombardieren. ◆**bom'bardment,** *s.* Bombardierung *f.* ◆'**bomber,** *s.* (*aircraft*) Bomber *m;* (*pers.*) Bombenleger *m.* ◆'**bombing,** *s.* (*a*) Bombardierung *f* (aus der Luft); (*b*) Bombenattentat *n* (auf ein Gebäude usw.). ◆'**bombshell,** *s. F:* **this was a b. to us all,** wir waren alle wie vom Schlag getroffen.

**bombastic** [bɔm'bæstik], *adj.* (*of style*) geschwollen.

**bona fide** ['bəunə'faidi], *adj.* echt.

**bond** [bɔnd], *s.* **1.** Fessel *f;* Band *n.* **2.** *Fin:* Obligation *f*.

**bone** [bəun]. **I.** *s.* **1.** Knochen *m;* (*of fish*) Gräte *f; Fig:* **b. of contention,** Zankapfel *m;* **to have a b. to pick with s.o.,** mit j-m ein Hühnchen zu rupfen haben; **b. dry,** knochentrocken; **b. idle,** stinkfaul. **2.** *pl.* (*of the dead*) Gebeine *npl.* **II.** *v.tr.* (Fleisch) vom Knochen lösen; (einen Fisch) entgräten. ◆'**boneless,** *adj.* ohne Knochen; (*of fish*) ohne Gräten. ◆'**bony,** *adj.* (*of face etc.*) knochig; (*of pers., animal*) mager.

**bonfire** ['bɔnfaiər], *s.* Feuer *n* (im Freien).

**bonnet** ['bɔnit], *s.* **1.** *Cl:* Haube *f.* **2.** *Aut:* Motorhaube *f*.

**bonus,** *pl.* **-uses** ['bəunəs, -əsiz], *s.* Bonus *m;* (*on savings*) Prämie *f;* **no claims b.,** Schadenfreiheitsrabatt *m*.

**boo** [bu:]. **I.** *int.* huh! buh! **II.** *v.* **1.** *v.tr.* auspfeifen. **2.** *v.i.* buhen.

**book** [buk]. **I.** *s.* **1.** Buch *n.* **2.** (*a*) **exercise b.,** Schulheft *n;* (*b*) *pl. Com:* **to keep the books,** die Bücher führen; *F:* **to be in s.o.'s bad books,** bei j-m schlecht angeschrieben sein. **II.** *v.tr.* (ein Zimmer, Taxi usw.) bestellen. ◆'**bookable,** *adj.* vorbestellbar; (*of tickets*) im Vorverkauf erhältlich. ◆'**bookcase,** *s.* Bücherregal *n.* ◆'**bookie,** *s. F:* Buchmacher *m.* ◆'**booking,** *s.* (*a*) Buchung *f;* (*b*) *Th: etc:* Vorbestellung *f;* **b. office,** Fahrkartenschalter *m; Th:* Theaterkasse *f.* ◆'**book-keeper,** *s.* Buchhalter *m.* ◆'**book-keeping,** *s.* Buchhaltung *f.* ◆'**booklet,** *s.* Broschüre *f.*

◆'**bookmaker,** *s.* Buchmacher *m.* ◆'**bookmark,** *s.* Lesezeichen *n.* ◆'**bookseller,** *s.* Buchhändler *m;* (*secondhand*) **b.,** Antiquar *m.* ◆'**bookshelf,** *s.* Bücherregal *n;* (*single shelf*) Bücherbord *n.* ◆'**bookshop,** *s.* Buchhandlung *f.* ◆'**bookstall,** *s.* Bücherstand *m;* (*on station*) Zeitungskiosk *m.* ◆'**bookworm,** *s.* Bücherwurm *m.*

**boom** [bu:m]. **I.** *s.* **1.** (*of guns etc.*) Dröhnen *n.* **2.** Aufschwung *m; Fin:* Hochkonjunktur *f;* **to be enjoying a b.,** sich großer Beliebtheit erfreuen. **II.** *v.i.* (*a*) dröhnen; (*b*) (*of business*) blühen.

**boomerang** ['bu:məraŋ], *s.* Bumerang *m.*

**boon** [bu:n], *s.* Segen *m.*

**boorish** ['buəriʃ], *adj.* lümmelhaft.

**boost** [bu:st]. **I.** *v.tr.* (*a*) (etwas) fördern, *Com:* ankurbeln; (*b*) *E: El:* (den Druck, die Spannung) erhöhen; (ein Signal) verstärken. **II.** *s.* Auftrieb *m; Fin:* **to give s.o., sth. a b.,** j-m, etwas *dat* Auftrieb geben. ◆'**booster,** *s.* **1.** *Med:* Nachimpfung *f.* **2. b.** (**rocket**), Startrakete *f.*

**boot** [bu:t]. **I.** *s.* **1.** Stiefel *m.* **2.** *Aut:* Kofferraum *m.* **II.** *v.tr. F:* **to b. s.o. out,** j-n rausschmeißen.

**booty** ['bu:ti], *s.* Beute *f.*

**booze** [bu:z]. **I.** *s. P:* Alkohol *m.* **II.** *v.i. P:* saufen. ◆'**boozer,** *s. P:* **1.** (*pers.*) Säufer *m.* **2.** (*pub*) Kneipe *f.*

**border** ['bɔ:dər]. **I.** *s.* **1.** Grenze *f.* **2.** (*a*) *Cl:* Kante *f;* (*b*) **flower b.,** Blumenrabatte *f.* **II.** *v.i.* grenzen (**on sth.,** an etwas *acc*). ◆'**borderline,** *s.* Grenzlinie *f;* **b. case,** Grenzfall *m.*

**bore**[1] [bɔ:r]. **I.** *v.tr. & i.* (ein Loch usw.) bohren. **II.** *s.* Kaliber *n* (einer Feuerwaffe).

**bore**[2] [bɔ:r]. **I.** *v.tr.* (j-n) langweilen; **to be bored (stiff/to death),** sich (zu Tode) langweilen. **II.** *s.* langweiliger Mensch *m.* ◆'**boredom,** *s.* Langeweile *f.* ◆'**boring,** *adj.* langweilig.

**born** [bɔ:n], *p.p.* geboren; **he was b. in 1970,** er wurde 1970 geboren.

**borough** ['bʌrə], *s.* Stadtgemeinde *f;* (*in city*) Bezirk *m.*

**borrow** ['bɔrəu], *v.tr.* **to b. sth. from s.o.,** etwas von j-m borgen. ◆'**borrower,** *s.* Entleiher *m.* ◆'**borrowing,** *s.* Borgen *n.*

**bosom** ['buzəm], *s.* Busen *m.*

**boss** [bɔs]. **I.** *s. F:* **the b.,** der Chef. **II.** *v.tr. F:* **to b. s.o. around,** j-n herumkommandieren. ◆'**bossy,** *adj. F:* herrisch.

**botany** ['bɔtəni], *s.* Botanik *f.* ◆**bo'tanical** [-'tænik], *adj.* botanisch. ◆'**botanist,** *s.* Botaniker/in *m(f)*.

**botch** [bɔtʃ], *v.tr. F:* verpfuschen.

**both** [bəuθ]. **I.** *adj. & pron.* beide; beides; **b. (of) their children,** ihre beiden Kinder; **they b. came,** sie sind (alle) beide gekommen. **II.** *adv.* **b. you and I,** wir beide; **b. ... and ...,** sowohl ... als auch ...

**bother** ['bɔðər]. **I.** *v.* **1.** *v.tr.* belästigen; **that doesn't b. him,** das stört ihn nicht; **I can't be bothered (to do it),** das ist mir zu viel Mühe. **2.** *v.i.* **to b. about s.o., sth.,** sich um j-n, etwas *acc* kümmern; **don't b.!** mach dir keine Mühe! **II.** *s.* Mühe *f.* ◆**'bothered,** *adj.* **hot and b.,** in Aufregung versetzt; **she isn't b.,** das ist ihr egal.

**bottle** ['bɔtl]. **I.** *s.* Flasche *f;* **b. opener,** Flaschenöffner *m.* **II.** *v.tr.* (etwas) in Flaschen abfüllen; (Obst) einmachen. ◆**'bottling,** *s.* Abfüllen *n.* ◆**'bottle-'feed,** *v.tr.* (ein Baby) mit der Flasche aufziehen. ◆**'bottleneck,** *s.* Flaschenhals *m; Fig:* Engpaß *m.* ◆**'bottle 'up,** *v.tr.* unterdrücken.

**bottom** ['bɔtəm]. **I.** *s.* **1.** (*a*) Fuß *m* (eines Hügels, der Treppe, einer Seite usw.); (*b*) Grund *m* (eines Flusses); Boden *m* (einer Tasse usw.); **at/on the b.,** unten; **at the b. of the garden,** am hinteren Ende des Gartens; **to be at the b. of sth.,** hinter etwas *dat* stecken; **to get to the b. of a mystery,** hinter ein Geheimnis kommen. **2.** *Anat: F:* Hintern *m.* **II.** *adj.* unterste; *Aut:* **b. gear,** erster Gang; *Sch:* **he is b. in French,** er ist der Schlechteste in Französisch. ◆**'bottomless,** *adj.* bodenlos.

**boulder** ['bəuldər], *s.* Felsblock *m.*

**bounce** [bauns]. **I.** *v.* **1.** *v.i.* springen; (*a*) (*of ball etc.*) (*up*) aufprallen; (*back*) zurückprallen; (*b*) *F:* **his cheque bounced,** sein Scheck platzte. **2.** *v.tr.* (einen Ball) aufprallen lassen. **II.** *s.* Sprung *m;* (*of ball*) Aufprall *m.* ◆**'bouncer,** *s. F:* Rausschmeißer *m.*

**bound**[1] [baund], *s.* (*usu.pl.*) **out of bounds,** Betreten verboten. ◆**'boundless,** *adj.* unbegrenzt; grenzenlos.

**bound**[2] [baund], *adj.* unterwegs (**for,** nach + *dat*); **homeward b.,** auf der Heimreise.

**bound**[3] [baund], *s.* Sprung *m;* **by leaps and bounds,** sprunghaft.

**bound**[4] [baund], *adj.* **he's b. to be late,** er kommt sicher/garantiert zu spät; **it was b. to happen,** es mußte so kommen.

**boundary** ['baund(ə)ri], *s.* Grenze *f.*

**bouquet** [bu'kei], *s.* **1.** Blumenstrauß *m.* **2.** Bukett *f* (des Weins).

**bout** [baut], *s.* **1.** *Sp:* Kampf *m.* **2.** (*illness*) Anfall *m.*

**bow**[1] [bəu], *s.* **1.** Bogen *m.* **2.** (*knot*) Schleife *f.* ◆**'bow-'legged,** *adj.* O-beinig. ◆**'bow-'tie,** *s.* Fliege *f.*

**bow**[2] [bau]. **I.** *s.* Verbeugung *f.* **II.** *v.* **1.** *v.i.* sich verbeugen; **to b. to s.o.'s wishes,** sich j-s Wünschen fügen. **2.** *v.tr.* (den Kopf) neigen.

**bow**[3] [bau], *s. Nau:* (*often pl.*) Bug *m.*

**bowel** ['bauəl], *s.* usu. pl. **bowels,** Darm *m.*

**bowl**[1] [bəul], *s.* **1.** Schüssel *f;* (*small, shallow*) Schale *f;* (*for animal*) Napf *m.*

**bowl**[2] [bəul]. **I.** *v.tr. & i.* (in cricket) wer-

fen. **II.** *s.* Kugel *f.* ◆**'bowler**[1], *s.* Werfer *m.* ◆**'bowling,** *s.* (*a*) Bowlsspiel *n;* (*b*) (*indoors*) Bowling *n;* **b. alley,** Kegelbahn *f.* ◆**'bowl 'over,** *v.tr.* umwerfen. ◆**bowls,** *s.* Bowlsspiel *m.*

**bowler**[2] ['bəulər], *s.* **b. (hat),** Melone *f.*

**box**[1] [bɔks], *s.* **1.** Schachtel *f;* (*small wooden or metal*) Kasten *m;* (*large wooden*) Kiste *f;* (*cardboard*) Karton *m;* **b. number,** Chiffre *f;* **P.O. Box,** Postfach *n.* **2.** (*a*) *Th:* Loge *f;* (*b*) (*in stable*) Box *f;* (*c*) *Jur:* **witness b.,** Zeugenstand *m.* ◆**'Boxing Day,** *s.* zweiter Weihnachtstag *m.* ◆**'box-office,** *s.* Kasse *f.*

**box**[2] [bɔks], *v.i.* boxen. ◆**'boxer,** *s.* Boxer *m.* ◆**'boxing,** *s.* Boxen *n;* **b. gloves,** Boxhandschuhe *mpl;* **b. match,** Boxkampf *m.*

**boy** [bɔi], *s.* Junge *m;* **b. scout,** Pfadfinder *m.* ◆**'boyfriend,** *s.* Freund *m.* ◆**'boyish,** *adj.* jungenhaft.

**boycott** ['bɔikɔt]. **I.** *v.tr.* boykottieren. **II.** *s.* Boykott *m.*

**bra** [brɑː], *s.* Büstenhalter *m, F:* BH *m.*

**brace** [breis]. **I.** *s.* **1.** (*a*) (*support*) Stütze *f;* (*b*) (*for teeth*) Zahnspange *f.* **2.** *pl. Cl:* Hosenträger *mpl.* **II.** *v.tr.* **to b. oneself for sth.,** sich auf etwas *acc* gefaßt machen. ◆**'bracing,** *adj.* **b. climate,** Reizklima *n.*

**bracelet** ['breislit], *s.* Armband *n.*

**bracken** ['bræk(ə)n], *s.* Farnkraut *n.*

**bracket** ['brækit]. **I.** *s.* **1.** *E:* Träger *m; Arch:* Konsole *f;* (*wall*) **b.,** Wandarm *m.* **2.** (*a*) Klammer *f;* **round/square brackets,** runde/eckige Klammern; (*b*) **the middle income b.,** die mittlere Einkommensklasse. **II.** *v.tr.* (einen Ausdruck, Zahlen) einklammern.

**brag** [bræg], *v.i.* prahlen (**about sth.,** mit etwas *dat*).

**braid** [breid], *s.* Borte *f;* **gold b.,** goldene Tresse *f.*

**braille** [breil], *s.* Blindenschrift *f.*

**brain** [brein], *s.* Gehirn *n;* **b. damage,** Gehirnschaden *m;* **to rack one's brain(s),** sich *dat* den Kopf zerbrechen. ◆**'brainchild,** *s.* Geistesprodukt *n.* ◆**'brainless,** *adj.* geistlos. ◆**'brainwash,** *v.tr.* (j-n) einer Gehirnwäsche unterziehen. ◆**'brainwashing,** *s.* Gehirnwäsche *f.* ◆**'brainwave,** *s.* Geistesblitz *m.* ◆**'brainy,** *adj. F:* gescheit.

**braise** [breiz], *v.tr.* schmoren.

**brake** [breik]. **I.** *s.* Bremse *f;* **b. fluid,** Bremsflüssigkeit *f;* **b. lining,** Bremsbelag *m;* **b. shoe,** Bremsbacke *f;* **to put on/apply the brakes,** bremsen. **II.** *v.tr. & i.* bremsen.

**bramble** ['bræmbl], *s.* Brombeerstrauch *m.*

**bran** [bræn], *s.* Kleie *f.*

**branch** [brɑːn(t)ʃ]. **I.** *s.* **1.** Ast *m* (eines Baumes). **2.** (*a*) Arm *m* (eines Flusses); (*b*) Zweig *m* (einer Familie); (*c*) *Com:* Filiale *f* (einer Firma). **II.** *v.i.* **to b. out,**

neue Wege gehen; *Com:* in eine neue Branche einsteigen; *(of road etc.)* **to b. (off),** abzweigen.

**brand** [brænd]. **I.** *s.* *(a) Com:* Marke *f;* *(b)* Sorte *f.* **II.** *v.tr.* *(a)* (einem Tier) ein Zeichen einbrennen; *(b)* **to b. s.o. as a liar,** j-n zum Lügner stempeln. ◆'**branded,** *adj.* **b. goods,** Markenartikel *mpl.* ◆'**brand(-)'new,** *adj.* nagelneu.

**brandish** ['brændiʃ], *v.tr.* (hin und her) schwingen.

**brandy** ['brændi], *s.* Weinbrand *m;* *(French)* Kognak *m.*

**brass** [brɑːs], *s.* Messing *n;* **b. band** Blaskapelle *f.*

**brassiere** ['bræsiɛər], *s.* Büstenhalter *m.*

**brat** [bræt], *s. F:* Balg *m & n.*

**bravado** [brə'vɑːdəu], *s.* (gespielte) Kühnheit *f.*

**brave** [breiv]. **I.** *adj.* tapfer. **II.** *v.tr.* (etwas *dat*) mutig entgegentreten. ◆'**bravery,** *s.* Tapferkeit *f.*

**bravo** [brɑː'vəu], *int.* bravo!

**brawl** [brɔːl]. **I.** *s.* Handgemenge *n.* **II.** *v.i.* zanken; raufen.

**brawn** [brɔːn], *s.* Muskelkraft *f.* ◆'**brawny,** *adj.* kräftig.

**bray** [brei], *v.i. (of donkey)* iahen.

**brazen** ['breizən], *adj.* unverschämt.

**Brazil** [brə'zil]. *Pr.n.* Brasilien *n;* **B. nut,** Paranuß *f.* ◆**Brazilian** [brə'ziljən]. **I.** *adj.* brasilianisch. **II.** *s.* Brasilianer(in) *m(f).*

**breach** [briːtʃ], *s.* **1.** Bruch *m* (eines Vertrages, des Versprechens usw.); Verstoß *m* (gegen Vorschriften usw.); *Jur:* **b. of the peace,** Friedensbruch *m.* **2.** Bresche *f* (in einer Mauer).

**bread** [bred], *s.* Brot *n;* **b. and butter,** Butterbrot *n.* ◆'**breadcrumbs,** *s.pl.* Brotkrümel *mpl; Cu:* Paniermehl *n.* ◆'**breadwinner,** *s.* Brotverdiener *m.*

**breadth** [bredθ], *s.* Breite *f.*

**break** [breik]. **I.** *s.* **1.** Bruch *m;* *(gap)* Lücke *f;* **lucky b.,** Glücksfall *m;* **give him a b.,** (i) gib ihm eine Chance; (ii) laß ihn in Ruhe. **2.** *(a) Sch: etc:* Pause *f;* **the coffee b.,** die Kaffeepause; *(b)* **you need a b.,** du brauchst Urlaub; **weekend b.,** Wochenendurlaub *m.* **3.** **b. of day,** Tagesanbruch *m.* **II.** *v.irr.* **1.** *v.tr. (a)* brechen; (eine Tasse usw.) zerbrechen; (ein Spielzeug usw.) kaputtmachen; **to b. one's arm,** sich *dat* den Arm brechen; *(b)* **to b. (out of) gaol,** aus dem Gefängnis ausbrechen; *(c) (interrupt)* (eine Reise, einen Stromkreis) unterbrechen; **the tree broke his fall,** sein Fall wurde vom Baum gebremst; *(d)* **to b. s.o.,** j-n ruinieren; *(e)* **b. it to her gently,** bring es ihr schonend bei. **2.** *v.i.* brechen; *(of glass etc.)* zerbrechen; *(of rope etc.)* zerreißen; *(b) (of waves)* sich brechen; *(of storm)* losbrechen; *(of day)* anbrechen; **to b. into a house,** in ein Haus einbrechen. ◆'**breakable,** *adj.* zerbrechlich. ◆'**breakage,** *s.* Bruch *m.* ◆'**break**

**a'way,** *v.* **1.** *v.tr.* abbrechen. **2.** *v.i. (of rock etc.)* losbrechen; *(of pers.)* sich losreißen; *Pol: (of group)* sich lossagen; *Pol:* **b.-a. group,** Splitterpartei *f.* ◆'**break 'down,** *v.* **1.** *v.tr. (a)* (eine Tür) einbrechen; (Widerstand) brechen; *(b)* (etwas) (in Kategorien) aufteilen. **2.** *v.i. (a) (of pers., system)* zusammenbrechen; *(of plan, negotiations)* scheitern; *(b) (of machine)* versagen; *(of car)* eine Panne haben. ◆'**breakdown,** *s.* **1.** *(a)* Zusammenbruch *m;* **(nervous) b.,** Nervenzusammenbruch *m;* *(b)* Scheitern *n* (der Verhandlungen usw.); *(c)* Versagen *n* (einer Maschine); *Aut:* Panne *f;* **b. lorry,** Abschleppwagen *m.* **2.** Aufgliederung *f.* ◆'**breaker,** *s. (wave)* Brecher *m.* ◆'**break 'even,** *v.i.* seine Kosten decken. ◆'**break 'in,** *v.* **1.** *v.tr.* (ein Tür usw.) aufbrechen. **2.** *v.i.* **to b. in(to a house),** (in ein Haus) einbrechen. ◆'**break-in,** *s.* Einbruch *m.* ◆'**break 'loose,** *v.i.* sich losreißen. ◆'**breakneck,** *adj.* **at b. speed,** in halsbrecherischem Tempo. ◆'**break 'off,** *v.* **1.** *v.tr.* (Verbindungen usw.) abbrechen; (eine Verlobung) lösen. **2.** *v.i.* abbrechen. ◆'**break 'open,** *v.tr.* aufbrechen. ◆'**break 'out,** *v.i.* ausbrechen. ◆'**break 'through,** *v.tr. & i.* (durch etwas *acc*) durchbrechen. ◆'**breakthrough,** *s.* Durchbruch *m.* ◆'**break 'up,** *v.* **1.** *v.tr. (a)* zerbrechen, zerstören; *(b) (scrap)* (ein Auto, ein Schiff) verschrotten; *(c)* (eine Menge) auseinandertreiben; (einen Kampf) abbrechen. **2.** *v.i. (a) (of marriage)* scheitern; *(of crowd)* sich auflösen; *(b) (of couple)* sich trennen; *(c) (of school)* in die Ferien gehen. ◆'**breakwater,** *s.* Buhne *f.*

**breakfast** ['brekfəst], *s.* Frühstück *n;* **to have b.,** frühstücken.

**breast** [brest], *s.* Brust *f;* **b. stroke,** Brustschwimmen *n.* ◆'**breast-'feed,** *v.tr.* stillen.

**breath** [breθ], *s.* Atem *m;* **a b.,** ein Atemzug *m;* **to hold one's b.,** den Atem anhalten; **to waste one's b.,** in den Wind reden; **out of b.,** außer Atem; **to go out for a b. of air,** frische Luft schöpfen gehen. ◆'**breathalyse,** *v.tr. F:* (j-n) (ins Röhrchen) pusten lassen. ◆'**breathless,** *adj.* atemlos.

**breathe** [briːð], *v.* **1.** *v.i.* atmen; **to b. in/out,** einatmen/ausatmen. **2.** *v.tr.* **to b. a sigh of relief,** erleichtert aufatmen. ◆'**breather,** *s. F:* Verschnaufpause *f.* ◆'**breathing,** *s.* Atmen *n;* **b. space,** Atempause *f.*

**breed** [briːd]. **I.** *v.irr.* **1.** *v.tr. (a)* (Tiere) züchten; *(b)* (Gewalt, Haß usw.) hervorrufen. **2.** *v.i.* sich vermehren. **II.** *s.* Rasse *f.* ◆**bred** [bred], *adj.* **well b.,** gut erzogen. ◆'**breeder,** *s.* **1.** *Agr:* Züchter *m.* **2.** **b. reactor,** Brutreaktor *m.* ◆'**breeding,** *s.* **1.** Züchtung *f;* Zucht *f;* **b. ground,** Nährboden *m.* **2.** Bildung *f.*

**breeze** [briːz], s. Brise f. ◆**'breezy,** adj.
1. (of day) windig. 2. (of pers., manner)
lebhaft.

**brevity** ['breviti], s. Kürze f.

**brew** [bruː]. I. s. Gebräu n. II. v. 1. v.tr.
(Bier) brauen; (Tee) kochen. 2. v.i. (a)
(of tea) ziehen; (b) there's a storm brewing, ein Gewitter ist im Anzug.
◆**'brewer,** s. Brauer m. ◆**'brewery,** s.
Brauerei f.

**bribe** [braib]. I. s. Bestechung f; (money)
Schmiergeld n; to take a b., sich bestechen lassen. II. v.tr. (j-n) bestechen.
◆**'bribery,** s. Bestechung f.

**brick** [brik], s. Ziegel m; (esp. red) Back-
stein m. ◆**'bricklayer,** s. Maurer m.

**bride** [braid], s. Braut f; the b. and
groom, das Brautpaar. ◆**'bridal,** adj.
Braut-. ◆**'bridegroom,** s. Bräutigam
m. ◆**'bridesmaid,** s. Brautjungfer f.

**bridge**¹ [bridʒ]. I. s. 1. Brücke f. 2. Nau:
Kommandobrücke f. II. v.tr. (eine
Schwierigkeit usw.) überbrücken; to b. a
gap, eine Lücke füllen.

**bridge**² [bridʒ], s. (game) Bridge n.

**bridle** [braidl]. I. s. Zaum m; b. path,
Reitweg m. II. v.tr. (ein Pferd) zäumen;
(eine Leidenschaft usw.) zügeln.

**brief** [briːf]. I. adj. kurz; in b., kurz (gesagt). II. s. 1. (a) Jur: Com: Instruktionen fpl; (b) Jur: (case) Mandat n. 2.
Cl: briefs, Slip m. III. v.tr. to b. s.o.,
j-m seine Instruktionen geben.
◆**'briefcase,** s. Aktentasche f.
◆**'briefing,** s. 1. Anweisung f. 2. Jur:
Instruktion f. ◆**'briefness,** s. Kürze f.

**brigade** [bri'geid], s. Brigade f. ◆**briga-
dier** [brigə'diər], s. Brigadegeneral m.

**bright** [brait], adj. 1. (a) hell; b. eyes,
klare Augen; (b) (of weather) heiter; (of
colour) leuchtend; to look on the b. side,
die Sache(n) optimistisch betrachten. 2.
(of pers.) gescheit; a b. idea, ein guter/
kluger Einfall. ◆**'brighten,** v. 1. v.tr.
aufhellen. 2. v.i. to b. (up), (of weather,
pers.) sich aufheitern. ◆**'brightness,** s.
Helle f; Klarheit f.

**brilliant** ['briljənt], adj. glänzend; (gifted)
hochbegabt; (intellectually) b., geistreich. ◆**'brilliance,** s. (a) (shine) Glanz
m; (b) (of pers.) hohe Begabung f; (intellectual) b., hohe Intelligenz f.

**brim** [brim]. I. s. Rand m; (of hat) Krempe f. II. v.i. to b. over, überfließen.

**brine** [brain], s. Salzwasser n, Sole f.

**bring** [briŋ], v.tr.irr. (a) bringen (to s.o.,
j-m); I cannot b. myself to do it, ich
kann es nicht über mich bringen; (b) (b.
along) mitbringen. ◆**'bring a'bout,**
v.tr. (etwas) verursachen; (einen Vorgang) bewirken. ◆**'bring a'long,** v.tr.
mitbringen. ◆**'bring 'back,** v.tr. zu-
rückbringen; to b. back memories, Erinnerungen wachrufen. ◆**'bring 'down,**
v.tr. (a) herunterbringen; (of storm) (ei-
en Baum usw.) umwerfen; (eine Regierung usw.) stürzen; (b) (den Preis) herab-

setzen. ◆**'bring 'forward,** v.tr. (einen
Termin) vorverlegen. ◆**'bring 'in,** v.tr.
(a) hereinbringen; die Polizei usw.) einschalten; (b) Com: to b. in interest, Zinsen tragen; (c) (introduce) (eine Maßnahme) einführen. ◆**'bring 'off,** v.tr. zustande bringen. ◆**'bring 'out,** v.tr. (etwas, ein Buch) herausbringen; (eine Eigenschaft) zutage bringen; (eine Farbe)
zur Geltung bringen. ◆**'bring 'over,**
v.tr. hinüberbringen. ◆**'bring 'round,**
v.tr. (a) (j-n) wieder zu sich bringen; (b)
(persuade) (j-n) überreden; (c) (die Konversation) lenken (to a subject, auf ein
Thema). ◆**'bring to'gether,** v.tr.
(Menschen) zusammenbringen; (eine
Sammlung) zusammenstellen. ◆**'bring
'up,** v.tr. (a) heraufbringen; (vomit) erbrechen; (b) (Kinder) erziehen; (c) to b.
up a subject, ein Thema zur Sprache
bringen.

**brink** [briŋk], s. Rand m.

**brisk** [brisk], adj. (a) (lively) lebhaft; (b)
(quick) schnell. ◆**'briskness,** s. Lebhaftigkeit f.

**bristle** [brisl]. I. s. Borste f. II. v.i. (a)
(of hair etc.) sich sträuben; (b) to b. with
sth., von etwas dat strotzen. ◆**'bristly,**
adj. borstig; (to touch) stachelig.

**Britain** ['britn]. Pr.n. (Great) B.,
Großbritannien n.

**British** ['britiʃ], adj. britisch; s.pl. the
British, die Briten. ◆**'Briton,** s. Brite
m; Britin f.

**brittle** [britl], adj. spröde.

**broach** [brəutʃ], v.tr. (ein Thema) anschneiden.

**broad** [brɔːd], adj. breit; Fig: it's as b.
as it's long, es ist gehüpft wie gesprungen; in b. outline, in groben Umrissen;
-ly, adv. b. speaking, allgemein gesprochen. ◆**'broadcast.** I. v.tr. (ein Programm) senden. II. s. Sendung f. III.
adj. übertragen. ◆**'broadcaster,**
s. Rundfunksprecher(in) m(f).
◆**'broadcasting,** s. Rundfunkwesen n.
◆**'broaden,** v.tr. & i. (sich) verbreitern. ◆**'broad-'minded,** adj. tolerant.
◆**'broad-'shouldered,** adj. breitschul-
trig.

**brocade** [brə(u)'keid], s. Brokat m.

**broccoli** ['brɔkəli], s. Brokkoli pl.

**brochure** [brɔ'ʃuər, 'brəuʃər], s. Prospekt
m.

**broiler** ['brɔilər], s. Brathuhn n.

**broke** [brəuk], adj. F: pleite.

**broken** ['brəuk(ə)n], adj. (of stick, leg
etc.) gebrochen; (of cup etc.) zerbrochen;
F: kaputt; b. English, gebrochenes Englisch; b. down, außer Betrieb; F: kaputt. ◆**'broken-'hearted,** adj. untröstlich.

**broker** ['brəukər], s. Makler m.

**bromide** ['brəumaid], s. Bromid n.

**bronchitis** [brɔŋ'kaitis], s. Bronchitis f.

**bronze** [brɔnz], s. Bronze f.

**brooch** [brəutʃ], s. Brosche f.

**brood** [bru:d]. **I.** s. Brut f. **II.** v.i. brüten; **to b. over sth.**, über etwas acc grübeln. ◆**'broody**, adj. brütend.

**brook** [bruk], s. Bach m.

**broom** [bru:m], s. Besen m.

**broth** [brɔθ], s. Brühe f.

**brothel** [brɔθl], s. Bordell n.

**brother** ['brʌðər], s. Bruder m; **brothers and sisters**, Geschwister npl. ◆**'brotherhood**, s. Brüderschaft f. ◆**'brother-in-law**, s. Schwager m.

**brow** [brau], s. (a) Anat: Stirn f; (b) (of hill) Kuppe f. ◆**'browbeat**, v.tr. einschüchtern.

**brown** [braun]. **I.** adj. (a) braun; **b. bread** = approx. Grahambrot n; (b) (of pers.) gebräunt. **II.** v. **1.** v.tr. bräunen; F: **to be browned off**, es satt haben. **2.** v.i. braun werden.

**brownie** ['brauni], s. **1.** junge Pfadfinderin f. **2.** N.Am: Schokoladenschnitte f.

**browse** [brauz], v.i. in Büchern blättern.

**bruise** [bru:z]. **I.** s. Quetschung f; F: blauer Fleck m. **II.** v.tr. quetschen.

**brunette** [bru:'net], s. Brünette f.

**brunt** [brʌnt], s. **to bear the b.** (of the work), die Hauptlast tragen; **to bear the b.** of his anger, seinen vollen Zorn zu spüren bekommen.

**brush** [brʌʃ]. **I.** s. (a) Bürste f; (b) (paint) b., Pinsel m. **II.** v. **1.** v.tr. (a) (Kleider) abbürsten; sich dat (die Haare) bürsten, (die Zähne) putzen; (b) (touch) streifen. **2.** v.i. **to b. against sth.**, (gegen) etwas acc streifen. ◆**'brush a'side**, v.tr. (-jn) beiseite schieben. ◆**'brush 'up**, v.tr. **to b. up one's German**, seine Deutschkenntnisse auffrischen. ◆**'brushwood**, s. Gestrüpp n.

**brusque** [bru:(:)sk], adj. schroff.

**Brussels** ['brʌslz]. Pr.n. Brüssel n; **B. sprouts**, Rosenkohl m.

**brute** [bru:t], s. Rohling m; Unmensch m; **b. force**, rohe Gewalt. ◆**'brutal**, adj. brutal. ◆**bru'tality**, s. Brutalität f.

**bubble** ['bʌbl]. **I.** s. Blase f. **II.** v.i. sprudeln. ◆**'bubbly**. **I.** adj. schäumend. **II.** s. F: Champagner m.

**buck** [bʌk]. **I.** s. **1.** (male deer) Bock m. **2.** N.Am: F: Dollar m. **3.** **to pass the b.**, die Verantwortung abschieben. **II.** v.i. (of horse) bocken. ◆**'buck 'up**, v.i. sich zusammenreißen.

**bucket** ['bʌkit], s. Eimer m; F: **to kick the b.**, abkratzen. ◆**'bucketful**, s. Eimervoll m.

**buckle** ['bʌkl]. **I.** s. Schnalle f. **II.** v. **1.** v.tr. (a) (einen Gürtel) zuschnallen; (b) (Metall) krümmen. **2.** v.i. **to b. (up)**, (of metal etc.) sich verbiegen.

**bud** [bʌd]. **I.** s. Knospe f. **II.** v.i. knospen. ◆**'budding**, adj. **a b. artist**, ein angehender Künstler.

**Buddhism** ['budiz(ə)m], s. Buddhismus m. ◆**'Buddhist**. **I.** s. Buddhist m. **II.** adj. buddhistisch.

**buddy** ['bʌdi], s. esp. N.Am: F: Kumpel m.

**budge** [bʌdʒ], v. **1.** v.tr. (etwas) (vom Fleck) bewegen. **2.** v.i. **he refused to b.**, er rührte sich nicht von der Stelle.

**budget** ['bʌdʒit]. **I.** s. Budget n; Pol: Haushaltsplan m. **II.** v.i. den Haushaltsplan aufstellen; **to b. for sth.**, etwas einkalkulieren.

**buff** [bʌf]. **I.** s. opera b., Opernfreund m. **II.** adj. sandfarben.

**buffalo**, pl. -oes ['bʌfələu, -əuz], s. Büffel m.

**buffer** ['bʌfər], s. esp.pl. (on carriage) Puffer m; (at end of line) Prellbock m.

**buffet**[1] ['bufei], s. Büfett n.

**buffet**[2] ['bʌfit], v.tr. stoßen.

**buffoon** [bʌ'fu:n], s. Clown m.

**bug** [bʌg]. **I.** s. **1.** (a) Wanze f; (b) N.Am: F: Insekt n, esp. Käfer m. **2.** F: **the flu b.**, der Grippebazillus m. **3.** (verstecktes) Abhörgerät n, F: Wanze f. **II.** v.tr. **to b. a room**, in einem Zimmer ein Abhörgerät verstecken.

**bugle** ['bju:gl], s. Signalhorn n.

**build** [bild]. **I.** v.tr.irr. bauen. **II.** s. Körperbau m; Figur f. ◆**'builder**, s. Baumeister m. ◆**'build 'in**, v.tr. einbauen. ◆**'building**, s. **1.** Gebäude n. **2.** b. (trade), Bauwesen n; b. site, Baustelle f; b. society, Bausparkasse f. ◆**'build 'up**, v.tr. (a) aufbauen; built up area, bebautes Gebiet; Aut: Adm: geschlossene Ortschaft; (b) (eine Sammlung) zusammenstellen. ◆**'build-up**, s. (preparation) Vorbereitung f; (publicity) einleitende Propaganda f.

**bulb** [bʌlb], s. **1.** Bot: Zwiebel f. **2.** El: Birne f.

**Bulgaria** [bʌl'geəriə]. Pr.n. Bulgarien n. ◆**Bul'garian**. **I.** adj. bulgarisch. **II.** s. Bulgare m; Bulgarin f.

**bulge** [bʌldʒ]. **I.** s. Ausbuchtung f; (long) Wulst m; (in body) Fettpolster m. **II.** v.i. **to b. (out)**, bauschen. ◆**'bulging**, adj. bauschig; (full) vollgestopft; (projecting) hervorstehend.

**bulk** [bʌlk], s. **1.** Masse f; **in b.**, en gros; b. buying, Großeinkauf m. **2.** (majority) Mehrheit f. ◆**'bulky**, adj. (large) umfangreich; (awkward shape) unförmig; (of goods etc.) sperrig.

**bull** [bul], s. Stier m. ◆**'bulldog**, s. Bulldogge f. ◆**'bulldozer**, s. Planierraupe f. ◆**'bullfight**, s. Stierkampf m. ◆**'bullfighter**, s. Stierkämpfer m. ◆**'bullock**, s. Ochse m. ◆**'bullring**, s. Stierkampfarena f. ◆**'bull's-eye**, s. Zentrum n (der Zielscheibe); **to score a b.-e.**, ins Schwarze treffen.

**bullet** ['bulit], s. Kugel f. ◆**'bulletproof**, adj. kugelsicher.

**bulletin** ['bulitin], s. (a) news b., Nachrichtensendung f; (b) (on sick person) Meldung f (über j-s Befinden).

**bullion** ['buljən], s. (gold) (Gold-/Silber)barren m.

**bully** ['buli]. **I.** s. Tyrann m. **II.** v.tr. tyrannisieren.

**bumble-bee** ['bʌmblbiː], s. Hummel f.

**bump** [bʌmp]. I. s. 1. (blow) Stoß m; (sound) Bums m. 2. Beule f; (in road etc.) holprige Stelle f. II. v. 1. v.tr. (j-n, etwas) anstoßen. 2. v.i. **to b. into sth.**, gegen etwas acc stoßen; (of vehicle) etwas anfahren; F: **to b. into s.o.**, j-n zufällig treffen. ◆**bumpy**, adj. holprig; (of ride) holpernd.

**bumper** ['bʌmpər]. I. s. Stoßstange f. II. adj. Rekord-; **b. crop**, Rekordernte f.

**bun** [bʌn], s. 1. (currant) b., Korinthenbrötchen n. 2. (hair) Knoten m.

**bunch** [bʌntʃ], s. (a) Strauß m (Blumen); **b. of grapes**, Traube f; **b. of keys**, Schlüsselbund m; (b) (people) Gruppe f.

**bundle** ['bʌndl]. I. s. Bündel n (Wäsche, Holz usw.); Stoß m (Papier usw.). II. v.tr. **to b. sth. up**, etwas (zusammen)bündeln.

**bung** [bʌŋ], v.tr. F: schmeißen; **to b. sth. up**, etwas verstopfen.

**bungalow** ['bʌŋɡələu], s. Bungalow m.

**bungle** ['bʌŋɡl], v.tr. verpfuschen.

**bunk¹** [bʌŋk], s. Schlafkoje f; **b. beds**, Etagenbetten npl.

**bunk²**, s. F: **to do a b.**, abhauen.

**bunker** ['bʌŋkər], s. Bunker m.

**bunting** ['bʌntiŋ], s. Flaggenschmuck m.

**buoy** [bɔi]. I. s. Boje f. II. v.tr. **to b. s.o. up**, j-n stärken. ◆**buoyancy**, s. 1. Schwimmfähigkeit f; (of water) Auftrieb m. 2. Fig: (of pers.) Schwung m. ◆**buoyant**, adj. 1. schwimmfähig; (of water) tragend. 2. (of pers.) munter; Com: (of market etc.) lebhaft.

**burden** ['bəːdn]. I. s. Last f; esp. Fig: Bürde f. II. v.tr. **to b. s.o. with sth.**, j-m etwas aufbürden.

**bureau**, pl. **-eaux** ['bjuərəu, -əuz], s. 1. (desk) Sekretär m. 2. (office) Büro n. ◆**bureaucracy** [bjuə'rɔkrəsi], s. Bürokratie f. ◆**bureaucrat** ['bjuərəkræt], s. Bürokrat m. ◆**bureau'cratic**, adj. bürokratisch.

**burglar** ['bəːɡlər], s. Einbrecher m; **b. alarm**, Alarmanlage f. ◆**burglarize**, v.tr. N.Am: = burgle. ◆**burglary**, s. Einbruch m. ◆**burgle**, v.tr. **they have been burgled**, bei ihnen ist eingebrochen worden.

**burial** ['beriəl], s. Begräbnis n.

**burly** ['bəːli], adj. stämmig.

**Burma** ['bəːmə]. Pr.n. Birma n.

**burn** [bəːn]. I. v.irr. 1. v.tr. verbrennen. 2. v.i. (of light, fire etc.) brennen; (of food) anbrennen. II. s. (a) (in carpet etc.) Brandstelle f; (b) Med: Verbrennung f. ◆**burner**, s. Brenner m. ◆**burn 'down**, v.tr. & i. niederbrennen. ◆**burnt**, adj. verbrannt; (of food) angebrannt. ◆**burn 'up**, v.tr. (Kohlen usw.) verbrennen; (Energie) verbrauchen.

**burp** [bəːp], v.i. F: rülpsen.

**burrow** ['bʌrəu]. I. s. Bau m. II. v.i. (of rabbits etc.) einen Bau/(of pers.) einen

Tunnel graben.

**bursar** ['bəːsər], s. Quästor m.

**burst** [bəːst]. I. v.irr. 1. v.i. **to b. into tears**, in Tränen ausbrechen; F: **I'm bursting**, ich muß dringend aufs Klo. 2. v.tr. (einen Ballon usw.) platzen lassen; **the river b. its banks**, der Fluß trat über die Ufer. II. s. **b. of fire**, Feuersalve f; **b. of activity**, Ausbruch m von Geschäftigkeit; **b. of speed**, Spurt m. ◆**burst 'in**, v.i. hereinstürmen. ◆**burst 'open**, v.i. (of door) auffliegen; (of parcel etc.) aufgehen. ◆**burst 'out**, v.i. **to b. out laughing**, in Gelächter ausbrechen.

**bury** ['beri], v.tr. (j-n) begraben, beerdigen; (etwas) vergraben.

**bus**, pl. **buses** [bʌs, 'bʌsiz], s. (Auto)bus m; **b. conductor**, Autobusschaffner m; **b. station**, Autobusbahnhof m; **b. stop**, Bushaltestelle f.

**bush** [buʃ], s. (a) Strauch m; **to beat about the b.**, um den heißen Brei herumreden; (b) pl. Gebüsch n. ◆**bushy**, adj. buschig.

**business** ['biznis], s. 1. (matter) Angelegenheit f, Sache f; **it's none of your b.**, das geht dich nichts an; **to get down to b.**, zur Sache kommen. 2. (firm) Betrieb m; Firma f; (b) coll. Geschäfte npl; **he's here on b.**, er ist geschäftlich hier; **to do b. with s.o.**, mit j-m geschäftlich zu tun haben; **to mean b.**, es ernst meinen; **b. hours**, Geschäftszeiten fpl. ◆**businesslike**, adj. (of pers.) geschäftstüchtig; praktisch veranlagt. 2. (of manner) sachlich. ◆**businessman**, s. Geschäftsmann m.

**bust¹** [bʌst], s. 1. Art: Büste f. 2. Anat: Busen m; **b. measurement**, Brustumfang m.

**bust²**. I. v. 1. v.tr. kaputtmachen. 2. v.i. kaputtgehen. II. adj. kaputt; F: **to go b.**, Bankrott machen.

**bustle** ['bʌsl]. I. v.i. **to b. (about)**, (herum)hantieren. II. s. (geschäftiges) Treiben n. ◆**bustling**, adj. geschäftig.

**busy** ['bizi]. I. adj. (a) (of pers.) (sehr) beschäftigt; (b) (of activity etc.) geschäftig; **a b. day**, ein anstrengender Tag; **a b. street**, eine belebte Straße. II. v.tr. **to b. oneself**, sich beschäftigen (with sth., mit etwas dat; **-ily**, adv. emsig. ◆**busybody**, s. Wichtigtuer(in) m(f).

**but** [bʌt]. I. conj. (a) aber; (b) (after negative) sondern; **he is not English b. German**, er ist kein Engländer, sondern ein Deutscher. II. adv. nur; **one can b. try**, man kann es wenigstens versuchen. III. conj. & prep. (a) (except) **all b. him**, alle außer ihm; **the last b. one**, der vorletzte; (b) **b. for**, ohne + acc.

**butcher** ['butʃər]. I. s. Fleischer m, Metzger m; **b.'s shop**, Fleischerei f, Metzgerei f. II. v.tr. abschlachten.

**butler** ['bʌtlər], s. Butler m.

**butt¹** [bʌt], s. 1. (of cigarette) (Zigaretten)stummel m. 2. (of rifle) (Ge-

wehr)kolben *m*.
**butt²**, *s. Fig: (target)* Zielscheibe *f*.
**butt³.** I. *s.* Stoß *m*. II. *v.tr. & i.* (j-n) mit dem Kopf stoßen; **to b. in,** unterbrechen.
**butter** ['bʌtər]. I. *s.* Butter *f*; **b. dish,** Butterdose *f*. II. *v.tr.* (Brot usw.) mit Butter bestreichen. ◆'**buttercup**, *s.* Butterblume *f*. ◆'**butter-fingers**, *s. F:* Dussel *m*.
**butterfly** ['bʌtəflai], *s.* Schmetterling *m*; **b. (stroke),** Schmetterlingsschwimmen *n*.
**buttock** ['bʌtək], *s.* Hinterbacke *f*; *pl.* **buttocks,** Gesäß *n*.
**button** ['bʌtn]. I. *s.* Knopf *m*. II. *v.tr.* **to b. sth. (up),** etwas zuknöpfen. ◆'**buttonhole**, *s.* Knopfloch *n*; **to wear a b.,** eine Blume im Knopfloch tragen.
**buttress** ['bʌtris], *s.* Strebepfeiler *m*; **flying b.,** Strebebogen *m*.
**buy** [bai], *v.tr.irr.* kaufen. ◆'**buyer**, *s.* Käufer *m*; *Com:* Einkäufer *m*. ◆'**buy 'out**, *v.tr.* (einen Teilhaber) auszahlen. ◆'**buy 'up**, *v.tr.* aufkaufen.
**buzz** [bʌz]. I. *s.* Summen *n*. II. *v.i.* summen. ◆'**buzz 'off**, *v.i. P:* abhauen. ◆'**buzzer**, *s.* Summer *m*. ◆'**buzzing**, *s.* Summen *n*; **b. in the ears,** Ohrensausen *n*.

**buzzard** ['bʌzəd], *s.* Bussard *m*.
**by** [bai]. I. *prep.* 1. *(near)* bei + *dat*; **by oneself,** alleine. 2. *(a)* **by car,** mit dem Auto; *(b)* **to go by s.o.,** *(pass)* an j-m vorbeigehen. 3. *(a)* **by night,** nachts; **by day,** am Tage; *(b)* **by this afternoon,** bis heute nachmittag; **by then,** bis dahin. 4. *(agency)* von + *dat*; durch + *acc*; **he is a baker by trade,** er ist Bäcker von Beruf. 5. *(a)* **he won by five seconds/ten metres,** er gewann mit einem Vorsprung von fünf Sekunden/zehn Metern; *(b)* **I am paid by the hour,** ich werde pro Stunde bezahlt. 6. **a room six metres by four,** ein Zimmer sechs Meter mal vier. II. *adv.* dabei; **close by,** in der Nähe; **by and large,** im großen und ganzen. ◆'**by-election**, *s.* Nachwahl *f*. ◆'**bygone**, *adj.* vergangen; **to let bygones be bygones,** den Streit beilegen. ◆'**by-law**, *s.* Statut *n*. ◆'**bypass**. I. *s.* Umgehungsstraße *f*. II. *v.tr.* umfahren. ◆'**by-product**, *s.* Nebenprodukt *n*. ◆'**bystander**, *s.* Zuschauer(in) *m(f)*. ◆'**byword**, *s.* Inbegriff *m* (**for,** von + *dat*).
**bye** [bai], *int. F:* (**b.**) **b.!** tschüs!

# C

**C, c** [si:], *s.* (der Buchstabe) C, c *n*.
**cab** [kæb], *s.* 1. Taxi *n*. 2. *(of lorry etc.)* Führerhaus *n*. ◆'**cabdriver**, *F:* '**cabby**, *s.* Taxifahrer *m*.
**cabaret** ['kæbərei], *s.* Kabarett *n*.
**cabbage** ['kæbidʒ], *s.* Kohl *m*.
**cabin** ['kæbin], *s.* 1. Hütte *f*. 2. *Nau: Av:* Kabine *f*.
**cabinet** ['kæbinit], *s.* 1. Schrank *m*; **glass c.,** Vitrine *f*; **c. maker,** Möbeltischler *m*. 2. *Pol:* the C., das Kabinett.
**cable** ['keibl]. I. *s.* 1. *(a)* Tau *n*; *(b)* *(metal)* Drahtseil *n*; *(c) El:* Kabel *n*. 2. *Tel:* **c.(gram),** Überseetelegramm *n*. II. *v.tr.* (j-m, etwas *acc*) telegrafieren.
**caboodle** [kə'bu:dl], *s. F:* **the whole c.,** *(things)* der ganze Klimbim.
**cache** [kæʃ], *s.* geheimes Lager *n*.
**cackle** ['kækl]. I. *s.* 1. *(of hen)* Gegacker *n*. 2. *(laughter)* Gekicher *n*. II. *v.i.* *(a)* gackern; *(b)* (laut) kichern.
**cactus,** *pl.* **-ti** ['kæktəs, -tai], *s.* Kaktus *m*.
**caddie** ['kædi], *s.* Golfjunge *m*.
**caddy,** *pl.* **-ies** ['kædi, -iz], *s.* (**tea-**)**c.,** Teedose *f*.
**cadet** [kə'det], *s.* Kadett *m*.
**cadge** [kædʒ], *v.tr.&i. F:* (etwas) schnorren.
**caesarean** [si:'zeəriən], *s.* Kaiserschnitt *m*.
**café** ['kæfei], *s.* Café *n*. ◆**cafeteria** [kæfi'tiəriə], *s.* Selbstbedienungsrestaurant *n*; *(snack bar)* Schnellimbiß *m*.

**caffeine** ['kæfi:n], *s.* Koffein *n*.
**cage** [keidʒ], *s.* Käfig *m*.
**cagey** ['keidʒi], *adj. F:* **he was very c.,** er wollte nichts verraten.
**cajole** [kə'dʒəul], *v.tr.* (j-m) gut zureden; **to c. s.o. into doing sth.,** j-n dazu überreden, etwas zu tun.
**cake** [keik]. I. *s.* Kuchen *m*; **c. shop,** Konditorei *f*; *F:* **it's a piece of c.,** es ist kinderleicht; **to be selling like hot cakes,** wie warme Semmeln weggehen; **c. of soap,** Riegel *m* Seife. II. *v.i.* sich verkrusten; **caked with mud,** mit Schmutz verkrustet.
**calamity** [kə'læmiti], *s.* Katastrophe *f*.
**calcium** ['kælsiəm], *s.* Kalzium *n*.
**calculate** ['kælkjuleit], *v.* 1. *v.i. Mth:* rechnen. 2. *v.tr. & i. Com:* (etwas) kalkulieren. 3. *v.tr.* (etwas) berechnen. ◆'**calculated**, *adj. (of effect etc.)* berechnet; *(of insult)* beabsichtigt; *(of lie etc.)* bewußt; **to take a c. risk,** sich bewußt auf ein Risiko einlassen. ◆'**calculating.** I. *adj. (of pers.)* berechnend. II. *(also* **calculation**) *s.* Berechnung *f*. ◆'**calculator**, *s.* Rechenmaschine *f*; (**pocket**) **c.,** Taschenrechner *m*.
**calendar** ['kælindər], *s.* Kalender *m*; **c. year,** Kalenderjahr *n*.
**calf,** *pl.* **calves¹** [kɑːf, kɑːvz], *s.* Kalb *n*.
**calf,** *pl.* **calves²**, *s. (of leg)* Wade *f*.
**calibre** ['kælibər], *s.* Kaliber *n*.
**call** [kɔːl]. I. *s.* 1. *(shout)* Ruf *m*; **c. for help,** Hilferuf *m*. 2. **telephone c.,** Anruf

*m.* **3. to be on c.**, Bereitschaftsdienst haben. **4.** (*visit*) Besuch *m;* **to pay a c. on s.o.**, j-m einen Besuch abstatten. **II.** *v.* **1.** *v.tr.* (*a*) (j-n, ein Tier) rufen; (*b*) (*telephone*) (j-n) anrufen; (*c*) (*wake*) (j-n) wekken; (*d*) **to c. s.o. a liar** etc., j-n einen Lügner usw. nennen; **to be called X**, X heißen; (*e*) **to c. a meeting**, eine Versammlung einberufen; **to c. a strike**, einen Streik ausrufen. **2.** *v.i.* vorbeikommen; *Tel:* anrufen. ◆'call 'back, *v.tr.* (j-n) zurückrufen. ◆'call-box, *s.* Telefonzelle *f.* ◆'caller, *s.* (*a*) Besucher *m;* (*b*) *Tel:* Anrufer *m.* ◆'call for, *v.tr.* (*a*) **to c. for s.o.**, nach j-m rufen; **to c. for help**, um Hilfe rufen; (*b*) (j-n, etwas) abholen; (*c*) **this calls for an explanation**, das verlangt eine Erklärung. ◆'callgirl, *s.* Callgirl *n.* ◆'call 'off, *v.tr.* (*a*) (*not start*) (etwas) absagen; (*b*) (*stop*) (etwas) abbrechen. ◆'call on, *v.tr.* (*a*) (*visit*) (j-n) besuchen; (*b*) (*invite*) (j-n) auffordern(, etwas zu tun). ◆'call 'out, *v.* **1.** *v.i.* rufen. **2.** *v.tr.* (Namen usw.) aufrufen. ◆'call 'up, *v.tr.* (*a*) *Tel: esp. N.Am:* (j-n) anrufen; (*b*) *Mil:* (j-n) einberufen.

**callous** ['kæləs], *adj.* gefühllos.

**calm** [kɑːm]. **I.** *adj.* (*a*) (*of pers.*) ruhig; (*b*) (*of wind* etc.) still. **II.** *s.* (*a*) Stille *f;* (*b*) (*of pers.*) Ruhe *f.* **III.** *v.* **1.** *v.tr.* **to c. s.o.** (**down**), j-n beruhigen. **2.** *v.i.* **to c.** (**down**), sich beruhigen.

**calorie** ['kæləri], *s.* Kalorie *f.*

**camber** ['kæmbər], *s.* Wölbung *f.*

**Cambodia** [kæm'bəudiə]. *Pr.n.* Kambodscha *n.*

**camel** ['kæməl], *s.* Kamel *n.*

**camera** ['kæm(ə)rə], *s.* Kamera *f.* ◆'cameraman, *pl.* -men, *s.* Kameramann *m.*

**camomile** ['kæməmail], *s.* Kamille *f.*

**camouflage** ['kæmuflɑːʒ]. **I.** *s.* Tarnung *f.* **II.** *v.tr.* tarnen.

**camp** [kæmp]. **I.** *s.* Lager *n; Mil:* Feldlager *n;* c. bed, Feldbett *n;* c. site, Campingplatz *m;* (*for tent*) Zeltplatz *m.* **II.** *v.i.* kampieren; (*in tent*) zelten; *Mil:* lagern. ◆'camper, *s.* **1.** Camper *m.* **2.** *Aut:* Reisemobil *n.* ◆'camping, *s.* Camping *n;* **to go c.**, zelten gehen.

**campaign** [kæm'pein]. **I.** *s. Mil:* Feldzug *m; Pol: etc:* Kampagne *f;* **election c.**, Wahlkampf *m.* **II.** *v.i.* (*a*) *Mil:* einen Feldzug unternehmen; (*b*) *Pol:* eine Kampagne führen; *Fig:* sich einsetzen; **to c. against sth.**, gegen etwas *acc* zu Felde ziehen.

**campus**, *pl.* -es ['kæmpəs, -iz], *s.* Universitätsgelände *n.*

**can¹** [kæn]. **I.** *s.* (*tin*) Dose *f;* c. opener, Dosenöffner *m.* **II.** *v.tr.* (in Büchsen) konservieren. ◆'canned, *adj.* **1.** Büchsen-; c. fruit, Obstkonserven *fpl.* **2.** *P:* (*drunk*) besoffen.

**can²** *modal aux. v.irr.* (*a*) (*ability*) können; (*b*) (*permission*) dürfen; **c. I go now?** darf

ich jetzt gehen?

**Canada** ['kænədə]. *Pr.n.* Kanada *n.* ◆**Canadian** [kə'neidjən]. **I.** *adj.* kanadisch. **II.** *s.* Kanadier(in) *m(f).*

**canal** [kə'næl], *s.* Kanal *m.*

**canary** [kə'nɛəri], *s.* Kanarienvogel *m;* **the C. Islands**, die Kanarischen Inseln *fpl.*

**cancel** ['kæns(ə)l], *v.tr.* (*a*) (eine Abmachung) rückgängig machen; (eine Schuld) tilgen; (*b*) (eine Veranstaltung) absagen; (*of performance*) **to be cancelled**, ausfallen; **to c. an appointment**, absagen; **to c. an order (for sth.)**, (etwas) abbestellen; (*c*) (Briefmarken, Fahrkarten) entwerten; (*d*) (*of two things*) **they c. one another out**, sie gleichen sich aus. ◆**cance'llation**, *s.* Absage *f;* **have you got a c.?** hat jemand abgesagt/abbestellt?

**cancer** ['kænsər], *s. Med: Astr:* Krebs *m.*

**candid** ['kændid], *adj.* offen.

**candidate** ['kændidit], *s.* (*a*) Kandidat(in) *m(f);* (*b*) (*for job*) Bewerber(in) *m(f);* (*c*) **examination c.**, Prüfling *m.*

**candle** ['kændl], *s.* Kerze *f.* ◆'candlestick, *s.* Kerzenständer *m.*

**candour** ['kændər], *s.* Offenheit *f.*

**candy**, *pl.* -ies ['kændi, -iz], *s.* **1.** (*sugar*) Kandiszucker *m.* **2.** *N.Am:* Bonbons *npl.* ◆'candyfloss, *s.* Zuckerwatte *f.*

**cane** [kein]. **1.** *s.* (*of bamboo, sugar*) Rohr *n;* c. chair, Rohrstuhl *m;* c. sugar, Rohrzucker *m.* **2.** (*a*) (*for punishment*) Rohrstock *m;* (*b*) (*walking stick*) Spazierstock *m.* *v.tr.* (j-n) mit dem Rohrstock züchtigen.

**canister** ['kænistər], *s.* Kanister *m.*

**cannibal** ['kænibəl], *s.* Kannibale *m.* ◆'cannibalism, *s.* Kannibalismus *m.*

**cannon** ['kænən], *s.* Kanone *f.*

**canoe** [kə'nuː], *s.* Paddelboot *n; Sp:* Kanu *n.*

**canon** ['kænən], *s.* **1.** Regel *f.* **2.** *Ecc:* (*a*) (*of bible*) Kanon *m;* (*b*) (*pers.*) Domherr *m.* ◆'canonize, *v.tr.* heiligsprechen.

**canopy**, *pl.* -ies ['kænəpi, -iz], *s.* Baldachin *m.*

**cantankerous** [kæn'tæŋkərəs], *adj.* streitsüchtig.

**canteen** [kæn'tiːn], *s.* Kantine *f.*

**canter** ['kæntər]. **I.** *s.* Kanter *m.* **II.** *v.i.* im Handgalopp reiten.

**canvas** ['kænvəs], *s.* **1.** Segeltuch *n.* **2.** *Art:* Leinwand *f.*

**canvass** ['kænvəs], *v.i.* Stimmen werben. ◆'canvassing, *s.* Stimmenwerbung *f.*

**canyon** ['kænjən], *s.* Cañon *m.*

**cap** [kæp]. **I.** *s.* **1.** Mütze *f.* **2.** (*cover*) Deckel *m;* (*of pen*) Kappe *f;* (*of bottle*) Kapsel *f.* **II.** *v.tr.* (*outdo*) übertreffen.

**capable** ['keipəbl], *adj.* (*a*) (*of pers.*) fähig (**of**, *gen/zu* + *inf*); **a c. teacher**, ein tüchtiger Lehrer. **2. to be c. of doing sth.**, (*of pers.*) imstande sein, etwas zu tun; (*of thing*) etwas tun können; -ably, *adv.* gekonnt. ◆**capa'bility**, *s.* Fähigkeit *f.*

**capacity** [kə'pæsiti], *s.* **1.** (*a*) *Ph:* Volu-

men *n*; (*b*) (*of a container*) Fassungs-vermögen *n*; (*of hall, train etc.*) **filled to c.**, voll besetzt; **c. audience**, ausverkauf-tes Haus. **2.** (*a*) (*of pers.*) Fähigkeit *f*; (*b*) (*of machine*) (**working**) **c.**, Leistungsvermögen *n*. **3.** (*position*) **in my c. as...**, in meiner Eigenschaft als ...
**cape**[1] [keip], *s. Cl:* Cape *n*, Umhang *m*.
**cape**[2], *s.* Kap *n*.
**caper** ['keipər], *s. Cu:* Kaper *f*.
**capital** ['kæpitl]. **I.** *adj.* **c. city**, Haupt-stadt *f*; **c. punishment**, Todesstrafe *f*; **c. letter**, Großbuchstabe *m*. **II.** *s.* **1.** *Fin:* Kapital *n*. **2.** (*city*) Hauptstadt *f*.
◆'**capitalism**, *s.* Kapitalismus *m*.
◆'**capitalist**, *s.* Kapitalist *m*.
◆'**capitalize**, *v.i.* **to c. on sth.**, aus et-was *dat* Nutzen ziehen.
**capitulate** ['kæ'pitjuleit], *v.i.* kapitulieren.
**capricious** [kə'priʃəs], *adj.* launenhaft.
**Capricorn** ['kæprikɔ:n], *s.* Steinbock *m*.
**capsize** [kæp'saiz], *v.i.* kentern.
**capsule** ['kæpsju:l], *s.* Kapsel *f*.
**captain** ['kæptin]. **I.** *s.* **1.** (*a*) *Mil:* Haupt-mann *m*; *Nau:* Kapitän *m*; (*b*) *Sp:* Mann-schaftskapitän *m*. **II.** *v.tr.* (*a*) (*Mil:* eine Kompanie, *Nau:* ein Schiff) kommandie-ren; (*b*) *Sp:* (eine Mannschaft) führen.
**caption** ['kæpʃ(ə)n], *s.* (*a*) (*of picture*) Bildunterschrift *f*; (*b*) (*heading*) Über-schrift *f*.
**captivate** ['kæptiveit], *v.tr.* bezaubern.
**captive** ['kæptiv]. **I.** *adj.* gefangen. **II.** *s.* Gefangene(r) *f(m)*. ◆**cap'tivity**, *s.* Ge-fangenschaft *f*. ◆**capture** ['kæptʃər]. **I.** *s.* Gefangennahme *f*; Eroberung *f* (einer Stadt). **II.** *v.tr.* (*a*) (ein Tier) fangen; (*b*) (j-n) gefangennehmen; (*c*) (eine Stadt usw.) erobern; **to c. the mood**, die Stimmung einfangen.
**car** [kɑːr], *s.* **1.** Auto *n*; **c. ferry**, Autofäh-re *f*; **c. park**, Parkplatz *m*; (*multistorey*) Parkhaus *n*; (*underground*) Tiefgarage *f*. **2.** *Rail: esp. N.Am:* Wagen *m*; **dining c.**, Speisewagen *m*.
**carafe** [kə'rɑːf, -æf], *s.* Karaffe *f*.
**caramel** ['kærəməl], *s.* (*a*) Karamel *m*; (*b*) (*sweet*) Karamelbonbon *n & m*.
**carat** ['kærət], *s.* Karat *n*; **eighteen c. gold**, achtzehnkarätiges Gold.
**caravan** ['kærəvæn], *s.* (*trailer*) Wohnwa-gen *m*.
**caraway** ['kærəwei], *s.* Kümmel *m*.
**carbohydrate** ['kɑːbəu'haidreit], *s.* Kohl-ehydrat *n*.
**carbon** ['kɑːbən], *s.* **1.** Kohlenstoff *m*; **c. dioxide**, Kohlendioxyd *n*. **2.** *attrib.* Kohle-; **c.** (**paper**), Kohlepapier *n*; **c. copy**, Durchschlag *m*.
**carburettor** [kɑːbjuretər], *s.* Vergaser *m*.
**carcass** ['kɑːkəs], *s.* **1.** (*corpse*) Kadaver *m*. **2.** Rumpf *m* (eines geschlachteten Tie-res).
**card** [kɑːd], *s.* **1.** Karte *f*; **playing c.**, Spielkarte *f*; **on the cards**, durchaus möglich; (**visiting**) **c.**, Visitenkarte *f*. **2.** (*material*) Karton *m*. ◆'**cardboard**, *s.*

Pappe *f*.
**cardiac** ['kɑːdiæk], *adj.* Herz-; **c. arrest**, Herzstillstand *m*.
**cardigan** ['kɑːdigən], *s.* Strickjacke *f*.
**cardinal** ['kɑːdin(ə)l]. **I.** *adj.* grundsätz-lich; **c. number**, Kardinalzahl *f*. **II.** *s.* Kardinal *m*.
**care** [kɛər]. **I.** *s.* **1.** (*worry*) Sorge *f*. **2.** (*caution*) Vorsicht *f*; **to take c.**, vorsichtig sein; **to take c. that ...**, darauf achten, daß ... **3.** (*trouble*) Sorgfalt *f*. **4. to take c. of s.o.**, für j-n sorgen; **dental c.**, Zahnpflege *f*; **the child was taken into c.**, das Kind kam in Fürsorge; (*on letter*) **c. of** (*abbr.* c/o), bei. **II.** *v.i.* (*a*) (*feel con-cern*) sich *dat* etwas daraus machen; **I don't c.!** das ist mir (völlig) egal! **for all I c. ...**, meinetwegen ...; (*b*) (*like*) **to c. for s.o.**, j-n mögen; **would you c. for a drink?** möchten Sie etwas trinken? (*c*) (*look after*) **to c. for s.o., sth.**, j-n, etwas pflegen. ◆'**carefree**, *adj.* sorgenfrei.
◆'**careful**, *adj.* **1.** (*cautious*) vorsichtig; (**be**) **c.!** paß auf! **2.** (*thorough*) sorgfältig.
◆'**careless**, *adj.* nachlässig.
◆'**carelessness**, *s.* Nachlässigkeit *f*.
◆'**caretaker**, *s.* (*a*) (*in schools, flats*) Hausmeister *m*; (*b*) (*in museum etc.*) Auf-seher *m*.
**career** [kə'riər]. **I.** *s.* (*a*) Laufbahn *f*; (**successful**) **c.**, Karriere *f*; (*b*) (*profes-sion*) Beruf *m*; **careers adviser** Berufsbe-rater(in) *m(f)*. **II.** *v.i.* **to c. (along)**, da-hinrasen.
**caress** [kə'res]. **I.** *s.* Liebkosung *f*. **II.** *v.tr.* liebkosen.
**cargo**, *pl.* **-oes** ['kɑːgəu, -əuz], *s.* Ladung *f*; **c. plane**, Transportflugzeug *n*.
**Caribbean** [kæri'bi(ː)ən], *adj.* **C.** (**Sea**), Karibisches Meer *n*.
**caricature** ['kærikətjuər]. **I.** *s.* Karikatur *f*. **II.** *v.tr.* karikieren.
**carnage** ['kɑːnidʒ], *s.* Gemetzel *n*.
**carnal** ['kɑːnəl], *adj.* fleischlich.
**carnation** [kɑː'neiʃən], *s.* Nelke *f*.
**carnival** ['kɑːniv(ə)l], *s.* Karneval *m*; *South G:* Fasching *m*.
**carnivorous** [kɑː'nivərəs], *adj.* fleisch-fressend.
**carol** ['kærəl], *s.* **Christmas c.**, Weih-nachtslied *n*.
**carp**[1] [kɑːp], *s. inv.* Karpfen *m*.
**carp**[2], *v.i.* etwas auszusetzen haben (**at**, an + *dat*).
**carpenter** ['kɑːpintər], *s.* (*a*) Tischler *m*; (*b*) (*working on buildings*) Zimmermann *m*. ◆'**carpentry**, *s.* Tischlerei *f*.
**carpet** ['kɑːpit]. **I.** *s.* Teppich *m*. **II.** *v.tr.* (ein Zimmer) mit (einem) Teppich ausle-gen.
**carriage** ['kæridʒ], *s.* **1.** Transport *m*; (*cost*) Transportkosten *pl.* **2.** (*posture*) Haltung *f*. **3.** (*a*) (*horsedrawn*) Kutsche *f*; (*b*) (*railway*) Eisenbahnwagen *m*. ◆'**carriageway**, *s.* Fahrbahn *f*; **dual c.**, zweibahnige Straße.
**carrier** ['kæriər], *s.* **1.** (*pers.*) (*a*) Träger *m*;

Überbringer *m* (von Nachrichten usw.); (*b*) *Med:* Krankheitsüberträger *m;* (*c*) *Com:* Spediteur *m.* 2. (*on bicycle etc.*) Gepäckträger *m;* **c. bag,** Tragtasche *f.*
**carrion** ['kæriən], *s.* Aas *n.*
**carrot** ['kærət], *s.* Karotte *f.*
**carry** ['kæri], *v.tr.* (*a*) tragen; (*of pers.*) (eine Botschaft) überbringen; (*b*) *Com:* (Waren) befördern; (*of pipe*) (Wasser, Öl) führen; (*c*) (*of newspaper*) (einen Artikel, Bericht) bringen; (*d*) *Fig:* **to c. sth. too far,** etwas zu weit treiben; (*e*) *Mth:* **c. five,** merke fünf; (*f*) *Parl: etc:* (*of motion*) **to be carried,** angenommen werden; (*g*) *abs.* **his voice carries well,** seine Stimme trägt gut. ◆'**carry a'way,** *v.tr.* **I was quite carried away,** ich war ganz hingerissen. ◆'**carrycot,** *s.* Babytragetasche *f.* ◆'**carry 'forward,** *v.tr.* (eine Summe) übertragen; (**amount**) **carried f.,** Übertrag *m.* ◆'**carry 'off,** *v.tr.* (*a*) (einen Preis) gewinnen; (*b*) **he carried it off well,** er hat es gut geschafft. ◆'**carry 'on,** *v.* **1** *v.tr.* (ein Geschäft, ein Gespräch) führen. **2.** *v.i.* (*a*) (*behave*) sich aufführen; (*fuss*) Theater machen; (*b*) (*continue*) (eine Tradition usw.) fortführen; **c. on!** weitermachen! nur weiter! **to c. on with sth.,** etwas weitermachen. ◆'**carry 'out,** *v.tr.* (*a*) hinaustragen; (*b*) (einen Plan, einen Befehl usw.) ausführen. ◆'**carry 'through,** *v.tr.* (einen Plan) durchführen.
**cart** [kɑːt]. **I.** *s.* (*a*) (*horsedrawn*) Wagen *m;* (*b*) (*handcart*) Karren *m.* **II.** *v.tr.* schleppen. ◆'**carthorse,** *s.* Zugpferd *n.*
**carton** ['kɑːtən], *s.* (*a*) (*material*) Pappe *f;* (*b*) (*box*) Pappschachtel *f;* **a c. of cream,** ein Becher *m* Sahne.
**cartoon** [kɑː'tuːn], *s.* **1.** Karikatur *f;* (*strip*) Comic strip *m;* *Cin:* **c. film,** Zeichentrickfilm *m.* **2.** *Art:* Karton *m.* ◆**car'toonist,** *s.* Karikaturist *m.*
**cartridge** ['kɑːtridʒ], *s.* **1.** Patrone *f.* **2. c. paper,** Zeichenpapier *n.*
**carve** [kɑːv], *v.tr.* (*a*) (*in wood*) (etwas) schnitzen; (*in stone*) (ein Bild) (in/aus Stein) hauen; (*b*) **to c. meat,** Fleisch aufschneiden; **to c. sth. up,** etwas in Stücke zerteilen. ◆'**carving,** *s.* **1.** Schnitzerei *f.* **2.** Aufschneiden *n;* **c. knife,** Tranchiermesser *n.*
**cascade** [kæs'keid]. **I.** *s.* Wasserfall *m.* **II.** *v.i.* herabstürzen.
**case¹** [keis], *s.* (*also Med: Gram: Jur:*) Fall *m;* **as the c. may be,** je nach Sachlage; **just in c.,** für alle Fälle; **in c. he comes,** falls er kommt; **in c. of a breakdown,** im Falle einer Panne; **in any c. it's too late,** es ist sowieso zu spät; **c. history,** Krankengeschichte *f; Jur:* **he has a good c.,** er hat schlüssige Beweise; **to make out a c. for sth.,** etwas begründen.
**case²,** *s.* **1.** (*a*) (*box*) Kasten *m;* (*small*) Kästchen *n;* (*suitcase*) Koffer *m;* **cigarette c.,** Zigarettenetui *n;* (*b*) (*soft*) **spectacle**

**c., Brillenfutteral** *n;* **pillow c.,** Kopfkissenbezug *m.* **2.** (*housing*) Gehäuse *n;* **glass c.,** Vitrine *f.*
**cash** [kæʃ]. **I.** *s. no pl.* **1.** Bargeld *n;* **to pay c.,** (in) bar bezahlen; **c. desk,** Kasse *f;* **c. box,** Geldkassette *f;* **c. register,** Registrierkasse *f;* **c. on delivery,** per Nachnahme. **2.** *F:* Geld *n;* **to be short of c.,** knapp bei Kasse sein. **II.** *v.tr.* (einen Scheck usw.) einlösen; **to c. in on sth.,** von etwas dat profitieren. ◆**ca'shier,** *s.* Kassierer(in) *m(f).*
**casino,** *pl.* **-os** [ke'siːnəu, -əuz], *s.* Kasino *n.*
**cask** [kɑːsk], *s.* Faß *n.*
**casserole** ['kæsərəul], *s.* **1.** (*container*) Schmortopf *m.* **2.** (*food*) Fleischeintopf *m.*
**cassette** [kæ'set], *s.* Kassette *f;* **c. recorder,** Kassettenrecorder *m.*
**cast** [kɑːst]. **I.** *s.* **1.** **plaster c.,** Gipsverband *m.* **2.** *Th:* Besetzung *f.* **II.** *v.tr.* (*a*) (die Angel, das Netz) auswerfen; **to c. anchor,** den Anker auswerfen; (*b*) **to c. light/shadow on sth.,** Licht/einen Schatten auf etwas *acc* werfen; (*c*) **to c. one's vote,** seine Stimme abgeben; (*d*) (Metall, eine Statue) gießen; **c. iron,** Gußeisen *n;* **c. iron proof,** hieb- und stichfester Beweis *m;* (*e*) **to c. s.o. as X/for the part of X.,** j-m die Rolle des X geben. ◆'**cast-away,** *s.* Schiffbrüchige(r) *f(m).* ◆'**casting,** *adj.* **c. vote,** entscheidende Stimme *f.* ◆'**cast 'off,** *v.* **1.** *v.tr.* (etwas) wegwerfen; **c. off clothes,** abgelegte Kleider. **2.** *v.i. Nau:* ablegen.
**castanets** [kæstə'nets], *s.* Kastagnetten *fpl.*
**castle** ['kɑːsl], *s.* **1.** Burg *f;* (*mansion*) Schloß *n.* **2.** (*in chess*) Turm *m.*
**castor¹** ['kɑːstər], *s.* Laufrolle *f.*
**castor²,** *s.* **c. oil,** Rizinusöl *n.*
**castrate** [kæs'treit], *v.tr.* kastrieren.
**casual** ['kæʒju(ə)l], *adj.* **1.** (*a*) (*chance*) zufällig; (*b*) (*not permanent*) Gelegenheits-. **2.** (*a*) (*informal*) ungezwungen; **c. clothes,** zwanglose Kleidung; (*b*) (*uninvolved*) gleichgültig; **a c. remark,** eine beiläufige Bemerkung.
**casualty,** *pl.* **-ies** ['kæʒjuəlti, -iz], *s.* (*injured*) Verletzte(r) *f(m);* (*dead*) Todesopfer *n;* **c. ward,** Unfallstation *f.*
**cat** [kæt], *s.* Katze *f;* **to let the c. out of the bag,** die Katze aus dem Sack lassen.
**catalogue** ['kætələg]. **I.** *s.* Katalog *m.* **II.** *v.tr.* (Bücher usw.) katalogisieren.
**catalyst** ['kætəlist], *s. Ch:* Katalysator *m; Fig:* auslösendes Moment *n.*
**catapult** ['kætəpʌlt]. **I.** *s.* Katapult *n.* **II.** *v.tr.* schleudern.
**cataract** ['kætərækt], *s. Med:* grauer Star *m.*
**catarrh** [kə'tɑːr], *s.* Katarrh *m.*
**catastrophe** [kə'tæstrəfi], *s.* Katastrophe *f.* ◆**catastrophic** [kætə'strɔfik], *adj.* katastrophal.
**catch** [kætʃ]. **I.** *v.irr.* **1.** *v.tr.* (*a*) fangen;

*(capture)* (Tiere) einfangen; *(in falling)* (j-n, etwas) auffangen; *(c. up with)* (j-n) einholen; *(b) (surprise)* (j-n) überraschen; *(c) (be in time for)* (einen Bus, einen Zug) erreichen, F: erwischen; *(d) (hear, understand)* **I didn't quite c. that,** das habe ich nicht ganz mitgekriegt; *(e) Med:* sich *dat* (eine Krankheit) zuziehen; **to c. a cold,** sich erkälten; *(f)* **to c. a dress on a nail,** mit dem Kleid an einem Nagel hängenbleiben; **to c. one's finger in a door,** sich *dat* den Finger in der Tür klemmen. **2.** *v.i. (stick)* **the door is catching,** die Tür klemmt; **her dress caught on a nail,** ihr Kleid blieb an einem Nagel hängen. **II.** *s.* **1.** *(action)* Fangen n. **2.** *(of fish)* Fang m. **3.** *(trap)* Falle f; **there's a c. in it,** die Sache hat einen Haken. **4.** *(closure)* Verschluß m; *(latch)* Klinke f. ◆**'catching,** *adj.* ansteckend. ◆**'catch 'on,** *v.i. (a) (be accepted)* Anklang finden; *(b) (understand)* **he caught on immediately,** er hat es sofort begriffen. ◆**'catch 'out,** *v.tr. (of pers.)* (j-n) hereinlegen; **his question caught me out,** seine Frage hat mich überrumpelt. ◆**'catch 'up,** *v.tr. & i. (a)* **to c. s.o., sth. up/c. up with s.o., sth.,** j-n, etwas einholen; **to c. up on one's work,** seine Arbeit nachholen; *(b)* **caught up in sth.,** (i) *(involved)* in etwas *acc* verwickelt; (ii) *(carried away)* von etwas *dat* mitgerissen.

**catechism** ['kætikiz(ə)m], *s.* Katechismus m.

**categorical** [kætə'gɔrik(ə)l], *adj.* kategorisch. ◆**category** ['kætigəri, *N.Am:* -gɔri], *s.* Kategorie f.

**cater** ['keitər], *v.i. (a)* Lebensmittel liefern; **to c. for s.o.,** j-n mit Lebensmitteln versorgen; *(b) Fig:* **to c. for s.o., sth.,** j-n, etwas berücksichtigen. ◆**'caterer,** *s.* Lebensmittellieferant m. ◆**'catering,** *s. c. (industry),** Gaststättengewerbe n; **who's doing the c.?** wer liefert das Essen?

**caterpillar** ['kætəpilər], *s.* Raupe f.

**cathedral** [kə'θi:drəl], *s.* Kathedrale f.

**catholic** ['kæθ(ə)lik]. **I.** *adj.* **1.** umfassend; **c. tastes,** weite Sympathien. **2.** *Ecc:* katholisch. **II.** *s.* Katholik(in) m(f). ◆**catholicism** [kə'θɔlisiz(ə)m], *s.* Katholizismus m.

**cattle** ['kætl], *s. inv.* Vieh n.

**catty** ['kæti], *adj. F:* gehässig.

**cauliflower** ['kɔliflauər], *s.* Blumenkohl m.

**cause** [kɔːz]. **I.** *s.* **1.** *(origin)* Ursache f. **2.** *(reason)* Grund m *(for sth.,* zu etwas *dat);* **no c. for complaint,** kein Grund zur Klage; **to have good c. for doing sth.,** seine guten Gründe für etwas *acc* haben. **3.** *(a) (purpose)* Zweck m; **it's all in a good c.,** es ist für einen guten Zweck; *(b)* Sache f; **in the c. of freedom,** um der Freiheit willen; **a lost c.,** eine verlorene Sache. **II.** *v.tr. (a)* (etwas) verursachen; *(b)* **to c. s.o. to do sth.,** j-n veranlassen,

etwas zu tun.

**causeway** ['kɔːzwei], *s.* Damm m.

**caustic** ['kɔːstik], *adj.* **1.** *Ch:* ätzend; *Ätz-.* **2.** *Fig:* beißend.

**cauterize** ['kɔːtəraiz], *v.tr. Med:* (eine Wunde usw.) ausbrennen.

**caution** ['kɔːʃ(ə)n]. **I.** *s.* **1.** *(care)* Vorsicht f; **to proceed with c.,** vorsichtig vorgehen. **2.** *(warning)* Warnung f; *Jur: etc:* Verwarnung f. **II.** *v.tr.* (j-n) warnen; *Jur: etc:* (j-n) verwarnen. ◆**'cautious,** *adj.* vorsichtig.

**cavalier** [kævə'liər], *adj.* anmaßend; **c. treatment,** arrogante Behandlung.

**cavalry** ['kæv(ə)lri], *s.* Kavallerie f.

**cave** [keiv]. **I.** *s.* Höhle f. **II.** *v.i.* **to c. in,** einstürzen.

**cavern** ['kævən], *s.* Höhle f. ◆**'cavernous,** *adj.* **1.** höhlenartig. **2.** *Fig:* hohl; *(of cheeks)* eingefallen.

**caviar(e)** ['kæviɑːr], *s.* Kaviar m.

**cavity** ['kævəti], *s.* Hohlraum m; *Anat:* Höhle f; *(in tooth)* Loch n.

**cavort** [kə'vɔːt], *v.i.* herumtollen.

**cease** [siːs], *v.* **1.** *v.tr.* (mit etwas *dat)* aufhören; (die Zahlung, das Feuer, die Arbeit usw.) einstellen; **it has ceased to exist,** es existiert nicht mehr. **2.** *v.i. (of rain etc.)* aufhören; *(of production etc.)* eingestellt werden. ◆**'ceasefire,** *s.* Waffenruhe f. ◆**'ceaseless,** *adj.* unaufhörlich.

**cedar** ['siːdər], *s.* Zeder f.

**cede** [siːd], *v.tr.* (etwas) abtreten *(to s.o.,* an j-n).

**ceiling** ['siːliŋ], *s.* **1.** Decke f (eines Zimmers). **2.** *(limit)* (oberste) Grenze f. **price c.,** oberste Preisgrenze f.

**celebrate** ['selibreit], *v.tr.* feiern. ◆**'celebrated,** *adj.* berühmt. ◆**cele'bration,** *s.* Feier f. ◆**celebrity** [sə'lebriti], *s.* Berühmtheit f.

**celery** ['seləri], *s.* Stangensellerie m & f.

**celestial** [si'lestiəl], *adj.* himmlisch.

**celibacy** ['selibəsi], *s.* Zölibat n. ◆**celibate** ['selibət], *adj.* enthaltsam.

**cell** [sel], *s.* Zelle f.

**cellar** ['selər], *s.* Keller m.

**cellist** ['tʃelist], *s.* Cellist(in) m(f). ◆**cello,** *pl.* **-os** ['tʃeləu, -əuz], *s.* Cello n.

**cellophane** ['seləfein], *s.* Zellophan n.

**cement** [si'ment]. **I.** *s.* Zement m. **II.** *v.tr. (a)* (etwas) zementieren; *(b) Fig:* **to c. a friendship,** eine Freundschaft festigen.

**cemetery** ['semətri], *s.* Friedhof m.

**censor** ['sensər]. **I.** *s.* Zensor m. **II.** *v.tr.* zensieren. ◆**'censorship,** *s.* Zensur f.

**censure** ['senʃər]. **I.** *s.* Tadel m; **vote of c.,** Mißtrauensvotum n. **II.** *v.tr.* (j-n) tadeln.

**census** ['sensəs], *s.* Volkszählung f.

**cent** [sent], *s.* **1.** *(coin)* Cent m; **I haven't a c.,** ich habe keinen Pfennig. **2. per c.,** Prozent n.

**centenary** [sen'tiːnəri], *s.* Hundertjahrfeier f.

**centigrade** ['sentigreid], *adj.* **20 degrees c.**, 20 Grad Celsius.

**centimetre** ['sentimi:tər], *s.* Zentimeter *m*.

**central** ['sentr(ə)l], *adj.* **1.** (*a*) zentral; (*of house*) zentral gelegen; **c. heating**, Zentralheizung *f*; (*b*) *Geog:* Mittel-; **C. America**, Mittelamerika *n*; (*c*) **c. reservation**, Mittelstreifen *m* (einer Autobahn). **2.** (*main*) Haupt-; **c. (station)**, Hauptbahnhof *m*; *Pol:* **c. government**, Zentralregierung *f*; **-ly**, *adv.* zentral. ◆**'centralize**, *v.tr.* zentralisieren.

**centre** ['sentər]. **I.** *s.* Zentrum *n*; **town c.**, Innenstadt *f*. **II.** *attrib.* Mittel-; *Sp:* **c. forward**, Mittelstürmer *m*; **c. half**, Mittelläufer *m*; *Pol:* **c. party**, Partei *f* der Mitte. **III.** *v.* **1.** *v.tr.* (*a*) *Tchn:* (etwas) zentrieren; (*b*) **to be centred in London**, London als Zentrum haben. **2.** *v.i.* **to c. on sth.**, sich auf etwas *acc* konzentrieren.

**century** ['sentʃəri], *s.* Jahrhundert *n*.

**ceramic** [si'ræmik], *adj.* keramisch.

**cereal** ['siəriəl], *s.* **1.** (*usu. pl.*) Getreide *n*. **2. (breakfast) c.**, Cornflakes, Haferflocken *usw.*

**ceremony** ['seriməni], *s.* **1.** Zeremonie *f*. **2.** (*formality*) Förmlichkeit *f*; **without c.**, ohne Umstände; **to stand on c.**, sehr formell sein. ◆**cere'monial. I.** *adj.* feierlich. **II.** *s.* Zeremoniell *n*. ◆**cere'monious**, *adj.* zeremoniell.

**certain** ['sə:t(ə)n], *adj.* **1.** sicher; **I know for c.**, ich weiß es genau/ganz bestimmt. **2.** (*not named*) gewiß; **on a c. day**, an einem bestimmten Tag; **-ly**, *adv.* bestimmt; **c.!** aber sicher! **c. not**, das kommt nicht in Frage. ◆**'certainty**, *s.* (*in one's mind*) Gewißheit *f*; (*factual*) Sicherheit *f*.

**certificate** [sə'tifikit], *s.* **1.** Bescheinigung *f*; (*paper*) Schein *m*; **medical c.**, ärztliches Attest *n*. **2.** *Sch:* Diplom *n*.

**certify** ['sə:tifai], *v.tr.* (*a*) (*confirm*) (einen Tod usw.) bestätigen; (*b*) (etwas) bescheinigen; (eine Abschrift) beglaubigen; **this is to c. that ...**, hiermit wird bescheinigt, daß ...; **to c. s.o. (as being insane)**, j-n wegen Geisteskrankheit entmündigen.

**cervix** ['sə:viks], *s.* Gebärmutterhals *m*.

**chafe** [tʃeif], *v.tr.* (*a*) (*of rope, skin etc.*) (an etwas *dat*) scheuern; (*b*) (*make sore*) (die Haut usw.) wund reiben.

**chaffinch** ['tʃæfin(t)ʃ], *s.* Buchfink *m*.

**chain** [tʃein]. **I.** *s.* Kette *f*; (*in WC*) **to pull the c.**, ziehen; **c. reaction**, Kettenreaktion *f*; **c. smoker**, Kettenraucher *m*; **c. store**, Kettengeschäft *n*. **II.** *v.tr.* anketten.

**chair** [tʃɛər]. **I.** *s.* **1.** Stuhl *m*; **c. lift**, Sessellift *m*. **2. to be in the/take the c.**, den Vorsitz führen. **3.** (*professorship*) Lehrstuhl *m*. **II.** *v.tr.* **to c. a meeting**, bei einer Versammlung den Vorsitz führen. ◆**'chairman, 'chairwoman**, *s.* (*a*) (*of a meeting etc.*) (*also* **chairperson**) Vorsitzen-

de(r) *f(m)*; (*b*) (*of a firm*) Generaldirektor *m*.

**chalet** ['ʃælei], *s.* (*Swiss*) Chalet *n*; (*for holidays*) Ferienhaus *n*.

**chalk** [tʃɔ:k], *s.* Kreide *f*.

**challenge** ['tʃælin(d)ʒ]. **I.** *s.* Herausforderung *f*. **II.** *v.tr.* (*a*) (j-n) herausfordern; **to c. s.o. to a duel**, j-n zum Duell fordern; (*b*) (*of sentry*) (j-n) anrufen; (*c*) (eine Behauptung usw.) bestreiten. ◆**'challenger**, *s.* Herausforderer *m*. ◆**'challenging**, *adj.* herausfordernd.

**chamber** ['tʃeimbər], *s.* **1.** Kammer *f*; **c. maid**, Zimmermädchen *n*; **c. pot**, Nachttopf *m*; **c. music**, Kammermusik *f*; **c. of horrors**, Gruselkabinett *n*. **2.** **C. of Commerce**, Handelskammer *f*. **3.** *Parl:* **Lower C.**, Unterhaus *n*; **Upper C.**, Oberhaus *n*.

**chameleon** [kə'mi:ljən], *s.* Chamäleon *n*.

**chamois** ['ʃæmwɑ], *s.* Gemse *f*; **c.**/*F:* **chammy** ['ʃæmi] **leather**, Waschleder *n*.

**champagne** [ʃæm'pein], *s.* Champagner *m*; (*German*) Sekt *m*.

**champion** ['tʃæmpjən]. **I.** *s.* **1.** Verfechter *m* (einer Sache). **2.** *Sp:* Meister(in) *m(f)*; **boxing c.**, Boxmeister *m*. **II.** *v.tr.* **to c. sth.**, sich für etwas *acc* einsetzen. ◆**'championship**, *s.* Meisterschaft *f*.

**chance** [tʃɑ:ns]. **I.** *s.* **1.** (*accident*) Zufall *m*; **by c.**, zufällig. **2.** (*luck*) Glück *n*; **to take no chances**, nichts riskieren. **3.** (*prospect*) Chance *f*; Aussichten *pl*; **on the off c.**, auf gut Glück; **the chances are that ...**, aller Wahrscheinlichkeit nach ...; **to stand a good/fair c. of sth.**, gute Aussichten auf etwas *acc* haben. **4.** (*opportunity*) Gelegenheit *f*; **to give s.o. a c.**, j-m eine Chance geben. **5.** *attrib.* Zufalls-; zufällig. **II.** *v.* **1.** *v.i.* **to c. (up)on s.o., sth.**, auf j-n, etwas *acc* stoßen. **2.** *v.tr.* **we'll have to c. it**, wir müssen es riskieren. ◆**'chancy**, *adj.* *F:* riskant.

**chancellor** ['tʃɑ:nsələr], *s.* Kanzler *m*; *Brit:* **C. of the Exchequer**, Schatzkanzler *m*.

**chandelier** [ʃændə'liər], *s.* Kronleuchter *m*.

**change** [tʃein(d)ʒ]. **I.** *s.* **1.** (*a*) (*alteration*) (Ver)änderung *f*; **c. of heart**, Gesinnungswandel *m*; (*b*) (*innovation*) Neuerung *f*. **2.** (*a*) (*replacement*) Wechsel *m*; **c. of clothes**, Kleider zum Wechseln; (*b*) (*transition*) Übergang *m*. **3.** (*variety*) Abwechslung *f*; **for a c.**, zur Abwechslung; **to need a c.**, Abwechslung nötig haben. **4.** (*money*) Wechselgeld *n*; **small c.**, Kleingeld *n*; **to give c. for a pound**, auf ein Pfund herausgeben. **II.** *v.* **1.** *v.tr.* (*a*) (*alter*) ändern; (j-n, seine Stimme, die Welt, usw.) verändern; **he has changed his mind**, er hat sich anders entschlossen; (*b*) (*swop*) wechseln; **to c. hands**, den Besitzer wechseln; **to c. sth. for sth. else**, etwas gegen etwas anderes (um)tauschen; **to c. trains**, umsteigen; **to**

c. **pounds into marks,** Pfund in Mark umwechseln; **to c. gear,** (den Gang) schalten; (c) **to c. one's clothes,** sich umziehen; **to c. the baby,** das Baby trokkenlegen; (d) (transform) **to c. sth. into sth.,** etwas in etwas acc verwandeln. 2. v.i. (a) (of pers., weather etc.) sich (ver)ändern; (b) **to c. into a frog,** sich in einen Frosch verwandeln; (c) Cl: sich umziehen; (d) Rail: etc: umsteigen; **all c.!** alles aussteigen! (e) **to c. from red to green,** von rot auf grün wechseln; (f) Aut: **to c. into third (gear),** in den dritten Gang schalten. ◆'**changeable,** adj. (of weather) veränderlich; (of pers.) wankelmütig. ◆'**changing,** s. **c. room,** Umkleideraum m. ◆'**change 'down,** v.i. Aut: herunterschalten (**into,** in + acc). ◆'**change 'up,** v.i. Aut: hinaufschalten (**into,** in + acc).

**channel** ['tʃænl]. I. s. 1. (a) (natural) Rinne f; (man-made) Kanal m; (navigation) c., Fahrrinne f (eines Flusses, Hafens usw.); (b) Geog: **the (English) C.,** der Ärmelkanal, F: der Kanal; **the C. Islands,** die Kanalinseln fpl. 2. Fig: Weg m; **through (the) official channels,** auf dem Amtsweg. 3. Rad: TV: Kanal m. II. v.tr. (Energie, Kräfte usw.) lenken.

**chant** [tʃɑ:nt]. I. s. (liturgischer) Gesang m. II. v.tr. (Schlagworte usw.) rhythmisch rufen.

**chaos** ['keiɔs], s. Chaos n. ◆**cha'otic,** adj. chaotisch.

**chap¹** [tʃæp], v.i. (of skin, lips etc.) aufspringen.

**chap²,** s. F: Kerl m.

**chapel** ['tʃæpl], s. Kapelle f.

**chaperon** ['ʃæpərəun]. I. s. Anstandsdame f. II. v.tr. (j-n) als Anstandsdame begleiten.

**chaplain** ['tʃæplin], s. Ecc: Kaplan m; (in hospital, school) Hausgeistlicher m.

**chapter** ['tʃæptər], s. Kapitel n.

**char¹** [tʃɑ:r], v. tr. & i. (Holz usw.) verkohlen.

**char².** I. s. F: Putzfrau f. II. v.i. F: als Putzfrau arbeiten.

**character** ['kæriktər], s. 1. Charakter m; **that is quite out of c. for him,** das ist untypisch für ihn. 2. (person) (a) (in play etc.) Person f; (b) **he's (quite) a c.,** er ist ein Original. ◆**character'istic.** I. adj. charakteristisch. II. s. (a) (trait) Merkmal n; (b) (quality) Eigenschaft f; **-ally,** adv. charakteristischerweise.

◆'**characterize,** v.tr. (j-n) charakterisieren. ◆'**characterless,** adj. charakterlos.

**charcoal** ['tʃɑ:kəul], s. (a) Holzkohle f; (b) Art: Zeichenkohle f.

**charge** [tʃɑ:dʒ]. I. s. 1. Ladung f (einer Bombe usw.); **explosive c.,** Sprengladung f. 2. (fee) Gebühr f; **bank charges,** Bankspesen pl; **free of c.,** kostenlos; **there is no c. for that,** das kostet nichts. 3. **to take c.,** die Verantwortung

übernehmen (**of sth.,** für etwas acc); **to be in c. of sth.,** für etwas acc verantwortlich sein. 4. Jur: (accusation) Beschuldigung f; (in criminal law) Anklage f; **on a c. of theft,** des Diebstahls beschuldigt. 5. Mil: Sturmangriff m. II. v.tr. (a) El: (eine Batterie usw.) aufladen; (b) Jur: **to c. s.o. with a crime,** j-n eines Verbrechens anklagen; (c) Com: etc: (eine Gebühr) erheben; **to c. sth. to s.o.,** j-m etwas berechnen; **to c. three pounds an hour,** pro Stunde drei Pfund berechnen.

◆'**charger,** s. (battery) c., Ladegerät n.

**chariot** ['tʃæriət], s. Kampfwagen m.

**charity** ['tʃæriti], s. 1. (quality) Nächstenliebe f. 2. c. (organisation), karitative Einrichtung; Hilfswerk n; **for c.,** zu Wohltätigkeitszwecken; **c. bazaar,** Wohltätigkeitsbasar m. ◆'**charitable,** adj. 1. (of pers.) gebefreudig; (of institution) karitativ. 2. (lenient) nachsichtig.

**charm** [tʃɑ:m]. I. s. 1. (magic) (a) Zaubermittel n; (b) Amulett n. 2. Charme m, Reiz m (einer Person, eines Ortes usw.). II. v.tr. (j-n) bezaubern. ◆'**charming,** adj. reizend, charmant.

**chart** [tʃɑ:t], s. 1. Nau: Seekarte f. 2. (sheet of information) Tabelle f. 3. Mus: F: **the charts** pl, die Hitparade.

**charter** ['tʃɑ:tər]. I. s. Chartern n (eines Schiffes, Flugzeugs); **c. plane,** Chartermaschine f. II. v.tr. (a) (j-n) konzessionieren; **chartered accountant,** Wirtschaftsprüfer m; (b) (ein Flugzeug) chartern.

**charwoman,** pl. **-women** ['tʃɑ:wumən, -wimin], s. Putzfrau f.

**chary** ['tʃɛəri], adj. **to be c. about doing sth.,** zögern, etwas zu tun.

**chase** [tʃeis]. I. v.tr. & i. jagen. II. s. Verfolgung f; (hunt) Jagd f.

**chasm** ['kæz(ə)m], s. Kluft f.

**chassis** ['ʃæsi], s. Fahrgestell n.

**chaste** [tʃeist], adj. keusch. ◆**chastity** ['tʃæstiti], s. Keuschheit f.

**chastise** [tʃæs'taiz], v.tr. (j-n) züchtigen.

**chat** [tʃæt]. I. v.i. plaudern; F: **to c. s.o. up,** sich an j-n heranmachen. II. s. Plauderei f, F: Plausch m.

**chatter** ['tʃætər]. I. v.i. (a) (of pers.) schwätzen; (of child) plappern; (b) (of teeth) klappern. II. s. Geschwätz n; Geplapper n (eines Kindes usw.).

**chauffeur** ['ʃəufər], s. Chauffeur m.

**cheap** [tʃi:p], adj. billig.

**cheat** [tʃi:t]. I. v. 1. v.tr. (j-n) beschwindeln. 2. v.i. (at games etc.) mogeln. II. s. (pers.) (a) Betrüger m; (b) (at games) Mogler m. ◆'**cheating,** s. 1. Schwindeln n. 2. (at games) Mogelei f.

**check¹** [tʃek]. I. v. 1. v.tr. (a) (den Fluß, eine Entwicklung usw.) hemmen; (den Feind, den Fortschritt usw.) aufhalten; (eine Krankheit usw.) in Schach halten; (b) (examine) (eine Rechnung, Liste usw.) prüfen; (eine Übersetzung, eine Maschine, den Ölstand usw.) überprüfen. 2. v.i.

nachprüfen; (by looking) nachsehen. **II.** s.
**1. to keep a c. on s.o., sth.,** j-n, etwas
unter Kontrolle halten; **to keep one's
feelings in c.,** sich beherrschen. **2.** (a)
Kontrolle f (von Fahrkarten, Gepäck
usw); (examination) Prüfung f (einer
Rechnung usw.); **c. list,** Checkliste f; (b)
N.Am: (bill) Rechnung f. **3.** N.Am: (cheque) Scheck m. ◆'**check 'in,** v.i. (a) (in
hotel) sich anmelden; (b) Av: einchecken.
◆'**checkmate,** s. Matt n; int. Schachmatt! ◆'**check 'out,** v. **1.** v.i. (at hotel)
sich abmelden. **2.** v.tr. esp. N.Am: (ein
Gerät) überprüfen; (eine Tatsache) nachprüfen. ◆'**check-out,** s. (in supermarket)
Kasse f. ◆'**checkpoint,** s. Kontrollpunkt m. ◆'**checkup,** s. Kontrolluntersuchung f. ◆'**check 'up,** v.i. nachprüfen; (by looking) nachsehen.
**check²,** s. (pattern) Karo n.
◆'**check(ed),** adj. (of pattern) kariert.
◆'**checkers,** s. N.Am: Damespiel n.

**cheek** [tʃiːk], s. **1.** Backe f. **2.** F: (impudence) Frechheit f. ◆'**cheeky,** adj.
frech.

**cheer** [tʃiər]. **I.** s. **1.** Frohsinn m. **2.** (a)
(applause) Hurra n; **three cheers for X,**
ein dreifaches Hoch auf X acc; (b) int.
**cheers!** Prost! **II.** v. **1.** v.tr. (a) **to c. s.o.
(up),** j-n aufmuntern; (b) (of crowd) (j-m)
zujubeln. **2.** v.i. (a) **to c. up,** (of pers.)
fröhlicher werden; (b) (of crowd) Beifall
rufen. ◆'**cheerful,** adj. (of pers.) heiter;
**c. news,** erfreuliche Nachrichten; **-ly,**
adv. (willingly) gern. ◆'**cheeri'o!** int.
F: tschüs! ◆'**cheerless,** adj. trostlos.
◆'**cheery,** adj. heiter.

**cheese** [tʃiːz]. **I.** s. Käse m. **II.** v.tr. P: **to
be cheesed off,** angeödet sein.
◆'**cheesecake,** s. Käsekuchen m.

**chef** [ʃef], s. (head cook) Küchenchef m;
(cook) Koch m.

**chemical** ['kemik(ə)l]. **I.** adj. chemisch.
**II.** s. pl. **chemicals,** Chemikalien fpl.
◆**chemist** ['kemist], s. **1.** (expert in chemistry) Chemiker(in) m(f). **2.** (non-dispensing) Drogist(in) m(f); (dispensing)
c., Apotheker(in) m(f); **chemist's shop,**
(non-dispensing) Drogerie f; (dispensing)
Apotheke f. ◆**chemistry** ['kemistri], s.
Chemie f.

**cheque** [tʃek], s. Scheck m (for £10, über
10 Pfund); **c. book,** Scheckheft n.

**chequered** ['tʃekəd], adj. Fig: **c. career,**
abwechslungsreiche Karriere.

**cherish** ['tʃeriʃ], v.tr. (einen Wunsch) hegen.

**cherry** ['tʃeri], s. Kirsche f; **c. tree,**
Kirschbaum m.

**chess** [tʃes], s. Schach n.
◆'**chessboard,** s. Schachbrett n.

**chest** [tʃest], s. **1.** Truhe f; **c. of drawers,**
Kommode f. **2.** Anat: Brust f; F: **to get
sth. off one's c.,** sich dat etwas von der
Seele reden.

**chestnut** ['tʃesnʌt], s. Kastanie f.

**chew** [tʃuː], v.tr. kauen. ◆'**chewing**

**gum,** s. Kaugummi m.

**chic** [ʃiːk], adj. schick.

**chick** [tʃik], s. Küken n. ◆'**chick-pea,** s.
Kichererbse f.

**chicken** ['tʃikin], s. Huhn n.
◆'**chickenpox,** s. Windpocken fpl.

**chicory** ['tʃikəri], s. Zichorie f; (as vegetable) Chicorée f.

**chief** [tʃiːf]. **I.** s. (a) Mil: **c. of staff,** Chef
m des Generalstabs; (b) Häuptling m (eines Stammes). **II.** adj. Haupt-; **c. constable,** Polizeipräsident m; **-ly,** adv. **1.**
(mostly) meistens. **2.** (mainly) hauptsächlich.

**chiffon** ['ʃifɔn], s. Chiffon m.

**chilblain** ['tʃilblein], s. Frostbeule f.

**child,** pl. **children** [tʃaild, 'tʃildrən], s.
Kind n; **that's c.'s play,** das ist ein Kinderspiel; **c. benefit,** Kindergeld n.
◆'**childbirth,** s. Entbindung f.
◆'**childhood,** s. Kindheit f.
◆'**childish,** adj. kindisch. ◆'**childless,** adj. kinderlos. ◆'**childlike,**
adj. kindlich. ◆'**childminder,** s. Tagesmutter f.

**Chile** ['tʃili]. Pr.n. Chile n. ◆**Chilean**
['tʃiliən]. **I.** s. Chilene m; Chilenin f. **II.**
adj. chilenisch.

**chill** [tʃil]. **I.** s. **1.** Verkühlung f; **to catch
a c.,** sich verkühlen. **2.** Kälte f; **to take
the c. off sth.,** etwas anwärmen. **II.** v.tr.
abkühlen. ◆'**chilly,** adj. **1.** (of pers.)
**to feel c.,** frösteln; (b) (of wind, air etc.)
frisch. **2.** (unfriendly) frostig.

**chime** [tʃaim]. **I.** s. Klang m (einer Glokke); Schlag m (einer Uhr). **II.** v.tr. & i.
(eine Glocke) läuten; **a chiming clock,**
eine schlagende Uhr; F: **to c. in,** einfallen.

**chimney** ['tʃimni], s. Schornstein m.
◆'**chimney-pot,** s. Schornsteinaufsatz
m. ◆'**chimney-sweep,** s. Schornsteinfeger m.

**chimpanzee** [tʃimpæn'ziː], s. Schimpanse
m.

**chin** [tʃin], s. Kinn n.

**china** ['tʃainə]. **1.** s. Porzellan n. **2.** Pr.n.
**C.,** China n. ◆**Chinese** [tʃai'niːz]. **I.** s.
**1.** Chinese m; Chinesin f. **2.** (language)
Chinesisch n. **II.** adj. chinesisch.

**chink¹** [tʃiŋk], s. Ritze f (in einer Wand,
einer Tür usw.).

**chink².** **I.** s. Geklirr n (von Glas); Klimpern n (von Münzen). **II.** v.i. (of glasses)
klirren; (of coins) klimpern.

**chip** [tʃip]. **I.** s. **1.** Span m (von Holz,
Metall); Fig: **to have a c. on one's
shoulder,** einen Komplex haben. **2.** (damaged place) angeschlagene Stelle f (eines
Tellers, einer Tasse usw.). **3.** Cu: **chips,**
Pommes frites pl. **II.** v. **1.** v.tr. (Porzellan) anschlagen. **2.** v.i. (of paint) absplittern.

**chiropodist** [ki'ropədist], s. Fußpfleger(in) m(f). ◆**chi'ropody,** s. Fußpflege f.

**chirp** ['tʃəːp], v.i. (of bird) zwitschern.

**chisel** ['tʃizl], s. Meißel m.
**chivalrous** ['ʃivəlrəs], adj. ritterlich.
◆**'chivalry**, s. Ritterlichkeit f.
**chives** [tʃaivz], s. Schnittlauch m.
**chloride** ['klɔːraid], s. Chlorid n.
◆**chlorine** ['klɔːriːn], s. Chlor n.
◆**chlorinate** ['klɔːrineit], v.tr. (Wasser) chloren.
**chloroform** ['klɔrəfɔːm], s. Chloroform n.
**choc-ice** ['tʃɔkais], s. Eis n mit Schokoladenüberzug.
**chocolate** ['tʃɔk(ə)lit]. I. s. (a) Schokolade f; (b) a c., eine Praline. II. adj. Schokoladen-; c. cake, Schokoladenkuchen m.
**choice** [tʃɔis]. I. s. (a) Wahl f; to make a c., eine Wahl treffen; (b) (selection) Auswahl f. II. adj. (of food, fruit etc.) auserlesen.
**choir** ['kwaiər], s. Chor m. ◆**'choirboy**, s. Chorknabe m.
**choke** [tʃəuk]. I. v. 1. v.tr. (strangle) (j-n) erwürgen; (stifle) (j-n) ersticken. 2. v.i. (of pers.) ersticken; to c. on a bone, an einem Knochen würgen. II. s. Aut: Choke m.
**cholesterol** [kə'lestərɔl], s. Cholesterin n.
**choose** [tʃuːz], v.tr.irr. wählen.
◆**'choos(e)y**, adj. F: (of pers.) wählerisch.
**chop** [tʃɔp]. I. s. 1. (a) Schlag m (mit der Axt, mit dem Fleischerbeil); (b) Hieb m (mit der flachen Hand). 2. Cu: Kotelett n. II. v. 1. v.tr. hacken. 2. v.i. to c. and change, (of pers.) es sich dat dauernd anders überlegen. ◆**'chop 'down**, v.tr. (einen Baum) fällen. ◆**'choppy**, adj. (of sea) bewegt. ◆**'chop 'off**, v.tr. abhauen. ◆**'chopstick**, s. Stäbchen n. ◆**'chop 'up**, v.tr. (Holz, Fleisch) in Stücke hacken.
**choral** ['kɔːr(ə)l], adj. Chor-; c. music, Chormusik f; c. society, Gesangverein m.
**chord** [kɔːd], s. Akkord m.
**chore** [tʃɔːr], s. lästige Arbeit f; to do the chores, die Hausarbeit machen.
**choreography** [kɔri'ɔgrəfi], s. Choreographie f.
**chorus** [kɔːrəs], pl. -uses ['kɔːrəs, -əsiz], s. 1. Mus: Th: Chor m. 2. Mus: Refrain m (eines Liedes usw.).
**Christ** [kraist]. Pr.n. Christus m.
**christen** ['krisn], v.tr. (j-n) taufen. ◆**'christening**, s. Taufe f.
**Christian** ['kristiən]. I. s. Christ(in) m(f). II. adj. christlich; C. name, Vorname m. ◆**Christianity** [-'æniti], s. Christentum n.
**Christmas** ['krisməs], s. Weihnachten pl; C. Day, der erste Weihnachtstag; C. Eve, Heiligabend m.
**chromium** ['krəumiəm], s. Chrom n; c. plating, Verchromung f.
**chronic** ['krɔnik], adj. 1. Med: chronisch. 2. F: mies.

**chronicle** ['krɔnikl]. I. s. Chronik f. II. v.tr. to c. events, Ereignisse aufzeichnen.
**chronological** [krɔnə'lɔdʒik(ə)l], adj. chronologisch.
**chrysalis** [kri'sælis], pl. -es ['krisəlis, -iz], s. Puppe f.
**chrysanthemum** [kri'sænθ(ə)məm], s. Chrysantheme f.
**chuck** [tʃʌk], v.tr. F: (a) (etwas) schmeißen; (b) to c. in/up one's job, seinen Job an den Nagel hängen.
**chuckle** ['tʃʌkl]. I. v.i. in sich hineinlachen; F: glucksen. II. s. F: Glukser m.
**chuff** [tʃʌf], v.i. F: to be chuffed, sich sehr freuen.
**chug** [tʃʌg], v.i. (of engine) tuckern.
**chunk** [tʃʌŋk], s. Klumpen m; Klotz m (Holz); großes Stück n (Brot).
**church** [tʃəːtʃ], s. Kirche f; to go to c., in die Kirche gehen. ◆**'churchyard**, s. Kirchhof m.
**churlish** ['tʃəːliʃ], adj. it would be c. to refuse, es wäre unhöflich abzulehnen.
**churn** [tʃəːn]. I. s. Butterfaß n; milk c., Milchkanne f. II. v.tr. to c. out sth., etwas am laufenden Band produzieren.
**chute** [ʃuːt], s. (for coal etc.) Schacht m; (on playground) Rutsche f.
**cider** ['saidər], s. approx. Apfelmost m.
**cigar** [si'gɑːr], s. Zigarre f.
**cigarette** [sigə'ret], s. Zigarette f; c. end, Zigarettenstummel m; c. lighter, Feuerzeug n.
**cinder** ['sindər], s. Asche f.
**cine-camera** ['sinikæm(ə)rə], s. Filmkamera f.
**cinema** ['sinimə], s. 1. (medium) Film m. 2. (building) Kino n.
**cinnamon** ['sinəmən], s. Zimt m.
**cipher** ['saifər], s. (code) Chiffre f; in c., chiffriert.
**circle** ['səːkl]. I. s. 1. Kreis m; N.Am: traffic c., Kreisverkehr m; to come full c., an den Ausgangspunkt zurückkehren; vicious c., Teufelskreis m. 2. Th: Balkon m; dress c., erster Rang; upper c., zweiter Rang. II. v. 1. v.tr. (etwas) umkreisen. 2. v.i. kreisen. ◆**circuit** ['səːkit], s. 1. El: Stromkreis m; c. diagram, Schaltbild n. 2. (race track) Rennstrecke f. ◆**circuitous** [-'kjuːitəs], adj. c. route, Umweg m. ◆**circular** ['səːkjulər], adj. (of arrangement, shape etc.) kreisförmig; c. letter, Rundschreiben n. ◆**circulate** ['səːkjuleit], v. 1. v.tr. (etwas) herumgehen lassen; (ein Gerücht usw.) in Umlauf setzen. 2. v.i. umgehen; (of money, bad news etc.) kursieren; (of blood) kreisen. ◆**circu'lation**, s. (a) Anat: etc: Kreislauf m; (b) Umlauf m (von Zahlungsmitteln); Kursieren n (des Geldes, eines Gerüchts); (c) Auflage f (einer Zeitung).
**circumcise** ['səːkəmsaiz], v.tr. (j-n) beschneiden. ◆**circum'cision**, f Beschneidung f.
**circumference** [sə'kʌmf(ə)rəns], s. Um-

fang *m.*

**circumstances** ['sə:kəmstənsiz, -stænsiz], *s. pl.* Umstände *mpl;* **in the c.,** unter den Umständen; **in/under no c.,** auf keinen Fall. ◆**circum'stantial,** *adj.* **c. evidence,** Indizienbeweis *m.*

**circus,** *pl.* **-uses** ['sə:kəs, -əsiz], *s.* Zirkus *m.*

**cirrhosis** [si'rəusis], *s.* Zirrhose *f.*

**cistern** ['sistən], *s. (of WC)* Wasserkasten *m.*

**citadel** ['sitədel], *s.* Zitadelle *f.*

**cite** [sait], *v.tr.* zitieren.

**citizen** ['sitizən], *s. (a) (in a town)* Bürger(in) *m(f); (b) (of a state)* Staatsbürger(in) *m(f).* ◆**'citizenship,** *s.* Staatsangehörigkeit *f.*

**citric** ['sitrik], *adj.* **c. acid,** Zitronensäure *f.*

**citrus** ['sitrəs], *adj.* **c. fruit,** Zitrusfrucht *f.*

**city** ['siti], *s.* Stadt *f; (large)* Großstadt *f.*

**civic** ['sivik]. **I.** *adj. Adm: (a) (citizen's)* bürgerlich; **c. rights,** Bürgerrechte *npl; (b) (town)* **the c. authorities,** die städtischen Behörden; **c. centre,** Stadthalle *f.* **II.** *s. pl. Sch:* civics, Staatsbürgerkunde *f.*

**civil** ['sivil], *adj.* **1.** *(a)* bürgerlich; **c. rights,** Bürgerrechte *npl;* **c. war,** Bürgerkrieg *m; (b)* **c. engineer,** Tiefbauingenieur *m;* **c. engineering,** Tiefbau *m; (c)* **c. service,** Staatsdienst *m;* **c. servant,** Staatsbeamte(r) *m.* **2.** *(polite)* höflich. ◆**ci'vilian. I.** *adj.* Zivil-; **in c. life,** im Zivilleben. **II.** *s.* Zivilist(in) *m(f).* ◆**'civilize** [-aiz], *v.tr.* zivilisieren. ◆**'civilized,** *adj.* zivilisiert. ◆**civili'zation,** *s.* Zivilisation *f.*

**claim** [kleim]. **I.** *s.* **1.** *(demand)* Forderung *f.* **2.** *(right)* Anspruch *m* **(to sth.,** auf etwas *acc);* **to lay c. to sth.,** etwas (für sich *acc)* beanspruchen; *Fig:* **to stake one's c.,** sein Anrecht geltend machen. **II.** *v.tr. (a)* (ein Recht, eine Pension) beanspruchen; *(demand)* (Schadenersatz) fordern; *(b) (recognize)* **does anyone c. this umbrella?** gehört dieser Schirm jemandem? *(c)* **he claims to represent young people,** er gibt vor, die Jugend zu vertreten; **to c. that ...,** behaupten, daß ...; *(d)* **to c. one's baggage,** sein Gepäck abholen.

**clairvoyant** [klɛə'vɔiənt], *s.* Hellseher(in) *m(f).*

**clam** [klæm], *s.* Venusmuschel *f.*

**clamber** ['klæmbər], *v.i.* klettern.

**clammy** ['klæmi], *adj.* feuchtkalt.

**clamour** ['klæmər]. **I.** *s. (protest)* Aufschrei *m;* **c. for sth.,** Schrei *m* nach etwas *dat.* **II.** *v.i.* **to c. for sth.,** nach etwas *dat* schreien; *Fig:* auf etwas *acc* drängen.

**clamp** [klæmp]. **I.** *s. (with screws)* Schraubzwinge *f; (small)* Klammer *f.* **II.** *v.* **1.** *v.tr.* **to c. sth. to sth.,** etwas an etwas *acc* festklammern. **2.** *v.i. Fig:* **to c. down on s.o., sth.,** gegen j-n, etwas *acc*

scharf vorgehen.

**clan** [klæn], *s.* Sippe *f.*

**clandestine** [klæn'destin, -ain], *adj.* heimlich.

**clang** [klæŋ]. **I.** *s.* metallischer Ton *m; (of bell)* tiefes Tönen *n.* **II.** *v.i.* laut schallen; *(of bell)* tönen. ◆**'clanger,** *s. F:* **to drop a c.,** ins Fettnäpfchen treten.

**clank** [klæŋk]. **I.** *s.* Klirren *n.* **II.** *v.tr. & i.* klirren.

**clap** [klæp]. **I.** *s.* **1.** Klatschen *n;* **to give s.o. a c.,** j-m Beifall spenden. **2.** **c. of thunder,** Donnerschlag *m.* **II.** *v.* **1.** *v.tr. (a)* **to c. one's hands,** klatschen; *(b)* **to c. eyes on s.o.,** j-n zu Gesicht bekommen. **2.** *v.i.* (Beifall) klatschen. ◆**'clapping,** *s.* Klatschen *n.*

**claret** ['klærət], *s.* Bordeaux-Rotwein *m.*

**clarify** ['klærifai], *v.tr.* klären.

**clarinet** [klæri'net], *s.* Klarinette *f.*

**clarity** ['klæriti], *s.* Klarheit *f.*

**clash** [klæʃ]. **I.** *s.* Kollision *f* (von Ansichten, Interessen usw.). **II.** *v.i. (a) (of opinions etc.)* aufeinanderprallen; *(of armies)* zusammenprallen; *(of pers.)* **to c. with s.o.,** mit j-m aneinandergeraten; *(b) (of colours)* sich beißen; *(c) (of events)* zusammenfallen.

**clasp** [klɑːsp]. **I.** *s.* Schließe *f* (eines Mantels, usw.). **II.** *v.tr.* greifen.

**class** [klɑːs], *s.* Klasse *f;* **the middle c.,** der Mittelstand; **first/second c.,** erste/ zweite Klasse; **first c.,** erstklassig. ◆**classifi'cation** [klæ-], *s.* Klassifikation *f.* ◆**'classify** ['klæ-], *v.tr.* klassifizieren; **classified advertisements,** Kleinanzeigen *fpl.* ◆**'classroom,** *s.* Klassenzimmer *n.* ◆**'classy,** *adj. F:* vornehm; *(of clothes etc.)* schick.

**classic** ['klæsik]. **I.** *adj.* klassisch; *(of garment etc.)* zeitlos. **II.** *s. pl.* Classics, Altphilologie *f.* ◆**'classical,** *adj.* klassisch; **c. education,** humanistische Bildung.

**clatter** ['klætər]. **I.** *s.* Geklapper *n.* **II.** *v.i.* klappern.

**clause** [klɔːz], *s.* **1.** *Jur: etc:* Klausel *f.* **2.** *Gram:* Satzteil *n.*

**claustrophobia** [klɔːstrə'fəubiə], *s.* Platzangst *f.*

**claw** [klɔː]. **I.** *s.* Kralle *f.* **II.** *v.tr.* **to c. at sth.,** etwas mit den Krallen bearbeiten.

**clay** [klei], *s. (earth)* Lehm *m; (for pottery)* Ton *m.*

**clean** [kliːn]. **I.** *adj. (a) (free of dirt)* sauber; *(of shirt, linen etc.)* frisch; *(of pers., animal etc.)* reinlich; **c. copy,** Reinschrift *f; (b) (of cut, break)* glatt; *(c) Aut:* **c. licence,** Führerschein *m* ohne Strafeintrag; *(d)* **to come c.,** *F:* *(of pers.)* Farbe bekennen. **II.** *adv.* ganz; völlig; **I had c. forgotten (about) it,** das hatte ich glatt vergessen; **they got c. away,** sie sind spurlos verschwunden. **III.** *v.* **1.** *v.tr.* säubern; **to c. one's teeth,** sich *dat* die Zähne putzen. **2.** *v.i.* saubermachen. ◆**'cleaner,** *s.* **1.** *(pers.)* Raumpfleger(in) *m(f); (char)* Putzfrau *f; (dry)* **cleaner's,**

chemische Reinigung *f*. 2. (*fluid*) Putz-
mittel *n*. ◆'**cleaning**, *s*. dry c., chemische Reinigung *f*. ◆'**clean 'out**, *v.tr*.
(ein Zimmer, einen Schreibtisch usw.)
ausräumen. ◆'**clean-'shaven**, *adj*.
glattrasiert.
**cleanse** [klenz], *v.tr*. reinigen.
◆'**cleansing**, *adj*. c. cream, Reini-
gungscreme *f*.
**clear** [kliər]. I. *adj*. klar; **a c. sky**, ein
heiterer Himmel; **a c. conscience**, ein
reines Gewissen; **c. profit**, reiner Gewinn; **c. majority**, absolute Mehrheit;
**three c. days**, drei volle Tage; **-ly**, *adv*.
(*a*) (*distinctly*) deutlich; (*b*) (*obviously*) offensichtlich. II. *adj. & adv*. **to steer/keep
c. of s.o., sth.**, j-m, etwas *dat* aus dem
Wege gehen; **stand c. of the doors!** Türe
freihalten! III. *v*. 1. *v.tr*. (*a*) **to c. the
air**, (*after row*) die Lage entspannen; (*b*)
(j-n) freisprechen; (*c*) (*empty*) (einen Saal)
räumen; (eine Straße von Schnee usw.)
freimachen; (ein Zimmer, einen Schrank
usw.) ausräumen; (einen Wald) roden; **to
c. the table**, den Tisch (nach dem Essen)
abräumen; **to c. one's throat**, sich räuspern; (*d*) (*remove*) (Teller vom Tisch
usw.) wegräumen; (Unkraut usw.) entfernen; **50 pence to c.**, Restposten für 50
Pence; (*e*) (*extend beyond*) (über etwas
*acc*) hinausragen; (*not hit*) (an einem Vorsprung usw.) gerade noch vorbeikom-
men. 2. *v.i*. (*of weather*) **to c. (up)**, sich
aufheitern; (*of mist*) **to c. (away)**, sich
auflösen. ◆'**clearance**, *s*. 1. (*removal*)
Beseitigung *f*; (*b*) (*customs*) *c*., Zollab-
fertigung *f*; (*b*) Rodung *f* (von Land,
Wald); (*c*) **c. sale**, Räumungsverkauf *m*.
2. (*space*) Zwischenraum *m*. ◆'**clear
a'way**, *v*. 1. *v.tr*. (etwas) wegräumen;
(Teller usw.) abräumen. 2. *v.i*. den Tisch
abräumen. ◆'**clear-'cut**, *adj*. scharf umrissen; **-c. distinction**, deutlicher
Unterschied. ◆'**clearing**, *s*. Lichtung *f*.
◆'**clear 'off**, *v.i*. *F*: (*of pers.*) abhauen.
◆'**clear 'up**, *v*. 1. *v.tr*. (ein Problem
usw.) klarstellen. 2. *v.i*. (*a*) (*of weather*)
sich aufklären; (*b*) (*tidy up*) aufräumen.
**cleavage** ['kli:vidʒ], *s*. Brustansatz *m*.
**clench** [klen(t)ʃ], *v.tr*. (die Zähne) zusammenbeißen; (die Faust) ballen.
**clergy** ['klɔ:dʒi], *s. coll*. Geistliche *mpl*;
**the c.**, die Geistlichkeit. ◆'**clergyman**,
*pl*. -**men**, *s*. Geistlicher *m*.
**clerical** ['klerik(ə)l], *adj*. 1. *Ecc*: geistlich.
2. **c. work**, Schreibarbeit *f*; **c. staff**,
Schreibkräfte *fpl*.
**clerk** [klɑ:k, *N.Am*: klə:k], *s*. 1. (*in office*)
Büroangestellte(r) *f(m)*; **bank c.**, Bankan-
gestellte(r) *f(m)*. 2. *N.Am*: (*sales person*)
Verkäufer(in) *m(f)*.
**clever** ['klevər], *adj*. 1. (*skilful*) geschickt.
2. (*intelligent*) klug.
**cliché** ['kli:ʃei], *s*. Klischee *n*.
**click** [klik]. I. *s*. (*sound*) Klicken *n*. II.
*v.i*. (*a*) **the door swung shut**, die Tür
fiel ins Schloß; (*b*) *F*: **it suddenly**

**clicked**, auf einmal fiel der Groschen.
**client** ['klaiənt], *s*. Kunde *m*, Kundin *f*.
◆'**clientele** [klaiən'tel, kli:ɑ̃:'tel], *s*.
Kundschaft *f*.
**cliff** [klif], *s*. Klippe *f*.
**climate** ['klaimət], *s*. Klima *n*.
**climax** ['klaimæks], *s*. Höhepunkt *m*.
**climb** [klaim]. I. *s*. Aufstieg *m*. II. *v*. 1.
*v.tr*. (einen Berg usw.) besteigen; (einen
Berg, eine Leiter, Mauer usw.) erklimmen. 2. *v.i*. steigen; (*clamber*) klettern.
◆'**climb 'down**, *v*. 1. *v.tr. & i*. (einen
Berg usw.) herabsteigen. 2. *v.i*. *F*: klein
beigeben. ◆'**climber**, *s*. 1. Bergstei-
ger(in) *m(f)*. 2. *Pej*: **social c.**, Karriere-
macher *m*. ◆'**climbing**. I. *adj*. **c. plant**,
Kletterpflanze *f*. II. *s*. Klettern *n*;
(*mountain*) *s*., Bergsteigen *n*.
**clinch** [klin(t)ʃ], *v.tr*. *F*: **to c. a deal**, ein
Geschäft festmachen.
**cling** [kliŋ], *v.i.irr*. (*of dirt etc.*) anhaften
(**to**, *dat*); (*of pers.*) **to c. to s.o./Fig: to a
hope**, sich an j-n/*Fig*: eine Hoffnung
klammern.
**clinic** ['klinik], *s*. Klinik *f*. ◆'**clinical**,
*adj*. klinisch.
**clink**[1] [kliŋk]. I. *s*. Geklirr *n*. II. *v.i*. klirren.
**clink**[2], *s*. *P*: (*prison*) Kittchen *n*.
**clip**[1] [klip]. I. *s*. Klammer *f*; **paper c.**,
Büroklammer *f*. II. *v.tr*. (etwas) an-
klammern (**to sth.**, an etwas *acc*).
**clip**[2]. I. *s* Ausschnitt *m* (aus einem Film).
II *v.tr*. (*a*) (ein Schaf) scheren; (eine
Hecke usw.) schneiden; (*b*) (*punch*) (eine
Fahrkarte usw.) knipsen.
**clique** [kli:k], *s*. Clique *f*.
**cloak** [kləuk], *s*. Umhang *m*.
◆'**cloakroom**, *s*. 1. *Th: etc*: Garderobe
*f*. 2. (*toilet*) Toilette *f*; (*washroom*) Waschraum *m*.
**clobber** ['klɔbər]. I. *v.tr*. *F*: (j-n) hauen.
II. *s*. *F*: Kram *m*.
**clock** [klɔk]. I. *s*. Uhr *f*; **it's two o'c.**, es
ist zwei Uhr; **to work round the c.**, rund
um die Uhr arbeiten. II. *v.i*. **to c. in/out**,
stempeln. ◆'**clockface**, *s*. Zifferblatt *n*.
◆'**clockwise**, *adj. & adv*. im Uhrzeigersinn *m*. ◆'**clockwork**, *s*. Uhrwerk *n*.
**clog** [klɔg]. I. *v.tr*. (ein Rohr usw.) verstopfen. II. *s*. Holzschuh *m*; (*modern*)
Clog *m*.
**cloister** ['klɔistər], *s*. Kreuzgang *m*.
**close**[1] [kləus]. I. *adj*. 1. nahe (**to**, + *dat*);
**c. together**, nahe/dicht beieinander. 2.
(*of atmosphere*) stickig; (*of weather*)
schwül. 3. (*a*) (*of connection etc.*) eng; **a
c. friend** ein enger Freund; (*b*) **on closer
examination**, bei näherer Betrachtung.
II. *adv*. **c.** (**by/at hand**), nahe, nahe dabei; **he lives c. to the station**, er wohnt
nahe beim Bahnhof; **-ly**, *adv*. eng; genau;
**to check sth. c.**, etwas genau nachprüfen; **c. related**, eng verwandt.
◆'**close-up**, *s*. Nahaufnahme *f*.
**close**[2] [kləuz]. I. *v*. 1. *v.tr*. (*a*) (*shut*)
(eine Tür, ein Geschäft, die Augen usw.)

schließen; (eine Straße usw.) sperren; (eine Fabrik, eine Eisenbahnlinie) stillegen; (b) (bring to an end) (eine Rede, eine Debatte usw.) beenden. 2. v.i. (of door, shop etc.) schließen. II. s. to draw to a c., sich dem Ende nähern; to bring sth. to a c., etwas beenden. ◆'close 'down, v. 1. v.tr. (einen Betrieb, Rail: eine Strecke) stillegen. 2. v.i. stillgelegt werden; Rad: TV: we c.d. at 11.30 p.m., wir haben um 23.30 Uhr Sendeschluß. ◆'closed, adj. 1. geschlossen; road c., Straße gesperrt. 2. c. circuit television, (for security) Fernseh-Überwachungssystem n. 3. c. shop, Gewerkschaftszwang m. ◆'closing, adj. schließend; Schluß-; c. remark, Schlußbemerkung f; c. date, Schlußtermin m; (for competition) Einsendeschluß m; c. time, (of shop) Ladenschluß m; (of pub) Polizeistunde f; Fin: c. price, Schlußkurs m. ◆'closure [-ʒər], s. Stillegung f (einer Fabrik usw.).

clot [klɔt]. I. s. 1. Med: blood c., Blutgerinnsel n. 2. P: (pers.) Hornochse m. II. v.i. gerinnen.

cloth [klɔθ], pl. cloths [klɔθs], s. 1. Tuch n. 2. (a) (rag) Lappen m; (b) (table) c., Tischtuch n.

clothe [kləuð], v.tr. (j-n) kleiden. ◆clothes [kləuðz], s.pl. Kleider npl; to put on/take off one's c., sich anziehen/ ausziehen; c. brush, Kleiderbürste f; c. line, Wäscheleine f; c. peg, Wäscheklammer f. ◆'clothing, s. (articles of) c., Kleidungsstücke npl; the c. industry/ trade, die Bekleidungsindustrie f.

cloud [klaud]. I. s. Wolke f. II. v.i. (of sky) to c. over, sich bewölken. ◆'cloudburst, s. Wolkenbruch m. ◆'cloudless, adj. wolkenlos. ◆'cloudy, adj. (of sky) bewölkt; (of liquid) trübe.

clove¹ [kləuv], s. Gewürznelke f.

clove², s. c. of garlic, Knoblauchzehe f.

clover ['kləuvər], s. Klee m.

clown [klaun], s. Clown m.

club [klʌb]. I. s. 1. (a) (heavy stick) Keule f; (b) (golfc.) Schläger m. 2. pl. (in cards) Kreuz n. 3. Verein m; esp. Sp: Klub m. II. v. 1. v.tr. (j-n) mit einer Keule schlagen. 2. v.i. to c. together, sich zusammentun. ◆'clubhouse, s. Klubhaus n.

cluck [klʌk], v.i. glucken.

clue [klu:], s. Anhaltspunkt m; (in crossword) Stichwort n; F: I haven't a c., ich habe keinen Schimmer. ◆'clueless, adj. F: doof.

clump [klʌmp], s. c. of trees, Baumgruppe f; c. of bushes, Gebüsch n.

clumsy ['klʌmzi], adj. (of pers., manner etc.) ungeschickt; (awkward) linkisch.

clutch [klʌtʃ]. I. s. 1. to be in s.o.'s clutches, in j-s Gewalt sein. 2. Aut: Kupplung f. II. v. 1. v.tr. festhalten. 2. v.i. to c. at sth., nach etwas dat greifen.

clutter ['klʌtər]. I. s. Kram m. II. v.tr. to

c. (up) a room with sth., ein Zimmer mit etwas dat vollstopfen.

co- [kəu-], prefix Mit-; co-author, Mitverfasser m; Av: co-pilot, Kopilot m.

coach [kəutʃ]. I. s. 1. (a) (motor) Omnibus m; (b) Rail: Wagen m; (c) (horsedrawn) Kutsche f. 2. Sp: Trainer m. II. v.tr. (a) (j-m) Nachhilfestunden geben; (b) Sp: (j-n) trainieren.

coagulate [kəu'ægjuleit], v.tr. & i. gerinnen.

coal [kəul], s. Kohle f. ◆'coalfield, s. Kohlenrevier n. ◆'coalmine, s. Kohlenbergwerk n.

coalesce [kəuə'les], v.i. (grow together) aneinanderwachsen; (fuse) verschmelzen.

coalition [kəuə'liʃ(ə)n], s. Koalition f.

coarse [kɔːs], adj. grob; (of joke) derb. ◆'coarseness, s. Grobheit f.

coast [kəust], s. Küste f; F: the c. is clear, die Luft ist rein. ◆'coastal, adj. Küsten-; c. waters, Küstengewässer npl. ◆'coaster, s. 1. Nau: Küstenfahrzeug n. 2. (small mat) Untersetzer m. ◆'coastguard, s. Küstenwacht f. ◆'coastline, s. Küstenlinie f.

coat [kəut]. I. s. 1. Mantel m. 2. c. of arms, Wappen n. 3. Fell n (einer Katze usw.). 4. (layer) Schicht f; (of paint) Anstrich m. II. v.tr. (einen Keks, eine Pille mit Schokolade, Zucker usw.) überziehen. ◆'coat(-)hanger, s. Kleiderbügel m. ◆'coating, s. (of sugar, chocolate) Überzug m.

coax [kəuks], v.tr. (j-m) gut zureden; (persuade) (j-n) überreden.

cob [kɔb], s. corn on the c., Maiskolben m.

cobble [kɔbl], s. c. (stone), Kopfstein m; cobbles, Kopfsteinpflaster n. ◆'cobbled, adj. c. street, Straße f mit Kopfsteinpflaster. ◆'cobbler, s. A: Flickschuster m.

cobra ['kəubrə], s. Kobra f.

cobweb ['kɔbweb], s. Spinngewebe n.

cocaine [kəu'kein], s. Kokain n.

cock [kɔk], s. (fowl) Hahn m. ◆'cocky, adj. großspurig.

cockerel ['kɔk(ə)rəl], s. Hähnchen n.

cock-eyed ['kɔkaid], adj. F: schief.

cockle ['kɔkl], s. Herzmuschel f.

cockney ['kɔkni], s. Cockney m.

cockpit ['kɔkpit], s. Cockpit n.

cockroach ['kɔkrəutʃ], s. Küchenschabe f.

cocktail ['kɔkteil], s. Cocktail m.

cocoa ['kəukəu], s. Kakao m.

coconut ['kəukənʌt], s. Kokosnuß f.

cocoon [kə'ku:n], s. Kokon m.

cod [kɔd], s. c.(-fish), Kabeljau m; c.-liver oil, Lebertran m.

code [kəud], s. 1. (system of rules) Code m; highway c., Straßenverkehrsordnung f. 2. c. word, Codewort n; a message written in c., eine chiffrierte Mitteilung.

co-education ['kəuedju'keiʃ(ə)n], s. Koedukation f.

**coerce** [kəu'əːs], *v.tr.* (j-n) zwingen (**into doing sth.**, etwas zu tun). ◆**coercion** [-'əːʃən], *s.* Zwang *m.*

**co-existence** ['kəuig'zistəns], *s.* **peaceful c.**, friedliche Koexistenz.

**coffee** ['kɔfi], *s.* Kaffee *m;* **white c.**, Kaffee mit Milch; **instant c.**, löslicher Kaffee *m;* **c. pot**, Kaffeekanne *f;* **c. break**, Kaffeepause *f;* **c. table**, Couchtisch *m.*

**coffin** ['kɔfin], *s.* Sarg *m.*

**cog** [kɔg], *s.* Zahn *m.* ◆**'cogwheel**, *s.* Zahnrad *n.*

**cognac** ['kɔnjæk], *s.* Kognak *m.*

**coherent** [kəu'hiərənt], *adj.* (*a*) zusammenhängend; (*of argument*) konsequent; (*b*) (*comprehensible*) verständlich.

**coil** [kɔil], **I.** 1. (*of rope etc.*) Rolle *f.* 2. *El:* Spule *f; Aut:* (**ignition**) **c.**, Zündspule *f.* 3. *Med:* Spirale *f.*

**coin** [kɔin]. **I.** *s.* Münze *f.* **II.** *v.tr.* (Geld, *Fig:* einen Ausdruck) prägen. ◆**'coinbox**, *s.* **c. telephone**, Münzfernsprecher *m.*

**coincide** [kəuin'said], *v.i.* (*a*) (*of events etc.*) zusammenfallen; (*b*) (*of ideas etc.*) übereinstimmen. ◆**coincidence** [kəu'insidəns], *s.* Zufall *m.*

**coke¹** [kəuk], *s.* Koks *m.*

**coke²**, *s. F:* (*abbr. for R.t.m* **coca-cola**) Cola *f.*

**colander** ['kʌləndər], *s.* Durchschlag *m* (für Gemüse).

**cold** [kəuld]. **I.** *adj.* 1. kalt; **I feel/I am c.**, mir ist (es) kalt; *F:* **he got c. feet**, er hat kalte Füße gekriegt. 2. (*a*) (*unfriendly*) kühl; *F:* **to give s.o. the c. shoulder**, j-m die kalte Schulter zeigen; (*b*) (*unfeeling*) kalt; **that leaves me c.**, das läßt mich kalt; **in c. blood**, kaltblütig. **II.** *s.* 1. Kälte *f.* 2. *Med:* Erkältung *f;* **c. in the head**, Schnupfen *m;* **to catch (a) cold**, sich erkälten. ◆**'cold-'blooded**, *adj.* kaltblütig.

**collaborate** [kə'læbəreit], *v.i.* zusammenarbeiten. ◆**collabo'ration**, *s.* Mitarbeit *f.* ◆**co'llaborator**, *s.* Mitarbeiter(in) *m(f)* (an einem Projekt).

**collapse** [kə'læps]. **I.** *s.* (*a*) Einsturz *m* (eines Gebäudes usw.); (*b*) Zusammenbruch *m* (eines Reiches usw.). **II.** *v.i.* (*of building, wall*) einstürzen; (*of plans etc.*) auffliegen; (*of pers.*) zusammenbrechen. ◆**co'llapsible**, *adj.* zusammenklappbar.

**collar** ['kɔlər]. **I.** *s.* 1. Kragen *m.* 2. (*for dog etc.*) Halsband *n.* **II.** *v.tr.* **to c. s.o.**, j-n anhalten; (*of police*) j-n erwischen. ◆**'collar-bone**, *s.* Schlüsselbein *n.*

**collate** [kɔ'leit], *v.tr.* zusammentragen.

**colleague** ['kɔliːg], *s.* Kollege *m;* Kollegin *f.*

**collect** [kə'lekt]. *v.* 1. *v.tr.* (*a*) sammeln; (*take in*) (Schulhefte usw.) einsammeln; (*pick up*) (Papierabfälle usw.) auflesen; (*b*) (Beiträge, Schulden usw.) einkassieren; **to c. taxes**, Steuern einziehen; (*c*) (*of pers.*) (seine Gedanken) sammeln; **to c. oneself**, sich aufraffen; (*d*) (*fetch*) abholen. 2. *v.i.* (*of crowd, dust, water etc.*) sich ansammeln. 3. *attrib. N.Am:* **c. call**, R-Gespräch *n.* ◆**co'llected**, *adj.* (*a*) **c. works**, gesammelte Werke; (*b*) (*of pers.*) **calm and c.**, ruhig und gefaßt. ◆**co'llection**, *s.* 1. Sammlung *f.* 2. Leerung *f* (eines Briefkastens). 3. (*a*) *Ecc:* Kollekte *f;* (*b*) (*for charity*) Sammlung *f.* ◆**co'llective**, *adj.* (*of property, efforts etc.*) gemeinsam. ◆**co'llector**, *s.* Sammler(in) *m(f).*

**college** ['kɔlidʒ], *s.* 1. *Brit:* Hochschule *f;* **c. of technology**, *approx.* technische Hochschule *f;* **c. of further education**, *approx.* Volkshochschule *f.* 2. *N.Am:* (kleiner) Universität *f.*

**collide** [kə'laid], *v.i.* zusammenstoßen. ◆**collision** [kə'liʒ(ə)n], *s.* Zusammenstoß *m.*

**colliery** ['kɔljəri], *s.* Kohlengrube *f.*

**colloquial** [kə'ləukwiəl], *adj.* umgangssprachlich.

**collusion** [kə'ljuːʒ(ə)n], *s.* Kollusion *f;* **to act in c. with s.o.**, in geheimer Absprache mit j-m handeln.

**Cologne** [kə'ləun], *Pr.n.* Köln *n.*

**Colombia** [kə'lɔmbiə], *Pr.n.* Kolumbien *n.*

**colon** [kəulən], *s.* 1. Doppelpunkt *m.* 2. *Anat:* Dickdarm *m.*

**colonel** ['kəːnl], *s.* Oberst *m.*

**colony** ['kɔləni], *s.* Kolonie *f.* ◆**colonial** [kə'ləunjəl], *adj.* kolonial. ◆**'colonist**, *s.* Kolonist *m.* ◆**coloni'zation**, *s.* Kolonisation *f.* ◆**'colonize**, *v.tr.* (ein Land usw.) kolonisieren; (ein Gebiet) besiedeln.

**color**, *s. N.Am:* = **colour**.

**colossal** [kə'lɔs(ə)l], *adj.* riesig.

**colour** ['kʌlər]. **I.** *s.* (*a*) Farbe *f;* **c. scheme**, Farbkombination *f;* **c. film**, Farbfilm *m;* **c. television**, Farbfernsehen *n;* (*b*) *F:* **off c.**, nicht ganz auf der Höhe. **II.** *v.tr.* färben. ◆**'colourblind**, *adj.* farbenblind. ◆**'coloured**. **I.** *adj.* (*a*) farbig; (**brightly**) **c.**, bunt; (*b*) *Fig:* (*biased*) gefärbt. **II.** *s. pl.* **coloureds**, Buntwäsche *f.* ◆**'colourful**, *adj.* farbenfroh. ◆**'colouring**, *s.* (*dye*) Farbstoff *m.* ◆**'colourless**, *adj.* farblos.

**colt** [kəult], *s.* Hengstfohlen *n.*

**column** ['kɔləm], *s.* 1. *Arch:* Säule *f; Anat:* **spinal c.**, Wirbelsäule *f.* 2. *Mil:* Kolonne *f.* 3. (*a*) (*in newspaper*) Spalte *f;* (*b*) **c. of figures**, Kolonne *f* von Zahlen. ◆**'columnist**, *s.* Kolumnist(in) *m(f).*

**coma** ['kəumə], *s.* Koma *n.*

**comb** [kəum]. **I.** *s.* Kamm *m.* **II.** *v.tr.* kämmen; **to c. one's hair**, sich *dat* die Haare kämmen; *Fig:* **to c. the district**, die Gegend absuchen.

**combat** ['kɔmbæt]. **I.** *s.* Kampf *m.* **II.** *v.tr.* bekämpfen.

**combine.** **I.** [kəm'bain], *v.* 1. *v.tr.* (Eigenschaften usw.) kombinieren; **to c. forces**, die Kräfte vereinigen; **to c. business with pleasure**, das Angenehme mit dem Nützlichen verbinden. 2. *v.i.* sich zusammenschließen. II. ['kɔmbain] *s.* **c. harvester,** Mähdrescher *m.* ◆**combination** [kɔmbi'neiʃ(ə)n], *s.* Kombination *f.* ◆**com'bined,** *adj.* **c. efforts,** gemeinsame Anstrengungen *fpl.*

**combustion** [kəm'bʌstʃ(ə)n], *s.* Verbrennung *f;* **c. engine,** Verbrennungsmotor *m.*

**come** [kʌm], *v.i.irr.* kommen; *F:* he had it coming to him, er hat es durchaus verdient; **c. to that,** in dem Fall; **that's what comes of doing nothing,** das kommt davon, wenn man nichts tut; **to c. to nothing,** zu nichts führen; **nothing will c. of this,** da wird nichts draus; **it comes to £5,** das macht £5; **c. to think of it,** wenn ich's mir überlege; **that comes easily to him,** das fällt ihm leicht; **in years to c.,** in späteren Jahren. '◆**come a'bout,** *v.i.* geschehen. ◆'**come a'cross,** *v.tr.* auf (j-n, etwas *acc*) stoßen. ◆'**come-back,** *s.* Comeback *n.* ◆'**come 'back,** *v.i.* zurückkommen (**to sth.,** auf etwas *acc*). ◆'**come 'by,** *v.* 1. *v.tr.* (etwas) auftreiben; (*by accident*) zu (etwas *dat*) kommen. 2. *v.i.* vorbeikommen. ◆'**come 'down,** *v.i.* (*of ceiling etc.*) herunterfallen; (*of rain, prices etc.*) fallen; **it all comes d. to his pride,** es ist alles auf seinen Stolz zurückzuführen. ◆'**come 'forward,** *v.i.* (*report*) sich melden. ◆'**come 'in,** *v.i.* (*a*) hereinkommen; (*of train etc.*) einfahren; *Com:* (*of mail, order etc.*) eingehen; (*answer to knock*) **c. in!** herein! (*b*) **that will c. in handy,** das wird mir zugute kommen; (*c*) **to c. in for criticism,** Kritik einstecken müssen. ◆'**come 'off,** *v.* 1. *v.tr. F:* **c. off it!** das glaubst du doch nicht im Ernst! 2. *v.i.* (*a*) (*of thing*) loskommen; (*of button etc.*) abgehen; (*b*) (*of attempt*) **it came off,** es hat geklappt; (*c*) (*of pers.*) **to c. off badly,** schlecht abschneiden. ◆'**come 'on,** *v.i.* (*a*) (*make progress*) Fortschritte machen; (*b*) *int.* **c. on!** (i) komm schon! (ii) (*in disbelief*) na hör mal! ◆'**come 'out,** *v.i.* (*a*) herauskommen; (*of stars, book*) erscheinen; **to c. out with the truth,** mit der Wahrheit herausrücken; (*b*) *Ind:* (*of workers*) **to c. out (on strike),** streiken; (*c*) (*of stain*) herausgehen; **how did the pictures c. out?** wie sind die Bilder geworden? ◆'**come 'over,** *v.i.* **what has c. o. you?** was ist in dich gefahren? ◆'**come 'round,** *v.i.* (*a*) **you must c. r. and see us,** Sie müssen uns besuchen kommen; (*b*) (*regain consciousness*) (wieder) zu sich *dat* kommen. ◆'**come 'to,** *v.i.* zu sich *dat* kommen. ◆'**come 'up,** *v.i.* (*a*) heraufkommen; (*b*) **to c. up to s.o.,** an j-n herantreten; (*c*) (*of seeds*) sprießen; (*d*) **to c. up (for discussion),** zur Diskussion kommen; (*e*) **to c. up to s.o.'s expectations,** j-s Erwartungen erfüllen; (*f*) **to c. up against difficulties,**

auf Schwierigkeiten stoßen; (*g*) (*reach*) **the water comes up to my waist,** das Wasser reicht mir bis zur Taille. ◆'**coming. I.** *adj.* kommend; **the c. year,** das kommende Jahr. II. *s.* **a lot of c. and going,** viel Hin und Her.

**comedy** ['kɔmədi], *s.* Komödie *f.* ◆**comedian** [kə'mi:diən], *s.* Komiker *m.*

**comet** ['kɔmit], *s.* Komet *m.*

**comfort** ['kʌmfət]. I. *s.* 1. Trost *m;* **to take c.,** Trost finden. 2. (*a*) **the comforts of life,** die Annehmlichkeiten des Lebens; (*b*) (*luxury*) Komfort *m.* II. *v.tr.* (j-n) trösten. ◆**comfortable** ['kʌmftəbl], *adj.* bequem; **-ably,** *adv.* bequem; **c. off,** wohlhabend. ◆'**comforting,** *adj.* tröstlich. ◆'**comfy,** *adj. F:* bequem.

**comic** ['kɔmik]. I. *adj.* komisch; **c. strip,** Comic Strip *m.* II. *s.* (*a*) (*pers.*) Komiker *m;* (*b*) Comic-Heft *n.*

**comma** ['kɔmə], *s.* Komma *n.*

**command** [kə'mɑ:nd]. I. *s.* 1. (*order*) Befehl *m.* 2. *Mil: etc:* Kommando *n;* **to be in c.,** das Kommando haben. 3. **c.** Beherrschung *f* (einer Sprache, einer Situation usw.). II. *v.tr.* (*a*) (j-m) befehlen(, etwas zu tun); (*b*) (ein Regiment usw.) führen; (*c*) (über ein großes Wissen, große Geldsummen usw.) verfügen; **to c. respect,** Achtung gebieten. ◆**comman'deer,** *v.tr.* beschlagnahmen. ◆**co'mmander,** *s.* Befehlshaber *m.* ◆**co'mmanding,** *adj.* **c. officer,** befehlshabender Offizier; (*of battalion*) Kommandeur *m.* ◆**co'mmandment,** *s.* Gebot *n.* ◆**co'mmando,** *s.* Mitglied *n* einer Kommandotruppe.

**commemorate** [kə'meməreit], *v.tr.* das Andenken (von j-m, etwas *dat*) feiern.

**commence** [kə'mens], *v.tr. & i.* anfangen. ◆**co'mmencement,** *s.* Anfang *m.*

**commend** [kə'mend], *v.tr.* (*a*) (*praise*) (j-n) loben; (*b*) (*recommend*) (j-m etwas) empfehlen; ◆**co'mmendable,** *adj.* lobenswert. ◆**commen'dation,** *s.* 1. Lob *n.* 2. Empfehlung *f.*

**commensurate** [kə'menʃərət], *adj.* angemessen (**to/with sth.,** etwas *dat*).

**comment** ['kɔment]. I. *s.* Bemerkung *f;* **no c.!** Kommentar überflüssig! II. *v.i.* (*casually*) Bemerkungen machen (**on sth.,** über etwas *acc*); **to c. on a text,** einen Text kommentieren. ◆'**commentary,** *s.* Kommentar *m.* ◆'**commentator,** *s.* Kommentator *m.*

**commerce** ['kɔmə:s], *s.* Handel *m.* ◆**co'mmercial. I.** *adj.* Handels-; **c. traveller,** Handelsreisende(r) *m;* **c. vehicle,** Nutzfahrzeug *n.* II. *s. TV:* Werbespot *m;* (*script*) Werbetext *m.* ◆**co'mmercialize,** *v.tr.* kommerzialisieren.

**commiserate** [kə'mizəreit], *v.i.* **to c. with s.o.,** j-m sein Mitgefühl aussprechen.

**commission** [kə'miʃ(ə)n. **I.** s. **1.** (*board of enquiry*) Kommission f. **2.** Mil: Offizierspatent n. **3.** (*order etc.*) Auftrag m. **4.** **my car is out of c.**, mein Auto ist außer Betrieb. **5.** Com: Provision f; **to work on c.**, auf Provision arbeiten. **II.** v.tr. (einen Künstler usw.) beauftragen; (ein Porträt usw.) in Auftrag geben. ◆**commis'sionaire**, s. Portier m. ◆**co'mmissioner**, s. **c. of police**, approx. Polizeikommissar m.

**commit** [kə'mit], v.tr. (a) (ein Verbrechen, Selbstmord usw.) begehen; (b) **to c. oneself**, sich festlegen; **a committed person**, ein engagierter Mensch; (c) **to c. sth. to memory**, sich dat etwas einprägen; **to c. s.o. for trial**, j-n dem Gericht überweisen. ◆**co'mmitment**, s. (*to cause, career etc.*) Engagement n; (*obligation*) Verpflichtung f.

**committee** [kə'miti], s. Ausschuß m.

**commodity** [kə'mɔditi], s. Gebrauchsartikel m; pl. Gebrauchsgüter npl.

**common** ['kɔmən]. **I.** adj. **1.** (*of property, interests etc.*) gemeinsam; **c. ground**, Diskussionsgrundlage f; **fur: c. law**, Gewohnheitsrecht n; **C. Market**, Gemeinsamer Markt; **c. room**, Lehrerzimmer n. **2.** (a) (*ordinary*) gewöhnlich; **the c. man**, der einfache Mann; F: **c. or garden**, ganz gewöhnlich; (b) (*frequent*) häufig; (*of views, practice etc.*) verbreitet; (*of expression, word*) geläufig; (c) **c. sense**, gesunder Menschenverstand. **3.** Pej: (*of pers., manners etc.*) ordinär. **II.** s. **1. to have sth. in c. with s.o.**, etwas mit j-m gemeinsam haben. **2. c. (land)**, Gemeindeland n. ◆**commoner**, s. Bürgerliche(r) f(m). ◆**commonplace**, adj. banal; (*frequent*) häufig. ◆**commons**, s. pl. **the (House of) C.**, das (britische) Unterhaus n. ◆**commonwealth**, s. **the C.**, das (britische) Commonwealth n.

**commotion** [kə'məuʃ(ə)n], s. Aufruhr f.

**communal** ['kɔmjun(ə)l], adj. **1.** (*shared*) gemeinschaftlich. **2.** (*community*) Gemeinde-.

**communicate** [kə'mju:nikeit], v. **1.** v.tr. (eine Nachricht, seine Gefühle usw.) mitteilen (**to s.o.**, j-m). **2.** v.i. (a) (*contact*) sich in Verbindung setzen; (b) (*make oneself understood*) sich verständigen. ◆**communication** [-i'keiʃ(ə)n], s. **1.** Verständigung f; **c. cord**, Notbremse f. **2.** (*message*) Mitteilung f. **3.** pl. communications, (a) (*transport*) Verkehrsverbindungen fpl; Mil: **lines of c.**, Nachschublinien fpl; (b) (*telephone etc.*) Nachrichtenwesen n. ◆**co'mmunicative** [-ikətiv], adj. mitteilsam. ◆**co'mmunion** [-jən], s. (**Holy**) **C.**, das (heilige) Abendmahl; (*Catholic*) Kommunion f.

**communism** ['kɔmjunizm], s. Kommunismus m. ◆**communist. I.** s. Kommunist m. **II.** adj. kommunistisch.

**community** [kə'mju:niti], s. Gemein-

schaft f; **c. centre**, Freizeitzentrum n.

**commute** [kə'mju:t], v.i. pendeln. ◆**co'mmuter**, s. Pendler m.

**compact**[1] [kəm'pækt], adj. kompakt.

**compact**[2] ['kɔmpækt], s. (**powder**) **c.**, Puderdose f.

**companion** [kəm'pænjən], s. Gefährte m; Gefährtin f. ◆**com'panionship**, s. Kameradschaft f; Gesellschaft f.

**company** ['kʌmpəni], s. **1.** (a) Gesellschaft f; **to keep s.o. c.**, j-m Gesellschaft leisten; **to part c. (with s.o.)**, sich (von j-m) trennen; (b) **we are expecting c.**, wir erwarten Besuch. **2.** Com: Gesellschaft f; (*firm*) Firma f; (*large company*) Konzern n. **3.** (a) Th: Schauspielertruppe f; (b) **ship's c.**, Besatzung f. **4.** Mil: Kompanie f.

**compare** [kəm'pɛər], v. **1.** v.tr. (j-n, etwas) vergleichen (**to/with**, mit + dat). **2.** v.i. **to c. badly with s.o., sth.**, gegen j-n, etwas acc schlecht abschneiden. ◆**comparable** ['kɔmp(ə)rəbl], adj. vergleichbar (**to/with**, mit + dat). ◆**com'parative**, adj. **1.** (*linguistics etc.*) vergleichend. **2.** (*of wealth etc.*) relativ; **-ly**, adv. verhältnismäßig. ◆**com'parison**, s. Vergleich m; **in c. to**, im Vergleich zu + dat.

**compartment** [kəm'pɑ:tmənt], s. **1.** Rail: Abteil n. **2.** (*of cupboard etc.*) Fach n; (*larger*) Abteilung f.

**compass** ['kʌmpəs], s. **1.** Kompaß m. **2.** (**pair of**) **compasses**, Zirkel m.

**compassion** [kəm'pæʃ(ə)n], s. Mitleid n. ◆**com'passionate**, adj. mitleidig; (*of pers., deed etc.*) erbarmungsvoll.

**compatible** [kəm'pætibl], adj. (a) (*of things*) vereinbar; (b) (*of pers.*) **they are very c.**, sie passen gut zusammen; (c) (*computers*) kompatibel. ◆**compati'bility**, s. (a) (*of things*) Vereinbarkeit f; (b) Verträglichkeit f; (c) Kompatibilität f.

**compatriot** [kəm'pætriət], s. Landsmann m; Landsmännin f.

**compel** [kəm'pel], v.tr. (j-n) zwingen (etwas zu tun). ◆**com'pelling**, adj. (*of story, film etc.*) fesselnd.

**compensate** ['kɔmpənseit], v. **1.** v.tr. (j-n) entschädigen. **2.** v.i. **to c. for a disadvantage**, einen Nachteil ausgleichen. ◆**compen'sation**, s. Entschädigung f.

**compère** ['kɔmpɛər], s. Conférencier m.

**compete** [kəm'pi:t], v.i. (a) konkurrieren; (b) **to c. for a prize**, sich um einen Preis bewerben.

**competent** ['kɔmpitənt], adj. **1.** (*of worker etc.*) tüchtig. **2.** fur: Adm: etc: kompetent. ◆**competence**, s. **1.** Tüchtigkeit f. **2.** fur: Adm: Kompetenz f.

**competition** [kɔmpə'tiʃ(ə)n], s. **1.** Com: etc: Konkurrenz f. **2.** Wettbewerb m; (*in magazine etc.*) Preisausschreiben n. ◆**com'petitive**, adj. (a) Wettbewerbs-; (b) (*of prices, products etc.*) konkurrenzfähig. ◆**com'petitor**, s. Konkurrent m; Sp: Teilnehmer m.

**compile** [kəm'pail], *v.tr.* zusammenstellen. ◆**compi'lation,** *s.* Zusammenstellung *f.*

**complacent** [kəm'pleis(ə)nt], *adj.* selbstzufrieden. ◆**com'placency,** *s.* Selbstzufriedenheit *f.*

**complain** [kəm'plein], *v.i.* (*a*) klagen; (*b*) (*formally*) sich beschweren. ◆**com'plaint,** *s.* 1. Klage *f.* 2. Beschwerde *f;* to lodge a c. against s.o., sth., gegen j-n, über etwas *acc* Beschwerde führen. 3. (*illness*) Leiden *n.*

**complement** ['kɔmplimənt]. I. *s.* 1. full c., volle Anzahl/Menge. 2. Ergänzung *f.* II. *v.tr.* ergänzen. ◆**comple'mentary,** *adj.* ergänzend.

**complete** [kəm'pli:t]. I. *adj.* 1. (*a*) vollständig; (*b*) (*concluded*) abgeschlossen. 2. he is a c. stranger to me, er ist mir völlig fremd; it came as a c. surprise to me, es kam für mich ganz überraschend. II. *v.tr.* (*a*) (eine Sammlung usw.) vervollständigen; (eine Arbeit, ein Buch usw.) abschließen; (*b*) to c. a form, ein Formular ausfüllen; **-ly,** *adv.* völlig. ◆**com'pletion,** *s.* 1. Fertigstellung *f;* it is nearing c., es wird bald fertig. 2. *Jur: Com:* on c. of contract, nach Vertragserfüllung.

**complex** ['kɔmpleks]. I. *adj.* (*of situation etc.*) verwickelt; (*of structure etc.*) komplex. II. *s.* Komplex *m;* inferiority c., Minderwertigkeitskomplex *m.* ◆**com'plexity,** *s.* Kompliziertheit *f.*

**complexion** [kəm'plekʃ(ə)n], *s.* Teint *m.*

**complicate** ['kɔmplikeit], *v.tr.* (etwas) komplizieren. ◆**'complicated,** *adj.* kompliziert. ◆**compli'cation,** *s.* Komplikation *f.*

**complicity** [kəm'plisiti], *s.* Mitschuld *f.*

**compliment** ['kɔmplimənt]. I. *s.* Kompliment *n;* to pay s.o. a c., j-m ein Kompliment machen; with compliments, mit besten Empfehlungen. II. *v.tr.* (j-m) ein Kompliment machen; to c. s.o. on his success, j-n zu seinem Erfolg beglückwünschen. ◆**complimentary** [-'ment(ə)ri], *adj.* (*a*) (*of remark etc.*) schmeichelhaft; (*b*) c. ticket, Freikarte *f.*

**comply** [kəm'plai], *v.i.* to c. with a rule, sich einer Regel fügen; to c. with a request, einer Bitte nachkommen.

**component** [kəm'pəunənt]. I. *s.* Bestandteil *m.* II. *adj.* c. parts, Einzelteile *npl.*

**compose** [kəm'pəuz], *v.tr.* (*a*) *Mus:* komponieren; (*b*) to c. oneself, sich fassen. ◆**com'posed,** *adj.* 1. (*of pers.*) gefaßt; (*of manner etc.*) gelassen. 2. to be c. of sth., aus etwas *dat* bestehen. ◆**com'poser,** *s.* Komponist *m.* ◆**composition** [kɔmpə'ziʃ(ə)n], *s.* 1. Komposition *f;* (*essay*) Aufsatz *m.* 2. Zusammensetzung *f* (eines Stoffes, einer Arznei usw.). ◆**composure** [-'pəuʒər], *s.* Gelassenheit *f.*

**compost** ['kɔmpɔst], *s.* Kompost *m.*

**compound** ['kɔmpaund]. I. *adj.* zusammengesetzt; c. fracture, komplizierter Bruch; c. interest, Zinseszins *m.* II. *s. Ch:* Verbindung *f.*

**comprehend** [kɔmpri'hend], *v.tr.* begreifen. ◆**comprehension** [kɔmpri'henʃ(ə)n], *s.* Verständnis *n;* (*capacity*) Fassungsvermögen *n.* ◆**comprehensible,** *adj.* verständlich. ◆**compre'hensive,** *adj.* umfassend; c. school, Gesamtschule *f;* c. insurance, Vollkasko *n.*

**compress.** I. [kəm'pres], *v.tr.* verdichten; compressed air, Druckluft *f.* II. ['kɔmpres], *s.* Kompresse *f.* ◆**compression** [-'preʃ(ə)n], *s.* Kompression *f.*

**comprise** [kəm'praiz], *v.tr.* to c. sth., aus etwas *dat* bestehen.

**compromise** ['kɔmprəmaiz]. I. *s.* Kompromiß *m.* II. *v.* 1. *v.tr.* (j-n) kompromittieren. 2. *v.i.* einen Kompromiß schließen. ◆**'compromising,** *adj.* kompromittierend.

**compulsion** [kəm'pʌlʃ(ə)n], *s.* Zwang *m.* ◆**com'pulsive** [-siv], *adj.* Zwangs-. ◆**com'pulsory** [-səri], *adj.* obligatorisch; Pflicht-.

**computer** [kəm'pju:tər], *s.* Computer *m,* Rechner *m.*

**comrade** ['kɔmreid, -rid], *s.* (*a*) Kamerad *m,* Kameradin *f;* (*b*) *Pol:* Genosse *m,* Genossin *f.*

**con** [kɔn]. *P:* I. *adj.* c. man, Hochstapler *m.* II. *v.tr.* (j-n) reinlegen; to c. s.o. into sth., j-m etwas andrehen.

**concave** ['kɔnkeiv], *adj.* konkav.

**conceal** [kən'si:l], *v.tr.* verbergen (from s.o., vor j-m). ◆**con'cealed,** *adj.* versteckt; c. lighting, indirekte Beleuchtung.

**concede** [kən'si:d], *v.tr.* to c. that ..., einräumen/zugeben, daß ...; to c. a point, in einem Punkt nachgeben.

**conceit** [kən'si:t], *s.* Eingebildetheit *f.* ◆**con'ceited,** *adj.* eingebildet.

**conceive** [kən'si:v], *v.tr.* (*a*) (ein Kind) empfangen; (*b*) sich *dat* (einen Plan usw.) ausdenken; (*c*) (*understand*) begreifen. ◆**con'ceivable,** *adj.* denkbar; the worst c. result, das denkbar schlechteste Ergebnis; **-ably,** *adv.* he could (not) c. ..., es ist (nicht) möglich/denkbar, daß er ...

**concentrate** ['kɔnsəntreit], *v.* 1. *v.tr.* konzentrieren. 2. *v.i.* to c. (on sth.), sich (auf etwas *acc*) konzentrieren. ◆**concen'tration,** *s.* Konzentration *f.*

**concept** ['kɔnsept], *s.* Begriff *m.*

**conception** [kən'sepʃ(ə)n], *s.* 1. Empfängnis *f* (eines Kindes). 2. (*idea*) Vorstellung *f.*

**concern** [kən'sə:n]. I. *s.* 1. (*matter*) Angelegenheit *f.* 2. (*worry*) Besorgnis *f.* 3. *Com:* Unternehmen *n.* II. *v.tr.* (*a*) (j-n) angehen; as far as I'm concerned, was mich betrifft; the persons concerned, die Beteiligten; (b) (worry) (j-n) beunruhigen; **we are concerned for her safety,** wir sind um ihre Sicherheit besorgt. ◆**con'cerning,** prep. bezüglich gen.

**concert** ['kɔnsət], s. Konzert n; **c. hall,** Konzertsaal m. ◆**concerted** [kən'sɑ:tid], adj. **c. efforts,** vereinte Anstrengungen.

**concertina** [kɔnsə'ti:nə], s. Konzertina f.

**concerto** [kən'tʃɑːtəu], s. Konzert n.

**concession** [kən'seʃ(ə)n], s. **to make a c. to s.o.,** j-m ein Zugeständnis machen.

**conciliatory** [kən'siliət(ə)ri], adj. (calming) beschwichtigend; (reconciling) versöhnend.

**concise** [kən'sais], adj. knapp (gefaßt); (of style, expression) prägnant.

**conclude** [kən'klu:d], v. 1. v.tr. abschließen. 2. v.i. (a) (finish) beenden; (b) (deduce) folgern. ◆**con'clusion** [-ʒən], s. 1. Abschluß m (einer Rede, eines Vertrags usw.). 2. Folgerung f; **to come to the c. that ...,** zu dem Schluß kommen, daß ... ◆**con'clusive** [-siv], adj. entscheidend.

**concoct** [kən'kɔkt], v.tr. (a) (ein Gericht) selber erfinden; (ein Getränk) zusammenbrauen; (b) (einen Plan usw.) aushecken. ◆**con'coction,** s. 1. (dish) selbsterfundenes Gericht n; (drink) Gebräu n. 2. (tale) Lügengeschichte f.

**concrete** ['kɔnkri:t]. I. adj. 1. (of form, proposal) konkret. 2. (of surface etc.) betoniert; **c. pillar,** Betonpfeiler m. II. s. Beton m; **reinforced c.,** Stahlbeton m.

**concur** [kən'kəːr], v.i. (agree) übereinstimmen.

**concussion** [kən'kʌʃ(ə)n], s. Gehirnerschütterung f.

**condemn** [kən'dem], v.tr. (a) (j-n) verurteilen; (b) (ein Haus usw.) für untauglich erklären. ◆**condem'nation,** s. Verurteilung f.

**condense** [kən'dens], v. 1. v.tr. (einen Bericht) zusammenfassen. 2. v.i. (of vapour) sich kondensieren. ◆**conden'sation,** s. (moisture) Kondensat n; (process) Kondensation f. ◆**con'densed,** adj. **c. milk,** Kondensmilch f.

**condescend** [kɔndi'send], v.i. sich herablassen (**to do sth.,** etwas zu tun). ◆**condes'cending,** adj. herablassend.

**condition** [kən'diʃ(ə)n]. I. s. 1. (requirement) Bedingung f; **on c. that,** unter der Bedingung, daß ... 2. pl. (circumstances) Verhältnisse npl. 3. (state) Zustand m. II. v.tr. (einen Stoff, j-n) konditionieren. ◆**con'ditional,** adj. (a) (of agreement etc.) bedingt; (b) **c. on sth.,** von etwas dat abhängig. ◆**con'ditioner,** s. (a) (hair) c., Haarkur f; (fabric) c., Weichspüler m.

**condolence** [kən'dəuləns], s. **to offer s.o. one's condolences,** j-m sein Beileid aussprechen.

**condone** [kən'dəun], v.tr. (etwas) stillschweigend dulden.

**conducive** [kən'dju:siv], adj. **to be c. to sth.,** etwas dat förderlich sein.

**conduct** I. ['kɔndʌkt], s. (behaviour) Benehmen n; Verhalten n; Sch: Betragen n. II. [kən'dʌkt], v.tr. (a) (j-n) führen; **conducted tour (of a town etc.),** Führung f (durch eine Stadt usw.); (b) **to c. s.o.'s affairs,** j-s Geschäfte führen; (c) (ein Orchester) dirigieren; (d) (Wärme, Strom) leiten. ◆**con'ductor,** s. 1. (a) Mus: Dirigent m; (b) (of conductress) (on bus) Schaffner(in) m(f). 2. El: Leiter m; **lightning c.,** Blitzableiter m.

**cone** [kəun], s. 1. Kegel m; (ice-cream) c., Tüte f. 2. Bot: Zapfen m.

**confectioner** [kən'fekʃ(ə)nər], s. Konditor m. ◆**confectionery** [kən'fekʃ(ə)n(ə)ri], s. Süßwaren fpl.

**confederation** [kənfedə'reiʃ(ə)n], s. Bund m; esp. Staatenbund m.

**confer** [kən'fəːr], v. 1. v.tr. **to c. a title etc. on s.o.,** j-m einen Titel usw. verleihen. 2. v.i. sich beraten. ◆**conference** ['kɔnfərəns], s. Konferenz f; **press c.,** Pressekonferenz f.

**confess** [kən'fes], v.tr. & i. (a) **to c. to a crime,** ein Verbrechen gestehen; (b) (admit) (etwas) zugeben; **I must c. that ...,** ich muß gestehen, daß ...; (c) Ecc: (seine Sünden) beichten. ◆**con'fessed,** adj. (self-)c., erklärt. ◆**confession** [-'feʃ(ə)n], s. 1. Geständnis n. 2. Ecc: Beichte f.

**confide** [kən'faid], v.i. **to c. in s.o.,** sich j-m anvertrauen. ◆**confidence** ['kɔnfid(ə)ns], s. (a) Vertrauen n (**in,** zu + dat); **in c.,** im Vertrauen; (b) (self-)c., Selbstvertrauen n. ◆**'confident,** adj. (a) (self-)c., selbstbewußt; (b) (optimistic) zuversichtlich; **to be c. that ...,** überzeugt sein, daß ... ◆**confidential** [-'denʃ(ə)l], adj. vertraulich; **-ly,** adv. im Vertrauen.

**confine** [kən'fain], v.tr. (a) **confined to bed,** ans Bett gefesselt; (b) **confined space,** enger Raum; (c) **to confine oneself to doing sth.,** sich darauf beschränken, etwas zu tun. ◆**con'finement,** s. 1. **solitary c.,** Einzelhaft f. 2. (of pregnant woman) Niederkunft f.

**confirm** [kən'fəːm], v.tr. (a) (ein Gerücht, einen Auftrag usw.) bestätigen; (b) Ecc: (j-n) konfirmieren. ◆**confirmation** [kɔnfə'meiʃ(ə)n], s. 1. Bestätigung f. 2. Ecc: Konfirmation f. ◆**con'firmed,** adj. **c. bachelor,** eingefleischter Junggeselle.

**confiscate** ['kɔnfiskeit], v.tr. beschlagnahmen. ◆**confis'cation,** s. Beschlagnahmung f.

**conflagration** [kɔnflə'greiʃ(ə)n], s. Feuersbrunst f.

**conflict** I. ['kɔnflikt]. I. s. 1. (fight) Kampf m. 2. Konflikt m (von Interessen usw.). II. [kən'flikt] v.i. **to c. with sth.,** zu etwas dat im Widerspruch stehen. ◆**con'flicting,** adj. sich widersprechend; (of feelings) widerstreitend.

**conform** [kən'fɔ:m], *v.i.* sich anpassen (**to**, *dat*). ◆**con'formity**, *s.* Anpassung *f* (**to**, an + *dat*).

**confront** [kən'frʌnt], *v.tr.* (einer Gefahr usw.) ins Auge sehen; **to c. s.o. with the truth**, j-n mit der Wahrheit konfrontieren. ◆**confron'tation** [kon-], *s.* Konfrontation *f*.

**confuse** [kən'fju:z], *v.tr.* (*a*) (eine Sache mit einer anderen) verwechseln; (*b*) (j-n) verwirren. ◆**con'fused**, *adj.* (*of pers.*) verwirrt; (*of report etc.*) verworren; **to get c.**, in Verwirrung geraten. ◆**con'fusion** [-ʒ(ə)n], *s.* Verwirrung *f*.

**congeal** [kən'dʒi:l], *v.i.* (*of blood*) gerinnen.

**congenital** [kən'dʒenitl], *adj.* angeboren.

**conger** ['kɔŋgər], *s.* **c. eel**, grauer Meeraal.

**congested** [kən'dʒestid], *adj.* (*of roads, nose*) verstopft; (*of traffic*) gestaut; (*overcrowded*) überfüllt. ◆**congestion**, [-'dʒestʃ(ə)n], *s.* Verstopfung *f*; (**traffic**) **c.**, Verkehrsstauung *f*.

**conglomeration** [kənglɔmə'reiʃ(ə)n], *s.* Ansammlung *f*; *Pej:* (*hotchpotch*) Mischmasch *m*.

**congratulate** [kən'grætjuleit], *v.tr.* (j-m) gratulieren (**on sth.**, zu etwas *dat*). ◆**congratu'lations**, *s. pl.* **c.!** herzlichen Glückwunsch!

**congregate** ['kɔŋgrigeit], *v.i.* sich versammeln. ◆**congre'gation**, *s.* (versammelte) Gemeinde *f*.

**congress** ['kɔŋgres], *s.* Kongreß *m*. ◆**'congressman**, *s. N.Am: Pol:* Mitglied *n* des Repräsentantenhauses.

**conical** ['kɔnikl], *adj.* kegelförmig.

**conifer** ['kɔnifər], *s.* Nadelbaum *m*.

**conjecture** [kən'dʒektʃər]. **I.** *s.* Mutmaßung *f*; **pure c.**, reine Vermutung *f*. **II.** *v.i.* Vermutungen anstellen.

**conjunction** [kən'dʒʌŋkʃ(ə)n], *s.* **1.** *Gram:* Konjunktion *f*. **2.** **in c. with**, in Verbindung mit + *dat*.

**conjunctivitis** [kən(d)ʒʌŋkti'vaitis], *s.* Bindehautentzündung *f*.

**conjure** ['kʌndʒər], *v.* **1.** *v.tr.* **to c. up memories** etc., Erinnerungen usw. heraufbeschwören. **2.** *v.i.* zaubern. ◆**'conjuring**, *s.* Zauberei *f*. ◆**'conjurer**, *s.* Zauberkünstler *m*.

**conk** [kɔŋk], *v.i. P:* **to c. out**, den Geist aufgeben.

**conker** ['kɔŋkər], *s. F:* Roßkastanie *f*.

**connect** [kə'nekt], *v.tr.* (*a*) verbinden; (zwei Teile usw. aneinander) anschließen; **to c. sth. to sth.**, etwas mit etwas *dat* verbinden; *esp. Tchn:* etwas an etwas *acc* anschließen; (*b*) (*associate*) (etwas) verknüpfen. ◆**co'nnecting**, *adj.* verbindend; **c. train**, Anschlußzug *m*. ◆**connection** [kə'nekʃ(ə)n], *s.* (*a*) Verbindung *f*; *El: Tel: Rail:* Anschluß *m*; (*b*) (*context*) Zusammenhang *m*; **in c. with my application**, bezüglich meiner Bewerbung; (*c*) **to have connections**, Be-

ziehungen haben (**with**, zu + *dat*).

**connoisseur** [kɔnə'sə:r], *s.* Kenner *m*.

**conquer** ['kɔŋkər], *v.tr.* (*a*) (j-n, ein Land) erobern; (*b*) (seiner Eifersucht *gen* usw.) Herr werden. ◆**'conqueror**, *s.* Sieger *m*. ◆**conquest** ['kɔŋkwest], *s.* Eroberung *f*.

**conscience** ['kɔnʃəns], *s.* Gewissen *n*; **to have sth. on one's c.**, etwas auf dem Gewissen haben. ◆**conscientious** [-ʃi'enʃəs], *adj.* gewissenhaft; **c. objector**, Kriegsdienstverweigerer *m*.

**conscious** ['kɔnʃəs], *adj.* **1. to be c. of sth.**, (sich *dat*) etwas *gen* bewußt sein; **c. attempt**, bewußter Versuch. **2. to be c.**, bei Bewußtsein sein. ◆**'consciousness**, *s.* **to lose c.**, das Bewußtsein verlieren; **to regain c.**, (wieder) zu Bewußtsein kommen.

**conscript** ['kɔnskript], *s.* Einberufene(r) *f(m)*. ◆**con'scription**, *s.* Einberufung *f*.

**consecrate** ['kɔnsikreit], *v.tr.* weihen.

**consecutive** [kən'sekjutiv], *adj.* **on three c. days**, an drei aufeinanderfolgenden Tagen; *adv.* hintereinander.

**consensus** [kən'sensəs], *s.* Übereinstimmung *f*.

**consent** [kən'sent]. **I.** *v.i.* **to c. to sth.**, in etwas *acc* einwilligen. **II.** *s.* **to give (one's) c.**, seine Zustimmung geben; **by common c.**, nach allgemeiner Ansicht; **age of c.**, sexuelle Mündigkeit *f*.

**consequence** ['kɔnsikwəns], *s.* **1.** Folge *f*; **to take the consequences**, die Folgen/die Konsequenzen tragen. **2.** (*importance*) **it's of no c.**, es hat keinerlei Bedeutung. ◆**'consequent**, *adj.* daraus folgend; **-ly**, *adv. & conj.* folglich.

**conserve** [kən'sə:v], *v.tr.* **to c. energy**, Kräfte sparen. ◆**conservation** [kɔnsə'veiʃ(ə)n], *s.* (**of the environment**), Umweltschutz *m*. ◆**con'servative** [-'sə:tiv]. **I.** *adj.* (*a*) *Pol: etc:* konservativ; (*b*) **at a c. estimate**, niedrig geschätzt. **II.** *s.* Konservative(r) *f(m)*. ◆**con'servatory** [-ətri], *s.* Wintergarten *m*.

**consider** [kən'sidər], *v.tr.* (*a*) (*examine*) (eine Frage usw.) erwägen; sich *dat* (eine Möglichkeit usw.) überlegen; (ein Angebot, eine Bewerbung usw.) berücksichtigen; **when you c. that ...**, wenn man bedenkt, daß ... (*b*) (*take into account*) (j-s Alter usw.) berücksichtigen, in Betracht ziehen; **all things considered**, wenn man alles in Betracht zieht; (*c*) (*think*) **I c. him crazy**, ich halte ihn für verrückt; **to c. oneself lucky**, sich glücklich schätzen. ◆**con'siderable**, *adj.* beträchtlich. ◆**con'siderate**, *adj.* rücksichtsvoll. ◆**consider'ation**, *s.* **1. to take sth. into c.**, etwas berücksichtigen; **after careful c.**, nach reiflicher Überlegung; **that is a c.**, das ist schon eine Erwägung. **2.** (*thoughtfulness*) Rücksicht *f*; **out of c. for s.o.**, aus Rücksicht auf j-n. **3.** (*payment*) **for a small c.**, gegen ein geringes Ent-

gelt. ◆con'sidered, adj. my c. opinion, meine wohlüberlegte Meinung.
◆con'sidering. I. prep. c. his age, in
Anbetracht seines Alters. II. adv. F: it's
not so bad, c., unter den Umständen ist
das gar nicht so schlecht.
consignment [kən'sainmənt], s. Lieferung f.
consist [kən'sist], v.i. to c. of sth., aus
etwas dat bestehen. ◆con'sistent, adj.
1. (a) (argument etc.) konsequent; (b) (un-
varying) gleichmäßig. 2. c. with, (im
Einklang/vereinbar mit + dat.
◆con'sistency, s. 1. (a) Konsequenz f;
(b) Gleichmäßigkeit f (der Leistungen).
2. (thickness etc.) Konsistenz f.
console [kən'səul], v.tr. trösten.
◆consolation [kɔnsə'leiʃ(ə)n], s. Trost
m; c. prize, Trostpreis m.
consolidate [kən'sɔlideit], v.tr. konsoli-
dieren.
consonant ['kɔnsənənt], s. Konsonant m.
consortium [kən'sɔːtiəm], s. Konsortium
n.
conspicuous [kən'spikjuəs], adj. auffallend; it is very c., es fällt sehr auf; to be
c. by one's absence, durch Abwesenheit
glänzen.
conspire [kən'spaiər], v.i. sich verschwö-
ren. ◆conspiracy ['-spirəsi], s. Verschwörung f. ◆con'spirator, s. Ver-
schwörer m.
constable ['kʌnstəbl], s. Polizist m.
◆constabulary [kən'stæbjuləri], s. Polizei f.
constant ['kɔnst(ə)nt]. I. adj. ständig. II.
s. Konstante f; -ly, adv. ständig.
constellation [kɔnstə'leiʃ(ə)n], s. Stern-
bild n.
consternation [kɔnstə'neiʃ(ə)n], s. Bestürzung f.
constipation [kɔnsti'peiʃ(ə)n], s. Verstopfung f.
constituent [kən'stitjuənt], s. Pol: Wähler m. ◆constituency, s. Wahlkreis m.
constitute ['kɔnstitjuːt], v.tr. (a) (represent) darstellen; (b) (make up) (eine Summe usw.) ausmachen. ◆consti'tution,
s. 1. Pol: Verfassung f. 2. (physical) Konstitution f. ◆consti'tutional, adj.
verfassungsmäßig.
constraint [kən'streint], s. Zwang m.
construct [kən'strʌkt], v.tr. bauen.
◆con'struction, s. Bau m; under c. im
Bau. ◆con'structive, adj. konstruktiv.
consul ['kɔns(ə)l], s. Konsul m.
◆'consulate [-julət], s. Konsulat n.
consult [kən'sʌlt], v.tr. (j-n) zu Rate ziehen; to c. a book/a timetable, in einem
Buch/einem Fahrplan nachsehen.
◆con'sultant, s. Berater m; Med:
Facharzt m. ◆consultation
[kɔnsəl'teiʃ(ə)n], s. Beratung f.
consume [kən'sjuːm], v.tr. (a) (Essen,
Getränke) zu sich dat nehmen; (b) (Kräfte, Geld) verbrauchen; he is consumed
with envy, ihn frißt der Neid.

◆con'sumer, s. Verbraucher m; c.
goods, Verbrauchsgüter npl; c. protection, Verbraucherschutz m.
consummate [kən'sʌmət], adj. with c.
ease, mit größter Leichtigkeit.
consummation [kɔnsə'meiʃ(ə)n], s. Voll-
ziehung f (einer Ehe).
consumption [kən'sʌm(p)ʃ(ə)n], s. Genuß m (von alkoholischen Getränken
usw.); Verbrauch m (Aut: von Benzin
usw.).
contact ['kɔntækt]. I. s. Kontakt m; to
come into c. with s.o., sth., mit j-m, etwas dat in Berührung kommen; to make
c., Kontakt aufnehmen; c. lens, Kon-
taktlinse f; he is a business c. of mine,
ich kenne ihn geschäftlich. II. v.tr. to c.
s.o., sich mit j-m in Verbindung setzen.
contagious [kən'teidʒəs], adj. anstek-
kend.
contain [kən'tein], v.tr. (a) enthalten; (b)
(restrain) (Gefühle usw.) unterdrücken; to
c. oneself, sich beherrschen.
◆con'tainer, s. Behälter m; Com: Container m; c. port, Containerhafen m.
contaminate [kən'tæmineit], v.tr. (Wasser usw.) verseuchen.
◆contami'nation, s. Verseuchung f.
contemplate ['kɔntempleit], v.tr. (a) (regard) (etwas) betrachten; (der Zukunft)
entgegensehen; (b) (consider) (an etwas
acc) denken. ◆contemplation, s.
Nachsinnen n.
contemporary [kən'temp(ə)rəri]. I. adj.
zeitgenössisch. II. s. Zeitgenosse m, Zeit-
genossin f.
contempt [kən'tem(p)t], s. 1. Verachtung
f. 2. Jur: c. of court, Mißachtung f des
Gerichts. ◆con'temptible, adj. verachtenswert. ◆con'temptuous, adj. geringschätzig.
contend [kən'tend], v.tr. to c. with s.o.,
sth., mit j-m, etwas dat kämpfen.
content¹ ['kɔntent], s. also pl. contents,
Inhalt m.
content² [kən'tent]. I. v.tr. to c. oneself
with sth., sich mit etwas dat begnügen.
II. adj. zufrieden. III. s. to one's heart's
c., nach Herzenslust. ◆con'tented,
adj. zufrieden. ◆con'tentment, s. Zu-
friedenheit f.
contention [kən'tenʃ(ə)n], s. bone of c.,
Zankapfel m.
contest. I. [kɔn'test], v.tr. (ein Testament) anfechten. II. ['kɔntest], s. (a) Sp:
Wettkampf m; (b) (competition) Wettbewerb m. ◆con'testant, s. Bewerber(in)
m(f); (in competition) Teilnehmer(in) m(f).
context ['kɔntekst], s. Zusammenhang m.
continent ['kɔntinənt], s. 1. Kontinent
m. 2. Brit: on the C., auf dem europä-
ischen Festland. ◆conti'nental, adj.
(a) Kontinental-; c. drift, Kontinental-
verschiebung f; (b) Brit: kontinentaleuro-
päisch; c. quilt, Federbett n.
contingent [kən'tindʒənt], s. Kontingent
n; F: Schub m (von Menschen).

◆**con'tingency**, *s. c.* **plan**, Eventualplan *m.*

**continue** [kən'tinju(:)], *v.* **1.** *v.tr.* (*a*) (etwas) fortsetzen; (*b*) **to c. to do sth./doing sth.**, in etwas *dat* fortfahren; **he continued to work/to read**, er arbeitete/las weiter. **2.** *v.i.* (*of speaker etc.*) fortfahren; (*of weather etc.*) anhalten; (*on a journey*) weiterfahren; (*with a job*) weitermachen. ◆**con'tinual**, *adj.* dauernd; **-ly**, *adv.* dauernd; (*repeatedly*) immer wieder. ◆**continu'ation**, *s.* Fortsetzung *f.* ◆**continuity** [kɔnti'nju(:)iti], *s.* (logische) Folge *f*; **there's no c.**, es fehlt der Zusammenhang. ◆**con'tinuous**, *adj.* ununterbrochen.

**contour** ['kɔntuər], *s.* Kontur *f*; **c. line**, Höhenlinie *f.*

**contraband** ['kɔntrəbænd], *s.* Schmuggelware *f.*

**contraception** [kɔntrə'sepʃ(ə)n], *s.* Empfängnisverhütung *f.* ◆**contra'ceptive** [-tiv]. **I.** *s.* Empfängnisverhütungsmittel *n.* **II.** *adj.* empfängnisverhütend.

**contract. I.** [kən'trækt], *v.* **1.** *v.i.* sich zusammenziehen. **2.** *v.tr.* **to c. an illness**, sich *dat* eine Krankheit zuziehen. **II.** ['kɔntrækt], *s.* Vertrag *m*; **breach of c.**, Vertragsbruch *m.* ◆**con'traction**, *s.* Zusammenziehung *f.* ◆**con'tractor**, *s.* Unternehmer *m.* ◆**con'tractual**, *adj.* vertraglich.

**contradict** [kɔntrə'dikt], *v.tr.* (j-m, etwas *dat*) widersprechen. ◆**contra'diction**, *s.* Widerspruch *m.* ◆**contra'dictory**, *adj.* widersprüchlich.

**contralto**, *pl.* **-os** [kən'træltəu, -trɑːltəu, -əuz], *s.* Alt *m.*

**contraption** [kən'træpʃ(ə)n], *s.* F: Pej: primitiver Apparat *m*; Machwerk *n.*

**contrary** ['kɔntrəri]. **I.** *adj.* entgegengesetzt (**to**, *dat*). **II.** *s.* Gegenteil *n*; **on the c.**, im Gegenteil; **proof to the c.**, gegenteilige Beweise. **III.** *adv.* **c. to**, gegen + *acc*; **c. to expectation(s)**, wider Erwarten.

**contrast. I.** [kən'trɑːst], *v.* **1.** *v.i.* **to c. with sth.**, einen Gegensatz zu etwas *dat* bilden; (*of colours*) gegen etwas *acc* abstechen. **2.** *v.tr.* **to c. sth. with sth.**, etwas einer Sache *dat* gegenüberstellen. **II.** ['kɔntrɑːst], *s.* Gegensatz *m*; **in c. with**, im Gegensatz zu.

**contravene** [kɔntrə'viːn], *v.tr.* (gegen ein Gesetz usw.) verstoßen.

**contribute** [kən'tribju(:)t], *v.* **1.** *v.tr.* (etwas) beitragen (**to**, zu + *dat*). **2.** *v.i.* (dazu) beitragen (, etwas zu tun). ◆**contri'bution** [kɔn-], *s.* Beitrag *m*; **to make a c.**, einen Beitrag leisten. ◆**con'tributor**, *s.* Beiträger *m.* ◆**con'tributory**, *adj.* **c. factor**, Mitursache *f.*

**contrite** ['kɔntrait], *adj.* Lit: reuig.

**contrive** [kən'traiv], *v.* **1.** *v.tr.* (einen Plan usw.) aushecken. **2.** *v.i.* **to c. to do sth.**, es fertigbringen, etwas zu tun.

◆**con'trived**, *adj.* gewollt.

**control** [kən'trəul]. **I.** *s.* **1.** (*mastery*) Beherrschung *f*; (*power*) Gewalt *f*; **due to circumstances beyond our c.**, wegen nicht vorauszusehender Umstände; **out of/under c.**, außer/unter Kontrolle; **he lost c. of/over his car**, er verlor die Herrschaft über seinen Wagen. **2.** (*regulation*) **under government c.**, unter Staatsaufsicht; **import controls**, Importbeschränkungen *fpl.* **3.** **at the controls**, (*of car*) am Steuer; **c. panel**, Schalttafel *f*; **c. tower**, Kontrollturm *m*; **volume c.**, Lautstärkeregler *m.* **II.** *v.tr.* (etwas) kontrollieren; Kontrolle (über j-n, etwas *acc*) haben; (den Verkehr, die Wirtschaft, ein Flugzeug usw.) lenken; **to c. oneself**, sich beherrschen.

**controversial** [kɔntrə'vəːʃ(ə)l], *adj.* (*of issue, figure etc.*) umstritten; (*of writings, critic etc.*) polemisch; **c. question**, Streitfrage *f.* ◆**controversy** [kɔntrəvəːsi, kən'trɔvəsi], *s.* Meinungsstreit *m*; **a subject of great c.**, ein heiß umstrittenes Thema.

**convalesce** [kɔnvə'les], *v.i.* sich erholen. ◆**conva'lescence**, *s.* Erholungszeit *f.*

**convene** [kən'viːn], *v.* **1.** *v.tr.* (eine Versammlung usw.) einberufen. **2.** *v.i.* sich versammeln.

**convenience** [kən'viːnjəns], *s.* **1.** Bequemlichkeit *f*; **at your c.**, wann (immer) es Ihnen paßt; **a c. food**, ein Schnellgericht *n.* **2.** (*public*) **c.**, (öffentliche) Toilette *f.* **3.** **with all conveniences**, mit allen Annehmlichkeiten. ◆**con'venient**, *adj.* (*of time*) gelegen; (*of arrangement etc.*) praktisch; **if it is c. for you**, wenn es Ihnen paßt.

**convent** ['kɔnvənt], *s.* Kloster *n.*

**convention** [kən'venʃ(ə)n], *s.* **1.** Tagung *f*; *N. Am:* Pol: Parteitag *m.* **2.** Pol: Konvent *m.* **3.** (*custom*) Sitte *f*; **social conventions**, gesellschaftliche Formen *fpl.* ◆**con'ventional**, *adj.* konventionell; (*customary*) herkömmlich.

**converge** [kən'vəːdʒ], *v.i.* (*of lines, roads*) zusammenlaufen.

**converse** [kən'vəːs], *v.i.* sich unterhalten. ◆**conver'sation**, *s.* Gespräch *n.*

**convert. I.** [kən'vəːt], *v.tr.* (*a*) (j-n) bekehren; (*b*) (etwas) umwandeln (**into** sth., in etwas *acc*); **to c. a house into flats**, ein Haus in Wohnungen umbauen. **II.** ['kɔnvəːt], *s.* Bekehrte(r) *f(m)*. ◆**con'version**, *s.* **1.** *Eccl:* Bekehrung *f.* **2.** Umwandlung *f* (von Wasser in Dampf usw.); Umbau *m* (eines Gebäudes). ◆**con'vertible**, *s.* Kabriolett *n.*

**convex** ['kɔnveks], *adj.* konvex.

**convey** [kən'vei], *v.tr.* (*a*) (Güter, Personen usw.) befördern; (Wasser, Strom usw.) leiten; (*b*) (den Sinn, seine Meinung usw.) ausdrücken. ◆**con'veyor**, *s.* **c. belt**, Förderband *n.*

**convict. I.** [kən'vikt], *v.tr.* (j-n) verurteilen; **to c. s.o. (of a crime)**, j-n (eines

Verbrechens) für schuldig befinden. **II.** ['kɔnvikt], s. Strafgefangene(r) *f(m)*. ◆**con'viction**, *s.* **1.** *Jur:* Verurteilung *f.* **2.** *(belief)* Überzeugung *f.*

**convince** [kən'vins], *v.tr.* (j-n) überzeugen **(of sth.,** von etwas *dat).* ◆**con'vincing**, *adj.* überzeugend.

**convoy** ['kɔnvɔi], *s.* (a) *(escort)* Geleit *n;* (b) *(escorted ships)* Geleitzug *m.*

**convulsion** [kən'vʌlʃ(ə)n], *s. Med:* **to get convulsions,** Krämpfe bekommen.

**cook** [kuk]. **I.** *v.* **1.** *v.tr.* (a) kochen; *(roast, fry)* (Fleisch, Würste usw.) braten; **is it cooked?** ist es gar? (b) *F: Com:* **to c. the books,** die Bücher frisieren. **2.** *v.i.* kochen. **II.** *s.* Koch *m;* Köchin *f.* ◆**'cookbook,** *s. N.Am:* Kochbuch *n.* ◆**'cooker,** *s.* Herd *m.* ◆**'cookery,** *s.* Kochen *n; c.* **book,** Kochbuch *n.* ◆**'cookie,** *s. N.Am:* Plätzchen *n.* ◆**'cooking,** *s.* Kochen *n.* **II.** *adj.* **c. apple,** Kochapfel *m;* **c. utensil,** Küchengerät *n.*

**cool** [ku:l]. **I.** *adj.* kühl; *(calm)* ruhig; gelassen. **II.** *s.* **1.** Kühle *f.* **2.** *F:* **to keep one's c.,** die Ruhe bewahren. **III.** *v.tr. & i.* abkühlen; **to c. down,** sich abkühlen; *Fig:* *(of pers.)* sich beruhigen; **to c. off,** *(of enthusiasm etc.)* abkühlen.

**coop** [ku:p]. **I.** *s.* Hühnerstall *m.* **II.** *v.tr.* **to c. s.o., sth. up,** j-n, etwas einsperren.

**co-operate** [kəu'ɔpəreit], *v.i.* zusammenarbeiten. ◆**co-ope'ration,** *s.* Zusammenarbeit *f;* *(help)* Mithilfe *f.* ◆**co-'operative.** **I.** *adj.* **1.** *(of pers.)* hilfsbereit. **2.** *(of organization etc.)* genossenschaftlich. **II.** *s.* Genossenschaft *f.*

**co-ordinate** [kəu'ɔ:dineit], *v.tr.* (etwas) koordinieren. ◆**co-ordi'nation,** *s.* Koordination *f.*

**cop** [kɔp], *s. P:* **1.** *(policeman)* Polyp *m;* **the cops,** die Polente *f.* **2.** **it's not much c.,** damit ist es nicht weit her.

**cope** [kəup], *v.i.* **to c. with s.o., sth.,** mit j-m, etwas *dat* fertig werden.

**copper** ['kɔpər], *s.* **1.** Kupfer *n.* **2.** *attrib.* kupfern. **3.** *P: (policeman)* Polyp *m.*

**copse** [kɔps], *s.* Gehölz *n.*

**copulate** ['kɔpjuleit], *v.i.* sich begatten; *(of male)* begatten. ◆**copu'lation,** *s.* Begattung *f.*

**copy** ['kɔpi]. **I.** *v.* **1.** *v.tr.* (a) kopieren; **to c. sth. (down/out),** etwas abschreiben; (b) *(imitate)* nachahmen. **2.** *v.i. Sch:* abschreiben. **II.** *s.* **1.** Kopie *f.* **2.** *(written or typed)* Abschrift *f;* **rough c.,** Kladde *f;* **fair c.,** Reinschrift *f;* **carbon c.,** Durchschlag *m.* **3.** *(of book etc.)* Exemplar *n;* *(of newspaper)* Nummer *f.* ◆**'copyright,** *s.* Copyright *n.*

**coral** ['kɔrəl]. **I.** *s.* Koralle *f.* **II.** *adj.* **c. reef,** Korallenriff *n.*

**cord** [kɔ:d], *s.* **1.** Strick *m.* **2.** **vocal cords,** Stimmbänder *npl.* **3.** *Cl: F:* **cords,** Cordhose *f.*

**cordial** ['kɔ:djəl]. **I.** *adj.* herzlich. **II.** *s.* Fruchtsirup *m.*

**cordon** ['kɔ:dən]. **I.** *s.* Kette *f;* **police c.,** Polizeikette *f.* **II.** *v.tr.* **to c. off an area etc.,** eine Gegend usw. absperren.

**corduroy** ['kɔ:dərɔi], *s.* Cord *m.*

**core** [kɔ:r], *s.* Kern *m;* *(of apple etc.)* Kerngehäuse *n.*

**cork** [kɔ:k]. **I.** *s.* **1.** *(material)* Kork *m.* **2.** *(for a bottle etc.)* Korken *m.* **II.** *adj.* Kork-. ◆**'corkscrew,** *s.* Korkenzieher *m.*

**corn¹** [kɔ:n], *s.* Korn *n; N.Am:* Mais *m;* **c. on the cob,** Maiskolben *m.* ◆**'cornflour,** *s.* Stärkemehl *n.*

**corn²,** *s. Med:* Hühnerauge *n.*

**cornea** ['kɔ:niə], *s.* Hornhaut *f.*

**corned** [kɔ:nd], *adj.* **c. beef,** Corned beef *n.*

**corner** ['kɔ:nər]. **I.** *s.* **1.** Ecke *f; F:* **c. shop,** Tante-Emma-Laden *m; Fb:* **c. (kick),** Eckball *m; Fig:* **to be in a tight c.,** in der Klemme sitzen. **2.** *(bend)* Kurve *f.* **II.** *v.* **1.** *v.tr.* (j-n) in die Enge treiben; *Com:* **to c. the market,** den Markt aufkaufen. **2.** *v.i. Aut:* eine/die Kurve nehmen.

**cornet** ['kɔ:nit], *s.* **1.** *Mus:* Kornett *n.* **2.** *(ice-cream)* **c.,** Eistüte *f.*

**corny** ['kɔ:ni], *adj. F:* (a) *(of joke)* abgedroschen; (b) *(of film etc.)* kitschig.

**coronary** ['kɔrənəri], *adj. Med:* **c. (thrombosis),** Koronarthrombose *f.*

**coronation** [kɔrə'neiʃ(ə)n], *s.* Krönung *f.*

**coroner** ['kɔrənər], *s.* richterliche(r) Beamte(r) *m* für die Leichenschau.

**corporal¹** ['kɔ:p(ə)r(ə)l], *s. Mil:* Stabsunteroffizier *m.*

**corporal²,** *adj.* **c. punishment,** körperliche Züchtigung *f.*

**corporation** [kɔ:pə'reiʃ(ə)n], *s.* Aktiengesellschaft *f.*

**corpse** [kɔ:ps], *s.* Leiche *f.*

**corpuscle** ['kɔ:pʌsl], *s.* Körperchen *n.*

**correct** [kə'rekt]. **I.** *v.tr.* (j-n, etwas) korrigieren. **II.** *adj.* (a) richtig; (b) *(of pers., dress etc.)* korrekt. ◆**co'rrection,** *s.* Korrektur *f.*

**correspond** [kɔris'pɔnd], *v.i.* (a) sich entsprechen; *(of two accounts etc.)* sich decken; **to c. with/to sth.,** etwas *dat* entsprechen; (b) **to c. with s.o.,** mit j-m korrespondieren. ◆**corres-'pondence,** *s.* Briefwechsel *m;* **to deal with one's c.,** seine Post erledigen; **c. course,** Fernkurs *m.* ◆**corres'pondent,** *s.* **1.** *(regular)* Briefpartner(in) *m(f).* **2.** *(reporter)* Korrespondent(in) *m(f).* ◆**corres'ponding,** *adj.* entsprechend.

**corridor** ['kɔridɔ:r], *s.* Korridor *m.*

**corroborate** [kə'rɔbəreit], *v.tr.* (eine Aussage usw.) bestätigen.

**corrode** [kə'rəud], *v.* **1.** *v.tr.* (a) *(of rust etc.)* (Metall usw.) zerfressen; *(of chemical etc.)* (Metall usw.) ätzen. **2.** *v.i.* korrodieren. ◆**co'rrosion** [-ʒ(ə)n], *s.* Korrosion *f.* ◆**co'rrosive** [-siv]. **I.** *s.* Ätzmittel *n.* **II.** *adj.* zerfressend.

**corrugated** ['korəgeitid], *adj.* gewellt; **c. iron,** Wellblech *n.*
**corrupt** [kə'rʌpt]. **I.** *v.tr.* (Jugendliche) verderben. **II.** *adj.* korrupt.
◆**co'rruption,** *s.* Korruption *f.*
**corset** ['kɔːsit], *s.* Mieder *n; esp. Med:* Korsett *n.*
**cosh** [kɔʃ]. **I.** *s.* Knüppel *m.* **II.** *v.tr.* (j-n) mit einem Knüppel schlagen.
**cosmetic** [kɔz'metik]. **I.** *adj.* kosmetisch. **II.** *s.pl.* **cosmetics,** Kosmetika *npl.*
**cosmopolitan** [kɔzmə'polit(ə)n], *adj.* kosmopolitisch; *(of city)* international; *(of pers.)* weltbürgerlich.
**cost** [kɔst]. **I.** *v.* 1. *v.i.* kosten; **it c. him five pounds,** es hat ihn fünf Pfund gekostet. 2. *v.tr.* **to c. a project,** eine Kostenberechnung für ein Projekt anstellen. **II.** *s.* Kosten *pl;* **c. of living,** Lebenshaltungskosten *pl;* **c. price,** Selbstkostenpreis *m; Fig:* **I know that to my c.,** das weiß ich aus bitterer Erfahrung; **at all costs,** um jeden Preis; **whatever the c.,** koste es, was es wolle. ◆**'costly,** *adj.* kostspielig.
**costume** ['kɔstjuːm], *s.* 1. **(national) c.,** Tracht *f.* 2. *(fancy dress)* Kostüm *n.*
**cosy** ['kəuzi]. **I.** *adj.* gemütlich. **II.** *s.* **(tea-)c.,** Teewärmer *m.*
**cot** [kɔt], *s.* Kinderbett *n; (with bars)* Gitterbett *n.*
**cottage** ['kɔtidʒ], *s.* Häuschen *n,* Cottage *f;* **c. cheese,** Hüttenkäse *m;* **c. industry,** Heimindustrie *f.*
**cotton** ['kɔtn]. **I.** *s.* Baumwolle *f;* **(sewing-)c.,** Nähgarn *n;* **c. reel,** Garnrolle *f;* **c. wool,** Watte *f.* **II.** *adj.* baumwollen.
**couch** [kautʃ], *s.* Couch *f.*
**cough** [kɔf]. **I.** *s.* Husten *m.* **II.** *v.i.* *(a)* husten; *(b) F: (pay)* **to c. up,** blechen.
**could** [kud], *see* **can²**.
**council** ['kauns(i)l], *s.* *(a) (assembly)* Rat *m;* **town c.,** Stadtrat *m;* *(b) (local authority)* Gemeinde *f;* **c. flat,** Sozialwohnung *f.* ◆**'councillor,** *s.* **(town) c.,** Rat *m;* Stadtrat *m.*
**counsel** ['kauns(ə)l]. **I.** *s.* 1. *(advice)* Rat *m.* 2. *Jur:* Anwalt *m;* **c. for the defence,** Verteidiger *m;* **c. for the prosecution,** Anklagevertreter *m.* **II.** *v.tr.* (j-n) beraten; **to c. caution,** zu Vorsicht raten. ◆**'counsellor,** *s.* Berater *m.* ◆**'counsellor,** *s. N.Am:* Anwalt *m.*
**count¹** [kaunt]. **I.** *v.* 1. *v.tr.* *(a)* zählen; *(b)* **to c. oneself lucky,** sich glücklich schätzen; **to c. on s.o.,** sich auf j-n verlassen; **to c. on sth.** mit etwas rechnen. 2. *v.i.* zählen. **II.** *s.* Zählung *f.* ◆**'count-down,** *s.* Countdown *m.* ◆**'countless,** *adj.* unzählig.
**count²,** *s.* Graf *m.*
**counter¹** ['kauntər], *s.* 1. *(a) (in shop)* Ladentisch *m;* *(b) (in bank, post office)* Schalter *m.* 2. *E:* Zähler *m.*
**counter²,** *v.* 1. *v.tr.* (einen Angriff) erwi-

dern; *(j-s* Plänen usw.) entgegenarbeiten. 2. *v.i.* kontern. ◆**counter'act,** *v.tr.* (etwas *dat)* entgegenwirken. ◆**'counterattack.** **I.** *s.* Gegenangriff *m.* **II.** *v.tr. & i.* einen Gegenangriff (gegen j-n) unternehmen. ◆**'counter-'espionage,** *s.* Gegenspionage *f.* ◆**counterfeit** ['kauntəfit]. **I.** *adj.* gefälscht. **II.** *v.tr.* (Geld usw.) fälschen. ◆**'counterfoil,** *s.* Kontrollabschnitt *m.* ◆**'counterpart,** *s.* Gegenstück *n.* ◆**'counter'sign,** *v.tr.* (einen Scheck usw.) gegenzeichnen.
**countess** ['kauntis], *s.* Gräfin *f.*
**country** ['kʌntri], *s.* 1. *(a)* Land *n; Pol:* Staat *m;* *(countryside)* **in the c.,** auf dem Land; **c. house,** Landhaus *n;* *(b) (terrain)* Gelände *n.* ◆**'countryside,** *s.* Landschaft *f.*
**county** ['kaunti], *s.* 1. *Brit:* Grafschaft *f;* **c. council,** Grafschaftsrat *m.* 2. *N.Am:* Verwaltungsbezirk *m.*
**coup** [kuː], *s.* Coup *m.*
**couple** ['kʌp(ə)l], *s.* 1. Paar *n;* **married c.,** Ehepaar *n.* 2. *(a few)* ein paar; **a c. of days,** ein paar Tage.
**coupon** ['kuːpɔn], *s.* 1. *(form)* Coupon *m.* 2. *(voucher)* Gutschein *m.*
**courage** ['kʌridʒ], *s.* Mut *m;* **to pluck up c.,** Mut aufbringen. ◆**courageous** [kə'reidʒəs], *adj.* mutig.
**courgette** [kuə'ʒet], *s.* Zucchini *f.*
**courier** ['kuriər], *s.* 1. Reiseleiter *m.* 2. *(messenger)* Kurier *m.*
**course** [kɔːs], *s.* 1. *(a)* Lauf *m* (der Ereignisse usw.); **in the c. of time,** im Laufe der Zeit; **in due c.,** zu seiner Zeit; **to let things take their c.,** den Dingen ihren Lauf lassen; *(b)* **of c.,** natürlich, selbstverständlich; **of c. not,** natürlich nicht; **a matter of c.,** eine Selbstverständlichkeit. 2. *(a) Sch:* Kurs *m;* Lehrgang *m;* *(b) Med:* **c. of treatment,** Behandlung *f.* 3. *(a)* Richtung *f; Nau:* Kurs *m;* *(b)* **to follow a c. of action,** eine Linie verfolgen. 4. *Cu:* Gang *m.* 5. *(a)* **golf c.,** Golfplatz *m;* *(b)* **race c.,** Rennstrecke *f.*
**court** [kɔːt]. **I.** *s.* 1. *(royal)* Hof *m.* 2. *Jur:* Gericht *n.* 3. **tennis c.,** Tennisplatz *m.* **II.** *v.tr.* (einer Frau) den Hof machen; **to c. disaster,** Unheil herausfordern. ◆**courteous** ['kɔːtjəs], *adj.* höflich. ◆**courtesy** ['kɔːtisi], *s.* Höflichkeit *f.* ◆**'court-'martial.** **I.** *s.* Militärgericht *n.* **II.** *v.tr.* (j-n) vor ein Militärgericht stellen. ◆**'courtship,** *s.* Werbung *f* (**of,** um + *acc).* ◆**'courtyard,** *s.* Hof *m.*
**cousin** ['kʌzn], *s.* *(male)* Vetter *m;* *(female)* Kusine *f.*
**cove** [kəuv], *s.* kleine Bucht *f.*
**cover** ['kʌvər]. **I.** *s.* 1. **cushion c.,** Kissenbezug *m;* *(lid)* Deckel *m* (eines Kochtopfs usw.). 2. *(a)* Deckel *m* (eines Buches); *(b)* Titelseite *f* (einer Zeitschrift); **c. girl,** Covergirl *n.* 4. **under separate c.,** mit getrennter Post. 5. *(protection)* Schutz *m;* **to take c.,** Schutz suchen, *Mil:* in Deckung gehen; *(insurance)*

c. note, Deckungszusage f. II. v.tr. (a) bedecken; (b) (eine Strecke) zurücklegen; (c) (den Bedarf, die Kosten) decken; (d) (ein Thema usw.) (umfassend) behandeln; (in media) (über etwas acc) berichten. ◆'coverage, s. (in media) Berichterstattung f. ◆'cover 'up, v.tr. (a) zudecken; (b) (eine Spur, einen Fehler usw.) verbergen; (eine peinliche Angelegenheit usw.) vertuschen.

**cow** [kau], s. Kuh f. ◆'cowboy, s. Cowboy m.

**coward** ['kauəd], s. Feigling m. ◆'cowardice, s. Feigheit f. ◆'cowardly, adj. feige.

**cower** ['kauər], v.i. sich ducken.

**cowslip** ['kauslip], s. Schlüsselblume f.

**cox** [kɔks], s. Nau: Steuermann m.

**coy** [kɔi], adj. (a) scheu; (b) (affectedly modest) zimperlich.

**crab** [kræb], s. Krabbe f.

**crack** [kræk]. I. s. 1. (of gun, whip etc.) Knall m. 2. Riß m; (in glass etc.) Sprung m. 3. F: I'll have a c. at it, ich werde es mal versuchen. II. adj. F: erstklassig; c. shot, Meisterschütze m. III. v. 1. v.tr. (a) (eine Nuß) knacken; to c. a plate, einen Sprung in einen Teller machen; (b) F: (einen Safe, einen Kode) knacken; (c) to c. jokes, Witze reißen. 2. v.i. (of glass etc.) einen Sprung bekommen; (of wall etc.) einen Riß/Risse bekommen; F: get cracking, mach dich dran; (hurry) mach fix! ◆'cracked, adj. (a) (of glass etc.) gesprungen; (of wall, skin etc.) rissig; (b) F: (of person) übergeschnappt. ◆'crack 'down, v.tr. to c. down on sth., harte Maßnahmen gegen etwas acc treffen. ◆'crack 'up, v. 1. v.tr. F: he's not all he's cracked up to be, er ist nicht so gut wie sein Ruf. 2. v.i. (of pers.) zusammenbrechen.

**crackle** ['krækl]. I. v.i. (of fire etc.) knistern. II. s. Knistern n. ◆'crackling n. knusprige Schwarte f (des Schweinebratens).

**cradle** ['kreidl], s. Wiege f.

**craft¹** [krɑ:ft], s. Handwerk n. ◆'craftsman, pl. -men, s. Handwerker m. ◆'craftsmanship, s. handwerkliches Geschick n. ◆'crafty, adj. schlau; Pej: (hinter)listig.

**craft²**, s. Fahrzeug n; coll. Fahrzeuge npl.

**crag** [kræg], s. Felszacke f.

**cram** [kræm], 1. v.tr. (etwas in einen Koffer, in den Mund usw.) hineinstopfen. 2. v.i. (a) sich hineinzwängen; (b) F: to c. for an examination, für eine Prüfung pauken.

**cramp** [kræmp]. I. s. Krampf m. II. v.tr. F: to c. s.o.'s style, hemmend auf j-n wirken. ◆'cramped, adj. eng.

**crane** [krein]. I. s. 1. Z: Kranich m. 2. Tchn: Kran m. II. v.tr. to c. one's neck, den Hals recken.

**crank** [kræŋk], s. verschrobener Typ m; Sonderling m. ◆'crankshaft, s. Kurbel-

**welle** f.

**crash** [kræʃ]. I. s. 1. Krach m. 2. Fin: Sturz m. 3. (a) Aut: Rail: Unglück n; (collision) Zusammenstoß m; c. helmet, Sturzhelm m; (b) Av: Absturz m. 4. attrib. c. course, Intensivkurs m. II. v.i. (a) krachen; (b) Aut: Rail: verunglücken; (of two cars) zusammenstoßen; to c. into a tree, gegen einen Baum fahren; (c) Av: abstürzen. ◆'crash-land, v.i. Av: eine Bruchlandung machen.

**crate** [kreit], s. Kiste f.

**crater** ['kreitər], s. (a) Krater m; (b) (bomb) c., Trichter m.

**craving** ['kreiviŋ], s. Begierde f, (of pregnant woman) Gelüste npl (for, nach + dat).

**crawl** [krɔːl]. I. v.i. (a) (of worm, car, pers.) kriechen; (of baby) krabbeln; (b) to be crawling with vermin, von Ungeziefer wimmeln. II. s. (swimming) Kraulen n; to do the c., kraulen.

**crayon** ['kreiən,-ɔn], s. Farbstift m.

**craze** [kreiz], s. F: Masche f. ◆'crazy, adj. verrückt; to be c. about s.o., verrückt nach j-m sein.

**creak** [kriːk]. I. v.i. knarren. II. s. Knarren n.

**cream** [kriːm], s. 1. Sahne f; c. cheese, Rahmkäse m. 2. Elite f; the c. of society, die Spitzen der Gesellschaft. 3. (face c.) Creme f. 4. attrib. c.(-coloured), cremefarben. ◆'creamy, adj. sahnig.

**crease** [kriːs]. I. v. 1. v.tr. (a) (Papier usw.) falten; (b) (ein Kleid usw.) zerknittern. 2. v.i. (of material etc.) knittern. II. s. Falte f.

**create** [kriˈeit], v.tr. schaffen; (einen Eindruck) machen; (Schwierigkeiten usw.) hervorrufen. ◆cre'ation, s. Schöpfung f. ◆cre'ative, adj. schöpferisch. ◆cre'ator, s. Schöpfer m. ◆creature ['kriːtʃər], s. 1. Geschöpf n. 2. c. comforts, Bequemlichkeiten fpl.

**crèche** [kreiʃ], s. Kinderkrippe f.

**credentials** [kriˈden(t)(ə)lz], s.pl. 1. Papiere npl; (references) Zeugnisse npl. 2. Fig: (qualifications) Voraussetzungen fpl.

**credible** ['kredibl], adj. glaubwürdig. ◆credi'bility, s. Glaubwürdigkeit f.

**credit** ['kredit]. I. s. 1. Com: Kredit m; to buy sth. on c., etwas auf Kredit kaufen; c. note, Gutschein m; c. card, Kreditkarte f. 2. Ehre f; it does him c., es macht ihm Ehre; to take the c. for sth., sich dat etwas als Verdienst anrechnen. II. v.tr. (a) to c. s.o. with a sum, j-m einen Betrag gutschreiben; (b) I credited you with more sense, ich hielt dich für vernünftiger. ◆'creditor, s. Gläubiger m.

**creed** [kriːd], s. Kredo n.

**creep** [kriːp]. I. v.i.irr. schleichen. II. s. F: it gives me the creeps, mir gruselt es davor. ◆'creepy, adj. gruselig.

**cremate** [kriˈmeit], v.tr. einäschern.

◆**cre'mation**, s. Einäscherung f.

◆**crematorium** [kremə'tɔːriəm], s. Krematorium n.

**crêpe** [kreip], s. **1. c. bandage**, elastische Binde f. **2. c.(-rubber) sole**, Kreppsohle f.

**cress** [kres], s. Kresse f; **water-c.**, Brunnenkresse f.

**crest** [krest], s. **1.** (of bird) Haube f. **2.** (of hill, wave) Kamm m. **3.** (coat of arms) Wappen n. ◆**'crestfallen**, adj. (of pers.) betreten.

**Crete** [kriːt], Pr.n. Kreta n.

**crew** [kruː], s. **1.** Besatzung f. **2.** Pej: Bande f. **3. c. cut**, Bürstenschnitt m.

**crib** [krib]. **1.** s. Krippe f. **2. (baby's) c.**, Kinderbett n.

**crick** [krik], s. **to have a c. in one's neck/back**, sich dat den Hals/den Rücken verrenkt haben.

**cricket** ['krikit], s. Sp: Kricket n. ◆**'cricketer**, s. Kricketspieler m.

**crime** [kraim], s. Verbrechen n. ◆**criminal** ['kriminl]. **I.** adj. kriminell; (punishable) strafbar; **to have a c. record**, vorbestraft sein. **II.** s. Verbrecher m.

**crimson** ['krimz(ə)n], adj. purpurrot.

**cringe** [krindʒ], v.i. (in fear) sich ducken.

**crinkle** ['kriŋkl], v.tr. & i. (Papier) knittern.

**cripple** ['kripl]. **I.** s. Krüppel m. **II.** v.tr. (a) (j-n) zum Krüppel machen; **crippled with arthritis**, durch Arthritis gelähmt; (b) Fig: lähmen.

**crisis**, pl. **crises** ['kraisis, -iːz], s. Krise f.

**crisp** [krisp]. **I.** adj. **1.** knusprig. **2.** (of air, weather) frisch. **3.** (of literary style) knapp. **II.** s. (potato) crisps, Chips pl.

**criterion**, pl. **-ia** [krai'tiəriən, -iə], s. Kriterium n.

**critic** ['kritik], s. Kritiker m. ◆**'critical**, adj. kritisch; **-ly**, adv. **c. ill**, schwerkrank. ◆**'criticism** [-isiz(ə)m], s. Kritik f. ◆**'criticize** [-isaiz], v.tr. kritisieren.

**croak** [krəuk]. **I.** v.i. (of frog) quaken; (of raven, pers.) krächzen. **II.** s. Krächzer m. ◆**'croaky**, adj. krächzend.

**crochet** ['krəuʃei], v.tr. & i. häkeln.

**crockery** ['krɔkəri], s. Geschirr n.

**crocodile** ['krɔkədail], s. Krokodil n.

**crocus** ['krəukəs], pl. **crocuses** [krəukəs, -əsiz], s. Krokus m.

**crony** ['krəuni], s. P: Kumpan m.

**crook** [kruk], s. F: Gauner m. ◆**crooked** ['krukid], adj. **1.** (bent) krumm; (at the wrong angle) schief. **2.** Fig: (of pers.) unehrlich.

**crop** [krɔp], s. **1.** Ernte f. **2. (riding) c.**, Reitstock m. ◆**'crop 'up**, v.i. F: auftauchen.

**cross** [krɔs]. **I.** s. **1.** Kreuz n. **2.** Bot: Z: Kreuzung f. **II.** v. **1.** v.tr. (a) (die Straße usw.) überqueren; (die Wüste) durchqueren; **it crossed my mind that …** der Ge-

danke ging mir durch den Kopf, daß …; (b) (die Beine) übereinanderschlagen …; **to keep one's fingers crossed for s.o.**, j-m die Daumen drücken; (c) (Tierrassen usw.) kreuzen; (d) **crossed cheque** Verrechnungsscheck m. **2.** v.i. (a) (of lines, roads etc.) sich kreuzen; (b) **to c. from Dover to Calais**, die Überfahrt von Dover nach Calais machen. **III.** adj. **1.** F: böse. **2.** (in compounds) Quer-. ◆**'cross-'country**. **I.** adv. querfeldein. **II.** s. s.c. (run), Geländelauf m. ◆**'cross-exami'nation**, s. Kreuzverhör n. ◆**'cross-e'xamine**, v.tr. (j-n) ins Kreuzverhör nehmen. ◆**'cross-eyed**, adj. schielend. ◆**'crossfire**, s. Kreuzfeuer n. ◆**'crossing**, s. **1.** (sea journey) Überfahrt f. **2.** (road, railway) Kreuzung f; **level c.**, Bahnübergang m; **(pedestrian) c.**, Fußgängerübergang m. ◆**'cross-legged**, adv. mit gekreuzten Beinen. ◆**'cross-'purposes**, s. **to talk at c.-p.**, aneinander vorbeireden. ◆**'crossroads**, s. Straßenkreuzung f. ◆**'crossword**, s. c. (puzzle), Kreuzworträtsel n.

**crotchet** ['krɔtʃit], s. Viertelnote f. ◆**'crotchety**, adj. mürrisch.

**crouch** [krautʃ], v.i. hocken.

**crow** [krəu], s. Krähe f; **as the c. flies**, in der Luftlinie.

**crowd** [kraud]. **I.** s. Menge f. **II.** v. **1.** v.i. **to c. (together)**, sich drängen. **2.** v.tr. **to c. (into) a room**, sich in ein Zimmer hineindrängen. ◆**'crowded**, adj. überfüllt.

**crown** [kraun]. **I.** s. Krone f. **II.** v.tr. **to c. s.o. king**, j-n zum König krönen.

**crucial** ['kruːʃ(ə)l], adj. entscheidend.

**crucifix** ['kruːsifiks], s. Kruzifix n. ◆**crucifixion** [-'fikʃ(ə)n], s. Kreuzigung f. ◆**'crucify**, v.tr. kreuzigen.

**crude** [kruːd], adj. **1.** (of raw material) roh; **c. oil**, Rohöl n. **2.** (of pers., manners etc.) grob; (of structure etc.) primitiv. ◆**'crudeness/'crudity**, s. primitive Art f; (of pers., language etc.) Grobheit f.

**cruel** ['kruəl], adj. grausam. ◆**'cruelty**, s. Grausamkeit f; **c. to animals**, Tierquälerei f.

**cruet** ['kru(ː)it], s. H: **c.(-stand)** Menage f.

**cruise** [kruːz]. **I.** s. Nau: Kreuzfahrt f. **II.** v.i. Nau: kreuzen; **cruising speed**, Reisegeschwindigkeit f. ◆**'cruiser**, s. (a) Nau: Kreuzer m; (b) **motor c./(cabin) c.**, Kajütboot n.

**crumb** [krʌm], s. Krümel m. ◆**crumble** ['krʌmbl], v.tr. & i. (Brot usw.) krümeln; (of walls, Fig: of empire) zerfallen.

**crumpet** ['krʌmpit], s. salziges Hefegebäck n.

**crumple** ['krʌmpl], v.tr. (etwas) zerdrücken; (ein Kleid, Papier usw.) zerknittern.

**crunch** [krʌn(t)ʃ]. **I.** v. **1.** v.tr. (einen Keks usw.) geräuschvoll essen. **2.** v.i. (of snow, gravel etc.) knirschen. **II.** s. F:

**when it comes to the c.**, wenn es darauf ankommt.

**crusade** [kruːˈseid], s. Kreuzzug m.

**crush** [krʌʃ]. I. v.tr. zerdrücken. II. s. 1. (crowd) Gedränge n. 2. F: **to have a c. on s.o.**, für j-n schwärmen. ◆'**crushing**, adj. (of defeat, reply etc.) vernichtend.

**crust** [krʌst], s. Kruste f. ◆'**crusty**, adj. (of bread etc.) krustig.

**crutch** [krʌtʃ], s. (for disabled) Krücke f.

**crux** [krʌks], s. **the c. (of the matter)**, der springende Punkt.

**cry** [krai]. I. v. 1. v.i. (a) (weep) weinen; (b) **to c. (out)**, schreien; (c) (exclaim) rufen. 2. v.tr. weinen. II. s. 1. Ruf m. 2. **to have a good c.**, sich ausweinen.

**cryptic** [ˈkriptik], adj. rätselhaft.

**crystal** [ˈkristl], s. 1. Kristall m. 2. **c. (-glass)**, Kristall n; **c. ball**, Kristallkugel f; **c.-clear**, kristallklar. ◆'**crystallize**, v.i. kristallisieren; (of plan etc.) feste Form annehmen.

**cub** [kʌb], s. 1. Junge(s) n; **bear c.**, Bärenjunge(s) n. 2. (scout) Wölfling m.

**cube** [kjuːb], s. Würfel m. ◆'**cubic**, adj. Kubik-; **c. meter**, Kubikmeter m & n; **c. capacity**, Kubikinhalt m; Aut: Hubraum m.

**cubicle** [ˈkjuːbikl], s. Kabine f.

**cubism** [ˈkjuːbiz(ə)m], s. Kubismus m.

**cuckoo** [ˈkukuː], s. Kuckuck m.

**cucumber** [ˈkjuːkʌmbər], s. Gurke f.

**cuddle** [ˈkʌdl], v. 1. v.tr. (ein Kind usw.) herzen. 2. v.i. **to c. up to s.o.**, sich an j-n kuscheln. ◆'**cuddly**, adj. F: kuschelig; **c. toy**, Kuscheltier n.

**cue¹** [kjuː], s. Th: Stichwort n.

**cue²**, s. **billiard c.**, Billardqueue n.

**cuff** [kʌf], s. 1. (of shirt etc.) Manschette f; F: **off the c.**, aus dem Stegreif. 2. N.Am: **trouser c.**, Hosenaufschlag m. ◆'**cuff-links**, s.pl. Manschettenknöpfe mpl.

**cuisine** [kwiˈziːn], s. Kochkunst f.

**cul-de-sac** [ˈkʌldəsæk], s. Sackgasse f.

**culinary** [ˈkʌlinəri], adj. kulinarisch.

**culminate** [ˈkʌlmineit], v.i. **to c. in sth.**, in etwas dat gipfeln. ◆culmiˈnation, s. Gipfelpunkt m.

**culprit** [ˈkʌlprit], s. Täter m.

**cult** [kʌlt], s. Kult m.

**cultivate** [ˈkʌltiveit], v.tr. (a) (das Land) bebauen; (Getreide, Wein usw.) anbauen; (b) (die Musik usw.) pflegen. ◆'**cultivated**, adj. (of pers.) kultiviert. ◆culti'**vation**, s. Kultivierung f.

**culture** [ˈkʌltʃər], s. Kultur f. ◆'**cultural**, adj. kulturell. ◆'**cultured**, adj. kultiviert.

**cumbersome** [ˈkʌmbəsəm], adj. unhandlich.

**cumulative** [ˈkjuːmjulətiv], adj. kumulativ.

**cunning** [ˈkʌniŋ]. I. s. Schlauheit f. II. adj. schlau; Pej: listig.

**cup** [kʌp], s. 1. Tasse f; **a c. of tea**, eine

Tasse Tee; F: **that's not my c. of tea**, das ist nicht mein Fall. 2. Sp: Pokal m; **c. final**, Pokalendspiel n. ◆'**cupful**, s. **c. of sugar**, Tasse f Zucker.

**cupboard** [ˈkʌbəd], s. Schrank m.

**curator** [kjuəˈreitər], s. Kustos m (eines Museums usw.).

**curb** [kəːb]. I. s. = **kerb**. II. v.tr. (sich, seinen Zorn usw.) im Zaum halten.

**curdle** [ˈkəːdl], v. 1. v.i. (of milk etc.) gerinnen. 2. v.tr. zum Gerinnen bringen.

**cure** [ˈkjuər]. I. v.tr. (a) heilen; (b) (smoke) räuchern; (salt) einsalzen. II. s. 1. (process) Heilung f. 2. (a) (treatment) Kur f; (b) (remedy) Heilmittel n (for, gegen + acc).

**curfew** [ˈkəːfjuː], s. Ausgehverbot n.

**curiosity** [kjuəriˈɔsiti], s. Neugier f. ◆'**curious**, adj. 1. (of pers.) neugierig. 2. (strange) merkwürdig.

**curl** [kəːl]. I. s. (of hair) Locke f. II. v. 1. v.tr. **to c. one's hair**, sich dat Locken drehen. 2. v.i. sich locken. ◆'**curler**, s. Lockenwickler m. ◆'**curl 'up**, v.i. (of cat etc.) sich zusammenrollen; (of pers.) F: es sich gemütlich machen. ◆'**curly**, adj. lockig.

**currant** [ˈkʌrənt], s. Korinthe f.

**currency** [ˈkʌrənsi], s. Währung f; **foreign c.**, Devisen pl.

**current** [ˈkʌrənt]. I. s. 1. (in water, also Fig:) Strömung f. 2. (electric) c., (elektrischer) Strom m. II. adj. 1. (of words etc.) geläufig; (of opinions etc.) herrschend. 2. (present) gegenwärtig; (topical) aktuell; **c. affairs**, aktuelle Fragen; **c. account**, Girokonto; **-ly**, adv. gegenwärtig.

**curriculum** [kəˈrikjuləm], s. (a) Lehrplan m; (b) **c. vitae**, Lebenslauf m.

**curry¹** [ˈkʌri], s. Curry n.

**curry²**, v.tr. **to c. favour with s.o.**, sich in j-s Gunst einschmeicheln.

**curse** [kəːs]. I. s. Fluch m. II. v. 1. v.tr. (j-n) verfluchen. 2. v.i. fluchen.

**cursory** [ˈkəːsəri], adj. flüchtig.

**curt** [kəːt], adj. barsch.

**curtail** [kəːˈteil], v.tr. abkürzen.

**curtain** [ˈkəːt(ə)n], s. (a) Gardine f; (b) Th: Vorhang m.

**curve** [kəːv]. I. s. Kurve f. II. v.i. sich biegen. ◆'**curved**, adj. gebogen.

**cushion** [ˈkuʃ(ə)n]. I. s. Kissen n. II. v.tr. (einen Stoß) dämpfen. ◆cushy [ˈkuʃi], adj. F: bequem.

**custard** [ˈkʌstəd], s. Vanillesoße f.

**custody** [ˈkʌstədi], s. 1. Obhut f; Sorgerecht n (**of a child**, über ein Kind). 2. Jur: Haft f. ◆custodian [-ˈtəudiən], s. Wächter m.

**custom** [ˈkʌstəm], s. 1. (tradition) Brauch m; (habit) Gepflogenheit f. 2. Com: Kundschaft f. 3. **customs**, Zoll m. ◆'**customary**, adj. gewohnt; (of walk, drink etc.) gewohnheitsmäßig. ◆'**custom-'built**, adj. in Sonderausführung gebaut. ◆'**customer**, s. Kunde m.

◆'custom-'made, adj. in Sonderausführung; (of clothes) maßgeschneidert.

cut [kʌt]. I. v.irr. 1. v.i. (of knife etc.) schneiden; (Gras, Getreide usw.) mähen; (Holz) hacken; (einen Schlüssel) anfertigen; (ein Stück Kuchen) abschneiden; to. c. one's finger, sich dat in den Finger schneiden; (b) (Preise, Steuern usw.) herabsetzen; (j-s Gehalt usw.) kürzen; (c) to c. (the cards), abheben; (d) to c. s.o. (dead), j-n schneiden; Fig: to c. corners, es sich leicht machen; (of builder etc.) an allen Ecken und Enden sparen. II. s. 1. Schnitt m; (wound) Schnittwunde f. 2. (reduction) Kürzung f (in salary etc., des Gehalts usw.); power c., Stromsperre f. 3. Schnitt m (eines Anzuges usw.). 4. Cu: c. (of meat), Fleischstück m. 5. short c., Abkürzung f. 6. F: (share) Anteil m. III. adj. c. glass, Kristall n; c. and dried, (of opinion) vorgefaßt; (of plans etc.) fix und fertig. ◆'cutback, s. Kürzung f (in expenditure, der Ausgaben). ◆'cut 'down, v.tr. (a) (einen Baum) fällen; (b) (seine Ausgaben usw.) reduzieren. ◆'cut 'in, v.i. (a) Aut: to c. in on s.o., j-n schneiden; (b) to c. in on a conversation, ein Gespräch unterbrechen. ◆'cut 'off, v.tr. abschneiden; Tel: we've been c. o., wir sind unterbrochen worden. ◆'cut 'out, v. 1. v.i. (of engine) aussetzen. 2. v.tr. (a) ausschneiden; (ein Kleid usw.) zuschneiden;

(b) Fig: (of pers.) to be c. o. for sth., zu etwas dat geeignet sein; F: c. it o.! laß das sein! ◆'cut 'short, v.tr. abkürzen; to c. a long story s., um es kurz zu machen. ◆'cutting. I. s. 1. Ausschnitt m. 2. (of plant) Ableger m. II. adj. also Fig: schneidend; c. edge, Schneide f; c. remark, bissige Bemerkung. ◆'cut 'up, v.tr. (a) (Fleisch, Wurst) aufschneiden; (Papier, Stoff usw.) zerschneiden; (b) F: to c. up rough, aggressiv werden.

cute [kju:t], adj. niedlich.

cutlery ['kʌtləri], s. Besteck n.

cutlet ['kʌtlit], s. Kotelett n.

cyanide ['saiənaid], s. Zyanid n.

cycle ['saikl]. I. s. 1. Zyklus m. 2. (bicycle) Fahrrad n; c. track, Radweg m. II. v.i. (mit dem Rad) fahren. ◆'cyclist, s. Radfahrer m.

cyclone ['saikləun], s. Zyklon m.

cylinder ['silindər], s. (a) Zylinder m; (b) oxygen c., Sauerstoffflasche f. ◆cy'lindrical, adj. zylindrisch.

cynic ['sinik], s. Zyniker m. ◆'cynical, adj. zynisch. ◆'cynicism, s. Zynismus m.

cypress ['saiprəs], s. Zypresse f.

Cyprus ['saiprəs]. Pr.n. Zypern n.

cyst [sist], s. Zyste f.

Czech [tʃek]. I. s. 1. Tscheche m; Tschechin f. 2. (language) Tschechisch n. II. adj. tschechisch. ◆Czechoslovakia [ˈtʃekəˌsləu(ˈ)vækiə]. Pr.n. die Tschechoslowakei f.

# D

D, d [di:], s. (der Buchstabe) D, d n.

dab [dæb]. I. s. 1. (tap) Tupfer m. 2. (of paint etc.) Klecks m. 3. F: to be a d. hand at sth., in etwas dat sehr geschickt sein. II. v.tr. abtupfen.

dabble ['dæbl], v.i. F: to d. in law/politics, sich oberflächlich mit Recht/Politik befassen.

dachshund ['dækshund], s. Dackel m.

dad [dæd], daddy ['dædi], s. F: Vati m. ◆'daddy-'long-legs, s. (a) Brit: Schnake f; (b) N.Am: Weberknecht m.

daffodil ['dæfədil], s. Osterglocke f; gelbe Narzisse f.

daft [dɑ:ft], adj. F: verrückt; P: doof.

dagger ['dægər], s. Dolch m.

dahlia ['deiliə], s. Dahlie f.

daily ['deili], adj. & adv. täglich; Tages-; d. (paper), Tageszeitung f.

dainty ['deinti], adj. zierlich.

dairy ['dɛəri], s. 1. Molkerei f; d. farming, Milchwirtschaft f; d. produce, Molkereiprodukte npl. 2. (shop) Milchgeschäft n.

daisy ['deizi], s. Gänseblümchen n; (large) Margerite f.

dam [dæm]. I. s. Staudamm m; (across

valley) Talsperre f. II. v.tr. to d. (up) a river etc., einen Fluß usw. stauen.

damage ['dæmidʒ]. I. s. 1. Schaden m. 2. pl. Jur: Schadenersatz m. II. v.tr. beschädigen; Fig: (einer Person, dem Ruf) schaden. ◆'damaged, adj. beschädigt. ◆'damaging, adj. schädlich.

damn [dæm]. I. s. P: I don't give a d., das kümmert mich einen Dreck. II. adj. P: verdammt; this d. job! diese Scheißarbeit! III. int. d. it! verdammt! IV. v.tr. verdammen. ◆'damned, adj. 1. verdammt. 2. F: (a) what a d. nuisance, verflucht unangenehm; to do one's damnedest, sein möglichstes tun; (b) adv. (intensive) it's d. hard! es ist verflucht schwer! a d. sight better, bei weitem besser. ◆'damning, adj. (of criticism etc.) vernichtend.

damp [dæmp]. I. s. Feuchtigkeit f. II. adj. feucht. ◆'dampen, v.tr. (Eifer usw.) dämpfen. ◆'damper. s. to put a d. on the celebrations, den Festlichkeiten einen Dämpfer aufsetzen.

dance [dɑ:ns]. I. s. 1. Tanz m. 2. (occasion) Tanzabend m; (smart) Ball m. II. v.tr. & i. tanzen. ◆'dancer, s. Tänzer(in) *m(f)*. ◆'**dancing,** *s.* Tanzen *n.*

**dandelion** ['dændilaiən], *s.* Löwenzahn *m.*

**dandruff** ['dændrʌf], *s.* Schuppen *pl.*

**Dane** [dein], *s.* **1.** Däne *m*; Dänin *f.* **2.** *(dog)* **(Great) D.,** Dänische Dogge *f.* ◆'**Danish. I.** *adj.* dänisch; **D. pastry,** Hefeteilchen *n*; *(coiled)* Schnecke *f.* **II.** *s. (language)* Dänisch *n.*

**danger** ['deindʒər], *s.* Gefahr *f* (**to sth.,** für etwas *acc*). ◆'**dangerous,** *adj.* gefährlich.

**dangle** ['dæŋgl], *v.* **1.** *v.i.* baumeln. **2.** *v.tr.* (etwas) baumeln lassen; (Beine, Arme) schlenkern.

**Danube** ['dænju:b]. *Pr.n.* **the D.,** die Donau.

**dare** [dɛər], *v.* **1.** *modal aux.* (es) wagen; **how d. you!** was fällt dir ein! **I d. say (that)** ..., ich glaube schon, daß ... **2.** *v.tr.* (a) **to d. to do sth.,** (es) wagen, etwas zu tun; (b) **to d. s.o. to do sth.,** j-n herausfordern, etwas zu tun. ◆'**daredevil,** *s.* Draufgänger *m.* ◆'**daring. I.** *adj.* (a) *(of pers.)* kühn; (b) *(of action)* gewagt. **II.** *s.* Kühnheit *f.*

**dark** [dɑ:k]. **I.** *adj.* dunkel; *(sombre)* düster; (pitch) **d.,** finster; **d. green,** dunkelgrün; *F:* **to keep sth. d.,** etwas geheimhalten; **d. horse,** unbekannte Größe. **II.** *s.* **1.** Dunkelheit *f.* **2.** *F:* **to keep s.o. in the d.,** j-n im Ungewissen lassen. ◆'**darken. 1.** *v.tr.* verdunkeln. **2.** *v.i.* sich verdunkeln. ◆'**darkness,** *s.* Dunkelheit *f*; (pitch) **d.,** Finsternis *f.*

**darling** ['dɑ:liŋ], *s.* Liebling *m.*

**darn** [dɑ:n], *v.tr.* stopfen.

**dart** [dɑ:t]. **1.** *s.* Pfeil *m.* **II.** *v.i.* **to d. in/out,** herein-/hinausflitzen.

**dash** [dæʃ]. **1.** *s.* **1.** Schuß *m* (Rum, Whisky); **d. of colour,** Farbklecks *m.* **2.** *(line)* Strich *m*; Gedankenstrich *m.* **3.** (a) *(rush)* Sturz *m*; **to make a d. for sth.,** sich auf etwas *acc* stürzen; (b) *N.Am: Sp:* Sprint *m.* **II.** *v.i.* (sich) stürzen; **I have to d.,** ich muß lossausen. ◆'**dashboard,** *s.* Armaturenbrett *n.* ◆'**dash 'off,** *v.* **1.** *v.i.* lossausen. **2.** *v.tr.* (einen Aufsatz usw.) hinhauen.

**data** ['dɑ:tə, 'deitə], *s.pl.* Daten *pl*; **d. processing,** Datenverarbeitung *f.*

**date¹** [deit], *s.* *(fruit)* Dattel *f.*

**date².** **I.** *s.* **1.** Datum *n*; **what's the d. today?** der wievielte ist heute? **to fix a d.,** einen Termin festsetzen; **to be up to d.,** auf dem laufenden sein; **to bring sth. up to d.,** etwas auf den neuesten Stand bringen; **out of d.,** (i) überholt; veraltet; (ii) *(expired)* ungültig; **to d.,** bis heute. **2.** *F:* Verabredung *f*; **to have a d. with s.o.,** mit j-m verabredet sein. **II.** *v.* **1.** *v.tr.* (einen Brief, ein Kunstwerk usw.) datieren. **2.** *v.i.* **to d. back to,** zurückreichen bis. ◆'**dated,** *adj.* (a) *(of letter etc.)* datiert; (b) *(old-fashioned)* veraltet.

**dative** ['deitiv], *s.* Dativ *m.*

**daub** [dɔ:b], *v.tr.* beschmieren; *(Farbe)* schmieren.

**daughter** ['dɔ:tər], *s.* Tochter *f.* ◆'**daughter-in-law,** *s.* Schwiegertochter *f.*

**daunting** ['dɔ:ntiŋ], *adj.* überwältigend; **d. task,** gewaltige Aufgabe.

**dawdle** ['dɔ:dl], *v.i.* trödeln.

**dawn** [dɔ:n]. **I.** *s.* Morgengrauen *n*; **at d.,** bei Tagesanbruch. **II.** *v.i.* (a) *(of day)* anbrechen; (b) *Fig:* **at last it dawned on me that** ..., endlich kam es mir zum Bewußtsein, daß ... ◆'**daybreak,** *s.* Tagesanbruch *m.* ◆'**daydream. I.** *s.* Wachtraum *m.* **II.** *v.i.* Luftschlösser bauen. ◆'**daylight,** *s.* Tageslicht *n*; **in broad d.,** am hellichten Tag. ◆'**daytime,** *s.* Tageszeit *f*; **in the d.,** bei Tage.

**day** [dei], *s.* **1.** (a) Tag *m*; **to call it a d.,** für heute Schluß machen; **that made my d.,** da habe ich mich königlich gefreut; **that'll be the d.!** das möchte ich mal erleben! (b) *attrib.* **d. shift,** Tagschicht *f*; **d. return (ticket),** Tagesrückfahrkarte *f.* **2. those were the days!** das waren noch Zeiten! **in our d.,** zu unserer Zeit; **I was a student in those days,** damals war ich Student; **these days,** heutzutage.

**daze** [deiz], *s.* **in a d.,** benommen.

**dazzle** ['dæzl], *v.tr.* (j-n) blenden. ◆'**dazzling,** *adj.* blendend.

**dead** [ded]. **I.** *adj.* **1.** (a) tot; *(of flower)* verwelkt; **d. body,** Leiche *f*; (b) *(of limb)* **to go d.,** taub werden; **Cologne is d. at weekends,** Köln ist am Wochenende wie ausgestorben. **2.** *(complete)* völlig; ganz; **d. loss,** Totalverlust *m*; **d. on time,** auf die Minute pünktlich; **d. heat,** totes Rennen. **II.** *s.* **1.** *pl.* **the d.,** die Toten *mpl.* **2. at d. of night,** mitten in der Nacht; **in the d. of winter,** im tiefsten Winter. **III.** *adv.* (a) völlig; ganz; **d. tired/***F:* **beat,** todmüde; (b) **to d. stop d.,** plötzlich stehenbleiben; (c) **I am d. against it,** ich bin ganz dagegen. *(Also Schall usw.)* dämpfen; (Schmerz) betäuben. ◆'**deaden,** *v.tr.* *(den Schall usw.)* dämpfen; (Schmerz) betäuben. ◆'**dead-'end,** *s.* (a) Sackgasse *f*; (b) *attrib.* ohne Ausweg; ohne Chancen. ◆'**deadline,** *s.* (äußerster) Termin *m.* ◆'**deadlock,** *s.* **to reach d.,** sich festfahren. ◆'**deadly,** *adj.* tödlich. ◆'**dead'pan,** *adj.* ausdruckslos.

**deaf** [def], *adj.* taub. ◆'**deafen,** *v.tr.* (j-n) taub machen. ◆'**deafening,** *adj.* ohrenbetäubend. ◆'**deaf-'mute,** *s.* Taubstumme(r) *f(m).* ◆'**deafness,** *s.* Taubheit *f.*

**deal¹** [di:l], *s.* (a) *(part)* **a good d. of the time,** ein Großteil der Zeit; (b) *(amount)* **a great d. of money,** eine Menge Geld; **he is a good d. better,** ihm geht es viel besser.

**deal².** **I.** *v.irr.* **1.** *v.tr.* (a) **to d. out (gifts etc.),** (Geschenke usw.) austeilen; (b) **to d. s.o. a blow,** j-m einen Schlag versetzen; (c) (Karten) geben. **2.** *v.i.* (a) **to deal with sth.,** (i) *(of book etc.)* von etwas *dat* handeln; (ii) (of pers.) etwas erledigen; **to d. with s.o.**, mit j-m fertig werden; *Com:* **to d. with a firm**, mit einer Firma Geschäfte machen; (b) (at cards) geben. **II.** s. Geschäft n; (agreement) Abmachung f; *F:* **it's a d.!** abgemacht! **he got a raw d.**, er hat schlecht dabei abgeschnitten. ◆**'dealer**, s. **1.** (at cards) Kartengeber m. **2.** *Com:* Händler m. ◆**'dealing**, s. pl. **to have dealings with s.o.**, mit j-m (geschäftlich) zu tun haben.

**dean** [di:n], s. Dekan m.

**dear** [diər]. **I.** adj. **1.** lieb; (in letter) **D. Mr. Smith**, Sehr geehrter Herr Smith; **D. David**, Lieber David. **2.** (expensive) teuer; **-ly**, adv. **to love s.o., sth. d.**, j-n, etwas sehr lieben. **II.** s. Liebe(r,s) f(m,n); **my d.**, mein Lieber m, meine Liebe f. **III.** int. *F:* **d. me!** du meine Güte! **oh d.!** ach je!

**dearth** [də:θ], s. Mangel m (of, an + dat).

**death** [deθ], s. **1.** Tod m; **frozen to d.**, erfroren; **burnt to d.**, verbrannt; **d. penalty**, Todesstrafe f; *F:* **d. trap**, Todesfalle f. **2.** (with number) **five deaths**, fünf Todesfälle mpl; (in accident) fünf Todesopfer npl. ◆**'deathbed**, s. Sterbebett n.

**debate** [di'beit]. **I.** s. Debatte f. **II.** v. **1** v.tr. (ein Thema) debattieren. **2.** v.i. **to d. whether to do sth.**, überlegen, ob man etwas tun sollte. ◆**de'batable**, adj. (of question) strittig; **it's d.**, es ist fraglich.

**debauched** [di'bɔ:tʃt], adj. liederlich.

**debility** [di'biliti], s. Entkräftung f.

**debit** ['debit]. **I.** s. Soll n; (amount) Debetposten m. **II.** v.tr. **to d. s.o./s.o.'s account with a sum**, j-s Konto mit einer Summe belasten.

**debris** ['debri:], s. Trümmer npl.

**debt** [det], s. Schuld f; **to be in d.**, verschuldet sein. ◆**'debtor**, s. Schuldner m.

**debut** ['deibju:, de-], s. Debüt n.

**decade** ['dekeid], s. Jahrzehnt n.

**decadence** ['dekəd(ə)ns], s. Dekadenz f. ◆**'decadent**, adj. dekadent.

**decaffeinated** [di'kæfineitid], adj. koffeinfrei.

**decanter** [di'kæntər], s. Karaffe f.

**decay** [di'kei]. **I.** s. **1.** (decline) Verfall m. **2.** (of matter, teeth) Fäulnis f. **II.** v.i. (a) verkommen; (of building) verfallen; (b) (of vegetable matter, teeth) verfaulen; (of flesh) verwesen.

**deceased** [di'si:st], s. **the d.**, der/die Verstorbene.

**deceit** [di'si:t], s. Betrug m. ◆**de'ceitful**, adj. falsch; (cunning) hinterlistig.

**deceive** [di'si:v], v. **1.** v.tr. (a) betrügen; (b) (mislead) täuschen. **2.** v.i. täuschen.

**December** [di'sembər], s. Dezember m.

**decent** ['di:s(ə)nt], adj. anständig; *F:* **are you d.?** bist du angezogen? **the food is quite d.**, das Essen ist ganz annehmbar. ◆**'decency** [-si], s. Anstand m; **he**

**didn't even have the d. to thank me**, hat es nicht einmal für nötig gehalten, mir zu danken.

**deception** [di'sepʃ(ə)n], s. (a) Betrug m; (b) (misleading) Täuschung f. ◆**de'ceptive**, adj. trügerisch; (misleading) irreführend.

**decibel** ['desibel], s. Dezibel n.

**decide** [di'said], v. **1.** v.tr. entscheiden; **to d. to do sth.**, beschließen, etwas zu tun. **2.** v.i. sich entschließen; **to d. on sth.**, sich zu etwas dat entschließen. ◆**de'cidedly**, adv. **d. fat**, entschieden zu fett. ◆**de'ciding**, adj. entscheidend.

**deciduous** [di'sidjuəs], adj. **d. tree**, Laubbaum m.

**decimal** ['desim(ə)l]. **I.** adj. dezimal; **d. point**, Dezimalpunkt m; **to three d. places** auf drei Dezimalstellen. **II.** s. Dezimalzahl f.

**decipher** [di'saifər], v.tr. entziffern; (in nen Code) entschlüsseln.

**decision** [di'siʒ(ə)n], s. **1.** (a) (of pers.) Entscheidung f; (resolve) Entschluß m; **to reach a d.**, zu einem Entschluß kommen; **to take/make a d.**, (i) einen Entschluß fassen; (ii) eine Entscheidung treffen; (b) (of group, assembly) Beschluß m; *Jur:* Urteil n. **2.** (manner) Entschlossenheit f. ◆**decisive** [-'saisiv], adj. **1.** ausschlaggebend; (of action etc.) entscheidend. **2.** (of pers., manner) entschlossen; **-ly**, adv. entscheidend.

**deck** [dek], s. Deck n; **a d. of cards**, ein Spiel Karten. ◆**'deck-chair**, s. Liegestuhl m.

**declare** [di'kleər], v.tr. & i. erklären; (at customs) **have you anything to d.?** haben Sie etwas zu verzollen? **to d. s.o. the winner**, j-n zum Sieger erklären. ◆**declaration** [deklə'reiʃ(ə)n], s. Erklärung f; (statement) Behauptung f.

**decline** [di'klain]. **I.** s. (a) Niedergang m (eines Reiches usw.); Abfall m (der Preise); **to go into a d./be on the d.**, zur Neige gehen; (b) (deterioration) Verschlechterung f (in morals, der Moral); **d. in standards**, Abfall m des Niveaus; *Sch:* Leistungsabfall m. **II.** v. **1.** v.tr. ablehnen; **he declined to comment**, er enthielt sich eines Kommentars. **2.** v.i. sinken; (of prices) abfallen.

**decode** [di:'kəud], v.tr. entschlüsseln.

**decompose** [di:kəm'pəuz], v.i. verwesen. ◆**decomposition** [-kɔmpə'ziʃ(ə)n], s. Verwesung f.

**décor** ['deikɔ:r], s. Dekor m. ◆**decorate** ['dekəreit], v.tr. (a) (etwas) schmücken; (eine Torte usw.) verzieren; (b) (ein Zimmer) neu streichen (und tapezieren); (c) (j-n) (mit einem Orden) auszeichnen. ◆**deco'ration**, s. **1.** (a) Verzierung f; (b) Dekoration f; **interior d.**, Innenausstattung f. **2.** (medal) Auszeichnung f. ◆**'decorative**, adj. dekorativ. ◆**'decorator**, s. (a) **interior d.**, Innenarchitekt m; (b) **painter and d.**, Maler und Tapezierer *m.*

**decoy** ['di:kɔi], *s.* (*object*) Köder *m;* (*pers., bird*) Lockvogel *m.*

**decrease I.** ['di:kri:s], *s.* (*in size*) Abnahme *f;* (*in number, price*) Rückgang *m.* **II.** [di:'kri:s], *v.* 1. *v.tr.* (den Preis) herabsetzen; (etwas) verringern. 2. *v.i.* (*in size*) abnehmen; (*in number*) weniger werden; (*of numbers*) sinken. ◆**de'creasing,** *adj.* abnehmend; **-ly,** *adv.* in abnehmendem Maße.

**decree** [di'kri:]. **I.** *s.* 1. *Adm:* Erlaß *m.* 2. *Jur:* Entscheid *m;* (*judgement*) Urteil *n.* **II.** *v.tr.* (etwas) verordnen.

**decrepit** [di'krepit], *adj.* 1. (*of pers.*) altersschwach. 2. (*of thing*) heruntergekommen; (*of house etc.*) verfallen.

**dedicate** ['dedikeit], *v.tr.* (*a*) (ein Gebäude) einweihen; (*b*) to d. sth. to s.o., j-m etwas widmen. ◆**dedi'cation,** *s.* 1. Einweihung *f* (einer Kirche usw.). 2. Widmung *f* (eines Buches usw.). 3. (*sense of*) d., Hingabe *f.*

**deduce** [di'dju:s], *v.tr.* folgern (from, aus + *dat*).

**deduct** [di'dʌkt], *v.tr.* (einen Betrag) abziehen. ◆**de'duction,** *s.* 1. Abzug *m.* 2. (*conclusion*) Folgerung *f.*

**deed** [di:d], *s.* 1. Tat *f.* 2. *Jur:* Urkunde *f.*

**deep** [di:p], *adj. & adv.* tief; **d. sleep,** fester Schlaf; **d. blue,** tiefblau. ◆**'deepen,** *v.* 1. *v.tr.* (*a*) vertiefen; (*b*) (ein Gefühl) verstärken. 2. *v.i.* sich vertiefen; (*strengthen*) sich verstärken. ◆**'deep-'freeze,** *s.* Tiefkühltruhe *f.* ◆**'deep-'fry,** *v.tr.* in tiefem Fett ausbacken. ◆**'deeply,** *adv.* **d. hurt,** schwer gekränkt. ◆**'deep-'rooted,** *adj.* tief verwurzelt. ◆**'deep-'seated,** *adj.* tiefsitzend.

**deer** [diər], *s. inv.* Hirsch *m.*

**deface** [di'feis], *v.tr.* beschädigen; (etwas Schriftliches) unleserlich machen.

**defamation** [defə'meiʃ(ə)n], *s.* Verleumdung *f.* ◆**defamatory** [di'fæmətri], *adj.* verleumderisch.

**default** [di'fɔ:lt]. **I.** *s.* *Jur:* **by d.,** durch Nichterscheinen *n* (des Gegners). **II.** *v.i.* (*a*) (seinen Verpflichtungen usw.) nicht nachkommen; (*b*) *Jur: etc:* nicht erscheinen.

**defeat** [di'fi:t]. **I.** *s.* Niederlage *f.* **II.** *v.tr.* (*a*) (j-n, eine Armee) besiegen; *Sp:* (j-n) schlagen; (*b*) *Parl:* (einen Vorschlag) ablehnen; (die Regierung) überstimmen. ◆**de'featist. I.** *s.* Defätist *m.* **II.** *adj.* defätistisch.

**defect¹** ['di:fekt], *s.* Fehler *m;* **physical d.,** Gebrechen *n.* ◆**de'fective,** *adj.* mangelhaft; **d. brakes,** defekte Bremsen.

**defect²** [di'fekt], *v.i.* (zu einer anderen Partei usw.) übertreten; abtrünnig werden.

**defence** [di'fens], *s.* (*a*) Verteidigung *f;* (*justification*) Rechtfertigung *f;* (*b*) *Sp:* Abwehr *f.* ◆**de'fenceless,** *adj.* wehrlos.

**defend** [di'fend], *v.tr.* (j-n, etwas) verteidigen (**from/against,** gegen + *acc*); (eine Tat) rechtfertigen. ◆**de'fendant,** *s. Jur:* Angeklagte(r) *f(m).* ◆**de'fender,** *s.* Verteidiger *m; Sp:* Abwehrspieler *m;* (*of title*) Titelverteidiger *m.* ◆**de'fensive. I.** *adj.* defensiv; **d. measure,** Abwehrmaßnahme *f.* **II.** *s.* Defensive *f;* **to go on to the d.,** in die Defensive gehen.

**defer** [di'fə:r], *v.tr.* verschieben. ◆**de'ferment,** *s.* Aufschub *m.*

**deference** ['def(ə)rəns], *s.* Ehrerbietung *f.* ◆**deferential** ['refənʃ(ə)l], *adj.* ehrerbietig.

**defiance** [di'faiəns], *s.* Trotz *m;* (*act of*) d., Herausforderung *f.* ◆**de'fiant,** *adj.* trotzig.

**deficiency** [di'fiʃənsi], *s.* 1. Mangel *m* (**of/in,** an + *dat*). 2. (*quality*) Mangelhaftigkeit *f.* ◆**de'ficient,** *adj.* ungenügend; (*of work*) mangelhaft; **to be d. in,** mangeln an + *dat.*

**deficit** ['defisit], *s.* Defizit *n.*

**define** [di'fain], *v.tr.* (*a*) definieren; **to d. one's position,** seinen Standpunkt klarstellen; (*b*) (Grenzen) festlegen; (*c*) (*of outlines, ideas*) **clearly defined,** klar umrissen. ◆**definite** ['definit], *adj.* bestimmt; **is that d.?** ist das sicher? **-ly,** *adv.* bestimmt. ◆**defi'nition,** *s.* 1. Definition *f* (eines Wortes). 2. Schärfe *f* (des Bildes, des Tones).

**deflate** [di:'fleit], *v.tr.* (*a*) (aus einem Reifen usw.) die Luft ablassen; (*b*) *F:* **that's deflated him!** das hat ihm den Wind aus den Segeln genommen! ◆**de'flation,** *s. Fin:* Deflation *f.*

**deflect** [di'flekt], *v.tr.* ablenken.

**deformed** [di'fɔ:md], *adj.* mißgestaltet. ◆**de'formity,** *s.* Mißbildung *f.*

**defraud** [di'frɔ:d], *v.tr.* **to d. s.o. of sth.,** j-n um etwas *acc* betrügen.

**defray** [di'frei], *v.tr.* **to d. the cost of sth.,** die Kosten von etwas *dat* tragen.

**defrost** [di:'frɔst], *v.tr.* (den Kühlschrank) abtauen; (Tiefgekühltes) auftauen lassen.

**deft** [deft], *adj.* geschickt, gewandt.

**defunct** [di'fʌŋkt], *adj.* (*of firm, railway etc.*) stillgelegt; **to be d.,** nicht mehr bestehen.

**defy** [di'fai], *v.tr.* (*a*) (j-m, etwas *dat*) trotzen; (*challenge*) (j-n) herausfordern; (*b*) **to d. description,** jeder Beschreibung spotten.

**degenerate. I.** [di'dʒenəreit], *v.i.* degenerieren. **II.** [di'dʒen(ə)rit], *adj.* entartet; (*of pers.*) degeneriert.

**degradation** [degrə'deiʃ(ə)n], *s.* Entwürdigung *f.* ◆**de'grading,** *adj.* entwürdigend.

**degree** [di'gri:], *s.* Grad *m;* **by degrees,** allmählich, nach und nach; **to get a d.,** sein Studium abschließen.

**dehydrate** [di:'haidreit], *v.tr.* (etwas *dat*) das Wasser entziehen; (Gemüse) dörren.

◆**dehy'dration**, s. Wasserentzug m.
**de-ice** ['di:'ais], v.tr. enteisen. ◆'**de-'icer**, s. Enteisungsmittel n.

**deign** [dein], v.tr. to d. to do sth., sich herablassen, etwas zu tun.

**dejected** [di'dʒektid], adj. niedergeschlagen. ◆**de'jection**, s. Niedergeschlagenheit f.

**delay** [di'lei]. I. s. 1. Verzögerung f; **without (further) d.**, unverzüglich. 2. (lateness) Verspätung f. II. v. 1. v.tr. (a) verzögern; (eine Zahlung usw.) aufschieben; (b) (j-n) aufhalten. 2. v.i. zögern. ◆**de'layed**, adj. verspätet; **to be d.**, sich verzögern; (of pers.) aufgehalten werden.

**delegate. I.** ['deligit], s. Delegierte(r) f(m). **II.** ['deligeit], v.tr. (j-n) delegieren; **to d. sth. to s.o.**, j-m etwas anvertrauen. ◆**dele'gation**, s. Delegation f.

**delete** [di'li:t], v.tr. streichen. ◆**de'letion**, s. Streichung f.

**deliberate. I.** [di'lib(ə)rit], adj. 1. (intentional) absichtlich; (conscious) bewußt. 2. (of pers., manner) bedächtig; (of speech, tread) gemessen. **II.** [di'libəreit], v.tr. & i. nachdenken (**on**, über + acc); (of group) sich beraten (**on**, über + acc). ◆**delibe'ration**, s. (a) Überlegung f; (b) pl. Beratung f (einer Versammlung usw.).

**delicacy** ['delikəsi], s. Cu: Delikatesse f. ◆**delicate** ['delikit], adj. (a) (of colours, feelings etc.) zart; (b) (tricky) heikel; (c) (of health, mechanism, pers.) empfindlich; (d) a d. taste, ein feiner Geschmack.

**delicatessen** [delikə'tes(ə)n], s. (shop) Feinkostgeschäft n.

**delicious** [di'liʃəs], adj. köstlich; (of food) lecker.

**delight** [di'lait]. I. s. Freude f. II. v. 1. v.tr. (j-n) erfreuen. 2. v.i. to d. in doing sth., sich damit vergnügen, etwas zu tun. ◆**de'lighted**, adj. to be d. with/at sth., sich über etwas acc freuen; (I shall be) d., mit dem größten Vergnügen. ◆**de'lightful**, adj. entzückend.

**delinquency** [di'liŋkwənsi], s. Kriminalität f. ◆**de'linquent. I.** adj. straffällig. **II.** s. Straftäter m.

**delirious** [di'liriəs], adj. (im Fieber) phantasierend; **d. with joy**, außer sich dat vor Freude. ◆**de'lirium**, s. Delirium n.

**deliver** [di'livər], v.tr. (a) (Waren usw.) liefern; (ein Paket) abgeben; (Post) zustellen; F: **to d. the goods**, seinen Verpflichtungen nachkommen; (b) **to d. a speech**, eine Rede halten. ◆**de'liverance**, s. Erlösung f. ◆**de'livery**, s. 1. Lieferung f (von Waren); Zustellung f (von Post). 2. Med: Entbindung f.

**delta** ['deltə], s. Flußdelta n.

**delude** [di'lju:d], v.tr. (j-n) täuschen; **to d. oneself**, sich dat Illusionen machen. ◆**de'lusion**, s. Täuschung f.

**deluge** ['delju:dʒ]. I. s. (a) Wolkenbruch m; (b) Fig: Flut f (von Briefen usw.). II. v.tr. (j-n) überschwemmen.

**de luxe** [də'luks]. adj. Luxus-; **d. 1. version/model**, Luxusausführung f.

**delve** [delv], v.i. to d. into sth., sich in etwas acc vertiefen.

**demand** [di'ma:nd]. I. s. 1. Forderung f; **on d.**, auf Verlangen. 2. Com: Nachfrage f; **in d.**, gefragt. 3. pl. **to make (many) demands on s.o.'s time**, j-n sehr in Anspruch nehmen. II. v.tr. verlangen.

**demented** [di'mentid], adj. wahnsinnig.

**democracy** [di'mɔkrəsi], s. Demokratie f. ◆**democrat** ['deməkræt], s. Demokrat(in) m(f). ◆**demo'cratic**, adj. demokratisch.

**demolish** [di'mɔliʃ], v.tr. zerstören; (Gebäude usw.) niederreißen. ◆**demolition** [demə'liʃ(ə)n], s. Abbruch m.

**demon** ['di:mən], s. Dämon m.

**demonstrate** ['demənstreit], v. 1. v.tr. (a) (etwas Wahres) beweisen; (b) (ein System) darlegen; Com: (ein Gerät, ein Auto) vorführen. 2. v.i. Pol: demonstrieren. ◆**demon'stration**, s. (a) Beweis m; (b) Darlegung f; Com: Vorführung f. 2. Pol: Demonstration f. ◆**demonstrative** [di'mɔnstrətiv], adj. demonstrativ; **she's not very d.**, sie zeigt selten ihre Gefühle. ◆'**demonstrator**, s. Pol: Demonstrant m.

**demoralize** [di'mɔrəlaiz], v.tr. entmutigen.

**demote** [di'məut], v.tr. degradieren.

**den** [den], s. 1. (a) Höhle f; (b) Bau m (eines Fuchses usw.). 2. (room) Bude f.

**denial** [di'naiəl], s. Leugnung f; (refusal) Verweigerung f; Ablehnung f (einer Bitte); **official d.**, Dementi n.

**Denmark** ['denma:k]. Pr.n. Dänemark n.

**denim** ['denim], s. Jeansstoff m; **denims**, Jeans pl.

**denomination** [dinɔmi'neiʃ(ə)n], s. 1. Ecc: Bekenntnis n. 2. Nennwert m (von Münzen usw.). ◆**de'nominator**, s. Nenner m.

**denote** [di'nəut], v.tr. bedeuten.

**denounce** [di'nauns], v.tr. (j-n, etwas) öffentlich verurteilen.

**dense** [dens], adj. 1. dicht. 2. F: (of pers.) schwer von Begriff; dumm. ◆'**density**, s. Dichte f.

**dent** [dent]. I. s. (in metal) Beule f; (also in wood etc.) Delle f. II. v.tr. (etwas) einbeulen; **dented**, verbeult.

**dental** ['dentl], adj. dental, Zahn-. ◆'**dentist**, s. Zahnarzt m. ◆'**dentistry**, s. Zahnheilkunde f. ◆'**denture**, s. Zahnprothese f, F: Gebiß n.

**deny** [di'nai], v.tr. (a) (eine Tat) leugnen; (ein Gerücht) dementieren; (esp. with neg.) (ein Gefühl) abstreiten; **there's no denying (the fact) that** ..., es läßt sich nicht leugnen, daß ...; (b) (refuse) **to d. s.o. sth.**, j-m etwas verweigern; **to d.**

oneself sth., sich *dat* etwas nicht gönnen.

**deodorant** [diː'əudərənt], *s.* Deo(dorant) *n.*

**depart** [di'pɑːt], *v.i.* (*a*) (*of pers.*) abreisen; (*of train*) abfahren; (*b*) **to d. (from a rule etc.)**, (von einer Regel usw.) abweichen. ◆**de'parture**, *s.* **1.** Abreise *f*, Abfahrt *f.* **2.** Abweichung *f*; **a new d.**, eine Neuerung.

**department** [di'pɑːtmənt], *s.* **1.** (*a*) Abteilung *f*; **d. store**, Kaufhaus *n*; (*b*) (*at university*) Institut *n.* **2.** *Pol:* Ministerium *n*; *N.Am:* **State D.**, Außenministerium *n.* ◆**depart'mental**, *adj.* **1.** Abteilungs-. **2.** *Pol:* Ministerial-.

**depend** [di'pend], *v.i.* (*a*) abhängen (**on** sth., von etwas *dat*); **depending on ...**, je nach + *dat*; (*b*) (*rely*) **to d. (up)on s.o., sth.**, sich auf j-n, etwas *acc* verlassen. ◆**de'pendable**, *adj.* (*of pers.*) verläßlich; (*of source etc.*) zuverlässig. ◆**de'pendant**, *s.* = **dependent II.** ◆**de'pendence**, *s.* **1.** Abhängigkeit *f* (**on**, von + *dat*). **2.** (*trust*) Vertrauen *n* (**on**, auf + *acc*). ◆**de'pendent. I.** *adj.* angewiesen (**on**, auf + *acc*). **II.** *s. Adm:* Unterhaltsberechtigte(r) *f (m).*

**depict** [di'pikt], *v.tr.* schildern.

**deplete** [di'pliːt], *v.tr.* (Vorräte usw.) aufbrauchen; (Reserven) verzehren. ◆**de'pletion**, *s.* Schwund *m* (von Reserven).

**deplore** [di'plɔːr], *v.tr.* bedauern. ◆**de'plorable**, *adj.* bedauernswert; (*disgraceful*) schändlich.

**deploy** [di'plɔi], *v.tr.* (*use*) einsetzen; (*position*) verteilen; (*base*) stationieren.

**deport** [di'pɔːt], *v.tr.* ausweisen. ◆**depor'tation**, *s.* Ausweisung *f.*

**depose** [di'pəuz], *v.tr.* vom Thron absetzen.

**deposit** [di'pɔzit]. **I.** *s.* **1.** (*safe*) **d.**, Depot *n*; **d. account**, Sparkonto *n.* **2.** (*a*) (*down payment*) Anzahlung *f* (**on**, auf + *acc*); (*b*) (*guarantee*) Pfand *n.* **3.** (*left by liquid*) Bodensatz *m.* **4.** Vorkommen *n* (von Erz usw.). **II.** *v.tr.* **to d. valuables (with a bank)**, Wertgegenstände (bei einer Bank) hinterlegen.

**depot** ['depəu, *N.Am.* 'diːpəu], *s.* (*a*) Depot *n*; (*b*) bus **d.**, Autobusgarage *f*; *Rail:* **goods d.**, Güterbahnhof *m*; (*building*) Güterhalle *f.*

**depraved** [di'preivd], *adj.* (*moralisch*) verdorben. ◆**depravity** [-'præv-], *s.* Verdorbenheit *f.*

**depreciate** [di'priːʃieit], *v.i. Fin:* an Wert verlieren. ◆**depreci'ation**, *s.* Wertverlust *m.*

**depress** [di'pres], *v.tr.* (*a*) (einen Knopf, ein Pedal usw.) herunterdrücken; (*b*) (j-n) deprimieren; (*c*) *Com:* (den Markt, Handel) ungünstig beeinflussen. ◆**de'pressed**, *adj.* (*of pers.*) deprimiert; (*of market etc.*) flau; **d. area**, (wirtschaftliches) Notstandsgebiet *n.* ◆**de'pressing**,

*adj.* deprimierend. ◆**de'pression**, *s.* **1.** *Fin:* Wirtschaftskrise *f.* **2.** (*of pers.*) Depression *f.*

**deprive** [di'praiv], *v.tr.* **to d. s.o. of sth.**, j-n etwas *gen* berauben. ◆**de'prived**, *adj.* benachteiligt. ◆**deprivation** [depri'veiʃ(ə)n], *s.* Entbehrung *f.*

**depth** [depθ], *s.* **1.** Tiefe *f.* **2.** (*a*) Stärke *f* (von Farben, Gefühlen usw.); (*b*) (*of study etc.*) **in d.**, gründlich, eingehend. **3. in the depths of despair**, in tiefster Verzweiflung.

**deputation** [depju(ː)'teiʃ(ə)n], *s.* Deputation *f.* ◆**'deputize**, *v.i.* **to d. for s.o.**, j-n vertreten. ◆**'deputy**, *s.* Stellvertreter(in) *m(f)*; **d. chairman**, stellvertretende(r) Vorsitzende(r) *f(m).*

**derail** [di'reil], *v.tr.* **to be derailed**, entgleisen. ◆**de'railment**, *s.* Entgleisung *f.*

**derange** [di'rein(d)ʒ], *v.tr.* **he is deranged**, er ist geistesgestört.

**derelict** ['derilikt], *adj.* verlassen.

**derision** [di'riʒ(ə)n], *s.* Hohn *m*, Spott *m.* ◆**de'risive** *adj.* höhnisch.

**derive** [di'raiv], *v.tr. & i.* (*a*) **to d. sth. from sth.**, etwas aus etwas *dat* gewinnen; (Nutzen usw.) aus etwas *dat* ziehen; **to d. pleasure from sth.**, Freude an etwas *dat* haben; (*b*) **to be derived/d. from sth.**, von etwas *dat* stammen. ◆**deri'vation** [deri-], *s.* Abstammung *f.* ◆**de'rivative** [di'rivətiv]. **I.** *adj.* (*a*) (*of substance*) abgeleitet; (*b*) (*of style etc.*) eklektisch. **II.** *s.* Ableitung *f*; *Ch:* Derivat *n.*

**dermatologist** [dəːmə'tɔlədʒist], *s.* Hautarzt *m.*

**derogatory** [di'rɔgət(ə)ri], *adj.* abträglich; (*of remark*) abfällig; (*of word*) abwertend.

**descend** [di'send], *v.* **1.** *v.i.* (*of thing*) herunterkommen; (*drop*) herunterfallen; (*of pers.*) heruntersteigen; **to be descended from s.o.**, von j-m abstammen. **2.** *v.tr.* (eine Treppe) hinuntergehen. ◆**de'scendant**, *s.* Nachkomme *m.* ◆**de'scent**, *s.* **1.** Abstieg *m.* **2.** (*in family etc.*) Abstammung *f.*

**describe** [dis'kraib], *v.tr.* beschreiben; **to d. s.o. as ...**, j-n als ... bezeichnen. ◆**des'cription**, *s.* Beschreibung *f*; **people of this d.**, Leute dieser Art. ◆**des'criptive**, *adj.* (*a*) beschreibend; (*b*) (*quality*) anschaulich.

**desert¹** ['dezət], *s.* Wüste *f.*

**desert²** [di'zəːt], *v.* **1.** *v.i.* **to d. (from the army)**, (vom Heer) desertieren. **2.** *v.tr.* (j-n) verlassen. ◆**de'serted**, *adj.* verlassen; (*of home etc.*) leer. ◆**de'serter**, *s.* Deserteur *m.* ◆**de'sertion**, *s.* Fahnenflucht *f.*

**deserts** [di'zəːts], *s. pl.* **to get one's just deserts**, seinen wohlverdienten Lohn empfangen.

**deserve** [di'zəːv], *v.tr.* verdienen. ◆**de'serving**, *adj.* verdienstvoll. ◆**de'servedly** [-idli], *adv.* verdienter-

maßen; (*rightly*) mit Recht.
**design** [di'zain]. **I.** *s.* **1.** (*intention*) Absicht *f*; **by d.**, absichtlich. **2.** (*a*) (*pattern*) Muster *n*; (*b*) (*shape*) Form *f*. **3.** *Ind: etc:* (*a*) (*plan*) Entwurf *m*; (*b*) Bauart *f*; *E: etc:* Konstruktion *f*; **the latest d.**, die neueste Ausführung. **II.** *v.tr.* (ein Kleid, eine Maschine usw.) entwerfen; (eine Brücke usw.) konstruieren; **that's not what it is designed for**, es ist nicht zu diesem Zweck bestimmt. ◆**de'signer**, *s. Ind:* Konstrukteur *m*; *Cl:* Modedesigner(in) *m(f).*
**designate** ['dezigneit], *v.tr. usu. Adm:* (*a*) **to d. s.o. (as) sth.**, j-n zu etwas *dat* ernennen; (*b*) (etwas) bezeichnen; (Bedingungen usw.) nennen; (Grenzen) kennzeichnen.
**desire** [di'zaiər]. **I.** *s.* **1.** (*a*) (*particular wish*) Wunsch *m*; (*b*) (*craving*) Verlangen *n* (**for**, nach + *dat*); **I have no d. to travel**, ich habe keine Lust zum Reisen. **2.** (*sensual*) **d.**, Begierde *f.* **II.** *v.tr.* (etwas) wünschen, *esp. Lit:* begehren; **it leaves much to be desired**, es läßt viel zu wünschen übrig. ◆**de'sirable**, *adj.* (*a*) (*of thing*) begehrenswert; (*attractive*) reizvoll; (*b*) (*of action*) wünschenswert.
**desk** [desk], *s.* (*in office etc.*) Schreibtisch *m; Sch:* Pult *n*.
**desolate** ['desəlat], *adj.* (*of place*) wüst, trostlos.
**despair** [dis'peər]. **I.** *s.* Verzweiflung *f* (**at**, über + *acc*). **II.** *v.i.* verzweifeln.
**desperate** ['desp(ə)rət], *adj.* **1.** (*a*) (*of illness etc.*) gefährlich; (*b*) (*extreme*) äußerst; **d. need**, dringendes Bedürfnis. **2.** (*of pers.*) verwegen; zu allem fähig; (*of conflict, attempt etc.*) verzweifelt; **-ly**, *adv.* sehr; (*urgently*) dringend; **to want sth. d.**, etwas unbedingt (haben) wollen. ◆**despe'ration**, *s.* **in d.**, aus Verzweiflung.
**despicable** ['despikəbl, dis'pik-], *adj.* verachtenswert. ◆**despise** [dis'paiz], *v.tr.* verachten.
**despite** [dis'pait], *prep.* trotz ( + *gen*).
**despondent** [dis'pɒndənt], *adj.* verzagt.
**despotic** [des'pɒtik], *adj.* despotisch.
**dessert** [di'zə:t], *s.* Nachtisch *m*; **d. spoon**, Dessertlöffel *m*.
**destination** [desti'neiʃ(ə)n], *s.* (*of train etc.*) Bestimmungsort *m*; (*of pers.*) Reiseziel *n*.
**destine** ['destin], *v.tr.* **to be destined for sth.**, zu etwas *dat* bestimmt sein. ◆'**destiny**, *s.* Schicksal *n*.
**destitute** ['destitju:t], *adj.* notleidend; (*poor*) verarmt.
**destroy** [dis'trɔi], *v.tr.* zerstören; (Papiere, Ungeziefer, eine Armee) vernichten; (ein Tier) töten. ◆**de'stroyer**, *s.* Zerstörer *m.* ◆**destruction** [dis'trʌkʃ(ə)n], *s.* Vernichtung *f*; Zerstörung *f* (eines Gebäudes usw.). ◆**des'tructive**, *adj.* destruktiv.
**detach** [di'tætʃ], *v.tr.* entfernen; **to d.**

**itself/become detached**, sich (los)lösen. ◆**de'tachable**, *adj.* abnehmbar. ◆**de'tached**, *adj.* **1.** abgetrennt; **d. house**, Einfamilienhaus *n.* **2.** (*of pers.*) distanziert; (*uninvolved*) unbeteiligt; (*unbiased*) objektiv. ◆**de'tachment**, *s.* **1.** (*of pers.*) Distanziertheit *f*; Objektivität *f.* **2.** *Mil: etc:* Abteilung *f.*
**detail** ['di:teil, *N.Am:* di'teil], *s.* Detail *n*; **in d.**, ausführlich; **to go into d.**, näher auf etwas *acc* eingehen.
**detain** [di'tein], *v.tr.* (*a*) *Jur:* (j-n) in Haft behalten; (*b*) (*delay*) (j-n) aufhalten. ◆**detai'nee**, *s.* Häftling *m*.
**detect** [di'tekt], *v.tr.* (*a*) (*find out*) entdecken; (*b*) (*notice*) wahrnehmen. ◆**de'tection**, *s.* (*a*) Entdeckung *f*; (*b*) Wahrnehmung *f.* ◆**de'tective**, *s.* Detektiv *m*; **d. story**, Kriminalroman *m.* ◆**de'tector**, *s.* Suchgerät *n.*
**detente** [dei'tɑ:t], *s.* Entspannung *f.*
**detention** [di'tenʃ(ə)n], *s. Jur:* Haft *f*; *Sch:* Nachsitzen *n*.
**deter** [di'tə:r], *v.tr.* abhalten.
**detergent** [di'tə:dʒ(ə)nt], *s.* Waschmittel *n.*
**deteriorate** [di'tiəriəreit], *v.i.* (*become worse*) sich verschlechtern. ◆**deterio'ration**, *s.* Verschlechterung *f.*
**determine** [di'tə:min], *v.tr.* (*a*) (*fix*) bestimmen; (*discover*) (das Wesen einer Sache) ermitteln; **to d. the sex of a baby**, das Geschlecht eines Babys feststellen; (*b*) (*decide*) **to d. to do sth.**, sich entschließen, etwas zu tun. ◆**de'termined**, *adj.* (*of pers.*) resolut; entschlossen. ◆**determi'nation**, *s.* (*of pers.*) Entschlossenheit *f.*
**deterrent** [di'terənt], *s.* Abschreckungsmittel *n.*
**detest** [di'test], *v.tr.* verabscheuen.
**detonate** ['detəneit], *v.tr.* explodieren lassen. ◆**deto'nation**, *s.* Detonation *f.* ◆'**detonator**, *s.* Sprengkapsel *f.*
**detour** ['di:tuər], *s.* Umweg *m.*
**detract** [di'trækt], *v.i.* **to d. from sth.**, etwas beeinträchtigen.
**detriment** ['detrimənt], *s.* Nachteil *m*; (*damage*) Schaden *m*; **to the d. of ...**, zum Schaden + *gen.* ◆**detri'mental**, *adj.* schädlich (**to**, für).
**deuce** [dju:s], *s.* (*Tennis*) Einstand *m.*
**devalue** [di:'vælju], *v.tr.* abwerten. ◆**devalu'ation**, *s.* Abwertung *f.*
**devastate** ['devəsteit], *v.tr.* verwüsten. ◆'**devastating**, *adj.* verheerend. ◆**devas'tation**, *s.* Verwüstung *f.*
**develop** [di'veləp], *v.* **1.** *v.tr.* entwickeln; **to d. a district**, ein Gebiet erschließen; **to d. an illness**, eine Krankheit bekommen. **2.** *v.i.* sich entwickeln; **to d. into sth.**, zu etwas *dat* werden. ◆**de'veloper**, *s.* (*pers.*) (*a*) Erschließer *m* (eines Gebiets); *Pej:* Spekulant *m*; (*b*) **late d.**, Spätentwickler *m.* ◆**de'veloping**, *adj.* **d. country**, Entwicklungsland *n.* ◆**de'velopment**, *s.* **1.**

Entwicklung f. 2. Erschließung f (eines Gebiets).

**deviate** ['di:vieit], v.i. abweichen. ◆**devi'ation**, s. Abweichung f.

**device** [di'vais], s. 1. to leave s.o. to his own devices, j-n sich dat selbst überlassen. 2. (apparatus) Gerät n.

**devil** ['devl], s. Teufel m; what the d. are you doing? was zum Teufel machst du da? talk of the d.! wenn man vom Teufel spricht! be a d.! wag's doch mal!

**devious** ['di:viəs], adj. 1. (complex) umständlich. 2. (of pers.) hinterlistig.

**devise** [di'vaiz], v.tr. (einen Plan) ersinnen; (eine Methode, ein Gerät) erfinden.

**devoid** [di'void], adj. d. of, frei von + dat; (neg. sense) bar + gen.

**devote** [di'vout], v.tr. (Zeit, ein Buch usw.) widmen (to s.o., sth., j-m, etwas dat); to d. oneself to sth., sich etwas dat widmen. ◆**de'voted**, adj. ergeben (to, dat); (loving) liebevoll. ◆**de'votion**, s. Hingabe f (to sth., an etwas dat); Liebe f (to s.o., für j-n).

**devour** [di'vauər], v.tr. verschlingen.

**devout** [di'vaut], adj. fromm.

**dew** [dju:], s. Tau m.

**dexterity** [deks'teriti], s. Geschicklichkeit f.

**diabetes** [daiə'bi:ti:z], s. Zuckerkrankheit f. ◆**diabetic** [-'betik]. I. adj. zuckerkrank; d. chocolate, Diabetikerschokolade f. II. s. Diabetiker(in) m(f).

**diabolical** [daiə'bɔlik(ə)l], adj. teuflisch.

**diagnose** ['daiəgnəuz], v.tr. (eine Krankheit) diagnostizieren ◆**diagnosis**, pl. -oses [-'nəusis, -əusi:z], s. Diagnose f.

**diagonal** [dai'ægənəl], adj. diagonal; -ly, adv. schräg.

**diagram** ['daiəgræm], s. Diagramm n.

**dial** ['daiəl]. I. s. Wählscheibe f (eines Telefons). II. v.tr. (eine Nummer) wählen; can I d. America? kann ich nach Amerika durchwählen? ◆**dialling**, s. d. tone, Amtszeichen n.

**dialect** ['daiəlekt], s. Dialekt m.

**dialogue** ['daiəlɔg], s. Dialog m.

**diameter** [dai'æmitər], s. Durchmesser m. ◆**dia'metrically**, adv. d. opposed, genau entgegengesetzt.

**diamond** ['daiəmənd], s. 1. Diamant m. 2. (a) (shape) Raute f; (b) (in cards) Karo n. ◆**diamond-shaped**, adj. rautenförmig.

**diaper** ['daiəpər], s. N.Am: Windel f.

**diarrhoea** [daiə'riə], s. Durchfall m.

**diary** ['daiəri], s. 1. (written record) Tagebuch n. 2. (for appointments etc.) Kalender m.

**dice** [dais], s. pl. Würfel m.pl.

**dictate** [dik'teit]. I. v.tr. & i. diktieren; (Maßnahmen usw.) vorschreiben. II. s. usu. pl. Gebot n. ◆**dic'tation**, s. Diktat n. ◆**dic'tator**, s. Diktator m. ◆**dicta'torial**, adj. (of power) diktatorisch; (of tone) gebieterisch. ◆**dic'tatorship**, s. Diktatur f.

**dictionary** ['dikʃ(ə)nri], s. Wörterbuch n.

**diddle** ['didl], v.tr. F: (j-n) übers Ohr hauen.

**die** [dai], v.i. (a) (of pers.) sterben (of sth., an etwas dat); (of plants, animals) eingehen; (of flowers) verwelken; (b) F: I am dying of thirst, ich verdurste; to be dying to do sth., darauf brennen, etwas zu tun; (c) F: (of car, machine) it died on me, es hat den Geist aufgegeben. ◆**'die a'way**, v.i. verhallen. ◆**'die 'down**, v.i. (of fire) ausgehen; (of wind) nachlassen. ◆**'diehard**, s. Hartnäckige(r) f(m). ◆**'die 'out**, v.i. aussterben.

**diesel** ['di:z(ə)l], s. d. (oil), Diesel(öl) n; d. engine, (i) E: Dieselmotor m; (ii) Rail: Diesellok f.

**diet** ['daiət]. I. s. 1. (food) Kost f. 2. (regime) Diät f; to be on a d., (to slim) eine Schlankheitskur machen. II. v.i. eine Schlankheitskur machen.

**differ** ['difər], v.i. (a) sich unterscheiden (from, von + dat); (b) (disagree) to d. about sth., über etwas acc anderer Meinung sein. ◆**'difference** ['difr(ə)ns], s. (a) Unterschied m; d. in age/colour, Alters-/Farbunterschied m; it makes no d. (to me), es ist (mir) gleich; (b) d. (of opinion), Meinungsverschiedenheit f. ◆**'different**, adj. (pred.) anders (from, als + nom); (attrib.) andere(r,s); (with pl.) (distinct, various) verschieden; they are d., (i) (both) sie sind anders; (ii) (from one another) sie sind verschieden. ◆**differentiate** [-'renʃieit], v.tr. & i. unterscheiden.

**difficult** ['difikəlt], adj. schwierig. ◆**'difficulty**, s. Schwierigkeit f.

**diffidence** ['difid(ə)ns], s. Schüchternheit f. ◆**'diffident**, adj. schüchtern.

**dig** [dig]. I. s. to give s.o. a d. in the ribs, j-m einen Rippenstoß geben. II. v.irr. 1. v.tr. (a) (Erde, ein Beet) umgraben; (b) (ein Loch) graben. 2. v.i. graben (for sth., nach etwas dat); (in garden) umgraben. ◆**digs**, s.pl. F: Bude f; to live in d., in Untermiete wohnen. ◆**'dig 'up**, v.tr. (a) (eine Pflanze, eine Schatz) ausgraben; (den Garten) umgraben; (b) F: (Informationen) ans Licht bringen.

**digest** [dai'dʒest], v.tr. (a) (Essen) verdauen; (b) (Tatsachen) verarbeiten. ◆**di'gestible**, adj. verdaulich. ◆**di'gestion**, s. Verdauung f.

**dignify** ['dignifai], v.tr. ehren. ◆**'dignified**, adj. würdevoll. ◆**'dignitary**, s. Würdenträger m. ◆**'dignity**, s. Würde f; beneath his d., unter seiner Würde.

**digress** [dai'gres], v.i. abschweifen. ◆**di'gression**, s. Abschweifung f.

**dike** [daik], s. Deich m.

**dilapidated** [di'læpideitid], adj. verwahrlost. ◆**dilapi'dation**, s. Verwahrlosung f.

**dilatory** ['dilət(ə)ri], adj. säumig.

**dilemma** [di'lemə], *s.* Dilemma *n.*
**diligence** ['dilidʒ(ə)ns], *s.* Fleiß *m.*
◆**'diligent,** *adj.* fleißig.
**dilute** [dai'lju:t], *v.tr.* verdünnen.
**dim** [dim]. **I.** *adj.* **1.** (a) (*of light*) trübe; (*of image*) verblaßt; **to grow d.,** (*of light, sight*) trübe werden; (*of recollection*) verblassen; (b) *F:* **to take a d. view of sth.,** von etwas *dat* nicht erbaut sein. **2.** *F:* (*of pers.*) dumm; **-ly,** *adv.* **d. lit,** mit düsterer Beleuchtung. **II.** *v.* **1.** *v.tr.* (ein Licht) abblenden. **2.** *v.i.* (*of light, sight*) trübe werden; (*of outlines*) verblassen.
**dimension** [di'menʃ(ə)n, dai-] *s.* (a) Dimension *f;* *pl.* Maße *npl* (eines Zimmers usw.); (b) *Fig:* Seite *f* (eines Problems usw.). ◆**di'mensional,** *adj.* **two-/three-d.,** zwei-/dreidimensional.
**diminish** [di'miniʃ], *v.* **1.** *v.tr.* vermindern. **2.** *v.i.* sich vermindern. ◆**di'minutive,** *adj.* winzig.
**dimple** ['dimpl], *s.* Grübchen *n.*
**din** [din], *s.* Krawall *m.*
**dine** [dain], *v.i.* speisen; **to d. out,** auswärts essen. ◆**'diner,** *s.* **1.** (*pers.*) Tischgast *m.* **2.** *N.Am:* Speiselokal *n;* *Rail:* Speisewagen *m.* ◆**'dining,** *s.* **d. room,** Speisezimmer *n;* **d. table,** Eßtisch *m;* *Rail:* **d. car,** Speisewagen *m.*
**dinghy** ['diŋ(g)i], *s.* Dingi *n;* **rubber d.,** Schlauchboot *n;* **sailing d.,** kleines Segelboot *n.*
**dingy** ['dindʒi], *adj.* düster; (*dark*) dunkel.
**dinner** ['dinər], *s.* (*evening meal*) Abendessen *n;* (*midday meal*) Mittagessen *n;* (*banquet*) Festessen *n;* **to give a d. party,** eine Gesellschaft zum Abendessen einladen; **d. jacket,** Smoking *m.*
**dinosaur** ['dainəsɔ:r], *s.* Dinosaurier *m.*
**dip** [dip]. **I.** *s.* **1.** *F:* **to go for/have a d.,** (kurz) schwimmen gehen. **2.** (*in road*) Mulde *f;* (*in landscape*) Senke *f.* **II.** *v.* **1.** *v.tr.* (a) (*into liquid*) (ein)tauchen; (b) *Aut:* **to d. the headlights,** abblenden. **2.** *v.i.* (a) (*of sun etc.*) sich senken; (b) **to d. into one's pocket,** in die Tasche greifen. ◆**'dipstick,** *s.* Ölmeßstab *m.*
**diphtheria** [dif'θiəriə], *s.* Diphtherie *f.*
**diploma** [di'pləumə], *s.* Diplom *n.*
**diplomacy** [di'pləuməsi], *s.* Diplomatie *f.* ◆**diplomat** ['dipləmæt], *s.* Diplomat *m.* ◆**diplo'matic,** *adj.* diplomatisch.
**dire** ['daiər], *adj.* **1.** (*urgent*) dringend; **to be in d. need of sth.,** etwas dringend brauchen. **2.** (*terrible*) entsetzlich.
**direct** [dai'rekt, di-]. **I.** *v.tr.* (a) (ein Unternehmen) leiten; **to d. a play/film,** bei einem Stück/Film Regie führen; (b) (Aufmerksamkeit, Anstrengungen) lenken (**to sth.,** auf etwas *acc*); (c) **could you d. me to the station?** können Sie mir den Weg zum Bahnhof sagen? (d) **to d. s.o. to do sth.,** j-m Anweisungen geben, etwas zu tun. **II.** *adj. & adv.* **1.** direkt; (a) (*of cause, taxes etc.*) unmittelbar; (b) (*of train*) durchgehend; **d. hit,** Voll-

treffer *m;* **d. current,** Gleichstrom *m.* **2.** (*exact*) genau; **the d. opposite,** das genaue Gegenteil; **-ly,** *adv.* (*exactly*) genau; (*time*) **he's coming d.,** er kommt sofort/gleich. ◆**di'rection,** *s.* **1.** Richtung *f;* **sense of d.,** Orientierungssinn *m.* **2.** Leitung *f* (eines Unternehmens usw.); *Th: etc:* Regie *f.* **3.** (*instructions*) Anleitungen *fpl;* **directions for use,** Gebrauchsanweisung *f.* ◆**di'rector,** *s.* Direktor *m;* *Th: Cin:* Regisseur *m;* *Com:* (*board member*) Vorstandsmitglied *n.* ◆**di'rectory** [-t(ə)ri], *s.* *Tel:* Telefonbuch *n;* *Com:* **trade d.,** Firmenverzeichnis *n.*
**dirt** [də:t], *s.* Schmutz *m;* **it's d. cheap,** es ist spottbillig. ◆**'dirty. I.** *adj.* schmutzig; *F:* dreckig; **d. mind,** dreckige Phantasie; **d. old man,** Lustmolch *m;* **d. trick,** Gemeinheit *f;* **to do the d. on s.o.,** j-m übel mitspielen; **d. look,** mißbilligender Blick. **II.** *v.tr.* schmutzig machen.
**disability** [disə'biliti], *s.* (**physical**) **d.,** körperliche Behinderung *f.*
**disable** [dis'eibl], *v.tr.* (j-n) untauglich machen. ◆**dis'abled,** *adj.* körperbehindert; (*of serviceman*) kriegsversehrt.
**disadvantage** [disəd'vɑ:ntidʒ], *s.* Nachteil *m;* **to be at a d.,** im Nachteil sein. ◆**disadvan'tageous,** *adj.* nachteilig (**to,** für + *acc*).
**disagree** [disə'gri:], *v.i.* (a) nicht übereinstimmen; (*of two reports etc.*) sich widersprechen; (b) (*of pers.*) anderer Meinung sein; (c) (*argue*) sich streiten; (d) **cherries d. with me,** Kirschen bekommen mir nicht. ◆**disa'greeable,** *adj.* unangenehm; (*of pers.*) unfreundlich. ◆**disa'greement,** *s.* **1.** (*between statements, etc.*) Widerspruch *m.* **2.** (*between people*) Meinungsverschiedenheit *f;* (*quarrel*) Streit *m.*
**disappear** [disə'piər], *v.i.* verschwinden. ◆**disa'ppearance,** *s.* Verschwinden *n.*
**disappoint** [disə'pɔint], *v.tr.* enttäuschen. ◆**disa'ppointing,** *adj.* enttäuschend. ◆**disa'ppointment,** *s.* Enttäuschung *f.*
**disapprove** [disə'pru:v], *v.i.* **to d. of sth.,** etwas mißbilligen. ◆**disa'pproval,** *s.* Mißbilligung *f;* **look of d.,** mißbilligender Blick.
**disarm** [dis'ɑ:m], *v.i.* abrüsten. ◆**dis'arming,** *adj.* entwaffnend. ◆**dis'armament,** *s.* Abrüstung *f.*
**disarray** [disə'rei], *s.* Unordnung *f.*
**disaster** [di'zɑ:stər], *s.* Katastrophe *f.* ◆**di'sastrous,** *adj.* katastrophal.
**disbelief** [disbi'li:f], *s.* Unglaube *m.*
**disc** [disk], *s.* (a) Scheibe *f;* **slipped d.,** Bandscheibenschaden *m;* (b) (*record*) Schallplatte *f;* **d. jockey,** Diskjockey *m.*
**discard** [dis'kɑ:d], *v.tr.* (Kleider, Karten usw.) ablegen; (einen Plan) aufgeben.
**discern** [di'sə:n], *v.tr.* erkennen. ◆**dis'cernible,** *adj.* erkennbar. ◆**dis'cerning,** *adj.* (*of pers.*) scharfsinnig; (*of taste*) erlesen; **a d. eye,** ein Kennerblick.

**discharge. I.** ['dist∫ɑːdʒ], s. **1.** (a) Abfluß m (von Wasser); Ausstoß m (von Rauch); (b) El: Entladung f; (c) Med: Ausfluß m; (from wound) Eiterung f. **2.** Entlassung f (eines Angestellten, Jur: eines Gefangenen, Med: eines Patienten). **II.** [dis't∫ɑːdʒ], v.tr. (a) Med: (Eiter usw.) absondern; (b) (einen Angestellten; Med: einen Patienten, Jur: einen Gefangenen) entlassen; (c) (eine Aufgabe) erfüllen; (einer Pflicht) nachkommen; (eine Schuld) begleichen.

**disciple** [di'saipl], s. Jünger m.

**discipline** ['disiplin]. **I.** s. Disziplin f. **II.** v.tr. **to d. s.o.,** j-n strafen.

**disclaimer** [dis'kleimər], s. Widerruf m.

**disclose** [dis'kləuz], v.tr. bekanntgeben; (ein Geheimnis) enthüllen. ◆**dis'closure** [-ʒər], s. Bekanntgabe f (einer Nachricht); Enthüllung f (eines Geheimnisses usw.).

**disco** ['diskəu], s. F: Diskothek f.

**discomfort** [dis'kʌmfət], s. (a) (inconvenience) Unbequemlichkeit f; (b) (slight pain etc.) Unbehagen n.

**disconcert** [diskən'səːt], v.tr. (j-n) aus der Fassung bringen. ◆**discon'certing,** adj. beunruhigend.

**disconnect** [diskə'nekt], v.tr. (a) trennen; (b) El: etc: (den Strom, das Telefon) abschalten. ◆**dis'connected,** adj. **1.** (a) getrennt; (b) El: etc: abgeschaltet. **2.** (of thoughts, speech) zusammenhanglos.

**disconsolate** [dis'kɔnsəlit], adj. untröstlich.

**discontent** [diskən'tent], s. Unzufriedenheit f. ◆**discon'tented,** adj. unzufrieden.

**discontinue** [diskən'tinju:], v.tr. (a) beenden; (b) Com: (ein Produkt) nicht mehr führen.

**discord** ['diskɔːd], s. Zwietracht f.

**discotheque** ['diskətek], s. Diskothek f.

**discount. I.** ['diskaunt], s. Rabatt m; **to sell sth. at a d.,** etwas mit Rabatt verkaufen. **II.** [dis'kaunt], v.tr. (j-s Meinung) nicht beachten; (eine Möglichkeit) ausschließen.

**discourage** [dis'kʌridʒ], v.tr. (a) (of future etc.) (j-n) entmutigen; (b) (of pers.) (j-m) abraten (from doing sth., etwas zu tun). ◆**dis'couraging,** adj. entmutigend; (of difficulty etc.) abschreckend. ◆**dis'couragement,** s. (a) (state) Entmutigung f; (b) (process, thing) Abschreckung f.

**discover** [dis'kʌvər], v.tr. entdecken. ◆**dis'covery,** s. Entdeckung f.

**discredit** [dis'kredit], v.tr. (a) (eine Theorie usw.) umstoßen; (b) (j-n) in Mißkredit bringen.

**discreet** [dis'kriːt], adj. diskret. ◆**dis'cretion** [-'kre∫(ə)n], s. **1.** (judgement) Ermessen n. **2.** (tact) Diskretion f.

**discrepancy** [dis'krepənsi], s. Diskrepanz f.

**discriminate** [dis'krimineit], v.i. (a) **to d.**

**between two things,** zwischen zwei Dingen unterscheiden; (b) **to d. against s.o.,** j-n benachteiligen. ◆**discrimi'nation,** s. (unfair) d., Benachteiligung f; **racial d.,** Rassendiskriminierung f.

**discuss** [dis'kʌs], v.tr. (etwas) besprechen; (eine Frage) erörtern. ◆**dis'cussion** [-∫(ə)n], s. Besprechung f; Diskussion f; **to be under d.,** zur Debatte stehen.

**disdain** [dis'dein], s. Verachtung f. ◆**dis'dainful,** adj. verächtlich.

**disease** [di'ziːz], s. Krankheit f.

**disembark** [disem'bɑːk], v.i. an Land gehen.

**disfigure** [dis'figər], v.tr. (j-s Gesicht) entstellen; (eine Landschaft usw.) verunstalten. ◆**dis'figurement,** s. Entstellung f; Verunstaltung f.

**disgrace. I.** s. Schande f; (object) Schandfleck m; **in d.,** in Ungnade. **II.** v.tr. (etwas dat) Schande machen; **to d. oneself,** sich blamieren. ◆**dis'graceful,** adj. schändlich; F: unerhört.

**disgruntled** [dis'grʌntld], adj. verstimmt (at sth., über etwas acc).

**disguise** [dis'gaiz]. **I.** s. Verkleidung f; **in d.,** verkleidet, Fig: getarnt. **II.** v.tr. (j-n, sich) verkleiden; (etwas) tarnen; (seine Stimme usw.) verstellen; (conceal) (Gefühle) verhehlen.

**disgust** [dis'gʌst], s. **1.** (physical) Abscheu m, Ekel m (at sth., vor etwas dat). **2.** (intense annoyance) Empörung f; **in d.,** empört. ◆**dis'gusting,** adj. (horrible) widerlich; (physically) ekelhaft.

**dish** [di∫]. **I.** v.tr. (a) **to d. up** (a meal), (das Essen) auftragen; (b) F: **to d. out money etc.,** Geld usw. austeilen. **II.** s. **1.** (a) (shallow) Platte f; (usu. glass) Schale f; (deeper) Schüssel f; **the dishes,** coll. das Geschirr. **2.** (food) Gericht n. ◆**'dishcloth,** s. Spültuch n. ◆**'dishwasher,** s. Geschirrspülmaschine f.

**dishearten** [dis'hɑːtn], v.tr. (j-n) entmutigen. ◆**dis'heartening,** adj. entmutigend; (of task) deprimierend.

**dishevelled** [di'∫ev(ə)ld], adj. **1.** (of hair) zerzaust. **2.** (of clothes) schlampig.

**dishonest** [dis'ɔnist], adj. unehrlich. ◆**dis'honesty,** s. Unehrlichkeit f.

**dishonour** [dis'ɔnər], v.tr. entehren.

**disillusion** [disi'lju:ʒ(ə)n], v.tr. (j-n) desillusionieren; (disappoint) (j-n) enttäuschen.

**disinfect** [disin'fekt], v.tr. desinfizieren. ◆**disin'fectant,** s. Desinfektionsmittel n.

**disinherit** [disin'herit], v.tr. enterben.

**disintegrate** [dis'intigreit], v.i. zerfallen; (of structure) auseinanderfallen. ◆**disinte'gration,** s. Zerfall m.

**disinterested** [dis'intristid], adj. selbstlos; (unbiased) unparteiisch.

**disjointed** [dis'dʒɔintid], adj. (of style,

*speech*) unzusammenhängend.

**disk** [disk], *s.* (*a*) *see* **disc**; (*b*) *Data-pr:* Diskette *f*.

**dislike** [dis'laik]. **I.** *s.* Abneigung *f* (**of/for s.o., sth.,** gegen j-n, etwas *acc*). **II.** *v.tr.* (j-n, etwas) nicht mögen; **to d. doing sth.,** etwas ungern tun.

**dislocate** ['disləkeit], *v.tr.* sich *dat* (ein Glied) ausrenken.

**dislodge** [dis'lɔdʒ], *v.tr.* verschieben.

**dismal** ['dizməl], *adj.* trübe, trist.

**dismantle** [dis'mæntl], *v.tr.* auseinander-nehmen.

**dismay** [dis'mei]. **I.** *s.* Bestürzung *f*. **II.** *v.tr.* (j-n) bestürzen.

**dismiss** [dis'mis], *v.tr.* (*a*) (j-n aus einer Stellung) entlassen; (j-n von einem Amt) absetzen; (*b*) (*let go*) (j-n) entlassen; (eine Versammlung) auflösen; *Mil:* **d.!** wegtre-ten! (*c*) *Fig:* **to d. sth. as worthless,** et-was als wertlos abtun; (*d*) (einen Vor-schlag) zurückweisen; *Jur:* **to d. a case,** eine Klage abweisen. ◆**dis'missal,** *s.* Entlassung *f* (aus einer Stellung); Abset-zung *f* (von einem Amt).

**dismount** [dis'maunt], *v.i.* (vom Pferd usw.) absteigen.

**disobey** [disə'bei], *v.tr.* (j-m) nicht gehor-chen. ◆**diso'bedience,** *s.* Ungehorsam *m* (**to s.o.,** j-m gegenüber). ◆**diso'bedient,** *adj.* ungehorsam.

**disorder** [dis'ɔːdər], *s.* **1.** Unordnung *f*. **2.** (*riot*) (*civil*) *u.* öffentliche Unruhen *fpl*. **3.** *Med:* Störung *f*. ◆**dis'orderly,** *adj.* **1.** unordentlich. **2.** (*a*) *Jur:* (*of pers.*) zuchtlos; (*b*) (*of crowd*) aufrührerisch.

**disorganize** [dis'ɔːgənaiz], *v.tr.* (etwas) durcheinanderbringen; **she's completely disorganized,** sie ist völlig unorganisiert.

**disown** [dis'əun], *v.tr.* (ein Kind) versto-ßen.

**disparaging** [dis'pæridʒiŋ], *adj.* verächt-lich.

**dispatch** [dis'pætʃ]. **I.** *v.tr.* (*a*) (Waren) absenden; (j-n, etwas) wegschicken; (*b*) (j-n, ein Tier) töten. **II.** *s.* **1.** Versand *m* (von Waren); Abschicken *n* (von Post); *Com:* **d. note,** Versandanzeige *f*. **2. d. ri-der,** Meldefahrer *m*.

**dispel** [dis'pel], *v.tr.* (Zweifel usw.) ver-treiben.

**dispense** [dis'pens], *v.i.* **to d. with sth.,** auf etwas *acc* verzichten. ◆**dis'pensary,** *s.* Apotheke *f*. ◆**dis'pensing,** *s.* **d. chemist,** Apotheker(in) *m(f)*.

**disperse** [dis'pəːs], *v.* **1.** *v.tr.* zerstreuen. **2.** *v.i.* (*of crowd*) sich zerstreuen.

**dispirited** [dis'piritid], *adj.* niedergeschla-gen.

**display** [dis'plei]. **I.** *s.* **1.** (*a*) Ausstellung *f* (von Waren); (*b*) (*demonstration*) Vorfüh-rung *f*; **air d.,** Flugschau *f*. **2.** Zurschau-stellung *f* (von Wissen, Zuneigung usw.). **II.** *v.tr.* (*a*) (Waren usw.) ausstellen; **to d. a notice,** eine Bekanntmachung aus-hängen; (*b*) (Dummheit, Wissen, Zunei-gung) zur Schau stellen; (Wissen) zeigen.

**displeasure** [dis'pleʒər], *s.* Mißfallen *n*.

**dispose** [dis'pəuz], *v.i.* **to d. of,** (etwas) loswerden; (eine Leiche usw.) wegschaf-fen; (eine Bombe) unschädlich machen; (Probleme) beseitigen. ◆**dis'posable,** *adj.* Wegwerf-; Einweg-. ◆**dis'posal,** *s.* **1.** (*a*) (*throwing away*) Wegwerfen *n*; (*re-moval*) Beseitigung *f*; (*b*) Ablagerung *f* (von Müll). **2. to be at s.o.'s d.,** j-m zur Verfügung stehen. ◆**dis'posed,** *adj.* **to be well/ill d. towards s.o.,** j-m gut/schlecht gesinnt sein. ◆**dispo'sition,** *s.* Veranlagung *f*; **he is of a nervous d.,** er ist nervös veranlagt.

**disproportionate** [disprə'pɔːʃənit], *adj.* übermäßig.

**disprove** [dis'pruːv], *v.tr.* widerlegen.

**dispute** [dis'pjuːt]. **I.** *s.* Streit *m*; **indus-trial d.,** Arbeitskonflikt *m*. **II.** *v.tr.* (*a*) (eine Frage) erörtern; (*b*) (eine Feststel-lung) anfechten.

**disqualify** [dis'kwɔlifai], *v.tr.* (j-n) dis-qualifizieren; **to d. s.o. from driving,** j-m den Führerschein entziehen.

**disregard** [disri'gɑːd]. **I.** *s.* Nichtbeach-tung *f* (einer Vorschrift usw.); Gleichgül-tigkeit *f* (**for,** gegenüber + *dat*). **II.** *v.tr.* ignorieren; **to d. a rule,** eine Vorschrift nicht beachten.

**disrepair** [disri'peər], *s.* **to fall into d.,** verfallen; **in a state of d.,** baufällig.

**disrepute** [disri'pjuːt], *s.* **to bring sth. into d.,** etwas in Verruf bringen. ◆**disreputable** [dis'repjutəbl], *adj.* (*of pers.*) in schlechtem Ruf stehend; (*of area etc.*) verrufen.

**disrespect** [disri'spekt], *s.* Respektlosig-keit *f*. ◆**disre'spectful,** *adj.* respektlos.

**disrupt** [dis'rʌpt], *v.tr.* unterbrechen.

**dissatisfaction** [dissætis'fækʃ(ə)n], *s.* Un-zufriedenheit *f*. ◆**dis'satisfied,** *adj.* un-zufrieden.

**dissent** [di'sent], *v.i.* **to d. (about sth.),** (über etwas *acc*) anderer Meinung sein.

**disservice** [di(s)'səːvis], *s.* **to do s.o. a d.,** j-m einen schlechten Dienst erweisen.

**dissident** ['disidənt]. **I.** *adj.* andersden-kend. **II.** *s.* Dissident *m*.

**dissipate** ['disipeit], *v.tr.* **to d.** (Angst, Zweifel) zerstreuen. ◆**'dissipated,** *adj.* aus-schweifend.

**dissociate** [di'səuʃieit], *v.tr.* **to d. oneself from a statement etc.,** sich von einer Äußerung usw. distanzieren.

**dissolute** ['disəl(j)uːt], *adj.* ausschwei-fend.

**dissolve** [di'zɔlv], *v.* **1.** *v.tr.* auflösen. **2.** *v.i.* sich auflösen.

**dissuade** [di'sweid], *v.tr.* (j-m) abraten.

**distance** ['distəns], *s.* (*a*) Entfernung *f*; **from a d.,** aus einiger Entfernung; **in the d.,** in der Ferne; (*also Fig:*) **to keep one's d.,** Distanz halten; (*b*) Strecke *f*; **to cover a long/short d.,** eine lange/kurze Strecke zurücklegen. ◆**distant** ['distənt], *adj.* **1.** (*of place, country*) ent-fernt, fern; **a d. relation,** ein entfernter

Verwandter. 2. (*of pers.*) zurückhaltend; (*of manner*) kühl.

**distaste** [dis'teist], *s.* Abneigung *f* (for, gegen + *acc*). ◆**dis'tasteful**, *adj.* widerwärtig.

**distil** [dis'til], *v.tr.* destillieren; (Schnaps usw.) brennen. ◆**dis'tillery**, *s.* Branntweinbrennerei *f*.

**distinct** [dis'tiŋ(k)t], *adj.* 1. (*different*) verschieden. 2. (*clear*) deutlich; -ly, *adv.* deutlich; **to remember d.**, sich genau erinnern. ◆**dis'tinction**, *s.* 1. (*difference*) Unterschied *m.* 2. (*excellence*) Auszeichnung *f.* ◆**dis'tinctive**, *adj.* charakteristisch.

**distinguish** [dis'tiŋgwiʃ], *v.* 1. *v.tr.* (*a*) (*discern*) (etwas) erkennen; (*b*) (etwas) unterscheiden; **to d. oneself**, sich auszeichnen. 2. *v.i.* unterscheiden. ◆**dis'tinguished**, *adj.* a d. writer, ein Schriftsteller von Rang.

**distort** [dis'tɔːt], *v.tr.* (*a*) (das Gesicht, *Rad: TV:* den Ton, das Bild usw.) verzerren; (Metall) verformen; (*b*) (Wahrheit, Tatsachen) verfälschen/(*unintentionally*) entstellen.

**distract** [dis'trækt], *v.tr.* (Aufmerksamkeit usw.) ablenken. ◆**dis'traction**, *s.* Ablenkung *f*; **noise is a d.**, Lärm lenkt ab.

**distraught** [dis'trɔːt], *adj.* verzweifelt.

**distress** [dis'tres], *s.* 1. (*grief*) Kummer *m.* 2. (*of ship*) **in d.**, in Seenot; **d. signal**, Notsignal *n.* ◆**dis'tressing**, *adj.* peinlich; **to be d. (to s.o.)**, (j-m) Kummer machen.

**distribute** [dis'tribju(ː)t], *v.tr.* verteilen (to/among, an + *acc*); (Waren) vertreiben. ◆**distri'bution**, *s.* Verteilung *f*; *Com:* Vertrieb *m.* ◆**dis'tributor**, *s.* 1. *Cin:* Verleiher *m*; *Com:* Vertreter *m.* 2. *El: Aut:* Verteiler *m.*

**district** ['distrikt], *s.* 1. Gegend *f.* 2. *Adm:* Bezirk *m*; **d. nurse**, Bezirkskrankenschwester *f.*

**distrust** [dis'trʌst]. I. *s.* Mißtrauen *n.* II. *v.tr.* (j-m, etwas *dat*) mißtrauen. ◆**dis'trustful**, *adj.* mißtrauisch.

**disturb** [dis'təːb], *v.tr.* (*a*) stören; (*b*) (*worry*) (j-n) beunruhigen. ◆**dis'turbance**, *s.* 1. Störung *f.* 2. *Pol:* Unruhe *f*; Aufruhr *m.* ◆**dis'turbed**, *adj.* (*a*) gestört; (*of child*) verhaltensgestört; (*b*) (*worried*) beunruhigt. ◆**dis'turbing**, *adj.* beunruhigend.

**disuse** [dis'juːs], *s.* **to fall into d.**, außer Gebrauch kommen. ◆**disused** [-'juːzd], *adj.* außer Gebrauch; **d. mine**, stillgelegtes Bergwerk.

**ditch** [ditʃ]. I. *s.* Graben *m.* II. *v.tr. F:* (*a*) (*in* Flugzeug) notwassern; (*b*) **she ditched him**, sie hat ihn abgehängt.

**dither** ['diðər], *v.i. F:* zaudern.

**ditto** ['ditəu], *adv.* ebenfalls, ebenso.

**dive** [daiv]. I. *s.* (*under water*) Tauchen *n*; (*of pers. into water*) Kopfsprung *m.* II. *v.i.* (*a*) **to d. into the water**, einen Kopfsprung ins Wasser machen; **he dived into the bushes**, er stürzte sich ins Gebüsch; (*b*) (*of submarine, diver*) tauchen. ◆**'diver**, *s.* (*a*) Taucher *m*; (*b*) (*from board*) Kunstspringer *m.* ◆**'diving**, *s.* (*a*) Tauchen *n*; **d. suit**, Taucheranzug *m*; (*b*) **d. board**, Sprungbrett *n.*

**diverge** [dai'vəːdʒ], *v.i.* (*of opinions etc.*) auseinandergehen; **to d. from sth.**, von etwas *dat* abweichen.

**diverse** [dai'vəːs], *adj.* verschiedenartig. **diversion** [dai'vəːʃ(ə)n], *s.* Umleitung *f* (des Verkehrs, eines Flusses); Ablenkung *f* (der Aufmerksamkeit); **to create a d.**, ein Ablenkungsmanöver durchführen. ◆**divert** [dai'vəːt], *v.tr.* (einen Fluß, den Verkehr usw.) umleiten; (die Aufmerksamkeit) ablenken.

**divide** [di'vaid], *v.* 1. *v.tr.* (*a*) (etwas) teilen; (*b*) (eine Zahl) dividieren (by, durch + *acc*); (*c*) (*separate*) (etwas) trennen (from, von + *dat*). 2. *v.i.* (*of thing*) sich teilen. ◆**dividend** ['dividend], *s.* Dividende *f*; *Fig:* Bonus *m*; *Fig:* **to pay dividends**, sich bezahlt machen.

**divine** [di'vain], *adj.* göttlich.

**division** [di'viʒ(ə)n], *s.* 1. Spaltung *f* (**into several parts**, in mehrere Teile). 2. Aufteilung *f* (von Besitz, der Arbeit usw.). 3. *Mth:* Division *f.* 4. (*a*) *Mil:* Abteilung *f*; (*b*) *Mil:* Division *f*; (*c*) *Sp:* Liga *f.* ◆**divisible** [-'vizəbl], *adj.* teilbar.

**divorce** [di'vɔːs]. I. *s.* Scheidung *f*; **to get a d.**, sich scheiden lassen. II. *v.tr.* **to d. one's husband/wife**, sich von seinem Mann/seiner Frau scheiden lassen. ◆**divorcee** [-'siː], *s.* Geschiedene(r) *f(m)*.

**divulge** [di'vʌldʒ], *v.tr.* ausplaudern.

**dizziness** ['dizinis], *s.* Schwindel *m.* ◆**'dizzy**, *adj.* 1. schwindlig; **I feel d.**, mir ist schwindlig. 2. (*of heights etc.*) schwindelnd.

**do** [duː]. I. *v.* 1. *v.tr. & i.* machen, tun; **what do you do (for a living)?** was machen Sie (beruflich)? **well done!** gut gemacht! **he was doing over a hundred**, er fuhr mit mehr als hundert; **to do s.o. out of sth.**, j-n um etwas *acc* bringen; (*after making a bargain*) **done!** abgemacht! **how do you do?** (i) wie geht es Ihnen? (ii) (*on being introduced*) sehr erfreut; (*suffice*) **that will do**, das genügt; **this room will do for an office**, dieses Zimmer kann als Büro dienen. 2. *verb substitute* **he writes better than I do**, er schreibt besser als ich; **may I open these letters? – please do**, darf ich die Briefe öffnen? – bitte; **I like coffee – do you?** ich mag Kaffee – Sie auch? **you like him, don't you?** Sie mögen ihn, nicht wahr? **don't!** nein! **you like London? so do I**, Sie mögen London? ich auch. 3. *v.aux.* (*a*) (*emphasis*) **he did go**, er ist doch hingegangen; **do sit down!** bitte setzen Sie sich doch! (*b*) **do you see him?** sehen Sie ihn? **we do not know,** wir wissen es nicht. **4. to have to do with s.o., sth.,** mit j-m, etwas *dat* zu tun haben; **I could do with a cup of tea,** ich könnte eine Tasse Tee gebrauchen; **to do without sth.,** auf etwas *acc* verzichten. **II.** *s. F:* (*event*) Party *f;* Veranstaltung *f;* **a big do,** eine große Angelegenheit. ◆**do a'way,** *v.i.* **to do away with sth.,** etwas abschaffen. ◆**'doing,** *s.* **that takes some d.,** da gehört schon allerhand dazu; **that was your d.,** das war Ihr Werk. ◆**do-it-yourself** [du:itjɔ:'self]. **I.** *s. F:* Eigenbau *m;* Heimwerken *n.* **II.** *adj.* Heimwerker-; **d.-i.-y. shop,** Heimwerkerladen *m.* ◆**'do 'up,** *v.tr. F:* (*a*) (ein Haus usw.) renovieren, *F:* aufmöbeln; **to do oneself up,** sich herausputzen; (*b*) (etwas) einpacken; (*button*) (einen Mantel usw.) zuknöpfen; (Knöpfe) zumachen.

**docile** ['dəusail], *adj.* fromm.

**dock**[1] [dɔk], **I.** *s.* Dock *n;* **the docks,** die Hafenanlagen *fpl.* **II.** *v.i.* ins Dock gehen. ◆**'docker,** *s.* Hafenarbeiter *m.* ◆**'dockyard,** *s.* Werft *f.*

**dock**[2], *s. Jur:* Anklagebank *f.*

**doctor** ['dɔktər], *s.* (*abbr.* **Dr.**) Doktor *m; Med:* Arzt *m;* **woman d.,** Ärztin *f.*

**doctrine** ['dɔktrin], *s.* Lehre *f.*

**document** ['dɔkjumənt], *s.* Dokument *n; pl.* Papiere *f.* ◆**docu'mentil.** **I.** *adj.* dokumentarisch. **II.** *s.* Dokumentarfilm *m.*

**dodge** [dɔdʒ], *v.tr.* (*a*) (einem Schlag) ausweichen; (*b*) **to d. a task,** sich vor einer Aufgabe drücken. ◆**'dodgy,** *adj. F:* (*a*) (*tricky*) knifflig; (*b*) (*faulty*) defekt.

**dog** [dɔg]. **I.** *s.* Hund *m.* **II.** *v.tr.* (j-n) verfolgen. ◆**'dog-'tired,** *adj.* hundemüde. ◆**'dog-house,** *s. F:* **to be in the d.-h.,** in Ungnade sein.

**dogged** ['dɔgid], *adj.* verbissen.

**dogmatic** [dɔg'mætik], *adj.* dogmatisch.

**dole** [dəul]. **I.** *s. F:* Arbeitslosenunterstützung *f;* **to go on the d.,** stempeln gehen. **II.** *v.tr.* **to d. sth. out,** etwas austeilen.

**doll** [dɔl]. **I.** *s.* Puppe *f.* **II.** *v.tr. F:* **to d. oneself up,** sich herausputzen.

**dollar** ['dɔlər], *s.* Dollar *m.*

**dolphin** ['dɔlfin], *s.* Delphin *m.*

**dome** [dəum], *s.* Kuppel *f.*

**domestic** [də'mestik], *adj.* (*a*) Haus-; **d. animal,** Haustier *n;* (*b*) (*d. in character*) häuslich; **d. bliss,** häusliches Glück; (*c*) *Econ: etc:* (*of produce, news*) inländisch; **d. flight,** Inlandsflug *m.* ◆**do'mesticate,** *v.tr.* (ein Tier) zähmen. ◆**do'mesticated,** *adj.* (*of pers.*) häuslich.

**dominant** ['dɔminənt], *adj.* (vor)herrschend. ◆**'dominance,** *s.* Vorherrschaft *f.* ◆**'dominate** ['dɔmineit], *v.* **1.** *v.tr.* (*a*) (j-n) beherrschen; (über etwas *acc*) dominieren; (*b*) (einen Ort usw.) überragen. **2.** *v.i.* dominieren. ◆**domi'nation,** *s.* Beherrschung *f.*

**domineering** [dɔmi'niəriŋ], *adj.* herrisch.

**donate** [də'neit, dəu-], *v.tr.* spenden. ◆**do'nation,** *s.* Spende *f.* ◆**donor** ['dəunər], *s.* Spender *m.*

**donkey** ['dɔŋki], *s.* Esel *m; Fig:* **d. work,** Schwerarbeit *f; F:* **donkey's years,** eine Ewigkeit.

**doodle** ['du:dl]. **I.** *v.i.* kritzeln. **II.** *s.* Gekritzel *n.*

**doomed** [du:md], *adj.* (*of plan etc.*) **d. to failure,** zum Scheitern verurteilt.

**door** [dɔ:r], *s.* **1.** (*a*) Tür *f;* **next d.,** nebenan; **d. to d. selling,** Hausieren *n;* (*b*) **out of doors,** im Freien. **2.** (*entrance*) Eingang *m;* **tickets at the d.,** Karten beim Eingang. ◆**'doorbell,** *s.* Türklingel *f.* ◆**'doorhandle,** *s.* Türklinke *f.* ◆**'doorknob,** *s.* **1.** (*turning*) Türgriff *m.* **2.** (*fixed*) Türknopf *m.* ◆**'doorman,** *s.* Portier *m.* ◆**'doormat,** *s.* Abtreter *m.* ◆**'doorstep,** *s.* Schwelle *f.* ◆**'doorway,** *s.* Türöffnung *f;* **in the d.,** in der Tür.

**dope** [dəup]. **I.** *s. F:* Rauschgift *n.* **II.** *v.tr. F:* **to d. oneself,** Drogen nehmen. ◆**'dop(e)y,** *adj.* **1.** (*a*) (dazed) benommen; (*b*) (sleepy) schläfrig. **2.** (*stupid*) dämlich.

**dormitory** ['dɔ:mitri], *s.* Schlafsaal *m.*

**dose** [dəus]. **I.** *s.* Dosis *f.* **II.** *v.tr.* **to d. s.o. with sth.,** j-m eine (starke) Dosis von etwas *dat* verabreichen.

**dot** [dɔt]. **I.** *s.* Punkt *m; F:* **he arrived on the d.,** er kam auf die Minute; **on the d. of two,** Punkt zwei. **II.** *v.tr.* **dotted line,** punktierte Linie; *Fig:* **a hillside dotted with houses,** ein Berghang mit vereinzelten Häusern.

**dote** [dəut], *v.i.* **to d. on/upon s.o.,** j-n vernarrt sein.

**double** [dʌbl]. **I.** *adj.* **1.** doppelt; **d. bed,** französisches Bett; **d. room,** Doppelzimmer *n.* **2.** (*twice*) doppelt; **the number,** die doppelte Anzahl, zweimal soviel. **II.** *adv.* **to see d.,** doppelt sehen. **III.** *s.* **1.** **the d.,** im Laufschritt *m; Fig:* schnellstens. **2.** *Sp:* **doubles,** Doppel *n.* **IV.** *v.* **1.** *v.tr.* verdoppeln. **2.** *v.i.* sich verdoppeln. ◆**'double-'bass,** *s.* Kontrabaß *m.* ◆**'double-'breasted,** *adj.* (*of suit*) zweireihig. ◆**'double-'cross,** *v.tr. F:* (j-n) hintergehen. ◆**'double-'decker,** *s.* (*bus*) Doppeldecker *f.* ◆**'double-park,** *v.tr. & i.* doppelreihig parken.

**doubt** [daut]. **I.** *v.* **1.** *v.tr.* (j-s Worte) anzweifeln; **I d. whether he will come,** ich zweifle, ob er kommen wird. **2.** *v.i.* zweifeln. **II.** *s.* Zweifel *m;* **no d.,** zweifellos. ◆**'doubtful,** *adj.* **1.** (*of thing*) zweifelhaft. **2.** (*of pers.*) nicht sicher; **to be d.** (**about sth.**), (an etwas *dat*) zweifeln. ◆**'doubtless,** *adv.* zweifellos.

**dough** [dəu], *s.* Teig *m.* ◆**'doughnut,** *s.* Berliner *m; South G:* Krapfen *m.*

**dove** [dʌv], *s.* Taube *f.*

**dowdy** ['daudi], *adj.* unschick.

**down** [daun]. **I.** *adv.* **1.** (*a*) (*direction*) hinunter; (b) **£100 d.**, £100 als Anzahlung; (c) (written) **did you get it d.**? hast du alles mitschreiben können? (d) int. **d. with the traitors!** nieder mit den Verrätern! (to a dog) **d.!** sitz! **2.** (position) (on the ground) am Boden; **d. below**, unten; F: **d. there**, dort unten; **face d.**, mit dem Gesicht/(of thing) der Vorderseite nach unten; F: **d. under**, in Australien. **3.** (as far as) **d. to here**, bis hier herunter; **I'm d. to my last cigarette**, ich habe nur noch eine Zigarette. **4.** F: **d. and out**, verkommen. **II.** prep. (a) hinab; **d. the mountain**, den Berg hinunter; (b) (along) **d. the street**, die Straße entlang; (c) N.Am: **d. town**, im/(direction) ins Stadtzentrum. **III.** adj. **d. payment**, Anzahlung f. **IV.** s. **ups and downs**, Höhen und Tiefen. **V.** v.tr. (a) **to d. tools**, die Arbeit niederlegen; (b) (drink) F: **to d. a gin**, sich dar einen Gin hinter die Binde gießen. ◆**'down-at-'heel**, adj. heruntergekommen. ◆**'downcast**, adj. niedergeschlagen. ◆**'downfall**, s. Untergang m (eines Reiches usw.); **love of drink was his d.**, die Trunksucht war sein Verderben. ◆**'down'hill. I.** adv. **to go d.**, (of road) abwärts führen; (of car etc.) bergab fahren; Fig: **he's going d.**, es geht bergab mit ihm. **II.** adj. Sp: **d. race**, Abfahrtslauf m. ◆**'downpour**, s. Platzregen m. ◆**'downright. I.** adj. ausgesprochen; **d. lie**, glatte Lüge. **II.** adv. **d. rude**, ausgesprochen frech. ◆**down'stairs. I.** adv. unten; **to go d.**, (die Treppe) hinuntergehen. **II.** adj. **the d. rooms**, die Zimmer im Erdgeschoß. ◆**'down-to-'earth**, adj. sachlich. ◆**'downward**, adj. abwärts führend; **d. slope**, Abhang m; **d. trend** (of prices), fallende Tendenz f (der Preise). ◆**'downwards**, adv. abwärts; (downhill) bergab.

**doze** [dəuz], v.i. dösen; **to d. off**, einnicken.

**dozen** ['dʌzn], s. Dutzend n; **half a d.**, ein halbes Dutzend; **dozens of people**, ein Haufen Leute.

**drab** [dræb], adj. (colour) graubraun; Fig: eintönig.

**draft** [drɑːft]. **I.** s. **1.** Mil: N.Am: Einberufung f. **2.** Com: Tratte f. **3.** Skizze f (eines Planes usw.); Entwurf m (eines Briefes usw.). **II.** v.tr. (Truppen) einberufen; (einen Brief usw.) aufsetzen; (einen Plan usw.) skizzieren.

**drag** [dræg]. **I.** v. **1.** v.tr. schleppen. **2.** v.i. (of conversation, lawsuit etc.) sich in die Länge ziehen. **II.** s. **1.** F: **an awful d.**, eine schreckliche Plage. **2.** in d., als Frau gekleidet. ◆**'drag 'on**, v.i. sich (in die Länge) ziehen.

**dragon** ['drægən], s. Drache m. ◆**'dragonfly**, s. Libelle f.

**drain** [drein]. **I.** s. **1.** Abfluß m; (underground) Kanal m; **d. pipe**, Abflußrohr n; Kanalrohr n. **2.** Fig: Verlust m; **d. on** one's strength, Kräfteverschleiß m; Fin: **d. on reserves**, Abfluß m von Geldern. **II.** v. **1.** v.tr. (a) (away), Wasser ableiten; (b) (ein Glas usw.) austrinken; (Land) entwässern; (einen Teich, Aut: den Kühler usw.) ablassen; Med: (eine Wunde) dränieren. **2.** v.i. (of water etc.) **to d.** (away), versickern. ◆**'drainage**, s. main d., Kanalisation f. ◆**'draining**, s. H: **d. board**, Abtropfbrett n.

**drama** ['drɑːmə], s. **1.** Schauspiel n. **2.** (event) Drama n. ◆**dramatic** [drə'mætik], adj. dramatisch. ◆**'dramatist**, s. Dramatiker m. ◆**'dramatize**, v.tr. (etwas) dramatisieren; (einen Roman usw.) für die Bühne bearbeiten.

**drastic** ['dræstik], adj. drastisch.

**draught** [drɑːft], s. **1.** pl. **draughts**, Damespiel n; **d. board**, Damebrett n. **2.** (in a room) Zugluft f. **3.** **beer on d./d. beer**, Bier n vom Faß. ◆**'draughty**, adj. zugig; **it's d.**, es zieht.

**draughtsman**, pl. **-men** ['drɑːftsmən], s. technischer Zeichner m.

**draw** [drɔː]. **I.** s. **1.** Ziehung f (einer Lotterie); Verlosung f (bei einer Tombola). **2.** (of pers., event) Attraktion f; (of play) **to be a** (box office) **d.**, ein Kassenschlager sein. **3.** Sp: Unentschieden n; **to end in a d.**, unentschieden ausgehen. **II.** v. **1.** v.tr. irr. (a) (pull) (den Vorhang usw.) zuziehen; (of horse etc.) (einen Wagen usw.) ziehen; **to d. water**, Wasser holen; **to d. breath**, (ein)atmen; (b) (attract) (Zuhörer, Kunden usw.) anziehen; **to d. attention to sth.**, die Aufmerksamkeit auf etwas acc lenken; (c) Com: (Geld) abheben; (einen Scheck) einlösen; (d) (ein Bild, einen Plan usw.) zeichnen; (e) Sp: **the game was drawn**, das Spiel war unentschieden. **2.** v.i. (a) **to d. near** (to s.o.), j-m nahekommen; (of train) **to d. into a station**, in einen Bahnhof einfahren; (b) **to d. to an end**, dem Ende entgegengehen; (of day etc.) sich neigen; (c) **to let the tea d.**, den Tee ziehen lassen. ◆**'draw a'head**, v.i. einen Vorsprung gewinnen. ◆**'draw a'side**, v.tr. (a) (j-n) beiseite nehmen; (b) (einen Vorhang usw.) zur Seite ziehen. ◆**'draw 'back**, v. **1.** v.tr. (einen Vorhang, seine Hand usw.) zurückziehen. **2.** v.i. sich zurückziehen. ◆**'drawback**, s. Nachteil m. ◆**'drawer**, s. Schublade f; **chest of drawers**, Kommode f. ◆**'draw 'in**, v.i. **the days are drawing in**, die Tage werden kürzer. ◆**'drawing**, s. Zeichnung f; **d. board**, Reißbrett n; **d. pin**, Reißzwecke f. ◆**'drawing-room**, s. Salon m. ◆**drawn**, adj. **1.** (of pers.) tired and d., müde und abgespannt. **2.** Sp: **d. match**, unentschiedenes Spiel. ◆**'draw 'on**, v.tr. (Reserven) angreifen; **he can d. on fifty years' experience**, er kann auf die Erfahrung von fünfzig Jahren zurückgreifen. ◆'draw 'out, *v.tr.* (*a*) (etwas aus etwas *dat*) herausholen; **I could not d. her o.**, ich konnte nichts aus ihr herauslocken; (*b*) (eine Diskussion usw.) hinauszienen. ◆'draw 'up, *v.* 1. *v.tr.* (ein Dokument) aufsetzen; (eine Liste) aufstellen. 2. *v.i.* (*of vehicle*) halten.

**dread** [dred], *v.tr.* fürchten. ◆'dreadful, *adj.* furchtbar.

**dream** [driːm]. I. *s.* Traum *m*; **to have a d.**, träumen; **like a d.**, traumhaft; **my d. house**, mein Traumhaus. II. *v.tr. & i. irr.* träumen (**about/of**, von + *dat*); *F:* **I shouldn't d. of doing it**, das würde mir nicht im Traum einfallen.

**dreary** ['driəri], *adj.* (*of weather etc.*) trostlos; (*of work etc.*) langweilig.

**dregs** [dregz], *s.pl.* Bodensatz *m*.

**drench** [dren(t)ʃ], *v.tr.* (j-n) durchnässen, **drenched**, klatschnaß.

**dress** [dres]. I. *s.* 1. (*a*) Kleidung *f*; (*b*) **d. circle**, erster Rang; **d. rehearsal**, Generalprobe *f.* 2. (*women's d.*) Kleid *n*; **d. designer**, Modedesigner(in) *m(f)*; (*creating fashions*) Modeschöpfer(in) *m(f)*. II. *v.* 1. *v.tr.* (*a*) (sich) anziehen; (*b*) (*decorate*) schmücken; (*c*) (eine Wunde) verbinden. 2. *v. refl. & i.* **to d.** (**oneself**), sich anziehen. ◆'dresser, *s. H:* Anrichte *f*; (**kitchen**) (Küchenbüfett *n* mit) Tellerbord *n.* ◆'dressing, *s.* 1. Ankleiden *n.* 2. *Cu:* (**salad**) *d.*, Salatsoße *f.* 3. *Med:* Verband *m.* 4. *attrib.* **d. gown**, Morgenrock *m*; **d. room**, (i) Ankleideraum *m*; (ii) *Th:* Garderobe *f*; **d. table**, Frisiertisch *m.* ◆'dressmaker, *s.* Schneiderin *f.* ◆'dressmaking, *s.* Schneidern *f.* ◆'dress 'up, *v.i.* (*of pers.*) (*a*) sich festlich anziehen; (*b*) sich auftakeln; (*b*) **to d. up as X**, sich als X verkleiden.

**dribble** ['dribl], *v.tr. & i.* (*a*) (*of baby etc.*) sabbern; (*b*) *Sp:* **to d.** (**the ball**), (mit dem Ball) dribbeln.

**dried** [draid], *adj.* getrocknet; **d. fruit**, Dörrobst *n*; **d. milk**, Trockenmilch *f.*

**drift** [drift]. I. *s.* 1. (*of argument*) Gedankengang *m*; Tendenz *f.* 2. (**snow-)d.**, Schneewehe *f.* II. *v.i.* (*a*) (*of pers.*) sich treiben lassen; (*of thing*) getrieben werden; *Nau: Av:* abgetrieben werden; (*of couple*) **to d. apart**, sich auseinanderleben; (*b*) (*of snow*) Wehen bilden.

**drill** [dril]. I. *s.* 1. *Tchn:* Bohrer *m.* 2. *Mil:* Exerzieren *n.* II. *v.* 1. *v.tr.* (*a*) (ein Loch) bohren; (*b*) (j-n) drillen. 2. *v.i.* bohren (**for sth.**, nach etwas *dat*).

**drink** [driŋk]. I. *s.* 1. (*a*) **food and d.**, Essen und Trinken; (*b*) **to give s.o. a d.**, j-m etwas zu trinken geben; **to have a d.**, etwas trinken. 2. Getränk *n*; **soft d.**, alkoholfreies Getränk; (**alcoholic**) *d.*, Drink *m.* 3. Alkohol *m*; **the worse for d.**, betrunken. II. *v.tr. irr.* trinken; **to d. to s.o.**, auf j-s Wohl trinken. ◆'drinkable, *adj.* trinkbar. ◆'drinker, *s.* Trinker(in) *m(f).* ◆'drinking, *s.* **d. fountain**, Trinkbrunnen *m*; **d. water**,

Trinkwasser *n.* ◆'drink 'up, *v.tr. & i.* austrinken.

**drip** [drip]. I. *s.* 1. (*a*) Tropfen *m*; (*b*) *Med:* Infusion *f.* 2. *F:* (*pers.*) Niete *f.* II. *v.i.* tropfen. ◆'drip-'dry, *adj.* bügelfrei.

**drive** [draiv]. I. *s.* 1. Fahrt *f*; **to go for a d.**, spazierenfahren; **an hour's d.**, eine Stunde Fahrt. 2. (*entrance*) Auffahrt *f*; (*short*) Einfahrt *f.* 3. **left-hand d.**, Linkssteuerung *f.* 4. *E:* **d. shaft**, Antriebswelle *f.* 5. (*of pers.*) Energie *f*; **to have plenty of d.**, viel Tatkraft haben. II. *v.irr.* 1. *v.tr.* (*a*) (Vieh) treiben; (*b*) (ein Fahrzeug) fahren; **to d. s.o. home**, j-n nach Hause fahren; **can you d.?** kannst du Auto fahren? (*c*) (einen Motor, ein Fahrzeug) betreiben; (*d*) **to d. s.o. to sth.**, j-n zu etwas *dat* treiben; **to d. s.o. mad** j-n zum Wahnsinn treiben. 2. *v.i.* fahren; **to d. on the right**, rechts fahren. ◆'drive at, *v.tr.* **what are you driving at?** worauf willst du hinaus? ◆'drive a'way, *v.* 1. *v.tr.* vertreiben. 2. *v.i.* abfahren. ◆'drive 'back, *v.* 1. *v.tr.* (*a*) (j-n, ein Heer) zurücktreiben; (*b*) (ein Auto) zurückfahren. 2. *v.i.* zurückfahren. ◆'drive-in, *s.* **d.-i.** (**cinema**), Autokino *n.* ◆'driver, *s.* Fahrer *m* (eines Autos usw.); Führer *m* (einer Lokomotive). ◆'driveway, *s.* Auffahrt *f.* ◆'drive 'up, *v.i.* vorfahren. ◆'driving. I. *adj.* **d. force**, treibende Kraft; **d. rain**, strömender Regen. II. *s.* Fahren *n*; **d. school**, Fahrschule *f*; **d. test**, Fahrprüfung *f*; **d. licence**, Führerschein *m.*

**drizzle** ['drizl]. I. *s.* Sprühregen *m.* II. *v.i.* **it is drizzling**, es nieselt.

**droop** [druːp], *v.i.* (*a*) (*of eyelids*) sich senken; (*b*) (*of flowers*) verwelken.

**drop** [drɔp]. I. *s.* 1. (*liquid*) Tropfen *m.* 2. (*fall*) Abfall *m*; **d. in prices**, Preissenkung *f*; **sudden d. in temperature**, plötzlicher Temperatursturz; *Fig:* **at the d.** **of a hat**, auf der Stelle. II. *v.* 1. *v.i.* (*a*) (*of leaves, blossom etc.*) fallen; (*of ground*) abfallen; (*b*) (*of pers.*) umfallen; (*c*) (*of prices*) sinken; (*of wind*) nachlassen; (*of voice*) leiser werden. 2. *v.tr.* (*a*) (etwas) fallen lassen; (Bomben) abwerfen; **to** (**let**) **d. a remark**, eine Bemerkung fallen lassen; (*b*) *F:* (*set down*) **I'll d. you at the station**, ich setze Sie am Bahnhof ab; (*c*) (*omit*) (eine Silbe, j-n) auslassen; (*give up*) (eine Idee usw.) aufgeben; (*d*) (die Stimme, die Augen) senken. ◆'drop 'in, *v.i.* vorbeikommen. ◆'drop 'off, *v.i.* (*a*) (*of thing*) abfallen; (*b*) (*of pers.*) einnicken. ◆'drop 'out, *v.i.* (*of pers.*) **to d. o. of a contest**, aus einem Wettkampf ausscheiden.

**drought** [draut], *s.* Dürre *f.*

**drown** [draun], *v.* 1. *v.tr.* (*a*) (ein Tier usw.) ertränken; **to be drowned**, ertrinken; (*b*) (einen Laut) übertönen. 2. *v.i.* ertrinken.

**drowse** [drauz], *v.i.* dösen. ◆'drowsy, *adj.* schläfrig.

**drudgery** ['drʌdʒəri], s. Schinderei f.
**drug** [drʌg]. I. s. 1. Med: Droge f. 2.
Rauschgift n; **d. addict**, Rauschgiftsüch-
tige(r) f(m). II. v.tr. (j-m) Drogen verabreichen. ◆'**druggist**, s. N.Am: Apo-
theker(in) m(f). ◆'**drugstore**, s. N.Am:
Drugstore m.
**drum** [drʌm]. I. s. Trommel f; coll. **the
drums**, das Schlagzeug. II. v. 1. v.i. (of
rain, fingers etc.) trommeln. 2. v.tr. **to d.
sth. into s.o.**, j-m etwas einpauken.
◆'**drummer**, s. Schlagzeuger m.
◆'**drumstick**, s. Mus: Trommelschlegel
m.
**drunk** [drʌŋk], adj. **to get d.**, sich betrin-
ken. ◆'**drunkard**, s. Säufer(in) m(f).
◆'**drunken**, adj. betrunken; **in a d. stupor**, sinnlos betrunken. ◆'**drunkenness**, s. Rausch m.
**dry** [drai]. I. adj. 1. trocken. 2. Fig: (a)
(boring) langweilig; (b) **a d. sense of humour**, ein trockener Humor. II. v. 1.
v.tr. (a) trocknen; **to d. the dishes**, das
Geschirr abtrocknen; **to d. one's eyes**,
die Tränen abwischen; (b) (Obst) dörren.
2. v.i. trocknen. ◆'**dry-'clean**, v.tr.
chemisch reinigen. ◆'**dry 'cleaner's**, s.
chemische Reinigung f. ◆'**dry 'off**, v.i.
trocknen. ◆'**dry 'out**, v.i. austrocknen.
◆'**dry-'rot**, s. Hausschwamm m. ◆'**dry
'up**, v.i. (a) (of spring) versiegen; (b) (of
ideas etc.) sich erschöpfen; (c) F: (dishes)
abtrocknen.
**dual** ['dju(:)əl], adj. doppelt; **d. carriageway**, zweispurige Straße.
**dubious** ['dju:biəs], adj. (a) (of pers.) unsicher; (b) (of undertaking) zweifelhaft.
**duchess** ['dʌtʃis], s. Herzogin f.
**duck** [dʌk]. I. s. Ente f. II. v.i. sich duk-
ken. ◆'**duckling**, s. Entlein n; Cu: junge Ente f.
**dud** [dʌd], F: adj. wertlos; **d. cheque**,
ungedeckter Scheck.
**due** [dju:]. I. adj. 1. (a) (of payment etc.)
fällig; **the balance d. to us**, der uns ge-
schuldete Saldo; (b) **the train is d. at two
o'clock**, der Zug soll (laut Fahrplan) um
zwei Uhr ankommen. 2. (appropriate) angemessen; **in d. course**, zu gegebener
Zeit; **with d. respect**, bei aller Achtung.
3. **d. to**, wegen + gen. 4. adv. **d. north**,
genau nördlich. II. s. 1. **to give him his
d.** he can really sing, er kann schon singen, das muß man ihm lassen. 2. pl.
(fees) abstumpfen fpl.
**duel** ['dju(:)əl], s. Duell n.
**duet** [dju(:)'et], s. Duett n.
**duke** [dju:k], s. Herzog m.
**dull** [dʌl]. I. adj. 1. (a) (of day, weather,
light) trüb; (of colour) matt; (b) (of sound,
pain) dumpf; (of sight, hearing) schwach.
2. (boring) langweilig. II. v.tr. (die Sinne
usw.) abstumpfen; (Schmerz) mildern.
**duly** ['dju:li], adv. 1. (correctly) ord-
nungsgemäß. 2. (punctually) rechtzeitig.
**dumb** [dʌm], adj. 1. stumm. 2. F: esp.
N.Am: dumm.

**dummy** ['dʌmi], s. 1. Attrappe f; (tailor's) **d.**, Schneiderpuppe f; (in window)
Schaufensterpuppe f. 2. (for baby)
Schnuller m. 3. **d. run**, Probe f.
**dump** [dʌmp]. I. s. 1. Abladeplatz m;
(rubbish) **d.**, (small) Müllhaufen m; (big)
Müllhalde f. 2. F: **what a d.!** was für ein
trauriger Laden! II. v.tr. (a) (Müll usw.)
deponieren; (b) F: (etwas) hinschmeißen.
**dumps** [dʌmps], s.pl. F: **down in the d.**,
deprimiert, (esp. after failure etc.) niedergeschlagen.
**dunce** [dʌns], s. Ignorant m; F: Niete f.
**dune** [dju:n], s. Düne f.
**dung** [dʌŋ], s. Mist m.
**dungarees** [dʌŋgə'ri:z], s.pl. Latzhose f.
**dungeon** ['dʌn(d)ʒ(ə)n], s. Verlies n.
**duplicate. I.** ['dju:plikət], **1.** adj.
Duplikat-; **d. key**, Nachschlüssel m. **2.** s.
Duplikat n; **in d.**, in doppelter Ausfertigung. II. ['dju:plikeit], v.tr. (a) (one copy)
(ein Dokument usw.) kopieren; (several
copies) (Schriftstücke) vervielfältigen; (b)
(etwas) wiederholen. ◆'**duplicator**, s.
Vervielfältigungsapparat m.
**durable** ['djuərəbl], adj. haltbar; (of material) strapazierfähig. ◆**dura'bility**, s.
Haltbarkeit f.
**duration** [dju(ə)'reiʃ(ə)n], s. Dauer f.
**during** ['djuəriŋ], prep. während + gen.
**dusk** [dʌsk], s. Dämmerung f; **at d.**, bei
Einbruch der Dunkelheit.
**dust** [dʌst]. I. s. Staub m; F: **to bite the
d.**, ins Gras beißen. II. v.tr. (Möbel
usw.) abstauben. ◆'**dustbin**, s. Müll-
tonne f. ◆'**dust-cart**, s. Müll(abfuhr)-
wagen m. ◆'**duster**, s. Staubtuch n.
◆'**dustman**, pl. **-men**, s. Müllmann m;
**the dustmen**, die Müllabfuhr.
◆'**dustpan**, s. Müllschippe f.
◆'**dusty**, adj. staubig.
**Dutch** [dʌtʃ]. I. adj. holländisch; Fig: **to
go D.**, getrennte Kasse machen. II. s. 1.
**the Dutch**, die Holländer pl. 2. Holländisch n. ◆'**Dutchman**, pl. **-men**, Holländer m.
**duty** ['dju:ti], s. 1. Pflicht f. 2. (a) (task)
**duties**, Aufgaben fpl; **to take up one's
duties**, sein Amt antreten; (b) **to be on
d.**, Dienst haben; **off d.**, dienstfrei. 3.
(customs) **d.**, Zoll m. ◆'**dutiable**, adj.
zollpflichtig. ◆'**dutiful**, adj. pflichtbe-
wußt; **-ly**, adv. pflichtgemäß. ◆'**duty-
'free**, adj. zollfrei.
**duvet** ['duvei], s. Daunendecke f.
**dwarf** [dwɔ:f]. I. s. Zwerg m. II. v.tr. (etwas) winzig erscheinen lassen.
**dwell** [dwel], v.i.irr. **to d. on a subject**,
bei einem Thema verweilen.
**dwindle** ['dwindl], v.i. dahinschwinden.
**dye** [dai]. I. s. Farbstoff m. II. v.tr. färben.
**dyke** [daik], s. see dike.
**dynamic** [dai'næmik], adj. dynamisch.
**dynamite** ['dainəmait], s. Dynamit n.
**dynamo**, pl **-os** ['dainəməu, -əuz], s. Dynamo.

**dynasty** ['dinəsti], s. Dynastie f.
**dysentery** ['disəntri], s. Ruhr f.
**dyslexia** [dis'leksiə], s. Legasthenie f.

◆**dys'lexic**, adj. legasthenisch.
**dyspepsia** [dis'pepsiə], s. Verdauungsstörung f.

# E

**E, e** [iː], s. (der Buchstabe) E, e n.
**each** [iːtʃ]. **I.** adj. jeder, jede, jedes; e. year, jedes Jahr; e. one of us, jede(r) (einzelne) von uns. **II.** pron. 1. (ein) jeder, (eine) jede, (ein) jedes; they earn £10 e./e. earn £10, jeder von ihnen verdient zehn Pfund. 2. e. other, einander; to be afraid of e. other, Angst voreinander haben; they hate e. other, sie hassen sich. **III.** adv. je; (of pers.) pro Person; (of thing) pro Stück; 10 pence e., je zehn Pence/zehn Pence pro Stück.
**eager** ['iːgər], adj. eifrig. ◆'**eagerness**, s. Eifer m.
**eagle** ['iːgl], s. Adler m.
**ear¹** ['iər], s. Ohr n; to play by e., nach dem Gehör spielen; F: to play it by e., je nach Lage der Dinge entscheiden. ◆'**earache**, s. Ohrenschmerzen mpl. ◆'**eardrum**, s. Trommelfell n. ◆'**earlobe**, s. Ohrläppchen n. ◆'**earmark**, v.tr. to e. funds for a purpose, Gelder für einen Zweck vorsehen. ◆'**earphones**, s.pl. Kopfhörer m. ◆'**earplug**, s. Ohrenwatte f. ◆'**earring**, s. Ohrring m. ◆'**earshot**, s. within e., in Hörweite. ◆'**earwig**, s. Ohrwurm m.
**ear²**, s. (of corn) Ähre f.
**earl** [əːl], s. Graf m.
**early** ['əːli]. **I.** adj. früh; **II.** adv. früh; to come (too) e., zu früh kommen.
**earn** [əːn], v.tr. verdienen. ◆'**earnings**, s.pl. 1. (of pers.) Einkommen n. 2. (profit) Ertrag m.
**earnest** ['əːnist]. **I.** adj. ernst. **II.** s. in e., im Ernst.
**earth** [əːθ], s. Erde f; F: where on e. have you been? wo in aller Welt bist du gewesen? **down to e.**, nüchtern. ◆'**earthenware**, s. Töpferwaren fpl. ◆'**earthly**, adj. 1. irdisch. 2. there is no e. reason for this, es besteht kein erdenklicher Grund dafür. ◆'**earthquake**, s. Erdbeben n.
**ease** [iːz]. **I.** s. 1. at e., behaglich; ill at e., unbehaglich. 2. Leichtigkeit f; with e., mühelos. **II.** v. 1. v.tr. (a) (das Gemüt) beruhigen; (Schmerzen) lindern; (b) (die Spannung, Belastung) erleichtern; (c) to e. sth. into position, etwas vorsichtig in die richtige Lage bringen. 2. v.i. (a) (of situation) sich entspannen; (b) (of storm etc.) to e. off, nachlassen.
**easel** ['iːzl], s. Staffelei f.
**east** [iːst]. **I.** s. Osten m; the Far/Middle E., der Ferne/Nahe Osten. **II.** adv. nach Osten. **III.** adj. Ost-, östlich; **e. wind**, Ostwind m. ◆'**easterly**, adj. = east **III.**

◆'**eastern**, adj. östlich; (oriental) orientalisch; **E. Bloc**, Ostblock m. ◆'**eastwards**, adv. ostwärts, nach Osten.
**Easter** ['iːstər], s. Ostern n; **E. egg**, Osterei n.
**easy** ['iːzi]. **I.** adj. leicht; **on e. terms**, auf Raten; **-ily**, adv. 1. leicht. 2. **e. the best**, bei weitem das Beste. **II.** adv. F: to take it/things e., sich schonen; sich dat Ruhe gönnen. ◆'**easy-chair**, s. Lehnstuhl m. ◆'**easy-'going**, adj. (a) unbekümmert; (b) (lax) lässig.
**eat** [iːt], v.irr. 1. v.tr. (of pers.) essen; (of animal) fressen. 2. v.i. (a) to e. out, auswärts essen; (b) to e. into sth., etwas allmählich wegfressen. ◆'**eating**. **I.** s. Essen n. **II.** adj. attrib. (apple, Eßapfel m; e. habits, Eßgewohnheiten fpl. ◆'**eat 'up**, v.tr. (a) (eine Speise) aufessen; (b) F: (Benzin, Geld usw.) fressen.
**eaves** [iːvz], s.pl. Dachüberhang m.
**eavesdrop** ['iːvzdrɔp], v.i. lauschen. ◆'**eavesdropper**, s. Lauscher(in) m(f).
**ebb** [eb]. **I.** s. 1. e. (tide), Ebbe f. 2. Fig: things were at a low e., es herrschte Tiefstand. **II.** v.i. (of tide) zurückgehen; (of life etc.) to e. away, dahinschwinden.
**ebony** ['ebəni], s. Ebenholz n.
**eccentric** [ek'sentrik, ik-]. **I.** adj. exzentrisch. **II.** s. (pers.) Sonderling m. ◆**eccen'tricity**, s. (of pers.) Verschrobenheit f; (eccentric act) Exzentrizität f.
**echo** ['ekəu]. **I.** s. (pl. echoes) Echo n. **II.** v. 1. v.tr. (einen Ton usw.) widerhallen lassen; (j-s Worte) nachbeten. 2. v.i. widerhallen.
**eclipse** [i'klips]. **I.** s. Finsternis f; **e. of the moon**, Mondfinsternis f. **II.** v.tr. (einen Stern) verfinstern; Fig: (j-n) in den Schatten stellen.
**ecology** [iː'kɔlədʒi], s. Ökologie f.
**economic** [iːkə'nɔmik], adj. wirtschaftlich. ◆**eco'nomical**, adj. sparsam. ◆**eco'nomics**, s. pl. Volkswirtschaft f. ◆**economist** [i(ː)'kɔnəmist], s. Volkswirt m. ◆**e'conomize**, v.i. sparen (on, an + dat). ◆**e'conomy**, s. 1. (of pers., car etc.) Sparsamkeit f; **e. (measure)**, Sparmaßnahme f. 2. (of country) Wirtschaft f; (political), Volkswirtschaft f.
**ecstasy** ['ekstəsi], s. Ekstase f.
**edge** [edʒ]. **I.** s. 1. (of a blade) Schneide f; Fig: to take the e. off sth., etwas dat die Schärfe nehmen; **on e.**, (of pers.) nervös; **to have the e. (on s.o.)**, (j-m) gerade noch voraus sein. 2. Rand m (des Waldes usw.); Kante f (des Tisches usw.). **II.** v.tr. & i. (a) the street was

**edged with trees,** die Straße war mit Bäumen eingesäumt; (b) **to e. one's way forwards,** Schritt für Schritt vorrücken; **to e. away,** sich zurückziehen. ◆**'edgeways,** adv. seitlich; F: **I can't get a word in e.,** ich kann kein Wort anbringen. ◆**'edgy,** adj. F: nervös.

**edible** ['edibl], adj. genießbar.

**edit** ['edit], v.tr. (a) (ein Buch, eine Zeitung) herausgeben; (b) (einen Text) redigieren; (c) (einen Film, eine Aufnahme) schneiden. ◆**edition** [i'diʃən], s. 1. Ausgabe f. 2. (printing) Auflage f. ◆**editor** ['editər], s. 1. Herausgeber m (eines Buches, einer Zeitung). 2. Redakteur m (bei einer Zeitung, bei einem Verlag). ◆**edi'torial. I.** adj. redaktionell; e. **staff,** Redaktion f. **II.** s. Leitartikel m.

**educate** ['edjukeit], v.tr. (a) bilden; (of university etc.) ausbilden; (b) (bring up) erziehen. ◆**education** [edju'keiʃən], s. 1. Sch: Bildung f; (at university) Ausbildung f. 2. (upbringing) Erziehung f. ◆**edu'cational,** adj. 1. (a) (of methods etc.) pädagogisch; (b) (valuable) pädagogisch wertvoll. 2. Bildungs-; e. **film,** Lehrfilm m.

**eel** [iːl], s. Aal m.

**eerie, eery** ['iəri], adj. 1. (of feeling, story) unheimlich. 2. (of house, atmosphere) gespenstisch.

**effect** [i'fekt]. **I.** s. 1. Wirkung f; **to have an e. on s.o.,** auf j-n wirken; **to take e.,** (i) wirksam werden; (ii) (of regulation) in Kraft treten; (iii) (of drugs) wirken; **to no e.,** ohne Resultat; **calculated for e.,** auf Effekt berechnet. 2. (meaning) **words to that e.,** Worte in diesem Sinne. 3. pl. **personal effects,** persönliche Habe f. 4. **in e.,** in Wirklichkeit. **II.** v.tr. bewirken. ◆**e'ffective,** adj. 1. wirkungsvoll. 2. (impressive) eindrucksvoll.

**effeminate** [i'feminit], adj. unmännlich.

**effervescent** [efə'vesənt], adj. sprudelnd.

**efficiency** [i'fiʃənsi], s. (a) (of pers.) Tüchtigkeit f; (b) (of firm, machinery etc.) Leistungsfähigkeit f. ◆**e'fficient,** adj. (a) (of pers.) tüchtig; (b) (of firm, factory) leistungsfähig; **-ly,** adv. **to work e.,** (of machine) rationell/(of pers.) tüchtig arbeiten.

**effort** ['efət], s. (a) Anstrengung f; **to make an e.,** sich anstrengen; (b) pl Bemühungen fpl. ◆**'effortless,** adj. mühelos.

**effusive** [i'fjuːsiv], adj. (of feelings, thanks etc.) überschwenglich.

**egg¹** [eg], s. Ei n; e. **yolk,** Eidotter n; e. **cup,** Eierbecher m. ◆**'eggshell,** s. Eierschale f.

**egg²,** v.tr. **to e. s.o. on,** j-n anstacheln.

**egoism** ['egəuizəm], s. Egoismus m. ◆**'egoist,** s. Egoist(in) m(f).

**Egypt** ['iːdʒipt]. Pr.n. Ägypten n. ◆**E'gyptian** [i'dʒipʃ(ə)n]. **I.** adj. ägyptisch. **II.** s. Ägypter(in) m(f).

**eiderdown** ['aidədaun], s. Daunendecke

f.

**eight** [eit], num. adj. acht. ◆**eighteen** [ei'tiːn], num. adj. achtzehn. ◆**eigh'teenth,** num. adj. achtzehnte(r,s). ◆**eighth** ['eitθ]. **I.** num. adj. achte(r,s). **II.** s. Achtel n. ◆**eighty** ['eiti], num. adj. achtzig.

**either** ['aiðər]. **I.** adj. jeder, jede, jedes (von zweien). **II.** pron. (a) eine(r,s) (von zweien); **e. of them,** einer von den beiden. **III.** conj. e. ... **or,** entweder ... oder. **IV.** adv. F: **not ... e./nor ... e.,** (und) auch nicht.

**ejaculate** [i'dʒækjuleit], v.tr. (also Biol:), ausstoßen. ◆**ejacu'lation,** s. 1. Ausruf m. 2. Biol: Ejakulation f.

**eject** [i'dʒekt], v.tr. hinauswerfen.

**eke** [iːk]. v.tr. **e. out,** (Vorräte usw.) strecken; **to e. out a meagre existence,** sich dürftig durchschlagen.

**elaborate.** **I.** [i'læbərit], adj. (a) kompliziert; (b) (of decoration) kunstvoll. **II.** [i'læbəreit], v. 1. v.tr (einen Plan) sorgfältig ausarbeiten. 2. v.i. **can you e.?** können Sie ausführlicher sein?

**elapse** [i'læps], v.i. verstreichen.

**elastic** [i'læstik]. **I.** adj. elastisch; e. **band,** Gummiband n. **II.** s. Gummiband n.

**elbow** ['elbəu], s. Ellbogen m. ◆**elbow-room,** s. Bewegungsfreiheit f.

**elder** ['eldər]. **I.** adj. älter. **II.** s. (der, die) Ältere m, f. ◆**elderly,** adj. ältlich. ◆**eldest,** adj. älteste(r,s).

**elect** [i'lekt]. **I.** v.tr. (a) **to e. to do sth.,** sich entschließen, etwas zu tun; (b) (j-n zu einem Amt) wählen. **II.** adj. **President e.,** zukünftiger Präsident. ◆**e'lection,** s. Wahl f; e. **campaign,** Wahlkampf m. ◆**e'lectorate,** s. Wählerschaft f.

**electric** [i'lektrik], adj. elektrisch; e. **motor,** Elektromotor m; e. **shock,** elektrischer Schlag. ◆**e'lectrical,** adj. elektrisch. ◆**electrician** [-'triʃ(ə)n], s. Elektriker m. ◆**electricity** [-'trisiti], s. Elektrizität f; (current) Strom m. ◆**e'lectrocute,** v.tr. **to be electrocuted,** durch einen elektrischen Schlag getötet werden. ◆**e'lectrode,** s. Elektrode f. ◆**elec'trolysis,** s. Elektrolyse f. ◆**e'lectron,** s. Elektron n. ◆**elec'tronic. I.** adj. elektronisch. **II.** s.pl. **electronics,** Elektronik f.

**elegance** ['eligəns], s. Eleganz f. ◆**'elegant,** adj. elegant.

**element** ['elimənt], s. (a) Element n; (b) **an e. of truth,** ein Körnchen Wahrheit. ◆**elementary** [-'ment(ə)ri], adj. elementar; (simple) einfach; e. **school,** Grundschule f.

**elephant** ['elifənt], s. Elefant m.

**elevate** ['eliveit], v.tr. (a) (etwas) hochheben; (b) (j-n in Rang) erhöhen (**to,** zu + dat). ◆**'elevated,** adj. 1. (of position) hoch (angebracht). 2. (of thought) erhaben. ◆**'elevator,** s. N.Am: Fahrstuhl m.

**eleven** [i'levn]. **I.** num. adj. elf. **II.** s.pl.

**elevenses,** *approx.* zweites Frühstück.
◆**e'leventh,** *num. adj.* elfte(r,s); **at the e. hour,** in letzter Minute.
**elicit** [i'lisit], *v.tr.* **to e. the facts,** die Tatsachen ans Licht bringen; **to e. a reply from s.o.,** j-m eine Antwort entlocken.
**eligible** ['elidʒibl], *adj.* berechtigt; **e. for a pension,** pensionsberechtigt; **e. bachelor,** gute Partie.
**eliminate** [i'limineit], *v.tr.* beseitigen; *Sp:* **to be eliminated in the first round,** in der ersten Runde ausscheiden.
◆**elimi'nation,** *s.* Beseitigung *f; Sp:* Ausscheiden *n.*
**elm** [elm], *s.* Ulme *f.*
**elocution** [elə'kjuːʃ(ə)n], *s.* Sprechtechnik *f.*
**elongate** [i'lɒŋgeit], *v.tr.* verlängern.
**elope** [i'ləup], *v.i.* durchgehen.
**eloquence** ['elɒkwəns], *s.* Beredsamkeit *f.* ◆**'eloquent,** *adj.* (*of pers.*) beredt.
**else** [els], *adv.* **1.** sonst; **do as I say, or e.!** tu, was ich sage, sonst passiert was! **2.** *adj. or adv.* **did you see anybody e.?** hast du sonst noch jemand gesehen? **something e.,** etwas anderes; (*in shop*) **anything e.?** sonst noch etwas? **someone e.,** jemand anders; **nothing e.,** sonst nichts; **everything e.,** alles andere; **somewhere e.,** irgendwo anders; **nowhere e.,** sonst nirgends. ◆**'else'where,** *adv.* anderswo; **to go e.,** woandershin gehen.
**elucidate** [i'luːsideit], *v.tr.* (ein Problem usw.) erläutern.
**elude** [i'ljuːd], *v.tr.* (*a*) ausweichen; (*b*) (*escape*) (j-m) entkommen.
**elusive** [i'ljuːsiv], *adj.* schwer erfaßbar.
**emaciated** [i'meiʃieitid], *adj.* abgezehrt.
**emancipate** [i'mænsipeit], *v.tr.* emanzipieren.
**embalm** [im'bɑːm], *v.tr.* (einen Leichnam) einbalsamieren.
**embankment** [im'bæŋkmənt], *s.* Böschung *f;* **railway e.,** Bahndamm *m.*
**embargo,** *pl.* **-oes** [em'bɑːgəu, -əuz], *s.* Embargo *n;* **trade e.,** Handelssperre *f.*
**embark** [im'bɑːk], *v.i.*(*a*) (*of pers.*) sich einschiffen; (*b*) **to e. on sth.,** mit etwas *dat* beginnen.
**embarrass** [im'bærəs], *v.tr.* (j-n) in Verlegenheit bringen. ◆**em'barrassed,** *adj.* (*of pers.*) verlegen. ◆**em'barrassing,** *adj.* peinlich. ◆**em'barrassment,** *s.* Verlegenheit *f.*
**embassy** ['embəsi], *s.* Botschaft *f.*
**embellish** [im'beliʃ], *v.tr.* (*a*) verschönern; (*b*) (eine Geschichte) ausschmücken. ◆**em'bellishment,** *s.* **1.** Verschönerung *f.* **2.** *Fig:* Ausschmükkung *f.*
**embers** ['embəz], *s.pl.* glühende Kohlen *fpl.*
**embezzle** [im'bezl], *v.tr.* unterschlagen.
**embittered** [im'bitərd], *adj.* verbittert.
**emblem** ['embləm], *s.* (*symbol*) Sinnbild *n;* (*of town etc.*) Wahrzeichen *n.*
**embody** [im'bɒdi], *v.tr.* verkörpern.

◆**em'bodiment,** *s.* Verkörperung *f.*
**embrace** [im'breis]. **I.** *v.tr.* (*a*) (j-n) umarmen; (*b*) (*include*) (etwas) umfassen; (*c*) **to e. a cause,** sich einer Sache annehmen. **II.** *s.* Umarmung *f.*
**embroider** [im'brɔidər], *v.tr.* (*a*) (ein Muster) sticken; (*b*) (eine Geschichte usw.) ausschmücken. ◆**em'broidery,** *s.* Stikkerei *f.*
**embryo,** *pl.* **-os** ['embriəu, -əuz], *s.* Embryo *m.*
**emerald** ['emərəld]. **I.** *s.* Smaragd *m.* **II.** *adj.* smaragdgrün.
**emerge** [i'məːdʒ], *v.i.* (*a*) (aus dem Wasser usw.) auftauchen; (aus einem Zimmer usw.) herauskommen; (*b*) (*be discovered*) zum Vorschein kommen; (*c*) (*come into being*) entstehen. ◆**e'mergence,** *s.* Entstehung *f* (einer Theorie usw.).
**emergency** [i'məːdʒənsi], *s.* Notfall *m;* **in (case of) an e.,** im Notfall; **e. exit,** Notausgang *m;* **state of e.,** Ausnahmezustand *m;* **e. landing,** Notlandung *f.*
**emery** ['eməri], *s.* **e. board,** Sandblattfeile *f.*
**emigrant** ['emigrənt], *s.* Auswanderer *m.* ◆**emigrate** ['emigreit], *v.i.* auswandern. ◆**emi'gration,** *s.* Auswanderung *f.*
**eminence** ['eminəns], *s.* hoher Rang *m.* ◆**'eminent,** *adj.* berühmt; **-ly,** *adv.* eminent.
**emit** [i'mit], *v.tr.* (*a*) (Strahlen, Wärme, usw.) ausstrahlen; (Rauchwolken usw.) ausstoßen; (*b*) (*of pers.*) (einen Seufzer, einen Ton) von sich geben.
**emotion** [i'məuʃ(ə)n], *s.* **1.** (*feeling*) Gefühl *n.* **2.** (state of) e., Erregung *f.* ◆**e'motional,** *adj.* (*of pers., voice*) erregt; (*of attitude etc.*) gefühlsbetont; **-ly,** *adv.* (*with adj.*), gefühlsmäßig; (*with verb*) erregt. ◆**e'motive,** *adj.* gefühlsgeladen.
**emperor** ['empərər], *s.* Kaiser *m.*
**emphasis** ['emfəsis], *s.* Betonung *f.* ◆**'emphasize,** *v.tr.* betonen. ◆**emphatic** [im'fætik], *adj.* betont; (*of warning etc.*) nachdrücklich; (*of refusal, denial*) entschieden.
**empire** ['empaiər], *s.* Reich *n.*
**employ** [im'plɔi], *v.tr.* (*a*) (j-n) beschäftigen; (*take on*) (j-n) anstellen; (*b*) (etwas) verwenden. ◆**em'ployee,** *s.* Arbeitnehmer(in) *m(f).* ◆**em'ployer,** *s.* Arbeitgeber(in) *m(f).* ◆**em'ployment,** *s.* (*a*) (*work*) Beschäftigung *f;* **e. agency,** Stellenvermittlungsbüro *n;* **full e.,** Vollbeschäftigung *f;* (*b*) (*taking on*) Anstellung *f* (von Arbeitskräften).
**empress** ['empris], *s.* Kaiserin *f.*
**empty** ['empti]. **I.** *v.* **1.** *v.tr.* (etwas) (aus)leeren; (einen Tank) ablassen; (ein Zimmer usw.) ausräumen. **2.** *v.i.* sich leeren. **II.** *adj.* leer; **on an e. stomach,** auf nüchternen Magen. ◆**'empty-'handed,** *adj.* mit leeren Händen. ◆**'emptiness,** *s.* Leere *f.*

**enable** [i'neibl], *v.tr.* **to e. s.o. to do sth.,** es j-m ermöglichen, etwas zu tun.
**enamel** [i'næməl], *s.* Email *n.*
**enamoured** [i'næməd], *adj.* angetan (**of**, von + *dat*).
**enchant** [in'tʃɑːnt], *v.tr.* (j-n) bezaubern.
◆**en'chanting**, *adj.* entzückend.
◆**en'chantment**, *s.* Zauber *m.*
**encircle** [in'səːkl], *v.tr.* (j-n, etwas) umzingeln; (den Feind usw.) einkreisen.
**enclose** [in'kləuz], *v.tr.* (*a*) (*surround*) (etwas mit etwas *dat*) umgeben; (ein Grundstück) einfrieden; (*b*) **to e. sth. with a letter,** etwas einem Brief beifügen.
◆**en'closure** [-ʒər], *s.* (*a*) (*paddock*) Koppel *f;* (*in zoo etc.*) Gehege *n;* (*b*) *Com:* Anlage *f.*
**encompass** [in'kʌmpəs], *v.tr.* umfassen.
**encore** [ɔŋ'kɔːr], *int. & s.* Zugabe *f.*
**encounter** [in'kauntər]. **I.** *v.tr.* (j-m, etwas *dat*) begegnen; (auf Schwierigkeiten usw.) stoßen. **II.** *s.* Begegnung *f.*
**encourage** [in'kʌridʒ], *v.tr.* (*a*) (j-n) ermutigen (**to do sth.**, etwas zu tun); (*b*) (die Forschung usw.) fördern. ◆**en'couragement**, *s.* **1.** (*act*) Ermutigung *f;* (*thing*) Ansporn *m.* **2.** Förderung *f.* ◆**en'couraging**, *adj.* ermutigend.
**encroach** [in'krəutʃ], *v.i.* übergreifen (**on s.o.'s property,** auf j-s Besitz; **on s.o.'s rights,** in j-s Rechte).
**encyclopaedia** [insaiklə'piːdiə], *s.* Enzyklopädie *f.*
**end** [end]. **I.** *s.* **1.** Ende *n;* **to put an e. to sth./make an e. of sth.,** mit etwas *dat* Schluß machen; **to come to an e.,** enden; **in the e.,** zum Schluß; **for two hours on e.,** zwei Stunden lang ununterbrochen; **my hair stood on e.,** mir standen die Haare zu Berge; **cigarette e.,** Zigarettenstummel *m; Aut:* **big e.,** Pleuelfuß *m.* **2.** (*purpose*) Zweck *m;* **to this e.,** zu diesem Zweck; **for his own ends,** für seine eigenen Zwecke. **II.** *v.* **1.** *v.tr.* beenden. **2.** *v.i.* (*a*) enden; (*b*) **to e. up with sth.,** zum Schluß etwas bekommen; **you'll e. up in jail,** du wirst noch im Gefängnis landen.
**endanger** [in'deindʒər], *v.tr.* gefährden.
**endear** [in'diər], *v.tr.* beliebt machen.
◆**en'dearing**, *adj.* gewinnend.
**endeavour** [in'devər]. **I.** *s.* Bemühen *n.* **II.** *v.i.* **to e. to do sth.,** sich darum bemühen, etwas zu tun.
**endorse** [in'dɔːs], *v.tr.* (*a*) (j-s Meinung usw.) bestätigen; (*b*) (einen Scheck) indossieren. ◆**en'dorsement**, *s.* Strafvermerk *m* (auf einem Führerschein).
**endow** [in'dau], *v.tr.* **endowed with great talents,** mit großem Talent ausgestattet. ◆**en'dowment**, *s.* **e. insurance,** Erlebensfallversicherung *f.*
**endure** [in'djuər], *v.tr.* aushalten.
◆**en'durance,** *s.* (**powers of**) **e.,** Durchhaltevermögen *n.*
**enemy** ['enəmi], *s.* Feind *m.*
**energetic** [enə'dʒetik], *adj.* energisch.

◆**energy** ['enədʒi], *s.* Energie *f.*
**enforce** [in'fɔːs], *v.tr.* (ein Gesetz) durchführen; (eine Vorschrift) in Kraft setzen.
◆**en'forcement**, *s.* Durchführung *f.*
**engage** [in'geidʒ], *v.* **1.** *v.tr.* (*a*) (*employ*) (j-n) anstellen; (*b*) **to e. s.o. in conversation**, j-n ins Gespräch ziehen. **2.** *v.i.* (*a*) (*of pers.*) sich befassen (**in**, mit + *dat*); (*b*) (*of gears etc.*) ineinandergreifen.
◆**en'gaged**, *adj.* **1.** (*a*) (*of couple*) verlobt; **to get e.,** sich verloben; (*b*) (*occupied*) beschäftigt (**in sth.**, mit etwas *dat*). **2.** *Tel:* besetzt. ◆**en'gagement**, *s.* **1.** (*appointment*) Verabredung *f.* **2.** (*to be married*) Verlobung *f;* **e. ring,** Verlobungsring *m.* ◆**en'gaging**, *adj.* (*of manner etc.*) gewinnend.
**engine** ['endʒin], *s.* **1.** *Rail:* Lokomotive *f;* **e. driver,** Lokomotivführer *m.* **2.** (*of car etc.*) Motor *m.* ◆**engineer** [endʒi'niər]. **I.** *s.* Ingenieur *m.* **II.** *v.tr.* organisieren, arrangieren.
◆**engi'neering**, *s.* Ingenieurwesen *n;* (**mechanical**) **e.,** Maschinenbau *m.*
**England** ['iŋglənd]. *Pr.n.* England *n.*
◆**English** [iŋgliʃ]. **I.** *adj.* englisch. **II.** *s.* **1.** Englisch *n.* **2.** **the E.,** die Engländer. ◆**'Englishman**, *pl.* **-men,** *s.* Engländer *m.* ◆**'Englishwoman**, *pl.* **-women,** *s.* Engländerin *f.*
**engrave** [in'greiv], *v.tr.* eingravieren.
**engross** [in'grəus], *v.tr.* **to be engrossed in sth.,** in etwas *acc* vertieft sein.
**engulf** [in'gʌlf], *v.tr.* überschütten.
**enhance** [in'hɑːns], *v.tr.* (den Wert) erhöhen; (Aussehen) verschönern.
**enigma** [i'nigmə], *s.* Rätsel *n.*
◆**enigmatic** [enig'mætik], *adj.* rätselhaft.
**enjoy** [in'dʒɔi], *v.tr.* (*a*) (an etwas *dat*) Vergnügen finden; **to e. oneself,** sich gut unterhalten; **to e. doing sth.,** etwas gern machen; (*b*) (Rechte usw.) genießen.
◆**en'joyable**, *adj.* erfreulich.
◆**en'joyment**, *s.* Vergnügen *n;* Unterhaltung *f.*
**enlarge** [in'lɑːdʒ], *v.* **1.** *v.tr.* vergrößern. **2.** *v.i.* **to e. upon a subject,** sich über ein Thema verbreiten. ◆**en'largement**, *s.* Vergrößerung *f.*
**enlighten** [in'laitn], *v.tr.* aufklären.
**enlist** [in'list], *v.* **1.** *v.tr.* (Soldaten) anwerben; **to e. s.o.'s aid,** j-n zu Hilfe ziehen. **2.** *v.i.* sich (zum Militärdienst) melden.
**enmity** ['enmiti], *s.* Feindschaft *f;* **e. towards/for s.o.,** Feindseligkeit *f* gegen j-n.
**enormous** [i'nɔːməs], *adj.* riesig; **an e. success,** ein Riesenerfolg.
**enough** [i'nʌf], *adj. & adv.* genug; **e. money,** genug Geld; **that's e.,** (*no more thanks*) das genügt; **that's e.!** das reicht!; **good e.,** gut genug.
**enquire** [in'kwaiər], *v.* **1.** *v.tr.* **to e. the way etc.,** sich nach dem Weg usw. erkundigen. **2.** *v.i.* sich erkundigen

(about/after s.o., sth., nach j-m, etwas dat). ◆**en'quiry**, s. 1. Nachfrage f; to make enquiries (about s.o., sth.), (über j-n, etwas acc) Erkundigungen einziehen. 2. (by police etc.) Untersuchung f.

**enrich** [in'ritʃ], v.tr. bereichern.

**enroll(l)** [in'raul], v.i. (of students) sich immatrikulieren.

**en route** [ã:(n)'ru:t], adv. unterwegs.

**enslave** [in'sleiv], v.tr. versklaven.

**ensue** [in'sju:], v.i. folgen; the ensuing discussion, die darauf folgende Diskussion.

**ensure** [in'ʃuər], v.tr. gewährleisten; to e. that ..., dafür sorgen, daß ...

**entail** [in'teil], v.tr. (Folgen) mit sich bringen; (Ausgaben) verursachen.

**enter** ['entər], v. 1. v.i. (a) eintreten; (b) to e. for a competition, sich an einem Wettbewerb beteiligen. 2. v.tr. (a) (ein Haus, ein Zimmer) betreten; (b) to e. university, auf die Universität gehen; (c) to e. a name on a list, einen Namen in eine Liste eintragen.

**enterprise** ['entəpraiz], s. 1. (project, firm) Unternehmen n; private e., Privatwirtschaft f. 2. (spirit of) e., Unternehmungsgeist m. ◆**'enterprising**, adj. unternehmungslustig.

**entertain** [entə'tein], v. 1. v.tr. (a) (amuse) (j-n) unterhalten; (b) (einen Gast) bewirten; (c) (einen Vorschlag) in Erwägung ziehen. 2. v.i. Gäste empfangen. ◆**enter'taining**, adj. unterhaltend. ◆**enter'tainment**, s. Unterhaltung f.

**enthuse** [in'θju:z], v.i. to e. about/over s.o., sth., für j-n, etwas acc schwärmen. ◆**en'thusiasm**, s. Begeisterung f. ◆**en'thusiast**, s. Enthusiast m; Anhänger m (einer Sportart); football e., Fußballfreund m. ◆**enthusi'astic**, adj. begeistert.

**entice** [in'tais], v.tr. (j-n) verlocken; to e. s.o. into sth., j-n zu etwas dat verleiten.

**entire** [in'taiər], adj. ganz; (of amount, population etc.) gesamt; (of confidence, attention) voll; -ly, adv. völlig. ◆**entirety** [in'taiə(rə)ti], s. Gesamtheit f; the population in its e., die gesamte Bevölkerung.

**entitle** [in'taitl], v.tr. to e. s.o. to sth., j-n zu etwas dat berechtigen. ◆**en'titled**, adj. to be e. to sth., ein Anrecht auf etwas acc haben; to be e. to do sth., dazu berechtigt sein, etwas zu tun.

**entrance** ['entrəns], s. 1. (of pers.) Eintritt m. 2. (a) (of building, cave etc.) Eingang m; (b) (for vehicle) Einfahrt f.

**entreat** [in'tri:t], v.tr. (j-n) anflehen.

**entrust** [in'trʌst], v.tr. to e. a secret, a child etc. to s.o., j-m ein Geheimnis, ein Kind usw. anvertrauen.

**entry** ['entri], s. 1. (a) (of pers.) Eintritt m; (b) (into country) Einreise f; e. visa, Einreisevisum n; no e., (i) (for traffic) keine Einfahrt; (ii) (for people) Zutritt verboten. 2. (in list etc.) Eintrag m; Com:

Buchung f.

**enunciate** [i'nʌnsieit], v. 1. v.tr. (Meinungen, Worte) aussprechen. 2. v.i. to e. clearly, eine deutliche Aussprache haben. ◆**enunci'ation**, s. Aussprache f.

**envelop** [en'veləp], v.tr. einhüllen (in sth., in etwas acc). ◆**envelope** ['envələup], s. Umschlag m.

**enviable** ['enviəbl], adj. beneidenswert. ◆**envious** ['enviəs], adj. neidisch (of, auf + acc).

**environment** [in'vaiərənmənt], s. Umwelt f; (surroundings) Umgebung f. ◆**environ'mental**, adj. Umwelt-.

**envisage** [in'vizidʒ], v.tr. voraussehen.

**envoy**, pl. -s ['envɔi, -z], s. Gesandte(r) m.

**envy** ['envi]. I. s. Neid m (of, auf + acc); she is the e. of her friends, sie wird von ihren Bekannten beneidet. II. v.tr. to e. s.o. sth., j-n um etwas acc beneiden.

**epic** ['epik], s. Epos n.

**epidemic** [epi'demik]. I. adj. epidemisch. II. s. Epidemie f.

**epilepsy** ['epilepsi], s. Epilepsie f. ◆**epi'leptic**, adj. epileptisch.

**episode** ['episəud], s. (a) Episode f; (b) TV: in four episodes, in vier Folgen.

**epitaph** ['epita:f], s. Grabinschrift f.

**epitome** [i'pitəmi], s. Verkörperung f.

**epoch** ['i:pɔk], s. Epoche f.

**equal** ['i:kwəl]. I. adj. 1. (a) gleich; (b) to be e. to the occasion/to a task, den Anlaß/einer Aufgabe gewachsen sein; -ly, adv. gleich; e. good, gleich/genauso gut; e., ..., gleichermaßen ... II. s. Gleichgestellte(r) f(m). III. v.tr. (j-m, etwas dat) gleichen; to e. s.o./be s.o.'s e., j-m gleichkommen. ◆**equality** [i'kwɔliti], s. Gleichheit f. ◆**'equalize**, v. 1. v.tr. gleichmachen. 2. v.i. Sp: ausgleichen. ◆**'equalizer**, s. Sp: Ausgleichstreffer m.

**equanimity** [ekwə'nimiti], s. Gleichmut m.

**equate** [i'kweit], v.tr. to e. sth. with sth., etwas mit etwas dat gleichsetzen. ◆**e'quation**, s. Gleichung f.

**equator** [i'kweitər], s. Äquator m. ◆**equatorial** [ekwə'tɔ:riəl], adj. äquatorial.

**equilibrium** [i:kwi'libriəm], s. Gleichgewicht n.

**equinox** ['ekwinɔks], s. Tagundnachtgleiche f.

**equip** [i'kwip], v.tr. ausrüsten; (ein Labor, eine Fabrik usw.) ausstatten. ◆**e'quipment**, s. 1. Ausrüstung f. 2. (apparatus) Geräte npl; Apparatur f.

**equitable** ['ekwitəbl], adj. gerecht.

**equity** ['ekwiti], s. 1. Gerechtigkeit f. 2. equities, Dividendenpapiere npl.

**equivalent** [i'kwivələnt]. I. adj. (of equal value) gleichwertig; (b) (corresponding) entsprechend. II. s. Entsprechung f; (in value) Gegenwert m; (counterpart) Gegenstück n.

**era** ['iərə], s. Zeitalter n.

**eradicate** [i'rædikeit], *v.tr.* ausrotten.

**erase** [i'reiz], *v.tr.* (Geschriebenes) ausradieren; (eine Aufnahme) löschen. ◆**e'raser,** *s.* Radiergummi *m.*

**erect** [i'rekt]. **I.** *adj.* aufrecht. **II.** *v.tr.* (a) (einen Mast usw.) aufrichten; (b) (ein Gebäude) errichten. ◆**e'rection,** *s.* **1.** Errichtung *f.* **2.** *Anat:* Erektion *f.*

**erode** [i'rəud], *v.tr.* (by water) auswaschen, (by wind etc.) aushöhlen. ◆**erosion** [i'rəuʒ(ə)n], *s.* Erosion *f.*

**erotic** [i'rɔtik], *adj.* erotisch.

**errand** ['erənd], *s.* Botengang *m; to run errands,* Besorgungen machen.

**erratic** [i'rætik], *adj.* (of things) unregelmäßig; (of pers., conduct) unberechenbar.

**error** ['erər], *s.* Irrtum *m; (tangible mistake)* Fehler *m.* ◆**erroneous** [i'rəuniəs], *adj.* (of opinion etc.) irrig; (of accusation) falsch; **-ly,** *adv.* irrtümlich.

**erudite** ['erudait], *adj.* gelehrt.

**erupt** [i'rʌpt], *v.i.* ausbrechen. ◆**e'ruption,** *s.* Ausbruch *m.*

**escalate** ['eskəleit], *v.tr. & i.* (sich) eskalieren. ◆**esca'lation,** *s.* Eskalation *f.* ◆**'escalator,** *s.* Rolltreppe *f.*

**escape** [is'keip]. **I.** *s.* **1.** (a) Flucht *f; to* **have a narrow e.,** gerade noch davonkommen; **e. route,** Fluchtweg *m; e.* **clause,** Ausweichklausel *f;* (b) **fire e.,** Feuerleiter *f;* (c) (of gas, fluid) Ausströmen *n* 2. *Fig:* Ausweg *m* (aus einer Situation). **II.** *v.* **1.** *v.i.* (a) (of pers.) entkommen; **to e. from prison,** aus dem Gefängnis entfliehen; (b) (of gas) entweichen; (of liquid) ausströmen. **2.** *v.tr.* (j-m) entkommen; (einer Gefahr usw.) entgehen; **to e. notice,** unbemerkt bleiben; **the name escapes me,** der Name fällt mir nicht ein. ◆**'escapade,** *s.* Eskapade *f.* ◆**es'capism,** *s.* Flucht *f* vor der Wirklichkeit.

**escarpment** [is'kɑ:pmənt], *s.* Böschung *f.*

**escort. I.** ['eskɔ:t], *s.* (of several pers.) Geleit *n;* (individual) Begleiter(in) *m(f).* **II.** [is'kɔ:t], *v.tr.* geleiten.

**especially** [i'speʃəli], *adv.* besonders.

**espionage** ['espjənɑ:ʒ], *s.* Spionage *f.*

**essay** ['esei], *s.* Aufsatz *m.*

**essence** ['esəns], *s.* (a) (of thing) Wesen *n; in e.,* im wesentlichen; (b) *Ch: Cu:* Essenz *f.* ◆**essential** [i'senʃəl]. **I.** *adj.* (a) (unbedingt) notwendig; (of qualifications) erforderlich; (of pers.) unentbehrlich; (of food, industry) lebenswichtig; (b) (of feature etc.) wesentlich. **II.** *s.* **the essentials,** das Wesentliche; **-ly,** *adv.* im wesentlichen; (chiefly) hauptsächlich.

**establish** [is'tæbliʃ], *v.tr.* (a) (set up) (eine Organisation) bilden; (ein Geschäft) gründen; (Ordnung) schaffen; **to e. oneself,** (i) (settle) sich niederlassen; (ii) (achieve fame) sich dat einen Namen machen; (b) (prove) beweisen. ◆**es'tablishment,** *s.* **1.** Bildung *f,* Gründung *f.* **2. educational e.,** Bildungs-

anstalt *f.* **3. the E.,** das Establishment.

**estate** [is'teit], *s.* (land) Gut *n;* (housing) **e.,** Wohnsiedlung *f; e.* **agent,** Grundstücksmakler *m; e.* **car,** Kombiwagen *m.*

**esteem** [is'ti:m], *s.* Achtung *f.*

**estimate. I.** ['estimət], *s.* Schätzung *f; (of cost)* Kostenvoranschlag *m.* **II.** ['estimeit], *v.tr.* schätzen. ◆**esti'mation,** *s.* **1.** Schätzung *f.* **2. in my e.,** meiner Ansicht nach.

**estuary** ['estjuəri], *s.* Flußmündung *f.*

**etching** ['etʃiŋ], *s.* Radierung *f.*

**eternal** [i'tə:nl], *adj.* ewig. ◆**e'ternity,** *s.* Ewigkeit *f.*

**ether** ['i:θər], *s.* Äther *m.*

**ethics** ['eθiks], *s.pl.* Ethik *f.* ◆**'ethical,** *adj.* (of values etc.) ethisch; (of conduct etc.) sittlich.

**Ethiopia** [i:θi'əupjə]. *Pr.n.* Äthiopien *n.*

**etiquette** ['etiket], *s.* Etikette *f.*

**etymology** [eti'mɔlədʒi], *s.* Etymologie *f.*

**euphemism** ['ju:fimiz(ə)m], *s.* Euphemismus *m.*

**Europe** ['juərəp]. *Pr.n.* Europa *n.* ◆**Euro'pean. I.** *adj.* europäisch. **II.** *s.* Europäer(in) *m(f).*

**evacuate** [i'vækjueit], *v.tr.* (a) (Personen, Truppen) evakuieren; (b) (ein Gebäude, ein Stadtteil usw.) räumen.

**evade** [i'veid], *v.tr.* ausweichen; sich (um eine Frage) drücken; (j-s Wachsamkeit) entgehen; **to e. the issue,** dem Streitpunkt umgehen.

**evaluate** [i'væljueit], *v.tr.* den Wert (von etwas dat) berechnen; (eine Leistung) bewerten.

**evangelical** [i:væn'dʒelik(ə)l], *adj.* evangelisch. ◆**e'vangelist,** *s.* Evangelist *m.*

**evaporate** [i'væpəreit], *v.tr.* (eine Flüssigkeit) verdunsten lassen; **evaporated milk,** Kondensmilch *f.* **2.** *v.i.* verdunsten.

**evasion** [i'veiʒən], *s.* Ausweichen *n.* ◆**e'vasive,** *adj.* (of answer) ausweichend.

**eve** [i:v], *s.* Vorabend *m; on the e. of his departure,* am Vortag seiner Abreise.

**even**[1] ['i:vən], *adv.* **1.** (a) sogar, selbst; **e. his enemies,** sogar seine Feinde; **e. so,** trotzdem; **e. if,** selbst/auch wenn; (b) **not e.,** nicht einmal. **2. e. better,** noch besser.

**even**[2]. **I.** *adj.* **1.** (level) eben. **2.** (a) (of breathing) regelmäßig; (b) (of temperament) ausgeglichen. **3.** (equal) gleich; (of two people) **to be e.,** quitt sein; *Fig:* **to get e. with s.o.,** es j-m heimzahlen. **4. e. number,** gerade Zahl. **II.** *v.tr.* **to e. things out,** das Gleichgewicht wiederherstellen.

**evening** ['i:vniŋ], *s.* Abend *m; in the e.,* abends; **e. dress,** Abendtoilette *f; (man's)* Abendanzug *m; (lady's)* Abendkleid *n; e.* **class,** Abendkurs *m.*

**event** [i'vent], *s.* **1.** (case) Fall *m; in the e.,* wie es sich herausstellte. **2.** (happening) Ereignis *n;* **the course of events,**

der Verlauf der Dinge. **3.** *esp. Sp:* **(type of) e.,** Disziplin *f.* ◆**e'ventful,** *adj.* ereignisreich. ◆**eventual** [i'ventjuəl], *adj.* **it led to his e. ruin,** es führte schließlich zu seinem Untergang; **-ly,** *adv.* schließlich. ◆**eventu'ality,** *s.* Möglichkeit *f;* **for all eventualities,** für alle Fälle.

**ever** ['evər], *adv.* **1.** *(a)* je; **have you e. been to Munich?** waren Sie schon einmal in München? **he hardly e. smokes,** er raucht fast nie; **it was raining harder than e.,** es regnete stärker denn je; *(b)* **e. since then,** seitdem. **2.** *(a)* immer; **for e.,** für immer; *(b)* **e. larger,** immer größer. **3.** *F:* **e. so difficult,** furchtbar schwer. ◆**'evergreen. I.** *adj. Bot:* immergrün. **II.** *s. Bot:* immergrüne Pflanze *f.* ◆**ever'lasting,** *adj.* ewig.

**every** ['evri], *adj.* jeder, jede, jedes. ◆**'everybody/'everyone,** *indef. pron.* jeder. ◆**'everyday,** *adj.* alltäglich. ◆**'everything,** *s. indef. pron.* alles. ◆**'everywhere,** *adv.* überall.

**evict** [i(:)'vikt], *v.tr.* auf die Straße setzen. ◆**e'viction,** *s.* Vertreibung *f.*

**evidence** ['evidəns], *s.* **1.** **much in e.,** überall zu sehen. **2.** *(sign)* Anzeichen *n; (trace)* Spur *f.* **3.** *Jur:* *(a) (proof)* Beweis *m; (b) (statement)* Zeugenaussage *f;* **to give e.,** (als Zeuge) aussagen. ◆**'evident,** *adj.* offensichtlich.

**evil** ['i:v(ə)l]. **I.** *adj.* böse; *(of pers., character, reputation etc.)* übel. **II.** *s.* **1.** Übel *n.* **2.** *(forces of e.)* das Böse.

**evoke** [i'vəuk], *v.tr.* (ein Bild usw.) heraufbeschwören; (Gefühle) wachrufen. ◆**evocative** [i'vɔkətiv], *adj.* **an e. picture,** ein Bild, das Erinnerungen wachruft.

**evolve** [i'vɔlv], *v.* **1.** *v.tr.* (etwas) entwickeln. **2.** *v.i.* *(a)* sich entwickeln **(into,** zu + *dat*); *(b) (come into being)* entstehen **(from,** aus + *dat*). ◆**evolution** [i:və'lu:ʃ(ə)n], *s.* Entwicklung *f; Biol:* Evolution *f.*

**ewe** [ju:], *s.* Mutterschaf *n.*

**ex-** [eks-], *prefix* ex-, Ex-.

**exact** [ig'zækt, ig-]. **I.** *adj.* genau; **the e. opposite,** das genaue Gegenteil. **II.** *v.tr.* (ein Versprechen usw.) erzwingen; **-ly,** *adv.* **1.** genau; **not e. ideal,** nicht gerade ideal. **2.** *(as answer)* eben! genau! ◆**e'xacting,** *adj.* anspruchsvoll.

**exaggerate** [ig'zædʒəreit], *v.tr. & i.* übertreiben. ◆**exagge'ration,** *s.* Übertreibung *f.*

**exam** [eg'zæm, ig-], *s. Sch: F:* = **examination 2.** *(a).* ◆**exami'nation,** *s.* **1.** *(investigation)* Untersuchung *f.* **2.** *(a) Sch:* Prüfung *f,* Examen *n; (b) Jur:* Verhör *n.* ◆**e'xamine,** *v.tr.* *(a)* untersuchen; *(b) Sch:* (einen Kandidaten) prüfen. ◆**e'xaminer,** *s.* Prüfer(in) *m(f).*

**example** [ig'zɑ:mpl], *s.* Beispiel *n* **(of,** für + *acc*); **for e.,** zum Beispiel; **to set an e.,** ein (gutes) Beispiel geben; **to make**

an **e. of s.o.,** an j-m ein Exempel statuieren.

**exasperate** [ig'zɑ:spəreit], *v.tr.* (j-n) zur Verzweiflung bringen. ◆**e'xasperated,** *adj.* außer sich *dat.* ◆**exaspe'ration,** *s.* Verzweiflung *f.*

**excavate** ['ekskəveit], *v.tr.* ausgraben. ◆**exca'vation,** *s.* Ausgrabung *f.*

**exceed** [ek'si:d, ik-], *v.tr.* *(a)* (eine Grenze usw.) überschreiten; (eine Summe, eine Zahl) übersteigen; *(b)* (j-s Erwartungen) übertreffen. ◆**ex'ceedingly,** *adv.* äußerst.

**excel** [ek'sel, ik-], *v.* **1.** *v.tr.* **he excelled himself,** er hat sich selbst übertroffen. **2.** *v.i.* sich auszeichnen. ◆**excellence** ['eks(ə)ləns], *s.* Vorzüglichkeit *f;* hervorragende Qualität *f.* ◆**'excellency,** *s.* **Your E.,** (Ihre) Exzellenz *f.* ◆**'excellent,** *adj.* ausgezeichnet.

**except** [ek'sept, ik-], *prep.* außer + *dat;* **e. for a few corrections,** bis auf einige Korrekturen; **e. that ...,** außer daß ... ◆**ex'ception,** *s.* **1.** Ausnahme *f;* **with the e. of,** mit Ausnahme von + *dat,* bis auf + *acc.* **2. to take e. to sth.,** an etwas *dat* Anstoß nehmen. ◆**ex'ceptional,** *adj.* *(a)* außergewöhnlich; *(b) (unusual)* ungewöhnlich.

**excerpt** ['eksɔ:pt], *s.* Auszug *m.*

**excess** [ik'ses], *s.* **1.** Übermaß *n* (**of,** an + *dat*); *(surplus)* Überschuß *m;* **to e.,** übermäßig; **in e. of,** über + *dat.* **2.** *attrib.* **e. baggage,** Übergewicht *n;* **e. fare,** Zuschlag *m* (zum Fahrpreis). **3.** *pl.* **excesses,** Ausschreitungen *fpl.* ◆**ex'cessive,** *adj.* übermäßig; *(of caution, cleanliness etc.)* übertrieben.

**exchange** [iks'tʃeindʒ, iks-]. **I.** *s.* **1.** *(of goods, students etc.)* Austausch *m; (of purchased article etc.)* Umtausch *m;* **in e. (for sth.),** im Tausch (gegen etwas *acc*). **2.** *Fin:* **rate of e.,** Wechselkurs *m.* **3.** *(telephone)* **e.,** Fernsprechzentrale *f.* **II.** *v.tr.* *(a)* tauschen **(for,** gegen + *acc*); (Worte) wechseln; *(b)* (Geld) wechseln **(for,** gegen + *acc*).

**exchequer** [iks'tʃekər], *s.* **the E.,** der Fiskus; **the Chancellor of the E.,** der Schatzkanzler.

**excite** [ik'sait], *v.tr.* aufregen. ◆**ex'citable,** *adj.* leicht erregbar. ◆**ex'citement,** *s.* *(a)* Aufregung *f; (b)* **(state of) e.,** Erregung *f.* ◆**ex'citing,** *adj.* erregend.

**exclaim** [iks'kleim, iks-], *v.i.* ausrufen. ◆**exclamation** [eksklə'meiʃ(ə)n], *s.* Ausruf *m;* **e. mark,** Ausrufezeichen *n.*

**exclude** [eks'klu:d], *v.tr.* ausschließen; **excluding,** mit Ausnahme von + *dat.* ◆**ex'clusion,** *s.* Ausschluß *m.* ◆**ex'clusive,** *adj.* **1.** *(excluding)* ausschließlich. **2.** *(elitist)* exklusiv; **-ly,** *adv.* ausschließlich.

**excommunicate** [ekskə'mju:nikeit], *v.tr.* exkommunizieren.

**excruciating** [iks'kru:ʃieitiŋ, eks-], *adj.*

grauenhaft.

**excursion** [eks'kə:ʃs(ə)n, iks-], s. Ausflug m.

**excuse. I.** [iks'kju:s], s. 1. Entschuldigung f. 2. (pretext) Vorwand m. **II.** [iks'kju:z], v.tr. entschuldigen; **e. me!** entschuldigen Sie bitte! ◆**ex'cusable** [-zəbl], adj. zu entschuldigen.

**execute** ['eksikju:t], v.tr. (a) (etwas) ausführen; (b) (einen Verbrecher) hinrichten. ◆**exe'cution**, s. 1. Ausführung f. 2. Hinrichtung f (eines Verbrechers). ◆**exe'cutioner**, s. Scharfrichter m. ◆**executive** [ig'zekjutiv]. **I.** adj. Pol: etc: **e. power**, ausübende Gewalt. **II.** s. 1. (body) Verwaltung f; Pol: Exekutive f. 2. (pers.) Adm: Verwaltungsbeamte(r) m; Com: Manager m.

**exemplary** [ig'zempləri], adj. 1. (of conduct etc.) musterhaft. 2. (of punishment) exemplarisch. ◆**exemplify** [ig'zemplifai], v.tr. **to e. sth.**, für etwas acc als Beispiel dienen.

**exempt** [ig'zem(p)t, eg-]. **I.** v.tr. befreien. **II.** adj. (von etwas dat) befreit; **e. from taxation**, steuerfrei. ◆**e'xemption**, s. Befreiung f.

**exercise** ['eksəsaiz]. **I.** s. 1. (movement) Bewegung f; **physical exercises**, Leibesübungen pl. 2. (a) Sch: Mus: etc: Übung f; **e. book**, Schulheft n; (b) Mil: Manöver n. **II.** v.tr. (a) (einen Beruf, ein Amt usw.) ausüben; (Geduld) üben; **to e. one's right**, von seinem Recht Gebrauch machen; (b) (ein Bein usw.) bewegen.

**exert** [ig'zə:t, eg-], v.tr. (a) (eine Kraft, einen Einfluß) ausüben; (b) **to e. oneself**, sich anstrengen. ◆**e'xertion**, s. Anstrengung f.

**exhaust** [ig'zɔ:st, eg-]. **I.** v.tr. erschöpfen. **II.** s. Aut: e. (system), Auspuff m; **e. pipe**, Auspuffrohr n. ◆**e'xhausted**, adj. erschöpft. ◆**e'xhausting**, adj. erschöpfend. ◆**e'xhaustion**, s. Erschöpfung f. ◆**e'xhaustive**, adj. eingehend.

**exhibit** [ig'zibit, eg-]. **I.** s. (a) Ausstellungsstück n; (b) Jur: Beweisstück n. **II.** v.tr. ausstellen. ◆**exhibition** [eksi'biʃ(ə)n], s. Ausstellung f.

**exhilarating** [ig'ziləreitiŋ], adj. aufregend. ◆**exhila'ration**, s. freudige Erregung f.

**exile** ['eksail]. **I.** s. 1. Exil n. 2. (pers.) Verbannte(r) f(m). **II.** v.tr. verbannen.

**exist** [ig'zist, eg-], v.i. existieren. ◆**e'xistence**, s. (of pers.) Dasein n, Existenz f; (of thing) Vorhandensein n; **in e.**, vorhanden. ◆**e'xisting**, adj. vorhanden; (of law etc.) gegenwärtig.

**exit** ['eksit], s. 1. Abgang m; Th: **e. visa**, Ausreisevisum n. 2. (door) Ausgang m.

**exonerate** [ig'zɔnəreit, eg-], v.tr. entlasten.

**exorbitant** [ig'zɔ:bit(ə)nt, eg-], adj. unverschämt; **e. price**, Wucherpreis m.

**exotic** [eg'zɔtik], adj. exotisch.

**expand** [iks'pænd, eks-], v. 1. v.tr. ver-

größern, ausdehnen. 2. v.i. sich ausdehnen. ◆**ex'panding**, adj. **an e. market**, ein wachsender Markt. ◆**expanse** [-'pæns], s. Weite f. ◆**ex'pansion**, s. Ausdehnung f.

**expatriate. I.** [eks'pætrieit], v.tr. ausbürgern. **II.** [eks'peitriət], s. Ausgebürgerte(r) f(m). **III.** adj. ausgebürgert.

**expect** [iks'pekt, ek-], v.tr. (a) erwarten; F: **she's expecting**, sie ist in anderen Umständen; (b) (demand) **I e. you to be punctual**, ich erwarte Pünktlichkeit von dir; **to e. a lot of s.o.**, j-m viel zumuten; (c) **I e. so**, ich denke schon. ◆**ex'pectant**, adj. erwartungsvoll; **e. mother**, werdende Mutter. ◆**expec'tation**, s. 1. Erwartung f. 2. usu.pl. **expectations**, Aussichten fpl.

**expediency** [iks'pi:diənsi, eks-], s. Zweckmäßigkeit f. ◆**ex'pedient**, adj. zweckmäßig.

**expel** [iks'pel, eks-], v.tr. (einen Ausländer) aus einem Land ausweisen; (einen Schüler) von der Schule verweisen.

**expendable** [iks'pendəbl, eks-], adj. entbehrlich. ◆**ex'penditure**, s. Ausgaben fpl. ◆**ex'pense**, s. 1. Ausgaben fpl; **at my e.**, auf meine Kosten. 2. pl. Spesen pl; **e. account**, Spesenkonto n. ◆**ex'pensive**, adj. teuer.

**experience** [iks'piəriəns, eks-]. **I.** s. 1. Erfahrung f. 2. **an e.**, ein Erlebnis n. **II.** v.tr. erleben. ◆**ex'perienced**, adj. erfahren.

**experiment** [iks'perimənt, eks-]. **I.** s. Experiment n. **II.** v.i. experimentieren. ◆**experi'mental**, adj. Versuchs-; **e. car**, Versuchsauto n.

**expert** ['ekspə:t]. **I.** adj. sachkundig; (of professional) fachkundig. **II.** s. Fachmann m. ◆**expertise** [-'ti:z], s. Sachkenntnis f; (professional) Fachkenntnis f.

**expire** [iks'paiər, eks-], v.i. (of period, licence) ablaufen. ◆**ex'piry**, s. Ablauf m.

**explain** [iks'plein, eks-], v.tr. erklären. ◆**explanation** [eksplə'neiʃ(ə)n], s. Erklärung f. ◆**explanatory** [iks'plænətri, eks-], adj. erklärend.

**explicable** [eks'plikəbl, iks-], adj. erklärlich.

**explicit** [iks'plisit, eks-], adj. (of answer etc.) deutlich; (of command etc.) ausdrücklich; **-ly**, adv. ausdrücklich.

**explode** [iks'pləud, eks-], v. 1. v.tr. (a) (eine Bombe usw.) explodieren; (b) Fig: (eine Theorie usw.) umstoßen. 2. v.i. explodieren.

**exploit¹** ['eksplɔit], s. Großtat f.

**exploit²** [iks'plɔit, eks-], v.tr. ausnutzen. ◆**exploi'tation**, s. Ausnutzung f.

**explore** [iks'plɔ:r, eks-], v.tr. (a) (ein Land usw.) erforschen; (b) (Möglichkeiten usw.) untersuchen. ◆**explo'ration**, s. Erforschung f. ◆**exploratory** [eks'plɔrətri, iks-], adj. **e. talks**, Sondierungsgespräche npl. ◆**ex'plorer**, s. Forscher m.

**explosion** [iks'pləuʒ(ə)n, eks-], s. Explosion f. ◆**ex'plosive** [-ziv]. I. adj. explosiv. II. s. Sprengstoff m.

**export.** I. [eks'pɔːt], v.tr. exportieren. II. ['ekspɔːrt], s. Export m. ◆**expor'tation**, s. Export m. ◆**ex'porter**, s. Exporteur m.

**expose** [iks'pəuz, eks-], v.tr. (a) (etwas) bloßlegen; (b) (j-n) aussetzen (**to sth.**, et-was dat); (c) (ein Verbrechen) aufdecken; (einen Betrüger) entlarven. ◆**ex'posed**, adj. **an e. position**, eine ungeschützte Lage. ◆**exposure** ['-pəuʒər], s. (a) **to die of e.**, erfrieren; (b) Phot: Belichtung f; **e. meter**, Belichtungsmesser m; (on film) **36 exposures**, 36 Aufnahmen.

**express¹** [iks'pres, eks-]. I. adj. 1. ausdrücklich; 2. **e. train**, Schnellzug m; **e. letter**, Eilbrief m. II. adv. durch Eilboten. III. s. Schnellzug m; -**ly**, adv. ausdrücklich.

**express²**, v.tr. ausdrücken. ◆**expression** ['-preʃ(ə)n], s. Ausdruck m; (**facial**) **e.**, Gesichtsausdruck m. ◆**ex'pressive**, adj. ausdrucksvoll.

**expulsion** [iks'pʌlʃ(ə)n, eks-], s. Ausweisung f (aus einem Lande); Verweisung f (von der Schule).

**exquisite** [eks'kwizit], adj. auserlesen.

**extend** [iks'tend, eks-]. I. v.tr. (a) verlängern; (Grenzen, j-s Einfluß usw.) ausdehnen; (einen Betrieb) vergrößern; (ein Haus) ausbauen; (b) (die Hand) ausstrecken. II. v.i sich ausdehnen. ◆**ex'tension**, s. 1. Verlängerung f (einer Frist, einer Straße usw.). 2. (on house) Anbau m. 3. Tel: Nebenanschluß m; **e. lead**, Verlängerungsschnur f. ◆**ex'tensive**, adj. **e. knowledge**, umfassendes Wissen; **e. research**, weitreichende Forschungen; -**ly**, adv. weitgehend.

**extent** [iks'tent, eks-], s. Ausdehnung f; Weite f (einer Fläche); Umfang m (eines Schadens usw.); **to some/a certain e.**, gewissermaßen.

**extenuating** [eks'tenjueitiŋ, iks-], adj. **e. circumstances**, mildernde Umstände.

**exterior** [eks'tiəriər]. I. adj. äußere(r,s), Außen-. II. s. (a) das Äußere; (outside) Außenseite f; **on the e.**, außen; (b) (appearance) Erscheinung f.

**exterminate** [eks'təːmineit], v.tr. ausrotten. ◆**extermi'nation**, s. Ausrottung f.

**external** [eks'təːn(ə)l], adj. äußere(r,s), Außen-; -**ly**, adv. äußerlich.

**extinct** [iks'tiŋ(k)t, eks-], adj. (a) (of volcano) erloschen; (b) (of species) ausgestorben. ◆**ex'tinction**, s. Aussterben n.

**extinguish** [iks'tiŋgwiʃ, eks-], v.tr. lö-

schen. ◆**ex'tinguisher**, s. Feuerlöscher m.

**extort** [iks'tɔːt, eks-], v.tr. erpressen. ◆**ex'tortion**, s. Erpressung f. ◆**ex'tortionate**, adj. **e. price**, Wucherpreis m.

**extra** ['ekstrə]. I. adj. zusätzlich; **e. charge**, Zuschlag m. II. adv. (a) extra; **you have to pay e. for the wine**, der Wein ist nicht im Preis inbegriffen; (b) besonders; F: **e. strong**, besonders stark. III. s. (a) (payment) Zuschlag m; (b) Cin: Statist m; (c) pl. **extras**, Nebenausgaben fpl.

**extract.** I. ['ekstrækt], s. 1. Extrakt m. 2. (from a book etc). Auszug m. II. v.tr. [iks'trækt, eks-], herausziehen; (einen Zahn) ziehen. ◆**ex'traction**, s. 1. Herausziehen n. 2. (origin) Herkunft f.

**extradition** [ekstrə'diʃ(ə)n], s. Auslieferung f.

**extraordinary** [iks'trɔːd(i)nri, eks-], adj. (a) außerordentlich; (b) F: (amazing) erstaunlich.

**extravagance** [iks'trævəgəns, eks-], s. Verschwendung f. ◆**ex'travagant**, adj. (of pers. etc.) verschwenderisch; (of claims, actions etc.) extravagant.

**extreme** [iks'triːm, eks-]. I. adj. (a) extrem; (b) Pol: etc: radikal. II. s. Extrem n; **in the e.**, äußerst; **to go to extremes**, es zu weit treiben; -**ly**, adv. äußerst. ◆**extremity** [iks'tremiti, eks-], s. 1. äußerstes Ende n (eines Seils usw.). 2. in **an e.**, im äußersten Notfall. 3. **one's extremities**, seine Gliedmaßen fpl.

**extricate** ['ekstrikeit], v.tr. befreien.

**extrovert** ['ekstrəuvəːt]. I. adj. extrovertiert. II. s. extrovertierter Mensch.

**exuberance** [ig'zuːbərəns, eg-], s. Ausgelassenheit f. ◆**e'xuberant**, adj. ausgelassen.

**eye** [ai]. I. s. 1. Auge n; **keep your eyes open! paß gut auf! to be up to one's eyes in work**, bis über die Ohren in Arbeit stecken; **to set eyes on sth.**, etwas zu Gesicht bekommen; **to see e. to e. with s.o.**, mit j-m gleicher Meinung sein; **to keep an e. on sth.**, (i) auf etwas acc aufpassen; (ii) etwas im Auge behalten. 2. (of needle) Öhr n. II. v.tr. **to e. s.o.**, j-n mustern. ◆**'eyeball**, s. Augapfel m. ◆**'eyebrow**, s. Augenbraue f. ◆**'eyelash**, s. Augenwimper f. ◆**'eyelid**, s. Augenlid n. ◆**'eye-opener**, s. Überraschung f. ◆**'eyeshadow**, s. Lidschatten m. ◆**'eyesight**, s. **good/bad e.**, gute/ schlechte Augen pl. ◆**'eyesore**, s. **that house is an e.**, das Haus ist ein Schandfleck. ◆**'eyewitness**, s. Augenzeuge m.

# F

F, f [ef], (der Buchstabe) F,f n.
fable ['feibl], s. Fabel f. ◆'fabulous
['fæbjuləs], adj. F: fantastisch.
fabric ['fæbrik], s. 1. Gefüge n (der Gesellschaft). 2. (material) Stoff m.
◆'fabricate, v.tr. (eine Geschichte
usw.) erfinden.
facade [fæ'sɑːd], s. Fassade f.
face [feis]. I. s. 1. Gesicht n; to be f. to f.
with s.o., j-m gegenüberstehen; attrib. f.
cloth/f. flannel, Waschlappen m. 2. (expression) Gesichtsausdruck m; (put on)
Miene f; to make/pull faces, Gesichter
schneiden; to keep a straight f., ernst
bleiben. 3. on the f. of it, auf den ersten
Blick; Fin: f. value, Nennwert m; Fig: I
took it at its f. value, ich habe es für
bare Münze genommen; to lose f., das
Gesicht verlieren. 4. (surface) Fläche f;
Zifferblatt n (einer Uhr). II. v.tr. & i. (a)
(of pers.) (j-m, etwas dat) gegenüberstehen; (j-m, der Gefahr) ins Gesicht sehen;
to be faced with sth., mit etwas dat kon-
frontiert werden; (b) (of house etc.) to f.
the street/the sea, auf die Straße/das
Meer hinausgehen. ◆'face-lift s. 1. Ge-
sichtsstraffung f. 2. to give sth. a f.-l.,
etwas aufmöbeln.
facet ['fæsit], s. 1. Schliff m (eines Edelsteins). 2. Aspekt m (eines Problems).
facetious [fə'siːʃəs], adj. (of remark etc.)
scherzhaft.
facial ['feiʃəl], adj. Gesichts-.
facile ['fæsail], adj. oberflächlich.
facilitate [fə'siliteit], v.tr. erleichtern.
facility [fə'siliti], s. 1. (a) (ease) Leichtigkeit f; (b) (skill) Gewandtheit f. 2. esp.pl.
Möglichkeiten fpl, Einrichtungen fpl.
fact [fækt], s. Tatsache f; in f./in point of
f., tatsächlich; (actually) eigentlich.
faction ['fækʃ(ə)n], s. Splittergruppe f.
factor ['fæktər], s. Faktor m.
factory [fæktəri], s. Fabrik f.
factual ['fæktjuəl], adj. sachlich; f. report, Tatsachenbericht m.
faculty ['fæk(ə)lti], s. 1. Fähigkeit f. 2.
(department) Fakultät f.
fad [fæd], s. F: Marotte f.
fade [feid], v.i. verblassen; (of flowers,
beauty) verwelken; (of hope) schwinden;
(of memory) verblassen; to f. (away), (of
sound) verklingen.
fag [fæg], s. F: 1. Schinderei f. 2. (cigarette) Glimmstengel m. ◆fagged 'out, adj.
F: völlig k.o.
fail [feil]. I. adv.phr. without f., unbedingt; was auch geschieht. II. v. 1. v.i.
(a) (of attempt, plan) scheitern; (of crops)
mißraten; if all else fails, wenn alle
Stricke reißen; (b) (of pers., voice,
machinery, heart etc.) versagen; Sch:
durchfallen; he failed to persuade her,
es gelang ihm nicht, sie zu überreden; (c)

(of memory, eyesight etc.) nachlassen; (of
health) sich verschlechtern; the light is
failing, es dämmert; (d) (of business)
Konkurs machen. 2. v.tr. to f. s.o., j-n
im Stich lassen; (in exam) j-n durchfallen
lassen; to f. an examination, bei einer
Prüfung durchfallen. ◆'failing. I. s. (of
pers.) Fehler m. II. prep. mangels + gen.
◆'failure, s. 1. Versagen n (der Nieren,
einer Maschine usw.); f. to appear,
Nichterscheinen n. 2. (pers.) Versager m.
3. (thing) Mißerfolg m.
faint [feint]. I. adj. 1. (a) (of light, Fig:
comfort) schwach; (b) (of colour) zart; a f.
sound, ein leises Geräusch; I haven't the
faintest idea, ich habe keine blasse Ahnung. 2. I feel f., ich werde gleich ohnmächtig. II. s. Ohnmacht f. III. v.i. ohnmächtig werden; -ly, adv. leise (sprechen, klingen); schwach (leuchten); f.
visible, kaum sichtbar. ◆'faintness, s.
(of sound, light etc.) Schwäche f.
fair¹ ['feər], s. (a) Jahrmarkt m; (b)
(trade) f. Messe f.
fair². I. adj. 1. (of skin) hell; (of hair)
blond. 2. (just) gerecht; F: f. enough, na
gut. 3. (quite good) ziemlich gut. 4. f.
copy, Reinschrift f. II. adv. to play f.,
fair spielen; -ly, adv. 1. (justly) gerecht.
2. (honestly) ehrlich. 3. (quite) ziemlich.
◆'fair-'haired, adj. blond. ◆'fairness,
s. Fairneß f; in all f., um gerecht zu
sein.
fairy ['feəri], s. Fee f; f. tale, Märchen n.
◆'fairyland, s. Märchenland n.
faith ['feiθ], s. 1. (a) Vertrauen n; to have
f. in s.o., zu j-m Vertrauen haben; (b)
the Christian f., der christliche Glaube.
2. in good f., gutgläubig. ◆'faithful. I.
adj. (a) (of friend) treu; (b) (of reproduction, translation) genau. II. s. Ecc: the f.,
die Gläubigen mpl; -ly, adv. 1. treu;
Com: yours f., hochachtungsvoll m. 2.
genau. ◆'faithfulness, s. Treue f (to
s.o., zu j-m). ◆'faithless, adj. treulos.
fake [feik]. I. s. Fälschung f. II. v.tr. fälschen.
falcon ['fɔːlkən], s. Falke m.
fall [fɔːl]. I. s. 1. Fall m; (heavy) Sturz m;
a heavy f. of snow, starker Schneefall. 2.
N.Am: the f., der Herbst. 3. Sinken n
(der Preise, der Temperaturen). 4.
Untergang m (eines Menschen); Pol:
Sturz m (einer Regierung). II. v. i. irr. (a)
(of thing) (herunter)fallen; (of building) to
f. (in), einstürzen; to f. to pieces, zusammenfallen; (b) (of pers.) (hin)fallen;
(heavily) stürzen; night is falling, die
Nacht bricht an; his face fell, er machte
ein langes Gesicht; (c) Christmas falls on
a Thursday, Weihnachten fällt auf einen
Donnerstag; (d) (of barometer, price) sinken; (of wind) nachlassen; (e) to f. ill,

krank werden; ◆'**fall** '**back**, *v.i.* to f. b. on sth., auf etwas *acc* zurückgreifen. ◆'**fall be'hind**, *v.i.* (hinter j-m) zurückbleiben; (*with work*) in Rückstand geraten. ◆**fall** '**down**, *v.i.* (*a*) (*of pers.*) hinfallen; (*of object*) hinunterfallen; (*b*) (*of building*) einstürzen. ◆'**fall for**, *v.i.* F: (*a*) to f. f. a trick, auf einen Trick reinfallen; (*b*) to f. f. s.o., sth., sich in j-n, etwas verlieben. ◆'**fall** '**in**, *v.i.* (*a*) (*of roof etc.*) einstürzen; (*b*) Mil: (in Linie) antreten; (*c*) to f. in with s.o., mit j-m gemeinsame Sache machen. ◆'**fall** '**off**, *v.* 1. *v.tr.* to f. o. (a wall), (von einer Mauer) herunterfallen. 2. *v.i.* nachlassen; (*in numbers*) weniger werden. ◆'**fall** '**out**, *v.i.* (*a*) to f. o. (of a window), (zum Fenster) hinausfallen; (*b*) (*of hair*) ausfallen; (*c*) Mil: wegtreten; (*d*) (*disagree*) in Streit geraten. ◆'**fallout**, *s.* (**radioactive**) f., (radioaktiver) Niederschlag *m.* ◆**fall** '**over**, *v.* 1. *v.tr.* to f. o. sth., über etwas *acc* stolpern. 2. *v.i.* (*of pers.*) umfallen; (*of jug, glass etc.*) umkippen. ◆'**fall** '**through**, *v.i.* ins Wasser fallen.

**fallacy** ['fæləsi], *s.* irrige Ansicht *f.*

**false** [fɔls], *adj.* 1. (*wrong*) falsch; 2. (*artificial*) (*of hair, teeth*) künstlich; f. teeth, (künstliches) Gebiß *n.* ◆'**falsehood**, *s.* Unwahrheit *f.* ◆'**falsify**, *v.tr.* fälschen.

**falter** ['fɔltər], *v.i.* (*esp. of voice*) stocken; (*of pers.*) zögern.

**fame** [feim], *s.* Ruhm *m.*

**familiar** [fə'miliər], *adj.* (*a*) (*intimate*) vertraut; (*b*) (*known*) bekannt (**to**, dat). (*c*) **to be f. with sth.**, mit etwas *dat* vertraut sein. ◆**famili'arity**, *s.* 1. Vertraulichkeit *f.* 2. Vertrautheit *f* (**with sth.**, mit etwas *dat.*). ◆**fa'miliarize**, *v.tr.* to f. oneself/s.o. with sth., sich/j-n mit etwas *dat* vertraut machen.

**family** ['fæmili], *s.* Familie *f*; f. doctor, Hausarzt *m*; f. man, Familienvater *m*; f. tree, Stammbaum *m*; f. allowance, Kindergeld *n*; f. planning, Familienplanung *f.*

**famine** ['fæmin], *s.* Hungersnot *f.* ◆'**famished**, *adj.* ausgehungert.

**famous** ['feiməs], *adj.* berühmt.

**fan**[1] [fæn], *s.* 1. Fächer *m.* 2. (*mechanical*) Ventilator *m*; f. belt, Keilriemen *m.* II. *v.* 1. *v.tr.* to f. oneself, sich fächeln. 2. *v.i.* to f. (out), sich (fächerförmig) ausbreiten.

**fan**[2], *s.* F: Fan *m*; f. mail, Verehrerpost *f.*

**fanatic** [fə'nætik], *s.* Fanatiker(in) *m(f).* ◆**fa'natical**, *adj.* fanatisch. ◆**fa'naticism**, *s.* Fanatismus *m.*

**fancy** ['fænsi]. I. *s.* to **take a f.** to s.o., sth., an j-m, etwas *dat* Gefallen finden. II. *adj.* (*a*) f. cake, Törtchen *n* (mit Zuckerguß usw.); (*b*) f. dress, Kostüm *n*; f.-dress ball, Kostümfest *n*; (*c*) Pej: (*of ideas etc.*) ausgefallen; f. prices, Phantasiepreise *mpl.* III. *v.tr.* (*a*) f. that! was Sie nicht sagen! (*b*) I f. a biscuit, ich

hätte Lust auf einen Keks; (*c*) F: he fancies himself, er hält sich für weiß Gott wen. ◆'**fanciful**, *adj.* phantastisch.

**fanfare** ['fænfɛər], *s.* Fanfare *f.*

**fang** [fæŋ], *s.* (*a*) Reißzahn *m*; (*b*) (*of snake*) Giftzahn *m.*

**fantasy** ['fæntəsi,-zi], *s.* Phantasie *f*; f. world, Phantasiewelt *f.* ◆**fan'tastic**, *adj.* F: fantastisch.

**far** [fɑːr]. I. *adv.* 1. (*a*) (*of place*) weit; f. away/off, weit entfernt; Fig: he will go f., er wird es weit bringen; (*b*) as f. as I know, soviel ich weiß; in so f. as, insofern; f. from it, keineswegs. 2. (*of time*) so f., bisher. 3. viel; it's f. better, es ist viel besser; by f., weitaus. II. *adj.* at the f. end of the street, am anderen Ende der Straße; the Far East, der Ferne Osten. ◆'**faraway**, *adj.* weit entfernt. ◆'**far-'fetched**, *adj.* an den Haaren herbeigezogen. ◆'**far-'reaching**, *adj.* weitreichend. ◆'**far-'sighted**, *adj.* weitblikkend.

**farce** [fɑːs], *s.* Farce *f.* ◆'**farcical**, *adj.* lächerlich.

**fare** ['fɛər], *s.* 1. (*a*) (*cost*) Fahrpreis *m*; (*b*) (*money*) Fahrgeld *n.* 2. (*food*) Kost *f.*

**farewell** [fɛə'wel]. *int. & s.* Lebewohl *n*; **to bid s.o./sth. f.**, von j-m/etwas *dat* Abschied nehmen.

**farm** [fɑːm]. I. *s.* Bauernhof *m*; f. labourer, Landarbeiter *m*; f. produce, landwirtschaftliche Produkte *npl.* II. *v.* 1. *v.tr.* (Land) bewirtschaften. 2. *v.i.* Landwirtschaft betreiben. ◆'**farmer**, *s.* Bauer *m.* ◆'**farmhouse**, *s.* Bauernhaus *n.* ◆'**farming**, *s.* Landwirtschaft *f.* ◆'**farmyard**, *s.* Hof *m.*

**fart** [fɑːt], P: I. *s.* Furz *m.* II. *v.i.* furzen.

**farther** ['fɑːðər]. I. *adv.* f. (than), weiter (als). II. *adj.* entfernt. ◆'**farthest**, *adv.* am weitesten.

**fascinate** ['fæsineit], *v.tr.* faszinieren. ◆'**fascinating**, *adj.* faszinierend. ◆**fasci'nation**, *s.* Faszination *f.*

**fascism** ['fæʃiz(ə)m], *s.* Faschismus *m.* ◆'**fascist**, *s.* Faschist *m.*

**fashion** ['fæʃ(ə)n]. I. *s.* 1. (*manner*) Art *f.* 2. Cl: *etc:* Mode *f*; in f., (in) Mode; out of f., unmodern; f. magazine, Modejournal *n.* II. *v.tr.* formen. ◆'**fashionable**, *adj.* modern; (*of clothes, resort*) modisch.

**fast**[1] [fɑːst]. I. *s.* Fasten *n.* II. *v.i.* fasten.

**fast**[2]. I. *adj.* 1. schnell; the clock is f., die Uhr geht vor. II. *adv.* 1. f. asleep, in tiefem Schlaf. 2. schnell.

**fasten** [fɑːsn], *v.* 1. *v.tr.* befestigen (**to** sth., an etwas *dat*). 2. *v.i.* the dress fastens at the back, das Kleid ist hinten zuzumachen. ◆'**fastener**, '**fastening**, *s.* Verschluß *m.*

**fastidious** [fæs'tidiəs], *adj.* wählerisch.

**fat** [fæt]. I. *adj.* 1. (*of pers., cigar etc.*) dick. 2. (*of meat*) fett. II. *s.* Fett *m.*

**fatal** [feit(ə)l], *adj.* 1. (*of disease, accident*) tödlich. 2. f. mistake, verhängnisvoller Irrtum; -ly, *adv.* f. injured, tödlich ver-

letzt. ◆**fatality** [fə'tæliti], s. Todesopfer n. ◆**fate** [feit], s. Schicksal n. ◆**'fated**, adj. (a) f. (to do sth.) vom Schicksal bestimmt(, etwas zu tun); (b) F: (of plan) zum Scheitern verurteilt.
**father** ['fɑ:ðər], s. Vater m. ◆**'fatherland**, s. Vaterland n. ◆**'father-in-law**, s. Schwiegervater m. ◆**'fatherless**, adj. vaterlos. ◆**'fatherly**, adj. väterlich.
**fathom** ['fæðəm]. I. s. Klafter f. II. v.tr. (a) (Wasser) loten; (b) Fig: (etwas) begreifen.
**fatigue** [fə'ti:g]. I. s. Ermüdung f. II. v.tr. ermüden. ◆**'fatiguing**, adj. ermüdend.
**fatten** ['fæt(ə)n], v. 1. v.tr. (Tiere) mästen. 2. v.i. fett werden. ◆**'fattening**, adj. that's f., das macht dick. ◆**'fatty**, adj. fett; f. foods, fetthaltige Nahrungsmittel.
**fatuous** ['fætjuəs], adj. albern.
**faucet** ['fɔ:sət], s. N.Am: Wasserhahn m.
**fault** [fɔlt]. I. s. 1. (a) (defect) Fehler m; (b) Tchn: Defekt m; TV: etc: Störung f. 2. to be at f., im Unrecht sein; it's your f., es ist Ihre Schuld. 3. Geog: Verwerfung f. II. v.tr. (j-m) einen Fehler nachweisen. ◆**'faultfinding**, s. Krittelei f. ◆**'faultless**, adj. fehlerfrei; f. German, tadelloses Deutsch. ◆**'faulty**, adj. fehlerhaft; f. brakes, defekte Bremsen.
**fauna** ['fɔ:nə], s. Fauna f.
**favour** ['feivər]. I. s. 1. to find f. (with s.o.) (j-m) gefallen; in f. of sth., für etwas acc. 2. (act) Gefallen m; to do s.o. a f., j-m einen Gefallen tun. II. v.tr. (a) to f. sth., für etwas acc sein; (b) (prefer) bevorzugen. ◆**'favourable**, adj. günstig. ◆**'favourite**. I. adj. Lieblings-; f. dish, Leibgericht n. II. s. (a) (pers.) Liebling m; (b) Sp: Favorit(in) m(f). ◆**'favouritism**, s. (unfaire) Bevorzugung f.
**fawn**¹ [fɔ:n]. I. s. Hirschkalb n; Rehkitz n. II. adj. rehbraun.
**fawn**², v.i. to f. on s.o., sich bei j-m einschmeicheln. ◆**'fawning**, adj. kriecherisch.
**fear** ['fiər]. I. s. Angst f; Furcht f (of s.o., sth., vor j-m, etwas dat); F: no f.! keine Angst! fears, Befürchtungen f. II. v. 1. v.tr. to f. the worst, das Schlimmste befürchten. 2. v.i. fürchten (for sth., um etwas acc). ◆**'fearful**, adj. 1. (terrible) furchtbar. 2. (apprehensive) furchtsam. ◆**'fearless**, adj. furchtlos. ◆**'fearlessness**, s. Furchtlosigkeit f.
**feasible** ['fi:zəbl], adj. durchführbar. ◆**feasi'bility**, s. Durchführbarkeit f; f. study, Durchführbarkeitsanalyse f.
**feast** [fi:st]. I. s. 1. Ecc: f. (day), Fest n. 2. (meal) Festessen n. II. v.i. to f. on sth., etwas ausgiebig genießen.
**feat** [fi:t], s. Großtat f; (achievement) Leistung f.
**feather** ['feðər], s. Feder f.

◆**'featherbrained**, adj. she is f., sie hat ein Spatzenhirn.
**feature** ['fi:tʃər]. I. s. 1. esp. pl. (of face) Gesichtszüge mpl. 2. (characteristic) Merkmal n. 3. (article) Bericht m; f. (film), Hauptfilm m. II. v. 1. v.tr. Cin: TV: etc: (j-n, einen Bericht usw.) bringen. 2. v.i. (of things) vorkommen; (of pers.) eine (führende) Rolle spielen.
**February** ['februəri], s. Februar m.
**fed** [fed], adj. F: to be f. up, es satt haben.
**federal** ['fedərəl], adj. Bundes-; the F. Republic of Germany, die Bundesrepublik Deutschland. ◆**fede'ration**, s. Bund m.
**fee** [fi:], s. Gebühr f.
**feeble** ['fi:bl], adj. (a) schwach; (of old pers.) gebrechlich; (b) (of excuse etc.) lahm; (c) F: (bad) mies. ◆**'feeble-'minded**, adj. schwachsinnig. ◆**'feebleness**, s. Schwäche f.
**feed** [fi:d]. I. s. (for animal) Futter n; (for baby) Nahrung f. II. v. irr. 1. v.tr. (a) (ein Tier, ein Kind) füttern (on sth., mit etwas dat); (einem Menschen) zu essen geben; (b) to f. sth. into the computer, etwas in den Computer eingeben. 2. v.i. fressen; to f. on sth., (of pers.) sich von etwas dat ernähren; (of animal) etwas fressen. ◆**'feedback**, s. 1. El: Rückkopplung f. 2. Reaktionen fpl (auf eine Umfrage usw.). ◆**'feedpipe**, s. Tchn: Zuleitungsrohr n. ◆**'feed 'up**, v.tr. (ein Tier) mästen.
**feel** [fi:l]. I. s. (a) it has a rough f., es fühlt sich rauh an; (b) to get the f. of sth., sich an etwas acc gewöhnen. II. v. irr. 1. v.tr. (a) (physically) fühlen; (Kälte, eine Bewegung, eine Wirkung) spüren; (Schmerz) empfinden. to f. one's way forward, sich nach vorn tasten; (b) (emotionally) (Liebe, Abscheu usw.) empfinden; (c) (consider) meinen. 2. v.i. (of pers.) (a) sich (wohl, besser, glücklich, fremd usw.) fühlen; I f. cold/ill, mir ist kalt/schlecht; (b) I felt like crying, ich hätte weinen können; I f. like a cup of tea, ich hätte Lust auf eine Tasse Tee; (c) to f. for s.o., mit j-m Mitleid haben; (d) to f. for sth., nach etwas dat tasten; (e) to f. up to sth., sich für etwas acc stark genug fühlen. ◆**'feeling**, s. Gefühl n.
**feign** [fein], v.tr. vortäuschen.
**fell** [fel], v.tr. (einen Baum) fällen.
**fellow** ['feləu], s. 1. f. citizen, Mitbürger m; f. countryman, Landsmann m; f. traveller, Mitreisende(r) f (m); Fig: Mitläufer m; F: Kerl m. ◆**'fellowship**, s. Forschungsstipendium n.
**felony** ['feləni], s. schweres Verbrechen n.
**felt** [felt], s. Filz m; f. pen, Filzstift m.
**female** ['fi:meil]. I. adj. weiblich. II. s. Weibchen n. ◆**feminine** ['feminin], adj. weiblich; (of dress etc.) feminin. ◆**'feminism**, s. Feminismus m.

◆'feminist. I. s. Feminist(in) m(f). II. adj. feministisch.

fence [fens]. I. s. Zaun m. II. v. 1. v.tr. to f. in sth., etwas einzäunen. 2. v.i. Sp: fechten. ◆'fencing, s. 1. Sp: Fechten n. 2. (material) Zaun m.

fend [fend], v. 1. v.tr. to f. off an attack, einen Angriff abwehren. 2. v.i. to f. for oneself, sich allein durchschlagen.

fender ['fendər], s. (a) Kaminvorsetzer m; (b) N. Am: Aut: Kotflügel m.

ferment. I. s. ['fə:ment]. I. Aufruhr m. II. [fə'ment]. v.i. gären. ◆fermen'tation, s. Gärung f.

fern [fə:n], s. Farnkraut n.

ferocious [fə'rəuʃəs], adj. (of pers.) grimmig; (of animal) wild; a f. attack, ein heftiger Angriff. ◆ferocity [-'rɔsiti], s. Wildheit f Heftigkeit f.

ferret ['ferit]. I. s. Z: Frettchen n. II. v.i. to f. about, herumsuchen.

ferry ['feri]. I. s. f. (boat), Fähre f. II. v.tr. übersetzen.

fertile ['fə:tail], adj. fruchtbar; f. imagination, reiche Phantasie. ◆fertility [-'tiliti], s. Fruchtbarkeit f ◆fertilization [-ilai'zeiʃ(ə)n], s. Befruchtung f. ◆'fertilize, v.tr. (a) befruchten; (b) (den Boden) düngen. ◆'fertilizer, s. Dünger m.

fervent ['fə:vənt], adj. leidenschaftlich; (of request etc.) inständig; ◆'fervour, s. Leidenschaft f.

fester ['festər], v.i. eitern.

festival ['festivəl], s. Fest n; Mus: Th: Festspiele npl; film f., Filmfestival n. ◆'festive, adj. festlich; the f. season = Weihnachten n. ◆fes'tivity, s. the festivities, die Festlichkeiten fpl.

fetch [fetʃ], v.tr. (a) (etwas) holen; (j-n) abholen; (b) to f. a good price, einen guten Preis erzielen. ◆'fetch 'back, v.tr. zurückholen. ◆'fetch 'down, v.tr. herunterholen. ◆'fetch 'in, v.tr. hereinbringen. ◆'fetching, adj. attraktiv; (of smile) gewinnend.

fête [feit], s. Fest n.

fetish ['fetiʃ], s. Fetisch m.

fetter ['fetər], s. usu. pl. fetters, Fesseln fpl.

feud [fju:d], s. Fehde f.

feudal ['fju:dəl], adj. feudal.

fever ['fi:vər], s. Fieber n. ◆'feverish, adj. fieberhaft; Med: fiebrig.

few [fju:], adj. (a) wenige; (b) (several) a f. (books etc.), ein paar (Bücher usw.); a f. more, noch ein paar; quite a f., ziemlich viele. ◆'fewer, adj. weniger. ◆'fewest, adj. he had the f. points, er hatte die wenigsten Punkte; I got (the) f., ich bekam am wenigsten.

fiancé [fi'ã:nsei], s. Verlobte(r) m. ◆fi'ancée, s. Verlobte f.

fiasco, pl. -os [fi'æskəu, -əuz], s. Fiasko n.

fib [fib]. I. s. F: kleine Lüge f. II. v.i. F: flunkern.

fibre ['faibər], s. (a) Faser f; (b) moral f., moralische Stärke f. ◆'fibreglass, s. Glasfaser f.

fickle [fikl], adj. unbeständig; (of pers.) wankelmütig. ◆'fickleness, s. Unbeständigkeit f; Wankelmut m.

fiction ['fikʃ(ə)n], s. 1. (not truth) Erfindung f. 2. (art, category) Belletristik f; (works of) f., Unterhaltungsliteratur f. ◆fic'titious, adj. (frei) erfunden.

fiddle [fidl]. I. s. 1. Mus: F: Geige f. 2. F: Schwindel m. II. v. 1. v.i. F: to f. with sth., mit etwas dat herumspielen. 2. v.tr. F: (etwas) arrangieren; to f. the accounts, die Bücher frisieren. ◆'fiddler, s. 1. Mus: Geiger m. 2. F: Schwindler m. ◆'fiddling, adj. geringfügig. ◆'fiddly, adj. F: knifflig.

fidelity [fi'deliti], s. Treue f.

fidget ['fidʒit]. I. s. F: Zappelphilipp m. II. v.i. to f. (about), (herum)zappeln. ◆'fidgeting, s. Zappelei f. ◆'fidgety, adj. zappelig.

field [fi:ld], s. 1. Feld n. to have a f. day, einen erfolgreichen Tag haben. 2. (area of study etc.) Gebiet n. ◆'fieldglasses, s.pl. Feldstecher m. ◆'Field-'Marshal, s. Feldmarschall m. ◆'fieldmouse, s. Feldmaus f.

fiend [fi:nd], s. (a) Teufel m; (b) (pers.) Unmensch m; (c) F: (enthusiast) Fanatiker m. ◆'fiendish, adj. teuflisch.

fierce ['fiəs], adj. (a) (of battle, competition etc.) heftig; (b) (of animal) bösartig. ◆'fierceness, s. Heftigkeit f; Bösartigkeit f.

fiery ['faiəri], adj. feurig.

fifteen [fif'ti:n], num. adj. fünfzehn. ◆'fif'teenth, num. adj. fünfzehnte(r,s).

fifth [fifθ]. I. num. adj. fünfte(r,s). II. s. Fünftel n.

fifty ['fifti], num. adj. fünfzig; let's go f.-f., machen wir's halbe-halbe.

fig [fig], s. Feige f.

fight [fait]. I. s. Kampf m; (brawl) Schlägerei f. II. v. 1. v.i. (a) kämpfen (for/over/about sth., um etwas acc); (b) (brawl) sich prügeln; (of children) sich raufen; to f. back, sich wehren. 2. v.tr. bekämpfen; (gegen j-n) kämpfen. ◆'fighter, s. 1. Kämpfer m. 2. Av: Jagdflugzeug n. ◆'fighting, s. 1. Kämpfen n; Mil: fierce f., heftige/schwere Kämpfe. 2. (brawling) Prügelei f.

figment ['figmənt], s. a f. of your imagination, ein Auswuchs m Ihrer Phantasie.

figure ['figər]. I. s. 1. (shape) Figur f. 2. (a) (pers. of importance) Persönlichkeit f; (b) a ghostly f., eine gespenstische Gestalt. 3. (a) (number) Zahl f; to be good at figures, gut im Rechnen sein; (b) (amount) Betrag m. 4. (in book) Abbildung f. II. v. 1. v.tr. (a) (auf einer Liste usw.) vorkommen; (b) N. Am: meinen. 2. v.tr. I can't f. him/it out, ich kann ihn/es nicht begreifen. ◆'figurative, *adj.* metaphorisch; **f. meaning,** übertragene Bedeutung; **-ly,** *adv.* to speak f., bildlich sprechen.

**filament** ['filəmənt], *s.* 1. *Bot:* Staubfaden *m.* 2. *El:* Glühfaden *m.*

**file¹** [fail]. **I.** *s.* (*tool*) Feile *f.* **II.** *v.tr.* feilen.

**file²**. **I.** *s.* **1.** (*containing documents etc.*) Ordner *m.* 2. (*dossier*) Akten *fpl;* **on f.,** bei den Akten. **3.** *Data-pr:* Datei *f.* **II.** *v.tr.* (etwas) zu den Akten legen, (*sort*) (ein)ordnen. ◆**'filing,** *s.* Einordnen *n;* **f. cabinet,** Aktenschrank *m.*

**file³**. **I.** *s.* **in single f.,** im Gänsemarsch. **II.** *v.i.* **to f. in/out,** einer nach dem anderen hinein-/hinaustreten.

**filial** ['filiəl], *attrib. adj.* Kindes-; **f. devotion,** Liebe *f* zu den Eltern.

**filibuster** ['filibʌstər], *v.i. N. Am:* Obstruktion treiben.

**fill** [fil]. **I.** *s.* **to eat one's f.,** sich satt essen; **to have one's f. of sth.,** genug von etwas *dat* haben. **II.** *v.* **1.** *v.tr.* (*a*) füllen; **to be filled with admiration,** von Bewunderung erfüllt sein; (*b*) (einen Posten) besetzen. **2.** *v.i.* sich füllen. ◆**'fill 'in,** *v.tr.* (*a*) (ein Loch) ausfüllen, (einen Graben) zuschütten; (*b*) (ein Formular) ausfüllen; (das Datum) einsetzen. ◆**'filling. I.** *adj.* sättigend. **II.** *s.* **1.** (*in tooth, food*) Füllung *f.* 2. *Aut:* **f. station,** Tankstelle *f.* ◆**'fill 'out,** *v. v.tr. esp. N.Am:* (ein Formular) ausfüllen. ◆**'fill 'up,** *v.* **1.** *v.tr.* (*a*) (ein Glas usw.) füllen; *Aut:* **to f. a car up (with petrol),** ein Auto volltanken; (*b*) (ein Loch, ein Formular) ausfüllen. **2.** *v.i.* (*a*) sich füllen; (*b*) *Aut:* volltanken.

**fillet** ['filit]. **I.** *s.* Filet *n.* **II.** *v.tr.* in Filets zerlegen.

**filly** ['fili], *s.* Jungstute *f.*

**film** [film]. **I.** *s.* **1.** (*layer*) (dünne) Schicht *f.* 2. Film *m;* **to make a f.,** einen Film drehen; **f. star,** Filmstar *m.* **II.** *v.* **1.** *v.tr.* (eine Szene) drehen. **2.** *v.i.* filmen.

**filter** ['filtər]. **I.** *s.* Filter *m.* **II.** *v.* **1.** *v.tr.* filtern. **2.** *v.i.* (*of news etc.*) **to f. through,** durchsickern.

**filth** [filθ], *s.* Dreck *m.* ◆**'filthy,** *adj.* dreckig.

**fin** [fin], *s.* Flosse *f.*

**final** ['fainl]. **I.** *adj.* (*a*) letzte(r,s); End-; (*b*) (*of decision etc.*) endgültig. **II.** *s.* **1.** *Sp:* Endspiel *n.* **2.** *Sch:* **finals,** Abschlußprüfung *f;* **-ly,** *adv.* schließlich. ◆**finale** [fi'nɑːli], *s.* Finale *n.* ◆**'finalist,** *s. Sp:* Finalist(in) *m(f).* ◆**'finalize,** *v.tr.* (etwas) vollenden; (Vorbereitungen usw. *dat*) abschließen.

**finance** [fai'næns]. **I.** [fai'næns]. *s.* **1.** Finanz *f.* 2. *pl* Finanzen *pl.* **II.** [fi'næns, 'fai-], *v.tr.* finanzieren. ◆**fi'nancial,** *adj.* finanziell; **f. year,** (i) *Com:* Geschäftsjahr *n;* (ii) *Pol:* Finanzjahr *n.* ◆**fi'nancier,** *s.* Finanzmann *m.*

**finch** [finʃ], *s.* Fink *m.*

**find** [faind]. **I.** *s.* Fund *m.* **II.** *v.tr. irr.* finden; **they will f. it easy/difficult,** es wird

ihnen leicht-/schwerfallen; **to f. s.o. guilty,** j-n für schuldig befinden. ◆**'find 'out,** *v.* **1.** *v.tr.* herausfinden. **2.** *v.i.* **to f. out (about sth.),** (*learn*) (etwas) erfahren; (*discover*) (etwas) entdecken.

**fine¹** [fain]. **I.** *s.* Geldstrafe *f.* **II.** *v.tr.* (j-n) mit einer Geldstrafe belegen; **to be fined (£50),** eine Geldstrafe (von £50) bekommen.

**fine²**. **I.** *adj.* **1.** (*of weather etc.*) schön; *F:* **that's f.!** (i) (*OK*) das geht in Ordnung; (ii) (*excellent*) das ist prima! **that's f. with me,** das paßt mir gut; (*of health*) **I'm f.,** mir geht's gut. **2.** (*a*) (*of mesh etc.*) fein; (*b*) (*of fabric, skin*) zart; **f. distinction,** feiner Unterschied. **II.** *adv.* fein; *F:* **to cut it f.,** sich *dat* recht wenig Zeit lassen; **-ly,** *adv.* **f. chopped,** fein gehackt. **III.** *int.* **f.!** gut!

**finger** ['fingər]. **I.** *s.* Finger *m;* **he wouldn't lift a f. (to help them),** er würde keinen Finger rühren (, ihnen zu helfen). **II.** *v.tr.* betasten. ◆**'fingernail,** *s.* Fingernagel *m.* ◆**'fingerprint,** *s.* Fingerabdruck *m.* ◆**'fingertip,** *s.* Fingerspitze *f;* **to have sth. at one's fingertips,** etwas griffbereit haben.

**finicky** ['finiki], *adj. F:* (*of pers.*) heikel; (*pedantic*) übertrieben genau.

**finish** ['finiʃ]. **I.** *s.* **1.** Ende *n.* 2. *Sp:* Ziel *n.* **3.** (*of products etc.*) Ausführung *f.* **II.** *v.* **1.** *v.tr.* (eine Arbeit usw.) beenden; (ein Buch) zu Ende lesen; (Essen) aufessen; (ein Getränk) austrinken. **2.** *v.i.* (*a*) (*of period, performance etc.*) zu Ende gehen; (*b*) (*of pers.*) fertig werden; (*c*) *Sp:* **to f. third,** als dritter durchs Ziel gehen. ◆**'finished,** *adj.* **1.** *Ind:* **f. goods/products,** Fertigprodukte *npl.* 2. **beautifully f.,** schön gearbeitet/lackiert (*of paintwork*). **3.** *F:* (*of pers.*) erledigt. ◆**'finishing,** *adj.* **f. touch,** der letzte Schliff; **f. line,** Ziellinie *f.* ◆**'finish 'off,** *v.tr.* (eine Aufgabe) zu Ende führen; (*eat up*) (etwas) aufessen. ◆**'finish 'up,** *v.i. F:* **we finished up in a pub,** zum Schluß landeten wir in einer Kneipe.

**finite** ['fainait], *adj.* begrenzt.

**Finland** ['finlənd]. *Pr. n.* Finnland *n.* ◆**Finn,** *s.* Finne *m,* Finnin *f.* ◆**'Finnish. I.** *adj.* finnisch. **II.** *s.* Finnisch *n.*

**fir** [fəːr], *s.* Tanne *f.*

**fire** ['faiər]. **I.** *s.* **1.** (*a*) Feuer *n;* **electric f.,** elektrischer Ofen *m;* (*b*) (*conflagration*) Brand *m;* **to catch f.,** Feuer fangen; **to set f. to a house,** ein Haus in Brand stecken; **to be on f.,** brennen; **in Flammen stehen; f. alarm,** Feueralarm *m;* **f. brigade,** Feuerwehr *f;* **f. engine,** Feuerwehrauto *n;* **f. escape,** Feuertreppe *f;* **f. extinguisher,** Feuerlöscher *m;* **f. station,** Feuerwache *f.* 2. *Mil:* **to cease f.,** das Feuer einstellen. **II.** *v.* **1.** *v.tr* (*a*) *Fig:* **to be fired with enthusiasm (for sth.),** von Begeisterung (für etwas *acc*) erfüllt sein; (*b*) **to f. a revolver at s.o.,** mit einem

Revolver auf j-n schießen; **to f. a shot,** einen Schuß abfeuern; **to f. questions at s.o.,** j-n mit Fragen bombardieren; (c) *F:* (einen Angestellten) entlassen, *F:* feuern. 2. *v.i.* schießen (**at s.o.,** auf j-n). ◆**'firearm,** *s.* Schußwaffe *f.* ◆**'fire a'way,** *v.i. F:* f. a.! leg los! ◆**'firefighter,** *s.* Feuerwehrmann *m.* ◆**'firefighting,** *s.* Brandbekämpfung *f.* ◆**'fireguard,** *s.* Schutzgitter *n.* ◆**'firelight,** *s.* Feuerschein *m.* ◆**'firelighter,** *s.* Feueranzünder *m.* ◆**'fireman,** *s.* Feuerwehrmann *m.* ◆**'fireplace,** *s.* Kamin *m.* ◆**'fireproof,** *adj.* (*of dish etc.*) feuerfest; *Cl:* feuerbeständig; **f. door,** feuersichere Tür. ◆**'fireside,** *s.* **by/at the f.,** am Kamin. ◆**'firewood,** *s.* Brennholz *n.* ◆**'firework,** *s.* Feuerwerkskörper *m; pl* **fireworks,** Feuerwerk *n.*

**firm**[1] [fəːm], *s.* Firma *f.*

**firm**[2] **I.** *adj.* (a) fest; (b) (*strict*) streng; **-ly,** *adv.* fest. ◆**'firmness,** *s.* Festigkeit *f;* (*of pers., treatment*) Strenge *f.*

**first** [fəːst]. **I.** *adj.* erste(r,s); **in the f. place,** erstens; (*to start with*) gleich am Anfang; **f. thing (in the morning),** zuallererst (nach dem Aufstehen); **f. aid,** Erste Hilfe *f; Aut:* **f. (gear),** erster Gang. **II.** *s.* **1.** (the) **first,** der, die, das Erste; **to be the f. to do sth.,** etwas als erster tun; *Sp:* **to be f.,** Erster sein. 2. **at first,** zuerst. **III.** *adv.* (a) erstens, zuerst; **f. of all,** zuallererst; (b) **when I f. saw him,** als ich ihn zum ersten Mal sah; **he arrived f.,** er kam als erster an; **-ly,** *adv.* erstens. ◆**'first(-)'class. I.** *adj.* erstklassig; **a f.-c. compartment** erster Klasse. **II.** *adv.* **to travel f.-c.,** erster Klasse reisen. ◆**'first-'rate,** *adj.* erstklassig.

**fish** [fiʃ]. **I.** *s.* Fisch *m;* **f. and chips,** Bratfisch *m* mit Pommes Frites. **II.** *v.i.* fischen; (*with rod*) angeln. ◆**'fishbone,** *s.* Fischgräte *f.* ◆**'fisherman,** *s.* Fischer *m.* ◆**'fishery,** *s.* Fischerei *f.* ◆**'fish-hook,** *s.* Angelhaken *m.* ◆**'fishing,** *s.* Fischen *n;* (*with rod*) Angeln *n;* **f. boat,** Fischerboot *n;* **f. limit,** Fischereigrenze *f;* **f. net,** Fischnetz *n;* **f. tackle,** Angelgeräte *npl;* **f. line,** Angelschnur *f;* **f. rod,** Angel(rute) *f.* ◆**'fishmonger,** *s.* Fischhändler *m;* **f.'s** (**shop**), Fischgeschäft *n.* ◆**'fishy,** *adj.* verdächtig.

**fission** ['fiʃ(ə)n], *s.* Spaltung *f.*

**fissure** ['fiʃər], *s.* Spalte *f.*

**fist** [fist], *s.* Faust *f;* **to clench one's fists,** die Fäuste ballen.

**fit**[1] [fit], *s.* (a) *Med: etc:* Anfall *m;* (b) **to be in fits of laughter,** sich vor Lachen krümmen; *Fig:* **f. of generosity etc.,** Anwandlung *f* von Großzügigkeit usw.; (c) **by fits and starts,** schubweise (arbeiten, vorwärtskommen). ◆**'fitful,** *adj.* unbeständig; (*of sleep*) unruhig.

**fit**[2]. **I.** *adj.* **1.** (a) (*suitable*) geeignet (**for sth.,** zu etwas *dat*); (b) **f. to eat/drink,**

eßbar/trinkbar. 2. (*healthy*) (gut) in Form, *esp.Sp:* fit; **to keep f.,** sich in Form halten. **II.** *s.* Sitz *m;* **to be a tight/loose f.,** knapp/lose sitzen; (*of dress*) **to be a good/bad f.,** gut/schlecht sitzen. **III.** *v.* **1.** *v.tr.* (a) (*suit*) (j-m) passen; (b) (*attach*) (etwas) anbringen (**to sth.,** an etwas *acc*); (Reifen usw.) montieren. 2. (*suit*) passen; **your dress fits well,** Ihr Kleid sitzt gut. ◆**'fit 'in,** *v.i.* **to f. in (with sth.),** (zu etwas *dat*) dazupassen; **he doesn't f. in here,** er paßt nicht hierher; **I will have to f. you/it in somehow,** ich werde Sie/es irgendwie einschieben müssen. ◆**'fitness,** *s.* **1.** (*of pers.*) Tauglichkeit *f* (**for sth.,** zu etwas *dat*). 2. (**physical**) **f.,** Form *f, Sp:* Fitneß *f.* ◆**'fitted,** *adj. Cl:* tailliert; **f. carpet,** Teppichboden *m;* **f. cupboard,** Einbauschrank *m.* ◆**'fitter,** *s.* Installateur *m.* ◆**'fitting. I.** *adj.* (*suitable*) passend; (*of remark*) treffend. **II.** *s.* **1.** (a) Anbringung *f, E:* Montage *f;* (b) *Cl:* Anprobe *f.* 2. *esp. pl.* **fittings,** Einrichtungen *fpl.*

**five** [faiv], *num.adj.* fünf. ◆**'fiver,** *s. Brit: F:* Fünfpfundschein *m; N.Am:* Fünfdollarschein *m.*

**fix** [fiks]. **I.** *s.* **1.** *F:* Klemme *f;* **to be in a f.,** in der Klemme sitzen. 2. *P:* (*drugs*) **to have a f.,** fixen. **II.** *v.tr.* (a) (etwas) befestigen (**to sth.,** an etwas *dat*); (b) (*decide*) (einen Termin, einen Preis usw.) festsetzen; **how are you fixed for money?** wie stehen deine Finanzen? (c) *F:* (*arrange*) **he'll f. it,** er wird's schon machen/organisieren; (d) (*repair*) **to f. sth.,** etwas herrichten; (e) *N.Am:* (*prepare*) (eine Mahlzeit) zubereiten. ◆**'fixed,** *adj. f.* **smile,** starres Lächeln. ◆**'fixture,** *s.* **1.** eingebautes Möbelstück *n; pl.* **fixtures,** eingebautes Mobilar *n.* 2. *Sp:* Veranstaltung *f.* ◆**'fix 'up,** *v.tr.* **to** organisieren; **to f. s.o. up with sth.,** etwas für j-n besorgen.

**fizz** [fiz], *v.i.* sprudeln. ◆**'fizzle 'out,** *v.i.* sich im Sand verlaufen. ◆**'fizzy,** *adj.* sprudelnd.

**flabbergast** ['flæbəgɑːst], *v.tr.* erstaunen; **I was flabbergasted,** ich war erstaunt/*F:* platt.

**flabby** ['flæbi], *adj.* schlaff.

**flag**[1] [flæg], *s.* Fahne *f; esp. Nau:* Flagge *f.* ◆**'flagship,** *s.* Flaggschiff *n.* ◆**'flag-signal,** *s.* Flaggensignal *n.* ◆**'flagstaff,** *s.* Fahnenstange *f.*

**flag**[2], *v.i.* (*of zeal, energy*) nachlassen; (*of conversation*) erlahmen.

**flagrant** ['fleigrənt], *adj.* (*of offence*) schamlos; **f. injustice,** schreiende Ungerechtigkeit.

**flair** ['flɛər], *s.* (a) (*gift*) Talent *n;* (b) (*instinct*) Flair *m.*

**flake** [fleik]. **I.** *s.* (a) (*of snow, oatmeal*) Flocke *f;* (b) (*of rust*) Schuppe *f.* **II.** *v.i.* (*of paint etc.*) **to f.** (**away/off**), abblättern. ◆**'flaky,** *adj.* **f. pastry,** Blätterteig *m.*

flamboyant [flæm'bɔiənt], adj. (of pers., style) extravagant; (of clothing) auffallend.

flame [fleim], s. Flamme f; to burst into/ go up in flames, in Flammen aufgehen.
◆'flameproof, adj. flammensicher.
◆'flamethrower, s. Flammenwerfer m.
◆'flaming, adj. (a) f. row, heftiger Streit; (b) P: verdammt.

flamingo, pl. -o(e)s [flə'miŋgəu, -əuz], s. Flamingo m.

flan [flæn], s. Torte f.

flange [flændʒ], s. (on pipe etc.) Flansch m.

flank [flæŋk]. I. s. Flanke f. II. v.tr. flankieren.

flannel ['flæn(ə)l], s. (a) Flanell m; f. trousers/flannels, Flanellhosen fpl; (b) face f., Waschlappen m.

flap [flæp]. I. s. 1. F: to get in a f., sich aufregen. 2. (of table, envelope etc.) Klappe f. II. v. 1. v.tr. (of bird) to f. its wings, mit den Flügeln schlagen. 2. v.i. (a) (of sail, flag) flattern; (b) F: (of pers.) sich aufregen.

flare ['flɛər].flare I. s. 1. (signal) Leuchtsignal n. 2. pl. flares, ausgestellte Hosen fpl. II. v.i. to f. up, s. (of flame etc.) (auf)lodern; (of pers.) aufbrausen. ◆'flared, adj. Cl: ausgestellt. ◆'flareup, s. (of pers.) Wutausbruch m.

flash [flæʃ]. I. s. (a) Blitz m; f. bulb, Blitzlicht n; Fig: f. of inspiration, Erleuchtung f; F: Geistesblitz m; in a f., im Nu m; a f. in the pan, ein Strohfeuer; (b) (news) f., Sondermeldung f. II. v. 1. v.i. blitzen. 2. v.tr. to f. (one's lights) at s.o., j-n anblinken. ◆'flashback. s. Rückblende f. ◆'flashing, adj. (of eyes) funkelnd; f. light, Blinklicht n. ◆'flashy, adj. auffällig; F: knallig.

flask [flɑːsk], s. Flasche f.

flat [flæt]. I. adj. 1. flach; to have a f. tyre, Reifenpanne f haben. 2. Fig: a f. refusal, eine glatte Absage. 3. (of conversation etc.) langweilig; (of drink) schal; f. battery, leere Batterie. 4. f. rate, Einheitspreis m. 5. Mus: A f., As; B f., B; D f., Des; E f., Es. II. adv. 1. flach. 2. F: to be f. broke, völlig pleite sein. 3. Fig: to fall f., (of performance etc.) danebengehen; (of idea, joke) verpuffen. 4. to sing f., zu tief singen; -ly, adv. entschieden; he f. refused, er weigerte sich glattweg. III. s. 1. Aut: F: Reifenpanne f. 2. Wohnung f. ◆'flatlet, s. Kleinwohnung f. ◆'flatness, s. (a) Flachheit f (einer Fläche); (b) Eintönigkeit f (des Lebens usw.). ◆'flatten, v.tr. (etwas) flachmachen; (den Boden) einebnen; F: to f. s.o., (j-n) k.o. schlagen.

flatter ['flætər], v.tr. (j-m) schmeicheln. ◆'flatterer, s. Schmeichler(in) m(f). ◆'flattering, adj. schmeichelhaft. ◆'flattery, s. Schmeichelei f.

flaunt [flɔːnt], v.tr. to f. sth., mit etwas dat protzen.

flavour ['fleivər]. I. s. Geschmack m; pl

Geschmacksrichtungen fpl. II. v.tr. würzen; vanilla-flavoured, mit Vanillegeschmack. ◆'flavouring, s. Würzstoff m. ◆'flavourless, adj. geschmacklos.

flaw [flɔː], s. Defekt m; (in material, Fig: character) Fehler m; (in argument) Lücke f. ◆'flawless, adv. tadellos.

flea [fliː], s. Floh m. ◆'fleabite, s. 1. Flohstich m. 2. Fig: Bagatelle f.

fleck [flek], s. (of colour) Tupfen m; (mark) Fleck m; f. of dust, Staubkorn n.

fledg(e)ling ['fledʒliŋ], s. Orn: eben flügge gewordener Vogel m.

flee [fliː], v.tr. & i. irr. to f. (from) s.o., sth., vor j-m, etwas dat fliehen.

fleece [fliːs], s. Schaffell n. ◆'fleecy, adj. (of lining etc.) wollig.

fleet [fliːt], s. 1. Flotte f. 2. (firm's) f., (cars) Wagenpark m.

fleeting ['fliːtiŋ], adj. flüchtig.

Flemish ['flemiʃ], I. adj. (a) (people) flämisch; (b) (land) flandrisch. II. s. Flämisch n.

flesh [fleʃ], s. 1. Fleisch n. 2. in the f., in Person. ◆'fleshy, adj. fleischig.

flex [fleks]. I. v.tr. (Muskeln) spielen lassen. II. s. Schnur f. ◆flexi'bility, s. Biegsamkeit f; (of pers.) Anpassungsfähigkeit f. ◆'flexible, adj. (of material) biegsam; (b) (adaptable) anpassungsfähig. ◆'flexitime, s. Gleitzeit f.

flick [flik]. I. s. Schnippen n. II. v.tr. schnippen.

flicker ['flikər], v.i. (a) flackern; El: flimmern; (b) (of eyelid) zucken.

flight [flait], s. 1. (a) (flying) Flug m; an hour's f., eine Flugstunde; f. path, Flugbahn f; f. recorder, Flug(daten)schreiber m; (b) Fig: f. of fancy, Phantasiegebilde n. 2. f. of stairs, Treppenflucht f. 3. (escape) Flucht f.

flimsy ['flimzi], adj. (a) schwach; (of structure) wackelig; (of material, paper) dünn; (b) (of excuse) fadenscheinig.

flinch [flintʃ], v.i. zurückzucken.

fling [fliŋ], v.tr. irr. (a) (etwas) schleudern; (b) to f. oneself, sich stürzen (at s.o., auf j-n).

flint [flint], s. Feuerstein m.

flip [flip], v. 1. v.tr. to f. sth. into the air, etwas hochschnellen. 2. v.i. to f. through a book, ein Buch schnell durchblättern.

flippant ['flipənt], adj. leichtfertig. ◆'flippancy, s. Leichtfertigkeit f.

flirt [fləːt]. I. s. Flirt m. II. v.i. flirten. ◆flir'tation, s. Flirt m.

float [fləut]. I. v. 1. v.i. (a) (of thing) schwimmen; (of swimmer, boat) treiben; (b) (in air) schweben. 2. v.tr. (a) (ein Schiff) flottmachen; (b) to f. a company, eine Gesellschaft gründen. II. s. 1. Schwimmer m. 2. (in procession) Wagen m. ◆'floating, adj. treibend; schwimmend; (in air) schwebend; f. voter, Wechselwähler m.

flock [flɔk]. I. s. (of animals) Herde f; (of

*birds*) Schwarm *m*; (*of people, geese etc.*) Schar *f*. II. *v.i.* **everyone is flocking to see the exhibition,** alle strömen in die Ausstellung.

**flog** [flɔg], *v.tr.* (*a*) auspeitschen; *Fig:* **to f. a subject to death,** ein Thema zu Tode reiten; (*b*) *F:* (*sell*) verschachern.

**flood** [flʌd]. I. *s.* (*a*) (*disaster*) Überschwemmung *f*; (*b*) f. of tears, Tränenstrom *m*. II. *v.* 1. *v.tr.* (ein Gebiet, *Com:* den Markt) überschwemmen. 2. *v.i.* (*of river*) über die Ufer treten. ◆'**flooding,** *s.* Überschwemmung *f*. ◆'**floodlight,** *s.* Flutlicht *n*.

**floor** [flɔːr], *s.* 1. Fußboden *m*. 2. (*storey*) Stock *m*; **ground f.,** Erdgeschoß *n*; **first f.,** (i) erster Stock *m*; (ii) *N.Am:* Erdgeschoß *n*. ◆'**floorboard,** *s.* Dielenbrett *n*. ◆'**floorcloth,** *s.* Scheuertuch *n*. ◆'**floorshow,** *s.* Kabarettvorstellung *f*.

**flop** [flɔp]. I. *s. Th:* Durchfall *m*. II. *v.i.* (*a*) (*of pers.*) **to f.** (down), (hin)plumpsen; (*b*) *F:* (*fail*) durchfallen. ◆'**floppy 'disk,** *s.* Diskette *f*.

**florid** ['flɔrid], *adj.* überladen.

**florist** ['flɔrist], *s.* Blumenhändler *m*; **florist's** (**shop**), Blumengeschäft *n*.

**flotilla** [flə'tilə], *s.* Flottille *f*.

**flounce** [flauns]. I. *s. Cl:* Volant *m*. II. *v.i.* **to f. out of a room,** (gereizt) aus einem Zimmer rauschen.

**flounder** ['flaundər], *s.* I. Flunder *f*. II. *Fig: F:* schwimmen.

**flour** ['flauər], *s.* Mehl *n*.

**flourish** ['flʌriʃ], *v.i.* (*of plant, pers. etc.*) gedeihen; (*of trade, arts etc.*) blühen.

**flout** [flaut], *v.tr.* mißachten.

**flow** [fləu]. I. *s.* Fluß *m*. II. *v.i.* fließen.

**flower** ['flauər]. I. *s.* Blume *f*; **f. bed,** Blumenbeet *n*; **f. pot,** Blumentopf *m*. II. *v.i.* blühen. ◆'**flowering,** *s.* Blüte *f*.

**flu** [fluː], *s. F:* Grippe *f*.

**fluctuate** ['flʌktjueit], *v.i.* schwanken. ◆'**fluctuating,** *adj.* schwankend. ◆**fluctu'ation,** *s.* Schwankung *f*.

**fluency** ['fluːənsi], *s.* Geläufigkeit *f*. ◆'**fluent,** *adj.* fließend.

**fluff** [flʌf], *s.* (*a*) (*on clothes etc.*) Fussel *f*; (*b*) (*down, soft fur*) Flaum *m*. ◆'**fluffy,** *adj.* flaumig; **f. toy,** Plüschtier *n*.

**fluid** ['fluːid]. I. *s.* Flüssigkeit *f*. II. *adj.* flüssig; **a f. situation,** eine veränderliche Lage.

**fluke** [fluːk], *s. F:* Zufall *m*.

**fluoride** ['fluːəraid], *s.* Fluor *n*.

**flurry** ['flʌri], *s.* 1. (*of wind*) Windstoß *m*; **snow f.,** Schneegestöber *n*. 2. (*agitation*) Aufregung *f*.

**flush**[1] [flʌʃ]. I. *s.* (*in face*) Erröten *n*; **hot flushes,** Wallungen *fpl*. II. *v.i.* (*a*) (*of face*) erröten; (*b*) (*in WC*) spülen. ◆'**flushed,** *adj.* errötet.

**flush**[2], *adj.* 1. *F:* **to be f.** (**with money**), gut bei Kasse sein. 2. **f. with the floor,** in gleicher Ebene mit dem Fußboden.

**fluster** ['flʌstər]. I. *s.* Verwirrung *f*. II. *v.tr.* (j-n) aus der Fassung bringen.

◆'**flustered,** *adj.* verwirrt.

**flute** [fluːt], *s.* Flöte *f*.

**flutter** ['flʌtər], *v.i.* flattern.

**fly**[1] [flai], *s.* Fliege *f*.

**fly**[2], *s.* (*also* **flies**) Hosenschlitz *m*.

**fly**[3], *v. irr.* 1. *v.i.* fliegen. **time flies,** die Zeit verfliegt; **the door flew open,** die Tür flog auf; **to f. into a rage,** in Wut geraten. 2. *v.tr.* (*a*) (eine Fahne) hissen; (einen Drachen) steigen lassen; (*b*) (ein Flugzeug) fliegen. ◆'**flying,** *adj.* (*a*) **f. boat,** Flugboot *n*; **f. saucer,** fliegende Untertasse *f*; **f. fish,** fliegender Fisch *m*; (*b*) (*police*) **f. squad,** Überfallkommando *n*; (*c*) **f. jump,** Sprung *m* (mit Anlauf); *Sp:* **f. start,** fliegender Start *m*; *F:* **f. visit,** Stippvisite *f*. ◆'**flyover,** *s.* Überführung *f*. ◆'**flypast,** *s.* Flugparade *f*.

**foal** [fəul], *s.* Fohlen *n*.

**foam** [fəum]. I. *s.* Schaum *m*; **f. rubber,** Schaumgummi *m*. II. *v.i.* schäumen.

**focal** ['fəukəl], *adj.* **f. point,** Brennpunkt *m*. ◆'**focus** ['fəukəs]. I. *s.* Brennpunkt *m*; **in f.,** scharf eingestellt; **out of f.,** unscharf. II. *v.* 1. *v.tr.* (*a*) (ein Fernrohr, einen Fotoapparat) scharf einstellen; (*b*) **to f. attention on sth.,** die Aufmerksamkeit auf etwas *acc* konzentrieren. 2. *v.i.* **to f. on an object,** einen Gegenstand fixieren. ◆'**focusing,** *s.* Scharfeinstellung *f*.

**fodder** ['fɔdər], *s.* Futter *n*.

**foetus** ['fiːtəs], *s.* Fötus *m*.

**fog** [fɔg], *s.* (dichter) Nebel *m*. ◆'**foggy,** *adj.* nebelig. ◆'**foghorn,** *s.* Nebelhorn *n*. ◆'**foglamp,** *s.* Nebelscheinwerfer *m*.

**foil**[1] [fɔil], *s.* Folie *f*; *Cu:* **baking f.,** Alufolie *f*.

**foil**[2], *s. Sp:* Florett *n*.

**foil**[3], *v.tr.* vereiteln.

**foist** [fɔist], *v.tr. F:* **to f. sth. on s.o.,** j-m etwas andrehen.

**fold** [fəuld]. I. *s.* Falte *f*. II. *v.tr.* (*a*) falten; (*b*) **to f. sth. in sth.,** etwas in etwas *dat* einwickeln; (*c*) **to f. one's arms,** die Arme verschränken. ◆'**folder,** *s.* Mappe *f*. ◆'**folding,** *adj.* Klapp-; **f. chair,** Klappstuhl *m*. ◆'**fold 'up,** *v.* 1. *v.tr.* (etwas) zusammenklappen; (Papier usw.) zusammenfalten. 2. *v.i. F:* (*of firm*) pleite gehen.

**foliage** ['fəuliidʒ], *s.* (*of trees*) Laub *n*; (*of plants*) Blätter *npl*.

**folk** [fəuk], *s.* (*a*) Leute *pl*; (*b*) *Mus:* **f. dance,** Volkstanz *m*; **f.** (**music**), Volksmusik *f*; **f. klore,** *s.* Folklore *f*. ◆'**folksong,** *s.* Volkslied *n*.

**follow** ['fɔləu], *v.* 1. *v.tr.* (*a*) (j-m, etwas *dat*) folgen; (*b*) (*of period etc.*) auf (etwas *acc*) folgen; (*c*) **to f. s.o.'s advice,** j-s Rat befolgen; **to f. instructions,** Anweisungen *dat* Folge leisten; (*d*) *F:* **I don't quite f. you,** da komm ich nicht ganz mit. 2. *v.i.* (nach)folgen; **as follows,** wie folgt. ◆'**follower,** *s.* Anhänger *m*. ◆'**following.** I. *adj.* folgend; **the f. day,** am nächsten Tag. II. *s.* Anhängerschaft f. ◆'follow 'up. I. v.tr. to f. up a matter, eine Sache weiterverfolgen. II. 'f.-up, s. Nachfassen n.

folly ['fɔli], s. Torheit f.

fond [fɔnd], adj. 1. (a) (loving) liebevoll; (b) to be f. of s.o., sth., j-n, etwas gern haben. 2. (of hope, belief etc.) töricht. ◆'fondness, s. (a) Liebe f (for s.o., zu j-m); (b) Schwäche f (for sth., für etwas acc).

fondle ['fɔndl], v.tr. liebkosen.

food [fu:d], s. (a) Nahrung f; (at meal) Essen n; (for animals) Futter n; f. poisoning, Lebensmittelvergiftung f; f. for thought, Grund m zum Nachdenken; (b) (fare, diet) Kost f; (c) (groceries) Lebensmittel pl; f. shop, Lebensmittelgeschäft n. ◆'foodstuff, s. Nahrungsmittel n.

fool [fu:l]. I. s. Narr m, Dummkopf m; to make a f. of s.o./oneself, j-n/sich lächerlich machen. II. 1. v.i. I was only fooling, ich habe es nicht ernst gemeint. 2. v.tr. (j-n) betrügen; you could have fooled me, was du nicht sagst! ◆'foolery, s. Dummheiten fpl. ◆'foolhardy, adj. tollkühn. ◆'foolish, adj. dumm. ◆'foolishness, s. Dummheit f. ◆'foolproof, adj. narrensicher.

foot [fut]. I. s. (pl feet [fi:t]). 1. Fuß m; on f., zu Fuß; to put one's f. down, (i) ein Machtwort sprechen; (ii) Aut: F: aufs Gas treten; F: to put one's f. in it, ins Fettnäpfchen treten. 2. Fußende n (des Bettes); Fuß m (eines Strumpfes, eines Berges usw.). II. v.tr. F: to f. the bill, für die Rechnung aufkommen. ◆'football, s. Fußball m; f. pitch, Fußballfeld n. ◆'footballer, s. Fußballspieler m. ◆'footbridge, s. Fußgängerbrücke f. ◆'footing, s. to be on a good f. with s.o., sich mit j-m gut stehen. ◆'footlights, s.pl. Rampenlicht n. ◆'footmark, s. Fußabdruck m. ◆'footnote, s. Fußnote f. ◆'footpath, s. Pfad m. ◆'footprint, s. Fußabdruck m. ◆'footstep, s. Schritt m; F: to follow in s.o.'s footsteps, in j-s Fußstapfen treten. ◆'footwear, s. Schuhwerk n.

for [fɔːr]. I. prep. 1. für + acc. to eat sth. f. supper, etwas zum Abendbrot essen; 2. (purpose) what f.? wozu? to jump f. joy, vor Freude hüpfen. 3. (time) I'm going away f. a fortnight, ich verreise für vierzehn Tage; he was missing f. a fortnight, er war vierzehn Tage (lang) verschwunden; I've been here f. three days, ich bin seit drei Tagen hier. II. conj. denn.

forage ['fɔridʒ], v.i. to f. for sth., nach etwas dat suchen.

forbearance [fɔː'bɛərəns], s. Nachsicht f. ◆for'bearing, adj. nachsichtig.

forbid [fə'bid], v.tr. verbieten; to f. s.o. to do sth., j-m verbieten, etwas zu tun. ◆for'bidden, adj. verboten.

◆for'bidding, adj. abschreckend.

force [fɔːs]. I. s. 1. by f. of habit, aus alter Gewohnheit. 2. (a) (of pers.) Kraft f; Wucht f (eines Schlages, Sturms usw.); to use f., Gewalt anwenden; (b) f. of gravity, Schwerkraft f. 3. Mil: etc: Verband m (von Truppen); to join the Forces, zum Militär gehen; to join forces with s.o., sich mit j-m zusammentun. (of law) to come into f., in Kraft treten. II. v.tr. (a) (j-n) zwingen; (b) (eine Tür) aufbrechen; (c) to f. sth. on s.o., j-m etwas aufdrängen. ◆'force 'back, v.tr. zurückdrängen. ◆'forced, adj. (a) erzwungen; f. labour, Zwangsarbeit f; f. landing, Notlandung f; (b) (of laugh, smile) gezwungen. ◆'forceful, adj. 1. (of pers.) energisch. 2. (of language) eindringlich. 3. (of argument) überzeugend. ◆'forcible, adj. gewaltsam.

ford [fɔːd], s. Furt f.

fore [fɔːr], to come to the f., in den Vordergrund treten. ◆'forearm, s. Unterarm m. ◆fore'boding, s. (böse) Vorahnung f. ◆'forecast. I. s. Voraussage f; weather f., Wetterbericht m. II. v.tr. (etwas) voraussagen. ◆'forecourt, s. (of building) Vorhof m; (of garage) Vorplatz m. ◆'forefather, s. Vorfahr m. ◆'forefinger, s. Zeigefinger m. ◆'forefront, s. in the f., in der vordersten Reihe; Fig: führend. ◆'foregoing, adj. (in book, letter) obig; the f., das Vorangehende. ◆'foregone, adj. it was a f. conclusion (that...), es war von vornherein klar (, daß...). ◆'foreground, s. Vordergrund m. ◆'forehand, s. Vorhand f. ◆forehead ['fɔrid,'fɔːhed], s. Stirn f. ◆'foreleg, s. Vorderbein n. ◆'foreman, s. Vorarbeiter m. ◆'foremost. I. adj. (of place) vorderste(r,s); the f. authority, der führende Experte (on sth., für etwas acc). II. adv. first and f., zuallererst. ◆'forename, s. esp. N.Am: Vorname m. ◆'forerunner, s. Vorläufer m. ◆fore'see, v.tr. voraussehen. ◆fore'shadow, v.tr. (ein Ereignis) voraushnen lassen. ◆'foresight, s. Voraussicht f. ◆fore'stall, v.tr. (j-m, j-s Plänen) zuvorkommen. ◆'foretaste, s. Vorgeschmack m. ◆fore'tell, v.tr.irr. (etwas) voraussagen. ◆'foreword, s. Vorwort n.

foreign ['fɔrin], adj. 1. (abroad) ausländisch; f. language, Fremdsprache f; f. currency, Devisen fpl; f. trade, Außenhandel m; f. affairs, auswärtige Angelegenheiten; the F. Office, das (britische) Außenministerium. 2. (strange) fremd; f. body, Fremdkörper m. ◆'foreigner, s. Ausländer(in) m(f).

forensic [fə'rensik], adj. gerichtlich; f. medicine, Gerichtsmedizin f.

forest ['fɔrist], s. Wald m; f. fire, Waldbrand m; esp. N.Am: f. ranger, Förster m. ◆'forestry, s. Forstwirtschaft f.

forfeit ['fɔːfit]. I. s. Pfand n. II. v.tr. verwirken.

**forge¹** [fɔːdʒ]. **I.** *s.* Schmiede *f.* **II.** *v.tr.* (*a*) schmieden; (*b*) (eine Unterschrift, Banknoten usw.) fälschen. ◆**'forger**, *s.* Fälscher *m.* ◆**'forgery**, *s.* Fälschung *f.*

**forge²**, *v.i.* to f. **ahead**, große Fortschritte machen.

**forget** [fə'get], *v.tr. irr.* vergessen. ◆**for'getful**, *adj.* vergeßlich. ◆**for'getfulness**, *s.* Vergeßlichkeit *f.* ◆**for'get-me-not**, *s.* Vergißmeinnicht *n.*

**forgive** [fə'giv], *v.tr. irr.* to f. **s.o.** for **sth.**, j-m etwas verzeihen/vergeben. ◆**for'givable**, *adj.* verzeihlich. ◆**for'giveness**, *s.* Verzeihung *f.* ◆**for'giving**, *adj.* versöhnlich.

**forgo** [fɔː'gəu], *v.tr. irr.* to f. **sth.**, auf etwas *acc* verzichten.

**fork** [fɔːk]. **I.** *s.* 1. Gabel *f.* 2. Gabelung *f* (einer Straße). **II.** *v.* 1. *v.i.* (*of road*) sich gabeln. 2. *v.tr. P:* to f. **out**/*N.Am:* to f. **over/up money**, blechen. ◆**fork-'lift 'truck**, *s.* Gabelstapler *m.*

**forlorn** [fə'lɔːn], *adj.* verlassen.

**form** [fɔːm]. **I.** *s.* 1. Form *f; F:* **you know the f.**, du weißt schon, wie das geht; **to be in (good) f.**/off f., in Form/nicht in Form sein. 2. (*printed*) Formular *n.* **II.** *v.* 1. *v.tr.* (*a*) (*mould*) formen (**into sth.**, zu etwas *dat*); (*b*) (*create*) (einen Kreis, Wörter, Sätze, eine Regierung usw.) bilden; (*c*) (eine Firma) gründen; (*d*) (einen Plan usw.) ausarbeiten. 2. *v.i.* (*a*) (*take on a particular shape*) sich formen; (*of idea, plans*) Gestalt annehmen; (*b*) (*come into being*) sich bilden. ◆**for'mation**, *s.* Formung *f;* Bildung *f;* Gründung *f; Av:* Formation *f.* ◆**'formative**, *adj.* **f. years**, Entwicklungsjahre *npl.*

**formal** ['fɔːm(ə)l], *adj.* (*following conventions, impersonal*) formell; (*of occasion, dress*) feierlich; (*of design*) symmetrisch. ◆**for'mality**, *s.* 1. (*social convention*) Förmlichkeit *f.* 2. *Adm: etc:* Formalität *f.*

**former** ['fɔːmər], *adj.* 1. ehemalig; **in f. times**, in früheren Zeiten. **2. the f.**, der, die, das erstere; **-ly**, *adv.* früher.

**formidable** ['fɔːmidəbl], *adj.* 1. (*of pers., character*) ehrfurchtgebietend. 2. (*of opponent, task etc.*) gewaltig.

**formula** ['fɔːmjulə], *s.* Formel *f.* ◆**'formulate**, *v.tr.* formulieren.

**forsake** [fə'seik], *v.tr. irr.* (*a*) (j-n, etwas) verlassen; (*b*) (*give up*) (etwas) aufgeben.

**fort** [fɔːt], *s.* Fort *n.*

**forth** [fɔːθ], *adv.* **back and f.**, hin und her; **and so f.**, und so weiter. ◆**forth'coming**, *adj.* 1. bevorstehend; (*of book*) in Kürze erscheinend. 2. (*of pers.*) mitteilsam.

**fortify** ['fɔːtifai], *v.tr.* (*a*) (eine Stadt) befestigen; (*b*) (j-n) stärken. ◆**fortifi'cation**, *s.* Festungswerk *n.*

**fortitude** ['fɔːtitjuːd], *s.* Standhaftigkeit *f.*

**fortnight** ['fɔːtnait], *s.* vierzehn Tage *mpl.* ◆**'fortnightly**. **I.** *adj.* vierzehntägig. **II.** *adv.* alle vierzehn Tage.

**fortress** ['fɔːtrəs], *s.* Festung *f.*

**fortuitous** [fɔː'tjuːitəs], *adj.* zufällig.

**fortune** ['fɔːtʃən,-tjuːn], *s.* 1. (*a*) (*luck*) Glück *n;* **by good f.**, durch glücklichen Zufall; (*b*) (*fate*) Schicksal *n;* **to tell fortunes**, wahrsagen; **f. teller**, Wahrsager(in) *m(f).* 2. (*wealth*) Vermögen *n.* ◆**'fortunate**, *adj.* glücklich; **to be f.**, Glück haben. **-ly**, *adv.* glücklicherweise.

**forty** ['fɔːti], *num.adj.* vierzig.

**forward** ['fɔːwəd]. **I.** *adj.* 1. **f. movement**, Vorwärtsbewegung *f.* 2. (*of pers.*) keck. **II.** *adv.* (*also* **forwards**) 1. vorwärts. 2. (*of pers.*) **to come f.**, sich melden. **III.** *s. Fb:* Stürmer *m.* **IV.** *v.tr.* (einen Brief) nachschicken.

**fossil** ['fɔs(ə)l], *s.* Fossil *n.*

**foster** ['fɔstər], *v.tr.* (*a*) (ein Kind) in Pflege nehmen; (*b*) (eine Hoffnung, einen Wunsch) hegen. ◆**'fosterchild**, *s.* Pflegekind *n.* ◆**'foster-mother**, *s.* Pflegemutter *f.*

**foul** [faul]. **I.** *adj.* 1. (*a*) (*putrid*) (*of smell, taste*) faulig; (*b*) (*nasty*) (*of taste, pers. etc.*) widerlich; (*c*) (*of language*) unflätig. 2. *adv.* **to fall f. of s.o.**, es sich *dat* mit j-m verderben. **3. f. play**, verbrecherische Absichten *fpl.* **II.** *s. Sp:* Foul *n.* **III.** *v.tr.* (*a*) (die Luft usw.) verschmutzen; (*b*) *Sp:* (j-n) foulen; (*c*) (*of dog etc.*) (den Gehsteig) beschmutzen.

**found** [faund], *v.tr.* (eine Firma, Schule, Gesellschaft usw.) gründen. ◆**foun'dation**, *s.* 1. Gründung *f* (einer Stadt usw.). 2. Grundmauer *f* (eines Gebäudes). 3. *Fig:* Grundlage *f;* (*of rumour*) **without f.**, unbegründet. ◆**'founder¹**, *s.* Gründer *m.*

**founder²** ['faundər], *v.i.* (*of ship*) sinken.

**foundry** ['faundri], Gießerei *f.*

**fountain** ['fauntin], *s.* (*a*) (*artificial*) Springbrunnen *m;* (*natural*) Quelle *f;* (**drinking**) **f.**, Trinkbrunnen *m;* (*b*) **f. pen**, Füllfederhalter *m.*

**four** [fɔːr], *num.adj.* vier. **to go on all fours**, auf allen Vieren gehen. ◆**'fourfold**, *adj. & adv.* vierfach. ◆**'four-'footed**, *adj. Hum:* **f.-f. friend**, Vierbeiner *m.* ◆**'four-'seater**, *s. Aut:* Viersitzer *m.* ◆**'fourteen**, *num.adj.* vierzehn. ◆**'fourteenth**, *num.adj.* vierzehnte(r, s). ◆**'fourth. I.** *num.adj.* vierte(r, s). **II.** *s.* Viertel *n.*

**fowl** [faul], *s. coll.* Geflügel *n.*

**fox** [fɔks]. **I.** *s.* Fuchs *m.* **II.** *v.tr.* (j-n) verblüffen; (*deceive*) täuschen. ◆**'foxglove**, *s.* Fingerhut *m.* ◆**'foxhound**, *s.* Meutehund *m.* ◆**'foxhunt(ing)**, *s.* Fuchsjagd *f.* ◆**fox-'terrier**, *s.* Fox(terrier) *m.* ◆**foxtrot**, *s.* Foxtrott *m.*

**foyer** ['fɔiei], *s.* Foyer *n.*

**fraction** ['frækʃ(ə)n], *s.* Bruchteil *m.*

**fracture** ['fræktʃər]. **I.** *s.* Bruch *m;* (**point of**) **f.**, Bruchstelle *f.* **II.** *v.tr.* brechen.

**fragile** ['frædʒail], *adj.* zerbrechlich.

**fragment** ['frægmənt], s. Fragment n.

**fragrance** ['freigrəns], s. Duft m. ◆'**fragrant**, adj. duftend.

**frail** [freil], adj. gebrechlich.

**frame** [freim]. I. s. 1. (a) Rahmen m; (b) Fassung f (einer Brille). 2. (a) (of pers.) Körperbau m; (b) f. of mind, Gemütsverfassung f. II. v.tr. (a) (ein Bild) einrahmen; (b) P: to f. s.o., j-m ein Verbrechen anhängen. ◆'**frame-up**, s. P: abgekartetes Spiel n. ◆'**framework**, s. 1. (of building) Gerippe n. 2. Fig: Gefüge n (der Regierung usw.); (structure) Aufbau m; **within the f. of the United Nations,** im Rahmen der Vereinten Nationen.

**France** [frɑːns]. Pr.n. Frankreich n.

**franchise** ['fræn(t)ʃaiz], s. Pol: Wahlrecht n; Com: Lizenz f.

**frank**[1] [fræŋk], adj. offen; **to be f./-ly,** adv. offen gestanden. ◆'**frankness**, s. Offenheit f.

**frank**[2], v.tr. (einen Brief) frankieren.

**frankfurter** ['fræŋkfə:tər], s. Frankfurter Würstchen n.

**frantic** ['fræntik], adj. (a) **to be f.,** außer sich dat sein (**with** joy/fear etc., vor Freude/Angst usw.); (b) **f. efforts,** verzweifelte Bemühungen fpl.

**fraternal** [frə'tə:nl], adj. brüderlich. ◆**fraternize** ['frætənaiz], v.i. fraternisieren.

**fraud** [frɔːd], s. Schwindel m; esp. Jur: Betrug m. ◆'**fraudulent**, adj. betrügerisch.

**fraught** [frɔːt], adj. **f. with danger,** gefahrvoll.

**fray**[1] [frei], s. Schlägerei f.

**fray**[2], v.tr. & i. ausfransen. ◆**frayed**, adj. (a) Cl: ausgefranst; (b) **f. tempers,** erhitzte Gemüter npl.

**freak** [fri:k], s. (a) einmaliges Phänomen n; (b) (pers.) Mißgeburt f; **f. storm,** ungeheurer Sturm.

**freckle** ['frekl], s. Sommersprosse f.

**free** [fri:]. I. adj. 1. frei; **to set s.o. f.,** (i) (of government) j-n freilassen; (ii) (of rescuer etc.) j-n befreien; **he is not f. to do it,** es steht ihm nicht frei, das zu tun; **f. from pain,** ohne Schmerzen; **f. from worry,** sorgenfrei; **duty f.,** zollfrei; **f. enterprise,** Privatwirtschaft f. 2. (no cost) kostenlos; **f. gift/sample,** Gratisprobe f; **-ly,** adv. (a) frei; **to move f.,** sich frei bewegen; **to speak f.,** offen reden; (b) (voluntarily) freiwillig. II. v.tr. (a) (j-n, ein Volk usw.) befreien; **to f. a prisoner,** (of government) einen Gefangenen freilassen; (by force etc.) einen Gefangenen befreien; (b) (etwas Verklemmtes) freibekommen. ◆'**freedom,** s. Freiheit f; **f. of speech,** Redefreiheit f. ◆'**freehand,** adj. **f. drawing,** Freihandzeichnen n. ◆'**freehold,** s. freier Grundbesitz. ◆'**freelance,** adj. freiberuflich. ◆'**freemason,** s. Freimaurer m. ◆'**freemasonry,** s. Freimaurerei f. ◆'**freestyle,** s. Freistilschwimmen n.

◆'**freeway,** s. N.Am: Schnellstraße f.

**freeze** [fri:z]. I. v.irr. 1. v.i. (a) (of liquid etc.) frieren; (b) (of pers.) **to f. to death,** erfrieren. 2. v.tr. (Obst usw.) tiefkühlen; (b) **to f. wages,** Löhne stoppen. II. s. **wage f.,** Lohnstopp m. ◆'**freezer,** s. (upright) Tiefkühlschrank m; (chest) f., Tiefkühltruhe f. ◆'**freezing.** I. adj. f. **temperatures,** Temperaturen fpl unter dem Nullpunkt; **f. fog,** Eisnebel m; F: **it's f.,** es ist eiskalt. II. s. **above/below f.,** über/unter Null; **f. point,** Gefrierpunkt m.

**freight** [freit], s. Fracht f; esp. N.Am: f. **train,** Güterzug m; **air f.,** Luftfracht f.

**French** [fren(t)ʃ]. I. adj. französisch; F: **bread,** Stangenbrot n; F. **dressing,** Salatsoße f nach französischer Art; F: **fries,** Pommes frites fpl; F. **window,** Glastür f (zum Garten); F. **horn,** Horn n. II. s. 1. Französisch n. 2. pl. **the F.,** die Franzosen. ◆'**Frenchman,** s. Franzose m. ◆'**Frenchwoman,** s. Französin f.

**frequency** ['fri:kwənsi], s. 1. Häufigkeit f. 2. Ph: Frequenz f. ◆**frequent.** I. adj. ['fri:kwənt]. 1. häufig; **-ly,** adv. oft. II. v.tr. [fri'kwent] (eine Kneipe usw.) (regelmäßig) aufsuchen.

**fresh** [freʃ]. I. adj. 1. frisch. 2. (cheeky) F: frech. ◆'**freshen,** v. 1. v.i. (of wind) frischer werden. 2. v.tr. (das Gedächtnis) auffrischen. ◆'**freshman,** F: **fresher,** s. Sch: Student m im ersten Jahr. ◆'**freshness,** s. Frische f. ◆'**freshwater,** adj. Süßwasser-; **f. fish,** Süßwasserfisch m.

**fret** [fret], v.i. sich sorgen. ◆'**fretful,** adj. weinerlich.

**friar** ['fraiər], s. Mönch m.

**friction** ['frikʃ(ə)n], s. 1. Reibung f. 2. Fig: Reiberei f.

**Friday** ['fraidi], s. Freitag m; **Good F.,** Karfreitag m.

**fridge** [fridʒ], s. F: Kühlschrank m.

**friend** [frend], s. 1. Freund(in) m(f); (acquaintance) Bekannte(r) f(m); **to make friends (with s.o.),** sich (mit j-m) anfreunden. ◆'**friendless,** adj. ohne Freund. ◆'**friendliness,** s. Freundlichkeit f. ◆'**friendly,** adj. freundlich; **to be f. with s.o.,** mit j-m befreundet sein; Sp: **f. match,** Freundschaftsspiel n. ◆'**friendship,** s. Freundschaft f.

**frieze** ['fri:z], s. Arch: Fries m; (on wallpaper) Zierstreifen m.

**frigate** ['frigət], s. Fregatte f.

**fright** [frait], s. Schreck(en) m; **to give s.o. a f.,** j-n erschrecken. ◆'**frighten,** v.tr. (j-m) Angst machen; (startle) (j-n) erschrecken. ◆'**frightening,** adj. erschreckend. ◆'**frightful,** adj. F: schrecklich; **-ly,** adv. F: **f. nice,** furchtbar nett.

**frigid** ['fridʒid], adj. frigide.

**frill** [fril], s. 1. Cl: Rüsche f. 2. F: **frills,** Verzierungen fpl; **a meal without frills,** ein einfaches Essen.

**fringe** [frindʒ], s. **1.** Franse f. **2.** (edge) Rand m; f. **benefits**, zusätzliche Sozialaufwendungen fpl.

**frisk** [frisk], v.tr. (j-n) durchsuchen, F: filzen. ◆'**frisky**, adj. lebhaft.

**fritter**¹ ['fritər], s. Fettgebäck n; **apple f.**, Apfelkrapfen m.

**fritter**², v.tr. **to f. (away)**, (Zeit, Geld usw.) verplempern.

**frivolous** ['frivələs], adj. leichtfertig; frivol. ◆**frivolity** [-'vɔliti], s. Leichtfertigkeit f; Frivolität f.

**frizz(l)y** ['friz(l)i], adj. kraus.

**frock** [frɔk], s. Kleid n.

**frog** [frɔg], s. Frosch m; **f.'s legs**, Froschschenkel mpl. ◆'**frogman**, s. Froschmann m.

**frolic** ['frɔlik], v.i. herumtollen.

**from** [frɔm, frəm], prep. **1.** von + dat; f. **now on**, von nun an. **2.** (a) (out of, with place) aus + dat; **to take a glass f. the cupboard**, ein Glas aus dem Schrank nehmen; **he comes f. London**, er stammt aus London; **made f. wood**, aus Holz (gemacht). **3.** f. **what I hear**, nach dem, was ich höre.

**front** [frʌnt]. **I.** s. **1.** Vorderseite f; **at the f. of the train**, vorn im Zug; **in f. of**, vor + dat; (opposite) gegenüber + dat; **in f./at the f.**, vorne. **2.** Mil: Meteor: Front f. **3.** (seafront) Strandpromenade f. **4.** Com: etc: (cover-up) Tarnorganisation f. **II.** adj. vorder, Vorder-; **f. door**, Haustür f; **f. page**, Titelseite f; **f. seat**, Vordersitz m; **f. line**, Front(linie) f. ◆'**frontage**, s. Front f.

**frontier** ['frʌntiər], s. Grenze f.

**frost** [frɔst], s. Frost m; ◆'**frostbite**, s. Erfrierung f. ◆'**frostbitten**, adj. erfroren. ◆'**frosted**, adj. (a) f. over, vereist; (b) f. **glass**, Milchglas n.

**froth** [frɔθ]. **I.** s. Schaum m. **II.** v.i. schäumen. ◆'**frothy**, adj. schaumig.

**frown** [fraun]. **I.** s. finsterer Blick m. **II.** v.i. die Stirn runzeln; **to f. at s.o.**, j-n finster anblicken.

**frozen** ['frəuzən], adj. (a) gefroren; F: f. **to death**, völlig erfroren; **I'm f.**, mir ist eiskalt; (b) (of food) tiefgekühlt; f. **food**, Tiefkühlkost f.

**frugal** ['fru:g(ə)l], adj. (of pers.) sparsam; (of meal etc.) kärglich.

**fruit** [fru:t], s. **1.** coll. Obst n. f. **juice**, Obstsaft m; f. **salad**, Obstsalat m. **2.** Bot: & Fig: Frucht f. ◆'**fruiterer**, s. Obsthändler m. ◆**fruitful**, adj. (also Fig:) fruchtbar. ◆**fru'ition**, s **to come to f.**, in Erfüllung gehen. ◆**fruitless**, adj. fruchtlos; f. **efforts**, vergebliche Mühe/Bemühungen. ◆**fruit-machine**, s. F: Spielautomat m.

**frumpish** ['frʌmpiʃ], adj. unmodisch (gekleidet).

**frustrate** [frʌs'treit], v.tr. (j-n) frustrieren. ◆**frus'trating**, adj. frustrierend. ◆**frus'tration**, s. Frustration f.

**fry** [frai], v. **1.** v.tr. (in der Pfanne) bra-

ten; **fried egg**, Spiegelei n. **2.** v.i. braten.

**frying pan**, Bratpfanne f.

**fuddled** ['fʌdld], adj. (a) (tipsy) beschwipst; (b) (confused) konfus.

**fuel** ['fjuəl], s. **1.** (for fire) Brennstoff m. **2.** (for engine) Kraftstoff m; Aut: f. **gauge**, Benzinuhr f.

**fug** [fʌg], s. F: Mief m.

**fugitive** ['fju:dʒitiv], s. Flüchtling m.

**fulfil** [ful'fil], v.tr. (a) (etwas) erfüllen; (of wish) **to be fulfilled**, in Erfüllung gehen; (b) (ein Versprechen) einlösen. ◆**ful'filment**, s. Erfüllung f.

**full** [ful]. **I.** adj. voll; (a) f. **of**, voller + gen, voll mit + dat; (b) f. (**up**), (of bus) voll besetzt; (of pers.) satt; (c) (of report) ausführlich; (d) (complete) ganz; f. **moon**, Vollmond m; f. **stop**, Punkt m. **II.** s. (a) **in f.**, vollständig; (b) **to enjoy sth. to the f.**, etwas in vollen Zügen genießen. ◆**full'back**, s. Verteidiger m. ◆**full-'blown**, adj. vollwertig. ◆**full-'length**. **I.** adj. (of skirt) lang; f.-l. **portrait**, ganzes Porträt; f.-l. **film**, abendfüllender Film. **II.** adv. **to lie f.-l. on the floor**, voll ausgestreckt auf dem Fußboden liegen. ◆**fullness**, s. **1.** Fülle f; **in the f. of time**, zur gegebenen Zeit. **2.** Weite f (eines Rocks). **3.** Ausführlichkeit f (eines Berichts usw.). ◆**full-'scale**, adj. (of rescue etc.) großangelegt; (thorough) gründlich; f.-s. **attack**, Großangriff m. ◆**full-'time**. **I.** adj. f.-t. **work**, ganztägige Arbeit F: **it's a f.t. job**, es läßt keine Zeit übrig. **II.** adv. ganztags. ◆**fully**, adv. völlig.

**fumble** ['fʌmbl], v.i. (mit den Fingern) fummeln; **to f. with sth.**, an etwas dat herumfummeln.

**fume** [fju:m]. **I.** s. usu.pl. **fumes**, Dämpfe mpl; Aut: **exhaust fumes**, Abgase npl. **II.** v.i. F: (of pers.) vor Wut kochen. ◆**fuming**, adj. wütend.

**fun** [fʌn], s. Spaß m; **to make f. of s.o.**, j-n zum besten halten; **for/in f.**, zum Spaß; **it's good/great f.**, es macht viel Spaß; **to have f. doing sth.**, sich bei etwas dat gut unterhalten. ◆**funfair**, s. Jahrmarkt m.

**function** ['fʌŋkʃ(ə)n]. **I.** s. **1.** Funktion f. **2.** (party etc.) (a) (private) Feier f; (b) (public) (öffentliche) Veranstaltung f; (reception) Empfang m. **II.** v.i. funktionieren. ◆**functional**, adj. zweckmäßig.

**fund** [fʌnd]. **I.** s. **1.** (a) Fonds m; **pension f.**, Pensionskasse f; (b) pl **funds**, Geldmittel npl; **to be in funds**, gut bei Kasse sein. **2.** Fig: (store) Vorrat m. **II.** v.tr. (etwas) finanzieren; (für ein Projekt) aufkommen.

**fundamental** [fʌndə'mentl]. **I.** adj. grundlegend; (essential) wesentlich (to, für + acc). **II.** s. Grundsatz m; -**ly**, adv. grundsätzlich.

**funeral** ['fju:n(ə)rəl], s. Begräbnis n; f. **service**, Trauergottesdienst m; f. **procession**, Leichenzug m.

**fungus**, *pl* **fungi** ['fʌŋgəs, -gai], *s.* Pilz *m.*

**funicular** [fju'nikjulər], *adj. & s.* **f.** (**railway**), Seilbahn *f.*

**funk** [fʌnk], *s. P:* Schiß *m;* **to be in a blue f.**, einen Mordsschiß haben.

**funnel** ['fʌnl], *s.* **1.** (*for pouring*) Trichter *m.* **2.** (*of ship etc.*) Schornstein *m.*

**funny** ['fʌni], *adj.* komisch; **-ily**, *adv.* **f. enough**, komischerweise.

**fur** [fəːr], *s.* (*a*) (*on animal*) Fell *n;* (*b*) *Cl:* Pelz *m;* **f. coat**, Pelzmantel *m.*

**furious** ['fjuːriəs], *adj.* (*a*) (*angry*) wütend (**with s.o.**, auf j-n); (*b*) (*violent*) heftig; **at a f. pace**, mit rasender Geschwindigkeit.

**furnace** ['fəːnis], *s.* (*a*) Brennofen *m;* **blast f.**, Hochofen *m;* (*b*) *Fig:* Backofen *m.*

**furnish** ['fəːniʃ], *v.tr.* (*a*) (eine Wohnung usw.) einrichten; **furnished room**, möbliertes Zimmer; (*b*) **to f. evidence/an example**, Beweise/ein Beispiel liefern. ◆**'furnishings**, *spl* Einrichtungsgegenstände *mpl.* ◆**furniture** ['fəːnitʃər], *s.* Möbel *npl;* **piece of f.**, Möbelstück *n.*

**furrow** ['fʌrəu], *s.* Furche *f.* ◆**'furrowed**, *adj.* **f. brow**, gerunzelte Stirn *f.*

**further** ['fəːðər]. **I.** *adv.* **1.** weiter. **2.** (*besides*) ferner. **II.** *adj.* weiter. **III.** *v.tr.* fördern. ◆**further'more**, *adv.* außerdem. ◆**'furthest. I.** *adj.* am weitesten entfernt. **II.** *adv.* am weitesten.

**furtive** ['fəːtiv], *adj.* verstohlen.

**fury** ['fjuəri], *s.* (*a*) (*anger*) Wut *f;* (*b*) *Fig:* Heftigkeit *f.*

**fuse** ['fjuːz]. **I.** *s. El:* Sicherung *f;* **f. box**, Sicherungskasten *m; f.* **wire**, Sicherungsdraht *m;* **the f. has gone/blown**, die Sicherung ist durchgebrannt. **II.** *v.i.* (*a*) **the lights have fused**, die Sicherung für das Licht ist durchgebrannt; (*b*) *Fig:* verschmelzen. ◆**fusion** ['fjuːʒ(ə)n], *s.* **1.** *Ph:* Fusion *f.* **2.** *Fig:* Vereinigung *f.*

**fuselage** ['fjuːzilɑːʒ], *s.* Rumpf *m.*

**fusillade** [fjuːzi'leid], *s.* Gewehrsalve *f.*

**fuss** [fʌs]. **I.** *s.* **1.** Getue *n;* **to make a f.**, Umstände/*F:* Theater machen. **2. to make a f. of s.o.**, viel Aufhebens um j-n machen; (*spoil*) j-n verhätscheln. **II.** *v.i.* Umstände/*F:* Theater machen. ◆**'fussiness**, *s.* Umständlichkeit *f.* ◆**'fussy**, *adj.* umständlich; (*particular*) heikel.

**fusty** ['fʌsti], *adj.* moderig; (*of smell*) muffig.

**futile** ['fjuːtail], *adj.* sinnlos. ◆**futility** [-'tiliti], *s.* Sinnlosigkeit *f.*

**future** ['fjuːtʃər]. **I.** *adj.* künftig. **II.** *s.* Zukunft *f.* ◆**futu'ristic**, *adj.* futuristisch.

**fuzzy** ['fʌzi], *adj.* **1.** (*of hair*) kraus. **2.** (*of outlines, photo*) unscharf.

# G

**G, g** [dʒiː], *s.* (der Buchstabe) G, g *n.*

**gab** [gæb], *s. F:* **to have the gift of the g.**, ein gutes Mundwerk haben.

**gabble** ['gæbl], *v.i.* plappern.

**gable** ['geibl], *s.* Giebel *m.*

**gadget** ['gædʒit], *s.* (kleines) Gerät *n.*

**Gaelic** ['geilik]. **I.** *adj.* gälisch. **II.** *s.* Gälisch *n.*

**gag** [gæg]. **I.** *s.* **1.** Knebel *m.* **2.** *F:* (*joke*) Gag *m*, Witz *m.* **II.** *v.tr.* (j-n) knebeln.

**gaily** ['geili], *adv.* fröhlich; **g. coloured**, farbenfroh.

**gain** [gein]. **I.** *s.* **1.** (*profit*) Gewinn *m;* (*advantage*) Vorteil *m.* **2.** (*in resources, capital etc.*) Zuwachs *m.* **II.** *v.* **1.** *v.tr.* (*a*) (etwas, einen Freund usw.) gewinnen; (*b*) **to g. strength, popularity** etc., an Stärke, Beliebtheit usw. gewinnen; **to g. weight**, zunehmen. **2.** *v.i.* (*a*) (*catch up*) aufholen; (*b*) (*of clock*) vorgehen.

**gala** ['gɑːlə], *s.* Fest *n;* **swimming g.**, Schauschwimmen *n;* **g. performance**, Galavorstellung *f.*

**galaxy** ['gæləksi], *s.* Milchstraße *f.*

**gale** [geil], *s.* (*a*) Sturm *m;* (*b*) *Fig:* **g. of laughter**, Lachsalve *f.*

**gall** [gɔːl], *s.* Galle *f;* **g. bladder**, Gallenblase *f.* ◆**'galling**, *adj.* ärgerlich; **it's g. to me**, es wurmt mich. ◆**'gallstone**, *s.* Gallenstein *m.*

**gallant** ['gælənt], *adj.* galant. ◆**'gallant**

**ry**, *s.* Tapferkeit *f.*

**gallery** ['gæləri], *s.* Galerie *f.*

**galley** ['gæli], *s.* **1.** *Hist:* Galeere *f.* **2.** *Nau:* Kombüse *f.*

**gallon** ['gælən], *s.* Gallone *f.*

**gallop** ['gæləp]. **I.** *s.* Galopp *m.* **II.** *v.i.* galoppieren.

**gallows** ['gæləuz], *s.* Galgen *m.*

**galore** [gə'lɔːr], *adv.* in Hülle und Fülle.

**gamble** ['gæmbl]. **I.** *s.* Risiko *n.* **II.** *v.tr. & i.* (um Geld) spielen; **to g. away a fortune**, ein Vermögen verspielen. ◆**'gambler**, *s.* Spieler(in) *m(f).* ◆**'gambling**, *s.* Spielen *n.*

**game** [geim]. **I.** *s.* **1.** Spiel *n;* (*a*) (*of cards, chess* etc.) Partie *f;* (*b*) *Sch:* **games**, Sport *m.* **2.** (*Hunting*) Wild *n.* **III.** *adj.* **g. for anything**, bereit, alles mit zumachen; *F:* **I'm g.**, ich mache mit. ◆**'gamekeeper**, *s.* Wildhüter *m.*

**gammon** ['gæmən], *s.* (geräucherter) Schinken *m.*

**gang** [gæŋ]. **I.** *s.* (*a*) Kolonne *f* (von Arbeitern); (*b*) Bande *f* (von Verbrechern, Kindern). **II.** *v.i. F:* **to g. up on s.o.**, sich gegen j-n zusammenrotten. ◆**'gangster**, *s.* Gangster *m.*

**gangrene** ['gæŋgriːn], *s.* Wundbrand *m.*

**gangway** ['gæŋwei], *s.* (*a*) Gang *m;* **g. please!** Platz machen, bitte! (*b*) *Nau:* Fallreep *n.*

**gaol** [dʒeil]. **I.** *s.* Gefängnis *n*; *F:* Kittchen *n.* **II.** *v.tr.* (j-n) ins Gefängnis werfen. ◆**'gaoler,** *s.* Gefängniswärter *m.*

**gap** [gæp], *s.* **1.** (*space with sth. missing*) Lücke *f.* **2.** Fin: trade g., Handelsdefizit *n*; to close the g., den Vorsprung aufholen. **3.** (*time*) Zwischenraum *m.*

**gape** [geip], *v.i.* (a) (*of things*) gähnen; (*of hole*) klaffen; (b) (*of pers.*) den Mund aufreißen; (*in surprise etc*) gaffen; **to g. at s.o., sth.,** j-n, etwas begaffen. ◆**'gaping,** *adj.* (*of wound, hole*) klaffend.

**garage** ['gærɑːʒ], *s.* (a) (*for storage*) Garage *f*; (b) (*for repairs*) Werkstatt *f*; (c) (*for petrol*) Tankstelle *f.*

**garbage** ['gɑːbidʒ], *s.* Müll *m*; *esp. N. Am:* Küchenabfälle *mpl*; **g. can,** Mülleimer *m.*

**garble** ['gɑːbl], *v.tr.* (einen Text) entstellen; (eine Nachricht) verstümmeln.

**garden** ['gɑːdn]. **I.** *s.* Garten *m*; **public gardens,** öffentliche Anlagen *fpl.*; **g. produce,** Gartenbauerzeugnisse *npl.* **II.** *v.i.* im Garten arbeiten. ◆**'gardener,** *s.* Gärtner(in) *m(f).* ◆**'gardening,** *s.* Gartenarbeit *f.*

**gargle** ['gɑːgl], *v.i.* gurgeln.

**garish** ['gɛəriʃ], *adj.* grell.

**garland** ['gɑːlənd], *s.* Girlande *f.*

**garlic** ['gɑːlik], *s.* Knoblauch *m.*

**garment** ['gɑːmənt], *s.* Kleidungsstück *n.*

**garnish** ['gɑːniʃ]. **I.** *v.tr.* garnieren. **II.** *s.* Garnierung *f.*

**garrison** ['gærisən], *s.* Garnison *f.*

**garrulous** ['gærələs, -juləs], *adj.* geschwätzig.

**garter** ['gɑːtər], *s.* (a) Strumpfband *n*; (b) *N. Am:* Sockenhalter *m.*

**gas** [gæs]. **I.** *s.* **1.** Gas *n*; **g. cooker,** Gasherd *m*; **g. fire,** Gasofen *m*; **g. meter,** Gasuhr *f.* **2.** *N.Am:* Benzin *n*; **g. station,** Tankstelle *f.* **II.** *v.tr.* (j-n) vergasen; **to g. oneself,** sich mit Gas umbringen. ◆**'gasoline,** *s. N. Am:* Benzin *n.* ◆**'gasworks,** *s. pl.* Gaswerk *n.*

**gash** [gæʃ]. **I.** *s.* (tiefe) Schnittwunde *f.* **II.** *v.tr.* (j-m) eine tiefe Schnittwunde zufügen; **he gashed his arm,** er hat sich tief in den Arm geschnitten.

**gasket** ['gæskit], *s.* Dichtung *f.*

**gasp** [gɑːsp]. **I.** *s.* Keuchen *n.* **II.** *v.i.* keuchen; **to g. for breath,** nach Luft schnappen.

**gastric** ['gæstrik], *adj.* Magen-. ◆**gas'tritis,** *s.* Gastritis *f.*

**gate** [geit], *s.* (a) Tor *n* (eines Gartens, einer Stadt usw.); (*of farm, across road etc.*) Gatter *n*; (b) *Av:* Flugsteig *m.* ◆**'gatecrash,** *v.tr.* (eine Party) uneingeladen mitmachen. ◆**'gatecrasher,** *s.* Eindringling *m.* ◆**'gateway,** *s.* (*also Fig:*) Tor *n.*

**gather** ['gæðər], *v.* **1.** *v.tr.* (a) (etwas) sammeln; (Blumen) pflücken; (Beeren) lesen; (Weizen, Heu usw.) ernten; **to g. strength,** Kräfte sammeln; **to g. speed,**

in Fahrt kommen; **to g. dust,** Staub fangen; (b) (*conclude*) (etwas) folgern; (*understand*) (Gesagtes, einen Namen usw.) mitkriegen. **2.** *v.i.* (a) (*of crowd etc.*) sich versammeln; (b) **a storm is gathering,** ein Gewitter zieht sich zusammen. ◆**'gathering,** *s.* Versammlung *f*; family g., Familientreffen *n.*

**gaudy** ['gɔːdi], *adj.* bunt; *Pej:* grell.

**gauge** [geidʒ]. **I.** *s.* (a) Meßinstrument *n*; *Mec. E:* Lehre *f*; (b) (*indicator*) Anzeiger *m*; petrol g., Benzinuhr *f.* **II.** *v.tr.* Fig: schätzen.

**gaunt** [gɔːnt], *adj.* hager.

**gauze** [gɔːz], *s.* Gaze *f.*

**gay** [gei], *adj.* **1.** (*of pers.*) (a) lustig; (b) *F:* (*homosexual*) schwul. **2.** (*of things*) heiter; **g. colours,** bunte Farben.

**gaze** [geiz]. **I.** *s.* (starrer) Blick *m.* **II.** *v.i.* **to g. at s.o., sth.,** j-n, etwas anstarren.

**gazelle** [gə'zel], *s.* Gazelle *f.*

**gazetteer** [gæzə'tiər], *s.* geographisches Namenverzeichnis *n.*

**gear** [giər]. **I.** *s.* **1.** *coll.* (a) Gerät *n*; Zubehör *n*; camping g., Campingausrüstung *f*; swimming g., Badesachen *fpl*; all my g., mein ganzes Zeug; (b) *F:* (*clothes*) Kluft *f.* **2.** *Aut:* Gang *m*; in g., mit eingelegtem Gang; to change g., (den Gang) schalten; g. lever, Schalthebel *m.* **II.** *v.tr.* (etwas) anpassen (to sth., etwas dat). ◆**'gearbox,** *s.* Getriebe *n.*

**Geiger** ['gaigər], *s.* G. counter, Geigerzähler *m.*

**gelatine** ['dʒelətiːn], *s.* Gelatine *f.*

**gelignite** ['dʒelignait], *s.* Gelatinedynamit *n.*

**gem** [dʒem], *s.* Edelstein *m*; *esp. Fig:* Juwel *n.*

**Gemini** ['dʒeminai]. *Pr. n. pl.* Zwillinge *mpl.*

**gen** [dʒen], *s. P:* Informationen *fpl.* ◆**'genned up,** *adj. phr. P:* to be g. up, Bescheid wissen.

**gender** ['dʒendər], *s.* Geschlecht *n.*

**gene** [dʒiːn], *s.* Gen *n.* ◆**genealogy** [dʒiːni'ælədʒi], *s.* Genealogie *f.* ◆**genealogical** [-ə'lɔdʒikl], *adj.* genealogisch.

**general** ['dʒen(ə)rəl]. **I.** *adj.* allgemein; the g. public, die breite Öffentlichkeit; g. knowledge, Allgemeinbildung *f*; g. practitioner, praktischer Arzt; (b) in g., im allgemeinen, im großen und ganzen. **II.** *s. Mil:* General *m.* ◆**generali'zation,** *s.* Verallgemeinerung *f.* ◆**'generalize,** *v.i.* verallgemeinern. ◆**'generally,** *adv.* allgemein.

**generate** ['dʒenəreit], *v.tr.* erzeugen. ◆**gene'ration,** *s.* **1.** (a) (*people*) Generation *f*; g. gap, Generationsunterschied *m*; (*time*) Menschenalter *n.* **2.** Erzeugung *f.* ◆**'generator,** *s.* Generator *m.*

**generous** ['dʒenərəs], *adj.* großzügig. ◆**generosity** [-'rɔsiti], *s.* Großzügigkeit *f.*

**genetics** [dʒə'netiks], s. Genetik f.
**Geneva** [dʒə'niːvə]. Pr. n. Genf n.
**genial** ['dʒiːniəl], adj. jovial.
**genitals** ['dʒenitlz], s. pl. (äußere) Geschlechtsteile npl.
**genius** ['dʒiːniəs], s. (pers.) Genie n; (quality) Genialität f; **work of g.**, geniale Arbeit.
**gent** [dʒent], s. abbr. P: = gentleman; F: **the gents,** die Herrentoilette f.
**gentle** ['dʒentl], adj. sanft; **g. hint,** zarter Wink. ◆**'gently,** adv. sachte; (carefully) vorsichtig.
**gentleman,** pl. -men ['dʒentlmən, -men] , s. **1.** (smart man) Gentleman m. **2.** (any man) Herr m; **Gentlemen,** Herren.
**gentry** ['dʒentri], s. (niederer) Adel m; **landed g.,** Landadel m.
**genuine** ['dʒenjuin], adj. (a) echt; (b) (of pers.) aufrichtig; **-ly,** adv. wirklich.
**geography** [dʒi'ɔgrəfi], s. Geographie f. ◆**geographical** [-ə'græfikl], adj. geographisch.
**geology** [dʒi'ɔlədʒi], s. Geologie f. ◆**geological** [-ə'lɔdʒikl], adj. geologisch. ◆**ge'ologist,** s. Geologe m, Geologin f.
**geometry** [dʒi'ɔmətri], s. Geometrie f. ◆**geometrical** [-ə'metrikl], adj. geometrisch.
**geranium** [dʒə'reinjəm], s. Geranie f.
**geriatric** [dʒeri'ætrik], adj. geriatrisch.
**germ** [dʒəːm], s. **1.** Biol: Bot: Keim m. **2.** Med: Bakterie f. ◆**germi'nation,** s. Keimung f. ◆**'germinate** v.i. keimen.
**German** ['dʒəːmən]. **I.** adj. deutsch; **G. measles,** Röteln f. **II.** s. **1.** Deutsche(r) f(m). **2.** (language) Deutsch n; **in G.,** auf deutsch. ◆**'Germany,** Pr. n. Deutschland n; **West G.,** die Bundesrepublik Deutschland; **East G.,** Ostdeutschland n; (official name) die Deutsche Demokratische Republik, usu. abbr. DDR f.
**gesticulate** [dʒes'tikjuleit], v.i. gestikulieren.
**gesture** ['dʒestʃər]. **I.** s. Geste f. **II.** v.i. gestikulieren.
**get** [get], v. irr.**1.** v.tr. (a) (receive) (etwas, eine Krankheit) bekommen, F: kriegen; (einen Brief) erhalten; (b) (obtain) (etwas) besorgen, F: kriegen; (c) (catch) (einen Dieb) fassen; F: **that really gets me** das macht mich wild; **what's got (into) him?** was ist in ihn gefahren? (d) F: (understand) (j-n, etwas) verstehen; (e) (fetch) **to (go and) g. s.o., sth.,** j-n, etwas holen (gehen); (f) (j-m etwas) zukommen lassen; **how can I g. it to you?** wie kann ich es dir zukommen lassen? **to g. lunch (ready),** das Mittagessen zubereiten; (g) **to g. s.o. to do sth.,** (i) j-n etwas tun lassen; (ii) (by persuasion) j-n dazu bringen, etwas zu tun; **to g. the house painted,** das Haus streichen lassen; (h) **what have you got there?** was hast du da? (i) (obligation) **you've got to do it,**

du mußt es (unbedingt) tun. **2.** v.i. (a) (become) (reich, alt usw.) werden; (b) (arrive) **he'll g. here tomorrow,** er wird morgen hier ankommen. ◆**'get a'cross,** v.tr. F: **he couldn't g. it across,** er hat es nicht klarmachen können. ◆**'get at,** v.tr. & i. **difficult to g. at,** schwer zugänglich; F: **what are you getting at?** worauf willst du hinaus? **to g. at s.o.,** es auf j-n abgesehen haben. ◆**'get a'long,** v.i. **they g. a. very well together,** sie kommen gut miteinander aus. ◆**'get a'way,** v.i. (a) (escape) entkommen; **to g. a. with it,** ungeschoren davonkommen. ◆**'getaway,** s. Flucht f; **g. car,** Fluchtauto n. ◆**'get 'back,** v. **1.** v.i. **to g. b. (home),** (nach) Hause zurückkommen. **2.** v.tr. (etwas) zurückbekommen; F: **to g. one's own b.,** sich revanchieren. ◆**'get 'by,** v.i. sich zurechtfinden; F: durchkommen. ◆**'get 'down,** v. **1.** v.i. (a) absteigen (from, von + dat); (b) **to g. d. to work/business,** sich an die Arbeit machen. **2.** v.tr. (a) (from shelf etc.) (etwas) herunterholen; (b) (write) (etwas) aufschreiben; (c) (swallow) (etwas) herunterschlucken; (d) F: **it gets you d.,** es ist deprimierend. ◆**'get 'in,** v. **1.** v.i. (a) (i. car etc.) einsteigen; (b) **when does the train g. in?** wann kommt der Zug an? (c) Pol: gewählt werden. **2.** v.tr. (a) (die Wäsche usw.) hereinholen; (die Ernte) einbringen. ◆**'get 'into,** v.tr. **to g. i. a car** etc., in einen Wagen usw. einsteigen; **to g. i. bad company,** in schlechte Gesellschaft geraten. ◆**'get 'off,** v. **1.** v.tr. & i. (a) **to g. o. (the bus/train),** (aus dem Bus/Zug) aussteigen; (b) davonkommen; **to g. o. lightly,** glimpflich davonkommen; (c) (leave) abfahren; (leave work) Feierabend machen. **2.** v.tr. (a) (ein Paket) abschicken; (b) **to g. the day o.,** den Tag freibekommen. ◆**'get 'on,** v. **1.** v.tr. (Kleider) anziehen. **2.** v.i. **time's getting on,** die Zeit vergeht; **to be getting on for forty,** auf die Vierzig zugehen; (b) **she is getting on well,** sie macht gute Fortschritte; **how are you getting on?** wie geht's? (c) **to g. on well with s.o.,** gut mit j-m auskommen. ◆**'get 'out,** v. **1.** v.tr. (a) (einen Nagel usw.) herausziehen, F: herauskriegen; (b) **to g. sth. o. of the drawer,** etwas aus der Schublade herausnehmen; **I got nothing o. of it,** ich hatte nichts davon. **2.** v.i. **to g. o. of sth.,** aus etwas dat herauskommen. ◆**'get 'over,** v.tr. & i. (a) **to g. o. a wall,** über eine Mauer klettern; (b) **to g. sth. o. with,** etwas hinter acc bringen; (c) über (eine Krankheit, eine Überraschung usw.) hinwegkommen. ◆**'get 'round,** v.i. **I never g. r. to it,** ich komme nie dazu. ◆**'get 'through,** v.tr. & i. (a) Tel: Anschluß bekommen; (b) (eine Arbeit) erledigen. ◆**'get together,** s. (meeting) Zusammenkunft f; (social) zwangloses Beisammensein n.

◆**'get 'up,** *v.i.* aufstehen. ◆**'getup,** *s.*
*F:* Aufmachung *f.*

**geyser** ['giːzər, *N. Am:* gaizər], *s.* **1.** Geysir *m.* **2.** *H:* Durchlauferhitzer *m.*

**ghastly** ['gɑːstli], *adj.* gräßlich.

**gherkin** ['gəːkin], *s.* Essiggurke *f.*

**ghetto** *pl.* **-os** ['getəu, -əuz], *s.* Getto *n.*

**ghost** [gəust], *s.* **1.** Gespenst *n;* **g. story,**
Gespenstergeschichte *f;* **g. town,** Geisterstadt *f.* **2. the Holy G.,** der Heilige
Geist. ◆**'ghostly,** *adj.* geisterhaft.

**giant** ['dʒaiənt]. **I.** *s.* Riese *m.* **II.** *adj.* riesig.

**gibe** [dʒaib], *s.* Seitenhieb *m; pl.* **gibes,**
Spott *m.*

**giblets** ['dʒiblits], *s. pl.* Geflügelklein *n.*

**giddy** ['gidi], *adj.* schwindlig; **I feel g.,**
mir ist schwindlig. ◆**'giddiness,** *s.*
Schwindelgefühl *n.*

**gift** [gift], *s.* (*a*) Geschenk *n; Com:* **free
g.,** Zugabe *f;* (*b*) Begabung *f;* **he has a g.
for languages,** er ist sprachbegabt.
◆**'gifted,** *adj.* begabt.

**gigantic** [dʒai'gæntik], *adj.* riesig.

**giggle** ['gigl]. **I.** *s.* Gekicher *n.* **II.** *v.i.* kichern.

**gild** [gild], *v.tr.* vergolden. ◆**gilt. I.** *adj.*
vergoldet. **II.** *s.* Vergoldung *f.*

**gill** [gil], *s. Z:* Kieme *f.*

**gimmick** ['gimik], *s. F:* Trick *m;* **advertising g.,** Reklamegag *m.*

**gin** [dʒin], *s.* Gin *m.*

**ginger** ['dʒindʒər]. **I.** *s.* Ingwer *m.* **II.**
*adj.* rotblond. ◆**'gingerly,** *adv.* vorsichtig.

**gipsy** ['dʒipsi], *s.* Zigeuner(in) *m(f).*

**giraffe** [dʒi'rɑːf], *s.* Giraffe *f.*

**girder** ['gəːdər], *s.* Tragbalken *m.*

**girdle** ['gəːdl], *s.* Mieder *n.*

**girl** [gəːl], *s.* Mädchen *n;* **g. guide,** Pfadfinderin *f;* **his g./g. friend,** seine Freundin. ◆**'girlish,** *adj.* mädchenhaft.

**giro** ['dʒaiərəu], *s.* Giro *n.*

**girth** [gəːθ] *s.* Umfang *m;* (*of pers.*) Taille
*f.*

**gist** [dʒist], *s.* Hauptinhalt *m;* **I got the g.
of it,** ich habe das Wesentliche mitgekriegt.

**give** [giv]. **I.** *v.* **1.** *v.tr.* (*a*) geben; **to g.
sth. to s.o./ s.o. sth.,** j-m etwas geben;
(einen Vortrag) halten. **2.** *v.i.* (*a*) geben;
(*b*) (*yield*) nachgeben. **II.** *s.* **g. and take,**
Kompromiß *m.* ◆**'give a'way,** *v.tr.* (*a*)
(etwas) verschenken; (*b*) (*betray*) (j-n, etwas) verraten; *F:* **to g. the game a.,** alles
verraten. ◆**'give 'back,** *v.tr.* zurückgeben. ◆**'give 'in,** *v.* **1.** *v.i.* nachgeben
(**to s.o., sth.,** j-m, etwas *dat*). **2.** *v.tr.*
(Bücher, eine Arbeit) einreichen.
◆**'given,** *adj.* **1.** (*a*) (*particular*) bestimmt. (*b*) *N. Am:* **g. name,** Vorname
*m.* **2.** (*of pers.*) ergeben (**to,** *dat*). ◆**'give
'off,** *v.tr.* (Gas, Dampf usw.) abgeben.
◆**'give 'out,** *v.* **1.** *v.tr.* (Bücher, Preise
usw.) verteilen; (eine Mitteilung) bekanntgeben. **2.** *v.i.* (*of supplies etc.*) ausgehen. ◆**'give 'up,** *v.tr.* (*a*) (Hoffnung,

einen Plan usw.) aufgeben; (*b*) **to g. oneself up,** sich (freiwillig) ergeben; (*to police*) sich der Polizei stellen. ◆**'give
'way,** *v.i.* (*a*) nachgeben (**to s.o.,** j-m; **to
temptation, pressure etc.,** der Versuchung, dem Druck usw.); **the roof gave
w.,** das Dach stürzte ein; **her love gave
w. to hatred,** ihre Liebe verwandelte sich
in Haß; (*b*) *Aut:* Vorfahrt gewähren.

**glacier** ['glæsiər], *s.* Gletscher *m.*

**glad** [glæd], *adj.* froh (**of/at,** über + *acc*);
**-ly,** *adv.* gern(e).

**glamour** ['glæmər], *s.* Glanz *m;* (*of person*)
Reiz *m.* ◆**'glamorous,** *adj.* (*of girl*)
traumhaft schön; (*of job etc.*) glanzvoll.

**glance** [glɑːns]. **I.** *s.* (*fleetiger*) Blick *m.*
**II.** *v.i.* (*a*) **to g. at s.o.,** einen Blick auf
j-n werfen; **to g. through a text,** einen
Text überfliegen; (*b*) **to g. off,** abprallen.

**gland** [glænd], *s.* Drüse *f.* ◆**'glandular,**
*adj.* **g. fever,** Drüsenfieber *n.*

**glare** [glɛər]. **I.** *s.* **1.** (*dazzle*) Blenden *n;*
grelles Licht *f* (der Sonne). **2.** (*look*) wütender Blick *m.* **II.** *v.i.* (*a*) grell
leuchten; (*b*) **to g. at s.o.,** j-n böse anstarren. ◆**'glaring,** *adj.* **1.** (*of sun etc.*)
grell. **2.** (*of injustice*) schreiend; (*of example, mistake*) kraß.

**glass** [glɑːs], *s.* **1.** Glas *n.* **2.** (**a pair of)
glasses,** eine Brille.

**glaze** [gleiz]. **I.** *v.tr.* (*a*) (ein Fenster
usw.) verglasen; (*b*) (eine Oberfläche, ein
Gemälde) lasieren; *Fig:* **glazed look,** glasiger Blick. **II.** *s.* Lasur *f.* ◆**'glazier,** *s.*
Glaser *m.*

**gleam** [gliːm]. **I.** *s.* (*a*) Schimmer *m;*
(schwacher) Schein *m;* (*b*) Glänzen *n* (eines Messers, der Augen). **II.** *v.i.* schimmern; (*of water, eyes*) glänzen.

**glean** [gliːn], *v.tr.* (Informationen) entnehmen.

**glib** [glib], *adj.* zungenfertig; (*superficial*)
oberflächlich.

**glide** [glaid], *v.i.* gleiten; (*of glider*) segeln. ◆**'glider,** *s.* Segelflugzeug *n.*
◆**'gliding,** *s. Av:* Segelfliegen *n.*

**glimmer** ['glimər], *s.* Glimmen *n;* **g. of
hope,** Hoffnungsschimmer *m.*

**glimpse** [glimps]. **I.** *s.* flüchtiger Blick *m;*
**to catch a g. of s.o., sth.,** j-n, etwas
flüchtig zu sehen bekommen. **II.** *v.tr.*
(etwas, j-n) flüchtig sehen.

**glint** [glint]. **I.** *s.* Schimmer *m.* **II.** *v.i.*
schimmern.

**glisten** [glisn], *v.i.* glitzern.

**glitter** ['glitər]. **I.** *s.* Glitzern *n.* **II.** *v.i.*
glitzern.

**gloat** [gləut], *v.i.* **to g. (over sth.),** sich
hämisch (über etwas *acc*) freuen.

**globe** [gləub], *s.* Globus *m;* **g. artichoke,**
Artischocke *f.* ◆**'global,** *adj.* global.

**gloom** [gluːm], *s.* **1.** Dunkelheit *f.* **2.**
(*state of mind*) Schwermut *f;* Trübsinn *m.*
◆**'gloomy,** *adj.* **1.** (*dark*) dunkel, düster. **2.** (*a*) (*of pers.*) schwermütig; (*b*)
pessimistisch.

**glory** ['glɔːri], *s.* **1.** Ruhm *m.* **2.** (*splen-*

*dour*) Pracht *f*. ◆'**glorify**, *v.tr.* verherrlichen. ◆'**glorified**, *adj.* F: it was only a g. **shed**, es war nur eine bessere Hütte. ◆'**glorious**, *adj.* 1. prächtig. 2. (*of victory etc.*) glorreich.

**gloss** [glɔs], *v.tr.* to g. **over**, (Fehler, Wahrheiten) vertuschen. ◆'**glossy**, *adj.* glänzend; g. **magazine**, Illustrierte *f*. ◆'**glossary** ['glɔsəri], *s.* Glossar *n*.

**glove** [glʌv], *s.* Handschuh *m*; g. **compartment**, Handschuhfach *n*.

**glow** [gləu]. I. *s.* Glühen *n*. II. *v.i.* (*a*) (*of metal, coal*) glühen; (*b*) to be glowing **with health**, vor Gesundheit strotzen. ◆'**glowing**, *adj.* (*of coals etc.*) glühend; (*of face etc.*) strahlend; g. **report**, begeisterter Bericht.

**glucose** ['glu:kəuz, -əus], *s.* Traubenzucker *m*.

**glue** [glu:]. I. *s.* Klebstoff *m*. II. *v.tr.* (etwas) kleben (**to sth.**, an etwas *acc*).

**glum** [glʌm], *adj.* trübsinnig.

**glut** [glʌt], *s.* Überfluß *m* (**of sth.**, an etwas *dat*).

**glutton** ['glʌtn], *s.* Vielfraß *m*; you're a g. **for punishment!** du kannst nie genug kriegen!

**gnarled** [nɑ:ld], *adj.* (*of tree*) knorrig; (*of hands etc.*) knotig.

**gnash** [næʃ], *v.tr.* to g. **one's teeth**, mit den Zähnen knirschen.

**gnat** [næt], *s.* Mücke *f*.

**gnaw** [nɔ:], *v.tr. & i.* to g. **(at) sth.**, an etwas *dat* nagen.

**go** [gəu]. I. *v.i.* irr. 1. (*a*) (*walk*) gehen; (*b*) (*travel*) fahren; **the train goes at 10**, der Zug fährt um 10 Uhr; (*c*) (*lead*) **this road goes to Munich**, diese Straße führt nach München. 2. (*of machinery*) gehen, funktionieren. 3. (*leave*) (fort)gehen; (*on a journey*) abreisen; **it's all gone**, es ist nichts mehr übrig; **a fuse went**, eine Sicherung brannte durch. 4. **all has gone well so far**, bisher ist alles glatt verlaufen. 5. **are you going to make a speech?** werden Sie eine Rede halten? **I was going to walk there but it was too far**, ich wollte zu Fuß hingehen, aber es war zu weit. 6. **it won't go into my case**, es geht/paßt nicht in meinen Koffer; **the key won't go into the lock**, der Schlüssel will nicht ins Schloß; **where does this book go?** wohin gehört dieses Buch? 7. (*become*) to go **mad**, verrückt werden. 8. **to let (sth.) go**, (etwas) loslassen. II. *s.* F: 1. **to be always on the go**, immer auf Trab sein. 2. (*a*) (*try*) Versuch *m*; **to have a go at sth.**, etwas probieren; (*b*) (*turn*) **it's your go**, du bist dran; **at one go**, auf einmal. 3. **he made a go of it**, er machte einen Erfolg daraus. ◆'**go a'bout**, *v.i. v.tr.* **how do you go a. it?** wie nimmst man das in Angriff? ◆'**go-ahead**. I. *adj.* fortschrittlich. II. *s.* **to give s.o. the g.-a.**, j-m grünes Licht geben. ◆'**go a'way**, *v.i.* fortgehen. ◆'**go 'back**, *v.i.* zurückgehen. ◆'**go-**

**between**, *s.* Vermittler(in) *m(f)*. ◆'**go 'by**, *v.tr. & i.* (*a*) (*pass*) vorbeigehen; (*of time*) vergehen; (*b*) to go by **appearances**, nach dem äußeren Schein urteilen. ◆'**go 'down**, *v.i.* (*a*) hinuntergehen; (*of ship, sun*) untergehen; (*of prices*) sinken; (*b*) (*in quality*) sich verschlechtern; (*of area*) herunterkommen; (*c*) **the suggestion went down well**, der Vorschlag hat Anklang gefunden. ◆'**go for**, *v.tr.* (*attack*) losgehen; auf j-n losgehen. ◆'**go 'in**, *v.i.* (*a*) (*into room*) eintreten; (*into house*) hineingehen; (*b*) to go **in for sth.**, sich mit etwas befassen. ◆'**going**. I. *adj.* a g. **concern**, ein gutgehendes Unternehmen; **the g. price**, der Marktpreis. II. *s.* (*a*) **while the g. is good**, solange es geht; (*b*) F: **goings on**, Vorfälle *mpl*; Pej: Umtriebe *mpl*. ◆'**go 'off**, *v.i.* (*a*) (*of pers.*) fortgehen; (*b*) (*of gun*) losgehen; (*of bomb*) explodieren; (*c*) **everything went o. well**, alles ist gut verlaufen; (*d*) F: (*of food*) verderben; (*e*) F: I've **gone o. Gruyere**, Schweizer Käse schmeckt mir nicht mehr. ◆'**go 'on**, *v.i.* (*a*) weitergehen; **to go on speaking, working etc.**, weitersprechen, weiterarbeiten usw.; **go on!** weiter! (*b*) **what's going on here?** was geht hier vor? (*c*) F: **to go on at s.o.**, mit j-m dauernd schimpfen. ◆'**go 'out**, *v.i.* (*a*) (*into garden etc.*) hinausgehen; (*with friend etc.*) ausgehen; (*b*) (*of fire*) ausgehen; (*c*) (*of tide*) zurückgehen. ◆'**go 'over**, *v.tr.* (eine Arbeit, ein Dokument) durchsehen. ◆'**go 'round**, *v.i.* (*of wheel etc.*) sich drehen; (*of pers.*, *rumours*) herumgehen. ◆'**go-'slow**, *s.* Bummelstreik *m*. ◆'**go 'through**, *v.* 1. *v.tr.* (*a*) (durch eine Tür usw.) durchgehen; (*b*) (Dokumente) durchsehen; (*c*) (Erlebnisse) durchmachen. 2. *v.i.* durchgehen. ◆'**go 'up**, *v.i.* (*of pers.*) hinaufgehen; (*of prices*) steigen; ◆'**go with'out**, *v.* 1. *v.tr.* (auf etwas *acc*) verzichten. 2. *v.i.* ohne (es) auskommen. ◆'**go 'wrong**, *v.i.* (*of plan etc.*) schiefgehen.

**goal** [gəul], *s.* 1. (*aim*) Ziel *n*. 2. *Sp:* Tor *n*; **to score a g.**, ein Tor schießen. ◆'**goalkeeper**, *s.* Torwart *m*. ◆'**goalpost**, *s.* Torpfosten *m*.

**goat** [gəut], *s.* Ziege *f*.

**gobble** [gɔbl], *v.tr.* gierig herunterschlingen.

**god** [gɔd], *s.* Gott *m*; **thank G.!** Gott sei Dank! **for God's sake**, um Gottes willen; F: **G. knows how**, weiß Gott, wie. ◆'**godchild**, *pl.* -**children**, *s.* Patenkind *n*. ◆'**goddaughter**, *s.* Patentochter *f*. ◆'**goddess**, *s.* Göttin *f*. ◆'**godfather**, *s.* Pate *m*. ◆'**godforsaken**, *adj.* gottverlassen. ◆'**godmother**, *s.* Patin *f*. ◆'**godparents**, *s.pl.* Paten *pl*. ◆'**godsend**, *s.* Geschenk *n* des Himmels; F: Segen *m*. ◆'**godson**, *s.* Patensohn *m*.

**goggles,** ['gɔglz], s. pl. Schutzbrille f.

**gold** [gəuld], s. Gold n. ◆**'golden,** adj.
golden; Gold-; **g. handshake,** Abfindung
f (eines abgehenden Direktors); **g. rule,**
goldene Regel. ◆**'goldfish,** s. Goldfisch
m. ◆**'gold-mine,** s. Goldmine f.
◆**'gold-plated,** adj. vergoldet.

**golf** [gɔlf], s. Golf(spiel) n; **g. club,** (i)
Golfschläger m; (ii) Golfklub m; **g.
course,** Golfplatz m. ◆**'golfball,** s.
Golfball m. ◆**'golfer,** s. Golfspieler(in)
m(f).

**gong** [gɔŋ], s. Gong m.

**good** [gud]. **I.** adj. gut; **g. morning/
evening!** guten Morgen/Abend! **g. at
French,** gut in Französisch; **a g. hour,**
eine gute Stunde; **a g. 10 kilometres,**
gute zehn Kilometer; **a g. deal,** ziemlich
viel; **to make g.,** (einen Schaden, Verlust
usw.) wiedergutmachen. **II.** s. 1. das
Gute n, Gutes n; (a) (of pers.) **to do g.,**
Gutes tun; **he's up to no g.,** er führt
nichts Gutes im Schilde; (b) (of thing) **to
do s.o. g.** j-m guttun; **that isn't much
g.,** das taugt/nützt nicht viel; **it's no g.!**
da ist nichts zu machen! es hilft nichts!
**no g. talking about it,** es hat keinen
Sinn, darüber zu reden; (c) adv. phr. **for
g. (and all),** für immer; **he is leaving the
country for g.,** er geht endgültig ins
Ausland. 2. pl. Com: Güter npl; Waren
fpl; **to deliver the goods,** F: Wort halten; **goods train,** Güterzug m.
◆**good'bye,** int. auf Wiedersehen!
◆**'good-'looking,** adj. gutaussehend.
◆**'good-'natured,** adj. gutmütig.
◆**'goodness. I.** s. (a) (kindness) Güte f;
(b) (virtue) Tugend f. **II.** int. **(my) g.!** du
meine Güte! **for g. sake!** um Gottes willen! **thank g.,** Gott sei Dank.

**goose,** pl **geese** [guːs, giːs], s. Gans f.
◆**'gooseflesh,** s. **'goosepimples/**
N.Am: F: **'goose bumps,** s.pl. Gänse-
haut f.

**gooseberry** ['guzbəri], s. Stachelbeere f.

**gory** ['gɔːri], adj. blutig; (of story etc.)
blutrünstig.

**gorgeous** ['gɔːdʒəs], adj. herrlich.

**gorilla** [gə'rilə], s. Gorilla m.

**gormless** ['gɔːmləs], adj. F: begriffsstutzig.

**gosh** [gɔʃ], int. F: mein Gott! Mensch!

**gospel** ['gɔspəl], s. Evangelium n; Fig: **to
take sth. as g. (truth),** etwas für bare
Münze nehmen.

**gossip** ['gɔsip], I. s. 1. (pers.) Klatschbase
f. 2. Klatsch m; **g. column,** Klatschspalte
f. **II.** v.i. klatschen.

**Gothic** ['gɔθik], adj. gotisch.

**gourmet** ['guəmei], s. Feinschmecker m.

**gout** [gaut] s. Gicht f.

**govern** ['gʌvən], v.tr. (a) (ein Land) regieren; (b) (determine) (seine Haltung
usw.) bestimmen. ◆**'government,** s.
Regierung f. ◆**'governor,** s. Gouver-
neur m; Statthalter m (einer Provinz);
Sch: etc: Vorstandsmitglied n.

**gown** [gaun]. 1. **evening g.,** Abendkleid
n. 2. Talar m (der Professoren, Richter
usw.); **dressing g.,** Morgenrock m.

**grab** [græb], v. 1. v.tr. (a) (etwas) packen;
**to g. hold of sth.,** etwas (hastig) ergreifen; (b) P: **how does that g. you?** wie
findest du das? 2. v.i. **to g. at sth.,** nach
etwas dat greifen.

**grace** [greis], **I.** s. 1. (of movement) Anmut
f; **social graces,** (gute) Umgangsformen
fpl. 2. **to say g.,** das Tischgebet sprechen; F: **to have ten days' g.,** zehn Tage
Aufschub haben. ◆**'graceful,** adj. an-
mutig. ◆**'gracious** ['greiʃəs], adj. (a)
(with condescension) gnädig; (kind) gütig;
(b) **g. living,** luxuriöser Lebensstil.

**grade** [greid]. **I.** s. 1. (also Sch:) Klasse f;
**good grades,** gute Noten fpl; F: **to make
the g.,** es schaffen. 2. (incline) N. Am:
Gefälle n. **II.** v.tr. (Waren usw.) eintei-
len; (Schularbeiten) bewerten.

**gradient** ['greidiənt], s. **up(ward) g.,**
Steigung f; **down(ward) g.,** Gefälle n.

**gradual** ['grædju(ə)l], adj. allmählich.

**graduate. I.** ['grædjuət] s. Hochschulab-
solvent m. **II.** ['grædjueit] v.i. graduie-
ren.

**graft** [grɑːft]. **I.** s. 1. Med: Transplantat
n; (process) Transplantation f. 2. (work)
Schwerarbeit f, F: Schufterei f. **II.** v.tr.
(Haut) verpflanzen.

**grain** [grein], s. 1. Korn n; coll. Getreide
n. 2. Maserung f (von Holz); F: **it goes
against the g.,** es geht (mir) gegen den
Strich.

**gram(me)** [græm], s. Gramm n.

**grammar** ['græmər], s. Grammatik f; **g.
school,** approx. Gymnasium n.

**gramophone** ['græməfəun], s. Grammophon n.

**grand** [grænd], adj. 1. (large) (a) groß;
(main) Haupt-; **g. piano,** Flügel m; (b) **g.
total,** Gesamtsumme f. 2. (magnificent)
grandios; (smart) vornehm; (elaborate)
prunkvoll. **3.** F: wunderbar.
◆**'grandchild,** pl. **-children,** s. En-
kelkind n. ◆**'granddaughter,** s. Enke-
lin f. ◆**grandeur** ['grændjər], s. Herr-
lichkeit f. ◆**'grandfather,** s. Großvater
m; **g. clock,** Standuhr f. ◆**'grandma,**
F: Oma f. ◆**grandiose** ['grændiəus],
adj. grandios. ◆**'grandpa,** F: Opa m.
◆**'grandmother,** s. Großmutter f.
◆**'grandparents,** s. pl. Großeltern pl.
◆**'grandson,** s. Enkel m.
◆**'grandstand,** s. (überdachte) Tribüne
f.

**granite** ['grænit], s. Granit m.

**granny** ['græni], s. F: Oma f.

**grant** [grɑːnt]. **I.** s. (finance) (finanzielle)
Unterstützung f; Sch: Studienbeihilfe f.
**II.** v.tr. (a) (j-m etwas) gewähren; (j-m
Erlaubnis) erteilen; (b) **to take sth. for
granted,** etwas als selbstverständlich hinnehmen; (c) (eine Bitte) erfüllen; (d) (admit) (etwas) zugeben.

**grape** [greip], s. Weintraube f. ◆**'grape-**

**graph** 431 **grocer**

fruit, *s.* Grapefruit *f.* ◆'grapevine, *s.*
F: I heard it through the g., ich habe es
munkeln hören.

graph [grɑːf], *s.* Diagramm *n;* graphische
Darstellung *f;* g. paper, Millimeterpapier
*n.* ◆graphic ['græfik], *adj.* graphisch;
g. description, anschauliche Beschreibung.

grapple ['græpl], *v.i.* ringen (with s.o.,
sth., mit j-m, etwas *dat*); to g. with a
problem, sich mit einem Problem auseinandersetzen.

grasp [grɑːsp]. I. *s.* (a) within his g., in
seiner Reichweite; (b) to have a thorough g. of a subject, eine Sache beherrschen. II. *v.tr.* (a) (etwas) ergreifen; (b)
(*understand*) (etwas) begreifen.
◆'grasping, *adj.* habgierig.

grass [grɑːs], *s.* (a) Gras *n;* (b) (*lawn*) Rasen *m.* ◆'grasshopper, *s.* Heuschrecke
*f.* ◆'grassy, *adj.* grasbedeckt.

grate¹ [greit], *s.* Kamin *m.* ◆'grating, *s.*
Gitter *n.*

grate², *v.* 1. *v.tr.* (a) (Käse) reiben; (b) to
g. one's teeth, mit den Zähnen knirschen. 2. *v.i.* knirschen. ◆'grater, *s.*
Reibe *f.*

grateful ['greitful], *adj.* dankbar (to s.o.
for sth.), j-m für etwas *acc*).
◆gratitude ['grætitjuːd], *s.* Dankbarkeit *f.*

gratifying, ['grætifaiiŋ], *adj.* erfreulich.

gratuity [grə'tjuiti], *s.* Trinkgeld *n.*
◆gra'tuitous, *adj.* überflüssig.

grave [greiv]. I. *s.* Grab *n.* II. *adj.* ernst;
g. mistake, schwerwiegender Fehler; -ly,
*adv.* g. ill, schwer krank.
◆'gravestone, *s.* Grabstein *m.*
◆'graveyard, *s.* Friedhof *m.*

gravel ['grævəl], *s.* Kies *m.*

gravity ['græviti], *s.* 1. Ernst *m.* 2. Ph:
(force of) g., Schwerkraft *f.* ◆'gravi-
tate, *v.i.* to g. towards sth., allmählich
zu etwas *dat* tendieren.

gravy ['greivi], *s.* Soße *f* (zum Braten
usw.); (*juice*) Bratensaft *m.*

gray [grei] *see* grey.

graze¹ [greiz], *v.i.* (of *animal*) weiden.

graze², I. *s.* Abschürfung *f.* II. *v.tr.* (a)
(die Haut, den Finger) abschürfen; (b)
(*touch lightly*) (j-n, etwas) streifen.

grease [griːs]. I. *s* Fett *n.* II. *v.tr.* (mit
Fett) schmieren. ◆'grease-proof, *adj.*
g.-p. paper, Butterbrotpapier *n.*
◆'greasy, *adj.* fettig; Pej: schmierig.

great [greit], *adj.* (a) groß; G. Britain,
Großbritannien *n; n;* a g. many people,
sehr viele Leute; (b) (*important*) bedeutend; g. occasion, wichtiger Anlaß; (c)
F: that's g.! das ist großartig! -ly, *adv.*
sehr. ◆'great-'aunt, *s.* Großtante *f.*
◆'great-'grandfather, *s.* Urgroßvater
*m.* ◆'great-'grandmother, *s.* Urgroß-
mutter *f.* ◆'greatness, *s.* Größe *f;* (*importance*) Bedeutung *f.* ◆'great-'uncle,
*s.* Großonkel *m.*

Greece [griːs]. *Pr. n.* Griechenland *n.*

◆Greek. I. *adj.* griechisch. II. *s.* Grie-
che *m,* Griechin *f.* III. *s.* Griechisch *n.*

greed [griːd], *s.* (a) Gier *f;* Habsucht *f;*
(b) (*for food*) Gefräßigkeit *f.* ◆'greedy,
*adj.* (a) gierig; (*covetous*) habsüchtig; (b)
gefräßig.

green [griːn]. I. *adj.* grün; Fig: g. with
envy, gelb vor Neid. II. *s.* (a) (*colour*)
Grün *n;* (b) greens, grünes Gemüse *n;* (c)
(*lawn etc.*) Grünfläche *f;* village g., Dorf-
wiese *f.* ◆'greenery, *s.* F: Grün *n;* (*foliage*) Laub *n.* ◆'greengage, *s.* Rene-
klode *f.* ◆'greengrocer, *s.* Obst- und
Gemüsehändler *m.* ◆'greenhouse, *s.*
Gewächshaus *n.*

greet [griːt], *v.tr.* (a) (j-n) grüßen; (b)
(*welcome*) (j-n, etwas) begrüßen.
◆'greeting, *s.* Gruß *m.*

gregarious [gri'gɛəriəs], *adj.* gesellig.

grenade [grə'neid], *s.* (hand) g., Handgranate *f.*

grey [grei], *adj.* grau. ◆'grey-'haired
*adj.* grauhaarig. ◆'greyhound, *s.*
Windhund *m.*

grid [grid], *s.* 1. (iron) g., Gitter *n.* 2. El:
(national) g., Überlandleitungsnetz *n.* 3.
(*for maps*) Gitternetz *n.*

grief [griːf], *s.* (*worry*) Kummer *m;* (*pain*)
Leid *n;* to come to g., verunglücken; (of
*plan*) scheitern. ◆'grievance, *s.* Beschwerde *f.* ◆grieve, *v.* 1. *v.tr.* (j-n)
betrüben. 2. *v.i.* sich *dat* Kummer machen (over, über + *acc*); to g. for s.o.,
um j-n trauern.

grill [gril]. I. *s.* 1. (*appliance*) Grill *m.* 2.
(*meat etc.*) (mixed) g., Gemischtes vom
Grill. II. *v.tr.* (Fleisch usw.) grillen.

grim [grim], *adj.* grimmig; g. determination, eiserne Entschlossenheit.

grimace ['griməs]. I. *s.* Grimasse *f.* II.
*v.i.* Grimassen schneiden.

grime [graim], *s.* (eingefressener)
Schmutz *m.* ◆'grimy, *adj.* schmutzig.

grin [grin]. I. *s.* Grinsen *n.* II. *v.i.* grinsen; F: to g. and bear it, gute Miene
zum bösen Spiel machen.

grind [graind]. I. *s.* F: Schinderei *f.* II. *v.*
*irr.* 1. *v.tr.* (a) (Kaffee usw.) mahlen; (b)
(Metall, Glas, Klingen) schleifen; to g.
one's teeth, mit den Zähnen knirschen;
(c) N.Am: (Fleisch) durchdrehen. 2. *v.i.*
to g. to a halt, zum Stillstand kommen.

grip [grip]. I. *s.* Griff *m;* Fig: to get/keep
a g. on oneself, sich beherrschen; to
come to grips with a problem, sich mit
einem Problem auseinandersetzen. II.
*v.tr.* (etwas) festhalten. ◆'gripping,
*adj.* fesselnd.

gristle ['grisl], *s.* Knorpel *m.*

grit [grit]. I. *s.* 1. Sand *m;* road g., Streu-
gut *n.* 2. Fig: Mut *m,* F: Schneid *m.* II.
*v.tr.* (a) (Straßen) streuen; (b) to g. one's
teeth, die Zähne zusammenbeißen.

groan [groun]. I. *s.* Stöhnen *n.* II. *v.i.*
stöhnen.

grocer ['grəusər], *s.* Lebensmittelhändler
*m;* g.'s (shop), Lebensmittelgeschäft *n.*

◆**'groceries**, s. pl. Lebensmittel npl.

**groin** [grɔin], s. Leiste f.

**groom** [gruːm]. **I.** s. **1.** Pferdeknecht m. **2.** (at wedding) Bräutigam m. **II.** v.tr. (j-n) (als Nachfolger usw.) einarbeiten.

**groove** [gruːv], s. Furche f; (in wood, record) Rille f.

**grope** [grəup], v.i. tasten (**for sth.**, nach etwas dat); **to g. one's way**, sich vorwärtstasten.

**gross** [grəus], adj. **1.** (of error, negligence) grob. **2.** Com: etc: Brutto-; **-ly**, adv. höchst; **g. exaggerated**, stark übertrieben.

**grotty** ['grɔti], adj. P: schäbig; (of area) heruntergekommen.

**grotesque** [grəu'tesk], adj. grotesk.

**ground**[1] [graund], adj. gemahlen; N.Am: **g. beef**, gehacktes Rindfleisch.

**ground**[2]. **I.** s. **1.** (a) Boden m; **g. floor**, Erdgeschoß n; **g. control**, Flugleitung f; **to hold/stand one's g.**, nicht nachgeben; **to gain/lose g.**, Boden gewinnen/ verlieren; **to break new g.**, Neuland betreten; (b) sports **g.**, Sportplatz m; (large) Sportgelände n; (c) pl. **grounds**, Anlagen fpl (eines Schlosses usw.). **2.** (reason) Grund m; **g. for complaint**, Anlaß m zur Klage; **on what grounds?** mit welcher Begründung? **4.** N. Am: El: Erde f. **II.** v.tr. (einem Flugzeug) Startverbot erteilen. ◆**'grounding**, s. Grundlage f (in einem Fach). ◆**'groundless**, adj. grundlos. ◆**'groundsheet**, s. Bodenplane f. ◆**'groundwork**, s. Vorarbeiten fpl.

**group** [gruːp]. **I.** s. Gruppe f. **II.** v.tr. (etwas) gruppieren.

**grove** [grəuv], s. Hain m.

**grovel** ['grɔv(ə)l], v.i. (of pers., dog) kriechen (**to s.o.**, vor j-m).

**grow** [grəu], v. irr. **1.** v.i. (a) (of pers., animals, plants etc.) wachsen; (b) (increase) zunehmen (**in sth.**, an etwas dat); (c) **this music grows on you**, mit der Zeit gefällt einem diese Musik doch; (d) (become) werden; **to g. old**, alt werden. **2.** v.tr. (a) (Getreide, Gemüse) anbauen; (Rosen usw.) züchten; (b) **to g. a beard**, sich dat einen Bart wachsen lassen. ◆**'grown-up**, s. Erwachsene(r) f(m). ◆**'growth**, s. **1.** (process) Wachsen n. **2.** (increase) Wachstum n; (in numbers) Zunahme f; **g. industry**, Wachstumsindustrie f. **3.** Wuchs m (der Haare usw.) **4.** Med: Tumor m. ◆**'grow 'up**, v.i. (of pers.) aufwachsen; (of town etc.) entstehen.

**growl** [graul], v.i. (dog) knurren; (bear) brummen.

**grub** [grʌb], s. P: Futter n. ◆**'grubby**, adj. F: schmuddelig; (filthy) dreckig.

**grudge** [grʌdʒ]. **I.** s. Groll m; **to bear s.o. a g.**, einen Groll gegen j-n hegen. **II.** v.tr. **to g. s.o. his success**, j-m seinen Erfolg mißgönnen. ◆**'grudging**, adj. (of nature etc.) mißgünstig; (of praise, gift etc.) widerwillig.

**gruelling** ['gruːəliŋ], adj. strapaziös.

**gruesome** ['gruːsəm], adj. schauerlich.

**gruff** [grʌf], adj. (ill-tempered) barsch; (of voice) rauh.

**grumble** ['grʌmbl], v.i. murren.

**grumpy** ['grʌmpi], adj. mürrisch.

**grunt** [grʌnt]. v.i. knurren; (of pig etc.) grunzen.

**guarantee** [gærən'tiː]. **I.** s. Garantie f; (document) Garantieschein m. **II.** v.tr. garantieren.

**guard** [gɑːd]. **I.** s. **1.** (a) Wache f; (pers.) Mil: etc: Wachposten m; (in prison) Wärter m; **to be on g./stand g.**, Wache stehen; **g. dog**, Wachhund m; (b) **to be on one's g.**, auf der Hut sein; **to be caught off one's g.**, überrumpelt werden. **2.** Rail: Zugführer m; **g.'s van**, Dienstwagen m. **3.** (on machine) Schutzblech n; (fire) **g.**, Kamingitter n. **II.** v. **1.** v.tr. (a) (Gefangene, ein Lager usw.) bewachen; (b) (protect) (einen Mechanismus, seinen Ruf usw.) schützen. **2.** v.i. **to g. against sth.**, sich vor etwas dat hüten. ◆**'guarded**, adj. behutsam; **g. answer**, vorsichtige Antwort. ◆**'guardian**, s. **1.** Vormund m (eines Minderjährigen); **g. angel**, Schutzengel m.

**guer(r)illa** [gə'rilə], s. Guerillakämpfer m.

**guess** [ges]. **I.** s. Vermutung f; **at a g.**, schätzungsweise. **II.** v. **1.** v.tr. (etwas) erraten. **2.** v.i. (a) raten; (b) N.Am: glauben, denken. ◆**'guesswork**, s. (reine) Vermutung f.

**guest** [gest], s. Gast m. ◆**'guesthouse**, s. Pension f.

**guidance** ['gaidəns], s. **1.** Leitung f; Führung f. **2.** (a) (information) Orientierung f; (b) (advice) Rat m. ◆**guide**. **I.** s. **1.** (pers.) Führer m; **girl g.**, Pfadfinderin f. **2.** (book) travel **g.**, Reiseführer m. **3.** (guideline) Richtlinie f; (model) Vorbild n. **II.** v.tr. (j-n) führen, leiten; (etwas) lenken. ◆**'guidebook**, s. Führer m; esp. (travel) **g.**, Reiseführer m. ◆**'guided**, adj. (a) **g. tour**, Führung f (durch ein Schloß usw.); (b) **g. missile**, Fernlenkgeschoß n. ◆**'guide-dog**, s. Blindenhund m. ◆**'guideline**, s. Richtlinie f.

**guillotine** [gilə'tiːn]. s. Guillotine f; (for paper) Schneidemaschine f.

**guilt** [gilt], s. Schuld f. ◆**'guilty**, adj. schuldig (**of**, + gen); **g. conscience**, schlechtes Gewissen.

**guinea-pig** ['ginipig], s. **1.** Meerschweinchen n. **2.** F: (pers.) Versuchskaninchen n.

**guitar** [gi'tɑːr], s. Gitarre f. ◆**gui'tarist**, s. Gitarrenspieler(in) m(f).

**gulf** [gʌlf], s. **1.** Geog: Golf m. **2.** Fig: Kluft f.

**gull** [gʌl], s. Möwe f.

**gullible** ['gʌləbl], adj. leichtgläubig.

**gulp** [gʌlp]. **I.** s. Schluck m. **II.** v. **to g. sth. (down)**, etwas hinunterschlucken.

**gum**[1] [gʌm]. **I.** s. **1.** (adhesive) Klebstoff

*m.* **2. (chewing) g.,** Kaugummi *m.* **II.**
*v.tr.* (*a*) (Papier) gummieren; (*b*) (etwas)
kleben (**on/to,** an + *acc*).

**gum²,** *s.* Zahnfleisch *n.*

**gun** [gʌn]. **I.** *s.* **1.** (*a*) (*large*) Geschütz *n;*
(*b*) (*rifle*) Gewehr *n;* (*c*) Revolver *m.* **II.**
*v.tr.* **to g. s.o. down,** j-n niederschießen.
◆**'gunfire,** *s.* Geschützfeuer *n.*
◆**'gunman,** *pl.* **-men,** *s.* bewaffneter
Bandit *m.* ◆**'gunpoint,** *s.* **at g.,** (*threatening*) mit vorgehaltener Pistole.
◆**'gunpowder,** *s.* Schießpulver *n.*
◆**'gunshot,** *s.* Gewehrschuß *m;* **g.
wound,** Schußwunde *f.*

**gurgle** ['gəːgl], *v.i.* gluckern.

**gush** [gʌʃ], *v.i.* **to g. (out),** heraus-
strömen. ◆**'gushing,** *adj.* (*of pers.,
praise*) überschwenglich.

**gust** [gʌst], *s.* Windstoß *m;* (*at sea*) Bö *f.*

**gusto** ['gʌstəu], *s. F:* **with g.,** mit Genuß;
(*singing*) aus voller Kehle.

**gut** [gʌt]. **I.** *s.* (*a*) Darm *m; guts,* Eingeweide *npl;* (*b*) *F:* **to have guts,** Schneid
haben. **II.** *v.tr.* (*a*) (Fisch, Geflügel) ausnehmen; (*b*) (*of house*) **gutted by fire,**
völlig ausgebrannt.

**gutter** ['gʌtər], *s.* **1.** Dachrinne *f.* **2.** (*in
street*) Gosse *f;* Rinnstein *m; F:* **g. press,**
Schmutzpresse *f.*

**guttural** ['gʌtərəl], *adj.* kehlig.

**guy** [gai], *s. F:* Kerl *m.*

**gym** [dʒim], *s. F:* **1.** Turnhalle *f.* **2.** Turnen *n;* **g. shoes,** Turnschuhe *mpl.*
◆**gymnasium** ['-neiziəm], *s.* Turnhalle
*f.* ◆**'gymnast** [-næst], *s.* Turner(in)
*m(f).* ◆**gym'nastics,** *s. pl.* Gymnastik
*f,* Turnen *n;* (*in competition*) Kunstturnen
*n.*

**gynaecology** [gaini'kɔlədʒi], *s.* Gynä-
kologie *f.* ◆**gynae'cologist,** *s.* Gynä-
kologe *m,* Frauenarzt *m,* Frauenärztin
*f.*

# H

**H, h** [eitʃ], *s.* (der Buchstabe) H, h *n.*

**haberdashery** ['hæbədæʃəri], *s.* Kurz-
waren *fpl; N. Am:* Herrenartikel *mpl.*

**habit** ['hæbit], *s.* **1.** Gewohnheit *f;* **to be
in the h. of doing sth.,** die Gewohnheit
haben/gewöhnt sein, etwas zu tun; **to get
into the h.** (**of doing sth.**), es sich *dat*
angewöhnen ( , etwas zu tun). **2.** *Ecc:* Habit *n.* ◆**habitual** [hə'bitjuəl], *adj.* gewohnt; (*automatic*) gewohnheitsmäßig;
**-ly,** *adv.* aus Gewohnheit; (*constantly*)
ständig.

**habitable** ['hæbitəbl], *adj.* bewohnbar.
◆**'habitat,** *s.* Habitat *m.*

**hack** [hæk], *v.tr. & i.* (etwas) hacken; **to
h. sth. to pieces,** etwas zerhacken/in
Stücke hacken. ◆**'hacking,** *adj.* **h.
cough,** trockener Husten.

**hackneyed** ['hæknid], *adj.* abgedroschen.

**haddock** ['hædək], *s.* Schellfisch *m.*

**haemorrhage** ['heməridʒ], *s.* Blutung *f.*

**haggard** ['hægəd], *adj.* abgezehrt; (*from
worry*) abgehärmt.

**haggle** ['hægl], *v.i.* feilschen (**over,**
um + *acc*).

**Hague (the)** [ðə'heig]. *Pr. n.* Den Haag.

**hail¹** [heil]. **I.** *s.* Hagel *m.* **II.** *v.i.* hageln.
◆**'hailstone,** *s.* Hagelkorn *n.*

**hail²,** *v.* **1.** *v.tr.* (*a*) (ein Taxi usw.) rufen;
(*b*) (*greet*) (j-n, etwas) begrüßen; *Fig:* **he
was hailed as the new star,** man feierte
ihn als den neuen Star. **2.** *v.i.* **he hails
from X,** er stammt aus X.

**hair** ['hɛər], *s.* (*human*) Haar *n; coll.* Haare *npl;* **to do one's h.,** sich frisieren; **h.
dryer,** Fön *m;* **by a h.'s breadth,** um
Haaresbreite. ◆**'hairbrush,** *s.* Haarbür-
ste *f.* ◆**'haircut,** *s.* Haarschnitt *m;* **to
have a h.,** sich *dat* die Haare schneiden
lassen. ◆**'hairdo,** *s. F:* Frisur *f.*
◆**'hairdresser,** *s.* Friseur *m,* Friseuse *f.*

◆**'hairpin,** *s.* Haarnadel *f;* (*in road*) **h.
bend,** Haarnadelkurve *f.* ◆**'hair-
raising,** *adj.* haarsträubend.
◆**'hairspray,** *s.* Haarspray *n.*
◆**'hairstyle,** *s.* Frisur *f.* ◆**'hairy,** *adj.*
(*a*) behaart; (*b*) *F:* (*of situation*) brenzlig.

**half,** *pl.* **halves** [hɑːf, hɑːvz]. **I.** *s.* (*a*)
Hälfte *f;* **to cut sth. in h.,** etwas halbieren; (*b*) **one and a h.,** eineinhalb, anderthalb; (*c*) *Fb: etc:* **the first h.,** die erste
Halbzeit. **II.** *adj.* halb; **h. an hour,** eine
halbe Stunde. **III.** *adv.* (*a*) halb; **zur
Hälfte; the glass was h. full,** das Glas
war halb voll; **not h.!** und wie! (*b*) **it's h.
past two,** es ist halb drei; (*c*) **h. as big,**
halb so groß. ◆**'half-and'half,** *adv.*
halb und halb. ◆**'half-brother,** *s.* Halb-
bruder *m.* ◆**'half-caste. I.** *adj.* halbblü-
tig. **II.** *s.* Mischling *m.* ◆**'half-fare,** *s.*
halber Fahrpreis *m.* ◆**'half-'hearted,**
*adj.* zaghaft; (*of pers.*) lustlos. ◆**'half-
'hourly,** *adj. & adv.* halbstündlich.
◆**halfpenny** ['heipni], *s. A:* halber Penny *m.* ◆**'half-sister,** *s.* Halbschwester *f.*
◆**'half-'term,** *s. Brit:* schulfreie Tage in
der Mitte eines Trimesters. ◆**'half-
'time,** *s. Fb: etc:* Halbzeit *f.* ◆**'half-
'way,** *adj. & adv.* **1.** auf halbem Weg;
**we have only got h.-w.,** wir
haben erst den halben Weg
zurückgelegt/(*with work*) nur die Hälfte
gemacht; *Fig:* **to meet s.o. h.-w.,** j-m
auf halbem Weg entgegenkommen; **2.** *N.
Am:* **'halfway,** halbwegs; **h. decent,** eini-
germaßen anständig. ◆**'halfwit,** *s.* Ein-
faltspinsel *m.*

**halibut** ['hælibət], *s.* Heilbutt *m.*

**hall** [hɔːl], *s.* **1.** (*for concerts etc.*) Saal *m;*
(*dining*) **h.,** Speisesaal *m.* **2.** (**entrance-)-
h.,** Flur *m;* (*large*) Diele *f.* **3.** **h. of residence,** Studentenheim *n.* ◆**'hallmark,**

*s.* (*a*) (*on gold*, *silver*) Beschauzeichen *n*; (*b*) *Fig:* Kennzeichen *n* (eines Genies usw.).

**hallo** *see* **hello.**

**hallowed** ['hæləud], *adj.* geheiligt.

**Hallowe'en** ['hæləu'iːn], *s.* Abend *m* vor Allerheiligen.

**hallucination** [həljuːsi'neiʃən], *s.* Halluzination *f.*

**halo**, *pl.* -oes ['heiləu, -əuz], *s.* Heiligenschein *m.*

**halt** [hɔlt]. **I.** *s.* Stillstand *m; Mil: etc:* Halt *m;* **II.** *v.* **1.** *v.tr.* (j-n, etwas) anhalten; (den Verkehr) zum Stehen bringen. **2.** *v.i.* haltmachen; *int. Mil: etc:* halt! ◆**'halting**, *adj.* zögernd.

**halve** [hɑːv], *v.tr.* (*a*) (*cut in two*) (etwas) halbieren; (*b*) (*cut down*) (etwas) um die Hälfte reduzieren.

**ham** [hæm], *s.* **1.** *Cu:* Schinken *m;* **h. sandwich**, Schinkenbrot *n.* **2.** *F:* (*a*) (**actor**), Kulissenreißer *m;* (*b*) (**radio**) **h.**, Hobbyfunker *m.*

**hamburger** ['hæmbəːgər], *s.* Hamburger *m.*

**hammer** ['hæmər]. **I.** *s.* Hammer *m.* **II.** *v.* **1.** *v.tr.* hämmern. **2.** *v.i.* **to h. at the door**, an die Tür hämmern.

**hammock** ['hæmək], *s.* Hängematte *f.*

**hamper** ['hæmpər],, *v.tr.* behindern.

**hamster** ['hæmstər], *s.* Hamster *m.*

**hamstring** ['hæmstriŋ], *s.* Kniesehne *f.*

**hand** [hænd]. **I.** *s.* **1.** Hand *f;* **hands up!** Hände hoch! **hands off!** Hände weg! **to give s.o. a h.**, j-m behilflich sein. **2.** (*a*) (**near**) **at h.**, nahe; **the matter in h.**, die in Bearbeitung befindliche Sache; **on the one h.**, einerseits; **on the other h.**, andererseits; **to get out of h.**, außer Kontrolle geraten; **to win hands down**, spielend gewinnen; **to live from h. to mouth**, von der Hand in den Mund leben. **3.** (*pers.*) *F:* **to be an old h. at sth.**, in etwas *dat* sehr geübt sein. **4.** *F:* (*applause*) Beifall *m;* **to give s.o. a big h.**, j-m begeistert Beifall spenden. **5.** (*in cards*) **to have a good/bad h.**, gute/schlechte Karten haben. **6.** (*of watch, clock*) Zeiger *m.* **II.** *v.tr.* **to h. sth. to s.o.**, j-m etwas reichen; *F:* **you've got to hand it to him**, das muß man ihm lassen. ◆**'handbag**, *s.* Handtasche *f.* ◆**'handbrake**, *s.* Handbremse *f.* ◆**'handbook**, *s.* **1.** (*manual*) Handbuch *n.* **2.** (*guide*) Führer *m.* ◆**'handcuff**, *v.tr.* (j-m) Handschellen anlegen. ◆**'handcuffs**, *s.pl.* Handschellen *fpl.* ◆**'handful**, *s.* Handvoll *f.* ◆**'hand-grenade**, *s. Mil:* Handgranate *f.* ◆**'hand 'in**, *v.tr.* (ein Paket usw.) abgeben; (ein Formular, ein Gesuch usw.) einreichen. ◆**handkerchief** ['hæŋkətʃiːf], *s.* Taschentuch *n.* ◆**'hand-'made**, *adj.* handgemacht. ◆**'hand 'out**, *v.tr.* (etwas) austeilen. ◆**'handout**, *s.* **1.** (*publicity*) Werbezettel *m.* **2.** (*charity*) Almosen *n.* ◆**'hand 'over**, *v.tr.* (etwas) übergeben (**to s.o.**,

an j-n) . ◆**'hand 'round**, *v.tr.* (eine Flasche usw.) herumreichen; (Bonbons usw.) austeilen. ◆**'handshake**, *s.* Händedruck *m.* ◆**'handwriting**, *s.* Handschrift *f.* ◆**'handwritten**, *adj.* handgeschrieben. ◆**'handy**, *adj.* **1.** (*a*) (*convenient*) praktisch; zweckmäßig; (*b*) (*of pers.*) geschickt. **2. to keep sth. h.**, etwas zur Hand haben. ◆**'handyman**, *pl.* -**men**, *s.* Mann *m,* der allerlei (kleine) Arbeiten verrichtet.

**handicap** ['hændikæp]. **I.** *s.* Handikap *n;* (*mental or physical*) Behinderung *f;* (*disadvantage*) Nachteil *n.* **II.** *v.tr.* **to be mentally/physically handicapped**, geistig/körperlich behindert sein.

**handicraft** ['hændikrɑːft], *s.* (*a*) (*craft*) Handwerk *n;* (*b*) (*work*) Handarbeit *f;* **handicrafts**, Handarbeiten *fpl.*

**handle** ['hændl]. **I.** *s.* (*of tool, weapon etc.*) Griff *m;* (*of door*) Klinke *f;* (*of cup*) Henkel *m;* (*of broom etc.*) Stiel *m.* **II.** *v.* **1.** *v.tr.* (*a*) (etwas) handhaben; (*touch*) (etwas) anfassen, berühren; (*b*) (eine Angelegenheit) handhaben. **2.** *v.i.* **this car handles well/badly**, der Wagen fährt sich gut/schwer. ◆**'handlebar**, *s.* Lenkstange *f.*

**handsome** ['hænsəm], *adj.* (*a*) gutaussehend; (*b*) (*of reward etc.*) großzügig.

**hang** [hæŋ]. **I.** *v.irr.* **1.** *v.tr.* (*a*) (etwas) hängen (**on/from sth.**, an etwas *acc*); **to h.** (**down**) **one's head**, den Kopf hängen lassen; (*b*) (*p. & p.p.* **hanged**) (einen Verbrecher) hängen; **to h. oneself**, sich erhängen. **2.** *v.i.* (*a*) hängen (**on/from sth.**, an etwas *dat*); (*b*) (*of criminal*) gehängt werden. **II.** *s. F:* **to get the h. of sth.**, kapieren, wie etwas funktioniert/wie man etwas macht. ◆**'hang a'bout/a'round**, *v.i.* herumstehen; *F:* herumlungern; (*wait*) warten. ◆**'hang 'back**, *v.i.* zurückbleiben; *F:* zögern. ◆**'hang 'down**, *v.i.* herunterhängen. ◆**'hanger**, *s.* (*a*) (*on coat etc.*) Aufhänger *m;* (*b*) (*for coat etc.*) Kleiderbügel *m.* ◆**'hanger-'on**, *s.* (*pers.*) *Pol: etc:* Mitläufer *m.* ◆**'hang-glider**, *s.* Drachenflieger *m.* ◆**'hang-gliding**, *s.* Drachenfliegen *n.* ◆**'hanging**, *s.* (*execution*) Hinrichtung *f* am Galgen. ◆**'hang 'on**, *v.i.* (*a*) sich festhalten (**to sth.**, an etwas *dat*); **to h. on to one's job**, seine Stelle behalten; (*b*) (*persevere, wait*) **can you h. on until I come?** kannst du warten, bis ich komme? *F:* **h. on!** Moment mal! ◆**'hang 'out**, *v.tr.* (Wäsche usw.) (draußen) aufhängen. ◆**'hang 'over**, *v.* *F:* Kater *m.* ◆**'hang 'up**, *v.* **1.** *v.tr.* (*a*) (etwas) aufhängen; (*b*) *P:* **hung up**, gehemmt. **2.** *v.i. Tel:* auflegen. ◆**'hangup**, *s. F:* Komplex *m.*

**hangar** ['hæŋər], *s.* Hangar *m.*

**hanker** ['hæŋkər], *v.i.* sich sehnen (**after sth.**, nach etwas *dat*).

**haphazard** [hæp'hæzəd], *adj.* willkürlich; (*accidental*) zufällig.

**happen** ['hæpən], v.i. (a) (of accident etc.) passieren; (of event etc.) geschehen; (b) **what's happened to him?** was ist mit ihm passiert/aus ihm geworden? (c) **the house happened to be empty,** zufällig stand das Haus leer; **do you h. to know whether ... ?** wissen Sie zufällig, ob ... ? **as it happens,** zufälligerweise; (d) to h. **upon sth.,** (zufällig) auf etwas acc stoßen; (e) (take place) stattfinden. ◆'**happening,** s. Ereignis n.

**happy** ['hæpi], adj. (a) glücklich; (b) (satisfied) zufrieden; **-ily,** adv. glücklich; (luckily) glücklicherweise. ◆'**happiness,** s. Glück n.

**harass** ['hærəs], v.tr. (j-n) plagen; (mentally) quälen.

**harbour** ['hɑːbər]. I. s. Hafen m. II. v.tr. (a) (einem Verbrecher usw.) Obdach gewähren; (b) Fig: (Gefühle) hegen.

**hard** [hɑːd]. I. adj. 1. (of pers.) hart. 2. (difficult) schwer; **h. of hearing,** schwerhörig. 3. (a) **to be h. on s.o.,** streng mit j-m sein; (b) **h. facts,** nackte Tatsachen fpl; **h. luck,** Pech n. II. adv. 1. (a) (with effort) kräftig; **to try h./harder,** sich dat große/mehr Mühe geben; **to think h.,** scharf nachdenken; **to work h./be h. at work,** schwer arbeiten; **it's raining h.,** es regnet heftig/stark; (b) F: **to be h. up,** knapp bei Kasse sein. 2. **hard-earned wages,** schwer/sauer verdienter Lohn. ◆'**hardboard,** s. Hartfaserplatte f. ◆'**hard-'boiled,** adj. hartgekocht. ◆'**harden.** 1. v.tr. (a) (Metalle, Fette usw.) härten; (b) (of pers.) **to h. oneself,** sich abhärten; **hardened to sth.,** an etwas acc gewöhnt. 2. v.i. hart werden. ◆'**hard-'hearted,** adj. hartherzig. ◆'**hardly,** adv. kaum. ◆'**hardness,** s. Härte f. ◆'**hardship,** s. Not f; (privation) Entbehrung f. ◆'**hardware,** s. 1. Haushaltswaren fpl. 2. Tchn: Hardware f. ◆'**hard-'wearing,** adj. (of material etc.) dauerhaft; (of clothes etc.) strapazierfähig. ◆'**hard-'won,** adj. schwer erkämpft. ◆'**hard-'working,** adj. fleißig. ◆'**hardy,** adj. (a) (of pers.) abgehärtet; (b) (of plant) ausdauernd; mehrjährig.

**hare** ['hɛər], s. Z: Hase m. ◆'**harelip,** s. Hasenscharte f.

**harm** [hɑːm]. I. s. Schaden m; **out of h.'s way,** in Sicherheit. II. v.tr. (j-m, etwas dat) schaden. ◆'**harmless,** adj. harmlos. ◆'**harmful,** adj schädlich.

**harmony** ['hɑːməni], s. Harmonie f. ◆'**har'monious,** adj. harmonisch. ◆'**harmonize.** 1. v.tr. (eine Melodie) harmonisieren. 2. v.i. (of colour etc.) harmonieren (**with sth.,** mit etwas dat).

**harness** ['hɑːnis]. I. s. (of horse etc.) Geschirr n. II. v.tr. (a) (ein Pferd usw.) anschirren; (b) (Wasserkraft) nutzbar machen.

**harp** [hɑːp], s. Harfe f.

**harpoon** [hɑː'puːn], s. Harpune f.

**harrowing** ['hærəuiŋ], adj. grauenvoll.

**harsh** [hɑːʃ], adj. 1. (of texture, sound etc.) rauh; (of colour) grell. 2. (of pers., Jur: sentence etc.) hart. ◆'**harshness,** s. 1. Rauheit f. 2. Härte f.

**harvest** ['hɑːvist]. I. s. Ernte f. II. v.tr. ernten. ◆'**harvester,** s. **combine h.,** Mähdrescher m.

**hash** [hæʃ], s. 1. F: **to make a h. of sth.,** etwas vermasseln/verpfuschen. 2. F: (drug) Hasch n.

**hassle** ['hæsəl], s. F: Ärger m.

**haste** [heist], s. Eile f. ◆'**hasten,** v.i. eilen, sich beeilen. ◆'**hasty,** adj. (of departure) hastig; (of decision) übereilt.

**hat** [hæt], s. Hut m; **that's old h.,** das sind olle Kamellen.

**hatch¹** [hætʃ], s. 1. Nau: etc: Luke f. 2. **service h.,** Durchreiche f. ◆'**hatchback,** s. Wagen m mit Hecktür.

**hatch²,** v. 1. v.tr. (Eier, Fig: einen Plan) ausbrüten. 2. v.i. **to h. (out),** ausschlüpfen.

**hatchet** ['hætʃit], s. Beil n; **to bury the h.,** das Kriegsbeil begraben.

**hate** [heit]. I. s. Haß m. II. v.tr. (a) (j-n, etwas) hassen; (b) **to h. to do sth.,** etwas sehr ungern tun. ◆'**hateful,** adj. hassenswert. ◆'**hatred,** s. Haß m (**for/of s.o., sth.,** gegen j-n, etwas acc).

**haughty** ['hɔːti], adj. hochmütig.

**haul** [hɔːl]. I. v.tr. ziehen, (with effort) schleppen. II. s. 1. (of robber) Beute f. 2. (distance) Strecke f. ◆'**haulage,** s. 1. Spedition f; **h. contractor,** Spediteur m. 2. (cost) Frachtkosten fpl. ◆'**haulier,** s. Spediteur m.

**haunt** [hɔːnt]. I. s. Lieblingsaufenthalt m. II. v.tr. **this house is haunted,** in diesem Haus spukt es; (of pers.) **to be haunted by memories (of sth.),** von Erinnerungen (an etwas acc) verfolgt werden.

**have** [hæv], v.tr.irr. haben; F: **he's had it,** mit ihm ist es aus; **to h. sth. done,** etwas machen lassen; **to h. to do sth.,** etwas tun müssen; **I h. come,** ich bin gekommen; **he has burnt it,** er hat es verbrannt; **I h. lived in London for three years,** ich wohne seit drei Jahren in London; **I had better say nothing,** ich sage lieber nichts. ◆'**have 'in,** v.tr. **to h. it in for s.o.,** es auf j-n abgesehen haben. ◆'**have 'on,** v.tr. (a) **to h. a coat on,** einen Mantel anhaben; **to h. nothing on,** unbekleidet sein; (b) **I h. nothing on tonight,** ich bin heute abend frei; **what do you h. on this evening?** was haben Sie heute Abend auf dem Programm? (c) F: **to h. s.o. on,** j-n anführen. ◆'**have 'out,** v.tr. **to h. it o. with s.o.,** j-n zur Rede stellen. ◆'**have 'up,** v.tr. F: **to be had up for sth.,** wegen etwas gen vors Gericht kommen.

**haven** ['heivn], s. (a) Hafen m; (b) (refuge) Zufluchtsort m.

**haversack** ['hævəsæk], s. Rucksack m.

**havoc** ['hævək], s. Chaos n; Fig: **to cause**

h., eine verheerende Wirkung haben.
**hawk** [hɔːk], s. Falke m.
**hawthorn** ['hɔːθɔːn], s. Hagedorn m.
**hay** [hei], s. Heu n. ◆'**hay-fever,** s. Heuschnupfen m. ◆'**haystack,** s. Heuschober m. ◆'**haywire,** adj. F: durcheinander; **to go h.,** durcheinandergeraten.
**hazard** ['hæzəd]. **I.** s. Gefahr f (**to health** etc., für die Gesundheit usw.); (risk) Risiko n. **II.** v.tr. (etwas) riskieren. ◆'**hazardous,** adj. riskant.
**haze** [heiz], s. Dunst m. ◆'**hazy,** adj. (of weather etc.) dunstig; Fig: (of ideas etc.) unklar.
**hazel-nut** ['heizlnʌt], s. Haselnuß f.
**he** [hiː], pers. pron. er.
**head** [hed]. **I.** s. **1.** Kopf m; **they put their heads together,** sie steckten die Köpfe zusammen; **it's above my h.,** das geht über meinen Verstand; **to keep one's h.,** etwas m.? Kopf nicht verlieren. **2.** Spitze f (eines Zuges usw.); Kopfende n (eines Tisches, eines Betts); (on beer) Blume f; **at the h. of the list,** (ganz) oben auf der Liste; Fig: **to come to a h.,** sich zuspitzen. **3.** (a) (pers.) Oberhaupt n (einer Familie); Sch: Direktor(in) m(f); (b) attrib. Haupt-; **h. office,** Hauptsitz m; **h. waiter,** Oberkellner m. **5.** thirty **h.** of cattle, dreißig Stück Vieh; **to pay so much per h./a h.,** soundsoviel pro Person zahlen. **6.** (of coin) **heads or tails?** Kopf oder Wappen? F: **I can't make h. or tail of this,** daraus werde ich nicht schlau. **II.** v. **1.** v.tr. (a) (lead) (eine Partei, Kolonne usw.) anführen; (b) **to h. the ball,** den Ball köpfen. **2.** v.i. **to h. for sth.,** auf etwas acc zugehen/Nau: & Fig: zusteuern. ◆'**headache,** Kopfschmerzen mpl. ◆'**header,** s. Fb: Kopfball m. ◆'**head-'first,** adv. kopfüber. ◆'**heading,** s. Überschrift f; (of letter) Briefkopf m. ◆'**headlamp,** '**headlight,** s. Scheinwerfer m. ◆'**headline,** s. Schlagzeile f; **to hit the headlines,** Schlagzeilen machen. ◆'**headlong,** adv. kopfüber. ◆**head'master,** s. Schulleiter m. ◆**head'mistress,** s. Schulleiterin f. ◆'**head-'on,** adj. frontal. ◆'**headphones,** s.pl. Kopfhörer m. ◆**head'quarters,** s.pl. **1.** Mil: Hauptquartier n. **2.** (of bank, police etc.) Zentrale f. ◆'**headrest,** s. Kopfstütze f. ◆'**headscarf,** s. Kopftuch n. ◆'**headstrong,** adj. eigenwillig. ◆'**headway,** s. **to make h.,** Fortschritte machen.
**heal** [hiːl], v.tr. & i. heilen.
**health** [helθ], s. **1.** Gesundheit f; **h. foods,** Reformkost f; **h. food store,** Reformhaus n; **h. insurance,** Krankenversicherung f; **h. resort,** Kurort m. **2.** **to drink (to) the h. of s.o.,** auf j-s Wohl trinken. ◆'**healthy,** adj. gesund.
**heap** [hiːp]. **I.** s. (a) Haufen m; (b) F: pl. (large number) jede Menge f; **heaps of time,** jede Menge Zeit. **II.** v.tr. (Sachen)

aufhäufen; **to h. s.o.'s plate with strawberries,** Erdbeeren auf j-s Teller häufen; **heaped spoonful,** gehäufter Löffel; Fig: **to h. praises/insults on s.o.,** j-n mit Lob/Beleidigungen überschütten.
**hear** [hiər], v.irr. **1.** v.tr. (a) hören; (b) (listen to) (j-m) zuhören. **2.** v.i. (a) **to h. from s.o.,** von j-m hören; (b) **to h. of/ about sth.,** etwas erfahren; **to have heard of s.o.,** von j-m gehört haben; **father won't h. of it,** Vater will nichts davon wissen. ◆'**hearing,** s. (a) Jur: etc: Verhandlung f; (b) Gehör n; **h. aid,** Hörgerät n. ◆'**hearsay,** s. Hörensagen n.
**hearse** [hɜːs], s. Leichenwagen m.
**heart** [hɑːt], s. Herz n. **1.** **h. attack,** Herzanfall m; **at h.,** im Grunde; **to have a change of h.,** seine Meinung ändern; **I did not have the h. to disturb him,** ich konnte es nicht über mich bringen, ihn zu stören; F: **have a h.!** sei nicht so! **to take h.,** sich dat ein Herz fassen; **to lose h.,** den Mut verlieren; **to know sth. by h.,** etwas auswendig können. **2.** (core) the h. of the matter, der Kern der Sache; **in the h. of,** im Herzen + gen. **3.** (in cards) **hearts,** Herz n. ◆'**heartbeat,** s. Herzschlag m. ◆'**heartbreaking,** adj. herzzerreißend. ◆'**heartbroken,** adj. untröstlich. ◆'**heartburn,** s. Sodbrennen n. ◆'**hearten,** v.tr. (j-n) ermutigen. ◆'**heartfelt,** adj. herzlich. ◆'**heartless,** adj. herzlos. ◆'**heartrending,** adj. herzzerreißend. ◆'**hearty,** adj. **1.** (of feeling etc.) herzlich. **2.** (of meal, appetite) herzhaft; **-ily,** adv. **1.** herzlich (empfinden). **2.** herzhaft (essen).
**hearth** [hɑːθ], s. Herd m.
**heat** [hiːt]. **I.** s. **1.** Wärme f; (intense) Hitze f. **2.** **it happened in the h. of the moment,** es geschah in der Hitze des Gefechts. **3.** Sp: (i) (in sprinting etc.) Vorlauf m; (ii) (in swimming etc.) Runde f. **II.** v.tr. (a) (etwas) heiß machen; (Wasser, Metall usw.) erhitzen; (b) (ein Zimmer usw.) heizen. ◆'**heated,** adj. (a) (of water etc.) erhitzt; (b) (of room etc.) geheizt; (c) (of discussion) hitzig. ◆'**heater,** s. Heizgerät n; (in car etc.) Heizanlage f. ◆'**heating,** s. Heizung f. ◆'**heatwave,** s. Hitzewelle f.
**heath** [hiːθ], s. Heide f.
**heathen** ['hiːðən]. **I.** adj. heidnisch. **II.** s. Heide m; Heidin f.
**heather** ['heðər], s. Heidekraut n.
**heave** [hiːv], v. **1.** v.tr. (a) (lift) (eine Last) (mit großer Anstrengung) heben; (b) **to h. a sigh,** einen Seufzer ausstoßen. **2.** v.i. (a) (of sea, breast) sich heben (und senken); (b) **to h. at a rope,** an einem Tau ziehen.
**heaven** ['hev(ə)n], s. Himmel m; **for h.'s sake,** um Himmels willen; **h. knows where it is,** der Himmel weiß wo das ist. ◆'**heavenly,** adj. himmlisch.

**heavy** ['hevi], *adj.* (*a*) schwer; (*b*) (*of traffic, eating etc.*) stark; (*c*) (*of style, tread*) schwerfällig; **-ily**, *adv.* schwer; **to sleep h.**, tief schlafen. ◆'**heavyweight**. *Sp:* **I.** *adj.* Schwergewichts-. **II.** *s.* Schwergewichtler *m.*

**Hebrew** ['hi:bru:]. **I.** *adj.* hebräisch. **II.** *s.* (*language*) Hebräisch *n.*

**heckle** ['hekl], *v.tr.* (den Redner) (durch Zwischenrufe) unterbrechen. ◆'**heckler**, *s.* Zwischenrufer *m.*

**hectic** ['hektik], *adj.* hektisch.

**hedge** [hedʒ]. **I.** *s.* Hecke *f.* **II.** *v.i.* Ausreden suchen. ◆'**hedgehog**, *s.* Igel *m.*

**heed** [hi:d]. **I.** *v.tr.* beachten. **II.** *s.* **to take h. of s.o., sth.**, j-m, etwas *dat* Beachtung schenken.

**heel** [hi:l]. **I.** *s.* (*a*) Ferse *f*; (*of shoe*) Absatz *m*; **down at h.**, heruntergekommen. **II.** *v.tr.* **to h. a shoe**, einen Absatz an einen Schuh machen.

**hefty** ['hefti], *adj. F*: (*of pers.*) stämmig; (*of blow*) schwer; **a h. sum**, eine saftige Summe.

**height** [hait], *s.* **1.** (*a*) Höhe *f*; (*b*) (*of pers.*) Größe *f.* **2.** *Fig*: Höhepunkt *m* (einer Karriere usw.); **the h. of fashion**, die neueste Mode.

**heir** ['eər], *s.* Erbe *m.* ◆'**heiress**, *s.* Erbin *f.* ◆'**heirloom**, *s.* Erbstück *n.*

**helicopter** ['helikɔptər], *s.* Hubschrauber *m.*

**helium** ['hi:ljəm], *s.* Helium *n.*

**hell** [hel], *s.* Hölle *f*; **what the h. do you want?** was zum Teufel wollen Sie? **oh h.!** verdammt! ◆'**hellish**, *adj.* teuflisch; **-ly**, *adv. F*: **h. difficult**, verdammt schwierig.

**hello** ['heləu], *int.* (*a*) (guten) Tag/ Morgen/Abend; (*b*) *Tel*: hallo.

**helm** [helm], *s.* Ruder *m.*

**helmet** ['helmit], *s.* Helm *m.*

**help** [help]. **I.** *s.* Hilfe *f.* **II.** *v.tr.* (*a*) (j-m) helfen; **h. yourself**, bedienen Sie sich; (*b*) **if I can h. it**, wenn ich es vermeiden kann; **I can't h. it**, ich kann nichts dafür; **I couldn't h. laughing**, ich mußte lachen. ◆'**helper**, *s.* Helfer(in) *m(f).* ◆'**helpful**, *adj.* (*a*) (*of pers.*) hilfsbereit; (*b*) (*of advice etc.*) nützlich. ◆'**helping. I.** *adj.* **to lend (s.o.) a h. hand**, j-m *dat* behilflich sein. **II.** *s.* Portion *f* (einer Speise). ◆'**helpless**, *adj.* hilflos. ◆'**helplessness**, *s.* Hilflosigkeit *f.* ◆'**help out**, *v.tr.* (j-m) aushelfen.

**hem** [hem]. **I.** *s.* Saum *m.* **II.** *v.tr.* (*a*) (ein Kleid) säumen; (*b*) **to h. in**, (j-n, etwas) umzingeln.

**hemisphere** ['hemisfiər], *s.* Hemisphäre *f.*

**hen** [hen], *s.* **1.** (*fowl*) Huhn *n.* **2.** (*female*) Henne *f*; *F*: **h. party**, Damengesellschaft *f.* ◆'**henpecked**, *adj. F*: **h. husband**, Pantoffelheld *m.*

**hence** [hens], *adv.* **1.** (*from now*) **five years h.**, in fünf Jahren. **2.** (*thus*) daher.

**hepatitis** [hepə'taitis], *s.* Leberentzündung *f.*

**her** [hər, hə:r]. **I.** *pers. pron.* **1.** (*object*) (*a*) *acc* sie; **for h.**, für sie; (*b*) *dat* ihr; **give h. this**, gib ihr das. **2. it's h.**, sie ist es. **II.** *poss. adj.* ihr.

**heraldry** ['herəldri], *s.* Heraldik *f.*

**herb** [hə:b], *s.* (*a*) *Bot:* Kraut *n*; (*b*) *Cu:* Gewürz *n.* ◆'**herbal**, *adj.* Kräuter-; **h. remedy**, Kräuterkur *f.*

**herd** [hə:d]. **I.** *s.* Herde *f.* **II.** *v.tr.* (Vieh usw.) hüten.

**here** [hiər], *adv.* hier. **h. goes!** also los! **h. you are**, das ist für Sie; **h. we are**, da sind wir; **that's neither h. nor there**, das ist völlig belanglos.

**hereditary** [hi'reditri], *adj.* erblich.

**heresy** ['herəsi], *s.* Ketzerei *f.* ◆'**heretic**, *s.* Ketzer *m.*

**heritage** ['heritidʒ], *s.* Erbe *n.*

**hermit** ['hə:mit], *s.* Einsiedler *m.*

**hernia** ['hə:niə], *s.* Bruch *m.*

**hero**, *pl.* **-oes** ['hiərəu, -əuz], *s.* Held *m.* ◆**heroic** [hə'rəuik], *adj.* heldenhaft. ◆**heroine** ['herəuin], *s.* Heldin *f.* ◆'**heroism**, *s.* Heldentum *n.*

**heroin** ['herəuin], *s.* Heroin *n.*

**heron** ['herən], *s.* Reiher *m.*

**herring** ['heriŋ], *s.* Hering *m*; *F*: **a red h.**, eine falsche Fährte.

**hers** [hə:z], *poss. pron.* ihrer, ihre, ihres; *pl.* ihre.

**herself** [hə:'self], *pers. pron.* (*a*) selbst; (*b*) (*refl.*) sich.

**hesitate** ['heziteit], *v.i.* zögern. ◆'**hesitant**, *adj.* zögernd. ◆**hesi'tation**, *s.* Zögern *n.*

**hey-day** ['heidei], *s.* Blütezeit *f*; Glanzzeit *f.*

**hibernate** ['haibəneit], *v.i.* Winterschlaf halten. ◆**hiber'nation**, *s.* Winterschlaf *m.*

**hiccup, hiccough** ['hikʌp]. **I.** *s.* **1.** Schluckauf *m.* **2.** *F:* (*hitch*) Stockung *f.* **II.** *v.i.* Schluckauf haben.

**hide**[1] [haid], *v.irr.* **1.** *v.tr.* (j-n, etwas) verstecken (**from s.o.**, vor j-m). **2.** *v.i.* sich verstecken. ◆'**hide-and-'seek**, *s.* Versteckspiel *n.* ◆'**hide-out**, *s.* Versteck *n.* ◆'**hiding**[1], *s.* **to go into h.**, sich verstecken; **to be in h.**, sich versteckt halten; **h. place**, Versteck *n.*

**hide**[2], *s.* (*skin*) Haut *f.* ◆'**hiding**[2], **to give s.o. a h.**, j-n verdreschen.

**hideous** ['hidiəs], *adj.* (*ugly*) scheußlich; (*of crime, noise etc.*) gräßlich.

**hierarchy** ['haiərɑ:ki], *s.* Hierarchie *f.*

**high** [hai]. **I.** *adj.* hoch; **a wall two metres h.** eine zwei Meter hohe Mauer; **h. jump**, Hochsprung *m*; *F*: **it's h. time he started school**, es ist höchste Zeit, daß er in die Schule kommt; **-ly**, *adv.* **1. to think h. of s.o.**, j-n sehr schätzen. **2. h. amusing**, höchst amüsant; **h. paid**, sehr gut bezahlt. **3. h. strung**, nervös. **II.** *adv.* hoch; **feelings ran h.**, die Gemüter erhitzten sich. ◆'**high-'heeled**, *adj.* mit hohen Absätzen. ◆'**highlands**, *s.pl.* **the H. of Scotland**, das Schottische Hochland. ◆**'high-'level**, *attrib. adj.* (Besprechung usw.) auf höchster Ebene. ◆**'highlight. I.** *s.* **1.** (*in hair*) helle Strähne *f.* **2.** Höhepunkt *m* (von etwas). **II.** *v.tr.* (etwas) hervorheben. ◆**'Highness**, *s.* **His H.**, Seine Hoheit *f.* ◆**'high-'pitched**, *adj.* (*of voice*) hoch; (*of scream*) schrill. ◆**'high-'ranking**, *adj.* ranghoch. ◆**'high-rise**, *adj.* **h.-r. flats**, Hochhäuser *npl.* ◆**'highway**, *s.* Landstraße *f; N.Am:* Schnellstraße *f;* the **H. Code**, die Straßenverkehrsordnung.

**hijack** ['haidʒæk], *v.tr.* entführen. ◆**'hijacker**, *s.* Entführer *m;* (*of aircraft*) Luftpirat *m.* ◆**'hijacking**, *s.* Entführung *f* (eines Flugzeuges usw.).

**hike** [haik]. **I.** *s.* Wanderung *f.* **II.** *v.i.* wandern. ◆**'hiker**, *s.* Wanderer *m.* ◆**'hiking**, *s.* Wandern *n.*

**hilarious** [hi'lɛəriəs], *adj.* urkomisch. ◆**hilarity** [-'læriti], *s.* Gelächter *n.*

**hill** [hil], *s.* **1.** Hügel *m.* **2.** (*incline*) Steigung *f.* ◆**'hillside**, *s.* Hang *m.* ◆**'hilly**, *adj.* hügelig.

**hilt** [hilt], *s.* Griff *m* (eines Schwertes usw.); *Fig:* to the h., voll und ganz.

**him** [him], *pers. pron. object.* **1.** (*a*) (*acc*) ihn; **for h.**, für ihn; (*b*) (*dat*) ihm; **give h. this**, gib ihm das. **2.** **it's h.**, er ist es. ◆**him'self**, *pers. pron.* (*a*) selbst; (*b*) (*refl.*) sich.

**hind** [haind], *adj.* **h. leg**, Hinterbein *n.* ◆**'hindsight**, *s.* verspätete Einsicht *f;* **with h.**, rückblickend.

**hinder** ['hindər], *v.tr.* (j-n, etwas) hindern; (eine Entwicklung) hemmen. ◆**'hindrance**, *s.* Hindernis *n.*

**Hindi** ['hindiː], *s.* (*language*) Hindi *n.* ◆**Hindu** [hin'duː]. **I.** *s.* (*pers.*) Hindu *m.* **II.** *adj.* Hindu-. ◆**'Hinduism**, *s.* Hinduismus *m.*

**hinge** [hindʒ]. **I.** *s.* Scharnier *n;* (*large*) Angel *f* (einer Tür usw.). **II.** *v.i.* abhängen (**on sth.**, von etwas *dat*).

**hint** [hint]. **I.** *s.* **1.** (*a*) Wink *m;* **to drop a h.**, eine Andeutung fallen lassen; (*b*) (*tip*) Hinweis *m.* **II.** *v.i.* **to h. at sth.**, auf etwas *acc* anspielen.

**hip** [hip], *s.* Hüfte *f.*

**hippopotamus**, *pl.* **-muses, -mi** [hipə'potəməs, -masiz, -mai], *s.* Nilpferd *n.*

**hire** ['haiər]. **I.** *s.* (*action*) Verleih *m;* **h. car**, Mietwagen *m;* **for h.**, zu mieten; (*of taxi*) frei; **h. purchase**, Ratenkauf *m;* **to buy sth. on h. purchase**, etwas auf Raten/Abzahlung kaufen. **II.** *v.tr.* (*a*) (ein Auto, einen Saal usw.) mieten; (Arbeiter usw.) einstellen; (*b*) **to h. out**, verleihen.

**his** [hiz]. **I.** *poss. adj.* sein(e). **II.** *poss. pron.* seiner, seine, seines; *pl.* seine; **this is h.**, das ist seins.

**hiss** [his]. **I.** Zischen *n.* **II.** *v.tr. & i.* zischen.

**history** ['histəri], *s.* Geschichte *f.* ◆**historian** [-'tɔːriən], *s.* Historiker(in) *m(f).* ◆**historic** [-'tɔrik], *adj.* historisch.

◆**his'torical**, *adj.* geschichtlich.

**hit** [hit]. **I.** *v.irr.* **1.** *v.tr.* (*a*) (j-n) schlagen; (*b*) (*missile, stone etc.*) (j-n, etwas) treffen; **hard h. by financial losses**, durch finanzielle Verluste schwer getroffen. **II.** *s.* **1.** (*a*) Schlag *m; direct* **h.**, Volltreffer *m;* (*b*) *F:* (*song, play*) Hit *m.* ◆**'hit 'off**, *v.tr.* **to h. it off with s.o.**, mit j-m gut auskommen. ◆**'hit 'on**, *v.tr.* **to h. on an idea**, auf eine Idee kommen. ◆**'hit 'out**, *v.i. Fig:* **to h. o. at s.o.**, **sth.**, über j-n, etwas *acc* herziehen.

**hitch** [hitʃ]. **I.** *s.* Störung *f;* **to go without a h.**, reibungslos/ *F:* wie geschmiert gehen; **technical h.**, Panne *f.* **II.** *v.tr.* (*a*) **to h. sth. (on) to sth.**, etwas an etwas *acc* festhaken; (*b*) **to h. (up) one's trousers**, sich *dat* die Hose hochziehen. ◆**'hitch-hike**, *v.i.* trampen, per Anhalter fahren. ◆**'hitch-hiker**, *s.* Tramper *m.*

**hive** [haiv], *s.* (bee)**h.**, Bienenkorb *m.*

**hoard** [hɔːd]. **I.** *s.* Hort *m.* **II.** *v.tr.* horten.

**hoarding** ['hɔːdiŋ], *s.* Bauzaun *m;* **advertisement h.**, Reklamewand *f.*

**hoarse** [hɔːs], *adj.* heiser.

**hoax** [həuks], *s.* (*false alarm*) blinder Alarm *m;* (*false report*) Ente *f.*

**hobble** ['hɔbl], *v.i.* humpeln.

**hobby** ['hɔbi], *s.* Hobby *n.*

**hockey** ['hɔki], *s.* Hockey *n.*

**hoe** [həu]. **I.** *s.* Hacke *f.* **II.** *v.tr. & i.* hacken.

**hog** [hɔg]. **I.** *s.* (*pig*) Schwein *n; Fig:* **to go the whole h.**, aufs Ganze gehen. **II.** *v.tr. F:* **to h. sth.**, auf etwas *dat* sitzen.

**hoist** [hɔist], *v.tr.* (*a*) (eine Fahne, Flagge) hissen; (*b*) **to h. sth. (up)**, etwas hochziehen.

**hold¹** [həuld]. **I.** *v.irr.* **1.** *v.tr.* (*a*) (j-n, etwas) halten; (*b*) (*contain*) fassen; (*c*) (*conduct*) (eine Sitzung, Ausstellung usw.) abhalten; (ein Fest usw.) veranstalten; (*d*) (den Atem) anhalten; **h. it!** halt! Moment! (*e*) (*consider*) **to h. s.o. responsible**, j-n verantwortlich machen; **to h. (the view) that ...**, die Meinung vertreten, daß ...; (*f*) (*possess*) (einen Titel, Land, Aktien) haben; **to h. an office**, ein Amt bekleiden. **2.** *v.i.* (*a*) (*of glue, rope etc.*) halten; (*b*) (*of weather*) anhalten; **to h. good (for sth.)**, (für etwas *acc*) gelten. **II.** *s.* Halt *m;* **to have a h. over s.o.**, j-n in seiner Hand haben; **to take h. of sth.**, etwas fassen; *F:* **to get h. of sth.**, etwas auftreiben; **to get h. of s.o.**, (*on phone etc.*) j-n erreichen. ◆**'hold-all**, *s.* Reisetasche *f.* ◆**'hold'back**, *v.tr.* (etwas) zurückhalten. **2.** *v.i.* sich zurückhalten. ◆**'holder**, *s.* **1.** (*pers.*) Inhaber *m* (einer Karte, Lizenz); Träger *m* (eines Titels usw.). **2.** (*device*) Halter *m.* ◆**'hold 'off**, *v.* **1.** *v.tr.* (den Feind) abwehren. **2.** *v.i.* (*of rain etc.*) ausbleiben. ◆**'hold 'on**, *v.i.* **to h. on to sth.**, sich an etwas *dat* festhalten; **h. on!** (i) festhalten! (ii) *F:* (warten Sie) einen Augenblick. ◆'hold 'out, v. 1. v.tr. (etwas) hinhalten. 2. v.i. (of pers.) durchhalten. ◆'hold 'up, v. 1. v.tr. (a) (die Hand usw.) hochheben; (b) (delay) (den Verkehr usw.) aufhalten; (c) (of robber) (j-n) überfallen. 2. v.i. (of story, evidence) stichhaltig sein. ◆'hold-up, s. 1. Stockung f (des Verkehrs usw.). 2. Überfall m (auf j-n, eine Bank usw.).

hold², s. Laderaum m (eines Schiffes).

hole [həul], s. Loch n.

holiday ['hɔlidei], s. (a) (day) (public) h., Feiertag m; to take a h., (i) sich dat einen Tag frei nehmen; (ii) Urlaub machen; (b) (period) Urlaub m; (esp. school) holidays, Ferien pl; on h., auf Urlaub. ◆'holidaymaker, s. Urlauber m.

Holland ['hɔlənd]. Pr. n. Holland n.

hollow ['hɔləu], adj. hohl.

holly ['hɔli], s. Stechpalme f.

holster ['həulstər], s. Pistolentasche f.

holy ['həuli], adj. heilig.

homage ['hɔmidʒ], s. Huldigung f; to pay h. to s.o., j-m huldigen.

home [həum]. I. s. 1. (a) Heim n; (b) at h., zu Hause; make yourself at h., fühlen Sie sich wie zu Hause. 2. (birthplace) Heimat f. 3. (institution or place) Heim n; old people's h., Altersheim n. II. adv. 1. nach Hause. 2. to bring sth. h. to s.o., j-m etwas klarmachen. III. adj. 1. h. address, Privatadresse f; h. help, Haushaltshilfe f; h. game, Heimspiel n; h. truth, ungeschminkte Wahrheit. 2. h. affairs, innere Angelegenheiten fpl; Brit: H. Office, Innenministerium n; H. Secretary, Innenminister m. ◆'homeland, s. Heimatland n. ◆'homeless, adj. obdachlos. ◆'homely, adj. 1. (of house, pers.) gemütlich; (of food) bürgerlich. 2. N. Am: (of pers.) unscheinbar. ◆'home-'made, adj. (of food) hausgemacht; (of object) selbstgemacht; (amateurish) (selbst)-gebastelt. ◆'homesick, adj. she's h., sie hat Heimweh. ◆'homesickness, s. Heimweh n. ◆'homework, s. Hausaufgaben fpl.

homicide ['hɔmisaid], s. Totschlag m; (murder) Mord m. ◆homi'cidal, adj. mörderisch.

homosexual [hɔməu'seksjuəl]. I. adj. homosexuell. II. s. Homosexuelle(r) m.

honest ['ɔnist], adj. aufrichtig; (of pers., intentions) ehrlich; an h. opinion, eine offene Meinung; -ly, adv. ehrlich; int. h.! wirklich! ◆'honesty, s. Ehrlichkeit f.

honey ['hʌni], s. Honig m. ◆'honeycomb, s. Honigwabe f. ◆'honeymoon, s. (period) Flitterwochen fpl; (trip) Hochzeitsreise f. ◆'honeysuckle, s. Geißblatt n.

honorary ['ɔnərəri], adj. (of position) ehrenamtlich.

honour ['ɔnər]. I. s. 1. Ehre f; in s.o.'s h., zu j-s Ehren; word of h., Ehrenwort n. 2. (award, medal etc.) Auszeichnung f.

II. v.tr. ehren. ◆'honourable, adj. ehrenhaft.

hood [hud], s. 1. Kapuze f. 2. Aut: N. Am: Kühlerhaube f.

hoof [hu:f], pl. -s, hooves [hu:f, -s, hu:vz], s. Huf m.

hook [huk]. I. s. Haken m. II. v.tr. (a) to h. sth. to sth., etwas an etwas acc festhaken; (b) (einen Fisch usw.) angeln. ◆'hooked, adj. F: to be h. on sth., etwas dat verfallen sein.

hooligan ['hu:ligən], s. Rowdy m.

hoop [hu:p], s. Reifen m.

hoot [hu:t], v.i. (a) (of owl etc.) rufen; (b) Aut: hupen. ◆'hooter, s. Sirene f (einer Fabrik); Aut: Hupe f.

hoover ['hu:vər]. I. s. R.t.m. Staubsauger m. II. v.tr. & i. saugen.

hop¹ [hɔp], s. Bot: Hopfen m.

hop², I. s. Hüpfer m. II. v.i. hüpfen. ◆'hopping, adj. F: h. mad, wütend.

hope [həup]. I. v.tr. & i. hoffen; to h. for sth., auf etwas acc hoffen. II. s. Hoffnung f; (prospect) Aussicht f. ◆'hopeful, adj. hoffnungsvoll; -ly, adv. hoffentlich. ◆'hopeless, adj. hoffnungslos; (of situation) aussichtslos. ◆'hopelessness, s. Hoffnungslosigkeit f.

horde [hɔːd], s. Horde f.

horizon [hə'raiz(ə)n], s. Horizont m.

horizontal [hɔri'zɔnt(ə)l], adj. horizontal.

hormone ['hɔːməun], s. Hormon n.

horn [hɔːn], s. 1. (of animal) Horn n. 2. Mus: (French) h., Horn n. 3. Aut: Hupe f.

hornet ['hɔːnit], s. Hornisse f.

horoscope ['hɔrəskəup], s. Horoskop n.

horrible ['hɔribl], adj. schrecklich.

horrid ['hɔrid], adj. scheußlich.

horrify ['hɔrifai], v.tr. entsetzen. ◆ho'rrific, adj. gruselig. ◆horror ['hɔrər], s. Entsetzen n; h. story, Schauergeschichte f; h. film, Horrorfilm m.

horse [hɔːs], s. Pferd n; h. racing, Pferderennen n. ◆'horseback, s. on h., zu Pferde. ◆'horseman, s. Reiter m. ◆'horsewoman, s. Reiterin f. ◆'horseplay, s. Herumalbern n. ◆'horsepower, s. Pferdestärke f (abbr. PS). ◆'horseradish, s. Meerrettich m. ◆'horseshoe, s. Hufeisen n.

horticulture ['hɔːtikʌltʃər], s. Gartenbau m.

hose [həuz]. I. s. Schlauch m. II. v.tr. (den Garten usw.) spritzen. ◆'hosiery, s. Strumpfwaren pl.

hospitable [hɔs'pitəbl], adj. gastfreundlich. ◆hospi'tality, s. Gastfreundschaft f.

hospital ['hɔspitl], s. Krankenhaus n.

host¹ [həust], s. Gastgeber m. ◆'hostess, s. Gastgeberin f; air h., Stewardeß f.

host², s. Ecc: Hostie f.

hostage ['hɔstidʒ], s. Geisel f.

**hostel** ['hɔstəl], s. (a) (for students etc) Heim n; (b) **youth h.**, Jugendherberge f.

**hostile** ['hɔstail], adj. feindselig (**to**, gegen + acc). ◆**hos'tility**, s. 1. (a) (enmity) Feindschaft f (**to**, gegen); (b) (animosity) Feindseligkeit f. 2. pl. Mil: Feindseligkeiten fpl.

**hot** [hɔt]. I. adj. 1. (a) heiß; (of water, meal etc.) warm; **I am h.**, mir ist heiß; (b) Cu: (of curry etc.) scharf. 2. **to be h. on discipline**, auf Disziplin scharf sein; **he's not very h. on geography**, Geographie ist nicht seine Stärke. II. v.tr. **to h. sth. up**, etwas erhitzen. ◆**'hot-'tempered**, adj. (of pers.) hitzig, jähzornig. ◆**'hot-'water 'bottle**, s. Wärmflasche f.

**hotel** [həu'tel], s. Hotel n.

**hound** [haund]. I. s. Jagdhund m. II. v.tr. jagen.

**hour** ['auər], s. Stunde f, F: **to take hours over sth.**, eine Ewigkeit für etwas acc brauchen; **office hours**, Dienststunden fpl; Bürozeit f; **after (working) hours**, nach Dienstschluß m; **in the small hours**, in den frühen Morgenstunden. ◆**'hourly**. I. adj. stündlich. II. adv. stündlich, jede Stunde.

**house**, pl. **-ses** [haus, 'hauziz]. I. s. 1. (a) Haus n; **at/in my h.**, bei mir; **to my h.**, zu mir; **to move h.**, umziehen; **h. plant**, Zimmerpflanze f; (b) **a drink on the h.**, ein Glas auf Kosten des Hauses. 2. Th: **h. full**, ausverkauft. II. v.tr. [hauz] unterbringen. ◆**'houseboat**, s. Hausboot n. ◆**'housecoat**, s. Morgenrock m. ◆**'household**, s. Haushalt m. ◆**'house-hunting**, s. Haussuche f. ◆**'housekeeper**, s. Haushälterin f. ◆**'housekeeping**, s. **h. money/F: h.**, Haushaltsgeld n. ◆**'house-warming**, s. **h.-w. party**, Einzugsfeier f. ◆**'housewife**, pl. **-wives**, s. Hausfrau f. ◆**'housework**, s. Hausarbeit f. ◆**'housing** ['hauziŋ], s. 1. coll. Wohnungen fpl; Häuserbestand m (einer Stadt); **h. estate**, Wohnsiedlung f; **the h. problem**, das Wohnungsproblem. 2. Tchn: Gehäuse n.

**hovel** ['hɔvl], s. Schuppen m.

**hover** ['hɔvər], v.i. (a) (of hawk etc.) rütteln; (b) (of pers.) zögernd herumstehen. ◆**'hovercraft**, s. Luftkissenfahrzeug n.

**how** [hau], adv. 1. wie; **h. are you?** wie geht es Ihnen? **h. do you do?** sehr erfreut; (Sie kennenzulernen); **h. about a drink?** wie wär's mit einem Drink? 2. (a) **h. much**, wieviel; **h. many**, wie viele; (b) **h. I wish I could!** wenn ich doch nur könnte!

**however** [hau'evər]. I. adv. wie ... auch; **h. good his work is**, wie gut seine Arbeit auch ist. II. conj. (je)doch.

**howl** [haul]. I. v.i. heulen. II. s. Heulen n. ◆**'howler**, s. F: Schnitzer m.

**hub** [hʌb], s. 1. Nabe f. 2. Fig: Mittelpunkt m. ◆**'hub-cap**, s. Radkappe f.

**hubbub** ['hʌbʌb], s. Tumult m.

**huddle** ['hʌdl]. I. v.i. **to h. (together)**, sich zusammendrängen; **to be huddled together**, dicht zusammengedrängt sein. II. s. Häufchen n.

**huff** [hʌf], s. F: **to be in a h.**, die gekränkte Leberwurst spielen.

**hug** [hʌg]. I. v.tr. umarmen. II. s. Umarmung f.

**huge** [hju:dʒ], adj. riesig; **-ly**, adv. **h. enjoyable**, höchst unterhaltsam.

**hull** [hʌl], s. Rumpf m.

**hum** [hʌm], v.tr. & i. summen.

**human** ['hju:mən], adj. menschlich; **h. (being)**, Mensch m; **-ly**, adv. **everything h. possible**, alles menschenmögliche. ◆**humane** [hju:'mein], adj. (a) (of methods etc.) human; (b) (of pers.) menschlich. ◆**humanity** [-'mæniti], s. 1. (quality) Menschlichkeit f. 2. (mankind) die Menschheit. 3. pl. Sch: Geisteswissenschaften fpl.

**humble** ['hʌmbl]. I. adj. (a) demütig; (b) (of circumstances, house etc.) bescheiden. II. v.tr. (j-n) demütigen.

**humdrum** ['hʌmdrʌm], adj. eintönig.

**humid** ['hju:mid], adj. feucht. ◆**hu'midity**, s. Feuchtigkeit f, esp. (atmospheric) h., Luftfeuchtigkeit f.

**humiliate** [hju:(')milieit], v.tr. (j-n) erniedrigen. ◆**humili'ation**, s. Erniedrigung f. ◆**hu'mility**, s. Demut f.

**humour** ['hju:mər]. I. s. 1. Humor m; **to have a sense of h.**, Humor haben. 2. (state of mind) Laune f; **to be in a good/bad h.**, guter/schlechter Laune sein. II. v.tr. **to h. s.o.**, j-m seinen Willen lassen. ◆**'humorist**, s. Humorist m. ◆**'humorous**, adj. (of pers.) humorvoll; (of writer) humoristisch.

**hump** [hʌmp], s. Buckel m; (of camel) Höcker m.

**hunch** [hʌn(t)ʃ], s. F: **I have a h. that ...**, ich habe so eine Ahnung, daß ... ◆**'hunchback**, s. (pers.) Bucklige(r) f(m).

**hundred** ['hʌndrəd]. I. num. adj. hundert. II. s. 1. (unit) Hundert n; **hundreds of people**, Hunderte von Menschen. ◆**'hundredth**. I. adj. hundertste(r, s). II. s. (fraction) Hundertstel n. ◆**'hundredweight**, s. Zentner m.

**Hungarian** [hʌŋ'gɛəriən]. I. s. 1. Ungar(in) m(f). 2. Ungarisch n. II. adj. ungarisch. ◆**Hungary** ['hʌŋgəri]. Pr. n. Ungarn m.

**hunger** ['hʌŋgər], s. Hunger m; **h. strike**, Hungerstreik m. ◆**'hungry**, adj. hungrig.

**hunt** [hʌnt]. I. s. Jagd f; (by police) Fahndung f (for, nach + dat). II. v.tr. & i. (a) jagen; (b) **to h. for sth.**, etwas eifrig suchen; **to h. a criminal**, nach einem Verbrecher fahnden. ◆**'hunter**, s. Jäger m. ◆**'hunt 'down**, v.tr. (a) (ein Tier) hetzen; (b) (einen Verbrecher) zur Strecke bringen. ◆**'hunting**, s. Jagd f.

**hurdle** ['hə:dl], *s.* (a) *Sp:* Hürde *f;* **100 metres hurdles**, 100-Meter-Hürdenlauf *m;* (b) (*obstacle*) Hindernis *n.*
**hurl** [hə:l], *v.tr.* (etwas) schleudern (**at s.o., sth.**, gegen j-n, etwas *acc.*).
**hurrah** [hu'rɑ:], **hurray** [hu'rei], *int.* hurra!
**hurricane** ['hʌrikən], *s.* Orkan *m.*
**hurry** ['hʌri]. **I.** *v.* **1.** *v.tr.* (j-n) antreiben; (etwas) beschleunigen. **2.** *v.i.* (a) sich beeilen; **h. up!** beeile dich! (b) **to h. somewhere**, irgendwohin eilen. **II.** *s.* Eile *f;* **to be in a h.**, es eilig haben. ◆'**hurried**, *adj.* eilig; (*superficial*) flüchtig.
**hurt** [hə:t], *v.irr.* **1.** *v.tr.* (a) (*bodily*) (j-n, sich) verletzen; **to get h.**, verletzt werden; (b) (*feelings*) (j-n) kränken; **to h. s.o.'s feelings**, j-s Gefühle verletzen. **2.** *v.i.* schmerzen; **does it h.?** tut es weh? **my foot hurts** mir tut der Fuß weh. ◆'**hurtful**, *adj.* verletzend.
**husband** ['hʌzbənd], *s.* Ehemann *m;* **my h.**, mein Mann.
**hush** [hʌʃ]. **I.** *s.* Schweigen *n.* **II.** *int.* still! ◆'**hush-'hush**, *adj. F:* streng geheim. ◆'**hush 'up**, *v.tr.* vertuschen.
**husk** [hʌsk], *s.* Hülse *f;* Spelze *f* (von Getreide).
**husky**[1] ['hʌski], *adj.* heiser.
**husky**[2], *s.* (*dog*) Eskimohund *m.*
**hut** [hʌt], *s.* Hütte *f.*
**hutch** [hʌtʃ], *s.* (rabbit-)h., Kaninchenstall *m.*
**hyacinth** ['haiəsinθ], *s.* Hyazinthe *f.*
**hybrid** ['haibrid], *s.* **1.** *Biol:* Hybride *f.* **2.**

(*thing*) Mischling *m.*
**hydrant** ['haidrənt], *s.* Hydrant *m.*
**hydraulic** [hai'drɔ:lik], *adj.* hydraulisch.
**hydroelectric** ['haidrəui'lektrik], *adj.* hydroelektrisch.
**hydrofoil** ['haidrəufɔil], *s.* Tragflächenboot *n.*
**hydrogen** ['haidrədʒ(ə)n], *s.* Wasserstoff *m.*
**hyena** [hai'i:nə], *s.* Hyäne *f.*
**hygiene** ['haidʒi:n], *s.* Hygiene *f.* ◆**hy'gienic**, *adj.* hygienisch.
**hymn** [him], *s.* Kirchenlied *n;* **h.-book**, Gesangbuch *n.*
**hyper-** ['haipə], *prefix* über-; **hypercritical**, *adj.* überkritisch; **hypersensitive**, *adj.* überempfindlich.
**hyphen** ['haif(ə)n], *s.* Bindestrich *m.*
**hypnosis** [hip'nəusis], *s.* Hypnose *f.* ◆'**hypnotism** [-nətizm], *s.* Hypnotismus *m.* ◆'**hypnotize** [-nətaiz], *v.tr.* hypnotisieren.
**hypochondriac** [haipəu'kɔndriæk], *s.* Hypochonder *m.*
**hypocrisy** [hi'pɔkrisi], *s.* Heuchelei *f.* ◆'**hypocrite** [-əkrit], *s.* Heuchler *m.* ◆**hypo'critical**, *adj.* heuchlerisch.
**hypothesis**, *pl.* **-ses** [hai'pɔθisis, -si:z], *s.* Hypothese *f.* ◆**hypothetical** [haipə'θetikl], *adj.* theoretisch.
**hysteria** [his'tiəriə], *s.* Hysterie *f.* ◆**hysterical** [-'terikl], *adj* hysterisch. ◆**hys'terics**, *s.pl.* hysterischer Anfall *m; F:* (*laughter*) **we were in h.**, wir haben uns gerollt vor Lachen.

# I

**I**[1], **i** [ai], *s.* (der Buchstabe) I, i *n.*
**I**[2], *pers.pron. ich.*
**ice** [ais]. **I.** *s.* Eis *n;* **i. hockey**, Eishockey *n;* **i. rink**, Eisbahn *f;* **i. skating**, Schlittschuhlaufen *n.* **II.** *v.* **1.** *v.tr.* **to i. a cake**, einen Kuchen mit Zuckerguß überziehen. **2.** *v.i.* (*of window etc.*) **to i. up**, vereisen. ◆'**iceberg**, *s.* Eisberg *m.* ◆'**icebox**, *s. N.Am:* Kühlschrank *m.* ◆'**ice-'cream**, *s.* Eis *m.* ◆'**ice-cube**, *s.* Eiswürfel *m.* ◆'**icicle**, *s.* Eiszapfen *m.* ◆'**icing**, *s. Cu:* Zuckerguß *m.* ◆'**icy**, *adj.* eiskalt; (*of wind, welcome etc.*) eisig; **i. road**, vereiste Straße.
**Iceland** ['aislənd]. *Pr.n.* Island *n.*
**icon** ['aikɔn], *s.* Ikone *f.*
**idea** [ai'diə]. **1.** Idee *f.* **2.** (*concept*) Vorstellung *f;* **he hasn't the faintest i.**, er hat keine blasse Ahnung. **3.** (*intention*) Absicht *f.*
**ideal** [ai'di:əl]. **I.** *adj.* ideal. **II.** *s.* Ideal *n; -ly, adv.* ideal. ◆**i'dealist**, *s.* Idealist(in) *m(f).* ◆**i'dealize**, *v.tr.* idealisieren.
**identical** [ai'dentik(ə)l], *adj.* identisch (**with/to**, mit + *dat*). ◆**identifi'cation**,

*s.* Identifizierung *f.* ◆**i'dentify**, *v.* **1.** *v.tr.* (a) identifizieren; (b) **to i. oneself**, sich ausweisen. **2.** *v.i.* (*of pers.*) **to i. with s.o., sth.**, sich mit j-m, etwas *dat* identifizieren. ◆**i'dentity**, *s.* Identität *f;* **i. card**, Personalausweis *m;* **mistaken i.**, Personenverwechslung *f.*
**ideology** [aidi'ɔlədʒi], *s.* Ideologie *f.* ◆**ideo'logical**, *adj.* ideologisch.
**idiom** ['idiəm], *s.* Redewendung *f.* ◆**idio'matic**, *adj.* idiomatisch.
**idiosyncrasy** [idiəu'siŋkrəsi], *s.* persönliche Eigenart *f.*
**idiot** ['idiət], *s.* Idiot *m.* ◆**idiotic** [-'ɔtik], *adj.* idiotisch.
**idle** ['aidl]. **I.** *adj.* **1.** (a) (*of pers.*) untätig; (*of worker*) **to be i.**, nicht arbeiten; (b) (*of machines etc.*) **standing i.**, außer Betrieb. **2.** (*lazy*) faul. **3.** **i. threats**, leere Drohungen. **II.** *v.i.* (a) (*of pers.*) faulenzen; (b) (*of engine*) leer laufen. ◆'**idly**, *adv.* **to stand i. by**, untätig dastehen.
**idol** ['aidl], *s.* Idol *n.* ◆'**idolize**, *v.tr.* (j-n) vergöttern.
**idyll** ['idil], *s.* Idylle *f.* ◆**i'dyllic**, *adj.* idyllisch.

**if** [if]. **I.** *conj.* **1.** wenn; **if not,** wenn nicht; **you'll only get five pence for it, if that,** dafür bekommst du höchstens fünf Pence; **if only I had known!** wenn ich das bloß gewußt hätte! **as if,** als ob. **2.** (=*whether*) ob. **II.** *s.* **with no ifs and buts,** ohne Wenn und Aber.

**igloo** ['iglu:], *s.* Iglu *m & n.*

**ignite** [ig'nait], *v.* **1.** *v.tr.* (etwas) entzünden. **2.** *v.i.* sich entzünden; (*catch fire*) Feuer fangen. ◆**ignition** [-'niʃən], *s.* Zündung *f*; **i. key,** Zündschlüssel *m.*

**ignorance** ['ignərəns], *s.* Unkenntnis *f* (of sth., + *gen*); Unwissenheit *f* (**on/about sth.,** über etwas *acc*). ◆**'ignorant,** *adj.* unwissend. ◆**ignore** [ig'nɔːr], *v.tr.* ignorieren.

**ill** [il]. **I.** *adj.* krank; **i. health,** schlechte Gesundheit; **i. effects,** schädliche Auswirkungen; **of i. repute,** von üblem Ruf. **II.** *s.* Übel *n.* **III.** *adv.* schlecht; **he is i. at ease,** er fühlt sich unbehaglich. ◆**ill-ad'vised,** *adj.* (*of action*) nicht ratsam; (*foolish*) unklug. ◆**'ill-'fated,** *adj.* unglückselig; (*of attempt*) mißglückt. ◆**ill-'feeling,** *s.* Feindseligkeit *f*. ◆**'ill-'gotten,** *adj.* **i.-g. gains,** unredlich erworbenes Geld. ◆**'illness,** *s.* Krankheit *f.* ◆**'ill-'timed,** *adj.* ungelegen. ◆**ill-'treat,** *v.tr.* schlecht behandeln, (*maltreat*) mißhandeln. ◆**'ill-'treatment,** *s.* schlechte Behandlung; Mißhandlung *f.* ◆**'ill-'will,** *s.* böses Blut *n.*

**illegal** [i'li:g(ə)l], *adj.* illegal.

**illegible** [i'ledʒibl], *adj.* unleserlich.

**illegitimate** [ili'dʒitimit], *adj.* (*of child*) unehelich.

**illicit** [i'lisit], *adj.* (gesetzlich) unerlaubt.

**illiteracy** [i'lit(ə)rəsi], *s.* Analphabetentum *n.* ◆**i'lliterate,** *adj.* des Lesens und Schreibens unkundig.

**illogical** [i'lɔdʒik(ə)l], *adj.* unlogisch.

**illuminate** [i'l(j)u:mineit], *v.tr.* beleuchten. ◆**il'luminating,** *adj.* (*of talk etc.*) aufschlußreich. ◆**illumi'nation,** *s.* Beleuchtung *f*; *pl.* festliche Beleuchtung *f.*

**illusion** [i'lu:ʒ(ə)n], *s.* Illusion *f.* ◆**i'llusionist,** *s.* Zauberer *m.* ◆**i'llusory,** *adj.* trügerisch.

**illustrate** ['iləstreit], *v.tr.* (*a*) (eine Lehre usw.) veranschaulichen; (*b*) (Bücher usw.) illustrieren. ◆**illus'tration,** *s.* **1.** (erklärendes) Beispiel *n.* **2.** Illustration *f.*

**image** ['imidʒ], *s.* **1.** Bild *n*; (*of saints etc.*) Bildnis *n.* **2.** *Fig:* **to improve one's i.,** sein Image aufpolieren.

**imagine** [i'mædʒin], *v.tr.* (*a*) (*sth. possible*) sich *dat* (j-n, etwas) vorstellen; (*b*) (*sth. untrue*) sich *dat* (etwas) einbilden. ◆**i'maginary,** *adj.* imaginär. ◆**imagi'nation,** *s.* Phantasie *f.* ◆**i'maginative,** *adj.* phantasievoll; (*of work etc.*) einfallsreich.

**imbecile** ['imbəsi:l], *s.* Schwachsinnige(r) *f(m).*

**imitate** ['imiteit], *v.tr* nachahmen.

◆**imi'tation,** *s.* Nachahmung *f*; **i. jewellery,** falscher Schmuck.

**immaculate** [i'mækjulit], *adj.* makellos, (*perfect*) tadellos.

**immaterial** [imə'tiəriəl], *adj.* unwichtig.

**immature** [imə'tjuər], *adj.* unreif.

**immediate** [i'mi:djət], *adj.* **1.** unmittelbar. **2.** (*at once*) unverzüglich; **-ly. I.** *adv.* (*a*) (*place etc.*) unmittelbar; (*b*) (*time*) sofort. **II.** *conj.* **i. he received the money,** sobald er das Geld bekam.

**immense** [i'mens], *adj.* enorm; ungeheuer; **-ly,** *adv.* **to enjoy oneself i.,** sich prächtig unterhalten.

**immerse** [i'mɔːs], *v.tr.* (j-n, etwas) untertauchen, (*dip*) eintauchen. ◆**i'mmersion,** *s.* **i. heater,** Wasserboiler *m.*

**immigrate** ['imigreit], *v.i.* einwandern. ◆**'immigrant. I.** *adj.* eingewandert. **II.** *s.* Einwanderer *m*; Immigrant(in) *m(f).* ◆**immi'gration,** *s.* Einwanderung *f.*

**imminent** ['iminənt], *adj.* unmittelbar bevorstehend.

**immobile** [i'məubail], *adj.* unbeweglich. ◆**i'mmobilize,** *v.tr.* bewegungsunfähig machen; (den Verkehr) lahmlegen.

**immodest** [i'mɔdist], *adj.* unbescheiden.

**immoral** [i'mɔrəl], *adj.* unmoralisch. ◆**immo'rality,** *s.* Unmoral *f.*

**immortal** [i'mɔːtl], *adj.* unsterblich. ◆**immor'tality,** *s.* Unsterblichkeit *f.* ◆**i'mmortalize,** *v.tr.* unsterblich machen.

**immune** [i'mju:n], *adj.* immun (**to,** gegen + *acc*); *Fig:* gefeit (**to,** gegen + *acc*). ◆**i'mmunity,** *s.* Immunität *f.* ◆**immuni'zation,** *s.* Immunisierung *f.* ◆**'immunize,** *v.tr.* (j-n) immunisieren.

**impact** ['impækt], *s.* **1.** Aufprall *m* (**against/on sth.,** auf etwas *acc*); (*of two moving objects*) Zusammenprall *m.* **2.** Wucht *f* (einer Explosion usw.). **3.** *Fig:* Wirkung *f* (**on s.o.,** auf j-n).

**impair** [im'pɛər], *v.tr.* (etwas *dat*) schaden; (Beziehungen) verschlechtern.

**impartial** [im'pɑːʃ(ə)l], *adj.* unparteiisch.

**impatient** [im'peiʃənt], *adj.* ungeduldig. ◆**im'patience,** *s.* Ungeduld *f.*

**impeccable** [im'pekəbl], *adj.* tadellos.

**impede** [im'pi:d], *v.tr.* (j-n) hindern; (*prevent*) (j-n, etwas) behindern. ◆**impediment** [im'pedimənt], *s.* (**speech**) **i.,** Sprachfehler *m.*

**impending** [im'pendiŋ], *adj.* (nahe) bevorstehend.

**impenetrable** [im'penitrəbl], *adj.* undurchdringlich.

**imperative** [im'perətiv]. **I.** *adj.* unerläßlich. **II.** *s. Gram:* Imperativ *m.*

**imperceptible** [impə'septəbl], *adj.* nicht wahrnehmbar.

**imperfect** [im'pə:fikt]. **I.** *adj.* fehlerhaft. **II.** *s. Gram:* Imperfekt *n.* ◆**imper'fection,** *s.* Fehler *m.*

**imperial** [im'piəriəl], *adj.* kaiserlich. ◆**im'perialism,** *s.* Imperialismus *m.*

**imperious** [im'piəriəs], *adj.* anmaßend.

**impersonal** [im'pə:sənəl], *adj.* unpersönlich.

**impersonate** [im'pə:səneit], *v.tr.* **to i. s.o.**, sich für j-n ausgeben; *Th:* j-n imitieren. ◆**imperso'nation**, *s.* Nachahmung *f.* ◆**im'personator**, *s.* Imitator *m.*

**impertinence** [im'pə:tinəns], *s.* Unverschämtheit *f.* ◆**im'pertinent**, *adj.* unverschämt.

**impervious** [im'pə:viəs], *adj.* **1.** (*of materials etc.*) undurchlässig. **2.** *Fig:* (*of pers.*) **i. to criticism**, keiner Kritik zugänglich.

**impetuous** [im'petjuəs], *adj.* (*of pers.*) ungestüm; (*of action*) unbesonnen.

**impetus** ['impitəs], *s.* Auftrieb *m.*

**impinge** [im'pindʒ], *v.i.* einwirken (**on/ upon**, auf + *acc*).

**implant** [im'plɑ:nt], *v.tr.* einpflanzen.

**implement¹** ['implimənt], *s.* Gerät *n;* (*tool*) Werkzeug *n.*

**implement²** [im'pliment], *v.tr.* (einen Plan usw.) ausführen; (einen Vertrag) erfüllen.

**implicate** ['implikeit], *v.tr.* (j-n) verwickeln (**in sth.**, in etwas *acc*). ◆**impli'cation**, *s.* Implikation *f.*

**implicit** [im'plisit], *adj.* **1.** inbegriffen (**in sth.**, in etwas *dat*); (*unexpressed*) unausgesprochen. **2. i. faith**, blinder Glaube. **-ly**, *adv.* **to obey (s.o.) i.**, (j-m) bedingungslos gehorchen.

**implore** [im'plɔ:r], *v.tr.* anflehen.

**imply** [im'plai], *v.tr.* (*a*) (*assume*) voraussetzen; (*b*) (*indicate*) andeuten.

**impolite** [impə'lait], *adj.* unhöflich.

**import** I. *s.* [im'pɔ:t]. Einfuhr *f,* Import *m;* (*article*) Einfuhrartikel *m.* II. *v.tr.* [im'pɔ:t]. einführen, importieren. ◆**im'porter**, *s.* Importeur *m.*

**importance** [im'pɔ:t(ə)ns], *s.* Wichtigkeit *f;* (*significance*) Bedeutung *f.* ◆**im'portant**, *adj.* wichtig; (*significant*) bedeutend.

**impose** [im'pəuz], *v.* **1.** *v.tr.* (eine Steuer, Bedingungen usw.) auferlegen; (eine Geldstrafe) verhängen. **2.** *v.i.* **to i. on s.o.**, sich j-m aufdrängen. ◆**im'posing**, *adj.* eindrucksvoll. ◆**impo'sition**, *s.* (*a*) Auferlegung *f;* Verhängung *f;* (*b*) **it's an i.**, es ist eine Zumutung.

**impossible** [im'pɔsəbl], *adj.* unmöglich. ◆**impossi'bility**, *s.* Unmöglichkeit *f.*

**impostor** [im'pɔstər], *s.* Hochstapler *m.*

**impotence** ['impət(ə)ns], *s.* (*a*) Unfähigkeit *f;* (*b*) *Med:* Impotenz *f.* ◆**'impotent**, *adj.* (*a*) unfähig; (*b*) *Med:* impotent.

**impoverished** [im'pɔv(ə)riʃt], *adj.* verarmt.

**impracticable** [im'præktikəbl], *adj.* (*a*) (*of plan etc.*) undurchführbar; (*b*) (*of design*) unpraktisch.

**impress** [im'pres], *v.tr.* (j-n) beeindrucken; **to i. sth. upon s.o.**, j-m etwas

einschärfen. ◆**im'pression**, *s.* · **1.** Eindruck *m.* **2.** Abdruck *m* (eines Siegels usw.). ◆**im'pressionable**, *adj.* leicht beeinflußbar. ◆**im'pressionist**, *s.* Impressionist(in) *m(f).* ◆**im'pressive**, *adj.* eindrucksvoll.

**imprison** [im'prizn], *v.tr.* (j-n) ins Gefängnis bringen. ◆**im'prisonment**, *s.* Haft *f.*

**improbable** [im'prɔbəbl], *adj.* unwahrscheinlich.

**impromptu** [im'prɔm(p)tju:]. I. *adj.* **i. speech**, Stegreifrede *f.* II. *adv.* aus dem Stegreif.

**improper** [im'prɔpər], *adj.* **1.** (*wrong*) falsch. **2.** (*unseemly*) ungehörig; (*unfitting*) unpassend; **-ly**, *adv.* **1. a word i. used**, ein falsch gebrauchtes Wort. **2. to behave i.**, sich ungehörig benehmen.

**improve** [im'pru:v], *v.* **1.** *v.tr.* verbessern. **2.** *v.i.* (*of pers.*) sich bessern; **to i. (up)on sth.**, (etwas) übertreffen. ◆**im'provement**, *s.* Verbesserung *f;* (*in health*) Besserung *f.*

**improvise** ['imprəvaiz], *v.tr.* improvisieren. ◆**improvi'sation**, *s.* Improvisation *f.*

**imprudent** [im'pru:dənt], *adj.* unklug. ◆**im'prudence**, *s.* Unklugheit *f.*

**impudent** ['impjudənt], *adj.* unverschämt. ◆**'impudence**, *s.* Unverschämtheit *f.*

**impulse** ['impʌls], *s.* Impuls *m.* ◆**im'pulsive**, *adj.* impulsiv.

**impunity** [im'pju:niti], *s.* Straffreiheit *f;* **with i.**, ungestraft.

**impure** [im'pjuər], *adj.* **1.** (*of air etc.*) unrein. **2.** (*of thoughts etc.*) unsittlich. ◆**im'purity**, *s.* Unreinheit *f;* **impurities**, Verunreinigungen *fpl* (im Blut usw.).

**in** [in]. I. *prep.* **1.** (*of place*) (*a*) (*position*) in + *dat;* (*b*) (*into*) in + *acc.* **2.** (*of time*) **in the evening**, am Abend; (*every evening*) abends; **in August**, im August; (*since*) **not in 6 years** seit 6 Jahren nicht mehr; **to do sth. in three hours**, etwas in drei Stunden erledigen. **3.** (*manner*) **in this way**, auf diese Weise; **in English**, auf Englisch. **4.** (*while*) bei + *dat;* **in coming downstairs he tripped and fell**, beim Herunterkommen stolperte er und fiel. II. *adv.* **1.** zu Hause. **2. to be (well) in with s.o.**, mit j-m auf gutem Fuße stehen. **3.** *F:* **he is in for it!** der kann sich auf etwas gefaßt machen! **4.** (*a*) **day in, day out**, tagein, tagaus; (*b*) **all in**, alles zusammen. III. *s.* **he knows the ins and outs (of the matter)**, er ist mit allen Feinheiten (der Sache) vertraut.

**inability** [inə'biliti], *s.* Unfähigkeit *f.*

**inaccessible** [inæk'sesəbl], *adj.* (*of place, pers.*) unzugänglich.

**inaccurate** [in'ækjurit], *adj.* ungenau.

**inactive** [in'æktiv], *adj.* untätig. ◆**inac'tivity**, *s.* Untätigkeit *f.*

**inadequate** [in'ædikwit], *adj.* unzulänglich; (*of number, quantity*) ungenügend; **to**

**feel i.**, sich der Situation nicht gewachsen fühlen.

**inadmissible** [inəd'misəbl], *adj.* unzulässig.

**inadvertent** [inəd'vəːt(ə)nt], *adj.* unbeabsichtigt.

**inadvisable** [inəd'vaizəbl], *adj.* nicht ratsam.

**inane** [i'nein], *adj.* albern.

**inanimate** [in'ænimit], *adj.* leblos.

**inappropriate** [inə'prəupriit], *adj.* unpassend.

**inarticulate** [inɑː'tikjulit], *adj. (of speech)* undeutlich; *(of pers.)* **to be i.**, sich nicht ausdrücken können.

**inattentive** [inə'tentiv], *adj.* unaufmerksam.

**inaudible** [in'ɔːdəbl], *adj.* unhörbar.

**inaugurate** [i'nɔːgjureit], *v.tr. (a)* (eine Veranstaltung) eröffnen; (ein Gebäude usw.) einweihen; *(b)* (einen Präsidenten) ins Amt einsetzen. ◆**i'naugural**, *adj.* Eröffnungs-.

**incalculable** [in'kælkjuləbl], *adj.* unermeßlich.

**incapable** [in'keipəbl], *adj.* unfähig, *(of, + gen).* ◆**incapa'bility**, *s.* Unfähigkeit *f.*

**incapacitate** [inkə'pæsiteit], *v.tr.* (j-n) untauglich machen, *(for work)* arbeitsunfähig machen.

**incendiary** [in'sendjəri], *s.* **i. (bomb)**, Brandbombe *f.*

**incense¹** ['insens], *s.* Weihrauch *m.*

**incense²** [in'sens], *v.tr.* (j-n) in Wut bringen. ◆**in'censed**, *adj.* wütend.

**incentive** [in'sentiv], *s.* Anreiz *m.*

**incessant** [in'sesnt], *adj.* unaufhörlich.

**incest** ['insest], *s.* Blutschande *f.*

**inch** [in(t)ʃ], *s.* Zoll *m* (2,54 cm); *Fig:* **not to give an i.**, keinen Fußbreit nachgeben.

**incidence** ['insidəns], *s.* Vorkommen *n* (einer Krankheit usw.).

**incident** ['insidənt], *s.* Zwischenfall *m.* ◆**inci'dental**, *adj.* beiläufig, Neben-; **-ly**, *adv.* übrigens.

**incinerator** [in'sinəreitər], *s.* Müllverbrennungsofen *m.*

**incipient** [in'sipiənt], *adj.* beginnend.

**incision** [in'siʒən], *s.* Einschnitt *m.*

**incisive** [in'saisiv], *adj. (of mind)* scharf; *(of remark)* scharfsinnig; *(of style)* prägnant.

**incite** [in'sait], *v.tr.* (j-n) aufhetzen (**to sth.**, zu etwas *dat*). ◆**in'citement**, *s.* Aufhetzung *f.*

**inclement** [in'klemənt], *adj. (of weather, climate)* unfreundlich.

**inclination** [inkli'neiʃən], *s.* Neigung *f.* ◆**incline** ['inklain], *s.* Hang *m.* ◆**in'clined**, *adj.* **1.** *(of pers.)* geneigt; **she's i.** to be lazy, sie neigt zur Faulheit. **2.** *(of thing)* schräg.

**include** [in'kluːd], *v.tr. (a)* (j-n, etwas) einschließen **(in,** in + *acc)*; (j-n) einbeziehen **(in a conversation,** in ein Gespräch); *(b)* **to i. s.o. in a team/a fact in a book,** j-n in eine Mannschaft/eine Tatsache in ein Buch aufnehmen. ◆**in'cluding,** *adj.* einschließlich; **i. VAT,** inklusive Mehrwertsteuer. ◆**in'clusion** [-ʒən], *s.* **1.** Einbeziehung *f.* **2.** Aufnahme *f* (in eine Mannschaft usw.). ◆**in'clusive** [-siv], *adj.* einschließlich **(of, +** *gen).*

**incognito** [inkɔg'niːtəu], *adv.* inkognito.

**incoherent** [inkəu'hiərənt], *adj. (of statement, talk etc.)* zusammenhanglos; *(of pers.)* **to be i.**, wirres Zeug reden.

**income** ['inkʌm], *s.* Einkommen *n*; **i. tax,** Einkommensteuer *f.*

**incoming** ['inkʌmiŋ], *adj.* **i. mail,** Posteingang *m*; *Tel:* **i. call,** Gespräch *n* von auswärts.

**incomparable** [in'kɔmp(ə)rəbl], *adj.* unvergleichlich.

**incompatible** [inkəm'pætibl], *adj. (of views, proposals etc.)* unvereinbar; *(of drugs, blood groups)* unverträglich; *(of people)* **they are i.**, sie passen nicht zueinander.

**incompetent** [in'kɔmpitənt], *adj. (of pers.)* unfähig; *(of worker)* untauglich. ◆**in'competence,** *s.* Unfähigkeit *f;* Untauglichkeit *f.*

**incomplete** [inkəm'pliːt], *adj.* unvollständig.

**incomprehensible** [inkɔmpri'hensibl], *adj.* unverständlich.

**inconceivable** [inkən'siːvəbl], *adj.* undenkbar.

**inconclusive** [inkən'kluːsiv], *adj. (of negotiations)* ergebnislos; *(of result, evidence)* nicht schlüssig.

**incongruous** [in'kɔŋgruəs], *adj.* unpassend.

**inconsiderate** [inkən'sid(ə)rit], *adj.* rücksichtslos.

**inconsistent** [inkən'sistənt], *adj. (a) (contradicting)* widersprüchlich; unvereinbar **(with the evidence,** mit den Beweisen); *(b) (of pers.)* unbeständig; *(illogical)* inkonsequent. ◆**incon'sistency,** *s. (a)* Unvereinbarkeit *f* **(with sth.,** mit etwas *dat*); *(b) (of pers.)* Unbeständigkeit *f.*

**inconspicuous** [inkən'spikjuəs], *adj.* unauffällig.

**inconvenience** [inkən'viːnjəns]. **I.** *s.* Unannehmlichkeit *f.* **II.** *v.tr.* (j-m) Umstände machen. ◆**incon'venient,** *adj.* ungünstig.

**incorporate** [in'kɔːpəreit], *v.tr. (a)* (einen Staat, ein Gebiet) einverleiben **(into, +** *dat);* *(b)* (einen Vorschlag usw.) aufnehmen **(in a plan,** in einen Plan).

**incorrect** [inkə'rekt], *adj.* falsch.

**incorrigible** [in'kɔridʒəbl], *adj.* unverbesserlich.

**increase. I.** *s.* ['inkriːs] Erhöhung *f* (von Preisen usw.); Zunahme *f* (der Bevölkerung usw.); Steigerung *f* (von Leistungen usw.); **to be on the i.**, zunehmen. **II.** *v.* [in'kriːs] **1.** *v.i. (a) (in size)* wachsen; *(of* *price etc.*) steigen; (*of population etc.*) zunehmen; **to i. in value,** im Wert steigen; (*b*) (*in number*) (*of difficulties etc.*) sich vermehren. **2.** *v.tr.* (Preise usw.) erhöhen; (die Leistung) steigern. ◆**in'creasingly,** *adv.* immer mehr; **it is becoming i.** difficult, es wird immer schwieriger.

**incredible** [in'kredibl], *adj.* unglaublich; **-ibly,** *adv.* **i. he was unharmed,** wie durch ein Wunder blieb er unverletzt; *F:* **i. hot,** unglaublich warm.

**incredulous** [in'kredjuləs], *adj.* ungläubig.

**increment** ['inkrimənt], *s.* Lohnerhöhung *f.*

**incriminate** [in'krimineit], *v.tr.* belasten. ◆**in'criminating,** *adj.* belastend.

**incubation** [inkju'beiʃən], *s.* Ausbrüten *n;* **i. period,** Inkubationszeit *f.* ◆**'incubator,** *s.* Brutkasten *m.*

**incur** [in'kə:r], *v.tr.* sich *dat* (j-s Unwillen usw.) zuziehen; **to i. debts,** Schulden machen.

**incurable** [in'kjuərəbl], *adj.* (*of disease*) unheilbar; **i. optimist,** unverbesserlicher Optimist.

**indebted** [in'detid], *adj.* (zu Dank) verpflichtet (**to s.o.,** j-m); **to be i. to s.o. for sth.,** j-m für etwas *acc* Dank schulden.

**indecent** [in'di:sənt], *adj.* anstößig; *Jur:* unzüchtig.

**indecision** [indi'siʒən], *s.* Unentschlossenheit *f.*

**indecisive** [indi'saisiv], *adj.* unentschlossen.

**indeed** [in'di:d], *adv.* (*a*) tatsächlich; (*b*) (*intensifying*) **I'm very glad i.,** ich bin wirklich sehr froh; (*c*) (*as comment*) **i.?** wirklich? **yes i.!** tatsächlich!

**indefinite** [in'definit], *adj.* unbestimmt.

**indent** [in'dent], *v.tr.* (eine Zeile usw.) einrücken.

**independence** [indi'pendəns], *s.* Unabhängigkeit *f.* ◆**inde'pendent,** *adj.* unabhängig (**of,** von + *dat*).

**indescribable** [indis'kraibəbl], *adj.* unbeschreiblich.

**indestructible** [indis'trʌktəbl], *adj.* unzerstörbar.

**indeterminate** [indi'tə:minit], *adj.* unbestimmt.

**index** ['indeks], *s. pl.* **-es** *& Mth: Tchn:* **indices** [-isi:z]. **1. i.** (**finger**) Zeigefinger *m.* **2.** (*in book*) Register *n.* **3.** (**card**) i., Kartei *f;* **i. card,** Karteikarte *f.* **4. cost of living** i., Lebenshaltungsindex *m.* ◆**'index-'linked,** *adj.* dem Lebenshaltungsindex angepaßt; **i.-l. pension,** dynamische Rente.

**India** ['indjə]. *Pr.n.* Indien *n.* ◆**'Indian. I.** *adj.* **1.** indisch. **2.** *N. & S.Am:* indianisch. **II.** *s.* **1.** Inder(in) *m(f).* **2.** *N. & S.Am:* Indianer(in) *m(f).*

**indicate** ['indikeit], *v.tr.* (*a*) (*show*) (etwas) zeigen; (*of instrument*) (einen Wert)

anzeigen; (*b*) (*point out*) (auf etwas *acc*) hinweisen. ◆**indi'cation,** *s.* **1.** (*sign*) Anzeichen *n; Med:* Indikation *f.* **2.** (*hint*) Hinweis *m.* ◆**in'dicative. I.** *adj.* **to be i. of sth.,** auf etwas *acc* hindeuten. **II.** *s. Gram:* Indikativ *m.* ◆**'indicator,** *s.* (*device*) Anzeiger *m; Aut:* Blinker *m.*

**indictment** [in'daitmənt], *s. Jur:* Anklage *f; Fig:* **i. of government policy,** Verurteilung der Regierungspolitik.

**Indies** ['indiz]. *Pr.n.* **the West I.,** die Antillen *fpl.*

**indifferent** [in'difr(ə)nt], *adj.* **1.** (*of pers.*) gleichgültig. **2.** (*of thing*) mittelmäßig. ◆**in'difference,** *s.* Gleichgültigkeit *f.*

**indigenous** [in'didʒinəs], *adj.* einheimisch.

**indigestion** [indi'dʒestʃ(ə)n], *s.* Verdauungsstörung *f.* ◆**indi'gestible,** *adj.* unverdaulich.

**indignant** [in'dignənt], *adj.* empört (**at,** über + *acc*). ◆**indig'nation,** *s.* Empörung *f.*

**indignity** [in'digniti], *s.* Demütigung *f.*

**indirect** [indi'rekt, indai-], *adj.* indirekt.

**indiscreet** [indis'kri:t], *adj.* (*of disclosure*) indiskret; (*of remark*) taktlos. ◆**indis'cretion,** *s.* Indiskretion *f;* Taktlosigkeit *f.*

**indiscriminate** [indis'kriminit], *adj.* wahllos.

**indispensable** [indis'pensəbl], *adj.* unentbehrlich.

**indisposed** [indis'pəuzd], *adj.* **to be i.,** sich nicht wohl fühlen.

**indistinct** [indis'tiŋkt], *adj.* undeutlich.

**indistinguishable** [indis'tiŋgwiʃəbl], *adj.* nicht zu unterscheiden.

**individual** [indi'vidjuəl]. **I.** *adj.* individuell; **i. case,** Einzelfall *m.* **II.** *s.* Individuum *n.* ◆**individu'ality,** *s.* Individualität *f.* ◆**indi'vidually,** *adv.* einzeln.

**indoctrinate** [in'dɔktrineit], *v.tr.* (j-n) indoktrinieren. ◆**indoctri'nation,** *s.* Indoktrination *f.*

**indolence** ['indələns], *s.* Faulheit *f.* ◆**'indolent,** *adj.* faul.

**Indonesia** [ində(u)'ni:zjə]. *Pr.n.* Indonesien *n.* ◆**Indo'nesian,** *adj.* indonesisch.

**indoor** ['indɔ:r], *adj.* (*a*) Innen-; **i. plant,** Zimmerpflanze *f;* (*b*) *Sp:* Hallen-; **i.** (**swimming**) **pool,** Hallenbad *n.* ◆**in'doors,** *adv.* (*a*) im Hause. (*b*) ins Haus; **to go i.,** ins Haus gehen.

**induce** [in'dju:s], *v.tr.* (*a*) (j-n) dazu bewegen (**to do sth.,** etwas zu tun); (*b*) *Med:* **to i. labour,** die Wehen einleiten. ◆**in'ducement,** *s.* Anreiz *m.*

**indulge** [in'dʌldʒ], *v.* **1.** *v.tr* (einer Neigung usw.) nachgeben; **to i. oneself,** sich verwöhnen. **2.** *v.i.* **to i. in sth.,** sich etwas *dat* hingeben. ◆**in'dulgence,** *s.* **i. in drink,** übermäßiges Trinken. ◆**in'dulgent,** *adj.* nachsichtig.

**industrial** [in'dʌstriəl], *adj.* industriell, Industrie-, Betriebs-; **i. dispute,** Arbeitskonflikt *m;* **i. estate,** Industriegelände *n.*

◆**in'dustrialist,** s. Industrieller m.
◆**in'dustrious,** adj. fleißig.
◆**industry** ['indəstri], s. **1.** (of pers.)
Fleiß m. **2.** Industrie f.
**ineffective** [ini'fektiv], **ineffectual**
[ini'fektju(ə)l], adj. unwirksam; (of pers.)
untauglich.
**inefficient** [ini'fiʃənt], adj. **1.** (of pers.)
untüchtig; nicht leistungsfähig. **2.** (of
firm, factory) unwirtschaftlich.
◆**ine'fficiency,** s. **1.** (of pers.) Untüch-
tigkeit f; mangelnde Leistungsfähigkeit f.
**2.** Com: Unwirtschaftlichkeit f.
**inept** [i'nept], adj. ungeschickt.
◆**i'neptitude,** s. Ungeschicktheit f.
**inequality** [ini:'kwɔliti], s. Ungleichheit f.
**inert** [i'nəːt], adj. (of pers.) reglos; Ph:
träge. ◆**inertia** [i'nəːʃ(i)ə], s. Trägheit
f.
**inescapable** [inis'keipəbl], adj. unent-
rinnbar; (of conclusion etc.) unvermeidlich.
**inevitable** [in'evitəbl], adj. unvermeidlich. ◆**inevita'bility,** s. Unvermeid-
lichkeit f.
**inexcusable** [iniks'kjuːzəbl], adj. unverzeihlich.
**inexorable** [in'eksərəbl], adj. unerbittlich.
**inexpensive** [iniks'pensiv] adj. preisgün-
stig.
**inexperienced** [iniks'piəriənst], adj.
unerfahren.
**inexplicable** [ineks'plikəbl], adj. unerklärlich.
**infallible** [in'fæləbl], adj. unfehlbar.
**infamous** ['infəməs], adj. berüchtigt.
**infant** ['infənt], s. (a) Kleinkind n; Baby
n; i. mortality, Säuglingssterblichkeit f;
(b) i. school, Anfängerstufe f der Grundschule. ◆**infancy** [-si], s. (a) frühe
Kindheit f; (b) Fig: Anfangsstadium n.
◆**infantile,** adj. kindisch.
**infantry** ['infəntri], s. Infanterie f.
**infatuated** [in'fætjueitid], adj. vernarrt
(with s.o., in j-n). ◆**infatu'ation,** s.
Vernarrtheit f; (blind) Betörung f.
**infect** [in'fekt], v.tr. (also Fig:) (j-n) anstecken; Med: (j-n, eine Wunde, ein Tier
usw.) infizieren. ◆**in'fection,** s. Infektion f. ◆**in'fectious,** adj. ansteckend.
**infer** [in'fəːr], v.tr. (conclude) (daraus)
schließen; (gather) entnehmen (from,
aus + dat). ◆**'inference** [-fərəns], s.
Folgerung f.
**inferior** [in'fiəriər], adj. **1.** i. to s.o. (in
rank etc.), j-m (im Rang usw.) untergeordnet. **2.** (a) (of thing) minderwertig;
(b) (of pers.) unterlegen. ◆**inferi'ority,**
s. Unterlegenheit f; i. complex, Minderwertigkeitskomplex m.
**infernal** [in'fəːnəl], adj. höllisch, Höllen-;
F: i. row, Höllenlärm m.
**inferno,** pl. -os [in'fəːnəu, -əuz], s. Inferno n.
**infested** [in'festid], adj. verseucht.
**infidelity** [infi'deliti], s. (eheliche) Un-

treue f.
**in-fighting** ['infaitiŋ], s. (interne) Quere-
len fpl.
**infiltrate** ['infiltreit], v.tr. (ein Land, eine
Partei) unterwandern. ◆**infil'tration,** s.
Unterwanderung f.
**infinite** ['infinit], adj. unendlich.
◆**infini'tesimal,** adj. unendlich klein.
◆**in'finitive,** s. Infinitiv m. ◆**in'finity,**
s. Unendlichkeit f.
**infirmary** [in'fəːməri], s. **1.** Krankenhaus
n. **2.** (room) Krankenzimmer n.
◆**in'firmity,** s. Gebrechlichkeit f.
**inflame** [in'fleim], v.tr. (eine Wunde
usw.) entzünden. ◆**in'flammable,** adj.
brennbar; (esp. as warning) feuergefähr-
lich. ◆**infla'mmation,** s. Entzündung
f. ◆**in'flammatory,** adj. (of speech etc.)
aufrührerisch.
**inflate** [in'fleit], v.tr. (einen Luftballon
usw.) aufblasen; (einen Gummireifen)
aufpumpen. ◆**in'flatable,** adj. aufblas-
bar. ◆**in'flated,** adj. aufgeblasen.
◆**in'flation,** s. Inflation f.
◆**in'flationary,** adj. inflationär.
**inflexible** [in'fleksəbl], adj. unnachgiebig.
**inflict** [in'flikt], v.tr. (eine Wunde, ein
Leid usw.) zufügen (on s.o., j-m).
**influence** ['influəns]. **I.** s. Einfluß m
(upon/over s.o., sth., auf j-n, etwas acc.)
**II.** v.tr. beeinflussen. ◆**influ'ential,**
adj. einflußreich.
**influenza** [influ'enzə], s. Grippe f.
**influx** ['inflʌks], s. Zustrom m (von Menschen); Zufuhr f (von Waren).
**inform** [in'fɔːm], v.tr. informieren; to i.
s.o. of sth., j-m etwas mitteilen.
◆**in'formant,** s. Informant m.
◆**information** [infə'meiʃ(ə)n], s. Information f; (piece of) i., Auskunft f; (several items) Informationen fpl.
◆**in'formative,** adj. aufschlußreich.
◆**in'formed,** adj. informiert.
◆**in'former,** s. police i., Polizeispitzel
m.
**informal** [in'fɔːməl], adj. zwanglos; (of
meeting, Sp: match) inoffiziell; -ally, adv.
informell. ◆**infor'mality,** s. Zwang-
losigkeit f.
**infra-red** ['infrə'red], adj. infrarot.
**infrastructure** ['infrəstrʌktʃər], s. Infra-
struktur f.
**infrequent** [in'friːkwənt], adj. selten.
**infringe** [in'frindʒ], v. **1.** v.tr. (gegen ein
Gesetz usw.) verstoßen; (ein Patent) verletzen. **2.** v.i. to i. on/upon s.o.'s rights,
in j-s Rechte eingreifen.
◆**in'fringement,** s. Verstoß m (of,
gegen + acc); i. (of the law) Gesetzes-
übertretung f.
**infuriate** [in'fjuərieit], v.tr. (j-n) wütend
machen. ◆**in'furiating,** adj. sehr ärgerlich.
**ingenious** [in'dʒiːnjəs], adj. (of pers.) einfallsreich; (of thing) raffiniert.
◆**inge'nuity** [-dʒi'njuːiti], s. Einfalls-
reichtum m; Raffiniertheit f.

**ingenuous** [in'dʒenjuəs], *adj.* naiv.

**ingot** [iŋgət], *s.* Barren *m.*

**ingratiate** [in'greiʃieit], *v.tr.* to i. oneself with s.o., sich bei j-m einschmeicheln.

**ingratitude** [in'grætitjuːd], *s.* Undankbarkeit *f.*

**ingredient** [in'griːdiənt], *s.* Bestandteil *m;* **ingredients of a cake,** Backzutaten *fpl;* *Fig:* **the ingredients of success,** die Voraussetzungen für den Erfolg.

**inhabit** [in'hæbit], *v.tr.* bewohnen. ◆**in'habitant,** *s.* Einwohner(in) *m(f).*

**inhale** [in'heil], *v.tr.* einatmen.

**inherent** [in'hiər(ə)nt], *adj.* innewohnend (**in,** + *dat*).

**inherit** [in'herit], *v.tr.* erben. ◆**in'heritance,** *s.* Erbe *n;* Erbschaft *f.*

**inhibit** [in'hibit], *v.tr.* hemmen; **inhibited,** (*of pers.*) gehemmt. ◆**inhi'bition,** *s.* Hemmung *f.*

**inhospitable** [inhɔs'pitəbl], *adj.* unwirtlich.

**inhuman** [in'hjuːmən], *adj.* unmenschlich.

**initial** [i'niʃəl]. **I.** *adj.* anfänglich, Anfangs-. **II.** *s.* (s.o.'s) **initials,** (j-s) Initialen *pl;* **-ally,** *adv.* am Anfang.

**initiate I.** [i'niʃieit], *v.tr.* (*a*) (etwas) beginnen; (*b*) to i. s.o. into a mystery, j-n in ein Geheimnis einweihen. **II.** [i'niʃiit], *s.* Eingeweihte(r) *f(m).* ◆**initi'ation,** Einführung *f,* *Fig:* Einweihung *f.* ◆**initiative** [i'niʃətiv], *s.* Initiative *f;* to **act on one's own i.,** aus eigener Initiative handeln; **to take the i.,** die Initiative ergreifen.

**inject** [in'dʒekt], *v.tr.* to i. s.o. with a drug, j-m ein Medikament injizieren. ◆**in'jection,** *s.* Injektion *f;* *Fig:* i. of capital, Kapitalspritze *f.*

**injunction** [in'dʒʌŋkʃən], *s.* einstweilige Verfügung *f.*

**injure** [in'dʒuər], *v.tr.* verletzen. ◆**'injured. I.** *adj.* verletzt. **II.** *s.* the i., die Verletzten *pl.* ◆**'injury,** *s.* Verletzung *f;* to **add insult to i.,** das Maß vollmachen.

**injustice** [in'dʒʌstis], *s.* Ungerechtigkeit *f;* **you do him an i.,** Sie tun ihm unrecht.

**ink** [iŋk], *s.* (*a*) (*for writing*) Tinte *f;* (*for drawing*) Tusche *f.* ◆**'inkwell,** *s.* Tintenfaß *n.*

**inkling** [iŋkliŋ], *s.* (leise) Ahnung *f.*

**inland. I.** *adj.* [inlənd] (*a*) binnenländisch; Binnen-; i. **waterways,** Binnengewässer *npl;* (*b*) *Brit:* **I. Revenue,** Steuerbehörde *f.* **II.** [in'lænd], *adv.* landeinwärts.

**in-laws** [inlɔːz], *s.pl. F:* Schwiegereltern *pl.*

**inlet** [inlet], *s.* **1.** Einlaß *m.* **2.** *Geog:* Meeresarm *m.*

**inmate** [inmeit], *s.* Insasse *m,* Insassin *f.*

**inn** [in], *s.* Wirtshaus *n.*

**innate** [i'neit], *adj.* angeboren.

**inner** [inər], *adj.* innere(r,s), Innen-; i.

**tube,** Luftschlauch *m.*

**innings** [iniŋz], *s.* Spielzeit *f.*

**innocent** [inəsənt], *adj.* (*a*) (*not guilty*) unschuldig; (*b*) (*unsuspecting*) arglos; (*ingenuous*) naiv. ◆**'innocence,** *s.* (*a*) Unschuld *f* (eines Angeklagten); (*b*) Arglosigkeit *f.*

**innocuous** [i'nɔkjuəs], *adj.* harmlos.

**innovation** [inəu'veiʃ(ə)n], *s.* Neuerung *f.*

**innuendo,** *pl.* **-oes** [inju(ː)'endəu, -əuz], *s.* versteckte Anspielung *f.*

**innumerable** [i'njuːmərəbl], *adj.* zahllos.

**inoculate** [i'nɔkjuleit], *v.tr.* impfen. ◆**inocu'lation,** *s.* Impfung *f.*

**inoffensive** [inə'fensiv], *adj.* harmlos.

**inopportune** [in'ɔpətjuːn], *adj.* ungelegen; (*of remark etc.*) unpassend.

**inordinate** [i'nɔːdinit], *adj.* unmäßig.

**input** [input], *s.* *Data-pr:* Eingabe *f.*

**inquest** [inkwest], *s.* *Jur:* amtliche Untersuchung *f* (zur Feststellung der Todesursache).

**inquire** [in'kwaiər], *v.* **1.** *v.tr.* sich (nach dem Preis, Weg usw.) erkundigen. **2.** *v.i.* sich erkundigen (**about/after s.o., sth.,** nach j-m, etwas *dat*); to i. **into sth.,** etwas untersuchen. ◆**in'quiring,** *adj.* fragend. ◆**in'quiry,** *s.* **1.** Nachfrage *f;* to **make inquiries (about s.o.),** (über j-n) Erkundigungen einziehen. **2.** (police) i., (polizeiliche) Untersuchung *f.* **3.** *Tel:* Inquiries, Auskunft *f.*

**inquisitive** [in'kwizitiv], *adj.* neugierig.

**insane** [in'sein], *adj.* (*a*) geisteskrank; (*b*) *F:* verrückt. ◆**in'sanity** [-'sæniti], *s.* Geisteskrankheit *f.*

**insanitary** [in'sænit(ə)ri], *adj.* unhygienisch.

**insatiable** [in'seiʃəbl], *adj.* unersättlich.

**inscription** [in'skripʃ(ə)n], *s.* Inschrift *f;* Gravur *f* (auf einer Münze).

**inscrutable** [in'skruːtəbl], *adj.* unergründlich.

**insect** [insekt], *s.* Insekt *n.* ◆**in'secticide,** *s.* Insektengift *n.*

**insecure** [insi'kjuər], *adj.* unsicher. ◆**inse'curity,** *s.* Unsicherheit *f.*

**insemination** [insemi'neiʃ(ə)n], *s.* **artificial i.,** künstliche Befruchtung *f.*

**insensitive** [in'sensitiv], *adj.* gefühllos. ◆**insensi'tivity,** *s.* Gefühllosigkeit *f.*

**inseparable** [in'sep(ə)rəbl], *adj.* untrennbar; (*of friends*) unzertrennlich.

**insert** [in'səːt], *v.tr.* (etwas) einfügen; **to i. a coin,** eine Münze einwerfen.

**inside** [in'said]. **I.** *s.* (*a*) Innenseite *f;* (*inner surface*) Innenfläche *f;* **on the i.,** innen; i. **out,** verkehrt herum; **turned i. out,** (*of pockets*) umgestülpt; *Fig:* to **know sth. i. out,** etwas in- und auswendig kennen; (*b*) (das) Innere *n* (eines Hauses usw.). **II.** *adj.* Innen-, innere(r,s); i. **information,** vertrauliche Informationen; i. **job,** *F:* von Angestellten begangener Diebstahl. **III.** *adv.* im Innern, innen. **IV.** *prep.* innerhalb + *gen.*

◆in'sider, *s.* Eingeweihte(r) *f* (*m*).
**insidious** [in'sidiəs], *adj.* heimtückisch.
**insight** ['insait], *s.* (*a*) Einblick *m*; **to gain an i. into sth.**, Einblick in eine Sache gewinnen; (*b*) (*realization*) Einsicht *f*.
**insignificant** [insig'nifikənt], *adj.* unbedeutend.
**insincere** [insin'siər], *adj.* unaufrichtig; (*of smile etc.*) falsch. ◆**insincerity** [-'seriti], *s.* Unaufrichtigkeit *f*.
**insinuate** [in'sinjueit], *v.tr.* andeuten. ◆**insinu'ation**, *s.* Andeutung *f*.
**insipid** [in'sipid], *adj.* (*of food*) geschmacklos; (*of book etc.*) langweilig.
**insist** [in'sist], *v.i.* bestehen (**on/upon**, auf + *acc*); **to i. on doing sth.**, darauf bestehen, etwas zu tun. ◆**in'sistence**, *s.* Beharren *n* (**on**, auf + *acc*). ◆**in'sistent**, *adj.* (*a*) beharrlich; (*b*) (*pushing*) aufdringlich.
**insolent** ['insələnt], *adj.* frech. ◆**'insolence**, *s.* Frechheit *f*.
**insoluble** [in'soljubl], *adj.* **1.** *Ch: etc:* unlöslich. **2.** (*of problem etc.*) unlösbar.
**insomnia** [in'somniə], *s.* Schlaflosigkeit *f*.
**inspect** [in'spekt], *v.tr.* (*a*) (Lebensmittel, Maschinen usw.) prüfen; (*b*) (eine Schule, *Hum:* ein Haus usw.) inspizieren; *Mil:* **to i. troops**, die Parade abnehmen. ◆**in'spection** [-'spekʃ(ə)n], *s.* Inspektion *f*; (*examination*) Überprüfung *f*. ◆**in'spector**, *s.* Inspektor(in) *m(f)*.
**inspire** [in'spaiər], *v.tr.* (j-n) inspirieren; **to i. s.o. with confidence**, j-m Vertrauen einflößen. ◆**inspiration** [-spi'reiʃ(ə)n], *s.* Inspiration *f*. ◆**in'spired**, *adj.* genial.
**instability** [instə'biliti], *s.* (*a*) (*of boat, car etc.*) Unausgewogenheit *f*; (*b*) *Fig:* Unbeständigkeit *f*; (*esp. of character*) Labilität *f*.
**install** [in'stɔ:l], *v.tr.* installieren. ◆**installation** [instə'leiʃ(ə)n], *s.* (*a*) Installierung *f*; (*b*) (*system*) Anlage *f*.
**instalment** [in'stɔ:lmənt], *s.* **1.** (*of serial etc.*) Fortsetzung *f*. **2.** (*part payment*) Rate *f*.
**instance** ['instəns], *s.* Beispiel *n* (**of sth.**, für etwas *acc*); (*case*) Fall *m*; **for i.**, zum Beispiel.
**instant** ['instənt]. **I.** *s.* Moment *m*. **II.** *adj.* sofortig; **i. coffee**, Schnellkaffee *m*. ◆**instan'taneous**, *adj.* unverzüglich.
**instead** [in'sted]. **I.** *prep.* **i. of s.o.**, anstelle von j-m, etwas *dat*; **i. of him**, an seiner Stelle. **II.** *adv.* statt dessen.
**instigate** ['instigeit], *v.tr.* (j-n, etwas) anregen; (etwas Böses) anstiften. ◆**insti'gation**, *s.* (*a*) Anregung *f*; **at his i.**, auf seine Anregung (hin); (*b*) Anstiftung *f* (von etwas Bösem). ◆**'instigator**, *s.* Anstifter(in) *m(f)*.
**instil** [in'stil], *v.tr.* **to i. sth. into s.o.**, j-m etwas einflößen.
**instinct** ['instiŋ(k)t], *s.* Instinkt *m*. ◆**in'stinctive**, *adj.* instinktiv.
**institute** ['institju:t]. **I.** *v.tr.* (einen Brauch, eine Vorschrift usw.) einführen;

*Jur:* **to i. an inquiry**, eine Untersuchung einleiten. **II.** *s.* Institut *n*. ◆**insti'tution**, *s.* (*a*) (*tradition*) Brauch *m*; (*b*) Anstalt *f*.
**instruct** [in'strʌkt], *v.tr.* (*a*) (j-n) unterrichten; (*b*) (j-n) anweisen (**to do sth.**, etwas zu tun). ◆**in'struction**, *s.* **1.** (*teaching*) Unterricht *m*; (*training*) Ausbildung *f*. **2.** *usu.pl.* Anweisung *f*. ◆**in'structive**, *adj.* aufschlußreich. ◆**in'structor**, *s.* Lehrer(in) *m(f)*.
**instrument** ['instrəmənt], *s.* Instrument *n*. ◆**instru'mental**, *adj.* **1. to be i. in doing sth.**, eine entscheidende Rolle bei etwas *dat* spielen. **2. i. music**, Instrumentalmusik *f*.
**insubordinate** [insəbɔ:'dinit], *adj.* ungehorsam. ◆**insubordi'nation**, *s.* Gehorsamsverweigerung *f*.
**insufferable** [in'sʌf(ə)rəbl], *adj.* unerträglich.
**insufficient** [insə'fiʃənt], *adj.* ungenügend.
**insular** ['insjulər], *adj.* (*a*) insular, Insel-; (*b*) (*of pers.*) engstirnig.
**insulate** ['insjuleit], *v.tr.* isolieren. ◆**insu'lation**, *s.* Isolierung *f*. ◆**'insulating**, *adj.* **i. tape**, Isolierband *n*.
**insulin** ['insjulin], *s.* Insulin *n*.
**insult.** **I.** ['insʌlt] *s.* Beleidigung *f*. **II.** [in'sʌlt] *v.tr.* (j-n) beleidigen. ◆**in'sulting**, *adj.* beleidigend.
**insuperable** [in'sju:p(ə)rəbl], *adj.* unüberwindlich.
**insure** [in'ʃuər], *v.tr.* (*a*) versichern; (*b*) (*guarantee*) (Erfolg usw.) gewährleisten. ◆**in'surance**, *s.* Versicherung *f*; **i. policy**, Versicherungspolice *f*.
**insurmountable** [insə(:)'mauntəbl], *adj.* unüberwindlich.
**insurrection** [insə'rekʃən], *s.* Aufstand *m*.
**intact** [in'tækt], *adj.* unversehrt.
**intake** ['inteik], *s.* **1.** (*opening*) Einlaß *m*, Einlaßöffnung *f*. **2.** (*amount admitted*) **food i.**, Nahrungsaufnahme *f*.
**integral** ['intigrəl], *adj.* wesentlich. ◆**'integrate** [-greit], *v.* **1.** *v.tr.* (j-n) integrieren (**into society etc.**), in die Gesellschaft usw.). **2.** *v.i.* sich integrieren. ◆**inte'gration**, *s.* Integration *f*.
**integrity** [in'tegriti], *s.* Integrität *f*.
**intellect** ['intəlekt], *s.* Verstand *m*. ◆**inte'llectual.** **I.** *adj.* intellektuell; (*of work etc.*) geistig. **II.** *s.* Intellektuelle(r) *f(m)*.
**intelligence** [in'telidʒəns], *s.* **1.** Intelligenz *f*. **2.** *esp. Mil:* (*service*) Nachrichtendienst *m*. ◆**in'telligent**, *adj.* intelligent.
**intelligible** [in'telidʒəbl], *adj.* verständlich.
**intend** [in'tend], *v.tr.* **to i. to do sth.**, beabsichtigen, etwas zu tun. ◆**in'tended**, *adj.* **1.** (*a*) beabsichtigt; (*of journey etc.*) geplant; (*b*) (*intentional*) absichtlich. **2. i. for s.o.**, für j-n gedacht;

*(of remark etc.)* an j-n gerichtet.

**intense** [in'tens], *adj. (a) (of colour, feelings etc.)* intensiv, stark; *(b) (of pers., expression)* angespannt; **-ly,** *adv.* äußerst; höchst; ◆**in'tensify,** *v.* 1. *v.tr. (a)* (eine Wirkung, einen Kontrast usw.) steigern; *(b)* **to i. one's efforts/a search,** seine Bemühungen/eine Suche intensivieren. 2. *v.i. (of feelings etc.)* stärker werden. ◆**in'tensity,** *s.* Intensität *f.* ◆**in'tensive,** *adj.* intensiv; **i. care unit,** Intensivstation *f.*

**intent** [in'tent]. **I.** *adj.* **to be i. on sth.,** in etwas *acc* ganz vertieft sein; **to be i. on doing sth.,** fest entschlossen sein, etwas zu tun. **II.** *s.* 1. Absicht *f.* 2. **to all intents and purposes,** so gut wie. ◆**intention** [in'tenʃən], *s.* Absicht *f.* ◆**in'tentional,** *adj.* absichtlich.

**interact** [intər'ækt], *v.i.* aufeinander wirken. ◆**inter'action,** *s.* Wechselwirkung *f.*

**intercede** [intə(:)'siːd], *v.i.* **to i. with s.o. for s.o.,** bei j-m für j-n Fürsprache einlegen.

**intercept** [intə(:)'sept], *v.tr.* abfangen. ◆**inter'ception,** *s.* Abfangen *n.*

**interchange. I.** ['intətʃeindʒ], *s. (of ideas etc.)* Austausch *m;* **traffic i.,** Kreuzung *f.* **II.** [intə'tʃeindʒ], *v.tr.* austauschen. ◆**inter'changeable,** *adj.* austauschbar.

**intercom** ['intəkɔm], *s.* Sprechanlage *f.*

**intercontinental** [intəkɔnti'nentl], *adj.* interkontinental.

**intercourse** ['intə(:)kɔːs], *s. (a)* **social i.,** gesellschaftlicher Umgang *m; (b)* **(sexual) i.,** Geschlechtsverkehr *m.*

**interest** ['int(ə)rest]. **I.** *s.* 1. *s.* Interesse *n* (**in music etc.,** an der Musik *dat* usw.); **to take an i. in sth.,** sich für etwas *acc* interessieren; *(b) (advantage)* Vorteil *m;* **to act in one's own i.,** zum eigenen Vorteil handeln. 2. *Com:* Beteiligung *f* (**in a firm,** an einer Firma). 3. *Fin:* Zinsen *mpl;* **i. rate,** Zinssatz *m.* **II.** *v.tr.* (j-n) interessieren (**in sth.,** für etwas *acc*). ◆**'interested,** *adj.* interessiert (**in sth.,** an etwas *dat*); **to be i. in sth.,** sich für etwas *acc* interessieren. ◆**'interesting,** *adj.* interessant.

**interface** ['intəfeis], *s. Data-pr:* Schnittstelle *f.*

**interfere** [intə'fiər], *v.i.* (in einen Streit usw.) eingreifen; **to i. in other people's business,** sich in fremde Angelegenheiten einmischen. ◆**inter'ference,** *s.* 1. Eingreifen *n;* Einmischung *f* (**in sth.,** in etwas *acc*). 2. *Rad:* Störung *f.* ◆**inter'fering,** *adj.* **he's very i.,** er mischt sich dauernd ein.

**interim** ['intərim]. **I.** *s.* **in the i.,** in der Zwischenzeit. **II.** *adj.* Zwischen-.

**interior** [in'tiəriər]. **I.** *adj.* inner, Innen-; **i. decorator,** Innenarchitekt *m.* **II.** *s. (space)* Innenraum *m; (of country)* Binnenland *n.*

**interlude** ['intəljuːd], *s.* Zwischenspiel *n.*

**intermediary** [intə'miːdjəri], *s.* Vermittler(in) *m(f).*

**intermediate** [intə'miːdiət], *adj.* Zwischen-.

**interminable** [in'təːminəbl], *adj.* endlos.

**intermission** [intə'miʃən], *s.* Pause *f.*

**intermittent** [intə'mitənt], *adj.* in Abständen (auftretend/erscheinend).

**internal** [in'təːnəl], *adj.* 1. innere(r, s); **i. combustion engine,** Verbrennungsmotor *m.* 2. Innen-; inländisch; **i. trade,** Binnenhandel *m; N.Am:* **i. revenue,** inländische Steuereinnahmen; **-ally,** *adv.* innen; **to bleed i.,** innerlich bluten.

**international** [intə'næʃ(ə)nəl], *adj.* international.

**interplay** ['intəplei], *s.* Wechselspiel *n.*

**interpret** [in'təːprit], *v.tr. (a)* (einen Text usw.) auslegen; *Mus:* (ein Stück) interpretieren; *(b) (translate)* (ein Gespräch usw.) dolmetschen. ◆**interpre'tation,** *s.* 1. Interpretation *f.* 2. (mündliche) Übersetzung *f.* ◆**in'terpreter,** *s.* Dolmetscher(in) *m(f).*

**interrogate** [in'terəgeit], *v.tr.* (j-n) ausfragen; *Jur:* (Zeugen usw.) verhören. ◆**interro'gation,** *s.* Vernehmung *f,* Verhör *n.*

**interrupt** [intə'rʌpt], *v.tr.* unterbrechen; *(disturb)* (j-n) stören. ◆**inte'rruption,** *s.* Unterbrechung *f;* Störung *f.*

**interval** ['intəvəl], *s. (a)* Zwischenraum *m;* **at intervals,** in Abständen; *(b) Meteor:* **bright i.,** kurze Aufheiterung *f; (c) Th: etc:* Pause *f.*

**intervene** [intə'viːn], *v.i. (a) (of pers.)* eingreifen (**in,** in + *acc*); *Pol: Mil: etc:* intervenieren; *(b) (of events)* dazwischenkommen; *(c) (of time)* **ten years intervened,** zehn Jahre lagen dazwischen. ◆**intervention** [-'venʃ(ə)n], *s.* Eingreifen *n; Pol: Mil: etc:* Intervention *f.*

**interview** ['intəvjuː]. **I.** *s. (a) TV:* Interview *n; (b) (for job)* Vorstellungsgespräch *n.* **II.** *v.tr. (a)* (j-n) interviewen; *(b)* (mit j-m) ein Vorstellungsgespräch führen. ◆**'interviewer,** *s.* Interviewer *m.*

**intestine** [in'testin], *s.* Darm *m.*

**intimacy** ['intiməsi], *s.* Intimität *f.* ◆**intimate**[1] ['intimit], *adj. (a)* vertraut; *(of room etc.)* intim; *(of manner, talk)* vertraulich; *(b) (of knowledge etc.)* gründlich; **-ly,** *adv.* **to know sth. i.,** etwas genau kennen.

**intimate**[2] ['intimeit], *v.tr.* (etwas) zu verstehen geben.

**intimidate** [in'timideit], *v.tr.* (j-n) einschüchtern. ◆**in'timidating,** *adj.* einschüchternd. ◆**intimi'dation,** *s.* Einschüchterung *f.*

**into** ['intu, 'intə], *prep.* in + *acc,* in ... hinein.

**intolerable** [in'tɔl(ə)rəbl], *adj.* unerträglich. ◆**in'tolerant,** *adj.* intolerant.

**intoxicate** [in'tɔksikeit], *v.tr.* berauschen. ◆**in'toxicated,** *adj.* berauscht; *(drunk)* betrunken. ◆**intoxi'cation,** *s.* Rausch *m.*

**intravenous** [intrə'vi:nəs], *adj.* intravenös.

**intrepid** [in'trepid], *adj.* unerschrocken.

**intricate** ['intrikit], *adj.* kompliziert; *F:* (*tricky*) knifflig. ◆**in'tricacy,** *s.* Kompliziertheit *f;* Kniffligkeit *f.*

**intrigue. I.** *v.* [in'tri:g]. **1.** *v.i.* intrigieren. **2.** *v.tr.* **to i. s.o.,** j-n faszinieren. **II.** *s.* ['intri:g] Intrige *f.* ◆**in'triguing,** *adj.* faszinierend.

**intrinsic** [in'trinsik], *adj.* innere(r,s); (*real*) wirklich.

**introduce** [intrə'dju:s], *v.tr.* (*a*) (etwas Neues) einführen; (*b*) **he introduced me to her,** er stellte mich ihr vor; **to i. s.o. to sth.,** j-n in etwas *acc* einführen. ◆**intro'duction,** *s.* **1.** Einführung *f.* **2.** (*of pers.*) Vorstellung *f.* ◆**intro'ductory,** *adj.* einführend; Einführungs-.

**introspective** [intrə'spektiv], *adj.* (*of pers.*) introspektiv.

**introvert** ['intrəuvə:t], *s.* introvertierter Mensch *m.*

**intrude** [in'tru:d], *v.i.* **to i. on s.o.,** sich bei j-m eindrängen. ◆**in'truder,** *s.* Eindringling *m.* ◆**in'trusion,** *s.* Eindringen *n;* (*disturbance*) Störung *f.* ◆**in'trusive,** *adj.* aufdringlich.

**intuition** [intju:(')'iʃən], *s.* Intuition *f.* ◆**in'tuitive,** *adj.* intuitiv.

**inundate** ['inʌndeit], *v.tr.* **inundated with tourists,** von Touristen überlaufen; **inundated with requests,** mit Bitten überhäuft.

**invade** [in'veid], *v.tr.* einfallen. ◆**in'vader,** *s.* Eindringling *m.*

**invalid**[1] [in'vælid], *adj.* ungültig. ◆**in'validate,** *v.tr.* (eine Behauptung usw.) entkräften; *Jur:* (einen Vertrag) nichtig machen.

**invalid**[2] ['invəlid, -li:d]. **I.** *adj.* (*of pers.*) krank. **II.** *s.* Invalide *m.*

**invaluable** [in'vælju(ə)bl], *adj.* unbezahlbar.

**invariable** [in'vɛəriəbl], *adj.* unveränderlich; **-ly,** *adv.* ständig; (*each time*) jedes Mal.

**invasion** [in'veiʒən], *s.* Invasion *f.*

**invective** [in'vektiv], *s.* Beschimpfungen *fpl.*

**invent** [in'vent], *v.tr.* erfinden. ◆**in'vention,** *s.* Erfindung *f.* ◆**in'ventive,** *adj.* erfinderisch. ◆**in'ventor,** *s.* Erfinder(in) *m(f).*

**inventory** ['invəntri], *s.* Bestandsaufnahme *f.*

**inverse** ['in'və:s], *adj.* umgekehrt. ◆**invert** [in'və:t], *v.tr.* umkehren; **inverted commas,** Anführungszeichen *npl.*

**invertebrate** [in'və:tibreit], *s.* wirbelloses Tier *n.*

**invest** [in'vest], *v.tr. & i.* investieren (**in sth.,** in etwas *acc*). ◆**in'vestment,** *s.* **1.** Investition *f.* **2.** (*money etc.*) Anlage *f.* ◆**in'vestor,** *s.* Kapitalanleger *m;* **small**

i., Kleinsparer *m.*

**investigate** [in'vestigeit], *v.tr.* untersuchen. ◆**investi'gation,** *s.* Untersuchung *f.* ◆**in'vestigator,** *s.* Ermittlungsbeamte(r) *m.*

**inveterate** [in'vet(ə)rit], *adj.* **i. gambler,** Gewohnheitsspieler *m.*

**invigorating** [in'vigəreitiŋ], *adj.* belebend.

**invincible** [in'vinsəbl], *adj.* unbesiegbar.

**invisible** [in'vizəbl], *adj.* unsichtbar.

**invite** [in'vait], *v.tr.* einladen. ◆**invitation** [-vi'teiʃ(ə)n], *s.* Einladung *f.* ◆**in'viting,** *adj.* einladend; (*of food*) appetitlich.

**invoice** ['invɔis]. **I.** *s.* Rechnung *f.* **II.** *v.tr.* **to i. s.o. for an amount,** j-m einen Betrag in Rechnung stellen.

**involuntary** [in'vɔlənt(ə)ri], *adj.* unwillkürlich.

**involve** [in'vɔlv], *v.tr.* (*a*) (*often passive*) (j-n) hineinziehen (**in sth.,** in etwas *acc*); **to be involved in a dispute/in a plot,** an einem Streit/an einer Verschwörung beteiligt sein; **the car involved (in the accident),** das (an dem Unfall) beteiligte Auto; (*b*) (*entail*) (Unkosten usw.) mit sich bringen. ◆**in'volved,** *adj.* kompliziert. ◆**in'volvement,** *s.* Beteiligung *f.*

**inwardly** ['inwəli], *adv.* innerlich. ◆**'inwards,** *adv.* nach innen (gerichtet).

**iodine** ['aiədi:n], *s.* Jod *n.*

**Iran** [i'ra:n]. *Pr.n.* Iran *m.* ◆**Iranian** [i'reinjən]. **I.** *adj.* iranisch. **II.** *s.* Iraner(in) *m(f).*

**Iraq** [i'ra:k]. *Pr.n.* Irak *m.* ◆**I'raqi. I.** *adj.* irakisch. **II.** *s.* Iraker(in) *m(f).*

**irate** [ai'reit], *adj.* wütend.

**Ireland** ['aiələnd]. *Pr.n.* Irland *n.*

**iris** ['aiəris], *s. Anat: Bot:* Iris *f.*

**Irish** ['aiəriʃ]. **I.** *adj.* irisch. **II.** *s.* **1.** (*language*) Irisch *n.* **2.** *pl.* **the I.,** die Iren *mpl.* ◆**'Irishman,** *pl.* **-men,** *s.* Ire *m.* ◆**'Irishwoman,** *pl.* **-women,** *s.* Irin *f.*

**irksome** ['ə:ksəm], *adj.* lästig.

**iron** ['aiən]. **I.** *s.* **1.** (*a*) Eisen *n;* **i. ore,** Eisenerz *n;* (*b*) **I. Curtain,** eiserner Vorhang *m.* **2.** *H:* Bügeleisen *n.* **II.** *v.tr.* (Wäsche) bügeln. ◆**'ironing,** *s.* Bügeln *n;* **i. board,** Bügelbrett *n.* ◆**'ironmonger,** *s.* Eisenwarenhändler *m.*

**irony** ['aiərəni], *s.* Ironie *f.* ◆**i'ronical,** *adj.* ironisch.

**irrational** [i'ræʃənəl], *adj.* irrational.

**irreconcilable** [irekən'sailəbl], *adj.* (*a*) (*of enemy etc.*) unversöhnlich; (*b*) (*of ideas*) unvereinbar (**with,** mit).

**irrefutable** [iri'fju:təbl], *adj.* unwiderlegbar.

**irregular** [i'regjulər], *adj.* **1.** (*a*) (*of bus service etc.*) unregelmäßig; (*b*) (*of surface*) uneben. **2.** (*of conduct etc.*) ungehörig; (*against rules*) unvorschriftsmäßig. ◆**irregu'larity,** *s.* **1.** Unregelmäßigkeit *f.* **2.** (*a*) Ungehörigkeit *f;* (*b*) (*infringement*) Verstoß *m* (gegen eine Vorschrift).

**irrelevance** [i'relivəns], s. Nebensächlichkeit f. ◆**i'rrelevant**, adj. nebensächlich; that's i., das hat nichts damit zu tun.
**irreparable** [i'rep(ə)rəbl], adj. nicht wiedergutzumachen.
**irreplaceable** [iri'pleisəbl], adj. unersetzlich.
**irrepressible** [iri'presəbl], adj. he is i., er ist nicht unterzukriegen.
**irresistible** [iri'zistəbl], adj. unwiderstehlich.
**irresolute** [i'rezəl(j)u:t], adj. unentschlossen.
**irrespective** [iris'pektiv], adj. & adv. i. of, ungeachtet + gen.
**irresponsible** [iris'pɔnsəbl], adj. (of pers.) verantwortungslos; (of action) unverantwortlich.
**irreverent** [i'rev(ə)rənt], adj. ehrfurchtslos.
**irrevocable** [i'revəkəbl], adj. unwiderruflich.
**irrigate** ['irigeit], v.tr. bewässern. ◆**irri'gation**, s. Bewässerung f.
**irritate** ['iriteit], v.tr. (a) (die Haut usw.) reizen; (b) (j-n) irritieren. ◆**irritable**, adj. reizbar; ◆**irritant**, s. Reizmittel n. ◆**irritating**, adj. irritierend. ◆**irri'tation**, s. 1. Ärger m. 2. Med: Reizung f.
**Islamic** [iz'læmik], adj. islamisch.
**island** ['ailənd], s. Insel f. ◆**isle**, s. (esp.in Pr.n.) Insel f.
**isobar** ['aisəubɑ:], s. Isobare f.
**isolate** ['aisəleit], v.tr. isolieren ◆**iso'lation**, s. Isolierung f.
**Israel** ['izrei(ə)l]. Pr.n. Israel n. ◆**Is'raeli**. I. adj. israelisch. II. s. Israeli m.
**issue** ['isju:]. I. s. 1. Frage f; (in argu-

ment) Streitfrage f; to force the i., eine Entscheidung erzwingen. 2. (a) Ausgabe f (von Münzen, Briefmarken usw.); Ausstellung f (eines Passes usw.); Emission f (von Aktien); (b) Nummer f (einer Zeitschrift). II. v.tr. (a) herausgeben; (Pässe, Schecks usw.) ausstellen; (Aktien) ausgeben; (b) Mil: to i. an order, einen Befehl erteilen.
**it** [it], pers.pron. 1. (a) (subject) es n; er m; sie f; (b) (direct object) es n; ihn m; sie f; (c) (indirect object) ihm m, n; ihr f. 2. it's me, ich bin's; it's the children, es sind die Kinder; that's just it! das ist es ja gerade! it's said that..., man sagt, daß...
**Italian** [i'tæljən]. I. adj. italienisch. II. s. (a) Italiener(in) m(f); (b) Italienisch n. ◆**Italy** ['itəli]. Pr.n. Italien n.
**italics** [i'tæliks], s.pl. Kursivschrift f.
**itch** [itʃ]. I. v.i. jucken; Fig: to be itching to do sth., darauf brennen, etwas zu tun. II. s. (also itching) Jucken n. ◆**itchy**, adj. juckend.
**item** ['aitəm], s. 1. (a) (object) Gegenstand m; i. of clothing, Kleidungsstück n; (b) (matter) Sache f. 2. (a) (on agenda etc.) Punkt m; (b) Com: etc: (in budget etc.) Posten m. 3. news i., (einzelne) Nachricht f; (article) Artikel m.
**itinerary** [i'tinərəri,ai-], s. Reiseroute f.
**its** [its], poss.adj. n, m sein; f ihr.
**it's** [its]. F: = 1. it is. 2. it has.
**itself** [it'self], pers.pron. 1. (reflexive) sich. 2. (emphatic) selbst.
**I've** [aiv]. F: = I have.
**ivory** ['aiv(ə)ri], s. 1. Elfenbein n. 2. attrib. (a) elfenbeinern; (b) (colour) elfenbeinfarbig.
**ivy** ['aivi], s. Efeu m.

# J

**J, j** [dʒei], s. (der Buchstabe) J, j n.
**jab** [dʒæb]. I. v.tr. & i. (j-n) stoßen, (with sth. sharp) stechen. II. s. 1. Knuff m. 2. Med: F: Spritze f.
**jack** [dʒæk], s. 1. (in cards) Bube m. 2. Aut: Wagenheber m. ◆**jackdaw**, s. Dohle f. ◆**jackknife**, v.i. the trailer jackknifed, der Anhänger scherte aus und stellte sich quer. ◆**jackpot**, s. Hauptgewinn m; F: to hit/win the j., den Haupttreffer machen; Fig: den Vogel abschießen. ◆**jack'up**, v.tr. (ein Auto usw.) aufbocken.
**jackal** ['dʒækɔ:l], s. Schakal m.
**jacket** ['dʒækit], s. 1. (a) Jacke f; (b) j. potatoes, gebackene Kartoffeln fpl. 2. book j., Schutzumschlag m.
**jade** [dʒeid], s. Jade m.
**jaded** ['dʒeidid], adj. abgekämpft.
**jagged** ['dʒægid], adj. zackig; (of rock, coastline) zerklüftet.
**jail** [dʒeil], s. see gaol.

**jam¹** [dʒæm]. I. v. 1. v.tr. (a) F: (etwas) hineinzwängen; to get one's finger jammed, sich dat den Finger einquetschen; (b) F: to j. on the brakes, (heftig) auf die Bremsen steigen; (c) (block) (eine Maschine) blockieren. 2. v.i. (a) (stick) klemmen; (b) (of key etc.) steckenbleiben. II. s. (a) (traffic) j., Verkehrsstauung f; (b) F: to be in a j., in der Klemme sitzen.
**jam²**, s. Marmelade f.
**Jamaica** [dʒəmeikə]. Pr. n. Jamaika n. ◆**Ja'maican. I.** adj. jamaikisch. II. s. Jamaikaner(in) m(f).
**jangle** ['dʒæŋgl], v. 1. v.i. klimpern. 2. v.tr. to j. the keys, mit den Schlüsseln klimpern.
**janitor** ['dʒænitər], s. Hausmeister m.
**January** ['dʒænjuəri], s. Januar m.
**Japan** [dʒə'pæn]. Pr. n. Japan n. ◆**Japa'nese. I.** adj. japanisch. II. s. 1. Japaner(in) m(f). 2. Japanisch n.

**jar¹** [dʒɑːr], *v.* **1.** *v.i.* nicht harmonieren. **2.** *v.tr.* (die Nerven, das Rückgrat usw.) erschüttern.

**jar²**, *s.* Glas *n.*

**jargon** ['dʒɑːgən], *s.* Jargon *m.*

**jasmine** ['dʒæzmin], *s.* Jasmin *m.*

**jaundice** ['dʒɔːndis], *s.* Gelbsucht *f.*

**jaunt** [dʒɔːnt], *s.* Spritztour *f.*

**javelin** ['dʒævlin], *s.* (*a*) Speer *m;* (*b*) (*event*) Speerwurf *m.*

**jaw** [dʒɔː], *s.* Kiefer *m.*

**jay** [dʒei], *s.* Eichelhäher *m.* ◆'**jaywalker,** *s.* leichtsinniger Fußgänger.

**jazz** [dʒæz], *s.* Jazz *m.* ◆'**jazz 'up,** *v.tr.* verjazzen. ◆'**jazzy,** *adj.* (*of music*) verjazzt; *F:* (*of tie etc.*) poppig; *Pej:* schreiend.

**jealous** ['dʒeləs], *adj.* eifersüchtig (*of,* auf + *acc.*). ◆'**jealousy,** *s.* Eifersucht *f.*

**jeans** [dʒiːnz], *s. pl.* Jeans *pl.*

**jeep** [dʒiːp], *s.* Jeep *m.*

**jeer** [dʒiər]. **I.** *v.i.* (*of crowd*) johlen; (*of pers.*) **to j. at s.o., sth.,** j-n, etwas verhöhnen. **II.** *s.* Hohnruf *m.* ◆'**jeering.** **I.** *adj.* johlend; (*scornful*) höhnisch. **II.** *s.* Johlen *n.*

**jelly** ['dʒeli], *s.* Gelee *n.* ◆'**jelly-fish,** *s.* Qualle *f.*

**jeopardize** ['dʒepədaiz], *v.tr.* gefährden. ◆'**jeopardy,** *s.* Gefahr *f.*

**jerk** [dʒəːk]. **I.** *s.* **1.** Ruck *m.* **2.** *P: Pej:* (*pers.*) Lümmel *m.* **II.** *v.* **1.** *v.tr.* (etwas) ruckweise ziehen. **2.** *v.i.* einen Ruck geben. ◆'**jerky,** *adj.* ruckartig.

**jerry-built** ['dʒeribilt], *adj.* schlecht gebaut.

**jersey** ['dʒəːzi], *s.* Pullover *m.*

**jest** [dʒest], *s.* Scherz *m.*

**jet** [dʒet], *s.* **1.** Strahl *m;* **j. of water,** Wasserstrahl *m.* **2.** (**plane**) Düsenflugzeug *n;* **j. engine,** Strahltriebwerk *n;* **j. fighter,** Düsenjäger *m.*

**jettison** ['dʒetis(ə)n], *v.tr.* über Bord werfen.

**jetty** ['dʒeti], *s.* Landungssteg *m.*

**Jew** [dʒuː], *s.* Jude *m.* ◆'**Jewish,** *adj.* jüdisch.

**jewel** ['dʒuːəl], *s.* (*a*) Edelstein *m; esp. Fig:* Juwel *n;* (*b*) *pl.* Schmuck *m.* ◆'**jeweller,** *s.* Juwelier *m.* ◆'**jewel(l)ery,** *s.* Schmuck *m.*

**jiffy** ['dʒifi], *s.* **in a j.,** im Nu; (*soon*) gleich.

**jigsaw** ['dʒigsɔː], *s.* **j. (puzzle),** Puzzle(-spiel) *n.*

**jilt** ['dʒilt], *v.tr. F:* (einem Mann) den Laufpaß geben; (ein Mädchen) sitzenlassen.

**jingle** ['dʒiŋgl], *v.* **1.** *v.i.* klingeln; (*of keys, money*) klimpern. **2.** *v.tr.* (etwas) klingeln lassen; (mit Geld, Schlüsseln) klimpern.

**jitter** ['dʒitər], *s. F:* **to get the jitters,** Schiß kriegen. ◆'**jittery,** *adj.* nervös.

**job** [dʒɔb], *s.* **1.** (*a*) Arbeit *f;* Aufgabe *f; F:* **it's a good j. you came,** es ist gut,

daß du gekommen bist; (*b*) *F:* **I had a (hard) j. to convince him,** ich konnte ihn nur mit Mühe überzeugen. **2.** (*position etc.*) Stellung *f; F:* Job *m.*

**jockey** ['dʒɔki], *s.* Jockei *m.*

**jocular** ['dʒɔkjulər], *adj.* scherzhaft.

**jodhpurs** ['dʒɔdpəːz], *s.pl.* Reithosen *fpl.*

**jog** [dʒɔg], *v.tr. & i.* (*a*) (**shake**) (j-n) durchrütteln; (*b*) (**knock**) j-n stupsen; **to j. s.o.'s memory,** j-s Gedächtnis auffrischen. ◆'**jogging,** *s.* Jogging *n.*

**join** [dʒɔin]. **I.** *s.* Verbindungsstelle *f.* **II.** *v.* **1.** *v.tr.* (*a*) (etwas) verbinden (**to sth.,** mit etwas *dat*); (zwei Teile) zusammenfügen; (*b*) (j-m) Gesellschaft leisten; (*c*) (einem Verein, einer Partei usw.) beitreten; (in eine Firma) eintreten; **to j. the army,** zur Armee gehen. **2.** *v.i.* (*of lines*) zusammenlaufen; (*of roads*) sich treffen. ◆'**joiner,** *s.* Tischler *m.* ◆'**joinery,** *s.* Tischlerarbeit *f.* ◆'**join 'in,** *v.* **1.** *v.i.* mitmachen. **2.** *v.tr.* sich (an etwas *dat*) beteiligen. ◆'**joint.** **I.** *s.* **1.** (*a*) *Tchn:* Fuge *f;* (*b*) *Anat:* Gelenk *n.* **2.** *Cu:* Braten *m.* **3.** *F: esp. N. Am:* Lokal *n; Pej:* Bude *f.* **III.** *adj.* **1.** gemeinsam; **j. account,** Gemeinschaftskonto *n.* **2.** Mit-; **j. owner,** Miteigentümer *m.* ◆'**join 'up,** *v.* **1.** *v.i. a) Mil:* zum Militär gehen; (*b*) (*of lines etc.*) zusammenlaufen. **2.** *v.tr.* (zwei Sachen) zusammenfügen.

**joist** [dʒɔist], *s.* Dielenbalken *m; pl.* Gebälk *n.*

**joke** [dʒəuk]. **I.** *s.* Scherz *m;* Witz *m;* (**practical**) **j.,** Streich *m; F:* **it's no j.!** das ist keine Kleinigkeit! **II.** *v.i.* scherzen; (*tell jokes*) Witze reißen; **you must be joking!** das meinst du doch nicht im Ernst! ◆'**joker,** *s.* **1.** Spaßvogel *m.* **2.** (*in cards*) Joker *m.* ◆'**joking,** *s.* **j. apart,** Scherz beiseite.

**jolly** ['dʒɔli]. **I.** *adj.* fröhlich; lustig. **II.** *adv. F:* **j. glad,** sehr froh.

**jolt** [dʒəult]. **I.** *s.* Ruck *m.* **II.** *v.* **1.** *v.tr.* (j-m, etwas *dat*) einen Ruck geben. **2.** *v.i.* holpern.

**Jordan** ['dʒɔːd(ə)n]. *Pr. n.* Jordanien *n.*

**jostle** ['dʒɔsl], *v.tr. & i.* drängeln.

**jot** [dʒɔt], *v.tr.* **to j. sth. down,** sich *dat* etwas notieren.

**journal** ['dʒəːn(ə)l], *s.* **1.** Journal *n* (einer Reise usw.); (*diary*) Tagebuch *n.* **2.** (*periodical*) Zeitschrift *f.* ◆'**journalism,** *s.* Journalismus *m.* ◆'**journalist,** *s.* Journalist(in) *m(f).*

**journey** ['dʒəːni], *s.* Reise *f.*

**jovial** ['dʒəuvjəl], *adj.* jovial.

**joy** [dʒɔi], *s.* Freude *f.* ◆'**joyful,** *adj.* freudig. ◆'**joy-ride,** *s. F:* Spritztour *f.* ◆'**joy-stick,** *s.* Steuerknüppel *m.*

**jubilant** ['dʒuːbilənt], *adj.* hocherfreut. ◆**jubi'lation,** *s.* Jubel *m.*

**jubilee** ['dʒuːbiliː], *s.* Jubiläum *n.*

**judge** [dʒʌdʒ]. **I.** *s. Jur:* Richter *m.* **2.** *Sp:* Schiedsrichter *m.* **II.** *v.* **1.** *v.tr.* (*a*) *Jur:* (einen Fall) entscheiden; (*b*) (eine Sache) beurteilen; **to j. a competition,** in einem Wettbewerb entscheiden; (c) (eine Entfernung usw.) schätzen. 2. v.i. urteilen **(by/from,** nach + dat). ◆'**judg(e)ment,** s. 1. Urteil n. 2. (ability) Urteilsvermögen n. ◆**judicial** [dʒuː'diʃəl], adj. gerichtlich. ◆**ju'dicious,** adj. klug.

**jug** [dʒʌg], s. Krug m; (for milk etc.) Kanne f; (small) Kännchen n.

**juggle** ['dʒʌgl], v.i. jonglieren. ◆'**juggler,** s. Jongleur m.

**Jugoslavia** [juːgə(u)'slɑːvjə]. Pr. n. Jugoslawien n.

**juice** [dʒuːs], s. Saft m.

**jukebox** ['dʒuːkbɔks], s. Musikbox f.

**July** [dʒu'lai], s. Juli m.

**jumble** ['dʒʌmbl]. I. v.tr. to j. sth. up, etwas durcheinanderbringen. II. s. Durcheinander n; j. **sale,** approx. = Flohmarkt m.

**jumbo** ['dʒʌmbəu], s. j. **(jet),** Jumbo-Jet m.

**jump** [dʒʌmp]. I. s. 1. Sprung m. 2. (fence) Hindernis n. II. v. 1. v.i. (a) springen; **you made me j.!** du hast mich erschreckt! (b) to j. **to conclusions,** voreilig Schlüsse ziehen. 2. v.tr. (etwas) überspringen; to j. **the queue,** sich vordrängen. ◆'**jump at,** v.tr. (a) to j. **at sth.,** sich auf etwas acc stürzen; (b) F: to j. **at an offer,** ein Angebot sofort ergreifen. ◆'**jumper,** s. Pullover m. ◆'**jump-'lead,** s. Starthilfekabel n. ◆'**jumpy,** adj. F: nervös.

**junction** ['dʒʌŋk(ʃ)(ə)n], s. 1. Verbindungsstelle f. 2. (a) (road) j., Kreuzung f; T-j., Einmündung f; (b) Rail: Bahnknotenpunkt m.

**juncture** ['dʒʌŋ(k)tʃər], s. at this j., in diesem Augenblick.

**June** [dʒuːn], s. Juni m.

**jungle** ['dʒʌŋgl], s. Dschungel m.

**junior** ['dʒuːnjər]. I. s. (a) Junior m. (b) **he is two years my j.,** er ist zwei Jahre jünger als ich. II. adj. jünger; j. **school,** Grundschule f; j. **events,** Juniorenwettkampf m.

**junk** [dʒʌŋk], s. Pej: Ramsch m; j. **shop,** Trödlerladen m.

**jurisdiction** [dʒuəris'dikʃ(ə)n], s. (authority) Gerichtsbarkeit f; (area of authority) Kompetenzbereich m.

**jury** ['dʒuəri], s. 1. Jur: the j., die Geschworenen pl. 2. (of competition) Jury f. ◆'**juror, 'juryman,** s. Geschworener m.

**just** [dʒʌst]. I. adj. (a) (fair) gerecht; (b) (deserved) verdient; **-ly,** adv. j. **famous,** mit Recht berühmt. II. adv. 1. gerade; I **saw him j. now/have j. seen him,** ich habe ihn gerade gesehen; j. **as he was leaving,** gerade als er wegging. 2. (exactly) genau; **it's j. the same,** es ist genau das gleiche; **he can do it j. as well,** er kann es ebenso gut. 3. I **was (only) j. in time/F: I only j. made it,** ich habe es gerade noch geschafft; **only j. enough,** gerade noch genug. 4. (only) nur; j. **tell me,** sag's mir doch. 5. F: j. **marvellous,** einfach großartig.

**justice** ['dʒʌstis], s. Gerechtigkeit f; **to do s.o. j.** j-m gerecht werden.

**justify** ['dʒʌstifai], v.tr. rechtfertigen. ◆**justi'fiable,** adj. berechtigt; (of action) zu rechtfertigen; (of conduct) entschuldbar. ◆**justifi'cation,** s. Rechtfertigung f. ◆'**justified,** adj. (of decision etc.) gerechtfertigt; (of pers.) to be j. **in doing sth.,** berechtigt sein, etwas zu tun.

**jut** [dʒʌt], v.i. to j. **(out),** vorspringen.

**juvenile** ['dʒuːvənail], adj. jugendlich; Jugend-; j. **court,** Jugendgericht n; j. **delinquent,** jugendlicher Straftäter m.

# K

**K, k** [kei], s. (der Buchstabe) K, k n.

**kaleidoscope** [kə'laidəskəup], s. Kaleidoskop n.

**kangaroo** [kæŋgə'ruː], s. Z: Känguruh n.

**kayak** ['kaiæk], s. Kajak m.

**keel** [kiːl]. I. s. Kiel m. II. v.i. to k. **over,** kentern.

**keen** [kiːn], adj. 1. (of interest, feeling) stark; Com: k. **competition,** scharfe Konkurrenz. 2. (of pers.) eifrig; **to be k. on sth.,** von etwas dat begeistert sein. 3. (of eye, ear) scharf.

**keep** [kiːp]. I. v.irr. 1. v.tr. (a) (retain) (etwas) behalten; **to k. a seat for s.o.,** einen Platz für j-n freihalten; **to k. a secret,** ein Geheimnis bewahren; (b) (look after) (Geflügel, Schweine usw.) halten; **to k. a hotel,** ein Hotel führen; **to k. one's parents,** für seine Eltern sorgen; (c) (hold up) (j-n) aufhalten; **to k. s.o. waiting,** j-n warten lassen; **the noise kept**

me from sleeping, der Lärm ließ mich nicht schlafen; (d) **to k. a promise,** ein Versprechen halten; (e) **to k. sth. secret,** etwas geheimhalten; (f) (store) (etwas) aufbewahren. 2. v.i. (a) **to k. doing sth.,** (i) etwas immer wieder machen; (ii) (continue) etwas weitermachen; (b) (on sign) **k. left,** links halten; (c) (of food etc.) sich halten; (d) **to k. warm/well/fit, warm/ gesund/fit bleiben; F: how are you keeping?** wie geht es Ihnen? II. s. **to earn one's k.,** seinen Unterhalt verdienen. ◆'**keep a'way,** v. 1. v.tr. (j-n, etwas) fernhalten. 2. v.i. sich fernhalten. ◆'**keep 'back,** v. 1. v.tr. (a) (den Feind, die Menge) zurückhalten; (b) (die Wahrheit) verschweigen; (of money) (zurück)behalten. 2. v.i. k. **back!** zurücktreten! ◆'**keeper,** s. (of zoo, lighthouse) Wärter m; (of park etc.) Wächter m. ◆'**keep 'in,** v. 1. v.tr. (a) (j-n) nicht hinauslassen; (b) (Zorn usw.) zurückhalten; (c) **to k. one's hand in,** in Übung bleiben. 2. *v.i.* (a) (*on road*) sich am Rand halten; (b) **to k. in with s.o.,** mit j-m auf gutem Fuß bleiben. ◆'**keeping,** *s.* 1. Aufbewahrung *f;* **for (your) safe k.,** zur Verwahrung. 2. **in k. with sth.,** etwas *dat* entsprechend. ◆'**keep 'off,** *v.tr.* (etwas) nicht anrühren; **k. o. the grass!** Betreten des Rasens verboten! **k. your hands o.!** Hände weg! ◆'**keep 'on,** *v.* 1. *v.tr.* (a) (seinen Hut) aufbehalten; (b) (j-n) (in einer Stellung) behalten. 2. *v.i.* **to k. on doing sth.,** (i) (*repeat*) etwas immer wieder machen; (ii) (*continue*) etwas weitermachen; *F:* **to k. on at s.o.,** an j-m dauernd herumnörgeln. ◆'**keep 'out,** *v.* 1. *v.tr.* (j-n) nicht hereinlassen. 2. *v.i.* **to k. o. of the way,** sich fernhalten; **K. o.!** Betreten verboten! *F:* **k. o. of this!** misch dich nicht ein! ◆'**keep to,** *v.tr.* (a) **to k. to a rule/promise,** sich an eine Regel/ein Versprechen halten; (b) **to k. to the left,** sich links halten; **he keeps (himself) to himself,** er ist ein Einzelgänger. ◆'**keep 'up,** *v.* 1. *v.tr.* (a) (*look after*) (einen Garten usw.) instandhalten; (b) **he won't be able to k. it up,** er wird es nicht durchhalten können; **k. it up!** nur so weiter! nicht nachlassen! (c) (*maintain*) (Interessen, eine Freundschaft usw.) aufrechterhalten; (d) **to k. s.o. up,** j-n vom Schlafen abhalten. 2. *v.i.* schritthalten (**with,** mit + *dat*).

**kennel** ['ken(ə)l], *s.* (a) Hundehütte *f;* (b) *pl.* (*for boarding*) Tierpension *f.*

**kerb** [kə:b], *s.* Bordkante *f.*

**kernel** ['kə:n(ə)l], *s.* Kern *m;* (*of cereal*) Korn *n.*

**ketchup** ['ketʃəp], *s.* Ketchup *m & n.*

**kettle** ['ketl], *s.* Kessel *m.*

**key** [ki:], *s.* 1. Schlüssel *m.* **k. ring,** Schlüsselring *m; Fig:* **k. word,** Schlüsselwort *n.* 2. *Mus:* Tonart *f.* 3. Taste *f* (einer Schreibmaschine, des Klaviers usw.). ◆'**keyboard,** *s.* (*of typewriter, piano*) Tastatur *f.* ◆'**keyhole,** *s.* Schlüsselloch *n.*

**khaki** ['kɑ:ki]. I. *adj.* khakifarben. II. *s.* (*material*) Khaki *m.*

**kick** [kik]. I. *v.* 1. *v.i.* (*of pers.*) treten; (*of baby*) strampeln; (*of horse etc.*) ausschlagen. 2. *v.tr.* (j-m, etwas *dat*) einen Fußtritt geben; **to k. the ball,** den Ball treten. II. *s.* 1. Tritt *m.* 2. *F: P:* (*just*) **for kicks,** nur zum Spaß. ◆'**kick 'off,** *v.i.* (a) *Fb:* anstoßen; (b) *F:* (*start*) loslegen. ◆'**kick-off,** *s.* Anstoß *m.* ◆'**kick 'out,** *v.tr. F:* (j-n) rausschmeißen. ◆'**kick 'up,** *v.tr. F:* **to k. up a fuss,** Theater machen.

**kid¹** [kid], *s.* 1. *Z:* Kitz *n.* 2. **k. gloves,** Glacéhandschuhe *mpl.* 3. *F:* Kind *n.*

**kid²,** *v.tr. F:* (j-n) foppen; **don't k. yourself,** mach dir nichts vor.

**kidnap** ['kidnæp], *v.tr.* (j-n) entführen; *F:* (j-n) kidnappen. ◆'**kidnapper,** *s.* Ent-

führer *m; F:* Kidnapper *m.*

**kidney** ['kidni], *s.* Niere *f.*

**kill** [kil], *v.tr.* töten; **to k. oneself,** sich umbringen; **to k. time,** die Zeit totschlagen. ◆'**killer,** *s.* 1. (*murderer*) Mörder *m.* 2. *F:* (*of drug*) **to be a k.,** tödlich sein; **k. disease,** tödliche Krankheit. 2. **k. whale,** Schwertwal *m.* ◆'**killing,** *s.* 1. Tötung *f* (eines Menschen); Schlachten *n* (eines Tieres). 2. Morden *n.*

**kiln** [kiln], *s.* Brennofen *m.*

**kilogram(me)** ['kiləʊgræm], *s.* Kilogramm *n.*

**kilometre** ['kiləʊmi:tər, ki'lɔmitər], *s.* Kilometer *m.*

**kilt** [kilt], *s.* Kilt *m.*

**kin** [kin], *s.* **next of k.,** nächste(r) Verwandte(r) *f(m).*

**kind¹** [kaind], *s.* Art *f;* **this k. of music,** diese Art Musik; *F:* **I k. of expected it,** ich habe das irgendwie schon erwartet.

**kind²,** *adj.* nett; gut. ◆'**kind-'hearted,** *adj.* gutherzig. ◆'**kindly.** I. *adj.* (*of pers.*) gütig. II. *adv.* freundlicherweise; **will you k. remove your foot!** nimm gefälligst deinen Fuß weg! ◆'**kindness,** *s.* Güte *f;* (*helpfulness*) Gefälligkeit *f.*

**kindergarten** ['kindəga:tn], *s.* Vorschule *f.*

**kindle** ['kindl], *v.tr.* (a) (ein Feuer usw.) anzünden; (b) (Leidenschaft) entflammen.

**king** [kiŋ], *s.* König *m.* ◆'**kingdom,** *s.* 1. Königreich *n;* **the United K.,** das Vereinigte Königreich. 2. Reich *n;* **animal k.,** Tierreich *n.* ◆'**kingfisher,** *s.* Eisvogel *m.* ◆'**king-size(d),** *adj.* im Großformat.

**kink** [kiŋk], *s.* Knick *m.* ◆'**kinky,** *adj. P:* abnorm.

**kiosk** ['ki:ɔsk], *s.* Kiosk *m.*

**kipper** ['kipər], *s.* Räucherhering *m.*

**kiss** [kis]. I. *s.* Kuß *m.* II. *v.tr.* küssen.

**kit** [kit], *s.* 1. (*equipment*) Ausrüstung *f.* 2. (*set of parts*) Bausatz *m;* (**model**) **k.,** Baukasten *m.* ◆'**kit-bag,** *s.* Seesack *m.*

**kitchen** ['kitʃən], *s.* Küche *f;* **k. unit,** Küchenelement *n;* **k. sink,** Spülbecken *n.*

**kite** [kait], *s.* Drachen *m.*

**kitten** [kitn], *s.* Kätzchen *n.*

**kitty** [ ], *s.* Kasse *f.*

**knack** [næk], *s.* Kniff *m; F:* Dreh *m.*

**knapsack** ['næpsæk], *s.* Rucksack *m; Mil:* Tornister *m.*

**knead** [ni:d], *v.tr.* kneten.

**knee** [ni:], *s.* Knie *n.* ◆'**knee-cap,** *s.* Kniescheibe *f.*

**kneel** [ni:l], *v.i.irr.* knien.

**knickers** ['nikəz], *s.pl.* Damenschlüpfer *m.*

**knife,** *pl.* **knives** [naif, naivz]. I. *s.* Messer *n.* II. *v.tr.* (j-n, etwas) mit dem Messer stechen.

**knight** [nait]. I. *s.* 1. *Hist:* Ritter *m.* 2. (*in chess*) Springer *m.* II. *v.tr.* (j-n) in den Adelsstand erheben. ◆'**knighthood,** *s.* **to receive a k.,** in den Adelsstand erho-

ben werden.
**knit** [nit], *v.tr & i.* stricken. ◆**'knitting,**
*s.* **1.** (*action*) Stricken *n.* **2.** Strickarbeit *f;*
**k. machine,** Strickmaschine *f.*
◆**'knitting-needle,** *s.* Stricknadel *f.*
◆**knitwear,** *s.* Strickwaren *fpl.*
**knob** [nɔb], *s.* **1.** (*on door etc.*) Griff *m;*
(*on drawer, radio etc.*) Knopf *m.* **2.** Stückchen *n* (Butter usw.).
**knock** [nɔk]. **I.** *s.* Klopfen *n;* (*blow*)
Schlag *m;* **there was a k.** (**at the door**),
es hat geklopft. **II.** *v.* **1.** *v.tr.* (*a*) (j-n, etwas) schlagen; (*b*) *F:* (*criticize*) **to k. sth.,**
etwas heruntermachen. **2.** *v.i.* (*a*) **to k.**
**against sth.,** gegen etwas *acc* stoßen; (*b*)
(*of pers., Aut: of engine*) klopfen.
◆**'knock 'down,** *v.tr.* (*a*) (j-n) niederschlagen; (etwas) umstoßen; **to be**
**knocked down by a car,** von einem Auto
angefahren werden; (*b*) (ein Haus) niederreißen. ◆**'knocker,** *s.* Türklopfer *m.*
◆**'knocking,** *s.* Klopfen *n.* ◆**'knock-**
**'kneed,** *adj.* X-beinig. ◆**'knock 'off,**
*v.* **1.** *v.tr. F:* **to k. off an essay etc.,**
einen Aufsatz usw. schnell hinhauen.
**2.** *v.i. F:* Feierabend machen.
◆**'knock 'out,** *v.tr.* (*a*) (einen Zahn)
(her)ausschlagen; (*b*) (j-n) k.o. schlagen.

◆**'knock 'over,** *v.tr.* (j-n, etwas) umstoßen.
**knot** [nɔt]. **I.** *s.* Knoten *m.* **II.** *v.tr.* (eine
Schnur) verknoten.
**know** [nəu]. **I.** *v.tr. & i.irr.* (*a*) (j-n, einen
Ort, ein Buch usw.) kennen; **to get to k.**
**s.o., sth.,** j-n, etwas kennenlernen; (*b*)
(etwas) wissen; **as far as I k.,** soviel ich
weiß; (*c*) **to k. about sth.,** über etwas *acc*
Bescheid wissen; **I k. nothing about it,**
davon weiß ich nichts. **II.** *s. F:* **to be in**
**the k.,** im Bilde sein. ◆**'know-all,** *s. F:*
Besserwisser *m.* ◆**'know-how,** *s. F:*
Sachkenntnis *f;* Technik *f.* ◆**'knowing.**
**I.** *adj.* wissend; **-ly,** *adv.* **1.** (*intentionally*)
wissentlich. **2. to look k. at s.o.,** j-m
einen wissenden Blick zuwerfen. **II.** *s.*
**there's no k. what will happen,** es ist
nicht vorauszusehen, was jetzt geschieht.
◆**knowledge** ['nɔlidʒ], *s.* **1.** (*in general*)
Wissen *n.* **2.** (*of sth. particular*) Kenntnisse *fpl.* ◆**'knowledgeable** *adj.* bewandert (**about,** in + *dat*).
**knuckle** [nʌkl], *s.* Fingerknöchel *m.*
**Korea** [kə'riə]. *Pr. n.* Korea *n.*
◆**Ko'rean. I.** *adj.* koreanisch. **the K.**
**War,** der Koreakrieg. **II.** *s.* Koreaner(in)
*m(f).*

# L

**L, l** [el], *s.* (der Buchstabe) L, l *n;* **L**
**plate,** Fahrschülerschild *n.*
**lab** [læb], *s. F:* Labor *n.*
**label** ['leibl]. **I.** *s.* **1.** Etikett *n;* (*tag*)
Schildchen *n;* (*luggage*) l., (*tie-on*) Ge-
päckanhänger *m.* **II.** *v.tr.* (*a*) (Flaschen
usw.) etikettieren; (*b*) (j-n als etwas) bezeichnen.
**laboratory** [lə'bɔrətri], *s.* Labor *n.*
**laborious** [lə'bɔːriəs], *adj.* mühsam.
**labour** ['leibər], *s.* **1.** (*work, task*) Arbeit
*f.* **2.** (*a*) (*workers*) *coll.* Arbeiter *mpl;* **l.**
**force,** Arbeiterschaft *f;* (*b*) *Pol:* **the L.**
**party,** die Labour Party. **3.** *Med:*
(**pains**), Geburtswehen *fpl.* ◆**'labourer,**
*s.* (ungelernter) Arbeiter *m.*
◆**'laboursaving,** *adj.* arbeitssparend.
**labyrinth** ['læbirinθ], *s.* Labyrinth *n.*
**lace** [leis]. **I.** *s.* **1.** (*for tying*) Schnürband
*n;* (*shoe*) l., Schnürsenkel *m.* **2.** (*material*) Spitze *f.* **II.** *v.tr.* **to l.** (**up**) **one's**
**shoes,** sich *dat* die Schuhe zuschnüren.
**lacerate** ['læsəreit], *v.tr.* zerfleischen.
**lack** [læk]. **I.** *s.* Mangel *m* (**of,** an + *dat*);
**II.** *v.tr. & i.* **he lacks/is lacking in ex-**
**perience,** es fehlt ihm an Erfahrung.
**lacquer** ['lækər], *s.* Lack *m;* **hair l.,** Haarspray *m.*
**lad** [læd], *s.* Junge *m,* (junger) Bursche *m.*
**ladder** ['lædər]. **I.** *s.* **1.** Leiter *f.* **2.** (*in*
*stocking*) Laufmasche *f.* **II.** *v.i.* Laufma-
schen bekommen.
**ladle** ['leidl], *s.* Schöpflöffel *m.*
**lady** ['leidi], *s.* (*a*) Dame *f;* (*in title*) Lady

*f;* **l. in waiting,** Hofdame *f;* (*b*) *F:* **the la-**
**dies',** die Damentoilette. ◆**'ladybird,** *s.*
Marienkäfer *m.* ◆**'ladylike,** *adj.* damen-
haft.
**lag** [læg], *v.i.* **to l. behind** (**s.o.**), (mit
j-m) nicht Schritt halten; (j-m) nachhin-
ken.
**lager** ['lɑːgər], *s.* Lagerbier *n.*
**lagoon** [lə'guːn], *s.* Lagune *f.*
**lair** [leər], *s.* Lager *n.*
**lake** [leik], *s.* See *m.*
**lamb** [læm], *s.* Lamm *n.*
**lame** [leim], *adj.* lahm.
**lament** [lə'ment]. **I.** *s.* Klage *f.* **II.** *v.tr.*
beklagen. ◆**lamentable** ['læməntəbl],
*adj.* beklagenswert. ◆**lamentation**
[-'teifən], *s.* Wehklage *f.*
**lamp** [læmp], *s.* Lampe *f.* ◆**'lamp-post,**
*s.* Laternenpfahl *m.* ◆**'lampshade,** *s.*
Lampenschirm *m.*
**lance** [lɑːns]. **I.** *s.* Lanze *f.* **II.** *v.tr. Med:*
aufschneiden.
**land** [lænd]. **I.** *s.* Land *n.* **II.** *v.* **1.** *v.tr.*
(*a*) (ein Flugzeug) landen; (*b*) *F:* (eine
Stellung) kriegen. **2.** *v.i.* landen.
◆**'landing,** *s.* **1.** Landung *f.* **2.** (*in hou-*
*se*) Treppenflur *m;* (**half**) l., Treppenab-
satz *m.* ◆**'landlady,** *s.* Wirtin *f.*
◆**'landlord,** *s.* (*a*) Hauseigentümer *m;*
(*of estate*) Grundbesitzer *m;* (*b*) (*of pub*)
Wirt *m.* ◆**'landmark,** *s.* Orientierungs-
punkt *m;* (*famous building*) Wahrzeichen
*n; Fig:* Markstein *m* (**in history etc.,** der
Geschichte usw.). ◆**'landowner,** *s.*

Grundbesitzer *m.* ◆'**landscape,** *s.*
Landschaft *f;* **l. gardener,** Gartenarchitekt *m.* ◆'**landslide,** *s.* 1. Erdrutsch *m.*
2. *Pol:* **l. victory,** überwältigender Wahlsieg.

**lane** [lein], *s.* 1. (*a*) (*in town*) Gasse *f;* (*b*) (*in country*) enge Landstraße *f;* Weg *m.* 2. (*a*) *Aut:* Spur *f;* (*b*) *Sp:* Bahn *f* (einer Rennbahn).

**language** ['læŋgwidʒ], *s.* Sprache *f.*

**languid** ['læŋgwid], *adj.* träge.

**lanky** ['læŋki], *adj.* schlaksig.

**lantern** ['læntən], *s.* Laterne *f.*

**lap¹** [læp], *s.* Schoß *m.*

**lap²,** *s. Sp:* Runde *f.*

**lap³,** *v.* 1 *v.tr. F:* **he lapped it up,** *Fig:* (*praise etc.*) er hat sich darin gesonnt. *v.i.* (*of water*) plätschern.

**lapel** [lə'pell], *s.* Aufschlag *m.*

**lapse** [læps], *s.* 1. (*a*) (*slip*) Versehen *n;* (*b*) (*moral*) Fehltritt *m.* 2. (*of time*) Verlauf *m;* Zeitspanne *f.*

**larceny** ['lɑːsəni], *s.* Diebstahl *m.*

**lard** [lɑːd], *s.* Schmalz *n.*

**larder** ['lɑːdər], *s.* Speisekammer *f.*

**large** [lɑːdʒ]. **I.** *adj.* groß. **II.** *s.* **at l.,** auf freiem Fuß; **the people at l.,** die breite Masse. **III.** *adv.* **by and l.,** im großen und ganzen; **-ly,** *adv.* größtenteils. ◆'**large-'scale,** *adj.* großangelegt.

**lark¹** [lɑːk], *s. Orn:* Lerche *f.*

**lark². I.** *s. F:* Jux *m.* **II.** *v.i. F:* **to l.** (**about**), herumtollen.

**larva,** *pl.* **-ae** ['lɑːvə, -viː], *s.* Larve *f.*

**larynx** ['læriŋks], *s.* Kehlkopf *m.* ◆**laryngitis** [lærin'dʒaitis], *s.* Kehlkopfentzündung *f.*

**laser** ['leizər], *s.* Laser *m.*

**lash¹** [læʃ]. **I.** *s.* Peitschenhieb *m.* **II.** *v.tr. & i.* peitschen. ◆'**lash 'out,** *v.i.* (*a*) um sich *acc* schlagen; (*verbally*) to l. o. (**against/at s.o., sth.**), (über j-n, etwas *acc*) herfallen; (*b*) *F:* es sich *dat* was kosten lassen.

**lash²,** *v.tr.* (*tie*) festbinden.

**lass** [læs], *esp. Scot:* **lassie** ['læsi], *s.* Mädel *n.*

**lasso** [læ'suː, 'læsuː, -uːz]. **I.** *s.* Lasso *n & m.* **II.** *v.tr.* mit einem Lasso einfangen.

**last¹** [lɑːst]. **I.** *adj.* letzte(r,s); **she was the l. to arrive,** sie kam als letzte; **the l. but one,** der/die/das vorletzte; **l. night,** gestern abend. **II.** *adv.* (*a*) **when I saw him l./l. saw him,** als ich ihn das letzte Mal sah; (*b*) **he came l.,** er kam als letzter (*Sp:* ans Ziel); **-ly,** *adv.* zuletzt.

**last²,** *v.i.* dauern; (*of food, weather etc.*) sich halten. ◆'**lasting,** *adj.* (*of peace, friendship etc.*) dauernd, von Dauer; (*of effect etc.*) anhaltend.

**latch** [lætʃ], *s.* Klinke *f;* **on the l.,** (nur) eingeklinkt; nicht verschlossen.

**late** [leit]. **I.** *adj.* 1. (*too l.*) (zu) spät; **the train is ten minutes l.,** der Zug hat zehn Minuten Verspätung. 2. (*not early*) spät. 3. **my l. father,** mein verstorbener Vater. 4. **of l.,** in letzter Zeit; **the latest model,** das neueste Modell. **II.** *adv.* (*a*) **to arrive too l./an hour l.,** zu spät/mit einer Stunde Verspätung ankommen; (*b*) **to stay up l.,** bis spät (in die Nacht) aufbleiben; **l. in life,** im vorgerückten Alter; **at the latest,** spätestens; **-ly,** *adv.* in letzter Zeit. ◆'**latecomer,** *s.* Nachzügler *m.*

**latent** ['leit(ə)nt], *adj.* verborgen; *Psy: Ph:* latent.

**lateral** ['lætərəl], *adj.* seitlich.

**lathe** [leið], *s.* Drehbank *f.*

**lather** ['læðər]. **I.** *s.* Seifenschaum *m.* **II.** *v.i.* schäumen.

**Latin** ['lætin]. **I.** *s.* Latein *n.* **II.** *adj.* 1. lateinisch. 2. (*of temperament*) südländisch; **L. America,** Lateinamerika *n.*

**latitude** ['lætitjuːd], *s.* 1. Spielraum *m.* 2. *Geog:* Breite *f.*

**latter** ['lætər], *adj.* 1. **the l.,** der/die/das letztere. 2. **the l. half of June,** die zweite Junihälfte.

**laudable** ['lɔːdəbl], *adj.* lobenswert.

**laugh** [lɑːf]. **I.** *s.* Lachen *n.* **II.** *v.* 1. *v.i.* (*a*) lachen; **to l. at s.o.,** j-n auslachen. 2. *v.tr.* **he tried to l. the matter off,** er versuchte, die Sache mit einem Scherz abzutun. ◆'**laughable,** *adj.* lächerlich. ◆'**laughing. I.** *adj.* lachend. **II.** *s.* Lachen *n;* **it's no l. matter,** da gibt's nichts zu lachen. ◆'**laughing-stock,** *s.* **to be a l.-s.,** ausgelacht werden. ◆'**laughter,** *s.* Gelächter *n.*

**launch** [lɔːntʃ]. **I.** *s.* Barkasse *f.* **II.** *v.tr.* (*a*) (eine Rakete usw.) abschießen; (*b*) (ein neues Schiff) vom Stapel lassen; (*c*) *Mil:* **to l. an attack,** einen Angriff starten; (*d*) *esp. Com:* (ein neues Erzeugnis, Modell usw.) herausbringen; (ein Unternehmen) starten. ◆'**launching,** *s.* 1. (*a*) Stapellauf *m* (eines Schiffes); (*b*) Abschuß *m* (*einer Rakete*); **l. pad,** Abschußrampe *f.* 2. Herausbringen *n* (eines Erzeugnisses usw.).

**laundry** ['lɔːndri], *s.* 1. (*place*) Wäscherei *f.* 2. (*clothes etc.*) Wäsche *f.* ◆**launderette** [lɔːn'dret], *s.* Waschsalon *m.*

**laurel** ['lɔrəl], *s.* Lorbeer *m.*

**lava** ['lɑːvə], *s.* Lava *f.*

**lavatory** ['lævətri], *s.* Toilette *f.*

**lavender** ['lævindər], *s.* Lavendel *m.*

**lavish** ['læviʃ]. **I.** *adj.* 1. (*of pers.*) verschwenderisch. 2. (*of entertainment etc.*) aufwendig. **II.** *v.tr.* **to l. attention on s.o.,** j-n mit Aufmerksamkeit überschütten; **-ly,** *adv.* **to entertain l.,** mit viel Aufwand empfangen.

**law** [lɔː], *s.* 1. Gesetz *n.* 2. (*subject*) Jura *npl;* **l. school,** Rechtsakademie *f.* 3. (*justice*) Recht *n;* **under British l.,** nach britischem Recht. ◆'**law-abiding,** *adj.* gesetzestreu. ◆'**lawless,** *adj.* gesetzlos. ◆'**lawsuit,** *s.* Prozeß *m.* ◆'**lawyer,** *s.* Rechtsanwalt *m;* Jurist *m.*

**lawn** [lɔːn], *s.* Rasen *m.* ◆'**lawnmower,** *s.* Rasenmäher *m.*

**lax** [læks], *adj.* (*of morals, discipline etc.*)

locker; (of pers. etc.) nachlässig.
◆'laxative, s. Abführmittel n.

lay¹ [lei], attrib. adj. laienhaft; Laien-.
◆'layman, pl. -men, s. Laie m.

lay², v.irr. 1. v.tr. legen; (einen Teppich,
Rohre usw.) verlegen; (eine Falle) aufstellen; to l. the table, den Tisch dek-
ken. 2. v.i. (of hen) Eier legen.
◆'layabout, s. Faulenzer m. ◆'layby,
s. (large) Rastplatz m; (small) Parkstreifen
m. ◆'lay 'down, v.tr. (a) hinlegen; to
l. d. one's arms, die Waffen niederlegen;
(b) (Grundsätze, Regeln) festsetzen; (Bedingungen) stellen. ◆'layer, s. Schicht
f; (of clothing) Lage f. ◆'lay 'into, v.tr.
F: to l. i. s.o., auf j-n losgehen; (criticize) über j-n herziehen. ◆'lay 'off, v.tr.
(Arbeiter) entlassen. ◆'lay 'on, v.tr.
(Gas, Wasser usw.) anlegen; (ein Essen)
bereitstellen. ◆'lay 'out, v.tr. (a) (einen
Leichnam) aufbahren; (b) (Geld) ausle-
gen; (c) (einen Garten) anlegen; (d) (with
blow) (j-n) niederstrecken. ◆'layout, s.
Anordnung f; (of magazine etc.) Layout n
(einer Seite usw.).

laziness ['leizinəs], s. Faulheit f. ◆'lazy,
adj. faul. ◆'lazybones, s. F: Faulpelz
m.

lead¹ [led], s. Blei n.

lead² [li:d]. I. v.tr. & i.irr. führen. II. s.
1. Führung f; to take the l., die Führung übernehmen. 2. (clue) Anhaltspunkt
m; (of police) Hinweis m. 3. Th: Hauptrolle f. 4. (for dog) Leine f. 5. (flex) Kabel n. ◆'lead a'stray, v.tr. verführen.
◆'lead a'way, v.tr. wegführen.
◆'lead 'back, v.tr. zurückführen.
◆'leader, s. 1. Führer m; Anführer m
(eines Aufruhrs usw.). 2. (in newspaper)
Leitartikel m. ◆'leadership, s. Führung f. ◆'leading, adj. 1. l. question,
Suggestivfrage f. 2. führend; l. article,
Leitartikel m; l. man (lady), Hauptdar-
steller(in) m(f). ◆'lead 'up, v.i. to l. up
to a subject, auf ein Thema hinführen; I
know what you are leading up to, ich
weiß, worauf Sie hinauswollen.

leaf, pl. leaves [li:f, li:vz], s. 1. Blatt n.
2. (of table) Klappe f. ◆'leaflet, s. Com:
Prospekt m; Pol: Flugblatt n. ◆'leafy,
adj. belaubt.

league [li:g], s. Liga f; in l. with s.o.,
mit j-m verbündet.

leak [li:k]. I. s. undichte Stelle f; (hole)
Loch n; (in ship etc.) Leck n. II. v. 1.
v.i. (of joint) undicht sein; (of tank, ship)
ein Leck haben; to l. away, auslaufen;
the roof is leaking, das Dach läßt den
Regen durch. 2. v.tr. (Nachrichten)
durchsickern lassen. ◆'leak 'out, v.i.
(of news) durchsickern. ◆'leaky, adj. (of
ship, tank) leck; (of roof, shoes etc.) undicht.

lean¹ [li:n], adj. mager.

lean², v.irr. 1. v.i. (a) sich lehnen
(against/on sth., an etwas acc); (position)
he is/was leaning on the wall, er lehnt/

lehnte an der Wand; (b) (bend over) sich
beugen; to l. out of the window, sich
zum Fenster hinauslehnen; to l. back,
sich zurücklehnen; (c) (of wall etc.) schief
stehen. 2. v.tr. to l. a ladder against a
wall, eine Leiter an eine Mauer anlehnen. ◆'leaning, adj. schief. ◆'lean-
to, s. (shed) angebauter Schuppen m.

leap [li:p]. I. s. Sprung m. II. v. 1. v.i.
irr. springen. 2. v.tr. (einen Graben)
überspringen. ◆'leapfrog, s. Bock-
sprung m; to (play at) l., bockspringen.
◆'leap-year, s. Schaltjahr n.

learn [lə:n], v.tr.irr. (a) lernen; (b) (einen
Beruf usw.) erlernen; (c) (Nachrichten
usw.) erfahren. ◆'learned ['lə:nid], adj.
gelehrt. ◆'learner, s. 1. to be a quick
l., leicht lernen. 2. Anfänger(in) m(f); l.
driver,　　　Fahrschüler(in)　　　m(f).
◆'learning, s. 1. (process) Lernen n. 2.
(knowledge) Wissen n; (erudition) Gelehrt-
heit f.

lease [li:s]. I. s. Pacht f; (rental agreement)
Mietvertrag m. II. v.tr. (a) verpachten (to
s.o., an j-n); (b) (take on l.) pachten; (ein
Auto) mieten. ◆'leasehold, s. 1. flat,
Pachtwohnung f. ◆'leaseholder, s.
Pächter m.

leash [li:ʃ], s. Hundeleine f.

least [li:st]. I. adj. geringste(r,s). II. s.
das Geringste/Wenigste/Mindeste; at l.
£10, mindestens zehn Pfund; I can at l.
try, ich kann's wenigstens versuchen. III.
adv. am wenigsten.

leather ['leðər], s. Leder n.

leave [li:v]. I. s. 1. (permission) Erlaubnis
f. 2. Mil: etc: l. (of absence) Urlaub m;
on l., auf Urlaub. 3. to take one's l.,
Abschied nehmen. II. v.irr. 1. v.tr. (a)
(j-n, etwas) lassen; (Essen) stehenlassen;
(b) (eine Nachricht, Spur) hinterlassen;
(eine Narbe) zurücklassen; to l. one's
money to s.o., j-m sein Geld
vermachen/hinterlassen; (c) (forget) I left
it in the office, ich habe es im Büro liegenlassen; (d) to l. a decision etc. to
s.o., j-m eine Entscheidung usw. überlassen; (e) is there any left? ist etwas
übrig? (f) (j-n, seine Frau, eine Stellung,
ein Zimmer) verlassen. 2. v.i. (of pers.)
abreisen; (of train, bus etc.) abfahren; (of
plane) starten; (of employee) he is leaving
next week, er geht nächste Woche (ab).
◆'leave be'hind, v.tr. (a) (j-n) zurücklassen; (b) (forget) (etwas) liegenlassen.
◆'leave 'out, v.tr. (a) (j-n) übergehen;
(b) (etwas) auslassen.

Lebanon ['lebənən]. Pr.n. der Libanon.

lecherous ['letʃ(ə)rəs], adj. lüstern.

lecture ['lektʃər]. I. s. Vortrag m; (at university) Vorlesung f (on, über + acc). II.
v.i. einen Vortrag/eine Vorlesung halten
(on, über + acc). ◆'lecturer, s. Vortra-
gende(r) f(m); (university) l., Dozent(in)
m(f).

ledge [ledʒ], s. (window l.) Sims m; (on
rock) Felsvorsprung m.

**ledger** ['ledʒər], s. Hauptbuch n.
**lee** [liː], s. Nau: Lee(seite) f; **in the l. of a rock**, im Windschatten eines Felsens. ◆'**leeway**, s. (freedom) Spielraum m.
**leech** [liːtʃ], s. Blutegel m.
**leek** [liːk], s. Lauch m, Porree m.
**leer** ['liər]. I. s. lüsterner Blick m. II. v.i. **to l. at s.o.**, lüstern/boshaft nach j-m schielen.
**left¹** [left]. I. adj. linke(r,s). II. adv. links. III. s. Linke f; (a) **on the l.**, links, auf der linken Seite; **from/to the l.**, von/ nach links; (b) Pol: **the L.**, die Linke. ◆'**left-hand**, adj. **on the l.-h. side**, auf der linken Seite. ◆'**left-'handed**, adj. linkshändig. ◆'**leftist**. I. s. Linksgerichtete(r) m. II. adj. linksgerichtet. ◆'**left-'wing**, adj. linksgerichtet.
**left²**, adj. & p.p. of **leave** q.v. ◆'**leftovers**, s.pl. Reste mpl. ◆'**left-'luggage (office)**, s. Gepäckaufbewahrung f.
**leg** [leg], s. 1. Bein n; **to pull s.o.'s leg**, j-n auf den Arm nehmen. 2. Cu: Keule f. 3. Sp: **the first l.**, die erste Etappe. ◆'**leg-room**, s. Knieraum m.
**legacy** ['legəsi], s. Erbschaft f.
**legal** ['liːg(ə)l], adj. gesetzlich; **is it l.?** ist es (gesetzlich) erlaubt? l. **documents**, Rechtsurkunden fpl; -**ly**, adv. l. **binding/ valid**, rechtskräftig. ◆**le'gality**, s. Gesetzlichkeit f; (of claim etc.) Rechtmäßigkeit f. ◆'**legalize**, v.tr. legalisieren.
**legend** ['ledʒənd], s. Legende f. ◆'**legendary**, adj. legendär.
**legible** ['ledʒibl], adj. leserlich.
**legion** ['liːdʒ(ə)n], s. Legion f.
**legislate** ['ledʒisleit], v.i. Gesetze erlassen. ◆**legis'lation**, s. Gesetzgebung f. ◆'**legislative** [-lətiv], adj. gesetzgebend. ◆'**legislator**, s. Gesetzgeber m.
**legitimacy** [li'dʒitiməsi], s. Rechtmäßigkeit f; Ehelichkeit f (eines Kindes). ◆**le'gitimate**, adj. 1. Jur: rechtmäßig; (of child) ehelich. 2. (justified) berechtigt.
**leisure** ['leʒər, N.Am: liː-], s. (restful) Muße f; (spare time) Freizeit f; **at l.**, mit Muße. ◆'**leisurely**, adj. gemächlich.
**lemon** ['lemən]. I. s. Zitrone f. II. adj. zitronengelb. ◆**lemo'nade**, s. Zitronenlimonade f.
**lend** [lend], v.tr.irr. (a) (Geld, Bücher usw.) leihen (**to s.o.**, j-m); (b) **this style lends itself to imitation**, dieser Stil läßt sich leicht nachahmen. ◆'**lender**, s. Verleiher m; (of loan) Darlehensgeber m. ◆'**lending**, s. Leihen n; l. **library**, Leihbücherei f.
**length** [leŋθ], s. 1. (distance) Länge f. 2. l. **of time**, Zeitspanne f, Zeit f; l. **of service**, Dienstalter n; **at l.**, (i) (at last) endlich; (ii) (in detail) ausführlich. 3. **to go to great lengths**, sich dat viel Mühe geben. ◆'**lengthen**, v. 1. v.tr. verlängern. 2. v.i. länger werden. ◆'**lengthways**, '**lengthwise**, adj. der Länge nach. ◆'**lengthy**, adj. langwierig.
**leniency** ['liːniənsi], s. Nachsicht f; Milde

f (einer Strafe). ◆'**lenient**, adj. (of pers.) nachsichtig; (of sentence) mild.
**lens** [lenz], s. Linse f; Phot: Objektiv n.
**Lent** [lent], s. Fastenzeit f.
**lentil** ['lentil], s. Linse f.
**Leo** ['liːəu], s. Astr: Löwe m.
**leopard** ['lepəd], s. Leopard m.
**leper** ['lepər], s. Aussätzige(r) f(m). ◆'**leprosy**, s. Lepra f.
**lesbian** ['lezbiən]. I. s. Lesbierin f. II. adj. lesbisch.
**less** [les]. I. adj. weniger; (smaller) geringer. II. prep. **purchase price l. 10%**, Kaufpreis weniger/abzüglich 10%. III. adv. weniger. ◆'**lessen**, v. 1. v.i. abnehmen; (of wind, resistance etc.) nachlassen. 2. v.tr. verringern. ◆'**lesser**, adj. geringer.
**lesson** ['les(ə)n], s. (a) Sch: Stunde f; (in book) Lektion f; (b) Fig: Lehre f; (c) Ecc: Bibellesung f.
**let¹** [let], v.tr.irr. I. v.tr. lassen; **to l. s.o. do sth.**, j-n etwas tun lassen; **to l. s.o. through/past** etc., j-n durchlassen/ vorbeilassen usw.; **to l. go of sth.**, etwas loslassen; Fig: **to l. oneself go**, sich gehenlassen. II. v. aux. **let's hurry!** beeilen wir uns! ◆'**let a'lone**, prep. geschweige denn. ◆'**let 'down**, v.tr. (a) Th: (den Vorhang) herunterlassen; (b) (ein Kleid) verlängern; (c) F: (j-n) im Stich lassen, (disappoint) enttäuschen. ◆'**letdown**, s. F: Reinfall m. ◆'**let 'in**, v.tr. (j-n, etwas) hereinlassen. ◆'**let 'off**, v.tr. (a) (Feuerwerk, eine Schußwaffe) abfeuern; (b) **to l. s.o. o.**, j-n laufen-lassen. ◆'**let 'on**, v.tr. & i. F: (etwas) verraten. ◆'**let 'out**, v.tr. herauslassen. ◆'**let 'up**, v.i. nachlassen. ◆'**letup**, s. Pause f.
**let²**, v.tr. (ein Haus usw.) vermieten (**to s.o.**, an j-n).
**lethal** ['liːθəl], adj. tödlich.
**lethargic** [le'θɑːdʒik], adj. träge.
**letter** ['letər], s. 1. (of alphabet) Buchstabe m. 2. (message) Brief m; l. **box**, Briefkasten m.
**lettuce** ['letis], s. Kopfsalat m.
**leukaemia** [luː'kiːmiə], s. Leukämie f.
**level** ['lev(ə)l]. I. s. 1. (height) Höhe f; (also Fig:) Ebene f; (standard) Niveau n; Med: Spiegel m (von Zucker usw.). 2. **on the l.**, (i) auf der Ebene; (ii) F: (of pers.) ehrlich. II. adj. (a) (flat) eben; l. **crossing**, Bahnübergang m; (b) l. **with**, auf gleicher Höhe mit + dat. III. v.tr. (a) (den Erdboden) ebnen; (b) **to l. a gun/ Fig: a criticism at s.o.**, ein Gewehr/ Kritik gegen j-n richten. ◆'**level-'headed**, adj. vernünftig; nüchtern.
**lever** ['liːvər]. I. s. Hebel m. II. v.tr. **to l. sth. up/open**, etwas mit einem Hebel heben/öffnen.
**levy** ['levi]. I. s. **capital l.**, Kapitalabgabe f. II. v.tr. (a) (Steuern usw.) erheben; (b) (Truppen) ausheben.
**lewd** [ljuːd], adj. unzüchtig.

**liable** ['laiəbl], *adj.* 1. (*responsible*) haftbar; **to be l.**, haften (**for sth.**, für etwas *acc*). 2. (*inclined*) **to be l. to do sth.**, dazu neigen, etwas zu tun; **difficulties are l. to occur**, man muß mit Schwierigkeiten rechnen. ◆**lia'bility**, *s.* 1. (*a*) Haftung *f*; (*b*) *pl.* Schulden *fpl.* 2. *F:* **he is a l.**, er ist eine Belastung.

**liaison** [li'eizɔn], *s.* Verbindung *f.* ◆**li'aise**, *v.i.* eine Verbindung aufnehmen (**with s.o.**, mit j-m).

**liar** ['laiər], *s.* Lügner(in) *m(f).*

**libel** ['laibl]. I. *s.* (schriftliche) Verleumdung *f.* II. *v.tr.* (j-n) (schriftlich) verleumden. ◆**'libellous**, *adj.* verleumderisch.

**liberal** ['lib(ə)rəl]. I. *adj.* liberal; (*open-minded*) aufgeschlossen; **l. education**, Allgemein **-ly**, *adv.*, reichlich. II. *s.* Liberale(r) *f(m).* ◆**'liberalism**, *s.* Liberalismus *m.*

**liberate** ['libəreit], *v.tr.* befreien. ◆**libe'ration**, *s.* Befreiung *f.*

**liberty** ['libəti], *s.* Freiheit *f.*

**Libra** ['li:brə], *s. Astr:* Waage *f.*

**library** ['laibrəri], *s.* Bibliothek *f*; (*public*) **lending l.**, Leihbücherei *f.* ◆**librarian** [lai'brɛəriən], *s.* Bibliothekar(in) *m(f).*

**Libya** ['libiə]. *Pr. n.* Libyen *n.*

**licence** ['lais(ə)ns], *s.* 1. (*a*) Lizenz *f*; (*permit*) Genehmigung *f*; (*b*) (*actual form*) Schein *m*; (*driving*) l., Führerschein *m.* 2. *poetic* l., dichterische Freiheit *f.* ◆**'license**, *v.tr.* (etwas) amtlich genehmigen; *Com:* (einen Händler usw.) konzessionieren. **licensed premises**, Schankwirtschaft *f.* ◆**licentious** ['-'senʃəs], *adj.* unzüchtig.

**lick** [lik]. I. *v.* 1. *v.tr. & i.* lecken. II. *s.* Lecken *n.*

**lid** [lid], *s.* Deckel *m.*

**lie**[1] [lai]. I. *s.* Lüge *f.* II. *v.i.* lügen; **to l. to s.o.**, j-n belügen.

**lie**[2], *v.i.irr.* liegen. ◆**'lie 'down**, *v.i.* sich hinlegen. ◆**'lie-in**, *s. F:* **to have l.-i.**, ausschlafen.

**lieutenant** [lef'tənənt, *N.Am:* lu:-], *s.* Oberleutnant *m.*

**life**, *pl.* **lives** [laif, laivz], *s.* Leben *n*; **l. assurance/insurance**, Lebensversicherung *f*; **for l.**, auf Lebenszeit; **l. sentence**, lebenslängliche Freiheitsstrafe. ◆**'lifebelt**, *s.* Rettungsring *m.* ◆**'lifeboat**, *s.* Rettungsboot *m.* ◆**'lifeguard**, *s.* Rettungsschwimmer *m.* ◆**'lifejacket**, *s.* Schwimmweste *f.* ◆**'lifeless**, *adj.* leblos. ◆**'lifelike**, *adj.* naturgetreu. ◆**'lifeline**, *s. Nau:* Rettungsleine *f*; *Fig:* Lebensader *f.* ◆**'life-size(d)**, *adj.* lebensgroß. ◆**'lifetime**, *s.* **in his l.**, zu seinen Lebzeiten.

**lift** [lift]. I. *v.* 1. *v.tr. (a)* **to l. s.o., sth. up**, j-n, etwas aufheben/(*above head*) hochheben; (*b*) **to l. a ban etc.**, ein Verbot usw. aufheben. 2. *v.i. (of fog etc.)* sich lichten. II. *s.* 1. *Aut:* **to give s.o. a l., j-n** (im Auto) mitnehmen; **to get a l.**, mitgenommen werden. 2. Aufzug *m*; (*skilift*) Lift *m.* 3. *Av:* Auftrieb *m.*

**light**[1] [lait]. I. *s.* 1. Licht *n*; (*of crime*) **to come to l.**, ans Licht kommen; **to bring sth. to l.**, etwas ans Licht bringen; **to throw l. on sth.**, eine Sache aufklären; **in the l. of your remarks**, angesichts Ihrer Bemerkungen. 2. (*electric etc.*) (*a*) (*lamp*) Lampe *f*; (*head-, spotlight*) Scheinwerfer *m*; (*b*) (*traffic*) l./ **lights**, Ampel *f*; (*c*) *Fig:* (*pers.*) **a leading l. in science**, eine Leuchte der Wissenschaft. 3. **have you got a l.?** haben Sie Feuer? II. *v.irr.* 1. *v.tr. (a)* (eine Lampe, eine Zigarette, ein Feuer usw.) anzünden; (*b*) (*illuminate*) (einen Saal usw.) erleuchten; (eine Treppe usw.) beleuchten. 2. *v.i.* **to l. up**, (*of eyes, face, etc.*) aufleuchten. III. *adj.* (*of sky, colour, hair etc.*) hell; **l. green**, hellgrün. ◆**'lighten**[1], *v.tr.* heller machen. ◆**'lighter**, *s.* Feuerzeug *n.* ◆**'lighthouse**, *s.* Leuchtturm *m.* ◆**'lighting**, *s.* Beleuchtung *f.*

**light**[2]. I. *adj.* (*not heavy*) leicht. II. *adv.* **to travel l.**, mit wenig Gepäck reisen; **-ly**, *adv.* leicht; **to get off l.**, billig davonkommen. ◆**'lighten**[2], *v.tr.* leichter machen. ◆**'light-'headed**, *adj.* schwindlig. ◆**'light-'hearted**, *adj.* sorglos, unbeschwert. ◆**'lightweight**, *adj.* leicht.

**lightning** ['laitniŋ], *s.* Blitz *m*; **l. conductor**, Blitzableiter *m.*

**like**[1] [laik]. I. *prep.* (*resembling*) wie; **what is he/the weather l.?**, wie ist er/das Wetter?; **l. this**, so. II. *s.* **the l.**, dergleichen; *F:* **the likes of us**, unsereins. ◆**'likelihood**, *s.* Wahrscheinlichkeit *f.* ◆**'likely**. I. *adj. (a)* wahrscheinlich; (*b*) (*suitable*) geeignet. II. *adv.* **most l./very l./as l. as not**, höchstwahrscheinlich; *F:* **not l.!** kommt nicht in Frage! ◆**'like-'minded**, *adj.* gleichgesinnt. ◆**'likeness**, *s.* 1. (*similarity*) Ähnlichkeit *f.* 2. (*portrait*) Porträt *n.* ◆**'likewise**, *adv.* gleichfalls.

**like**[2]. I. *v.tr.* 1. (*with noun*) (j-n, etwas) mögen, gern haben; **I l. that**, das gefällt mir; **as much as you l.**, soviel du willst. 2. **to l. to do/doing sth.**, etwas gern tun; **I would/I'd l. to come too**, ich möchte mitkommen; **as you l.**, wie Sie wollen. II. *s.* **likes and dislikes**, Neigungen und Abneigungen *fpl.* ◆**'likable**, *adj.* sympathisch. ◆**'liking**, *s.* Vorliebe *f.*

**lilac** ['lailək]. I. *s.* Flieder *m.* II. *adj.* lila.

**lily** ['lili], *s.* 1. Lilie *f.* 2. **l. of the valley**, Maiglöckchen *n.*

**limb** [lim], *s.* 1. Glied *n.* 2. Ast *m* (eines Baumes); *Fig:* **out on a l.**, für sich allein.

**limber** ['limbər], *v.i.* **to l. up**, Lockerungsübungen machen.

**limbo** ['limbəu], *s. Fig:* **in l.**, in der Schwebe.

**lime**[1] [laim], *s.* Kalk *m. m.* ◆**'limestone**, *s.* Kalkstein *m.*

**lime²**, s. Limone f; **l. juice**, Limonensaft m.

**lime³**, s. l. (tree), Linde f.

**limelight** ['laimlait], s. Rampenlicht n.

**limit** ['limit]. **I.** s. Grenze f; (time) l., Frist f; F: **that's the l.!** da hört doch alles auf! **II.** v.tr. beschränken (**to**, **auf** + acc). ◆'**limited**, p.p. & adj. beschränkt; **l. company**, Gesellschaft f mit beschränkter Haftung. ◆**limi'tation**, s. Beschränkung f. ◆'**limitless**, adj. grenzenlos.

**limousine** ['limu(:)zi:n], s. Limousine f.

**limp¹** [limp]. **I.** s. Hinken n; **to have a l.**, hinken. **II.** v.i. hinken.

**limp²**, adj. schlaff.

**limpet** ['limpit], s. Napfschnecke f; Fig: Klette f.

**line¹** [lain]. **I.** s. 1. (a) Nau: Leine f; **fishing l.**, Angelschnur f; **washing l.**, Wäscheleine f; (b) Tel: Leitung f; **a bad l.**, eine schlechte Verbindung; **hold the l.**, bleiben Sie am Apparat. 2. (a) (on paper etc) Linie f; **enemy lines**, feindliche Stellungen fpl; (b) (row) Reihe f; esp. N.Am: (queue) Schlange f; **in/out of l.**, in einer/außerhalb der Reihe; **this is in l. with my ideas**, das steht im Einklang mit meinen Ideen; (c) (wrinkle) Falte f; (d) (writing) Zeile f; F: **to drop s.o. a l.**, j-m ein paar Zeilen schreiben; Th: **to learn/forget one's lines**, seine Rolle lernen/vergessen; (e) **railway l.**, Eisenbahnlinie f; (route) Eisenbahnstrecke f; (tracks) Gleise npl; (f) (family) Geschlecht n; (g) **l. of argument**, Beweisführung f; **I take the l. that ...**, ich vertrete den Standpunkt, daß ...; (h) (principles) pl. **along/on the right lines**, nach den richtigen Grundsätzen. 3. **l. of business**, Branche f. **II.** v.tr. **to l. the street**, die Straße säumen. ◆'**liner**, s. Linienschiff n. ◆'**linesman**, s. Linienrichter m. ◆'**line 'up**, v.i. (a) sich in einer Reihe aufstellen; (b) (queue) Schlange stehen.

**line²**, v.tr. Cl: füttern. ◆'**lining**, s. Futter n.

**linen** ['linin], s. 1. (cloth) Leinen n. 2. (washing) Wäsche f.

**linger** ['liŋgər], v.i. verweilen. ◆'**lingering**, adj. (of glance) sehnsüchtig; **a l. doubt**, ein nicht zu verdrängender Zweifel.

**lingerie** ['lɛ̃:ʒəri(:)], s. Damenunterwäsche f.

**linguist** ['liŋgwist], s. Linguist m. ◆**lin'guistics**, s.pl. Linguistik f.

**link** [liŋk]. **I.** s. (a) Glied n (einer Kette); (b) Fig: (connection) Verbindung f. **II.** v. 1. v.tr. (etwas) verbinden (**with**, mit + dat). 2. v.i. **to l. up with s.o.**, **sth.**, sich j-m, an etwas acc anschließen.

**linoleum** [li'nəuliəm], F: **lino** ['lainəu], s. Linoleum n.

**linseed** ['linsi:d], s. **l. oil**, Leinöl n.

**lint** [lint], s. Mull m.

**lion** ['laiən], s. Löwe m. ◆'**lioness**, s.

Löwin f.

**lip** [lip], s. 1. Lippe f. 2. Rand m (einer Tasse usw.); Schnauze f (eines Krugs). ◆'**lip-read**, v.tr. & i. (Worte) von den Lippen ablesen. ◆'**lip-service**, s. **to pay l.-s. to sth.**, zu etwas dat ein Lippenbekenntnis ablegen. ◆'**lipstick**, s. Lippenstift m.

**liqueur** [li'kjuər], s. Likör m.

**liquid** ['likwid]. **I.** adj. flüssig. **II.** s. Flüssigkeit f. ◆'**liquidate**, v.tr. liquidieren. ◆**liqui'dation**, s. Fin: Liquidation f. ◆'**liquidizer**, s. (elektrischer) Mixer m.

**liquor** ['likər], s. esp. N.Am: Alkohol m; **l. store**, Wein- und Spirituosenhandlung f.

**liquorice** ['likəris], s. Lakritze f.

**lisp** [lisp]. **I.** s. Lispeln n. **II.** v.i. lispeln.

**list¹** [list]. **I.** s. Liste f. **II.** v.tr. (enter) (etwas) (in eine Liste) eintragen; (mention) (Sachen, Vorteile usw.) aufführen.

**list²**, v.i. (of ship) Schlagseite haben.

**listen** ['lisn], v.i. **to l. to s.o.**, **sth.**, j-m, etwas dat zuhören. ◆'**listen 'in**, v.i. **to l. i. (to the radio)**, Radio hören; **to l. i. to a telephone conversation etc.**, ein Telefongespräch usw. mithören. ◆'**listener**, s. Zuhörer(in) m(f); Rad: Hörer(in) m(f).

**listless** ['listlis], adj. teilnahmslos.

**literate** ['litərət], adj. des Lesens und Schreibens kundig; (educated) gebildet.

**literal** ['litərəl], adj. wörtlich; **-ly**, adv. wörtlich; **they l. starved to death**, sie sind buchstäblich verhungert.

**literary** ['litərəri], adj. literarisch; **l. language**, Schriftsprache f. ◆**literature** ['litrətʃər], s. Literatur f.

**lithe** [laið], adj. geschmeidig.

**litigation** [liti'geiʃən], s. Prozeß m, Rechtsstreit m.

**litre** ['li:tər], s. Liter m.

**litter** ['litər], s. 1. (of waste paper etc.) Abfälle mpl. 2. Z: Wurf m. **II.** v.tr. **to l. the room with papers/l. papers all over the room**, Papiere (überall) im Zimmer verstreuen.

**little** ['litl]. **I.** adj. 1. (of size) klein. 2. (of amount) wenig; **l. money**, wenig Geld; **a l. money**, ein wenig/F: ein bißchen Geld. **II.** s. **I see very l. of him**, ich sehe ihn (sehr) selten; **l. by l.**, nach und nach.

**live. I.** adj. [laiv] 1. lebend; **l. broadcast**, Live-Sendung f. 2. (a) El: unter Strom; attrib. stromführend; (b) Mil: (of ammunition) scharf. **II.** v. [liv] 1. v.i. (a) (be alive) leben; **to l. on sth.** von etwas leben; (b) (reside) wohnen. 2. v.tr. **to l. a happy life**, ein glückliches Leben führen. ◆'**live 'down**, v.tr. **he'll never l. this d.**, man wird es ihm nie vergessen lassen. ◆**livelihood** ['laivlihud], s. Lebensunterhalt m. ◆'**lively** ['laivli], adj. lebhaft. ◆'**liven** ['laivən] '**up**, v. 1. v.i. (of pers.) in Stimmung kommen; **the party is livening up**, jetzt kommt die Party in Schwung. 2. v.tr. (etwas) beleben.

◆**livestock** ['laivstɔk], s. Vieh n.
◆**'live 'up**, v.i. to l. up to one's reputation, seinem Ruf gerecht werden; **to l. it up**, ein tolles Leben führen. ◆**living** ['liviŋ]. I. adj. lebend. II. s. **to earn/make one's l.**, seinen Lebensunterhalt verdienen; **l. wage**, Existenzminimum n. ◆**'living-room**, s. Wohnzimmer n.

**liver** ['livər], s. Leber f.

**livid** ['livid], adj. (angry) wütend.

**lizard** ['lizəd], s. Eidechse f.

**llama** ['lɑːmə], s. Lama n.

**load** [ləud]. I. s. 1. Last f; (cargo) Ladung f; **work l.**, Arbeitsbelastung f; Fig: **that's a l. off my mind**, mir ist ein Stein vom Herzen gefallen. 2. F: **loads of money**, ein Haufen Geld. II. v. 1. v.tr. (a) **to l. s.o., sth. with sth.**, j-n, etwas mit etwas dat beladen; (b) (ein Gewehr usw.) laden; (einen Film, eine Kassette) einlegen; (c) P: **he's loaded**, er hat Geld wie Heu. 2. v.i. **to l. (up), (auf)laden.

**loaf**[1], pl. **loaves** [ləuf, ləuvz], s. 1. Brot n. 2. P: (head) **use your l.!** streng mal dein Hirn an!

**loaf**[2], v.i. **to l. (about)**, herumlungern.

**loan** [ləun]. I. s. 1. Leihgabe f. 2. Fin: Darlehen n. II. v.tr. **to l. s.o. sth.**, j-m etwas leihen.

**loath** [ləuθ], adj. **to be l. to do sth.**, etwas nur ungern tun.

**loathe** [ləuð], v.tr. (j-n, etwas) verabscheuen, nicht ausstehen können. ◆**'loathing**, s. Abscheu m. ◆**'loathsome**, adj. abscheulich.

**lobby** ['lɔbi]. I. s. (a) Vorraum m; Pol: Interessengruppe f, Lobby f. II. v.tr. **to l. M.P.s**, Parlamentsabgeordnete zu beeinflussen versuchen.

**lobster** ['lɔbstər], s. Hummer m.

**local** ['ləuk(ə)l]. I. adj. örtlich, Orts-; **l. government**, Kommunalverwaltung f; **l. authority**, Ortsbehörde f; **l. call**, Ortsgespräch n; **l. anaesthetic**, örtliche Betäubung. II. s. (a) **l. (inhabitant)**, Ortsansässige(r) f(m); **the locals**, die Hiesigen pl; (b) F: **the l.**, die Kneipe um die Ecke; **-ly**, adv. **well-known l.**, allgemein bekannt in der Gegend. ◆**lo'cality**, s. Gegend f. ◆**lo'cate**, v.tr. (a) (find) ausfindig machen; (b) (place) plazieren; (in building) unterbringen; **to be located**, sich befinden. ◆**lo'cation**, s. (situation) Lage f; Cin: **shot on l.**, als Außenaufnahme gedreht.

**lock**[1] [lɔk], s. (of hair) Locke f.

**lock**[2]. I. s. 1. (of door, rifle etc.) Schloß n. 2. (on canal etc.) Schleuse f. II. v. 1. v.tr. (a) (die Tür usw.) zuschließen; **to l. (up) the house**, das Haus abschließen; **to l. s.o. into a room**, j-n in ein Zimmer einschließen; (b) Tchn: (ein Teil) sperren. 2. v.i. (a) (of door etc.) sich verschließen lassen; (b) (of moving parts) sperren; (of wheels, brakes) blockieren. ◆**'locker**, s. kleiner Schrank m; Nau: Mil: Spind m; (on station etc.) Schließfach m; ◆**'lock-**out**, s. Aussperrung f. ◆**'locksmith**, s. Schlosser m. ◆**'lock 'up**, v.tr. (a) (j-n) einsperren; (b) (das Haus) abschließen.

**locket** ['lɔkit], s. Medaillon n.

**locomotive** [ləukə'məutiv], s. Lokomotive f.

**locust** ['ləukəst], s. Heuschrecke f.

**lodge** [lɔdʒ]. I. s. Loge f. II. v. 1. v.tr. **to l. a complaint**, eine Beschwerde einreichen. 2. v.i.i. (a) (of pers.) (bei j-m) logieren; (b) (of thing) steckenbleiben. ◆**'lodger**, s. Untermieter m. ◆**'lodgings**, s.pl. möblierte Zimmer npl.

**loft** [lɔft], s. Dachboden m.

**log** [lɔg], s. 1. Holzscheit n; **l. cabin**, Blockhütte f; F: **to sleep like a l.**, wie ein Sack schlafen. 2. **l. (book)**, Logbuch n; Aut: **l. book**, approx. Zulassungsschein m.

**logarithm** ['lɔgəriθ(ə)m], s. Logarithmus m.

**loggerheads** ['lɔgəhedz], s. **they are constantly at l.**, sie liegen sich ständig in den Haaren.

**logic** ['lɔdʒik], s. Logik f. ◆**'logical**, adj. logisch.

**loin** [lɔin], s. (usu. pl.) Lenden fpl.

**loiter** ['lɔitər], v.i. herumlungern.

**loll** [lɔl], v.i. (sich) lümmeln.

**lollipop** ['lɔlipɔp], F: **lolly** ['lɔli], s. Lutscher m; **ice l.**, Eis n am Stiel.

**lone** [ləun], adj. einsam. ◆**'lonely**, adj. einsam; **a l. spot**, eine abgelegene Stelle. ◆**'loneliness**, s. Einsamkeit f. ◆**'lonesome**, adj. einsam.

**long**[1] [lɔŋ]. I. adj. lang; **a l. time**, lange; **for a l. time**, seit langem. II. s. 1. **the l. and the short of it is ...**, mit einem Wort/kurzum ... 2. **before l.**, bald; **it's not for l.**, es dauert nicht lange. III. adv. 1. **has he been gone l.?** ist er schon lange fort? **I won't be long**, ich bin bald wieder da; **as l. as I live**, solange ich lebe. 2. **all day l.**, den ganzen Tag. 3. **no longer**, nicht mehr; **how much longer?** wie lange noch? ◆**'long-'distance**, adj. **l.-d. runner**, Langstreckenläufer m; **l.-d. call**, Ferngespräch n. ◆**'long-'haired**, adj. langhaarig. ◆**'long 'jump**, n. Weitsprung m. ◆**'long-'playing**, adj. **l.-p. record**, Langspielplatte f. ◆**'long-'range**, adj. (a) (long-distance) Langstrecken-; **l.-r. missile**, Ferngeschoß n; (b) (of plan, forecast) auf lange Sicht. ◆**'long-'sighted**, adj. weitsichtig. ◆**'long-'standing**, adj. seit langem bestehend. ◆**'long-'suffering**, adj. geduldig. ◆**'long-'term**, adj. langfristig. ◆**'long-'winded**, adj. langatmig; (lengthy) langwierig.

**long**[2], v.i. sich sehnen (**for s.o., sth.**, nach j-m, etwas dat). ◆**'longing**. I. s. Sehnsucht f. II. adj. sehnend.

**longitude** ['lɔŋgitjuːd, 'lɔndʒi-], s. Länge f.

**loo** [luː], s. F: Klo n.

**look** [luk]. **I.** s. **1.** (*glance*) Blick m; (*expression*) Miene f; **to have a l. at sth.,** sich dat etwas ansehen. **2.** (*appearance*) (*a*) Anschein m; **by the l. of it,** allem Anschein nach; (*b*) F: pl **good looks,** gutes Aussehen n. **II. 1.** v.tr. & i. sehen; *South G:* schauen; *North G:* gucken; F: **l. here!** na hör mal! **2.** v.i. (*appear*) aussehen (**like,** nach + dat). ◆**'look 'after,** v.tr. **to l. a. s.o.,** sth., sich um j-n, etwas acc kümmern; (*carefully*) (etwas) pflegen; **please l. a. my bag for a moment,** bitte passen Sie einen Augenblick auf meine Tasche auf. ◆**'look a'round,** v. **1.** v.i. sich umsehen (**for sth.,** nach etwas dat). **2.** v.tr. **to l. a. a place,** sich in einem Ort umsehen. ◆**'look 'at,** v.tr. (j-n, etwas) ansehen; (j-n) anblicken. ◆**'look 'a'way,** v.i. den Blick abwenden. ◆**'look 'back,** v.i. zurückblicken (**at s.o.,** sth., auf j-n, etwas acc). ◆**'look 'down,** v.i. (*also Fig:*) herabsehen (**on s.o.,** sth., auf j-n, etwas acc). ◆**'look 'for,** v.tr. suchen. ◆**'look 'forward,** v.i. **l. l. f. to sth.,** sich auf etwas acc freuen. ◆**'look-in,** s. F: **he won't get a l.-i.,** dabei springt nichts für ihn heraus. ◆**'look 'into,** v.tr. (eine Angelegenheit) untersuchen. ◆**'look 'on,** v.i. zusehen. ◆**'look 'out,** v.i. (*a*) hinaussehen; **to l. o. of the window,** zum Fenster hinaussehen/hinausblicken; **a room that looks out on the garden,** ein Zimmer mit Ausblick auf den Garten; (*b*) Ausschau halten (**for s.o.,** nach j-m); (*c*) (*take care*) aufpassen; **l. o.!** Vorsicht! ◆**'look-out,** s. **1.** to be on the **l.-o. for s.o.,** sth., nach j-m, etwas dat Ausschau halten. **2.** F: **that's his l.-o.,** das ist seine Angelegenheit. ◆**'look 'round,** v.tr. & i. **to l. r.** (**a museum** etc), sich (in einem Museum usw.) umsehen; **don't l. r.,** dreh dich nicht um. ◆**'look 'up,** v. **1.** v.i. (*a*) aufblicken (*Fig:* **to s.o.,** zu j-m); (*b*) (*improve*) sich bessern. **2.** v.tr. (*a*) (ein Wort usw.) nachschlagen; (*b*) (*visit*) (j-n) aufsuchen.

**loom¹** [lu:m], s. Webstuhl m.

**loom²,** v.i. (*plötzlich*) aufragen.

**loop** [lu:p], s. Schleife f; (*of rope etc.*) Schlinge f. ◆**'loophole,** s. Fig: Lücke f; F: Hintertürchen n.

**loose** [lu:s]. *adj.* **1.** (*a*) (*detached, undone*) lose; **l. change,** Kleingeld n; (*b*) (*free*) frei. **2.** (*slack*) locker; **-ly,** adv. **1. l. tied,** locker gebunden. **2. l. translated,** frei übersetzt. ◆**'loose-'leaf,** adj. **l.-l. binder,** Schnellhefter m. ◆**'loosen,** v. **1.** v.tr. lockern; (einen Knoten usw.) lösen. **2.** v.i. sich lockern.

**loot** [lu:t]. **I.** s. Beute f. **II.** v. **1.** v.tr. (eine Stadt) ausplündern. **2.** v.i. plündern.

**lop** [lɔp], v.tr. **to l. off a branch,** einen Ast absägen. ◆**'lop-'sided,** adj. schief.

**lord** [lɔːd], s. **1.** (*master, also Ecc:*) Herr m; **the L.'s Prayer,** das Vaterunser. **2.**

(*title*) Lord m. ◆**'lordship,** s. **Your L.,** Euer Gnaden.

**lorry** ['lɔri], s. Lastwagen m, F: Laster m; **l. driver,** Lastwagenfahrer m.

**lose** [lu:z], v.tr.irr. (*a*) verlieren; **to l. in value,** an Wert verlieren; *Sp:* **to l. by 2 goals to 1,** 2 zu 1 verlieren; **to l. weight,** abnehmen; **to l. oneself/one's way,** sich verirren; (*of car driver*) sich verfahren; (*b*) (*of clock etc.*) nachgehen. ◆**'lose 'out,** v.i. verlieren. ◆**'loser,** s. Verlierer m. ◆**'lost,** adj. (*a*) (*of thing*) verloren; **to get l.,** verlorengehen; **l. property office,** Fundbüro n; (*of pers.*) verirrt; **to get l.,** sich verirren; **I am l.,** ich habe mich verirrt; (*c*) *Mil:* (*of pers.*) verschollen; (*of ship*) untergegangen.

**loss** [lɔs], s. Verlust m; **to be at a l.,** nicht weiter wissen.

**lot** [lɔt], s. **1.** (*fate*) Los n; **to draw lots for sth.,** um etwas acc losen. **2.** (*a*) (*at auction*) Posten m; (*b*) F: **the l.,** alles, das Ganze. **3.** F: **a l.,** viel(e), eine Menge; **a l. of money,** viel Geld, eine Menge Geld; **I see quite a l. of him,** ich sehe ihn ziemlich oft; adv. **times have changed a l.,** die Zeiten haben sich sehr geändert. **4.** F: **lots,** jede Menge.

**lotion** ['ləuʃ(ə)n], s. Lotion f.

**lottery** ['lɔtəri], s. Lotterie f; **l. ticket,** Los n.

**loud** [laud], adj. laut; **-ly,** adv. laut; **to protest l.,** lautstark protestieren. ◆**'loudness,** s. Lautstärke f. ◆**'loud'speaker,** s. Lautsprecher m.

**lounge** [laundʒ]. **I.** s. (*in house*) Wohnzimmer n; (*in hotel*) Gesellschaftsraum m. **II.** v.i. sich lümmeln.

**louse,** pl. **lice** [laus, lais], s. Laus f. ◆**'lousy** ['lauzi], adj. F: miserabel.

**lout** [laut], s. Flegel m.

**love** [lʌv]. **I.** s. Liebe f; **in l.,** verliebt; **to fall in l. with s.o.,** sich in j-n verlieben; **to make l.,** zusammen schlafen; **l. letter,** Liebesbrief m; **l. song,** Liebeslied n; **l. story,** Liebesgeschichte f; **l. affair,** (Liebes)verhältnis n. **2.** (*pers.*) **my l.,** mein Schatz; mein Liebster, meine Liebste. **3.** *Sp:* Null f. **II.** v.tr. lieben; F: **to l. doing sth.,** etwas schrecklich gern tun. ◆**'lovable,** adj. liebenswert. ◆**'lovely,** adj. (*a*) (*of girl, picture etc.*) reizend; (*b*) F: (*of party, meal etc.*) großartig. ◆**'lover,** s. **1.** Geliebte(r) f(m); esp. Th: Liebhaber m. **2.** Freund m (der Künste usw.); **music l.,** Musikfreund m. ◆**'loving,** adj. liebevoll.

**low** [ləu]. **I.** adj. (*a*) niedrig; **l. speed,** geringe Geschwindigkeit; **supplies are (running) l.,** die Vorräte werden knapp; (*b*) (*of note, sound*) tief; (*soft*) leise; (*c*) Fig: (*mean*) niederträchtig; (*d*) Fig: (*bad*) **l. opinion,** schlechte Meinung. **II.** adv. (*a*) tief (fliegen, liegen, sinken usw.); **to lie l.,** sich versteckt halten; (*b*) **the lowest paid workers,** die am schlechtesten bezahlten Arbeiter. **III.** s. **all-time l.,** ab-

soluter Tiefstand *m.* ◆'**low-down**, *s.*
*P:* to give s.o. the l.-d.,
j-n aufklären (on sth., über etwas *acc*).
◆'**lower**, *v.tr.* (*a*) (j-n, etwas) herunterlassen; (eine Fahne) niederholen; (*b*) (die
Augen, den Preis usw.) senken.
**loyal** ['lɔiəl], *adj.* treu (to s.o., sth., j-m,
etwas *dat*). ◆'**loyalty**, *s.* Treue *f.*
**lozenge** ['lɔzindʒ], *s.* Pastille *f.*
**lubricate** ['lu:brikeit], *v.tr.* schmieren.
◆'**lubricant**, *s.* Schmiermittel *n.*
◆**lubri'cation**, *s.* Schmierung *f.*
**lucid** ['lu:sid], *adj.* klar; (*of pers., mind*)
scharfsichtig.
**luck** [lʌk], *s.* 1. (*fortune*) (good) l., Glück
*n;* bad/ F: hard/tough l., Pech *n;* good
l.! viel Glück! piece/stroke of l., Glücksfall *m;* worse l.! leider! 2. (*chance*) Zufall
*m.* ◆'**lucky**, *adj.* glücklich; (*of thing*)
glückbringend; to be l., (*of pers.*) Glück
haben; (*of thing*) Glück bringen; l. day,
Glückstag *m;* -ily, *adv.* zum Glück.
**lucrative** ['lu:krətiv], *adj.* lukrativ.
**ludicrous** ['lu:dikrəs], *adj.* lächerlich.
**lug** [lʌg], *v.tr.* F: schleppen.
**luggage** ['lʌgidʒ], *s.* Gepäck *n;* l. rack,
Gepäcknetz *n;* l. locker, Schließfach *n.*
**lugubrious** [lu:'gu:briəs], *adj.* düster.
**lukewarm** ['lu:kwɔ:m], *adj.* lauwarm.
**lull** [lʌl]. I. *s.* (*in a storm*) kurze Flaute *f;*
a l. in the conversation, eine Gesprächs-
pause. II. *v.tr. Fig:* to be lulled into a
(false) sense of security, sich in einem
Sicherheitsgefühl wiegen. ◆**lullaby**
['lʌləbai], *s.* Wiegenlied *n.*
**lumbago** [lʌm'beigəu], *s.* Hexenschuß *m.*
**lumber** ['lʌmbər], *v.tr.* F: (j-n) belasten
(**with** sth., mit etwas *dat*).
◆'**lumberjack**, *s.* Holzfäller *m.*
**luminous** ['lu:minəs], *adj.* leuchtend,
Leucht-.
**lump** [lʌmp]. I. *s.* (*a*) (*of clay, wood etc.*)
Klumpen *m;* l. of sugar, Zuckerwürfel
*m;* l. sum, Pauschalbetrag *m;* (*b*) (*swelling etc.*) Schwellung *f.* II. *v.tr.* F: to l.
everything together, alles in einen Topf
werfen. ◆'**lumpy**, *adj.* (*of sauce*) klum-
pig.
**lunacy** ['lu:nəsi], *s.* Wahnsinn *m.*
◆'**lunatic**. I. *s.* Verrückte(r) *f(m).* II.
*adj.* wahnsinnig.
**lunar** ['lu:nər], *adj.* Mond-; l. module,
Mondfähre *f.*
**lunch** [lʌn(t)ʃ], *s.* Mittagessen *n;* l. hour,
Mittagspause *f.* ◆'**luncheon**, *s.* Mittagessen *n;* l. voucher, Essensbon *m.*
**lung** [lʌŋ], *s.* Lunge *f.*
**lunge** [lʌndʒ], *v.i.* vorwärts stoßen.
**lupin** ['lu:pin], *s.* Lupine *f.*
**lurch**[1] [lə:tʃ], *s.* to leave s.o. in the l.,
j-n im Stich lassen.
**lurch**[2], *v.i.* (*a*) (*of vehicle*) einen Ruck geben; (*b*) (*of ship*) schlingern; (*c*) (*of pers.*)
taumeln.
**lure** ['ljuər]. I. *s. Fig:* Verlockung *f.* II.
*v.tr.* (*a*) (ein Fisch, Tier) ködern; (*b*)
(j-n, ein Tier) anlocken.
**lurid** ['ljuərid], *adj.* 1. (*of colours*) grell. 2.
(*of film etc.*) reißerisch.
**lurk** [lə:k], *v.i.* lauern.
**luscious** ['lʌʃəs], *adj.* köstlich.
**lush** [lʌʃ], *adj.* üppig.
**lust** [lʌst], *s.* (*a*) (geschlechtliche) Begierde *f;* (*b*) l. for power, Machtgier *f.*
**lusty** ['lʌsti], *adj.* rüstig.
**lute** [lu:t], *s.* Laute *f.*
**luxuriant** [lʌg'zjuəriənt], *adj.* üppig.
◆**lux'urious**, *adj.* luxuriös. ◆**luxury**
['lʌkʃəri], *s.* Luxus *m.*
**lynch** [lin(t)ʃ], *v.tr.* (j-n) lynchen.
**lyric** ['lirik]. I. *adj.* lyrisch; l. poetry, Lyrik *f.* II. *s.* (*a*) lyrisches Gedicht *n;* (*b*)
*Mus:* lyrics, Text *m.* ◆'**lyrical**, *adj.*
lyrisch.

# M

**M, m** [em], *s.* (der Buchstabe) M, m *n.*
**mac** [mæk], *s. abbr.* F: = mackintosh.
**macabre** [mə'ka:br], *adj.* makaber.
**macaroni** [mækə'rəuni], *s.* Makkaroni *pl.*
**machinations** [mæki'neiʃ(ə)nz], *s.pl.* Ma-
chenschaften *pl.*
**machine** [mə'ʃi:n], *s.* (*a*) Maschine *f;* m.
tool, Werkzeugmaschine *f;* (*b*) (*small device*) Apparat *m.* ◆**ma'chinery**, *s.* Ma-
schinerie *f;* (*mechanism*) Mechanismus *m.*
**mackerel** ['mæk(ə)rəl], *s.* Makrele *f.*
**mackintosh** ['mækintɔʃ], *s.* Regenmantel
*m.*
**mad** [mæd], *adj.* 1. verrückt. 2. F: m.
about/on sth., auf etwas *acc* versessen;
m. about s.o., in j-n vernarrt. 3. (*angry*)
böse. ◆'**maddening**, *adj.* aufreizend.
◆'**madness**, *s.* Wahnsinn *m.*
**madam** ['mædəm], *s.* gnädige Frau.
**magazine** [mægə'zi:n], *s.* Zeitschrift *f;*

(*illustrated*) Illustrierte *f.*
**maggot** ['mægət], *s.* Made *f.*
**magic** ['mædʒik]. I. *s.* Zauber *m.* II. *adj.*
magisch. ◆'**magical**, *adj.* zauberhaft.
◆**magician** [mə'dʒiʃ(ə)n], *s.* Zauberkünstler *m.*
**magistrate** ['mædʒistreit], *s.* Friedensrichter *m.*
**magnanimous** [mæg'næniməs], *adj.*
großmütig.
**magnate** ['mægneit], *s.* Magnat *m.*
**magnet** ['mægnit], *s.* Magnet *n.*
◆**magnetic** [-'netik], *adj.* magnetisch.
◆'**magnetism** [-nətizm], *s.* Magnetis-
mus *m; Fig:* (*personal*) m., Anziehungs-
kraft *f.*
**magnify** ['mægnifai], *v.tr.* (ein Bild usw.)
vergrößern; **magnifying glass**, Vergröße-
rungsglas *n.*
**magnificent** [mæg'nifisənt], *adj.* herrlich.

**magnitude** ['mægnitju:d], s. **1.** Größe f.
**2.** Fig: Ausmaß n (einer Katastrophe).
**magpie** ['mægpai], s. Elster f.
**mahogany** [mə'hɔgəni], s. Mahagoni n.
**maid** [meid], s. **1.** Dienstmädchen n. **2.**
old m., alte Jungfer f. ◆'**maiden,** attrib. adj. **1.** (unmarried) m. aunt, unverheiratete Tante f; m. name, Mädchenna-
me m. **2.** (first) m. voyage, Jungfernfahrt
f; m. speech, Jungfernrede f.
**mail** [meil]. **I.** s. Post f; m. order firm,
Versandhaus n. **II.** v.tr. esp. N.Am: (etwas) mit der Post schicken; (einen Brief)
aufgeben. ◆'**mailbag,** s. Postsack m.
◆'**mailbox,** s. N.Am: Briefkasten m.
**maim** [meim], v.tr. verstümmeln.
**main** [mein]. **I.** s. **1.** in the m., im ganzen; im wesentlichen. **2.** (a) (water) m.,
Hauptwasseranschluß m; (b) (gas m.)
Hauptleitung f; El: Stromnetz n. **II.** attrib. adj. Haupt-; m. road, Hauptstraße
f; m. thing, Hauptsache f; **-ly,** adv.
hauptsächlich; (mostly) größtenteils.
◆'**mainland,** s. Festland f.
◆'**mainstay,** s. Fig: Hauptstütze f.
**maintain** [mein'tein], v.tr. (a) (Recht und
Ordnung, Kontakt usw.) aufrechterhalten; (eine Geschwindigkeit) beibehalten;
(b) (Straßen, Anlagen usw.) instand halten; (eine Maschine) warten; (c) (j-n, eine
Familie) unterhalten; (d) he maintained
that ..., er behauptete, daß ...
◆'**maintenance** [-tinəns], s. Instandhaltung f; Aut: etc: Wartung f.
**maisonette** [meizə'net], s. Maisonette-
wohnung f.
**maize** [meiz], s. Mais m.
**majesty** ['mædʒisti], s. Majestät f.
◆**majestic** [mə'dʒestik], adj. majestä-
tisch.
**major¹** ['meidʒər], s. Major m.
**major²,** adj. **1.** (a) (larger) Haupt-; the m.
part, der größte Teil; (b) (serious) ernst;
m. operation, schwere Operation; (c)
(important) bedeutend; a m. change, eine
große Veränderung. **2.** m. road, Haupt-
verkehrsstraße f; (having priority) Vorfahrtsstraße f. **3.** Mus: Dur; in A m., in
A-Dur. ◆**majority** [mə'dʒɔriti], s.
Mehrheit f.
**make** [meik]. **I.** s. Marke f. **II.** v.irr. **1.**
v.tr. (etwas) machen; (earn) verdienen;
(reach) (eine Stadt usw.) erreichen; to m.
sth. into sth., etwas zu etwas dat machen; to m. s.o. do sth., j-n veranlassen,
etwas zu tun; F: we've made it! wir haben's geschafft! **2.** v.i. what do you m.
of it? was halten Sie davon? ◆'**make
'do,** v.i. sich begnügen (with s.o., sth.,
mit j-m, etwas dat). ◆'**make 'for,** v.i.
(a) (aim for) he was making f. London,
sein Ziel war London; where are you
making f.? wohin wollen Sie? (b) (contribute to) it makes for good relations, es
fördert gute Beziehungen. ◆'**make 'off,**
v.i. F: sich davonmachen (with s.o.,
sth., mit j-m, etwas dat). ◆'**make 'out,**

v.tr. (a) (einen Scheck) ausstellen; (b)
(eine Handschrift) entziffern; I cannot
m. it o., ich werde nicht klug daraus; (c)
I could not m. o. his features in the
dark, ich konnte seine Züge im Dunkeln
nicht erkennen. ◆'**makeshift,** adj. behelfsmäßig; a m. shelter, eine Notunter-
kunft f. ◆'**make 'up,** v. **1.** v.tr. (a) to
m. up lost ground, Versäumtes nachholen; (in race) aufholen; (b) to m. up a
prescription, eine verschriebene Arznei
zubereiten; (c) Cl: (einen Anzug) anfertigen; (d) (invent) (eine Geschichte) erfinden; (e) (form) (ein Ganzes usw.) bilden;
(f) to m. (s.o., oneself) up, (j-n, sich)
schminken; (g) to m. up one's mind,
sich entschließen; (h) to m. it up with
s.o., sich mit j-m versöhnen. **2.** v.i. to
m. up for sth., etwas wiedergutmachen;
to m. up for lost time, verlorene Zeit
aufholen. ◆'**make-up,** s Make-up n;
Th: (result) Maske f.
**malaria** [mə'lɛəriə], s. Malaria f.
**male** [meil]. **I.** s. **1.** Mann m; (animal)
Männchen n. **II.** adj. männlich.
**malfunction** [mæl'fʌŋkʃ(ə)n], s. Funk-
tionsstörung f.
**malice** ['mælis], s. Bosheit f.
◆**ma'licious,** adj. (of damage etc.) bös-
willig; (of remarks) boshaft.
**malign** [mə'lain], v.tr. (j-n) verleumden.
◆**malignant** [mə'lignənt], adj. m. tumour, bösartige Geschwulst f.
**mallet** ['mælit], s. Holzhammer m.
**malnutrition** [mælnju'triʃ(ə)n], s. Unterernährung f.
**malpractice** [mæl'præktis], s. Mißbrauch
m.
**malt** [mɔːlt], s. Malz n.
**mammal** ['mæməl], s. Säugetier n.
**mammoth** ['mæməθ]. **I.** s. Z: Mammut
n. **II.** adj. Fig: riesig, ungeheuer.
**man** [mæn]. **I.** s. pl. **men** [men]. **1.** (human) Mensch m; the m. in the street,
der Durchschnittsmensch. **2.** (male)
Mann m. **II.** v.tr. (ein Schiff usw.) be-
mannen. ◆'**manhole,** s. Einsteige-
schacht m. ◆'**manhood,** s. Mannesalter
n. ◆**man'kind,** s. die Menschheit.
◆'**manpower,** s. coll. Arbeitskräfte fpl.
◆'**manslaughter,** s. Totschlag m.
**manage** ['mænidʒ], v. **1.** v.tr. (a) (einen
Betrieb, ein Hotel) führen, leiten; (b) F:
(etwas) schaffen; she managed to see
him, es gelang ihr, ihn zu sehen. **2.** v.i.
zurechtkommen. ◆'**manageable,** adj.
**1.** (of tool etc.) handlich. **2.** (of pers.) füg-
sam. ◆'**management,** s. **1.** (a) (manag-
ers) Leitung f (eines Geschäfts, usw.);
(b) (practice) Geschäftsführung f. **2.**
(handling) Handhabung f (einer Angelegenheit). ◆'**manager,** s. Leiter m, Manager m. ◆'**manageress,** s. Geschäfts-
führerin f (eines Restaurants usw.); Lei-
terin f (einer Abteilung); Direktorin f
(einer Firma). ◆**mana'gerial,** adj. führend, leitend; m. staff, Führungskräfte

*fpl.* ◆'**managing,** *adj.* m. director, Geschäftsführer *m.*

**mandarin(e)** ['mændərin], *s.* Mandarine *f.*

**mandate** ['mændeit], *s.* Mandat *n; Jur:* Vollmacht *f.* ◆'**mandatory** [-dətri], *adj.* verbindlich.

**mane** [mein], *s.* Mähne *f.*

**mangle** ['mæŋgl]. I. *s.* Mangel *f.* II. *v.tr.* verstümmeln.

**mango,** *pl.* **-oes** ['mæŋgəu, -əuz], *s.* Mango *f.*

**mania** ['meiniə], *s.* Manie *f.* ◆'**maniac,** *s. F:* Verrückte(r) *f(m)*; **sex m.,** *(a)* Triebtäter *m*; *(b) Hum:* Lustmolch *m.*

**manicure** ['mænikjuər]. I. *s.* Maniküre *f.* II. *v.tr.* maniküren.

**manifest** ['mænifest]. I. *adj.* offensichtlich. II. *v.tr.* (etwas) aufweisen; **to m. itself,** sich zeigen. ◆**manifes'tation,** *s.* Erscheinung *f.* ◆**mani'festo,** *pl.* **-os,** *s.* election m., Wahlprogramm *n.*

**manipulate** [mə'nipjuleit], *v.tr.* manipulieren. ◆**manipu'lation,** *s.* Manipulation *f.*

**manner** ['mænər], *s.* 1. *(a)* Weise *f*; **in this m.,** auf diese Weise; *(b) (of pers.)* Art *f.* 2. *pl.* Manieren *pl*; **(good) manners,** gute Manieren/gutes Benehmen. ◆'**mannerism,** *s.* Tick *m.*

**manoeuvre** [mə'nu:vər]. I. *s.* Manöver *n.* II. *v.tr. & i.* manövrieren.

**manor** ['mænər], *s.* m. **(house),** Herrenhaus *n;* Schloß *n.*

**mansion** ['mænʃən], *s.* Schloß *n.*

**mantelpiece** ['mæntlpi:s], *s.* Kaminsims *m.*

**manual** ['mænjuəl]. I. *adj.* manuell; Hand-. II. *s.* Handbuch *n.*

**manufacture** [mænju'fæktʃər]. I. *s.* Herstellung *f*; **country of m.,** Herstellungsland *n.* II. *v.tr.* herstellen; **manufactured goods,** Industriewaren *fpl.* ◆**manu'facturer,** *s.* Hersteller *m.*

**manure** [mə'njuər], *s.* Dünger *m*; **(farmyard) m.,** Mist *m.*

**manuscript** ['mænjuskript], *s.* Manuskript *n.*

**many** ['meni]. I. *adj.* 1. viel(e); **how m.?** wie viele? 2. *Lit:* **m. a,** mancher, manche, manches. II. *s.* viele *pl.*

**map** [mæp]. I. *s.* Landkarte; *(of town)* Stadtplan *m.* II. *v.tr.* kartieren.

**maple** ['meipl], *s.* Ahorn *m*; **m. syrup,** Ahornsirup *m.*

**mar** [mɑ:r], *v.tr.* verderben.

**marathon** ['mærəθən], *s.* Marathonlauf *m.*

**marble** ['mɑ:bl], *s.* 1. Marmor *m.* 2. Murmel *f.*

**March**[1] [mɑ:tʃ], *s.* März *m.*

**march**[2]. I. *s.* Marsch *m.* II. *v.* 1. *v.i.* marschieren. 2. *v.tr.* **to m. s.o. off,** j-n abführen. ◆'**marching,** *s.* **m. orders,** Marschbefehl *m.*

**mare** [mɛər], *s.* Stute *f.*

**margarine** [mɑ:dʒə'ri:n], *s.* Margarine *f.*

**margin** ['mɑ:dʒin], *s.* 1. Rand *m* (einer Seite usw.). 2. **m. of error,** Fehlerbereich *m*; **profit m.,** Gewinnspanne *f.* ◆'**marginal,** *adj. (a)* am Rande; **m. note,** Randbemerkung *f*; *(b) (slight)* geringfügig; **m. seat,** Wahlkreis *m* mit knapper Mehrheit.

**marigold** ['mærigəuld], *s.* Ringelblume *f.*

**marijuana** [mæri'(h)wɑːnə], *s.* Marihuana *n.*

**marinade** [mæri'neid], *s.* Marinade *f.* ◆'**marinate,** *v.tr.* marinieren.

**marine** [mə'ri:n]. I. *adj. (a) (sea)* Meeres-; *(b) (shipping)* See-. II. *s.* Marinesoldat *m.*

**marital** ['mæritl], *adj.* ehelich; **m. status,** Familienstand *m.*

**maritime** ['mæritaim], *adj.* See-.

**marjoram** ['mɑ:dʒ(ə)rəm], *s.* Majoran *n.*

**mark**[1] [mɑ:k]. I. *s.* 1. *(target)* **to hit the m.,** ins Schwarze treffen; **to be wide of the m.,** danebentreffen. 2. *(trace)* Spur *f*; **(dirty) m.,** Fleck *m*; **birth m.,** Muttermal *n.* 3. *(a) (sign)* Zeichen *n*; *(b) (feature)* Kennzeichen *n.* 4. *Sch:* Note *f.* II. *v.tr. (a)* (eine Grenze usw.) markieren; *(b)* (Schularbeiten) benoten; *(c)* **to m. time,** Zeit schinden; *(d)* **(you) m. my words!** paß nur auf! du wirst noch an meine Worte denken! *(e) Fb:* (einen Spieler) decken. ◆'**marked,** *adj.* **a. m. improvement,** eine merkliche Besserung. ◆'**markup,** *s.* Kalkulationsaufschlag *m.*

**mark**[2], *s. (money)* Mark *f*; **ten marks,** zehn Mark.

**market** ['mɑ:kit]. I. *s.* Markt *m*; **m. place,** Marktplatz *m*; **m. research,** Marktforschung *f.* II. *v.tr. (a) (introduce)* (etwas) auf den Markt bringen; *(b) (sell)* (etwas) vertreiben. ◆'**marketable,** *adj.* marktfähig. ◆'**marketing,** *s.* Marketing *n; (sale)* Vertrieb *m.*

**marksman,** *pl.* **-men** ['mɑ:ksmən], *s.* Scharfschütze *m.*

**marmalade** ['mɑ:məleid], *s.* Orangenmarmelade *f.*

**maroon**[1] [mə'ru:n], *adj.* dunkelrot.

**maroon**[2], *v.tr.* **to be marooned,** *(on an island)* ausgesetzt werden; *F: (be stuck)* festsitzen.

**marquee** [mɑ:'ki:], *s.* Festzelt *n.*

**marriage** ['mæridʒ], *s. (a) (state)* Ehe *f*; **m. guidance,** Eheberatung *f*; *(b) (ceremony)* Trauung *f*; **m. certificate,** Heiratsurkunde *f*; *(c) (act of marrying)* Heirat *f*; **m. bureau,** Ehevermittlung *f.* ◆'**married,** *adj.* verheiratet; **m. couple,** Ehepaar *n.* ◆'**marry,** *v.tr & i.* heiraten.

**marrow** ['mærəu], *s.* 1. **bone m.,** Knochenmark *m.* 2. **(vegetable) m.,** Speisekürbis *m.*

**marsh** [mɑ:ʃ], *s.* Sumpf *m.*

**marshal** ['mɑ:ʃəl]. I. *s.* **field m.,** Feldmarschall *m.* II. *v.tr.* (Truppen usw.) aufstellen; (Gedanken, Tatsachen) ordnen.

**martial** ['mɑːʃ(ə)l], *adj.* **m. law**, Kriegs-recht *n.*
**Martian** ['mɑːʃən], *s.* Marsmensch *m.*
**martyr** ['mɑːtər]. **I.** *s.* Märtyrer(in) *m(f).* **II.** *v.tr.* (j-n) zum Märtyrer machen. ◆'**martyrdom**, *s.* Martyrium *n.*
**marvel** ['mɑːv(ə)l]. **I.** *s.* Wunder *n.* **II.** *v.i.* sich wundern (**at sth.**, über etwas *acc*). ◆'**marvellous**, *adj.* wunderbar; *F:* fabelhaft.
**Marxist** ['mɑːksist]. **I.** *s.* Marxist(in) *m(f).* **II.** *adj.* marxistisch.
**marzipan** [mɑːzi'pæn], *s.* Marzipan *n.*
**mascara** [mæs'kɑːrə], *s.* Wimperntusche *f.*
**mascot** ['mæskət], *s.* Maskottchen *n.*
**masculine** ['mæskjulin], *adj.* männlich.
**mash** [mæʃ], *v.tr.* (etwas) zu Brei zer-drücken; **mashed potatoes**, Kartoffelbrei *m.*
**mask** [mɑːsk]. **I.** *s.* Maske *f.* **II.** *v.tr.* maskieren. ◆'**masking**, *adj.* **m. tape**, Abdeckband *n.*
**masochist** ['mæsəkist], *s.* Masochist *m.*
**mason** ['meisən], *s.* **1.** Steinmetz *m.* **2.** *(freemason)* Freimaurer *m.* ◆**masonic** [mə'sɒnik], *adj.* freimaurerisch. ◆'**masonry**, *s.* Mauerwerk *n.*
**masquerade** [mæskə'reid]. **I.** *s.* Maske-rade *f.* **II.** *v.i.* **to m. as s.o.**, sich für j-n ausgeben.
**mass¹** [mæs], *s.* *Ecc:* Messe *f.*
**mass²**, *s.* Masse *f;* **m. production**, Mas-senproduktion *f.* ◆'**mass-pro'duce**, *v.tr.* (einen Artikel) in Massenproduktion herstellen.
**massacre** ['mæsəkər]. **I.** *s.* Massaker *n.* **II.** *v.tr.* massakrieren.
**massage** ['mæsɑːʒ]. **I.** *s.* Massage *f.* **II.** *v.tr.* massieren.
**massive** ['mæsiv], *adj.* massiv.
**mast** [mɑːst], *s.* Mast *m.*
**master** ['mɑːstər]. **I.** *s.* **1.** Herr *m.* **2.** *Sch:* (a) *(teacher)* Lehrer *m;* (b) Rektor *m* (ei-nes Colleges). **3.** *(of subject etc.)* Meister *m;* **m. copy**, Original *n;* **m. key**, Haupt-schlüssel *m.* **II.** *v.tr.* (eine Aufgabe, Schwierigkeiten) meistern; (ein Fach usw.) beherrschen. ◆'**masterful**, *adj.* gebieterisch. ◆'**masterly**, *adj.* meister-haft. ◆'**mastermind**, *v.tr.* **to m. a pro-ject**, der führende Kopf eines Projekts sein. ◆'**masterpiece**, *s.* Meisterwerk *n.* ◆'**mastery**, *s.* Beherrschung *f.*
**masturbate** ['mæstəbeit], *v.i.* onanieren.
**mat** [mæt], *s.* (a) Matte *f;* **(door) m.**, Ab-treter *m;* (b) *(rug)* Vorleger *m;* (c) *(under plates, vases etc.)* Untersetzer *m;* **beer m.**, Bierdeckel *m.* ◆'**matted**, *adj.* verfilzt.
**match¹** [mætʃ]. **I.** *s.* **1.** *Sp:* Spiel *n.* **2.** **to be a m. for s.o., sth.**, j-m, etwas *dat* ge-wachsen sein; **to meet one's m.**, seinen Meister finden. **3. these colours are a good m.**, diese Farben passen gut zusammen/vertragen sich gut. **II.** *v.tr. & i.* (a) **he can m. anyone for speed**, er kann es mit jedem an Schnelligkeit auf-

nehmen; **to be evenly matched (for strength etc.)**, einander (an Stärke usw.) gleich sein; (b) *(adapt)* *(Tchn:* Teile) auf-einander abstimmen; (c) **the curtains m. the carpet**, die Vorhänge passen zum Teppich. ◆'**matching**, *adj.* zusammen-passend. ◆'**matchless**, *adj.* unver-gleichlich.
**match²**, *s.* Streichholz *n.* ◆'**matchbox**, *s.* Streichholzschachtel *f.*
**mate** [meit]. **I.** *s.* (a) *(assistant)* Gehilfe *m* (eines Arbeiters); (b) *P:* Kumpel *m.* **II.** *v.i.* sich paaren. ◆'**mating**, *s.* *Z:* Paa-rung *f;* **m. season**, Paarungszeit *f.*
**material** [mə'tiəriəl]. **I.** *adj.* materiell. **II.** *s.* **1.** *(fabric)* Stoff *m.* **2.** (a) *(basis)* Mate-rial *n;* **raw m.**, Rohstoff *m;* **building m.**, Baumaterial *n;* (b) usw. *pl.* **writing mater-ials**, Schreibmaterialien *npl;* **teaching materials**, Lehrmittel *npl.* ◆**ma'terialist**, *s.* Materialist *m.* ◆**materia'listic**, *adj.* materialistisch. ◆**ma'terialize**, *v.i.* (a) *(of idea, project etc.)* sich verwirklichen; (b) *F: (of pers.)* **to fail to m.**, nicht auftauchen.
**maternal** [mə'tɜːnəl], *adj.* mütterlich. ◆**ma'ternity**, *s.* Mutterschaft *f;* **m. dress**, Umstandskleid *n.*
**mathematics** [mæθə'mætiks], *s.pl.* Ma-thematik *f.* ◆**mathe'matical**, *adj.* ma-thematisch. ◆**mathema'tician**, *s.* Mathematiker *m.* ◆'**maths**, *adj.* *Fam:* Mathe *f.*
**matinée** ['mætinei], *s.* Matinee *f.*
**matrimony** ['mætriməni], *s.* Ehestand *m.*
**matron** ['meitrən], *s.* (in school etc.) Hausmutter *f;* (in hospital) Oberin *f.*
**matter** ['mætər]. **I.** *s.* **1.** (a) *(material)* Materie *f;* (b) **reading m.**, Lesestoff *m.* **2. no m. how**, egal wie. **3.** *(affair)* Sache *f,* Angelegenheit *f;* **as a m. of course**, selbstverständlich; **as a m. of fact**, in der Tat; eigentlich; **for that m.**, was das an-belangt; **what is the m.?** was ist los? **to make matters worse ...**, zu allem Un-glück ...; und obendrein ... **II.** *v.i.* von Bedeutung sein (**to s.o.**, für j-n *acc*); **it doesn't m.**, es spielt keine Rolle; **it doesn't m. to me**, es macht mir nichts aus. ◆'**matter-of-'fact**, *adj.* sachlich.
**mattress** ['mætris], *s.* Matratze *f.*
**mature** [mə'tjuər]. **I.** *adj.* reif. **II.** *v.tr. & i.* (a) reifen; (b) *(of policy etc.)* fällig wer-den. ◆**ma'turity**, *s.* Reife *f.*
**mauve** [məuv], *adj.* lila.
**maxim** ['mæksim], *s.* Maxime *f;* *(princi-ple)* Grundsatz *m.*
**maximize** ['mæksimaiz], *v.tr.* steigern. ◆'**maximum**. **I.** *s.* Maximum *n.* **II.** *adj.* maximal; **m. speed**, Höchst-geschwindigkeit *f.*
**may¹** [mei], *v. aux.* (a) *(possibility)* kön-nen; **be that as it may**, wie dem auch sei; (b) *(permission)* dürfen; **m. I?** darf ich? (c) *(wish)* mögen. ◆'**maybe**, *adv.* viel-leicht.
**May²**, *s.* Mai *m.*

**mayonnaise** [meiə'neiz], s. Mayonnaise f.

**mayor** ['mɛər], s. Bürgermeister m. ◆'**mayoress**, s. Bürgermeisterin f.

**maze** [meiz], s. Irrgarten m; esp. Fig: Labyrinth n.

**me** [mi:], pers. pron. 1. (object) (a) acc mich; **for me**, für mich; (b) dat mir; **he gave me money**, er gab mir Geld. 2. **it's me**, ich bin's.

**meadow** ['medəu], s. Wiese f.

**meagre** ['mi:gər], adj. dürftig.

**meal**, s. Mahlzeit f.

**mean**[1] [mi:n], adj m. **temperature**, mittlere Temperatur f. ◆**means**, s. **the m.**, das/die Mittel; **by all m.**, aber natürlich; **by m. of sth.**, durch etwas acc.

**mean**[2], adj. 1. (small) gering. 2. (unkind) gemein. 3. (miserly) geizig. ◆'**meanness**, s. 1. Gemeinheit f. 2. Geiz m.

**mean**[3], v.tr.irr. (a) (intend) (etwas) beabsichtigen; (esp. with remark) (etwas) meinen; **he didn't m. (to do) it**, er hat es nicht absichtlich getan; **to m. well** es gut meinen; **do you m. me?** meinen Sie mich? **this book was meant for you**, dieses Buch war für dich gedacht/bestimmt; (b) (signify) bedeuten; **what does this m.?** was bedeutet das? ◆'**meaning. I.** adj. well-m., (of pers.) wohlmeinend; (of action, words) wohlgemeint. **II.** s. 1. (of Bedeutung f (eines Wortes usw.); Sinn m (eines Satzes, einer Rede usw.). ◆'**meaningful**, adj. sinnvoll. ◆'**meaningless**, adj. bedeutungslos.

**meander** [mi'ændər], v.i. sich schlängeln.

**meantime** ['mi:ntaim]/**meanwhile** ['mi:n(h)wail], s. & adv. (**in the) m.**, inzwischen.

**measles** ['mi:zlz], s.pl. Masern pl.

**measure** ['meʒər]. **I.** s. 1. Maß n. **made to m.**, nach Maß gearbeitet. 2. (action) Maßnahme f. **II.** v. 1. v.tr. (a) messen; (ein Zimmer) ausmessen; (b) **to m. s.o. (for a suit)**, j-m (für einen Anzug) Maß nehmen. 2. v.i. (a) **the table measures three metres by two**, der Tisch mißt drei mal zwei Meter; (b) **to m. up to expectations**, den Erwartungen entsprechen. ◆'**measurement**, s. 1. (act) Messung f; **to take measurements**, Messungen vornehmen. 2. (length etc.) Maß n; **to take s.o.'s measurements**, j-m Maß nehmen.

**meat** [mi:t], s. Fleisch n.

**mechanic** [mi'kænik], s. 1. Mechaniker m; **motor m.**, Autoschlosser m. 2. pl. **mechanics**, Mechanik f. ◆**me'chanical**, adj. mechanisch; (by machine) maschinell.

**mechanism** ['mekənizm], s. Mechanismus m. ◆'**mechanize** [-naiz], v.tr. mechanisieren.

**medal** ['medl], s. Sp: etc: Medaille f; Mil: Orden m. ◆'**medallist**, s. Medaillengewinner(in) m(f). ◆**medallion** [-'dæljən],

s. Medaillon n.

**meddle** ['medl], v.i. (a) (interfere) sich einmischen (**in/with sth.**, in etwas acc); (b) (mess about) **who has been meddling with my papers?** wer hat sich an meine Papiere herangemacht?

**media** ['mi:diə], s. **the (mass) m.**, die (Massen)medien.

**medi(a)eval** [medi'i:vəl], adj. mittelalterlich.

**mediate** ['mi:dieit], v.i. vermitteln. ◆'**mediator**, s. Vermittler m. ◆**medi'ation**, s. Vermittlung f.

**medical** ['medik(ə)l]. **I.** adj. ärztlich; **m. certificate**, ärztliches Attest; **m. student**, Medizinstudent(in) m(f); **m. practitioner**, praktischer Arzt m; **the m. profession**, die Ärzteschaft. **II.** s. F: ärztliche Untersuchung; -**ly**, adv. ärztlich. ◆**medicine** ['meds(i)n], s. Medizin f; **medicines**, Medikamente npl. ◆**medicinal** [-'disinl], adj. medizinisch.

**mediocre** [mi:di'iəukər], adj. mittelmäßig. ◆**mediocrity** [-'ɔkriti], s. Mittelmäßigkeit f.

**meditate** ['mediteit], v.i. meditieren. ◆**medi'tation**, s. Meditation f.

**Mediterranean** [meditə'reiniən], adj. **the M. (Sea)**, das Mittelmeer.

**medium** ['mi:diəm]. **I.** s.pl. -**s**, -**ia** [-iə]. 1. Mitte f. 2. (means) Mittel n. 3. (spiritualist) Medium m. **II.** adj. mittlere(r,s), Mittel-.

**medley** ['medli], s. Potpourri m.

**meek** [mi:k], adj. Pej: duckmäuserisch.

**meet** [mi:t], v.irr. 1. v.tr. (a) (j-n) treffen; (by chance) (j-m) begegnen; (b) (for the first time) (j-n) kennenlernen; (c) (Gefahren, Schwierigkeiten usw. dat) begegnen. (d) (fulfil) (einer Anforderung) entsprechen; (eine Bedingung) erfüllen; (einer Verpflichtung) nachkommen. 2. v.i. (a) sich treffen; (b) **to m. with sth.**, etwas erleben. ◆'**meeting**, s. 1. (by chance) Begegnung f; (arranged) Treffen n; **m. place**, Treffpunkt m. 2. (gathering) Versammlung f; (of committee etc.) Sitzung f.

**melancholy** ['melənkəli]. **I.** s. Melancholie f. **II.** adj. melancholisch.

**mellow** ['meləu]. **I.** adj. (a) (of wine) ausgereift; (b) (of sound, colour) sanft. **II.** v.i. ausreifen; Fig: (of pers.) milder werden.

**melodious** [mi'ləudiəs], adj. melodiös. ◆**melody** ['melədi], s. Melodie f.

**melodrama** ['melədrɑːmə], s. Melodrama n. ◆**melodra'matic**, adj. melodramatisch.

**melon** ['melən], s. Melone f.

**melt** [melt], v. 1. v.i. schmelzen. 2. v.tr. (etwas) schmelzen lassen; **to m. down metals**, Metalle einschmelzen. ◆'**melting**, s. **m. point**, Schmelzpunkt m.

**member** ['membər], s. Mitglied n; **M. of Parliament**, Parlamentsabgeordnete(r) f(m). ◆'**membership**, s. 1. Mitgliedschaft f; **m. card**, Mitgliedskarte f. 2.

(*number*) Mitgliederzahl *f*.

**memento,** *pl.* **-o(e)s** [mə'mentəu, -əuz], *s.* Andenken *n*.

**memo,** *pl.* **-os** ['meməu, -əuz], *s. F*: (*abbr. of* **memorandum**) Mitteilung *f*.

**memoirs** ['memwɑːrz], *s.pl.* Memoiren *fpl*.

**memorable** ['mem(ə)rəbl], *adj.* denkwürdig.

**memorandum,** *pl.* **-da, -dums** [memə'rændəm, -də, -dəmz], *s.* 1. Memorandum *n*. 2. (*note*) Mitteilung *f*.

**memorial** [mə'mɔːriəl]. I. *s.* Denkmal *n*. II. *attrib. adj.* Gedächtnis-. ◆'**memorize,** *v.tr.* auswendig lernen. ◆**memory** ['meməri], *s.* 1. (*faculty*) Gedächtnis *n*. 2. (*thing remembered*) Erinnerung *f*.

**menace** ['menəs, -nis], *s.* (*threat*) Drohung *f*; (*danger*) drohende Gefahr *f*. ◆'**menacing,** *adj.* drohend; (*of silence*) bedrohlich.

**menagerie** [mə'nædʒəri], *s.* Menagerie *f*.

**mend** [mend], *v.tr.* reparieren; (Kleider) ausbessern; (Löcher, Strümpfe) stopfen.

**menial** ['miːniəl], *adj.* niedrig.

**meningitis** [menin'dʒaitis], *s.* Gehirnhautentzündung *f*.

**menopause** ['menəupɔːz], *s.* Wechseljahre *npl*.

**menstruate** ['menstrueit], *v.i.* die Regel haben. ◆**menstru'ation,** *s.* Menstruation *f*, monatliche Regel *f*.

**mental** ['ment(ə)l], *adj.* geistig. **m. illness,** Geisteskrankheit *f*; **m. hospital/home,** Krankenhaus *n*/Heim *n* für Geisteskranke; **-ly,** *adv.* geistig. ◆**mentality** [-'tæliti], *s.* Mentalität *f*.

**mention** ['menʃ(ə)n]. I. *s.* Erwähnung *f*. II. *v.tr.* erwähnen; **not to m. ...,** ganz zu schweigen von ... *dat*; *F*: **don't m. it!** gern geschehen!

**menu** ['menjuː], *s.* Speisekarte *f*.

**mercantile** ['məːk(ə)ntail], *adj.* kaufmännisch; Handels-.

**mercenary** ['məːsin(ə)ri]. I. *s.* Söldner *m*. II. *adj.* gewinnsüchtig.

**merchant** ['məːtʃ(ə)nt]. I. *s.* Kaufmann *m*; (*dealer*) Händler *m*. 2. *attrib.* Handels-; **m. bank,** Handelsbank *f*; **m. navy,** Handelsmarine *f*. ◆'**merchandise,** *s.* Handelsgüter *npl*; Waren *fpl*.

**Mercury** ['məːkjuri]. 1. *Pr.n.* Merkur. 2. **m.,** *s. Ch:* Quecksilber *n*.

**mercy** ['məːsi], *s.* Barmherzigkeit *f*; *Ecc: etc:* Gnade *f*; **to be at s.o.'s m.** j-m ausgeliefert sein. ◆'**merciful,** *adj.* barmherzig; **-ly,** *adv.* zum Glück. ◆'**merciless,** *adj.* erbarmungslos.

**mere** ['miər], *adj.* (*a*) bloß; **the m. thought,** der bloße Gedanke; (*b*) (*pure*) rein; **-ly,** *adv.* bloß.

**merge** [məːdʒ], *v.* 1. *v.tr.* (Firmen) fusionieren. 2. *v.i.* (*a*) (*of roads etc.*) zusammenlaufen; (*of rivers etc.*) zusammenfließen; (*b*) **to m. into sth.,** in etwas *dat* verschmelzen. ◆'**merger,** *s.* Fusion *f*.

**meringue** [mə'ræŋ], *s.* Baiser *n*.

**merit** ['merit]. I. *s.* 1. (*a*) *usu. pl.* (*of person*) Verdienst *m*; (*b*) (*advantage*) Vorteil *m*. 2. (*worth*) Wert *m*. II. *v.tr.* verdienen.

**mermaid** ['məːmeid], *s.* Meerjungfrau *f*.

**merry** ['meri], *adj.* (*a*) fröhlich; (*b*) (*tipsy*) angeheitert.

**mesh** [meʃ], *s.* (*of net etc.*) Masche *f*.

**mess** [mes], *s.* 1. Unordnung *f*, (*muddle*) Durcheinander *n*; **to make a m. of a job,** eine Arbeit verpfuschen. 2. (*dirt*) Dreck *m*. 3. *Mil:* Messe *f*. ◆**mess a'bout,** *v.* 1. *v.i. F*: herummurksen; **to m. a. with sth.,** mit etwas *dat* herumspielen. 2. *v.tr. F*: (j-n) hinhalten. ◆**mess 'up,** *v.tr. F*: (*a*) (etwas) dreckig machen; (*b*) (Pläne usw.) durcheinanderbringen. ◆'**messy,** *adj.* 1. (*untidy*) unordentlich. 2. (*dirty*) dreckig.

**message** ['mesidʒ], *s.* Botschaft *f*; **to give s.o. a m.,** j-m etwas ausrichten. ◆'**messenger** ['mesindʒər], *s.* Bote *m*.

**metabolism** [me'tæbəlizm], *s.* Metabolismus *m*.

**metal** [metl], *s.* Metall *n*. ◆**metallic** [mi'tælik], *adj.* metallisch. ◆me'**tallurgy** [mi'tælik], *adj.* metallisch. ◆me'**tallurgy,** *s.* Metallurgie *f*.

**metaphor** ['metəfər], *s.* Metapher *f*. ◆**metaphorical** [-'fɔrikl], *adj.* metaphorisch.

**meteor** ['miːtiər], *s.* Meteor *m*. ◆**meteoric** [-'ɔrik], *adj.* **m. rise,** kometenhafter Aufstieg.

**meteorology** [miːtjə'rɔlədʒi], *s.* Meteorologie *f*.

**meter** ['miːtər], *s.* Meßgerät *n*; **parking m.,** Parkuhr *f*; **electricity/gas m.,** Stromzähler/Gaszähler *m*.

**methane** ['miːθein], *s.* Methan *n*.

**method** ['meθəd], *s.* Methode *f*. ◆**methodical** [mi'θɔdikl], *adj.* systematisch.

**methylated** ['meθileitid], *adj.* **m. spirits,** *F*: **meths,** Brennspiritus *m*.

**meticulous** [mi'tikjuləs], *adj.* äußerst genau.

**metre** ['miːtər], *s.* Meter *m & n*. ◆**metric** ['metrik], *adj.* metrisch.

**Mexico** ['meksikəu]. *Pr. n.* Mexiko *n*. ◆'**Mexican,** *s.* Mexikaner(in) *m(f)*.

**miaow** [mi(ː)'au]. I. *s.* Miau *n*. II. *v.i.* miauen.

**micro-** ['maikrəu-], *comb.fm.* Mikro-; **microfilm,** Mikrofilm *m*; **microprocessor,** Mikroprozessor *m*.

**microbe** ['maikrəub], *s.* Mikrobe *f*.

**microphone** ['maikrəfəun], *s.* Mikrofon *n*.

**microscope** ['maikrəskəup], *s.* Mikroskop *n*. ◆**microscopic** [-'skɔpik], *adj.* mikroskopisch klein.

**microwave** ['maikrəuweiv], *s.* **m. oven,** Mikrowellenherd *m*.

**mid** [mid], *attrib. adj.* **in m. air,** in der Luft; **in m. June,** Mitte Juni; **he is in his m.-fifties,** er ist Mitte fünfzig. ◆'**mid'day,** *s.* Mittag *m*. ◆**middle**

['midl]. **I.** *adj.* mittlere(r,s), Mittel-; **the m. class(es)**, der Mittelstand; **m. aged/in m. age**, im mittleren Alter; **the M. Ages**, das Mittelalter; **the M. East**, der Nahe Osten. **II.** *s.* (*a*) Mitte *f*; **in the m. of**, in der Mitte von, mitten in + *dat*; (*b*) *F:* (*waist*) Taille *f*. ◆**'the 'Midlands**, *s.pl.* Mittelengland *n.* ◆**'midnight**, *s.* Mitternacht *f.* ◆**midst**, *s.* **in the m. of**, mitten in + *dat.* ◆**'mid'stream**, *s.* **in m.**, in der Mitte des Flusses/Stromes. ◆**'mid'summer**, *s.* Hochsommer *m.* ◆**'mid'way**, *adv.* auf halbem Wege; **m. between**, in der Mitte zwischen + *dat.* ◆**'mid'week**, *s. & adv.* Mitte *f* der Woche. ◆**'mid'west**. *Pr. n.* Mittelwesten *m* (von Amerika).

**midwife**, *pl.* **-wives** ['midwaif, -waivz], *s.* Hebamme *f.* ◆**midwifery** ['-'wif(ə)ri], *s.* Geburtshilfe *f.*

**might¹** [mait], *s.* Macht *f.*

**might²**, *v. aux.* (*past tense of* may) könnte(n); **you m. have asked!** Sie hätten doch fragen können! ◆**'mighty. I.** *adj.* (*powerful*) mächtig; (*enormous*) gewaltig. **II.** *adv.* höchst.

**migraine** ['mi:grein], *s.* Migräne *f.*

**migrate** [mai'greit], *v.i.* (*of pers.*) abwandern; (*of birds*) ziehen. ◆**'migrant. I.** *adj.* wandernd; **m. worker**, Wanderarbeiter *m;* (*from abroad*) Gastarbeiter *m.* **II.** *s.* Wanderer *m;* (*pers.*) Umsiedler(in) *m(f).* ◆**mi'gration**, *s.* (*of pers.*) Abwanderung *f;* (*of peoples*) Völkerwanderung *f;* (*of birds, fish*) Zug *m.*

**mike** [maik], *s. F:* Mikro *n.*

**Milan** [mi'læn]. *Pr.n.* Mailand *n.*

**mild** [maild], *adj.* mild; (*of illness, cigar etc.*) leicht; **-ly**, *adv.* leicht; **to put it m.**, gelinde gesagt. ◆**'mildness**, *s.* Milde *f.*

**mile** [mail], *s.* Meile *f; F:* **he's miles faster**, er ist viel schneller. ◆**'mileage**, *s.* (*zurückgelegte*) Meilenzahl *f;* (*of car*) Meilenstand *m;* **unlimited m.**, unbegrenzte                    Kilometerleistung. ◆**'milestone**, *s.* Meilenstein *m.*

**militant** ['militənt]. **I.** *adj.* militant. **II.** *s.* Kämpfer *m; Pol:* Aktivist *m.* ◆**'military. I.** *adj.* militärisch, Militär-. **II.** *s.* **the m.**, das Militär.

**milk** [milk]. **I.** *s.* Milch *f.* **II.** *v.tr.* melken. ◆**'milkman**, *s.* Milchmann *m.*

**mill** [mil]. **I.** *s.* Mühle *f.* **II.** *v.* **1.** *v.tr.* mahlen. **2.** *v.i.* **to m. (about)**, hin- und hertreiben.

**milligramme** ['miligræm], *s.* Milligramm *n.* ◆**'millimetre** ['milimetr], *s.* Millimeter *m.*

**million** ['miljən], *s.* Million *f.* ◆**millio'naire**, *s.* Millionär(in) *m(f).* ◆**'millionth**, *adj.* millionste(r,s).

**mime** [maim], *v.tr. & i.* mimen.

**mimic** ['mimik]. **I.** *s.* Imitator *m* (von Stimmen). **II.** *v.tr.* nachäffen. ◆**'mimicry**, *s.* Nachäffung *f.*

**mince** [mins]. **I.** *s. Cu:* Hackfleisch *n.* **2. m. pie**, mit 'mincemeat' gefüllte Pastete. **II.** *v.tr.* (*a*) (Fleisch usw.) durchdrehen; **minced meat**, Hackfleisch *n;* (*b*) *Fig:* **not to m. one's words**, kein Blatt vor den Mund nehmen. ◆**'mincemeat**, *s.* Pastetenfüllung *f* aus Rosinen, Korinthen, Äpfeln usw; *Fig:* **to make m. of s.o.**, aus j-m Hackfleisch machen. ◆**'mincer**, *s.* Fleischwolf *m.*

**mind** [maind]. **I.** *s.* **1.** Sinn *m;* Kopf *m;* (*intellect*) Geist *m;* **you're/you must be out of your m.!** du bist (wohl) nicht bei Trost! **2. to bear/keep sth. in m.**, sich *dat* etwas merken; (*consider*) etwas berücksichtigen; *F:* **it went clean out of my m.**, ich habe es total vergessen. **3.** (*opinion*) Meinung *f;* **to my m.**, meiner Ansicht nach; **to give s.o. a piece of one's m.**, j-m gehörig die Meinung sagen; **to make up one's m.**, sich entschließen; **to change one's m.**, sich *dat* anders überlegen; **to have an open m.**, unvoreingenommen sein. **4.** (*attention*) **to take his m. off it**, um ihn davon abzulenken. **II.** *v.* **1.** *v.tr.* (*a*) (*look after*) **to m. s.o., sth.**, sich um j-n, etwas *acc* kümmern; **m. your own business**, kümmere dich um deine eigenen Angelegenheiten; (*b*) (*look out*) **m. the step!** Achtung Stufe! **m. (that) you don't lose it**, paß auf/gib acht, daß du es nicht verlierst; (*c*) (*object*) **do you m. my smoking?** stört es Sie, wenn ich rauche? **would you m. shutting the door?** würden Sie bitte die Tür schließen? **I don't m.**, mir macht es nichts aus; **never m.**, mach dir nichts draus; (*d*) **the dirt is bad enough**, **never m. the noise**, der Schmutz ist schlimm genug, von dem Lärm ganz zu schweigen. **2.** *v.i. F:* **to m.** (out), aufpassen; **m. out!** Achtung! ◆**'minded**, *adj.* gesinnt.

**mine¹** [main], *poss. pron.* meiner, meine, mein(e)s; *pl.* meine.

**mine². I.** *s.* **1.** Bergwerk *n;* (coal) m., Kohlengrube *f; Fig:* **a m. of information**, eine Fundgrube des Wissens. **2.** *Mil:* Mine *f.* **II.** *v.tr.* (*a*) **to m. coal, ores etc.**, Kohle, Erze usw. abbauen; (*b*) *Mil:* verminen. ◆**'minefield**, *s. Mil:* Minenfeld *n.* ◆**'miner**, *s.* Bergarbeiter *m.* ◆**mining**, *s.* Bergbau *m.*

**mineral** ['minərəl], *s.* **1.** Mineral *n.* **2. m. water**, Mineralwasser *n.*

**mingle** ['mingl], *v.i.* sich mischen.

**mini** ['mini]. **I.** *s. m.* (**skirt**) Minirock *m.* **II.** *adj. & prefix* klein, Mini-; **minibus**, Kleinbus *m.*

**miniature** ['minitʃər, 'minjətʃər], *adj.* Klein-.

**minimal** ['miniməl], *adj.* minimal. ◆**'minimize**, *v.tr.* (etwas) auf ein Minimum beschränken. ◆**'minimum. I.** *s.* Minimum *n* (of, an + *dat*). **II.** *attrib. adj.* Mindest-; **m. wage**, Mindestlohn *m.*

**minister** ['ministər], *s.* **1.** *Pol:* Minister *m.* **2.** *Ecc:* Pastor *m.* ◆**minis'terial**, *adj.* ministeriell; **at m. level**, auf Ministerebene. ◆**'ministry**, *s.* Ministerium *n.*

**mink** [miŋk], s. Nerz m.

**minor** ['mainər]. **I.** adj. **1.** (a) klein(er); (negligible) geringfügig; **m. injury,** leichte Verletzung; **a m. offence,** ein leichtes Vergehen; (b) (less important) unbedeutend, Neben-; **m. matter/point,** Nebensache f. **2.** Mus: Moll; **A m.,** a-Moll. **II.** s. Minderjährige(r) f(m). ◆**mi'nority,** s. Minderheit f.

**mint¹** [mint]. **I.** adj. **in m. condition,** in neuwertigem Zustand. **II.** v.tr. prägen.

**mint²,** s. (a) Bot: Minze f; (b) (peppermint) Pfefferminzbonbon n.

**minus** ['mainəs], prep. (a) minus, weniger; (b) F: ohne + acc; (c) **it is m. 10 degrees,** es ist 10 Grad unter Null.

**minute¹** ['minit], s. **1.** Minute f; F: **wait a/just a m.!** Moment mal! einen Augenblick! **2.** pl. **minutes,** Protokoll n (einer Sitzung).

**minute²** [mai'nju:t], adj. winzig.

**miracle** ['mirəkl], s. Wunder n. ◆**miraculous** [-'rækjuləs], adj. wunderbar; **to have a m. escape/recovery,** wie durch ein Wunder entkommen/genesen.

**mirage** ['mira:ʒ], s. Fata Morgana f.

**mirror** ['mirər]. **I.** s. Spiegel m. **II.** v.tr. wiederspiegeln.

**misapprehension** [misæpri'henʃ(ə)n], s. Mißverständnis n.

**misbehave** [misbi'heiv], v.i. & refl. **to m. (oneself),** sich schlecht benehmen.

**miscalculate** [mis'kælkjuleit], v. **1.** v.tr. (etwas) falsch berechnen. **2.** v.i. sich verrechnen.

**miscarriage** [mis'kærid3], s. **1. m. of justice,** Justizirrtum m. **2.** Med: Fehlgeburt f.

**miscellaneous** [misə'leiniəs], adj. (of writings etc.) vermischt; (of goods etc.) divers.

**mischief** ['mistʃif], s. Unfug m; **to get up to m.,** Unfug anstellen. ◆**'mischievous,** adj. **m.** child, Schlingel m; **a m. smile,** ein schelmisches Lächeln.

**misconception** ['miskən'sepʃən], s. falsche Auffassung f.

**misdemeanour** ['misdi'mi:nər], s. Vergehen n.

**miser** ['maizər], s. Geizhals m. ◆**'miserly,** adj. geizig.

**miserable** ['miz(ə)rəbl], adj. (a) (of existence etc.) elend; (b) (of pers.) trübsinnig; (c) F: Pej: (of pay, weather etc.) miserabel; **-ably,** adv. **to fail m.,** kläglich versagen. ◆**'misery,** s. (a) Elend n; (b) F: (pers.) Miesepeter m.

**misfire** [mis'faiər], v.i. (a) (of gun) versagen; (of engine) fehlzünden; (of joke, plan) danebengehen.

**misfit** ['misfit], s. Außenseiter m.

**misfortune** [mis'fɔ:tʃ(ə)n, -tju:n], s. Unglück n; pl. Unglücksfälle mpl.

**misgiving** [mis'givin], s. Bedenken n.

**mishap** [mishæp], s. Mißgeschick n.

**misinform** ['misin'fɔ:m], v.tr. (j-n) falsch unterrichten.

**misjudge** ['misdʒʌdʒ], v.tr. falsch beurteilen.

**mislay** [mis'lei], v.tr.irr. verlegen.

**mislead** [mis'li:d], v.tr.irr. (j-n) irreführen; (misinform) (j-n) falsch unterrichten. ◆**mis'leading,** adj. irreführend.

**misplace** [mis'pleis], v.tr. verlegen. ◆**mis'placed,** adj. unangebracht.

**misprint** ['misprint], s. Druckfehler m.

**misrepresent** ['misrepri'zent], v.tr. (Tatsachen usw.) falsch darstellen.

**miss¹** [mis]. **I.** s. (blow) Fehlschlag m; (shot) Fehlschuß m; (throw) Fehlwurf m; **I'll give that film a m.,** den Film werde ich mir schenken. **II.** v. **1.** v.tr. (a) (einen Schlag, das Ziel usw.) verfehlen; (eine Verabredung, eine Gelegenheit, einen Zug usw.) verpassen; F: **to m. the boat,** den Anschluß verpassen; (b) **to m. the point,** nicht begreifen, worum es eigentlich geht; (c) (j-n, etwas) vermissen; (d) (escape) **he just missed being run over,** er wäre fast überfahren worden; (e) **to m. (out) s.o., sth.,** j-n etwas auslassen. **2.** v.i. (a) das Ziel verfehlen; (of shot) danebengehen; (b) F: **he feels he's missing out on something,** er glaubt, er versäumt etwas. ◆**'missing,** adj. **1.** fehlend; **to be m.,** fehlen. **2.** (of pers., esp. soldier) vermißt.

**miss²,** s. Fräulein n.

**missile** ['misail], s. (thrown) Wurfgeschoß n; (fired) Geschoß n.

**mission** ['miʃ(ə)n], s. **1.** (a) (task) Aufgabe f; (b) Mil: Av: Einsatz m. **2.** Ecc: Mission f. ◆**'missionary,** s. Missionar m.

**mist** [mist]. **I.** s. (haze) Dunst m; (thick) Nebel m. **II.** v.i. (of glass) **to m. up/over,** beschlagen; **misted up,** beschlagen. ◆**'misty,** adj. neblig; (hazy) dunstig.

**mistake** [mis'teik]. **I.** s. Fehler m; (abstract) Irrtum m; **by m.,** irrtümlich. **II.** v.tr.irr. (j-n, etwas) verwechseln (**for s.o., sth.,** mit j-m, etwas dat). ◆**mis'taken,** adj. **1. to be m.,** sich irren (**about sth.,** in etwas dat). **2. m. opinion,** irrtümliche Meinung; (**case of**) **m. identity,** Personenverwechslung f; **-ly,** adv. irrtümlicherweise.

**mistletoe** ['misltəu], s. Mistel f.

**mistress** ['mistris], s. **1.** (a) Herrin f; (b) Sch: Lehrerin f; **2.** (lover) Geliebte f.

**mistrust** [mis'trʌst]. **I.** s. Mißtrauen n. **II.** v.tr. (j-m, etwas dat) mißtrauen.

**misunderstand** ['misʌndə'stænd], v.tr.irr. mißverstehen. ◆**'misunder'standing,** s. Mißverständnis n.

**misuse. I.** [mis'ju:s], s. Mißbrauch m. **II.** ['mis'ju:z], v.tr. (a) mißbrauchen; (b) (Worte, Werkzeuge usw.) falsch anwenden.

**mitten** ['mit(ə)n], s. Fausthandschuh m.

**mix** [miks]. **I.** s. Mischung f. **II.** v. **1.** v.tr. mischen. **2.** v.i. (of substance) sich mischen; (b) (of pers.) **to m. (with other people),** mit anderen Leuten verkehren. ◆**mixed,** adj. gemischt.

◆'**mixer,** s. **1.** H: Küchenmaschine f. **2.** (of pers.) **a good/bad m.,** ein geselliger/ungeselliger Mensch.
◆**mixture** ['mikstʃər], s. Mischung f.
◆'**mix'up,** v.tr. (a) (Papiere usw.) durcheinanderbringen; (b) (j-n, etwas) verwechseln; (c) **to be mixed up in sth.,** in etwas dat verwickelt sein; (d) F: **mixed up,** (confused) verwirrt. ◆'**mix-up,** s. Durcheinander n; Verwechslung f.

**moan** [məun]. **I.** s. (a) (groan) Stöhnen n; (b) F: (complaint) Klage f. **II.** v.i. (a) ächzen; (groan) stöhnen; (b) F: (complain) jammern.

**moat** [məut], s. Burggraben m.

**mob** [mɔb]. **I.** s. (wilde) Horde f. **II.** v.tr. (a) (of angry crowd) (j-n) anpöbeln; (b) **he was mobbed by his fans,** er wurde von seinen Fans umdrängt.

**mobile** ['məubail], adj. (a) (of pers.) beweglich; (b) (of thing) fahrbar; **m. home,** Wohnmobil n. ◆**mobility** ['məubiliti], s. Beweglichkeit f. ◆'**mobilize,** v.tr. & i. mobilisieren.

**mock** [mɔk]. **I.** attrib. adj. (a) (false) falsch; (b) (pretend) Schein-. **II.** v.tr. & i. **to m. (at) s.o., sth.,** j-n, etwas verspotten. ◆'**mockery,** s. **1.** Spott m. **2.** (travesty) Farce f.

**mode** [məud], s. (Art und) Weise f.

**model** ['mɔdl]. **I.** s. **1.** Modell n; **m.** aeroplane, Modellflugzeug n. **2.** (for imitation) (a) Vorbild n; (b) (ideal) Muster n; **m. husband,** Mustergatte m. **3.** (pers.) Mannequin n; **male m.,** Dressman m. **II.** v.tr. (a) (in clay etc.) (einen Kopf usw.) modellieren; (b) (Kleider) vorführen.

**moderate I.** adj. ['mɔd(ə)rət], (a) mäßig; (of views etc.) gemäßigt; (b) (medium) mittlere(r, s). **II.** v.tr. ['mɔdəreit], mäßigen; **-ly,** adv. mäßig. ◆**mode'ration,** s. Mäßigung f; **everything in m.,** alles mit Maß.

**modern** ['mɔdən], adj. modern; **m. languages,** neuere Sprachen. ◆'**modernize,** v.tr. modernisieren.

**modest** ['mɔdist], adj. bescheiden; (of price) mäßig. ◆'**modesty,** s. Bescheidenheit f.

**modify** ['mɔdifai], v.tr. (einen Entwurf) modifizieren; (Pläne) ändern.

**module** ['mɔdju:l], s. (space m.) Raumkapsel f; **lunar m.,** Mondfähre f.

**moist** [mɔist], adj. feucht. ◆**moisten** ['mɔisən], v.tr. befeuchten. ◆'**moisture,** s. Feuchtigkeit f. ◆'**moisturizer,** s. Feuchtigkeitscreme f. ◆'**moisturizing,** adj. **m. cream,** Feuchtigkeitscreme f.

**mole¹** [məul], s. (on skin) Leberfleck m.

**mole²,** s. Z: Maulwurf m.

**molecule** ['mɔlikju:l], s. Molekül n. ◆**molecular** [-'lekjulər], adj. molekular.

**molest** [mə(u)'lest], v.tr. belästigen.

**mollycoddle** ['mɔlikɔdl], v.tr. F: verhätscheln.

**moment** ['məumənt], s. Moment m, Augenblick m. ◆'**momentary,** adj. vorübergehend; **-ily,** adv. einen Augenblick (lang). ◆**mo'mentous,** adj. bedeutsam. ◆**mo'mentum,** s. Moment n; **to gather m.,** esp. Fig: allmählich in Fahrt kommen.

**monarch** ['mɔnək], s. Monarch m. ◆'**monarchy,** s. Monarchie f.

**monastery,** ['mɔnəstri], s. Kloster n. ◆**mo'nastic,** adj. mönchisch.

**Monday** ['mʌndi], s. Montag m.

**monetary** ['mʌnit(ə)ri], adj. Geld-; **m.** policy, Währungspolitik f.

**money** ['mʌni], s. Geld n. ◆'**money-box,** s. Sparbüchse f. ◆'**moneylender,** s. Geldverleiher m. ◆'**money-spinner,** s. F: Kassenschlager m.

**Mongolia** [mɔŋ'gəuliə]. Pr. n. Mongolei f.

**mongrel** ['mʌŋgrəl], s. (dog) Bastard m; F: Promenadenmischung f.

**monitor** ['mɔnitər]. **I.** s. **1.** Monitor m. **II.** v.tr. (Ereignisse, Entwicklungen) verfolgen.

**monk** [mʌŋk], s. Mönch m.

**monkey** ['mʌŋki], s. Affe m; **m. wrench,** Engländer m.

**monocle** ['mɔnəkl], s. Monokel n.

**monogram** ['mɔnəgræm], s. Monogramm n.

**monologue** ['mɔnələg], s. Monolog m.

**monopolize** [mə'nɔpəlaiz], v.tr. monopolisieren. ◆**mo'nopoly,** s. Monopol n.

**monotone** ['mɔnətəun], s. **in a m.,** mit monotoner Stimme. ◆**monotonous** [mə'nɔtənəs], adj. monoton; (of landscape) eintönig; (boring) langweilig. ◆**mo'notony,** s. Monotonie f; Eintönigkeit f.

**monsoon** [mɔn'su:n], s. Monsun m.

**monster** ['mɔnstər], s. (a) Ungeheuer n; (b) Pej: (pers.) Scheusal n. ◆**monstrosity** [-'strɔsiti], s. Mißgeburt f. ◆'**monstrous,** adj. unerhört.

**month** [mʌnθ], s. Monat m; **once a m.,** einmal im Monat; **for (several) months,** monatelang. ◆'**monthly. I.** adj. & adv. monatlich; **m. season (ticket),** Monatskarte f. **II.** s. (periodical) Monatsheft n.

**monument** ['mɔnjumənt], s. Denkmal n. ◆**monu'mental,** adj. monumental.

**moo** [mu:]. **I.** s. Muh n. **II.** v.i. muhen.

**mood** [mu:d], s. (of pers.) Laune f; (esp. of group) Stimmung f; **in a good/bad m.,** gut/schlecht gelaunt; **I am not in the m. for it,** mir ist nicht danach zumute. ◆'**moody,** adj. **1.** (fickle) launenhaft. **2.** (gloomy) mürrisch.

**moon** [mu:n], s. Mond m; F: **over the m.,** im siebten Himmel. ◆'**moonlight. I.** s. Mondlicht n; **in the/by m.,** im Mondschein. **II.** v.i. eine Nebenbeschäftigung haben.

**moor¹** [muər], s. Heide f.

**moor²,** v.tr. (ein Schiff) festmachen. ◆'**moorings,** s.pl. Anlegestelle f.

**moose** [muːs], s. Elch m.

**moot** [muːt], s. it's a m. point, darüber läßt sich streiten.

**mop** [mɔp]. I. s. 1. Mop m. 2. m. of hair, Wuschelkopf m. II. v.tr. (den Fußboden) wischen. ◆'mop 'up, v.tr. aufwischen.

**mope** [məup], v.i. Trübsal blasen.

**moped** ['məuped], s. Moped n.

**moral** ['mɔrəl]. I. adj. 1. sittlich. 2. (of life, tone, support etc.) moralisch. II. s. 1. Moral f (einer Geschichte). 2. pl. morals, Moral f; -ly, adv. moralisch. ◆mo'rality, s. Sittlichkeit f. ◆'moralize, v.i. Moral predigen.

**morale** [mɔ'raːl], s. Moral f.

**morass** [mə'ræs], s. Morast m.

**morbid** ['mɔːbid], adj. morbid; (pathological) krankhaft.

**more** [mɔːr]. I. adj. (a) mehr; (b) (additional) noch; one m. week, noch eine Woche. II. s. is there any m.? gibt es noch etwas davon? what is m., außerdem/noch dazu. III. adv. (a) m. and m., immer mehr; m. or less, mehr oder weniger; (b) (again) noch; once m., noch einmal; I don't want to go there any m., ich will nicht wieder/nicht mehr dort hingehen; (c) (comparative) m. critically, kritischer; even m. beautiful, noch schöner. ◆more'over, adv. außerdem.

**morning** ['mɔːniŋ], s. Morgen m; (later part) Vormittag m; tomorrow m., morgen früh; yesterday/this m., gestern/heute morgen; in the m., am Morgen; am Vormittag.

**Morocco** [mə'rɔkəu]. Pr. n. Marokko n.

**moron** ['mɔːrɔn], s. F: Idiot m.

**morose** [mə'rəus], adj. (grumpy) mürrisch; griesgrämig; (sullen) verstockt.

**Morse** [mɔːs], s. M. (code), Morsealphabet n.

**mortal** ['mɔːt(ə)l], adj. (a) sterblich; (b) (causing death) a m. blow, ein tödlicher Schlag; -ly, adv. tödlich (verletzt, beleidigt). ◆'mor'tality, s. Sterblichkeit f.

**mortar** ['mɔːtər], s. 1. (bowl, also Mil:) Mörser m. 2. (cement) Mörtel m.

**mortgage** ['mɔːgidʒ]. I. s. Hypothek f. II. v.tr. (ein Haus usw.) mit einer Hypothek belasten.

**mortician** [mɔː'tiʃən], s. N.Am: Leichenbestatter m.

**mortify** ['mɔːtifai], v.tr. (j-n) demütigen.

**mortuary** ['mɔːtjuəri], s. Leichenhalle f.

**mosaic** [mə(u)'zeiik], s. Mosaik n.

**Moscow** ['mɔskəu]. Pr. n. Moskau n.

**mosque** [mɔsk], s. Moschee f.

**mosquito**, pl. -oes [məs'kiːtəu, -əuz], s. Moskito m.

**moss** [mɔs], s. Moos m. ◆'mossy, adj. moosig.

**most** [məust]. I. adj. meist; m. people, die meisten Leute; for the m. part, zum größten Teil. II. s. & indef. pron. (a) she won m., sie hat am meisten gewonnen; m. of my friends, die meisten meiner

Freunde; m. of the work, der größte Teil der Arbeit; to make the m. of an opportunity, das Beste aus einer Gelegenheit machen; (b) twenty at (the) m., höchstens zwanzig. III. adv. 1. (comparison) (a) (with verb) am meisten; (b) (with adj. & adv.) the m. beautiful woman, die schönste Frau. 2. (intensive) höchst; (extremely) äußerst; -ly, adv. (a) (in most cases) meistens; (b) (for the most part) zum größten Teil.

**motel** [məu'tel], s. Motel n.

**moth** [mɔθ], s. 1. Nachtfalter m. 2. (clothes) m., Motte f. ◆'motheaten, adj. mottenzerfressen.

**mother** ['mʌðər], s. 1. Mutter f; m.-in-law, Schwiegermutter f. II. v.tr. (j-n) bemuttern. ◆'motherhood, s. Mutterschaft f. ◆'motherly, adj. mütterlich.

**motif** [məu'tiːf], s. Motiv n.

**motion** ['məuʃ(ə)n]. I. s. 1. (a) (movement) Bewegung f; (b) (sign) Zeichen n. 2. Pol: etc: Antrag m. II. v.tr. & i. to m. (to) s.o. to do sth., j-m ein Zeichen geben, etwas zu tun. ◆'motionless, adj. bewegungslos.

**motive** ['məutiv], s. 1. Motiv n (einer Handlung). 2. (motif) Motiv n. ◆'motivate, v.tr. (eine Handlung) motivieren. ◆moti'vation, s. Motivation f.

**motley** ['mɔtli], adj. bunt gemischt.

**motor** ['məutər], s. (a) Motor m; (b) m. car, Automobil n; m. vehicle, Kraftfahrzeug n. ◆'motorboat, s. Motorboot n. ◆'motorcycle, F: 'motorbike, s. Motorrad n. ◆'motorcyclist, s. Motorradfahrer m. ◆'motorist, s. Autofahrer m. ◆'motorize, v.tr. motorisieren. ◆'motorway, s. Autobahn f.

**motto**, pl. -o(e)s ['mɔtəu, -əuz], s. Motto n.

**mould**[1] [məuld], I. s. Form f. II. v.tr. formen (into sth., zu etwas dat).

**mould**[2], s. (on food, wall) Schimmel m. ◆'mouldy, adj. schimm(e)lig.

**moult** [məult], v.i. (of birds etc.) sich mausern.

**mound** [maund], s. (of earth) Erdhügel m; (of stones) Steinhaufen m.

**mount** [maunt], v. 1. v.i. (rise) steigen; (grow) wachsen. 2. v.tr. (a) (ein Pferd usw.) besteigen; (of car) to m. the pavement, auf den Bürgersteig hinauffahren; (b) Tchn: (einen Apparat usw.) montieren; (on sth., auf etwas acc); (c) (ein Bild, ein Juwel) einfassen; (d) to m. guard, Wache halten. ◆'mounted, adj. (on horse etc.) beritten. ◆'mount 'up, v.i. sich häufen.

**mountain** ['mauntin], s. Berg m; m. range, Gebirgskette f. ◆mountai'neer, s. Bergsteiger m. ◆mountai'neering, s. Bergsteigen n. ◆'mountainous, adj. gebirgig.

**mourn** [mɔːn], v. 1. v.i. trauern (for/over s.o., sth., um j-n, etwas acc). 2. v.tr. betrauern. ◆'mourner, s. Trauernde(r) *f(m)*; **the mourners,** die Leidtragenden *mpl.* ◆**'mournful,** *adj.* trauervoll; *(sad)* traurig. ◆**'mourning,** *s.* Trauer *f; (dress)* Trauerkleidung *f.*

**mouse,** *pl.* **mice** [maus, mais], *s.* Maus *f.* ◆**'mousetrap,** *s.* Mausefalle *f.* ◆**'mousy,** *adj.* graubraun.

**moustache** [məs'tɑ:ʃ], *s.* Schnurrbart *m.*

**mouth.** I. [mauθ], *s.* **1.** Mund *m.* **2.** Z: Maul *n; (of dog etc.)* Schnauze *f.* **3.** Mündung *f* (eines Flusses, Gewehrs); Öffnung *f* (einer Flasche usw.); Eingang *m* (eines Tunnels, einer Höhle); Einfahrt *f* (eines Hafens). II. [mauð], *v.tr.* (Worte) lautlos formen. ◆**'mouthful,** *s.* (a) Mundvoll *m; (b) (word)* Zungenbrecher *m.* ◆**'mouth-organ,** *s.* Mundharmonika *f.* ◆**'mouthpiece,** *s.* **1.** Mundstück *n* (eines Blasinstruments); *Tel:* Sprechmuschel *f* (eines Telefons). **2.** *(speaker)* Sprachrohr *n.*

**move** [mu:v]. I. *s.* **1.** (a) *(in game)* Zug *m; (b) Fig:* Schritt *m;* **what is the next m.?** was machen wir jetzt? **2.** *(movement)* **on the m.,** unterwegs; **to make a m.,** aufbrechen; *F:* **to get a m. on,** sich beeilen. **3.** *(moving house)* Umzug *m.* II. *v.* **1.** *v.tr.* (a) *(shift)* (etwas) von der Stelle bewegen; (einen Stuhl usw.) rücken; *(misplace)* (eine Vase usw.) verrücken; *(remove)* (etwas) entfernen; *(to another place)* (Möbel) umstellen; **to m. house,** umziehen; *(b) (set in motion)* (den Kopf, die Hand usw.) bewegen; *(c) (emotionally)* (j-n) rühren. **2.** *v.i.* (a) sich bewegen; *(b) (move house)* umziehen. ◆**move a'way,** *v.i.* wegrücken (**from,** von + *dat*); *(move house)* wegziehen. ◆**'move 'forward,** *v.tr. & i.* vorrücken. ◆**'move 'in,** *v.i.* (in ein Haus) einziehen. ◆**'movement,** *s.* Bewegung *f.* ◆**'move 'out,** *v.i.* (aus einem Haus) ausziehen. ◆**'movie,** *s. F: esp N.Am:* Film *m.* ◆**'moving,** *adj.* **1.** **m. parts,** bewegliche Teile. **2.** *(of book, play etc.)* ergreifend.

**mow** [məu], *v.tr.irr.* mähen. ◆**'mower,** *s.* **(lawn) m.,** Rasenmäher *m.*

**Mrs** ['misiz], *s.* **Mrs. Smith,** Frau Smith.

**Mr** ['mistər], *s.* **Mr. Smith,** Herr Smith.

**Ms** [məz], *s.* **Ms Brown,** Frau Brown.

**much** [mʌtʃ]. I. *adj.* viel; **how m. bread?** wieviel Brot? II. *adv.* viel; **m. better,** viel besser; **m. as I like him,** so gern ich ihn auch mag; **m. to my surprise,** sehr zu meiner Überraschung. III. *s.* (a) *(a lot)* viel; *(many things)* vieles; *(b)* **as/so m.,** soviel; **so m. the better,** umso besser; *(c)* **too m.,** zuviel. ◆**'muchness,** *s. F:* **much of a m.,** ziemlich das gleiche.

**muck** [mʌk]. I. *s. (dung)* Schlamm *m; F: (filth)* Dreck *m.* II. *v.* **1.** *v.tr. F:* **to m. up a job,** eine Arbeit verpfuschen. **2.** *v.i. F:* **to m. about,** herumspielen. ◆**'mucky,** *adj. F:* dreckig.

**mud** [mʌd], *s. (liquid)* Schlamm *m; (sticky)* Morast *m; (on street etc.)* Kot *m; (on clothes)* Schmutz *m; F:* Dreck *m.*

◆**'muddy,** *adj. (of river etc.)* schlammig; *(of liquid)* trüb; *(of floor, shoes, colour etc.)* schmutzig. ◆**'mudguard,** *s.* Schutzblech *n.*

**muddle** ['mʌdl]. I. *s.* Durcheinander *n.* II. *v.tr.* (Dinge) durcheinanderbringen. ◆**'muddled,** *adj.* durcheinander; *(of pers.)* verwirrt; *(of thinking, situation)* verworren. ◆**'muddle 'through,** *v.i.* sich durchwursteln.

**muffle** ['mʌfl], *v.tr.* dämpfen. ◆**'muffler,** *s.* **1.** *(scarf)* (dicker) Schal *m.* **2.** *N.Am:* Aut: Auspufftopf *m.*

**mug1** [mʌg], *s.* Becher *m* (mit Henkel).

**mug2,** *s. (fool)* Trottel *m.*

**mug3,** *v.tr.* überfallen. ◆**'mugging,** *s.* Straßenraub *m.*

**muggy** ['mʌgi], *adj. F:* schwül.

**mule** [mju:l], *s.* Maultier *n.*

**mull** [mʌl], *v.tr.* (a) **to m. sth. over,** über etwas *acc* nachdenken; *(b)* **mulled wine,** Glühwein *m.*

**multi** ['mʌlti], *prefix* viel-, mehr-; **multilingual,** mehrsprachig; **multimillionaire,** Multimillionär *m.*

**multicoloured** ['mʌltikʌləd], *adj.* vielfarbig.

**multiple** ['mʌltipl], *adj.* vielfach; *(with pl)* mehrere; **m. sclerosis,** multiple Sklerose *f.* ◆**multipli'cation,** *s.* Multiplikation *f.* ◆**'multiply,** *v.* **1.** *v.tr. & i. Mth:* multiplizieren. **2.** *v.i.* sich vermehren.

**multistorey** ['mʌlti'stɔ:ri], *adj.* **m. car park,** Parkhaus *n.*

**multitude** ['mʌltitju:d], *s.* Menge *f.*

**mum** [mʌm], *s. F:* Mama *f.*

**mumble** ['mʌmbl], *v.tr. & i.* undeutlich sprechen.

**mummy1** ['mʌmi], *s. (in tomb)* Mumie *f.*

**mummy2,** *s. F:* Mutti *f.*

**mumps** [mʌmps], *s.pl.* Mumps *m.*

**mundane** [mʌn'dein], *adj.* alltäglich.

**municipal** [mju(:)'nisip(ə)l], *adj.* städtisch; **m. council,** Stadtrat *m;* **m. elections,** Gemeindewahlen *fpl.*

**mural** ['mjuərəl], *s.* Wandmalerei *f.*

**murder** ['mə:dər]. I. *s.* Mord *m;* Ermordung *f* **(of s.o.,** j-s). II. *v.tr.* (j-n) ermorden. ◆**'murderer,** *s.* Mörder *m.* ◆**'murderous,** *adj.* mörderisch.

**murky** ['mə:ki], *adj.* düster; *(dark)* finster.

**murmur** ['mə:mər]. I. *s.* Gemurmel *n.* II. *v.tr. & i.* murmeln.

**muscle** ['mʌsl], *s.* Muskel *m.* ◆**muscular** ['mʌskjulər], *adj.* **1.** Muskel-. **2.** *(of pers., body etc.)* muskulös.

**museum** [mju:('):'zi:əm], *s.* Museum *n.*

**mushroom** ['mʌʃrum]. I. *s. (eßbarer)* Pilz *m, esp.* Champignon *m.* II. *v.i. F: (of buildings etc.)* aus dem Boden schießen.

**music** ['mju:zik], *s.* (a) Musik *f; (b) (printed)* Noten *fpl.* ◆**'musical.** I. *adj.* **1.** musikalisch; *(of sound)* melodisch; **m. instrument,** Musikinstrument *n.* II. *s.* Musical *n;* **-ly,** *adv.* musikalisch.

◆**'music-hall**, s. Varieté(theater) n.
◆**musician** [mju:'ziʃən], s. Musiker(in) m(f).
**Muslim** ['muzləm]. I. s. Mohammedaner(in) m(f). II. adj. mohammedanisch.
**mussel** ['mʌsl], s. Muschel f.
**must** [mʌst]. I. modal aux. v. 1. müssen. 2. neg. you m. not do that, das darfst du nicht tun. II. s. F: it's a m., man muß es einfach tun/sehen usw.
**mustard** ['mʌstəd], s. Senf m.
**muster** ['mʌstər], v.tr. (Kraft, Mut) aufbringen.
**mute** [mju:t], adj. stumm.
**mutilate** ['mju:tileit], v.tr. verstümmeln. ◆**muti'lation**, s. Verstümmelung f.
**mutiny** ['mju:tini]. I. s. Meuterei f. II. v.i. meutern. ◆**muti'neer**, s. Meuterer m.
**mutter** ['mʌtər], v.tr. & i. murmeln.
**mutton** ['mʌt(ə)n], s. Hammelfleisch n.

**mutual** ['mju:tjuəl], adj. (a) (reciprocal) gegenseitig; (b) (shared) gemeinsam.
**muzzle** ['mʌzl]. 1. s. 1. (of dog etc.) (a) Schnauze f; (b) (guard) Maulkorb m. 2. (of gun) Mündung f. II. v.tr. (a) (einem Hund) einen Maulkorb anlegen; (b) F: (die Presse usw.) knebeln.
**my** [mai], poss. adj. mein.
**myself** [mai'self], pers. pron. (a) selbst; (b) refl. mich (selbst).
**mystery** ['mistəri], s. Geheimnis n; (puzzle) Rätsel n. ◆**mysterious** [-'tiəriəs], adj. geheimnisvoll; (puzzling) rätselhaft.
**mystic** ['mistik], s. Mystiker m. ◆**'mysticism**, s. Mystik f.
**mystify** ['mistifai], v.tr. it mystified me, es war mir ein Rätsel. ◆**'mystified**, adj. perplex.
**myth** [miθ], s. Mythos m. ◆**'mythical**, adj. mythisch. ◆**my'thology**, s. Mythologie f.

# N

**N, n** [en], s. (der Buchstabe) N; n n.
**nab** [næb], v.tr. F: schnappen.
**nag** [næg], v.tr. & i. meckern (about sth., über etwas acc); to n. (at) s.o., an j-m dauernd herumnörgeln. ◆**'nagging**, adj. (of pers.) meckernd; (of doubt, pain) nagend.
**nail** [neil]. I. s. Anat: Tchn: Nagel m; n. file, Nagelfeile f; n. scissors, Nagelschere f; n. varnish, Nagellack m. II. v.tr. (etwas) nageln (to sth., an/auf etwas acc). ◆**'nailbrush**, s. Nagelbürste f.
**naïve** [nɑː'iːv, nai-], adj. naiv.
**naked** ['neikid], adj. nackt. ◆**'nakedness**, s. Nacktheit f.
**name** [neim]. I. s. 1. Name m; Christian/first/N.Am: given n., Vorname m; my n. is..., ich heiße...; to call s.o. names, j-n beschimpfen. 2. (reputation) Ruf m. II. v.tr. nennen. ◆**'nameless**, adj. namenlos. ◆**'namely**, adv. nämlich. ◆**'namesake**, s. Namensvetter m.
**nanny** ['næni], s. 1. Kindermädchen n. 2. F: n. goat, Ziege f.
**nap** [næp]. I. s. F: Nickerchen n; to have a n., ein Nickerchen machen. II. v.i. F: to catch s.o. napping, j-n überrumpeln.
**nape** [neip], s. n. of the neck, Nacken m.
**napkin** ['næpkin], s. (a) (table) n., Serviette f; (b) (baby's) n., Windel f.
**Naples** ['neiplz]. Pr. n. Neapel n.
**nappy** ['næpi], s. F: Windel f.
**narcotic** [nɑː'kɔtik], s. Betäubungsmittel n.
**nark** [nɑːk], v.tr. F: to be/feel narked, verschnupft sein.
**narrate** [nə'reit], v.tr. (etwas) erzählen. ◆**narrative** ['nærətiv], s. Erzählung f. ◆**na'rrator**, s. Erzähler m.
**narrow** ['nærəu]. I. adj. (a) (not wide) eng; (b) (with a small margin) knapp; to

have a n. escape, mit knapper Not davonkommen; (c) (of pers., views) engstirnig. II. v. 1. v.i. (Sp: of lead, gap) kleiner werden; (of pipe, road etc) sich verengen. 2. v.tr. (eine Straße usw.) enger machen; (ein Arbeitsgebiet) einengen. -ly, adv. (with a small margin) he n. escaped death, er entging mit knapper Not dem Tod. ◆**'narrow-'minded**, adj. engstirnig.
**nasal** ['neiz(ə)l], adj. nasal.
**nasturtium** [nəs'tə:ʃəm], s. Kapuzinerkresse f.
**nasty** ['nɑːsti], adj. 1. ekelhaft; a n. job, eine unangenehme Arbeit; n. accident, schwerer Unfall; n. cold, üble Erkältung; 2. (of pers.) gemein (to s.o., zu j-m); F: a n. piece of work, ein Ekel.
**nation** ['neiʃ(ə)n], s. Nation f; (people) Volk n. ◆**national** ['næʃ(ə)nəl]. I. adj. national, National-; n. anthem, Nationalhymne f. II. s. Staatsbürger(in) m(f); -ly, adv. national. ◆**'nationalism**, s. Nationalismus m. ◆**'nationalist**, s. Nationalist m. ◆**natio'nality**, s. Staatsangehörigkeit f. ◆**nationali'zation**, s. Verstaatlichung f. ◆**'nationalize**, v.tr. verstaatlichen. ◆**'nationwide**, adj. & adv. überregional; (in W. Germany) bundesweit.
**native** ['neitiv]. I. adj. (a) (of quality, talent etc.) angeboren; (b) (of place) Geburts-; n. tongue, Muttersprache f; (c) (of population etc.) einheimisch. II. s. Einheimische(r) f(m); a n. of Munich, ein gebürtiger Münchner.
**nativity** [nə'tiviti], s. Christi Geburt f.
**Nato** ['neitəu], s. Nato f.
**natter** ['nætər], v.i. schwatzen.
**natural** ['nætʃər(ə)l], adj. natürlich; n. gas, Erdgas n; -ly, adv. natürlich.

◆**'naturalist**, *s.* Naturwissenschaftler *m.* ◆**naturali'zation**, *s.* Einbürgerung *f.* ◆**'naturalize**, *v.tr.* einbürgern.

**nature** ['neitʃər], *s.* Natur *f*; **by n.,** von Natur aus; **something of that n.,** etwas in der Art.

**naughty** ['nɔ:ti], *adj.* (*of child*) ungezogen.

**nausea** ['nɔ:siə], *s.* Brechreiz *m.* ◆**'nauseate**, *v.tr.* (j-n) anekeln. ◆**'nauseating**, *adj.* ekelerregend.

**nautical** ['nɔ:tik(ə)l], *adj.* nautisch, See-; **n. mile,** Seemeile *f.*

**naval** ['neiv(ə)l], *adj.* Marine-; **n. officer,** Marineoffizier *m.*

**nave** [neiv], *s.* Kirchenschiff *n.*

**navel** ['neiv(ə)l], *s.* Nabel *m.*

**navigable** ['nævigəbl], *adj.* schiffbar. ◆**'navigate**, *v.* 1. *v.i.* (*a*) navigieren; (*b*) (*map-read*) die Karte lesen. 2. *v.tr.* (*a*) (einen Fluß) befahren; (*b*) (ein Schiff, Flugzeug) navigieren. ◆**navi'gation**, *s.* Navigation *f.* ◆**'navigator**, *s.* Navigator *m.*

**navvy** ['nævi], *s.* Bauarbeiter *m.*

**navy** ['neivi], *s.* Marine *f*; **n. blue,** Marineblau *n.*

**Nazi** ['nɑ:tsi]. I. *s.* Nazi *m.* II. *adj.* nazistisch, Nazi-. ◆**'Nazism**, *s.* Nazismus *m.*

**near** ['niər]. I. *adv.* nah(e); **n. at hand,** (ganz) in der Nähe; **to come/draw n. to s.o.,** sth., sich j-m, etwas *dat* nähern. II. *prep.* (etwas *dat*) nahe; in der Nähe (von etwas *dat*); **n. the end,** (*of period*) kurz vor dem Ende; (*of line etc.*) fast am Ende; **n. (to) the shops,** in der Nähe der Geschäfte. III. *adj.* nah; **the nearest hospital,** das nächste Krankenhaus; *Aut:* **the n. side,** die rechte Seite; *Brit:* die linke Seite. IV. *v.tr.* sich (dem Ende, Ziel usw.) nähern; -**ly,** *adv.* fast, beinahe. ◆**'nearby.** I. ['niəbai] *adj.* nahegelegen. II. [niə'bai] *adv.* in der Nähe. ◆**'near-'sighted**, *adj.* kurzsichtig.

**neat** [ni:t], *adj.* 1. (*unmixed*) pur. 2. (*tidy*) ordentlich; (*of pers.*) gepflegt; **n. solution,** elegante Lösung; -**ly,** *adv.* ordentlich. ◆**'neatness**, *s.* Ordentlichkeit *f.*

**necessary** ['nesis(ə)ri, -seri], *adj.* (*a*) nötig, notwendig (**for sth.,** zu etwas *dat*); **if n.,** notfalls; (*b*) (*inevitable*) zwangsläufig; -**arily** [also -'serili], *adv.* (*of necessity*) notwendigerweise; (*inevitably*) zwangsläufig. ◆**'necessitate** [nə'sesiteit], *v.tr.* (er)fordern. ◆**ne'cessity**, *s.* Notwendigkeit *f*; **of n.,** notwendigerweise; **for me a car is a n.,** ein Auto ist für mich unentbehrlich.

**neck** [nek]. I. *s.* 1. (*a*) Hals *m*; **to run n. and n.,** Kopf an Kopf laufen; **low n.,** tiefer Ausschnitt. 2. (*a*) Hals *m* (einer Flasche); (*b*) (*of land*) Landenge *f.* II. *v.i. P:* knutschen. ◆**'necklace**, *s.* Halskette *f.* ◆**'neckline**, *s.* Ausschnitt *m.* ◆**'necktie**, *s.* *N.Am:* Schlips *m.*

**nectarine** ['nektəri(:)n], *s.* Nektarine *f.*

**née** [nei], *adj.* **n. Meyer,** geborene Meyer.

**need** [ni:d]. I. *s.* 1. (*a*) Notwendigkeit *f*; **there's no n. to go there,** es ist nicht nötig, hinzugehen; (*b*) Bedarf *m* (**of sth.,** an etwas *dat*); **to have n./be in n. of sth.,** etwas benötigen. 2. (*suffering, starvation etc.*) Not *f*; **those in n.,** die Notleidenden. 3. (*particular n.*) Bedürfnis *n.* II. *v.* 1. *v.tr.* (etwas) brauchen, (*formal*) benötigen. 2. *aux. v.* **n. he go?** muß er gehen? **you needn't wait,** du brauchst nicht zu warten. ◆**'needless**, *adj.* unnötig; (*superfluous*) überflüssig; **n. to say,** selbstverständlich. ◆**'needy**, *adj.* notleidend.

**needle** ['ni:dl], *s.* Nadel *f.* ◆**'needlework**, *s.* Handarbeit *f.*

**negative** ['negətiv]. I. *adj.* negativ. II. *s.* 1. **to answer in the n.,** eine negative Antwort geben. 2. *Phot:* Negativ *n.*

**neglect** [ni'glekt]. I. *s.* Vernachlässigung *f* (**of s.o., sth.,** j-s, etwas *gen*); **in a state of n.** in einem Zustand der Verwahrlosung. II. *v.tr.* (*a*) (j-n, etwas) vernachlässigen; (*pass over*) (j-n) übersehen; (*b*) (eine Pflicht, eine Gelegenheit usw.) versäumen. ◆**ne'glected**, *adj.* verwahrlost.

**negligence** ['neglidʒəns], *s.* Nachlässigkeit *f*; *Jur:* Fahrlässigkeit *f.* ◆**'negligent**, *adj.* nachlässig; *Jur:* fahrlässig. ◆**'negligible**, *adj.* unbedeutend; (*of quantity, sum*) geringfügig.

**negotiate** [ni'gəuʃieit], *v.* 1. *v.tr.* (einen Vertrag, Bedingungen usw.) aushandeln. 2. *v.i.* verhandeln (**for/about sth.,** über etwas *acc*). ◆**ne'gotiable**, *adj.* **salary n.,** Gehalt nach Vereinbarung. ◆**negoti'ation**, *s.* Verhandlung *f.* ◆**ne'gotiator**, *s.* Unterhändler *m.*

**negress** ['ni:grəs], *s.* Negerin *f.* ◆**negro**, *pl.* **-oes** ['ni:grəu, -əuz]. I. *adj.* Neger-. II. *s.* Neger *m.*

**neigh** [nei], *v.i.* wiehern.

**neighbour** ['neibər], *s.* Nachbar(in) *m(f)*. ◆**'neighbourhood**, *s.* Nachbarschaft *f.* ◆**'neighbouring**, *adj.* benachbart; Nachbar-. ◆**'neighbourly**, *adj.* nachbarlich.

**neither** ['naiðər, *N.Am:* 'ni:ðər]. I. *adv. & conj.* **n. ... nor ...** weder ... noch ...; **she was not there and n. was her sister,** sie war nicht da und ihre Schwester auch nicht. II. *adj. & pron.* **in n. case,** in keinem der Fälle; **n. of them has come,** keine(r) von beiden ist gekommen.

**neon** ['ni:ɔn], *s.* Neon *n*; **n. light,** Neonlicht *n*; **n. sign,** Leuchtschrift *f*; (*advert*) Leuchtreklame *f.*

**nephew** ['nevju:, nef-], *s.* Neffe *m.*

**nerve** [nə:v], *s.* **to get on s.o.'s nerves,** j-m auf die Nerven gehen; **to lose one's n.,** die Nerven verlieren; **what a n.!** so eine Frechheit! ◆**'nerve-racking**, *adj.* nervenaufreibend. ◆**'nervous**, *adj.* 1. **n. system,** Nervensystem *n.* 2. (*of pers.*) (*a*) (*on edge*) nervös; (*b*) (*timid*) ängstlich; **to be n.,** Angst haben. ◆'**nervousness**, s. (a) Nervosität f; (b) Ängstlichkeit f.

**nest** [nest]. **I.** s. Nest n; **n. of tables**, Dreisatztisch m. **II.** v.i. nisten.

**nestle** ['nesl], v.i. es sich dat bequem machen; **to n. up to s.o.**, sich an j-n kuscheln.

**net**[1] [net]. **I.** s. Netz n. **II.** v.tr. (Fische, Vögel usw.) mit dem Netz fangen. ◆'**netting**, s. wire n., Maschendraht m. ◆'**network**, s. Netz n; **road n.**, Straßennetz n.

**net**[2], adj. netto, Netto-; **£250 n.**, £250 netto.

**Netherlands** ['neðələndz]. Pr. n. the N., die Niederlande.

**nettle** ['netl], s. Nessel f.

**neuralgia** [njuə'rældʒə], s. Neuralgie f.

**neurology** [njuə'rɔlədʒi], s. Neurologie f. ◆**neu'rologist**, s. Neurologe m.

**neurosis**, pl. -ses [njuə'rəusis, -siːz], s. Neurose f. ◆**neurotic** [-'rɔtik], adj. neurotisch.

**neuter** ['njuːtər]. **I.** adj. sächlich. **II.** s. Neutrum n. **III.** v.tr. (einen Kater usw.) kastrieren; (eine Katze usw.) sterilisieren. ◆'**neutral**. **I.** adj. neutral. **II.** s. Aut: in n., im Leerlauf. ◆**neu'trality**, s. Neutralität f. ◆'**neutralize**, v.tr. neutralisieren.

**never** ['nevər], adv. nie; **n. again**, nie wieder; **he'll n. believe that**, das glaubt er dir doch nie; F: **well I n.!** na, so was! **n. mind**, mach dir nichts draus, macht doch nichts. ◆'**never-'ending**, adj. endlos. ◆'**never-'never**, s. F: **to buy sth. on the n.-n.**, etwas auf Pump kaufen. ◆'**nevertheless**, adv. trotzdem.

**new** [njuː], adj. neu; **n. moon**, Neumond m; Com: **as n.**, neuwertig; -ly, adv. neu; **a n. painted door**, eine frisch gestrichene Tür; **n.-weds**, frischgebackenes Ehepaar n. ◆'**newborn**, adj. neugeboren. ◆'**newcomer**, s. Neuankömmling m. ◆**New 'England**. Pr. n. Neuengland n. ◆'**new-'laid**, adj. **n.-l. eggs**, frische Eier. ◆'**newness**, s. Neuheit f. ◆**New 'Year**, s. das Neue Jahr; N. Y.'s Day, Neujahr n; N. Y.'s Eve, Silvester n. ◆**New 'Zealand**. Pr. n. Neuseeland n.

**news** [njuːz], s. **1.** Neuigkeit f; **we have had no n. from him**, wir haben nichts von ihm gehört; **have you heard the n.?** haben Sie das Neueste gehört? **what (is the) n.?** was gibt's Neues? **a sad piece of n.**, eine traurige Nachricht. **2.** Rad: TV: Nachrichten pl; in. **flash**, Kurzmeldung f. ◆'**newsagent**, s. Zeitungshändler m. ◆'**newspaper** ['njuːs-], s. Zeitung f.

**next** [nekst]. **I.** adj. nächste(r,s); **the n. room**, das nächste Zimmer; **n. to**, neben + dat; **the n. day she went home**, am nächsten Tag fuhr sie nach Hause; **the week after n.**, übernächste Woche; **this time n. year**, heute in einem Jahr; **the n. time I see him**, das nächste Mal,

wenn ich ihn sehe; **who's n.?** wer ist als nächster dran? **II.** adv. **what shall we do n.?** was wollen wir als nächstes machen? **when I n. saw him**, als ich ihn das nächste Mal sah. ◆'**next(-)'door**, adv. nebenan.

**nib** [nib], s. Feder f.

**nibble** ['nibl], v.tr. & i. **to n. (at) sth.**, an etwas dat knabbern.

**nice** [nais], adj. esp. F: (a) (of pers.) nett; sympathisch; **to be n. to s.o.**, zu j-m nett sein; (b) (of thing) nett; (of weather) schön; **a n. meal**, ein gutes Essen; **it's n. and warm**, es ist schön warm; -ly, adv. F: **that will do n.**, das paßt ausgezeichnet; **he is doing n.**, (i) (of patient) er macht gute Fortschritte; (ii) (financially) es geht ihm nicht schlecht; (in job) er macht sich. ◆**nicety** ['naisəti], s. pl niceties feine Unterschiede mpl.

**niche** [niːʃ], s. Nische f.

**nick** [nik]. **I.** s. **1.** (notch) Kerbe f. **2.** Fig: **in the n. of time**, im letzten Augenblick. **II.** v.tr. P: (etwas) klauen.

**nickel** ['nikl], s. **1.** Nickel n. **2.** N.Am: Fünfcentstück n.

**nickname** ['nikneim]. **I.** s. Spitzname m. **II.** v.tr. **to n. s.o. X**, j-m den Spitznamen X geben.

**nicotine** ['nikətiːn], s. Nikotin n.

**niece** [niːs], s. Nichte f.

**Nigeria** [nai'dʒiəriə]. Pr. n. Nigeria n.

**nigger** ['nigər], s. Pej: Neger m.

**niggle** ['nigl], v.tr. (j-n) ärgern, reizen. ◆'**niggling**, adj. **n. details**, belanglose Einzelheiten.

**night** [nait], s. Nacht f; **last n.**, heute/letzte Nacht; (up to bedtime) gestern abend; **the n. before**, am Abend vorher; (late) in der Nacht davor; **ten o'clock at n.**, zehn Uhr abends; **good n.!** gute Nacht! **at/by n.**, nachts; **in the n.**, in der Nacht; **n. watchman**, Nachtwächter m; **n. school**, Abendschule f; **n. shift**, Nachtschicht f; Th: **first n.**, Premiere. ◆'**nightcap**, s. Schlaftrunk m. ◆'**nightclub**, s. Nachtklub m. ◆'**nightdress**, s. Nachthemd n. ◆'**nightfall**, s. **at n.**, bei Einbruch der Dunkelheit. ◆'**nightie**, s. Nachthemd n. ◆'**nightingale**, s. Nachtigall f. ◆'**nightly**. **I.** adj. nächtlich. **II.** adv. jede Nacht; (evening) jeden Abend. ◆'**nightmare**, s. Alptraum m. ◆**nightshade**, s. **deadly n.**, Belladonna f.

**nil** [nil], s. null.

**nine** [nain], num. adj. neun. ◆'**nine'teen**, num. adj. neunzehn. ◆'**nine'teenth**, num. adj. neunzehnte(r,s). ◆'**ninety**, num. adj. neunzig. ◆**ninth**. **I.** num. adj. neunte(r,s). **II.** s. (fraction) Neuntel n.

**ninny** ['nini], s. Trottel m.

**nip** [nip]. **I.** s. **1.** (pinch) Kniff m; (bite) kleiner Biß m; Fig: **there was a n. in the air**, die Luft war merklich kühl. **II.** v. **1.**

*v.tr.* (j-n in den Arm usw.) kneifen. 2.
*v.i. F:* **n. round to the baker's,** lauf mal
schnell zum Bäcker. ◆**'nippy,** *adj.* it's
a bit n. **today,** es ist ziemlich kalt heute.
**nipple** ['nipl], *s.* Brustwarze *f.*
**nitrate** ['naitreit], *s.* Nitrat *n.* ◆**'nitric,**
*adj.* **n. acid,** Salpetersäure *f.*
◆**'nitrogen** [-rədʒən], *s.* Stickstoff *m.*
**no** [nəu]. **I.** *adj.* kein(e). **no admittance,**
kein Eintritt; Betreten verboten; **no
smoking,** Rauchen verboten; **it's no
good/use,** es nützt nichts; **in no time,** im
Nu; **no one=nobody.** **II.** *adv.* **I am no
richer than he is,** ich bin nicht reicher
als er; **he is no longer here,** er ist nicht
mehr hier. **III.** *adv.* nein; **to answer no,**
mit einem Nein antworten.
**noble** ['nəubl]. **I.** *adj.* **1.** (*aristocratic*) ad-
lig. **2.** (*of sentiments, bearing etc.*) edel. **II.**
*s.* Adlige(r) *f(m).* ◆**no'bility,** *s.* Adel *m.*
**nobody** ['nəubɔdi], *pron.* niemand; kei-
ne(r) *f(m);* **n. else** keiner sonst.
**nod** [nɔd]. **I.** *s.* Nicken *n;* **he gave me a
friendly n.,** er nickte mir freundlich zu.
**II.** *v.* **1.** *v.i.* nicken; *F:* **to n. off,**
einnicken. **2.** *v.tr.* **he nodded his
head,** er nickte mit dem Kopf.
**noise** [nɔiz], *s.* **1.** (*loud*) Lärm *m;* **to
make a n.,** Lärm/*F:* Krach machen. **2.**
Geräusch *n.* ◆**'noiseless,** *adj.* geräuschlos. ◆**'noisy,** *adj.* laut.
**nomad** ['nəumæd], *s.* Nomade *m.*
◆**no'madic,** *adj.* nomadisch.
**nominal** ['nɔmin(ə)l], *adj.* **1.** nominell; **n.
value,** Nennwert *m.* **2.** (*of amount*) unbedeutend.
**nominate** ['nɔmineit], *v.tr.* (*a*) (j-n) ernennen (**as director etc.,** zum Direktor
usw.); (*b*) (j-n als Kandidat) aufstellen.
◆**nomi'nation,** *s.* (*a*) **his n. for the
post of/as minister,** seine Ernennung
zum Minister; (*b*) Aufstellen *n* (einer
Person) als Kandidat. ◆**nomi'nee,** *s.* **1.**
(**for president etc.,** zum Präsidenten
usw.) Ernannte(r) *f(m).* **2.** aufgestellter
Kandidat *m.*
**non** [nɔn], *comb. fm.* nicht-; -los.
**non-alcoholic** ['nɔnælkə'hɔlik], *adj.* al-
koholfrei.
**nonchalant** ['nɔnʃələnt], *adj.* (*a*) (*of
pers.*) gleichgültig; *Pej:* sorglos; (*b*) (*of
gesture etc.*) lässig.
**non-commissioned** ['nɔnkə'miʃ(ə)nd],
*adj. Mil:* **n.-c. officer,** Unteroffizier *m.*
**noncommittal** ['nɔnkə'mit(ə)l], *adj.* **he
was n.,** er legte sich nicht fest.
**nondescript** ['nɔndiskript], *adj.* nichts-
sagend; **a n. person,** ein unscheinbarer
Mensch.
**none** [nʌn]. **I.** *pron.* keiner, keine,
kein(e)s; **how much money have you
got? — n. at all,** wieviel Geld hast du?
— gar kein; **I know n. of them,** ich
kenne keinen von ihnen; **have you any
apples? — no, n.,** haben Sie Äpfel? —
nein, keine; **n. of your impudence!** laß
die Frechheiten! **II.** *adv.* (*a*) **I like him n.**

**the worse for it,** ich mag ihn deshalb
nicht weniger; (*b*) **he came n. too soon,**
er kam keine Minute zu früh.
**nonentity** [nɔ'nentiti], *s.* (*pers.*) Null *f.*
**nonexistent** ['nɔnig'zist(ə)nt], *adj.* nicht
vorhanden.
**non-fiction** ['nɔn'fikʃən], *s.* Sachliteratur
*f.*
**non-iron** ['nɔn'aiən], *adj.* bügelfrei.
**nonplus** ['nɔn'plʌs], *v.tr.* **to be nonplussed,** verblüfft/perplex sein.
**nonsense** ['nɔnsəns], *s.* Unsinn *m; F:*
Quatsch *m;* **no n.!** nur keinen Blödsinn!
◆**non'sensical,** *adj.* unsinnig; *F:* blöd-
sinnig.
**non-skid** ['nɔn'skid], *adj.* rutschfest.
**non-smoker** ['nɔn'sməukər], *s.* Nicht-
raucher *m.*
**nonstop** ['nɔn'stɔp]. **I.** *adj.* Nonstop-; **n.
train,** durchgehender Zug *m.* **II.** *adv.* **to
talk n.,** ununterbrochen reden.
**non-union** ['nɔn'juːniən], *adj.* (*of workers*) nicht gewerkschaftlich organisiert.
**non-violent** ['nɔn'vaiələnt], *adj.* gewalt-
los.
**noodles** ['nuːdlz], *s.* Nudeln *pl.*
**nook** [nuk], *s.* Ecke *f; Fig:* Schlupfwinkel
*m.*
**noon** [nuːn], *s.* Mittag *m; at* **12 o'clock
n.,** um zwölf Uhr mittags.
**noose** [nuːs], *s.* Schlinge *f.*
**nor** [nɔːr], *conj.* **he was not hungry, n.
was I,** er hatte keinen Hunger, und ich
auch nicht.
**norm** [nɔːm], *s.* Norm *f;* **above the n.,**
über dem Durchschnitt. ◆**'normal. I.**
*adj.* normal. **II.** *s.* Normalzustand *m;* **to
get back to n.,** sich normalisieren; **-ly,**
*adv.* normalerweise.
**north** [nɔːθ]. **I.** *s.* Norden *m;* **in the n.,**
im Norden; **to the n. (of),** nördlich
(+ *gen*). **II.** *adv.* nördlich; **n. of London,**
nördlich von London; **to travel n.,** nach
Norden fahren; **the window faces n.,** das
Fenster geht nach Norden. **III.** *adj.*
Nord-; **the N. Sea,** die Nordsee; **the N.
Pole,** der Nordpol. ◆**'north-'east. I.** *s.*
Nordosten *m.* **II.** *adj.* Nordost-. **III.**
*adv.* nordöstlich. ◆**northerly** ['nɔːðəli],
*adj.* nördlich. ◆**northern** ['nɔːð(ə)n],
*adj.* nördlich; **N. Ireland,** Nordirland *n;*
**n. lights,** Nordlicht *n.* ◆**'northwards,**
*adv.* nach Norden. ◆**'north'west. I.** *s.*
Nordwesten *m.* **II.** *adj.* Nordwest-. **III.**
*adv.* nordwestlich. ◆**'north-'western,**
*adj.* nordwestlich.
**Norway** ['nɔːwei], *Pr.n.* Norwegen *n.*
**Nor'wegian** [nɔː'wiːdʒən]. **I.** *adj.* norwegisch. **II.** *s.* **1.** Norweger(in) *m(f).* **2.**
(*language*) Norwegisch *n.*
**nose** [nəuz]. **I.** *s.* **1.** Nase *f; Fig:* **to have
a (keen) n. for sth.,** eine feine Nase/*F:*
einen guten Riecher für etwas *acc* haben.
**II.** *v.* **1.** *v.tr. F:* **to n. out** (a secret etc.),
(ein Geheimnis usw.) ausschnüffeln. **2.**
*v.i.* **to n. about/around,** herumschnüf-
feln. ◆**'nosebleed,** *s.* Nasenbluten *n.*

◆**'nosedive**, s. Sturzflug m. ◆**'nosy**, adj. F: neugierig; **a n. parker**, ein Schnüffler.

**nostalgia** [nɔs'tældʒiə], s. Nostalgie f; Sehnsucht f (for, nach + dat). ◆**nos'talgic**, adj. nostalgisch.

**nostril** ['nɔstril], s. Nasenloch n.

**not** [nɔt], adv. nicht. 1. **she is n./F: isn't here**, sie ist nicht da; **n. at all**, gar nicht; **thank you very much — n. at all**, vielen Dank — nichts zu danken; **n. including the wine**, Wein nicht inbegriffen; F: **n. to worry!** keine Sorge! das macht nichts! **n. that I am afraid of him**, nicht etwa, daß ich Angst vor ihm habe. 2. **n. any/n. a(n)**, kein(e); **n. a hope**, keine Chance.

**notable** ['nəutəbl], adj. (of fact etc.) bemerkenswert; (of pers.) bedeutend; **-ably**, adv. (a) bemerkenswert; (b) **many politicians, n. the Prime Minister**, viele Politiker, insbesondere der Premierminister.

**notch** [nɔtʃ], s. Kerbe f.

**note** [nəut]. I. s. 1. Mus: Note f; (sound) Ton m. 2. usu. pl. **notes**, Notizen fpl; **to make a n. of sth.**, sich dat etwas notieren; **to leave a n. for s.o.**, j-m einen Zettel hinlegen. 3. (commentary) Anmerkung f. 4. **credit n.**, Gutschein m; **bank n.**, Banknote f; **ten mark n.**, Zehnmarkschein m. 5. **to take n. of sth.**, von etwas dat Notiz nehmen. II. v.tr. (a) (pay attention to) zur Kenntnis nehmen; (b) (write down) aufschreiben. ◆**'notebook**, s. Notizbuch n. ◆**'notecase**, s. Brieftasche f. ◆**'noted**, adj. bekannt. ◆**'notepaper**, s. Briefpapier n. ◆**'noteworthy**, adj. bemerkenswert.

**nothing** ['nʌθiŋ]. I. s. nichts; **to say n. of the others**, von den anderen ganz zu schweigen; **she is n. if not discreet**, diskret ist sie auf jeden Fall; **n. new**, nichts Neues; **n. much**, nicht viel; **n. but**, nichts als; **he does n. but complain**, er beschwert sich dauernd; **for n.**, umsonst; **he is n. to me**, er bedeutet mir nichts. II. adv. **n. near/n. like as good**, längst nicht so gut.

**notice** ['nəutis]. I. s. 1. (public) Anschlag m; **official n.**, amtliche Bekanntmachung f; (b) (in newspaper) Anzeige f; **n. of birth/death**, Geburtsanzeige/Todesanzeige f. 2. (warning) Kündigung f; **to give an employee a month's n.**, einem Angestellten mit einmonatiger Frist kündigen; (of employee) **to give in one's n.**, kündigen; **without n.**, ohne Warnung; (of dismissal) fristlos; **at short n.**, kurzfristig; **until further n.**, bis auf weiteres. 3. (attention) **to take n. of s.o., sth.**, auf j-n, etwas acc achten. II. v.tr. (j-n, etwas) bemerken; **to n. that ...**, merken, daß ... ◆**'noticeable**, adj. bemerkbar; **it's not n.**, es fällt nicht auf. ◆**'notice-board**, s. Anschlagtafel f; Sch: etc: schwarzes Brett n.

**notify** ['nəutifai], v.tr. (j-n) benachrichtigen (**of sth.**, von etwas dat).

◆**notifi'cation**, s. Benachrichtigung f (der Polizei usw.).

**notion** ['nəuʃ(ə)n], s. Idee f; **he has no n. of time**, er hat keinen Zeitbegriff.

**notorious** [nəu'tɔːriəs], adj. berüchtigt. ◆**notoriety** [-tə'raiəti], s. schlechter Ruf m.

**nought** [nɔːt], s. Mth: Null f.

**noun** [naun], s. Substantiv n.

**nourish** ['nʌriʃ], v.tr. (a) (j-n) ernähren, (eine Pflanze usw.) nähren; (b) Fig: (Hoffnungen usw.) hegen. ◆**'nourishing**, adj. nahrhaft. ◆**'nourishment**, s. Nahrung f.

**novel**[1] ['nɔv(ə)l], s. Roman m. ◆**'novelist**, s. Romanschriftsteller m.

**novel**[2], adj. neuartig; (original) originell. ◆**'novelty**, s. Neuheit f.

**November** [nəu'vembər], s. November m.

**novice** ['nɔvis], s. 1. Neuling m. 2. Ecc: Novize m/Novizin f.

**now** [nau]. I. adv. jetzt; **in three days from n.**, heute in drei Tagen; **it is going to begin n.**, es wird (jetzt) gleich beginnen; **I saw him just n.**, ich habe ihn eben gesehen; **n. here, n. there**, einmal hier, einmal dort; **n. and then**, hin und wieder; **come n.!** nun hör mal; **n. then! what's all this about?** nanu, was ist denn hier los? II. conj. **n. that I am older**, jetzt, wo ich älter bin. ◆**'nowadays**, adv. heutzutage.

**nowhere** ['nəuwɛər], adv. nirgends; **n. near as pretty as ...**, nicht annähernd so hübsch wie ...

**nozzle** ['nɔzl], s. Düse f.

**nucleus** ['njuːkliəs], s. Kern m. ◆**'nuclear**, adj. nuklear, Kern-; **n. power station**, Kernkraftwerk n.

**nude** [njuːd]. I. adj. nackt; **n. photograph**, Aktaufnahme f. II. s. (a) in the n., nackt; (b) (pers.) Nackte(r) f(m); Art: Akt m. ◆**'nudist**, s. Nudist m. ◆**'nudity**, s. Nacktheit f.

**nudge** [nʌdʒ]. I. v.tr. (j-n) mit dem Ellbogen anstoßen. II. s. Stoß m.

**nuisance** ['njuːs(ə)ns], s. (a) (pers.) lästiger Mensch; (tormentor) Quälgeist m; **to make a n. of oneself**, lästig/aufdringlich werden; (b) (thing) Plage f; **public n.**, öffentliches Ärgernis n; **what a n.!** wie ärgerlich!

**null** [nʌl], adj. Jur: **n. and void**, nichtig. ◆**'nullify**, v.tr. für nichtig erklären.

**numb** [nʌm]. I. adj. (of limb etc.) gefühllos; esp. pred. taub. II. v.tr. betäuben.

**number** ['nʌmbər]. I. s. 1. Mth: (a) Zahl f; (b) (numeral) Ziffer f. 2. (quantity) Anzahl f; **a n. of people voted for him**, mehrere Leute stimmten für ihn; **in large/small numbers**, in großer/geringer Anzahl. 3. (of room, house etc.) Nummer f; **telephone n.**, Telefonnummer f; Aut: **(registration) n.**, Kennzeichen n; **n. plate**, Nummernschild n. 4. (of periodical) Ausgabe f. II. v.tr. (a) numerieren;

(b) **I n. him among my friends,** ich zähle ihn zu meinen Freunden; (c) **his days are numbered,** seine Tage sind gezählt. ◆'**numberless,** adj. zahllos.

**numeral** ['njuːmərəl], s. Ziffer f. ◆**nu'merical,** adj. numerisch; **in n. order,** zahlenmäßig geordnet. ◆'**numerous,** adj. zahlreich.

**nun** [nʌn], s. Nonne f.

**nuptial** ['nʌpʃ(ə)l], adj. Hochzeits-.

**nurse** [nəːs]. I. s. (a) Krankenschwester f; **male n.,** Krankenpfleger m; (b) (**children's**) **n.,** Kindermädchen n. II. v.tr. (a) pflegen; (b) (Zweifel, Verdacht usw.) hegen. ◆'**nursemaid,** s. Kindermädchen n. ◆'**nursery,** s. 1. Kinderzimmer n; **n. rhyme,** Kinderreim m; **day n.,** Kindertagesstätte f; **n. school,** Vorschule f. 2. (for flowers) Gärtnerei f; (for trees) Baumschu-

le f. ◆'**nursing,** s. Krankenpflege f; **n. home,** Privatklinik f.

**nurture** ['nəːtʃər], v.tr. (j-n, ein Tier) nähren; (Gefühle) hegen.

**nut** [nʌt], s. 1. Nuß f. 2. F: **she's nuts,** sie spinnt. 3. Tchn: Mutter f. ◆'**nutcase,** s. F: **he's a n.,** er spinnt. ◆'**nutcracker,** s. Nußknacker m. ◆'**nutmeg,** s. Muskat m. ◆'**nutshell,** s. Nußschale f; Fig: **in a n.,** kurz gesagt.

**nutrient** ['njuːtriənt], s. Nährstoff m. ◆**nu'trition,** s. Ernährung f. ◆**nu'tritious,** adj. nahrhaft. ◆'**nutritive,** adj. **n. value,** Nährwert m.

**nylon** ['nailɔn], s. Nylon n.

**nymph** [nimf], s. Nymphe f. ◆**nymphomaniac** [nimfəu'meinjæk], s. Nymphomanin f.

# O

**O, o** [əu], s. 1. (der Buchstabe) O, o n. 2. Tel: Null f.

**oaf** [əuf], s. Lümmel m.

**oak** [əuk], s. o. (tree), Eiche f.

**oar** [ɔːr], s. Ruder n. ◆'**oarsman,** s. Ruderer m.

**oasis,** pl. **oases** [əu'eisis, əu'eisiːz], s. Oase f.

**oat** [əut], s. usu. pl. Hafer m; Fig: **to sow one's wild oats,** sich dat die Hörner abstoßen. ◆'**oatmeal,** s. Hafermehl n.

**oath** [əuθ], pl. **oaths** [əuðz], s. 1. Eid m; **to take an o.,** einen Eid leisten. 2. (curse) Fluch m.

**obdurate** ['ɔbdjurət], adj. verstockt; (stubborn) starrköpfig.

**obedience** [ə'biːdjəns], s. Gehorsam m. ◆**o'bedient,** adj. gehorsam.

**obese** [əu'biːs], adj. fettleibig.

**obey** [ə'bei], v.tr. & i. (j-m, einem Befehl) gehorchen.

**obituary** [ə'bitjuəri], s. Todesanzeige f.

**object.** I. ['ɔbdʒikt] s 1. (a) (also Gram:) Objekt n; (b) (purpose) Zweck m; **the o. of the exercise,** der Sinn der Sache; (c) **expense is no o.,** Geld spielt keine Rolle. II. [əb'dʒekt] v.i. **to o. to s.o., sth.,** gegen j-n, etwas acc sein; **do you o. to my smoking?** haben Sie etwas dagegen, wenn ich rauche? ◆**ob'jection,** s. Einwand m; **I've no o. to that,** ich habe nichts dagegen. ◆**ob'jectionable,** adj. widerwärtig. ◆**ob'jective.** I. adj. objektiv. II. s. (aim) Ziel n. ◆**objec'tivity,** s. Objektivität f. ◆**ob'jector,** s. Gegner(in) m(f) (**to,** gen).

**oblige** [ə'blaidʒ], v.tr. **to o. s.o. to do sth.,** j-n zwingen/nötigen, etwas zu tun; **to be obliged to do sth.,** etwas tun müssen; **much obliged!** danke bestens! ◆**obligation** [ɔbli'geiʃ(ə)n], s. Verpflichtung f; **without o.,** unverbindlich. ◆**obligatory** [ə'bligətri], adj. obligato-

risch. ◆**o'bliging,** adj. entgegenkommend.

**oblique** [ə'bliːk], adj. schräg.

**obliterate** [ə'blitəreit], v.tr. (efface) (etwas) auslöschen; (Geschriebenes) ausstreichen. ◆**oblite'ration,** s. Auslöschung f.

**oblivion** [ə'bliviən], s. Vergessenheit f.

**oblong** ['ɔblɔŋ]. I. adj. länglich; Mth: rechteckig. II. s. Rechteck n.

**obnoxious** [əb'nɔkʃəs], adj. widerwärtig.

**oboe** ['əubəu], s. Oboe f.

**obscene** [əb'siːn, ɔb-], adj. obszön. ◆**obscenity** [-'seniti], s. Obszönität f.

**obscure** [əb'skjuər]. I. adj. 1. (of argument etc.) unklar. 2. (of writer etc.) unbekannt; (forgotten) vergessen; Pej: unbedeutend. II. v.tr. (etwas) verdunkeln; (hide) verbergen. ◆**ob'scurity,** s. 1. (darkness) Dunkelheit f. 2. Unklarheit f. 3. Unbekanntheit f; **to sink into o.,** in Vergessenheit geraten.

**obsequious** [əb'siːkwiəs], adj. (of pers.) unterwürfig; (of manner) kriecherisch.

**observe** [əb'zəːv], v.tr. (a) (einen Brauch) pflegen; (b) (watch) (j-n, etwas) beobachten; (notice) (etwas) bemerken. ◆**ob'servant,** adj. aufmerksam; **he's very o.,** er merkt alles. ◆**obser'vation,** s. 1. Beobachtung f. 2. (remark) Bemerkung f. ◆**ob'servatory,** s. Sternwarte f. ◆**ob'server,** s. Beobachter m.

**obsess** [əb'ses], v.tr. **to be obsessed with an idea/a fear,** von einer Idee/Angst besessen sein. ◆**ob'session,** s. (state) Besessenheit f; (idea) Zwangsvorstellung f. ◆**ob'sessive,** adj.

**obsolete** ['ɔbsəliːt], adj. veraltet. ◆**obsolescent** [-'lesənt], adj. veraltend.

**obstacle** ['ɔbstəkl], s. Hindernis n; Sp: **o. race,** Hindernisrennen n.

**obstetrics** [əb'stetriks], s. pl. Geburtshilfe f.

**obstinate** ['ɔbstinət], adj. starrköpfig; störrisch. ◆**'obstinacy**, s. Starrsinn m.

**obstreperous** [əb'strep(ə)rəs], adj. aufsässig.

**obstruct** [əb'strʌkt], v.tr. (a) (eine Straße usw.) versperren; (eine Einfahrt, ein Rohr usw.) blockieren; **to o. s.o.'s view,** j-m die Sicht versperren; (b) hemmen; **to o. the police,** die Polizei behindern. ◆**ob'struction,** s. 1. (a) Versperrung f; Blockierung f; (b) Hemmung f; Behinderung f; (c) Pol: (**policy of**) o., Obstruktion f. 2. (obstacle) Hindernis n ◆**ob'structive,** adj. hinderlich.

**obtain** [əb'tein], v.tr. erhalten; (get for oneself) sich dat (etwas) verschaffen. ◆**ob'tainable,** adj. erhältlich.

**obtrusive** [əb'tru:siv], adj. aufdringlich.

**obtuse** [əb'tju:s], adj. 1. Mth: stumpf. 2. (of pers.) begriffsstutzig.

**obviate** ['ɔbvieit], v.tr. vermeiden. ◆**'obvious,** adj. offensichtlich; **o. fact,** selbstverständliche Tatsache; **-ly,** adv. offensichtlich.

**occasion** [ə'keiʒ(ə)n], s. (a) Gelegenheit f; **on this o.,** bei dieser Gelegenheit; (b) Anlaß m; **to rise to the o.,** sich der Lage gewachsen zeigen. ◆**o'ccasional,** adj. gelegentlich; **o. showers,** vereinzelte Regenschauer mpl; **-ly,** adv. hin und wieder.

**occupant** ['ɔkjupənt], s. Bewohner m. ◆**occu'pation,** s. 1. Mil: Besetzung f (eines Landes). 2. (task) Beschäftigung f; (profession) Beruf m. ◆**occu'pational,** adj. Berufs-. ◆**'occupied,** adj. (a) (busy) beschäftigt; (b) (taken) besetzt. ◆**'occupier,** s. Bewohner m. ◆**'occupy,** v.tr. (a) (live in) (ein Haus usw.) bewohnen; Mil: besetzen; (b) (Zeit) in Anspruch nehmen; (Platz) einnehmen; (c) (keep busy) (j-n, sich) beschäftigen.

**occur** [ə'kə:r], v.i. (a) geschehen, sich ereignen; (b) **the word only occurs twice,** das Wort kommt nur zweimal vor; (c) **it occurs to me that ...,** es fällt mir ein, daß ... ◆**o'ccurrence,** s. (event) Ereignis n.

**ocean** ['əuʃ(ə)n], s. Ozean m. ◆**oceanic** [əuʃi'ænik], adj. ozeanisch. ◆**ocean'ography,** s. Meereskunde f.

**ochre** ['əukər], s. Ocker m.

**o'clock** [ə'klɔk], adv. **one/six o'clock,** ein/sechs Uhr.

**octagon** ['ɔktəgən], s. Achteck n. ◆**octagonal** [-'tægən(ə)l], adj. achteckig.

**octave** ['ɔktiv], s. Mus: Oktave f.

**October** [ɔk'təubər], s. Oktober m.

**octogenarian** [ɔktəudʒi'nɛəriən], s. Achtzigjährige(r) f(m).

**octopus,** pl. -ses ['ɔktəpəs, -siz], s. Krake m.

**oculist** ['ɔkjulist], s. Augenarzt m.

**odd** [ɔd], adj. 1. (a) (of number) ungerade; (b) **fifty o.,** über fünfzig; **to be the o. man/one out,** überzählig/(exception) die

Ausnahme sein. 2. (a) (single) einzeln; (b) **at o. times,** hin und wieder; bei Gelegenheit; **o. job man,** Gelegenheitsarbeiter m. 3. (unusual) seltsam; F: komisch; **-ly,** adv. **o. (enough),** seltsamerweise. ◆**'oddity,** s. 1. (characteristic) Eigenart f. 2. (thing) etwas Seltsames/Komisches. ◆**'oddness,** s. Seltsamkeit f. ◆**odds,** s.pl. 1. (a) (chances) Aussichten fpl; **the o. are in his favour,** er hat gute Chancen; (b) 2. **o. and ends,** Kram m.

**ode** [əud], s. Ode f.

**odious** ['əudjəs], adj. (of pers.) verhaßt; (of task etc.) widerlich.

**odour** ['əudər], s. (a) (smell) Geruch m; (b) (scent) Duft m. ◆**'odourless,** adj. geruchlos.

**of** [accented ɔv, unaccented əv], prep. 1. gen or von + dat; (a) (belonging to) **the head of the horse,** der Kopf des Pferdes; **the Queen of England,** die Königin von England; (b) (by) **the works of Shakespeare,** die Werke Shakespeares/von Shakespeare; (c) (quantity) **many of these mistakes,** viele dieser Fehler; (d) (from) **south of the river,** südlich des Flusses; (e) (characteristic) **a matter of principle,** eine Prinzipienfrage; **it's very kind of you,** das ist sehr nett von Ihnen; (f) **a glass of wine,** ein Glas Wein; **the first of June,** der erste Juni. 2. **to die of sth.,** an etwas dat sterben; **to think of sth.,** an etwas acc denken. 3. (made of) aus + dat; **a fence of wood,** ein Zaun aus Holz.

**off** [ɔf]. I. adv. 1. (away) (a) (position) weg; (specific distance) entfernt; **a long way o.,** weit weg; (b) (movement) fort; **I must be o.,** ich muß gehen; (c) (down) **to fall o.,** herunterfallen. 2. (a) (switched) o., El: ausgeschaltet; (of gas, water) abgestellt; (b) Cl: ausgezogen; (c) (in restaurant) **chicken is o.,** Huhn gibt es nicht mehr; (d) F: (of deal etc.) **it's all o.,** die ganze Sache ist abgeblasen; (e) **the meat is o./has gone o.,** das Fleisch ist schlecht (geworden). 3. **well o.,** gut dran; (rich) reich. II. prep. 1. (a) von + dat; **to fall o. a horse,** vom Pferd fallen; **to take sth. o. the table,** etwas vom Tisch nehmen; (b) **a street o. Oxford Street,** eine Seitenstraße von Oxford Street; **o. Dover,** vor der Küste bei Dover. 2. (a) F: **to be o. one's food,** keinen Appetit haben; (b) **to have a day o.,** einen Tag frei haben. III. adj. (a) Aut: **o. side,** rechts; (when driving on the right) links; (b) **an o. day,** ein schlechter Tag; **on the o. chance,** aufs Geratewohl. ◆**'off'hand.** I. adv. **I don't know o.,** das kann ich nicht so ohne weiteres sagen. II. adj. (a) (of pers.) brüsk; (of answer) kurz angebunden; (b) (casual) lässig. ◆**'off-licence,** s. (shop) Wein- und Spirituosengeschäft n. ◆**'off-'peak,** adj. außerhalb der Stoßzeit. ◆**'offset,** v.tr.irr. (Verlust usw.) wettmachen. ◆**offshore** [ɔf'ʃɔːr], adv. vor der Küste. ◆**'off'side.** Fb: adj.

& *adv.* abseits. ◆'**offspring,** *s.* 1. *coll.* Nachkommen *mpl.* 2. *F:* (*child*) Sprößling *m.*

**offal** ['ɔf(ə)l], *s.* Innereien *fpl* (vom Rind usw.).

**offence** [ə'fens], *s.* 1. **to take o. at sth.,** an etwas *dat* Anstoß nehmen; **no o. (meant)!** nichts für ungut! 2. (*crime*) Vergehen *n.* 3. (*attack*) Angriff *m.* ◆o'**ffend,** *v.tr.* beleidigen. ◆o'**ffender,** *s.* Täter(in) *m(f); Jur:* Straffällige(r) *f(m).* ◆o'**ffending,** *adj.* (*a*) (*of thing*) anstößig; (*b*) (*of words etc.*) beleidigend. ◆o'**ffensive. I.** *adj.* (*a*) anstößig (**to s.o.,** für j-n); (*b*) (*of smell etc.*) ekelhaft. **II.** *s. Mil:* Offensive *f.*

**offer** ['ɔfər]. **I.** *s.* Angebot *n;* **o. of marriage,** Heiratsantrag *m.* **II.** *v.tr.* **to offer s.o. sth.,** j-m etwas anbieten; **to o. resistance,** Widerstand leisten. ◆'**offering,** *s. Ecc:* Spende *f;* (*to god*) Opfer *n.* ◆'**offertory,** *s.* Kollekte *f.*

**office** ['ɔfis], *s.* 1. (*a*) Büro *n;* head o., Hauptgeschäftsstelle *f;* **o. hours,** Bürostunden *fpl;* (*b*) *Brit: Pol:* **Foreign/Home O.,** Außen/Innenministerium *n.* 2. (*post*) Amt *n.* ◆**officer** ['ɔfisər], *s.* 1. (*official*) Beamte(r) *f(m);* (**police**) o., Polizist *m;* **medical o.,** Amtsarzt *m.* 2. *Mil:* Offizier *m.* ◆**official** [ə'fiʃ(ə)l]. **I.** *adj.* (*a*) **on o. business,** dienstlich; (*b*) (*of news etc.*) offiziell. **II.** *s.* Funktionär *m;* (*state employee*) Beamter, Beamtin *f.* ◆**officia'lese,** *s. F:* Amtssprache *f.* ◆o'**fficiate,** *v.i.* (*a*) fungieren (**as host etc.,** als Gastgeber usw.)); (*b*) *Ecc:* den Gottesdienst leiten. ◆o'**fficious,** *adj.* diensteifrig. ◆o'**fficiousness,** *s.* (übertriebener) Diensteifer *m.*

**often** ['ɔftən, 'ɔfn], *adv.* oft; **every so o.,** von Zeit zu Zeit.

**oh** [əu], *int.* oh! **oh, I see!** ach so!

**oil** [ɔil]. **I.** *s.* Öl *n;* (**mineral**) o., Erdöl *n;* **o. well,** Erdölquelle *f;* **o. rig,** Bohrinsel *f;* **o. slick,** Ölteppich *m;* **o. level,** Ölstand *m;* **o. can,** Ölkanne *f;* **o. colours/ paints, oils,** Ölfarben *fpl;* **o. painting,** Ölgemälde *n; Fig:* **to pour o. on troubled waters,** Öl auf die Wogen gießen. **II.** *v.tr.* (eine Maschine usw.) ölen; *P:* (*of pers.*) **well oiled,** besoffen. ◆'**oilfield,** *s.* Ölfeld *n.* ◆'**oilskins,** *s. pl. Cl:* Ölzeug *n.* ◆'**oily,** *adj.* (*a*) ölig; (*b*) *Fig:* (*of manner*) aalglatt.

**ointment** ['ɔintmənt], *s.* Salbe *f.*

**OK** (*also* **okay**) [əu'kei]. *F:* **I.** *int.* in Ordnung! okay! **II.** *adj.* **that's OK,** das geht in Ordnung.

**old** [əuld], *adj.* alt; **to grow o.,** alt werden; altern; **an o. maid,** eine alte Jungfer; **o. age,** das Alter. ◆**o. age pensioner,** Rentner *m; F:* **the/my o. man/woman,** mein Alter/meine Alte; *F:* **an o. flame,** eine alte Flamme. ◆'**old-'fashioned,** *adj.* 1. altmodisch; (*clothes*) unmodern. 2. (*of ideas*) überholt; (*of pers.*) rückständig. ◆'**old-'hat,** *adj. F:* unmodern.

**olive** ['ɔliv]. **I.** *s.* 1. Olive *f;* **o. oil,** Olivenöl *n;* **o.** (**tree**), Ölbaum *m;* **o. branch,** Ölzweig *m; Fig:* **to hold out the o. branch,** ein Friedensangebot machen. 2. *Cu:* **beef o.,** Rindsroulade *f.* **II.** *adj.* **o.(-green),** olivgrün.

**Olympic** [ə'limpik]. **I.** *adj.* olympisch; **the O. Games,** die Olympischen Spiele. **II.** *s.* **the Olympics,** die Olympiade.

**omelet(te)** ['ɔmlit], *s. Cu:* Omelett *n.*

**omen** ['əumen], *s.* Omen *n.* ◆**ominous** ['ɔminəs], *adj.* ominös; (*evil*) unheilvoll.

**omit** [ə'mit], *v.tr.* (*a*) (etwas) auslassen; (j-n) übergehen; (*b*) **to o. to do sth.,** es unterlassen, etwas zu tun. ◆o'**mission,** *s.* (*of thing*) Weglassung *f;* (*of action*) Unterlassung *f.*

**omnipotence** [ɔm'nipətəns], *s.* Allmacht *f.* ◆**om'nipotent,** *adj.* allmächtig.

**omniscient** [ɔm'nisiənt], *adj.* allwissend.

**omnivorous** [ɔm'nivərəs], *adj.* allesfressend.

**on** [ɔn]. **I.** *prep.* 1. (*a*) auf + *dat/* (*motion*) + *acc;* **it is on the table,** es liegt auf dem Tisch; **it fell on the roof,** es fiel auf das Dach; *F:* **have you enough (money) on you?** haben Sie genug Geld bei sich? **on the shore, on the strand; to hang on the wall,** an der Wand hängen; (*b*) (*direction*) **on the left/right,** links/ rechts; **on the way,** auf dem Weg, unterwegs; (*c*) (*means*) **on the train/bus,** mit dem Zug/Bus; **on foot,** zu Fuß; **on the radio,** im Radio; **on television,** im Fernsehen. 2. (*time*) **on Monday,** am Montag; **on Mondays,** montags; **on time,** pünktlich; **on** (**his**) **arrival in Helsinki,** bei seiner Ankunft in Helsinki; **on waking up,** beim Aufwachen. 3. *F:* **the drinks are on me,** die Drinks gehen auf meine Rechnung. 4. (*concerning*) über + *acc;* **a talk on Luther,** ein Vortrag über Luther. 5. (*condition*) unter + *dat;* **on this condition,** unter dieser Bedingung; **on no account,** auf keinen Fall. **II.** *adv.* 1. (*a*) (*of event*) **to be on,** stattfinden; **what's on at the cinema?** was wird im Kino gespielt? **have you anything on tonight?** haben Sie heute abend etwas vor? (*b*) (*of switch, apparatus*) eingeschaltet; **don't leave the light on,** laß das Licht nicht brennen; *Tchn:* '**on-off**', 'Ein-Aus'. 2. **to have a coat on,** einen Mantel anhaben. 3. (*continuation*) (*a*) **to work on,** weiterarbeiten; **and so on,** und so weiter; **on and on,** immer weiter; (*b*) **later on,** später; **from then on,** von dem Zeitpunkt an.

**once** [wʌns], *adv.* 1. einmal; **not o.,** kein einziges Mal; **o. more,** noch einmal; **for o.,** ausnahmsweise; **o. in a while,** hin und wieder; **o. and for all,** ein für allemal; **o.** (**upon a time**) **there was ...,** es war einmal .... 2. **at o.,** (i) (*immediately*) sofort; (ii) (*at the same time*) auf einmal.

**oncoming** ['ɔnkʌmiŋ], *adj.* **o. traffic,** Gegenverkehr *m.*

**one** [wʌn]. **I.** *adj.* ein, eine; **o. day,** eines

Tages. **II.** s. **1.** (*number*) eins. **2.** (*a*) **there's only o. left,** es ist nur einer/eine/ eins übrig; **all in o.,** alles in einem; (*b*) **at o. (o'clock),** um ein Uhr/*F:* um eins. **III.** *dem. pron.* (*a*) **this o.,** dieser/diese/dieses; **which o. do you like best?** welcher/ welche/welches gefällt dir am besten? (*b*) **a red dot and a blue o.,** ein roter Punkt und ein blauer. **IV.** *indef. pron.* **1.** (*pl.* **some, any**) einer/eine/ein(e)s; **I haven't a pencil, have you got o.?** ich habe keinen Bleistift, hast du einen? **o. of them,** einer von ihnen; **not o. (of them),** keiner (von ihnen); **o. by o.,** einer nach dem anderen. **2.** (*you*) (*a*) (*subject*) man; (*object*) einen; **o. never knows,** man weiß nie; (*b*) **one's,** sein(e); **to cut one's finger,** sich in den Finger schneiden. ◆'**one- 'armed,** *adj. F:* **o.-a. bandit,** Spielauto- mat *m.* ◆'**one-'eyed,** *adj.* einäugig. ◆'**one-'horse,** *adj. F:* **o.-h. town,** arm- seliges Nest. ◆'**one-'parent,** *adj.* **o.-p. family,** Halbfamilie *f.* ◆**one'self,** *pron.* (*a*) *refl.* sich; **to talk to o.,** mit sich selbst reden; **by o.,** allein; (*b*) **one must do it o.,** man muß es selber machen. ◆'**one- 'sided,** *adj.* einseitig. ◆'**one-'track,** *adj.* **to have a o.-t. mind,** immer nur das eine im Kopf haben. ◆'**one-'up,** *adj.* (*a*) *Sp:* **to be o.-up,** einen Punkt/*Fb:* ein Tor usw. voraus sein; (*b*) **to be o.-up on s.o.,** j-m voraus sein. ◆**one'upmanship,** *s. Hum:* Kunst *f,* den anderen immer voraus zu sein. ◆'**one-'way,** *adj.* Einbahn-; **o.-w. street,** Einbahnstraße *f.*

**onerous** ['ɔnərəs, 'əun-], *adj.* (*of task*) mühsam; (*of duties*) lästig.

**onion** ['ʌnjən], *s.* Zwiebel *f;* **o. skin,** Zwiebelschale *f.*

**onlooker** ['ɔnlukər], *s.* Zuschauer(in) *m(f).*

**only** ['əunli]. **I.** *adj.* einzig; **o. son,** einzi- ger Sohn. **II.** *adv.* (*a*) nur; **I've o. three,** ich habe nur drei; (*b*) (*with time*) erst; **o. just,** gerade erst; **o. yesterday,** erst ge- stern. **III.** *conj.* aber; **o. it's too big,** es ist nur zu groß.

**onslaught** ['ɔnslɔːt], *s.* (heftiger) Angriff *m.*

**onus** ['əunəs], *s.* Last *f;* (*responsibility*) Verantwortung *f.*

**onward(s)** ['ɔnwəd(z)], *adv.* (*a*) (*for- wards*) vorwärts; (*b*) **from tomorrow o.,** ab morgen.

**ooze** [uːz]. **I.** *s.* (*mud*) Schlamm *m.* **II.** *v.i.* sickern.

**op** [ɔp], *s. F:* **1.** *Med:* Operation *f.* **2.** *Mil:* **combined op(s),** vereintes Unter- nehmen *n.*

**opal** ['əup(ə)l], *s.* Opal *m.*

**opaque** [əu'peik], *adj.* undurchsichtig.

**open** ['əup(ə)n]. **I.** *adj.* **1.** offen; (*of shop etc.*) geöffnet; **o. to the public,** für die Öffentlichkeit zugänglich. **2.** (*a*) **in the o.** (**air**), im Freien; **on the o. road,** auf freier Strecke; **the o. sea,** das offene

Meer; (*b*) *Fig:* **o. to question,** fraglich; (*of verdict*) anfechtbar. **3.** (*frank*) offen; **to keep an o. mind,** sich nicht beeinflussen lassen. **4. the job is still open,** die Stelle ist noch frei. **II.** *v.* **1.** *v.tr.* (*a*) öffnen; (ein Buch usw.) aufschlagen; (*b*) (ein Land, neue Märkte usw.) erschließen; **to o.** (**up**) **a way/path through sth.,** sich *dat* einen Weg durch etwas *acc* bahnen; (*c*) (ein Fest, ein Geschäft, ein Gespräch, ein Konto usw.) eröffnen. **2.** *v.i.* (*of flower etc.*) sich öffnen; (*of shop etc.*) öffnen/*F:* aufmachen; **the door opens into the gar- den,** die Tür führt in den Garten; **-ly,** *adv.* offen; **to speak o. about sth.,** offen über etwas *acc* sprechen. ◆'**open-'air,** *adj.* Frei-; **o.- a. pool,** Freibad *n;* **o.-a. theatre,** Freilichtbühne *f.* ◆'**opener,** *s.* **can/tin o.,** Büchsenöffner *m.* ◆'**open- 'heart,** *adj. Med:* **o.-h. surgery,** Eingriffe *mpl* am offenen Herzen. ◆'**opening,** *s.* **1.** (*a*) Öffnen *n* (einer Flasche, der Post usw.); (*b*) Eröffnung *f* (von Verhandlun- gen, von einem Gebäude usw.); **o. speech,** Eröffnungsrede *f.* **2.** (*gap*) Öff- nung *f;* (*in a forest*) Lichtung *f.* **3.** (*poss- ibility, esp. job*) Möglichkeit *f.* ◆'**open- 'minded,** *adj.* aufgeschlossen. ◆'**openness,** *s.* Offenheit *f.* ◆'**open- 'plan,** *adj. Arch:* ohne Trennwände. ◆'**open 'out,** *v.* **1.** *v.tr.* (ein Blatt Pa- pier usw.) ausbreiten. **2.** *v.i.* (*of valley etc.*) sich ausbreiten; (*of view*) sich er- strecken. ◆'**open 'up,** *v.* **1.** *v.tr.* (ein Land, einen Markt usw.) erschließen. **2.** *v.i.* **o. up!** aufmachen!

**opera** ['ɔp(ə)rə], *s.* Oper *f;* **o. glasses,** Opernglas *n.* ◆**ope'ratic,** *adj.* (*for ope- ra*) Opern-; **o. music,** Opernmusik *f.*

**operate** ['ɔpəreit], *v.* **1.** *v.i.* (*a*) (*of machi- ne*) in Betrieb sein; (*b*) *Med:* **to o.** (**on s.o.**), (j-n) operieren. **2.** *v.tr.* (*of pers.*) (eine Maschine) bedienen; (eine Bremse, einen Hebel) betätigen. ◆'**operating,** *s. Ind: etc:* Betrieb *m;* **o. instructions,** Be- dienungsanleitung *f;* **o. theatre,** Opera- tionssaal *m.* ◆**ope'ration,** *s.* **1.** (*run- ning*) Betrieb *m;* (*control*) Bedienung *f* (einer Maschine); Betätigung *f* (einer Bremse usw.). **2.** (*single process*) Arbeits- vorgang *m; Mth:* Prozeß *m.* **3.** *Med:* Ope- ration *f;* **to have an o.,** operiert werden. ◆**ope'rational,** *adj.* (*ready for use*) betriebsfertig/*Mil:* einsatzfähig; (*in use*) im Betrieb/*Mil:* Einsatz. ◆**operative** ['ɔp(ə)rətiv], *adj.* (*a*) (*effective*) wirksam; (*of law etc.*) **to become o.,** in Kraft tre- ten; (*b*) (*relevant*) zutreffend. ◆'**operator,** *s.* (*a*) *Ind:* Maschinist *m;* (*b*) *Tel:* Telefonist(in) *m(f);* *Nau: Av: etc:* **radio o.,** Funker *m.*

**opinion** [ə'pinjən], *s.* Meinung *f;* **in my o.,** meiner Meinung nach; **that's a mat- ter of o.,** das ist Ansichtssache *f;* **o. poll,** Meinungsumfrage *f.* ◆**o'pinionated,** *adj.* rechthaberisch.

**opium** ['əupjəm], *s.* Opium *n.*

opponent [ə'pəunənt], s. Gegner m.

oppor'tunity [ɔpə'tjuːniti], s. Gelegenheit f.

oppose [ə'pəuz], v.tr. (a) sich (j-m, etwas dat) widersetzen; (eine Ansicht, eine Bewegung usw.) bekämpfen; (b) (compare) gegenüberstellen. ◆o'pposed, adj. abgeneigt; to be o. to sth., gegen etwas acc sein. ◆o'pposing, adj. entgegengesetzt. ◆opposite ['ɔpəzit, -sit]. I. adj. (a) (facing) gegenüberstehend; the house o., das Haus gegenüber; (b) (of directions, poles, meaning etc.) entgegengesetzt; the o. sex, das andere Geschlecht. II. s. Gegenteil n. III. adv. gegenüber; she lives o., sie wohnt gegenüber. IV. prep. gegenüber + dat. ◆oppo'sition, s. (a) Widerstand m; (b) Pol: Opposition f.

oppress [ə'pres], v.tr. (a) (ein Volk) unterdrücken; (b) (of anxiety, heat etc.) (j-n) bedrücken. ◆o'ppression, s. 1. Unterdrückung f. 2. (feeling) Bedrücktheit f. ◆o'ppressive, adj. 1. (of rule etc.) tyrannisch. 2. (of atmosphere) bedrückend; (of weather, heat) schwül. ◆o'ppressor, s. Unterdrücker m.

'optical ['ɔptikəl, adj. optisch. ◆op'tician, s. Optiker m. ◆'optics, s. pl. Optik f.

optimist ['ɔptimist], s. Optimist(in) m(f). ◆'optimism, s. Optimismus m. ◆opti'mistic, adj. optimistisch.

option ['ɔpʃ(ə)n], s. (choice) Wahl f; Alternative f; to leave one's options open, sich nicht festlegen. ◆'optional, adj. wahlweise.

opulence ['ɔpjuləns], s. Üppigkeit f. ◆'opulent, adj. üppig.

or [ɔːr], conj. oder; he can't read or write, er kann weder lesen noch schreiben.

oracle ['ɔrəkl], s. Orakel n.

oral ['ɔːr(ə)l]. I. adj. mündlich. II. s. Sch: F: mündliche Prüfung.

orange ['ɔrin(d)ʒ]. I. s. Apfelsine f, Orange f. II. adj. orange(farben).

oration [ə'reiʃ(ə)n], s. feierliche Rede f. ◆orator ['ɔrətər], s. Redner(in) m(f). ◆'oratory, s. Redekunst f.

oratorio, pl. -os [ɔrə'tɔːriəu, -əuz], s. Mus: Oratorium n.

orbit ['ɔːbit]. I. s. Umlaufbahn f (eines Satelliten); to go into o., in die Umlaufbahn gelangen; II. v.tr. (einen Planeten) umkreisen.

orchard ['ɔːtʃəd], s. Obstgarten m.

orchestra ['ɔːkistrə], s. Orchester n. ◆or'chestral [-'kes-, -tras], adj. Orchester-. ◆'orchestrate, v.tr. (ein Werk) orchestrieren. ◆orche'stration, s. Orchesterbearbeitung f.

orchid ['ɔːkid], s. Orchidee f.

ordain [ɔː'dein], v.tr. (a) Ecc: to o. s.o. priest, j-n zum Priester weihen; (b) (decree) (etwas) verfügen, Fig: (of fate etc.) bestimmen.

ordeal [ɔː'diːl], s. (schwere) Probe f; Fig:

Feuerprobe f.

order ['ɔːdər]. I. s. 1. Ordnung f; (sequence) Reihenfolge f; in o., in Ordnung; out of o., (of machine) außer Betrieb; (defective) defekt; in good o., in gutem Zustand. 2. in o. to, um zu + inf; in o. that, damit. 3. (class, also medal) Orden m. 4. (a) (command) Befehl m; until further orders, bis auf weiteren Befehl; (b) Com: Auftrag m; (act of ordering) Bestellung f; o. form, Bestellschein m; (c) money/postal o., Postanweisung f. II. v.tr. (a) to o. s.o. to do sth., j-m befehlen, etwas zu tun; (b) (Waren, Essen, ein Taxi usw.) bestellen; (in restaurant) have you ordered? haben Sie schon bestellt? ◆'orderly. I. adj. (a) (tidy) ordentlich; (of life) geordnet; (b) (of crowd etc.) friedlich. II. s. medical o., Krankenwärter m; Mil: Sanitäter m.

ordinal ['ɔːdin(ə)l], adj. o. (number), Ordnungszahl f.

ordinary ['ɔːdin(ə)ri]. adj. normal; (also Pej:) gewöhnlich; -ily, adv. normalerweise.

ordnance ['ɔːdnəns], s. 1. Mil: Artillerie f. 2. Brit: O. Survey map, Meßtischblatt n (der Nationalen Landesvermessung).

ore [ɔːr], s. Erz n.

organ ['ɔːgən], s. 1. Mus: Orgel f. 2. Anat: Organ n. ◆organic [ɔ'gænik], adj. organisch. ◆'organism, s. Organismus m. ◆'organist, s. Mus: Organist m. ◆organi'zation, s. Organisation f. ◆'organize, v.tr. organisieren. ◆'organizer, s. Organisator m; (of event) Veranstalter m.

orgy ['ɔːdʒi], s. Orgie f.

orient ['ɔːriənt], s. the O., der Orient. ◆ori'ental. I. adj. orientalisch. II. s. Orientale m; Orientalin f. ◆'orientate, v.tr. to o. oneself, sich orientieren.

origin ['ɔridʒin], s. Ursprung m; (source) Quelle f (eines Gerüchts usw.); (of pers.) Herkunft f; country of o., Herkunftsland n. ◆original [ə'ridʒ-]. I. adj. (a) (first) ursprünglich; (unaltered) original; (b) (new) originell. II. s. Original n (eines Bildes usw.). ◆origi'nality, s. Originalität f. ◆o'riginate, v. 1. v.tr. (create) (etwas) schaffen; (found) (eine Bewegung, Stilrichtung) begründen. 2. v.i. (of thing) entstehen (from/in, aus + dat); (of war, quarrel etc.) seinen Ausgang nehmen.

Orkneys ['ɔːkniz], Pr.n.pl. the O., die Orkneyinseln fpl.

ornament ['ɔːnəmənt]. I. s. Ornament n; Fig: (pers. etc.) Zierde f. II. v.tr. (etwas) verzieren. ◆orna'mental, adj.

ornate [ɔː'neit], adj. (of style) überladen; (of object) reich verziert, verschnörkelt; (of language) blumig.

ornithology [ɔːni'θɔlədʒi], s. Vogelkunde f.

orphan ['ɔːf(ə)n], s. Waise f; ◆'orphanage, s. Waisenhaus n.

orthodox ['ɔːθədɔks], adj. orthodox.

**orthography** [ɔːˈθɔgrəfi], *s.* Rechtschreibung *f.*

**orthopaedic** [ɔːθəˈpiːdik], *adj.* orthopädisch.

**oscillate** [ˈɔsileit], *v.i.* schwingen; *(of needle etc.)* ausschlagen. ◆**osciˈllation**, *s.* Schwingung *f.*

**ostensible** [ɔsˈtensibl], *adj.* angeblich; *(apparent)* scheinbar.

**ostentation** [ɔstenˈteiʃ(ə)n], *s.* Protzigkeit *f.* ◆**ostenˈtatious**, *adj.* protzig.

**osteopath** [ˈɔstiəpæθ], *s.* Osteopath *m.*

**ostracism** [ˈɔstrəsizm], *s.* Achtung *f.* ◆**ˈostracize**, *v.tr.* (j-n) ächten.

**ostrich** [ˈɔstritʃ], *s.* Strauß *m.*

**other** [ˈʌðər]. I. *adj.* (a) andere(r,s); **the o. one**, der/die/das andere; (b) **the o. night**, neulich abends/nachts; (c) *(alternate)* **every o. day**, jeden zweiten Tag; (d) *(different)* **o. than**, anders als. II. *pron.* andere(r,s); **one after the o.**, einer nach dem anderen; **the others**, die anderen; **each o.**, einander; *F:* **someone or o.**, irgend jemand. ◆**ˈotherwise**, *adv.* 1. *(differently)* anders. 2. *(in other respects)* sonst; **o. he's quite sane**, sonst ist er ganz normal.

**otter** [ˈɔtər], *s.* Otter *m.*

**ought** [ɔːt], *v. aux.* sollte(n); **you o. to go now**, Sie sollten jetzt gehen; **you o. to see the exhibition**, Sie sollten sich die Ausstellung ansehen; **that o. to be enough for three**, das müßte für drei Personen genügen.

**our** [uːr, ˈauər], *poss. adj.* unser. ◆**ours**, *poss. pron* unsere, unsere, unseres; **this is o.**, das gehört uns; **a friend of o.**, ein Freund von uns. ◆**ourˈselves**, *pers. pron. pl.* selbst.

**oust** [aust], *v.tr.* (j-n) verdrängen.

**out** [aut]. *adv.* hinaus; (a) **to go o.**, hinausgehen; **to come o.**, herauskommen; **o. you go!** raus mit dir! (b) *(away)* weg; **to throw sth. o.**, etwas wegwerfen; (c) **my father is o.**, mein Vater ist nicht zu Hause. 2. *(wrong)* **to be o. in one's calculations**, sich verrechnet haben. 3. *(of fire)* ausgegangen. 4. *(finished)* zu Ende. 5. **o. of**, (a) aus + *dat*; **o. of the window**, aus dem Fenster/zum Fenster hinaus; **o. of doors**, im Freien; **o. of the way**, (i) *int.* aus dem Weg! (ii) *(of place)* abgelegen; (b) *(outside)* **a mile o. of (the) town**, eine Meile außerhalb der Stadt. ◆**ˈoutback**, *s. Austral:* **the o.**, das Landesinnere. ◆**outˈbid**, *v.tr.irr.* *(at auction)* (j-n) überbieten. ◆**ˈoutboard**, *adj.* **o. motor**, Außenbordmotor *m.* ◆**ˈoutbreak**, *s.* Ausbruch *m* (einer Krankheit usw.). ◆**ˈoutbuilding**, *s.* Nebengebäude *n.* ◆**ˈoutburst**, *s.* Ausbruch *m* (von Zorn usw.). ◆**ˈoutcast**. I. *s.* Ausgestoßene(r) *f(m).* II. *adj.* ausgestoßen. ◆**ˈoutcome**, *s.* Ergebnis *n.* ◆**ˈoutcry**, *s.* (lautstarker) Protest *m.* ◆**outˈdistance**, *v.tr. Sp:* (j-n) weit hinter sich *dat* lassen. ◆**outˈdo**, *v.tr.irr.*

(j-n) übertreffen. ◆**ˈoutdoor**, *adj.* im Freien. ◆**ˈouter**, *adj.* äußere(r,s), Außen-; **o. space**, Weltraum *m.* ◆**ˈoutfit**, *s.* Ausrüstung *f.* ◆**ˈoutgoings**, *s.pl.* Ausgaben *fpl.* ◆**ˈoutgrow**, *v.tr.irr.* herauswachsen (aus Kleidern usw.); *(Gewohnheiten)* ablegen. ◆**ˈouting**, *s.* Ausflug *m.* ◆**outˈlandish**, *adj.* *(of dress)* ausgefallen; *(of behaviour, ideas)* seltsam. ◆**ˈoutlaw**. I. *s.* Geächtete(r) *f(m).* II. *v.tr.* (a) (j-n) ächten; (b) *Fig:* (etwas) verbieten. ◆**ˈoutlay**, *s.* Auslagen *fpl.* ◆**ˈoutline**. I. *s.* Umriß *m.* II. *v.tr.* (etwas) umreißen; **to o. sth. roughly**, etwas in groben Zügen darstellen. ◆**outˈlive**, *v.tr.* (j-n, etwas) überleben. ◆**ˈoutlook**, *s.* (a) *(view)* Aussicht *f*; (b) *Fig:* *(prospect)* Aussichten *fpl*; *(opinion)* Ansicht *f.* ◆**ˈoutlying**, *adj.* *(of villages etc.)* entlegen. ◆**outˈnumber**, *v.tr.* (dem Feind usw.) zahlenmäßig überlegen sein. ◆**ˈoutput**, *s.* (a) *Ind:* Produktion *f*; *Min:* Ertrag *m*; *Lit: etc:* Werk *n*; (b) *(of engine, machine etc.)* Leistung *f.* ◆**ˈoutrage**. *s.* 1. *(atrocity)* Greueltat *f.* 2. *(sth. shocking)* Unverschämtheit *f.* ◆**outˈrageous**, *adj.* unerhört; *(of prices)* unverschämt; *(of remark)* empörend. ◆**ˈoutright**, *adv.* glatt; **to refuse o.**, glattweg ablehnen. ◆**ˈoutset**, *s.* Anfang *m.* ◆**outˈshine**, *v.tr.irr.* (j-n, etwas) in den Schatten stellen. ◆**ˈoutside**. I. *s.* Außenseite *f.* II. *adj.* äußere(r,s); Außen-; *Fb:* **o. right**, Rechtsaußen *m.* III. *adv.* *(viewed from inside)* draußen. IV. *prep.* außerhalb + *gen.* ◆**outˈsider**, *s.* Außenseiter *m.* ◆**ˈoutskirts**, *s.pl.* Rand *m*; *(of town)* Stadtrand *m.* ◆**outˈstanding**, *adj.* 1. *(excellent)* hervorragend. 2. *(not paid)* ausstehend; **o. debts**, Außenstände *mpl*; (b) *(of work etc.)* unerledigt. ◆**outˈstay**, *v.tr.* **to o. one's welcome**, länger als erwünscht bleiben. ◆**outˈstretched**, *adj.* ausgestreckt. ◆**outˈvote**, *v.tr.* (j-n) überstimmen. ◆**ˈoutward**. I. *adj.* (a) Hin-; **o. journey**, Hinreise *f*; (b) *(external)* äußerlich; *(attrib. only)* äußere(r, s). II. *adv.* nach außen, **-ly**, *adv.* *(apparently)* allem Anschein nach. ◆**ˈoutwards**, *adv.* nach außen. ◆**outˈwit**, *v.tr.* (j-n) überlisten.

**oval** [ˈəuv(ə)l]. I. *adj.* oval. II. *s.* Oval *n.*

**ovary** [ˈəuvəri], *s.* Eierstock *m.*

**ovation** [əuˈveiʃ(ə)n], *s.* Ovation *f.*

**oven** [ˈʌv(ə)n], *s.* 1. *(baker's etc.)* Backofen *m*; *(of cooker)* Backrohr *n.* 2. *(kiln)* Ofen *m.* ◆**ˈovenware**, *s.* feuerfestes Geschirr *n.*

**over** [ˈəuvər]. I. *prep.* (a) über + *dat/ (motion) + acc*; *(beyond)* **o. the frontier**, über die Grenze; **the house o. the road**, das Haus gegenüber; (b) *(more than)* über + *acc*; *(during)* **o. the weekend**, übers Wochenende; (c) *(about)* **to worry o. sth.**, sich wegen etwas *gen* Sorgen machen. II. *adv.* 1. **all o.**, (i) *(of pers.)* am ganzen Körper; (ii) (*of thing*) an der ganzen Oberfläche; **all o. again,** wieder von vorne; **o. and o. again,** immer wieder. **2.** (*a*) (*away*) hinüber; **to cross o.,** die Straße überqueren; (*b*) **o. there,** (da) drüben; (*c*) (*towards speaker*) herüber; *F:* **come o. to our place,** komm rüber zu uns. **3.** (*more*) **children of 12 and o.,** Kinder über 12 Jahre. **4.** (*past*) vorbei; (*at an end*) zu Ende; **it's all o. with me,** mit mir ist es aus. ◆**over'all. I.** [ˈəuvərˈɔːl] *adj.* gesamt; Gesamt-. **II.** [ˈəuvərɔːl] *s.* Kittelschürze *f.* ◆**over'bearing,** *adj.* an o. manner, eine herrische Art. ◆**'overboard,** *adv.* über Bord. ◆**over'burden,** *v.tr.* überlasten. ◆**over'cast,** *adj.* (*of sky*) bedeckt. ◆**over'charge,** *v.tr. & i.* **to o.** (s.o.), (j-m) zu viel berechnen. ◆**'overcoat,** *s.* Mantel *m.* ◆**over'come. I.** *v.tr.irr.* überwinden. **II.** *adj.* **to be o. with/by sth.,** von etwas *dat* übermannt werden. ◆**over'crowded,** *adj.* überfüllt. ◆**over'crowding,** *s.* Überfüllen *n.* ◆**over'do,** *v.tr.irr.* (etwas) zu weit treiben; (*exaggerate*) übertreiben. ◆**'overdose,** *s.* Überdosis *f.* ◆**'overdraft,** *s.* **I have an o.,** ich habe mein Konto überzogen. ◆**over'draw,** *v.tr.irr.* (das Konto) überziehen. ◆**'overdrive,** *s. Aut:* Schongang *m.* ◆**over'due,** *adj.* überfällig. ◆**over'eat,** *v.i.irr.* (*of pers.*) sich übersessen. ◆**over'estimate. I.** *s.* Überschätzung *f.* **II.** *v.tr.* (etwas) überschätzen. ◆**overflow. I.** [ˈəuvəfləu] *s.* **1.** (*of liquid etc.*) Überlaufen *n.* **2.** (*pipe*) Überlauf *m.* **II.** [ˌəuvəˈfləu] *v.* **1.** *v.tr.* (*of river*) **to o. its banks,** über die Ufer treten. **2.** *v.i.* (*of water etc.*) überfließen; (*of cup etc.*) überlaufen. ◆**over'grown,** *adj.* überwuchert. ◆**overhaul. I.** [ˈəuvəhɔːl] *s.* Überholung *f* (einer Maschine usw.). **II.** [ˌəuvəˈhɔːl] *v.tr.* (eine Maschine usw.) überholen. ◆**over-'head,** *adv.* oben. ◆**over'hear,** *v.tr.irr.* (eine Konversation usw.) zufällig mit anhören. ◆**over'heat,** *v.* **1.** *v.tr.* überhitzen. **2.** *v.i.* (*of bearing etc.*) heißlaufen. ◆**'over'land,** *adv.* auf dem Landweg. ◆**overlap** [ˈəuvəˈlæp], *v.tr. & i.* **to o.** (one another), sich überschneiden. ◆**overload. I.** [ˌəuvəˈləud] *v.tr.* (*a*) überladen; (*b*) (einen Motor usw., *El:* das Netz) überlasten. **II.** [ˈəuvələud] *s.* Überlastung *f.* ◆**over'look,** *v.tr.* (*a*) (das Meer usw.) überblicken; (*b*) (j-n, eine Tatsache) übersehen; **we'll o. it,** wir werden darüber hinwegsehen. ◆**over'night. I.** *adv.* über Nacht; **to stay o.,** übernachten. **II.** *adj.* **o. stay/stop,** Übernachtung *f* (at, in + *dat*). ◆**'overpass,** *s.* Überführung *f.* ◆**over'power,** *v.tr.* überwältigen. ◆**over'powering,** *adj.* überwältigend. ◆**over'rate,** *v.tr.* (etwas) überbewerten; (j-n) überschätzen. ◆**'overrider,** *s. Aut:*

Stoßstangenhorn *n.* ◆**over'rule,** *v.tr.* (*a*) (j-n) überstimmen; (*b*) (einen Einwand) zurückweisen; *Jur:* (ein Urteil) verwerfen. ◆**over'run,** *v.tr.* (*a*) *Mil:* (über etwas) herfallen; (*b*) **the house is o. with mice,** in dem Haus wimmelt es von Mäusen; (*c*) (die Zeit, die Grenzen) überschreiten. ◆**over'seas. I.** *adv.* nach Übersee; **to go o.,** ins Ausland fahren. **II.** *adj.* Übersee-; **o. trade,** Überseehandel *m.* ◆**over'shadow,** *v.tr.* überschatten. ◆**'over'shoot,** *v.tr.irr.* **to o. a turning,** an einer Abzweigung (versehentlich) vorbeifahren. ◆**over'sleep,** *v.i.irr.* verschlafen. ◆**over'steer,** *s.* Übersteuerung *f.* ◆**'over'step,** *v.tr.* (die Grenzen, seine Befugnisse) überschreiten. ◆**over'take,** *v.tr.irr.* (*a*) überholen; (*b*) *Lit:* (*of accident*) (j-n) ereilen. ◆**'over'taking,** *s.* Überholen *n;* **no o.,** Überholverbot *n.* ◆**over'tax,** *v.tr.* (*a*) *Fin:* (j-n) übersteuern; (*b*) (j-n) überbeanspruchen. ◆**over'throw** *v.tr.irr.* (eine Regierung usw.) stürzen; (einen Plan) zunichte machen. ◆**'overtime. I.** *s. Ind:* Überstunden *fpl.* **II.** *adv.* **to work o.,** Überstunden machen. ◆**over'whelm,** *v.tr.* (*a*) (den Feind, j-n) überwältigen; **to be overwhelmed with work,** mit Arbeit überhäuft sein. ◆**over'whelming,** *adj.* (*of majority etc.*) überwältigend. ◆**'over'work. I.** *s.* Überlastung *f.* **II.** *v.* **1.** *v.tr.* (j-n) mit Arbeit überlasten. **2.** *v.i.* (*of pers.*) sich überarbeiten.

**overture** [ˈəuvətjuər], *s.* **1.** *Mus:* Ouvertüre *f.* **2.** *usu. pl.* **to make overtures to s.o.,** bei j-m Annäherungsversuche machen.

**owe** [əu], *v.tr.* (*a*) **to o. s.o. money/o. money to s.o.,** j-m Geld schulden/schuldig sein; (*b*) *v.i.* **I still o. you for the petrol,** ich bin Ihnen noch das Benzin schuldig; (*c*) (j-m sein Leben, seinen Erfolg usw.) verdanken; **I o. you an explanation,** ich bin Ihnen eine Erklärung schuldig. ◆**'owing,** *prep.* **o. to,** wegen + *gen;* **o. to the rain,** wegen des Regens.

**owl** [aul], *s.* Eule *f.*

**own** [əun]. **I.** *v.tr.* (etwas) besitzen. **II.** *adj.* eigen; **the house is my o.,** das Haus gehört mir. **III.** *s.* (*a*) **he has a copy of his o.,** er hat ein eigenes Exemplar; *F:* **to get one's o. back,** sich revanchieren; (*b*) **to be (all) on one's o.,** (ganz) allein sein. ◆**'owner,** *s.* Besitzer(in) *m(f);* Eigentümer(in) *m(f)* (eines Hauses, einer Firma); **parking at o.'s risk,** Parken auf eigene Gefahr.

**ox,** *pl.* **oxen** [ɔks, ˈɔks(ə)n], *s.* Ochse *m; Cu:* **o. tongue,** Ochsenzunge *f* ◆**'oxtail,** *s.* Ochsenschwanz *m.*

**oxide** [ˈɔksaid], *s.* Oxyd *m.* ◆**oxidize** [ˈɔksidaiz], *v.tr. & i.* oxydieren.

**oxygen** ['ɔksidʒən], s. Sauerstoff m.
**oyster** ['ɔistər], s. Auster f; Orn: o.

**catcher,** Austernfischer m.
**ozone** ['əuzəun], s. Ozon n.

# P

**P, p** [pi:], s. (der Buchstabe) P, p n.
**pace** [peis]. **I.** s. 1. (step) Schritt m. 2.
(speed) Tempo n; **at a walking p.,** im
Schrittempo; Sp: etc: **to set the p.,** das
Tempo angeben. **II.** v.i. **to p. up and
down,** auf und ab schreiten. ◆'**pacemaker,** s. Med: & Sp: Schrittmacher m.
**pacific** [pə'sifik], s. **the P. (Ocean),** der
Pazifik, der Stille Ozean. ◆'**pacifism,**
s. Pazifismus m. ◆'**pacifist,** s. Pazifi-
st(in) m(f). ◆**pacify** ['pæsifai], v.tr. (j-n)
beruhigen; (Zorn, Ärger) beschwichtigen.
**pack** [pæk]. **I.** v.tr. (a) (Kleider usw.) einpacken; Ind: (Waren) verpacken; **packed
lunch,** Lunchpaket n; **to p. one's
suitcase/abs.** to p., (den Koffer) packen;
(b) (fill) **to p. sth. with sth.,** etwas mit
etwas dat vollstopfen; (c) (squeeze) stopfen; **the hall was packed,** der Saal war
gerammelt voll; (d) P: **I'm packing it in,**
ich schmeiße den Kram/die Arbeit hin.
**II.** s. 1. Pack m; (on back) Tornister m;
Mil: Gepäck n. 2. (of people) Pack n,
Bande f; (of hounds, wolves etc.) Meute f;
**a p. of cards,** ein Kartenspiel n; Fig: **to
tell s.o. a p. of lies,** j-m die Hucke voll
lügen. ◆'**package. I.** s. (parcel, also
Pol: etc.) Paket n; Com: Packung f; **p.
tour,** Pauschalreise f. **II.** v.tr. Com:
(Waren) verpacken. ◆'**packaging,** s.
(material) Verpackung f. ◆'**packet,** s.
Päckchen n; **a p. of cigarettes,** ein Päckchen Zigaretten. ◆'**packing,** s. 1. (a)
(action) Verpacken n; (b) (wrappings) Verpackung f; **p. case,** Kiste f.
**pact** [pækt], s. Pol: Mil: etc: Pakt m.
**pad** [pæd]. **I.** s. 1. Cl: etc: Polster n. 2.
**writing p.,** Schreibblock m. **II.** v.tr. (a)
(einen Stuhl usw.) polstern; (eine Jacke
in den Schultern) auspolstern; (b) Fig:
(eine Rede usw.) mit Füllwörtern usw.
strecken. ◆'**padding,** s. (a) Polsterung
f; Cl: Wattierung f; (b) F: (in book etc.)
Füllsel n.
**paddle**[1] ['pædl]. **I.** s. 1. Paddel n. 2. (on
wheel) Schaufel f; **p. steamer,** Raddamp-
fer m. **II.** v.tr. & i. (ein Kanu) paddeln.
**paddle**[2], v.i. planschen; **paddling pool,**
Planschbecken n.
**paddock** ['pædək], s. (a) (field) Koppel f;
(b) Rac: Führring m.
**paddy** ['pædi], s. **p. field,** Reisfeld n.
**padlock** ['pædlɔk], s. Vorhängeschloß n.
**paediatrician** [pi:diə'triʃ(ə)n], s. Kinde-
rärztin f.
**pagan** ['peigən]. **I.** s. Heide m, Heidin f.
**II.** adj heidnisch.
**page**[1] [peidʒ], s. **p.-boy,** Hotelpage m.
**page**[2], s. Seite f; **on p. 6,** auf Seite 6; **p.
by p.,** Seite für Seite.

**pageant** ['pædʒənt], s. Festzug m.
**paid** [peid], adj. bezahlt.
**pail** [peil], s. Eimer m.
**pain** [pein]. s. 1. (physical, also Fig:)
Schmerz m; (mental) Qual f; **to be in
great p.,** starke Schmerzen haben; F:
**he's a p. in the neck,** er ist nicht auszu-
halten. 2. pl. Mühe f; **to take pains,** sich
dat Mühe geben (over sth., bei etwas
dat). ◆'**painful,** adj. (of wound, treatment etc.) schmerzhaft; (of memories etc.)
schmerzlich. ◆'**painkiller,** s. schmerz-
stillendes Mittel n. ◆'**painless,** adj.
schmerzlos. ◆'**painstaking,** adj. **he is
very p.,** er scheut keine Mühe; **p. work,**
mühsame Kleinarbeit.
**paint** [peint]. **I.** s. (a) Farbe f; **coat of p.,**
Anstrich m; (notice) **wet p.** frisch gestrichen! **II.** v. 1. v.tr. (ein Zimmer usw.)
streichen; (ein Bild) malen; **to p.** (of artist etc.) malen. ◆'**paintbrush,** s. Farb-
pinsel m. ◆'**painter,** s. 1. (artist) Ma-
ler(in) m(f). 2. (house) p., Anstreicher m.
◆'**painting,** s. 1. (art) Malerei f. 2. (picture) Gemälde n. ◆'**paintwork,** s. Aut:
Lack m.
**pair** [pɛər], s. Paar n.
**Pakistan** [pɑːkis'tɑːn, pæk-]. Pr. n. Pakistan n. ◆**Pakis'tani. I.** adj. pakista-
nisch. **II.** s. Pakistaner(in) m(f).
**pal** [pæl], s. F: (guter) Freund m.
**palace** ['pælis], s. Schloß n; (royal) Kö-
nigsschloß n.
**palate** ['pælit], s. Anat: Gaumen m.
◆'**palatable** [-ətəbl], adj. wohl-
schmeckend.
**palatial** [pə'leiʃ(ə)l], adj. prunkvoll.
**pale** [peil], adj. (a) (of face etc.) blaß; (of
moonlight etc.) fahl; (b) (of colour) hell.
**Palestine** ['pælistain]. Pr. n. Palästina n.
◆**Pales'tinian. I.** adj. palästinensisch.
**II.** s. Palästinenser(in) m(f).
**palings** ['peilinz], s.pl. Lattenzaun m.
**pall** [pɔːl]. s. p. bearer, Sargträger m.
**pallet** ['pælit], s. Ind: & Paint: Palette f.
**palliative** ['pæliətiv], s. schmerzlindern-
des Mittel n.
**pallid** ['pælid], adj. (of face, light etc.)
blaß; (of sky) fahl.
**pallor** ['pælər], s. Blässe f.
**palm**[1] [pɑːm], s. 1. p. (tree), Palme f. 2.
Ecc: **P. Sunday,** Palmsonntag m.
**palm**[2], s. Handfläche f. ◆'**palmistry,** s.
Handlesekunst f.
**palpable** ['pælpəbl], adj. (of result etc.)
greifbar; (of difference, relief etc.) fühlbar;
(of error) eindeutig.
**palpitate** ['pælpiteit], v.i. (a) (of heart)
heftig klopfen; wild schlagen.
◆**palpi'tation,** s. Herzklopfen n.

**paltry** ['pɔːltri], *adj.* dürftig; *(of excuse)* fadenscheinig.

**pamper** ['pæmpər], *v.tr.* verhätscheln.

**pamphlet** ['pæmflit], *s.* Broschüre *f; esp. Pol:* Flugblatt *n.*

**pan** [pæn], *s. Cu:* Kochtopf *m;* **frying p.,** Bratpfanne *f.* ◆**'pancake,** *s.* Pfannkuchen *m;* **P. Day,** Faschingsdienstag *m.*

**panacea** [pænə'siːə], *s.* Allheilmittel *n.*

**panache** [pə'næʃ], *s.* Schwung *m; (elegance)* Eleganz *f.*

**pancreas** ['pænkriəs], *s.* Bauchspeicheldrüse *f.*

**panda** ['pændə], *s. Z:* Panda *m; F:* **p. car,** Streifenwagen *m.*

**pander** ['pændər], *v.i.* frönen (**to sth.,** etwas *dat*).

**pane** [pein], *s.* Fensterscheibe *f.*

**panel** ['pæn(ə)l]. **I.** *s.* **1.** *(wood)* Holztafel *f; (glass)* Glasscheibe *f; (in door)* Türfüllung *f; (metal)* Verkleidungsblech *n.* **2.** *(committee)* Ausschuß *m; TV: Rad: etc:* Team *n; (in quiz)* Rateteam *n.* **II.** *v.tr.* (eine Wand usw.) täfeln. ◆**'panelling,** *s.* Täfelung *f.*

**pang** [pæŋ], *s.* **pangs of conscience,** Gewissensbisse.

**panic** ['pænik]. **I.** *s.* Panik *f.* **II.** *v.i.* von Panik erfaßt werden. ◆**'panicky,** *adj. F: (of pers.)* in Panikstimmung.

**panorama** [pænə'rɑːmə], *s.* Panorama *n.* ◆**panoramic** [-'ræmik], *adj.* **p. view,** Rundblick *m.*

**pansy** ['pænzi], *s. Bot:* Stiefmütterchen *n.*

**pant** [pænt], *v.i.* keuchen.

**panther** ['pænθər], *s.* Panther *m.*

**panties** ['pæntiz], *s. pl.* Damenslip *m.*

**pantomime** ['pæntəmaim], *s. Th:* Märchenspiel *n* (im Varietéstil).

**pantry** ['pæntri], *s.* Speisekammer *f.*

**pants** [pænts], *s. pl.* (a) **(pair of) p.,** Unterhose *f; (b) N.Am:* Hose *f.*

**papal** ['peipəl], *adj.* päpstlich.

**paper** ['peipər]. **I.** *s.* **1.** Papier *n;* **piece of p.,** Zettel *m; (large)* Bogen *m;* **p. clip,** Büroklammer *f;* **p. mill,** Papierfabrik *f;* **p. weight,** Briefbeschwerer *m.* **2.** *(a) (esp. pl.) (documents)* Dokumente *npl; (records)* Akten *fpl; (proving identity etc.)* Papiere *npl.* **3.** *(newspaper)* Zeitung *f.* **4.** **(wall)p.,** Tapete *f.* **II.** *v.tr.* (ein Zimmer usw.) tapezieren. ◆**'paperback,** *s.* Taschenbuch *n.* ◆**'paperwork,** *s.* Schreibarbeit *f; F:* Papierkrieg *m.*

**par** [pɑːr], *s.* **1.** Gleichheit *f;* (a) **to be on a p. with s.o.,** j-m gleichstehen; *(b) F:* **to feel below p.,** nicht ganz auf der Höhe sein. **2.** *(Golf)* Par *n.*

**parable** ['pærəbl], *s.* Gleichnis *n.*

**parachute** ['pærəʃuːt]. **I.** *s.* Fallschirm *m.* **II.** *v.i.* mit dem Fallschirm abspringen.

**parade** [pə'reid]. **I.** *s. Mil: etc: (static)* Parade *f; (marching)* Aufmarsch *m; (procession)* Festzug *m.* **II.** *v.i. Mil:* vorbeimarschieren.

**paradise** ['pærədais], *s.* Paradies *n.*

**paradox** ['pærədɔks], *s.* Paradox *n.*

◆**para'doxical,** *adj.* paradox; **-ally,** *adv.* paradoxerweise.

**paraffin** ['pærəfin], *s.* Paraffin *n.*

**paragon** ['pærəgən], *s.* Muster *n.* **p. of virtue,** Ausbund *m* der Tugend.

**paragraph** ['pærəgrɑːf], *s.* Absatz *m.*

**parallel** ['pærəlel]. **I.** *adj.* parallel (**with/to, zu + *dat*).** **II.** *s. (comparison)* Parallele *f,* Vergleich *m.*

**paralyse** ['pærəlaiz], *v.tr.* lähmen. ◆**pa'ralysis,** *s.* Lähmung *f.*

**paramount** ['pærəmaunt], *adj.* höchste(r,s); oberste(r,s).

**parapet** ['pærəpit], *s.* Brüstung *f; (railing)* Geländer *n.*

**paraphernalia** [pærəfə'neiliə], *s.pl. F:* Kram *m; (personal)* Siebensachen *fpl.*

**paraphrase** ['pærəfreiz]. **I.** *s.* Paraphrase *f,* Umschreibung *f.* **II.** *v.tr.* umschreiben.

**parasite** ['pærəsait], *s.* Parasit *m.*

**paratrooper** ['pærətruːpər], *s.* Fallschirmjäger *m.* ◆**'paratroops,** *s.pl. Mil:* Fallschirmtruppen *fpl.*

**parcel** ['pɑːs(ə)l], *s.* Paket *n.*

**parch** [pɑːtʃ], *v.tr. (of sun, wind)* (etwas) austrocknen; *F:* **I'm parched!** ich komme um vor Durst!

**parchment** ['pɑːtʃmənt], *s.* Pergament *n.*

**pardon** ['pɑːd(ə)n]. **I.** *s. (a)* **to beg s.o.'s p.,** j-n um Verzeihung bitten; **I beg your p.!** Entschuldigung! *(b) Jur:* **free p.,** Begnadigung *f.* **II.** *v.tr. (a)* (j-m) vergeben, verzeihen; *(b) Jur:* (j-n) begnadigen.

**parent** ['pɛərənt], *s.* Elternteil *m; pl.* **parents,** Eltern *pl.*

**parenthesis,** *pl.* **-eses** [pə'renθəsis, -əsiːz], *s.* Parenthese *f;* **in parentheses,** in Klammern.

**Paris** ['pæris]. *Pr. n.* Paris *n.* ◆**Parisian** [pə'riziən]. **I.** *adj.* Pariser. **II.** *s.* Pariser(in) *m(f).*

**parish** ['pæriʃ], *s. Ecc:* Gemeinde *f.*

**parity** ['pæriti], *s. Com: Fin:* Parität *f.*

**park** [pɑːk]. **I.** *s.* Park *m.* **II.** *v.tr.* (ein Auto usw.) parken. ◆**'parking,** *s.* Parken *n;* **no p.,** Parken verboten; **p. space,** Parklücke *f;* **p. meter,** Parkuhr *f;* **p. ticket,** Strafzettel *m.*

**parliament** ['pɑːləmənt], *s.* Parlament *n.* ◆**parlia'mentary,** *adj.* parlamentarisch.

**parlour** ['pɑːlər], *s.* **1. beauty p.,** Schönheitssalon *m.* **2.** *A: (best room)* gute Stube *f.*

**parochial** [pə'rəukiəl], *adj.* **1.** *Ecc:* parochial. **2.** *Pej:* provinzlerisch.

**parody** ['pærədi]. **I.** *s.* Parodie *f* (**on/of** auf + *acc*). **II.** *v.tr.* parodieren.

**parole** [pə'rəul], *s.* **on p.,** auf Ehrenwort.

**parquet** ['pɑːkei], *s.* Parkett *n.*

**parrot** ['pærət], *s.* Papagei *m.*

**parsimonious** [pɑːsi'məuniəs], *adj.* sparsam; *(miserly)* knauserig.

**parsley** ['pɑːsli], *s.* Petersilie *f.*

**parsnip** ['pɑːsnip], *s.* Pastinake *f.*

**parson** ['pɑːs(ə)n], *s.* Gemeindepfarrer *m.* ◆**'parsonage,** *s.* Pfarrhaus *n.*

**part** [pɑːt]. **I.** *s.* **1.** *(a)* Teil *m & n;* **in p.,**

zum Teil/teilweise; *Ind:* spare parts, Ersatzteile *npl;* (b) *Gram:* **p. of speech,** Wortart *f;* (c) *(in newspaper etc.)* Fortsetzung *f* (eines Romans usw.); *(volume)* Band *m;* (d) **p.-time work,** Teilzeitarbeit *f;* **to work p.-time,** halbtags arbeiten. 2. (a) **to take p. in sth.,** an etwas *dat* teilnehmen; (b) *Th:* Rolle *f;* (c) *Mus:* Partie *f.* 3. **on the p. of,** seitens + *gen.* **II.** *adv.* teilweise. **III.** *v.* 1. *v.tr. (separate)* (etwas) trennen; **to p. one's hair,** sich *dat* einen Scheitel ziehen. 2. *v.i* sich trennen. ◆**'parting. I.** *s.* (a) Trennung *f;* (b) *(farewell)* Abschied *m.* 2. *(in the hair)* Scheitel *m.*

**partial** ['pɑ:ʃ(ə)l], *adj.* **1.** (a) *(biased)* voreingenommen; *Jur:* befangen; (b) **to be p. to sth.,** eine Schwäche für etwas *acc* haben. 2. Teil–; teilweise; **p. acceptance,** Teilakzept *n.*

**participate** [pɑ:'tisipeit], *v.i.* **to p. in sth.,** an etwas *dat* teilnehmen. ◆**partici'pation,** *s.* Teilnahme *f* (**in,** an + *dat*).

**participle** ['pɑ:tisipl], *s. Gram:* Partizip *n.*

**particle** ['pɑ:tikl], *s.* **1.** *Gram:* Partikel *f.* 2. *Ph: etc:* Teilchen *n.*

**particular** [pə'tikjulər]. **I.** *adj.* **1.** *(special)* besondere(r,s); **in p.,** besonders. 2. *(fussy)* eigen; **-ly,** *adv.* besonders. **II.** *s. esp. pl.* **particulars,** Einzelheiten *fpl.*

**partisan** [pɑ:ti'zæn]. *s.* Partisan *m.*

**partition** [pɑ:'tiʃ(ə)n]. **I.** *s.* Trennwand *f.* **II.** *v.tr.* (a) (ein Feld, Land usw.) teilen; (b) *(ein Zimmer)* aufteilen.

**partly** ['pɑ:tli], *adv.* zum Teil, teilweise.

**partner** ['pɑ:tnər], *s.* **1.** Partner(in) *m(f).* 2. *Com:* Teilhaber(in) *m(f).* ◆**'partnership,** *s.* **1.** Partnerschaft *f;* *(combination)* Kombination *f.* 2. *Com:* Assoziation *f.*

**partridge** ['pɑ:tridʒ], *s.* Rebhuhn *n.*

**party** ['pɑ:ti], *s.* **1.** *Pol:* Partei *f.* 2. Party *f;* **birthday p.,** Geburtstagsfeier *f.* 3. *(group of people)* Gesellschaft *f;* Gruppe *f;* **rescue p.,** Rettungsmannschaft *f.* 4. **a third p.,** ein Dritter.

**pass** [pɑ:s]. **I.** *v.* **1.** *v.i.* (a) *(of pers.)* vorbeigehen; *(in vehicle)* vorbeifahren; **to let s.o. p.,** j-n vorbeilassen; **if you're passing this way,** falls Sie hier vorbeikommen; **to let a remark p.,** eine Bemerkung durchgehen lassen; (b) *(of time)* **to p. (by),** vergehen; (c) *(in examination, test)* bestehen. 2. *v.tr.* (a) **to p. s.o., sth.,** an j-m, etwas *dat* vorbeigehen/*(in vehicle)* vorbeifahren; (b) *(exceed)* überschreiten; (c) *Sch:* (eine Prüfung) bestehen; *Parl:* **to p. a bill,** ein Gesetz verabschieden; (d) *(hand)* (j-m etwas) reichen; *Fb:* **to p. the ball to s.o.,** j-m den Ball zuspielen; *Med:* **to p. water,** Wasser lassen; (e) **to p. the time,** die Zeit verbringen. **II.** *s.* **1.** *(mountain)* **p.,** (Gebirgs)paß *m.* 2. *(document)* *Adm:* Passierschein *m.* 3. *Fb: etc:* Vorlage *f.* ◆**'passable,** *adj.* (a) passabel; (b) *(of road)* passierbar.

◆**passage** ['pæsidʒ], *s.* **1.** *(in a building)* Flur *m,* Korridor *m;* *(between buildings etc.)* Durchgang *m.* 2. *(in music, book etc.)* Stelle *f.* ◆**passenger** ['pæsindʒər], *s.* Passagier *m.* ◆**passer-'by,** *(pl* passers-by), *s.* Passant *m.* ◆**'passing. I.** *adj. (of remark etc.)* beiläufig; **a p. fancy,** eine (vorübergehende) Laune. **II.** *s. (death)* Hinscheiden *n.* ◆**'pass 'off,** *v.* **1.** *v.i.* ablaufen. 2. *v.tr.* **to p. oneself o. as an actor,** sich als Schauspieler ausgeben. ◆**'pass 'on,** *v.* **1.** *v.tr.* (Informationen, ein Buch usw.) weitergeben. 2. *v.i. Fig: (die)* hinscheiden. ◆**'pass 'out,** *v.i.* ohnmächtig werden. ◆**'pass 'over,** *v.i. (end)* sich legen. ◆**'Passover,** *s. Ecc:* Passah *m.* ◆**'passport,** *s.* Paß *m.* ◆**'pass 'round,** *v.tr.* **to p. r. the wine etc.,** die Weinflasche usw. herumreichen. ◆**'password,** *s. Mil: etc:* Kennwort *n.*

**passion** ['pæʃ(ə)n], *s.* Leidenschaft *f.* ◆**'passionate,** *adj.* leidenschaftlich.

**passive** ['pæsiv]. **I.** *adj.* passiv. **II.** *s. Gram:* Passiv *n.*

**past¹** [pɑ:st]. **I.** *adj.* (a) vergangen; **in times p.,** in früheren Zeiten; (b) *Gram:* **p. participle,** Partizip Perfekt *n.* **II.** *s.* Vergangenheit *f;* **in the p.,** früher.

**past².** **I.** *prep.* (a) an ... *dat* vorbei; **to walk p. s.o.,** an j-m vorbeigehen; (b) **a quarter p. four,** Viertel nach vier; *F:* **to be p. it,** zu alt dafür sein. **II.** *adv.* **to walk/go p.,** vorbeigehen.

**pasta** ['pæstə], *s.* Teigwaren *fpl.*

**paste** [peist]. **I.** *s. (for sticking paper etc.)* Kleister *m.* **II.** *v.tr.* **to p. sth. in/on sth.,** etwas in/auf etwas *acc* festkleben.

**pastel** ['pæst(ə)l], **p. shades,** Pastelltöne *mpl.*

**pasteurize** ['pɑ:stjəraiz], *v.tr.* (Milch) pasteurisieren.

**pastime** ['pɑ:staim], *s.* Zeitvertreib *m.*

**pastor** ['pɑ:stər], *s. Ecc:* Pastor *m.* ◆**'pastoral,** *adj. Art:* **p. scene,** ländliche Szene.

**pastry** ['peistri], *s.* **1.** *(dough)* Teig *m.* 2. *(cake)* Gebäck *n.*

**pasture** ['pɑ:stʃər], *s.* Weide *f.*

**pasty¹** ['peisti], *F:* **to look p.,** käseweiß sein.

**pasty²** ['pæsti], *s. Cu:* Pastete *f.*

**pat** [pæt]. **I.** *s.* **1.** Klaps *m.* 2. **p. of butter,** Stückchen *n* Butter. **II.** *v.tr.* (j-n, ein Tier) tätscheln. **III.** *adv.* **to have an answer off p.,** eine Antwort parat haben.

**patch** [pætʃ]. **I.** *s.* **1.** *(for repair)* Flicken *m.* 2. *(small area)* (a) Fleck *m;* (b) *(land)* (kleines) Stück *n.* 3. *(on eye)* Augenklappe *f.* **II.** *v.tr.* (ein Kleid, einen Reifen usw.) flicken; *F:* **to p. it up with s.o.,** sich wieder aussöhnen (mit j-m). ◆**'patchy,** *adj.* (a) fleckig; **p. fog,** strichweise Nebel; (b) *Fig: (uneven)* ungleichmäßig; *(of knowledge etc.)* lückenhaft.

**pâté** ['pæteij], *s.* Pastete *f.*

**patent** ['pætənt, 'peitənt]. **I.** *adj.* **1.** p.

**medicine,** Markenpräparat *n;* **p. leather,** Lackleder *n.* 2. *(obvious)* offensichtlich; **-ly,** *adv.* offensichtlich. **II.** *s.* Patent *n;* **p. pending,** Patent angemeldet. **III.** *v.tr.* (eine Erfindung usw.) patentieren.

**paternal** [pə'tə:nl], *adj.* väterlich. ◆**pa'ternity,** *s.* Vaterschaft *f.*

**path,** *pl.* [pɑːθ], *s.* **1.** Pfad *m; esp. Fig:* Weg *m.* 2. Bahn *f* (der Sonne, eines Planeten usw.).

**pathetic** [pə'θetik], *adj.* **1.** mitleiderregend; **a p. sight,** ein rührender Anblick. 2. *F: Pej:* **p. effort,** ein kläglicher Versuch.

**pathology** [pə'θɔlədʒi], *s.* Pathologie *f.* ◆**pa'thologist,** *s.* Pathologe *m.*

**pathos** ['peiθɔs], *s.* **the p. of the situation,** das Rührende an der Situation.

**patience** ['peiʃ(ə)ns], *s.* **1.** Geduld *f.* 2. *(game)* Patience *f.* ◆**'patient. I.** *adj.* geduldig; **to be p.,** Geduld haben. **II.** *s. Med:* Patient(in) *m(f).*

**patriot** ['peitriət, 'pæ-], *s.* Patriot(in) *m(f).* ◆**patri'otic,** *adj.* patriotisch. ◆**'patriotism,** *s.* Patriotismus *m.*

**patrol** [pə'trəul]. **I.** *s. (a) Mil: etc:* Patrouille *f; (b) (police)* Streife *f;* **p. car,** Streifenwagen *m.* **II.** *v.* **1.** *v.i.* auf Patrouille/*(police)* Streife gehen. **2.** *v.tr.* patrouillieren.

**patron** ['peitrən], *s.* **1.** *(a)* Förderer *m* (der Künste usw.); *(b)* Schirmherr *m* (einer Wohltätigkeitsveranstaltung usw.); *(c) Ecc:* **p. saint,** Schutzheilige(r) *f(m).* 2. *Com: Th: Cin:* Besucher *m* (eines Kinos usw.); Kunde *m* (eines Geschäfts). ◆**patronage** ['pætrənidʒ], *s.* Förderung *f.* ◆**patronize** ['pæ-], *v.tr.* **to p. s.o.,** j-n herablassend behandeln. ◆**'patronizing,** *adj.* **p. tone,** herablassender Ton.

**patter** ['pætər]. **I.** *v.i. (of feet)* trappeln; *(of rain, hail etc.)* prasseln. **II.** *s.* Getrappel *n; (hesitate)* zögern.

**pattern** ['pætən], *s.* Muster *n.*

**paunch** [pɔ:n(t)ʃ], *s.* Wanst *m.*

**pause** [pɔːz]. **I.** *s.* Pause *f.* **II.** *v.i.* eine Pause machen; *(in conversation)* innehalten; *(hesitate)* zögern.

**pave** [peiv], *v.tr.* (eine Straße) pflastern; *Fig:* **to p. the way for s.o., sth.,** j-m, etwas *dat* den Weg bahnen. ◆**'pavement,** *s.* Bürgersteig *m.* ◆**'paving,** *s.* Pflaster *n;* **p. stone,** Pflasterstein *m.*

**pavilion** [pə'viljən], *s. Sp:* Klubhaus *n.*

**paw** [pɔː]. **I.** *s. Z: (also F:=hand)* Pfote *f.* **II.** *v.tr. (a)* (of cat, dog etc.) mit den Pfoten stupsen; *(b) F: (of pers.)* betasten.

**pawn¹** [pɔːn], *v.tr.* (Wertsachen) verpfänden. ◆**'pawnbroker,** *s.* Pfandleiher *m.*

**pawn²,** *s. (in chess)* Bauer *m.*

**pay** [pei]. **I.** *v.irr.* **1.** *v.tr. (a)* bezahlen; (j-m eine Summe) zahlen; *(b)* **to p. attention to sth.,** etwas *dat* Aufmerksamkeit schenken; **p. attention!** aufpassen! **to p. s.o. the honour,** j-m die Ehre erweisen.

2. *v.i. (a) (of pers.)* zahlen, bezahlen; *(b) (of thing)* sich lohnen; **crime doesn't p.,** Verbrechen zahlt sich nicht aus. **II.** *s.* Lohn *m;* **p. packet,** Lohntüte *f.* ◆**'payable,** *adj.* zahlbar; **to become p.,** fällig werden. ◆**'pay 'back,** *v.tr.* zurückzahlen. ◆**'pay-day,** *s.* Zahltag *m.* ◆**pay'ee,** *s.* Zahlungsempfänger *m.* ◆**'pay 'for,** *v.tr.* (etwas) bezahlen; *F:* **you'll p. for this!** das wird dir teuer zu stehen kommen! ◆**'pay 'in,** *v.tr.* (einen Scheck usw.) einzahlen **(into an account,** auf ein Konto). ◆**'payload,** *s.* Nutzlast *f* (eines Flugzeugs, eines Schiffs usw.). ◆**'payment,** *s. (act, amount)* Zahlung *f; (of pers.)* Bezahlung *f.* ◆**'pay 'off,** *v.* **1.** *v.tr.* (Schulden usw.) abzahlen. **2.** *v.i.* **it'll p. off in the end,** am Ende macht sich das bezahlt. ◆**'pay 'out,** *v.tr.* (Geld) ausgeben. ◆**'payroll,** *s.* Gehaltsliste *f.* ◆**'payslip,** *s.* Lohnzettel *m.* ◆**'pay 'up,** *v.i.* zahlen.

**pea** [piː], *s.* Erbse *f.*

**peace** [piːs], *s.* **1.** Frieden *m; (of country etc.)* **at p.,** im Frieden **(with,** mit + *dat).* 2. *Jur:* **to keep the p.,** den (öffentlichen) Frieden aufrechterhalten. **3. p. and quiet,** Ruhe *f.* ◆**'peaceful,** *adj.* friedlich. ◆**'peacefulness,** *s.* Friedlichkeit *f.* ◆**'peacetime,** *s.* Friedenszeiten *fpl.*

**peach** [piːtʃ], *s.* Pfirsich *m.*

**peacock** ['piːkɔk], *s.* Pfau *m.*

**peak** [piːk]. *s.* **1.** Schirm *m* (einer Mütze). 2. *(a)* Gipfel *m* (eines Berges usw.); *Fig:* Höhepunkt *m; (b) attrib.* Höchst-; **p. hours,** Stoßzeit *f.*

**peal** [piːl]. **I.** *s.* **1.** **p. of bells,** Glockengeläut *n.* 2. **p. of laughter,** Lachsalve *f.*

**peanut** ['piːnʌt], *s.* Erdnuß *f.*

**pear** [pɛər], *s.* Birne *f.*

**pearl** [pɔːl], *s.* Perle *f.*

**peasant** ['pez(ə)nt], *s.* Bauer *m.*

**peat** [piːt], *s.* Torf *m.*

**pebble** ['pebl], *s.* Kieselstein *m.* ◆**'pebbly,** *adj.* kiesig.

**peck** [pek], *v.tr. (of bird etc.)* hacken **(at,** nach + *dat).* ◆**'peckish,** *adj. F:* **to feel (a bit) p.,** (ein bißchen) Appetit haben.

**peculiar** [pi'kjuːliər], *adj.* **1.** besondere(r,s). 2. *(odd)* eigenartig. ◆**peculi'arity,** *s.* **1.** Besonderheit *f.* 2. *(also* pe'culiarness) Eigenartigkeit *f.*

**pedal** ['pedl]. **I.** *s.* Pedal *n.* **II.** *v.i.* in die Pedale treten.

**pedantic** [pe'dæntik], *adj.* pedantisch.

**peddle** ['pedl], *v.* **1.** *v.i.* hausieren. 2. *v.tr. Pej:* **to p. drugs etc.,** mit Drogen usw. handeln. ◆**'peddler/'pedlar,** *s.* Hausierer *m.*

**pedestal** ['pedist(ə)l], *s.* Sockel *m; Fig:* **to put s.o. on a p.,** j-n aufs Podest stellen.

**pedestrian** [pi'destriən]. **I.** *adj.* prosaisch; *(unimaginative)* einfallslos. **II.** *s.* Fußgänger *m;* **p. precinct,** Fußgängerzone *f;* **p. crossing,** Fuß-gängerübergang *m.*

**pedigree** ['pedigriː], *s. (a)* Stammbaum *m; (b)* **p. dog,** Rassehund *m.*

**peel** [pi:l]. **I.** s. Schale f. **II.** v. **1.** v.tr. (eine Frucht, Kartoffeln usw.) schälen. **2.** v.i. (of paint etc.) abblättern; (of skin, nose etc.) sich schälen. ◆**'peeler,** s. **potato p.,** Kartoffelschäler m. ◆**peelings,** s.pl. Schalen fpl.

**peep** [pi:p]. **I.** s. (glance) verstohlener Blick m; F: **to get a p. at sth.,** etwas kurz zu Gesicht bekommen. **II.** v.i. **to p. at sth.,** etwas kurz angucken; **to p. out,** hervorgucken.

**peer** [piər], v.i. **to p. over the wall,** über die Mauer spähen.

**peerage** ['piərid3], s. Brit: (a) Peerswürde f; (b) Adelsstand m.

**peeved** [pi:vd], adj. verärgert.

**peewit** ['pi:wit], s. Kiebitz m.

**peg** [peg]. **I.** s. (a) (for tent etc.) Pflock m; (b) (hat, coat) p., Haken m; **clothes p.,** Wäscheklammer f; Cl: **off the p.,** von der Stange. **II.** v.tr. (etwas) anpflocken **(to, an + acc).**

**pejorative** [pi'd3ɔrətiv], adj. abwertend.

**pelican** ['pelikən], s. Pelikan m.

**pellet** ['pelit], s. **1.** Kügelchen n. **2.** (for gun) Schrotkugel f.

**pelt** [pelt]. **I.** v. **1.** v.tr. (j-n) bewerfen **(with stones,** mit Steinen). **2.** v.i. (of rain etc.) **to p. (down),** niederprasseln. **II.** s. (skin) Balg m.

**pelvis** ['pelvis], s. Becken n.

**pen¹** [pen], s. (for sheep etc.) Pferch m.

**pen²**, s. (for writing) Feder f; **p. friend,** Brieffreund(in) m(f).

**penal** ['pi:n(ə)l], adj. Straf-; **p. code,** Strafgesetzbuch n. ◆**'penalize,** v.tr. (punish) (j-n) bestrafen; Sp: Strafpunkte geben. ◆**penalty** ['pen(ə)lti], s. **1.** Strafe f; **to pay the p. (for sth.),** (für etwas acc) büßen (müssen). **2.** Fb: Elfmeter m.

**penance** ['penəns], s. Buße f; **to do p.,** Buße tun.

**pence** [pens], s.pl. Pence mpl.

**pencil** ['pens(i)l], s. Bleistift m.

**pending** ['pendiŋ], prep. bis auf + acc; **p. further instructions,** bis auf weiteres.

**pendulum** ['pendjuləm], s. Pendel n.

**penetrate** ['penitreit], v.tr. & i. (in etwas acc) eindringen; (permeate) (etwas) durchdringen. ◆**'penetrating,** adj. durchdringend; (of pers.) scharfsinnig.

**penguin** ['peŋgwin], s. Pinguin m.

**penicillin** [peni'silin], s. Penizillin n.

**peninsula** [pe'ninsjulə], s. Halbinsel f.

**penis** ['pi:nis], s. Penis m.

**penitence** ['penit(ə)ns], s. Reue f. ◆**'penitent,** adj. reuig.

**penknife** ['pennaif], s. Taschenmesser n.

**penny** ['peni], s. Penny m; Fig: **he hasn't a p. to his name,** er hat keinen Pfennig; **the penny's dropped,** der Groschen ist gefallen. ◆**'penniless,** adj. mittellos.

**pension** ['penʃ(ə)n]. **I.** s. Rente f; (from employer/fund) Pension f. **II.** v.tr. **to p. s.o. off,** j-n pensionieren. ◆**'pensionable,** adj. **p. age,** Pensionsalter n. ◆**'pensioner,** s. Pensionär(in)

m(f); **(old-age) p.,** Rentner(in) m(f).

**pensive** ['pensiv], adj. nachdenklich.

**pentagon** ['pentəgən], s. Fünfeck n.

**penthouse** ['penthaus], s. Dachterrassenwohnung f.

**penultimate** [pən'ʌltimət], adj. vorletzte(r,s).

**people** ['pi:pl]. **I.** s. coll. (with pl. construction) **1.** (a) Leute pl; (esp. with number) Menschen mpl; **a thousand p.,** tausend Menschen; (b) (impers.) **p. say,** man sagt. **2.** Pol: Volk n. **II.** v.tr. (ein Land usw.) bevölkern.

**pep** [pep], s. F: Schwung m; **p. talk,** anspornende Rede f.

**pepper** ['pepər], s. **1.** Cu: Pfeffer m. **2.** Bot: **(green, red) p.,** (grüner, roter) Paprika m; (single fruit) Paprikaschote f. ◆**'peppercorn,** s. Pfefferkorn n. ◆**'peppermill,** s. Pfeffermühle f. ◆**'peppermint,** s. Pfefferminz(bonbon) m.

**per** [pər], prep. **1.** (a) pro; **ten pence p. pound,** zehn Pence das Pfund; **sixty kilometres p. hour,** sechzig Kilometer in der Stunde. **2.** gemäß + gen; **as p. invoice,** gemäß Rechnung.

**perceive** [pə'si:v], v.tr. Lit: wahrnehmen. ◆**per'ceptible,** adj. wahrnehmbar. ◆**per'ception,** s. **1.** Wahrnehmung f. **2.** (faculty) Auffassungsvermögen n. ◆**per'ceptive,** adj. aufmerksam; (astute) scharfsinnig; (understanding) einsichtig.

**percentage** [pə'sentid3], s. Prozentsatz m.

**perch¹** [pə:tʃ]. **I.** s. (for birds) Vogelstange f. **II.** v.i. (a) (of birds etc.) sitzen; (b) **the hut is perched on the mountainside,** die Hütte liegt hoch am Berghang.

**perch²**, s. (fish) Barsch m.

**percolate** ['pə:kəleit], v.i. (of liquid) durchsickern; (of coffee) durchlaufen. ◆**'percolator,** s. Kaffeemaschine f.

**percussion** [pə'kʌʃ(ə)n], s. Mus: Schlagzeug n.

**perennial** [pə'renjəl]. **I.** adj. immer wiederkehrend. **II.** s. Bot: perennierende Pflanze f.

**perfect. I.** ['pə:fikt] adj. **1.** (a) perfekt; (ideal) ideal; (b) F: (complete) völlig. **2.** Gram: **p. (tense)** Perfekt n. **II.** [pə'fekt] v.tr. (eine Maschine usw.) perfektionieren; (Sprachkenntnisse usw.) vervollkommnen. ◆**per'fection,** s. Perfektion f.

**perforate** ['pə:fəreit], v.tr. perforieren. ◆**perfo'ration,** s. Perforation f.

**perform** [pə'fɔ:m], v. **1.** v.tr. (a) (eine Bewegung) ausführen; (einen Dienst) leisten; (eine Aufgabe, eine Pflicht) erfüllen; (b) Th: Mus: aufführen; Th: (eine Rolle) spielen; Mus: (ein Lied usw.) vortragen. **2.** v.i. (a) (of actor) spielen; (b) (of machine) funktionieren. ◆**per'formance,** s. **1.** Leistung f (eines Arbeiters, eines Sportlers, einer Maschine usw.). **2.** Th: Mus: Aufführung f; Th:

Vorstellung *f.* ◆**per'former**, *s. Th: etc:* *Darsteller(in) m(f).*
**perfume**, *s.* ['pə:fju:m] Parfüm *n.*
**perfunctory** [pə'fʌŋkt(ə)ri], *adj.* flüchtig.
**perhaps** [pə'hæps, præps], *adv.* vielleicht.
**peril** ['peril], *s.* Gefahr *f;* **at your p.**, auf eigene Gefahr. ◆**'perilous**, *adj.* gefährlich.
**perimeter** [pə'rimitər], *s.* Umgrenzung *f.*
**period** ['piəriəd], *s.* **1.** *(time) (a)* Zeitraum *m,* Zeitspanne *f; (fixed)* Frist *f; (b) Sch:* Schulstunde *f.* **2.** Epoche *f; Art: etc:* Periode *f.* **3.** *Gram:* Punkt *m.* **4.** *Med:* (monatliche) Regel *f* (einer Frau). ◆**peri'odical. I.** *adj. (also* peri'odic) periodisch; **-ly,** *adv.* von Zeit zu Zeit. **II.** *s. (publication)* Zeitschrift *f.*
**periscope** ['periskəup], *s.* Periskop *n.*
**perish** ['periʃ], *v.i. (a) A: (die)* umkommen; *(b) (of goods etc.)* verderben; *(of rubber)* altern. ◆**'perishable**, *adj. (of goods etc.)* leicht verderblich. ◆**'perishing**, *adj.* F: it's p., es ist saukalt.
**perjure** ['pə:dʒər], *v.tr. Jur:* to p. one-self, einen Meineid leisten. ◆**'perjury**, *s.* Meineid *m.*
**perk** [pə:k]. **I.** *s.* F: Vorteil *m* (in einer Stellung). **II.** *v.i.* F: to p. (up), wieder aufleben.
**perm** [pə:m], *s.* F: Dauerwelle *f.*
**permanent** ['pə:mənənt], *adj. (a) (lasting)* bleibend; *esp. Tchn:* Dauer-; **p. address,** ständiger Wohnsitz; *(b) (constant) (of fear etc.)* ständig; **-ly,** *adv.* auf immer (und ewig); **p. employed,** fest angestellt. ◆**'permanence**, *s.* Dauerhaftigkeit *f.*
**permeate** ['pə:mieit], *v.tr. & i.* to p. (through) sth., *(of moisture, flavour)* in etwas *acc* einziehen.
**permissible** [pə'misibl], *adj.* zulässig. ◆**per'mission**, *s.* Erlaubnis *f.* ◆**per'missive**, *adj.* p. society, permissive Gesellschaft.
**permit. I.** [pə'mit] *v.tr.* (j-m etwas) erlauben. **II.** ['pə:mit] *s.* Genehmigung *f;* **work p.,** Arbeitserlaubnis *f.*
**pernicious** [pə'niʃəs], *adj.* schädlich.
**pernickety** [pə'nikiti], *adj. F:* pingelig.
**perpendicular** [pə:pən'dikjulər], *adj. Mth:* senkrecht (**to,** zu + *dat*).
**perpetrate** ['pə:pitreit], *v.tr.* (ein Verbrechen usw.) begehen. ◆**'perpetrator**, *s.* Täter *m.*
**perpetual** [pə'pətjuəl], *adj.* ewig; *(unending)* endlos; *(not stopping)* unaufhörlich. ◆**per'petuate**, *v.tr.* (eine Lage usw.) fortbestehen lassen.
**perplex** [pə'pleks], *v.tr.* (j-n) verblüffen. ◆**per'plexed**, *adj. (of pers.)* perplex, verblüfft. ◆**per'plexing**, *adj.* verblüffend.
**persecute** ['pə:sikju:t], *v.tr.* (j-n) verfolgen. ◆**perse'cution**, *s.* Verfolgung *f.* ◆**'persecutor**, *s.* Verfolger *m.*

**persevere** [pə:si'viər], *v.i.* durchhalten; **to p. with sth.**, mit etwas *dat* (beharrlich) weitermachen. ◆**perse'verance**, *s.* Ausdauer *f.*
**Persia** ['pə:ʃə]. *Pr. n.* Persien *n.* ◆**'Persian. I.** *adj.* persisch. **II.** *s.* Perser(in) *m(f).*
**persist** [pə'sist], *v.i. (a) (of pers.)* to p. in sth., auf etwas *dat* beharren; *(b) (of condition etc.)* anhalten. ◆**per'sistence**, *s.* **1.** *(of pers.)* Beharrlichkeit *f.* **2.** Anhalten *n* (des Fiebers usw.). ◆**per'sistent**, *adj.* **1.** *(of rain, fever)* anhaltend. **2.** *(of pers.)* beharrlich; *(obstinate)* hartnäckig; *(importunate)* aufdringlich.
**person** ['pə:s(ə)n], *s.* Person *f;* **in p.,** persönlich. ◆**'personable**, *adj. (of pers.)* gutaussehend. ◆**'personage**, *s.* Persönlichkeit *f.* ◆**'personal**, *adj.* persönlich; **-ly,** *adv.* persönlich. ◆**perso'nality**, *s.* Persönlichkeit *f.* ◆**personifi'cation**, *s.* Verkörperung *f.* ◆**per'sonify**, *v.tr.* (etwas) verkörpern; **he was innocence personified,** er war die Unschuld in Person. ◆**perso'nnel**, *s.* Personal *n.*
**perspective** [pə'spektiv], *s.* Perspektive *f.*
**perspire** [pə'spaiər], *v.i.* schwitzen. ◆**perspiration** [pə:spi'reiʃ(ə)n], *s. (sweat)* Schweiß *m.*
**persuade** [pə'sweid], *v.tr. (a)* to p. s.o. of sth., j-n von etwas *dat* überzeugen; *(b)* to p. s.o. to do sth., j-n überreden, etwas zu tun; **he persuaded me not to,** er redete es mir aus. ◆**per'suasion**, *s. (a)* Überredung *f; (powers of)* p., Überredungskünste *fpl; (b) (conviction)* Überzeugung *f.* ◆**per'suasive**, *adj.* überzeugend.
**pertinent** ['pə:tinənt], *adj. (of remark)* zur Sache; *(of literature etc.)* einschlägig.
**perturb** [pə'tə:b], *v.tr.* (j-n) beunruhigen.
**Peru** [pə'ru:]. *Pr. n.* Peru *n.* ◆**Pe'ruvian. I.** *adj.* peruanisch. **II.** *s.* Peruaner(in) *m(f).*
**peruse** [pə'ru:z], *v.tr.* (ein Buch usw.) durchlesen.
**pervade** [pə'veid], *v.tr.* (durch etwas *acc*) durchdringen. ◆**per'vasive**, *adj.* durchdringend.
**perverse** [pə'və:s], *adj. (of pers., idea etc.)* pervers. ◆**per'versity**, *s.* Perversität *f.* ◆**per'version**, *s.* Perversion *f.* ◆**pervert. I.** [pə'və:t] *v.tr.* (j-n) pervertieren; *(etwas)* entstellen. **II.** ['pə:və:t] *s.* Perverse(r) *f(m).*
**pessimism** ['pesimizm], *s.* Pessimismus *m.* ◆**'pessimist**, *s.* Pessimist(in) *m(f).* ◆**pessi'mistic**, *adj.* pessimistisch.
**pest** [pest], *s. (nuisance)* Plage *f; (child, animal etc.)* Quälgeist *m.* ◆**'pester**, *v.tr.* (j-n) belästigen. ◆**'pesticide**, *s.* Schädlingsbekämpfungsmittel *n.*
**pet** [pet]. **I.** *s.* **1.** *(a)* Haustier *n;* **to have a p. rabbit**, ein Kaninchen als Haustier halten; *(b) (child)* Engel *m.* **2.** *attrib. (favourite)* Lieblings-. **II.** *v.tr.* streicheln. ◆**'petting**, *s.* Petting *n.*

**petal** ['pet(ə)l], s. Bot: Blütenblatt n.

**peter** ['piːtər], v.i. **to p. out**, sich im Sande verlaufen.

**petition** [pi'tiʃ(ə)n], s. Jur: etc: Gesuch n; **p. for divorce**, Scheidungsklage f.

**petrify** ['petrifai], v.tr. (a) (etwas) versteinern; (b) (terrify) (j-n) entsetzen; **I was petrified**, ich war starr vor Entsetzen.

**petrol** ['petr(ə)l], s. Benzin n; **p. station**, Tankstelle f.

**petticoat** ['petikəut], s. Unterrock m.

**petty** ['peti], adj. 1. (a) geringfügig; **p. theft**, Bagatelldiebstahl m; (b) **p. (-minded)**, kleinlich. 2. Com: **p. cash**, Kleingeld n. 3. Nau: **p. officer**, Bootsmann m. ◆'**pettiness**, s. Kleinlichkeit f.

**petulant** ['petjulənt], adj. launisch; (irritated) gereizt.

**pew** [pjuː], s. Kirchenbank f.

**pewter** ['pjuːtər], s. Zinn n.

**phantom** ['fæntəm], s. Phantom n.

**pharmaceutical** [fɑːmə'sjuːtik(ə)l], adj. pharmazeutisch. ◆'**pharmacist**, s. Pharmazeut m. ◆'**pharmacy**, s. Pharmazie f; (shop) Apotheke f.

**phase** [feiz]. I. s. Phase f. II. v.tr. esp. Com: **to p. out a model etc.**, ein Modell usw. auslaufen lassen.

**pheasant** ['feznt], s. Fasan m.

**phenomenon**, pl. **-ena** [fi'nɔminən, -inə], s. (everyday) Erscheinung f; (remarkable) Phänomen n. ◆**phe'nomenal**, adj. phänomenal.

**philanthropy** [fi'lænθrəpi], s. Philanthropie f. ◆**phi'lanthropist**, s. Menschenfreund m.

**philately** [fi'lætəli], s. Philatelie f. ◆**phi'latelist**, s. Philatelist m.

**Philippines** ['filipiːnz]. Pr. n. **the P.**, die Philippinen fpl.

**philology** [fi'lɔlədʒi], s. Philologie f.

**philosopher** [fi'lɔsəfər], s. Philosoph m. ◆**philo'sophical**, adj. 1. philosophisch. 2. Fig: (of pers.) gelassen. ◆**phi'losophy**, s. Philosophie f.

**phobia** ['fəubjə], s. Phobie f.

**phone** [fəun]. I. s. F: Telefon n. II. v.tr. & i. F: anrufen.

**phonetic** [fə'netik], adj. phonetisch. ◆**pho'netics**, s.pl. (sing. constr.) Phonetik f.

**phoney** ['fəuni], adj. F: unecht; (forged) gefälscht.

**phosphorus** ['fɔsf(ə)rəs], s. Phosphor m.

**photo** ['fəutəu]. I. s. F: Foto n. II. comb. fm. Foto-, foto-. ◆'**photocopier**, s. Fotokopiergerät n. ◆'**photocopy**, s. 1. Fotokopie f. II. v.tr. (etwas) fotokopieren. ◆**photogenic** [-'dʒiːnik], adj. fotogen. ◆'**photograph**. I. s. Fotografie f; **to take a p.**, eine Aufnahme machen. II. v.tr. fotografieren. ◆**photographer** [fə'tɔgrəfər], s. Fotograf m. ◆**photographic** [-'græfik], adj. fotografisch. ◆**photography** [fə'tɔgrəfi], s. Fotografie f.

**phrase** [freiz]. I. s. Ausdruck m; **set p.**, Redewendung f; **turn of p.**, Ausdrucksweise f. II. v.tr. (etwas) in Worte fassen, formulieren.

**physical** ['fizik(ə)l], adj. (a) Ph: physikalisch; (b) physisch; (bodily) körperlich; **p. training** Leibesübungen fpl. **-ly**, adv. (a) physikalisch; (b) physisch; **p. impossible**, praktisch unmöglich; **p. handicapped**, körperbehindert. ◆**physician** [fi'ziʃ(ə)n], s. Arzt m, Ärztin f. ◆**physics** ['fiziks], s.pl. (sing. constr.) Physik f. ◆'**physicist**, s. Physiker(in) m(f).

**physiognomy** [fizi'ɔnəmi], s. Physiognomie f.

**physiological** [fiziəu'lɔdʒikəl], adj. physiologisch.

**physiotherapy** ['fiziəu'θerəpi], s. Krankengymnastik f. ◆'**physio'therapist**, s. Krankengymnast(in) m(f).

**physique** [fi'ziːk], s. Körperbau m.

**piano**, pl. **-os** ['piænəu, -əuz], s. Klavier n; **grand p.**, Konzertflügel m. ◆**pianist** ['piːənist], s. Pianist(in) m(f).

**pick** [pik]. I. v.tr. & i. (a) (choose) (j-n, etwas) auswählen; **to p. and choose**, wählerisch sein; **to p. a quarrel**, Streit suchen; (b) (Blumen, Obst usw.) pflücken; (lift) aufheben (off, von + dat); (c) **to p. at one's food**, im Essen herumstochern; **to p. one's nose**, in der Nase bohren; Fig: **I've a bone to p. with you**, mit dir habe ich noch ein Hühnchen zu rupfen; (d) **to p. a lock**, ein Schloß knacken. II. s. 1. Spitzhacke f. 2. (thing) das Beste. ◆'**pickaxe**, s. Spitzhacke f. ◆'**pick on**, v.tr. sich dat (j-n) aufs Korn nehmen. ◆'**pick out**, v.tr. (select) (j-n, etwas) aussuchen. ◆'**pickpocket**, s. Taschendieb(in) m(f). ◆'**pick 'up**, v. 1. v.tr. (a) (etwas) (vom Boden) aufheben; (b) (collect) (eine Warensendung usw.) abholen; **to p. s.o. up**, (i) j-n (im Auto) mitnehmen/(fetch) abholen; (ii) F: j-n aufgabeln; (c) Rad: (Signale usw.) auffangen; (d) (learn) (eine Sprache, Ausdrücke usw.) lernen; (e) (of vehicle) **to p. up speed**, beschleunigen. 2. v.i. (of pers.) (wieder) zu Kräften kommen; **business is picking up**, das Geschäft erholt sich. ◆'**pick-up**, s. 1. F: (pers.) Gelegenheitsbekanntschaft f; (prostitute) Flittchen n. 2. (collection) Abholung f. 3. Rec: Tonabnehmer m.

**picket** ['pikit]. I. s. Ind: (strike) p., Streikposten m. II. v.tr. & i. Ind: **to p. (a factory etc.)**, (vor einer Fabrik usw.) Streikposten stehen.

**pickle** ['pikl]. I. s. Marinade f. II. v.tr. (Gurken, Zwiebeln, Fisch usw.) einlegen; (Fleisch) pökeln.

**picnic** ['piknik]. I. s. Picknick n. II. v.i. picknicken.

**picture** ['piktʃər]. I. s. (a) Bild n; (painting) Gemälde n; **he's the p. of health**, er strotzt vor Gesundheit; Fig: **to be in the p.**, im Bilde sein; (b) Cin: Film m; **to go**

**to the pictures**, ins Kino gehen. **II.** *v.tr.* (*imagine*) sich *dat* (j-n, etwas) vorstellen. ◆**pictu'resque**, *adj.* malerisch.

**pie** [pai], *s.* Pastete *f*; **p. crust**, Kruste *f*.

**piebald** ['paibɔ:ld], *adj.* gescheckt.

**piece** [pi:s]. **I.** *s.* 1. Stück *n*; **a p. of news**, eine Neuigkeit; **a p. of information**, eine Information; **a p. of furniture**, ein Möbelstück; *Fig:* **I gave him a p. of my mind**, ich habe ihm gehörig die Meinung gesagt. 2. (*part*) Teil *m & n*; **in pieces**, zerlegt; (*broken*) zerbrochen; **to take sth. to pieces**, etwas auseinandernehmen/zerlegen; **to come to pieces**, (i) zerlegbar sein; (ii) (*fall apart*) auseinanderfallen; *Fig:* **she went to pieces**, sie brach zusammen. 3. (*a*) (*coin*) Münze *f*; **50p p.**, 50-Pence-Stück *n*; (*b*) (*in chess*) Figur *f*. **II.** *v.tr.* **to p. together**, zusammenstückeln. ◆**'piecemeal**, *adv.* stückweise.

**pier** ['piər], *s.* 1. (*a*) *Brit:* Pier *m*; (*b*) (*landing*) **p.**, Landungsbrücke *f.* 2. *Civ.E:* Pfeiler *m* (einer Brücke usw.).

**pierce** ['piəs], *v.tr.* (*a*) (*enter*) (in etwas *acc*) hineinstechen; (*b*) (*go through*) (etwas) durchstechen; (*of light*) **to p. the darkness**, die Dunkelheit durchdringen. ◆**'piercing**, *adj.* (*of scream etc.*) durchdringend.

**piety** ['paiəti], *s.* Frömmigkeit *f*.

**pig** [pig], *s.* Schwein *n.* ◆**'piggy-bank**, *s.* Sparschwein *n.* ◆**'pig'headed**, *adj. F:* störrisch. ◆**'piglet**, *s.* Ferkel *n.* ◆**'pigsty**, *s.* Schweinestall *m.* ◆**'pigtail**, *s.* Zopf *m.*

**pigeon** ['pidʒin], *s.* Taube *f.* ◆**'pigeon-hole**, *s.* Brieffach *n.*

**pigment** ['pigmənt], *s.* Pigment *n.*

**pike** [paik], *s.* Hecht *m.*

**pile1** [pail], *s.* (*for building*) Pfahl *m.*

**pile2. I.** *s.* Haufen *m*; (*tidy*) Stapel *m.* **II.** *v.* 1. *v.tr.* **to p. up**, (Holz usw.) aufschichten; (Bücher, Kisten) stapeln; (*amass*) (Vermögen usw.) anhäufen. 2. *v.i.* **to p. up**, sich häufen. ◆**'pile-up**, *s. Aut: F:* Karambolage *f.*

**pile3**, *s.* (*of velvet, carpet etc.*) Flor *m.*

**piles** [pailz], *s.pl. Med:* Hämorrhoiden *fpl.*

**pilfer** ['pilfər], *v.tr.* (etwas) stehlen, *F:* klauen.

**pilgrim** ['pilgrim], *s.* Pilger *m.* ◆**'pilgrimage**, *s.* Pilgerfahrt *f.*

**pill** [pil], *s.* Pille *f*; (*sugar-coated*) Dragée *n*; *F:* **to be on the p.**, die Pille nehmen.

**pillage** ['pilidʒ], *v.tr. & i.* plündern.

**pillar** ['pilər], *s.* Pfeiler *m*; (*round*) Säule *f*; *Fig:* (*pers.*) **a p. of society**, eine Stütze der Gesellschaft. ◆**'pillar-box**, *s.* Briefkasten *m.*

**pillion** ['piliən], *s.* Soziussitz *m*; **p. passenger**, Soziusfahrer(in) *m(f).*

**pillow** ['piləu], *s.* Kopfkissen *n*; **p.-case**, Kopfkissenbezug *m.*

**pilot** ['pailət]. **I.** *s.* 1. (*a*) *Av:* Pilot(in) *m(f)*; (*b*) *Nau:* Lotse *m.* 2. **p. light**, (*gas*)

Zündflamme *f.* 3. **p. scheme**, Modellversuch *m*; **p. study**, Pilotstudie *f.* **II.** *v.tr.* (*a*) *Av:* (ein Flugzeug) führen; (*b*) *Nau:* (ein Schiff, *Fig:* j-n) lotsen.

**pimento** [pi'mentəu], *s.* Piment *m & n.*

**pimp** [pimp], *s.* Zuhälter *m.*

**pimple** ['pimpl], *s.* Pickel *m.*

**pin** [pin]. **I.** *s.* 1. (Steck)nadel *f*; **p. cushion**, Nadelkissen *n*; **I have pins and needles**, mir kribbelt es. 2. *Sp:* (*in bowling*) Kegel *m.* **II.** *v.tr.* (*a*) (etwas) mit einer Nadel heften; *Fig:* **to p. one's hope on sth.**, seine Hoffnung auf etwas *acc* setzen; (*b*) (j-n) (am Boden, gegen die Wand usw.) festhalten; *Fig:* **to p. s.o. down**, j-n (auf ein Angebot usw.) festnageln. ◆**'pinpoint**, *v.tr.* (*a*) (ein Flugzeug usw.) genau orten; (*b*) (etwas) genau feststellen. ◆**'pinprick**, *s.* Nadelstich *m.* ◆**'pinstripe**, *s.* Nadelstreifen *m.*

**pinafore** ['pinəfɔ:r], *s.* **p.** (**dress**), Trägerrock *m.*

**pincer** ['pinsər], *s.* (*a*) **pair of pincers**, Kneifzange *f*; (*b*) *Z:* Schere *f.*

**pinch** [pin(t)ʃ]. **I.** *v.tr.* (*a*) (j-n) kneifen; *abs.* (*of shoe*) drücken; (*b*) *F:* (*steal*) (etwas) klauen. **II.** *s.* (*a*) Kneifen *n*; *Fig:* **at a p.**, im Notfall; (*b*) **a p.** (**of salt etc.**), eine Prise (Salz usw.); *Fig:* **to take sth. with a p. of salt**, etwas nicht für bare Münze nehmen.

**pine1** [pain], *s.* **p.**(**-tree**), Kiefer *f*; **p. cone**, Kienapfel *m.*

**pine2**, *v.i.* **to p. away**, sich (vor Leid usw.) verzehren; **to p. for s.o., sth.**, sich nach j-m, etwas *dat* sehnen.

**pineapple** ['painæpl], *s.* Ananas *f.*

**pink** [pink], *adj.* rosa *inv.*

**pinnacle** ['pinəkl], *s.* 1. (*summit*) Gipfel *m*; (*rock*) Felsnadel *f.* 2. *Arch:* Spitzturm *m.*

**pint** [paint], *s. Meas:* Pint *n* (*Brit:* 0·568 Liter); **a p. of beer**, *approx.* eine Halbe (Bier).

**pioneer** [paiə'niər], *s.* Pionier *m.*

**pious** ['paiəs], *adj.* fromm.

**pip** [pip], *s.* (*in fruit*) Obstkern *m.*

**pipe** [paip]. **I.** *s.* 1. (*for liquid, gas*) Rohr *n*; (*mains*) Leitung *f*; **burst p.**, Rohrbruch *m.* 2. *Mus:* Pfeife *f*; *pl.* (**bag**)**pipes**, Dudelsack *m.* 3. (*for tobacco*) Pfeife *f*; **p. dream**, Wunschtraum *m.* **II.** *v.tr.* (Wasser, Gas usw.) durch Rohre leiten. ◆**'pipeline**, *s.* Pipeline *f.* ◆**'piping**, *adj.* **p. hot**, kochend heiß.

**piquant** ['pi:kənt], *adj.* pikant.

**pique** [pi:k], *s.*; **in a fit of p.**, pikiert.

**pirate** ['paiərət]. **I.** *s.* Pirat *m.* **II.** *adj. Rad:* **p. station**, Piratensender *m*; (*book etc.*) **pirate(d) edition**, Raubdruck *m.* ◆**'piracy**, *s.* Piraterie *f.*

**Pisces** ['paisi:z], *s.pl. Astr:* Fische *mpl.*

**piss** [pis]. **I.** *s. V:* Pisse *f.* **II.** *v.i. V:* pissen; **p. off!** hau ab! ◆**'pissed**, *adj. P:* stockbesoffen.

**pistachio** [pis'ta:ʃiəu], *s.* Pistazie *f.*

**pistol** ['pist(ə)l], *s.* Pistole *f.*

**piston** ['pistən], s. Kolben m.

**pit** [pit]. **I.** s. (hole in ground, mine) Grube f; Th: etc: orchestra p., Orchesterraum m. **II.** v.tr. to p. one's wits, strength etc. against s.o., seinen Geist, seine Kraft usw. mit j-m messen. ◆'**pitted**, adj. (of metal) angefressen; (of skin) narbig.

**pitch¹** [pitʃ], s. Pech n; p. black, pechschwarz; it is p. dark, es ist stockdunkel.

**pitch²** [pitʃ]. **I.** v. 1. v.tr. (a) (ein Zelt, Lager) aufschlagen; pitched battle, F: regelrechte Schlacht; (b) Sp: (einen Ball usw.) schleudern. 2. v.i. F: to p. into sth., sich über etwas acc hermachen. **II.** s. 1. (a) Mus: (of voice) Tonhöhe f (einer Stimme); Tonlage f (eines Instruments); (b) Fig: (degree) Grad m. 2. (throw) Wurf m. 3. Sp: Spielfeld n; football p., Fußballfeld n. 4. (slope) Gefälle n (eines Daches usw.). ◆'**pitchfork**, s. Heugabel f.

**piteous** ['pitiəs], adj. kläglich.

**pitfall** ['pitfɔːl], s. esp. Fig: Falle f.

**pith** [piθ], s. das Weiße (einer Orangenschale). ◆'**pithy**, adj. (of style) markig.

**pittance** ['pit(ə)ns], s. Hungerlohn m.

**pity** ['piti]. **I.** s. (a) Mitleid n; to take/have p. on s.o., sth., mit j-m, etwas dat Erbarmen haben; to feel p. for s.o., Mitleid mit j-m haben; (b) what a p.! wie schade! **II.** v.tr. (j-n) bedauern. ◆'**pitiful**, adj. (a) (of sight etc.) jämmerlich; it's p. to see him, es jammert einen, wenn man ihn so sieht; (b) Pej: kläglich.

**pivot** ['pivət]. **I.** s. Drehpunkt m. **II.** v.i. sich drehen (on an axis, um eine Achse).

**placard** ['plækɑːd], s. Plakat n.

**placate** plə'keit], v.tr. (j-n) beschwichtigen.

**place** [pleis]. **I.** s. 1. (a) (village, town) Ort m; (small town) Ortschaft f; the most expensive hotel in the p., das teuerste Hotel am Ort; (b) F: (restaurant etc.) Lokal n; F: at our p., bei uns zu Hause; (c) p. of business, Geschäftssitz m; Adm: p. of residence, Wohnsitz m. 2. (a) Platz m; books are spread all over the p., Bücher liegen überall herum; out of p., fehl am Platze; (b) (square) Platz m. 3. (seat at table etc.) Platz m; p. mat, Set m & n; to change places with s.o., mit j-m den Platz tauschen. 4. (position) (a) (also Mth:) Stelle f; in your p., an deiner Stelle; in (the) p. of ..., anstelle von ... dat; (b) he knows his p., er weiß, wo er hingehört; (c) Sp: in first/second p., auf dem ersten/zweiten Platz. **II.** v.tr. (etwas) stellen, legen (on, in etc., auf, in usw. + acc); to p. an order, einen Auftrag erteilen; to be well placed, (well able) gut imstande sein (to ..., zu ...); Sp: to be placed, sich plazieren.

**placid** ['plæsid], adj. (of pers.) gelassen; (of child) friedlich.

**plagiarism** ['pleidʒiərizm], s. Plagiat n.

**plague** [pleig]. **I.** s. 1. (nuisance) Plage f.

2. Med: Pest f. **II.** v.tr. (j-n) plagen.

**plaice** [pleis], s. Scholle f.

**plain** [plein]. **I.** adj. 1. (clear) klar, deutlich; it's as p. as day es liegt auf der Hand/ist sonnenklar; p. speaking, unverblümte Worte. 2. (simple) (a) (of style, dress etc.) einfach, schlicht; p. truth, ungeschminkte Wahrheit; (b) (of material etc.) einfarbig; (c) p. chocolate, Bitterschokolade f. 3. (of pers.) unansehnlich; **-ly**, adv. klar; (obviously) offensichtlich; I can see it p., ich sehe es genau. **II.** s. Geog: etc: Ebene f. ◆'**plain-'clothes**, adj. p.-c. policeman, Polizeibeamter m in Zivil. ◆'**plainness**, s. (a) (of pers.) unvorteilhaftes Aussehen n.; (b) Einfachheit f, Schlichtheit f.

**plaintiff** ['pleintif], s. Kläger(in) m(f).

**plaintive** ['pleintiv], adj. klagend.

**plait** [plæt]. **I.** s. Zopf m. **II.** v.tr. (Haare usw.) flechten.

**plan** [plæn]. **I.** s. Plan m; (of building) Grundriß m; according to p., planmäßig/nach Plan. **II.** v.tr. (etwas) planen; to p. to do sth., vorhaben, etwas zu tun. ◆'**planning**, s. Planung f; p. permission, Baugenehmigung f.

**plane¹** [plein], s. Mth: etc: Ebene f.

**plane²** [plein]. **I.** s. Tchn: Hobel m. **II.** v.tr. (Holz) hobeln.

**plane³**, s. p.(-tree), Platane f.

**plane⁴**, s. Av: F: Flugzeug n.

**planet** ['plænit], s. Planet m.

**plank** [plæŋk], s. Planke f.

**plant** [plɑːnt]. **I.** s. 1. Pflanze f. 2. Ind: (factory) Werk n; (b) (machinery) Maschinen fpl. **II.** v.tr. (a) pflanzen; (b) to p. a bomb, eine Bombe legen. ◆**plan'tation**, s. Plantage f.

**plaque** [plɑːk, plæk], s. 1. (tablet) Gedenktafel f. 2. (on teeth) Zahnbelag m.

**plaster** ['plɑːstər]. **I.** s. 1. Med: sticking p., Kleb(e)pflaster n. 2. (a) Arch: Putz m; (b) Med: p. (of paris), Gips m; his leg is in p., sein Bein ist in Gips/in einem Gipsverband. **II.** v.tr. (a) Arch: (eine Wand, Decke usw.) verputzen; (b) (cover) bedecken; (c) P: plastered, besoffen. ◆'**plasterer**, s. Arch: etc: Gipser m.

**plastic** ['plæstik]. **I.** adj. 1. Med: surgery, plastische Chirurgie f. 2. Plastik-; p. cup, Plastiktasse f. **II.** s. Kunststoff m, esp. Plastik n.

**plate** [pleit]. **I.** s. 1. (for food) Teller m; F: he has a lot on his p., er hat viel um die Ohren. 2. (sheet of metal etc.) (a) Platte f; p. glass, Schaufensterglas n; (b) (with name etc.) Schild n; Aut: (number) p., Nummernschild n. 3. (book illustration) Bildtafel f. **II.** v.tr. (chromium) (etwas) verchromen; (silver) (etwas) versilbern. ◆'**plateful**, s. Tellervoll m. ◆'**plating**, s. silver p., Versilberung f.

**plateau**, pl. **-x, -s** ['plætəu, -z], s. Plateau n.

**platform** ['plætfɔːm], s. 1. (a) (for speaker) Podium n; (stage) Bühne f; **drilling**

p., Bohrinsel *f; (b) Rail:* Bahnsteig *m.*
**platinum** ['plætinəm], *s.* Platin *n.*
**platitude** ['plætitju:d], *s.* Gemeinplatz *m.*
**platoon** [plə'tu:n], *s. Mil:* Zug *m.*
**plausible** ['plɔ:zibl], *adj. (a) (of theory)* plausibel; **p. explanation**, glaubwürdige Erklärung; *(of pers.)* überzeugend.
**play** [plei]. **I.** *s.* 1. Spiel *n;* **p. on words,** Wortspiel *n; Sp:* **p. began at one o'clock,** das Spiel begann um ein Uhr. 2. *Th:* Stück *n.* **II.** *v. tr. & i.* spielen; **to p. safe,** sichergehen. ◆**'play 'at,** *v.tr. (a)* (Karten usw.) spielen; *(b) F:* **what are they playing at?** was treiben denn die da? ◆**'play 'back,** *v.tr.* (ein Tonband) überspielen. ◆**'play 'down,** *v.tr.* bagatellisieren. ◆**'player,** *s.* Spieler *n.* ◆**'playful,** *adj. (of pers.)* zum Spielen aufgelegt; *(of kitten, child)* verspielt; *(of remark)* neckend. ◆**'playground,** *s.* Spielplatz *m; Sch:* Schulhof *m.* ◆**'plaything,** *s.* Spielzeug *n.* ◆**'play 'up,** *v.i. (give trouble)* Mätzchen machen. ◆**'playwright,** *s.* Dramatiker *m.*
**plea** [pli:], *s.* 1. *Jur:* Bekenntnis *f* (**of guilty,** zur Schuld). 2. *(request)* Bitte *f;* **p. for mercy,** Gnadengesuch *n.*
**plead** [pli:d], *v.* *v.i. (a) Jur:* (of barrister) plädieren (**for s.o.,** für j-n); *(of prisoner)* **to p. guilty/not guilty,** sich schuldig/nicht schuldig bekennen; to p. **with s.o.,** j-n anflehen; **to p. for mercy,** um Gnade bitten. 2. **to p. ignorance,** sich auf Unwissenheit berufen.
**pleasant** ['plez(ə)nt], *adj.* angenehm; *(of pers.)* freundlich, *F:* nett.
**please** [pli:z], *v.tr. (a)* (j-m) gefallen; *(satisfy)* (j-n) zufriedenstellen; **p. yourself!** (ganz) wie Sie wünschen/wollen! *(b)* bitte; **p. tell me …,** bitte sagen Sie mir …; **may I?—p. do!** darf ich?—bitte sehr! ◆**pleased,** *adj.* erfreut; *(satisfied)* zufrieden (with, mit + dat); **he's very p. about it,** er freut sich sehr darüber; **I'm p. to see you,** es freut mich, Sie zu sehen. ◆**'pleasing,** *adj.* angenehm; *(of result etc.)* erfreulich. ◆**pleasure** ['pleʒər], *s.* Vergnügen *n; pl* Freuden *fpl;* **with p.,** gern.
**pleat** [pli:t]. **I.** *s. Cl: etc:* Falte *f.* **II.** *v.tr.* (einen Rock, Stoff usw.) in Falten legen; **pleated skirt,** Faltenrock *m.*)
**pledge** [pledʒ]. **I.** *s. (promise)* Versprechen *n.* **II.** *v.tr.* **pledged to do sth.,** verpflichtet, etwas zu tun.
**plenty** ['plenti], *s.* Überfluß *m;* **p. of time/shirts,** reichlich Zeit/viele Hemden; **there's p. more,** es ist noch viel übrig; **five will be p.,** fünf sind mehr als genug. ◆**'plentiful,** *adj.* reichlich vorhanden.
**pliable** ['plaiəbl], *adj.* biegsam.
**pliers** ['plaiəz], *s.pl.* Zange *f.*
**plight** [plait], *s.* Notlage *f.*
**plinth** [plinθ], *s. Arch:* Plinthe *f.*
**plod** [plɔd], *v.i.* schwerfällig gehen; **to p. on,** mühsam weitermachen.
**plonk¹** [plɔŋk], *v.tr. F:* (etwas) hinpflan-

zen.
**plonk²,** *s. F:* Gesöff *n, esp.* billiger Wein *m.*
**plot** [plɔt]. **I.** *s.* 1. (kleines) Grundstück *n.* 2. Handlung *f* (eines Romans usw.). 3. *(conspiracy)* Verschwörung *f.* **II.** *v.* 1. *v.tr. (a) Mth: etc:* (eine Kurve usw.) konstruieren; graphisch darstellen; **to p. a course,** einen Kurs abstecken; *(b)* (plan) (einen Mord usw.) planen. 2. *v.i.* **to p. against s.o., sth.,** gegen j-n, etwas intrigieren.
**plough** [plau]. **I.** *s.* Pflug *m.* **II.** *v.tr. (a)* (einen Acker) pflügen; *(b) F:* **to p. through a book etc.,** ein Buch usw. durchackern.
**ploy** [plɔi], *s. F:* Trick *m.*
**pluck** [plʌk]. *v.tr. (a)* (Geflügel) rupfen; (Augenbrauen) (aus)zupfen; *Mus:* (eine Saite usw.) zupfen; *(b) Lit:* (Früchte, Blumen) pflücken. ◆**'pluck 'up,** *v.tr.* **to p. up (one's) courage,** sich *dat* ein Herz fassen.
**plug** [plʌg]. **I.** *s.* 1. *(in basin etc.)* Stöpsel *m.* 2. *(a) El:* Stecker *m; (b) Aut:* **(spark) p.,** Zündkerze *f.* **II.** *v.* 1. *v.tr. (a)* (ein Loch) zustopfen; *(b) Com: F:* **to p. a product,** die Werbetrommel für ein Produkt rühren; *(c)* **to p. in the TV,** den Fernseher einstecken. 2. *v.i.* **to p. away,** sich abplagen (**at sth.,** mit etwas *dat*).
**plum** [plʌm], *s.* Pflaume *f.*
**plumage** ['plu:midʒ], *s.* Gefieder *n.*
**plumb** [plʌm]. **I.** *s.* **p. line,** Lotleine *f.* **II.** *adv.* **p. in the middle,** genau in der Mitte. ◆**'plumber,** *s.* Installateur *m.* ◆**'plumbing,** *s.* Rohrleitungen *fpl* (in einem Haus).
**plump** [plʌmp]. **I.** *adj. (of child, woman)* mollig; *(of man, woman)* rundlich; *(of chicken, arm etc.)* fleischig. **II.** *v.i. F:* **to p. for s.o., sth.,** sich für j-n, etwas *acc* entscheiden.
**plunder** ['plʌndər]. **I.** *s. (booty)* Beute *f.* **II.** *v.tr.* (eine Stadt usw.) plündern.
**plunge** [plʌn(d)ʒ]. **I.** *v.* 1. *v.tr.* (etwas ins Wasser usw.) tauchen; **plunged into darkness,** in Dunkelheit getaucht. 2. *v.i. (a)* (ins Wasser usw.) tauchen; *Fig:* sich (in ein Abenteuer usw.) stürzen; *(c) (drop) (of cliff)* (steil) abfallen; *(of prices)* stark fallen. **II.** *s.* Sturz *m; (dive)* Tauchen *n; Fig:* **to take the p.,** den Sprung wagen.
**pluperfect** [plu:'pə:fikt], *adj. & s.* **p. (tense),** Plusquamperfekt *n.*
**plural** ['pluər(ə)l], *adj. & s.* Plural *m.*
**plus** [plʌs], *prep.* plus; **p. VAT,** zuzüglich Mehrwertsteuer.
**plush** [plʌʃ]. *adj. F:* luxuriös; *(smart)* vornehm.
**ply¹** [plai], *v.tr. (a)* **to p. a trade,** ein Gewerbe betreiben; *(b)* **to p. s.o. with drink,** j-m Alkohol aufdrängen.
**ply²,** *s.* **three p. wool,** dreifache Wolle. ◆**'plywood,** *s.* Sperrholz *n.*
**pneumatic** [nju:'mætik], *adj.* pneuma-

tisch; **p. drill,** Preßluftbohrer *m.*
**pneumonia** [nju(ː)'məuniə], *s.* Lunge-
nentzündung *f.*
**poach¹** [pəutʃ], *v.tr. Cu:* (Eier) pochie-
ren; **poached eggs,** verlorene Eier.
**poach²,** *v.tr. & i.* **to p.** (game), wildern.
◆**'poacher,** *s.* Wilderer *m.*
**pocket** ['pɔkit]. **I.** *s.* 1. Tasche *f;* **p. edition,** Taschenausgabe *f;* **p. knife,** Taschenmesser *n;* **p. money,** Taschengeld
*n.* 2. *(in billiards etc.)* Loch *n.* **II.** *v.tr.*
(Geld usw.) einstecken.
**pod** [pɔd], *s.* Schote *f; (of seeds)* Hülse *f.*
**poem** ['pəuim], *s.* Gedicht *n.* ◆**poet**
['pəuit], *s.* Dichter *m.* ◆**po'etic,** *adj.*
poetisch; **p. licence,** dichterische Freiheit. ◆**'poetry,** *s.* Gedichte *npl;* **(lyric)
p.,** Lyrik *f.*
**poignant** ['pɔinjənt], *adj.* rührend.
**point** [pɔint]. **I.** *s.* 1. Punkt *m; (a) (place)*
Stelle *f;* **p. of view,** Gesichtspunkt *m;
(attitude)* Standpunkt *m; (b)* Frage *f,* Sache *f;* **p. at issue,** Streitpunkt *m;* **to
make one's p.,** seinen Standpunkt klarmachen; **to make a p. of doing sth.,** darauf bedacht sein, etwas zu tun; **that's the
p.,** darum geht es ja; *(c) (sense)* **what
would be the p. of ...,** welchen Sinn hätte es, zu ...; **there's no p.,** es hat keinen
Zweck; *(d)* **to be on the p. of doing sth.,**
im Begriff sein, etwas zu tun; *(e) (degree)*
**up to a (certain) p.,** bis zu einem gewissen Grad; *(f)* **to refuse p. blank,** glatt
ablehnen. 2. *(end)* Spitze *f* (einer Nadel
usw.); *Geog:* Landspitze *f.* 3. *Rail: pl*
**points,** Weiche *f.* **II.** *v.* 1. *v.tr.* (eine
Waffe usw.) richten **(at s.o.,** auf j-n). 2.
*v.i. (a)* **to p. at s.o., sth.,** auf j-n, etwas
*acc* zeigen; *Fig:* **all the evidence points
to him,** alle Beweise deuten auf ihn; *(b)*
**to p. sth. out,** auf etwas *acc* hinweisen.
◆**'pointed,** *adj. (sharp, also of remark)*
spitz. ◆**'pointer,** *s. (a)* Zeiger *m* (eines
Meßgerätes); *(b) F:* Tip *m.* ◆**'pointing,**
*s.* Ausfugung *f* (einer Mauer).
◆**'pointless,** *adj.* sinnlos.
**poise** [pɔiz]. **I.** *s. (balance)* Gleichgewicht
*n; (attitude)* Haltung *f* (des Körpers). **II.**
*v.tr.* balancieren.
**poison** ['pɔiz(ə)n]. **I.** *s.* Gift *n.* **II.** *v.tr.*
*(a)* (j-n) vergiften; *(b) Fig:* (j-s Charakter,
ein Verhältnis usw.) verderben. ◆**'poisoning,** *s.* Vergiftung *f.* ◆**'poisonous,**
*adj.* giftig.
**poke** [pəuk]. 1. *v.tr. (a)* (j-n) anstoßen;
*(b)* (das Feuer) schüren; *(c)* (einen
Schirm usw.) (in etwas *acc*) stecken; *(d)*
**to p. fun at s.o.,** sich über j-n lustig machen. 2. *v.i.* **to p. about,** herumstochern.
◆**'poker¹,** *s.* Schürhaken *m.*
**poker²** ['pəukər], *s. (game)* Poker *n.*
**Poland** ['pəulənd]. *Pr. n.* Polen *n.*
**polar** ['pəulər], *adj.* polar, Polar-; **p.
bear,** Eisbär *m.*
**Pole¹** ['pəul], *s.* Pole *m,* Polin *f.*
**pole²,** *s.* Stange *f; (post)* Pfahl *m; (for flag
etc.)* Mast *m; Sp:* **p. vault,** Stabhoch-

sprung *m.*
**pole³,** *s. Geog:* Pol *m; Fig:* **poles apart,**
grundverschieden.
**police** [pə'liːs], *s.* **the p. (force),** die Polizei; **p. officer,** Polizist(in) *m(f);* **p. station,** Polizeiwache *f.* ◆**po'liceman,** *pl.*
**-men,** *s.* Polizist *m.* ◆**po'licewoman,**
*pl.* **-women,** *s.* Polizeibeamtin *f,* Polizi-
stin *f.*
**policy** ['pɔlisi], *s.* 1. *(a)* Politik *f;* **foreign
p.,** Außenpolitik *f; (b) Com: adj:* Grundsatz *m.* 2. *Ins:* **(insurance) p.,** Police *f.*
**polio** ['pəuliəu], *s.* Kinderlähmung *f.*
**polish** ['pɔliʃ]. **I.** *s.* Politur *f; (shine)*
Hochglanz *m;* **shoe p.,** Schuhcreme *f.* **II.**
*v.tr.* polieren. ◆**'polished,** *adj.* poliert;
*Fig: (of style, manners etc.)* geschliffen.
◆**'polish 'off,** *v.tr. F:* (eine Arbeit) hinhauen; (Essen) wegputzen. ◆**'polish
'up,** *v.tr.* **to p. up one's French,** sein
Französisch auffrischen.
**Polish** ['pəuliʃ]. **I.** *adj. Geog:* polnisch. **II.**
*s. (language)* Polnisch *n.*
**polite** [pə'lait], *adj.* höflich.
◆**po'liteness,** *s.* Höflichkeit *f.*
**politics** ['pɔlitiks], *s.pl.* Politik *f.* ◆**political** [pə'litik(ə)l], *adj.* politisch.
◆**poli'tician,** *s.* Politiker(in) *m(f).*
**poll** [pəul], *s.* 1. Wahl *f;* **to go to the
polls,** zur Wahl gehen. 2. **(opinion) p.,**
Meinungsumfrage *f.* ◆**'polling,** *s.* **p.
station,** Wahllokal *n.*
**pollen** ['pɔlin, -ən], *s.* Blütenstaub *m.*
**pollute** [pə'l(j)uːt], *v.tr.* verschmutzen.
◆**po'llution,** *s.* **(environmental) p.,**
Umweltverschmutzung *f.*
**polo** ['pəuləu], *s.* 1. *Sp:* Polo *n.* 2. *Cl:* **p.
neck,** Rollkragen *m.*
**polystyrene** [pɔli'stairiːn], *s.* Polystyrol
*n.*
**polytechnic** [pɔli'teknik], *s. approx.*
Technische Hochschule *f.*
**polythene** ['pɔliθiːn], *s.* **p. bag,** Plastik-
beutel *m.*
**pomegranate** ['pɔm(i)grænit], *s.* Granat-
apfel *m.*
**pompous** ['pɔmpəs], *adj. (a) (of style etc.)*
schwülstig; *(b) (of pers.)* aufgeblasen.
**pond** [pɔnd], *s.* Teich *m.*
**ponder** ['pɔndər], *v.tr.* (etwas) überlegen.
◆**'ponderous,** *adj.* schwerfällig.
**pony** ['pəuni], *s.* Pony *n;* **p. tail,** Pferde-
schwanz *m.*
**poodle** ['puːdl], *s.* Pudel *m.*
**pool** [puːl]. **I.** *s. (a) (natural)* Weiher *m;
(small)* Tümpel *m; (b) (man-made)* Becken
*m;* **(swimming) p.,** Schwimmbad *n; (c)* **p.
of blood/oil,** Blutlache/Ollache *f. (d)*
**(football) pools,** Fußballtoto *m & n.* **II.**
*v.tr.* (Gewinne, Gelder usw.) zusammen-
legen; **to p. one's resources,** sich zusammentun.
**poor** [puər, pɔːr], *adj.* 1. *(needing money
or help)* arm; **the p.,** die Armen. 2. *(bad)*
schlecht; **p. excuse,** faule Ausrede; **to
have a p. opinion of s.o., sth.,** nicht viel
von j-m, etwas *dat* halten. ◆**'poorly. I.**

*adv.* schlecht. **II.** *adj.* (*ill*) unpäßlich; **he is p.**, es geht ihm nicht gut.

**pop¹** [pɔp]. **I.** *v.i.* (*a*) (*of cork etc.*) knallen; (*b*) **to p. in to see s.o.**, bei j-m vorbeischauen; **to p. out**, (i) (*jump*) hinausspringen; (ii) (*go out*) einen Moment weggehen. **II.** *s.* Knall *m* (eines Korkens).
◆**'popcorn**, *s.* Popkorn *n.* ◆**'popgun**, *s.* Platzpistole *f.*

**pop²**, *adj.* **p.** (*music*) Popmusik *f;* **p. song**, Schlager *m.*

**pop³**, *s.* F: (*drink*) Brause *f.*

**pope** ['pəup], *s.* Papst *m.*

**poplar** ['pɔplər], *s.* Pappel *f.*

**poppy** ['pɔpi], *s.* Mohnblume *f.*

**popular** ['pɔpjulər], *adj.* (*a*) (*of the people*) Volks-; (*b*) (*much liked*) beliebt; (*c*) (*prevalent*) **p. view**, herrschende Meinung; **-ly**, *adv.* **it is p. believed that ...**, man nimmt allgemein an, daß ... ◆**popu'larity**, *s.* Beliebtheit *f.* ◆**'popularize**, *v.tr.* popularisieren.

**populate** ['pɔpjuleit], *v.tr.* (ein Land usw.) bevölkern; **densely populated**, dicht bevölkert. ◆**popu'lation**, *s.* Bevölkerung *f.*

**porcelain** ['pɔːslin], *s.* Porzellan *n.*

**porch** [pɔːtʃ], *s.* (*a*) (*on houses*) Windfang *m;* (*b*) *N.Am:* Veranda *f.*

**porcupine** ['pɔːkjupain], *s.* Stachelschwein *n.*

**pore¹** [pɔːr], *s.* Pore *f.*

**pore²**, *v.i.* **to p. over a book**, über einem Buch hocken.

**pork** [pɔːk], *s.* Schweinefleisch *n.*

**pornography** [pɔːˈnɔɡrəfi], *s.* Pornographie *f.*

**porous** ['pɔːrəs], *adj.* porös.

**porpoise** ['pɔːpəs], *s.* Tümmler *m.*

**porridge** ['pɔridʒ], *s.* Haferbrei *m;* **p. oats**, Haferflocken *fpl.*

**port¹** [pɔːt], *s. Nau:* Hafen *m.*

**port²**, *s. Nau:* (*direction*) Backbord *m.*

**port³**, *s.* (*wine*) Portwein *m.*

**portable** ['pɔːtəbl], *adj.* tragbar.

**porter¹** ['pɔːtər], *s.* (*doorman*) Pförtner *m.*

**porter²**, *s. Rail: etc:* Gepäckträger *m;* (*in hotels*) Hoteldiener *m.*

**portfolio**, *pl.* **-oes** [pɔːtˈfəuljəu, -z], *s.* (*folder*) Mappe *f.*

**porthole** ['pɔːthəul], *s. Nau:* Bullauge *n.*

**portion** ['pɔːʃ(ə)n]. **I.** *s.* (*a*) Teil *m;* (*share*) Anteil *m* (**of sth.**, von etwas *dat*); (*b*) *Cu:* Portion *f* (von Speisen). **II.** *v.tr.* **to p. sth. out**, etwas austeilen.

**portly** ['pɔːtli], *adj.* beleibt.

**portrait** ['pɔːtrit], *s.* Porträt *n;* (*description*) Schilderung *f.* ◆**por'tray**, *v.tr.* darstellen; (*describe*) schildern.

**Portugal** ['pɔːtjuɡ(ə)l]. *Pr. n.* Portugal *n.* ◆**Portu'guese** ['giːz]. **I.** *adj.* portugiesisch. **II.** *s.* (*a*) Portugiese *m*, Portugiesin *f;* (*b*) (*language*) Portugiesisch *n.*

**pose** [pəuz]. **I.** *s.* Pose *f.* **II.** *v.* **1.** *v.tr.* (eine Frage) stellen; **this poses a problem**, das ist problematisch. **2.** *v.i.* (*a*) *Art:* **to p. for s.o.**, für j-n Modell stehen;

(*b*) **to p. as a Frenchman**, sich als Franzose ausgeben.

**posh** [pɔʃ], *adj.* F: vornehm.

**position** [pəˈziʃ(ə)n]. **I.** *s.* (*a*) Position *f; Stellung f* (des Körpers, *Tchn:* eines Hebels usw.); (*mental attitude*) Standpunkt *m;* (*b*) (*situation*) Lage *f* (eines Hauses usw.); Standort *m* (eines Schiffes usw.); **in p.**, an der richtigen Stelle; (*c*) (*relative to others*) Stellung *f; Sp:* Stelle *f;* **in first p.**, an erster Stelle; (*d*) (*job*) Stelle *f.* **II.** *v.tr.* (etwas) in die richtige Lage/Stellung bringen.

**positive** ['pɔzitiv], *adj.* **1.** (*of result, reply etc.*) positiv. **2.** (*a*) (*certain*) **are you p.?** sind Sie ganz sicher? (*b*) F: (*definite*) **a p. advantage**, ein eindeutiger/ausgesprochener Vorteil; **-ly**, *adv.* **1.** sicher, mit Gewißheit. **2.** F: ganz, völlig.

**possess** [pəˈzes], *v.tr.* (*a*) (*own*) (etwas) besitzen; (*b*) **what possessed you?** was ist in Sie gefahren? **like a man possessed**, wie ein Besessener. ◆**po'ssession**, *s.* **1. to take p. of sth.**, etwas in Besitz nehmen. **2. all my possessions**, mein ganzes Hab und Gut. ◆**po'ssessive**, *adj.* (*a*) (*jealous*) eifersüchtig; (*b*) *Gram:* Possessiv-.

**possible** ['pɔsəbl], *adj.* möglich; **as many details as p.**, möglichst viele Einzelheiten. ◆**'possibly**, *adv.* **1.** (*emphatic*) **I cannot p. do it**, das kann ich unmöglich tun. **2.** (*perhaps*) **yes**, **p.**, ja, vielleicht. ◆**possi'bility**, *s.* Möglichkeit *f.*

**post¹** [pəust], *s.* Pfosten *m;* (*stake*) Pfahl *m;* (*tall*) Mast *m; Fig:* **as deaf as a p.**, stocktaub; **starting p.**, Startpfosten *m;* **winning p.**, Ziel *n.*

**post²**. **I.** *s.* **1.** *Mil:* Posten *m;* **at his p.**, auf seinem Posten. **2.** (*job*) Stelle *f;* (*office*) Amt *n.* **II.** *v.tr. Mil:* (*a*) **to p. sentries**, Wachen aufstellen; (*b*) **to be posted to Germany**, nach Deutschland versetzt werden.

**post³**. **I.** *s.* (*mail, service, post office*) Post *f;* (*a*) **by return of p.**, postwendend; **to send sth. by p.**, etwas mit der Post schicken; **p. office**, Postamt *n;* **p. box**, Briefkasten *m;* **P.O. Box**, Postfach *n.* **II.** *v.tr.* (*a*) **to p. a letter**, einen Brief zur Post bringen/(*in letter box*) einwerfen; (*b*) *Fig:* **to keep s.o. posted**, j-n auf dem laufenden halten. ◆**'postage**, *s.* Porto *n;* **p. stamp**, Briefmarke *f.* ◆**'postal**, *adj.* Post-; **p. code**, Postleitzahl *f.* ◆**'postcard**, *s.* Postkarte *f.* ◆**'postman**, *s.* Briefträger *m.* ◆**'postmark**, *s.* Poststempel *m.*

**post-** [pəust-], *prefix* Nach-. ◆**'post'mortem**, *s.* Obduktion *f.* ◆**'post-'war**, *adj.* Nachkriegs-.

**poster** ['pəustər], *s.* Plakat *n*, Poster *n.*

**posterity** [pɔsˈteriti], *s.* die Nachwelt; (*s.o.'s descendants*) Nachkommenschaft *f.*

**posthumous** ['pɔstjuməs], *adj.* postum.

**postpone** [pəusˈpəun], *v.tr.* (etwas) aufschieben.

**postscript** ['pəusskript], s. Nachschrift f.

**posture** ['pɔstʃər]. s. (pose) Positur f; (position) Stellung f.

**pot** [pɔt]. I. s. (a) Topf m; (for tea, coffee) Kanne f; **a p. of jam,** ein Glas n Marmelade; (b) P: **to go to p.,** auf den Hund kommen. II. v.tr. (Pflanzen) eintopfen. ◆**'potted,** adj. **p. plant,** Topfpflanze f. ◆**'pot-hole,** s. (in road) Schlagloch n. ◆**'pot-'luck,** s. F: **to take p.-l.,** mit dem vorliebnehmen, was es gerade gibt.

**potash** ['pɔtæʃ], s. Kali n.

**potassium** [pə'tæsiəm], s. Kalium n.

**potato,** pl. **-oes** [pə'teitəu, -əuz], s. Kartoffel f; **p. crisps,** Chips mpl.

**potency** ['pəutənsi], s. Stärke f (eines Drinks, eines Motors usw.); Wirksamkeit f (eines Medikaments). ◆**'potent,** adj. stark; (of drug) wirksam; Fig: (of argument) stichhaltig. ◆**po'tential. I.** adj. potentiell. II. s. esp. Potential n; (of pers.) Fähigkeiten fpl; **-ly,** adv. **p. dangerous,** unter Umständen gefährlich.

**potter¹** ['pɔtər], v.i. **to p.** (about), (aimlessly) herumtrödeln; (in house, garden) herumhantieren.

**potter²,** s. Töpfer(in) m(f); **p.'s wheel,** Töpferscheibe f. ◆**'pottery,** s. 1. (workshop) Töpferei f. 2. (vessels etc.) Töpferwaren fpl.

**potty** ['pɔti], s. F: (for child) Töpfchen n.

**pouch** [pautʃ], s. Beutel m.

**poultry** ['pəultri], s. coll. Geflügel n.

**pounce** [pauns], v.i. sich stürzen (**on** auf + acc).

**pound¹** [paund], s. (weight, money) Pfund n; (a) **by the p.,** pfundweise; (b) **p. note,** Pfundnote f.

**pound²,** v.i. (of heart) pochen.

**pour** [pɔːr], v. 1. v.tr. (eine Flüssigkeit) gießen (**into/over sth.,** in/über etwas acc). 2. v.i. (a) **it's pouring** (with rain), es gießt; es regnet in Strömen; (b) (of water, Fig: of people etc.) strömen (**into,** in + acc; **out of,** aus + dat). ◆**'pour 'in,** v. 1. v.i. (of applications etc.) in großen Mengen eintreffen. 2. v.tr. (eine Flüssigkeit) eingießen. ◆**'pour 'out,** v.tr. Fig: **to p. out one's heart,** sein Herz ausschütten.

**pout** [paut], v.i. (of pers.) schmollen.

**poverty** ['pɔvəti], s. Armut f. ◆**'poverty-'stricken,** adj. verarmt.

**powder** ['paudər]. I. s. Pulver n; (cosmetic) Puder m. II. v.tr. (a) **to p. one's face,** sich dat das Gesicht pudern; (b) **powdered milk,** Trockenmilch f.

**power** ['pauər]. I. s. 1. Macht f; **it is beyond my p.,** es liegt nicht in meiner Macht; **to fall into s.o.'s p.,** in j-s Gewalt kommen; Pol: (of party) **in p.,** an der Macht. 2. (ability) Fähigkeit f; **p. of speech,** Sprechvermögen n. 3. (strength, force) (a) Tchn: etc: Stärke f (eines Motors); (of vehicle) **under its own p.,** mit eigener Kraft; (b) El: Strom m; **p. cable/line,** Starkstromleitung f; **p. point,**

Steckdose f; **p. station,** Kraftwerk n. 4. F: **the powers that be,** Vater Staat. 5. Mth: **three to the p. of four,** drei hoch vier. II. v.tr. (eine Maschine usw.) antreiben. ◆**'powerful,** adj. (a) (of engine, pers., animal etc.) stark; (of car) leistungsfähig; (of blow) heftig; (b) (influential) mächtig. ◆**'powerless,** s. (without influence) machtlos.

**practicable** ['præktikəbl], adj. (of plan, idea) durchführbar; (possible) möglich.

**practical** ['præktik(ə)l], adj. praktisch; **p. joke,** Streich m; **-ly,** adv. 1. praktisch. 2. F: (virtually) fast.

**practice** ['præktis], s. 1. (action) Praxis f; **in p.,** in der Praxis. 2. (a) (habit) Gewohnheit f; (custom) Brauch m; (b) **illegal p.,** illegale Handlungsweise. 3. (repeated exercise) (a) Übung f; **out of p.,** aus der Übung; **choir p.,** Chorprobe f; (b) Sp: etc: Training n. 4. Jur: Med: etc: Praxis f. ◆**'practise** ['præktis], v.tr. (a) (Klavier, Schwimmen) üben; **to p. what one preaches,** seine Lehren in die Tat umsetzen; (b) (einen Beruf) ausüben. ◆**prac'titioner,** s. Med: **general p.,** praktischer Arzt m.

**pragmatic** [præg'mætik], adj. pragmatisch.

**prairie** ['prɛəri], s. Prärie f.

**praise** [preiz]. I. s. Lob n; **in p. of s.o., sth.,** j-m, etwas dat zu Ehren. II. v.tr. loben. ◆**'praiseworthy,** adj. lobenswert.

**pram** [præm], s. Kinderwagen m.

**prance** [prɑːns], v.i. (of child etc.) hüpfen; (of horse) tänzeln.

**prank** [præŋk], s. Streich m.

**prawn** [prɔːn], s. Garnele f.

**pray** [prei], v.tr. & i. beten (**for sth.,** um etwas acc). ◆**'prayer,** s. Gebet n; **the Lord's P.** das Vaterunser.

**pre-** [priː-], prefix Vor-.

**preach** [priːtʃ], v. 1. v.tr. **to p. a sermon,** eine Predigt halten. 2. v.i. predigen (**about sth.,** von etwas dat). ◆**'preacher,** s. Prediger m.

**precarious** [pri'kɛəriəs], adj. unsicher; (dangerous) gefährlich.

**precaution** [pri'kɔːʃ(ə)n], s. Vorsichtsmaßnahme f; **to take precautions,** Vorsichtsmaßnahmen treffen; **as a p.,** vorsichtshalber.

**precede** [pri(ː)'siːd], v.tr. (j-m, einer Sache) vorausgehen. ◆**precedence** ['presidəns], s. **to take p.,** den Vorrang haben (**over s.o.,** vor j-m). ◆**precedent** ['presid(ə)nt], s. Präzedenzfall m. ◆**preceding** [pri'siːdiŋ]. I. adj. vorhergehend; **the p. day,** der vorige Tag. II. prep. **the week p. the match,** die Woche vor dem Spiel.

**precept** ['priːsept], s. Gebot n.

**precinct** ['priːsiŋkt], s. Gelände n; **shopping p.,** Einkaufszentrum n; **pedestrian p.,** Fußgängerzone f.

**precious** ['preʃəs]. I. adj. (a) (of great value) kostbar; **p. stones,** Edelsteine mpl.

**II.** *adv.* **p. little,** herzlich wenig.
**precipice** ['presipis], *s.* Steilwand *f.*
◆**pre'cipitous,** *adj. (of cliff)* abschüssig.
**precipitate I.** [pri'sipiteit] *v.tr. (hasten)* **(in order) to p. matters,** um die Sache zu beschleunigen. **II.** [-itit] *adj.* übereilt.
◆**precipi'tation,** *s. Meteor: & Ch:* Niederschlag *m.*
**precise** [pri'sais], *adj.* genau; **you must be p.,** Sie müssen präzise sein.
◆**precision** [-'siʒ(ə)n], *s.* Genauigkeit *f;* **p. engineering,** Feinmechanik *f.*
**precocious** [pri'kauʃəs], *adj.* frühreif; *Pej: (of small child)* altklug.
**preconceived** [pri:kən'si:vd], *adj.* **p. idea** *(also* **precon'ception),** vorgefaßte Meinung *f.*
**precursor** [pri(:)'kə:sər], *s.* Vorläufer(in) *m(f).*
**predator** ['predət(ə)r], *s.* Raubtier *n.*
**predecessor** ['pri:disesər], *s.* Vorgänger(in) *m(f).*
**predetermine** ['pri:di'tə:min], *v.tr.* vorherbestimmen.
**predicament** [pri'dikəmənt], *s.* mißliche Lage *f.*
**predict** [pri'dikt], *v.tr.* voraussagen.
◆**pre'dictable,** *adj.* leicht vorauszusagen. ◆**pre'diction,** *s.* Voraussage *f.*
**predilection** [pri:di'lekʃ(ə)n], *s.* Vorliebe *f.*
**predispose** [pri:dis'pəuz], *v.tr.* **predisposed to sth.,** zu etwas *dat* geneigt.
◆**predispo'sition,** *s.* Neigung *f* **(to,** zu + *dat).*
**predominate** [pri:'dɔmineit], *v.i. (numerically)* überwiegen; *(of feature)* vorherrschen. ◆**pre'dominance,** *s. (in numbers)* Überwiegen *n.*
**preeminent** [pri(:)'eminənt], *adj.* **to be p.,** den Vorrang haben.
**prefabricated** [pri:'fæbrikeitid], *adj.* **p. house,** Fertighaus *n.*
**preface** ['prefis], *s. (of book)* Vorwort *n.*
**prefect** ['pri:fekt], *s. Sch: Brit:* Aufsichtsschüler(in) *m(f).*
**prefer** [pri'fə:r], *v.tr. (etwas)* vorziehen; **I would p. to go without,** ich würde lieber darauf verzichten. ◆**preferable** ['pref-], *adj.* **p. (to sth.),** *(etwas dat)* vorzuziehen; **-ably,** *adv.* vorzugsweise. ◆**preference** ['pref-], *s.* Vorliebe *f* **(for sth.,** für etwas *acc).* ◆**prefe'rential** [pref-], *adj.* **p. treatment,** Vorzugsbehandlung *f.*
**prefix** ['pri:fiks], *s.* Präfix *n;* Vorsilbe *f.*
**pregnancy** ['pregnənsi], *s.* Schwangerschaft *f.* ◆**'pregnant,** *adj.* schwanger.
**prehistoric** [pri:hi'stɔrik], *adj.* vorgeschichtlich.
**prejudice** ['predʒudis]. **I.** *s.* **1.** Vorurteil *n.* **II.** *v.tr.* **to p. s.o. for/against sth.,** j-n für/gegen etwas *acc* beeinflussen.
◆**'prejudiced,** *adj. (of pers.)* voreingenommen **(for/against s.o., sth.,** für/gegen j-n, etwas *acc); (of judge, judgement)* befangen.

**preliminary** [pri'liminəri], *adj.* Vor-; *(preparatory)* vorbereitend; **p. remarks,** einleitende Bemerkungen.
**prelude** ['prelju:d], *s. Mus:* Vorspiel *n; Fig:* Auftakt *m* **(to,** zu + *dat).*
**premature** ['premətjuər], *adj.* frühzeitig; **p. birth,** Frühgeburt *f.*
**premeditated** [pri:'mediteitid], *adj.* vorsätzlich. ◆**premier** ['premiər]. **I.** *adj.* führend. **II.** *s. Pol:* Premierminister *m.*
**première** [pri'premiɛər], *s. Th:* Premiere *f,* Uraufführung *f.*
**premises** ['premisiz], *s.pl.* Räumlichkeiten *fpl; (restaurant)* Lokal *n;* **business p.,** Geschäftslokal *n;* **on the p.,** im Hause.
**premium** ['pri:miəm], *s.* **1.** *insurance* **p. 2. to be at a p.,** sehr gesucht sein.
**premonition** [pri:mə'niʃ(ə)n], *s.* Vorahnung *f.*
**preoccupation** [pri:ɔkju'peiʃ(ə)n], *s. (distraction)* Zerstreutheit *f;* Vertieftsein *n* **(with sth.,** in etwas *dat).*
◆**pre'occupied,** *adj.* in Gedanken vertieft.
**prepaid** ['pri:'peid], *adj.* im Voraus bezahlt.
**prepare** [pri'pɛər], *v.* **1.** *v.tr.* vorbereiten; *(ein Gericht)* zubereiten; **to p. to do sth.,** sich anschicken, etwas zu tun. **2.** *v.i.* **to p. for sth.,** sich auf etwas *acc* vorbereiten. ◆**prepa'ration,** *s.* Vorbereitung *f.* ◆**pre'paratory.** *adj.* vorbereitend. ◆**pre'pared,** *adj. (ready)* bereit.
**preponderance** [pri'pɔnd(ə)rəns], *s.* Überwiegen *n.*
**preposition** [prepə'ziʃ(ə)n], *s.* Präposition *f.*
**prepossessing** [pri:pə'zesiŋ], *adj.* anziehend.
**preposterous** [pri'pɔst(ə)rəs], *adj.* absurd.
**prerequisite** [pri:'rekwizit], *s.* Vorbedingung *f.*
**prescribe** [pri'skraib], *v.tr. Med:* **to p. sth. for s.o.,** j-m etwas verordnen/verschreiben. ◆**prescription** [-'skripʃ(ə)n], *s. Med:* Rezept *n.*
**presence** ['prez(ə)ns], *s.* Gegenwart *f,* Anwesenheit *f;* **in the p. of danger,** angesichts der Gefahr; **p. of mind,** Geistesgegenwart *f.* ◆**present**[1]. **I.** *adj.* **1.** *(place) (of pers.)* anwesend **(at,** bei + *dat);* **the people p.,** die Anwesenden *mpl;* **to be p. at a ceremony,** einer Zeremonie beiwohnen. **2.** *(time)* gegenwärtig; *(a)* **at the p. time,** zur Zeit; *(b) (existing, current)* jetzig; *(c) Gram:* **p. tense,** Gegenwart *f;* **-ly,** *adv. (soon)* bald. **II. s. the p.,** die Gegenwart; **up to the p.,** bis heute; **at p.,** zur Zeit; **for the p.,** vorläufig.
**present**[2]. **I.** ['prez(ə)nt] *s. (gift)* Geschenk *n.* **II.** [pri'zent] *v.tr. (a) (hand over) (ein* Gesuch usw.) einreichen; **to p. sth. to s.o.,** j-m etwas überreichen; *(b) (offer)* (eine Gelegenheit, Schwierigkeiten usw.) bieten; *Th:* **to p. a play,** ein Stück dar-

bieten; (c) (*introduce*) (j-n, sich) vorstellen; (ein Thema, eine Geschichte usw.) darstellen. ◆**pre'sentable** [pri-], *adj.* präsentabel. ◆**presen'tation** [prezə-], *s.* 1. *Th: etc:* Darbietung *f.* 2. (feierliche) Überreichung *f* (eines Preises usw.).

**presentiment** [pri'zentimənt], *s.* (böse) Vorahnung *f.*

**preserve** [pri'zəːv]. I. *v.tr.* (a) (ein Gebäude, den Frieden usw.) erhalten; (Dokumente) aufbewahren; **well preserved,** gut erhalten; (b) (Obst usw.) einmachen. II. *s usu. pl. Cu:* Eingemachtes *n;* (*jam*) Konfitüre *f.* ◆**pre'servative,** *s.* 1. (*in foods*) Konservierungsmittel *n.* 2. (*for wood etc.*) Schutzmittel *n.*

**preside** [pri'zaid], *v.i.* den Vorsitz haben (**at/over a meeting,** über eine Versammlung). ◆**'president,** *s.* (a) *N.Am: Com:* Vorsitzende(r) *m* (eines Konzerns); (b) *Pol:* Präsident *m.*

**press** [pres]. I. *s.* (*also newspapers*) Presse *f;* **p. cutting,** Zeitungsausschnitt *m;* **to have a good/bad p.,** eine gute/schlechte Presse haben; **to go to p.,** in Druck gehen. II. *v.* 1. *v.tr.* (a) (etwas) drücken; (Trauben usw.) keltern; **to p. the button,** auf den Knopf drücken; **to p. clothes,** Kleider bügeln; (b) (j-n) bedrängen; **to be pressed for time,** unter Zeitdruck stehen; **hard pressed,** schwer unter Druck. 2. *v.i.* **to p. on sth.,** auf etwas *acc* drücken; **to p. for sth.,** etwas fordern. ◆**'pressing,** *adj.* (*urgent*) dringend. ◆**'press 'on,** *v.i.* (a) (*walking*) weitergehen; (b) (*working*) weitermachen. ◆**pressure** ['preʃər], *s.* Druck *m;* **to bring s.o. to bear,** Druck ausüben. ◆**'pressurize,** *v.tr.* unter Druck setzen.

**prestige** [pres'tiːʒ], *s.* Prestige *n.*

**presume** [pri'zjuːm], *v.tr.* (a) (etwas) vermuten; (b) **to p. to do sth.,** sich *dat* erlauben, etwas zu tun. ◆**pre'sumably,** *adv.* vermutlich. ◆**pre'sumption,** *s.* Vermutung *f.* ◆**pre'sumptuous,** *adj.* anmaßend.

**presuppose** [priːsə'pəuz], *v.tr.* (etwas) voraussetzen.

**pretence** [pri'tens], *s.* Vortäuschung *f;* **by false pretences,** unter Vorspiegelung falscher Tatsachen. ◆**pre'tend** I. *v.tr.* (*feign*) (etwas) vortäuschen; **to p. to be sth.,** vorgeben, etwas zu sein; **he pretended to be in pain,** er tat, als ob er Schmerzen hätte; **he does not p. to be an expert,** er gibt sich nicht als Experte aus. 2. *v.i.* **he's only pretending,** er tut nur so. ◆**pre'tentious,** *adj.* überheblich.

**pretext** ['priːtekst], *s.* Vorwand *m;* **on the p. of consulting me,** unter dem Vorwand, mich zu Rate zu ziehen.

**pretty** ['priti]. I. *adj.* hübsch. II. *adv. F:* ziemlich; **p. well finished/the same,** so ziemlich fertig/das gleiche.

**prevail** [pri'veil], *v.i.* (a) **to p. on s.o. to do sth.,** j-n dazu bringen, etwas zu tun;

(b) (*of situation etc.*) herrschen; **calm prevails,** es herrscht Ruhe. ◆**pre'vailing,** *adj.* **p. winds,** vorherrschende Winde. ◆**'prevalent,** *adj.* vorherrschend.

**prevaricate** [pri'værikeit], *v.i.* Ausflüchte machen.

**prevent** [pri'vent], *v.tr.* (a) (j-n) hindern (**from doing sth.,** an etwas *dat*); (b) (etwas) verhindern; (einen Unfall usw.) verhüten. ◆**pre'vention,** *s.* Verhinderung *f;* **p. of accidents,** Unfallverhütung *f.* ◆**pre'ventive,** *adj.* vorbeugend.

**preview** ['priːvjuː], *s.* Vorbesichtigung *f* (einer Ausstellung usw.); *Th: Cin:* Vorschau *f.*

**previous** ['priːviəs], *adj.* (a) vorhergehend; **on the p. day,** am Tag vorher; (b) (*earlier*) früher; **-ly,** *adv.* vorher; (*formerly*) früher.

**pre-war** ['priːwɔːr], *adj.* Vorkriegs-.

**prey** [prei]. I. *s.* Beute *f;* **bird of p.,** Raubvogel *m.* II. *v.i.* **to p. upon insects etc.,** Insekten usw. jagen; *Fig:* **something is preying on his mind,** etwas bedrückt ihn/*F:* liegt ihm im Magen.

**price** [prais]. I. *s.* Preis *m;* **p. list,** Preisliste *f;* **p. reduction,** Preissenkung *f.* II. *v.tr.* den Preis (einer Ware) festsetzen; (*estimate*) schätzen. ◆**'priceless,** *adj.* (a) von un schätzbarem Wert; (b) *F:* (*of pers., story etc.*) unbezahlbar.

**prick** [prik]. I. *s.* Stich *m.* II. *v.tr.* (a) **to p. one's finger,** sich *dat* in den Finger stechen; (b) **to p. up one's ears,** die Ohren spitzen. ◆**'prickle.** I. *s.* Stachel *m.* II. *v.i.* stechen; (*of skin etc.*) prickeln. ◆**'prickly,** *adj.* stachlig; *Fig:* (*of pers., temper*) reizbar.

**pride** [praid]. I. *s.* Stolz *m;* **to take a p. in sth.,** auf etwas *acc* stolz sein. II. *v.tr.* **to p. oneself on sth.,** auf etwas *acc* stolz sein.

**priest** [priːst], *s.* Priester *m;* (*parish*) *p.,* Pfarrer *m.* ◆**'priesthood,** *s.* (a) *coll.* **the p.,** der Klerus; (b) (*office*) Priesteramt *n.*

**priggish** ['prigiʃ], *adj.* selbstgefällig.

**prim** [prim], *adj.* (*of pers.*) spröde; (*of manner*) geziert.

**primary** ['praiməri]. I. *adj.* 1. (*basic*) Grund-; **p. colours,** Grundfarben *fpl;* **p. school,** Grundschule *f.* 2. (*main*) Haupt-; **p. concern,** Hauptsorge *f.*

**prime¹** [praim]. I. *adj.* 1. (*first*) Haupt-; **of p. importance,** von höchster Wichtigkeit; **P. Minister,** Premierminister *m.* 2. *Mth:* **p. number,** Primzahl *f.* II. *s.* Blütezeit *f;* **in the p. of life,** in den besten Jahren.

**prime²,** *v.tr.* (a) *Mil:* (eine Bombe, Handgranate) scharfmachen; (b) (*in decorating etc.*) (etwas) grundieren.

**primitive** ['primitiv], *adj. esp. Pej:* primitiv; (*original*) ursprünglich.

**primrose** ['primrəuz], *s. Bot:* Primel *f.*

**prince** [prins], *s.* (*royal*) Prinz *m;* (*nobleman & Fig:*) Fürst *m.* ◆**prin'cess,** *s.*

Prinzessin *f.* ◆**princi'pality**, *s.* Fürstentum *n.*

**principal** ['prinsip(ə)l]. **I** *adj.* Haupt-; **-ly**, *adv.* hauptsächlich. **II.** *s.* **1.** (*a*) *Sch: etc:* Direktor *m;* (*b*) *Th:* Hauptdarsteller(in) *m(f).* **2.** *Fin:* Kapital *n.*

**principle** ['prinsipl], *s.* Prinzip *n;* **in p.,** im Prinzip; grundsätzlich; **to do sth. on p.,** etwas aus Prinzip tun.

**print** [print]. **I.** *s.* **1.** Druck *m;* **in p.,** im Druck; (*available*) vorrätig; **out of p.,** vergriffen. **2.** (*mark*) Abdruck *m.* **3.** *Phot:* Abzug *m.* **II.** *v.tr.* (*a*) (ein Buch, eine Zeitung) drucken; **printed matter,** Drucksache *f;* (*b*) (*write in capitals*) in Druckbuchstaben schreiben. ◆**'printer**, *s.* Drucker *m.* ◆**'printing**, *s.* (*process*) Drucken *n;* **p. press,** Druckerpresse *f;* **p. works,** Druckerei *f.* ◆**'print-out**, *s. Data-pr:* Ausdruck *m.*

**prior** ['praiər]. **I.** *adj.* früher (**to,** als). **II.** *adv.* **p. to,** vor + *dat;* **p. to my departure,** bevor/ehe ich abreise. ◆**priority** [prai'ɔriti], *s.* Priorität *f; Aut:* Vorfahrt *f;* **to give sth. p.,** etwas *dat* den Vorrang geben.

**priory** ['praiəri], *s. Ecc:* Priorat *n.*

**prism** ['prizm], *s.* Prisma *n.*

**prison** ['priz(ə)n], *s.* Gefängnis *n;* **to send s.o. to p.,** j-n ins Gefängnis stecken, j-n einsperren. ◆**'prisoner**, *s.* Gefangene(r) *f(m);* **to take s.o. p.,** j-n gefangennehmen.

**pristine** ['pristiːn], *adj.* unberührt; **in p. condition,** makellos.

**private** ['praivit]. **I.** *adj.* privat; Privat-; (*confidential*) vertraulich; **to keep a matter p.,** etwas für sich *acc* behalten; **p. parts,** Geschlechtsteile *npl;* (*on notice*) **P.,** kein Zutritt! **-ly,** *adv.* privat; (*secretly*) insgeheim; **p. owned,** in Privatbesitz. **II.** *s.* **1. in p.,** privat; (*of conversation*) unter vier Augen; (*of meeting*) hinter geschlossenen Türen. **2.** *Mil:* einfacher Soldat *m;* **P. Smith,** Soldat Smith. ◆**privacy** ['praivəsi, 'pri-], *s.* Zurückgezogenheit *f;* **in the p. of one's home,** bei sich zu Hause.

**privet** ['privit], *s.* Liguster *m.*

**privilege** ['privilidʒ], *s.* Privileg *n;* (*honour*) Ehre *f.* ◆**'privileged**, *adj.* privilegiert; **to be p. to do sth.,** die Ehre haben, etwas zu tun.

**prize** [praiz]. **I.** *s.* Preis *m.* **II.** *v.tr.* (j-n), etwas) schätzen. ◆**prizewinner**, *s.* Preisträger(in) *m(f).*

**pro1** [prəu]. **I.** *prep.* **1.** *F:* für + *acc;* **the pros and cons,** das Für und Wider. **2. p. rata,** anteilmäßig. **II.** *prefix* -freundlich; **p. German,** deutschfreundlich.

**pro2**, *s. Sp: F:* Profi *m.*

**probable** ['prɔbəbl], *adj.* wahrscheinlich; **the p. answer,** die vermutliche Antwort. ◆**proba'bility**, *s.* Wahrscheinlichkeit *f;* **in all p.,** höchstwahrscheinlich. ◆**'probably**, *adv.* wahrscheinlich.

**probation** [prəu'beiʃ(ə)n], *s.* Probezeit *f;*

*Jur:* Bewährung *f;* **on p.,** auf Probe/*Jur:* Bewährung; **p. officer,** Bewährungshelfer *m.* ◆**pro'bationary**, *adj.* Probe-; **p. period,** Probezeit *f.*

**probe** [prəub]. **I.** *v.* **1.** *v.tr.* (einen Gegenstand) forschend untersuchen; (eine Angelegenheit) erforschen. **2.** *v.i.* **to p. into sth.,** etwas forschend untersuchen. **II.** *s.* (*investigation*) Untersuchung *f.*

**problem** ['prɔbləm], *s.* Problem *n.* ◆**proble'matic**, *adj.* problematisch.

**procedure** [prə'siːdʒər], *s.* Verfahren *n.*

**proceed** [prə'siːd], *v.i.* (*a*) (*go*) sich (irgendwohin) begeben; (*continue*) (i) weiterfahren; (ii) (*on foot*) weitergehen; (*b*) (*act*) verfahren; **how shall we p.?** wie sollen wir verfahren/(*continue*) weitermachen? **to p. with a job,** (*start*) eine Arbeit in Angriff nehmen; (*c*) (*of thing*) vor sich gehen; **things are proceeding as usual,** alles geht seinen üblichen Gang. ◆**pro'ceedings**, *s.pl.* (*a*) *Parl: etc:* Vorgänge *mpl; Jur:* **legal p.,** Gerichtsverfahren *n;* **to take p. against s.o.,** gegen j-n gerichtlich vorgehen. ◆**proceeds** ['prəusiːdz], *s.pl.* Erlös *m* (**of a sale,** aus einem Verkauf).

**process** ['prəuses]. **I.** *s.* Vorgang *m; esp. Ind:* Verfahren *n;* **he is in the p. of moving,** er ist gerade dabei, umzuziehen. **II.** *v.tr.* (*a*) *Ind:* (Rohstoffe) verarbeiten; (*b*) *Phot:* (einen Film) entwickeln; (*c*) *Adm:* (einen Fall, eine Anmeldung) bearbeiten.

**procession** [prə'seʃ(ə)n], *s.* Umzug *m; Ecc: etc:* Prozession *f.*

**proclaim** [prə'kleim], *v.tr.* proklamieren. ◆**proclamation** [prɔklə'meiʃ(ə)n], *s.* Proklamation *f.*

**procrastinate** [prəu'kræstineit], *v.i.* (*of pers.*) zaudern.

**procure** [prə'kjuər], *v.* **1.** *v.tr.* (*a*) (Arbeit usw.) beschaffen. **2.** *v.i. Jur:* kuppeln.

**prod** [prɔd]. **I.** *v.tr.* (*a*) **to p. s.o., sth.,** j-n, etwas stoßen/*F:* knuffen; (*b*) *Fig:* (j-n) anspornen (**into doing sth.,** zu etwas *dat*). **II.** *s.* leichter Stoß *m.*

**prodigal** ['prɔdig(ə)l], *adj.* verschwenderisch; **the p. son,** der verlorene Sohn.

**prodigy** ['prɔdidʒi], *s.* **child/infant p.,** Wunderkind *n.* ◆**pro'digious**, *adj.* erstaunlich.

**produce. I.** [prə'djuːs] *v.tr.* (*a*) (*bring out*) (den Paß usw.) vorzeigen; (ein Taschentuch usw.) herausholen; (*b*) *Th:* (ein Stück) inszenieren; *Rad: TV:* (ein Programm) leiten; *Cin:* (bei einem Film) Regie führen; (*c*) (*manufacture*) (Waren usw.) produzieren, herstellen; (Blüten, Früchte) hervorbringen; (*d*) *Fig:* (eine Wirkung) erzielen; (eine Stimmung, ein Gefühl usw.) hervorrufen. **II.** ['prɔdjuːs] *s.* Produkte *npl.* ◆**pro'ducer**, *s.* **1.** *Com:* Erzeuger *m.* **2.** *Th:* Regisseur *m; Cin:* Produzent *m; Rad:* Spielleiter *m.* ◆**product** ['prɔdʌkt], *s.* Produkt *n.* ◆**pro'duction**, *s.* **1.** *Ind:* Herstellung *f;* Produktion *f;* **p. line,** Fließband *n;* **to be**

in p., hergestellt werden. 2. *Th:* Inszenierung *f.* ◆**pro'ductive,** *adj.* (*of activity*) produktiv; (*of mine, period etc.*) ergiebig. ◆**produc'tivity,** *s.* Produktivität *f.*

**profane** [prə'fein], *adj.* (*a*) (*of language*) lästerlich; (*b*) (*not sacred*) profan.

**profess** [prə'fes], *v.tr.* (seine Liebe usw.) erklären; (seine Unschuld usw.) beteuern; **I do not p. to be a scholar,** ich gebe mich nicht als Gelehrter aus. ◆**profession** [-'feʃ(ə)n], *s.* **1.** (*declaration*) Erklärung *f* (der Liebe). **2.** (*occupation*) Beruf *m;* **by p.,** von Beruf; **the professions,** die freien Berufe. ◆**pro'fessional. I.** *adj.* (*a*) beruflich; Berufs-; (*of practice etc.*) professionell; (*piece of work etc.*) fachmännisch. **II.** *s.* Fachmann *m; Sp: & F:* Profi *m.* ◆**pro'fessor,** *s.* Professor *m.* ◆**pro'fessorship,** *s.* Professur *f.*

**proficient** [prə'fiʃənt], *adj.* tüchtig; **to be p. in sth.,** in etwas *dat* bewandert sein. ◆**pro'ficiency,** *s.* Fertigkeit *f.*

**profile** ['prəufail], *s.* **1.** Profil *n.* **2.** (*article*) Porträt *n.*

**profit** ['prɔfit]. **I.** *s.* (*gain*) Gewinn *m;* (*advantage*) Vorteil *m;* **to sell at a p.,** etwas mit Gewinn verkaufen. **II.** *v.i.* **to p. by sth.,** aus etwas *dat* Gewinn ziehen. ◆**'profitable,** *adj.* rentabel; (*advantageous*) vorteilhaft.

**profound** [prə'faund], *adj.* (*a*) (*deep*) tief; (*b*) (*of knowledge*) gründlich; (*of thought etc.*) tiefgründig; **p. respect,** größte Hochachtung; **-ly,** *adv.* sehr, stark.

**profuse** [prə'fju:s], *adj.* überschwenglich; **-ly,** *adv.* **to perspire p.,** übermäßig schwitzen. ◆**pro'fusion,** *s.* Fülle *f.*

**program(me)** ['prəugræm]. **I.** *s.* Programm *n.* **II.** *v.tr.* (einen Computer usw.) programmieren. ◆**'programmer,** *s. Data-pr:* Programmierer *m.*

**progress. I.** ['prəugres] *s.* Fortschritt *m;* **to make p.,** Fortschritte machen; **to make quick/slow p.,** schnell/langsam vorankommen; **in p.,** im Gange. **II.** [prə'gres] *v.i.* (*a*) (*proceed*) (*of work etc.*) weitergehen; (*b*) (*make progress*) vorwärtskommen; (*develop*) sich entwickeln. ◆**pro'gression,** *s.* (*a*) Fortschritt *m* (von einer Sache zur anderen); (*sequence*) Folge *f;* (*b*) (*movement*) Fortbewegung *f.* ◆**pro'gressive,** *adj.* (*a*) (*in ideas*) fortschrittlich; (*b*) (*increasing*) progressiv; **-ly,** *adv.* zunehmend.

**prohibit** [prə'hibit], *v.tr.* (etwas) verbieten; **to p. s.o. from doing sth.,** j-m verbieten, etwas zu tun; **smoking prohibited,** Rauchen verboten. ◆**prohibition** [prəuhi'biʃ(ə)n], *s.* Verbot *n; N.Am. Hist:* Prohibition *f.* ◆**pro'hibitive,** *adj.* unerschwinglich.

**project. I.** [prə'dʒekt] *v.* **1.** *v.tr.* (*a*) *Phot:* (Dias, ein Bild) projizieren; *Th:* **to p. (one's voice),** seine Stimme weit tragen lassen. **2.** *v.i.* vorstehen; **to p. from/out of sth.,** aus etwas *dat* hervorragen. **II.**

['prɔdʒekt] *s.* Projekt *n.* ◆**pro'jection,** *s.* **1.** Projektion *f.* **2.** (*forecast*) Vorhersage *f.* **3.** (*sticking out*) Vorsprung *m;* (*rock*) Überhang *m.* ◆**pro'jector,** *s.* Projektor *m.*

**proletariat** [prəuli'tɛəriət], *s.* Proletariat *n.*

**prolific** [prə'lifik], *adj.* (*of writer etc.*) produktiv; (*of period etc.*) fruchtbar.

**prologue** ['prəulɔg], *s.* Prolog *m.*

**prolong** [prə'lɔŋ], *v.tr.* (ein Treffen usw.) verlängern. ◆**pro'longed,** *adj.* anhaltend; **a p. period,** eine längere Zeit.

**promenade** [prɔmən'ɑːd], *s.* Promenade *f.*

**prominence** ['prɔminəns], *s.* (*fame*) Berühmtheit *f;* (*importance*) Bedeutung *f.* ◆**'prominent,** *adj.* (*noticeable*) auffallend; (*projecting*) vorstehend; (*of pers.*) prominent; **p. position,** (*of pers.*) führende Stellung; **a p. figure,** eine wichtige Persönlichkeit.

**promiscuity** [prɔmisk'juiti], *s.* Promiskuität *f.*

**promise** ['prɔmis]. **I.** *s.* (*a*) Versprechen *n* (**to help etc.,** zu helfen usw.); (*b*) (*prospect*) Aussicht *f;* **to show great p.,** viel versprechen. **II.** *v.* **1.** *v.tr.* (*a*) **to p. s.o. sth.,** j-m etwas versprechen; (*b*) *Fig:* (etwas) in Aussicht stellen. **2.** *v.i.* **I p.,** ich verspreche es. ◆**'promising,** *adj.* vielversprechend.

**promontory** ['prɔmənt(ə)ri], *s.* Küstenvorsprung *m.*

**promote** [prə'məut], *v.tr.* (*a*) (j-n) befördern (**to the rank of,** zu + *dat*); (*b*) (eine Sache, gute Beziehungen, die Künste usw.) fördern; *Com:* **to p. a product,** für ein Produkt werben. ◆**pro'motion,** *s.* **1.** Beförderung *f* (von j-m); **to gain p.,** befördert werden. **2.** Förderung *f* (einer Sache); *Com:* Werbung *f* (für ein Produkt); **sales p.,** Absatzförderung *f.*

**prompt** [prɔm(p)t]. **I.** *adj.* (*a*) (*immediate*) prompt; (*b*) (*punctual*) pünktlich. **II.** *v.tr.* (*a*) **to p. s.o. to do sth.,** j-n veranlassen/ (*persuade*) dazu animieren, etwas zu tun; (*b*) *Th:* (einem Schauspieler) soufflieren.

**prone** [prəun], *adj.* **to be p. to sth.,** zu etwas *dat* neigen.

**prong** [prɔŋ], *s.* Zinke *f* (einer Gabel); (*sharp point*) Zacke *f.* ◆**'pronged,** *adj.* **two-/three p.,** zwei-/dreizinkig.

**pronoun** ['prəunaun], *s. Gram:* Pronomen *n,* Fürwort *n.*

**pronounce** [prə'nauns], *v.tr.* (*a*) (*declare*) (etwas) erklären; **to p. s.o. fit,** j-n für gesund erklären; *Jur:* (ein Urteil) verkünden; (*c*) (ein Wort usw.) aussprechen. ◆**pro'nounced,** *adj.* (*a*) (*noticeable*) auffallend; (*b*) (*distinct*) deutlich; **p. improvement,** ausgesprochene Verbesserung. ◆**pro'nouncement,** *s.* **1.** *Jur:* Verkündigung *f.* **2.** Erklärung *f.* ◆**pronunci'ation** [-nʌn-], *s.* Aussprache *f.*

**proof** [pruːf]. **I.** *s.* **1.** Beweis *m*. **2.** (*of alcohol*) Alkoholgehalt *m*. **3.** (*a*) p. (**stage**), Korrektur *f*; (**galley**) p., Korrekturfahne *f*; (*b*) *Phot*: Probeabzug *m*. **II.** *adj.* -fest; **p. against the weather**, wetterfest.

**prop¹** [prɔp]. **I.** *s.* Stütze *f*. **II.** *v.tr.* **to p.** (**up**) **sth.**, etwas stützen.

**prop²**, *s. Th*: *usu. pl.* **props**, Requisiten *npl*.

**propaganda** [prɔpəˈɡændə], *s.* Propaganda *f*.

**propel** [prəˈpel], *v.tr.* (j-n, etwas) (vorwärts)treiben; **propelled by steam**, mit Dampfantrieb. ◆**proˈpeller**, *s.* Propeller *m*.

**propensity** [prəˈpensiti], *s.* Hang *m* (**for/to sth.**, zu etwas *dat*).

**proper** [ˈprɔpər], *adj.* richtig; **they're very p.**, sie sind sehr korrekt; **p. name**, Eigenname *m*; **in the hotel p.**, im Hotel selbst; **-ly**, *adv.* richtig; **not p. shut**, nicht richtig geschlossen; **to behave p.**, sich anständig benehmen.

**property** [ˈprɔpəti], *s.* **1.** (*a*) (*thing owned*) Eigentum *n*; **lost p.**, Fundsachen *fpl*; (*b*) (*house etc.*) Besitz *m*; (*small*) Haus *n*; (*c*) *coll.* (*land, buildings*) Immobilien *pl*. **2.** (*attribute*) Eigenschaft *f* (eines Stoffes).

**prophecy** [ˈprɔfisi], *s.* Prophezeiung *f*. ◆ˈ**prophesy** [-sai], *v.tr. & i.* prophezeien. ◆**prophet** [-fit], *s.* Prophet *m*.

**proportion** [prəˈpɔːʃ(ə)n]. **I.** *s.* **1.** (*a*) (*part*) Teil *m*; (*b*) *Ch: Cu: etc:* (*amount in mixture*) Anteil *m*. **2.** (*relation*) Verhältnis *n*; Proportion *f*; **in p.**, im richtigen Verhältnis; **to lose all sense of p.**, jeglichen Maßstab/Überblick verlieren. **3.** *pl.* **a debt of enormous proportions**, eine Schuld von gewaltigem Ausmaß. **II.** *v.tr.* **well proportioned**, gut proportioniert. ◆**proˈportional**, *adj.* proportional (**to**, zu + *dat*); (*of figures*) **to be p.**, im Verhältnis zueinander stehen; *Pol:* **p. representation**, Verhältniswahlrecht *n*. ◆**proˈportionate**, *adj.* im richtigen Verhältnis; **to be p. to sth.**, etwas *dat* entsprechen.

**propose** [prəˈpəuz], *v.* **1.** *v.tr.* (*a*) (*suggest*) (j-n, etwas) vorschlagen; **to p. a toast**, einen Toast ausbringen; (*b*) (*intend*) (etwas) vorhaben; **how do you p. to do it?** wie wollen Sie es tun? **2.** *v.i.* **to p. to a girl**, einem Mädchen einen Heiratsantrag machen. ◆**proˈposal**, *s.* (*suggestion*) Vorschlag *m*. ◆**proposition** [prɔpəˈziʃ(ə)n], *s.* (*suggestion*) Vorschlag *m*; (*plan*) Vorhaben *n*; (*in debate*) Antrag *m*.

**proprietor** [prəˈpraiətər], *s.* Besitzer *m*.

**propriety** [prəˈpraiəti], *s.* **1.** Anstand *m*. **2.** (*rightness*) Angemessenheit *f* (einer Bemerkung usw.).

**propulsion** [prəˈpʌlʃ(ə)n], *s.* Antrieb *m*.

**prosaic** [prəuˈzeiik], *adj.* prosaisch.

**prose** [prəuz]. **I.** *s.* **1.** Prosa *f*. **2.** *Sch:* Übersetzung *f* (in eine Fremdsprache).

**prosecute** [ˈprɔsikjuːt], *v.tr. & i. Jur:* to

p. s.o., gegen j-n gerichtlich vorgehen. ◆**proseˈcution**, *s. Jur:* (*a*) (*action*) strafrechtliche Verfolgung *f* (eines Verbrechens); (*b*) (*prosecuting party*) Anklagevertretung *f*. ◆ˈ**prosecutor**, *s. Jur:* Ankläger *m*.

**prospect** [ˈprɔspekt], *s.* Aussicht *f*; **job with good prospects**, Stellung mit guten Aufstiegsmöglichkeiten. ◆**prosˈpective**, *adj.* (*future*) künftig; (*possible*) eventuell; **p. client**, potentieller Kunde.

**prospectus**, *pl* **-uses** [prəˈspektəs, -əsiz], *s.* Prospekt *m*.

**prosper** [ˈprɔspər], *v.i.* (*of business etc.*) blühen. ◆**prosˈperity**, *s.* Wohlstand *m*. ◆ˈ**prosperous**, *adj.* (*of pers.*) wohlhabend; (*of business*) erfolgreich.

**prostitute** [ˈprɔstitjuːt], *s.* Prostituierte *f*. ◆**prostiˈtution**, *s.* Prostitution *f*.

**prostrate** [ˈprɔstreit], *adj.* **1.** **p. on the floor**, auf dem Boden hingestreckt. **2.** *Fig:* **p. with grief**, vor Gram gebrochen.

**protagonist** [prəuˈtæɡənist], *s.* Hauptfigur *f*.

**protect** [prəˈtekt], *v.tr.* (j-n, etwas) schützen (**from sth.**, vor etwas *dat*); **to p. one's interests**, seine Interessen wahren. ◆**proˈtection**, *s.* Schutz *m*. ◆**proˈtective**, *adj.* (*a*) Schutz-; **p. layer**, Schutzschicht *f*; (*b*) (*of pers.*) schützend. ◆**proˈtector**, *s.* Schützer *m*.

**protein** [ˈprəutiːn], *s.* Eiweiß *n*.

**protest I.** [ˈprəutest] *s.* Protest *m*; **to make a p.**, protestieren; *Jur:* Einspruch erheben; **under p.**, unter Protest. **II.** [prəˈtest] *v.* **1.** *v.i.* protestieren. **2.** *v.tr.* **to p. one's innocence**, seine Unschuld beteuern. ◆**Protestant** [ˈprɔtistənt]. **I.** *s.* Protestant(in) *m(f)*. **II.** *adj.* protestantisch.

**protocol** [ˈprəutəkɔl], *s.* Protokoll *n*.

**protract** [prəˈtrækt], *v.tr.* (Verhandlungen usw.) in die Länge ziehen. ◆**proˈtracted**, *adj.* langwierig.

**protrude** [prəˈtruːd], *v.i.* hervorstehen; (*of ears*) abstehen; (*of teeth*) vorstehen. ◆**proˈtrusion**, *s.* Vorsprung *m*.

**proud** [praud], *adj.* **1.** stolz (**of s.o., sth.**, auf j-n, etwas *acc*). **2.** *Pej:* hochmütig.

**prove** [pruːv], *v.irr.* **1.** *v.tr.* (*a*) (Schuld, eine Tatsache) beweisen; (seine Identität usw.) nachweisen; (*b*) (*confirm*) (etwas) bestätigen; (*c*) **to p. itself/oneself**, sich bewähren; **to p. oneself to be a good friend**, sich als treuer Freund erweisen. **2.** *v.i.* sich herausstellen.

**proverb** [ˈprɔvəːb], *s.* Sprichwort *n*. ◆**proˈverbial** [prəˈvəːbjəl], *adj.* sprichwörtlich; (*in negative contexts*) notorisch.

**provide** [prəˈvaid], *v.* **1.** *v.i.* **to p. for**, (*foresee*) (eine Möglichkeit) voraussehen; (*satisfy*) (Bedürfnisse) befriedigen; (Kosten) decken; **to p. for a family**, für eine Familie sorgen. **2.** *v.tr.* (Unterstützung usw.) zur Verfügung stellen; (eine Gelegenheit) bieten; **to p. s.o., sth. with sth.**, j-n, etwas mit etwas *dat* versehen/

(*supply*) beliefern. ◆**pro'vided**, *conj.* p. **(that)** ..., vorausgesetzt, (daß) ...

**providence** ['prɔvid(ə)ns], *s.* Vorsehung *f.*

**province** ['prɔvins], *s.* Provinz *f.* ◆**provincial** [prə'vinʃ(ə)l], *adj.* provinziell; **p. town**, Provinzstadt *f.*

**provision** [prə'viʒ(ə)n]. **I.** *s.* **1.** (*a*) (*providing*) Versehen *n* (of sth., mit etwas *dat*); (*b*) **to make p. for sth.**, Vorkehrungen für etwas *acc* treffen. **2.** *pl* Lebensmittel *npl*; (*supplies*) Vorräte *mpl*. **3.** *Jur:* Bestimmung *f* (eines Vertrags usw.). ◆**pro'visional**, *adj.* provisorisch.

**proviso**, *pl.* -**oes** [prə'vaizəu, -əuz], *s.* Vorbehalt *m.*

**provocation** [prɔvə'keiʃən], *s.* Provokation *f*; Herausforderung *f.* ◆**provocative** [prə'vɔk-], *adj.* herausfordernd. ◆**provoke** [prə'vəuk], *v.tr.* (j-n) provozieren; **to p. s.o. to do sth.**, j-n dazu herausfordern, etwas zu tun.

**prowess** ['prauis], *s.* (*skill*) Tüchtigkeit *f.*

**prowl** [praul]. **I.** *v.i.* **to p. (around)**, herumschleichen. **II.** *s.* **to be on the p.**, herumstreifen.

**proximity** [prɔk'simiti], *s.* Nähe *f.*

**proxy** ['prɔksi], *s.* **by p.**, in Vertretung.

**prude** [pru:d], *s.* Prüde(r) *f(m)*. ◆**'prudish**, *adj.* prüde.

**prudence** ['pru:d(ə)ns], *s.* Umsicht *f.* ◆**'prudent**, *adj.* umsichtig; **-ly**, *adv.* klugerweise.

**prune¹** [pru:n], *s.* Backpflaume *f.*

**prune²**, *v.tr.* (einen Baum usw.) beschneiden.

**Prussia** ['prʌʃə]. *Pr. n.* Preußen *n.* ◆**'Prussian**. **I.** *adj.* preußisch. **II.** *s.* Preuße *m*, Preußin *f.*

**pry** [prai], *v.i.* **to p. into sth.**, seine Nase in etwas *acc* stecken.

**psalm** [sɑ:m], *s.* Psalm *m.*

**pseudo** ['sju:dəu]. **I.** *prefix* pseudo-. **II.** *adj. F:* unecht.

**pseudonym** ['sju:dənim], *s.* Pseudonym *n.*

**psychiatry** [sai'kaiətri], *s.* Psychiatrie *f.* ◆**psy'chiatrist**, *s.* Psychiater *m.*

**psychic** ['saikik], *adj.* (*of phenomena*) übersinnlich.

**psychoanalysis** [saikəuə'nælisis], *s.* Psychoanalyse *f.*

**psychology** [sai'kɔlədʒi], *s.* Psychologie *f.* ◆**psycho'logical**, *adj.* psychologisch; (*of illness, pressure, reasons etc.*) psychisch. ◆**psy'chologist**, *s.* Psychologe *m*, Psychologin *f.*

**pub** [pʌb], *s.* (= **public house**) *F:* Wirtschaft *f*; **p. crawl**, Kneipenrunde *f.*

**puberty** ['pju:bəti], *s.* Pubertät *f.*

**public** ['pʌblik]. **I.** *adj.* öffentlich; **p. demand**, allgemeine Nachfrage *f*; **p. house**, Wirtshaus *n*; **p. relations**, Öffentlichkeitsarbeit *f.* **II.** *s.* **1.** **the** (**general**) **p.**, die (breite) Öffentlichkeit; **in p.**, in der Öffentlichkeit. **2.** (*audience*) Publikum *n.*

**publican** ['pʌblikən], *s.* Wirt *m.*

**publication** [pʌbli'keiʃ(ə)n], *s. Lit: etc:* Veröffentlichung *f.*

**publicity** [pʌb'lisiti], *s.* Publicity *f*; Werbung *f.* ◆**'publicize**, *v.tr.* (*a*) (etwas) öffentlich bekanntmachen; (*b*) (*advertize*) Reklame machen (für etwas *acc*).

**publish** ['pʌbliʃ], *v.tr.* (einen Roman usw.) veröffentlichen. ◆**'publisher**, *s.* Verleger *m.* ◆**'publishing**, *s.* **p. house**, Verlag *m.*

**pudding** ['pudiŋ], *s.* **1.** *Cu:* Pudding *m*; **rice p.**, Milchreis *m.* **2.** (*dessert*) Nachtisch *m.*

**puddle** ['pʌdl], *s.* Pfütze *f.*

**puerile** ['pjuərail], *adj.* infantil.

**puff** [pʌf]. **I.** *s.* **1.** (*a*) **p. of wind**, leichter Windstoß *m*; (*b*) Zug *m* (an einer Zigarette); **p. of smoke**, Rauchwölkchen *n.* **2.** *Cu:* **p. pastry**, Blätterteig *m.* **II.** *v.* **1.** *v.i.* (*a*) (*of smoker*) paffen; (*b*) (*of pers., steam train*) keuchen. **2.** *v.tr.* **to p.** (**out**) **smoke**, Rauch ausstoßen. ◆**puffed**, *adj.* (*of pers.*) außer Atem. ◆**'puffy**, *adj.* (*of face*) aufgedunsen.

**pugnacious** [pʌg'neiʃəs], *adj.* kampflustig.

**puke** [pju:k], *v.i. P:* kotzen.

**pull** [pul]. **I.** *s.* Zug *m*; **to give sth. a p.**, an etwas *dat* ziehen. **II.** *v.* **1.** *v.tr.* (*a*) (etwas) ziehen; (*b*) **to p. a muscle**, sich *dat* einen Muskel zerren. **2.** *v.i.* ziehen. ◆**'pull 'down**, *v.tr.* (ein Gebäude) niederreißen. ◆**'pull 'in**, *v.i.* (*of train*) einfahren; *Aut:* **to p. in** (**to the kerb**), (am Randstein) anhalten. ◆**'pull 'off**, *v.* **1.** *v.tr. F:* **to p. o. a victory**, den Sieg erringen. **2.** *v.i. Aut:* (*start*) losfahren. ◆**'pull 'out**, *v.* **1.** *v.tr.* (einen Zahn usw.) herausziehen. **2.** *v.i.* (*of train*) abfahren; (*of car etc.*) ausscheren. ◆**'pullover**, *s. Cl:* Pullover *m.* ◆**'pull 'round/'through**, *v.i.* (*of patient*) durchkommen. ◆**'pull to'gether**, *v.tr.* **to p. oneself t.**, sich zusammennehmen. ◆**'pull 'up**, *v.* **1.** *v.tr.* (die Rolläden usw.) hochziehen. **2.** *v.i.* (*of rider, vehicle*) anhalten.

**pulley** ['puli], *s.* Rolle *f.*

**pulp** [pʌlp], *s.* **1.** (*of fruit*) Fruchtfleisch *n.* **2.** (*paper*) **p.**, Papierbrei *m.*

**pulpit** ['pulpit], *s.* Kanzel *f.*

**pulse** [pʌls], *s.* Puls *m*; **to feel s.o.'s p.**, j-m den Puls fühlen. ◆**pul'sate**, *v.i.* pulsieren.

**pulverize** ['pʌlvəraiz], *v.tr.* (eine Substanz) pulverisieren; (Gestein) zerkleinern.

**pumice** ['pʌmis], *s.* **p.** (-**stone**), Bimsstein *m.*

**pump** [pʌmp]. **I.** *s.* Pumpe *f*; *Aut:* **p. attendant**, Tankwart *m.* **II.** *v.tr.* (*a*) (Wasser usw.) pumpen; *Aut:* **to p.** (**up**) **a tyre**, einen Reifen aufpumpen; (*b*) *F:* **to p. s.o.**, j-n ausfragen.

**pumpkin** ['pʌm(p)kin], *s.* Kürbis *m.*

**pun** [pʌn], *s.* Wortspiel *n.*

**punch¹** [pʌntʃ]. **I.** *s.* **1.** (*tool*) Stempel *m*;

(*for paper etc.*) Locher *m.* 2. (*blow*) Faustschlag *m.* **II.** *v.tr.* (*a*) (Papier usw.) lochen; (*b*) (j-n, etwas) mit der Faust schlagen; **to p. s.o.'s face**, j-m eine ins Gesicht geben/langen. ◆'**punch-up**, *s. F:* Schlägerei *f.*

**punch²,** *s.* (*drink*) Punsch *m.*

**punctual** ['pʌŋktju(ə)l], *adj.* pünktlich.

**punctuate** ['pʌŋktjueit], *v.tr. & i.* (einen Text) interpunktieren. ◆**punctu'ation**, *s.* Interpunktion *f.*

**puncture** ['pʌŋktʃər]. **I.** *s. Aut: etc:* Reifenpanne *f;* **to mend a p.**, einen Reifen flicken. **II.** *v.tr.* (ein Luftkissen usw.) durchstechen.

**pungent** ['pʌndʒənt], *adj.* **1.** (*of smell*) stechend. **2.** (*of remark, satire etc.*) beißend.

**punish** ['pʌniʃ], *v.tr.* (*a*) bestrafen; (*b*) *Fig:* (einen Motor usw.) strapazieren. ◆'**punishable**, *adj.* strafbar; **it is p. by a fine**, darauf steht eine Geldstrafe. ◆'**punishing**, *adj.* strapazierend. ◆'**punishment**, *s.* Strafe *f;* (*process*) Bestrafung *f.*

**punk** [pʌŋk], *s.* (*a*) (*Pers.*) Punker *m;* (*b*) (*music*) Punk *m.*

**punter** ['pʌntər], *s. Sp:* Wetter *m.*

**puny** ['pju:ni], *adj.* kümmerlich.

**pupil¹** ['pju:p(i)l], *s. Sch:* Schüler(in) *m(f).*

**pupil²,** *s.* Pupille *f* (des Auges).

**puppet** ['pʌpit], *s.* Marionette *f.*

**puppy** ['pʌpi], *s.* junger Hund *m; Pej:* **p. fat**, Babyspeck *m.*

**purchase** ['pə:tʃəs]. **I.** *s.* Kauf *m;* (*article*) Anschaffung *f;* **p. price**, Kaufpreis *m.* **II.** *v.tr.* (etwas) kaufen; **purchasing power**, Kaufkraft *f.* ◆'**purchaser**, *s.* Käufer(in) *m(f).*

**pure** [pjuər], *adj.* rein.

**purgatory** ['pə:gət(ə)ri], *s.* Fegefeuer *n.*

**purge** [pə:dʒ]. **I.** *s. esp. Pol:* Säuberungsaktion *f.* **II.** *v.tr.* (ein Land, eine politische Partei usw.) säubern. ◆'**purgative** [-gə-], *s. Med:* Abführmittel *n.*

**purify** ['pjuərifai], *v.tr.* (etwas) reinigen. ◆purifi'cation, *s.* Reinigung *f.* ◆'**purist**, *s.* Purist *m.* ◆'**purity**, *s.* Reinheit *f.*

**Puritan** ['pjuərit(ə)n]. **I.** *s.* Puritaner(in) *m(f).* **II.** *adj.* (*also* puri'tanical) puritanisch.

**purl** [pə:l], *s.* **p. stitch**, Linksmasche *f.*

**purple** ['pə:pl]. **I.** *s.* Purpur *m.* **II.** *adj.* purpurrot.

**purpose** ['pə:pəs], *s.* (*aim*) Zweck *m;* (*intention*) Absicht *f;* **on p.**, absichtlich; **for this**, zu diesem Zweck. ◆'**purposeful**, *adj.* zielbewußt. ◆'**purposely**, *adv.* absichtlich.

**purr** [pə:r], *v.i.* (*of cat*) schnurren.

**purse** [pə:s]. **I.** *s.* **1.** Portemonnaie *n.* **II.** *v.tr.* **to p. one's lips**, die Lippen schürzen. ◆'**purser**, *s. Nau:* Zahlmeister *m.*

**pursue** [pə'sju:], *v.tr.* (j-n, etwas) verfolgen; (dem Vergnügen, seinem Studium

usw.) nachgehen. ◆**pur'suit**, *s.* (*a*) Verfolgung *f;* (*b*) Ausübung *f* (eines Gewerbes); Betreiben *n* (von Studien); *Fig:* **the p. of happiness**, die Jagd nach dem Glück.

**purveyor** [pə'veiər], *s.* Lieferant *m.*

**pus** [pʌs], *s.* Eiter *m.*

**push** [puʃ]. **I.** *s.* **1.** Stoß *m; F:* **to give s.o. the p.**, j-n rausschmeißen. **2.** *F:* **at a p.**, im Notfall. **II.** *v.* **1.** *v.tr.* (*a*) (etwas) schieben; **p. the button**, (auf) den Knopf drücken; **to p. oneself forward**, sich nach vorne drängen; (*b*) *F:* **I'm pushed (for time)**, ich stehe unter Zeitdruck; (*c*) *F:* **he's pushing forty**, er wird (bald) vierzig. **2.** *v.i.* drängen. ◆'**pusher**, *s.* (*drug*) **p.**, Rauschgifthändler *m.* ◆'**push-bike**, *s. F:* Fahrrad *n.* ◆'**push 'off**, *v.i. F:* (*leave*) abhauen.

**puss/pussy** [pus, 'pusi], *s. F:* Miezekatze *f.*

**put** [put], *v.tr.* (*a*) (*place*) (etwas) setzen, stellen, *F:* tun (**on/in**, auf/in + *acc*); **p. it on the table**, setzen/legen/stellen Sie es auf den Tisch; **to p. sth. in a cupboard**, etwas in einen Schrank stecken/*F:* tun; **to p. milk in one's tea**, Milch in seinen Tee tun; **to p. the matter right**, die Angelegenheit ins reine bringen; **to p. a law into operation**, ein Gesetz in Kraft setzen; **to stay p.**, sich nicht vom Fleck rühren; (*b*) (*express*) (etwas) ausdrücken; **to p. it mildly**, gelinde gesagt; **to p. a question to s.o.**, j-m eine Frage stellen; **I'll p. it to him**, ich werde es ihm vorschlagen; (*c*) (*estimate*) **I p. the population at 10,000**, ich schätze die Bevölkerung auf 10 000. ◆'**put a'cross**, *v.tr.* (eine Idee usw.) verständlich machen. ◆'**put a'way**, *v.tr.* (*a*) (seine Sachen) wegräumen; (*b*) *F:* **to p. s.o. a.**, j-n einsperren. ◆'**put 'back**, *v.tr.* (etwas) zurückstecken (**in sth.**, in etwas *acc*); (etwas) zurücklegen (**on sth.**, auf etwas *acc*). ◆'**put 'by**, *v.tr.* (etwas) weglegen; (Geld) auf die hohe Kante legen. ◆'**put 'down**, *v.tr.* (*a*) (etwas) niedersetzen; (*b*) (*write*) (etwas) aufschreiben; (*c*) (*attribute*) **you can p. it d. to his ignorance**, man kann es seiner Unwissenheit zuschreiben; (*d*) **to p. d. an animal**, ein Tier einschläfern. ◆'**put 'forward**, *v.tr.* (j-n, einen Plan usw.) vorschlagen; (einen Vorschlag) unterbreiten. ◆'**put 'in** *v.* **1.** *v.tr.* (etwas) hineinsetzen. **2.** *v.i.* (*a*) *Nau:* **to p. in to a port**, in einen Hafen einlaufen; (*b*) **to p. in for a post**, sich um eine Stelle bewerben. ◆'**put 'off**, *v.* **1.** *v.tr.* (*a*) (*postpone*) (etwas) verschieben (**for a week, um eine Woche**); (*b*) **to p. s.o. o. with an excuse**, j-n mit einer Ausrede abspeisen; (*c*) *F:* (*dissuade*) **to p. s.o. o. doing sth.**, j-n von etwas *dat* abbringen; **the noise puts me o.**, der Lärm stört mich. ◆'**put 'on**, *v.tr.* (*a*) **to p. the kettle/the potatoes on**, Wasser/die Kartoffeln aufsetzen; **to p. on a record/a**

**tape,** eine Platte auflegen/ein Band spielen; (*b*) (*organize*) (eine Ausstellung usw.) veranstalten; *Th:* (ein Stück) aufführen; (*c*) (*switch on*) (ein Licht usw.) einschalten; *Aut:* to p. the brakes on, bremsen; (*d*) (Kleider, Schuhe) anziehen; to p. on one's clothes, sich anziehen; to p. on one's hat, den Hut aufsetzen; (*e*) to p. on weight, zunehmen. ◆'put 'out, *v.tr.* (*a*) (*stretch out*) (die Hand usw.) ausstrecken; (*b*) (*switch off*) (das Licht usw.) ausschalten; he p. himself o. for me, er machte sich meinetwegen viel Mühe. ◆'put 'over, *v.tr.* = put across. ◆'put 'through, *v.tr. Tel:* can you p. me t. to X? können Sie mich bitte mit X verbinden? ◆'put to'gether, *v.tr.* (*a*) (mehrere Teile) zusammensetzen; (*b*) (*assemble*) (eine Maschine usw.) zusammenbauen; *Fig:* to p. two and two t., seine Schlüsse ziehen. ◆'put 'up, *v.tr.* (*a*) (einen Schirm) aufspannen; (einen Vorhang usw.) aufhängen; (*b*) (ein Plakat usw.) anbringen; (*c*) (*increase*) (Preise) erhöhen; (*d*) (*accommodate*) (j-n) unterbringen; (*e*) to p. up with sth., sich mit etwas *dat* abfinden; (*f*) to p. s.o. up to sth., j-n zu etwas *dat* anstiften; (*g*) (ein Gebäude) errichten; (ein Zelt) aufschlagen. ◆'put u'pon, *p.p. only* to be p. u., ausgenutzt werden.

**putrefy** ['pju:trifai], *v.i.* (*of object*) faulen.
**putrid** ['pju:trid], *adj.* (*of food etc.*) faulig.
**putt** [pʌt]. I. *s.* (*in golf*) Putt *m.* II. *v.i.* putten.
**putty** ['pʌti], *s.* Kitt *m.*
**puzzle** ['pʌzl]. I. *s.* Rätsel *n;* (jigsaw) p., Puzzlespiel *n.* II. *v.tr.* (j-n) verdutzen; it puzzles me, es ist mir ein Rätsel. ◆'puzzled, *adj.* verdutzt. ◆'puzzling, *adj.* rätselhaft.
**pygmy** ['pigmi], *s.* Pygmäe *m*, Pygmäin *f.*
**pyjamas** [pi'dʒɑ:məz], *s.pl.* Schlafanzug *m.*
**pylon** ['pailən], *s.* Hochspannungsmast *m.*
**pyramid** ['pirəmid], *s.* Pyramide *f.*
**Pyrenees** [pirə'ni:z], *Pr. n.* the P., die Pyrenäen *pl.*
**python** ['paiθ(ə)n], *s.* Pythonschlange *f.*

# Q

**Q, q** [kju:], *s.* (der Buchstabe) Q, q *n.*
**quack¹** [kwæk], *v.i.* (*of duck*) quaken.
**quack²,** *s.* (*a*) q. (doctor), Kurpfuscher *m;* (*b*) (*charlatan*) Scharlatan *m.*
**quad** [kwɔd], *s. F: abbr.* (*child*) Vierling *m.*
**quadrangle** ['kwɔdræŋgl], *s. Arch:* (viereckiger) Hof *m.*
**quadruped** ['kwɔdruped], *s.* Vierfüßler *m.*
**quadruple** ['kwɔdrupl]. I. *adj.* vierfach; (*in four parts*) vierteilig. II. *v.tr.* vervierfachen. ◆'quadruplet, *s.* Vierling *m.*
**quagmire** ['kwægmaiər, 'kwɔg-], *s.* Morast *m.*
**quail** [kweil], *s.* Wachtel *f.*
**quaint** [kweint], *adj.* (*a*) (*of house, village*) malerisch; (*b*) (*curious*) kurios; *N.Am:* drollig.
**quake** [kweik], *v.i.* zittern, (with fear, vor Angst).
**Quaker** ['kweikər], *s.* Quäker *m.*
**qualify** ['kwɔlifai], *v.* 1. *v.tr.* (*a*) to q. s.o. for sth., (*entitle*) j-n zu etwas *dat* berechtigen; (*make suitable*) j-n für etwas *acc* geeignet machen; (*b*) (*modify*) to q. a statement etc., eine Behauptung einschränken. 2. *v.i.* (*a*) (*be suitable*) sich eignen (for, zu + *dat*); to q. for assistance, zur Unterstützung berechtigt sein; (*b*) (*train, pass test*) sich qualifizieren (as an engineer, zum Ingenieur). ◆qualification [-i'keiʃ(ə)n], *s.* Qualifikation *f.* ◆'qualified, *adj.* (*a*) (*of pers.*) qualifiziert; geeignet; (*b*) (*entitled*) berechtigt.
**quality** ['kwɔliti], *s.* 1. Qualität *f* (einer Ware usw.); *Com:* q. goods, Qualitätswaren *fpl;* of good/bad q., von guter/schlechter Qualität. 2. (*characteristic*) Eigenschaft *f;* (*consistency*) Beschaffenheit *f.*
**qualm** [kwɑ:m], *s.* to have no qualms about doing sth., keine Bedenken haben, etwas zu tun.
**quandary** ['kwɔndəri], *s.* to be in a q., sich in einem Dilemma befinden.
**quantity** ['kwɔntiti], *s.* (*a*) Quantität *f;* (*amount*) Menge *f;* (*number*) Anzahl *f;* (*b*) q. surveyor, Baukostensachverständige(r) *m.*
**quarantine** ['kwɔrənti:n]. I. *s.* Quarantäne *f.* II. *v.tr.* (j-n, ein Tier) unter Quarantäne stellen.
**quarrel** ['kwɔrəl]. I. *s.* Streit *m;* to have a q., sich streiten. II. *v.i.* (*sich*) streiten (with s.o. over/about sth., mit j-m über etwas *acc*). ◆'quarrelsome, *adj.* streitsüchtig.
**quarry** ['kwɔri]. I. *s.* Steinbruch *m.* II. *v.tr.* (Steine) brechen.
**quart** [kwɔ:t], *s. Meas:* Quart *n* (*Brit:* = 1,14 Liter; *N.Am:* = 0,95 Liter).
**quarter** ['kwɔ:tər]. I. *s.* 1. (*a*) (*also district*) Viertel *n;* three quarters of our food, drei Viertel unserer Nahrungsmittel; (*b*) *Z:* hind quarters, Hinterteil *n.* 2. (*a*) (*three months*) Quartal *n;* Vierteljahr *n;* (*b*) q. of an hour, Viertelstunde *f;* three quarters of an hour, eine Dreiviertelstunde; *:*q. to/past eight, Viertel vor/ nach acht. 3. at close quarters, dicht beieinander; seen at/from close quarters, aus der Nähe betrachtet. 4. *pl. Mil:* Quartiere *npl.* II. *v.tr.* (*a*) (einen Apfel

usw.) vierteln; (b) Mil: (Truppen) einquartieren. ◆'quarter-'final, s. Sp:
Viertelfinale n. ◆'quarterly. I. adj. (of
payment etc.) vierteljährlich. II. s. (publication) Vierteljahresschrift f.
quartet [kwɔː'tet], s. Mus: Quartett n.
quartz [kwɔːts], s. Quarz m.
quash [kwɔʃ], v.tr. (a) Jur: (ein Urteil)
widerrufen; (b) (einen Aufstand) niederschlagen.
quaver ['kweivər] I. s. Mus: Achtelnote f.
II. v.i. zittern.
quay [kiː], s. Kai m.
queasy ['kwiːzi], adj. unwohl; (sick) übel.
queen ['kwiːn], s. 1. Königin f. 2. (in
cards, chess) Dame f.
queer ['kwiər], adj. 1. (strange) seltsam;
F: komisch. 2. (homosexual) P: schwul; a
q., ein Schwuler.
quell [kwel], v.tr. Lit: (einen Aufstand,
Fig: Gefühle) unterdrücken.
quench [kwen(t)ʃ], v.tr. to q. one's
thirst, seinen Durst löschen.
query ['kwiəri]. I. s. Frage f; (on work
done) Rückfrage f; to raise a q., eine
Frage aufwerfen. II. v.tr. (eine Behauptung) in Frage stellen.
quest [kwest], s. Suche f (for,
nach + dat).
question ['kwestʃ(ə)n]. I. s. Frage f; (a)
to ask s.o. a q., j-m eine Frage stellen;
q. mark, Fragezeichen n; without q.,
zweifellos; (b) (matter) that's out of the
q. das kommt nicht in Frage; a q. of
time, eine Frage der Zeit. II. v.tr. (a)
(j-n) befragen; (of police) (j-n) verneh-
men; Jur: (einen Zeugen, Angeklagten)
verhören; (b) (etwas) bezweifeln.
◆'questionable, adj. fragwürdig; it is
q. whether ..., es ist fraglich, ob ...
◆questio'nnaire, s. Fragebogen m.
queue [kjuː]. I. s. Schlange f (von Menschen, Autos). II. v.i. to q. (up), Schlange stehen, (sich) anstellen.
quibble ['kwibl], v.i. kritteln.
quick [kwik]. I. adj. schnell; a q. child,
ein aufgewecktes Kind; q. wit, schlagfer-
tiger Humor; she has a q. temper, sie ist
jähzornig. II. s. Fig: cut to the q., im
Innersten getroffen. ◆'quick-'acting,
adj. schnellwirkend. ◆'quicken, v. 1.
v.tr. (a) (den Gang) beschleunigen. 2. v.i.
(of pulse etc.) sich beschleunigen.
◆'quicksand, s. Treibsand m.
◆'quick-'tempered, adj. jähzornig.
◆'quick-'witted, adj. aufgeweckt; (of

answer etc.) schlagfertig.
quid [kwid], s. F: Pfund n.
quiet ['kwaiət]. I. s. 1. (rest, peace) Ruhe
f; (silence) Stille f; (privacy) Ungestörtheit
f. 2. F: on the q., heimlich. II. adj. ruhig; (a) (silent) still; (of talk, voice) leise;
be q.! (shut up) sei still! (b) keep it q.,
behalte es für dich. ◆'quieten, v. 1.
v.tr. (j-n, ein Kind) beruhigen, (pacify)
besänftigen. 2. v.i. to q. down, sich beruhigen. ◆'quietness, s. (a) Ruhe f;
Stille f; (b) Besonnenheit f (eines Menschen usw.).
quill [kwil], s. q. (pen), Federkiel m.
quilt [kwilt], s. Steppdecke f.
quintet [kwin'tet], s. Mus: Quintett n.
quintuple ['kwintjupl]. I. adj. fünffach.
II. v.tr. verfünffachen. ◆'quintuplet, s.
Fünfling m.
quirk [kwɜːk], s. Fig: Laune f (der Natur,
des Schicksals usw.).
quit [kwit]. I. adj. F: to be quits, quitt
sein. II. v. 1. v.tr. (j-n, einen Ort) verlassen; to q. doing sth., mit etwas dat aufhören. 2. v.i. F: (of employee) seine Stellung aufgeben.
quite [kwait], adv. (a) ganz; (fairly) ziemlich; (entirely) völlig; q. new, ganz/
ziemlich neu; not q. as much, nicht ganz
so viel; q. enough, schon genug; I don't
q. know what he will do, ich weiß nicht
recht, was er tun wird; (b) (with noun) q.
a surprise, eine ziemliche Überraschung.
quiver ['kwivər], v.i. (of voice, movement)
zittern (with, vor + dat).
quiz [kwiz], pl. quizzes [kwiz, 'kwiziz]. I. s.
Quiz n. II. v.tr. (j-n) ausfragen.
quizzical ['kwizik(ə)l], adj. (teasing) (of remark, manner) neckisch; (of look, smile)
spöttisch.
quorum ['kwɔːrəm], s. Quorum n.
quota ['kwəutə], s. (of money, immigrants)
Quote f; (of goods) Kontingent n.
quote [kwəut]. I. v.tr. (a) (einen Schriftsteller, eine Stelle usw.) zitieren; to q.
(from) the Bible, aus der Bibel zitieren;
to q. an instance of sth., ein Beispiel für
etwas acc anführen; Com: please q. this
number/reference, bitte geben Sie diese
Nummer/dieses Zeichen an; (b) Com:
(einen Preis) nennen. II. v.i. to q. for
sth. einen Preis für etwas acc nennen.
III. s. F: = quotation. ◆quo'tation, s.
1. Zitat n; q. marks, Anführungszeichen
npl. 2. Com: (estimate) Kostenvoranschlag
m; (of price) Preisangabe f.

# R

R, r [ɑːr], s. (der Buchstabe) R, r n.
rabbi ['ræbai], s. Rabbiner m.
rabbit ['ræbit], s. Kaninchen n; (N.Am:
also) Hase m; r. hole, Kaninchenbau m;
r. hutch, Kaninchenstall m.
rabble ['ræbl], s. (a) (mob) Pöbel m; (b)

Pej: Gesindel n.
rabies ['reibiːz], s. Tollwut f.
race¹ [reis]. I. s. Sp: Rennen n; to go to
the races, zum Pferderennen gehen; r.
meeting, (horse r.) Renntag m; Fig: r.
against time, Wettlauf m mit der Zeit;

**arms r.**, Wettrüsten *n*. **II.** *v*. 1. *v.i.* (*a*) an einem Rennen teilnehmen; (*b*) (*of car etc.*) **to r. along**, dahinrasen. 2. *v.tr.* **to r. s.o.**, mit j-m um die Wette laufen; (*b*) (ein Pferd) rennen lassen. ◆'**racecourse,** *s*. Rennplatz *m*. ◆'**racehorse,** *s*. Rennpferd *n*. ◆'**race-track,** *s*. Rennbahn *f*; (*for motor racing*) Rennstrecke *f*. ◆'**racing,** *s*. (*a*) (*activity*) Rennen *n*; (*sport*) Rennsport *m*; (*b*) *attrib.* Renn-; **r. driver**, Rennfahrer *m*; **r. car**, Rennwagen *m*. ◆'**racy,** *adj*. (*a*) (*of car etc.*) sportlich; (*b*) (*of style*) spritzig.

**race²**, *s*. Rasse *f*; **the human r.**, das Menschengeschlecht. ◆'**racial** ['reiʃ(ə)l], *adj*. rassisch; **r. discrimination**, Rassendiskriminierung *f*; **r. minorities**, Rassenminderheiten *fpl*. ◆'**racialism/racism** ['reisizm], *s*. Rassismus *m*. ◆'**racialist/ 'racist. I.** *s*. Rassist *m*. **II.** *adj*. rassistisch.

**rack¹** [ræk], *s*. (*frame*) Gestell *n*; (*stand*) Ständer *m*; *Rail*: **luggage r.**, Gepäckablage *f*.

**rack²**, *v.tr.* **to r. one's brains**, sich *dat* den Kopf zerbrechen.

**racket¹** ['rækit], *s*. *Sp*: Schläger *m*.

**racket²**, *s*. F. 1. (*noise*) Krach *m*. 2. (*shady business*) Schiebergeschäft *n*; **it's a r.!** das ist ein Schwindel! ◆'**racke'teer,** *s*. Schieber *m*.

**radar** ['reidɑːr], *s*. Radar *n*, *m*.

**radiance** ['reidjəns], *s*. strahlender Glanz *m*. ◆'**radiant,** *adj*. strahlend. ◆**radiate** ['reidieit], *v*. 1. *v.i.* ausstrahlen (**from**, aus + *dat*); (*emit rays*) Strahlen aussenden; (*of lines, roads etc.*) strahlenförmig (von einem Punkt) ausgehen. 2. *v.tr.* ausstrahlen. ◆**radi'ation,** *s*. Strahlung *f*; *nuclear r.*, Kernstrahlung *f*. ◆'**radiator,** *s*. 1. (*for heating*) Heizkörper *m*. 2. *Aut*: Kühler *m*.

**radical** ['rædik(ə)l]. **I.** *adj*. radikal. **II.** *s*. (*pers.*) Radikale(r) *f(m)*.

**radio** ['reidiəu], *s*. (*a*) Radio *n*; **on the r.**, im Radio; (*b*) (*institution*) Rundfunk *m*; **r. station**, Rundfunksender *m*; **r. play**, Hörspiel *n*. ◆'**radio'active,** *adj*. radioaktiv. ◆'**radioac'tivity,** *s*. Radioaktivität *f*. ◆**radi'ographer,** *s*. Röntgenassistent(in) *m(f)*. ◆**radi'ologist,** *s*. Röntgenologe *m*. ◆**radi'ology,** *s*. Röntgenologie *f*.

**radish** ['rædiʃ], *s*. (*red*) Radieschen *n*.

**radium** ['reidiəm], *s*. Radium *n*.

**radius**, *pl*. **-ii** ['reidiəs, -iai], *s*. *Mth*: Radius *m*; **within a r. of three kilometres**, im Umkreis von drei Kilometern.

**raffle** ['ræfl], *s*. Tombola *f*; **r. ticket**, Los *n*.

**raft** [rɑːft], *s*. Floß *n*.

**rafter** ['rɑːftər], *s*. Dachsparren *m*.

**rag¹** [ræg], *s*. (*a*) (*torn piece*) Fetzen *m*, Lumpen *m*; (*b*) (*for cleaning*) Lappen *m*. ◆'**ragamuffin** ['rægəmʌfin], *s*. zerlumpter Kerl *m*; (*esp. child*) Strolch *m*.

◆**ragged** ['rægid], *adj*. zerlumpt.

**rag²**, *s*. (*students'*) Studentenkarneval *m*.

**rage** [reidʒ]. **I.** *s*. Wut *f*; (*fit of*) **r.**, Wutanfall *m*; **to be in a r.** (**with** s.o.), (auf j-n) wütend sein; **to fly into a r.**, in Wut geraten; **to be all the r.**, große Mode sein. **II.** *v.i. Fig*: (*of storm, wind*) toben; (*of epidemic*) wüten.

**raid** [reid]. **I.** *s*. Raubzug *m* (von Banditen); Razzia *f* (der Polizei); *Mil: etc*: Überfall *m*; **air r.**, Luftangriff *m*. **II.** *v.tr. Mil*: (ein Lager usw.) überfallen; (*of police*) **to r. an area**, eine Razzia auf ein Viertel vornehmen.

**rail** [reil], *s*. 1. (*for clothes etc.*) Stange *f*; Geländer *n* (einer Treppe usw.). 2. (*fence*) *Nau*: Reling *f*; *esp. pl.* Gitterzaun *m*. 3. *Rail*: (*a*) (*track*) Schiene *f*; *pl.* **rails**, Gleise *npl*; *F*: (*of pers.*) **to go off the rails**, aus dem Gleis kommen; (*b*) (*railway*) **to go/travel by r.**, mit der Bahn fahren. ◆'**railings,** *s.pl.* Gitter *n*; Gitterzaun *m*; (*on bridge*) Geländer *n*. ◆'**railway,** *N.Am:* '**railroad,** *s*. Eisenbahn *f*; **r. station**, Bahnhof *m*.

**rain** [rein]. **I.** *s*. Regen *m*. **II.** *v.tr. & i.* (*a*) regnen; *F*: **to r. cats and dogs**, gießen, in Strömen regnen; *Sp: etc*: **to be rained off**, wegen Regen abgesagt werden; (*b*) *Fig*: (*of blows etc.*) **to r. (down)**, niederprasseln. ◆'**rainbow,** *s*. Regenbogen *m*. ◆'**raincoat,** *s*. Regenmantel *m*. ◆'**raindrop,** *s*. Regentropfen *m*. ◆'**rainfall,** *s*. Regenfälle *mpl*; (*quantity*) Niederschlagsmenge *f*.

**rainy,** *adj*. regnerisch; **to keep sth. for a r. day**, etwas für den Notfall aufheben.

**raise** [reiz]. **I.** *v.tr.* (*a*) (*lift*) (die Hand, den Arm usw.) heben; (eine Last) hochheben, (*with crane*) hochwinden; (Rolläden, den Vorhang usw.) hochziehen; (sein Glas, seinen Kopf, den Blick usw.) erheben; (*b*) (*erect*) **to r. a monument to s.o.**, j-m ein Denkmal setzen; (*c*) (*bring up*) (eine Familie) aufziehen; (Tiere) züchten; (*d*) **to r. false hopes**, falsche Hoffnungen erwecken; (*e*) **to r. one's voice**, seine Stimme erheben; **to r. the alarm**, Alarm schlagen; (*f*) (eine Frage) aufwerfen; **to r. an objection**, Einspruch erheben; (*g*) (*increase*) (j-s Gehalt, einen Preis usw.) erhöhen; (*h*) **to r. money**, Geld aufbringen; (*for charity*) Geld auftreiben. **II.** *s*. *N.Am*: Gehaltserhöhung *f*.

**raisin** ['reizn], *s*. Rosine *f*.

**rake** [reik]. **I.** *s*. Harke *f*. **II.** *v.tr.* (*a*) (Blätter) zusammenharken; (den Boden, einen Weg) (glatt) harken; (*b*) (das Feuer) schüren. ◆'**rake 'in**, *v.tr. F*: **to r. in money**, Geld scheffeln. ◆'**rake 'up**, *v.tr. Fig*: **to r. up s.o.'s past**, j-s Vergangenheit aufwärmen.

**rally** ['ræli]. **I.** *s*. 1. Zusammenkunft *f*; (*demonstration*) Massenkundgebung *f*; *Aut*: (*car*) **r.**, Rallye *f*. 2. (*in tennis*) Ballwechsel *m*. **II.** *v*. 1. *v.tr.* (Truppen, Anhänger usw.) zusammenrufen. 2. *v.i.* (*of* *troops, supporters etc.*) zusammenkommen; **they rallied round their leader,** sie scharten sich um ihren Führer.

**ram** [ræm]. **I.** *s. Z:* Widder *m.* **II.** *v.tr.* to r. (in) a post etc., einen Pfahl usw. einrammen; *Aut:* **to r. another car,** einen anderen Wagen rammen.

**ramble** ['ræmbl]. **I.** *s.* (*hike*) Wanderung *f.* **II.** *v.i.* (*a*) (*hike*) wandern; (*b*) *Fig:* vom Thema abschweifen. ◆'**rambling,** *adj.* **1.** (*of story, speech*) weitschweifig; (*incoherent*) unzusammenhängend. **2.** r. house, weitläufiges Haus.

**ramifi'cation** [ræmifi'keiʃ(ə)n], *s.* **ramifications of a problem,** Verwicklungen *fpl* eines Problems.

**ramp** [ræmp], *s.* Rampe *f;* (*for loading*) Laderampe *f.*

**rampage** [ræm'peidʒ], *s.* **to be on the r.,** randalieren.

**rampant** ['ræmpənt], *adj.* (*of evils etc.*) um sich greifend; (*unrestrained*) zügellos.

**rampart** ['ræmpɑːt], *s.* Wall *m.*

**ramshackle** ['ræmʃækl], *adj.* baufällig.

**ranch** [rɑːn(t)ʃ], *s. N.Am:* Ranch *f.*

**rancid** ['rænsid], *adj.* ranzig.

**random** ['rændəm]. **I.** *s.* at r., aufs Geratewohl; **to hit out at r.,** blindlings drauflosschlagen. **II.** *adj.* ziellos; (*chance*) zufällig; r. sample, Stichprobe *f.*

**range** [reindʒ]. **I.** *s.* **1.** (*a*) r. of mountains/hills, Gebirgskette *f*/Hügelkette *f;* (*b*) (*selection*) *Com:* Auswahl *f* (of, an + *dat*); wide r., große Auswahl. **2.** (*distance, area*) (*a*) *Mil:etc:* Schußweite *f* (einer Kanone usw.); Reichweite *f* (einer Rakete, eines Autos usw.); Flugbereich *m* (eines Flugzeugs); **at a r. of 800 metres,** in einer Entfernung von 800 Metern; (*b*) *Fig:* Bereich *m;* (*c*) *Com:* price r., Preislage *f;* (*d*) *Mus:* Umfang *m* (einer Stimme, eines Instruments). **II.** *v.i.* (*extend*) sich erstrecken, (from ... to ..., von ... *dat* bis ... *dat*); **the temperatures r. from ten to thirty degrees,** die Temperaturen liegen zwischen zehn und dreißig Grad.

**rank¹** [ræŋk]. **I.** *s.* **1.** *Mil:* Reihe *f,* Linie *f; Pol:* the party r. and file, das Fußvolk der Partei. **2.** (*position*) *Mil: etc:* Rang *m.* **3.** taxi r., Taxistand *m.* **II.** *v.* **1.** *v.tr.* (j-n) zählen (with/among the great writers etc., zu den großen Schriftstellern usw.); *Sp:* **he is ranked fifth,** er steht an fünfter Stelle. **2.** *v.i.* zählen (among/with, zu + *dat*); **to r. as ...,** als ... gelten; **to r. above s.o.,** vor j-m rangieren.

**rank²,** *adj.* übelriechend; (*rancid*) ranzig.

**rankle** ['ræŋkl], *v.i.* **his undeserved success rankles with me,** sein unverdienter Erfolg wurmt mich.

**ransack** ['rænsæk], *v.tr.* (*a*) (ein Zimmer, eine Schublade usw.) durchwühlen; (*b*) (eine Stadt) plündern.

**ransom** ['rænsəm]. **I.** *s.* (*sum*) Lösegeld *n;* **to be held to r.,** gegen Lösegeld gefangengehalten werden. **II.** *v.tr.* (j-n) freikaufen.

**rant** [rænt], *v.i.* (*in anger*) toben.

**rap** [ræp]. **I.** *s.* Klaps *m;* (*knock*) lautes Klopfen *n; Fig:* **to take the r.,** die Schuld auf sich *acc* nehmen. **II.** *v.tr. & i.* klopfen (**at,** an + *acc;* **on,** auf + *acc*).

**rapacious** [rə'peiʃəs], *adj.* habgierig.

**rape** [reip]. **I.** *s.* Vergewaltigung *f.* **II.** *v.tr.* vergewaltigen.

**rapid** ['ræpid]. **I.** *adj.* schnell; **-ly,** *adv.* schnell. **II.** *s.* (*usu. pl.*) (*in river*) Stromschnelle *f.* ◆**ra'pidity,** *s.* Schnelligkeit *f.*

**rapt** [ræpt], *adj.* hingerissen. ◆**rapture** ['ræptʃər], *s.* Entzücken *n.* ◆'**rapturous,** *adj.* r. applause, stürmischer Beifall.

**rare** ['rɛər], *adj.* **1.** (*infrequent*) selten; (*valuable*) rar. **2.** (*of air*) dünn. **3.** (*of meat*) nicht gar; (*of steak*) englisch. ◆'**rarefied** [-ifaid], *adj.* (*of air*) verdünnt.

**rascal** ['rɑːsk(ə)l], *s.* Gauner *m;* (*esp. child*) Schlingel *m.*

**rash¹** [ræʃ], *s. Med:* Hautausschlag *m.*

**rash²,** *adj.* (*hasty*) übereilt; (*ill-considered*) unüberlegt; (*risky*) leichtsinnig. ◆'**rashness,** *s.* Überstürztheit *f;* Unbesonnenheit *f;* Leichtsinn *m.*

**rasher** ['ræʃər], *s. Cu:* r. of bacon, Scheibe *f* Speck.

**rasp** [rɑːsp], *v.i.* (*of voice etc.*) krächzen; (*of sound*) schnarren.

**raspberry** ['rɑːsb(ə)ri, 'rɑːz-], *s.* Himbeere *f.*

**rat** [ræt], *s.* **1.** *Z:* Ratte *f.* **2.** *Pej:* (*pers.*) Schuft *m.*

**ratchet** ['rætʃit], *s. Tchn:* Ratsche *f;* (*bar*) Sperrstange *f.*

**rate** [reit]. **I.** *s.* **1.** (*a*) Rate *f;* Satz *m;* r. of growth, Wachstumsrate *f;* birth/death r., Geburtenziffer *f*/Sterblichkeitsziffer *f; Fin:* r. of interest, Zinssatz *m;* (*b*) (*fixed charge*) Tarif *m;* postal rates, Postgebühren *fpl.* **2.** (*speed*) Geschwindigkeit *f; F:* Tempo *n;* (*b*) at this r., wenn es so weitergeht; **at any r.,** jedenfalls. **3.** *pl.* rates, (*tax*) Gemeindeabgaben *fpl.* **4.** (*class*) **first/second r.,** erstrangig/zweitrangig. **II.** *v.tr.* (*estimate*) einschätzen. ◆'**rating,** *s.* (*a*) (*valuation*) Bewertung *f;* (*b*) *TV:* **programme r.,** Einschaltquote *f* (eines Programms).

**rather** ['rɑːðər], *adv.* **1.** ziemlich; r. pretty, recht hübsch. **2.** lieber (**than,** als); **I'd r. not,** (ich möchte) lieber nicht. **3.** eher; **he is r. to be pitied than feared,** er ist eher/vielmehr zu bemitleiden als zu fürchten; **or r., I did have it,** genauer gesagt, ich hatte es.

**ratify** ['rætifai], *v.tr.* (einen Vertrag) ratifizieren; (eine Abmachung) bestätigen. ◆**ratifi'cation,** *s.* Ratifizierung *f,* Bestätigung *f.*

**ratio,** *pl.* **ratios** ['reiʃiəu, -əuz], *s.* Verhältnis *n.*

**ration** ['ræʃ(ə)n]. **I.** *s.* Ration *f;* (*allowance*) Zuteilung *f.* **II.** *v.tr.* (Lebensmittel rationieren.

**rational** ['ræʃən(ə)l], *adj.* 1. *(of pers.)* vernünftig; *(sane)* zurechnungsfähig. 2. *(of thought etc.)* rational, *(of explanation)* vernunftgemäß.

**rattle** ['rætl]. I. *s.* 1. *(toy)* Klapper *f.* 2. *(a) (noise)* Geklapper *n;* Rasseln *n* (von Ketten usw.); *(b)* death r., Röcheln *n.* II. *v.* 1. *v.i.* klappern. 2. *v.tr. (a)* to r. chains, mit Ketten rasseln; *(b)* F: (j-n) aus der Fassung bringen. ◆'**rattlesnake,** *s.* Klapperschlange *f.*

**raucous** ['rɔːkəs], *adj. (of voice)* rauh; r. laughter, rohes Gelächter.

**ravage** ['rævidʒ]. I. *v.tr.* (ein Land, eine Stadt, *Fig:* ein Gesicht) verwüsten. II. *s. usu. pl.* verheerende Wirkung *f* (der Zeit usw.).

**rave** [reiv], *v.i. (a) (of madman)* phantasieren; **a raving lunatic,** ein Rasender; *(b)* F: to r. about sth., von etwas *dat* schwärmen. ◆'**raving,** *s. usu. pl* irres Gerede *n.*

**raven** ['reiv(ə)n], *s.* Rabe *m.*

**ravenous** ['ræv(ə)nəs], *adj.* heißhungrig; *F:* to be r., einen Bärenhunger haben.

**ravine** [rə'viːn], *s.* Schlucht *f.*

**ravishing** ['rævifiŋ], *adj.* hinreißend (schön).

**raw** [rɔː], *adj.* 1. *(uncooked)* roh; r. state, Rohzustand *m.* 2. *Ind:* Roh-; r. material, Rohstoff *m.* 3. *(a) (sore)* wund; r. wound, offene Wunde; *(b)* r. weather, naßkaltes Wetter; *(c) F:* to get a r. deal, unfair behandelt werden.

**ray** [rei], *s.* Strahl *m;* r. of light, Lichtstrahl *m;* a r. of hope, ein Hoffnungsschimmer *m.*

**rayon** ['reiɔn], *s.* Kunstseide *f.*

**raze** [reiz], *v.tr.* to r. to the ground, dem Erdboden gleichmachen.

**razor** ['reizər], *s. (a)* (cut-throat) r., Rasiermesser *n; (b)* (safety) r., Rasierapparat *m;* r. blade, Rasierklinge *f.*

**re¹** [riː], *prep. Com:* betrifft; *abbr.* betr.; re your letter of June 10th, mit Bezug auf Ihren Brief vom 10. Juni.

**re²** ['riː-], *prefix* wieder, noch einmal; to re-read sth., etwas noch einmal lesen.

**reach** [riːtʃ]. I. *s.* 1. within s.o.'s r., in j-s Reichweite; out of r., außer Reichweite; within easy r. of the station, vom Bahnhof leicht zu erreichen. 2. Flußstrecke *f* (zwischen zwei Krümmungen). II. *v.* 1. *v.tr. (a)* erreichen; to r. agreement/a conclusion, zu einer Einigung/zu einem Schluß gelangen; *(b)* *(come as far as)* bis zu (etwas *dat*) reichen; *(c)* to r. out, (die Hand usw.) ausstrecken. 2. *v.i. (a)* sich erstrecken, reichen (to/as far as, bis/bis zu + *dat*); will it r. (this far)? reicht es (bis dahin)? *(b) (of pers.)* hinkommen; *(c)* to r. out for sth., nach etwas *dat* greifen.

**react** [ri'ækt], *v.i.* reagieren (to, auf + *acc*). ◆**re'action,** *s.* Reaktion *f;* *(statement)* Stellungnahme *f.*

◆**re'actionary.** I. *adj.* reaktionär. II. *s.* Reaktionär *m.* ◆**re'actor,** *s.* Reaktor *m.*

**read** [riːd]. I. *v.tr. & i. irr. (a)* (etwas) lesen; to r. to s.o., j-m vorlesen; *El:* to r. the meter, den Zähler ablesen; *(b) (study)* to r. up a subject, über eine Sache nachlesen; *(at university)* he's reading French, er studiert Französisch; *(c)* this sentence does not r. well, dieser Satz liest sich nicht gut; *(d) Tchn: (of instrument)* anzeigen. II. *s. F:* Lektüre *f;* this book is a good r., das Buch liest sich gut. III. *adj.* [red] well-r., belesen; bewandert. ◆'**readable,** *adj.* 1. *(legible)* lesbar; *(of writing)* leserlich. 2. *(enjoyable)* lesenswert. ◆'**reader,** *s.* 1. Leser(in) *m(f).* 2. *Sch:* Lesebuch *n.* ◆'**readership,** *s.* Leserkreis *m.* ◆'**reading,** *s.* 1. *(action)* Lesen *n;* Lektüre *f.* 2. *(figure etc.)* Anzeige *f* (eines Meßinstruments). ◆'**reading-matter,** *s.* Lesestoff *m.*

**readjust** [riːə'dʒʌst], *v.* 1. *v.tr. (a)* to r. sth. (to sth.), etwas (etwas *dat*) wieder anpassen; *(b) Tchn:* (etwas) neu einstellen. 2. *v.i. (of pers.)* to r. (to sth.), sich (etwas *dat*) wieder anpassen. ◆**rea'djustment,** *s. (a)* Wiederanpassung *f; (b) Tchn:* Neueinstellung *f.*

**ready** ['redi]. I. *adj.* 1. *(a) (mentally prepared) (of pers.)* bereit (to do sth., etwas zu tun); to get r., sich vorbereiten (for sth., auf etwas *acc); (b) (finished) (of pers., thing)* fertig; lunch is r., das Mittagessen ist fertig; *Sp:* r., steady, go! Achtung, fertig, los! 2. *(quick) (of answer)* prompt. II. *adv.* r. made, fertig; *Cu:* Fertig-; r. cooked, fertig gekocht; -ily, *adv.* 1. *(willingly)* gern. 2. *(easily)* leicht. ◆'**readiness,** *s.* 1. to be r., bereit sein. 2. Bereitwilligkeit *f* (to do sth., etwas zu tun).

**real** ['riəl]. 1. *adj.* wirklich; *(genuine)* echt; *(true)* wahr; r. silk, echte Seide; in r. life, im wirklichen Leben. 2. *Jur:* r. estate, Immobilien *pl;* -ly, *adv. (a) (genuinely)* wirklich; *(b) (emphatic)* you r. must go there, Sie müssen unbedingt hingehen. ◆'**realism,** *s.* Realismus *m.* ◆'**realist,** *s.* Realist(in) *m(f).* ◆**rea'listic,** *adj.* realistisch; *(of model etc.)* wirklichkeitsgetreu. ◆**reality** [ri'æliti], *s.* Wirklichkeit *f.*

**realize** ['riəlaiz], *v.tr. (a) (achieve)* (eine Ambition usw.) verwirklichen; *(b) (recognize)* (etwas) einsehen, erkennen; I r. that, das sehe ich schon ein. ◆**reali'zation,** *s.* 1. Verwirklichung *f* (eines Plans). 2. Einsicht *f;* Erkenntnis *f.*

**realm** [relm], *s.* 1. Königreich *n.* 2. *Fig: (sphere)* Bereich *m.*

**ream** [riːm], *s. (paper)* Ries *n.*

**reap** [riːp], *v.tr.* (Getreide usw.) ernten; (ein Feld) mähen.

**reappear** ['riːə'piər], *v.i.* wieder erscheinen. ◆'**rea'ppearance,** *s.* Wiedererscheinen *n.*

**rear¹** ['riər]. **I.** s. (a) hinterer Teil m; Rückseite f (eines Hauses usw.); Heck n (eines Autos); (b) **he stood at the r.** (of the crowd), er stand ganz hinten (in der Menge). **II.** adj. hinter, Hinter-; r. **light,** Hecklicht n; r.- **view mirror,** Rückspiegel m. ◆**'rear-'admiral,** s. Konteradmiral m.

**rear²,** v. **1.** v.tr. (a) (ein Kind) aufziehen; (Tiere) züchten; (b) Fig: **to r. its ugly head,** (of question) sich erheben; (of jealousy etc.) erwachen. **2.** v.i. (of horse) sich aufbäumen.

**rearm** ['ri:'ɑ:m], v.tr. aufrüsten. ◆**'re'armament,** s. Aufrüstung f.

**re-arrange** ['ri:ə'reindʒ], v.tr. (differently) (etwas) umstellen; (again) (etwas) neu ordnen.

**reason** ['ri:z(ə)n]. **I.** s. **1.** Grund m (for, gen); (cause) Ursache f (for, gen); (occasion) Anlaß m (for, zu + dat); **with (good) r.,** mit Recht. **2.** (mental powers) Verstand m. **3.** (good sense) Vernunft f; **it stands to r. that...,** es leuchtet ein, daß... **II.** v. **1.** v.i. **to r. with s.o.,** j-m zureden. **2.** v.tr. **to r. that...,** folgern, daß... ◆**'reasonable,** adj. **1.** (sensible) vernünftig; (understanding) verständig. **2.** (a) (of article) preiswert; (of price) angemessen; (low) niedrig; (b) **in r. condition,** in ganz gutem Zustand. **-bly,** adv. **1.** vernünftig. **2.** (quite) ziemlich; **I know him r. well,** ich kenne ihn ganz gut. ◆**'reasoning,** s. Argumentation f.

**reassemble** ['ri:ə'sembl], v. **1.** v.tr. (eine Maschine usw.) wieder zusammenbauen. **2.** v.i. (of people) wieder zusammenkommen.

**reassure** ['ri:ə'ʃuər], v.tr. (j-n) beruhigen; **he reassured me that...,** er versicherte mir (nochmals), daß... ◆**rea'ssuring,** adj. beruhigend.

**rebate** ['ri:beit], s. (a) (discount) Rabatt m; (b) (on tax, rent) Rückvergütung f.

**rebel. I.** ['reb(ə)l]. s. Rebell(in) m(f). **II.** [ri'bel] v.i. rebellieren. ◆**re'bellion,** s. Rebellion f. ◆**re'bellious,** adj. rebellisch.

**rebirth** ['ri:'bə:θ], s. Wiedergeburt f.

**rebound.** **I.** [ri'baund] v.i. zurückprallen. **II.** ['ri:baund] s. **on the r.,** Fig: als Reaktion.

**rebuff** [ri'bʌf]. **I.** s. Abfuhr f. **II.** v.tr. (j-n) abweisen; (of girl) (j-n) abblitzen lassen.

**rebuild** ['ri:'bild], v.tr.irr. wiederaufbauen.

**rebuke** [ri'bju:k]. **I.** s. Rüge f. **II.** v.tr. (j-n) rügen.

**recall** [ri'kɔ:l]. **I.** s. (memory) Erinnerungsvermögen n. **II.** v.tr. (a) (j-n) zurückrufen; (einen Botschafter) abberufen; (b) **I don't r. his name,** ich kann mich nicht an seinen Namen erinnern.

**recapitulate** [ri:kə'pitjuleit], F: **recap** ['ri:kæp] v.tr. & i. (Hauptpunkte einer Rede) rekapitulieren, wiederholen.

◆**'recapitu'lation,** F: **'recap,** s. Rekapitulation f.

**recapture** ['ri:'kæptʃər]. **I.** v.tr. (einen Verbrecher) wieder gefangennehmen; (eine Stadt usw.) zurückerobern. **II.** s. Wiederergreifung f; Wiedereinnahme f (einer Stadt usw.).

**recede** [ri'si:d], v.i. (of flood etc.) zurückgehen. ◆**re'ceding,** adj. **1.** zurückgehend. **2.** (of forehead) fliehend.

**receipt** [ri'si:t], s. **1.** Empfang m; **on r. of this letter,** nach Erhalt/Com: Eingang dieses Briefes. **2.** Com: pl. **receipts,** Einnahmen fpl. **3.** (document) (for goods) Empfangsbestätigung f; (for money) Quittung f; (from till) Kassenzettel m; **to give. a r. for a sum/a payment,** eine Geldsumme/Zahlung quittieren.

**receive** [ri'si:v], v.tr. (a) erhalten; (eine Wunde, Rad: eine Sendung; Ecc: das Sakrament usw.) empfangen; (b) (greet) (Gäste) empfangen. ◆**re'ceiver,** s. **1.** (in bankruptcy) Konkursverwalter m. **2.** (a) Tel: Hörer m; (b) Rad: Empfänger m.

**recent** ['ri:s(ə)nt], adj. (of event) unlängst/vor kurzem stattgefunden; **in r. years,** in den letzten Jahren; **r. events,** die jüngsten Ereignisse; **-ly,** adv. kürzlich, neulich; **he has r. become lazy,** er ist in letzter Zeit faul geworden.

**receptacle** [ri'septəkl], s. Behälter m.

**reception** [ri'sep ʃ(ə)n], s. Empfang m; (in hotel etc.) r. **(desk),** Empfang m, Rezeption f. ◆**re'ceptionist,** s. (in hotel etc.) Empfangsdame f; (male) Empfangschef m; Med: Sprechstundenhilfe f. ◆**receptive** [ri'septiv], adj. (of pers.) empfänglich **(to,** für + acc).

**recess,** pl. **-esses** [ri'ses, 'ri:ses, -esiz], s. **1.** (in wall) Nische f. **2.** Ferien pl (des Parlaments usw.). ◆**re'cession,** s. Com: Konjunkturrückgang m.

**recipe** ['resipi], s. Rezept n.

**recipient** [ri'sipiənt], s. Empfänger(in) m(f).

**reciprocate** [ri'siprəkeit], v.tr. **to r. s.o.'s feelings/good wishes,** j-s Gefühle/Glückwünsche erwidern. ◆**re'ciprocal,** adj. gegenseitig.

**recite** [ri'sait], v.tr. & i. (ein Gedicht usw.) aufsagen, (in public) vortragen. ◆**re'cital,** s. Mus: Solistenkonzert n. ◆**recitation** [resi'teiʃ(ə)n], s. Vortrag m.

**reckless** ['reklis], adj. (of driving etc.) rücksichtslos; (of behaviour) leichtsinnig.

**reckon** ['rek(ə)n], v.tr. & i. (a) (calculate) (Kosten) berechnen; (b) (estimate) (Kosten, den Wert) schätzen; (c) (think) meinen; (rate) (j-n, etwas) einschätzen; (d) **to r. on sth.,** auf etwas acc rechnen. ◆**'reckoning,** s. **to be out in one's r.,** sich verrechnet haben; **day of r.,** Tag der Abrechnung.

**reclaim** [ri'kleim] v.tr. (a) (claim back) (Eigentum) zurückfordern; (b) **to r. land from the sea,** Neuland vom Meer gewinnen. **II.** ['ri:kleim] *s. Av:* **baggage r.**, Gepäckausgabe *f.*

**recline** [ri'klain], *v.i.* liegen (**on/upon**, auf + *dat*); **reclining on a couch,** ausgestreckt auf einer Couch; **reclining seats,** Liegesitze *mpl.*

**recluse** [ri'klu:s], *s.* Einsiedler(in) *m(f).*

**recognize** ['rekəgnaiz], *v.tr.* (a) (j-n, etwas) erkennen (**by sth.**, an etwas *dat*); (b) (einen Staat, j-s Rechte, Leistungen) anerkennen. ◆**recog'nition,** *s.* **1.** Erkennen *n.* **2.** Anerkennung *f* (eines Staates usw.). ◆**'recognizable,** *adj.* erkennbar. ◆**'recognized,** *adj.* (of expert etc.) anerkannt.

**recoil I.** ['ri:koil] *s.* Rückstoß *m* (eines Gewehrs); Rücklauf *m* (eines Geschützes). **II.** [ri'koil] *v.i.* (a) (of firearm) zurückstoßen; (b) (of pers.) zurückspringen; (in horror) zurückschrecken (**from,** vor + *dat*).

**recollect** [rekə'lekt], *v.tr.* **to r. sth.**, sich an etwas *acc* erinnern. ◆**reco'llection,** *s.* Erinnerung *f.*

**recommend** [rekə'mend], *v.tr.* **to r. sth. to s.o.**, j-m etwas empfehlen; **to r. s.o. to do sth.**, j-m empfehlen/raten, etwas zu tun. ◆**recommen'dation,** *s.* Empfehlung *f.*

**recompense** ['rekəmpens]. **I.** *s.* Belohnung *f;* Entschädigung *f* (für einen Verlust usw.). **II.** *v.tr.* (j-n) belohnen (**for sth.,** für etwas *acc*).

**reconcile** ['rekənsail], *v.tr.* (a) (zwei Personen miteinander) versöhnen; **to become reconciled,** sich versöhnen; **to r. oneself to sth.,** sich mit etwas *dat* abfinden; (b) (Gegensätze usw.) in Einklang bringen. ◆**recon'cilable,** *adj.* (of pers.) versöhnbar; (of things) vereinbar. ◆**reconcili'ation** [-sili-], *s.* Versöhnung *f* (zwischen zwei Personen).

**recondition** ['ri:kən'diʃ(ə)n], *v.tr.* (etwas) überholen.

**reconnaissance** [ri'kənis(ə)ns], *s. Mil: etc:* Erkundung *f* (der feindlichen Stellungen); Aufklärung *f.*

**reconnoitre** [rekə'nɔitər], *v.* **1.** *v.tr.* (ein Gelände) erkunden. **2.** *v.i.* Erkundungen anstellen.

**reconsider** ['ri:kən'sidər], *v.tr.* sich *dat* (eine Frage usw.) nochmals überlegen.

**reconstruct** ['ri:kən'strʌkt], *v.tr.* (ein Gebäude usw.) wiederaufbauen. ◆**'recon'struction,** *s.* (a) Wiederaufbau *m;* (b) Rekonstruktion *f* (eines Verbrechens usw.).

**record. I.** ['rekɔ:d] *s.* **1.** (a) Aufzeichnung *f* (von Tatsachen usw.); (document) Aktenstück *n;* (list) Register *n;* **to make/keep a r. of sth.,** etwas protokollieren/aufzeichnen; (b) *pl.* **records,** Akten *fpl; Hist:* Archiv *n.* **2.** (reputation) Leumund *m;* **to have a criminal r.,** vorbestraft sein. **3.** *Sp: etc:* Rekord *m;* **4.** *Rec:* Schallplatte, *F:* Platte *f;* **r. player,** Plattenspieler *m.* **II.** [ri'kɔ:d] *v.tr.* (a) (eine

Tat, ein Geschehen) aufzeichnen; (b) *Tchn:* (of meter etc.) (einen Wert) registrieren; (c) **recorded delivery,** approx.=Einschreiben *n;* (d) *Rec:* (etwas) aufnehmen. ◆**re'corder,** *s.* **1.** *Rec:* (**tape) r.,** Tonbandgerät *n;* **cassette r.,** Kassettenrecorder *m.* **2.** *Mus:* Blockflöte *f.* ◆**re'cording,** *s. Rec:* Aufnahme *f.*

**recount**[1] [ri'kaunt], *v.tr.* (etwas) erzählen.

**recount**[2] **I.** ['ri:'kaunt] *v.tr.* (Stimmen usw.) nachzählen. **II.** ['ri:kaunt] *s. Pol:* nochmalige Zählung *f* (der Stimmen).

**recoup** [ri'ku:p], *v.tr.* **to r. one's losses,** seine Verluste wiedergutmachen.

**recourse** [ri'kɔ:s], *s.* **to have r. to sth.,** Zuflucht zu etwas *dat* nehmen.

**recover** [ri'kʌvər], *v.* **1.** *v.tr.* (einen verlorenen Gegenstand) zurückbekommen; (eine Schuld) eintreiben; (einen Verlust) wiedergutmachen. **2.** *v.i.* sich erholen. ◆**re'covery,** *s.* **1.** (of sth. lost etc) Wiedererlangung *f.* **2.** (of pers.) Erholung *f;* (from illness) Genesung *f.*

**recreation** [rekri'eiʃ(ə)n], *s.* Erholung *f;* (entertainment) Unterhaltung *f;* (pastime) Zeitvertreib *m.*

**recrimination** [rikrimi'neiʃ(ə)n], *s. usu. pl.* gegenseitige Beschuldigungen *fpl.*

**recruit** [ri'kru:t]. **I.** *s.* Rekrut *m.* **II.** *v.tr.* (a) *Mil:* rekrutieren; (b) (neue Mitglieder) werben. ◆**re'cruitment,** *s. Com:* Anwerbung *f* (von Arbeitskräften usw.).

**rectangle** ['rektæŋgl], *s.* Rechteck *n.* ◆**rec'tangular,** *adj.* rechteckig.

**rectify** ['rektifai], *v.tr.* (einen Fehler) korrigieren; (eine Aussage) richtigstellen; (Mißstände) beseitigen.

**rector** ['rektər], *s.* **1.** *Ecc:* Pfarrer *m.* **2.** (of university) Rektor *m.*

**recumbent** [ri'kʌmbənt], *adj.* liegend.

**recuperate** [ri'kju:pəreit], *v.i.* (of pers.) sich erholen.

**recur** [ri'kə:r], *v.i.* (of event, problem etc.) wiederkehren; (be repeated) sich wiederholen. ◆**re'currence,** *s.* Wiederkehr *f,* Wiederauftreten *n* (einer Krankheit usw.). ◆**re'current,** *adj.* immer wieder auftretend.

**recycle** ['ri:'saikl], *v.tr.* wiederverwerten.

**red** [red]. **I.** *adj.* (a) rot; **r. light district,** Bordellviertel *n;* (b) *F:* **r. herring,** (action) Ablenkungsmanöver *n;* (clue) falsche Spur *f;* (c) *Adm:* **r. tape,** Bürokratie *f.* **II.** *s.* (a) (colour) Rot *n;* (b) *F:* **to be in the r.,** in den roten Zahlen stecken. ◆**'redden,** *v.i.* (of sky, leaves etc.) rot werden; (of pers.) erröten (**at,** über + *acc;* **with,** vor + *dat*). ◆**'reddish,** *adj.* rötlich. ◆**'red-'haired,** *adj.* rothaarig. ◆**'red-'handed,** *adj.* **to catch s.o. r.-h.,** j-n auf frischer Tat ertappen. ◆**'redhead,** *s.* Rothaarige(r) *f(m).* ◆**'red-'hot,** *adj.* (of metal) glühend heiß. ◆**'redness,** *s.* Röte *f.*

**redecorate** ['ri:'dekəreit], *v.tr.* neu streichen (und tapezieren).

**redeem** [ri'di:m], *v.tr.* (a) *Ecc:* (j-n) erlösen; (*b*) (Fehler usw.) ausgleichen; (*save*) (seinen guten Ruf usw.) wiederherstellen. ◆**re'deemer**, *s.* the R., der Erlöser. ◆**re'deeming**, *adj.* the only r. feature is that..., das einzig Gute daran ist, daß ... ◆**redemption** [ri'dempʃ(ə)n], *s. Ecc:* Erlösung *f* (der Menschheit).

**redirect** ['riːdai'rekt, -di-], *v.tr.* (einen Brief usw.) nachsenden.

**redress** [ri'dres], *v.tr.* (*a*) (ein Unrecht) wiedergutmachen; (einen Mißstand) beseitigen; (*b*) **to r. the balance**, das Gleichgewicht wiederherstellen.

**reduce** [ri'djuːs], *v.tr.* (etwas) reduzieren, (*in length*) verkürzen, (*scale down*) verkleinern (**to**, auf + *acc*); (eine Zahl) vermindern; (die Temperatur) senken; (den Preis) herabsetzen; *Fig:* **to r. s.o. to silence/despair**, j-n zum Schweigen/zur Verzweiflung bringen. ◆**re'duced**, *adj.* reduziert; (*of speed, number*) vermindert; **r. fare**, ermäßigter Fahrpreis. ◆**reduction** [ri'dʌkʃ(ə)n], *s.* Verminderung *f*, Reduzierung *f*; Herabsetzung *f* (der Preise); Rückgang *m* (der Temperatur); *Com: Rail: etc:* Ermäßigung *f*.

**redundant** [ri'dʌndənt], *adj.* überschüssig; (*of worker*) überzählig; **to be made r.**, entlassen werden. ◆**re'dundancy**, *s. Com:* Entlassung *f* (von überzähligen Arbeitern); **r. pay(ment)**, Abfindung *f*.

**reed** [riːd]reed, *s.* **1.** *Bot:* Schilfrohr *n; esp. pl.* **reeds**, Schilf *n.* **2.** *Mus:* Rohrblatt *n.*

**reef** [riːf], *s.* Riff *n;* **coral r.**, Korallenriff *n.*

**reek** [riːk]. **I.** *s.* Gestank *m.* **II.** *v.i.* stinken (**of** nach).

**reel** [riːl]. **I.** *s.* (*a*) **r. of cotton**, Garnrolle *f;* (*b*) (*for fishing*) Rolle *f;* (*c*) *Rec: Cin:* Spule *f;* (*d*) *Mus:* schottischer Reigentanz *m.* **II.** *v.* **1.** *v.tr. F:* **to r. off answers etc.**, Antworten usw. herunterrasseln. **2.** *v.i.* taumeln.

**re-elect** ['riːi'lekt], *v.tr.* (j-n) wiederwählen. ◆**re-e'lection**, *s.* Wiederwahl *f.*

**re-enter** ['riː'entər], *v.tr. & i.* wieder eintreten.

**refectory** [ri'fektəri], *s.* Speisesaal *m; (for students)* Mensa *f.*

**refer** [ri'fəːr], *v.* **1.** *v.tr.* **to r. a matter to s.o./to a tribunal etc.**, eine Sache an j-n/ein Gericht usw. weiterleiten; **his doctor referred him to a specialist**, sein Arzt überwies ihn zu einem Facharzt. **2.** *v.i.* (*a*) **to r. to s.o., sth.**, auf j-n, etwas *acc* hinweisen; (*mention*) j-n, etwas erwähnen; (*b*) **to r. to s.o., sth.** (as one's authority), sich auf j-n, etwas *acc* berufen. ◆**referee** [refə'riː]. **I.** *s.* **1.** *Sp:* Schiedsrichter *m.* **2.** **to give s.o. as a r.**, j-n als Referenz angeben. **II.** *v.tr.* (ein Spiel) als Schiedsrichter leiten. ◆**reference** ['ref(ə)rəns], *s.* **1.** Verweisung *f* (einer Frage usw.) (**to**, an + *acc*). **2.** (*a*) (*mention*) Erwähnung *f* (**to**, *gen*); Hinweis *m* (**to**, auf + *acc*); **with r. to...**,

mit Hinsicht auf + *acc; Com:* bezugnehmend auf + *acc;* (*b*) *Com: Adm:* (*on letter, file etc.*) Aktenzeichen *n.* **3.** **r. work**, Nachschlagewerk *n.* **4.** (*for job*) Referenz *f.* ◆**refe'rendum**, *s.* Volksentscheid *m.*

**refill. I.** ['riː'fil] *v.tr.* (etwas) nachfüllen. **II.** ['riːfil] *s.* Nachfüllung *f;* (*for ballpoint*) (neue) Mine *f.*

**refine** [ri'fain], *v.tr.* (*a*) (Zucker, Petroleum usw.) raffinieren; (*b*) (seinen Geschmack, Methoden usw.) verfeinern. ◆**re'fined**, *adj.* (*of taste etc.*) verfeinert; (*of pers.*) kultiviert. ◆**re'finement**, *s.* (*quality*) Feinheit *f* (der Sprache, Manieren usw.). ◆**re'finery**, *s.* Raffinerie *f.*

**reflect** [ri'flekt], *v.* **1.** *v.tr.* (*of surface*) (Licht, ein Bild) wiederspiegeln; (Hitze, Strahlen) reflektieren. **2.** *v.i.* (*a*) (*meditate*) nachdenken (**on/upon sth.**, über etwas *acc*); (*b*) (*of action*) **to r. on s.o.**, ein schlechtes Licht auf j-n werfen. ◆**re'flection**, *s.* **1.** (*a*) (*process*) Wiederspiegelung *f;* (*image*) Spiegelbild *n;* (*b*) Reflexion *f* (von Strahlen usw.). **2.** (*thought*) Überlegung *f;* **on r.**, wenn ich es mir überlege.

**reflex** ['riːfleks], *s.* Reflex *m.*

**reflexive** [ri'fleksiv], *adj. Gram:* **r. pronoun**, Reflexivpronomen *n.*

**reform** [ri'fɔːm]. **I.** *v.* **1.** *v.tr.* (Verwaltung usw.) reformieren. **2.** *v.i.* sich bessern. **II.** *s.* Reform *f; pl* Reformbestrebungen *fpl.* ◆**reformation** [refə'meiʃ(ə)n], *s.* **1.** Reformierung *f;* Besserung *f* (des Charakters usw.). **2.** *Hist:* the R., die Reformation. ◆**re'former**, *s.* Reformer(in) *m(f); Ecc: Hist:* Reformator *m.*

**refrain** [ri'frein], *v.i.* **to r. from sth.**, von etwas *dat* absehen; **he could not r. from smiling**, er konnte sich des Lächelns nicht enthalten.

**refresh** [ri'freʃ], *v.tr.* (*a*) (j-n) erfrischen; (*b*) **to r. oneself**, sich erfrischen; (*with drink, food*) sich stärken. ◆**re'freshing**, *adj.* erfrischend; (*of sleep*) erquickend. ◆**re'freshment**, *s.* Erfrischung *f.*

**refrigerate** [ri'fridʒəreit], *v.tr.* (Nahrungsmittel) kühlen. ◆**re'frigerator**, *s.* Kühlschrank *m.*

**refuel** ['riː'fjuəl], *v.tr. Nau: Av:* (ein Schiff, ein Flugzeug) betanken.

**refuge** ['refjuːdʒ], *s.* **1.** Zuflucht *f;* (*protection*) Schutz *m* (**from**, vor + *dat*); **to seek/take r. with s.o.**, Zuflucht bei j-m nehmen. **2.** (*place*) Zufluchtsort *m;* (*home*) Zufluchtsstätte *f;* Asyl *n.* ◆**refu'gee**, *s.* Flüchtling *m.*

**refund. I.** [riː'fʌnd] *v.tr.* (Geld) zurückzahlen (**to s.o.**, an j-n). **II.** ['riːfʌnd] *s.* Rückzahlung *f.*

**refurbish** [riː'fəːbiʃ], *v.tr.* (ein Haus usw.) renovieren.

**refuse**[1] ['refjuːs], *s.* Müll *m;* **garden r.**, Gartenabfälle *mpl;* **r. collection**, Müllabfuhr *f;* **r. tip**, Müllkippe *f.*

**refuse**[2] [ri'fjuːz], *v.tr.* (*a*) **to r. s.o. sth.**, j-m etwas verweigern; **to r. an applica-tion, a gift** etc., einen Antrag, ein Ge-schenk usw. ablehnen; (b) **to r. to do sth.**, sich weigern, etwas zu tun. ◆re'fusal, s. Ablehnung f (eines An-trags usw.); Verweigerung f (einer Bitte usw.).

**refute** [ri'fjuːt], v.tr. widerlegen.

**regain** [ri(ː)'gein], v.tr. (die Freiheit usw.) wiedergewinnen; **to r. consciousness**, wieder zu Bewußtsein kommen.

**regal** ['riːg(ə)l], adj. königlich.

**regard** [ri'gɑːd]. I. s. 1. **with/having r. to**, hinsichtlich + gen; **with r. to payment**, was die Zahlung betrifft ... 2. (considera-tion) Rücksicht f (**for**, auf + acc); (con-cern) Beachtung f (**for**, gen); **without r. for expense**, ohne Rücksicht auf die Ko-sten. 3. (a) (esteem) Achtung f; (b) (end of letter) **regards, Peter**, herzliche Grüße, Peter. **II.** v.tr. (a) (etwas) ansehen (**as**, als); (b) (concern) (j-n) betreffen; **as re-gards the money**, was das Geld betrifft; (c) (j-s Wünsche) berücksichtigen. ◆re'garding, prep. hinsichtlich + gen; **r. your enquiry**, mit Bezug auf Ihre An-frage. ◆re'gardless, adj. **r. of**, un-geachtet + gen.

**regenerate** [riː'dʒenəreit], v.tr. Fig: (et-was) neu beleben.

**regent** ['riːdʒənt], s. Regent(in) m(f). ◆'regency, s. Regentschaft f.

**regime** [rei'ʒiːm], s. Pol: Regime n.

**regiment** ['redʒimənt], s. Regiment n.

**region** ['riːdʒ(ə)n], s. 1. (a) Gebiet n, Re-gion f; (b) (district) Gegend f; Adm: Be-zirk m. 2. (sphere) Bereich m; **a sum in the r. of £1000**, eine Summe von unge-fähr 1000 Pfund. ◆'regional, adj. re-gional.

**register** ['redʒistər]. I. s. 1. (list) Register n; Sch: (class) r., Klassenbuch n. 2. (vo-cabulary etc.) Sprachgebrauch m (eines Fachbereichs usw.). **3. cash r.**, Regi-strierkasse f. II. v. 1. v.tr. (a) (einen Na-men) einschreiben; (eine Geburt) anmel-den; (b) (of meter) (einen Wert) anzeigen. 2. v.i. (a) sich (in ein Register) eintra-gen; sich (bei der Polizei usw.) anmel-den; (b) F: **it didn't r. (with her)**, sie hat es nicht mitgekriegt. ◆'registered, adj. (of letter etc.) eingeschrieben. ◆regis'trar, s. 1. (r. of births etc.) Stan-desbeamte(r) m. 2. (at university) Regi-sterführer m. 3. Med: Oberarzt m. ◆regis'tration, s. Eintragung f; **r. number**, (polizeiliches) Kennzeichen n. ◆'registry, s. **r. office**, Standesamt n.

**regret** [ri'gret]. I. s. Bedauern n; **to have no regrets** keine Reue empfinden. II. v.tr. (a) (etwas) bedauern; **I r. to have to tell/inform you that ...**, ich muß Ihnen leider mitteilen, daß ...; (b) (eine Tat, Vergangenes) bereuen. ◆re'grettable, adj. bedauerlich. ◆re'gretful, adj. be-dauernd; (sad) traurig; (remorseful) reue-voll; **-ly**, adv. mit Bedauern.

**regular** ['regjulər]. I. adj. (a) regelmäßig; (b) (systematic) geregelt, geordnet; (c) (usual) üblich; Gram: **r. verb**, regelmäßi-ges Verb; (d) **r. staff**, ständiges Personal. **II.** s. F: (in shop) Stammkunde m, Stammkundin f; (in pub) Stammgast m. ◆regu'larity, s. Regelmäßigkeit f. ◆'regulate, v.tr. regulieren; (den Ver-kehr, die Geschwindigkeit usw.) regeln. ◆regu'lation, s. (rule) Vorschrift f; at-trib. vorschriftsmäßig.

**rehabilitate** [riːhə'biliteit], v.tr. (a) (j-n) rehabilitieren; (b) (Versehrte, Flücht-linge, Verbrecher) wieder (in die Gesell-schaft) eingliedern. ◆rehabili'tation, s. Rehabilitierung f; Wiedereingliederung f (in die Gesellschaft).

**rehearse** [ri'hɜːs], v.tr. & i. (ein Stück) proben. ◆re'hearsal, s. Probe f.

**reign** [rein]. I. s. Herrschaft f; **r. of ter-ror**, Schreckensherrschaft f. II. v.i. regie-ren (**over**, über + acc).

**reimburse** [riːim'bɜːs], v.tr. **to r. s.o. (for his costs)/s.o.'s costs**, j-m die Ko-sten rückerstatten.

**rein** [rein], s. Zügel m; Fig: **to give free r. to sth.**, etwas dat freien Lauf lassen.

**reindeer** ['reindiər], s. Rentier n.

**reinforce** [riːin'fɔːs], v.tr. (einen Bau, einen Stoff, Mil: eine Besatzung usw.) verstärken; **reinforced concrete**, Stahlbe-ton m. ◆rein'forcement, s. Mil: usu. pl. Verstärkungstruppen fpl.

**reinstate** [riːin'steit], v.tr. (j-n) wieder-einstellen.

**reiterate** [riː'itəreit], v.tr. (etwas) wieder-holen.

**reject.** I. [ri'dʒekt] v.tr. (of pers.) (etwas) ablehnen; (eine Methode, ein Urteil) ver-werfen; (einen Freier, einen Kandidaten usw.) abweisen. II. ['riːdʒekt] s. Aus-schußware f. ◆re'jection, s. Ablehnung f; Verwerfung f; Zurückweisung f.

**rejoice** [ri'dʒɔis], v.i. sich (sehr) freuen, (**at/over sth.**, über etwas acc).

**rejoin** [riː'dʒɔin], v.tr. sich (j-m) wieder anschließen.

**rejuvenate** [ri'dʒuːvineit], v.tr. (sich, j-n) verjüngen.

**relapse** [ri'læps], s. Rückfall m.

**relate** [ri'leit], v. 1. v.tr. (a) (etwas) er-zählen; (Tatsachen) berichten; (b) (zwei Sachen) aufeinander beziehen, in Bezie-hung bringen. 2. v.i. **to r. to sth.**, (i) sich auf etwas acc beziehen; (ii) (of pers.) eine Beziehung zu etwas dat haben. ◆re'lated, adj. **1.** (of things) verbunden (**to**, mit + dat). **2.** (of pers.) verwandt (**to**, mit + dat). ◆re'lation, s. **1.** (relation-ship) Beziehung f; Verhältnis n; **in r. to**, im Verhältnis zu + dat. **2.** (pers.) Ver-wandte(r) f(m). ◆re'lationship, s. (a) Verhältnis n (**to/with**, zu + dat); (b) (to relative) Verwandtschaft f.

**relative** ['relətiv]. **I.** adj. **1.** (a) (of terms, success etc.) verhältnismäßig; (b) **r. to sth.**, im Verhältnis zu etwas dat. **2.**

*Gram:* **r. pronoun,** Relativpronomen *n.*
**II.** *s.* Verwandte(r) *f(m);* **-ly,** *adv.* verhältnismäßig; **r. happy,** ganz/ziemlich glücklich.

**relax** [ri'læks], *v.* **1.** *v.tr.* (den Griff, die Disziplin, ein Verbot usw.) lockern; (Muskeln) entspannen. **2.** *v.i.* sich entspannen. ◆**relax'ation,** *s.* Lockerung *f;* Entspannung *f.* ◆**re'laxing,** *adj.* entspannend.

**relay. I.** [ri'lei] *v.tr.irr.* (eine Nachricht) weitergeben; *Rad:* übertragen. **II.** ['ri:lei] *s. (relief team)* Ablösung *f;* **to work in relays,** sich (bei der Arbeit) ablösen; *Sp:* **r. (race),** Staffellauf *m.*

**release** [ri'li:s]. **I.** *s.* **1.** *(of pers.)* Befreiung *f;* Freilassung *f* (eines Gefangenen). **2.** *(a)* Freigabe *f (Com:* eines neuen Modells, *Cin:* eines Films); *(b)* (press) *r.,* Verlautbarung *f.* **II.** *v.tr. (a)* (j-n) befreien; (einen Gefangenen) freilassen; *(b)* *(Com:* einen neuen Wagen usw., *Cin:* einen Film) freigeben; *(publish)* (einen Text usw.) veröffentlichen; *(c) (let go)* loslassen; (die Bremse) lösen.

**relegate** ['religeit], *v.tr.* (j-n, etwas) verbannen **(to,** in + *acc*); *Fb:* **to be relegated,** absteigen **(to,** in + *acc*).

**relent** [ri'lent], *v.i.* sich erweichen lassen. ◆**re'lentless,** *adj. (of pers.)* schonungslos; *(pitiless)* erbarmungslos; **r. struggle,** erbitterter Kampf.

**relevant** ['relivənt], *adj.* einschlägig; **to be r. to sth.,** sich auf etwas *acc* beziehen. ◆**'relevance,** *s.* Relevanz *f.*

**reliable** [ri'laiəbl], *adj.* zuverlässig; *(trustworthy)* vertrauenswürdig; *(of machine)* betriebssicher. ◆**relia'bility,** *s.* Zuverlässigkeit *f;* Vertrauenswürdigkeit *f;* Betriebssicherheit *f* (einer Maschine usw.). ◆**re'liant** [ri'laiənt], *adj.* **to be r. on s.o.,** sich auf j-n verlassen müssen.

**relic** ['relik], *s.* **1.** *Ecc:* Reliquie *f.* **2.** *(remains)* Überrest *m;* **relics of the past,** Altertümer *npl.*

**relief¹** [ri'li:f], *s.* **1.** Erleichterung *f.* **2.** *(a)* *(aid)* **r. fund,** Unterstützungsfonds *m;* *(b) (substitute)* Entlastung *f;* *(c) Mil: etc:* Ablösung *f* (einer Wache usw.). **3.** *Fin:* **tax r.,** Steuererleichterung *f.* ◆**re'lieve,** *v.tr. (a)* (Leiden) erleichtern; (Schmerzen) lindern; (j-s Gewissen) beruhigen; *(b) Mil:* **to r. a town/fortress,** eine Stadt/Festung entsetzen; **to r. s.o. of a duty/responsibility,** j-n von einer Pflicht/Verantwortung entbinden. ◆**re'lieved,** *adj.* erleichtert.

**relief²,** *s.* **to stand out in (sharp) r.,** sich scharf abheben **(against sth.,** von etwas *dat*).

**religion** [ri'lidʒən], *s.* Religion *f; Fig:* Kult *m.* ◆**re'ligious,** *adj.* religiös; *(pious)* fromm.

**relinquish** [ri'liŋkwiʃ], *v.tr.* einen Plan usw. aufgeben; (auf ein Amt) verzichten.

**relish** ['reliʃ]. **I.** *s.* **1.** *(spice)* Würze *f.* **2.** *Fig:* **with great r.,** mit großem Vergnü-

gen. **II.** *v.tr.* **to r. doing sth.,** etwas sehr gern/mit Vergnügen tun.

**reluctance** [ri'lʌktəns], *s.* Widerwille *m;* Abneigung *f* (, etwas zu tun). ◆**re'luctant,** *adj.* **1.** *(of pers.)* **r. to do sth.,** abgeneigt, etwas zu tun. **2.** *(of consent etc.)* widerwillig; *(hesitant)* zögernd; **-ly,** *adv.* widerstrebend.

**rely** [ri'lai], *v.i.* **to r. (up)on s.o., sth.,** sich auf j-n, etwas *acc* verlassen.

**remain** [ri'mein], *v.i.* bleiben; **only ten r.,** es sind nur noch zehn übrig; **to r. sitting/seated,** sitzen bleiben; **to r. behind,** zurückbleiben. ◆**re'mainder.** *s.* **the r.,** der Rest; *coll.* die Übrigen *pl;* **the r. of his life,** der Rest seines Lebens; ◆**re'maining,** *adj.* übrig; *(surviving)* übriggeblieben. ◆**re'mains,** *s.pl.* Reste *mpl;* Überbleibsel *npl* (einer Mahlzeit); Überreste *mpl,* Spuren *fpl* (einer Zivilisation usw.).

**remand** [ri'mɑːnd], *s. Jur:* **on r.,** in Untersuchungshaft.

**remark** [ri'mɑːk]. **I.** *s.* Bemerkung *f.* **II.** *v.* **1.** *v.tr.* bemerken. **2.** *v.i.* **to r. on sth.,** auf etwas    *acc*    hinweisen. ◆**re'markable,** *adj.* bemerkenswert; *(strange)* merkwürdig; *(extraordinary)* außerordentlich.

**remedial** [ri'mi:djəl], *adj.* Hilfs-. ◆**remedy** ['remidi]. **I.** *s.* **(a)** Abhilfe *f;* Mittel *n* **(for/against,** gegen + *acc*); *(b) Med:* Heilmittel *n.* **II.** *v.tr.* (etwas *dat*) abhelfen, in Ordnung bringen; (einen Mißstand) beseitigen.

**remember** [ri'membər], *v.tr. (a)* **to r. s.o., sth.,** sich an j-n, etwas *acc* erinnern; **as far as I r.,** soviel/soweit ich mich entsinne; *(b) (make a mental note of)* sich *dat* (etwas) merken; *(c) (bear in mind)* (etwas) bedenken. ◆**re'membrance,** *s.* Andenken *n;* **in r. of s.o.,** zur Erinnerung/*(on grave etc.)* zum Andenken an j-n; **R. Day,** Heldengedenktag *m.*

**remind** [ri'maind], *v.tr.* **to r. s.o. of s.o., sth.,** j-n an j-n, etwas *acc* erinnern; **that reminds me (...)!** dabei fällt mir ein (,...)! ◆**re'minder,** *s.* Mahnung *f.*

**reminisce** [remi'nis], *v.i.* in Erinnerungen schwelgen. ◆**remi'niscence,** *s.* Erinnerung *f.* ◆**remi'niscent,** *adj.* **to be r. of s.o., sth.,** an j-n, etwas *acc* erinnern.

**remit** [ri'mit], *v.tr. Com: (pay)* (j-m eine Summe) überweisen. ◆**re'mittance,** *s. Com:* Überweisung *f.*

**remnant** ['remnənt], *s.* (letzter) Rest *m.*

**remonstrate** ['remənstreit], *v.i.* protestieren **(against sth.,** gegen etwas *acc*).

**remorse** [ri'mɔːs], *s.* Reue *f.* ◆**re'morseful,** *adj.* reumütig. ◆**re'morseless,** *adj. (a)* reuelos; *(b) (pitiless)* erbarmungslos.

**remote** [ri'məut], *adj.* **1.** *(a) (distant)* fern; *(weit)* entfernt; *Rad:* **r. control,** Fernlenkung *f;* *(b) (of situation)* abgelegen. 2. *Fig:* a r. resemblance, eine entfernte Ähnlichkeit.

**remove** [ri'mu:v], *v.tr.* (*a*) (*take off*) abnehmen; (ein Kleidungsstück) ablegen; (*take away*) (etwas) wegnehmen/entfernen; (*b*) (*eliminate*) (Flecken) entfernen; (Fehler, ein Hindernis usw.) beseitigen; (Schwierigkeiten, einen Mißstand) beheben. ◆**re'movable**, *adj.* abnehmbar. ◆**re'moval**, *s.* 1. Entfernen *n* (eines Flecks usw.); Beseitigung *f* (eines Mißstandes). 2. (*to another house*) Umzug *m;* **furniture** r., Möbelspedition *f.* ◆**re'mover**, *s.* (*liquid*) Entferner *m;* **paint** r., Abbeizmittel *n.*

**remunerate** [ri'mju:nəreit], *v.tr.* (*pay*) (j-n) bezahlen; (*reward*) belohnen (for, für + *acc*). ◆**remune'ration**, *s.* Bezahlung *f;* Belohnung *f* (for, für + *acc*).

**renaissance** [re'neis(ə)ns], *s.* **the R.**, die Renaissance.

**render** ['rendər], *v.tr.* (*a*) **to r. a service to s.o.**, j-m einen Dienst erweisen; (*b*) (*with adj.*) (j-n, etwas) ... machen; **to r. sth. unusable**, etwas unbrauchbar machen.

**rendezvous** ['rɔndivu:], *s.* Rendezvous *n;* (*place*) Treffpunkt *m.*

**renew** [ri'nju:], *v.tr.* (etwas) erneuern; (*at library*) (ein Buch) verlängern; (eine Bekanntschaft) wieder aufnehmen. ◆**re'newal**, *s.* Erneuerung *f;* Wiederaufnahme *f.*

**renounce** [ri'nauns], *v.tr.* (auf ein Recht, einen Titel usw.) verzichten.

**renovate** ['renəuveit], *v.tr.* renovieren. ◆**reno'vation**, *s.* Renovierung *f.*

**renown** [ri'naun], *s.* Berühmtheit *f.* ◆**re'nowned**, *adj.* berühmt (for, für + *acc*).

**rent** [rent]. I. *s.* (*for house etc.*) Miete *f.* II. *v.tr.* (*a*) (*let*) (ein Haus) vermieten; (*b*) (*hire*) (eine Wohnung) mieten; (ein Fernsehgerät usw.) leihen. ◆**'rental**, *s.* (*amount*) Miete *f.*

**reopen** ['ri:'əup(ə)n], *v.tr.* (*a*) wieder aufmachen; (*b*) (Verhandlungen usw.) wiedereröffnen.

**reorganize** ['ri:'ɔ:gənaiz], *v.tr.* (etwas) neu organisieren, (*alter*) umorganisieren.

**rep** [rep], *s. F:* Com: Vertreter(in) *m* (*f*).

**repair** [ri'peər]. I. *s.* Reparatur *f* (einer Maschine usw.); Ausbesserung *f* (von Kleidern usw.). II. *v.tr.* (etwas) reparieren; (Kleider) ausbessern; (einen Reifen) flicken; **to r. damage/a loss**, Schaden/einen Verlust wiedergutmachen. ◆**re'pairable**, *adj.* reparierbar; *pred.* zu reparieren.

**repatriate** [ri:'pætrieit], *v.tr.* (j-n) repatriieren.

**repay** [ri:'pei], *v.tr.irr.* (*a*) (Geld, eine Schuld) zurückzahlen; (j-n) entschädigen; **to r. s.o. for sth.**, j-m etwas vergelten; (*b*) **to r. a favour**, eine Gefälligkeit erwidern. ◆**re'payment**, *s.* (*a*) Rückzahlung *f;* (*b*) Entschädigung *f.*

**repeal** [ri'pi:l]. I. *s.* Aufhebung *f* (eines Gesetzes). II. *v.tr.* (ein Gesetz) aufheben.

**repeat** [ri'pi:t]. I. *v.tr.* (etwas) wiederholen. II. *s.* Wiederholung *f;* Com: r. order, Nachbestellung *f.* ◆**re'peated**, *adj.* wiederholt.

**repel** [ri'pel], *v.tr.* (den Feind usw.) zurücktreiben; (einen Angriff, einen Schlag) abwehren; (Insekten) vertreiben. ◆**re'pellent**, *adj.* abstoßend; **water** r., wasserabstoßend.

**repent** [ri'pent], *v.* 1. *v.tr.* (etwas) bereuen. 2. *v.i.* Reue empfinden. ◆**re'pentance**, *s.* Reue *f.* ◆**re'pentant**, *adj.* reuig.

**repercussion** [ri:pə'kʌʃ(ə)n], *s.* Rückwirkung *f.*

**repertoire** ['repətwɑ:r], *s.* Repertoire *n.* ◆**repertory** ['repət(ə)ri], *s. Th:* Repertoire *n.*

**repetition** [repi'tiʃ(ə)n], *s.* Wiederholung *f.*

**replace** [ri'pleis], *v.tr.* (*a*) (etwas) wieder an seinen Platz stellen/setzen; (*b*) (*substitute*) (j-n, etwas) ersetzen (**by/with**, durch + *acc*); (Maschinenteile) auswechseln. ◆**re'placeable**, *adj.* ersetzbar; *Tchm:* auswechselbar. ◆**re'placement**, *s.* Ersatz *m;* (*a*) (*pers.*) (*temporary*) Stellvertreter(in) *m*(*f*); (*b*) *Ind:* r. (part), Ersatzteil *n.*

**replay** ['ri:plei], *s.* 1. *Sp:* Wiederholungsspiel *n.* 2. *Rec:* Abspielen *n.*

**replenish** [ri'pleniʃ], *v.tr.* (ein Glas, einen Tank usw.) wieder auffüllen (**with**, mit + *dat*); **to r. one's supplies**, neue Vorräte anlegen.

**replica** ['replikə], *s.* (*genaue*) Kopie *f; Art:* Replik *f.*

**reply** [ri'plai]. I. *s.* Antwort *f.* II. *v.i.* antworten (**to sth.**, auf etwas *acc*; **to s.o.**, j-m).

**report** [ri'pɔ:t]. I. *s.* Bericht *m* (**on**, über + *acc*); (*verbal*) Meldung *f;* **to make a r.**, Bericht erstatten (**on sth.**, über etwas *acc*). II. *v.* 1. *v.tr.* (*a*) (eine Tatsache) berichten/(*on radio*) melden; (*b*) **to r. an accident to the police**, einen Unfall der Polizei melden; (*c*) *Gram:* **reported speech**, indirekte Rede. 2. *v.i.* (*a*) **to r. on sth.**, über etwas *acc* Bericht erstatten/berichten; (*b*) **to r. to s.o.**, sich bei j-m melden. ◆**re'porter**, *s.* Reporter *m.*

**repose** [ri'pəuz]. I. *s.* Ruhe *f.* II. *v.i.* ruhen.

**reprehensible** [repri'hensəbl], *adj.* tadelnswert.

**represent** [repri'zent], *v.tr.* (*a*) (*portray*) (etwas, *Th:* eine Rolle usw.) darstellen; (*b*) (*act for*) (eine Firma, einen Wahlbezirk usw.) vertreten. ◆**represen'tation**, *s.* 1. (*portrayal*) Darstellung *f.* 2. *Com: etc:* Vertretung *f.* ◆**repre'sentative**. I. *adj.* 1. (*symbolical*) symbolisch (**of**, für + *acc*). 2. (*typical*) repräsentativ. II. *s. esp. Com:* Vertreter(in) *m*(*f*); *Jur:* Beauftragte(r) *m & f.*

**repress** [ri'pres], *v.tr.* (einen Aufstand, Emotionen) unterdrücken; (Wünsche, Gedanken) verdrängen. ◆**re'pression,** *s.* Unterdrückung *f;* Verdrängung *f.* ◆**re'pressive,** *adj.* repressiv.

**reprieve** [ri'priːv]. **I.** *s. Jur: etc: (temporary)* Aufschub *m; (permanent)* Begnadigung *f.* **II.** *v.tr. (a) (permanently)* (j-n) begnadigen; *(b) Fig:* (j-m) eine Gnadenfrist geben.

**reprimand** ['reprimɑːnd]. **I.** *s.* Verweis *m.* **II.** *v.tr.* (j-m) einen Verweis erteilen.

**reprint. I.** ['riːprint] *v.tr.* (ein Buch) neu auflegen. **II.** ['riːprint] *s.* Neuauflage *f.*

**reprisal** [ri'praiz(ə)l], *s.* Vergeltungsmaßnahme *f.*

**reproach** [ri'prəutʃ]. **I.** *s.* Vorwurf *m;* beyond r., ohne Tadel. **II.** *v.tr.* to r. s.o. about sth., j-m wegen etwas *gen* Vorwürfe machen. ◆**re'proachful,** *adj.* vorwurfsvoll.

**reproduce** ['riːprə'djuːs], *v.* **1.** *v.tr.* (ein Modell usw.) nachbilden; (Musik) wiedergeben; (ein Bild) nachdrucken. **2.** *v.i. (multiply)* sich vermehren. ◆'**repro'duction,** *s.* **1.** Reproduktion *f* (eines Gemäldes, der menschlichen Rasse); *Rec: etc:* Wiedergabe *f* (von Tönen, Farben usw.). **2.** Nachbildung *f.*

**reptile** ['reptail], *s.* Reptil *n.*

**republic** [ri'pʌblik], *s.* Republik *f.* ◆**re'publican. I.** *adj.* republikanisch. **II.** *s.* Republikaner(in) *m(f).*

**repudiate** [ri'pjuːdieit], *v.tr.* (eine Beschuldigung usw.) zurückweisen; (j-s Autorität) nicht anerkennen.

**re'pugnant** [ri'pʌgnənt], *adj.* widerlich; to be r. to s.o., j-m zuwider sein.

**repulse** [ri'pʌls], *v.tr.* (einen Feind) zurücktreiben; (einen Angriff) abwehren. ◆**re'pulsion,** *s.* Abscheu *f* (to/for s.o., sth., vor j-m, etwas *dat).* ◆**re'pulsive,** *adj.* widerlich.

**reputable** ['repjutəbl], *adj.* angesehen; *(respectable)* anständig. ◆**repu'tation,** *s.* Ruf *m.* ◆**re'puted,** *adj. (supposed)* vermeintlich.

**request** [ri'kwest]. **I.** *s.* Bitte *f* (for, um + *acc); (formal)* Ersuchen *n* (for, um + *acc);* on/by r., auf Wunsch; *Rad: etc:* r. programme, Wunschsendung *f.* **II.** *v.tr.* (um etwas *acc)* bitten; to r. sth. from s.o., j-n um etwas *acc* ersuchen.

**require** [ri'kwaiər], *v.tr. (a) (demand)* to r. sth. of s.o., etwas von j-m verlangen; *(b) (need)* (etwas) brauchen, nötig haben. ◆**re'quired,** *adj. (necessary)* nötig; *(desired)* gewünscht; if r., notfalls. ◆**re'quirement,** *s.* **1.** *(demand)* Forderung *f.* **2.** *(need)* Bedürfnis *n; pl.* Bedarf *m.* **3.** *(condition)* Voraussetzung *f.*

**requisite** ['rekwizit], *adj. (necessary)* erforderlich. ◆**requi'sition,** *v.tr. Mil: etc:* beschlagnahmen.

**rescind** [ri'sind], *v.tr. Jur: Adm:* (ein Gesetz usw.) aufheben; (einen Vertrag) für

ungültig erklären.

**rescue** ['reskjuː]. **I.** *s.* Rettung *f;* Bergung *f* (von Schiffbrüchigen); to come to s.o.'s r., j-m zu Hilfe kommen. **II.** *v.tr.* retten, *Nau:* bergen (from, aus + *dat).*

**research** [ri'səːtʃ]. **I.** *s.* Forschung *f* (on/into sth., über etwas *acc).* **II.** *v.* **1.** *v.i.* to r. (into a subject), Forschung (über eine Sache) betreiben. **2.** *v.tr.* (ein Gebiet) erforschen.

**resemble** [ri'zembl], *v.tr.* (j-m, etwas *dat)* ähnlich sein. ◆**re'semblance,** *s.* Ähnlichkeit *f* (to, mit + *dat).*

**resent** [ri'zent], *v.tr.* (etwas) übelnehmen; (j-n) ablehnen. ◆**re'sentful,** *adj.* to be r. of sth., etwas nicht vertragen können. ◆**re'sentment,** *s.* Ressentiment *n* (against/at, gegen + *acc).*

**reserve** [ri'zəːv]. **I.** *v.tr.* (einen Platz) reservieren; to r. the right to do sth., sich *dat* das Recht vorbehalten, etwas zu tun. **II.** *s.* **1.** Reserve *f* (von Geld, Energie usw.); *(store)* Vorrat *m* (von Lebensmitteln). **2.** *Sp:* Reservespieler *m.* **3.** *(area)* nature r., Naturschutzgebiet *n.* **4.** *(reticence)* Zurückhaltung *f.* ◆**reser'vation** [rezə-], *s.* **1.** Reservierung *f.* **2.** *(doubt)* Bedenken *n;* without r., ohne Vorbehalt. **3.** *(for animals)* Naturschutzgebiet *n.* ◆**re'served,** *adj.* **1.** r. seats, reservierte Plätze. **2.** *(of pers.)* zurückhaltend. ◆**reservoir** ['rezəvwɑːr], *s.* Reservoir *n; (container)* Speicher *m.*

**reshuffle** [riː'ʃʌfl], *s. Pol:* Umbildung *f.*

**reside** [ri'zaid], *v.i.* wohnen. ◆**residence** ['rezidəns], *s. (a)* (place of) r., Wohnsitz *m; (b) (house etc.)* Wohnung *f;* Residenz *f* (eines Fürsten); (students') hall of r., Studentenheim *n.* ◆'**resident. I.** *adj.* r. in X, wohnhaft in X. **II.** *s.* Einwohner(in) *m(f); (in hotel)* Hotelgast *m.* ◆**resi'dential,** *adj.* Wohn-; r. area, Wohnviertel *n.*

**residue** ['rezidjuː], *s.* Rest *m; Ch:* Rückstand *m.*

**resign** [ri'zain]. **I.** *s.* **1.** *v.tr. (a)* (eine Stelle) aufgeben; *(b)* to r. oneself to doing sth., sich damit abfinden, etwas tun zu müssen. **2.** *v.i.* (von einem Posten) zurücktreten; (aus einem Verein) austreten. ◆**resignation** [rezig'neiʃ(ə)n], *s.* **1.** Rücktritt *m* (from a post, von einem Posten). **2.** *(state of mind)* Resignation *f.* ◆**re'signed,** *adj.* resigniert.

**resilient** [ri'ziliənt], *adj.* elastisch; *(of pers.)* nicht unterzukriegen.

**resin** ['rezin], *s.* Harz *n.*

**resist** [ri'zist], *v.tr. & i. (a)* (etwas *dat)* widerstehen; *(b) (oppose)* (j-m) Widerstand leisten; sich (einem Projekt usw.) widersetzen. ◆**re'sistance,** *s.* Widerstand *m* (to, gegen + *acc);* Widerstandsfähigkeit *f* (von Stahl usw.). ◆**re'sistant,** *adj. (of material)* widerstandsfähig; **heat-**r., hitzebeständig.

**resolute** ['rezəl(j)uːt], *adj. (of pers., man-*

*ner)* resolut; *(of resistance etc.)* fest.

**reso'lution,** *s.* **1.** *(a) (corporate decision)* Beschluß *m* (einer Versammlung); *(b) (personal decision)* Entschluß *m;* **good resolutions,** gute Vorsätze *mpl.* **2.** *(decisiveness)* Entschlossenheit *f.* **3. r. of a problem,** Lösung *f* eines Problems. ◆**resolve** [ri'zɔlv]. **I.** *s. (decisiveness)* Entschlossenheit *f.* **II.** *v.* **1.** *v.tr. (solve)* (ein Problem) lösen; (einen Zweifel) beseitigen. **2.** *v.i.* sich entschließen (**to do sth.,** etwas zu tun).

**resonant** ['rezənənt], *adj.* resonant.

**resort** [ri'zɔːt]. **I.** *s.* **1. as a last r.,** als letzter Ausweg, *F:* wenn alle Stricke reißen. **2.** *(holiday)* r., Ferienort *m;* **seaside r.,** Seebad *n.* **II.** *v.i.* **to r. to violence, force etc.,** Gewalt, Zwang usw. anwenden.

**resound** [ri'zaund], *v.i.* erschallen; widerhallen. ◆**re'sounding,** *adj. (of success etc.)* glänzend; **r. blow,** heftiger/*Fig:* schwerer Schlag; **r. victory,** überwältigender Sieg.

**resource** [ri'sɔːs], *s.* **1.** Hilfsmittel *n; Sch:* Lehrmittel *n.* **2.** *pl. (money, labour etc.)* Mittel *npl; (wealth)* Reichtümer *mpl* (eines Landes); **natural resources,** Naturschätze *mpl; (minerals)* Bodenschätze *mpl.* ◆**re'sourceful,** *adj.* findig.

**respect** [ri'spekt]. **I.** *s.* **1.** *(aspect)* Hinsicht *f;* **with r. to/in r. of,** hinsichtlich + *gen.* **2.** *(esteem)* Achtung *f;* **to have r. for s.o.,** j-n respektieren. **II.** *v.tr.* (j-n) respektieren; **to r. s.o.'s wishes,** j-s Wünsche berücksichtigen. ◆**respecta'bility,** *s. (status)* Ansehen *n; (quality)* Anständigkeit *f.* ◆**re'spectable,** *adj. (of pers., firm etc.)* solide; **-ably,** *adv.* **r. dressed,** anständig gekleidet. ◆**re'spectful,** *adj.* ehrerbietig; *(of pers.)* respektvoll (**towards,** gegen + *acc*); **-ly,** *adv.* höflichst. ◆**re'spective,** *adj.* jeweilig; **-ly,** *adv.* **the concerts are in London and Manchester r.,** die Konzerte finden jeweils in London und Manchester statt.

**respiration** [respi'reiʃ(ə)n], *s.* Atmung *f.*

**respite** ['respait, 'respit], *s. (breathing space)* Atempause *f; (rest)* Ruhepause *f.*

**resplendent** [ri'splendənt], *adj.* prächtig.

**respond** [ri'spɔnd], *v.i. (a) (of pers.)* antworten (**to a question etc.,** auf eine Frage usw.); *(react)* reagieren (**to sth.,** auf etwas *acc*,); *(b) (of machine, instrument)* ansprechen (**to sth.,** auf etwas *acc*); *(of illness, patient)* **to r. to treatment,** auf die Behandlung ansprechen. ◆**re'sponse,** *s. (answer)* Antwort *f; (to advertisement etc.)* Zuschrift *f; coll.* Reaktion *f.* ◆**responsi'bility,** *s.* Verantwortung *f.* ◆**re'sponsible,** *adj.* **1.** *(accountable)* verantwortlich (**to s.o. for sth.,** j-m für etwas *acc*). **2.** *(of job, attitude etc.)* verantwortungsvoll; *(of pers.)* verantwortungsbewußt; *(reliable)* zuverlässig. ◆**re'sponsive,** *adj.* empfänglich (**to in-**

**fluences,** für Einflüsse); *(of audience)* mitgehend.

**rest**[1] [rest]. **I.** *s.* **1.** *(a) (repose)* Ruhe *f; Fig:* **to set s.o.'s mind at r.,** j-n beruhigen; *(b) (halt)* Rast *f; (break)* Ruhepause *f* **(from,** von + *dat*); **to have/take a r.,** sich ausruhen; *(take a break)* Pause machen. **2.** *Mus:* Pause *f.* **3.** *(support)* Stütze *f.* **II.** *v.* **1.** *v.i. (a)* ruhen; *(in bed etc.)* sich ausruhen; *(b)* **to r. on sth.,** sich auf/gegen etwas *acc* stützen/lehnen. **2.** *v.tr. (a)* (die Augen, die Stimme) schonen; *Sp:* (einen Spieler) aussetzen lassen; *(b) (support)* (die Ellbogen usw.) stützen. ◆**'restful,** *adj.* erholsam; *(peaceful)* ruhig, friedlich. ◆**'restless,** *adj.* ruhelos; *(uneasy)* unruhig. ◆**'restlessness,** *s.* Ruhelosigkeit *f;* Unruhe *f.*

**rest**[2], *s. (a)* Rest *m;* **the r. of the money,** das übrige Geld; *(b) (pers.)* pl. die Übrigen; **the r. of us,** wir anderen.

**restaurant** ['rest(ə)rɔŋ], *s.* Restaurant *n.*

**restive** ['restiv], *adj.* unruhig; *(on edge)* nervös.

**restore** [ri'stɔːr], *v.tr. (a) (return)* (etwas Gestohlenes usw.) wiedergeben (**to s.o.,** j-m); *(b) (renovate)* (ein Gebäude, Gemälde usw.) restaurieren; (Möbel) erneuern; *(c) (re-establish)* (die öffentliche Ordnung) wiederherstellen. ◆**restoration** [restə'reiʃ(ə)n], *s.* **1.** Rückerstattung *f* (von Eigentum). **2.** Restaurierung *f* (eines Kunstwerkes usw.). **3.** Wiederherstellung *f* (der Gesundheit, Ordnung usw.).

**restrain** [ri'strein], *v.tr.* (j-n, sich) zurückhalten; (einen Hund) bändigen; *Fig:* (Gefühle) unterdrücken; *(limit)* (Freigebigkeit usw.) einschränken; **to r. s.o. from doing sth.,** j-n davon abhalten, etwas zu tun. ◆**re'strained,** *adj. (of expression etc.)* verhalten; *(of pers., manner)* zurückhaltend. ◆**re'straint,** *s. (a)* Beschränkung *f* (der Freiheit, des Handels); *(b) (manner)* Zurückhaltung *f.*

**restrict** [ri'strikt], *v.tr. (a)* beschränken (**to,** auf + *acc*); *(of things)* (Bewegungen) hemmen. ◆**re'stricted,** *adj.* beschränkt; *(of movements)* gehemmt. ◆**re'striction,** *s. (a)* Beschränkung *f;* **speed r.,** Geschwindigkeitsbegrenzung *f; (b)* Hemmung *f* (der Bewegungen usw.). ◆**re'strictive,** *adj.* einschränkend.

**result** [ri'zʌlt]. **I.** *s. (a)* Ergebnis *n; (consequence)* Folge *f; (b)* **to produce results,** Erfolg bringen; **the desired r.,** die gewünschte Wirkung. **II.** *v.i. (a)* sich ergeben **(from,** aus + *dat*); *(b)* enden (**in,** in + *dat*). ◆**re'sultant,** *adj.* resultierend.

**resume** [ri'zjuːm], *v.* **1.** *v.tr. (a)* (Verhandlungen, Beziehungen usw.) wiederaufnehmen; *(b)* (den Kampf, das Spiel) fortsetzen. **2.** *v.i.* wieder anfangen. ◆**resumption** [ri'zʌmpʃən], *s.* Wiederaufnahme *f;* Fortsetzung *f* (eines Spiels usw.).

**resurface** ['riː'səːfis], *v.* **1.** *v.tr.* **to r. the**

**road,** den Straßenbelag erneuern. **2.** *v.i.* (*of diver, submarine*) wieder auftauchen.

**resurrection** [rezə'rekʃ(ə)n], *s.* Auferstehung *f.*

**resuscitate** [ri'sʌsiteit], *v.tr.* (j-n) wiederbeleben.

**retail** ['ri:teil], *s.* **r. (trade),** Einzelhandel *m.*

**retain** [ri'tein], *v.tr.* (*a*) (etwas) behalten; (eine Sitte, eine Gewohnheit usw.) beibehalten; (*b*) (*remember*) (etwas im Gedächtnis) behalten; (*c*) (Wasser usw.) zurückhalten. ◆**re'tainer,** *s.* (*fee*) Honorar *n.*

**retaliate** [ri'tælieit], *v.i.* sich revanchieren. ◆**retali'ation,** *s.* Vergeltung *f;* (*act*) Vergeltungsmaßnahme *f.*

**retarded** [ri'tɑ:did], *adj.* **(mentally)** r., zurückgeblieben.

**retention** [ri'tenʃ(ə)n], *s.* Behalten *n;* Beibehaltung *f* (alter Bräuche usw.); (*memory*) Merkfähigkeit *f.*

**reticent** ['retis(ə)nt], *adj.* (*of character*) zurückhaltend. ◆**'reticence,** *s.* Verschwiegenheit *f.*

**retire** [ri'taiər], *v.* **1.** *v.i.* (*a*) sich zurückziehen (**from,** von + dat); (*b*) (*stop working*) aufhören zu arbeiten; (*esp. of civil servant*) in den Ruhestand treten. **2.** *v.tr.* (j-n) pensionieren. ◆**re'tired,** *adj.* im Ruhestand. ◆**re'tirement,** *s.* Ruhestand *m.* ◆**re'tiring,** *adj.* (*of pers.*) zurückhaltend.

**retort** [ri'tɔ:t]. **I.** *s.* (schlagfertige) Antwort *f.* **II.** *v.tr.* schlagfertig antworten (**to sth.,** auf etwas *acc*).

**retrace** [ri'treis], *v.tr.* (j-s Bewegungen) zurückverfolgen; **to r. one's steps,** denselben Weg zurückgehen.

**retract** [ri'trækt], *v.tr.* (*a*) (die Klauen, *Av:* das Fahrgestell) einziehen; (*b*) (eine Anklage) zurückziehen; (eine Aussage) widerrufen; (eine Behauptung) zurücknehmen.

**retreat** [ri'tri:t]. **I.** *s. Mil:* Rückzug *m; Fig:* **to beat a hasty r.,** eiligst das Feld räumen. **II.** *v.i.* sich zurückziehen.

**retribution** [retri'bju:ʃ(ə)n], *s.* Vergeltung *f.*

**retrieve** [ri'tri:v], *v.tr.* (*a*) (*recover*) (Verlorenes) wiederbekommen; (*from awkward position*) (etwas) herausholen (**from,** aus + dat); *Data-pr:* (Informationen) abfragen; (*b*) (*put right*) (einen Verlust) wettmachen. ◆**re'trieval,** *s.* Wiedergewinnung *f; Data-pr:* Abfragen *n.* ◆**re'triever,** *s.* (*dog*) Apportierhund *m.*

**retrospect** ['retrəuspekt], *s.* **in r.,** rückblickend, im Rückblick.

**return** [ri'tɔ:n]. **I.** *s.* **1.** Rückkehr *f;* Heimkehr *f* (aus dem Krieg); (*recurrence*) Wiederkehr *f* (*Mus:* eines Themas usw.); **many happy returns (of the day)!** herzlichen Glückwunsch zum Geburtstag! **r. journey,** Rückreise *f;* **r. ticket,** Rückfahrkarte *f.* **2.** (*profit*) *Com: esp. pl.* Ertrag *m.* **3.** (*a*) (*giving back*) Rückgabe *f;* (*sending back*) Rücksendung *f.* **4. tax r.,**

Steuererklärung *f.* **II.** *v.* **1.** *v.i.* zurückkehren; (*recur*) wiederkehren; **to r. home,** heimkehren. **2.** *v.tr.* (*a*) (etwas Geborgtes usw.) zurückgeben, (*send back*) zurückschicken; (Geld) zurückzahlen (**to s.o.,** j-m); (*b*) (Dank, einen Gruß, einen Schlag) erwidern. ◆**re'turnable,** *adj.* rückgabepflichtig; (*of deposit etc.*) rückzahlbar; (*of goods*) umtauschbar.

**reunion** [ri:'ju:njən], *s.* Treffen *n* (von ehemaligen Schülern usw.).

**rev** [rev]. **I.** *s. F: Aut: etc:* (*abbr. of* **revolution**) Umdrehung *f* (pro Minute). **II.** *v. F: Aut:* **1.** *v.tr.* **to r. up the engine,** den Motor auf Touren bringen. **2.** *v.i.* auf Touren kommen.

**reveal** [ri'vi:l], *v.tr.* (ein Geheimnis usw.) enthüllen; (*betray*) (seine Absicht, ein Versteck usw.) verraten. ◆**re'vealing,** *adj.* aufschlußreich; *Hum:* (*of dress*) offenherzig. ◆**revelation** [revə'leiʃ(ə)n], *s.* Offenbarung *f.*

**reveille** [ri'væli], *s. Mil:* Wecksignal *n.*

**revel** ['rev(ə)l], *v.i.* (*celebrate*) feiern; (*carouse*) zechen. ◆**'reveller,** *s.* Feiernde(r) *f(m);* Zecher *m.* ◆**'revelry,** *s.* Feiern *n;* (*drinking*) Gelage *n.*

**revenge** [ri'vendʒ]. **I.** *s.* Rache *f;* (*in games etc.*) Revanche *f;* **to get one's r. on s.o. for sth.,** sich an j-m für etwas *acc* rächen. **II.** *v.tr.* (j-n, ein Unrecht usw.) rächen; **to r. oneself/be revenged** (**on s.o.,** an j-m; **for sth.,** für etwas *acc*).

**revenue** ['revinju:], *s.* Einnahmen *fpl, esp.* (*of state*) Staatseinnahmen *fpl.*

**reverberate** [ri'və:b(ə)reit], *v.i.* (*of sound*) hallen; (*echo*) widerhallen. ◆**reverbe'ration,** *s.* Widerhall *m.*

**revere** [ri'viər], *v.tr.* (j-n) verehren. ◆**reverence** ['rev(ə)rəns], *s.* Ehrfurcht *f.* ◆**'reverend,** *adj.* ehrwürdig; *Ecc:* (*as title*) **the (Very) R. Father Brown,** Hochwürden Brown. ◆**'reverent,** *adj.* ehrfürchtig.

**reverie** ['revəri], *s.* Träumerei *f.*

**reversal** [ri'və:s(ə)l], *s.* (*a*) Umkehrung *f* (der Reihenfolge usw.); (*b*) Umstoßung *f* (einer Entscheidung, *Jur:* eines Urteils). ◆**reverse** [ri'və:s]. **I.** *adj.* (*of order etc.*) umgekehrt; (*of direction*) entgegengesetzt. **II.** *s.* **1.** (*opposite*) Gegenteil *n.* **2.** (*back*) Rückseite *f* (eines Blatts); Kehrseite *f* (einer Münze usw.). **3.** *Aut:* **r. (gear),** Rückwärtsgang *m.* **III.** *v.tr.* (*a*) (*turn over*) (etwas) umdrehen; (*b*) (*change to opposite*) (die Reihenfolge) umkehren; (eine Entscheidung, *Jur:* ein Urteil) umstoßen; (*c*) *Aut:* **to r. (one's car),** rückwärts fahren; (*d*) *Tel:* **to r. the charges,** ein R-Gespräch führen. ◆**re'versible,** *adj.* umkehrbar.

**revert** [ri'və:t], *v.i.* (*a*) (*of property*) heimfallen (**to s.o.,** an j-m); (*b*) **to r. to a custom etc.,** in einen Brauch usw. zurückfallen.

**review** [ri'vju:]. **I.** *s.* **1.** *Mil:* Parade *f.* **2.**

(a) (of past events) Rückschau f; (b) (survey) Übersicht f; (report) Bericht m; (c) Rezension f (eines Buches, Films usw.); **good/bad r.**, gute/schlechte Kritik f; (d) (periodical) Rundschau f. **II.** v.tr. (a) (Truppen usw.) inspizieren; (b) Gehälter, die Lage usw.) überprüfen; (c) (ein Buch, einen Film) besprechen.

**revile** [ri'vail], v.tr. (j-n) schmähen.

**revise** [ri'vaiz], v.tr. (a) (alter) (seine Meinung) ändern; (b) (correct) (eine Sach usw.) überarbeiten. ◆**revision** [ri'viʒ(ə)n], s. Revision f.

**revive** [ri'vaiv], v. 1. v.i. (regain consciousness) wieder zu sich dat kommen. 2. v.tr. (a) (j-n) wiederbeleben; (b) (einen alten Brauch) wieder einführen. ◆**re'vival**, s. Neubelebung f (einer Kunst, des Handels); Wiederbelebung f (eines Gefühls usw.); Wiedereinführung f (eines Brauches usw.); Th: Wiederaufnahme f.

**revoke** [ri'vəuk], v.tr. (eine Anordnung usw.) widerrufen; (einen Befehl usw.) aufheben; (einen Vertrag) annullieren.

**revolt** [ri'vəult]. **I.** s. Aufstand m. **II.** v. 1. v.i. revoltieren. 2. v.tr. (disgust) (j-n) anwidern; (make indignant) empören. ◆**re'volting**, adj. widerlich.

**revolution** [revə'lju:ʃ(ə)n], s. 1. (rotation) Umdrehung f. 2. Pol: etc: Revolution f. ◆**revo'lutionary. I.** adj. revolutionär. **II.** s. Revolutionär(in) m(f).

**revolve** [ri'vɔlv], v. 1. v.tr. (a) (ein Rad usw.) drehen. 2. v.i. kreisen (**round** sth., um etwas acc); (of wheel etc.) sich drehen. ◆**re'volving**, adj. **r. door**, Drehtür f.

**revolver** [ri'vɔlvər], s. Revolver m.

**revulsion** [ri'vʌlʃ(ə)n], s. (feeling of) r., Ekel m.

**reward** [ri'wɔ:d]. **I.** s. Belohnung f; (to finder) Finderlohn m. **II.** v.tr. (j-n) belohnen.

**rewrite** [ri:'rait], v.tr.irr. überarbeiten.

**rhetoric** ['retərik], s. 1. Rhetorik f. 2. Pej: Schwulst m. ◆**rhetorical** [ri'tɔrik(ə)l], adj. (of question etc.) rhetorisch; (of style) hochtrabend, Pej: schwülstig.

**rheumatism** ['ru:mətizm], s. Rheuma n. ◆**rheumatic** [-'mætik], adj. rheumatisch; (of pers.) rheumakrank.

**Rhine** [rain]. Pr. n. the R., der Rhein.

**rhinoceros** [rai'nɔsərəs], F: **rhino** ['rainəu], s. Z: Nashorn n.

**rhubarb** ['ru:bɑ:b], s. Rhabarber m.

**rhyme** [raim]. **I.** s. Reim m; in r., gereimt. **II.** v.i. sich reimen.

**rhythm** ['rið(ə)m], s. Rhythmus m.

**rib** [rib]. **I.** s. Rippe f. **II.** v.tr. F: (j-n) necken.

**ribbon** ['ribən], s. (a) Band n; (b) (of typewriter) Farbband n.

**rice** [rais], s. Reis m; **r. pudding**, Milchreis m.

**rich** [ritʃ], adj. 1. reich (**in**, an + dat). 2. (a) (of soil) fruchtbar; (of harvest) ergiebig; (b) (of food) gehaltvoll; (fatty) fett;

(c) (of colours) satt; (of sound) voll.

**rick** [rik], s. r. of hay, Heuschober m.

**rickets** ['rikits], s. Med: Rachitis f. ◆**'rickety**, adj. F: (of house) baufällig; (of furniture) wackelig.

**ricochet** ['rikəʃei], v.i. abprallen.

**rid** [rid], v.tr.irr. (j-n, etwas) befreien (**of s.o., sth.**, von j-m, etwas dat); **to get r. of s.o., sth.**, j-n, etwas loswerden. ◆**'riddance**, s. **good r.!** den/die/das sind wir glücklich los!

**ridden** ['rid(ə)n], comb. fm. von … dat geplagt; **bed-r.**, bettlägerig.

**riddle**[1] ['ridl], s. Rätsel n.

**riddle**[2], v.tr. **riddled with holes**, ganz durchlöchert.

**ride** [raid]. **I.** s. (on horse) Ritt m; (in car, train etc.) Fahrt f. **II.** v. 1. v.i. (a) reiten; (b) **to r. on a bicycle**, mit dem Rad fahren; **to r. in a bus/car/train**, im Autobus/Auto/Zug fahren. 2. v.tr. **to r. a horse**, ein Pferd reiten; **to r. a bicycle/ motorcycle**, radfahren/Motorrad fahren. ◆**'rider**, s. Reiter(in) m(f) (eines Pferdes); Fahrer(in) m(f) (eines Fahrrads, Motorrads). ◆**'riding**, s. Reiten n.

**ridge** [ridʒ], s. Rücken m (der Nase, eines Berges usw.); (raised area) Erhöhung f; (line of hills) Hügelkette f.

**ridicule** ['ridikju:l]. **I.** s. Spott m. **II.** v.tr. (j-n) lächerlich machen. ◆**ri'diculous**, adj. lächerlich.

**rife** [raif], adj. (of disease) **to be r.**, grassieren.

**rifle**[1] ['raifl], v.tr. **to r. through** sth. etwas durchwühlen.

**rifle**[2], s. Gewehr n.

**rift** [rift], s. (a) (gap) Ritze f; (b) Fig: (between friends) Riß m.

**rig**[1] [rig]. **I.** s. **oil/drilling r.**, Bohrinsel f. **II.** v.tr. (ein Schiff) auftakeln. ◆**'rigging**, s. Nau: (a) (type) Takelung f; (b) coll. Takelage f. ◆**'rig 'out**, v.tr. (sich, j-n) ausstaffieren. ◆**'rig 'up**, v.tr. F: (einen Apparat usw.) aufstellen, (amateurishly) zusammenbasteln.

**rig**[2], v.tr. F: manipulieren; **the fight was rigged**, der Kampf war ein abgekartetes Spiel.

**right** [rait]. **I.** adj. 1. **r. angle**, rechter Winkel. 2. (a) (appropriate) recht; (just) gerecht; **the r. thing (to do)**, das Richtige; (b) (correct) richtig; (exact) genau; **to be r.**, (of pers.) recht haben; (of amount, remark etc.) stimmen; (of watch etc.) richtig gehen. 3. (in order) **to put things r.**, die Dinge (wieder) in Ordnung bringen. 4. (direction) rechte(r,s); **on the r. (hand) side**, auf der rechten Seite; Pol: **r. wing**, rechter Flügel. 5. int. **r.!** also gut! **-ly**, adv. (correctly) richtig; (justly) mit Recht; **I can't r. say**, das kann ich nicht genau sagen. **II.** s. 1. (justice) Recht n. 2. (a) (claim) Anrecht n (**to** sth., auf etwas acc); **what gives you the r. to do this?** was berechtigt Sie dazu? **in one's own r.**, von sich aus; **r. of way**, Vorfahrt f; (b) pl.

**rights,** Rechte *npl*. 3. (*right hand & Pol:*) Rechte *f*; **on the r.,** rechts/zur Rechten; **to the r.,** nach rechts; **to the r. of,** rechts von + *dat*. **III.** *adv*. 1. (*a*) **go r. on,** gehen Sie immer geradeaus; (*b*) **r. away,** sofort; (*c*) ganz; **to sink r. to the bottom,** bis auf den Grund sinken; **r. at the top,** ganz oben; **r. in the middle,** genau in der Mitte. 2. **to answer/guess r.,** richtig antworten/raten. **IV.** *v.tr.* (*a*) (ein Unrecht) wiedergutmachen; (*b*) (ein Boot usw.) aufrichten. ◆**'righteous** ['raitʃəs], *adj*. (*of pers.*) rechtschaffen; *Pej:* (*self-r.*) selbstgerecht. ◆**'righteousness,** *s*. Rechtschaffenheit *f*. ◆**'rightful,** *adj*. rechtmäßig. ◆**'right-'hand,** *adj*. (*a*) rechte(r,s); **the r.-h. drawer,** die rechte Schublade; (*b*) nach rechts, Rechts-. ◆**'right-handed,** *adj*. rechtshändig. ◆**'right-'wing,** *adj*. *Pol:* rechtsgerichtet; **he's very r.-w.,** er steht sehr weit rechts.

**rigid** ['ridʒid], *adj*. starr; *Fig:* (*of pers.*) unbeugsam.

**rigour** ['rigər], *s*. Strenge *f*. ◆**'rigorous,** *adj*. streng.

**rim** [rim], *s*. 1. Felge *f* (eines Rades). 2. Rand *m* (einer Vase usw.).

**rind** [raind], *s*. (*of cheese*) Rinde *f*; (*of fruit*) Schale *f*; (*of bacon*) Schwarte *f*.

**ring¹** [riŋ], *s*. Ring *m*; **r. road,** Umgehungsstraße *f*. ◆**'ringleader,** *s*. Rädelsführer *m*. ◆**'ringlet,** *s*. Ringellocke *f*.

**ring².** **I.** *s*. 1. (*sound*) (*a*) Klang *m* (der Gläser, der Stimme); (*b*) **there's a r. at the door,** es läutet/klingelt. 2. *F:* **I'll give you a r.,** ich werde dich anrufen. **II.** *v.* 1. *v.i.* (*a*) (*of bells*) läuten; (*of small bell*) klingeln; **to r. for service,** nach der Bedienung klingeln; (*b*) (*echo*) ertönen (**with,** von + *dat*). 2. *v.tr.* **to r. the bell,** (i) (*large*) die Glocke läuten; (ii) (*doorbell*) läuten. ◆**'ring 'up,** *v.tr. Tel:* (j-n) anrufen.

**rink** [riŋk], *s*. (*skating*) r., Eisbahn *f*.

**rinse** [rins]. **I.** *v.tr.* spülen. **II.** *s*. Spülen *n*; (*colour*) r., Tönung *f*.

**riot** ['raiət]. **I.** *s*. Aufruhr *f*; **r. police,** Bereitschaftspolizei *f*. **to run r.,** (*of children*) sich austoben. **II.** *v.i.* aufständisch werden; (*football fans*) randalieren. ◆**'rioter,** *s*. Aufrührer *m*. ◆**'rioting,** *s*. Unruhen *fpl*. ◆**'riotous,** *adj*. (*a*) (*of crowd*) aufrührerisch; (*b*) (*of laughter*) ausgelassen; (*hilarious*) urkomisch.

**rip** [rip]. **I.** *s*. Riß *m*. **II.** *v.tr. & i.* (etwas) reißen. ◆**'rip 'off,** *v.tr. Fig: F:* **to r. s.o. off,** j-n übers Ohr hauen.

**ripe** [raip], *adj*. (*of fruit*) reif. ◆**'ripen,** *v.* 1. *v.tr.* (Obst usw.) reifen lassen. 2. *v.i.* reifen; *esp. Fig:* zur Reife kommen.

**ripple** ['ripl]. **I.** *v.* 1. *v.i.* sich kräuseln. 2. *v.tr.* (Wasser) kräuseln. **II.** *s*. Kräuselung *f*; kleine Welle *f*.

**rise** [raiz]. **I.** *v.i.* sich erheben; (*of sun etc., Th: curtain*) aufgehen; (*of temperature, prices etc.*) steigen. **II.** *s*. (*a*) (in

ground) Erhebung *f*; (*small hill*) Anhöhe *f*; (*b*) (*increase*) Erhöhung *f* (der Preise usw); (*c*) (*cause*) **to give r. to sth.,** Anlaß zu etwas *dat* geben; etwas veranlassen. ◆**'rising.** **I.** *adj*. (*of prices, temperature etc.*) steigend. **II.** *s*. (*revolt*) Aufstand *m*.

**risk** [risk]. **I.** *s*. Risiko *n*; Gefahr *f*; **to take/run a r.,** ein Risiko eingehen; **at one's own r.,** auf eigene Gefahr. **II.** *v.tr.* (etwas) riskieren. ◆**'risky,** *adj*. riskant; (*dangerous*) gefährlich.

**rite** [rait], *s*. Ritus *m*; *Ecc:* **the last rites,** die Sterbesakramente *npl*. ◆**'ritual** ['ritjuəl]. **I.** *adj*. rituell. **II.** *s*. Ritual *n*.

**rival** ['raiv(ə)l]. **I.** *s*. Rivale *m*, Rivalin *f*; (*competitor*) Konkurrent(in) *m(f)*. **II.** *adj*. rivalisierend; *Com:* Konkurrenz-. **III.** *v.tr.* (j-m) Konkurrenz machen. ◆**'rivalry,** *s*. Rivalität *f*.

**river** ['rivər], *s*. Fluß *m*; (*large*) Strom *m*; **down/up** the r., flußabwärts/flußaufwärts; stromabwärts/stromaufwärts.

**rivet** ['rivit]. **I.** *s. Tchn:* Niete *f*. **II.** *v.tr.* (etwas) nieten. ◆**'riveting,** *adj. Fig:* fesselnd.

**road** [rəud], *s*. Straße *f*; *esp. Fig:* Weg *m*; **r. transport,** Straßentransport *m*; **r. surface,** Fahrbahn *f*; **r. sign,** Straßenschild *n*. ◆**'road-block,** *s*. Straßensperre *f*. ◆**'roadside,** *s*. Straßenrand *m*. ◆**'roadway,** *s*. Fahrbahn *f*. ◆**'roadworks,** *s.pl*. Straßenbauarbeiten *fpl*. ◆**'roadworthy,** *adj*. fahrtüchtig.

**roam** [rəum], *v.i.* wandern; (*stray*) streunen.

**roar** [rɔːr]. **I.** *s*. 1. Gebrüll *n* (eines Löwen usw.). 2. Donnern *n* (einer Kanone); Toben *n* (des Meeres, des Sturms). **II.** *v.i.* brüllen; (*of sea, storm*) toben; (*of thunder*) krachen; (*of fire*) lodern; *Aut: Av:* **to r. past,** vorbeibrausen.

**roast** [rəust]. **I.** *v.* 1. *v.tr.* (*a*) (Fleisch, Kartoffeln) (im Ofen) braten; (*b*) (Kaffee, Kastanien) rösten. 2. *v.i. Cu: & Fig:* (*of pers.*) braten. **II.** *s:* **I'm roasting,** ich komme um vor Hitze. **II.** *s. Cu:* Braten *m*; **r. beef,** Rinderbraten *m*, Roastbeef *n*.

**rob** [rɔb], *v.tr.* (j-n) bestehlen; (eine Bank usw.) ausrauben. ◆**'robber,** *s*. Räuber *m*. ◆**'robbery,** *s*. Raub *m*; *F:* **it's sheer r.,** das ist der reinste Wucher.

**robe** [rəub], *s*. (*loose garment*) Gewand *n*; (*ceremonial*) Robe *f*.

**robin** ['rɔbin], *s*. **r.** (*redbreast*), Rotkehlchen *n*.

**robot** ['rəubɔt], *s*. Roboter *m*.

**robust** [rəu'bʌst], *adj*. robust; (*of structure*) stabil.

**rock¹** [rɔk], *s*. 1. (*a*) Felsen *m*; (*in sea*) Klippe *f*; (*b*) (*material*) Gestein *n*. 2. (*a*) (*sweet*) Zuckerstange *f*. 3. *attrib*. **r. plant,** Steinpflanze *f*. ◆**'rock-'bottom,** *s*. **to touch r.-b.,** den Tiefpunkt erreichen. ◆**'rockery,** *s*. Steingarten *m*. ◆**'rocky,** *adj*. felsig.

**rock²,** *v.* 1. *v.tr.* (die Wiege, ein Kind usw.) schaukeln. 2. *v.i.* (*of cradle etc.*)

schaukeln; (of building etc.) schwanken.
◆'rocking, adj. r. chair, Schaukelstuhl
m.
rocket ['rɔkit], s. Rakete f.
rod [rɔd], s. Stange f; (bar, short stick)
Stab m; (stick) Rute f; (fishing) r., Angel-
rute f.
rodent ['rəud(ə)nt], s. Nagetier n.
roe¹ [rəu], s. Z: r. (deer), Reh n.
roe², s. (of fish) Rogen m.
rogue [rəug], s. (a) Pej: Schurke m; (b)
Schelm m.
rôle [rəul], s. Th: etc: Rolle f.
roll [rəul]. I. s. 1. (a) (of paper, film etc.)
Rolle f; (b) (of bread) Brötchen n. 2. (list)
Liste f, esp. Namenliste f. II. v. 1. v.tr.
rollen; (eine Zigarette) drehen; rolled
gold, Dubleegold n. 2. v.i. (a) (forwards,
down) rollen; (b) (sideways) (of ship, car)
schlingern. ◆'roller, s. Tchn: Rolle f;
(cylinder) Walze f. ◆'roller-'skate. I. s.
Rollschuh m. II. v.i. Rollschuh laufen.
◆'rolling. I. adj. (a) r. country, hügeli-
ge Gegend; (b) F: to be r. (in money),
im Geld schwimmen. II. s. Cu: r. pin,
Teigrolle f; Rail: r. stock, rollendes Material. ◆'roll 'over, v. 1. v.tr. (j-n, etwas) umdrehen. 2. v.i. (of pers.) sich (im
Liegen) umdrehen; (of dog) sich auf den
Rücken wälzen.
Roman ['rəumən]. I. s. Römer(in) m(f).
II. adj. römisch; R. numerals, römische
Ziffern; R. Catholic, (römisch)-katho-
lisch; (pers.) Katholik(in) m(f).
romance [rəu'mæns], s. Romanze f; (love
story) Liebesgeschichte f. ◆ro'mantic,
adj. romantisch; Art: Lit: R. Movement, Romantik f.
Rome [rəum]. Pr.n. Rom n.
romp [rɔmp], v.i. (of children) to r.
(about), herumtoben.
roof [ruːf], s. Dach n; Aut: r. rack, Dach-
gepäckträger m.
rook¹ [ruk], s. Orn: Krähe f; esp. Saatkrä-
he f.
rook², s. (in chess) Turm m.
room [ruːm, rum], s. 1. Zimmer n; (esp.
very large) Raum m; r. mate, Zimmerge-
nosse -(genossin) m(f). 2. (space) Platz m.
◆'roomy, adj. geräumig.
roost [ruːst]. I. s. (of birds) Sitzplatz m;
(of hens) Hühnerstange f; to rule the r.,
das Regiment führen. II. v.i. (of hens)
auf der Stange sitzen.
root [ruːt]. I. s. 1. Wurzel f; to take r.,
Wurzel fassen; r. cause, Grundursache f.
2. Mth: square r., Quadratwurzel f.
◆'rooted, adj. (of prejudice etc.) deeply
r., tief verwurzelt.
rope [rəup], s. Seil n; esp. Nau: Tau n;
(hangman's) Strick m. ◆'rope 'in, v.tr.
F: they roped me in, sie haben mich
rangekriegt. ◆'ropey, adj. P: mies.
rosary ['rəuzəri], s. Ecc: Rosenkranz m.
rose [rəuz]. I. s. 1. Rose f; r. bush, Ro-
senstrauch m; r. hip, Hagebutte f. 2.
Brause f (einer Gießkanne). 3. (colour)

Rosa n. II. adj. r. (coloured), rosa.
◆'rosemary, s. Bot: Rosmarin m.
◆'rosy, adj. rosig.
rosette [rəu'zet], s. Rosette f.
rosin ['rɔzin], s. Kolophonium n.
roster ['rɔstər], s. Dienstplan m.
rostrum ['rɔstrəm], s. Podium n.
rot [rɔt]. I. s. Fäule f. II. v.i. faulen; (of
corpse) verwesen. ◆'rotten, adj. (of
fruit, egg etc.) faul; verfault; (of wood)
morsch; (b) F: miserabel; I feel r., mir
ist mies.
rota ['rəutə], s. abwechselnder Dienst;
duty r., Dienstplan m.
rotate [rəu'teit], v. 1. v.i. sich drehen. 2.
v.tr. (ein Rad usw.) drehen. ◆'rotary,
adj. drehend. ◆ro'tation, s. Drehung
f; in r., der Reihe nach. ◆'rotor, s.
Läufer m (einer Turbine); Av: Rotor m
(eines Hubschraubers).
rote [rəut], s. to learn by r., auswendig
lernen.
rotund [rəu'tʌnd], adj. rundlich.
rough [rʌf]. I. adj. 1. (a) (of surface,
sound) rauh; (coarse) grob; (b) (of road)
holprig; (of ground) uneben; F: to feel
pretty r., sich ziemlich mies fühlen. 2.
(a) (stormy) stürmisch; r. sea, bewegte
See; (b) (of treatment, manner) grob. 3. (a)
(approximate) grob, annähernd; I can
give you a r. idea, ich kann es Ihnen
ungefähr/(of scheme) in groben Umrissen
sagen; (b) r. copy, Konzept n; -ly, adv.
1. grob. 2. (approximately) ungefähr; r.
speaking, so ungefähr. II. s. (in golf) to
get into the r., den Ball ins lange Gras
schlagen. III. adv. to live/sleep r., im
Freien leben/schlafen. IV. v.tr. F: to r.
it, auf Bequemlichkeit verzichten.
◆'roughage, s. grobe Nahrung f; Bal-
laststoffe mpl. ◆'rough-and-'ready,
adj. primitiv. ◆'roughen, v.tr. (eine
Fläche) aufrauhen.
roulette [ruː'let], s. Roulett(e) n.
round [raund]. I. adj. rund. II. s. 1. Sp:
etc: Runde f; to stand a r. of drinks,
eine Runde ausgeben; (of doctor, postman
etc.) to do one's rounds, seine Runde
machen; r. of applause, Beifallssturm m.
2. Mil: Salve f; r. (of ammunition),
Schuß m. 3. Mus: Kanon m. III. adv. 1.
(a) to turn r., sich umdrehen; r. and r.,
im Kreis; to go r., (i) (not straight there)
herumgehen; (ii) (rotate) sich drehen; (iii)
(to see s.o.) vorbeigehen; (b) to hand r.
the cake, den Kuchen herumreichen;
there isn't enough to go r., es reicht
nicht für alle; (c) all the year r., das ganze Jahr hindurch; r. about, rund herum.
IV. prep. um + acc (herum); (a) r. the table, rings um den Tisch; um der Tisch
herum; r. the world, rund um die Welt;
to go r. the corner, um die Ecke gehen;
(b) (approximately) r. (about) £100, ungefähr £100. V. v.tr. (a) (etwas) rund machen; (eine Kante) abrunden; (b) to r. a
bend, um eine Kurve fahren.

◆'**roundabout. I.** s. **1.** (*at fair*) Karussell n. **2.** *Aut:* Kreisverkehr m. **II.** adj. (*of pers. etc.*) umständlich. ◆'**rounded**, adj. (ab)gerundet. ◆'**round 'off**, v.tr. (eine Rede usw.) abschließen. ◆'**round 'up**, v.tr. (a) (eine Herde) zusammentreiben; (*Verbrecher*) einfangen; (b) (Ziffern) aufrunden.

**rouse** [rauz], v.tr. (a) **to r. s.o.** (**from sleep**), j-n (aus dem Schlaf) wecken; (b) *Fig:* (j-n) aufrütteln; **to r. oneself,** sich aufraffen; (c) (*anger*) (j-n) aufbringen. ◆'**rousing**, adj. **r. speech,** mitreißende Rede.

**rout** [raut], v.tr. *Mil:* (eine Armee) in die Flucht schlagen.

**route** [ru:t], s. Route f; (*itinerary*) Reiseroute f; *Av:* Rail: Strecke f.

**routine** [ru:'ti:n], s. (a) Routine f; (b) attrib. routinemäßig; *Pej:* (*of performance etc.*) schablonenhaft.

**row¹** [rəu], s. Reihe f; **in rows,** in Reihen, reihenweise.

**row²**, v.tr. & i. (ein Boot) rudern. ◆'**rower**, s. Ruderer m. ◆'**rowing**, s. Rudern n; *Sp:* Rudersport m; **r. boat,** Ruderboot n.

**row³** [rau], s. **1.** (*noise*) Krach m. **2.** (*quarrel*) Streit m; **to have a r.,** sich streiten.

**rowdy** ['raudi], adj. rauflustig; (*noisy*) randalierend.

**royal** ['rɔiəl], adj. königlich. ◆'**royalty**, s. **1.** (a) königliche Person(en) f(pl); (b) (*status etc.*) Königswürde f. **2.** *esp. pl.* (*for publication etc.*) Tantiemen fpl.

**rub** [rʌb], v. **1.** v.tr. (j-n, etwas) reiben; *Fig:* **to r. shoulders with s.o.,** mit j-m zusammenkommen. **2.** v.i. (sich) reiben (**against,** gegen + acc.). ◆'**rubber**, s. Gummi m & n; (**India**) r., Radiergummi m; **r. band,** Gummiband n. ◆'**rub 'down**, v.tr. (a) abreiben; (*with sandpaper*) abschmirgeln. ◆'**rub 'in**, v.tr. (eine Salbe usw.) einreiben; *F:* **don't r. it in!** du brauchst es mir nicht unter die Nase zu reiben! ◆'**rub 'out**, v.tr. (etwas) ausradieren.

**rubbish** ['rʌbiʃ], s. **1.** (a) (*waste*) Abfälle mpl; (*refuse*) Müll m; (*debris*) Schutt m; **r. bin,** Abfalleimer m; **r. dump,** Müllkippe f; (b) (*worthless goods*) Ausschußware f; *F:* Mist m. **2.** (*nonsense*) Unsinn m; *F:* Quatsch m.

**rubble** ['rʌbl], s. (*debris*) Schutt m; (*for roadmaking etc.*) Bruchstein m.

**ruby** ['ru:bi], s. **1.** Rubin m. **2.** (*colour*) Rubinrot n.

**rucksack** ['rʌksæk], s. Rucksack m.

**rudder** ['rʌdər], s. Ruder n.

**ruddy** ['rʌdi], adj. **1.** (a) (*of cheeks*) rot; **r. complexion,** frische Gesichtsfarbe; (b) rötlich. **2.** *P:* verdammt.

**rude** [ru:d], adj. **1.** (a) (*impolite*) unhöflich (**to s.o.,** zu j-m); (b) (*indecent*) unanständig; *Hum:* **r. drawing,** obszöne Zeichnung. **2.** (*abrupt*) unsanft.

**rudiments** ['ru:dimənts], s.pl. Anfänge

---

mpl; Grundbegriffe mpl (einer Wissenschaft). ◆**rudi'mentary**, adj. (*of knowledge*) elementar; (*simple*) einfach.

**ruffian** ['rʌfjən], s. Rohling m.

**ruffle** ['rʌfl], v.tr. (a) (Haare, Federn) zerzausen; (b) *Fig:* (j-n) aus der Fassung bringen; **ruffled,** gereizt.

**rug** [rʌg], s. **1.** (*blanket*) Decke f. **2.** (*on floor*) kleiner Teppich m; (*by bed*) Bettvorleger m.

**rugby** ['rʌgbi], s. **r.** (**football**), *F:* rugger ['rʌgər], Rugby n.

**rugged** ['rʌgid], adj. (a) (*of terrain*) wild; (*of cliffs*) zerklüftet; (b) **r. features,** markante Züge.

**ruin** ['ru:in]. **I.** s. **1.** (*building etc.*) Ruine f; **to be in ruins,** eine Ruine sein; *Fig:* (*of plan*) völlig zerstört sein. **2.** (*esp. of pers.*) Ruin m. **II.** v.tr. ruinieren; (Pläne) vereiteln. ◆**rui'nation,** s. Vernichtung f; (*of pers.*) Ruin m. ◆'**ruinous,** adj. (*causing ruin*) ruinös.

**rule** [ru:l]. **I.** s. **1.** (*regulation*) Regel f; **as a** (**general**) **r.,** in der Regel, im allgemeinen; **r. of thumb,** Faustregel f; **rules and regulations,** Vorschriften fpl. **2.** (*government*) Regierung f (einer Partei); (*domination*) Herrschaft f. **II.** v. **1.** v.tr. (ein Land, ein Volk) regieren; **to r. over a country,** über ein Land herrschen. ◆'**ruler,** s. **1.** (*pers.*) Herrscher(in) m(f). **2.** *Mth:* Lineal n. ◆'**ruling. I.** adj. herrschend; **the r. class,** die herrschende Schicht. **II.** s. (*amtliche/gerichtliche*) Verordnung f. ◆'**rule 'out,** v.tr. (j-n, eine Möglichkeit) ausschließen.

**rum** [rʌm], s. Rum m.

**Rumania** [ru(:)'meiniə]. *Pr. n.* Rumänien n. ◆**Ru'manian. I.** adj. rumänisch. **II.** s. **1.** (*pers.*) Rumäne m, Rumänin f. **2.** (*language*) Rumänisch n.

**rumble** ['rʌmbl], **1.** s. Grollen n (des Donners); Rumpeln n (eines Lastwagens); *Rec:* Rumpelgeräusch n. **II.** v.i. (*of thunder etc.*) grollen; (*of stomach*) knurren.

**ruminate** ['ru:mineit], v.i. (a) (*of cow*) wiederkäuen; (b) (*of pers.*) grübeln (**on/ over sth.,** über etwas acc).

**rummage** ['rʌmidʒ], v.i. **to r. through old papers,** alte Papiere durchstöbern.

**rumour** ['ru:mər], s. Gerücht n. ◆'**rumoured,** adj. **it is r. that...,** man munkelt, daß...

**rump** [rʌmp], s. (*of cattle*) Hinterteil n; **r. steak,** Rumpsteak n.

**rumple** ['rʌmpl], v.tr. (Papier) zerknüllen; (ein Kleid) zerknittern; (Haare) zerraufen.

**rumpus** ['rʌmpəs], s. *F:* (a) (*noise*) Krawall m; (b) (*fuss*) Spektakel m.

**run** [rʌn]. **I.** v. **1.** v.i. (a) (*of pers.*) laufen; (*fast, in race*) rennen; (b) *Sp:* teilnehmen (**in a race,** an einem Rennen); *Pol:* **to r. for an office,** für ein Amt kandidieren; (c) (*travel*) fahren; **this train is not run-**

**ning today,** dieser Zug verkehrt heute nicht; (d) (flow) fließen; (of eyes) tränen; (of tap, nose, colour) laufen; Fig: **it runs in the family,** es liegt in der Familie; (e) (work) funktionieren, laufen; (f) (stretch) sich erstrecken; (of road) verlaufen. 2. v.tr. (a) **to r. a race,** um die Wette laufen; (b) (drive) (j-n, ein Auto) fahren; **to r. s.o. into town,** j-n in die Stadt fahren; (c) (einen Motor, einen Hahn usw.) laufen lassen; (ein Bad) einlaufen lassen; (d) (manage) (ein Geschäft usw.) führen. II. s. (a) Lauf m; (of criminal) **to be on the r.,** auf der Flucht sein; (in cricket, baseball) **to score/make a r.,** einen Lauf machen; (b) Aut: etc: Fahrt f; **to go for a r.,** eine Spazierfahrt machen; **trial r.,** Probefahrt f; (c) (succession) Reihe f; Th: **to have a long/short r.,** lange/kurze Zeit laufen. ◆'**run a'cross,** v.i. (meet etc) (j-m) zufällig begegnen. ◆'**run a'way,** v.i. davonlaufen. ◆'**runaway,** s. Ausreißer m. ◆'**run 'down,** v. 1. v.i. (of clock) ablaufen. 2. v.tr. (a) (die Straße, den Berg usw.) hinunterlaufen; (b) Aut: (j-n) anfahren; (c) (criticize) herabsetzen; (d) (einen Betrieb) abbauen; Fig: (of pers.) **run down,** (gesundheitlich) herunter. ◆'**run-down,** s. (report) Bericht m. ◆'**run 'into,** v.i. (a) **to r. i. sth.,** in etwas acc hineinrennen/(of car) hineinfahren; (b) **to r. i. difficulties,** auf Schwierigkeiten stoßen. ◆'**runner,** s. 1. (athlete) Läufer(in) m(f); (competitor, horse etc.) Teilnehmer(in) m(f). 2. Bot: (shoot) Trieb m; **r. bean,** Stangenbohne f. 3. Kufe f (eines Schlittens usw.). ◆'**runner-'up,** s. Sp: Zweite(r) f(m). ◆'**running. I.** adj. (of commentary, expenses etc.) laufend; (one after another) nacheinander; **three days r.,** drei Tage hintereinander. II. s. 1. Sp: & Fig: **to be in/out of the r.,** Aussichten/keine Aussichten haben. 2. (a) (operation) Betrieb m (einer Maschine, usw.); Laufen n (eines Motors). ◆'**runny,** adj. flüssig; (of nose) laufend; ◆'**run**

'**off,** v.i. (a) davonrennen; (b) (of water) ablaufen. ◆'**run 'out,** v.i. (of supplies) ausgehen; **time is running out,** die Zeit wird knapp. ◆'**run 'over,** v.tr. Aut: (j-n) überfahren. ◆'**run 'through,** v.tr. (ein Dokument usw.) schnell durchlesen. ◆'**run 'up,** v. 1. v.i. (approach) herbeilaufen; **to come running up,** herangelaufen kommen. 2. v.tr. (eine Schuld) auflaufen lassen; **to r. up a bill,** eine Rechnung anwachsen lassen; ◆'**runway,** s. Av: (for take-off) Startbahn f; (for landing) Landebahn f.

**rung** [rʌŋ], s. Sprosse f (einer Leiter).

**rupture** ['rʌptʃər]. I. s. (all senses) Bruch m. II. v.tr. & i. (etwas) brechen.

**rural** ['ruərəl], adj. ländlich.

**ruse** [ruːz], s. List f.

**rush**[1] [rʌʃ], s. (reed) Binse f.

**rush**[2]. I. s. 1. Ansturm m (for sth., auf etwas acc); **r. hour,** Stoßzeit f; **r. hour traffic,** Stoßverkehr m. 2. (hurry) Eile f. II. v. 1. v.i. stürzen (at s.o., auf j-n). 2. v.tr. (hurry) (j-n) drängen.

**rusk** [rʌsk], s. Zwieback m.

**russet** ['rʌsit], adj. rostbraun.

**Russia** ['rʌʃə]. Pr. n. Rußland n. ◆'**Russian. I.** s. (a) Russe m, Russin f; (b) (language) Russisch n. II. adj. russisch.

**rust** [rʌst]. I. s. Rost m. II. v.i. verrosten. ◆'**rusty,** adj. rostig; F: Fig: **I am r.,** ich bin aus der Übung.

**rustic** ['rʌstik], adj. ländlich; (of furniture, pers.) rustikal; esp. Hum: bäuerlich.

**rustle** ['rʌsl], v. 1. v.i. (of wind etc.) rauschen; (of leaves) rascheln; (of paper, silk) knistern. 2. v.tr. (a) F: **to r. up a meal,** ein Essen herzaubern; (b) N.Am: (Vieh) stehlen.

**rut** [rʌt], s. Furche f; Fig: (of pers.) **to be in a r.,** im alten Gleis festgefahren sein.

**ruthless** ['ruːθlis], adj. mitleidlos; (relentless) rücksichtslos. ◆'**ruthlessness,** s. Rücksichtslosigkeit f.

**rye** [rai], s. Roggen m; **r. bread,** Roggenbrot n.

# S

**S, s** [es], s. (der Buchstabe) S, s n.

**Sabbath** ['sæbəθ], s. Sabbat m.

**sable** ['seibl], s. (animal/fur) Zobel m.

**sabotage** ['sæbətɑːʒ]. I. s. Sabotage f. II. v.tr. (ein Projekt, Maschinen usw.) sabotieren. ◆**sabo'teur,** s. Saboteur m.

**saccharin** ['sækərin], s. Saccharin n.

**sachet** ['sæʃei], s. (plastic) Sachet n.

**sack**[1] [sæk]. I. s. Sack m. II. v.tr. F: **to s. s.o.,** j-n an die Luft setzen.

**sack**[2], v.tr. (eine Stadt usw.) plündern.

**sacrament** ['sækrəmənt], s. Ecc: Sakrament n.

**sacred** ['seikrid], adj. heilig; **s. music,** geistliche Musik.

**sacrifice** ['sækrifais]. I. s. Opfer n; **to make sacrifices,** Opfer bringen. II. v.tr. (etwas) opfern.

**sacrilege** ['sækrilidʒ], s. Sakrileg n. ◆**sacri'legious,** adj. frevlerisch; (blasphemous) gotteslästerlich.

**sacrosanct** ['sækrəusæŋkt], adj. sakrosankt; (untouchable) unantastbar.

**sad** [sæd], adj. traurig; (of colours etc.) trist; (dilapidated) verkommen; **-ly,** adv. (a) traurig; (b) (before statement) traurigerweise. ◆'**sadden,** v.tr. (j-n) betrüben. ◆'**sadness,** s. Traurigkeit f.

**saddle** ['sædl]. I. s. (seat) Sattel m. II. v.tr. (a) (ein Pferd) satteln; F: **to s. s.o.**

with sth., j-m etwas aufbürden.
**sadism** ['seidizm], s. Sadismus m.
◆**'sadist**, s. Sadist m. ◆**sadistic**
[sə'-], adj. sadistisch.
**safari** [sə'fɑːri], s. Safari f.
**safe** [seif]. I. adj. sicher; (unhurt) heil; **s.
and sound**, wohlbehalten; **-ly**, adv. sicher; **to arrive s.**, wohlbehalten ankommen. II. s. Safe m. ◆**'safeguard**. I. s.
Vorsichtsmaßnahme f; (protection) Schutz
m (against, gegen + acc). II. v.tr. (etwas)
sicherstellen; (Rechte, Interessen) schützen. ◆**safe'keeping**, s. (sichere) Aufbewahrung f. ◆**'safety**, s. Sicherheit f; **s.
measures**, Sicherheitsmaßnahmen fpl; **s.
pin**, Sicherheitsnadel f; Aut: Av: **s. belt**,
Sicherheitsgurt m.
**saffron** ['sæfrən]. I. s. Safran m. II. adj.
**s. (yellow)**, safrangelb.
**sag** [sæg], v.i. (of roof, bed etc.) durchhängen.
**sage** [seidʒ], s. Bot: Salbei m.
**Sagittarius** [sædʒi'teəriəs], s. Astr: Schütze m.
**sago** ['seigəu], s. Sago m.
**sail** [seil]. I. s. 1. Nau: (a) Segel n; **to set
s.**, in See stechen; (b) (trip) Segelfahrt f.
2. Flügel m (einer Windmühle). II. v.i.
segeln; (of steamer etc.) fahren.
◆**'sailing**. I. adj. **s. dinghy**, (kleines)
Segelboot; **s. ship**, Segelschiff n. II. s.
Segeln n; F: **it was all plain s.**, es ging
alles ganz glatt. ◆**'sailor**, s. Matrose m.
**saint** [seint], s. (a) Heilige(r) f(m); Fig:
**the patience of a s.**, eine Engelsgeduld;
(b) attrib. **St. Peter**, der Heilige Petrus.
◆**'saintly**, adj. heilig; (of smile etc.) engelhaft.
**sake** [seik], s. **for the s. of**, wegen + gen;
**for s.o.'s s.**, j-m zuliebe; **for my/your/her
s.**, um meinetwillen/deinetwillen/
ihretwillen; **for heaven's/God's/
goodness's s.**, um Gottes willen.
**salad** ['sæləd], s. Salat m; **s. dressing**, Salatsoße f.
**salary** ['sæləri], s. Gehalt n.
**sale** [seil], s. Verkauf m; (a) **for s.**, zu
verkaufen; (b) Com: pl. Absatz m; (c)
(clearance) s., Ausverkauf m; **summer
s.**, Sommerschlußverkauf m; attrib.
**sales**, Verkaufs-; F: **sales talk**, Verkaufsjargon n. ◆**'salesgirl**, s. Verkäuferin f.
◆**'salesman**, pl. **-men**, s. Verkäufer m;
(travelling) s., Handelsreisende(r) m.
**salient** ['seiliənt], adj. hervorstehend; **s.
point**, springender Punkt.
**saline** ['seilain], adj. salzhaltig.
**saliva** [sə'laivə], s. Speichel m.
**sallow** ['sæləu], adj. gelblich(-blaß).
**salmon** ['sæmən]. I. s. Lachs m. II. adj.
**s. pink**, lachsfarben.
**saloon** [sə'luːn], s. (a) N.Am: Schankwirtschaft f; F: Kneipe f; Brit: **s. bar**,
(vornehmere) Bar f; (b) Aut: **s. (car)**, Limousine f.
**salt** [sɔlt]. I. s. (a) Cu: Salz n; Fig: **to
take a story with a pinch of s.**, eine Ge-

schichte nicht wörtlich nehmen. II. adj.
salzig; **s. water**, Salzwasser n. III. v.tr.
(etwas) salzen. ◆**'salty**, adj. salzig; Cu:
versalzen.
**salubrious** [sə'luːbriəs], adj. gesund.
**salutary** ['sæljut(ə)ri], adj. heilsam.
**salute** [sə'l(j)uːt]. I. s. esp. Mil: Gruß m.
II. v.tr. (j-n) grüßen; abs. Mil: salutieren.
**salvage** ['sælvidʒ]. I. s. 1. (a) Bergung f
(eines Schiffes usw.); (b) Wiederverwertung f (von Abfällen, Resten usw.). 2.
(property saved) Bergungsgut n. II. v.tr.
(ein Schiff usw.) bergen; (Abfälle usw.)
wiederverwerten.
**salvation** [sæl'veiʃ(ə)n], s. Rettung f;
Ecc: Erlösung f; **S. Army**, Heilsarmee f.
**same** [seim], I. adj. gleiche(r,s); **the s.
...**, derselbe/dieselbe/dasselbe ...; der/
die/das gleiche ...; **the s. thing**, dasselbe;
das gleiche; **he's the s. age as I am**, er
ist ebenso alt wie ich; **it's all the s. to
me**, es ist mir gleich/egal; **the s. to you!**
gleichfalls! II. adv. **gleich** (aussehen
usw.); **all the s.**, immerhin.
◆**'sameness**, s. 1. Gleichheit f. 2.
(dullness) Eintönigkeit f.
**sample** ['sɑːmpl]. I. s. 1. (specimen) Probe
f (eines Minerals, von Blut usw.); Kostprobe f (von Wein usw.). 2. (example)
Beispiel n. II. v.tr. (etwas) probieren; (try
out) (eine neues Restaurant usw.) ausprobieren.
**sanctify** ['sæŋ(k)tifai], v.tr. (j-n, etwas)
heiligen. ◆**sanctimonious** [-'məuniəs],
adj. frömmelnd. ◆**'sanctuary**, s. 1.
Heiligtum n. 2. (refuge) Zufluchtsort m.
3. **bird s.**, Vogelschutzgebiet n.
**sanction** ['sæŋ(k)ʃ(ə)n]. I. s. 1. (punishment) Bestrafung f; Pol: Sanktion f. 2.
(approval) Billigung f; (permission) Erlaubnis f. II. v.tr. billigen.
**sand** [sænd]. I. s. 1. Sand m. 2. (also pl.
**sands**) (beach) Sandstrand m. II. v.tr. **to
s. sth. (down)**, etwas abschmirgeln/
abschleifen. ◆**'sandbag**, s. Sandsack m.
◆**'sandbank**, s. Sandbank f. ◆**'sand-
dune**, s. Sanddüne f. ◆**'sandpaper**, s.
Sandpapier n. ◆**'sandpit**, s. Sandkasten
m. ◆**'sandstone**, s. Sandstein m.
◆**'sandy**, adj. (of soil, beach etc.) sandig.
**sandal** ['sænd(ə)l], s. Sandale f.
**sandwich** ['sænwidʒ, -witʃ]. I. s. (a)
Sandwich n; ham s., Schinkenbrot n; (b)
Sch: **s. course**, Lehrgang m mit theoretischem und praktischem Teil. II. v.tr.
(j-n) einklemmen.
**sane** [sein], adj. vernünftig; (of pers.) bei
Verstand. ◆**sanity** ['sæniti], s. Vernunft
f; **to lose one's s.**, den Verstand verlieren.
**sanguine** ['sæŋgwin], adj. (of temperament) heiter; (of views, policy etc.) zuversichtlich.
**sanitation** [sæni'teiʃ(ə)n], s. sanitäre Einrichtungen fpl. ◆**'sanitary**, adj. sanitär;
**s. towel**, Damenbinde f.

**Santa Claus** ['sæntəklɔːz]. *Pr.n. Brit:* der Weihnachtsmann.

**sap** [sæp]. **I.** *s.* Saft *m* (eines Baumes usw.). **II.** *v.tr.* **to s. s.o.'s strength,** an j-s Kräften zehren.

**sapling** ['sæpliŋ], *s.* junger Baum *m.*

**sapphire** ['sæfaiər], *s.* Saphir *m.*

**sarcasm** ['saːkæzm], *s.* Sarkasmus *m.* ◆**sar'castic,** *adj.* sarkastisch.

**sardine** [saː'diːn, 'saː-], *s.* Sardine *f.*

**Sardinia** [saː'diniə]. *Pr. n.* Sardinien *n.*

**sardonic** [saː'dɔnik], *adj.* sardonisch.

**sash** [sæʃ], *s. (clothing)* Schärpe *f.*

**satanic** [sə'tænik], *adj.* satanisch.

**satchel** ['sætʃ(ə)l], *s.* Schulranzen *m.*

**satellite** ['sætilait], *s.* Satellit *m;* **s. town,** Trabantenstadt *f.*

**satiate** ['seiʃieit], *v.tr.* (j-n) sättigen; *(to excess)* übersättigen.

**satin** ['sætin], *s.* Satin *m.*

**satire** ['sætaiər], *s.* Satire *f.* ◆**satirical,** [sə'tirik(ə)l] *adj.* satirisch.

**satisfaction** [sætis'fækʃ(ə)n], *s.* **1.** *(action)* Befriedigung *f* (eines Gläubigers). **2.** *(a) (state)* Befriedigung *f; (b) (feeling)* Genugtuung *f* (**at/with,** über + *acc.*) ◆**satis'factory,** *adj.* zufriedenstellend; *(just good enough)* befriedigend; **not s.,** unbefriedigend. ◆**satisfy** ['sætisfai], *v.tr. (a) (fulfil)* (einer Verpflichtung) nachkommen; *(eine Bedingung, einen Wunsch)* erfüllen; *(Ansprüche)* befriedigen; *(b) (make content)* (j-n) befriedigen; **to s. one's hunger,** sich sättigen; *(c) (convince)* (j-n) überzeugen. ◆**satisfied,** *adj.* **1.** zufrieden. **2.** *(convinced)* überzeugt. ◆**satisfying,** *adj.* befriedigend; *(of food)* sättigend; *(of arguments, reasons)* überzeugend.

**saturate** ['sætjureit], *v.tr. (a) (wet)* (etwas) durchtränken; *(b) (Ch:* eine Substanz, *Com:* den Markt) sättigen.

**Saturday** ['sætədi], *s.* Samstag *m,* Sonnabend *m.*

**sauce** [sɔːs], *s. Cu:* Soße *f.* ◆**'saucepan,** *s.* Kochtopf *m.* ◆**'saucer,** *s.* Untertasse *f.* ◆**'saucy,** *adj. F:* frech.

**Saudi Arabia** ['saudi ə'reibiə]. *Pr. n.* Saudi-Arabien *n.*

**sauna** ['sɔːnə], *s.* Sauna *f.*

**saunter** ['sɔːntər]. **I.** *v.i.* **to s. (along),** (dahin)schlendern. **II.** *s.* Bummel *m.*

**sausage** ['sɔsidʒ], *s.* Wurst *f;* **s. meat,** Bratwurstmasse *f.*

**savage** ['sævidʒ]. **I.** *adj. (a) (of people, tribe etc.)* wild; primitiv; *(b) (fierce) (of animal)* bösartig; *(of pers., attack etc.)* brutal; **-ly,** *adv.* brutal; bösartig. **II.** *s.* Wilde(r) *f(m).* **III.** *v.tr. (of animal)* (j-n, ein Tier) anfallen.

**save** [seiv]. **I.** *v.tr. (a) (rescue)* (j-n, etwas) retten (**from sth.,** vor etwas *dat*); **to s. s.o.'s life,** j-m das Leben retten; *(b) (keep)* (etwas) aufheben; *(c) (economize)* (Geld, Zeit usw.) sparen; **I'm saving (up) for a new car,** ich spare auf ein neues Auto; *(d) (avoid)* **that will s. us a lot of**

**trouble,** das erspart uns viel Mühe. **II.** *s. Fb: etc:* Abwehraktion *f;* **to make a s.,** den Ball abwehren. ◆**'saving. I.** *adj. (a)* sparend; **labour-s.,** arbeitssparend; *(b)* **it's his s. grace,** das ist ein versöhnender Zug an ihm. **II.** *s. (a)* Ersparnis *f;* **s. of time,** Zeitersparnis *f; (b) pl.* **savings,** Ersparnisse *fpl;* **savings bank,** Sparkasse *f.*

**saviour** ['seivjər], *s.* **the S.,** der Heiland.

**savour** ['seivər], *v.tr. Lit:* (Wein, eine Speise) kosten/*(enjoy)* genießen. ◆**'savoury,** *adj. Cu: (a) (tasty)* schmackhaft; *(b) (spicy)* pikant.

**saw** [sɔː]. **I.** *s.* Säge *f.* **II.** *v.tr. & i.* (Holz usw.) sägen. ◆**'sawdust,** *s.* Sägemehl *n.* ◆**'sawmill,** *s.* Sägemühle *f.*

**Saxon** ['sæksən]. **I.** *s.* Sachse *m;* Sächsin *f.* **II.** *adj.* sächsisch. ◆**'Saxony.** *Pr. n.* Sachsen *n.*

**saxophone** ['sæksəfəun], *s.* Saxophon *n.*

**say** [sei]. **I.** *v.tr.irr. (a)* sagen; **it said on the radio ...,** im Radio wurde gemeldet ...; *(in book etc.)* **it says here ...,** hier heißt es ...; **people s./they s.** es heißt/man sagt; **there's a lot to be said for it,** es spricht vieles dafür; **that's to s.,** das heißt; *(let's)* **s. you are alone,** nehmen wir an, Sie sind allein; *(b) (speak)* (ein Gebet) sprechen; *(ein Gedicht)* aufsagen. **II.** *s.* **to have a s.,** ein Wort mitzureden haben. ◆**'saying,** *s.* **1.** **it goes without s. that ...,** es versteht sich ganz von selbst, daß ... **2.** *(common)* **s.,** Sprichwort *n.*

**scab** [skæb], *s.* **1.** *(on wound)* Schorf *m.* **2.** *F: (pers.)* Streikbrecher *m.*

**scaffold** ['skæf(ə)ld], *s.* **1.** Baugerüst *n.* **2.** *(for executions)* Schafott *n.* ◆**'scaffolding,** *s.* Baugerüst *n.*

**scald** [skɔːld], *v.tr.* **to s. oneself/one's foot,** sich/sich *dat* den Fuß verbrühen. ◆**'scalding,** *adj.* **s. hot,** brühheiß.

**scale**[1] [skeil]. **I.** *s.* **1.** Schuppe *f* (eines Fisches). **2.** *(a) (in boiler etc.)* Kesselstein *m; (b) (on teeth)* Zahnstein *m.* **II.** *v.tr.* (einen Fisch) schuppen.

**scale**[2]. **I.** *s.* **1.** *(a)* Skala *f; (of a map, model etc.)* Maßstab *m;* **to a s. of 1:10,** im Maßstab von 1:10; **s. model,** maßstabgetreues Modell; *(b) (relative size)* Umfang *m* (einer Katastrophe usw.); **(on a) large/small s.,** im Großen/im Kleinen. **2.** *Mus:* Tonleiter *f.* **II.** *v.tr.* **scaled down,** in verkleinertem Maßstab.

**scale**[3], *v.tr. (climb)* (eine Mauer usw.) erklimmen; (einen Berg) besteigen.

**scales** [skeilz], *s.pl. (pair of)* **s.,** Waage *f.*

**scallop** ['skɔləp], *s. Z:* Kammuschel *f.*

**scalp** [skælp], *s.* Kopfhaut *f.*

**scalpel** ['skælp(ə)l], *s.* Skalpell *n.*

**scamper** ['skæmpər], *v.i.* huschen; **to s. off,** weghuschen.

**scan** [skæn]. **I.** *v.* **1.** *v.tr. & i.* (einen Vers) skandieren. **2.** *v.tr. (a) (horizon)* absuchen (**for sth.,** nach etwas *dat*); (die Zeitung usw.) durchsehen. **II.** *s.* Abta-

stung *f; Med:* Scan *m.*
**scandal** ['skænd(ə)l], *s.* **1.** (*action*) Skandal *m.* **2.** (*gossip*) Klatsch *m.*
◆**'scandalize,** *v.tr.* (j-n) schockieren.
◆**'scandalous,** *adj.* skandalös.
**Scandinavia** [skændi'neivjə]. *Pr. n.* Skandinavien *n.* ◆**Scandi'navian. I.** *adj.* skandinavisch. **II.** *s.* Skandinavier(in) *m(f).*
**scant** [skænt], *adj.* recht wenig. ◆**'scanty,** *adj.* dürftig; (*of vegetation etc.*) kärglich; **-ily,** *adv.* **s. dressed,** dürftig/spärlich bekleidet.
**scapegoat** ['skeipgəut], *s.* Sündenbock *m.*
**scar** [skɑ:r]. **I.** *s.* Narbe *f.* **II.** *v.* **1.** *v.tr.* (*a*) (ein Gesicht usw.) mit Narben entstellen; (*b*) *Fig:* (*damage*) (etwas) beschädigen. **2.** *v.i.* eine Narbe hinterlassen.
**scarce** ['skɛəs], *adj.* (*rare*) selten; (*not plentiful*) knapp; *F:* **make yourself s.!** verdufte! **-ly,** *adv.* kaum. ◆**'scarcity/ 'scarceness,** *s.* Knappheit *f;* (*lack*) Mangel *m.*
**scare** ['skɛər]. **I.** *s.* (*a*) (*fright*) Schrecken *m;* (*b*) Alarm *m;* (*hoax*) blinder Alarm; **bomb s.,** Bombenalarm *m.* **II.** *v.tr.* (j-n) erschrecken; **to s. s.o./an animal away,** j-n/ein Tier verscheuchen. ◆**'scarecrow,** *s.* Vogelscheuche *f.* ◆**'scared,** *adj.* ängstlich; **to be s.** (**of** *sth.*), Angst (vor etwas *dat*) haben; **to be s. to death,** Todesangst haben. ◆**'scaremonger,** *s.* Bangemacher *m.* ◆**'scary,** *adj. F:* gruselig.
**scarf** [skɑ:f], *s.* Schal *m;* (*headscarf*) Kopftuch *n.*
**scarlet** ['skɑ:lət], *adj.* scharlachrot; **s. fever,** Scharlach *m.*
**scathing** ['skeiðiŋ], *adj.* kritisch; (*of criticism etc.*) vernichtend.
**scatter** ['skætər], *v.* **1.** *v.tr.* (*a*) (*make run/fly away*) (Vögel, Leute usw.) zerstreuen; (*b*) (Konfetti usw.) streuen; (Samen) ausstreuen. **2.** *v.i.* (*of crowd*) sich zerstreuen. ◆**'scatterbrained,** *adj.* (*of pers.*) zerstreut. ◆**scattered,** *s.* showers, vereinzelte Schauer. ◆**'scatty,** *adj. F:* verrückt.
**scavenger** ['skævindʒər], *s* Aasfresser *m.*
**scenario,** *pl.* **-os** [si'nɑ:riəu,-əuz], *s. Cin: etc:* Drehbuch *n; Th:* Textbuch *n.*
**scene** [si:n]. **1.** *Th: etc:* Szene *f;* **behind the scenes,** hinter den Kulissen. **2.** (*place*) Schauplatz *m;* **s. of the crime,** Tatort *m;* **s. of the accident/disaster,** Unfallort *m.* **3.** (*view, sight*) **a touching s.,** ein rührender Anblick. **4.** (*emotional outburst*) Szene *f.* ◆**'scenery,** *s.* **1.** *Th:* Kulissen *fpl;* (*design*) Bühnenbild *n.* **2.** (*landscape*) Landschaft *f.* ◆**'scenic,** *adj.* landschaftlich schön.
**scent** [sent]. **I.** *s.* **1.** (*pleasant smell*) Duft *m;* (*perfume*) Parfüm *n.* **2.** Witterung *f* (eines Tieres); (*track*) Fährte *f;* (*of hounds, police etc.*) **to be on the right s.,** auf der richtigen Spur sein. **II.** *v.tr.* (*a*)

(ein Tier) wittern; (*b*) (etwas) parfümieren; (die Luft) mit Duft erfüllen.
**sceptic** ['skeptik], *s.* Skeptiker(in) *m(f).* ◆**'sceptical,** *adj.* skeptisch. ◆**'scepticism,** *s.* Skepsis *f.*
**sceptre** ['septər], *s.* Zepter *n.*
**schedule** ['ʃedju:l, *esp. N.Am:* 'ske-]. **I.** *s.* **1.** (*list*) Verzeichnis *n.* **2.** (*a*) Plan *m;* **to work to s.,** nach Plan arbeiten; **on s.,** (*of train etc.*) fahrplanmäßig; **to be behind s. with sth.,** mit etwas *dat* zurück sein; (*b*) (*of pers.*) Programm *n;* **crowded s.,** volles Programm. **II.** *v.tr.* (etwas) planen; *Rail:* **scheduled service,** fahrplanmäßiger Verkehr *m.*
**scheme** [ski:m]. **I.** *s.* **1.** (*combination*) Schema *n;* (*system*) System *n.* **2.** (*a*) (*plan*) Plan *m;* (*b*) (*dishonest*) Intrige *f.* **II.** *v.* *v.i.* planen (**to do sth.,** etwas zu tun); **to s. against s.o.,** gegen j-n intrigieren. **2.** *v.tr.* Ränke schmieden; ein Komplott anzetteln. ◆**'scheming. I.** *adj.* intrigant. **II.** *s.* Intrigieren *n.*
**schizophrenic** [skitsəu'frenik]. **I.** *adj.* schizophren. **II.** *s.* Schizophrene(r) *f(m).*
**scholar** ['skɔlər], *s.* **1.** (*student*) Studierende(r) *f(m); A:* (*pupil*) Schüler(in) *m(f).* **2.** (*pers. with much knowledge*) Gelehrte(r) *f(m).* ◆**'scholarly,** *adj.* gelehrt. ◆**'scholarship,** *s.* **1.** Gelehrsamkeit *f.* **2.** *Sch:* Stipendium *n.*
**school** [sku:l], *s.* Schule *f;* **s. leaver,** Schulabgänger *m;* **driving s.,** Fahrschule *f; Fig:* **s. of thought,** Denkart *f.* ◆**'schoolboy,** *s.* Schüler *m.* ◆**'schoolgirl,** *s.* Schülerin *f.* ◆**'schooling,** *s.* (*education*) Ausbildung *f;* (*instruction*) Schulunterricht *m.* ◆**'schoolteacher,** *s.* Lehrer(in) *m(f).*
**science** ['saiəns], *s.* Wissenschaft *f; esp.* Naturwissenschaft *f;* **s. fiction,** Science-Fiction *f.* ◆**scien'tific,** *adj.* (*a*) naturwissenschaftlich; (*b*) (*of method*) wissenschaftlich; (*of pers.*) systematisch. ◆**'scientist,** *s.* Naturwissenschaftler(in) *m(f).*
**scintillate** ['sintileit], *v.i. Fig:* (*of wit etc.*) sprühen; *Th: etc:* **scintillating performance,** glänzende Aufführung.
**scissors** ['sizəz], *s.pl.* (**pair of**) **s.,** Schere *f.*
**scoff**[1] [skɔf], *v.i.* spotten (**at s.o., sth.,** über j-n, etwas *acc*)
**scoff**[2], *v. P:* (*eat*) **1.** *v.i.* fressen. **2.** *v.tr.* (etwas) verputzen.
**scold** [skəuld], *v.tr.* ausschimpfen.
**scone** [skɔn, skəun], *s. approx.* Milchbrötchen *n.*
**scoop** [sku:p]. **I.** *v.tr.* **to s.** (**out**), (Wasser usw.) ausschöpfen; **to s. up,** (etwas) aufschaufeln. **II.** *s.* **1.** (*kleine*) Schaufel *f.* **2.** *F:* (*report*) Exklusivmeldung *f.*
**scooter** ['sku:tər], *s.* Roller *m.*
**scope** [skəup], *s.* (*a*) (*range*) Bereich *m;* (*extent*) Umfang *m;* (*b*) (*opportunity*) **to give s.o. plenty of s.,** j-m viel Spielraum geben; **it leaves s. for improvement,** es

ließe sich noch verbessern.

**scorch** [skɔːtʃ], v.tr. (etwas) versengen. ◆'**scorching**, adj. & adv. sengend; s. hot, glutheiß.

**score** [skɔːr]. I. s. 1. (scratch) Kratzer m; (notch) Kerbe f; (cut) Einkerbung f. 2. Sp: (no. of points) Punkt(e)zahl f; (position of game) Spielstand m; (result) Ergebnis n; what's the s.? wie steht das Spiel? 3. (debt) Fig: to settle/pay off old scores, alte Rechnungen begleichen. 4. Mus: Partitur f. 5. (a) A: (inv. in pl.) a s., zwanzig; (b) pl. jede Menge; scores of people, Scharen pl von Menschen. II. v. 1. v.tr. (a) (mark with cuts) (Metall, Stein usw.) ritzen; (b) Sp: (Punkte usw.) erzielen; Fb: to s. a goal, ein Tor schießen. 2. v.i. (a) Sp: die Punkte anschreiben; (b) Sp: (of player) Punkte erzielen. ◆'**scoreboard**, s. Sp: etc: Anzeigetafel f. ◆'**scorer**, s. Fb: Torschütze m.

**scorn** [skɔːn]. I. s. Hohn m. II. v.tr. verhöhnen; (reject) (ein Angebot usw.) verschmähen. ◆'**scornful**, adj. höhnisch.

**Scorpio** ['skɔːpiəu], s. Astr: Skorpion m.

**scorpion** ['skɔːpjən], s. Skorpion m.

**Scot** [skɔt], s. Schotte m; Schottin f; to get off s.(-)free, straffrei ausgehen. ◆**Scotch** [skɔtʃ]. I. adj. schottisch. II. s. (whisky) Schottischer Whisky m, Scotch m. III. v.tr. (j-s Pläne usw.) durchkreuzen. ◆**Scotland** ['skɔtlənd]. Pr.n. Schottland n. ◆**Scots**, adj. schottisch. ◆'**Scotsman**, pl. -men, s. Schotte m. ◆'**Scotswoman**, pl. -women, s. Schottin f. ◆'**Scottish**, adj. schottisch.

**scoundrel** ['skaundrəl], s. Schuft m.

**scour**[1] ['skauər], v.tr. (Töpfe usw.) scheuern.

**scour**[2], v.tr. to s. the district for s.o., sth., die Gegend nach j-m, etwas dat absuchen.

**scourge** [skɔːdʒ], s. Geißel f; Fig: Plage f.

**scout** [skaut]. I. s. (a) Mil: Kundschafter m; (b) (boy) s., Pfadfinder m II. v.i. to s. about/around for sth., nach etwas dat herumsuchen.

**scowl** [skaul]. I. s. finsterer Blick m. II. v.i. finster blicken; to s. at s.o., j-n finster anblicken.

**scraggy** ['skrægi], adj. mager.

**scramble** ['skræmbl]. I. v. 1. v.i. (climb) klettern; (b) to s. for the ball, sich um den Ball raufen. 2. v.tr. (a) (code) (eine Nachricht) verschlüsseln; (b) Cu: scrambled eggs, Rührei n. II. s. (rush) Hetze f; Gedränge n (for sth., um etwas acc).

**scrap**[1] [skræp]. I. s. 1. (a) (small piece) Stückchen n; (of cloth, paper) Fetzen m; (b) (fragment) Bruchstück n. 2. (a) pl. scraps, (remains) Überbleibsel npl; (uneaten food) Reste mpl (einer Mahlzeit); (b) s. (metal), Schrott m; s. heap, Schrotthaufen m. II. v.tr. (a) (etwas) wegwerfen;

(ein Auto usw.) verschrotten; (b) (einen Plan usw.) aufgeben. ◆'**scrappy**, adj. bruchstückhaft.

**scrap**[2]. s. (fight) F: Rauferei f; (quarrel) Streit m.

**scrape** [skreip]. I. s. 1. Kratzen n; (result) Schramme f. 2. (awkward situation) F: to be in a s., in der Klemme sitzen. II. v. 1. v.tr. (a) (Schmutz, Farbe usw.) abkratzen; (b) (damage) (Möbel, Lackierung usw.) schrammen; to s., sich dat das Knie usw. aufschürfen. 2. v.i. kratzen; to s. through an exam, ein Examen mit knapper Not bestehen. ◆'**scraper**, s. Schabmesser n.

**scratch** [skrætʃ]. I. s. 1. (a) (mark) Kratzer m; (b) (wound) Schramme f. 2. (a) to start from s., ganz von vorne anfangen; (b) to come up to s., den Erwartungen entsprechen. II. v.tr. (a) (j-n, etwas) kratzen; Fig: to s. the surface (of a subject), ein Thema nur oberflächlich berühren; (b) (of animal) (im Sand usw.) scharren. ◆'**scratchy**, adj. (of wool etc.) kratzig.

**scrawl** [skrɔːl]. I. v.tr. to s. sth. on sth., etwas auf etwas acc kritzeln/schmieren. II. s. Kritzelei f.

**scream** [skriːm]. I. s. (gellender) Schrei m; s. of pain, Schmerzensschrei m. II. v.i. schreien (with fright, vor Angst).

**scree** [skriː], s. Geröllhalde f.

**screech** [skriːtʃ]. I. s. gellender Schrei m. II. v.i. kreischen.

**screen** [skriːn]. I. s. 1. (shield) Schirm m; (against draughts) Wandschirm m. 2. (a) Phot: Cin: Leinwand f; (medium) the s., der Film; s. test, Probeaufnahmen fpl; (b) TV: etc: Bildschirm m. II. v.tr. (a) (hide, protect) (etwas) abschirmen (from sth., gegen etwas acc); (b) Cin: (einen Roman usw.) verfilmen; TV: (ein Programm) (auf dem Bildschirm) zeigen. ◆'**screening**, s. 1. (protection, also El:) Abschirmung f (from/against, gegen + acc). 2. Pol: Durchleuchten n. ◆'**screenplay**, s. Cin: Drehbuch n.

**screw** [skruː]. I. s. 1. Schraube f. 2. P: (warder) Gefängniswärter m. II. v.tr. (a) to s. sth. (on) to sth., etwas an etwas acc schrauben; (b) to s. up one's handkerchief, sein Taschentuch zusammenknüllen; to s. up one's eyes, die Augen zusammenkneifen; (c) V: (copulate) (j-n) ficken. ◆'**screwdriver**, s. Schraubenzieher m.

**scribble** ['skribl]. I. v.tr. (etwas) kritzeln. II. s. Gekritzel n.

**script** [skript], s. 1. (a) (manuscript) Manuskript n; (b) Cin: Drehbuch n; s. writer, Drehbuchautor m. 2. (alphabet) Schrift f.

**scripture** ['skriptʃər], s. (Holy) S., Heilige Schrift f.

**scroll** [skrəul], s. Schriftrolle f.

**scrounge** [skraundʒ], v.tr. & i. F: (beg) (etwas) schnorren. ◆'**scrounger**, s.

Schnorrer *m*.
**scrub** [skrʌb], *v.tr.* (den Fußboden usw.) schrubben. ◆'**scrubbing-brush,** *s*. Scheuerbürste *f*.
**scruff** [skrʌf], *s*. **1. to seize s.o. by the s. of the neck,** j-n beim Kragen packen. ◆'**scruffy,** *adj. F*: ungepflegt.
**scrum** [skrʌm], *s. Sp: & F*: Gedränge *n*.
**scruple** ['skru:pl], *s*. Skrupel *m*; *pl*. **scruples,** Bedenken *npl*. ◆'**scrupulous,** *adj.* (*a*) (*conscientious*) gewissenhaft (**about to,** mit + *dat*); (*b*) (*precise*) genau.
**scrutinize** ['skru:tinaiz], *v.tr.* (j-n, etwas) prüfend ansehen. ◆'**scrutiny,** *s*. Untersuchung *f*.
**scuffle** ['skʌfl]. **I.** *s*. Rauferei *f*. **II.** *v.i.* raufen.
**scullery** ['skʌləri], *s*. Spülküche *f*.
**sculptor** ['skʌlptər], *s*. Bildhauer *m*. ◆'**sculpture,** *s. Art*: Plastik *f*.
**scum** [skʌm], *s*. Schaum *m*; *Pej*: (*people*) Abschaum *m* (der Menschheit).
**scurrilous** ['skʌriləs], *adj.* gemein; (*of language etc.*) unflätig.
**scurry** ['skʌri], *v.i.* huschen; **to s. off/ away,** davonhasten.
**scuttle**[1] ['skʌtl], *s*. (**coal**) **s.,** Kohlenschütte *f*.
**scuttle**[2], *v.tr.* (ein Schiff) versenken.
**scuttle**[3], *v.i.* **to s. off** = scurry off.
**scythe** [saið], *s*. Sense *f*.
**sea** [si:], *s*. **1.** (*a*) Meer *n*; See *f*; **at s.,** auf See; **by the s.,** am Meer; **by s.,** auf dem Seeweg; (*b*) (*motion of sea*) **heavy s.,** schwerer Seegang *m*. **2.** *Fig*: (*expanse*) **a s. of faces,** ein Meer von Gesichtern. ◆'**sea-breeze,** *s*. Seebrise *f*. ◆'**seafarer,** *s*. Seefahrer *m*. ◆'**seafood,** *s*. Meeresfrüchte *fpl*. ◆'**seafront,** *s*. Strandpromenade *f*. ◆'**seagull,** *s*. Möwe *f*. ◆'**seashell,** *s*. Muschel *f*. ◆'**seashore,** *s*. Meeresstrand *m*. ◆'**sea-sickness,** *s*. Seekrankheit *f*. ◆'**seaside,** *s*. Meeresküste *f*; **at the s.,** am Meer; **s. resort,** Seebad *n*. ◆'**sea-water,** *s*. Meerwasser *n*. ◆'**seaweed,** *s*. Seetang *m*. ◆'**seaworthy,** *adj.* seetüchtig.
**seal**[1] [si:l], *s*. Seehund *m*.
**seal**[2]. **I.** *s*. (*a*) (*on document, letter etc.*) Siegel *n*; **to give sth. the s. of approval,** etwas *dat* persönlich billigen; (*b*) (*closure*) Verschluß *m*. **II.** *v.tr.* (*with wax*) versiegeln; (*gum down*) (einen Brief usw.) zukleben; (*make airtight*) luftdicht verschließen. ◆'**seal off,** *v.tr.* (ein Gebiet) abriegeln.
**seam** [si:m], *s*. **1.** Naht *f*; *Fig*: **bursting at the seams,** zum Bersten voll. **2.** *Min*: (*of coal*) Flöz *n*; (*of ore*) Ader *f*.
**search** [sə:tʃ]. **I.** *s*. **1.** Suche *f*; (*for s.o. missing*) Suchaktion *f*; (*manhunt*) Fahndung *f*; **s. party,** Suchtrupp *m*; (*b*) *Jur*: Haussuchung *f*; **s. warrant,** Haussuchungsbefehl *m*. **2.** (*examination*) Durchsuchung *f* (von Gepäck usw.). **II.** *v.* **1.** *v.tr.* (*a*) (eine Schublade usw.) durchsu-

chen, (j-n, einen Ort) absuchen (**for sth., nach etwas** *dat*); *Jur*: (Gepäck, ein Haus usw.) durchsuchen; (*b*) *P*: **s. me!** keine Ahnung! **2.** *v.i.* **to s.** (**for sth.**), (nach etwas *dat*) suchen. ◆'**searchlight,** *s*. Suchscheinwerfer *m*.
**season** ['si:z(ə)n]. **I.** *s*. **1.** Jahreszeit *f*; **holiday s.,** Urlaubszeit *f*; **to be in s.,** (*of fruit*) reif sein. **2.** *Th: Sp: etc*: Saison *f*; *Rail: etc*: **s.** (**ticket**), Zeitkarte *f*. **II.** *v.tr.* (*a*) (eine Speise) würzen; (*b*) (Holz) ablagern. ◆'**seasonal,** *adj.* saisonbedingt. ◆'**seasoned,** *adj.* **1.** gewürzt. **2.** (*of timber*) abgelagert; *Fig*: (*of pers.*) erfahren. ◆'**seasoning,** *s. Cu*: Würze *f*.
**seat** [si:t]. **I.** *s*. (*a*) Sitz *m*; *Rail: etc*: Sitzplatz *m*; *Th*: Platz *m*; *Aut*: **s. belt,** Sicherheitsgurt *m*; (*b*) (*part of body*) Gesäß *n*; **s. of trousers,** Hosenboden *m*; (*c*) **s. of government,** Regierungssitz *m*. **II.** *v.tr.* (j-n, sich) setzen; **to be seated,** sitzen; **please be seated,** nehmen Sie bitte Platz; (*of building*) **to s. 500,** 500 Sitzplätze haben. ◆'**seating,** *s*. (*seats*) Sitzplätze *mpl*; **s. capacity,** Zahl *f* der Sitzplätze.
**secluded** [si'klu:did], *adj.* (*of place etc.*) ruhig gelegen; (*lonely*) einsam. ◆**seclusion** [-'klu:ʒ(ə)n], *s*. Ruhe *f*; ruhige Lage *f* (eines Hauses).
**second**[1] ['sekənd], *s*. Sekunde *f*.
**second**[2]. **I.** *adj.* zweiter, zweite, zweites; **the s. of January,** der zweite Januar; **the s. largest,** der/die/das zweitgrößte; *Sp*: **to come s.** (**to s.o.**), den zweiten Platz (hinter j-m) belegen; **to have s. thoughts,** es sich *dat* anders überlegen; **-ly,** *adv.* zweitens. **II.** *s*. **1.** Zweite *m f & n*; **Charles the S.,** Karl der Zweite. **2.** *Com*: **seconds,** Waren *fpl* zweiter Wahl. **III.** *v.tr. Pol*: **to s. a motion,** einen Vorschlag befürworten. ◆'**secondary,** *adj.* **1.** sekundär; **of s. importance,** nebensächlich. **2.** *Sch: Brit*: **s. school/ education,** höhere Schule/Schulbildung. ◆'**second(-)hand,** *adj.* aus zweiter Hand; **s.-h. car,** Gebrauchtwagen *m*. ◆'**second-rate,** *adj.* zweitrangig; (*mediocre*) mittelmäßig.
**secret** ['si:krit]. **I.** *adj.* (*a*) (*officially*) geheim; (*b*) (*of whisper, smile, feeling etc.*) heimlich; **-ly,** *adv.* heimlich. **II.** *s*. Geheimnis *n*; **in s.,** heimlich; **to let s.o. into a s.,** j-n in ein Geheimnis einweihen. ◆'**secrecy,** *s*. (*a*) Heimlichkeit *f* (eines Planes usw.); (*b*) **sworn to s.,** zur Verschwiegenheit verpflichtet. ◆**secrete** [si'kri:t], *v.tr.* (*a*) *Biol*: (ein Sekret) absondern; (*b*) (*hide*) (j-n, etwas) verbergen (**from,** von + *dat*). ◆'**secretive,** *adj.* (*of pers.*) geheimtuerisch.
**secretary** ['sekrətri], *s*. Sekretär(in) *m(f)*; *Pol*: **S. of State,** (i) *Brit*: Minister *m*; (ii) *N.Am*: Außenminister *m*.
**sect** [sekt], *s*. Sekte *f*.
**section** ['sekʃ(ə)n], *s*. **1.** (*a*) (*part*) Teil *m*;

*(b)* Abschnitt *m* (eines Textes usw.); *Rail:* Streckenabschnitt *m; (c) (department)* Abteilung *f; Mil:* Gruppe *f; (d) Jur:* Paragraph *m* (eines Gesetzes). 2. *Mth: Med:* Schnitt *m;* **(cross) s.,** Querschnitt *m.*

**sector** ['sektər], *s.* Sektor *m.*

**secular** ['sekjulər], *adj.* weltlich.

**secure** [si'kjuər]. **I.** *adj.* 1. *(safe, certain)* sicher **(against,** vor + *dat);* **to feel s.,** sich geborgen fühlen. 2. *(firm)* fest. **II.** *v.tr. (a) (make safe)* (etwas) sichern; *(protect)* schützen **(against/from,** gegen + *acc); (b) (fix)* (etwas) festmachen **(to,** an + *acc); (c) (obtain)* sich *dat* (einen Platz, j-s Dienste usw.) beschaffen. ◆**se'curity,** *s.* 1. Sicherheit *f.* 2. *(a) (guarantee)* Bürgschaft *f; (b) Com: (deposit)* Kaution *f; (for loan etc.)* Sicherheit *f; (c) Fin: usu. pl.* **securities,** Wertpapiere *npl.*

**sedate** [si'deit], *adj.* gesetzt.

**sedative** ['sedətiv]. **I.** *s.* Beruhigungsmittel *n.* **II.** *adj.* beruhigend.

**sedentary** ['sedəntri], *adj.* sitzend.

**sediment** ['sedimənt], *s. (a)* Sediment *n; (b) (in wine etc.)* Bodensatz *m.*

**sedition** [si'diʃ(ə)n], *s.* Aufruhr *m.* ◆**se'ditious,** *adj.* aufrührerisch.

**seduce** [si'dju:s], *v.tr.* (j-n) verführen. ◆**seduction** [-'dʌkʃ(ə)n], *s.* Verführung *f.* ◆**se'ductive,** *adj.* verführerisch.

**see** [si:], *v.tr. & i.irr. (a)* (j-n, etwas) sehen; **see you on Thursday!** bis Donnerstag! *F:* **I'll go and s.,** ich werde mal nachsehen; *(b) (visit)* **to go to/F: go and s. s.o.,** j-n besuchen; *(c)* (einen Besucher) empfangen; **I can't s. him today,** ich kann ihn heute nicht sprechen; *(d) (accompany)* (j-n) begleiten; **I'll s. you home/to the door,** ich begleite Sie nach Hause/(bis) zur Tür; *(e) (recognize)* (etwas) erkennen; *(understand)* (etwas) verstehen; *(f)* **to s. that everything is in order,** danach sehen/dafür sorgen, daß alles in Ordnung ist. ◆**see a'bout,** *v.tr.* **to s. a. sth.,** sich um etwas *acc* kümmern. ◆**see 'off,** *v.tr.* **to s. s.o. off on a train/a plane,** j-n zur Bahn/zum Flughafen bringen. ◆**see 'through,** *v.tr. (a) Fig:* (j-s Absichten usw.) durchschauen; *(b) (support)* **to s. s.o. t.,** j-m (bis zum Ende) durchhelfen; **to s. it t.,** (die Sache) durchhalten. ◆**see 'to,** *v. tr.* (nach j-m, etwas *dat*) sehen. ◆**seeing,** *s.* Sehen *n;* **worth s.,** sehenswert. **II.** *conj. phr.* **s. that ...,** angesichts der Tatsache, daß ...

**seed** [si:d], *s.* 1. Samen *m; coll.* Saat *f;* **s. potato,** Saatkartoffel *f;* **to go to s.,** *F: (of pers.)* herunterkommen. 2. *Sp:* gesetzter Spieler *m.* ◆**'seedy,** *adj. F: (of pers., place etc.)* schäbig.

**seek** [si:k], *v.tr. (a) (look for)* (etwas) suchen; *(b) (ask for)* **to s. sth. from s.o.,** etwas von j-m erbitten.

**seem** [si:m], *v.i.* scheinen; *(a)* **how does**

**it s. to you?** wie erscheint Ihnen das? wie kommt Ihnen das vor? *(b) impers.* **it seems as though/as if,** es scheint, als ob. ◆**'seeming,** *adj.* **-ly,** *adv. (not real)* scheinbar; *(perhaps real)* anscheinend.

**seep** [si:p], *v.i.* sickern; *(s. through)* durchsickern.

**see-saw** ['si:sɔː]. **I.** *s.* Wippe *f.* **II.** *v.i.* wippen.

**seethe** [si:ð], *v.i. (of place)* wimmeln **(with,** von + *dat);* **to be seething with anger,** vor Wut kochen.

**segment** ['segmənt], *s.* Abschnitt *m;* **orange s.,** Orangenspalte *f.*

**segregate** ['segrigeit], *v.tr.* trennen.

**seize** [si:z], *v.* 1. *v.tr. (a)* sich (etwas gen) bemächtigen; *(take possession of) Jur:* beschlagnahmen; *(b) (capture)* (j-n) festnehmen; *Mil:* (eine Stadt usw.) einnehmen; *(c) (take hold of)* (etwas) packen; *Fig:* **to s. the opportunity,** die Gelegenheit ergreifen; **to s. power,** die Macht an sich reißen. 2. *v.i. (of piston etc.)* **to s. (up),** sich festfressen. ◆**seizure** ['si:ʒər], *s.* 1. Beschlagnahme *f* (von Waren). 2. *Med:* plötzlicher Anfall *m.*

**seldom** ['seldəm], *adv.* selten.

**select** [si'lekt]. **I.** *v.tr.* (etwas) auswählen *(from,* aus + *dat).* **II.** *adj. (of school etc.)* ausgesucht; Elite-. ◆**se'lection,** *s.* Auswahl *f;* **to make a s.,** eine Auswahl treffen. ◆**se'lective,** *adj.* selektiv.

**self,** *pl.* **selves** [self, selvz], *s.* Selbst *n; F:* **he's his old s. again,** er ist wieder der alte. ◆**'self-a'ssertive,** *adj.* selbstbehauptend. ◆**'self-a'ssurance,** *s.* Selbstsicherheit *f.* ◆**'self-a'ssured,** *adj.* selbstsicher. ◆**'self-'centred,** *adj.* selbstsüchtig. ◆**'self-con'fessed,** *adj.* erklärt. ◆**'self-'confidence,** *s.* Selbstbewußtsein *n.* ◆**'self-'conscious,** *adj.* verlegen. ◆**'self-'consciousness,** *s.* Befangenheit *f.* ◆**'self-con'tained,** *adj.* 1. *(independent)* unabhängig. 2. **s.-c. flat,** abgeschlossene Wohnung *f.* ◆**'self-con'trol,** *s.* Selbstbeherrschung *f.* ◆**'self-de'fence,** *s.* Selbstverteidigung *f; Jur:* Notwehr *f.* ◆**'self-em'ployed,** *adj.* selbständig. ◆**'self-es'teem,** *s.* Selbstachtung *f.* ◆**'self-'evident,** *adj.* selbstverständlich. ◆**'self-'government,** *s.* Selbstverwaltung *f.* ◆**'self-im'portant,** *adj.* überheblich. ◆**'self-in'dulgent,** *adj. (of pers.)* genüßsüchtig. ◆**'self-in'flicted,** *adj.* **s.-i. wound,** Selbstverstümmelung *f.* ◆**'self-'interest,** *s.* Eigennutz *m.* ◆**selfish,** *adj.* selbstsüchtig. ◆**'selfishness,** *s.* Selbstsucht *f.* ◆**'self-po'ssessed,** *adj.* selbstbewußt. ◆**'self-re'liance,** *s.* Selbständigkeit *f.* ◆**'self-re'spect,** *s.* Selbstachtung *f.* ◆**'self-'same,** *adj.* genau der/die/dasselbe. ◆**'self-'service.** **I.** *s.* Selbstbedienung *f.* **II.** *adj.* **s.-s. shop,** Selbstbedienungsgeschäft *n.* ◆**'self-su'fficient,** *adj.* sich selbst versorgend **(in,** mit + *dat).*

**sell** [sel], *v.irr.* 1. *v.tr.* verkaufen (**to**, an + *acc.*). 2. *v.i.* **will it s.?** wird es sich gut verkaufen? **the picture sold for £500**, das Bild wurde für £500 verkauft. ◆'**seller**, *s.* (*a*) (*pers.*) Verkäufer(in) *m(f)*; (*b*) (*article*) **a good s.**, eine gutgehende Ware. ◆'**selling**, *s.* Verkauf *m*; **s. price**, Verkaufspreis *m.* ◆'**sell 'off**, *v.tr.* Com: (Waren usw.) unter Preis abstoßen. ◆'**sell 'out**, *v.tr.* Com: (Waren) ausverkaufen.

**sellotape** ['seləuteip], *s. R.t.m.* = Tesafilm *m R.t.m.*

**semaphore** ['seməfɔːr], *s.* (*signals*) Winkzeichen *npl.*

**semblance** ['sembləns], *s.* Anschein *m.*

**semi** ['semi], *prefix* halb-. ◆'**semi-auto'matic**, *adj.* halbautomatisch. ◆'**semicircle**, *s.* Halbkreis *m.* ◆'**semi'circular**, *adj.* halbkreisförmig. ◆'**semi'colon**, *s.* Semikolon *n.* ◆**semi'conscious**, *adj.* halb bei Bewußtsein. ◆'**semi-de'tached**, *adj.* **s.-d. house**, Doppelhaus *n.* ◆'**semi-'final**, *s.* Halbfinale *n.* ◆'**semi-'skilled**, *adj.* (*of worker*) angelernt.

**seminary** ['seminəri], *s.* Priesterseminar *n.*

**semolina** [seməˈliːnə], *s.* Grieß *m.*

**senate** ['senit], *s.* Senat *m.* ◆'**senator**, *s.* Senator *m.*

**send** [send], *v.tr.irr.* (*a*) schicken; **she sent me for bread**, sie schickte mich Brot holen; **to s. sth. crashing to the ground**, etwas zusammenstürzen lassen. ◆'**send a'way**, *v.tr.* (j-n) fortschicken. ◆'**sender**, *s.* Absender *m* (eines Briefes usw.). ◆'**send 'for**, *v.tr.* (j-n) holen lassen; **I shall s. f. it**, ich werde es mir schicken lassen/(*order it*) es bestellen. ◆'**send 'off**. I. *v.tr.* (j-n) fortschicken; (*b*) (einen Brief usw.) abschicken. II. *s. F:* **they gave him a terrific s.-o.**, sie haben ihn ganz groß verabschiedet. ◆'**send 'on**, *v.tr.* (j-m einen Brief usw.) nachschicken. ◆'**send 'up**, *v.tr. F:* **to s. up s.o., sth.**, j-n, etwas verulken. ◆'**send-up**, *s. F:* Karikatur *f*; (*performance*) Parodie *f.*

**senile** ['siːnail], *adj.* senil.

**senior** ['siːnjər]. I. *adj.* ältere(r, s); **s. citizen**, Senior *m*; (*pensioner*) Rentner *m*; **William Jones S.**, William Jones senior; (*b*) **s. (in rank)**, ranghöher. II. *s.* **to be s.o.'s s.**, (*in age*) älter als j-d sein; (*in rank*) j-s Vorgesetzter sein. ◆**seniority** [-ˈɔriti], *s.* 1. (*in age*) höheres Alter; *Adm: Com: etc:* Dienstalter *n.* 2. (*in rank*) höherer Rang.

**sensation** [sen'seiʃ(ə)n], *s.* 1. (*feeling*) Gefühl *n* 2. Sensation *f*; **to create/cause a s.**, Sensation machen. ◆**sen'sational**, *adj.* sensationell.

**sense** [sens]. I. *s.* 1. (*a*) Sinn *m*; **a keen s. of smell**, ein feiner Geruchssinn; (*b*) (*feeling*) Gefühl *n* (der Freude, der Sicherheit usw.); **s. of justice**, Gerechtigkeitssinn

*m.* 2. (*a*) *pl.* **to come to one's senses**, (i) Vernunft annehmen; (ii) (*regain consciousness*) wieder zu Bewußtsein kommen; **to bring s.o. to his senses**, j-n zur Besinnung bringen; (*b*) (*reason*) Vernunft *f*; **common s.**, gesunder Menschenverstand; **there is no s. in (doing) that**, das hat keinen Sinn. 3. (*meaning*) Bedeutung *f* (eines Wortes). II. *v.tr.* (etwas) spüren. ◆'**senseless**, *adj.* (*pointless*) sinnlos. ◆'**sensible**, *adj.* vernünftig. ◆'**sensitive** ['sensitiv], *adj.* (*a*) (*of pers., skin, tooth etc.*) empfindlich; **s. to cold**, kälteempfindlich; (*b*) (*positive sense*) (*of pers.*) sensibel. ◆**sensual** ['sensjuəl], *adj.* sinnlich. ◆**sensu'ality**, *s.* Sinnlichkeit *f.* ◆'**sensuous**, *adj.* (*of pleasure etc.*) sinnlich; (*voluptuous*) wollüstig.

**sentence** ['sentəns]. I. *s.* 1. *Gram:* Satz *m.* 2. *Jur:* (*a*) (*statement*) Urteil *n*; **to pass s.**, das Urteil sprechen (**on s.o.**, über j-n); (*b*) (*punishment*) Strafe *f*; **s. of death**, Todesstrafe *f.* II. *v.tr. Jur:* (j-n) verurteilen.

**sentiment** ['sentimənt], *s.* 1. (*a*) (*feeling*) Gefühl *n*; (*b*) *esp. pl.* Ansicht *f*; **my sentiments entirely!** ganz meine Meinung! 2. (*sentimentality*) Sentimentalität *f.* ◆**senti'mental**, *adj.* sentimental; *Pej:* (*of book, film*) rührselig; **s. value**, Erinnerungswert *m.*

**sentry** ['sentri], *s.* Posten *m.* ◆'**sentry-box**, *s. Mil:* Schilderhaus *n.*

**separate.** I. ['sep(ə)rət] *adj.* (*a*) (*not connected*) getrennt (**from**, von + *dat*); (*b*) (*different*) verschieden; **a s. question**, eine andere Frage; **-ly**, *adv.* getrennt; (*individually*) einzeln. II. ['sepəreit] *v.tr. & i.* (j-n, etwas) trennen; (*of two or more people*) sich trennen. ◆**sepa'ration**, *s.* 1. Trennung *f.* 2. (*distance*) Entfernung *f.*

**September** [sep'tembər], *s.* September *m.*

**septic** ['septik], *adj. Med:* septisch; **s. tank**, Senkgrube *f.*

**sequel** ['siːkwəl], *s.* (*a*) Fortsetzung *f* (eines Romanes usw.); (*b*) (*consequence*) Folge *f.*

**sequence** ['siːkwəns], *s.* 1. Folge *f*; (*order*) Reihenfolge *f*; **in s.**, der Reihe nach. 2. (*series*) Reihe *f*; *Cin: etc:* Stelle *f.*

**serenade** [serə'neid], *s.* 1. Serenade *f.* II. *v.tr.* **to s.** (s.o.), (j-m) ein Ständchen bringen.

**serene** [sə'riːn], *adj.* (*of pers.*) abgeklärt; (*unperturbed*) gelassen; (*of sky, landscape etc.*) heiter. ◆**serenity** [-'reniti], *s.* Abgeklärtheit *f*; heitere Gelassenheit *f.*

**sergeant** ['sɑːdʒənt], *s.* Feldwebel *m.* ◆'**sergeant-'major**, *s. Mil:* Hauptfeldwebel *m.*

**serial** ['siəriəl]. I. *adj.* **s. number**, laufende Nummer *f.* II. *s.* **s.** (*story*) Fortsetzungsgeschichte *f.* ◆**series** ['siəriːz], *s. inv.* Serie *f*; *Rad: TV:* Sendereihe *f.*

**serious** ['siəriəs], *adj.* (*a*) ernst; (*earnest*) ernsthaft; (*of offer*) ernstgemeint; **I'm s.**, ich meine es im Ernst; (*b*) **s. injury**, schwere Verletzung; **s. mistake,** schwerwiegender Fehler; **-ly,** *adv.* (*a*) **to take sth. s.,** etwas ernst nehmen; (*b*) **s. ill,** schwer krank. ◆**'seriousness,** *s.* (*a*) Ernst *m* (einer Lage usw.); (*of pers.*) Ernsthaftigkeit *f*; **in all s.,** allen Ernstes; (*b*) Schwere *f* (einer Krankheit usw.).

**sermon** ['sə:mən], *s.* **1.** *Ecc:* Predigt *f.* **2.** *F:* Moralpredigt *f.*

**serpent** ['sə:p(ə)nt], *s. Z:* Schlange *f.*

**serrated** [sə'reitid], *adj.* gezackt.

**serum** ['siərəm], *s.* Serum *n.*

**serve** [sə:v], *v.* **1.** *v.tr.* (*a*) (*of pers.*) **to s. a master/a cause,** einem Herrn/einer Sache dienen; (*b*) (*of thing*) (etwas *dat*) dienlich sein; **it will s. the purpose/abs. it will s.,** es erfüllt den Zweck; (*c*) (*in shop, at table*) (j-n) bedienen; **to s. the soup,** die Suppe servieren; (*d*) *F:* **it serves you right!** es geschieht dir recht! **2.** *v.i.* (*a*) dienen (**as,** als); *Adm:* amtieren; (*b*) (*in tennis*) aufschlagen. ◆**'servant,** *s.* (**domestic**) s., Diener(in) *m(f).* ◆**'service. I.** *s.* **1.** Dienst *m*; (*a*) **I'm at your s.,** ich stehe Ihnen zur Verfügung; (*b*) (*regular transport*) Verkehr *m*; **railway s.,** Eisenbahnverbindung *f*; (*c*) *esp. pl.* (**public**) **services,** (öffentliche) Einrichtungen *fpl*; **social services,** Sozialeinrichtungen *fpl.* **2.** (*a*) (*in shop, hotel etc.*) Bedienung *f*; **s. charge,** Bedienungsgeld *n*; (*b*) *Aut:* Wartung *f.* **3.** *Ecc:* Gottesdienst *m.* **4.** (*in tennis*) Aufschlag *m.* **5.** (*china*) **tea/dinner s.,** Teeservice/Speiseservice *n.* **II.** *v.tr.* (ein Auto usw.) warten. ◆**'serviceman,** *s. Mil:* Soldat *m*; *pl.* **servicemen,** Militärpersonal *n.*

**serviette** [sə:vi'et], *s.* Serviette *f.*

**servile** ['sə:vail], *adj.* (*of pers.*) unterwürfig.

**servitude** ['sə:vitju:d], *s.* Knechtschaft *f.*

**session** ['seʃ(ə)n], *s.* Sitzung *f.*

**set** [set]. **I.** *s.* **1.** (*a*) Satz *m*; Set *n* (von Unterwäsche); (*china*) Service *n*; **s. of teeth,** Gebiß *n*; *TV: Rad:* Apparat *m*; (*c*) *Sp:* Satz *m*; (*d*) (*series*) Reihe *f.* **2. shampoo and s.,** Waschen und Legen *n.* **3.** *Cin:* Filmkulisse *f*; *Th:* Bühnenbild *n.* **II.** *v.* **1.** *v.tr.* (*a*) (*put*) (etwas auf etwas *acc*) stellen/setzen; **to s. the table,** den Tisch decken; (*b*) (*adjust*) einstellen (**to,** auf + *acc*); (eine Falle, den Wecker, eine Aufgabe usw.) stellen; (*c*) **to s. sth. on fire,** etwas in Brand stecken; **to s. s.o. free,** j-n befreien; **to s. the fashion,** den Ton angeben; *Th:* **the scene is s. in the street,** die Handlung spielt sich auf der Straße ab; (*d*) *Mus:* (ein Gedicht usw.) vertonen. **2.** *v.i.* (*a*) (*of sun*) untergehen; (*b*) (*of jelly, cement etc.*) fest werden; (*c*) **to s. to work,** sich an die Arbeit machen. **III.** *adj.* fest; **s. phrase,** stehende Wendung; **he's s. in his ways,** er ist von Gewohnheitsmensch; *F:* **to be all s.,** ganz bereit sein. ◆**'set a'bout,** *v.i.* (*a*) **to s. a. (doing)** sth., etwas in Angriff nehmen; (*b*) **to s.**

**a. s.o.,** über j-n herfallen. ◆**'set a'side,** *v.tr.* (*save*) (Geld) beiseite legen. ◆**'setback,** *s.* Rückschlag *m.* ◆**'set 'back,** *v.tr.* (*a*) (*move back*) (etwas) zurückstellen; (*b*) (*delay*) verzögern; (j-n) aufhalten; (*c*) *F:* **it set me b. £20,** es hat mich um £20 ärmer gemacht. ◆**'set 'down,** *v.tr.* (etwas) hinsetzen; (einen Fahrgast) absetzen. **2.** *v.tr.* (Gründe usw.) darlegen. ◆**'set 'in,** *v.i.* (*start*) einsetzen. ◆**'set 'off,** *v.* **1.** *v.tr.* (eine Bombe usw.) zur Explosion bringen. **2.** *v.i.* sich aufmachen (**on a journey,** zu einer Reise). ◆**'set 'out,** *v.tr.* (*a*) (*display*) (Waren usw.) auslegen, (*arrange*) anordnen; (eine Gründe) darlegen; (*b*) **to s. o. to do sth.,** sich *dat* vornehmen, etwas zu tun. ◆**'set-square,** *s.* Zeichendreieck *n.* ◆**'setting,** *s.* **1.** (*a*) Schauplatz *m* (eines Romans usw.); Milieu *n*; (*b*) Fassung *f* (eines Edelsteins usw.). **2.** *Mus:* Vertonung *f* (eines Gedichtes usw.). **3.** (*adjustment*) Einstellung *f* (eines Gerätes usw.). ◆**'set-to,** *s. F:* Schlägerei *f.* ◆**'set 'up,** *v.tr.* aufstellen; (eine Maschine) montieren; **to s. up house,** einen (eigenen) Hausstand gründen; **to s. up a business/in business,** ein Geschäft etablieren. ◆**'set-up,** *s. F:* (*structure*) Aufbau *m* (einer Firma usw.); **what's the s.-up here?** wie ist das hier organisiert?

**settee** [se'ti:], *s.* Sofa *n.*

**setter** ['setər], *s.* (*dog*) Setter *m.*

**settle** ['setl], *v.* **1.** *v.tr.* (*a*) (*colonize*) (ein Land usw.) besiedeln; (*b*) (*decide*) regeln; (einen Streit) beilegen; **that settles it!** das wär's! (*c*) (*calm*) beruhigen; (*d*) (*fix*) festsetzen; (*e*) (*pay*) eine Rechnung usw.) begleichen; **to s. (up) with s.o.,** mit j-m abrechnen. **2.** *v.i.* (*a*) (*of pers., bird etc.*) **to s. somewhere,** sich irgendwo niederlassen; (*b*) (*of dust*) sich legen; (*c*) (*of liquid*) sich klären; (*of dregs, sediment*) sich absetzen; (*d*) (*of foundations, soil*) sich senken; (*d*) (*decide*) **to s. on/for sth.,** sich für etwas *acc* entscheiden, (*agree*) sich auf etwas *acc* einigen. ◆**'settled,** *adj.* (*a*) (*of weather etc.*) beständig; (*b*) (*decided*) entschieden; (*of matter*) erledigt; (*c*) (*of pers.*) ruhig. ◆**'settle 'down,** *v.i.* sich niederlassen. ◆**'settlement,** *s.* **1.** (*a*) (*act*) Besiedlung *f* (eines Landes usw.); (*b*) (*place*) Siedlung *f.* **2.** Erledigung *f* (einer Angelegenheit); Begleichung *f* (einer Schuld usw.); **they have reached a s.,** sie haben sich geeinigt.

**seven** ['sev(ə)n]. **I.** *num. adj.* sieben. **II.** *s.* Sieben *f.* ◆**seven'teen.** **I.** *num. adj.* siebzehn. **II.** *s.* Siebzehn *f.* ◆**'seventeenth.** **I.** *num. adj.* siebzehnte(r, s). **II.** *s.* Siebzehntel *n.* ◆**'seventh.** **I.** *num. adj.* siebente(r, s). **II.** *s.* Siebentel *n.* ◆**'seventieth.** **I.** *num. adj.* siebzigste(r, s). **II.** *s.* Siebzigstel *n.* ◆**'seventy.** **I.** *num. adj.* siebzig. **II.** *s.* Siebzig *f*; **in the seventies,** in den siebziger Jahren.

**sever** ['sevər], *v.tr.* (etwas) abtrennen.

**several** ['sev(ə)rəl], *adj.* mehrere.
**severe** [si'viər], *adj.* **1.** (*strict*) streng; (*of criticism, punishment etc.*) hart. **2.** (*of pain, storm*) stark; (*of weather*) rauh; **s. illness,** schwere Krankheit; **-ly,** *adv.* **1.** streng. **2.** stark. ◆**severity** [-'veriti], *s.* **1.** Strenge *f.* **2.** Stärke *f,* Heftigkeit *f* (*Med:* eines Anfalls usw.).
**sew** [səu], *v.tr.irr.* nähen; **to s. on a button,** einen Knopf annähen. ◆**'sewing,** *s.* **1.** Nähen *n;* **s. machine,** Nähmaschine *f.* **2.** Näharbeit *f.*
**sewage** ['s(j)u:idʒ], *s.* Abwasser *n;* **s. works,** Kläranlage *f.* ◆**'sewer** ['s(j)u:ər], *s.* Abwasserkanal *m.* ◆**'sewerage,** *s.* Kanalisation *f.*
**sex** [seks], *s.* Sex *m;* (*gender*) Geschlecht *n;* **s. education,** Sexualaufklärung *f; Sch:* Sexualkunde *f.* ◆**'sexual,** *adj.* geschlechtlich; **s. intercourse,** Geschlechtsverkehr *m.* ◆**'sexy,** *adj. F:* (*of film, book etc.*) erotisch; (*of girl*) sexy.
**sextet** [seks'tet], *s.* Sextett *n.*
**shabby** ['ʃæbi], *adj.* schäbig.
**shade** [ʃeid]. **I.** *s.* **1.** Schatten *m.* **2.** (*a*) **s.** (*of a colour*), Farbton *m;* (*nuance*) Schattierung *f; Fig:* **s. of meaning,** Nuance *f;* (*b*) (*slightly*) **a s. too big,** eine Spur zu groß. **3.** (*lamp*) **s.,** Lampenschirm *m.* **II.** *v.tr.* (*a*) (einen Ort) beschatten; (*make dark*) (etwas) überschatten; (*b*) (*screen*) (ein Licht, die Augen) abschirmen. ◆**'shading,** *s.* Schattierung *f.* ◆**'shady,** *adj.* **1.** schattig. **2.** *F:* zwielichtig; (*suspicious pers.*) verdächtig; **a s. business,** eine anrüchige Sache.
**shadow** ['ʃædəu]. **I.** *s.* Schatten *m.* **II.** *v.tr. Fig:* (follow) **to s. s.o.,** j-n beschatten. ◆**'shadowy,** *adj.* (*a*) schattenhaft; (*b*) (*shady*) schattig.
**shaft** [ʃɑ:ft], *s.* **1.** Stiel *m* (eines Werkzeuges usw.); Schaft *m* (eines Pfeiles). **2.** (*ray*) Strahl *m* (der Sonne usw.). **3.** *Tchn:* (*spindle, axle*) Welle *f.* **4.** (*of mine, lift*) Schacht *m.*
**shaggy** ['ʃægi], *adj.* (*of hair etc.*) struppig; (*of dog*) zottig.
**shake** [ʃeik]. **I.** *s.* **1.** Schütteln *n.* **2.** (*milk*) **s.,** Milchshake *m.* **II.** *v.irr.* **1.** *v.tr.* (*a*) schütteln; **to s. one's head,** den Kopf schütteln; **to s. hands with s.o.,** j-m die Hand schütteln; (*b*) *Fr:* (j-n, j-s Glauben usw.) erschüttern. **2.** *v.i.* beben; (*of building etc.*) wackeln; (*tremble*) (*of pers., voice*) zittern. ◆**'shaken,** *adj.* (*of pers.*) erschüttert; (*trembling*) zitterig; **badly s.** (**up**), stark mitgenommen. ◆**'shake off,** *v.tr.* (einen Verfolger, etwas) abschütteln. ◆**'shake 'up,** *v.tr.* (*a*) (eine Flüssigkeit) (gut) schütteln; (*b*) *Fig:* (j-n) aufrütteln. ◆**'shake-up,** *s. F:* (*of pers.*) Aufrüttelung *f;* **a big s.-up,** eine große Umwälzung. ◆**'shaky,** *adj.* (*a*) (*of pers.*) zitterig; (*of hand, voice*) zitternd; (*of chair etc.*) wackelig; (*b*) (*uncertain*) unsicher; *F:* wackelig.
**shall** [ʃæl, ʃ(ə)l], *modal aux. v.* (*p.* **should**

[ʃud], *q.v.*) (*a*) (*command*) sollen; **s. I open the window?** soll ich das Fenster öffnen? (*b*) *1st pers. future* werde(n).
**shallow** ['ʃæləu]. **I.** *adj.* (*of water, also Fig:*) seicht; (*of dish etc.*) flach. **II.** *s.pl.* **shallows,** Untiefen *fpl.* ◆**'shallowness,** *s.* Seichtheit *f.*
**sham** [ʃæm]. **I.** *adj.* (*a*) (*pretend*) vorgetäuscht; (*b*) (*false*) falsch. **II.** *s.* (*a*) (*thing*) Täuschung *f;* (*b*) (*pers.*) Scharlatan *m.*
**shamble** ['ʃæmbl], *s.pl.* **shambles** (*with sing. constr.*) *F:* (*mess*) Schlamassel *m;* (*fiasco*) Reinfall *m.*
**shame** [ʃeim]. **I.** *s.* (*a*) (*disgrace*) Schande *f;* **to my s.,** zu meiner Schande; **have you no sense of s.?** schämen Sie sich nicht? **to put s.o. to s.,** j-n beschämen; (*b*) *F:* **what a s.!** wie schade! **II.** *v.tr.* (j-n) beschämen. ◆**'shamefaced,** *adj.* beschämt. ◆**'shameful,** *adj.* schändlich. *F:* ◆**'shameless,** *adj.* schamlos.
**shampoo** [ʃæm'pu:]. **I.** *s.* Shampoo *n.* **II.** *v.tr.* (Haar) schamponieren.
**shamrock** ['ʃæmrɔk], *s.* irischer Dreiblattklee *m.*
**shandy** ['ʃændi], *s.* approx. = North *G:* Alsterwasser *n, South G:* Radler *m.*
**shan't** [ʃɑ:nt], = **shall not.**
**shanty** ['ʃænti], *s.* **1. s. town,** Barackenvorstadt *f.* **2.** (*song*) (*sea*) **s.,** Seemannslied *n.*
**shape** [ʃeip]. **I.** *s.* **1.** (*a*) (*outer form*) Form *f;* (*of plan, structure etc.*) **to take s.,** Gestalt annehmen; (*b*) (*pers. or being*) Gestalt *f.* **2.** *F:* (*state*) Zustand *m; Sp: etc:* Kondition *f;* **in good/poor s.,** (*of pers., team etc.*) gut/schlecht in Form. **II.** *v.* **1.** *v.tr.* (Ton usw.) formen. **2.** *v.i.* (*develop*) sich entwickeln. ◆**'shapeless,** *adj.* formlos. ◆**'shapely,** *adj.* (*of thing*) formschön; (*of pers.*) gut proportioniert.
**share** [ʃeər]. **I.** *s.* **1.** (*a*) Anteil *m;* **fair s.,** gerechter Anteil; (*b*) (*part played*) Beteiligung *f;* **he doesn't do his s.,** er trägt sein Teil nicht bei. **2.** *Fin:* Aktie *f;* **s. prices,** Börsenkurse *mpl.* **II.** *v.* **1.** *v.tr.* (etwas, *Fig:* Ansichten usw.) teilen; **to s. sth. out,** etwas aufteilen; **to s. (in) sth.,** an etwas *dat* teilnehmen. ◆**'shareholder,** *s. Fin:* Aktionär(in) *m(f).*
**shark** [ʃɑ:k], *s.* Hai *m; F:* (*pers.*) Gauner *m.*
**sharp** [ʃɑ:p]. **I.** *adj.* (*a*) scharf; (*of point*) spitz; (*of drop*) steil; (*b*) *Fig:* (*of pers.*) scharfsinnig; *Pej:* gerissen; **s. practices,** unsaubere Geschäftsmethoden; Gaunerei *f;* (*c*) (*of wind*) schneidend; (*d*) (*of sound*) durchdringend; schrill; (*e*) (*of taste*) herb; (*f*) *Mus:* zu hoch; **C s., F s.** etc., Cis, Fis usw.; **-ly,** *adv.* scharf; **the road dips s.,** die Straße fällt steil ab; **to answer s.o. s.,** j-m schroff antworten. **II.** *adv.* **1.** scharf. **2.** pünktlich; **at four o'clock s.,** pünktlich um vier Uhr. ◆**'sharpen,** *v.tr.* schärfen; (einen Bleistift) spitzen.

◆'sharpness, s. Schärfe f; (severity) Heftigkeit f (des Schmerzes); (of pers.) Scharfsinn m; (cunning) Schlauheit f.
◆'sharp-'witted, adj. scharfsinnig.

shatter ['ʃætər], v. 1. v.tr. (Glas usw.) zerschmettern; Fig: (Hoffnungen usw.) zerstören; (Nerven usw.) zerrütten. 2. v.i. zersplittern. ◆'shattering, adj. a s. blow, ein vernichtender Schlag.

shave [ʃeiv]. I. s. 1. to have a s., sich rasieren. 2. to have a close/narrow s., mit knapper Not davonkommen. II. v. 1 v.tr. (a) (j-n, sein Kinn usw.) rasieren; to s. (oneself), sich rasieren; (b) (Holz) abschälen; to s. sth. off, etwas abschaben. 2 v.i. sich rasieren. ◆'shaven, adj. clean-s., glatt rasiert. ◆'shaving, s. 1. s. brush, Rasierpinsel m. 2. usu. pl. shavings, Späne mpl (von Holz usw.).

shawl [ʃɔːl], s. Dreieckstuch n.

she [ʃi, ʃiː]. pers. pron. f. 1. (pers.) sie. 2. (car, ship) es; she sails tomorrow, es/das Schiff fährt morgen ab.

sheaf, pl. sheaves [ʃiːf, ʃiːvz], s. Garbe f (von Korn usw.).

shear [ʃiər], v.tr. (ein Schaf usw.) scheren. ◆shears, s.pl. (pair of) s., große Schere f.

sheath [ʃiːθ], s. (a) Scheide f (eines Schwertes usw.); Futteral n (eines Messers usw.); (b) Tchn: Hülle f; (contraceptive) s., Kondom n. ◆sheathe ['ʃiːð], v.tr. (ein Schwert usw.) in die Scheide stecken.

shed [ʃed], v.tr. (a) (of tree) (Laub) verlieren; (of lorry etc.) to s. its load, seine Ladung verlieren; (b) (Tränen, Blut) vergießen; Fig: to s. light on a matter, eine Sache aufklären.

sheen [ʃiːn], s. Glanz m.

sheep [ʃiːp], s. inv. Schaf n; coll. Schafe npl. ◆'sheepdog, s. Schäferhund m. ◆'sheepish, adj. 1. (feeling foolish) verlegen. 2. (timid) furchtsam; (shy) schüchtern. ◆'sheepskin, s. Schaffell n.

sheer ['ʃiːər], adj. 1. (complete) völlig; (b) (of rock) senkrecht; (of drop) jäh.

sheet [ʃiːt], s. 1. (for bed) Bettuch n. 2. (paper) Bogen m; (small) Blatt n. 3. s. metal, Blech n.

sheik(h) [ʃeik], s. Scheich m.

shelf, pl. shelves [ʃelf, ʃelvz], s. Brett n, Bord n; (in cupboard) Fach n; (set of) shelves, Regal n (für Bücher usw.).

shell [ʃel]. I. s. 1. Schale f (eines Eies, einer Muschel, einer Nuß usw.); Haus n (einer Schnecke); Panzer m (einer Schildkröte). 2. (outer structure) Rohbau m (eines Gebäudes). 3. Mil: Granate f. II. v.tr. (a) (Erbsen) enthülsen; (b) Mil: beschießen. ◆'shellfish, s. coll. Schalentiere npl.

shelter ['ʃeltər]. I. s. 1. (concept) Obdach n; (protection) Schutz m; (place) Unterschlupf m. 2. (hut) Schutzhütte f; (roof) Schutzdach n. II. v. 1. v.tr. (j-n, etwas) schützen (from, vor + dat); (take into

one's home) (j-m) Obdach geben. 2. v.i. Schutz suchen (from, vor + dat); sich unterstellen. ◆'sheltered, adj. geschützt (against/from, vor + dat).

shelve [ʃelv], v.tr. (einen Plan usw.) aufschieben. ◆'shelving, s. Regale npl.

shepherd ['ʃepəd], s. Schäfer m.

sheriff ['ʃerif], s. N.Am: Sheriff m.

sherry ['ʃeri], s. Sherry m.

Shetland ['ʃetlənd]. Pr. n. the Shetlands/S. Islands, die Shetlandinseln fpl.

shield [ʃiːld]. I. s. Schild m; Fig: Schutz m. II. v.tr. (j-n, seine Augen usw.) abschirmen (from, gegen + acc); (protect) (j-n) schützen (from, vor + dat).

shift [ʃift]. I. s. 1. (movement) Verschiebung f; (change) Veränderung f; Wechsel m. 2. Ind: Schicht f; s. work, Schichtarbeit f. II. v. 1. v.tr. (move) (etwas) verschieben; (eine Last usw.) verlagern; (Möbel usw.) umstellen; Th: to s. the scenery, die Kulissen schieben. 2. v.i. (move) (of cargo etc.) sich verschieben; (of wind) umspringen. ◆'shifty, adj. (of pers.) verschlagen; s. look, ausweichender Blick.

shimmer ['ʃimər], v.i. schimmern.

shin [ʃin], s. Anat: s. (bone), Schienbein n.

shine [ʃain]. I. v.i.irr. (a) (of sun etc.) scheinen; (of eyes etc.) strahlen; (of polished surface, hair etc.) glänzen; (of sun, lamp etc.) to s. on sth., etwas anstrahlen; (illuminate) etwas beleuchten; (b) Fig: (of pers.) glänzen. II. v. 1. Schein m (der Sonne usw.). 2. (polish) Glanz m. ◆'shining, adj. glänzend; a s. example, ein leuchtendes Beispiel. ◆'shiny, adj. glänzend.

shingle ['ʃingl], s. Strandkies m.

shingles ['ʃinglz], s.pl. Med: Gürtelrose f.

ship [ʃip]. I. s. Schiff n. II. v.tr. (a) (load) (eine Fracht usw.) verladen; (b) (send) (Güter) verschiffen/(by air) befördern/(by road, rail) verfrachten. ◆'shipbuilding, s. Schiffbau m. ◆'shipment, s. 1. (a) (loading) Einschiffung f; (b) (sending) Verschiffung f. 2. (a) (shipload) Schiffsladung f; (b) (batch of goods) Lieferung f. ◆'shipping, s. 1. Verfrachtung f; (in ship) Verschiffung f. s. company/line, Reederei f; s. lane/route, Schiffahrtsstraße f. 2. coll. Schiffe pl. ◆'shipshape, adj. in tadelloser Ordnung; (spotless) blitzsauber. ◆'shipwreck. I. s. (a) Schiffbruch m; (b) (ship) Wrack n. II. v.tr. to be shipwrecked, schiffbrüchig werden; shipwrecked sailors, Schiffbrüchige pl.

shirk [ʃəːk], v.tr. to s. a task, sich vor einer Aufgabe drücken.

shirt [ʃəːt], s. Hemd n; in (one's) s. sleeves, in Hemdsärmeln.

shit [ʃit]. I. s. V: Scheiße f. II. v.i. V: scheißen.

shiver ['ʃivər]. I. v.i. zittern (with cold/fear, vor Kälte/Angst). II. s. Schauer m.

◆**'shivery**, *adj. F:* to feel s., frösteln.

**shoal** [ʃəul], *s.* Schwarm *m* (von Fischen, *Fig:* von Menschen).

**shock** [ʃɔk]. **I.** *s.* **1.** *(jolt)* Stoß *m;* **s. wave**, Druckwelle *f; Aut:* **s. absorber**, Stoßdämpfer *m.* **2.** *(a) Med: Fig:* Schock *m;* **to be suffering from s.**, unter Schock stehen; *(b) Fig: (fright)* Schreck *m; (blow)* Schlag *m.* **3.** *El:* (elektrischer) Schlag *m.* **II.** *v.tr. (a)* (j-n) schockieren; *(b) (frighten)* (j-n) erschrecken. ◆**'shocking**, *adj.* schockierend; **it's s.**, es ist entsetzlich.

**shoddy** ['ʃɔdi], *adj.* schäbig, *(bad)* minderwertig.

**shoe** [ʃuː]. **I.** *s.* **1.** Schuh *m;* **s. polish**, Schuhcreme *f.* **2.** *(horse)* **s.**, Hufeisen *n.* **II.** *v.tr.irr.* (ein Pferd) beschlagen. ◆**'shoebrush**, *s.* Schuhbürste *f.* ◆**'shoehorn**, *s.* Schuhlöffel *m.* ◆**'shoelace**, *s.* Schnürsenkel *m.*

**shoot** [ʃuːt]. **I.** *v.irr.* **1.** *v.i. (a) (with gun, also Fb:)* schießen (**at s.o., sth.**, auf j-n, etwas *acc*); *(b) (move fast)* schießen; *(of car etc.)* **to s. (along)**, (dahin)rasen. **2.** *v.tr.* (ein Tier usw.) schießen; (eine Pistole, *Fig:* Fragen usw.) abfeuern (**at s.o.**, auf j-n); **to s. s.o. dead**, j-n erschießen; *(b) Cin:* (einen Film) drehen. **II.** *s. Bot:* Schößling *m.* ◆**'shoot 'down**, *v.tr.* abschießen. ◆**'shooting. I.** *adj.* **s. star**, Sternschnuppe *f;* **s. pain**, stechender Schmerz. **II.** *s. (a)* Erschießung *f* (von j-m); **s. incident**, Schießerei *f; (b) Cin:* Dreharbeiten *fpl.* ◆**'shoot 'up**, *v.i. (of flames etc.)* emporschießen; *(of prices)* (rapide) in die Höhe gehen; *(of plant)* schnell wachsen.

**shop** [ʃɔp]. **I.** *s.* **1.** Laden *m;* Geschäft *n:* **s. assistant**, Verkäufer(in) *m(f);* **s. window**, Schaufenster *n.* **2.** *Ind:* Werkstatt *f;* **s. steward**, Vertrauensmann *m* (der Gewerkschaft); **on the s. floor**, in der Fabrikhalle; unter den Arbeitern. **3.** *F:* to **talk s.**, fachsimpeln. **II.** *v.i.* einkaufen. ◆**'shopkeeper**, *s.* Ladenbesitzer(in) *m(f),* Geschäftsinhaber(in) *m(f).* ◆**'shoplifter**, *s.* Ladendieb *m.* ◆**'shoplifting**, *s.* Ladendiebstahl *m.* ◆**'shopping**, *s. (a) (purchases)* Einkäufe *mpl; (b) (activity)* Einkaufen *n;* **to go s.**, einkaufen gehen; **s. centre**, Einkaufszentrum *n.* ◆**'shop-soiled**, *adj. Com:* (leicht) angeschmutzt.

**shore¹** [ʃɔːr], *s.* Ufer *n* (eines Sees); *(sea)* **s.**, Strand *m;* Küste *f* (des Meeres); *Nau:* **on s.**, an Land; **(two miles) off s.**, (zwei Meilen) vor der Küste.

**shore²**, *v.tr.* **to s. (sth.) up**, (etwas) abstützen.

**short** [ʃɔːt]. **I.** *adj.* kurz; **a s. man**, ein kleiner Mann; **at s. range**, aus kurzer Entfernung; *El:* **s. circuit**, Kurzschluß *m;* **at s. notice**, kurzfristig; **you have a s. memory**, Sie vergessen schnell; **a s. time ago**, vor kurzem; **s. story**, Kurzgeschichte *f;* **in s.**, kurz; **to have a s. temper**, leicht aufbrausen/in Zorn geraten; **s.**

**weight/measure**, Fehlgewicht *n;* **s. (of money)**, knapp bei Kasse; **I'm 20p s.**, mir fehlen 20 Pence; **to be s. of breath**, außer Atem sein; **-ly**, *adv. (soon)* bald; **s. after(wards)**, kurz danach. **II.** *s. (a) Cl:* **shorts**, Shorts *pl; (b) Cin: F:* Kurzfilm *m.* **III.** *adv.* **1. to stop s.**, plötzlich stehenbleiben; *(in speaking)* innehalten; **to cut s.o. s.**, j-m das Wort abschneiden. **2. to fall s. of sth.**, etwas nicht erreichen; *(not fulfil)* etwas *dat* nicht nachkommen. ◆**'shortage**, *s.* Knappheit *f* **(of food**, an Nahrungsmitteln); Mangel *m* **(of labour, money** etc.**,** an Arbeitskräften, Geld usw.). ◆**'shortbread/'shortcake**, *s.* (Art) Mürbeteiggebäck *n.* ◆**'short-'circuit**, *v.tr. El:* (einen Kreis usw.) kurzschließen. ◆**'shortcomings**, *s.pl.* Mängel *mpl.* ◆**'shorten**, *v.* **1.** *v.tr.* (etwas) verkürzen; (Kleider) kürzen. **2.** *v.i.* kürzer werden. ◆**'shorthand**, *s.* Kurzschrift *f;* **s.-typist**, Stenotypistin *f.* ◆**'short-'lived**, *adj. (of fashion etc.)* kurzlebig. ◆**'shortness**, *s.* Kürze *f.* ◆**'short-'sighted**, *adj.* kurzsichtig. ◆**'short-'tempered**, *adj.* reizbar. ◆**'short-'term**, *adj.* kurzfristig.

**shot** [ʃɔt], *s.* **1.** *(discharge)* Schuß *m; Fig:* **a long s.**, reine Vermutung; **not by a long s.**, noch lange nicht. **2.** *(missile)* Geschoß *n; (small)* **s.**, Schrot *m.* **3.** *Sp: (a) Fb:* Schuß *m; (throw)* Wurf *m; (b) (heavy ball)* Kugel *f.* **4.** *Phot:* Aufnahme *f.* **5.** *F: (try)* Versuch *m;* **I'll have a s. at it**, ich werde es mal probieren. ◆**'shotgun**, *s.* Schrotbüchse *f.*

**should** [ʃud]. **1.** *pret. of* **shall** *(ought to)* sollte(n), solltest, sollte; **you s. do it at once!** Sie sollten es sofort tun! **you s. have seen him**, Sie hätten ihn sehen sollen. **2. s. the occasion arise**, sollte sich die Gelegenheit ergeben.

**shoulder** ['ʃuldər]. **I.** *s.* Schulter *f;* **s. blade**, Schulterblatt *n;* **s. strap**, Schulterriemen *m; (on bra etc.)* Träger *m; (on motorway)* **hard s.**, Randstreifen *m.* **II.** *v.tr. Fig:* **to s. a responsibility**, eine Verantwortung auf sich *acc* nehmen.

**shout** [ʃaut]. **I.** *s. (a) (loud call)* Ruf *m; (b) (loud cry)* Schrei *m.* **II.** *v.* **1.** *v.i. (speak loudly)* schreien; *(call out)* rufen; **to s. at s.o.**, j-n anschreien; **to s. for joy**, jauchzen. **2.** *v.tr.* (etwas) schreien; **to s. s.o. down**, j-n überschreien. ◆**'shouting**, *s.* Geschrei *n.*

**shove** [ʃʌv]. **I.** *s.* Schubs *m.* **II.** *v.tr.* schubsen; **to s. sth. into a drawer**, etwas in eine Schublade hineinstopfen.

**shovel** ['ʃʌv(ə)l]. **I.** *s.* Schaufel *f.* **II.** *v.tr.* schaufeln.

**show** [ʃəu]. **I.** *s.* **1.** *(a) Ind: Com: (display)* Ausstellung *f* (von Waren); **motor s.**, Automobilausstellung *f;* **fashion s.**, Modenschau *f; (b) Th:* Vorstellung *f; esp. Cin: TV:* Show *f.* **2.** *(appearance)* Schau *f;* **it's only for s.**, es ist nur fürs Auge. **II.** *v.irr.* **1.** *v.tr.* (etwas) zeigen **(s.o./to**

s.o., j-m); (a) (Fahrkarten usw.) vorzeigen; **to s. s.o. how to do sth.** (*teach*) j-m
etwas beibringen; (b) (*exhibit*) (etwas)
ausstellen; (*demonstrate*) (etwas) vorführen; (c) (*indicate*) (etwas) anzeigen; **to s.
a profit**, einen Gewinn aufweisen; (d) **to
s. s.o. to his room**, j-n zu seinem Zimmer bringen; (e) (*prove*) **he showed himself to be unreliable**, er erwies sich als
unzuverlässig. 2. *v.i.* (a) (*of thing*) her-
vorsehen (**under sth.**, unter etwas *dat*); **it
shows**, man sieht es; (b) (*of film*) **to be
showing**, laufen. ◆'**showdown**, *s.*
(endgültige) Auseinandersetzung *f*; (*trial
of strength*) Kraftprobe *f*. ◆'**show 'in**,
*v.tr.* (j-n) hereinführen. ◆'**showing**, *s.*
1. *Cin:* Vorstellung *f*. 2. *Sp: etc:* **on this
s.**, nach dieser Leistung zu urteilen.
◆'**show-jumping**, *s.* Springreiten *n*.
◆'**show 'off**, *v.* 1. *v.tr.* (j-s Vorzüge)
zur Geltung kommen lassen; *Pej:* (mit
einem Auto usw.) angeben. 2. *v.i.* (*of
pers.*) angeben. ◆'**show-off**, *s. F:* An-
geber *m*. ◆'**showroom**, *s.* Ausstel-
lungsraum *m*. ◆'**show 'up**, *v.* 1. *v.tr.*
(j-n, j-s Heuchelei usw.) bloßstellen. 2.
*v.i.* (*of feature*) hervortreten; *F:* (*of visitor
etc.*) auftauchen. ◆'**showy**, *adj.* auffällig; (*splendid*) prunkvoll; (*of performance
etc.*) effektvoll.

**shower** ['ʃauər]. I. *s.* (a) Schauer *m* (von
Regen usw.); **heavy s.**, Regenguß *m*; (b)
**s. (bath)**, Dusche *f*; **to take a s.**, duschen. II. *v.tr.* j-n (mit Wasser usw.)
übergießen; **to s. compliments/presents
on s.o.**, j-n mit Komplimenten/
Geschenken überschütten. ◆'**showery**,
*adj.* (*of weather*) mit häufigen Schauern.

**shred** [ʃred]. I. *s.* Streifen *m*; Fetzen *m*
(von Stoff, Papier usw.); **to tear sth. to
shreds**, etwas in kleine Stücke zerreißen;
*Fig:* **there isn't a s. of evidence**, man
hat keinen einzigen Beweis. II. *v.tr.* (a)
(etwas) in Stücke schneiden; (b) (*tear*)
zerreißen; (*Gemüse*) raspeln.

**shrewd** [ʃru:d], *adj.* (*of pers.*) scharfsinnig; klug. ◆'**shrewdness**, *s.* Scharfsinn
*m*; Klugheit *f*.

**shriek** [ʃri:k]. I. *s.* (schriller) Schrei *m*;
**shrieks of laughter**, kreischendes Gelächter *n*. II. *v.i.* schrill aufschreien; kreischen (**with laughter**, vor Lachen).

**shrill** [ʃril], *adj.* schrill.

**shrimp** [ʃrimp], *s.* Garnele *f*.

**shrine** [ʃrain], *s.* Schrein *m* (eines Heiligen).

**shrink** [ʃiŋk], *v.i.irr.* (a) schrumpfen; (*of
clothes etc.*) einlaufen; (*of other materials*)
sich zusammenziehen; (b) (*of pers.*) **to s.
(back) from danger etc.**, vor einer Gefahr usw. zurückschrecken.

**shrivel** ['ʃriv(ə)l], *v.i.* schrumpfen; **to s.
up**, zusammenschrumpfen; (*of skin etc.*)
runzelig werden.

**shroud** [ʃraud], *s.* Leichentuch *n*.
◆'**shrouded**, *adj.* eingehüllt.

**Shrove** [ʃrəuv], *adj.* **S. Tuesday**, Fast-

nachtsdienstag *m*.

**shrub** [ʃrʌb], *s.* Strauch *m*.
◆'**shrubbery**, *s.* Gesträuch *n*; (*planted*)
Sträucherrabatte *f*.

**shrug** [ʃrʌg]. I. *v.tr.* **to s. (one's shoulders)**, mit den Achseln zucken. II. *s.*
Achselzucken *n*.

**shrunken** ['ʃrʌŋk(ə)n], *adj.* geschrumpft.

**shudder** ['ʃʌdər]. I. *s.* Zittern *n*; Beben
*n*; Schauder *m* (von Entsetzen, Furcht
usw.). II. *v.i.* (*tremble*) zittern; (*shake*)
beben (**with horror, fear etc.**, vor Entsetzen, Furcht usw.).

**shuffle** ['ʃʌfl], *v.* 1. *v.i.* **to s. (along)**,
(dahin)schlurfen. 2. *v.tr. & i.* **to s. one's
feet**, mit den Füßen scharren. 3. *v.tr.*
(*Karten*) mischen.

**shun** [ʃʌn], *v.tr.* (j-n, etwas) meiden.

**shunt** [ʃʌnt], *v.tr.* *Rail:* rangieren.

**shut** [ʃʌt], *v.irr.* 1. *v.tr.* schließen, zumachen; **to be s.**, zusein; **the shops are shut**,
die Geschäfte sind/haben zu. ◆'**shut
'down**, *v.tr. & i.* (eine Fabrik usw.)
schließen. ◆'**shut-down**, *s.* Schließung
*f* (einer Fabrik usw.). ◆'**shut 'in**, *v.tr.*
einschließen; (*lock in*) einsperren.
◆'**shut 'off**, *v.tr.* (a) (Strom, Wasser
usw.) absperren; (b) (j-n) absondern
(**from**, von *dat*). ◆'**shut 'out**, *v.tr.* (a)
(*exclude*) (j-n) ausschließen; (b) (*lock out*)
(j-n) aussperren. ◆'**shut 'up**, *v.* 1. *v.tr.*
(a) (j-n, etwas) einschließen; (b) (ein
Haus usw.) verschließen; (c) *F:* **to s. s.o.
up**, j-m das Maul stopfen. 2. *v.i. F:* **s.
up!** halt's Maul! ◆'**shutter**, *s.* 1. Fen-
sterladen *m*. 2. *Phot:* Verschluß *m*.

**shuttle** ['ʃʌtl], *s.* **s. service**, Pendelver-
kehr *m*. ◆'**shuttlecock**, *s.* Federball *m*.

**shy¹** [ʃai], *v.i.* (*of horse*) scheuen.

**shy²**, *adj.* (*of pers.*) scheu; (*timid*) schüchtern. ◆'**shyness**, *s.* Scheu *f*; Schüchternheit *f*.

**Siberia** [sai'biəriə]. *Pr. n.* Sibirien *n*.
◆**Si'berian**, *adj.* sibirisch.

**Sicily** ['sisili]. *Pr. n.* Sizilien *n*.
◆**Si'cilian**. I. *s.* Sizilianer(in) *m(f)*. II.
*adj.* sizilianisch.

**sick** [sik], *adj.* 1. krank. 2. **to be s.**, (*vomit*) sich übergeben; **I feel s.**, mir ist
schlecht. 3. *F:* **to be s. of sth.**, etwas
satt haben; **it makes you s.**, es ekelt ein-
en an; *P:* es ist zum Kotzen. ◆'**sicken**,
*v.* 1. *v.i.* erkranken (**with**, an + *dat*);
**he's sickening for sth.**, er brütet etwas
aus. 2. *v.tr.* (j-n) anekeln. ◆'**sickening**,
*adj.* widerlich; **it's s.**, es ekelt einen an.
◆'**sickly**, *adj.* (a) (*of pers. etc.*) kränklich; (*weakly*) schwächlich; (b) **s. smell/
taste**, widerlich süßer Geruch/Geschmack
*m*. ◆'**sickness**, *s.* 1. Krankheit *f*.
2. (*vomiting*) Übelkeit *f*.

**sickle** ['sikl], *s.* Sichel *f*.

**side** [said]. I. *s.* 1. Seite *f*; **by s.o.'s s.**, an
j-s Seite, neben j-m; **s. by s.**, Seite an
Seite, nebeneinander; **s. of bacon**,
Speckseite *f*; **to move to one s.**, zur Seite treten; **to put sth. on one s.**, etwas

beiseite legen/(*save*) auf die hohe Kante legen; *F:* **to make sth. on the s.**, etwas nebenbei verdienen; **the right/wrong s.**, die Oberseite/Rückseite (eines Stoffs usw.); **to get on the right s. of s.o.**, sich mit j-m gut stellen; **you must look on the bright s.**, Sie müssen das Gute an der Sache sehen. **2.** (*a*) **he's on our s.**, er ist auf unserer Seite; **to take sides (with s.o.)**, (j-s) Partei ergreifen; (*b*) *Sp: etc:* Partei *f*; (*team*) Mannschaft *f*; (*c*) **on his mother's/father's s.**, mütterlicherseits/väterlicherseits. **3.** *attrib.* (*a*) seitlich; Seiten-; **s. entrance**, Seiteneingang *m*; (*b*) (*secondary*) Neben-; **s. issue**, Nebenfrage *f*; *Med:* **s. effect**, Nebenwirkung *f*. **II.** *v.i.* **to s. with s.o.**, j-s Partei ergreifen. ◆'**sideboard**, *s.* Büfett *n*; Anrichte *f* (in einem Eßzimmer). ◆'**sideburns**, *s.pl.* Koteletten *fpl*. ◆'**sidelight**, *s. Aut:* Standlicht *n*. ◆'**sideline**, *s.* **as a s.**, nebenbei. ◆'**sidestep**, *v.tr. & i.* (einem Schlag usw.) ausweichen. ◆'**side-street**, *s.* Seitenstraße *f*, Nebenstraße *f*. ◆'**sidewalk**, *s. N.Am:* Bürgersteig *m*. ◆'**sideways**, *adv.* seitwärts. ◆'**siding**, *s.* Abstellgleis *n*.

**sidle** ['saidl], *v.i.* **to s. up to s.o.**, sich an j-n heranschleichen.

**siege** [si:dʒ], *s.* Belagerung *f*.

**sieve** [siv]. **I.** *s.* Sieb *n*. **II.** *v.tr.* sieben.

**sift** [sift], *v.tr.* (*a*) (etwas) sieben; (*b*) (Beweismaterial usw.) sichten.

**sigh** [sai]. **I.** *s.* Seufzer *m.* **II.** *v.i.* seufzen.

**sight** [sait]. **I.** *s.* **1.** (*a*) Sehvermögen *n*; **short s.**, Kurzsichtigkeit *f*; **to lose one's s.**, erblinden; (*b*) **to catch s. of s.o., sth.**, j-n, etwas erblicken; **to lose s. of s.o., sth.**, j-n, etwas aus den Augen verlieren; **at first s.**, zunächst; **to know s.o. by s.**, j-n (nur) vom Sehen kennen; (*c*) **to come into s.**, sichtbar werden; **out of s.**, außer Sicht; unsichtbar. **2.** (*a*) (*sth. seen*) Anblick *m*; (*b*) **to see the sights**, die Sehenswürdigkeiten besichtigen. **3.** *Mil:* Visier *n* (eines Gewehrs usw.). **II.** *v.tr.* (j-n, etwas) erblicken; **to s. land**, Land sichten. ◆'**sighting**, *s.* Sichten *n*; Sichtung *f* (von Vögeln usw.). ◆'**sight-read**, *v.tr. & i. Mus:* (ein Stück) vom Blatt singen/spielen. ◆'**sightseeing**, *s.* Besichtigung *f*; **to go s.**, Sehenswürdigkeiten besichtigen.

**sign** [sain]. **I.** *s.* **1.** Zeichen *n*. **2.** (*a*) (*indication*) Anzeichen *n*; (*trace*) Spur *f*; (*b*) (*proof*) Beweis *m*; **as a s. of confidence**, als Vertrauensbeweis. **3.** (*a*) (*notice*) Schild *n*; Aushängeschild *n* (eines Wirtshauses); (*road*) **s.**, Verkehrszeichen *n*; **s. of the Zodiac**, Tierkreiszeichen *n*. **II.** *v.tr.* (einen Brief usw.) unterschreiben; (ein Gemälde) signieren. ◆'**sign 'on**, *v.* **1.** *v.tr.* (Arbeiter usw.) einstellen. **2.** *v.i.* sich (in eine Liste) eintragen; (*take a job*) sich verpflichten (eine Stellung anzunehmen); (*of unemployed pers.*) stempeln gehen. ◆'**signpost**. **I.** *s.* Wegweiser *m.* **II.**

*v.tr.* (eine Straße) ausschildern.

**signal** ['signəl]. **I.** *s.* Signal *n*; (*indication, gesture*) Zeichen *n*; *Rail:* **s. box**, Stellwerk *n*. **II.** *v.i.* ein Signal/Zeichen geben, (*wave*) winken (**to s.o.**, j-m). ◆'**signalman**, *pl* **-men**, *s. Rail:* Weichensteller *m*.

**signature** ['signətʃər], *s.* Unterschrift *f*; *Rad: etc:* **s. tune**, Kennmelodie *f*; Indikativ *n*.

**signify** ['signifai], *v.tr.* (*a*) (*mean*) bedeuten; (*b*) (*indicate*) (Zustimmung usw.) zu verstehen geben. ◆**significance** [-'nifikəns], *s.* Bedeutung *f*; **of (no) s.**, von (keinerlei) Bedeutung. ◆**sig'nificant**, *adj.* bedeutend; (*typical*) bezeichnend; **-ly**, *adv.* bezeichnenderweise; **to change s.**, sich bedeutend/erheblich ändern.

**silence** ['sailəns]. **I.** *s.* Stille *f*; (*esp. of pers.*) Schweigen *n*; (*command*) **s.!** Ruhe! **II.** *v.tr.* (j-n) zum Schweigen bringen; (*by force etc.*) (j-n) mundtot machen. ◆'**silencer**, *Aut:* Auspufftopf *m*. ◆'**silent**, *adj.* (*a*) (*of mechanism, steps etc.*) geräuschlos; (*of night, countryside*) still; *Cin:* **s. film**, Stummfilm *m*; (*b*) (*of pers.*) schweigsam; **to keep s. about sth.**, über etwas *acc* schweigen; **-ly**, *adv.* geräuschlos; schweigend.

**silhouette** [silu(:)'et]. **I.** *s.* (*a*) (*outline*) Umrisse *mpl*; (*b*) *Art:* Silhouette *f*. **II.** *v.tr.* **to be silhouetted against the sky**, sich gegen den Himmel abheben.

**silicon** ['silikən], *s. Ch:* Silizium *n*; **s. chip**, Siliziumchip *m*.

**silk** [silk], *s.* (*a*) Seide *f*; (*b*) *attrib.* Seiden-. ◆'**silkworm**, *s.* Seidenraupe *f*. ◆'**silky**, *adj.* seidig; (*soft*) seidenweich.

**sill** [sil], *s.* (*window*) **s.**, Fenstersims *m*; (*internal*) Fensterbank *f*.

**silly** ['sili], *adj.* dumm; *F:* blöd; **don't do anything s.**, mach keine Dummheiten. ◆'**silliness**, *s.* Dummheit *f*.

**silt** [silt]. **I.** *s.* Schlick *m.* **II.** *v.tr. & i.* (*of river, harbour*) **to s. up**, verschlammen.

**silver** ['silvər], *s.* **1.** (*metal, also articles*) Silber *n*. **2.** *attrib.* silbern, Silber-; **s. spoon**, Silberlöffel *m*; **s.-plated**, versilbert. **3.** (*coins*) Silber *n*; (*change*) Kleingeld *n*.

**similar** ['similər], *adj.* ähnlich (**to**, *dat*). ◆**similarity** [-'læriti], *s.* Ähnlichkeit *f*.

**simile** ['simili], *s.* Gleichnis *n*.

**simmer** ['simər], *v.i.* (*a*) *Cu:* sanft kochen; (*b*) *Fig:* (*of revolt*) schwelen; (*of pers.*) **to s. down**, sich beruhigen.

**simple** ['simpl], *adj.* **1.** (*of thing, problem*) einfach; (*plain*) schlicht; (*not complicated*) unkompliziert. **2.** (*of pers.*) einfältig. ◆'**simple-'minded**, *adj.* (*of pers.*) einfältig. ◆**sim'plicity**, *s.* (*a*) Einfachheit *f* (einer Methode, eines Problems usw.); Unkompliziertheit *f* (eines Charakters); (*b*) Schlichtheit *f* (eines Kleides usw.). **2.** (*of pers.*) Einfalt *f*. ◆'**simplify**, *v.tr.* (etwas) vereinfachen. ◆'**simply**, *adv.* **1.**

einfach. 2. (a) F: (absolutely) **you s. must go,** du mußt unbedingt gehen; (b) (only) nur; **I s. said that ...,** ich sagte nur, daß ...

**simulate** ['simjuleit], v.tr. simulieren.

**simultaneous** [sim(ə)l'teiniəs], adj. gleichzeitig.

**sin** [sin]. **I.** s. Sünde f; Hum: **to live in s.,** in wilder Ehe leben. **II.** v.i. sündigen. ◆**'sinful,** adj. (of pers.) sündig; (of act, waste etc.) sündhaft.

**since** [sins]. **I.** adv. (a) seitdem; **ever s.,** von der Zeit an; **it is many years s.,** es ist viele Jahre her; (b) (meanwhile) inzwischen. **II.** prep. seit + dat; **he's been up s. dawn,** er ist schon seit der Morgendämmerung auf; **s. then,** seitdem. **III.** conj. (a) (time) seitdem; seit; **s. I've been here,** seit(dem) ich hier bin; (b) (consequence) da; weil.

**sincere** [sin'siər], adj. (of pers., feelings etc.) aufrichtig; (warm) herzlich; **-ly,** adv. aufrichtig; (in letter) **yours s.,** mit freundlichen Grüßen. ◆**sincerity** [-'seriti], s. Aufrichtigkeit f; Herzlichkeit f.

**sinew** ['sinju:], s. Sehne f.

**sing** [siŋ], v.tr. & i.irr. singen. ◆**'singer,** s. Sänger(in) m(f). ◆**'singing. I.** adj. singend. **II.** s. Gesang m.

**singe** [sindʒ], v.tr. (Haare usw.) versengen.

**single** ['siŋgl]. **I.** adj. 1. (a) (only one) einzig; (of payment) einmalig; **not a s. one,** kein einziger; (b) (individual) einzeln; **every s. one of us,** jeder einzelne von uns. 2. (a) (for one pers.) Einzel-; **s. bed,** Einzelbett n; Rail: **s. ticket,** einfache Fahrkarte; (b) (of pers.) ledig; alleinstehend. **II.** s. Sp: **singles,** Einzel n. **III.** v.tr. **to s. s.o., sth. out,** j-n, etwas auslesen. ◆**single-'breasted,** adj. Cl: einreihig. ◆**'single-'handed,** adj. allein; **he did it s.-h.,** er hat es im Alleingang gemacht. ◆**'single-'minded,** adj. (of pers.) zielstrebig. ◆**single-'track,** adj. (a) Rail: eingleisig; (b) (of road) einspurig. ◆**'singly,** adv. 1. (separately) getrennt; einzeln. 2. (alone) allein.

**singlet** ['siŋglit], s. 1. (vest) Unterhemd n. 2. Sp: Trikot n.

**singular** ['siŋgjulər]. **I.** adj. (uncommon) einzigartig; (remarkable) merkwürdig. **II.** s. Gram: Einzahl f, Singular m.

**sinister** ['sinistər], adj. finster; **s. story,** unheimliche Geschichte.

**sink¹** [siŋk], s. Spülbecken n.

**sink²,** v.irr. **I.** v.i. 1. (a) sinken; (of ship, sun) untergehen; **his heart sank,** der Mut verließ ihn; (b) (of ground) sich senken, (slope) abfallen; (c) **to s. (in value),** im Wert sinken. 2. v.tr. (a) (in ship) versenken; (b) (einen Pfahl usw.) einsenken; Min: (einen Schacht) abteufen. ◆**'sink 'in,** v.i. (of words) Wirkung haben; **it hasn't sunk in yet,** er/sie hat es noch nicht ganz begriffen.

**sinuous** ['sinjuəs], adj. gewunden.

**sinus** ['sainəs], s. Nebenhöhle f. ◆**sinu'sitis,** s. Nebenhöhlenentzündung f.

**sip** [sip]. **I.** s. kleiner Schluck m. **II.** v.tr. (etwas) in kleinen Schlucken trinken.

**siphon** ['saif(ə)n]. **I.** s. Siphon m. **II.** v.tr. **to s. (off) a liquid,** eine Flüssigkeit absaugen.

**sir** [sə:r, sər], s. Herr; (in letter) **(Dear) Sir,** Sehr geehrter Herr!

**siren** ['saiərən], s. Sirene f.

**sister** ['sistər], s. Schwester f; Med: **(ward) s.,** Oberschwester f. ◆**'sister-in-law,** s. Schwägerin f.

**sit** [sit], v.irr. 1. v.i. (a) sitzen; (b) **to s. on a committee,** in einem Ausschuß tätig sein; **to s. for an exam(ination),** eine Prüfung ablegen; (c) (of court, assembly etc.) tagen. 2. v.tr. (ein Kind auf einen Stuhl usw.) setzen. ◆**'sit 'back,** v.i. sich zurücklehnen. ◆**'sit 'down,** v.i. sich (auf einen Stuhl usw.) setzen; **please s. d.,** nehmen Sie bitte Platz. ◆**'sit-in,** s. Sit-in n. ◆**'sitting. I.** s. Sitzung f. **II.** adj. sitzend; **s. target,** leichte Beute. ◆**'sitting-room,** s. Wohnzimmer n. ◆**'sit 'up,** v.i. (a) aufrecht sitzen; (b) (not go to bed) aufbleiben.

**site** [sait], s. (of building, town etc.) Lage f; **camping s.,** Campingplatz m; (building) **s.,** Baustelle f.

**situated** ['sitjueitid], adj. **the house is s. by the sea,** das Haus liegt am Meer; **pleasantly s.,** schön gelegen. ◆**situ'ation,** s. 1. Lage f. 2. (job) Stelle f; **situations vacant,** Stellenangebote npl.

**six** [siks]. **I.** num. adj. sechs. **II.** s. Sechs f. ◆**six'teen. I.** num. adj. sechzehn. **II.** s. Sechzehn f. ◆**six'teenth. I.** num. adj. sechzehnte(r, s). **II.** s. Sechzehntel n. ◆**sixth. I.** num. adj. sechste(r, s). **II.** s. (fraction) Sechstel m. ◆**'sixtieth. I.** num. adj. sechzigste(r, s). **II.** s. Sechzigstel n. ◆**'sixty.** num. adj. sechzig; (of pers.) **in his sixties,** in den Sechzigern; **in the sixties** (=1960s), in den sechziger Jahren.

**size** [saiz]. **I.** s. Größe f; Umfang m (eines Problems); (of book, paper) Format n. **II.** v.tr. **to s. s.o., sth. up,** sich dat über j-n, etwas acc eine Meinung bilden. ◆**'siz(e)able,** adj. **a s. sum,** eine beträchtliche Summe.

**sizzle** ['sizl], v.i. (of sausages etc.) brutzeln.

**skate¹** [skeit], s. (fish) Glattrochen m.

**skate². I.** s. Schlittschuh m. **II.** v.i. Schlittschuh laufen. ◆**'skateboard,** s. Rollbrett n, Skateboard n. ◆**'skater,** s. Schlittschuhläufer m. ◆**'skating,** s. **s. rink,** Eisbahn f.

**skeleton** ['skelit(ə)n], s. (a) Skelett n; (b) **s. key,** Nachschlüssel m; (c) **s. staff/ crew,** Minimalbelegschaft f.

**sketch** [sketʃ]. **I.** s. 1. Skizze f; **to give a s. of sth.** (in words), etwas kurz umreißen. 2. Th: Sketch m. **II.** v.tr. (eine Szene usw.) skizzieren. ◆'**sketchy**, *adj.* (*of description etc.*) skizzenhaft; (*of knowledge etc.*) oberflächlich.

**skewer** ['skju(:)ər], *s.* Spieß *m.*

**ski** [ski:]. I. *s.* Ski *m*; **s. jumping,** Skispringen *n*; **s. lift,** Skilift *m.* II. *v.i.* skilaufen. ◆'**skier**, *s.* Skiläufer *m.* ◆'**skiing**, *s.* Skilaufen *n*; **s. instructor,** Skilehrer *m.*

**skid** [skid]. I. *s.* Rutschen *n*; *Aut:* Schleudern *n.* II. *v.i.* rutschen; *Aut:* schleudern.

**skill** [skil], *s.* Geschick *n.* ◆'**skilful**, *adj.* geschickt. ◆'**skilfulness**, *s.* Geschicklichkeit *f.* ◆'**skilled**, *adj.* (*of pers.*) geschickt (at sth., in etwas *dat*); *Ind:* **s. worker,** gelernter Arbeiter.

**skim** [skim], *v.* 1. *v.tr.* (den Rahm usw.) abschöpfen; **skimmed milk,** Magermilch *f.* 2. *v.i.* **to s. through a letter,** einen Brief flüchtig durchlesen.

**skimp** [skimp], *v.* 1. *v.tr.* (an Material, am Essen usw.) sparen. 2. *v.i.* knausern. ◆'**skimpy**, *adj.* (*of meal*) mager; (*of garment*) dürftig.

**skin** [skin]. I. *s.* 1. Haut *f*; (*with fur*) Fell *n.* 2. (*of fruit*) Schale *f.* II. *v.tr.* (ein Tier) häuten. ◆'**skinflint**, *s.* Geizhals *m.* ◆'**skinny**, *adj.* mager. ◆**skin-'tight**, *adj.* hauteng.

**skint** [skint], *adj. F:* pleite.

**skip** [skip]. I. *v.* 1. *v.i.* (*a*) hüpfen; (*b*) (*with rope*) seilspringen. 2. *v.tr.* (ein Kapitel im Buch usw.) überspringen. II. *s. Ind: etc:* Kübel *m.*

**skirmish** ['skə:miʃ], *s.* Geplänkel *n.*

**skirt** [skə:t]. I. *s. Cl:* Rock *m.* II. *v.tr.* (eine Stadt, einen Wald usw.) umranden. ◆'**skirting**, *adj.* **s. board,** Fußleiste *f.*

**skittle** ['skitl], *s.* Kegel *m*; **to play skittles,** kegeln. ◆'**skittle alley,** *s.* Kegelbahn *f.*

**skulk** [skʌlk], *v.i.* sich versteckt halten; (*with evil purpose*) lauern.

**skull** [skʌl], *s.* Schädel *m*; **s. and crossbones,** Totenkopf *m.*

**skunk** [skʌŋk], *s. Z:* Stinktier *n.*

**sky** [skai], *s.* Himmel *m*; **in the s.,** am Himmel. ◆'**sky-'blue**, *adj.* himmelblau. ◆'**skylight**, *s.* Dachluke *f.* ◆'**skyline**, *s.* Horizont *m*; Skyline *f.* ◆'**skyscraper**, *s.* Wolkenkratzer *m.*

**slab** [slæb], *s.* (*a*) (*of stone etc.*) Platte *f*; (*b*) (*slice*) dicke Scheibe *f.*

**slack** [slæk]. I. *s.* (*of rope*) Lose *n*; **to take up the s.,** (ein Seil usw.) straffen. II. *adj.* 1. (*of pers.*) nachlässig (at, in + *dat*); (*of attitude etc.*) lässig; (*of discipline, morals*) locker. 2. (*not tight*) lose; (*of rope*) schlaff. 3. (*of business etc.*) flau. III. *v.i.* (*of pers.*) *F:* faulenzen. ◆'**slacken**, *v.i.* (*of rope etc.*) sich lockern. ◆'**slacken off,** *v.i.* nachlassen. ◆'**slackness**, *s.* 1. (*of pers.*) Nachlässigkeit *f*; (*of attitude etc.*) Lässigkeit *f.* 2. (*of rope etc.*) Schlaffheit *f.* 3. (*of business etc.*) Flauheit *f.*

**slag** [slæg], *s.* Schlacke *f*; **s. heap,** Halde *f.*

**slam** [slæm]. I. *s.* (*of door etc.*) Knall *m.* II. *v.* 1. *v.i.* (*of door etc.*) knallen. 2. *v.tr.* (eine Tür usw.) zuknallen.

**slander** ['slɑ:ndər]. I. *s.* Verleumdung *f.* II. *v.tr.* (j-n) verleumden. ◆'**slanderous**, *adj.* verleumderisch.

**slang** [slæŋ], *s.* Slang *m.*

**slant** [slɑ:nt]. I. *s.* 1. Schräge *f*; **at a s.,** schräg. 2. *F:* (*point of view*) Blickwinkel *m.* II. *v.* 1. *v.i.* schräg sein; (*of surface etc.*) sich neigen. 2. *v.tr.* (*a*) (etwas) neigen; (*b*) *Fig:* (einen Bericht usw.) färben. ◆'**slanting**, *adj.* schräg.

**slap** [slæp]. I. *s.* 1. Klaps *m.* II. *v.tr.* (ein Kind usw.) klapsen; **to s. s.o.'s face,** j-m eine Ohrfeige geben. ◆'**slapdash/** ◆'**slap-happy**, *adj.* liederlich. ◆'**slapstick**, *s.* **s.** (*comedy*), Slapstick *m.* ◆'**slap-up**, *adj.* **s.-up meal,** feudales Essen.

**slash** [slæʃ]. I. *s.* 1. Hieb *m* (mit dem Messer usw.). 2. (*cut*) Hiebwunde *f.* II. *v.tr.* (*a*) **to s. s.o.'s face,** j-m das Gesicht zerschneiden; (*b*) *Fig:* (Preise usw.) stark herabsetzen.

**slat** [slæt], *s.* Latte *f.*

**slate** [sleit], *s.* Schiefer *m*; **s. roof,** Schieferdach *n.*

**slaughter** ['slɔ:tər]. I. *s.* (*a*) (*act*) Schlachten *n* (von Vieh); Abschlachten *n* (von Menschen); (*b*) (*carnage*) Gemetzel *n.* II. *v.tr.* (Vieh) schlachten; (Menschen) abschlachten. ◆'**slaughterhouse,** *s.* Schlachthaus *n.*

**Slav** [slɑ:v]. I. *s.* Slawe *m*, Slawin *f.* II. *adj.* slawisch. ◆**Slavonic** [sləˈvɔnik], *adj.* slawisch.

**slave** [sleiv]. I. *s.* Sklave *m*; Sklavin *f.* II. *v.i.* **to s.** (**away**) **at sth.,** sich mit etwas *dat* abschinden/abplagen. ◆'**slavery**, *s.* Sklaverei *f.*

**slay** [slei], *v.tr.irr. A: & Lit:* (j-n) umbringen.

**sleazy** ['sli:zi], *adj. F:* verkommen.

**sledge** [sledʒ]. I. *s.* Schlitten *m.* II. *v.i.* **to s./go sledging,** Schlitten fahren.

**sledge-hammer** ['sledʒhæmər], *s.* Vorschlaghammer *m.*

**sleek** [sli:k], *adj.* (*a*) (*of hair etc.*) seidenglänzend; (*b*) **s. lines,** schnittige Form (eines Autos usw.).

**sleep** [sli:p]. I. *s.* Schlaf *m*; (*of pers., F: of leg etc.*) **to go to s.,** einschlafen; **to put an animal to s.,** ein Tier einschläfern. II. *v.* 1. *v.i.* (*a*) schlafen; (*b*) (*spend night*) (im Hotel usw.) übernachten. 2. (*accommodate*) (Leute) unterbringen; **the hotel sleeps 100,** das Hotel bietet Schlafgelegenheiten für 100 Personen. ◆'**sleeper**, *s.* 1. **to be a light/heavy s.,** einen leichten/tiefen Schlaf haben. 2. *Rail:* (*on track*) Schwelle *f.* 3. *Rail:* Schlafwagen *m.* ◆'**sleep 'in,** *v.i.* (*intentionally*) ausschlafen; (*unintentionally*) verschlafen. ◆'**sleepiness**, *s.* 1. Schläfrigkeit *f.* 2. (*lethargy*) Verschlafenheit *f.* ◆'**sleeping.**

**I.** *adj.* schlafend; *Com:* **s. partner,** stiller Teilhaber *m.* **II.** *s.* Schlafen *n;* **s. bag,** Schlafsack *m; Rail:* **s. pill,** Schlaftablette *f.* ◆**'sleep-walking,** *s.* Schlafwandeln *n.* ◆**'sleepy,** *adj.* verschlafen.

**sleet** [sli:t], *s.* Schneeregen *m.*

**sleeve** [sli:v], *s.* **1.** Ärmel *m.* **2. (record) s.,** Plattenhülle *f.*

**sleigh** [slei], *s.* Pferdeschlitten *m.*

**sleight** [slait], *s.* **s. of hand,** Fingerfertigkeit *f.*

**slender** ['slendər], *adj.* **1.** *(of pers.)* schlank. **2.** *(a) (of income etc.)* schmal; *(b) (of hope, excuse etc.)* schwach.

**slice** [slais]. **I.** *s.* Scheibe *f.* **II.** *v.tr.* (Brot usw.) (in Scheiben) schneiden.

**slick** [slik]. **I.** *s.* **(oil) s.,** Ölteppich *m.* **II.** *adj.* *(a) (of businessman etc.)* clever; *(b) (of performance)* routiniert.

**slide** [slaid]. **I.** *s.* **1.** *(action)* Rutschen *n; (landslide)* Erdrutsch *m.* **2.** *(on ice, in playground)* Rutschbahn *f.* **3.** *Phot:* F: Dia *n; (for microscope)* Objektträger *m.* **4.** *(a)* **(hair) s.,** Haarspange *f; (b) Tchn:* Schieber *m; Mth:* **s. rule,** Rechenschieber *m.* **II.** *v.irr.* **1.** *v.i. (a) (of bolt, drawer etc.)* gleiten; *(of pers.) (on ice etc.)* rutschen; *(by accident)* ausrutschen. **2.** *v.tr.* (etwas) schieben. ◆**'sliding,** *adj.* gleitend; **s. door,** Schiebetür *f.*

**slight** [slait]. **I.** *adj.* **1.** *(of pers., build)* zierlich; *(frail-looking)* schmächtig. **2.** *(not great)* leicht; *(insignificant)* gering(fügig); **s. smell,** schwacher Geruch; **-ly,** *adv.* **1.** *(of pers.)* **s. built,** von zierlichem Körperbau. **2.** leicht; **s. better,** ein bißchen/ etwas besser. **II.** *s.* Kränkung *f.*

**slim** [slim]. **I.** *adj. (a) (of pers.)* schlank; *(b) (of chance, hope etc.)* gering. **II.** *v.i. (lose weight)* abnehmen. ◆**'slimline,** *adj. (of TV etc.)* superflach.

**slime** [slaim], *s. (mud)* Schlamm *m.* ◆**'slimy,** *adj.* **1.** *(muddy)* schlammig. **2.** *(slippery, also Fig:)* schleimig.

**sling** [sliŋ]. **I.** *s. (weapon)* Schleuder *f.* **2.** *Med:* Armschlinge *f.* **II.** *v.tr.irr. (a)* (einen Ball usw.) schleudern; *(b)* **to s. a rifle over one's shoulder,** ein Gewehr umhängen.

**slink** [sliŋk], *v.i.irr.* schleichen; **to s. off,** wegschleichen. ◆**'slinky,** *adj. (of dress)* verführerisch; *(tight)* hauteng.

**slip** [slip]. **I.** *s.* **1.** *(a) (on ice etc.)* Rutsch *m; (b)* **to give s.o. the s.,** j-m entkommen. **2.** *(mistake)* Versehen *n; (conduct)* Fehltritt *m;* **it was a s. of the tongue,** ich habe mich versprochen. **3.** **(pillow-)-s.,** Kopfkissenbezug *m.* **4.** *Cl:* Unterrock *m.* **5.** **s. of paper,** Zettel *m.* **II.** *v.* **1.** *v.i. (a) (move out of position)* rutschen; *(slide)* gleiten; *(b) F: (go quickly)* **to s. away,** davonschleichen; **to s. into a dress,** in ein Kleid schlüpfen; *(c) F:* **he's slipping,** er hat nachgelassen; *(of time)* **to s. by,** verstreichen. **2.** *v.tr.* **to s. off a ring/a dress,** einen Ring/ein Kleid abstreifen; *(b)* **it slipped my mind,** es ist mir entfal-

len; *(c)* **he slipped it into his pocket,** er ließ es in die Tasche gleiten. ◆**'slipper,** *s.* Hausschuh *m; (bedroom)* s., Pantoffel *m.* ◆**'slippery,** *adj.* **1.** *(of liquid)* glitschig; *(icy)* glatt. **2.** F: *(of pers.)* gerissen. ◆**'sliproad,** *s.* Zufahrtstraße *f.* ◆**'slip 'up,** *v.i.* einen Schnitzer machen. ◆**'slip-up,** *s.* F: Panne *f.* ◆**'slipway,** *s.* Helling *f.*

**slit** [slit]. **I.** *s.* Schlitz *m.* **II.** *v.tr.* (j-m die Kehle) aufschneiden; **to s. open a sack etc.,** einen Sack usw. aufschlitzen.

**slither** ['sliðər], *v.i.* glitschen; *(of snake etc.)* gleiten.

**sliver** ['slivər], *s. (of wood etc.)* Streifchen *n; (of cheese etc.)* hauchdünne Scheibe *f.*

**slob** [slob], *s.* F: Lümmel *m.*

**slobber** ['slobər], *v.i.* geifern.

**slog** [slog]. **I.** *v.i.* **to s. away at sth.,** sich mit etwas *dat* abplagen. **II.** *s.* **hard s.,** Schinderei *f.*

**slogan** ['slougən], *s.* Slogan *m.*

**slop** [slop]. **I.** *s.pl.* **slops,** Schmutzwasser *n.* **II.** *v.* **1.** *v.i. (of liquid)* **to s. (over),** überschwappen. **2.** *v.tr.* (Bier, Wasser usw.) verschütten. ◆**'sloppy,** *adj.* F: *(a) (untidy)* schlampig; *(b) (sentimental)* rührselig.

**slope** [sloup]. **I.** *s. (a) (gradient)* Neigung *f;* **on/at a s.,** geneigt; *(b) (sloping ground)* Hang *m.* **II.** *v.* **1.** *v.i. (a) (of ground)* sich neigen; **to s. down,** abfallen; **to s. upwards,** ansteigen; *(b) (of writing)* **to s. forwards/ backwards,** sich nach rechts/links neigen. **2.** *v.tr.* (etwas) neigen. ◆**'sloping,** *adj. (of ground etc.)* geneigt; *(of writing etc.)* schräg; *(of shoulders)* abfallend.

**slot** [slot], *s.* **1.** *(for money etc.)* Einwurf *m;* **s. machine,** Münzautomat *m.* **2.** *(for peg etc.)* Kerbe *f.*

**slouch** [slautʃ], *v.i.* mit hängenden Schultern stehen/sitzen/gehen.

**slovenly** ['slʌv(ə)nli], *adj.* liederlich.

**slow** [slou]. **I.** *adj.* **1.** langsam; **s. train,** Personenzug *m; F:* Bummelzug *m; Cin: TV:* **in s. motion,** in Zeitlupe. **2.** *(mentally)* schwerfällig. **3.** **business is s.,** das Geschäft geht schleppend. **4.** **the clock is (ten minutes) s.,** die Uhr geht (10 Minuten) nach. **III.** *v.* **1.** *v.i.* **to s. up/down,** langsamer fahren/gehen. **2.** *v.tr.* **to s. sth. down/up,** etwas verlangsamen; **-ly,** *adv.* langsam. ◆**'slowness,** *s.* Langsamkeit *f.*

**slug** [slʌg], *s.* Nacktschnecke *f.*

**sluggish** ['slʌgiʃ], *adj. (of pers., engine)* träge. ◆**'sluggishness,** *s.* Trägheit *f.*

**sluice** [slu:s]. *s.* Schleuse *f;* **s. gate,** Schleusentor *n.*

**slum** [slʌm], *s.* Elendsviertel *n.*

**slumber** ['slʌmbər], *s.* Schlummer *m.*

**slump** [slʌmp]. **I.** *s. Com:* Kurssturz *m;* **economic s.,** Konjunkturrückgang *m.* **II.** *v.i. (a) (of pers.)* sacken; *(b) Com: (of prices etc.)* (plötzlich) stürzen.

**slur**[1] [slə:r], *s.* Makel *m;* **to cast a s. upon s.o.** j-s Ehre beflecken.

**slur**[2], *v.tr.* (Buchstaben, Silben) verschleifen; **to s. one's words,** mit schwerer Zunge reden. ◆**'slurred,** adj. undeutlich.

**slush** [slʌʃ], s. **1.** Matsch m. **2.** Fig: Kitsch m. **3.** F: s. **fund,** Schmiergelder pl. ◆**'slushy,** adj. **1.** matschig. **2.** Fig: kitschig.

**slut** [slʌt], s. Schlampe f.

**sly** [slai], adj. (of pers., look etc.) listig.

**smack¹** [smæk], v.i. **to s. of sth.,** leicht nach etwas dat schmecken.

**smack².** I. s. **1.** (sound) Klatsch m. **2.** (slap) Klaps m; **s. in the face,** Ohrfeige f. **II.** v.tr. (a) **to s. s.o.,** j-m einen Klaps geben; (b) **to s. one's lips,** (mit den Lippen) schmatzen.

**small** [smɔːl]. **I.** adj. klein; **s. number,** geringe Anzahl; **the s. print,** das Kleingedruckte; **s. business,** Kleinbetrieb m; **s. talk,** Geplauder n; **a s. matter,** eine Kleinigkeit; **on a s. scale,** in kleinem Maßstab; **to make s.o. look s.,** j-n blamieren; **to feel s.,** sich schämen. **II.** s. Anat: **s. of the back,** Kreuz n. ◆**'smallpox,** s. Med: Pocken fpl. ◆**'small-'scale,** adj. (of model) in verkleinertem Maßstab (angefertigt).

**smart** [smɑːt]. **I.** v.i. (of wound, eyes etc.) brennen. **II.** adj. **1.** (of pers., clothes) elegant; F: schick. **2.** (clever) klug; **s. answer,** fixe Antwort. **3.** (brisk) **s. pace,** flottes Tempo. **4.** (of blow) hart; **-ly,** adv. **s. dressed,** elegant/flott angezogen. ◆**'smarten,** v. v.tr. (a) **to s. sth. up,** etwas aufmöbeln; **to s. s.o./oneself up,** j-n/sich feinmachen. ◆**'smartness,** s. (of clothes, pers. etc.) Schick m.

**smash** [smæʃ]. **I.** s. **1.** (loud noise) Krach m; (blow) (heftiger) Schlag m. **2.** (crash) (heftiger) Zusammenstoß m; **car s.,** Autounfall m. **II.** v. **1.** v.tr. (a) **to s. sth. (to pieces),** etwas zerschlagen/(shatter) zerschmettern; (b) (den Feind) vernichtend schlagen. **2.** v.i. (a) (of window etc.) zerbrechen; (b) (of car) **to s. into a wall,** gegen eine Wand prallen. ◆**'smashing,** adj. F: klasse. ◆**'smash 'up,** v.tr. (etwas) zertrümmern; F: (ein Auto) zu Schrott fahren.

**smattering** ['smæt(ə)riŋ], s. oberflächliche Kenntnisse fpl (of, in + dat).

**smear** [smiːər]. **I.** s. **1.** Klecks m; Fig: **s. campaign,** Verleumdungskampagne f. **2.** Med: Abstrich m. **II.** v.tr. (a) (j-n, etwas) beschmieren; (b) (Tinte usw.) verwischen.

**smell** [smel]. **I.** s. Geruch m; (bad) s., Gestank m. **II.** v.irr. **1.** v.tr. (a) (involuntarily) (etwas) riechen; (b) (voluntarily) **to s. a flower,** an einer Blume riechen. **2.** v.i. **to s. nice/bad,** gut/ schlecht riechen; **to s. of garlic,** nach Knoblauch dat riechen. ◆**'smelly,** adj. stinkend.

**smelt** [smelt], v.tr. (Erz) schmelzen.

**smile** [smail]. **I.** s. Lächeln n. **II.** v.i. lächeln; **to s. at s.o.,** j-m zulächeln.

**smirk** [sməːk]. **I.** s. (selbstgefälliges)

Grinsen n. **II.** v.i. feixen.

**smith** [smiθ], s. Schmied m.

**smithereens** [smiðə'riːnz], s.pl. F: **to be smashed to s.,** in tausend Stücke zerspringen.

**smock** [smɔk], s. Hänger(kleid) m(n).

**smog** [smɔg], s. Smog m.

**smoke** [sməuk]. **I.** s. Rauch m. **II.** v. **1.** v.tr. (a) (eine Zigarette usw.) rauchen; (b) (Fleisch usw.) räuchern. **2.** v.i. rauchen. ◆**'smokeless,** adj. **s. fuel,** raucharmer Brennstoff. ◆**'smoking,** s. Rauchen n; **no s.,** Rauchen verboten; Rail: **s. compartment,** Raucherabteil n. ◆**'smoky,** adj. rauchig.

**smooth** [smuːð]. **I.** adj. glatt; (of flight, crossing) ruhig; (of drink) mild. **II.** v.tr. **to s. sth. (down/out),** etwas glätten; **-ly,** adv. glatt; **to run s.,** (i) (of machine) ruhig laufen; (ii) (of event etc.) reibungslos verlaufen. ◆**'smoothness,** s. Glätte f; ruhiger Verlauf m (eines Fluges usw.); Laufruhe f (einer Maschine usw.).

**smother** ['smʌðər], v.tr. (j-n, etwas) ersticken.

**smoulder** ['sməuldər], v.i. schwelen.

**smudge** [smʌdʒ]. **I.** s. Schmutzfleck m; (in writing etc.) verwischte Stelle f. **II.** v. **1.** v.tr. (etwas) beschmutzen; (die Unterschrift, Farben usw.) verwischen. **2.** v.i. (of ink, paint etc.) schmieren.

**smug** [smʌg], adj. selbstgefällig.

**smuggle** ['smʌgl], v.tr. & i. schmuggeln. ◆**'smuggling,** s. Schmuggel m.

**smut** [smʌt], s. Schmutz m. ◆**'smutty,** adj. schmutzig.

**snack** [snæk], s. Imbiss m; **to have a s.,** eine Kleinigkeit essen. ◆**'snack-bar,** s. Schnellimbiß m.

**snag** [snæg], s. F: Haken m; **that's the s.,** das ist der Haken (dabei/daran).

**snail** [sneil], s. Schnecke f; **at a s.'s pace,** im Schneckentempo.

**snake** [sneik], s. Schlange f.

**snap** [snæp]. **I.** s. **1.** (a) (bite) Schnappen n. (b) (sound) Knacks m. **2. cold s.,** Kälteeinbruch m. **3.** Phot: **s.(shot),** Schnappschuß m. **II.** adj. **to make a s. decision/judgement,** Knall und Fall entscheiden/urteilen. **III.** v. **1.** v.tr. (a) **to s. sth. shut,** etwas zuklappen; (b) **to s. one's fingers,** mit den Fingern schnalzen; (c) (break) (etwas) durchbrechen; (d) Phot: F: (j-n, etwas) knipsen. **2.** v.i. (a) **to s. at s.o.,** (of dog) nach j-m schnappen; (of pers.) j-n anfahren; (b) (of lock etc.) **to s. to/shut,** zuschnappen; (c) (break) entzweibrechen; (of rope) reißen. ◆**'snap 'up,** v.tr. (etwas) ergattern.

**snare** ['snɛər]. **I.** s. Falle f. **II.** v.tr. (ein Tier usw.) in einer Falle fangen.

**snarl** [snɑːl]. **I.** v.i. (of animal, pers.) knurren; **to s. at s.o.,** j-n anknurren. **II.** s. Knurren n. ◆**'snarl 'up,** v. **1.** v.i. (of traffic etc.) einen Stau bilden. **2.** v.tr. (den Verkehr usw.) zum Stocken bringen.

**snatch** [snætʃ], v. 1. v.i. greifen (at, nach + dat). 2. v.tr. (a) (j-n, etwas) weg- reißen; (b) Fig: (eine Gelegenheit) ergrei- fen.

**sneak** [sni:k], v. 1. v.i. to s. about, her- umschleichen; to s. off, wegschleichen. 2. v.tr. F: (etwas) hinterhältig klauen. ◆'sneakers, s. (shoes) N.Am: F: Leise- treter mpl. ◆'sneaking, adj. a s. suspi- cion, ein leiser Verdacht. ◆'sneaky, adj. hinterhältig.

**sneer** [sniər]. I. s. spöttisches Lächeln n. II. v.i. spöttisch lächeln; to s. at s.o., sth., über j-n, etwas acc spotten.

**sneeze** [sni:z]. I. s. Niesen n. II. v.i. nie- sen.

**sniff** [snif]. I. s. Schnüffeln n. II. v. 1. v.i. schnüffeln; to s. at sth., (of pers.) an etwas dat riechen; (of animal) etwas be- schnuppern. 2. v.tr. (of pers.) (an etwas dat) riechen; (of animal) (etwas) be- schnuppern. ◆'sniffle, v.i. schnüffeln.

**snigger** ['snigər]. I. s. Kichern n. II. v.i. kichern.

**snip** [snip]. I. v.tr. to s. (at) sth., (an et- was dat) schnippeln. II. s. (a) (cut) Schnitt m; (b) (piece) Schnipsel m.

**sniper** ['snaipər], s. Heckenschütze m.

**snivel** ['snivl], v.i. a (with runny nose) schnüffeln; (b) (cry) wimmern. ◆'snivelling, adj. (a) schnüffelnd; (b) wimmernd; (of child) weinerlich.

**snob** [snɔb], s. Snob m. ◆'snobbery s. Snobismus m. ◆'snobbish, adj. snobi- stisch.

**snooker** ['snu:kər], s. Snooker n.

**snoop** [snu:p], v.i. to s. (around), (her- um)schnüffeln. ◆'snooper, s. Schnüff- ler m.

**snooty** ['snu:ti], adj. F: hochnäsig.

**snooze** [snu:z], v.i. ein Nickerchen ma- chen.

**snore** [snɔːr], v.i. schnarchen.

**snorkel** ['snɔːkl], s. Schnorchel m.

**snort** [snɔːt], v.i. schnauben.

**snout** [snaut], s. Schnauze f.

**snow** [snəu]. I. s. Schnee m. II. v. impers. schneien; F: I'm snowed under with work, ich bin mit Arbeit überhäuft. ◆'snowball. I. s. Schneeball m. II. v.i. Fig: (grow quickly) lawinenartig anwach- sen. ◆'snowbound, adj. eingeschneit. ◆'snowdrift, s. Schneewehe f. ◆'snowdrop, s. Schneeglöckchen n. ◆'snowfall, s. Schneefall m. ◆'snowflake, s. Schneeflocke f. ◆'snowplough, s. Schneepflug m. ◆'snowy, adj (of landscape etc.) schnee- bedeckt.

**snub¹** [snʌb]. I. s. schroffe Abweisung f. II. v.tr. (j-n) schroff abweisen.

**snub²**, adj. F: s.-nose, Stupsnase f.

**snuff** [snʌf], s. Schnupftabak m.

**snug** [snʌg], adj. gemütlich; (of bed etc.) mollig warm; -ly, adv. gemütlich; (of gar- ment etc.) to fit s., wie angegossen pas- sen.

**snuggle** ['snʌgl], v.i. to s. up to s.o., sich an j-n anschmiegen; to s. down in bed, sich ins Bett kuscheln.

**so** [səu]. I. adv. 1. so; so much, so (sehr); so far, so weit; so far as I know, soviel ich weiß; so that, so viel; (unspe- cified quantity) so many articles at 10 marks, soundsoviele Artikel zu 10 Mark; so much so that ..., derart/dermaßen, daß ... 2. (a) and s. on, und so weiter; (b) I think so, ich glaube (schon); I don't think so, ich glaube nicht; so to speak, sozusagen; is that so? tatsächlich? (c) (also) he is clever and so is she, er ist intelligent und sie auch. 3. conj. phr. so that ..., (i) (result) so daß ...; (ii) (intent) damit ...; so as to ..., damit ...; he hur- ried, so as not to be late/so that he would not be late, er beeilte sich, um nicht zu spät zu kommen. 4. (about) a week or so, ungefähr eine Woche. II. conj. also; he wasn't there, so I came back, er war nicht da, also/daher bin ich zurückgekommen; F: so what? na und? ◆'so-called, adj. sogenannt. ◆'so-'so, adv. F: he's s., es geht ihm so lala.

**soak** [səuk], v. 1. v.tr. (a) (Brot, Wäsche usw.) einweichen (in, in + dat); (b) (et- was) durchtränken (in sth., mit etwas dat); (of rain) (j-n, etwas) durchnässen; soaked to the skin, völlig durchnäßt. 2. v.i. (a) (of washing etc.) eingeweicht wer- den; (b) (of moisture) to s. through, durchkommen. ◆'soaking, s. (of pers.) to get a good s., völlig durchnäßt wer- den. ◆'soak 'up, v.tr. (of sponge etc.) (Wasser usw.) aufsaugen.

**soap** [səup]. I. s. Seife f. II. v.tr. einsei- fen; s. powder, Waschpulver n. ◆'soapy, adj. seifig.

**soar** [sɔːr], v.i. (of bird, plane etc.) in die Höhe steigen; (of spire etc.) hochragen; (of prices) in die Höhe schnellen.

**sob** [sɔb]. I. s. Schluchzer m. II. v.i. schluchzen.

**sober** ['səubər]. I. adj. nüchtern; (matter of fact) sachlich. II. v. 1. v.i. to s. up, nüchtern werden. 2. v.tr. to s. s.o. up/ down, j-n ernüchtern. ◆so'briety [-'braiəti], s. Nüchternheit f.

**soccer** ['sɔkər], s. Fußball m.

**sociable** ['səuʃəbl], adj. gesellig.

**social** ['səuʃ(ə)l]. I. adj. (a) (of society) ge- sellschaftlich; Gesellschafts-; s. class, Gesellschaftsschicht f; (b) (aiding society) sozial; s. security, Sozialversicherung f; s. worker, Sozialarbeiter(in) m(f); s. ser- vices, Sozialeinrichtungen fpl; -ly, adv. to meet s., sich gesellschaftlich zusammen- kommen. II. s. geselliges Beisammensein n.

**socialism** ['səuʃəlizm], s. Sozialismus m. ◆'socialist. I. s. Sozialist m. II. adj. so- zialistisch.

**society** [sə'saiəti], s. Gesellschaft f; (club) Verein m.

**sock** [sɔk], s. Socken m; long/knee s.,

Kniestrumpf *m*.
**socket** ['sɔkit], *s*. **(power) s.**, Steckdose *f*.
**soda** ['səudə], *s*. Soda *n*; **baking-s.**, (doppeltkohlensaures) Natron *n*.
**sodden** ['sɔdn], *adj*. durchnäßt.
**sofa** ['səufə], *s*. Sofa *n*.
**soft** [sɔft], *adj*. 1. weich. 2. (*a*) (*of voice, light, breeze etc.*) sanft; (*b*) (*quiet*) leise; **s. music**, gedämpfte Musik. 3. **to have a s. spot for s.o.**, für j-n etwas übrig haben. 4. **s. drugs**, weiche Drogen; **s. drinks**, alkoholfreie Getränke. 5. (*of pers.*) F: (*a*) **s. (in the head)**, schwachsinnig; (*b*) (*physically*) verweichlicht; **-ly**, *adv*. **to speak/tread s.**, leise sprechen/gehen. ◆**soften** ['sɔfn], *v*. 1. *v.tr*. (etwas) weich machen; (das Licht, die Musik usw.) dämpfen. 2. *v.i.* weich werden; (*of pers.*) sich erweichen lassen. ◆**'soft-'hearted**, *adj*. weichherzig. ◆**'softness**, *s*. Weichheit *f*; (*of voice etc.*) Sanftheit *f*. ◆**'software**, *s*. Datapr: Software *f*.
**soggy** ['sɔgi], *adj*. matschig; (*soaked*) durchnäßt.
**soil**[1] [sɔil], *s*. Boden *m*.
**soil**[2], *v.tr*. (etwas) beschmutzen. ◆**'soiled**, *adj*. schmutzig.
**solar** ['səulər], *adj*. Sonnen-; **s. system**, Sonnensystem *n*.
**solder** ['sɔldər, 'sɔldər]. I. *s*. Lötmittel *n*. II. *v.tr*. löten.
**soldier** ['səuldʒər], *s*. Soldat *m*.
**sole**[1] [səul]. I. *s*. Sohle *f*; **s. of the foot**, Fußsohle *f*. II. *v.tr*. (Schuhe usw.) besohlen.
**sole**[2], *s*. Seezunge *f*.
**sole**[3], *adj*. einzig; **-ly**, *adv*. einzig und allein; (*merely*) lediglich.
**solemn** ['sɔləm], *adj*. 1. (*of music, ceremony etc.*) feierlich. 2. (*of pers., mood etc.*) ernst. ◆**solemnity** [-'lemniti], *s*. Feierlichkeit *f*.
**solicit** [sə'lisit], *v.tr. & i.* (*a*) **to s. (for) sth.**, um etwas *acc* werben; (*b*) (*of prostitute*) sich anbieten. ◆**so'licitor**, *s*. Rechtsanwalt *m*.
**solid** ['sɔlid]. I. *adj*. 1. (*not liquid*) fest. 2. (*not hollow*) massiv. 3. (*firm, reliable*) (*of pers., thing*) solid(e). 4. (*of argument, proof etc.*) handfest. 5. **a s. hour**, eine volle Stunde. II. *s*. 1. Ph: Ch: fester Körper *m*. 2. *pl*. (*food*) **solids**, feste Nahrung *f*; **-ly**, *adv*. 1. **s. built**, (i) (*of pers.*) kräftig gebaut; (ii) (*of building etc.*) stabil gebaut. 2. **they are s. behind us**, sie stehen geschlossen hinter uns. ◆**soli'darity**, *s*. Solidarität *f*. ◆**so'lidify**, *v*. 1. *v.i.* fest werden. 2. *v.tr*. fest werden lassen.
**soliloquy** [sə'liləkwi], *s*. Selbstgespräch *n*; Th: Monolog *m*.
**solitary** ['sɔlit(ə)ri], *adj*. (*only one*) einzig; (*lonely*) einsam; **s. confinement**, Einzelhaft *f*. ◆**'solitude**, *s*. Einsamkeit *f*.
**solo**, *pl.* **-os** ['səuləu, -əuz]. I. *s*. Solo *n*. II. *adj*. Solo-. III. *adv*. Mus: **to play s.**,

solo spielen. ◆**'soloist**, *s*. Solist(in) *m*(*f*).
**solstice** ['sɔlstis], *s*. Sonnenwende *f*.
**soluble** ['sɔljubl], *adj*. 1. Ph: Ch: löslich. 2. (*of problem*) lösbar. ◆**solution** [sə'lu:ʃ(ə)n], *s*. Lösung *f*.
**solve** [sɔlv], *v.tr*. (ein Problem usw.) lösen. ◆**'solvent**. I. *adj*. Com: (*of firm*) zahlungsfähig. II. *s*. Ch: etc: Lösungsmittel *n*.
**some** [sʌm]. I. *adj*. 1. (*usu. not translated*) **I bought s. coffee**, ich habe (etwas) Kaffee gekauft; **s. more meat**, noch (etwas) Fleisch. 2. (*a certain amount*) einige(r, s); **after s. time**, nach einiger Zeit; **s. days ago**, vor einigen Tagen. 3. (*about*) etwa; **s. twenty people**, etwa zwanzig Leute; **in s. cases**, in manchen Fällen. 4. (*unspecified*) **s. man (or other)**, irgendein Mann; **s. time**, irgendwann. 5. F: N.Am: toll; **that was s. party!** das war vielleicht eine Party! II. *pron*. 1. (*partitive*) welche(s); **take s. bread – I've already got s.**, nimm dir Brot – ich habe schon welches; **take s.!** nimm (dir) davon! 2. (*not all*) einige; **s. of them**, einige von ihnen/ (*things*) davon.
**somebody** ['sʌmbədi], *pron*. jemand; **s. or other**, irgend jemand.
**somehow** ['sʌmhau], *adv*. **s. (or other)**, irgendwie.
**someone** ['sʌmwʌn], *pron. & s.* = **somebody**.
**somersault** ['sʌməsɔ:lt]. I. *s*. Purzelbaum *m*, Sp: Salto *m*. II. *v.i.* (*a*) einen Purzelbaum schlagen; Gym: einen Salto machen; (*b*) (*accidentally*) (*of pers., car etc.*) sich überschlagen.
**something** ['sʌmθiŋ]. I. *pron*. etwas; F: was; **s. nice**, etwas Schönes; **s. to drink**, etwas zu trinken; **s. or other**, irgend etwas; **s. which you ought to know**, etwas, was Sie wissen sollten; F: **he is an architect or s.**, er ist Architekt oder so was (Ähnliches). II. *adv*. **it looks s. like a rose**, es sieht so ähnlich wie eine Rose aus.
**sometime** ['sʌmtaim], *adv*. **s. (or other)**, irgendwann; F: **see you s.**, bis dann.
**sometimes** ['sʌmtaimz], *adv*. manchmal.
**somewhat** ['sʌmwɔt], *adv*. (*a*) (*with adj.*) etwas; (*b*) **s. of a surprise**, eine ziemliche Überraschung.
**somewhere** ['sʌmwɛər], *adv*. **s. (or other)**, irgendwo; **s. else**, (irgend)wo anders.
**son** [sʌn], *s*. Sohn *m*. ◆**'son-in-law**, *s*. Schwiegersohn *m*.
**sonata** [sə'nɑːtə], *s*. Sonate *f*.
**song** [sɔŋ], *s*. Lied *n*. ◆**'songwriter**, *s*. Liedermacher *m*; (*classical*) Liederkomponist *m*.
**sonic** ['sɔnik], *adj*. Schall-.
**sonnet** ['sɔnit], *s*. Sonett *n*.
**sonorous** ['sɔnərəs], *adj*. (*of voice etc.*) klangvoll.
**soon** [suːn], *adv*. 1. bald; **s. after**, bald

darauf/danach; **as s. as possible**, möglichst bald. **2.** (*early*) **too s.**, zu früh; **how s. can you be ready?** wie schnell kannst du fertig sein? **3.** (*a*) **I would just as s. stay**, ich würde ebensogern bleiben; (*b*) **sooner**, (*rather*) lieber.

**soot** [sut], *s.* Ruß *m.* ◆**'sooty**, *adj.* rußig.

**soothe** [suːð], *v.tr.* (*a*) (j-n, j-s Zorn usw.) beruhigen; (*b*) (Schmerzen usw.) lindern.

**soppy** ['sɔpi], *adj.* F: (*silly*) doof; (*sentimental*) kitschig.

**sophisticated** [sə'fistikeitid], *adj.* **1.** (*of pers.*) weltklug; (*of tastes etc.*) verfeinert, anspruchsvoll; *Cl: etc:* hochelegant. **2.** (*of machine etc.*) hochentwickelt; (*of system*) raffiniert. ◆**sophisti'cation**, *s.* **1.** (*of pers.*) Weltklugheit *f.* **2.** Raffiniertheit *f*; hochentwickelter Stand (der Technik).

**soporific** [sɔpə'rifik]. **I.** *s.* Schlafmittel *n.* **II.** *adj.* einschläfernd.

**soprano**, *pl.* **-os** [sə'prɑːnəu, -əuz], *s. Mus:* (*a*) (*voice*) Sopran *m*; (*b*) (*pers.*) Sopranistin *f.*

**sorcerer** ['sɔːsərər], *s.* Zauberer *m.* ◆**'sorcery**, *s.* Zauberei *f.*

**sordid** ['sɔːdid], *adj.* elend; (*dirty*) dreckig; (*of story*) trist; (*unpleasant*) unschön.

**sore** [sɔːr]. **I.** *adj.* **1.** wund; **my finger is s.**, mein Finger tut weh. **2.** F: (*a*) (*of pers.*) ärgerlich; (*hurt*) gekränkt. **II.** *s.* wunde Stelle *f*; **-ly**, *adv.* sehr; **s. needed**, dringend gebraucht.

**sorrow** ['sɔrəu], *s.* (*a*) (*suffering*) Leid *n*; Kummer *m*; (*b*) (*regret*) Bedauern *n.* ◆**'sorrowful**, *adj.* kummervoll; (*of expression etc.*) traurig. ◆**'sorry**, *adj.* **l. he is s. that ...**, es tut ihm leid, daß ...; er bedauert, daß ...; **he was s. for her**, sie tat ihm leid; **I am s. to say**, ich muß leider sagen. **2.** (**I'm s.**)**!** Entschuldigung! **3.** (*pitiable*) **a s. sight/state**, ein erbärmlicher Anblick/Zustand.

**sort** [sɔːt]. **I.** *s.* **1.** (*a*) (*kind*) Sorte *f*; **two sorts of apple**, zwei Sorten Äpfel; **all sorts of people**, allerlei Leute; (*b*) Art *f*; **what s. of car have you got?** was für ein Auto haben Sie? **something of that s.**, etwas in der Art; (*c*) F: **s. of hot**, ziemlich warm. **2.** (*of pers.*) **he/she is a good s.**, er/sie ist ein guter Kerl. **3.** F: **out of sorts**, (i) (*health*) nicht ganz auf der Höhe; (ii) (*temper*) schlecht gelaunt. **II.** *v.tr.* (Gegenstände, Briefe usw.) sortieren. ◆**'sort 'out**, *v.tr.* (*a*) (etwas) aussortieren; (*b*) (eine Angelegenheit, Frage usw.) erledigen. ◆**'sorting**, *s.* Sortieren *n*; **s. office**, Sortierstelle *f.*

**soul** [səul], *s.* **1.** Seele *f*; **to put one's heart and s. into it**, mit Leib und Seele dabei sein; **he was the life and s. of the party**, er hielt die Party in Schwung. **2.** (*person*) **there wasn't a s. to be seen**, es war keine Menschenseele zu sehen; **poor s.!** armes Geschöpf! ◆**'soul-**

**destroying**, *adj.* geisttötend. ◆**'soulful**, *adj.* (*of eyes, look etc.*) traurig; (*of music*) gefühlvoll; *Pej:* gefühlsselig.

**sound¹** [saund]. **I.** *s.* **1.** (*a*) (*noise*) Geräusch *n*; (*b*) Schall *m* (einer Glocke usw.); *esp. Cin:* Ton *m*; **s. track**, Tonspur *f*; (*recording*) Filmmusik *f*; (*c*) (*uttered by pers. or animal*) Laut *m*; (*d*) (*tone*) Klang *m* (einer Stimme, eines Instruments usw.) **2. I don't like the s. of it**, es gefällt mir nicht. **II.** *v.* **1.** *v.i.* (*a*) (*of trumpet etc.*) schallen; (*of music*) erklingen; (*b*) klingen; **that sounds good**, das hört sich gut an; **it sounds like Mozart**, es klingt nach Mozart. **2.** *v.tr.* **to s. the alarm**, Alarm läuten. ◆**'soundless**, *adj.* lautlos. ◆**'soundproof**. **I.** *adj.* schalldicht. **II.** *v.tr.* (einen Raum usw.) schalldicht machen.

**sound²**, *v.tr. Nau:* (die Wassertiefe usw.) loten. ◆**'sounding**, *s.* **to take soundings**, loten.

**sound³**, *s. Geog:* Meerenge *f*; (*with name*) Sund *m.*

**sound³**, *adj.* **1.** (*healthy*) gesund. **2.** (*a*) (*sensible*) vernünftig; (*of judgement etc.*) folgerichtig; (*of argument etc.*) stichhaltig; **s. advice**, guter Rat; (*b*) *Com: Fin:* (*of investment*) solide; (*c*) (*thorough*) tüchtig. **3.** (*of sleep*) fest.

**soup** [suːp], *s.* Suppe *f*; **clear s.**, Bouillon *f*; **s. plate**, Suppenteller *m.*

**sour** [sauər]. **I.** *adj.* sauer; **to turn s.**, sauer werden. **II.** *v.tr.* (*a*) (etwas) säuern; (*b*) (j-n) verbittern. ◆**'sourness**, *s.* **1.** (*of fruit etc.*) Säure *f.* **2.** (*of pers.*) mürrisches Wesen *n.*

**source** [sɔːs], *s.* Quelle *f* (eines Flusses, *Fig:* der Freude usw.); (*origin*) Ursprung *m.*

**south** [sauθ]. **I.** *s.* **in the s.**, im Süden; **to the s. (of)**, südlich ( + *gen*). **II.** *adv.* südlich; **s. of London**, südlich von London; **to travel s.**, nach (dem) Süden fahren. **III.** *adj.* Süd-; **S. Africa**, Südafrika *n*; **S. African**, (i) *adj.* südafrikanisch; (ii) **s.** Südafrikaner(in) *m(f).* ◆**'south'east**. **I.** *s.* Südosten *m.* **II.** *adj.* Südost-; (*of wind*) südöstlich. **III.** *adv.* südöstlich (**of**, + *gen*/**with** *Pr. n.* von + *dat*); (*direction*) nach Südosten. ◆**'south-'eastern**, *adj.* südöstlich. ◆**'southerly** ['sʌðəli], *adj.* südlich. ◆**'southern** ['sʌðən], *adj.* südlich; ◆**'south-'west**. **I.** *s.* Südwesten *m.* **II.** *adj.* Südwest-. **III.** *adv.* südwestlich (**of**, + *gen*/**with** *Pr. n.* von + *dat*); (*direction*) nach Südwesten. ◆**'south-'western**, *adj.* südwestlich.

**souvenir** [suːvə'niːər], *s.* Andenken *n.*

**sovereign** ['sɔvrin]. **I.** *s.* **1.** Herrscher(in) *m(f).* **2.** (*gold coin*) Sovereign *m.* **II.** *adj.* **s. state**, unabhängiger Staat. ◆**'sovereignty**, *s.* Souveränität *f.*

**Soviet** ['səuviət, 'sɔvjət], *s.* Sowjet *m*; **S. Union**, Sowjetunion *f*; **Union of S.**

**Socialist Republics (USSR),** Union *f* der Sozialistischen Sowjetrepubliken (UdSSR).

**sow¹** [sǝu], *v.tr.irr.* säen.

**sow²** [sau], *s. Z:* Sau *f.*

**soya** ['sɔiǝ], *s. Cu:* **s. bean,** Sojabohne *f.*

**spa** [spɑ:], *s.* Kurort *m.*

**space** [speis]. **I. s. 1.** (*a*) (*concept*) Raum *m;* (*between objects, lines*) Abstand *m;* **blank s.,** Lücke *f;* (*b*) (*room*) Platz *m;* (*c*) (*area*) Fläche *f;* **in a confined s.,** auf engem Raum. **2.** (**outer**) **s.,** Weltraum *m;* **s. travel,** Weltraumfahrt *f.* **3. s.** (**of time**), Zeitraum *m;* **in the s. of a few minutes,** innerhalb weniger Minuten. **II.** *v.tr.* (*etwas*) in regelmäßigen Abständen verteilen. ◆**'spaceman,** *pl.* **-men,** *s.* Raumfahrer *m.* ◆**'spaceship,** *s.* Raumschiff *n.* ◆**'spacing,** *s.* Abstand *m* (zwischen den Zeilen usw.); **single/double s.,** einfacher/doppelter Zeilenabstand. ◆**'spacious** [-ʃǝs], *adj.* geräumig.

**spade¹** [speid], *s.* Spaten *m.*

**spade²,** *s.* Pik *n;* **queen of spades,** Pikdame *f.*

**spaghetti** [spǝ'geti], *s.* Spaghetti *pl.*

**Spain** [spein]. *Pr. n.* Spanien *n.*

**span** [spæn]. **I. s. 1.** Spannweite *f* (einer Brücke usw.). **2. s.** (**of time**), Zeitspanne *f;* **life s.,** Lebensdauer *f.* **II.** *v.tr.* (*a*) (*of bridge etc.*) **to s. sth.,** sich über etwas *acc* spannen; (*b*) (*of life, reign etc.*) (*einen Zeitraum*) umspannen.

**Spaniard** ['spænjǝd], *s.* Spanier(in) *m(f).*

**spaniel** ['spænjǝl], *s.* Spaniel *m.*

**Spanish** ['spæniʃ]. **I.** *adj.* spanisch. **II.** *s.* Spanisch *n.*

**spank** [spæŋk], *v.tr.* **to s. a child,** einem Kind den Hintern versohlen.

**spanner** ['spænǝr], *s.* Schraubenschlüssel *m.*

**spar** [spɑ:r], *v.i.* (*a*) *Sp:* sparren; (*b*) *Fig:* **to s. with s.o.,** mit j-m argumentieren.

**spare** [speǝr]. **I.** *adj.* (*a*) überschüssig; **s. time,** Freizeit *f;* **s. room,** Gästezimmer *n;* (*b*) *Aut: etc:* **s. part,** Ersatzteil *n;* **s. wheel,** Reserverad *n.* **II.** *v.tr.* (*a*) (*do without*) (*etwas*) entbehren; **to have nothing to s.,** nichts übrig haben; (*b*) (*not hurt*) (j-n, j-s Gefühle usw.) schonen; (*c*) (*save*) **to s. you the trouble,** um Ihnen die Mühe zu (er)sparen. **III.** *s. Aut: etc:* Ersatzteil *n.* ◆**'sparing,** *adj.* sparsam.

**spark** [spɑ:k]. **I. s.** (*a*) Funke *m;* (*b*) *Fig:* Funken *m.* **II.** *v.i.* funken; **s. plug,** Zündkerze *f.* ◆**'spark 'off,** *v.tr.* (*etwas*) auslösen.

**sparkle** ['spɑ:kl]. **I. s.** Funkeln *n.* **II.** *v.i.* funkeln; (*of wine*) perlen. ◆**'sparkling,** *adj.* funkelnd; **s. wine,** Schaumwein *m.*

**sparrow** ['spærǝu], *s.* Spatz *m.*

**sparse** [spɑ:s], *adj.* (*a*) (*of population etc.*) dünn; **s. hair,** schütteres Haar; **s. vegetation,** spärlicher Pflanzenwuchs; (*b*) (*rare*) selten; **-ly,** *adv.* dünn.

**spasm** ['spæz(ǝ)m], *s. Med:* Krampf *m.* ◆**spas'modic,** *adj.* (*a*) *Med:* krampfar-

tig; (*b*) unregelmäßig; **-ally,** *adv.* hin und wieder.

**spastic** ['spæstik]. *Med:* **I.** *adj.* spastisch; (*of pers.*) spastisch gelähmt. **II.** *s.* Spastiker *m.*

**spate** [speit], *s.* **1. the river is in (full) s.,** der Fluß führt Hochwasser. **2.** *Fig:* Flut *f* (von Worten, Briefen usw.).

**spatial** ['speiʃ(ǝ)l], *adj.* räumlich.

**spatter** ['spætǝr], *v.tr.* bespritzen.

**spatula** ['spætjulǝ], *s.* Spachtel *m.*

**spawn** [spɔ:n]. **I. s.** Laich *m;* **frog s.,** Froschlaich *m.* **II.** *v.* **1.** *v.i.* (*of fish, frog etc.*) laichen. **2.** *v.tr.* (*of fish, frog etc.*) (*Eier*) ablegen.

**speak** [spi:k], *v.irr.* **1.** *v.i.* (*a*) sprechen; **to s. to s.o.,** (i) (*address*) j-n ansprechen; (ii) (*converse with*) mit j-m sprechen (**about,** über + *acc*); *Tel:* **who is (it) speaking?** wer ist am Apparat? (*b*) *generally speaking,* im allgemeinen; *strictly speaking,* genaugenommen; (*c*) (*make a speech*) sprechen; eine Rede halten. **2.** *v.tr.* (*a*) **to s. the truth,** die Wahrheit sagen; (*b*) **to s. German,** Deutsch sprechen. ◆**'speaker,** *s.* Redner *m;* **to be a fluent s.,** flüssig reden; *Pol: Brit:* **the S.,** der Präsident (des Unterhauses). ◆**'speak 'for,** *v.i.* (*a*) **to s. f. s.o.,** (*support*) j-n unterstützen; (*on behalf of*) in j-s Namen spechen; **s. f. yourself!** das ist (wohl) Ihre Meinung! ◆**'speaking,** *adj.* **English-s.,** englischsprechend. ◆**'speak of,** *v.i.* (j-n, etwas) erwähnen. ◆**'speak 'out,** *v.i.* seine Meinung offen sagen. ◆**'speak 'up,** *v.i.* (*a*) lauter sprechen; (*b*) **to s. up for s.o.,** für j-n eintreten.

**spear** ['spiǝr]. **I. s.** Speer *m.* **II.** *v.tr.* mit dem Speer durchbohren.

**special** ['speʃ(ǝ)l]. **I.** *adj.* besondere(r, s) Sonder-; **s. case,** Sonderfall *m; Com:* **s. offer,** Sonderangebot *n.* **II. s. 1.** Sondernummer *f* (einer Zeitung usw.). **2.** (*train*) Sonderzug *m.* **3.** (*in restaurant*) *F:* **today's s.,** Spezialität *f* des Tages; **-ly,** *adv.* (*a*) besonders; **s. good,** besonders gut; (*b*) **I came s.,** ich bin extra gekommen. ◆**'specialist,** *s.* Spezialist *m.* ◆**speciality** [-i'æliti], *s.* Spezialität *f.* ◆**specialization** [-ǝlai'zeiʃ(ǝ)n], *s.* Spezialisierung *f;* (*subject*) Spezialfach *n.* ◆**'specialize,** *v.i.* sich spezialisieren (**in,** auf + *acc*).

**species** ['spi:si:z], *s. Z: etc:* Art *f.*

**specific** [spǝ'sifik], *adj.* (*of statement, orders etc.*) genau; **a s. purpose,** ein bestimmter Zweck; **-ally,** *adv.* genau; **he s. mentioned it,** er hat es ausdrücklich erwähnt. ◆**specifi'cation,** *s.* (*a*) Spezifizierung *f;* (*description*) Beschreibung *f;* (*b*) (*data*) **technical s.,** technische Daten. ◆**specify** ['spesifai], *v.tr.* (*a*) (*state*) (Zweck usw.) genau angeben; (*state Gründe usw.*) nennen; (*b*) (*prescribe*) (etwas) vorschreiben.

**specimen** ['spesimin], *s.* (*a*) (*example*) Exemplar *n;* (*b*) (*sample*) Probe *f.*

**speck** [spek], *s.* (kleiner) Fleck *m;* **s. of dust,** Staubkorn *n.* ◆**'speckled,** *adj.* gesprenkelt.

**spectacle** ['spektəkl], *s.* **1.** (*a*) (*public show*) Schau *f;* Fig: Schauspiel *n;* **to make a s. of oneself,** sich auffällig benehmen/kleiden; (*b*) (*sight*) Anblick *m.* **2. (pair of) spectacles,** Brille *f.* ◆**spectacular** [-'tækjulər], *adj.* spektakulär. ◆**spectator** [-'teitər], *s.* Zuschauer(in) *m(f)*.

**spectre** ['spektər], *s.* Gespenst *n.*

**spectrum,** *pl.* **-tra** ['spektrəm, -trə], *s.* Spektrum *n.*

**speculate** ['spekjuleit], *v.i.* (*a*) **to s. about sth.,** Mutmaßungen über etwas *acc* anstellen; (*b*) Fin: spekulieren (**on,** auf + *acc*). ◆**specu'lation,** *s.* **1.** Mutmaßung *f* (**about,** über + *acc*). **2.** Fin: Spekulation *f.* ◆**'speculative** [-lətiv], *adj.* (*a*) (*of pers., mood etc.*) grüblerisch; (*b*) Fin: spekulativ.

**speech** ['spi:tʃ], *s.* **1.** (*a*) Sprache *f;* **freedom of s.,** Redefreiheit *f;* (*b*) (*way of talking*) Sprechweise *f;* (*c*) Gram: **indirect s.,** indirekte Rede; **part of s.,** Wortart *f.* **2.** (*address*) Rede *f;* **to make a s.,** eine Rede halten. ◆**'speechless,** *adj.* sprachlos (**with,** vor + *dat*).

**speed** [spi:d]. **I.** *s.* **1.** Geschwindigkeit *f;* **at s.,** in voller Fahrt. **2.** Aut: etc: (*gear*) Gang *m.* *n* **II.** *v.i.irr* schnell fahren; F: sausen; **to s. along,** dahinsausen. ◆**'speedboat,** *s.* Schnellboot *n.* ◆**'speeding,** *s.* Überschreitung *f* der zulässigen Geschwindigkeit. ◆**spee'dometer,** *s.* Tachometer *m.* ◆**'speed 'up, *v.i.* 1.** schneller werden; (*accelerate*) beschleunigen. **2.** *v.tr.* **to s. sth. up,** etwas beschleunigen. ◆**'speedy,** *adj.* zügig; (*fast*) schnell; **s. reply/recovery,** baldige Antwort/Genesung.

**spell¹** [spel], *s.* Zauberspruch *m;* Fig: Bann *m;* **to cast a s. over s.o.,** j-n verzaubern. ◆**'spellbound,** *adj.* (wie) gebannt.

**spell²** [spel], *v.tr.irr.* **1.** *v.tr.* (*a*) (*in Wort*) schreiben; **how do you s. it?** wie wird es geschrieben? **to s. a word (out),** (*aloud*) ein Wort buchstabieren; (*b*) (*mean*) bedeuten. **2.** *v.i.* rechtschreiben. ◆**'spelling,** *s.* Rechtschreibung *f.* ◆**'spell 'out,** *v.tr.* (*Worte*) buchstabieren; (*b*) (*etwas*) im einzelnen darlegen.

**spell³,** *s.* Periode *f;* **cold s.,** Kältewelle *f;* **for a s.,** eine Zeitlang.

**spend** [spend], *v.tr.* (*a*) (*Geld*) ausgeben (**on,** für + *acc*); (*b*) **to s. a lot of time on sth.,** etwas *dat* viel Zeit widmen; (*c*) (*Zeit*) verbringen. ◆**'spending,** *s.* Ausgeben *n* (von Geld); **s. power,** Kaufkraft *f.* ◆**'spendthrift,** *s.* Verschwender *m.* ◆**spent,** *adj.* (*of pers., powers etc.*) erschöpft; (*of bullet etc.*) verbraucht.

**sperm** [spə:m], *s.* Samen *m.* ◆**'spermwhale,** *s.* Pottwal *m.*

**spew** [spju:], *v.tr.* **to s. sth. (out),** etwas ausspeien.

**sphere** ['sfi(:)ər], *s.* **1.** Mth: Kugel *f.* **2.** Bereich *m;* **in the political s.,** in der politischen Sphäre; **s. of activity,** Tätigkeitsbereich *m.* ◆**spherical** ['sfe-], *adj.* kugelförmig.

**spice** [spais]. **I.** *s.* Gewürz *n.* ◆**'spicy,** *adj.* (*a*) (*of food*) würzig; (*b*) (*of story etc.*) pikant.

**spick and span** ['spik ən(d) 'spæn], *adj.* (*of room etc.*) blitzblank; (*of pers.*) geschniegelt.

**spider** ['spaidər], *s.* Spinne *f.*

**spike** [spaik], *s.* (*on railing, stick etc.*) Spitze *f;* (*on barbed wire etc.*) Stachel *m.* ◆**'spiky,** *adj.* stachelig; (*pointed*) spitz.

**spill** [spil], *v.irr.* **1.** *v.tr.* (Wasser, Milch usw.) verschütten. **2.** *v.i.* (*of liquid*) verschüttet werden.

**spin** [spin]. **I.** *v.irr.* **1.** *v.tr.* (*a*) (Garn usw.) spinnen. **2.** *v.i.* (*of top, wheel etc.*) sich drehen; (*of aircraft*) trudeln; (*of pers.*) **to s. round,** sich plötzlich umdrehen. **II.** *s.* Sp: Drall *m;* **to put s. on the ball,** dem Ball einen Drall geben. ◆**'spin-'drier,** *s.* Wäscheschleuder *f.* ◆**'spinning,** *s.* Spinnen *n;* Ind: Spinnerei *f;* **s. wheel,** Spinnrad *n.* ◆**'spin-off,** *s.* Abfallprodukt *m;* Fig: Nebenwirkung *f.* ◆**'spin 'out,** *v.tr.* (eine Geschichte) in die Länge ziehen.

**spinach** ['spinidʒ], *s.* Spinat *m.*

**spindle** [spindl], *s.* Spindel *f;* (*shaft*) Welle *f.*

**spine** [spain], *s.* **1.** Anat: Wirbelsäule *f.* **2.** (*of book*) Rücken *m.* **3.** (*prickle*) Stachel *m.* ◆**'spine-chilling,** *adj.* gruselig. ◆**'spineless,** *adj.* **he's s.,** er hat kein Rückgrat.

**spinster** ['spinstər], *s.* unverheiratete Frau *f;* (*old*) alte Jungfer *f.*

**spiral** ['spaiərəl]. **I.** *s.* Spirale *f.* **II.** *adj.* gewunden; **s. staircase,** Wendeltreppe *f.* **III.** *v.i.* (in Spiralen) hochwirbeln; (*of prices etc.*) in die Höhe schießen.

**spire** ['spaiər], *s.* Turmspitze *f.*

**spirit** ['spirit]. **I.** *s.* **1.** Geist *m;* (*of pers.*) **kindred spirits,** verwandte Seelen. **2.** (*a*) (*mood*) Stimmung *f;* **to enter into the s. of sth.,** etwas mit Hingabe mitmachen; (*b*) *pl.* **spirits,** Gemütsverfassung *f;* **in high spirits,** übermütig. **3.** (*alcohol*) *usu. pl.* Spirituosen *pl;* **surgical s.,** Wundbenzin *n.* **II.** *v.tr.* **to s. s.o., sth. away,** j-n, etwas wegzaubern. ◆**'spirited,** *adj.* (*of pers.*) temperamentvoll; (*of discussion*) lebhaft; (*of bravade, defence, speech*) feurig. ◆**'spiritual. I.** *adj.* **1.** (*of the spirit*) geistig. **2.** Ecc: geistlich. **II.** *s.* (*negro*) **s.,** Spiritual *n.* ◆**'spiritualism,** *s.* Spiritismus *m.*

**spit¹** [spit], *s.* **1.** Cu: Bratspieß *m.* **2.** Geog: Landzunge *f.*

**spit²,** *v.i.irr.* spucken; (*of cat*) fauchen; **it's spitting (with rain),** es tröpfelt. ◆**'spittle,** *s.* Speichel *m.*

**spite** [spait]. **I.** *s.* **1.** Bosheit *f.* **2.** *prep. phr.* **in s. of**, trotz + *gen*; **in s. of everything**, trotz allem. **II.** *v.tr.* **he did it to s. her**, er tat es ihr zum Trotz. ◆'**spiteful**, *adj.* gehässig.

**splash** [splæʃ]. **I.** *s.* **1.** (*a*) (*sound*) Klatsch *m*; Platschen *n*; (*b*) (*mark*) Spritzer *m.* **2.** (*of colour, light*) Fleck *m.* **II.** *v.* **1.** *v.i.* (*of waves etc.*) klatschen; (*of tap*) spritzen; **to s. about**, planschen. **2.** *v.tr.* (j-n, etwas, sich) bespritzen. ◆'**splash 'down**, *v.tr.* (*of spacecraft*) wassern. ◆'**splash-down**, *s.* Wasserung *f.*

**splendid** ['splendid], *adj.* herrlich; (*magnificent*) prächtig. ◆'**splendour**, *s.* Pracht *f.*

**splint** [splint], *s.* Schiene *f.*

**splinter** ['splintər]. **I.** *s.* Splitter *m.* **II.** *v.i.* splittern.

**split** [split]. **I.** *s.* Riß *m* (im Stoff usw.); *Pol:* **a s. in the party**, eine Spaltung innerhalb der Partei; *Sp:* **to do the splits**, Spagat machen. **II.** *v.irr.* **1.** *v.tr.* (*a*) spalten; (*when bargaining*) **to s. the difference**, sich in der Mitte treffen. **2.** *v.i.* (*of wood etc.*) sich spalten; (*of seam etc.*) platzen. **III.** *adj.* gespalten; **s. peas**, geschälte Erbsen. ◆'**split-'level**, *adj.* auf zwei Ebenen. ◆'**split 'up**, *v.* **1.** *v.i.* (*of couple*) auseinandergehen. **2.** *v.tr.* (etwas) aufteilen (**into**, in + *acc*).

**splutter** ['splʌtər], *v.i.* (*of pers., engine*) stottern.

**spoil** [spɔil]. **I.** *v.irr.* **1.** *v.i.* (*a*) (*of food*) schlecht werden; (*b*) (*of pers.*) **spoiling for a fight**, streitlustig. **2.** *v.tr.* (*a*) (etwas) verderben; (*b*) (ein Kind usw.) verwöhnen. **II.** *s.* *usu.* *pl.* Beute *f.* ◆'**spoilsport**, *s.* Spielverderber *m.* ◆'**spoilt**, *adj.* verdorben; **a s. child**, ein verwöhntes Kind.

**spoke** [spəuk], *s.* (*of wheel*) Speiche *f.*

**spoken** ['spəukən], *adj. Hum:* **s. for**, vergeben.

**spokesman**, *pl.* **-men** ['spəuksmən, -men], *s.* Wortführer *m*; **government s.**, Regierungssprecher *m.*

**sponge** [spʌn(d)ʒ]. **I.** *s.* **1.** Schwamm *m.* **2.** *Cu:* **s.**(-**cake**), Biskuitkuchen *m.* **II.** *v.tr.* (etwas) mit einem Schwamm abwischen. ◆'**sponger**, *s. F:* Schmarotzer *m.* ◆'**spongy**, *adj.* schwammig; (*of ground*) sumpfig.

**sponsor** ['spɔnsər]. **I.** *s.* (*backer*) Förderer *m*; *Com:* Bürge *m*; (*in advertising, Sp:*) Sponsor *m.* **II.** *v.tr.* (j-n, etwas) fördern; *Com:* (für j-n) bürgen; *Rad: TV:* (eine Sendung) (als Sponsor) finanzieren; *Sp:* (j-n, eine Mannschaft usw.) sponsern. ◆'**sponsorship**, *s.* Unterstützung *f*; *Com:* Bürgschaft *f*; *Sp:* Sponsern *n.*

**spontaneous** [spɔn'teinjəs], *adj.* spontan. ◆**spontaneity** [spɔntə'ni:iti]/ ◆**spon'taneousness**, *s.* Spontaneität *f.*

**spool** [spu:l], *s.* Spule *f.*

**spoon** [spu:n]. **I.** *s.* Löffel *m.* **II.** *v.tr.* **to s. sth.** (**up**), etwas löffeln. ◆'**spoonful**,

**s. a s. of soup**, ein Löffel Suppe.

**sporadic** [spɔ'rædik], *adj.* sporadisch.

**sport** [spɔ:t]. **I.** *s.* **1.** (*a*) Sport *m*; (**type of**) **s.**, Sportart *f*; (*b*) *attrib.* Sport-; **sports car**, Sportwagen *m*; **sports jacket**, Sakko *m.* **2.** (*fun*) Spaß *m.* **3.** (*pers.*) **a good s.**, ein guter Kerl. **II.** *v.tr.* (eine Blume im Knopfloch usw.) tragen. ◆'**sporting**, *adj.* sportlich; **s. chance**, ziemlich gute Chance. ◆'**sportsman**, *pl.* **-men**, *pl.* **-woman**, *pl.* **-women**, *s.* **1.** Sportler(in) *m(f).* **2.** (*fair player*) Sportsmann *m.* ◆'**sporty**, *adj.* sportlich.

**spot** [spɔt]. **I.** *s.* **1.** Punkt *m*; Fleck *m.* **2.** (*a*) (*place*) Ort *m*; (*b*) (*exact position*) Stelle *f*; **on the s.**, (i) zur Stelle; (ii) (*there and then*) an Ort und Stelle; (iii) (*immediately*) auf der Stelle; **s. check**, Stichprobe *f*; *F:* **to put s.o. on the s.**, j-n in Verlegenheit bringen. **3.** (*on face etc.*) Pickel *m*; (*rash*) Ausschlag *m.* **4.** (*drop*) Tropfen *m* (Regen). **II.** *v.* **1.** *v.i.* **it's spotting with rain**, es tröpfelt. **2.** *v.tr.* (*catch sight of*) (j-n, etwas) erkennen. ◆'**spotless**, *adj.* fleckenlos; (*immaculate*) makellos. ◆'**spotlight**. **I.** *s. Th: etc:* Spotlight *n.* **II.** *v.tr. Fig:* (j-n, etwas) herausstellen. ◆'**spot-'on**, *adj.* genau richtig. ◆'**spotted**, *adj.* (*of material*) getupft; (*of animal*) gefleckt; (*speckled*) gesprenkelt. ◆'**spotty**, *adj.* (*of face etc.*) pickelig.

**spouse** [spauz], *s. Jur:* Ehepartner(in) *m(f)*; *Hum:* Gatte *m*, Gattin *f.*

**spout** [spaut]. **I.** *s.* **1.** Schnauze *f* (einer Kanne usw.); (*for rainwater*) Ausguß *m*; (*of pump*) Hahn *m.* **II.** *v.i.* (heraus)spritzen.

**sprain** [sprein]. **I.** *s.* Verstauchung *f.* **II.** *v.tr.* **to s. one's ankle/wrist**, sich *dat* den Fuß/die Hand verstauchen.

**sprat** [spræt], *s.* Sprotte *f.*

**sprawl** [sprɔ:l], *v.i.* (*of pers.*) (behaglich) ausgestreckt liegen/sitzen; *F:* (sich) rekeln; (*b*) (*of town*) sich weit ausdehnen.

**spray¹** [sprei], *s.* **s. of flowers**, Blütenzweig *m.*

**spray²**. **I.** *s.* **1.** (*of sea etc.*) Gischt *f.* **2.** (*a*) (*for hair, plants etc.*) Spray *m* or *n*; (*b*) (*atomizer*) Sprühdose *f.* **II.** *v.* **1.** *v.i.* (*of liquid*) sprühen. **2.** *v.tr.* (*a*) (eine Flüssigkeit) zerstäuben; (*b*) *Agr:* (Bäume, Getreide usw.) spritzen; *Ind:* (ein Auto usw.) spritzen.

**spread** [spred]. **I.** *s.* **1.** *Fig:* (*range*) Umfang *m.* **2.** (*process*) Verbreitung *f* (des Wissens, der Krankheit usw.). **3.** *F:* (*meal*) Schmaus *m.* **4.** (*on bread*) Aufstrich *m.* **II.** *v.irr.* **1.** *v.i.* (*of news, disease etc.*) sich verbreiten; (*of fire, area of land*) sich ausbreiten. **2.** *v.tr.* (*a*) **to s.** (**out**), etwas ausbreiten; (*b*) (Krankheit, eine Nachricht usw.) verbreiten; (*c*) (Brot mit Butter usw.) bestreichen; **to s. butter on bread**, Butter aufs Brot streichen.

**spree** [spri:], *s.* **shopping s.**, Einkaufsbummel *m.*

**sprig** [sprig], *s.* Zweig *m.*

**sprightly** ['spraitli], *adj.* lebhaft; (*of old pers.*) rüstig.

**spring** [spriŋ]. **I.** *s.* 1. (*jump*) Sprung *m.* 2. (*of water*) Quelle *f.* 3. (*season*) Frühling *m.* 4. **s. tide**, Springflut *f.* 5. (*a*) (*elasticity*) Elastizität *f;* (*b*) (*device*) Feder *f.* **II.** *v.irr.* 1. *v.i.* (*a*) springen; (*b*) (*arise*) entstammen (**from**, *dat*). 2. *v.tr.* (*a*) **to s. sth. on s.o.**, j-n mit etwas *dat* überraschen; (*b*) **to s. a leak**, ein Leck bekommen. ◆**'springboard**, *s.* Sprungbrett *n.* ◆**'spring-'cleaning**, *s.* Frühjahrsputz *m.* ◆**'spring 'up**, *v.i.* (*of breeze, Fig: doubt etc.*) aufkommen; (*of plant*) aufschießen. ◆**'springy**, *adj.* (*of gait etc.*) federnd.

**sprinkle** ['spriŋkl], *v.tr.* (*a*) (Wasser usw.) sprengen; (Sand, Zucker) streuen; (*b*) **to s. s.o., sth. with water**, j-n, etwas mit Wasser besprengen/berieseln. ◆**'sprinkler**, *s.* Sprinkler *m.*

**sprint** [sprint]. **I.** *s.* (*a*) (*race*) Sprint *m;* (*b*) (*spurt*) Spurt *m.* **II.** *v.i.* (*a*) sprinten; (*b*) (*spurt*) spurten. ◆**'sprinter**, *s.* Sprinter *m;* Kurzstreckenläufer *m.*

**sprout** [spraut]. **I.** *v.i.* (*a*) (*of seed*) treiben; (*of plant*) sprießen; (*b*) (*of plant etc.*) hochschießen. **II.** *s.* Sproß *m;* (**Brussels**) **sprouts**, Rosenkohl *m.*

**spruce** [spru:s], *s.* (*tree*) Fichte *f.*

**sprung** [sprʌŋ], *adj.* **well/badly s.**, gut/ schlecht gefedert.

**spur** [spə:r]. **I.** *s.* 1. Sporn *m.* 2. (*incitement*) Ansporn *m;* **on the s. of the moment**, ganz spontan; (*of decision*) plötzlich. 3. *Geog:* Ausläufer *m.* **II.** *v.tr. Fig:* **to s. s.o. on**, j-n anspornen.

**spurious** ['spjuəriəs], *adj.* falsch.

**spurn** [spə:n], *v.tr.* verschmähen.

**spurt** [spə:t]. **I.** *v.i.* (*a*) (*of liquid, flames etc.*) **to s. out**, hervorschießen; **to s. up**, emporschießen; (*b*) *Sp:* spurten. **II.** *s.* 1. **s. of water**, plötzlich hervorschießender Wasserstrahl; **s. of energy**, plötzlicher Tatendrang. 2. *Sp:* Spurt *m.*

**spy** [spai]. **I.** *s.* Spion(in) *m(f).* **II.** *v.* 1. *v.i.* spionieren; **to s. on s.o.**, j-m nachspionieren. 2. *v.tr.* (*see*) erspähen. ◆**'spying**, *s.* Spionage *f.*

**squabble** ['skwɔbl]. **I.** *v.i.* zanken. **II.** *s.* Zank *m.* ◆**'squabbling**, *s.* Gezänk *n.*

**squad** [skwɔd], *s.* 1. *Mil: etc:* Kommando *n;* **firing s.**, Exekutionskommando *n.* 2. Mannschaft *f.*

**squadron** ['skwɔdrən], *s.* (*a*) *Mil:* (*armoured*) Kompanie *f;* (*cavalry*) Schwadron *n;* (*b*) *Nau:* Geschwader *n;* (*c*) *Av:* Staffel *f.*

**squalid** ['skwɔlid], *adj.* elend. ◆**'squalor**, *s.* Elend *n.*

**squall** [skwɔ:l], *s.* Bö *f.* ◆**'squally**, *adj.* böig.

**squander** ['skwɔndər], *v.tr.* vergeuden.

**square** [skwɛər]. **I.** *s.* (*a*) (*figure*) Quadrat *n;* (*on chessboard, map etc.*) Feld *n.* 2. (*in town*) Platz *m.* 3. *Mth:* **the s. of a number**, die zweite Potenz einer Zahl. 4. (**set**) **s.**, Winkel *m.* **II.** *adj.* 1. (*a*) quadratisch; (*b*) (*of shoulders, chin etc.*) eckig. 2. *Mth:* Quadrat-; **s. root**, Quadratwurzel *f;* **two metres s.**, zwei Meter im Quadrat. 3. (*a*) **to get things s.**, alles in Ordnung bringen; (*b*) **to give s.o. a s. deal**, j-n fair behandeln; (*c*) **a s. meal**, ein ordentliches Essen. **III.** *adv. Fig:* **fair and s.**, (*above-board*) einwandfrei. **IV.** *v.* 1. *v.tr.* (*a*) *Mth:* (eine Zahl) zur zweiten Potenz erheben; (*b*) (etwas mit etwas *dat*) in Einklang bringen. 2. *v.i.* **to s. up with s.o.**, mit j-m abrechnen. ◆**squared**, *adj.* **s. paper**, kariertes Papier.

**squash** [skwɔʃ]. **I.** *v.* 1. *v.tr.* (etwas) zerdrücken. 2. *v.i.* (*a*) (*of fruit etc.*) zerdrückt werden; (*b*) (*of people*) sich quetschen (**into a car etc.**, in einen Wagen usw.). **II.** *s.* 1. Gedränge *n.* 2. **orange s.**, Orangengetränk *n.* 3. *Sp:* **s. (rackets)**, Squash *n.*

**squat** [skwɔt]. **I.** *v.i.* (*a*) hocken; **to s. down**, sich hinkauern; (*b*) **to s. in a house**, ein Haus besetzt haben. **II.** *adj.* untersetzt. ◆**'squatter**, *s.* Hausbesetzer *m.*

**squawk** [skwɔ:k]. **I.** *v.i.* kreischen. **II.** *s.* Kreischen *n.*

**squeak** [skwi:k]. **I.** *v.i.* (*a*) (*of mouse etc.*) piepsen; (*b*) (*of hinge, shoes, etc.*) quietschen. **II.** *s.* (*a*) Piepser *m;* (*b*) Quietschen *n.*

**squeal** [skwi:l], *v.i.* (*a*) (*of child etc.*) quietschen; **to s. with fear**, vor Angst schreien; (*b*) (*of pig*) quieken; (*c*) *P:* (*turn informer*) singen.

**squeamish** ['skwi:miʃ], *adj.* überempfindlich.

**squeeze** [skwi:z], *v.tr.* (*a*) drücken; (Saft, eine Zitrone usw.) auspressen; (*b*) (*force*) (etwas in einen Koffer usw.) quetschen.

**squelch** [skweltʃ], *v.i.* **to s. through the mud**, durch den Morast quatschen.

**squib** [skwib], *s.* Knallfrosch *m.*

**squint** [skwint], **I.** *v.i.* schielen (**at**, auf + *acc*). **II.** *s.* Schielen *n.*

**squirm** [skwə:m], *v.i.* (*of worm, Fig: of pers. etc.*) sich winden.

**squirrel** ['skwirəl], *s.* Eichhörnchen *n.*

**squirt** [skwə:t]. **I.** *v.* 1. *v.i.* (*of liquid*) **to s. (out)**, (heraus)spritzen. 2. *v.tr.* (Wasser, Sahne usw.) spritzen. **II.** *s.* (*jet*) Strahl *m;* **a s. of soda**, ein Spritzer *m* Soda.

**stab** [stæb]. **I.** *v.tr.* (mit) **to s. s.o.**, auf j-n einstechen; **to s. s.o. to death**, j-n erstechen. **II.** *s.* Stoß *m* (mit dem Dolch usw.); (*wound*) Stichwunde *f; Fig:* **s. in the back**, Dolchstoß *m.*

**stable[1]** ['steibl]. **I.** *s.* Stall *m.* **II.** *v.tr.* (ein Pferd) einstallen.

**stable[2]**, *adj.* stabil; (*lasting*) dauerhaft; (*of pers.*) ausgeglichen. ◆**stability** [stə'biliti], *s.* Stabilität *f;* Ausgeglichenheit *f* (einer Person). ◆**'stabilize**, *v.tr.* stabilisieren.

**stack** [stæk]. **I.** *s.* 1. **s. of wood/books**

etc., Stapel *m* Holz/Bücher usw. 2.
Schornstein *m*; *(of factory)* Fabrikschlot
*m*. **II.** *v.tr.* **to s. sth. (up)**, etwas
(auf)stapeln.

**stadium**, *pl.* **-ia, -iums** ['steidiəm, -iə,
-iəmz], *s.* Stadion *n*.

**staff** [stɑːf], *s.* **1.** *(pole)* Stab *m*. **2.** *(a)* Personal *n*; *Sch:* **(teaching) s.**, Lehrkörper
*m*; **editorial s.**, Redaktion *f*; *(b) Mil:*
Stab *m*. **II.** *v.tr.* (ein Büro usw.) mit Personal besetzen.

**stag** [stæg], *s.* Hirsch *m*.

**stage** [steidʒ]. **I.** *s.* **1.** *Th:* Bühne *f*; **s.
directions**, Bühnenanweisungen *fpl*; **s.
fright**, Lampenfieber *n*. **2.** *(a)* Stadium *n*;
*(in development)* Entwicklungsstufe *f*; **at
an early s.**, in einem frühen Stadium; *(b)*
Etappe *f* (einer Reise, eines Rennens); **by
(easy) stages**, etappenweise. **3. landing
s.**, Landungssteg *m*. **II.** *v.tr.* (ein Stück,
eine Demonstration usw.) inszenieren.

**stagger** ['stægər], *v.* **1.** *v.i.* schwanken;
*(nearly fall)* taumeln. **2.** *v.tr.* *(a)* (j-n) erschüttern; *(b) Tchn:* (etwas) versetzt anordnen. ◆**'staggered**, *adj.* *(a)* erstaunt;
*(b) (of hours, holidays)* gestaffelt; *(c) Tchn:*
versetzt. ◆**'staggering**, *adj.* *(of news)*
umwerfend.

**stagnant** ['stægnənt], *adj.* *(a)* **s. water**,
stehendes Wasser; *(b) (of trade etc.)* **to be
s.**, stocken. ◆**stag'nate**, *v.i.* *(of water,
also Fig:)* stagnieren; *(of pers.)* geistig abstumpfen.

**staid** [steid], *adj.* *(of pers.)* gesetzt.

**stain** [stein]. **I.** *s.* **1.** *(a)* Fleck *m*; **s. remover**, Fleckenentferner *m*; *(b) Fig:* Ma-
kel *m* (**on**, an + *dat*). **2.** *(for wood)* Beize
*f*. **II.** *v.tr.* *(a)* (ein Kleid, Fig: j-s Ruf)
beflecken; *(b)* (Glas usw.) färben; (Holz)
beizen; **stained glass**, bemaltes Glas.
◆**'stainless**, *adj.* unbefleckt; **s. steel**,
rostfreier Stahl.

**stair** [steər], *s.* *(a)* Stufe *f*; *(b) pl.* **stairs**
*(also staircase)* Treppe *f*.

**stake** [steik]. **I.** *s.* **1.** *(post)* Pfahl *m*. **2.**
*(money)* Einsatz *m*; **to have a s. in sth.**,
an etwas *dat* (finanziell) beteiligt sein;
*Fig:* **to be at s.**, auf dem Spiel stehen.
**II.** *v.tr.* (eine Geldsumme usw.) setzen
(**on**, auf + *acc*).

**stalactite** ['stæləktait], *s.* Stalaktit *m*.

**stalagmite** ['stæləgmait], *s.* Stalagmit *m*.

**stale** [steil], *adj.* *(a) (of bread)* alt(backen);
*(of beer)* abgestanden; *(of air)* verbraucht;
*(b) (of smell etc.)* muffig. ◆**'stalemate**,
*s.* (*in chess*) Patt *n*. **2.** *Fig:* **the talks
have reached a s.**, die Verhandlungen
sind in eine Sackgasse geraten.

**stalk**¹ [stɔːk], *v.* **1.** *v.i.* stolzieren. **2.** *v.tr.*
sich (an j-n, etwas *acc*) anschleichen.

**stalk**², *s.* Stiel *m*.

**stall** [stɔːl]. **I.** *s.* **1.** *(for horses & at market
etc.)* Stand *m*. **2.** *Ecc:* Stuhl *m*. **3.** *Th:*
**stalls**, Parkett *n*. **II.** *v.* **1.** *v.tr.* *(a) Aut:*
(den Motor) abwürgen; *(b) Fig:* **to s. s.o.**,
j-n hinhalten. **2.** *v.i.* *(a) Aut:* *(of engine)*
absterben; *(b) Fig:* *(of pers.)* Ausflüchte

machen.

**stallion** ['stæljən], *s.* Hengst *m*.

**stamina** ['stæminə], *s.* Durchhaltevermögen *n*; *esp. Sp:* Ausdauer *f*.

**stammer** ['stæmər]. **I.** *v.i.* stottern. **II.** *s.*
Stottern *n*.

**stamp** [stæmp]. **I.** *s.* **1.** *(mark, instrument)*
Stempel *m*; **date s.**, Datumsstempel *m*.
**2.** *(postage)* **s.**, Briefmarke *f*. **II.** *v.* **1.**
*v.tr.* *(a)* **to s. one's foot**, mit dem Fuß
aufstampfen; *(b)* (einen Brief, einen Paß)
(ab)stempeln; *(c) (affix stamp)* **to s. a letter**, einen Brief freimachen. **2.** *v.i.*
stampfen; **to s. about**, herumtrampeln;
**to s. on sth.**, etwas zertrampeln.
◆**'stamped**, *adj.* **s. addressed envelope**, frankierter Rückumschlag.
◆**'stamping**, *s.* **s.-ground**, Lieblingsaufenthalt *m* (eines Tieres, einer Person).
◆**'stamp 'out**, *v.tr.* (ein Feuer) austreten; (einen Aufstand) niederschlagen;
(eine Epidemie) ausrotten.

**stampede** [stæm'piːd]. **I.** *s.* *(a) (of animals)* panische Flucht *f*; *(of people)*
Ansturm *m* **II.** *v.i.* *(a) (of animals)* (in
wilder Flucht) davonstürmen; *(b) (of people)* losstürmen (**for/towards**, auf + *acc.*).

**stance** [stæns, stɑːns], *s.* Haltung *f*; *Fig:*
**to take up a s.**, einen Standpunkt beziehen.

**stand** [stænd]. **I.** *s.* **1.** *Fig:* **to take a firm
s.**, eine entschlossene Haltung einneh-
men. **2.** *(support)* Ständer *m*; **hat s.**, Klei-
derständer *m*. **3.** *(at market, exhibition
etc.)* Stand *m*; **news s.**, Zeitungsstand *m*.
**4.** *(for spectators)* Tribüne *f*. **II.** *v.irr.* **1.**
*v.i.* *(a) (of pers., building etc.)* stehen; **to
s. still**, (i) *(cease to move)* stehenbleiben;
(ii) *(not fidget)* still stehen; **to s. firm/fast**,
nicht nachgeben; *(b) (remain valid) (of offer etc.)* bestehenbleiben; *Sp:* **the record
stands at 5 metres**, der Rekord liegt bei
5 Metern; **I'd like to know where I s.**,
ich möchte wissen, woran ich bin; **as
things s./as it stands at the moment**,
wie die Dinge stehen/zur Zeit liegen; **to
s. as candidate**, sich als Kandidat aufstellen lassen; *(c)* **it stands to reason that
…**, es liegt auf der Hand/ist nur natürlich, daß … **2.** *v.tr.* *(a) (place)* stellen;
*(b) (bear)* (etwas) ertragen; **I can't s. the
heat**, ich kann die Hitze nicht vertragen;
**I can't s. him**, ich kann ihn nicht ausstehen; *(c)* **he stands a good/poor chance**,
seine Chancen stehen gut/schlecht.
◆**'stand a'side**, *v.i.* zur Seite treten.
◆**'stand 'back**, *v.i.* *(of pers.)* zurücktreten. ◆**'stand 'by**, *v.* **1.** *v.i.* *(of troops
etc.)* in Alarmbereitschaft stehen. **2.** *v.tr.*
*(a)* (j-m) beistehen; *(b)* **to s. by a promise**, ein Versprechen einhalten.
◆**'standby**, *s.* *(a) Av:* **s. flight**,
Standby-Flug *m*; *(b)* Reserve *f*; **s. troops**,
Reservetruppen *fpl*; *Rail:* **s. engine**, Er-
satzlokomotive *f*. ◆**'stand 'down**, *v.i.*
**to s. d. in favour of s.o. else**, zugunsten
eines anderen zurücktreten. ◆**'stand**

**'for,** *v.tr.* (*a*) (*of abbreviation*) (etwas) bedeuten; (*b*) (*tolerate*) sich *dat* (etwas) gefallen lassen. ◆**'stand 'in,** *v.i.* **to s. i.
for s.o.,** für j-n einspringen.
◆**'stand-in,** *s. Sp: etc:* Ersatzmann
*m; Cin:* Double *n.* ◆**'standing.
I.** *adj.* **1. to be left s.,** überhaupt
nicht mithalten können. **2.** (*permanent*)
**to become a s. joke,** sprichwörtlich werden; *Fin:* **s. order,** Dauerauftrag *m.* **II.** *s.*
**1.** (*in bus etc.*) **s. room for three passengers,** drei Stehplätze. **2.** (*a*) (*position*)
Rang *m;* **social s.,** gesellschaftlicher
Rang; (*b*) (**high**) **s.,** Ansehen *n.* **3.** Dauer
*f;* **of long s.,** langjährig.
◆**'stand'offish,** *adj. F:* (*of pers.*) unfreundlich, kühl. ◆**'stand 'out,** *v.i.* (*a*)
(*of pers., thing*) sich abheben (**against,**
gegen + *acc;* **from,** von + *dat*); **he stands
o. among his contemporaries,** er ragt
unter seinen Zeitgenossen hervor.
◆**'standpoint,** *s.* Standpunkt *m.*
◆**'standstill,** *s.* Stillstand *m;* **to come
to a s.,** zum Stillstand kommen; (*of car*)
stehenbleiben. ◆**'stand 'up,** *v.i.* (*a*)
aufstehen; (*b*) *Fig:* **to s. up for s.o.,**
**sth.,** für j-n, etwas *acc* eintreten; **to s. up
to s.o.,** sich gegen j-n wehren; (*of materials etc.*) **to s. up to hard use,** strapazierfähig sein; (*c*) *F:* **to s. s.o. up,** j-n sitzenlassen.
**standard** ['stændəd], *s.* **1.** *Mil:* Fahne *f.*
**2.** *Meas:* Eichmaß *n; Ind:* Norm *f;* **to
apply/set high standards,** hohe Maßstäbe
anlegen/setzen; **to be up to s.,** den
Anforderungen/*Ind:* der Norm entsprechen; **below s.,** ungenügend; (*of goods*)
von minderwertiger Qualität. **3.** (*level of
achievement*) Niveau *n;* **s. of living,** Le-
bensstandard *m;* (*c*) *pl.* (*values*) **moral
standards,** moralische Werte. **4.** *attrib.*
(*a*) Standard-; **s. work,** Standardwerk *n;*
(*b*) *Ind:* (*of equipment etc.*) serienmäßig.
**5. lamp s.,** Laternenpfahl *m; H:* **s. lamp,**
Stehlampe *f.* ◆**standardi'zation,** *s.*
Standardisierung *f; Ind:* Normierung *f;*
*Meas:* Eichung *f.* ◆**'standardize,** *v.tr.*
(etwas) standardisieren; *Ind:* (Produkte
usw.) normieren.
**stanza** ['stænzə], *s.* Strophe *f.*
**staple**[1] ['steipl]. **I.** *s.* Klammer *f.* **II.** *v.tr.*
(mit einer Klammer) zusammenheften.
◆**'stapler,** *s.* Heftmaschine *f.*
**staple**[2], *adj.* Haupt-; **s. diet,** Hauptnah-
rung *f.*
**star** [stɑːr]. **I.** *s.* **1.** Stern *m.* **2.** *Cin: Th:
etc:* Star *m;* **s. part,** Starrolle *f.* **II.** *v.* **1.**
*v.tr. Cin: Th:* **a film starring X,** ein Film
mit X in der Hauptrolle. **2.** *v.i.* (*of actor
usw.*) die Hauptrolle spielen (**in** einem
Film usw.). ◆**'starlight,** *s.* Sternenlicht
*n.* ◆**'starlit,** *adj.* sternhell. ◆**'starry,**
*adj.* (*of sky, night etc.*) sternklar; (*of eyes*)
leuchtend; **s.-eyed,** (*naive*) blauäugig.
**starboard** ['stɑːbəd], *s. Nau:* Steuerbord
*n;* **to s./the s. side,** nach Steuerbord.
**starch** [stɑːtʃ]. **I.** *s.* Stärke *f.* **II.** *v.tr.*

(Wäsche) stärken.
**stare** [steər]. **I.** *s.* starrer Blick. **II.** *v.i.*
starren; **to s. at s.o.,** j-n anstarren.
**stark** [stɑːk]. **I.** *adj.* (*bare*) kahl; **in s.
contrast with ...,** in scharfem Gegensatz
zu ... *dat.* **II.** *adv.* **s. naked,** splitter-
nackt.
**starling** ['stɑːliŋ], *s.* Star *m.*
**start** [stɑːt]. **I.** *s.* **1.** (*a*) Anfang *m; Rac:*
Start *m;* **for a s.,** erstens; **from s. to
finish,** von Anfang bis Ende; (*b*) *Aut:* Antritt
*m* (einer Reise); Abfahrt *f;* (*c*) *Sp:* **to give
s.o. twenty metres s.,** j-m zwanzig Me-
ter Vorsprung geben. **2.** (*a*) (*fright*) **to
give s.o. a s.,** j-n erschrecken; (*b*) **by fits
and starts,** schubweise (arbeiten); ruckweise (vorwärtskommen). **II.** *v.* **1.** *v.i.*
(*a*) anfangen (**doing sth./to do sth.,** etwas zu tun; **on sth.,** mit etwas *dat*); **to s.
with,** (i) (*at the beginning*) zuerst; (ii) (*in
the first place*) erstens; (*b*) *Aut:* (*of engine*) anspringen; (*c*) (*in race*) starten; (*on
journey*) **to s.** (**out**), aufbrechen; (*of bus
etc.*) losfahren. **2.** *v.tr.* (*a*) (eine Arbeit
usw.) anfangen; (*b*) **to s.** (**up**) **a business,** ein Unternehmen gründen; **to s. a
fire,** (i) (*of thing*) einen Brand verursachen; (ii) (*of pers.*) (*arson*) Feuer legen;
(*c*) *Sp:* **to s. a race,** ein Rennen starten;
(*d*) *Aut:* (das Auto) starten; **to s. the engine,** den Motor anlassen; *Ind: etc:* **to s.
(up) a machine,** eine Maschine in Gang
setzen. ◆**'starter,** *s. Sp:* Starter *m*
(eines Rennens). **2.** *Aut:* Anlasser *m.* **3.**
(*a*) *Cu:* Vorspeise *f.* (*b*) **that'll do for
starters,** das genügt für den Anfang.
◆**'starting,** *s. attrib.* **s. point,** Ausgangspunkt *m; Sp:* **s. post,** Startpfosten
*m.*
**startle** ['stɑːtl], *v.tr.* (j-n) erschrecken.
◆**'startling,** *adj.* alarmierend; (*amazing*)
erstaunlich; (*of resemblance*) frappant.
**starve** [stɑːv], *v.* **1.** *v.i.* hungern; **to s. to
death,** verhungern. **2.** *v.tr.* (j-n) hungern
lassen. ◆**star'vation,** *s.* Hungern *n.*
◆**'starved,** *adj.* ausgehungert; **to be s.
of sth.,** nach etwas *dat* hungern.
**state** [steit]. **I.** *s.* **1.** (*condition*) Zustand *m*
(einer Person, eines Gegenstands); **s. of
health,** Gesundheitszustand *m.* **2.** (*status*)
**married s.,** Ehestand *m.* **3.** (*ceremony*)
Pomp *m;* (*of body*) **to lie in s.,** feierlich
aufgebahrt sein. **4.** (*nation*) Staat *m;*
**Head of S.,** Staatsoberhaupt *n;* **affairs of
s.,** Staatsangelegenheiten *fpl;* **the United
States (of America)/***F:* **the States,** die
Vereinigten Staaten (von Amerika); **s.
school,** staatliche Schule. **II.** *v.tr.* (seinen
Namen, seine Gründe usw.) angeben;
(Tatsachen) feststellen; (seine Meinung)
äußern; **he stated that ...,** er sagte, daß
... ◆**'stated,** *adj.* **on s. days,** an fest-
gesetzten Tagen. ◆**'stateless,** *adj.* (*of
pers.*) staatenlos. ◆**'stately,** *adj.* (*of
pers., building etc.*) stattlich; (*of manner,
walk etc.*) gemessen; **s. home,** herrschaft-
liches Haus, *esp.* Landschloß *n.*

◆**'statement**, s. Feststellung f; (remark) Behauptung f; esp. Jur: Aussage f; **public s.**, öffentliche Erklärung f; Fin: **s. of account/bank s.**, Kontoauszug m.
◆**'statesman**, pl. -men, s. Staatsmann m.

**static** ['stætik]. **I.** adj. (a) Ph: El: statisch; (b) (immobile) unbeweglich. **II.** s. Ph: statische Elektrizität; Rad: atmosphärische Störung.

**station** ['steiʃ(ə)n]. **I.** s. **1.** (position) Platz m; Fig: **s. in life**, gesellschaftliche Stellung. **2.** (a) Rad: Sender m; (b) (police) **s.**, Polizeiwache f; **lifeboat s.**, Rettungsstation f; Pol: **polling s.**, Wahllokal n; **weather s.**, Wetterwarte f. **3.** (railway) **s.**, Bahnhof m; **bus/coach s.**, Omnibusbahnhof m; **underground/F: tube s.**, U-Bahnhof m. **II.** v.tr. (a) (j-n, sich) aufstellen; (b) Mil: **to s. troops**, Truppen stationieren. ◆**'stationary**, adj. unbeweglich; **to be s.**, (still) stehen; **a s. car**, ein haltendes Auto. ◆**'station-master**, s. Bahnhofsvorsteher m.

**stationer** ['steiʃənər], s. Schreibwarenhändler m. ◆**'stationery**, s. Schreibwaren fpl; (paper) Schreibpapier n; **office s.**, Bürobedarf m.

**statistics** [stə'tistiks], s.pl. Statistik f.
◆**sta'tistical**, adj. statistisch.
◆**statisti'cian** [stætis'tiʃ(ə)n], s. Statistiker m.

**statue** ['stætju:], s. Standbild n.
◆**statuesque** [-ju'esk], adj. wie eine Statue.

**stature** ['stætʃər], s. Gestalt f.

**status** ['steitəs], s. (a) Adm: **marital s.**, Familienstand m; Jur: **legal s.**, Rechtsstellung f; **with no official s.**, nicht amtlich anerkannt; (b) **social s.**, gesellschaftlicher Rang; **s. symbol**, Statussymbol n; (c) **s. quo**, Status quo m.

**statute** ['stætju:t], s. (a) Jur: Gesetz n; (b) (of corporation etc.) Satzung f.
◆**'statutory**, adj. gesetzlich; **s. requirement**, Vorschrift f.

**staunch** [stɔ:n(t)ʃ], adj. treu.

**stave** [steiv]. **I.** s. Mus: Notensystem n. **II.** v.tr. **to s. off danger/a disaster**, eine Gefahr/eine Katastrophe abwenden.

**stay** [stei]. **I.** s. Aufenthalt m. **II.** v. **1.** v.i. (a) bleiben; (b) sich aufhalten (**in a place**, an einem Ort; **with s.o.**, bei j-m); **to s. at a hotel**, in einem Hotel wohnen. **2.** v.tr. (of pers., horse) **to s. the course/distance**, (bis zum Schluß) durchhalten. ◆**'stay a'way**, v.i. wegbleiben. ◆**'stay 'in**, v.i. zu Hause bleiben. ◆**'staying**, s. **s. power**, Ausdauer f. ◆**'stay 'on**, v.i. länger bleiben. ◆**'stay 'out**, v.i. ausbleiben; Ind: **the men are staying o.**, die Arbeiter setzen den Streik fort. ◆**'stay 'up**, v.i. **to s. up late**, lange aufbleiben.

**stead** [sted], s. **1. to stand s.o. in good s.**, j-m zustatten kommen. **2. in his s.**, an seiner Stelle.

**steadfast** ['stedfɑ:st], adj. (of pers.) beständig (**in**, in + dat); (in courage etc.) standfest.

**steady** ['stedi]. **I.** adj. **1.** fest; (of table, ladder etc.) standfest; (of voice) ruhig; **to have a s. hand**, eine sichere Hand haben. **2.** (unchanging) gleichmäßig; (of prices etc.) stabil; (continuous) ständig; **s. girlfriend**, feste Freundin; **s. job**, regelmäßige Arbeit. **3.** (of pers.) solide; (reliable) zuverlässig. **II.** v. **1.** v.tr. (a) (ein Boot, einen Tisch usw.) festhalten; **to s. oneself against sth.**, sich auf etwas acc stützen; (b) (j-n, sich, die Nerven) beruhigen. **2.** v.i. (of prices, etc.) sich festigen; **-ily**, adv. **1.** fest; **he looked at her s.**, er sah sie mit ruhigem Blick an. **2.** ständig; **to work s. at sth.**, beharrlich an etwas dat arbeiten. ◆**'steadiness**, s. **1.** Festigkeit f (der Hand, der Stimme usw.). **2.** Gleichmäßigkeit f; Com: Stabilität f (der Preise).

**steak** [steik], s. Steak n.

**steal** [sti:l], v.irr. **1.** v.tr. **to s. sth. from s.o.**, j-m etwas stehlen. **2.** v.i. **to s. away/off**, sich davonschleichen/wegstehlen. ◆**'stealing**, s. Stehlen n.

**stealthy** ['stelθi], adj. verstohlen.

**steam** [sti:m]. **I.** s. Dampf m; **to let off s.**, Fig: seinen Gefühlen Luft machen; **s. engine**, (i) Dampfmaschine f; (ii) Rail: Dampflokomotive f. **II.** v. **1.** v.tr. (Fisch, Gemüse usw.) dünsten. **2.** v.i. (a) (emit steam) dampfen; (b) (of glass) **to s. up**, (sich) beschlagen. ◆**'steamer**, s. Nau: Dampfer m. ◆**'steamroller**, s. Dampfwalze f. ◆**'steamy**, adj. dampfig; (of climate) feuchtheiß.

**steel** [sti:l]. **I.** s. Stahl m. **II.** v.tr. **to s. oneself to do sth.**, sich überwinden, etwas zu tun. ◆**'steelworks**, s.pl. Stahlwerk n.

**steep¹** [sti:p], adj. steil; **s. drop**, jäher Abfall.

**steep²**, v.tr. (a) (etwas) einweichen (**in sth.**, mit etwas dat); (b) Fig: **steeped in tradition**, traditionsreich.

**steeple** [sti:pl], s. (spitzer) Kirchturm m; (spire) Kirchturmspitze f.
◆**'steeplejack**, s. Turmarbeiter m.

**steer** ['stiːər], v.tr. & i. (a) (ein Auto usw.) lenken; (ein Schiff) steuern; (b) Fig: **to s. clear of sth.**, etwas vermeiden. ◆**'steering**, s. (a) Nau: Steuerung f; (b) Aut: Lenkung f; **s. wheel**, Lenkrad n.

**stem¹** [stem]. **I.** s. **1.** Bot: Stengel m. **2.** Stiel m (eines Glases, einer Pfeife). **3.** Stamm m (eines Wortes usw.). **II.** v.i. **to s. from sth.**, von etwas dat herstammen.

**stem²**, v.tr. **to s. the flow**, den Fluß dämmen; (of blood) das Blut stillen.

**stench** [sten(t)ʃ], s. Gestank m.

**stencil** ['stens(i)l]. **I.** s. (a) (plate) Schablone f; (b) (design) Schablonenzeichnung f. **II.** v.tr. (a) (etwas) schablonieren.

**step¹** [step]. **I.** s. **1.** (a) (walking) Schritt m; **to take a s.**, einen Schritt machen; **s.**

**by s.**, Schritt für Schritt; (b) *Fig:* **a big s. forward**, ein großer Fortschritt. **2.** (*measure*) Maßnahme f; **to take the necessary steps**, die erforderlichen Maßnahmen ergreifen/treffen. **3.** Stufe f (einer Treppe); (*door*) **s.**, Schwelle f. **II.** v.i. treten; **s. this way**, folgen Sie mir bitte. ◆'**stepladder**, s. Stehleiter f, (*small*) Trittleiter f. ◆'**step 'up**, v.tr. (Produktion usw.) steigern.

**step-²**, *prefix* Stief-; **stepbrother**, Stiefbruder m; **stepchild**, Stiefkind n.

**stereo** ['steriəu, 'stiəriəu]. **I.** s. (a) **in s.**, in Stereo; (b) *F:* (*system*) Stereoanlage f. **II.** adj. Stereo-. ◆**stereo'phonic**, adj. stereophon. ◆'**stereotype**, s. **1.** *Print:* Druckplatte f. **2.** *Fig:* Klischee n. ◆'**stereotyped**, adj. stereotyp; **s. phrase**, Klischee n.

**sterile** ['sterail], adj. steril; (*germ-free*) keimfrei. ◆**sterility** [stə'riliti], s. Sterilität f. ◆'**sterilize**, v.tr. (j-n, etwas) sterilisieren. ◆'**sterilizer**, s. Sterilisator m.

**sterling** ['stə:liŋ], adj. **1.** Sterling-; **s. silver**, Standardsilber n. **2. pound s.**, Pfund n Sterling.

**stern¹** [stə:n], adj. streng.

**stern²**, s. *Nau:* Heck n.

**stethoscope** ['steθəskəup], s. Stethoskop n.

**stew** [stju:]. **I.** s. Eintopf m. **II.** v. **1.** v.tr. (Fleisch) schmoren; (Obst) kochen. **2.** v.i. (*of meat*) schmoren. ◆**stewed**, adj. **s. meat**, Schmorfleisch n; **s. fruit**, Kompott n.

**steward** ['stju:əd], s. **1.** (*estate manager*) Verwalter m. **2.** (*attendant*) *Nau: Av:* Steward m; *Rail:* Kellner m. **3.** (*official*) Ordner m. ◆**stewar'dess**, s. Stewardeß f.

**stick¹** [stik], s. **1.** (a) (*for walking, hitting etc.*) Stock m; (*for peas, beans etc.*) Stange f; **hockey s.**, Hockeyschläger m; (b) (*drumstick*) Schlegel m; (c) pl. **sticks**, Kleinholz n; (*firewood*) Reisig n. **2.** Stange f (Sellerie, Rhabarber usw.). **3.** *Av:* (**control**) **s.**, Steuerknüppel m.

**stick²**, v.irr. **1.** v.tr. (a) (eine Nadel usw.) (hinein)stechen (**into** sth., in etwas acc); **to s. a knife into s.o.**, j-n mit einem Messer stechen; (b) *F:* (*put*) (etwas) stecken (**in/on** etc., in/auf usw. + acc); (c) (*fix with glue etc.*) (etwas) kleben (**to**, an + acc); (d) *F:* (*bear*) (j-n, etwas) ertragen; **to s. it out**, es durchhalten. **2.** v.i. (a) (*of lid, drawer etc.*) festsitzen; (*of door*) klemmen; (b) kleben (**to** sth., an etwas acc); **to s. to a friend/one's word**, einem Freund/seinem Wort treu bleiben; **to s. together**, (*of people*) zusammenhalten; **to s. to the subject/point**, bei der Sache bleiben; (c) **to s./be stuck**, steckenbleiben; (*between two objects*) (fest) eingeklemmt sein. ◆'**sticker**, s. Aufkleber m. ◆'**stickiness**, s. Klebrigkeit f. ◆'**sticking**, adj. **s. plaster**, Heftpflaster

n. ◆'**stick-in-the-mud**, s. *F:* Rückschrittler m. ◆'**stick 'on**, v.tr. (a) (*affix*) (eine Briefmarke usw.) aufkleben; (b) *F:* (*add*) (eine weitere Summe) dazurechnen. ◆'**stick 'out**, v. **1.** v.tr. **to s. o. one's tongue**, die Zunge herausstrecken. **2.** v.i. (a) vorstehen; (*of ears*) abstehen; **to s. o. beyond** sth., über etwas acc hinausragen; (b) *Fig:* (*be noticeable*) auffallen. ◆'**stick 'up**, v. **1.** v.tr. (*hang up*) (etwas) aufhängen; (*put up*) (etwas) anbringen. **2.** v.i. (a) **to s. up** (**above** sth.), über etwas acc) hinausragen; (b) *F:* **to s. up for** s.o., sich für j-n einsetzen. ◆'**sticky**, adj. **1.** (a) klebrig; (b) (*gummed*) Klebe-; **s. tape**, Klebestreifen m; (c) *Fig:* **s. weather**, schwüles Wetter. **2.** *F:* (*difficult*) schwierig.

**stickler** ['stiklər], s. Pedant m.

**stiff** [stif]. **I.** adj. (a) steif; (*of fingers*) **s. with cold**, starr vor Kälte; **s. breeze**, steife Brise; (b) *Fig:* **s. competition**, scharfe Konkurrenz; (c) (*difficult*) schwierig. **II.** s. *P:* (*corpse*) Leiche f. ◆'**stiffen**, v. **1.** v.tr. (etwas) versteifen. **2.** v.i. (a) sich versteifen; (*of pers.*) (plötzlich) erstarren; (b) (*of wind*) auffrischen. ◆'**stiffness**, s. (a) Steifheit f; (b) (*difficulty*) Schwierigkeit f.

**stifle** ['staifl], v. **1.** v.tr. (a) (j-n, ein Feuer usw.) ersticken; (b) (*suppress*) (ein Gefühl) unterdrücken. **2.** v.i. ersticken. ◆'**stifling**, adj. stickig; **it's s. in here**, hier ist es zum Ersticken (heiß).

**stigma** ['stigmə], s. Stigma n; (*disgrace*) Schande f.

**stile** [stail], s. Zauntritt m.

**still¹** [stil]. **I.** adj. still; (*quiet*) ruhig; (*of cider etc.*) nicht schäumend; **to stand s.**, stillstehen; *Art:* **s. life**, Stilleben n. **II.** s. *Cin:* Standfoto n. ◆'**stillborn**, adj. totgeboren. ◆'**stillness**, s. Stille f.

**still²**. **I.** adv. (a) noch; **he's s. here**, er ist (immer) noch da; (b) (*even so*) **you s. have to pay**, Sie müssen trotzdem zahlen; (c) **s. better**, noch besser. **II.** conj. dennoch; **but s.**, **I did see her**, aber wenigstens habe ich sie gesehen.

**still³**, s. Destillierapparat m.

**stilt** [stilt], s. (**pair of**) **stilts**, Stelzen fpl. ◆'**stilted**, adj. steif; **s. language**, gezierte Sprache.

**stimulate** ['stimjuleit], v.tr. stimulieren; (den Handel) ankurbeln. ◆'**stimulant**, s. Anregungsmittel n. ◆'**stimulating**, adj. stimulierend. ◆**stimu'lation**, s. Anregung f. ◆'**stimulus**, s. Antrieb m; *Psy:* Reiz m.

**sting** [stiŋ]. **I.** s. **1.** Stachel m (einer Biene usw.). **2.** (*wound*) Stich m. **II.** v. **1.** v.tr. (a) (*of bee etc.*) (j-n) stechen; (b) *F:* **to s. s.o. for a fiver**, j-n um £5 neppen. **2.** v.i. **my eyes were stinging**, mir brannten die Augen. ◆'**stinging**, adj. stechend; **s. nettle**, Brennessel f.

**stingy** ['stin(d)ʒi], adj. knauserig.

**stink** [stiŋk]. **I.** s. Gestank m. **II.** v.i. stin-

ken (*of*, nach + *dat*). ◆'**stinking**, *adj.*
stinkend; *Pej*: (*awful*) widerlich; *F*: **s.
rich**, steinreich.

**stint** [stint]. **I.** *v.tr.* (*a*) **to s. oneself**, sich
einschränken; (*b*) **to s. (on) sth.**, mit et-
was *dat* knausern. **II.** *s.* **to do one's s.**,
seinen Teil beitragen.

**stipulate** ['stipjuleit], *v.* **1.** *v.tr.* (eine Bedingung usw.) voraussetzen; (einen Ter-
min usw.) festsetzen. **2.** *v.i.* **he stipu-
lated that ...**, er machte es zur Bedingung, daß ... ◆**stipu'lation**, *s.* Bedingung *f*.

**stir** [stəːr]. **I.** *s.* **1.** (*a*) (*movement*) Bewegung *f*; (*b*) (*excitement*) Aufregung *f*. **II.**
*v.* **1.** *v.tr.* (*a*) (Kaffee, Teig usw.) rühren;
(*b*) (*move*) (etwas) bewegen; (*c*) *Fig*: **to s.
up trouble**, böses Blut machen. **2.** *v.i.*
sich rühren. ◆'**stirring**, *adj.* (*of tune,
speech etc.*) mitreißend; **s. times**, aufre-
gende Zeiten.

**stirrup** ['stirəp], *s.* Steigbügel *m*.

**stitch** [stitʃ]. **I.** *s.* **1.** (*a*) (*in sewing*) Stich
*m*; (*b*) (*in knitting*) Masche *f*; (*c*) *Med*: **to
put stitches in a wound**, eine Wunde nä-
hen. **2. s. (in the side)**, Seitenstechen *n*.
**II.** *v.tr.* (ein Kleidungsstück, *Med*: eine
Wunde) nähen; **to s. up a tear**, einen
Riß flicken.

**stoat** [stəut], *s.* Hermelin *m*.

**stock** [stɔk]. **I.** *s.* **1.** (*race*) Stamm *m*. **2.**
(*store*) Vorrat *m*; *Com*: Lagerbestand *m*;
**in/out of s.**, vorrätig/nicht vorrätig; **to
take s.**, *Fig*: Bilanz ziehen; **to take s. of
the situation**, die Lage abschätzen. **3.**
*Agr*: (**live**)**s.**, Vieh *n*; Viehbestand *m*. **4.**
(*for soup*) Brühe *f*. **5.** *Fin*: Aktien *fpl*;
**stocks and shares**, Wertpapiere *npl*; **the
S. Exchange**, die Börse. **II.** *v.* **1.** *v.tr.* (*a*)
*Com*: (*of shop*) (eine Ware) führen; (*b*)
(einen Bach usw.) (mit Fischen) beset-
zen. **2.** *v.i.* **to s. up (with sth.)**, sich (mit
etwas *dat*) eindecken. ◆'**stockbroker**,
*s.* Börsenmakler *m*. ◆'**stockist**, *s.* Fach-
händler *m* (**of**, für + *acc*). ◆'**stockpile.
I.** *s.* großer Vorrat *m*. **II.** *v.* **1.** *v.tr.*
(Waren) aufstapeln. **2.** *v.i.* einen großen
Vorrat anlegen. ◆'**stocktaking**, *s. Com*:
Inventur *f*. ◆'**stocky**, *adj.* (*of pers.*)
untersetzt; (*strong*) stämmig.

**stocking** ['stɔkiŋ], *s.* Strumpf *m*.

**stodge** [stɔdʒ], *s. F*: Mehlpampe *f*.
◆'**stodgy**, *adj.* (*of food*) schwer verdaulich.

**stoical** ['stəuikəl], *adj.* stoisch.
◆'**stoicism** [-sizm], *s.* Stoizismus *m*.

**stoke** [stəuk], *v.tr.* (ein Feuer) schüren;
(einen Ofen) bedienen.

**stolid** ['stɔlid], *adj.* stur.

**stomach** ['stʌmək]. **I.** *s.* (*a*) Magen *m*;
(*b*) (*belly*) Bauch *m*. **II.** *v.tr.* vertragen.

**stone** [stəun]. **I.** *s.* (*a*) Stein *m*; **s. quarry**,
Steinbruch *m*; **a s.'s throw**, ein Kat-
zensprung *m*; (**precious**) **s.**, Edelstein *m*;
(*b*) (*in fruit*) Kern *m*, Stein *m*; **cherry s.**,
Kirschkern *m*; (*c*) *Meas*: = 6,35 Kilo; (*d*)
**s. cold**, eiskalt; *Fig*: **a heart of s.**, ein

steinernes Herz. **II.** *v.tr.* (*a*) **to s. s.o. (to
death)**, j-n (zu Tode) steinigen; (*b*)
(*Obst*) entsteinen; (Kirschen, Datteln)
entkernen. ◆**stoned**, *adj.* **1.** *P*: besoffen. **2.** (*of fruit*) entsteint. ◆'**stone-
mason**, *s.* Steinmetz *m*. ◆'**stonework**,
*s.* Mauerwerk *n*. ◆'**stony**, *adj.* **1.** (*of
path etc.*) steinig. **2.** *Fig*: steinern; **s. silence**, eisiges Schweigen.

**stool** [stuːl], *s.* **1.** Hocker *m*; **folding s.**,
Klappstuhl *m*; **wooden (foot)s.**, Schemel
*m*. **2.** *Med*: Stuhl *m*; (*bowel movement*)
Stuhlgang *m*.

**stoop** [stuːp]. **I.** *s.* krumme Haltung *f*; **to
walk with a s.**, krumm gehen. **II.** *v.i.* (*a*)
sich bücken; (*habitually*) sich krumm halten; (*b*) *Fig*: **I won't s. to (doing) that**,
ich werde mich nicht dazu erniedrigen.

**stop** [stɔp]. **I.** *s.* **1.** (*a*) (*state*) Stillstand *m*;
**to put a s. to sth.**, (mit) etwas *dat* ein
Ende machen; (*during journey*) Halt
*m*; (*longer*) Aufenthalt *m*; **to make a s.**,
haltmachen; (*c*) (*for bus etc.*) Haltestelle *f*.
**2.** (**full**) **s.**, Punkt *m*. **3.** (**organ**) **s.**, Register *n*. **4.** *Phot*: Blende *f*. **II.** *v.* **1.** *v.tr.*
(*a*) (j-n, einen Wagen, den Verkehr)
anhalten/(*briefly*) aufhalten; (eine Tätigkeit) einstellen; (den Ball, eine Uhr)
stoppen; (eine Maschine, *Aut*: den Motor) abstellen; (den Kampf) abbrechen;
(einem Vorgang) ein Ende machen; **to s.
doing sth.**, aufhören, etwas zu tun; **to s.
s.o. doing sth.**, j-n daran hindern, etwas
zu tun; *Fin*: **to s. a cheque**, einen
Scheck sperren; (*b*) (*fill, block*) (ein Loch)
zustopfen; (eine Lücke) ausfüllen. **2.** *v.i.*
(*a*) (*stop moving*) (*of car etc.*) halten; (*of
pers., watch*) stehenbleiben; (*b*) (*stop action*) aufhören; (*stop talking*) innehalten;
(*c*) *F*: **to s. at home**, zu Hause bleiben.
◆'**stopcock**, *s.* Absperrhahn *m*.
◆'**stopgap**, *s.* Lückenbüßer *m*.
◆'**stoplight**, *s. Aut*: Stopplicht *n*.
◆'**stoppage**, *s.* **1.** Stockung *f* (des Verkehrs usw.). **2.** (*interruption*) Unterbrechung *f*; *Ind*: (*by workers*) Arbeitseinstel-
lung *f*. ◆'**stopper**, *s.* Verschluß *m*.
◆'**stopping**, *s.* **s. place**, (*for tourists
etc.*) Aufenthaltsort *m*; (*for bus etc.*) Haltestelle *f*. ◆'**stopwatch**, *s.* Stoppuhr *f*.

**storage** ['stɔːridʒ], *s.* **1.** (*storing*) Lagerung *f* (von Waren); Speicherung *f* (von
Energie usw.); **to take goods out of s.**,
Waren auslagern; *El*: **s. heating**, Spei-
cherheizung *f*. **2.** (*space*) Lagerraum *m*.

**store** [stɔːr]. **I.** *s.* **1.** (*a*) Vorrat *m* (**of sth.**,
an etwas *dat*); (*b*) (*warehouse*) Lagerhaus
*n*; (*furniture*) **s.**, Möbeldepot *n*; **s. room**,
Lagerraum *m*. **2.** (*shop*) esp. *N.Am*: Geschäft *n*; (*department*) **s.**, Kaufhaus *n*.
**II.** *v.tr.* lagern. ◆'**storehouse**, *s.* (*a*)
Lagerhaus *n*; (*b*) *Fig*: Schatzkammer *f*.

**storey** ['stɔːri], *s.* Stockwerk *n*; **on the
third s.**/*N.Am*: **on the fourth s.**, im dritten Stock.

**stork** [stɔːk], *s.* Storch *m*.

**storm** [stɔːm]. **I.** *s.* **1.** Sturm *m*; (**thun-**

der)s., Gewitter n. 2. *Mil:* to take a town by s., eine Stadt im Sturm nehmen. II *v.tr. & i.* stürmen. ◆'stormy, *adj.* stürmisch; s. wind, Sturmwind *m;* s. sky, drohender Himmel.

story¹ ['stɔːri], *s.* Geschichte *f;* (*plot*) Handlung *f* (eines Romans usw.). ◆'storyline, *s.* Handlung *f.* ◆'storyteller, *s.* Erzähler *m.*

story², *s. N.Am:* = storey.

stout¹ [staut], *adj.* 1. (*strong*) stark; (*of shoes*) fest. 2. (*fat*) beleibt; -ly, *adv.* s. built, fest gebaut.

stout², *s.* Stout *n* (dunkles Starkbier).

stove [stəuv], *s.* (*a*) (*for heating*) Ofen *m;* (*b*) (*cooker*) Herd *m.*

stow [stəu], *v.* 1. *v.tr.* to s. (away) goods, cargo etc., Güter, die Ladung usw. verstauen. 2. *v.i.* to s. away, als blinder Passagier fahren. ◆'stowaway, *s.* blinder Passagier *m.*

straddle ['strædl], *v.tr.* to s. a horse/a chair, rittlings auf einem Pferd/einem Stuhl sitzen; (*of bridge*) to s. a river etc., einen Fluß usw. überspannen.

straggle ['strægl], *v.i.* (*of pers.*) umherstreifen; (*of plants*) wuchern; to s. (behind), hinterherzotteln. ◆'straggling, *adj.* (*of hair*) strähnig.

straight [streit]. I. *adj.* 1. gerade; s. hair, glattes Haar; with a s. face, mit ernstem Gesicht; to put sth. s., etwas geradestellen. 2. (*of pers.*) aufrichtig. 3. s. whisky, Whisky pur; *Th:* s. play, (konventionelles) Theaterstück *n.* II. *s. Sp:* Gerade *f.* III. *adv.* 1. gerade; to keep s. on, immer geradeaus gehen. 2. (*a*) direkt; to look s.o.s. in the face/the eye, j-m gerade ins Gesicht sehen; to come s. to the point, direkt zur Sache kommen; (*b*) (*at once*) gleich; I'll come s. back, ich bin gleich wieder da. ◆'straighten, *v.* 1. *v.tr. (a)* (etwas) geradestellen/(*by bending*) geradebiegen; (*b*) (*tidy*) (ein Zimmer, eine Angelegenheit usw.) in Ordnung bringen; to s. out a problem, ein Problem regeln. 2. *v.i.* (*of pers.*) to s. (up), sich aufrichten. ◆'straight'forward, *adj.* (*a*) (*frank*) offen; (*b*) (*uncomplicated*) einfach; a s. answer, eine direkte Antwort. ◆'straight'forwardness, *s.* (*a*) Offenheit *f;* (*b*) Einfachheit *f.*

strain¹ [strein]. I. *s.* 1. Spannung *f* (eines Seils); *Tchn: Fig:* (*physical*) Anstrengung *f* (on s.o., für j-n); Belastung *f* (eines Teils); to reduce the s. on a part, ein Teil entlasten; mental/nervous s., nervliche Überanstrengung *f. Med:* Zerrung *f.* II. *v.* 1. *v.tr. (a)* (ein Seil usw.) spannen; to s. one's ears, angestrengt lauschen; (*b*) *Med:* (einen Muskel) zerren; (ein Gelenk) verstauchen; (das Herz, die Augen) überanstrengen; (die Flüssigkeit) filtrieren. 2. *v.i.* zerren (at, an+*dat*). ◆'strained, *adj.* 1. s. relations, gespannte Beziehungen; *Med:* s. muscle, Muskelzerrung *f.* ◆'strainer, *s.* Sieb *n.*

strain², *s.* 1. Zug *m;* a s. of weakness/mysticism, ein Hang zur Schwäche/zur Mystik. 2. (*a*) (*breed*) Rasse *f;* (*b*) (*plant, virus*) Art *f.*

strait [streit], *s.* (*a*) Meeresstraße *f;* the Straits of Dover, die Straße von Dover; (*b*) in dire straits, in einer Notlage. ◆'straitjacket, *s.* Zwangsjacke *f.* ◆'strait'laced, *adj.* sittenstreng; prüde.

strand [strænd], *s.* Strang *m* (eines Seils usw.); s. of hair, Haarsträhne *f.*

stranded ['strændid], *adj.* (*a*) (*of ship*) (auf Grund) aufgelaufen; (*b*) (*of pers.*) to be s., auf dem trockenen sitzen; *Aut:* steckengeblieben sein.

strange [strein(d)ʒ], *adj.* 1. (*alien*) fremd; (*unfamiliar*) unbekannt. 2. (*peculiar*) seltsam; -ly, *adv.* s. dressed, seltsam angezogen; s. (enough), seltsamerweise. ◆'stranger, *s.* Fremde(r) *f(m);* I'm a s. here, ich bin hier fremd.

strangle ['stræŋgl], *v.tr.* (j-n) erwürgen. ◆'strangu'lation, *s.* Strangulierung *f.*

strap [stræp]. I. *s.* Riemen *m;* (*for watch*) Armband *n;* (*over shoulder*) Träger *m.* II. *v.tr.* to s. sth. (down), (etwas) (mit einem Riemen) festschnallen. ◆'strapping, *adj. F:* stramm.

strategic [strə'tiːdʒik], *adj.* strategisch. ◆'strategy ['strætədʒi], *s.* Strategie *f.*

stratum, *pl.* -a ['strɑːtəm, -ə], *s.* Schicht *f.*

straw [strɔː], *s.* 1. *coll.* Stroh *n.* 2. (*single s.*) Strohhalm *m; Fig:* to clutch at straws, sich an einen Strohhalm klammern.

strawberry ['strɔːb(ə)ri], *s.* Erdbeere *f;* s. jam, Erdbeermarmelade *f.*

stray [strei]. I. *adj.* (*of dog etc.*) streunend; s. bullet, verirrte Kugel. II. *s.* streunendes Tier. III. *v.i.* (*of pers., animal*) streunen; (*of thoughts*) abschweifen; (*b*) to s. from the point, vom Thema abschweifen.

streak [striːk]. I. *s.* 1. (*strip*) Streifen *m.* 2. (*a*) (*element*) s. of cowardice, feiger Zug; (*b*) a s. of luck/bad luck, eine Glückssträhne/Pechsträhne. II. *v.i.* to s. past, vorbeisausen. ◆'streaked, *adj.* s. with red, mit roten Streifen. ◆'streaky, *adj.* streifig; s. bacon, durchwachsener Speck.

stream [striːm]. I. *s.* (*a*) Bach *m;* (*b*) (*current & Fig:*) Strom *m;* in a continuous s., unaufhörlich. II. *v.i.* strömen. ◆'streamer, *s.* (*paper*) streamers, Papierschlangen *fpl.* ◆'streamline, *v.tr.* (*a*) (etwas *dat*) eine Stromlinienform geben; (*b*) eine Firma usw.) rationalisieren. ◆'streamlined, *adj.* stromlinienförmig.

street [striːt], *s.* Straße *f;* in the s., auf der Straße; s. lighting, Straßenbeleuchtung *f;* s. sweeper, (*pers.*) Straßenkehrer *m.* ◆'streetcar, *s. N.Am:* Straßenbahn *f.*

strength [streŋθ], *s.* 1. (*a*) Stärke *f;*

(*physical*) Kraft *f*; **with all one's s.**, mit aller Kraft; (*b*) Intensität *f* (der Farbe, des Gefühls). **2. to be present in great s.**, in großen Mengen anwesend sein. ◆'**strengthen**, *v.tr.* stärken; (eine Mauer usw.) verstärken.

**strenuous** ['strenjuəs], *adj.* anstrengend; **-ly**, *adv.* energisch.

**stress** [stres]. **I.** *s.* **1.** (*a*) *Tchn:* (starke) Beanspruchung *f*; (*load*) Belastung *f*; (*pressure*) Druck *m*; (*b*) *Psy:* Streß *m*. **2.** (*emphasis*) (*a*) Nachdruck *m*; (*b*) **s. (accent)**, Betonung *f*. **II.** *v.tr.* (*a*) *Tchn:* (ein Teil) (stark) beanspruchen; (*b*) (den Wert von etwas, eine Silbe usw.) betonen.

**stretch** [stretʃ]. **I.** *s.* **1.** (*a*) (*road, rail etc.*) Strecke *f*; **s. of water**, Gewässer *n*; **s. of forest**, Waldgebiet *n*; (*b*) (*time*) Zeitspanne *f*; **at a/one s.**, ununterbrochen. **2.** (*quality*) Elastizität *f*; *attrib.* elastisch; *Cl:* Stretch-. **II.** *v.* **1.** *v.tr.* (*a*) (*expand*) dehnen; (*stretch tight*) (ein Tuch usw.) spannen; (*b*) **that's stretching it a bit!** das ist ein bißchen übertrieben! **2.** *v.i.* (*a*) (*of elastic etc.*) sich dehnen; **material that stretches**, dehnbarer Stoff; (*b*) (*of landscape etc.*) sich erstrecken; (*c*) (*of pers.*) sich strecken; **to s. for sth.**, nach etwas *dat* langen. ◆'**stretcher**, *s. Med:* Tragbahre *f*. ◆'**stretch 'out**, *v.* **1.** *v.tr.* (sich, die Beine, die Hand) ausstrecken. **2.** *v.i.* (*reach*) langen **for sth.**, nach etwas *dat*).

**strict** [strikt], *adj.* streng; (*precise*) genau; **-ly**, *adv.* **s. (speaking)**, genaugenommen; **s. forbidden/prohibited**, strengstens verboten. ◆'**strictness**, *s.* Strenge *f*.

**stride** [straid]. **I.** *s.* langer Schritt *m*. **II.** *v.i.* (*of pers.*) mit langen Schritten gehen; **to s. along**, dahinschreiten.

**strident** ['straidənt], *adj.* (*of voice*) kreischend; (*of sound*) schrill.

**strife** [straif], *s.* Streit *m*.

**strike** [straik]. **I.** *s.* **1.** *Ind:* Streik *m*; **to go on/come out on s.**, in Streik treten. **2.** *Mil:* Angriff *m*. **II.** *v.irr.* **1.** *v.tr.* (*a*) (*hit*) schlagen; (das Ziel) treffen; **his head struck the pavement**, sein Kopf ist aufs Pflaster aufgeschlagen; **to s. a match**, ein Streichholz anzünden; **to s. oil**, auf Öl stoßen; *F:* **to s. lucky**, Glück haben; *Fig:* **to s. terror into s.o.**, j-m Schrecken einjagen; (*c*) (*impress*) (j-m) auffallen; (*d*) **to s. a balance**, das Gleichgewicht herstellen; **to s. a bargain**, einen Handel abschließen; (*e*) (*delete*) **to s. (off/out)**, (etwas) streichen. **2.** *v.i.* (*a*) (*of clock, hour*) schlagen; (*b*) (*of enemy*) zuschlagen; **to s. back**, zurückschlagen; **to s. out**, losschlagen; (*in words*) loslegen; (*c*) (*of employees*) streiken. ◆'**striker**, *s. Ind:* Streikende(r) *f(m)*. **2.** *Fb:* Stürmer *m*. ◆'**striking**, *adj.* (*a*) (*of similarity etc.*) auffallend; (*b*) (*impressive*) eindrucksvoll. ◆'**strike 'up**, *v.* **1.** *v.tr.* (eine Bekanntschaft usw.) anknüpfen. **2.** *v.tr. & i. Mus:* **to s. up (a tune)**, (mit einer Melo-

die) einsetzen.

**string** [striŋ]. **I.** *s.* **1.** Schnur *f*; *Fig:* **to pull strings**, seine Beziehungen spielen lassen; **s. vest**, Netzhemd *n*. **2.** *Mus:* Saite *f*; *Mus: coll.* **the strings**, die Streicher *mpl*; **s. instrument**, Streichinstrument *n*. **3.** (*a*) **s. of beads**, Perlenkette *f*; (*b*) (*queue*) Schlange *f*; Kolonne *f* (von Autos usw.). **II.** *v.* **1.** *v.tr.* (*a*) *Fig:* (of *pers.*) **highly strung**, nervös; (*b*) (Perlen) (auf eine Schnur) aufziehen; (*c*) *F:* **to s. s.o. along**, (*deceive*) j-n an der Nase herumführen. **2.** *v.i. F:* **to s. along with s.o.**, sich mit j-m auf kurz oder lang zusammentun. ◆'**stringy**, *adj.* (*of meat*) sehnig.

**stringent** ['strin(d)ʒ(ə)nt], *adj.* streng. ◆'**stringency**, *s.* Strenge *f*.

**strip** [strip]. **I.** *s.* **1.** Streifen *m*; **s. cartoon/comic s.**, Comic-strip *m*; **s. lighting**, Neonröhren *fpl*. **2.** *Fb:* Dreß *m*. **II.** *v.* **1.** *v.tr.* (*a*) (j-n) ausziehen; (*violently*) (j-m) die Kleider vom Leibe reißen; **stripped to the waist**, mit nacktem Oberkörper; (*b*) **to s. s.o. of sth.**, j-n etwas *gen* berauben; (*c*) (ein Bett) abziehen; (ein Zimmer) ausräumen; (*burgle*) ausplündern; (Farbe, Lack) abziehen, (*with liquid*) abbeizen; (eine Maschine, ein Gewehr) auseinandernehmen. **2.** *v.i.* (*of pers.*) sich ausziehen. ◆'**stripper**, *s.* **1.** (*pers.*) Stripperin *f.* **2.** (*paint s.*) Abbeizmittel *n.*

**stripe** [straip], *s.* Streifen *m*. ◆'**striped/ 'stripy**, *adj.* gestreift.

**strive** [straiv], *v.i.irr.* **to s. (to do sth.)**, sich bemühen, ( etwas zu tun); **to s. after/for sth.**, nach etwas *dat* streben.

**stroke** [strəuk]. **I.** *s.* (*a*) (*blow*) Schlag *m*; (*with whip*) Hieb *m*; (*b*) (*in swimming*) Schwimmart *f*; (*c*) **s. of the brush/pen**, Pinselstrich/Federstrich *m*; (*d*) *Med:* Schlaganfall *m*. **II.** *v.tr.* (j-n, etwas) streicheln.

**stroll** [strəul]. **I.** *s.* Spaziergang *m*; *F:* (*sightseeing etc.*) Bummel *m*. **II.** *v.i.* schlendern; (*go for a s.*) bummeln.

**strong** [strɔŋ]. **I.** *adj.* (*a*) stark; (*of colour, health, expression, voice etc.*) kräftig; **s. feelings**, feste Überzeugungen; (*b*) **s. cheese**, scharfer Käse. **II.** *adv. F:* (*machine etc.*) **it's still going s.**, es funktioniert noch tadellos; **-ly**, *adv.* (*a*) **I feel s. that ...**, ich bin fest davon überzeugt, daß ... (*b*) stark (riechen, schmecken). ◆'**stronghold**, *s. Mil:* Festung *f*; *Fig:* Hochburg *f*. ◆'**strong-'minded**, *adj.* willensstark. ◆'**strongroom**, *s.* Tresor *m*.

**stroppy** ['strɔpi], *adj. F:* ungehalten.

**structure** ['strʌktʃər], *s.* Struktur *f*; (*manner of construction*) Bauart *f* (eines Hauses); Bauweise *f*; (*building*) Bauwerk *n*; (*social*) Struktur *f*; **s. of a sentence**, Satzbau *m*. ◆'**structural**, *adj.* Struktur-; baulich; Bau-; **s. engineering**, Hochbau *m*.

**struggle** ['strʌgl]. **I.** s. Kampf m. **II.** v.i. kämpfen (**for sth.,** um etwas acc); **we struggled through,** wir haben uns durchgekämpft.

**strum** [strʌm], v.tr. & i. **to s. (on) the piano/the guitar,** auf dem Klavier/auf der Gitarre klimpern.

**strut¹** [strʌt]. **I.** s. stolzer Gang m. **II.** v.i. stolzieren.

**strut²,** s. (for building) Strebe f.

**stub** [stʌb]. **I.** s. (short piece) Stummel m; (of tree) Baumstumpf m; (ticket) s., Kontrollabschnitt m. **II.** v.tr. (a) **to s. one's toe,** sich dat die Zehe anstoßen; (b) **to s. out a cigarette,** eine Zigarette ausdrücken. ◆**'stubby,** adj. kurz und dick; **s. fingers,** Wurstfinger mpl.

**stubble** ['stʌbl], s. Stoppel f. ◆**'stubbly,** adj. stoppelig.

**stubborn** ['stʌbən], adj. hartnäckig; Pej: (of pers.) eigensinnig.

**stucco** ['stʌkəu], s. Stuck m.

**stud¹** [stʌd]. s. **1.** (nail) Nagel m; Fb: (on boot) Stollen m. **2. collar** s., Kragenknopf m. ◆**'studded,** adj. mit Nägeln beschlagen.

**stud²,** s. s. **(farm),** Gestüt n; (stallion) Zuchthengst m.

**student** ['stju:d(ə)nt], s. Student(in) m(f).

**studio,** pl. -os [stju:diəu, -əuz], s. Studio n.

**studious** ['stju:diəs], adj. lernbegierig.

**study** ['stʌdi]. **I.** s. **1.** (a) Studie f; **to make a s. of sth.,** etwas studieren; **the s. of physics,** das Studium der Physik; (b) pl. **studies,** Studium n. **2.** Mus: Etüde f. **3.** (room) Arbeitszimmer n. **II.** v.tr. & i. studieren; **to s. for an examination,** sich auf eine Prüfung vorbereiten. ◆**'studied,** adj. absichtlich.

**stuff** [stʌf]. **I.** s. F: Zeug n; **he knows his s.,** er kennt sich aus; (b) **have you got all your s.?** hast du deine ganzen Sachen? **II.** v.tr. (a) (fill) (etwas) vollstopfen; (ein Kissen, Cu: Geflügel usw.) füllen; (ein Sofa) polstern; (of taxidermist) (ein Tier) ausstopfen; (b) **to s. up a hole,** ein Loch zustopfen; (c) **to s. sth. into sth.,** etwas in etwas acc stopfen. ◆**'stuffing,** s. (all senses) Füllung f.

**stuffy** ['stʌfi], adj. (a) (of air) stickig; (of room) muffig; (b) (of pers.) spießig.

**stumble** ['stʌmbl], v.i. (a) stolpern; **to s. (in one's speech),** sich verhaspeln; Fig: **stumbling block,** (obstacle) Hindernis n; (b) **to s. on s.o., sth.,** zufällig auf j-n, etwas acc stoßen.

**stump** [stʌmp]. **I.** s. **1.** (of tree, tooth etc.) Stumpf m; (of pencil, cigar etc.) Stummel m. **2.** (in cricket) Torstab m. **II.** v.tr. F: (j-n) verblüffen; **to be stumped,** aufgeschmissen sein. ◆**'stumpy,** adj. stumpfartig; (of pers.) untersetzt.

**stun** [stʌn], v.tr. betäuben; **the news stunned me,** ich war von der Nachricht wie betäubt. ◆**'stunning,** adj. F: toll.

**stunt¹** [stʌnt], v.tr. **to s. the growth of**

s.o., sth., j-n, etwas im Wachstum hemmen. ◆**'stunted,** adj. (of pers. etc.) verkümmert.

**stunt²,** s. s. **flying,** Kunstflug m; Cin: **s. man,** Stuntman m; Pej: **publicity** s., Werbetrick m.

**stupefy** ['stju:pifai], v.tr. (j-n) erstaunen.

**stupendous** [stju:'pendəs], adj. umwerfend.

**stupid** ['stju:pid], adj. dumm, F: blöd. ◆**stu'pidity,** s. Dummheit f.

**stupor** ['stju:pər], s. Betäubung f; **to be in a s.,** betäubt sein.

**sturdy** ['stə:di], adj. kräftig; (of pers.) robust; (of structure) stabil.

**stutter** ['stʌtər]. **I.** s. **1.** Stottern n. **II.** v.tr. & i. (etwas) stottern.

**sty,** pl. **sties** [stai, staiz], s. (pig) s., Schweinestall m.

**sty(e)** [stai], s. Med: Gerstenkorn n.

**style** [stail]. **I.** s. **1.** Stil m; (kind) Art f; (manner) Weise f; Cl: **the latest s.,** die neueste Mode; **to live in s.,** auf großem Fuß leben. **II.** v.tr. (das Haar) modisch frisieren; (for men) (Haare) im Fassonschnitt schneiden. ◆**'stylish,** adj. schick. ◆**'stylist,** s. (hair) s., Friseur m, Friseuse f. ◆**'stylize,** v.tr. (etwas) stilisieren.

**sub-** [sʌb]. **I.** prefix Unter-. **II.** s. Nau: F: U-Boot n.

**subconscious** [sʌb'kɔnʃəs], adj. unterbewußt; **-ly,** adv. im Unterbewußtsein.

**subcontract** [sʌb'kɔntrækt], s. Nebenvertrag m. ◆**subcon'tractor,** s. Unterkontrahent m; (supplier) Lieferant m.

**subdivide** [sʌbdi'vaid], v. **1.** v.tr. (etwas) unterteilen. **2.** v.i. sich unterteilen. ◆**subdi'vision,** s. (category) Unterabteilung f.

**subdue** [səb'dju:], v.tr. (a) (j-n, etwas) unterwerfen; (b) (das Licht usw.) dämpfen. ◆**sub'dued,** adj. (a) (quiet) ruhig; (gloomy) bedrückt; (b) (of colour, lighting etc.) gedämpft.

**sub-edit** ['sʌb'edit], v.tr. redigieren. ◆**'sub-'editor,** s. zweiter (zweite) Redakteur(in) m(f).

**subheading** ['sʌbhediŋ], s. Untertitel m.

**subject. I.** s. **1.** (pers.) Staatsbürger(in) m(f). **2.** Gram: Subjekt n. **3.** (a) Thema n (eines Aufsatzes usw.); **s. (matter),** Gegenstand m (eines Buches usw.); (b) Sch: Fach n. **II.** ['sʌbdʒikt] adj. **1. s. to s.o.,** j-m unterworfen. **2.** Adm: -pflichtig; **s. to modification,** Änderungen vorbehalten. **III.** [səb'dʒekt] v.tr. (ein Volk) unterwerfen; **to s. s.o. to sth.,** j-n etwas dat aussetzen. ◆**sub'jective,** adj. subjektiv.

**subjunctive** [səb'dʒun(k)tiv], s. Gram: Konjunktiv m.

**sublet** ['sʌb'let], v.tr. (ein Zimmer usw.) untervermieten.

**sublime** [sə'blaim], adj. (a) (lofty) erhaben; (extremely beautiful) himmlisch; (b) **s. ignorance,** selige Unwissenheit.

◆**sublimate** ['sʌblimeit], *v.tr.* (Gefühle) sublimieren.

**submarine** ['sʌbməri:n], *s.* Unterseeboot *n*, U-Boot *n*.

**submerge** [səb'mə:dʒ], *v.* **1.** *v.tr.* (a) untertauchen; (b) (flood) (ein Feld usw.) überschwemmen. **2.** *v.i.* (of submarine, diver) tauchen. ◆**sub'merged**, *adj.* unter Wasser; (by flood) überschwemmt. ◆**sub'mersion**, *s.* Untertauchen *n*.

**submission** [səb'miʃ(ə)n], *s.* **1.** (a) Unterwerfung *f* (von Rebellen usw.); (b) (obedience) Ergebenheit *f.* **2.** Unterbreitung *f* (einer Frage usw.); Vorlegen *n* (einer Sache). **3.** (claim) Behauptung *f.* ◆**sub'missive**, *adj.* (servile) unterwürfig. ◆**sub'mit**, *v.* **1.** *v.i.* sich fügen (**to s.o., sth.**, j-m, etwas *dat*). **2.** *v.tr.* **to s. sth. to s.o.**, j-m etwas vorlegen; **to s. a question**, eine Frage unterbreiten.

**subnormal** [sʌb'nɔ:m(ə)l], *adj.* (of pers.) geistig zurückgeblieben.

**subordinate** [sə'bɔ:dinət]. **I.** *adj.* untergeordnet (**to s.o.**, j-m); *Gram:* **s. clause**, Nebensatz *m.* **II.** *s.* Untergebene(r) *f(m).*

**subpoena** [sʌb'pi:nə], *Jur: esp. N.Am:* *v.tr.* (j-n) unter Strafandrohung vorladen.

**subscribe** [səb'skraib], *v.* **1.** *v.tr.* (eine Summe) spenden; **to s. £10, £10** stiften. **2.** *v.i.* (a) **to s. to a charity**, einem Wohltätigkeitsverein einen Beitrag zahlen; (b) **to s. to a newspaper**, eine Zeitung abonnieren. ◆**sub'scriber**, *s.* **1.** (to newspaper etc.) Abonnent(in) *m(f).* **2.** (telephone) **s.**, Teilnehmer(in) *m(f).* ◆**subscription** [-'skripʃ(ə)n], *s.* **1.** (member's) **s.**, Mitgliedsbeitrag *m.* **2.** (for theatre, magazine etc.) Abonnement *n.*

**subsequent** ['sʌbsikwənt], *adj.* folgend; (later) später; **-ly**, *adv.* später; (as a result) infolgedessen.

**subside** [səb'said], *v.i.* (a) (of ground) sich senken; (b) (of water level) sinken; (c) (of storm, anger, fever, noise) nachlassen. ◆**subsidence** [sʌbsidəns], *s.* Bodensenkung *f.*

**subsidiary** [səb'sidjəri]. **I.** *adj.* untergeordnet. **II.** *s.* *Com:* Filiale *f;* Tochtergesellschaft *f.*

**subsidy** ['sʌbsidi], *s.* Subvention *f;* government **s.**, Staatszuschuß *m.* ◆**'subsidize**, *v.tr.* subventionieren.

**subsistence** [səb'sistəns], *s.* Lebensunterhalt *m;* **s. allowance**, Unterhaltsbeihilfe *f.*

**substance** ['sʌbstəns], *s.* **1.** Substanz *f;* *Fig:* **the s.** (of an argument etc.), das Wesentliche *n* (an einem Argument usw.). **2.** (wealth) **a man of s.**, ein wohlhabender Mann. ◆**substantial** [səb'stænʃ(ə)l], *adj.* **1.** (real) wirklich. **2.** (large) beträchtlich. **3.** (a) **a s. meal**, ein reichliches Essen; (b) (of structure) solide; **-ally**, *adv.* (a) beträchtlich; (b) (essentially) **s. the same**, im wesentlichen gleich. ◆**sub'stantiate**, *v.tr.* (einen Anspruch

usw.) begründen.

**substandard** ['sʌb'stændəd], *adj.* unter der Norm.

**substitute** ['sʌbstitju:t]. **I.** *s.* **1.** (pers.) Stellvertreter *m; Fb:* Auswechselspieler *m.* **2.** (material, foodstuff) Ersatz *m;* **coffee s.**, Kaffee-Ersatz *m.* **II.** *v.tr.* **s. concrete for stone**, Stein durch Beton ersetzen.

**subterfuge** ['sʌbtəfju:dʒ], *s.* List *f;* (evasion) Ausflucht *f.*

**subterranean** [sʌbtə'reiniən], *adj.* unterirdisch.

**subtitle** ['sʌbtaitl], *s.* Untertitel *m.*

**subtle** ['sʌtl], *adj.* **1.** fein. **2.** (a) (ingenious) raffiniert; (b) (crafty) schlau. ◆**'subtlety**, *s.* (a) Feinheit *f;* (b) Raffiniertheit *f;* Schlauheit *f.*

**subtract** [səb'trækt], *v.tr.* (eine Zahl usw.) abziehen, *Mth:* subtrahieren (**from**, von + *dat*). ◆**sub'traction**, *s. Mth:* Subtraktion *f.*

**suburb** ['sʌbə:b], *s.* Vorort *m.* ◆**su'burban** [sə-], *adj.* vorstädtisch; Vorstadt-. ◆**su'burbia**, *s. usu. Pej:* Vorstadt *f.*

**subversion** [səb'və:ʃ(ə)n], *s. Pol:* Staatsgefährdung *f; Fig:* Untergrabung *f* (der Moral usw.). ◆**sub'versive**, *adj.* subversiv.

**subway** ['sʌbwei], *s.* **1.** Unterführung *f* (für Fußgänger). **2.** *N.Am: Rail:* U-Bahn *f.*

**succeed** [sək'si:d], *v.* **1.** *v.tr.* **to s. s.o. (in office)**, j-m (im Amt) nachfolgen. **2.** *v.i.* (a) (of project) gelingen; (of pers.) **if I s.**, wenn es mir gelingt. ◆**suc'ceeding**, *adj.* (nächst)folgend. ◆**suc'cess**, *s.* Erfolg. ◆**suc'cessful**, *adj.* (of pers.) erfolgreich; **he was s. (in doing sth.)**, es gelang ihm(, etwas zu tun). ◆**suc'cession**, *s.* **1.** (a) (sequence) Folge *f;* **in s.**, hintereinander; (b) (series) Reihe *f.* **2.** (to title etc.) Erbfolge *f;* **s. to the throne**, Thronfolge *f.* ◆**suc'cessive**, *adj.* aufeinanderfolgend; **-ly**, *adv.* **to win two games s.**, zwei Spiele nacheinander gewinnen. ◆**suc'cessor**, *s.* Nachfolger(in) *m(f);* **s. to s.o.**, j-s Nachfolger.

**succinct** [sʌk'siŋ(k)t], *adj.* prägnant.

**succulent** ['sʌkjulənt], *adj.* saftig.

**succumb** [sə'kʌm], *v.i.* **to s. to an illness**, *Fig:* temptation etc., einer Krankheit, *Fig:* einer Versuchung usw. erliegen.

**such** [sʌtʃ], *adj. & adv.* **1.** solch; **s. a man**, so ein Mann; **he drives at s. a speed that ...**, er fährt so schnell, daß ...; **s. a thing**, so etwas, *F:* so was; **s. big houses**, so große/solche große Häuser; **s. a long time**, so lange; **s. was his courage that ...**, so groß war sein Mut, daß ...; **some s. plan**, irgend so ein Plan. **2.** **s. as**, (so) wie; **men s. as you/s. men as you**, Männer wie Sie; *F:* **s. as?** zum Beispiel? ◆**'suchlike**. **I.** *adj. F:* derartig. **II.** *pron. usu. pl.* **and s.**, und dergleichen.

**suck** [sʌk], *v.tr. & i.* (*a*) (etwas) saugen (**out of**, aus + *dat*); (*b*) **to s. sweets/an ice-cream**, Bonbons/ein Eis lutschen. ◆'**suck** '**down**, *v.tr.* (*of current, bog etc.*) (j-n, etwas) hinunterziehen. ◆'**sucker**, *s. P:* (*pers.*) Dussel *m.* ◆'**suckle**, *v.tr.* (ein Jungtier) säugen; (ein Baby) stillen. ◆'**suck** '**up**, *v.* 1. *v.tr.* (Flüssigkeit usw.) aufsaugen. 2. *v.i. F:* **to s. up to s.o.**, j-m um den Bart gehen. ◆'**suction**, *s.* (*action*) Saugen *n*; (*effect*) Saugwirkung *f*; **s. pump**, Saugpumpe *f.*

**Sudan** [suːˈdæn, suːˈdɑːn]. *Pr. n.* **the S.**, der Sudan *m.* ◆**Sudanese** [-dəˈniːz]. I. *adj.* sudanesisch. II. *s.* Sudanese *m*; Sudanesin *f.*

**sudden** [ˈsʌdn]. I. *adj.* plötzlich. II. *adv. phr.* **all of a s.**, ganz plötzlich; **-ly**, *adv.* plötzlich.

**suds** [sʌdz], *s.pl.* (**soap-**)**s.**, Seifenlauge *f.*

**sue** [suː, sjuː], *v.tr. Jur:* **to s. s.o.**, gegen j-n gerichtlich vorgehen.

**suede** [sweid], *s.* Wildleder *n.*

**suet** [ˈsjuːit], *s.* Rindertalg *m.*

**suffer** [ˈsʌfər], *v.* 1. *v.tr.* (*a*) (Verluste, Schmerzen, den Tod usw.) erleiden; **to s. damage**, beschädigt werden; (*b*) (*bear*) (j-s Launen usw.) ertragen. 2. *v.i.* leiden (**from an illness**, an einer Krankheit; **from neglect** etc., unter Vernachlässigung usw.). ◆'**sufferer**, *s.* Leidende(r) *f(m).* ◆'**suffering**. I. *adj.* leidend. II. *s.* Leiden *n.*

**suffice** [səˈfais], *v.i.* genügen; **s. it to say**, kurz und gut. ◆**su'fficient**, *adj.* genügend; **£100 will be s.**, hundert Pfund werden genügen/reichen.

**suffix** [ˈsʌfiks], *s. Gram:* Nachsilbe *f.*

**suffocate** [ˈsʌfəkeit], *v.tr. & i.* ersticken. ◆'**suffocating**, *adj.* erstickend. ◆**suffo'cation**, *s.* Ersticken *n.*

**suffrage** [ˈsʌfridʒ], *s.* Wahlrecht *n.*

**sugar** [ˈʃugər]. I. *s.* Zucker *m*; **s. cane**, Zuckerrohr *n*; **s. lump**, Stück *n* Zucker. II. *v.tr.* zuckern. ◆'**sugary**, *adj.* (*a*) zuckrig; (**too**) **s.**, zu süß; (*b*) *Pej:* (*of smile, words etc.*) zuckersüß.

**suggest** [səˈdʒest], *v.tr.* (*a*) **to s. sth. to s.o.**, j-m etwas vorschlagen/(*recommend*) nahelegen; (*b*) (*indicate*) (*of evidence etc.*) (auf etwas *acc*) hindeuten; **this shape suggests a rabbit**, diese Form erinnert an ein Kaninchen; (*c*) (*assert*) (etwas) behaupten. ◆**su'ggestion**, *s.* (*a*) Vorschlag *m*; **to make a s.**, etwas vorschlagen; **at his s.**, auf seinen Vorschlag hin; (*b*) Behauptung *f*; (*c*) (*trace*) Spur *f.* ◆**su'ggestive**, *adj.* (*a*) vielsagend; (*b*) (*of remark etc.*) zweideutig.

**suicide** [ˈsjuːˌisaid], *s.* (*act*) Selbstmord *m*; **to commit s.**, Selbstmord begehen; **attempted s.**, Selbstmordversuch *m.* ◆**sui'cidal**, *adj.* **s. tendencies**, selbstmörderische Neigungen; *F:* **I feel s.**, ich könnte mich umbringen.

**suit** [suːt, sjuːt]. I. *s.* 1. *Jur:* Klage *f.* 2. *Cl:* (*man's*) Anzug *m*; (*woman's*) Kostüm *n.* 3. (*in cards*) Farbe *f*; **to follow s.**, *Fig:* dasselbe tun. II. *v.tr.* (*a*) (*of pers.*) **to be suited to sth.**, für etwas *acc* geeignet sein; (*b*) (*of thing*) (j-m) passen; **I shall do it when it suits me**, ich werde es tun, wenn es mir paßt; **this colour suits you**, diese Farbe steht Ihnen gut. ◆**suita'bility**, *s.* Eignung *f*; Schicklichkeit *f* (einer Bemerkung, des Benehmens usw.). ◆'**suitable**, *adj.* passend; **to be s. to/for sth.**, zu etwas *dat*/für etwas *acc* geeignet sein/passen. ◆'**suitcase**, *s.* Koffer *m.*

**suite** [swiːt], *s.* 1. (*a*) **s. of rooms**, Zimmerflucht *f*; (*in hotel*) Suite *f*; (*b*) **s. of furniture**, Möbelgarnitur *f*; **lounge s.**, Sitzgarnitur *f.* 2. *Mus:* Suite *f.*

**sulk** [sʌlk], *v.i.* schmollen. ◆'**sulky**, *adj.* mürrisch; (*of temperament*) verdrießliche Miene.

**sullen** [ˈsʌlən], *adj.* verdrossen; **s. expression**, verdrießliche Miene.

**sulphur** [ˈsʌlfər], *s.* Schwefel *m.* ◆'**sulphate**, *s.* Sulfat *n.* ◆**sulphuric** [-ˈfjuːrik], *adj.* Schwefel-.

**sultan** [ˈsʌltən], *s.* 1. Sultan *m.* ◆**sultana** [-ˈtɑːnə], *s.* 1. Sultanin *f.* 2. (*raisin*) Sultanine *f.*

**sultry** [ˈsʌltri], *adj.* schwül; (*of temperament*) heißblütig.

**sum** [sʌm], *s.* 1. (*a*) (*total*) Summe *f*; **s. total**, Gesamtsumme *f*; (*b*) **s.** (*of money*), Betrag *m*, Summe *f.* 2. *Mth: F:* Rechenaufgabe *f*; **to do sums**, rechnen. ◆'**summarize**, *v.tr.* (eine Rede usw.) zusammenfassen. ◆'**summary**. I. *adj.* (*immediate*) unverzüglich; (*of dismissal*) fristlos; *Jur:* summarisch. II. *s.* Zusammenfassung *f.* ◆'**sum** '**up**, *v.tr.* (*a*) (kurz) zusammenfassen; (*b*) **to s. up I would like to say ...**, zusammenfassend möchte ich sagen, ...

**summer** [ˈsʌmər], *s.* Sommer *m*; **in** (**the**) **s.**, im Sommer. ◆'**summertime**, *s.* Sommerzeit *f.* ◆'**summery**, *adj.* sommerlich.

**summit** [ˈsʌmit], *s.* Gipfel *m*; *Pol:* **s. meeting**, Gipfeltreffen *n.*

**summon** [ˈsʌmən], *v.tr.* (*a*) j-n (zu sich *dat*) bestellen; (die Feuerwehr usw.) rufen; *Jur:* **to s. s.o.** (**as a witness**), j-n (als Zeugen) vorladen; (*b*) **to s. a meeting**, eine Versammlung einberufen; (*c*) **to s. up one's courage/all one's strength**, seinen Mut/seine ganzen Kräfte zusammenraffen. ◆'**summons**, *s.* 1. Aufforderung *f* (**to s.o.**, zu j-m zu kommen). 2. *Jur:* Vorladung *f.*

**sumptuous** [ˈsʌm(p)tjuəs], *adj.* (*of clothes, feast*) prächtig; **a. meal**, ein üppiges Mahl.

**sun** [sʌn]. I. *s.* Sonne *f.* II. *v.tr.* **to s. oneself**, sich sonnen. ◆'**sunbathe**, *v.tr.* sich sonnen. ◆'**sunbathing**, *s.* Sonnenbaden *n.* ◆'**sunbeam**, *s.* Sonnenstrahl *m.* ◆'**sunburn**, *s.* Sonnenbrand *m.*

◆'**sunburnt,** *adj.* (*tanned*) sonnengebräunt; (*esp. excessively*) sonnenverbrannt. ◆'**Sunday,** *s.* Sonntag *m.*
◆'**sundial,** *s.* Sonnenuhr *f.*
◆'**sunflower,** *s.* Sonnenblume *f.*
◆'**sunglasses,** *s.pl.* Sonnenbrille *f.*
◆'**sunlight,** *s.* Sonnenlicht *n.*
◆'**sunlit,** *adj.* sonnenbeschienen.
◆'**sunny,** *adj.* sonnig. ◆'**sunrise,** *s.* Sonnenaufgang *m.* ◆'**sunset,** *s.* Sonnenuntergang *m.* ◆'**sunshine,** *s.* Sonnenschein *m;* **in the s.,** in der Sonne.
◆'**sunstroke,** *s.* Sonnenstich *m.*
◆'**suntan,** *s.* Sonnenbräune *f.*
◆'**suntanned,** *adj.* sonnengebräunt.

**sundry** ['sʌndri]. **I.** *adj.* verschiedene; **s. expenses,** diverse Unkosten. **II.** *s.* (*a*) **all and s.,** jedermann; (*b*) *pl.* **sundries,** Verschiedenes *n;* (*with meal*) Beilagen *fpl.*

**sunken** ['sʌŋkən], *adj.* (*of wreck etc.*) versunken; (*of garden, bath etc.*) versenkt.

**super** ['suːpər]. **I.** *adj. F:* toll. **II.** *prefix* Super-. (*See also* ...)

**superannuation** [suːpərænjuˈeiʃən], *s.* Pension *f.*

**superb** [suːˈpəːb], *adj.* (*outstanding*) hervorragend; (*beautiful*) herrlich.

**supercilious** [suːpəˈsiliəs], *adj.* (*of manner*) hochnäsig; (*of remark*) geringschätzig.

**superficial** [suːpəˈfiʃ(ə)l], *adj.* oberflächlich.

**superfluous** [suːˈpəːfluəs], *adj.* überflüssig.

**superimpose** [suːpərimˈpəuz], *v.tr.* (etwas) darüberlegen; **to s. sth. on sth.,** etwas über etwas *acc* legen.

**superintendent** [suːpərinˈtendənt], *s.* Direktor *m; Adm:* Aufsichtsbeamte(r) *m;* **police s.,** Polizeikommissar *m.*

**superior** [suːˈpiəriər]. **I.** *adj.* **1.** (*better*) (*of pers.*) überlegen (**to s.o.,** j-m); (*of thing*) besser (**to,** als). **2.** (*higher*) *Mil: etc:* **s. officer,** Vorgesetzter *m; Jur: etc:* **s. court,** höhere Instanz. **3.** (*supercilious*) überheblich. **II.** *s.* (*a*) (*at work etc.*) Vorgesetzte(r) *f(m);* (*b*) *Ecc:* **Mother S.,** Oberin *f.* ◆**superiority** [-ˈɔriti], *s.* **1.** Überlegenheit *f* (**over,** über + *dat*); **s. in strength,** Übermacht *f.* **2.** Überheblichkeit *f.*

**superlative** [suːˈpəːlətiv]. **I.** *adj.* unübertrefflich. **II.** *s. Gram:* Superlativ *m.*

**superman,** *pl.* **-men** ['suːpəmæn, -men], *s.* Übermensch *m.*

**supermarket** ['suːpəmaːkit], *s.* Supermarkt *m.*

**supernatural** [suːpəˈnætʃ(ə)rəl], *adj.* übernatürlich.

**superpower** ['suːpəpauər], *s. Pol:* Supermacht *f.*

**supersede** [suːpəˈsiːd], *v.tr.* (etwas) ersetzen (**by sth.,** durch etwas *acc*); **a method now superseded,** eine jetzt überholte Methode.

**supersonic** [suːpəˈsɔnik], *adj.* Überschall-.

**superstition** [suːpəˈstiʃ(ə)n], *s.* Aberglau-

be *m.* ◆**super'stitious,** *adj.* abergläubisch.

**superstructure** ['suːpəstrʌktʃər], *s.* Oberbau *m; Nau:* Aufbauten *mpl.*

**supervise** ['suːpəvaiz], *v.tr.* beaufsichtigen. ◆**supervision** [-ˈviʒ(ə)n], *s.* Beaufsichtigung *f;* **under police s.,** unter Polizeiaufsicht *f.* ◆'**supervisor,** *s.* Aufseher *m.*

**supper** ['sʌpər], *s.* Abendessen *n;* **to have s.,** zu Abend essen; *Ecc:* **the Last S.,** das letzte Abendmahl.

**supple** ['sʌpl], *adj.* geschmeidig; (*flexible*) biegsam.

**supplement. I.** ['sʌplimənt] *s.* **1.** (*addition*) Ergänzung *f* (**to,** *gen*). **2.** (*a*) Beilage *f;* (*to book, report*) Nachtrag *m;* (*b*) *Rail: etc:* (*to fare*) Zuschlag *m.* **II.** ['sʌplimənt] *v.tr.* **to s. one's income by sth.,** sein Einkommen durch etwas *acc* ergänzen. ◆**supple'mentary,** *adj.* zusätzlich.

**supply** [səˈplai]. **I.** *s.* **1.** (*act*) Versorgung *f* (**of,** mit + *dat*); (*delivery*) Lieferung *f; Tchn:* Zufuhr *f* (von Öl usw.); **in short s.,** knapp. **2.** (*store*) Vorrat *m* (**of,** an + *dat*); **supplies,** Vorräte *mpl;* (*food*) Proviant *m;* **office supplies,** Bürobedarf *m.* **II.** *v.tr.* (*a*) **to s. s.o. with sth./sth. to s.o.,** j-n mit etwas *dat* versorgen; (*b*) *Com:* (j-n) beliefern; (Waren) liefern. ◆**su'pplier,** *s.* Lieferant *m* (von Waren).

**support** [səˈpɔːt]. **I.** *s.* **1.** (*a*) (*act*) Unterstützung *f;* **to be without means of s.,** mittellos sein. **2.** (*object*) Stütze *f;* (*of arch etc.*) Träger *m.* **II.** *v.tr.* (*a*) (*einen Bogen etc.*) stützen; (*b*) *Fig:* (*with money, help*) unterstützen; (*with comfort*) (j-m) beistehen; (eine Theorie, einen Anspruch) bestätigen; (*c*) (j-n, eine Familie) erhalten/(*feed*) ernähren. ◆**su'pporter,** *s.* Verfechter *m* (einer Sache); *Fb: etc:* Anhänger *m.* ◆**su'pporting,** *adj.* (*a*) stützend; Stütz-; **s. wall,** Stützmauer *f;* (*b*) *Th: Cin:* **s. cast,** Mitspieler *mpl;* **s. role,** Nebenrolle *f.*

**suppose** [səˈpəuz], *v.tr.* (*a*) (*treat as fact*) (etwas) annehmen; **s./supposing (that) ...** angenommen, daß ...; (*b*) (*imagine*) (etwas) vermuten, (*think*) glauben, **I s. so,** es ist wohl anzunehmen; (*c*) **to be supposed to do sth.,** etwas tun sollen; **I'm not really supposed to be here,** eigentlich dürfte ich nicht hier sein. ◆**su'pposed,** *adj.* vermeintlich; **-ly,** *adv.* vermutlich. ◆**supposition** [sʌpəˈziʃ(ə)n], *s.* Vermutung *f;* (*assumption*) Annahme *f.*

**suppress** [səˈpres], *v.tr.* unterdrücken; (eine Veröffentlichung) verbieten; (einen Skandal, die Wahrheit) vertuschen. ◆**su'ppression,** *s.* **1.** Unterdrückung *f.* **2.** Verbot *m;* (*hushing up*) Vertuschung *f.* ◆**su'ppressor,** *s.* **1.** Unterdrücker *m.* **2.** *El:* Entstörer *m.*

**supreme** [suˈ(ː)priːm], *adj.* (*a*) (*highest*) höchste(r,s); (*in rank*) oberste(r,s); (*b*) (*unbeatable*) unübertrefflich; *Sp:* unschlagbar; (*c*) (*ultimate*) äußerste(r,s). ◆**supremacy** ['-'preməsi], *s.* Vorherrschaft *f* (**over**, über + *acc*); Oberhoheit *f* (der Kirche, des Staates).

**surcharge** ['sɜːtʃɑːdʒ], *s.* Zuschlag *m.*

**sure** [ʃuər]. I. *adj.* sicher; **s. of oneself**, selbstsicher; **he's s. to know**, er wird es bestimmt wissen; **to make s. of sth.**, sich einer Sache vergewissern; (*check*) etwas prüfen; **just to make s.**, (einfach) um sicherzugehen; **s. footing**, fester Halt. II. *adv.* **s. enough he was there**, er war wie erwartet/tatsächlich da; **-ly**, *adv.* 1. sicher; **slowly but s.**, langsam aber sicher. 2. (*intensive*) doch; **s. you don't believe that!** das glauben Sie doch nicht im Ernst! ◆**'sure-'footed**, *adj.* mit sicherem Tritt.

**surf** [sɜːf]. I. *s.* Brandung *f.* II. *v.i.* wellenreiten. ◆**'surfboard**, *s.* Surfbrett *n.* ◆**'surfing**, *s.* Wellenreiten *n*, Surfing *n.*

**surface** ['sɜːfis]. I. *s.* 1. (*top, exterior*) Oberfläche *f*; (**road**) *s.* Straßendecke *f.* 2. (*area*) Fläche *f.* II. *v.* 1. *v.tr.* (eine Straße) asphaltieren. 2. *v.i.* auftauchen.

**surge** [sɜːdʒ]. I. *s.* (*a*) Schwall *m* (des Wassers usw.); **s. of power**, Kräftestoß *m*; (*b*) *Fig:* Aufwallung *f* (von Freude, Zorn usw.). II. *v.i.* (*of sea*) wogen; (*of crowd*) **to s. forward**, nach vorn drängen.

**surgeon** ['sɜːdʒən], *s.* Chirurg *m.* ◆**'surgery**, *s.* 1. Chirurgie *f*; **further s. is not necessary**, weitere chirurgische Eingriffe sind nicht nötig. 2. (*place*) Praxis *f*; **s.** (**hours**), Sprechstunden *fpl.* ◆**'surgical**, *adj.* chirurgisch; **s. appliances**, Sanitätsartikel *mpl.*

**surly** ['sɜːli], *adj.* griesgrämig; (*in speech*) schroff; (*rude*) grob.

**surmise** [sə(ː)'maiz], *v.tr.* (etwas) vermuten.

**surmount** [sə(ː)'maunt], *v.tr.* überwinden.

**surname** ['sɜːneim], *s.* Familienname *m.*

**surpass** [sə(ː)'pɑːs], *v.tr.* übertreffen.

**surplice** ['sɜːplis], *s.* Chorhemd *n.*

**surplus** ['sɜːpləs], *s.* (*a*) Überschuß *m* (of sth., an etwas *dat*); (*b*) *attrib.* überschüssig; Über-.

**surprise** [sə'praiz]. I. *s.* Überraschung *f*; **to take s.o. by s.**, j-n überraschen/*Mil:* überrumpeln; **s. visit**, unerwarteter Besuch. II. *v.tr.* (j-n) überraschen; **surprised at sth.**, von etwas *dat* überrascht; **I'm surprised at you!** ich staune über Sie! ◆**sur'prising**, *adj.* überraschend.

**surrealism** [sə'ri:əlizm], *s.* Surrealismus *m.* ◆**su'rrealist**. I. *s.* Surrealist(in) *m(f).* II. *adj.* surrealistisch.

**surrender** [sə'rendər]. I. *s.* 1. (*handing over*) Übergabe *f* (einer Sache, *Mil:* einer Festung usw.); Auslieferung *f* (von Gefangenen usw.). 2. *Mil:* Kapitulation *f* (eines Heeres). II. *v.* 1. *v.tr.* (*a*) (etwas) übergeben; (Gefangene usw.) ausliefern; (*b*) (*give up*) (einen Besitz) aufgeben; **to**

**s. a right**, auf ein Recht verzichten. 2. *v.i.* **to s.** (**to the enemy**), sich (dem Feind) ergeben; **to s.** (**to the police**), sich (der Polizei) stellen.

**surreptitious** [sʌrəp'tiʃəs], *adj.* heimlich.

**surround** [sə'raund]. I. *s.* Umrandung *f.* II. *v.tr.* (*a*) (j-n, etwas) umgeben; (*b*) *Mil:* umzingeln. ◆**su'rrounding**, *adj.* umliegend. ◆**su'rroundings**, *s.pl.* Umgebung *f.*

**surveillance** [sə(ː)'veiləns], *s.* Überwachung *f.*

**survey.** I. ['sɜːvei] *s.* 1. (*a*) (*esp. written*) Übersicht *f* (**of**, über + *acc*); (*b*) (*examination*) Untersuchung *f*; (*c*) (*opinion poll*) Umfrage *f.* 2. (*of land etc.*) Vermessung *f*; **air/aerial s.**, Luftbildmessung *f.* II. [sə(ː)'vei] *v.tr.* (*a*) (*from high point*) überblicken; (*b*) (*examine*) (etwas) untersuchen; (*c*) (Land usw.) vermessen. ◆**sur'veying**, *s.* Vermessung *f.* ◆**sur'veyor**, *s.* (**land**) *s.*, Landvermesser *m.*

**survival** [sə'vaiv(ə)l], *s.* Überleben *n.* ◆**sur'vive**, *v.tr. & i.* überleben. ◆**sur'vivor**, *s.* Überlebende(r) *f(m).*

**susceptible** [sə'septibl], *adj.* empfindlich; **s. to pain**, schmerzempfindlich; **s. to a disease**, für eine Krankheit anfällig. ◆**suscepti'bility**, *s.* Anfälligkeit *f* (**to an illness etc.**, gegen/für eine Krankheit usw.); **s. to impressions**, Empfänglichkeit *f* für Eindrücke.

**suspect.** I. ['sʌspekt]. 1. *adj.* (*a*) (*of pers.*) verdächtig; (*b*) (*of thing*) suspekt. 2. *s.* Verdächtige(r) *f(m).* II. [sə'spekt] *v.tr.* (*a*) verdächtigen (**of a murder etc.**, eines Mordes usw.); (*b*) (etwas) vermuten.

**suspend** [sə'spend], *v.tr.* (*a*) (*hang*) (etwas) aufhängen; **suspended in midair**, in der Luft hängend; (*b*) (*stop*) (Zahlungen, ein Verfahren usw.) einstellen; *Jur:* **suspended sentence**, Urteil *n* mit Bewährung; (*b*) (*ban*) (ein Mitglied) suspendieren; *Sp:* (einen Sportler) sperren. ◆**sus'pender**, *s.* (*a*) Strumpfhalter *m*; **s. belt**, Strumpfbandgürtel *m*; (*b*) *pl.* *N.Am:* Hosenträger *mpl.* ◆**sus'pense**, *s.* Spannung *f.* ◆**sus'pension**, *s.* 1. (*a*) **s. bridge**, Hängebrücke *f*; (*b*) *Aut:* Radaufhängung *f.* 2. Ausschließen *n* (eines Vereinsmitglieds usw.); *Sp:* Sperrung *f* (eines Spielers).

**suspicion** [sə'spiʃ(ə)n], *s.* 1. (*a*) Verdacht *m*; (*b*) (*state*) Mißtrauen *n*; **to regard s.o. with s.**, j-n mit Mißtrauen betrachten. 2. (*trace*) Spur *f.* ◆**sus'picious**, *adj.* (*a*) (*of behaviour etc.*) verdächtig; (*b*) (*of glance, attitude, pers.*) mißtrauisch (**about s.o., sth.**, gegen j-n, etwas *acc*); **to be s. of s.o.**, j-n verdächtigen; **-ly**, *adv.* (*a*) **to behave s.**, sich verdächtig benehmen; (*b*) **to look s. at s.o.**, j-n mißtrauisch ansehen.

**sustain** [sə'stein], *v.tr.* (*a*) (*keep going*) (j-n) erhalten; (*b*) (*suffer*) (eine Niederlage, eine Verletzung usw.) erleiden; (*c*) (*withstand*) (einen Druck usw.) aushalten; (einem Angriff) standhalten. ◆**sus'tained**, *adj.* Dauer-; (*of interest etc.*) anhaltend.

**sustenance** ['sʌstinəns], *s.* (*food*) Nahrung *f.*

**swab** [swɔb]. **I.** *s. Med:* (*a*) Tupfer *m;* (*b*) (*specimen*) Abstrich *m.* **II.** *v.tr.* (das Deck) schrubben.

**swagger** ['swægər]. **I.** *s.* 1. stolzierender Gang *m.* 2. (*boasting*) Prahlerei *f.* **II.** *v.i.* (*a*) stolzieren; (*b*) (*boast*) prahlen.

**swallow**[1] ['swɔləu]. **I.** *s.* Schluck *m.* **II.** *v.tr.* (*a*) schlucken; *Fig:* (eine Beleidigung, seinen Stolz usw.) herunterschlukken; (*b*) **to s. sth. (up)**, (*also Fig:*) etwas verschlingen.

**swallow**[2], *s. Orn:* Schwalbe *f.*

**swamp** [swɔmp]. **I.** *s.* Sumpf *m.* **II.** *v.tr.* überschwemmen; (*of waves*) **to s. a boat**, über einem Boot zusammenschlagen; *Fig:* (*of pers.*) **to be swamped with work**, mit Arbeit überhäuft sein.

**swan** [swɔn], *s.* Schwan *m.*

**swap** [swɔp]. **I.** *s.* Austausch *m.* **II.** *v.tr.* **to s. sth. for sth.**, etwas gegen etwas *acc* austauschen; **shall we s.?** tauschen wir?

**swarm** [swɔːm]. **I.** *s.* Schwarm *m;* **s. of bees**, Bienenschwarm *m.* **II.** *v.i.* (*a*) (*of bees*) schwärmen; (*of people, ants*) strömen; (*b*) **to s. with sth.**, von etwas *dat* wimmeln.

**swarthy** ['swɔːði], *adj.* dunkelhäutig.

**swastika** ['swɔstikə], *s.* Hakenkreuz *n.*

**swat** [swɔt], *v.tr.* (eine Fliege usw.) totschlagen.

**swathe** [sweið], *v.tr.* (j-n, etwas) einwickeln.

**sway** [swei]. **I.** *s.* 1. Schwanken *n.* 2. *Lit:* (*rule*) Herrschaft *f;* (*influence*) Einfluß *m;* **to hold s.**, herrschen (**over**, über + *acc*). **II.** *v.* 1. *v.i.* schwanken; (*gently*) sich wiegen; (*of boat*) schaukeln. 2. *v.tr.* (j-n, j-s Meinung) beeinflussen; (das Publikum) mitreißen.

**swear** [sweər], *v.irr.* 1. *v.tr.* (einen Eid, Treue usw.) schwören; **to s. to do sth.**, sich (eidlich) verpflichten, etwas zu tun; **to be sworn in**, vereidigt werden. 2. *v.i.* (*a*) schwören; **to s. by s.o., sth.**, auf j-n, etwas *acc* schwören; (*b*) (*curse*) fluchen; **to s. at s.o.**, auf j-n schimpfen. ◆**'swear-word**, *s.* Fluch *m.*

**sweat** [swet]. **I.** *s.* Schweiß *m;* **to be in a s.**, schwitzen. **II.** *v.tr. & i.* (*a*) schwitzen; *F:* **to s. it out**, es (mit Hangen und Bangen) durchstehen; (*b*) (*work*) **to s. blood**, Blut schwitzen. **III.** *s. Cl:* Pullover *m.* ◆**'sweaty**, *adj.* verschwitzt.

**Sweden** ['swiːd(ə)n]. *Pr.n.* Schweden *n.* ◆**Swede**, *s.* 1. (*pers.*) Schwede *m;* Schwedin *f.* 2. *Agr:* **s.**, Kohlrübe *f.* ◆**'Swedish. I.** *adj.* schwedisch. **II.** *s.* Schwedisch *n.*

**sweep** [swiːp]. **I.** *s.* 1. *Fig:* **to make a clean s.**, reinen Tisch machen. 2. (*movement*) (*a*) Schwung *m* (des Arms usw.);

(*b*) (*of radar*) Abtasten *n.* 3. (*a*) geschwungene Kurve *f* (einer Bucht, Straße usw.); (*b*) (*stretch*) weite Strecke *f.* 4. (*pers.*) (**chimney**) **s.**, Schornsteinfeger *m.* **II.** *v.tr.* 1. *v.tr.* (*a*) (das Zimmer, den Schornstein usw.) kehren, fegen; (*b*) (*of current*) **to s. s.o., sth. along**, j-n, etwas mitreißen; **to s. away obstacles etc.**, Hindernisse usw. aus dem Weg räumen; **I was swept off my feet**, ich war ganz hingerissen. 2. *v.i.* (*with broom*) kehren, fegen; (*of wind, rain*) fegen; (*of water*) strömen; (*of pers., vehicle*) **to s. (along)**, dahinfegen; **to s. into/out of a room**, in ein Zimmer hineinrauschen/aus einem Zimmer hinausrauschen; **to s. past**, vorbeirauschen. ◆**'sweeper**, *s.* (*for street, carpet etc.*) Kehrmaschine *f.* ◆**'sweeping. I.** *adj.* (*grand*) großangelegt; (*far-reaching*) weitgehend; **s. gesture**, weit ausholende Geste; **s. statement**, Verallgemeinerung *f;* **s. changes**, tiefgreifende Änderungen. ◆**'sweepstake**, *s.* Sweepstake *n.*

**sweet** [swiːt]. **I.** *adj.* süß; (*a*) *F:* **to have a s. tooth**, ein Leckermaul sein; (*b*) **s.-(smelling)**, wohlriechend; (*c*) (*of food, water*) frisch; (*of sound*) wohlklingend; (*e*) (*of child, girl*) lieb, süß. **II.** *s.* (*a*) Bonbon *n & m;* **sweets**, Süßigkeiten *fpl;* (*b*) (*course*) Nachtisch *m; -ly, adv.* 1. süß. 2. (*of machine*) **to run s.**, glatt laufen. ◆**'sweeten**, *v.tr.* (ein Getränk usw.) süßen. ◆**'sweetener/'sweetening**, *s.* Süßstoff *m.* ◆**'sweetheart**, *s.* Schatz *m.* ◆**'sweetie**, *s.* Bonbon *n & m.* ◆**'sweetness**, *s.* Süße *f.* ◆**'sweet-'tempered**, *adj.* gutmütig.

**swell** [swel]. **I.** *s. Nau:* Dünung *f.* **II.** *adj. esp. N.Am: F:* klasse. **III.** *v.irr.* 1. *v.tr.* (*a*) **the river was swollen with floodwater**, der Fluß war vom Hochwasser angeschwollen; (*b*) (*increase*) (eine Anzahl) erhöhen; (eine Menschenmenge) vergrößern. 2. *v.i.* anschwellen; (*of sail etc.*) blähen; (*grow in number*) sich vermehren; (*of numbers*) ansteigen. ◆**'swelling**, *s. Med:* Schwellung *f.*

**swelter** ['sweltər], *v.i.* (*of pers.*) vor Hitze verschmachten/*F:* kochen. ◆**'sweltering**, *adj.* drückend heiß.

**swerve** [swəːv]. **I.** *s.* Abschwenkung *f;* (*skid*) Schleudern *n.* **II.** *v.i.* (*of pers., vehicle*) (plötzlich) abschwenken.

**swift** [swift]. **I.** *adj.* schnell. **II.** *s. Orn:* Segler *m.*

**swig** [swig]. *F:* **I.** *s.* tüchtiger Schluck *m.* **II.** *v.tr.* (etwas) (gierig) saufen.

**swill** [swil]. **I.** *s.* (**pig**) **s.**, Schweinefutter *n.* **II.** *v.tr.* (*a*) (den Fußboden) abschwemmen; **to s. (out) a glass**, ein Glas ausspülen; (*b*) *P:* (ein Glas Bier usw.) saufen.

**swim** [swim]. **I.** *s.* **to go for a s.**, schwimmen gehen. **II.** *v.tr. & i.irr.* schwimmen; **to s. (across) the river**, den Fluß durchschwimmen. ◆**'swimmer**, *s.*

Schwimmer(in) *m(f)*. ◆'**swimming**, *s.* Schwimmen *n*; **s. pool**, *(complex)* Schwimmbad *n*; *(actual pool)* Schwimmbecken *n*; *(outdoor)* Freibad *n*; *(indoor)* *(also* **s. bath(s)**), Hallenbad *n*; **s. trunks**, Badehose *f.* ◆'**swimsuit**, *s.* Badeanzug *m.*

**swindle** ['swindl]. **I.** *s.* Schwindel *m.* **II.** *v.tr.* **to s. s.o. (out of sth.)**, j-n (um etwas *acc*) betrügen. ◆'**swindler**, *s.* Schwindler(in) *m(f)*.

**swine** [swain], *s. inv. (also Pej: of pers.)* Schwein *n*; *Pej:* **dirty s.!** Drecksau!

**swing** [swiŋ]. **I. s.** **1.** *(a)* Schwingen *n*; *(one movement)* Schwung *m*; *(b)* *(change)* Umschwung *m* (der öffentlichen Meinung). **2.** *(rhythm etc.)* Schwung *m*; **to be in full s.**, in vollem Gang sein. **3.** *(child's)* **s.**, Schaukel *f.* **4.** *Mus:* Swing *m.* **II** *v.irr.* **1.** *v.i.* *(a)* schwingen; *(of hanging object)* baumeln; *(of pers. on swing)* schaukeln; *(of door)* **to s. open**, aufgehen; *(b)* *(turn)* **to s. round**, sich umdrehen; **he swung round the corner**, er schwenkte um die Ecke; *(c)* **to s. at s.o.**, zum Schlag gegen j-n ausholen. **2.** *v.tr.* *(a)* (etwas) schwingen; *(above one's head)* (ein Schwert usw.) schwenken; *(seine Beine) baumeln lassen; **to s. one's arms**, mit den Armen schlenkern; *(b)* *(turn)* (etwas) drehen; **to s. sth. round**, etwas umdrehen. ◆'**swing-bridge**, *s.* Drehbrücke *f.* ◆'**swing-door**, *s.* Pendeltür *f.* ◆'**swinging**, *adj.* *(a)* schwingend; *(b)* *F:* flott, schwungvoll.

**swipe** [swaip]. **I.** *s.* (wuchtiger) Schlag *m.* **II.** *v.tr.* *(a)* *Sp:* (den Ball) (mit Wucht) schlagen; *(b)* *P:* **to s. sth. (from s.o.)**, (j-m) etwas klauen.

**swirl** [swəːl]. **I.** *s.* Wirbel *m*; *(water)* (kleiner) Strudel *m.* **II.** *v.i.* *(of dust etc.)* wirbeln; *(of water)* strudeln.

**swish** [swiʃ]. **I.** *s.* Rascheln *n* (von Seide usw.); Zischen *n* (einer Peitsche, eines Stocks). **II.** *v.i.* *(rustle)* rascheln; *(of whip, stick)* zischen. **III.** *adj.* *F:* nobel.

**Swiss** [swis]. **I.** *adj.* schweizerisch, Schweizer; **S. German**, Schweizerdeutsch *n.* **II. s.** *inv.* Schweizer(in) *m(f)*.

**switch** [switʃ]. **I. s.** **1.** *(stick)* Gerte *f.* **2.** *El:* Schalter *m.* **3.** *(change)* Wechsel *m.* **II.** *v.* **1.** *v.tr.* *(a)* *El:* **to s. sth. on/off**, etwas einschalten/ausschalten; *(b)* *(change)* (das Thema usw.) wechseln; (die Produktion) umstellen (**to**, auf + *acc*). **2.** *v.i.* *(a)* **to s. on/off**, einschalten/ausschalten; *(b)* *(change)* **to s. (over)**, sich umstellen (**to**, auf + *acc*). ◆'**switchboard**, *s.* *(a)* *(in office etc.)* Zentrale *f*; **s. operator**, Telefonist(in) *m(f)*; *(b)* *El:* Schaltbrett *n.*

**Switzerland** ['switsələnd]. *Pr. n.* die Schweiz.

**swivel** ['swiv(ə)l]. **I.** *v.* **1.** *v.i.* sich drehen. **2.** *v.tr.* (etwas) drehen, *(swing)* schwenken. **3.** *attrib.* **s. chair**, Drehstuhl *m.*

**swollen** ['swəulən], *adj.* geschwollen.

**swoop** [swuːp]. **I.** *s.* *(a)* *(of bird of prey)* Sturzflug *m*; *(b)* *(raid)* Überfall *m*; *(by police)* Razzia *f*; *Fig:* **at one fell s.**, mit einem Schlag. **II.** *v.i.* *(of bird)* **to s. on its prey**, auf seine Beute herabstoßen; *(of pers.)* **to s. (on sth.)**, *(auf etwas acc)* stürzen; *(of police)* **to s. on an area**, in einem Bezirk Razzia machen.

**sword** [sɔːd], *s.* Schwert *n.*

**sworn** [swɔːn], *adj.* geschworen; **s. enemies**, Todfeinde *mpl.*

**swot** [swɔt], *Sch: F:* **I.** *s.* Büffler *m.* **II.** *v.tr.* **to s. (up)** *maths*, Mathematik büffeln.

**syllable** ['siləbl], *s.* Silbe *f.*

**syllabus**, *pl.* **-uses** ['siləbəs, -əsiz], *s.* Lehrplan *m.*

**symbol** ['simb(ə)l], *s.* Symbol *n*; *Mth: etc:* Zeichen *n.* ◆**symbolic** [-'bɔlik], *adj.* symbolisch. ◆'**symbolism**, *s.* Symbolik *f.* ◆'**symbolize**, *v.tr.* symbolisieren.

**symmetry** ['simitri], *s.* Symmetrie *f.* ◆**symmetrical** [-'metrikl], *adj.* symmetrisch.

**sympathetic** [simpə'θetik], *adj.* *(a)* mitfühlend; *(b)* *(understanding)* verständnisvoll; **s. to new ideas**, für neue Ideen empfänglich; *(c)* *(congenial)* sympathisch. ◆'**sympathize**, *v.i.* **to s. (with s.o.)**, *(be sorry)* (mit j-m) Mitleid haben; *(understand)* (mit j-m) sympathisieren. ◆'**sympathizer**, *s.* Sympathisant(in) *m(f)*. ◆'**sympathy**, *s.* **1.** *(sorrow)* Mitleid *n*; *(concern)* Mitgefühl *n*; **to have s. for/with s.o.**, mit j-m Mitleid haben. **2.** Sympathie *f*; **popular s. is on his side**, er genießt die Sympathie der Öffentlichkeit.

**symphony** ['simfəni], *s.* Symphonie *f.*

**symptom** ['simptəm], *s.* Anzeichen *n*; *Med:* Symptom *n* (**of**, für + *acc*).

**synagogue** ['sinəgɔg], *s.* Synagoge *f.*

**synchronize** ['siŋkrənaiz], *v.tr.* synchronisieren; **s. your watches**, stimmen Sie Ihre Uhren aufeinander ab.

**syndicate** ['sindikit], *s.* Syndikat *n.*

**synonym** ['sinənim], *s.* Synonym *n.* ◆**synonymous** [-'nɔniməs], *adj.* synonym; **s. with sth.**, gleichbedeutend mit etwas *dat.*

**synopsis**, *pl.* **-ses** [si'nɔpsis, -siːz], *s.* Inhaltsangabe *f.*

**syntax** ['sintæks], *s.* Syntax *f.*

**synthesis**, *pl.* **-ses** ['sinθisis, -siːz], *s.* Synthese *f.*

**synthetic** [sin'θetik], *adj.* synthetisch, Kunst-; **s. fibre**, Kunstfaser *f.*

**syphilis** ['sifilis], *s.* Syphilis *f.*

**Syria** ['siriə]. *Pr. n.* Syrien *n.* ◆'**Syrian**. **I.** *s.* Syrer(in) *m(f)*. **II.** *adj.* syrisch.

**syringe** ['sirindʒ]. **I.** *s.* Spritze *f.* **II.** *v.tr.* *(a)* (eine Flüssigkeit) spritzen; *(b)* *Med:* (die Ohren) ausspritzen.

**syrup** ['sirəp], *s.* Sirup *m.*

**system** ['sistəm], *s.* *(a)* System *n*; *(b)* *(of railways, roads etc.)* Netz *n*; **motorway s.**, Autobahnnetz *n*; **one way s.**, Einbahnstraßensystem *n; Data-pr:* **systems analysis,** Systemanalyse *f; F:* **to get sth. out** | **of one's s.,** etwas ganz loswerden. ◆**syste'matic,** *adj.* systematisch.

# T

**T, t** [tiː], *s.* (der Buchstabe) T, t *n; Fig:* **it suits me to a T,** es paßt mir ausgezeichnet; **T-junction,** Einmündung *f* (in eine Vorfahrtsstraße).

**ta** [tɑː], *int. F:* danke.

**tab** [tæb], *s.* (*a*) (*material, cardboard*) Strippe *f;* (*metal*) Zunge *f;* (*b*) *Cl:* (*loop*) Schlaufe *f;* (*for hanging up*) Aufhänger *m;* (*c*) (*label*) Anhänger *m.*

**tabby** ['tæbi], *s.* **t. (cat),** getigerte Katze.

**tabernacle** ['tæbənækl], *s.* Tabernakel *m.*

**table** ['teibl]. I. *s.* 1. Tisch *m;* **to lay the t.,** den Tisch decken; **to clear the t.,** (den Tisch) abräumen; **t. mat,** Set *n;* **t. wine,** Tafelwein *m;* **t. tennis,** Tischtennis *n.* 2. (*list*) Tafel *f;* (*conversion etc.*) Tabelle *f.* II. *v.tr. Parl:* **to t. a motion,** einen Antrag einbringen. ◆**'tablecloth,** *s.* Tischtuch *n.* ◆**'tablespoon,** *s.* Eßlöffel *m.*

**tablet** ['tæblit], *s.* 1. *Med:* Tablette *f.* 2. **t. of soap,** Stück *n* Seife. 3. *N.Am:* Notizblock *m.*

**taboo** [tə'buː]. I. *s.* Tabu *n.* II. *adj.* tabu.

**tabulate** ['tæbjuleit], *v.tr.* (Resultate) in Tabellen aufzeichnen; (Ziffern) tabellarisch anordnen.

**tacit** ['tæsit], *adj.* stillschweigend. ◆**'taciturn,** *adj.* (*silent*) schweigsam; (*of few words*) wortkarg.

**tack** [tæk]. I. *s.* 1. (*nail*) Zwecke *f;* carpet t., Teppichnagel *m.* 2. *Cl:* Heftstich *m.* 3. *Nau:* **to be on a starboard t.,** auf Steuerbordhalsen liegen; *Fig:* **on the right/wrong t.,** auf dem richtigen/ falschen Wege. II. *v.* 1. *v.tr.* (*a*) **to t. sth. (down),** etwas festnageln; (*b*) *Cl:* (einen Saum usw.) heften. 2. *v.i. Nau:* kreuzen.

**tackle** ['tækl]. I. *s.* 1. Gerät *n;* (*equipment*) Ausrüstung *f;* **fishing t.,** Angelgerät *n.* 2. (*ropes*) *Nau:* Takel *f;* *Tchn:* block and t., Flaschenzug *m.* 3. *Fb:* Tackling *n.* II. *v.tr.* (*a*) (j-n) mit Fragen usw.) angehen; (ein Problem) anpacken; (*b*) *Fb:* angreifen.

**tacky** ['tæki], *adj.* klebrig.

**tact** [tækt], *s.* Takt *m,* Feingefühl *n.* ◆**'tactful,** *adj.* taktvoll. ◆**'tactless,** *adj.* taktlos. ◆**'tactlessness,** *s.* Taktlosigkeit *f.*

**tactical** ['tæktik(ə)l], *adj.* taktisch. ◆**tactician** [tæk'tiʃən], *s.* Taktiker *m.* ◆**'tactics,** *s. pl.* Taktik *f.*

**tadpole** ['tædpəul], *s.* Kaulquappe *f.*

**taffeta** ['tæfitə], *s.* Taft *m.*

**tag** [tæg]. I. *s.* 1. Anhängsel *n;* (*label*) Etikett *n;* **price t.,** Preisschild *n.* 2. (*quotation*) geflügeltes Wort *n.* 3. (*children's game*) Haschen *n.* II. *v.i.* **to t. along** (be-|hind), hinterherlaufen.

**tail** [teil]. I. *s.* (*a*) Schwanz *m; Schweif m* (eines Kometen); (*b*) *Aut:* **t. light,** Schlußlicht *n;* (*c*) **t. end,** Schluß *m* (einer Prozession usw.); Ende (der Saison). II. *v.tr.* **to t. s.o.,** j-m auf den Fersen folgen; (*of police*) j-n beschatten. ◆**'tailback,** *s. Aut:* Rückstau *m.* ◆**'tailgate,** *s. Aut:* Heckklappe *f.* ◆**'tail 'off,** *v.i.* abklingen, schwächer werden.

**tailor** ['teilər]. I. *s.* Schneider *m.* II. *v.tr.* (einen Anzug) nach Maß schneidern; **well tailored,** tadellos gearbeitet. ◆**'tailoring,** *s.* (*job*) Schneiderei *f;* (*process*) Schneidern *n.* ◆**'tailor-'made,** *adj. Cl: & Fig:* maßgeschneidert.

**taint** [teint], *v.tr.* (j-n, Fleisch) verderben; *esp. Fig:* (j-n) anstecken (**with sth.,** von etwas *dat*). ◆**'tainted,** *adj.* verdorben.

**take** [teik], *v.tr.irr.* nehmen; (*a*) **to t. sth. from s.o.,** j-m etwas (weg)nehmen; **to t. a passage from a book,** eine Stelle einem Buch entnehmen; **to t. an opportunity,** eine Gelegenheit wahrnehmen; (*b*) (*capture*) (j-n) festnehmen; *Mil:* (eine Stadt) einnehmen; **to t. s.o. prisoner,** j-n gefangennehmen; **to be taken ill,** erkranken; (*c*) **to t. a paper,** eine Zeitung abonnieren; (*of seat, table*) taken, besetzt; **t. a seat/your seats,** nehmen Sie bitte Platz; **to t. the wrong road,** die falsche Straße einschlagen; **to t. an examination,** eine Prüfung ablegen; (*d*) (einen Preis) gewinnen; (*e*) (Nahrung) zu sich nehmen; *Com:* **to t. £3000 per week,** £3000 wöchentlich einnehmen; **to t. a photograph,** eine Aufnahme machen; **to t. sth. to pieces,** etwas auseinandernehmen; (*f*) (*accept*) (ein Geschenk) annehmen; **the car can t. six people,** in dem Auto haben sechs Leute Platz; **t. it from me!** glaube (es) mir! **to t. sth. the wrong way,** etwas falsch auffassen; (*g*) (*assume*) **I t. it that you are coming,** ich nehme an, daß du kommst; **I took him for an Englishman,** ich hielt ihn für einen Engländer; **to t. a dislike to s.o.,** gegen j-n eine Abneigung entwickeln; (*h*) (*require*) (Geduld usw.) erfordern; (*last*) (eine Woche usw.) dauern; **the journey takes five days,** die Reise dauert fünf Tage; *Gram:* **this verb takes the dative,** dieses Verb wird mit dem Dativ konstruiert; (*i*) **to t. s.o. somewhere,** j-n irgendwohin führen/(in den Auto *etc.*) mitnehmen; **to t. s.o. to the hospital/to the station,** j-n ins Krankenhaus/zum Bahnhof bringen; **to t. sth. to s.o.,** etwas zu j-m hintragen; **t. it with you,** nehmen Sie es mit. ◆**'take**

'**after**, v.i. she doesn't t. a. her father, sie gerät nicht nach ihrem Vater. ◆'**take a'way**, v.tr. wegnehmen; (in café) **is it to t.a.?** ist es zum Mitnehmen? ◆'**takeaway**, s. (shop) Restaurant n mit Straßenverkauf. ◆'**take 'back**, v.tr. (a) (etwas) zurücknehmen (**to s.o.**, j-m); (b) (j-n) zurückführen; (einen Angestellten) wiedereinstellen. ◆'**take 'down**, v.tr. (a) (from shelf etc.) herunternehmen; (Vorhänge usw.) abnehmen; (b) (write) **to t. d. a few notes,** sich dat einige Notizen machen. ◆'**take 'in**, v.tr. (a) (admit) (j-n) einlassen; (ein Mitglied, einen Untermieter) aufnehmen; (b) **to t. in a dress at the waist,** ein Kleid in der Taille enger machen; (c) (include) (etwas) umfassen; (d) (grasp) (eine Idee) begreifen; (e) F: (j-n) reinlegen; **to be taken in,** reinfallen (**by sth.**, auf etwas acc). ◆'**take 'off**, v. 1. v.tr. (a) (etwas) wegnehmen; (b) (den Hut) abnehmen; (Kleider) ausziehen; **to t. o. one's clothes,** sich ausziehen; (c) (j-n) wegbringen; (d) F: (mimic) (j-n) nachäffen. 2. v.i. Av: starten. ◆'**take-off**, s. Av: Abflug m, Start m. ◆'**take 'on**, v.tr. (a) (eine Arbeit) annehmen; (einen Kampf) aufnehmen; (b) (engage) (einen Arbeiter) einstellen; (c) (Passagiere usw.) einsteigen lassen; (Fracht) laden. ◆'**take 'out**, v.tr. (a) herausnehmen; **to t. o. a stain,** einen Fleck entfernen; **to t. o. a tooth,** einen Zahn ziehen; (from bank) **to t. o. money,** Geld abheben; (from library) **to t. o. a book,** ein Buch ausleihen; (b) **the heat takes it o. of one,** die Hitze macht einen ganz matt; **don't t. it o. on me,** laß deine Wut nicht an mir aus; (c) (j-n, einen Hund) ausführen; (d) **to t. o. an insurance policy,** eine Versicherung abschließen. ◆'**take 'over**, v. 1. v.tr. (etwas) übernehmen. 2. v.i. **to t. o. from s.o.,** j-m (in einem Amt) nachfolgen; (relieve s.o.) j-n ablösen. ◆'**take-over**, s. (a) Com: etc: Übernahme f (eines Betriebes usw.); **t. bid,** Übernahmeangebot n; (b) Pol: Machtübernahme f. ◆'**take 'to**, v.i. (a) **to t. to flight/to one's heels,** die Flucht ergreifen; **to t. to the road,** losfahren; **to t. to one's bed,** das Bett hüten; (b) **to t. to drink,** sich dem Alkohol ergeben; (c) **to t. to s.o.,** sich zu j-m hingezogen fühlen. ◆'**take 'up**, v.tr. (a) (etwas) aufnehmen; (raise) heben; (einen Teppich) aufrollen; (eine Straße) aufreißen; (b) (einen Rock usw.) kürzer machen; (c) (absorb) (Wasser) aufsaugen; (d) (einen Beruf) ergreifen; (eine Tätigkeit) beginnen; (e) (Zeit, j-s Aufmerksamkeit, Platz usw.) in Anspruch nehmen. ◆'**taking,** adj. t. **ways,** gewinnende Art. ◆'**takings,** s.pl. Com: Einnahmen fpl.

**talc** [tælk], s. Talk m. ◆'**talcum,** s. t. **powder,** Körperpuder m.

**tale** [teil], s. (a) (story) Erzählung f; (b) (untruth) Lügengeschichte f.

**talent** ['tælənt], s. Talent n; (ability) Fähigkeit f; esp. Iron: Gabe f. ◆'**talented,** adj. begabt.

**talk** [tɔ:k]. I. s. 1. (a) (action) Reden n; (b) (what is said) Gerede n; (idle) t., Geschwätz n; (c) (conversation) Gespräch n; (casual) Plauderei f; **to have a t. with s.o.,** sich mit j-m unterhalten. 2. (lecture) Vortrag m. II. v. 1. v.i. (a) reden, sprechen (**on/about sth.**, über etwas acc; of sth., von etwas dat); **it's easy to t.!** du hast gut reden! (b) **talking of which...,** da wir gerade davon sprechen...; **t. about luck!** was für ein Glück! (c) **to t. to s.o.,** sich mit j-m unterhalten; (d) (give away a secret) reden; **somebody must have talked,** es muß einer geschwatzt haben. 2. v.tr. (a) (Deutsch, Französisch usw.) sprechen; (Unsinn, wirres Zeug) reden; (b) **to t. sense,** vernünftig reden; **to t. oneself hoarse,** sich heiser reden; **to t. s.o. into doing sth.,** j-m einreden, etwas zu tun; **to t. s.o. round/over,** j-n überreden. ◆'**talkative,** adj. geschwätzig. ◆'**talker,** s. Pej: Schwätzer(in) m(f); **he's a great t.,** er redet viel. ◆'**talking,** s. Reden n; no t. **please!** Ruhe bitte! F: **to give s.o. a good t. to,** j-m die Leviten lesen.

**tall** [tɔ:l], adj. 1. (of pers.) groß; (of thing) hoch. 2. F: **a t. story,** eine unglaubliche Geschichte; **that's a t. order!** das ist ein bißchen viel verlangt! ◆'**tallboy,** s. Aufsatzkommode f. ◆'**tallness,** s. Größe f, Höhe f.

**tallow** ['tæləu], s. Talg m.

**tally** ['tæli]. I. s. (bill etc.) Rechnung f. II. v.i. übereinstimmen.

**talon** ['tælən], s. Kralle f.

**tambourine** [tæmbə'ri:n], s. Tamburin n.

**tame** [teim]. I. adj. 1. (of animal) zahm; (tamed) gezähmt. 2. Fig: (of pers., affair etc.) lahm; (boring) fade. II. v.tr. (ein Tier) zähmen; (einen Löwen) bändigen. ◆'**tameness,** s. 1. Zahmheit f (eines Tieres). 2. Fig: Lahmheit f.

**tamper** ['tæmpər], v.i. **to t. with sth.,** an etwas dat herumhantieren; (alter) etwas unbefugt abändern.

**tan** [tæn]. I. s. 1. (colour) Hellbraun n. 2. (suntan) Bräune f. II. adj. hellbraun. III. v. 1. v.tr. (a) (Leder) gerben; (b) (die Haut) bräunen. 2. v.i. (of pers.) sich bräunen; **she tans easily,** sie wird schnell braun.

**tandem** ['tændəm], s. Tandem n.

**tang** [tæŋ], s. scharfer Beigeschmack m; (smell) Geruch m.

**tangent** ['tæn(d)ʒənt], s. Tangente f.

**tangerine** [tæn(d)ʒə'ri:n], s. Mandarine f.

**tangible** ['tæn(d)ʒibl], adj. konkret.

**tangle** ['tæŋgl]. I. s. Gewirr n; (in ball) wirrer Knäuel m (von Garn, Haaren); **in a t.,** ganz durcheinander. II. v.tr. durcheinanderbringen.

**tango** ['tæŋgəu]. s. Tango m.

**tank** [tæŋk], s. 1. (*container*) Tank m. 2. *Mil:* Panzer m. ◆'**tanker**, s. (*a*) *Nau:* Tanker m; (*b*) *Aut:* Tankwagen m.

**tankard** ['tæŋkəd], s. Bierkrug m; (*pewter*) t., Zinnkrug m.

**tantalize** ['tæntəlaiz], v.tr. (j-n) quälen; (*keep in suspense*) (j-n) zappeln lassen. ◆'**tantalizing**, adj. quälend; (*of smile*) provozierend.

**tantamount** ['tæntəmaunt], adj. t. to, gleichbedeutend mit + dat.

**tantrum** ['tæntrəm], s. Wutanfall m.

**tap¹** [tæp]. I. s. Hahn m. II. v.tr. anzapfen.

**tap²**. I. s. leichter Schlag m, Klaps m; t. **dance/dancing**, Steptanz m. II. v.tr. klopfen.

**tape** [teip]. I. s. 1. **Band** n; (*adhesive*) t., Klebestreifen m; *Rec:* (**recording**) t., Tonband n; t. **recorder**, Tonbandgerät n; t. **measure**, Bandmaß n. II. v.tr. *Rec:* (etwas) auf Tonband aufnehmen. ◆'**tapeworm**, s. Bandwurm m.

**taper** ['teipər]. I. s. (*candle*) dünne Wachskerze f. II. v.i. sich verjüngen. ◆'**tapering**, adj. spitz zulaufend; (*conical*) kegelförmig.

**tapestry** ['tæpistri], s. Gobelin m.

**tapioca** [tæpi'əukə], s. Tapioka f.

**tappet** ['tæpit], s. *Aut:* Ventilstößel m.

**tar** [tɑːr]. I. s. Teer m. II. v.tr. teeren.

**tarantula** [tə'ræntjulə], s. Tarantel f.

**target** ['tɑːgit], s. Ziel n; (*in archery etc.*) Schießscheibe f.

**tariff** ['tærif], s. 1. Zolltarif m. 2. (*price list*) Preisverzeichnis n.

**tarmac** ['tɑːmæk], s. *Av:* Rollfeld; t. (**surface**), Teerdecke.

**tarn** [tɑːn], s. (kleiner) Bergsee m.

**tarnish** ['tɑːniʃ], v.tr. trüben; *Fig:* (j-s Ruf usw.) beflecken.

**tarpaulin** [tɑː'pɔːlin], s. Plane f; *Nau:* Persenning f.

**tart¹** [tɑːt], s. 1. *Cu:* Torte f; (*small*) Törtchen n. 2. *F:* (*prostitute*) Dirne f.

**tart²**, adj. sauer; (*of answer*) bissig.

**tartan** ['tɑːt(ə)n], s. Schottenstoff m; (*pattern*) Schottenmuster n.

**tartar** ['tɑːtər], s. 1. *Ch:* Weinstein m. 2. *Med:* Zahnstein m. 3. *Cu:* t. **sauce**, Tatarsoße f.

**task** [tɑːsk], s. Aufgabe f; *Mil:* t. **force**, Spezialtruppe f.

**tassel** ['tæs(ə)l], s. Quaste f.

**taste** [teist]. I. s. Geschmack m; (*a*) (**sense of**) t., Geschmackssinn m; (*b*) (*small quantity*) kleiner Bissen m (Käse usw.); Schlückchen n (Wein); (*c*) (*liking*) **to have a t. for sth.**, eine Vorliebe für etwas acc haben; (*d*) **to have (good) t.**, (guten) Geschmack haben; **in bad t.**, geschmacklos; (*bad manners*) unangebracht. II. v. 1. v.tr. (a) (etwas) schmecken; (ein Gewürz usw.) herausschmecken; (b) (*sample*) (etwas) kosten; (Weine) probieren. 2. v.i. **to t. of sth.**, nach etwas dat schmecken. ◆'**tasteful**,

adj. geschmackvoll. ◆'**tasteless**, adj. 1. (*of food*) ohne Geschmack. 2. (*of furnishings etc.*) geschmacklos. ◆'**tastelessness**, s. Geschmacklosigkeit f. ◆'**tastiness**, s. Schmackhaftigkeit f (einer Speise). ◆'**tasty**, adj. schmackhaft.

**ta-ta** [tæ'tɑː], int. *F:* Wiedersehen!

**tatters** ['tætəz], s. pl. **in t.**, zerlumpt. ◆'**tattered**, adj. zerfetzt.

**tattoo¹** [tə'tuː], s. *Mil:* 1. (*drumming*) Zapfenstreich m. 2. (*entertainment*) Tattoo m.

**tattoo²**. I. s. (*on body*) Tätowierung f. II. v.tr. tätowieren.

**tatty** ['tæti], adj. *F:* schäbig.

**taunt** [tɔːnt]. I. s. spöttische Bemerkung f. II. v.tr. (j-n) verspotten.

**Taurus** ['tɔːrəs], s. *Astr:* Stier m.

**taut** [tɔːt], adj. (*of rope etc.*) straff; gespannt; (*of nerves*) angespannt.

**tavern** ['tævən], s. esp. A: Schenke f.

**tawdry** ['tɔːdri], adj. kitschig-bunt; geschmacklos.

**tawny** ['tɔːni], adj. gelbbraun; t. **owl**, Waldkauz m.

**tax** [tæks]. I. s. Steuer f; t. **collector**, Steuereinnehmer m; t. **return**, Steuererklärung f. II. v.tr. (a) (j-n, etwas) besteuern; (b) (*weary*) (j-n, j-s Kräfte, Geduld) strapazieren. ◆'**taxable**, adj. (*of income*) steuerpflichtig. ◆**tax'ation**, s. Besteuerung f; **subject to t.**, steuerpflichtig. ◆'**tax-'free**, adj. steuerfrei. ◆'**taxing**, adj. strapazierend. ◆'**taxpayer**, s. Steuerzahler m.

**taxi** ['tæksi]. I. s. Taxi n, Taxe f; t. **driver**, Taxifahrer m; t. **rank**/*Scot:* **stance**, Taxistand m. II. v.i. *Av:* rollen.

**taxidermy** ['tæksidəːmi], s. Taxidermie f. ◆'**taxidermist**, s. Tierpräparator m.

**tea** [tiː], s. Tee m; t. **break**, Teepause f; t. **service/set**, Teeservice n; (*afternoon*) t., Nachmittagstee m; (**high**) t., frühes Abendbrot n; t. **party**, Teegesellschaft f; t. **trolley**, Teewagen m. ◆'**teabag**, s. Teebeutel m. ◆'**teacaddy**, s. Teedose f. ◆'**teacake**, s. flaches, weiches Brötchen n. ◆'**teacloth**, s. 1. (kleine) Tischdecke f. 2. = tea towel. ◆'**teacosy**, s. Teewärmer m. ◆'**teacup**, s. Teetasse f. ◆'**tealeaf**, s. Teeblatt n. ◆'**teapot**, s. Teekanne f. ◆'**tearoom**, s. Teestube f. ◆**teashop**, s. 1. (*café*) Teestube f. 2. (*shop*) Teegeschäft n. ◆'**teaspoon**, s. Teelöffel m. ◆'**teaspoonful**, s. Teelöffel(voll) m. ◆'**teatowel**, s. Geschirrtuch n.

**teach** [tiːtʃ], v.tr.irr. (j-n, ein Fach) unterrichten, lehren; **to t. s.o. sth.**, j-m etwas lehren/*F:* beibringen; (*in school*) j-n in etwas dat unterrichten; *F:* **that will t. him!** das wird ihm eine Lehre sein! ◆'**teacher**, s. Lehrer(in) m(f). ◆'**teaching**, s. 1. Unterricht m; 2. esp. pl. **teachings** Lehren fpl.

**teak** [tiːk], s. Teakholz n.

**team** [tiːm], s. 1. *Sp: etc:* Mannschaft f;

t. **spirit,** Mannschaftsgeist *m.* 2. Gespann *n* (von Pferden usw.). ◆**'teamwork,** *s.* 1. Zusammenarbeit *f,* Teamwork *n.*

**tear¹** [tiər], *s.* Träne *f.* ◆**'tearful,** *adj.* *(of pers., voice)* weinerlich; *(of parting etc.)* tränenreich. ◆**'tear-gas,** *s.* Tränengas *n.*

**tear²** [tɛər]. I. *s.* Riß *m* (in einem Kleid usw.). II. *v.irr.* 1. *v.tr.* (a) (etwas) zerreißen; *Fig:* **torn between two possibilities,** zwischen zwei Möglichkeiten hin und her gerissen; *F:* **that's torn it!** jetzt ist alles im Eimer! (b) **to t. sth. (away) from s.o./out of s.o.'s hands,** j-m etwas entreißen. 2. *v.i.* (a) *(of paper etc.)* reißen; (b) *(rush)* **to t. along/down/up,** dahinrasen/hinunterrasen/hinaufrasen. ◆**'tear a'way,** *v.tr.* (etwas) wegreißen; **I could not t. myself a.,** ich konnte mich nicht losreißen. ◆**'tear 'down,** *v.tr.* herunterreißen; (ein Haus) niederreißen. ◆**'tearing,** *adj.* reißend; **to be in a t. hurry,** es furchtbar eilig haben. ◆**'tear 'up,** *v.tr.* (einen Brief usw.) zerreißen.

**tease** [tiːz], *v.tr.* (j-n) necken, *(maliciously)* aufziehen. ◆**'teaser,** *s.* *F:* *(problem)* harte Nuß *f.* ◆**'teasing.** I. *adj.* neckend. II. *s.* Neckerei *f.*

**teat** [tiːt], *s.* *Anat:* Brustwarze *f; Z:* Zitze *f; (on bottle)* Sauger *m.*

**technical** ['teknik(ə)l], *adj.* technisch; **t. terms,** Fachausdrücke *mpl,* **-ly,** *adv.* 1. technisch. 2. *(actually)* genaugenommen. ◆**techni'cality,** *s.* 1. *Tchn:* technische Einzelheit *f.* 2. *Jur: Adm: etc:* Formsache *f.* ◆**tech'nician,** *s.* Techniker *m.* ◆**technique** [tek'niːk], *s.* Technik *f.* ◆**tech'nology,** *s.* Technologie *f.*

**teddy (bear)** ['tedi (bɛər)], *s.* Teddy(bär) *m.*

**tedious** ['tiːdiəs], *adj.* langweilig. ◆**'tediousness/'tedium,** *s.* Langweiligkeit *f.*

**tee** [tiː], *s.* *Sp:* *(area)* Abschlag *m; (peg)* Aufsatz *m.*

**teem** [tiːm], *v.i.* **to be teeming with people, ants etc.,** von Leuten, Ameisen usw. wimmeln; **teeming rain,** strömender Regen.

**teens** [tiːnz], *s. pl.* Jugendjahre *npl.* ◆**'teenager,** *s.* Teenager *m.*

**teeter** ['tiːtər], *v.i.* taumeln, *(sway)* wanken.

**teeth** [tiːθ], *s. pl. of* **tooth** *q.v.* ◆**teethe** [tiːð], *v.i.* zahnen.

**teetotal** [tiː'təutl], *adj.* abstinent. ◆**tee'totaller,** *s.* Abstinenzler(in) *m(f).*

**telecommunications** [telikəmjuːni'keiʃ(ə)nz], *s. pl.* Fernmeldewesen *n.*

**telegram** ['teligræm], *s.* Telegramm *n.* ◆**telegraph** ['teligrɑːf], *s.* Telegraf *m;* **t. pole,** Telegrafenmast *m.* ◆**telegraphic** [-'græfik], *adj.* telegrafisch. ◆**telegraphy** [ti'legrəfi], *s.* Telegrafie *f.*

**telepathy** [ti'lepəθi], *s.* Gedankenübertragung *f.* ◆**telepathic**

[teli'pæθik], *adj.* telepathisch.

**telephone** ['telifəun]. I. *s.* Telefon *n;* **t. number,** Telefonnummer *f;* **t. box,** Telefonzelle *f;* **t. call,** Telefonanruf *m;* **t. directory,** Telefonbuch *n;* **t. exchange,** Telefonzentrale *f;* **t. operator,** Telefonist(in) *m(f).* II. *v.* 1. *v.i.* telefonieren. 2. *v.tr.* (eine Nachricht) telefonieren. ◆**telephonist** [ti'lefənist], *s.* Telefonist(in) *m(f).*

**telephoto** [teli'fəutəu], *s.* **t. (lens),** Teleobjektiv *n.*

**teleprinter** [teli'printər], *s.* Fernschreiber *m.*

**telescope** ['teliskəup]. I. *s.* Teleskop *n.* II. *v.tr.* (Teile) ineinanderschieben. ◆**telescopic** [-'skɔpik], *adj.* (a) teleskopisch; (b) *(collapsible)* ineinanderschiebbar; *(of aerial, strut)* ausziehbar.

**television** [teli'viʒ(ə)n], *s.* Fernsehen *n;* **on (the) t.,** im Fernsehen; **t. set,** Fernsehapparat *m;* **t. announcer,** Fernsehansager(in) *m(f).* ◆**'televise,** *v.tr.* (etwas) im Fernsehen übertragen.

**telex** ['teleks], *s.* Telex *n.*

**tell** [tel], *v.* 1. *v.tr.* (a) (etwas, die Wahrheit usw.) sagen; (etwas, eine Geschichte usw.) erzählen; **to t. a lie,** lügen; **to t. tales,** aus der Schule plaudern; *Sch: F:* petzen; **to t. s.o. sth.,** j-m etwas sagen/ erzählen; (b) *(pass on)* (eine Neuigkeit) mitteilen; (ein Geheimnis) verraten; (c) *(inform)* **to t. s.o. about sth.,** j-m von etwas *dat* erzählen; j-n über etwas *acc* informieren; (d) **to t. s.o. to do sth.,** j-m sagen/j-n bitten, etwas zu tun; (e) *(distinguish)* (etwas) unterscheiden; *(recognize)* erkennen; (f) *(know)* (etwas) wissen; **who can t.?** wer weiß? 2. *v.i.* (a) seine Wirkung haben; **this tells in his favour,** das spricht für ihn; (b) **to t. on s.o.,** j-n verpetzen; ◆**'teller,** *s.* 1. Erzähler(in) *m(f).* 2. *Com:* Kassierer(in) *m(f).* ◆**'telling,** *adj.* wirksam; **t. blow,** wuchtiger Schlag. ◆**'tell 'off,** *v.tr.* ausschimpfen. ◆**'telltale,** *adj.* **t. signs,** verräterische Zeichen.

**telly** ['teli], *s. F:* Flimmerkiste *f.*

**temerity** [ti'meriti], *s.* Kühnheit *f.*

**temper** ['tempər]. I. *s.* 1. (a) Temperament *n;* **to lose one's t.,** ärgerlich werden; *(lose patience)* die Geduld verlieren; (b) *(state of mind)* Laune *f;* **to be in a good/bad t.,** guter/schlechter Laune sein; (c) *(anger)* Zorn *m.* 2. *Tchn:* Härte *f* (des Stahls). II. *v.tr.* (a) (Stahl) härten; (b) (seinen Eifer usw.) mäßigen. ◆**'temperament,** *s.* 1. *(excitability)* Temperament *n.* 2. *(character)* Veranlagung *f.* ◆**tempera'mental,** *adj.* launenhaft.

**temperance** ['temp(ə)rəns], *s.* Mäßigkeit *f; (abstinence)* Enthaltsamkeit *f.* ◆**'temperate,** *adj. (of pers.)* mäßig; enthaltsam; *(of language, climate)* gemäßigt.

**temperature** ['tempritʃər], *s.* Temperatur *f; Med:* **to have a t.,** Fieber haben.

**tempest** ['tempist], *s. A: & Lit:* (wilder) Sturm *m.* ◆**tempestuous** [-'pestjuəs], *adj.* stürmisch; *(of pers., nature)* ungestüm.

**template** ['templit], *s. Tchn:* Schablone *f.*

**temple¹** ['templ], *s.* Tempel *m.*

**temple²**, *s. Anat:* Schläfe *f.*

**tempo** ['tempəu], *s.* Tempo *n.*

**temporal** ['tempərəl], *adj.* **1.** zeitlich. **2.** *(secular)* weltlich.

**temporary** ['temp(ə)rəri], *adj. (provisional)* vorläufig, provisorisch; **-ily,** *adv.* vorübergehend.

**tempt** [tem(p)t], *v.tr.* **to t. s.o. to do sth.,** j-n verlocken, etwas zu tun; **to be tempted,** in Versuchung kommen. ◆**temp'tation,** *s.* Versuchung *f.* ◆**'tempting,** *adj.* verführerisch; *(of offer, food)* verlockend.

**ten** [ten], *num. adj.* zehn.

**tenable** ['tenəbl], *adj. (of opinion)* vertretbar.

**tenacious** [tə'neiʃəs], *adj.* zäh. ◆**tenacity** [-'næsiti], *s.* Zähigkeit *f.*

**tenant** ['tenənt], *s. (of house etc.)* Mieter *m; (of estate)* Pächter *m.* ◆**'tenancy,** *s.* Mieten *n* (eines Hauses usw.); Pachtung *f* (eines Gutes usw.).

**tend¹** [tend], *v.tr.* (einen Garten, einen Kranken) pflegen; (eine Maschine) bedienen.

**tend²**, *v.i.* *(a)* **to t. towards sth.,** zu etwas *dat/*in eine gewisse Richtung tendieren; *(b)* **to t. to do sth.,** dazu neigen, etwas zu tun. ◆**'tendency,** *s.* Tendenz *f; (of pers.)* Neigung *f* (**to,** zu + *dat*).

**tender¹** ['tendər], *adj. (a)* zart; **t. meat,** zartes/weiches Fleisch; *(b) (of pers.)* zärtlich; *Fig:* **t. heart,** weiches/empfindsames Herz. ◆**'tenderness,** *s.* Zartheit *f; (of pers.)* Zärtlichkeit *f,* Weichherzigkeit *f.*

**tender²**. **I.** *s. Com:* Angebot *n.* **II.** *v.tr.* (seine Dienste) anbieten; **to t. one's resignation,** sein Abschiedsgesuch einreichen.

**tendon** ['tendən], *s. Anat:* Sehne *f.*

**tenement** ['tenimənt], *s.* Mietskaserne *f.*

**tenfold** ['tenfəuld], *adj. & adv.* zehnfach.

**tennis** ['tenis], *s.* Tennis *n;* **t. court,** Tennisplatz *m;* **t. racket,** Tennisschläger *m.*

**tenor** ['tenər], *s.* **1.** *Lit: (sense)* wesentlicher Sinn; *(content)* Inhalt *m.* **2.** *Mus:* Tenor *m; (voice)* Tenorstimme *f.*

**tense¹** [tens], *s. Gram:* Zeitform *f.*

**tense²**, *adj.* gespannt. ◆**'tenseness,** *s.* Gespanntheit *f* (des Muskels, der Verhältnisse); das Spannende (an einem Drama usw.). ◆**'tension** ['tenʃ(ə)n], *s.* **1.** *(also El:)* Spannung *f.* **2.** Gespanntheit *f* (der Muskeln).

**tent** [tent], *s.* Zelt *n;* **t. peg,** Zeltpflock *m.*

**tentacle** ['tentəkl], *s. Z:* Fühler *m.*

**tentative** ['tentətiv], *adj.* zögernd; *(provisional)* provisorisch; **-ly,** *adv.* versuchsweise.

**tenterhooks** ['tentəhuks], *s. pl. Fig:* **to be on t.,** auf die Folter gespannt sein.

**tenth** [tenθ], *num. adj.* zehnte(r, s). **2.** *(fraction)* Zehntel *n.*

**tenuous** ['tenjuəs], *adj. (of thread)* dünn; *(of distinction)* subtil.

**tenure** ['tenjər], *s.* Bekleidung *f* (eines Amtes); *(period)* Amtszeit *f.*

**tepid** ['tepid], *adj.* lauwarm.

**term** [təːm], *s.* **1.** *(a) (fixed)* Frist *f; (b) (period)* Zeit *f,* Dauer *f;* **in the short/long t.,** auf kurze/lange Sicht (gesehen); *(c) Sch: etc:* Trimester *n/*Semester *n; (d) Jur:* Sitzungsperiode *f.* **2.** *pl. (a) (conditions)* Bedingungen *fpl. Fig:* **to come to terms with death,** sich mit dem Tod abfinden; *(b) (relationship)* Beziehungen *fpl;* **to be on friendly/good terms with s.o.,** mit j-m befreundet sein/auf gutem Fuße stehen. **3.** *(expression) (a)* Ausdruck *m; (b)* **in terms of,** in Hinsicht auf + *acc.* ◆**'terminal. I.** *adj. (a)* End-; *(b) Med: (of illness)* unheilbar. **II.** *s. Rail:* Endstation *f; Av:* Terminal *m;* **coach t.,** Omnibusbahnhof *m.* ◆**'terminate,** *v.* **1.** *v.tr.* beenden. **2.** *v.i.* zum Abschluß kommen. ◆**termi'nation,** *s.* Ende *n;* Abschluß *m* (der Verhandlungen usw.); ◆**termi'nology,** *s.* Terminologie *f; (specialized)* Fachsprache *f.* ◆**'terminus,** *pl.* **-i, -uses** [-minəs, -miniː, -əsiz], *s. Rail:* Endstation *f.*

**termite** ['təːmait], *s.* Termite *f.*

**terrace** ['terəs, -ris], *s.* **1.** Terrasse *f.* **2.** Häuserreihe *f;* **t. house,** Reihenhaus *n.*

**terrain** [tə'rein], *s.* Gelände *n.*

**terrestrial** [ti'restriəl], *adj.* irdisch.

**terrible** ['teribl], *adj.* schrecklich, furchtbar; **-ibly,** *adv. F:* furchtbar, schrecklich.

**terrier** ['teriər], *s.* Terrier *m.*

**terrific** [tə'rifik], *adj. (a) (enormous)* enorm, ungeheuer; **-ally,** *adv.* enorm.

**terrify** ['terifai], *v.tr.* (j-n) in Angst und Schrecken versetzen. ◆**'terrifying,** *adj.* fürchterlich.

**territory** ['terit(ə)ri], *s.* Gebiet *n.* ◆**terri'torial,** *adj.* territorial; **t. waters,** Hoheitsgewässer *npl.*

**terror** ['terər], *s.* Schrecken *m* (**of,** vor + *dat*); ◆**'terrorism,** *s.* Terrorismus *m.* ◆**'terrorist,** *s.* Terrorist *m.* ◆**'terrorize,** *v.tr.* terrorisieren.

**terse** [təːs], *adj.* knapp; *(of pers.)* kurz und bündig; *(of sentences etc.)* gedrängt.

**test** [test]. **I.** *s.* **1.** Probe *f,* Test *m; (examination)* Untersuchung *f; (check)* Kontrolle *f;* **to put s.o., sth. to the t.,** j-n, etwas auf die Probe stellen; *Av:* **t. pilot,** Testpilot *m; Ch: etc:* **t. tube,** Reagenzglas *n;* **t. (match),** Länderspiel *n.* **2.** *Sch: etc:* Test *m; Prüfung f.* **II.** *v.tr.* (j-n, etwas) prüfen (**for sth.,** auf etwas *acc* hin); (etwas) einer Prüfung unterziehen; (eine Maschine usw.) testen, *(examine)* untersuchen; (ein Verfahren) auf die Probe stellen; *Ch:* (einen Stoff) analysieren; *Med:* (Blut) untersuchen.

**testament** ['testəmənt], *s.* Testament *n.*

**testicle** ['testikl], *s.* Hoden *m.*

**testify** ['testifai], *v.* 1. *v.tr.* (etwas) aussagen. 2. *v.i.* **to t. to sth.**, etwas bezeugen. ◆**testimonial** [-'məunjəl], *s.* (*evidence*) Zeugnis *n*; (*for job etc.*) Empfehlungsschreiben *n*. ◆**'testimony** [-məni], *s. Jur: etc:* Zeugnis *n*; (*statement*) (mündliche) Zeugenaussage *f*.

**testy** ['testi], *adj.* reizbar.

**tetanus** ['tetənəs], *s.* Wundstarrkrampf *m*.

**tether** ['teðər]. **I.** *s.* Haltestrick *m* (eines Pferdes usw.); *Fig:* **at the end of one's t.**, am Ende seiner Kräfte; (*impatient*) am Ende seiner Geduld. **II.** *v.tr.* (ein Tier) anbinden.

**text** [tekst], *s.* Text *m*. ◆**'textbook**, *s. Sch:* Lehrbuch *n*.

**textile** ['tekstail], *s.* Gewebe *n*; *pl.* **textiles**, Textilien *pl*. ◆**texture** ['tekstʃər], *s.* Beschaffenheit *f*.

**Thai** [tai]. **I.** *s.* Thailänder(in) *m(f)*. **II.** *adj.* thailändisch. ◆**'Thailand.** *Pr. n.* Thailand *n*.

**Thames** [temz]. *Pr. n.* Themse *f*.

**than** [ðæn, ðən], *conj.* als.

**thank** [θæŋk]. **I.** *s. pl.* **thanks**, Dank *m; F:* **thanks!** danke! **many thanks!** vielen Dank! (*b*) **thanks to**, dank + *gen.* **II.** *v.tr.* (*a*) (j-m) danken, sich (bei j-m) bedanken (**for sth.**, für etwas *acc*); **t. goodness!** Gott sei Dank! (*b*) **to have s.o. to t. for sth.**, j-m etwas zu verdanken haben. ◆**'thankful**, *adj.* dankbar. ◆**'thankfulness**, *s.* Dankbarkeit *f*. ◆**'thankless**, *adj.* undankbar. ◆**thanks'giving**, *s.* Danksagung *f; Ecc:* (**Harvest**) **T.**, Erntedankfest *n*. ◆**'thankyou**, *s.* Dankeschön *n*.

**that¹** [ðæt]. **I.** *dem. pron.* (*pl.* **those** [ðəuz]) 1. das, *pl.* die; **give me t.**, gib mir das; **how much are those?** wieviel kosten die (da)? **t. is (to say) ...**, das heißt, ...; **after t.**, danach, darauf; **what do you mean by t.?** was willst du damit sagen? **at t.**, noch dazu; **and t.'s t.!** und damit basta! 2. (*opposed to this*, **these**) jener, jene, jenes; **this is new, t. is old,** dies(es) ist neu, jenes ist alt. **II.** *dem. adj.* (*pl.* **those**) jener, jene, jenes; *pl.* jene; **t. one**, jenes dort; **everyone agrees on t. point,** alle sind sich in dem Punkt einig. **III.** *dem. adv.* **t. high,** so hoch.

**that²** [ðət], *rel. pron. sing. & pl.* der, die, das; **everything/all t. ...**, alles, was ...; **the best t. he could do,** das Beste, was er machen konnte.

**that³** [ðæt, ðət], *conj.* daß.

**thatch** [θætʃ], *v.tr.* (ein Dach) mit Stroh decken; **thatched cottage,** strohgedecktes Landhaus.

**thaw** [θɔː]. **I.** *s.* Tauwetter *n;* (*process*) Tauen *n.* **II.** *v.* 1. *v.tr.* (Schnee) tauen; (Fleisch usw.) auftauen. 2. *v.i.* (*of snow etc.*) tauen; (*of frozen food; Fig: of pers.*) auftauen.

**the** [ðə], *before vowel* [ðiː]. **I.** *def. art.* der, die, das; *pl.* die. **II.** *adv.* **so much**

**the better,** umso besser; **the sooner the better,** je eher, desto besser. ◆**theatre** ['θiətər], *s.* 1. Theater *n;* **to go to the t.,** ins Theater gehen. 2. *Med:* (**operating**) **t.,** Operationssaal *m*. ◆**'theatregoer,** *s.* Theaterbesucher(in) *m(f)*. ◆**theatrical** [θi'ætrik(ə)l], *adj.* 1. Theater-. 2. (*as in the theatre*) theatralisch.

**theft** [θeft], *s.* Diebstahl *m*.

**their** [ðɛər], *poss. adj.* ihr, ihre; ◆**theirs** [ðɛəz], *poss. pron.* ihrer, ihre, ihres; *pl.* ihre.

**them** [ðəm], *pers. pron. pl.* (*objective case*) (*acc*) sie; (*dat*) ihnen; **I like t.,** ich habe sie gern; **I shall tell t.,** ich werde es ihnen sagen; **it's t.!** sie sind's! ◆**them'selves**, *pers. pron.* 1. (*reflexive*) sich. 2. (*emphatic*) selbst.

**theme** [θiːm], *s.* Thema *n; t.* **song**, Titelmelodie *f*.

**then** [ðen], *adv.* dann; (*a*) (*at that time*) damals; **t. and there,** auf der Stelle, sofort; **now and t.**, dann und wann; (*b*) (*after that*) danach, darauf; **now t.!** (i) aufpassen! (ii) hören Sie mal! **before t.**, vorher; **by t.**, bis dahin; bis zu der Zeit; **till t.**, bis dahin.

**theology** [θi'ɔlədʒi], *s.* Theologie *f*. ◆**theologian** [θiə'ləudʒən], *s.* Theologe *m*. ◆**theological** [-'lɔdʒikl], *adj.* theologisch.

**theorem** ['θiərəm], *s.* Lehrsatz *m*. ◆**theoretical** ['θiə'retikl], *adj.* theoretisch. ◆**'theorize,** *v.i.* Theorien aufstellen. ◆**theory** ['θiəri], *s.* Theorie *f;* **in t.**, theoretisch.

**therapy** ['θerəpi], *s.* Therapie *f*. ◆**'therapist**, *s.* Therapeut(in) *m(f)*.

**there** [ðɛər]. **I.** *adv.* (*place*) dort, da; (*direction*) dorthin, dahin. 2. (*unstressed*) [ðər] **t. is/are,** es ist/sind; es gibt + *acc.* 3. da; **t. you are mistaken,** da irrst du dich. **II.** *int. da!* (*look*) sieh mal! **t. now! t. t. now!** na also! (*calming*) schon gut! **t.! t.! don't worry!** schon gut, mach dir keine Sorgen! ◆**'thereabouts**, *adv.* 1. in der Nähe. 2. (*with number*) so ungefähr. ◆**there'by**, *adv.* dadurch. ◆**'therefore**, *adv.* deswegen. ◆**thereu'pon**, *adv.* darauf(hin).

**thermal** ['θəːməl], *adj. esp. Ph:* Wärme-; **t. unit,** Wärmeeinheit *f*. ◆**thermometer** [θə'mɔmitər], *s.* Thermometer *n*. ◆**'thermos** *s. R.t.m.* (**flask**), Thermosflasche *f*. ◆**thermostat** ['θəːməstæt], *s.* Thermostat *m*.

**these** [ðiːz], *pl. of* **this** *q.v.*

**thesis** ['θiːsis], *pl.* **theses** ['θiːsis, 'θiːsiːz], *s.* These *f;* (*for doctorate*) Doktorarbeit *f*.

**they** [ðei]. 1. *pers. pron. nom. pl.* sie. 2. *indef. pron.* (= *one*) man.

**thick** [θik]. **I.** *adj.* 1. dick. 2. (*of forest, fog, hair etc.*) dicht; (*of crowd*) dichtgedrängt. 3. (*a*) (*of liquid*) dickflüssig; (*b*) *F:* **t.(-headed),** begriffsstutzig. **II.** *s.* **in the t. of it,** mittendrin. ◆**'thicken,** *v.* 1. *v.tr.* (etwas) dicker machen; *Cu:* (eine

Soße) eindicken. 2. *v.i.* dicker werden; (*of fog etc.*) dichter werden. ◆'**thicket**, *s.* Dickicht *n.* ◆'**thickness**, *s.* 1. (*a*) Dicke *f* (eines Gegenstandes); (*b*) Dichte *f* (des Nebels, eines Waldes usw.); Dichtheit *f* (der Haare usw.). 2. (*layer*) Schicht *f.* ◆'**thickset**, *adj.* (*of pers.*) untersetzt. ◆'**thick-skinned**, *adj.* dickhäutig; *F:* (*of pers.*) dickfellig.

**thief**, *pl.* **thieves** [θi:f, θi:vz], *s.* Dieb(in) *m(f)*; (*crook*) Gauner *m.* ◆'**thieve**, *v.tr. & i.* stehlen. ◆'**thieving**. I. *adj.* diebisch. II. *s.* Diebstahl *m.*

**thigh** [θai], *s.* Oberschenkel *m.*

**thin** [θin]. I. *adj.* dünn; (*of thread*) fein; (*of pers.*) mager; (*slim*) schlank; (*of population*) spärlich; *t.* **excuse**, fadenscheinige Entschuldigung. -**ly**, *adv.* dünn. II. *v.* 1. *v.tr.* (*a*) (einen Gegenstand) dünner machen; (*b*) (eine Farbe, Soße usw.) verdünnen. 2. *v.i.* (*a*) dünn(er) werden; (*of pers.*) abnehmen. ◆'**thinness**, *s.* Dünnheit *f*; Feinheit *f*; Magerkeit *f*; Schlankheit *f*; Spärlichkeit *f.*

**thing** [θiŋ], *s.* (*object*) Ding *n*; *pl. F:* (*possessions*) Sachen *fpl.* 2. (*matter*) Sache *f.* **last t. at night**, als letztes (vor dem Schlafengehen); **as things are**, wie die Dinge liegen.

**think** [θiŋk]. 1. *v.tr. & i.irr.* (*a*) denken; (*consider*) überlegen; (*meditate*) nachdenken; (*b*) (*believe*) glauben; **just t.!** stell dir nur vor! (*c*) (*express opinion*) meinen; **what do you t. I ought to do?** was sollte ich Ihrer Ansicht nach machen? **I t. she's pretty**, ich finde sie hübsch; **everyone thought he was mad**, jeder hielt ihn für verrückt; **I t. so**, ich glaube ja. 2. *v.tr.* **to t. of/about sth.**, an etwas *acc* denken; (*meditate*) über etwas *acc* nachdenken; (*imagine*) sich *dat* etwas vorstellen; **I can't t. of the right word**, ich komme nicht auf das richtige Wort; **the best I can t. of**, das beste, was mir einfällt; (*just*) **t. of that!** stell dir (nur) vor! **to t. of s.o.'s feelings**, Rücksicht auf j-s Gefühle nehmen; **to be thinking of doing sth.**, vorhaben, etwas zu tun; **what do you t. of/about it?** was halten Sie davon/meinen Sie dazu? ◆'**thinker**, *s.* Denker(in) *m(f).* ◆'**thinking**. I. *adj.* denkend. II. *s.* Denken *n.* ◆'**think 'over**, *v.tr.* (etwas) überdenken. ◆'**think 'up**, *v.tr.* sich (etwas) ausdenken.

**third** [θə:d]. I. *num. adj.* dritter, dritte, drittes; **t. person**, (*also* **t. party**) Dritte(r) *m*; **t. party insurance**, Haftpflichtversicherung *f.* II. *s.* (*fraction*) Drittel *n*; -**ly**, *adv.* drittens. ◆'**third-'rate**, *adj.* drittrangig.

**thirst** [θə:st], *s.* Durst *m*; *Fig:* **t. for knowledge**, Wißbegier *f.* ◆'**thirsty**, *adj.* durstig; **to be (very) t.**, (großen) Durst haben; **this is t. work**, diese Arbeit macht Durst/durstig.

**thirteen** [θə:'ti:n]. I. *num. adj.* dreizehn. II. *s.* Dreizehn *f.* ◆**thir'teenth**, *num.*

*adj.* dreizehnte(r,s).

**thirty** ['θə:ti], *num. adj.* dreißig. ◆'**thirtieth**, *num. adj.* dreißigste(r,s).

**this** [ðis]. I. *dem. pron. pl.* **these** [ði:z] 1. dies(es); *pl.* diese; II. *dem. adj.* (*pl.* **these**) dieser, diese, dieses; *pl.* diese; **t. one**, dieses; **t. evening**, heute abend. III. *dem. adv.* **t. high**, so hoch; **t. far**, bis hierher.

**thistle** ['θisl], *s.* Distel *f.*

**thong** [θɔŋ], *s.* Lederstreifen *m.*

**thorn** [θɔ:n], *s.* Dorn *m*; (*bush*) Dornbusch *m.* ◆'**thorny**, *adj.* dornig; *Fig:* **t. problem**, heikles Problem.

**thorough** ['θʌrə], *adj.* gründlich; (*of search*) eingehend; (*careful*) sorgfältig; -**ly**, *adv.* gründlich; (*completely*) vollkommen (begreifen); völlig (neu gestalten) **I t. enjoyed the meal**, das Essen schmeckte mir ausgezeichnet. ◆'**thoroughbred**, *s.* I. *adj.* (*of horse*) vollblütig, Vollblut-; (*of dog*) reinrassig. II. *s.* Vollblut(pferd) *n.* ◆'**thoroughfare**, *s. esp. Adm:* Durchgangsstraße *f.* ◆'**thoroughness**, *s.* Gründlichkeit *f*; (*care*) Sorgfalt *f*; (*completeness*) Vollkommenheit *f.*

**those** [ðəuz], *pron. & adj. pl. of* **that**[1].

**though** [ðəu], *conj.* 1. obwohl. 2. **as t.**, als ob + *subj.*

**thought** [θɔ:t], *s.* 1. Gedanke *m*; **the mere t. (of it)**, der bloße Gedanke (daran). 2. (*process*) Denken *n*; (*meditation*) Nachdenken *n*; **lost in t.**, in Gedanken vertieft. 3. (*idea*) Idee *f*; (*consideration*) Überlegung *f.* ◆'**thoughtful**, *adj.* 1. (*pensive*) nachdenklich. 2. (*considerate*) rücksichtsvoll; -**ly**, *adv.* (*pensively*) nachdenklich. ◆'**thoughtfulness**, *s.* 1. Nachdenklichkeit *f.* 2. Rücksicht(nahme) *f*; (*attention*) Aufmerksamkeit *f.* ◆'**thoughtless**, *adj.* (*a*) unüberlegt; (*b*) (*inconsiderate*) rücksichtslos; -**ly**, *adv.* rücksichtslos. ◆'**thoughtlessness**, *s.* (*a*) Unüberlegtheit *f*; (*b*) Rücksichtslosigkeit *f.*

**thousand** ['θauz(ə)nd]. I. *num. adj.* tausend. II. *s.* Tausend *n.* ◆'**thousandth**. I. *num. adj.* tausendste(r,s). II. *s.* (*fraction*) Tausendstel *n.*

**thrash** [θræʃ], *v.tr.* (*a*) (j-n) verprügeln; (*b*) *Sp: etc:* (j-n, eine Mannschaft) vernichtend schlagen. ◆'**thrashing**, *s.* a **t.**, eine Tracht Prügel. ◆'**thrash 'out**, *v.tr.* (ein Problem) ausführlich erörtern.

**thread** [θred]. I. *s.* 1. (*a*) Faden *m*; **sewing t.**, Nähfaden *m*; (*b*) *Cl:* Garn *n*; *Fig:* **to lose the t.**, den Faden verlieren. 2. Gewinde *n.* II. *v.tr. Tchn:* **to t. a needle**, (den Faden in) eine Nadel einfädeln. ◆'**threadbare**, *adj.* (*also Fig:*) fadenscheinig.

**threat** [θret], *s.* Drohung *f.* ◆'**threaten**, *v.tr.* **to t. s.o., sth. (with sth.)**, j-m, etwas *dat* (mit etwas *dat*) drohen; **to t. to do sth.**, drohen, etwas zu tun. ◆'**threatening**, *adj.* (*of tone*) drohend.

**three** [θri:]. I. *num. adj.* drei; **t.-**

**cornered,** dreieckig; *Cl:* **t.-piece suit,** dreiteiliger Anzug; *Aut:* **t.-wheeler,** Dreiradauto *n.* **II.** *s. (figure)* Drei *f.* ◆'**threefold,** *adj. & adv.* dreifach.
**thresh** [θreʃ], *v.tr.* (Weizen) dreschen. ◆'**thresher,** *s.* Dreschmaschine *f.*
**threshold** ['θreʃ(h)əuld], *s.* Schwelle *f.*
**thrift** [θrift], '**thriftiness,** *s.* Sparsamkeit *f.* ◆'**thrifty,** *adj. (economical)* sparsam.
**thrill** [θril]. **I.** *s.* **1.** *(trembling)* Zittern *n.* **2.** *(excitement)* Erregung *f.* **II.** *v.* **1.** *v.tr.* (a) *(excite)* (j-n) erregen; (b) *(delight)* (j-n, das Publikum) begeistern. **2.** *v.i.* beben (**with,** vor + *dat*). ◆'**thriller,** *s.* Thriller *m.* ◆'**thrilling,** *adj.* aufregend; *(tense)* spannend; *(of spectacle)* packend.
**thrive** [θraiv], *v.i.* *(of child, plant etc.)* gedeihen; *(of business)* blühen. ◆'**thriving,** *adj.* gedeihend; *(of pers., business)* blühend.
**throat** [θrəut], *s. (outside)* Hals *m;* *(inside)* Kehle *f;* *(of animal)* Rachen *m;* **to have a sore t.,** Halsschmerzen haben; **to clear one's t.,** sich räuspern.
**throb** [θrɔb]. **I.** *s.* Klopfen *n;* Pochen *n* (des Herzens). **II.** *v.i.* klopfen. ◆'**throbbing,** *s. (pain)* pochende/(*in the head)* hämmernde Schmerzen *mpl.*
**throes** [θrəuz], *s. pl.* **death** *s.,* Todeskampf *m;* *Fig:* **in the t. of,** mitten in + *dat.*
**thrombosis** [θrɔm'bəusis], *s.* Thrombose *f.*
**throne** [θrəun], *s.* Thron *m.*
**throng** [θrɔŋ]. **I.** *s. (people)* Menschenmenge *f;* *(crush)* Gedränge *n.* **II.** *v.i.* **to t. together,** sich zusammendrängen.
**throttle** ['θrɔtl]. **I.** *s. Aut: etc: (pedal)* Gaspedal *n.* **to open the t.,** Gas geben. **II.** *v.tr.* (j-n) erwürgen.
**through** [θru:]. **I.** *prep.* (a) durch + *acc;* (b) *(time)* während, hindurch; **all t. his life,** sein ganzes Leben hindurch; (c) *(because of)* wegen + *gen;* *(with emotions etc.)* aus + *dat.* **II.** *adv.* **1.** durch; *Tel:* **to get t.,** eine Verbindung bekommen; **you're t.,** Sie sind verbunden. **2.** *(finished)* fertig; **I'm t. with him,** ich will nichts mehr mit ihm zu tun haben. ◆**through'out.** **I.** *prep.* ... *acc* hindurch; **t. the year,** das ganze Jahr hindurch/während des ganzen Jahres. **II.** *adv. (all the time)* die ganze Zeit. ◆'**throughway,** *s. N.Am.* Autobahn *f.*
**throw** [θrəu]. **I.** *s.* Wurf *m.* **II.** *v.tr.irr.* werfen, *(hurl)* schleudern. ◆'**throw a'way,** *v.tr.* wegwerfen; *(waste)* (Worte, Zeit) verschwenden. ◆'**throwaway,** *adj.* Wegwerf-. ◆'**throw 'in,** *v.tr.* hineinwerfen; *Fb:* (den Ball) einwerfen. ◆'**throw 'out,** *v.tr.* hinauswerfen; (Hitze) ausstrahlen. ◆'**throw 'up,** *v.* **1.** *v.tr.* (etwas) in die Höhe werfen, hochwerfen; (die Hände) hochheben. **2.** *v.i.* *F: (vomit)* kotzen.
**thru** [θru:], *N.Am:* = **through.**
**thrush** [θrʌʃ], *s.* Drossel *f.*

**thrust** [θrʌst]. **I.** *s. (a)* Stoß *m;* *(Tchn)* Schubleistung *f.* **II.** *v.* **1.** *v.tr. (a)* (etwas) (heftig) stoßen; (j-n) schieben; **to t. one's hands into one's pockets,** die Hände in die Taschen stecken; *(b)* **to t. sth. on s.o.,** j-m etwas aufdrängen.
**thud** [θʌd], *s.* dumpfer Schlag *m.*
**thug** [θʌg], *s. F:* Schläger *m;* *(bully)* Tyrann *m.*
**thumb** [θʌm]. **I.** *s.* Daumen *m.* **II.** *v.tr.* (a) **to t. (through) a book,** ein Buch durchblättern; *(of book)* **well-thumbed,** abgegriffen; (b) *F:* **to t. a lift,** per Anhalter fahren. ◆'**thumbnail,** *s.* Daumennagel *m.* ◆'**thumbtack,** *s. N.Am:* Reißzwecke *f.*
**thump** [θʌmp]. **I.** *s.* dumpfer Schlag *m,* *F:* Plumps *m;* *(blow)* Puff *m.* **II.** *v.tr. & i.* (a) (j-n) schlagen; (b) *(of heart)* heftig pochen.
**thunder** ['θʌndər]. **I.** *s.* Donner *m.* **II.** *v.tr. & i. (also Fig:)* donnern. ◆'**thunderbolt,** *s.* Donnerkeil *m;* *Fig:* *(news)* Blitzstrahl *m.* ◆'**thundering,** *adj.* donnernd. ◆'**thunderous,** *adj. (of applause)* donnernd. ◆'**thunderstorm,** *s.* Gewitter *n.* ◆'**thunderstruck,** *adj.* wie vom Blitz getroffen. ◆'**thundery,** *adj. F: (of weather)* gewitterschwül.
**Thursday** ['θə:zdi], *s.* Donnerstag *m.*
**thus** [ðʌs], *adv.* **1.** *(in this way)* so. **2.** *(therefore)* also, folglich.
**thwart** [θwɔ:t], *v.tr.* (j-m) in die Quere kommen; **to t. s.o.'s plans,** j-s Pläne durchkreuzen; **to be thwarted,** gehindert sein.
**thyme** [taim], *s.* Thymian *m.*
**thyroid** ['θairɔid], *s.* **t. (gland),** Schilddrüse *f.*
**tiara** [ti'ɑ:rə], *s.* Diadem *n.*
**Tibet** [ti'bet]. *Pr. n.* Tibet *n.* ◆**Ti'betan.** **I.** *adj.* tibetisch. **II.** *s.* Tibeter(in) *m(f).*
**tick¹** [tik]. **I.** *s.* **1.** *(a) (sound)* Ticken *n;* (b) *F:* Moment *m;* **just a/half a t.!** ich komme gleich! **2.** *(mark)* Häkchen *n.* **II.** *v.* **1.** *v.i. (sound)* ticken. **2.** *v.tr.* abhaken. ◆'**ticking,** *s.* **1.** Ticken *n.* **2.** Bezugsstoff *m* (für Kissen usw.); (bed-) t., Inlett *n.* ◆'**tick 'over,** *v.i. (of engine)* leerlaufen.
**tick²,** *s. (insect)* Zecke *f.*
**tick³,** *s. F:* Kredit *m;* **to buy sth. on t.,** etwas auf Pump kaufen.
**ticket** ['tikit], *s.* **1.** Karte *f;* **(entrance) t.,** Eintrittskarte *f;* **(bus, train) t.,** Fahrkarte *f;* **left luggage t.,** Gepäckschein *m;* **cloakroom t.,** Garderobenmarke *f;* **lottery t.,** Los *n;* Lotterielos *n;* **t. collector,** Fahrkartenkontrolleur *m;* **t. machine,** Fahrkartenautomat *m;* **t. office,** Fahrkartenschalter *m.* **2.** *(label)* Etikett *n;* **(price) t.,** Preisschild *n;* *Aut: F:* **to get a (parking) t.,** einen Strafzettel bekommen.
**tickle** ['tikl]. **I.** *s.* Kitzel *m.* **II.** *v.tr.* (a) (j-n) kitzeln; *Fig:* **to t. s.o.'s fancy,** j-m zusagen; (b) *F:* (j-n) erheitern. ◆'**ticklish,** *adj.* **1.** *(of pers.)* kitzlig. **2.**

(*tricky*) heikel.

**tide** [taid], *s. esp. coll. or pl.* **tides,** Gezeiten *pl;* **high t.,** Flut *f;* **the t. is out/it is low t.,** es ist Ebbe *f.* ◆'**tidal,** *adj.* **1. t. wave,** Flutwelle *f.* 2. Gezeiten-. ◆'**tide 'over,** *v.tr.* **that will t. us over,** das wird uns solange über Wasser halten.

**tidy** ['taidi]. **I.** *adj.* ordentlich; (*orderly*) geordnet. **II.** *v.* **1.** *v.tr.* (etwas) ordnen, in Ordnung bringen; **to t. a room,** in einem Zimmer aufräumen; **to t. sth. away,** etwas wegräumen. 2. *v.i.* **to t. up,** aufräumen. ◆'**tidily,** *adv.* **t. dressed,** ordentlich angezogen. ◆'**tidiness,** *s.* Ordentlichkeit *f;* (*order*) Ordnung *f.*

**tie** [tai]. **I.** *s.* **1.** Band *n;* (*connection*) Verbindung *f;* **family ties,** Familienverpflichtungen *fpl.* 2. *Cl:* Krawatte *f;* **bow t.,** Fliege *f.* 3. *Sp: etc:* Gleichstand *m.* **II.** *v.* **1.** *v.tr.* (etwas) binden, (*tightly*) festbinden. 2. *v.i. Sp: etc:* punktgleich sein. ◆'**tie 'down,** *v.tr.* (*a*) (j-n) fesseln; (etwas) festbinden; (*b*) (j-n) festlegen (**to sth.,** auf etwas *acc*). ◆'**tie 'on,** *v.tr.* (etwas) anbinden (**to sth.,** an etwas *acc*). ◆'**tiepin,** *s.* Krawattennadel *f.* ◆'**tie 'up,** *v.tr.* (*a*) (Schnürsenkel, einen Knoten usw.) binden; (ein Paket) zubinden; (ein Bündel) zusammenbinden; (*bandage*) (einen verletzten Arm, usw.) verbinden; (*b*) (einen Hund) anbinden (**to a post,** an einen Pfahl); (j-n) fesseln; (*c*) **just now I'm tied up,** augenblicklich bin ich beschäftigt.

**tier** [tiər], *s.* Etage *f;* *Th: etc:* Rang *m;* **in tiers,** etagenförmig.

**tiff** [tif], *s.* kleine Unstimmigkeit *f,* *F:* Krach *m.*

**tiger** ['taigər], *s.* Tiger *m.* ◆'**tigress,** *s.* Tigerin *f.*

**tight** [tait]. **I.** *adj.* **1.** (*a*) (*of clothes etc.*) eng; **t. fit,** knapper Sitz *m;* (*b*) (*of money, time etc.*) knapp; (*c*) (*of cork, screw etc.*) fest; (*stiff*) steif; (*d*) (*taut*) gespannt. 2. *F:* blau; **II.** *adv.* (*of door, eyes etc.*) **shut t.,** fest geschlossen; **-ly,** *adv.* (*of clothes etc.*) **to fit t.,** eng anliegen; **t. packed,** dicht gedrängt. ◆'**tighten,** *v.* **1.** *v.tr.* (*a*) (eine Schraube usw.) festziehen; (einen Seil usw.) straff ziehen; (Muskeln, eine Feder) spannen; (*b*) **to t. restrictions,** Beschränkungen verschärfen. 2. *v.i.* (*of rope, muscle etc.*) sich spannen; (*of grip*) fester werden. ◆'**tight-'fisted,** *adj.* knauserig. ◆'**tight-'fitting,** *adj. Cl:* eng anliegend. ◆'**tightness,** *s.* (*a*) knapper Sitz *m* (einer Hose usw.); (*b*) Festigkeit *f,* Steifheit *f;* (*c*) Straffheit *f* (eines Seils usw.). ◆'**tightrope,** *s.* Seil *n;* **t. walker,** Seiltänzer(in) *m(f).* ◆'**tights,** *s. pl.* Strumpfhose *f;* *Th: etc:* Trikot *n.*

**tile** [tail], *s.* (*a*) (*floor*) **t.,** Fliese *f;* (*on walls etc.*) Kachel *f;* (*on roof*) Dachziegel *m;* **tiled roof,** Ziegeldach *n;* **tiled floor,** Fliesenboden *m.*

**till**[1] [til], *v.tr. A: & Lit:* (Land usw.) bestellen.

**till**[2], *s.* (*cash*) **t.,** Ladenkasse *f.*

**till**[3], *prep. & conj.* (*a*) bis; **t. now/then,** bis jetzt/dahin; (*b*) (*with noun*) bis zu + *dat;* **t. the next time,** bis zum nächsten Mal; (*c*) **he won't come t. after dinner,** er kommt erst nach dem Essen.

**tiller** ['tilər], *s. Nau:* Ruderpinne *f.*

**tilt** [tilt], *v.* **1.** *v.i.* (*of surface*) **to t. (up),** sich neigen; (*of pile*) **to t. over,** kippen; (*fall*) umkippen. 2. *v.tr.* (etwas) kippen.

**timber** ['timbər], *s.* Holz *n;* **standing t./t. trees,** Nutzholzbäume *mpl.*

**time** [taim]. **I.** *s.* (*a*) Zeit *f;* **in a short t.,** binnen kurzem; **in three weeks' t.,** in drei Wochen; **I haven't seen him for a long t.,** ich habe ihn (schon) lange/seit langem nicht gesehen; **for some t.** (*past*), seit einiger Zeit; **all the t.,** die ganze Zeit; **to take one's t.,** sich für etwas *acc* Zeit lassen; *F:* **I've no t. for him,** (i) ich habe keine Geduld mit ihm; (ii) er ist mir unsympathisch; (*b*) (*moment*) Zeit *f;* Zeitpunkt *m;* **at that t.,** zu der Zeit, damals; **at the present t.,** gegenwärtig; **at times,** manchmal; **some t. or other,** irgendwann einmal; **by the t. I got there,** bis ich dort ankam; **from t. to t.,** ab und zu; von Zeit zu Zeit; **what's the t.?** wieviel Uhr ist es? wie spät ist es? **to arrive on t.,** pünktlich ankommen; **in good t.,** rechtzeitig; **I was just in t.,** ich kam gerade (noch) rechtzeitig; **it's high t.,** es ist höchste Zeit; **we had a good t.,** wir haben uns bestens amüsiert; **next t.,** nächstes Mal; **several times over,** mehrere Male; **four times as big,** viermal so groß; **at the same t.,** gleichzeitig; **t. lag,** Verzögerung *f;* **t. limit,** Frist *f;* Zeitbeschränkung *f;* (*c*) *Mus:* Takt *m;* **to beat/keep t.,** (den) Takt schlagen. **II.** *v.tr.* (*a*) den Zeitpunkt festlegen/wählen für (etwas *acc*); **he didn't t. it right,** er hat den richtigen Zeitpunkt nicht erwischt; (*b*) *Sp:* **to t. s.o.,** j-n stoppen. ◆'**timekeeper,** *s. Sp:* Zeitnehmer *m.* ◆'**timeswitch,** *s.* Schaltuhr *f.* ◆'**timetable,** *s.* **1.** *Rail: etc:* Fahrplan *m.* 2. *Sch:* Stundenplan *m.* ◆'**timing,** *s.* **1.** (*ignition*) **t.,** Zündeinstellung *f.* 2. *Sp:* Zeitnahme *f.* 3. (*fixing of time*) Zeitbestimmung *f;* Zeitwahl *f.*

**timid** ['timid], *adj.* scheu. ◆**ti'midity,** *s.* Scheu *f.*

**timpani** ['timpəni], *s. pl.* Kesselpauken *fpl.* ◆'**timpanist,** *s.* Pauker *m.*

**tin** [tin], *s.* **1.** Zinn *n;* (*tinplate*) Blech *n;* 2. Dose *f;* **t. opener,** Dosenöffner *m.* ◆'**tinfoil,** *s.* Stanniol *n.* ◆'**tinny,** *adj.* (*of sound etc.*) blechern. ◆'**tin'plate,** *s.* Weißblech *n.*

**tinge** [tin(d)ʒ]. **I.** *s.* **1.** (zarte) Tönung *f;* **with a t. of red,** mit einem Stich ins Rote; rötlich getönt. 2. *Fig:* (*trace*) Spur *f;* **a t. of sadness,** ein Anflug *m* von Trauer. **II.** *v.tr.* (Haare usw.) leicht tönen.

**tingle** ['tiŋgl], *v.i.* prickeln; (*with cold*

*etc.*) (leicht) brennen.

**tinker** ['tiŋkər]. **I.** *s.* Kesselflicker *m.* **II.** *v.i.* to t. (about), herumpfuschen (**with,** an + *dat*).

**tinkle** ['tiŋkl]. **I.** *s.* (*also* **tinkling**) Geklingel *n.* **II.** *v.* 1. *v.i.* klingeln. 2. *v.tr.* (mit etwas *dat*) klingeln.

**tinsel** ['tins(ə)l], *s.* Lametta *n; (loose)* Flitter *m.*

**tint** [tint]. **I.** *s.* Farbton *m; Tönung f; (of black)* Schattierung *f.* **II.** *v.tr.* (Haar usw.) tönen.

**tiny** ['taini], *adj.* winzig.

**tip**[1] [tip], *s.* Spitze *f; Fig:* **it is on the t. of my tongue,** es liegt mir auf der Zunge. ◆'**tiptoe.** **I.** *s. & adv.* (**on**) t., auf Zehenspitzen *fpl.* **II.** *v.i.* auf Zehenspitzen gehen. ◆'**tip'top,** *adj. F:* klasse, prima.

**tip**[2]. **I.** *s.* 1. *(money)* Trinkgeld *n.* 2. *Sp: etc:* Tip *m.* **II.** *v.* 1. *v.tr.* (*a*) (j-n ins Wasser usw.) stoßen, *(tilt)* (etwas) kippen; *(knock over)* (etwas) umstoßen; (*b*) **to t. s.o. off,** j-m einen Wink geben; (*c*) (j-m) ein Trinkgeld geben. 2. *v.i.* kippen; **to t. over,** umkippen; **to t. up,** hochkippen. ◆'**tip-lorry**/*F:* '**tipper,** *s.* Kipper *m.* ◆'**tip-off,** *s. F:* Tip *m;* to give s.o. a/ the t.-o., j-m einen Wink geben.

**tipple** ['tipl]. **I.** *s. F:* Gesöff *n.* **II.** *v.i.* zechen.

**tipsy** ['tipsi], *adj.* beschwipst; **to get t.,** sich auf einen Schwips antrinken.

**tire**[1] ['taiər], *v.* 1. *v.tr.* (j-n, ein Tier) ermüden. 2. *v.i.* müde werden; **he soon tired of it,** ihm wurde es bald langweilig. ◆'**tired,** *adj.* müde; **t. out,** erschöpft; **to death,** todmüde; **to be t. of sth.,** etwas *gen* müde sein. ◆'**tiredness,** *s.* Müdigkeit *f.* ◆'**tireless,** *adj.* unermüdlich. ◆'**tiresome,** *adj.* aufreibend; *(of child)* lästig. ◆'**tiring,** *adj.* ermüdend, *(of day, pers. etc.)* anstrengend.

**tire**[2], *s. N. Am:* = **tyre.**

**tissue** ['tisju:], *s.* 1. *Anat: etc:* Gewebe *n.* 2. (**paper**) t., Papiertaschentuch *n;* **t. paper,** Seidenpapier *n.*

**tit**[1] [tit], *s. Orn:* Meise *f;* **blue t.** Blaumeise *f.*

**tit**[2], *s. F:* **t. for tat,** wie du mir, so ich dir.

**titbit** ['titbit], *s.* Leckerbissen *m.*

**titillate** ['titileit], *v.tr.* (den Gaumen, die Sinne usw.) kitzeln.

**titivate** ['titiveit], *v.tr.* sich schön machen.

**title** ['taitl], *s.* 1. Titel *m; Th:* **t. rôle,** Titelrolle *f.* 2. *Jur:* Rechtstitel *m; (to property)* Eigentumsrecht *n;* **t. deed,** Eigentumsurkunde *f.* ◆'**titled,** *adj.* adelig.

**titter** ['titər]. **I.** *s.* Kichern *n.* **II.** *v.i.* kichern. ◆'**tittering,** *s.* Gekicher *n.*

**to** [tu:]. **I.** *prep.* 1. zu + *dat; (esp. with town, country)* nach + *dat;* **he went to France/to the USA,** er reiste nach Frankreich/in die USA; **to go to school/ university,** in die Schule/auf die Universität gehen; **to clasp s.o. to one's heart,**

j-n ans Herz drücken; **to this end,** zu diesem Zweck; **to everyone's surprise,** zur Überraschung aller. 2. (*a*) *(until)* bis; **to this day,** bis heute, zum heutigen Tag; **ten (minutes) to six,** zehn (Minuten) vor sechs; (*b*) bis auf + *acc;* **soaked to the skin,** naß bis auf die Haut. 3. **to speak to s.o.,** mit j-m sprechen; **he said to me ...,** er sagte mir, ... **II.** *(with the infinitive)* zu; **(in order) to,** um zu; **he came to help me,** er kam, um mir zu helfen; **too hot to drink,** zu heiß zum Trinken; **he wants/is able to go,** er will/ kann gehen. **III.** *adv.* (*stressed*) 1. **to come t.,** (wieder) zu sich *dat* kommen. 2. **movement to and fro,** Hin- und Herbewegung *f.*

**toad** [toud], *s.* Kröte *f.* ◆'**toadstool,** *s.* Giftpilz *m.*

**toady** ['toudi], *v.i.* **to t. to s.o.,** vor j-m kriechen.

**toast** [toust]. **I.** *s.* 1. (**a piece of**) t., (eine Scheibe) Toast *m.* 2. Trinkspruch *m,* Toast *m.* **II.** *v.* 1. *v.tr.* (Brot) toasten. 2. *v.tr.* **to t. s.o.,** auf j-s Wohl trinken. ◆'**toaster,** *s.* Toaster *m.*

**tobacco** [tə'bækou], *s.* Tabak *m;* **t. pouch,** Tabak(s)beutel *m.* ◆**to'bacconist,** *s.* Tabakhändler *m;* **t.'s (shop),** Tabakwarenladen *m.*

**toboggan** [tə'bɔgən]. **I.** *s.* Rodelschlitten *m.* **II.** *v.i.* rodeln.

**today** [tə'dei], *adv. & s.* heute; **t./ today's,** heutig; **t.'s paper,** die Zeitung von heute.

**toddle** ['tɔdl], *v.i. (of child)* watscheln. ◆'**toddler,** *s.* Kleinkind *n.*

**toddy** ['tɔdi], *s.* Grog *m.*

**to-do** [tə'du:], *s. F: (fuss)* Getue *n; what a t.!* was für eine Aufregung!

**toe** [tou]. **I.** *s.* Zehe *f.* **II.** *v.tr. F:* **to t. the line,** sich an die Hausordnung/*Pol:* Parteilinie halten. ◆'**toecap,** *s.* Schuhspitze *f.* ◆'**toehold,** *s.* Halt *m* (für die Zehen). ◆'**toenail,** *s.* Zehennagel *m.*

**toffee** ['tɔfi], *s.* Toffee *n; (weiches)* Karamelbonbon *n.*

**together** [tə'geðər], *adv.* zusammen; **to go/belong t.,** zusammengehören; **t. with,** zusammen mit + *dat.*

**toggle** ['tɔgl], *s.* Knebel(verschluß) *m.*

**toil** [tɔil]. **I.** *s.* (mühselige) Arbeit *f.* **II.** *v.i.* sich abplagen.

**toilet** ['tɔilit], *s.* Toilette *f;* **t. soap,** Toilettenseife *f;* **t. paper,** Toilettenpapier *n;* **t. roll,** Rolle *f* Toilettenpapier.

**token** ['touk(ə)n], *s.* 1. Zeichen *n.* 2. *(for books, records)* Gutschein *m; (at games)* Spielmarke *f.*

**tolerable** ['tɔlərəbl], *adj.* (*a*) erträglich; (*b*) *(reasonable)* passabel; **-ably,** *adv.* ziemlich. ◆'**tolerance,** *s.* Toleranz *f.* ◆'**tolerant,** *adj.* tolerant. ◆'**tolerate,** *v.tr.* (*a*) (j-n, etwas) dulden; (Ansichten usw.) tolerieren; (*b*) *(bear)* (etwas) aushalten. ◆**tole'ration,** *s.* Duldung *f.*

**toll**[1] [toul], *s.* (*a*) Zoll *m;* **t. bridge/road,**

gebührenpflichtige Brücke/Straße; *(b)*
*Fig: (of epidemic etc.)* **to take a heavy t.,**
viele Opfer fordern.

**toll²,** *v.tr. & i.* (eine Glocke) läuten.

**tomato,** *pl.* **-oes** [tə'mɑːtəu, -əuz], *s.* Tomate *f.*

**tomb** [tuːm], *s.* Grab *n; (monument)* Grabmal *n; (vault)* Gruft *f.* ◆**'tombstone,** *s.* Grabstein *m.*

**tombola** [tɔm'bəulə, 'tɔmbələ], *s.* Tombola *f.*

**tomboy** ['tɔmbɔi], *s.* jungenhaftes Mädchen *n; F:* wilde Range *f.*

**tome** [təum], *s.* dicker Band *m, F:* Wälzer *m.*

**tomfool** ['tɔm'fuːl], *adj. F:* dämlich.
◆**tom'foolery,** *s. F:* Unfug *m.*

**tommy gun** ['tɔmi gʌn], *s. F:* Maschinenpistole *f.*

**tomorrow** [tə'mɔrəu]. **I.** *adv.* morgen; **t. evening,** morgen abend; **the day after t.,** übermorgen. **II.** *s.* Morgen *n; t.'s/of* t., von morgen.

**ton** [tʌn], *s.* Tonne *f; F:* **there's tons of it,** es gibt jede Menge davon.
◆**'tonnage,** *s. Nau: (a) (of ship)* Tonnage *f; (b) (duty)* Frachtgeld *n.*

**tonal** ['təunəl], *adj. Mus:* tonal.

**tone** [təun]. **I.** *s. (sound)* Ton *m; Fig:* **to set the t.,** den Ton angeben. **II.** *v.i.* **to t. with sth.,** mit etwas harmonieren. ◆**'tone 'down,** *v.tr.* (einen Ausdruck, Farben, usw.) abschwächen. ◆**'toneless,** *adj.* tonlos.

**tongs** [tɔŋz], *s.pl.* Zange *f;* **fire-t.,** Feuerzange *f.*

**tongue** [tʌŋ], *s.* **1.** Zunge *f;* **to put one's t. out at s.o.,** j-m die Zunge herausstrecken; **to hold one's t.,** den Mund halten; **t. in cheek,** nicht ernst gemeint. **2.** *A: (language)* Sprache *f.* ◆**'tongue-tied,** *adj.* sprachlos. ◆**'tongue-twister,** *s.* Zungenbrecher *m.*

**tonic** ['tɔnik]. **I.** *adj.* **t. water,** Tonic *m.* **II.** *s.* **1.** *Med:* Tonikum *n; Fig:* Stimulans *n.* **2.** *Mus:* Grundton *m.*

**tonight** [tə'nait], *adv. & s.* heute abend; *(after bedtime)* heute nacht.

**tonsil** ['tɔns(i)l], *s. Anat:* Mandel *f.*
◆**tonsillitis** [-'laitis], *s. Med:* Mandelentzündung *f.*

**too** [tuː], *adv.* **1.** zu; **t. much money,** zuviel Geld. **2.** *(as well)* auch; **I'm coming t.,** ich komme auch mit.

**tool** [tuːl], *s.* Werkzeug *n;* **gardening tools,** Gartengeräte *npl.* ◆**'toolbag,** *s.* Werkzeugtasche *f.* ◆**'toolbox,** *s.* Werkzeugkasten *m.*

**tooth,** *pl.* **teeth** [tuːθ, tiːθ], *s.* Zahn *m;* **set of teeth,** Gebiß *n;* **to have a t. out,** sich *dat* einen Zahn ziehen lassen.
◆**'toothache,** *s.* Zahnschmerzen *mpl.*
◆**'toothbrush,** *s.* Zahnbürste *f.*
◆**'toothless,** *adj.* zahnlos.
◆**'toothpaste,** *s.* Zahnpasta *f.*
◆**'toothpick,** *s.* Zahnstocher *m.*

**top¹** [tɔp]. **I.** *s* **1.** Spitze *f* (eines Daches usw.); Gipfel *m* (eines Berges usw.); Wipfel *m* (eines Baumes); **at the t.,** (ganz) oben; *Fig:* an der Spitze; *Fig:* **at the t. of his voice,** aus vollem Halse; **from t. to toe,** von Kopf bis Fuß; **on t.,** obenauf; **on t. of it (all),** noch dazu/ obendrein. **2.** *Aut: (gear)* höchster Gang *m.* **II.** *adj.* oberste(r,s), höchste(r,s); **t. coat,** letzter Anstrich; *m;* **t. speed,** Höchstgeschwindigkeit *f;* **t. secret,** streng geheim. **III.** *v.tr. (a) (lop)* (einen Baum usw.) kappen; *(b) (cover)* (etwas) bedecken, *(crown)* krönen; **and to t. it all...,** und um dem ganzen die Krone aufzusetzen...; *(c) (exceed)* (eine Zahl, Summe) übersteigen; *(d)* **to t. the list,** die Liste anführen; *Fig: (take priority)* den Vorrang haben. ◆**'top'heavy,** *adj.* kopflastig. ◆**'topless,** *adj. & adv.* oben ohne; *attrib.* Oben-ohne-. ◆**'top 'up,** *v.tr.* nachfüllen.

**top²,** *s.* Kreisel *m.*

**topaz** ['təupæz], *s.* Topas *m.*

**topic** ['tɔpik], *s.* Thema *n.* ◆**'topical,** *adj.* aktuell.

**topple** ['tɔpl], *v.* **1.** *v.i.* **to t. (down/ over),** umkippen; *(of tree, building etc.)* umstürzen. **2.** *v.tr.* **to t. sth. over,** etwas umstoßen.

**topsy-turvy** ['tɔpsi'təːvi], *adj. & adv.* verkehrt; *(confused)* durcheinander; **to turn everything t.-t.,** alles auf den Kopf stellen.

**torch** [tɔːtʃ], *s.* **1.** Fackel *f.* **2.** **(electric) t.,** Taschenlampe *f.*

**torment. I.** ['tɔːment] *s.* Qual *f.* **II.** [tɔː'ment] *v.tr.* (j-n) quälen.

**tornado,** *pl.* **-oes** [tɔː'neidəu, -əuz], *s.* Tornado *m.*

**torpedo,** **I.** *s. (pl.* **-oes)** [tɔː'piːdəu] [-əuz] Torpedo *m.* **II.** *v.tr.* (ein Schiff) torpedieren.

**torrent** ['tɔrənt], *s.* (reißender) Strom *m; (mountain stream)* Sturzbach *m.* ◆**torrential** [-'renʃ(ə)l], *adj. (of rain)* strömend.

**torrid** ['tɔrid], *adj. (a) (of heat, passion etc.)* glühend; *(b) (of land, plain etc.)* ausgedörrt.

**torso,** *pl.* **-os** ['tɔːsəu, -əuz], *s.* Rumpf *m.*

**tortoise** ['tɔːtəs], *s.* Schildkröte *f.*
◆**'tortoiseshell** ['tɔːtəʃel], *s.* Schildpatt *n.*

**tortuous** ['tɔːtjuəs], *adj.* **1.** *(of path etc.)* verschlungen. **2.** *Fig: (of argument)* spitzfindig.

**torture** ['tɔːtʃər]. **I.** *s.* Folter *f; Fig:* Marter *f.* **II.** *v.tr.* (j-n) foltern.

**toss** [tɔs]. **I.** *s.* Wurf *m* (einer Münze usw.). **II.** *v.* **1.** *v.tr. (a)* (einen Ball usw.) in die Luft werfen; **to t. a coin,** mit einer Münze knobeln **(for sth.,** um etwas *acc).* **2.** *v.i.* **to t. (about)/t. and turn in bed,** sich im Bett hin und her wälzen. ◆**'toss-up,** *s. (a)* Knobeln *n* (mit einer Münze); *(b) F:* **it's a t.-up,** es steht auf der Kippe.

**tot¹** [tɔt], s. 1. F: (*child*) **tiny t.**, kleiner Wicht m. 2. **a t. of rum**, ein Schluck m Rum.

**tot²**, v.tr. **to t. up**, (Zahlen, Ausgaben usw.) zusammenrechnen.

**total** ['təut(ə)l]. I. adj. (a) (*whole*) gesamt; **t. amount**, Gesamtsumme f; (b) (*complete*) völlig; (*of eclipse, war etc.*) total; **t. silence**, absolute Stille; **-ly**, adv. völlig. II. s. (a) (*money*) Gesamtbetrag m; **grand t.**, Gesamtsumme f; (b) (*number*) Endresultat n. III. v.tr. (Summen usw.) zusammenrechnen. ◆**totali'tarian** [təutæli'tɛəriən], adj. totalitär. ◆**totali'tarianism**, s. Totalitarismus m. ◆**totality** ['tæliti], s. Gesamtheit f.

**totalisator** ['təutəlaizeitər], F: **tote** [təut], s. Totalisator m.

**totem** ['təutəm], s. Totem n.

**totter** ['tɔtər], v.i. (a) (*of pers.*) taumeln; (b) (*of structure*) wanken, wackeln.

**touch** [tʌtʃ]. I. s. 1. (a) Berührung f; F: **it was t. and go**, es hing an einem Faden; (b) **to give sth. the finishing t.**, einer Sache den letzten Schliff geben. 2. (*sense of*) **t.**, Tastsinn m. 3. (*feature*) Zug m; **the t. of the master**, die Hand des Meisters; **personal t.**, persönliche Note. 4. **t. of garlic**, eine Spur Knoblauch; **with a t. of bitterness**, mit einem Anflug von Bitterkeit; **a t. of flu**, eine leichte Grippe. 5. Kontakt m; **to be in t. with s.o.**, mit j-m in Verbindung stehen/ Kontakt haben; 6. *Sp:* (*at rugby*) Malfeld n; *Fb:* Aus n; **t. line**, (*at rugby*) Mallinie f; *Fb:* Seitenlinie f. II. v.tr. (a) (j-n, etwas) berühren; (*esp. neg.*) (etwas) anrühren; **t. wood!** toi, toi, toi! *Fig:* **to t.** (**on**) **a subject**, ein Thema (kurz) berühren; (b) (j-n) rühren; **his kindness touched me deeply**, ich war von seiner Güte sehr gerührt. ◆**'touch 'down**, v.i. (a) *Av:* landen; (b) (*at rugby*) den Ball im gegnerischen Malfeld niederlegen. ◆**touched**, adj. (*of pers.*) (a) (*moved*) gerührt; (b) F: (*slightly mad*) nicht ganz richtig im Kopf. ◆**'touchiness**, s. Reizbarkeit f. ◆**'touching**, adj. rührend. ◆**'touch 'up**. v.tr. (Lack) ausbessern; *Phot:* (eine Aufnahme) retuschieren. ◆**'touchy**, adj. (*of pers.*) reizbar.

**tough** [tʌf]. I. adj. 1. (*strong*) stark, widerstandsfähig; (*of pers., meat*) zäh. 2. (*inflexible*) (*of pers.*) hart, unnachgiebig. 3. (*difficult*) F: **a t. job**, ein schwerer Job; **t. luck!** Pech! II. s. F: Rowdy m. ◆**'toughen**, v. 1. v.tr. (j-n) abhärten; (einen Stoff) fester machen. 2. v.i. sich abhärten. ◆**'toughness**, s. 1. Stärke f; Zäheit f. 2. Härte f. 3. Schwierigkeit f.

**tour** [tuər]. I. s. (a) Tour f, Reise f (of, durch + acc); **walking t.**, Wandertour f; (b) *Th: etc:* Tournee f (of, durch + acc). II. v.tr. & i. *Th: etc:* **to t. the provinces**, Gastspiele in der Provinz geben. ◆**'tourism**, s. Fremdenverkehr m. ◆**'tourist**, s. Tourist m; **t. office**, Verkehrsamt n.

**tournament** ['tuənəmənt], s. Turnier n.

**tousle** ['tauzl], v.tr. (Haare) zerzausen.

**tow** [təu]. I. s. **to take a ship/a car in t.**, ein Schiff ins Schlepptau nehmen/ein Auto abschleppen. II. v.tr. (ein Fahrzeug) abschleppen; (ein Schiff) schleppen. ◆**'towing**, s. Schleppen n; *Aut:* Abschleppen n. ◆**'towpath**, s. Leinpfad m. ◆**'tow-rope**, s. *Aut:* Abschleppseil n.

**towards** [tə'wɔːdz], prep. 1. auf ... acc zu; **he came t. me**, er kam auf mich zu/ mir entgegen; 2. (*for*) für + acc; **his feelings t. me**, seine Gefühle mir gegenüber; 3. (*time*) gegen + acc; **t. noon**, gegen Mittag.

**towel** ['tauəl], s. Handtuch n.

**tower** ['tauər]. I. s. Turm m; **t. block**, Hochhaus n; (*flats*) Wohnturm m; *Fig:* **he's a t. of strength**, er ist eine große Stütze. II. v.i. hochragen; **to t. over/ above s.o., sth**, j-n, etwas weit überragen/*Fig:* übertreffen. ◆**'towering**, adj. haushoch.

**town** [taun]. I. s. Stadt f; **to go into t.**, in die Stadt gehen; **t. council**, Stadtrat m; **t. hall**, Rathaus n; **t. planning**, Städteplanung f. ◆**'township**, s. (a) Stadtgemeinde f; (b) *N.Am:* Verwaltungsbezirk m.

**toxic** ['tɔksik], adj. giftig.

**toy** [tɔi]. I. s. Spielzeug n; **toys**, Spielsachen fpl. II. v.i. **to t. with an idea**, mit einem Gedanken spielen. ◆**'toyshop**, s. Spielwarengeschäft n.

**trace** [treis]. I. s. Spur f; **we lost all t. of them**, wir haben sie völlig aus den Augen verloren; **to disappear without (a) t.**, spurlos verschwinden. II. v.tr. (a) (*draw*) (Linien usw.) nachziehen; (Muster usw.) durchpausen; (b) (*find*) (j-n, etwas) aufspüren. ◆**'tracery**, s. Flechtwerk n; *Arch:* (*window*) Maßwerk n. ◆**'tracing**, s. (*act*) Durchpausen n; **t. paper**, Pauspapier n.

**track** [træk]. I. s. 1. (*trace*) Spur f; Fährte f (eines Tieres); **to follow in s.o.'s tracks**, in j-s Fußstapfen treten; **to keep t. of s.o.**, j-n nicht aus den Augen verlieren; F: **to make tracks**, sich auf den Weg machen (**for**, nach + dat). 2. (a) (*path*) Weg m; **it's off the beaten t.**, es liegt abseits; (b) *Sp:* Piste f; (**motor-racing**) **t.**, Rennstrecke f; **t. racing**, Rundstreckenrennen n. 3. *Rail:* Gleis n. II. v.tr. (einen Täter, eine Spur usw.) verfolgen; **to t. s.o. down**, j-n aufspüren. ◆**'tracker dog**, s. Spürhund m.

**tract¹** [trækt], s. **1. t. (of country)**, Landstrich m.

**tract²**, s. *Ecc:* Traktat n.

**tractor** ['træktər], s. *Agr:* Traktor m; (*for towing*) Zugmaschine f.

**trade** [treid]. I. s. Handel m; (*occupation*) Beruf m; (*craft*) Handwerk n; (*business*) Geschäft n, Gewerbe n; **t. directory**, Firmenverzeichnis n; **t. union**, Gewerkschaft *f;* **t. unionism,** Gewerkschaftswesen *n;* **t. unionist,** Gewerkschaftler *m;* **t. mark,** Warenzeichen *n;* **t. name,** Handelsbezeichnung *f.* **II.** *v.* 1. *v.i.* handeln (**in sth.,** mit etwas *dat*). 2. *v.tr. Com:* **to t. in one's old car,** sein altes Auto in Zahlung geben. ◆**'trader,** *s.* Händler *m.* ◆**'tradesman,** *pl.* **-men,** *s.* Händler *m;* (*shopkeeper*) Geschäftsinhaber *m.* ◆**'tradewind,** *s.* Passat *m.* ◆**'trading,** *s.* Handel *m;* **t. stamp,** Rabattmarke *f;* **t. estate,** Gewerbegebiet *n.*

**tradition** [trə'diʃ(ə)n], *s.* (*a*) Tradition *f;* (*custom*) Brauch *m;* (*b*) **oral t.,** mündliche Überlieferung *f.* ◆**tra'ditional,** *adj.* traditionell; **-ly,** *adv.* nach altem Brauch.

**traffic** ['træfik]. **I.** *s.* 1. (*trade*) Handel *m;* (*illegal*) Schleichhandel *m.* 2. Verkehr *m;* **t. jam,** Verkehrsstauung *f;* **t. lights,** Ampel *f;* **t. warden,** (*female*) Politesse *f;* (*male*) Hilfspolizist *m* (für den ruhenden Verkehr). **II.** *v.i. Pej:* **to t. in sth.,** mit etwas *dat* Schwarzhandel treiben.

**tragedy** ['trædʒidi], *s.* Tragödie *f.* ◆**'tragic,** *adj.* tragisch.

**trail** [treil]. **I.** *s.* 1. Spur *f;* **t. of smoke,** Rauchfahne *f.* 2. *esp. N.Am:* (unbefestigte) Straße *f;* Weg *m.* **II.** *v.* 1. *v.tr. (a)* **to t. sth. (along) behind one,** (etwas) hinter sich *dat* herschleppen; (*b*) (*follow*) (j-n) verfolgen; (*shadow*) (einen Verbrecher usw.) beschatten; **to t. an animal,** der Fährte eines Tieres folgen. 2. *v.i.* (*a*) **to t. (behind),** (i) *Sp:* (*drop back*) Boden verlieren; (ii) (*be far behind*) zurückliegen; (*b*) (*of pers.*) to t. along, sich dahinschleppen; (*of skirt*) **to t. along the ground,** am Boden schleifen; (*c*) (*of plant*) herunterhängen. ◆**'trailer,** *s.* 1. *Aut:* (*a*) Anhänger *m;* (*b*) *N.Am:* Wohnwagen *m.* 2. *Cin:* Voranzeige *f.*

**train** [trein]. **I.** *s.* 1. *Rail:* Zug *m;* **t. ferry,** Zugfähre *f.* 2. *Fig:* Folge *f* (von Ereignissen usw.); **t. of thought,** Gedankengang *m.* 3. *Cl:* Schleppe *f.* **II.** *v.* 1. *v.tr. (a)* (j-n) ausbilden; (ein Kind) erziehen; (ein Tier) dressieren; *Sp:* (j-n) trainieren; (*b*) (eine Pflanze) ziehen; (*c*) (eine Waffe, Kamera usw.) richten (**on,** auf + *acc*). 2. *v.i. Sp: etc:* trainieren (**for,** für + *acc*). ◆**trained,** *adj.* (*of soldier etc.*) ausgebildet; (*of animal*) dressiert; (*of eye etc.*) geschult; (*of athlete*) trainiert. ◆**trai'nee,** *s.* Lehrling *m.* ◆**'trainer,** *s.* 1. Dompteur *m* (eines Löwen usw.); Dresseur *m* (von Hunden). 2. *Sp:* Trainer *m.* ◆**'training,** *s.* (*a*) Ausbildung *f;* Schulung *f* (des Auges usw.); **(teacher) t. college,** Pädagogische Hochschule *f;* (*b*) *Sp:* Training *n;* **in t.,** in Kondition; (*c*) Dressur *f* (eines Tieres).

**traipse** [treips], *v.i. F:* latschen.

**trait** [trei], *s.* Charakterzug *m.*

**traitor** ['treitər], *s.* Verräter(in) *m(f).*

**trajectory** [trə'dʒektəri], *s.* Flugbahn *f.*

**tram** [træm], *s.* Straßenbahn *f.* ◆**'tramcar,** *s.* Straßenbahnwagen *m.*

◆**'tramline,** *s.* Straßenbahnschiene *f.*

**tramp** [træmp]. **I.** *s.* 1. (*sound*) Getrampel *n* (von Füßen, Hufen usw.). 2. Fußmarsch *m;* (*hike*) Wanderung *f.* 3. (*pers.*) (*a*) Landstreicher *m;* (*b*) *N.Am:* (*prostitute*) Straßenmädchen *n.* **II.** *v.i.* (*a*) trampeln (**on sth.,** auf etwas *dat*); (*b*) (*hike*) wandern; (*wander*) herumvagabundieren.

**trample** ['træmpl], *v.* 1. *v.i.* **to t. on s.o., sth.,** j-n, etwas mit Füßen treten. 2. *v.tr.* **to t. sth. underfoot,** etwas zertrampeln.

**trampoline** ['træmpəliːn], *s.* Trampolin *n.*

**trance** [trɑːns], *s.* Trance *f.*

**tranquil** ['træŋkwil], *adj.* ruhig; (*peaceful*) friedlich; (*of pers., attitude etc.*) gelassen. ◆**tran'quillity,** *s.* Ruhe *f.* ◆**'tranquillizer,** *s.* Beruhigungsmittel *n.*

**trans-** [træns, trænz], *prefix* trans-. ◆**transact** [træn'sækt], *v.tr.* (ein Geschäft) durchführen. ◆**tran'saction,** *s.* 1. Durchführung *f* (einer Sache). 2. (*a*) *Com:* (**business**) **t.,** Geschäft *n;* (*process*) Geschäftsvorgang *m;* (*b*) *pl.* (*negotiations*) Verhandlungen *fpl.* ◆**transatlantic** [trænzət'læntik], *adj.* (*a*) (*of flight etc.*) transatlantisch; (*b*) amerikanisch. ◆**transcend** [træn'send], *v.tr.* (*a*) (den Verstand, j-s Kräfte usw.) übersteigen; (*b*) (*excel*) (etwas) übertreffen. ◆**transcontinental** ['trænzkɔnti'nentl], *adj.* transkontinental. ◆**transcribe** [træn'skraib], *v.tr.* (*a*) (*copy*) (etwas Geschriebenes) abschreiben; (*b*) (Stenogramm, eine Aufnahme usw.) übertragen. ◆**'transcript/tran'scription,** *s.* (*a*) Abschrift *f;* Übertragung *f* (einer Aufnahme usw.); (*b*) (*recording*) Aufzeichnung *f.* ◆**transept** ['trænsept], *s.* Querschiff *n.* ◆**transfer. I.** [træns'fəːr] *v.* 1. *v.tr.* (*move*) (eine Geschäftsstelle usw.) verlegen (**to,** nach + *dat*); (Beamte usw.) versetzen (**to,** nach + *dat*); (*b*) (*hand over*) (ein Recht, ein Eigentum, *Fig:* Zuneigung usw.) übertragen (**to s.o.,** auf j-n); (Geld) überweisen (**to s.o.,** j-m). 2. *v.i.* übergehen (**to sth.,** zu etwas *dat*). **II.** ['trænsfər] *s.* 1. (*a*) Verlegung *f;* (*b*) Versetzung *f.* 2. (*a*) Übertragung *f* (von Eigentum); (*b*) Überweisung *f* (von Geld). 3. (*change*) Wechsel *m; Av: etc:* Umsteigen *n.* 4. (*picture*) Abziehbild *n.* ◆**trans'ferable,** *adj.* übertragbar (**to,** auf + *acc*). ◆**transform** [træns'fɔːm], *v.tr.* (*a*) verwandeln (**into sth.,** in etwas *acc*); (*b*) *Ch:* (Energie usw.) umsetzen; *El:* (Strom) umspannen. ◆**transfor'mation,** *s.* Verwandlung *f.* ◆**trans'former,** *s. El:* Transformator *m.* ◆**transfuse** [træns'fjuːz], *v.tr. Med:* (Blut) übertragen. ◆**trans'fusion,** *s.* (**blood**) **t.,** Bluttransfusion *f.* ◆**transient** ['trænziənt]. **I.** *adj.* vorübergehend; (*of happiness*) vergänglich. **II.** *s.pl. N.Am:* (*travellers*) Durchreisende *mpl.* ◆**transistor** [træn'sistə], *s. El:* Transistor *m;* **t. (radio),** Transistorradio n. ◆**transit** ['trænsit, -zit], s. Durchreise f; **passengers in t.,** Durchreisende mpl; **t. camp,** Durchgangslager n. ◆**transition** [træn'siʃən], s. Übergang m **(to,** zu + dat). ◆**tran'sitional,** adj. Übergangs-. ◆'**transitive,** adj. **t. verb,** transitives Verb. ◆'**transitory,** adj. vorübergehend. ◆**translate** [træns'leit], v.tr. übersetzen. ◆**trans'lation,** s. Übersetzung f. ◆**trans'lator,** s. Übersetzer(in) m(f). ◆**trans'lucent,** adj. lichtdurchlässig. ◆**transmission** [trænz'miʃ(ə)n], s. (a) Übertragung f; Übermittlung f (von Nachrichten usw.); (b) Aut: Getriebe n; (c) Rad: Übertragung f. ◆**trans'mit,** v.tr. (a) (Krankheiten, Rad: eine Sendung usw.) übertragen **(to,** auf + acc); (b) (Nachrichten usw.) übermitteln. ◆**trans'mitter,** s. Rad: etc: Sender m. ◆**transparency** [træns'pɛər(ə)nsi], s. 1. (quality) Durchsichtigkeit f. 2. Phot: Diapositiv n. ◆**trans'parent,** adj. durchsichtig; **-ly,** adv. **t. obvious,** ganz offensichtlich. ◆**transplant.** I. [træns'plɑ:nt] v.tr. (a) umpflanzen; (b) Med: transplantieren. II. ['trænsplɑ:nt] s. Med: Transplantation f. ◆**transport.** I. ['trænspɔ:t] s. (a) Transport m, Beförderung f; (b) **(means of) t.,** Transportmittel n. II. [træns'pɔ:t] v.tr. (a) transportieren, befördern. ◆**transpor'tation,** s. Transport m, Beförderung f. ◆**trans'porter,** s. (vehicle) Transporter m. ◆**transverse** ['trænzvə:s], adj. querlaufend; Quer-. ◆**transvestite** [trænz'vestait], s. Transvestit m.

**trap1** [træp]. I. s. 1. Falle f. 2. P: (mouth) Klappe f. II. v.tr. (a) (ein Tier usw.) (mit einer Falle) fangen; **trapped by the flames,** von den Flammen eingeschlossen; (b) (j-m) eine Falle stellen. ◆'**trapdoor,** s. Falltür f.

**trap2,** s. (pony) f.a., Ponywagen m.

**trapeze** [trə'pi:z], s. Trapez n.

**trappings** ['træpiŋz], s. pl. **all the t.,** das ganze Drum und Dran.

**trash** [træʃ], s. 1. N.Am: Abfälle mpl. 2. Pej: (literature) Schund m; (worthless stuff) Plunder m. ◆'**trashy,** adj. wertlos.

**traumatic** [trɔ:'mætik], adj. traumatisch; F: erschütternd.

**travel** ['trævl]. I. s. Reisen n; **t. agency,** Reisebüro n. II. v. 1. v.i. reisen. 2. v.tr. (eine Strecke) zurücklegen. ◆'**traveller,** s. Reisende(r) f(m); **t.'s cheque,** Reisescheck m. ◆'**travelling,** adj. reisend; **t. salesman,** Handelsreisende(r) m. II. s. Reisen n; **t. bag,** Reisetasche f. ◆'**travelogue,** s. Reisebeschreibung f.

**traverse** [trə'və:s], v.tr. durchqueren.

**trawler** ['trɔ:lər], s. Trawler m, Fischdampfer m.

**tray** [trei], s. Tablett n.

**treacherous** ['tretʃ(ə)rəs], adj. (of pers., disease etc.) heimtückisch; (of action) verräterisch; Fig: **a t. surface,** eine glitschige Fahrbahn. ◆'**treachery,** s. Verrat m.

**treacle** ['tri:kl], s. (dunkler) Sirup m.

**tread** [tred]. I. s. 1. Schritt m, Tritt m. 2. (of stair) Treppenstufe f. 3. Aut: etc: Profil n (eines Reifens). II. v.irr. 1. v.i. treten; **to t. on s.o.'s toes,** j-m auf die Zehen treten. 2. v.tr. **to t. under foot,** (etwas) mit Füßen treten.

**treason** ['tri:z(ə)n], s. Landesverrat m.

**treasure** ['treʒər]. I. s. Schatz m; **t. hunt,** Schatzsuche f. II. v.tr. (a) (etwas) (wie einen Schatz) hüten; (b) Fig: (j-s Freundschaft usw.) sehr schätzen. ◆'**treasurer,** s. Schatzmeister m. ◆'**treasury,** s. Schatzamt n; Brit: Adm: Finanzministerium n.

**treat** [tri:t]. I. s. (besonderes) Vergnügen n; (meal) Schmaus m; **to stand s.o. a t.,** j-m etwas spendieren; **school t.,** Schulausflug m. II. v.tr. (a) behandeln; (b) **to t. s.o. to sth.,** j-m etwas spendieren; **to t. oneself to sth.,** sich dat etwas gönnen. ◆'**treatise** ['tri:tiz], s. Abhandlung f (on, über + acc). ◆'**treatment,** s. Behandlung f. ◆'**treaty,** s. Vertrag m.

**treble** ['trebl]. I. adj. 1. dreifach. 2. Mus: **t. voice,** Sopranstimme f; **t. clef,** Diskantschlüssel m. II. s. 1. das Dreifache. 2. Mus: (a) (pers., voice) Sopran m; (b) (range) Diskant m. III. v.tr. (etwas) verdreifachen.

**tree** [tri:], s. Baum m. ◆'**treetop,** s. Baumkrone f; (tip) Baumwipfel m.

**trek** [trek]. I. s. Treck m. II. v.i. F: (irgendwohin) latschen.

**trellis** ['trelis], s. Gitter n; (for plants) Spalier n.

**tremble** ['trembl], v.i. zittern **(with,** vor + dat); (of voice etc.) beben. ◆'**trembling.** I. adj. zitternd. II. s. Zittern n; Beben n.

**tremendous** [tri'mendəs], adj. (a) enorm; (b) (splendid) prächtig.

**tremor** ['tremər], s. 1. Zittern n. 2. (earth) t., Erschütterungswelle f.

**trench** [tren(t)ʃ]. s. Graben m; Mil: Schützengraben m.

**trend** [trend]. I. s. Trend m. II. v.i. tendieren **(to/towards,** zu + dat). ◆'**trendy,** adj. F: modisch.

**trepidation** [trepi'deiʃ(ə)n], s. Angst f.

**trespass** ['trespəs], v.i. (ein Grundstück) unbefugt betreten. ◆'**trespasser,** s. **trespassers will be prosecuted,** unbefugtes Betreten wird strafrechtlich verfolgt.

**tress** [tres], s. Lit: Locke f.

**trestle** ['tresl], s. Bock m; **t. table,** (langer) Klapptisch m.

**trial** ['traiəl], s. 1. Jur: Prozeß m. 2. (test) Probe f; **on t.,** auf/zur Probe; **by t. and error,** durch wiederholtes Versuchen; Com: **t. order,** Probeauftrag m; Aut: **t. run,** Probefahrt f.

**triangle** ['traiæŋgl], s. 1. Dreieck n. 2. Mus: Triangel m. ◆**tri'angular,** adj. dreieckig.

**tribe** [traib], s. Volksstamm m. ◆**'tribal,** adj. Stammes-. ◆**'tribesman,** pl. **-men,** s. Stammesangehörige(r) m.

**tribulation** [tribju'leiʃən], s. Lit: Drangsal n.

**tribunal** [tr(a)i'bju:n(ə)l], s. Tribunal n; (for appeals) Appellationsgericht n; Ind: Arbeitsgericht n.

**tribute** ['tribju:t], s. (respect) Huldigung f; (praise) Lob n. ◆**'tributary,** s. Nebenfluß m.

**trice** [trais], s. **in a t.,** im Nu.

**trick** [trik]. **I.** s. **1.** Trick m; **to play a t. on s.o.,** j-m einen Streich spielen. **2.** (habit) Angewohnheit f; F: Tick m. **3.** (at cards) Stich m. **II.** v.tr. (j-n) betrügen. ◆**'trickery,** s. Betrug m. ◆**tricky,** adj. (of job etc.) kompliziert; (of situation etc.) heikel.

**trickle** ['trikl]. **I.** s. Rinnsal n; (drip) Tröpfeln n. **II.** v.i. rieseln; (seep) sickern; (of tap) tröpfeln.

**tricycle** ['traisikl], s. Dreirad n.

**tried** [traid], adj. (well) t., bewährt.

**trier** ['traiər], s. F: he's a (hard) t., er bemüht sich sehr.

**trifle** ['traifl], s. **1.** (a) Kleinigkeit f; (b) **a t. too short,** etwas zu kurz. **2.** Cu: Trifle n. ◆**'trifling,** adj. unbedeutend.

**trigger** ['trigər]. **I.** s. (a) (of gun) Abzug m; **to pull the t.,** abdrücken; (b) Phot: etc: Auslöser m. **II.** v.tr. **to t. sth. (off),** etwas auslösen.

**trigonometry** [trigə'nɔmitri], s. Trigonometrie f.

**trill** [tril]. **I.** s. Mus: Triller m. **II.** v.i. trillern.

**trilogy** ['trilədʒi], s. Trilogie f.

**trim** [trim]. **I.** s. **1.** (condition) (guter) Zustand m; **in good t.,** in gutem Zustand; (of pers.) in guter Form; Sp: **to get into t.,** in Kondition kommen. **2.** (cutting) **to give sth. a t.,** etwas (nach)schneiden. **II.** adj. (neat) ordentlich; sauber; (smart) schmuck; (of lawn, beard) gepflegt; **a t. figure,** eine schlanke Figur. **III.** v.tr. (a) (cut) (Haare usw.) (nach)schneiden; (eine Hecke, den Bart) stutzen; (einen Hund) trimmen; (b) (decorate) Cl: verzieren; **trimmed with lace,** mit Spitze besetzt; (c) Fig: **to t. one's sails to the wind,** sich nach dem Winde drehen. ◆**'trimming,** s. **1.** Cl: Besatz m. **2.** Cu: Garnierung f; F: **with all the trimmings,** mit allem Drum und Dran.

**Trinity** ['triniti], s. **the T.,** die Dreifaltigkeit; **T.** (Sunday), Dreifaltigkeitsfest n.

**trinket** ['triŋkit], s. (wertloses) Schmuckstück n.

**trio,** pl. **-os** ['tri:əu, -əuz], s. Trio n.

**trip** [trip]. **I.** s. **1.** (excursion) Ausflug m; (journey) Reise f; (short) Fahrt f; esp. N.Am: (holiday) Urlaubsreise f; Aut: **t. (recorder),** Kilometerzähler m (für kurze Entfernungen). **2.** (a) (stumble) Stolpern

n; (b) (tripping s.o.) Beinstellen n. **II.** v. **1.** v.i. (a) **to t. along,** dahertrippeln; (b) **to t. (up),** stolpern; Fig: **to t. up (badly),** einen (schweren) Fehler machen. **2.** v.tr. **to t. s.o. (up),** (i) j-m ein Bein/Fig: eine Falle stellen; (ii) (catch out) Fig: j-n bei einem Fehler ertappen. ◆**'tripper,** s. Ausflügler(in) m(f).

**tripe** [traip], s. **1.** Cu: Kutteln fpl. **2.** F: (rubbish) Mist m.

**triple** ['tripl], adj. dreifach. ◆**'triplet,** s. (pers.) Drilling m. ◆**'triplicate,** s. **in t.,** in dreifacher Ausfertigung.

**tripod** ['traipɔd], s. Dreifuß m; Phot: Stativ n.

**trite** [trait], adj. banal; (of phrase) abgedroschen.

**triumph** ['traiəmf, -ʌmf]. **I.** s. Triumph m; (victory) Sieg m. **II.** v.i. triumphieren. ◆**triumphal** [-'ʌmf(ə)l], adj. Triumph-. ◆**tri'umphant,** adj. triumphierend; (victorious) siegreich.

**trivial** ['triviəl], adj. unbedeutend; (a) (of reason, complaint etc.) geringfügig; (b) (of work of art) banal. ◆**trivi'ality,** s. (a) Unwichtigkeit f; (b) Banalität f.

**trolley** ['trɔli], s. (a) Handwagen m; shopping t., Einkaufswagen m; Rail: Av: **luggage t.,** Kofferkuli m; (b) (tea) t., Teewagen m. ◆**'trolleybus,** s. Oberleitungsbus m, F: O-Bus m.

**trombone** [trɔm'bəun], s. Mus: Posaune f.

**troop** [tru:p]. **I.** s. **1.** (group) Schar f. **2.** Mil: pl. **troops,** Truppen fpl; **t. ship,** Truppentransportschiff n. **II.** v.i. **to t. in/out/off,** in Scharen hereinströmen/hinausströmen/losziehen. ◆**'trooper,** s. Mil: Kavallerist m.

**trophy** ['trəufi], s. Trophäe f.

**tropic** ['trɔpik], s. (a) Wendekreis m (b) pl. **the tropics,** die Tropen pl. ◆**'tropical,** adj. tropisch.

**trot** [trɔt]. **I.** s. Trab m. **II.** v.i. traben.

**trouble** ['trʌbl]. **I.** s. **1.** (a) (worry) Sorge f; (b) (difficulties) Schwierigkeiten fpl; (unpleasantness) Unannehmlichkeiten fpl; **to get into t. with the police,** mit der Polizei in Konflikt kommen; **to be in t.,** in Nöten sein; **to make t.,** Unruhe stiften. **2.** (bother) Mühe f; **to take the t./go to the t. of doing sth.,** sich dat die Mühe machen, etwas zu tun; **it's not worth the t.,** das ist nicht der Mühe wert; **to go to a lot of t.,** sich dat viel Mühe machen; **it's no t.!** das ist nicht der Rede wert! **3.** (a) **he has heart t.,** er hat es mit dem Herzen; (b) **engine t.,** Maschinenschaden m; (c) pl. Pol: Unruhen fpl. **II.** v. **1.** v.tr. (a) (worry) (j-n) beunruhigen; **to be troubled about s.o.,** um j-n in Sorge sein; (b) (j-n) belästigen; **I'm sorry to t. you,** es tut mir leid, Sie stören zu müssen; **to t. (oneself) to do sth.,** sich dat die Mühe machen, etwas zu tun. **2.** v.i. (worry) beunruhigt sein (about, wegen + gen); **don't t. about it,** machen Sie sich keine Sorgen darum. ◆'**troubled**, *adj.* **1.** (*of water*) aufgewühlt. **2.** (*of sleep etc.*) unruhig; **t. period,** turbulente/ bewegte Zeit. ◆'**troublemaker,** *s.* Unruhestifter *m.* ◆'**troubleshooter,** *s.* (*a*) *Ind:* Störungssucher *m;* (*b*) *Fig:* (*peacemaker*) Friedensstifter *m.* ◆'**troublesome,** *adj.* **1.** lästig. **2.** (*of task*) mühsam.

**trough** [trɔf], *s.* **1.** Trog *m.* **2.** *Meteor:* **t. of low pressure,** Tiefdruckgebiet *n.*

**trounce** [trauns], *v.tr.* (j-n, eine Mannschaft) haushoch besiegen.

**troupe** [truːp], *s. Th: etc:* Truppe *f.*

**trousers** ['trauzəz], *s.pl.* (**pair of**) **t.,** Hose *f.*

**trousseau** ['truːsəu], *s.* Aussteuer *f.*

**trout** [traut], *s. inv.* Forelle *f.*

**trowel** ['trau(ə)l], *s.* Kelle *f.*

**truant** ['truːənt], *s. Sch:* Schwänzer *m;* **to play t.,** die Schule schwänzen.

**truce** [truːs], *s.* Waffenstillstand *m.*

**truck¹** [trʌk], *s.* **1. I have no t. with him,** mit ihm will ich nichts zu tun haben. **2.** *N.Am:* (**garden**) **t.,** Gemüse und Obst; **t. farmer,** Gemüsegärtner *m;* **t. farm,** Gemüsegärtnerei *f.*

**truck²,** *s.* (*a*) *Aut: esp. N.Am:* Lastwagen *m, F:* Laster *m;* **delivery t.,** Lieferwagen *m;* **t. driver,** Lastwagenfahrer *m;* (*b*) *Rail: esp. Brit:* Wagen *m;* **goods t.,** Güterwagen *m.*

**truculence** ['trʌkjuləns], *s.* Trotz *m.* ◆'**truculent,** *adj.* trotzig.

**trudge** [trʌdʒ]. *v.i.* (mühselig) stapfen.

**true** [truː]. *adj.* **1.** wahr; **that's t.!** das stimmt! **to come t.,** sich verwirklichen; (*of dream*) in Erfüllung gehen. **2.** (*real*) echt, wirklich; **a t. friend,** ein wahrer Freund. **3.** (*faithful*) treu (**to,** *dat*); **t. to one's word,** seinem Wort getreu; **t. to life,** lebensecht.

**truffle** ['trʌfl], *s.* Trüffel *f.*

**truly** ['truːli], *adv.* (*a*) treu, aufrichtig; (*b*) **I am t.** grateful to you, ich bin Ihnen wirklich dankbar; (*c*) **yours t.,** Ihr ergebener.

**trump** [trʌmp]. **I.** *s.* Trumpf *m.* **II.** *v.tr.* **to t. up an excuse,** eine Entschuldigung erfinden.

**trumpet** ['trʌmpit]. **I.** *s.* Trompete *f.* **II.** *v.i.* trompeten.

**truncheon** ['trʌn(t)ʃ(ə)n], *s.* Knüppel *m;* **rubber t.,** Gummiknüppel *m.*

**trundle** ['trʌndl], *v.* **1.** *v.tr.* (eine Schubkarre usw.) schieben. **2.** *v.i. Aut:* **to t. along,** dahingondeln.

**trunk** [trʌŋk], *s.* **1.** (*a*) Stamm *m* (eines Baumes); (*b*) (*of pers., animal*) Rumpf *m; Tel:* **t. call,** Ferngespräch *n.* **2.** (*large case*) Schrankkoffer *m.* **3.** Rüssel *m* (eines Elefanten). **4.** *pl. Cl:* Unterhose *f;* (*for swimming*) Badehose *f.*

**truss** [trʌs], *s. 1. Med:* Bruchband *n.* **II.** *v.tr.* **to t. s.o. up,** j-n fesseln.

**trust** [trʌst]. **I.** *s.* **1.** Vertrauen *n* (**in,** auf + *acc*). **2.** *Jur:* Treuhandverhältnis *n.* **II.** *v.tr.* (j-m) vertrauen; (j-m) trauen; **to**

**t. s.o. with sth./sth. to s.o.,** j-m etwas anvertrauen; **t. him to spend it all on drink!** das sieht ihm ähnlich, alles für Alkohol auszugeben! ◆'**trus'tee,** *s. Jur:* Treuhänder *m;* Verwalter *m* (eines Vermögens). ◆'**trustful/'trusting,** *adj.* vertrauensvoll. ◆'**trustworthiness,** *s.* **1.** Zuverlässigkeit *f.* **2.** Glaubwürdigkeit *f.* ◆'**trustworthy,** *adj.* **1.** zuverlässig. **2.** (*credible*) glaubwürdig. ◆'**trusty,** *adj.* zuverlässig; (*faithful*) treu.

**truth** [truːθ], *s.* **1.** Wahrheit *f;* **the t. is/to tell the t., I forgot,** ich habe es vergessen. ◆'**truthful,** *adj.* (*a*) (*of pers.*) wahrheitsliebend; (*b*) (*of story etc.*) wahrhaftig. ◆'**-ly,** *adv.* ehrlich, wahrhaftig. ◆'**truthfulness,** *s.* (*a*) Wahrheitsliebe *f;* (*b*) Wahrhaftigkeit *f.*

**try** [trai]. **I.** *s.* Versuch *m;* **to have a t. at doing sth,** es mit etwas *dat* versuchen. **II.** *v.* **1.** *v.tr.* (*a*) versuchen; (*b*) (*test*) ausprobieren; (*c*) *Fig:* (j-n, etwas) prüfen; (*d*) *Jur:* **to t. a case,** über eine Sache gerichtlich verhandeln. **2.** *v.i.* (*a*) (*take trouble*) **you're not trying,** du strengst dich nicht an; (*b*) (*es*) versuchen; **t. again,** versuch es noch einmal; **it's worth trying,** der Versuch lohnt sich; (*c*) **to t. for sth.,** sich um etwas *acc* bemühen. ◆'**trying,** *adj.* aufreibend; (*laborious*) mühsam. ◆'**try 'on,** *v.tr.* (ein Kleidungsstück) anprobieren. ◆'**try 'out,** *v.tr.* ausprobieren. ◆'**try-out,** *s.* Probe *f.*

**tsar** [zɑːr, tsɑːr], *s.* Zar *m.*

**tub** [tʌb], *s.* (*a*) (*for plants etc.*) Kübel *m;* **bath t.,** Badewanne *f;* (*b*) (*small*) Becher *m.* ◆'**tubby,** *adj. F:* (*of pers.*) pummelig.

**tuba** ['tjuːbə], *s.* Tuba *f.*

**tube** [tjuːb], *s.* **1.** Rohr *n,* Röhre *f; T.V:* Bildröhre *f;* (*flexible, also Aut:*) Schlauch *m.* **2. t. of toothpaste** etc., Tube *f* Zahnpasta usw. **3.** *Rail: F:* **the t.,** die U-Bahn; **t. station,** U-Bahnhof *m.* ◆'**tubeless,** *adj. Aut:* schlauchlos. ◆'**tubular,** *adj.* röhrenförmig.

**tuber** ['tjuːbər], *s. Bot:* Knolle *f.* ◆**tuberculosis** [tjubɜːkjuˈləusis], *s. Med:* Tuberkulose *f.*

**tuck** [tʌk], *s.* **1** *Cl:* Abnäher *m.* **2. t. shop,** Süßwarengeschäft *n.* **II.** *v.tr.* (*a*) *Cl:* Abnäher (in den Stoff) machen; (*b*) (etwas) (irgendwohin) stecken. ◆'**tuck a'way,** *v.tr.* (*a*) (etwas) wegstecken, (*hide*) verstecken; (*b*) *F:* (Essen) verdrücken. ◆'**tuck 'in,** *v.* **1.** *v.tr.* (*a*) (etwas) einstecken; **to t. in the sheet,** das Bettuch unterschlagen/feststecken; (*b*) **to t. the children in,** die Kinder im Bett gut zudecken. **2.** *v.i. F:* (tüchtig) zulangen. ◆'**tuck 'up,** *v.tr.* (*a*) (die Ärmel) hochkrempeln; (den Rock) schürzen; (*b*) (j-n) im Bett gut zudecken.

**Tuesday** ['tjuːzdi], *s.* Dienstag *m.*

**tuft** [tʌft], *s.* (*of hair, grass etc.*) Büschel *n.*

**tug** [tʌg]. **I.** *s.* **1.** Zerren *n; Sp:* (*also Fig:*)

t. of war, Tauziehen n. 2. Nau: t.
(boat), Schlepper m. II. v.tr. & i. ziehen;
to t. sth. along, etwas hinter sich dat
herziehen.
**tuition** [tju:(:)'iʃ(ə)n], s. Unterricht m.
**tulip** ['tju:lip], s. Tulpe f.
**tumble** ['tʌmbl]. I. s. Fall m, Sturz m; to
take a t., stürzen. II. v.i. (a) (fall) stürzen; (b) F: to t. to it, es kapieren.
◆'**tumbledown**, adj. baufällig.
◆'**tumble-'drier**, s. Wäschetrockner m.
◆'**tumbler**, s. (glass) Trinkglas n.
**tummy** ['tʌmi], s. F: Magen m; (belly)
Bauch m; t. ache, Bauchschmerzen pl.
**tumour** ['tju:mər], s. Tumor m.
**tumult** ['tju:mʌlt], s. Tumult m.
◆**tu'multuous**, adj. turbulent; (of applause etc.) stürmisch.
**tumulus**, pl. -li ['tju:mjuləs, -lai], s. Hü-
gelgrab n.
**tuna** ['tju:nə], s. Thunfisch m.
**tundra** ['tʌndrə], s. Tundra f.
**tune** [tju:n]. I. s. 1. Melodie f. 2. (a) the
piano is in t./out of t., das Klavier ist
gestimmt/verstimmt; (to sing/play) out of
t./in t., falsch/richtig (singen/spielen); (b)
Fig: to be in t./out of t. with one's surroundings, mit seiner Umwelt im
Einklang/im Widerspruch stehen. 3. Aut:
(of engine) (state of) t., Einstellung f. II.
v.tr. (a) (Instrument) stimmen; (b)
Aut: to t. (in ein Instrument) stimmen; (b)
Aut: to t. the ignition/engine etc., die
Zündung/den Motor usw. einstellen.
◆'**tuneful**, adj. (of voice etc.) melodisch;
(of music) melodienreich. ◆'**tuneless**,
adj. ohne Melodie. ◆'**tuner**, s. 1. piano
t., Klavierstimmer m. 2. Rad: Tuner m.
◆**tune 'in**, v.tr. & i. Rad: etc: (das Radio) einstellen (to a station, auf einen
Sender). ◆'**tune 'up**, v. 1. v.i. Mus: die
Instrumente stimmen. 2. v.tr. Aut: (den
Motor) frisieren. ◆'**tuning**, s. 1. Mus:
Stimmen n. 2. Aut: Einstellen n. 3. Rad:
Sendereinstellung f.
**tungsten** ['tʌŋstən], s. Wolfram n.
**tunic** ['tju:nik], s. 1. (of soldier, policeman)
Uniformjacke f. 2. (blouse) Kasack-Bluse
f.
**Tunisia** [tju:(:)'niziə]. Pr. n. Tunesien n.
◆**Tu'nisian. I.** adj. tunesisch. II. s. Tu-
nesier(in) m(f).
**tunnel** ['tʌn(ə)l]. I. s. Tunnel m. II. v.i.
einen Tunnel bohren. ◆'**tunnelling**, s.
Tunnelbau m.
**tunny(-fish)** ['tʌni(fiʃ)], s. Thunfisch m.
**turban** ['tə:bən], s. Turban m.
**turbid** ['tə:bid], adj. (a) (thick) zähflüssig;
(b) (not clear) trüb.
**turbine** ['tə:bain], s. Turbine f.
**turbot** ['tə:bət], s. Steinbutt m.
**turbulent** ['tə:bjulənt], adj. turbulent.
◆'**turbulence**, s. Turbulenz f.
**tureen** [tə'ri:n, tju-], s. Terrine f.
**turf**, pl. **turves** [tə:f, tə:vz]. s. 1. Rasen
m; (sod) Grassode f. 2. (peat) Torf m.
**turgid** ['tə:dʒid], adj. Med: & Fig: geschwollen.

**Turkey**[1] ['tə:ki]. Pr. n. die Türkei.
◆**Turk**, s. Türke m, Türkin f.
◆'**Turkish. I.** adj. türkisch; **T. bath**,
Dampfbad n; t. delight, Türkischer Honig m. II. s. (language) Türkisch n.
**turkey**[2], s. (bird) Truthahn m; Cu: Pute(r)
f (m).
**turmoil** ['tə:moil], s. Tumult m.
**turn** [tə:n]. I. s. 1. (revolution) Umdrehung f, Drehung f (eines Rades usw.). 2.
(a) (change of direction) Richtungswechsel
m; t. of the tide, Gezeitenwechsel m;
Fig: Wendepunkt m; (of tide, weather
etc.) to be on the t., umschlagen; (b) (in
road) Abbiegung f; (bend) Kurve f; (c)
(change of condition) Wendung f; at the t.
of the century, um die Jahrhundertwen-
de; to take a t. for the better/worse,
sich zum Guten/Schlechten wenden; (d)
F: the sight gave me quite a t., der Anblick versetzte mir einen ziemlichen
Schock. 3. (a) in t., der Reihe nach; by
turns, abwechselnd; they take (it in)
turns, sie wechseln sich ab; it is my t.,
ich bin an der Reihe/F: dran; (b) Th: etc:
Nummer f. 4. to do s.o. a good t., j-m
einen Gefallen tun. II. v. 1. v.tr. (a) (rotate) drehen; to t. a page, umblättern;
(b) they turned the whole house upside
down, sie haben das ganze Haus auf den
Kopf gestellt; (c) (direct) (Augen, Gedanken usw.) richten (to, towards,
auf + acc); (d) to t. the corner, um die
Ecke biegen; (of invalid etc.) über dem
Berg sein; (e) (j-n, etwas) machen (into,
zu + dat); this weather has turned the
milk sour, bei diesem Wetter ist die
Milch sauer geworden. 2. v.i. (a) (rotate)
(of wheel etc.) sich drehen; to toss and t.
in bed, sich im Bett hin und her wälzen;
(b) sich wenden (to, zu + dat); to t. to
the right/left, sich nach rechts/links drehen; Aut: nach rechts/links abbiegen; the
wind is turning, der Wind dreht sich; to
t. to s.o., j-m zuwenden; (c) (change) sich verwandeln (into, in + acc); (become) werden (zu + dat); the tide is turning, die Gezeiten schlagen um; the milk
has turned (sour), die Milch ist sauer geworden; the leaves are beginning to t.,
die Blätter verfärben sich. ◆'**turn
a'way**, v. 1. v.tr. (a) (das Gesicht, einen
Schlag usw.) abwenden; (b) (j-n, esp. Zuschauer) abweisen. 2. v.i. sich abwenden. ◆'**turn 'back**, v. 1. v.tr. (a) (j-n)
umkehren lassen; (b) (die Bettdecke
usw.) zurückschlagen. 2. v.i. umkehren.
◆'**turn 'down**, v.tr. (a) (die Bettdecke
usw.) zurückschlagen; (den Kragen usw.)
herunterschlagen; (eine Buchseite) um-
knicken; (b) (die Gasflamme usw.) kleiner stellen; (das Radio usw.) leiser stellen; (c) (j-n) ablehnen; to t. d. an offer
etc., ein Angebot usw. ablehnen.
◆'**turn 'in**, v.tr. (die Füße usw.) nach
innen drehen; (Stoff usw.) nach innen
falten. ◆'**turning. I.** adj. (sich) dre-

hend; *Fig:* t. **point,** Wendepunkt *m.* **II.**
*s.* Abbiegen *n;* **take the first t. to the**
**right,** die erste Straße rechts abbiegen.
◆**'turn 'off,** *v.* 1. *v.tr.* (das Wasser, den
Strom usw.) abstellen; (das Licht) ausmachen; (das Radio, den Fernseher usw.)
ausschalten; (den Wasserhahn usw.) zudrehen. 2. *v.i.* (von einer Straße) abbiegen. ◆**'turn 'on,** *v.tr.* (das Gas, den
Strom usw.) anstellen; (das Wasser) andrehen; (das Licht) anmachen; (ein Gerät) einschalten; (den Wasserhahn usw.)
aufdrehen. ◆**'turn 'out,** *v.* 1. *v.tr.* *(a)*
(j-n) hinauswerfen **(of/from,** aus + *dat);*
*(b)* (eine Schublade, ein Zimmer usw.)
ausräumen; *(c) Ind:* (Waren) herstellen;
*(d)* (das Licht usw.) ausmachen. 2. *v.i.*
**everything turned o. well in the end,** es
ist alles gut ausgegangen; **it turned out**
**that...,** es stellte sich heraus, daß...;
◆**'turn-out,** *s.* **there was a good t.-o.**
**at the meeting,** die Versammlung war
gut besucht. ◆**'turn 'over,** *v.tr.* *(a)* umdrehen; (eine Seite) umblättern;
◆**'turnover,** *s. Com:* Umsatz *m.*
◆**'turn 'round,** *v.* 1. *v.tr.* umdrehen. 2.
*v.i.* *(of pers., etc.)* sich umdrehen.
◆**'turnstile,** *s.* Drehkreuz *n.*
◆**'turntable,** *s.* 1. *Rail: etc:* Drehschei-
be *f.* 2. *Rec:* Plattenteller *m;* *(complete*
*unit)* Laufwerk *n.* ◆**'turn 'to,** *v.i.* **to t.**
**to s.o. (for help),** sich an j-n wenden.
◆**'turn 'up,** *v.* 1. *v.tr.* *(a)* nach oben
drehen; (den Kragen) hochschlagen;
**turned up nose,** Stupsnase *f;* *Fig:* **to t.**
**up one's nose at sth.,** über etwas *acc* die
Nase rümpfen; *(c)* **to t. up the gas,** das
Gashöher stellen; *Rad: etc:* **can you t. it/**
**the volume up?** können Sie es bitte lauter stellen? 2. *v.i. F: (appear)* auftauchen. ◆**'turn-up,** *s.* Aufschlag *m* (an
einer Hose usw.).
**turnip** ['tə:nip], *s.* (weiße) Rübe *f.*
**turpentine** ['tə:p(ə)ntain], *s.* Terpentin *n.*
**turquoise** ['tə:kwɔːz, -kwɔiz]. **I.** *s.* 1.
Türkis *m.* 2. *(colour)* Türkis *n.* **II.** *adj.*
türkisfarben.
**turret** ['tʌrit], *s.* Türmchen *n.*
**turtle** ['tə:tl], *s.* 1. Schildkröte *f;* **t. soup,**
Schildkrötensuppe *f.* 2. **t. dove,** Turteltaube *f.*
**tusk** [tʌsk], *s.* Stoßzahn *m.*
**tussle** ['tʌsl], *s.* Handgemenge *n.*
**tutor** ['tju:tər], *s.* 1. Tutor *m;* (private) t.,
Privatlehrer *m.* ◆**tu'torial,** *s.* Tutoren-
stunde *f.*
**tuxedo** [tʌk'si:dəu, -əuz], *s.*
*N.Am:* Smoking *m.*
**twaddle** ['twɔdl], *s. F:* Quatsch *m;* **to**
**talk t.,** quatschen.
**twang** [twæŋ]. **I.** *s.* 1. Vibrierton *m* (eines
Saiteninstruments). 2. **to talk with a na-**
**sal t.,** näseln. **II.** *v.* 1. *v.tr.* **to t. a gui-**
**tar,** auf der Gitarre zupfen. 2. *v.i. (of*
*string)* vibrieren.
**tweak** [twi:k], *v.tr.* (etwas) zwicken.
**tweed** [twi:d], *s.* Tweed *m.*

**tweezers** ['twi:zəz], *s.pl.* Pinzette *f.*
**twelve** [twelv], *num. adj.* zwölf.
◆**'twelfth,** *num. adj.* zwölfte(r, s).
**twenty** ['twenti], *num. adj.* zwanzig.
◆**'twentieth.** **I.** *num. adj.* zwanzigste(r,
s). **II.** *s. (fraction)* Zwanzigstel *n.*
**twerp** [twə:p], *s. P:* Blödian *m.*
**twice** [twais], *adv.* zweimal; **t. as big,**
doppelt so groß; **he's t. my age,** er ist
doppelt so alt wie ich.
**twig¹** [twig], *s.* Zweig *m.*
**twig²,** *v.tr. P:* (etwas) kapieren.
**twilight** ['twailait], *s.* *(evening)* Zwielicht
*n;* Abenddämmerung *f; occ. (morning)*
Morgendämmerung *f.*
**twin** [twin]. **I.** *s.* 1. Zwilling *m.* 2. **t.**
**beds,** zwei Einzelbetten; **t. town,** Part-
nerstadt *f.* **II.** *v.tr.* (zwei Städte) zu Part-
nerstädten machen. ◆**'twinning,** *s.*
Partnerschaft *f* (zweier Städte).
**twine** [twain]. **I.** *s.* Bindfaden *m.* **II.** *v.* 1.
*v.tr.* (Fäden usw.) drehen, *(together)* zu-
sammendrehen. 2. *v.i.* sich winden.
**twinge** [twin(d)ʒ], *s.* *(a)* Stich *m; (b)*
**twinges of conscience,** Gewissensbisse
*mpl.*
**twinkle** ['twiŋkl]. **I.** *s.* Funkeln *n.* **II.** *v.i.*
funkeln. ◆**'twinkling,** *s.* Funkeln *n; F:*
**in the t. of an eye/in a t.,** im Nu.
**twirl** [twə:l]. **I.** *s.* 1. *(action)* Drehen *n.* 2.
*(decoration)* Schnörkel *m.* **II.** *v.* 1. *v.tr.*
(Daumen, Locken usw.) drehen. 2. *v.i.*
sich drehen.
**twist** [twist]. **I.** *s.* Windung *f; (rotating)*
Drehung *f; also Fig:* Verdrehung *f;*
**strange t. of fate,** seltsame Wendung des
Schicksals. **II.** *v.* 1. *v.tr.* *(a)* drehen; *(b)*
*(out of shape)* (etwas, *Fig:* die Wahrheit)
verdrehen, verzerren; **to t. one's ankle,**
sich *dat* den Fuß verrenken. 2. *v.i. (of*
*worm, road etc.)* sich winden. ◆**'twisted,** *adj.* *(a) (contorted)* verzerrt;
*(of ankle etc.)* verrenkt; *(b) (of pers., views*
*etc.)* verdreht; *(esp. sexually)* pervers;
**t. mind,** perverse Veranlagung.
◆**'twister,** *s. F:* Gauner *m.*
**twit** [twit], *s. P:* Idiot *m.*
**twitch** [twitʃ]. **I.** *s.* Zucken *n.* **II.** *v.i.*
zucken.
**twitter** ['twitər]. **I.** *s.* Zwitschern *n.* **II.**
*v.i.* *(of bird etc.)* zwitschern.
◆**'twittering,** *s.* Gezwitscher *n.*
**two** [tu:]. **I.** *s.* 1. **the t. of us** wir zwei;
wir beide; **t. by t./in twos,** zu zweit; *Fig:*
**to put t. and t. together,** es sich *dat* zu-
sammenreimen. 2. *(figure)* Zwei *f.* **II.** *adj.*
zwei; **the t. boys,** die beiden Jungen;
*Fig:* **to be in t. minds about sth.,** über
etwas *acc* im Zwiespalt sein. ◆**'two-**
**'faced,** *adj.* heuchlerisch. ◆**'two-**
**'piece,** *adj.* zweiteilig. ◆**'two-'seater,**
*s.* Zweisitzer *m.* ◆**'two-stroke,** *adj.*
Zweitakt-. ◆**'two-'time,** *v.tr. esp.*
*N.Am:* (seinen Mann usw.) betrügen.
◆**'two-'way,** *adj. El:* **t.-w. adapter/***F:*
**plug,** Doppelstecker *m.*
**tycoon** [tai'ku:n], *s.* Industriemagnat *m.*

**type** ['taip]. **I.** *s.* **1.** Typ *m;* (*a*) (*of pers.*) **an unpleasant t.**, ein unangenehmer Typ; (*b*) (*of thing*) **that t. of thing**, etwas in dieser Art. **2.** (*in printing*) Type *f.* **II.** *v.tr. & i.* (*a*) (etwas) mit der Maschine schreiben, *F:* tippen; **typed**, maschinegeschrieben; (*b*) **to t. s.o.**, j-n typisieren. ◆'**typecast**, *v.tr. Th: etc:* (einem Schauspieler) eine Rolle zuordnen, die seinem Charakter entspricht. ◆'**typescript**, *s.* (Schreibmaschinen)manuskript *n.* ◆'**type-writer**, *s.* Schreibmaschine *f; n.* ◆'**typewritten**, *adj.* maschinegeschrieben, *F:* getippt. ◆'**typing**, *s.* Maschineschreiben *n, F:* Tippen *n;* ◆'**typist**, *s.* Stenotypist(in) *m(f).*

**typhoid** ['taifɔid], *s.* Typhus *m.*
**typhoon** [tai'fuːn], *s.* Taifun *m.*
**typhus** ['taifəs], *s.* Flecktyphus *m.*
**typical** ['tipik(ə)l], *adj.* typisch; **that's t. of him**, das ist typisch für ihn. ◆'**typify**, *v.tr.* (etwas) charakterisieren.
**tyranny** ['tirəni], *s.* Tyrannei *f.* ◆**tyrannical** [ti'rænik(ə)l] tyrannisch. ◆'**tyrannize**, *v.tr.* tyrannisieren. ◆**tyrant** ['taiər(ə)nt], *s.* Tyrann(in) *m(f).*
**tyre** ['taiər], *s.* Reifen *m;* **t. pressure**, Reifendruck *m.*
**Tyrol** [ti'rɔːl]. *Pr. n.* (**in**) **the T.**, (in) Tirol *n.* ◆**Tyrolean** [tirə'liːən] *adj.* **T. Alps**, Tiroler Alpen. ◆**Tyrolese** [tirə'liːz] *s.* Tiroler(in) *m(f).*

# U

**U, u** [juː], *s.* **1.** (der Buchstabe) U, u *n.* **2.** *F:* **U and non-U**, das Feine und das Unfeine.
**ubiquitous** [juː'bikwitəs], *adj.* allgegenwärtig.
**udder** ['ʌdər], *s.* Euter *n.*
**ugh** [uh], *int.* pfui!
**ugly** ['ʌgli], *adj.* häßlich; **in an u. mood**, übler Laune. ◆'**ugliness**, *s.* Häßlichkeit *f.*
**ulcer** ['ʌlsər], *s.* Geschwür *n.*
**ulterior** [ʌl'tiəriər], *adj.* **u. motive**, Hintergedanken *f.*
**ultimate** ['altimət], *adj.* äußerste(r, s); (*final*) endgültig; **-ly**, *adv.* (*a*) schließlich; (*b*) im Endeffekt. ◆**ultimatum** [ʌlti'meitəm], *s.* Ultimatum *f.*
**ultra-** ['ʌltrə], *prefix* Ultra-. ◆**ultra'sonic**, *adj.* Ultraschall-. ◆**ultra'violet**, *adj.* ultraviolett.
**umbilical** [ʌm'bilik(ə)l], *adj.* **u. cord**, Nabelschnur *f.*
**umbrage** ['ʌmbridʒ], *s.* Ärgernis *n;* **to take u. at sth.**, an etwas *dat* Anstoß nehmen.
**umbrella** [ʌm'brelə], *s.* Schirm *m.*
**umpire** ['ʌmpaiər]. **I.** *s. Sp:* Schiedsrichter *m.* **II.** *v.tr. Sp:* (ein Spiel) als Schiedsrichter leiten. ◆'**umpiring**, *s.* Schiedsrichtern *n.*
**umpteen** [ʌm(p)'tiːn], *adj. F:* zig; **u. times**, x-mal.
**un-** [ʌn], *prefix* un-, nicht.
**unabashed** [ʌnə'bæʃt], *adj.* unerschrocken.
**unabated** [ʌnə'beitid], *adj.* unvermindert.
**unable** [ʌn'eibl], *adj.* **to be u. to do sth.**, etwas nicht tun können.
**unacceptable** [ʌnək'septəbl], *adj.* unannehmbar.
**unaccompanied** [ʌnə'kʌmpənid], *adj.* unbegleitet.
**unaccountable** [ʌnə'kauntəbl], *adj.* unerklärlich; **-ably**, *adv.* unerklärlicher-

weise.
**unaccustomed** [ʌnə'kʌstəmd], *adj.* ungewohnt; **u. to sth.**, an etwas *acc* nicht gewöhnt.
**unadulterated** [ʌnə'dʌltəreitid], *adj.* unverfälscht, rein.
**unaffected** [ʌnə'fektid], *adj.* **1.** (*genuine*) ungekünstelt; (*of feelings*) aufrichtig; (*of pers., style*) natürlich. **2.** (*a*) (*of pers.*) (*unmoved*) unberührt; (*b*) (*unchanged*) unverändert.
**unaided** [ʌn'eidid], *adj.* ohne Hilfe; (**alone and**) **u.**, ganz allein.
**unaltered** [ʌn'ɔːltəd], *adj.* unverändert.
**unambitious** [ʌnæm'biʃəs], *adj.* **1.** (*of pers.*) nicht ehrgeizig. **2.** (*of project*) anspruchslos.
**unanimous** [juː(ː)'næniməs], *adj.* (*of decision*) einstimmig.
**unanswerable** [ʌn'ɑːnsərəbl], *adj.* (*of criticism*) unwiderlegbar; (*of question, problem*) unlösbar.
**unappetizing** [ʌn'æpitaiziŋ], *adj.* unappetitlich.
**unapproachable** [ʌnə'prəutʃəbl], *adj.* unzugänglich; (*of pers.*) unnahbar.
**unarmed** [ʌn'ɑːmd], *adj.* unbewaffnet.
**unashamed** [ʌnə'feimd], *adj.* schamlos.
**unasked** [ʌn'ɑːskt], *adv.* ungebeten.
**unassuming** [ʌnə'sjuːmiŋ], *adj.* anspruchslos; (*modest*) bescheiden.
**unattached** [ʌnə'tætʃt], *adj.* ungebunden.
**unattainable** [ʌnə'teinəbl], *adj.* unerreichbar.
**unattended** [ʌnə'tendid], *adj.* unbeaufsichtigt.
**unattractive** [ʌnə'træktiv], *adj.* unattraktiv.
**unauthorized** [ʌn'ɔːθəraizd], *adj.* unbefugt.
**unavoidable** [ʌnə'vɔidəbl], *adj.* unvermeidlich.
**unaware** [ʌnə'weər], *adj.* **to be u. of sth.**, sich *dat* einer Sache nicht bewußt

sein. ◆**una'wares**, *adv.* to take s.o. u., j-n überraschen.

**unbalanced** [ʌn'bælənst], *adj.* unausgeglichen; (*of mind*) gestört.

**unbearable** [ʌn'bɛərəbl], *adj.* unerträglich.

**unbeatable** [ʌn'biːtəbl], *adj.* unschlagbar.

**unbecoming** [ʌnbi'kʌmiŋ], *adj.* 1. unschicklich. 2. (*of garment*) unkleidsam.

**unbelievable** [ʌnbi'liːvəbl], *adj.* unglaublich.

**unbend** [ʌn'bend], *v.irr.* 1. *v.i.* sich gerade biegen; *Fig:* (*of pers.*) auftauen. 2. *v.tr.* (etwas) geradebiegen. ◆**un'bending**, *adj.* unbiegsam; *Fig:* (*of will etc.*) unbeugsam.

**unbias(s)ed** [ʌn'baiəst], *adj.* unparteiisch.

**unbounded** [ʌn'baundid], *adj.* unbegrenzt.

**unbreakable** [ʌn'breikəbl], *adj.* unzerbrechlich.

**unbridled** [ʌn'braidld], *adj.* (*of passion*) zügellos.

**unbroken** [ʌn'brəuk(ə)n], *adj.* (*a*) nicht gebrochen; (*b*) (*uninterrupted*) ununterbrochen; (*c*) *Sp:* u. record, unübertroffener Rekord.

**unbutton** [ʌn'bʌt(ə)n], *v.tr.* aufknöpfen.

**uncalled** [ʌn'kɔːld], *adj.* u. for, (*inappropriate*) fehl am Platze; (*unjustified*) unbegründet.

**uncanny** [ʌn'kæni], *adj.* unheimlich.

**uncared for** [ʌn'kɛəd fɔːr], *adj.* vernachlässigt.

**unceasing** [ʌn'siːsiŋ], *adj.* unaufhörlich.

**unceremonious** [ʌnseri'məuniəs], *adj.* (*of treatment*) unsanft; (*of pers., rebuke*) brüsk; -ly, *adv.* ohne viel Federlesens.

**uncertain** [ʌn'səːt(ə)n], *adj.* unsicher; (*of future etc.*) ungewiß; (*of time, amount*) unbestimmt; (*varying*) unbeständig; **I am u.** **whether ...**, ich bin nicht sicher, ob ... ◆**un'certainty**, *s.* Unsicherheit *f*; Ungewißheit *f*; Unbestimmtheit *f*; (*doubt*) Zweifel *m*.

**unchangeable** [ʌn'tʃein(d)ʒəbl], *adj.* unveränderlich. ◆**un'changed**, *adj.* unverändert. ◆**un'changing**, *adj.* gleichbleibend.

**uncharted** [ʌn'tʃɑːtid], *adj.* nicht kartiert.

**unchecked** [ʌn'tʃekt], *adj.* 1. (*not held up*) ungehemmt; (*of fire, epidemic*) **to continue u.**, unvermindert fortdauern. 2. (*not examined*) nicht kontrolliert.

**uncivil** [ʌn'sivl], *adj.* unhöflich. ◆**uncivilized** [ʌn'sivilaizd], *adj.* unzivilisiert; (*of conditions*) primitiv; (*of behaviour*) ungehobelt.

**unclaimed** [ʌn'kleimd], *adj.* (*of letter etc.*) nicht abgeholt.

**uncle** ['ʌŋkl], *s.* Onkel *m*.

**unclouded** [ʌn'klaudid], *adj.* (*of sky*) unbewölkt; (*of vision*) klar; (*of liquid*) ungetrübt.

**uncoil** [ʌn'kɔil], *v.* 1. *v.tr.* (ein Kabel usw.) abspulen. 2. *v.i.* (*of snake*) sich ausringeln.

**uncomfortable** [ʌn'kʌmf(ə)təbl], *adj.* (*of things*) unbequem; (*unpleasant*) unangenehm.

**uncommon** [ʌn'kɔmən], *adj.* ungewöhnlich; (*of word, bird, flower etc.*) selten; -ly, *adv.* außerordentlich.

**uncommunicative** [ʌnkə'mjuːnikətiv], *adj.* verschlossen.

**uncomplaining** [ʌnkəm'pleiniŋ], *adj.* nicht klagend; -ly, *adv.* klaglos.

**uncomplimentary** [ʌnkɔmpli'ment(ə)ri], *adj.* wenig schmeichelhaft.

**uncompromising** [ʌn'kɔmprəmaiziŋ], *adj.* kompromißlos; (*inflexible*) unnachgiebig.

**unconcerned** [ʌnkən'səːnd], *adj.* (*not worried*) unbesorgt; unbekümmert (**about,** wegen + *gen*).

**unconditional** [ʌnkən'diʃənəl], *adj.* vorbehaltlos.

**unconfirmed** [ʌnkən'fəːmd], *adj.* unbestätigt.

**uncongenial** [ʌnkən'dʒiːniəl], *adj.* (*of pers.*) unsympathisch.

**unconnected** [ʌnkə'nektid], *adj.* nicht miteinander verbunden; (*separate*) getrennt; (*not related*) nicht verwandt.

**unconscious** [ʌn'kɔnʃəs], *adj.* 1. (*unaware*) unbewußt (**of,** + *gen*); **the u.,** das Unbewußte. 2. (*senseless*) bewußtlos; **to become u.,** das Bewußtsein verlieren; -ly, *adv.* unbewußt. ◆**un'consciousness,** *s.* 1. Unbewußtheit *f*. 2. Bewußtlosigkeit *f*.

**uncontrollable** [ʌnkən'trəuləbl], *adj.* (*of child, anger*) unbändig; (*of desire*) unwiderstehlich; **u. laughter,** unbeherrschtes Gelächter.

**unconventional** [ʌnkən'venʃən(ə)l], *adj.* unkonventionell.

**unconvinced** [ʌnkən'vinst], *adj.* nicht überzeugt (**of sth.,** von etwas *dat*).

**uncooked** [ʌn'kukt], *adj.* ungekocht, roh.

**uncork** [ʌn'kɔːk], *v.tr.* entkorken.

**uncouth** [ʌn'kuːθ], *adj.* ungehobelt; (*of remark*) grob; (*awkward*) linkisch.

**uncover** [ʌn'kʌvər], *v.tr.* (*a*) (etwas) freilegen; (*uninteated*) entblößen; (*b*) *Fig:* **to u. a plot,** eine Verschwörung aufdecken.

**uncultivated** [ʌn'kʌltiveitid], *adj.* 1. (*of field*) unbebaut. 2. *Fig:* (*of pers.*) unkultiviert.

**undamaged** [ʌn'dæmidʒd], *adj.* unbeschädigt.

**undaunted** [ʌn'dɔːntid], *adj.* unverzagt.

**undecided** [ʌndi'saidid], *adj.* (*a*) (*of game, issue etc.*) unentschieden; (*b*) (*of pers.*) unschlüssig.

**undecipherable** [ʌndi'saif(ə)rəbl], *adj.* nicht zu entziffern.

**undefinable** [ʌndi'fainəbl], *adj.* undefinierbar. ◆**unde'fined,** *adj.* (*a*) nicht definiert; (*b*) (*vague*) unbestimmt.

**undemonstrative** [ʌndi'mɔnstrətiv], *adj.* zurückhaltend.

**undeniable** [ʌndi'naiəbl], *adj.* unbestreitbar.

**under** ['ʌndər]. **I.** *prep.* unter + *dat*/(*with motion*) + *acc*; **from u. the table**, unter dem Tisch hervor; **he's u. thirty**, er ist unter dreißig (Jahren); **u. age**, minderjährig; **u. these circumstances**, unter diesen Umständen; **u. construction**, im Bau; **to be u. repair**, in Reparatur sein. **II.** *adv.* unten. ◆**under'carriage**, *s. Av:* Fahrgestell *n.* ◆**'underclothes**, *s. pl.* /**'underclothing**, *s.* Unterwäsche *f.* ◆**'undercoat**, **I.** *s.* Grundierung *f.* **II.** *v.tr.* grundieren. ◆**'undercover**, *adj.* **u. agent**, Geheimagent *m.* ◆**'undercurrent**, *s.* Unterströmung *f.* ◆**under'cut**, *v.tr.irr.* (j-n im Preis) unterbieten. ◆**'underde'veloped**, *adj.* unterentwickelt; **u. countries**, Entwicklungsländer *npl.* ◆**'underdog**, *s.* **the u.**, der Unterlegene. ◆**under'done**, *adj.* nicht gar; (*of meat*) nicht durch(gebraten). ◆**under'estimate**. **I.** [-mət] *s.* Unterschätzung *f.* **II.** [-meit] *v.tr.* (j-n, etwas) unterschätzen. ◆**underex'pose**, *v.tr.* (einen Film) unterbelichten. ◆**under'fed**, *adj.* unterernährt. ◆**under'foot**, *adv.* unter den Füßen. ◆**under'go**, *v.tr.irr.* (eine Erfahrung, einen Prozeß usw.) durchmachen; (einen Verlust) erleiden; *Med:* **to u. an operation**, sich einer Operation unterziehen. ◆**under-'graduate/F:undergrad**, *s.* Student(in) *m(f)* (einer Universität). ◆**'underground**. **I.** *adj.* Untergrund-; **u. railway**, Untergrundbahn *f.* **II.** *s. Rail:* Untergrundbahn *f, F:* U-Bahn *f.* ◆**'undergrowth**, *s.* Unterholz *n;* Gestrüpp *n.* ◆**'underhand**, *adj.* hinterhältig. ◆**under'line**, *v.tr.* unterstreichen. ◆**'underling**, *s. Pej:* Handlanger *m.* ◆**under'lying**, *adj.* (*a*) darunterliegend; (*b*) *Fig:* zugrundeliegend. ◆**under'mine**, *v.tr.* (*a*) (etwas) unterminieren; (ein Ufer) aushöhlen; (*b*) *Fig:* (Autorität usw.) untergraben. ◆**under'neath**. **I.** *prep.* unter + *dat*/ (*with motion*) + *acc*; **from u. sth.**, unter etwas *dat* hervor. **II.** *adv.* (*a*) unten; (*b*) (*below*) darunter. **III.** *s.* Unterseite *f.* ◆**under'nourished**, *adj.* unterernährt. ◆**under'paid**, *adj.* unterbezahlt. ◆**'underpass**, *s.* Unterführung *f.* ◆**under'privileged**, *adj.* unterprivilegiert; (gesellschaftlich) benachteiligt. ◆**under'rate**, *v.tr.* unterschätzen. ◆**'underseal**, *s. Aut:* Bodenschutz *m.* ◆**'underside**, *s.* Unterseite *f.* ◆**under'signed**, *s.* **the u.**, der/die Unterzeichnete. ◆**'underskirt**, *s.* Unterrock *m.* ◆**under'stand**, *v.tr. & i.irr.* unterstehen; **to u. business**, sich in geschäftlichen Angelegenheiten auskennen; **I u. your impatience**, ich habe Ver-

ständnis für Ihre Ungeduld; **what do you u. by that?** was verstehen sie darunter? **am I to u. that ...?** wollen Sie damit sagen, daß ...? ◆**under'standable**, *adj.* verständlich; **-ably**, *adv.* begreiflicherweise. ◆**under'standing**. **I.** *s.* **1.** Verständnis *n* (**of**, für + *acc*); (*insight*) Einsicht *f* (**of**, in + *acc*). **2.** (*agreement*) Vereinbarung *f;* **on the u. that**, unter der Bedingung/Voraussetzung, daß ... **II.** *adj.* (*of pers.*) verständnisvoll. ◆**'under'statement**, *s.* Untertreibung *f.* ◆**under'stood**, *adj.* **1.** verstanden; **easily u.**, leicht verständlich; **to make oneself u.**, sich verständlich machen. **2.** (*agreed*) abgemacht. ◆**'understudy**. **I.** *s.* zweite Besetzung *f.* **II.** *v.tr.* (einen Schauspieler) vertreten. ◆**under'take**, *v.tr.irr.* (*a*) (eine Reise usw.) unternehmen; (eine Aufgabe) auf sich *acc* nehmen; (*b*) **to u. to do sth.**, sich verpflichten, etwas zu tun. ◆**'undertaker**, *s.* Leichenbestatter *m.* ◆**under'taking**, *s.* **1.** (*taking on*) Übernehmen *n* (einer Aufgabe); Unternehmen *n* (einer Reise usw.). **2.** (*a*) *Com:* (*business*) Unternehmen *n;* (*b*) (*task*) Aufgabe *f.* **3.** (*promise*) Verpflichtung *f.* ◆**under'value**, *v.tr.* unterbewerten. ◆**'underwear**, *s.* Unterwäsche *f.* ◆**'underworld**, *s.* **the** (*criminal*) **u.**, die Unterwelt. ◆**'under'write**, *v.tr.irr.* (eine Summe usw.) garantieren. ◆**'underwriter**, *s.* Versicherungsgeber *m.*

**undeserved** [ʌndi'zɔːvd], *adj.* unverdient; **-ly** [-idli], *adv.* unverdient(erweise).

**undesirable** [ʌndi'zaiərəbl], *adj.* unerwünscht.

**undies** ['ʌndiz], *s. pl. F:* Unterwäsche *f.*

**undignified** [ʌn'dignifaid], *adj.* würdelos.

**undiscovered** [ʌndis'kʌvəd], *adj.* unentdeckt.

**undiscriminating** [ʌndis'krimineitiŋ], *adj.* (*of pers., taste etc.*) anspruchslos.

**undisputed** [ʌndis'pjuːtid], *adj.* unbestritten.

**undistinguished** [ʌndis'tiŋwiʃt], *adj.* durch nichts ausgezeichnet; (*ordinary*) gewöhnlich.

**undisturbed** [ʌndis'tɔːbd], *adj.* ungestört.

**undo** [ʌn'duː], *v.tr.irr.* (*a*) (*destroy*) **to u. all the good**, alles zunichte machen; (*b*) (*open*) aufmachen; (*unbutton*) (ein Kleid) aufknöpfen. ◆**un'done**, *adj.* **1.** offen. **2.** (*of work etc.*) unerledigt; **what's done cannot be u.**, Geschehenes kann man nicht ungeschehen machen.

**undoubted** [ʌn'dautid], *adj.* unbestritten; **-ly**, *adv.* zweifellos.

**undress** [ʌn'dres], *v.* **1.** *v.i.* sich ausziehen. **2.** *v.tr.* ausziehen.

**undue** ['ʌndjuː], *adj.* ungebührlich; (*excessive*) übertrieben. ◆**un'duly**, *adv.* übermäßig.

**undulate** ['ʌndjuleit], *v.i.* wogen.

◆**'undulating**, *adj.* wogend.

**unearth** [ʌn'ɔ:θ], *v.tr.* (etwas) ausgraben; (ein Manuskript usw.) aufstöbern.

**unearthly** [ʌn'ɔ:θli], *adj.* (*supernatural*) übernatürlich; *F:* at an u. hour, in aller Herrgottsfrühe.

**uneasy** [ʌn'i:zi], *adj.* (*worried*) besorgt; (*embarrassed*) verlegen; he was u. (in his mind), ihm war unbehaglich zumute. ◆**un'easiness**, *s.* Unbehagen *n*; (*worry*) Unruhe *f*.

**uneatable** [ʌn'i:təbl], *adj.* ungenießbar.

**uneconomic** [ʌni:kə'nɔmik], *adj.* unwirtschaftlich. ◆**uneco'nomical**, *adj.* nicht sparsam.

**uneducated** [ʌn'edjukeitid], *adj.* ungebildet; (*of accent etc.*) unkultiviert.

**unem'ployed**, *adj.* (*a*) unbeschäftigt; (*b*) (*out of a job*) arbeitslos; the u., die Arbeitslosen *pl.* ◆**unem'ployment**, *s.* Arbeitslosigkeit *f; Adm:* u. benefit, Arbeitslosenunterstützung *f*.

**unending** [ʌn'endiŋ], *adj.* endlos.

**unenviable** [ʌn'enviəbl], *adj.* wenig beneidenswert.

**unequal** [ʌn'i:kwəl], *adj.* ungleich; to be u. to the task, der Aufgabe nicht gewachsen sein; **-ly**, *adv.* ungleich. ◆**un'equalled**, *adj.* einmalig; (*of pers.*) ohnegleichen.

**unerring** [ʌn'ɔ:riŋ], *adj.* unfehlbar; (*of sense*) untrüglich.

**uneven** [ʌn'i:v(ə)n], *adj.* (*a*) (*of surface*) uneben; (*bumpy*) holperig; (*b*) *Fig:* (*variable*) ungleichmäßig; (*of pulse*) nicht regelmäßig; *Mth:* u. number, ungerade Zahl.

**uneventful** [ʌni'ventful], *adj.* ereignislos; u. life, ruhiges Leben.

**unexpected** [ʌnik'spektid], *adj.* unerwartet; (*of result*) unvermutet; (*of meeting*) unverhofft.

**unexploded** ['ʌniks'spləudid], *adj.* nicht explodiert.

**unexpressed** [ʌniks'prest], *adj.* unausgesprochen.

**unfailing** [ʌn'feiliŋ], *adj.* unfehlbar.

**unfair** [ʌn'fɛər], *adj.* ungerecht, *also Sp:* unfair; **-ly**, *adv.* unfair; (*wrongly*) zu Unrecht; to act u., ungerecht handeln. ◆**un'fairness**, *s.* Ungerechtigkeit *f*.

**unfaithful** [ʌn'feiθfəl], *adj.* untreu. ◆**un'faithfulness**, *s.* Untreue *f*.

**unfamiliar** [ʌnfə'miljər], *adj.* (*a*) (*of thing*) unbekannt (to s.o., j-m); (*strange*) fremd; (*b*) (*of pers.*) to be u. with sth., etwas nicht kennen.

**unfashionable** [ʌn'fæʃ(ə)nəbl], *adj.* altmodisch; *esp. Cl:* unmodern.

**unfasten** [ʌn'fɑ:sn], *v.tr.* (*a*) (etwas) losmachen; (*b*) (*open*) aufmachen.

**unfavourable** [ʌn'feiv(ə)rəbl], *adj.* ungünstig; (*of terms etc.*) unvorteilhaft (for/to, für + *acc*).

**unfeeling** [ʌn'fi:liŋ], *adj.* gefühllos.

**unfinished** [ʌn'finiʃt], *adj.* nicht fertig; (*of work of art*) unvollendet.

**unfit** [ʌn'fit], *adj.* (*a*) ungeeignet (for

sth., für etwas *acc*); (*unworthy*) nicht würdig (to do sth., etwas zu tun); (*b*) (*in poor health*) bei schlechter Gesundheit, *Sp: & F:* nicht fit.

**unflagging** [ʌn'flægiŋ], *adj.* unermüdlich.

**unflappable** [ʌn'flæpəbl], *adj. F:* she is u., sie ist nicht aus der Ruhe zu bringen.

**unflattering** [ʌn'flæt(ə)riŋ], *adj.* wenig schmeichelhaft; (*of dress*) unvorteilhaft.

**unflinching** [ʌn'flin(t)ʃiŋ], *adj.* unerschütterlich; (*resolute*) entschlossen; **-ly**, *adv.* ohne mit der Wimper zu zucken.

**unfold** [ʌn'fəuld], *v.* 1. *v.tr.* (*a*) (etwas) entfalten; (eine Zeitung) ausbreiten; (*b*) (einen Plan) darlegen. 2. *v.i.* sich entfalten; (*of plot etc.*) sich entwickeln.

**unforeseeable** [ʌnfɔ:'si:əbl], *adj.* nicht voraussehbar. ◆**unfore'seen**, *adj.* unvorhergesehen.

**unforgettable** [ʌnfə'getəbl], *adj.* unvergeßlich.

**unforgivable** [ʌnfə'givəbl], *adj.* unverzeihlich.

**unfortunate** [ʌn'fɔ:tʃənət], *adj.* (*a*) (*of pers.*) unglücklich; to be u., Pech haben; (*b*) (*of mistake, coincidence etc.*) bedauerlich; **-ly**, *adv.* leider.

**unfounded** [ʌn'faundid], *adj.* unbegründet.

**unfriendly** [ʌn'frendli], *adj.* unfreundlich. ◆**un'friendliness**, *s.* Unfreundlichkeit *f*.

**unfurnished** [ʌn'fɔ:niʃt], *adj.* unmöbliert.

**ungainly** [ʌn'geinli], *adj.* unbeholfen.

**unget-at-able** ['ʌnget'ætəbl], *adj. F:* schwer erreichbar/zugänglich.

**ungodly** [ʌn'gɔdli], *adj.* 1. gottlos; (*sinful*) sündhaft. 2. *F:* at an u. hour, in aller Hergottsfrühe.

**ungracious** [ʌn'greiʃəs], *adj.* unliebenswürdig; (*impolite*) unhöflich.

**ungrateful** [ʌn'greitful], *adj.* undankbar.

**ungrudging** [ʌn'grʌdʒiŋ], *adj.* bereitwillig.

**unguarded** [ʌn'gɑ:did], *adj.* 1. unbewacht. 2. (*of pers., remark*) unachtsam.

**unhappy** [ʌn'hæpi], *adj.* unglücklich. ◆**un'happily**, *adv.* unglücklicherweise.

**unharmed** [ʌn'hɑ:md], *adj.* unversehrt.

**unhealthy** [ʌn'helθi], *adj.* (*a*) ungesund; (*b*) (*of pers.*) nicht gesund.

**unheard** [ʌn'hɔ:d], *adj.* 1. to go u., nicht gehört werden; (*be ignored*) nicht beachtet werden. 2. that's u. of, das ist noch nie dagewesen/(*outrageous*) unerhört.

**unhelpful** [ʌn'helpful], *adj.* (*of pers.*) nicht hilfsbereit, unfreundlich; (*of criticism*) nicht konstruktiv.

**unhesitating** [ʌn'heziteitiŋ], *adj.* prompt, unverzüglich.

**unhurt** [ʌn'hɔ:t], *adj.* unverletzt.

**unidentified** [ʌnai'dentifaid], *adj.* nicht identifiziert; u. flying object, unbekanntes Flugobjekt.

**unification** [ju:nifi'keiʃ(ə)n], *s.* Vereinigung *f*.

**uniform** ['ju:nifɔːm]. **I.** *adj.* (*same*) gleich; (*same shape*) gleichförmig; (*of dress etc.*) einheitlich. **II.** *s.* Uniform *f*. ◆**uni'formity,** *s.* Gleichförmigkeit *f*; Einheitlichkeit *f* (der Kleidung, des Stils usw.); *Pej:* Eintönigkeit *f*.

**unify** ['ju:nifai], *v.tr.* vereinigen.

**unilateral** [ju:ni'læt(ə)rəl], *adj.* einseitig.

**unimaginable** [ʌni'mædʒinəbl], *adj.* unvorstellbar. ◆**uni'maginative,** *adj.* phantasielos.

**unimportant** [ʌnim'pɔːtənt], *adj.* unwichtig.

**unimpressed** [ʌnim'prest], *adj.* nicht beeindruckt. ◆**unim'pressive,** *adj.* nicht eindrucksvoll; (*small*) unscheinbar.

**uninhabitable** [ʌnin'hæbitəbl], *adj.* unbewohnbar. ◆**unin'habited,** *adj.* unbewohnt.

**uninjured** [ʌn'in(d)ʒəd], *adj.* unverletzt.

**unintelligent** [ʌnin'telidʒənt], *adj.* unintelligent. ◆**unin'telligible,** *adj.* unverständlich.

**unintentional** [ʌnin'tenʃ(ə)nəl], *adj.* unabsichtlich.

**uninterested** [ʌn'intristid], *adj.* uninteressiert (**in,** an + *dat*); (*indifferent*) gleichgültig. ◆**un'interesting,** *adj.* uninteressant.

**uninterrupted** [ʌnintə'rʌptid], *adj.* ununterbrochen; (*of work*) ungestört (**by,** von + *dat*).

**uninviting** [ʌnin'vaitiŋ], *adj.* wenig verlockend.

**union** ['ju:njən], *s.* **1.** (*joining*) Vereinigung *f*; *Pol:* Zusammenschluß *m* (von Parteien usw.). **2.** (*body*) (*a*) Verein *m*; *Com:* Verband *m*; *Pol:* Union *f*; (*b*) *Ind:* (**trade**) **u.,** Gewerkschaft *f*. ◆**'Union 'Jack,** *s.* Union Jack *m* (*die britische Nationalflagge*).

**unique** [ju:'ni:k], *adj.* einmalig; (*of its kind*) einzigartig.

**unison** ['ju:nisən], *s. Mus:* (*a*) Einklang *m*; **in u.,** unisono; (*b*) *attrib.* einstimmig.

**unit** ['ju:nit], *s.* Einheit *f*; *Fin:* **u. trust,** Investmenttrust *m*; **u. furniture,** Anbaumöbel *pl*; **kitchen u.,** Küchenelement *n*.

**unite** [ju:'nait], *v.* **1.** *v.tr.* (*a*) vereinigen; (Elemente, Bestandteile) verbinden; (Eigenschaften) in sich vereinigen. **2.** *v.i.* (*a*) sich vereinigen; (*b*) (*of states*) sich verbünden. ◆**u'nited,** *adj.* vereint; (*esp. of states etc.*) vereinigt; **the U. Kingdom,** das Vereinigte Königreich; **the U. States** (**of America**), die Vereinigten Staaten (von Amerika); **the U. Nations,** die Vereinten Nationen. ◆**unity** ['ju:niti], *s.* (*a*) Einheit *f* (einer Partei, einer Nation usw.); Einheitlichkeit *f* (der Handlung eines Romans usw.); (*b*) (*agreement*) Einigkeit *f*; (*harmony*) Eintracht *f*.

**universe** ['ju:nivəːs], *s.*Universum *n*. ◆**uni'versal,** *s.* universal, Universal-; (*of knowledge*) allumfassend; (*of rule etc.*) allgemeingültig; **-ly,** *adv.* allgemein. ◆**uni'versity,** *s.* Universität *f*.

**unjust** [ʌn'dʒʌst], *adj.* ungerecht (**to,** gegen + *acc*); ◆**unjusti'fiable,** *adj.* nicht zu rechtfertigen(d). ◆**un'justified,** *adj.* ungerechtfertigt.

**unkempt** [ʌn'kem(p)t], *adj.* (*of hair*) zerzaust; (*of appearance*) ungepflegt; (*of garden*) verwahrlost.

**unkind** [ʌn'kaind], *adj.* lieblos; (*unfeeling*) gefühllos; (*cruel*) grausam; **that's u. of him,** das ist nicht nett von ihm. ◆**un'kindly,** *adv.* unfreundlich. ◆**un'kindness,** *s.* Lieblosigkeit *f*; Unfreundlichkeit *f*.

**unknown** [ʌn'nəun]. **I.** *adj.* unbekannt (**to,** dat). **II.** *adv.* **u. to me,** ohne mein Wissen. **III.** *s.* (*pers.*) Unbekannte(r) *f(m)*; *Mth:* Unbekannte *f*.

**unladen** [ʌn'leidn], *adj.* unbeladen; **weight u./u. weight,** Leergewicht *n*.

**unlawful** [ʌn'lɔːful], *adj.* ungesetzlich; (*of transaction etc.*) illegal.

**unleash** [ʌn'li:ʃ], *v.tr.* (j-n, etwas) entfesseln; (Hunde) loskoppeln.

**unless** [ʌn'les], *conj.* wenn/falls ... nicht; es sei denn, (daß + *subj.*); **u. I am mistaken,** wenn ich mich nicht irre.

**unlicensed** [ʌn'laisənst], *adj.* unbefugt; (*of action*) unerlaubt; *Com:* (*of sale etc.*) nicht konzessioniert.

**unlike** [ʌn'laik]. **I.** *adj.* verschieden. **II.** *prep.* **not u. s.o.,** j-m nicht unähnlich; **he, u. his father ...,** er, im Gegensatz zu seinem Vater ... ◆**un'likeable,** *adj.* unsympathisch. ◆**un'likely,** *adj.* unwahrscheinlich; **an u. tale,** eine unglaubwürdige Geschichte; **he's u. to come,** wahrscheinlich kommt er nicht.

**unlimited** [ʌn'limitid], *adj.* unbegrenzt; *Com:* (*of liability etc.*) unbeschränkt.

**unlined** [ʌn'laind], *adj.* (*a*) (*of clothes*) ungefüttert; (*b*) (*of paper*) unliniert; (*of face*) faltenlos.

**unload** [ʌn'ləud], *v.tr.* entladen; (eine Fracht) ausladen. ◆**un'loading,** *s.* Entladen *n*.

**unlock** [ʌn'lɔk], *v.tr.* aufschließen.

**unlucky** [ʌn'lʌki], *adj.* **1.** (*a*) (*of pers.*) unglücklich; **to be u.,** kein Glück haben; *F:* Pech haben; (*b*) (*of thing*) unglückbringend. ◆**un'luckily,** *adv.* unglücklicherweise.

**unmanageable** [ʌn'mænidʒəbl], *adj.* nicht zu handhaben; (*of child*) widerspenstig.

**unmarketable** [ʌn'mɑːkitəbl], *adj.* unverkäuflich.

**unmarried** [ʌn'mærid], *adj.* unverheiratet; **u. mother,** ledige Mutter.

**unmask** [ʌn'mɑːsk], *v.* **1.** *v.tr.* (j-n) demaskieren; *Fig:* (j-n) entlarven. **2.** *v.i.* sich demaskieren.

**unmerited** [ʌn'meritid], *adj.* unverdient.

**unmistakable** [ʌnmis'teikəbl], *adj.* unmißverständlich; (*easily recognized*) unverkennbar.

**unmitigated** [ʌn'mitigeitid], *adj.* (*undiminished*) ungemindert; (*thorough*) hundertprozentig.

**unnatural** [ʌn'nætʃrəl], *adj.* unnatürlich; (*of crime*) widernatürlich; (*of style etc.*) künstlich.

**unnecessary** [ʌn'nesis(ə)ri], *adj.* unnötig; (*superfluous*) überflüssig.

**unnoticed** [ʌn'nəutist], *adj.* unbemerkt.

**unobservant** [ʌnəb'zɔːvənt], *adj.* unaufmerksam. ◆**unob'served**, *adj.* unbemerkt.

**unobtainable** [ʌnəb'teinəbl], *adj.* nicht erhältlich.

**unobtrusive** [ʌnəb'truːsiv], *adj.* (*of pers., manner*) unaufdringlich; (*of thing*) unauffällig.

**unoccupied** [ʌn'ɔkjupaid], *adj.* 1. (*of pers.*) unbeschäftigt. 2. (*empty*) leerstehend; (*of house etc.*) unbewohnt; (*of seat*) frei.

**unofficial** [ʌnə'fiʃ(ə)l], *adj.* inoffiziell; (*of report*) unbestätigt.

**unopposed** [ʌnə'pəuzd], *adj.* (*of pers.*) ohne Konkurrenz; *Sp:* ohne Gegner; *Parl:* ohne Gegenkandidat(en); (*of proposal etc.*) unbeanstandet.

**unorthodox** [ʌn'ɔːθədɔks], *adj.* unorthodox.

**unostentatious** [ʌnɔsten'teiʃəs], *adj.* (*of building, dress*) schlicht; (*of pers., behaviour*) unauffällig.

**unpack** [ʌn'pæk], *v.tr. & i.* auspacken.

**unpaid** [ʌn'peid], *adj.* unbezahlt; (*honorary*) ehrenamtlich.

**unpalatable** [ʌn'pælitəbl], *adj.* nicht schmackhaft; *Fig:* (*of truth etc.*) unangenehm.

**unparalleled** [ʌn'pærəleld], *adj.* (*of intensity etc.*) unvergleichlich; (*of action*) beispiellos; (*of luck etc.*) ohnegleichen.

**unpardonable** [ʌn'pɑːdnəbl], *adj.* unverzeihlich.

**unperturbed** [ʌnpə'təːbd], *adj.* ungestört; (*calm*) gelassen.

**unpleasant** [ʌn'plez(ə)nt], *adj.* unangenehm; (*of sight, meeting etc.*) unerfreulich.

**unpolished** [ʌn'pɔliʃt], *adj.* unpoliert; (*of gem, marble etc., Fig:* of pers., style*) ungeschliffen.

**unpopular** [ʌn'pɔpjulər], *adj.* unbeliebt.

**unpractical** [ʌn'præktik(ə)l], *adj.* unpraktisch.

**unprecedented** [ʌn'presidentid], *adj.* beispiellos; noch nie dagewesen.

**unprejudiced** [ʌn'predʒudist], *adj.* vorurteilslos; (*of pers., judgement*) unparteiisch.

**unprepared** [ʌnpri'pɛəd], *adj.* unvorbereitet.

**unpretentious** [ʌnpri'tenʃəs], *adj.* anspruchslos; (*modest*) bescheiden.

**unprincipled** [ʌn'prinsipld], *adj.* skrupellos.

**unprofitable** [ʌn'prɔfitəbl], *adj.* unrentabel; *Fig:* (*of effort etc.*) unnütz.

**unprotected** [ʌnprə'tektid], *adj.* ungeschützt.

**unprovided for** [ʌnprə'vaidid fɔːr], *adj.* (*a*) (*of child etc.*) ohne Mittel; (*b*) (*of*

*eventuality*) nicht vorgesehen.

**unpunctual** [ʌn'pʌŋ(k)tju(ə)l], *adj.* unpünktlich.

**unpunished** [ʌn'pʌniʃt], *adj.* ungestraft; **to go u.**, (*of pers.*) straflos ausgehen; (*of deed*) ungestraft bleiben.

**unqualified** [ʌn'kwɔlifaid], *adj.* 1. (*of pers.*) unqualifiziert; (*not fully trained*) nicht ausgebildet. 2. (*unlimited*) uneingeschränkt; (*of statement*) ohne Vorbehalt; **not an u. success,** kein durchgreifender Erfolg.

**unquestionable** [ʌn'kwestʃənəbl], *adj.* unbestreitbar; **-ably,** *adv.* ohne jeden Zweifel. ◆**un'questioning,** *adj.* ohne Frage; (*absolute*) bedingungslos; **u. obedience,** blinder Gehorsam; **-ly,** *adv.* ohne zu fragen; ohne Zögern.

**unravel** [ʌn'ræv(ə)l], *v.tr.* (*a*) (Fäden) entwirren; (ein Gewebe, Gestricktes) auftrennen; (*b*) *Fig:* (ein Geheimnis) enträtseln.

**unreadable** [ʌn'riːdəbl], *adj.* (*a*) (*of handwriting*) unleserlich; (*b*) (*of book*) unlesbar.

**unreal** [ʌn'riːəl], *adj.* unwirklich; phantastisch. ◆**'unrea'listic,** *adj.* unrealistisch; (*of pers., attitude*) wirklichkeitsfremd. ◆**unreality** [-'æliti], *s.* Unwirklichkeit *f.*

**unreasonable** [ʌn'riːznəbl], *adj.* (*a*) (*of pers.*) **don't be so u.,** sei doch vernünftig; (*b*) (*of request etc.*) unzumutbar; **u. demands,** übertriebene Forderungen; **it's u. to expect that,** das ist zu viel verlangt.

**unrecognizable** [ʌn'rekəgnaizəbl], *adj.* unerkennbar; **he was u.,** er war nicht wiederzuerkennen.

**unrehearsed** [ʌnri'həːst], *adj.* (*a*) *Th:* ungeprobt; (*b*) (*of speech etc.*) aus dem Stegreif.

**unrelated** [ʌnri'leitid], *adj.* (*of facts, concepts*) nicht miteinander verbunden; (*of pers.*) nicht miteinander verwandt.

**unrelenting** [ʌnri'lentiŋ], *adj.* (*of. pers.*) unnachgiebig; (*of struggle*) unerbittlich; (*of persecution*) schonungslos; (*of pace*) unvermindert.

**unreliable** [ʌnri'laiəbl], *adj.* unzuverlässig; (*of character*) nicht vertrauenswürdig; (*of information*) nicht glaubwürdig.

**unrelieved** [ʌnri'liːvd], *adj.* 1. (*of pain*) ungemindert. 2. (*uniform*) einheitlich, (*monotonous*) monoton; (*of colour etc.*) ohne Abwechslung.

**unrepentant** [ʌnri'pentənt], *adj.* reuelos.

**unreserved** [ʌnri'zəːvd], *adj.* (*of praise, support etc.*) uneingeschränkt. 2. (*of pers., nature*) offenherzig. 3. **u. seats,** nicht reservierte Plätze; **-ly** [-idli], *adv.* ohne Vorbehalt.

**unresponsive** [ʌnris'pɔnsiv], *adj.* (*of pers.*) teilnahmslos.

**unrest** [ʌn'rest], *s.* Unruhe *f;* **industrial u.,** Unzufriedenheit *f* unter der Arbeiterschaft.

**unrestricted** [ʌnri'striktid], *adj.* uneingeschränkt; (*of speed*) unbegrenzt; (*of view*) ungehindert.

**unripe** [ʌn'raip], *adj.* (*of fruit etc.*) unreif.

**unrivalled** [ʌn'raiv(ə)ld], *adj.* unvergleichlich; (*of pers.*) ohne Rivalen; (*of ability, performance etc.*) unerreicht.

**unroll** [ʌn'rəul], *v.* **1.** *v.tr.* (einen Teppich usw.) aufrollen. **2.** *v.i.* (*of flag etc.*) sich aufrollen.

**unruffled** [ʌn'rʌfld], *adj.* (*of pers.*) gelassen; **u. composure,** unerschütterliche Gelassenheit.

**unruly** [ʌn'ru:li], *adj.* (*of child*) widerspenstig; (*wild*) ungestüm.

**unsafe** [ʌn'seif], *adj.* unsicher; (*of action*) gefährlich; (*of undertaking*) riskant; (*of pers.*) in Gefahr.

**unsaid** [ʌn'sed], *adj.* unausgesprochen.

**unsal(e)able** [ʌn'seiləbl], *adj.* unverkäuflich.

**unsanitary** [ʌn'sænit(ə)ri], *adj.* unhygienisch.

**unsatisfactory** [ʌnsætis'fækt(ə)ri], *adj.* unbefriedigend; (*of explanation*) nicht überzeugend. ◆**unsatisfied** [ʌn'sætisfaid], *adj.* **1.** (*of pers.*) unzufrieden. **2.** (*of desire etc.*) unbefriedigt; (*of appetite*) nicht gesättigt.

**unsavoury** [ʌn'seiv(ə)ri], *adj.* **1.** (*of dish*) unschmackhaft; **u. smell,** übler Geruch. **2.** (*of affair etc.*) zwielichtig; **u. reputation,** übler Ruf.

**unscrew** [ʌn'skru:], *v.tr.* abschrauben.

**unscrupulous** [ʌn'skru:pjuləs], *adj.* skrupellos.

**unseen** [ʌn'si:n]. **I.** *adj.* **1.** ungesehen. **2.** (*invisible*) unsichtbar. **II.** *s. Sch:* unvorbereitete Übersetzung *f.*

**unselfish** [ʌn'selfiʃ], *adj.* (*of pers.*) selbstlos. ◆**un'selfishness,** *s.* Selbstlosigkeit *f.*

**unsettle** [ʌn'setl], *v.tr.* (j-n) beunruhigen. ◆**un'settled,** *adj.* **1.** (*disturbed*) unruhig; (*of weather*) veränderlich. **2.** (a) (*undecided*) unentschlossen; (*of questions*) unentschieden; (b) (*of bill*) unbezahlt; (*of estate*) noch nicht abgewickelt.

**unshak(e)able** [ʌn'ʃeikəbl], *adj.* unerschütterlich.

**unshaven** [ʌn'ʃeivn], *adj.* unrasiert.

**unsightly** [ʌn'saitli], *adj.* häßlich.

**unskilful** [ʌn'skilful], *adj.* ungeschickt. ◆**un'skilled,** *adj.* ungeübt; *Ind:* **u. worker,** ungelernter Arbeiter.

**unsociable** [ʌn'səuʃəbl], *adj.* ungesellig.

**unsolved** [ʌn'sɔlvd], *adj.* ungelöst.

**unsophisticated** [ʌnsə'fistikeitid], *adj.* ungekünstelt; (*genuine*) unverfälscht; (*naive*) arglos; (*simple*) schlicht.

**unsound** [ʌn'saund], *adj.* (*defective*) fehlerhaft; (*of wood*) morsch; (*of fruit*) verdorben; (*of structure etc.*) unsicher, (*dangerous*) gefährlich; *esp. Jur:* of **u. mind,** unzurechnungsfähig.

**unsparing** [ʌn'spɛəriŋ], *adj.* **to be u. in one's efforts,** keine Mühe scheuen.

**unspeakable** [ʌn'spi:kəbl], *adj.* unbeschreiblich; *F:* (*terrible*) entsetzlich.

**unspoilt** [ʌn'spoilt], *adj.* unverdorben; (*of countryside*) unberührt.

**unspoken** [ʌn'spəuk(ə)n], *adj.* unausgesprochen; (*of agreement*) stillschweigend.

**unstable** [ʌn'steibl], *adj.* nicht stabil; (*of pers.*) labil.

**unsteady** [ʌn'stedi], *adj.* **1.** (*of object*) wacklig; (*of footsteps*) wankend; (*of hand*) unsicher; **u. on one's feet,** wacklig auf den Beinen. **2.** (*varying*) unbeständig; (*of prices*) schwankend; (*of pulse etc.*) unregelmäßig. ◆**un'steadiness,** *s.* **1.** Wackligkeit *f;* Wanken *n* (der Schritte); Unsicherheit *f* (der Hand). **2.** Unbeständigkeit *f;* Schwanken *n* (der Preise usw.). **3.** Unregelmäßigkeit *f* (des Pulses).

**unstinting** [ʌn'stintiŋ], *adj.* großzügig.

**unstuck** [ʌn'stʌk], **to come u.,** (i) (*of envelope*) aufgehen; (ii) *F:* (*of plan*) schiefgehen.

**unsuccessful** [ʌnsək'sesful], *adj.* **1.** erfolglos. **2.** (*of pers.*) nicht erfolgreich; (*in examination*) durchgefallen.

**unsuitable** [ʌn'sju:təbl], *adj.* **1.** (*of pers., thing*) ungeeignet (**for,** für + *acc*); (*of behaviour*) unangemessen. **2.** (*of thing*) unpassend; (*of several things, married couple*) nicht zusammenpassend.

**unsuspected** [ʌnsəs'pektid], *adj.* **1.** (*of pers.*) unverdächtigt. **2.** (*of qualities*) ungeahnt. ◆**unsus'pecting,** *adj.* ahnungslos; (*by nature*) nicht argwöhnisch; (*naive*) arglos.

**unswerving** [ʌn'swə:viŋ], *adj.* unbeirrbar; **u. devotion,** unerschütterliche Liebe.

**unsympathetic** [ʌnsimpə'θetik], *adj.* **1.** mitleidslos. **2.** (*uncongenial*) unsympathisch.

**untamed** [ʌn'teimd], *adj.* ungezähmt.

**untapped** [ʌn'tæpt], *adj.* unangezapft; **u. source,** ungenutzte Quelle.

**unthinkable** [ʌn'θiŋkəbl], *adj.* undenkbar; (*unimaginable*) unvorstellbar.

**untidy** [ʌn'taidi], *adj.* unordentlich. ◆**un'tidiness,** *s.* Unordentlichkeit *f.*

**untie** [ʌn'tai], *v.tr.* aufbinden; (einen Knoten) lösen; (ein Tier) losbinden.

**until** [ʌn'til]. **I.** *prep. & conj.* bis; **u. the evening,** bis zum Abend; **not u.,** erst; **he won't come u. two o'clock,** er wird erst um zwei Uhr kommen.

**untimely** [ʌn'taimli], *adj. & adv.* (*early*) (*of death etc.*) vorzeitig; (*of arrival etc.*) verfrüht.

**untiring** [ʌn'taiəriŋ], *adj.* unermüdlich.

**untold** [ʌn'təuld], *adj.* **1.** (*of story*) unerzählt. **2.** *Fig:* unzählbar.

**untoward** [ʌn'təwɔ:d], *adj.* (*of circumstances*) ungünstig; (*of accident*) unglücklich.

**untrained** [ʌn'treind], *adj.* ungeschult.

**untranslatable** [ˌʌntræns'leitəbl], *adj.* unübersetzbar.

**untried** [ʌn'traid], *adj.* ungeprüft; (*of*

*pers., method etc.*) unerprobt; **we left nothing u.**, wir haben alles versucht.
**untroubled** [ʌn'trʌbld], *adj.* (*of mind etc.*) ruhig; (*of happiness etc.*) ungestört.
**untrue** [ʌn'truː], *adj.* unwahr.
**untrustworthy** [ʌn'trʌstwəːði], *adj.* unzuverlässig; (*of witness etc.*) nicht vertrauenswürdig.
**untruth** [ʌn'truːθ], *s.* Unwahrheit *f.* ◆**un'truthful**, *adj.* (*of pers.*) lügnerisch; (*of statement etc.*) unwahr; (*of report*) falsch.
**unusable** [ʌn'juːzəbl], *adj.* unbrauchbar. ◆**un'used**, *adj.* ungebraucht; (*of stamp*) ungestempelt.
**unusual** [ʌn'juːʒju(ə)l, -ʒəl], *adj.* ungewöhnlich; (*rare*) selten; (*of word etc.*) ungebräuchlich; **nothing u.**, nichts Ungewöhnliches; **-ly**, *adv.* ungewöhnlich.
**unveil** [ʌn'veil], *v.tr.* enthüllen.
**unwanted** [ʌn'wɔntid], *adj.* unerwünscht.
**unwary** [ʌn'wɛəri], *adj.* unvorsichtig.
**unwavering** [ʌn'weivəriŋ], *adj.* unerschütterlich; **-ly**, *adv.* unbeirrt.
**unwelcome** [ʌn'welkəm], *adj.* unwillkommen; (*of news*) unangenehm.
**unwell** [ʌn'wel], *adj.* krank.
**unwholesome** [ʌn'houlsəm], *adj.* unbekömmlich; (*esp. of appearance*) unappetitlich.
**unwieldy** [ʌn'wiːldi], *adj.* **1.** (*of equipment, tool*) unhandlich; (*of package etc.*) sperrig. **2.** (*of structure*) unförmig; (*topheavy*) kopflastig.
**unwilling** [ʌn'wiliŋ], *adj.* (*of pers., agreement etc.*) widerwillig; **u. to do sth.**, unwillig, etwas zu tun. **-ly**, *adv.* ungern.
**unwind** [ʌn'waind], *v.irr.* **1.** *v.tr.* (ein Kabel usw.) abwickeln. **2.** *v.i. Fig:* (*of pers.*) sich entspannen.
**unwise** [ʌn'waiz], *adj.* unklug; (*foolish*) töricht.
**unwitting** [ʌn'witiŋ], *adj.* unbewußt; (*unintentional*) unabsichtlich; **-ly**, *adv.* unwissentlich.
**unworkable** [ʌn'wəːkəbl], *adj.* (*of plan*) undurchführbar.
**unworthy** [ʌn'wəːði], *adj.* unwürdig (**of**, + *gen*: **to do sth.**, etwas zu tun).
**unwrap** [ʌn'ræp], *v.tr.* (ein Geschenk) auspacken; (ein Paket usw.) aufmachen; (einen Verband usw.) abwickeln.
**unwritten** [ʌn'rit(ə)n], *adj.* ungeschrieben.
**unyielding** [ʌn'jiːldiŋ], *adj.* nicht nachgebend; (*of pers.*) unnachgiebig.
**up** [ʌp]. **I.** *adv.* **1.** nach oben; (*upwards*) aufwärts; (*into the air*) in die Höhe; **to go up**, hinaufgehen; (*explode*) in die Luft gehen; **to walk up and down**, auf und ab gehen. **2.** (*position*) oben; **up on the roof**, oben auf dem Dach; **halfway up**, in halber Höhe; **up above (sth.)**, oberhalb (von etwas *dat*); **the moon is up**, der Mond ist aufgegangen; **road up**, (Vorsicht) Bauarbeiten. **3.** (*a*) **to go up**, (*of*

*prices, temperature etc.*) steigen; (*b*) **his blood was up**, er war ganz aufgeregt/empört; (*c*) **to be up against s.o.**, es mit j-m zu tun haben; *F:* **to be up against it**, in der Klemme sein. **4.** (*not in bed*) auf; **is he up yet?** ist er schon aufgestanden? **to be up and about**, auf den Beinen sein; **to be/stay up all night**, die ganze Nacht aufbleiben. **5. what's up?** was ist los? **6.** (**your**) **time's up**, Ihre Zeit ist um; **his leave's up**, sein Urlaub ist zu Ende; *F:* **the game's up**, das Spiel ist aus; **it's all up with him**, mit ihm ist es aus. **7.** **up to**; (*a*) (*place, time*) bis; **to go up to s.o.**, auf j-n zugehen; **up to now**, bis jetzt; (*b*) **to be up to a task**, einer Aufgabe gewachsen sein; **he's up to something**, er führt etwas im Schilde; (*c*) **it's up to him to decide**, die Entscheidung liegt bei ihm. **II.** *prep.* **1. to go up a hill**, einen Berg hinaufsteigen/(*of car*) hinauffahren; **he went up the stairs**, er ging die Treppe hinauf; **the cat is up the tree**, die Katze ist (oben) auf dem Baum. **2. up the river**, den Fluß hinauf, flußaufwärts. **III.** *s. F:* **ups and downs**, das Auf und Ab. **IV.** *v.tr. F:* (Preise) erhöhen. ◆**'up-and-'coming**, *adj.* vielversprechend. ◆**'up-and-'up**, *s. F:* **he is on the up-a.-up**, er macht sich. ◆**upbringing** ['ʌpbriŋiŋ], *s.* Erziehung *f.* ◆**up-end** ['ʌp'end], *v.tr.* (etwas) hochkant stellen. ◆**up'grade** ['ʌp'greid], *v.tr.* (*a*) (*improve*) verbessern; (*b*) (*promote*) (j-n) befördern; (eine Stellung) höher einstufen. ◆**upheaval** [ʌp'hiːv(ə)l], *s.* (*a*) (*fuss*) Getue *n*; (*b*) (*violent*) Aufruhr *f*; *Pol: esp:* Umwälzung *f.* ◆**uphill** ['ʌp'hil]. **I.** *adj.* bergauf; *Fig:* (*of task*) mühsam. **II.** *adv.* bergauf. ◆**uphold** [ʌp'hould], *v.tr.irr.* (*a*) (eine Tradition) aufrechterhalten; (*b*) (*approve*) (j-s Verhalten, einen Einspruch) billigen; (eine Entscheidung) bestätigen. ◆**up'holstery**, *s.* Polsterung *f.* ◆**upkeep** ['ʌpkiːp], *s.* Instandhaltung *f.* ◆**up-market** [ʌp'mɑːkit], *adj. Com:* (*of product*) für höhere Ansprüche. ◆**upon** [ə'pɔn], *prep.* (*a*) *esp. Lit:* (on) auf + *dat*/(*motion*) + *acc*; **once u. a time**, es war einmal. ◆**upper** ['ʌpər]. **I.** *adj.* obere(r,s); Ober-; **u. jaw**, Oberkiefer *m*; **the u. storeys**, die oberen Stockwerke; **u. part**, Oberteil *m, n*; **the u. classes**, (i) die Oberschicht (der Gesellschaft); (ii) *Sch:* die Oberklassen; *Fig:* **to get the u. hand**, die Oberhand gewinnen. **II.** *s. usu. pl.* Oberleder *n* (am Schuh). ◆**uppermost** ['ʌpəməust]. **I.** *adj.* oberste(r,s). **II.** *adv.* zuoberst. ◆**upright** ['ʌprait]. **I.** *adj.* **1.** aufrecht; (*vertical*) senkrecht; (*straight*) gerade. **2.** (*of conduct*) aufrichtig; (*of pers.*) rechtschaffen. **II.** *adv.* aufrecht. ◆**uprising** ['ʌpraiziŋ], *s.* Aufstand *m.* ◆**uproar** ['ʌprɔːr], *s.* Tumult *m*; **the town is in an u.**, die Stadt ist in Aufruhr. ◆**uproot** [ʌp'ruːt], *v.tr.* (einen Baum, *Fig:* j-n) entwurzeln; (eine Pflanze) ausreißen. ◆**upset. I.** ['ʌpset] *s.* **1.** Umkippen *n* (eines Wagens usw.); Kentern *n* (eines Bootes); (*of pers.*) seelische Erschütterung *f.* **2.** (*confusion*) Verwirrung *f.* **II.** [ʌp'set] *v.tr.irr.* (*a*) (*knock over*) umkippen; (*b*) (*destroy*) (die Gesellschaftsordnung) umstürzen; (j-s Pläne) vereiteln; (*c*) (*disturb*) (Verhältnisse, j-s Pläne) stören; (*d*) (*confuse*) (j-n) verwirren. **III.** *adj.* (*a*) (*of pers.*) aufgeregt; aus der Fassung; (*b*) he has an u. stomach, er hat einen verdorbenen Magen. ◆**upshot** ['ʌpʃɔt], *s.* Ausgang *m;* the u. was that..., der Endeffekt war, daß... ◆**upside down** ['ʌpsai(d)'daun], *adv. phr.* auf den Kopf gestellt; (*in a muddle*) drunter und drüber. ◆**upstairs** [ʌp'stɛəz]. **I.** *adv.* (*a*) (*position*) oben; (*b*) to go u., nach oben gehen. **II.** *adj.* (*of room*) im oberen Stockwerk. ◆**upstart** ['ʌpstɑːt], *s.* Emporkömmling *m.* ◆**upstream** ['ʌpstriːm], *adv.* stromaufwärts. ◆**uptake** ['ʌpteik], *s.* slow on the u., schwer von Begriff; to be quick on the u., schnell begreifen. ◆**uptight** [ʌp'tait], *adj. F:* (*tense*) nervös; (*angry*) sauer. ◆**up-to-date** [ʌptə'deit], *adj.* (*of pers., clothes etc.*) modern; (*of report, subject*) aktuell; (*of attitude*) zeitgemäß; (*of machine*) auf dem neuesten Stand; to be/ keep up-to-d., auf dem laufenden sein. ◆**upturn** ['ʌptəːn], *s.* Aufwärtsbewegung *f* (der Preise usw.); *Fig:* (*in fortune*) Aufschwung *m.* ◆**upward** ['ʌpwəd], *adj.* Aufwärts-; u. movement, Aufwärtsbewegung *f;* an u. tendency, eine steigende Tendenz. ◆**upwards** ['ʌpwədz], *adv.* **1.** aufwärts. **2.** (*facing u.*) nach oben. **3.** (*more*) mehr; a hundred pounds and u., hundert Pfund und mehr; from ten (years old) u., ab zehn Jahren.

**Urals** ['juərəlz]. *Pr. n.* the U., der Ural.
**uranium** [ju'reiniəm], *s.* Uran *n.*
**urban** ['əːbən], *adj.* städtisch, Stadt-. ◆**urbani'zation,** *s.* Verstädterung *f.*
**urbane** [əː'bein], *adj.* weltmännisch; (*smart*) elegant.
**urchin** ['əːtʃin], *s.* **1.** (*boy*) Gassenjunge *m.* **2.** *Z:* sea u., Seeigel *m.*
**urge** [əːdʒ]. **I.** *s.* Drang *m.* **II.** *v.tr.* (*a*) to u. s.o./a horse (on), j-n/ein Pferd vorwärts treiben/anspornen; (*b*) to u. s.o. to do sth., j-n drängen, etwas zu tun. ◆'**urgent,** *adj.* dringend. ◆'**urgency,** *s.* Dringlichkeit *f.*
**urinal** ['juərainəl], *s.* (*a*) Pissoir *n;* (*b*) (*for invalid*) Urinflasche *f.* ◆**urine** ['juərin], *s.* Urin *m,* Harn *m.* ◆'**urinate,** *v.i.* urinieren.
**urn** [əːn], *s.* (*a*) Vase *f;* (*burial*) u., Urne *f;* (*b*) tea u., Teemaschine *f.*
**us** [ʌs], *pers. pron.* uns; he sees us, er sieht uns; give us some, gib uns davon; there are three of us, wir sind drei.

**usable** ['juːzəbl], *adj.* brauchbar. ◆**usage** ['juːsidʒ], *s.* **1.** (*treatment*) Behandlung *f.* **2.** (*custom*) Brauch *m.* **3.** (*of language*) Sprachgebrauch *m;* (*of word*) Wortgebrauch *m.*
**use. I.** [juːs], *s.* **1.** Gebrauch *m;* (*for a particular purpose*) Verwendung *f;* (*application*) Anwendung *f* (von Gewalt usw.); I'll find a u. for it, ich werde es schon irgendwie verwenden können; to make u. of sth., Gebrauch von etwas *dat* machen; not in u., nicht in Gebrauch; (*of lift etc.*) außer Betrieb; ready for u., gebrauchsfertig; directions for u., Gebrauchsanweisung *f.* **2.** (*ability, right*) he has the u. of the garden, er darf den Garten benutzen. **3.** (*help*) Nutzen *m;* of u., nützlich; it's no u., es hat keinen Sinn; to have no u. for sth., mit etwas *dat* nichts anfangen können; I have no u. for him, für ihn habe ich nichts übrig; what's the u.? wozu (das)? **II.** [juːz] *v.tr.* (etwas) gebrauchen; (ein Gerät, einen Gegenstand) benutzen; (*for a purpose*) verwenden; (Zeit usw.) nutzen; to u. sth. (up), etwas aufbrauchen/verbrauchen; this car uses a lot of petrol, dieses Auto (ver)braucht viel Benzin. ◆**used¹** [juːzd], *adj.* gebraucht; u. car, Gebrauchtwagen *m;* hardly u., fast neu; u. up, (*of supplies*) verbraucht. ◆**used²** [juːst], *adj.* to be u. to sth., an etwas *acc* gewöhnt sein; etwas gewohnt sein; to get u. to sth., sich an etwas *acc* gewöhnen. **II.** *aux.* I used to do it, ich habe es früher immer getan. ◆**useful** ['juːsful] *adj.* (*a*) nützlich; (*of clothing*) praktisch; (*b*) (*usable*) verwendbar. ◆'**usefulness,** *s.* Nützlichkeit *f,* Verwendbarkeit *f.* ◆**useless** ['juːslis], *adj.* (*unusable*) (*of object*) unbrauchbar; (*of pers., actions*) unnütz; (*pointless*) sinnlos; (*of efforts*) vergeblich. ◆'**uselessness,** *s.* Nutzlosigkeit *f.* ◆**user** ['juːzər], *s.* Benutzer(in) *m(f).*
**usher** ['ʌʃər]. *s.* Platzanweiser *m.* ◆**ushe'rette,** *s.* Platzanweiserin *f.*
**usual** ['juːʒu(ə)l], *adj.* gewöhnlich; (*generally accepted*) üblich; it's the u. practice, das ist gang und gäbe; as u., wie immer; -ly, *adv.* gewöhnlich; meistens.
**usurper** [ju'zəːpər], *s.* Besitzergreifer *m;* (*of throne*) Thronräuber *m.*
**usury** ['juːʒuri], *s.* Wucher *m.*
**utensil** [ju(ː)'tens(i)l], *s.* (*a*) Gerät *n;* (*b*) (*tool*) Werkzeug *n.*
**uterus** ['juːtərəs], *s.* Gebärmutter *f.*
**utilitarian** [juːtili'tɛəriən]. **I.** *adj.* utilitär. **II.** *s.* Utilitarist *m.* ◆**utility** [ju'tiliti], *s.* (*a*) (*usefulness*) Nutzen *m; Com:* u. goods, Gebrauchsgegenstände *mpl;* (*b*) public u./*N.Am:* u., gemeinnütziges Unternehmen *n.* ◆**utilization** [-ai'zeiʃ(ə)n], *s.* Verwendung *f;* Nutzbarmachung *f* (des Bodens, *Fig:* von Talenten usw.); Verwertung *f* (von Rohstoffen usw.) ◆'**utilize** [-aiz], *v.tr.* (*a*) (etwas) verwenden; (*b*) (*exploit*) (den Boden, *Fig:*

Talente usw.) nutzbar machen; (Zeit, eine Gelegenheit) ausnutzen.
**utmost** ['ʌtməust]. **I.** *adj.* (*of care etc.*) äußerste(r,s); (*of need etc.*) größte(r,s); **it is of the u. importance that…**, es ist äußerst wichtig, daß… **II.** *s.* das Äußerste; **to the u. of one's ability,** nach be-

sten Kräften.
**utter¹** ['ʌtər], *adj.* vollkommen; **u. bliss,** die höchste Seligkeit; **u. nonsense,** völliger Unsinn; **-ly,** *adv.* völlig. ◆'**uttermost,** *adj.* äußerste(r,s).
**utter²,** *v.tr.* (ein Wort, Gefühle, Gedanken) äußern, aussprechen.

# V

**V, v** [viː], *s.* (der Buchstabe) V, v *n; Cl:* **V neck,** V-Ausschnitt *m.*
**vacant** ['veik(ə)nt], *adj.* (a) (*empty*) leer; (*not occupied*) frei; (*of job*) offen; (b) *Fig:* (*of expression etc.*) geistlos. ◆'**vacancy,** *s.* 1. (*emptiness*) Leere *f.* 2. (a) (*on boarding house*) 'v.', Zimmer frei; (b) (*job*) offene Stelle *f.* ◆**vacate** [və'keit], *v.tr.* (a) (eine Stelle usw.) aufgeben; (b) (ein Zimmer usw.) räumen. ◆**va'cation,** *s.* (a) *Sch:* Ferien *fpl;* (b) *esp. N.Am:* Urlaub *m.*
**vaccinate** ['væksineit], *v.tr.* (j-n) impfen. ◆**vacci'nation,** *s.* Schutzimpfung *f.*
**vacuum** ['vækjuəm], *s. Ph: & Fig:* Vakuum *n; v.* **cleaner,** Staubsauger *m; v.* **flask,** Thermosflasche *f.*
**vagina** [və'dʒainə], *s.* Scheide *f.*
**vagrant** ['veigrənt], Landstreicher *m.*
**vague** [veig], *adj.* vage; (*unclear*) unklar; **v. outlines,** verschwommene Umrisse; **I haven't the vaguest idea,** ich habe nicht die geringste Ahnung; **-ly,** *adv. esp. F:* vage. ◆'**vagueness,** *s.* Vagheit *f;* Unklarheit *f;* (*of pers. etc.*) vage Art.
**vain** [vein], *adj.* 1. (*of pers.*) eitel. 2. (*of effort etc.*) vergeblich. 3. **in v.** (*also* **-ly,** *adv.*), vergeblich.
**valentine** ['væləntain], *s.* (*card*) Valentinsgruß *m.*
**valiant** ['væljənt], *adj.* tapfer; (*in attack*) mutig; (*of effort etc.*) heldenhaft.
**valid** ['vælid], *adj.* gültig; (*of argument, reason*) stichhaltig. ◆**va'lidity,** *s.* Gültigkeit *f* (eines Dokuments); Stichhaltigkeit *f* (eines Arguments, eines Grundes).
**valley** ['væli], *s.* Tal *n.*
**value** ['væljuː]. **I.** *s.* (a) Wert *m; v.* **added tax,** Mehrwertsteuer *f;* (b) **this is good v.,** das ist preiswert; **to get good v. for** (one's) **money,** preiswert einkaufen. **II.** *v.tr.* schätzen. ◆'**valuable. I.** *adj.* wertvoll. **II.** *s.pl.* **valuables,** Wertgegenstände *mpl.* ◆**valu'ation,** *s.* 1. (*value*) Schätzwert *m.* 2. (*process*) Bewertung *f.* ◆'**valueless,** *adj.* wertlos. ◆'**valuer,** *s.* Schätzer *m.*
**valve** [vælv], *s.* 1. *Tchn:* Ventil *m;* (*cock*) Hahn *m.* 2. *Anat: & Mus:* Klappe *f* (des Herzens, eines Instruments usw.). 3. *Rad:* Röhre *f.*
**vampire** ['væmpaiər], *s.* Vampir *m.*
**van** [væn], *s.* 1. *Aut:* (**delivery**) **v.,** Lieferwagen. 2. *Rail:* Güterwagen *m;* (**luggage**) **v.,** Gepäckwagen *m.*

**vandal** ['vænd(ə)l], *s.* Vandale *m.*
◆'**vandalism,** *s.* Vandalismus *m.*
◆'**vandalize,** *v.tr.* mutwillig beschädigen.
**vanilla** [və'nilə], *s.* Vanille *f.*
**vanish** ['væniʃ], *v.i.* verschwinden; *F:* **v. into thin air,** spurlos verschwinden.
**vanity** ['væniti], *s.* Eitelkeit *f; v.* **case,** Kosmetikkoffer *m.*
**vantage** ['vɑːntidʒ], *s.* (a) (*in tennis*) Vorteil *m;* (b) **v. point,** Aussichtspunkt *m.*
**vaporize** ['veipəraiz], *v.* 1. *v.tr.* verdampfen lassen. 2. *v.i.* (*of liquid*) verdampfen.
◆'**vapour,** *s.* Dampf *m; Av:* **v. trail,** Kondensstreifen *m.*
**variable** ['vɛəriəbl], *adj.* (a) veränderlich; (*of weather, mood*) wechselhaft; (*of cost*) schwankend; (b) *Tchn:* (*adjustable*) verstellbar. ◆'**variance,** *s.* **to be at v. with s.o.,** mit j-m uneinig sein. ◆'**variant,** *s.* (*change*) Variante *f.* ◆**vari'ation,** *s.* (*change*) Schwankung *f; v.* **of/in temperature,** Temperaturschwankung *f.*
**varicose** ['værikəus], *adj.* **v. veins,** Krampfadern *fpl.*
**variety** [və'raiəti], *s.* 1. (a) (*richness*) Abwechslung *f;* (b) (*large number*) Vielzahl *f;* (*selection*) Auswahl *f.* 2. (*type*) Art *f;* (*variant*) Variante *f.* 3. *Th:* Varieté *n; v.* **show,** Varietévorstellung *f.*
**various** ['vɛəriəs], *adj.* verschieden; **for v. reasons,** aus verschiedenen Gründen.
**vary** ['vɛəri], *v.* 1. *v.tr.* abändern; *Mus:* (ein Thema usw.) variieren. 2. *v.i.* (a) (*of temperature etc.*) schwanken; (b) (*be different*) verschieden sein; (*disagree*) nicht übereinstimmen; **opinions v. on this,** da teilen sich die Meinungen. ◆'**varied,** *adj.* verschiedenartig; (*of work, career etc.*) abwechslungsreich. ◆'**varying,** *adj.* (a) (*different*) verschieden; (*of weight, degree etc.*) unterschiedlich; (b) (*inconstant*) veränderlich; **v. prices,** schwankende Preise.
**vase** [vɑːz], *s.* Vase *f.*
**vast** [vɑːst], *adj.* riesig; (*of plain etc.*) ausgedehnt.
**vat** [væt], *s.* Bottich *m;* (*barrel*) Faß *n.*
**Vatican** ['vætikən]. *Pr. n.* **the V.,** der Vatikan.
**vault¹** [vɔː(ː)lt], *s.* 1. (*roof*) Gewölbe *n.* 2. (*underground*) Kellergewölbe *n;* (*of bank*) Tresorraum *m;* **wine v.,** Weinkeller *m.*
◆'**vaulted,** *adj.* gewölbt.
**vault².** **I.** *s. Sp:* Sprung *m.* **II.** *v.tr. & i.*

**to v. (over) sth.**, über etwas *acc* springen.

**vaunt** [vɔːnt], *v.tr. Lit:* (etwas) rühmen.

**veal** [viːl], *s.* Kalbfleisch *n.*

**veer** ['viər], *v.i.* (*of wind*) sich drehen; (*of ship*) abdrehen.

**vegetable** ['vedʒ(i)təbl]. *s.* Gemüse *n;* **v. garden,** Gemüsegarten *m.* ◆**vege'tarian. I.** *adj.* vegetarisch. **II.** *s.* Vegetarier(in) *m(f).* ◆**'vegetate,** *v.i.* vegetieren. ◆**vege'tation,** *s.* Vegetation *f.*

**vehemence** ['viːəməns], *s.* Heftigkeit *f.* ◆**'vehement,** *adj.* heftig.

**vehicle** ['viːikl], *s.* **1.** Fahrzeug *n.* **2.** *Fig:* Mittel *n.*

**veil** [veil]. **I.** *s.* Schleier *m.* **II.** *v.tr.* (das Gesicht) verschleiern; *Fig:* (seine Gefühle usw.) verhüllen.

**vein** [vein], *s.* **1.** *Anat:* Vene *f.* **2.** *Bot:* Rippe *f.* **3.** (*a*) (*in marble, wood*) Maser *f;* (*b*) *Min:* Ader *f* (von Erz usw.); (*seam*) Flöz *n.* **4.** *Fig:* (*a*) Stimmung *f;* (*b*) **poetic v.,** poetische Ader.

**velocity** [vi'lositi], *s.* Geschwindigkeit *f.*

**velvet** ['velvit], *s.* Samt *m.*

**vendetta** [ven'detə], *s.* Blutrache *f.*

**veneer** [və'ni(ː)ər]. *s.* **1.** Furnier *n.* **2.** *Fig:* Anschein *m.*

**venerable** ['ven(ə)rəbl], *adj.* ehrwürdig. ◆**'venerate** [-əreit], *v.tr.* (j-n) verehren. ◆**vene'ration,** *s.* Verehrung *f.*

**venereal** [vi'niəriəl], *adj.* **v. disease** (*abbr. F:* **VD**), Geschlechtskrankheit *f.*

**Venetian** [vi'niːʃ(ə)n]. **I.** *adj.* venezianisch; **v. blind,** Jalousie *f.* **II.** *s.* Venezianer(in) *m(f).*

**Venezuela** [vene'zweilə]. *Pr. n.* Venezuela *n.* ◆**Vene'zuelan. I.** *adj.* venezolanisch. **II.** *s.* Venezolaner(in) *m(f).*

**vengeance** ['ven(d)ʒəns], *s.* Rache *f;* **to take v. on s.o.,** sich an j-m rächen.

**Venice** ['venis]. *Pr. n.* Venedig *n.*

**venison** ['venizn], *s.* Reh(fleisch) *n;* **roast v.,** Rehbraten *m.*

**venom** ['venəm], *s.* (*a*) Schlangengift *n;* (*b*) *Fig:* Giftigkeit *f.* ◆**'venomous,** *adj.* giftig.

**vent** [vent]. **I.** *s.* **1.** (*round*) Luftloch *n;* (*long*) Luftschlitz *m;* (*in barrel*) Spundloch *n.* **2.** *Cl:* Schlitz *m* (an einem Jackett usw). **II.** *v.tr.* **to v. one's anger on s.o.,** seinen Ärger an j-m auslassen.

**ventilate** ['ventileit], *v.tr.* (*a*) (ein Zimmer usw.) lüften; (*b*) *Fig:* (eine Beschwerde, eine Frage) zur Sprache bringen. ◆**venti'lation,** *s.* **1.** Lüftung *f* (eines Zimmers usw.); (*intake*) Belüftung *f;* (*extraction*) Entlüftung *f.* **2.** Erörterung *f* (einer Frage). ◆**'ventilator,** *s.* Ventilator *m.*

**ventriloquist** [ven'triləkwist], *s.* Bauchredner *m.*

**venture** ['ventʃər]. **I.** *s.* Unternehmen *n.* **II.** *v.* **1.** *v.tr.* (*a*) (etwas) wagen; (*b*) (sein Leben, Geld) riskieren. **2.** *v.i.* **to v. out of doors,** sich hinauswagen.

**venue** ['venjuː], *s.* (*meeting place*) Treffpunkt *m;* (*of conference*) Tagungsort *m; Sp: etc:* (*scene of event*) Schauplatz *m.*

**veranda(h)** [və'rændə], *s.* Veranda *f.*

**verb** [vəːb], *s.* Verb *n.* ◆**'verbal,** *adj.* **1.** *Gram:* verbal. **2.** (*oral*) mündlich. **3.** (*literal*) wörtlich.

**verbatim** [vəː'beitim]. **I.** *adj.* wörtlich. **II.** *adv.* Wort für Wort.

**verdict** ['vəːdikt], *s.* Urteil *n.*

**verge** [vəːdʒ]. **I.** *s.* (*a*) Rand *m;* Einfassung *f* (eines Blumenbeets); (*beside road*) (**grass**) **v.,** Grasstreifen *m;* (*b*) **on the v. of tears,** den Tränen nahe. **II.** *v.i.* **to v. on sth.,** an etwas *acc* grenzen.

**verger** ['vəːdʒər], *s. Ecc:* Kirchendiener *m.*

**verify** ['verifai], *v.tr.* überprüfen. ◆**verification** [-fi'keiʃ(ə)n], *s.* Nachprüfung *f.*

**vermicelli** [vəːmi'tʃeli], *s.* Fadennudeln *fpl.*

**vermin** ['vəːmin], *s.* Ungeziefer *n; Fig:* Abschaum *m.*

**vermouth** ['vəːməθ], *s.* Wermut *m.*

**versatile** ['vəːsətail], *adj.* (*of pers. etc.*) vielseitig. ◆**versa'tility,** *s.* Vielseitigkeit *f.*

**verse** [vəːs], *s.* **1.** (*unit*) Strophe *f;* (*in bible*) Vers *m.* **2.** (*a*) Verse *mpl;* (**lyric**) **v.,** Lyrik *f;* (*b*) (*metre*) Versmaß *n.*

**version** ['vəːʃ(ə)n], *s.* **1.** (*a*) Fassung *f* (eines Werkes usw.); (*b*) *F:* (*of a story*) Version *f.* **2.** *Ind:* (*model*) Ausführung *f.*

**versus** ['vəːsəs], *prep.* gegen + *acc.*

**vertebra,** *pl.* **-brae** ['vəːtibrə, -briː], *s.* Wirbel *m.*

**vertical** ['vəːtik(ə)l]. *adj.* senkrecht, vertikal; *Av:* **v. take-off aircraft,** Senkrechtstarter *m.*

**vertigo** ['vəːtigəu], *s.* Schwindel *m.*

**verve** [vəːv], *s.* Schwung *m.*

**very** ['veri]. **I.** *adj.* (*a*) (*exact*) genau; **you're the v. man!** du bist genau der Richtige! **the v. opposite,** genau das Gegenteil; **at that v. moment,** genau in dem Augenblick; (*b*) (*emphatic*) **at the v. beginning/end,** ganz am Anfang/Ende; **caught in the v. act,** auf frischer Tat ertappt; (*c*) (*mere*) **the v. thought** (of it), der bloße Gedanke (daran). **II.** *adv.* sehr; **v. good,** sehr gut; **at the v. latest,** spätestens.

**vespers** ['vespəz], *s.pl.* Vesper *f.*

**vessel** ['vesl], *s.* **1.** Schiff *n.* **2.** (*container*) Gefäß *n.*

**vest** [vest], *s.* **1.** Unterhemd *n.* **2.** *N.Am:* Weste *f.*

**vested** [vestid], *adj.* **v. rights/interests,** angestammte Rechte.

**vestige** ['vestidʒ], *s.* Spur *f.*

**vestments** ['vestmənts], *s. pl. Ecc:* Meßgewand *n.* ◆**'vestry,** *s.* Sakristei *f.*

**vet** [vet]. **I.** *s. F:* Tierarzt *m.* **II.** *v.tr. F:* (j-s Arbeit usw.) überprüfen.

**veteran** ['vet(ə)rən]. **I.** *s.* Veteran *m.* **II.** *adj.* (*of things*) uralt.

**veterinary** ['vetrənri], *adj.* tierärztlich.

**veto** ['vi:təu]. I. *s.* Veto *n.* II. *v.tr.* (et-was) verbieten, (*reject*) durch ein Veto zurückweisen.

**vex** [veks], *v.tr.* (j-n) irritieren, (*annoy*) ärgern. ◆**vex'ation**, *s.* Ärger *m.* ◆**'vexing**, *adj.* ärgerlich; (*troublesome*) lästig.

**via** ['vaiə], *prep.* über + *acc.*

**viable** ['vaiəbl], *adj. Biol:* lebensfähig; *Fig:* (*of project etc.*) durchführbar.

**viaduct** ['vaiədΛkt], *s.* Viadukt *m.*

**vibrate** [vai'breit], *v.i.* vibrieren; (*of tone, string*) schwingen; (*of voice*) beben. ◆**vi'bration**, *s.* Vibration *f; Ph:* Schwingung *f.*

**vicar** ['vikər], *s.* Pfarrer *m.* ◆**'vicarage**, *s.* Pfarrhaus *n.*

**vice¹** [vais], *s.* Laster *n.*

**vice²**, *s. Tls:* Schraubstock *m.*

**vice-³**, *prefix* Vize-; **v.-chairman**, stellvertretender Vorsitzender; **v.-president**, Vizepräsident *m.*

**vice versa** ['vaisi'və:sə], *adv. phr.* umgekehrt.

**vicinity** [vi'siniti], *s.* Nähe *f;* nähere Umgebung *f* (der Stadt usw.).

**vicious** ['viʃəs], *adj.* (*a*) bösartig; (*of attack, criticism etc.*) gemein; (*b*) **v. kick**, boshafter Fußtritt; (*c*) *Fig:* **v. circle**, Teufelskreis *m.*

**victim** ['viktim], *s.* Opfer *n.* ◆**victimi'zation**, *s.* Schikane *f.* ◆**'victimize**, *v.tr.* (j-n) schikanieren.

**victor** ['viktər], *s.* Sieger *m.* ◆**victorious** [vik'tɔ:riəs], *adj.* siegreich. ◆**'victory**, *s.* Sieg *m.*

**Victorian** [vik'tɔ:riən], *adj.* viktorianisch.

**video** ['vidiəu], *s.* **v. tape**, Videoband *n;* **v. tape recorder**, Videorecorder *m;* **v. cassette**, Videokassette *f.*

**vie** [vai], *v.i.* **to v. with s.o.**, mit j-m wetteifern.

**Vienna** [vi'enə]. *Pr. n.* Wien *n.* ◆**Viennese** [viə'ni:z]. I. *adj.* Wiener; (*in character*) wienerisch. II. *s.* (*pers.*) Wiener(in) *m(f).*

**view** [vju:]. I. *s.* **1.** (*a*) Besichtigung *f;* (*b*) **in v.**, in Sicht; **to come into v.**, sichtbar werden. **2.** (*scene*) Aussicht *f;* (*particular aspect*) Ansicht *f;* **views of the town**, Blicke *mpl* auf die Stadt; (*pictures*) Bilder *npl*/Ansichten *fpl* von der Stadt. **3.** *Fig:* (*a*) **point of v.**, Gesichtspunkt *m;* (*b*) **in v. of the fact that…**, angesichts der Tatsache, daß… **4.** (*opinon*) Ansicht *f;* **in my v.**, meiner Ansicht/Meinung nach. II. *v.tr.* (*a*) ansehen; (eine Ausstellung usw.) besichtigen; (*b*) *Fig:* (j-n, etwas) betrachten (**as**, als). ◆**'viewer**, *s.* **1.** (*pers.*) Betrachter *m; TV:* Fernsehzuschauer *m.* **2.** *Phot:* Diabetrachter *m.* ◆**'viewfinder**, *s. Phot:* Sucher *m.* ◆**'viewpoint**, *s.* Gesichtspunkt *m.*

**vigilance** ['vidʒiləns], *s.* Wachsamkeit *f.* ◆**'vigilant**, *adj.* wachsam.

**vigour** ['vigər], *s.* Energie *f;* Vitalität *f; Fig:* Nachdruck *m.* ◆**'vigorous**, *adj.*

energisch.

**vile** ['vail], *adj.* **1.** (*of pers.*) widerwärtig. **2.** *F:* (*of weather, temper etc.*) scheußlich.

**villa** ['vilə], *s.* Villa *f.*

**village** ['vilidʒ], *s.* Dorf *n.* ◆**'villager**, *s.* Dorfbewohner(in) *m(f).*

**villain** ['vilən], *s.* Schurke *m.*

**vindicate** ['vindikeit], *v.tr.* (*a*) (j-n, Handlungen usw.) rechtfertigen; (*b*) (einen Anspruch) geltend machen.

**vindictive** [vin'diktiv], *adj.* (*vengeful*) rachsüchtig; (*unforgiving*) nachtragend.

**vine** [vain], *s.* Weinstock *m;* **v. grower**, Winzer *m;* **v. growing**, Weinbau *m.* ◆**vineyard** ['vinjəd], *s.* (*on hill*) Weinberg *m;* (*on flat*) Weingarten *m.*

**vinegar** ['vinigər], *s.* Essig *m.*

**vintage** ['vintidʒ], *s.* **1.** Weinlese *f;* (*crop*) Weinernte *f.* **2.** (*year*) Jahrgang *m;* **v. wine**, Qualitätswein *m.* **3.** **v. car**, Oldtimer *m.*

**viola** [vi'əulə], *s.* Bratsche *f.*

**violate** ['vaiəleit], *v.tr.* (*a*) (eine Regel) verletzen; (ein Gesetz) übertreten; (*b*) (*rape*) vergewaltigen. ◆**vio'lation**, *s.* (*a*) Verletzung *f;* Übertretung *f;* (*b*) Vergewaltigung *f.* ◆**'violence** ['vaiələns], *s.* **1.** (*action*) Gewalt *f.* **2.** (*quality*) Heftigkeit *f* (einer Reaktion, des Windes usw.). ◆**'violent**, *adj.* (*a*) heftig, stark; **v. temper**, tobend vor Wut; (*b*) (*of act, pers.*) gewaltsam.

**violet** ['vaiələt]. I. *s.* **1.** Veilchen *n.* **2.** (*colour*) Violett *n.* II. *adj.* violett.

**violin** [vaiə'lin], *s.* Violine *f,* Geige *f.* ◆**vio'linist**, *s.* Geiger(in) *m(f).*

**viper** ['vaipər], *s.* Giftschlange *f.*

**virgin** ['və:dʒin]. I. *s.* Jungfrau *f.* II. *adj.* jungfräulich; *Fig:* unberührt. ◆**vir'ginity**, *s.* Jungfräulichkeit *f.*

**Virgo** ['və:gəu], *s. Astr:* Jungfrau *f.*

**virile** ['virail], *adj.* (*a*) (*sexually*) viril; (*b*) robust; (*manly*) männlich. ◆**vi'rility**, *s.* (*a*) Virilität *f;* (*b*) Männlichkeit *f;* Robustheit *f.*

**virtual** ['və:tjuəl], *adj.* eigentlich; praktisch; **this was a v. confession**, das war praktisch ein Geständnis; **-ly**, *adv.* praktisch; (*nearly*) beinahe.

**virtue** ['və:tju:], *s.* **1.** Tugend *f.* **2.** *prep. phr.* **by v. of**, auf Grund + *gen.* ◆**'virtuous**, *adj.* tugendhaft; (*in character*) rechtschaffen.

**virtuoso**, *pl.* **-os** [və:tju'əuzəu, -əuz], *s.* Virtuose *m,* Virtuosin *f.*

**virulent** ['virjulənt], *adj. Med:* bösartig.

**virus** ['vaiərəs], *s.* Virus *m.*

**visa** ['vi:zə], *s.* Visum *n.*

**vis-à-vis** ['vi:za:'vi:]. *prep.* gegenüber + *dat.*

**viscount** ['vaikaunt], *s.* Vicomte *m.*

**visible** ['vizəbl, -ibl], *adj.* sichtbar. ◆**visi'bility**, *s.* (*a*) Sichtbarkeit *f;* (*b*) Sichtverhältnisse *npl.* ◆**vision** ['viʒ(ə)n], *s.* **1.** (*a*) Sehkraft *f* (eines Auges); **field of v.**, Blickfeld *n;* (*b*) *Fig:* **a man of v.**, ein Mann mit Weitblick. **2.**

(a) Traumbild n; (b) Ecc: etc: Vision f; **to see visions,** Visionen haben.

**visit** ['vizit]. **I.** s. Besuch m (**to,** in + dat); (stay) Aufenthalt m; **on a v.,** zu/auf Besuch; **to pay s.o. a v.,** j-n besuchen. **II.** v.tr. besuchen; (seek out) (j-n) aufsuchen. ◆**'visiting. I.** adj. zu/auf Besuch; Gast-; **v. professor,** Gastprofessor m. **II.** s. Besuchen n; **v. card,** Visitenkarte f. ◆**'visitor,** s. Besucher m (**to,** gen); (to house, restaurant) Gast m (**to,** in + dat); **she's got visitors,** sie hat Besuch; **visitors' book,** Gästebuch n.

**vista** ['vistə], s. Aussicht f.

**visual** ['vizju(ə)l, 'viʒ-], adj. visuell; Sch: **v. aids,** Anschauungsmaterial n. ◆**'visualize,** v.tr. **to v. s.o., sth.,** sich dat j-n, etwas vorstellen; **I can't v. it,** ich kann mir davon kein Bild machen.

**vital** ['vait(ə)l], adj. **1.** (essential) lebenswichtig. **2.** (full of life) vital. ◆**vitality** [-'tæliti], s. Vitalität f.

**vitamin** ['vitəmin, vait-], s. Vitamin n.

**vitiate** ['viʃieit], v.tr. (etwas) beeinträchtigen; (Argumente) hinfällig machen.

**vivacious** [vi'veiʃəs], adj. lebhaft. ◆**vi'vaciousness, vivacity** [-'væsiti], s. Lebhaftigkeit f.

**vivid** ['vivid], adj. (a) (bright) hell, leuchtend; **v. colours,** leuchtende Farben; (b) (clear) deutlich; (c) (lively) (of description etc.) lebhaft; (of picture) lebendig; **v. imagination,** rege Phantasie. ◆**'vividness,** s. Lebhaftigkeit f; Lebendigkeit f.

**vivisection** [vivi'sekʃ(ə)n], s. Vivisektion f.

**vizor** ['vaizər], s. **1.** Visier n. **2.** Aut: & Cl: (on cap) Blende m.

**vocabulary** [və'kæbjuləri], s. Wortschatz m; (list) Wörterverzeichnis n.

**vocal** ['vəuk(ə)l], adj. Stimm-, Gesang-; Anat: **v. cords,** Stimmbänder npl.

**vocation** [və(u)'keiʃ(ə)n], s. (a) (calling) Berufung f (**for,** zu + dat); (b) (aptitude) Begabung f (**for,** für + acc); (c) (profession) Beruf m. ◆**vo'cational,** adj. Berufs-; **v. guidance,** Berufsberatung f.

**vociferate** [və'sifəreit], v.i. (of pers.) schreien. ◆**vo'ciferous,** adj. lautstark.

**vogue** [vəug], s. Mode f; **to be in v.,** Mode sein.

**voice** [vɔis]. **I.** s. (a) Stimme f; **in a low v.,** mit leiser Stimme; **with one v.,** einstimmig; (b) Gram: **active/passive v.,** Aktiv n/Passiv n; **II.** v.tr. (eine Meinung, Zweifel usw.) äußern. ◆**voiced,** adj. stimmhaft.

**void** [vɔid]. **I.** adj. **1.** (empty) leer. **2.** Jur: **null and v.,** null und nichtig. **3. v. of,**

ohne + acc. **II.** s. Leere f.

**volatile** ['vɔlətail], adj. **1.** Ch: flüchtig. **2.** (of pers.) (excitable) überschäumend; (inconstant) flatterhaft.

**volcano,** pl. **-oes** [vɔl'keinəu, -əuz], s. Vulkan m. ◆**volcanic** [-'kænik], adj. vulkanisch.

**volition** [və'liʃ(ə)n], s. Willenskraft f; **of one's own v.,** aus freien Stücken.

**volley** ['vɔli], s. (a) Mil: Geschützsalve f; (b) Sp: Flugball m, Volley n. ◆**'volleyball,** s. Volleyball m.

**volt** [vəult], s. Volt n. ◆**'voltage,** s. Spannung f.

**voluble** ['vɔljubl], adj. redselig.

**volume** ['vɔlju:m], s. **1.** (book) Band m. **2.** (quantity) **the v. of exports,** das Ausfuhrvolumen. **3.** (measure) Ph: etc: Volumen n; Rauminhalt m. **4.** (loudness) Lautstärke f; **to turn up the v. of the radio,** das Radio lauter stellen.

**voluntary** ['vɔlənt(ə)ri]. adj. freiwillig. ◆**volunteer** [vɔlən'ti:ər]. **I.** s. Mil: Freiwillige(r) m. **II.** v.i. sich freiwillig melden (**for sth.,** zu etwas dat).

**voluptuous** [və'lʌptjuəs], adj. (of thoughts, pleasures etc.) wollüstig.

**vomit** ['vɔmit]. **I.** s. Erbrochenes n. **II.** v. **1.** v.tr. erbrechen. **2.** v.i. sich übergeben. ◆**'vomiting,** s. Erbrechen n.

**voracious** [və'reiʃəs], adj. gierig; **v. appetite,** unersättlicher Appetit.

**vote** [vəut]. **I.** s. (a) Abstimmung f; (b) (individual) Stimme f; **to have the/a v.,** das Stimmrecht haben. **II.** v.tr. & i. wählen; **to v. for s.o., s.th.,** für j-n, etwas stimmen. ◆**'voter,** s. Wähler m. ◆**'voting,** s. Abstimmung f; (at election) Wählen n.

**vouch** [vautʃ], v.i. **to v. for s.o./for the truth of sth.,** für j-n/für die Wahrheit von etwas dat bürgen. ◆**'voucher,** s. Gutschein m.

**vow** [vau]. **I.** s. Gelübde n. **II.** v.tr. geloben.

**vowel** ['vauəl], s. Vokal m; **v. sound,** Vokallaut m.

**voyage** ['vɔiidʒ]. s. Seereise f. ◆**'voyager,** s. Seereisende(r) f (m).

**vulgar** ['vʌlgər], adj. vulgär; (of language, pers.) ordinär. ◆**'vul'garity,** s. Gewöhnlichkeit f; **to lapse into v.,** ins Ordinäre verfallen.

**vulnerable** ['vʌln(ə)rəbl], adj. (leicht) verletzbar; Fig: anfällig (**to sth.,** für etwas acc). ◆**vulnera'bility,** s. Verletzbarkeit f; Fig: Anfälligkeit f (**to,** für + acc).

**vulture** ['vʌltʃər], s. Geier m.

# W

**W, w** ['dʌblju:], s. (der Buchstabe) W, w n.

**wad** [wɔd], s. (a) (ball) Ball m; Knäuel n (Papier); (pad) Polster n; **w. of cotton wool**, Wattebausch m; (b) **w. of (bank)notes**, Bündel n Banknoten.

**waddle** ['wɔdl], v.i. watscheln.

**wade** [weid], v.i. (durch einen Bach usw.) waten.

**wafer** ['weifər], s. **1.** (biscuit) Waffel f. **2.** Ecc: Hostie f.

**waft** [wɑ:ft], v.tr. & i. **a scent (was) wafted into the room**, ein Duft wehte ins Zimmer.

**wag** [wæg], v.tr. **the dog wagged its tail**, der Hund wedelte mit dem Schwanz.

**wage¹** [weidʒ], s. (sing. or pl.) Lohn m; **w. earner**, Lohnempfänger m; **w. packet**, Lohntüte f; **w. freeze**, Lohnstopp m.

**wage²**, v.tr. **to w. war/a campaign**, Krieg/einen Feldzug führen.

**wager** ['weidʒər]. **I.** v.i. wetten. **II.** s. Wette f.

**waggle** ['wægl], v.tr. **to w. its tail**, mit dem Schwanz wedeln.

**wag(g)on** ['wæg(ə)n], s. **1.** (cart) Pferdewagen m. **2.** Rail: **(goods) w.**, Güterwagen m.

**wail** [weil]. **I.** v.i. (a) (of child, siren etc.) heulen; (b) (lament) klagen. **II.** s. (a) Heulen n; (b) Klage f.

**waist** [weist], s. (of pers., dress) Taille f. ◆**'waistcoat**, s. Weste f. ◆**'waistline**, s. Taille f; **to watch one's w.**, auf die Linie achten.

**wait** [weit]. **I.** v.i. (a) warten; **to w. for s.o., sth.**, auf j-n, etwas acc warten; **w. and see!** nur Geduld! (threat) **just you w.!** warte nur! (b) **to w. (at table)**, (bei Tisch) bedienen. **II.** s. Wartezeit f. ◆**'waiter**, s. Kellner m; (calling) **w.!** Herr Ober! ◆**'waiting**, s. **w. list**, Warteliste f; **w. room**, (at doctor's etc.) Wartezimmer n; Rail: Wartesaal m. ◆**'waitress**, s. Kellnerin f; (calling) **w.!** Fräulein!

**waive** [weiv], v.tr. **to w. a claim/one's rights**, auf einen Anspruch/seine Rechte verzichten.

**wake¹** [weik], v.irr. **1.** v.i. **to w. (up)**, aufwachen. **2.** v.tr. **to w. s.o. (up)**, j-n wecken. ◆**'waken**, v. **1.** v.i. aufwachen; Fig: erwachen. **2.** v.tr. (a) (j-n) wecken; (b) (Gefühle usw.) wecken; (Erinnerungen) wachrufen.

**wake²**, s. (a) Nau: Kielwasser n; (b) Fig: **in the w. of the storm**, unmittelbar nach dem Sturm; (c) (for dead) Totenwache f.

**walk** [wɔ:k]. **I.** v.i. **1.** v.i. gehen; (for pleasure) spazierengehen; (longer distances) wandern. **2.** v.tr. **to w. a dog**, einen Hund spazierenführen. **II.** s. Weg m; **it's an hour's w. from here**, von hier aus geht man eine Stunde zu Fuß. **2.** Spaziergang m; **to go for a w.**, spazierengehen. **3.** (gait) Gang m. **4.** (in garden etc.) Spazierweg m. **5. people from all walks of life**, Angehörige pl aller Gesellschaftsschichten. ◆**'walker**, s. Spaziergänger m; (hiker) Wanderer m. ◆**'walkie-'talkie**, s. tragbares Funksprechgerät n, Walkie-talkie n. ◆**'walking**, s. Gehen n; Laufen n; (for pleasure) Spazierengehen n; (hiking) Wandern n; **w. stick**, Spazierstock m. ◆**'walkout**, s. Ind: spontane Arbeitsniederlegung f. ◆**'walk 'over**, v.i. **to w. o. to s.o.**, zu j-m hinübergehen. ◆**'walkover**, s. Sp: leichter Sieg m.

**wall** [wɔ:l]. **I.** s. (a) Mauer f; (b) (of building, room) Wand f. **II.** v.tr. **to w. sth. (in)**, etwas ummauern. ◆**'wallflower**, s. (a) Bot: Goldlack m; (b) F: (at dance) **to be a w.**, Mauerblümchen spielen. ◆**'wallpaper**, s. Tapete f.

**wallet** ['wɔlit], s. Brieftasche f.

**wallow** ['wɔləu]. v.i. (a) (of animal) **to w. in the mud**, sich im Schlamm wälzen; (b) (of pers.) Fig: **to w. in sentiment etc.**, in Gefühlen usw. schwelgen.

**walnut** ['wɔ:lnʌt], s. (a) Walnuß f; (b) (tree) Nußbaum m; (c) (wood) Nußbaumholz n.

**walrus** ['wɔ:lrəs], s. Walroß n.

**waltz** [wɔ:l(t)s]. **I.** s. Walzer m. **II.** v.i. Walzer tanzen.

**wan** [wɔn], s. (a) (of pers., face) bleich; (b) (of light, sky) fahl.

**wand** [wɔnd], s. **(magic) w.**, Zauberstab m.

**wander** ['wɔndər], v.i. wandern; **to w. about**, herumschweifen; (stray) irren; **to w. from the subject**, vom Thema abschweifen. ◆**'wanderer**, s. Wanderer m. ◆**'wandering**. **I.** adj. wandernd. **II.** s. Wandern n.

**wane** [wein], v.i. abnehmen; (of interest etc.) nachlassen; (of beauty) schwinden.

**want** [wɔnt]. **I.** v.tr. (a) (desire) (etwas) wollen, wünschen; **he wants a bike for Christmas**, er wünscht sich ein Fahrrad zu Weihnachten; **you're wanted (on the phone)**, Sie werden (am Telefon) verlangt; (b) **to w. to do sth.**, etwas tun wollen; **he wants me to go with him**, er will, daß ich mitgehe; (c) (need) (j-n, etwas) brauchen; **have you got everything you w.?** haben Sie alles, was Sie brauchen? (d) (seek) (eine Stelle, einen Verbrecher) suchen; **cook wanted**, Koch/ Köchin gesucht. **II.** s. **1.** (lack) Mangel m (**of**, an + dat.); **for w. of anything better**, mangels eines Besseren. **2.** (poverty) Not f; **to be in w.**, Not leiden. **3.** (need) Bedürfnis n; (desire) Wunsch m. ◆**'wanting**, adj. **he is w. in intelli-**

gence, tact etc., es fehlt ihm an Intelligenz, Takt usw.

**wanton** ['wɔntən], *adj.* 1. (*wilful*) **w. destruction,** mutwillige Zerstörung. 2. (*unchaste*) unkeusch.

**war** [wɔːr], *s.* Krieg *m;* **to make w. on s.o.,** gegen j-n Krieg führen. ◆'**warfare,** *s.* Kriegführung *f.* ◆'**warhead,** *s.* Sprengkopf *m;* **nuclear w.,** Atomsprengkopf *m.*

**warble** ['wɔːbl]. I. *v.i.* (*of bird*) trillern. II. *s.* Triller *m.* ◆'**warbler,** *s.* Grasmücke *f.*

**ward** [wɔːd]. I. *s.* 1. *Jur:* Mündel *n.* 2. (*in hospital*) Station *f;* **w. sister,** Stationsschwester *f.* II. *v.tr.* **to w. off a blow, a danger etc.,** einen Schlag, eine Gefahr usw. abwehren. ◆'**warden,** *s.* Aufseher *m;* Leiter *m* (eines Studentenheims); (*of youth hostel*) Herbergsvater *m;* (*female*) Herbergsmutter *f;* **traffic w.,** (*male*) Verkehrspolizist *m;* (*female*) Politesse *f.* ◆'**warder/'wardress,** *s.* Gefängniswärter(in) *m(f).* ◆'**wardrobe,** *s.* 1. Kleiderschrank *m.* 2. (*clothes*) Garderobe *f.*

**ware** [wɛər], *s.* Waren *fpl;* (*china etc.*) Geschirr *n.* ◆'**warehouse,** *s.* Lager.

**warm** [wɔːm]. I. *adj.* warm; **I am w.,** mir ist warm; **to give s.o. a w. welcome/reception,** j-m einen warmen/herzlichen Empfang bereiten. II. *v.* 1. *v.tr.* (ein Zimmer, eine Flüssigkeit usw.) wärmen, (*gradually*) erwärmen. 2. *v.i.* sich erwärmen; **-ly,** *adv.* 1. **w. dressed,** warm angezogen. 2. **to thank s.o. w.,** j-m herzlich danken. ◆'**warm'hearted,** *adj.* warmherzig. ◆'**warmth,** *s.* 1. Wärme *f.* 2. (*cordiality*) Herzlichkeit *f* (eines Empfanges usw.). ◆'**warm 'up,** *v.* 1. *v.tr.* (etwas) erwärmen; (Speisen) aufwärmen. 2. *v.i.* warm werden; (*of engine*) warmlaufen.

**warn** [wɔːn], *v.tr.* (j-n) warnen (**of/against,** vor + *dat*). ◆'**warning.** I. *adj.* warnend; **w. light,** Warnlicht *n.* II. *s.* Warnung *f;* **to arrive without w.,** unangemeldet kommen.

**warp** [wɔːp], *v.i.* (*of wood*) sich verziehen. ◆'**warped,** *adj.* 1. (*of wood*) verzogen. 2. (*of mind, humour etc.*) verdreht.

**warrant** ['wɔrənt]. *s.* (*order*) Befehl *m;* (*authority*) Vollmacht *f;* *Jur:* **w. of arrest,** Haftbefehl *m.* ◆'**warranty,** *s. Com:* Garantie *f.*

**warren** ['wɔrən], *s.* (**rabbit**) **w.,** Kaninchenbau *m.*

**warrior** ['wɔriər], *s.* Krieger *m.*

**Warsaw** ['wɔːsɔː]. *Pr. n.* Warschau *n.*

**wart** [wɔːt], *s.* Warze *f.*

**wary** ['wɛəri], *adj.* vorsichtig; **to be w. of doing sth.,** sich hüten, etwas zu tun; **-ily,** *adv.* vorsichtig; **to tread w.,** behutsam vorgehen.

**wash** [wɔʃ]. I. *v.* 1. *v.tr.* (*a*) (etwas) waschen; **to w. oneself,** sich waschen; **to w. one's hands/hair,** sich *dat* die Hände/Haare waschen; (*b*) (*of sea*) (Felsen) um-

spülen. 2. *v.i.* (*of pers.*) sich waschen. II. *s.* (*a*) (*of pers.*) **to have a w.,** sich waschen; **to give sth. a w.,** etwas waschen; (*b*) (*dirty clothes etc.*) Wäsche *f.* ◆'**washable,** *adj.* waschbar. ◆'**wash a'way,** *v.tr.* (etwas) wegspülen. ◆'**wash-basin,** *N.Am:* '**washbowl,** *s.* Waschbecken *n.* ◆'**washcloth,** *s. N.Am:* Waschlappen *m.* ◆'**washer¹,** *s.* 1. (*pers.*) **w. up,** Tellerwäscher *m.* 2. *Aut:* (**windscreen**/*N.Am:* **windshield**) **w.,** Scheibenwaschanlage *f.* ◆'**washing,** *s.* 1. Waschen *n.* 2. (*a*) Wäsche *f;* **dirty w.,** Schmutzwäsche *f;* **w. machine,** Waschmaschine *f* (eine Flasche usw.) ausspülen. ◆'**washout,** *s. F:* (*of event etc.*) Pleite *f;* (*of pers.*) Niete *f.* ◆'**washroom,** *s.* Waschraum *m.* ◆'**washstand,** *s.* Waschtisch *m.* ◆'**wash 'up,** *v.* 1. *v.tr.* (*a*) (das Geschirr usw.) abwaschen; (*b*) (*of sea*) (etwas) an Land spülen. 2. *v.i.* abwaschen.

*(b)* Aut: **w. bay,** Waschanlage *f.* 3. **w.-up,** Abwasch *m;* **to do the w.-up,** den Abwasch machen. ◆'**wash-leather,** *s.* Waschleder *n.* ◆'**wash 'out,** *v.tr.* (*a*) (*remove*) (einen Fleck usw.) auswaschen; (*b*) (*rinse*) (eine Flasche usw.) ausspülen. *(abové inline — reordered)*

**washer²,** *Tchn:* Dichtungsring *m.*

**wasp** [wɔsp], *s.* Wespe *f.*

**waste** [weist]. I. *v.* 1. *v.tr.* (Geld usw.) verschwenden; (seine Kräfte usw.) vergeuden (**on,** an + *acc*). 2. *v.i.* (*of pers.*) **to w. away,** dahinschwinden, (*die*) dahinsiechen. II. *adj.* 1. **w. land/ground,** wüstes/unbebautes Gelände. 2. Abfall-; **w. paper,** Altpapier *n;* **w. paper basket,** Papierkorb *m.* III. *s.* 1. Verschwendung *f* (von Geld, Licht usw.); **w. of time/space,** Zeit/Platzvergeudung *f.* 2. (*rubbish*) Abfälle *mpl;* **w. disposal unit,** (*chute*) Müllschlucker *m;* (*in sink*) Abfallzerkleinerer *m.* 3. *usu. pl.* (*deserted land*) Einöde *f.* ◆'**wastage,** *s.* Verschwendung *f.* ◆'**wasteful,** *adj.* (*of pers.*) verschwenderisch; (*of methods etc.*) unwirtschaftlich.

**watch** [wɔtʃ]. I. *s.* 1. (*also Nau:*) Wache *f;* **to be on the w. for s.o., sth.,** nach j-m, etwas *dat* Ausschau halten; **to keep w. over s.o., sth.,** auf/j-n, etwas *acc* aufpassen. 2. (*for time*) Uhr *f.* II. *v.* 1. *v.tr.* (*a*) (j-n, etwas) beobachten; **to w. s.o. do sth.,** beobachten, wie j-d etwas macht; **to w. television,** fernsehen; (*b*) **could you w. the baby for a moment?** würdest du einen Moment auf das Baby aufpassen? *F:* **w. your step! w. it!** paß auf! Vorsicht! 2. *v.i.* (*a*) **to w.** (**out**) **for s.o., sth.,** nach j-m, etwas *dat* ausschauen; (*wait*) j-n, etwas abwarten; (*b*) (*take care*) **to w. out,** aufpassen; **w. out!** Vorsicht! paß auf! ◆'**watchdog,** *s.* Wachhund *m.* ◆'**watchful,** *adj.* wachsam. ◆'**watchmaker,** *s.* Uhrmacher *m.* ◆'**watchman,** *s.* Wächter *m;* **night w.,** Nachtwächter *m.*

**water** ['wɔːtər]. **I.** s. Wasser n; pl **waters**, Gewässer npl (eines Sees, eines Flusses usw.); **w. level**, Wasserstand m; **w. lily**, Seerose f; **w. melon**, Wassermelone f; **w. polo**, Wasserball m; **w. skiing**, Wasserski n. **II.** v. **1.** v.tr. (a) (die Blumen, den Garten usw.) gießen; (of river etc.) (eine Landschaft) bewässern; (b) to **w. sth. down**, etwas verwässern; (c) (Tiere) tränken. **2.** v.i. (a) (of eyes) tränen; (b) **my mouth watered**, das Wasser lief mir im Mund zusammen. ◆**'water-colour**, s. **1.** (paint) Wasserfarbe f. **2.** (painting) Aquarell n. ◆**'watercress**, s. Brunnenkresse f. ◆**'waterfall**, s. Wasserfall m. ◆**'waterhole**, s. Wasserstelle f (in den Tropen). ◆**'watering**, s. Gießen n (der Blumen usw.); **w. can**, Gießkanne f. ◆**'waterline**, s. Wasserlinie f (eines Schiffes). ◆**'waterlogged**, adj. (of boat) voll Wasser; (of ground, wood) (von Wasser) durchtränkt. ◆**'waterproof. I.** adj. wasserdicht. **II.** v.tr. (etwas) imprägnieren. ◆**'watershed**, s. (a) Geog: Wasserscheide f; (b) Fig: Wendepunkt m. ◆**'watertight**, adj. (a) wasserdicht; (b) Fig: (of argument etc.) stichhaltig. ◆**'waterworks**, s. Wasserwerk n. ◆**'watery**, adj. wässerig.

**watt** [wɔt], s. Watt n.

**wave** [weiv]. **I.** s. **1.** (also Ph: & Fig:) Welle f; **permanent w.**, Dauerwelle f. **2.** Winken n; **to give s.o. a w.**, j-m mit der Hand (zu)winken. **II.** v. **1.** v.i. (a) (of flag etc.) wehen; (b) **to w. to s.o.**, j-m zuwinken; (c) (of hair) sich wellen. **2.** v.tr. (die Arme, eine Fahne usw.) schwenken; **to w. one's hand**, mit der Hand winken; **to w. goodbye to s.o.**, j-m zum Abschied zuwinken. ◆**'wavelength**, s. Rad: & Fig: Wellenlänge f. ◆**'wavy**, adj. wellig; gewellt.

**waver** ['weivər], v.i. (a) (of flame etc.) flackern; (b) (of pers.) schwanken; (of courage) wanken.

**wax¹** [wæks]. **I.** s. Wachs n; **ear w.**, Ohrenschmalz m. **II.** v.tr. wachsen. ◆**'waxwork**, s. Wachsfigur f; **waxworks**, Wachsfigurenkabinett n. ◆**'waxy**, adj. (a) (pale) wachsbleich; (b) (waxlike) wachsartig.

**wax²**, v.i. (of moon) zunehmen.

**way** [wei], s. **1.** (path) **Weg** m; (road) Straße f; **over/across the w.**, gegenüber; **which is the best w. to the station?** wie kommt man am besten zum Bahnhof? **to lose one's w.**, sich verirren; **to go the wrong w.**, (i) (on foot) sich verlaufen; (ii) (in car etc.) sich verfahren; **to find one's w.**, den Weg finden; **to know one's w. about**, sich auskennen; **on the w.**, unterwegs (**to**, nach + dat); **on the w. home/to school**, auf dem Heimweg/Schulweg; **to go out of one's w.**, einen Umweg machen; Fig: **to go out of one's w. to help s.o.**, sich dat besondere Mühe geben, j-m zu helfen; (of village etc.) **out of the w.**,

abgelegen; **by the w.**, übrigens; **w. in**, Eingang m; **w. out**, Ausgang m; **it's a long w. (from here)**, es liegt weit weg/ weit entfernt (von hier); **all the w.**, den ganzen Weg; **to be in s.o.'s w.**, j-m im Wege stehen; **to keep out of s.o.'s w.**, j-m aus dem Wege gehen; **to make w. for s.o.**, j-m Platz machen; **give w.!** Vorfahrt beachten! **2.** (direction) (a) Richtung f; **which w. are you going?** in welche Richtung gehen Sie? (b) **the wrong w. round**, verkehrt herum; (of photograph etc.) seitenverkehrt; **the other w. round**, anders herum. **3.** (manner) Weise f; Art f; **in this w.**, auf diese Weise; so; **is this the w. to do it?** macht man es so? **no w.!** ganz ausgeschlossen! **to get one's own w.**, seinen Willen durchsetzen; **if I had my w.**, wenn es nach mir ginge; (respect) **in many ways**, in vieler Hinsicht. **4.** **what have you got in the w. of drinks?** was haben Sie an Getränken? **5.** (motion) Fahrt f; **under w.**, (of ship) in Fahrt; (of work) im Gange. ◆**'way'lay**, v.tr.irr. (j-m) auflauern. ◆**'wayward**, adj. (capricious) launenhaft; (self-willed) eigensinnig.

**we** [wiː], pers. pron. wir.

**weak** [wiːk], adj. schwach. ◆**'weaken**, v. **1.** v.tr. (j-n, etwas) schwächen; (j-n, ein Argument) entkräften. **2.** v.i. schwach/schwächer werden; (of power, influence etc.) nachlassen. ◆**'weakling**, s. Schwächling m. ◆**'weakly. I.** adv. schwach. **II.** adj. kränklich. ◆**'weakness**, s. Schwäche f; Unzulänglichkeit f (einer Leistung).

**wealth** [welθ], s. **1.** Reichtum m. **2. a w. of material/ideas**, eine Fülle von Material/Anregungen. ◆**'wealthy**, adj. reich, wohlhabend.

**wean** [wiːn], v.tr. entwöhnen.

**weapon** ['wepən], s. Waffe f.

**wear** [weər]. **I.** v.irr. **1.** v.tr. (einen Hut, ein Kleid, eine Brille) tragen; **what shall I w.?** was soll ich anziehen? **2.** v.i. (a) (of tyres etc.) sich abnutzen; (b) (of material etc.) **to w. well**, strapazierfähig sein; **these shoes have worn well**, diese Schuhe haben gut gehalten. **II.** s. **1.** (clothes) **men's w.**, Herrenkleidung f. **2.** (a) **there's still a lot of w. in this dress**, dieses Kleid läßt sich noch lange tragen; (b) Abnutzung f; Tchn: Verschleiß m; **fair w. and tear**, (normale) Abnutzung. ◆**'wear a'way**, v. **1.** v.tr. (etwas) abnutzen; (Farbe) abtragen; (eine Inschrift usw.) wegwischen. **2.** v.i. abgenutzt werden; (of steps) ausgetreten werden; (of rocks etc.) ausgewaschen werden. ◆**'wear 'down**, v. **1.** v.tr. (a) (etwas) abnutzen; (Absätze) abtreten; (b) **to w. d. s.o.'s resistance**, j-n zermürben. **2.** v.i. abgenutzt werden; (of heels) abgetreten werden. ◆**'wearer**, s. Träger(in) m(f) (eines Mantels usw.). ◆**'wearing**, adj. (of thing) ermüdend; (of pers.) an-

strengend. ◆'wear 'off, v. 1. v.tr. (etwas) abtragen. 2. v.i. (a) abgetragen werden; (of pile etc.) sich abwetzen; (b) (of
effect etc.) nachlassen; **the novelty will
soon w. o.,** der Reiz der Neuheit wird
sich bald verlieren. ◆'wear 'out, v. 1.
v.i. (of things) abgenutzt werden. 2. v.tr.
(a) (etwas) abnutzen; (Kleider) abtragen;
(b) **to w. oneself o.,** sich erschöpfen.
**weary** ['wiəri]. I. adj. müde (of
sth., + gen); w. of life, lebensmüde. II.
v. 1. v.tr. (j-n) ermüden. 2. v.i. **to w. of
sth.,** etwas gen müde/überdrüssig werden. ◆'weariness, s. Müdigkeit f.
◆'wearisome, 'wearying, adj. ermüdend; (tedious) langweilig.
**weasel** ['wi:z(ə)l], s. Wiesel n.
**weather** ['weðər]. I. s. Wetter n; **w. forecast,** Wettervorhersage f; F: (of pers.)
**under the w.,** unpäßlich; nicht ganz auf
der Höhe. II. v. 1. v.tr. (a) (Holz) austrocknen; (b) **to w. a storm,** (of ship)
einen Sturm abwettern; Fig: (of pers.)
eine Krise überstehen. 2. v.i. (of stone
etc.) verwittern. ◆'weatherbeaten,
adj. (of building etc.)
vom Wetter angegriffen; (of face) ver-
wittert. ◆'weathercock, s. Wetterhahn
m.
**weave** [wi:v], v.irr. 1. v.tr. (a) (Stoff) weben; (b) (Körbe usw.) flechten; (c) (of
pers., river etc.) sich winden. 2. v.i. (a)
weben; (b) F: **get weaving!** mach dich
dran! ◆'weaver, s. Weber m.
◆'weaving, s. Weberei f.
**web** [web], s. 1. spider's w., Spinnennetz
n; Fig: Gewebe n. 2. Z: (of webbed foot)
Schwimmhaut f; (of bat's wing) Flughaut
f. ◆'webbed, adj. Z: w. foot,
Schwimmfuß m. ◆'webbing, s. Cl:
Gurt m.
**wed** [wed], v. 1. v.tr. Lit: (a) (j-n) heiraten; (b) (of priest) (ein Brautpaar) trauen.
2. v.i. (of pers.) heiraten. ◆'wedding,
s. (a) Hochzeit f; (ceremony) Trauung f;
**silver/golden w.,** silberne/goldene Hochzeit; (b) attrib. Hochzeits-; **w. day,**
Hochzeitstag m; **w. ring,** Trauring m.
**wedge** [wedʒ], s. 1. Keil m. 2. a w. of
cake, ein Stück Kuchen. 3. w. heel,
Keilabsatz m. II. v.tr. **to w. sth. into
sth.,** etwas in etwas acc hineinzwängen;
**wedged in position,** festgeklemmt.
**Wednesday** ['wenzdi], s. Mittwoch m.
**wee** [wi:], adj. esp. Scot: klein.
**weed** [wi:d]. I. s. Unkraut n. II. v.i. Unkraut jäten. ◆'weedkiller, s. Unkraut-
vertilgungsmittel n. ◆'weedy, adj. 1.
(of garden) von Unkraut bewachsen. 2.
(of pers.) schmächtig.
**week** [wi:k], s. 1. Woche f; once a w., einmal in der Woche; **a w. from now/today
w.,** heute in acht Tagen. ◆'weekday,
s. Wochentag m. ◆'weekend, s. Wochenende n. ◆'weekly. I. adj. & adv.
wöchentlich; **w. wage,** Wochenlohn m.
II. s. (newspaper) Wochenzeitung f.

**weep** [wi:p]. I. v.i.irr. weinen (over/
about, über + acc). II. s. **to have a good
w.,** sich ausweinen.
**weigh** [wei], v. 1. v.tr. (a) wiegen; (b)
Nau: to w. anchor, den Anker lichten.
2. v.i. **how much do you w.?** wieviel
wiegen Sie? ◆'weighbridge, s. Brük-
kenwaage f. ◆'weigh 'down, v.tr. (etwas) niederdrücken. ◆'weight, s. (a)
Gewicht n; (of pers.) **to lose w.,** abnehmen; **to gain/put on w.,** zunehmen; (b)
(burden) Last f; Fig: **that's a great w. off
my mind,** damit ist mir ein Stein vom
Herzen gefallen. ◆'weightlessness, s.
Schwerelosigkeit f. ◆'weight-'lifter, s.
Gewichtheber m. ◆'weighty, adj.
schwer; Fig: (of reason etc.) schwerwie-
gend. ◆'weight-'watcher, s. Linienbe-
wußte(r) f(m). ◆'weigh 'up, v.tr. **to w.
up advantages and disadvantages,** Vor-
und Nachteile abwägen; **to w. s.o. up,**
j-n abschätzen.
**weir** ['wiər], s. Wehr n.
**weird** ['wiəd], adj. (a) (uncanny) unheimlich; (b) (strange) seltsam; (of pers.) verschroben; F: komisch.
**welcome** ['welkəm]. I. adj. (a) willkommen; **to make s.o. w.,** j-n freundlich aufnehmen; (b) int. **w.!** herzlich willkommen! **thank you – you're w.!** vielen
Dank – nichts zu danken! II. s. **to give
s.o. a warm/hearty w.,** j-n freundlich/
herzlich aufnehmen. III. v.tr. (j-n) willkommen heißen.
**weld** [weld]. I. v.tr. schweißen; **welded
seam,** Schweißnaht f. II. s. Schweißstelle
f. ◆'welder, s. Schweißer m.
◆'welding, s. Schweißen n.
**welfare** ['welfeər], s. (of state etc.) Wohl-
fahrt f; (of pers.) Wohlergehen n; (social)
**w.,** öffentliche Fürsorge; **the W. State,**
der Wohlfahrtsstaat.
**well**[1] [wel], s. 1. Brunnen m. 2. **oil w.,**
Ölquelle f.
**well**[2]. I. adv. 1. (a) gut; **to behave w.,**
sich gut benehmen; **you would do w. to
forget about it,** am besten vergißt du
das; **to wish s.o. w.,** j-m alles Gute wünschen; (b) **to think w. of s.o.,** j-n schätzen. 2. (a) **you may w. laugh,** du hast
gut lachen; (b) **we might (just) as w.
have stayed at home,** wir hätten ebenso-
gut zu Hause bleiben können. 3. (intensifying) he's w. over fifty, er ist weit über
fünfzig. 4. **as w.,** auch. 5. **w. off,**
gut dran; (rich) wohlhabend. II. adj. 1.
(healthy) gesund; **I'm not w.,** es geht
mir nicht gut. 2. **all is w.,** es ist alles in
Ordnung. III. int. **w! w. I never!**
na, so was! (oh) **w., it can't be helped,**
na ja, das ist nun mal so. ◆'well-
ad'vised, adj. (of pers.) **you would be
w.-a. to forget this,** es wäre ratsam, das
zu vergessen. ◆'well-be'haved, adj.
artig. ◆'well-'being, s. Wohlergehen
n (eines Einzelnen); Wohl n (der Familie,
des Staates usw.); **a feeling of w.-b.,** ein

Wohlgefühl n. ◆**'well-'bred**, adj. gut erzogen. ◆**'well-'known**, adj. bekannt. ◆**'well-'read**, adj. (of pers.) belesen. ◆**'well-'timed**, adj. it was w.-t., es geschah gerade im richtigen Augenblick. ◆**'well-to-'do**, adj. wohlhabend. ◆**'well-wisher**, s. Wohlgesinnte(r) f(m).

**wellington** ['weliŋtən], s. w. boots/wellingtons/F: wellies, Gummistiefel mpl.

**Welsh** [welʃ]. I. adj. walisisch; Cu: W. rabbit/rarebit, überbackener Käsetoast m. II. s. (a) the W., die Waliser; (b) (language) Walisisch. ◆**'Welshman**, s. Waliser m. ◆**'Welshwoman**, s. Waliserin f.

**west** [west]. I. s. Westen m; to the w. (of), westlich + gen/(with names) von+II. adj. West-; the w. coast, die Westküste; W. Indian, (a) adj. westindisch; (b) s. Westinder(in) m(f). III. adv. the room faces w., das Zimmer geht nach Westen. ◆**'westerly**, adj. in a w. direction, in westlicher Richtung. ◆**'western**. I. adj. westlich; W. Europe, Westeuropa n. II. s. F: Cin: Western m. ◆**'westwards**, adv. nach Westen.

**wet** [wet]. I. adj. (a) naß; w. paint, frisch gestrichen; (b) w. weather, Regenwetter n; F: (pers.) a w. blanket, ein Spielverderber. II. v.tr. (etwas) naß machen. ◆**'wetness**, s. Nässe f. ◆**'wet-suit**, s. Kälteschutzanzug m (für Taucher).

**whack** [wæk]. I. v.tr. F: (a) to w. s.o., (thrash) j-n verprügeln; (hit) j-m eine langen; (b) Sp: (seine Gegner) in die Pfanne hauen. II. s. Schlag m. ◆**'whacking**, s. to give s.o. a w., j-m eine Tracht Prügel verabreichen.

**whale** [weil], s. 1. Wal m. 2. F: we had a w. of a time, wir hatten einen Mordsspaß. ◆**'whaling**, s. Walfang m. ◆**'whaler**, s. (pers., ship) Walfänger m.

**wharf** pl. -ves ['wɔːf -vz], s. Kai m.

**what** [wɔt]. I. adj. welche(r, s); he gave me w. money he had, er gab mir alles, was er an Geld hatte; w. size do you take? welche Größe haben Sie? w. good/use is it? wozu dient es/ist es gut? w. sort of (an) animal is that? was ist das für ein Tier? w. an idea! was für eine Idee! w. a lovely picture! welch ein schönes Bild! II. pron. was. w. I have just said ..., das, was ich eben gesagt habe ...; w. are you doing here? was machst du denn hier? what's his name? wie heißt er? w. is the weather like? wie ist das Wetter? w. about a cup of tea? wie wär's mit einer Tasse Tee? w. about you? wie steht's mit Ihnen? well, w. about it? ja, und? w. if it rains? was geschieht, wenn es regnet? w. did you say? wie bitte? w. with? womit? w. on? worauf? over w.? worüber? w. for? (purpose) wozu? (reason) wieso? warum? F: so w.? na, und? ◆**what'ever**. I. pron. w. happens, was auch geschieht; w. hap-

pened to Susan? was in aller Welt ist aus Susan geworden? II. adj. w. price they are asking, welchen Preis sie auch immer verlangen; no hope w., gar/überhaupt keine Hoffnung; is there any hope w.? gibt es überhaupt noch Hoffnung?

**wheat** [wiːt], s. Weizen m.

**wheedle** ['wiːdl], v.tr. to w. sth. out of s.o., j-m etwas abschmeicheln.

**wheel** [wiːl]. I. s. (a) Rad n; Nau: Steuerrad n; Aut: (steering) w., Lenkrad n; at the w., am Steuer; (b) potter's w., Töpferscheibe f. II. v. 1. v.tr. (ein Fahrrad, eine Karre usw.) schieben. 2. v.i. (a) (of bird) kreisen; (b) (of pers.) to w. round, sich jäh umdrehen. ◆**'wheelbarrow**, s. Schubkarre(n) f(m). ◆**'wheelchair**, s. Rollstuhl m.

**wheeze** [wiːz]. I. v.i. pfeifend atmen. II. s. pfeifender Atemzug m. ◆**'wheezy**, adj. (of breath) pfeifend; (of pers.) asthmatisch.

**when** [wen]. I. adv. 1. interrog. wann? 2. rel. the days w. the shops are closed, die Tage, an denen die Geschäfte geschlossen sind; the time w. ..., die Zeit, wo ... II. conj. 1. (in the past) als; w. he saw her, als er sie sah. 2. (whenever) wenn; we always had fun w. he came, wir hatten immer viel Spaß, wenn er kam. 3. (future) I find it I'll let you know, sobald ich es finde, sage ich dir Bescheid. ◆**when'ever**, adv. (a) (any time that) wann immer; (b) (each time that) immer wenn.

**where** [wɛər], adv. 1. interrog. wo? w. (to)? wohin? w. from? woher? w. do you live? wo wohnen Sie? w. are you going? wohin gehen Sie? w. do you come from? woher kommen Sie? 2. rel. wo; (direction) wohin; (at the place) w. it happened, an der Stelle/dort, wo es passiert ist; he doesn't know w. to go, er weiß nicht, wohin er gehen soll. ◆**whereabouts**. I. [wɛərə'bauts] interrog. adv. w. do you live? wo wohnen Sie? II. ['wɛər-] s. Aufenthaltsort m. ◆**where'as**, conj. während. ◆**wher'ever**, adv. w. he is, wo (immer) er auch ist. w. you go you see them, überall, wo man hinkommt, sieht man sie.

**whet** [wet], v.tr. Fig: to w. the appetite, den Appetit anregen.

**whether** ['weðər], conj. ob.

**which** [witʃ], adj. & pron. 1. interrog. welche(r, s); w. have you chosen? welche/welchen/welches hast du gewählt? 2. rel. (a) der, die, das; the house w. is for sale, das Haus, das zu verkaufen ist; (b) (with prep.) about w., worüber; for w., wofür; (c) (referring to a clause) was; I have lost my money, w. is very annoying, ich habe mein Geld verloren, was sehr ärgerlich ist. ◆**which'ever**, adj. & pron. welche(r,s) auch; take w. book you like, nehmen Sie sich welches Buch Sie wollen.

**whiff** [wif]. *s.* (leichter) Hauch *m*; *(scent)* Duft *m*; *(smell)* Geruch *m.*

**while** [wail]. **I.** *s.* **1.** Weile *f*; **for a w.,** eine Zeitlang; **once in a w.,** hin und wieder. **2. it's not worth your w.,** es ist nicht der Mühe wert; es lohnt sich nicht (für Sie). **II.** *conj.* *(time)* während.

**whim** [wim], *s.* Laune *f.* ◆**'whimsical,** *adj.* *(of pers.)* launenhaft; *(of ideas)* schrullig.

**whimper** ['wimpər]. **I.** *v.i.* wimmern; *(esp. of dog)* winseln. **II.** *s.* Wimmern *n*; Winseln *n.*

**whine** [wain]. **I.** *v.i.* *(of engine etc.)* heulen; *(complain)* (wehleidig) jammern; *(of child)* quengeln; *(of dog)* jaulen. **II.** *s.* *(also 'whining)* Geheul *n*; Gejammer *n*; Quengelei *f*; Jaulen *n.*

**whip** [wip]. **I.** *v.tr.* (*a*) (j-n, ein Pferd) peitschen; (*b*) *Cu:* (Sahne usw.) schlagen; **whipped cream,** Schlagsahne *f*; (*c*) **he whipped the revolver out of his pocket,** er riß die Pistole aus der Tasche. **II.** *s.* **1.** Peitsche *f.* **2.** *Parl:* *(pers.)* Einpeitscher *m.* ◆**'whip 'round. I.** *v.i.* sich blitzartig umdrehen. **II.** *s.* *F:* **to have a quick 'w.-r.,** den Hut herumgehen lassen. ◆**'whip 'up,** *v.tr.* (Leidenschaften) aufpeitschen.

**whirl** [wə:l]. **I.** *v.tr. & i.* (herum)wirbeln. **II.** *s.* Wirbel *m.* ◆**'whirlpool,** *s.* Wasserstrudel *m.* ◆**'whirlwind,** *s.* Wirbelwind *m.*

**whirr** [wə:r]. **I.** *s.* Schwirren *n* (der Flügel); Brummen *n* (einer Maschine); Surren *n* (eines Propellers). **II.** *v.i.* schwirren; *(of machinery etc.)* brummen; *(of propeller etc.)* surren.

**whisk** [wisk]. **I.** *v.tr.* (Eiweiß, Sahne) schlagen. **II.** *s.* *Cu:* Schneebesen *m.*

**whisker** ['wiskər], *s.* Schnurrhaar *n* (einer Katze usw.); *F:* *(of pers.)* **whiskers,** Backenbart *m.*

**whisk(e)y** ['wiski], *s.* Whisky *m.*

**whisper** ['wispər]. **I.** *s.* Flüstern *n.* **II.** *v.tr. & i.* flüstern (to s.o., mit j-m).

**whist** [wist], *s.* Whist *n*; **w. drive,** Whistturnier *n.*

**whistle** ['wisl]. **I.** *s.* **1.** *(sound)* Pfeifen *n*; *(single)* Pfiff *m.* **2.** *(instrument)* Pfeife *f.* **II.** *v.tr. & i.* pfeifen.

**white** [wait]. **I.** *adj.* (*a*) weiß; **w. coffee,** Milchkaffee *m*; **w. horse,** Schimmel *m*; a **w. man,** ein Weißer; (*b*) *(pale)* **w. face,** ein bleiches/blasses Gesicht; (*c*) *Fig:* **w. lie,** Notlüge *f.* **II. 1.** Weiß *n*; **dressed (all) in w.,** (ganz) in Weiß gekleidet; (ganz) weiß angezogen. **2.** *(pers.)* Weiße(r) *f(m).* **3.** *Cu:* **w. of egg,** Eiweiß *n.* ◆**'whitebait,** *s.* Breitling *m.* ◆**'white-'collar,** *adj.* **w.-c. worker,** Büroangestellte(r) *f(m).* ◆**'whiten,** *v.tr.* (etwas) weiß machen; *(whitewash)* (eine Mauer usw.) weißen; *(bleach)* (Kleider usw.) bleichen. ◆**'whiteness,** *s.* **1.** Weiße *f.* **2.** *(pallor)* Blässe *f.* ◆**'whitewash. I.** *s.* Tünche *f.* **II.** *v.tr.*

(*a*) (eine Mauer usw.) weißen; (*b*) *Fig:* (j-n) (von einer Anschuldigung) reinwaschen.

**whiting** ['waitiŋ], *s.* Merlan *m.*

**Whitsun(tide)** ['witsən(taid)], *s.* Pfingsten *n.*

**whittle** ['witl], *v.tr.* (*a*) **to w. away,** (Ersparnisse usw.) allmählich aufzehren; (*b*) **to w. down,** (etwas) stark reduzieren.

**whizz** [wiz], *v.i.* sausen; **to w. past,** vorbeisausen; *(of bullet etc.)* vorbeizischen; **to w. along,** dahinflitzen. ◆**'whizzkid,** *s.* *F:* Senkrechtstarter *m.*

**who** [hu:], *nom. pron.* **1.** *interrog.* wer? **2.** *rel.* der, die, das; **the friend w. came yesterday,** der Freund, der gestern gekommen ist. ◆**who'dunit,** *s.* *F:* Krimi *m.* ◆**who'ever,** *pron.* wer (auch) immer; **w. finds it may keep it,** wer es findet, darf es behalten.

**whole** [həul]. **I.** *adj.* ganz. **II.** *s.* **the w.,** das Ganze; **to form a w.,** ein Ganzes/eine Einheit bilden; **on the w.,** im großen und ganzen. ◆**'whole-'hearted,** *adj.* aufrichtig; **w. support,** rückhaltlose Unterstützung; **-ly,** *adv.* von ganzem Herzen; **I agree w.,** ich bin ganz Ihrer Meinung. ◆**'wholemeal,** *adj.* **w. bread,** Vollkornbrot *n.* ◆**'wholesale. I.** *adj. Com:* **1.** Großhandels- **2. w. slaughter,** Massenmord *m.* **II.** *adv.* im Großhandel, en gros. ◆**'wholesaler,** *s.* Großhändler *m.* ◆**'wholly,** *adv.* *(entirely)* ganz völlig.

**wholesome** ['həulsəm], *adj.* gesund; *(of food, drink)* bekömmlich.

**whom** [hu:m], *pron.* **1.** *interrog. acc* wen; *dat* wem; **w. did you see?** wen haben Sie gesehen? **of w. ...?** von wem/*(whose)* wessen ...? **2.** *rel. acc.* den, die, das; *dat* dem, der; *pl* denen; **the man w. you saw,** der Mann, den du gesehen hast; **the friend to w. I lent the book,** der Freund, dem ich das Buch geliehen habe; **of w.,** von dem/*pl.* denen; *(whose)* dessen, *pl.* denen.

**whoop** [hu:p] *v.i.* keuchen. ◆**'whooping cough,** *s.* Keuchhusten *m.*

**whopper** ['wɔpər], *s.* *P:* Mordsding *n*; *(giant)* Riese *m.* ◆**'whopping,** *adj.* *P:* enorm; **w. lie,** faustdicke Lüge.

**whore** [hɔ:r]. **I.** *s.* Hure *f.* **II.** *v.i.* huren.

**whose** [hu:z], *poss. pron.* **1.** *interrog.* wessen? **w. daughter are you?** wessen Tochter bist du? **2.** *rel.* dessen; *pl. & f* deren; **the pupil about w. work I complained,** der Schüler, über dessen Arbeit ich mich beklagt habe.

**why** [wai]. **I.** *adv.* warum; **the reason w.** (he came), der Grund (, weshalb er gekommen ist). **II.** *int.* **w., of course!** aber natürlich!

**wick** [wik], *s.* Docht *m.*

**wicked** ['wikid], *adj.* (*a*) *(of pers., intentions)* böse; *(of remarks)* boshaft; (*b*) *(of child)* schlimm. ◆**'wickedness,** *s.* Bosheit *f*.

**wicker** ['wikər], *s*. w. (work), Flechtwerk *n*; (*articles*) Korbwaren *fpl*.

**wicket** ['wikit], *s*. 1. Pförtchen *n*. 2. (*in cricket*) Dreistab *m*; Tor *n*; w. keeper, Torhüter *m*.

**wide** [waid]. I. *adj*. 1. (*of river, road*) breit; how w. is the room? welche Breite hat das Zimmer? 2. (*extensive*) weit; the w. world, die weite Welt; *Fig*: w. experience, reiche Erfahrung; w. reading, große Belesenheit. II. *adv*. weit; w. apart, weit auseinander; far and w., weit und breit; open w.! weit aufmachen! w. awake, hellwach; -ly, *adv*. weit; w. known, weit und breit bekannt; he has travelled w., er ist ein weit gereister Mann. ◆'wide-'angle, *adj*. w.-a. lens, Weitwinkelobjektiv *n*. ◆'widen, *v*. 1. *v.tr*. (*a*) (etwas) breiter machen; (eine Straße) verbreitern; (*b*) (ein Loch) ausweiten; (*c*) *Fig*: to w. one's horizons, seinen Gesichtskreis erweitern. 2. *v.i*. breiter werden. ◆'widespread, *adj*. weitverbreitet. ◆width [widθ], *s*. Breite *f*.

**widow** ['widəu], *s*. Witwe *f*. ◆'widowed, *adj*. verwitwet. ◆'widower, *s*. Witwer *m*.

**wield** [wi:ld], *v.tr*. (ein Schwert usw.) handhaben.

**wife**, *pl*. **wives** [waif, waivz], *s*. Frau *f*; (*formal*) Gattin *f*.

**wig** [wig], *s*. Perücke *f*.

**wiggle** ['wigl], *v*. 1. *v.i*. (*a*) (*of path etc.*) sich schlängeln; (*b*) (*move*) wackeln. 2. *v.tr*. to w. one's toes, hips, etc., mit den Zehen, Hüften usw. wackeln.

**wigwam** ['wigwæm], *s*. Wigwam *m*.

**wild** [waild]. I. *adj*. (*a*) wild; (*of plants*) to grow w., wild wachsen; (*b*) (*of wind*) heftig; a w. night, eine stürmische Nacht; (*c*) (*untamed*) ungezähmt; w. animals, wilde Tiere; (*d*) (*of pers.*) ausgelassen; it makes me w., das macht mich wild/wütend; (*of girl*) w. about s.o., verrückt nach j-m; (*e*) (*of idea etc.*) verrückt. II. *s*. (*a*) in the w., in der Natur; (*b*) *pl* the wilds, die Wildnis; -ly, *adv*. wild; (*at random*) aufs Geratewohl. ◆'wildcat, *adj*. *Ind*: w. strike, wilder Streik. ◆wilderness ['wildənis], *s*. Wildnis *f*; (*desert*) Wüste *f*. ◆'wildfire, *s*. to spread like w., sich wie ein Lauffeuer verbreiten. ◆'wildfowl, *s*. Wildvögel *mpl*. ◆'wild 'goose, *s*. Wildgans *f*; *F*: w.-g. chase, nutzloses Unterfangen. ◆'wildlife, *s*. Tiere *npl* (in der freien Natur); w. sanctuary, Tierschutzgebiet *n*. ◆'wildness, *s*. Wildheit *f*; Toben *n* (eines Sturmes); Unsinnigkeit *f* (der Ideen, des Geredes).

**wilful** ['wilful], *adj*. 1. (*of pers.*) eigensinnig. 2. (*intentional*) absichtlich.

**will** [wil]. I. *s*. 1. *a* (*a*) Wille *m*; strength of w., Willensstärke *f*; (*b*) (*desire*) Wunsch *m*; of one's own free w., aus freien

Stücken. 2. *Jur*: Testament *n*; to leave s.o. sth. in one's w., j-m etwas testamentarisch vermachen. II. *modal aux. v*. (*a*) (*want*) wollen; the engine won't start, der Motor will nicht anspringen; (*b*) (*future*) werden; I w./F: I'll come, ich werde kommen. ◆'willing, *adj*. to be w., to do sth., bereit sein, etwas zu tun; -ly, *adv*. bereitwillig; I would w. go, but ..., ich würde gerne hingehen, aber ... ◆'willingness, *s*. Bereitschaft *f* (etwas zu tun). ◆'willpower, *s*. Willenskraft *f*.

**willow** ['wiləu], *s*. w. (tree), Weide *f*.

**wilt** [wilt], *v.i*. (*a*) (*of plant*) verwelken; (*b*) (*of pers.*) schlapp werden.

**wily** ['waili], *adj*. listig; *F*: gerissen.

**win** [win]. I. *v.tr. & i.irr*. gewinnen. II. *s*. Sieg *m*. ◆'winner, *s*. Gewinner(in) *m(f)*; *Sp*: Sieger(in) *m(f)*. ◆'winning. I. *adj*. 1. (*of pers., team*) siegreich; (*in lottery etc.*) w. number, Gewinnnummer *f*. 2. (*of pers.*) w. ways, anziehendes Wesen. II. *s*. 1. Sieg *m*; w. post, Ziel *n*. 2. *pl* winnings, Gewinn *m* (beim Spiel, Toto usw.). ◆'win 'over, *v.tr*. (j-n) für sich *acc* gewinnen. ◆'win 'through, *v.i*. to w. t. in the end, sich am Ende durchsetzen.

**wince** [wins]. I. *v.i*. (vor Schmerz) zusammenzucken; (*make a face*) das Gesicht verziehen (at, bei + *dat*). II. *s*. Zusammenzucken *n*.

**winch** [wintʃ], *s*. Winde *f*.

**wind**[1] [wind]. I. *s*. 1. Wind *m*; to get w. of sth., etwas wittern; to put the w. up s.o., j-m angst und bange machen. 2. (*a*) (*breath*) Atem *m*; to get one's second w., wieder zu Atem kommen; (*b*) (*flatulence*) Blähungen *fpl*. 3. *Mus*: w. instrument, Blasinstrument *n*. II. *v.tr*. it winded me, es hat mir den Atem verschlagen. ◆'windbreak, *s*. Windschutz *m*. ◆'windcheater, *s*. Windjacke *f*. ◆'windfall, *s*. 1. (*fruit*) windfalls, Fallobst *n*. 2. *Fig*: unverhoffter Gewinn. ◆'windless, *adj*. windstill. ◆'windmill, *s*. Windmühle *f*. ◆'windpipe, *s*. Luftröhre *f*. ◆'windscreen/*N.Am*: 'windshield, *s*. *Aut*: Windschutzscheibe *f*; w. wiper, Scheibenwischer *m*. ◆'windswept, *adj*. dem Wind ausgesetzt; (*of sea etc.*) windgepeitscht. ◆'windward, *adj*. Wind-/*Nau*: Luv-. ◆'windy, *adj*. windig; (*of day, weather*) stürmisch.

**wind**[2] [waind]. I. *v.irr*. 1. *v.i*. sich winden. 2. *v.tr*. (*a*) (etwas) winden (round sth., um etwas *acc*); to w. wool into a ball, Wolle zu einem Knäuel wickeln; (*b*) (eine Uhr) aufziehen. II. *s*. Windung *f*; (*single bend*) Biegung *f*. ◆'winding. I. *adj*. sich schlängelnd; (*of road*) kurvenreich; w. staircase, Wendeltreppe *f*. II. *s*. Aufziehen *n* (einer Uhr). ◆'wind 'up, *v*. 1. *v.tr*. (*a*) (ein Seil usw.) aufwinden; (Garn) aufwickeln; (eine Uhr) aufziehen; (*b*) (*finish*) (eine Rede usw.)

schließen; *Com:* (eine Firma) liquidieren.
**2.** *v.i.* enden.
**windlass** ['windləs], *s.* Winde *f; Nau:* Ankerspill *n.*
**window** ['windəu], *s.* (*a*) Fenster *n;* w. pane, Fensterscheibe *f;* w. ledge/sill, Fenstersims *n;* (*internal*) Fensterbrett *n;* w. box, Blumenkasten *m;* (*b*) (shop) w., Schaufenster *n;* w. shopping, Schaufensterbummel *m.*
**wine** [wain], *s.* Wein *m;* w. production, Weinbau *m;* w. cellar, Weinkeller *m;* w. list, Weinkarte; w. merchant, Weinhändler *m;* w. tasting, Weinprobe *f;* w. waiter, Weinkellner *m.* ◆'**wineglass**, *s.* Weinglas *n.*
**wing** [wiŋ], *s.* (*a*) Flügel *m;* (*b*) *Th:* the wings, die Kulissen *fpl;* (*c*) *Fb: etc:* (*pers.*) Außenstürmer *m.*
**wink** [wiŋk]. **I.** *s.* Wink *m* (mit den Augen); with a w., mit einem Zwinkern; *F:* to have forty winks, ein Nickerchen machen. **II.** *v.i.* (*a*) (*of pers.*) zwinkern; to w. at s.o., j-m zuzwinkern; (*b*) (*of light*) blinken. ◆'**winking**, *s.* Zwinkern *n.*
**winkle** ['wiŋkl], *s.* Strandschnecke *f.*
**winter** ['wintər]. **I.** *s.* Winter *m;* w. clothes, Winterkleidung *f;* w. sports, Wintersport *m.* **II.** *v.i.* überwintern. ◆'**wintry**, *adj.* winterlich.
**wipe** [waip]. **I.** *v.tr.* (etwas) wischen; (eine Fläche) abwischen; to w. sth. clean/dry, etwas sauberwischen/abtrocknen. **II.** *s.* Wischen *n;* give it a w.! wisch es ein bißchen ab! ◆'**wiper**, *s. Aut:* (windscreen/*N.Am:* windshield) w., Scheibenwischer *m.* ◆'**wipe 'out**, *v.tr.* (*a*) (eine Schuld) tilgen; (*b*) (*erase*) (ein Bild, Wörter) ausradieren; (*destroy*) (eine Armee usw.) vernichten; (eine Rasse, Tierart) ausrotten.
**wire** ['waiər]. **I.** *s.* Draht *m;* (*a*) (barbed) w., Stacheldraht *m;* (*b*) (telephone) w., Telefonleitung *f;* w. tapping, Anzapfen *n* von Telefonleitungen; (*c*) (*telegram*) Telegramm *n.* **II.** *v.tr.* (eine Nachricht) telegrafieren. ◆'**wireless**, *s.* w. (set), Radio(apparat) *n(m);* on the w., im Rundfunk. ◆'**wirepulling**, *s. Fig:* Drahtzieherei *f.* ◆'**wiry**, *adj.* drahtig.
**wisdom** ['wizdəm], *s.* Weisheit *f;* w. tooth, Weisheitszahn *m.* ◆**wise** [waiz], *adj.* weise; (*in particular instance*) klug; -ly, *adv.* klugerweise, vernünftigerweise. ◆'**wisecrack**, *s.* Witz *m.*
**wish** [wiʃ]. **I.** *v.tr.* (*a*) to w. to do sth., etwas tun wollen; I don't w. you to do it, ich möchte nicht, daß du es tust; I w. I were in your place, ich wollte, ich wäre an deiner Stelle; (*b*) (*greeting*) (j-m etwas) wünschen. **II.** *s.* Wunsch *m;* my best wishes on your retirement/for a rapid recovery, die besten Wünsche zu Ihrer Pensionierung/für eine baldige Genesung; (*end of letter*) all best wishes, herzliche Grüße. ◆'**wishful**, *adj. F:* that's w. thinking, das ist reines

Wunschdenken.
**wishy-washy** ['wiʃiwɔsi], *adj. F:* (*of soup etc.*) wäßrig; (*of colour*) verwaschen; (*of idea*) vage; (*of book etc.*) seicht.
**wisp** [wisp], *s.* w. of hair, Haarsträhne *f;* w. of smoke, Rauchfahne *f.*
**wistful** ['wistful], *adj.* wehmütig; (*longing*) sehnsüchtig.
**wit** [wit], *s.* **1.** *pl.* wits, Verstand *m;* to have one's wits about one, geistesgegenwärtig sein; to be at one's wits' end, am Ende seiner Weisheit sein. **2.** (*pers.*) Witzbold *m.*
**witch** [witʃ], *s.* Hexe *f;* w. doctor, Medizinmann *m.* ◆'**witchcraft**, *s.* Hexerei *f.*
**with** [wið], *prep.* mit + *dat;* he stays with his mother, er wohnt bei seiner Mutter; I'll be w. you in a moment, ich komme gleich; *Fig:* I'm not quite w. you, ich komme nicht ganz mit; it's a habit w. me, das ist Gewohnheit bei mir; have you a pencil w. you? hast du einen Bleistift bei dir? (*in spite of*) w. all his faults, trotz aller seiner Fehler; to tremble w. rage, vor Wut zittern.
**withdraw** [wið'drɔ:], *v.irr.* **1.** *v.tr.* (*remove*) (etwas) entfernen, wegnehmen; (die Hand, *Jur:* eine Klage, *Com:* ein Angebot usw.) zurückziehen (from, von/ aus + *dat);* to w. money from the bank, Geld von der Bank abheben. **2.** *v.i.* (*of pers.*) sich zurückziehen (from, von/ aus + *dat);* *Sp:* (*of competitor*) to w. from a competition, aus einem Wettkampf ausscheiden. ◆**with'drawal**, *s.* Zurückziehen *n;* Abhebung *f* (von Geld); Zurücknahme *f* (eines Angebotes usw.); *Mil:* Rückzug *m;* *Sp:* Ausscheiden *n;* w. symptoms, Entzugserscheinungen *fpl.*
**wither** ['wiðər], *v.i.* (*of plant*) verwelken; (*dry up*) verdorren. ◆'**withered**, *adj. Bot:* verwelkt. ◆'**withering**, *adj. Fig:* w. look, vernichtender Blick.
**withhold** [wið'həuld], *v.tr.irr.* (*a*) (*refuse*) (seine Einwilligung usw.) verweigern; (*b*) (Tatsachen usw.) vorenthalten.
**within** [wið'in], *prep.* innerhalb + *gen;* w. one's four walls, innerhalb seiner vier Wände; w. sight, in Sichtweite; w. a week, innerhalb einer Woche.
**without** [wið'aut], *prep.* ohne + *acc;* w. seeing me, ohne mich zu sehen; that goes w. saying, das versteht sich von selbst; to do w. sth., auf etwas *acc* verzichten.
**withstand** [wið'stænd], *v.tr.irr.* (Schmerzen usw.) aushalten; *Mil:* (einem Angriff) widerstehen.
**witness** ['witnis]. **I.** *s.* Zeuge *m;* Zeugin *f;* w. box/*N.Am:* stand, Zeugenbank *f.* **II.** *v.tr.* (*a*) to w. an occurrence, bei einem Vorfall zugegen sein; (*b*) (eine Unterschrift) beglaubigen.
**witty** ['witi], *adj.* witzig, geistreich. ◆'**witticism**, *s.* witzige Bemerkung *f.*
**wizard** ['wizəd], *s.* Zauberer *m.* ◆'**wizardry**, *s.* Zauberei *f.*

**wizened** ['wizənd], *adj.* runz(e)lig; (*shrunken*) zusammengeschrumpft.

**wobble** ['wɔbl], *v.i.* wackeln; (*sway*) schwanken. ◆'**wobbly**, *adj. F:* wack(e)lig.

**woe** [wəu], *s.* Leid *n*, Kummer *m.* ◆'**woebegone**, *adj.* jammervoll.

**wog** [wɔg], *s. P: Pej:* (*esp. Arab*) Kameltreiber *m*; (*black*) Nigger *m.*

**wolf**, *pl.* **wolves** [wulf, wulvz]. **I.** *s.* 1. Wolf *m*; (*she*) *w.,* Wölfin *f*; *Fig:* **to cry w.,** blinden Alarm schlagen. 2. (*pers.*) *F:* Schürzenjäger *m.* **II.** *v.tr.* **to w. one's food,** sein Essen hinunterschlingen.

**woman**, *pl.* **women** ['wumən, 'wimin], *s.* Frau *f*; **women's libber,** Frauenrechtlerin *f*; **w. doctor,** Ärztin *f*; **w. friend,** Freundin *f.*

**womb** [wuːm], *s.* Gebärmutter *f.*

**wonder** ['wʌndər]. **I.** *s.* 1. (*miracle*) Wunder *n*; **no w.!** kein Wunder! 2. (*surprise*) Erstaunen *n.* **II.** *v.* 1. *v.i.* sich wundern; erstaunt sein (**at/about,** über + *acc*); **I don't w. at it,** das wundert mich nicht. 2. *v.tr.* **I w. whether he will come,** ich frage mich/bin gespannt, ob er kommen wird. ◆'**wonderful**, *adj.* wunderbar. ◆'**wonderment**, *s.* Verwunderung *f.*

**wood** [wud], *s.* 1. Wald *m*; **we're not out of the w. yet,** wir sind noch nicht über den Berg. 2. (*material*) Holz *n.* ◆'**wood-carving**, *s.* Holzschnitzerei *f.* ◆'**woodcut**, *s.* Holzschnitt *m.* ◆'**wood-cutter**, *s.* Holzfäller *m.* ◆'**wooded**, *adj.* (*of area, slope*) bewaldet. ◆'**wooden**, *adj.* hölzern, Holz-; **w.-headed,** begriffsstutzig. ◆'**woodland**, *s.* Wald *m*; (*area*) Waldfläche *f.* ◆'**woodlouse**, *s.* Kellerassel *f.* ◆'**woodman**, *pl.* **-men**, *s.* 1. Förster *m.* 2. (*lumberjack*) Holzfäller *m.* ◆'**woodpecker**, *s.* Specht *m*; **spotted w.,** Buntspecht *m.* ◆'**woodshed**, *s.* Holzschuppen *m.* ◆'**woodwind**, *s. Mus:* die Holzbläser *mpl* (eines Orchesters); **w. instrument,** Holzblasinstrument *n.* ◆'**woodwork**, *s.* Holzarbeit *f.* ◆'**woodworm**, *s.* Holzwurm *m.*

**wool** [wul], *s.* Wolle *f.* ◆'**woollen**, *adj.* wollen; **w. goods,** Wollwaren *fpl.* ◆'**woollens**, *s. pl.* (*materials*) Wollstoffe *mpl*; (*goods*) Wollwaren *fpl.* ◆'**woolly**, *adj.* wollig; *Fig:* (*of ideas etc.*) verschwommen.

**word** [wəːd]. **I.** *s.* Wort *n*; **in other words,** mit anderen Worten; anders ausgedrückt; **a man of few words,** ein wortkarger Mensch; **to have words with s.o.,** eine Auseinandersetzung mit j-m haben; **by w. of mouth,** mündlich; (*news*) **to send s.o. w. of sth.,** j-n (brieflich) über etwas *acc* benachrichtigen; **to keep/break one's w.,** sein Wort halten/brechen. **II.** *v.tr.* (etwas) formulieren. ◆'**wording**, *s.* (*a*) Wortlaut *m* (eines Dokuments); (*b*) (*choice of words*) Wortwahl *f*; (*manner*) Formulierung *f.*

**work** [wəːk]. **I.** *s.* 1. Arbeit *f*; **at w.,** bei der Arbeit; (*in office*) im Büro; **to set to w.,** sich an die Arbeit machen; **out of w.,** arbeitslos; **a piece of w.,** (*task*) eine Aufgabe; (*completed*) eine Leistung. 2. *Lit: Mus: etc:* Werk *n*; **a w. of art,** ein Kunstwerk. 3. **road works,** Straßenbauarbeiten *fpl.* 4. (*machinery*) Räderwerk *n*; (*gears*) Getriebe *n*; **the works of a watch,** ein Uhrwerk. 5. *pl.* (*factory*) Werk *n*, Betrieb *m.* **II.** *v.* 1. *v.i.* (*a*) arbeiten (**on sth.,** an etwas *dat*); **to w. hard,** schwer/fleißig arbeiten; (*b*) (*of machine etc.*) funktionieren; (*c*) **this medicine really works,** diese Medizin wirkt garantiert; **his plan didn't w.,** sein Plan ist nicht gelungen/*F:* hat nicht geklappt. 2. *v.tr.* **to w. one's way up,** sich nach oben arbeiten; **he worked his way through college,** er verdiente sich *dat* sein Studium. ◆'**workable**, *adj.* (*of project*) durchführbar. ◆'**workbench**, *s.* Werkbank *f*; (*small*) Arbeitstisch *m.* ◆'**worker**, *s.* Arbeiter(in) *m(f).* ◆'**working**, *adj.* 1. (*of pers.*) berufstätig; **the w. class,** die Arbeiterklasse. 2. (*a*) (*of machine*) **w./in w. order,** betriebsfähig; **not w.,** außer Betrieb. ◆'**workman**, *s.* Arbeiter *m.* ◆'**workmanship**, *s.* Arbeit *f*, Ausführung *f.* ◆'**work 'off**, *v.tr.* (*a*) (Schulden usw.) abarbeiten; (*b*) **to w. o. one's energy,** überflüssige Energie loswerden. ◆**work on**, *v.* 1. *v.i.* ['wəːk'ɔn] weiterarbeiten. 2. *v.tr.* ['wəːkɔn] **to w. on a project,** an einem Projekt arbeiten. ◆'**work 'out**, *v.* 1. *v.tr.* (*a*) (eine Idee, einen Plan usw.) ausarbeiten; (*b*) (ein Problem) lösen. 2. *v.i.* (*a*) (gut/schlecht) ausgehen; (*b*) (*of sum*) **how much does it w. o. at?** auf wieviel beläuft es sich? ◆'**workshop**, *s.* Werkstatt *f.* ◆'**work 'up**, *v.tr.* (*a*) (*develop*) (einen Gedanken, eine Situation usw.) entwickeln; (ein Geschäft) hochbringen; (*b*) (*excite*) (j-n, das Publikum) aufregen; **to w. oneself up into a rage,** sich in Wut hineinsteigern; *F:* **don't get worked up,** reg dich nicht auf.

**world** [wəːld], *s.* Welt *f*; **all over the w./ the w. over,** in der ganzen Welt; **what in the w. is the matter with you?** was in aller Welt fehlt dir? **w. war,** Weltkrieg *m*; *Sp:* **w. record,** Weltrekord *m*; **man of the w.,** Mann von Welt; **to feel on top of the w.,** in bester Form sein; **that will do you a w. of good,** das wird dir ungemein gut tun; **to think the w. of s.o.,** j-n sehr hoch einschätzen; **she is/means the w. to him,** sie ist sein ein und alles. ◆'**world-'famous**, *adj.* weltberühmt. ◆'**worldly**, *adj.* weltlich. ◆'**world'wide**, *adj.* weltweit; **w. reputation,** Weltruf *m.*

**worm** [wəːm]. **I.** *s.* 1. Wurm *m*; *esp.* (**earth**) **w.,** Regenwurm *m*; *Fig:* **w.'s eye view,** Froschperspektive *f.* 2. **w. gear,**

Schneckengetriebe *n*. **II.** *v.tr.* **to w. a secret out of s.o.,** j-m ein Geheimnis entlocken. ◆'**wormeaten,** *adj.* (*a*) wurmstichig; (*b*) *Fig:* uralt.

**worn** [wɔːn], *adj.* (*of clothes*) abgetragen; **w. out,** (i) (*of thing*) (ganz) abgenutzt; (ii) (*of pers.*) erschöpft.

**worry** ['wʌri]. **I.** *v.* 1. *v.tr.* (*a*) (j-n) beunruhigen; (*pester*) belästigen; **to w. oneself,** sich *dat* Sorgen/Kummer machen; (*b*) (*of dog*) (Schafe usw.) hetzen. 2. *v.i.* sich *dat* Sorgen machen; **don't w.!** mach dir keine Sorgen! **it's not worth worrying about,** es lohnt sich nicht, sich *dat* darüber Gedanken zu machen. **II.** *s.* Sorge *f*; (*stronger*) Kummer *m*. ◆'**worried,** *adj.* besorgt. ◆'**worrying,** *adj.* (*of thing*) beunruhigend.

**worse** [wəːs]. **I.** *adj.* schlechter, schlimmer. **II.** *s.* 1. Schlimmeres *n*, Schlechteres *n*; **to change for the w.,** sich zum Schlechteren wenden. **III.** *adv.* schlechter, schlimmer. ◆'**worsen,** *v.* 1. *v.tr.* (Beziehungen usw.) verschlechtern. 2. *v.i.* sich verschlechtern.

**worship** ['wəːʃip]. **I.** *v.tr.* anbeten. **II.** *s.* Anbetung *f*; *Ecc:* Kult *m*. ◆'**worshipper,** *s.* Anbeter(in) *m(f)*; *Ecc:* Kirchgänger(in) *m(f)*.

**worst** [wəːst]. **I.** *adj.* schlechteste(r, s); schlimmste(r, s); **his w. enemy,** sein ärgster Feind; **the w. part of it/about it is that …,** das Schlimmste daran ist, daß … **II.** *s.* **the w.,** der, die, das Schlechteste/Schlimmste; **that's the w. of cheap shoes,** das ist der Nachteil von billigen Schuhen; **at the w.,** schlimmstenfalls; **if the w. comes to the w.,** wenn alle Stricke reißen. **III.** *adv.* am schlechtesten/schlimmsten.

**worsted** ['wustid], *s.* Kammgarn *n*.

**worth** [wəːθ]. **I.** *adj.* (*a*) **to be w. £10,** £10 wert sein; **it's not w. that much,** so viel ist es nicht wert; (*b*) **it's w. the trouble/w. it,** es lohnt sich; es ist der Mühe wert; **nothing w. mentioning,** nichts Erwähnenswertes. **II.** *s.* Wert *m*; **five pounds' w.** of petrol, für fünf Pfund Benzin; **to get one's money's w.,** auf seine Kosten kommen. ◆'**worthless,** *adj.* wertlos. ◆'**worth'while,** *adj.* der Mühe wert, lohnend.

**worthy** ['wəːði], *adj.* würdig; (*esp. of thing*) wert (**of** sth., etwas *gen*).

**would** [wud], *aux. v.* **what w. you like?** was möchten Sie? **he w. come if he were invited,** er käme schon, wenn man ihn einladen würde; **she w. often come home tired out,** oft kam sie total erschöpft nach Hause. ◆**would-be** ['wudbi], *adj.* (*a*) (*unsuccessful*) **w. assassin,** erfolgloser Attentäter *m*; (*b*) (*so-called*) sogenannt.

**wound** [wuːnd]. **I.** *s.* Wunde *f*. **II.** *v.tr.* (j-n) verwunden; *Fig:* (j-s Gefühle) verletzen.

**woven** ['wəuv(ə)n], *adj.* **w. goods,** Web-waren *fpl*.

**wrangle** ['ræŋgl]. **I.** *v.i.* sich streiten. **II.** *s.* Zank *m*, Streit *m*.

**wrap** [ræp]. **I.** *v.tr.* (*a*) **to w. sth.** (**up**), (etwas) einwickeln; (*b*) **to w.** (**oneself**) **up,** sich warm anziehen; (*c*) *Fig:* **wrapped up in one's work,** ganz in seine Arbeit vertieft; (*d*) **he wrapped his arms round her,** er hielt sie umschlungen. **II.** *s.* (*scarf*) Schal *m*; (*rug*) Decke *f*. ◆'**wrapper,** *s.* Hülle *f*; Umschlag *m* (eines Buches). ◆'**wrapping,** *s.* Hülle *f*; *esp. pl.* Verpackung *f*; **w. paper,** Packpapier *n*.

**wreath** [riːθ], *s.* Kranz *m*; (*flowers*) Girlande *f*.

**wreck** [rek]. **I.** *s.* 1. (*a*) (*ship, car*) Wrack *n*; (*building*) Ruine *f*; **my car's a complete w.,** mein Wagen hat Totalschaden; (*b*) *Fig:* (*of pers.*) **to be a nervous w.,** ein Nervenbündel sein. 2. (*occurrence*) Schiffbruch *m*. **II.** *v.tr.* (ein Schiff) zum Wrack machen; (ein Auto) zu Schrott fahren; (ein Gebäude usw.) (total) zerstören; **to be wrecked,** (*of ship*) auflaufen; (*of pers.*) Schiffbruch erleiden. ◆'**wreckage,** *s.* Wrackteile *npl* (eines Schiffes); Trümmer *pl* (eines Autos, Flugzeugs usw.).

**wren** [ren], *s. Orn:* Zaunkönig *m*.

**wrench** [rentʃ]. **I.** *s.* 1. (heftiger) Ruck *m*; **he gave his ankle a w.,** er hat sich *dat* den Knöchel verstaucht; *Fig:* **it will be a w. to leave,** man trennt sich schweren Herzens. 2. *Tchn:* Schraubenschlüssel *m*. **II.** *v.tr.* (*a*) (etwas) mit Wucht drehen; (*tear away*) plötzlich wegreißen; **to w. oneself free (from s.o.),** sich gewaltsam (von j-m) befreien; (*b*) **to w. one's ankle/shoulder,** sich *dat* den Knöchel/die Schulter verrenken.

**wrestle** [resl], *v.i.* ringen; *Fig:* **to w. with difficulties** etc., mit Schwierigkeiten usw. kämpfen. ◆'**wrestler,** *s.* Ringer *m*. ◆'**wrestling,** *s.* Ringen *n*.

**wretch** [retʃ], *s.* (**poor**) **w.,** armer Teufel. ◆'**wretched** [-id], *adj.* 1. (*of pers.*) elend. 2. *Pej:* **where's my w. umbrella?** wo ist denn der blöde Schirm?

**wriggle** [rigl], *v.* 1. *v.i.* sich winden; (*of child etc.*) zappeln; **he tried to w. out of it,** er versuchte, sich davor zu drücken. 2. *v.tr.* **to w. one's way into/through sth.,** sich in etwas *acc* einschleichen/ durch etwas *acc* durchschlängeln. ◆'**wriggly,** *adj.* zappelig.

**wring** [riŋ], *v.tr.irr.* **to w. (out) the washing,** die Wäsche (aus)wringen; **to w. the neck of a chicken,** einem Huhn den Hals abdrehen. ◆'**wringing,** *adj.* **w. wet,** *F:* klatschnaß.

**wrinkle** ['riŋkl]. **I.** *s.* (*a*) (*on face*) Runzel *f*, Falte *f*; (*furrow*) Furche *f*; (*b*) (*in clothes*) Falte *f*. **II.** *v.* 1. *v.tr.* (in etwas *dat*) Falten machen, (*crumple*) (etwas) zerknittern; **to w. one's forehead,** die Stirn runzeln. 2. *v.i.* Falten werfen; (*of face*) runzelig werden. ◆'**wrinkled,** *adj.*

faltig; (*crumpled*) zerknittert; (*of face*) runzelig.

**wrist** [rist], s. Handgelenk *n*; **w. watch,** Armbanduhr *f.*

**writ** [rit], s. gerichtlicher Befehl *m*; **to serve a w. on s.o.,** j-n vorladen.

**write** [rait], *v.tr. & i.irr.* schreiben; **he writes for a living,** er ist von Beruf Schriftsteller; **he wrote to me yesterday,** er hat mir gestern geschrieben. ◆**'write 'down,** *v.tr.* (etwas) aufschreiben. ◆**'write 'off,** *v.* 1. *v.tr.* (*a*) Fin: (eine Summe usw.) abschreiben; (*b*) F: **to w. off a car,** ein Auto zu Schrott fahren. 2. *v.i.* **to w. off for sth.,** sich schriftlich um etwas *acc* bewerben. ◆**'write-off,** *s.* Totalverlust *m*; **the car's a w.-o.,** der Wagen hat Totalschaden. ◆**'writer,** *s.* Schriftsteller(in) *m(f)*; (*author*) Verfasser(in) *m(f)*. ◆**'write 'up,** *v.tr.* (über ein Ereignis usw.) berichten; (ein Thema) behandeln. ◆**'write-up,** *s.* Bericht *m* (über ein Ereignis). ◆**'writing,** *s.* 1. (*process*) Schreiben *n.* 2. Schrift *f*; **w. paper,** Schreibpapier *n, esp.* Briefpapier *n.* 3. **writings,** Schriften *fpl.* ◆**'written** [ritn], *adj.* geschrieben; (*in writing*) schriftlich.

**writhe** [raið], *v.i.* sich krümmen (**in/with**

**pain,** vor Schmerzen).

**wrong** [rɔŋ]. I. *adj.* 1. unrecht; **it's w. (of him) to do that,** es ist unrecht (von ihm), das zu tun. 2. (*incorrect*) (*a*) (*of fact etc.*) falsch; (*of view*) irrig; (*b*) (*of pers.*) **to be w.,** sich irren; unrecht haben; (*c*) **in the w. place,** am falschen Ort/Platz; **your sweater's w. side out,** du hast den Pullover verkehrt herum an; (*d*) **what's w. with you?** was hast du? **there's something w. with this car,** etwas stimmt nicht an diesem Auto. **-ly,** *adv.* (*a*) (*unjustly*) zu Unrecht; (*by mistake*) irrtümlicherweise; (*b*) (*incorrectly*) falsch. II. *s.* (*injustice*) Unrecht *n*; **to do s.o. w.,** j-m unrecht tun/ein Unrecht zufügen; **to be in the w.,** unrecht haben; im Unrecht sein. III. *adv.* 1. falsch. **2. to go w.,** (i) (*of pers.*) sich verlaufen; (ii) (*of plan*) schiefgehen; (*of machinery*) nicht richtig funktionieren. IV. *v.tr.* (j-m) unrecht tun. ◆**'wrong'doer,** *s.* Übeltäter(in) *m(f)*. ◆**'wrongful,** *adj.* ungerecht.

**wrought** [rɔːt], *adj.* **w. iron,** Schmiedeeisen *n.*

**wry** [rai], *adj.* **a w. smile,** ein ironisches Lächeln; **w. humour,** trockener Humor; **to pull a w. face,** ein schiefes Gesicht ziehen.

# X

**X, x** [eks], *s.* (der Buchstabe) X, x *n.*

**Xmas** ['eksməs], *s.* F: Weihnachten *fpl.*

**X-ray** ['eksrei]. I. *s.* Röntgenstrahl *m*; **to**

**have an X-r.,** sich röntgen lassen. II. *v.tr.* (j-n, ein Organ) röntgen.

**xylophone** ['zailəfəun], *s.* Xylophon *n.*

# Y

**Y, y** [wai], *s.* (der Buchstabe) Y, y *n.*

**yacht** [jɔt], *s.* Jacht *f*; **y. club,** Jachtklub *m.* ◆**'yachting,** *s.* Segelsport *m.* ◆**'yachtsman,** *s.* Sportsegler *m.*

**yank**[1] [jæŋk]. F: I. *v.tr.* (an etwas *dat*) zerren; (j-n) (aus dem Bett usw.) zerren; **to y. out a tooth etc.,** einen Zahn usw. mit einem Ruck herausziehen. II. *s.* Ruck *m.*

**Yank**[2], **Yankee** ['jæŋki], *s.* F: Ami *m.*

**yap** [jæp]. I. *v.i.* kläffen. II. *s.* Kläffen *n.* ◆**'yapping,** *s.* Gekläff *n.*

**yard**[1] [jɑːd], *s. Meas:* Yard *n* (=0,914 m).

**yard**[2], *s.* Hof *m*; *Scotland* Y., die Londoner Kriminalpolizei, Scotland Yard.

**yarn** [jɑːn], *s.* 1. Garn *n.* 2. *Fig:* (*story*) Seemannsgarn *n.*

**yawn** [jɔːn]. I. *v.i.* (*of pers. & Fig: gap*) gähnen. II. *s.* Gähnen *n.*

**year** [jəːr, jiər], *s.* Jahr *n*; **in the y. 1850,** im Jahre 1850; **y. after y.,** Jahr für Jahr; (*of wine etc.*) **a good y.,** ein guter Jahrgang. ◆**'yearbook,** *s.* Jahrbuch *n.* ◆**'yearly,** *adj.* jährlich.

**yearn** [jəːn], *v.i.* **to y. for sth.,** sich nach

etwas *dat* sehnen. ◆**'yearning,** *s.* Sehnen *n* (**for,** nach + *dat*).

**yeast** [jiːst], *s.* Hefe *f.*

**yell** [jel]. I. *v.tr. & i.* (etwas) schreien. II. *s.* (gellender) Schrei *m.*

**yellow** ['jeləu]. I. *adj.* (*a*) gelb; *Med:* **y. fever,** Gelbfieber *n*; (*b*) F: (*of pers.*) feige. II. *s.* Gelb *n.* ◆**'yellowhammer,** *s.* Goldammer *f.*

**yelp** [jelp]. I. *v.i.* (*of dog*) kläffen; (*in pain*) jaulen. II. *s.* Kläffen *n*; Jaulen *n.*

**yes** [jes]. I. *adv.* ja; **y. man,** Jasager *m.* II. *s.* Ja *n*; (*esp. to proposal*) Jawort *n.*

**yesterday** ['jestədi]. I. *adv.* gestern. II. *s.* **yesterday's paper,** die gestrige Zeitung/ Zeitung von gestern; **the day before y.,** vorgestern.

**yet** [jet]. I. *adv.* (*a*) noch; **has he gone y.?** ist er schon gegangen? **not y.,** noch nicht; **he'll win y.,** er wird schon noch gewinnen; (*b*) (*even*) **y. further,** noch weiter; **y. again,** schon wieder. II. *conj.* dennoch; **(and) y. I like him,** (und) trotzdem mag ich ihn.

**yew** [juː], *s.* **y. (tree),** Eibe *f*; (*wood*) Eibenholz n.

**Yiddish** ['jidiʃ]. **I.** adj. jiddisch. **II.** s. (language) Jiddisch n.

**yield** [ji:ld]. **I.** s. Ertrag m; (a) (harvest) Ernte f; (b) Fin: (interest) Zinsertrag m. **II.** v. 1. v.tr. Agr: Min: etc: (Getreide, Kohlen, Öl usw.) liefern; Fin: (einen Gewinn) abwerfen; (eine Ernte) einbringen; Fin: to **y. interest,** Zinsen tragen. 2. v.i. nachgeben (to s.o., -j-m). ◆'yielding. **I.** adj. nachgebend; (of pers.) nachgiebig. **II.** s. Nachgeben n; Fig: Nachgiebigkeit f.

**yodel** ['jəudl], v.i. jodeln.

**yoga** ['jəugə], s. Joga n.

**yoghurt** ['jɔgət, 'jəu-], s. Joghurt m.

**yoke** [jəuk], s. Joch n.

**yolk** [jəuk], s. Eidotter n, Eigelb n.

**you** [ju:], pers. pron. 1. (subject) Sie; (to close friend, relative, child, animal etc.) du/pl ihr; **y. poor thing!** Sie/du Ärmste(r)! **y. poor things!** Sie/ihr Ärmsten! **y. Germans,** ihr Deutschen. 2. (object) (a) acc Sie, dich; pl Sie, euch; **I love y.,** ich liebe dich; (b) dat Ihnen, dir; pl Ihnen, euch; **I'll give y. this,** ich gebe Ihnen/dir/euch das; **between y. and me,** unter uns. 3. refl. **have y. any money on y.?** haben Sie Geld bei sich? hast du Geld bei dir? habt ihr Geld bei euch? 4. (indefinite) man; acc einen; dat einem; **it does y. good,** es tut gut. ◆**you'd**=you

**would.** ◆**you'll**=you will.

**young** [jʌŋ]. **I.** adj. jung; **y. children,** kleine Kinder; **y. people,** Jungendliche/ junge Leute. **II.** s. inv. **the y.,** die Jugend. ◆'**youngster,** s. Jugendliche(r) f(m); (boy) Junge m.

**your** [jɔ:r], poss. adj. Ihr(e); (familiar) sing. dein(e); pl. euer, eure. ◆**yours,** poss. pron. Ihrer, Ihre, Ihres; pl Ihre; (familiar) deiner, deine, deines; pl deine; (familiar pl.) eurer, eure, eures; pl eure; **this is y.,** das gehört Ihnen/dir/euch; **a friend of y.,** ein Freund von Ihnen/dir/ euch. ◆**your'self,** pl. **your'selves,** pers. pron. (a) selbst; **you said so y./ yourselves,** Sie haben/du hast/ihr habt es selbst gesagt; (b) refl. sich dat & acc; dich acc; dir dat; euch dat & acc; **you have hurt y./yourselves,** Sie haben sich/du hast dich/ihr habt euch verletzt; (c) **you're not quite y.,** Sie sind/du bist nicht ganz auf der Höhe.

**youth,** pl. -s [ju:θ, pl. ju:ðz], s. 1. (period) Jugend f. 2. (pers.) Jugendliche(r) f(m). 3. coll. junge Leute, die Jugend; **y. hostel,** Jugendherberge f. ◆'**youthful,** adj. (of pers.) jugendlich. ◆**youthfulness,** s. Jugendlichkeit f.

**Yugoslavia** [ju:gəu'sla:viə]. Pr. n. Jugoslawien n. ◆'**Yugoslav. I.** adj. jugoslawisch. **II.** s. Jugoslawe m, Jugoslawin f.

# Z

**Z, z** [zed, N.Am: zi:], s. (der Buchstabe) Z, z n.

**Zambia** ['zæmbiə]. Pr.n. Sambia n. ◆'**Zambian. I.** s. Sambier m. **II.** adj. sambisch.

**zany** ['zeini], adj. F: burlesk.

**zeal** [zi:l], s. Eifer m. ◆**zealous** ['zeləs], adj. eifrig.

**zebra** ['zebrə, 'zi:brə], s. Zebra n; **z. crossing,** Zebrastreifen m.

**zenith** ['zeniθ], s. Zenit m; Fig: Höhepunkt m.

**zero,** pl. -os ['ziərəu, -əuz], s. (number) Null f; (point on scale etc.) Nullpunkt m; **z. hour,** die Stunde Null.

**zest** [zest], s. (enthusiam) Begeisterung f; (verve) Schwung m; **to eat with z.,** mit Genuß essen.

**zigzag** ['zigzæg]. s. Zickzack m; **in zigzags,** im Zickzack.

**zinc** [ziŋk], s. Zink n.

**Zionism** ['zaiənizm], s. Zionismus m.

**zip** [zip]. **I.** s. 1. Surren n (einer Kugel usw.). 2. **z. (fastener),** Reißverschluß m. 3. N.Am: **z. code,** Postleitzahl f. **II.** v. 1. v.i. (of bullet etc.) surren. 2. v.tr. F: **can you z. me up?** kannst du mir den Reißverschluß zumachen?

**zither** ['ziðər], s. Zither f.

**zodiac** ['zəudiæk], s. Tierkreis m.

**zombie** ['zɔmbi], s. F: apathischer Typ m; (moron) Schwachkopf m.

**zone** [zəun]. s. Zone f.

**zoo** [zu:], s. Zoo m. ◆**zoology** [zu:'ɔlədʒi], s. Zoologie f. ◆**zoo'logical** [zu:(ə)-], adj. zoologisch. ◆**zoologist** [zu:'ɔ-], s. Zoologe m, Zoologin f.

**zoom** [zu:m]. **I.** s. Phot: **z. (lens),** Zoom(objektiv) n. **II.** v.i. F: **to z. along,** dahinbrausen.

**Zurich** ['zjuərik]. Pr. n. Zürich n.

# Deutsche Abkürzungen
## German Abbreviations

**A** *Ampere* ampere

**AA** *Auswärtiges Amt approx.* Foreign Office

**a.a.O.** *am angeführten Ort* loc.cit.

**Abb.** *Abbildung* illustration, figure, *abbr.* fig.

**Abf.** *Abfahrt* departure

**Abg.** *Abgeordnete(r)* deputy; *West G:* member of the Bundestag/Landtag

**Abk.** *Abkürzung* abbreviation, *abbr.* abbr.

**Abs.** 1. *Absatz* paragraph, *abbr.* par. 2. *Absender* sender

**Absch.** *Abschnitt* section

**Abt.** *Abteilung* department, *abbr.* dept.

**abzgl.** *abzüglich* less

**a.D.** 1. *außer Dienst* retired. 2. *an der Donau* on the Danube

**ADAC** *Allgemeiner Deutscher Automobilclub* (W.German motoring association)

**Adr.** *Adresse* address

**AG** *Aktiengesellschaft* joint-stock company

**akad.** *akademisch* academic, university (trained)

**allg.** *allgemein* general

**a.M.** *am Main* on the Main

**amtl.** *amtlich* official

**Angest.** *Angestellte(r)* employee

**Anh.** *Anhang* appendix

**Ank.** *Ankunft* arrival

**Anm.** *Anmerkung* note

**Antw.** *Antwort* answer

**a.O.** *an der Oder* on the Oder

**AOK** *Allgemeine Ortskrankenkasse* local health insurance

**a.o.Prof.** *außerordentlicher Professor approx.* associate professor

**a.Rh.** *am Rhein* on the Rhine

**ARD** *Arbeitsgemeinschaft der öffentlichen Rundfunkanstalten der BRD* (umbrella organization of West German radio and TV)

**ärztl.** *ärztlich* medical

**ASTA** *Allgemeiner Studentenausschuß* (student's union)

**A.T.** *Altes Testament* Old Testament

**AT-Motor** *Austauschmotor* exchange reconditioned engine

**atü** *Atmosphärenüberdruck* pressure above atmospheric pressure

**AUA** Austrian Airlines

**Aufl.** *Auflage* edition

**ausschl.** *ausschließlich* exclusive(ly)

**AvD** *Automobilclub von Deutschland* (W.German motoring association)

**a.W.** *ab Werk* ex works

**Az** *Aktenzeichen* file number, reference

**B** *Bundesstraße* Federal Highway, main road

**BASF** *Badische Anilin- und Sodafabrik* (leading W.German chemical firm)

**Bauj.** *Baujahr* year of manufacture

**Bd., Bde.,** *Band, Bände* volume, volumes

**BDI** *Bundesverband der Deutschen Industrie* Confederation of (West) German Industry (employers' organization)

**Bearb.** *Bearbeitung;* **in B.,** being dealt with

**Bed.** *Bedarf* demand

**befr.** *Sch: befriedigend* satisfactory, *approx.* C

**begl.** *beglaubigt* certified

**beisp.** *beispielsweise* for example

**bes.** *besonders* especially

**Betr.** *Betreff* reference, *abbr.* re

**betr.** *betreffend* concerning, *abbr.* re

**Bez.** *Bezirk* district

**BGB** *Bürgerliches Gesetzbuch* (W.German Civil Code)

**BH** *Cl: F: Büstenhalter* bra

**Bhf.** *Bahnhof* station

**BM** *Bundesministerium* Federal Ministry

**BND** *Bundesnachrichtendienst* W.German Intelligence Service

**BP** *Bundespost* Federal Post Office

**BRD** *Bundesrepublik Deutschland* Federal Republic of Germany

**BRT** *Bruttoregistertonnen* gross tonnage

**b.w.** *bitte wenden* please turn over, *abbr.* P.T.O.

**bzgl.** *bezüglich* with reference to

**bzw.** *beziehungsweise* and . . . respectively; or

**C** *Celsius* centigrade

**cal** *(Gramm-)Kalorie* calorie

**cand.** *Kandidat* candidate

**cbm** *Kubikmeter* cubic metre

**ccm** *Kubikzentimeter* cubic centimetre, *abbr.* c.c.

**CDU** *Pol: Christlich-Demokratische Union* Christian Democratic Union

**Cie.** *Com: Kompanie* company

**cm** *Zentimeter* centimetre, *abbr.* cm

**Co.** *Com: Kompanie* company

**CSU** *Pol: Christlich-Soziale Union* Christian Social Union

**c.t.** *cum tempore* starting a quarter of an hour later

**CVJM** *Christlicher Verein Junger Männer* Young Men's Christian Association, *abbr.* Y.M.C.A.

**d.** 1. *Mth: Durchmesser* diameter. 2. *der/die/das* the

**DB** *Deutsche Bundesbahn* Federal German Railways

**DBP** *Deutsche Bundespost* Federal Post Office

**DDR** *Deutsche Demokratische Republik* German Democratic Republic, *abbr.* GDR

**DER** *Deutsches Reisebüro* (West) German Travel Agency

**DGB** *Deutscher Gewerkschaftsbund* Federation of (West) German Trade Unions

**d.h.** *das heißt* that is, *abbr.* i.e.

**Di** *Dienstag* Tuesday, *abbr.* Tues.

**DIN** *Deutsche Industrienorm* German Industrial Standard

**Dipl.** (*a*) *Diplom* diploma; (*b*) *Diplom-* holding a diploma, (academically) qualified; **Dipl.Kfm.** *Diplomkaufmann* person with a commercial diploma; **Dipl.Ing.** *Diplomingenieur* fully trained engineer

**Dir.** 1. *Direktor* director. 2. *Mus: Dirigent* conductor

**Diss.** *Dissertation*

**DJH** *Deutsches Jugendherbergswerk* German Youth Hostel Association

**DM** *Deutsche Mark* (West) German mark

**dm** *Dezimeter* decimetre (10 cm)

**d.M.** *dieses Monats* of this month, *Com:* instant

**DNA** *Deutscher Normenausschuß* German Standards Committee

**do.** *dito* ditto

**Do** *Donnerstag* Thursday, *abbr.* Thurs.

**Doz.** *Dozent* university lecturer

**dpa** *Deutsche Presseagentur* German Press Agency

**d.Red.** *die Redaktion* the editor(s)

**Dr.** *Doktor* Doctor; **Dr.h.c.** *Doctor honoris causa* honorary doctorate; **Dr.jur.** *Doctor juris* doctor of law, *abbr.* LLD; **Dr.med.** *Doctor medicinae* Doctor of Medicine, *abbr.* M.D.; **Dr.phil.** *Doktor der Philosophie* Doctor of Philosophy, *abbr.* Ph.D.

**DRK** *Deutsches Rotes Kreuz* (West) German Red Cross

**DSG** *Deutsche Schlafwagen- und Speisewagengesellschaft* (West) German Sleeping and Dining Car Company

**ds.J.** *dieses Jahres* of this year

**dz.** *derzeit* at present

**E** *Eilzug* semi-fast train

**Ed.** *Edition* edition

**EG** *Europäische Gemeinschaft* European Community

**e.h.** *ehrenhalber;* **Dr. e.h.** honorary doctor

**ehem.** *ehemals* formerly

**eigtl.** *eigentlich* in fact, strictly speaking

**einschl.** *einschließlich* inclusive of

**EKG** *Elektrokardiogramm* electrocardiogram

**Empf.** 1. *Empfänger* addressee. 2. *adj. empfohlen* recommended

**entspr.** *entsprechend* corresponding(ly)

**entw.** *entweder* either

**erstkl.** *erstklassig* first-rate

**Eßl.** *Eßlöffel* tablespoon

**etw.** 1. *etwaig* possible. 2. *etwas* something

**ev.** *evangelisch* protestant

**e.V.** *eingetragener Verein* registered society

**EVP** *Einzelhandelsverkaufspreis/ Endverbraucherpreis* retail price

**evtl.** *eventuell* perhaps, possibly

**E-Werk** *Elektrizitätswerk* power station

**EWG** *Europäische Wirtschaftsgemeinschaft* European Economic Community

**exkl.** *exklusive* exclusive of

**f.** 1. *für* for. 2. (*und*) *folgende (Seite)* and following page

**Fa.** *Firma* firm; *Fa. X* Messrs. X

**Fak.** *Fakultät* faculty

**Fam.** *Familie* family

**F.A.Z.** *Frankfurter Allgemeine Zeitung* (leading West German daily newspaper)

**FC** *Fußballclub* Football Club

**FDGB** *Freier Deutscher Gewerkschaftsbund* (East German Trade Union Federation)

**FDJ** *Freie Deutsche Jugend* Free German Youth (East German youth organization)

**FDP** *Pol: Freie Demokratische Partei* Free Democratic Party (West German centre party)

**Fernschr.** *Fernschreiber* telex

**F.f.** *Fortsetzung folgt* to be continued

**ff** *sehr fein* extra fine (quality)

**FHZ** *Freihandelszone* Free Trade Area

**Fil.** *Com: Filiale* branch

**FKK** *Freikörperkultur* nudism; **FKK-Kolonie** nudist colony

**fl.W.** *fließendes Wasser* running water

**Forts.** *Fortsetzung* continuation

**Fr.** 1. *Frau* Mrs. 2. *Freitag* Friday, *abbr.* Fri.

**fr.** *franko* post-paid

**Frfr.** *Freifrau* Baroness

**Frhr.** *Freiherr* Baron

**Frl.** *Fräulein* Miss

**frz.** *französisch* French

**FU** *Freie Universität* Free University (of Berlin)

**g** 1. *Meas: Gramm* gram. 2. *Aus: Groschen* groschen (smallest Austrian coin)

**geb.** (*a*) *geboren* born; (*b*) *geborene* née

**Gebr.** *Com: Gebrüder* Brothers

**gefl.** *Com: gefällig* kind

**gegr.** *gegründet* founded

**gem.** *gemäß* according to

**Gem.** *Gemeinde* municipality; (*kleine Ortschaft*) parish

**Gen.** *Genossenschaft* co-operative society

**Geogr.** *Geographie* geography

**gepr.** *geprüft* tested

**Ges.** *Gesellschaft* company

**gesch.** *geschieden* divorced

**ges.gesch.** *gesetzlich geschützt* patented (invention); registered (trade mark)

**geschl.** *geschlossen* closed; private (performance etc.)

**Geschw.** 1. *Geschwister* brother(s) and sister(s). 2. *Geschwindigkeit* speed

**gest.** *gestorben* deceased; (*mit Datum*) died

**gez.** *gezeichnet* signed

**GG** *Grundgesetz* Basic (constitutional) Law

**GmbH** *Gesellschaft mit beschränkter Haftung* limited (liability) company; *abbr. (nach dem Firmennamen)* Co.Ltd.

**Gymn.** *Gymnasium approx.* grammar/*N.Am:* high school

**gzj.** *ganzjährig* all year (round)

**h** *Stunde* hour

**H** *(Schild) Haltestelle* (bus/tram) stop

**ha** *Meas: Hektar* hectare

**habil.** *habilitiert* qualified as a university teacher

**Hbf.** *Hauptbahnhof* main railway station

**h.c.** *honoris causa* as an honour, honorary

**herg.** *hergestellt* manufactured

**HF** *Hochfrequenz* high frequency

**HG** *Handelsgesellschaft* trading company

**HGB** *Jur: Handelsgesetzbuch* commercial code

**hj.** *halbjährlich* half-yearly

**hl** *Meas: Hektoliter* 100 litres

**Hl., hl.** *heilige;* **der hl. Martin** St.Martin

**HO** *East G: Handelsorganisation (a)* State Trading Organization; *(b) F:* state-owned shop

**Hochw.** *Ecc: Hochwürden* Reverend

**höfl.** *höflichst* kindly

**Hptst.** *Hauptstadt* capital

**Hr.** *Herr* Mr

**Hrsg.** *Herausgeber* editor; **hrsg. v.** *herausgegeben von* edited by

**HTL** *Höhere Technische Lehranstalt approx.* polytechnic

**Hz** *Ph:Rad: Hertz* hertz

**i.** *in/im* in/in the

**i.A.** . . . *im Auftrag* on behalf of . . . , *abbr.* p.p.

**i.allg.** *im allgemeinen* in general

**i.D.** *im Durchschnitt* on average

**IG** *Industriegewerkschaft* industrial union

**i.J.** *im Jahre* in (the year)

**ill.** *illustriert* illustrated

**inbegr.** *inbegriffen* included

**Ing.** *Ingenieur* engineer

**Inh.** *Inhaber* owner

**inkl.** *inklusive* including, inclusive of

**Insp.** *Inspektor* inspector

**Inst.** 1. *Instanz* instance. 2. *Institut* institute

**int.** *international* international

**inzw.** *inzwischen* in the meantime

**IR-** *Infrarot-* infra red

**i.R.** *im Ruhestand* retired

**i.V.** 1. *in Vertretung* per pro, *abbr.* p.p. 2. *in Vorbereitung* in preparation

**i.W.** *in Worten* in words

**Jb.** *Jahrbuch* yearbook

**Jg.** *Jahrgang* year/age group

**JH** *Jugendherberge* youth hostel

**Jh** *Jahrhundert* century

**jun.** *junior* junior

**jur.** *juristisch* legal

**kath.** *katholisch* catholic

**Kfm.** *Kaufmann* business man

**Kfz** *Kraftfahrzeug* motor vehicle

**KG** *Kommanditgesellschaft* limited partnership

**kg** *Kilogramm* kilogram

**kgl.** *königlich* royal

**khz** *Kilohertz* kilocycles per second, kilohertz

**k.J.** *künftigen Jahres* of next year

**Kl.** *Klasse* class

**k.M.** *künftigen Monats* of next month

**km** *Kilometer* kilometre(s), *abbr.* km; **km/h** *Kilometer pro Stunde* kilometres per hour, *abbr.* k.p.h.

**kn** *Nau: Knoten* knot(s)

**kompl.** *komplett* complete

**Konf.** *Konfession* denomination

**Kpt** *Kapitän* captain

**Kr.** *Adm: Kreis* administrative district

**Kt.** *Kanton* Canton

**k.u.k.** *Aus:Hist: kaiserlich und königlich* Imperial and Royal, i.e. Austro-Hungarian

**kv.** *kriegsverwendungsfähig* fit for war service

**KW** *Kurzwelle* short wave

**kW** *Kilowatt* kilowatt(s), *abbr.* kW

**kWh** *Kilowattstunde(n)* kilowatt hour(s), *abbr.* kWh

**KZ** *Hist: Konzentrationslager* concentration camp

**Kzf.** *Kurzform* abbreviated form

**l** 1. *Meas: Liter* litre. 2. *links* on the left

**landw.** *landwirtschaftlich* agricultural

**Ldkr.** *Landkreis* rural district

**led.** *ledig* unmarried, single

**lfd.** *laufend* current

**LG** *Landgericht* District Court

**Lit.** *Literatur* literature

**Lkw., LKW** *Lastkraftwagen* lorry

**LPG** *East G: landwirtschaftliche Produktionsgenossenschaft* agricultural co-operative

**lt.** *laut* according to

**luth.** *Ecc: lutherisch* Lutheran

**LW** *Rad: Langwelle* long wave

**M** *East G: Mark* mark(s)

**m** *Meas: Meter* metre; **m²** square metre; **m³** cubic metre

**MA.** *Mittelalter* middle ages

**ma.** *mittelalterlich* medieval

**Mag.** *Magister* Master (degree)

**Math.** *Mathematik* mathematics

**m.a.W.** *mit anderen Worten* in other words

**max.** *maximal* maximum

**mb** *Millibar* millibar

**mdal.** *mundartlich* dialect

**MdB** *Mitglied des Bundestages* Member of the Bundestag (West German parliament)

**mdl.** *mündlich* verbal(ly)

**m.E.** *meines Erachtens* in my opinion

**mech.** *mechanisch* mechanical

**med.** *medizinisch* medical

**mehrf.** *mehrfach* multiple; *adv.* several times

**MEZ** *Mitteleuropäische Zeit* Central European Time

**mfG** *mit freundlichen Grüßen* kind regards

**mg** *Milligramm* milligram(s)

**MG** *Maschinengewehr* machine gun

**MHz** *Megahertz* megahertz

**Mi** *Mittwoch* Wednesday, *abbr.* Wed.

**Mill.** *Million(en)* million(s)

**Min.** *Minute(n)* minute(s)

**min.** *minimal* minimum

**ml** *Milliliter* millilitre

**mm** *Millimeter* millimetre

**Mo** *Montag* Monday, *abbr.* Mon.

**möbl.** *möbliert* furnished

**Mrd.** *Milliarde* thousand million, *N.Am:* billion

**mtl.** *monatlich* monthly

**M-und-S, M + S** *Aut: Matsch-und-Schnee (Reifen)* snow (tyres)

**MWSt.** *Mehrwertsteuer* value-added tax, *abbr.* VAT

**Mz.** *Mehrzahl* plural

**N** *Nord* north

**Nachf.** *Com: Nachfolger* successor

**nachm.** *nachmittags* in the afternoon, *abbr.* p.m.

**nat.** *national* national

**n.Br.** *nördlicher Breite* of northern latitude

**n.Chr.** *nach Christus* after Christ, *abbr.* A.D.

**NDR** *Norddeutscher Rundfunk* North German Radio

**NF** 1. *Niederfrequenz* low frequency. 2. *East G:Pol: Nationale Front* National Front

**n.J.** *nächsten Jahres* of next year

**n.M.** *nächsten Monats* of next month

**N.N.** *Name unbekannt* name unknown

**NO** *Nordost* northeast

**NR** *Aus: Mitglied des Nationalrats* Member of the National Assembly

**Nr.** *Nummer* number

**NS** 1. *Nachschrift* postscript, *abbr.* PS. 2. *Hist: nationalsozialistisch* National Socialist, Nazi

**N.T.** *Neues Testament* New Testament

**NW** *Nordwest* northwest

**O** *Ost* east

**o.** 1. *oder* or. 2. *ohne* without. 3. *oben* above

**ö.** *öffentlich* public

**o.a.** *oben angeführt* above-mentioned

**o.ä.** *oder ähnlich* or similar

**o.A.** *ohne Adresse* of no fixed abode

**ÖAMTC** *Österreichischer Auto-, Motorrad- und Touring-Club* Austrian Automobile, Motorcycle and Touring Club

**OB** 1. *Oberbürgermeister* first mayor. 2. *Mil: Oberbefehlshaber* commander-in-chief, *abbr.* C.-in-c.

**o.B.** *Med: ohne Befund* (test) result negative

**Obb.** *Oberbayern* Upper Bavaria

**ÖBB** *Österreichische Bundesbahnen* Austrian Federal Railways

**od.** *oder* or

**OEZ** *Osteuropäische Zeit* East European time

**öff(entl).** *öffentlich* public

**OHG** *Offene Handelsgesellschaft* general partnership

**o.J.** *ohne Jahr* no date

**ö.L.** *östlicher Länge* of eastern longitude

**OÖ.** *Oberösterreich* Upper Austria

**OP** 1. *Originalpackung* original pack. 2. *Med: Operationssaal* operating theatre

**o.Pr.** *ordentlicher Professor* full professor

**ORF** *Österreichischer Rundfunk* Austrian Radio

**örtl.** *örtlich* local(ly)

**o.V.** *ohne Verfasser* author unknown, *abbr.* anon.

**ÖVP** *Österreichische Volkspartei* Austrian Peoples' Party

**P.** *Ecc:* 1. *Pastor* pastor. 2. *Pater* Father

**p.A(dr).** *per Adresse* care of, *abbr.* c/o

**Part.** *Parterre* ground floor

**pat.** *patentiert* patented

**Pf** *Pfennig* pfennig(s)

**Pfd.** *Pfund* pound (weight)

**PH** *Pädagogische Hochschule* teachers' training college

**pharm.** *pharmazeutisch* pharmaceutical

**phot.** *photographisch* photographic

**Pkt.** *Punkt* point

**PKW, Pkw.** *Personenkraftwagen* passenger car

**Pl.** *Platz* square

**pl., Pl.** *Plural* plural

**pol.** 1. *politisch* political. 2. *polizeilich* police

**pop.** *populär* popular

**Postf.** *Postfach* post-office box

**P.P.** *praemissis praemittendis* to whom it may concern

**p.p., p.pa., ppa.** *per procura* per pro, *abbr.* p.p.

**Präp.** *Präposition* preposition

**priv.** *privat* private

**Prof.** *Professor* professor

**prot.** *protestantisch* Protestant

**Prov.** *Provinz* province

**PS** 1. *Pferdestärke(n)* horse-power. 2. *postscriptum, Nachschrift* postscript

**qkm** *Quadratkilometer* square kilometre, *abbr.* sq.km.

**qm** *Quadratmeter* square metre, *abbr.* sq.m.

**Quitt.** *Quittung* receipt

**r.** 1. *rechts* on the right. 2. *Mth: Radius* radius

**rd.** *rund* roughly

**Red.** *Redakteur* editor; *Redaktion* editorial staff

**Reg.** 1. *Regierung* government. 2. *Register* register

**Reg.Bez.** *Regierungsbezirk* administrative district

**Rel.** *Religion* religion

**Rep.** *Republik* republic

**resp.** *respektive* or . . . as the case may be

**Rhld.** *Rheinland* Rhineland

**RIAS** *Rundfunk im amerikanischen Sektor* Radio in the American Sector (of Berlin)

**rk., r.-k.** *römisch-katholisch* Roman Catholic

**rm** *Raummeter* cubic metre

**röm.** *römisch* Roman
**Rzpt.** *Med: Rezept* prescription
**S** *Süd* south
**S. 1.** *Seite* page. **2.** *Aus: Schilling* schilling
**s.** *siehe* see, *abbr.* v.; **s.a.** *siehe auch* see also
**Sa** *Samstag* Saturday, *abbr.* Sat.
**S-Bahn** *Schnellbahn* urban railway
**SB** *Selbstbedienung* self-service
**SBB** *Schweizerische Bundesbahn* Swiss Federal
　Railways
**s.Br.** *südlicher Breite* of southern latitude
**s.d.** *siehe dies* see this
**SDR** *Süddeutscher Rundfunk* South German
　Radio
**SED** *East G:Pol: Sozialistische Einheitspartei
　Deutschlands* Socialist Unity Party (of Ger-
　many)
**Sek., sek.** *Sekunde* second
**Sekr.** *Sekretär(in)* secretary
**Sem.** *(a) Semester* term; *(b) Seminar* seminar
**Sen.** *Senator* senator
**sen.** *senior* senior
**SFB** *Sender Freies Berlin* Free Berlin Radio
**sfr., sFr.** *Schweizer Franken* Swiss francs
**sm** *Seemeile* nautical mile
**SO** *Südost* south-east, *abbr.* SE
**s.o.** *siehe oben* see above
**So** *Sonntag* Sunday, *abbr.* Sun.
**sog.** *sogenannt* so-called
**SOS** *internationales Notsignal* SOS
**soz.** *sozial(istisch)* social, socialist
**SPD** *Sozialdemokratische Partei Deutschlands*
　Social Democratic Party of Germany
**spez.** *(a) speziell* special(ly); *(b) spezifisch* specif-
　ic(ally)
**SPÖ** *Sozialistische Partei Österreichs* Socialist
　Party of Austria
**SR** *Saarländischer Rundfunk* Saar Radio
**SSD** *East G: Staatssicherheitsdienst* State Secur-
　ity Service
**St. 1.** *Stück* piece. **2.** *Sankt* Saint
**staatl.gepr.** *staatlich geprüft* who has passed a
　state examination
**städt.** *städtisch* urban, municipal
**Std.** *Stunde* hour
**stdl.** *stündlich* every hour
**stellv.** *stellvertretend* assistant
**StGB** *Strafgesetzbuch* Penal Code
**StKl.** *Steuerklasse* tax class
**StPO** *Strafprozeßordnung* Code for Criminal
　Proceedings
**Str.** *Straße* street, road
**stud.** *studiosus, Student* student
**StVO** *Straßenverkehrsordnung* traffic regulations
**s.t.** *sine tempore* sharp, on time
**s.u.** *siehe unten* see below
**SV** *Sportverein* sports club
**svw.** *soviel wie* as good as; much the same as
**SW** *Südwest* south-west, *abbr.* SW.
**SWF** *Südwestfunk* South-West German Radio

**s.Z.** *seinerzeit* at that time
**SZ** *Sommerzeit* summer time
**t** *Tonne* ton
**TA 1.** *Rec: Tonabnehmer* pick-up. **2.** *Aus:
　Tierarzt* veterinary surgeon
**Tab.** *Tabelle* table, chart
**tägl.** *täglich* daily, per day
**Tb, Tbc** *Tuberkulose* tuberculosis
**TEE** *Trans-Europ-Express* Trans-European Ex-
　press
**Teilh.** *Teilhaber* partner
**Teilz.** *Teilzahlung* part-payment
**Tel.** *(a) Telefon* telephone; *(b) Telegramm* tele-
　gram
**Temp.** *Temperatur* temperature
**TF-Boot** *Tragflächenboot* hydrofoil
**TH** *Technische Hochschule* technical university
**Tsd.** *Tausend* thousand
**TSV** *Turn- und Sportverein* gymnastics and
　sports club
**TU** *Technische Universität* Technical University
**TÜV** *Technischer Überwachungsverein* Associa-
　tion for Technical Inspection; *(Prüfung)*
　*approx. Brit:* MOT test
**TV 1.** *Turnverein* gymnastics club. **2.** *Tarifver-
　trag* wage agreement. **3.** *Television* television
**u.** *und* and
**u.a.** *und andere/anderes* and others/other things;
　*unter anderem/anderen* among other things
**u.ä.** *und ähnliche(s)* and the like
**u.A.w.g.** *um Antwort wird gebeten* an answer is
　requested, *abbr.* R.S.V.P.
**Übers.** *Übersetzer* translator
**übl.** *üblich* usual
**u.dsgl.(m)./u.dgl.(m).** *und desgleichen/
　dergleichen (mehr)* and things like that
**u.d.M./ü.d.M.** *unter/über dem Meeresspiegel* be-
　low/above sea level
**UdSSR** *Union der Sozialistischen Sowjet-
　republiken* Union of Soviet Socialist
　Republics
**u.E.** *unseres Erachtens* in our opinion
**UHF** *Rad: Ultra-Hochfrequenz* ultra high fre-
　quency
**UKW** *Rad: Ultrakurzwelle* very high frequency,
　*abbr.* VHF
**ult.** *ultimo* on the last day of (the month)
**U/min.** *Umdrehungen in der Minute* revolutions
　per minute, *abbr.* r.p.m.
**Univ.** *Universität* university
**unverk.** *unverkäuflich* not for sale
**urspr.** *ursprünglich* original(ly)
**US(A)** *Vereinigte Staaten (von Amerika)* United
　States (of America)
**usf.** *und so fort* and so forth
**usw.** *und so weiter* and so on, *abbr.* etc.
**u.U.** *unter Umständen* circumstances permitting
**UV-** *ultraviolett* ultra-violet
**u.v.a.** *und viele(s) andere* and many others
**u.W.** *unseres Wissens* as far as we know

**v.** *von, vom* of; from; by
**V** 1. *Volt* volt. 2. *Volumen* volume
**V.** *Vers* line, verse
**VAR** *Vereinigte Arabische Republik* United Arab Republic
**var.** *variabel* variable
**v.Chr.** *vor Christus* before Christ, *abbr.* B.C.
**VDS** *Verband deutscher Studentenschaften* Association of German Students
**VEB** *East G: Volkseigener Betrieb* nationalized/people's concern
**verb.** *verbessert* corrected
**Verf., Vf.** *Verfasser* author
**verh.** *verheiratet* married
**Verl.** (a) *Verlag* publishing firm; (b) *Verleger* publisher
**Verm.** *Vermerk* note
**versch.** 1. *verschieden* different. 2. *verschollen* missing
**verst.** *verstorben* deceased
**vgl.** *vergleiche* compare, *abbr.* cf.
**v.H., vH** *vom Hundert* per cent
**VHS** *Volkshochschule approx.* College of Further Education
**v.J.** *vorigen Jahres* of last year
**v.l.n.r.** *von links nach rechts* from left to right
**v.M.** *vorigen Monats* of last month
**v.o.** *von oben* from above
**Vollm.** *Vollmacht* authority
**vollst.** *vollständig* complete
**vorl.** *vorläufig* provisional
**vorm.** 1. *vormittags* in the morning, *abbr.* a.m. 2. *vormals* formerly
**Vors.** *Vorsitzender* chairman
**VR** *Volksrepublik* People's Republic
**v.r.n.l.** *von rechts nach links* from right to left
**v.T., vT** *vom Tausend* per thousand
**W** 1. *West* west. 2. *El: Watt* watt(s)
**Wb.** *Wörterbuch* dictionary
**WDR** *Westdeutscher Rundfunk* West German Radio

**WEU** *Westeuropäische Union* Western European Union
**WEZ** *westeuropäische Zeit* West European time, Greenwich mean time
**Whg.** *Wohnung* flat
**Wkst.** (a) *Werkstatt* workshop; (b) *Werkstück* workpiece
**w.L.** *westlicher Länge* of western longitude
**w.o.** *wie oben* as above
**WSP** *Wasserschutzpolizei* river police
**Wwe.** *Witwe* widow
**Wwr.** *Witwer* widower
**Wz.** *Warenzeichen* trademark
**Z.** 1. *Zahl* number. 2. *Zeile* line
**z.** *zu, zum* at; to
**z.A.** *zur Ansicht* for inspection; (sent) on approval
**z.B.** *zum Beispiel* for instance, *abbr.* e.g.
**z.d.A.** *zu den Akten* to be filed
**ZDF** *Zweites Deutsches Fernsehen* Second Channel of West German Television
**zgl.** *zugleich* at the same time
**z.H(d).** *Com: zu Händen* for the attention of
**Zi** *Zimmer* room
**Ziff.** *Ziffer* figure
**ZK** *Pol: Zentralkomitee* Central Committee
**z.K.** *zur Kenntnisnahme* for information
**ZPO** *Jur: Zivilprozeßordnung* Code for Civil Actions
**z.S.** *zur See* naval
**z.T.** *zum Teil* partly
**Ztg.** *Zeitung* newspaper
**Ztr.** *Zentner approx.* hundredweight
**Zub.** *Zubehör* accessories
**zuf.** *zufolge* as a result of
**zus.** *zusammen* together
**z.V.** *zum Verkauf* for sale
**zw.** *zwischen* between, among
**zzgl.** *zuzüglich* plus
**z.Z(t).** *zur Zeit* at the time; (*jetzt*) at present

# English Abbreviations
# Englische Abkürzungen

**A.A.** *Automobile Association* (britischer Automobilclub)
**A.A.A.** 1. *N.Am: American Automobile Association* (führender Automobilclub) 2. *Brit: Amateur Athletics Association* Leichtathletikverband *m*
**ABC** 1. *American Broadcasting Company* (amerikanische Rundfunkgesellschaft). 2. *Australian Broadcasting Corporation* Australischer

Rundfunk
**AC** *El: alternating current* Wechselstrom *m*
**a/c** *account* Konto *n*
**A.D.** *anno Domini* nach Christi Geburt, *abbr.* n.Chr.
**AFN** *American Forces Network* Rundfunk der amerikanischen Streitkräfte
**A.G.M.** *Annual General Meeting* Jahresvollver-

sammlung *f*
**a.m.** *ante meridiem* vormittags
**anon** *anonymous* Autor unbekannt
**appro.** *Com: on appro.* = *on approval* zur Ansicht/Probe
**approx.** *approximately* ungefähr
**arr.** *Rail: etc: arrive(s)* . . . an, Ankunft . . .
**ASAP** *as soon as possible* sobald wie möglich
**ass(oc).** *association* Verband *m*
**asst.** *assistant* Mitarbeiter *m; attrib.* stellvertretend
**Aug.** *August* August *m*
**Av., Ave.** *Avenue* Chaussee *f*
**b.** *born* geboren, *abbr.* geb.
**B.A.** 1. *Bachelor of Arts* (Grad). 2. *Av: British Airways* Britische Fluggesellschaft
**b. & b.** *bed & breakfast* Zimmer mit Frühstück
**Bart** *Baronet* Baron *m*
**B.A.O.R.** *British Army of the Rhine* Britische Rheinarmee
**BBC** *British Broadcasting Corporation* Britische Rundfunkgesellschaft
**BC** *before Christ* vor Christi Geburt, *abbr.* v.Chr.
**B.C.G.** *Bilié de Calmette et Guérin* (TBC-Impfstoff)
**Beds.** *Bedfordshire* (Grafschaft)
**Berks.** *Berkshire* (Grafschaft)
**B.F.N.** *Rad: British Forces Network* Rundfunk der Britischen Streitkräfte
**b.h.p.** *Mec.E: brake horse power* Brems-PS
**bldg(s).** *building(s)* Gebäude *n*
**B.M.A.** *British Medical Association* Britischer Ärzteverband
**B.O.** *F: body odour* Körpergeruch *m*
**Br.** *Ecc: Brother* Frater *m*
**BR** *British Rail* Britische Eisenbahngesellschaft
**Bros.** *Com: Brothers* Gebrüder
**BS** *British Standard approx.* = DIN
**B.Sc.** *Bachelor of Science* (Grad)
**B.S.I.** *British Standards Institution* Britisches Normungsinstitut
**B.S.T.** *British Summer Time* Britische Sommerzeit
**bt. fwd.** *Com: brought forward* Übertrag
**B.T.U.** *British Thermal Unit* Britische Wärmeeinheit
**Bucks.** *Buckinghamshire* (Grafschaft)
**C** *Ph: centigrade* Celsius
**c.** 1. *N.Am: etc: cent* Cent *m.* 2. *circa* zirka
**Cantab.** *Cantabrigiensis* = *of Cambridge* von Cambridge
**Capt.** *captain Mil:* Hauptmann *m; Nau:* Kapitän *m*
**CB** *Rad: Citizens' Band* Privatfunk (CB)
**CBC** *Canadian Broadcasting Company* Kanadischer Rundfunk
**C.B.E.** *Commander of the (Order of the) British Empire* Komtur des Ordens des British Empire
**C.B.I.** *Confederation of British Industries* Briti-

scher Industrieverband
**C.B.S.** *Columbia Broadcasting System* (amerikanische Rundfunkgesellschaft)
**C.C.** 1. *County Council* Verwaltung der Grafschaft. 2. *Cricket Club*
**c.c.** *cubic centimetre(s)* Kubikzentimeter *m*
**C.D.** 1. *Civil Defence* ziviler Bevölkerungsschutz. 2. *corps diplomatique* diplomatisches Korps
**Cdr.** *Nau: Commander* Fregattenkapitän *m*
**cent.** *hundred* hundert
**cert.** *certificate* Bescheinigung *f; Sch:* Zeugnis *n,* Zertifikat *n*
**CET** *Central European Time* Mitteleuropäische Zeit, *abbr.* MEZ
**cf.** *confer* vergleiche, *abbr.* vgl.
**C.H.** *Companion of Honour* Mitglied des Ehrenordens
**chw.** *constant hot water* fließendes Warmwasser zu jeder Tages- und Nachtzeit
**C.I.** *Channel Islands* Kanalinseln *fpl*
**C.I.A.** *Central Intelligence Agency* (amerikanischer Geheimdienst)
**C.I.D.** *Brit: Criminal Investigation Department* Kriminalpolizei *f*
**C-in-C.** *Commander-in-Chief* Oberbefehlshaber *m*
**cl.** *Meas: centilitre* Zentiliter *m*
**cm** *Meas: centimetre* Zentimeter *m*
**CND** *Campaign for Nuclear Disarmament* Bewegung für atomare Abrüstung
**C.O.** *Commanding Officer* Kommandeur *m*
**c/o** *(on letter) care of* bei
**Co.** *Company* Gesellschaft
**COD** *cash on delivery* per Nachnahme
**C. of E.** *Church of England* anglikanische Kirche
**Col.** *Mil: Colonel* Oberst *m*
**Cons.** *Pol: Conservative* konservativ
**cp.** *compare* vergleiche, *abbr.* vgl.
**cr.** *Fin: credit* Haben
**Cres.** *Crescent* (bogenförmig geschwungene Straße)
**cu.** *cubic* kubik
**c.v.** *curriculum vitae* Lebenslauf *m*
**cwt.** *Meas: hundredweight* Zentner *m*
**d.** 1. *deceased* gestorben. 2. *A: (coin) penny/pl pence* Penny
**D.A.** *N.Am: district attorney* Bezirksstaatsanwalt *m*
**D.C.** 1. *El: direct current* Gleichstrom *m.* 2. *N.Am: Geog:* District of Columbia
**deb.** *Fin: debit* Soll *n*
**Dec.** *December* Dezember *m*
**dep.** *departure* Abfahrt *f*
**Dept.** *Department* Abteilung *f*
**Dip.Ed.** *Diploma of Education* Lehrerdiplom *n*
**DIY** *do-it-yourself* Heimwerken *n; DIY shop* Heimwerkerladen *m*
**D.J.** *dinner jacket* Smoking *m*
**do.** *ditto* dito, desgleichen

**dol.** *dollar* Dollar *m*
**doz.** *dozen* Dutzend *n*
**D.Phil.** *doctor of Philosophy* Doktor der Philosophie
**Dr.** *doctor* Doktor *m*
**D.S.C.** *Distinguished Service Cross* (militärisches Verdienstkreuz)
**D.S.O.** *Distinguished Service Order* (militärischer Verdienstorden)
**D.T.** *delirium tremens* Delirium tremens *n*
**E.** *East* Ost
**E. & O.E.** *Com: errors and omissions excepted* Irrtümer und Auslassungen vorbehalten
**E.C.** *European Community* Europäische Gemeinschaft, *abbr.* EG
**E.C.G.** *electrocardiogram* Elektrokardiogramm *n*, *abbr.* EKG
**Ed.** *Editor* Redakteur *m*
**ed(it).** *edited (by)* herausgegeben (von)
**E.E.C.** *European Economic Community* Europäische Wirtschaftsgemeinschaft, *abbr.* EWG
**EFTA** *European Free Trade Association* Europäische Freihandelszone
**e.g.** *for example* zum Beispiel, *abbr.* z.B.
**encl.** *Com: enclosure(s)* Anlage *f*
**eng(r).** *engineer* Ingenieur, *abbr.* Ing.
**Esq.** *Esquire;* (*in address*) *J. Smith Esq.* Herrn J. Smith
**est.** *established* gegründet
**E.T.A.** *Estimated Time of Arrival* geschätzte Ankunftszeit
**et. al.** *et alia* und andere
**etc.** *etcetera* und so weiter, *abbr.* usw.
**Euratom** *European Atomic Energy Community* Europäische Atomgemeinschaft
**ex.** *example* Beispiel *n*
**Exc.** *Excellency* Exzellenz *f*
**excl.** *exclusive* ausschließlich
**F** *Meas: Fahrenheit* (Temperaturskala)
**F.A.** *Football Association* Fußballbund *m*
**F.B.I.** *N.Am: Federal Bureau of Investigation* Bundeskriminalamt *n*
**F.C.** *football club* Fußballclub *m*
**Feb.** *February* Februar *m*
**fem.** *feminine* weiblich
**ff.** (*and*) *following (pages etc.)* (und) folgende (Seiten usw.)
**fig.** 1. *figure* Abbildung *f.* 2. *figurative* figurativ, übertragen
**fl.** *florin* Florin *m*
**FM** *frequency modulation* Frequenzmodulation *f*; *Rad:* (=*VHF*) UKW
**F.O.** *Foreign Office* (britisches) Außenministerium *n*
**f.o.b.** *Com: free on board* frei Schiff
**f.o.c.** *Com: free of charge* franko
**Fr.** *Ecc: Father* Pater *m*
**F.R.G.** *Federal Republic of Germany* Bundesrepublik Deutschland
**Fri.** *Friday* Freitag *m*, *abbr.* Fr.

**F.R.S.** *Fellow of the Royal Society* Mitglied der königlichen Gesellschaft (für Naturwissenschaften)
**ft.** *Meas: foot* Fuß *m*
**fwd.** *forward;* (*amount*) *brought fwd.* Übertrag *m*
**gal.** *Meas: gallon* Gallone *f*
**G.B.** *Great Britain* Großbritannien *n*
**G.C.** *George Cross* (Tapferkeitsorden für die Zivilbevölkerung)
**Gdn(s).** *Garden(s)* (in Straßennamen)
**G.D.R.** *German Democratic Republic* Deutsche Demokratische Republik, *abbr.* DDR
**Gen.** *Mil: etc: General* General *m*
**G.I.** *N.Am: general infantryman* einfacher Soldat
**G.L.C.** *Greater London Council* Verwaltungsrat für Groß-London
**G.M.T.** *Greenwich Mean Time* westeuropäische Zeit, *abbr.* WEZ
**G.N.P.** *gross national product* Bruttosozialprodukt *n*
**govt.** *government* Regierung *f*
**G.P.** *general practitioner* praktischer Arzt *m*
**G.P.O.** *A: General Post Office* Britische Postverwaltung
**gr.** *Meas: gram* Gramm *n*
**h.** *hour(s)* Stunde(n) *f(pl)*
**h. & c.** *hot and cold* fließendes Warm- und Kaltwasser
**Hants.** *Hampshire* (Grafschaft)
**hect.** *Meas: hectolitre* Hektoliter, *abbr.* hl.
**Herts.** *Hertfordshire* (Grafschaft)
**H.F.** *high frequency* Hochfrequenz *f*
**H.M.** *His/Her Majesty* Seine/Ihre Majestät
**H.M.S.** *His/Her/Majesty's Ship* Schiff der königlichen Marine
**H.M.S.O.** *His/Her Majesty's Stationery Office* Staatsdruckerei und -verlag
**Hon.** (*in titles*) *Honourable* ehrenwert (jüngerer Sohn eines Adligen)
**H.P.** *Hire Purchase* Ratenkauf *m*
**h.p.** *Mec: horsepower* Pferdestärke, *abbr.* PS
**H.Q.** *Mil: headquarters* Hauptquartier *n*
**H.R.H.** *His/Her Royal Highness* Seine/Ihre Königliche Hoheit
**ibid.** *ibidem* ebenda
**i/c** *in charge; to be i/c* die Leitung/Verantwortung haben
**ID** *identity/identification* Identität *f*/ Identitätsausweis *m*
**i.e.** *id est = that is to say* das heißt
**I.L.O.** *International Labour Organization* Internationale Arbeitsorganisation
**I.M.F.** *International Monetary Fund* Internationaler Währungsfonds
**in./ins.** *Meas: inch/inches* Zoll *m(pl)*
**Inc.** *Incorporated (of company etc.)* eingetragen
**incl.** *inclusive* inklusive, einschließlich
**Ind.** *Pol: Independent* Unabhängige(r) *f(m)*
**inst.** *Com: instant* dieses Monats

**I.O.M.** *Isle of Man* die Insel Man
**I.O.U.** *I owe you* Schuldschein *m*
**I.O.W.** *Isle of Wight* die Insel Wight
**I.Q.** *intelligence quotient* Intelligenzquotient *m*, *abbr.* IQ *m*
**IRA** *Irish Republican Army* Irisch-Republikanische Armee, *abbr.* IRA *f*
**ITV** *Independent Television* Unabhängiges Fernsehen

**Jan.** *January* Januar *m*
**J.C.** *Jesus Christ* Jesus Christus
**J.P.** *Justice of the Peace* Friedensrichter *m*
**Jul.** *July* Juli *m*
**Jr.** *Junior* Junior *m*
**k.** *kilogram* Kilogramm *n*, *abbr.* kg
**kc.** *El: kilocycle* Kilohertz *n*, *abbr.* kHz
**K.C.B.** *Knight Commander of the Order of the Bath* Großmeister *m* des Bath-Ordens
**KHz** *kilohertz* Kilohertz *n*, *abbr.* kHz
**km** *kilometre* Kilometer *m*, *abbr.* km
**K.O.** *knockout* K.O. *n*
**k.p.h.** *kilometres per hour* Stundenkilometer *pl*, *abbr.* km/h
**kv** *El: kilovolt* Kilovolt *n*, *abbr.* kV
**kw** *El: kilowatt* Kilowatt *n*, *abbr.* kW
**l. 1.** *Meas:* litre Liter *m abbr.* l. **2.** *left* links
**Lab.** *Pol: Labour* Labour(partei *f*)
**lat.** *Geog: latitude* geographische Breite
**lb.** *Meas: pound* Pfund *n* (Gewicht)
**l.b.w.** *(Cricket) leg before wicket* (unerlaubtes) Schützen des Tores durch die Beine
**Leics.** *Leicestershire* (Grafschaft)
**L.F.** *low-frequency* Niederfrequenz *f*
**l.h.** *lefthand* linke(r, s)
**Lib.** *Pol: Liberal* Liberale(r) *f(m)*
**Lieut.** *Mil: Lieutenant* Oberleutnant *m*
**Lieut.-Col.** *Mil: Lieutenant-Colonel* Oberstleutnant *m*
**Lincs.** *Lincolnshire* (Grafschaft)
**loc.cit.** *loco citato = at the place cited* am angeführten Orte, *abbr.* a.a.O.
**long.** *Geog: longitude* geographische Länge
**L.P.** *long-playing record* Langspielplatte *f*
**L.P.O.** *London Philharmonic Orchestra* Londoner Philharmoniker *pl*
**L.S.D.** *lysergic acid diethylamide* LSD *n*
**L.S.E.** *London School of Economics* Londoner Wirtschaftshochschule *f*
**L.S.O.** *London Symphony Orchestra* Londoner Symphonieorchester *n*
**Lt.** *Mil: Lieutenant* Oberleutnant *m*
**Ltd.** *Com: Limited (company)* approx. (Gesellschaft *f*) mit beschränkter Haftung, *abbr.* GmbH *f*
**m. 1.** *male, Gram: masculine* männlich, *abbr.* m. **2.** *Meas:* (a) *metre* Meter *m*, *abbr.* m; **m²** *square metre* Quadratmeter *m*, *abbr.* m²; **m³** *cubic metre* Kubikmeter *m*, *abbr.* m³; (b) *mile(s)* Meile(n) *f(pl)*
**M.A.** *Master of Arts* (Magistergrad)

**Maj.** *Mil: Major* Major *m*
**masc.** *masculine* männlich
**math** *N.Am:/maths Brit: mathematics* Mathematik *f*
**max.** *maximum* Maximum *n*
**M.C.** *Master of Ceremonies* Zeremonienmeister *m*
**M.C.C.** *Marylebone Cricket Club* (führender Cricketverein)
**M.D.** *Medicinae Doctor = Doctor of Medicine* Doktor *m* der Medizin, *abbr.* Dr.med.
**mg.** *Meas: milligram* Milligramm *n*, *abbr.* mgr
**Mgr.** *Ecc: Monsignor* Monsignore *m*, *abbr.* Mgr.
**Middx.** *Middlesex* (Grafschaft)
**min.** *minimum* Minimum *n*
**mm** *Meas: millimetre(s)* Millimeter *m*, *abbr.* mm
**M.O.** *Mil: Medical officer* Stabsarzt *m*
**mod.cons.** *modern conveniences* (moderner) Komfort
**Mon.** *Monday* Montag *m*, *abbr.* Mo
**M.O.T.** (a) *A: Ministry of Transport* Transportministerium *n*; (b) *Aut:F: MOT (test)* approx. TUV *m*
**M.P. 1.** *Member of Parliament* Parlamentsabgeordnete(r) *f(m)*. **2.** *Military Police* Militärpolizei *f*
**m.p.g.** *Aut: miles per gallon* Meilen pro Gallone
**m.p.h.** *miles per hour* Meilen pro Stunde
**MS.** *manuscript* Manuskript *n*; **MSS.** *manuscripts* Manuskripte *npl*
**MS** *Nau: Motor Ship* Motorschiff *n*
**Mt.** *Mount* Berg *m* (in Eigennamen)
**N.** *north* Nord, *abbr.* N
**NASA** ['næsə] *N.Am: National Aeronautics and Space Administration* Nationale Luft- und Raumfahrtbehörde
**NATO** ['neitəu] *North Atlantic Treaty Organization* Nato *f*
**N.B.** *nota bene* wohlgemerkt
**NBC** *National Broadcasting Corporation* (amerikanische Rundfunkgesellschaft)
**N.C.O.** *Mil: non-commissioned officer* Unteroffizier *m*
**NE, N.E.** *north-east* Nordost, *abbr.* NO
**N.H.S.** *Adm: National Health Service* Staatlicher Gesundheitsdienst
**no.** *number* Nummer *f*, *abbr.* Nr.
**Northants.** *Northamptonshire* (Grafschaft)
**Notts.** *Nottinghamshire* (Grafschaft)
**Nov.** *November* November *m*
**nr.** *near (in address)* bei
**N.S.P.C.C.** *National Society for the Prevention of Cruelty to Children* Kinderschutzbund *m*
**N.T.** *New Testament* Neues Testament
**NUJ** *National Union of Journalists* (Journalistengewerkschaft)
**NUR** *National Union of Railwaymen* (Eisenbahnergewerkschaft)
**NUS** *National Union of Students* (Studentengewerkschaft)

**NUT** *National Union of Teachers* (Lehrergewerkschaft)

**NW** *north-west* Nordwest, *abbr.* NW

**N.Y.** *New York*

**N.Y.C.** *New York City*

**N.Z.** *New Zealand* Neuseeland *n*

**OAP** *old age pensioner* Rentner *m*

**OAS** *Organization of American States* Organisation der amerikanischen Staaten

**OAU** *Organization of African Unity* Organisation der afrikanischen Einheit

**ob.** *obit* gestorben, *abbr.* gest.

**O.B.E.** *(Officer of the) Order of the British Empire* (Auszeichnung für Beamte und Zivilisten)

**Oct.** *October* Oktober *m*

**OECD** *Organization for Economic Cooperation and Development* Organisation für wirtschaftliche Zusammenarbeit und Entwicklung

**OHMS** *On His/Her Majesty's Service* im Dienste seiner/ihrer Majestät; *(Post)* Dienstsache

**O.M.** *Order of Merit* (hohe Auszeichnung)

**o.n.o.** *or nearest offer* oder höchstes Angebot

**op.** *Mus: opus* Opus

**op.cit.** *opere citato = in the work quoted* im zitierten Werk, *abbr.* op.cit.

**ord.** *ordinary* gewöhnlich, normal

**Oxon.** 1. *Oxoniensis = of Oxford* von Oxford. 2. *Oxfordshire* (Grafschaft)

**oz.** *Meas: ounce* Unze *f*

**p.** 1. *page* Seite. 2. *per* pro. 3. *(money) pence* Pence *pl*

**p.a.** *per annum* pro Jahr

**P.A.** *Press Association* Presseverband *m*

**P.A.Y.E.** *pay as you earn* direkt einbehaltene Einkommensteuer

**P.C.** 1. *police constable* Polizist *m*, Schutzmann *m*. 2. *postcard* Postkarte *f*. 3. *personal computer* Personal Computer *m*

**p.c.** 1. *per cent* Prozent. 2. *postcard* Postkarte *f*

**P.D.S.A.** *People's Dispensary for Sick Animals* tierärztliche Fürsorge für weniger wohlhabende Tierhalter

**P.E.** *Physical Education* Leibesübungen und Sport

**Ph.D.** *Doctor of Philosophy* Doktor der Philosophie

**PLC/plc** *public limited company* Gesellschaft *f* mit beschränkter Haftung, *abbr.* GmbH *f* (mit börsenfähigen Aktien)

**P.L.O.** *Palestine Liberation Organization* Vereinigung für die Befreiung Palästinas

**P.M.** *Prime Minister* Premierminister *m*

**p.m.** *post meridiem* nachmittags, abends

**P.O.** *Post Office* Postamt *n*

**P.O.W.** *prisoner of war* Kriegsgefangene(r) *m*

**pp.** *pages* Seiten *fpl*

**p.p.** *per pro(curationem)* in Auftrag, *abbr.* i.A.

**P.R.** *public relations* Öffentlichkeitsarbeit *f*

**pr(s).** *pair(s)* Paar(e) *n(pl)*

**Pres.** *president* Präsident *m*

**Prof.** *professor* Professor *m*

**P.S.** *postscript* Postskriptum *n*, Nachschrift *f*, *abbr.* PS

**P.T.** *physical training* Leibesübungen *fpl*

**P.T.A.** *Parent-Teacher Association* Elternvereinigung *f*, Elternbeirat *m*

**Pte.** *Mil: Private* einfacher Soldat

**P.T.O.** *please turn over* bitte wenden, *abbr.* b.w.

**pub.** *published* veröffentlicht

**PVC** *polyvinylchloride* PVC *n*

**PX** *N.Am:Mil: Post Exchange* (Geschäft für das Militär)

**Q.C.** *Jur: Queen's Council* Justizrat *m*

**Q.E.D.** *quad erat demonstrandum* was zu beweisen war, *abbr.* q.e.d.

**q.v.** *which see* siehe unten, *abbr.* s.u.

**R.** 1. *River* Fluß *m*. 2. *Road* Straße *f*

**r.** *right* rechts

**R.A.** *Royal Academy* Königliche Kunstakademie

**R.A.C.** *Royal Automobile Club* (britischer Automobilclub)

**RADA** ['rɑ:də] *Royal Academy of Dramatic Art* Königliche Schauspielschule

**R.A.F.** *Royal Air Force* (Britische Luftwaffe)

**R.C.** *Roman Catholic* römisch-katholisch

**Rd.** *road* Straße *f*, *abbr.* Str.

**R.E.** 1. *Mil: Royal Engineers* (Pioniertruppe). 2. *Sch: religious education* Religion *f* (als Fach)

**ref.** *reference* Aktenzeichen *n*; *(on letter) your ref.*, Ihr Zeichen

**regd.** *registered* eingetragen; *(of letter)* eingeschrieben

**REME** *Royal Electrical and Mechanical Engineers* auf Elektronik und Mechanik spezialisierte Pioniertruppe

**rep.** *representative Com:* Vertreter *m*

**retd.** *retired* in Pension

**Rev.** *Ecc: Reverend* Hochwürden

**rev.** *revolution* Umdrehung *f*

**r.h.** *righthand* rechte(r,s)

**rly.** *railway* Eisenbahn *f*

**rm(s).** *room(s)* Zimmer *n(pl)*

**R.N.** *Royal Navy* Königliche Marine

**R.N.L.I.** *Royal National Lifeboat Institution* Königlich-Nationales Institut für Rettungsboote

**r.p.m.** *revolutions per minute* Umdrehungen pro Minute

**R.P.O.** *Royal Philharmonic Orchestra* Königliches Philharmonisches Orchester

**RSPCA** *Royal Society for the Prevention of Cruelty to Animals* Königlicher Tierschutzverein

**R.S.V.P.** *répondez s'il vous plaît* um Antwort wird gebeten, *abbr.* u.A.w.g.

**Rt.Hon.** *Right Honourable* Sehr Ehrenwert

**S.** *south* Süd

**s.a.e.** *stamped addressed envelope* frankierter Umschlag mit Adresse

**SALT** [sɔlt] *Strategic Arms Limitation Treaty* Vertrag über die Beschränkung von strategischen Waffen
**SDP** *Social Democratic Party* Sozialdemokratische Partei
**SE** *south-east* Südost, *abbr.* SE
**SEATO** ['siːtəu] *South East Asia Treaty Organization* Südostasienpakt-Organisation *f*
**sec.** 1. *second* Sekunde *f.* 2. *secretary* Schriftführer(in) *m(f)*
**Sen.** 1. *(with names) Senior* Senior, der Älteste. 2. *N.Am: Senator* Senator *m*
**Sept.** *September* September *m*
**S.F.** *science fiction* Science-fiction *f*
**Sgt.** *sergeant* Feldwebel *m*
**SLR** *Phot: single-lens reflex* (einäugige) Spiegelreflexkamera *f*
**SNP** *Scottish National Party* Schottisch-Nationale Partei
**snr.** *senior* Senior, ꞏder Älteste
**Soc.** *Society* Gesellschaft *f,* *(club)* Verein *m*
**Som.** *Somerset* (Grafschaft)
**S.O.S.** SOS *n* (Seenotzeichen)
**Sq.** *Square* Platz *m*
**sq.** *square* Quadrat *n*
**SRN** *state-registered nurse* staatlich anerkannte Krankenschwester
**St.** 1. *Saint* Sankt. 2. *Street* Straße *f*
**Sta.** *station* Bahnhof *m*
**Staffs.** *Staffordshire* (Grafschaft)
**S.T.D.** *Subscriber Trunk Dialling* Selbstwählferndienst *m*
**sub.** *subscription* Beitrag *m*
**Sun.** *Sunday* Sonntag *m*
**Supt.** *superintendent (of police) approx.* Kommissar *m*
**SW.** *south-west* Südwest, *abbr.* SW
**t.** *Meas: ton* Tonne *f*
**T.B.** *Med: tuberculosis* Tuberkulose *f*
**tel.** *telephone (number)* Telefon(nummer) *n (f)*
**temp.** 1. *temperature* Temperatur *f.* 2. *F: temporary secretary* Aushilfssekretärin *f*
**Ter(r).** *Terrace* Häuserreihe *f*
**Thurs.** *Thursday* Donnerstag, *abbr.* Do
**TNT** *trinitrotoluene* TNT *n*
**Tues.** *Tuesday* Dienstag, *abbr.* Di
**TUC** *Trade Union Congress* (britischer) Gewerkschaftsbund *m*
**TV** *television* Fernsehen *n,* TV *n*
**U.A.R.** *United Arab Republic* Vereinigte Arabische Republik
**UFO** ['juːfəu] *unidentified flying object* unbekanntes Flugobjekt, *abbr.* UFO *n*
**UHF** *ultra high frequency* Ultra-Hochfrequenz *f*
**U.K.** *Geog: United Kingdom* Vereinigtes Königreich
**ult.** *ultimo* des letzten Monats
**UN, U.N.** *United Nations* Vereinte Nationen *pl, abbr.* UNO *f*
**UNESCO** *United Nations Educational, Scientific*

*and Cultural Organization* Organisation der Vereinten Nationen für Erziehung, Wissenschaft und Kultur
**UNICEF** *United Nations International Children's Emergency Fund* Kinderhilfswerk *n* der Vereinten Nationen
**Univ.** *university* Universität *f*
**UNO** *United Nations Organization* Organisation der Vereinten Nationen, *abbr.* UNO *f*
**US** *United States* Vereinigte Staaten *pl, abbr.* US(A) *pl*
**USA** *United States of America* Vereinigte Staaten von Amerika, *abbr.* USA *pl*
**USAF** *United States Air Force* US-Luftwaffe *f*
**USN** *United States Navy* US-Marine *f*
**USS** *United States Ship* US-Schiff *n*
**USSR** *Union of Socialist Soviet Republics* Union der Sozialistischen Sowjetrepubliken, *abbr.* UdSSR *f*
**v.** 1. *El: volt* Volt *n.* 2. *Sp: & Jur: versus* gegen *acc.* 3. *vide* siehe. 4. *Poet: verse* Vers *m*
**V. & A.** *F: Victoria and Albert Museum* (Kunstmuseum in London)
**VAT** *value added tax* Mehrwertsteuer *f, abbr.* MWSt.
**V.C.** 1. *Vice-Chancellor* Vizekanzler *m.* 2. *Victoria Cross* (höchste Tapferkeitsmedaille)
**VD** *venereal disease* Geschlechtskrankheit *f*
**VDU** *visual display unit* Sichtgerät *n*
**VHF** *Rad: very high frequency* Ultrakurzwelle *f, abbr.* UKW
**VIP** *F: very important person* hohes Tier
**viz.** *videlicet* nämlich
**vocab.** *F: vocabulary* Wortschatz *m; (with translations)* Glossar *n*
**vol.** *volume* Band *m;* **vols.** *volumes* Bände *pl*
**vs.** *versus* gegen *acc*
**W.** *(a) west* West; *(b) adj. western* West-, westlich
**W., w.** *El: watt(s)* Watt *n(pl)*
**WC** *water closet* WC *n*
**Wed.** *Wednesday* Mittwoch *m, abbr.* Mi
**WHO** *World Health Organization* Weltgesundheitsorganisation *f*
**Worcs.** *Worcestershire* (Grafschaft)
**wpm** *words per minute* Worte pro Minute
**WRAF** *Women's Royal Air Force* (Frauendienst der Luftwaffe)
**WRNS** *Women's Royal Naval Service* (Frauendienst der Marine)
**yd.** *Meas: yard* Yard *n* (0.914 m)
**YHA** *Youth Hostel Association* Jugendherbergsverband *m*
**YMCA** *Young Men's Christian Association* Christlicher Verein junger Männer, *abbr.* CVJM
**YWCA** *Young Women's Christian Association* Christlicher Verein junger Frauen, *abbr.* CVJF
**yrs.** *(in letter) yours* Ihr(e), Dein(e)